W9-AOA-881

WITHDRAWN

Features

Guide to Tabular Presentation *p. xi*

Telephone and Internet Contacts *p. xiii*

Guide to Sources of Statistics *p. 879*

Guide to State Statistical Abstracts *p. 895*

Guide to Foreign Statistical Abstracts *p. 899*

Metropolitan and Micropolitan Area Concepts
and Components *p. 901*

Index by Subject *p. 950*

Visit us on the Web at
http://www.census.gov/statab/www/

ACKNOWLEDGEMENTS

Lars B. Johanson was responsible for the technical supervision and coordination of this volume under the general direction of **Glenn W. King**, Chief, Statistical Compendia Branch. Assisting in the research and analytical phases of assigned sections and in the development aspects of new tables were **Rosemary E. Clark, Richard P. Kersey, Stacey M. Lowe,** and **Jean F. Maloney. Catherine Lavender** provided primary editorial assistance. Other editorial assistance was rendered by **Susan Antroinen, Connie Nadzadi, Samuel E. Santos,** and **Barbara Shugart**.

Maps were designed and produced by **Connie Beard** and **Jessica Dobrowolski** of the Cartographic Operations Branch within the Geography Division.

Patricia Edwards, Wanda Cevis, Melanie Koserowski, Jamie Peters, Shirley Clark, Linda Chen, and **Diane Oliff-Michael** of the Administrative and Customer Services Division, **Walter C. Odom**, Chief, provided publications and printing management, graphics design and composition, and editorial review for print and electronic media. General direction and production management were provided by **James R. Clark**, Assistant Division Chief, and **Susan L. Rappa**, Chief, Publications Services Branch.

The cooperation of many contributors to this volume is gratefully acknowledged. The source note below each table credits the various government and private sector agencies that have collaborated in furnishing the information for the *Statistical Abstract*.

Statistical Abstract of the United States: 2004-2005

124th Edition

The National Data Book

Issued October 2004

U.S. Department of Commerce
Donald L. Evans,
Secretary

Theodore W. Kassinger,
Deputy Secretary

Economics and Statistics Administration
Kathleen B. Cooper,
Under Secretary for Economic Affairs

U.S. CENSUS BUREAU
Charles Louis Kincannon,
Director

SUGGESTED CITATION

U.S. Census Bureau,
Statistical Abstract of the United States: 2004–2005
(124th Edition)
Washington, DC,
2004

ECONOMICS
AND STATISTICS
ADMINISTRATION

Economics
and Statistics
Administration

Kathleen B. Cooper,
Under Secretary
for Economic Affairs

U.S. CENSUS BUREAU

Charles Louis Kincannon,
Director

Hermann Habermann,
Deputy Director and
Chief Operating Officer

Vacant,
Principal Associate Director
and Chief Financial Officer

Ted A. Johnson, Associate Director
for Finance and Administration

Walter C. Odom, Chief, Administrative
and Customer Services Division

U.S. GOVERNMENT PRINTING OFFICE OFFICIAL EDITION NOTICE

This is the Official U.S. Government edition of this publication and is
herein identified to certify its authenticity. The Superintendent of Documents of the U.S. Government Printing Office requests that any reprinted
edition clearly be labeled as a copy of the authentic work. Use of the 0-16
ISBN prefix is for U.S. Government Printing Office Official Editions only.

ISBN: 0-16-072331-0

NATIONAL BIBLIOGRAPHY METADATA/CATALOGING-IN-PUBLICATION

Statistical Abstract of the United States : 2004–2005.—124 ed.
  p. cm.
  Includes index.
  ISBN 0-16-072331-0   3 9082 09640 6379
  ISSN 0081-4741
1. United States—Statistics. I. United States. Census Bureau.

HA 202.S8 2005
317.3

Library of Congress Card No. 0418089

http://purl.access.gpo.gov/GPO/LPS2878

Printed by the U.S. Government Printing Office on acid-free paper that
meets the American National Standards Institute Z39048 standard.

U.S. GOVERNMENT PRINTING OFFICE
U.S. Superintendent of Documents   Washington, DC 20402-0001

Preface

The *Statistical Abstract of the United States,* published since 1878, is the standard summary of statistics on the social, political, and economic organization of the United States. It is designed to serve as a convenient volume for statistical reference and as a guide to other statistical publications and sources. The latter function is served by the introductory text to each section, the source note appearing below each table, and Appendix I, which comprises the Guide to Sources of Statistics, the Guide to State Statistical Abstracts, and the Guide to Foreign Statistical Abstracts.

This volume includes a selection of data from many statistical publications, both government and private. Publications cited as sources usually contain additional statistical detail and more comprehensive discussions of definitions and concepts than can be presented here. Data not available in publications issued by the contributing agency but obtained from unpublished records are identified in the source notes as unpublished data. More information on the subjects covered in the tables so noted may generally be obtained from the source.

Except as indicated, figures are for the United States as presently constituted. Although emphasis in the *Statistical Abstract* is primarily given to national data, many tables present data for regions and individual states and a smaller number for metropolitan areas and cities. Appendix II, Metropolitan Area Concepts and Components, presents explanatory text, a complete current listing and population data for metropolitan and micropolitan areas defined as of December 2003. Statistics for the Commonwealth of Puerto Rico and for island areas of the United States are included in many state tables and are supplemented by information in Section 29. Additional information for states, cities, counties, metropolitan areas, and other small units, as well as more historical data are available in various supplements to the *Abstract* (see inside back cover).

Statistics in this edition are generally for the most recent year or period available by summer 2004. Each year over 1,400 tables and charts are reviewed and evaluated; new tables and charts of current interest are added, continuing series are updated, and less timely data are condensed or eliminated. Text notes and appendices are revised as appropriate.

USA Statistics in Brief, a pocket-size pamphlet highlighting many statistical series in the *Abstract* is available. Copies can be obtained free from U.S. Census Bureau, Customer Services, Call Center, Washington, DC 20233 (telephone 301-763-INFO (4636)). We attempt to update the pamphlet several times during the year. The latest data can be found on our Web site: <http://www.census.gov/statab/www/brief.html>.

Changes in this edition—Long-time users of the Statistical Abstract will notice that this edition covers two years in the title, 2004-2005. We instituted this change so that the year in which most of the sales occur will be reflected in the title. This will conform with common practice for many private almanacs and yearbooks. The next edition of the Statistical Abstract will show only one year, 2006.

We have introduced 68 new tables in this edition. These cover a variety of topics including the social and economic characteristics of the Native Hawaiian and other Pacific Islander population, statistics for the largest public school districts, computer and internet use by children and adolescents, the percentage of students who reported carrying a weapon, private sector job gains and losses, asset ownership rates for households, science and engineering degree recipients and transit ridership in the 50 largest urbanized areas. In addition, a number of new tables have been added that contain data from the 2002 Economic Census. For a complete list of new tables, see Appendix VI, p. 947.

v

Statistical Abstract on other media— The *Abstract* is available on the Internet and on CD-ROM. Both versions contain the same material as the book, except for a few copyrighted tables for which we did not receive permission to release in these formats. Our Internet site, <http://www .census.gov/statab/www> contains this 2004 edition plus selected earlier editions in Adobe Acrobat .pdf format. The CD-ROM version also includes spread-sheet files for each table in the book and links to the Web sites of each source. Many of the spreadsheet files on the CD-ROM contain more historical and/or detailed data than are found in the book.

Statistics for counties and cities— Extensive data for counties can be found in the *County and City Data Book: 2000.* It features 191 data items covering every-thing from age and agriculture to water use and wholesale trade for all states and counties with U.S. totals for comparison. Also included are 103 data items for cities with population of 25,000 or more. The primary sources are Census 2000 and the 1997 Economic Census. Two tables present 11 data items from Census 2000 for all places and minor civil divisions with a population of 2,500 or more.

This publication, as well as selected rank-ings, is available on our Internet site at <http://www.census.gov/statab /www/ccdb.html>. Some data items that appear in the book from private sources are not available on the Internet or CD-ROM versions, because we did not receive copyright permission to release the data items in these formats. For a database with over 5,000 county items, check out USA Counties at <http://www .census.gov/statab/www/county.html>.

Statistics for states and metropolitan areas—Extensive data for the states and metropolitan areas of the United States can be found in the *State and Metropoli-tan Area Data Book: 1997-98.*

This publication minus some data items, as well as selected rankings of the states and metropolitan areas, is available on our Internet site at <http://www.census .gov/statab/www/smadb.html>. The CD-ROM version is also available. See the inside back cover for more information.

Limitations of the data—The contents of this volume were taken from many sources. All data from either censuses and surveys or from administrative records are subject to error arising from a number of factors: Sampling variability (for statis-tics based on samples), reporting errors in the data for individual units, incomplete coverage, nonresponse, imputations, and processing error. (See also Appendix III, pp. 923.) The Census Bureau cannot accept the responsibility for the accuracy or limitations of the data presented here, other than those for which it collects. The responsibility for selection of the material and for proper presentation, however, rests with the Census Bureau.

For additional information on data presented—Please consult the source publications available in local libraries or write to the agency indicated in the source notes. Write to the Census Bureau only if it is cited as the source.

Suggestions and comments—Users of the Statistical Abstract and its supple-ments (see inside back cover) are urged to make their data needs known for con-sideration in planning future editions. Suggestions and comments for improving coverage and presentation of data should be sent to the Director, U.S. Census Bureau, Washington, DC 20233.

Contents

[Numbers following subjects are page numbers]

	Page
Guide to Tabular Presentation	xi
Telephone and Internet Contacts	xiii

Sec. 1. Population (Tables 1 - 69) ... 1
Fig. 1.1. Center of Population: 1790 to 2000 ... 19
Immigration ... 8
Estimates by age, sex, race and Hispanic origin ... 12
States, metro. areas, cities ... 20
Profiles of elderly, racial and Hispanic origin populations ... 35
Native and Foreign-born populations ... 43
Ancestry languages ... 46
Marital status and households ... 48
Religion ... 55

Sec. 2. Vital Statistics (Tables 70 - 113) ... 57
Fig. 2.1. Infant Mortality Rates by State: 2001 ... 59
Births ... 60
Life expectancy ... 71
Deaths ... 74

Sec. 3. Health and Nutrition (Tables 114 - 201) ... 89
Fig. 3.1. Number of Retail Drug Prescriptions: 1995 to 2003 ... 91
Health expenditures, insurance ... 92
Health measures ... 119
Food consumption, nutrition ... 129

Sec. 4. Education (Tables 202-288) ... 133
Education projections ... 136
Educational attainment ... 141
Internet access ... 159
Degrees conferred ... 179

Sec. 5. Law Enforcement, Courts, and Prisons (Tables 289 - 345) ... 183
Fig. 5.1. Violent Crime Rates per 100,000 Population by State: 2002 ... 186
Crime arrests, and victimizations ... 193
Courts ... 202
Juveniles, child abuse ... 205
Prisoners and inmates ... 206

Sec. 6. Geography and Environment (Tables 346 - 383) ... 211
Land and water ... 213
Air quality ... 221
Hazardous waste sites ... 225
Climate ... 230

Sec. 7. Elections (Tables 384 - 416) ... 237
Fig. 7.1. Vote Cast for President by Major Political Party: 1992 to 2000 ... 238
Vote results ... 239
Campaign finances ... 259

Sec. 8. State and Local Government Finances and Employment (Tables 417 - 460) ... 261
Governmental units ... 262
State government finances ... 281

U.S. Census Bureau, Statistical Abstract of the United States: 2004-2005

Local government finances. 288
Employment and payroll 298

Sec. 9. Federal Government Finances and Employment (Tables 461 - 491) . . . 305
Fig. 9.1. Federal Budget Summary: 1980 to 2004 307
Budget receipts, outlays, debt 308
Federal employment and payroll 320

Sec. 10. National Defense and Veterans Affairs (Tables 492 - 517) 325
Fig. 10.1. National Defense Outlays 326
Fig. 10.2. Department of Defense Manpower: 2003 326
Fig. 10.3. Living Veterans by Age: 2003 337
National defense outlays 327
Military manpower 330

Sec. 11. Social Insurance and Human Services (Tables 518 - 568). 339
Fig. 11.1. Government Transfer Payments to Individuals by State: 2002 343
*Fig. 11.2. Old-age and Survivors Insurance (OASI) Benefits and Assets: 1990 to
2003* 343
Government transfer payments 342
Social Security 348
Public aid, federal food programs 357
Child care, child support 359

Sec. 12. Labor Force, Employment, and Earnings (Tables 569 - 640) 367
Labor force status 371
Multiple jobholding 382
Projections 390
Productivity 405
Minimum wage. 413
Union membership. 419

Sec. 13. Income, Expenditures, and Wealth (Tables 641 - 696) 421
Gross domestic product 425
Consumer expenditures 438
Money income of families 446
Poverty status 452

Sec. 14. Prices (Tables 697 - 715) 459
Fig. 14.1. Annual Percent Change in Consumer Price Indexes: 1990 to 2003 462
*Fig. 14.2. Annual Percent Change in Producer Price Indexes by Stage of Process-
ing: 1990 to 2003* 462
Purchasing power of the dollar. 461
Cost of living index 466

Sec. 15. Business Enterprise (Tables 716 - 763) 481
Sole proprietors, partnerships, corporations 483
Establishments, employees, payroll 491
Bankruptcies, mergers and acquisitions 498
Patents, trademarks, copyrights. 500
Investment, capital expenditures 501
Economic indicators. 503
Profits 506
Multinationals 507

Sec. 16. Science and Technology (Tables 764 - 786) 509
R&D funds, outlays. 512
Space program. 518

Sec. 17. Agriculture (Tables 787 - 840). 521
Fig. 17.1. Farms by Size: 1997 and 2002. 523
Fig. 17.2. Age of Principal Operator. 523

Farms and farmland 524
Farm balance sheet, income 529
Foreign trade 534
Crops, livestock 538

Sec. 18. Natural Resources (Tables 841 - 881) 547
Timber, lumber 551
Fishery 554
Petroleum, gas 562

Sec. 19. Energy (Tables 882 - 917) 569
Fig. 19.1. Energy Production, Trade, and Consumption: 1980 to 2002 573
Fig. 19.2. Top Suppliers of U.S. Crude Oil Imports: 2003 573
Energy consumption, expenditures 574
Crude oil 580
Electric utilities, nuclear 582
Gas utilities 588

Sec. 20. Construction and Housing (Tables 918 - 971) 591
Construction spending 595
Home sales 602
Homeownership 612
Home remodeling 622

Sec. 21. Manufactures (Tables 972 - 1015) 625
Fig. 21.1. GDP in Manufacturing by Industry: 2002 627
Fig. 21.2. Manufacturing as a Percent of Total Gross Domestic Product: 1998 to
   2003 627
Fig. 21.3. Employment in Top Five Manufacturing Industries: 1990 to 2003 627
Manufacturing summary 630
Steel 644
Machine tools 645
Computers, electronics 647

Sec. 22. Domestic Trade (Tables 1016 - 1044) 651
Fig. 22.1. Retail E-Commerce Sales: 2002 653
Fig. 22.2. Merchant Wholesale E-Commerce Trade Sales: 1998-2002 653
Retail trade 656
Wholesale merchant 667

Sec. 23. Transportation (Tables 1045 - 1112) 669
Transportation outlays 675
Air transportation 678
Port traffic 685
Motor vehicle registrations 692
Motor vehicle accidents 697
Transit ridership 705

Sec. 24. Information and Communications (Tables 1113 - 1153) 711
Information technologies 715
Newspapers 718
Book purchasing 722
Recording media 724
Telecommunications 726
Internet access and use 731

Sec. 25. Banking, Finance, and Insurance (Tables 1154 - 1223) 733
Establishments, receipts 735
Flow of funds, financial assets 736
Financial institutions 740
Mortgage debt, consumer credit 744
Money stock, interest rates 748

U.S. Census Bureau, Statistical Abstract of the United States: 2004-2005

Stocks and bonds, equity ownership 750
Mutual funds securities industry 757
Insurance, real estate 760

Sec. 26. Arts, Entertainment and Recreation (Tables 1224 - 1261) 763
Performing arts 767
Leisure activities 771
NCAA sports. 777
Travel 780

Sec. 27. Accommodation, Food Services, and Other Services (Tables 1262 -
    1277). 785
Fig. 27.1. Advertising Expenditures: 1990 to 2003. 786
Advertising 793
Administrative and support and waste management 794

Sec. 28. Foreign Commerce and Aid (Tables 1278 - 1302) 795
Fig. 28.1. U.S. International Transaction Balances: 1990 to 2003 798
*Fig. 28.2. Top Purchasers of U.S. Exports and Suppliers of U.S. General Imports:
    2003* 798
International transactions. 799
Foreign investments. 803
Foreign grants and credits 807
Exports and imports. 814

Sec. 29. Puerto Rico and the Island Areas (Tables 1303 - 1317) 821
Fig. 29.1. Selected Island Areas of the United States 822
Population 823

Sec. 30. Comparative International Statistics (Tables 1318 - 1385) 829
Fig. 30.1. Net Additions to the World: 2003 839
World maps 832
World population; vital statistics 840
Economic measures 852
Finance 871

Appendix I.
Guide to Sources of Statistics. 879
Guide to State Statistical Abstracts. 895
Guide to Foreign Statistical Abstracts. 899

Appendix II.
Metropolitan and Micropolitan Statistical Areas: Concepts, Components,
    and Population. 901

Appendix III.
Limitations of the Data. 923

Appendix IV.
Weights and Measures 943

Appendix V.
Tables Deleted From the 2003 Edition of the Statistical Abstract 944

Appendix VI.
New Tables. 947

Index 950

Guide to Tabular Presentation

Example of Table Structure

No. 313. Immigration and Naturalization Service Enforcement Activities: 1990 to 2000

[For fiscal years ending in year shown. See text, Section 8]

Item	Unit	1990	1994	1995	1996	1997	1998	1999	2000
Deportable aliens located.	1,000	1,169.9	1,094.7	1,394.6	1,650.0	1,536.5	1,679.4	1,714.0	1,814.7
Border Patrol	1,000	1,103.4	1,031.7	1,324.2	1,549.9	1,413.0	1,555.8	1,579.0	1,676.4
Southwestern border	1,000	(NA)	979.1	1,271.4	1,507.0	1,368.7	1,516.7	1,537.0	1,643.7
Mexican.	1,000	1,054.8	999.9	1,293.5	1,523.1	1,387.7	1,522.9	1,534.5	1,636.9
Canadian	1,000	5.7	3.4	3.5	2.7	2.9	2.3	2.7	2.2
Other	1,000	42.8	28.4	27.2	24.0	22.4	30.5	41.8	37.3
Number of seizures by									
Border Patrol	Number. . .	17,275	9,134	9,327	11,129	11,792	14,401	16,803	17,269
Value of seizures by Border Patrol.	Mil. dol. . . .	843.6	1,622.0	2,011.8	1,256.0	1,094.6	1,405.0	2,004.0	1,945.0
Narcotics.	Mil. dol. . . .	797.8	1,555.7	1,965.3	1,208.8	1,046.3	1,340.0	1,919.0	1,848.0
Aliens expelled:									
Formal removals [1]	1,000	30.0	45.7	45.2	69.7	114.4	173.0	180.3	184.8
Voluntary departures [2]	1,000	1,022.5	1,029.1	1,313.8	1,573.4	1,440.7	1,570.1	1,574.5	1,675.3

NA Not available. [1] Include deportations, exclusions, and removals. [2] Includes aliens under docket control required to depart and voluntary departures not under docket control.

Source: U.S. Bureau of Citizenship and Immigration Services, *Statistical Yearbook*, annual. See also <http://www.immigration .gov/graphics/shared/aboutus/statistics/index.htm>.

Headnotes immediately below table titles provide information important for correct interpretation or evaluation of the table as a whole or for a major segment of it.

Footnotes below the bottom rule of tables give information relating to specific items or figures within the table.

Unit indicators show the *specified quantities* in which data items are presented. They are used for two primary reasons. Sometimes data are not available in absolute form and are estimates (as in the case of many surveys). In other cases we round the numbers in order to save space to show more data, as in the case above.

EXAMPLES OF UNIT INDICATOR INTERPRETATION FROM TABLE

Year	Item	Unit Indicator	Number shown	Multiplier
1990	Deportable aliens located	Thousands	1,169.9	1,000
1990	Value of seizures by Border Patrol . .	$ Millions	843.6	1,000,000

To Determine the Figure It Is Necessary to Multiply the Number Shown by the Unit Indicator:

Deportable aliens located - 1,169.9 x 1,000 = 1,169,900 (over 1 million)

Value of seizures by Border Patrol - 843.6 x $1,000,000 - $843,600,000 (over $843 million).

When a table presents data with more than one unit indicator, they are found in the headnotes and column headings (Tables 2 and 27), spanner (Table 40), stub (Table 23), or unit column (shown above). When the data in a table are shown in the same unit indicator, it is shown in boldface as the first part of the headnote (Table 2). If no unit indicator is shown, data presented are in absolute form (Table 1).

Vertical rules are used to separate independent sections of a table, (Table 1), or in tables where the stub is continued into one or more additional columns (Table 2).

Averages—An average is a single number or value that is often used to represent the "typical value" of a group of numbers. It is regarded as a measure of "location" or "central tendency" of a group of numbers.

The *arithmetic mean* is the type of average used most frequently. It is derived by summing the individual item values of a particular group and dividing the total by the number of items. The arithmetic mean is often referred to as simply the "mean" or "average."

The *median* of a group of numbers is the middle number or value when each item in the group is arranged according to size (lowest to highest or visa versa); it generally has the same number of items above it as well as below it. If there is an even number of items in the group, the median is taken to be the average of the two middle numbers.

Per capita (or per person) quantities. A per capita figure represents an average computed for every person in a specified group (or population). It is derived by taking the total for an item (such as income, taxes, or retail sales) and dividing it by

U.S. Census Bureau, *Statistical Abstract of the United States: 2004-2005*

the number of persons in the specified population.

Index numbers—An index number is the measure of difference or change, usually expressed as a percent, relating one quantity (the variable) of a specified kind to another quantity of the same kind. Index numbers are widely used to express changes in prices over periods of time, but may also be used to express differences between related subjects for a single point in time.

To compute a price index, a base year or period is selected. The base year price (of the commodity or service) is then designated as the base or reference price to which the prices for other years or periods are related. Many price indexes use the year 1982 as the base year; in tables this is shown as "1982=100." A method of expressing the price relationship is: The price of a set of one or more items for a related year (e.g. 1990) **divided by** the price of the same set of items for the base year (e.g. 1982). The result multiplied by 100 provides the index number. When 100 is subtracted from the index number, the result equals the percent change in price from the base year.

Average annual percent change— Unless otherwise stated in the *Abstract* (as in Section 1, Population), average annual percent change is computed by use of a *compound interest formula.* This formula assumes that the rate of change is constant throughout a specified compounding period (1 year for average annual rates of change). The formula is similar to that used to compute the balance of a savings account that receives compound interest. According to this formula, at the end of a compounding period the amount of accrued change (e.g. school enrollment or bank interest) is added to the amount that existed at the beginning of the period. As a result, over time (e.g., with each year or quarter), the same rate of change is applied to a larger and larger figure.

The *exponential formula,* which is based on continuous compounding, is often used to measure population change. It is preferred by population experts, because they view population and population-related subjects as changing without interruption, ever ongoing. Both exponential and compound interest formulas assume a constant rate of change. The former, however, applies the amount of change continuously to the base rather than at the end of each compounding period. When the average annual rates are small (e.g., less than 5 percent) both formulas give virtually the same results. For an explanation of these two formulas as they relate to population, see U.S. Census Bureau, *The Methods and Materials of Demography,* Vol. 2, 3d printing (rev.), 1975, pp. 372-381.

Current and constant dollars— Statistics in some tables in a number of sections are expressed in both current and constant dollars (see, for example, Table 653 in Section 13, Income, Expenditures, and Wealth). Current dollar figures reflect actual prices or costs prevailing during the specified year(s). Constant dollar figures are estimates representing an effort to remove the effects of price changes from statistical series reported in dollar terms. In general, constant dollar series are derived by dividing current dollar estimates by the appropriate price index for the appropriate period (for example, the Consumer Price Index). The result is a series as it would presumably exist if prices were the same throughout, as in the base year—in other words, as if the dollar had constant purchasing power. Any changes in this constant dollar series would reflect only changes in real volume of output, income, expenditures, or other measure.

Explanation of Symbols

The following symbols, used in the tables throughout this book, are explained in condensed form in footnotes to the tables where they appear:

- Represents zero or rounds to less than half the unit of measurement shown.

B Base figure too small to meet statistical standards for reliability of a derived figure.

D Figure withheld to avoid disclosure pertaining to a specific organization or individual.

NA Data not enumerated, tabulated, or otherwise available separately.

S Figure does not meet publication standards for reasons other than that covered by symbol B, above.

X Figure not applicable because column heading and stub line make entry impossible, absurd, or meaningless.

Z Entry would amount to less than half the unit of measurement shown.

In many tables, details will not add to the totals shown because of rounding.

Telephone and Internet Contacts

To help *Abstract* users find more data and information about statistical publications, we are issuing this list of contacts for federal agencies with major statistical programs. The intent is to give a single, first-contact point-of-entry for users of statistics. These agencies will provide general information on their statistical programs and publications, as well as specific information on how to order their publications. We are also including the Internet (World Wide Web) addresses for many of these agencies. These URLs were current in July 2004.

Executive Office of the President
Office of Management and Budget
Administrator
Office of Information and Regulatory Affairs
Office of Management and Budget
725 17th Street, NW
Washington, DC 20503
Information: 202-395-3080
Internet address:
http://www.whitehouse.gov/omb

Department of Agriculture
Economic Research Service
Information Center
U.S. Department of Agriculture
1800 M Street, NW
Washington, DC 20036-5831
Information and Publications:
202-694-5050
Internet address:
http://www.ers.usda.gov/

National Agricultural Statistics Service
National Agricultural Statistics Service
USDA-NASS
Room 5829-South
Washington, DC 20250
Information hotline: 1-800-727-9540
Internet address:
http://www.usda.gov/nass/

Department of Commerce
U.S. Census Bureau
Customer Services Branch
U.S. Census Bureau
4700 Silver Hill Road
Washington, DC 20233-0001
Information and Publications:
301-763-4636
Internet address:
http://www.census.gov/

Department of Commerce —Con.
Bureau of Economic Analysis
Bureau of Economic Analysis
1441 L Street, NW
Washington, DC 20230
Information and Publications:
202-606-9900
Internet address: http://www.bea.gov/
International Trade Administration
Trade Statistics Division
Office of Trade and Economic Analysis
International Trade Administration
Room 2814 B
U.S. Department of Commerce
Washington, DC 20230
Information and Publications:
202-482-2185
Internet address:
http://www.ita.doc.gov/td/industry/otea

National Oceanic and Atmospheric Administration
National Oceanic and Atmospheric Administration Central Library
U.S. Department of Commerce
1315 East-West Highway
2nd Floor, SSMC3
Silver Spring, MD 20910
Library: 301-713-2600
Internet address:
http://www.lib.noaa.gov/

Department of Defense
Department of Defense
Office of the Assistant Secretary of Defense, Public Affairs, (DPO)
Room 3A750
Attention: Press Operations
1400 Defense Pentagon
Washington, DC 20301-1400
Information: 703-697-5131
Internet address:
http://www.defenselink.mil

U.S. Census Bureau, Statistical Abstract of the United States: 2004-2005

Department of Education
National Library of Education
U.S. Department of Education
400 Maryland Avenue, SW
Washington, DC 20202-5621
Education Information and Statistics
1-800-424-1616
Education Publications: 1-877-433-7827
Internet address: http://www.ed.gov/

Department of Energy
Energy Information Administration
National Energy Information Center
U.S. Department of Energy
1000 Independence Ave., SW
Room EI-30
Washington, DC 20585
Information and Publications:
202-586-8800
Internet address:
http://www.eia.doe.gov/

Department of Health and Human Services
Health Resources and Services Administration
HRSA Office of Communications
Parklawn Building
5600 Fishers Lane
Rockville, MD 20857
Information Center: 1-888-275-4772
Internet address: http://www.hrsa.gov/

Substance Abuse and Mental Health Services Administration
U.S. Department of Health and Human Services
Parklawn Building, Room 12-105
5600 Fishers Lane
Rockville, MD 20857
Information: 301-443-4795
Publications: 1-800-729-6686
Internet address:
http://www.samhsa.gov/

Centers for Disease Control and Prevention
Public Inquiries/MASO
Mail Stop F07
1600 Clifton Road
Atlanta, GA 30333
Public Inquiries: 1-800-311-3435
Internet address: http://www.cdc.gov/

Department of Health and Human Services —Con.
Centers for Medicare and Medicaid Services (CMS)
Office of Public Affairs
U.S. Department of Health and Human Services
Room 303D, Humphrey Building
200 Independence Ave., SW
Washington, DC 20201
Media Relations: 202-690-6145
Internet address:
http://www.cms.hhs.gov/

National Center for Health Statistics
U.S. Department of Health and Human Services - Centers for Disease Control and Prevention
National Center for Health Statistics
Hyattsville, MD 20782
301-458-4000
Internet address:
http://www.cdc.gov/nchs

Department of Homeland Security
U.S. Citizenship and Immigration Services
425 I Street, NW
Washington, DC 20536
Information and Publications:
202-305-1613
Internet address:
http://uscis.gov/graphics/ index.htm

U.S. Department of Housing and Urban Development
Office of the Assistant Secretary for Community Planning and Development
451 7th Street, SW
Washington, DC 20410
Information and Publications:
1-800-998-9999
Internet address: http://www.hud.gov/

Department of the Interior
U.S. Geological Survey
Earth Science Information Center
U.S. Geological Survey
U.S. Department of the Interior
12201 Sunrise Valley Drive
Reston, VA 20192
Information and Publications:
1-888-275-8747
Internet address for minerals:
http://minerals.usgs.gov/
Internet address for other materials:
http://ask.usgs.gov/

Department of Justice

Bureau of Justice Statistics

Statistics Division
810 7th Street, NW
Washington, DC 20531
Information and Publications:
1-800-851-3420
Datasets and Codebooks:
1-800-999-0960
Internet address:
http://www.ojp.usdoj.gov/bjs/

National Criminal Justice Reference Service

P.O. Box 6000
Rockville, MD 20849-6000
Information and Publications:
301-519-5500
Publications: 1-800-851-3420
Internet address: http://www.ncjrs.org/

Federal Bureau of Investigation

U.S. Department of Justice
J. Edgar Hoover FBI Building
935 Pennsylvania Ave., NW
Washington, DC 20535-0001
National Press Office: 202-324-3000
Internet address: http://www.fbi.gov/

Department of Labor

Bureau of Labor Statistics

Office of Publications and Special Studies
Services
Bureau of Labor Statistics
Postal Square Building
2 Massachusett Ave., NE
Washington, DC 20212-0001
Information and Publications:
202-691-5200
Internet address: http://www.bls.gov/

Employment and Training Administration

Office of Outreach
U.S. Department of Labor
Francis Perkins Building
200 Constitution Ave., NW
Washington, DC 20210
Information and Publications:
202-693-3965
Internet address: http://www.doleta.gov/

Department of Transportation

Federal Aviation Administration

U.S. Department of Transportation
800 Independence Ave., SW
Washington, DC 20591
Information and Publications:
202-267-3484
Internet address: http://www.faa.gov/

Bureau of Transportation Statistics

400 7th Street, SW, Room 3103
Washington, DC 20590
Products and Statistical Information:
800-853-1351
Internet address: http://www.bts.gov/

Department of Transportation —Con.

Federal Highway Administration

Office of Public Affairs
Federal Highway Administration
U.S. Department of Transportation
400 7th Street, SW
Washington, DC 20590
Information: 202-366-0660
Internet address:
http://www.fhwa.dot.gov/

National Highway Traffic Safety Administration

Office of Public & Consumer Affairs
National Highway Traffic Safety
Administration
U.S. Department of Transportation
400 7th Street, SW
Washington, DC 20590
Information: 202-366-4000
Publications: 202-366-8892/9550
Internet address:
http://www.nhtsa.dot.gov/

Department of the Treasury

Internal Revenue Service

Statistics of Income Division
Internal Revenue Service
P.O. Box 2608
Washington, DC 20013-2608
Information and Publications:
202-874-0410
Internet address:
http://www.irs.gov/taxstats/

Department of Veterans Affairs

Office of Public Affairs
Department of Veterans Affairs
810 Vermont Ave., NW
Washington, DC 20420
Information: 202-273-6482
Internet address: http://www.va.gov/

Independent Agencies

Administrative Office of the U.S. Courts

Statistics Division
1 Columbus Circle, NE
Washington, DC 20544
Information: 202-502-1455
Internet address:
http://www.uscourts.gov/

Environmental Protection Agency

Environmental Protection Agency Library
1301 Constitution Ave., NW Room 3340
EPA NW
Washington, DC 20229
Information: 202-566-0556
Internet address: http://www.epa.gov/

Independent Agencies —Con.

Federal Reserve Board
Division of Research and Statistics
Federal Reserve Board
20th & C Street, NW
Washington, DC 20551
Information: 202-452-3301
Publications: 202-452-3245
Internet address:
http://www.federalreserve.gov/

National Science Foundation
Office of Legislation and Public Affairs
National Science Foundation
4201 Wilson Boulevard
Arlington, Virginia 22230
Information: 703-292-8070
Publications: 703-292-8129
Internet address: http://www.nsf.gov/

Independent Agencies —Con.

Securities and Exchange Commission
Office of Public Affairs
Securities and Exchange Commission
450 5th St., NW
Washington, DC 20549
Information: 202-942-8088
Publications: 202-942-4040
Internet address: http://www.sec.gov/

Social Security Administration
Social Security Administration
Office of Research, Evaluation and Statistics
4-C-15 Operations Building
6401 Security Boulevard
Baltimore, MD 21235
Information and Publications:
1-800-772-1213
Internet Address:
http://www.socialsecurity.gov/

Section 1
Population

This section presents statistics on the growth, distribution, and characteristics of the U.S. population. The principal source of these data is the U.S. Census Bureau, which conducts a decennial census of population, a monthly population survey, a program of population estimates and projections, and a number of other periodic surveys relating to population characteristics. For a list of relevant publications, see the Guide to Sources of Statistics in Appendix I.

Decennial censuses—The U.S. Constitution provides for a census of the population every 10 years, primarily to establish a basis for apportionment of members of the House of Representatives among the states. For over a century after the first census in 1790, the census organization was a temporary one, created only for each decennial census. In 1902, the Census Bureau was established as a permanent federal agency, responsible for enumerating the population and also for compiling statistics on other population and housing characteristics.

Historically, the enumeration of the population has been a complete count. That is, an attempt is made to account for every person, for each person's residence, and for other characteristics (sex, age, family relationships, etc.). Since the 1940 census, in addition to the complete count information, some data have been obtained from representative samples of the population. In the 1990 and 2000 censuses, variable sampling rates were employed. For most of the country, 1 in every 6 households (about 17 percent) received the long form or sample questionnaire; in governmental units estimated to have fewer than 2,500 inhabitants, every other household (50 percent) received the sample questionnaire to enhance the reliability of sample data for small areas. Exact agreement is not to be expected between sample data and the 100-percent count. Sample data may be used with confidence where large numbers are involved and assumed to indicate trends and relationships where small numbers are involved.

Current Population Survey (CPS)—This is a monthly nationwide survey of a scientifically selected sample representing the noninstitutional civilian population. The sample is located in 754 areas with coverage in every state and the District of Columbia and is subject to sampling error. At the present time, about 60,000 occupied households are eligible for interview every month; of these between 6 and 7 percent are, for various reasons, unavailable for interview.

While the primary purpose of the CPS is to obtain monthly statistics on the labor force, it also serves as a vehicle for inquiries on other subjects. Using CPS data, the Bureau issues a series of publications under the general title of *Current Population Reports,* which cover population characteristics (P20), consumer income (P60), special studies (P23), and other topics.

Estimates of population characteristics based on the CPS will not agree with the counts from the census because the CPS and the census use different procedures for collecting and processing the data for racial groups, the Hispanic population, and other topics. Caution should also be used when comparing estimates for various years because of the periodic introduction of changes into the CPS. Beginning in January 1994, a number of changes were introduced into the CPS that effect all data comparisons with prior years. These changes included the results of a major redesign of the survey questionnaire and collection methodology and the introduction of 1990 census population controls, adjusted for the estimated undercount. Beginning with the 2001 CPS Annual Demographic Supplement the independent estimates used as control totals for the CPS are based on civilian population benchmarks consistent with Census 2000. In March 2002, the sample size of the Annual Demographic Supplement was increased to approximately

78,000. In 2003 the name of the March supplement was changed to Annual Social and Economic Supplement. These changes in population controls had relatively little impact on derived measures such as means, medians, and percent distribution, but did have a significant impact on levels.

Population estimates and projections—Estimates of the United States population are derived by updating the resident population enumerated in Census 2000 with information on the components of population change: births, deaths, and net international migration. The April 1, 2000, population used in these estimates reflects modifications to the Census 2000 population as documented in the Count Question Resolution program.

Registered births and deaths are estimated from data supplied by the National Center for Health Statistics. The net international migration component in the population estimates includes: legal immigration to the United States, emigration of foreign born and native people from the United States, net movement between the United States and Puerto Rico, estimates of temporary migrants, and estimates of net residual foreign-born population, which include unauthorized migration.

For the first time, the estimates of the international migration component incorporated data available from the Census 2000 Supplementary Survey (C2SS) and the 2001 Supplementary Survey (SS01) along with estimates developed from the Demographic Analysis and Population Estimates (DAPE) project (See Deardorff and Blumerman, 2001, "Evaluation Components of International Migration: Estimates of the Foreign-Born Population by Migrant Status in 2000," Population Division Working Paper Series, No. 58).

Estimates for state and county areas are based on the same components of change data and sources as the national estimates with the addition of net internal migration. School enrollment statistics from state departments of education and parochial school systems, federal income tax returns from the Internal Revenue Service, group quarters data from the Federal-State Cooperative Program, and medicare data from the Centers of Medicare and Medicaid Services are also included.

The population by age for April 1, 1990, (shown in Table 11) reflects modifications to the 1990 census data counts. The review of detailed 1990 information indicated that respondents tended to report age as of the date of completion of the questionnaire, not as of April 1, 1990. In addition, there may have been a tendency for respondents to round up their age if they were close to having a birthday. A detailed explanation of the age modification procedure appears in 1990 Census of Population and Housing, Data Paper Listing CPH-L74.

Population estimates and projections are available on the Census Bureau Internet site <http://www.census.gov>. These estimates and projections are consistent with official decennial census figures with no adjustment for estimated net census coverage. However, the categories for these estimates and projections by race have been modified and are not comparable to the census race categories (see section below under "Race"). For details on methodology, see the sources cited below the individual tables.

Immigration—Immigration (migration *to* a country) is one component of international migration; the other component is emigration (migration *from* a country). In its simplest form, international migration is defined as any movement across a national border. In the United States, federal statistics on international migration are produced primarily by the U.S. Census Bureau and the Office of Immigration Statistics (located in the Department of Homeland Security).

The Census Bureau collects data used to estimate international migration through its decennial censuses and numerous surveys of the U.S. population. The Office of Immigration Statistics publishes immigration data in the *Yearbook of Immigration Statistics* and collects these data from several administrative records such as the Immigrant Visa and Alien Registration (OF-155, U.S. State Department) for new arrivals, and the Memorandum of Creation of Record of Lawful Permanent Residence (I-181, INS) for persons adjusting migrant status. Immigrants are aliens admitted for legal permanent residence in the United States. The category, immigrant, includes persons who may have entered the United States as nonimmigrants or refugees, but who subsequently changed their status to that of a permanent resident. Nonresident aliens admitted to the United States for a temporary period are nonimmigrants. Refugees are considered nonimmigrants when initially admitted into the United States but are not included in nonimmigrant admission data. A refugee is an alien outside the United States who is unable or unwilling to return to his or her country of nationality because of persecution or a well-founded fear of persecution.

U.S. immigration law gives preferential immigration status to persons with a close family relationship with a U.S. citizen or legal permanent resident, persons with needed job skills, or persons who qualify as refugees. Immigration to the United States can be divided into two general categories: (1) those subject to the annual worldwide limitation and (2) those exempt from it. Numerical limits are imposed on visas issued and not on admissions. The maximum number of visas allowed to be issued under the preference categories in 2002 was 368,632—226,000 for family-sponsored immigrants and 142,632 for employment-based immigrants. There are nine categories among which the family-sponsored and employment-based immigrant visas are distributed, beginning in fiscal year 1992. Within the overall limitations the per-country limit for independent countries is set to 7 percent of the total family-sponsored and employment-based limits, while dependent areas are limited to 2 percent of the total. The 2002 limit allowed no more than 25,804 preference visas for any independent country and 7,373 for any dependency. Those exempt from the worldwide limitation include immediate relatives of U.S. citizens, refugees and asylees adjusting to permanent residence, and other various classes of special immigrants (see Table 6).

The Refugee Act of 1980 provides for a uniform admission procedure for refugees of all countries, based on the United Nations' definition of refugees. Authorized admission ceilings are set annually by the President in consultation with Congress. After 1 year of residence in the United States, refugees are eligible for immigrant status.

Metropolitan Areas—The United States Office of Management and Budget (OMB) defines metropolitan and micropolitan statistical areas according to published standards that are applied to Census Bureau data. The general concept of a metropolitan or micropolitan statistical area is that of a core area containing a substantial population nucleus, together with adjacent communities having a high degree of economic and social integration with that core. Currently defined metropolitan and micropolitan statistical areas are based on application of 2000 standards to 2000 decennial census data. The term "metropolitan area" (MA) was adopted in 1990 and referred collectively to metropolitan statistical areas (MSAs), consolidated metropolitan statistical areas (CMSAs), and primary metropolitan statistical areas (PMSAs). The term "core based statistical area" (CBSA) became effective in 2000 and refers collectively to metropolitan and micropolitan statistical areas.

Over time, new statistical areas are created and the components of others change. Because of historical changes in geographic definitions, users must be cautious in comparing data for these statistical areas from different dates. For some purposes, comparisons of data for areas as defined at given dates may be appropriate; for other purposes, it may be preferable to maintain consistent area definitions. For descriptive details and a listing of titles and components of metropolitan and micropolitan areas, see Appendix II.

Urban and rural—For Census 2000, the Census Bureau classified as urban all territory, population, and housing units located within urbanized areas (UAs) and urban clusters (UCs). A UA consists of densely settled territory that contains 50,000 or more people, while a UC consists of densely settled territory with at least 2,500 people but fewer than 50,000 people. (UCs are a new type of geographic entity for Census 2000.) Prior to Census 2000—from the 1950 census through the 1990 census—the urban population consisted of all people living in UAs and most places outside of UAs with a census population of 2,500 or more.

U.S. Census Bureau, Statistical Abstract of the United States: 2004-2005

UAs and UCs encompass territory that generally consists of:

- A cluster of one or more block groups or census blocks each of which has a population density of at least 1,000 people per square mile at the time.
- Surrounding block groups and census blocks each of which has a population density of at least 500 people per square mile at the time.
- Less densely settled blocks that form enclaves or indentations, or are used to connect discontiguous areas with qualifying densities.

They also may include an airport located adjacent to qualifying densely settled area if it has an annual enplanement (aircraft boarding) of at least 10,000 people.

"Rural" for Census 2000 consists of all territory, population, and housing units located outside of UAs and UCs. Prior to Census 2000, rural consisted of all territory, population, and housing outside of UAs and outside of other places designated as "urban." For Census 2000, many more geographic entities, including metropolitan areas, counties, county subdivisions, and places, contain both urban and rural territory, population, and housing units.

Residence—In determining residence, the Census Bureau counts each person as an inhabitant of a usual place of residence (i.e., the place where one usually lives and sleeps most of the time). While this place is not necessarily a person's legal residence or voting residence, the use of these different bases of classification would produce the same results in the vast majority of cases.

Race—For the 1990 census, the Census Bureau collected and published racial statistics as outlined in Statistical Policy Directive No. 15 issued by the U.S. Office of Management and Budget (OMB). This directive provided standards on ethnic and racial categories for statistical reporting to be used by all federal agencies. According to the directive, the basic racial categories were American Indian or Alaskan Native, Asian or Pacific Islander, Black, and White. (The directive identified Hispanic origin as an ethnicity.) The question on race for Census 2000 was different from the one for the 1990 census in

several ways. Most significantly, respondents were given the option of selecting one or more race categories to indicate their racial identities. Because of these changes, the Census 2000 data on race are not directly comparable with data from the 1990 census or earlier censuses. Caution must be used when interpreting changes in the racial composition of the U.S. population over time. Census 2000 adheres to the federal standards for collecting and presenting data on race and Hispanic origin as established by OMB in October 1997. Starting with Census 2000, the OMB requires federal agencies to use a minimum of five race categories: White, Black or African American, American Indian or Alaska Native, Asian, and Native Hawaiian or Other Pacific Islander. For respondents unable to identify with any of these five race categories, OMB approved and included a sixth category— "Some other race" on the Census 2000 questionnaire. The Census 2000 question on race included 15 separate response categories and three areas where respondents could write in a more specific race group. The response categories and write-in answers can be combined to create the five minimum OMB race categories plus "Some other race." People who responded to the question on race by indicating only one race are referred to as the *race alone* population, or the group that reported only one race category. Six categories make up this population: White alone, Black or African American alone, American Indian and Alaska Native alone, Asian alone, Native Hawaiian and Other Pacific Island alone, and Some other race alone. Individuals who chose more than one of the six race categories are referred to as the *Two or more races* population, or as the group that reported more than one race. Additionally, respondents who reported one race together with those who reported the same race plus one or more other races are combined to create the *race alone or in combination* categories. For example, the *White alone or in combination group* consists of those respondents who reported White combined with one or more other race groups, such as "White and Black or African American," or "White and Asian and American Indian and Alaska Native." Another way to think of the group who reported White alone or in combination is as the total number of people who identified entirely or partially as White. This group is also described as people who reported White, whether or not they reported any other race.

The *alone or in combination* categories are tallies of *responses* rather than *respondents*. That is, the alone or in combination categories are not mutually exclusive. Individuals who reported two races were counted in two separate and distinct alone or in combination race categories, while those who reported three races were counted in three categories, and so on. Consequently, the sum of all alone or in combination categories equals the number of races reported (i.e., responses) which exceeds the total population.

The concept of race, as used by the Census Bureau, reflects self-identification by people according to the race or races with which they most closely identify. These categories are sociopolitical constructs and should not be interpreted as being scientific or anthropological in nature. Furthermore, the race categories include both racial and national-origin groups.

Data for the population by race for April 1, 2000, (shown in Tables 13 through 15) are modified counts and are not comparable to Census 2000 race categories. These numbers were computed using Census 2000 data by race that had been modified to be consistent with the 1997 Office of Management and Budget's, "Revisions to the Standards for the Classification of Federal Data on Race and Ethnicity," (Federal Register Notice, Vol. 62, No 210, October 1997). A detailed explanation of the race modification procedure appears on the Census Web page, <http://eire.census.gov/popest/data/national/tables/files/mod_race.php>.

In the CPS and other household sample surveys in which data are obtained through personal interview, respondents are asked to classify their race as: (1) White; (2) Black, African American or Negro; (3) American Indian or Alaska Native; (4) Asian; (5) Native Hawaiian or Other Pacific Islander. Beginning January 2003, respondents were allowed to report more than one race to indicate their mixed racial heritage.

Hispanic population—The Census Bureau collected data on the Hispanic origin population in the 2000 census by using a self-identification question. Persons of Spanish/Hispanic origin are those who classified themselves in one of the specific Hispanic origin categories listed on the questionnaire— Mexican, Puerto Rican, Cuban, as well as those who indicated that they were of Other Spanish/Hispanic origin. Persons of Other Spanish/Hispanic origin are those whose origins are from Spain, the Spanish-speaking countries of Central or South America, or the Dominican Republic.

In the CPS information on Hispanic persons is gathered by using a self-identification question. Persons classify themselves in one of the Hispanic categories in response to the question: "What is the origin or descent of each person in this household?" Hispanic persons in the CPS are persons who report themselves as Mexican-American, Chicano, Mexican, Puerto Rican, Cuban, Central or South American (Spanish countries), or other Hispanic origin.

Traditional and current data collection and classification treat race and Hispanic origin as two separate and distinct concepts in accordance with guidelines from the OMB. Race and Hispanic origin are two separate concepts in the federal statistical system. People who are Hispanic may be of any race and people in each race group may be either Hispanic or Not Hispanic. Also, each person has two attributes, their race (or races) and whether or not they are Hispanic. The overlap of race and Hispanic origin is the main comparability issue. For example, Black Hispanics (Hispanic Blacks) are included in both the number of Blacks and in the number of Hispanics. For further information, see Census Web page, <http://www.census.gov/population/www/socdemo/compraceho.html>.

Foreign-born and native populations—The Census Bureau separates the U.S. resident population into two groups based on whether or not a person was a U.S. citizen at the time of birth. Anyone born in the United States or a U.S. Island Area (such as Puerto Rico) or born abroad to a U.S. citizen parent is a U.S. citizen at the time of birth and consequently included in the *native population*. The term *foreign-born population* refers to anyone who is not a U.S. citizen at birth. This includes naturalized U.S. citizens, legal permanent resident aliens (immigrants), temporary migrants (such as students), humanitarian migrants (such as refugees), and people illegally present in the United States. The Census Bureau provides a variety of demographic, social, economic, geographic, and housing information on the foreign-born population in the United States. More information on the foreign-born population collected from censuses and surveys is available at the Foreign-Born Population page, <http://www.census.gov/population/www/socdemo/foreign.html>.

Mobility status—The U.S. population is classified according to mobility status on the basis of a comparison between the place of residence of each individual at the time of the survey or census and the place of residence at a specified earlier date. Nonmovers are all persons who were living in the same house or apartment at the end of the period as at the beginning of the period. Movers are all persons who were living in a different house or apartment at the end of the period than at the beginning of the period. Movers are further classified as to whether they were living in the same or different county, state, or region or were movers from abroad. Movers from abroad include all persons, either U.S. citizens or noncitizens, whose place of residence was outside the United States at the beginning of the period; that is, in Puerto Rico, another U.S. Island Area, or a foreign country.

Living arrangements—Living arrangements refer to residency in households or in group quarters. A "household" comprises all persons who occupy a "housing unit," that is, a house, an apartment or other group of rooms, or a single room that constitutes "separate living quarters." A household includes the related family members and all the unrelated persons, if any, such as lodgers, foster children, wards, or employees who share the housing unit. A person living alone or a group of unrelated persons sharing the same housing unit is also counted as a household. See text, Section 20, Construction and Housing, for definition of housing unit.

All persons not living in housing units are classified as living in group quarters. These individuals may be institutionalized, e.g., under care or custody in juvenile facilities, jails, correctional centers, hospitals, or nursing homes; or they may be residents in noninstitutional group quarters such as college dormitories, group homes, or military barracks.

Householder—The householder is the person in whose name the home is owned or rented. If a home is owned or rented jointly by a married couple, either the husband or the wife may be listed first. Prior to 1980, the husband was always considered the householder in married-couple households.

Family—The term family refers to a group of two or more persons related by birth, marriage, or adoption and residing together in a household. A family includes among its members the householder.

Subfamily—A subfamily consists of a married couple and their children, if any, or one parent with one or more never-married children under 18 years old living in a household. Subfamilies are divided into "related" and "unrelated" subfamilies. A related subfamily is related to, but does not include, the householder. Members of a related subfamily are also members of the family with whom they live. The number of related subfamilies, therefore, is not included in the count of families. An unrelated subfamily may include persons such as guests, lodgers, or resident employees and their spouses and/or children; none of whom is related to the householder.

Married couple—A married couple is defined as a husband and wife living together in the same household, with or without children and other relatives.

Statistical reliability—For a discussion of statistical collection and estimation, sampling procedures, and measures of statistical reliability applicable to Census Bureau data, see Appendix III.

No. 1. Population and Area: 1790 to 2000

[Area figures represent area on indicated date including in some cases considerable areas not then organized or settled, and not covered by the census. Total area figures for 1790 to 1970 have been recalculated on the basis of the remeasurement of states and counties for the 1980 census, but not on the basis of the 1990 census. The land and water area figures for past censuses have not been adjusted and are not strictly comparable with the total area data for comparable dates because the land areas were derived from different base data, and these values are known to have changed with the construction of reservoirs, draining of lakes, etc. Density figures are based on land area measurements as reported in earlier censuses]

Census date	Resident population				Area (square miles)		
	Number	Per square mile of land area	Increase over preceding census		Total	Land	Water [1]
			Number	Percent			
1790 (Aug. 2)	3,929,214	4.5	(X)	(X)	891,364	864,746	24,065
1800 (Aug. 4)	5,308,483	6.1	1,379,269	35.1	891,364	864,746	24,065
1810 (Aug. 6)	7,239,881	4.3	1,931,398	36.4	1,722,685	1,681,828	34,175
1820 (Aug. 7)	9,638,453	5.5	2,398,572	33.1	1,792,552	1,749,462	38,544
1830 (June 1)	12,866,020	7.4	3,227,567	33.5	1,792,552	1,749,462	38,544
1840 (June 1)	17,069,453	9.8	4,203,433	32.7	1,792,552	1,749,462	38,544
1850 (June 1)	23,191,876	7.9	6,122,423	35.9	2,991,655	2,940,042	52,705
1860 (June 1)	31,443,321	10.6	8,251,445	35.6	3,021,295	2,969,640	52,747
1870 (June 1)	[2]39,818,449	[2]11.2	8,375,128	26.6	3,612,299	3,540,705	52,747
1880 (June 1)	50,189,209	14.2	10,370,760	26.0	3,612,299	3,540,705	52,747
1890 (June 1)	62,979,766	17.8	12,790,557	25.5	3,612,299	3,540,705	52,747
1900 (June 1)	76,212,168	21.5	13,232,402	21.0	3,618,770	3,547,314	52,553
1910 (Apr. 15)	92,228,496	26.0	16,016,328	21.0	3,618,770	3,547,045	52,822
1920 (Jan. 1)	106,021,537	29.9	13,793,041	15.0	3,618,770	3,546,931	52,936
1930 (Apr. 1)	123,202,624	34.7	17,181,087	16.2	3,618,770	3,551,608	45,259
1940 (Apr. 1)	132,164,569	37.2	8,961,945	7.3	3,618,770	3,551,608	45,259
1950 (Apr. 1)	151,325,798	42.6	19,161,229	14.5	3,618,770	3,552,206	63,005
1960 (Apr. 1)	179,323,175	50.6	27,997,377	18.5	3,618,770	3,540,911	74,212
1970 (Apr. 1)	[3]203,302,031	[3]57.5	23,978,856	13.4	[3]3,536,855	[3]3,536,855	[3]78,444
1980 (Apr. 1)	[4]226,542,199	64.0	23,240,168	11.4	3,618,770	3,539,289	79,481
1990 (Apr. 1)	[5]248,718,302	70.3	22,176,103	9.8	[6]3,717,796	[6]3,536,278	[6]181,518
2000 (Apr. 1)	[7]281,423,231	79.6	32,704,929	13.1	3,794,083	3,537,439	256,645

X Not applicable. [1] Data for 1790 to 1980 cover inland water only. Data for 1990 comprise Great Lakes, inland, and coastal water. Data for 2000 comprise Great Lakes, inland, territorial and coastal water. [2] Revised to include adjustments for underenumeration in southern states; unrevised number is 38,558,371 (10.9 per square mile). [3] Figures corrected after 1970 final reports were issued. [4] Total population count has been revised since the 1980 census publications. Numbers by age, race, Hispanic origin, and sex have not been corrected. [5] The April 1, 1990 census count includes count question resolution corrections processed through December 1997, and does not include adjustments for census coverage errors. [6] Data reflect corrections made after publication of the results. [7] Reflects modifications to the Census 2000 population as documented in the Count Question Resolution program.

Source: U.S. Census Bureau, *1990 Census of Population and Housing, Population and Housing Unit Counts* (CPH-2); 1990 Census of Population and Housing Listing (1990 CPH-L-157); "Table NA-2003EST-01 - Monthly Population Estimates for the United States: April 1, 2000 to March 1, 2004"; published: 28 May 2004; <http://eire.census.gov/popest/data/national/tables/NA-EST2003-01.php>. Area data: 2000 Census of Population and Housing, *Summary Population and Housing Characteristics*, Series PHC-1; and unpublished data from TIGER (R).

No. 2. Population: 1960 to 2003

[In thousands, except percent (180,671 represents 180,671,000). Estimates as of July 1. Total population includes Armed Forces abroad; civilian population excludes Armed Forces. For basis of estimates, see text of this section]

Year	Total		Resident popula- tion	Civilian popula- tion	Year	Total		Resident popula- tion	Civilian popula- tion
	Popula- tion	Percent change [1]				Popula- tion	Percent change [1]		
1960	180,671	1.60	179,979	178,140	1982	232,188	0.97	231,664	229,995
1961	183,691	1.67	182,992	181,143	1983	234,307	0.91	233,792	232,097
1962	186,538	1.55	185,771	183,677	1984	236,348	0.87	235,825	234,110
1963	189,242	1.45	188,483	186,493	1985	238,466	0.90	237,924	236,219
1964	191,889	1.40	191,141	189,141	1986	240,651	0.92	240,133	238,412
1965	194,303	1.26	193,526	191,605	1987	242,804	0.89	242,289	240,550
1966	196,560	1.16	195,576	193,420	1988	245,021	0.91	244,499	242,817
1967	198,712	1.09	197,457	195,264	1989	247,342	0.95	246,819	245,131
1968	200,706	1.00	199,399	197,113	1990	250,132	1.13	249,623	247,983
1969	202,677	0.98	201,385	199,145	1991	253,493	1.34	252,981	251,370
1970	205,052	1.17	203,984	201,895	1992	256,894	1.34	256,514	254,929
1971	207,661	1.27	206,827	204,866	1993	260,255	1.31	259,919	258,428
1972	209,896	1.08	209,284	207,511	1994	263,436	1.22	263,126	261,714
1973	211,909	0.96	211,357	209,600	1995	266,557	1.18	266,278	264,927
1974	213,854	0.92	213,342	211,636	1996	269,667	1.17	269,394	268,108
1975	215,973	0.99	215,465	213,789	1997	272,912	1.20	272,647	271,394
1976	218,035	0.95	217,563	215,894	1998	276,115	1.17	275,854	274,633
1977	220,239	1.01	219,760	218,106	1999	279,295	1.15	279,040	277,841
1978	222,585	1.06	222,095	220,467	2000	282,388	1.11	282,178	280,954
1979	225,055	1.11	224,567	222,969	2001	285,321	1.04	285,094	283,879
1980	227,726	1.19	227,225	225,621	2002	288,205	1.01	287,974	286,728
1981	229,966	0.98	229,466	227,818	2003	291,049	0.99	290,810	289,558

[1] Percent change from immediate preceding year.

Source: U.S. Census Bureau, *Current Population Reports*, P25-802 and P25-1095; "Table CO-EST2001-12-00 - Time Series of Intercensal State Population Estimates: April 1, 1990 to April 1, 2000"; published 11 April 2002; <http://eire.census.gov/popest/data/counties/tables/CO-EST2001-12/CO-EST2001-12-00.php>; "Table NA-2003EST-01 - Monthly Population Estimates for the United States: April 1, 2000 to March 1, 2004"; published: 28 May 2004; <http://eire.census.gov/popest/data/national/tables/NA-EST2003-01.php>. and unpublished data.

No. 3. Resident Population Projections: 2004 to 2050

[292,801 represents 292,801,000. As of July 1. The projections are based on assumptions about future childbearing, mortality, and migration. The level of childbearing among women is assumed to remain close to present levels, with differences by race and Hispanic origin diminishing over time. Mortality is assumed to decline gradually with less variation by race and Hispanic origin than at present. International migration is assumed to vary over time and decrease generally relative to the size of the population]

Year	Number (1,000)	Percent change [1]	Year	Number (1,000)	Percent change [1]	Year	Number (1,000)	Percent change [1]
2004	292,801	0.9	2020	335,805	0.8	2036	380,716	0.7
2005	295,507	0.9	2021	338,490	0.8	2037	383,537	0.7
2006	298,217	0.9	2022	341,195	0.8	2038	386,348	0.7
2007	300,913	0.9	2023	343,921	0.8	2039	389,151	0.7
2008	303,598	0.9	2024	346,669	0.8	2040	391,946	0.7
2009	306,272	0.9	2025	349,439	0.8	2041	394,734	0.7
2010	308,936	0.9	2026	352,229	0.8	2042	397,519	0.7
2011.	311,601	0.9	2027	355,035	0.8	2043	400,301	0.7
2012	314,281	0.9	2028	357,862	0.8	2044	403,081	0.7
2013	316,971	0.9	2029	360,711	0.8	2045	405,862	0.7
2014	319,668	0.9	2030	363,584	0.8	2046	408,646	0.7
2015	322,366	0.8	2031	366,466	0.8	2047	411,435	0.7
2016	325,063	0.8	2032	369,336	0.8	2048	414,230	0.7
2017	327,756	0.8	2033	372,196	0.8	2049	417,035	0.7
2018	330,444	0.8	2034	375,046	0.8	2050	419,854	0.7
2019	333,127	0.8	2035	377,886	0.8			

[1] Percent change from immediate preceding year. 2004, change from 2003.

Source: U.S. Census Bureau, International Data Base, Table 094; published: 10 October 2002; <http://www.census.gov/ipc/www.idbprint.html>.

No. 4. Components of Population Change: 2000 to 2003

[In thousands (281,423 represents 281,423,000), except as indicated. Resident population]

Period	Population as of beginning of period	Net increase				Net international migration [2]	Population as of end of period
		Total	Per-cent [1]	Births	Deaths		
April 1, 2000 to July 1, 2000.	281,423	755	0.3	989	561	326	282,178
July 1, 2000 to July 1, 2001	282,178	2,916	1.0	4,047	2,419	1,288	285,094
July 1, 2001 to July 1, 2002	285,094	2,880	1.0	4,023	2,432	1,290	287,974
July 1, 2002 to July 1, 2003	287,974	2,836	1.0	4,027	2,477	1,286	290,810

[1] Percent of population at beginning of period.   [2] Includes legal migration, emigration, temporary migration, net movement from Puerto Rico, and net change in the residual foreign-born population (including unauthorized migration). Includes federal civilian movement.

Source: U.S. Census Bureau, "Table NA-EST2003-05 - Components of National Population Change: 2002 to 2003"; published 18 December 2003; <http://eire.census.gov/popest/data/states/tables/NST-EST2003-05.php>; "Table NA-EST2003-01 - Annual Population Estimates: 2000 to 2003"; published 18 December 2003; <http://eire.census.gov/popest/data/states/tables/NST-EST2003-01.php>; and "National and State population, population change, and estimated components of population change - downloadable dataset" <http://eire.census.gov/popest/natstdataset.csv>.

No. 5. Immigration: 1901 to 2002

[In thousands, except rate (8,795 represents 8,795,000). For fiscal years ending in year shown; see text, Section 8. For definition of immigrants, see text of this section. Data represent immigrants admitted. Rates based on Census Bureau estimates as of July 1 for resident population through 1929 and for total population thereafter (excluding Alaska and Hawaii prior to 1959)]

Period	Number	Rate [1]	Year	Number	Rate [1]
1901 to 1910	8,795	10.4	1990	1,536	6.1
1911 to 1920	5,736	5.7	1991	1,827	7.2
1921 to 1930	4,107	3.5	1992	974	3.8
			1993	904	3.5
1931 to 1940	528	0.4	1994	804	3.1
1941 to 1950	1,035	0.7	1995	720	2.7
1951 to 1960	2,515	1.5	1996	916	3.4
			1997	798	2.9
1961 to 1970	3,322	1.7	1998	654	2.4
1971 to 1980	4,493	2.1	1999	647	2.3
			2000	850	3.0
1981 to 1990	7,338	3.1	2001	1,064	3.7
1991 to 2000	9,095	3.4	2002	1,064	3.7

[1] Annual rate per 1,000 U.S. population. Rate computed by dividing sum of annual immigration totals by sum of annual U.S. population totals for same number of years.

Source: U.S. Dept. of Homeland Security, Office of Immigration Statistics, 2002 Yearbook of Immigration Statistics. See also <http://uscis.gov/graphics/shared/aboutus/statistics/ybpage.htm>.

No. 6. Immigrants Admitted by Class of Admission: 1990 to 2002

[For fiscal year ending September 30. For definition of immigrants, see text of this section]

Class of admission	1990	1995	1999	2000	2001	2002
Immigrants, total................	**1,536,483**	**720,461**	**646,568**	**849,807**	**1,064,318**	**1,063,732**
New arrivals......................	435,729	380,291	401,775	407,402	411,059	384,427
Adjustments......................	1,100,754	340,170	244,793	442,405	653,259	679,305
Preference immigrants, total.................	272,742	323,458	273,700	342,304	411,338	362,037
Family-sponsored immigrants, total...........	214,550	238,122	216,883	235,280	232,143	187,069
Unmarried sons/daughters of U.S. citizens and their children...............	15,861	15,182	22,392	27,707	27,098	23,567
Spouses, unmarried sons/daughters of alien residents, and their children	107,686	144,535	108,007	124,595	112,260	84,860
Married sons/daughters of U.S. citizens [1]......	26,751	20,876	24,040	22,833	24,878	21,072
Brothers or sisters of U.S. citizens [1]........	64,252	57,529	62,444	60,145	67,907	57,570
Employment-based immigrants, total...........	58,192	85,336	56,817	107,024	179,195	174,968
Priority workers [1]...................	(X)	17,339	14,898	27,706	41,801	34,452
Professionals with advanced degrees [1].......	(X)	10,475	8,581	20,304	42,620	44,468
Skilled workers, professionals, unskilled workers [1]..........	(X)	50,245	27,966	49,736	86,058	88,555
Special immigrants [1].................	4,463	6,737	5,086	9,052	8,523	7,344
Employment creation [1]...............	(X)	540	286	226	193	149
Professional or highly skilled immigrants [1] [2]....	26,546	(X)	(X)	(X)	(X)	(X)
Needed skilled or unskilled workers [1] [2].......	27,183	(X)	(X)	(X)	(X)	(X)
Immediate relatives......................	231,680	220,360	258,584	347,870	443,035	485,960
Spouses of U.S. citizens.................	125,426	123,238	127,988	197,525	270,545	294,798
Children of U.S. citizens..................	46,065	48,740	69,113	82,726	91,526	97,099
Orphans................	7,088	9,384	16,037	18,120	19,087	21,100
Parents of U.S. citizens	60,189	48,382	61,483	67,619	80,964	94,063
Refugees and asylees......................	97,364	114,664	42,852	65,941	108,506	126,084
Refugee adjustments...................	92,427	106,827	39,495	59,083	97,305	115,832
Asylee adjustments	4,937	7,837	3,357	6,858	11,201	10,252
Immigration Reform and Control Act of 1986 legalization adjustments...................	880,372	4,267	8	421	263	55
Other immigrants	54,325	57,712	71,424	93,271	101,176	89,596
Diversity Programs [3]................	29,161	47,245	47,571	50,945	42,015	42,829
Amerasians (P.L. 100-202) [4]..............	13,059	939	239	943	376	348
Children born abroad to alien residents........	2,410	1,894	978	1,009	929	788
Legalization dependents [5]...............	(X)	277	-	55	37	57
Nicaraguan Adjustment and Central American Relief Sec. 202 entrants (P.L. 105-100)	(X)	(X)	11,267	23,641	18,926	9,495
Cancellation of removal [6]	889	3,168	9,032	12,349	22,506	23,827
Other................................	8,806	4,189	2,337	4,329	16,387	12,252

- Represents zero.   X Not applicable.   [1] Includes spouses and children.   [2] Category was eliminated in 1992 by the Immigration Act of 1990.   [3] Includes categories of immigrants admitted under three laws intended to diversify immigration: P.L. 99-603, P.L. 100-658, and P.L. 101-649.   [4] Under Public Law 100-202, Amerasians are aliens born in Vietnam between January 1, 1962, and January 1, 1976, who were fathered by U.S. citizens.   [5] Spouses and children of persons granted permanent resident status under provisions of the Immigration Reform and Control Act of 1986.   [6] Was suspension of deportation prior to April 1, 1997.

Source: U.S. Dept. of Homeland Security, Office of Immigration Statistics, *2002 Yearbook of Immigration Statistics.* See also <http://uscis.gov/graphics/shared/aboutus/statistics/ybpage.htm>.

No. 7. Estimated Unauthorized Immigrants by Selected States and Countries of Origin: 2000

[In thousands (7,000 represents 7,000,000). As of January. Unauthorized immigrants refer to foreign-born persons who entered without inspection or who violated the terms of a temporary admission and who have not acquired legal permanent resident status or gained temporary protection against removal by applying for an immigration benefit. The estimates were derived using the residual technique: the legally resident population was estimated and then subtracted from the census-based foreign-born population, leaving estimated unauthorized residents as a residual. The estimates rely primarily on data from two sources: 1) annual INS statistics (immigrants admitted, deportable aliens removed, and nonimmigrant residents admitted); and 2) data for the foreign-born population from the 2000 Census. Estimates were derived separately for: (1) unauthorized residents who entered the United States in the 1990s; and (2) those who entered before 1990 and still lived here illegally in January 2000]

State	Number	Country	Number
United States, total [1]	**7,000**	**Total [1]**..................	**7,000**
California	2,209	Mexico	4,808
Texas.................	1,041	El Salvador	189
New York	489	Guatemala...............	144
Illinois	432	Colombia................	141
Florida	337	Honduras................	[2]138
Arizona.................	283	China	115
Georgia	228	Ecuador	108
New Jersey	221	Dominican Republic..........	91
North Carolina............	206	Philippines..............	85
Colorado................	144	Brazil	77
Washington...............	136	Haiti	76
Virginia.................	103	India	70
Nevada	101	Peru	61
Oregon.................	90	Korea	55
Massachusetts.............	87	Canada	47

[1] Includes other states and countries not shown separately.   [2] Includes 105,000 Hondurans granted temporary protected status in December 1998.

Source: U.S. Dept. of Homeland Security, Office of Immigration Statistics, *2002 Yearbook of Immigration Statistics.* See also <http://uscis.gov/graphics/shared/aboutus/statistics/ybpage.htm>.

Population 9

No. 8. Immigrants by Country of Birth: 1981 to 2002

[In thousands (7,338.1 represents 7,338,100). For fiscal years ending Sept. 30. For definition of immigrants, see text of this section]

Country of birth	1981-1990, total	1991-2000, total	2001	2002	Country of birth	1981-1990, total	1991-2000, total	2001	2002
All countries	7,338.1	9,095.4	1,064.3	1,063.7	Taiwan	([4])	106.4	12.2	9.8
Europe [1]	705.6	1,311.4	175.4	174.2	Thailand	64.4	48.4	4.3	4.2
Armenia	(X)	[2]26.6	1.8	1.8	Turkey	20.9	26.3	3.2	3.4
Belarus	(X)	[2]29.0	2.9	2.9	Vietnam	401.4	421.1	35.5	33.6
Bosnia and Herzegovina	(X)	[2]39.1	23.6	25.4	Africa [1]	192.3	383.0	53.9	60.3
France	23.1	27.5	4.6	3.8	Egypt	31.4	46.7	5.2	4.9
Germany	70.1	67.7	9.9	9.0	Ethiopia	27.2	49.3	5.1	7.6
Greece	29.1	13.6	1.2	1.0	Ghana	14.9	35.6	4.0	4.3
Ireland	32.8	59.0	1.5	1.4	Nigeria	35.3	67.3	8.3	8.1
Italy	32.9	22.6	3.1	2.6	South Africa	15.7	22.6	4.1	3.9
Poland	97.4	169.6	11.8	12.7	Oceania [1]	(NA)	48.0	6.1	5.6
Portugal	40.0	22.8	1.7	1.3	North America [1]	3,125.0	3,917.4	407.9	404.4
Romania	38.9	57.5	6.6	4.9	Canada	119.2	137.6	21.9	19.5
Russia	(X)	[2]128.0	20.4	20.8	Mexico	1,653.3	2,251.4	206.4	219.4
Soviet Union [3]	84.0	103.9	2.7	2.4	Caribbean [1]	892.7	996.1	103.5	96.5
Ukraine	(X)	[2]141.3	21.0	21.2	Cuba	159.2	180.9	27.7	28.3
United Kingdom	142.1	135.8	18.4	16.4	Dominican Republic	251.8	340.9	21.3	22.6
Yugoslavia [3]	19.2	25.9	6.2	10.4	Haiti	140.2	181.8	27.1	20.3
Asia [1]	2,817.4	2,892.2	349.8	342.1	Jamaica	213.8	173.5	15.4	14.9
Afghanistan	26.6	17.4	1.2	1.8	Trinidad and Tobago	39.5	63.3	6.7	5.8
Bangladesh	15.2	66.0	7.2	5.5	Central America [1]	458.7	531.8	75.9	69.0
Cambodia	116.6	18.5	2.5	2.8	El Salvador	214.6	217.4	31.3	31.2
China	[4]388.8	424.6	56.4	61.3	Guatemala	87.9	103.1	13.6	16.2
Hong Kong	63.0	74.0	8.3	6.1	Honduras	49.5	66.8	6.6	6.5
India	261.9	383.3	70.3	71.1	Nicaragua	44.1	97.7	19.9	10.9
Iran	154.8	112.6	10.5	13.0	Panama	29.0	24.0	1.9	1.7
Iraq	19.6	40.7	5.0	5.2	South America [1]	455.9	539.9	68.9	74.5
Israel	36.3	32.0	3.8	3.9	Argentina	25.7	24.3	3.3	3.7
Japan	43.2	61.5	9.6	8.3	Brazil	23.7	52.3	9.5	9.5
Jordan	32.6	39.7	4.6	4.0	Chile	23.4	16.9	1.9	1.9
Korea	338.8	171.3	20.7	21.0	Colombia	124.4	131.0	16.7	18.8
Laos	145.6	43.6	1.4	1.3	Ecuador	56.0	76.4	9.7	10.6
Lebanon	41.6	43.5	4.6	4.0	Guyana	95.4	73.9	8.3	10.0
Pakistan	61.3	124.6	16.4	13.7	Peru	64.4	105.7	11.1	12.0
Philippines	495.3	505.6	53.2	51.3	Venezuela	17.9	29.9	5.2	5.3
Syria	20.6	26.1	3.4	2.6					

NA Not available.   X Not applicable.   [1] Includes countries not shown separately.   [2] Covers years 1992-2000.   [3] Prior to 1992, data include independent republics; beginning in 1992, data are for unknown republic only.   [4] Data for Taiwan included with China.

Source: U.S. Dept. of Homeland Security, Office of Immigration Statistics, *2002 Yearbook of Immigration Statistics*. See also <http://uscis.gov/graphics/shared/aboutus/statistics/ybpage.htm>.

No. 9. Immigrants Admitted as Permanent Residents Under Refugee Acts by Country of Birth: 1991 to 2002

[For fiscal years ending September 30]

Country of birth	1991-2000, total	2001	2002	Country of birth	1991-2000, total	2001	2002
Total [1]	1,021,266	108,506	126,084	Afghanistan	9,725	257	1,044
Europe [1]	426,565	55,825	62,911	Cambodia	6,388	75	47
Albania	3,255	114	170	China [4]	7,608	813	695
Azerbaijan	[2]12,072	476	497	India	2,544	942	1,558
Belarus	[2]24,581	1,548	1,446	Iran	24,313	1,364	4,806
Bosnia and Herzegovina	[2]37,591	23,303	25,033	Iraq	22,557	3,060	3,434
Croatia	1,807	2,337	3,315	Laos	37,265	520	374
Georgia	[2]2,593	178	174	Thailand	22,759	653	498
Germany	1,309	1,345	1,889	Vietnam	206,857	10,351	6,926
Kazakhstan	[2]4,269	659	648	Africa [1]	51,649	6,906	13,454
Latvia	2,757	175	154	Ethiopia [5]	17,865	881	1,897
Moldova	[2]11,717	1,322	1,336	Liberia	3,839	976	1,680
Poland	7,500	71	54	Somalia	16,837	2,484	4,084
Romania	15,708	119	85	Sudan	5,191	593	1,987
Russia	60,404	4,758	5,089	Oceania [1]	291	19	33
Soviet Union [3]	90,533	1,621	1,508	North America [1]	185,333	24,696	26,807
Tajikistan	[2]2,546	100	53	Cuba	144,612	22,687	24,893
Ukraine	[2]109,739	11,130	10,601	Haiti	9,364	735	769
Uzbekistan	[2]19,539	1,099	1,038	El Salvador	4,073	195	187
Yugoslavia [3]	6,274	4,190	8,556	Nicaragua	22,486	350	281
Asia [1]	351,347	19,992	21,414	South America [1]	5,857	936	1,222
				Peru	2,507	399	402

[1] Includes other countries and unknown, not shown separately.   [2] Covers years 1992-2000.   [3] Prior to 1992, data include independent republics; beginning in 1992, data are for unknown republic only.   [4] Includes Taiwan.   [5] Prior to 1993, data include Eritrea.

Source: U.S. Dept. of Homeland Security, Office of Immigration Statistics, *2002 Yearbook of Immigration Statistics*. See also <http://uscis.gov/graphics/shared/aboutus/statistics/ybpage.htm>.

No. 10. Immigrants Admitted by State and Leading Country of Birth: 2002

[For year ending September 30. For definition of immigrants, see text of this section]

State and other area	Total [1]	Mexico	India	China	Philip-pines	Vietnam	El Salvador	Cuba	Bosnia and Herze-govina
Total	1,063,732	219,380	71,105	61,282	51,308	33,627	31,168	28,272	25,373
Alabama.	2,570	396	215	212	110	103	10	23	43
Alaska	1,564	99	16	66	462	17	26	2	4
Arizona.	17,719	8,415	651	519	425	356	127	183	1,189
Arkansas	2,535	1,163	200	92	58	92	148	3	5
California	291,216	105,699	18,265	19,494	21,971	13,126	13,497	548	901
Colorado.	12,060	3,808	606	703	225	468	119	14	390
Connecticut.	11,243	276	968	577	315	234	67	34	621
Delaware	1,862	135	324	119	106	17	12	7	2
District of Columbia	2,723	29	115	148	180	46	521	3	16
Florida	90,819	3,822	1,652	1,022	1,897	887	665	22,262	2,074
Georgia	20,555	3,008	1,616	758	408	1,191	175	129	1,494
Hawaii	5,503	67	14	538	2,800	210	1	1	1
Idaho	2,236	678	66	161	40	39	4	-	370
Illinois	47,235	11,461	5,197	2,768	2,451	594	266	128	1,926
Indiana.	6,853	1,465	531	494	216	140	101	11	380
Iowa	5,591	1,005	211	186	154	293	74	5	1,658
Kansas.	4,508	1,650	334	310	139	283	100	9	75
Kentucky	4,681	441	275	207	121	101	23	506	840
Louisiana	3,199	197	195	190	86	379	25	90	67
Maine.	1,269	6	44	89	83	42	11	2	56
Maryland	23,751	616	1,785	1,755	1,209	467	1,514	43	138
Massachusetts.	31,615	284	2,323	2,780	441	1,471	866	92	427
Michigan.	21,787	1,325	2,756	1,448	560	396	34	305	1,667
Minnesota.	13,522	756	1,001	704	399	601	132	21	442
Mississippi	1,155	182	98	91	78	74	5	16	7
Missouri	8,610	838	484	554	271	339	62	54	1,828
Montana.	422	24	9	29	24	7	-	1	-
Nebraska	3,657	1,352	175	128	58	210	75	11	174
Nevada	9,499	3,452	167	317	1,186	142	474	491	179
New Hampshire.	3,009	73	304	219	118	53	9	2	345
New Jersey.	57,721	1,209	9,683	2,966	3,111	557	933	1,274	293
New Mexico	3,399	1,988	86	124	96	117	19	96	13
New York	114,827	2,250	4,728	9,872	2,319	760	5,123	449	1,483
North Carolina	12,910	2,247	1,005	612	456	615	245	74	460
North Dakota.	776	6	8	15	18	7	-	1	210
Ohio	13,875	543	1,734	1,100	372	359	29	16	828
Oklahoma	4,229	1,524	261	145	148	310	25	6	17
Oregon.	12,125	3,111	523	795	361	651	74	251	211
Pennsylvania.	19,473	883	2,473	1,650	482	957	54	108	737
Rhode Island.	3,067	65	64	118	57	30	61	5	6
South Carolina.	2,966	288	310	188	157	116	13	14	12
South Dakota	902	59	41	49	22	13	7	2	96
Tennessee	5,694	791	426	308	219	249	43	87	211
Texas.	88,365	44,694	4,294	2,561	2,258	3,704	3,289	660	1,041
Utah	4,889	1,288	102	207	99	146	71	6	643
Vermont	1,007	9	45	67	19	41	1	-	269
Virginia.	25,411	749	2,928	1,527	1,247	1,017	1,878	88	532
Washington.	25,704	3,650	1,108	1,586	1,573	1,499	131	10	659
West Virginia.	636	31	89	65	50	7	3	-	-
Wisconsin.	6,498	1,123	568	452	185	84	14	14	333
Wyoming	281	80	7	26	8	1	-	-	-
Guam	1,698	-	7	59	1,351	4	-	-	-
Northern Mariana Islands	138	-	-	23	74	-	-	-	-
Puerto Rico.	3,071	67	-	86	11	2	12	112	-
Virgin Islands.	994	2	18	2	2	1	-	3	-
Armed Services posts . . .	100	1	-	1	21	2	-	-	-
Unknown	8	-	-	-	1	-	-	-	-

- Represents zero. [1] Includes other countries, not shown separately.

Source: U.S. Dept. of Homeland Security, Office of Immigration Statistics, *2002 Yearbook of Immigration Statistics*. See also <http://uscis.gov/graphics/shared/aboutus/statistics/ybpage.htm>.

Population 11

No. 11. Resident Population by Age and Sex: 1980 to 2003

[In thousands, except as indicated (226,546 represents 226,546,000). 1980, 1990, and 2000 data are enumerated population as of April 1; data for other years are estimated population as of July 1. Excludes Armed Forces overseas. For definition of median, see Guide to Tabular Presentation]

Age group	1980 Total[1]	1980 Male	1980 Female	1990[2] Total	1990[2] Male	1990[2] Female	1995 total	1996 total	1997 total	1998 total	1999 total	2000 Total	2000 Male	2000 Female	2001 total	2002 total	2003 Total	2003 Male	2003 Female
Total	226,546	110,053	116,493	248,791	121,284	127,507	266,278	269,394	272,647	275,854	279,040	281,422	136,054	143,368	285,094	287,974	290,810	143,037	147,773
Under 5 years .	16,348	8,362	7,986	18,765	9,603	9,162	19,627	19,408	19,233	19,145	19,136	19,176	9,811	9,365	19,364	19,576	19,769	10,105	9,664
5 to 9 years .	16,700	8,539	8,161	18,042	9,236	8,806	19,438	19,861	20,254	20,510	20,606	20,550	10,523	10,026	20,238	19,960	19,775	10,120	9,655
10 to 14 years .	18,242	9,316	8,926	17,067	8,742	8,325	19,207	19,435	19,601	19,825	20,213	20,528	10,520	10,008	20,882	21,094	21,193	10,857	10,337
15 to 19 years .	21,168	10,755	10,413	17,893	9,178	8,714	18,374	18,920	19,398	19,840	20,085	20,220	10,391	9,829	20,477	20,348	20,477	10,519	9,959
20 to 24 years .	21,319	10,663	10,655	19,143	9,749	9,394	18,300	17,877	17,910	18,167	18,591	18,964	9,688	9,276	19,777	20,330	20,728	10,664	10,064
25 to 29 years .	19,521	9,705	9,816	21,336	10,708	10,629	19,680	19,864	19,899	19,804	19,575	19,381	9,799	9,583	19,168	18,902	18,969	9,773	9,196
30 to 34 years .	17,561	8,677	8,884	21,838	10,866	10,973	22,372	21,945	21,446	20,953	20,603	20,510	10,322	10,189	20,714	20,813	20,705	10,450	10,255
35 to 39 years .	13,965	6,862	7,104	19,851	9,837	10,014	22,492	22,786	22,904	22,926	22,883	22,707	11,319	11,388	22,259	21,806	21,408	10,727	10,681
40 to 44 years .	11,669	5,708	5,961	17,593	8,679	8,914	20,219	20,766	21,325	21,822	22,194	22,442	11,129	11,313	22,791	22,942	22,963	11,407	11,555
45 to 49 years .	11,090	5,388	5,702	13,747	6,741	7,006	17,624	18,611	18,687	19,114	19,654	20,092	9,890	10,203	20,779	21,264	21,761	10,731	11,030
50 to 54 years .	11,710	5,621	6,089	11,315	5,494	5,821	13,856	14,189	15,491	16,118	16,924	17,586	8,608	8,978	18,421	18,765	19,043	9,313	9,731
55 to 59 years .	11,615	5,482	6,133	10,489	5,009	5,480	11,182	11,481	11,905	12,589	13,085	13,469	6,509	6,961	14,188	14,973	15,794	7,661	8,133
60 to 64 years .	10,088	4,670	5,418	10,627	4,947	5,679	10,138	10,109	10,194	10,422	10,693	10,805	5,137	5,669	11,112	11,596	12,106	5,764	6,342
65 to 74 years .	15,581	6,757	8,824	18,048	7,908	10,140	18,866	18,824	18,684	18,570	18,419	18,391	8,303	10,088	18,329	18,293	18,337	8,349	9,988
75 to 84 years .	7,729	2,867	4,862	10,014	3,745	6,268	11,222	11,524	11,812	12,016	12,225	12,361	4,879	7,482	12,579	12,744	12,869	5,154	7,714
85 years and over ..	2,240	682	1,559	3,022	841	2,181	3,681	3,795	3,905	4,033	4,154	4,240	1,227	3,013	4,430	4,570	4,713	1,445	3,269
5 to 13 years ..	31,159	15,923	15,237	31,839	16,301	15,538	34,825	35,375	35,915	36,454	36,804	37,025	18,964	18,061	37,059	36,952	36,752	18,816	17,936
14 to 17 years ..	16,247	8,298	7,950	13,345	6,860	6,485	15,013	15,443	15,769	15,829	16,007	16,093	8,285	7,808	16,181	16,319	16,522	8,469	8,053
18 to 24 years ..	30,022	15,054	14,969	26,961	13,744	13,217	25,482	25,275	25,479	26,059	26,685	27,143	13,874	13,270	27,919	28,461	28,900	14,875	14,025
18 years and over ..	162,791	77,473	85,321	184,841	88,519	96,322	196,814	199,169	201,730	204,426	207,094	209,128	100,994	108,134	212,490	215,127	217,766	105,647	112,119
55 years and over ..	47,253	20,458	26,796	52,200	22,450	29,748	55,089	55,733	56,501	57,630	58,576	59,266	26,055	33,211	60,638	62,176	63,819	28,373	35,446
65 years and over ..	25,550	10,306	15,245	31,084	12,494	18,589	33,769	34,143	34,402	34,619	34,798	34,992	14,410	20,582	35,338	35,608	35,919	14,948	20,971
75 years and over ..	9,969	3,549	6,421	13,036	4,586	8,449	14,903	15,319	15,718	16,049	16,379	16,601	6,106	10,494	17,009	17,314	17,582	6,599	10,983
Median age (years) ..	30.0	28.8	31.3	32.8	31.6	34.0	34.2	34.4	34.7	34.9	35.2	35.3	34.0	36.5	35.5	35.7	35.9	34.5	37.1

[1] Total population count has been revised since the 1980 census publications. Numbers by age and sex have not been corrected. [2] The data shown have been modified from the official 1990 census counts. See text of this section for explanation. The April 1, 1990, estimates base (248,790,925) includes count resolution corrections processed through August 1997. It generally does not include adjustments for census coverage errors. However, it includes adjustments estimated for the 1995 Test Census in various localities in California, New Jersey, and Louisiana; and the 1998 census dress rehearsals in localities in California and Wisconsin. These adjustments amounted to a total of 81,052 persons.

Source: U.S. Census Bureau, Current Population Reports, P25-1095; and "Intercensal Estimates of the United States Resident Population by Age Groups and Sex, 1990-2000"; published 13 September 2002; <http://eire.census.gov/popest/data/national/tables/intercensal/US-EST90INT-04.php>; and "Table NC-EST2003-01 - Annual Estimates of the Population by Sex and Five-Year Age Groups for the United States: April 1, 2000 to July 1, 2003;" and "Table NC-EST2003-02 - Annual Estimates of the Population by Sex and Selected Age Groups for the United States: April 1, 2000 to July 1, 2003;" published 10 June 2004; <http://eire.census.gov/popest/data/national/tables/NC-EST2003-as.php>.

No. 12. Resident Population Projections by Sex and Age: 2005 to 2050

[In thousands, except as indicated (295,507 represents 295,507,000). As of July. Data shown are for middle series; for assumptions, see Table 3. For definition of median, see Guide to Tabular Presentation]

Age	2005			2010			2015	2020	2025	2030	2035	2040	2045	2050	Percent distribution									
	Total	Male	Female	Total	Male	Female									2005	2010	2015	2020	2025	2030	2035	2040	2045	2050
Total	295,507	145,113	150,394	308,936	151,815	157,121	322,366	335,805	349,439	363,584	377,886	391,946	405,862	419,854	100.0	100.0	100.0	100.0	100.0	100.0	100.0	100.0	100.0	100.0
Under 5 years	20,495	10,471	10,024	21,426	10,947	10,479	22,358	22,932	23,518	24,272	25,262	26,299	27,233	28,080	6.9	6.9	6.9	6.8	6.7	6.7	6.7	6.7	6.7	6.7
5 to 9 years	19,467	9,954	9,512	20,706	10,575	10,131	21,623	22,564	23,163	23,790	24,562	25,550	26,586	27,521	6.6	6.7	6.7	6.7	6.6	6.5	6.5	6.5	6.6	6.6
10 to 14 years	20,838	10,670	10,167	19,767	10,109	9,658	20,984	21,914	22,888	23,539	24,186	24,953	25,938	26,974	7.1	6.4	6.5	6.5	6.5	6.5	6.4	6.4	6.4	6.4
15 to 19 years	21,172	10,862	10,310	21,336	10,938	10,398	20,243	21,478	22,052	23,503	24,182	24,824	25,534	26,572	7.2	6.9	6.3	6.4	6.3	6.5	6.4	6.3	6.3	6.3
20 to 24 years	20,823	10,657	10,166	21,676	11,075	10,602	21,810	20,751	22,457	23,136	24,227	24,897	25,587	26,297	7.0	7.0	6.8	6.2	6.4	6.4	6.4	6.4	6.3	6.3
25 to 29 years	19,753	10,016	9,737	21,375	10,868	10,507	22,195	21,478	21,390	22,810	23,943	25,024	25,690	26,327	6.7	6.9	6.9	6.4	6.1	6.3	6.3	6.4	6.3	6.3
30 to 34 years	19,847	9,987	9,860	20,271	10,238	10,034	21,858	22,704	22,361	22,125	23,605	24,731	25,808	26,477	6.7	6.5	6.8	6.8	6.4	6.1	6.2	6.3	6.4	6.3
35 to 39 years	20,869	10,449	10,420	20,137	10,091	10,046	20,543	22,143	22,955	23,399	23,669	24,101	25,223	26,300	7.1	6.5	6.4	6.6	6.6	6.4	6.3	6.2	6.2	6.3
40 to 44 years	22,735	11,282	11,452	20,984	10,462	10,523	20,250	20,673	22,305	23,277	23,350	23,747	24,376	25,496	7.7	6.8	6.3	6.2	6.4	6.4	6.2	6.1	6.0	6.1
45 to 49 years	22,453	11,076	11,377	22,654	11,190	11,464	20,926	20,219	20,678	23,669	24,241	23,001	23,001	24,466	7.6	7.3	6.5	6.0	5.9	6.5	6.4	5.9	5.7	5.8
50 to 54 years	19,983	9,771	10,212	22,173	10,874	11,299	22,376	20,702	20,043	23,350	23,641	24,376	23,001	22,917	6.8	7.2	6.9	6.2	5.8	6.4	6.3	6.2	6.0	5.5
55 to 59 years	17,359	8,415	8,944	19,507	9,456	10,051	21,649	21,876	20,291	22,352	20,241	23,747	24,376	23,384	5.9	6.3	6.7	6.5	5.8	6.1	5.4	6.1	6.0	5.6
60 to 64 years	13,017	6,203	6,814	16,679	7,982	8,696	18,761	20,856	21,128	20,550	19,156	21,910	21,370	22,384	4.4	5.4	5.8	6.2	6.0	5.7	5.1	5.6	5.3	5.3
65 to 69 years	10,123	4,712	5,412	12,172	5,686	6,486	15,621	17,618	19,647	19,702	18,683	19,719	18,829	20,444	3.4	3.9	4.8	5.2	5.6	5.4	4.9	5.0	4.6	4.9
70 to 74 years	8,500	3,804	4,697	9,097	4,111	4,987	10,987	14,161	16,041	17,968	18,350	17,233	16,879	17,499	2.9	2.9	3.4	4.2	4.6	4.9	4.7	4.4	4.2	4.2
75 to 79 years	7,376	3,094	4,282	7,186	3,066	4,120	7,761	9,450	12,268	13,989	15,764	16,192	15,304	15,067	2.5	2.3	2.4	2.8	3.5	3.8	4.3	4.1	3.8	3.6
80 to 84 years	5,576	2,117	3,459	5,665	2,206	3,459	5,600	6,134	7,557	9,914	11,414	12,978	13,449	12,835	1.9	1.8	1.7	1.8	2.2	2.7	3.1	3.3	3.3	3.1
85 to 89 years	3,206	1,072	2,135	3,713	1,274	2,439	3,857	3,897	4,353	5,451	7,259	8,476	9,768	10,254	1.1	1.2	1.2	1.2	1.2	1.5	1.9	2.1	2.4	2.4
90 to 94 years	1,431	397	1,034	1,727	510	1,218	2,069	2,221	2,312	2,651	3,395	4,621	5,510	6,473	0.5	0.6	0.6	0.7	0.7	0.7	0.9	1.2	1.4	1.5
95 to 99 years	412	91	321	569	137	432	723	909	1,018	1,102	1,310	1,731	2,430	2,984	0.1	0.2	0.2	0.3	0.3	0.3	0.3	0.5	0.6	0.7
100 years and over	71	12	58	114	21	93	173	241	327	399	467	581	790	1,150	(Z)	(Z)	0.1	0.1	0.1	0.1	0.1	0.1	0.2	0.3
5 to 13 years	35,968	18,402	17,566	36,439	18,618	17,821	38,418	40,148	41,501	42,627	43,922	45,536	47,379	49,138	12.2	11.8	11.9	12.0	11.9	11.7	11.6	11.6	11.7	11.7
14 to 17 years	17,175	8,809	8,366	16,566	8,492	8,074	16,243	17,220	18,079	18,800	19,311	19,847	20,505	21,330	5.8	5.4	5.0	5.1	5.2	5.2	5.1	5.1	5.1	5.1
18 to 24 years	29,156	14,931	14,225	30,481	15,587	14,894	30,000	29,339	30,980	32,533	33,924	34,841	35,763	36,895	9.9	9.9	9.3	8.7	8.9	8.9	9.0	8.9	8.8	8.8
16 years and over	230,335	111,774	118,561	242,936	118,082	124,854	253,361	264,085	275,339	287,281	299,051	310,182	320,974	331,940	77.9	78.6	78.6	78.6	78.8	79.0	79.1	79.1	79.1	79.1
18 years and over	221,868	107,430	114,438	234,504	113,758	120,746	245,347	255,505	266,341	277,877	289,391	300,264	310,746	321,305	75.1	75.9	76.1	76.1	76.2	76.4	76.6	76.6	76.5	76.5
16 to 64 years	193,639	96,475	97,164	202,693	101,071	101,622	206,570	209,453	211,815	215,828	222,410	230,132	238,015	245,234	65.5	65.6	64.1	62.4	60.6	59.4	58.9	58.7	58.7	58.4
55 years and over	67,072	29,916	37,156	76,429	34,450	41,980	87,201	97,363	104,944	110,831	116,039	121,679	127,245	132,427	22.7	24.7	27.1	29.0	30.0	30.5	30.7	31.0	31.4	31.5
65 years and over	36,696	15,299	21,397	40,244	17,011	23,233	46,791	54,632	63,524	71,453	76,641	80,050	82,959	86,706	12.4	13.0	14.5	16.3	18.2	19.7	20.3	20.4	20.4	20.7
75 years and over	18,072	6,783	11,289	18,974	7,214	11,761	20,183	22,852	27,835	33,506	39,609	44,579	47,251	48,763	6.1	6.1	6.3	6.8	8.0	9.2	10.5	11.4	11.6	11.6
85 years and over	5,120	1,572	3,548	6,123	1,942	4,182	6,822	7,269	8,011	9,603	12,430	15,409	18,498	20,861	1.7	2.0	2.1	2.2	2.3	2.6	3.3	3.9	4.6	5.0
Median age (years)	35.2	34.0	36.6	36.0	34.6	37.4	36.4	37.0	37.5	38.0	38.2	38.1	38.1	38.1	(X)	(X)	(X)	(X)	(X)	(X)	(X)	(X)	(X)	(X)

X Not applicable. Z Less than 0.05 percent.

Source: U.S. Census Bureau, International Data Base; published 10 October 2002; <http://www.census.gov/ipc/www/idbprint.html>.

No. 13. Resident Population by Sex, Race, and Hispanic Origin Status: 2000 to 2003

[281,422 represents 281,422,000. **As of July, except as noted**. Data shown are modified race counts; see text of this section]

Characteristic	Number (1,000) 2000 (April 1)	2000	2001	2002	2003	Percent change, 2000 to 2003
BOTH SEXES						
Total	281,422	282,178	285,094	287,974	290,810	3.3
One race	277,524	278,250	281,040	283,794	286,502	3.2
White	228,104	228,610	230,502	232,369	234,196	2.7
Black or African American	35,704	35,810	36,247	36,676	37,099	3.9
American Indian and Alaska Native	2,664	2,673	2,711	2,749	2,787	4.6
Asian	10,589	10,691	11,105	11,515	11,925	12.6
Native Hawaiian and Other Pacific Islanders	463	465	475	485	495	7.1
Two or more races	3,898	3,928	4,053	4,180	4,308	10.5
Race alone or in combination: [1]						
White	231,434	231,968	233,973	235,956	237,899	2.8
Black or African American	37,104	37,228	37,742	38,248	38,749	4.4
American Indian and Alaska Native	4,225	4,236	4,280	4,323	4,366	3.3
Asian	12,007	12,121	12,584	13,043	13,503	12.5
Native Hawaiian and Other Pacific Islanders	907	911	927	943	960	5.8
Not Hispanic or Latino	246,116	246,528	248,032	249,486	250,911	1.9
One race	242,710	243,096	244,496	245,845	247,164	1.8
White	195,575	195,757	196,314	196,833	197,326	0.9
Black or African American	34,313	34,410	34,811	35,205	35,593	3.7
American Indian and Alaska Native	2,097	2,104	2,130	2,155	2,180	4.0
Asian	10,357	10,457	10,865	11,269	11,673	12.7
Native Hawaiian and Other Pacific Islanders	367	369	376	383	391	6.4
Two or more races	3,406	3,431	3,536	3,640	3,747	10.0
Race alone or in combination: [1]						
White	198,476	198,680	199,332	199,945	200,535	1.0
Black or African American	35,498	35,610	36,076	36,534	36,989	4.2
American Indian and Alaska Native	3,456	3,462	3,491	3,518	3,546	2.6
Asian	11,632	11,743	12,194	12,641	13,089	12.5
Native Hawaiian and Other Pacific Islanders	752	755	767	779	791	5.2
Hispanic or Latino	35,306	35,650	37,062	38,488	39,899	13.0
One race	34,814	35,153	36,544	37,949	39,338	13.0
White	32,529	32,853	34,187	35,536	36,870	13.3
Black or African American	1,391	1,400	1,436	1,471	1,506	8.2
American Indian and Alaska Native	566	570	582	594	606	7.1
Asian	232	234	240	246	251	8.2
Native Hawaiian and Other Pacific Islanders	95	96	99	102	105	9.7
Two or more races	491	497	518	539	561	14.1
Race alone or in combination: [1]						
White	32,959	33,288	34,641	36,011	37,364	13.4
Black or African American	1,606	1,618	1,666	1,713	1,760	9.6
American Indian and Alaska Native	770	774	789	805	820	6.6
Asian	375	378	390	402	414	10.3
Native Hawaiian and Other Pacific Islanders	155	156	160	165	169	9.0
MALE						
Total	138,054	138,456	140,009	141,533	143,037	3.6
One race	136,143	136,531	138,019	139,480	140,919	3.5
White	112,476	112,754	113,796	114,819	115,821	3.0
Black or African American	16,971	17,025	17,245	17,459	17,672	4.1
American Indian and Alaska Native	1,333	1,338	1,357	1,376	1,396	4.7
Asian	5,128	5,178	5,379	5,579	5,779	12.7
Native Hawaiian and Other Pacific Islanders	235	236	242	247	252	7.2
Two or more races	1,910	1,926	1,990	2,053	2,118	10.9
Race alone or in combination: [1]						
White	114,114	114,406	115,506	116,586	117,648	3.1
Black or African American	17,643	17,706	17,965	18,218	18,471	4.7
American Indian and Alaska Native	2,088	2,094	2,116	2,138	2,160	3.4
Asian	5,834	5,890	6,117	6,341	6,566	12.5
Native Hawaiian and Other Pacific Islanders	456	458	466	475	483	5.8
Not Hispanic or Latino	119,892	120,109	120,912	121,682	122,438	2.1
Hispanic or Latino	18,162	18,348	19,097	19,852	20,599	13.4
FEMALE						
Total	143,368	143,721	145,085	146,441	147,773	3.1
One race	141,381	141,719	143,021	144,314	145,583	3.0
White	115,628	115,856	116,705	117,550	118,375	2.4
Black or African American	18,733	18,785	19,002	19,217	19,427	3.7
American Indian and Alaska Native	1,331	1,336	1,354	1,373	1,391	4.5
Asian	5,462	5,514	5,726	5,936	6,146	12.5
Native Hawaiian and Other Pacific Islanders	227	229	233	238	243	7.0
Two or more races	1,987	2,002	2,064	2,126	2,189	10.2
Race alone or in combination: [1]						
White	117,321	117,562	118,468	119,369	120,251	2.5
Black or African American	19,461	19,522	19,777	20,029	20,278	4.2
American Indian and Alaska Native	2,137	2,142	2,164	2,185	2,206	3.2
Asian	6,173	6,231	6,467	6,702	6,937	12.4
Native Hawaiian and Other Pacific Islanders	451	453	461	469	477	5.8
Not Hispanic or Latino	126,224	126,419	127,120	127,804	128,473	1.8
Hispanic or Latino	17,144	17,302	17,965	18,637	19,300	12.6

[1] 'In combination' means in combination with one or more other races. The sum of the five race groups adds to more than the total population because individuals may report more than one race.

Source: U.S. Census Bureau, "Annual Estimates of the Population by Sex, Race and Hispanic or Latino Origin for the United States: April 1, 2000 to July 1, 2003 (NC-EST2003-03)"; published 14 June 2004; <http://eire.census.gov/popest/data/national/tables/NC-EST2003-srh.php>.

No. 14. Resident Population by Race, Hispanic Origin, and Age: 2000 and 2003

[In thousands (281,422 represents 281,422,000); except as indicated. 2000 as of April and 2003 as of July. For definition of median, see Guide to Tabular Presentation. See headnote, Table 13]

Age group	Total		White alone		Black or African American alone		American Indian, Alaska Native alone		Asian alone		Native Hawaiian, Other Pacific Islander alone		Two or more races		Hispanic or Latino origin [1]		Not Hispanic or Latino White alone	
	2000	2003	2000	2003	2000	2003	2000	2003	2000	2003	2000	2003	2000	2003	2000	2003	2000	2003
Total	281,422	290,810	228,104	234,196	35,704	37,099	2,664	2,787	10,589	11,925	463	495	3,898	4,308	35,306	39,899	195,575	197,326
Under 5 years	19,176	19,769	14,656	15,119	2,925	2,998	233	208	708	777	41	35	613	632	3,718	4,158	11,287	11,250
5 to 9 years	20,550	19,775	15,687	15,098	3,320	3,048	258	239	716	767	44	43	524	579	3,624	3,830	12,392	11,614
10 to 14 years	20,528	21,193	15,842	16,192	3,221	3,415	264	270	715	769	42	45	443	503	3,163	3,661	12,961	12,857
15 to 19 years	20,220	20,477	15,746	15,862	3,024	3,115	251	261	776	778	44	43	380	418	3,172	3,247	12,837	12,891
20 to 24 years	18,964	20,728	14,827	16,135	2,729	3,023	218	247	848	912	46	48	297	363	3,409	3,747	11,682	12,680
25 to 29 years	19,381	19,168	15,217	14,944	2,645	2,624	204	213	1,019	1,062	42	46	254	279	3,385	3,799	12,077	11,419
30 to 34 years	20,510	20,705	16,348	16,263	2,710	2,739	202	208	980	1,195	39	42	231	257	3,125	3,580	13,451	12,938
35 to 39 years	22,707	21,408	18,371	17,076	2,910	2,800	217	209	937	1,053	38	39	233	231	2,825	3,175	15,752	14,130
40 to 44 years	22,442	22,963	18,346	18,628	2,772	2,875	202	214	870	975	38	37	219	233	2,304	2,741	16,213	16,087
45 to 49 years	20,092	21,761	16,615	17,844	2,330	2,600	169	191	770	887	33	31	183	208	1,775	2,170	14,972	15,835
50 to 54 years	17,586	19,043	14,793	15,794	1,846	2,134	135	155	641	766	27	25	149	169	1,361	1,649	13,530	14,267
55 to 59 years	13,469	15,794	11,479	13,395	1,332	1,559	95	117	443	572	21	19	106	132	960	1,215	10,581	12,264
60 to 64 years	10,805	12,106	9,214	10,329	1,082	1,169	70	83	350	418	15	13	78	93	750	873	8,511	9,513
65 to 69 years	9,534	9,746	8,238	8,335	895	943	52	60	279	330	11	10	61	68	599	683	7,675	7,695
70 to 74 years	8,857	8,591	7,799	7,480	742	747	38	44	224	260	8	7	49	52	477	539	7,348	6,972
75 to 79 years	7,416	7,453	6,634	6,601	557	581	27	31	159	193	6	5	36	40	327	397	6,325	6,227
80 to 84 years	4,945	5,416	4,466	4,856	350	390	15	20	90	121	4	5	22	26	180	244	4,296	4,626
85 to 89 years	2,790	3,003	2,525	2,715	200	203	8	10	43	59	2	3	12	14	98	119	2,432	2,603
90 to 94 years	1,113	1,296	1,007	1,164	82	97	3	5	15	23	1	2	4	6	39	54	970	1,112
95 to 99 years	287	355	254	315	27	30	1	1	4	6	1	1	-	2	11	16	243	300
100 years and over	50	60	41	50	7	8	-	-	1	1	-	-	-	1	3	4	39	47
5 to 13 years	37,025	36,752	28,381	28,057	5,923	5,792	471	455	1,288	1,381	78	79	885	988	6,186	6,807	22,753	21,861
14 to 17 years	16,093	16,522	12,522	12,745	2,426	2,565	205	211	590	614	33	34	315	352	2,438	2,624	10,290	10,350
18 to 24 years	27,143	28,900	21,199	22,486	3,944	4,244	315	351	1,178	1,230	64	66	444	523	4,744	5,054	16,829	17,831
16 years and over	217,149	225,953	178,789	184,615	25,633	26,996	1,857	2,017	8,305	9,457	328	363	2,237	2,505	24,204	27,594	156,351	159,032
18 years and over	209,128	217,766	172,545	178,276	24,430	25,744	1,755	1,912	8,003	9,153	311	346	2,084	2,335	22,964	26,310	151,244	153,865
16 to 64 years	182,157	190,034	147,826	153,099	22,773	23,997	1,713	1,844	7,490	8,464	305	336	2,051	2,295	22,470	25,538	127,023	129,451
55 years and over	59,266	63,819	51,656	55,241	5,274	5,727	310	372	1,608	1,984	48	59	371	436	3,444	4,143	48,421	51,358
65 years and over	34,992	35,919	30,964	31,516	2,860	2,999	144	172	815	994	23	27	186	210	1,734	2,055	29,329	29,581
75 years and over	16,601	17,583	14,927	15,701	1,223	1,309	55	68	312	404	8	10	77	90	657	833	14,306	14,914
85 years and over	4,240	4,713	3,827	4,244	316	338	13	17	63	89	2	3	18	23	151	193	3,685	4,062
Median age (yrs)	35.3	35.9	36.6	37.3	30.0	30.6	27.7	28.9	32.5	33.7	26.8	28.5	19.8	20.3	25.8	26.7	38.6	39.6

- Represents or rounds to zero.   [1] Persons of Hispanic origin may be of any race.

Source: U.S. Census Bureau, "National Sex, Age, Race and Hispanic Origin Population Estimates," published 10 June 2004; <http://eire.census.gov/popest/data/national/tables/NC-EST2003-asrh.php>.

No. 15. Resident Population by Race, Hispanic Origin, and Single Years of Age: 2003

[In thousands, except as indicated (290,810 represents 290,810,000). As of July 1. Resident population. For derivation of estimates, see text of this section]

Age	Total	Race						Hispanic or Latino origin [1]	Not Hispanic or Latino White alone
		White alone	Black or African American alone	American Indian, Alaska Native alone	Asian alone	Native Hawaiian and Other Pacific Islander alone	Two or more races		
Total	**290,810**	**234,196**	**37,099**	**2,787**	**11,925**	**495**	**4,308**	**39,899**	**197,326**
Under 5 yrs. old . .	19,769	15,119	2,998	208	777	35	632	4,158	11,250
Under 1 yr. old .	4,004	3,061	612	39	159	6	127	866	2,245
1 yr. old	4,005	3,063	613	39	159	6	124	876	2,237
2 yrs. old	4,040	3,088	619	39	164	7	123	856	2,282
3 yrs. old	3,879	2,974	575	44	149	8	129	789	2,253
4 yrs. old	3,842	2,933	579	47	146	8	129	772	2,234
5-9 yrs. old.	19,775	15,098	3,048	239	767	43	579	3,830	11,614
5 yrs. old	3,868	2,950	588	47	150	8	124	768	2,253
6 yrs. old	3 865	2,953	585	47	154	8	118	761	2,261
7 yrs. old	3,969	3,038	604	47	155	8	116	772	2,335
8 yrs. old	4,005	3,057	623	48	155	9	112	767	2,359
9 yrs. old	4,069	3,101	648	50	153	9	108	762	2,407
10-14 yrs. old. . . .	21,193	16,192	3,415	270	769	45	503	3,661	12,857
10 yrs. old	4,139	3,152	669	52	153	9	105	760	2,459
11 yrs. old	4,226	3,223	684	54	153	9	104	754	2,536
12 yrs. old	4,293	3,282	692	55	154	9	101	741	2,607
13 yrs. old	4,318	3,302	699	55	154	9	99	721	2,645
14 yrs. old	4,217	3,233	672	54	155	9	94	684	2,610
15-19 yrs. old. . . .	20,477	15,862	3,115	261	778	43	418	3,247	12,891
15 yrs. old	4,118	3,172	641	53	155	9	89	656	2,573
16 yrs. old	4,095	3,167	629	53	151	8	86	645	2,579
17 yrs. old	4,092	3,172	623	52	153	9	83	639	2,588
18 yrs. old	4,095	3,183	614	52	157	9	81	646	2,590
19 yrs. old	4,077	3,168	608	52	161	9	79	661	2,561
20-24 yrs. old. . . .	20,728	16,135	3,023	247	912	48	363	3,747	12,680
20 yrs. old	4,121	3,208	608	52	167	9	77	700	2,564
21 yrs. old	4,165	3,243	609	51	177	10	76	736	2,565
22 yrs. old	4,215	3,278	617	50	186	10	74	761	2,577
23 yrs. old	4,201	3,270	611	49	191	10	70	781	2,549
24 yrs. old	4,026	3,136	579	46	191	10	65	769	2,425
25-29 yrs. old. . . .	19,168	14,944	2,624	213	1,062	46	279	3,799	11,419
25 yrs. old	3,929	3,067	553	45	192	10	61	770	2,355
26 yrs. old	3,819	2,983	526	43	199	9	58	765	2,273
27 yrs. old	3,797	2,959	519	43	213	9	55	764	2,250
28 yrs. old	3,837	2,987	518	42	228	9	54	764	2,277
29 yrs. old	3,786	2,948	508	40	230	9	52	735	2,263
30-34 yrs. old. . . .	20,705	16,263	2,739	208	1,195	42	257	3,580	12,938
30 yrs. old	3,851	2,988	522	41	241	8	51	731	2,308
31 yrs. old	4,066	3,175	545	42	243	9	52	731	2,495
32 yrs. old	4,250	3,346	560	42	241	9	53	718	2,680
33 yrs. old	4,378	3,458	574	43	242	9	52	725	2,785
34 yrs. old	4,159	3,296	538	40	228	8	49	675	2,669
35-39 yrs. old. . . .	21,408	17,076	2,800	209	1,053	39	231	3,175	14,130
35 yrs. old	4,079	3,237	532	40	217	8	46	656	2,627
36 yrs. old	4,076	3,245	533	40	206	8	45	633	2,658
37 yrs. old	4,211	3,353	557	41	206	8	46	632	2,767
38 yrs. old	4,484	3,580	592	44	213	8	47	639	2,987
39 yrs. old	4,558	3,661	587	44	211	8	47	615	3,091
40-44 yrs. old. . . .	22,963	18,628	2,875	214	975	37	233	2,741	16,087
40 yrs. old	4,543	3,662	577	43	206	8	48	591	3,114
41 yrs. old	4,584	3,717	574	43	196	8	47	567	3,191
42 yrs. old	4,601	3,741	573	43	191	7	46	546	3,234
43 yrs. old	4,711	3,822	594	43	196	8	47	543	3,319
44 yrs. old	4,524	3,686	557	41	187	7	45	494	3,229
45-49 yrs. old. . . .	21,761	17,844	2,600	191	887	31	208	2,170	15,835
45 yrs. old	4,534	3,705	554	41	184	7	44	478	3,262
46 yrs. old	4,435	3,630	536	39	180	6	43	453	3,211
47 yrs. old	4,336	3,552	520	38	178	6	42	432	3,152
48 yrs. old	4,311	3,537	512	37	178	6	41	419	3,150
49 yrs. old	4,145	3,420	479	35	166	6	39	388	3,060

U.S. Census Bureau, Statistical Abstract of the United States: 2004-2005

No. 15. Resident Population by Race, Hispanic Origin, and Single Years of Age: 2003—Con.

[In thousands, except as indicated (290,810 represents 290,810,000). As of July 1. Resident population. For derivation of estimates, see text of this section]

| Age | Total | Race | | | | | | Hispanic or Latino origin [1] | Not Hispanic or Latino White alone |
		White alone	Black or African American alone	American Indian, Alaska Native alone	Asian alone	Native Hawaiian and Other Pacific Islander alone	Two or more races		
50-54 yrs. old	19,043	15,794	2,134	155	766	25	169	1,649	14,267
50 yrs. old	4,009	3,319	452	34	162	5	36	361	2,985
51 yrs. old	3,914	3,251	438	32	154	5	35	343	2,933
52 yrs. old	3,742	3,100	423	31	150	5	33	326	2,798
53 yrs. old	3,763	3,111	427	31	156	5	33	324	2,810
54 yrs. old	3,616	3,013	393	28	145	5	31	295	2,740
55-59 yrs. old	15,794	13,395	1,559	117	572	19	132	1,215	12,264
55 yrs. old	3,662	3,093	370	28	136	4	31	281	2,832
56 yrs. old	3,495	2,978	333	26	125	4	29	260	2,736
57 yrs. old	3,064	2,598	303	23	111	4	26	241	2,373
58 yrs. old	2,785	2,351	282	21	104	4	23	224	2,142
59 yrs. old	2,788	2,376	270	20	96	3	23	209	2,181
60-64 yrs. old	12,106	10,329	1,169	83	418	13	93	873	9,513
60 yrs. old	2,742	2,347	260	19	92	3	22	195	2,165
61 yrs. old	2,608	2,233	247	18	87	3	20	183	2,062
62 yrs. old	2,337	1,989	228	16	82	3	18	170	1,830
63 yrs. old	2,259	1,917	226	15	82	3	18	169	1,759
64 yrs. old	2,160	1,843	209	14	75	2	16	156	1,697
65-69 yrs. old	9,746	8,335	943	60	330	10	68	683	7,695
65 yrs. old	2,101	1,794	204	14	72	2	15	150	1,653
66 yrs. old	1,987	1,698	192	12	69	2	14	141	1,565
67 yrs. old	1,947	1,665	188	12	66	2	14	137	1,536
68 yrs. old	1,912	1,634	187	11	65	2	13	133	1,510
69 yrs. old	1,799	1,545	171	10	59	2	12	121	1,431
70-74 yrs. old	8,591	7,480	747	44	260	7	52	539	6,972
70 yrs. old	1,761	1,513	168	10	57	2	12	116	1,404
71 yrs. old	1,752	1,522	155	9	53	1	11	111	1,417
72 yrs. old	1,725	1,510	144	9	51	1	10	107	1,409
73 yrs. old	1,715	1,499	145	9	52	1	10	107	1,398
74 yrs. old	1,638	1,437	136	8	47	1	9	98	1,344
75-79 yrs. old	7,453	6,601	581	31	193	5	40	397	6,227
75 yrs. old	1,614	1,423	129	7	44	1	9	92	1,336
76 yrs. old	1,551	1,371	123	7	41	1	9	85	1,291
77 yrs. old	1,480	1,310	117	6	38	1	8	79	1,235
78 yrs. old	1,445	1,283	111	6	37	1	8	74	1,212
79 yrs. old	1,362	1,215	101	5	33	1	7	67	1,152
80-84 yrs. old	5,416	4,856	390	20	121	3	26	244	4,626
80 yrs. old	1,249	1,115	93	5	30	1	6	61	1,057
81 yrs. old	1,197	1,073	86	4	27	1	6	55	1,021
82 yrs. old	1,117	1,007	76	4	24	1	5	49	961
83 yrs. old	961	860	71	4	22	-	5	43	819
84 yrs. old	892	802	64	3	18	-	4	36	768
85-89 yrs. old	3,003	2,715	203	10	59	2	14	119	2,603
90-94 yrs. old	1,296	1,164	97	5	23	1	6	54	1,112
95-99 yrs. old	355	315	30	1	6	-	2	16	300
100 yrs. old and over	60	50	8	-	1	-	1	4	47
Median age (yr.) . .	35.9	37.3	30.6	28.9	33.7	28.5	20.3	26.7	39.6

- Represents or rounds to zero.   [1] Persons of Hispanic origin may be of any race.

Source: U.S. Census Bureau, "National Population Estimates for the 2000s, Monthly Postcensal Resident Population, by single year of age, sex, race, and Hispanic origin;" published 10 June 2004; <http://eire.census.gov/popest/data/national/asrodetail1.php>.

Population   17

[In thousands (295,507 represents 295,507,000), except as indicated. As of July. For definition of median, see Guide to Tabular Presentation. Projections are based on middle series of assumptions; see headnote, Table 3]

Age group	Total 2005	Total 2010	White alone 2005	White alone 2010	Black alone 2005	Black alone 2010	Asian alone 2005	Asian alone 2010	All other races alone 2005	All other races alone 2010	Hispanic origin [1] 2005	Hispanic origin [1] 2010	Non-Hispanic White alone 2005	Non-Hispanic White alone 2010
Total	295,507	308,936	236,924	244,995	38,056	40,454	12,419	14,241	8,108	9,246	41,801	47,756	198,451	201,112
Under 5 years	20,495	21,426	15,503	15,995	3,113	3,332	833	919	1,046	1,181	4,397	4,824	11,528	11,647
5 to 9 years	19,467	20,706	14,862	15,639	2,941	3,127	763	888	901	1,052	3,892	4,515	11,330	11,553
10 to 14 years	20,838	19,767	15,881	15,049	3,332	2,976	787	834	838	909	3,853	4,057	12,370	11,361
15 to 19 years	21,172	21,336	16,281	16,203	3,306	3,396	815	886	770	851	3,576	4,162	13,013	12,401
20 to 24 years	20,823	21,676	16,153	16,591	3,078	3,357	898	943	695	785	3,604	3,878	12,836	12,992
25 to 29 years	19,753	21,375	15,375	16,495	2,807	3,130	985	1,041	584	709	3,781	3,927	11,881	12,919
30 to 34 years	19,847	20,271	15,466	15,654	2,678	2,856	1,190	1,166	514	595	3,666	3,973	12,060	11,977
35 to 39 years	20,869	20,137	16,538	15,597	2,732	2,701	1,117	1,319	482	520	3,297	3,769	13,480	12,096
40 to 44 years	22,735	20,984	18,318	16,566	2,892	2,724	1,033	1,208	492	486	2,926	3,343	15,606	13,466
45 to 49 years	22,453	22,654	18,312	18,213	2,736	2,844	948	1,105	457	492	2,375	2,939	16,113	15,489
50 to 54 years	19,983	22,173	16,499	18,066	2,276	2,657	828	997	379	453	1,823	2,371	14,812	15,870
55 to 59 years	17,359	19,507	14,582	16,102	1,788	2,176	685	857	305	372	1,393	1,806	13,289	14,431
60 to 64 years	13,017	16,679	11,075	14,004	1,250	1,674	480	706	212	295	978	1,365	10,161	12,736
65 to 69 years	10,123	12,172	8,629	10,357	972	1,127	370	489	152	199	745	941	7,931	9,477
70 to 74 years	8,500	9,097	7,348	7,767	767	838	275	355	110	138	571	694	6,811	7,117
75 to 79 years	7,376	7,186	6,506	6,226	591	622	200	244	79	94	433	510	6,097	5,747
80 to 84 years	5,576	5,665	4,993	5,005	407	440	125	158	51	61	275	359	4,733	4,666
85 to 89 years	3,206	3,713	2,890	3,321	231	274	59	83	26	34	135	204	2,763	3,128
90 to 94 years	1,431	1,727	1,286	1,546	112	136	22	31	11	14	60	84	1,230	1,467
95 to 99 years	412	569	366	503	37	53	5	8	3	4	18	28	349	476
100 years and over	71	114	60	98	9	14	1	1	1	1	3	6	57	92
5 to 13 years	35,968	36,439	27,432	27,613	5,575	5,491	1,389	1,550	1,571	1,786	6,975	7,760	21,091	20,580
14 to 17 years	17,175	16,566	13,150	12,589	2,735	2,597	648	695	642	685	2,956	3,291	10,453	9,586
18 to 24 years	29,156	30,481	22,594	23,280	4,347	4,768	1,226	1,307	990	1,125	4,994	5,611	18,005	18,142
16 years and over . .	230,335	242,936	187,339	195,194	27,964	30,383	9,874	11,427	5,159	5,933	28,904	33,541	160,572	164,179
18 years and over . .	221,868	234,504	180,839	188,799	26,632	29,034	9,549	11,077	4,848	5,594	27,473	31,881	155,378	159,300
18 to 64 years	193,639	202,693	155,261	160,372	24,837	26,877	8,816	10,056	4,725	5,387	26,663	30,715	130,601	132,007
55 years and over . .	67,072	76,429	57,734	64,928	6,165	7,355	2,223	2,934	950	1,213	4,611	5,997	53,421	59,339
65 years and over . .	36,696	40,244	32,078	34,821	3,127	3,505	1,058	1,371	433	546	2,240	2,826	29,971	32,171
75 years and over . .	18,072	18,974	16,101	16,698	1,388	1,540	413	527	171	209	924	1,191	15,228	15,577
85 years and over . .	5,120	6,123	4,602	5,467	390	478	87	125	41	54	216	322	4,398	5,163
Median age (yrs)	35.2	36.0	36.7	37.6	29.9	30.5	33.8	35.7	22.6	23.0	26.1	27.1	39.3	40.3

[1] Persons of Hispanic origin may be of any race.

Source: U.S. Census Bureau, International Data Base; published 10 October 2002; <http://www.census.gov/ipc/www/idbprint.html>.

Figure 1.1
Center of Population: 1790 to 2000

[Prior to 1960, excludes Alaska and Hawaii. The median center is located at the intersection of two median lines, a north-south line constructed so that half of the nation's population lives east and half lives west of it, and an east-west line selected so that half of the nation's population lives north and half lives south of it. The mean center of population is that point at which an imaginary, flat, weightless, and rigid map of the United States would balance if weights of identical value were placed on it so that each weight represented the location of one person on the date of the census]

Year	Median center		Mean center		
	Latitude-N	Longitude	Latitude-N	Longitude-W	Approximate location
1790 (August 2)	(NA)	(NA)	39 16 30	76 11 12	In Kent County, MD, 23 miles E of Baltimore MD
1850 (June 1)..	(NA)	(NA)	38 59 00	81 19 00	In Wirt County, WV, 23 miles SE of Parkersburg, WV[1]
1900 (June 1)..	40 03 32	84 49 01	39 09 36	85 48 54	In Bartholomew County, IN, 6 miles SE of Columbus, IN
1950 (April 1)..	40 00 12	84 56 51	38 50 21	88 09 33	In Richland County, IL, 8 miles NNW of Olney, IL
1960 (April 1)..	39 56 25	85 16 60	38 35 58	89 12 35	In Clinton County, IL, 6.5 miles NW of Centralia, IL
1970 (April 1)	39 47 43	85 31 43	38 27 47	89 42 22	In St. Clair County, IL, 5.3 miles ESE of Mascoutah, IL
1980 (April 1)..	39 18 60	86 08 15	38 08 13	90 34 26	In Jefferson County, MO, .25 mile W of DeSoto, MO
1990 (April 1)..	38 57 55	86 31 53	37 52 20	91 12 55	In Crawford County, MO, 10 miles SE of Steelville, MO
2000 (April 1)..	38 45 23	86 55 51	37 41 49	91 48 34	In Phelps County, MO, 3 miles E of Edgar Springs, MO

NA Not available.   [1]West Virginia was set off from Virginia, Dec. 31, 1862, and admitted as a state, June 19, 1863.

U.S. Census Bureau, Statistical Abstract of the United States: 2004-2005

No. 17. Resident Population—States: 1980 to 2003

[In thousands (226,546 represents 226,546,000). 1980, 1990, and 2000 data as of April 1, data for other years as of July 1. Insofar as possible, population shown for all years is that of present area of state. See Appendix III]

State	1980 [1]	1990 [2]	1995	1998	1999	2000 [3]	2001	2002	2003
United States	226,546	248,791	266,278	275,854	279,040	281,423	285,094	287,974	290,810
Alabama.	3,894	4,040	4,297	4,405	4,430	4,447	4,466	4,479	4,501
Alaska	402	550	604	620	625	627	633	641	649
Arizona.	2,718	3,665	4,432	4,883	5,024	5,131	5,298	5,441	5,581
Arkansas	2,286	2,351	2,535	2,626	2,652	2,673	2,692	2,706	2,726
California	23,668	29,811	31,697	32,988	33,499	33,872	34,533	35,002	35,484
Colorado.	2,890	3,294	3,827	4,117	4,226	4,302	4,429	4,501	4,551
Connecticut.	3,108	3,287	3,324	3,365	3,386	3,406	3,433	3,459	3,483
Delaware	594	666	730	763	775	784	796	806	817
District of Columbia	638	607	581	565	570	572	573	569	563
Florida	9,746	12,938	14,538	15,487	15,759	15,983	16,355	16,692	17,019
Georgia	5,463	6,478	7,328	7,864	8,046	8,187	8,395	8,544	8,685
Hawaii	965	1,108	1,197	1,215	1,210	1,212	1,225	1,241	1,258
Idaho	944	1,007	1,177	1,252	1,276	1,294	1,321	1,343	1,366
Illinois	11,427	11,431	12,008	12,272	12,359	12,420	12,517	12,586	12,654
Indiana.	5,490	5,544	5,851	5,999	6,045	6,081	6,126	6,157	6,196
Iowa	2,914	2,777	2,867	2,903	2,918	2,926	2,932	2,936	2,944
Kansas.	2,364	2,478	2,601	2,661	2,678	2,689	2,700	2,712	2,724
Kentucky	3,661	3,687	3,887	3,985	4,018	4,042	4,067	4,090	4,118
Louisiana	4,206	4,222	4,379	4,440	4,461	4,469	4,466	4,476	4,496
Maine.	1,125	1,228	1,243	1,259	1,267	1,275	1,285	1,295	1,306
Maryland	4,217	4,781	5,070	5,204	5,255	5,296	5,383	5,451	5,509
Massachusetts.	5,737	6,016	6,141	6,272	6,317	6,349	6,400	6,422	6,433
Michigan.	9,262	9,295	9,676	9,848	9,897	9,938	10,005	10,043	10,080
Minnesota.	4,076	4,376	4,660	4,813	4,873	4,919	4,985	5,025	5,059
Mississippi	2,521	2,575	2,723	2,805	2,828	2,845	2,858	2,867	2,881
Missouri	4,917	5,117	5,378	5,522	5,562	5,597	5,636	5,670	5,704
Montana.	787	799	877	892	898	902	906	910	918
Nebraska	1,570	1,578	1,657	1,696	1,705	1,711	1,719	1,728	1,739
Nevada	800	1,202	1,582	1,853	1,935	1,998	2,095	2,167	2,241
New Hampshire.	921	1,109	1,158	1,206	1,222	1,236	1,259	1,274	1,288
New Jersey.	7,365	7,748	8,083	8,287	8,360	8,414	8,504	8,575	8,638
New Mexico	1,303	1,515	1,720	1,793	1,808	1,819	1,829	1,852	1,875
New York	17,558	17,991	18,524	18,756	18,883	18,977	19,075	19,134	19,190
North Carolina.	5,882	6,632	7,345	7,809	7,949	8,046	8,195	8,306	8,407
North Dakota.	653	639	648	648	644	642	636	634	634
Ohio	10,798	10,847	11,203	11,312	11,335	11,353	11,386	11,409	11,436
Oklahoma.	3,025	3,146	3,308	3,405	3,437	3,451	3,467	3,490	3,512
Oregon.	2,633	2,842	3,184	3,352	3,394	3,421	3,473	3,520	3,560
Pennsylvania.	11,864	11,883	12,198	12,246	12,264	12,281	12,298	12,329	12,365
Rhode Island.	947	1,003	1,017	1,031	1,040	1,048	1,059	1,068	1,076
South Carolina.	3,122	3,486	3,749	3,919	3,975	4,012	4,060	4,104	4,147
South Dakota	691	696	738	746	750	755	758	760	764
Tennessee	4,591	4,877	5,327	5,570	5,639	5,689	5,746	5,790	5,842
Texas.	14,229	16,986	18,959	20,158	20,558	20,852	21,341	21,737	22,119
Utah	1,461	1,723	2,014	2,166	2,203	2,233	2,280	2,319	2,351
Vermont	511	563	589	600	605	609	613	616	619
Virginia.	5,347	6,189	6,671	6,901	7,000	7,078	7,193	7,288	7,386
Washington.	4,132	4,867	5,481	5,770	5,843	5,894	5,993	6,067	6,131
West Virginia.	1,950	1,793	1,824	1,816	1,812	1,808	1,802	1,805	1,810
Wisconsin	4,706	4,892	5,185	5,298	5,333	5,364	5,405	5,440	5,472
Wyoming	470	454	485	491	492	494	494	499	501

[1] See footnote 4, Table 1.   [2] The April 1, 1990, census counts include corrections processed through August 1997, results of special censuses and test censuses, and do not include adjustments for census coverage errors.   [3] Reflects modifications to the Census 2000 population as documented in the Count Question Resolution program, updates to the Boundary and Annexation Survey, and geographic program revisions.

Source: U.S. Census Bureau, 1990 Census of Population and Housing, *Population and Housing Unit Counts* (CPH-2); "Table CO-EST2001-12-00 - Time Series of Intercensal State Populaton Estimates: April 1, 1990 to April 1, 2000"; published 11 April 2002; <http://eire.census.gov/popest/data/counties/tables/CO-EST2001-12/CO-EST2001-12-00.php>; and "Table NST-EST2003-01 - Annual Estimates of the Population for the United States and States, and for Puerto Rico: April 1, 2000 to July 1, 2003"; published 18 December 2003; <http://eire.census.gov/popest/data/states/tables/NST-EST2003-01.php>.

No. 18. State Population—Rank, Percent Change, and Population Density: 1980 to 2003

[As of April 1, except 2003 as of July 1. Insofar as possible, population shown for all years is that of present area of state. For area figures of states, see Table 346. Minus sign (-) indicates decrease. See Appendix III]

State	Rank 1980	Rank 1990	Rank 2000	Rank 2003	Percent change 1980-1990	Percent change 1990-2000	Percent change 2000-2003	Population per sq. mile of land area[1] 1990	Population per sq. mile of land area[1] 2000	Population per sq. mile of land area[1] 2003
United States.....	(X)	(X)	(X)	(X)	9.8	13.1	3.3	70.3	79.6	82.2
Alabama.........	22	22	23	23	3.8	10.1	1.2	79.6	87.6	88.7
Alaska..........	50	49	48	47	36.9	14.0	3.5	1.0	1.1	1.1
Arizona.........	29	24	20	18	34.8	40.0	8.8	32.3	45.2	49.1
Arkansas........	33	33	33	32	2.8	13.7	2.0	45.1	51.3	52.3
California........	1	1	1	1	26.0	13.6	4.8	191.1	217.2	227.5
Colorado........	28	26	24	22	14.0	30.6	5.8	31.8	41.5	43.9
Connecticut......	25	27	29	29	5.8	3.6	2.3	678.5	702.9	719.0
Delaware........	47	46	45	45	12.1	17.6	4.3	341.0	401.1	418.5
District of Columbia...	(X)	(X)	(X)	(X)	-4.9	-5.7	-1.5	9,884.4	9,316.4	9,175.6
Florida	7	4	4	4	32.7	23.5	6.5	239.9	296.4	315.6
Georgia.........	13	11	10	9	18.6	26.4	6.1	111.9	141.4	150.0
Hawaii	39	41	42	42	14.9	9.3	3.8	172.6	188.6	195.8
Idaho	41	42	39	39	6.7	28.5	5.6	12.2	15.6	16.5
Illinois..........	5	6	5	5	(Z)	8.7	1.9	205.6	223.4	227.6
Indiana.........	12	14	14	14	1.0	9.7	1.9	154.6	169.5	172.7
Iowa...........	27	30	30	30	-4.7	5.4	0.6	49.7	52.4	52.7
Kansas.........	32	32	32	33	4.8	8.5	1.3	30.3	32.9	33.3
Kentucky........	23	23	25	26	0.7	9.6	1.9	92.8	101.7	103.7
Louisiana........	19	21	22	24	0.4	5.9	0.6	96.9	102.6	103.2
Maine..........	38	38	40	40	9.2	3.8	2.4	39.8	41.3	42.3
Maryland........	18	19	19	19	13.4	10.8	4.0	489.1	541.9	563.6
Massachusetts......	11	13	13	13	4.9	5.5	1.3	767.4	809.8	820.6
Michigan........	8	8	8	8	0.4	6.9	1.4	163.6	175.0	177.5
Minnesota.......	21	20	21	21	7.4	12.4	2.8	55.0	61.8	63.6
Mississippi.......	31	31	31	31	2.2	10.5	1.3	54.9	60.6	61.4
Missouri	15	15	17	17	4.1	9.4	1.9	74.3	81.2	82.8
Montana	44	44	44	44	1.6	12.9	1.7	5.5	6.2	6.3
Nebraska	35	36	38	38	0.5	8.4	1.6	20.5	22.3	22.6
Nevada	43	39	35	35	50.1	66.3	12.2	10.9	18.2	20.4
New Hampshire	42	40	41	41	20.5	11.4	4.2	123.7	137.8	143.6
New Jersey	9	9	9	10	5.2	8.6	2.7	1,044.5	1,134.4	1,164.6
New Mexico.......	37	37	36	36	16.3	20.1	3.1	12.5	15.0	15.4
New York	2	2	3	3	2.5	5.5	1.1	381.0	401.9	406.5
North Carolina	10	10	11	11	12.8	21.3	4.5	136.2	165.2	172.6
North Dakota	46	47	47	48	-2.1	0.5	-1.3	9.3	9.3	9.2
Ohio...........	6	7	7	7	0.5	4.7	0.7	264.9	277.3	279.3
Oklahoma........	26	28	27	28	4.0	9.7	1.8	45.8	50.3	51.1
Oregon.........	30	29	28	27	7.9	20.4	4.0	29.6	35.6	37.1
Pennsylvania	4	5	6	6	0.2	3.4	0.7	265.1	274.0	275.9
Rhode Island	40	43	43	43	5.9	4.5	2.7	960.3	1,003.2	1,029.9
South Carolina	24	25	26	25	11.7	15.1	3.4	115.8	133.2	137.7
South Dakota	45	45	46	46	0.8	8.5	1.3	9.2	9.9	10.1
Tennessee........	17	17	16	16	6.2	16.7	2.7	118.3	138.0	141.7
Texas..........	3	3	2	2	19.4	22.8	6.1	64.9	79.6	84.5
Utah...........	36	35	34	34	17.9	29.6	5.3	21.0	27.2	28.6
Vermont	48	48	49	49	10.0	8.2	1.7	60.8	65.8	66.9
Virginia........	14	12	12	12	15.8	14.4	4.3	156.3	178.8	186.6
Washington	20	18	15	15	17.8	21.1	4.0	73.1	88.6	92.1
West Virginia	34	34	37	37	-8.0	0.8	0.1	74.5	75.1	75.2
Wisconsin	16	16	18	20	4.0	9.6	2.0	90.1	98.8	100.8
Wyoming.........	49	50	50	50	-3.4	8.9	1.5	4.7	5.1	5.2

X Not applicable.   Z Less than 0.05 percent.   [1] Persons per square mile were calculated on the basis of land area data from the 2000 census.

Source: U.S. Census Bureau, 1990 Census of Population and Housing, *Population and Housing Unit Counts* (CPH-2); "ST-99-3 State Population Estimates: Annual Time Series, July 1, 1990, to July 1, 1999"; published 29 December 1999; <http://www.census.gov/population/estimates/state/st-99-3.txt>; *Population Change and Distribution: 1990 to 2000, Census 2000 Brief,* (C2KBR/01-2), April 2001; and "Table NST-EST2003-02 - Cumulative Estimates of Population Change for the United States and States, and for Puerto Rico and National Rankings of States: April 1, 2000 to July 1, 2003"; published 18 December 2003; <http://eire.census.gov/popest/data/states/tables/NST-EST2003-02.php>.

No. 19. State Resident Population—Components of Change: 2000-2003

[Covers period April 1, 2000, to July 1, 2003. Minus sign (-) indicates net decrease]

State	Numeric population change [1]	Births	Deaths	Natural increase (births minus deaths)	Net internal migration	Net international migration
United States	9,386,546	13,085,539	7,889,270	5,196,269	(X)	4,190,277
Alabama.	53,652	198,297	149,646	48,651	-9,826	16,549
Alaska	21,887	32,190	10,102	22,088	-3,737	3,620
Arizona.	450,179	278,744	136,492	142,252	194,704	111,543
Arkansas	52,316	122,012	92,026	29,986	8,550	14,210
California	1,612,800	1,701,252	756,758	944,494	-277,188	937,831
Colorado.	248,691	217,234	93,256	123,978	48,023	74,258
Connecticut.	77,788	137,197	97,971	39,226	-9,220	50,574
Delaware	33,891	35,263	23,141	12,122	14,922	7,386
District of Columbia	-8,675	25,698	19,520	6,178	-28,520	13,622
Florida	1,036,248	675,642	543,406	132,236	540,529	349,333
Georgia	498,198	438,289	212,673	225,616	140,009	127,050
Hawaii	46,071	59,044	29,180	29,864	-2,541	19,338
Idaho.	72,376	66,337	32,085	34,252	27,169	9,479
Illinois	233,974	598,234	347,071	251,163	-238,404	217,631
Indiana.	115,137	277,808	181,651	96,157	-14,924	36,229
Iowa	17,680	121,048	91,168	29,880	-29,728	19,335
Kansas.	34,693	125,734	80,523	45,211	-35,605	25,497
Kentucky	75,618	177,581	130,520	47,061	12,740	17,753
Louisiana	27,376	219,361	135,991	83,370	-67,774	12,630
Maine.	30,805	43,434	40,920	2,514	25,722	3,126
Maryland	212,424	241,352	144,272	97,080	38,668	72,453
Massachusetts.	84,325	265,871	185,556	80,315	-102,905	108,737
Michigan.	141,505	428,261	285,979	142,282	-78,251	82,169
Minnesota.	139,890	216,100	122,759	93,341	-1,154	47,425
Mississippi	36,625	141,826	92,710	49,116	-18,171	6,410
Missouri	107,801	245,375	180,689	64,686	16,967	28,149
Montana.	15,426	35,234	27,673	7,561	6,564	1,343
Nebraska	28,026	80,474	50,477	29,997	-15,857	14,878
Nevada	242,897	102,521	53,711	48,810	146,688	43,954
New Hampshire	51,901	47,194	32,188	15,006	29,628	7,454
New Jersey.	224,049	370,057	240,899	129,158	-92,699	192,044
New Mexico	55,568	87,305	45,302	42,003	-4,383	18,188
New York	213,294	835,326	515,916	319,410	-551,672	442,800
North Carolina.	360,797	386,343	235,328	151,015	107,641	102,905
North Dakota.	-8,363	24,648	19,620	5,028	-15,662	2,374
Ohio	82,655	493,802	354,822	138,980	-103,400	50,359
Oklahoma	60,878	162,253	115,649	46,604	-8,671	24,310
Oregon.	138,164	145,101	100,483	44,618	47,780	47,963
Pennsylvania	84,401	464,646	424,782	39,864	-16,472	68,935
Rhode Island.	27,845	40,114	31,964	8,150	8,024	12,549
South Carolina.	135,304	182,193	122,447	59,746	54,719	23,056
South Dakota	9,465	33,914	22,917	10,997	-3,606	2,492
Tennessee	152,486	255,980	181,364	74,616	46,771	32,816
Texas.	1,266,719	1,190,484	475,020	715,464	106,964	439,765
Utah	118,269	154,257	42,133	112,124	-29,648	33,271
Vermont.	10,280	20,066	16,774	3,292	4,624	2,890
Virginia.	307,847	321,528	184,285	137,243	77,716	90,536
Washington.	237,304	255,338	144,509	110,829	39,235	88,929
West Virginia.	2,004	66,283	68,098	-1,815	2,406	2,098
Wisconsin.	108,595	220,988	153,446	67,542	13,943	30,643
Wyoming	7,460	20,306	13,398	6,908	-688	1,388

X Not applicable.   [1] The estimated components of population change will not sum to the numerical population change due to the process of controlling to national totals.

Source: U.S. Census Bureau, "Table NST-EST2003-02 - Cumulative Estimates of Population Change for the United States and States, and for Puerto Rico and National Rankings of States: April 1, 2000 to July 1, 2003"; published 18 December 2003; <http://eire.census.gov/popest/data/states/tables/NST-EST2003-02.php>; and "Table NST-EST2003-04 - Cumulative Estimates of the Components of Population Change for the United States and States: April 1, 2000 to July 1, 2003"; published 18 December 2003; <http://eire.census.gov/popest/data/states/tables/NST-EST2003-04.php>.

U.S. Census Bureau, Statistical Abstract of the United States: 2004-2005

No. 20. Resident Population by Age and State: 2003

[In thousands, except percent (290,810 represents 290,810,000). **As of July**. Includes Armed Forces stationed in area]

State	Total	Under 5 years	5 to 17 years	18 to 24 years	25 to 34 years	35 to 44 years	45 to 54 years	55 to 64 years	65 to 74 years	75 to 84 years	85 years and over	Percent 65 years and over
U.S.	290,810	19,769	53,274	28,900	39,873	44,371	40,805	27,900	18,337	12,869	4,713	12.4
AL	4,501	297	811	454	596	654	636	461	318	203	71	13.2
AK........	649	49	141	70	82	104	106	57	25	12	3	6.3
AZ........	5,581	436	1,083	553	803	785	692	514	382	252	81	12.8
AR........	2,726	186	496	276	354	385	368	283	198	131	49	13.9
CA........	35,484	2,544	6,876	3,569	5,297	5,560	4,779	3,094	1,919	1,357	489	10.6
CO.	4,551	328	825	455	716	718	664	404	235	152	54	9.7
CT........	3,483	211	624	303	417	574	522	362	221	176	74	13.5
DE	817	54	145	82	107	127	114	83	57	37	12	13.1
DC........	564	34	75	64	109	85	75	55	34	24	9	12.0
FL	17,019	1,055	2,869	1,494	2,112	2,517	2,295	1,780	1,458	1,068	372	17.0
GA........	8,685	659	1,638	889	1,349	1,386	1,167	770	455	275	97	9.5
HI	1,258	85	212	125	165	184	185	132	83	64	22	13.5
ID	1,366	102	270	153	179	191	188	128	80	54	21	11.4
IL.........	12,654	887	2,344	1,255	1,805	1,929	1,755	1,172	752	544	212	11.9
IN	6,196	430	1,174	634	816	916	871	591	386	276	101	12.3
IA	2,944	182	512	317	362	422	427	289	204	159	70	14.7
KS........	2,724	189	506	296	352	393	384	249	170	129	55	13.0
KY........	4,118	271	723	412	562	623	593	421	274	177	62	12.4
LA........	4,496	324	853	501	592	652	626	424	279	184	62	11.7
ME........	1,306	67	220	121	146	207	211	146	96	67	25	14.4
MD.	5,509	365	1,014	507	721	909	817	552	325	223	77	11.3
MA........	6,433	398	1,089	597	889	1,046	927	630	408	321	128	13.3
MI	10,080	648	1,891	992	1,313	1,537	1,478	984	622	452	162	12.3
MN........	5,059	326	923	521	674	802	737	468	295	219	95	12.0
MS........	2,881	211	551	323	382	406	387	272	186	119	44	12.1
MO	5,704	373	1,035	578	738	850	803	568	386	270	103	13.3
MT........	918	54	162	96	104	129	148	100	64	44	17	13.6
NE........	1,739	121	320	188	226	248	244	160	112	84	36	13.4
NV........	2,241	163	418	199	344	344	297	225	148	81	22	11.2
NH........	1,288	73	233	120	150	220	204	134	79	55	21	12.0
NJ	8,638	568	1,564	726	1,116	1,431	1,249	860	556	416	153	13.0
NM........	1,875	133	369	198	231	266	266	186	122	76	27	12.0
NY........	19,190	1,215	3,318	1,827	2,671	3,039	2,716	1,916	1,250	896	343	13.0
NC........	8,407	590	1,497	824	1,228	1,282	1,150	820	547	350	119	12.1
ND........	634	37	110	76	78	87	93	59	44	34	16	14.8
OH........	11,436	740	2,075	1,120	1,465	1,709	1,677	1,133	761	559	196	13.3
OK........	3,512	244	634	382	461	494	484	351	242	161	58	13.1
OR........	3,560	224	626	347	501	512	535	362	221	166	66	12.7
PA........	12,365	705	2,126	1,181	1,476	1,859	1,839	1,279	909	727	266	15.4
RI	1,076	62	183	114	137	169	156	106	68	59	23	14.0
SC........	4,147	277	746	427	560	611	583	430	279	174	58	12.3
SD........	764	52	144	85	90	107	108	70	52	39	17	14.3
TN........	5,842	383	1,012	571	820	887	837	604	391	248	87	12.4
TX........	22,119	1,807	4,433	2,352	3,284	3,318	2,892	1,857	1,180	741	255	9.8
UT........	2,351	230	513	314	380	290	260	162	107	71	25	8.6
VT........	619	31	106	64	71	97	102	69	41	28	11	12.9
VA........	7,386	491	1,308	736	1,017	1,183	1,074	745	445	289	99	11.3
WA........	6,131	390	1,107	619	854	956	917	598	344	249	97	11.3
WV	1,810	101	290	175	224	254	282	207	145	99	33	15.3
WI	5,472	339	994	566	686	848	803	524	349	257	106	13.0
WY	501	31	90	56	60	70	81	53	32	20	7	12.0

Source: U.S. Census Bureau, "Table ST-EST2003-01res - Annual Estimates of the Resident Population by Selected Age Groups for the United States and States: July 1, 2003 and April 1, 2000;" published 10 March 2004; <http://eire.census.gov/popest/data/states/ST-EST2003-01.php> and unpublished data.

Population   23

No. 21. Resident Population by Race, Hispanic or Latino Origin, and State: 2003

[In thousands (290,810 represents 290,810,000). As of July. Persons of Hispanic or Latino origin may be of any race. Due to the complexities associated with the production of detailed characteristics estimates at the state and county levels, the values of the estimates at lower levels of geography may not necessarily sum to estimates at higher levels of geography. In addition, further complications arise when producing characteristics estimates for the District of Columbia. Due to its unique status, the population total presented here is the sum of the characteristics for the District of Columbia and does not match the official population total previously released]

State		One race						Hispanic or Latino origin	Non-Hispanic White alone
	Total population	White alone	Black or African American alone	American Indian, Alaska Native alone	Asian alone	Native Hawaiian and Other Pacific Islander alone	Two or more races		
U.S....	290,810	234,196	37,099	2,787	11,925	495	4,308	39,899	197,326
AL.......	4,501	3,211	1,189	23	38	2	39	89	3,132
AK.......	649	460	25	103	27	4	31	30	436
AZ.......	5,581	4,893	185	294	117	10	82	1,550	3,424
AR.......	2,726	2,208	441	19	25	2	31	100	2,115
CA.......	35,484	27,505	2,442	413	4,148	145	830	12,176	16,043
CO.......	4,551	4,105	190	51	117	6	80	847	3,314
CT.......	3,483	2,975	349	11	102	2	44	352	2,667
DE.......	817	624	159	3	21	(Z)	10	43	587
DC.......	564	205	332	2	18	(Z)	8	53	160
FL.......	17,019	13,710	2,703	69	327	13	197	3,160	10,739
GA.......	8,685	5,859	2,497	27	212	6	85	541	5,368
HI.......	1,258	326	30	4	529	116	252	95	289
ID.......	1,366	1,304	8	20	15	2	18	119	1,192
IL.......	12,654	10,055	1,920	39	501	8	131	1,727	8,415
IN.......	6,196	5,508	530	17	74	3	64	243	5,283
IA.......	2,944	2,793	67	10	47	1	26	92	2,707
KS.......	2,724	2,431	163	26	57	2	44	213	2,233
KY.......	4,118	3,717	313	9	37	2	39	72	3,653
LA.......	4,496	2,889	1,481	26	64	2	36	117	2,788
ME.......	1,306	1,267	8	7	11	(Z)	11	11	1,258
MD.......	5,509	3,616	1,547	18	248	3	77	262	3,390
MA.......	6,433	5,612	433	18	285	5	80	478	5,225
MI.......	10,080	8,211	1,447	60	217	4	142	357	7,890
MN.......	5,059	4,563	199	58	168	3	69	165	4,413
MS.......	2,881	1,764	1,064	13	22	1	17	43	1,728
MO.......	5,704	4,869	659	26	76	4	71	131	4,750
MT.......	918	834	4	60	6	1	14	20	818
NE.......	1,739	1,602	73	16	28	1	18	107	1,502
NV.......	2,241	1,885	154	33	106	10	53	491	1,424
NH.......	1,288	1,240	12	3	20	(Z)	12	23	1,220
NJ.......	8,638	6,681	1,257	26	565	6	103	1,254	5,576
NM.......	1,875	1,591	42	187	24	2	27	810	818
NY.......	19,190	14,127	3,425	105	1,242	18	272	3,132	11,613
NC.......	8,407	6,234	1,838	108	143	5	80	467	5,810
ND.......	634	586	5	31	5	(Z)	6	8	579
OH.......	11,436	9,770	1,334	26	165	4	136	232	9,568
OK.......	3,512	2,754	276	280	58	3	141	200	2,575
OR.......	3,560	3,233	64	49	122	10	82	326	2,930
PA.......	12,365	10,687	1,279	21	263	5	110	423	10,330
RI.......	1,076	960	64	6	29	1	15	103	877
SC.......	4,147	2,806	1,246	15	44	2	34	114	2,706
SD.......	764	679	6	64	6	(Z)	9	12	669
TN.......	5,842	4,721	978	17	70	3	54	146	4,588
TX.......	22,119	18,490	2,555	147	678	23	225	7,557	11,169
UT.......	2,351	2,202	23	33	45	18	31	233	1,982
VT.......	619	600	4	2	6	(Z)	7	6	595
VA.......	7,386	5,462	1,475	24	310	5	110	395	5,111
WA.......	6,131	5,243	216	100	369	27	175	508	4,779
WV.......	1,810	1,720	59	4	12	(Z)	15	13	1,709
WI.......	5,472	4,933	325	50	107	2	54	215	4,736
WY.......	501	475	5	12	3	(Z)	6	34	443

Z Less than 500.

Source: U.S. Census Bureau, "Annual Estimates of the Population by Race Alone and Hispanic or Latino Origin for the United States and States: July 1, 2003 (SC-EST2003-04);" published 30 September 2004; <http://www.census.gov/popest/states/asrh/SC-EST2003-04.html>.

No. 22. Resident Population by Region, Race, and Hispanic Origin: 2000

[As of April (281,422 represents 281,422,000). For composition of regions, see map, inside front cover]

Race and Hispanic origin	Population (1,000)					Percent distribution				
	United States	North-east	Mid-west	South	West	United States	North-east	Mid-west	South	West
Total population	281,422	53,594	64,393	100,237	63,198	100.0	19.0	22.9	35.6	22.5
One race.	274,596	52,366	63,370	98,390	60,470	100.0	19.1	23.1	35.8	22.0
White	211,461	41,534	53,834	72,819	43,274	100.0	19.6	25.5	34.4	20.5
Black or African American . . .	34,658	6,100	6,500	18,982	3,077	100.0	17.6	18.8	54.8	8.9
American Indian and Alaska Native	2,476	163	399	726	1,188	100.0	6.6	16.1	29.3	48.0
Asian	10,243	2,119	1,198	1,922	5,004	100.0	20.7	11.7	18.8	48.8
Asian Indian	1,679	554	293	441	391	100.0	33.0	17.5	26.3	23.3
Chinese	2,433	692	212	343	1,186	100.0	28.4	8.7	14.1	48.8
Filipino	1,850	202	151	245	1,253	100.0	10.9	8.2	13.2	67.7
Japanese	797	76	63	77	580	100.0	9.6	7.9	9.7	72.8
Korean	1,077	246	132	224	474	100.0	22.9	12.3	20.8	44.0
Vietnamese.	1,123	115	107	336	564	100.0	10.3	9.5	29.9	50.3
Other Asian [1]	1,285	233	239	257	556	100.0	18.2	18.6	20.0	43.2
Native Hawaiian and Other Pacific Islander	399	21	22	51	304	100.0	5.2	5.6	12.8	76.3
Native Hawaiian	141	4	6	12	118	100.0	3.2	4.1	8.9	83.8
Guamanian or Chamorro . .	58	5	5	15	34	100.0	7.9	7.9	25.1	59.1
Samoan	91	4	5	9	73	100.0	4.2	5.6	9.7	80.5
Other Pacific Islander [2] . . .	109	8	7	15	79	100.0	7.3	6.4	14.0	72.2
Some other race	15,359	2,430	1,417	3,889	7,623	100.0	15.8	9.2	25.3	49.6
Two or more races	6,826	1,228	1,022	1,847	2,728	100.0	18.0	15.0	27.1	40.0
Hispanic or Latino (of any race).	35,306	5,254	3,125	11,587	15,341	100.0	14.9	8.8	32.8	43.5
Mexican.	20,641	479	2,200	6,548	11,413	100.0	2.3	10.7	31.7	55.3
Puerto Rican	3,406	2,075	325	759	247	100.0	60.9	9.6	22.3	7.2
Cuban.	1,242	169	45	921	106	100.0	13.6	3.6	74.2	8.5
Other Hispanic or Latino. . . .	10,017	2,531	554	3,358	3,574	100.0	25.3	5.5	33.5	35.7
Not Hispanic or Latino	246,116	48,340	61,268	88,650	47,857	100.0	19.6	24.9	36.0	19.4
White alone	194,553	39,327	52,386	65,928	36,912	100.0	20.2	26.9	33.9	19.0

[1] Other Asian alone, or two or more Asian categories.   [2] Other Pacific Islander alone, or two or more Native Hawaiian and Other Pacific Islander categories.

Source: U.S. Census Bureau, "Demographic Profiles: Census 2000"; <http://www.census.gov/Press-Release/www/2001/demoprofile.html>.

No. 23. Population in Coastal Counties: 1970 to 2003

[Population as of April 1, except as indicated (3,536 represents 3,536,000). Areas as defined by U.S. National Oceanic and Atmospheric Agency, 1992. Covers 673 counties and equivalent areas with at least 15 percent of their land area either in a coastal watershed (drainage area) or in a coastal cataloging unit (a coastal area between watersheds)See Appendix III]

Year		Counties in coastal regions					Balance of United States
	Total	Total	Atlantic	Gulf of Mexico	Great Lakes	Pacific	
Land area, 1990 (1,000 sq. mi.)	3,536	888	148	114	115	510	2,649
POPULATION							
1970 (mil.).	203.3	110.0	51.1	10.0	26.0	22.8	93.3
1980 (mil.).	226.5	119.8	53.7	13.1	26.0	27.0	106.7
1990 (mil.).	248.7	133.4	59.0	15.2	25.9	33.2	115.3
2000 (mil.).	281.4	148.3	65.2	18.0	27.3	37.8	133.1
2001 (July 1) (mil.)	285.1	150.2	66.0	18.3	27.4	38.5	134.9
2002 (July 1) (mil.)	288.0	151.6	66.6	18.6	27.5	38.9	136.4
2003 (July 1) (mil.)	290.8	152.9	67.1	18.9	27.5	39.4	137.9
1970 (percent)	100	54	25	5	13	11	46
1980 (percent)	100	53	24	6	11	12	47
1990 (percent)	100	54	24	6	10	13	46
2000 (percent)	100	53	23	6	10	13	47
2003 (July 1) (percent)	100	53	23	6	9	14	47

Source: U.S. Census Bureau, U.S. Census of Population: 1970; 1980 Census of Population, Vol. 1, Chapter A (PC80-1-A-1), U.S. Summary; 1990 Census of Population and Housing (CPH1); and unpublished data.

U.S. Census Bureau, Statistical Abstract of the United States: 2004-2005

[1990 and 2000, as of April 1; beginning 2001 as of July 1 (658 represents 658,000). Covers metropolitan statistical areas with 250,000 and over population in 2003 as defined by the U.S. Office of Management and Budget as of December 2003. For definitions and components of all metropolitan and micropolitan areas, see Appendix II. Minus sign (-) indicates decrease]

Metropolitan statistical area	Number (1,000)					Percent change		Rank, 2003
	1990	2000	2001	2002	2003	1990- 2000	2000- 2003	
Akron, OH.	658	695	699	700	702	5.7	1.0	69
Albany-Schenectady-Troy, NY	810	826	830	835	841	2.0	1.8	59
Albuquerque, NM	599	730	739	752	765	21.7	4.8	64
Allentown-Bethlehem-Easton, PA-NJ	687	740	749	758	768	7.8	3.7	63
Anchorage, AK	266	320	326	333	339	20.1	6.2	140
Ann Arbor, MI	283	323	329	334	339	14.1	4.9	141
Asheville, NC.	308	369	374	378	382	19.9	3.4	124
Atlanta-Sandy Springs-Marietta, GA.	3,069	4,248	4,405	4,510	4,610	38.4	8.5	9
Atlantic City, NJ	224	253	255	259	263	12.6	4.3	165
Augusta-Richmond County, GA-SC	436	500	503	507	511	14.7	2.4	89
Austin-Round Rock, TX	846	1,250	1,321	1,347	1,378	47.7	10.2	38
Bakersfield, CA	545	662	676	692	713	21.4	7.8	67
Baltimore-Towson, MD	2,382	2,553	2,580	2,599	2,616	7.2	2.5	19
Baton Rouge, LA	624	706	710	716	723	13.2	2.4	66
Beaumont-Port Arthur, TX	361	385	383	382	383	6.6	-0.6	123
Binghamton, NY.	264	252	252	252	251	-4.6	-0.5	170
Birmingham-Hoover, AL.	957	1,052	1,060	1,065	1,073	10.0	1.9	48
Boise City-Nampa, ID	320	465	485	499	511	45.4	9.9	90
Boston-Cambridge-Quincy, MA-NH	4,134	4,391	4,432	4,440	4,440	6.2	1.1	11
Boulder, CO [1]	209	270	277	279	278	29.1	3.1	160
Bridgeport-Stamford-Norwalk, CT	828	883	890	895	899	6.6	1.9	52
Brownsville-Harlingen, TX	260	335	344	353	363	28.9	8.3	130
Buffalo-Niagara Falls, NY.	1,189	1,170	1,165	1,161	1,159	-1.6	-0.9	45
Canton-Massillon, OH.	394	407	407	407	407	3.3	-	112
Cape Coral-Fort Myers, FL.	335	441	459	476	492	31.6	11.6	97
Charleston-North Charleston, SC	507	549	555	563	572	8.3	4.1	85
Charleston, WV	308	310	307	307	307	0.6	-0.9	147
Charlotte-Gastonia-Concord, NC-SC	1,024	1,330	1,374	1,406	1,437	29.9	8.0	37
Chattanooga, TN-GA	433	477	480	483	486	10.0	2.0	98
Chicago-Naperville-Joliet, IL-IN-WI	8,182	9,098	9,200	9,269	9,334	11.2	2.6	3
Cincinnati-Middletown, OH-KY-IN	1,845	2,010	2,027	2,037	2,047	8.9	1.9	24
Cleveland-Elyria-Mentor, OH	2,102	2,148	2,144	2,142	2,140	2.2	-0.4	23
Colorado Springs, CO.	409	537	557	565	572	31.3	6.5	84
Columbia, SC	549	647	656	663	671	17.9	3.7	71
Columbus, GA-AL	266	282	283	286	287	5.7	1.9	154
Columbus, OH.	1,405	1,613	1,640	1,656	1,675	14.8	3.8	31
Corpus Christi, TX	368	403	402	405	407	9.7	0.9	114
Dallas-Fort Worth-Arlington, TX.	3,989	5,162	5,349	5,476	5,590	29.4	8.3	5
Davenport-Moline-Rock Island, IA-IL	368	376	375	375	375	2.1	-0.3	127
Dayton, OH.	844	848	846	845	846	0.5	-0.2	57
Deltona-Daytona Beach-Ormond Beach, FL	371	443	452	460	469	19.6	5.7	101
Denver-Aurora, CO [1]	1,667	2,179	2,244	2,277	2,301	30.7	5.6	22
Des Moines, IA	416	481	489	496	503	15.6	4.4	95
Detroit-Warren-Livonia, MI	4,249	4,453	4,473	4,477	4,484	4.8	0.7	10
Duluth, MN-WI.	269	275	277	276	276	2.3	0.2	162
Durham, NC	345	426	435	442	447	23.7	4.8	104
El Paso, TX.	592	680	688	695	705	14.9	3.8	68
Erie, PA.	276	281	281	280	280	1.9	-0.3	158
Eugene-Springfield, OR.	283	323	325	327	331	14.2	2.3	143
Evansville, IN-KY	325	343	343	344	346	5.5	0.8	137
Fayetteville-Springdale-Rogers, AR-MO	239	347	358	367	378	44.9	8.9	126
Fayetteville, NC	298	337	337	339	342	13.1	1.5	139
Flint, MI	430	436	439	441	442	1.3	1.4	105
Fort Collins-Loveland, CO	186	251	260	264	267	35.1	6.0	163
Fort Smith, AR-OK	234	273	276	278	280	16.7	2.4	159
Fort Wayne, IN	354	390	394	397	400	10.1	2.5	117
Fresno, CA.	667	799	815	832	850	19.8	6.4	56
Grand Rapids-Wyoming, MI.	646	740	750	757	762	14.6	2.9	65
Green Bay, WI.	244	283	286	289	291	16.0	3.1	152
Greensboro-High Point, NC.	540	643	652	656	662	19.1	2.8	72
Greenville, SC.	472	560	568	573	578	18.6	3.3	83
Harrisburg-Carlisle, PA	474	509	511	514	517	7.3	1.6	88
Hartford-West Hartford-East Hartford, CT	1,124	1,149	1,158	1,169	1,178	2.2	2.6	44
Hickory-Morganton-Lenoir, NC	292	342	347	348	350	16.9	2.4	135
Honolulu, HI	836	876	883	893	903	4.8	3.0	51
Houston-Baytown-Sugar Land, TX.	3,767	4,715	4,845	4,969	5,076	25.2	7.6	8
Huntington-Ashland, WV-KY-OH	288	289	287	287	287	0.2	-0.7	156
Huntsville, AL	293	342	348	353	358	16.8	4.5	133
Indianapolis, IN	1,294	1,525	1,554	1,575	1,595	17.8	4.6	34
Jackson, MS	447	497	501	505	510	11.2	2.6	92
Jacksonville, FL.	925	1,123	1,150	1,176	1,203	21.4	7.1	42
Kalamazoo-Portage, MI	293	315	316	318	320	7.3	1.7	145
Kansas City, MO-KS.	1,637	1,836	1,864	1,887	1,905	12.2	3.8	27
Killeen-Temple-Fort Hood, TX.	269	331	335	339	343	23.0	3.8	138
Kingsport-Bristol-Bristol, TN-VA.	276	298	298	299	300	8.3	0.4	149
Knoxville, TN.	535	616	623	630	637	15.2	3.4	76
Lakeland, FL	405	484	492	500	510	19.4	5.5	91
Lancaster, PA	423	471	475	478	483	11.3	2.6	99
Lansing-East Lansing, MI	433	448	451	454	456	3.5	1.8	103

See footnotes at end of table.

26   Population

No. 24. Large Metropolitan Statistical Areas—Population: 1990 to 2003-Con.

[1990 and 2000, as of April 1; beginning 2001 as of July 1 (658 represents 658,000). Covers metropolitan statistical areas with 250,000 and over population in 2003 as defined by the U.S. Office of Management and Budget as of December 2003. For definitions and components of all metropolitan and micropolitan areas, see Appendix II. Minus sign (-) indicates decrease]

Metropolitan statistical area	Number (1,000)					Percent change		Rank, 2003
	1990	2000	2001	2002	2003	1990-2000	2000-2003	
Las Vegas-Paradise, NV	741	1,376	1,456	1,516	1,577	85.6	14.6	35
Lexington-Fayette, KY	348	408	413	416	422	17.2	3.4	109
Lincoln, NE	229	267	270	274	278	16.5	4.1	161
Little Rock-North Little Rock, AR	535	611	617	622	628	14.1	2.9	80
Los Angeles-Long Beach-Santa Ana, CA	11,274	12,366	12,550	12,694	12,829	9.7	3.7	2
Louisville, KY-IN	1,056	1,162	1,172	1,180	1,190	10.0	2.4	43
Lubbock, TX	230	250	253	254	257	8.6	3.0	167
Madison, WI	432	502	511	520	527	16.1	5.0	87
Manchester-Nashua, NH	336	381	389	392	395	13.4	3.6	119
McAllen-Edinburg-Pharr, TX	384	569	591	613	636	48.5	11.6	77
Memphis, TN-MS-AR	1,067	1,205	1,216	1,227	1,239	12.9	2.8	41
Miami-Fort Lauderdale-Miami Beach, FL	4,056	5,008	5,118	5,209	5,289	23.5	5.6	6
Milwaukee-Waukesha-West Allis, WI	1,432	1,501	1,505	1,510	1,514	4.8	0.9	36
Minneapolis-St. Paul-Bloomington, MN-WI	2,539	2,969	3,025	3,057	3,084	16.9	3.9	16
Mobile, AL	379	400	400	399	400	5.6	-	116
Modesto, CA	371	447	465	481	492	20.6	10.1	96
Montgomery, AL	305	347	349	351	353	13.6	1.7	134
Naples-Marco Island, FL	152	251	264	276	287	65.3	14.0	155
Nashville-Davidson—Murfreesboro, TN	1,048	1,312	1,337	1,353	1,371	25.1	4.5	39
New Haven-Milford, CT	804	824	830	836	842	2.5	2.2	58
New Orleans-Metairie-Kenner, LA	1,264	1,317	1,312	1,314	1,318	4.1	0.1	40
New York-Northern New Jersey-Long Island, NY-NJ-PA	16,846	18,323	18,480	18,569	18,641	8.8	1.7	1
Norwich-New London, CT	255	259	261	262	264	1.6	1.9	164
Ocala, FL	195	259	265	272	280	32.9	8.3	157
Oklahoma City, OK	971	1,095	1,107	1,120	1,133	12.8	3.4	47
Ogden-Clearfield, UT	352	443	452	460	469	25.8	5.9	100
Omaha-Council Bluffs, NE-IA	686	767	776	783	793	11.8	3.4	60
Orlando, FL	1,225	1,645	1,708	1,756	1,803	34.3	9.6	29
Oxnard-Thousand Oaks-Ventura, CA	669	753	769	781	791	12.6	5.0	61
Palm Bay-Melbourne-Titusville, FL	399	476	487	496	506	19.4	6.2	93
Pensacola-Ferry Pass-Brent, FL	344	412	418	424	429	19.7	4.1	108
Peoria, IL	359	367	365	366	366	2.3	-0.2	129
Philadelphia-Camden-Wilmington, PA-NJ-DE	5,436	5,687	5,714	5,743	5,773	4.6	1.5	4
Phoenix-Mesa-Scottsdale, AZ	2,238	3,252	3,383	3,490	3,593	45.3	10.5	14
Pittsburgh, PA	2,468	2,431	2,422	2,416	2,410	-1.5	-0.9	21
Port St. Lucie-Fort Pierce, FL	251	319	327	337	349	27.2	9.1	136
Portland-South Portland, ME	441	488	495	500	505	10.5	3.7	94
Portland-Vancouver-Beaverton, OR-WA	1,524	1,928	1,976	2,013	2,040	26.5	5.8	25
Poughkeepsie-Newburgh-Middletown, NY	567	622	634	643	654	9.6	5.2	75
Providence-New Bedford-Fall River, RI-MA	1,510	1,583	1,598	1,612	1,623	4.8	2.5	33
Provo-Orem, UT	269	377	391	401	407	39.9	8.0	113
Raleigh-Cary, NC	544	797	833	859	884	46.5	11.0	54
Reading, PA	337	374	378	381	385	11.0	3.1	121
Reno-Sparks, NV	257	343	355	365	374	33.3	9.2	128
Richmond, VA	949	1,097	1,111	1,125	1,138	15.6	3.8	46
Riverside-San Bernardino-Ontario, CA	2,589	3,255	3,383	3,502	3,642	25.7	11.9	13
Roanoke, VA	269	288	289	289	290	7.4	0.8	153
Rochester, NY	1,002	1,038	1,039	1,040	1,041	3.5	0.3	49
Rockford, IL	284	320	324	327	331	12.9	3.3	142
Sacramento—Arden-Arcade—Roseville, CA	1,481	1,797	1,867	1,926	1,975	21.3	9.9	26
Salem, OR	278	347	352	358	363	24.9	4.5	131
Salinas, CA	356	402	408	411	414	13.0	3.2	110
Salt Lake City, UT	768	969	985	995	1,005	26.1	3.8	50
San Antonio, TX	1,408	1,712	1,749	1,786	1,821	21.6	6.4	28
San Diego-Carlsbad-San Marcos, CA	2,498	2,814	2,863	2,905	2,931	12.6	4.2	17
San Francisco-Oakland-Fremont, CA	3,684	4,124	4,179	4,164	4,157	11.9	0.8	12
San Jose-Sunnyvale-Santa Clara, CA	1,534	1,736	1,747	1,733	1,735	13.1	-0.1	30
San Luis Obispo-Paso Robles, CA	217	247	251	252	253	13.6	2.6	168
Santa Barbara-Santa Maria-Goleta, CA	370	399	401	402	403	8.0	0.9	115
Santa Cruz-Watsonville, CA	230	256	255	253	252	11.3	-1.6	169
Santa Rosa-Petaluma, CA	388	459	466	466	467	18.1	1.8	102
Sarasota-Bradenton-Venice, FL	489	590	606	620	634	20.5	7.4	78
Savannah, GA	258	293	297	301	304	13.6	3.9	148
Scranton—Wilkes-Barre, PA	575	561	556	554	552	-2.6	-1.5	86
Seattle-Tacoma-Bellevue, WA	2,559	3,044	3,095	3,122	3,142	18.9	3.2	15
Shreveport-Bossier City, LA	360	376	376	377	378	4.5	0.6	125
South Bend-Mishawaka, IN-MI	297	317	317	318	318	6.8	0.3	146
Spartanburg, SC	227	254	257	259	261	11.9	3.0	166
Spokane, WA	361	418	423	427	431	15.7	3.1	107
Springfield, MA	673	680	680	685	688	1.0	1.2	70
Springfield, MO	299	368	374	379	385	23.3	4.4	122
Stockton, CA	481	564	593	613	633	17.3	12.3	79

See footnotes at end of table.

Population 27

No. 24. Large Metropolitan Statistical Areas—Population: 1990 to 2003—Con.

[1990 and 2000, as of April 1; beginning 2001 as of July 1 (658 represents 658,000). Covers metropolitan statistical areas with 250,000 and over population in 2003 as defined by the U.S. Office of Management and Budget as of December 2003. For definitions and components of all metropolitan and micropolitan areas, see Appendix II. Minus sign (-) indicates decrease]

Metropolitan statistical area	Number (1,000)					Percent change		Rank, 2003
	1990	2000	2001	2002	2003	1990-2000	2000-2003	
St. Louis, MO-IL.	2,600	2,699	2,736	2,747	2,759	4.7	1.4	18
Syracuse, NY	660	650	651	652	654	-1.5	0.6	74
Tallahassee, FL	259	320	323	325	328	23.6	2.4	144
Tampa-St. Petersburg-Clearwater, FL.	2,068	2,396	2,444	2,489	2,532	15.9	5.7	20
Toledo, OH	654	659	660	660	661	0.8	0.3	73
Trenton-Ewing, NJ	326	351	355	358	362	7.7	3.2	132
Tucson, AZ	667	844	862	879	893	26.5	5.8	53
Tulsa, OK	761	860	868	876	880	12.9	2.4	55
Utica-Rome, NY.	317	300	298	298	298	-5.3	-0.6	150
Vallejo-Fairfield, CA	339	395	404	410	412	16.2	4.5	111
Virginia Beach-Norfolk-Newport News, VA-NC.	1,451	1,576	1,591	1,614	1,637	8.7	3.9	32
Visalia-Porterville, CA	312	368	374	381	391	18.0	6.2	120
Washington-Arlington-Alexandria, DC-VA-MD-WV.	4,122	4,796	4,926	5,013	5,090	16.3	6.1	7
Wichita, KS.	511	571	575	580	583	11.7	2.0	82
Wilmington, NC	200	275	281	287	293	37.2	6.8	151
Winston-Salem, NC	361	422	428	433	438	16.7	3.7	106
Worcester, MA.	710	751	762	770	777	5.8	3.4	62
York-Hanover, PA.	340	382	386	389	395	12.4	3.4	118
Youngstown-Warren-Boardman, OH-PA	614	603	599	596	593	-1.7	-1.6	81

- Represents or rounds to zero.   [1] Broomfield County, CO was formed from parts of Adams, Boulder, Jefferson, and Weld Counties, CO on November 15, 2001 and is coextensive with Broomfield city. For purposes of defining and presenting data for metropolitan statistical areas, Broomfield city is treated as if it were a county at the time of the 1990 and 2000 censuses.

Source: U.S. Census Bureau, "Ranking Tables for Population of Metropolitan Statistical Areas, Micropolitan Statistical Areas, Combined Statistical Areas, New England City and Town Areas, and Combined New England City and Town Areas: 1990 and 2000 (Areas defined by the Office of Management and Budget as of June 6, 2003.) (PHC-T-29)"; published 30 December 2003; <http://www.census.gov/population/www/cen2000/phc-t29.html> and unpublished data.

No. 25. Urban and Rural Population by State: 1990 and 2000

[In thousands, except percent (248,718 represents 248,718,000). As of April 1. Resident population. Based on current urban definition; see text, this section]

State	Total	Urban		Rural	State	Total	Urban		Rural
		Number	Percent				Number	Percent	
1990, total . . .	[1]248,718	194,097	78.0	54,613	MS	2,845	1,387	48.8	1,457
2000, total . .	281,422	222,361	79.0	59,061	MO	5,595	3,883	69.4	1,712
					MT	902	488	54.1	414
AL.	4,447	2,466	55.4	1,981	NE.	1,711	1,194	69.8	518
AK.	627	411	65.6	216	NV.	1,998	1,829	91.5	170
AZ.	5,131	4,524	88.2	607	NH .	1,236	732	59.3	503
AR.	2,673	1,404	52.5	1,269					
CA.	33,872	31,990	94.4	1,882	NJ.	8,414	7,939	94.4	475
					NM.	1,819	1,364	75.0	456
CO	4,301	3,633	84.5	668	NY.	18,976	16,603	87.5	2,374
CT.	3,406	2,988	87.7	418	NC.	8,049	4,849	60.2	3,200
DE.	784	628	80.1	156	ND.	642	359	55.9	283
DC	572	572	100.0	-					
FL.	15,982	14,270	89.3	1,712	OH	11,353	8,782	77.4	2,571
					OK	3,451	2,255	65.3	1,196
GA .	8,186	5,864	71.6	2,322	OR	3,421	2,694	78.7	727
HI .	1,212	1,108	91.5	103	PA.	12,281	9,464	77.1	2,817
ID .	1,294	859	66.4	434	RI .	1,048	953	90.9	95
IL .	12,419	10,910	87.8	1,510					
IN .	6,080	4,304	70.8	1,776	SC.	4,012	2,427	60.5	1,585
					SD.	755	391	51.9	363
IA .	2,926	1,787	61.1	1,139	TN.	5,689	3,620	63.6	2,069
KS.	2,688	1,921	71.4	768	TX.	20,852	17,204	82.5	3,648
KY.	4,042	2,254	55.8	1,788	UT.	2,233	1,970	88.2	263
LA .	4,469	3,246	72.6	1,223					
ME .	1,275	513	40.2	762	VT.	609	232	38.2	376
					VA.	7,079	5,170	73.0	1,909
MD .	5,296	4,559	86.1	738	WA .	5,894	4,831	82.0	1,063
MA .	6,349	5,801	91.4	548	WV .	1,808	833	46.1	976
MI .	9,938	7,419	74.7	2,519	WI .	5,364	3,664	68.3	1,700
MN .	4,919	3,490	70.9	1,429	WY .	494	321	65.1	172

- Represents zero.   [1] Count has been revised since the publication of the 1990 census reports.

Source: U.S. Census Bureau, 2000 Census of Population and Housing, *Population and Housing Unit Counts* PHC-3.

No. 26. Incorporated Places by Population Size: 1980 to 2003

[140.3 represents 140,300,000. See Appendix III]

Population size	Number of incorporated places				Population (mil.)				Percent of total			
	1980	1990	2000	2003	1980	1990	2000	2003	1980	1990	2000	2003
Total	19,097	19,262	19,452	19,450	140.3	152.9	173.5	179.8	100.0	100.0	100.0	100.0
1,000,000 or more. . . .	6	8	9	9	17.5	20.0	22.9	23.3	12.5	13.0	13.2	13.0
500,000 to 999,999 . . .	16	15	20	22	10.9	10.1	12.9	14.0	7.8	6.6	7.4	7.8
250,000 to 499,999 . . .	33	41	37	37	11.8	14.2	13.3	13.3	8.4	9.3	7.7	7.4
100,000 to 249,999 . . .	114	131	172	177	16.6	19.1	25.5	26.8	11.8	12.5	14.7	14.9
50,000 to 99,999.	250	309	363	397	17.6	21.2	24.9	27.5	12.3	13.9	14.3	15.3
25,000 to 49,999.	526	567	644	665	18.4	20.0	22.6	23.2	13.1	13.0	13.0	12.9
10,000 to 24,999.	1,260	1,290	1,435	1,460	19.8	20.3	22.6	22.9	14.1	13.3	13.0	12.8
Under 10,000	16,892	16,901	16,772	16,683	28.0	28.2	28.7	28.7	20.0	18.4	16.6	16.0

Source: U.S. Census Bureau, *Census of Population: 1980*, Vol. I; *1990 Census of Population and Housing, Population and Housing Unit Counts* (CPH-2-1); *County and City Data Book 2000*; and "Table 4: Annual Estimates of the Population for Incorporated Places, Listed Alphabetically: April 1, 2000 to July 1, 2003;" published 23 June 2004; http://eire.census.gov/popest/data/cities/tables/SUB-EST2003-04.php>.

No. 27. Incorporated Places With 100,000 or More Inhabitants in 2003—Population, 1980 to 2003, and Land Area, 2000

[Population: As of April 1, except 2003 as of July 1 (98 represents 98,000). 2003 data refer to boundaries in effect on January 1, 2003; 1990 and 2000 data, boundaries in effect on January 1, 2000; 1980 data, boundaries in effect for 1980 census. Minus sign (-) indicates decrease. See Appendix III]

Incorporated place	1980, total popula- tion (1,000)	1990, total popula- tion (1,000)	Population, 2000		Population, 2003			Land area, 2000 (square miles)
			Total (1,000)	Percent change, 1990-2000	Total (1,000)	Rank	Percent change [1], 2000-2003	
Abilene, TX	98	107	116	8.4	115	204	-0.9	105.1
Akron, OH	237	223	217	-2.7	212	86	-2.2	62.1
Albuquerque, NM	332	387	449	15.9	472	33	5.1	180.6
Alexandria, VA	103	111	128	15.4	129	173	0.5	15.2
Allentown, PA.	104	105	107	1.1	106	222	-0.6	17.7
Amarillo, TX.	149	158	174	10.0	179	120	2.9	89.9
Anaheim, CA	219	267	328	23.0	332	52	1.3	48.9
Anchorage, AK	174	226	260	15.0	271	67	4.1	1,697.2
Ann Arbor, MI.	108	110	114	3.5	114	205	0.3	27.0
Antioch, CA	43	62	91	45.6	101	242	11.7	26.9
Arlington, VA [2]	153	171	189	10.9	188	113	-0.8	26.0
Arlington, TX	160	262	333	27.1	355	49	6.6	95.8
Arvada, CO	85	90	102	13.8	102	238	-0.3	32.7
Athens-Clarke County, GA [3]	(NA)	87	100	15.9	102	233	2.2	117.8
Atlanta, GA	425	394	416	5.8	423	41	1.6	131.7
Augusta-Richmond County, GA [3].	(NA)	186	195	4.8	193	110	-1.0	302.1
Aurora, CO	159	222	276	24.6	290	59	5.3	142.5
Aurora, IL	81	100	143	42.6	162	131	13.3	38.5
Austin, TX	346	494	657	32.8	672	16	2.4	251.5
Bakersfield, CA	106	184	247	34.3	271	66	11.5	113.1
Baltimore, MD	787	736	651	-11.5	629	18	-3.5	80.8
Baton Rouge, LA	220	222	228	2.5	225	79	-1.5	76.8
Beaumont, TX	118	114	114	-0.5	112	208	-1.3	85.0
Bellevue, WA	74	99	110	11.1	112	209	-0.1	30.7
Berkeley, CA	103	103	103	-0.1	102	237	-0.7	10.5
Birmingham, AL	284	266	243	-8.7	237	74	-2.5	149.9
Boise City, ID.	102	135	186	37.5	190	112	2.2	63.8
Boston, MA	563	574	589	2.6	582	23	-1.3	48.4
Bridgeport, CT	143	142	140	-1.4	140	164	0.1	16.0
Brownsville, TX	85	115	140	21.3	156	136	11.8	80.4
Buffalo, NY	358	328	293	-10.8	285	60	-2.6	40.6
Burbank, CA	87	94	100	7.1	103	231	3.0	17.3
Cambridge, MA	95	96	101	5.7	102	239	0.2	6.4
Cape Coral, FL.	32	75	102	36.1	119	195	16.1	105.2
Carrollton, TX.	41	83	110	32.7	117	201	6.5	36.5

See footnotes at end of table.

Population 29

No. 27. Incorporated Places With 100,000 or More Inhabitants in 2003—Population, 1980 to 2003, and Land Area, 2000–Con.

[Population: As of April 1 (98 represents 98,000), except 2003 as of July 1. 2003 data refer to boundaries in effect on January 1, 2003; 1990 and 2000 data, boundaries in effect on January 1, 2000; 1980 data, boundaries in effect for 1980 census. Minus sign (-) indicates decrease. See Appendix III]

Incorporated place	1980, total population (1,000)	1990, total population (1,000)	Population, 2000			Population, 2003			Land area, 2000 (square miles)
			Total (1,000)	Percent change, 1990-2000	Total (1,000)	Rank	Percent change [1] 2000-2003	
Cedar Rapids, IA	110	109	121	10.9	123	189	1.0	63.1
Chandler, AZ	30	91	177	94.7	211	87	19.6	57.9
Charleston, SC	70	80	97	20.9	101	243	4.5	97.0
Charlotte, NC	315	427	541	26.7	585	21	4.8	242.3
Chattanooga, TN	170	153	156	1.8	155	137	-0.5	135.2
Chesapeake, VA	114	152	199	31.1	211	88	5.8	340.7
Chicago, IL	3,005	2,784	2,896	4.0	2,869	3	-0.9	227.1
Chula Vista, CA	84	135	174	28.3	199	95	14.7	48.9
Cincinnati, OH	385	365	331	-9.1	317	56	-4.2	78.0
Clarksville, TN	55	77	103	35.2	108	220	4.3	94.9
Clearwater, FL	85	97	109	11.9	108	217	-0.6	25.3
Cleveland, OH	574	505	478	-5.4	461	35	-3.4	77.6
Colorado Springs, CO	215	283	361	27.5	370	48	2.6	185.7
Columbia, SC	101	114	116	1.6	117	198	0.9	125.2
Columbus, GA	[3]169	[3]179	[3]186	4.0	186	114	-0.3	216.1
Columbus, OH	565	636	711	11.8	728	15	2.4	210.3
Concord, CA	104	111	122	9.5	125	182	2.5	30.1
Coral Springs, FL	37	79	118	48.5	127	178	8.0	23.9
Corona, CA	38	76	125	64.0	142	160	13.7	35.1
Corpus Christi, TX	232	258	277	7.4	279	63	0.6	154.6
Costa Mesa, CA	83	97	109	12.3	110	214	0.7	15.6
Dallas, TX	905	1,007	1,189	18.1	1,208	9	1.7	342.5
Daly City, CA	79	92	104	12.4	101	244	-2.7	7.6
Dayton, OH	194	182	166	-8.9	162	132	-2.7	55.8
Denver, CO	493	468	555	18.6	557	26	0.7	153.4
Des Moines, IA	191	193	199	2.8	196	102	-1.3	75.8
Detroit, MI	1,203	1,028	951	-7.5	911	10	-4.2	138.8
Downey, CA	83	91	107	17.3	110	213	2.8	12.4
Durham, NC	101	148	187	26.0	198	96	5.9	94.6
El Monte, CA	79	106	116	9.2	122	191	5.0	9.6
El Paso, TX	425	516	564	9.3	584	22	3.6	249.1
Elizabeth, NJ	106	110	121	9.5	123	188	2.2	12.2
Erie, PA	119	109	104	-4.6	101	241	-2.3	22.0
Escondido, CA	64	109	134	22.5	136	167	1.8	36.3
Eugene, OR	106	114	138	21.1	142	161	2.8	40.5
Evansville, IN	130	126	122	-3.6	118	197	-3.0	40.7
Fairfield, CA	58	79	96	22.1	103	232	6.8	37.7
Fayetteville, NC	60	113	121	7.4	124	185	-0.5	58.8
Flint, MI	160	141	125	-11.6	120	192	-3.7	33.6
Fontana, CA	37	88	129	46.7	152	142	17.8	36.1
Fort Collins, CO	65	89	119	33.5	126	181	5.9	46.5
Fort Lauderdale, FL	153	149	152	2.4	163	129	5.7	31.7
Fort Wayne, IN	172	203	206	1.3	219	80	-0.4	79.0
Fort Worth, TX	385	448	535	19.3	585	20	8.1	292.5
Fremont, CA	132	173	203	17.3	205	91	0.5	76.7
Fresno, CA	217	355	428	20.3	451	36	5.3	104.4
Fullerton, CA	102	113	126	11.1	131	171	4.2	22.2
Gainesville, FL	81	85	95	12.2	109	215	-2.0	48.2
Garden Grove, CA	123	144	165	15.0	167	127	1.1	18.0
Garland, TX	139	181	216	19.3	218	82	1.0	57.1
Gilbert, AZ	6	30	110	265.6	145	152	32.1	43.0
Glendale, AZ	97	151	219	45.0	233	76	6.4	55.7
Glendale, CA	139	180	195	8.3	200	92	2.8	30.6
Grand Prairie, TX	71	99	127	28.1	137	166	7.3	71.4
Grand Rapids, MI	182	190	198	4.3	196	103	-1.1	44.6
Green Bay, WI	88	97	102	5.8	101	240	-1.3	43.9
Greensboro, NC	156	192	224	16.9	229	77	2.3	104.7
Hampton, VA	123	134	146	9.5	147	150	0.3	51.8
Hartford, CT	136	137	122	-11.4	124	184	0.2	17.3
Hayward, CA	94	115	140	22.1	141	162	0.9	44.3
Henderson, NV	24	65	175	169.4	215	85	22.5	79.7
Hialeah, FL	145	188	226	20.5	226	78	(Z)	19.2
Hollywood, FL	121	123	139	13.5	143	156	2.8	27.3
Honolulu, HI [2]	365	377	372	-1.4	380	45	2.3	85.7
Houston, TX	1,595	1,698	1,954	15.1	2,010	4	2.9	579.4
Huntington Beach, CA	171	183	190	3.7	194	107	2.4	26.4
Huntsville, AL	143	160	158	-1.3	164	128	3.6	174.0
Independence, MO	112	112	113	0.8	112	210	-1.1	78.3
Indianapolis, IN [3]	701	732	782	6.9	783	12	0.2	361.5
Inglewood, CA	94	110	113	1.9	115	203	2.3	9.1

See footnotes at end of table.

U.S. Census Bureau, Statistical Abstract of the United States: 2004-2005

No. 27. Incorporated Places With 100,000 or More Inhabitants in 2003—Population, 1980 to 2003, and Land Area, 2000–Con.

[Population: As of April 1 (98 represents 98,000), except 2003 as of July 1. 2003 data refer to boundaries in effect on January 1, 2003; 1990 and 2000 data, boundaries in effect on January 1, 2000; 1980 data, boundaries in effect for 1980 census. Minus sign (-) indicates decrease. See Appendix III]

Incorporated place	1980, total population (1,000)	1990, total population (1,000)	Population, 2000 Total (1,000)	Population, 2000 Percent change, 1990-2000	Population, 2003 Total (1,000)	Population, 2003 Rank	Population, 2003 Percent change [1] 2000-2003	Land area, 2000 (square miles)
Irvine, CA	62	111	143	28.4	171	124	19.2	46.2
Irving, TX	110	155	192	23.5	194	106	1.5	67.2
Jackson, MS	203	197	184	-6.3	180	119	-2.5	104.9
Jacksonville, FL	541	635	736	15.8	774	13	5.2	757.7
Jersey City, NJ	224	228	240	5.1	239	73	-0.4	14.9
Joliet, IL	78	79	106	35.2	124	187	15.9	38.1
Kansas City, KS	161	151	147	-3.0	146	151	-0.8	124.3
Kansas City, MO	448	435	442	1.5	443	38	0.3	313.5
Knoxville, TN	175	173	174	0.4	173	123	-0.7	92.7
Lafayette, LA	81	103	110	7.5	112	212	0.2	47.6
Lakewood, CO	114	126	144	14.2	142	159	-1.2	41.6
Lancaster, CA	48	98	119	20.6	126	180	6.0	94.0
Lansing, MI	130	127	119	-6.1	118	196	-0.8	35.0
Laredo, TX	91	125	177	41.2	197	98	11.4	78.5
Las Vegas, NV	165	260	478	84.1	517	30	7.8	113.3
Lexington-Fayette, KY	204	225	261	15.6	267	68	2.4	284.5
Lincoln, NE	172	193	226	17.0	236	75	4.4	74.6
Little Rock, AR	159	177	183	3.4	184	115	0.5	116.2
Long Beach, CA	361	430	462	7.4	475	32	3.0	50.4
Los Angeles, CA	2,969	3,485	3,695	6.0	3,820	2	3.4	469.1
Louisville, KY	299	270	256	-5.0	249	69	-2.9	62.1
Lowell, MA	92	103	105	1.7	104	227	-0.8	13.8
Lubbock, TX	174	187	200	6.9	206	90	3.5	114.8
Madison, WI	171	191	208	9.0	218	81	4.6	68.7
Manchester, NH	91	99	107	7.9	109	216	1.7	33.0
McAllen, TX	66	86	106	24.3	117	202	9.5	46.0
Memphis, TN	646	619	650	5.0	646	17	-0.6	279.3
Mesa, AZ	152	290	396	36.6	432	40	8.7	125.0
Mesquite, TX	67	102	125	22.4	129	172	3.8	43.4
Miami, FL	347	360	362	0.7	377	46	4.0	35.7
Milwaukee, WI	636	628	597	-5.0	587	19	-1.7	96.1
Minneapolis, MN	371	368	383	3.9	373	47	-2.5	54.9
Mobile, AL	200	198	199	0.3	193	109	-2.9	117.9
Modesto, CA	107	166	189	13.5	207	89	9.5	35.8
Montgomery, AL	178	191	202	5.6	200	93	-0.7	155.4
Moreno Valley, CA	(4)	119	142	19.9	157	135	10.3	51.2
Naperville, IL	43	87	128	47.6	138	165	7.4	35.4
Nashville-Davidson, TN [3]	456	488	546	11.7	545	27	-0.1	473.3
New Haven, CT	126	130	124	-5.0	125	183	0.7	18.9
New Orleans, LA	558	497	485	-2.5	469	34	-3.2	180.6
New York, NY	7,072	7,323	8,008	9.4	8,086	1	1.0	303.3
Newark, NJ	329	275	274	-0.6	278	64	2.0	23.8
Newport News, VA	145	171	180	5.1	182	116	0.8	68.3
Norfolk, VA	267	261	234	-10.3	242	72	3.1	53.7
North Las Vegas, NV	43	48	115	140.8	145	153	25.1	78.5
Norwalk, CA	85	94	103	9.7	107	221	2.7	9.7
Oakland, CA	339	400	399	-0.1	399	43	-0.2	56.1
Oceanside, CA	77	129	161	25.2	167	126	3.8	40.6
Oklahoma City, OK	404	445	506	13.8	523	29	3.4	607.0
Olathe, KS	37	63	93	46.5	105	226	13.2	54.2
Omaha, NE	314	358	390	9.0	404	42	3.4	115.7
Ontario, CA	89	133	158	18.6	167	125	5.9	49.8
Orange, CA	91	111	129	16.4	132	170	2.6	23.4
Orlando, FL	128	163	186	13.8	199	94	4.4	93.5
Overland Park, KS	82	112	149	33.3	160	133	7.3	56.7
Oxnard, CA	108	142	170	19.6	181	117	6.2	25.3
Palmdale, CA	12	77	117	50.9	128	175	9.4	105.0
Pasadena, CA	118	132	134	1.7	141	163	5.4	44.2
Pasadena, TX	113	119	142	18.7	144	154	1.9	23.1
Paterson, NJ	138	158	149	-5.6	151	147	1.0	8.4
Pembroke Pines, FL	36	65	137	110.0	149	148	8.4	33.1
Peoria, AZ	12	51	108	111.8	128	176	17.4	138.2
Peoria, IL	124	114	113	-0.8	113	207	-0.1	44.4
Philadelphia, PA	1,688	1,586	1,518	-4.3	1,479	5	-2.5	135.1
Phoenix, AZ	790	989	1,321	33.6	1,388	6	5.1	474.9
Pittsburgh, PA	424	370	335	-9.6	325	54	-2.8	55.6
Plano, TX	72	129	222	72.8	242	71	9.0	71.6
Pomona, CA	93	132	149	13.0	154	138	3.1	22.8
Port St. Lucie, FL	15	56	89	59.2	106	224	18.8	75.5
Portland, OR	368	486	529	8.9	539	28	1.8	134.3

See footnotes at end of table.

U.S. Census Bureau, Statistical Abstract of the United States: 2004-2005

[Population: As of April 1 (98 represents 98,000), except 2003 as of July 1. 2003 data refer to boundaries in effect on January 1, 2003; 1990 and 2000 data, boundaries in effect on January 1, 2000; 1980 data, boundaries in effect for 1980 census. Minus sign (-) indicates decrease. See Appendix III]

Incorporated place	1980, total population (1,000)	1990, total population (1,000)	Population, 2000 Total (1,000)	Population, 2000 Percent change, 1990-2000	Population, 2003 Total (1,000)	Population, 2003 Rank	Population, 2003 Percent change[1], 2000-2003	Land area, 2000 (square miles)
Providence, RI	157	160	174	8.3	176	121	1.6	18.5
Provo, UT	74	87	105	20.7	105	225	(Z)	39.6
Pueblo, CO	102	99	102	3.1	104	229	1.5	45.1
Raleigh, NC	150	220	276	25.3	317	57	12.0	114.6
Rancho Cucamonga, CA	55	101	128	26.0	152	145	18.7	37.4
Reno, NV	101	135	180	33.9	194	108	7.2	69.1
Richmond, CA	75	86	99	15.5	102	235	3.1	30.0
Richmond, VA	219	203	198	-2.4	195	105	-1.5	60.1
Riverside, CA	171	227	255	12.6	282	61	10.3	78.1
Rochester, NY	242	231	220	-4.8	215	84	-2.1	35.8
Rockford, IL	140	144	150	4.3	152	143	0.9	56.0
Sacramento, CA	276	395	407	3.0	445	37	9.4	97.2
Salem, OR	89	109	137	25.8	143	157	4.3	45.7
Salinas, CA	80	109	151	38.8	148	149	3.6	19.0
Salt Lake City, UT	163	160	182	13.6	180	118	-1.0	109.1
San Antonio, TX	786	997	1,145	14.8	1,215	8	5.5	407.6
San Bernardino, CA	119	171	185	8.3	195	104	5.5	58.8
San Buenaventura (Ventura), CA.	74	94	101	7.8	104	228	3.2	21.1
San Diego, CA	876	1,111	1,223	10.1	1,267	7	3.5	324.3
San Francisco, CA	679	724	777	7.3	752	14	-3.2	46.7
San Jose, CA	629	783	895	14.2	898	11	0.4	174.9
Santa Ana, CA	204	294	338	14.8	343	51	1.3	27.1
Santa Clara, CA	88	93	102	9.7	102	236	-0.3	18.4
Santa Clarita, CA	(4)	124	151	22.2	163	130	7.7	47.8
Santa Rosa, CA	83	120	148	22.5	153	140	3.7	40.1
Savannah, GA	142	138	132	-4.4	128	177	-3.2	74.7
Scottsdale, AZ	89	130	203	55.8	218	83	7.6	184.2
Seattle, WA	494	516	563	9.1	569	24	1.0	83.9
Shreveport, LA	206	198	200	0.9	198	97	-0.9	103.1
Simi Valley, CA	78	100	111	11.0	117	199	5.2	39.2
Sioux Falls, SD	81	101	124	22.2	134	169	7.5	56.3
South Bend, IN	110	106	108	1.6	106	223	-2.2	38.7
Spokane, WA	171	178	196	9.8	197	101	0.5	57.8
Springfield, IL	100	107	111	3.9	114	206	1.8	54.0
Springfield, MA	152	157	152	-3.1	152	141	(Z)	32.1
Springfield, MO	133	141	152	7.4	151	146	-0.6	73.2
Stamford, CT	102	108	117	8.3	120	193	2.6	37.7
Sterling Heights, MI	109	118	124	5.7	126	179	1.4	36.6
Stockton, CA	150	211	244	15.3	271	65	11.4	54.7
St. Louis, MO	453	397	348	-12.3	332	53	-4.6	61.9
St. Paul, MN	270	272	287	5.5	280	62	-2.2	52.8
St. Petersburg, FL	239	240	248	3.3	248	70	-0.3	59.6
Sunnyvale, CA	107	117	132	12.3	129	174	-2.5	21.9
Syracuse, NY	170	164	147	-10.1	144	155	-1.7	25.1
Tacoma, WA	159	177	194	9.1	197	100	1.7	50.1
Tallahassee, FL	82	125	151	20.1	154	139	1.7	95.7
Tampa, FL	272	281	303	8.1	318	55	4.7	112.1
Tempe, AZ	107	142	159	11.7	159	134	0.2	40.1
Thousand Oaks, CA	77	104	117	12.5	124	186	6.1	54.9
Toledo, OH	355	333	314	-5.8	309	58	-1.5	80.6
Topeka, KS	119	121	122	1.3	122	190	-0.7	56.0
Torrance, CA	130	133	138	3.5	143	158	3.4	20.5
Tucson, AZ	331	417	487	16.7	508	31	4.2	194.7
Tulsa, OK	361	367	393	7.0	388	44	-1.4	182.6
Vallejo, CA	80	111	117	5.3	120	194	2.5	30.2
Vancouver, WA	43	105	144	37.3	152	144	5.6	42.8
Virginia Beach, VA	262	393	425	8.2	439	39	3.3	248.3
Visalia, CA	50	76	92	21.0	101	245	9.4	28.6
Waco, TX	101	104	114	9.4	117	200	2.6	84.2
Warren, MI	161	145	138	-4.7	136	168	-1.6	34.3
Washington, DC	638	607	572	-5.7	563	25	-1.5	61.4
Waterbury, CT	103	108	107	-0.9	108	219	0.8	28.6
West Covina, CA	80	96	105	9.6	108	218	3.0	16.1
West Valley City, UT	(4)	87	109	25.2	112	211	2.6	35.4
Westminster, CO	50	74	101	36.1	103	230	2.4	31.5
Wichita, KS	280	309	344	11.5	355	50	1.0	135.8
Wichita Falls, TX	94	97	104	7.7	102	234	-1.8	70.7
Winston-Salem, NC	132	167	186	11.1	190	111	2.4	108.9
Worcester, MA	162	170	173	1.8	176	122	1.8	37.6
Yonkers, NY	195	188	196	4.2	197	99	0.7	18.1

NA Not available.   Z Less than 0.05 percent.   [1] Based on the April 1, 2000 Population Estimates Base which reflects modifications to the Census 2000 population as documented in the Count Question Resolution program, updates from the Boundary and Annexation Survey, and geographic program revisions.   [2] The population shown is for the census designated place (CDP).   [3] Represents the portion of a consolidated city that is not within one or more separately incorporated places.   [4] Not incorporated.

Source: U.S. Census Bureau, 1990 Census of Population and Housing, Population and Housing Unit Counts, (CPH-2); "Population Estimates for Cities with Populations of 10,000 and Greater (Sorted Within State by 1999 Population Size): July 1, 1999 (includes April 1, 1990 Population Estimates Base)"; published 20 October 2000; <http://www.census.gov/population/estimates/metrocity/SC10K-T3.txt>; and "Incorporated Place Population Estimates, Sorted Alphabetically: April 1, 2000 to July 1, 2003"; published 24 June 2004; <http://eire.census.gov/popest/data/cities/tables/SUB-EST2003.php>.

No. 28. Mobility Status of the Population by Selected Characteristics: 1980 to 2003

[As of March (221,641 represents 221,641,000). For persons 1 year old and over. Excludes members of the Armed Forces except those living off post or with their families on post. Based on Current Population Survey; see text of this section and Appendix III. For composition of regions, see map, inside front cover]

Mobility period and characteristic	Total (1,000)	Percent distribution						
			Movers (different house in United States)					Movers from abroad
		Non-movers	Total	Same county	Different county			
					Total	Same state	Different state	
1980-1981	221,641	83	17	10	6	3	3	1
1990-1991	244,884	83	16	10	6	3	3	1
2000-2001	275,611	86	14	8	6	3	3	1
2001-2002	278,160	85	14	9	5	3	2	1
2002-2003, total	282,556	86	14	8	5	3	3	(Z)
1 to 4 years old	16,408	79	21	14	7	4	3	1
5 to 9 years old	19,708	84	15	10	6	3	3	(Z)
10 to 14 years old	21,190	87	13	8	5	2	2	(Z)
15 to 19 years old	20,182	86	14	8	5	3	2	(Z)
20 to 24 years old	19,884	70	29	18	11	6	6	1
25 to 29 years old	18,721	72	27	16	11	5	5	1
30 to 44 years old	64,595	85	15	9	6	3	3	1
45 to 64 years old	67,633	92	8	4	3	1	2	(Z)
65 to 74 years old	18,111	96	4	2	2	1	1	(Z)
75 to 84 years old	12,576	96	4	2	2	1	1	(Z)
85 years old and over	3,547	96	4	2	1	1	(Z)	(Z)
Northeast	53,547	89	11	6	4	2	2	(Z)
Midwest	63,846	87	13	8	5	3	3	(Z)
South	100,582	85	14	8	6	3	3	1
West	64,581	83	17	10	6	3	3	1
Persons 16 years and over	221,141	86	13	8	5	3	3	(Z)
Civilian labor force	145,616	85	15	9	6	3	3	(Z)
Employed	136,277	85	14	9	6	3	3	(Z)
Unemployed	9,339	78	21	12	9	4	4	1
Armed Forces	856	68	29	10	19	6	13	3
Not in labor force	74,668	90	10	5	4	2	2	1
Employed civilians, 16 years and over	136,277	85	14	9	6	3	3	(Z)
Management, business, and financial	20,115	88	11	6	5	3	2	(Z)
Professional	27,457	85	14	8	6	3	3	(Z)
Service	21,893	82	17	11	6	3	3	1
Sales	15,899	85	15	9	6	3	3	(Z)
Office and administrative support	19,601	86	14	9	5	3	2	(Z)
Farming, fishing, and forestry	877	85	14	9	5	3	2	1
Construction and extraction	7,867	83	17	11	6	3	3	(Z)
Installation, maintenance, and repair	4,913	86	14	9	5	3	2	(Z)
Production	9,536	86	13	9	5	2	2	(Z)
Transportation and material moving	8,117	84	15	10	5	3	2	(Z)
Tenure:								
Owner-occupied units	200,627	93	7	4	3	2	1	(Z)
Renter-occupied units	81,929	69	30	18	11	6	6	1

Z Less than 0.5 percent.

Source: U.S. Census Bureau, "Geographic Mobility: 2003; Detailed Tables for P20-549"; published 23 March 2004; <http://www.census.gov/population/www/socdemo/migrate/p20-549.html>, and earlier Current Population Reports.

No. 29. Mobility Status of Households by Household Income: 2002-2003

[As of March (111,298 represents 111,298,000). Covers householders 15 years old and over. Excludes members of the Armed Forces except those living off post or with their families on post. Based on Current Population Survey; see text of this section and Appendix III]

Household income in 2002	Total (1,000)	Percent distribution						
			Movers (different house in United States)					Movers from abroad
		Non-movers	Total	Same county	Different county			
					Total	Same state	Different state	
Householders, 15 years and over	111,298	86	13	8	5	3	3	(Z)
Less than $5,000	3,533	77	21	12	8	4	5	3
$5,000 to $9,999	6,557	84	16	10	5	3	3	(Z)
$10,000 to $14,999	7,838	84	15	9	7	3	3	(Z)
$15,000 to $24,999	14,651	84	16	10	6	3	3	(Z)
$25,000 to $34,999	13,673	84	15	10	6	3	3	(Z)
$35,000 to $49,999	16,817	86	14	8	6	3	3	(Z)
$50,000 to $74,999	16,862	88	12	8	5	2	2	(Z)
$75,000 and over	31,367	90	10	5	5	2	2	(Z)

Z Less than 0.5 percent.

Source: U.S. Census Bureau, "Geographic Mobility: 2003; Detailed Tables for P20-549"; published 23 March 2004; <http://www.census.gov/population/www/socdemo/migrate/p20-549.html>.

Population   33

No. 30. Mobility Status of Resident Population by State: 2000

[In thousands, except percent (262,375 represents 262,375,000). As of April 1. Based on comparison of place of residence in 1995 and 2000. Based on sample data from the 2000 Census of Population and Housing; see text of this section and Appendix III]

State	Population 5 years and over	Same house in 1995	Different house in United States in 1995						
			Total		Same county	Different county			
			Number	Percent of population 5 yrs. and over		Total	Same state	Different state	Elsewhere in 1995
U.S. . . .	262,375	142,027	112,852	43.0	65,435	47,417	25,327	22,089	7,496
AL.	4,152	2,385	1,719	41.4	1,027	692	366	326	49
AK.	580	268	299	51.6	160	139	43	96	13
AZ.	4,753	2,104	2,466	51.9	1,456	1,009	213	796	183
AR.	2,492	1,327	1,131	45.4	618	513	261	252	34
CA.	31,417	15,758	14,251	45.4	9,714	4,537	3,088	1,449	1,408
CO	4,006	1,769	2,103	52.5	920	1,183	539	644	135
CT.	3,185	1,853	1,228	38.6	799	429	168	261	104
DE.	732	410	305	41.7	187	118	17	101	17
DC	540	269	240	44.5	127	113	(X)	113	30
FL.	15,044	7,352	7,039	46.8	3,866	3,173	1,312	1,861	653
GA	7,594	3,736	3,615	47.6	1,605	2,010	1,045	966	243
HI	1,134	644	444	39.1	295	149	24	125	47
ID	1,197	594	582	48.6	286	296	113	183	21
IL	11,548	6,558	4,635	40.1	3,011	1,624	959	665	354
IN	5,658	3,111	2,472	43.7	1,444	1,028	576	451	75
IA	2,738	1,558	1,142	41.7	637	504	290	215	38
KS.	2,500	1,310	1,139	45.5	606	533	256	277	51
KY.	3,776	2,112	1,618	42.8	933	686	367	319	46
LA	4,153	2,452	1,659	39.9	1,017	642	388	254	42
ME	1,204	717	476	39.5	276	201	93	108	11
MD	4,945	2,752	2,046	41.4	1,085	960	465	495	147
MA	5,954	3,482	2,267	38.1	1,356	911	464	447	206
MI.	9,269	5,307	3,802	41.0	2,324	1,478	1,010	468	160
MN	4,591	2,618	1,889	41.1	934	955	600	355	85
MS	2,641	1,545	1,071	40.6	595	476	249	227	25
MO	5,226	2,803	2,355	45.1	1,229	1,126	653	473	67
MT	847	454	386	45.6	191	195	84	112	7
NE.	1,595	872	694	43.5	373	321	167	154	28
NV.	1,854	693	1,086	58.6	567	519	53	466	75
NH	1,160	642	501	43.2	259	242	80	162	17
NJ.	7,856	4,697	2,847	36.2	1,628	1,219	684	535	312
NM	1,690	920	731	43.3	400	331	126	205	39
NY.	17,749	10,961	6,067	34.2	3,876	2,190	1,464	726	721
NC	7,513	3,980	3,337	44.4	1,679	1,658	739	919	196
ND	603	342	253	42.0	131	122	62	60	7
OH	10,600	6,096	4,384	41.4	2,793	1,591	1,002	589	121
OK	3,216	1,650	1,510	47.0	808	702	379	323	55
OR	3,199	1,497	1,619	50.6	863	756	357	399	83
PA.	11,556	7,334	4,057	35.1	2,513	1,544	875	669	165
RI	985	572	387	39.3	240	147	50	97	26
SC	3,749	2,097	1,592	42.5	837	755	313	442	59
SD	704	392	305	43.3	149	156	83	73	7
TN.	5,316	2,866	2,372	44.6	1,341	1,032	464	568	78
TX.	19,242	9,545	8,970	46.6	5,204	3,766	2,403	1,363	726
UT.	2,024	998	961	47.5	538	422	180	242	65
VT.	575	340	228	39.6	122	106	36	70	7
VA.	6,619	3,453	2,960	44.7	1,197	1,763	942	822	205
WA	5,501	2,676	2,650	48.2	1,511	1,139	521	618	176
WV	1,707	1,081	618	36.2	359	259	120	138	8
WI.	5,022	2,836	2,121	42.2	1,233	888	550	338	65
WY	463	238	220	47.6	111	109	36	73	5

X Not applicable.

Source: U.S. Census Bureau, 2000 Census of Population and Housing, *Profiles of General Demographic Characteristics*; See also <http://www.census.gov/Press-Release/www/2002/demoprofiles.html>.

No. 31. Persons 65 Years Old and Over—Characteristics by Sex: 1990 to 2003

[As of March, except as noted (29.6 represents 29,600,000). Covers civilian noninstitutional population. Excludes members of Armed Forces except those living off post or with their families on post. Data for 1990 are based on 1980 census population controls; 1995 and 2000 data based on 1990 census population controls; 2003 data based on 2000 census population controls and an expanded sample of households. Based on Current Population Survey; see text of this section and Appendix III]

Characteristic	Total				Male				Female			
	1990	1995	2000	2003	1990	1995	2000	2003	1990	1995	2000	2003
Total (million)	29.6	31.7	32.6	34.2	12.3	13.2	13.9	14.5	17.2	18.5	18.7	19.7
PERCENT DISTRIBUTION												
Marital status:												
Never married	4.6	4.2	3.9	3.9	4.2	4.2	4.2	4.3	4.9	4.2	3.6	3.7
Married....................	56.1	56.9	57.2	56.5	76.5	77.0	75.2	74.4	41.4	42.5	43.8	43.3
Spouse present...........	54.1	54.7	54.6	53.8	74.2	74.5	72.6	71.2	39.7	40.6	41.3	41.0
Spouse absent...........	2.0	2.2	2.6	2.7	2.3	2.5	2.6	3.2	1.7	1.9	2.5	2.3
Widowed...................	34.2	33.2	32.1	31.6	14.2	13.5	14.4	14.3	48.6	47.3	45.3	44.3
Divorced..................	5.0	5.7	6.7	8.0	5.0	5.2	6.1	7.0	5.1	6.0	7.2	8.7
Educational attainment:												
Less than ninth grade	28.5	21.0	16.7	15.4	30.0	22.0	17.8	15.7	27.5	20.3	15.9	15.1
Completed 9th to 12th grade, but no high school diploma	[1]16.1	15.2	13.8	13.2	[1]15.7	14.5	12.7	12.3	[1]16.4	15.6	14.7	13.8
High school graduate...........	[2]32.9	33.8	35.9	36.2	[2]29.0	29.2	30.4	31.3	[2]35.6	37.1	39.9	39.7
Some college or associate degree ..	[3]10.9	17.1	18.0	17.9	[3]10.8	17.1	17.8	17.8	[3]11.0	17.0	18.2	18.0
Bachelor's or advanced degree	[4]11.6	13.0	15.6	17.4	[4]14.5	17.2	21.4	22.8	[4]9.5	9.9	11.4	13.3
Labor force participation: [5]												
Employed	11.5	11.7	12.4	13.5	15.9	16.1	16.9	17.8	8.4	8.5	9.1	10.2
Unemployed	0.4	0.5	0.4	0.5	0.5	0.7	0.6	0.7	0.3	0.3	0.3	0.4
Not in labor force	88.1	87.9	87.2	86.0	83.6	83.2	82.5	81.4	91.3	91.2	90.6	89.4
Percent below poverty level [6]	11.4	11.7	10.2	10.4	7.8	7.2	6.9	7.7	13.9	14.9	11.8	12.4

[1] Represents those who completed 1 to 3 years of high school. [2] Represents those who completed 4 years of high school.
[3] Represents those who completed 1 to 3 years of college. [4] Represents those who completed 4 years of college or more.
[5] Annual averages of monthly figures. Source: U.S. Bureau of Labor Statistics, *Employment and Earnings*, January issues. See footnote 2, Table 569. [6] Poverty status based on income in preceding year.

Source: Except as noted, U.S. Census Bureau, *Current Population Reports*, P20-546, and earlier reports; P60-222; and "Educational Attainment in the United States: 2003 Detailed Tables for Current Population Report, P20-550;" published 29 June 2004; <http://www.census.gov/population/www/socdemo/education/cps2003.html>; and "Table PINC-02. Marital Status—People 18 Years Old and Over, by Total Money Income in 2002, Work Experience in 2002, Age, Race, Hispanic Origin and Sex;" published 29 October 2003; <http://ferret.bls.census.gov/macro/032003/perinc/new02000.htm>.

No. 32. Persons 65 Years Old and Over—Grandparents, Disability Status, and Language Spoken at Home: 2000

[As of April 1 (5,772 represents 5,772,000). Based on the 2000 Census of Population and Housing; see text of this section and Appendix III]

Subject	Number (1,000)	Percent
GRANDPARENTS AS CAREGIVERS		
Grandparent living in household with one or more own grandchildren under 18 years	5,772	100.0
Grandparent responsible for grandchildren	2,427	42.0
DISABILITY STATUS OF THE CIVILIAN NONINSTITUTIONALIZED POPULATION		
Population 65 years and over	33,347	100.0
With a disability [1]	13,978	41.9
Sensory disability	4,738	14.2
Physical disability	9,546	28.6
Mental disability [2]	3,593	10.8
Self-care disability [3]	3,184	9.5
Go-outside-home disability [4]	6,796	20.4
With no disability	19,369	58.1
LANGUAGE SPOKEN AT HOME		
Population 65 years and over	34,979	100.0
English only	30,564	87.4
Language other than English	4,415	12.6
Speak English less than "very well"	2,341	6.7
Spanish	1,677	4.8
Speak English less than "very well"	1,030	2.9
Other Indo-European languages	1,932	5.5
Speak English less than "very well"	774	2.2
Asian and Pacific Island languages	630	1.8
Speak English less than "very well"	456	1.3
Other languages...	177	0.5
Speak English less than "very well"	81	0.2

[1] Persons with one or more disabilities. [2] Learning, remembering, or concentrating. [3] Dressing, bathing, or getting around inside the home. [4] Going outside the home alone to shop or visit a doctor's office.

Source: U.S. Census Bureau, 2000 Census of Population, Summary File 3, <http://www.census.gov/Press-Release/www/2002/sumfile3.html>.

Population 35

No. 33. Social and Economic Characteristics of the White and Black Populations: 1990 to 2003

[As of March, except labor force status, annual average (134,687 represents 134,687,000). Excludes members of Armed Forces except those living off post or with their families on post. Data for 1990 are based on 1980 census population controls; 2000 data based on 1990 census population controls; 2003 data based on 2000 census population controls and an expanded sample of households. Based on Current Population Survey; see text of this section and Appendix III]

Characteristic	Number (1,000)						Percent distribution			
	White		White alone [1]	Black		Black alone [1]	White,	White alone [1],	Black,	Black alone [1],
	1990	2000	2003	1990	2000	2003	2000	2003	2000	2003
EDUCATIONAL ATTAINMENT										
Persons 25 years old and over	134,687	147,067	153,188	16,751	20,036	20,527	100.0	100.0	100.0	100.0
Less than ninth grade	14,131	10,035	10,084	2,701	1,417	1,311	6.8	6.6	7.1	6.4
Completed 9th to 12th grade, but no high school diploma	[2]14,080	12,153	12,691	[2]2,969	2,899	2,798	8.3	8.3	14.5	13.6
High school graduate	[3]52,449	49,105	49,332	[3]6,239	7,050	7,234	33.4	32.2	35.2	35.2
Some college or associate degree	[4]24,350	37,353	38,774	[4]2,952	5,366	5,625	25.4	25.3	26.8	27.4
Bachelor's or advanced degree	[5]29,677	38,421	42,308	[5]1,890	3,303	3,558	26.1	27.6	16.5	17.3
LABOR FORCE STATUS [6]										
Civilians 16 years old and over	160,625	176,220	181,292	21,477	24,902	25,686	100.0	100.0	100.0	100.0
Civilian labor force	107,447	118,545	120,546	13,740	16,397	16,526	67.3	66.5	65.8	64.3
Employed	102,261	114,424	114,235	12,175	15,156	14,739	64.9	63.0	60.9	57.4
Unemployed	5,186	4,121	6,311	1,565	1,241	1,787	2.3	3.5	5.0	7.0
Unemployment rate [7]	4.8	3.5	5.2	11.4	7.6	10.8	(X)	(X)	(X)	(X)
Not in labor force	53,178	57,675	60,746	7,737	8,505	9,161	32.7	33.5	34.2	35.7
FAMILY TYPE										
Total families	56,590	60,251	62,297	7,470	8,664	8,928	100.0	100.0	100.0	100.0
With own children [8]	26,718	28,107	28,641	4,378	4,782	4,958	46.6	46.0	55.2	55.5
Married couple	46,981	48,790	49,915	3,750	4,144	4,165	81.0	80.1	47.1	46.7
With own children [8]	21,579	21,809	21,980	1,972	2,093	2,082	36.2	35.3	24.2	23.3
Female householder, no spouse present	7,306	8,380	8,881	3,275	3,814	4,000	13.9	14.3	45.1	44.8
With own children [8]	4,199	4,869	5,155	2,232	2,409	2,591	8.1	8.3	27.8	29.0
Male householder, no spouse present	2,303	3,081	3,500	446	706	762	5.1	5.6	7.8	8.5
With own children [8]	939	1,429	1,506	173	280	284	2.4	2.4	3.2	3.2
FAMILY INCOME IN PREVIOUS YEAR IN CONSTANT (2002) DOLLARS										
Total families [9]	56,590	60,256	62,313	7,470	8,664	8,932	100.0	100.0	100.0	100.0
Less than $5,000	(NA)	(NA)	1,218	(NA)	(NA)	540	(NA)	2.0	(NA)	6.0
$5,000 to $9,999	(NA)	(NA)	1,455	(NA)	(NA)	589	(NA)	2.3	(NA)	6.6
$10,000 to $14,999	(NA)	(NA)	2,364	(NA)	(NA)	723	(NA)	3.8	(NA)	8.1
$15,000 to $24,999	(NA)	(NA)	6,604	(NA)	(NA)	1,462	(NA)	10.6	(NA)	16.4
$25,000 to $34,999	(NA)	(NA)	7,091	(NA)	(NA)	1,316	(NA)	11.4	(NA)	14.7
$35,000 to $49,999	(NA)	(NA)	9,543	(NA)	(NA)	1,400	(NA)	15.3	(NA)	15.7
$50,000 or more	(NA)	(NA)	34,039	(NA)	(NA)	2,901	(NA)	54.6	(NA)	32.5
Median income (dol.) [10]	(NA)	(NA)	54,633	(NA)	(NA)	33,525	(X)	(X)	(X)	(X)
POVERTY										
Families below poverty level [11]	4,409	4,377	4,862	2,077	1,898	1,923	7.3	7.8	21.9	21.5
Persons below poverty level [11]	20,785	21,922	23,466	9,302	8,360	8,602	9.8	10.2	23.6	24.1
HOUSING TENURE										
Total occupied units	80,163	87,671	91,645	10,486	12,849	13,465	100.0	100.0	100.0	100.0
Owner-occupied	54,094	62,077	66,070	4,445	6,055	6,422	70.8	72.1	47.1	47.7
Renter-occupied	24,685	24,253	24,321	5,862	6,563	6,823	27.7	26.5	51.1	50.7
No cash rent	1,384	1,340	1,254	178	231	220	1.5	1.4	1.8	1.6

NA Not available.   X Not applicable.   [1] The 2003 Current Population Survey asked respondents to choose one or more races. Refers to people who reported specified race and did not report any other race category.   [2] Represents those who completed 1 to 3 years of high school.   [3] Represents those who completed 4 years of high school.   [4] Represents those who completed 1 to 3 years of college.   [5] Represents those who completed 4 years of college or more.   [6] Source: U.S. Bureau of Labor Statistics, *Employment and Earnings*, January issues. See footnote 2, Table 569.   [7] Total unemployment as percent of civilian labor force.   [8] Children under 18 years old.   [9] Includes families in group quarters.   [10] For definition of median, see Guide to Tabular Presentation.   [11] For explanation of poverty level, see text, Section 13.

Source: Except as noted, U.S. Census Bureau, Current Population Reports, P20-550, P60-221, P60-222, and earlier reports; and unpublished data.

No. 34. Selected Characteristics of the White and Black Populations: 2000

[As of April 1 (143,086 represents 143,086,000). Based on a sample from the 2000 Census of Population and Housing; see text of this section and Appendix III]

Characteristic	White alone		Black or African American alone		White alone, not Hispanic or Latino	
	Number (1,000)	Percent	Number (1,000)	Percent	Number (1,000)	Percent
EDUCATIONAL ATTAINMENT						
Population 25 years and over	143,086	100.0	19,858	100.0	133,786	100.0
Less than 9th grade	8,440	5.9	1,576	7.9	6,133	4.6
9th to 12th grade, no diploma	15,059	10.5	3,932	19.8	13,327	10.0
High school graduate (includes equivalency)	42,217	29.5	5,910	29.8	40,148	30.0
Some college, no degree	30,764	21.5	4,464	22.5	29,233	21.9
Associate degree	9,316	6.5	1,145	5.8	8,885	6.6
Bachelor's degree	23,735	16.6	1,877	9.5	22,977	17.2
Graduate or professional degree	13,557	9.5	954	4.8	13,084	9.8
Percent high school graduate or higher.	83.6	(X)	72.3	(X)	85.5	(X)
Percent bachelor's degree or higher.	26.1	(X)	14.3	(X)	27.0	(X)
DISABILITY STATUS [1]						
Population 5 to 20 years.	44,855	100.0	9,573	100.0	40,138	100.0
With a disability	3,384	7.5	957	10.0	2,966	7.4
Population 21 to 64 years.	121,289	100.0	18,054	100.0	112,171	100.0
With a disability	21,012	17.3	5,005	27.7	18,753	16.7
Percent employed	58.0	(X)	51.2	(X)	58.4	(X)
No disability.	100,277	82.7	13,050	72.3	93,418	83.3
Percent employed	79.4	(X)	70.7	(X)	80.3	(X)
Population 65 years and over	28,957	100.0	2,670	100.0	27,842	100.0
With a disability	11,762	40.6	1,409	52.8	11,237	40.4
RESIDENCE IN 1995						
Population 5 years and over	198,544	100.0	31,617	100.0	183,343	100.0
Same house in 1995.	111,546	56.2	16,224	51.3	104,404	56.9
Different house in the U.S. in 1995	83,438	42.0	14,678	46.4	76,844	41.9
Same county	46,420	23.4	9,679	30.6	41,908	22.9
Different county.	37,017	18.6	4,999	15.8	34,936	19.1
Same state.	19,785	10.0	2,670	8.4	18,648	10.2
Different state	17,232	8.7	2,329	7.4	16,287	8.9
Elsewhere in 1995	3,561	1.8	715	2.3	2,095	1.1
NATIVITY AND PLACE OF BIRTH						
Total population	211,354	100.0	34,362	100.0	194,514	100.0
Native.	197,978	93.7	32,262	93.9	187,674	96.5
Born in United States.	195,813	92.6	31,985	93.1	186,344	95.8
State of residence	130,796	61.9	23,216	67.6	123,194	63.3
Different state	65,017	30.8	8,770	25.5	63,150	32.5
Born outside United States	2,164	1.0	276	0.8	1,330	0.7
Foreign born	13,376	6.3	2,100	6.1	6,841	3.5
Entered 1990 to March 2000	5,231	2.5	869	2.5	2,287	1.2
Naturalized citizen.	5,756	2.7	934	2.7	3,729	1.9
Not a citizen.	7,620	3.6	1,165	3.4	3,111	1.6
COMMUTING TO WORK						
Workers 16 years and over	101,306	100.0	12,820	100.0	94,935	100.0
Car, truck, or van — drove alone	79,815	78.8	8,442	65.9	75,704	79.7
Car, truck, or van — carpooled	10,782	10.6	2,048	16.0	9,479	10.0
Public transportation (including taxicab)	3,184	3.1	1,567	12.2	2,711	2.9
Walked	2,726	2.7	413	3.2	2,497	2.6
Other means	1,104	1.1	159	1.2	979	1.0
Worked at home.	3,693	3.6	190	1.5	3,565	3.8
Mean travel time to work (minutes)	24.8	(X)	29.0	(X)	24.7	(X)
OCCUPATION						
Employed civilian population 16 yrs and over	102,325	100.0	13,002	100.0	95,834	100.0
Management, professional, and related occupations	36,433	35.6	3,281	25.2	35,035	36.6
Service occupations	13,661	13.4	2,861	22.0	12,314	12.8
Sales and office occupations	27,667	27.0	3,545	27.3	26,101	27.2
Farming, fishing, and forestry occupations.	646	0.6	49	0.4	514	0.5
Construction, extraction, and maintenance occupations	10,014	9.8	849	6.5	9,198	9.6
Production, transportation, and material moving occupations	13,903	13.6	2,417	18.6	12,673	13.2

X Not applicable.   [1] Civilian noninstitutionalized population.

Source: U.S. Census Bureau, Tables DP-2: Profile of Selected Social Characteristics: 2000 and DP-3: Profile of Selected Economic Characteristics: 2000; 2000 Census of Population, Summary File 4 (SF 4); <http://www.census.gov/Press-Release /www/2003/SF4.html>.

No. 35. American Indian and Alaska Native Population by Tribe: 2000

[As of April. This table shows data for American Indian and Alaska Native tribes alone or in combination of tribes or races. Respondents who identified themselves as American Indian or Alaska Native were asked to report their enrolled or principal tribe. Therefore, data shown here reflect the written tribal entries reported on the questionnaire. Some of the entries (for example, Iroquois, Sioux, Colorado River, and Flathead) represent nations or reservations. The information on tribe is based on self-identification and includes federally- or state-recognized tribes, as well as bands and clans]

American Indian and Alaska Native tribe	Number	American Indian and Alaska Native tribe	Number
Total persons [1]	4,119,301	Osage	15,897
Apache	96,833	Ottawa	10,677
Blackfeet	85,750	Paiute	13,532
Cherokee	729,533	Pima	11,493
Cheyenne	18,204	Potawatomi	25,595
Chickasaw	38,351	Pueblo	74,085
Chippewa	149,669	Puget Sound Salish	14,631
Choctaw	158,774	Seminole	27,431
Colville	9,393	Shoshone	12,026
Comanche	19,376	Sioux	153,360
Cree	7,734	Tohono O'odham	20,087
Creek	71,310	United Houma Nation	8,713
Crow	13,394	Ute	10,385
Delaware	16,341	Yakama	10,851
Iroquois	80,822	Yaqui	22,412
Kiowa	12,242	Yuman	8,976
Latin American Indian	180,940	Alaskan Athabascan	18,838
Lumbee	57,868	Aleut	10,548
Menominee	9,840	Eskimo	54,761
Navajo	298,197	Tlingit-Haida	22,365

[1] Includes other tribes not shown separately.

Source: U.S. Census Bureau, *The American Indian and Alaska Native Population: 2000*, Census 2000 Brief (C2KBR/01-15), February 2002.

No. 36. Population Living on Selected Reservations and Trust Lands: 2000

[As of April. OTSA=Oklahoma Tribal Statistical Area; SDAISA=State Designated American Indian Statistical Area; ANRC=Alaska Native Regional Corporation]

Reservation, Trust Land, or Other Area	Total population	American Indian and Alaska Native population alone	American Indian and Alaska Native population alone or in combination with one or more races
Navajo Nation Reservation and Off-Reservation Trust Land, AZ—NM—UT	180,462	173,987	175,228
Cherokee OTSA, OK	462,327	76,041	104,482
Creek OTSA, OK	704,565	51,296	77,253
Lumbee SDAISA, NC	474,100	58,238	62,327
Choctaw OTSA, OK	224,472	29,521	39,984
Cook Inlet ANRC, AK	364,205	24,923	35,972
Chickasaw OTSA, OK	277,416	22,946	32,372
Calista ANRC, AK	23,032	19,617	20,353
United Houma Nation SDAISA, LA	839,880	11,019	15,305
Sealaska ANRC, AK	71,507	11,320	15,059
Pine Ridge Reservation and Off-Reservation Trust Land, SD—NE	15,521	14,304	14,484
Doyon ANRC, AK	97,190	11,182	14,128
Kiowa-Comanche-Apache-Fort Sill Apache OTSA, OK	193,260	9,675	13,045
Fort Apache Reservation, AZ	12,429	11,702	11,854
Citizen Potawatomi Nation-Absentee Shawnee OTSA, OK	106,624	6,733	10,617
Gila River Reservation, AZ	11,257	10,353	10,578
Cheyenne-Arapaho OTSA, OK	157,869	7,402	10,310
Tohono O'odham Reservation and Off-Reservation Trust Land, AZ	10,787	9,718	9,794
Osage Reservation, OK	44,437	6,410	9,209
Rosebud Reservation and Off-Reservation Trust Land, SD	10,469	9,040	9,165
San Carlos Reservation, AZ	9,385	8,921	9,065
Blackfeet Reservation and Off-Reservation Trust Land, MT	10,100	8,507	8,684
Yakama Reservation and Off-Reservation Trust Land, WA	31,799	7,411	8,193
Turtle Mountain Reservation and Off-Reservation Trust Land, MT—ND—SD	8,331	8,009	8,043
Flathead Reservation, MT	26,172	6,999	7,883
Zuni Reservation and Off-Reservation Trust Land, NM—AZ	7,758	7,426	7,466
Bering Straits ANRC, AK	9,196	6,915	7,274
Sac and Fox OTSA, OK	55,690	5,334	7,232
Eastern Cherokee Reservation, NC	3,092	6,665	6,898
Wind River Reservation and Off-Reservation Trust Land, WY	23,250	6,544	6,864
Hopi Reservation and Off-Reservation Trust Land, AZ	6,946	6,573	6,633
Fort Peck Reservation and Off-Reservation Trust Land, MT	10,321	6,391	6,577
Cheyenne River Reservation and Off-Reservation Trust Land, SD	8,470	6,249	6,346
NANA ANRC, AK	7,208	5,944	6,181
Standing Rock Reservation, SD—ND	8,250	5,964	6,054
Bristol Bay ANRC, AK	7,892	5,336	5,749
Arctic Slope ANRC, AK	7,385	5,050	5,453
Crow Reservation and Off-Reservation Trust Land, MT	6,894	5,165	5,275
Red Lake Reservation, MN	5,162	5,071	5,087

Source: U.S. Census Bureau, 2000 Census of Population and Housing, *Profiles of General Demographic Characteristics*. See also <http://factfinder.census.gov/home/aian/aianaff2000.html>.

No. 37. Selected Characteristics of the American Indian, Alaska Native, Asian, and Native Hawaiian and Other Pacific Islander Populations: 2000

[As of April 1 (1,351 represents 1,351,000). Based on a sample from the 2000 Census of Population and Housing; see text of this section and Appendix III]

Characteristic	American Indian and Alaska Native alone		Asian alone		Native Hawaiian and Other Pacific Islander alone	
	Number (1,000)	Percent	Number (1,000)	Percent	Number (1,000)	Percent
EDUCATIONAL ATTAINMENT						
Population 25 years and over	1,351	100.0	6,641	100.0	207	100.0
Less than 9th grade	150	11.1	709	10.7	16	7.5
9th to 12th grade, no diploma	243	18.0	590	8.9	29	14.2
High school graduate (includes equivalency)	395	29.2	1,051	15.8	70	33.7
Some college, no degree	319	23.6	928	14.0	49	23.6
Associate degree	89	6.6	436	6.6	15	7.2
Bachelor's degree	103	7.6	1,772	26.7	20	9.7
Graduate or professional degree	53	3.9	1,154	17.4	8	4.1
Percent high school graduate or higher.	70.9	(X)	80.4	(X)	78.3	(X)
Percent bachelor's degree or higher.	11.5	(X)	44.1	(X)	13.8	(X)
DISABILITY STATUS [1]						
Population 5 to 20 years.	729	100.0	2,239	100.0	112	100.0
With a disability	75	10.3	133	5.9	9	8.2
Population 21 to 64 years.	1,326	100.0	6,444	100.0	208	100.0
With a disability	379	28.6	1,124	17.4	46	22.2
Percent employed	48.3	(X)	62.5	(X)	57.4	(X)
No disability.	946	71.4	5,320	82.6	162	77.8
Percent employed	67.7	(X)	70.4	(X)	70.8	(X)
Population 65 years and over	132	100.0	772	100.0	18	100.0
With a disability	76	57.6	315	40.8	9	48.5
RESIDENCE IN 1995						
Population 5 years and over	2,243	100.0	9,520	100.0	347	100.0
Same house in 1995.	1,132	50.5	4,374	45.9	156	44.9
Different house in the U.S. in 1995	1,070	47.7	3,790	39.8	163	47.1
Same county	595	26.5	2,136	22.4	96	27.6
Different county.	475	21.2	1,653	17.4	67	19.4
Same state	279	12.4	825	8.7	30	8.7
Different state	196	8.7	829	8.7	37	10.7
Elsewhere in 1995	41	1.8	1,357	14.2	28	8.1
NATIVITY AND PLACE OF BIRTH						
Total population	2,448	100.0	10,172	100.0	379	100.0
Native.	2,317	94.6	3,160	31.1	303	80.1
Born in United States.	2,297	93.8	3,036	29.9	254	67.0
State of residence	1,688	69.0	2,310	22.7	176	46.6
Different state	609	24.9	726	7.1	77	20.4
Born outside United States	20	0.8	123	1.2	50	13.1
Foreign born	131	5.4	7,012	68.9	75	19.9
Entered 1990 to March 2000.	60	2.5	3,050	30.0	33	8.8
Naturalized citizen	40	1.6	3,502	34.4	30	8.0
Not a citizen	91	3.7	3,510	34.5	45	11.9
COMMUTING TO WORK						
Workers 16 years and over	900	100.0	4,712	100.0	157	100.0
Car, truck, or van — drove alone.	612	68.0	3,112	66.0	102	64.9
Car, truck, or van — carpooled	167	18.5	739	15.7	32	20.4
Public transportation (including taxicab)	34	3.8	480	10.2	10	6.2
Walked	41	4.6	210	4.5	6	4.0
Other means	22	2.4	57	1.2	3	2.1
Worked at home.	24	2.7	113	2.4	4	2.5
Mean travel time to work (minutes)	25.1	(X)	28.2	(X)	26.1	(X)
OCCUPATION						
Employed civilian population 16 yrs and over	914	100.0	4,787	100.0	157	100.0
Management, professional, and related occupations	222	24.3	2,133	44.6	37	23.3
Service occupations	189	20.6	675	14.1	33	20.8
Sales and office occupations	219	24.0	1,149	24.0	45	28.8
Farming, fishing, and forestry occupations.	12	1.3	14	0.3	1	0.9
Construction, extraction, and maintenance occupations	118	12.9	173	3.6	15	9.6
Production, transportation, and material moving occupations	154	16.8	643	13.4	26	16.5

X Not applicable.   [1] Civilian noninstitutionalized population.

Source: U.S. Census Bureau, Tables DP-2: Profile of Selected Social Characteristics: 2000 and DP-3: Profile of Selected Economic Characteristics: 2000; 2000 Census of Population, Summary File 4 (SF 4); <http://www.census.gov/Press-Release /www/2003/SF4.html>.

Population   39

No. 38. Social and Economic Characteristics of the Asian Alone Population: 2003

[As of March, except labor force status, annual average (11,558 represents 11,558,000). Excludes members of Armed Forces except those living off post or with their families on post. Based on the Current Population Survey, Annual Social and Economic Supplement (ASEC); see text of this section]

Characteristic	Number (1,000)	Percent distribution	Characteristic	Number (1,000)	Percent distribution
Total persons	**11,558**	**100.0**	Female householder, no spouse present	337	11.8
Under 5 years old	753	6.5	Male householder, no spouse present	223	7.8
5 to 14 years old	1,477	12.8			
15 to 44 years old	5,815	50.3	**FAMILY INCOME IN 2002**		
45 to 64 years old	2,536	21.9			
65 years old and over	977	8.5	**Total families**	**2,845**	**100.0**
			Less than $5,000	69	2.4
EDUCATIONAL ATTAINMENT			$5,000 to $9,999	38	1.3
Persons 25 years old and over	**9,328**	**100.0**	$10,000 to $14,999	90	3.2
Elementary: 0 to 8 years	659	7.1	$15,000 to $24,999	247	8.7
Completed ninth to twelfth grade, but no high school diploma	906	9.7	$25,000 to $34,999	284	10.0
High school graduate	1,762	18.9	$35,000 to $49,999	389	13.7
Some college or associate degree	1,986	21.3	$50,000 or more	1,728	60.7
Bachelor's or advanced degree	4,016	43.1	Median income [3]	60,984	(X)
LABOR FORCE STATUS [1]			POVERTY		
Civilians 16 years old and over	**9,220**	**100.0**			
Civilian labor force	6,122	66.4	Families below poverty level [4]	210	7.4
Employed	5,756	62.4	Persons below poverty level [4]	1,161	10.1
Unemployed	366	4.0			
Unemployment rate [2]	6.0	(X)	HOUSING TENURE		
Not in labor force	3,098	33.6			
			Total occupied units	**3,917**	**100.0**
FAMILY TYPE			Owner-occupied	2,220	56.7
			Renter-occupied	1,657	42.3
Total families	**2,845**	**100.0**	No cash rent	40	1.0
Married couple	2,286	80.4			

X Not applicable. [1] Source: U.S. Bureau of Labor Statistics, *Employment and Earnings*, January 2004. [2] Total unemployment as percent of civilian labor force. [3] For definition of median, see Guide to Tabular Presentation. [4] For explanation of poverty level, see text, Section 13.

Source: Except as noted: U.S. Census Bureau, unpublished data.

No. 39. Social and Economic Characteristics of the Native Hawaiian and Other Pacific Islander Alone Population: 2000

[As of April 1 (79 represents 79,000). Based on a sample from the 2000 Census of Population and Housing; see text of this section and Appendix III]

Characteristic	Number (1,000)	Percent distribution	Characteristic	Number (1,000)	Percent distribution
FAMILY TYPE			$15,000 to $24,999	9	11.5
			$25,000 to $34,999	10	12.5
Total families	**79**	**100.0**	$35,000 to $49,999	14	17.4
With own children [1]	50	62.5	$50,000 or more	36	45.6
Married couple	56	71.2			
With own children [1]	36	45.5	Median income (dol.) [2]	45,915	(X)
Female householder, no spouse present	15	19.5			
With own children [1]	9	11.9	POVERTY		
Male householder, no spouse present	7	9.3	Families below poverty level [3]	12	14.6
With own children [1]	4	5.1	Persons below poverty level [3]	65	17.7
FAMILY INCOME IN 1999			HOUSING TENURE		
Total families	**79**	**100.0**	**Total occupied units**	**99**	**100.0**
Less than $10,000	6	7.9	Owner-occupied	45	45.5
$10,000 to $14,999	4	5.0	Renter-occupied	54	54.5

X Not applicable. [1] Children under 18 years old. [2] For definition of median, see Guide to Tabular Presentation. [3] For explanation of poverty level, see text, Section 13.

Source: U.S. Census Bureau, Tables PCT27. Family Type by Presence of Own Children Under 18 Years by Age of Own Children; PCT112. Family Income in 1999; PCT113. Median Family Income in 1999; PCT142. Poverty Status in 1999 by Sex by Age; PCT159. Poverty Status in 1999 of Families by Disability Status of Householder; and HCT2. Tenure; 2000 Census of Population, Summary File 4 (SF4); <http://www.census.gov/Press-Release/www/2003/SF4.html>.

No. 40. Social and Economic Characteristics of the Hispanic Population: 2002

[As of March, except labor force status, annual average (37,438 represents 37,438,000). Excludes members of the Armed Forces except those living off post or with their families on post. Based on Current Population Survey; see text of this section and Appendix III]

Characteristic	Number (1,000)						Percent distribution					
	His-panic, total	Mexi-can	Puerto Rican	Cuban	Central and South Ameri-can	Other His-panic	His-panic, total	Mexi-can	Puerto Rican	Cuban	Central and South Ameri-can	Other His-panic
Total persons	37,438	25,074	3,222	1,376	5,349	2,416	100.0	100.0	100.0	100.0	100.0	100.0
Under 5 years	3,841	2,888	251	72	413	217	10.3	11.5	7.8	5.2	7.7	9.0
5 to 14 years old	7,246	5,208	579	154	829	474	19.4	20.7	18.0	11.2	15.5	19.7
15 to 44 years old	19,114	12,852	1,565	507	3,031	1,158	50.9	51.3	48.6	36.8	56.7	47.9
45 to 64 years old	5,341	3,135	611	331	849	416	14.3	12.5	19.0	24.0	15.8	17.2
65 years old and over	1,896	992	214	312	226	153	5.1	4.0	6.6	22.6	4.2	6.3
EDUCATIONAL ATTAINMENT												
Persons 25 years old and over	19,670	12,380	1,831	1,017	3,135	1,308	100.0	100.0	100.0	100.0	100.0	100.0
High school graduate or more	11,206	6,268	1,223	720	2,028	968	57.0	50.6	66.8	70.8	64.7	74.0
Bachelors degree or more	2,181	935	257	189	542	258	11.1	7.6	14.0	18.6	17.3	19.7
LABOR FORCE STATUS [1]												
Civilians 16 years old and over	25,963	16,420	2,484	1,141	4,147	1,771	100.0	100.0	100.0	100.0	100.0	100.0
Civilian labor force	17,943	11,542	1,546	635	3,024	1,196	69.1	70.3	62.2	55.6	72.9	67.5
Employed	16,590	10,673	1,401	592	2,817	1,107	63.9	65.0	56.4	51.9	67.9	62.5
Unemployed	1,353	869	145	43	208	88	5.2	5.3	5.8	3.8	5.0	5.0
Unemployment rate [2]	7.5	7.5	9.4	6.7	6.9	7.4	(X)	(X)	(X)	(X)	(X)	(X)
Male	7.2	7.1	9.4	6.5	6.7	7.5	(X)	(X)	(X)	(X)	(X)	(X)
Female	8.0	8.2	9.4	7.1	7.0	7.2	(X)	(X)	(X)	(X)	(X)	(X)
Not in labor force	8,020	4,878	938	507	1,123	574	30.9	29.7	37.8	44.4	27.1	32.4
HOUSEHOLDS												
Total	10,499	6,537	1,128	511	1,566	757	100.0	100.0	100.0	100.0	100.0	100.0
Family households	8,516	5,441	834	358	1,275	608	81.1	83.2	73.9	70.1	81.4	80.3
Married-couple families [3]	5,778	3,818	436	268	854	401	55.0	58.4	38.7	52.4	54.5	53.0
Male householder, no spouse present	817	544	79	28	119	46	7.8	8.3	7.0	5.5	7.6	6.1
Female householder, no spouse present	1,922	1,078	319	62	301	161	18.3	16.5	28.3	12.1	19.2	21.3
Nonfamily households	1,982	1,097	293	153	291	149	18.9	16.8	26.0	29.9	18.6	19.7
Male householder	1,108	636	166	67	169	71	10.6	9.7	14.7	13.1	10.8	9.4
Female householder	874	461	128	86	122	78	8.3	7.1	11.3	16.8	7.8	10.3
Size:												
One person	1,385	731	221	122	192	118	13.2	11.2	19.6	23.9	12.3	15.6
Two people	2,329	1,271	314	176	354	214	22.2	19.4	27.8	34.5	22.6	28.3
Three people	2,092	1,295	230	92	330	146	19.9	19.8	20.4	18.0	21.1	19.3
Four people	2,210	1,403	205	82	368	152	21.1	21.5	18.2	16.1	23.5	20.1
Five people	1,342	942	103	22	187	88	12.8	14.4	9.1	4.3	11.9	11.7
Six people	639	482	37	11	85	23	6.1	7.4	3.3	2.2	5.5	3.0
Seven people or more	500	413	17	5	50	15	4.8	6.3	1.5	1.0	3.2	2.0
FAMILY INCOME IN 2001												
Total families [4]	8,516	5,441	834	358	1,275	608	100.0	100.0	100.0	100.0	100.0	100.0
Less than $5,000	350	218	42	13	54	23	4.1	4.0	5.1	3.7	4.2	3.8
$5,000 to $14,999	1,080	678	157	47	130	69	12.7	12.5	18.9	13.0	10.2	11.2
$15,000 to $24,999	1,503	999	159	61	185	99	17.6	18.4	19.1	17.0	14.6	16.3
$25,000 to $34,999	1,381	932	108	58	202	81	16.2	17.1	12.9	16.1	15.9	13.4
$35,000 to $49,999	1,471	970	119	54	237	91	17.3	17.8	14.2	15.1	18.6	14.9
$50,000 to $74,999	1,427	903	126	51	231	116	16.8	16.6	15.1	14.3	18.1	19.1
$75,000 and over	1,304	742	124	75	235	129	15.3	13.6	14.8	20.9	18.4	21.2
POVERTY												
Families below poverty level [5]	1,649	1,110	202	47	191	99	19.4	20.4	24.2	13.1	15.0	16.3
Persons below poverty level [5]	7,997	5,698	839	226	806	427	21.4	22.8	26.1	16.5	15.2	17.7
HOUSING TENURE												
Total occupied units	10,499	6,537	1,128	511	1,566	757	100.0	100.0	100.0	100.0	100.0	100.0
Owner-occupied	4,984	3,268	398	290	644	384	47.5	50.0	35.3	56.9	41.1	50.8
Renter-occupied [6]	5,514	3,269	730	220	922	373	52.5	50.0	64.7	43.1	58.9	49.2

X Not applicable. [1] Source: U.S. Bureau of Labor Statistics, *Employment and Earnings*, January 2003. [2] Total unemployment as percent of civilian labor force. [3] In married-couple families, Hispanic origin refers to the householder. [4] Includes families in group quarters. [5] For explanation of poverty level, see text, Section 13. [6] Includes no cash rent.

Source: Except as noted, U.S. Census Bureau, Current Population Reports, P20-545 and "The Hispanic Population in the United States: March 2002 Detailed Tables (PPL-165);" published 18 June 2003; <http://www.census.gov/population/www/socdemo/hispanic/ppl-165.html>.

Population 41

No. 41. Selected Characteristics of the Hispanic or Latino Populations: 2000

[In thousands, except as noted (18,270 represents 18,270,000). As of April 1. Persons of Hispanic origin may be of any race. Based on a sample from the 2000 Census of Population and Housing; see text of this section and Appendix III]

Characteristic	Hispanic or Latino [1]		Mexican	Puerto Rican	Cuban	Central American	South American
	Number	Percent					
EDUCATIONAL ATTAINMENT							
Population 25 yrs and over..........	18,270	100.0	10,178	1,843	935	1,082	940
Less than 9th grade	5,076	27.8	3,435	289	173	369	105
9th to 12th grade, no diploma	3,617	19.8	2,080	388	173	215	119
High school graduate (includes equivalency) .	4,039	22.1	2,123	483	187	207	226
Some college, no degree	2,848	15.6	1,423	345	149	147	192
Associate degree	782	4.3	358	108	54	41	62
Bachelor's degree.	1,216	6.7	513	152	108	67	137
Graduate or professional degree	692	3.8	246	78	90	36	100
Percent high school graduate or higher	52.4	(X)	45.8	63.3	62.9	46.0	76.1
Percent bachelor's degree or higher.......	10.4	(X)	7.5	12.5	21.2	9.5	25.2
DISABILITY STATUS [2]							
Population 5 to 20 years	10,524	100.0	6,578	1,006	202	424	299
With a disability	954	9.1	559	126	15	40	23
Population 21 to 64 years..........	18,857	100.0	10,883	1,825	738	1,188	958
With a disability	4,727	25.1	2,659	536	166	291	190
Percent employed	54.2	(X)	56.1	44.5	51.3	62.7	61.7
No disability	14,131	74.9	8,224	1,288	572	896	768
Percent employed	65.7	(X)	65.2	66.6	70.3	67.8	69.2
Population 65 years and over........	1,660	100.0	783	181	228	54	74
With a disability	806	48.5	380	100	104	24	29
RESIDENCE IN 1995							
Population 5 years and over	31,570	100.0	18,514	3,091	1,189	1,678	1,342
Same house in 1995................	14,047	44.5	8,152	1,416	595	642	512
Different house in the U.S. in 1995	14,495	45.9	8,515	1,463	486	788	567
Same county	10,030	31.8	6,082	914	340	560	360
Different county	4,465	14.1	2,433	549	146	228	208
Same state.	2,454	7.8	1,389	265	78	110	104
Different state	2,011	6.4	1,044	283	69	119	104
Elsewhere in 1995	3,027	9.6	1,846	212	108	247	263
NATIVITY AND PLACE OF BIRTH							
Total population.	35,238	100.0	20,900	3,404	1,250	1,812	1,420
Native	21,081	59.8	12,223	3,356	394	439	333
Born in United States.	19,414	55.1	12,045	2,032	380	417	312
State of residence	15,807	44.9	10,118	1,457	275	343	225
Different state	3,607	10.2	1,927	575	105	74	87
Born outside United States	1,667	4.7	178	1,325	14	22	21
Foreign born	14,158	40.2	8,677	47	856	1,372	1,087
Entered 1990 to March 2000........	6,489	18.4	4,228	20	226	612	513
Naturalized citizen.	3,940	11.2	1,930	20	517	360	400
Not a citizen.	10,218	29.0	6,747	27	339	1,013	688
COMMUTING TO WORK							
Workers 16 years and over........	13,099	100.0	7,638	1,209	531	853	691
Car, truck, or van — drove alone........	7,950	60.7	4,632	710	397	446	402
Car, truck, or van — carpooled	2,944	22.5	1,965	187	72	207	112
Public transportation (including taxicab)	1,162	8.9	451	204	29	126	115
Walked.	523	4.0	279	69	14	38	33
Other means	284	2.2	189	19	7	23	11
Worked at home.	236	1.8	121	20	13	15	19
Mean travel time to work (minutes)	27.2	(X)	25.9	29.5	29.0	30.3	29.8
OCCUPATION							
Employed civilian population 16 yrs and over.................	13,348	100.0	7,785	1,219	543	869	705
Management, professional, and related occupations......................	2,411	18.1	1,164	295	172	116	195
Service occupations	2,906	21.8	1,709	241	78	245	151
Sales and office occupations	3,090	23.1	1,629	363	159	165	171
Farming, fishing, and forestry occupations. . .	357	2.7	310	5	2	11	2
Construction, extraction, and maintenance occupations.....................	1,755	13.1	1,171	99	53	131	63
Production, transportation, and material moving occupations................	2,831	21.2	1,802	217	79	200	122

X Not applicable.   [1] Includes other Hispanic groups not shown separately.   [2] Civilian noninstitutionalized population.

Source: U.S. Census Bureau, Tables DP-2: Profile of Selected Social Characteristics: 2000 and DP-3: Profile of Selected Economic Characteristics: 2000; 2000 Census of Population, Summary File 4 (SF 4); <http://www.census.gov/Press-Release /www/2003/SF4.html>.

No. 42. Native and Foreign-Born Population by State: 1980 to 2000

[In thousands, except percent (212,466 represents 212,466,000). As of April. Data are based on a sample from the census; for details, see text of this section and Appendix III. For definition of foreign-born, see headnote, table 44]

State	Native population	Foreign-born population Number	Percent of total population	Percent entered 1990 to March 2000	State	Native population	Foreign-born population Number	Percent of total population	Percent entered 1990 to March 2000
1980	212,466	14,080	6.2	(X)	MO	5,444	151	2.7	52.4
1990	228,943	19,767	7.9	(X)	MT	886	16	1.8	29.0
2000, U.S. ...	250,314	31,108	11.1	42.4	NE	1,637	75	4.4	57.8
AL	4,359	88	2.0	53.0	NV	1,682	317	15.8	44.0
AK	590	37	5.9	39.7	NH	1,182	54	4.4	37.3
AZ	4,474	656	12.8	48.4					
AR	2,600	74	2.8	55.3	NJ	6,938	1,476	17.5	41.6
CA	25,007	8,864	26.2	36.9	NM	1,669	150	8.2	39.1
CO	3,931	370	8.6	54.4	NY	15,108	3,868	20.4	40.4
CT	3,036	370	10.9	39.0	NC	7,619	430	5.3	62.4
DE	739	45	5.7	47.2	ND	630	12	1.9	52.3
DC	498	74	12.9	51.0	OH	11,014	339	3.0	42.2
FL	13,312	2,671	16.7	38.6	OK	3,319	132	3.8	53.0
GA	7,609	577	7.1	59.7	OR	3,132	290	8.5	50.0
HI	999	212	17.5	34.1	PA	11,773	508	4.1	41.1
ID	1,230	64	5.0	47.7	RI	929	119	11.4	34.8
IL	10,890	1,529	12.3	45.0	SC	3,896	116	2.9	52.4
IN	5,894	187	3.1	52.2	SD	741	13	1.8	55.0
IA	2,835	91	3.1	57.5	TN	5,530	159	2.8	57.7
KS	2,554	135	5.0	55.1	TX	17,952	2,900	13.9	46.1
KY	3,961	80	2.0	58.8	UT	2,075	159	7.1	57.2
LA	4,353	116	2.6	37.0					
ME	1,238	37	2.9	28.3	VT	586	23	3.8	35.3
MD	4,778	518	9.8	44.1	VA	6,508	570	8.1	47.2
MA	5,576	773	12.2	40.4	WA	5,280	614	10.4	46.6
MI	9,415	524	5.3	44.9	WV	1,789	19	1.1	35.7
MN	4,659	260	5.3	54.5	WI	5,170	194	3.6	46.8
MS	2,805	40	1.4	49.6	WY	483	11	2.3	37.8

X Not applicable.

Source: U.S. Census Bureau, *1990 Census of Population Listing* (1990CPH-L-121) and "2000 Census of Population and Housing, Profiles of General Demographic Characteristics"; <http://www.census.gov/Press-Release/www/2002/demoprofiles.html>.

No. 43. Nativity and Place of Birth of Resident Population—25 Largest Cities: 2000

[In thousands except percent (656 represents 656,000). As of April. See headnote, Table 42]

City	Total population	Native population Total	Born in United States	Born outside United States	Foreign-born population Total Number	Percent of total population	Entered 1990 to March 2000 Number	Percent of foreign-born population
Austin, TX	656	547	537	10	109	16.6	66	60.6
Baltimore, MD	651	622	617	4	30	4.6	14	47.4
Boston, MA	589	437	418	19	152	25.8	74	48.5
Chicago, IL	2,896	2,267	2,206	61	629	21.7	292	46.4
Columbus, OH	712	664	659	5	48	6.7	30	63.7
Dallas, TX	1,188	898	888	9	290	24.4	174	60.0
Denver, CO	555	458	452	6	97	17.4	60	62.4
Detroit, MI	951	906	899	6	46	4.8	26	56.5
El Paso, TX	564	417	405	12	148	26.1	45	30.3
Houston, TX	1,955	1,439	1,420	19	516	26.4	269	52.2
Indianapolis, IN [1]	782	746	741	5	36	4.6	22	60.5
Jacksonville, FL	736	692	678	14	44	5.9	19	43.1
Los Angeles, CA	3,695	2,182	2,150	32	1,513	40.9	570	37.7
Memphis, TN	650	624	620	3	26	4.0	17	66.4
Milwaukee, WI	597	551	540	11	46	7.7	24	52.2
Nashville-Davidson, TN [1].	546	507	502	5	39	7.1	26	67.7
New York, NY	8,008	5,137	4,763	374	2,871	35.9	1,225	42.7
Philadelphia, PA	1,518	1,380	1,332	48	137	9.0	64	46.4
Phoenix, AZ	1,321	1,064	1,051	13	257	19.5	150	58.4
San Antonio, TX	1,145	1,011	989	22	134	11.7	47	35.4
San Diego, CA	1,223	909	889	20	314	25.7	118	37.4
San Francisco, CA	777	491	479	12	286	36.8	106	37.2
San Jose, CA	894	564	554	11	330	36.9	145	44.1
Seattle, WA	563	468	459	10	95	16.9	44	46.5
Washington, DC	572	498	491	7	74	12.9	38	51.0

[1] Represents the portion of a consolidated city that is not within one or more separately incorporated places.

Source: U.S. Census Bureau, "2000 Census of Population and Housing, Profiles of General Demographic Characteristics"; <http://www.census.gov/Press-Release/www/2002/demoprofiles.html>.

Population   43

No. 44. Foreign-Born Populations—Selected Characteristics by Region of Origin: 2003

[In thousands (33,471 represents 33,471,000). As of March. The term foreign-born refers to anyone who is not a U.S. citizen at birth. This includes naturalized U.S. citizens, legal permanent residents (immigrants), temporary migrants (such as foreign students), humanitarian migrants (such as refugees), and persons illegally present in the United States. Based on Current Population Survey; see text of this section and Appendix III]

Characteristic	Total foreign-born	Europe	Asia	Latin America				Other areas
				Total	Carib-bean	Central America [1]	South America	
Total	33,471	4,593	8,372	17,840	3,373	12,346	2,121	2,667
Under 5 years old	321	36	83	174	18	133	23	28
5 to 14 years old.	1,756	153	369	1,098	149	804	144	137
15 to 24 years old	4,338	372	885	2,787	371	2,152	263	295
25 to 34 years old	7,691	564	1,856	4,632	527	3,688	418	639
35 to 44 years old	7,404	790	1,887	4,105	736	2,840	528	622
45 to 54 years old	5,096	709	1,527	2,462	607	1,485	371	398
55 to 64 years old	3,172	681	908	1,312	419	690	203	272
65 to 74 years old	2,176	660	579	786	318	340	127	151
75 to 84 years old	1,122	453	205	376	169	169	38	89
85 years old and over	394	175	73	109	60	44	5	36
EDUCATIONAL ATTAINMENT								
Persons 25 years old and over	27,055	4,033	7,035	13,781	2,834	9,257	1,690	2,207
Less than ninth grade	5,822	423	540	4,637	504	3,936	197	222
Ninth to twelfth grade (no diploma) .	3,047	185	347	2,372	385	1,834	153	143
High school graduate	6,626	1,244	1,456	3,383	921	1,936	526	542
Some college or associate degree .	4,194	752	1,173	1,790	511	942	337	479
Bachelor's degree	4,656	803	2,173	1,146	356	458	331	534
Advanced degree	2,712	626	1,346	453	156	151	145	287
High school graduate or more	18,187	3,425	6,148	6,772	1,944	3,487	1,341	1,842
Bachelor's degree or more	7,367	1,429	3,519	1,598	513	609	477	821
INCOME IN 2002								
Total families	10,700	1,529	2,641	5,698	1,169	3,859	670	832
Under $15,000	1,265	134	203	841	193	575	73	85
$15,000 to $24,999	1,548	154	236	1,061	196	767	99	96
$25,000 to $34,999	1,482	188	239	959	167	702	90	96
$35,000 to $49,999	1,728	224	341	1,024	204	707	113	138
$50,000 to $74,999	1,968	304	549	952	164	650	138	163
$75,000 and over	2,710	524	1,073	859	244	458	157	253
Median income (dol.) [2]	42,980	53,184	61,792	34,798	36,771	32,526	44,563	50,009
POVERTY STATUS IN 2002 [3]								
Persons at or below poverty level. .	5,558	400	928	3,855	638	2,910	308	375
Persons above poverty level	27,879	4,192	7,444	13,955	2,732	9,415	1,808	2,289

[1] Includes Mexico.   [2] For definition of median, see Guide to Tabular Presentation.   [3] Persons for whom poverty status is determined. Excludes unrelated individuals under 15 years old.

Source: U.S. Census Bureau, Current Population Reports, P20-551.

No. 45. Foreign-Born Population by Place of Birth and Citizenship Status: 2002

[In thousands, except percent (33,049 represents 33,049,000). The term foreign-born refers to anyone who is not a U.S. citizen at birth. This includes naturalized U.S. citizens, legal permanent residents (immigrants), temporary migrants (such as foreign students), humanitarian migrants (such as refugees), and persons illegally present in the United States. Data based on twelve monthly samples from the 2002 Supplementary Survey and subject to sampling variability. The survey universe is limited to the household population and excludes the population living in institutions, college dormitories, and other group quarters]

Region	Foreign-born popula-tion, total	Natural-ized citi-zen	Not U.S. citizen		Region	Foreign-born popula-tion, total	Natural-ized citi-zen	Not U.S. citizen	
			Number	Percent of foreign-born				Number	Percent of foreign-born
Total	33,049	13,536	19,513	59	South America . .	2,239	878	1,361	61
Latin America.	17,281	5,345	11,937	69	Asia	8,880	4,723	4,158	47
Caribbean	3,057	1,626	1,432	47	Europe	4,858	2,706	2,151	44
Central America	11,985	2,841	9,144	76	Africa	1,014	346	668	66
Mexico.	9,856	2,205	7,651	78	Northern America . .	821	352	469	57
Other Central America . . .	2,129	636	1,493	70	Oceania	194	64	130	67
					Born at sea	(Z)	(Z)	-	-

- Represents zero.   Z Less than 500.

Source: U.S. Census Bureau, American FactFinder, 2002 American Community Survey Summary Tables, P039. Place of Birth by Citizenship Status for The Foreign-Born Population; (accessed: 11 May 2004).

No. 46. Native and Foreign-Born Populations by Selected Characteristics: 2003

[In thousands (285,933 represents 285,933,000). As of March. The foreign-born population includes anyone who is not a U.S. citizen at birth. This includes legal permanent residents (immigrants), temporary migrants (such as students), humanitarian migrants (such as refugees), and persons illegally present in the United States. Based on Current Population Survey which includes the civilian noninstitutional population plus Armed Forces living off post or with their families on post; see text of this section and Appendix III]

Characteristic	Total population	Native population	Foreign-born population			
			Total	Natural-ized citizen	Not U.S. citizen	Year of entry: 1990 to March 2003
Total	**285,933**	**252,463**	**33,471**	**12,837**	**20,634**	**16,771**
Under 5 years old	19,786	19,465	321	84	237	321
5 to 14 years old	40,898	39,142	1,756	242	1,514	1,705
15 to 24 years old	40,066	35,728	4,338	784	3,554	3,424
25 to 34 years old	39,242	31,552	7,691	1,724	5,967	5,350
35 to 44 years old	44,074	36,669	7,404	2,840	4,564	3,202
45 to 54 years old	40,234	35,137	5,096	2,653	2,443	1,461
55 to 64 years old	27,400	24,227	3,172	1,972	1,200	642
65 to 74 years old	18,111	15,935	2,176	1,431	745	427
75 to 84 years old	12,576	11,453	1,122	812	311	202
85 years old and over	3,547	3,153	394	295	99	35
Median age (years) [2]	35.7	35.1	38.4	47.7	33.4	30.3
Male	139,876	123,059	16,817	6,043	10,774	8,593
Female	146,057	129,403	16,654	6,794	9,860	8,177
MARITAL STATUS						
Persons 15 years old and over	**225,250**	**193,856**	**31,393**	**12,511**	**18,883**	**14,745**
Married	120,349	101,200	19,149	8,293	10,856	8,264
Widowed	14,001	12,463	1,538	968	571	352
Divorced	21,665	19,822	1,843	958	885	553
Separated	4,731	3,818	913	298	615	385
Never married	64,503	56,553	7,950	1,993	5,957	5,191
EDUCATIONAL ATTAINMENT						
Persons 25 years old and over	**185,183**	**158,128**	**27,055**	**11,727**	**15,329**	**11,320**
Not high school graduate	28,599	19,731	8,869	2,660	6,208	3,836
High school grad/some college	106,202	95,382	10,820	5,341	5,479	4,077
Bachelor's degree	33,213	28,558	4,656	2,382	2,273	2,130
Advanced degree	17,169	14,457	2,712	1,344	1,368	1,277
EARNINGS IN 2002 [1]						
Persons 15 yrs old and over with earnings	**100,621**	**85,789**	**14,832**	**6,058**	**8,774**	**6,680**
Under $15,000	9,498	7,055	2,443	552	1,890	1,394
$15,000 to $24,999	20,276	16,150	4,125	1,265	2,861	2,159
$25,000 to $34,999	20,442	17,725	2,717	1,206	1,511	1,138
$35,000 to $49,999	21,227	18,913	2,314	1,173	1,141	901
$50,000 to $74,999	16,642	14,910	1,732	985	747	575
$75,000 and over	12,536	11,035	1,501	877	624	514
Median earnings (dol.) [2]	35,038	35,956	27,045	35,032	22,687	23,109
HOUSEHOLD SIZE [3]						
Total households	**111,278**	**97,365**	**13,912**	**6,423**	**7,490**	**5,390**
One person	29,431	26,943	2,488	1,304	1,184	803
Two persons	37,078	33,649	3,429	1,693	1,736	1,292
Three persons	17,889	15,315	2,574	1,151	1,423	1,111
Four persons	15,967	13,257	2,710	1,171	1,538	1,153
Five persons	7,029	5,541	1,488	655	833	534
Six persons	2,521	1,837	684	260	424	293
Seven persons or more	1,364	824	540	189	352	204
INCOME IN 2002						
Total families	**75,596**	**64,896**	**10,700**	**4,927**	**5,773**	**4,177**
Under $15,000	6,775	5,511	1,265	437	828	590
$15,000 to $24,999	8,196	6,649	1,548	544	1,003	690
$25,000 to $34,999	8,855	7,373	1,482	592	890	635
$35,000 to $49,999	11,669	9,941	1,728	717	1,011	693
$50,000 to $74,999	15,961	13,993	1,968	1,005	964	721
$75,000 and over	24,139	21,429	2,710	1,633	1,077	848
Median income (dol.) [2]	52,704	54,686	42,980	53,393	36,580	37,492
POVERTY STATUS IN 2002 [4]						
Persons at or below poverty level	34,570	29,012	5,558	1,285	4,273	3,427
Persons above poverty level	250,747	222,868	27,879	11,547	16,332	13,310
HOUSING TENURE [3][5]						
Owner-occupied unit	75,909	68,807	7,102	4,349	2,752	1,706
Renter-occupied unit	33,799	27,166	6,632	1,992	4,640	3,621

[1] Covers only year-round full-time workers. [2] For definition of median, see Guide to Tabular Presentation. [3] Based on citizenship of householder. [4] Persons for whom poverty status is determined. Excludes unrelated individuals under 15 years old. [5] Excludes occupiers who paid no cash rent.

Source: U.S. Census Bureau, Current Population Reports, P20-551

Population 45

No. 47. Population by Selected Ancestry Group and Region: 2000

[In thousands (281,422 represents 281,422,000). As of April. Covers single and multiple ancestries. Based on sample data from the 2000 Census of Population and Housing; see text of this section and Appendix III. For composition of regions, see map, inside front cover]

Ancestry group	Total (1,000)	North-east	Mid-west	South	West	Ancestry group	Total (1,000)	North-east	Mid-west	South	West
		Percent distribution by region						Percent distribution by region			
Total population	281,422	19	23	36	22	Norwegian	4,478	6	50	11	33
Total ancestries						Polish	8,977	35	38	16	11
reported	287,305	21	24	32	23	Portuguese	1,177	48	3	10	39
Arab	1,203	28	24	26	22	Russian.	2,652	39	17	19	25
British	1,086	16	17	38	29	Scotch-Irish	4,319	15	19	44	22
Czech	1,263	11	50	24	16	Scottish	4,891	18	21	34	27
Danish	1,431	9	33	13	45	Slovak.	798	45	35	12	7
Dutch	4,542	17	36	25	22	Subsaharan African [1].	1,782	24	18	43	16
English	24,515	18	22	34	26	African.	1,183	19	19	46	15
European.	1,969	12	19	35	34	Swedish	3,998	14	40	15	32
French (except						Swiss	912	16	35	18	31
Basque).	8,310	25	24	30	20	Ukrainian	893	45	21	15	18
French Canadian . . .	2,350	42	20	23	15	United States or					
German.	42,885	17	40	23	20	American	20,625	11	21	55	13
Greek	1,153	36	23	22	19	Welsh	1,754	21	24	27	28
Hungarian	1,399	33	32	19	17	West Indian [1][2]	1,870	52	4	39	5
Irish	30,528	28	25	29	19	Jamaican	737	53	5	37	5
Italian	15,724	48	17	19	16						

[1] Includes other groups not shown separately.   [2] Excludes Hispanic groups.

Source: U.S. Census Bureau, American FactFinder, QT-P13. Ancestry: 2000, Census 2000 Summary File 3 (SF 3) - Sample Data (accessed 9 February 2004).

No. 48. Languages Spoken at Home by Age Group and Language: 2000

[In thousands (262,375 represents 262,375,000). As of April. Based on sample data from the 2000 Census of Population and Housing; see text of this section and Appendix III]

Language	Total, 5 years old and over	5 to 17 years old	18 years old and over	Language	Total, 5 years old and over	5 to 17 years old	18 years old and over
Total.	262,375	53,096	209,279	Other Indic languages	439	79	360
Speak only English	215,424	43,316	172,107	Other Indo-European			
Speak other language	46,952	9,780	37,172	languages	328	55	273
				Asian and Pacific Island			
Spanish or Spanish Creole. . . .	28,101	6,830	21,271	languages	6,960	1,159	5,801
Other Indo-European				Chinese	2,022	317	1,705
languages	10,018	1,445	8,573	Japanese	478	56	422
French (incl Patois,				Korean	894	156	738
Cajun).	1,644	233	1,411	Mon-Khmer, Cambodian. . . .	182	58	124
French Creole	453	113	341	Miao, Hmong	168	83	85
Italian	1,008	68	940	Thai	120	14	106
Portuguese or Portuguese				Laotian	149	38	111
Creole.	565	85	479	Vietnamese	1,010	205	805
German.	1,383	165	1,218	Other Asian languages.	398	53	346
Yiddish	179	39	140	Tagalog.	1,224	128	1,096
Other West Germanic				Other Pacific Island			
languages.	251	47	205	languages	314	51	263
Scandinavian languages. . . .	162	15	147				
Greek	365	39	327	Other languages	1,872	346	1,527
Russian.	706	118	589	Navajo	178	43	135
Polish.	667	76	592	Other Native North			
Serbo-Croatian.	234	41	192	American languages	203	40	163
Other Slavic languages	301	37	264	Hungarian	118	8	110
Armenian.	203	36	166	Arabic.	615	124	490
Persian	312	54	258	Hebrew	195	40	155
Gujarathi	236	42	194	African languages	419	68	350
Hindi.	317	41	276	Other and unspecified			
Urdu.	263	62	201	languages	145	23	122

Source: U.S. Census Bureau, "Table 5. Detailed List of Languages Spoken at Home for the Population 5 Years and Over by State: 2000"; published 25 February 2003; <http://www.census.gov/population/cen2000/phc-t20/tab05.pdf> and American Fact-Finder, PCT10. Age by Language Spoken At Home For The Population 5 Years and Over; Census 2000 Summary File 3 (SF 3) - Sample Data (accessed 11 March 2003).

No. 49. Language Spoken at Home by Resident Population by State: 2000

[In thousands, except percent (262,375 represents 262,375,000). As of April. Based on sample data from the 2000 Census of Population and Housing; see text of this section and Appendix III]

State	Population 5 years and over	English only	Language other than English — Number	Language other than English — Percent of population 5 yrs and over	State	Population 5 years and over	English only	Language other than English — Number	Language other than English — Percent of population 5 yrs and over
U.S...	262,375	215,424	46,952	17.9	MO	5,226	4,962	264	5.1
AL	4,152	3,990	162	3.9	MT......	847	803	44	5.2
AK......	580	497	83	14.3	NE......	1,595	1,469	126	7.9
AZ......	4,753	3,523	1,229	25.9	NV	1,854	1,426	428	23.1
AR......	2,492	2,368	124	5.0	NH.....	1,160	1,064	96	8.3
CA.....	31,417	19,015	12,402	39.5	NJ	7,856	5,855	2,002	25.5
CO.....	4,006	3,402	604	15.1	NM.....	1,690	1,073	617	36.5
CT.....	3,185	2,601	584	18.3	NY.....	17,749	12,786	4,963	28.0
DE.....	732	663	70	9.5	NC.....	7,513	6,910	604	8.0
DC.....	540	449	90	16.8	ND.....	603	565	38	6.3
FL.....	15,044	11,570	3,474	23.1	OH.....	10,600	9,951	648	6.1
GA.....	7,594	6,843	751	9.9	OK.....	3,216	2,977	239	7.4
HI	1,134	832	302	26.6	OR.....	3,199	2,811	389	12.1
ID	1,197	1,085	112	9.3	PA.....	11,556	10,583	972	8.4
IL......	11,548	9,327	2,221	19.2	RI	985	789	197	20.0
IN	5,658	5,296	362	6.4	SC.....	3,749	3,552	196	5.2
IA	2,738	2,578	160	5.8	SD.....	704	658	46	6.5
KS.....	2,500	2,282	219	8.7	TN.....	5,316	5,059	257	4.8
KY.....	3,776	3,628	148	3.9	TX.....	19,242	13,231	6,011	31.2
LA.....	4,153	3,771	382	9.2	UT.....	2,024	1,771	253	12.5
ME.....	1,204	1,110	94	7.8	VT.....	575	541	34	5.9
MD.....	4,945	4,322	623	12.6	VA.....	6,619	5,884	735	11.1
MA.....	5,954	4,839	1,116	18.7	WA.....	5,501	4,731	771	14.0
MI	9,269	8,487	781	8.4	WV	1,707	1,661	46	2.7
MN.....	4,591	4,202	390	8.5	WI	5,022	4,653	369	7.3
MS.....	2,641	2,546	96	3.6	WY	463	433	29	6.4

Source: U.S. Census Bureau, "2000 Census of Population and Housing, Profiles of General Demographic Characteristics"; <http://www.census.gov/Press-Release/www/2002/demoprofiles.html>.

No. 50. Language Spoken at Home by Resident Population—25 Largest Cities: 2000

[In thousands except percent (610 represents 610,000). As of April. See headnote, Table 49]

City	Population 5 years and over	English only	Language other than English, total [1] — Number	Language other than English, total [1] — Percent of population 5 yrs and over	Language other than English, total [1] — Speak English less than "very well"	Spanish	Other Indo-European languages	Asian and Pacific Island languages
Austin, TX..........	610	420	190	31.1	85	149	17	21
Baltimore, MD	609	562	47	7.8	18	18	18	7
Boston, MA........	557	371	186	33.4	91	76	68	35
Chicago, IL	2,679	1,727	952	35.5	494	625	213	83
Columbus, OH.......	659	593	66	10.0	28	19	19	17
Dallas, TX..........	1,090	686	404	37.1	237	348	23	22
Denver, CO.........	517	378	139	27.0	75	109	15	11
Detroit, MI..........	875	795	80	9.2	38	43	18	6
El Paso, TX.........	517	148	369	71.3	159	357	7	4
Houston, TX	1,795	1,053	742	41.3	395	597	54	71
Indianapolis, IN [2] ..	725	672	53	7.3	25	30	14	6
Jacksonville, FL.....	682	617	65	9.5	23	28	18	14
Los Angeles, CA	3,413	1,439	1,974	57.8	1,113	1,422	225	278
Memphis, TN........	600	558	42	7.0	20	23	9	7
Milwaukee, WI.......	550	462	87	15.9	42	55	16	13
Nashville-Davidson, TN [2].	509	458	51	10.1	25	26	13	8
New York, NY.......	7,476	3,921	3,555	47.6	1,769	1,832	1,046	515
Philadelphia, PA.......	1,420	1,168	252	17.7	114	110	79	50
Phoenix, AZ........	1,207	819	388	32.2	206	326	30	17
San Antonio, TX.......	1,053	561	492	46.7	171	463	14	12
San Diego, CA.......	1,142	714	427	37.4	199	244	44	126
San Francisco, CA	746	405	341	45.7	186	90	50	195
San Joce, CA	826	403	423	51.2	222	187	49	178
Seattle, WA.........	538	429	108	20.2	50	22	21	56
Washington, DC......	540	449	90	16.8	38	49	24	9

[1] Includes other language groups not shown separately.   [2] Represents the portion of a consolidated city that is not within one or more separately incorporated places.

Source: U.S. Census Bureau, "2000 Census of Population and Housing, Profiles of General Demographic Characteristics"; <http://www.census.gov/Press-Release/www/2002/demoprofiles.html>.

Population   47

No. 51. Marital Status of the Population by Sex, Race, and Hispanic Origin: 1990 to 2003

[In millions, except percent (181.8 represents 181,800,000). As of **March. Persons 18 years old and over.** Excludes members of Armed Forces except those living off post or with their families on post. Population controls for 2003 based on Census 2000 and an expanded sample of households. Based on Current Population Survey, see text of this section and Appendix III]

Marital status, race, and Hispanic origin	Total				Male				Female			
	1990	1995	2000	2003	1990	1995	2000	2003	1990	1995	2000	2003
Total [1]	181.8	191.6	201.8	212.4	86.9	92.0	96.9	102.3	95.0	99.6	104.9	110.1
Never married	40.4	43.9	48.2	51.9	22.4	24.6	26.1	28.6	17.9	19.3	22.1	23.3
Married	112.6	116.7	120.1	124.9	55.8	57.7	59.6	62.1	56.7	58.9	60.4	62.8
Widowed	13.8	13.4	13.7	14.0	2.3	2.3	2.6	2.7	11.5	11.1	11.1	11.3
Divorced	15.1	17.6	19.8	21.6	6.3	7.4	8.5	9.0	8.8	10.3	11.3	12.7
Percent of total	100.0	100.0	100.0	100.0	100.0	100.0	100.0	100.0	100.0	100.0	100.0	100.0
Never married	22.2	22.9	23.9	24.4	25.8	26.8	27.0	27.9	18.9	19.4	21.1	21.2
Married	61.9	60.9	59.5	58.8	64.3	62.7	61.5	60.7	59.7	59.2	57.6	57.1
Widowed	7.6	7.0	6.8	6.6	2.7	2.5	2.7	2.6	12.1	11.1	10.5	10.3
Divorced	8.3	9.2	9.8	10.2	7.2	8.0	8.8	8.8	9.3	10.3	10.8	11.5
White [2], **total**	155.5	161.3	168.1	174.5	74.8	78.1	81.6	85.0	80.6	83.2	86.6	89.5
Never married	31.6	33.2	36.0	38.6	18.0	19.2	20.3	21.9	13.6	14.0	15.7	16.5
Married	99.5	102.0	104.1	106.7	49.5	50.6	51.8	53.3	49.9	51.3	52.2	53.4
Widowed	11.7	11.3	11.5	11.6	1.9	1.9	2.2	2.3	9.8	9.4	9.3	9.4
Divorced	12.6	14.8	16.5	17.8	5.4	6.3	7.2	7.6	7.3	8.4	9.3	10.2
Percent of total	100.0	100.0	100.0	100.0	100.0	100.0	100.0	100.0	100.0	100.0	100.0	100.0
Never married	20.3	20.6	21.4	22.1	24.1	24.6	24.9	25.8	16.9	16.9	18.1	18.4
Married	64.0	63.2	62.0	61.1	66.2	64.9	63.5	62.7	61.9	61.7	60.3	59.7
Widowed	7.5	7.0	6.8	6.6	2.6	2.5	2.7	2.7	12.2	11.3	10.8	10.5
Divorced	8.1	9.1	9.8	10.2	7.2	8.1	8.8	8.9	9.0	10.1	10.7	11.3
Black [2], **total**	20.3	22.1	24.0	24.4	9.1	9.9	10.7	10.8	11.2	12.2	13.3	13.5
Never married	7.1	8.5	9.5	9.5	3.5	4.1	4.3	4.5	3.6	4.4	5.1	5.1
Married	9.3	9.6	10.1	10.3	4.5	4.6	5.0	5.0	4.8	4.9	5.1	5.3
Widowed	1.7	1.7	1.7	1.7	0.3	0.3	0.3	0.3	1.4	1.4	1.4	1.4
Divorced	2.1	2.4	2.8	2.9	0.8	0.8	1.1	1.0	1.3	1.5	1.7	1.9
Percent of total	100.0	100.0	100.0	100.0	100.0	100.0	100.0	100.0	100.0	100.0	100.0	100.0
Never married	35.1	38.4	39.4	38.9	38.4	41.7	40.2	41.6	32.5	35.8	38.3	37.2
Married	45.8	43.2	42.1	42.2	49.2	46.7	46.7	46.3	43.0	40.4	38.3	38.7
Widowed	8.5	7.6	7.0	7.0	3.7	3.1	2.8	2.8	12.4	11.3	10.5	10.2
Divorced	10.6	10.7	11.5	11.9	8.8	8.5	10.3	9.3	12.0	12.5	12.8	13.9
Hispanic, [3] **total**	13.6	17.6	21.1	26.0	6.7	8.8	10.4	13.4	6.8	8.8	10.7	12.6
Never married	3.7	5.0	5.9	7.9	2.2	3.0	3.4	4.8	1.5	2.1	2.5	3.1
Married	8.4	10.4	12.7	15.2	4.1	5.1	6.2	7.6	4.3	5.3	6.5	7.7
Widowed	0.5	0.7	0.9	0.9	0.1	0.2	0.2	0.2	0.4	0.6	0.7	0.7
Divorced	1.0	1.4	1.6	1.9	0.4	0.6	0.7	0.8	0.6	0.8	1.0	1.1
Percent of total	100.0	100.0	100.0	100.0	100.0	100.0	100.0	100.0	100.0	100.0	100.0	100.0
Never married	27.2	28.6	28.0	30.4	32.1	33.8	32.3	35.8	22.5	23.5	23.4	24.6
Married	61.7	59.3	60.2	58.5	60.9	57.9	59.7	56.7	62.4	60.7	60.7	61.1
Widowed	4.0	4.2	4.2	3.5	1.5	1.8	1.6	1.4	6.5	6.6	6.5	5.5
Divorced	7.0	7.9	7.6	7.3	5.5	6.6	6.4	5.9	8.5	9.2	9.3	8.7

[1] Includes persons of other races, not shown separately. [2] The 2003 Current Population Survey (CPS) allowed respondents to choose more than one race. Beginning 2003 data represent persons who selected this race group only and exclude persons reporting more than one race. The CPS in prior years only allowed respondents to report one race group. See also comments on race in the text for this section. [3] Hispanic persons may be of any race.

Source: U.S. Census Bureau, *Current Population Reports*, P20-547, and earlier reports; and unpublished data.

No. 52. Married Couples by Race and Hispanic Origin of Spouses: 1980 to 2003

[In thousands (49,714 represents 49,714,000). As of March. **Persons 15 years old and over.** Persons of Hispanic origin may be of any race. Based on Current Population Survey; see headnote, Table 51 and Appendix III]

Race and origin of spouses	1980	1990	2000	2003
Married couples, total [1]	49,714	53,256	56,497	58,586
Interracial married couples, total	651	964	1,464	2,094
White [2]/Black [2]	167	211	363	416
Black husband/White wife	122	150	268	275
White husband/Black wife	45	61	95	141
White [2]/other race [3]	450	720	1,051	1,546
Black [2]/other race [3]	34	33	50	132
HISPANIC ORIGIN				
Hispanic/Hispanic	1,906	3,085	4,739	5,706
Hispanic/other origin (not Hispanic)	891	1,193	1,743	1,888
All other couples (not of Hispanic origin)	46,917	48,979	50,015	50,992

[1] Includes other married couples not shown separately. [2] See footnote 2, Table 51. [3] "Other race," is any race other than White or Black, such as American Indian, Japanese, Chinese, etc. This total excludes combinations of other races by other races.

Source: U.S. Census Bureau, Table MS-3. Interracial Married Couples: 1980 to Present; published 12 June 2003; <http://www.census.gov/population/www/socdemo/hh-fam.html>; and unpublished data.

No. 53. Marital Status of the Population by Sex and Age: 2003

[As of March (102,313 represents 102,313,000). See headnote, Table 51]

Sex and age	Number of persons (1,000)					Percent distribution				
	Total	Never married	Married	Wid-owed	Divorced	Total	Never married	Married	Wid-owed	Divorced
Male	102,313	28,577	62,087	2,692	8,957	100.0	27.9	60.7	2.6	8.8
18 to 19 years old	3,858	3,794	61	2	2	100.0	98.3	1.6	-	0.1
20 to 24 years old	9,953	8,563	1,297	-	93	100.0	86.0	13.0	-	0.9
25 to 29 years old	9,366	5,112	3,914	14	327	100.0	54.6	41.7	0.1	3.5
30 to 34 years old	10,177	3,371	6,105	21	678	100.0	33.1	59.9	0.2	6.7
35 to 39 years old	10,503	2,289	7,142	21	1,051	100.0	21.8	68.0	0.2	10.0
40 to 44 years old	11,199	1,953	7,896	67	1,284	100.0	17.4	70.4	0.6	11.5
45 to 54 years old	19,578	2,117	14,439	202	2,821	100.0	10.8	73.8	1.0	14.4
55 to 64 years old	13,158	757	10,430	292	1,679	100.0	5.8	79.3	2.2	12.8
65 to 74 years old	8,268	383	6,415	726	744	100.0	4.6	77.6	8.8	9.0
75 years old and over...	6,253	239	4,390	1,347	277	100.0	3.8	70.2	21.5	4.4
Female	110,115	23,333	62,834	11,288	12,660	100.0	21.2	57.1	10.3	11.5
18 to 19 years old	3,689	3,486	198	-	5	100.0	94.5	5.4	-	0.1
20 to 24 years old	9,903	7,463	2,274	16	150	100.0	75.4	23.0	0.2	1.5
25 to 29 years old	9,330	3,760	5,028	36	505	100.0	40.3	53.9	0.4	5.4
30 to 34 years old	10,329	2,349	6,995	58	928	100.0	22.7	67.8	0.6	9.0
35 to 39 years old	10,766	1,544	7,617	134	1,471	100.0	14.3	70.8	1.2	13.7
40 to 44 years old	11,556	1,411	8,199	185	1,762	100.0	12.2	71.0	1.6	15.2
45 to 54 years old	20,617	1,797	14,521	640	3,658	100.0	8.7	70.4	3.1	17.7
55 to 64 years old	14,229	801	9,463	1,487	2,478	100.0	5.6	66.5	10.4	17.4
65 to 74 years old	9,831	337	5,505	2,888	1,101	100.0	3.4	56.1	29.4	11.2
75 years old and over...	9,864	383	3,034	5,844	602	100.0	3.9	30.8	59.2	6.1

- Represents or rounds to zero.

No. 54. Living Arrangements of Persons 15 Years Old and Over by Selected Characteristics: 2003

[In thousands (225,057 represents 225,057,000). As of March. See headnote, Table 51]

Living arrangement	Total	15 to 19 years old	20 to 24 years old	25 to 34 years old	35 to 44 years old	45 to 54 years old	55 to 64 years old	65 to 74 years old	75 years old and over
Total [1]	225,057	20,176	19,856	39,201	44,025	40,196	27,387	18,099	16,117
Alone	29,431	152	1,388	3,809	4,210	4,819	4,505	4,201	6,347
With spouse..........	117,172	257	3,181	20,426	28,633	27,299	18,949	11,398	7,029
With other persons	78,454	19,767	15,287	14,966	11,182	8,078	3,933	2,500	2,741
White [2]	184,361	15,707	15,579	30,935	35,580	33,239	23,358	15,558	14,406
Alone	24,111	105	1,040	2,892	3,324	3,814	3,647	3,575	5,714
With spouse..........	101,412	230	2,745	17,234	24,268	23,548	16,751	10,155	6,481
With other persons	58,838	15,372	11,794	10,809	7,988	5,877	2,960	1,828	2,211
Black [2]	26,224	2,973	2,777	5,000	5,435	4,582	2,627	1,660	1,196
Alone	3,984	37	219	567	668	803	681	505	504
With spouse..........	8,527	12	266	1,578	2,317	2,054	1,228	736	337
With other persons	13,738	2,925	2,292	2,855	2,450	1,725	718	419	355
Hispanic origin [3]	27,936	3,201	3,569	7,424	5,926	3,661	2,101	1,223	830
Alone	1,600	8	102	322	315	263	232	186	174
With spouse..........	13,300	91	811	3,781	3,805	2,346	1,385	726	356
With other persons	13,036	3,102	2,656	3,321	1,806	1,052	484	311	300

[1] Includes other races and persons not of Hispanic origin, not shown separately.   [2] See footnote 2, Table 51.   [3] Persons of Hispanic origin may be of any race.

Source of Tables 53 and 54: U.S. Census Bureau, Current Population Reports, P20-547 and earlier reports; and unpublished data.

No. 55. Unmarried-Partner Households by Sex of Partners: 2000

[As of April. For definitions of household and family, see text of this section. See Appendix III]

Item	Number
Total households	**105,480,101**
Unmarried-partner households.	5,475,768
Male householder and male partner	301,026
Male householder and female partner	2,615,119
Female householder and female partner	293,365
Female householder and male partner.	2,266,258
All other households	100,004,333

Source: U.S. Census Bureau, American FactFinder, PCT14. Unmarried-Partner Households by Sex of Partners; Census 2000 Summary File 1 (SF 1) 100-Percent Data (accessed 20 March 2002).

Population   49

No. 56. Households, Families, Subfamilies, and Married Couples: 1980 to 2003

[In thousands, except as indicated (80,776 represents 80,776,000). As of March. Excludes members of Armed Forces except those living off post or with their families on post. Beginning 2001 population controls based on Census 2000 and an expanded sample of households. Based on Current Population Survey, see text of this section and Appendix III. Minus sign (-) indicates decrease]

Type of unit	1980	1990	1995	2000	2001	2002	2003	Percent change 1980-1990	Percent change 1990-2000	Percent change 2000-2003
Households	80,776	93,347	98,990	104,705	108,209	109,297	111,278	16	12	6
Average size	2.76	2.63	2.65	2.62	2.58	2.58	2.57	(X)	(X)	(X)
Family households	59,550	66,090	69,305	72,025	73,767	74,329	75,596	11	9	5
Married couple	49,112	52,317	53,858	55,311	56,592	56,747	57,320	7	6	4
Male householder [1]	1,733	2,884	3,226	4,028	4,275	4,438	4,656	66	40	16
Female householder [1]	8,705	10,890	12,220	12,687	12,900	13,143	13,620	25	17	7
Nonfamily households	21,226	27,257	29,686	32,680	34,442	34,969	35,682	28	20	9
Male householder	8,807	11,606	13,190	14,641	15,345	15,579	16,020	32	26	9
Female householder	12,419	15,651	16,496	18,039	19,097	19,390	19,662	26	15	9
One person	18,296	22,999	24,732	26,724	28,207	28,775	29,431	26	16	10
Families	59,550	66,090	69,305	72,025	73,767	74,329	75,596	11	9	5
Average size	3.29	3.17	3.19	3.17	3.14	3.15	3.13	(X)	(X)	(X)
With own children [2]	31,022	32,289	34,296	34,605	35,355	35,705	35,968	4	7	4
Without own children [2]	28,528	33,801	35,009	37,420	38,412	38,623	39,628	18	11	6
Married couple	49,112	52,317	53,858	55,311	56,592	56,747	57,320	7	6	4
With own children [2]	24,961	24,537	25,241	25,248	25,980	25,792	25,914	-2	3	3
Without own children [2]	24,151	27,780	28,617	30,062	30,612	30,955	31,406	15	8	4
Male householder [1]	1,733	2,884	3,226	4,028	4,275	4,438	4,656	66	40	16
With own children [2]	616	1,153	1,440	1,786	1,836	1,903	1,915	87	55	7
Without own children [2]	1,117	1,731	1,786	2,242	2,438	2,535	2,741	55	30	22
Female householder [1]	8,705	10,890	12,220	12,687	12,900	13,143	13,620	25	17	7
With own children [2]	5,445	6,599	7,615	7,571	7,538	8,010	8,139	21	15	8
Without own children [2]	3,261	4,290	4,606	5,116	5,362	5,133	5,481	32	19	7
Unrelated subfamilies	360	534	674	571	568	474	525	48	7	-8
Married couple	20	68	64	37	44	43	34	(B)	(B)	(B)
Male reference persons [1]	36	45	59	57	70	59	84	(B)	(B)	(B)
Female reference persons [1]	304	421	550	477	455	371	407	39	13	-15
Related subfamilies	1,150	2,403	2,878	2,984	3,118	2,986	3,089	109	24	4
Married couple	582	871	1,015	1,149	1,202	1,129	1,232	50	32	7
Father-child [1]	54	153	195	201	251	269	260	(B)	31	29
Mother-child [1]	512	1,378	1,668	1,634	1,665	1,588	1,596	169	19	-2
Married couples	49,714	53,256	54,937	56,497	57,838	57,919	58,586	7	6	4
With own household	49,112	52,317	53,858	55,311	56,592	56,747	57,320	7	6	4
Without own household	602	939	1,079	1,186	1,246	1,172	1,266	56	26	7
Percent without	1.2	1.8	2.0	2.1	2.2	2.0	2.2	(X)	(X)	(X)

B Not shown; base less than 75,000.   X Not applicable.   [1] No spouse present.   [2] Under 18 years old.

Source: U.S. Census Bureau, Current Population Reports, P20-547 and earlier reports; and unpublished data.

No. 57. Households and Persons Per Household by Type of Household: 1990 to 2003

[As of March (93,347 represents 93,347,000). See headnote, Table 56]

Type of household	Households Number (1,000)			Households Percent distribution			Persons per household		
	1990	2000	2003	1990	2000	2003	1990	2000	2003
Total households	93,347	104,705	111,278	100	100	100	2.63	2.62	2.57
Family households	66,090	72,025	75,596	71	69	68	3.22	3.24	3.19
Married couple family	52,317	55,311	57,320	56	53	52	3.25	3.26	3.22
Male householder, no spouse present	2,884	4,028	4,656	3	4	4	3.04	3.16	3.11
Female householder, no spouse present	10,890	12,687	13,620	12	12	12	3.10	3.17	3.12
Nonfamily households	27,257	32,680	35,682	29	31	32	1.22	1.25	1.24
Living alone	22,999	26,724	29,431	25	26	26	1.00	1.00	1.00
Male householder	11,606	14,641	16,020	12	14	14	1.33	1.34	1.32
Living alone	9,049	11,181	12,511	10	11	11	1.00	1.00	1.00
Female householder	15,651	18,039	19,662	17	17	18	1.14	1.17	1.17
Living alone	13,950	15,543	16,919	15	15	15	1.00	1.00	1.00

Source: U.S. Census Bureau, Current Population Reports, P20-547, and earlier reports; and unpublished data.

No. 58. Households by Age of Householder and Size of Household: 1980 to 2003

[In millions (80.8 represents 80,800,000). As of March. Based on Current Population Survey; see headnote, Table 56]

Age of householder and size of household	1980	1990	1995	2000	2002	2003 Total [1]	2003 White [2]	2003 Black [2]	2003 Hispanic [3]
Total	80.8	93.3	99.0	104.7	109.3	111.3	91.6	13.5	11.3
Age of householder:									
15 to 24 years old	6.6	5.1	5.4	5.9	6.4	6.6	5.0	1.1	1.1
25 to 29 years old	9.3	9.4	8.4	8.5	8.4	8.5	6.7	1.2	1.4
30 to 34 years old	9.3	11.0	11.1	10.1	10.6	10.5	8.3	1.4	1.6
35 to 44 years old	14.0	20.6	22.9	24.0	24.0	24.1	19.4	3.1	3.1
45 to 54 years old	12.7	14.5	17.6	20.9	22.2	22.6	18.6	2.8	1.9
55 to 64 years old	12.5	12.5	12.2	13.6	15.2	16.3	13.8	1.8	1.2
65 to 74 years old	10.1	11.7	11.8	11.3	11.5	11.4	9.8	1.2	0.7
75 years old and over	6.4	8.4	9.6	10.4	11.0	11.3	10.2	0.9	0.4
One person	18.3	23.0	24.7	26.7	28.8	29.4	24.1	4.0	1.6
Male	7.0	9.0	10.1	11.2	12.0	12.5	10.2	1.7	0.8
Female	11.3	14.0	14.6	15.5	16.8	16.9	14.0	2.3	0.8
Two persons	25.3	30.1	31.8	34.7	36.2	37.0	31.7	3.7	2.6
Three persons	14.1	16.1	16.8	17.2	17.7	17.9	14.3	2.5	2.2
Four persons	12.7	14.5	15.3	15.3	15.8	16.0	12.9	1.9	2.4
Five persons	6.1	6.2	6.6	7.0	6.9	7.0	5.7	0.8	1.4
Six persons	2.5	2.1	2.3	2.4	2.4	2.5	2.0	0.3	0.7
Seven persons or more	1.8	1.3	1.4	1.4	1.4	1.4	1.0	0.2	0.5

[1] Includes other races, not shown separately.   [2] The 2003 Current Population Survey (CPS) allowed respondents to choose more than one race. Beginning 2003 data represent persons who selected this race group only and exclude persons reporting more than one race. The CPS in prior years only allowed respondents to report one race group. See also comments on race in the text for this section.   [3] Hispanic persons may be of any race.

Source: U.S. Census Bureau, Current Population Reports, P20-547, and earlier reports; and unpublished data.

No. 59. Family Groups with Children Under 18 Years Old by Race and Hispanic Origin: 1980 to 2003

[In thousands. As of March (32,150 represents 32,150,000). Family groups comprise family households, related subfamilies, and unrelated subfamilies. Excludes members of Armed Forces except those living off post or with their families on post. Population controls for 2003 based on Census 2000 and an expanded sample of households. Based on Current Population Survey, see text of this section and Appendix III]

Race and Hispanic origin of householder or reference person	1980	1990	2000	2003 Total	2003 Family households	2003 Subfamilies Total	2003 Subfamilies Related	2003 Subfamilies Unrelated
All races, total [1]	32,150	34,670	37,496	38,847	35,968	2,878	2,375	503
Two-parent family groups	25,231	24,921	25,771	26,445	25,914	531	519	12
One-parent family groups	6,920	9,749	11,725	12,402	10,054	2,348	1,857	491
Maintained by mother	6,230	8,398	9,681	10,142	8,139	2,003	1,596	407
Maintained by father	690	1,351	2,044	2,260	1,915	344	260	84
White [2], total	27,294	28,294	30,079	30,639	28,641	1,998	1,595	403
Two-parent family groups	22,628	21,905	22,241	22,409	21,980	429	417	12
One-parent family groups	4,664	6,389	7,838	8,230	6,661	1,569	1,178	391
Maintained by mother	4,122	5,310	6,216	6,471	5,155	1,316	1,003	313
Maintained by father	542	1,079	1,622	1,758	1,506	253	175	78
Black [2], total.	4,074	5,087	5,530	5,597	4,957	640	576	64
Two-parent family groups	1,961	2,006	2,135	2,120	2,082	39	39	-
One-parent family groups	2,114	3,081	3,396	3,477	2,876	602	538	64
Maintained by mother	1,984	2,860	3,060	3,124	2,591	533	475	58
Maintained by father	129	221	335	353	285	68	62	6
Hispanic [3], total	2,194	3,429	5,503	6,468	5,704	763	674	89
Two-parent family groups	1,626	2,289	3,625	4,211	4,001	209	200	9
One-parent family groups	568	1,140	1,877	2,257	1,703	553	473	80
Maintained by mother	526	1,003	1,565	1,807	1,357	451	390	61
Maintained by father	42	138	313	450	346	104	84	20

- Represents or rounds to zero.   [1] Includes other races, not shown separately.   [2] The 2003 Current Population Survey (CPS) allowed respondents to choose more than one race. Beginning 2003 data represent persons who selected this race group only and exclude persons reporting more than one race. The CPS in prior years allowed respondents to report only one race group. See also comments on race in the text for this section.   [3] Hispanic persons may be of any race.

Source: U.S. Census Bureau, Current Population Reports, P20-547, and earlier reports; and unpublished data.

Population   51

No. 60. Families by Number of Own Children Under 18 Years Old: 1980 to 2003

[As of March (59,550 represents 59,550,000). Based on Current Population Survey; see headnote, Table 59]

Race, Hispanic origin, and year	Number of families (1,000)					Percent distribution				
	Total	No chil- dren	One child	Two chil- dren	Three or more chil- dren	Total	No chil- dren	One child	Two chil- dren	Three or more children
ALL FAMILIES [1]										
1980...................	59,550	28,528	12,443	11,470	7,109	100	48	21	19	12
1990...................	66,090	33,801	13,530	12,263	6,496	100	51	20	19	10
2000...................	72,025	37,420	14,311	13,215	7,080	100	52	20	18	10
2003, total............	75,596	39,628	15,183	13,539	7,245	100	52	20	18	10
Married couple	57,320	31,406	9,875	10,520	5,519	100	55	17	18	10
Male householder [2]	4,656	2,741	1,174	534	208	100	59	25	11	4
Female householder [2]	13,620	5,481	4,134	2,486	1,519	100	40	30	18	11
WHITE FAMILIES [3]										
1980...................	52,243	25,769	10,727	9,977	5,769	100	49	21	19	11
1990...................	56,590	29,872	11,186	10,342	5,191	100	53	20	18	9
2000...................	60,251	32,144	11,496	10,918	5,693	100	53	19	18	9
2003, total............	62,297	33,656	11,913	10,993	5,735	100	54	19	18	9
Married couple	49,915	27,935	8,258	8,983	4,739	100	56	17	18	9
Male householder [2]	3,500	1,994	922	428	156	100	57	26	12	4
Female householder [2]	8,881	3,726	2,733	1,583	841	100	42	31	18	9
BLACK FAMILIES [3]										
1980...................	6,184	2,364	1,449	1,235	1,136	100	38	23	20	18
1990...................	7,470	3,093	1,894	1,433	1,049	100	41	25	19	14
2000...................	8,664	3,882	2,101	1,624	1,058	100	45	24	19	12
2003, total............	8,928	3,970	2,219	1,636	1,103	100	44	25	18	12
Married couple	4,165	2,083	851	760	471	100	50	20	18	11
Male householder [2]	762	478	176	72	37	100	63	23	9	5
Female householder [2]	4,000	1,409	1,192	805	595	100	35	30	20	15
HISPANIC FAMILIES [4]										
1980...................	3,029	946	680	698	706	100	31	22	23	23
1990...................	4,840	1,790	1,095	1,036	919	100	37	23	21	19
2000...................	7,561	2,747	1,791	1,693	1,330	100	36	24	22	18
2003, total............	9,090	3,385	2,097	2,032	1,575	100	37	23	22	17
Married couple	6,189	2,188	1,307	1,501	1,194	100	35	21	24	19
Male householder [2]	872	526	181	111	54	100	60	21	13	6
Female householder [2]	2,029	672	609	420	327	100	33	30	21	16

[1] Includes other races, not shown separately. [2] No spouse present. [3] The 2003 Current Population Survey (CPS) allowed respondents to choose more than one race. Beginning 2003 data represent persons who selected this race group only and exclude persons reporting more than one race. The CPS in prior years only allowed respondents to report one race group. See also comments on race in the text for this section. [4] Hispanic persons may be of any race.

Source: U.S. Census Bureau, Current Population Reports, P20-547, and earlier reports; and unpublished data.

No. 61. Families by Size and Presence of Children: 1980 to 2003

[In thousands, except as indicated (59,550 represents 59,550,000). As of March . Excludes members of Armed Forces except those living off post or with their families on post. Population controls for 2003 based on Census 2000 and an expanded sample of households. Based on Current Population Survey, see text of this section and Appendix III]

Characteristic	Number					Percent distribution				
	1980	1990	1995	2000	2003	1980	1990	1995	2000	2003
Total............	59,550	66,090	69,305	72,025	75,596	100	100	100	100	100
Size of family:										
Two persons	23,461	27,606	29,176	31,455	33,706	39	42	42	44	45
Three persons	13,603	15,353	15,903	16,073	16,652	23	23	23	22	22
Four persons........	12,372	14,026	14,624	14,496	15,149	21	21	21	20	20
Five persons	5,930	5,938	6,283	6,526	6,619	10	9	9	9	9
Six persons.........	2,461	1,997	2,106	2,226	2,298	4	3	3	3	3
Seven or more persons..	1,723	1,170	1,213	1,249	1,173	3	2	2	2	2
Average per family	3.29	3.17	3.19	3.17	3.13	(X)	(X)	(X)	(X)	(X)
Own children under age 18:										
None	28,528	33,801	35,009	37,420	39,628	48	51	51	52	52
One	12,443	13,530	14,088	14,311	15,183	21	20	20	20	20
Two	11,470	12,263	13,213	13,215	13,539	19	19	19	18	18
Three	4,674	4,650	5,044	5,063	5,290	8	7	7	7	7
Four or more	2,435	1,846	1,951	2,017	1,955	4	3	3	3	3
Own children under age 6:										
None	46,063	50,905	53,695	57,039	60,012	77	77	77	79	79
One	9,441	10,304	10,733	10,454	10,734	16	16	15	15	14
Two or more	4,047	4,882	4,876	4,533	4,850	7	7	7	6	6

X Not applicable.

Source: U.S. Census Bureau, Current Population Reports, P20-547, and earlier reports; and unpublished data.

No. 62. Families by Type, Race, and Hispanic Origin: 2003

[In thousands, except as indicated (75,596 represents 75,596,000). As of March. Excludes members of Armed Forces except those living off post or with their families on post or with their families on post. Population controls based on Census 2000 and an expanded sample of households. Based on Current Population Survey, see text of this section and Appendix III]

Characteristic	All families	Married couple families — All races[1]	Married — White[2]	Married — Black[2]	Married — Hispanic[3]	Female family householder[4] — All races[1]	Female — White[2]	Female — Black[2]	Female — Hispanic[3]	Male family householder[4], all races	Pct — All families	Pct — Married couple families	Pct — Female family householder[4]	Pct — Male family householder[4]
All families........	75,596	57,320	49,915	4,165	6,189	13,620	8,881	4,000	2,029	4,656	100	100	100	100
Age of householder:														
Under 25 years old	3,551	1,379	1,198	115	361	1,383	817	471	272	789	5	2	10	17
25 to 34 years old	13,438	9,536	8,138	722	1,645	2,892	1,696	1,044	518	1,011	18	17	21	22
35 to 44 years old	18,741	14,001	11,927	1,107	1,861	3,652	2,387	1,087	593	1,087	25	24	27	23
45 to 54 years old	16,863	13,297	11,511	1,032	1,099	2,644	1,788	705	339	922	22	23	19	20
55 to 64 years old	11,261	9,543	8,483	623	689	1,305	896	336	146	413	15	17	10	9
65 to 74 years old	6,908	5,865	5,224	394	369	845	587	207	97	199	9	10	6	4
75 years old and over	4,833	3,700	3,433	171	163	898	709	152	64	235	6	6	7	5
Without own children under 18	39,628	31,406	27,935	2,083	2,188	5,481	3,726	1,409	672	2,741	52	55	40	59
With own children under 18	35,968	25,914	21,980	2,082	4,001	8,139	5,155	2,591	1,357	1,915	48	45	60	41
One own child under 18	15,183	9,875	8,258	851	1,307	4,134	2,733	1,192	609	1,174	20	17	30	25
Two own children under 18	13,539	10,520	8,983	760	1,501	2,486	1,583	805	420	534	18	18	18	11
Three or more own children under 18	7,245	5,519	4,739	471	1,194	1,519	841	595	327	208	10	10	11	4
Average per family with own children under 18	1.83	1.89	1.87	1.93	2.06	1.72	1.58	1.92	1.90	1.50	(X)	(X)	(X)	(X)
Age of own children:														
Of any age	46,255	31,694	26,839	2,621	4,598	11,741	7,667	3,468	1,770	2,820	61	55	86	61
Under 25 years	41,392	29,511	25,067	2,381	4,330	9,527	6,069	2,981	1,548	2,354	55	51	70	51
Under 12 years	26,251	19,168	16,256	1,513	3,243	5,788	3,571	1,946	1,028	1,295	35	33	42	28
Under 6 years	15,584	11,743	9,970	896	2,152	3,111	1,859	1,076	586	729	21	20	23	16
Under 3 years	9,081	7,014	6,018	485	1,283	1,615	924	600	287	452	12	12	12	10
Under 1 year	2,917	2,255	1,932	152	371	481	274	170	80	181	4	4	4	4
Members 65 and older:														
Without members 65 and older	60,988	45,868	39,728	3,428	5,443	11,289	7,183	3,505	1,775	3,830	81	80	83	82
With members 65 and older	14,608	11,451	10,187	737	746	2,331	1,698	495	254	826	19	20	17	18
Marital status of householder:														
Married, spouse present	57,320	57,320	49,915	4,165	6,189	(X)	(X)	(X)	(X)	(X)	76	100	(X)	(X)
Married, spouse absent	2,697	(X)	(X)	(X)	(X)	2,064	1,308	614	490	632	4	(X)	15	14
Separated	1,933	(X)	(X)	(X)	(X)	1,560	1,003	464	361	373	3	(X)	11	8
Other	764	(X)	(X)	(X)	(X)	504	305	150	129	259	1	(X)	4	6
Widowed	2,628	(X)	(X)	(X)	(X)	2,182	1,609	444	213	446	3	(X)	16	10
Divorced	6,269	(X)	(X)	(X)	(X)	4,839	3,681	943	524	1,430	8	(X)	36	31
Never married	6,683	(X)	(X)	(X)	(X)	4,535	2,284	1,999	802	2,148	9	(X)	33	46

X Not applicable. [1] Includes other races not shown separately. [2] The 2003 Current Population Survey (CPS) allowed respondents to choose more than one race. Beginning 2003 data represent persons who selected this race group only and exclude persons reporting more than one race. The CPS in prior years only allowed respondents to report one race group. See also comments on race in the text for this section. [3] Persons of Hispanic origin may be of any race. [4] No spouse present.

Source: U.S. Census Bureau, Current Population Reports, unpublished data.

Population 53

No. 63. Family Households With Own Children Under Age 18 by Type of Family, 1990 to 2003, and by Age of Householder, 2003

[As of March (32,289 represents 32,289,000). Excludes members of Armed Forces except those living off post or with their families on post. Population controls for 2003 based on Census 2000 and an expanded sample of households. Based on Current Population Survey, see text of this section and Appendix III]

Family type	1990	2000	2003						
			Total	15 to 24 years old	25 to 34 years old	35 to 44 years old	45 to 54 years old	55 to 64 years old	65 years old and over
NUMBER (1,000)									
Family households with children . . .	32,289	34,605	35,968	1,955	10,110	15,053	7,634	1,040	176
Married couple	24,537	25,248	25,914	845	6,931	11,218	5,960	842	118
Male householder [1]	1,153	1,786	1,915	160	537	732	398	72	15
Female householder [1]	6,599	7,571	8,139	949	2,642	3,102	1,276	126	43
HOUSEHOLDS WITH CHILDREN, AS A PERCENT OF ALL FAMILY HOUSEHOLDS BY TYPE									
Family households with children, total	49	48	48	55	75	80	45	9	1
Married couple	47	46	45	61	73	80	45	9	1
Male householder [1]	40	44	41	20	53	67	43	17	3
Female householder [1]	61	60	60	69	91	85	48	10	2

[1] No spouse present.

Source: U.S. Census Bureau, Current Population Reports, P20-537 and earlier reports; and unpublished data.

No. 64. Nonfamily Households by Sex and Age of Householder: 2003

[In thousands (16,020 represents 16,020,000). As of March. See headnote, Table 63]

Item	Male householder					Female householder				
	Total	15 to 24 yr. old	25 to 44 yr. old	45 to 64 yr. old	65 yr. old and over	Total	15 to 24 yr. old	25 to 44 yr. old	45 to 64 yr. old	65 yr. old and over
Total	16,020	1,507	6,621	4,994	2,898	19,662	1,552	4,325	5,765	8,020
One person (living alone) . .	12,511	722	4,785	4,280	2,725	16,919	818	3,235	5,044	7,824
Nonrelatives present	3,510	785	1,836	715	174	2,742	735	1,090	721	196
Never married	7,919	1,444	4,579	1,481	414	6,150	1,496	2,894	1,300	460
Married [1]	1,463	29	551	590	293	1,070	32	304	462	271
Widowed	1,782	-	43	255	1,483	7,247	4	113	1,103	6,025
Divorced	4,855	35	1,446	2,665	709	5,193	20	1,012	2,898	1,263

- Represents or rounds to zero. [1] No spouse present.

Source: U.S. Census Bureau, unpublished data.

No. 65. Persons Living Alone by Sex and Age: 1990 to 2003

[As of March (22,999 represents 22,999,000). Excludes members of Armed Forces except those living off post or with their families on post. Beginning 2002 population controls based on Census 2000 and an expanded sample of households. Based on Current Population Survey, see text of this section and Appendix III]

Sex and age	Number of persons (1,000)					Percent distribution				
	1990	1995	2000	2002	2003	1990	1995	2000	2002	2003
Both sexes	22,999	24,732	26,724	28,775	29,431	100	100	100	100	100
15 to 24 years old	1,210	1,196	1,144	1,292	1,540	5	5	4	4	5
25 to 34 years old	3,972	3,653	3,848	3,923	3,809	17	15	14	14	13
35 to 44 years old	3,138	3,663	4,109	4,103	4,210	14	15	15	14	14
45 to 64 years old	5,502	6,377	7,842	8,992	9,324	24	26	29	31	32
65 to 74 years old	4,350	4,374	4,091	4,279	4,201	19	18	15	15	14
75 years old and over	4,825	5,470	5,692	6,187	6,347	21	22	21	22	22
Male	9,049	10,140	11,181	12,004	12,511	39	41	42	42	43
15 to 24 years old	674	623	556	601	722	3	3	2	2	2
25 to 34 years old	2,395	2,213	2,279	2,322	2,212	10	9	9	8	8
35 to 44 years old	1,836	2,263	2,569	2,613	2,573	8	9	10	9	9
45 to 64 years old	2,203	2,787	3,422	3,904	4,280	10	11	13	14	15
65 to 74 years old	1,042	1,134	1,108	1,225	1,291	5	5	4	4	4
75 years old and over	901	1,120	1,247	1,339	1,434	4	5	5	5	5
Female	13,950	14,592	15,543	16,771	16,919	61	59	58	58	57
15 to 24 years old	536	572	588	691	818	2	2	2	2	3
25 to 34 years old	1,578	1,440	1,568	1,601	1,597	7	6	6	6	5
35 to 44 years old	1,303	1,399	1,540	1,490	1,638	6	6	6	5	6
45 to 64 years old	3,300	3,589	4,420	5,087	5,044	14	15	17	18	17
65 to 74 years old	3,309	3,240	2,983	3,054	2,911	14	13	11	11	10
75 years old and over	3,924	4,351	4,444	4,848	4,913	17	18	17	17	17

Source: U.S. Census Bureau, Current Population Reports, P20-547, and earlier reports; and unpublished data.

No. 66. Population in Group Quarters by Sex, Age, and Group Quarters Type: 2000

[In thousands (7,779 represents 7,779,000). As of April. For definitions of group quarters, see text, this section]

Group quarters type	Total popula- tion	Male				Female			
		Total	Under 18 years	18 to 64 years	65 years and over	Total	Under 18 years	18 to 64 years	65 years and over
Total	7,779	4,502	215	3,740	548	3,276	108	1,722	1,446
Institutionalized population	4,059	2,534	122	1,968	444	1,525	36	292	1,197
Correctional institutions.........	1,976	1,806	19	1,773	14	170	2	166	2
Nursing homes	1,721	488	-	88	401	1,232	-	75	1,157
Hospitals/wards and hospices for chronically ill..............	40	20	1	10	9	20	1	6	14
Mental (psychiatric) hospitals or wards	79	50	7	37	6	29	4	18	7
Juvenile institutions	128	101	88	13	-	27	24	2	-
Other institutions	115	68	8	47	14	47	5	25	18
Noninstitutionalized population	3,720	1,968	93	1,772	104	1,751	72	1,431	249
College dormitories [1]	2,064	958	5	952	-	1,107	5	1,101	-
Military quarters	355	307	1	306	-	48	1	47	-
Other noninstitutional group quarters..................	1,300	703	86	513	104	597	66	283	249

- Represents or rounds to zero.   [1] Includes college quarters off campus.

Source: U.S. Census Bureau, American FactFinder, PCT17. Group Quarters Population by Sex by Age by Group Quarters Type, Census 2000 Summary File 1 (SF 1) 100-Percent Data.

No. 67. Self-Described Religious Identification of Adult Population: 1990 and 2001

[In thousands (175,440 represents 175,440,000). The American Religious Identification Survey (ARIS) 2001 was based on a random digit-dialed telephone survey of 50,281 American residential households in the continental U.S.A (48 states). Respondents were asked to describe themselves in terms of religion with an open-ended question. Interviewers did not prompt or offer a suggested list of potential answers. Moreover, the self-description of respondents was not based on whether established religious bodies, institutions, churches, mosques or synagogues considered them to be members. Quite the contrary, the survey sought to determine whether the respondents themselves regarded themselves as adherents of a religious community. Subjective rather than objective standards of religious identification were tapped by the surveys]

Religious group	1990	2001	Religious group	1990	2001
Adult population, total [1]	175,440	207,980	Fundamentalist	27	61
			Salvation Army	27	25
Total Christian	151,496	159,506	Independent Christian Church	25	71
Catholic......................	46,004	50,873			
Baptist......................	33,964	33,830	Total other religions.	5,853	7,740
Protestant - no denomination supplied. .	17,214	4,647	Jewish......................	3,137	2,831
Methodist/Wesleyan	14,174	14,150	Muslim/Islamic.................	527	1,104
Lutheran	9,110	9,580	Buddhist	401	1,082
Christian - no denomination supplied. . .	8,073	14,150	Unitarian/Universalist	502	629
Presbyterian	4,985	5,596	Hindu	227	766
Pentecostal/Charismatic	3,191	4,407	Native American	47	103
Episcopalian/Anglican.............	3,042	3,451	Scientologist	45	55
Mormon/Latter-Day Saints..........	2,487	2,787	Baha'l	28	84
Churches of Christ...............	1,769	2,593	Taoist	23	40
Jehovah's Witness...............	1,381	1,331	New Age	20	68
Seventh-Day Adventist	668	724	Eckankar	18	26
Assemblies of God...............	660	1,106	Rastafarian...................	14	11
Holiness/Holy	610	569	Sikh	13	57
Congregational/United Church of Christ .	599	1,378	Wiccan	8	134
Church of the Nazarene	549	544	Deity	6	49
Church of God	531	944	Druid.......................	(NA)	33
Orthodox (Eastern)	502	645	Santeria	(NA)	22
Evangelical [2].................	242	1,032	Pagan	(NA)	140
Mennonite	235	346	Spiritualist	(NA)	116
Christian Science................	214	194	Ethical Culture.................	(NA)	4
Church of the Brethren	206	358	Other unclassified	837	386
Born Again [2]	204	56			
Nondenominational [2]	195	2,489	No religion specified, total	14,331	29,481
Disciples of Christ	144	492	Atheist.....................	(NA)	902
Reformed/Dutch Reform	161	289	Agnostic.....................	1,186	991
Apostolic/New Apostolic	117	254	Humanist	29	49
Quaker	67	217	Secular	(NA)	53
Full Gospel...................	51	168	No religion	13,116	27,486
Christian Reform	40	79			
Foursquare Gospel	28	70	Refused to reply to question.	4,031	11,246

NA Not available.   [1] Refers to the total number of adults in all fifty states. All other figures are based on projections from surveys conducted in the continental United States (48 states).   [2] Because of the subjective nature of replies to open-ended question, these categories are the most unstable as they do not refer to clearly identifiable denominations as much as underlying feelings about religion. Thus they may be the most subject to fluctuation over time.

Source: 1990 data, Barry A. Kosmin and Seymour P. Lachman, "One Nation Under God: Religion in Contemporary American Society", 1993; 2001 data, The Graduate Center of the City University of New York, New York, NY, Barry A. Kosmin, Egon Mayer and Ariela Keysar, American Religious Identification Survey, 2001 (copyright).

Population   55

No. 68. Religious Bodies—Selected Data

[**Membership data: 2,500 represents 2,500,000.** Includes the self-reported membership of religious bodies with 750,000 or more as reported to the *Yearbook of American and Canadian Churches*. Groups may be excluded if they do not supply information. The data are not standardized so comparisons between groups are difficult. The definition of "church member" is determined by the religious body]

Religious body	Year reported	Churches reported	Membership (1,000)	Pastors serving parishes [1]
African Methodist Episcopal Church.	1999	(NA)	2,500	7,741
African Methodist Episcopal Zion Church	2002	3,226	1,431	3,235
American Baptist Churches in the U.S.A.	2002	5,836	1,484	4,325
Assemblies of God	2002	12,133	2,687	19,005
Baptist Bible Fellowship International	2002	4,500	1,200	(NA)
Christian Church (Disciples of Christ) in the United States and Canada	2002	3,691	786	3,362
Christian Churches and Churches of Christ.	1988	5,579	1,072	5,525
Christian Methodist Episcopal Church	2002	3,300	850	3,001
Church of God (Cleveland, Tennessee)	2002	6,623	945	5,084
Church of God in Christ, The	1991	15,300	5,500	28,988
Church of Jesus Christ of Latter-day Saints, The	2002	11,879	5,411	35,657
Churches of Christ	1999	15,000	1,500	14,500
Episcopal Church	2001	7,344	2,334	6,057
Evangelical Lutheran Church in America.	2002	10,721	5,038	7,354
Greek Orthodox Archdiocese of America	(NA)	510	1,500	599
Jehovah's Witnesses	2002	11,876	1,022	(NA)
Lutheran Church—Missouri Synod (LCMS), The	2002	6,142	2,513	5,217
National Baptist Convention of America, Inc.	2000	(NA)	3,500	(NA)
National Baptist Convention, U.S.A., Inc.	(NA)	9,000	5,000	(NA)
National Missionary Baptist Convention of America.	1992	(NA)	2,500	(NA)
Orthodox Church in America, The	2002	725	900	792
Pentecostal Assemblies of the World, Inc.	1998	1,750	1,500	4,500
Presbyterian Church (U.S.A.)	2002	11,097	3,407	8,725
Progressive National Baptist Convention, Inc.	1995	2,000	2,500	(NA)
Roman Catholic Church, The	2002	19,484	66,407	(NA)
Seventh-day Adventist Church	2002	4,619	919	2,589
Southern Baptist Convention	2002	42,775	16,248	94,231
United Church of Christ.	2002	5,850	1,331	4,295
United Methodist Church, The	2002	35,102	8,251	24,273

NA Not available.   [1] Does not include retired clergy or clergy not working with congregations.
Source: National Council of Churches, New York, NY, *2004 Yearbook of American and Canadian Churches*, annual (copyright). (For more info visit <www.ncccusa.org> or call 888-870-3325.)

No. 69. Christian Church Adherents, 2000, and Jewish Population, 2002—States

[**133,377 represents 133,377,000.** Christian church adherents were defined as "all members, including full members, their children and the estimated number of other regular participants who are not considered as communicant, confirmed or full members." The Jewish population includes Jews who define themselves as Jewish by religion as well as those who define themselves as Jewish in cultural terms. Data on Jewish population are based primarily on a compilation of individual estimates made by local Jewish federations. Additionally, most large communities have completed Jewish demographic surveys from which the Jewish population can be determined]

State	Christian adherents, 2000		Jewish population, 2002		State	Christian adherents, 2000		Jewish population, 2002	
	Number (1,000)	Percent of population [1]	Number (1,000)	Percent of population [1]		Number (1,000)	Percent of population [1]	Number (1,000)	Percent of population [1]
U.S.	133,377	47.4	6,155	2.2	MO	2,813	50.3	62	1.1
AL	2,418	54.4	9	0.2	MT	401	44.4	1	0.1
AK	210	33.6	3	0.5	NE	995	58.2	7	0.4
AZ	1,946	37.9	82	1.6	NV	604	30.2	77	3.8
AR	1,516	56.7	2	0.1	NH	571	46.2	10	0.8
CA	14,328	42.3	999	2.9	NJ	4,262	50.7	485	5.8
CO.	1,604	37.3	73	1.7	NM	1,041	57.2	11	0.6
CT	1,828	53.7	111	3.3	NY	9,569	50.4	1,657	8.7
DE	299	38.2	14	1.7	NC	3,598	44.7	26	0.3
DC	331	57.8	26	4.5	ND	468	72.9	(Z)	0.1
FL	5,904	36.9	620	3.9	OH	4,912	43.3	149	1.3
GA	3,528	43.1	94	1.1	OK	2,079	60.3	5	0.1
HI	431	35.6	7	0.6	OR	1,029	30.1	32	0.9
ID	624	48.3	1	0.1	PA	6,751	55.0	282	2.3
IL	6,457	52.0	270	2.2	RI	646	61.7	16	1.5
IN	2,578	42.4	18	0.3	SC	1,874	46.7	11	0.3
IA	1,698	58.0	6	0.2	SD	510	67.6	(Z)	(Z)
KS	1,307	48.6	14	0.5	TN	2,867	50.4	18	0.3
KY	2,141	53.0	11	0.3	TX	11,316	54.3	131	0.6
LA	2,599	58.2	16	0.4	UT	1,659	74.3	4	0.2
ME.	450	35.3	9	0.7	VT	230	37.8	6	0.9
MD.	2,012	38.0	213	4.0	VA	2,807	39.7	66	0.9
MA.	3,725	58.7	275	4.3	WA	1,872	31.8	43	0.7
MI	3,970	39.9	110	1.1	WV	646	35.7	2	0.1
MN.	2,974	60.5	42	0.9	WI	3,198	59.6	28	0.5
MS.	1,549	54.5	1	0.1	WY	229	46.4	(Z)	0.1

Z Fewer than 500 or .05 percent.   [1] Based on U.S. Census Bureau data for resident population enumerated as of April 1, 2000, and estimated as of July 1, 2002.
Source: Christian church adherents—Dale E. Jones, Sherri Doty, Clifford Grammich, James E. Horsch, Richard Houseal, John P. Marcum, Kenneth M. Sanchagrin, and Richard H. Taylor, *Religious Congregations and Membership in the United States: 2000*, Glenmary Research Center, Nashville, TN , 2002 (copyright); Jewish population—American Jewish Committee, New York, NY, *American Jewish Year Book, 2002* (copyright).

Section 2
Vital Statistics

This section presents vital statistics data on births, deaths, abortions, fetal deaths, fertility, life expectancy, marriages, and divorces. Vital statistics are compiled for the country as a whole by the National Center for Health Statistics (NCHS) and published in its annual report, *Vital Statistics of the United States,* in certain reports of the *Vital and Health Statistics* series, and in the *National Vital Statistics Reports* (formerly *Monthly Vital Statistics Report).* Reports in this field are also issued by the various state bureaus of vital statistics. Data on fertility, on age of persons at first marriage, and on marital status and marital history are compiled by the U.S. Census Bureau from its Current Population Survey (CPS; see text, Section 1) and published in *Current Population Reports,* P20 Series. Data on abortions are published by the Alan Guttmacher Institute, New York, NY, in selected issues of *Family Planning Perspectives.*

Registration of vital events—The registration of births, deaths, fetal deaths, and other vital events in the United States is primarily a state and local function. The civil laws of every state provide for a continuous and permanent birth- and death-registration system. Many states also provide for marriage- and divorce-registration systems. Vital events occurring to U.S. residents outside the United States are not included in the data.

Births and deaths—The live-birth, death, and fetal-death statistics prepared by NCHS are based on vital records filed in the registration offices of all states, New York City, and the District of Columbia. The annual collection of death statistics on a national basis began in 1900 with a national death-registration area of ten states and the District of Columbia; a similar annual collection of birth statistics for a national birth-registration area began in 1915, also with ten reporting states and the District of Columbia. Since 1933, the birth- and death-registration areas have comprised the entire United States, including Alaska

(beginning 1959) and Hawaii (beginning 1960). National statistics on fetal deaths were first compiled for 1918 and annually since 1922.

Prior to 1951, birth statistics came from a complete count of records received in the Public Health Service (now received in NCHS). From 1951 through 1971, they were based on a 50-percent sample of all registered births (except for a complete count in 1955 and a 20- to 50-percent sample in 1967). Beginning in 1972, they have been based on a complete count for states participating in the Vital Statistics Cooperative Program (VSCP) (for details, see the technical appendix in *Vital Statistics of the United States*) and on a 50-percent sample of all other areas. Beginning in 1986, all reporting areas participated in the VSCP. Mortality data have been based on a complete count of records for each area (except for a 50-percent sample in 1972). Beginning in 1970, births to and deaths of nonresident aliens of the United States and U.S. citizens outside the United States have been excluded from the data. Fetal deaths and deaths among Armed Forces abroad are excluded. Data based on samples are subject to sampling error; for details, see annual issues of *Vital Statistics of the United States.*

Mortality statistics by cause of death are compiled in accordance with World Health Organization regulations according to the *International Classification of Diseases* (ICD). The ICD is revised approximately every 10 years. The tenth revision of the ICD was employed beginning in 1999. Deaths for prior years were classified according to the revision of the ICD in use at the time. Each revision of the ICD introduces a number of discontinuities in mortality statistics; for a discussion of those between the ninth and tenth revisions of the ICD, see *National Vital Statistics Reports,* Vol. 49, Nos. 2 and 8. Preliminary mortality data are based on a percentage of death records weighted up to the total number of deaths reported for the given year; for a discussion of preliminary data, see *National Vital Statistics Reports*, Vol. 49, No. 3. Information on tests of statistical significance, differences between death rates, and standard errors can also be found in the reports mentioned above.

Some of the tables present age-adjusted death rates in addition to crude death rates. Age-adjusted death rates shown in this section were prepared using the direct method, in which age-specific death rates for a population of interest are applied to a standard population distributed by age. Age adjustment eliminates the differences in observed rates between points in time or among compared population groups that result from age differences in population composition.

Fertility and life expectancy—The total fertility rate, defined as the number of births that 1,000 women would have in their lifetime if, at each year of age, they experienced the birth rates occurring in the specified year, is compiled and published by NCHS. Other data relating to social and medical factors that affect fertility rates, such as contraceptive use and birth expectations, are collected and made available by both NCHS and the Census Bureau. NCHS figures are based on information in birth and fetal death certificates and on the periodic National Surveys of Family Growth; Census Bureau data are based on decennial censuses and the CPS.

Data on life expectancy, the average remaining lifetime in years for persons who attain a given age, are computed and published by NCHS. For details, see *National Vital Statistics Reports*, Vol. 52, No. 3.

Marriage and divorce—The compilation of nationwide statistics on marriages and divorces in the United States began in 1887-88, when the National Office of Vital Statistics prepared estimates for the years 1867-86. Although periodic updates took place after 1888, marriage and divorce statistics were not collected and published annually until 1944 by that office. In 1957 and 1958, respectively, the same office established marriage- and divorce-registration areas. Beginning in 1957, the marriage-registration area comprised 30 states, plus Alaska, Hawaii, Puerto Rico, and the Virgin Islands; it currently includes 42 states and the District of Columbia. The divorce-registration area, starting in 1958 with 14 states, Alaska, Hawaii, and the Virgin Islands, currently includes a total of 31 states and the Virgin Islands. Procedures for estimating the number of marriages and divorces in the registration states are discussed in *Vital Statistics of the United States*, Vol. III—Marriage and Divorce. Total counts of events for registration and nonregistration states are gathered by collecting already summarized data on marriages and divorces reported by state offices of vital statistics and by county offices of registration. The collection and publication of detailed marriage and divorce statistics (for example: by age and race) was suspended beginning in January 1996. For additional information contact the National Center for Health Statistics online at <http://www.cec.gov/nchs/releases/96facts/mardiv.htm>.

Vital statistics rates—Except as noted, vital statistics rates computed by NCHS are based on decennial census population figures as of April 1 for 1940, 1950, 1960, 1970, 1980, and 1990; and on mid-year population figures for other years, as estimated by the Census Bureau (see text, Section 1).

Race—Data by race for births, deaths, marriages, and divorces from NCHS are based on information contained in the certificates of registration. The Census Bureau's Current Population Survey obtains information on race by asking respondents to classify their race as (1) White, (2) Black, (3) American Indian, Eskimo, or Aleut, or (4) Asian or Pacific Islander.

Beginning with the 1989 data year, NCHS is tabulating its birth data primarily by race of the mother. In 1988 and prior years, births were tabulated by race of the child, which was determined from the race of the parents as entered on the birth certificate.

Trend data by race shown in this section are by race of mother beginning with the 1980 data. Hispanic origin of the mother is reported and tabulated independently of race. Thus, persons of Hispanic origin may be of any race. In 1994, 91 percent of women of Hispanic origin were reported as White.

Figure 2.1
Infant Mortality Rates by State: 2001

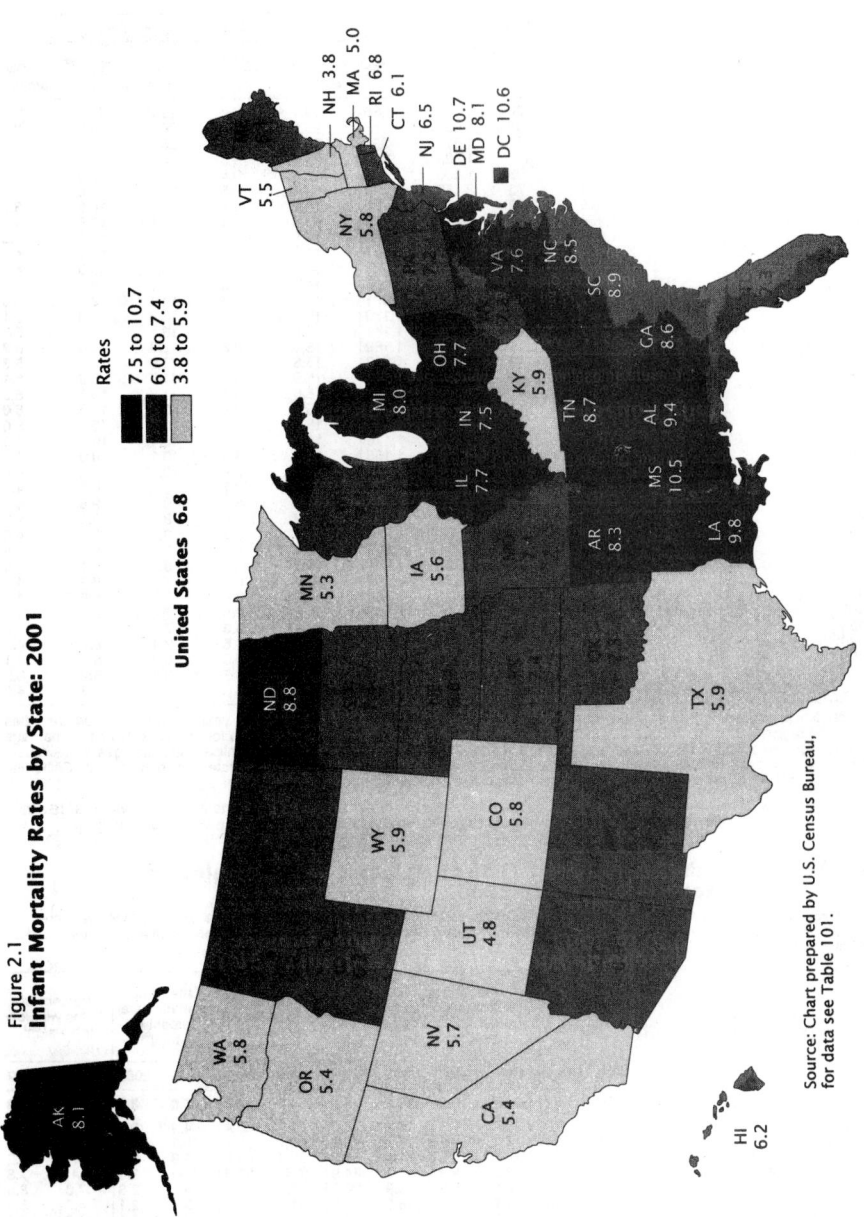

Rates

◼ 7.5 to 10.7
◼ 6.0 to 7.4
◻ 3.8 to 5.9

United States 6.8

NH 3.8
MA 5.0
RI 6.8
CT 6.1
NJ 6.5
DE 10.7
MD 8.1
◼ DC 10.6

VT 5.5
NY 5.8
VA 7.6
NC 8.5
SC 8.9
GA 8.6
OH 7.7
KY 5.9
TN 8.7
AL 9.4
IN 7.5
IL 7.7
MS 10.5
AR 8.3
LA 9.8
MI 8.0
MN 5.3
IA 5.6
ND 8.8
WY 5.9
CO 5.8
UT 4.8
TX 5.9
WA 5.8
OR 5.4
NV 5.7
CA 5.4
AK 8.1
HI 6.2

Source: Chart prepared by U.S. Census Bureau,
for data see Table 101.

Vital Statistics 59

No. 70. Live Births, Deaths, Marriages, and Divorces: 1950 to 2002

[3,632 represents 3,632,000. Prior to 1960, excludes Alaska and Hawaii. Beginning 1970, excludes births to, and deaths of nonresidents of the United States. See Appendix III]

Year	Number (1,000)					Rate per 1,000 population				
		Deaths		Mar-riages [3]	Div-orces [4]		Deaths		Mar-riages [3]	Div-orces [4]
	Births [1]	Total	Infant [2]			Births [1]	Total	Infant [2]		
1950	3,632	1,452	104	1,667	385	24.1	9.6	29.2	11.1	2.6
1955	4,097	1,529	107	1,531	377	25.0	9.3	26.4	9.3	2.3
1957	4,300	1,633	112	1,518	381	25.3	9.6	26.3	8.9	2.2
1960	4,258	1,712	111	1,523	393	23.7	9.5	26.0	8.5	2.2
1965	3,760	1,828	93	1,800	479	19.4	9.4	24.7	9.3	2.5
1970	3,731	1,921	75	2,159	708	18.4	9.5	20.0	10.6	3.5
1971	3,556	1,928	68	2,190	773	17.2	9.3	19.1	10.6	3.7
1972	3,258	1,964	60	2,282	845	15.6	9.4	18.5	10.9	4.0
1973	3,137	1,973	56	2,284	915	14.8	9.3	17.7	10.8	4.3
1974	3,160	1,934	53	2,230	977	14.8	9.1	16.7	10.5	4.6
1975	3,144	1,893	51	2,153	1,036	14.6	8.8	16.1	10.0	4.8
1976	3,168	1,909	48	2,155	1,083	14.6	8.8	15.2	9.9	5.0
1977	3,327	1,900	47	2,178	1,091	15.1	8.6	14.1	9.9	5.0
1978	3,333	1,928	46	2,282	1,130	15.0	8.7	13.8	10.3	5.1
1979	3,494	1,914	46	2,331	1,181	15.6	8.5	13.1	10.4	5.3
1980	3,612	1,990	46	2,390	1,189	15.9	8.8	12.6	10.6	5.2
1981	3,629	1,978	43	2,422	1,213	15.8	8.6	11.9	10.6	5.3
1982	3,681	1,975	42	2,456	1,170	15.9	8.5	11.5	10.6	5.1
1983	3,639	2,019	41	2,446	1,158	15.6	8.6	11.2	10.5	5.0
1984	3,669	2,039	40	2,477	1,169	15.6	8.6	10.8	10.5	5.0
1985	3,761	2,086	40	2,413	1,190	15.8	8.8	10.6	10.1	5.0
1986	3,757	2,105	39	2,407	1,178	15.6	8.8	10.4	10.0	4.9
1987	3,809	2,123	38	2,403	1,166	15.7	8.8	10.1	9.9	4.8
1988	3,910	2,168	39	2,396	1,167	16.0	8.9	10.0	9.8	4.8
1989	4,041	2,150	40	2,403	1,157	16.4	8.7	9.8	9.7	4.7
1990	4,158	2,148	38	2,443	1,182	16.7	8.6	9.2	9.8	4.7
1991	4,111	2,170	37	2,371	1,187	16.2	8.6	8.9	9.4	4.7
1992	4,065	2,176	35	2,362	1,215	15.8	8.5	8.5	9.3	4.8
1993	4,000	2,269	33	2,334	1,187	15.4	8.8	8.4	9.0	4.6
1994	3,953	2,279	31	2,362	1,191	15.0	8.8	8.0	9.1	4.6
1995	3,900	2,312	30	2,336	1,169	14.6	8.7	7.6	8.9	4.4
1996	3,891	2,315	28	2,344	1,150	14.4	8.6	7.3	8.8	4.3
1997	3,881	2,314	28	2,384	1,163	14.2	8.5	7.2	8.9	4.3
1998 [5]	3,942	2,337	28	2,244	1,135	14.3	8.5	7.2	8.4	4.2
1999 [5]	3,959	2,391	28	2,358	(NA)	14.2	8.6	7.1	8.6	4.1
2000 [5]	4,059	2,403	28	2,329	(NA)	14.4	8.5	6.9	8.2	4.1
2001 [5]	4,026	2,416	28	2,345	(NA)	14.1	8.5	6.8	8.2	3.9
2002 [5]	4,022	2,448	28	2,254	(NA)	13.9	8.5	7.0	7.8	4.0

NA Not available. [1] Prior to 1960, data adjusted for underregistration. [2] Infants under 1 year, excluding fetal deaths; rates per 1,000 registered live births. [3] Includes estimates for some states through 1965 and also for 1976 and 1977 and marriage licenses for some States for all years except 1973 and 1975. Beginning 1978, includes nonlicensed marriages in California. [4] Includes reported annulments and some estimated state figures for all years. [5] Divorce rate excludes data for California, Colorado, Indiana, and Louisiana; population for this rate also excludes these states.

Source: U.S. National Center for Health Statistics, *Vital Statistics of the United States*, annual; and *National Vital Statistics Reports (NVSR)* (formerly *Monthly Vital Statistics Report*); and unpublished data. See also <http://www.cdc.gov/nchs>.

No. 71. Live Births by Race and Type of Hispanic Origin—Selected Characteristics: 1990 and 2002

[4,158 represents 4,158,000. Represents registered births. Excludes births to nonresidents of the United States. Data are based on Hispanic origin of mother and race of mother. Hispanic origin data are available from only 48 States and the District of Columbia in 1990]

Race and Hispanic origin	Number of births (1,000)		Births to teen-age mothers, percent of total		Births to unmarried mothers, per-cent of total		Prenatal care beginning first trimester percent of total		Late or no prenatal care percent of total		Percent of births with low birth weight [1]	
	1990	2002	1990	2002	1990	2002	1990	2002	1990	2002	1990	2002
Total	4,158	4,022	12.8	10.8	26.6	34.0	74.2	83.7	6.0	3.6	7.0	7.8
White	3,290	3,175	10.9	9.8	16.9	28.5	77.7	85.4	4.9	3.1	5.7	6.8
Black	684	594	23.1	18.0	66.7	68.2	60.7	75.2	10.9	6.2	13.3	13.3
American Indian, Eskimo, Aleut	39	42	19.5	18.5	53.6	59.7	57.9	69.8	12.9	8.0	6.1	7.2
Asian and Pacific Islander [2]	142	211	5.7	3.8	13.2	14.9	(NA)	84.8	(NA)	3.1	(NA)	7.8
Filipino	26	33	6.1	4.5	15.9	20.0	77.1	85.4	4.5	2.8	7.3	8.6
Chinese	23	34	1.2	0.9	5.0	9.0	81.3	87.2	3.4	2.1	4.7	5.5
Japanese	9	9	2.9	1.7	9.6	10.3	87.0	90.5	2.9	2.1	6.2	7.6
Hawaiian	6	7	18.4	14.6	45.0	50.4	65.8	78.1	8.7	4.7	7.2	8.1
Hispanic origin [3]	595	877	16.8	14.9	36.7	43.5	60.2	76.7	12.0	5.5	6.1	6.5
Mexican	386	628	17.7	15.9	33.3	42.1	57.8	75.7	13.2	5.8	5.5	6.2
Puerto Rican	59	57	21.7	17.8	55.9	59.1	63.5	79.9	10.6	4.1	9.0	9.7
Cuban	11	14	7.7	8.1	18.2	29.8	84.8	92.0	2.8	1.3	5.7	6.5
Central and South American	83	126	9.0	8.5	41.2	44.4	61.5	78.7	10.9	4.9	5.8	6.5
Other and unknown Hispanic	56	51	(NA)	16.7	(NA)	44.4	(NA)	76.7	(NA)	5.3	(NA)	7.9

NA Not available. [1] Births less than 2,500 grams (5 lb.-8 oz.). [2] Includes other races not shown separately. [3] Hispanic persons may be of any race. Includes other types, not shown separately.

Source: U.S. National Center for Health Statistics; *Vital Statistics of the United States*, annual; *National Vital Statistics Report (NVSR) (formerly Monthly Vital Statistics Report)*; and unpublished data.

60 Vital Statistics

No. 72. Births and Birth Rates by Race, Sex, and Age: 1980 to 2002

[Births in thousands. (3,612 represents 3,612,000). Births by race of mother. Excludes births to nonresidents of the United States. For population bases used to derive these data, see text this section, and Appendix III]

Item	1980	1985	1990	1995	1996	1997	1998	1999	2000	2001	2002
Live births [1]	3,612	3,761	4,158	3,900	3,891	3,881	3,942	3,959	4,059	4,026	4,022
White	2,936	3,038	3,290	3,099	3,093	3,073	3,119	3,133	3,194	3,178	3,175
Black	568	582	684	603	595	600	610	606	623	606	594
American Indian, Eskimo, Aleut	29	34	39	37	38	39	40	41	42	42	42
Asian or Pacific Islander	74	105	142	160	166	170	173	182	201	200	211
Male	1,853	1,928	2,129	1,996	1,990	1,986	2,016	2,028	2,077	2,058	2,058
Female	1,760	1,833	2,029	1,903	1,901	1,895	1,925	1,934	1,982	1,968	1,964
Males per 100 females	105	105	105	105	105	105	105	106	105	105	105
Age of mother:											
Under 20 years old	562	478	533	512	503	493	494	485	478	454	433
20 to 24 years old	1,226	1,141	1,094	966	945	942	965	982	1,018	1,022	1,022
25 to 29 years old	1,108	1,201	1,277	1,064	1,071	1,069	1,083	1,078	1,088	1,058	1,060
30 to 34 years old	550	696	886	905	898	887	889	892	929	943	951
35 to 39 years old	141	214	318	384	400	410	425	434	452	452	454
40 to 44 years old	(NA)	(NA)	(NA)	(NA)	72	76	81	83	90	93	96
45 to 49 years old	(NA)	(NA)	(NA)	(NA)	3	3	4	4	4	5	5
Birth rate per 1,000 population	15.9	15.8	16.7	14.6	14.4	14.2	14.3	14.2	14.4	14.1	13.9
White	15.1	15.0	15.8	14.1	13.9	13.7	13.8	13.7	13.9	13.7	13.5
Black	21.3	20.4	22.4	17.8	17.3	17.1	17.1	16.8	17.0	16.3	15.7
American Indian	20.7	19.8	18.9	15.3	14.9	14.7	14.8	14.2	14.0	13.7	13.8
Asian or Pacific Islander	19.9	18.7	19.0	16.7	16.5	16.2	15.9	15.9	17.1	16.4	16.5
Plural birth ratio [2]	19.3	21.0	23.3	26.1	27.4	28.6	30.0	30.7	31.1	32.0	33.0
White	18.5	20.4	22.9	26.0	27.5	28.7	30.2	30.9	31.2	32.1	33.0
Black	24.1	25.3	27.0	28.8	29.8	30.9	32.0	32.9	34.0	34.6	35.4
Fertility rate per 1,000 women [3]	68.4	66.2	70.9	64.6	64.1	63.6	64.3	64.4	65.9	65.3	64.8
White [3]	65.6	64.1	68.3	63.6	63.3	62.8	63.6	64.0	65.3	65.0	64.8
Black [3]	84.9	78.8	84.8	71.0	69.2	69.0	69.4	68.5	70.0	67.6	65.8
American Indian [3]	82.7	78.6	76.2	63.0	61.8	60.8	61.3	59.0	58.7	58.1	58.0
Asian or Pacific Islander [3]	73.2	68.4	69.6	62.6	62.3	61.3	60.1	60.9	65.8	64.2	64.1
Age of mother:											
10 to 14 years old	1.1	1.2	1.4	1.3	1.2	1.1	1.0	0.9	0.9	0.8	0.7
15 to 19 years old	53.0	51.0	59.9	56.0	53.5	51.3	50.3	48.8	47.7	45.3	43.0
20 to 24 years old	115.1	108.3	116.5	107.5	107.8	107.3	108.4	107.9	109.7	106.2	103.6
25 to 29 years old	112.9	111.0	120.2	108.8	108.6	108.3	110.2	111.2	113.5	113.4	113.6
30 to 34 years old	61.9	69.1	80.8	81.1	82.1	83.0	85.2	87.1	91.2	91.9	91.5
35 to 39 years old	19.8	24.0	31.7	34.0	34.9	35.7	36.9	37.8	39.7	40.6	41.4
40 to 44 years old	3.9	4.0	5.5	6.6	6.8	7.1	7.4	7.4	8.0	8.1	8.3
45 to 49 years old	0.2	0.2	0.2	0.3	0.3	0.4	0.4	0.4	0.5	0.5	0.5

NA Not available. [1] Includes other races not shown separately. [2] Number of multiple births per 1,000 live births. [3] Number of live births per 1,000 women, 15 to 44 years old in specified group. The rate for age of mother 45 to 49 years old computed by relating births to mothers 45 years old and over to women 45 to 49 years old.

Source: U.S. National Center for Health Statistics, *Vital Statistics of the United States*, annual; *National Vital Statistics Report* (NVSR) (formerly *Monthly Vital Statistics Report*); and unpublished data.

No. 73. Teenagers—Births and Birth Rates by Race and Age: 1990 to 2002

[Birth rates per 1,000 women in specified group, see text, this section]

Item	1990	1994	1995	1996	1997	1998	1999	2000	2001	2002
NUMBER OF BIRTHS										
All races, total [1]	521,826	505,488	499,873	494,272	489,211	484,975	476,050	468,990	445,944	425,493
15-17 years	183,327	195,169	192,508	186,762	183,324	173,252	163,588	157,209	145,324	138,731
18-19 years	338,499	310,319	307,365	307,509	305,886	311,724	312,462	311,781	300,620	286,762
White	354,482	348,081	349,635	346,509	342,620	340,894	337,888	333,013	318,563	305,988
15-17 years	114,934	126,388	127,165	124,031	121,864	116,699	111,624	106,786	99,192	95,864
18-19 years	239,548	221,693	222,470	222,477	220,164	224,195	226,264	226,227	219,371	210,124
Black	151,613	140,968	133,694	131,059	130,401	126,865	121,166	118,954	110,843	103,795
15-17 years	62,881	62,563	59,112	56,218	54,883	50,062	45,919	44,618	40,842	37,889
18-19 years	88,732	78,405	74,582	74,841	75,518	76,803	75,247	74,336	70,001	65,906
BIRTH RATE										
All races, total [1]	59.9	58.2	56.0	53.5	51.3	50.3	48.8	47.7	45.3	43.0
15-17 years	37.5	37.2	35.5	33.3	31.4	29.9	28.2	26.9	24.7	23.2
18-19 years	88.6	90.2	87.7	84.7	82.1	80.9	79.1	78.1	76.1	72.8
White	50.8	50.5	49.5	47.5	45.5	44.9	43.2	43.2	41.2	39.4
15-17 years	29.5	30.4	29.7	28.0	26.6	25.6	24.5	23.3	21.4	20.5
18-19 years	78.0	81.0	80.0	77.4	74.8	73.9	72.8	72.3	70.8	68.0
Black	112.8	102.9	94.4	89.6	86.3	83.5	79.1	77.4	71.8	66.6
15-17 years	82.3	75.2	68.6	63.4	59.4	55.5	50.7	49.0	43.9	40.0
18-19 years	152.9	145.8	134.6	130.1	127.4	124.3	120.1	118.8	114.0	107.6

[1] Includes races other than white and black.

Source: U.S. National Center for Health Statistics, *Vital Statistics of the United States*, annual; *National Vital Statistics Report* (NVSR) (formerly *Monthly Vital Statistics Report*), and unpublished data. See also <http://www.cdc.gov/nchs.htm>.

Vital Statistics　61

No. 74. Live Births by State: 2002

[Number of births, except rate. Registered births. Excludes births to nonresidents of the United States. By race of mother. See Appendix III]

State	All races [1]	White	Black	Asian or Pacific Islander	American Indian, Eskimo, Aleut	Hispanic [2]	Birth rate [3]	Fertility rate [4]
United States. .	4,021,726	3,174,760	593,691	210,907	42,368	876,642	13.9	64.8
Alabama.	58,967	39,978	18,292	533	164	2,569	13.1	61.2
Alaska	9,938	6,377	432	691	2,438	799	15.4	73.5
Arizona.	87,837	77,043	2,779	2,314	5,701	37,938	16.1	77.8
Arkansas	37,437	29,209	7,427	544	257	3,050	13.8	66.6
California	529,357	428,549	32,653	65,122	3,033	263,061	15.1	68.3
Colorado.	68,418	62,425	2,934	2,397	662	21,029	15.2	69.3
Connecticut.	42,001	34,654	5,195	1,928	224	6,982	12.1	58.8
Delaware	11,090	7,925	2,708	428	29	1,316	13.7	62.2
Dist of Columbia . . .	7,498	2,677	4,620	194	7	954	13.1	52.9
Florida	205,579	152,855	46,238	5,411	1,075	51,619	12.3	62.5
Georgia	133,300	85,809	42,777	4,388	326	16,819	15.6	68.4
Hawaii	17,477	3,953	475	12,878	171	2,422	14.0	68.6
Idaho.	20,970	20,151	103	339	377	2,788	15.6	73.8
Illinois	180,622	140,163	31,833	8,362	264	41,022	14.3	66.1
Indiana.	85,081	74,309	9,332	1,283	157	6,169	13.8	64.8
Iowa	37,559	35,112	1,263	950	234	2,390	12.8	61.7
Kansas.	39,412	34,904	2,890	1,170	448	5,023	14.5	68.7
Kentucky	54,233	48,399	4,943	788	103	1,630	13.3	60.5
Louisiana	64,872	36,757	26,659	1,044	412	1,383	14.5	65.4
Maine.	13,559	13,049	174	220	116	167	10.5	49.8
Maryland	73,323	45,198	24,214	3,672	239	6,062	13.4	60.6
Massachusetts. . . .	80,645	66,689	8,344	5,421	191	9,592	12.5	56.7
Michigan.	129,967	102,590	22,440	4,254	683	7,265	12.9	60.7
Minnesota.	68,025	58,023	4,862	3,782	1,358	4,646	13.6	62.0
Mississippi	41,518	22,618	18,202	430	268	823	14.5	65.7
Missouri	75,251	62,374	11,028	1,496	353	3,267	13.3	62.1
Montana.	11,049	9,512	37	105	1,395	382	12.1	60.3
Nebraska	25,383	22,980	1,442	558	403	3,313	14.7	69.5
Nevada	32,571	26,979	2,611	2,441	540	11,386	15.0	72.5
New Hampshire. . . .	14,442	13,691	225	478	48	503	11.3	52.4
New Jersey.	114,751	84,493	19,952	10,134	172	24,664	13.4	63.5
New Mexico	27,753	23,281	511	413	3,548	14,623	15.0	70.7
New York	251,415	181,212	49,590	19,920	693	54,700	13.1	59.8
North Carolina	117,335	85,210	27,571	2,897	1,657	15,064	14.1	65.4
North Dakota.	7,757	6,762	90	90	815	149	12.2	58.7
Ohio	148,720	122,887	22,547	2,998	288	4,817	13.0	61.7
Oklahoma.	50,387	39,508	4,704	1,015	5,160	5,259	14.4	68.8
Oregon.	45,192	41,047	941	2400	804	8,040	12.8	61.9
Pennsylvania	142,850	117,817	20,265	4,415	353	8,696	11.6	56.4
Rhode Island.	12,894	11,036	1,145	556	157	2,328	12.1	54.6
South Carolina.	54,570	35,373	18,183	846	168	3,175	13.3	60.7
South Dakota	10,698	8,657	103	133	1,805	318	14.1	68.3
Tennessee	77,482	59,627	16,304	1,394	157	4,348	13.4	62.2
Texas.	372,450	317,150	41,642	12,824	834	178,968	17.1	77.1
Utah	49,182	46,572	339	1586	685	6,952	21.2	90.6
Vermont	6,387	6,239	44	94	10	32	10.4	48.9
Virginia.	99,672	71,415	22,084	6,048	125	9,790	13.7	61.9
Washington.	79,028	66,519	3,393	7,196	1,920	12,349	13.0	60.2
West Virginia.	20,712	19,877	679	145	11	84	11.5	57.0
Wisconsin.	68,560	58,979	6,418	2,112	1,051	5,295	12.6	59.0
Wyoming	6,550	6,147	54	70	279	622	13.1	63.6
Puerto Rico	52,747	47,811	4,925	(NA)	(NA)	(NA)	13.7	61.6
Virgin Islands	1,634	326	1,222	(NA)	86	323	15.0	71.1
Guam	3,212	260	41	2,909	2	54	19.9	88.3
American Samoa .	1,627	8	(NA)	1,619	(NA)	(NA)	28.2	126.7
Northern Marianas	1,290	17	1	1,272	(NA)	(NA)	17.4	45.1

NA Not available   [1] Includes other races not shown separately.   [2] Persons of Hispanic origin may be of any race. Births by Hispanic origin of mother.   [3] Per 1,000 estimated population.   [4] Number of births per 1,000 women aged 15-44 years estimated.

Source: U.S. National Center for Health Statistics, *Vital Statistics of the United States,* annual; and *National Vital Statistics Reports (NVSR)*Vol. 52, No.10. (formerly *Monthly Vital Statistics Report*). See also: <http://www.cdc.gov/nchs/nvss.htm>.

No. 75. Total Fertility Rate by Race: 1970 to 2002

[Based on race of child and registered births only, thru 1979. Beginning 1980, based on race of mother. Excludes births to nonresidents of United States. The *total fertility rate* is the number of births that 1,000 women would have in their lifetime if, at each year of age, they experienced the birth rates occurring in the specified year. A total fertility rate of 2,110 represents "replacement level" fertility for the total population under current mortality conditions (assuming no net immigration). See also Appendix III]

Year	Total [1]	White	Black [2]	Year	Total [1]	White	Black [2]
1970	2,480	2,385	3,067	1987	1,872	1,805	2,198
1971	2,267	2,161	2,920	1988	1,934	1,857	2,298
1972	2,010	1,907	2,628	1989	2,014	1,931	2,433
1973	1,879	1,783	2,443	1990	2,081	2,003	2,480
1974	1,835	1,749	2,339	1991	2,063	1,988	2,462
1975	1,774	1,686	2,276	1992	2,046	1,978	2,416
1976	1,738	1,652	2,223	1993	2,020	1,962	2,351
1977	1,790	1,703	2,279	1994	2,002	1,958	2,259
1978	1,760	1,668	2,265	1995	1,978	1,955	2,128
1979	1,808	1,716	2,310	1996	1,976	1,961	2,089
1980	1,840	1,773	2,177	1997	1,971	1,955	2,092
1981	1,812	1,748	2,118	1998	1,999	1,991	2,112
1982	1,828	1,767	2,107	1999	2,008	2,008	2,083
1983	1,799	1,741	2,066	2000	2,056	2,051	2,129
1984	1,807	1,749	2,071	2001	2,034	2,040	2,051
1985	1,844	1,787	2,109	2002	2,013	2,028	1,991
1986	1,838	1,776	2,136				

[1] Includes other races, not shown separately.   [2] Data for 1984 and earlier includes races other than Black.

Source: U.S. National Center for Health Statistics, *Vital Statistics of the United States*, annual; and unpublished data. See also <http://www.cdc.gov/nchs/>.

No. 76. Projected Fertility and Birth Rates by Race, Origin, and Age Group: 2010

[For definition of total fertility rate, see headnote, Table 75. Birth rates represent live births per 1,000 women in age group indicated. Projections are based on middle fertility assumptions. For explanations of methodology, see text, Section 1, Population]

Age Group	All races [1]	White	Black	American Indian, Eskimo, Aleut	Asian and Pacific Islander	Hispanic [2]
Total fertility rate	2,123	2,098	2,140	2,451	2,252	2,818
Birth rates:						
10 to 14 years old	1.3	0.9	3.5	2.0	0.7	2.3
15 to 19 years old	60.2	54.3	95.6	93.6	29.6	95.7
20 to 24 years old	115.8	112.6	137.1	159.6	83.7	175.2
25 to 29 years old	115.7	118.5	95.5	118.6	134.5	146.7
30 to 34 years old	87.8	90.0	63.4	77.3	128.2	91.6
35 to 39 years old	36.7	36.6	28.9	33.7	59.0	41.9
40 to 44 years old	7.3	7.1	6.0	7.4	13.8	9.9
45 to 49 years old	0.3	0.3	0.3	0.3	0.9	0.6

[1] Includes other races not shown separately.   [2] Persons of Hispanic origin may be of any race.

Source: U.S. Census Bureau, Population Division Working Paper No. 38. See also <http://www.census.gov/population/www/techpap.html>.

No. 77. Birth Rates by Live-Birth Order and Race: 1990 to 2002

[Births per 1,000 women 15 to 44 years old in specified racial group. Live-birth order refers to number of children born alive. Figures for births of order not stated are distributed. See also headnote, Table 72. See Appendix III]

Live-birth order	All races [1]					White					Black				
	1990	1995	2000	2001	2002	1990	1995	2000	2001	2002	1990	1995	2000	2001	2002
Total	70.9	64.6	65.9	65.3	64.8	68.3	63.6	65.3	65.0	64.8	86.8	71.0	70.0	67.6	65.8
First birth	29.0	26.9	26.5	26.0	25.8	28.4	26.6	26.3	25.9	25.7	32.4	28.2	26.2	25.4	24.8
Second birth	22.8	20.7	21.4	21.3	21.1	22.4	20.9	21.5	21.6	21.5	25.6	20.4	20.8	19.9	19.2
Third birth	11.7	10.3	11.0	11.0	10.9	11.1	10.2	11.0	11.0	11.0	15.6	11.8	12.5	12.1	11.7
Fourth birth	4.5	4.0	4.2	4.3	4.3	4.0	3.7	4.0	4.1	4.1	7.4	5.6	5.8	5.6	5.5
Fifth birth	1.7	1.5	1.6	1.6	1.5	1.4	1.3	1.4	1.4	1.4	3.2	2.6	2.5	2.5	2.4
Sixth and seventh	1.0	0.9	0.9	0.9	0.9	0.8	0.7	0.8	0.8	0.8	2.0	1.8	1.7	1.6	1.6
Eighth and over	0.3	0.3	0.3	0.3	0.3	0.2	0.2	0.2	0.2	0.2	0.6	0.6	0.6	0.5	0.5

[1] Includes other races not shown separately.

Source: U.S. National Center for Health Statistics, *Vital Statistics of the United States*, annual; and *National Vital Statistics Reports (NVSR)* (formerly *Monthly Vital Statistics Report*).

Vital Statistics   63

No. 78. Births to Teens, Unmarried Mothers, and Prenatal Care: 1990 to 2002

[In percent. Represents registered births. See headnote, Table 71. See Appendix III]

Characteristics	1990	1995	1998	1999	2000	2001	2002
Percent of births to teenage mothers	**12.8**	**13.1**	**12.5**	**12.3**	**11.8**	**11.3**	**10.8**
White	10.9	11.5	11.1	10.9	10.6	10.2	9.8
Black	23.1	23.1	21.5	20.7	19.7	18.9	18.0
American Indian, Eskimo, Aleut	19.5	21.4	20.9	20.2	19.7	19.3	18.5
Asian and Pacific Islander [1]	5.7	5.6	5.4	5.1	4.5	4.3	3.8
Filipino	6.1	6.2	6.2	5.9	5.3	5.1	4.5
Chinese	1.2	0.9	0.9	0.9	0.9	1.0	0.9
Japanese	2.9	2.5	2.4	2.1	1.9	1.7	1.7
Hawaiian	18.4	19.1	18.8	18.2	17.4	16.2	14.6
Other	(NA)	6.3	5.8	5.5	4.8	4.6	4.0
Hispanic origin [2]	16.8	17.9	16.9	16.7	16.2	15.6	14.9
Mexican	17.7	18.8	17.5	17.4	17.0	16.5	15.9
Puerto Rican	21.7	23.5	21.9	21.1	20.0	19.2	17.8
Cuban	7.7	7.7	6.9	7.7	7.5	7.5	8.1
Central and South American	9.0	10.6	10.3	10.0	9.9	9.4	8.5
Other and unknown Hispanic	(NA)	20.1	20.2	19.5	18.8	17.3	16.7
Percent births to unmarried mothers	**26.6**	**32.2**	**32.8**	**33.0**	**33.2**	**33.5**	**34.0**
White	16.9	25.3	26.3	26.8	27.1	27.7	28.5
Black	66.7	69.9	69.1	68.9	68.5	68.4	68.2
American Indian, Eskimo, Aleut	53.6	57.2	59.3	58.9	58.4	59.7	59.7
Asian and Pacific Islander [1]	13.2	16.3	15.6	15.4	14.8	14.9	14.9
Filipino	15.9	19.5	19.7	21.1	20.3	20.4	20.0
Chinese	5.0	7.9	6.4	6.9	7.6	8.4	9.0
Japanese	9.6	10.8	9.7	9.9	9.5	9.2	10.3
Hawaiian	45.0	49.0	51.1	50.4	50.0	50.6	50.4
Hispanic origin [2]	36.7	40.8	41.6	42.2	42.7	42.5	43.5
Mexican	33.3	38.1	39.6	40.1	40.7	40.8	42.1
Puerto Rican	55.9	60.0	59.5	59.6	59.6	58.9	59.1
Cuban	18.2	23.8	24.8	26.4	27.3	27.2	29.8
Central and South American	41.2	44.1	42.0	43.7	44.7	44.3	44.8
Percent of mothers beginning prenatal care 1st trimester	**74.2**	**81.3**	**82.8**	**83.2**	**83.2**	**83.4**	**83.7**
White	77.7	83.6	84.8	85.1	85.0	85.2	85.4
Black	60.7	70.4	73.3	74.1	74.3	74.5	75.2
American Indian, Eskimo, Aleut	57.9	66.7	68.8	69.5	69.3	69.3	69.8
Asian and Pacific Islander [1]	(NA)	79.9	83.1	83.7	84.0	84.0	84.8
Filipino	77.1	80.9	84.2	84.2	84.9	85.0	85.4
Chinese	81.3	85.7	88.5	88.5	87.6	87.0	87.2
Japanese	87.0	89.7	90.2	90.7	91.0	90.1	90.5
Hawaiian	65.8	75.9	78.8	79.6	79.9	79.1	78.1
Hispanic origin [2]	60.2	70.8	74.3	74.4	74.4	75.7	76.7
Mexican	57.8	69.1	72.8	73.1	72.9	74.6	75.7
Puerto Rican	63.5	74.0	76.9	77.7	78.5	79.1	79.9
Cuban	84.8	89.2	91.8	91.4	91.7	91.8	92.0
Central and South American	61.5	73.2	78.0	77.6	77.6	77.4	78.7
Percent of mothers beginning prenatal care 3d trimester or no care	**6.0**	**4.2**	**3.9**	**3.8**	**3.9**	**3.7**	**3.6**
White	4.9	3.5	3.3	3.2	3.3	3.2	3.1
Black	10.9	7.6	7.0	6.6	6.7	6.5	6.2
American Indian, Eskimo, Aleut	12.9	9.5	8.5	8.2	8.6	8.2	8.0
Asian and Pacific Islander [1]	(NA)	4.3	3.6	3.5	3.3	3.4	3.1
Filipino	4.5	4.1	3.1	2.8	3.0	3.0	2.8
Chinese	3.4	3.0	2.2	2.0	2.2	2.4	2.1
Japanese	2.9	2.3	2.1	2.1	1.8	2.0	2.1
Hawaiian	8.7	5.1	4.7	4.0	4.2	4.8	4.7
Hispanic origin [2]	12.0	7.4	6.3	6.3	6.3	5.9	5.5
Mexican	13.2	8.1	6.8	6.7	6.9	6.2	5.8
Puerto Rican	10.6	5.5	5.1	5.0	4.5	4.6	4.1
Cuban	2.8	2.1	1.2	1.4	1.4	1.3	1.3
Central and South American	10.9	6.1	4.9	5.2	5.4	5.7	4.9
Percent of births with low birth weight [3]	**7.0**	**7.3**	**7.6**	**7.6**	**7.6**	**7.7**	**7.8**
White	5.7	6.2	6.5	6.6	6.5	6.7	6.8
Black	13.3	13.1	13.0	13.1	13.0	13.0	13.3
American Indian, Eskimo, Aleut	6.1	6.6	6.8	7.1	6.8	7.3	7.2
Asian and Pacific Islander [1]	(NA)	6.9	7.4	7.4	7.3	7.5	7.8
Filipino	7.3	7.8	8.2	8.3	8.5	8.7	8.6
Chinese	4.7	5.3	5.3	5.2	5.1	5.3	5.5
Japanese	6.2	7.3	7.5	7.9	7.1	7.3	7.6
Hawaiian	7.2	6.8	7.2	7.7	6.8	7.9	8.1
Hispanic origin [2]	6.1	6.3	6.4	6.4	6.4	6.5	6.5
Mexican	5.5	5.8	6.0	5.9	6.0	6.1	6.2
Puerto Rican	9.0	9.4	9.7	9.3	9.3	9.3	9.7
Cuban	5.7	6.5	6.5	6.8	6.5	6.5	6.5
Central and South American	5.8	6.2	6.5	6.4	6.3	6.5	6.5

NA Not available. [1] Includes other races not shown separately. [2] Hispanic persons may be of any race. Includes other types, not shown separately. [3] Births less than 2,500 grams (5 lb.-8 oz.).

Source: U.S. National Center for Health Statistics, *Vital Statistics of the United States*, annual; and *National Vital Statistics Reports (NVSR)* (formerly *Monthly Vital Statistics Report*).

No. 79. Births to Unmarried Women by Race of Child and Age of Mother: 1990 to 2002

[Excludes births to nonresidents of United States. Marital status is inferred from a comparison of the child's and parents' surnames on the birth certificate for those states that do not report on marital status. No estimates included for misstatements on birth records or failures to register births. See also Appendix III]

Race of child and age of mother	1990	1995	2000	2001	2002	Race of child and age of mother	1990	1995	2000	2001	2002
NUMBER (1,000)						30 to 34 years	10.1	10.6	9.7	10.0	10.2
Total live births [1]	1,165	1,254	1,347	1,349	1,366	35 to 39 years	(NA)	5.8	6.0	4.8	4.8
White	647	785	866	880	904	40 years and over.	(NA)	(NA)	1.2	1.3	1.3
Black	473	421	427	415	405						
Under 15 years	11	11	8	7	7	AS PERCENT OF ALL					
15 to 19 years	350	376	369	352	340	BIRTHS IN RACIAL					
20 to 24 years	404	432	504	515	528	GROUPS					
25 to 29 years	230	229	255	258	268	Total [1]	26.6	32.2	33.2	33.5	34.0
30 to 34 years	118	133	130	135	139	White	16.9	25.3	27.1	27.7	28.5
35 to 39 years	(NA)	60	65	65	66	Black	66.7	69.9	68.5	68.4	68.2
40 years and over.	(NA)	13	16	17	17						
						BIRTH RATE [2]					
PERCENT						Total [1] [3]	43.8	44.3	44.0	43.8	43.7
DISTRIBUTION						White [3]	32.9	37.0	38.2	38.2	38.9
Total [1]	100.0	100.0	100.0	100.0	100.0	Black [3]	90.5	74.5	70.5	68.2	66.2
White	55.6	62.6	64.3	65.2	66.2	15 to 19 years	42.5	43.8	39.0	37.0	35.4
Black	40.6	33.6	31.7	30.7	29.6	20 to 24 years	65.1	68.7	72.1	71.2	70.5
Under 15 years	0.9	0.9	0.6	0.6	0.5	25 to 29 years	56.0	54.3	58.5	59.5	61.5
15 to 19 years	30.0	30.0	27.4	26.1	24.9	30 to 34 years	37.6	38.9	39.3	40.4	40.8
20 to 24 years	34.7	34.5	37.4	38.2	38.6	35 to 39 years	17.3	19.3	19.7	20.4	20.8
25 to 29 years	19.7	18.2	18.9	19.1	19.7	40 to 44 years	3.6	4.7	5.0	5.3	5.4

NA Not available. [1] Includes other races not shown separately. [2] Rate per 1,000 unmarried women (never-married, widowed, and divorced) estimated as of July 1. [3] Covers women aged 15 to 44 years.

Source: U.S. National Center for Health Statistics, *Vital Statistics of the United States*, annual; and *National Vital Statistics Reports (NVSR)* (formerly *Monthly Vital Statistics Report*).

No. 80. Live Births and Ratios by Plurality of Birth and Race of Mother: 1995 to 2002

Plurality and race of mother	1995	1998	1999	2000	2001	2002
NUMBER						
Live births, total [1]	3,899,589	3,941,553	3,959,417	4,058,814	4,025,933	4,021,726
White	3,098,885	3,118,727	3,132,501	3,194,005	3,177,626	3,174,760
Black	603,139	609,902	605,970	622,598	606,156	593,691
Live births in single deliveries [1]	3,797,880	3,823,258	3,837,789	3,932,573	3,897,216	3,889,191
White	3,018,184	3,024,693	3,035,757	3,094,219	3,075,683	3,069,915
Black	585,787	590,372	586,027	601,451	585,189	572,659
Live births in twin deliveries [1]	96,736	110,670	114,307	118,916	121,246	125,134
White	76,196	87,163	90,191	93,235	95,315	98,304
Black	17,000	19,001	19,374	20,626	20,414	20,423
Live births in higher-order multiple deliveries [1] . . .	4,973	7,625	7,321	7,325	7,471	7,401
White	4,505	6,871	6,553	6,551	6,628	6,541
Black	352	529	569	521	553	609
RATIO PER 1,000 LIVE BIRTHS						
All multiple births [1]	26.1	30.0	30.7	31.1	32.0	33.0
White	26.0	30.2	30.9	31.2	32.1	33.0
Black	28.8	32.0	32.9	34.0	34.6	35.4
Twin births [1]	24.8	28.1	28.9	29.3	30.1	31.1
White.	24.6	27.9	28.8	29.2	30.0	31.0
Black.	28.2	31.2	32.0	33.1	33.7	34.4
RATIO PER 100,000 LIVE BIRTHS						
Higher-order multiple births [1]	127.5	193.5	184.9	180.5	185.6	184.0
White	145.4	220.3	209.2	205.1	208.6	206.0
Black	58.4	86.7	93.9	83.7	91.2	102.6

[1] Includes races other than White and Black.

Source: U.S. National Center for Health Statistics, *Advance Report of Final Natality Statistics*, and *National Vital Statistics Reports (NVSR)* (formerly *Monthly Vital Statistics Report*).

No. 81. Low Birth Weight and Births to Teenage Mothers and to Unmarried Women—States and Outlying Areas: 1990 to 2002

[Represents registered births. Excludes births to nonresidents of the United States. Based on 100 percent of births in all states and the District of Columbia. See Appendix III]

State and outlying area	Percent of births with low birth weight [1]			Births to teenage mothers percent of total [2]			Births to unmarried women percent of total		
	1990	2000	2002	1990	2000	2002	1990	2000	2002
U.S.	7.0	7.6	7.8	12.8	11.8	10.8	26.6	33.2	34.0
AL	8.4	9.7	9.9	18.2	15.7	14.6	30.1	34.3	34.8
AK	4.8	5.6	5.8	9.7	11.8	10.9	26.2	33.0	34.0
AZ	6.4	7.0	6.8	14.2	14.3	13.2	32.7	39.3	40.4
AR	8.2	8.6	8.6	19.7	17.3	15.5	29.4	35.7	37.1
CA	5.8	6.2	6.4	11.6	10.6	9.6	31.6	32.7	33.0
CO	8.0	8.4	8.9	11.3	11.7	10.7	21.2	25.0	26.8
CT	6.6	7.4	7.8	8.2	7.8	7.0	26.6	29.3	29.1
DE	7.6	8.6	9.9	11.9	12.3	11.1	29.0	37.9	40.6
DC	15.1	11.9	11.6	17.8	14.2	12.8	64.9	60.3	56.5
FL	7.4	8.0	8.4	13.9	12.6	11.5	31.7	38.2	39.3
GA	8.7	8.6	8.9	16.7	13.9	12.4	32.8	37.0	37.8
HI	7.1	7.5	8.3	10.5	10.3	8.9	24.8	32.2	33.6
ID	5.7	6.7	6.1	12.3	11.6	10.0	16.7	21.6	21.9
IL	7.6	7.9	8.2	13.1	11.4	10.3	31.7	34.5	34.8
IN	6.6	7.4	7.6	14.5	12.5	11.4	26.2	34.7	36.4
IA	5.4	6.1	6.6	10.2	10.0	9.1	21.0	28.0	29.3
KS	6.2	6.9	7.0	12.3	12.0	11.1	21.5	29.0	31.1
KY	7.1	8.2	8.6	17.5	14.1	12.9	23.6	31.0	33.2
LA	9.2	10.3	10.4	17.6	17.0	15.9	36.8	45.6	47.0
ME	5.1	6.0	6.3	10.8	9.4	8.5	22.6	31.0	32.6
MD	7.8	8.6	9.0	10.5	9.9	9.1	29.6	34.6	34.8
MA	5.9	7.1	7.5	8.0	6.6	5.8	24.7	26.5	26.8
MI	7.6	7.9	8.0	13.5	10.5	9.6	26.2	33.3	34.1
MN	5.1	6.1	6.3	8.0	8.3	7.6	20.9	25.8	27.4
MS	9.6	10.7	11.2	21.3	18.8	17.2	40.5	46.0	47.1
MO	7.1	7.6	8.0	14.4	13.1	11.9	28.6	34.6	35.2
MT	6.2	6.2	6.8	11.5	11.6	11.5	23.7	30.8	32.8
NE	5.3	6.8	7.2	9.8	10.2	9.5	20.7	27.2	28.6
NV	7.2	7.2	7.5	12.6	12.7	11.4	25.4	36.4	37.4
NH	4.9	6.3	6.3	7.2	6.8	6.1	16.9	24.7	24.6
NJ	7.0	7.7	8.0	8.4	7.1	6.5	24.3	28.9	29.3
NM	7.4	8.0	8.0	16.3	17.4	16.6	35.4	45.6	46.9
NY	7.6	7.7	7.9	9.1	8.2	7.4	33.0	36.6	35.7
NC	8.0	8.8	9.0	16.2	13.0	12.0	29.4	33.3	34.7
ND	5.5	6.4	6.3	8.6	9.2	8.5	18.4	28.3	29.0
OH	7.1	7.9	8.3	13.8	12.1	10.7	28.9	34.6	35.4
OK	6.6	7.5	8.0	16.2	15.9	14.8	25.2	34.3	36.4
OR	5.0	5.6	5.8	12.0	11.3	9.9	25.7	30.1	30.9
PA	7.1	7.7	8.2	10.9	9.9	9.2	28.6	32.7	33.4
RI	6.2	7.2	7.9	10.5	10.2	9.4	26.3	35.5	35.7
SC	8.7	9.7	10.0	17.1	15.3	13.7	32.7	39.8	40.4
SD	5.1	6.2	7.2	10.8	11.6	10.7	22.9	33.5	35.0
TN	8.2	9.2	9.2	17.6	14.7	13.5	30.2	34.5	36.2
TX	6.9	7.4	7.7	15.6	15.3	14.3	17.5	30.5	32.4
UT	5.7	6.6	6.4	10.3	8.9	7.3	13.5	17.3	17.2
VT	5.3	6.1	6.4	8.5	8.0	8.4	20.1	28.1	31.9
VA	7.2	7.9	7.9	11.7	9.9	9.2	26.0	29.9	30.3
WA	5.3	5.6	5.9	10.8	10.2	9.0	23.7	28.2	28.8
WV	7.1	8.3	9.0	17.8	15.9	12.8	25.4	31.7	32.9
WI	5.9	6.5	6.6	10.2	10.2	9.5	24.2	29.3	30.0
WY	7.4	8.3	8.4	13.6	13.5	12.4	19.8	28.8	30.3
PR	(NA)	10.8	11.5	(NA)	(NA)	(NA)	(NA)	49.7	52.0
VI	(NA)	9.1	11.8	(NA)	(NA)	(NA)	(NA)	66.7	67.3
GU	(NA)	7.6	8.0	(NA)	(NA)	(NA)	(NA)	54.8	55.4
AS	(NA)	2.7	3.9	(NA)	(NA)	(NA)	(NA)	35.5	32.0
MP	(NA)	8.9	6.9	(NA)	(NA)	(NA)	(NA)	(NA)	59.7

NA Not available.   [1] Less than 2,500 grams (5 pounds-8 ounces).   [2] Defined as mothers who are 19 years of age or younger.

Source: U.S. National Center for Health Statistics, *Vital Statistics of the United States*, annual; and *National Vital Statistics Reports (NVSR)* (formerly *Monthly Vital Statistics Report*). See also <http://www.cdc.gov/nchs/>.

No. 82. Live Births by Place of Delivery, Median and Low Birth Weight, and Prenatal Care: 1990 to 2002

[4,110 represents 4,110,000. Represents registered births. Excludes births to nonresidents of the United States. For total number of births, see Table 72. See Appendix III]

Item	1990	1995	1997	1998	1999	2000	2001	2002
Births attended (1,000):								
In hospital [1]	4,110	3,861	3,881	3,904	3,923	4,021	3,990	3,986
By physician, not in hospital . . .	14	6	5	6	5	5	4	4
By midwife and other, not in hospital [2]	21	21	20	21	21	21	22	22
Median birth weight	7 lb.-7 oz.	(NA)	7 lb.-7 oz.	7 lb.-7 oz.	(NA)	7 lb.-7 oz.	7 lb.-6 oz.	7 lb.-6oz.
Percent of births with low birth weight	7.0	7.3	7.5	7.6	7.6	7.6	7.7	7.8
White	5.7	6.2	6.5	6.5	6.6	6.5	6.7	6.8
Black	13.3	13.1	13.0	13.0	13.1	13.0	13.0	13.3
Hispanic [3]	6.1	6.3	6.4	6.4	6.4	6.4	6.5	6.5
Percent of births by period in which prenatal care began:								
1st trimester	74.2	81.3	82.5	82.8	83.2	83.2	83.4	83.7
3d trimester or no prenatal care.	6.0	4.2	3.9	3.9	3.8	3.9	3.7	3.6

NA Not available.   [1] Includes all births in hospitals or institutions and in clinics.   [2] Includes births with attendant not specified.   [3] Hispanic persons may be of any race.

Source: U.S. National Center for Health Statistics, *Vital Statistics of the United States,* annual; and *National Vital Statistics Reports* (NVSR) (formerly *Monthly Vital Statistics Report*), and unpublished data. See also <http://www.cdc.gov/nchs/births.htm>.

No. 83. Method of Delivery by Race: 1990 to 2002

[In thousands (4,111 represents 4,111,000), except rate. 1990 excludes data for Oklahoma, which did not report method of delivery on the birth certificate. See Appendix III]

Age of mother	1990	2000	2002	Age of mother	1990	2000	2002
Births, total	4,111	4,059	4,022	Not stated	16	4	3
Vaginal	3,111	3,108	2,958				
After previous cesarean	84	90	59	Hispanic births	595	816	877
Cesarean deliveries	914	924	1,044	Vaginal	458	633	654
Primary	575	578	634	After previous cesarean	10	17	13
Repeat	339	346	409	Cesarean deliveries	123	180	220
Not stated	85	27	19	Primary	76	105	123
White births	3,252	3,194	3,175	Repeat	47	75	97
Vaginal	2,454	2,449	2,341	Not stated	14	3	3
After previous cesarean	67	70	46				
Cesarean deliveries	733	723	818	Cesarean delivery rate [1]	22.7	22.9	26.1
Primary	459	449	493	White	23.0	22.8	25.9
Repeat	274	274	325	Black	22.1	24.3	27.6
Not stated	66	22	16	Primary [2]	16.0	16.1	18.0
Black births	679	623	594	White	16.1	15.9	17.7
Vaginal	517	468	428	Black	15.7	17.3	19.4
After previous cesarean	13	14	10				
Cesarean deliveries	146	150	163	Rate of vaginal birth after previous cesarean [3]	19.9	20.6	12.6
Primary	93	95	101	White	19.7	20.4	12.4
Repeat	53	56	63	Black	20.3	20.5	13.2

[1] Cesarean rates are the number of cesarean deliveries per 100 total deliveries for specified category.   [2] Number of primary cesareans per 100 live births to women who have not had a previous cesarean.   [3] Number of vaginal births after previous cesarean delivery per 100 live births to women with a previous cesarean delivery.

Source: U.S. National Center for Health Statistics, *Vital Statistics of the United States,* annual.

No. 84. Percent Low Birthweight by Smoking Status, Age, and Race of Mother: 2002

[Low birthweight is defined as weight of less than 2,500 grams (5 lb. 8 oz.). Excludes California, Indiana, New York State (but includes New York City), and South Dakota, which did not require reporting of tobacco use during pregnancy]

Smoking status and race of mother	All ages	Age of mother							
		Under 15 years	15-19 years			20-24 years	25-29 years	30-34 years	35-39 years
			Total	15-17 years	18-19 years				
All races [1]	8.0	13.8	9.9	10.7	9.5	8.2	7.1	7.4	8.8
Smoker.	12.2	12.9	11.5	12.2	11.2	11.0	11.4	13.7	16.7
Nonsmoker.	7.5	13.7	9.5	10.5	9.1	7.6	6.6	6.9	8.1
White	7.0	12.5	8.4	9.1	8.0	6.9	6.2	6.6	7.8
Smoker.	11.0	13.3	10.9	11.6	10.6	10.2	10.4	12.0	14.6
Nonsmoker.	6.4	12.3	7.7	8.6	7.3	6.1	5.7	6.1	7.2
Black.	13.4	15.2	14.0	14.5	13.7	13.0	12.5	13.4	15.3
Smoker.	20.1	(B)	16.9	17.8	16.5	17.1	18.8	25.7	28.7
Nonsmoker.	12.7	15.2	13.8	14.3	13.4	12.5	11.8	12.4	13.8

B Base figure too small to meet statistical standards for reliability of a derived figure.   [1] Includes races other than White and Black.

Source: U.S. National Center for Health Statistics, *National Vital Statistics Reports (NVSR)Vol. 52, No.10* (formerly *Monthly Vital Statistics Report*). See also <http://www.cdc.gov/nchs/nvss.htm>.

Vital Statistics   67

No. 85. Women Who Have Had a Child in the Last Year by Age: 1990 to 2002

[3,913 represents 3,913,000. As of June. Excludes births to nonresidents of the United States. Data are by place of residence. See headnote, Table 86.]

Age of mother	Women who had a child in last year (1,000)			Total births per 1,000 women			First births per 1,000 women		
	1990	2000	2002	1990	2000	2002	1990	2000	2002
Total	3,913	3,934	3,766	67.0	64.6	61.4	26.4	26.7	23.1
15 to 29 years old	2,568	2,432	2,318	90.8	85.9	80.7	43.2	43.1	35.4
15 to 19 years old . .	338	586	549	39.8	59.7	55.9	30.1	38.7	27.7
20 to 24 years old . .	1,038	850	872	113.4	91.8	90.0	51.8	47.1	45.3
25 to 29 years old . .	1,192	996	897	112.1	107.9	97.2	46.2	43.7	33.2
30 to 44 years old . .	1,346	1,502	1,448	44.7	46.1	44.4	10.6	12.5	12.2
30 to 34 years old . .	892	871	859	80.4	87.9	83.6	21.9	27.5	26.4
35 to 39 years old . .	377	506	452	37.3	45.1	41.9	6.5	9.6	7.9
40 to 44 years old . .	77	125	137	8.6	10.9	11.9	1.2	2.3	3.6

Source: U.S. Census Bureau, Current Population Reports, P20-375, P20-543RV, and P20-548.

No. 86. Characteristics of Women Who Have Had a Child in the Last Year: 2000 and 2002

[As of June. Covers civilian noninstitutional population. Since the number of women who had a birth during the 12-month period was tabulated and not the actual numbers of births, some small underestimation of fertility for this period may exist due to the omission of: (1) Multiple births, (2) Two or more live births spaced within the 12-month period (the woman is counted only once), (3) Women who had births in the period and who did not survive to the survey date, (4) Women who were in institutions and therefore not in the survey universe. These losses may be somewhat offset by the inclusion in the CPS of births to immigrants who did not have their children born in the United States and births to nonresident women. These births would not have been recorded in the vital registration system. Based on Current Population Survey (CPS) The 2003 Current Population Survey (CPS) allowed respondents to choose more than one race. Beginning 2003 data represent persons who selected this race group only and exclude persons reporting more than one race. The CPS in prior years allowed respondents to report only one race group. See also comments on race in the text for Section 1, Population and Appendix III]

Characteristic	2000			2002		
	Women who have had a child in the last year			Women who have had a child in the last year		
	Number of women (1,000)	Total births per 1,000 women	First births per 1,000 women	Number of women (1,000)	Total births per 1,000 women	First births per 1,000 women
Total [1]	60,873	64.6	26.7	61,361	61.4	23.1
White	48,506	65.4	27.2	48,481	61.0	22.9
Black	8,939	63.2	21.9	8,846	64.6	22.3
Hispanic [2]	8,002	95.1	38.6	9,141	82.0	30.4
Currently married	30,497	88.8	35.5	30,274	82.8	28.6
Married, spouse present	28,215	90.8	37.0	27,828	85.6	29.6
Married, spouse absent [3]	2,282	64.5	16.6	2,446	50.5	17.0
Widowed or divorced	5,281	31.0	6.8	5,303	26.9	6.6
Never married	25,095	42.3	20.2	25,782	43.3	19.9
Educational attainment:						
Less than high school	13,006	70.7	29.5	13,096	62.0	20.1
High school, 4 years	17,205	70.0	29.5	16,644	60.4	22.8
College: 1 or more years	30,662	59.0	24.0	31,621	61.6	24.4
No degree	12,603	51.6	19.2	12,451	60.2	24.0
Associate degree.	4,955	60.6	23.6	5,113	43.2	15.5
Bachelor's degree	9,926	61.7	27.7	10,592	64.5	25.1
Graduate or professional degree .	3,178	77.7	32.0	3,465	84.9	36.8
Labor force status:						
Employed	41,369	47.7	20.7	40,150	46.5	18.4
Unemployed	2,493	79.4	31.1	3,210	58.8	32.9
Not in labor force	17,011	103.7	40.6	18,001	95.0	31.6
Occupation of employed women:						
Managerial-professional	12,481	52.2	22.9	13,021	55.0	23.8
Technical, sales, admin support. . . .	16,561	44.0	20.3	17,163	44.8	19.0
Service workers	8,102	51.0	20.1	9,102	47.9	18.1
Farming, forestry, and fishing	473	69.6	21.8	493	33.3	4.8
Precision prod, craft, repair.	880	42.3	15.1	819	45.7	16.3
Operators, fabricators, laborers	2,872	38.1	17.2	2,884	40.9	13.2
Family income:						
Under $10,000	4,249	86.8	32.5	4,203	84.5	30.5
$10,000 to $19,999	6,203	74.8	25.3	5,760	81.9	34.8
$20,000 to $24,999	3,439	76.2	37.3	3,348	64.3	21.9
$25,000 to $29,999	3,761	78.9	34.0	3,464	56.1	15.9
$30,000 to $34,999	3,572	62.4	27.3	3,612	73.2	23.1
$35,000 to $49,999	8,864	64.9	25.3	8,477	53.9	19.0
$50,000 to $74,999	10,646	61.2	26.8	10,613	52.2	23.3
$75,000 and over	12,506	60.1	24.3	13,771	60.0	21.4

[1] Includes women of other races and women with family income not reported, not shown separately. [2] Persons of Hispanic origin may be of any race. [3] Includes separated women.

Source: U.S. Census Bureau, Current Population Reports, P20-543RV, P20-548, and unpublished data.

No. 87. Women Who Have Had a Child in the Last Year by Age and Labor Force Status: 1980 to 2002

[3,247 represents 3,247,000. See headnote, Table 86. See Appendix III]

Year	Total, 18 to 44 years old			18 to 29 years old			30 to 44 years old		
	Number (1,000)	In the labor force		Number (1,000)	In the labor force		Number (1,000)	In the labor force	
		Number (1,000)	Percent		Number (1,000)	Percent		Number (1,000)	Percent
1980	3,247	1,233	38	2,476	947	38	770	287	37
1981	3,381	1,411	42	2,499	1,004	40	881	407	46
1982	3,433	1,508	44	2,445	1,040	43	988	469	48
1983	3,625	1,563	43	2,682	1,138	42	942	425	45
1984	3,311	1,547	47	2,375	1,058	45	936	489	52
1985	3,497	1,691	48	2,512	1,204	48	984	488	50
1986	3,625	1,805	50	2,452	1,185	48	1,174	620	53
1987	3,701	1,881	51	2,521	1,258	50	1,180	623	53
1988	3,667	1,866	51	2,384	1,177	49	1,283	688	54
1990 [1]	3,913	2,068	53	2,568	1,275	50	1,346	793	59
1992 [1]	3,688	1,985	54	2,346	1,182	50	1,342	802	60
1994 [1]	3,890	2,066	53	2,389	1,209	51	1,501	857	57
1995 [1]	3,696	2,034	55	2,252	1,150	51	1,444	884	61
1998 [1]	3,671	2,155	59	2,274	1,275	56	1,397	880	63
2000 [1]	3,934	2,170	55	2,432	1,304	54	1,502	866	58
2002 [1]	3,766	2,056	55	2,318	1,175	51	1,448	881	61

[1] Lower age limit is 15 years old.

Source: U.S. Census Bureau, Current Population Reports, P20-543; and unpublished data.

No. 88. Contraceptive Use by Women, 15 to 44 Years of Age: 1995

[60,201 represents 60,201,000. Based on samples of the female population of the United States; see source for details]

Contraceptive status and method	Age				Race			Marital status		
	All women [1]	15-24 years	25-34 years	35-44 years	Non-Hispanic		His-panic	Never mar-ried	Cur-rently mar-ried	For-merly married
					White	Black				
All women (1,000)	60,201	18,002	20,758	21,440	42,522	8,210	6,702	22,679	29,673	7,849
PERCENT DISTRIBUTION										
Sterile [2]	29.7	2.6	25.0	57.0	30.2	31.5	28.4	6.9	43.2	45.1
Surgically sterile	27.9	1.8	23.6	54.0	28.5	29.7	26.3	5.7	41.1	42.5
Nonsurgically sterile [3]	1.7	0.7	1.3	2.8	1.6	1.8	2.0	1.1	2.0	2.2
Pregnant, postpartum	4.6	5.9	6.9	1.3	4.3	4.5	6.3	3.1	6.4	1.9
Seeking pregnancy	4.0	2.1	6.2	3.5	3.7	4.6	4.0	1.5	6.4	2.1
Other nonusers	22.3	44.4	13.3	12.6	21.1	23.1	26.3	46.8	4.7	18.4
Never had intercourse	10.9	30.8	3.4	1.4	10.4	8.9	12.1	28.9	-	-
No intercourse in last month [4]	6.2	7.0	5.3	6.5	5.7	7.2	8.6	11.5	0.5	12.7
Had intercourse in last month [4]	5.2	6.6	4.6	4.7	5.0	7.0	5.6	6.4	4.2	5.7
Nonsurgical contraceptors	39.7	45.0	49.1	26.1	41.2	36.1	35.1	41.8	39.7	32.4
Pill	17.3	23.1	23.7	6.3	18.8	14.8	13.6	20.4	15.6	14.6
IUD	0.5	0.1	0.6	0.8	0.5	0.5	0.9	0.3	0.7	0.4
Diaphragm	1.2	0.2	1.2	2.0	1.5	0.5	0.4	0.5	1.8	0.9
Condom	13.1	13.9	15.0	10.7	13.0	12.5	12.1	13.9	13.3	10.1
Periodic abstinence	1.5	0.5	1.8	2.0	1.6	0.7	1.3	0.6	2.3	0.7
Natural family planning	0.2	-	0.3	0.3	0.3	-	0.1	-	0.4	-
Withdrawal	2.0	1.6	2.3	1.9	2.1	0.9	2.0	1.5	2.3	1.8
Other methods [5]	3.9	5.6	4.2	2.1	3.4	6.2	4.7	4.6	3.3	3.9

- Represents or rounds to zero.   [1] Includes other races, not shown separately.   [2] Total sterile includes male sterile for unknown reasons.   [3] Persons sterile from illness, accident, or congenital conditions.   [4] Data refer to no intercourse in the 3 months prior to interview.   [5] Includes implants, injectables, morning-after-pill, suppository, Today(TM) sponge and less frequently used methods.

Source: U.S. National Center for Health Statistics, special tabulations from the 1995 National Survey of Family Growth.

No. 89. Abortions—Number, Rate, and Ratio by Race: 1972 to 2000

	All races				White				Black and other			
	Women 15-44 years old (1,000)	Abortions			Women 15-44 years old (1,000)	Abortions			Women 15-44 years old (1,000)	Abortions		
Year		Number (1,000)	Rate per 1,000 women	Ratio per 1,000 live births[1]		Number (1,000)	Rate per 1,000 women	Ratio per 1,000 live births[1]		Number (1,000)	Rate per 1,000 women	Ratio per 1,000 live births[1]
1972 ..	44,588	587	13.2	184	38,532	455	11.8	175	6,056	132	21.7	223
1975 ..	47,606	1,034	21.7	331	40,857	701	17.2	276	6,749	333	49.3	565
1976 ..	48,721	1,179	24.2	361	41,721	785	18.8	296	7,000	394	56.3	638
1977 ..	49,814	1,317	26.4	400	42,567	889	20.9	333	7,247	428	59.0	679
1978 ..	50,920	1,410	27.7	413	43,427	969	22.3	356	7,493	440	58.7	665
1979 ..	52,016	1,498	28.8	420	44,266	1,062	24.0	373	7,750	435	56.2	625
1980 ..	53,048	1,554	29.3	428	44,942	1,094	24.3	376	8,106	460	56.5	642
1981 ..	53,901	1,577	29.3	430	45,494	1,108	24.3	377	8,407	470	55.9	645
1982 ..	54,679	1,574	28.8	428	46,049	1,095	23.8	373	8,630	479	55.5	646
1983 [2] ..	55,340	1,575	28.5	436	46,506	1,084	23.3	376	8,834	491	55.5	670
1984 ..	56,061	1,577	28.1	423	47,023	1,087	23.1	366	9,038	491	54.3	646
1985 ..	56,754	1,589	28.0	422	47,512	1,076	22.6	360	9,242	513	55.5	659
1986 [2] ..	57,483	1,574	27.4	416	48,010	1,045	21.8	350	9,473	529	55.9	661
1987 ..	57,964	1,559	27.1	405	48,288	1,017	21.1	338	9,676	542	56.0	648
1988 ..	58,192	1,591	27.3	401	48,325	1,026	21.2	333	9,867	565	57.3	638
1989 [2] ..	58,365	1,567	26.8	380	48,104	1,006	20.9	309	10,261	561	54.7	650
1990 [2] ..	58,700	1,609	27.4	389	48,224	1,039	21.5	318	10,476	570	54.4	655
1991 ..	59,305	1,557	26.2	379	48,560	982	20.2	303	10,745	574	53.5	661
1992 ..	59,417	1,529	25.7	380	48,435	943	19.5	298	10,982	585	53.3	681
1993 [2] ..	59,712	1,495	25.0	376	48,497	908	18.7	290	11,215	587	52.4	698
1994 [2] ..	60,020	1,423	23.7	362	48,592	856	17.6	275	11,429	567	49.6	696
1995 ..	60,368	1,359	22.5	350	48,719	817	16.8	265	11,648	542	46.6	684
1996 ..	60,704	1,360	22.4	349	48,837	797	16.3	258	11,867	563	47.5	699
1997 ..	61,041	1,335	21.9	341	48,942	777	15.9	251	12,099	558	46.1	684
1998 ..	61,326	1,319	21.5	334	49,012	762	15.5	244	12,313	557	45.2	678
1999 ..	61,475	1,315	21.4	327	48,974	743	15.2	234	12,501	572	45.8	674
2000 ..	61,631	1,313	21.3	324	48,936	733	15.0	230	12,695	580	45.7	676

[1] Live births are those which occurred from July 1 of year shown through June 30 of the following year (to match time of conception with abortions). Births are classified by race of child 1972-1988, and by race of mother after 1988. [2] Total numbers of abortions in 1983 and 1986 have been estimated by interpolation; 1989, 1990, 1993, and 1994 have been estimated using trends in CDC data.

No. 90. Abortions by Selected Characteristics: 1990 to 2000

[Number of abortions from surveys conducted by source; characteristics from the U.S. Centers for Disease Control's (CDC) annual abortion surveillance summaries, with adjustments for changes in states reporting data to the CDC each year. Total number of abortions in 1990 have been estimated using trends in CDC data]

Characteristic	Number (1,000)			Percent distribution			Abortion ratio [1]		
	1990	1995	2000	1990	1995	2000	1990	1995	2000
Total abortions	1,609	1,359	1,313	100	100	100	280	259	245
Age of woman:									
Less than 15 years old	13	11	9	1	1	1	515	479	512
15 to 19 years old	351	263	235	22	19	18	403	347	339
20 to 24 years old	532	441	430	33	32	33	328	317	296
25 to 29 years old	360	308	303	22	23	23	224	224	220
30 to 34 years old	216	196	190	13	14	15	196	179	169
35 to 39 years old	108	109	110	7	8	8	249	219	195
40 years old and over	29	32	37	2	2	3	354	309	276
Race of woman:									
White	1,039	817	733	65	60	56	241	209	187
Black and other	570	542	580	35	40	44	396	406	403
Marital status of woman: [2]									
Married	341	268	246	21	20	19	104	93	84
Unmarried	1,268	1,091	1,067	79	80	81	516	466	443
Number of prior live births:									
None	780	612	533	49	45	41	316	276	248
One	396	358	361	25	26	28	230	223	216
Two	280	247	260	17	18	20	292	285	278
Three	102	94	104	6	7	8	279	283	285
Four or more	50	48	56	3	4	4	223	228	250
Number of prior induced abortions:									
None	891	719	699	55	53	53	(NA)	(NA)	(NA)
One	443	382	355	28	28	27	(NA)	(NA)	(NA)
Two or more	275	259	259	17	19	20	(NA)	(NA)	(NA)
Weeks of gestation:									
Less than 9 weeks	825	726	757	51	53	58	(NA)	(NA)	(NA)
9 to 10 weeks	416	316	266	26	23	20	(NA)	(NA)	(NA)
11 to 12 weeks	195	152	138	12	11	11	(NA)	(NA)	(NA)
13 weeks or more	173	145	153	11	11	12	(NA)	(NA)	(NA)

NA Not available. [1] Number of abortions per 1,000 abortions and live births. Live births are those which occurred from July 1 of year shown through June 30 of the following year (to match time of conception with abortions). [2] Separated women included with unmarried.

Source of Tables 89 and 90: S.K. Henshaw and J. Van Vort, eds., *Abortion Factbook, 1992 Edition: Readings, Trends, and State and Local Data to 1988*, The Alan Guttmacher Institute, New York, NY, 1992 (copyright); S.K. Henshaw and J. Van Vort, *Abortion Services in the United States, 1991 and 1992. Family Planning Perspectives*, 26:100, 1994; L.B. Finer and S.K. Henshaw, Abortion Incidence and Services in the United States, 2000, *Perspectives on Sexual and Reproductive Health*, 356, 2003; and unpublished data.

No. 91. Abortions—Number and Rate by State: 1992 and 2000

[Number of abortions from surveys of hospitals, clinics, and physicians identified as providers of abortion services conducted by The Alan Guttmacher Institute. Abortion rates are computed per 1,000 women 15 to 44 years of age on July 1 of specified year]

State	Number (1,000)		Rate [1]		State	Number (1,000)		Rate [1]	
	1992	2000	1992	2000		1992	2000	1992	2000
U.S.	1,529	1,313	25.7	21.3	MO	14	8	11.5	6.6
AL	17	14	18.1	13.5	MT	3	3	18.4	13.5
AK	2	2	16.5	11.7	NE	6	4	15.6	11.6
AZ	21	18	23.5	16.5	NV	13	14	43.3	32.2
AR	7	6	13.5	9.8	NH	4	3	14.6	11.2
CA	304	236	41.8	31.2	NJ	55	66	30.4	36.3
CO	20	16	23.6	15.9	NM	6	6	17.6	14.7
CT	20	15	26.0	21.1	NY	195	165	45.6	39.1
DE	6	5	34.9	31.3	NC	36	38	22.2	21.0
DC	21	10	133.1	68.1	ND	1	1	10.7	9.9
FL	85	103	29.3	31.9	OH	50	40	19.5	16.5
GA	40	32	23.7	16.9	OK	9	7	12.5	10.1
HI	12	6	46.0	22.1	OR	16	17	23.9	23.5
ID	2	2	7.2	7.0	PA	50	37	18.6	14.3
IL	68	64	25.2	23.2	RI	7	6	29.5	24.1
IN	16	12	12.0	9.4	SC	12	8	14.2	9.3
IA	7	6	11.3	9.8	SD	1	1	6.9	5.5
KS	13	12	22.4	21.4	TN	19	19	16.1	15.2
KY	10	5	11.4	5.3	TX	97	89	23.1	18.8
LA	14	13	13.4	13.0	UT	4	4	9.2	6.6
ME	4	3	14.9	9.9	VT	3	2	21.5	12.7
MD	31	35	26.2	29.0	VA	35	29	22.6	18.1
MA	41	30	28.1	21.4	WA	33	26	27.7	20.3
MI	56	46	25.1	21.6	WV	3	3	7.8	6.8
MN	16	15	15.6	13.5	WI	15	11	13.5	9.6
MS	8	4	12.4	5.9	WY	(Z)	(Z)	4.4	0.9

Z Less than 500. [1] Rate per 1,000 women, 15 to 44 years old.

Source: S.K. Henshaw and J. Van Vort, *Abortion Services in the United States, 1991 and 1992, Family Planning Perspectives,* 26:100, 1994; and L.B. Finer and S.K. Henshaw, *Abortion Incidence and Services in the United States in 2000, Perspectives on Sexual and Reproductive Health,* 35:6, 2003; and unpublished data.

No. 92. Expectation of Life at Birth, 1970 to 2001, and Projections, 2005 and 2010

[In years. Excludes deaths of nonresidents of the United States. See Appendix III]

Year	Total			White			Black		
	Total	Male	Female	Total	Male	Female	Total	Male	Female
1970	70.8	67.1	74.7	71.7	68.0	75.6	64.1	60.0	68.3
1975	72.6	68.8	76.6	73.4	69.5	77.3	66.8	62.4	71.3
1980	73.7	70.0	77.4	74.4	70.7	78.1	68.1	63.8	72.5
1982	74.5	70.8	78.1	75.1	71.5	78.7	69.4	65.1	73.6
1983	74.6	71.0	78.1	75.2	71.6	78.7	69.4	65.2	73.5
1984	74.7	71.1	78.2	75.3	71.8	78.7	69.5	65.3	73.6
1985	74.7	71.1	78.2	75.3	71.8	78.7	69.3	65.0	73.4
1986	74.7	71.2	78.2	75.4	71.9	78.8	69.1	64.8	73.4
1987	74.9	71.4	78.3	75.6	72.1	78.9	69.1	64.7	73.4
1988	74.9	71.4	78.3	75.6	72.2	78.9	68.9	64.4	73.2
1989	75.1	71.7	78.5	75.9	72.5	79.2	68.8	64.3	73.3
1990	75.4	71.8	78.8	76.1	72.7	79.4	69.1	64.5	73.6
1991	75.5	72.0	78.9	76.3	72.9	79.6	69.3	64.6	73.8
1992	75.8	72.3	79.1	76.5	73.2	79.8	69.6	65.0	73.9
1993	75.5	72.2	78.8	76.3	73.1	79.5	69.2	64.6	73.7
1994	75.7	72.3	79.0	76.4	73.2	79.6	69.6	64.9	74.1
1995	75.8	72.5	78.9	76.5	73.4	79.6	69.6	65.4	74.0
1996	76.1	73.0	79.0	76.8	73.8	79.6	70.3	66.1	74.2
1997	76.5	73.6	79.4	77.1	74.3	79.9	71.1	67.2	74.7
1998 [1]	76.7	73.8	79.5	77.3	74.5	80.0	71.3	67.6	74.8
1999	76.7	73.9	79.4	77.3	74.6	79.9	71.4	67.8	74.7
2000	77.0	74.3	79.7	77.6	74.9	80.1	71.7	68.3	75.2
2001 [2]	77.2	74.4	79.8	77.7	75.0	80.2	72.2	68.6	75.5
Projections [3]:									
2005	77.8	74.9	80.7	78.3	75.4	81.1	73.5	69.9	76.8
2010	78.5	75.6	81.4	79.0	76.1	81.8	74.5	70.9	77.8

[1] The 1998 life table values are based upon an 85 percent sample of deaths. [2] Preliminary data.
[3] Based on middle mortality assumptions; for details, see source. Source: U.S. Census Bureau, Population Division Working Paper No. 38.

Source: Except as noted, U.S. National Center for Health Statistics, *Vital Statistics of the United States,* annual, and *National Vital Statistics Reports (NVSR)* (formerly *Monthly Vital Statistics Reports*).

No. 93. Selected Life Table Values: 1979 to 2001

[See Appendix III]

Age and sex	Total [1]								White								Black							
	1979-1981	1985	1990	1995	1998	1999	2000	2001	1979-1981	1985	1990	1995	1998	1999	2000	2001	1979-1981	1985	1990	1995	1998	1999	2000	2001
AVERAGE EXPECTATION OF LIFE IN YEARS																								
At birth: Male	70.1	71.1	71.8	72.5	73.8	73.9	74.3	74.4	70.8	71.8	72.7	73.4	74.5	74.6	74.9	75.0	64.1	65.0	64.5	65.4	67.6	67.8	68.3	68.6
Female	77.6	78.2	78.8	78.9	79.5	79.4	79.7	79.8	78.2	78.7	79.4	79.6	80.0	79.9	80.1	80.2	72.9	73.4	73.6	74.0	74.8	74.7	75.2	75.5
Age 20: Male	51.9	52.6	53.3	53.8	55.0	55.0	55.3	55.5	52.5	53.2	54.0	54.5	55.5	55.6	55.6	55.9	46.4	47.1	46.7	47.3	49.5	49.6	50.0	50.3
Female	59.0	59.3	59.1	59.9	60.3	60.2	60.5	60.6	59.4	59.8	60.3	60.3	60.8	60.7	60.9	60.9	54.9	55.2	55.3	55.5	56.2	56.2	56.6	56.8
Age 40: Male	33.6	34.2	35.1	35.6	36.4	36.4	36.7	37.0	34.0	34.7	35.6	36.1	36.8	36.9	37.1	37.3	29.5	29.8	30.1	30.6	31.5	31.9	32.3	32.6
Female	39.8	40.0	40.6	40.7	41.1	41.0	41.0	41.3	40.2	40.4	41.0	41.0	41.4	41.3	41.5	41.6	36.3	36.4	36.8	37.0	37.5	37.4	37.8	38.0
Age 50: Male	25.0	25.5	26.4	27.0	27.6	27.7	27.9	28.2	25.3	25.8	26.7	27.3	27.9	28.0	28.2	28.4	22.0	22.1	22.5	23.1	23.9	24.0	24.2	24.5
Female	30.7	30.8	31.3	31.4	31.7	31.7	32.0	32.1	31.0	31.1	31.6	31.7	32.0	32.0	32.2	32.3	27.8	27.8	28.2	28.5	28.8	28.7	29.1	29.4
Age 65: Male	14.2	14.5	15.1	15.6	16.0	16.1	16.2	16.4	14.3	14.5	15.2	15.7	16.1	16.1	16.3	16.5	13.3	13.0	13.2	13.7	14.3	14.3	14.2	14.4
Female	18.4	18.5	18.9	18.9	19.2	19.1	19.3	19.4	18.6	18.7	19.1	19.0	19.3	19.2	19.4	19.5	17.1	16.9	17.2	17.2	17.4	17.3	17.7	17.9
EXPECTED DEATHS PER 1,000 ALIVE AT SPECIFIED AGE [2]																								
At birth: Male	13.9	12.0	10.3	8.3	8.0	7.7	7.5	6.8	12.3	10.6	8.6	7.0	6.5	6.4	6.2	6.2	23.0	19.9	19.7	16.2	15.8	15.9	15.6	15.4
Female	11.2	9.4	8.2	6.8	6.6	6.4	6.2	5.7	9.7	8.0	6.6	5.6	5.4	5.2	5.1	5.1	19.3	16.5	16.3	13.8	12.9	13.2	12.7	12.5
Age 20: Male	1.8	1.5	1.6	(NA)	1.3	1.3	1.3	1.2	1.8	1.4	1.4	(NA)	1.2	1.2	1.2	1.2	3.2	1.9	2.7	(NA)	2.1	2.1	2.0	2.1
Female	0.6	0.5	0.5	(NA)	0.4	0.5	0.5	.4	0.6	0.5	0.5	(NA)	0.4	0.4	0.4	0.4	0.7	0.6	0.7	(NA)	0.6	0.6	0.6	0.6
Age 40: Male	3.0	2.8	3.1	(NA)	2.5	2.6	2.5	2.4	2.6	2.5	2.7	(NA)	2.3	2.3	2.4	2.4	6.9	6.5	7.1	(NA)	4.5	4.8	4.6	4.3
Female	1.6	1.4	1.4	(NA)	1.4	1.4	1.4	1.3	1.4	1.3	1.2	(NA)	1.2	1.2	1.3	1.3	3.2	2.9	3.1	(NA)	2.8	2.9	2.8	2.9
Age 50: Male	7.8	6.8	6.2	(NA)	5.1	5.6	5.2	5.2	7.1	6.2	5.6	(NA)	4.7	5.1	5.2	5.2	14.9	13.3	12.8	(NA)	9.6	11.3	11.2	10.6
Female	4.2	3.8	3.5	(NA)	3.1	3.1	3.1	2.9	3.8	3.5	3.2	(NA)	2.8	2.9	3.2	2.9	7.7	6.8	6.6	(NA)	5.5	6.0	6.2	6.2
Age 65: Male	28.2	26.1	22.9	(NA)	16.2	20.5	19.5	19.4	27.4	25.2	23.0	(NA)	16.0	19.8	19.2	18.5	38.5	38.5	36.8	(NA)	19.3	30.5	29.6	30.0
Female	14.3	14.1	13.5	(NA)	11.0	12.8	12.7	12.3	13.6	13.5	12.8	(NA)	10.7	12.3	12.2	11.8	21.6	21.4	21.4	(NA)	14.2	18.3	18.2	18.0
NUMBER SURVIVING TO SPECIFIED AGE PER 1,000 BORN ALIVE																								
Age 20: Male	973	977	979	981	(NA)	984	984	986	975	979	981	981	(NA)	986	986	986	961	966	963	967	(NA)	971	973	973
Female	982	985	986	987	(NA)	989	989	991	984	986	988	987	(NA)	990	990	991	972	976	976	978	(NA)	980	981	982
Age 40: Male	933	941	938	940	(NA)	952	952	958	940	946	946	940	(NA)	958	958	958	885	897	880	885	(NA)	917	918	920
Female	965	970	971	971	(NA)	974	978	978	969	973	975	971	(NA)	977	978	978	941	948	944	944	(NA)	954	955	957
Age 50: Male	890	902	899	899	(NA)	917	917	925	901	911	912	899	(NA)	926	925	925	801	820	801	803	(NA)	850	855	859
Female	941	948	950	950	(NA)	954	954	959	947	953	957	950	(NA)	960	960	959	896	908	904	902	(NA)	915	915	918
Age 65: Male	706	727	741	750	(NA)	777	779	799	724	744	760	750	(NA)	793	794	799	551	571	571	581	(NA)	633	640	656
Female	835	844	851	855	(NA)	863	863	875	848	855	864	855	(NA)	874	874	875	733	746	751	758	(NA)	777	780	796

NA Not available. [1] Includes other races not shown separately. [2] See footnote 1, Table 94.

Source: U.S. National Center for Health Statistics, U.S. Life Tables and Actuarial Tables, 1959-61, 1969-71, and 1979-81; Vital Statistics of the United States, annual; and unpublished data.

No. 94. Expectation of Life and Expected Deaths by Race, Sex, and Age: 2001

[See Appendix III]

Age (years)	Expectation of life in years					Expected deaths per 1,000 alive at specified age [1]				
		White		Black			White		Black	
	Total	Male	Female	Male	Female	Total	Male	Female	Male	Female
At birth	77.2	75.0	80.2	68.6	75.5	6.84	6.21	5.06	15.43	12.47
1	76.7	74.5	79.6	68.6	75.4	0.52	0.50	0.42	0.88	0.72
2	75.7	73.5	78.7	67.7	74.5	0.34	0.36	0.28	0.52	0.39
3	74.8	72.6	77.7	66.7	73.5	0.26	0.27	0.20	0.40	0.33
4	73.8	71.6	76.7	65.8	72.5	0.21	0.23	0.17	0.33	0.24
5	72.8	70.6	75.7	64.8	71.5	0.17	0.17	0.15	0.29	0.18
6	71.8	69.6	74.7	63.8	70.6	0.16	0.16	0.14	0.24	0.18
7	70.8	68.6	73.7	62.8	69.6	0.14	0.14	0.14	0.16	0.17
8	69.8	67.6	72.7	61.8	68.6	0.14	0.15	0.12	0.24	0.15
9	68.8	66.6	71.7	60.8	67.6	0.15	0.14	0.12	0.27	0.21
10	67.9	65.6	70.8	59.8	66.6	0.15	0.16	0.11	0.29	0.15
11	66.9	64.7	69.8	58.9	65.6	0.16	0.16	0.12	0.30	0.17
12	65.9	63.7	68.8	57.9	64.6	0.18	0.19	0.14	0.29	0.19
13	64.9	62.7	67.8	56.9	63.6	0.21	0.25	0.16	0.35	0.18
14	63.9	61.7	66.8	55.9	62.6	0.27	0.32	0.20	0.36	0.30
15	62.9	60.7	65.8	54.9	61.7	0.54	0.43	0.25	0.64	0.27
16	61.9	59.7	64.8	54.0	60.7	0.54	0.66	0.39	0.89	0.30
17	61.0	58.8	63.8	53.0	59.7	0.69	0.89	0.44	1.25	0.43
18	60.0	57.8	62.9	52.1	58.7	0.83	1.13	0.41	1.78	0.50
19	59.1	56.9	61.9	51.2	57.8	0.92	1.30	0.43	1.98	0.55
20	58.1	56.0	60.9	50.3	56.8	0.91	1.25	0.43	2.10	0.60
21	57.2	55.0	60.0	49.4	55.8	1.00	1.39	0.45	2.34	0.68
22	56.2	54.1	59.0	48.5	54.9	0.95	1.30	0.40	2.41	0.69
23	55.3	53.2	58.0	47.6	53.9	0.95	1.24	0.43	2.42	0.81
24	54.3	52.2	57.0	46.7	52.9	0.95	1.23	0.46	2.60	0.71
25	53.4	51.3	56.1	45.8	52.0	0.92	1.18	0.47	2.37	0.83
26	52.4	50.4	55.1	45.0	51.0	0.95	1.24	0.46	2.52	0.81
27	51.5	49.4	54.1	44.1	50.1	0.95	1.20	0.50	2.46	0.97
28	50.5	48.5	53.1	43.2	49.1	1.00	1.28	0.52	2.48	1.06
29	49.6	47.6	52.2	42.3	48.2	0.99	1.22	0.53	2.51	1.18
30	48.6	46.6	51.2	41.4	47.2	1.04	1.28	0.60	2.67	1.08
31	47.7	45.7	50.2	40.5	46.3	1.03	1.27	0.57	2.43	1.13
32	46.7	44.7	49.2	39.6	45.3	1.11	1.32	0.68	2.69	1.38
33	45.8	43.8	48.3	38.7	44.4	1.21	1.46	0.72	2.87	1.59
34	44.8	42.9	47.3	37.8	43.5	1.29	1.56	0.77	2.92	1.71
35	43.9	41.9	46.3	36.9	42.5	1.41	1.70	0.83	3.23	1.86
36	43.0	41.0	45.4	36.0	41.6	1.48	1.76	0.93	3.15	1.97
37	42.0	40.1	44.4	35.1	40.7	1.65	1.96	1.04	3.74	2.00
38	41.1	39.1	43.5	34.3	39.8	1.81	2.15	1.15	3.85	2.42
39	40.2	38.2	42.5	33.4	38.9	1.92	2.23	1.27	4.22	2.57
40	39.2	37.3	41.6	32.5	38.0	2.07	2.45	1.35	4.30	2.94
41	38.3	36.4	40.6	31.7	37.1	2.17	2.53	1.39	4.79	2.97
42	37.4	35.5	39.7	30.8	36.2	2.36	2.75	1.52	5.24	3.40
43	36.5	34.6	38.7	30.0	35.3	2.61	3.04	1.69	5.78	3.77
44	35.6	33.7	37.8	29.2	34.4	2.83	3.30	1.85	6.33	3.99
45	34.7	32.8	36.9	28.4	33.6	3.05	3.52	2.00	7.01	4.17
46	33.8	31.9	36.0	27.5	32.7	3.24	3.77	2.10	7.60	4.49
47	32.9	31.0	35.0	26.8	31.8	3.56	4.23	2.32	8.33	4.62
48	32.0	30.2	34.1	26.0	31.0	3.80	4.56	2.40	8.95	5.13
49	31.1	29.3	33.2	25.2	30.2	4.13	4.83	2.69	9.81	5.85
50	30.3	28.4	32.3	24.4	29.3	4.41	5.20	2.86	10.60	6.16
51	29.4	27.6	31.4	23.7	28.5	4.62	5.42	3.05	10.96	6.14
52	28.5	26.7	30.5	23.0	27.7	5.08	5.81	3.48	12.16	6.93
53	27.7	25.9	29.6	22.2	26.9	5.37	6.15	3.79	12.42	7.51
54	26.8	25.0	28.7	21.5	26.1	6.14	7.16	4.32	14.16	8.29
55	26.0	24.2	27.8	20.8	25.3	6.11	7.09	4.30	14.05	8.15
56	25.1	23.4	26.9	20.1	24.5	7.10	8.28	5.08	15.36	9.46
57	24.3	22.6	26.1	19.4	23.7	7.75	8.94	5.63	17.43	10.15
58	23.5	21.8	25.2	18.7	23.0	8.77	10.24	6.39	19.36	11.08
59	22.7	21.0	24.4	18.1	22.2	8.96	10.33	6.59	19.82	11.78
60	21.9	20.2	23.5	17.5	21.5	10.15	12.06	7.49	20.55	11.99
61	21.1	19.4	22.7	16.8	20.7	10.87	12.68	8.07	22.79	13.44
62	20.3	18.7	21.9	16.2	20.0	12.07	14.20	9.04	24.23	14.94
63	19.6	18.0	21.1	15.6	19.3	13.16	15.50	9.99	25.35	15.70
64	18.8	17.2	20.3	15.0	18.6	14.33	16.96	10.76	27.68	17.53
65	18.1	16.5	19.5	14.4	17.9	15.58	18.55	11.76	29.97	17.98
70	14.6	13.2	15.7	11.7	14.7	23.67	28.73	18.49	41.64	26.15
75	11.5	10.2	12.3	9.3	11.7	36.75	45.27	29.29	61.00	39.89
80	8.8	7.7	9.3	7.3	9.2	57.07	69.53	48.43	85.82	56.79

[1] Based on the proportion of the cohort who are alive at the beginning of an indicated age interval who will die before reaching the end of that interval. For example, out of every 1,000 people alive and exactly 50 years old at the beginning of the period, between 4 and 5 (4.44) will die before reaching their 51st birthdays.

Source: U.S. National Center for Health Statistics, *Vital Statistics of the United States*, annual; and *National Vital Statistics Report*, Vol. 52, No. 3, and unpublished data.

Vital Statistics 73

No. 95. Deaths and Death Rates by Sex and Race: 1970 to 2002

[1,921 represents 1,921,000. Rates are per 1,000 population for specified groups. Excludes deaths of nonresidents of the United States and fetal deaths. For explanation of age-adjustment, see text, this section. The standard population for age-adjustment is the projected year 2000 population of the United States. See Appendix III. Data for Hispanic origin and specified races other than white and black should be interpreted with caution because of inconsistencies between reporting Hispanic origin and race on death certificates and censuses and surveys.]

Sex and race	1970	1980	1990	1995	1996	1997	1998	1999	2000	2001	2002 [1]
Deaths [2] (1,000)	1,921	1,990	2,148	2,312	2,315	2,314	2,337	2,391	2,403	2,416	2,448
Male [2] (1,000)	1,078	1,075	1,113	1,173	1,164	1,154	1,157	1,175	1,178	1,183	1,201
Female [2] (1,000)	843	915	1,035	1,139	1,151	1,160	1,180	1,216	1,226	1,233	1,247
White (1,000)	1,682	1,739	1,853	1,987	1,993	1,996	2,016	2,061	2,071	2,080	2,108
Male (1,000)	942	934	951	997	992	987	990	1,005	1,007	1,011	1,027
Female (1,000)	740	805	902	990	1,001	1,010	1,026	1,056	1,064	1,068	1,080
Black (1,000)	226	233	265	286	282	277	278	285	286	288	289
Male (1,000)	128	130	145	154	149	144	143	146	145	146	146
Female (1,000)	98	103	120	132	133	132	135	139	141	142	143
American Indian, Eskimo, Aleut (1,000)	6	7	8	10	10	11	11	11	11	12	12
Male (1,000)	3	4	5	6	6	6	6	6	6	6	7
Female (1,000)	2	3	3	4	5	5	5	5	5	6	6
Asian and Pacific Islander (1,000)	(NA)	11	21	28	30	31	32	34	35	37	38
Male (1,000)	(NA)	7	12	16	17	17	18	18	19	20	20
Female (1,000)	(NA)	4	9	12	13	14	14	15	16	17	18
Hispanic origin (1,000)	(NA)	(NA)	(NA)	(NA)	(NA)	95	98	104	107	113	117
Male (1,000)	(NA)	(NA)	(NA)	(NA)	(NA)	54	56	58	60	63	66
Female (1,000)	(NA)	(NA)	(NA)	(NA)	(NA)	41	43	46	47	50	51
Death rates [2]	9.5	8.8	8.6	8.7	8.6	8.5	8.5	8.6	8.5	8.5	8.5
Male [2]	10.9	9.8	9.2	9.0	8.8	8.6	8.6	8.6	8.5	8.5	8.5
Female [2]	8.1	7.9	8.1	8.4	8.4	8.3	8.4	8.5	8.6	8.5	8.5
White	9.5	8.9	8.9	9.0	9.0	8.9	8.9	9.0	9.0	9.0	9.0
Male	10.9	9.8	9.3	9.3	9.1	8.9	8.9	8.9	9.1	8.8	8.9
Female	8.1	8.1	8.5	8.9	8.9	8.9	8.9	9.1	9.2	9.1	9.1
Black	10.0	8.8	8.7	8.5	8.2	7.9	7.8	7.9	7.8	7.7	7.7
Male	11.9	10.3	10.1	9.8	9.2	8.7	8.5	8.5	8.8	8.2	8.1
Female	8.3	7.3	7.5	7.6	7.3	7.2	7.2	7.3	7.6	7.3	7.2
American Indian, Eskimo, Aleut	(NA)	4.9	4.0	4.1	4.0	4.0	4.0	4.0	3.8	3.9	4.0
Male	(NA)	6.0	4.8	4.6	4.4	4.6	4.4	4.3	4.2	4.2	4.4
Female	(NA)	3.8	3.3	3.6	3.6	3.5	3.5	3.7	3.5	3.6	3.7
Asian and Pacific Islander	(NA)	3.0	2.8	2.9	2.9	2.9	2.9	3.0	3.0	3.0	3.0
Male	(NA)	3.8	3.3	3.4	3.4	3.4	3.4	3.3	3.3	3.4	3.3
Female	(NA)	2.2	2.3	2.5	2.5	2.5	2.5	2.6	2.6	2.7	2.7
Hispanic origin	(NA)	(NA)	(NA)	(NA)	(NA)	3.1	3.0	3.1	3.0	3.1	3.0
Male	(NA)	(NA)	4.1	(NA)	(NA)	3.4	3.3	3.7	3.3	3.3	3.3
Female	(NA)	(NA)	2.9	(NA)	(NA)	2.7	2.7	2.9	2.7	2.8	2.7
Age-adjusted death rates [2]	12.2	10.4	9.4	9.2	8.9	8.8	8.7	8.8	8.7	8.5	8.5
Male [2]	15.4	13.5	12.0	11.5	11.2	10.9	10.7	10.7	10.5	10.3	10.2
Female [2]	9.7	8.2	7.5	7.5	7.3	7.3	7.2	7.3	7.3	7.2	7.2
White	11.9	10.1	9.1	8.9	8.7	8.6	8.5	8.5	8.5	8.4	8.3
Male	15.1	13.2	11.7	11.1	10.8	10.6	10.4	10.4	10.3	10.1	10.0
Female	9.4	8.0	7.3	7.3	7.1	7.1	7.1	7.2	7.2	7.1	7.0
Black	15.2	13.1	12.5	12.2	11.8	11.4	11.3	11.4	11.2	11.0	10.8
Male	18.7	17.0	16.4	15.8	15.2	14.6	14.3	14.3	14.0	13.8	13.4
Female	12.3	10.3	9.8	9.7	9.4	9.2	9.2	9.3	9.3	9.1	9.0
American Indian, Eskimo, Aleut	(NA)	8.7	7.2	7.2	7.6	7.7	7.7	7.8	7.1	6.9	6.8
Male	(NA)	11.1	9.2	8.6	9.2	9.7	9.4	9.3	8.4	8.0	8.0
Female	(NA)	6.6	5.6	5.9	6.4	6.3	6.4	6.7	6.0	5.9	5.8
Asian and Pacific Islander	(NA)	5.9	5.8	6.2	5.4	5.3	5.2	5.2	5.1	4.9	4.7
Male	(NA)	7.9	7.2	7.9	6.8	6.6	6.5	6.4	6.2	6.0	5.8
Female	(NA)	4.3	4.7	4.9	4.4	4.3	4.3	4.3	4.2	4.1	4.0
Hispanic origin	(NA)	(NA)	(NA)	(NA)	(NA)	6.7	6.7	6.8	6.7	6.6	6.3
Male	(NA)	(NA)	8.9	(NA)	(NA)	8.4	8.3	7.4	8.2	8.0	7.7
Female	(NA)	(NA)	5.4	(NA)	(NA)	5.4	5.4	4.9	5.5	5.4	5.2

NA Not available.   [1] Preliminary data.   [2] Includes other races, not shown separately.

Source: U.S. National Center for Health Statistics, *Vital Statistics of the United States*, annual; and *National Vital Statistics Reports (NVSR)* (formerly *Monthly Vital Statistics Report*).

74   Vital Statistics

No. 96. Death Rates by Age: 1940 to 2002
[Rates per 100,000 population. See Appendix III]

Characteristic	All ages [1]	Under 1 year	1-4 years	5-14 years	15-24 years	25-34 years	35-44 years	45-54 years	55-64 years	65-74 years	75-84 years	85 years and older
MALE:												
1940	1,197.4	6,189.8	311.5	117.8	228.9	338.4	588.1	1,248.8	2,612.0	5,462.3	12,126.4	24,639.0
1950	1,106.1	3,728.0	151.7	70.9	167.9	216.5	428.8	1,067.1	2,395.3	4,931.4	10,426.0	21,636.0
1960	1,104.5	3,059.3	119.5	55.7	152.1	187.9	372.8	992.2	2,309.5	4,914.4	10,178.4	21,186.3
1970	1,090.3	2,410.0	93.2	50.5	188.5	215.3	402.6	958.5	2,282.7	4,873.8	10,010.2	17,821.5
1980	976.9	1,428.5	72.6	36.7	172.3	196.1	299.2	767.3	1,815.1	4,105.2	8,816.7	18,801.1
1990	918.4	1,082.8	52.4	28.5	147.4	204.3	310.4	610.3	1,553.4	3,491.5	7,888.6	18,056.6
2000 [2]	853.0	806.5	35.9	20.9	114.9	138.6	255.2	542.8	1,230.7	2,979.6	6,972.6	17,501.4
2002 [2]	847.8	758.7	35.3	20.0	117.3	142.3	256.8	546.8	1,185.6	2,862.2	6,774.3	16,295.3
White:												
1980	983.3	1,230.3	66.1	35.0	167.0	171.3	257.4	698.9	1,728.5	4,035.7	8,829.8	19,097.3
1985	963.6	1,056.5	52.8	30.1	134.2	158.8	243.1	611.7	1,625.8	3,770.7	8,486.1	18,980.1
1990	930.9	896.1	45.9	26.4	131.3	176.1	268.2	548.7	1,467.2	3,397.7	7,844.9	18,268.3
1995	932.1	717.5	38.8	24.5	122.3	177.7	287.7	534.6	1,330.8	3,199.0	7,320.6	18,152.9
1999	911.2	658.1	33.9	20.3	104.9	134.5	231.5	494.2	1,200.2	3,043.2	6,965.1	17,202.1
2000	887.8	667.6	32.6	19.8	105.8	124.1	233.6	496.9	1,163.3	2,905.7	6,933.1	17,716.4
2001	881.9	627.6	34.2	18.4	108.0	130.3	239.7	501.3	1,127.5	2,842.3	6,799.7	16,935.4
2002 [2]	885.9	651.6	31.6	18.4	109.9	128.5	238.8	505.0	1,120.6	2,804.4	6,756.0	16,519.4
Black:												
1980	1,034.1	2,586.7	110.5	47.4	209.1	407.3	689.8	1,479.9	2,873.0	5,131.1	9,231.6	16,098.8
1985	989.3	2,219.9	90.1	42.3	173.6	351.9	630.2	1,292.9	2,779.8	5,172.4	9,262.3	15,774.2
1990	1,008.0	2,112.4	85.8	41.2	252.2	430.8	699.6	1,261.0	2,618.4	4,946.1	9,129.5	16,954.9
1995	980.7	1,590.8	77.5	40.2	249.2	416.5	721.2	1,273.0	2,437.5	4,610.5	8,778.8	16,728.7
1999	880.0	1,694.0	66.0	34.6	185.6	268.4	473.6	1,081.9	2,244.0	4,182.8	8,352.6	16,047.8
2000	834.1	1,567.6	54.5	28.2	181.4	261.0	453.0	1,017.7	2,080.1	4,253.5	8,486.0	16,791.0
2001	823.9	1,426.4	53.2	27.7	180.7	259.2	445.0	996.1	2,025.3	4,166.6	8,355.9	16,439.9
2002 [2]	814.6	1,334.9	54.3	29.1	172.5	263.3	433.1	979.9	2,036.6	4,011.4	8,154.7	15,622.6
Hispanic [3]:												
1980	(NA)	(NA)	(NA)	(NA)	(NA)	(NA)	(NA)	(NA)	(NA)	(NA)	(NA)	(NA)
1985	374.6	1,044.6	53.8	23.0	147.5	202.1	290.1	495.7	1,129.4	2,484.9	5,696.1	12,156.2
1990	411.6	921.8	53.8	26.0	159.3	234.0	341.8	533.9	1,123.7	2,368.2	5,369.1	12,272.1
1995	(NA)	(NA)	(NA)	(NA)	(NA)	(NA)	(NA)	(NA)	(NA)	(NA)	(NA)	(NA)
1999	374.6	655.3	34.3	19.4	124.9	151.6	226.0	456.3	962.6	2,219.4	4,525.1	9,842.3
2000	331.3	637.1	31.5	17.9	107.7	120.2	211.0	439.0	965.7	2,287.9	5,395.3	13,086.2
2001	332.9	624.4	33.8	16.6	111.5	118.0	208.5	443.9	923.9	2,242.6	5,258.0	12,888.3
2002 [2]	327.8	643.3	34.1	17.2	113.5	112.0	190.8	418.6	936.3	2,205.2	5,043.5	11,649.0
Asian or Pacific Islander [3]:												
2002 [2]	330.5	453.5	27.4	14.1	58.2	54.6	99.1	246.6	599.7	1,486.7	4,063.1	10,908.7
American Indian [3]:												
2002 [2]	439.4	878.1	49.3	22.0	144.4	193.5	316.8	537.7	1,060.2	2,378.3	4,743.8	9,380.0
FEMALE:												
1940	954.6	4,774.3	267.0	89.1	181.1	274.3	452.2	860.7	1,800.4	4,222.2	10,368.6	22,759.1
1950	823.5	2,854.6	126.7	48.9	89.1	142.7	290.3	641.5	1,404.8	3,333.2	8,399.6	19,194.7
1960	809.2	2,321.3	98.4	37.3	61.3	106.6	229.4	526.7	1,196.4	2,871.8	7,633.1	19,008.4
1970	807.8	1,863.7	75.4	31.8	68.1	101.6	231.1	517.2	1,098.9	2,579.7	6,677.6	15,518.0
1980	785.3	1,141.7	54.7	24.2	57.5	75.9	159.3	412.9	934.3	2,144.7	5,440.1	14,746.9
1990	812.0	855.7	41.0	19.3	49.0	74.2	137.9	342.7	878.8	1,991.2	4,883.1	14,274.3
2000	855.0	663.4	28.7	15.0	43.1	63.5	143.2	312.5	772.2	1,921.2	4,814.7	14,719.2
2001	850.4	613.9	29.5	14.6	42.6	66.0	148.2	316.8	754.0	1,890.8	4,760.5	14,429.9
2002 [2]	849.9	625.3	27.0	14.8	43.7	64.0	148.8	316.7	739.3	1,870.2	4,770.9	14,240.5
White:												
1980	806.1	962.5	49.3	22.9	55.5	65.4	138.2	372.7	876.2	2,066.6	5,401.7	14,979.6
1985	840.1	799.3	40.0	19.5	48.1	59.4	121.9	341.7	869.1	2,027.1	5,111.6	14,745.4
1990	846.9	690.0	36.1	17.9	45.9	61.5	117.4	309.3	822.7	1,923.5	4,839.1	14,400.6
1995	891.3	571.6	31.2	16.6	44.3	64.3	125.8	294.4	788.4	1,924.5	4,831.1	14,639.1
1999	924.1	532.6	27.4	14.9	42.2	58.4	123.3	281.8	739.1	1,916.2	4,869.7	15,053.8
2000	912.3	550.5	25.5	14.1	41.1	55.1	125.7	281.4	730.9	1,868.3	4,785.3	14,890.7
2001	907.9	511.5	27.1	13.9	40.8	58.6	131.0	286.8	712.2	1,840.2	4,738.5	14,597.6
2002 [2]	909.5	520.1	24.5	13.8	42.5	56.9	133.4	286.8	700.5	1,826.4	4,757.2	14,420.6
Black:												
1980	733.3	2,123.7	84.4	30.5	70.5	150.0	323.9	768.2	1,561.0	3,057.4	6,212.1	12,367.2
1985	734.2	1,821.4	71.1	28.6	59.6	137.6	276.5	667.6	1,532.5	2,967.8	6,078.0	12,703.0
1990	747.9	1,735.5	67.6	27.5	68.7	159.5	298.6	639.4	1,452.6	2,865.7	5,688.3	13,309.5
1995	759.0	1,342.0	62.9	26.5	70.3	166.6	327.7	619.0	1,350.3	2,823.7	5,840.3	13,472.2
1999	761.3	1,403.3	51.5	22.6	60.1	122.0	282.6	581.0	1,255.7	2,732.1	6,002.7	14,262.9
2000	733.0	1,279.8	45.3	20.0	58.3	121.8	271.9	588.3	1,227.2	2,689.6	5,696.5	13,941.3
2001	727.7	1,176.3	41.7	18.7	54.9	117.9	278.0	579.1	1,215.5	2,616.1	5,591.6	13,849.9
2002 [2]	723.3	1,165.7	39.3	20.1	54.3	116.5	272.3	577.8	1,181.4	2,544.1	5,580.3	13,693.5
Hispanic [3]:												
1980	(NA)	(NA)	(NA)	(NA)	(NA)	(NA)	(NA)	(NA)	(NA)	(NA)	(NA)	(NA)
1985	251.9	791.4	42.3	16.0	36.2	56.3	100.0	251.3	619.7	1,449.5	3,551.8	10,228.6
1990	285.4	746.6	42.1	17.3	40.6	62.9	109.3	253.3	607.5	1,453.8	3,351.3	10,098.7
1995	(NA)	(NA)	(NA)	(NA)	(NA)	(NA)	(NA)	(NA)	(NA)	(NA)	(NA)	(NA)
1999	293.7	565.9	29.8	14.4	36.4	51.8	99.9	226.7	536.0	1,366.8	3,245.6	8,838.0
2000	274.6	553.6	27.5	13.4	31.7	43.4	100.5	223.8	548.4	1,423.2	3,624.5	11,202.8
2001	279.0	518.9	27.2	12.7	33.7	45.2	97.0	226.7	543.0	1,408.0	3,589.8	11,300.5
2002 [2]	273.5	536.1	24.9	13.3	34.1	40.1	95.2	218.7	520.0	1,372.2	3,515.1	10,185.2
Asian or Pacific Islander [3]:												
2002 [2]	270.1	405.6	19.3	10.1	24.3	26.6	53.1	151.2	372.9	1,019.7	2,721.9	8,402.5
American Indian [3]:												
2002 [2]	367.1	739.2	43.0	21.6	62.1	86.1	175.1	323.1	746.2	1,830.6	3,683.1	7,832.7

NA Not available. [1] Figures for age not stated are included in "All ages" but not distributed among age groups. [2] Preliminary data. [3] The death rates for Hispanic origin and specified races other than white and black should be interpreted with caution because of inconsistencies between reporting Hispanic origin and race on death certificates and censuses and surveys.

Source: U.S. National Center for Health Statistics, *Vital Statistics of the United States*, annual.

Vital Statistics 75

No. 97. Age-Adjusted Death Rates by Race and Sex: 1940 to 2002

[Age adjusted rates per 100,000 population; see headnote, Table 95. Populations enumerated as of April 1 for census years and estimated as of July 1 for all other years. Beginning 1970, excludes deaths of nonresidents of the United States. Data for specified races other than white and black should be interpreted with caution because of inconsistencies reporting race on death certificates and on censuses and surveys. See Appendix III]

Sex and Race	1940	1950	1960	1970	1980	1990	1995	2000	2001	2002 [1]
ALL RACES [2]										
Total	1,785.0	1,446.0	1,339.2	1,222.6	1,039.1	938.7	918.5	869.0	854.5	846.8
Male	1,976.0	1,674.2	1,609.0	1,542.1	1,348.1	1,202.8	1,150.3	1,053.8	1,029.1	1,015.3
Female	1,599.4	1,236.0	1,105.3	971.4	817.9	750.9	748.2	731.4	721.8	716.7
WHITE										
Total	1,735.3	1,410.8	1,311.3	1,193.3	1,012.7	909.8	890.0	849.8	836.5	831.0
Male	1,925.2	1,642.5	1,586.0	1,513.7	1,317.6	1,165.9	1,112.7	1,029.4	1,006.1	995.1
Female	1,550.4	1,198.0	1,074.4	944.0	796.1	728.8	726.6	715.3	706.7	703.2
BLACK										
Total	(NA)	(NA)	1,577.5	1,518.1	1,314.8	1,250.3	1,224.5	1,121.4	1,101.2	1,081.2
Male	(NA)	(NA)	1,811.1	1,873.9	1,697.8	1,644.5	1,582.3	1,403.5	1,375.0	1,338.4
Female	(NA)	(NA)	1,369.7	1,228.7	1,033.3	975.1	970.1	927.6	912.5	900.4
AMERICAN INDIAN [3]										
Total	(NA)	(NA)	(NA)	(NA)	867.0	716.3	716.5	709.3	686.7	677.6
Male	(NA)	(NA)	(NA)	(NA)	1,111.5	916.2	864.2	841.5	798.9	796.1
Female	(NA)	(NA)	(NA)	(NA)	662.4	561.8	592.8	604.5	594.0	580.7
ASIAN OR PACIFIC ISLANDER [4]										
Total	(NA)	(NA)	(NA)	(NA)	589.9	582.0	616.0	506.4	492.1	473.9
Male	(NA)	(NA)	(NA)	(NA)	786.5	716.4	788.1	624.2	597.4	576.5
Female	(NA)	(NA)	(NA)	(NA)	425.9	469.3	488.4	416.8	412.0	396.4

NA Not Available. [1] Preliminary data. [2] For 1940-91 includes deaths among races not shown separately; see Other races and, race not stated, in the Technical notes for information for 1992 to present. [3] Includes Aleuts and Eskimos. [4] Includes Chinese, Filipino, Hawaiian, Japanese, and Other Asian or Pacific Islander.

Source: U.S. National Center for Health Statistics, *Vital Statistics of the United States*, annual.

No. 98. Death Rates by Hispanic Origin, Age and Sex: 1985 to 2002

[Rates per 100,000 population. Rates are based on populations enumerated as of April 1 for census years and estimated as of July 1 for all other years. Excludes deaths of nonresidents of the United States. Data for Hispanic origin should be interpreted with caution because of inconsistencies between reporting Hispanic origin and race on death certificates and censuses and surveys.]

Year	Male						Female					
	1985	1990	1999	2000	2001	2002	1985	1990	1999	2000	2001	2002
Age adjusted [1] .	889.2	886.4	736.0	818.1	802.5	765.8	546.1	537.1	490.1	546.0	544.2	517.4
Crude.	374.6	411.6	367.9	331.3	332.9	327.8	251.9	285.4	293.7	274.6	279.0	273.5
Under 1	1,044.6	921.8	655.3	637.1	624.4	643.3	791.4	746.6	565.9	553.6	518.9	536.1
1-4 years	53.8	53.8	34.3	31.5	33.8	34.1	42.3	42.1	29.8	27.5	27.2	27.4
5-14 years . . .	23.0	26.0	19.4	17.9	16.6	17.2	16.0	17.3	14.4	13.4	12.7	13.3
15-24 years. . .	147.5	159.3	124.9	107.7	111.5	113.5	36.2	40.6	36.4	31.7	33.7	34.1
25-34 years. . .	202.1	234.0	151.6	120.2	118.0	112.0	56.3	62.9	51.8	43.4	45.2	40.1
35-44 years. . .	290.1	341.8	226.0	211.0	208.5	190.8	100.0	109.3	99.9	100.5	97.0	95.2
45-54 years. . .	495.7	533.9	456.3	439.0	443.9	418.6	251.3	253.3	226.7	223.8	226.7	218.7
55-64 years. . .	1,129.4	1,123.7	962.3	965.7	923.9	936.3	619.7	607.5	536.0	548.4	543.0	520.0
65-74 years. . .	2,484.9	2,368.2	2,219.4	2,287.9	2,242.6	2,205.2	1,449.5	1,453.8	1,366.8	1,423.2	1,408.0	1,372.2
75-84 years. . .	5,696.1	5,369.1	4,525.1	5,395.3	5,258.0	5,043.5	3,551.8	3,351.3	3,245.6	3,624.5	3,589.8	3,515.1
85 years and over	12,156.2	12,272.1	9,842.3	13,086.2	12,888.3	11,649.0	10,228.6	10,098.7	8,838.7	11,202.8	11,300.5	10,185.2

[1] See headnote, Table 95.

Source: U.S. National Center for Health Statistics, *Vital Statistics of the United States*, annual.

No. 99. Deaths and Death Rates by State and Outlying Areas: 1990 to 2002

[2,148 represents 2,148,000. By state of residence. Excludes deaths of nonresidents of the United States, except as noted. Caution should be used in comparing death rates by state; rates are affected by the population composition of the area. 2002 data is preliminary. See also Appendix III]

State	Number of deaths (1,000)							Rate per 1,000 population [1]						
	1990	1995	1998	1999	2000	2001	2002	1990	1995	1998	1999	2000	2001	2002
U.S..	2,148	2,312	2,337	2,391	2,403	2,416	2,448	8.6	8.7	8.5	8.6	8.5	8.5	8.5
Alabama	39	42	44	45	45	45	46	9.7	10.0	10.1	10.3	10.1	10.1	10.3
Alaska	2	3	3	3	3	3	3	4.0	4.2	4.2	4.4	4.6	4.7	4.7
Arizona	29	35	38	40	41	41	43	7.9	8.4	8.2	8.4	7.9	7.7	7.8
Arkansas.	25	27	28	28	28	28	29	10.5	10.8	10.8	10.9	10.6	10.3	10.5
California.	214	224	227	229	230	234	235	7.2	7.1	6.9	6.9	6.8	6.8	6.7
Colorado	22	25	27	27	27	28	29	6.6	6.7	6.7	6.7	6.3	6.4	6.5
Connecticut	28	29	30	29	30	30	30	8.4	9.0	9.1	9.0	8.8	8.7	8.7
Delaware.	6	6	7	7	7	7	7	8.7	8.8	8.8	8.8	8.8	8.9	8.5
Dist. of Columbia .	7	7	6	6	6	6	6	12.0	12.4	11.6	11.7	10.5	10.4	10.2
Florida	134	153	158	163	164	167	168	10.4	10.8	10.1	10.8	10.3	10.2	10.0
Georgia	52	58	60	62	64	64	65	8.0	8.1	7.9	8.0	7.8	7.7	7.6
Hawaii	7	8	8	8	8	8	9	6.1	6.4	6.8	7.0	6.8	6.8	7.1
Idaho	7	9	9	10	10	10	10	7.4	7.3	7.5	7.7	7.4	7.4	7.4
Illinois.	103	108	104	108	107	105	(NA)	9.0	9.2	8.7	8.9	8.6	8.4	(NA)
Indiana	50	53	53	55	55	55	55	8.9	9.2	9.1	9.3	9.1	9.0	9.0
Iowa.	27	28	28	28	28	28	28	9.7	9.9	9.9	9.9	9.6	9.5	9.5
Kansas	22	24	24	24	25	25	25	9.0	9.3	9.2	9.2	9.2	9.1	9.2
Kentucky.	35	37	38	39	40	40	41	9.5	9.6	9.6	9.9	9.8	9.8	10.1
Louisiana	38	40	40	41	41	42	42	8.9	9.1	9.2	9.4	9.2	9.3	9.4
Maine	11	12	12	12	12	12	13	9.0	9.5	9.8	9.8	9.7	9.7	9.8
Maryland.	38	42	42	43	44	44	44	8.0	8.3	8.2	8.3	8.3	8.1	8.1
Massachusetts . . .	53	55	55	56	57	57	57	8.8	9.1	9.0	9.0	8.9	8.9	8.9
Michigan	79	84	85	87	87	86	88	8.5	8.8	8.7	8.8	8.7	8.6	8.7
Minnesota	35	38	37	39	38	38	39	7.9	8.1	7.9	8.1	7.7	7.6	7.7
Mississippi.	25	27	28	28	29	28	29	9.8	10.0	10.1	10.2	10.1	9.9	10.0
Missouri	50	54	55	56	55	55	56	9.8	10.2	10.1	10.2	9.8	9.8	9.9
Montana	7	8	8	8	8	8	9	8.6	8.8	9.1	9.2	9.0	9.1	9.4
Nebraska	15	15	15	16	15	15	16	9.4	9.3	9.1	9.4	8.8	8.8	9.1
Nevada.	9	13	14	15	15	16	17	7.8	8.2	8.3	8.3	7.6	7.8	7.8
New Hampshire . .	8	9	9	10	10	10	10	7.7	8.0	8.0	7.9	7.8	7.8	7.7
New Jersey	70	74	72	74	75	75	74	9.1	9.3	8.8	9.1	8.9	8.8	8.6
New Mexico.	11	13	13	14	13	14	14	7.0	7.4	7.4	7.9	7.4	7.7	7.7
New York	169	168	157	160	158	159	159	9.4	9.3	8.6	8.8	8.3	8.3	8.3
North Carolina . . .	57	65	68	70	72	71	72	8.6	9.0	9.0	9.1	8.9	8.6	8.7
North Dakota	6	6	6	6	6	6	6	8.9	9.3	9.3	9.6	9.1	9.5	9.3
Ohio.	99	106	106	109	108	108	110	9.1	9.5	9.4	9.6	9.5	9.5	9.6
Oklahoma	30	33	34	35	35	35	36	9.7	10.0	10.1	10.3	10.2	10.0	10.2
Oregon	25	28	29	29	30	30	31	8.8	9.0	9.0	8.9	8.6	8.7	8.8
Pennsylvania	122	128	127	130	131	130	130	10.3	10.6	10.6	10.9	10.7	10.5	10.6
Rhode Island	10	10	10	10	10	10	10	9.5	9.8	9.8	9.8	9.6	9.5	9.6
South Carolina . . .	30	34	35	36	37	37	38	8.5	9.1	9.1	9.3	9.2	9.0	9.2
South Dakota	6	7	7	7	7	7	7	9.1	9.5	9.3	9.5	9.3	9.1	9.1
Tennessee.	46	51	53	54	55	55	57	9.5	9.8	9.8	9.8	9.7	9.6	9.8
Texas	125	138	143	147	150	153	159	7.4	7.4	7.2	7.3	7.2	7.1	7.3
Utah.	9	11	12	12	12	13	13	5.3	5.6	5.6	5.7	5.5	5.6	5.7
Vermont	5	5	5	5	5	5	5	8.2	8.5	8.4	8.4	8.4	8.5	8.2
Virginia	48	53	54	55	56	56	57	7.8	8.0	8.0	8.0	8.0	7.8	7.8
Washington	37	41	43	44	44	45	45	7.6	7.5	7.5	7.6	7.5	7.4	7.5
West Virginia	19	20	21	21	21	21	21	10.8	11.1	11.5	11.6	11.7	11.6	11.7
Wisconsin	43	45	46	47	46	47	47	8.7	8.8	8.8	8.9	8.7	8.6	8.6
Wyoming	3	4	4	4	4	4	4	7.1	7.7	8.0	8.4	7.9	8.2	8.4
Puerto Rico . . .	26	30	29	28	28	29	28	7.3	8.1	7.7	7.4	7.2	7.6	7.2
Virgin Islands . .	(NA)	1	1	1	1	1	1	4.6	5.8	5.2	5.5	5.3	5.6	5.7
Guam	1	1	1	1	1	1	1	3.9	4.1	4.2	4.6	4.2	4.2	4.0
American Samoa.	(NA)	(NA)	(NA)	(NA)	(NA)	(NA)	(NA)	(NA)	(NA)	3.9	3.9	3.3	4.2	5.1
Northern Marianas	(NA)	(NA)	(NA)	(NA)	(NA)	(NA)	(NA)	(NA)	(NA)	2.4	2.3	1.9	2.1	2.2

- Represents zero. NA Not available.   [1] Rates based on enumerated resident population as of April 1 for 1990 and 2000; estimated resident population as of July 1 for all other years.

Source: U.S. National Center for Health Statistics, Vital Statistics of the United States, annual; National Vital Statistics Reports (NVSR) (formerly Monthly Vital Statistics Report).

Vital Statistics   77

No. 100. Infant, Maternal, and Neonatal Mortality Rates by Race: 1980 to 2001

[Deaths per 1,000 live births, except as noted. Excludes deaths of nonresidents of the United States. Beginning 1989, race for live births tabulated according to race of mother, for maternal mortality rates and mortality rates. See also Appendix III]

Item	1980	1990	1995	1997	1998	1999 [1]	2000	2001
Infant deaths [2]	12.6	9.2	7.6	7.2	7.2	7.1	6.9	6.8
White	10.9	7.6	6.3	6.0	6.0	5.8	5.7	5.7
Black and other	20.2	15.5	12.6	11.8	11.9	11.9	11.4	11.3
Black	22.2	18.0	15.1	14.2	14.3	14.6	14.1	14.0
Maternal deaths [3]	9.2	8.2	7.1	8.4	7.1	9.9	9.8	9.9
White	6.7	5.4	4.2	5.8	5.1	6.8	7.5	7.2
Black and other	19.8	19.1	18.5	18.3	14.9	21.4	18.0	20.2
Black	21.5	22.4	22.1	20.8	17.1	25.4	22.0	24.7
Neonatal deaths [4]	8.5	5.8	4.9	4.8	4.8	4.7	4.6	4.5
White	7.4	4.8	4.1	4.0	4.0	3.9	3.8	3.8
Black and other	13.2	9.9	8.1	7.7	7.9	7.9	7.6	7.4
Black	14.6	11.6	9.8	9.4	9.5	9.8	9.4	9.2

[1] Beginning 1999, deaths are classified according to the Tenth Revision of the International Classification of Diseases; earlier years classified according to the revision in use at the time, see text, this section.   [2] Represents deaths of infants under 1 year old, exclusive of fetal deaths.   [3] Per 100,000 live births from deliveries and complications of pregnancy, childbirth, and the puerperium. Deaths are classified according to the tenth revision of the *International Classification of Diseases;* earlier years classified according to the revision in use at the time; see text, this section.   [4] Represents deaths of infants under 28 days old, exclusive of fetal deaths.
Source: U.S. National Center for Health Statistics, *Vital Statistics of the United States,* annual; *National Vital Statistics Reports (NVSR)* (formerly *Monthly Vital Statistics Report*).

No. 101. Infant Mortality Rates by Race—States: 1980 to 2001

[Deaths per 1,000 live births, by place of residence. Represents deaths of infants under 1 year old, exclusive of fetal deaths. Excludes deaths of nonresidents of the United States. See Appendix III]

State	Total [1]				White				Black			
	1980	1990	2000	2001	1980	1990	2000	2001	1980	1990	2000	2001
U.S.	12.6	9.2	6.9	6.8	10.9	7.6	5.7	5.7	22.2	18.0	14.1	14.0
Alabama	15.1	10.8	9.4	9.4	11.6	8.1	6.6	6.8	21.6	16.0	15.4	15.1
Alaska	12.3	10.5	6.8	8.1	9.4	7.6	5.8	5.8	19.5	(B)	(B)	(B)
Arizona	12.4	8.8	6.7	6.9	11.8	7.8	6.2	6.1	18.4	20.6	17.6	22.8
Arkansas	12.7	9.2	8.4	8.3	10.3	8.4	7.0	6.8	18.0	16.8	12.9	12.9
California	11.1	7.9	5.4	5.4	10.6	7.0	5.1	5.0	19.1	19.4	19.5	12.8
Colorado	10.1	8.8	6.2	5.8	9.8	7.8	5.6	5.5	19.1	17.6	14.4	16.9
Connecticut	11.2	7.9	6.6	6.1	10.2	6.3	5.6	4.7	27.9	20.1	14.8	19.9
Delaware	13.9	10.1	9.2	10.7	9.8	9.7	7.9	8.0	26.7	24.6	16.1	15.0
District of Columbia	25.0	20.7	12.0	10.6	17.8	(B)	(B)	(B)	26.7	24.6	16.1	15.0
Florida	14.6	9.6	7.0	7.3	11.8	6.7	5.4	5.5	22.8	16.8	12.6	13.5
Georgia	14.5	12.4	8.5	8.6	10.8	7.4	5.9	6.2	21.0	18.3	13.9	13.3
Hawaii	10.3	6.7	8.1	6.2	11.6	6.1	6.5	6.0	(B)	(B)	(B)	(B)
Idaho	10.7	8.7	7.5	6.2	10.7	8.6	7.5	6.3	(NA)	(B)	(B)	(B)
Illinois	14.8	10.7	8.5	7.7	11.7	7.9	6.6	6.0	26.3	22.4	17.1	15.5
Indiana	11.9	9.6	7.8	7.5	10.5	7.9	6.9	6.8	23.4	17.4	15.8	13.7
Iowa	11.8	8.1	6.5	5.6	11.5	7.9	6.0	5.5	27.2	21.9	21.1	(B)
Kansas	10.4	8.4	6.8	7.4	9.5	8.0	6.4	6.5	20.6	17.7	12.2	20.5
Kentucky	12.9	8.5	7.2	5.9	12.0	8.2	6.7	5.6	22.0	14.3	12.7	9.7
Louisiana	14.3	11.1	9.0	9.8	10.5	8.1	5.9	6.5	20.6	16.7	13.3	14.4
Maine	9.2	6.2	4.9	6.1	9.4	6.7	4.8	5.7	(B)	(B)	(B)	(B)
Maryland	14.0	9.5	7.6	8.1	11.6	6.8	4.8	5.5	20.4	17.1	13.2	13.7
Massachusetts	10.5	7.0	4.6	5.0	10.1	6.1	4.0	4.6	16.8	11.9	9.9	9.6
Michigan	12.8	10.7	8.2	8.0	10.6	7.4	6.0	6.1	24.2	21.6	18.2	17.0
Minnesota	10.0	7.3	5.3	5.3	9.6	6.7	4.8	4.8	20.0	23.7	14.6	9.6
Mississippi	17.0	12.1	10.7	10.5	11.1	7.4	6.8	7.0	23.7	16.2	15.3	14.9
Missouri	12.4	9.4	7.2	7.4	11.1	7.9	5.9	5.9	20.7	18.2	14.7	16.5
Montana	12.4	9.0	6.1	6.7	11.8	6.0	5.5	6.7	(NA)	(B)	(B)	(B)
Nebraska	11.5	8.3	7.3	6.8	10.7	6.9	6.4	6.4	25.2	18.9	20.3	(B)
Nevada	10.7	8.4	6.5	5.7	10.0	8.2	6.0	5.1	20.6	14.2	12.7	17.1
New Hampshire	9.9	7.1	5.7	3.8	9.9	6.0	5.5	3.8	22.5	(B)	(B)	(B)
New Jersey	12.5	9.0	6.3	6.5	10.3	6.4	5.0	5.1	21.9	18.4	13.6	14.2
New Mexico	11.5	9.0	6.6	6.4	11.3	7.6	6.3	6.3	23.1	(B)	(B)	(B)
New York	12.5	9.6	6.4	5.8	10.8	7.4	5.4	5.1	20.0	16.5	15.7	15.8
North Carolina	14.5	10.6	8.6	8.5	12.1	8.0	6.3	6.1	20.0	18.1	10.9	9.7
North Dakota	12.1	8.0	8.1	8.8	11.7	7.2	7.5	8.0	27.5	(B)	(B)	(B)
Ohio	12.8	9.8	7.6	7.7	11.2	7.8	6.3	6.2	23.0	19.5	15.4	16.4
Oklahoma	12.7	9.2	8.5	7.3	12.1	9.1	7.9	6.5	21.8	14.3	16.9	15.0
Oregon	12.2	8.3	5.6	5.4	12.2	7.0	5.5	5.5	15.9	(B)	(B)	(B)
Pennsylvania	13.2	9.6	7.1	7.2	11.9	7.4	5.8	6.1	23.1	20.5	15.7	14.4
Rhode Island	11.0	8.1	6.3	6.8	10.9	7.0	5.9	6.1	22.9	17.3	14.8	15.0
South Carolina	15.6	11.7	8.7	8.9	10.8	8.1	5.4	5.9	(NA)	(B)	(B)	(B)
South Dakota	10.9	10.1	5.5	7.4	9.0	8.0	4.3	6.1	19.3	17.9	18.0	16.2
Tennessee	13.5	10.3	9.1	8.7	11.9	7.3	6.8	6.7	18.8	14.7	11.4	12.0
Texas	12.2	8.1	5.7	5.9	11.2	6.7	5.1	5.2	27.3	(B)	(B)	(B)
Utah	10.4	7.5	5.2	4.8	10.5	6.0	5.1	4.9	(B)	(B)	(B)	(B)
Vermont	10.7	6.4	6.0	5.5	10.7	5.9	6.1	5.6	(B)	(B)	(B)	(B)
Virginia	13.6	10.2	6.9	7.6	11.9	7.4	5.4	5.4	16.4	20.6	9.4	12.9
Washington	11.8	7.8	5.2	5.8	11.5	7.3	4.9	5.7	21.5	(B)	(B)	(B)
West Virginia	11.8	9.9	7.6	7.2	11.4	8.1	7.4	7.2	21.5	(B)	(B)	(B)
Wisconsin	10.3	8.2	6.6	7.1	9.7	7.7	5.5	5.9	18.5	19.0	17.2	17.8
Wyoming	9.8	8.6	6.7	5.9	9.3	7.5	6.5	5.9	25.9	(B)	(B)	(B)

B Base figure too small to meet statistical standards for reliability.   NA Not available.   [1] Includes other races, not shown separately.
Source: U.S. National Center for Health Statistics, *Vital Statistics of the United States,* annual; and unpublished data.

No. 102. Deaths by Major Causes: 1960 to 2002

[Age-adjusted death rates per 100,000 population; see headnote, Table 95. See Appendix III]

Year	Heart disease	Cancer	Cerebro-vascular diseases	Chronic lower respira-tory diseases	Accidents	Diabetes mellitus	Influenza and pneumo-nia	Inten-tional self harm (suicide)	Chronic liver disease and cirrhosis	Assault (homicide)
1960	559.0	193.9	177.9	12.5	63.1	22.5	53.7	12.5	13.3	5.2
1961	545.3	193.4	173.1	12.6	60.6	22.1	43.4	12.2	13.3	5.2
1962	556.9	193.3	174.0	14.2	62.9	22.6	47.1	12.8	13.8	5.4
1963	563.4	194.7	173.9	16.5	64.0	23.1	55.6	13.0	14.0	5.4
1964	543.3	193.6	167.0	16.3	64.1	22.5	45.4	12.7	14.2	5.7
1965	542.5	195.6	166.4	18.3	65.8	22.9	46.8	13.0	14.9	6.1
1966	541.2	196.5	165.8	19.2	67.6	23.6	47.9	12.7	15.9	6.5
1967	524.7	197.3	159.3	19.2	66.2	23.4	42.2	12.5	16.3	7.5
1968	531.0	198.8	162.5	20.7	65.5	25.3	52.8	12.4	16.9	8.1
1969	516.8	198.5	155.4	20.9	64.9	25.1	47.9	12.7	17.1	8.3
1970	492.7	198.6	147.7	21.3	62.2	24.3	41.7	13.1	17.8	9.0
1971	492.9	199.3	147.6	21.8	60.3	23.9	38.4	13.1	17.8	9.8
1972	490.2	200.3	147.3	22.8	60.2	23.7	41.3	13.3	18.0	10.0
1973	482.0	200.0	145.2	23.6	59.3	23.0	41.2	13.1	18.1	10.2
1974	458.8	201.5	136.8	23.2	52.7	22.1	35.5	13.2	17.9	10.5
1975	431.2	200.1	123.5	23.7	50.8	20.3	34.9	13.6	16.7	10.2
1976	426.9	202.5	117.4	24.9	48.7	19.5	38.8	13.2	16.4	9.2
1977	413.7	203.5	110.4	24.7	48.8	18.2	31.0	13.7	15.8	9.2
1978	409.9	204.9	103.7	26.3	48.9	18.3	34.5	12.9	15.2	9.2
1979	401.6	204.0	97.1	25.5	46.5	17.5	26.1	12.6	14.8	9.9
1980	412.1	207.9	96.4	28.3	46.4	18.1	31.4	12.2	15.1	10.5
1981	397.0	206.4	89.5	29.0	43.4	17.6	30.0	12.3	14.2	10.1
1982	389.0	208.3	84.2	29.1	40.1	17.2	26.5	12.5	13.2	9.4
1983	388.9	209.1	81.2	31.6	39.1	17.6	29.8	12.4	12.8	8.4
1984	378.8	210.8	78.7	32.4	38.8	17.2	30.6	12.6	12.7	8.1
1985	375.0	211.3	76.6	34.5	38.5	17.4	34.5	12.5	12.3	8.0
1986	365.1	211.5	73.1	34.8	38.6	17.2	34.8	13.0	11.8	8.6
1987	355.9	211.7	71.6	35.0	38.2	17.4	33.8	12.8	11.7	8.3
1988	352.5	212.5	70.6	36.5	38.9	18.0	37.3	12.5	11.6	8.5
1989	332.0	214.2	66.9	36.6	37.7	20.5	35.9	12.3	11.6	8.8
1990	321.8	216.0	65.5	37.2	36.3	20.7	36.8	12.5	11.1	9.5
1991	313.8	215.8	63.2	38.0	34.9	20.7	34.9	12.3	10.7	10.1
1992	306.1	214.3	62.0	37.9	33.4	20.8	33.1	12.1	10.5	9.6
1993	309.9	214.6	63.1	40.9	34.5	22.0	35.2	12.2	10.3	9.8
1994	299.7	213.1	63.1	40.6	34.6	22.7	33.9	12.1	10.2	9.4
1995	296.3	211.7	63.9	40.5	34.9	23.4	33.8	12.0	10.0	8.6
1996	288.3	208.7	63.2	41.0	34.9	24.0	33.2	11.7	9.8	7.8
1997	280.4	205.7	61.8	41.5	34.8	24.0	33.6	11.4	9.6	7.3
1998	272.4	202.4	59.6	42.0	35.0	24.2	34.6	11.3	9.5	6.7
1999	267.8	202.7	61.8	45.8	35.9	25.2	23.6	10.7	9.7	6.2
2000	257.6	199.6	60.9	44.2	34.9	25.0	23.7	10.4	9.5	5.9
2001	247.8	196.0	57.9	43.7	35.7	25.3	22.0	10.7	9.5	7.1
2002 [1]	240.4	194.0	56.3	43.7	35.3	25.4	22.7	10.6	9.3	5.9

[1] Preliminary data.

Source: U.S. National Center for Health Statistics, *Vital Statistics of the United States,* annual.

U.S. Census Bureau, Statistical Abstract of the United States: 2004-2005

No. 103. Deaths and Death Rates by Selected Causes: 2001 and 2002

[Rates per 100,000 population. Figures are weighted data rounded to the nearest individual, so categories may not add to total or subtotal. Excludes deaths of nonresidents of the United States, except as noted. Deaths classified according to tenth revision of *International Classification of Diseases;* See also Appendix III]

Cause of death	2001 Number	2001 Rate	2001 Age-adjusted rate [1]	2002 [2] Number	2002 [2] Rate	2002 [2] Age-adjusted rate [1]
All causes..........................	2,416,425	848.5	854.5	2,447,862	848.9	846.8
Major cardiovascular diseases	922,334	323.9	326.5	917,839	318.3	317.1
Diseases of heart	700,142	245.8	247.8	695,754	241.3	240.4
Acute rheumatic fever and chronic rheumatic heart disease	3,489	1.2	1.2	3,743	1.3	1.3
Hypertensive heart disease	24,689	8.7	8.7	25,938	9.0	8.9
Hypertensive heart and renal disease	2,826	1.0	1.0	2,888	1.0	1.0
Ischemic heart disease.................	502,189	176.3	177.8	493,542	171.1	170.6
Other heart diseases	166,949	58.6	59.1	169,643	58.8	58.6
Essential (primary) hypertension and hypertensive renal disease......................	19,250	6.8	6.8	20,241	7.0	7.0
Cerebrovascular diseases	163,538	57.4	57.9	163,010	56.5	56.3
Atherosclerosis......................	14,086	4.9	5.0	13,942	4.8	4.8
Other disorders of circulatory system	4,665	1.6	1.6	4,679	1.6	1.6
Malignant neoplasms	553,768	194.4	196.0	558,847	193.8	194.0
Malignant neoplasms of lip, oral cavity, and pharynx .	7,702	2.7	2.7	7,732	2.7	2.7
Malignant neoplasms of colon, rectum and anus..	56,887	20.0	20.1	56,866	19.7	19.7
Malignant neoplasms of trachea, bronchus and lung .	156,058	54.8	55.3	158,258	54.9	55.1
Malignant neoplasm of breast	41,809	14.7	14.8	41,989	14.6	14.5
Malignant neoplasms of kidney and renal pelvis	12,078	4.2	4.3	12,184	4.2	4.2
Malignant neoplasms of lymphoid, hematopoietic and related tissue	56,341	19.8	20.0	56,377	19.6	19.6
Leukemia	21,451	7.5	7.6	21,575	7.5	7.5
Accidents (unintentional injuries)...............	101,537	35.7	35.7	102,303	35.5	35.3
Motor vehicle accidents	43,788	15.4	15.3	44,572	15.5	15.4
Accidental discharge of firearms	802	0.3	0.3	813	0.3	0.3
Accidental drowning and submersion	3,281	1.2	1.1	3,399	1.2	1.2
Accidental exposure to smoke, fire and flames.....	3,309	1.2	1.2	3,024	1.0	1.1
Accidental poisoning and exposure to noxious substances	14,078	4.9	4.9	14,670	5.1	5.1
Other acute lower respiratory infections	347	0.1	0.1	361	0.1	0.1
Chronic lower respiratory diseases	123,013	43.2	43.7	125,500	43.5	43.7
Bronchitis, chronic and unspecified	959	0.3	0.3	961	0.3	0.3
Emphysema......................	16,242	5.7	5.8	15,568	5.4	5.4
Asthma........................	4,269	1.5	1.5	4,157	1.4	1.5
Other chronic lower respiratory diseases........	101,543	35.7	36.1	104,814	36.3	36.5
Influenza and pneumonia.................	62,034	21.8	22.0	65,984	22.9	22.7
Influenza.......................	257	0.1	0.1	753	0.3	0.2
Pneumonia......................	61,777	21.7	21.9	65,231	22.6	22.5
Tuberculosis	764	0.3	0.3	802	0.3	0.3
Septicemia........................	32,238	11.3	11.4	33,881	11.7	11.7
Human immunodeficiency virus (HIV) disease	14,175	5.0	5.0	13,991	4.9	4.9
Anemias........................	4,627	1.6	1.6	4,601	1.6	1.6
Diabetes mellitus	71,372	25.1	25.3	73,119	25.4	25.4
Nutritional deficiencies.................	3,704	1.3	1.3	3,785	1.3	1.3
Meningitis........................	727	0.3	0.3	694	0.2	0.2
Parkinsons disease	16,544	5.8	5.9	16,961	5.9	5.9
Alzheimers disease....................	53,852	18.9	19.1	58,785	20.4	20.2
Chronic liver disease and cirrhosis	27,035	9.5	9.5	27,045	9.4	9.3
Alcoholic liver disease	12,207	4.3	4.3	11,965	4.1	4.1
Other chronic liver disease and cirrhosis	14,828	5.2	5.2	15,079	5.2	5.2
Nephritis, nephrotic syndrome and nephrosis........	39,480	13.9	14.0	41,018	14.2	14.2
Renal failure	38,784	13.6	13.7	40,272	14.0	13.9
Other disorders of kidney	29	(Z)	(Z)	34	(Z)	(Z)
Infections of kidney....................	748	0.3	0.3	792	0.3	0.3
Pregnancy, childbirth and the puerperium	416	0.1	0.1	358	0.1	0.1
Congenital malformations, deformations and chromosomal abnormalities	10,442	3.7	3.6	10,635	3.7	3.7
All other diseases (Residual)	186,406	65.5	65.9	193,974	67.3	66.9
Intentional self-harm (suicide)...............	30,622	10.8	10.7	30,646	10.6	10.6
Assault (homicide)	20,308	7.1	7.1	17,045	5.9	5.9
Legal intervention....................	396	0.1	0.1	365	0.1	0.1
Events of undetermined intent	4,198	1.5	1.5	4,423	1.5	1.5
Operations of war and their sequelae..........	17	(B)	(B)	21	(Z)	(Z)
Complications of medical and surgical care........	3,021	1.1	1.1	2,820	1.0	1.0
Injury by firearms [3]	29,573	10.4	10.3	29,737	10.3	10.3
Drug-induced deaths [3]	21,683	7.6	7.6	22,296	7.7	7.7
Alcohol-induced deaths [3].................	19,817	7.0	6.9	19,344	6.7	6.6
Injury at work......................	8,303	3.7	3.7	5,202	2.3	2.3

B Base figure too small to meet statistical standards for reliability; see text, this section.   Z Less than 0.05.   [1] See headnote, Table 95.   [2] Preliminary data.   [3] Included in selected categories.

Source: U.S. National Center for Health Statistics , *Vital Statistics of the United States,*annual; National Vital Statistics Reports (NVSR) (formerly *Monthly Statitics Report); and* unpublished data.

No. 104. Deaths by Selected Causes: 2000 and 2001

[Deaths in thousands (2,403 represents 2,403,000). Deaths are classified according to the Tenth Revision of the International Classification of Diseases. See Appendix III]

Cause of Death	2000												2001											
	All ages	Under 1 year	1-4 years	5-14 years	15-24 years	25-34 years	35-44 years	45-54 years	55-64 years	65-74 years	75-84 years	85 years over	All ages	Under 1 year	1-4 years	5-14 years	15-24 years	25-34 years	35-44 years	45-54 years	55-64 years	65-74 years	75-84 years	85 years over
All causes	2,403	28	5	7	31	40	90	160	241	441	700	658	2,416	28	5	7	32	42	92	168	244	431	702	666
Tuberculosis	1	-	-	-	-	-	-	-	-	-	-	-	1	-	-	-	-	-	-	-	-	-	1	-
Viral hepatitis	5	-	-	-	-	-	1	2	1	1	-	-	6	-	-	-	-	-	1	2	1	1	1	-
Human immunodeficiency virus (HIV) disease	14	-	-	-	-	2	6	4	1	-	-	-	14	-	-	-	-	2	6	4	1	-	-	-
Malignant neoplasms	553	-	-	1	2	4	17	48	89	150	165	77	554	-	-	1	2	4	17	50	90	147	165	78
Malignant neoplasms of colon, rectum and anus	57	-	-	-	-	-	1	4	8	14	18	11	57	-	-	-	-	-	1	5	8	14	18	11
Malignant neoplasms of trachea, bronchus and lung	156	-	-	-	-	-	3	12	30	52	46	13	156	-	-	-	-	-	3	12	30	51	47	13
Malignant neoplasm of breast	42	-	-	-	-	-	3	6	8	9	10	6	42	-	-	-	-	-	3	7	8	9	10	6
Leukemia	21	-	-	-	-	-	1	1	2	5	7	4	21	-	-	-	-	-	1	1	3	5	7	4
Diabetes mellitus	69	-	-	-	-	1	2	5	9	17	22	14	71	-	-	-	-	1	2	5	10	17	23	14
Nutritional deficiencies	4	-	-	-	-	-	-	-	-	-	1	2	4	-	-	-	-	-	-	-	-	1	1	2
Alzheimers disease	50	-	-	-	-	-	-	-	-	3	17	28	54	-	-	-	-	-	-	-	1	3	19	31
Major cardiovascular diseases	937	1	-	-	1	4	17	44	77	156	296	340	922	1	-	-	1	4	17	44	76	148	292	338
Diseases of heart	711	1	-	-	1	3	13	35	63	122	220	251	700	1	-	-	1	3	13	36	62	116	217	249
Hypertensive heart disease	24	-	-	-	-	-	-	2	3	4	6	8	25	-	-	-	-	-	-	2	3	4	6	8
Ischemic heart diseases	515	-	-	-	-	1	8	25	48	93	164	177	502	-	-	-	-	1	8	25	47	87	160	174
Acute myocardial infarction	193	-	-	-	-	1	3	11	21	38	62	57	185	-	-	-	-	1	3	11	20	35	59	56
Influenza and pneumonia	65	-	-	-	-	-	1	2	3	7	20	32	62	-	-	-	-	-	1	2	3	7	20	30
Chronic lower respiratory diseases	122	-	-	-	-	-	1	3	11	31	48	28	123	-	-	-	-	-	1	3	11	31	48	28
Chronic liver disease and cirrhosis	27	-	-	-	-	-	3	7	6	5	4	1	27	-	-	-	-	-	3	7	6	5	4	1
Accidents (unintentional injuries)	98	1	2	3	14	12	15	12	8	8	12	12	102	1	2	3	14	12	16	13	8	8	13	12
Transport accidents	47	-	1	2	11	7	8	6	4	3	3	1	47	-	1	2	11	7	8	6	4	3	4	1
Motor vehicle accidents	43	(X)	1	2	11	7	7	5	3	3	2	1	44	(X)	1	2	11	7	7	6	3	3	3	1
Intentional self-harm (suicide)	29	-	-	-	4	5	7	5	3	2	3	1	31	-	-	-	4	5	7	6	4	3	4	1
Assault (homicide)	17	-	1	-	5	4	3	2	1	1	-	-	20	-	1	-	5	5	4	2	1	1	-	-
Complications of medical and surgical care	3	-	-	-	-	-	-	-	-	-	1	1	3	-	-	-	-	-	-	-	-	-	1	1

- Represents or rounds to zero. X Not applicable.

Source: U.S. National Center for Health Statistics, *Vital Statistics of the United States*, annual; *National Vital Statistics Reports (NVSR)* (formerly *Monthly Vital Statistics Report*).

Vital Statistics 81

No. 105. Deaths and Death Rates by Leading Causes of Death and Age: 2001

[Data are based on the Tenth revision of the ICD. Rates per 100,000 population in specified group. Numbers are based on weighted data rounded to the nearest individual, so categories may not add to totals. See Appendix III]

Age	Number	Rate	Age	Number	Rate
ALL AGES [1]			Intentional self-harm (suicide)	6,635	14.7
			Human immunodeficiency virus		
All causes.	2,416,425	848.5	(HIV) disease	5,867	13.0
Diseases of heart	700,142	245.8			
Malignant neoplasms.	553,768	194.4	**45-54 YEARS**		
Cerebrovascular diseases	163,538	57.4			
Chronic lower respiratory diseases. . .	123,013	43.2	All causes.	168,065	428.9
			Malignant neoplasms.	49,562	126.5
1-4 YEARS			Diseases of heart	36,399	92.9
			Accidents	13,344	34.1
All causes.	5,108	33.3	Chronic liver disease and cirrhosis. . .	7,259	18.5
Accidents (unintentional injuries)	1,714	11.2	Intentional self-harm (suicide)	5,942	15.2
Congenital malformations.	557	3.6			
Malignant neoplasms.	420	2.7	**55-64 YEARS**		
Assault (homicide)	415	2.7			
Diseases of heart	225	1.5	All causes.	244,139	964.6
			Malignant neoplasms.	90,223	356.5
5-14 YEARS			Diseases of heart	62,486	246.9
			Chronic lower respiratory diseases. . .	11,166	44.1
All causes.	7,094	17.3	Cerebrovascular diseases	9,608	38.0
Accidents (unintentional injuries)	2,836	6.9	Diabetes mellitus	9,570	37.8
Malignant neoplasms.	1,008	2.5			
Congenital malformations	375	0.9	**65-74 YEARS**		
Assault (homicide)	326	0.8			
Diseases of heart	272	0.7	All causes.	430,960	2,353.3
Intentional self-harm (suicide)	189	0.7	Malignant neoplasms.	147,018	802.8
			Diseases of heart	116,299	635.1
15-24 YEARS			Chronic lower respiratory diseases. . .	30,751	167.9
			Cerebrovascular diseases	22,598	123.4
All causes.	32,252	17.3	Diabetes mellitus	16,731	91.4
Accidents (unintentional injuries)	14,411	36.1			
Assault (homicide)	5,297	13.3	**75-84 YEARS**		
Intentional self-harm (suicide)	3,971	9.9			
Malignant neoplasms.	1,704	4.3	All causes.	701,929	5,582.4
Diseases of heart	999	2.5	Diseases of heart	216,992	1,725.7
			Malignant neoplasms.	165,445	1,315.8
25-34 YEARS			Cerebrovascular diseases	55,822	443.9
			Chronic lower respiratory diseases. . .	47,762	379.8
All causes.	41,683	105.2	Diabetes mellitus	22,805	181.4
Accidents	11,839	29.9			
Assault (homicide)	5,204	13.1	**85 YEARS AND**		
Intentional self-harm (suicide)	5,070	12.2	**OVER**		
Malignant neoplasms.	3,994	10.1			
Diseases of heart	3,160	8.0	All causes.	665,531	15,112.8
			Diseases of heart	249,439	5,664.2
35-44 YEARS			Malignant neoplasms.	77,751	1,765.6
			Cerebrovascular diseases	66,066	1,500.2
All causes.	91,674	203.6	Alzheimers disease	31,281	710.3
Malignant neoplasms.	16,569	36.8	Influenza and pneumonia	30,191	685.6
Accidents	15,945	35.4			
Diseases of heart	13,326	29.6			

[1] Includes deaths under 1 year of age.

Source: U.S. National Center for Health Statistics, Vital Statistics of the United States, annual; and National Vital Statistics Reports (NVSR), Vol. 52, No. 9. See also <http://www.cdc.gov/nchs/data/nvsr/nvsr52_09.pdf\> (released 7 November 2003).

No. 106. Death Rates for Major Causes of Death—States and Outlying Areas: 2001

[Deaths per 100,000 resident population enumerated as of July 1. By place of residence. Excludes nonresidents of the United States. Causes of death classified according to tenth revisions of International Classification of Diseases. See Appendix III]

State and Outlying areas	Total	Heart disease	Cancer	Cerebro-vascular diseases	Acci-dents	Motor vehicle acci-dents	Chronic lower respira-tory dis-eases	Diabe-tes mellitus	HIV [1]	Inten-tional self-harm (suicide)	Assault (homi-cide)
United States .	**848.5**	**245.8**	**194.4**	**57.4**	**35.7**	**15.4**	**43.2**	**25.1**	**5.0**	**10.8**	**7.1**
AL.	1,014.0	295.5	219.3	67.1	49.5	23.2	49.3	30.1	4.8	11.5	9.5
AK.	469.4	95.2	108.7	24.9	54.4	16.3	23.2	12.6	(B)	16.1	6.0
AZ.	773.7	199.5	172.3	46.7	46.6	19.2	47.1	19.9	2.9	14.5	9.3
AR.	1,030.1	306.6	226.1	83.7	47.4	24.5	50.8	28.1	2.4	14.2	6.8
CA.	676.4	197.2	155.8	52.3	23.5	11.4	37.5	18.5	4.3	8.2	6.4
CO	638.5	142.0	138.7	41.2	38.8	17.1	41.4	15.1	2.1	16.3	3.8
CT.	868.4	249.9	206.5	58.3	30.7	9.2	43.3	22.1	5.6	8.2	5.0
DE.	892.8	255.2	224.2	48.1	36.4	15.3	38.4	27.4	8.4	13.6	4.1
DC	1,037.1	306.9	231.3	46.2	38.9	9.4	26.1	36.4	38.9	7.0	34.3
FL.	1,021.6	309.2	238.7	63.6	42.6	18.9	54.7	28.3	10.2	14.1	5.9
GA	767.2	207.9	164.4	51.3	40.4	19.4	36.8	17.5	8.6	11.1	8.1
HI	684.1	188.3	165.0	62.4	30.3	10.4	22.8	14.1	2.1	11.1	2.8
ID	738.5	188.5	158.5	59.1	43.0	19.4	44.0	24.1	(B)	15.9	3.1
IL	842.1	247.5	197.9	57.7	32.6	12.7	38.1	24.7	4.1	9.1	8.7
IN	900.9	256.0	209.4	63.3	35.7	15.8	51.2	27.4	1.9	11.7	7.1
IA	947.9	281.4	218.4	75.6	35.8	15.2	52.9	24.2	(B)	10.4	2.1
KS.	912.1	248.5	201.6	68.4	42.8	19.9	53.4	26.7	1.4	10.8	5.3
KY.	979.7	290.2	230.0	62.8	48.9	21.2	55.7	27.0	2.2	12.2	5.4
LA.	934.1	256.7	212.9	59.0	45.4	22.1	39.4	38.8	9.0	11.0	12.1
ME	967.0	254.7	237.1	64.0	38.1	15.6	62.3	31.0	(B)	12.5	1.6
MD	813.9	228.6	191.6	53.5	24.9	13.1	35.4	27.1	10.6	8.4	10.3
MA	886.6	236.6	214.8	55.2	23.5	8.8	43.9	22.2	3.9	6.7	3.8
MI	863.7	268.8	196.8	57.0	32.9	14.3	41.5	26.5	2.5	10.5	6.9
MN	757.0	175.7	179.9	54.7	36.1	12.6	38.3	24.3	1.1	9.6	2.5
MS	988.2	316.5	208.3	67.7	54.9	28.8	46.6	23.1	7.1	11.5	11.4
MO	975.3	295.1	219.3	67.3	43.5	19.6	51.1	27.2	2.6	12.9	7.8
MT	912.9	217.6	216.0	63.8	51.7	23.4	64.4	25.3	(B)	19.3	3.5
NE.	882.2	241.3	197.0	65.7	36.8	15.8	51.3	23.3	1.9	10.9	2.6
NV.	776.3	209.4	181.9	43.5	35.2	15.8	54.2	15.3	3.6	18.4	8.3
NH	779.4	225.1	190.4	50.3	29.7	10.8	48.9	23.1	(B)	13.3	2.2
NJ.	877.8	266.8	213.4	47.1	28.3	8.9	34.2	30.0	9.2	6.9	12.3
NM	771.7	187.0	158.4	45.0	55.7	23.5	42.3	29.4	2.1	19.8	7.1
NY.	834.4	296.8	193.7	40.4	26.1	8.8	36.2	20.1	10.9	6.6	14.8
NC	864.4	229.0	195.8	65.8	41.9	20.1	42.8	26.6	5.7	12.1	7.3
ND	950.1	267.1	218.5	79.6	37.4	18.1	48.4	30.8	(B)	12.4	(B)
OH	948.5	284.9	217.8	60.5	33.9	12.9	51.6	32.9	1.8	10.7	4.6
OK	999.6	312.4	213.6	68.7	49.0	21.0	55.4	30.7	2.9	14.8	6.1
OR	868.2	203.7	203.2	74.5	37.8	14.6	49.7	29.1	1.8	14.5	2.9
PA.	1,054.4	320.6	243.1	70.1	37.0	12.8	47.5	31.1	4.0	10.4	5.5
RI	945.7	290.3	226.3	57.9	27.7	9.2	48.2	25.0	2.8	8.3	3.5
SC.	901.3	233.2	203.6	69.7	48.3	24.6	42.6	26.8	7.6	11.5	8.6
SD.	912.9	261.8	209.7	64.6	50.4	24.3	47.7	28.0	(B)	13.8	(B)
TN.	959.2	272.9	212.7	70.2	47.1	22.7	51.2	30.4	4.8	12.4	7.9
TX.	714.9	202.1	156.7	49.7	37.1	18.5	36.2	25.5	4.9	10.4	6.6
UT.	555.7	127.1	101.5	38.2	28.2	13.1	23.0	22.3	(B)	14.1	3.4
VT.	848.5	233.1	203.8	52.7	37.5	14.4	49.8	25.3	(B)	11.7	(B)
VA.	782.0	207.2	185.4	57.4	33.8	13.4	38.1	22.4	3.8	11.1	7.1
WA	744.9	188.2	180.2	62.8	34.6	12.4	43.9	23.4	1.9	11.9	3.3
WV	1,164.2	351.2	260.1	70.6	46.3	20.7	70.7	44.5	1.6	15.9	3.8
WI	862.5	240.9	199.4	67.7	38.8	15.2	43.9	24.7	1.4	10.8	4.0
WY	816.0	199.5	186.9	52.7	55.1	28.4	54.7	24.3	(B)	16.8	(B)
PR	757.7	167.0	122.8	44.3	33.6	13.0	31.9	64.5	18.6	7.5	19.8
VI	556.3	158.2	104.8	43.2	36.8	(B)	28.5	28.5	(B)	(B)	25.7
GU	418.7	128.8	61.3	39.2	28.4	12.6	13.9	(B)	(B)	14.5	(B)
AS	415.4	88.7	59.1	(B)	(B)	(B)	(B)	36.5	(B)	(B)	(B)
MP	205.9	32.0	37.6	(B)	(B)	(B)	(B)	(B)	(B)	(B)	(B)

B Figure does not meet standards of reliability or precision. [1] Human immunodeficiency virus.

Source: U.S. National Center for Health Statistics, *National Vital Statistics Report (NVSR)*.

Vital Statistics 83

No. 107. Death Rates from Heart Disease by Sex and Age: 1990 to 2000

[Rates per 100,000 population. For explanation of age-adjustment, see headnote, Table 95. See Appendix III]

Characteristic	Male						Female					
	1990	1995	1997	1998	1999 [1]	2000	1990	1995	1997	1998	1999 [1]	2000
All ages, age adjusted	412.4	372.7	349.6	336.6	328.1	315.0	257.0	239.7	228.1	223.1	220.9	213.0
All ages, crude ..	297.6	282.7	272.2	268.0	263.8	256.1	281.8	278.8	271.1	268.3	268.0	260.2
Under 1 year ...	21.9	17.5	18.0	16.2	13.8	13.2	18.3	16.7	14.7	16.1	13.6	12.4
1-4 years......	1.9	1.7	1.5	1.5	1.3	1.4	1.9	1.5	1.2	1.3	1.1	1.0
5-14 years.....	0.9	0.8	0.9	1.0	0.8	0.8	0.8	0.7	0.7	0.7	0.6	0.6
15-24 years	3.1	3.6	3.6	3.5	3.4	3.2	1.8	2.2	2.4	2.1	2.2	2.1
25-34 years	10.3	11.4	10.8	10.8	10.6	10.3	5.0	5.6	5.8	5.8	5.6	5.5
35-44 years	48.1	47.2	43.7	44.0	43.3	41.6	15.1	17.1	16.5	17.3	17.6	17.2
45-54 years	183.0	168.6	157.7	152.2	145.7	142.7	61.0	56.0	54.3	52.8	51.9	50.3
55-64 years	537.3	465.4	434.6	411.1	391.6	378.6	215.7	193.9	182.1	173.9	167.5	160.4
65-74 years	1,250.0	1,102.3	1,031.1	997.3	961.6	909.2	616.8	557.8	529.4	522.6	503.2	479.9
75-84 years	2,968.2	2,615.0	2,443.6	2,377.2	2,308.9	2,210.1	1,893.8	1,715.2	1,616.6	1,579.5	1,562.5	1,501.5
85 years and over	7,418.4	7,039.6	6,658.5	6,330.6	6,313.3	6,100.8	6,478.1	6,267.8	6,013.7	5,876.6	5,913.8	5,740.1

[1] Starting with 1999 data, cause of death is coded according to ICD-10. For explanation, see text, this section.

Source: U.S. National Center for Health Statistics , *Vital Statistics of the United States*, annual; *National Vital Statistics Reports (NVSR) (formerly Monthly Statistics Report);* and unpublished data. <http://www.cdc.gov/nchs/data/nvsr/nvsr50/nvsr5015.pdf> (released 15 September 2002).

No. 108. Death Rates from Cerebrovascular Diseases by Race, Sex, and Age: 1950 to 2000

[Rates per 100,000 population. For explanation of age-adjustment, see headnote, Table 95. See Appendix III]

Characteristic	1950 [1]	1960 [1]	1970	1980	1985	1990	1995	1997	1998	1999 [2]	2000
All ages, age adjusted	180.7	177.9	147.7	96.4	76.6	65.5	63.9	61.8	59.6	61.8	60.9
Under 1 year	5.1	4.1	5.0	4.4	3.7	3.8	5.8	7.0	7.8	2.7	3.2
1-4 years.............	0.9	0.8	1.0	0.5	0.3	0.3	0.4	0.4	0.4	0.3	0.3
5-14 years............	0.5	0.7	0.7	0.3	0.2	0.2	0.2	0.2	0.2	0.2	0.2
15-24 years...........	1.6	1.8	1.6	1.0	0.8	0.6	0.5	0.5	0.5	0.5	0.5
25-34 years...........	4.2	4.7	4.5	2.6	2.2	2.2	1.8	1.7	1.7	1.5	1.6
35-44 years...........	18.7	14.7	15.6	8.5	7.2	6.5	6.5	6.3	6.0	5.7	5.8
45-54 years...........	70.4	49.2	41.6	25.2	21.3	18.7	17.6	16.9	16.5	15.5	16.2
55-64 years...........	194.2	147.3	115.8	65.2	54.8	48.0	46.1	44.4	42.6	41.3	41.5
65-74 years...........	554.7	469.2	384.1	219.5	172.8	144.4	137.2	134.8	130.0	132.2	130.2
75-84 years...........	1,499.6	1,491.3	1,254.2	788.6	601.5	499.3	481.4	462.0	455.4	472.8	463.1
85 years and over......	2,990.1	3,680.5	3,014.3	2,288.9	1,865.1	1,633.9	1,636.5	1,584.6	1,500.0	1,606.7	1,568.4
Male, all ages, age adjusted	186.4	186.1	157.4	102.4	80.2	68.7	66.3	63.9	60.1	62.4	61.1
Under 1 year	6.4	5.0	5.8	5.0	4.6	4.4	6.3	7.6	9.0	3.3	3.8
1-4 years.............	1.1	0.9	1.2	0.4	0.4	0.3	0.4	0.5	0.3	0.3	0.3
5-14 years............	0.5	0.7	0.8	0.3	0.2	0.2	0.2	0.2	0.2	0.2	0.2
15-24 years...........	1.8	1.9	1.8	1.1	0.7	0.7	0.5	0.6	0.6	0.5	0.5
25-34 years...........	4.2	4.5	4.4	2.6	2.2	2.1	1.9	1.7	1.7	1.6	1.7
35-44 years...........	17.5	14.6	15.7	8.7	7.4	6.8	7.1	6.5	6.2	5.6	5.8
45-54 years...........	67.9	52.2	44.4	27.3	23.2	20.5	19.8	19.2	18.5	17.1	17.8
55-64 years...........	205.2	163.8	138.7	74.7	63.5	54.4	53.4	51.4	49.5	47.6	48.1
65-74 years...........	589.6	530.7	449.5	259.2	201.4	166.8	155.9	153.1	145.7	149.0	146.8
75-84 years...........	1,543.6	1,555.9	1,361.6	868.3	661.2	552.7	517.1	488.7	474.7	494.5	482.5
85 years and over.......	3,048.6	3,643.1	2,895.2	2,199.2	1,730.1	1,533.2	1,537.7	1,500.7	1,347.2	1,455.5	1,408.3
Female, all ages, age adjusted	175.8	170.7	140.0	91.9	73.5	62.7	61.5	59.7	58.3	60.5	59.7
Under 1 year	3.7	3.2	4.0	3.8	2.7	3.1	5.2	6.3	6.6	2.0	2.7
1-4 years.............	0.7	0.7	0.7	0.5	0.3	0.3	0.3	0.3	0.4	0.3	0.4
5-14 years............	0.4	0.6	0.6	0.3	0.3	0.2	0.2	0.2	0.2	0.2	0.2
15-24 years...........	1.5	1.6	1.4	0.8	0.8	0.6	0.4	0.5	0.4	0.5	0.5
25-34 years...........	4.3	4.9	4.7	2.6	2.1	2.2	1.7	1.7	1.8	1.5	1.6
35-44 years...........	19.9	14.8	15.6	8.4	6.9	6.1	6.0	6.2	5.7	5.6	5.8
45-54 years...........	72.9	46.3	39.0	23.3	19.4	17.0	15.5	14.8	14.6	14.0	14.6
55-64 years...........	183.1	131.8	95.3	56.9	47.2	42.2	39.4	37.9	36.3	35.5	35.6
65-74 years...........	522.1	415.7	333.3	189.0	150.7	126.9	122.2	120.1	117.2	118.5	116.5
75-84 years...........	1,462.2	1,441.1	1,183.1	741.6	566.3	467.4	458.7	444.4	442.6	458.2	450.0
85 years and over.......	2,949.4	3,704.4	3,081.0	2,328.2	1,918.9	1,672.7	1,675.0	1,618.4	1,563.3	1,670.6	1,637.4
White male, age adjusted..	182.1	181.6	153.7	99.0	77.4	65.7	63.2	61.5	57.6	60.0	58.6
Black male, age adjusted..	228.8	238.5	206.4	142.1	112.7	102.5	96.7	88.5	86.3	87.4	87.1
White female, age adjusted	169.7	165.0	135.5	89.2	70.9	60.5	59.5	57.9	56.6	58.7	57.8
Black female, age adjusted.	238.4	232.5	189.3	119.8	99.4	84.0	81.0	76.1	75.3	78.1	78.1

[1] Includes deaths of persons who were not residents of the 50 States and the District of Columbia. [2] Starting with 1999 data, cause of death is coded according to ICD-10. For explanation, see text, this section.

Source: U.S. National Center for Health Statistics. *Vital Statistics of the United States,* annual; National Vital Statistics Reports (NVSR); and unpublished data.

No. 109. Death Rates from Malignant Neoplasms, by Race, Sex and Age: 1950 to 2000

[Rates per 100,000 population. For explanation of age-adjustment, see headnote, Table 95. See Appendix III]

Characteristic	1950 [1]	1960 [1]	1970	1980	1985	1990	1995	1997	1998	1999 [2]	2000
Total, age adjusted . .	**193.9**	**193.9**	**198.6**	**207.9**	**211.3**	**216.0**	**211.7**	**205.7**	**202.4**	**202.7**	**199.6**
Under 1 year	8.7	7.2	4.7	3.2	3.1	2.3	1.8	2.4	2.1	1.8	2.4
1-4 years	11.7	10.9	7.5	4.5	3.8	3.5	3.1	2.9	2.4	2.8	2.8
5-14 years	6.7	6.8	6.0	4.3	3.5	3.1	2.7	2.7	2.6	2.6	2.6
15-24 years	8.6	8.3	8.3	6.3	5.4	4.9	4.6	4.5	4.6	4.6	4.5
25-34 years	20.0	19.5	16.5	13.7	13.2	12.6	11.9	11.6	11.3	10.6	10.5
35-44 years	62.7	59.7	59.5	48.6	45.9	43.3	40.3	38.9	38.2	37.3	36.8
45-54 years	175.1	177.0	182.5	180.0	170.1	158.9	142.2	135.1	132.3	130.4	129.3
55-64 years	390.7	396.8	423.0	436.1	454.6	449.6	416.0	395.7	383.8	380.8	371.3
65-74 years	698.8	713.9	754.2	817.9	845.5	872.3	868.2	847.3	841.3	836.2	826.4
75-84 years	1,153.3	1,127.4	1,169.2	1,232.3	1,271.8	1,348.5	1,364.8	1,335.2	1,326.3	1,340.0	1,340.8
85 years and over	1,451.0	1,450.0	1,320.7	1,594.6	1,615.4	1,752.9	1,823.8	1,805.0	1,749.4	1,796.7	1,765.6
Male, all ages, age adjusted	208.1	225.1	247.6	271.2	274.4	280.4	268.8	258.0	252.4	251.6	247.4
Female, all ages, age adjusted	182.3	168.7	163.2	166.7	171.2	175.7	175.4	171.6	169.2	169.9	205.9
White male, all ages, age adjusted	210.0	224.7	244.8	265.1	267.1	272.2	261.8	251.9	246.9	246.5	242.5
Black male, all ages, age adjusted	178.9	227.6	291.9	353.4	373.9	397.9	372.8	354.7	343.1	340.5	333.2
White female, all ages, age adjusted	182.0	167.7	162.5	165.2	169.9	174.0	173.7	170.0	167.7	168.6	168.7
Black female, all ages, age adjusted	174.1	174.3	173.4	189.5	195.5	205.9	206.0	204.4	200.0	200.0	196.6
DEATH RATES FOR MALIGNANT NEOPLASM OF BREASTS FOR FEMALES											
All ages, age adjusted	31.9	31.7	32.1	31.9	33.0	33.3	30.8	28.6	27.9	27.0	27.1
All ages, crude	24.7	26.1	28.4	30.6	32.8	34.0	32.6	30.7	30.2	29.5	29.8
Under 25 years	(B)	(B)	(B)	(B)	(B)	(B)	(B)	(B)	(B)	(B)	(B)
25-34 years	3.8	3.8	3.9	3.3	3.0	2.9	2.7	2.6	2.6	2.3	2.5
35-44 years	20.8	20.2	20.4	17.9	17.5	17.8	15.0	14.0	13.4	12.1	12.5
45-54 years	46.9	51.4	52.6	48.1	47.1	45.4	41.4	37.8	35.8	33.5	33.4
55-64 years	69.9	70.8	77.6	80.5	84.2	78.6	69.8	64.4	62.2	59.9	59.7
65-74 years	95.0	90.0	93.8	101.1	107.8	111.7	103.3	94.1	93.3	89.9	89.4
75-84 years	139.8	129.9	127.4	126.4	136.2	146.3	142.0	132.2	131.4	131.3	131.2
85 years and over	195.5	191.9	157.1	169.3	178.5	196.8	203.7	198.5	194.7	202.6	206.4
DEATH RATES FOR MALIGNANT NEOPLASM OF TRACHEA BRONCHUS, AND LUNG											
All ages, age adjusted	15.0	24.1	37.1	49.9	54.6	59.3	58.9	58.1	57.6	56.0	56.5
All ages, crude	12.2	20.3	32.1	45.8	51.5	56.8	57.5	57.3	57.2	55.8	55.6
Under 25 years	0.1	-	0.1	-	-	-	-	-	-	-	-
25-34 years	0.8	1.0	0.9	0.6	0.6	0.7	0.7	0.6	0.6	0.5	0.5
35-44 years	4.5	6.8	11.0	9.2	7.8	6.8	6.0	6.2	6.1	6.1	6.1
45-54 years	20.4	29.6	43.4	54.1	50.9	46.8	38.0	34.6	33.3	31.9	32.1
55-64 years	48.7	75.3	109.1	138.2	153.8	160.6	142.9	134.3	131.4	125.5	124.0
65-74 years	59.7	108.1	164.5	233.3	261.2	288.4	297.1	295.7	296.7	284.6	287.6
75-84 years	55.8	91.5	163.2	240.5	282.0	333.3	361.4	368.5	367.7	364.4	372.2
85 years and over	42.3	65.6	101.7	176.0	195.2	242.5	284.0	297.6	289.9	295.5	298.1

- Represents zero or rounds to less than half the unit of measurement shown. B Base figure too small to meet statistical standards for reliability of a derived figure. [1] Includes deaths of persons who were not residents of the 50 States and the District of Columbia. [2] Starting with 1999 data, cause of death is coded according to ICD-10. For explanation, see text, this section.

Source: U.S. National Center for Health Statistics, *Vital Statistics of the United States*, annual; *National Vital Statistics Reports (NVSR)* ; and unpublished data.

No. 110. Death Rates From Suicide, by Sex and Race: 1950 to 2000

[Rates per 100,000 population. For explanation of age-adjustment, see headnote, Table 95. See Appendix III]

Characteristic	1950 [1]	1960 [1]	1970	1980	1985	1990	1995	1997	1998	1999 [3]	2000
All ages, age adjusted	13.2	12.5	13.1	12.2	12.5	12.5	12.0	11.4	11.3	10.7	10.4
All ages, crude	11.4	10.6	11.6	11.9	12.4	12.4	11.9	11.4	11.3	10.7	10.4
Under 1 year	(X)	(X)	(X)	(X)	(X)	(X)	(X)	(X)	(X)	(X)	(X)
1-4 years	(X)	(X)	(X)	(X)	(X)	(X)	(X)	(X)	(X)	(X)	(X)
5-14 years	0.2	0.3	0.3	0.4	0.8	0.8	0.9	0.8	0.8	0.6	0.7
15-24 years	4.5	5.2	8.8	12.3	12.8	13.2	13.3	11.4	11.1	10.1	10.2
25-44 years	11.6	12.2	15.4	15.6	15.0	15.2	15.3	14.8	14.6	13.6	13.4
25-34 years	9.1	10.0	14.1	16.0	15.3	15.2	15.4	14.3	13.8	12.7	12.0
35-44 years	14.3	14.2	16.9	15.4	14.6	15.3	15.2	15.3	15.4	14.3	14.5
45-64 years	23.5	22.0	20.6	15.9	16.3	15.3	14.1	14.2	14.1	13.2	13.5
45-54 years	20.9	20.7	20.0	15.9	15.7	14.8	14.6	14.7	14.8	13.9	14.4
55-64 years	26.8	23.7	21.4	15.9	16.8	16.0	13.3	13.5	13.1	12.2	12.1
65 years and over [2]	30.0	24.5	20.8	17.6	20.4	20.5	18.1	16.8	16.9	15.8	15.2
65-74 years	29.6	23.0	20.8	16.9	18.7	17.9	15.8	14.4	14.1	13.4	12.5
75-84 years	31.1	27.9	21.2	19.1	23.9	24.9	20.7	19.3	19.7	18.1	17.6
85 years and over	28.8	26.0	19.0	19.2	19.4	22.2	21.6	20.8	21.0	19.3	19.6
White male, all ages, age adjusted	22.3	21.1	20.8	20.9	22.4	22.8	21.9	20.6	20.6	19.4	19.1
Black male, all ages, age adjusted	7.5	8.4	10.0	11.4	11.8	12.8	12.5	11.4	10.6	10.4	10.0
White female, all ages, age adjusted	6.0	5.9	7.9	6.1	5.7	5.2	4.7	4.8	4.7	4.4	4.3
Black female, all ages, age adjusted	1.8	2.0	2.9	2.4	2.3	2.4	2.1	2.0	1.8	1.6	1.8

X Not applicable.   [1] Includes deaths of persons who were not residents of the 50 States and the District of Columbia.   [2] In 1950 rate is for the age group 75 years and over.   [3] Starting with 1999 data, cause of death is coded according to ICD 10.

Source: U.S. National Center for Health Statistics, *Vital Statistics of the United States*, annual; *National Vital Statistics Reports* (NVSR) (formerly Monthly Vital Statistics Report); and unpublished data.

No. 111. Death Rates from Human Immunodeficiency Virus (HIV) Disease by Race, Sex and Age: 1990 to 2000

[Rates per 100,000 population. For explanation of age-adjustment, see headnote, Table 95. See Appendix III]

Characteristic	1990	1993	1994	1995	1996	1997	1998	1999 [1]	2000
All ages, age adjusted	10.2	14.5	16.2	16.3	11.7	6.1	4.9	5.4	5.2
Under 1 year	2.7	2.2	2.5	1.5	1.1	(B)	(B)	(B)	(B)
1-4 years	0.8	1.3	1.3	1.3	0.9	0.4	0.2	0.2	(B)
5-14 years	0.2	0.4	0.5	0.5	0.5	0.3	0.1	0.2	0.1
15-24 years	1.5	1.7	1.8	1.7	1.1	0.8	0.5	0.5	0.5
25-34 years	19.7	27.0	29.3	29.1	19.9	10.1	7.5	7.2	6.5
35-44 years	27.4	39.1	44.1	44.4	31.4	16.1	12.9	13.9	13.2
45-54 years	15.2	22.6	25.6	26.3	19.3	10.4	9.0	10.9	11.1
55-64 years	6.2	8.8	10.4	11.0	8.4	4.9	4.3	4.9	5.2
65-74 years	2.0	2.9	3.1	3.6	2.7	1.8	1.6	2.2	2.2
75-84 years	0.7	0.8	0.9	0.7	0.8	0.6	0.5	0.6	0.7
85 years and over	(B)	(B)	(B)	(B)	(B)	(B)	(B)	(B)	(B)
Male, all ages, age adjusted	18.5	25.4	27.8	27.7	19.2	9.7	7.7	8.4	8.0
Under 1 year	2.4	2.1	2.1	1.7	1.1	(B)	(B)	(B)	(B)
1-4 years	0.8	1.3	1.2	1.2	0.9	0.3	(B)	(B)	(B)
5-14 years	0.3	0.4	0.5	0.5	0.5	0.3	0.1	0.2	0.1
15-24 years	2.2	2.3	2.3	2.1	1.3	0.8	0.5	0.5	0.5
25-34 years	34.5	46.0	48.5	47.1	31.4	15.1	10.7	10.2	8.6
35-44 years	50.2	68.5	76.2	75.9	51.8	25.5	20.1	21.1	19.9
45-54 years	29.1	41.7	46.3	46.9	33.6	17.4	15.2	17.9	18.1
55-64 years	12.0	16.5	19.1	19.9	14.9	8.5	7.3	8.5	8.9
65-74 years	3.7	5.4	5.8	6.4	5.1	3.4	2.9	3.9	3.8
75-84 years	1.1	1.4	1.4	1.3	1.5	1.0	0.9	1.0	1.3
85 years and over	(B)	(B)	(B)	(B)	(B)	(B)	(B)	(B)	(B)
Female age adjusted	2.2	3.9	4.9	5.3	4.3	2.7	2.3	2.6	2.6
Under 1 year	3.0	2.4	2.9	1.2	(B)	(B)	(B)	(B)	(B)
1-4 years	0.8	1.3	1.3	1.5	1.0	0.4	(B)	(B)	(B)
5-14 years	0.2	0.4	0.5	0.5	0.4	0.2	0.2	0.2	0.1
15-24 years	0.7	1.1	1.3	1.4	1.0	0.7	0.6	0.6	0.4
25-34 years	4.9	8.0	10.1	11.1	8.5	5.1	4.4	4.3	4.4
35-45 years	5.2	10.2	12.5	13.4	11.3	6.8	5.8	6.8	6.5
45-54 years	1.9	4.4	5.8	6.7	5.7	3.8	3.1	4.2	4.5
55-64 years	1.1	1.9	2.6	2.9	2.5	1.6	1.6	1.6	1.8
65-74 years	0.8	1.0	1.0	1.4	0.8	0.5	0.6	0.8	0.8
75-84 years	0.4	0.4	0.6	0.3	0.3	0.4	0.3	0.3	0.3
85 years and over	(B)	(B)	(B)	(B)	(B)	(B)	(B)	(B)	(B)
Race, age adjusted									
White male	15.7	20.0	21.2	20.7	13.2	6.0	4.6	5.0	4.6
Black male	46.3	74.5	87.2	90.4	71.5	41.7	34.0	37.1	35.1
White female	1.1	1.8	2.3	2.5	1.9	1.0	0.8	1.0	1.0
Black female	10.1	17.8	22.6	24.7	21.1	13.9	12.2	13.4	13.2

B Base figure too small to meet statistical standards for reliability of a derived figure.   [1] Starting with 1999 data, cause of death is coded according to ICD-10. For explanation, see text, this section.

Source: U.S. National Center for Health Statistics. *Vital Statistics of the United States*, annual; *National Vital Statistics Reports* (NVSR); and unpublished data.

No. 112. Deaths—Life Years Lost and Mortality Costs by Age, Sex, and Cause: 2000 and 2001

[**Life years lost:** Number of years person would have lived in absence of death. **Mortality cost:** value of lifetime earnings lost by persons who die prematurely, discounted at 6 percent]

Characteristic	Number of deaths (1,000)	Life years lost [1] Total (1,000)	Life years lost [1] Per death	Mortality cost [2] Total (mil. dol.)	Mortality cost [2] Per death (dol.)
Total, 2000	**2,403**	**38,843**	**16.2**	**431,992**	**179,772**
Under 5 yrs. old	33	2,522	76.4	30,421	921,471
5 to 14 yrs. old	7	513	69.2	8,331	1,123,778
15 to 24 yrs. old	31	1,835	58.6	43,039	1,374,751
25 to 44 yrs. old	130	5,604	43.1	144,409	1,108,713
45 to 64 yrs. old	346	10,555	30.5	168,201	486,146
65 yrs old and over	1,855	17,815	9.6	37,591	20,265
Heart disease	711	8,917	12.5	72,224	101,623
Cancer	553	10,028	18.1	107,501	194,367
Cerebrovascular diseases	168	1,934	11.5	12,103	72,187
Accidents and adverse effects	98	3,303	33.8	69,429	709,801
Other	874	14,661	16.8	170,736	195,408
Male	**1,177**	**20,415**	**17.3**	**316,850**	**269,135**
Under 5 yrs. old	19	1,373	74.0	19,287	1,040,197
5 to 14 yrs. old	4	295	67.0	5,540	1,258,796
15 to 24 yrs. old	23	1,319	57.2	34,230	1,483,692
25 to 44 yrs. old	85	3,549	41.7	107,638	1,263,555
45 to 64 yrs. old	244	6,098	25.0	123,301	505,917
65 yrs. old and over	802	7,781	9.7	26,853	33,467
Heart disease	345	4,709	13.7	56,883	164,989
Cancer	286	5,333	18.6	75,819	265,036
Cerebrovascular diseases	65	777	12.0	7,861	121,377
Accidents and adverse effects	64	2,259	35.4	55,756	874,831
Other	418	7,336	17.6	120,531	288,386
Female	**1,226**	**18,428**	**15.0**	**115,142**	**93,939**
Under 5 yrs. old	14	1,149	79.4	11,134	769,356
5 to 14 yrs. old	3	218	72.4	2,791	926,495
15 to 24 yrs. old	8	516	62.6	8,809	1,069,584
25 to 44 yrs. old	45	2,054	45.6	36,770	815,994
45 to 64 yrs. old	102	4,457	43.6	44,899	439,031
65 yrs. old and over	1,053	10,034	9.5	10,738	10,201
Heart disease	366	4,208	11.5	15,341	41,923
Cancer	267	4,695	17.6	31,681	118,653
Cerebrovascular diseases	103	1,157	11.2	4,241	41,223
Accidents and adverse effects	34	1,044	30.6	13,673	401,183
Other	456	7,325	16.1	50,205	110,150
Total, 2001	**2,416**	**39,682**	**16.4**	**471,777**	**195,272**
Under 5 yrs. old	33	2,506	76.7	31,596	966,975
5 to 14 yrs. old	7	493	69.5	8,339	1,175,347
15 to 24 yrs. old	32	1,897	58.8	46,136	1,430,483
25 to 44 yrs. old	133	5,777	43.4	154,920	1,161,695
45 to 64 yrs. old	357	10,987	30.8	186,400	522,503
65 yrs old and over	1,854	18,022	9.7	44,386	23,942
Heart disease	700	8,934	12.8	78,221	111,732
Cancer	554	10,184	18.4	117,621	212,404
Cerebrovascular diseases	164	1,912	11.7	12,917	78,983
Accidents and adverse effects	101	3,410	33.6	74,332	732,935
Other	897	15,243	17.0	188,687	210,303
Male	**1,183**	**20,791**	**17.6**	**337,965**	**285,663**
Under 5 yrs. old	18	1,366	74.3	19,652	1,069,443
5 to 14 yrs. old	4	280	67.2	5,396	1,294,601
15 to 24 yrs. old	24	1,376	57.4	36,514	1,523,772
25 to 44 yrs. old	87	3,649	42.0	113,870	1,310,046
45 to 64 yrs. old	250	6,327	25.3	133,493	534,387
65 yrs. old and over	800	7,794	9.7	29,039	36,306
Heart disease	339	4,686	13.8	59,848	176,518
Cancer	287	5,407	18.8	80,701	281,120
Cerebrovascular diseases	63	765	12.1	8,129	128,674
Accidents and adverse effects	66	2,329	35.3	58,991	894,405
Other	428	7,605	17.8	130,296	304,543
Female	**1,233**	**18,891**	**15.3**	**133,812**	**108,533**
Under 5 yrs. old	14	1,140	79.7	11,944	835,290
5 to 14 yrs. old	3	213	72.7	2,943	1,005,532
15 to 24 yrs. old	8	521	62.8	9,622	1,160,789
25 to 44 yrs. old	46	2,129	45.8	41,050	884,005
45 to 64 yrs. old	107	4,660	43.6	52,907	494,742
65 yrs. old and over	1,054	10,228	9.7	15,346	14,560
Heart disease	361	4,248	11.8	18,373	50,891
Cancer	267	4,777	17.9	36,920	138,437
Cerebrovascular diseases	100	1,147	11.4	4,788	47,703
Accidents and adverse effects	35	1,081	30.5	15,341	432,607
Other	469	7,638	16.3	58,390	124,401

[1] Based on life expectancy at year of death. [2] Cost estimates based on the person's age, sex, life expectancy at the time of death, labor force participation rates, annual earnings, value of homemaking services, and a 4 percent discount rate by which to convert to present worth the potential aggregate earnings lost over the years.

Source: Institute for Health and Aging, University of California, San Francisco, CA, unpublished data.

Vital Statistics   87

No. 113. Marriages and Divorces—Number and Rate by State: 1990 to 2001

[2443.0 represents 2,443,000. By place of occurence. See Appendix III]

State	Marriages [1]						Divorces [3]					
	Number (1,000)			Rate per 1,000 population [2]			Number (1,000)			Rate per 1,000 population [2]		
	1990	2000	2001	1990	2000	2001	1990	2000	2001	1990	2000	2001
U.S. [4]	2,443.0	2,329.0	2,345.0	9.8	8.2	8.2	1,182.0	(NA)	(NA)	4.7	4.1	3.9
Alabama	43.3	45.0	42.2	10.6	10.3	9.6	25.3	23.5	23.4	6.1	5.4	5.3
Alaska	5.7	5.6	5.1	10.2	8.9	8.2	2.9	2.7	2.6	5.5	4.4	4.1
Arizona	37.0	38.7	40.0	10.0	7.9	8.0	25.1	21.6	21.1	6.9	4.4	4.2
Arkansas	35.7	41.1	38.4	15.3	16.0	14.8	16.8	17.9	17.1	6.9	6.9	6.6
California [5]	236.7	196.9	224.2	7.9	5.9	6.6	128.0	(NA)	(NA)	4.3	(NA)	(NA)
Colorado	31.5	35.6	36.5	9.8	8.6	8.7	18.4	(NA)	(NA)	5.5	(NA)	(NA)
Connecticut	27.8	19.4	18.6	7.9	5.9	5.6	10.3	6.5	9.7	3.2	2.0	2.9
Delaware	5.6	5.1	5.2	8.4	6.7	6.7	3.0	3.2	3.1	4.4	4.2	4.0
Dist. of Columbia . .	4.7	2.8	3.5	8.2	5.4	6.8	2.7	1.5	1.2	4.5	3.0	2.3
Florida	142.3	141.9	151.3	10.9	9.3	9.7	81.7	81.9	84.6	6.3	5.3	5.4
Georgia	64.4	56.0	51.3	10.3	7.1	6.3	35.7	30.7	30.6	5.5	3.9	3.8
Hawaii	18.1	25.0	24.0	16.4	21.2	20.4	5.2	4.6	4.5	4.6	3.9	3.8
Idaho	15.0	14.0	14.7	13.9	11.0	11.4	6.6	6.9	7.2	6.5	5.4	5.6
Illinois	97.1	85.5	89.8	8.8	7.0	7.3	44.3	39.1	39.7	3.8	3.2	3.2
Indiana	54.3	34.5	34.1	9.6	5.8	5.7	(NA)	(NA)	(NA)	(NA)	(NA)	(NA)
Iowa	24.8	20.3	20.9	9.0	7.0	7.2	11.1	9.4	9.3	3.9	3.3	3.2
Kansas	23.4	22.2	20.3	9.2	8.3	7.6	12.6	10.6	8.7	5.0	4.0	3.2
Kentucky	51.3	39.7	36.6	13.5	10.0	9.1	21.8	21.6	22.0	5.8	5.4	5.5
Louisiana	41.2	40.5	37.5	9.6	9.3	8.6	(NA)	(NA)	(NA)	(NA)	(NA)	(NA)
Maine	11.8	10.5	11.4	9.7	8.3	9.0	5.3	5.8	4.9	4.3	4.6	3.9
Maryland	46.1	40.0	37.5	9.7	7.7	7.1	16.1	17.0	15.9	3.4	3.3	3.0
Massachusetts	47.8	37.0	40.0	7.9	6.0	6.4	16.8	18.6	14.8	2.8	3.0	2.4
Michigan	76.1	66.4	66.5	8.2	6.7	6.7	40.2	39.4	38.9	4.3	4.0	3.9
Minnesota	33.7	33.4	33.0	7.7	6.9	6.8	15.4	14.8	16.0	3.5	3.1	3.3
Mississippi	24.3	19.7	18.7	9.4	7.1	6.7	14.4	14.4	15.1	5.5	5.2	5.4
Missouri	49.3	43.7	42.2	9.6	7.9	7.6	26.4	26.5	23.8	5.1	4.8	4.3
Montana	7.0	6.6	6.4	8.6	7.4	7.2	4.1	2.1	2.3	5.1	2.4	2.6
Nebraska	12.5	13.0	13.6	8.0	7.8	8.1	6.5	6.4	6.2	4.0	3.8	3.7
Nevada	123.4	144.3	146.1	99.0	76.7	75.0	13.3	18.1	13.2	11.4	9.6	6.8
New Hampshire . . .	10.6	11.6	10.6	9.5	9.5	8.6	5.3	7.1	6.1	4.7	5.8	5.0
New Jersey	58.0	50.4	54.1	7.6	6.1	6.6	23.6	25.6	28.5	3.0	3.1	3.5
New Mexico	13.2	14.5	13.9	8.8	8.3	7.9	7.7	9.2	9.0	4.9	5.3	5.1
New York	169.3	162.0	145.5	8.6	8.9	7.9	57.9	62.8	54.1	3.2	3.4	3.0
North Carolina	52.1	65.6	61.1	7.8	8.5	7.8	34.0	36.9	34.9	5.1	4.8	4.5
North Dakota	4.8	4.6	4.1	7.5	7.3	6.6	2.3	2.0	1.7	3.6	3.2	2.7
Ohio	95.8	88.5	82.3	9.0	7.9	7.3	51.0	49.3	45.6	4.7	4.4	4.0
Oklahoma	33.2	15.6	16.6	10.6	4.6	4.9	24.9	12.4	11.5	7.7	3.7	3.4
Oregon	25.2	26.0	26.0	8.9	7.8	7.7	15.9	16.7	16.5	5.5	5.0	4.9
Pennsylvania	86.8	73.2	71.4	7.1	6.1	6.0	40.1	37.9	38.0	3.3	3.2	3.2
Rhode Island	8.1	8.0	8.6	8.1	8.0	8.6	3.8	3.1	3.3	3.7	3.1	3.3
South Carolina	55.8	42.7	36.8	15.9	10.9	9.3	16.1	14.4	13.8	4.5	3.7	3.5
South Dakota	7.7	7.1	6.7	11.1	9.6	9.1	2.6	2.7	2.5	3.7	3.6	3.4
Tennessee	66.6	88.2	77.7	13.9	15.9	13.9	32.3	33.8	28.8	6.5	6.1	5.2
Texas	182.8	196.4	194.9	10.5	9.6	9.4	94.0	85.2	85.4	5.5	4.2	4.1
Utah	19.0	24.1	23.2	11.2	11.1	10.6	8.8	9.7	9.7	5.1	4.5	4.4
Vermont	6.1	6.1	6.0	10.9	10.2	9.9	2.6	5.1	2.4	4.5	8.6	4.0
Virginia	71.3	62.4	63.4	11.4	9.0	9.0	27.3	30.2	30.2	4.4	4.3	4.3
Washington	48.6	40.9	42.2	9.5	7.0	7.2	28.8	27.2	26.3	5.9	4.7	4.5
West Virginia	13.2	15.7	14.2	7.2	8.7	7.9	9.7	9.3	9.3	5.3	5.2	5.2
Wisconsin	41.2	36.1	34.9	7.9	6.8	6.5	17.8	17.6	17.3	3.6	3.3	3.2
Wyoming	4.8	4.9	5.0	10.7	10.3	10.3	3.1	2.8	2.9	6.6	5.9	6.1

NA Not available. [1] Data are counts of marriages performed, except as noted. [2] Based on total population residing in area; population enumerated as of April 1 for 1990 and 2000; estimated as of July 1 for all other years. [3] Includes annulments. [4] U.S. totals for the number of divorces is an estimate which includes states not reporting (CA, CO, IN, and LA). [5] Marriage data include nonlicensed marriages registered.

Source: U.S. National Center for Health Statistics, *Vital Statistics of the United States*, annual; *National Vital Statistics Reports (NVSR)* (formerly *Monthly Vital Statistical Report*).

Section 3
Health and Nutrition

This section presents statistics on health expenditures and insurance coverage, including medicare and medicaid, medical personnel, hospitals, nursing homes and other care facilities, injuries, diseases, disability status, nutritional intake of the population, and food consumption. Summary statistics showing recent trends on health care and discussions of selected health issues are published annually by the U.S. National Center for Health Statistics (NCHS) in *Health, United States*. Data on national health expenditures, medical costs, and insurance coverage are compiled by the U.S. Centers for Medicare & Medicaid Services (CMS) (formerly Health Care Financing Administration), and appear on the CMS Web site at <http://www.cms.hhs.gov/statistics/nhe> and in the annual *Medicare and Medicaid Statistical Supplement* to the *Health Care Financing Review*. Statistics on health insurance are also collected by NCHS and are published in Series 10 of *Vital and Health Statistics*. U.S. Census Bureau also publishes data on utilization of insurance coverage. Statistics on hospitals are published annually by the Health Forum, L.L.C., an American Hospital Association Company, in *Hospital Statistics*. Primary sources for data on nutrition is the annual *Food Consumption, Prices, and Expenditures*, issued by the U.S. Department of Agriculture. NCHS also conducts periodic surveys of nutrient levels in the population, including estimates of food and nutrient intake, overweight and obesity, hypercholesterolemia, hypertension, and clinical signs of malnutrition.

National health expenditures—CMS compiles estimates of national health expenditures (NHE) to measure spending for health care in the United States. The NHE accounts are structured to show spending by type of expenditure (i.e., hospital care, physician and clinical care, dental care, and other professional care; home health care; retail sales of prescription drugs; other medical nondurables; vision products and other medical durables; nursing home care and other personal health expenditures; plus nonpersonal health expenditures for such items as public health, research, construction of medical facilities, administration, and the net cost of private health insurance) and by source of funding (e.g., private health insurance, out-of-pocket payments, and a range of public programs including medicare, medicaid, and those operated by the Department of Veterans Affairs (VA)).

Data used to estimate health expenditures come from existing sources, which are tabulated for other purposes. The type of expenditure estimates rely upon statistics produced by such groups as the American Hospital Association, the Census Bureau, and the Department of Health and Human Services (HHS). Source of funding estimates are constructed using administrative and statistical records from the medicare and medicaid programs, the Department of Defense and VA medical programs, the Social Security Administration, Census Bureau's *Governmental Finances,* state and local governments, other HHS agencies, and other nongovernment sources. More information and detailed descriptions of sources and methods are available on the CMS home page at <http://cms.hhs.gov/statistics /nhe/default.asp>.

Medicare and medicaid—Since July 1966, the federal medicare program has provided two coordinated plans for nearly all people age 65 and over: (1) A hospital insurance plan, which covers hospital and related services and (2) a voluntary supplementary medical insurance plan, financed partially by monthly premiums paid by participants, which partly covers physicians' and related medical services. Such insurance also applies, since July 1973, to disabled beneficiaries of any age after 24 months of entitlement to cash benefits under the social security or railroad retirement programs and to persons with end stage renal disease.

U.S. Census Bureau, Statistical Abstract of the United States: 2004-2005

Medicaid is a health insurance program for certain low-income people. These include: certain low-income families with children; aged, blind, or disabled people on supplemental security income; certain low-income pregnant women and children; and people who have very high medical bills. Medicaid is funded and administered through a state-federal partnership. Although there are broad federal requirements for medicaid, states have a wide degree of flexibility to design their program. States have authority to establish eligibility standards, determine what benefits and services to cover, and set payment rates. All states, however, must cover these basic services: inpatient and outpatient hospital services, laboratory and X-ray services, skilled nursing and home health services, doctor's services, family planning, and periodic health checkups, diagnosis and treatment for children.

Health resources—Hospital statistics based on data from the American Hospital Association's yearly survey are published annually in *Hospital Statistics* and cover all hospitals accepted for registration by the Association. To be accepted for registration, a hospital must meet certain requirements relating to number of beds, construction, equipment, medical and nursing staff, patient care, clinical records, surgical and obstetrical facilities, diagnostic and treatment facilities, laboratory services, etc. Data obtained from NCHS cover all U.S. hospitals that meet certain criteria for inclusion. The criteria are published in *Vital and Health Statistics* reports, Series 13. NCHS defines a hospital as a nonfederal short-term general or special facility with six or more inpatient beds with an average stay of less than 30 days.

Statistics on the demographic characteristics of persons employed in the health occupations are compiled by the U.S. Bureau of Labor Statistics and reported in *Employment and Earnings* (monthly) (see Table 597, Section 12, Labor Force, Employment, and Earnings). Data based on surveys of health personnel and utilization of health facilities providing long-term care, ambulatory care, and hospital

care are presented in NCHS Series 13, *Data on Health Resources Utilization and Advance Data from Vital and Health Statistics.* Statistics on patient visits to health care providers, as reported in health interviews, appear in NCHS Series 10, *National Health Interview Survey Data.*

The CMS's *Health Care Financing Review* and its annual *Medicare and Medicaid Statistical Supplement* present data for hospitals and nursing homes as well as extended care facilities and home health agencies. These data are based on records of the medicare program and differ from those of other sources because they are limited to facilities meeting federal eligibility standards for participation in medicare.

Disability and illness—General health statistics, including morbidity, disability, injuries, preventive care, and findings from physiological testing are collected by NCHS in its National Health Interview Survey and its National Health and Nutrition Examination Surveys and appear in *Vital and Health Statistics,* Series 10 and 11, respectively. The Department of Labor compiles statistics on occupational injuries (see Section 12, Labor Force, Employment, and Earnings). Annual incidence data on notifiable diseases are compiled by the Public Health Service (PHS) at its Centers for Disease Control and Prevention in Atlanta, Georgia, and are published as a supplement to its *Morbidity and Mortality Weekly Report.* The list of diseases is revised annually and includes those which, by mutual agreement of the states and PHS, are communicable diseases of national importance.

Nutrition—Statistics on annual per capita consumption of food and its nutrient value are estimated by the U.S. Department of Agriculture and published quarterly in *National Food Review.* Historical data can be found in *Food Consumption, Prices, and Expenditures,* and online at <http://www.ers.usda.gov /data/foodconsumption>. Statistics on food insufficiency and food and nutrient intake are collected by NCHS to estimate the diet of the nation's population. NCHS also collects physical examination data to assess the population's nutritional status,

90   Health and Nutrition

including growth, overweight/obesity, nutritional deficiencies, and prevalence of nutrition-related conditions, such as hypertension, hypercholesterolemia, and diabetes.

Statistical reliability—For discussion of statistical collection, estimation, and sampling procedures and measures of reliability applicable to data from NCHS and CMS, see Appendix III.

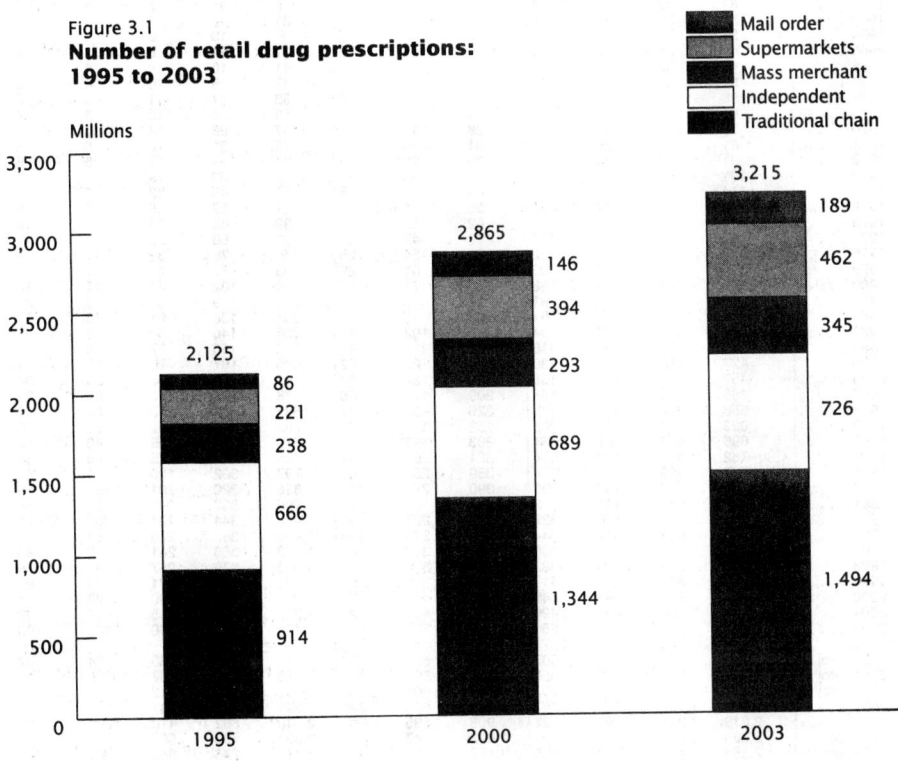

Figure 3.1
Number of retail drug prescriptions: 1995 to 2003

Legend:
- Mail order
- Supermarkets
- Mass merchant
- Independent
- Traditional chain

Millions

Year	Traditional chain	Independent	Mass merchant	Supermarkets	Mail order	Total
1995	914	666	238	221	86	2,125
2000	1,344	689	293	394	146	2,865
2003	1,494	726	345	462	189	3,215

Source: Chart prepared by U.S. Census Bureau. For data, see Table 122.

U.S. Census Bureau, Statistical Abstract of the United States: 2004-2005

No. 114. National Health Expenditures—Summary, 1960 to 2002, and Projections, 2003 to 2013

[In billions of dollars (27 represents $27,000,000,000). Excludes Puerto Rico and island areas]

Year	Private expenditures				Public expenditures			Health services and supplies				
	Total expendi-tures [1]	Total [2]	Out-of-pocket	Insur-ance	Total	Federal	State and local	Total [3]	Hospi-tal care	Physi-cian and clinical ser-vices	Pre-scrip-tion drugs	Nursing home care
1960	27	20	13	6	7	3	4	25	9	5	3	1
1961	29	21	13	7	7	3	4	27	10	6	3	1
1962	31	23	14	7	8	4	4	29	11	6	3	1
1963	34	25	15	8	9	4	5	31	12	7	3	1
1964	38	28	17	9	9	4	5	34	13	8	3	1
1965	41	31	18	10	10	5	6	37	14	8	4	2
1966	45	32	19	10	14	7	6	41	16	9	4	2
1967	51	32	19	11	19	12	7	47	18	10	4	2
1968	58	36	21	12	22	14	8	53	21	11	5	3
1969	65	40	23	13	24	16	9	59	24	12	5	4
1970	73	45	25	16	28	18	10	67	28	14	6	4
1971	81	50	26	18	31	20	11	75	31	16	6	5
1972	91	56	29	21	35	23	12	84	34	17	6	6
1973	101	61	32	23	39	25	14	93	39	19	7	6
1974	114	67	35	26	46	30	16	106	45	22	7	7
1975	130	75	37	30	55	36	19	121	52	25	8	9
1976	149	87	41	37	62	43	20	139	60	28	9	10
1977	169	99	45	45	70	47	23	160	68	33	9	12
1978	189	110	48	52	80	54	26	179	76	35	10	13
1979	214	124	53	60	90	61	29	203	87	41	11	15
1980	246	141	58	68	105	71	34	234	102	47	12	18
1981	285	164	66	81	121	83	39	271	119	55	13	20
1982	321	187	72	94	134	92	42	305	135	61	15	23
1983	354	206	79	104	148	102	46	336	146	68	17	26
1984	390	229	86	118	161	113	48	372	156	77	20	28
1985	427	252	96	130	175	122	52	409	167	90	22	31
1986	457	267	103	135	190	132	59	439	178	100	24	34
1987	498	289	109	148	209	143	66	478	192	112	27	36
1988	558	332	119	175	226	154	72	535	209	127	31	41
1989	623	371	126	205	252	172	79	599	229	142	35	46
1990	696	414	137	234	283	193	90	670	254	158	40	53
1991	762	441	142	254	321	222	99	735	280	175	45	58
1992	827	469	146	274	359	251	107	797	302	190	48	62
1993	888	498	147	298	390	274	116	856	320	201	51	66
1994	937	510	144	312	427	299	129	905	332	211	55	68
1995	990	533	146	329	458	324	134	958	344	221	61	75
1996	1,039	558	152	344	482	344	138	1,005	355	229	67	80
1997	1,093	589	162	360	504	360	143	1,056	368	241	76	85
1998	1,150	629	175	383	521	368	153	1,112	379	257	87	89
1999	1,223	670	184	413	553	386	166	1,182	393	271	104	90
2000	1,309	715	193	449	595	416	179	1,261	413	290	122	94
2001	1,421	768	201	496	652	460	192	1,370	444	315	141	99
2002	1,553	840	213	550	713	505	209	1,496	487	340	162	103
2003, proj ..	1,674	915	227	607	759	535	224	1,614	518	363	184	107
2004, proj ..	1,794	984	243	656	810	569	241	1,730	552	387	208	112
2005, proj ..	1,921	1,057	261	707	864	605	259	1,853	586	412	234	117
2006, proj ..	2,064	1,136	280	762	928	648	280	1,991	623	441	262	123
2007, proj ..	2,219	1,221	299	822	998	695	303	2,140	662	472	292	130
2008, proj ..	2,388	1,313	320	888	1,075	747	328	2,303	703	507	325	138
2009, proj ..	2,565	1,408	342	955	1,157	803	354	2,475	746	543	360	146
2010, proj ..	2,751	1,504	364	1,022	1,247	865	382	2,655	791	580	397	155
2011, proj ..	2,946	1,603	387	1,092	1,342	931	412	2,843	838	619	435	164
2012, proj ..	3,146	1,702	411	1,161	1,444	1,000	444	3,037	885	659	476	174
2013, proj ..	3,358	1,806	436	1,233	1,552	1,075	477	3,242	934	701	520	185

[1] Includes medical research and medical facilities construction, not shown separately. [2] Includes other private expenditures, not shown separately. [3] Includes other objects of expenditure, not shown separately.

Source: U. S. Centers for Medicare & Medicaid Services, Office of the Actuary, "Health Accounts" <http://www.cms.hhs.gov/statistics /nhe/default.asp>.

No. 115. National Health Expenditures by Type: 1990 to 2002

[In billions of dollars (696.0 represents $696,000,000,000), except percent. Excludes Puerto Rico and island areas]

Type of expenditure	1990	1995	1997	1998	1999	2000	2001	2002
Total	696.0	990.2	1,092.8	1,150.3	1,222.6	1,309.4	1,420.7	1,553.0
Annual percent change [1]	11.8	5.7	5.1	5.3	6.3	7.1	8.5	9.3
Percent of gross domestic product	12.0	13.4	13.1	13.1	13.2	13.3	14.1	14.9
Private expenditures	413.5	533.6	589.2	629.0	669.7	714.9	768.4	839.6
Health services and supplies	401.9	521.1	574.3	613.4	654.3	697.3	751.0	819.7
Out-of-pocket payments	137.3	146.5	162.1	175.3	184.5	192.6	200.5	212.5
Insurance premiums [2]	233.5	329.7	360.1	382.9	412.7	449.3	495.6	549.6
Other	31.1	44.9	52.1	55.2	57.2	55.3	54.9	57.7
Medical research	1.0	1.4	1.6	2.0	2.1	3.4	2.7	2.7
Medical facilities construction	10.7	11.1	13.3	13.6	13.3	14.2	14.7	17.1
Public expenditures	282.5	456.6	503.6	521.3	552.9	594.6	652.3	713.4
Percent federal of public	68.2	70.6	71.5	70.7	69.9	70.0	70.6	70.7
Health services and supplies	267.7	436.5	481.2	498.6	527.4	564.2	619.0	676.6
Medicare [3]	110.2	183.1	209.5	210.2	213.5	225.1	246.5	267.1
Public assistance medical payments [4] . .	78.7	149.5	164.7	176.6	191.7	209.3	232.2	259.6
Temporary disability insurance [5]	0.1	0.1	0.1	0.1	-	-	-	-
Workers' compensation (medical) [5]	17.5	21.9	20.5	20.7	22.8	25.3	27.6	30.0
Defense Dept. hospital, medical.	10.4	12.1	12.1	12.2	12.9	14.0	15.2	17.2
Maternal, child health programs.	1.8	2.2	2.3	2.4	2.6	2.7	2.8	2.8
Public health activities	20.2	31.4	35.4	38.0	43.7	45.8	48.3	51.2
Veterans' hospital, medical care.	11.3	15.4	16.3	16.9	17.7	19.1	21.7	22.3
Medical vocational rehabilitation.	0.5	0.7	0.7	0.8	0.8	0.8	0.8	0.8
State and local hospitals [6]	13.1	14.1	13.3	13.8	13.7	13.4	14.0	15.2
Other [7]	3.8	6.0	6.1	6.9	8.0	8.8	9.8	10.3
Medical research	11.7	15.7	17.1	18.6	21.3	25.4	28.8	31.6
Medical facilities construction	3.1	4.4	5.2	4.2	4.3	5.0	4.5	5.2

- Represents zero or rounds to zero. [1] Change from immediate prior year. For explanation of average annual percent change, see Guide to Tabular Presentation. [2] Covers insurance benefits and amount retained by insurance companies for expenses, additions to reserves, and profits (net cost of insurance). [3] Represents expenditures for benefits and administrative cost from Federal hospital and medical insurance trust funds under old-age, survivors, disability, and health insurance programs; see text, of this section. [4] Payments made directly to suppliers of medical care (primarily medicaid). [5] Includes medical benefits paid under public law by private insurance carriers, state governments, and self-insurers. [6] Expenditures not offset by other revenues. [7] Covers expenditures for Substance Abuse and Mental Health Services Administration, Indian Health Service; school health and other programs.

No. 116. National Health Expenditures by Object, 1990 to 2002, and Projections, 2003

[In billions of dollars (696.0 represents $696,000,000,000). Excludes Puerto Rico and island areas]

Object of expenditure	1990	1995	1997	1998	1999	2000	2001	2002	2003, proj.
Total	696.0	990.2	1,092.8	1,150.3	1,222.6	1,309.4	1,420.7	1,553.0	1,673.6
Spent by—									
Consumers	370.8	476.2	522.2	558.2	597.1	641.9	696.1	762.1	833.7
Out-of-pocket	137.3	146.5	162.1	175.3	184.5	192.6	200.5	212.5	227.0
Private insurance.	233.5	329.7	360.1	382.9	412.7	449.3	495.6	549.6	606.7
Public	282.5	456.6	503.6	521.3	552.9	594.6	652.3	713.4	759.0
Other [1]	42.8	57.4	67.0	70.8	72.6	72.9	72.3	77.5	80.9
Spent for—									
Health services and supplies.	669.6	957.6	1,055.5	1,112.1	1,181.7	1,261.4	1,370.0	1,496.3	1,613.6
Personal health care expenses	609.4	865.7	959.2	1,009.6	1,065.0	1,135.3	1,231.4	1,340.2	1,436.5
Hospital care	253.9	343.6	367.6	378.5	393.5	413.2	443.3	486.5	518.1
Physician and clinical services	157.5	220.5	241.0	256.8	270.9	290.3	315.1	339.5	362.8
Dental services	31.5	44.5	50.2	53.2	56.4	60.7	65.6	70.3	74.0
Other professional services [2]	18.2	28.6	33.4	35.5	36.7	38.8	42.6	45.9	48.3
Home health care.	12.6	30.5	34.5	33.6	32.3	31.7	33.7	36.1	38.3
Prescription drugs	40.3	60.8	75.7	87.3	104.4	121.5	140.8	162.4	184.1
Other nondurable medical products	22.5	25.6	27.9	28.6	30.3	30.8	31.0	31.7	33.6
Durable medical equipment [3]	10.6	14.2	16.2	16.9	17.2	17.7	18.2	18.8	19.6
Nursing home care	52.7	74.6	85.1	89.1	89.6	93.8	99.1	103.2	107.0
Other personal health care.	9.6	22.9	27.7	30.2	33.7	36.7	40.9	45.8	50.8
Public administration and net cost of private health insurance [4]	40.0	60.5	60.9	64.5	73.0	80.3	90.3	105.0	120.8
Public health activities	20.2	31.4	35.4	38.0	43.7	45.8	48.3	51.2	56.3
Medical research [5]	12.7	17.1	18.7	20.5	23.4	24.8	31.5	34.3	36.3
Medical facilities construction	13.7	15.5	18.5	17.7	17.6	19.2	19.2	22.4	23.7

[1] Includes nonpatient revenues, privately funded construction, and industrial inplant. [2] Includes services of registered and practical nurses in private duty, podiatrists, optometrists, physical therapists, clinical psychologists, chiropractors, naturopaths, and Christian Science practitioners. [3] Includes expenditures for eyeglasses, hearing aids, orthopedic appliances, artificial limbs, crutches, wheelchairs, etc. [4] Includes administrative expenses of federally financed health programs. [5] Research and development expenditures of drug companies and other manufacturers and providers of medical equipment and supplies are excluded from research expenditures, but are included in the expenditure class in which the product falls.

Source of Tables 115 and 116: U. S. Centers for Medicare & Medicaid Services, Office of the Actuary, "Health Accounts" <http://www.cms.hhs.gov/statistics/nhe/default.asp>.

Health and Nutrition 93

No. 117. Health Services and Supplies—Per Capita Consumer Expenditures by Object: 1990 to 2002

[In dollars, except percent. Based on Social Security Administration estimates of total U.S. population as of July 1, excluding Armed Forces and Federal employees abroad and civilian population of Puerto Rico and island areas. Excludes medical research and construction]

Object of expenditure	1990	1995	1997	1998	1999	2000	2001	2002
Total, national	**2,635**	**3,576**	**3,870**	**4,040**	**4,255**	**4,499**	**4,842**	**5,241**
Annual percent change [1]	10.6	4.8	4.0	4.4	5.3	5.7	7.6	8.2
Hospital care	999	1,283	1,348	1,375	1,417	1,474	1,570	1,704
Physician and clinical services	620	824	884	933	975	1,035	1,114	1,189
Dental services.	124	166	184	193	203	217	232	246
Other professional services [2]	72	107	122	129	132	138	151	161
Home health care	49	114	127	122	116	113	119	127
Prescription drugs	159	227	278	317	376	433	498	569
Other nondurable medical products	88	95	102	104	109	110	110	111
Durable medical equipment [2]	42	53	59	61	62	63	64	66
Nursing home care	207	278	312	324	323	334	350	361
Other personal health care	38	86	102	110	121	131	144	160
Public administration and net cost of private health insurance	157	226	223	234	263	286	319	368
Public health activities	80	117	130	138	157	163	171	179
Total, private consumer [3]	**1,459**	**1,778**	**1,915**	**2,028**	**2,150**	**2,289**	**2,460**	**2,669**
Hospital care	426	456	462	482	505	536	575	630
Physician and clinical services	386	497	532	561	579	617	659	705
Dental services.	120	158	175	184	193	205	218	230
Other professional services [2]	47	69	83	88	91	94	102	106
Home health care	20	37	49	54	53	50	46	46
Prescription drugs	132	181	220	250	296	338	386	442
Other nondurable medical products	86	91	98	100	105	105	104	106
Durable medical equipment [2]	33	38	42	44	44	44	43	42
Nursing home care	90	96	105	117	118	120	121	118
Net cost of private health insurance	117	153	150	148	166	181	206	246

[1] Change from immediate prior year.   [2] See footnotes for corresponding objects in Table 116.   [3] Represents out-of-pocket payments and private health insurance.

No. 118. Government Expenditures for Health Services and Supplies: 2002

[In millions of dollars (676,595 represents $676,595,000,000). Excludes Puerto Rico and island areas. Excludes medical research and construction]

Type of service	Total [1]	Federal	State and local	Medicare [2] (OASDHI)	Public assistance [3]	Other health services		
						Veterans	Defense Dept. [4]	Workers' compensation [5]
Total [1]	**676,595**	**476,463**	**200,132**	**267,105**	**259,597**	**22,255**	**17,238**	**30,013**
Hospital care	286,445	229,936	56,509	149,241	86,682	16,592	10,260	9,983
Physician and clinical services	114,814	94,742	20,072	68,828	26,326	1,420	3,605	9,039
Prescription drugs	36,239	20,866	15,373	2,634	31,153	72	1,214	975
Nursing home care	66,054	45,515	20,539	12,925	51,084	2,045	-	-
Public administration. . . .	33,269	18,968	14,301	8,006	17,458	93	587	6,781
Public health activities. . .	51,159	7,041	44,118	-	-	-	-	-

- Represents zero.   [1] Includes other items not shown separately.   [2] Covers hospital and medical insurance payments and administrative costs under old-age, survivors, disability, and health insurance program.   [3] Covers medicaid and other medical public assistance. Excludes funds paid into medicare trust fund by states to cover premiums for public assistance recipients and medically indigent persons.   [4] Includes care for retirees and military dependents.   [5] Medical benefits.

No. 119. Personal Health Care—Third Party Payments and Private Consumer Expenditures, 1990 to 2002, and Projections, 2003

[In billions of dollars (609.4 represents $609,400,000,000), except percent. See headnote, Table 120]

Item	1990	1995	1997	1998	1999	2000	2001	2002	2003, proj
Personal health care expenditures	609.4	865.7	959.2	1,009.6	1,065.0	1,135.3	1,231.4	1,340.2	1,436.5
Third party payments, total	**472.1**	**719.2**	**797.2**	**834.3**	**880.5**	**942.8**	**1,030.9**	**1,127.7**	**1,209.5**
Percent of personal health care	77.5	83.1	83.1	82.6	82.7	83.0	83.7	84.1	84.2
Private insurance payments	203.6	288.8	319.2	342.0	366.4	398.7	437.2	479.3	522.1
Public expenditures	237.9	386.2	426.6	437.9	457.9	489.8	540.0	592.2	628.9
Other [1]	30.6	44.2	51.4	54.4	56.2	54.2	53.7	56.2	58.5
Private consumer expenditures [2]	**340.9**	**435.3**	**481.3**	**517.3**	**550.9**	**591.3**	**637.8**	**691.8**	**749.1**
Percent met by private insurance	59.7	66.3	66.3	66.1	66.6	67.4	68.6	69.3	69.7
Hospital care	108.4	122.2	125.9	132.6	140.3	150.2	162.6	179.8	197.9
Percent met by private insurance	89.6	91.4	91.2	91.0	91.1	91.6	91.9	91.8	91.9
Physician and clinical services.	98.1	133.2	145.0	154.4	160.7	173.0	186.5	201.1	215.6
Percent met by private insurance	69.0	80.3	80.2	80.0	80.2	81.4	82.2	83.0	83.0
Prescription drugs	33.6	48.5	60.0	68.8	82.2	94.9	109.3	126.2	143.2
Percent met by private insurance	29.2	46.5	53.6	55.7	58.2	59.6	61.1	61.5	62.0

[1] Includes nonpatient revenues and industrial inplant health services.   [2] Includes expenditures not shown separately. Represents out-of-pocket payments and private health insurance benefits. Excludes net cost of insurance.
Source of tables 117-119: U. S. Centers for Medicare and Medicaid Services, Office of the Actuary, "Health Accounts" <http://cms.hhs.gov/statistics/nhe/default.asp>.

No. 120. Personal Health Care Expenditures by Object and Source of Payment: 2002

[In millions of dollars (1,340,226 represents $1,340,226,000,000). Excludes Puerto Rico and island areas. Covers all expenditures for health services and supplies, except net cost of insurance and administration, government public health activities, and expenditures of philanthropic agencies for fund raising activities]

Object of expenditure	Total	Private payments					Govern- ment	Third party pay- ments [2]
		Total	Consumer					
			Total	Out of pocket pay- ments	Private health insur- ance	Other [1]		
Total	1,340,226	748,059	691,843	212,510	479,333	56,216	592,167	1,127,716
Hospital care.	486,511	200,066	179,757	14,742	165,015	20,309	286,445	471,769
Physician and clinical services	339,544	224,730	201,136	34,258	166,878	23,594	114,814	305,286
Dental services	70,319	65,770	65,702	30,869	34,833	68	4,550	39,450
Other professional services [3]	45,852	33,208	30,206	13,046	17,160	3,003	12,644	32,806
Home health care.	36,129	14,278	13,226	6,493	6,734	1,051	21,852	29,637
Prescription drugs	162,413	126,173	126,173	48,605	77,569	-	36,239	113,808
Other non-durable medical products . .	31,733	30,139	30,139	30,139	-	-	1,594	1,594
Durable medical equipment	18,754	11,930	11,930	8,471	3,459	-	6,825	10,283
Nursing home care.	103,167	37,113	33,574	25,888	7,687	3,538	66,054	77,279
Other personal health care.	45,803	4,653	-	-	-	4,653	41,151	45,803

- Represents zero or rounds to zero.   [1] Includes nonpatient revenues and industrial plant.   [2] Covers private health insurance, other private payments, and government.   [3] See footnotes for corresponding items on Table 116.

Source: U. S. Centers for Medicare and Medicaid Services, Office of the Actuary, "Health Accounts" <http://cms.hhs.gov/statistics/nhe/default.asp>.

No. 121. Hospital Care, Physician and Clinical Service, and Nursing Home Care Expenditures by Source of Payment: 1990 to 2002

[In billions of dollars (253.9 represents $253,900,000,000)]

Source of payment	1990	1995	1996	1997	1998	1999	2000	2001	2002
Hospital care, total	253.9	343.6	355.2	367.6	378.5	393.5	413.2	444.3	486.5
Out-of-pocket payments	11.2	10.5	10.5	11.1	11.9	12.4	12.7	13.1	14.7
Third-party payments.	242.7	333.1	344.7	356.5	366.6	381.0	400.5	431.2	471.8
Private health insurance	97.1	111.7	111.9	114.8	120.7	127.9	137.5	149.5	165.0
Other private funds	10.3	14.7	15.8	18.0	19.7	20.5	20.2	19.1	20.3
Government	135.2	206.6	217.0	223.7	226.2	232.6	242.8	262.6	286.4
Federal	102.7	166.4	176.4	182.2	181.5	186.0	194.2	211.6	229.9
State and local	32.4	40.2	40.6	41.5	44.7	46.7	48.6	51.1	56.5
Medicare [1]	67.8	107.2	116.0	122.5	121.6	122.6	126.9	137.2	149.2
Medicaid [2]	27.6	54.5	56.9	58.1	61.0	66.5	70.2	75.3	83.5
Physician and clinical services, total	157.5	220.5	229.4	241.0	256.8	270.9	290.3	315.1	339.5
Out-of-pocket payments	30.4	26.2	26.9	28.7	30.9	31.8	32.1	33.1	34.3
Third-party payments.	127.1	194.3	202.4	212.2	225.9	239.1	258.2	282.0	305.3
Private health insurance	67.7	107.0	111.0	116.3	123.5	129.0	140.9	153.4	166.9
Other private funds	11.3	17.6	18.8	20.1	21.7	22.5	21.3	22.2	23.6
Government	48.2	69.8	72.6	75.9	80.8	87.7	96.0	106.4	114.8
Federal	38.7	56.4	59.2	62.3	66.8	72.7	79.7	88.1	94.7
State and local	9.4	13.3	13.5	13.5	14.0	15.0	16.4	18.3	20.1
Medicare [1]	30.2	41.9	44.2	47.1	50.5	54.5	59.4	65.1	68.8
Medicaid [2]	7.0	14.8	15.6	16.3	16.8	17.7	19.3	22.0	24.5
Nursing home care, total	52.7	74.6	79.9	85.1	89.1	89.6	93.8	99.1	103.2
Out-of-pocket payments	19.8	20.1	20.2	21.6	24.8	25.2	26.2	26.7	25.9
Third-party payments.	32.9	54.5	59.7	63.5	64.3	64.4	67.6	72.4	77.3
Private health insurance	3.1	5.6	6.7	7.0	7.4	7.5	7.3	7.6	7.7
Other private funds	3.9	4.8	5.0	5.2	4.5	4.5	4.1	3.7	3.5
Government	25.9	44.1	48.0	51.3	52.4	52.4	56.1	61.1	66.1
Federal	15.8	28.5	31.9	34.3	35.1	34.5	37.7	42.2	45.5
State and local	10.2	15.5	16.1	17.0	17.2	17.9	18.5	18.9	20.5
Medicare [1]	1.7	6.9	8.5	9.9	10.4	8.7	9.5	12.0	12.9
Medicaid [2]	23.2	35.4	37.7	39.6	40.1	41.8	44.6	46.9	50.9

[1] Medicare expenditures come from federal funds.   [2] Medicaid expenditures come from federal and state and local funds.

Source: U. S. Centers for Medicare and Medicaid Services, Office of the Actuary, "Health Accounts" <http://cms.hhs.gov/statistics/nhe/default.asp>.

Health and Nutrition 95

No. 122. Retail Prescription Drug Sales: 1995 to 2003

[2,125 represents 2,125,000,000]

Sales outlet	Unit	1995	1996	1997	1998	1999	2000	2001	2002	2003
Number of prescriptions	Mil. . . .	2,125	2,221	2,316	2,481	2,707	2,865	3,009	3,139	3,215
Traditional chain	Mil. . . .	914	969	1,038	1,129	1,246	1,344	1,415	1,474	1,494
Independent	Mil. . . .	666	660	646	651	680	689	700	708	726
Mass merchant	Mil. . . .	238	252	254	272	289	293	314	339	345
Supermarkets	Mil. . . .	221	242	269	306	357	394	418	444	462
Mail order.	Mil. . . .	86	98	109	123	134	146	161	174	189
Retail sales.	Bil. dol..	72.2	82.2	93.8	108.7	125.8	145.6	164.1	182.7	203.1
Traditional chain	Bil. dol..	28.8	32.8	38.2	45.5	53.8	61.2	67.7	75.9	85.4
Independent	Bil. dol..	21.1	22.3	23.7	26.1	28.9	31.4	33.9	35.4	38.3
Mass merchant	Bil. dol..	7.7	8.5	9.6	10.9	11.8	13.5	15.2	18.0	19.5
Supermarkets	Bil. dol..	7.4	8.8	10.3	13.8	13.8	17.4	19.8	23.1	25.1
Mail order.	Bil. dol..	7.4	9.8	11.9	14.3	17.4	22.1	27.6	30.2	34.9

Source: National Association of Chain Drug Stores, Alexandria, VA, *The Chain Pharmacy Industry Profile, 2004* (copyright). <http://www.nacds.org>

No. 123. Personal Health Care Expenditures by State: 1990 to 1998

[In millions of dollars (612,245 represents $612,245,000,000).This series of State Health Expenditures (SHE) uses the same definitions and, to the extent possible, the same data sources as does the national health expenditures series. For health services, this structure clusters spending according to the establishment providing those services. For retail purchases of medical products, it groups spending according to product classification. Thus, SHE is establishment-based, grouping services together according to place of service or of product sale rather than according to type of service. Establishment-based expenditures are those in which spending is located in the state of the provider rather than in the beneficiary's state of residence. Because people are able to cross state borders to receive health care services, health care spending by provider location is not necessarily an accurate reflection of spending on behalf of persons residing in that state]

State	1990	1995	1997	1998	State	1990	1995	1997	1998
U.S.	612,245	876,212	965,701	1,016,383	MO	12,690	18,024	19,783	20,911
					MT	1,628	2,445	2,680	2,838
AL	9,163	13,654	15,519	16,056	NE	3,531	5,091	5,721	6,095
AK	1,347	1,921	2,133	2,299	NV	2,806	4,471	5,170	5,606
AZ	8,562	12,352	13,834	14,782	NH	2,558	3,779	4,333	4,658
AR	4,925	7,149	8,033	8,463					
CA	74,369	99,215	105,790	110,057	NJ	20,169	29,504	31,580	32,695
					NM	2,917	4,430	5,075	5,344
CO	7,740	11,395	12,776	13,669	NY	53,926	75,183	81,100	85,785
CT	10,013	13,662	14,600	15,221	NC	13,748	21,966	25,584	27,327
DE	1,728	2,619	2,915	3,106	ND	1,639	2,373	2,542	2,680
DC	3,564	4,184	4,205	4,258					
FL	35,789	51,328	56,754	59,724	OH	26,896	37,246	40,552	42,581
					OK	6,357	9,454	10,419	10,988
GA	15,303	23,096	25,940	27,219	OR	6,247	9,182	10,259	10,840
HI	2,745	4,168	4,452	4,658	PA	32,635	45,050	48,853	51,322
ID	1,697	2,758	3,194	3,397	RI	2,728	3,783	4,149	4,515
IL	27,618	39,000	42,267	44,305					
IN	12,692	18,388	20,207	21,259	SC	6,806	10,616	12,363	13,204
					SD	1,513	2,301	2,635	2,842
IA	6,067	8,513	9,496	10,198	TN	12,213	18,820	21,154	22,021
KS	5,540	7,989	8,890	9,394	TX	37,682	56,504	64,245	67,750
KY	7,820	11,790	13,592	14,414	UT	3,233	4,807	5,622	5,944
LA	9,975	14,673	15,946	16,500					
ME	2,695	3,908	4,554	4,925	VT	1,172	1,762	1,933	2,066
					VA	13,252	18,712	21,103	22,261
MD	11,755	16,838	18,596	19,646	WA	11,276	16,810	18,214	19,292
MA	19,027	25,997	28,471	30,039	WV	3,930	6,024	6,692	7,037
MI	22,133	31,089	34,435	35,647	WI	11,441	16,739	18,738	19,945
MN	11,462	16,826	18,858	20,313	WY	793	1,179	1,313	1,407
MS	4,729	7,447	8,431	8,882					

Source: U. S. Centers for Medicare and Medicaid Services, Office of the Actuary, "Health Accounts" <http://cms.hhs.gov/statistics /nhe/default.asp>.

96   Health and Nutrition

No. 124. Consumer Price Indexes of Medical Care Prices: 1980 to 2003

[1982-1984=100. Indexes are annual averages of monthly data based on components of consumer price index for all urban consumers; for explanation, see text, Section 14. See Appendix III]

Year	Medical care, total	Medical care services		Professional services			Hospital and related services	Medical care commodities		Annual percent change [3]		
		Total [1]	Total [1]	Physicians	Dental			Total [2]	Prescription drugs and medical supplies	Medical care, total	Medical care services	Medical care commodities
1980....	74.9	74.8	77.9	76.5	78.9	69.2		75.4	72.5	11.0	11.3	9.3
1985....	113.5	113.2	113.5	113.3	114.2	116.1		115.2	120.1	6.3	6.1	7.2
1990....	162.8	162.7	156.1	160.8	155.8	178.0		163.4	181.7	9.0	9.3	8.4
1995....	220.5	224.2	201.0	208.8	206.8	257.6		204.5	235.0	4.5	5.1	1.9
1997....	234.6	239.1	215.4	222.9	226.6	278.4		215.3	249.3	2.8	2.9	2.3
1998....	242.1	246.8	222.2	229.5	236.2	287.5		221.8	258.6	3.2	3.2	3.0
1999....	250.6	255.1	229.2	236.0	247.2	299.5		230.7	273.4	3.5	3.4	4.0
2000....	260.8	266.0	237.7	244.7	258.5	317.3		238.1	285.4	4.1	4.3	3.2
2001....	272.8	278.8	246.5	253.6	269.0	338.3		247.6	300.9	4.6	4.8	4.0
2002....	285.6	292.9	253.9	260.6	281.0	367.8		256.4	316.5	4.7	5.1	3.6
2003....	297.1	306.0	261.2	267.7	292.5	394.8		262.8	326.3	4.0	4.5	2.5

[1] Includes other services not shown separately.   [2] Includes other commodities not shown separately.   [3] Percent change from the immediate prior year.
Source: U.S. Bureau of Labor Statistics, *CPI Detailed Report*, January 2004.

No. 125. Average Annual Expenditures Per Consumer Unit for Health Care: 1990 to 2002

[In dollars, except percent. See text, Section 13 and headnote, Table 660. For composition of regions, see map, inside front cover]

Item	Health care, total					Percent distribution		
	Amount	Percent of total expenditures	Health insurance	Medical services	Drugs and medical supplies [1]	Health insurance	Medical services	Drugs and medical supplies [1]
1990	1,480	5.2	581	562	337	39.3	38.0	22.8
1995	1,732	5.4	860	512	360	49.7	29.6	20.8
1998	1,903	5.4	913	542	448	48.0	28.5	23.5
1999	1,959	5.3	923	558	479	47.1	28.5	24.5
2000	2,066	5.4	983	568	515	47.6	27.5	24.9
2001	2,182	5.5	1,061	573	549	48.6	26.3	25.2
2002	2,350	5.8	1,168	590	592	49.7	25.1	25.2
Age of reference person:								
Under 25 years old	640	2.6	285	196	160	44.5	30.6	25.0
25 to 34 years old	1,417	3.5	762	391	264	53.8	27.6	18.6
35 to 44 years old	1,980	4.1	1,023	556	402	51.7	28.1	20.3
45 to 54 years old	2,550	5.2	1,180	768	602	46.3	30.1	23.6
55 to 64 years old	3,007	6.8	1,356	863	788	45.1	28.7	26.2
65 to 74 years old	3,588	11.1	1,921	635	1,032	53.5	17.7	28.8
75 years old and over	3,584	15.1	1,849	527	1,207	51.6	14.7	33.7
Race of reference person:								
White and other	2,490	5.9	1,226	637	627	49.2	25.6	25.2
Black	1,339	4.4	747	247	345	55.8	18.4	25.8
Origin of reference person:								
Hispanic	1,366	3.9	671	358	337	49.1	26.2	24.7
Non-Hispanic	2,452	5.9	1,219	614	619	49.7	25.0	25.2
Region of residence:								
Northeast	2,207	5.2	1,178	505	525	53.4	22.9	23.8
Midwest	2,383	5.9	1,185	566	631	49.7	23.8	26.5
South	2,431	6.5	1,196	597	638	49.2	24.6	26.2
West...................	2,310	5.2	1,096	676	538	47.4	29.3	23.3
Size of consumer unit:								
One person	1,522	6.3	759	330	434	49.9	21.7	28.5
Two or more persons.	2,696	5.7	1,339	699	659	49.7	25.9	24.4
Two persons.	3,010	7.2	1,491	700	819	49.5	23.3	27.2
Three persons	2,496	5.2	1,247	648	601	50.0	26.0	24.1
Four persons	2,472	4.6	1,240	740	492	50.2	29.9	19.9
Five persons or more	2,340	4.2	1,144	715	482	48.9	30.6	20.6
Income before taxes:								
Complete income reporters [2]...	2,410	5.7	1,185	605	620	49.2	25.1	25.7
Quintiles of income:								
Lowest 20 percent	1,402	7.4	702	239	461	50.1	17.0	32.9
Second 20 percent	2,183	8.0	1,107	414	662	50.7	19.0	30.3
Third 20 percent	2,506	6.8	1,212	652	643	48.4	26.0	25.7
Fourth 20 percent.......	2,692	5.3	1,354	725	614	50.3	26.9	22.8
Highest 20 percent......	3,262	4.1	1,548	994	721	47.5	30.5	22.1
Incomplete reporters of income .	2,095	6.3	1,088	521	485	51.9	24.9	23.2

[1] Includes prescription and nonprescription drugs.   [2] A complete reporter is a consumer unit providing values for at least one of the major sources of income.
Source: U.S. Bureau of Labor Statistics, *Consumer Expenditure Survey*, annual. <http://www.bls.gov/cex/>

No. 126. Medicare Enrollees: 1980 to 2003

[In millions (28.4 represents 28,400,000). As of July 1. Includes Puerto Rico and island areas and enrollees in foreign countries and unknown place of residence]

Item	1980	1985	1990	1995	2000	2001	2002	2003
Total	**28.4**	**31.1**	**34.3**	**37.6**	**39.7**	**40.1**	**40.5**	**41.0**
Aged	25.5	28.1	31.0	33.2	34.3	34.5	34.7	35.0
Disabled	3.0	2.9	3.3	4.4	5.4	5.6	5.8	6.0
Hospital insurance	28.0	30.6	33.7	37.2	39.3	39.7	40.1	40.6
Aged	25.0	27.7	30.5	32.7	33.8	34.0	34.3	34.6
Disabled	3.0	2.9	3.3	4.4	5.4	5.6	5.8	6.0
Supplementary medical insurance	27.3	29.9	32.6	35.6	37.3	37.7	38.0	38.5
Aged	24.6	27.2	29.6	31.7	32.6	32.7	32.9	33.1
Disabled	2.7	2.7	2.9	3.9	4.8	4.9	5.1	5.3

Source: U.S. Centers for Medicare and Medicaid Services, Office of the Actuary, "Medicare Enrollment Selected Years"; published September 2003; <http://www.cms.hhs.gov/statistics/enrollment/

No. 127. Medicare Disbursements by Type of Beneficiary: 1990 to 2002

[In millions of dollars (109,709 represents $109,709,000,000). For years ending Sept. 30. Distribution of benefits by type is estimated and subject to change]

Type of beneficiary	1990	1995	1997	1998	1999	2000	2001	2002
Total disbursements	**109,709**	**180,096**	**210,359**	**213,411**	**211,959**	**219,276**	**241,175**	**256,856**
Hospital insurance disbursements	66,687	114,883	137,836	137,140	131,441	130,284	141,723	148,031
Benefits	65,721	113,395	136,007	134,321	129,107	125,992	135,979	144,140
Aged	58,503	100,107	120,091	118,346	113,328	110,241	118,835	125,262
Disabled	7,218	13,288	15,916	15,975	15,779	15,751	17,144	18,878
Disabled	6,467	12,300	14,755	14,850	14,745	14,719	16,010	17,613
ESRD [1]	751	988	1,161	1,125	1,034	1,032	1,135	1,265
Home health transfer [2]	-	-	-	978	179	1,706	3,103	1,168
Peer review activity	191	189	168	188	177	236	274	259
Administrative expenses [3]	774	1,300	1,661	1,653	1,978	2,350	2,368	2,464
Supplementary medical insurance disbursements [1]	43,022	65,213	72,523	76,271	80,518	88,992	99,452	108,825
Benefits	41,498	63,491	71,102	75,815	79,187	88,918	100,569	108,163
Aged	36,837	54,830	60,957	65,115	67,963	76,334	86,093	91,660
Disabled	4,661	8,660	10,129	10,666	11,187	12,542	14,420	16,407
Disabled	3,758	7,363	8,683	9,279	9,850	11,063	12,753	14,510
ESRD [1]	903	1,297	1,446	1,387	1,337	1,479	1,667	1,898
Home health transfer [2]	-	-	-	-978	-179	-1,706	-3,103	-1,168
Peer review activity	-	2	16	33	36	43	55	95
Administrative expenses	1,524	1,722	1,420	1,435	1,510	1,780	1,986	1,830

- Represents zero. [1] Represents persons entitled because of End Stage Renal Disease only. Benefits for those who have ESRD but would be entitled due to their aged or disabled status are included in aged and disabled benefits. [2] Beginning 1998 home health agency transfers are excluded from total supplementary medical insurance disbursements and included in total hospital insurance disbursements. [3] Includes costs of experiments and demonstration projects. Includes costs of the health care fraud and abuse control program.

Source: U.S. Centers for Medicare and Medicaid Services, unpublished data.

No. 128. Medicare Benefits by Type of Provider: 1990 to 2002

[In millions of dollars (65,721 represents $65,721,000,000). For years ending Sept. 30. Distribution of benefits by type is estimated and subject to change]

Type of provider	1990	1995	1997	1998	1999	2000	2001	2002
Hospital insurance benefits, total	**65,721**	**113,395**	**136,007**	**134,321**	**129,107**	**125,992**	**135,979**	**144,140**
Inpatient hospital	57,012	81,095	88,991	87,519	86,394	87,060	93,391	101,677
Skilled nursing facility	2,761	8,684	12,104	13,200	11,194	10,229	12,475	15,251
Home health agency	3,295	15,715	17,771	13,716	8,590	4,422	3,812	4,830
Hospice	318	1,854	2,082	2,080	2,494	2,818	3,464	4,516
Managed care	2,335	6,047	15,059	17,807	20,435	21,463	22,837	17,865
Supplementary medical insurance benefits, total	**41,498**	**63,490**	**71,086**	**75,782**	**79,151**	**88,876**	**100,514**	**108,068**
Physician fee schedule	(NA)	31,110	31,958	32,339	33,389	35,958	40,442	44,199
Durable medical equipment	(NA)	3,576	4,112	4,103	4,270	4,577	5,228	6,145
Carrier lab [1]	(NA)	2,819	2,414	2,166	2,086	2,194	2,360	2,701
Other carrier [2]	(NA)	4,513	5,452	5,854	6,398	7,154	8,396	10,300
Hospital [3]	(NA)	8,448	9,208	8,926	8,455	8,520	11,787	13,454
Home health	(NA)	223	213	184	340	4,276	4,169	4,842
Intermediary lab [4]	(NA)	1,437	1,464	1,533	1,597	1,748	1,930	2,144
Other intermediary [5]	(NA)	5,110	6,373	6,545	5,645	6,100	6,953	8,230
Managed care	(NA)	6,253	9,893	14,132	16,970	18,348	19,249	16,052

NA Not available. [1] Lab services paid under the lab fee schedule performed in a physician's office lab or an independent lab. [2] Includes free-standing ambulatory surgical centers facility costs, ambulance, and supplies. [3] Includes the hospital facility costs for Medicare Part B services which are predominantly in the outpatient department. The physician reimbursement associated with these services is included on the "Physician Fee Schedule" line. [4] Lab fee services paid under the lab fee schedule performed in a hospital outpatient department. [5] Includes ESRD free-standing dialysis facility payments and payments to rural health clinics, outpatient rehabilitation facilities, psychiatric hospitals, and federally qualified health centers.

Source: U.S. Centers for Medicare and Medicaid Services, unpublished data.

No. 129. Medicare—Enrollment by State and Other Areas: 1995 to 2002

[(37,535 represents 37,535,000). Hospital and/or medical insurance enrollment as July 1]

State and area	1995	2000	2001	2002	State and area	1995	2000	2001	2002
All areas .	37,535	39,620	40,026	40,489	MO	833	861	867	874
U.S.	36,758	38,762	39,149	39,594	MT	130	137	138	140
					NE........	249	254	255	256
AL.........	642	685	695	706	NV	194	240	251	261
AK.........	34	42	44	46	NH	156	170	173	176
AZ.........	602	675	691	708	NJ	1,168	1,203	1,208	1,213
AR.........	423	439	442	446	NM........	211	234	238	244
CA.........	3,633	3,901	3,955	4,009	NY........	2,630	2,715	2,729	2,747
CO.........	421	467	476	484	NC........	1,027	1,133	1,155	1,178
CT.........	502	515	516	518	ND........	103	103	103	103
DE.........	101	112	114	116	OH........	1,666	1,701	1,705	1,713
DC.........	78	75	75	74	OK........	488	508	511	515
FL.........	2,628	2,804	2,838	2,876	OR.	469	489	496	504
GA.........	833	916	933	951	PA	2,071	2,095	2,095	2,101
HI	149	165	168	171	RI	168	172	172	172
ID	150	165	169	173	SC........	509	568	580	592
IL.........	1,617	1,635	1,640	1,646	SD........	117	119	120	121
IN	823	852	858	865	TN........	771	829	842	855
IA	474	477	478	479	TX........	2,080	2,265	2,300	2,338
KS.........	383	390	391	392	UT........	187	206	210	215
KY.........	586	623	630	637	VT........	83	89	90	91
LA.........	581	602	605	612	VA........	818	893	910	927
ME.........	201	216	219	223	WA........	688	736	746	759
MD.........	602	645	655	664	WV........	330	338	340	343
MA.........	933	961	961	963	WI	762	783	787	794
MI	1,347	1,403	1,414	1,426	WY	60	65	66	67
MN........	631	654	660	667	PR	477	537	550	562
MS........	397	419	423	429	Other areas .	300	321	327	25

Source: U.S. Centers for Medicare and Medicaid Services, "Medicare Beneficiaries enrolled as of July 1 of each year, 1995-1998", published July 1999. "Medicare Beneficiaries Enrolled by State as of July 1, 1999-2002"; published September 2003. <http://www.cms.hhs.gov/statistics>

No. 130. Medicare—Estimated Benefit Payments by State: 2001

[For the year ending September 30. In billions of dollars (236.5 represents $236,500,000,000). Medicare fee for service payments are based on the state of the provider. Managed care organization payments are distributed based on the state of the plan. Both types of payments are on a paid basis. This distribution may differ from similar tables based on the state of the beneficiary]

State and area	Estimated[1] payments, total	Fee for service	Managed care	State and area	Estimated[1] payments, total	Fee for service	Managed care
All areas	236.5	194.4	42.1	Missouri	4.8	3.8	1.0
U.S.	235.0	192.9	42.1	Montana	0.7	0.7	-
				Nebraska	1.4	1.3	0.1
Alabama	4.3	3.9	0.4	Nevada	1.3	0.7	0.6
Alaska	0.2	0.2	-	New Hampshire	0.7	0.7	-
Arizona.........	3.3	1.8	1.5	New Jersey	6.9	5.9	1.0
Arkansas........	2.4	2.3	0.1	New Mexico......	0.9	0.7	0.2
California.......	24.9	13.7	11.2	New York	20.4	17.1	3.4
Colorado........	2.7	1.8	0.9	North Carolina	6.8	6.5	0.3
Connecticut	3.1	2.6	0.5	North Dakota	0.6	0.6	-
Delaware........	0.5	0.5	-	Ohio........	10.7	9.1	1.6
District of Columbia.	0.8	0.6	0.2	Oklahoma	2.3	2.1	0.3
Florida	21.6	16.3	5.3	Oregon	2.2	1.2	1.0
Georgia	4.4	4.1	0.3	Pennsylvania	15.1	11.4	3.7
Hawaii	0.7	0.4	0.3	Rhode Island	1.1	0.8	0.4
Idaho	0.7	0.7	-	South Carolina	3.4	3.4	-
Illinois.........	8.0	7.0	1.0	South Dakota.....	0.6	0.6	-
Indiana........	5.0	4.9	0.1	Tennessee.	5.5	5.3	0.2
Iowa...........	1.6	1.6	-	Texas	16.3	14.6	1.7
Kansas........	2.1	2.1	0.1	Utah........	1.1	1.1	-
Kentucky........	3.6	3.5	0.1	Vermont	0.4	0.4	-
Louisiana	4.9	4.2	0.7	Virginia	3.9	3.9	-
Maine	0.9	0.9	-	Washington	3.2	2.3	0.9
Maryland........	4.6	4.3	0.3	West Virginia	1.8	1.8	-
Massachusetts	6.0	4.4	1.6	Wisconsin	4.0	3.8	0.2
Michigan........	7.0	6.5	0.6	Wyoming........	0.3	0.3	-
Minnesota.......	3.1	2.8	0.4	Puerto Rico	1.5	1.5	-
Mississippi......	2.1	2.1	-	Island areas	0.1	0.1	-

- Represents or rounds to zero. [1] Medicare fee for service estimated benefit payments are based on the state of the provider.

Source: U.S. Centers for Medicare and Medicaid, "Medicare Estimated Benefit Payments by State." <http://www.cms.hhs.gov/statistics/feeforservice/BenefitPayments01.pdf>

Health and Nutrition 99

No. 131. Medicare Trust Funds: 1990 to 2003

[In billions of dollars (72.1 represents $72,100,000,000)]

Type of trust fund	1990	1995	1997	1998	1999	2000	2001	2002	2003
HOSPITAL INSURANCE (HI)									
Net contribution income [1]	72.1	103.3	119.5	130.7	140.3	154.5	160.9	162.7	159.2
Interest received [2]	8.5	10.8	9.6	9.3	10.1	11.7	14.0	15.1	15.8
Benefit payments [3]	66.2	116.4	137.8	134.0	128.8	128.5	141.2	149.9	152.1
Assets, end of year	98.9	130.3	115.6	120.4	141.4	177.5	208.7	234.8	256.0
SUPPLEMENTARY MEDICAL INSURANCE (SMI)									
Net premium income	11.3	19.7	19.3	[4]20.9	[4]19.0	20.6	22.8	25.1	27.4
Transfers from general revenue	33.0	39.0	60.2	[4]64.1	[4]59.1	65.9	72.8	78.3	86.4
Interest received [2]	1.6	1.6	2.5	2.7	2.8	3.5	3.1	2.8	2.0
Benefit payments [3]	42.5	65.0	72.8	76.1	80.7	88.9	99.7	111.0	123.8
Assets, end of year	15.5	13.1	36.1	46.2	44.8	44.0	41.3	34.3	24.0

[1] Includes income from taxation of benefits beginning in 1994. Includes premiums from aged ineligibles enrolled in HI.
[2] Includes recoveries of amounts reimbursed from the trust fund. [3] Beginning 1998 monies transferred to the SMI trust fund for home health agency costs, as provided for by P.L. 105-33, are included in HI benefit payments but excluded from SMI benefit payments. [4] Premiums withheld from check and associated general revenue contributions that were to occur on Jan. 3, 1999 actually occurred on December 31, 1998. These amounts are therefore excluded from 1999 data.

Source: U.S. Centers for Medicare and Medicaid Services, *Annual Report of the Board of Trustees of the Federal Hospital Insurance Trust Fund* and *Annual Report of the Board of Trustees of the Federal Supplementary Medical Insurance Trust Fund.*

No. 132. Medicaid—Selected Characteristics of Persons Covered: 2002

[In thousands, except percent (32,985 represents 32,985,000). Represents number of persons as of March of following year who were enrolled at any time in year shown. Excludes unrelated individuals under age 15. Person did not have to receive medical care paid for by medicaid in order to be counted. See headnote, Table 547]

Poverty status	Total [1]	White	Black	Hispanic [2]	Under 18 years old	18-44 years old	45-64 years old	65 years old and over
Persons covered, total	**32,985**	**22,000**	**8,225**	**7,880**	**17,265**	**8,438**	**4,000**	**3,283**
Below poverty level	14,007	8,625	4,396	3,615	7,571	3,693	1,718	1,025
Above poverty level	18,978	13,375	3,829	4,265	9,694	4,745	2,282	2,258
Percent of population covered	11.6	9.6	23.1	20.1	23.8	7.6	5.9	9.6
Below poverty level	40.5	36.8	51.1	42.3	62.4	27.8	30.9	28.7
Above poverty level	6.7	5.8	10.7	10.9	13.3	4.3	3.4	6.6

[1] Includes other races not shown separately. [2] Persons of Hispanic origin may be of any race.

Source: U.S. Census Bureau, Health Insurance Coverage in the United States: 2002, P60-223. Health Insurance Coverage in the United States: 2002, P60-223. Tables HI02 and HI03. Health Insurance Coverage Status and Type of Coverage by Selected Characteristics for People in the Poverty University: 2002 <http://ferret.bls.census.gov/macro/032003/health/toc.htm>

No. 133. Medicaid—Recipients and Payments: 1990 to 2000

[For year ending September 30 (25,255 represents 25,255,000). Data through 1998 includes Puerto Rico and island areas. Data for 1999 and 2000 includes states only. Medical vendor payments are those made directly to suppliers of medical care]

Basis of eligibility and type of service	Recipients (1,000)					Payments (mil. dol.)				
	1990	1995	1998	1999	2000	1990	1995	1998	1999	2000
Total [1]	**25,255**	**36,282**	**40,649**	**40,184**	**42,763**	**64,859**	**120,141**	**142,318**	**153,479**	**168,307**
Age 65 and over	3,202	4,119	3,964	3,774	3,731	21,508	36,527	40,602	42,521	44,503
Blindness	83	92	(NA)	(NA)	(NA)	434	848	(NA)	(NA)	(NA)
Disabled [2]	3,635	5,767	6,638	6,697	6,889	23,969	48,570	60,375	65,850	72,742
AFDC [3] program	17,230	24,767	26,872	26,348	28,473	17,690	31,487	37,639	39,952	44,537
Other and unknown	1,105	1,537	3,176	3,365	3,671	1,257	2,708	3,702	5,156	6,525
Inpatient services in—										
General hospital	4,593	5,561	4,273	4,497	4,933	16,674	26,331	21,499	22,231	24,266
Mental hospital	92	84	135	97	99	1,714	2,511	2,801	1,758	1,768
Intermediate care facilities, mentally retarded	147	151	126	122	118	7,354	10,383	9,482	9,332	9,375
Nursing facility services [4]	1,461	1,667	1,646	1,617	1,703	17,693	29,052	31,892	33,251	34,432
Physicians	17,078	23,789	18,555	18,373	19,104	4,018	7,360	6,070	6,556	6,806
Dental	4,552	6,383	4,965	5,622	5,892	593	1,019	901	1,204	1,404
Other practitioner	3,873	5,528	4,342	3,986	4,735	372	986	587	470	658
Outpatient hospital	12,370	16,712	12,158	12,417	13,226	3,324	6,627	5,759	6,094	7,053
Clinic	2,804	5,322	5,285	6,746	7,667	1,688	4,280	3,921	5,801	6,174
Laboratory [5]	8,959	13,064	9,381	10,194	11,396	721	1,180	939	1,158	1,288
Home health [6]	719	1,639	1,225	814	995	3,404	9,406	2,702	2,906	3,119
Prescribed drugs	17,294	23,723	19,338	19,855	20,517	4,420	9,791	13,522	16,612	20,014
Family planning	1,752	2,501	2,011	(NA)	(NA)	265	514	449	(NA)	(NA)
Prepaid health care	(NA)	(NA)	20,203	20,687	21,261	(NA)	(NA)	19,296	21,514	24,413

NA Not available. [1] Recipient data do not add due to small number of recipients that are reported in more than one category. Includes recipients of, and payments for, other care not shown separately. [2] Permanently and totally. Beginning 1998, includes blind. [3] Aid to families with dependent children. From 1997 onwards Temporary Assistance to Needy Families which includes children, adults, and foster care children. [4] Nursing facility services includes skilled nursing facility services and intermediate care facility services for all other than the mentally retarded. [5] Includes radiological services. [6] Data for 2000 not comparable with earlier years.

Source: Centers for Medicare and Medicaid Services, OIS/EDG/DQCDD 1990 through 1998 Medicaid Statistical Report HCFA-2082; Beginning; 1999 Medicaid Statistical Information System, MSIS <http://www.cms.hhs.gov/medicaid/datasources.asp>.

100 Health and Nutrition

Medicaid—Summary by State and Other Areas: 1995 and 2000

[For year ending September 30 (36,282 represents 36,282,000). Data for 1995 includes Puerto Rico and island areas. 2000 data includes states only. Data for 2000 includes managed care recipients and capitation payments]

State and area	Recipients [1] (1,000) 1995	2000	Payments [2] (mil. dol) 1995	2000	State and area	Recipients [1] (1,000) 1995	2000	Payments [2] (mil. dol) 1995	2000
All areas .	36,282	(NA)	120,141	(NA)	MO	695	890	2,039	3,270
U.S.	35,210	42,763	119,885	168,307	MT........	99	104	326	433
					NE........	168	229	608	958
AL........	539	619	1,455	2,391	NV........	105	138	350	515
AK........	68	96	252	470	NH........	97	97	473	651
AZ........	494	681	218	2,112	NJ	790	822	3,813	4,707
AR........	353	489	1,376	1,510	NM.......	287	376	714	1,249
CA........	5,017	7,915	10,521	17,060	NY........	3,035	3,420	22,086	26,148
CO........	294	381	1,063	1,809	NC........	1,084	1,209	3,175	4,830
CT........	380	420	2,125	2,839	ND........	61	61	297	356
DE........	79	115	324	528	OH........	1,533	1,305	5,585	7,090
DC........	138	139	532	793	OK........	394	507	1,055	1,604
FL........	1,735	2,360	4,802	7,350	OR........	452	542	1,327	1,700
GA........	1,147	1,290	3,076	3,578	PA........	1,230	1,492	4,633	6,366
HI	52	204	258	535	RI	135	179	673	1,070
ID........	115	131	360	594	SC........	496	685	1,438	2,672
IL........	1,552	1,516	5,600	7,807	SD........	74	102	305	401
IN........	559	705	1,878	2,976	TN........	1,466	1,568	2,772	3,491
IA	304	314	1,036	1,476	TX........	2,562	2,603	6,565	9,075
KS........	256	263	831	1,226	UT........	160	224	464	959
KY........	641	771	1,945	2,913	VT........	100	139	320	479
LA........	785	761	2,708	2,631	VA........	681	627	1,833	2,484
ME........	153	192	760	1,307	WA	639	895	1,461	2,432
MD........	414	665	2,019	3,586	WV	389	335	1,169	1,392
MA........	728	1,047	3,972	5,397	WI	460	577	1,894	2,906
MI	1,168	1,352	3,409	4,881	WY	51	46	171	214
MN........	473	559	2,550	3,277	PR	1,055	(NA)	244	(NA)
MS........	520	605	1,266	1,807	VI	17	(NA)	12	(NA)

NA Not available. [1] Persons who had payments made on their behalf at any time during the fiscal year. [2] Payments are for fiscal year and reflect federal and state contribution payments. Data exclude disproportionate hospital share payments. Disproportionate share hospitals receive higher medicaid reimbursement than other hospitals because they treat a disproportionate share of Medicaid patients.

Source: U.S. Centers for Medicare and Medicaid Services, OIS/EDG/DQCDD Data before 1999 Medicaid Statistical Report HCFA 2082, 1999 data and onwards Medicaid Statistical Information System, MSIS <http://www.cms.hhs.gov/medicaid/datasources.asp>

No. 135. State Children's Health Insurance Program (SCHIP)-Enrollment and Expenditures by State: 2000 and 2003

[(3,334 represents 3,334,000). For year ending September 30. This program provides health benefits coverage to children living in families whose incomes exceed the eligibility limits for medicaid. Although it is generally targeted to families with incomes at or below 200 percent of the federal poverty level, each state may set its own income eligibility limits, within certain guidelines. States have three options: they may expand their medicaid programs, develop a separate child health program that functions independently of medicaid, or do a combination of both]

State	Enrollment [1] (1,000) 2000	2003	Expenditures [2] (mil. dol.) 2000	2003	State	Enrollment [1] (1,000) 2000	2003	Expenditures [2] (mil. dol.) 2000	2003
US	3,334	5,850	1,928.8	4,276.4	MO	74	151	41.2	71.6
AL......	38	79	31.9	71.3	MT......	8	13	4.3	12.0
AK......	13	23	18.1	24.0	NE......	11	45	6.1	24.9
AZ......	61	90	29.4	186.7	NV......	16	47	9.0	22.3
AR......	2	(NA)	1.5	32.7	NH......	4	10	1.6	4.4
CA......	478	955	187.3	565.0	NJ......	89	119	46.9	262.6
CO......	35	74	13.9	40.6	NM.....	6	19	3.4	18.2
CT......	19	21	12.8	17.4	NY......	769	795	401.0	352.2
DE......	4	10	1.5	4.6	NC......	104	150	65.5	130.7
DC......	2	6	5.8	6.0	ND......	3	5	1.8	5.1
FL......	227	443	125.7	357.7	OH......	111	208	53.1	138.5
GA......	121	252	48.7	179.7	OK......	58	92	51.3	38.3
HI	2	12	0.4	7.3	OR......	37	45	12.5	19.8
ID......	12	17	7.5	12.2	PA......	120	160	70.7	120.3
IL......	63	127	32.7	59.4	RI	12	25	10.4	38.7
IN	44	74	53.7	61.7	SC.....	60	76	46.6	44.9
IA	20	37	15.5	32.9	SD.....	6	12	3.1	9.1
KS.....	26	46	12.8	36.9	TN.....	15	(Z)	41.7	(NA)
KY.....	56	94	60.0	69.2	TX.....	131	726	41.4	405.6
LA.....	50	105	25.3	78.4	UT.....	25	38	12.8	20.1
ME.....	23	29	11.4	21.1	VT.....	4	6	1.4	3.1
MD.....	93	130	92.2	137.7	VA.....	38	84	18.6	51.3
MA.....	113	129	44.2	71.6	WA.....	3	10	0.6	16.2
MI.....	37	77	36.2	60.8	WV.....	22	35	9.7	27.0
MN.....	(Z)	(Z)	(Z)	(Z)	WI.....	47	68	21.4	94.9
MS.....	20	75	21.1	88.7	WY.....	3	5	1.0	3.9

NA Not Available. Z Less than 500 or $50,000. [1] Number of children ever enrolled in SCHIP. [2] Expenditures for which States are entitled to Federal reimbursement under Title XXI and which reconciles any advance of Title XXI Federal funds made on the basis of estimates.

Source: U.S. Centers for Medicare & Medicaid Services, The State Children's Health Insurance Program, Annual Enrollment Report and the Statement of Expenditures for the SCHIP Program (CMS-21) <http://www.cms.hhs.gov/schip/>

Health and Nutrition 101

[For year ending June 30. (33,373 represents 33,373,000)]

State and area	Total medi-caid (1,000)	Managed care enrollment Number (1,000)	Percent of total	State and area	Total medi-caid (1,000)	Managed care enrollment Number (1,000)	Percent of total	State and area	Total medi-caid (1,000)	Managed care enrollment Number (1,000)	Percent of total
1995	33,373	9,800	29.4	IL......	1,581	138	8.7	NC......	1,075	749	69.7
2000	33,690	18,786	55.8	IN	707	502	71.0	ND.....	54	36	66.0
2001	36,563	20,774	56.8	IA	267	244	91.5	OH.....	1,516	436	28.8
2003,				KS.....	246	141	57.3	OK.....	498	339	68.0
total ..	41,767	24,406	58.4	KY.....	663	612	92.3	OR.....	426	331	77.7
U.S. ..	40,794	23,548	57.7	LA.....	862	505	58.6	PA.....	1,492	1,192	79.9
AL.....	761	405	53.2	ME.....	250	148	59.3	RI	179	119	66.8
AK.....	95	-	-	MD.....	681	467	68.5	SC.....	862	71	8.3
AZ.....	902	809	89.7	MA.....	915	573	62.6	SD.....	93	91	97.3
AR.....	557	374	67.1	MI	1,322	1,315	99.4	TN.....	1,305	1,305	100.0
CA.....	6,272	3,259	52.0	MN.....	553	362	65.6	TX.....	2,559	1,066	41.7
CO.....	330	262	79.4	MS.....	720	-	-	UT.....	188	162	86.4
CT.....	405	294	72.7	MO.....	951	425	44.7	VT.....	131	86	65.4
DE.....	122	87	71.3	MT.....	80	55	68.9	VA.....	584	263	45.0
DC.....	128	85	66.6	NE.....	197	142	72.1	WA.....	1,060	855	80.7
FL.....	2,214	1,354	61.2	NV.....	164	75	45.7	WV.....	296	152	51.1
GA.....	1,449	1,213	83.7	NH.....	91	13	14.7	WI.....	739	349	47.2
HI.....	180	141	78.8	NJ.....	782	526	67.2	WY.....	56	-	-
ID	157	101	64.5	NM.....	404	261	64.5	PR.....	957	857	89.6
				NY.....	3,646	1,915	52.5	VI.....	16	-	-

- Represents zero.   [1] The Unduplicated Medicaid enrollment figures include individuals in state health care reform programs that expand eligiblity beyond traditional Medicaid eligibility standards.
Source: U.S. Centers for Medicare and Medicaid Services,"Medicaid Managed Care Enrollment Report";<http://www.cms.hhs .gov/medicaid/managedcare/enrolstats.asp>

No. 137. Health Maintenance Organizations (HMOs): 1990 to 2003

[As of January 1 (33.0 represents 33,000,000). An HMO is a prepaid health plan delivering comprehensive care to members through designated providers, having a fixed periodic payment for health care services, and requiring members to be in a plan for a specified period of time (usually 1 year). A group HMO delivers health services through a physician group that is controlled by the HMO unit or contracts with one or more independent group practices to provide health services. An individual practice association (IPA) HMO contracts directly with physicians in independent practice, and/or contracts with one or more associations of physicians in independent practice, and/or contracts with one or more multispecialty group practices. Data are based on a census of HMO's]

Model type	Number of plans						Enrollment [1] (mil.)					
	1990	1995	2000	2001	2002	2003	1990	1995	2000	2001	2002	2003
Total	572	550	568	541	500	454	33.0	46.2	80.9	79.5	76.1	71.8
IPA	360	323	278	257	229	203	13.7	17.4	33.4	33.1	31.6	28.0
Group	212	107	102	104	100	105	19.3	12.9	15.2	15.6	14.9	16.1
Mixed........	(NA)	120	188	180	171	146	(NA)	15.9	32.3	30.8	29.5	27.7

NA Not available.   [1] 1990-1995 exclude enrollees participating in open-ended plans; beginning 1999 includes open-ended enrollment.

No. 138. Persons Enrolled in Health Maintenance Organizations (HMOs) by State: 2000 and 2003

[71,673 represents 71,673,000. Data are based on a census of health maintenance organizations. Pure and open-ended enrollment as of January 1]

State	Number 2003 (1,000)	Percent of population 2000	2003	State	Number 2003 (1,000)	Percent of population 2000	2003	State	Number 2003 (1,000)	Percent of population 2000	2003
US [1] ..	71,673	29.7	24.9	KS	211	17.9	7.8	ND.....	2	2.5	0.4
AL.....	171	7.2	3.8	KY.....	1,278	31.5	31.2	OH.....	2,123	25.1	18.6
AK.....	-	-	-	LA.....	547	17.0	12.2	OK.....	486	14.7	13.9
AZ.....	1,161	30.9	21.3	ME....	274	22.3	21.1	OR.....	851	41.1	24.2
AR.....	192	10.4	7.1	MD....	1,340	43.9	30.6	PA.....	3,911	33.9	31.7
CA.....	17,026	53.5	48.5	MA....	2,489	53.0	38.7	RI	339	38.1	31.7
CO.....	1,366	39.5	30.3	MI	2,613	27.1	26.0	SC.....	266	9.9	6.5
CT.....	1,306	44.6	37.8	MN....	1,386	29.9	27.6	SD.....	81	6.7	10.6
DE.....	123	22.0	15.3	MS....	24	1.1	0.8	TN.....	1,046	33.0	18.0
DC.....	858	35.2	27.8	MO....	1,830	35.2	32.3	TX.....	2,789	18.5	12.8
FL.....	4,339	31.4	26.0	MT....	47	7.0	5.2	UT.....	600	35.3	25.9
GA.....	1,151	17.4	13.4	NE....	152	11.2	8.8	VT.....	61	4.6	9.9
HI	374	30.0	30.0	NH....	331	33.7	25.9	VA.....	852	18.5	16.5
ID	38	7.9	2.8	NJ.....	2,323	30.9	27.0	WA	917	15.2	15.1
IL......	1,852	21.0	14.7	NM....	562	37.7	30.3	WV	163	10.3	10.1
IN	731	12.4	11.9	NV....	459	23.5	21.1	WI	1,582	30.2	29.1
IA	279	7.4	9.5	NC....	963	17.8	11.6	WY	12	1.4	2.4

- Represents zero.   [1] Includes Guam and Puerto Rico.

Source of Tables 137 and 138: InterStudy Publications, St. Paul, MN. *The InterStudy Competitive Edge*, annual (copyright).

No. 139. Health Insurance Coverage Status by Selected Characteristics: 1990 to 2002

[Persons as of following year for coverage in the year shown (248.9 represents 248,900,000). Government health insurance includes medicare, medicaid, and military plans. Based on Current Population Survey; see text, Section 1, Population, and Appendix III]

		Number (mil.)						Percent			
		Covered by private or government health insurance					Not covered by health insurance	Covered by private or government health insurance			Not covered by health insurance
Characteristic	Total persons	Total[1]	Private		Government			Total[1]	Private		
			Total	Group health[2]	Medicare	Medicaid[3]				Medicaid[3]	
1990	248.9	214.2	182.1	150.2	32.3	24.3	34.7	86.1	73.2	9.7	13.9
1995	264.3	223.7	185.9	161.5	34.7	31.9	40.6	84.6	70.3	12.1	15.4
2000 [4][5]	279.5	239.7	201.1	177.8	37.7	29.5	39.8	85.8	71.9	10.6	14.2
2001 [4][5]	282.1	240.9	199.9	176.6	38.0	31.6	41.2	85.4	70.9	11.2	14.6
2002, total [4][5] . . .	285.9	242.4	199.0	175.3	38.4	33.2	43.6	84.8	69.6	11.6	15.2
Age:											
Under 18 years	73.3	64.8	49.5	46.2	0.5	17.5	8.5	88.4	67.5	23.9	11.6
Under 6 years . . .	23.7	21.1	15.0	14.2	0.2	6.9	2.6	89.1	63.4	29.1	10.9
6 to 11 years	24.3	21.6	16.5	15.6	0.2	5.8	2.7	89.0	68.1	24.0	11.0
12 to 17 years . . .	25.4	22.1	18.0	16.3	0.2	4.8	3.3	87.1	70.7	19.0	12.9
18 to 24 years	27.4	19.3	16.6	13.4	0.2	2.9	8.1	70.4	60.4	10.6	29.6
25 to 34 years	39.2	29.5	26.5	24.8	0.5	2.8	9.8	75.1	67.5	7.1	24.9
35 to 44 years	44.1	36.3	33.2	31.2	0.9	2.7	7.8	82.3	75.4	6.2	17.7
45 to 54 years	40.2	34.6	31.7	29.6	1.4	2.2	5.6	86.1	78.9	5.5	13.9
55 to 64 years	27.4	23.9	20.8	18.5	2.4	1.8	3.5	87.2	75.9	6.5	12.9
65 years and over . .	34.2	34.0	20.7	11.6	32.6	3.3	0.3	99.3	60.4	9.6	0.8
Sex: Male	139.9	116.5	97.4	87.0	16.6	14.7	23.3	83.3	69.6	10.5	16.7
Female	146.1	125.8	101.6	88.3	21.8	18.6	20.2	86.1	69.6	12.7	13.9
Race: White alone	230.8	198.1	167.2	145.2	33.1	22.2	32.7	85.8	72.4	9.6	14.2
Black alone.	35.8	28.6	19.3	18.0	3.8	8.3	7.2	79.8	54.0	23.2	20.2
Asian alone	11.6	9.4	7.9	6.9	1.0	1.2	2.1	81.6	68.7	10.4	18.5
Hispanic origin [6]	39.4	26.6	18.1	16.7	2.5	7.9	12.8	67.6	46.0	20.2	32.4
Household income:											
Less than $25,000 . .	63.0	48.2	23.7	15.3	18.0	18.7	14.8	76.5	37.7	29.6	23.5
$25,000-$49,999 . . .	75.9	61.3	49.8	43.0	11.5	9.2	14.6	80.7	65.6	12.2	19.3
$50,000-$74,999 . . .	58.6	51.7	47.7	44.0	4.5	3.0	6.9	88.2	81.3	5.2	11.8
$75,000 or more . . .	88.4	81.2	77.8	72.9	4.4	2.3	7.3	91.8	88.0	2.6	8.2
Persons below poverty .	34.6	24.1	8.7	5.6	5.0	14.0	10.5	69.7	25.3	40.5	30.4

[1] Includes other government insurance, not shown separately. Persons with coverage counted only once in total, even though they may have been covered by more than one type of policy. [2] Related to employment of self or other family members. [3] Beginning 1997 persons with no coverage other than access to Indian Health Service are no longer considered covered by health insurance; instead they are considered to be uninsured. The effect of this change on the overall estimates of health insurance coverage is negligible; however, the decrease in the number of people covered by medicaid may be partially due to this change. [4] Estimates reflect results of follow-up verification questions. [5] Implementation of Census 2000 based population controls. Sample expanded by 28,000 households. [6] Persons of Hispanic origin may be of any race.

No. 140. Persons With and Without Health Insurance Coverage by State: 2002

[242,360 represents 242,360,000. Based on the Current Population Survey and subject to sampling error; see text, Section 1, Population, and Appendix III]

State	Total persons covered (1,000)	Total persons not covered Number (1,000)	Total persons not covered Percent of total	Children not covered Number (1,000)	Children not covered Percent of total	State	Total persons covered (1,000)	Total persons not covered Number (1,000)	Total persons not covered Percent of total	Children not covered Number (1,000)	Children not covered Percent of total
U.S. . . .	242,360	43,574	15.2	8,531	11.6	MO	4,939	646	11.6	69	5.0
						MT.	767	139	15.3	32	15.0
AL	3,876	564	12.7	122	10.8	NE.	1,530	174	10.2	25	5.6
AK	516	119	18.7	26	13.3	NV	1,703	418	19.7	114	19.7
AZ	4,526	916	16.8	218	14.7	NH	1,141	125	9.9	15	4.8
AR	2,252	440	16.3	67	10.0	NJ	7,408	1,197	13.9	210	9.7
CA	28,761	6,398	18.2	1,352	14.0	NM.	1,452	388	21.1	73	14.5
CO.	3,756	720	16.1	165	14.4	NY	16,241	3,042	15.8	461	9.9
CT	3,027	356	10.5	71	8.1	NC	6,794	1,368	16.8	261	12.7
DE	719	79	9.9	19	9.8	ND	564	69	10.9	11	7.4
DC	498	74	13.0	10	8.6	OH	9,938	1,344	11.9	239	8.2
FL	13,586	2,843	17.3	563	14.5	OK.	2,876	601	17.3	102	11.6
GA	7,072	1,354	16.1	279	12.3	OR.	2,999	511	14.6	95	11.3
HI	1,101	123	10.0	24	7.4	PA	10,809	1,380	11.3	290	10.2
ID	1,067	233	17.9	50	13.6	RI	952	104	9.8	11	4.7
IL	10,737	1,767	14.1	373	11.3	SC	3,497	500	12.5	69	6.9
IN	5,303	797	13.1	158	9.8	SD	659	85	11.5	15	7.7
IA	2,626	277	9.5	42	5.9	TN	5,058	614	10.8	95	6.8
KS	2,404	280	10.4	57	8.1	TX	15,973	5,556	25.8	1,352	22.4
KY	3,498	548	13.6	122	12.6	UT.	2,000	310	13.4	71	9.3
LA	3,627	820	18.4	140	11.9	VT.	553	66	10.7	8	5.7
ME	1,125	144	11.3	22	7.9	VA	6,156	962	13.5	221	12.3
MD	4,728	730	13.4	140	9.9	WA	5,151	850	14.2	137	9.0
MA	5,827	644	9.9	88	5.9	WV	1,496	255	14.6	40	10.3
MI	8,752	1,158	11.7	175	6.9	WI	4,938	538	9.8	63	4.6
MN	4,657	397	7.9	72	5.8	WY	402	86	17.7	17	14.2
MS	2,322	465	16.7	83	10.9						

Source of Tables 139 and 140: U.S. Census Bureau; Current Population Reports, P60-223, and unpublished data.

No. 141. People Without Health Insurance for the Entire Year by Selected Characteristics: 2000 and 2002

[In thousands, except as noted (279,517 represents 279,517,000). Based on the Current Population Survey and subject to sampling error; see text, Section 1 and Appendix III]

Characteristic	2000			2002		
		Uninsured persons			Uninsured persons	
	Total persons	Number	Percent distribution	Total persons	Number	Percent distribution
Total [1]	279,517	39,804	100.0	285,933	43,574	100.0
Under 18 years	72,314	8,617	21.6	73,312	8,531	19.6
18 to 24 years	26,815	7,406	18.6	27,438	8,128	18.7
25 to 34 years	38,865	8,507	21.4	39,243	9,769	22.4
35 to 44 years	44,566	6,898	17.3	44,074	7,781	17.9
45 to 64 years	63,391	8,124	20.4	67,633	9,107	20.9
65 years and over.	33,566	251	0.6	34,234	258	0.6
Male.	136,559	20,791	52.2	139,876	23,327	53.5
Female	142,958	19,013	47.8	146,057	20,246	46.5
White	228,208	30,075	75.6	(NA)	(NA)	(NA)
Non-Hispanic	193,931	18,683	46.9	(NA)	(NA)	(NA)
Black	35,597	6,683	16.8	(NA)	(NA)	(NA)
Asian and Pacific Islander	12,693	2,287	5.7	(NA)	(NA)	(NA)
White alone [2]	(NA)	(NA)	(NA)	230,809	32,706	75.1
Black alone [2]	(NA)	(NA)	(NA)	35,806	7,228	16.6
Asian alone [2]	(NA)	(NA)	(NA)	11,558	2,132	4.9
Hispanic [3]	36,093	11,883	29.9	39,384	12,756	29.3

NA Not available.   [1] Includes other races not shown separately.   [2] Refers to person who indicated only a single race group.   [3] Persons of Hispanic origin may be of any race.

Source: U.S. Census Bureau, *Current Population Survey*, 2001 and 2003 Annual Demographic Supplements.

No. 142. Percent of Workers Participating in Health Care Benefit Programs and Percent of Participants Required to Contribute: 2003

[Based on National Compensation Survey, a sample survey of 2,924 private industry establishments of all sizes, representing nearly 102.2 million workers; see Appendix III. See also Table 630]

Characteristic	Percent of workers participating—			Single coverage medical care			Family coverage medical care		
	Medical care	Dental care	Vision care	Employee contributions not required (percent)	Employee contributions required (percent)	Average monthly contribution [1] (dol.)	Employee contributions not required (percent)	Employee contributions required (percent)	Average monthly contribution [1] (dol.)
Total	45	32	19	22	78	60.24	10	90	228.98
White-collar occupations .	50	37	21	20	80	61.95	8	92	236.17
Blue-collar occupations ..	51	33	20	27	73	55.22	13	87	208.18
Service occupations	22	15	9	(NA)	(NA)	(NA)	(NA)	(NA)	(NA)
Full time [2]	56	40	23	22	78	59.63	10	90	227.52
Part time [2]	9	6	5	(NA)	(NA)	(NA)	(NA)	(NA)	(NA)
Union [3]	60	51	37	41	59	49.40	31	69	174.60
Nonunion [3]	44	30	17	(NA)	(NA)	(NA)	(NA)	(NA)	(NA)

NA Not available.   [1] The average is presented for all covered workers and excludes workers without the plan provision. Averages are for plans stating a flat monthly cost.   [2] Employees are classified as working either a full-time or part-time schedule based on the definition used by each establishment.   [3] Union workers are those whose wages are determined through collective bargaining.

Source: U.S. Bureau of Labor Statistics, *National Compensation Survey: Employee Benefits in Private Industry in the United States, 2003*.

No. 143. Outpatient Prescription Drug Benefits—Selected Features: 2000

[In percent except as indicated. 50,464 represents 50,464,000. Covers only drug benefits for full-time employees. Based on National Compensation Survey, a sample survey of 1,436 private industry establishments of all sizes, representing over 107 million workers; see Appendix III. See also Table 630]

Characteristic	Full-time employees, total	Professional, technical, and related	Clerical and sales	Blue-collar and service
Number with coverage (1,000)	50,464	13,380	14,112	22,972
Percent with—				
Coverage for brand name drugs	99	99	99	99
Higher reimbursement for generic drugs	78	78	84	74
Coverage for mail order drugs [1]	64	64	64	65
Higher reimbursement for prescriptions filled at selected pharmacies	42	45	39	42

[1] Programs that provide drugs for maintenance purposes, that is, drugs required on a continuous basis.

Source: U.S. Bureau of Labor Statistics, *National Compensation Survey: Employee Benefits in Private Industry in the United States, 2000*, U. S. Department of Labor Bulletin 2555, January 2003; <www.bls.gov/ncs/ebs/>.

No. 144. Medical Care Benefits of Workers by Type and Amount of Employee Contribution: 2003

[In percent except as indicated (35,888 represents 35,888,000) . See head note, Table 142]

Type and amount of contribution	Individual coverage				Type and amount of contribution	Family coverage			
	All employees,	White-collar occupations,	Blue-collar occupations,	Service occupations		All employees	White-collar occupations,	Blue-collar occupations,	Service occupations
Number with contributory coverage (1,000)	35,888	21,174	11,207	3,507	Number with contributory coverage (1,000)	41,377	24,248	13,279	3,850
Total with contributory coverage	100	100	100	100	Total with contributory coverage	100	100	100	100
Flat monthly amount	72	73	72	67	Flat monthly amount	72	71	74	70
Less than $5.00	1	1	1	(Z)	Less than $25.00	1	1	2	2
$5.00-$9.99	2	1	2	2	$25.00-$49.99	3	2	5	2
$10.00-$14.99	2	2	3	1	$50.00-$74.99	4	3	6	7
$15.00-$19.99	2	1	3	1	$75.00-$99.99	5	5	4	3
$20.00-$29.99	8	8	8	9	$100.00-$124.99	6	6	7	4
$30.00-$39.99	10	9	11	7	$125.00-$149.99	5	5	7	1
$40.00-$49.99	10	9	11	9	$150.00-$174.99	7	7	7	7
$50.00-$59.99	9	10	8	9	$175.00-$199.99	6	6	6	4
$60.00-$69.99	8	8	6	9	$200.00-$224.99	5	5	4	7
$70.00-$79.99	6	6	7	4	$225.00-$249.99	4	4	5	2
$80.00-$89.99	2	3	3	2	$250.00-$274.99	4	5	3	4
$90.00-$99.99	3	3	3	4	$275.00-$299.99	2	3	2	2
$100.00-$124.99	6	8	3	3	$300.00-$324.99	4	4	4	3
$125.00 or more	4	5	3	6	$325.00-$349.99	2	2	3	3
Dollar amount unspecified .	-	-	-	-	$350.00 or more	13	15	11	21
Composite rate[1]	1	2	(Z)	(Z)	Composite rate[1]	1	1	(Z)	(Z)
Varies[2]	4	4	4	5	Varies[2]	3	3	3	3
Flexible benefits[3]	2	3	1	1	Flexible benefits[3]	2	2	1	1
Percent of earnings	(Z)	1	(Z)	1	Percent of earnings	(Z)	(Z)	(Z)	(Z)
Exists, but unknown	18	16	19	24	Exists, but unknown	19	19	18	22

- Represents zero.   Z Less than 0.5 percent.   [1] A composite rate is a set contribution covering more than one benefit area; for example, health care and life insurance. Cost data for individual plans cannot be determined.   [2] Based on worker attributes. For example, employee contributions may vary based on earnings, length of service, or age.   [3] Amount varies by options selected under a "cafeteria plan" or employer-sponsored reimbursement account.

Source: U.S. Bureau of Labor Statistics, *News*, USDL 03-489, September 19, 2003.

No. 145. Annual Receipts/Revenue for Health Care Industries: 1998 to 2002

[In millions of dollars (399,518 represents $399,518,000,000). Based on the North American Industry Classification System, 1997 (NAICS); see text, Section 15. All firms in NAICS 6211, 6212, 6213, and 6215 are defined as taxable. Estimates for the non-employer portion are derived from administrative records data provided by other federal agencies. These data are available only at the total revenue level. Estimates for tax-exempt firms are derived only from a sample of employer firms. See Appendix III]

Kind of business	NAICS code	Total, all firms [1]			Employer firms		
		1998	2000	2002	1998	2000	2002
Ambulatory health care services	621	399,518	443,510	519,145	374,348	415,962	486,698
Offices of physicians	6211	192,639	214,658	249,592	181,579	202,913	236,055
Offices of dentists	6212	53,156	60,726	70,833	51,476	58,812	68,630
Offices of other health practitioners [2]	6213	37,778	41,579	48,623	30,018	32,512	37,741
Offices of chiropractors	62131	7,907	8,691	10,283	6,946	7,576	8,982
Offices of optometrists	62132	7,454	8,607	9,411	6,885	7,941	8,672
Offices of PT/OT/speech therapy & audiology [3].	62134	10,173	9,869	12,384	9,003	8,531	10,743
Outpatient care centers	6214	52,447	60,255	72,249	51,851	59,571	71,487
Medical & diagnostic laboratories	6215	19,236	23,129	28,173	18,501	22,261	27,088
Home health care services	6216	31,942	30,019	34,447	30,579	28,325	32,168
Other ambulatory health care services	6219	12,321	13,144	15,228	10,345	11,568	13,520
Hospitals	622	397,373	430,329	507,206	397,373	430,329	507,206
General medical & surgical hospitals	6221	(NA)	(NA)	(NA)	370,862	402,578	475,453
Psychiatric & substance abuse hospitals	6222	(NA)	(NA)	(NA)	14,686	14,944	15,378
Other specialty hospitals	6223	(NA)	(NA)	(NA)	11,825	12,807	16,374
Nursing and residential care facilities	623	100,138	108,885	122,881	98,984	107,421	121,197
Nursing care facilities.	6231	(NA)	(NA)	(NA)	63,085	65,774	72,531
Residential mental retardation/health facilities [2] . .	6232	(NA)	(NA)	(NA)	12,479	14,353	16,614
Residential mental retardation facilities	62321	(NA)	(NA)	(NA)	8,287	9,301	10,687
Community care facilities for the elderly	6233	(NA)	(NA)	(NA)	18,041	21,504	25,477

NA Not available.   [1] Includes taxable nonemployer firms, not shown separately.   [2] Includes other kinds of business not shown separately.   [3] Offices of physical, occupational and speech therapists, and audiologists.

Source: U.S. Census Bureau, *Service Annual Survey, 2002*, SAS/02. See also <http://www.census.gov/prod/2004pubs/SAS-02.pdf>.

Health and Nutrition 105

No. 146. Receipts for Selected Health Service Industries by Source of Revenue: 2000 and 2002

[In millions of dollars (202,913 represents $202,913,000,000). Based on the 1997 North American Industry Classification System (NAICS), see text, Section 15. Based on a sample of employer firms only and does not include nonemployer revenue. See Appendix III]

Source of revenue	Offices of physicians (NAICS 6211) 2000	2002	Offices of dentists (NAICS 6212) 2000	2002	Hospitals (NAICS 622) 2000	2002	Nursing and residential care facilities (NAICS 623) 2000	2002
Total	202,913	236,065	58,812	68,630	430,329	507,204	107,421	121,197
Medicare	48,370	56,634	(S)	(S)	138,843	162,915	12,699	15,861
Medicaid	13,896	17,024	1,416	2,376	52,305	60,690	43,834	49,178
Other government [1]	2,025	2,356	(S)	(S)	22,687	27,106	7,157	8,868
Worker's compensation	7,419	7,982	(S)	(S)	4,720	5,524	(S)	(S)
Private insurance	97,193	115,000	30,232	35,344	155,206	187,964	6,231	6,936
Patient (out-of-pocket)	22,865	24,762	25,747	29,675	22,928	26,587	[2]27,019	[2]27,651
Other patient care sources, n.e.c [3]	7,299	8,228	(S)	(S)	10,622	12,094	3,300	2,733
Non-patient care revenue	3,846	4,079	(S)	(S)	23,019	24,324	6,910	3,142

S Figure does not meet publication standards.   [1] Veterans, National Institute of Health, Indian Affairs, etc.   [2] Represents payment from patients and their families plus patients' assigned social security benefits.   [3] N.e.c. represents not elsewhere classified.

Source: U.S. Census Bureau, *Service Annual Survey: 2002.*

No. 147. Employment in the Health Service Industries: 1990 to 2003

[In thousands (2,842 represents 2,842,000). See head note Table 613]

Industry	NAICS code [1]	1990	1995	2000	2001	2002	2003
Ambulatory health care services [2]	621	2,842	3,768	4,320	4,462	4,633	4,776
Offices of physicians	6211	1,278	1,540	1,840	1,911	1,968	2,004
Offices of dentists	6212	513	592	688	705	725	745
Offices of other health practitioners	6213	276	395	438	457	486	501
Medical and diagnostic laboratories	6215	129	146	162	170	175	180
Home health care services	6216	288	622	633	639	680	727
Hospitals	622	3,513	3,734	3,954	4,051	4,160	4,253
General medical and surgical hospitals	6221	3,305	3,520	3,745	3,833	3,930	4,013
Psychiatric and substance abuse hospitals	6222	113	101	86	87	90	91
Other hospitals	6223	95	112	123	132	140	148
Nursing and residential care facilities [2]	623	1,856	2,308	2,583	2,676	2,743	2,784
Nursing care facilities	6231	1,170	1,413	1,514	1,547	1,573	1,583

[1] Based on the North American Industry Classification System 2002 code; see text, Section 15.   [2] Includes other industries not shown separately.

Source: U.S. Bureau of Labor Statistics, *Employment and Earnings,* monthly, March 2004 issue.

No. 148. Registered Nurses by Employment Status: 1996 and 2000

[As of March (2,559 represents 2,559,000). Based on a sample and subject to sampling variability; see source for details]

Age, race and Hispanic origin status	Total (1,000)	Employed in nursing Number (1,000)	Percent distribution	Not employed in nursing (1,000)
1996	2,559	2,116	100.0	443
2000	2,697	2,202	100.0	495
Less than 25 years	66	65	2.9	2
25 to 29 years	177	166	7.5	11
30 to 34 years	248	225	10.2	24
35 to 39 years	360	316	14.4	44
40 to 44 years	464	409	18.6	55
45 to 49 years	465	406	18.5	58
50 to 54 years	342	288	13.1	55
55 to 59 years	238	180	8.2	58
60 to 64 years	156	87	4.0	69
65 years and over	154	41	1.9	113
Unknown age	25	19	0.8	6
White non-Hispanic	2,334	1,891	85.9	443
Black non-Hispanic	133	113	5.1	20
Asian non-Hispanic	93	83	3.8	11
Native Hawaiian/Pacific Islander	6	6	0.3	1
American Indian/Alaska Native	13	11	0.5	1
Hispanic [1]	55	48	2.2	7
Two or more races non-Hispanic	33	27	1.2	6
Unknown race/ethnic	29	23	1.1	6

[1] Persons of Hispanic origin may be of any race.

Source: U.S. Dept. of Health and Human Services, Health Resources and Services Administration, *The Registered Nurse Population, March 2000,* September 2001.

No. 149. Physicians by Selected Activity: 1980 to 2002

[In thousands (467.7 represents 467,700). As of Dec. 31, except 1990 as of Jan. 1, and as noted. Includes Puerto Rico and island areas]

Activity	1980	1990	1995	1999	2000	2001	2002
Doctors of medicine, total	467.7	615.4	720.3	797.6	813.8	836.2	853.2
Professionally active	435.5	560.0	646.0	720.9	737.5	751.7	768.5
Place of medical education:							
U.S. medical graduates	343.6	437.2	492.2	542.2	554.2	562.3	573.7
Foreign medical graduates [1]	91.8	122.8	153.8	178.7	183.4	189.4	194.8
Sex: Male	386.7	463.9	505.9	544.1	551.7	556.6	564.0
Female	48.7	96.1	140.1	176.7	185.8	195.1	204.5
Active nonfederal	417.7	539.5	624.9	702.8	718.1	731.7	748.3
Patient care	361.9	487.8	564.1	610.7	631.4	652.3	658.1
Office-based practice	271.3	359.9	427.3	473.2	490.4	514.0	516.2
General and family practice	47.8	57.6	59.9	66.2	67.5	70.0	71.7
Cardiovascular diseases	6.7	10.7	13.7	15.6	16.3	17.0	17.0
Dermatology	4.4	6.0	7.0	7.8	8.0	8.2	8.3
Gastroenterology	2.7	5.2	7.3	8.2	8.5	8.9	9.0
Internal medicine	40.5	57.8	72.6	84.6	88.7	94.7	96.5
Pediatrics	17.4	26.5	33.9	40.5	42.2	44.8	46.1
Pulmonary diseases	2.0	3.7	5.0	5.7	6.1	6.6	6.7
General surgery	22.4	24.5	24.1	26.8	24.5	25.6	24.9
Obstetrics and gynecology	19.5	25.5	29.1	31.1	31.7	32.6	32.7
Ophthalmology	10.6	13.1	14.6	15.2	15.6	16.0	16.1
Orthopedic surgery	10.7	14.2	17.1	17.0	17.4	17.8	18.1
Otolaryngology	5.3	6.4	7.1	7.3	7.6	7.9	8.0
Plastic surgery	2.4	3.8	4.6	5.1	5.3	5.5	5.6
Urological surgery	6.2	7.4	8.0	8.2	8.5	8.6	8.6
Anesthesiology	11.3	17.8	23.8	26.6	27.6	28.9	28.7
Diagnostic radiology	4.2	9.8	12.8	14.3	14.6	15.6	15.9
Emergency medicine	(NA)	8.4	11.7	13.9	14.5	15.8	16.9
Neurology	3.2	5.6	7.6	8.1	8.6	9.2	9.0
Pathology, anatomical/clinical	6.0	7.3	9.0	10.1	10.3	10.6	10.1
Psychiatry	15.9	20.0	23.3	24.4	25.0	25.7	25.4
Other specialty	31.9	28.8	35.0	36.4	42.0	44.1	41.0
Hospital-based practice	90.6	127.9	136.8	137.2	141.0	138.3	141.9
Residents and interns [2]	59.6	89.9	93.7	92.5	95.1	92.9	96.5
Full-time hospital staff	31.0	38.0	43.1	44.8	45.9	45.4	45.3
Other professional activity [3]	35.2	39.0	40.3	41.2	41.6	41.0	41.1
Not classified	20.6	12.7	20.6	50.9	45.1	38.3	49.1
Federal	17.8	20.5	21.1	18.1	19.4	20.0	20.2
Patient care	14.6	16.1	18.1	14.7	16.0	16.6	16.7
Other professional activity [3]	3.2	4.4	3.0	3.4	3.4	3.4	3.5
Inactive/unknown address	32.1	55.4	74.3	76.8	76.3	84.5	84.7
Doctors of osteopathy [4]	18.8	30.9	35.7	43.5	44.9	47.0	49.2

NA Not available.   [1] Foreign medical graduates received their medical education in schools outside the United States and Canada.   [2] Includes clinical fellows.   [3] Includes medical teaching, administration, research, and other.   [4] As of June 1. Total DOs. Data from American Osteopathic Association, Chicago, IL.

Source: Except as noted, American Medical Association, Chicago, IL, Physician Characteristics and Distribution in the U.S., annual (copyright).

No. 150. Active Nonfederal Physicians, 2002, and Nurses, 2001 by State

[As of December. Excludes doctors of osteopathy, federally-employed persons, and physicians with addresses unknown. Includes all physicians not classified according to activity status]

State	Physicians Total	Physicians Rate [1]	Nurses Total	Nurses Rate [1]	State	Physicians Total	Physicians Rate [1]	Nurses Total	Nurses Rate [1]
United States. .	738,076	256	2,262,020	793	Missouri	13,237	233	52,970	940
Alabama	9,054	202	36,400	814	Montana	1,960	215	7,620	842
Alaska	1,246	194	4,930	778	Nebraska	3,975	230	15,970	928
Arizona	10,648	196	34,880	657	Nevada	3,762	174	10,840	517
Arkansas	5,257	194	19,860	737	New Hampshire	3,205	251	11,190	889
California	88,045	252	185,550	536	New Jersey	26,183	305	71,500	840
Colorado.	10,627	236	33,510	756	New Mexico	4,103	222	11,630	635
Connecticut.	12,438	360	32,740	953	New York	73,710	385	165,580	868
Delaware	1,951	242	7,280	913	North Carolina	20,039	241	72,050	878
District of Columbia .	3,890	683	8,600	1,498	North Dakota	1,444	228	6,460	1,014
Florida	39,612	237	129,610	792	Ohio	28,314	248	103,870	912
Georgia	17,790	208	58,600	697	Oklahoma	5,705	163	22,890	660
Hawaii	3,474	280	8,680	707	Oregon	8,528	242	26,040	750
Idaho	2,158	161	8,400	636	Pennsylvania.	35,937	291	132,120	1,074
Illinois	33,341	265	104,830	837	Rhode Island.	3,638	341	11,160	1,053
Indiana	12,748	207	49,590	809	South Carolina	8,978	219	28,130	693
Iowa	5,232	178	30,190	1,030	South Dakota	1,531	201	8,440	1,114
Kansas	5,699	210	24,680	913	Tennessee	14,470	250	48,880	850
Kentucky	8,943	219	34,920	858	Texas.	44,315	204	129,710	607
Louisiana	11,570	258	36,690	821	Utah	4,638	200	13,830	607
Maine.	3,243	250	13,390	1,043	Vermont	2,131	346	5,820	949
Maryland	20,587	378	43,340	805	Virginia.	18,439	253	55,440	770
Massachusetts.	27,389	427	75,580	1,181	Washington	15,176	250	45,170	754
Michigan	23,072	230	83,950	839	West Virginia.	3,987	221	15,850	880
Minnesota	13,239	263	46,990	943	Wisconsin	13,915	256	49,610	918
Mississippi	4,891	171	22,290	779	Wyoming	878	176	3,780	765

[1] Per 100,000 resident population. Based on U.S. Census Bureau estimates as of July 1.

Source: Physicians: American Medical Association, Chicago, IL, Physician Characteristics and Distribution in the U.S., annual (copyright); Nurses: U.S. Dept. of Health and Human Services, Health Resources and Services Administration, unpublished data.

Health and Nutrition   107

No. 151. Health Professions—Practitioners and Schools: 1990 to 2002

[(573 represents 573,000). Data on the number of schools and total enrollment are reported as of the beginning of the academic year; all other school data are reported as of the end of the academic year. Data are based on reporting by health professions schools]

Year	Medi-cine	Oste-opathy	Registered nursing				Licensed practical nursing	Den-tistry [1]	Optom-etry	Phar-macy
			Total	Bacca-laureate	Associ-ate degree	Diploma				
ACTIVE PERSONNEL (1,000)										
1990	573	28	[2]1,790	682	1,107	([3])	441	148	26	168
1995	646	36	[2]2,116	881	1,235	([3])	399	159	29	181
2000	738	45	[2]2,249	983	1,267	([3])	374	168	32	196
2001	752	42	[2]2,262	1,000	1,262	([3])	(NA)	(NA)	(NA)	(NA)
NUMBER OF SCHOOLS [4]										
1990	126	15	1,470	489	829	152	1,154	56	17	74
1995	125	16	1,516	521	876	119	1,210	54	17	75
2000	125	19	(NA)	(NA)	(NA)	(NA)	(NA)	55	17	81
2001	125	19	(NA)	(NA)	(NA)	(NA)	(NA)	54	17	83
2002	125	19	(NA)	(NA)	(NA)	(NA)	(NA)	54	(NA)	83
TOTAL ENROLLMENT										
1990	65,016	6,615	201,458	74,865	106,175	20,418	46,720	16,412	4,723	23,013
1995	66,788	8,146	268,350	112,659	135,895	19,796	59,428	16,353	5,201	27,667
2000	66,377	10,388	192,202	89,508	95,598	7,096	(NA)	17,242	5,464	29,586
2001	66,160	10,817	(NA)	(NA)	(NA)	(NA)	(NA)	17,349	5,428	30,301
2002	66,253	11,101	(NA)	(NA)	(NA)	(NA)	(NA)	17,487	(NA)	31,769
GRADUATES										
1990	15,398	1,529	66,088	18,571	42,318	5,199	35,417	4,233	1,115	6,956
1995	15,883	1,843	97,052	31,254	58,749	7,049	44,234	3,908	1,219	7,837
2000	15,714	2,279	(NA)	(NA)	(NA)	(NA)	(NA)	4,171	1,315	7,260
2001	15,785	2,510	(NA)	(NA)	(NA)	(NA)	(NA)	4,367	1,310	7,000
2002	15,652	2,534	(NA)	(NA)	(NA)	(NA)	(NA)	4,349	(NA)	7,573

NA Not available. [1] Personnel data exclude dentists in military service, U.S. Public Health Service, and U.S. Dept. of Veterans Affairs. [2] Includes nurses with advanced degrees. [3] Diploma nurses included with associate degree nurses. [4] Some nursing schools offer more than one type of program. Numbers shown for nursing are number of nursing programs.

Source: U.S. Dept. of Health and Human Services, Bureau of Health Professions, unpublished data; American Medical Association, Chicago, IL, *Physician Characteristics and Distribution in the U.S.*, annual; and American Association of Colleges of Osteopathic Medicine, Rockville, MD, *Annual Statistical Report.*

No. 152. Percent Distribution of Number of Visits to Health Care Professionals by Selected Characteristics: 2001 and 2002

[Covers ambulatory visits to doctor's offices and emergency departments, and home health care visits during a 12-month period. Based on the redesigned National Health Interview Survey, a sample survey of the civilian noninstitutionalized population. See Appendix III]

Characteristic	None		1-3 visits		4-9 visits		10 or more visits	
	2001	2002	2001	2002	2001	2002	2001	2002
All persons [1]	16.5	15.9	45.8	45.5	24.4	25.2	13.3	13.4
Age:								
Under 6 years	5.5	5.6	45.8	47.0	37.9	37.1	10.8	10.4
6-17 years	14.6	13.0	58.9	59.0	20.5	22.3	6.1	5.7
18-44 years	23.3	22.6	46.1	45.7	18.9	19.4	11.8	12.4
45-64 years	15.6	14.8	42.9	41.9	25.7	26.9	15.9	16.4
65-74 years	8.1	9.1	35.8	33.7	33.5	36.8	22.6	20.5
75 years and over	5.8	7.3	28.2	28.6	38.1	35.8	27.9	28.3
Sex: [1]								
Male	21.3	20.6	46.5	46.5	21.6	22.2	10.7	10.7
Female	11.9	11.4	45.1	44.5	27.1	28.0	15.9	16.1
Race: [1][2]								
White only	15.9	15.6	45.7	45.1	24.8	25.4	13.5	13.8
Black only	16.4	15.3	46.4	45.8	24.0	26.0	13.2	13.0
American Indian or Alaska Native only	21.4	18.1	36.4	43.7	25.4	21.7	16.9	16.6
Asian only	20.8	21.2	48.3	49.7	22.3	20.3	8.6	8.8
Two or more races	18.0	13.5	41.2	43.7	23.5	27.3	17.3	15.4
Race and Hispanic origin: [1]								
Hispanic	27.0	25.7	40.2	41.5	20.7	21.1	12.0	11.7
White, non-Hispanic	14.3	14.0	46.4	45.8	25.4	26.1	13.9	14.2
Black, non-Hispanic	16.4	15.3	46.4	45.7	24.0	26.0	13.1	13.1

[1] Estimates are age adjusted to the year 2000 standard using six age groups: Under 18 years, 18-44 years, 45-54 years, 55-64 years, 65-74 years, and 75 years and over. [2] Estimates by race and Hispanic origin are tabulated using the 1997 Standards for Federal data on race and ethnicity. Estimates for specific race groups are shown when they meet requirements for statistical reliability and confidentiality. The categories "White only," "Black or African American only," "American Indian and Alaska Native (AI/AN) only," and "Asian only" include persons who reported only one racial group; and the category "2 or more races" includes persons who reported more than one of the five racial groups in the 1997 Standards or one of the five racial groups and "Some other race."

Source: U.S. National Center for Health Statistics, *Health, United States, 2004.*

No. 153. Medical Practice Characteristics by Selected Specialty: 1990 to 2001

[Dollar figures in thousands (164.3 represents $164,300). Based on a sample telephone survey of nonfederal office and hospital based patient care physicians, excluding residents. Survey not conducted for 2000. For details see source. For definition of mean, see Guide to Tabular Presentation]

Specialty	1990	1995	1996	1997	1998	1999	2001 [2]
MEAN PATIENT VISITS PER WEEK							
All physicians [1]	120.9	107.6	109.4	110.6	105.0	106.7	107.2
General/family practice	146.0	133.7	133.1	130.1	125.0	122.9	126.6
Internal medicine	112.0	99.7	104.7	106.4	102.8	103.0	102.7
Surgery	107.6	97.1	95.1	99.3	93.5	95.8	97.7
Pediatrics	134.0	125.9	121.1	125.5	110.9	120.5	111.0
Obstetrics/gynecology	120.0	94.0	104.2	103.8	99.3	101.8	101.2
MEAN HOURS IN PATIENT CARE PER WEEK							
All physicians [1]	53.3	51.3	53.4	53.2	51.7	51.6	52.8
General/family practice	55.0	52.9	53.5	53.1	51.3	50.6	50.7
Internal medicine	55.7	53.9	57.2	56.0	54.3	54.2	56.2
Surgery	53.1	53.2	54.2	55.0	51.7	53.3	53.1
Pediatrics	52.4	50.4	51.0	51.6	48.6	49.5	49.4
Obstetrics/gynecology	60.4	54.6	60.5	59.9	59.9	59.0	59.3
MEAN NET INCOME							
All physicians [1]	164.3	195.5	199.0	199.6	194.4	(NA)	205.7
General/family practice	102.7	131.2	139.1	140.9	142.5	(NA)	144.7
Internal medicine	152.5	185.7	185.7	193.9	182.1	(NA)	196.1
Surgery	236.4	269.4	275.2	261.4	268.2	(NA)	274.7
Pediatrics	106.5	140.5	140.6	143.5	139.6	(NA)	137.8
Obstetrics/gynecology	207.3	244.3	231.0	228.7	214.4	(NA)	227.0
MEAN LIABILITY PREMIUM							
All physicians [1]	14.5	15.0	14.1	14.2	16.8	(NA)	18.4
General/family practice	7.8	9.0	8.4	12.0	10.9	(NA)	13.8
Internal medicine	9.2	9.4	8.9	9.4	16.5	(NA)	13.7
Surgery	22.8	23.3	21.7	19.7	22.8	(NA)	23.6
Pediatrics	7.8	7.9	8.3	12.3	9.0	(NA)	11.6
Obstetrics/gynecology	34.3	38.6	35.2	33.0	35.8	(NA)	39.2

NA Not available. [1] Includes other specialties not shown separately. [2] Mean net income and mean liability premium are 2000 data.

Source: American Medical Association, Chicago IL, *Physician Socioeconomic Statistics* (copyright)

No. 154. Ambulatory Care Visits to Physicians' Offices and Hospital Outpatient and Emergency Departments: 2002

[1,083.5 represents 1,083,500,000. Based on the annual National Ambulatory Medical Care Survey and National Hospital Ambulatory Medical Care Survey and subject to sampling error; see source for details. For composition of regions, see map inside front cover]

Characteristic	Number of visits (mil.)				Visits per 100 persons			
	Total	Physician offices	Outpatient dept.	Emergency dept.	Total	Physician offices	Outpatient dept.	Emergency dept.
Total	1,083.5	890.0	83.3	110.2	382.7	314.4	29.4	38.9
Age:								
Under 15 years old	202.3	159.2	18.9	24.1	333.8	262.8	31.3	39.7
15 to 24 years old	98.9	71.9	9.8	17.2	250.4	181.9	24.9	43.6
25 to 44 years old	245.9	192.4	21.1	32.4	296.9	232.2	25.5	39.2
45 to 64 years old	283.5	242.1	21.4	19.9	428.3	365.8	32.4	30.1
65 to 74 years old	122.5	109.3	6.4	6.8	679.3	606.4	35.4	37.5
75 years old and over	130.4	115.0	5.6	9.7	818.3	722.2	35.1	61.1
Sex:								
Male	443.8	360.9	32.3	50.6	321.4	261.4	23.4	36.6
Female	639.7	529.1	51.0	59.6	441.2	364.9	35.2	41.1
Race:								
White	909.1	766.1	61.3	81.7	397.1	334.6	26.8	35.7
Black/African-American	133.0	89.5	18.7	24.9	376.0	252.9	52.8	70.3
Asian/Native Hawaiian/Other Pacific Islander	30.8	26.3	2.3	2.2	268.5	229.3	20.3	18.9
American Indian/Alaska Native	3.4	2.2	[1] 0.4	[1] 0.8	127.1	82.9	[1] 14.0	[1] 30.0
More than one race reported	2.8	[1] 2.4	0.2	0.2	67.9	[1] 59.0	5.0	4.2
Region:								
Northeast	246.1	205.7	21.5	18.9	460.8	385.2	40.2	35.4
Midwest	246.1	196.7	23.3	26.0	383.9	307.0	36.4	40.6
South	373.1	300.7	26.9	45.5	369.4	297.7	26.7	45.1
West	218.2	186.9	11.6	19.7	337.9	289.4	18.0	30.5
Primary source of payment:								
Private insurance	599.4	525.5	31.1	42.8	(X)	(X)	(X)	(X)
Medicare	217.2	188.2	12.0	17.0	(X)	(X)	(X)	(X)
Medicaid	111.6	67.1	22.7	21.8	(X)	(X)	(X)	(X)
Worker's compensation	17.8	14.7	1.0	2.1	(X)	(X)	(X)	(X)
Self pay	61.6	39.5	6.1	15.9	(X)	(X)	(X)	(X)
No charge	6.3	2.5	[1] 2.7	[1] 1.2	(X)	(X)	(X)	(X)
Other	27.0	21.5	3.0	2.6	(X)	(X)	(X)	(X)
Unknown	42.5	31.0	4.7	6.8	(X)	(X)	(X)	(X)

X Not applicable. [1] Figures do not meet standard of reliability or precision.

Source: U.S. National Center for Health Statistics, Advance Data, Nos. 340, 345, and 346; March 18, 2004; June 24, 2004; and August 26, 2004.

Health and Nutrition 109

No. 155. Visits to Office-Based Physicians and Hospital Outpatient Departments by Diagnosis: 2000 and 2002

[369.0 represents 369,000,000. See headnote, Table 154]

Leading diagnoses [1]	Number (mil.)		Rate per 1,000 persons [2]		Leading diagnoses [1]	Number (mil.)		Rate per 1,000 persons [2]	
	2000	2002	2000	2002		2000	2002	2000	2002
MALE					**FEMALE**				
All ages	369.0	393.2	2,760	2,848	All ages	537.8	580.1	3,829	4,001
Under 15 years old [3]	85.3	92.3	2,765	2,979	Under 15 years old [3]	75.4	85.8	2,556	2,901
Routine infant or child health check	17.9	19.6	580	632	Routine infant or child health check	17.5	18.1	593	613
Acute respiratory infections [4] .	8.5	8.3	276	268	Acute respiratory infections [4] .	8.1	7.6	276	256
Otitis media and Eustachian tube disorders . . . . : .	7.1	7.0	231	226	Otitis media and Eustachian tube disorders	6.6	6.8	222	231
Acute pharyngitis	1.9	2.9	61	95	Acute pharyngitis	2.3	3.4	78	116
Asthma	3.1	2.8	101	90					
					15 to 44 years old [3]	194.8	194.8	3,199	3,160
15 to 44 years old [3]	98.9	100.4	1,660	1,654	Normal pregnancy	24.5	19.7	402	320
General medical examination .	3.9	4.8	66	80	Gynecological examination . .	6.1	7.7	100	126
Acute respiratory infections [4] .	3.6	3.6	60	59	General medical examination .	6.6	6.2	108	100
Spinal disorders.	3.0	3.3	50	54	Acute respiratory infections [4] .	6.0	6.0	98	97
Rheumatism, excluding back .	3.3	2.7	55	45					
					45 to 64 years old [3]	141.0	157.3	4,511	4,611
45 to 64 years old [3]	96.5	106.3	3,294	3,313	Essential hypertension	8.3	11.4	264	335
Essential hypertension	6.8	10.2	233	318	Diabetes mellitus	5.6	5.6	181	165
Diabetes mellitus	5.8	5.7	199	179	Arthropathies and related disorders	6.6	5.6	212	165
Spinal disorders.	3.1	4.1	106	128	Rheumatism, excluding back .	4.6	4.5	146	132
Arthropathies and related disorders	2.9	3.9	99	121	Spinal disorders.	4.1	4.3	130	127
General medical examination .	2.3	3.0	79	94					
					65 years old and over [3]	126.6	142.1	6,736	7,238
65 years old and over [3]	88.2	94.3	6,340	6,578	Essential hypertension	11.8	16.9	628	860
Essential hypertension	6.6	8.0	478	557	Arthropathies and related disorders	6.3	7.2	333	369
Diabetes mellitus	4.8	6.3	344	440	Diabetes mellitus	6.0	6.3	318	321
Malignant neoplasms	7.1	5.5	507	382	Heart disease, excluding ischemic.	3.6	4.5	194	232
Ischemic heart disease	4.9	4.8	349	336	Malignant neoplasms	5.9	4.5	312	230
Heart disease, excluding ischemic.	4.1	3.6	296	252					

[1] Based on the International Classification of Diseases, 9th Revision, Clinical Modification, (ICD-9-CM). [2] Based on U.S. Census Bureau estimated civilian population as of July 1. [3] Includes other first-listed diagnoses, not shown separately. [4] Excluding pharyngitis.

Source: U.S. National Center for Health Statistics, Advance Data, Nos. 345 and 346; and June 24, 2004; and August 26, 2004.

No. 156. Visits to Hospital Emergency Departments by Diagnosis: 2002

[50,561 represents 50,561,000. See headnote, Table 154]

Leading diagnoses [1]	Number (1,000)	Rate per 1,000 persons [2]	Leading diagnoses [1]	Number (1,000)	Rate per 1,000 persons [2]
MALE			**FEMALE**		
All ages.	50,561	366	All ages.	59,594	411
Under 15 years old [3]	12,815	413	Under 15 years old [3]	11,262	381
Acute upper respiratory infections [4] . . .	1,301	42	Acute respiratory infections [4]	1,109	37
Otitis media and Eustachian tube disorders	1,127	36	Otitis media and Eustachian tube disorders	1,042	35
Open wound of head	802	26	Pyrexia of unknown origin	492	17
Contusions with intact skin surfaces . . .	629	20	Acute pharyngitis	483	16
15 to 44 years old [3]	22,039	363	15 to 44 years old [3]	27,608	448
Open wound, excluding head	1,557	26	Abdominal pain	1,681	27
Contusions with intact skin surfaces . . .	1,254	21	Complications of pregnancy, childbirth, and the puerperium	1,296	21
Strains and sprains, excluding ankle and back	885	15	Contusions with intact skin surfaces . . .	1,042	17
Strains and sprains of neck and back . .	819	13	Sprains and strains of neck and back . .	919	15
Spinal disorders	789	13	Acute upper respiratory infections [4] . . .	807	13
45 to 64 years old [3]	9,065	283	45 to 64 years old [3]	10,877	319
Chest pain	603	19	Chest pain	764	22
Open wound, excluding head	392	12	Abdominal pain	444	13
Spinal disorders	308	10	Contusions with intact skin surfaces . . .	403	12
Abdominal pain	285	9	Spinal disorders	381	11
65 years old and over [3]	6,641	463	65 years old and over [3]	9,847	502
Heart disease, excluding ischemic	450	31	Heart disease, excluding ischemic	690	35
Chest pain	369	26	Chest pain	494	25
Abdominal pain	191	13	Contusions with intact skin surfaces . . .	450	23
Open wound, excluding head	191	13	Cerebrovascular disease	361	18
Pneumonia.	176	12	Urinary tract infection, site not specified.	287	15

[1] Based on the International Classification of Diseases, 9th Revision, Clinical Modification, (ICD-9-CM). [2] Based on U.S. Census Bureau estimated civilian population as of July 1. [3] Includes other first-listed diagnoses, not shown separately. [4] Excluding pharyngitis.

Source: U.S. National Center for Health Statistics, Advance Data, No. 340; March 18, 2004.

110   Health and Nutrition

No. 157. Hospitals—Summary Characteristics: 1980 to 2002

[(1,365 represents 1,365,000). Covers hospitals accepted for registration by the American Hospital Association; see text, this section. Short-term hospitals have an average patient stay of less than 30 days; long-term, an average stay of longer duration. Special hospitals include obstetrics and gynecology; eye, ear, nose, and throat; rehabilitation; orthopedic; and chronic and other special hospitals except psychiatric, tuberculosis, alcoholism, and chemical dependency hospitals]

ITEM	1980	1990	1995	1997	1998	1999	2000	2001	2002
Number:									
All hospitals	6,965	6,649	6,291	6,097	6,021	5,890	5,810	5,801	5,794
With 100 beds or more	3,755	3,620	3,376	3,267	3,216	3,140	3,102	3,084	3,032
Nonfederal [1]	6,606	6,312	5,992	5,812	5,746	5,626	5,565	5,558	5,554
Community hospitals [2]	5,830	5,384	5,194	5,057	5,015	4,956	4,915	4,908	4,927
Nongovernmental nonprofit	3,322	3,191	3,092	3,000	3,026	3,012	3,003	2,998	3,025
For profit	730	749	752	797	771	747	749	754	766
State and local government	1,778	1,444	1,350	1,260	1,218	1,197	1,163	1,156	1,136
Long-term general and special	157	131	112	125	125	129	131	136	124
Psychiatric	534	757	657	601	579	516	496	491	477
Tuberculosis	11	4	3	4	3	4	4	4	4
Federal	359	337	299	285	275	264	245	243	240
Beds (1,000):									
All hospitals [3]	1,365	1,213	1,081	1,035	1,013	994	984	987	976
Rate per 1,000 population [4]	6.0	4.9	4.1	3.8	3.7	3.6	3.5	3.5	3.4
Beds per hospital	196	182	172	170	168	169	169	170	168
Nonfederal [1]	1,248	1,113	1,004	973	956	939	931	936	926
Community hospitals [2]	988	927	873	853	840	830	824	826	821
Rate per 1,000 population [4]	4.3	3.7	3.3	3.1	3.0	3.0	2.9	2.9	2.8
Nongovernmental nonprofit	692	657	610	591	588	587	583	585	582
For profit	87	102	106	115	113	107	110	109	108
State and local government	209	169	157	148	139	136	131	132	130
Long-term general and special	39	25	19	17	18	20	18	19	18
Psychiatric	215	158	110	100	95	87	87	89	85
Tuberculosis	2	(Z)	(Z)	(Z)	(Z)	(Z)	(Z)	(Z)	(Z)
Federal	117	98	78	62	57	55	53	53	50
Average daily census (1,000):									
All hospitals	1,060	844	710	673	662	657	650	658	662
Community hospitals [2]	747	619	548	528	525	526	526	533	540
Nongovernmental nonprofit	542	455	393	376	377	381	382	385	391
For profit	57	54	55	60	60	58	61	63	64
State and local government	149	111	100	92	87	86	83	85	84
Expenses (bil. dol.): [5]									
All hospitals	91.9	234.9	320.3	342.3	355.5	372.9	395.4	426.8	462.2
Nonfederal [1]	84.0	219.6	300.0	319.6	332.9	349.2	371.5	399.3	432.5
Community hospitals [2]	76.9	203.7	285.6	305.8	318.8	335.2	356.6	383.7	416.6
Nongovernmental nonprofit	55.8	150.7	209.6	225.3	238.0	251.5	267.1	287.3	312.7
For profit	5.8	18.8	26.7	31.2	31.7	31.2	35.0	37.3	40.1
State and local government	15.2	34.2	49.3	49.3	49.1	52.5	54.5	59.1	63.8
Long-term general and special	1.2	2.7	2.2	2.5	2.6	2.8	2.8	3.3	3.6
Psychiatric	5.8	12.9	11.7	11.0	11.2	11.0	11.9	13.2	12.1
Tuberculosis	0.1	0.1	0.4	0.1	(Z)	(Z)	(Z)	(Z)	(Z)
Federal	7.9	15.2	20.2	22.7	22.6	23.7	23.9	27.5	29.7
Personnel (1,000): [6]									
All hospitals	3,492	4,063	4,273	4,333	4,407	4,369	4,454	4,535	4,610
Nonfederal [1]	3,213	3,760	3,971	4,036	4,071	4,074	4,157	4,236	4,312
Community hospitals [2]	2,873	3,420	3,714	3,790	3,831	3,838	3,911	3,987	4,069
Nongovernmental nonprofit	2,086	2,533	2,702	2,765	2,834	2,862	2,919	2,971	3,039
For profit	189	273	343	385	383	362	378	379	380
State and local government	598	614	670	640	614	614	614	637	651
Long-term general and special	56	55	38	37	37	42	41	44	46
Psychiatric	275	280	215	204	198	191	200	201	193
Tuberculosis	3	1	1	1	1	1	1	1	1
Federal	279	303	301	296	336	295	297	299	299
Outpatient visits (mil.)	263.0	368.2	483.2	520.6	545.5	573.5	592.7	612.0	640.5
Emergency	82.0	92.8	99.9	97.4	99.0	103.8	106.9	109.8	114.2

Z Less than 500 beds or $50 million.   [1] Includes hospital units of institutions.   [2] Short term (average length of stay less than 30 days) general and special (e.g., obstetrics and gynecology; eye, ear, nose and throat; rehabilitation etc. except psychiatric, tuberculosis, alcoholism and chemical dependency). Excludes hospital units of institutions.   [3] Beginning 1990, number of beds at end of reporting period; prior years, average number in 12 month period.   [4] Based on Census Bureau estimated resident population as of July 1. Estimates reflect revisions based on the 2000 Census of Population.   [5] Excludes new construction.   [6] Includes full-time equivalents of part-time personnel.

Source: Health Forum, An American Hospital Association Company, Chicago, IL, *Hospital Statistics 2004 Edition*, and prior years (copyright). <http://www.healthforum.com/>.

Health and Nutrition   111

No. 158. Average Cost to Community Hospitals Per Patient: 1980 to 2002

[In dollars, except percent. Covers non-Federal short-term general or special hospitals (excluding psychiatric or tuberculosis hospitals and hospital units of institutions). Total cost per patient based on total hospital expenses (payroll, employee benefits, professional fees, supplies, etc.). Data have been adjusted for outpatient visits]

Type of expense and hospital	1980	1990	1995	1996	1997	1998	1999	2000	2001	2002
Average cost per day, total	245	687	968	1,006	1,033	1,067	1,103	1,149	1,217	1,290
Annual percent change [1]	12.9	7.8	4.0	4.0	2.6	3.3	3.3	4.2	5.9	6.0
Nongovernmental nonprofit	246	692	994	1,042	1,074	1,111	1,140	1,182	1,255	1,329
For profit	257	752	947	946	962	968	999	1,057	1,121	1,181
State and local government	239	635	878	903	914	949	1,007	1,064	1,114	1,188
Average cost per stay, total	1,851	4,947	6,216	6,225	6,262	6,386	6,512	6,649	6,980	7,346
Nongovernmental nonprofit	1,902	5,001	6,279	6,344	6,393	6,526	6,608	6,717	7,052	7,458
For profit	1,676	4,727	5,425	5,207	5,219	5,262	5,350	5,642	5,972	6,161
State and local government	1,750	4,838	6,445	6,419	6,475	6,612	6,923	7,106	7,400	7,773

[1] Change from immediate prior year.

No. 159. Community Hospitals—States: 1990 to 2002

[For beds, 928.1 represents 928,100. For definition of community hospitals see footnote 2, Table 157]

State	Number of hospitals			Beds (1,000)			Patients admitted (1,000)		Average daily census [1] (1,000)		Outpatient visits (mil.)	
	1990	2000	2002	1990	2000	2002	2000	2002	2000	2002	2000	2002
United States ...	5,384	4,915	4,927	928.1	823.6	820.7	33,089	34,478	525.7	538.9	521.4	556.4
Alabama	120	108	106	18.6	16.4	15.9	680	676	9.8	8.9	8.0	10.0
Alaska	16	18	19	1.2	1.4	1.4	47	48	0.8	0.8	1.3	1.3
Arizona	61	61	61	9.9	10.9	10.9	539	591	6.8	7.0	5.3	5.1
Arkansas	86	83	87	10.9	9.8	9.9	368	384	5.7	5.8	4.4	4.8
California	445	389	383	80.5	72.7	74.3	3,315	3,430	47.8	50.9	44.9	53.3
Colorado	69	69	68	10.4	9.4	9.6	397	427	5.4	6.0	6.7	7.0
Connecticut	35	35	35	9.6	7.7	7.7	349	376	5.8	6.1	6.7	6.6
Delaware	8	5	6	2.0	1.8	2.0	83	93	1.4	1.5	1.5	1.9
District of Columbia	11	11	10	4.5	3.3	3.4	129	137	2.5	2.6	1.3	1.5
Florida	224	202	202	50.7	51.2	51.2	2,119	2,315	31.0	33.7	21.8	22.5
Georgia	163	151	146	25.7	23.9	24.5	863	885	15.0	15.8	11.2	12.5
Hawaii	18	21	25	2.9	3.1	3.2	100	111	2.3	2.4	2.5	2.0
Idaho	43	42	39	3.2	3.5	3.3	123	123	1.8	1.8	2.2	2.4
Illinois	210	196	192	45.8	37.3	36.3	1,531	1,615	22.4	22.8	25.1	26.5
Indiana	113	109	112	21.8	19.2	19.0	700	716	10.8	11.2	14.1	14.1
Iowa	124	115	116	14.3	11.8	11.3	360	371	6.8	6.7	9.2	9.3
Kansas	138	129	132	11.8	10.8	10.9	310	329	5.7	5.9	5.3	5.7
Kentucky	107	105	104	15.9	14.8	15.1	582	602	9.1	9.3	8.7	8.6
Louisiana	140	123	128	19.1	17.5	17.9	654	692	9.8	10.6	10.0	10.7
Maine	39	37	37	4.5	3.7	3.7	147	146	2.4	2.4	3.2	3.7
Maryland	52	49	49	13.6	11.2	11.4	587	635	8.2	8.4	6.0	6.5
Massachusetts	101	80	78	21.7	16.6	16.0	740	766	11.7	11.9	16.7	19.0
Michigan	176	146	145	33.9	26.1	26.1	1,106	1,163	16.9	17.3	24.9	25.9
Minnesota	152	135	133	19.4	16.7	16.7	571	599	11.2	11.4	7.3	8.9
Mississippi	103	95	91	12.9	13.6	13.1	425	417	8.0	7.5	3.7	4.0
Missouri	135	119	119	24.3	20.1	18.9	773	809	11.7	11.6	14.8	14.9
Montana	55	52	53	4.6	4.3	4.3	99	107	2.9	2.9	2.6	2.7
Nebraska	90	85	86	8.5	8.2	8.1	209	206	4.8	4.7	3.4	3.5
Nevada	21	22	26	3.4	3.8	4.5	199	212	2.7	3.0	2.2	2.5
New Hampshire	27	28	28	3.5	2.9	2.9	111	118	1.7	1.8	2.8	3.0
New Jersey	95	80	81	28.9	25.3	24.1	1,074	1,095	17.3	17.0	16.3	15.9
New Mexico	37	35	36	4.2	3.5	3.6	174	180	2.0	2.3	3.1	4.2
New York	235	215	211	74.7	66.4	65.6	2,416	2,463	52.1	50.4	46.4	46.8
North Carolina	120	113	113	22.0	23.1	23.6	971	967	16.0	16.2	12.4	13.8
North Dakota	50	42	42	4.4	3.9	3.9	89	95	2.3	2.3	1.7	1.9
Ohio	190	163	168	43.1	33.8	33.7	1,404	1,476	20.6	21.0	26.9	28.4
Oklahoma	111	108	105	12.4	11.1	11.1	429	446	6.2	6.5	4.7	4.8
Oregon	70	59	60	8.1	6.6	6.8	330	345	3.9	4.1	7.3	8.2
Pennsylvania	238	207	201	52.6	42.3	40.5	1,796	1,798	28.8	28.3	31.8	32.4
Rhode Island	12	11	11	3.2	2.4	2.4	119	123	1.7	1.8	2.1	2.2
South Carolina	69	63	62	11.3	11.5	11.1	495	513	8.0	8.0	7.8	7.3
South Dakota	53	48	51	4.2	4.3	4.6	99	100	2.8	2.7	1.7	1.5
Tennessee	134	121	125	23.6	20.6	20.4	737	797	11.5	12.3	10.3	10.0
Texas	428	403	416	59.2	55.9	56.8	2,367	2,534	33.1	36.1	29.4	33.5
Utah	42	42	42	4.4	4.3	4.4	194	206	2.4	2.4	4.5	4.8
Vermont	15	14	14	1.7	1.7	1.6	52	52	1.1	1.0	1.2	1.5
Virginia	97	88	86	20.0	16.9	17.2	727	747	11.4	11.7	9.5	10.8
Washington	91	84	86	12.0	11.1	11.3	505	519	6.6	6.8	9.6	9.7
West Virginia	59	57	57	8.4	8.0	7.8	288	295	4.8	4.9	5.2	5.7
Wisconsin	129	118	120	18.6	15.3	14.6	558	580	9.1	9.3	10.9	11.6
Wyoming	27	24	24	2.2	1.9	1.9	48	49	1.1	1.0	0.9	0.9

[1] Inpatients receiving treatment each day; excludes newborn.

Source of tables 158 and 159: Health Forum, An American Hospital Association Company, Chicago, IL, Hospital Statistics 2004 Edition, and prior years (copyright). <http://www.healthforum.com>.

112 Health and Nutrition

No. 160. Hospital Use Rates by Type of Hospital: 1980 to 2002

Type of hospital	1980	1990	1995	1998	1999	2000	2001	2002
Community hospitals: [1]								
Admissions per 1,000 population [2]	159	125	116	115	116	117	118	120
Admissions per bed.	37	34	35	38	39	40	40	42
Average length of stay [3] (days)	7.6	7.2	6.5	6.0	5.9	5.8	5.7	5.7
Outpatient visits per admission . . . . ., ...	5.6	9.7	13.4	14.9	15.3	15.8	15.9	16.1
Outpatient visits per 1,000 population [2].	890	1,207	1,556	1,754	1,816	1,852	1,890	1,932
Surgical operations (million [4])	18.8	21.9	23.2	25.3	26.3	26.1	26.5	27.6
Number per admission	0.5	0.7	0.7	0.8	0.8	0.8	0.8	0.8
Nonfederal psychiatric:								
Admissions per 1,000 population [2]	2.5	2.9	2.7	2.7	2.4	2.4	2.6	2.5
Days in hospital per 1,000 population [2]	295	190	122	101	94	93	94	92

[1] For definition of community hospitals, see footnote 2, Table 157. [2] Based on U.S. Census Bureau estimated resident population as of July 1. Estimates reflect revisions based on the 2000 Census of Population. [3] Number of inpatient days divided by number of admissions. [4] 18.8 represents 18,800,000.

Source: Health Forum, An American Hospital Association Company, Chicago, IL, *Hospital Statistics 2004 Edition*, and prior years (copyright).

No. 161. Hospital Utilization Rates: 1990 to 2002

[30,788 represents 30,788,000. Represents estimates of inpatients discharged from noninstitutional, short-stay hospitals, exclusive of federal hospitals. Excludes newborn infants. Based on sample data collected from the National Hospital Discharge Survey, a sample survey of hospital records of patients discharged in year shown; subject to sampling variability]

Item and Sex	1990	1995	1996	1997	1998	1999	2000	2001	2002
Patients discharged (1,000).	30,788	30,722	30,545	30,914	31,827	32,132	31,706	32,653	33,727
Patients discharged per 1,000 persons, total [1]	122	116	114	114	117	117	114	115	118
Male	100	94	92	93	93	95	92	93	95
Female	143	136	135	135	139	138	135	137	139
Days of care per 1,000 persons, total [1] . .	784	620	597	582	589	581	560	562	572
Male	694	551	533	508	517	510	491	490	506
Female	869	686	657	653	658	649	627	631	635
Average stay (days).	6.4	5.4	5.2	5.1	5.1	5.0	4.9	4.9	4.9
Male	6.9	5.8	5.8	5.5	5.5	5.4	5.3	5.3	5.3
Female	6.1	5.0	4.9	4.8	4.7	4.7	4.6	4.6	4.6

[1] Based on U.S. Census Bureau estimated civilian population as of July 1. Beginning with 1997 data, rates are based on the U.S. Census Bureau estimates of the civilian population that have been adjusted for net underenumeration in the 1990 census. Population estimates based on the 2000 census were first used to calculate rates in 2001. The 2000 population estimates were based on the 1990 census.

Source: U.S. National Center for Health Statistics, *Vital and Health Statistics*, Series 13; and unpublished data.

No. 162. Hospital Discharges and Days of Care: 2001 and 2002

[32,653 represents 32,653,000. See headnote, Table 161. For composition of regions, see map, inside front cover]

Age, race and region	Discharges				Days of care per 1,000 persons [1]		Average stay (days)	
	Number (1,000)		Per 1,000 persons [1]					
	2001	2002	2001	2002	2001	2002	2001	2002
Total	32,653	33,727	115	118	562	572	4.9	4.9
Age:								
Under 1 year old	850	810	211	201	1,168	1,134	5.5	5.6
1 to 4 years old	731	713	48	46	157	159	3.3	3.5
5 to 14 years old	978	1,016	24	25	106	109	4.4	4.4
15 to 24 years old	2,968	3,083	76	77	265	266	3.5	3.5
25 to 34 years old	3,815	3,897	97	99	324	328	3.3	3.3
35 to 44 years old	3,560	3,757	80	84	345	368	4.3	4.4
45 to 64 years old	7,224	7,723	112	116	565	575	5.0	5.0
65 to 74 years old	4,692	4,642	256	254	1,450	1,412	5.7	5.6
75 years old and over. . . .	7,834	8,085	461	467	2,734	2,795	5.9	6.0
Race:								
White.	20,330	20,806	89	90	431	436	4.9	4.9
Black.	3,900	3,995	108	109	593	584	5.5	5.3
Asian/Pacific Islander . . .	438	538	40	45	210	243	5.2	5.4
American Indian/Eskimo/ Aleut	161	173	59	63	282	330	4.8	5.2
Region:								
Northeast	7,026	6,990	130	129	732	727	5.6	5.6
Midwest	7,429	7,503	115	115	499	512	4.3	4.4
South	12,744	12,994	126	127	621	618	4.9	4.9
West	5,453	6,239	85	96	385	430	4.5	4.5

[1] Based on U.S. Census Bureau estimated civilian population.

Source: U.S. National Center for Health Statistics, *Vital and Health Statistics*, Series 13; and unpublished data.

Health and Nutrition 113

No. 163. Hospital Discharges and Days of Care by Sex: 2002

[13,389 represents 13,389,000. Represents estimates of inpatients discharged from noninstitutional, short-stay hospitals, exclusive of federal hospitals. Diagnostic categories are based on the International Classification of Diseases, Ninth Revision, Clinical Modification. See head note, Table 161]

Age and first-listed diagnosis	Discharges Number (1,000)	Discharges Per 1,000 persons [1]	Days of care per 1,000 persons [1]	Average stay (days)	Age and first-listed diagnosis	Discharges Number (1,000)	Discharges Per 1,000 persons [1]	Days of care per 1,000 persons [1]	Average stay (days)
MALE					**FEMALE**				
All ages [2]	13,389	102.4	549.5	5.4	**All ages [2]**	20,338	132.9	596.0	4.5
Under 18 years [3]	1,615	43.3	198.1	4.6	Under 18 years [3]	1,547	43.5	192.1	4.4
Pneumonia	228	6.1	21.4	3.5	Pneumonia	183	5.2	19.8	3.8
Injuries and poisoning	180	4.8	20.3	4.2	Injuries and poisoning	120	3.4	14.1	4.2
Asthma	69	1.9	4.5	2.4	Asthma	42	1.2	2.6	2.2
18 to 44 years [3]	2,703	48.2	236.3	4.9	18 to 44 years [3]	7,411	132.6	431.9	3.3
Injuries and poisoning	445	7.9	36.9	4.7	Delivery	3,783	67.7	174.6	2.6
Serious mental illness [4]	361	6.4	51.5	7.9	Serious mental illness [4]	385	6.9	52.6	7.6
Alcohol and drug [5]	226	4.0	18.3	4.5	Injuries and poisoning	268	4.8	18.7	3.9
Diseases of heart	173	3.1	10.6	3.4					
					45 to 64 years [3]	3,968	116.0	553.4	4.8
45 to 64 years [3]	3,755	115.8	597.0	5.2	Diseases of heart	501	14.6	60.4	4.1
Diseases of heart	812	25.0	98.5	3.9	Injuries and poisoning	279	8.2	43.5	5.3
Injuries and poisoning	342	10.6	63.2	6.0	Malignant neoplasms	198	5.8	34.0	5.9
Malignant neoplasms	211	6.5	42.9	6.6	Serious mental illness [4]	207	6.1	51.6	8.5
Serious mental illness [4]	139	4.3	47.6	11.1					
Diabetes	98	3.0	17.3	5.7	65 to 74 years [3]	2,437	244.4	1,349.6	5.5
Cerebrovascular diseases	121	3.7	22.6	6.1	Diseases of heart	484	48.6	230.5	4.7
					Injuries and poisoning	173	17.3	99.5	5.7
65 to 74 years [3]	2,205	265.6	1,486.7	5.6	Malignant neoplasms	141	14.1	107.0	7.6
Diseases of heart	564	67.9	303.4	4.5	Cerebrovascular diseases	107	10.8	54.9	5.1
Injuries and poisoning	153	18.4	111.5	6.1	Pneumonia	114	11.4	69.7	6.1
Malignant neoplasms	154	18.5	136.8	7.4					
75 years old and older [3]	3,111	480.7	2,894.9	6.0	75 years old and older [3]	4,975	458.2	2,735.5	6.0
Diseases of heart	759	117.4	606.9	5.2	Diseases of heart	1,036	95.4	483.4	5.1
Pneumonia	251	38.8	241.0	6.2	Injuries and poisoning	526	48.4	279.6	5.8
Injuries and poisoning	211	32.7	212.4	6.5	Cerebrovascular diseases	274	25.2	130.5	5.2
Cerebrovascular diseases	174	26.8	155.3	5.8	Pneumonia	312	28.7	185.5	6.5
Malignant neoplasms	154	23.8	179.5	7.5	Malignant neoplasms	186	17.1	131.1	7.7

[1] Based on U.S. Census Bureau estimated civilian population as of July 1.   [2] Average length of stay and rates per 1,000 population are age-adjusted to the year 2000 standard using five age groups; Under 18 years, 18-44 years, 45-64 years, 65-74 years, and 75 years and over.   [3] Includes other first-listed diagnoses not shown separately.   [4] Excludes discharges from other types of facilities such as the Dept. of Veterans Affairs or long-term hospitals.   [5] Includes abuse, dependence, and withdrawal. Excludes discharges from other types of facilities such as the Dept. of Veterans Affairs or day treatment programs.

Source: U.S. National Center for Health Statistics, *Health, United States 2004.*

No. 164. Organ Transplants and Grafts: 1990 to 2003

[As of end of year. Based on reports of procurement programs and transplant centers in the United States, except as noted]

Procedure	Number of procedures 1990	1995	2000	2001	2002	2003	Number of centers 1990	2003	Number of people waiting, 2003	1-year patient survival rates, 2003 (percent)
Transplant: [1]										
Heart	2,095	2,342	2,172	2,202	2,153	2,057	148	134	3,518	87.1
Heart-lung	52	69	47	27	33	29	79	61	194	(NA)
Lung	203	869	955	1,054	1,042	1,085	70	69	3,925	82.2
Liver	2,631	3,818	4,816	5,177	5,326	5,671	85	122	17,497	84.9
Kidney	9,358	10,957	13,258	14,152	14,741	15,129	232	248	58,396	97.6
Kidney-pancreas	459	915	910	884	903	871	(NA)	(NA)	2,440	96.0
Pancreas	60	103	420	468	546	502	84	140	1,611	94.8
Intestine	1	21	29	112	107	116	(NA)	46	184	87.2
Multi-organ	71	124	213	228	309	342	(NA)	(NA)	(NA)	(NA)
Cornea grafts [2]	40,631	44,652	46,949	46,532	46,625	46,436	[3]107	[3]88	(NA)	(NA)
Bone grafts(1,000)	350	450	800	875	1,050	1,200	30	60	(X)	(NA)
Skin grafts [4]	5,500	5,500	15,000	20,000	30,000	35,000	25	40	(X)	(NA)

NA Not available.   X Not applicable.   [1] Kidney-pancreas and heart-lung transplants are each counted as one organ. All other multi-organ transplants, excluding kidney-pancreas and heart-lung, are included in the multi-organ row. Based on the Organ Procurement and Transplant Network (OPTN) as of June 4, 2004. The data have been supplied by UNOS under contract with HHS. This work was supported in part by Health Resources and Services Administration contract 231-00-0015. The authors alone are responsible for the reporting and interpretation of these data. Data subject to change based on future data submission or correction.   [2] 1990-1992, number of procedures and eye banks include Canada. From 1993 on, the data is for the U.S. only.   [3] Eye banks.   [4] Procedure data are shown in terms of square feet.

Source: U.S. Department of Health and Human Services, Health Resources and Services Administration, Office of Special Programs, Division of Transplantation, Rockville, MD; United Network for Organ Sharing (UNOS), Richmond, VA; University Renal Research and Education Association, Ann Arbor, MI; American Association of Tissue Banks, McLean, VA; and Eye Bank Association of America, Washington, DC; and unpublished data.

No. 165. Procedures for Inpatients Discharged From Short-Stay Hospitals: 1990 to 2002

[23,051 represents 23,051,000. Excludes newborn infants and discharges from federal hospitals. See head note, Table 161]

Sex and type of procedure	Number of procedures (1,000)				Rate per 1,000 population [1]			
	1990	1995	2000	2002	1990	1995	2000	2002
Surgical procedures, total [2][3]	23,051	22,530	23,244	25,255	92.4	86.2	83.6	88.0
Cardiac catheterization	995	1,068	1,221	1,328	4.0	4.1	4.4	4.6
Removal of coronary artery obstruction [3]	285	434	1,025	1,204	1.2	1.7	3.7	4.2
Reduction of fracture [4]	609	577	628	606	2.4	2.2	2.3	2.1
Coronary artery bypass graft	392	573	519	515	1.6	2.2	1.9	1.8
Male, total [2]	8,538	8,388	8,689	9,585	70.6	65.9	63.9	68.2
Cardiac catheterization	620	660	732	799	5.1	5.2	5.4	5.7
Removal of coronary artery obstruction [3]	200	285	655	802	1.7	2.2	4.8	5.7
Coronary artery bypass graft	286	423	371	373	2.4	3.3	2.7	2.7
Female, total [2]	14,513	14,142	14,556	15,670	113.0	105.3	102.4	106.9
Repair of current obstetric laceration	795	964	1,136	1,234	6.2	7.2	8.0	8.4
Cesarean section	945	785	855	1,059	7.4	5.8	6.0	7.2
Hysterectomy	591	583	633	669	4.6	4.3	4.5	4.6
Diagnostic and other nonsurgical procedures [5]	17,455	17,278	16,737	17,278	70.0	66.1	60.2	60.2
Angiocardiography and arteriography [6] . .	1,735	1,834	2,005	2,005	7.0	7.0	7.2	7.2
Respiratory therapy	1,164	1,127	991	1,070	4.7	4.3	3.6	3.7
Diagnostic ultrasound	1,608	1,181	886	773	6.4	4.5	3.2	2.7
CAT scan [7]	1,506	967	754	703	6.0	3.7	2.7	2.5
Male, total [5]	7,378	7,261	6,965	7,248	61.0	57.1	51.2	51.6
Angiocardiography and arteriography [6] . .	1,051	1,076	1,157	1,142	8.7	8.5	8.5	8.1
Respiratory therapy	586	572	507	546	4.9	4.5	3.7	3.9
CAT scan [7]	736	473	345	324	6.1	3.7	2.5	2.3
Female, total [5]	10,077	10,016	9,772	10,030	78.5	74.6	68.8	68.4
Manual assisted delivery	750	866	898	993	5.9	6.5	6.3	6.8
Fetal EKG and fetal monitoring	1,377	935	750	797	10.8	7.0	5.5	5.4
Diagnostic ultrasound	941	682	501	427	7.3	5.1	3.5	2.9

[1] Based on U.S. Census Bureau estimated civilian population as of July 1. Beginning in 1997 population figures are adjusted for net underenumeration in the 1990 Census using the 1990 National Population Adjustment Matrix from the Census Bureau. Since population estimates for the 2000 Census were not available when the 2000 hospital data were released, the population estimates used to compute hospital rates for this year were based on the 1990 Census. Beginning with the 2001 hospital data, rates were calculated using the 2000 Census. [2] Includes other types of surgical procedures not shown separately. [3] Beginning 1999 includes separately coded "insertion of stent". [4] Excluding skull, nose, and jaw. [5] Includes other nonsurgical procedures not shown separately. [6] Using contrast material. [7] Computerized axial tomography.

Source: U.S. National Center for Health Statistics, *Vital and Health Statistics*, series 13; and unpublished data.

No. 166. Hospital Utilization Measures for HIV Patients: 1985 to 2002

[HIV represents human immunodeficiency virus. See headnote, Table 161]

Measure of utilization	Unit	1985	1990	1995	2000	2001	2002
Number of patients discharged [1]	1,000	23	146	249	173	185	189
Rate of patient discharges [2]	Rate	1.0	5.8	9.4	6.2	6.5	6.6
Number of days of care	1,000	387	2,188	2,326	1,257	1,435	1,322
Rate of days of care [2]	Rate	16.3	86.9	87.6	45.2	50.6	46.0
Average length of stay	Days	17.1	14.9	9.3	7.3	7.8	7.0

[1] Comparisons beginning 1990 with data for earlier years should be made with caution as estimates of change may reflect improvements in the 1988 sample design rather than true changes in hospital use. [2] Per 10,000 population. Based on Census Bureau estimated civilian population as of July 1. Population estimates for the 1980's do not reflect revised estimates based on the 1990 Census of Population. Beginning 1998, rates are based on civilian population estimates that have been adjusted for net underenumeration in the 1990 census. Population estimates for the 2000 Census were first used to calculate rates in 2001. The 2000 population estimates were based on the 1990 Census.

Source: National Center for Health Statistics, *Vital and Health Statistics*, Series 13; and unpublished data.

No. 167. Skilled Nursing Facilities: 1980 to 2002

[436 represents 436,000. Covers facilities and beds certified for participation under Medicare as of midyear. Includes facilities which have transfer agreements with one or more participating hospitals, and are engaged primarily in providing skilled nursing care and related services for the rehabilitation of injured, disabled, or sick persons]

Item	Unit	1980	1985	1990	1995	1999	2000	2001	2002
Skilled nursing facilities	Number .	5,052	6,451	8,937	13,122	14,913	14,913	14,841	14,755
Beds	1,000 .	436	(NA)	509	652	837	837	939	1,050
Per 1,000 Medicare enrollees [1]	Rate . . .	15.6	(NA)	17.7	18.8	21.6	21.3	23.7	26.2

NA Not available. [1] Based on total number of beneficiaries enrolled in the medicare hospital insurance program as of July 1 of year stated.
Source: U.S. Centers for Medicare and Medicaid Services, Providers and Suppliers of Health Services, 1980; and unpublished data.

Health and Nutrition 115

No. 168. Home Health and Hospice Care Agencies by Selected Characteristics: 2000

[In percent, except as indicated (11.4 represents 11,400). Based on the National Home and Hospice Care Survey. Home health care is provided to individuals and families in their place of residence. Hospice care is available in both the home and inpatient settings. See source for details. For composition of regions, see map, inside front cover]

Agency characteristic		Current patients [1]			Discharges [2]		
	Agencies, total	Total	Home health care	Hospice care	Total	Home health care	Hospice care
Total (1,000).	11.4	1,460.8	1,355.3	105.5	7,800.1	7,179.0	621.1
PERCENT DISTRIBUTION							
Ownership:							
Proprietary.	44.7	33.2	34.1	22.3	24.2	25.0	15.8
Voluntary nonprofit	42.5	57.8	56.6	73.2	66.9	65.8	80.0
Government and other	12.8	9.0	9.3	4.4	8.9	9.3	4.2
Region:							
Northeast.	15.9	31.2	31.9	22.0	39.3	41.0	20.1
Midwest.	26.1	20.6	20.7	19.5	18.4	17.8	25.7
South	42.7	37.3	37.3	37.7	29.8	29.5	33.7
West.	15.3	10.9	10.1	20.8	12.5	11.7	20.6

[1] Patients on the rolls of the agency as of midnight the day prior to the survey.   [2] Patients removed from the rolls of the agency during the 12 months prior to the day of the survey. A patient could be included more than once if the individual had more than one episode of care during the year.

Source: U.S. National Center for Health Statistics, unpublished data.

No. 169. Home Health and Hospice Care Patients by Selected Characteristics: 2000

[In percent, except as indicated (1,460.8 represents 1,460,800). See head note, Table 168]

Item	Current patients [1]			Discharges [2]		
	Total	Home health care	Hospice care	Total	Home health care	Hospice care
Total (1,000).	1,460.8	1,355.3	105.5	7,800.1	7,179.0	621.1
PERCENT DISTRIBUTION						
Age: [3]						
Under 45 years old	13.2	13.9	4.5	13.7	14.5	3.9
45-54 years old	6.5	6.7	5.1	6.2	6.3	5.0
55-64 years old	8.9	8.9	8.9	10.2	10.0	11.5
65 years old and over	71.3	70.5	81.4	70.0	69.1	79.6
65-69 years old.	7.1	7.1	7.3	9.4	9.4	10.1
70-74 years old.	10.2	10.2	9.9	11.1	10.8	14.5
75-79 years old.	17.1	16.8	20.9	15.5	15.8	12.5
80-84 years old.	14.6	14.5	16.1	16.2	16.2	15.9
85 years old and over	22.3	21.9	27.2	17.8	17.0	26.5
Sex:						
Male.	35.8	35.2	42.6	37.3	36.2	49.8
Female	64.2	64.8	57.4	62.7	63.8	50.2
Race:						
White	76.3	76.0	82.8	79.5	79.1	84.1
Black and other [4]	14.6	14.8	12.3	12.2	12.4	10.3
Black.	12.4	12.6	10.6	9.8	10.0	8.1
Unknown.	9.0	9.4	5.0	8.3	8.5	5.5
Marital status: [3]						
Married	32.7	31.9	42.7	40.9	40.3	47.2
Widowed.	34.9	34.8	36.7	29.9	29.6	33.2
Divorced or separated	5.5	5.5	6.3	5.3	5.2	5.7
Never married	17.4	18.0	9.2	14.7	15.3	7.7
Unknown.	9.5	9.9	5.0	9.3	9.5	6.2
Primary admission diagnosis:						
Neoplasms	8.6	5.1	52.6	9.7	5.5	58.4
Endocrine, nutritional and metabolic and immunity disorders	8.8	9.5	0.3	5.8	6.2	0.3
Diseases of the nervous system and sense organs	2.3	2.4	0.4	0.7	0.7	0.2
Diseases of the circulatory system . .	23.0	23.6	15.6	21.4	22.3	11.7
Diseases of the respiratory system. .	6.8	9.8	6.5	9.2	9.4	6.9
Diseases of the musculoskeletal system and connective tissue	9.1	9.8	0.1	11.2	12.1	1.0
Injuries and poisoning	9.6	10.2	0.9	11.3	12.3	0.5

[1] Patients on the rolls of the agency as of midnight the day prior to the survey.   [2] Patients removed from the rolls of the agency during the 12 months prior to the day of the survey. A patient could be included more than once if the individual had more than one episode of care during the year.   [3] For current patients, current age or marital status; for discharged patients, age or marital status at time of discharge.   [4] Patients with multiple races are coded in the "other" category.

Source: U.S. National Center for Health Statistics, *Health, United States, 2002*

No. 170. Elderly Home Health Patients: 2000

[1,041 represents 1,041,000. Covers the civilian population 65 years old and over who are home health care patients. Age of patient is based on age at the time of interview. Home health care is provided to individuals and families in their place of residence. Based on the 2000 National Home and Hospice Care Survey]

Item	Current patients [1] Num-ber (1,000)	Current patients [1] Per-cent	Discharges [2] Num-ber (1,000)	Discharges [2] Per-cent	Item	Current patients [1] Num-ber (1,000)	Current patients [1] Per-cent	Discharges [2] Num-ber (1,000)	Discharges [2] Per-cent
Total 65 yrs. old & over	**1,041**	**100.0**	**5,456**	**100.0**	Own income	61	5.9	85	1.6
Received help with—					Medicare	705	67.8	4,867	89.2
Bathing or showering . .	544	52.3	2,172	39.8	Medicaid	141	13.5	150	2.8
Dressing	480	46.1	1,900	34.8					
Eating	166	15.9	537	9.9	Services rendered: [5]				
Transferring in/out of					Nursing services	782	75.1	4,672	85.6
a bed or chair	373	35.9	1,737	31.8	Social services	138	13.3	977	17.9
Using the toilet room . .	289	27.8	1,092	20.0	Counseling	37	3.6	255	4.7
Doing light housework .	379	36.4	1,031	18.9	Medications	106	10.2	599	11.0
Managing money	17	1.6	[3]30	[3]0.5	Physical therapy	285	27.4	2,216	40.6
Shopping for groceries									
or clothes	127	12.2	261	4.8	Homemaker-				
Using the telephone . .	31	3.0	113	2.1	household services . .	289	27.8	691	12.7
Preparing meals	227	21.8	549	10.1	Nutrition services	53	5.1	204	3.7
Taking medications . . .	216	20.7	1,017	18.6	Physician services	48	4.6	307	5.6
Primary source of payment: [4]					Occupational therapy . .	83	8.0	543	10.0
Private insurance	44	4.2	251	4.6	Speech therapy/ audiology	19	1.8	102	1.9

[1] Patients on the rolls of the agency as of midnight the day prior to the survey. [2] Patients removed from the rolls of the agency during the 12 months prior to the day of the survey. A patient could be included more than once if the individual had more than one episode of care during the year. [3] Figure does not meet standard of reliability or precision. [4] For current patients, the expected source; for discharges the actual source for the entire episode. [5] For current patients, services currently being provided; for discharges services provided during the 30 days prior to discharge.

Source: U.S. National Center for Health Statistics, unpublished data.

No. 171. Nursing Homes—Selected Characteristics: 1985 to 1999

[Beds: 1,624 represents 1,624,000. Covers licensed and/or certified nursing homes in the conterminous United States that had three or more beds. Based on the 1999 National Nursing Home Survey, a two-stage survey sample of nursing homes and their residents. Subject to sampling variability. For composition of regions, see map, inside front cover]

Characteristic	Beds Nursing homes	Beds Number (1,000)	Beds Per nursing home	Current residents Number (1,000)	Current residents Occu-pancy rate [1]	Full-time equivalent employment Administrative, medical, and therapeutic Number (1,000)	Full-time equivalent employment Administrative, medical, and therapeutic Rate per 100 beds	Full-time equivalent employment Nursing Number (1,000)	Full-time equivalent employment Nursing Rate per 100 beds
1985	19,100	1,624	85	1,491	91.8	89.4	5.5	704	43.4
1995	16,700	1,771	106	1,549	87.4	90.5	5.1	916	51.7
1997	17,000	1,821	107	1,609	88.4	100.0	5.5	950	52.2
1999, total	**18,000**	**1,965**	**109**	**1,627**	**82.8**	**96.6**	**4.9**	**961**	**48.9**
Ownership:									
Proprietary	12,000	1,291	108	1,048	81.2	60.2	4.6	597	46.2
Voluntary nonprofit	4,800	523	109	446	85.3	29.1	5.6	280	53.5
Government and other	1,200	151	126	133	88.1	7.4	4.7	84	55.6
Certification:									
Medicare and medicaid certified	14,700	1,698	116	1,414	83.3	83.2	4.9	842	49.6
Medicare only	[2]600	49	82	37	75.5	2.8	5.7	26	53.1
Medicaid only	2,100	177	89	143	80.8	9.0	5.1	75	42.4
Not certified	[2]500	40	80	33	82.5	1.6	4.0	18	45.0
Bed size:									
Less than 50 beds	2,000	72	36	59	81.9	7.1	9.9	43	59.7
50-99 beds	7,000	503	72	414	82.3	28.8	5.7	252	50.1
100-199 beds	7,500	998	133	826	82.8	45.0	4.5	476	47.7
200 beds or more	1,400	392	280	328	83.7	15.7	4.0	190	48.5
Region:									
Northeast	3,200	443	138	382	86.2	21.7	4.9	244	55.1
Midwest	6,000	619	103	498	80.4	28.3	4.6	272	43.9
South	6,000	652	109	531	81.6	30.5	4.7	311	47.7
West	2,800	251	90	215	85.7	16.1	6.4	133	53.0
Affiliation: [3]									
Chain	10,800	1,179	109	977	82.9	58.7	5.0	556	47.2
Independent	7,200	781	108	646	82.7	37.7	4.8	404	51.7

[1] Number of residents divided by number of available beds multiplied by 100. [2] Figure does not meet standards of reliability or precision. [3] Excludes a small number of homes, beds, and residents with unknown affiliation.

Source: U.S. National Center for Health Statistics, Vital and Health Statistics, Series 13, No. 152.

Health and Nutrition 117

No. 172. Nursing Home Residents 65 Years Old and Over by Selected Characteristics: 1999

[1,470 represents 1,470,000. Covers licensed and/or certified nursing homes in the conterminous United States that had three or more beds. Based on the National Nursing Home Survey, a two-stage sample survey of nursing homes and their residents. Subject to sampling variability]

Characteristic [1]	Number (1,000)	Percent distribution	Item	Percent of elderly residents	Functional status	Percent of elderly residents receiving assistance
Total [2].............	1,470	100.0	Type of aids used:		ADLs: [6]	
			Wheelchair........	62.6	Bathing, showering...	94.7
Male.....................	378	25.7	Walker...........	26.1	Dressing..........	87.5
Female..................	1,092	74.3			Eating	47.1
					Transferring in or	
65 to 74 years...........	195	13.3	Vision impaired.......	28.5	out of beds or chair .	30.2
75 to 84 years...........	518	35.2	Hearing impaired......	22.8	Using toilet room	57.6
85 years and over.........	757	51.5				
Living quarters before					IADLs: [7]	
admission:			Primary source		Care of personal	
Private residence	447	30.4	of payment: [3]		possessions	74.3
Retirement home........	23	1.6	Private sources [4]	26.3	Managing money	70.7
Board and care,			Medicare	32.8	Securing personal	
assisted living, and/or			Medicaid	37.5	items	72.9
residential facility......	81	5.5	Other [5]...........	3.4	Using telephone	62.2
Nursing home...........	164	11.1				
Hospital...............	679	46.2				
Other health facility	76	5.2				

[1] At time of survey. [2] Includes other and/or unknown, not shown separately. [3] At admission. [4] Includes private insurance, own income, family support, social security benefits, and retirement funds. [5] Includes supplemental security income, other government assistance or welfare, religious organizations, foundations, agencies, Veterans Administration contract, pensions, or other compensation, payment source not yet determined, and other and unknown sources. [6] Activities of daily living. [7] Instrumental activities of daily living.

Source: U.S. National Center for Health Statistics, *Vital and Health Statistics*, Series 13, No. 152.

No. 173. Mental Health Facilities—Summary by Type of Facility: 2000

[Beds: 215.2 represents 215,200. Facilities, beds and inpatients as of year-end; Excludes private psychiatric office practice and psychiatric service modes of all types in hospitals or outpatient clinics of federal agencies other than U.S. Dept. of Veterans Affairs. Excludes data from Puerto Rico, Virgin Islands, Guam, and other territories]

Type of facility	Number of facilities	Inpatient beds		Inpatients		Inpatient care episodes [2] (1,000)
		Total (1,000)	Rate [1]	Total (1,000)	Rate [1]	
Total	4,546	215.2	76.7	182.8	65.2	2,339
Mental hospitals:						
State and county	220	59.4	21.2	54.8	19.6	278
Private [3]	743	60.2	21.5	48.3	17.3	595
General hospitals [4]	1,373	37.7	13.4	25.8	9.2	1,052
Veterans Administration [5]	142	13.0	4.6	11.8	4.2	198
Other [6]	2,068	44.9	16.0	42.1	15.0	197

[1] Rate per 100,000 population. Based on U.S. Census Bureau estimated civilian population as of July 1. [2] "Inpatient care episodes" is defined as the number of residents in inpatient facilities at the beginning of the year plus the total additions to inpatient facilities during the year. [3] Includes residential treatment centers for emotionally disturbed children. [4] Non-federal hospitals with separate psychiatric services. [5] Includes U.S. Department of Veterans Affairs (VA) neuropsychiatric hospitals, VA general hospitals with separate psychiatric settings and VA freestanding psychiatric outpatient clinics. [6] Includes other multiservice mental health facilities with two or more settings, which are not elsewhere classified, as well as freestanding partial care facilities which only provide psychiatric partial care services. Number of facilities, expenditures, and staff data also include freestanding psychiatric partial care facilities.

Source: U.S. Substance Abuse and Mental Health Services Administration, Center for Mental Health Services, unpublished data.

No. 174. Injury and Poisoning Episodes and Conditions by Age and Sex: 2002

[23,661 represents 23,661,000. Covers all medically attended injuries and poisonings occurring during the 3-month period prior to the survey interview. Data were age-adjusted by the direct method to the 2000 projected population. Age adjustment is used to adjust for differences in the age distribution of populations being compared. The NCHS standard for age adjustment was recently changed from the 1940 standard to a 2000 standard. There may be more than one condition per episode. Based on the redesigned National Health Interview Survey, a sample survey of the civilian noninstitutionalized population; see Appendix III]

External cause and nature of injury	Total	Total, age adjusted [1]	Both sexes Under 12 years old	12 to 21 years old	22 to 44 years old	45 to 64 years old	65 years old and over	Male, total	Female, total
EPISODES									
Number (1,000)	23,661	(X)	3,763	5,264	7,695	4,352	2,586	12,645	11,016
Annual rate per 1,000 population, total [2]	84.9	82.2	77.8	129.9	83.5	67.3	78.2	92.9	77.2
Fall	25.4	24.8	27.7	30.6	18.9	20.9	42.6	23.4	27.3
Struck by or against a person or an object .	13.4	12.0	16.2	33.6	10.7	6.9	4.6	[4]17.9	9.1
Transportation [3]	13.4	13.3	9.4	20.1	17.3	10.2	6.6	14.6	12.4
Overexertion.	11.1	10.7	0.8	[4]19.7	13.5	12.6	5.6	13.9	8.4
Cutting, piercing instruments	6.0	5.9	5.1	9.4	7.1	3.7	4.6	7.4	4.7
Poisoning.	2.1	2.0	3.4	[4]2.6	[4]1.4	[4]1.9	[4]2.0	[4]1.3	2.9
CONDITIONS [5]									
Annual rate per 1,000 population, total [2]	107.4	105.2	88.9	150.3	111.9	92.3	98.9	112.5	102.5
Sprains/strains	20.9	20.2	5.5	37.5	26.3	20.1	9.7	20.9	20.9
Open wounds	12.7	12.4	17.2	17.1	12.6	8.0	10.0	16.7	8.8
Fractures	16.1	15.4	15.6	26.1	13.2	11.9	20.7	17.5	14.8
Contusions.	9.9	9.8	8.3	10.4	8.1	10.2	16.0	9.0	10.7

X Not applicable. [1] Data were age-adjusted by the direct method to the 2000 standard population. [2] Includes other items not shown separately. [3] Includes the categories "Motor vehicle traffic"; "Pedal cycle, other"; "Pedestrian, other"; and "Transport, other". [4] Figure does not meet standard of reliability or precision. [5] Poisoning episodes are assumed to have a single condition resulting from the episode.
Source: U.S. National Center for Health Statistics, unpublished data.

No. 175. Injuries Associated With Consumer Products: 2001

[For products associated with more than 20,000 injuries in 2001. Estimates calculated from a representative sample of hospitals with emergency treatment departments in the United States. Data are estimates of the number of emergency room treated cases nationwide associated with various products. Product involvement does not necessarily mean the product caused the accident. Products were selected from the U.S. Consumer Product Safety Commission's National Electronic Injury Surveillance System]

Product	Number	Product	Number
Home workshop equipment:		Other doors (excl. garage)	349,679
Saws (hand or power)	93,872	Ceilings and walls	319,011
Hammers.	43,055	Household cabinets, racks, and shelves . .	262,407
		Nails, screws, tacks, or bolts	179,757
Household packaging and containers:		Porches, balconies, open side floors	142,872
Household containers and packaging	220,118		
Bottles and jars.	83,753	Home entertainment equipment:	
		Televisions	47,210
Housewares:			
Knives.	460,580	Personal use items:	
Tableware and flatware.	116,125	Footwear.	118,501
Drinking glasses	91,979	Wheelchairs	93,873
		Jewelry	76,327
Home furnishing:			
Beds.	519,001	Yard and garden equipment:	
Chairs.	314,953	Lawn mowers.	87,506
Tables [1].	310,121		
Bathtubs and showers	211,250	Sports and recreation equipment:	
Ladders	175,179	Bicycles.	546,236
Sofas, couches, davenports, etc.	137,860	All-terrain vehicles	111,700
Carpets, rugs	112,779	Skateboards	104,449
		Scoters	99,812
Home structures, construction:		Trampolines	91,870
Stairs or steps	1,087,546	Playground climbing equipment	87,444
Floors or flooring materials	957,367		

[1] Includes accessories.

No. 176. Costs of Unintentional Injuries: 2002

[586.3 represents $586,300,000,000. Covers costs of deaths or disabling injuries together with vehicle accidents and fires]

Cost	Amount (bil. dol.) Total [1]	Motor vehicle	Work	Home	Other	Percent distribution Total [1]	Motor vehicle	Work	Home	Other
Total	586.3	242.7	146.6	126.7	88.3	100	100	100	100	100
Wage and productivity losses [2]	286.4	79.6	74.0	80.3	56.3	48.8	32.8	50.5	63.4	63.8
Medical expense	106.6	28.0	27.7	30.2	22.3	18.2	11.5	18.9	23.8	25.3
Administrative expenses [3]	88.7	62.0	26.3	5.5	4.3	15.1	25.5	17.9	4.3	4.9
Motor vehicle damage	71.1	71.1	2.8	(NA)	(NA)	12.1	29.3	1.9	(NA)	(NA)
Employer cost [4]	22.6	2.0	12.5	4.7	3.8	3.9	0.8	8.5	3.7	4.3
Fire loss	10.9	(NA)	3.3	6.0	1.6	1.9	(NA)	2.3	4.7	1.8

NA Not available. [1] Excludes duplication between work and motor vehicle ($18.0 billion in 2002). [2] Actual loss of wages and household production, and the present value of future earnings lost. [3] Home and other costs may include costs of administering medical treatment claims for some motor-vehicle injuries filed through health insurance plans. [4] Estimate of the uninsured costs incurred by employers, representing the money value of time lost by noninjured workers.
Source of Tables 175 and 176: National Safety Council, Itasca, IL, *Injury Facts, 2003 Edition* (copyright).

Health and Nutrition   119

No. 177. Specified Reportable Diseases—Cases Reported: 1980 to 2002

[190.9 represents 190,900. Figures should be interpreted with caution. Although reporting of some of these diseases is incomplete, the figures are of value in indicating trends of disease incidence. Includes cases imported from outside the United States]

Disease	1980	1985	1990	1995	1998	1999	2000	2001	2002
AIDS [1]	(²)	8,249	41,595	71,547	46,521	45,104	40,758	41,868	42,745
Botulism [3]	89	122	92	97	116	154	138	155	118
Brucellosis (undulant fever)	183	153	85	98	79	82	87	136	125
Chickenpox(Varicella) [4] (1,000)	190.9	178.2	173.1	120.6	82.5	46.0	27.4	22.5	22.8
Cholera	9	4	6	23	17	6	5	3	2
Cryptosporidiosis	(²)	(²)	(²)	(NA)	3,793	2,361	3,128	3,785	3,016
Diphtheria	3	3	4	-	1	1	1	2	1
Escherichia coli 0157:H7	(²)	(²)	(²)	2,139	3,161	4,513	4,528	3,287	3,840
Haemophilus influenza	(²)	(²)	(²)	1,180	1,194	1,309	1,398	1,597	1,743
Hansen disease (Leprosy)	223	361	198	144	108	108	91	79	96
Hepatitis: B (serum) (1,000)	19.0	26.6	21.1	10.8	10.3	7.7	8.0	7.8	7.9
A (infectious) (1,000)	29.1	23.2	31.4	31.6	23.2	17.0	13.4	10.6	8.7
C/Non-A, non-B (1,000) [5]	(²)	4.2	2.6	4.6	3.5	3.1	3.2	4.0	1.8
Legionellosis	(²)	830	1,370	1,241	1,355	1,108	1,127	1,168	1,321
Lyme disease	(²)	(²)	(²)	11,700	16,801	16,273	17,730	17,029	23,763
Malaria	2,062	1,049	1,292	1,419	1,611	1,666	1,560	1,544	1,430
Measles (1,000)	13.5	2.8	27.8	0.3	0.1	0.1	0.1	0.1	-
Meningococcal infections	2,840	2,479	2,451	3,243	2,725	2,501	2,256	2,333	1,814
Mumps (1,000)	8.6	3.0	5.3	0.9	0.7	0.4	0.3	0.3	-
Pertussis [6] (1,000)	1.7	3.6	4.6	5.1	7.4	7.3	7.9	7.6	9.7
Plague	18	17	2	9	9	9	6	2	2
Poliomyelitis, acute [7]	9	7	6	7	1	-	-	-	-
Psittacosis	124	119	113	64	47	16	17	25	18
Rabies, animal	6,421	5,565	4,826	7,811	7,259	6,730	6,934	7,150	7,609
Rabies, human	-	1	1	5	1	-	4	1	3
Rocky Mountain spotted fever	1,163	714	651	590	365	579	495	695	1,104
Rubella [8]	3,904	630	1,125	128	364	267	176	23	18
Salmonellosis [9] (1,000)	33.7	65.3	48.6	46.0	43.7	40.6	39.6	40.5	44.2
Shigellosis [10] (1,000)	19.0	17.1	27.1	32.1	23.6	17.5	22.9	20.2	23.5
Tetanus	95	83	64	41	41	40	35	37	25
Toxic-shock syndrome	(²)	384	322	191	138	113	135	127	109
Trichinosis	131	61	129	29	19	12	16	22	14
Tuberculosis [11] (1,000)	27.7	22.2	25.7	22.9	18.4	17.5	16.4	16.0	15.1
Typhoid fever	510	402	552	369	375	346	377	368	321
Sexually transmitted diseases:									
Gonorrhea (1,000)	1,004	911	690	393	356	360	359	362	351
Syphilis (1,000)	69	68	134	69	38	36	32	32	33
Chlamydia (1,000)	(²)	(²)	(²)	478	604	657	702	783	834
Chancroid	788	2,067	4,212	606	189	143	78	38	67

- Represents zero. [1] Acquired immunodeficiency syndrome was not a notifiable disease until 1984. Figures are shown for years in which cases were reported to the CDC. Beginning 1995, based on revised classification system and expanded surveillance case definition. [2] Disease was not notifiable. [3] Includes foodborne, infant, wound, and unspecified cases. [4] Chickenpox was taken off the nationally notifiable list in 1991 but many states continue to report. [5] Includes some persons positive for antibody to hepatitis C virus who do not have hepatitis. [6] Whooping cough. [7] Revised. Data subject to annual revisions. [8] German measles. Excludes rubella, congenital syndrome. [9] Excludes typhoid fever. [10] Bacillary dysentery. [11] Newly reported active cases.

Source: U.S. Centers for Disease Control and Prevention, Atlanta, GA, *Summary of Notifiable Diseases, United States, 2002, Morbidity and Mortality Weekly Report*, Vol. 51, No. 53, April 30, 2004.

No. 178. Children Immunized Against Specified Diseases: 1995 to 2002

[In percent. Covers civilian noninstitutionalized population ages 19 months to 35 months. Based on estimates from the National Immunization Survey. The health care providers of the children are contacted to verify and/or complete vaccination information. Results are based on race/ethnic status of the child]

Vaccination	1995, total	2000, total	2002					
			Total	White non-Hispanic	Hispanic	Black non-Hispanic	American Indian/ Alaskan Native [1]	Asian [1]
Diphtheria-tetanus-pertussis (DTP)/ diphtheria-tetanus:								
3+ doses	95	94	95	96	95	94	(NA)	98
4+ doses	79	82	82	84	79	76	(NA)	88
Polio: 3+ doses	88	90	90	91	90	87	(NA)	92
Hib [2]: 3+ doses	92	93	93	94	92	92	(NA)	95
Measles, mumps, rubella vaccine	90	91	92	93	91	90	84	95
Hepatitis B: 3+ doses	68	90	90	91	90	88	(NA)	94
Varicella [3]	(NA)	68	81	79	82	83	71	87
4+ DTP/3+ polio/1+ MCV [4]	76	78	79	81	77	72	(NA)	85
4+ DTP/3+ polio/1+ MCV/3+ Hib	74	76	78	80	76	71	(NA)	83

NA Not available. [1] Non-Hispanic. [2] Haemophilus B. [3] Data collection for varicella (chicken pox) began in July 1996. [4] MCV=Measles containing vaccine.

Source: U.S. Centers for Disease Control and Prevention, Atlanta, GA, *Morbidity and Mortality Weekly Report*, Vol. 52, No. 31, August 8, 2003; and "Immunization Coverage in the U.S."; <http://www.cdc.gov/nip/coverage/default.htm>.

No. 179. AIDS Cases Reported by Exposure Category and Sex: 1981 to 2002

[**Provisional.** For cases reported in the year shown. Includes Puerto Rico, Virgin Islands, Guam, and U.S. Pacific Islands. Acquired immunodeficiency syndrome (AIDS) is a specific group of diseases or conditions which are indicative of severe immunosuppression related to infection with the human immunodeficiency virus (HIV). Data are subject to retrospective changes and may differ from those data in Table 177]

Exposure category	2002			1981-2002 [1]		
	Total	Male	Female	Total	Male	Female
Persons 13 years old and over, total..................	43,792	32,513	11,279	849,780	697,718	152,060
Male-to-male sexual contact.....	14,545	14,545	(X)	384,784	384,784	(X)
Injection drug use...........	7,502	5,121	2,381	209,920	151,367	58,552
Men who have sex with men and injecting drug use...........	1,510	1,510	(X)	54,224	54,224	(X)
Hemophilia/coagulation disorder . .	90	79	11	5,371	5,067	304
Heterosexual contact	7,953	3,213	4,740	100,071	36,692	63,379
Sex with injection drug user ...	1,504	519	985	33,351	10,412	22,939
Sex with bisexual male	205	(X)	205	4,088	(X)	4,088
Sex with person with hemophilia..............	18	3	15	518	72	446
Sex with HIV-infected transfusion recipient........	59	27	32	1,132	472	660
Sex with HIV-infected person, risk not specified...........	6,167	2,664	3,503	60,982	25,736	35,246
Receipt of blood transfusion, blood components, or tissue........	265	147	118	9,152	5,164	3,988
Other/risk not reported or identified................	11,927	7,898	4,029	86,258	60,420	25,837

X Not applicable.   [1] Includes persons with characteristics unknown.

Source: U.S. Centers for Disease Control and Prevention, Atlanta, GA, *HIV/AIDS Surveillance Report*, Volume 14. <http://www.cdc.gov/hiv/stats/hasrlink.htm>

No. 180. Estimated Persons Living With Acquired Immunodeficiency Syndrome (AIDS) by Selected Characteristics and Year: 1998 to 2002

[These numbers do not represent actual cases of persons living with AIDS. Rather, these numbers are point estimates of persons living with AIDS that have been adjusted for reporting delays and for redistribution of cases in persons initially reported without an identified risk. The estimates have not been adjusted for incomplete reporting.]

Age and characteristic	1998	1999	2000	2001	2002
Total [1]	288,565	311,424	335,316	359,141	384,906
Age as of end of year					
Less than 13 years old	3,128	3,006	2,816	2,571	2,292
13 and 14 years old	372	438	513	642	732
15 to 24 years..........................	4,657	4,675	4,951	5,204	5,653
35 to 44 years	130,403	141,434	151,476	158,962	165,348
45 to 54 years..........................	66,105	77,334	89,716	102,991	116,927
55 to 64 years..........................	16,033	19,330	23,030	27,462	33,201
65 years old and over.....................	4,256	5,152	6,263	7,471	8,902
RACE/ETHNICITY					
White, not Hispanic......................	113,267	120,094	126,851	133,461	140,835
Black, not Hispanic	115,644	126,499	138,129	149,808	162,412
Hispanic.............................	55,980	60,767	65,823	70,865	76,052
Asian/Pacific Islander	2,314	2,578	2,858	3,189	3,574
American Indian/Alaska Native	989	1,074	1,198	1,316	1,450
MALE ADULT/ADOLESCENT EXPOSURE CATEGORY					
Males 13 years old and over, total	227,494	244,615	261,907	279,242	289,248
Male-to-male sexual contact	130,000	139,763	149,742	160,067	171,592
Injection drug use.......................	55,735	59,199	62,743	65,729	68,636
Male-to-male sexual contact and injection drug use ...	20,256	21,212	21,931	22,679	23,495
Heterosexual contact	17,656	20,433	23,328	26,420	29,973
Other [2]	3,846	4,008	4,164	4,348	4,553
FEMALE ADULT/ADOLESCENT EXPOSURE CATEGORY					
Females 13 years old and over, total	57,338	63,023	39,579	79,035	82,764
Injection drug use.......................	24,441	25,874	27,471	28,912	30,158
Heterosexual contact	31,175	35,295	40,072	44,895	50,174
Other [2]...............................	1,722	1,854	2,036	2,227	2,432
Child (under 13 years old) total..............	3,731	3,784	3,827	3,864	3,893
Perinatal..............................	3,577	3,635	3,680	3,716	3,748
Other [3]..............................	154	149	147	147	145

[1] Includes persons of unknown or multiple race and of unknown sex. [2] Includes hemophilia, blood transfusion, perinatal, and risk not reported or not identified. [3] Includes hemophilia, blood transfusion, and risk not reported or not indentified.

Source: U.S. Centers for Disease Control and Prevention, Atlanta, GA, *HIV/AIDS Surveillance Report*, Volume 14. See also <http://www.cdc.gov/hiv/stats/hasrlink.htm>

Health and Nutrition   121

No. 181. AIDS, Syphilis, and Tuberculosis Cases Reported by State: 2003

State	AIDS	Syphilis	Tuber-culosis	State	AIDS	Syphilis	Tuber-culosis	State	AIDS	Syphilis	Tuber-culosis
U.S. [1] ..	42,745	32,871	15,075	KS	70	77	89	ND.	3	-	6
				KY.	305	212	146	OH.	780	351	257
AL	432	700	233	LA	1,167	775	230	OK.	204	287	190
AK.	33	9	49	ME.	28	9	23	OR.	301	75	111
AZ.	630	1,085	263	MD.	1,854	839	306	PA	1,811	689	353
AR.	240	217	136	MA.	810	541	271	RI	107	67	49
CA.	4,364	3,912	3,169	MI	789	1,181	315	SC	833	619	256
CO.	332	174	104	MN.	161	148	237	SD	11	-	13
CT.	618	188	104	MS.	433	451	134	TN	792	1,074	308
DE.	193	62	25	MO	391	204	136	TX	3,140	4,110	1,550
DC.	927	431	82	MT.	17	4	12	UT.	94	71	31
FL	5,058	3,280	1,086	NE.	70	25	28	VT	12	2	8
GA.	1,471	1,893	524	NV.	314	113	85	VA	955	528	315
HI	128	59	148	NH.	41	24	19	WA	477	158	252
ID	31	23	14	NJ	1,436	1,062	530	WV	83	5	30
IL.	2,108	1,592	680	NM.	88	110	57	WI	187	134	78
IN	491	318	128	NY.	6,664	3,879	1,434	WY	12	1	3
IA	94	54	34	NC.	1,061	1,049	434				

- Represents zero.   [1] Includes cases among persons with unknown state of residence.

Source: U.S. Centers for Disease Control and Prevention, Atlanta, GA, *Summary of Notifiable Diseases, United States, 2002, Morbidity and Mortality Weekly Report*, Vol. 51, No. 53, April 30, 2004.

No. 182. Persons with Limitation of Activity Caused by Chronic Conditions: 2000 to 2002

[In percent. Limitation of activity is assessed by asking respondents a series of questions about limitations in their ability to perform activities usual for their age group because of a physical, mental, or emotional problem. Respondents are asked about limitations in activities of daily living, or instrumental activities of daily living, play, school, work, difficulty walking or remembering, and any other activity limitations. For reported limitations the causal health conditions are determined and respondents are considered limited if one or more of these conditions is chronic. Based on the National Health Interview Survey, a sample survey of the civilian noninstitutionalized population; see Appendix III]

Characteristic	2000	2001	2002	Characteristic	2000	2001	2002
Total [1] [2]	11.7	12.1	12.4	Male [2]	11.7	12.2	12.3
Under 18 years	6.0	6.7	7.1	Female [2]	11.5	11.9	12.3
18 to 44 years.	5.8	6.1	6.3				
45 to 54 years.	12.4	13.1	13.7	White, non-Hispanic [2].	11.5	11.8	12.1
55 to 64 years.	19.7	20.7	21.1	Black, non-Hispanic [2].	14.3	15.6	14.9
65 to 74 years.	26.1	26.0	25.2	Hispanic [2] [3]	10.3	10.6	10.7
75 years and over	45.1	44.7	45.1	Mexican	10.4	10.3	10.8

[1] Includes all other races not shown separately.   [2] Estimates for all persons are age adjusted to the year 2000 standard using six age groups: Under 18 years, 18-44 years, 45-54 years, 55-64 years. 65-74 years, and 75 years and over.   [3] Persons of Hispanic origin may be of any race.

Source: U.S. National Center for Health Statistics, *Health, United States, 2004.*

No. 183. Persons 65 Years Old and Over With Limitation of Activity Caused by Chronic Conditions: 2000 to 2002

[In percent. Covers noninstitutionalized persons 65 years old and over. To determine activities of daily living (ADL) limitations respondents were asked "Because of a physical, mental, or emotional problem, does (this person) need the help of other persons with personal care needs, such as eating, bathing, dressing, or getting around inside this home?" Instrumental activities of daily living (IADL) were determined by asking respondents "Because of a physical, mental, or emotional problem, does (this person) need the help of other persons in handling routine needs, such as everyday household chores, doing necessary business, shopping, or getting around for other purposes?" See also headnote, Table 182]

Characteristic	Percent with ADL limitation			Percent with IADL limitation		
	2000	2001	2002	2000	2001	2002
Total [1] [2]	6.3	6.4	6.1	12.7	12.6	12.2
65 to 74 years	3.3	3.4	2.7	6.6	6.7	6.0
75 years and over.	9.5	9.6	9.8	19.3	18.9	18.9
Male [2]	5.1	6.1	4.7	9.2	9.6	7.8
Female [2]	7.0	6.6	7.0	15.1	14.6	15.2
Hispanic or Latino [2] [3]	8.6	11.2	9.2	13.4	17.0	13.1
Mexican	9.4	10.6	10.1	16.3	17.0	13.9
Not Hispanic or Latino [2].	6.1	6.1	5.9	12.6	12.3	12.1
White	5.7	5.5	5.5	12.1	11.6	11.5
Black or African American.	10.1	11.8	9.9	19.1	18.7	18.4

[1] Includes other races not shown separately.   [2] Estimates are age adjusted to the year 2000 standard using two age groups: 65-74 years and 75 years and over.   [3] Persons of Hispanic origin may be of any race.

Source: U.S. National Center for Health Statistics, *Health, United States, 2004.*

No. 184. Disability Status of Population by State: 2000

[In thousands except percent (64,689 represents 64,689,000). As of April. Covers civilian noninstitutionalized population. A disability is a long-lasting physical, mental, or emotional condition. This condition can make it difficult for a person to do activities such as walking, climbing stairs, dressing, bathing, learning, or remembering. This condition can also impede a person from being able to go outside the home alone or to work at a job or business. Based on sample data from the 2000 Census of Population and Housing; see text, Section 1 and Appendix III]

State	Population 5 to 20 years			Population 21 to 64 years			Population 65 years and over		
		With a disability			With a disability			With a disability	
	Total	Number	Percent of total	Total	Number	Percent of total	Total	Number	Percent of total
U.S.	**64,689**	**5,214**	**8.1**	**159,132**	**30,554**	**19.2**	**33,347**	**13,978**	**41.9**
AL.........	1,018	91	9.0	2,498	579	23.2	555	275	49.5
AK.........	166	11	6.9	358	56	15.6	34	16	46.2
AZ.........	1,200	96	8.0	2,813	547	19.4	654	260	39.7
AR.........	613	58	9.4	1,474	345	23.4	355	173	48.9
CA.........	8,172	609	7.5	19,211	3,848	20.0	3,470	1,466	42.2
CO	977	73	7.4	2,550	407	15.9	399	159	40.0
CT.........	736	56	7.6	1,945	328	16.8	440	163	37.0
DE.........	177	16	8.9	443	80	18.0	97	37	37.7
DC	113	11	10.0	350	76	21.9	66	28	42.5
FL.........	3,264	285	8.7	8,746	1,915	21.9	2,720	1,076	39.5
GA	1,915	158	8.2	4,733	940	19.9	755	359	47.5
HI	260	17	6.6	670	119	17.7	158	64	40.6
ID	332	24	7.2	702	117	16.7	141	60	42.5
IL	2,881	222	7.7	7,053	1,204	17.1	1,416	574	40.5
IN	1,422	118	8.3	3,434	636	18.5	707	302	42.6
IA	681	50	7.3	1,602	244	15.2	404	153	37.8
KS.........	645	47	7.2	1,465	246	16.8	331	137	41.5
KY.........	897	81	9.0	2,322	558	24.0	477	235	49.3
LA.........	1,111	104	9.3	2,446	541	22.1	490	235	48.1
ME	279	25	9.0	733	141	19.2	175	72	41.1
MD	1,194	97	8.1	3,076	530	17.2	573	228	39.8
MA	1,356	116	8.6	3,698	663	17.9	807	305	37.8
MI	2,336	198	8.5	5,631	1,018	18.1	1,171	496	42.3
MN	1,168	83	7.1	2,804	392	14.0	554	204	36.9
MS	707	61	8.6	1,542	378	24.5	326	168	51.7
MO	1,289	103	8.0	3,121	567	18.2	711	303	42.6
MT	213	15	7.1	505	85	16.9	114	45	39.6
NE.........	409	27	6.7	936	143	15.2	217	80	37.1
NV.........	436	33	7.7	1,173	256	21.8	214	87	40.6
NH	282	24	8.4	725	117	16.1	139	54	38.5
NJ.........	1,807	134	7.4	4,864	845	17.4	1,064	411	38.6
NM	457	37	8.1	997	209	21.0	206	92	44.8
NY.........	4,198	371	8.8	10,933	2,295	21.0	2,334	941	40.3
NC	1,750	148	8.5	4,643	970	20.9	924	423	45.7
ND	154	11	7.2	345	53	15.4	87	34	38.5
OH	2,601	206	7.9	6,395	1,121	17.5	1,422	583	41.0
OK	810	70	8.7	1,886	405	21.5	430	201	46.7
OR	762	63	8.2	1,973	355	18.0	423	176	41.5
PA.........	2,690	202	7.5	6,837	1,197	17.5	1,809	713	39.4
RI	234	22	9.3	590	116	19.7	144	58	40.3
SC.........	917	82	9.0	2,270	515	22.7	466	213	45.8
SD.........	186	13	6.8	400	62	15.6	101	40	39.5
TN.........	1,256	110	8.8	3,291	720	21.9	668	320	47.8
TX.........	5,183	410	7.9	11,612	2,315	19.9	1,966	880	44.8
UT.........	639	44	6.9	1,176	181	15.4	184	73	39.9
VT.........	141	12	8.3	354	57	16.2	73	28	38.6
VA.........	1,550	126	8.1	4,074	712	17.5	754	317	42.1
WA	1,356	104	7.7	3,400	607	17.8	640	270	42.3
WV	377	34	9.1	1,039	247	23.8	266	129	48.6
WI	1,258	99	7.9	3,019	450	14.9	663	242	36.5
WY	119	9	7.7	277	46	16.8	55	21	39.3

Source: U.S. Census Bureau, "2000 Census of Population and Housing, Profiles of General Demographic Characteristics"; <http://www.census.gov/Press-Release/www/2002/demoprofiles.html>.

No. 185. Substance Abuse Treatment Facilities and Clients: 1995 to 2003

[As of October 1. Based on the Uniform Facility Data Set (UFDS) survey, a census of all known facilities that provide substance abuse treatment in the United States and associated jurisdictions. Selected missing data for responding facilities were imputed]

Primary focus	Number	Primary focus	Number	Type of care and type of problem	Number of clients
FACILITIES		**CLIENTS**		**2003, total [1]**	1,091,816
1995	10,746	1995.	1,009,127	Outpatient rehab	956,245
1996	10,641	1996.	940,141	Outpatient detoxification . .	11,761
1997	10,860	1997.	929,086	24 hour rehab.	107,695
1998	13,455	1998.	1,038,378	24 hour detoxification. . . .	16,115
1999	15,239	2000.	1,000,896		
2000	13,428	2002.	1,136,287		
2002	13,720				
2003 total	13,690	**2003 total**	1,091,816	Drug only.	358,165
Substance abuse		Substance abuse		Alcohol only	221,800
treatment services. . .	8,386	treatment services	743,971	Both alcohol & drug.	511,851
Mental health services .	1,168	Mental health services . .	56,159		
General health care . .	249	General health care	17,766	Total with a drug	
Both substance abuse .		Both substance abuse		problem [2]	870,016
and mental health . . .	3,614	and mental health	254,986	Total with an	
Other	273	Other	18,934	alcohol problem [3]	733,651

[1] Includes clients at facilities that did not provide data on type of substance abuse problem treated. [2] The sum of clients with a drug problem and clients with both diagnoses. [3] The sum of clients with an alcohol problem and clients with both diagnoses.

Source: U.S. Substance Abuse and Mental Health Services Administration, *Uniform Facility Data Set (UFDS): Annual surveys for 1995 - 1999* and National Survey of Substance Abuse Treatment Services (N-SSATS) 2000, 2002 and 2003.

No. 186. Drug Use by Type of Drug and Age Group: 2000 and 2002

[In percent. The 2002 Survey changed names from the National Household Survey on Drug Abuse to National Household Survey on Drug Use and Health (NSDUH). Due to the impact of Survey improvements, 2002 data should not be compared with data collected in 2001 or earlier years. Current users are those who used drugs at least once within month prior to this study. Based on a representative sample of the U.S. population age 12 and older, including persons living in households and in some group quarters such as dormitories and homeless shelters. Estimates are based on computer-assisted interviews of about 72,000 respondents. Subject to sampling variability; see source]

Age and type of drug	Ever used		Current user		Age and type of drug	Ever used		Current user	
	2000	2002	2000	2002		2000	2002	2000	2002
12 YEARS OLD AND OVER					**18 TO 25 YEARS OLD**				
Any illicit drug	38.9	46.0	6.3	8.3	Any illicit drug	51.2	59.8	15.9	20.2
Marijuana and hashish . . .	34.2	40.4	4.8	6.2	Marijuana and hashish . . .	45.7	53.8	13.6	17.3
Cocaine.	11.2	14.4	0.5	0.9	Cocaine.	10.9	15.4	1.4	2.0
Crack.	2.4	3.6	0.1	0.2	Hallucinogens.	19.3	24.2	1.8	1.9
Heroin.	1.2	1.6	0.1	0.1	Inhalants	12.8	15.7	0.6	0.5
Hallucinogens.	11.7	14.6	0.4	0.5	Any psychotherapeutic [1] . .	19.5	27.7	3.6	5.4
LSD.	8.8	10.4	0.2	-	Alcohol	84.0	86.7	56.8	60.5
PCP	2.6	3.2			"Binge" alcohol use [2] . . .	(NA)	(NA)	37.8	40.9
Inhalants	7.5	9.7	0.3	0.3	Cigarettes	67.3	71.2	38.3	40.8
Any psychotherapeutic [1] . . .	14.5	19.8	1.7	2.6	Smokeless tobacco	23.6	23.7	5.0	4.8
Pain relievers [1]	8.6	12.6	1.2	1.9	Cigars.	42.3	45.6	10.4	11.0
Tranquilizers [1]	5.8	8.2	0.4	0.8	**26 TO 34 YEARS OLD**				
Stimulants [1]	6.6	9.0	0.4	0.5	Any illicit drug	50.9	58.3	7.8	10.5
Methamphetamine [1] . .	4.0	5.3	0.2	0.3	Marijuana and hashish . . .	46.0	52.2	5.9	7.7
Sedatives [1]	3.2	4.2	0.1	0.2	Cocaine.	15.1	17.6	0.8	1.2
Alcohol	81.0	83.1	46.6	51.0	Hallucinogens.	15.8	20.6	0.4	0.5
"Binge" alcohol use [2]	(NA)	(NA)	20.6	22.9	Inhalants	11.0	14.1	0.2	0.1
Cigarettes	66.5	69.1	24.9	26.0	Any psychotherapeutic [1] . .	16.9	24.4	2.1	3.6
Smokeless tobacco	18.5	19.9	3.4	3.3	**35 YEARS OLD AND OVER**				
Cigars.	34.2	37.4	4.8	5.4	Any illicit drug	35.5	42.7	3.3	4.6
Pipes	16.4	17.0	1.0	0.8	Marijuana and hashish . . .	31.6	38.0	2.3	3.1
12 TO 17 YEARS OLD					Cocaine.	11.8	15.4	0.3	0.6
Any illicit drug	26.9	30.9	9.7	11.6	Hallucinogens.	10.1	12.6	-	0.1
Marijuana and hashish . . .	18.3	20.6	7.2	8.2	Inhalants	5.3	7.2	0.1	0.1
Cocaine.	2.4	2.7	0.6	0.6	Any psychotherapeutic [1] . .	13.5	18.0	1.0	1.6
Hallucinogens.	5.8	5.7	1.2	1.0	**26 YEARS OLD AND OVER.**				
Inhalants	8.9	10.5	1.0	1.2	Alcohol	85.8	88.0	49.0	53.9
Any psychotherapeutic [1] . . .	10.9	13.7	3.0	4.0	"Binge" alcohol use [2] . . .	(NA)	(NA)	19.1	21.4
Alcohol	41.7	43.4	16.4	17.6	Cigarettes	70.7	73.7	24.2	25.2
"Binge" alcohol use [2]	(NA)	(NA)	10.4	10.7	Smokeless tobacco	19.1	20.9	3.3	3.2
Cigarettes	34.6	33.3	13.4	13.0	Cigars.	35.2	39.0	3.9	4.6
Smokeless tobacco	8.6	8.0	2.1	2.0					
Cigars.	17.1	16.3	4.5	4.5					

- Represents or rounds to zero. NA Not available. [1] Nonmedical use of any prescription-type pain reliever, tranquilizer, stimulant, or sedative; does not include over-the-counter drugs. [2] Binge use is defined as drinking five or more drinks on the same occasion on at least one day in the past 30 days.

Source: U.S. Substance Abuse and Mental Health Services Administration, *Summary of Findings from the 2002 National Survey on Drug Use and Health.*

No. 187. Estimated Use of Selected Drugs by State: 2002

[**19,522 represents 19,522,000**. The 2002 Survey changed names from the National Household Survey on Drug Abuse to National Household Survey on Drug Use and Health (NSDUH). Due to the impact of Survey improvements, 2002 data should not be compared with data collected in 2001 or earlier years. Current users are those persons 12 years old and over who used drugs at least once within month prior to this study. Based on national sample of respondents (see also headnote, Table 186). The state estimates were produced by combining the prevalence rate based on the state sample data and the prevalence rate based on a national regression model applied to local-area county and census block group/tract-level estimates from the state. The parameters of the regression model are estimated from the entire national sample. For comparison purposes, the data shown here display estimates for all 50 States and the District of Columbia utilizing the modeled estimates for all 51 areas]

State	Estimated current users (1,000)					Current users as percent of population				
	Any illicit drug [1]	Marijuana	Any illicit drug other than marijuana [1]	Cigarettes	Binge alcohol [2]	Any illicit drug [1]	Marijuana	Any illicit drug other than marijuana [1]	Cigarettes	Binge alcohol [2]
U.S.	19,522	14,584	8,777	61,134	53,788	8.3	6.2	3.7	26.0	22.9
AL.	245	161	136	992	677	6.6	4.4	3.7	26.9	18.4
AK.	60	48	22	124	117	12.2	9.8	4.4	25.0	23.5
AZ.	372	242	212	1,205	1,071	8.5	5.5	4.9	27.6	24.6
AR.	170	120	86	700	464	7.7	5.4	3.9	31.6	20.9
CA.	2,565	1,914	1,104	5,754	6,084	9.1	6.8	3.9	20.4	21.5
CO	374	326	155	940	942	10.2	8.9	4.2	25.7	25.8
CT.	256	177	105	705	648	9.1	6.3	3.7	24.9	22.9
DE.	61	45	27	190	153	9.1	6.8	4.0	28.5	23.0
DC	60	52	21	117	130	12.4	10.8	4.4	24.2	26.9
FL.	1,222	909	529	3,374	3,121	8.8	6.6	3.8	24.4	22.6
GA.	488	352	244	1,899	1,336	7.1	5.1	3.6	27.8	19.5
HI	88	69	33	199	220	9.1	7.2	3.4	20.7	22.9
ID	75	60	40	270	228	7.0	5.6	3.7	25.1	21.2
IL	788	570	337	2,701	2,587	7.7	5.6	3.3	26.3	25.2
IN	428	321	185	1,459	1,215	8.5	6.4	3.7	29.1	24.2
IA	149	113	71	630	621	6.1	4.6	2.9	25.8	25.4
KS.	147	117	71	564	487	6.7	5.3	3.2	25.6	22.1
KY.	292	186	143	1,148	678	8.6	5.5	4.2	33.8	20.0
LA	319	230	155	1,032	849	8.8	6.4	4.3	28.6	23.5
ME	100	77	37	298	245	9.1	6.9	3.3	27.0	22.1
MD	368	254	174	1,062	1,010	8.3	5.7	3.9	23.9	22.7
MA	460	340	201	1,245	1,385	8.5	6.3	3.7	23.1	25.7
MI	747	586	309	2,299	2,010	9.1	7.1	3.7	27.9	24.4
MN	333	263	144	1,143	1,199	8.0	6.3	3.5	27.5	28.9
MS.	165	116	86	666	452	7.1	5.0	3.7	28.9	19.6
MO	421	282	192	1,468	1,090	9.0	6.1	4.1	31.5	23.4
MT	76	66	28	204	196	10.0	8.7	3.7	26.8	25.8
NE.	115	90	56	374	361	8.1	6.4	4.0	26.5	25.6
NV.	189	150	84	554	388	10.8	8.6	4.8	31.8	22.3
NH	118	105	40	290	253	11.0	9.9	3.8	27.2	23.7
NJ.	526	353	245	1,700	1,645	7.4	5.0	3.5	24.0	23.3
NM	110	88	58	362	353	7.3	5.9	3.9	24.1	23.5
NY.	1,494	1,194	558	4,052	3,997	9.4	7.5	3.5	25.5	25.2
NC	554	374	303	2,155	1,438	8.2	5.6	4.5	32.0	21.4
ND	37	29	17	141	158	7.1	5.6	3.3	26.7	30.0
OH	766	627	304	2,862	2,256	8.2	6.7	3.2	30.5	24.1
OK	222	148	129	796	520	7.8	5.2	4.6	28.2	18.4
OR	306	262	128	761	580	10.5	9.0	4.4	26.1	19.9
PA.	781	556	330	2,922	2,316	7.6	5.4	3.2	28.4	22.5
RI	97	85	40	252	246	10.8	9.5	4.5	28.1	27.4
SC.	220	167	110	952	753	6.5	5.0	3.2	28.2	22.3
SD.	44	35	21	164	163	7.0	5.7	3.4	26.5	26.3
TN.	328	223	178	1,359	875	6.9	4.7	3.7	28.5	18.4
TX.	1,149	838	616	4,210	4,041	6.7	4.9	3.6	24.5	23.5
UT.	113	83	68	342	300	6.2	4.6	3.7	18.9	16.6
VT.	58	53	19	134	131	11.0	10.0	3.6	25.4	25.0
VA.	478	377	209	1,455	1,210	8.2	6.4	3.6	24.8	20.6
WA	534	404	214	1,187	997	10.8	8.1	4.3	23.9	20.1
WV	101	76	45	433	303	6.6	5.0	2.9	28.4	19.8
WI	331	246	145	1,172	1,189	7.3	5.4	3.2	26.0	26.3
WY	29	21	15	117	97	6.9	5.2	3.7	28.3	23.4

[1] Any illicit drug indicates use at least once of marijuana/hashish, cocaine (including crack), inhalants, hallucinogens (including PCP and LSD), heroin, or any prescription-type psychotherapeutic used nonmedically. Any illicit drug other than marijuana indicates use at least once of any of these listed drugs, regardless of marijuana/hashish use; marijuana/hashish users who also have used any of the other listed drugs are included. [2] Binge use is defined as drinking five or more drinks on the same occasion on at least one day in the past 30 days. By "occasion" is meant the same time or within a couple hours of each other.

Source: U.S. Substance Abuse and Mental Health Services Administration, *National Household Survey on Drug Use and Health*, annual. <http://www.oas.samhsa.gov/nhsda.htm>

Health and Nutrition   125

No. 188. Current Cigarette Smoking: 1990 to 2002

[In percent. Prior to 1995, a current smoker is a person who has smoked at least 100 cigarettes and who now smokes. Beginning 1995, definition includes persons who smoke only "some days." Excludes unknown smoking status. Based on the National Health Interview Survey; for details, see Appendix III]

Sex, age, and race	1990	1995	2000	2002	Sex, age, and race	1990	1995	2000	2002
Total smokers, age-adjusted [1]	25.3	24.6	23.1	22.4	Black, total	32.5	28.5	26.1	27.0
Male	28.0	26.5	25.2	24.8	18 to 24 years	21.3	[2]14.6	20.8	22.8
Female	22.9	22.7	21.1	20.1	25 to 34 years	33.8	25.1	23.3	28.8
White male............	27.6	26.2	25.5	25.0	35 to 44 years	42.0	36.3	30.8	28.3
Black male............	32.8	29.4	25.7	26.7	45 to 64 years	36.7	33.9	32.2	29.9
White female	23.5	23.4	22.0	21.1	65 years and over.....	21.5	28.5	14.2	19.4
Black female..........	20.8	23.5	20.7	18.3	Female, total	22.8	22.6	21.0	20.0
Total smokers......	25.5	24.7	23.3	22.5	18 to 24 years........	22.5	21.8	25.1	24.6
Male, total	28.4	27.0	25.7	25.2	25 to 34 years........	28.2	26.4	22.5	21.6
18 to 24 years.........	26.6	27.8	28.5	32.4	35 to 44 years........	24.8	27.1	26.2	23.7
25 to 34 years.........	31.6	29.5	29.0	27.5	45 to 64 years........	24.8	24.0	21.6	21.1
35 to 44 years.........	34.5	31.5	30.2	29.7	65 years and over	11.5	11.5	9.3	8.6
45 to 64 years.........	29.3	27.1	26.4	24.5	White, total	23.4	23.1	21.6	20.7
65 years and over	14.6	14.9	10.2	10.1	18 to 24 years........	25.4	24.9	28.7	26.9
White, total	28.0	26.6	25.8	25.2	25 to 34 years........	28.5	27.3	25.1	24.1
18 to 24 years	27.4	28.4	30.9	34.5	35 to 44 years........	25.0	27.0	26.6	24.5
25 to 34 years	31.6	29.9	29.9	28.1	45 to 64 years........	25.4	24.3	21.4	21.5
35 to 44 years	33.5	31.2	30.6	29.7	65 years and over.....	11.5	11.7	9.1	8.5
45 to 64 years	28.7	26.3	25.8	24.4	Black, total	21.2	23.5	20.8	18.5
65 years and over.....	13.7	14.1	9.8	9.3	18 to 24 years	10.0	[2]8.8	14.2	17.1
					25 to 34 years	29.1	26.7	15.5	13.9
					35 to 44 years	25.5	31.9	30.2	24.0
					45 to 64 years	22.6	27.5	25.6	22.2
					65 years and over.....	11.1	13.3	10.2	9.4

[1] Estimates are age adjusted to the year 2000 standard using five age groups: 18-24 years, 25-34 years, 35-44 years, 45-64 years, 65 years and over.   [2] Data have a relative standard error of 20-30 percent.

Source: U.S. National Center for Health Statistics, *Health, United States*, annual.

No. 189. Current Cigarette Smoking by Sex and State: 2002

[In percent. Current cigarette smoking is defined as persons who reported having smoked 100 or more cigarettes during their lifetime and who currently smoke every day or some days. Based on the Behavioral Risk Factor Surveillance System, a telephone survey of health behaviors of the civilian, noninstitutionalized U.S. population, 18 years old and over; for details, see source]

State	Total	Male	Female	State	Total	Male	Female	State	Total	Male	Female
U.S.[1] ..	23.1	25.9	20.9	KS	22.1	23.2	20.9	ND......	21.5	23.1	20.0
				KY	32.6	34.8	30.5	OH......	26.6	28.4	25.0
AL......	24.4	27.5	21.6	LA	23.9	26.6	21.5	OK......	26.7	29.7	23.8
AK......	29.4	31.9	26.7	ME......	23.6	26.4	21.1	OR......	22.4	24.6	20.2
AZ......	23.5	27.0	20.1	MD......	22.0	25.7	18.6	PA	24.6	26.1	23.2
AR......	26.3	28.7	24.1	MA......	19.0	20.2	18.0	RI	22.5	24.3	20.9
CA......	16.4	19.7	13.3	MI	24.2	25.1	23.5	SC	26.6	29.1	24.4
CO.....	20.4	21.4	19.4	MN.....	21.7	24.3	19.4	SD......	22.6	25.6	19.7
CT.....	19.5	20.6	18.4	MS.....	27.4	33.2	22.2	TN......	27.8	31.0	24.9
DE.....	24.7	25.4	24.1	MO.....	26.6	29.6	23.9	TX......	22.9	26.8	19.1
DC.....	20.4	23.8	17.5	MT.....	21.3	21.3	21.4	UT......	12.7	14.2	11.3
FL......	22.1	23.6	20.7	NE.....	22.8	26.3	19.4	VT......	21.2	21.5	20.9
GA.....	23.3	26.8	20.0	NV.....	26.0	28.5	23.5	VA	24.6	28.5	20.9
HI	21.1	26.2	16.0	NH.....	23.2	23.9	22.6	WA	21.5	23.6	19.4
ID......	20.6	21.6	19.7	NJ......	19.1	20.4	17.9	WV	28.4	29.8	27.2
IL.......	22.9	26.1	19.8	NM.....	21.2	23.3	19.3	WI	23.4	25.4	21.4
IN......	27.7	29.8	25.8	NY.....	22.4	25.9	19.3	WY	23.7	25.3	22.0
IA	23.1	26.3	20.2	NC.....	26.4	30.7	22.3				

[1] Represents median value among the states and DC. For definition of median, see Guide to Tabular Presentations

Source: U.S. Centers for Disease Control and Prevention, Atlanta, GA, *Morbidity and Mortality Weekly Report*, Vol. 52, No. 53, January 9, 2004.

No. 190. Use of Mammography for Women 40 Years Old and Over by Patient Characteristics: 1990 to 2000

[Percent of women having a mammogram within the past 2 years. Covers civilian noninstitutional population. Based on National Health Interview Survey; see Appendix III]

Characteristic	1990	1994	2000	Characteristic	1990	1994	2000
Total [1]	51.4	60.9	70.3	Years of school completed:			
40 to 49 years old	55.1	61.3	64.2	Less than 12 years.........	36.4	48.2	57.7
50 years old and over.........	49.7	60.6	73.6	12 years	52.7	61.0	69.6
50 to 64 years old	56.0	66.5	78.6	13 years or more	62.8	69.7	76.1
65 years old and over	43.4	55.0	68.0	Poverty status: [3]			
White, non-Hispanic..........	52.7	61.3	72.1	Below poverty	28.7	44.4	55.2
Black, non-Hispanic	46.0	64.4	67.9	At or above poverty	54.8	64.8	72.2
Hispanic origin [2]	45.2	51.9	61.4				

[1] Includes all other races not shown separately and unknown education level and poverty status.   [2] Persons of Hispanic origin may be of any race.   [3] For explanation of poverty level, see text, Section 13.

Source: U.S. National Center for Health Statistics, *Health, United States*, annual.

No. 191. Cancer—Estimated New Cases, 2004, and Survival Rates, 1980-1982 to 1995-2000

[1,368 represents 1,368,000. The 5-year relative survival rate, which is derived by adjusting the observed survival rate for expected mortality, represents the likelihood that a person will not die from causes directly related to their cancer within 5 years. Survival data shown are based on those patients diagnosed while residents of an area listed below during the time periods shown. Data are based on information collected as part of the National Cancer Institute's Surveillance, Epidemiology and End Results (SEER) program, a collection of population-based registries in Connecticut, New Mexico, Utah, Iowa, Hawaii, Atlanta, Detroit, Seattle-Puget Sound, and San Francisco-Oakland]

Site	Estimated new cases, [1] 2004 (1,000)			5-year relative survival rates (percent)							
				White				Black			
	Total	Male	Female	1980-1982	1989-1991	1992-1994	1995-2000	1980-1982	1989-1991	1992-1994	1995-2000
All sites [2]	1,368	700	668	52.1	60.3	63.8	65.5	39.8	46.2	52.0	55.2
Lung.	174	93	81	13.5	14.4	15.1	15.4	12.1	10.8	11.8	13.2
Breast [3]	217	1	216	77.1	86.2	87.5	88.9	65.8	71.2	72.5	75.2
Colon and rectum	147	74	73	54.9	62.4	62.8	64.1	46.7	54.1	52.1	54.6
Colon	106	50	56	55.6	63.2	63.1	63.8	49.4	53.9	51.9	54.4
Rectum	41	23	17	53.1	60.5	62.0	64.6	38.3	54.5	52.7	55.2
Prostate	230	230	(X)	74.5	92.0	98.1	100.0	64.8	80.8	92.4	96.0
Bladder	60	45	16	78.9	82.2	82.3	82.7	58.5	62.0	64.2	61.9
Corpus uteri	40	(X)	40	82.8	85.7	86.3	86.1	55.2	57.8	56.1	63.1
Non-Hodgkin's lymphoma [4] .	54	29	26	51.9	52.1	54.4	60.3	50.5	43.7	42.3	50.5
Oral cavity and pharynx . . .	28	19	10	55.7	55.6	58.4	60.9	31.1	33.3	35.0	39.0
Leukemia [4]	33	19	14	39.5	46.4	49.2	47.8	32.9	34.9	39.4	38.6
Melanoma of skin	55	30	25	83.3	89.0	89.2	90.7	58.3	78.8	59.6	74.0
Pancreas.	32	16	16	2.8	4.1	4.7	4.2	4.5	3.9	3.7	3.8
Kidney	36	22	14	51.1	60.8	63.1	63.9	56.3	58.1	60.0	63.5
Stomach	23	14	9	16.5	18.4	21.0	21.5	19.1	24.8	18.9	24.2
Ovary	26	(X)	26	38.7	41.2	42.1	44.0	39.3	30.7	46.2	37.9
Cervix uteri [5]	11	(X)	11	68.2	72.5	72.6	74.0	61.5	62.6	57.7	65.7

X Not applicable.   [1] Estimates provided by American Cancer Society are based on rates from the National Cancer Institute's SEER program.   [2] Includes other sites not shown separately.   [3] Survival rates for female only.   [4] All types combined. [5] Invasive cancer only.

Source: U.S. National Institutes of Health, National Cancer Institute, *Cancer Statistics Review*, annual. <http://seer.cancer.gov/csr/>.

No. 192. Cancer—Estimated New Cases and Deaths by State: 2004

[In thousands (1,368.0 represents 1,368,000). Excludes basal and squamous cellskin cancers and in situ carcinomas except urinary bladder]

State	New cases [1]			Deaths			State	New cases [1]			Deaths		
	Total [2]	Lung	Female breast	Total [2]	Lung	Female breast		Total [2]	Lung	Female breast	Total [2]	Lung	Female breast
U.S. . .	1,368.0	173.8	216.0	563.7	160.4	40.1							
							MO	30.3	4.1	4.7	12.5	3.8	0.9
AL	24.3	3.4	4.0	10.0	3.1	0.7	MT	5.0	0.7	0.6	2.1	0.6	0.1
AK	1.9	0.2	0.3	0.8	0.2	(Z)	NE	8.3	1.0	1.3	3.4	1.0	0.2
AZ	23.6	2.8	4.0	9.7	2.6	0.7	NV	11.0	1.6	1.6	4.5	1.5	0.3
AR	14.8	2.2	2.1	6.1	2.1	0.4	NH	6.3	0.8	0.9	2.6	0.7	0.2
CA	134.3	15.7	21.9	55.3	14.5	4.1							
							NJ	43.8	5.1	8.0	18.1	4.7	1.5
CO	15.5	1.7	2.6	6.4	1.6	0.5	NM	7.6	0.8	1.0	3.1	0.7	0.2
CT	17.0	2.0	2.9	7.0	1.9	0.5	NY	88.2	10.0	15.2	36.3	9.3	2.8
DE	4.4	0.6	0.7	1.8	0.5	0.1	NC	40.2	5.7	5.9	16.6	5.3	1.1
DC	2.9	0.3	0.6	1.2	0.3	0.1	ND	3.3	0.4	0.5	1.3	0.3	0.1
FL	97.3	13.4	13.4	40.1	12.4	2.5							
							OH	59.4	7.7	10.1	24.5	7.1	1.9
GA	35.4	5.1	6.1	14.6	4.7	1.1	OK	18.5	2.6	2.9	7.6	2.4	0.5
HI	5.1	0.6	0.8	2.1	0.5	0.1	OR	17.3	2.1	2.8	7.1	2.0	0.5
ID	5.5	0.7	0.9	2.3	0.6	0.2	PA	72.6	8.6	11.2	29.9	7.9	2.1
IL	60.3	7.3	9.6	24.8	6.8	1.8	RI	6.0	0.8	0.9	2.5	0.7	0.2
IN	32.2	4.5	4.8	13.3	4.2	0.9							
							SC	21.5	3.0	3.3	8.9	2.7	0.6
IA	15.9	1.8	2.3	6.6	1.7	0.4	SD	4.0	0.5	0.5	1.7	0.4	0.1
KS	12.9	1.7	1.9	5.3	1.6	0.4	TN	30.9	4.7	4.3	12.7	4.3	0.8
KY	22.7	3.7	3.3	9.4	3.4	0.6	TX	84.5	10.5	13.0	34.8	9.7	2.4
LA	23.5	3.2	3.9	9.7	2.9	0.7	UT	6.4	0.5	1.1	2.6	0.4	0.2
ME	7.5	1.0	0.9	3.1	0.9	0.2							
							VT	3.2	0.4	0.6	1.3	0.4	0.1
MD	25.3	3.2	4.1	10.4	2.9	0.8	VA	31.2	4.1	6.4	12.9	3.7	1.2
MA	33.1	4.1	5.2	13.6	3.7	1.0	WA	27.4	3.5	4.0	11.3	3.3	0.8
MI	48.2	6.2	7.3	19.9	5.7	1.4	WV	11.4	1.8	1.6	4.7	1.6	0.3
MN	22.7	2.6	3.6	9.4	2.4	0.7	WI	26.2	3.1	4.0	10.8	2.8	0.8
MS	15.1	2.2	2.5	6.2	2.1	0.5	WY	2.4	0.3	0.3	1.0	0.3	(Z)

Z less than 50 deaths.   [1] Estimates are offered as a rough guide and should be interpreted with caution. They are calculated according to the distribution of estimated 2004 cancer deaths by state.   [2] Includes other types of cancer, not shown separately.

Source: American Cancer Society, Inc., Atlanta, Georgia, *Cancer Facts and Figures—2004* (copyright). <http://www.cancer.org>

Health and Nutrition 127

No. 193. Cumulative Percent Distribution of Population by Height and Sex: 1988-94

[Height was measured without shoes. Based on sample and subject to sampling variability; see source]

Height	Males 20-29 years	30-39 years	40-49 years	50-59 years	60-69 years	70-79 years	Females 20-29 years	30-39 years	40-49 years	50-59 years	60-69 years	70-79 years
Percent under—												
4'8"	-	-	-	-	-	-	0.6	0.1	-	-	0.2	1.7
4'9"	-	-	-	-	-	-	0.7	0.2	0.3	0.1	0.7	3.3
4'10"	-	-	-	-	0.1	-	1.2	0.7	0.7	1.9	1.7	4.9
4'11"	-	-	-	-	0.1	0.1	3.1	2.6	1.7	3.1	4.4	9.8
5'	0.1	-	0.2	-	0.4	0.1	6.0	5.5	5.3	6.6	9.9	15.4
5'1"	0.1	-	0.4	0.1	0.5	0.6	11.5	10.4	9.9	11.9	19.0	28.9
5'2"	0.5	0.8	0.7	0.2	0.7	1.9	21.8	18.5	18.8	24.4	34.3	45.6
5'3"	1.3	1.4	0.9	1.0	2.2	2.7	34.3	30.7	31.9	38.6	48.3	61.2
5'4"	3.4	2.2	1.7	2.5	5.8	7.8	48.9	42.9	49.2	52.6	65.5	74.5
5'5"	6.9	5.1	5.6	6.0	9.4	16.5	62.7	59.1	64.3	69.9	76.5	85.9
5'6"	11.7	10.1	12.1	11.7	15.8	27.3	74.0	71.8	77.0	81.6	87.8	93.9
5'7"	20.8	18.9	19.6	20.5	27.4	39.5	84.7	84.1	87.0	89.3	92.5	97.3
5'8"	32.0	28.3	28.0	32.6	38.6	53.4	92.4	91.6	94.5	95.6	96.7	99.2
5'9"	46.3	44.3	42.1	43.9	55.1	68.7	96.2	95.6	97.3	99.0	99.3	99.9
5'10"	58.7	58.0	58.1	60.6	68.8	79.5	98.6	98.1	98.9	99.6	99.8	100.0
5'11"	70.1	70.4	71.1	75.2	81.4	89.2	99.5	99.5	99.4	100.0	100.0	100.0
6'	81.2	79.7	81.5	85.4	90.0	94.1	100.0	100.0	100.0	100.0	100.0	100.0
6'1"	87.4	86.2	89.0	92.4	95.2	97.2	100.0	100.0	100.0	100.0	100.0	100.0
6'2"	94.7	92.4	94.4	96.4	98.2	99.3	100.0	100.0	100.0	100.0	100.0	100.0
6'3"	97.9	98.1	97.2	98.2	99.5	99.9	100.0	100.0	100.0	100.0	100.0	100.0

- Represents or rounds to zero.

Source: U.S. National Center for Health Statistics, unpublished data.

No. 194. Age-adjusted Percent Distributions of Body Mass Index (BMI) Among Persons 18 Years Old and Over, by Selected Characteristics: 2002

[Body Mass Index (BMI) is a measure that adjusts body weight for height. It is calculated as weight in kilograms divided by height in meters squared. For both men and women, underweight is indicated by a BMI under 18.5; healthy weight is indicated by a BMI greater than or equal to 18.5 and less than 25; overweight is indicated by those who have a BMI equal to 25 and less than 30. Percent who are obese represent those who have a BMI equal to or above 30. These estimates are based on definitions provided in the *Dietary Guidelines for Americans*, published by the U.S. Dept. of Agriculture and the U.S. Dept. of Health and Human Services. Based on the National Health Interview Survey; for details, see Appendix III]

Selected characteristic	Under-weight	Healthy weight	Above healthy weight Total	Over-weight	Obese
Total [1] (age-adjusted)	2.1	39.6	58.4	35.0	23.4
Total [1] (unadjusted)	2.0	39.4	58.5	35.0	23.5
Age: [2]					
18 to 44 years	2.5	44.2	53.3	31.9	21.4
45 to 64 years	1.1	32.1	66.9	39.1	27.8
65 to 74 years	1.7	31.7	66.6	39.3	27.3
75 years and over	3.5	45.4	51.0	35.1	15.9
Sex:					
Male	1.1	32.0	66.9	43.1	23.8
Female	3.0	46.9	50.0	27.1	22.9
Race:					
White alone[4]	2.0	40.5	57.5	35.3	22.2
Black or African American alone[4]	1.7	29.4	68.9	34.1	34.8
American Indian or Alaska Native alone[4]	[3]2.2	36.1	61.7	30.4	31.3
Asian alone[4]	5.6	59.9	34.5	27.5	7.0
Native Hawaiian or other Pacific Islander alone[4]	-	33.2	66.8	36.4	[3]30.4
2 or more races [5]	[3]2.6	39.1	58.3	30.9	27.4
Hispanic or Latino origin status [6]:					
Hispanic or Latino	1.4	33.4	65.2	39.8	25.4
Not Hispanic or Latino	2.2	40.4	57.4	34.3	23.1
Education: [7]					
Less than a high school diploma	1.5	32.1	66.4	36.7	29.7
High school diploma or GED	2.0	34.6	63.4	35.9	27.5
Some college	1.7	36.1	62.2	36.4	25.8
Bachelors degree or higher	1.7	43.6	54.7	37.3	17.4

- Represents zero. [1] Total includes other races not shown separately and persons with unknown characteristics. [2] Estimates for age groups are not age adjusted. [3] Base figure too small to meet statistical standards for reliability of a derived figure. [4] Refers to persons who indicated only a single race group. [5] The "two or more races" refers to all persons who indicated more than one race group. [6] Persons of Hispanic or Latino origin may be of any race. [7] Education is shown only for persons 25 years old and over.

Source: U.S. National Center for Health Statistics, Vital and Health Statistics, Series 10, Number 222, *Summary Health Statistics for U.S. Adults: National Health Interview Survey, 2002.*

No. 195. Percentage of Adults Engaging in Leisure-Time, Transportation-Related and Household-Related Physical Activity: 2003

[In percent. Covers persons 18 years old and over. Based on responses to questions about physical activity in prior month from the Behavioral Risk Factor Surveillance System. Estimates are age-adjusted to the year 2000 standard population. Based on a survey sample of approximately 257,000 persons in 50 states and the DC in 2003]

Characteristic	Persons who meet recom-mended activity [1]	Persons not meet-ing recom-mended activity [2]	Persons who are physically inactive [3]	Characteristic	Persons who meet recom-mended activity [1]	Persons not meet-ing recom-mended activity [2]	Persons who are physically inactive [3]
Total............	46.0	54.0	24.3	30 to 44 years old . . .	47.7	52.3	23.4
				45 to 64 years old . . .	42.6	57.4	26.7
Male..............	48.2	51.8	22.0	65 to 74 years old . . .	37.1	62.9	31.2
Female.............	44.0	56.0	26.3	75 years old and			
				over	27.6	72.4	42.0
White, non-Hispanic . . .	49.0	51.0	20.9				
Black, non-Hispanic. . . .	36.3	63.7	32.7	School years completed:			
Hispanic	37.5	62.5	36.0	Less than 12 years ..	33.8	66.2	45.7
Other	43.5	56.5	25.2	12 years	43.1	56.9	30.5
				Some college (13 to			
Males:				15 years)	47.5	52.5	21.0
18 to 29 years old . . .	57.8	42.2	17.1	College (16 or more			
30 to 44 years old . . .	48.7	51.3	20.7	years)	51.9	48.1	13.1
45 to 64 years old . . .	43.2	56.8	24.4				
65 to 74 years old . . .	45.7	54.3	24.9	Household income:			
75 years old and				Less than $10,000...	34.7	65.3	42.2
over	36.7	63.3	31.0	$10,000 to $19,999 ..	37.0	63.0	38.9
				$20,000 to $34,999 ..	43.6	56.4	29.4
Females:				$35,000 to $49,999 ..	47.3	52.7	21.9
18 to 29 years old . . .	50.1	49.9	21.9	$50,000 and over ...	53.6	46.4	13.6

[1] Recommended activity is physical activity at least 5 times/week x 30 minutes/time or vigorous physical activity for 20 minutes at a time at least 3 times/week.   [2] Persons whose reported physical activity does not meet recommended level or report no leisure-time, transporation-related, or household-related physical activity.   [3] Persons with no reported physical activity.

Source: U.S. National Center for Chronic Disease Prevention and Health Promotion, "Nutrition and Physical Activity"; and unpublished data. <http://www.cdc.gov/nccdphp/dnpa>

No. 196. Households and Persons Having Problems With Access to Food: 1999 to 2002

[104,684 represents 104,684,000. Food secure means that a household had access at all times to enough food for an active healthy life for all household members, with no need for recourse to socially unacceptable food sources or extraordinary coping behaviors to meet their basic food needs. Food insecure households had limited or uncertain ability to acquire acceptable foods in socially acceptable ways. Food insecure households with hunger were those with one or more household members who were hungry at least sometime during the period due to inadequate resources for food. The omission of homeless persons may be a cause of underreporting.The severity of food insecurity and hunger in households is measured through a series of questions about experiences and behaviors known to characterize households that are having difficulty meeting basic food needs. These experiences and behaviors generally occur in an ordered sequence as the severity of food insecurity increases. As resources become more constrained, adults in typical households first worry about having enough food, then they stretch household resources and juggle other necessities, then decrease the quality and variety of household members' diets, then decrease the frequency and quantity of adults' food intake, and finally decrease the frequency and quantity of children's food intake. All questions refer to the previous 12 months and include a qualifying phrase reminding respondents to report only those occurrences that resulted from inadequate financial resources. Restrictions to food intake due to dieting or busy schedules are excluded. Data are from the Food Security Supplement to the Current Population Survey (CPS); for details about the CPS, see text, Section 1 and Appendix III]

Household food security level	Number (1,000)				Percent distribution			
	1999	2000	2001	2002	1999	2000	2001	2002
Households, total.	104,684	106,043	107,824	108,601	100.0	100.0	100.0	100.0
Food secure	94,154	94,942	96,303	96,543	89.9	89.5	89.3	88.9
Food insecure	10,529	11,101	11,521	12,058	10.1	10.5	10.7	11.1
Without hunger............	7,420	7,786	8,010	8,259	7.1	7.3	7.4	7.6
With hunger..............	3,109	3,315	3,511	3,799	3.0	3.1	3.3	3.5
With hunger among children [1] ..	219	255	211	265	0.6	0.7	0.6	0.7
Adult members	198,900	201,922	204,340	206,493	100.0	100.0	100.0	100.0
In food secure households......	179,960	181,586	183,398	184,718	90.5	89.9	89.8	89.5
In food insecure households.....	18,941	20,336	20,942	21,775	9.5	10.1	10.2	10.5
Without hunger............	13,869	14,763	14,879	15,486	7.0	7.3	7.3	7.5
With hunger [2].............	5,072	5,573	6,063	6,289	2.5	2.8	3.0	3.0
Child members	71,418	71,763	72,321	72,542	100.0	100.0	100.0	100.0
In food secure households......	59,344	58,868	59,620	59,415	83.1	82.0	82.4	81.9
In food insecure households.....	12,074	12,895	12,701	13,127	16.9	18.0	17.6	18.1
Without hunger...........	11,563	12,334	12,234	12,560	16.2	17.2	16.9	17.3
With hunger among children [1]..	511	562	467	567	0.7	0.8	0.6	0.8

[1] One or more children in these households was hungry at sometime during the year because of the household's food insecurity. Percent distribution of households with hunger among children excludes households with no child from the denominator.   [2] One or more adults in these households was hungry at sometime during the year because of the household's food insecurity.

Source: U.S. Dept. of Agriculture, Economic Research Service, Household Food Security in the United States, 2002, Food Assistance and Nutrition Research Report No. 35; October 2003.

Health and Nutrition   129

No. 197. Nutrition—Nutrients in Foods Available for Civilian Consumption Per Capita Per Day: 1970 to 2000

[Computed by the Center for Nutrition Policy and Promotion (CNPP). Based on Economic Research Service (ERS) estimates of per capita quantities of food available for consumption from "Food Consumption, Prices, and, Expenditures", on imputed consumption data for foods no longer reported by ERS, and on CNPP estimates of quantities of produce from home gardens. Food supply estimates do not reflect loss of food or nutrients from further marketing or home processing. Enrichment and fortification levels of iron, zinc, thiamin, riboflavin, niacin, folate, vitamin A, vitamin B_6, vitamin B_{12}, and Vitamin C are included]

Nutrient	Unit	1970-79	1980-89	1990-99	1995	2000
Food energy	Calories	3,200	3,400	3,700	3,700	3,900
Carbohydrate	Grams	388	411	472	473	490
Dietary fiber	Grams	19	20	23	23	24
Protein	Grams	95	98	107	106	110
Total fat [1]	Grams	149	156	157	156	170
Saturated	Grams	51	52	50	50	54
Monounsaturated	Grams	60	63	67	66	72
Polyunsaturated	Grams	28	31	33	32	36
Cholesterol	Milligrams	440	420	410	400	430
Vitamin A	Micrograms RE [2]	1,240	1,210	1,250	1,260	1,260
Carotenes	Micrograms RE [3]	550	590	720	720	720
Vitamin E	Milligrams α-TE [4]	13.9	15.6	17.1	16.8	19.2
Vitamin C	Milligrams	110	117	126	126	126
Thiamin	Milligrams	2.2	2.5	2.9	2.9	2.9
Riboflavin	Milligrams	2.5	2.7	2.9	2.8	2.9
Niacin	Milligrams	24.0	28.0	31.0	31.0	32.0
Vitamin B_6	Milligrams	2.0	2.2	2.4	2.4	3.4
Total Folate [5] [6]	Micrograms	317	346	439	375	691
Folate	Micrograms DFE	332	375	505	401	907
Vitamin B_{12}	Micrograms	8.9	8.2	7.9	8.0	8.3
Calcium	Milligrams	910	920	960	960	960
Phosphorus	Milligrams	1,490	1,530	1,640	1,630	1,670
Magnesium	Milligrams	330	350	380	370	380
Iron	Milligrams	16.3	19.4	22.5	22.3	23.1
Zinc	Milligrams	12.9	13.9	14.8	14.7	14.9
Copper	Milligrams	1.6	1.7	1.9	1.8	1.9
Potassium	Milligrams	3,430	3,470	3,690	3,650	3,740
Selenium	Milligrams	130	139	160	156	176
Sodium [7]	Milligrams	1,350	1,340	1,350	1,340	1,330

[1] Includes other types of fat not shown separately. [2] Retinol activity equivalents. [3] Retinol equivalents. [4] Alpha-Tocopherol equivalents. [5] Dietary Folate Equivalents. [6] Reflects new terminology from Institute of Medicine's Dietary Reference Intakes reports. [7] Does not include amount from processed foods; underestimates actual availability.

Source: U.S. Dept. of Agriculture, Center for Nutrition Policy and Promotion, *Nutrient Content of the U.S. Food Supply, 1909-2000*, in press. Data also published by Economic Research Service in *Food Consumption, Prices, and Expenditures*, annual. <http://www.usda.gov/cnpp>.

No. 198. Sources of Calcium, Iron, and Cholesterol in the U.S. Food Supply: 1970 and 2000

[In percent. See headnote, Table 197]

Commodity group	Calcium		Commodity group	Iron		Commodity group	Cholesterol	
	1970	2000		1970	2000		1970	2000
Total	100	100	Total	100	100	Total	100	100
Whole milk	35	11	Grains and breakfast cereal	36	52	Meat, poultry, fish [1]	39	44
Low-fat and skim milk	11	21	Meat, poultry, fish [1]	32	24	Eggs	40	35
Cheese	11	26	Eggs	4	2	Whole milk	8	3
Other dairy	19	15	Vegetables	14	10	Low fat and skim milk	1	2
Vegetables	7	7	Fruits	3	2	Cheese	3	7
Other foods	17	20	Dairy products	2	2	Other dairy	3	4
			Other foods	9	8	Other foods	6	5

[1] Includes meat alternatives (legumes, nuts, and soy).

Source: U.S. Dept. of Agriculture, Center for Nutrition Policy and Promotion, *Nutrient Content of the U.S. Food Supply, 1909-2000*, 2002. <http://www.usda.gov/cnpp/>.

130   Health and Nutrition

No. 199. Per Capita Consumption of Major Food Commodities: 1980 to 2002

[In pounds, retail weight, except as indicated. Consumption represents the residual after exports, nonfood use and ending stocks are subtracted from the sum of beginning stocks, domestic production, and imports. Based on Census Bureau estimated population]

Commodity	Unit	1980	1985	1990	1995	2000	2001	2002
Red meat, total (boneless, trimmed weight) [1][2]	Pounds . . .	126.4	124.9	112.2	113.6	113.7	111.4	114.0
Beef	Pounds . . .	72.1	74.6	63.9	63.5	64.5	63.1	64.5
Veal	Pounds . . .	1.3	1.5	0.9	0.8	0.5	0.5	0.5
Lamb and mutton	Pounds . . .	1.0	1.1	1.0	0.9	0.8	0.8	0.9
Pork	Pounds . . .	52.1	47.7	46.4	48.4	47.8	46.9	48.2
Poultry (boneless, trimmed weight) [2]	Pounds . . .	40.8	45.5	56.2	62.1	66.9	67.8	70.7
Chicken	Pounds . . .	32.7	36.4	42.4	48.2	53.2	54.0	56.8
Turkey	Pounds . . .	8.1	9.1	13.8	13.9	13.7	13.8	14.0
Fish and shellfish (boneless, trimmed weight) . .	Pounds . . .	12.4	15.0	14.9	14.8	15.2	14.7	15.6
Eggs	Number. . .	271	255	234	232	250	253	255
Shell.	Number. . .	236	217	186	172	177	180	180
Processed	Number. . .	35	39	48	59	73	73	75
Dairy products, total [3]	Pounds . . .	543.2	593.7	568.0	576.2	592.8	586.5	585.3
Fluid milk products [4]	Gallons . . .	27.9	27.1	26.2	24.5	23.2	22.8	22.8
Beverage milks	Gallons . . .	27.6	26.7	25.7	23.9	22.5	22.0	21.9
Plain whole milk.	Gallons . . .	16.5	13.9	10.2	8.3	7.7	7.4	7.3
Plain reduced-fat milk (2%)	Gallons . . .	6.3	7.9	9.1	8.0	7.1	7.0	7.0
Plain light and skim milks.	Gallons . . .	3.1	3.2	4.9	6.1	6.1	5.9	5.8
Flavored whole milk	Gallons . . .	0.6	0.4	0.3	0.3	0.4	0.4	0.4
Flavored milks other than whole	Gallons . . .	0.6	0.7	0.8	0.8	1.0	1.0	1.2
Buttermilk	Gallons . . .	0.5	0.5	0.4	0.3	0.3	0.2	0.2
Yogurt (excl. frozen)	1/2 pints . .	4.6	7.3	7.4	9.2	12.0	13.0	13.7
Fluid cream products [5]	1/2 pints . .	10.5	13.5	14.3	15.6	18.4	20.0	19.7
Cream [6]	1/2 pints . .	6.3	8.2	8.7	9.4	11.7	12.8	12.1
Sour cream and dips	1/2 pints . .	3.4	4.3	4.7	5.4	6.1	6.5	6.7
Condensed and evaporated milks	Pounds . . .	7.0	7.5	7.9	6.8	5.8	5.4	6.0
Whole milk.	Pounds . . .	3.8	3.6	3.2	2.3	2.0	2.0	2.3
Skim milk.	Pounds . . .	3.3	3.8	4.8	4.5	3.8	3.5	3.7
Cheese [7]	Pounds . . .	17.5	22.5	24.6	26.9	29.8	30.0	30.5
American [8]	Pounds . . .	9.6	12.2	11.1	11.7	12.7	12.8	12.8
Cheddar.	Pounds . . .	6.9	9.8	9.0	9.0	9.7	9.9	9.6
Italian [8]	Pounds . . .	4.4	6.5	9.0	10.3	12.0	12.3	12.4
Mozzarella	Pounds . . .	3.0	4.6	6.9	8.0	9.3	9.7	9.7
Other [8]	Pounds . . .	3.4	3.9	4.5	5.0	5.1	4.9	5.3
Swiss	Pounds . . .	1.3	1.3	1.4	1.1	1.0	1.2	1.1
Cream and Neufchatel	Pounds . . .	1.0	1.2	1.7	2.0	2.4	2.3	2.4
Cottage cheese, total.	Pounds . . .	4.5	4.1	3.4	2.7	2.6	2.6	2.6
Lowfat	Pounds . . .	0.8	1.0	1.2	1.2	1.3	1.3	1.3
Frozen dairy products	Pounds . . .	26.4	27.9	28.4	29.0	28.0	26.9	26.4
Ice cream.	Pounds . . .	17.5	18.1	15.8	15.5	16.6	16.3	16.7
Lowfat ice cream.	Pounds . . .	7.1	6.9	7.7	7.4	7.3	7.3	6.5
Sherbet	Pounds . . .	1.2	1.3	1.2	1.3	1.2	1.1	1.1
Frozen yogurt	Pounds . . .	(NA)	(NA)	2.8	3.4	2.0	1.5	1.5
Fats and oils:								
Total, fat content only	Pounds . . .	56.9	64.1	63.0	65.4	74.5	(NA)	(NA)
Butter (product weight)	Pounds . . .	4.5	4.9	4.4	4.4	4.6	(NA)	(NA)
Margarine (product weight)	Pounds . . .	11.3	10.8	10.9	9.1	8.2	(NA)	(NA)
Lard (direct use)	Pounds . . .	2.3	1.6	1.6	1.6	2.0	(NA)	(NA)
Edible beef tallow (direct use)	Pounds . . .	1.1	2.0	0.6	2.7	4.0	(NA)	(NA)
Shortening	Pounds . . .	18.2	22.9	22.2	22.2	23.1	(NA)	(NA)
Salad and cooking oils	Pounds . . .	21.2	23.5	25.2	26.5	33.7	(NA)	(NA)
Other edible fats and oils	Pounds . . .	1.5	1.6	1.2	1.6	1.5	(NA)	(NA)
Flour and cereal products [9]	Pounds . . .	144.7	156.5	180.9	190.2	199.8	194.4	191.3
Wheat flour	Pounds . . .	116.9	124.6	135.9	140.0	146.3	141.1	136.7
Rice, milled	Pounds . . .	9.4	9.1	15.8	18.6	19.6	18.7	19.2
Corn products	Pounds . . .	12.9	17.2	21.4	24.9	28.4	29.0	29.7
Oat products	Pounds . . .	3.9	4.0	6.5	5.4	4.3	4.5	4.5
Caloric sweeteners, total [10]	Pounds . . .	123.0	128.8	132.4	143.8	148.9	147.1	146.1
Sugar, refined cane and beet	Pounds . . .	83.6	62.7	64.4	64.7	65.6	64.5	63.2
Corn sweeteners [11]	Pounds . . .	38.2	64.8	66.8	77.9	81.9	81.3	81.5
High-fructose corn syrup	Pounds . . .	19.0	45.2	49.6	57.6	62.7	62.6	62.8
Other:								
Cocoa beans	Pounds . . .	3.4	4.6	5.4	4.5	5.9	5.6	4.9
Coffee (green beans).	Pounds . . .	10.3	10.5	10.3	7.9	10.3	9.5	9.2
Peanuts (shelled)	Pounds . . .	4.8	6.3	6.0	5.6	5.8	5.8	5.8
Tree nuts (shelled)	Pounds . . .	1.8	2.5	2.4	1.9	2.5	2.8	3.1

NA Not available. [1] Excludes edible offals. [2] Excludes shipments to Puerto Rico and the other U.S. possessions.
[3] Milk-equivalent, milkfat basis. Includes butter. [4] Fluid milk figures are aggregates of commercial sales and milk produced and consumed on farms. [5] Includes eggnog, not shown separately. [6] Heavy cream, light cream, and half and half. [7] Excludes full-skim American, cottage, pot, and baker's cheese. [8] Includes other cheeses not shown separately. [9] Includes rye flour and barley products not shown separately. Excludes quantities used in alcoholic beverages. [10] Dry weight. Includes edible syrups (maple, molasses, etc.) and honey not shown separately. [11] Includes glucose and dextrose not shown separately.

Source: U.S. Department of Agriculture, Economic Research Service, *Food Consumption, Prices, and Expenditures, 1970-2002*; online at <http://www.ers.usda.gov/data/foodconsumption/>

Health and Nutrition 131

No. 200. Per Capita Utilization of Commercially Produced Fruits and Vegetables: 1980 to 2002

[In pounds, farm weight. Domestic food use of fresh fruits and vegetables reflects the fresh-market share of commodity production plus imports and minus exports]

Commodity	1980	1985	1990	1995	1998	1999	2000	2001	2002
Fruits and vegetables, total [1]	608.0	629.3	657.7	690.8	697.0	706.0	712.3	686.0	683.6
Fruits, total	270.5	270.0	272.1	283.6	284.1	292.3	287.1	272.8	271.7
Fresh fruits	104.8	110.6	116.2	122.5	128.8	129.6	127.2	125.4	125.6
Noncitrus	78.7	89.1	94.9	98.7	102.3	109.3	103.8	101.5	103.2
Apples	19.2	17.3	19.6	18.7	19.0	18.5	17.5	15.6	16.0
Bananas	20.8	23.5	24.3	27.1	28.0	30.7	28.4	26.6	26.8
Cantaloupes	5.8	8.5	9.2	9.0	10.7	11.5	10.8	11.2	11.3
Grapes	4.0	6.8	7.9	7.4	7.1	8.0	7.3	7.6	8.6
Peaches and nectarines	7.1	5.5	5.5	5.3	4.8	5.4	5.4	5.2	5.3
Pears	2.6	2.8	3.2	3.4	3.3	3.3	3.2	3.1	2.9
Pineapples	1.5	1.5	2.0	1.9	2.8	3.0	3.2	3.2	3.8
Plums and prunes	1.5	1.4	1.5	0.9	1.2	1.3	1.2	1.3	1.3
Strawberries	2.0	3.0	3.2	4.1	3.9	4.6	4.9	4.2	4.7
Watermelons	10.7	13.5	13.3	15.2	14.3	15.4	13.9	15.1	13.9
Other [2]	3.5	5.3	5.2	5.7	7.2	7.6	8.0	8.4	8.6
Fresh citrus	26.1	21.5	21.4	23.8	26.6	20.3	23.4	23.8	22.4
Oranges	14.3	11.6	12.4	11.8	14.6	8.4	11.7	11.9	10.6
Grapefruit	7.3	5.5	4.4	6.0	5.9	5.7	5.1	4.8	4.8
Other [3]	4.5	4.4	4.6	6.0	6.1	6.2	6.6	7.1	7.0
Processed fruits	165.7	159.5	155.9	161.0	155.3	162.7	159.9	147.4	146.0
Frozen fruits [4]	3.1	3.3	3.8	4.8	4.3	4.7	4.3	7.0	4.6
Dried fruits [5]	11.2	12.8	12.1	12.6	12.1	10.1	10.4	10.2	10.6
Canned fruits [6]	24.6	20.9	21.0	17.3	17.0	19.2	17.5	17.6	16.7
Fruit juices [7]	126.1	122.2	118.8	126.0	121.6	128.1	127.2	112.1	113.6
Vegetables, total	337.5	359.2	385.6	407.2	412.9	413.7	425.2	413.2	412.0
Fresh vegetables	150.4	157.4	170.2	180.9	186.5	191.3	200.4	196.7	193.4
Asparagus (all uses)	0.3	0.5	0.6	0.6	0.7	0.9	1.0	0.9	1.0
Broccoli	1.4	2.6	3.4	4.3	5.1	6.5	6.1	5.6	5.0
Cabbage	8.1	8.8	8.3	8.1	8.5	7.6	9.0	9.0	8.4
Carrots	6.2	6.5	8.3	11.2	12.7	10.9	10.4	10.7	9.5
Cauliflower	1.1	1.8	2.2	1.6	1.5	1.9	2.0	1.6	1.5
Celery (all uses)	7.4	6.9	7.2	6.9	6.5	6.6	6.4	6.6	6.5
Corn	6.5	6.4	6.7	7.8	9.3	9.1	9.2	9.4	9.0
Cucumbers	3.9	4.4	4.7	5.6	6.5	6.8	6.4	6.4	6.7
Head lettuce	25.6	23.7	27.7	22.2	21.6	23.9	23.4	23.5	22.4
Mushrooms	1.2	1.8	2.0	2.0	2.5	2.5	2.6	2.6	2.6
Onions	11.4	13.6	15.1	17.8	18.3	18.1	18.3	17.8	18.5
Snap beans	1.3	1.3	1.1	1.6	1.7	1.9	2.0	2.2	2.1
Bell peppers (all uses)	2.9	3.8	4.5	6.2	6.4	6.7	7.0	6.7	7.0
Potatoes	51.1	46.3	46.7	49.2	47.0	48.0	47.3	46.2	45.0
Sweetpotatoes (all uses)	4.4	5.4	4.4	4.2	3.8	3.7	4.2	4.4	3.7
Tomatoes	12.8	14.9	15.5	16.8	17.5	17.8	17.6	17.4	18.4
Other fresh vegetables [8]	4.8	8.7	11.8	14.8	16.9	18.4	27.5	25.7	26.1
Processed vegetables	187.1	201.8	215.5	226.3	226.4	222.4	224.7	216.5	218.6
Selected vegetables for freezing	51.5	64.5	66.8	78.8	80.4	80.9	79.6	78.2	78.0
Selected vegetables for canning	102.8	99.2	110.4	108.0	105.3	102.8	103.0	97.1	99.8
Vegetables for dehydrating [9]	10.5	12.8	14.6	14.5	17.7	14.7	17.8	15.7	15.7
Potatoes for chips	16.5	17.6	16.4	16.4	14.8	15.9	16.0	17.6	17.0
Pulses [10]	5.8	7.6	7.3	8.5	8.2	8.1	8.4	7.8	8.1

[1] Excludes wine grapes. [2] Apricots, avocados, cherries, cranberries, kiwifruit, mangoes, papayas, and honeydew melons.
[3] Lemons, limes, tangerines, and tangelos. [4] Apples, apricots, blackberries, blueberries, boysenberries, cherries, loganberries, peaches, plums, prunes, raspberries, and strawberries. [5] Apples, apricots, dates, figs, peaches, pears, prunes, and raisins.
[6] Apples, apricots, cherries, olives, peaches, pears, pineapples, plums, and prunes. [7] Apple, cranberry, grape, grapefruit, lemon, lime, orange, pineapple, and prunes. [8] Artichokes, brussels sprouts, eggplant, escarole, endive, garlic, romaine, leaf lettuce, radishes, spinach, and squash. Beginning 2000 includes collard greens, kale, mustard greens, okra, pumpkin, and turnip greens. [9] Onions and potatoes. [10] Dry peas, lentils, and dry edible beans.

No. 201. Per Capita Consumption of Selected Beverages by Type: 1980 to 2002

[In gallons. See headnote, Table 199]

Commodity	1980	1985	1990	1995	1998	1999	2000	2001	2002
Nonalcoholic	(NA)	(NA)	128.3	128.2	136.2	141.3	(NA)	(NA)	(NA)
Milk (plain and flavored)	27.6	26.7	25.7	23.9	23.0	22.9	23.3	22.0	21.9
Whole	17.0	14.3	10.5	8.6	8.1	8.2	8.4	7.8	7.7
Reduced-fat, light, and skim	10.5	12.3	15.2	15.3	14.9	14.8	15.0	14.2	14.2
Tea	7.3	7.1	6.9	7.9	8.3	8.2	7.8	8.2	7.8
Coffee	26.7	27.4	26.8	20.2	23.9	25.1	26.3	24.2	23.6
Bottled water	2.4	4.5	8.0	11.5	15.7	17.7	(NA)	(NA)	(NA)
Carbonated soft drinks	35.1	35.7	46.2	47.4	47.9	49.7	49.3	(NA)	(NA)
Diet	5.1	7.1	10.7	10.9	11.0	11.4	11.6	(NA)	(NA)
Regular	29.9	28.7	35.6	36.5	36.8	38.2	37.7	(NA)	(NA)
Fruit juices	7.4	7.8	8.0	8.6	8.8	9.0	9.1	8.0	8.0
Fruit drinks, cocktails, and ades	(NA)	(NA)	6.3	7.7	7.7	7.7	(NA)	(NA)	(NA)
Canned iced tea	(NA)	(NA)	0.1	0.7	0.7	0.7	(NA)	(NA)	(NA)
Vegetable juices	(NA)	(NA)	0.3	0.3	0.3	0.3	(NA)	(NA)	(NA)
Alcoholic	28.4	28.0	27.4	24.7	24.8	25.0	25.8	25.1	25.2
Beer	24.3	23.8	23.9	21.8	21.7	21.8	22.5	21.8	21.8
Wine [1]	2.1	2.4	2.0	1.7	1.9	2.0	2.0	2.0	2.1
Distilled spirits	2.0	1.8	1.5	1.2	1.2	1.2	1.3	1.3	1.3

NA Not available. [1] Beginning 1985, includes wine coolers.

Source of Tables 200 and 201: U.S. Dept. of Agriculture, Economic Research Service, *Food Consumption, Prices, and Expenditures*, annual; online at <http://www.ers.usda.gov/data/foodconsumption/>

Section 4

Education

This section presents data primarily concerning formal education as a whole, at various levels, and for public and private schools. Data shown relate to the school-age population and school enrollment, educational attainment, education personnel, and financial aspects of education. In addition, data are shown for charter schools, computer usage in schools, distance education, and adult education. The chief sources are the decennial census of population and the Current Population Survey (CPS), both conducted by the U.S. Census Bureau (see text, Section 1, Population); annual, biennial, and other periodic surveys conducted by the National Center for Education Statistics (NCES), a part of the U.S. Department of Education; and surveys conducted by the National Education Association.

The censuses of population have included data on school enrollment since 1840 and on educational attainment since 1940. The CPS has reported on school enrollment annually since 1945 and on educational attainment periodically since 1947.

The NCES is continuing the pattern of statistical studies and surveys conducted by the U.S. Office of Education since 1870. The annual *Digest of Education Statistics* provides summary data on pupils, staff, finances, including government expenditures, and organization at the elementary, secondary, and higher education levels. It is also a primary source for detailed information on federal funds for education, projections of enrollment, graduates, and teachers. *The Condition of Education*, issued annually, presents a summary of information on education of particular interest to policymakers. NCES also conducts special studies periodically.

The census of governments, conducted by the Census Bureau every 5 years (for the years ending in "2" and "7"), provides data on school district finances and state and local government expenditures for education. Reports published by the

Bureau of Labor Statistics contain data relating civilian labor force experience to educational attainment (see also Tables 573, 600, and 608 in Section 12, Labor Force, Employment, and Earnings).

Types and sources of data—The statistics in this section are of two general types. One type, exemplified by data from the Census Bureau, is based on direct interviews with individuals to obtain information about their own and their family members' education. Data of this type relate to school enrollment and level of education attained, classified by age, sex, and other characteristics of the population. The school enrollment statistics reflect attendance or enrollment in any regular school within a given period; educational attainment statistics reflect the highest grade completed by an individual, or beginning 1992, the highest diploma or degree received.

Beginning in 2001, the CPS used Census 2000 population controls. From 1994 to 2000, the CPS used 1990 census population controls plus adjustment for undercount. Also the survey changed from paper to computer assisted technology. For years 1981 through 1993, 1980 census population controls were used; 1971 through 1980, 1970 census population controls had been used. These changes had little impact on summary measures (e.g., medians) and proportional measures (e.g., enrollment rates); however, use of the controls may have significant impact on absolute numbers.

The second type, generally exemplified by data from the NCES and the National Education Association, is based on reports from administrators of educational institutions and of state and local agencies having jurisdiction over education. Data of this type relate to enrollment, attendance, staff, and finances for the nation, individual states, and local areas.

Education   133

Unlike the NCES, the Census Bureau does not regularly include specialized vocational, trade, business, or correspondence schools in its surveys. The NCES includes nursery schools and kindergartens that are part of regular grade schools in their enrollment figures. The Census Bureau includes all nursery schools and kindergartens. At the higher education level, the statistics of both agencies are concerned with institutions granting degrees or offering work acceptable for degree-credit, such as junior colleges.

School attendance—All states require that children attend school. While state laws vary as to the ages and circumstances of compulsory attendance, generally they require that formal schooling begin by age 6 and continue to age 16.

Schools—The NCES defines a school as "a division of the school system consisting of students composing one or more grade groups or other identifiable groups, organized as one unit with one or more teachers to give instruction of a defined type, and housed in a school plant of one or more buildings. More than one school may be housed in one school plant, as is the case when the elementary and secondary programs are housed in the same school plant."

Regular schools are those which advance a person toward a diploma or degree. They include public and private nursery schools, kindergartens, graded schools, colleges, universities, and professional schools.

Public schools are schools controlled and supported by local, state, or federal governmental agencies; private schools are those controlled and supported mainly by religious organizations or by private persons or organizations.

The Census Bureau defines *elementary* schools as including grades 1 through 8; *high* schools as including grades 9 through 12; and *colleges* as including junior or community colleges, regular 4-year colleges, and universities and graduate or professional schools. Statistics reported by the NCES and the National Education Association by type of organization, such as elementary level and secondary level, may not be strictly comparable with those from the Census Bureau because the grades included at the two levels vary, depending on the level assigned to the middle or junior high school by the local school systems.

School year—Except as otherwise indicated in the tables, data refer to the school year which, for elementary and secondary schools, generally begins in September of the preceding year and ends in June of the year stated. For the most part, statistics concerning school finances are for a 12-month period, usually July 1 to June 30. Enrollment data generally refer to a specific point in time, such as fall, as indicated in the tables.

Statistical reliability—For a discussion of statistical collection, estimation, and sampling procedures and measures of statistical reliability applicable to the Census Bureau and the NCES data, see Appendix III.

No. 202. School Enrollment: 1970 to 2012

[In thousands (59,838 represents 59,838,000). As of fall. Based on survey of state education agencies; see source for details.]

Year	All levels			K through grade 8		Grades 9 through 12		College [1]	
	Total	Public	Private	Public	Private	Public	Private	Public	Private
1970	59,838	52,322	7,516	32,558	4,052	13,336	1,311	6,428	2,153
1975	61,004	53,654	7,350	30,515	3,700	14,304	1,300	8,835	2,350
1980	58,305	50,335	7,971	27,647	3,992	13,231	1,339	9,457	2,640
1985	57,226	48,901	8,325	27,034	4,195	12,388	1,362	9,479	2,768
1990	60,269	52,061	8,208	29,878	4,084	11,338	1,150	10,845	2,974
1995	64,764	55,933	8,831	32,341	4,465	12,500	1,197	11,092	3,169
1996	65,744	56,733	9,011	32,764	4,551	12,847	1,213	11,121	3,247
1997	66,470	57,323	9,147	33,073	4,623	13,054	1,218	11,196	3,306
1998	66,983	57,677	9,306	33,346	4,702	13,193	1,235	11,138	3,369
1999	67,667	58,166	9,501	33,488	4,765	13,369	1,254	11,309	3,482
2000 [2]	68,698	58,976	9,722	33,709	4,875	13,514	1,287	11,753	3,560
2001, prel.	69,818	59,921	9,897	33,952	4,880	13,736	1,322	12,233	3,695
2002, proj.	70,262	60,272	9,990	33,942	4,885	13,976	1,356	12,354	3,749
2003, proj.	70,656	60,587	10,069	33,843	4,876	14,198	1,379	12,546	3,814
2004, proj.	70,922	60,802	10,120	33,669	4,871	14,506	1,408	12,627	3,841
2005, proj.	71,294	61,090	10,204	33,534	4,878	14,770	1,433	12,786	3,893
2006, proj.	71,794	61,467	10,327	33,589	4,933	14,936	1,449	12,942	3,945
2007, proj.	72,068	61,682	10,386	33,654	4,950	14,986	1,458	13,042	3,978
2008, proj.	72,292	61,843	10,449	33,791	4,975	14,899	1,459	13,153	4,015
2009, proj.	72,597	62,069	10,528	33,994	5,001	14,767	1,461	13,308	4,066
2010, proj.	72,927	62,322	10,605	34,243	5,040	14,648	1,455	13,431	4,110
2011, proj.	73,342	62,650	10,692	34,597	5,091	14,487	1,443	13,566	4,158
2012, proj.	73,872	63,083	10,789	35,006	5,148	14,361	1,430	13,716	4,211

[1] Data beginning 1996 based on new classification system. See footnote 1, Table 261.   [2] Public K-8 and 9-12 data preliminary.

Source: U.S. National Center for Education Statistics, *Digest of Education Statistics*, annual, and *Projections of Education Statistics*, annual.

No. 203. School Expenditures by Type of Control and Level of Instruction in Constant (2001-2002) Dollars: 1960 to 2002

[In millions of dollars (144,699 represents $144,699,000,000). For school years ending in year shown. Total expenditures for public elementary and secondary schools include current expenditures, interest on school debt and capital outlay. Data deflated by the Consumer Price Index, wage earners, and clerical workers through 1975; thereafter, all urban consumers, on a school year basis (supplied by the National Center for Education Statistics). See also Appendix III. Based on survey of state education agencies; see source for details]

Year	Elementary and secondary schools				Colleges and universities [2]		
	Total	Total	Public	Private [1]	Total	Public	Private
1960	144,699	101,356	94,685	6,671	43,343	23,673	19,670
1970	322,934	203,704	191,911	11,793	119,230	76,580	42,650
1975	373,863	236,867	223,105	13,762	136,996	92,779	44,217
1980	380,163	236,787	220,260	16,526	143,376	95,103	48,273
1985	417,243	251,703	230,812	20,891	165,539	107,328	58,213
1986	441,293	264,954	243,338	21,616	176,339	114,741	61,598
1987	467,731	280,664	257,756	22,908	187,068	119,430	67,638
1988	482,044	289,186	265,651	23,535	192,858	122,842	70,014
1989	510,033	307,854	283,740	24,113	202,179	128,076	74,102
1990	535,416	324,134	298,592	25,541	211,283	135,266	76,019
1991	549,081	331,230	305,283	25,947	217,851	138,960	78,890
1992	558,249	336,835	310,791	26,044	221,414	140,104	81,310
1993	570,201	342,987	316,231	26,755	227,214	143,990	83,224
1994	581,600	350,379	323,325	27,055	231,221	145,722	85,499
1995	597,010	358,260	330,537	27,722	238,751	151,163	87,586
1996	610,807	367,048	338,675	28,372	243,759	153,109	90,649
1997	631,063	380,307	351,152	29,155	250,756	156,563	94,193
1998	655,348	398,173	368,317	29,856	257,175	161,988	95,187
1999	686,846	415,897	385,357	30,539	270,950	168,177	102,773
2000	718,736	433,174	401,912	31,261	285,563	177,148	108,415
2001	750,983	450,455	418,804	31,651	300,528	190,209	110,319
2002	780,100	462,700	430,600	32,100	317,400	198,600	118,800

[1] Estimated.   [2] Data beginning 1996 based on new classification system. See footnote 1, Table 261.

Source: U.S. National Center for Education Statistics, *Digest of Education Statistics*, annual.

Education   135

No. 204. School Enrollment, Faculty, Graduates, and Finances— Projections: 2003 to 2009

[As of fall, except as indicated (54,296 represents 54,296,000)]

Item	Unit	2003	2004	2005	2006	2007	2008	2009
ELEMENTARY AND SECONDARY SCHOOLS								
School enrollment, total............	1,000...	54,296	54,455	54,615	54,907	55,049	55,124	55,223
Kindergarten through grade 8	1,000...	38,719	38,541	38,412	38,522	38,605	38,766	38,995
Grades 9 through 12	1,000...	15,577	15,914	16,203	16,385	16,445	16,358	16,228
Public	1,000...	48,040	48,175	48,304	48,524	48,640	48,690	48,761
Kindergarten through grade 8 ...	1,000...	33,843	33,669	33,534	33,589	33,654	33,791	33,994
Grades 9 through 12	1,000...	14,198	14,506	14,770	14,936	14,986	14,899	14,767
Private	1,000...	6,256	6,279	6,311	6,383	6,409	6,434	6,461
Kindergarten through grade 8 ...	1,000...	4,876	4,871	4,878	4,933	4,950	4,975	5,001
Grades 9 through 12	1,000...	1,379	1,408	1,433	1,449	1,458	1,459	1,461
Classroom teachers, total FTE [1]	1,000...	3,364	3,367	3,369	3,390	3,407	3,446	3,474
Public	1,000...	2,980	2,983	2,983	3,001	3,016	3,051	3,076
Private	1,000...	384	384	386	389	391	395	398
High school graduates, total [2]......	1,000...	3,002	3,037	3,101	3,172	3,262	3,274	3,262
Public	1,000...	2,698	2,728	2,785	2,850	2,931	2,942	2,930
Public schools: [2]								
Average daily attendance (ADA) ...	1,000...	44,548	44,674	44,793	44,997	45,105	45,151	45,217
Current dollars: [3]								
Teachers' average salary	Dol.....	46,303	47,471	49,080	50,607	(NA)	(NA)	(NA)
Current school expenditure	Bil. dol. .	390.8	408.6	432.0	452.7	(NA)	(NA)	(NA)
Per pupil in fall enrollment	Dol.....	8,135	8,482	8,942	9,329	(NA)	(NA)	(NA)
Constant (2001-2002) dollars: [4]								
Teachers' average salary	Dol.....	44,547	44,752	45,317	45,650	(NA)	(NA)	(NA)
Current school expenditure	Bil. dol. .	376.0	385.2	398.8	408.3	(NA)	(NA)	(NA)
Per pupil in fall enrollment	Dol.....	7,826	7,997	8,257	8,415	(NA)	(NA)	(NA)
HIGHER EDUCATION								
Enrollment, total..............	1,000...	16,361	16,468	16,679	16,887	17,020	17,168	17,374
Male.......................	1,000...	7,098	7,144	7,208	7,281	7,342	7,413	7,498
Full time.................	1,000...	4,484	4,502	4,551	4,612	4,657	4,709	4,775
Part time.................	1,000...	2,614	2,642	2,656	2,669	2,685	2,704	2,724
Female.....................	1,000...	9,263	9,324	9,471	9,606	9,679	9,755	9,876
Full time.................	1,000...	5,290	5,358	5,457	5,548	5,615	5,692	5,785
Part time.................	1,000...	3,972	3,966	4,015	4,058	4,064	4,063	4,091
Public.....................	1,000...	12,546	12,627	12,786	12,942	13,042	13,153	13,308
Four-year institutions	1,000...	6,611	6,658	6,748	6,838	6,896	6,961	7,051
Two-year institutions	1,000...	5,935	5,969	6,038	6,104	6,146	6,192	6,257
Private	1,000...	3,814	3,841	3,894	3,945	3,979	4,015	4,066
Four-year institutions	1,000...	3,540	3,565	3,614	3,661	3,692	3,725	3,772
Two-year institutions	1,000...	274	276	280	284	287	290	294
Undergraduate...............	1,000...	14,048	14,146	14,329	14,511	14,634	14,775	14,965
Graduate...................	1,000...	1,973	1,980	2,003	2,024	2,032	2,036	2,049
First-time professional	1,000...	340	342	347	352	355	357	360
Full-time equivalent............	1,000...	12,138	12,232	12,402	12,574	12,694	12,829	13,005
Public.....................	1,000...	8,926	8,993	9,117	9,243	9,329	9,429	9,557
Private....................	1,000...	3,212	3,238	3,285	3,331	3,364	3,401	3,448
Degrees conferred, total [2]	1,000...	2,624	2,659	2,719	2,743	2,765	2,789	2,813
Associate's	1,000...	660	669	675	676	681	684	688
Bachelor's	1,000...	1,333	1,352	1,397	1,413	1,425	1,441	1,456
Master's	1,000...	502	506	513	519	522	526	530
Doctorate's	1,000...	44	45	45	45	46	46	46
First-professional	1,000...	84	88	89	90	91	92	93
Public 4-year colleges: [2]								
FTE enrollment [1]	1,000...	5,502	5,545	5,625	5,706	5,761	5,825	5,909
Current dollars: [3]								
Current fund expenditures......	Bil. dol. .	153.3	160.9	170.3	180.0	(NA)	(NA)	(NA)
Per FTE................	Dol.....	27,871	29,015	30,283	31,550	(NA)	(NA)	(NA)
Constant (2001-02) dollars: [3][4]								
Current fund expenditures......	Bil. dol. .	147.5	151.7	157.3	162.4	(NA)	(NA)	(NA)
Per FTE................	Dol.....	26,814	27,353	27,962	28,459	(NA)	(NA)	(NA)
Public 2-year colleges: [2]								
FTE enrollment [1]	1,000...	3,424	3,448	3,432	3,537	3,568	3,604	3,648
Current dollars: [3]								
Current fund expenditures......	Bil. dol. .	31.9	33.7	36.5	39.0	(NA)	(NA)	(NA)
Per FTE................	Dol.....	9,329	9,781	10,442	11,019	(NA)	(NA)	(NA)
Constant (2001-02) dollars: [3][4]								
Current fund expenditures......	Bil. dol. .	30.7	31.8	33.7	35.2	(NA)	(NA)	(NA)
Per FTE................	Dol.....	8,975	9,221	9,642	9,940	(NA)	(NA)	(NA)

NA Not available. [1] Full-time equivalents (FTE). [2] For school year ending in June the following year. [3] Limited financial projections are shown due to the uncertain behavior of inflation over the long term. [4] Based on the Consumer Price Index (CPI) for all urban consumers, U.S. Bureau of Labor Statistics. CPI adjusted to school year basis by NCES.

Source: U.S. National Center for Education Statistics, *Projections of Education Statistics to 2013*, NCES 2004-013, October 2003.

No. 205. Federal Funds for Education and Related Programs: 2000 to 2002

[In millions of dollars (85,944.2 represents $85,944,200,000), except percent. For fiscal years ending in September. Figures represent on-budget funds]

Level, agency, and program	2000	2001 [1]	2002 [1]
Total, all programs	85,944.2	94,505.6	109,468.6
Percent of Federal budget outlays	4.8	5.1	5.4
Elementary/secondary education programs	43,790.8	48,530.1	54,624.1
Department of Education [2]	20,039.6	22,862.4	26,535.8
Grants for the disadvantaged	8,529.1	8,647.2	9,398.2
School improvement programs	2,550.0	2,925.2	4,700.5
Indian education	65.3	77.8	113.0
Special education	4,949.0	5,809.0	6,924.6
Vocational and adult education	1,463.0	2,262.2	1,995.0
Education reform—Goals 2000	1,243.5	1,737.9	1,792.7
Department of Agriculture [2]	10,051.3	10,140.5	10,894.0
Child nutrition programs	[3]9,554.0	[3]9,561.0	[3]10,324.0
Agricultural Marketing Service—commodities [4]	400.0	400.0	400.0
Special milk program	([3])	([3])	([3])
Department of Defense [2]	1,485.6	1,475.0	1,484.9
Overseas dependents schools	210.4	906.0	889.9
Section VI schools [5]	370.4	351.9	360.2
Department of Health and Human Services	6,011.0	6,958.0	7,315.9
Head Start	5,267.0	6,199.8	6,537.6
Social security student benefits	729.0	754.2	774.3
Department of the Interior [2]	725.4	890.5	941.4
Mineral Leasing Act and other funds	78.1	91.7	127.0
Indian Education	645.3	797.8	813.4
Department of Justice	224.8	380.6	406.4
Inmate programs	223.8	378.6	404.4
Department of Labor	4,683.2	5,189.0	6,351.0
Job Corps	1,256.0	1,369.0	1,431.0
Department of Veterans Affairs	445.1	487.4	510.4
Vocational rehab for disabled veterans	438.6	479.8	501.8
Other agencies and programs	124.8	146.5	184.2
Higher education programs	15,008.7	14,893.5	22,586.7
Department of Education [2]	10,727.3	9,840.7	16,808.7
Student financial assistance	9,060.3	10,161.0	11,992.5
Federal Family Education Loans	2,707.5	-2,404.8	2,651.6
Department of Agriculture	30.7	37.7	40.7
Department of Commerce	3.8	4.0	4.2
Department of Defense	1,147.8	1,299.2	1,376.3
Tuition assistance for military personnel	263.3	346.5	342.5
Service academies [6]	212.7	241.2	241.6
Senior ROTC	363.5	387.1	439.3
Professional development education	308.3	324.4	352.9
Department of Health and Human Services [2]	954.2	1,360.6	1,524.0
Health professions training programs	340.4	681.1	771.8
National Health Service Corps scholarships [7]	16.0	43.0	49.0
National Institutes of Health training grants [7]	550.2	589.7	654.5
Department of the Interior	187.2	149.4	199.0
Shared revenues, Mineral Leasing Act and other receipts—estimated education share	98.7	58.6	104.5
Indian programs	88.4	90.8	94.5
Department of State	319.0	316.8	291.0
Department of Transportation	60.3	80.5	82.2
Department of Veterans Affairs [2]	1,132.3	1,314.9	1,790.9
Post-Vietnam veterans	4.0	4.9	3.4
All-volunteer-force educational assistance	984.1	1,129.3	1,596.1
Other agencies and programs [2]	446.2	489.8	469.8
National Endowment for the Humanities	28.4	30.6	30.0
National Science Foundation	389.0	432.0	413.0
Other education programs [2]	5,484.6	5,880.0	6,399.8
Department of Education [2]	3,223.4	3,293.4	3,606.1
Administration	458.1	551.7	561.4
Rehabilitative services and handicapped research	2,755.5	2,730.3	3,026.1
Department of Agriculture	444.5	454.6	460.5
Department of Health and Human Services	214.0	243.0	282.0
Department of Justice	34.7	29.1	26.4
Department of State	69.3	73.3	96.6
Department of the Treasury [2]	83.0	88.0	139.0
Other agencies and programs [2]	1,415.7	1,698.7	1,789.2
Agency for International Development	299.0	452.0	431.0
Library of Congress	299.0	315.0	359.0
National Endowment for the Arts	4.0	4.6	5.1
National Endowment for the Humanities	70.8	74.1	72.0
Research programs at universities and related institutions [2]	21,660.1	25,202.0	25,857.9
Department of Agriculture	553.6	677.6	500.9
Department of Defense	1,891.7	2,507.0	1,888.0
Department of Energy	3,577.0	3,746.2	3,625.1
Department of Health and Human Services	10,491.6	12,167.2	13,736.5
National Aeronautics and Space Administration	2,071.0	2,195.2	2,060.3
National Science Foundation	2,566.2	2,865.6	2,817.8

[1] Estimated. [2] Includes other programs and agencies, not shown separately. [3] The Special Milk Program is included in the Child Nutrition Program. [4] Purchased under Section 32 of the Act of August 1935, for use in child nutrition programs. [5] Program provides for the education of dependents of Federal employees residing on federal property where free public education is unavailable in the nearby community. [6] Instructional costs only including academics, audiovisual, academic computer center, faculty training, military training, physical education, and libraries. [7] Includes alcohol, drug abuse, and mental health training programs.

Source: U.S. National Center for Education Statistics, *Digest of Education Statistics*, annual.

No. 206. School Enrollment by Age: 1970 to 2002

[As of October (60,357 represents 60,357,000). Covers civilian noninstitutional population enrolled in nursery school and above. Based on Current Population Survey, see text, Section 1 and Appendix III]

Age	1970	1980	1985	1990	1995	1998	1999	2000	2001	2002
ENROLLMENT (1,000)										
Total 3 to 34 years old	**60,357**	**57,348**	**58,013**	**60,588**	**66,939**	**69,277**	**69,601**	**69,560**	**70,271**	**71,003**
3 and 4 years old	1,461	2,280	2,801	3,292	4,042	4,164	4,273	4,097	4,030	4,187
5 and 6 years old	7,000	5,853	6,697	7,207	7,901	7,902	7,774	7,648	7,526	7,353
7 to 13 years old	28,943	23,751	22,849	25,016	27,003	27,846	28,209	28,296	28,570	28,525
14 and 15 years old.	7,869	7,282	7,362	6,555	7,651	7,653	7,741	7,885	7,914	8,022
16 and 17 years old.	6,927	7,129	6,654	6,098	6,997	7,456	7,611	7,341	7,483	7,669
18 and 19 years old.	3,322	3,788	3,716	4,044	4,274	4,914	4,840	4,926	4,871	5,007
20 and 21 years old.	1,949	2,515	2,708	2,852	3,025	3,197	3,256	3,314	3,570	3,696
22 to 24 years old	1,410	1,931	2,068	2,231	2,545	2,607	2,664	2,731	2,798	3,003
25 to 29 years old	1,011	1,714	1,942	2,013	2,216	2,216	2,018	2,030	2,140	2,196
30 to 34 years old	466	1,105	1,218	1,281	1,284	1,322	1,215	1,292	1,370	1,345
35 years old and over	(NA)	1,290	1,766	2,439	2,830	2,831	2,794	2,653	2,852	3,043
ENROLLMENT RATE										
Total 3 to 34 years old	**56.4**	**49.7**	**48.3**	**50.2**	**53.7**	**55.8**	**56.0**	**55.8**	**55.7**	**56.1**
3 and 4 years old	20.5	36.7	38.9	44.4	48.7	52.1	54.2	52.1	52.2	54.5
5 and 6 years old	89.5	95.7	96.1	96.5	96.0	95.6	96.0	95.6	95.3	95.2
7 to 13 years old.	99.2	99.3	99.2	99.6	98.9	98.9	98.7	98.2	98.3	98.3
14 and 15 years old.	98.1	98.2	98.1	99.0	98.9	98.4	98.2	98.7	98.1	98.4
16 and 17 years old.	90.0	89.0	91.7	92.5	93.6	93.9	93.6	92.8	93.4	94.3
18 and 19 years old.	47.7	46.4	51.6	57.3	59.4	62.2	60.6	61.2	61.0	63.3
20 and 21 years old.	31.9	31.0	35.3	39.7	44.9	44.8	45.3	44.1	45.5	47.8
22 to 24 years old	14.9	16.3	16.9	21.0	23.2	24.9	24.5	24.6	25.1	25.6
25 to 29 years old	7.5	9.3	9.2	9.7	11.6	11.9	11.1	11.4	11.7	12.1
30 to 34 years old	4.2	6.4	6.1	5.8	6.0	6.6	6.2	6.7	6.8	6.6
35 years old and over	(NA)	1.4	1.6	2.1	2.2	2.1	1.8	1.9	2.0	2.1

NA Not available.

Source: U.S. Census Bureau, Current Population Reports, PPL-148; and earlier PPL and P-20 reports; and data published on the Internet. See Internet site <http://www.census.gov/population/www/socdemo/school.html>.

No. 207. School Enrollment by Race, Hispanic Origin, and Age: 1980 to 2002

[47,673 represents 47,673,000. See headnote, Table 206]

Age	White			Black			Hispanic origin [1]		
	1980	1990	2002	1980	1990	2002	1980	1990	2002
ENROLLMENT (1,000)									
Total 3 to 34 years old	**47,673**	**48,899**	**55,117**	**8,251**	**8,854**	**11,225**	**4,263**	**6,073**	**11,224**
3 and 4 years old	1,844	2,700	3,213	371	452	702	172	249	609
5 and 6 years old	4,781	5,750	5,701	904	1,129	1,159	491	835	1,446
7 to 13 years old	19,585	20,076	22,116	3,598	3,832	4,770	2,009	2,794	5,023
14 and 15 years old	6,038	5,265	6,286	1,088	1,023	1,254	568	739	1,267
16 and 17 years old	5,937	4,858	6,002	1,047	962	1,216	454	592	1,092
18 and 19 years old	3,199	3,271	3,988	494	596	681	226	329	662
20 and 21 years old	2,206	2,402	2,921	242	305	468	111	213	333
22 to 24 years old.	1,669	1,781	2,283	196	274	391	93	121	344
25 to 29 years old.	1,473	1,706	1,652	187	162	329	84	130	294
30 to 34 years old.	942	1,090	955	124	119	255	54	72	153
35 years old and over	1,104	2,096	2,383	186	238	477	(NA)	145	320
ENROLLMENT RATE									
Total 3 to 34 years old	**48.9**	**49.5**	**55.4**	**53.9**	**51.9**	**59.6**	**49.8**	**47.4**	**49.9**
3 and 4 years old	36.3	44.9	53.9	38.2	41.6	57.5	28.5	29.8	41.0
5 and 6 years old	95.8	96.5	95.1	95.4	96.3	95.7	94.5	94.8	94.4
7 to 13 years old	99.2	99.6	98.3	99.4	99.8	98.1	99.2	99.4	98.0
14 and 15 years old	98.3	99.1	98.5	97.9	99.2	98.2	94.3	99.0	98.1
16 and 17 years old	88.6	92.5	94.6	90.6	91.7	93.3	81.8	85.4	90.9
18 and 19 years old	46.3	57.1	63.8	45.7	55.2	57.7	37.8	44.1	50.6
20 and 21 years old	31.9	41.0	47.4	23.4	28.4	43.5	19.5	27.2	24.6
22 to 24 years old.	16.4	20.2	24.6	13.6	20.0	23.5	11.7	9.9	15.3
25 to 29 years old.	9.2	9.9	11.4	8.8	6.1	13.6	6.9	6.3	8.4
30 to 34 years old.	6.3	5.9	5.9	6.8	4.4	9.8	5.1	3.6	4.4
35 years old and over	1.3	2.1	2.0	1.8	2.1	3.1	(NA)	2.1	2.4

NA Not available.   [1] Persons of Hispanic origin may be of any race.

Source: U.S. Census Bureau, Current Population Reports, PPL-148; and earlier PPL and P-20 reports; and data published on the Internet. See Internet site <http://www.census.gov/population/www/socdemo/school.html>

No. 208. Enrollment in Public and Private Schools: 1970 to 2002

[In millions (39.0 represents 39,000,000), except percent. As of October. For civilian noninstitutional population. For 1970 to 1985, persons 3 to 34 years old; beginning 1986, for 3 years old and over. For college enrollment 35 years old and over, see Table 264. See also headnote, Table 206]

Year	Public						Private					
	Total	Nursery	Kindergarten	Elementary	High School	College	Total	Nursery	Kindergarten	Elementary	High School	College
1970	52.2	0.3	2.6	30.0	13.5	5.7	8.1	0.8	0.5	3.9	1.2	1.7
1975	52.8	0.6	2.9	27.2	14.5	7.7	8.2	1.2	0.5	3.3	1.2	2.0
1980	(NA)	0.6	2.7	24.4	(NA)	(NA)	(NA)	1.4	0.5	3.1	(NA)	(NA)
1984	49.0	0.8	3.0	24.1	12.7	8.5	8.3	1.6	0.5	2.7	1.1	2.4
1985	49.0	0.9	3.2	23.8	12.8	8.4	9.0	1.6	0.6	3.1	1.2	2.5
1986 [1]	51.2	0.8	3.4	24.2	13.0	9.8	9.4	1.7	0.6	3.0	1.2	2.9
1987	51.7	0.8	3.4	24.8	12.7	10.0	8.9	1.7	0.6	2.8	1.1	2.8
1988	52.2	0.9	3.4	25.5	12.2	10.3	8.9	1.8	0.5	2.8	1.0	2.8
1989	52.5	0.9	3.3	25.9	12.1	10.3	8.9	1.9	0.6	2.7	0.8	2.9
1990	53.8	1.2	3.3	26.6	11.9	10.7	9.2	2.2	0.6	2.7	0.9	2.9
1991	54.5	1.1	3.5	26.6	12.2	11.1	9.4	1.8	0.6	3.0	1.0	3.0
1992	55.0	1.1	3.5	27.1	12.3	11.1	9.4	1.8	0.6	3.1	1.0	3.0
1993	56.0	1.2	3.5	27.7	12.6	10.9	9.4	1.8	0.7	2.9	1.0	3.0
1994	58.6	1.9	3.3	28.1	13.5	11.7	10.7	2.3	0.6	3.4	1.1	3.3
1995	58.7	2.0	3.2	28.4	13.7	11.4	11.1	2.4	0.7	3.4	1.2	3.3
1996	59.5	1.9	3.4	28.1	14.1	12.0	10.8	2.3	0.7	3.4	1.2	3.2
1997	61.6	2.3	3.3	29.3	14.6	12.1	10.5	2.2	0.7	3.1	1.2	3.3
1998	60.8	2.3	3.1	29.1	14.3	12.0	11.3	2.3	0.7	3.4	1.2	3.6
1999	60.8	2.3	3.2	29.2	14.4	11.7	11.4	2.3	0.7	3.6	1.3	3.5
2000	61.2	2.2	3.2	29.4	14.4	12.0	11.0	2.2	0.7	3.5	1.3	3.3
2001	62.4	2.2	3.1	29.8	14.8	12.4	10.8	2.1	0.6	3.4	1.2	3.5
2002	62.8	2.2	3.0	29.7	15.1	12.8	11.3	2.2	0.6	3.5	1.3	3.7
Percent White:												
1970.	84.5	59.5	84.4	83.1	85.6	90.7	93.4	91.1	88.2	94.1	96.1	92.8
1980.	(NA)	68.2	80.7	80.9	(NA)	(NA)	(NA)	89.0	87.0	90.7	(NA)	(NA)
1990.	79.8	71.7	78.3	78.9	79.2	84.1	87.4	89.6	83.2	88.2	89.4	85.0
1995.	78.0	71.3	76.9	77.5	76.9	81.9	85.0	88.7	84.1	86.1	86.0	81.1
2000.	77.0	69.4	77.3	76.7	78.0	78.0	83.5	84.9	82.8	85.9	84.6	79.8
2001.	76.5	68.7	76.1	76.7	77.4	76.5	83.1	84.3	84.4	85.6	86.7	78.4
2002.	76.6	71.8	75.3	76.5	77.9	76.2	83.8	83.6	87.5	84.1	86.4	82.1

NA Not available.   [1] Data beginning 1986 based on a revised edit and tabulation package.

Source: U.S. Census Bureau, Current Population Reports, PPL-148; and earlier PPL and P-20 reports; and data published on the Internet. See Internet site <http://www.census.gov/population/www/socdemo/school.html>

No. 209. School Enrollment by Sex and Level: 1970 to 2002

[In millions (46.3 represents 46,300,000). As of Oct. For the civilian noninstitutional population. 1970-1979, for persons 3 to 34 years old; beginning 1980, 3 years old and over. Elementary includes kindergarten and grades 1-8; high school, grades 9-12; and college, 2-year and 4-year colleges, universities, and graduate and professional schools. Data for college represent degree-credit enrollment. See headnote, Table 206]

Year	All levels [1]			Elementary			High school			College		
	Total	Male	Female	Total	Male	Female	Total	Male	Female	Total	Male	Female
1970	60.4	31.4	28.9	37.1	19.0	18.1	14.7	7.4	7.3	7.4	4.4	3.0
1975	61.0	31.6	29.4	33.8	17.3	16.5	15.7	8.0	7.7	9.7	5.3	4.4
1980	58.6	29.6	29.1	30.6	15.8	14.9	14.6	7.3	7.3	11.4	5.4	6.0
1983	59.3	30.1	29.2	30.6	15.7	14.8	14.1	7.1	7.0	12.4	6.0	6.3
1984	58.9	29.9	29.0	30.3	15.6	14.7	13.9	7.1	6.8	12.3	6.0	6.3
1985	59.8	30.0	29.7	30.7	15.7	15.0	14.1	7.2	6.9	12.5	5.9	6.6
1986 [2]	60.5	30.6	30.0	31.1	16.1	15.0	14.2	7.2	7.0	12.7	6.0	6.7
1987	60.6	30.7	29.9	31.6	16.3	15.3	13.8	7.0	6.8	12.7	6.0	6.7
1988	61.1	30.7	30.5	32.2	16.6	15.6	13.2	6.7	6.4	13.1	5.9	7.2
1989	61.5	30.8	30.7	32.5	16.7	15.8	12.9	6.6	6.3	13.2	6.0	7.2
1990	63.0	31.5	31.5	33.2	17.1	16.0	12.8	6.5	6.4	13.6	6.2	7.4
1991	63.9	32.1	31.8	33.8	17.3	16.4	13.1	6.8	6.4	14.1	6.4	7.6
1992	64.6	32.2	32.3	34.3	17.7	16.6	13.3	6.8	6.5	14.0	6.2	7.8
1993	65.4	32.9	32.5	34.8	17.9	16.9	13.6	7.0	6.6	13.9	6.3	7.6
1994	69.3	34.6	34.6	35.4	18.2	17.2	14.6	7.4	7.2	15.0	6.8	8.2
1995	69.8	35.0	34.8	35.7	18.3	17.4	15.0	7.7	7.3	14.7	6.7	8.0
1996	70.3	35.1	35.2	35.5	18.3	17.3	15.3	7.9	7.4	15.2	6.8	8.4
1997	72.0	35.9	36.2	36.3	18.7	17.6	15.8	8.0	7.7	15.4	6.8	8.6
1998	72.1	36.0	36.1	36.4	18.7	17.7	15.6	7.9	7.6	15.5	6.9	8.6
1999	72.4	36.3	36.1	36.7	18.8	17.9	15.9	8.2	7.7	15.2	7.0	8.2
2000	72.2	35.8	36.4	36.7	18.9	17.9	15.8	8.1	7.7	15.3	6.7	8.6
2001	73.1	36.3	36.9	36.9	19.0	17.9	16.1	8.2	7.8	15.9	6.9	9.0
2002	74.0	36.8	37.3	36.7	18.9	17.8	16.4	8.3	8.0	16.5	7.2	9.3

[1] Includes nursery schools, not shown separately.   [2] Revised. Data beginning 1986, based on a revised edit and tabulation package.

Source: U.S. Census Bureau, Current Population Reports, PPL-148; and earlier PPL and P-20 reports; and data published on the Internet. See Internet site <http://www.census.gov/population/www/socdemo/school.html>.

Education   139

No. 210. School Enrollment by Control and Level: 1980 to 2001

[In thousands (58,305 represents 58,305,000). As of fall. Data are for regular day schools and exclude independent nursery schools and kindergartens, residential schools for exceptional children, subcollegiate departments of colleges, federal schools for Indians, and federally operated schools on federal installations. College data include degree-credit and nondegree-credit enrollment. Based on survey of state education agencies. See source for details. For projections, see Table 202]

Control of school and level	1980	1990	1994	1995	1996	1997	1998	1999	2000 [1]	2001 prel.
Total...........	58,305	60,269	63,888	64,764	65,743	66,470	66,982	67,667	68,697	69,818
Public.............	50,335	52,061	55,245	55,933	56,732	57,323	57,677	58,166	58,976	59,921
Private............	7,971	8,208	8,643	8,831	9,011	9,147	9,306	9,501	9,722	9,897
Kindergarten through 8 ..	31,639	33,962	36,233	36,806	37,316	37,696	38,048	38,253	38,584	38,832
Public............	27,647	29,878	31,898	32,341	32,764	33,073	33,346	33,488	33,709	33,952
Private	3,992	4,084	4,335	4,465	4,551	4,623	4,702	4,765	4,875	4,880
Grades 9 through 12....	14,570	12,488	13,376	13,376	14,060	14,272	14,427	14,623	14,801	15,058
Public............	13,231	11,338	12,213	12,500	12,847	13,054	13,193	13,369	13,514	13,736
Private	1,339	1,150	1,163	1,197	1,213	1,218	1,235	1,254	1,287	1,322
College [2]	12,097	13,819	14,279	14,262	14,368	14,502	14,507	14,791	15,312	15,928
Public............	9,457	10,845	11,134	11,092	11,120	11,196	11,138	11,309	11,753	12,233
Private	2,640	2,974	3,145	3,169	3,247	3,306	3,369	3,482	3,560	3,695

[1] Public K-8 and 9-12 data preliminary.   [2] Data beginning 1996 reflects new classification system. See footnote 1, Table 261.

Source: U.S. National Center for Education Statistics, *Digest of Education Statistics,* annual.

No. 211. Students Who Are Foreign-Born or Who Have Foreign Born Parents: 2002

[In thousands (49,506 represents 49,506,000), except percent. As of October. Covers civilian noninstitutional population enrolled in elementary school and above. Based on Current Population Survey, see text, Section 1 and Appendix III]

Characteristic	All students	Students with at least one foreign-born parent					
		Total		Foreign-born student		Native student	
		Number	Percent	Number	Percent	Number	Percent
ELEMENTARY AND HIGH SCHOOL							
Total [1].....................	**49,506**	**10,477**	**21.2**	**2,799**	**5.7**	**7,679**	**15.5**
White........................	38,487	7,395	19.2	1,899	4.9	5,496	14.3
White, non-Hispanic.............	30,543	2.168	7.1	433	1.4	1,735	5.7
Black........................	8,102	1,079	13.3	285	3.5	794	9.8
Asian and Pacific Islander	2,154	1,830	85.0	590	27.4	1,239	57.5
Hispanic [2].......................	8,523	5,578	65.4	1,555	18.2	4,023	47.2
COLLEGE, 1 TO 4 YEARS							
Total [1].....................	**13,426**	**2,964**	**22.1**	**1,534**	**11.4**	**1,429**	**10.6**
White.......................	10,437	1,704	16.3	765	7.3	939	9.0
White, non-Hispanic.............	9,082	821	9.0	346	3.8	475	5.2
Black.......................	1,904	401	21.1	257	13.5	143	7.5
Asian and Pacific Islander	934	833	89.2	502	53.7	332	35.5
Hispanic [2].......................	1,446	949	65.6	454	31.4	495	34.2
GRADUATE SCHOOL							
Total [1].....................	**3,072**	**841**	**27.4**	**566**	**18.4**	**276**	**9.0**
White.......................	2,344	430	18.3	225	9.6	206	8.8
White, non-Hispanic.............	2,155	303	14.1	139	6.5	164	7.6
Black.......................	375	96	25.6	84	22.4	12	3.2
Asian and Pacific Islander	324	310	95.7	252	77.8	58	17.9
Hispanic [2].......................	210	141	67.1	93	44.3	48	22.9

[1] Includes other races, not shown separately.   [2] Persons of Hispanic origin may be of any race.

Source: U.S. Census Bureau, Current Population Survey, unpublished data. See Internet site <http://www.census.gov/population/www/socdemo/school.html>

140 Education

No. 212. Educational Attainment by Race and Hispanic Origin: 1960 to 2003

[In percent. For persons 25 years old and over. 1960, 1970, and 1980 as of April 1 and based on sample data from the censuses of population. Other years as of March and based on the Current Population Survey; see text, Section 1, Population, and Appendix III. See Table 213 for data by sex]

Year	Total [1]	White [2]	Black [2]	Asian and Pacific Islander [2]	Hispanic [3] Total [4]	Mexican	Puerto Rican	Cuban
HIGH SCHOOL GRADUATE OR MORE [5]								
1960	41.1	43.2	20.1	(NA)	(NA)	(NA)	(NA)	(NA)
1970	52.3	54.5	31.4	(NA)	32.1	24.2	23.4	43.9
1980	66.5	68.8	51.2	(NA)	44.0	37.6	40.1	55.3
1990	77.6	79.1	66.2	80.4	50.8	44.1	55.5	63.5
1995	81.7	83.0	73.8	(NA)	53.4	46.5	61.3	64.7
1999	83.4	84.3	77.0	84.7	56.1	49.7	63.9	70.3
2000	84.1	84.9	78.5	85.7	57.0	51.0	64.3	73.0
2001	84.1	84.8	78.8	87.6	56.8	50.7	64.6	72.2
2002	84.1	84.8	78.7	87.4	57.0	50.6	66.8	70.8
2003	84.6	85.1	80.0	[6]87.6	57.0	50.9	69.7	70.8
COLLEGE GRADUATE OR MORE [5]								
1960	7.7	8.1	3.1	(NA)	(NA)	(NA)	(NA)	(NA)
1970	10.7	11.3	4.4	(NA)	4.5	2.5	2.2	11.1
1980	16.2	17.1	8.4	(NA)	7.6	4.9	5.6	16.2
1990	21.3	22.0	11.3	39.9	9.2	5.4	9.7	20.2
1995	23.0	24.0	13.2	(NA)	9.3	6.5	10.7	19.4
1999	25.2	25.9	15.4	42.4	10.9	7.1	11.1	24.8
2000	25.6	26.1	16.5	43.9	10.6	6.9	13.0	23.0
2001	26.2	26.6	15.7	47.5	11.1	7.8	12.9	19.3
2002	26.7	27.2	17.0	47.2	11.1	7.6	14.0	18.6
2003	27.2	27.6	17.3	[6]49.8	11.4	7.8	12.3	21.6

NA Not available.   [1] Includes other races, not shown separately.   [2] The 2003 Current Population Survey (CPS) allowed respondents to choose more than one race. Beginning 2003 data represent persons who selected this race group only and exclude persons reporting more than one race. The CPS in prior years only allowed respondents to report one race group. See also comments on race in the text for Section 1.   [3] Persons of Hispanic origin may be of any race.   [4] Includes persons of other Hispanic origin, not shown separately.   [5] Through 1990, completed 4 years of high school or more and 4 years of college or more.   [6] Starting in 2003, data are for Asians only, excludes Pacific Islanders.

Source: U.S. Census Bureau, U.S. Census of Population, *U.S. Summary*, PC80-1-C1 and Current Population Report P20-550, and earlier reports, unpublished data, and data published on the Internet. See Internet site <http://www.census.gov/population/www/socdemo/educ-attn.html>.

No. 213. Educational Attainment by Race, Hispanic Origin, and Sex: 1960 to 2003

[In percent. See Table 212 for headnote and totals for both sexes]

Year	All races [1] Male	Female	White [2] Male	Female	Black [2] Male	Female	Asian and Pacific Islander [2] Male	Female	Hispanic [3] Male	Female
HIGH SCHOOL GRADUATE OR MORE [4]											
1960	39.5	42.5	41.6	44.7	18.2	21.8	(NA)	(NA)	(NA)	(NA)
1970	51.9	52.8	54.0	55.0	30.1	32.5	(NA)	(NA)	37.9	34.2
1980	67.3	65.8	69.6	68.1	50.8	51.5	(NA)	(NA)	67.3	65.8
1990	77.7	77.5	79.1	79.0	65.8	66.5	84.0	77.2	50.3	51.3
1995	81.7	81.6	83.0	83.0	73.4	74.1	(NA)	(NA)	52.9	53.8
1999	83.4	83.4	84.2	84.3	76.7	77.2	86.9	82.8	56.0	56.3
2000	84.2	84.0	84.8	85.0	78.7	78.3	88.2	83.4	56.6	57.5
2001	84.1	84.2	84.4	85.1	79.2	78.5	90.3	85.1	55.5	58.0
2002	83.8	84.4	84.3	85.2	78.5	78.9	89.5	85.5	56.1	57.9
2003	84.1	85.0	84.5	85.7	79.6	80.3	[5]89.5	[5]86.0	56.3	57.8
COLLEGE GRADUATE OR MORE [4]											
1960	9.7	5.8	10.3	6.0	2.8	3.3	(NA)	(NA)	(NA)	(NA)
1970	13.5	8.1	14.4	8.4	4.2	4.6	(NA)	(NA)	7.8	4.3
1980	20.1	12.8	21.3	13.3	8.4	8.3	(NA)	(NA)	9.4	6.0
1990	24.4	18.4	25.3	19.0	11.9	10.8	44.9	35.4	9.8	8.7
1995	26.0	20.2	27.2	21.0	13.6	12.9	(NA)	(NA)	10.1	8.4
1999	27.5	23.1	28.5	23.5	14.2	16.4	46.2	39.0	10.7	11.0
2000	27.8	23.6	28.5	23.9	16.3	16.7	47.6	40.7	10.7	10.6
2001	28.2	24.3	28.7	24.0	15.3	16.1	52.3	43.2	10.8	11.4
2002	28.5	25.1	29.1	25.4	16.4	17.5	50.9	43.8	11.0	11.2
2003	28.9	25.7	29.4	25.9	16.7	17.8	[5]53.9	[5]46.1	11.2	11.6

NA Not available.   [1] Includes other races, not shown separately.   [2] Beginning 2003, for persons who selected this race group only. See footnote 2, Table 212.   [3] Persons of Hispanic origin may be of any race.   [4] Through 1990, completed 4 years of high school or more and 4 years of college or more.   [5] Starting in 2003, data are for Asians only, excludes Pacific Islanders.

Source: U.S. Census Bureau, U.S. Census of Population, 1960, 1970, and 1980, Vol. 1; and Current Population Reports P20-550 and earlier reports; and data published on the Internet. See Internet site <http://www.census.gov/population/www/socdemo/educ-attn.html>.

Education   141

No. 214. Educational Attainment by Selected Characteristic: 2003

[For persons 25 years old and over (185,183 represents 185,183,000). As of March. Based on the Current Population Survey; see text, Section 1, and Appendix III. For composition of regions, see map inside front cover]

Characteristic	Population (1,000)	Not a high school graduate	High school graduate	Some college, but no degree	Associ- ate's degree [1]	Bachelor's degree	Advanced degree
				Percent of population—highest level			
Total persons	185,183	15.4	32.0	17.2	8.2	17.9	9.3
Age:							
25 to 34 years old.	39,243	12.9	29.0	19.4	8.6	22.5	7.5
35 to 44 years old.	44,074	12.0	31.5	17.4	9.7	20.2	9.2
45 to 54 years old.	40,234	11.0	30.9	18.1	9.5	18.8	11.6
55 to 64 years old.	27,399	14.8	33.5	17.0	7.7	15.5	11.5
65 to 74 years old.	18,111	25.1	37.2	13.7	5.0	11.3	7.8
75 years old or over	16,123	32.5	35.1	12.8	4.2	9.8	5.6
Sex:							
Male.	88,597	15.9	30.9	17.1	7.2	18.5	10.4
Female	96,586	15.0	33.1	17.2	9.1	17.5	8.2
Race:							
White [2]	153,188	14.9	32.2	17.0	8.3	18.2	9.5
Black [2]	20,527	20.0	35.2	19.9	7.5	12.2	5.1
Other	11,469	15.0	23.8	14.5	7.4	25.1	14.3
Hispanic origin:							
Hispanic	21,189	43.0	27.4	13.0	5.2	8.3	3.1
Non-Hispanic	163,994	11.9	32.6	17.7	8.6	19.2	10.1
Region:							
Northeast	36,182	14.3	35.0	12.8	7.7	19.0	11.3
Midwest	41,728	12.2	35.3	17.5	9.0	17.2	8.8
South	66,071	17.8	32.2	17.1	7.6	17.0	8.3
West	41,202	16.0	25.9	20.7	8.6	19.2	9.6
Marital status:							
Never married	28,694	15.1	30.1	18.5	7.4	20.2	8.7
Married spouse present.	113,748	13.0	31.1	16.8	8.7	19.8	10.7
Married spouse absent [3]	2,942	30.4	31.9	12.8	5.4	12.7	6.8
Separated	4,447	25.5	35.9	17.6	7.1	9.9	3.9
Widowed.	13,970	32.8	36.9	12.8	5.0	8.3	4.2
Divorced	21,382	13.5	35.6	20.6	9.4	13.9	7.1
Civilian labor force status:							
Employed	117,539	9.9	30.0	18.3	9.4	21.2	11.3
Unemployed	6,576	18.8	35.9	19.1	8.0	13.3	4.9
Not in the labor force	60,390	26.1	35.6	14.6	5.8	12.0	5.7

[1] Includes vocational degrees.   [2] For persons who selected this race group only. See footnote 2, Table 212.   [3] Excludes those separated.

Source: U.S. Census Bureau, Current Population Report P20-550; and data published on the Internet. See Internet site <http://www.census.gov/population/www/socdemo/educ-attn.html>.

No. 215. Mean Earnings by Highest Degree Earned: 2002

[In dollars. For persons 18 years old and over with earnings. Persons as of March the following year. Based on Current Population Survey; see text, Section 1, and Appendix III. For definition of mean, see Guide to Tabular Presentation]

Characteristic	Total persons	Not a high school graduate	High school graduate only	Some college, no degree	Asso- ciate's	Bache- lor's	Master's	Profes- sional	Doctorate
				Level of highest degree					
All persons [1]	36,308	18,826	27,280	29,725	34,177	51,194	60,445	112,845	89,734
Age:									
25 to 34 years old. . . .	32,527	19,235	26,278	28,879	30,662	42,623	48,598	75,247	62,190
35 to 44 years old. . . .	41,963	22,324	30,259	37,533	37,440	58,267	63,758	123,811	88,818
45 to 54 years old. . . .	45,392	21,231	31,251	40,225	39,167	60,680	67,096	126,230	112,538
55 to 64 years old. . . .	42,381	24,761	30,893	37,450	34,848	55,057	62,640	132,372	81,166
65 years old and over .	36,611	18,949	27,519	29,809	34,331	51,612	61,151	114,981	91,771
Sex:									
Male.	44,310	22,091	32,673	36,869	42,392	63,503	73,629	138,827	99,607
Female	27,271	13,459	21,141	22,292	27,341	37,909	47,368	61,583	66,426
White [2].	37,376	19,264	28,145	30,570	34,876	52,479	60,787	115,523	92,125
Male.	45,793	22,539	33,920	38,095	43,494	65,439	74,426	140,965	103,787
Female	27,512	13,354	21,388	22,452	27,480	37,903	47,209	60,944	64,106
Black [2].	28,179	16,516	22,823	26,711	30,391	42,285	51,974	96,368	69,780
Male.	31,790	19,294	25,582	31,858	36,028	47,018	60,647	(B)	(B)
Female	25,131	13,748	20,209	22,455	26,940	38,741	47,765	(B)	(B)
Hispanic [3].	25,824	18,981	24,163	26,459	31,710	40,949	58,814	81,186	(B)
Male.	29,084	21,611	27,992	31,545	37,365	46,115	59,901	90,767	(B)
Female	21,008	13,694	18,810	20,707	25,888	35,357	57,447	(B)	(B)

B Base figure too small to meet statistical standards for reliability of a derived figure.   [1] Includes other races, not shown separately.   [2] For persons who selected this race group only. See footnote 2, Table 212.   [3] Persons of Hispanic origin may be of any race.

Source: U.S. Census Bureau, Current Population Report P20-550 and data published on the Internet. See Internet site <http://www.census.gov/population/www/socdemo/educ-attn.html>

No. 216. Educational Attainment by State: 1990 to 2003

[In percent. As of March, except 1990 as of April. For persons 25 years old and over. Based on the 1990 Census of Population and the Current Population Survey; see text, Section 1, and Appendix III]

State	1990 High school graduate or more	1990 Bachelor's degree or more	1998 High school graduate or more	1998 Bachelor's degree or more	2000 High school graduate or more	2000 Bachelor's degree or more	2003 High school graduate or more	2003 Bachelor's degree or more
United States.......	75.2	20.3	82.8	24.4	84.1	25.6	84.6	27.2
Alabama..............	66.9	15.7	78.8	20.6	77.5	20.4	79.9	22.7
Alaska	86.6	23.0	90.6	24.2	90.4	28.1	90.6	24.0
Arizona..............	78.7	20.3	81.9	21.9	85.1	24.6	83.8	26.0
Arkansas	66.3	13.3	76.8	16.2	81.7	18.4	80.9	17.4
California	76.2	23.4	80.1	26.4	81.2	27.5	81.1	29.8
Colorado..............	84.4	27.0	89.6	34.0	89.7	34.6	88.7	36.0
Connecticut...........	79.2	27.2	83.7	31.4	88.2	31.6	87.5	33.5
Delaware	77.5	21.4	85.2	25.1	86.1	24.0	88.7	28.1
District of Columbia	73.1	33.3	83.8	36.5	83.2	38.3	86.0	46.4
Florida	74.4	18.3	81.9	22.5	84.0	22.8	84.7	25.8
Georgia	70.9	19.3	80.0	20.7	82.6	23.1	85.1	25.0
Hawaii	80.1	22.9	84.6	24.0	87.4	26.3	88.5	27.0
Idaho...............	79.7	17.7	82.7	20.3	86.2	20.0	88.2	22.5
Illinois	76.2	21.0	84.2	25.8	85.5	27.1	85.9	28.1
Indiana..............	75.6	15.6	83.5	17.7	84.6	17.1	86.4	22.2
Iowa	80.1	16.9	87.7	20.3	89.7	25.5	89.7	24.6
Kansas..............	81.3	21.1	89.2	28.5	88.1	27.3	88.6	31.0
Kentucky	64.6	13.6	77.9	20.1	78.7	20.5	82.8	21.3
Louisiana	68.3	16.1	78.6	19.5	80.8	22.5	79.8	22.3
Maine...............	78.8	18.8	86.7	19.2	89.3	24.1	86.6	23.7
Maryland	78.4	26.5	84.7	31.8	85.7	32.3	87.6	37.2
Massachusetts.........	80.0	27.2	85.6	31.0	85.1	32.7	87.1	37.6
Michigan.............	76.8	17.4	85.4	22.1	86.2	23.0	87.6	23.3
Minnesota............	82.4	21.8	89.4	31.0	90.8	31.2	91.6	32.7
Mississippi	64.3	14.7	77.3	19.5	80.3	18.7	81.2	19.3
Missouri	73.9	17.8	82.9	22.4	86.6	26.2	88.3	26.6
Montana.............	81.0	19.8	89.1	23.9	89.6	23.8	90.1	24.9
Nebraska	81.8	18.9	87.7	20.9	90.4	24.6	90.8	26.8
Nevada	78.8	15.3	89.1	20.6	82.8	19.3	85.6	21.2
New Hampshire	82.2	24.4	84.0	26.6	88.1	30.1	92.1	34.0
New Jersey............	76.7	24.9	86.5	30.1	87.3	30.1	86.2	33.4
New Mexico	75.1	20.4	79.6	23.1	82.2	23.6	81.7	23.7
New York	74.8	23.1	81.5	26.8	82.5	28.7	84.2	29.6
North Carolina.........	70.0	17.4	81.4	23.3	79.2	23.2	81.4	23.8
North Dakota..........	76.7	18.1	84.3	22.5	85.5	22.6	89.7	25.2
Ohio	75.7	17.0	86.2	21.5	87.0	24.6	87.2	25.0
Oklahoma............	74.6	17.8	84.6	20.5	86.1	22.5	85.7	24.3
Oregon..............	81.5	20.6	85.5	27.7	88.1	27.2	86.9	26.4
Pennsylvania..........	74.7	17.9	84.1	22.1	85.7	24.3	86.0	24.8
Rhode Island..........	72.0	21.3	80.7	27.8	81.3	26.4	81.0	27.6
South Carolina.........	68.3	16.6	78.6	21.3	83.0	19.0	80.8	22.3
South Dakota..........	77.1	17.2	86.3	21.8	91.8	25.7	88.7	23.9
Tennessee	67.1	16.0	76.9	16.9	79.9	22.0	81.0	23.5
Texas	72.1	20.3	78.3	23.3	79.2	23.9	77.2	24.7
Utah	85.1	22.3	89.3	27.6	90.7	26.4	89.4	28.4
Vermont	80.8	24.3	86.7	27.1	90.0	28.8	88.9	31.3
Virginia	75.2	24.5	82.6	30.3	86.6	31.9	87.8	34.2
Washington...........	83.8	22.9	92.0	28.1	91.8	28.6	89.1	28.8
West Virginia..........	66.0	12.3	76.4	16.3	77.1	15.3	78.7	15.3
Wisconsin............	78.6	17.7	88.0	22.3	86.7	23.8	88.6	24.1
Wyoming	83.0	18.8	90.0	19.8	90.0	20.6	90.9	20.7

Source: U.S. Census Bureau, 1990 Census of Population, CPH-L-96, and Current Population Reports, P20-550, and earlier reports; and data published on the Internet. See Internet site <http://www.census.gov/population/www/socdemo/educ-attn.html>.

U.S. Census Bureau, Statistical Abstract of the United States: 2004-2005

No. 217. Nonfatal Crimes Against Students: 2000 and 2001

[For students aged 12 through 18 (1,946.4 represents 1,946,400). For crimes occurring at school or going to or from school. Based on the National Crime Victimization Survey; see Appendix III]

Student characteristic	2000				2001			
			Violent				Violent	
	Total	Theft	Total	Serious [1]	Total	Theft	Total	Serious [1]
Total (1,000)............	1,946.4	1,246.6	699.8	128.4	2,001.3	1,237.6	763.7	160.9
RATE PER 1,000 STUDENTS								
Total [2]...............	72	46	26	5	73	45	28	6
Sex:								
Male.................	80	47	33	7	78	48	30	6
Female...............	62	45	18	[3]2	67	42	26	5
Age:								
12 to 14 years old.........	80	48	32	5	82	47	35	7
15 to 18 years old.........	65	45	21	5	66	43	22	5
Race/ethnicity:								
White, non-Hispanic	75	49	26	3	79	50	29	5
Black, non-Hispanic.........	72	46	26	[3]5	63	38	25	[3]7
Hispanic	63	34	29	11	64	31	33	9
Other, non-Hispanic.........	40	32	[3]8	[3]2	51	46	[3]4	[3]2
Urbanicity: [4]								
Urban.................	68	46	22	7	73	44	29	7
Suburban	74	47	28	4	76	48	28	6
Rural	70	44	26	[3]3	66	41	25	[3]5
Household income:								
Less than $7,500	61	32	[3]28	[3]6	57	29	[3]28	[3]10
$7,500 to $14,999.........	57	31	26	[3]5	55	33	22	[3]3
$15,000 to $24,999.........	81	55	27	[3]5	79	38	41	[3]9
$25,000 to $34,999.........	69	40	30	[3]6	68	40	28	[3]4
$35,000 to $49,999.........	81	49	33	[3]6	80	45	36	11
$50,000 to $74,999.........	86	58	27	[3]6	80	59	21	[3]5
$75,000 and over	74	54	21	[3]4	88	59	29	[3]4

[1] Includes rape, sexual assault, robbery and aggravated assault. [2] Includes those whose race/ethnicity or incomes are unknown. [3] Estimate based on fewer than 10 cases. [4] Urban: The largest city (or groupings of cities) of an MSA; suburban: those portions of metro areas outside central cities: rural: places outside MSAs.

Source: U.S. National Center for Education Statistics and U.S. Bureau of Justice Statistics, *Indicators of School Crime and Safety 2003*, October 2003, NCES 2004-004.

No. 218. Students Reporting Being Threatened or Injured With a Weapon on School Property: 1993 to 2001

[In percent. For students in grades 9 through 12 reporting incident in the prior 12 months. Based on the Youth Risk Behavior Surveillance System. See source for details. See also <http://www.cdc.gov/nccdphp/dash/yrbs/index.htm>]

Student characteristic	1993	1995	1997	1999	2001
Total.............................	7.3	8.4	7.4	7.7	8.9
Sex:					
Male..............................	9.2	10.9	10.2	9.5	11.5
Female............................	5.4	5.8	4.0	5.8	6.5
Race/ethnicity:					
White	(NA)	(NA)	(NA)	6.6	8.5
Black or African American.................	(NA)	(NA)	(NA)	7.6	9.3
Hispanic or Latino.....................	(NA)	(NA)	(NA)	9.8	8.6
Asian	(NA)	(NA)	(NA)	7.7	11.3
American Indian or Alaska Native............	(NA)	(NA)	(NA)	13.2	15.2
Native Hawaiian or other					
Pacific Islander......................	(NA)	(NA)	(NA)	15.6	24.8
Multiple...........................	(NA)	(NA)	(NA)	9.3	10.3
Grade:					
9th...............................	9.4	9.6	10.1	10.5	12.7
10th..............................	7.3	9.6	7.9	8.2	9.1
11th..............................	7.3	7.7	5.9	6.1	6.9
12th..............................	5.5	6.7	5.8	5.1	5.3

NA Not available.

Source: U.S. National Center for Education Statistics and U.S. Department of Justice, Bureau of Justice Statistics, *Indicators of School Crime and Safety 2002*, November 2002, NCES 2003-009.

144   Education

No. 219. Children Whose Parents Are Involved in School Activities: 1999

[In percent, except as Indicated (23,355 represents 23,355,000). Based on the Parent and Family Involvement Survey of the National Household Education Survey Program; see source and Appendix III for details. See also Tables 220 and 223]

Parental involvement	Students in grades K to 5					Students in grades 6 to 8				
	Total	Two-parent families	One-parent families			Total	Two-parent families	One-parent families		
			Total	Mother	Father			Total	Mother	Father
Total students (1,000)	23,355	15,841	7,514	6,634	880	11,252	7,747	3,506	3,010	496
Any adult attending a meeting	84.9	88.6	77.1	77.3	75.7	81.1	85.3	72.0	71.2	77.0
Only mother attended	39.4	25.7	68.2	77.3	(X)	38.7	28.5	61.2	71.2	(X)
Only father attended	5.7	4.1	8.9	(X)	75.7	6.9	5.1	10.9	(X)	77.0
Both attended	39.8	58.7	(X)	(X)	(X)	35.6	51.7	(X)	(X)	(X)
Any adult attending a conference	87.7	89.4	84.1	85.1	76.7	71.1	72.3	68.5	68.1	70.8
Only mother attended	52.0	41.0	75.1	85.1	(X)	41.0	33.1	58.8	68.1	(X)
Only father attended	6.4	5.1	9.0	(X)	76.7	7.1	5.8	10.0	(X)	70.8
Both attended	29.4	43.3	(X)	(X)	(X)	23.0	33.4	(X)	(X)	(X)
Any adult attending a class event	70.8	74.0	64.1	63.1	71.2	67.8	72.6	57.3	55.9	66.1
Only mother attended	31.5	20.0	55.7	63.1	(X)	24.6	14.1	48.0	55.9	(X)
Only father attended	5.1	3.6	8.3	(X)	71.2	5.3	3.5	9.3	(X)	66.1
Both attended	34.2	50.4	(X)	(X)	(X)	37.9	55.0	(X)	(X)	(X)
Any adult acted as a volunteer	48.9	55.5	34.8	36.3	23.1	31.7	36.1	21.9	22.1	20.6
Only mother attended	37.0	39.3	32.1	36.3	(X)	21.8	23.0	19.0	22.1	(X)
Only father attended	3.2	3.4	2.7	(X)	23.1	3.1	3.1	2.9	(X)	20.6
Both attended	8.6	12.7	(X)	(X)	(X)	6.8	9.9	(X)	(X)	(X)
Number of activities at least one parent participated in:										
None	3.5	2.2	6.5	6.2	8.3	7.3	4.4	13.7	14.1	11.2
One	7.4	5.7	11.0	11.1	10.3	11.7	11.0	13.4	13.9	10.8
Two	19.7	17.6	24.3	24.2	25.0	25.8	24.8	27.9	28.0	27.3
Three	32.0	31.7	32.5	31.7	39.0	32.2	33.5	29.2	28.5	33.5
Four	37.4	42.9	25.7	26.8	17.4	23.0	26.2	15.7	15.5	17.2
Number of activities both parents participated in:										
None	24.0	24.0	(X)	(X)	(X)	27.0	27.0	(X)	(X)	(X)
One	21.7	21.7	(X)	(X)	(X)	24.8	24.8	(X)	(X)	(X)
Two	26.0	26.0	(X)	(X)	(X)	24.2	24.2	(X)	(X)	(X)
Three	21.5	21.5	(X)	(X)	(X)	19.5	19.5	(X)	(X)	(X)
Four	6.7	6.7	(X)	(X)	(X)	4.5	4.5	(X)	(X)	(X)

X Not applicable.

Source: U.S. National Center for Education Statistics, *National Household Education Survey*, 1999. See Internet site <http://nces.ed.gov/pubsearch/getpubcats.asp?sid=004>.

No. 220. Children's Involvement in Home Literacy Activities: 1993 and 2001

[In percent, except number of children (8,579 represents 8,579,000). For children 3 to 5 years old not yet enrolled in kindergarten who participated in activities with a family member. Based on the School Readiness Survey of the National Education Household Education Survey Program; see source and Appendix III. See also Tables 219 and 223]

Characteristic	Children (1,000)		Read to [1]		Told a story [1]		Taught letters, words, or numbers [1]		Visited a library [2]	
	1993	2001	1993	2001	1993	2001	1993	2001	1993	2001
Total	8,579	8,551	78	84	43	54	58	74	38	36
Age:										
3 years old	3,889	3,795	79	84	46	54	57	71	34	35
4 years old	3,713	3,861	78	85	41	55	58	77	41	37
5 years old	976	896	76	81	36	52	58	75	38	37
Race/ethnicity:										
White, non-Hispanic	5,902	5,313	85	89	44	58	58	75	42	39
Black, non-Hispanic	1,271	1,251	66	77	39	51	63	78	29	31
Hispanic	1,026	1,506	58	71	38	42	54	68	26	30
Other	381	482	73	87	50	60	59	78	43	38
Mother's home language: [3]										
English	7,805	7,368	81	88	44	56	58	76	39	38
Not English	603	984	42	60	36	38	52	61	26	25
Mother's highest education: [3]										
Less than high school	1,036	996	60	69	37	43	56	67	22	21
High school	3,268	2,712	76	81	41	53	56	73	31	30
Vocational ed or some college	2,624	2,406	83	86	45	53	60	76	44	39
College degree	912	1,418	90	93	48	59	56	75	55	45
Graduate/professional training or degree	569	820	90	96	50	63	60	80	59	55
Family type:										
Two parents	6,226	6,416	81	87	44	55	57	74	41	38
None or one parent	2,353	2,135	71	76	41	51	59	73	30	30
Poverty status:										
Above threshold	6,323	6,499	82	87	44	55	57	75	41	39
Below threshold	2,256	2,053	68	74	39	51	59	72	28	27

[1] Three or more times in the past week. [2] At least once in the past month. [3] Excludes children with no mother in the household and no female guardian.

Source: U.S. National Center for Education Statistics, *Statistical Brief*, NCES 2000-026, November 1999; and unpublished data. See Internet site <http://nces.ed.gov/pubsearch/getpubcats.asp?sid=004>.

Education 145

No. 221. Children Who Speak a Language Other Than English at Home: 1979 to 1999

[In percent, except total. For children 5 to 17 years old (3.8 represents 3,800,000). For children reported to speak English less than "very well." Based on the Current Population Survey; see text Section 1, and Appendix III]

Characteristic	1979	1989	1992	1995 [1]	1999 [1]
Children who speak another language at home (mil) .	**3.8**	**5.3**	**6.4**	**6.7**	**8.8**
Percent of children 5 to 17 years old	8.5	12.6	14.2	14.1	16.7
Race and Hispanic origin:					
White, non-Hispanic	3.2	3.5	3.7	3.6	3.9
Black, non-Hispanic	1.3	2.4	4.2	3.0	4.5
Hispanic [2]	75.1	71.2	76.6	73.9	70.9
Other, non-Hispanic [3]	44.1	53.4	58.3	45.5	51.0
Region: [4]					
Northeast	10.5	13.5	16.2	15.1	17.7
Midwest	3.7	4.9	5.6	5.9	7.5
South	6.8	10.7	11.1	11.7	14.3
West	17.0	24.2	27.2	26.4	28.8
Children who speak another language at home and have difficulty speaking English (mil)	**1.3**	**1.9**	**2.2**	**2.4**	**2.6**
Percent of children 5 to 17 years old	2.8	4.4	4.9	5.1	5.0
Race and Hispanic origin:					
White, non-Hispanic	0.5	0.8	0.6	0.7	1.0
Black, non-Hispanic	0.3	0.5	1.3	0.9	1.0
Hispanic [2]	28.7	27.4	29.9	31.0	23.4
Other, non-Hispanic [3]	19.8	20.4	21.0	14.1	11.7
Region: [4]					
Northeast	2.9	4.8	5.3	5.0	4.4
Midwest	1.1	1.3	1.6	2.3	2.0
South	2.2	3.8	3.5	3.4	3.6
West	6.5	8.8	10.4	11.4	10.5

[1] Reflects revised interviewing techniques and/or change in population controls to the 1990 Census-based estimates.
[2] Persons of Hispanic origin may be of any race.   [3] Includes mostly Asian/Pacific Islanders, but also American Indian/Alaska Native children.   [4] For composition of regions, see map, inside front cover.

Source: Federal Interagency Forum on Child and Family Statistics, *America's Children: Key National Indicators of Well-Being, 2001*. See Internet site <http://www.childstats.gov/americaschildren/>

No. 222. Preprimary School Enrollment—Summary: 1970 to 2002

[As of October. Civilian noninstitutional population (10,949 represents 10,949,000). Includes public and nonpublic nursery school and kindergarten programs. Excludes 5 year olds enrolled in elementary school. Based on Current Population Survey; see text, Section 1, and Appendix III]

Item	1970	1975	1980	1985	1990	1995	2000	2001	2002
NUMBER OF CHILDREN (1,000)									
Population, 3 to 5 years old	10,949	10,183	9,284	10,733	11,207	12,518	11,858	11,653	11,481
Total enrolled [1]	**4,104**	**4,954**	**4,878**	**5,865**	**6,659**	**7,739**	**7,592**	**7,441**	**7,504**
Nursery	1,094	1,745	1,981	2,477	3,378	4,331	4,326	4,250	4,423
Public	332	570	628	846	1,202	1,950	2,146	2,126	2,205
Private	762	1,174	1,353	1,631	2,177	2,381	2,180	2,124	2,218
Kindergarten	3,010	3,211	2,897	3,388	3,281	3,408	3,266	3,191	3,081
Public	2,498	2,682	2,438	2,847	2,767	2,799	2,701	2,690	2,551
Private	511	528	459	541	513	608	565	501	530
White	3,443	4,105	3,994	4,757	5,389	6,144	5,861	5,678	5,799
Black	586	731	725	919	964	1,236	1,265	1,323	1,239
Hispanic [2]	(NA)	(NA)	370	496	642	1,040	1,155	1,218	1,263
3 years old	454	683	857	1,035	1,205	1,489	1,540	1,504	1,619
4 years old	1,007	1,418	1,423	1,765	2,086	2,553	2,556	2,526	2,568
5 years old	2,643	2,852	2,598	3,065	3,367	3,697	3,496	3,411	3,317
ENROLLMENT RATE									
Total enrolled [1]	**37.5**	**48.6**	**52.5**	**54.6**	**59.4**	**61.8**	**64.0**	**63.9**	**65.4**
White	37.8	48.6	52.7	54.7	59.7	63.0	63.2	63.2	65.0
Black	34.9	48.1	51.8	55.8	57.8	58.9	68.5	69.2	67.7
Hispanic [2]	(NA)	(NA)	43.3	43.3	49.0	51.1	52.6	53.9	56.1
3 years old	12.9	21.5	27.3	28.8	32.6	35.9	39.2	38.4	42.4
4 years old	27.8	40.5	46.3	49.1	56.0	61.6	64.9	66.4	66.6
5 years old	69.3	81.3	84.7	86.5	88.8	87.5	87.6	86.7	87.2

NA Not available.   [1] Includes races not shown separately.   [2] Persons of Hispanic origin may be of any race. The method of identifying Hispanic children was changed in 1980 from allocation based on status of mother to status reported for each child. The number of Hispanic children using the new method is larger.

Source: U.S. Census Bureau, Current Population Reports, PPL-148; and earlier PPL and P-20 reports; and data published on the Internet. See Internet site <http://www.census.gov/population/www/socdemo/school.html>

No. 223. Children's School Readiness Skills: 1993 and 2001

[In percent. For children 3 to 5 years old not yet enrolled in kindergarden. Based on the School Readiness Surey of the National Household Education Survey Program; see source for details. See also Tables 219 and 220]

Characteristic	Recognizes all letters		Counts to 20 or higher		Writes name		Reads or pretends to read storybooks		Has 3-4 skills	
	1993	2001	1993	2001	1993	2001	1993	2001	1993	2001
Total	21	23	52	57	50	53	72	71	35	39
Age:										
3 years old	11	12	37	39	22	23	66	64	15	16
4 years old	28	29	62	68	70	73	75	76	49	53
5 years old	36	38	78	82	84	89	81	80	65	71
Sex:										
Male	19	19	49	52	47	47	68	68	32	34
Female	23	27	56	61	53	58	76	74	39	43
Race/ethnicity:										
White, non-Hispanic	23	24	56	61	52	55	76	78	39	43
Black, non-Hispanic	18	23	53	57	45	52	63	64	31	35
Hispanic.	10	14	32	39	42	43	59	52	22	22
Other.	22	35	49	61	52	57	70	64	36	48
Mother's employment status:										
Employed.	23	23	57	60	52	56	75	74	39	42
Unemployed.	17	17	41	47	46	47	67	55	29	28
Not in the labor force	18	22	49	52	47	48	68	67	32	34
Family type:										
Two parents	22	24	54	58	51	54	74	74	37	41
None or one parent	18	17	49	51	47	48	65	61	31	31
Poverty status:										
Above threshold	24	25	57	61	53	55	74	75	40	44
Below threshold.	12	14	41	43	41	45	64	57	23	23

Source: U.S. National Center for Education Statistics, *Home Literacy Activities and Signs of Children's Emerging Literacy, 1993 and 1999*, NCES 2000-026, November 1999; and unpublished data. See Internet site <http://nces.ed.gov/pubsearch/getpubcats.asp?sid=004>

No. 224. Public Charter and Traditional Schools—Selected Characteristics: 1999-2000

[45,100 represents 45,100,000. A public charter school is a public school that, in accordance with an enabling state statue, has been granted a charter exempting it from selected state and local rules and regulations. All schools open as public charter schools during 1998-99 and still open in the 1999-2000 school year were surveyed. Based in the School and Staffing Survey; see source for details]

Characteristic	All schools		Elementary		Secondary		Combined	
	Tradi-tional	Public charter	Tradi-tional	Public charter	Tradi-tional	Public charter	Tradi-tional	Public charter
Number of schools	83,725	1,010	59,900	586	20,651	235	3,174	190
Enrollment (1,000).	45,100	267	29,050	159	15,201	58	848	50
PERCENT DISTRIBUTION OF STUDENTS								
Race/ethnicity.	100.0	100.0	100.0	100.0	100.0	100.0	100.0	100.0
White.	63.2	46.4	61.4	44.7	66.4	42.0	68.6	57.0
Black.	16.9	27.3	18.0	31.0	14.9	23.4	17.1	19.9
Hispanic.	14.9	20.8	15.8	19.5	13.6	28.9	9.1	15.5
Asian/Pacific Islander	3.7	3.2	3.6	3.3	4.1	2.8	1.7	3.5
American Indian/Alaskan Native	1.2	2.3	1.2	1.5	1.1	3.0	3.4	4.1
PERCENT DISTRIBUTION OF SCHOOLS								
Size of enrollment	100.0	100.0	100.0	100.0	100.0	100.0	100.0	100.0
Less than 300	28.5	72.2	25.5	69.3	31.1	80.2	69.9	71.4
300 to 599	39.4	16.5	46.4	18.6	22.6	10.9	16.5	16.9
600 to 999	21.8	8.4	23.4	9.9	19.2	3.9	10.3	9.2
1,000 or more	10.2	2.9	4.8	2.1	27.1	4.9	3.4	2.5
Percent minority enrollment.	100.0	100.0	100.0	100.0	100.0	100.0	100.0	100.0
Less than 10.0	38.2	17.8	36.8	18.5	43.3	14.3	32.0	20.1
10.0 to 24.9	17.4	19.5	17.1	19.0	19.0	18.2	12.2	22.9
25.0 to 49.9	16.5	14.6	16.9	13.7	15.5	14.3	15.4	17.5
50.0 to 74.9	11.6	13.0	12.1	11.9	9.9	17.8	15.0	10.4
75.0 or more	16.3	35.1	17.1	36.9	12.4	35.3	25.4	29.1
Percent of students eligible for free or reduced-price lunch	100.0	100.0	100.0	100.0	100.0	100.0	100.0	100.0
Less than 15.0	23.4	29.8	20.4	30.2	32.9	28.4	17.4	30.3
15.0 to 29.9	19.7	11.4	19.2	11.6	23.0	11.9	8.4	10.5
30.0 to 49.9	21.5	16.7	22.0	16.7	19.7	17.1	23.6	16.5
50.0 to 74.9	18.6	16.7	20.2	14.8	14.1	19.8	19.4	19.0
75.0 or more.	16.7	25.3	18.2	26.8	10.3	22.8	31.3	23.7

Source: U.S. National Center for Education Statistics, *Digest Education Statistics*, 2002.

No. 225. Public Elementary and Secondary Schools—Summary: 1980 to 2003

[For school year ending in year shown, except as indicated (48,041 represents 48,041,000). Data are estimates]

Item	Unit	1980	1985	1990	1995	2000	2002	2003
ENROLLMENT								
Population 5-17 years old [1]	1,000...	48,041	44,787	44,949	48,855	52,811	53,240	53,271
Percent of resident population	Percent .	21.4	19.0	18.2	18.6	18.9	18.5	18.5
Fall enrollment [2]	1,000...	41,778	39,354	40,527	43,898	46,581	47,345	47,781
Percent of population 5-17 years old	Percent .	87.0	87.9	90.2	89.9	88.2	88.9	89.7
Elementary [3]	1,000...	24,397	23,830	26,253	28,148	29,245	29,547	29,616
Secondary [4]	1,000...	17,381	15,524	14,274	15,750	17,336	17,799	18,165
Average daily attendance (ADA)	1,000...	38,411	36,530	37,573	40,792	43,269	44,119	44,643
High school graduates	1,000...	2,762	2,424	2,327	2,282	2,540	2,623	2,682
INSTRUCTIONAL STAFF								
Total [5]	1,000...	2,521	2,473	2,685	2,919	3,273	3,386	3,450
Classroom teachers	1,000...	2,211	2,175	2,362	2,565	2,891	2,984	3,035
Average salaries:								
Instructional staff	Dollar ..	16,715	24,666	32,638	38,349	43,837	46,723	48,050
Classroom teachers	Dollar ..	15,970	23,600	31,367	36,675	41,807	44,632	45,891
REVENUES								
Revenue receipts	Mil. dol. .	97,635	141,013	208,656	273,255	369,754	412,772	430,713
Federal	Mil. dol. .	9,020	9,533	13,184	18,764	26,346	30,871	34,739
State	Mil. dol. .	47,929	69,107	100,787	129,958	183,986	204,563	211,166
Local	Mil. dol. .	40,686	62,373	94,685	124,533	159,421	177,338	184,808
Percent of total:								
Federal	Percent .	9.2	6.8	6.3	6.9	7.1	7.5	8.1
State	Percent .	49.1	49.0	48.3	47.6	49.8	49.6	49.0
Local	Percent .	41.7	44.2	45.4	45.6	43.1	43.0	42.9
EXPENDITURES								
Total	Mil. dol. .	96,105	139,382	209,698	276,584	374,782	417,240	438,808
Current expenditures (day schools)	Mil. dol. .	85,661	127,230	186,583	242,995	320,954	356,608	376,262
Other current expenditures [6]	Mil. dol. .	1,859	2,109	3,341	5,564	6,618	7,454	7,807
Capital outlay	Mil. dol. .	6,504	7,529	16,012	21,646	37,552	41,847	42,992
Interest on school debt	Mil. dol. .	2,081	2,514	3,762	6,379	9,659	11,331	11,746
Percent of total:								
Current expenditures (day schools)	Percent .	89.1	91.3	89.0	87.9	85.6	85.5	85.7
Other current expenditures [6]	Percent .	1.9	1.5	1.6	2.0	1.8	1.8	1.8
Capital outlay	Percent .	6.8	5.4	7.6	7.8	10.0	10.0	9.8
Interest on school debt	Percent .	2.2	1.8	1.8	2.3	2.6	2.7	2.7
In current dollars:								
Revenue receipts per pupil enrolled	Dollar ..	2,337	3,583	5,149	6,225	7,938	8,718	9,014
Current expenditures per pupil enrolled	Dollar ..	2,050	3,233	4,604	5,535	6,890	7,532	7,875
In constant (2003) dollars: [7]								
Revenue receipts per pupil enrolled	Dollar ..	5,484	6,167	7,382	7,537	8,538	8,909	9,014
Current expenditures per pupil enrolled	Dollar ..	4,812	5,564	6,601	6,702	7,411	7,697	7,875

[1] Estimated resident population as of July 1 of the previous year, except 1980, 1990, and 2000 population enumertated as of April 1. Estimates reflect revisions based on the 2000 Census of Population. [2] Fall enrollment of the previous year. [3] Kindergarten through grade 6. [4] Grades 7 through 12. [5] Full-time equivalent. [6] Current expenses for summer schools, adult education, post-high school vocational education, personnel retraining, etc., when operated by local school districts and not part of regular public elementary and secondary day-school program. [7] Compiled by U.S. Census Bureau. Deflated by the Consumer Price Index, all urban consumers (for school year) supplied by U.S. National Center for Education Statistics.

Source: Except as noted, National Education Association, Washington, DC, Estimates of School Statistics Database (copyright).

No. 226. Public Elementary and Secondary Schools and Enrollment—States: 2001-2002

[For schools with membership (47,668 represents 47,668,000). Based on the Common Core of Data Program; see source for details]

State	Total number of schools with member-ship	Total number of students (1,000)	Type of school							
			Regular		Special education [1]		Vocational education [2]		Alternative education [3]	
			Number of schools	Percent of students	Number of schools	Percent of students	Number of schools	Percent of students	Number of schools	Percent of students
Total.........	**91,380**	**47,688**	**84,919**	**98**	**1,641**	**0.4**	**328**	**0.4**	**4,492**	**1.1**
Alabama.........	1,381	737	1,334	100	18	0.1	2	(Z)	27	0.3
Alaska.........	506	134	473	98	2	0.2	1	(Z)	30	2.0
Arizona.........	1,742	922	1,652	98	13	0.1	9	0.5	68	1.3
Arkansas........	1,129	450	1,125	100	-	-	-	-	4	0.1
California	8,914	6,249	7,667	97	122	0.5	-	-	1,125	2.8
Colorado.........	1,630	742	1,535	99	14	0.1	2	(Z)	79	1.4
Connecticut.......	1,073	570	992	96	23	0.7	17	1.9	41	1.0
Delaware	197	116	170	93	13	1.3	5	4.8	9	1.3
Dist. of Columbia ...	193	75	178	95	10	4.2	-	-	5	1.2
Florida..........	3,314	2,500	2,992	98	122	0.6	25	0.1	175	0.8
Georgia	1,969	1,471	1,940	100	1	(Z)	-	-	28	0.4
Hawaii	279	185	275	100	3	0.1	-	-	1	0.1
Idaho..........	654	247	589	98	5	0.1	-	-	60	1.7
Illinois	4,292	2,071	3,913	98	253	1.2	-	-	126	0.8
Indiana.........	1,891	996	1,832	100	11	0.1	-	-	48	0.4
Iowa..........	1,519	486	1,473	99	10	0.2	-	-	36	1.0
Kansas.........	1,423	470	1,423	100	-	-	-	-	-	-
Kentucky	1,387	654	1,228	99	9	0.1	2	(Z)	148	0.9
Louisiana	1,509	731	1,378	98	28	0.2	-	-	103	2.2
Maine..........	681	206	678	100	3	(Z)	-	-	-	-
Maryland	1,340	861	1,241	98	50	0.9	12	1.1	37	0.6
Massachusetts.....	1,889	973	1,811	96	1	(Z)	43	3.4	34	0.5
Michigan........	3,782	1,731	3,495	98	90	0.7	12	0.1	185	1.1
Minnesota........	2,119	851	1,606	97	195	1.2	1	(Z)	317	2.0
Mississippi	886	494	886	100	-	-	-	-	-	-
Missouri	2,274	910	2,158	99	55	0.4	-	-	61	0.3
Montana........	870	152	863	100	2	(Z)	-	-	5	0.1
Nebraska	1,280	285	1,229	99	51	0.7	-	-	-	-
Nevada	517	357	471	98	12	0.3	1	0.5	33	0.9
New Hampshire....	472	207	472	100	-	-	-	-	-	-
New Jersey......	2,410	1,342	2,271	98	83	0.7	38	1.2	18	0.4
New Mexico	792	320	720	98	15	0.6	-	-	57	1.8
New York	4,298	2,872	4,162	98	26	0.1	25	1.1	85	1.0
North Carolina.....	2,223	1,315	2,127	99	20	0.2	1	(Z)	75	0.4
North Dakota.....	529	106	529	100	-	-	-	-	-	-
Ohio	3,826	1,831	3,700	97	28	0.2	68	3.1	30	0.2
Oklahoma........	1,814	622	1,814	100	-	-	-	-	-	-
Oregon.........	1,273	551	1,193	99	11	0.1	-	-	69	1.3
Pennsylvania......	3,185	1,822	3,144	98	12	1.1	16	0.7	13	0.1
Rhode Island......	326	158	313	98	4	0.4	4	0.7	5	0.7
South Carolina.....	1,053	691	1,047	100	5	0.1	-	-	1	(Z)
South Dakota	749	128	720	99	4	0.1	-	-	25	0.9
Tennessee	1,610	925	1,574	100	15	0.1	3	0.1	18	0.1
Texas..........	7,646	4,163	6,715	98	133	0.1	25	0.1	773	1.4
Utah	791	485	719	98	19	0.4	-	-	53	1.4
Vermont	359	101	315	99	42	1.2	-	-	2	0.1
Virginia.........	1,839	1,163	1,793	99	10	0.1	-	-	36	0.6
Washington.......	2,170	1,009	1,834	97	79	0.3	10	0.1	247	3.1
West Virginia......	784	283	752	100	7	0.1	5	(Z)	20	0.3
Wisconsin.......	2,208	879	2,035	98	12	0.1	1	(Z)	160	2.2
Wyoming........	383	88	363	98	-	-	-	-	20	1.9

- Represents zero.   Z Less than 0.05 percent.   [1] Focuses on special education with materials and instructional approaches adapted to meet the students' needs.   [2] Focuses on vocational, technical, or career education and provides education and training in at least one semi-skilled or technical occupation.   [3] Adresses the needs of students that typically cannot be met in the regular school setting, and provides nontraditional education.

Source: U.S. National Center for Education Statistics, *Overview of Public Elementary and Secondary Schools and Districts: School Year 2001-02*, NCES 2003-411, May 2003.

Education   149

No. 227. Selected Statistics for the Largest Public School Districts: 2001-2002

[**For the 50 largest districts by enrollment size.** Excludes outlying areas. Based on reports from state educatuion agencies in the spring 2002. Data from the Common Core Data Program; see source for details. School district boundaries are not necessarily the same as city or county boundaries]

School district	City	County	Number of students [1]	Number of full-time equivalent (FTE) teachers	Number of completers [2]	Number of schools
New York City Public Schools, NY	Brooklyn	Kings	1,049,831	65,804	41,151	1,218
Los Angeles Unified, CA	Los Angeles	Los Angeles	735,058	36,115	27,579	663
City of Chicago School District, IL	Chicago	Cook	437,418	24,064	14,091	599
Dade County School District, FL	Miami	Dade	375,836	19,043	17,287	363
Broward County School District, FL	Fort Lauderdale	Broward	262,055	12,763	11,215	244
Clark County School District, NV	Las Vegas	Clark	245,659	12,514	10,138	275
Houston Independent School District, TX . . .	Houston	Harris	210,950	12,097	7,632	299
Philadelphia City School District, PA	Philadelphia	Philadelphia	197,083	10,686	9,362	263
Hawaii Department of Education, HI	Honolulu	Honolulu	184,546	11,007	10,323	279
Hillsborough County School District, FL . . .	Tampa	Hillsborough	169,789	9,975	7,845	219
Detroit City School District, MI	Detroit	Wayne	166,675	9,053	6,068	265
Dallas Independent School District, TX. . . .	Dallas	Dallas	163,562	10,562	6,008	226
Fairfax County Public Schools, VA.	Fairfax	Fairfax	160,584	12,310	10,657	198
Palm Beach County School District, FL . . .	West Palm Beach	Palm Beach	160,223	8,678	7,394	193
Orange County School District, FL.	Orlando	Orange	157,433	8,946	7,028	184
San Diego City Unified, CA	San Diego	San Diego	141,599	7,501	6,534	182
Montgomery County Public Schools, MD . .	Rockville	Montgomery	136,895	8,662	8,078	193
Prince Georges County Public Schools, MD	Upper Marlboro	Prince George's	135,039	8,067	7,490	196
Duval County School District, FL.	Jacksonville	Duval	127,392	6,478	4,962	178
Gwinnett County School District, GA	Lawrenceville	Gwinnett	116,339	7,598	6,102	86
Memphis City School District, TN	Memphis	Shelby	115,992	7,155	4,301	174
Pinellas County School District, FL	Largo	Pinellas	114,583	6,480	5,218	169
Baltimore County Public Schools, MD	Towson	Baltimore	107,212	6,857	6,592	170
Charlotte-Mecklenburg Schools, NC.	Charlotte	Mecklenburg	106,312	6,927	4,801	137
Wake County Schools, NC.	Raleigh	Wake	101,756	6,408	5,183	120
Cobb County School District, GA.	Marietta	Cobb	98,338	6,388	5,541	96
Baltimore City Public School System, MD. .	Baltimore	Baltimore City	97,817	6,303	4,365	177
Milwaukee School District, WI.	Milwaukee	Milwaukee	97,762	5,980	3,446	208
De Kalb County School District, GA.	Decatur	De Kalb	97,501	6,417	4,591	129
Long Beach Unified, CA	Long Beach	Los Angeles	96,488	4,581	4,396	90
Jefferson (KY) County, KY.	Louisville	Jefferson	93,516	5,374	5,213	172
Jefferson (CO) County, CO	Golden	Jefferson	88,460	4,724	5,155	166
Albuquerque Public Schools, NM	Albuquerque	Bernalillo	87,201	5,847	4,585	138
Polk County School District, FL.	Bartow	Polk	81,207	4,851	3,615	142
Fresno Unified, CA.	Fresno	Fresno	81,058	3,859	3,530	99
Fort Worth Independent School District, TX.	Fort Worth	Tarrant	80,597	5,024	3,259	143
Austin Independent School District, TX. . . .	Austin	Travis	77,684	5,304	3,619	111
Virginia Beach City Public Schools, VA. . . .	Virginia Beach	Virginia Beach City	75,970	5,213	4,504	85
Anne Arundel County Public Schools, MD. .	Annapolis	Anne Arundel	75,081	4,440	4,344	119
Mesa Unified District, AZ	Mesa	Maricopa	74,808	3,698	4,053	89
Jordan School District, UT	Sandy	Salt Lake	73,494	3,072	4,901	81
Orleans Parish School Board, LA	New Orleans	Orleans	73,185	4,552	3,672	130
Denver County, CO	Denver	Denver	72,361	4,376	2,585	134
Cleveland City School District, OH.	Cleveland	Cuyahoga	72,199	6,619	2,173	125
Granite School District, UT.	Salt Lake City	Salt Lake	72,082	3,423	4,337	98
Brevard County School District, FL	Viera	Brevard	71,781	3,914	3,630	109
Fulton County School District, GA	Atlanta	Fulton	69,841	4,639	3,520	77
District of Columbia Public Schools, DC . . .	Washington	District of Columbia	68,449	4,951	3,043	165
Nashville-Davidson County School District, TN.	Nashville	Davidson	67,689	4,700	2,801	123
Cypress-Fairbanks Independent School District, TX	Houston	Harris	67,562	4,453	3,673	57

[1] Number of students receiving educational services from the school district. [2] Includes high school diploma recipients and other completers (for example certificates of attendance) but does not include high school equivalents (GEDs).

Source: U.S. National Center for Education Statistics, *Characteristics of the 100 Largest Public Elementary and Secondary School Districts in the United States: 2001-02* NCES 2003-353, September 2003.

No. 228. Public Elementary and Secondary Schools by Type and Size of School: 2001-2002

[**Enrollment in thousands (47,519 represents 47,519,000).** Data reported by schools, rather than school districts. Based on the Common Core of Data Survey; see source for details.]

Enrollment size of school	Number of schools					Enrollment [1]				
	Total	Elementary [2]	Secondary [3]	Combined [4]	Other [5]	Total	Elementary [2]	Secondary [3]	Combined [4]	Other [5]
Total	94,112	65,228	22,180	5,288	1,416	47,519	30,946	15,215	1,275	82
PERCENT										
Total	100.0	100.0	100.0	100.0	100.0	100.0	100.0	100.0	100.0	100.0
Under 100 students.	10.76	6.21	15.63	45.31	58.53	0.94	0.64	1	6.36	18.57
100 to 199 students	9.77	8.73	11.18	16.27	21.07	2.81	2.77	2.28	8.82	21.59
200 to 299 students	11.52	12.85	8.14	8.66	9.03	5.59	6.83	2.83	7.93	15.91
300 to 399 students	13.32	15.67	7.73	7.22	4.52	8.96	11.5	3.75	9.38	11.22
400 to 499 students	13.14	15.89	6.73	5.36	3.85	11.34	14.95	4.20	8.93	12.11
500 to 599 students	10.94	13.11	6.04	4.34	0.84	11.51	15.03	4.63	8.80	3.30
600 to 699 students	8.13	9.43	5.48	3.09	0.50	10.11	12.78	4.95	7.40	2.36
700 to 799 students	5.76	6.38	4.80	2.25	0.50	8.27	9.98	5.01	6.18	2.80
800 to 999 students	6.92	6.90	8.08	2.97	0.33	11.82	12.79	10.07	9.73	2.10
1,000 to 1,499 students . . .	6.07	4.18	12.67	2.99	0.50	13.95	10.23	21.64	13.22	4.49
1,500 to 1,999 students . . .	2.15	0.53	7.40	0.95	-	7.08	1.87	17.78	6.08	-
2,000 to 2,999 students . . .	1.27	0.12	5.01	0.36	0.33	5.74	0.57	16.49	3.09	5.55
3,000 or more students . . .	0.27	0.01	1.09	0.23	-	1.87	0.07	5.37	4.07	-
Average enrollment	(X)	(X)	(X)	(X)	(X)	520	477	718	270	138

- Represents zero. X Not applicable. Z Less than 0.05 percent. [1] Data for those schools reporting enrollment. [2] Includes schools beginning with grade 6 or below and with no grade higher than 8. [3] Includes schools with no grade lower than 7. [4] Includes schools with both elementary and secondary grades. [5] Includes special education, alternative, and other schools not classified by grade span.

Source: U.S. National Center for Education Statistics, *Digest of Education Statistics*, annual.

No. 229. Students Who Are Homeschooled by Selected Characteristics: 1999

[**As of spring. (50,188 represents 50,188,000).** For students 5 to 17 with a grade equivalent of K-12. Homeschoolers are students whose parents reported them to be schooled at home instead of a public or private school. Excludes students who were enrolled in school for more than 25 hours a week or were homeschooled due to a temporary illness. Based on the Parent and Family Involvement Survey of the National Household Education Surveys Program; see source and Appendix III for details]

Characteristic	Number of students			Percent distribution		
	Total (1,000)	Home-schooled (1,000)	Percent home-schooled	All students	Home-schooled	Non-home-schooled
Total	50,188	850	1.7	100.0	100.0	100.0
Grade equivalent: [1]						
K-5	24,428	428	1.8	48.7	50.4	48.7
Kindergarten	3,790	92	2.4	7.6	10.8	7.5
Grades 1 to 3	12,692	199	1.6	25.3	23.5	25.3
Grades 4 to 5	7,946	136	1.7	15.8	16.0	15.8
Grades 6 to 8	11,788	186	1.6	23.5	21.9	23.5
Grades 9 to 12	13,954	235	1.7	27.8	27.7	27.8
Sex:						
Male	25,515	417	1.6	50.8	49.0	50.9
Female	24,673	434	1.8	49.2	51.0	49.1
Race/ethnicity:						
White, non-Hispanic	32,474	640	2.0	64.7	75.3	64.5
Black, non-Hispanic	8,047	84	1.0	16.0	9.9	16.1
Hispanic.	7,043	77	1.1	14.0	9.1	14.1
Other.	2,623	49	1.9	5.2	5.8	5.2
Number of children in the household:						
One child	8,226	120	1.5	16.4	14.1	16.4
Two children	19,883	207	1.0	39.6	24.4	39.9
Three or more children	22,078	523	2.4	44.0	61.6	43.7
Number of parents in the household:						
Two parents	33,007	683	2.1	65.8	80.4	65.5
One parent	15,454	142	0.9	30.8	16.7	31.0
Nonparental guardians	1,727	25	1.4	3.4	2.9	3.5
Parents' participation in the labor force:						
Two parents-one in labor force	9,628	444	4.6	19.2	52.2	18.6
Two parents-both in labor force	22,880	237	1.0	45.6	27.9	45.9
One parent in labor force	13,907	98	0.7	27.7	11.6	28.0
No parent in labor force	3,773	71	1.9	7.5	8.3	7.5
Household income:						
$25,000 or less	16,776	262	1.6	33.4	30.9	33.5
25,001 to 50,000	15,220	278	1.8	30.3	32.7	30.3
50,001 to 75,000	8,576	162	1.9	17.1	19.1	17.1
75,001 or more	9,615	148	1.5	19.2	17.4	19.2
Parents' highest educational attainment:						
High school diploma or less	18,334	160	0.9	36.5	18.9	36.8
Voc/tech degree or some college	15,177	287	1.9	30.2	33.7	30.2
Bachelor's degree	8,269	213	2.6	16.5	25.1	16.3
Graduate/professional school	8,407	190	2.3	16.8	22.3	16.7

[1] Excludes those ungraded.

Source: U.S. National Center for Education Statistics, *Homeschooling in the United States: 1999*, NCES 2001-033, July 2001.

Education 151

No. 230. Public Elementary and Secondary School Enrollment by State: 1980 to 2001

[In thousands (27,647 represents 27,647,000), except rate. As of fall. Includes unclassified students. Based on survey of state education agencies; see source for details]

State	Enrollment								Enrollment rate [2]			
	K through grade 8 [1]				Grades 9 through 12							
	1980	1990	2000, prel.	2001, prel.	1980	1990	2000, prel.	2001, prel.	1980	1990	2000, prel.	2001, prel.
United States ...	27,647	29,878	33,709	33,952	13,231	11,338	13,514	13,736	86.2	91.2	88.9	89.6
Alabama.........	528	527	539	536	231	195	201	202	87.6	93.2	89.5	90.3
Alaska	60	85	94	95	26	29	39	39	94.0	97.4	93.2	94.6
Arizona.........	357	479	641	672	157	161	237	251	88.9	93.3	89.1	89.5
Arkansas	310	314	318	318	138	123	132	132	90.3	95.8	90.2	90.4
California	2,730	3,615	4,409	4,480	1,347	1,336	1,733	1,769	87.1	92.6	90.8	91.0
Colorado........	374	420	517	529	172	154	208	213	92.2	94.6	90.2	90.0
Connecticut......	364	347	406	410	168	122	156	160	83.3	90.2	90.9	89.6
Delaware	62	73	81	81	37	27	34	34	79.5	87.2	80.2	82.4
District of Columbia .	71	61	54	58	29	19	15	17	91.8	100.6	83.6	94.7
Florida	1,042	1,370	1,760	1,797	468	492	675	703	84.4	92.6	90.2	89.6
Georgia	742	849	1,060	1,075	327	303	385	395	86.8	93.7	91.8	91.7
Hawaii	110	123	132	132	55	49	52	53	83.4	87.4	84.7	86.1
Idaho..........	144	160	170	171	59	61	75	75	95.4	96.9	90.3	90.8
Illinois.........	1,335	1,310	1,474	1,484	649	512	575	587	82.6	86.9	86.5	87.5
Indiana.........	708	676	703	711	347	279	286	285	88.0	90.4	85.9	85.8
Iowa	351	345	334	330	183	139	161	156	88.4	92.1	90.8	92.0
Kansas.........	283	320	323	322	133	117	147	148	88.7	92.5	89.8	91.3
Kentucky	464	459	472	473	206	177	194	181	83.7	90.5	91.3	93.5
Louisiana	544	586	547	537	234	199	197	194	80.2	88.1	82.3	83.0
Maine..........	153	155	146	144	70	60	61	62	91.6	96.5	89.8	93.5
Maryland	493	527	609	611	258	188	244	250	83.9	89.1	85.1	85.2
Massachusetts.....	676	604	703	699	346	230	273	274	88.6	88.8	88.4	89.7
Michigan........	1,227	1,145	1,256	1,223	570	440	488	508	86.9	90.3	90.6	90.6
Minnesota.......	482	546	578	573	272	211	277	278	87.2	91.3	89.2	90.4
Mississippi	330	372	364	362	147	131	134	132	79.6	91.3	87.2	88.3
Missouri	567	588	645	643	277	228	268	267	83.8	86.5	86.3	87.4
Montana	106	111	105	103	50	42	50	49	92.9	94.1	86.4	90.7
Nebraska	189	198	195	195	91	76	91	90	86.6	88.7	85.9	87.4
Nevada	101	150	251	262	49	51	90	94	93.4	98.6	93.1	90.2
New Hampshire....	112	126	147	144	55	46	61	62	85.3	89.1	89.1	88.4
New Jersey......	820	784	953	972	426	306	355	370	81.5	85.9	85.8	86.8
New Mexico	186	208	225	225	85	94	95	95	89.5	94.4	84.7	86.3
New York	1,838	1,828	2,029	2,017	1,033	770	853	855	80.8	86.6	83.5	84.2
North Carolina.....	786	783	945	956	343	304	348	359	90.1	94.8	90.8	90.0
North Dakota......	77	85	72	70	40	33	37	36	85.9	92.6	89.9	92.9
Ohio	1,312	1,258	1,294	1,287	645	514	541	544	84.8	88.0	86.0	86.3
Oklahoma........	399	425	445	446	179	154	178	176	92.9	95.1	95.0	97.0
Oregon.........	319	340	379	382	145	132	167	170	88.5	90.6	87.6	87.8
Pennsylvania......	1,231	1,172	1,258	1,255	678	496	556	567	80.4	83.5	82.7	84.0
Rhode Island.....	98	102	114	113	51	37	44	45	80.1	87.5	85.5	87.1
South Carolina.....	426	452	493	500	193	170	184	191	88.1	93.9	90.9	95.3
South Dakota	86	95	88	87	42	34	41	41	87.4	89.9	84.8	86.5
Tennessee	602	598	668	675	252	226	241	250	87.8	93.5	88.8	90.7
Texas..........	2,049	2,511	2,943	3,016	851	872	1,117	1,147	92.4	98.4	95.2	95.9
Utah	250	325	333	338	93	122	148	147	98.2	97.8	94.6	96.7
Vermont	66	71	70	69	29	25	32	32	87.9	94.3	89.9	92.5
Virginia.........	703	728	816	826	307	270	329	337	90.7	94.2	89.7	90.4
Washington.......	515	613	694	696	242	227	310	313	91.7	94.1	89.7	90.4
West Virginia......	270	224	201	200	113	98	85	83	92.6	95.7	95.3	95.9
Wisconsin........	528	566	595	592	303	232	285	288	82.1	86.1	85.7	86.7
Wyoming	70	71	60	59	28	27	30	29	97.3	97.7	91.8	93.8

[1] Data include a small number of prekindergarten students. [2] Percent of persons 5-17 years old. Based on enumerated resident population as of April 1, 1980, 1990, and 2000, and estimated resident population as of July 1 for 2001.

Source: U.S. National Center for Education Statistics, *Digest of Education Statistics*, annual.

No. 231. Public School Districts With Alternative Schools or Programs for at-Risk Students: 2000-2001

[For the school year. Alternative schools and programs are designed to address the needs of students that typically cannot be met in regular schools. The schools and programs in data shown here serve students who are typically at risk for educational failure (as indicated by poor grades or truancy, for example). Alternative schools are usually housed in a separate facility where students are removed from regular schools. Alternative programs are usually housed within regular schools. Based on the Fast Response Survey System; see source for details]

District characteristic	Percent of districts with schools or programs	Percent distribution of districts with schools or programs by—						
		Number of schools or programs			Percent of district students enrolled			
		One	Two	Three or more	Less than 1 percent	1 to 1.99 percent	2 to 2.99 percent	3 percent or more
Total	39	65	18	17	43	27	14	16
Metropolitan status: [1]								
Urban	66	33	15	52	36	30	17	16
Suburban	41	63	19	18	49	26	12	13
Rural	35	74	17	8	38	28	16	18
Enrollment size:								
Less that 2,500	26	82	11	7	39	26	15	20
2,500 to 9,999	69	58	26	16	46	29	13	12
10,000 or more	95	27	17	56	46	25	17	12
Percent minority enrollment:								
5 percent or less	26	75	15	10	49	26	11	14
6 to 20 percent	43	63	20	17	48	22	14	16
21 to 50 percent	51	63	16	22	38	32	18	12
More than 50 percent	62	58	20	22	34	28	16	22
Poverty concentration:								
10 percent or less	31	68	15	16	56	24	10	10
11 to 20 percent	43	59	22	20	40	27	17	16
More than 20 percent	45	71	15	14	38	29	15	18

[1] Urban: Primarily serves the central city of a Metropolitan Statistical Areas (MSA); suburban: serves an MSA, but not primarily the central city; rural: does not serve an MSA.

Source: U.S. National Center for Education Statistics, *Public School Alternative Schools and Programs for Students At Risk of Education Failure 2000-01*, September 2002, NCES 2002-004.

No. 232. Public Elementary and Secondary School Enrollment by Grade: 1980 to 2001

[In thousands (40,877 represents 40,877,000). As of fall of year. Kindergarten includes nursery schools. Based on survey of state education agencies; see source for details]

Grade	1980	1985	1990	1993	1994	1995	1996	1997	1998	1999	2000, prel.	2001, prel.
Pupils enrolled . . .	40,877	39,422	41,217	43,465	44,111	44,840	45,611	46,127	46,539	46,857	47,223	47,688
Kindergarten and grades 1 to 8 . .	27,647	27,034	29,878	31,504	31,898	32,341	32,764	33,073	33,346	33,488	33,709	33,952
Kindergarten	2,689	3,192	3,610	3,922	4,047	4,173	4,202	4,198	4,172	4,148	4,178	4,248
First	2,894	3,239	3,499	3,529	3,593	3,671	3,770	3,755	3,727	3,684	3,635	3,615
Second	2,800	2,941	3,327	3,429	3,440	3,507	3,600	3,689	3,681	3,656	3,633	3,595
Third	2,893	2,895	3,297	3,437	3,439	3,445	3,524	3,597	3,696	3,691	3,673	3,654
Fourth	3,107	2,771	3,248	3,361	3,426	3,431	3,454	3,507	3,592	3,686	3,708	3,696
Fifth	3,130	2,776	3,197	3,350	3,372	3,438	3,453	3,458	3,520	3,604	3,703	3,728
Sixth	3,038	2,789	3,110	3,356	3,381	3,395	3,494	3,492	3,497	3,564	3,658	3,770
Seventh	3,085	2,938	3,067	3,355	3,404	3,422	3,464	3,520	3,530	3,541	3,624	3,722
Eighth	3,086	2,982	2,979	3,249	3,302	3,356	3,403	3,415	3,480	3,497	3,532	3,619
Unclassified [1]	924	511	543	515	494	502	401	442	451	417	366	306
Grades 9 to 12	13,231	12,388	11,338	11,961	12,213	12,500	12,847	13,054	13,193	13,369	13,514	13,736
Ninth	3,377	3,439	3,169	3,487	3,604	3,704	3,801	3,819	3,856	3,935	3,958	4,013
Tenth	3,368	3,230	2,896	3,050	3,131	3,237	3,323	3,376	3,382	3,415	3,487	3,529
Eleventh	3,195	2,866	2,612	2,751	2,748	2,826	2,930	2,972	3,021	3,034	3,080	3,174
Twelfth	2,925	2,550	2,381	2,424	2,488	2,487	2,586	2,673	2,722	2,782	2,799	2,863
Unclassified [1]	366	303	282	248	242	245	206	214	212	203	189	157

[1] Includes ungraded and special education.

Source: U.S. National Center for Education Statistics, *Digest of Education Statistics*, annual.

Education 153

No. 233. School Enrollment Below Postseconday—Summary by Sex, Race, and Hispanic Origin: 2002

[In thousands (57,548 represents 57,548,000), except percent and rate. As of October. Covers civilian noninstitutional population enrolled in nursery school through high school. Based on Current Population Survey, see text, Section 1, and Appendix III]

Characteristic	Sex			Race and Hispanic origin				
				White			Asian and Pacific Islander	Hispanic [2]
	Total [1]	Male	Female	Total	Non-Hispanic	Black		
All students.................	57,548	29,540	28,008	44,720	35,489	9,424	2,529	9,888
Nursery.................	4,471	2,324	2,147	3,473	2,881	725	217	637
Full day.............	2,266	1,163	1,103	1,571	1,241	533	128	367
Part day.............	2,205	1,161	1,044	1,903	1,640	192	89	271
Kindergarten	3,571	1,845	1,725	2,760	2,065	598	157	727
Elementary	33,132	17,038	16,094	25,625	20,124	5,545	1,431	5,909
High school	16,374	8,332	8,042	12,862	10,419	2,558	723	2,614
Students in public schools	49,945	25,636	24,309	38,287	29,640	8,707	2,123	9,262
Nursery	2,246	1,211	1,035	1,613	1,172	503	85	476
Full day	1,190	609	580	749	513	362	52	263
Part day.............	1,057	601	455	864	658	142	33	213
Kindergarten............	2,976	1,545	1,431	2,240	1,585	543	137	688
Elementary...............	29,658	15,216	14,442	22,703	17,495	5,210	1,237	5,585
High school	15,064	7,664	7,401	11,730	9,388	2,451	664	2,513
Population 15 to 17 years old: Percent below modal grade [3] ..	30	36	24	30	28	36	19	36
Students, 10th to 12th grade: Annual dropout rate.........	3	4	3	3	2	4	2	5
Population 18 to 24 years old....	27,368	13,745	13,623	21,704	17,132	3,923	1,339	4,918
Dropouts.................	3,375	1,924	1,450	2,641	1,288	571	58	1,480
High school graduates	22,318	10,823	11,495	17,793	14,911	3,041	1,231	3,077
Enrolled in college	10,033	4,629	5,404	7,921	7,005	1,227	804	979

[1] Includes other races, not shown separately.   [2] Persons of Hispanic origin may be of any race.   [3] The modal grade is the grade most common for a given age.

Source: U.S. Census Bureau, Current Population Survey, unpublished data. See Internet site <http://www.census.gov/population/www/socdemo/school.html>

No. 234. Elementary and Secondary Schools—Teachers, Enrollment, and Pupil-Teacher Ratio: 1960 to 2002

[In thousands (1,600 represents 1,600,000), except ratios. As of fall. Data are for full-time equivalent teachers. Based on survey of state education agencies; see source for details]

Year	Teachers			Enrollment			Pupil-teacher ratio		
	Total	Public	Private	Total	Public	Private	Total	Public	Private
1960	1,600	1,408	192	42,181	36,281	5,900	26.4	25.8	30.7
1965	1,933	1,710	223	48,473	42,173	6,300	25.1	24.7	28.3
1970	2,292	2,059	233	51,257	45,894	5,363	22.4	22.3	23.0
1975	2,453	2,198	255	49,819	44,819	5,000	20.3	20.4	19.6
1976	2,457	2,189	268	49,478	44,311	5,167	20.1	20.2	19.3
1977	2,488	2,209	279	48,717	43,577	5,140	19.6	19.7	18.4
1978	2,479	2,207	272	47,635	42,550	5,085	19.2	19.3	18.7
1979	2,461	2,185	276	46,651	41,651	5,000	19.0	19.1	18.1
1980	2,485	2,184	301	46,208	40,877	5,331	18.6	18.7	17.7
1981	2,440	2,127	313	45,544	40,044	5,500	18.7	18.8	17.6
1982	2,458	2,133	325	45,165	39,566	5,600	18.4	18.6	17.2
1983	2,476	2,139	337	44,967	39,252	5,715	18.2	18.4	17.0
1984	2,508	2,168	340	44,908	39,208	5,700	17.9	18.1	16.8
1985	2,549	2,206	343	44,979	39,422	5,557	17.6	17.9	16.2
1986	2,592	2,244	348	45,205	39,753	5,452	17.4	17.7	15.7
1987	2,631	2,279	352	45,487	40,008	5,479	17.3	17.6	15.6
1988	2,668	2,323	345	45,430	40,189	5,242	17.0	17.3	15.2
1989	2,734	2,357	377	45,741	40,543	5,198	16.7	17.2	13.8
1990	2,753	2,398	355	46,451	41,217	5,234	16.9	17.2	14.7
1991	2,787	2,432	355	47,322	42,047	5,275	17.0	17.3	14.9
1992	2,822	2,459	363	48,145	42,823	5,322	17.1	17.4	14.7
1993	2,870	2,504	366	48,813	43,465	5,348	17.0	17.4	14.6
1994	2,926	2,552	374	49,609	44,111	5,498	17.0	17.3	14.7
1995	2,978	2,598	380	50,502	44,840	5,662	17.0	17.3	14.9
1996	3,054	2,667	387	51,375	45,611	5,764	16.8	17.1	14.9
1997	3,134	2,746	388	51,968	46,127	5,841	16.6	16.8	15.1
1998	3,221	2,830	391	52,475	46,539	5,937	16.3	16.4	15.2
1999 [1]	3,306	2,911	395	52,876	46,857	6,018	16.0	16.1	15.2
2000 [1]	3,332	2,941	390	53,385	47,223	6,162	16.0	16.0	15.8
2001 [1]	3,388	2,998	390	53,890	47,688	6,202	15.9	15.9	15.9
2002 proj.	3,369	2,983	385	54,158	47,918	6,241	16.1	16.1	16.2

[1] Public school enrollment data prelimiary.

Source: U.S. National Center for Education Statistics, *Digest of Education Statistics*, annual.

No. 235. Public Elementary and Secondary School Teachers—Selected Characteristics: 1999-2000

[For school year. **(509 represents 509,000)** Based on School and Staffing Survey and subject to sampling error; for details, see source Web site at <http://nces.ed.gov/surveys/sass/>. Excludes prekindergarten teachers. See Table 247 for similar data on private school teachers]

Characteristic	Unit	Age				Sex		Race/ethnicity		
		Under 30 years old	30 to 39 years old	40 to 49 years old	Over 50 years old	Male	Fe-male	White [1]	Black [1]	His-panic
Total teachers [2]	1,000 . .	509	661	953	879	754	2,248	2,532	228	169
Highest degree held:										
Bachelor's	Percent .	77.9	56.7	46.8	39.0	49.7	52.8	51.2	51.1	65.5
Master's	Percent .	20.4	38.5	46.9	51.4	42.7	41.6	43.0	40.3	28.5
Education specialist.	Percent .	1.2	3.8	4.9	7.3	4.7	4.8	4.6	6.2	4.1
Doctorate	Percent .	(Z)	0.4	0.7	1.5	1.4	0.5	0.6	1.6	1.2
Full-time teaching experience:										
Less than 3 years	Percent .	46.1	11.5	5.9	2.3	13.0	12.9	12.2	15.2	18.7
3 to 9 years	Percent .	53.9	51.5	19.3	7.5	28.1	29.1	28.1	27.6	39.1
10 to 20 years	Percent .	(X)	37.0	41.4	24.5	23.4	30.2	29.1	24.5	24.6
20 years or more	Percent .	(X)	(X)	33.4	65.7	35.6	27.9	30.6	32.7	17.7
Full-time teachers.	1,000 . .	475	600	863	805	700	2,042	2303	214	157
Earned income.	Dol. . .	33,583	38,468	44,375	50,278	46,891	41,596	43,032	43,150	41,241
Salary	Dol. . .	30,386	35,502	41,407	47,138	41,104	39,475	40,022	39,377	38,488

X Not applicable. Z Less than 0.05 percent. [1] Non-Hispanic. [2] Includes teachers with no degrees and associates degrees, not shown separately.

Source: U.S. National Center for Education Statistics, *Digest of Education Statistics, 2002.*

No. 236. Public Elementary and Secondary Schools—Number and Average Salary of Classroom Teachers, 1980 to 2003, and by State, 2003

[Estimates for school year ending in **June of year shown (2,211 represents 2,211,000).** Schools classified by type of organization rather than by grade-group; elementary includes kindergarten]

Year and state	Teachers [1] (1,000)			Avg. salary ($1,000)			Year and state	Teachers [1] (1,000)			Avg. salary ($1,000)		
	Total	Ele-men-tary	Sec-ond-ary	All teach-ers	Ele-men-tary	Sec-ond-ary		Total	Ele-men-tary	Sec-ond-ary	All teach-ers	Ele-men-tary	Sec-ond-ary
1980	2,211	1,206	1,005	16.0	15.6	16.5	LA	50.3	35.1	15.2	37.2	37.2	37.2
1985	2,175	1,212	963	23.6	23.2	24.2	ME	16.0	11.0	5.0	38.5	38.7	38.8
1990	2,362	1,390	972	31.4	30.8	32.0	MD	55.5	33.2	22.4	49.7	49.0	50.3
1992	2,429	1,466	963	34.1	33.5	34.8	MA	71.9	30.9	41.0	50.8	50.8	50.8
1993	2,466	1,496	970	35.0	34.4	35.9	MI	92.2	47.7	44.5	53.6	53.6	53.6
1994	2,512	1,517	995	35.7	35.2	36.6	MN	52.6	26.9	25.8	44.7	45.3	44.1
1995	2,565	1,517	1,048	36.7	36.1	37.5	MS	30.6	17.9	12.7	34.6	34.6	34.6
1996	2,605	1,543	1,062	37.6	37.1	38.4	MO	66.2	33.7	32.5	37.7	37.7	37.7
1997	2,671	1,586	1,086	38.4	38.0	39.2	MT	10.4	6.9	3.4	35.8	35.8	35.8
1998	2,746	1,630	1,116	39.4	39.0	39.9	NE	20.7	12.5	8.2	37.9	37.9	37.9
1999	2,814	1,650	1,164	40.5	40.1	41.3	NV	19.5	11.6	7.8	41.8	41.6	42.1
2000	2,891	1,696	1,195	41.8	41.3	42.5	NH	15.0	10.5	4.5	41.9	41.9	41.9
2001	2,941	1,727	1,214	43.4	42.9	44.0	NJ	105.4	39.5	65.9	54.2	52.8	55.0
2002	2,984	1,745	1,240	44.6	44.2	45.2	NM	21.0	14.8	6.2	37.0	36.6	37.7
2003, U.S. . .	**3,035**	**1,772**	**1,264**	**45.9**	**45.6**	**46.2**	NY	226.0	113.0	113.0	53.0	52.5	53.5
AL	46.5	27.1	19.4	38.2	38.2	38.2	NC	86.1	54.3	31.8	43.1	43.1	43.1
AK	8.1	5.2	2.8	49.7	49.5	50.0	ND	7.7	5.2	2.5	33.9	34.2	33.3
AZ	45.1	32.7	12.4	40.9	40.9	40.9	OH	122.2	81.7	40.5	45.5	45.4	45.7
AR	31.8	15.6	16.2	37.8	36.7	38.8	OK	40.6	21.1	19.5	34.9	34.7	35.1
CA	309.8	226.3	83.5	56.3	56.0	58.0	OR	27.1	17.4	9.7	47.6	47.1	47.9
CO	45.4	22.9	22.5	42.7	42.5	42.7	PA	118.3	61.9	56.5	51.4	51.5	51.3
CT	43.2	30.6	12.6	55.4	54.8	56.6	RI	13.4	8.1	5.3	51.1	51.1	51.1
DE	7.7	3.8	3.8	50.8	49.2	49.3	SC	44.5	31.6	12.9	40.4	38.4	39.0
DC	4.8	3.1	1.7	50.8	49.4	53.3	SD	9.0	6.3	2.7	32.4	32.4	32.4
FL	141.0	70.2	70.8	40.3	40.3	40.3	TN	58.3	42.3	16.0	39.7	39.5	39.7
GA	95.9	55.5	40.4	45.5	44.8	46.5	TX	288.4	147.1	141.3	40.0	39.6	40.4
HI	11.2	6.0	5.2	44.5	44.5	44.5	UT	21.6	11.5	10.0	38.3	38.2	38.6
ID	13.8	7.1	6.8	40.1	39.9	39.6	VT	8.8	4.5	4.2	41.5	41.2	41.8
IL	133.7	91.8	41.9	51.5	49.2	56.4	VA	93.1	55.8	37.3	43.2	43.2	43.2
IN	59.5	31.4	28.1	45.0	45.0	45.0	WA	53.1	29.6	23.5	45.0	45.0	44.9
IA	34.6	16.3	18.2	39.1	38.1	39.9	WV	19.9	14.6	5.4	38.5	38.2	39.3
KS	32.6	16.1	16.5	37.8	37.8	37.8	WI	60.0	41.4	18.6	42.8	42.6	43.2
KY	38.8	27.2	11.6	39.0	38.6	39.5	WY	6.5	3.1	3.4	38.8	38.9	38.8

[1] Full-time equivalent.

Source: National Education Association, Washington, DC, *Estimates of School Statistics Database* (copyright).

Education 155

No. 237. Average Salary and Wages Paid in Public School Systems: 1980 to 2003

[**In dollars.** For school year ending in year shown. Data reported by a stratified sample of school systems enrolling 300 or more pupils. Data represent unweighted means of average salaries paid school personnel reported by each school system]

Position	1980	1985	1990	1995	1999	2000	2001	2002	2003
ANNUAL SALARY									
Central-office administrators:									
Superintendent (contract salary)...	39,344	56,954	75,425	90,198	106,122	112,158	118,496	121,794	126,268
Deputy/assoc. superintendent	37,440	52,877	69,623	81,266	92,936	97,251	104,048	107,458	112,104
Assistant superintendent........	33,452	48,003	62,698	75,236	86,005	88,913	94,137	96,627	98,623
Administrators for—									
Finance and business........	27,147	40,344	52,354	61,323	71,387	73,499	77,768	80,132	81,451
Instructional services	29,790	43,452	56,359	66,767	75,680	79,023	82,725	82,418	84,640
Public relations/information	24,021	35,287	44,926	53,263	59,214	60,655	65,505	67,170	67,298
Staff personnel services	29,623	44,182	56,344	65,819	73,850	76,608	80,969	83,035	85,041
Technology	(X)	(X)	(X)	(X)	(X)	(X)	(X)	72,962	73,931
Subject area supervisors........	23,974	34,422	45,929	54,534	61,083	63,103	64,659	66,351	66,582
School building administrators:									
Principals:									
Elementary	25,165	36,452	48,431	58,589	67,348	69,407	72,587	73,114	75,291
Junior high/middle	27,625	39,650	52,163	62,311	71,499	73,877	77,382	78,176	80,708
Senior high	29,207	42,094	55,722	66,596	76,768	79,839	83,367	83,944	86,452
Assistant principals:									
Elementary	20,708	30,496	40,916	48,491	54,306	56,419	59,080	60,672	62,230
Junior high/middle	23,507	33,793	44,570	52,942	59,238	60,842	63,709	64,375	67,288
Senior high	24,816	35,491	46,486	55,556	62,691	64,811	67,593	67,822	70,847
Classroom teachers..........	15,913	23,587	31,278	37,264	41,351	42,213	43,658	43,802	45,026
Auxiliary professional personnel:									
Counselors................	18,847	27,593	35,979	42,486	47,287	48,195	50,003	50,022	51,706
Librarians................	16,764	24,981	33,469	40,418	45,680	46,732	49,007	48,741	49,611
School nurses..............	13,788	19,944	26,090	31,066	35,520	35,540	37,188	38,221	39,165
Secretarial/clerical personnel:									
Central office:									
Secretaries	10,331	15,343	20,238	23,935	27,540	28,405	29,514	30,039	31,295
Accounting/payroll clerks	10,479	15,421	20,088	24,042	27,630	28,498	29,898	30,551	32,154
Typists/data entry clerks	8,359	12,481	16,125	18,674	22,474	22,853	24,232	24,840	25,793
School building level:									
Secretaries	8,348	12,504	16,184	19,170	21,831	22,630	23,630	24,041	24,853
Library clerks.............	6,778	9,911	12,152	14,381	16,033	16,509	17,052	18,104	18,170
HOURLY WAGE RATE									
Other support personnel:									
Teacher aides:									
Instructional	4.06	5.89	7.43	8.77	9.80	10.00	10.41	10.68	10.93
Noninstructional............	3.89	5.60	7.08	8.29	9.31	9.77	10.15	10.42	10.98
Custodians................	4.88	6.90	8.54	10.05	11.22	11.35	11.85	11.96	12.40
Cafeteria workers	3.78	5.42	6.77	7.89	8.82	9.02	9.41	9.71	9.98
Bus drivers................	5.21	7.27	9.21	10.69	12.04	12.48	12.99	13.49	13.85

X Not applicable.

Source: Educational Research Service, Arlington, VA, *National Survey of Salaries and Wages in Public Schools*, annual. (All rights reserved. Copyright.)

No. 238. Public School Employment: 1982 and 2003

[**In thousands (3,082 represents 3,082,000).** Covers full-time employment. Excludes Hawaii. 1982 also excludes District of Columbia and New Jersey. 1982 based on sample survey of school districts with 250 or more students; 2003 based on sample survey based of school districts with 100 or more employees; see source for sampling variability]

Occupation	1982					2003				
	Total	Male	Female	White [1]	Black [1]	Total	Male	Female	White [1]	Black [1]
All occupations	3,082	1,063	2,019	2,498	432	3,876	1,018	2,858	3,119	517
Officials, administrators	41	31	10	36	3	56	28	27	46	6
Principals and assistant										
principals...............	90	72	19	76	11	111	54	58	78	16
Classroom teachers [2]	1,680	534	1,146	1,435	186	2,275	565	1,710	1,876	219
Elementary schools	798	129	669	667	98	1,157	162	995	943	108
Secondary schools	706	363	343	619	67	843	347	496	708	78
Other professional staff	235	91	144	193	35	166	36	130	134	19
Teachers aides [3]...........	215	14	200	146	45	403	45	358	268	81
Clerical, secretarial staff.......	210	4	206	177	19	248	8	239	187	30
Service workers [4]	611	316	295	434	132	618	281	337	530	145

[1] Excludes individuals of Hispanic origin. [2] Includes other classroom teachers, not shown separately. [3] Includes technicians. [4] Includes craftworkers and laborers.

Source: U.S. Equal Employment Opportunity Commission, *Elementary-Secondary Staff Information (EEO-5)*, biennial.

No. 239. Public Elementary and Secondary School Price Indexes: 1975 to 2001

[**1983=100. For years ending June 30.** Reflects prices paid by public elementary-secondary schools. For explanation of average annual percent change, see Guide to Tabular Presentation]

Year	Personnel compensation					Contracted services, supplies and equipment						
	Index, total	Total	Professional salaries	Nonprofessional salaries	Fringe benefits	Total	Services	Supplies and materials	Equipment replacement	Library materials and textbooks	Utilities	Fixed costs
1975 ..	52.7	53.4	56.0	55.6	40.9	50.4	55.7	58.0	53.7	53.8	34.5	45.2
1980 ..	76.6	75.9	76.7	77.8	71.0	79.2	77.4	85.9	79.6	82.1	71.1	77.9
1985 ..	112.1	113.7	113.4	111.3	117.1	106.0	112.4	103.2	107.2	111.0	96.1	110.8
1986 ..	118.5	121.1	121.4	117.6	123.3	108.3	117.4	103.0	109.3	120.8	93.7	116.2
1987 ..	123.3	127.4	128.4	121.9	128.8	107.5	123.7	101.5	112.9	126.5	75.3	122.7
1988 ..	129.8	134.5	135.5	127.5	137.0	111.7	126.1	105.9	113.4	140.0	78.1	128.4
1989 ..	136.3	141.6	142.2	133.3	147.0	116.1	131.8	112.0	116.0	149.4	75.1	134.6
1990 ..	144.5	150.0	150.1	139.4	159.3	123.5	137.7	119.2	121.2	171.7	82.1	140.3
1991 ..	152.3	158.3	158.1	146.5	169.8	129.6	142.5	122.7	125.7	189.5	92.6	144.9
1992 ..	158.5	165.5	165.9	152.4	175.8	131.9	148.0	122.5	128.5	199.8	90.8	148.9
1993 ..	162.2	169.6	169.3	155.1	184.5	133.9	151.5	121.9	131.8	205.6	90.4	153.8
1994 ..	167.1	175.2	175.1	159.3	190.2	136.5	154.0	122.7	135.4	218.6	90.6	158.8
1995 ..	170.9	179.2	178.9	163.7	194.9	139.3	157.2	124.4	138.7	230.4	89.7	163.9
1996 ..	177.5	185.6	185.7	169.2	200.3	146.6	161.8	138.1	143.2	243.0	91.0	169.1
1997 ..	182.0	190.2	190.2	174.5	204.2	150.8	165.2	137.2	145.2	263.7	100.1	172.9
1998 ..	184.9	193.3	193.3	177.9	207.6	152.7	168.0	137.6	144.2	278.7	98.1	177.0
1999 ..	189.5	199.2	199.1	184.5	213.4	152.3	172.1	135.2	145.6	295.8	87.5	178.3
2000 ..	194.2	204.1	203.5	189.3	220.2	156.1	175.5	136.4	147.9	312.5	92.6	182.1
2001 ..	201.8	211.4	210.8	197.6	226.3	165.6	177.4	143.2	149.4	334.0	118.4	186.7

Source: Research Associates of Washington, Arlington, VA, *Inflation Measures for Schools, Colleges, and Libraries*, periodic (copyright).

No. 240. Finances of Public Elementary and Secondary School Systems by Enrollment-Size Group: 2001-2002

[**In millions of dollars (419,798 represents $419,798,000,000), except as indicated.** Data are based on annual survey. For details, see source. See also Appendix III]

Item	All school systems	School systems with enrollment of—						
		50,000 or more	25,000 to 49,999	15,000 to 24,999	7,500 to 14,999	5,000 to 7,499	3,000 to 4,999	Under 3,000
Fall enrollment (1,000)	47,168	9,845	5,542	4,930	6,801	4,422	5,515	10,114
General revenue.	419,798	85,838	46,482	39,548	59,210	39,273	49,982	99,464
From federal sources	32,703	8,034	3,688	2,844	4,186	2,436	3,189	8,327
Through state	29,312	7,438	3,368	2,602	3,662	2,201	2,866	7,175
Child nutrition programs	7,089	1,933	910	719	925	570	709	1,324
Direct.	3,391	596	320	241	524	235	323	1,152
From state sources [1]	207,375	41,110	23,697	21,264	29,745	18,388	23,085	50,085
General formula assistance	141,089	25,912	15,750	15,230	20,610	12,810	16,003	34,775
Compensatory programs	4,454	558	1,059	563	776	417	391	691
Special education.	13,228	3,382	1,357	983	1,659	1,011	1,555	3,281
From local sources.	179,719	36,695	19,096	15,440	25,279	18,449	23,709	41,052
Taxes.	120,837	19,871	13,060	10,582	18,028	13,270	16,868	29,159
Contributions from parent government	30,449	12,378	2,781	2,104	3,292	2,548	3,424	3,923
From other local governments.	4,300	526	500	369	390	349	620	1,546
Current charges	10,693	1,677	1,092	1,062	1,558	1,003	1,292	3,010
School lunch	5,969	858	632	636	941	641	805	1,456
Other	13,439	2,244	1,663	1,323	2,011	1,279	1,505	3,415
General expenditure	435,315	90,716	47,866	41,011	61,231	40,484	51,187	102,820
Current spending.	370,534	76,841	40,572	35,128	51,958	34,548	43,624	87,862
By function:								
Instruction	224,815	47,435	24,568	21,483	31,836	21,224	26,681	51,587
Support services	125,479	24,853	13,715	11,674	17,348	11,580	14,735	31,576
Other current spending.	20,239	4,553	2,289	1,972	2,774	1,744	2,208	4,699
By object:								
Total salaries and wages	236,940	49,343	26,662	23,025	33,779	22,380	27,928	53,823
Total employee benefits	62,296	12,909	6,595	5,974	9,054	5,962	7,475	14,326
Other	71,298	14,589	7,315	6,129	9,124	6,207	8,221	19,713
Capital outlay	52,921	11,888	5,964	4,835	7,437	4,650	5,980	12,167
Interest on debt	10,157	1,862	1,116	1,007	1,524	1,032	1,356	2,260
Payments to other governments	1,703	125	215	41	312	253	227	530
Debt outstanding.	226,447	47,361	24,529	21,419	32,141	22,529	29,755	48,712
Long-term.	219,304	46,473	24,029	21,048	31,077	21,926	28,603	46,149
Short-term	7,143	889	501	371	1,064	603	1,152	2,563
Long-term debt issued	40,806	7,523	5,068	4,123	5,470	3,971	5,224	9,427
Long-term debt retired	18,738	2,149	2,117	1,645	2,595	2,064	3,090	5,078

[1] Includes other sources, not shown separately.

Source: U.S. Census Bureau, *Public Education Finances, 2002.* See Internet site <http://www.census.gov/govs/www/school.html>

Education 157

No. 241. Public Elementary and Secondary Estimated Finances, 1980 to 2003, and by State, 2003

[In millions of dollars (101,724 represents $101,724,000,000), except as noted. For school years ending in June of year shown]

Year and state	Receipts — Revenue receipts — Total	Source — Total	Source — Federal	Source — State	Source — Local	Non-revenue receipts [1]	Expenditures — Total [2]	Per capita [3] (dol.)	Current expenditures — Elementary and secondary day schools	Average per pupil in ADA [4] — Amount (dol.)	Rank
1980	101,724	97,635	9,020	47,929	40,686	4,089	96,105	427	85,661	2,230	(X)
1985	146,976	141,013	9,533	69,107	62,373	5,963	139,382	591	127,230	3,483	(X)
1990	218,126	208,656	13,184	100,787	94,685	9,469	209,698	850	186,583	4,966	(X)
1995	288,501	273,255	18,764	129,958	124,533	15,246	276,584	1,051	242,995	5,957	(X)
1996	306,189	286,600	19,319	137,488	129,793	19,588	292,378	1,098	254,483	6,137	(X)
1997	325,007	303,400	19,965	148,184	135,251	21,607	310,719	1,153	269,824	6,401	(X)
1998	349,787	324,429	21,668	159,596	143,164	25,359	330,952	1,214	285,213	6,666	(X)
1999	370,735	345,901	23,583	170,606	151,711	24,835	350,539	1,271	301,380	7,011	(X)
2000	390,861	369,754	26,346	183,986	159,421	21,106	374,782	1,343	320,954	7,418	(X)
2001	425,201	396,294	27,840	198,560	169,894	28,907	399,176	1,418	341,199	7,807	(X)
2002	440,137	412,772	30,871	204,563	177,338	27,365	417,240	1,464	356,608	8,083	(X)
2003, total	**458,788**	**430,713**	**34,739**	**211,166**	**184,808**	**28,076**	**438,808**	**1,524**	**376,262**	**8,428**	**(X)**
Alabama	6,340	5,684	654	3,296	1,733	656	4,915	1,097	3,910	5,646	48
Alaska	1,414	1,260	158	801	302	154	1,389	2,165	1,286	11,234	6
Arizona	6,988	6,817	604	3,406	2,807	172	6,036	1,109	4,887	5,459	49
Arkansas	3,139	2,846	244	1,749	853	292	3,186	1,177	2,577	6,148	47
California	55,869	53,869	6,369	30,272	17,228	2,000	52,754	1,507	45,233	7,523	35
Colorado	6,782	6,185	370	2,544	3,272	597	6,746	1,499	5,585	8,010	28
Connecticut	7,185	7,174	367	2,903	3,904	11	7,185	2,078	6,507	12,014	1
Delaware	1,445	1,300	106	880	314	145	1,355	1,681	1,194	10,869	7
Dist. of Columbia .	861	861	148	-	713	-	1,130	1,986	902	15,068	(X)
Florida	21,418	18,884	2,019	8,245	8,620	2,535	20,481	1,227	16,244	6,753	42
Georgia	13,829	13,404	1,084	6,350	5,970	425	14,308	1,675	12,471	8,964	18
Hawaii	1,965	1,900	172	1,695	33	65	1,497	1,207	1,370	8,071	26
Idaho	1,700	1,650	150	1,000	500	50	1,700	1,266	1,585	6,778	41
Illinois	21,619	20,094	1,804	6,451	11,839	1,525	23,549	1,871	19,593	10,312	10
Indiana	9,938	9,676	547	5,125	4,003	263	10,090	1,639	8,267	8,859	19
Iowa	4,213	4,013	236	1,993	1,785	200	3,919	1,335	3,363	7,358	36
Kansas	4,240	3,971	320	2,320	1,331	269	4,027	1,485	3,630	8,687	21
Kentucky	4,927	4,919	499	2,955	1,465	8	4,983	1,218	4,556	8,010	27
Louisiana	6,056	5,533	733	2,710	2,091	523	5,907	1,320	5,045	7,564	34
Maine	2,095	1,980	133	880	968	115	2,095	1,618	1,895	10,038	11
Maryland	8,466	8,173	506	2,944	4,723	293	7,957	1,460	7,042	8,689	20
Massachusetts . . .	10,694	10,693	709	4,067	5,916	1	11,095	1,728	10,177	11,307	5
Michigan	16,302	15,976	886	10,922	4,168	326	17,962	1,788	14,249	9,038	17
Minnesota	9,512	8,321	467	6,210	1,644	1,191	9,266	1,844	7,307	9,267	15
Mississippi	3,432	3,282	490	1,790	1,001	150	3,238	1,129	2,862	6,226	46
Missouri	8,503	7,605	624	2,697	4,284	898	7,451	1,314	6,303	7,674	31
Montana	1,234	1,209	139	576	495	25	1,173	1,288	1,105	8,097	25
Nebraska	2,150	2,129	152	860	1,118	20	2,299	1,331	2,014	7,671	32
Nevada	3,645	3,164	179	847	2,138	481	3,139	1,448	2,264	6,716	43
New Hampshire . .	2,116	1,947	91	990	867	169	1,903	1,493	1,692	8,683	22
New Jersey	17,360	17,206	492	6,722	9,992	154	15,865	1,850	15,181	11,643	3
New Mexico.	2,847	2,650	401	1,917	332	197	2,791	1,507	2,351	8,193	23
New York	37,474	36,550	1,550	17,500	17,500	924	37,101	1,939	32,967	11,910	2
North Carolina . . .	10,828	10,044	774	7,231	2,038	784	10,422	1,255	8,812	7,200	38
North Dakota	905	823	106	302	414	83	799	1,261	670	6,879	40
Ohio	21,009	18,059	1,171	8,105	8,783	2,949	18,361	1,609	15,868	9,563	14
Oklahoma	4,430	4,097	524	2,279	1,293	333	4,188	1,200	3,826	6,577	44
Oregon	4,515	4,170	442	2,177	1,551	345	4,678	1,329	4,005	8,185	24
Pennsylvania	17,963	17,962	903	7,175	9,883	2	15,915	1,291	15,135	9,047	16
Rhode Island	1,454	1,454	57	545	851	-	1,635	1,530	1,562	10,562	9
South Carolina . . .	6,696	5,796	521	2,900	2,376	900	6,225	1,517	4,976	7,898	29
South Dakota	1,006	953	139	342	472	52	1,039	1,367	865	7,292	37
Tennessee	5,835	5,539	583	2,651	2,305	296	5,813	1,004	5,506	6,470	45
Texas	39,018	34,445	3,488	13,947	17,010	4,573	36,552	1,682	30,170	7,684	30
Utah	2,949	2,948	258	1,722	968	1	2,941	1,268	2,361	5,287	50
Vermont	1,145	1,126	72	803	251	19	1,131	1,834	991	11,526	4
Virginia	12,002	11,296	653	5,114	5,530	706	8,333	1,143	7,431	6,915	39
Washington	9,329	8,519	779	5,374	2,366	810	9,184	1,514	7,168	7,579	33
West Virginia	2,790	2,632	285	1,579	768	158	2,790	1,546	2,495	9,584	13
Wisconsin	10,166	8,965	498	4,812	3,655	1,202	9,345	1,718	7,948	9,598	12
Wyoming	987	958	84	489	385	29	963	1,931	855	10,704	8

- Represents or rounds to zero.   X Not applicable.   [1] Amount received by local education agencies from the sales of bonds and real property and equipment, loans, and proceeds from insurance adjustments.   [2] Includes interest on school debt and other current expenditures not shown separately.   [3] Based on U.S. Census Bureau estimated resident population, as of July 1, the previous year, except 1980, 1990, and 2000 population enumerated as of April 1.   [4] Average daily attendance.

Source: National Education Association, Washington, DC, Estimates of School Statistics Database (copyright).

158   Education

No. 242. Public Schools With Internet Access: 1995 to 2002

[In percent. As of fall. Excludes special education, vocational education, and alternative schools. Based on the Fast Response Survey System and subject to sampling error; see source for details]

School characteristic	Percent of schools with Internet access				Percent of instructional classrooms with Internet access				Students per instructional computer with Internet access, 2002	Schools with Internet available to students outside of regular school hours, 2002
	1995	1999	2000	2002	1995	1999	2000	2002		
Total [1]	50	95	98	99	8	64	77	92	5	53
Instructional level:										
Elementary	46	94	97	99	8	62	76	92	5	47
Secondary	65	98	100	100	8	67	79	91	4	73
Size of enrollment:										
Less than 300	39	96	96	96	9	71	83	91	3	49
300 to 999	52	94	98	100	8	64	78	93	5	50
1,000 or more	69	96	99	100	4	58	70	89	5	79
Percent minority enrollment:										
Less than 6 percent	52	95	98	97	9	74	85	93	4	52
6 to 20 percent	58	97	100	100	10	78	83	94	5	50
21 to 49 percent.	55	96	98	99	9	64	79	91	5	54
50 percent or more.	39	92	96	99	3	43	64	89	5	54
Percent of students eligible for free or reduced-price lunch:										
Less than 35 percent	60	95	99	98	9	73	82	93	5	52
35 to 49 percent.	48	98	99	100	6	69	81	90	5	54
50 to 74 percent.	41	96	97	100	6	61	77	91	5	50
75 percent or more.	31	89	94	99	3	38	60	89	6	56

[1] Includes combined schools.

Source: U.S. National Center for Education Statistics, *Internet Access in U.S. Public Schools and Classrooms: 1994-2002*, NCES 2004-011, October 2003.

No. 243. Computers for Student Instruction in Elementary and Secondary Schools: 2003-2004

[54,426 represents 54,426,000. Market Data Retrieval collects student use computer information in elementary and secondary schools nationwide through a comprehensive annual technology survey that utilizes both mail, telephone, and Internet data methods]

Level	Total schools	Total enroll-ment (1,000)	Number of com-puters [1] (1,000)	Students per com-puter	Schools with a wireless network (percent)	Schools with distance learning programs (percent) [2]		Schools with lap-top com-puters [3]	Schools with high speed Internet access (percent) [4]
						For stu-dents	For teachers		
U.S. total	113,878	54,426	14,071	3.9	33.8	21.2	23.6	48.8	79.2
Public schools, total.	90,665	49,039	12,951	3.8	36.9	25.0	27.6	53.1	84.4
Elementary	52,863	23,762	5,627	4.2	32.4	17.2	21.9	48.3	81.2
Middle/junior high.	14,074	9,417	2,468	3.8	42.5	21.7	25.6	58.2	88.9
Senior high.	16,605	13,491	4,152	3.2	46.3	42.9	40.4	62.4	90.7
K to 12/other.	7,123	2,369	704	3.4	37.8	44.9	42.8	56.6	83.4
Catholic schools, total	7,974	2,581	513	5.0	22.6	5.1	7.2	35.6	63.0
Elementary	6,600	1,888	352	5.4	19.7	3.2	6.7	32.8	59.4
Secondary	1,208	630	148	4.3	36.5	15.8	9.8	51.4	81.6
K to 12/other.	166	62	12	5.0	39.0	6.8	8.5	37.3	67.9
Other private schools, total .	15,239	2,806	607	4.6	18.8	6.1	6.7	25.8	50.0
Elementary	7,417	1,173	220	5.3	16.6	1.7	4.7	24.6	48.1
Secondary	1,274	259	79	3.3	34.5	18.4	7.3	45.1	67.6
K to 12/other.	6,548	1,374	308	4.5	19.4	10.4	9.5	24.0	49.4

[1] Includes estimates for schools not reporting number of computers.   [2] Distance learning programs as determined by respondents.   [3] For student instruction.   [4] Statistics based on responses to those indicating type of Internet connection. High speed includes Internet connection types: T1, T3, cable modem, digital satellite.

Source: Market Data Retrieval, Shelton, CT, unpublished data (copyright).

Education 159

No. 244. Computer and Internet Use by Children and Adolescents: 2001

[For persons 5 to 17 years old (53,013 represents 53,013,000). As of September. Based on the Current Population Survey; see source and Appendix III for details]

User characteristics	Number of children (1,000)	Percent using computers at school	Percent using computers at home	Home use activity				
				Word processing	Connect to the Internet	E-mail	Complete school assignments	Play games
Total [1]	**53,013**	**80.7**	**65.2**	**32.4**	**45.6**	**34.4**	**44.2**	**59.2**
Age:								
5 to 7 years old	11,990	68.2	56.4	9.4	22.6	9.5	13.8	54.0
8 to 10 years old	12,455	83.1	62.7	23.8	39.5	23.9	37.7	58.8
11 to 14 years old	16,493	85.2	68.6	42.1	54.1	43.3	56.6	62.9
15 to 17 years old	12,075	84.5	72.0	50.9	62.9	57.7	64.2	59.6
Sex:								
Female	25,835	81.6	65.7	34.7	45.7	36.1	45.4	58.3
Male	27,178	79.9	64.8	30.3	45.5	32.7	43.1	60.0
Race/ethnicity:								
White, non-Hispanic	33,433	83.5	76.9	39.3	55.2	42.7	52.1	70.2
Black, non-Hispanic	8,275	79.8	41.0	18.9	27.3	18.8	28.3	37.7
Hispanic	8,400	71.8	40.6	17.0	23.1	15.1	26.7	35.6
Asian, non-Hispanic	2,268	76.1	75.7	40.4	57.3	43.7	54.3	64.3
American Indian, non-Hispanic	637	83.0	54.1	20.7	31.7	20.8	32.0	51.7
Disability status:								
Disabled	626	71.5	58.4	23.5	29.8	21.1	34.4	54.4
Not disabled	45,416	81.4	65.7	33.0	45.9	35.0	45.0	59.8
Parent educational attainment:								
Less than high school credential	5,450	70.6	26.2	11.1	14.5	10.4	18.3	22.8
High school credential	13,611	80.2	53.7	22.8	35.1	27.3	35.5	49.3
Some college	15,665	82.0	70.7	34.3	48.7	36.0	47.5	64.6
Bachelor's degree	6,712	84.8	80.8	42.8	60.8	45.2	55.5	72.9
Graduate education	9,114	85.0	90.2	52.2	67.6	52.1	62.5	81.7
Family/household type:								
Two parent household	37,230	81.5	73.3	36.6	51.6	38.8	49.6	66.6
Male householder	2,715	78.6	53.8	26.7	37.8	29.8	37.9	48.5
Female householder	12,440	79.6	44.1	21.9	29.7	22.4	30.3	40.1
Other arrangement	628	63.6	51.1	19.1	36.3	26.9	30.4	43.8
Household language:								
Spanish-only	2,549	64.2	29.2	12.0	14.5	10.7	19.1	23.5
Not Spanish-only	50,464	81.6	67.0	33.5	47.1	35.6	45.5	61.0
Poverty status:								
In poverty	9,277	75.2	31.9	12.5	17.2	12.1	20.1	28.7
Not in poverty	36,904	83.1	75.2	38.7	53.7	40.7	51.4	68.5
Family income:								
Under $20,000	8,344	75.3	31.2	13.1	16.8	11.8	20.0	28.3
20,000 to 34,999	8,852	78.3	50.9	21.0	30.8	22.7	31.4	46.3
35,000 to 49,999	7,438	83.1	70.7	32.1	47.7	34.9	46.7	65.6
50,000 to 74,999	9,530	83.9	80.1	40.0	56.9	42.6	55.2	73.8
75,000 or more	12,018	85.4	89.3	52.2	69.3	54.0	63.7	79.8

[1] Includes those whose characteristics were not reported. Includes other home activities, not shown separately.

Source: U.S. National Center for Education Statistics, *Computer and Internet Use by Children and Adolescents in 2001*, NCES 2004-014, October 2003.

No. 245. Children and Youth With Disabilities Served by Selected Programs: 1991 to 2002

[For school year ending in year shown. In thousands. (4,361.8 represents 4,361,800). Excludes outlying areas. Through 1995, includes children with disabilities served under Chapter 1 of of ESEA (Elementary and Secondary Education Act), SOP (State Operated Programs); beginning 1995, Individuals with Disabilities Act (IDEA), Parts B and C]

Disability	1991	1995	1997	1998	1999	2000	2001	2002
Total	**4,361.8**	**4,907.5**	**5,230.8**	**5,397.0**	**5,539.8**	**5,678.0**	**5,774.3**	**5,867.2**
Specific learning disabilities	2,144.0	2,510.2	2,674.4	2,754.5	2,815.6	2,867.8	2,881.9	2,887.2
Speech impairments	987.8	1,020.3	1,048.7	1,063.6	1,074.1	1,087.8	1,093.5	1,093.6
Mental retardation	551.5	570.5	593.6	603.3	610.7	614.3	613.5	605.3
Emotional disturbance	390.8	428.0	446.3	454.4	462.8	469.8	474.4	477.6
Multiple disabilities	97.6	89.6	99.4	107.3	107.8	113.0	123.0	128.6
Hearing impairments	59.2	65.2	68.8	69.8	70.9	71.4	70.8	71.2
Orthopedically impairments	49.3	60.5	66.3	67.4	69.4	71.4	73.0	73.8
Other health impairments	56.3	107.1	161.4	191.1	221.8	255.3	294.0	338.7
Visually impaired	23.7	24.7	25.8	26.0	26.1	26.4	26.0	25.8
Autism	(NA)	22.7	34.4	42.5	54.1	66.0	79.6	97.9
Deaf-blind	1.5	1.3	1.2	1.3	1.6	1.7	1.3	1.6
Traumatic brain injury	(NA)	7.3	10.5	11.9	13.0	13.9	14.9	20.7
Developmental delay [1]	(X)	(X)	(X)	3.8	11.9	19.3	28.6	45.1

NA Not available.   X Not applicable.   [1] States had the option of reporting children ages 3 to 9 under developmental delay beginning 1997-98.

Source: U.S. Department of Education, Office of Special Education Programs, Data Analysis System (DANS).

No. 246. Private Schools: 1999-2000

[5,163 represents 5,163,000. Based on the Private School Survey, conducted every 2 years; see source for details. For composition of regions, see map, inside front cover]

Characteristic	Schools				Students (1,000)				Teachers (1,000) [1]			
	Num-ber	Ele-mentary	Sec-ondary	Com-bined	Num-ber	Ele-mentary	Sec-ondary	Com-bined	Num-ber	Ele-mentary	Sec-ondary	Com-bined
Total	**27,223**	**16,530**	**2,538**	**8,155**	**5,163**	**2,831**	**807**	**1,525**	**395**	**188**	**63**	**145**
School type:												
Catholic.	8,102	6,707	1,114	282	2,511	1,815	608	89	150	101	41	8
Parochial	4,607	4,352	193	63	1,307	1,209	80	18	72	66	6	1
Diocesan	2,598	2,053	481	64	835	543	274	19	49	30	18	1
Private.	897	302	440	155	368	63	254	52	28	5	18	5
Other religious . . .	13,232	6,843	718	5,672	1,844	750	112	981	153	58	11	84
Conservative Christian	4,989	1,789	225	2,975	773	230	29	514	60	17	2	41
Affiliated.	3,531	2,200	287	1,044	554	275	52	226	47	23	5	19
Unaffiliated	4,712	2,853	206	1,653	517	245	31	240	45	18	3	23
Nonsectarian	5,889	2,981	707	2,201	808	267	87	455	93	29	11	53
Regular	2,494	1,396	262	837	547	163	56	328	58	16	7	35
Special emphasis	2,131	1,387	257	487	175	92	22	61	20	11	2	7
Special education	1,264	198	188	878	86	11	9	66	15	2	1	11
Program emphasis:												
Regular el/sec . . .	22,263	14,278	1,963	6,021	4,752	2,674	751	1,327	346	170	57	119
Montessori.	1,190	1,045	(B)	139	77	63	(B)	13	8	7	(B)	1
Special program emphasis	606	280	111	216	111	36	21	54	11	4	2	5
Special education .	1,409	232	202	975	95	13	10	72	16	2	2	12
Vocational/tech . . .	(B)	(B)	(B)	(B)	(B)	(B)	(B)	(B)	(B)	(B)	(B)	(B)
Alternative	1,617	579	254	784	120	39	23	58	13	4	2	6
Early childhood. . .	133	116	-	(B)	6	5	-	(B)	1	(B)	-	(B)
Size:												
Less than 150 . . .	15,303	8,961	1,103	5,240	912	557	63	293	98	53	8	37
150 to 299.	6,571	4,811	429	1,332	1,424	1,042	94	288	102	67	9	27
300 to 499.	3,219	2,019	419	782	1,229	768	164	297	84	45	13	26
500 to 749.	1,352	629	285	440	805	366	173	267	54	18	12	24
750 or more.	778	110	305	362	792	99	314	380	57	5	20	32
Region:												
Northeast	6,452	4,049	776	1,628	1,295	750	264	281	104	49	22	32
Midwest	6,991	5,001	622	1,367	1,345	892	244	210	91	55	17	19
South	8,240	4,131	594	3,515	1,576	652	159	764	131	49	13	70
West.	5,540	3,349	546	1,645	947	537	140	269	69	35	10	24

- Represents zero.　B Does not meet standard of reliability or precision.　[1] Full time equivalents.

Source: U.S. National Center for Education Statistics, *Private School Universe Survey*, NCES 2001-330, August 2001. See Internet site <http://nces.ed.gov/surveys/pss/>

No. 247. Private Elementary and Secondary School Teachers— Selected Characteristics: 1999-2000

[For school year (87 represents 87,000). Based on School and Staffing Survey and subject to sampling error; for details, see source Web site at <http://nces.ed.gov/surveys/sass/>. Data revised since originally published. See Table 235 for similar data on public school teachers]

Characteristic	Unit	Age				Sex		Race/ethnicity		
		Under 30 years old	30 to 39 years old	40 to 49 years old	Over 50 years old	Male	Fe-male	White [1]	Black [1]	His-panic
Total teachers [2] . . .	**1,000 . . .**	**87**	**101**	**131**	**131**	**107**	**342**	**402**	**17**	**21**
Highest degree held:										
Bachelor's	Percent .	75.7	58.9	56.0	45.8	48.2	60.4	57.8	58.9	54.6
Master's	Percent .	13.9	28.0	32.4	40.9	38.5	27.8	31.0	18.4	26.4
Education specialist .	Percent .	0.6	2.2	3.4	5.1	3.7	2.9	3.0	2.5	3.9
Doctorate	Percent .	0.3	1.6	1.3	3.4	4.9	0.8	1.8	0.7	1.5
Full-time teaching experience:										
Less than 3 years . .	Percent .	57.6	24.4	17.3	8.1	25.3	23.5	23.2	32.3	29.7
3 to 9 years	Percent .	42.1	46.5	30.6	12.3	28.2	31.9	31.0	30.1	33.0
10 to 20 years.	Percent .	(NA)	29.2	36.7	34.1	22.7	28.6	27.4	22.5	28.7
20 years or more . . .	Percent .	(NA)	(NA)	15.4	46.2	23.8	15.9	18.5	15.1	8.7
Full-time teachers . . .	1,000 . . .	76	81	104	105	86	280	327	14	17
Earned income	Dol.	25,289	29,841	29,638	33,278	36,524	27,771	29,942	27,593	29,508
Salary	Dol.	22,299	26,828	27,229	31,063	31,438	25,922	27,340	24,374	27,162

NA Not available.　[1] Non-Hispanic.　[2] Includes teachers with no degrees and associates degrees, not shown separately.

Source: U.S. National Center for Education Statistics, *Digest of Education Statistics, 2002*; and unpublished data.

Education　161

No. 248. SAT Scores and Characteristics of College-Bound Seniors: 1967 to 2003

[For school year ending in year shown. Data are for the SAT I: Reasoning Tests. SAT I: Reasoning Test replaced the SAT in March 1994. Scores between the two tests have been equated to the same 200-800 scale and are thus comparable. Scores for 1995 and prior years have been recentered and revised]

Type of test and characteristic	Unit	1967	1970	1975	1980	1985	1990	1995	2000	2002	2003
AVERAGE TEST SCORES [1]											
Verbal, total [2]	Point . . .	543	537	512	502	509	500	504	505	504	507
Male	Point . . .	540	536	515	506	514	505	505	507	507	512
Female.	Point . . .	545	538	509	498	503	496	502	504	502	503
Math, total [2].	Point . . .	516	512	498	492	500	501	506	514	516	519
Male	Point . . .	535	531	518	515	522	521	525	533	534	537
Female.	Point . . .	495	493	479	473	480	483	490	498	500	503
PARTICIPANTS											
Total [3].	1,000 . . .	(NA)	(NA)	996	922	977	1,026	1,068	1,260	1,328	1,406
Male	Percent .	(NA)	(NA)	49.9	48.2	48.3	47.8	46.4	46.2	46.4	46.4
White	Percent .	(NA)	(NA)	86.0	82.1	81.0	73.0	69.2	66.4	65.0	63.8
Black	Percent .	(NA)	(NA)	7.9	9.1	7.5	10.0	10.7	11.2	11.4	12
Obtaining scores [1] of—											
600 or above:											
Verbal	Percent .	(NA)	(NA)	(NA)	(NA)	(NA)	20.3	21.9	21.1	21.2	21.9
Math	Percent .	(NA)	(NA)	(NA)	(NA)	(NA)	20.4	23.4	24.2	25.3	26.2
Below 400:											
Verbal	Percent .	(NA)	(NA)	(NA)	(NA)	(NA)	17.3	16.4	15.9	16.3	15.3
Math	Percent .	(NA)	(NA)	(NA)	(NA)	(NA)	15.8	16.0	14.7	14.4	14.2
Selected intended area of study:											
Business and commerce	Percent .	(NA)	(NA)	11.5	18.6	21.0	20.9	13.3	13.6	13.7	13.4
Engineering	Percent .	(NA)	(NA)	6.7	11.1	11.7	10.2	8.8	8.5	8.9	9.3
Social science	Percent .	(NA)	(NA)	7.7	7.8	7.5	12.6	11.6	10.6	10.1	10.1
Education	Percent .	(NA)	(NA)	9.1	6.1	4.7	7.5	8.1	8.8	8.6	8.6

NA Not available.   [1] Minimum score 200; maximum score, 800.   [2] 1967 and 1970 are estimates based on total number of persons taking SAT.   [3] 996 represents 996,000.

Source: The College Entrance Examination Board, New York, NY, *College Bound Seniors*, (copyright). All rights reserved. See Internet site <http://www.collegeboard.com>

No. 249. ACT Program Scores and Characteristics of College-Bound Students: 1970 to 2003

[For academic year ending in year shown. Except as indicated, test scores and characteristics of college-bound students. Through 1980, data based on 10 percent sample; thereafter, based on all ACT tested graduating seniors]

Type of test and characteristic	Unit	1970	1975	1980	1985	1990 [1]	1995 [1]	2000 [1]	2001 [1]	2002 [1]	2003 [1]
TEST SCORES [2]											
Composite	Point . . .	19.9	18.6	18.5	18.6	20.6	20.8	21.0	21.0	20.8	20.8
Male.	Point . . .	20.3	19.5	19.3	19.4	21.0	21.0	21.2	21.1	20.9	21.0
Female	Point . . .	19.4	17.8	17.9	17.9	20.3	20.7	20.9	20.9	20.7	20.8
English.	Point . . .	18.5	17.7	17.9	18.1	20.5	20.2	20.5	20.5	20.2	20.3
Male.	Point . . .	17.6	17.1	17.3	17.6	20.1	19.8	20.0	20.0	19.7	19.8
Female	Point . . .	19.4	18.3	18.3	18.6	20.9	20.6	20.9	20.8	20.6	20.7
Math	Point . . .	20.0	17.6	17.4	17.2	19.9	20.2	20.7	20.7	20.6	20.6
Male.	Point . . .	21.1	19.3	18.9	18.6	20.7	20.9	21.4	21.4	21.2	21.2
Female	Point . . .	18.8	16.2	16.2	16.0	19.3	19.7	20.2	20.2	20.4	20.1
Reading [3]	Point . . .	19.7	17.4	17.2	17.4	(NA)	21.3	21.4	21.3	21.1	21.2
Male.	Point . . .	20.3	18.7	18.2	18.3	(NA)	21.1	21.2	21.1	20.9	21.0
Female	Point . . .	19.0	16.4	16.4	16.6	(NA)	21.4	21.5	21.5	21.3	21.4
Science reasoning [4]	Point . . .	20.8	21.1	21.1	21.2	(NA)	21.0	21.0	21.0	20.8	20.8
Male.	Point . . .	21.6	22.4	22.4	22.6	(NA)	21.6	21.6	21.6	21.3	21.3
Female	Point . . .	20.0	20.0	20.0	20.0	(NA)	20.5	20.6	20.6	20.4	20.4
PARTICIPANTS [5]											
Total [6].	1,000 . . .	788	714	822	739	817	945	1,065	1,070	1,116	1,175
Male	Percent .	52	46	45	46	46	44	43	43	44	44
White	Percent .	(NA)	77	83	82	79	75	76	75	74	73
Black	Percent .	4	7	8	8	9	10	11	11	12	12
Obtaining composite scores of—[7]											
27 or above	Percent .	14	14	13	14	12	13	14	14	13	14
18 or below	Percent .	21	33	33	32	35	34	32	33	35	35
Planned educational major:											
Business [8]	Percent .	18	21	20	21	20	14	11	11	11	11
Engineering	Percent .	8	6	8	9	9	9	6	6	6	5
Social science [9]	Percent .	10	6	6	7	10	9	8	9	9	9
Education	Percent .	16	12	9	6	8	9	9	9	9	9

NA Not available.   [1] Beginning 1990, not comparable with previous years because a new version of the ACT was introduced. Estimated average composite scores for prior years: 1989, 20.6; 1988, 1987, and 1986, 20.8.   [2] Minimum score, 1; maximum score, 36.   [3] Prior to 1990, social studies; data not comparable with previous years.   [4] Prior to 1990, natural sciences; data not comparable with previous years.   [5] Beginning 1985, data are for seniors who graduated in year shown and had taken the ACT in their junior or senior years. Data by race are for those responding to the race question.   [6] 788 represents 788,000.   [7] Prior to 1990, 26 or above and 15 or below.   [8] Includes political and persuasive (e.g. sales) fields through 1975; 1980 and 1985 business and commerce; thereafter, business and management and business and office.   [9] Includes religion through 1975.

Source: ACT, Inc., Iowa City, IA, *High School Profile Report*, annual.

No. 250. Proficiency Test Scores for Selected Subjects by Characteristic: 1977 to 2001

[Based on The National Assessment of Educational Progress (NAEP) Tests which are administered to a representative sample of students in public and private schools. Reading, writing, mathematics and science based on NAEP long-term trend assessments. Test scores can range from 0 to 500, except as indicated. For details, see source]

Test and year	Sex			Race			Parental education				
						His-panic origin	Less than high school	High school	More than high school		
	Total	Male	Fe-male	White [1]	Black [1]				Total	Some college	College gradu-ate
READING											
9 year olds:											
1979-80........	215	210	220	221	189	190	194	213	226	(NA)	(NA)
1987-88........	212	208	216	218	189	194	193	211	220	(NA)	(NA)
1998-99........	212	209	215	221	186	193	199	206	220	(NA)	(NA)
13 year olds:											
1979-80........	259	254	263	264	233	237	239	254	271	(NA)	(NA)
1987-88........	258	252	263	261	243	240	247	253	265	(NA)	(NA)
1998-99........	259	254	265	267	238	244	238	251	270	(NA)	(NA)
17 year olds:											
1979-80........	286	282	289	293	243	261	262	278	299	(NA)	(NA)
1987-88........	290	286	294	295	274	271	267	282	300	(NA)	(NA)
1998-99........	288	282	295	295	264	271	265	274	298	(NA)	(NA)
WRITING [2]											
4th graders:											
1983-84........	204	201	208	211	182	189	179	192	217	208	218
1987-88........	206	199	213	215	173	190	194	199	212	211	212
1995-96........	207	200	214	216	182	191	190	203	(NA)	205	214
8th graders:											
1983-84........	267	258	276	272	247	247	258	261	276	271	278
1987-88........	264	254	274	269	246	250	254	258	271	275	271
1995-96........	264	251	276	271	242	246	245	258	(NA)	270	274
11th graders:											
1983-84........	290	281	299	297	270	259	274	284	299	298	300
1987-88........	291	282	299	296	275	274	276	285	298	296	299
1995-96........	283	275	292	289	267	269	260	275	(NA)	287	291
MATHEMATICS											
9 year olds:											
1977-78........	219	217	220	224	192	203	200	219	231	230	231
1985-86........	222	222	222	227	202	205	201	218	231	229	231
1998-99........	232	233	231	239	211	213	214	224	(NA)	237	240
13 year olds:											
1977-78........	264	264	265	272	230	238	245	263	280	273	284
1985-86........	269	270	268	274	249	254	252	263	278	274	280
1998-99........	276	277	275	283	251	259	256	264	(NA)	279	286
17 year olds:											
1977-78........	300	304	297	306	268	276	280	294	313	305	317
1985-86........	302	305	299	308	279	283	279	293	310	305	314
1998-99........	308	310	307	315	283	293	289	299	(NA)	308	317
SCIENCE											
9 year olds:											
1976-77........	220	222	218	230	175	192	199	223	233	237	232
1985-86........	224	227	221	232	196	199	204	220	235	236	235
1998-99........	229	231	228	240	199	206	213	218	(NA)	234	237
13 year olds:											
1976-77........	247	251	244	256	208	213	224	245	264	260	266
1985-86........	251	256	247	259	222	226	229	245	262	258	264
1998-99........	256	259	253	266	227	227	229	243	(NA)	261	268
17 year olds:											
1976-77........	290	297	282	298	240	262	265	284	304	296	309
1985-86........	289	295	282	298	253	259	258	277	300	295	304
1998-99........	295	300	291	306	254	276	264	281	(NA)	297	307
HISTORY, 2001											
4th graders........	209	209	209	220	188	186	177	197	(NA)	214	216
8th graders........	262	264	261	271	243	243	241	251	(NA)	264	270
12th graders.......	287	288	286	292	269	274	263	276	(NA)	287	296
GEOGRAPHY, 2001											
4th graders........	209	212	207	222	181	184	186	197	(NA)	216	216
8th graders........	262	264	260	273	234	240	238	250	(NA)	265	272
12th graders.......	285	287	282	291	260	270	263	274	(NA)	286	294
CIVICS, 1997-98 [3]											
4th graders........	150	149	151	159	132	126	124	153	(NA)	150	153
8th graders........	150	148	152	159	133	127	123	144	(NA)	143	160
12th graders.......	150	148	152	158	131	130	124	140	(NA)	145	160

NA Not available.   [1] Non-Hispanic.   [2] Writing scores revised from previous years; previous writing scores were recorded on a 0 to 400 rather than 0 to 500 scale.   [3] Civics uses a scale of 0 to 300.

Source: U.S. National Center for Education Statistics, *Digest of Education Statistics*, annual, and *NAEP 1998 Civics Report Card for the Nation* ; and *NAEP 2001 Geography* and *History Report Card for the Nation.*

Education   163

No. 251. Advanced Placement Program—Summary: 2002 and 2003

[Includes exams taken by candidates abroad. In 2003, this represents 32,024 examinations taken by 19,067 students in 729 schools abroad. Minus sign (-) indicates decrease]

Item	Schools repre-sented, 2003	Program total Exams taken 2002	Program total Exams taken 2003	Percent change, 2002-03	2003 Grade level of test taker 10th grade	2003 Grade level of test taker 11th grade	2003 Grade level of test taker 12th grade	2003 Sex of test taker Male	2003 Sex of test taker Female
Exams taken, total [1]	(X)	1,578,412	1,737,231	10	122,778	609,618	946,524	791,597	945,634
By subject area:									
Art History	1,048	12,728	13,720	8	1,214	3,840	8,251	4,723	8,997
Biology	7,167	97,762	103,944	6	8,512	38,355	53,316	43,078	60,866
Calculus AB	10,484	157,524	166,821	6	1,770	25,156	135,180	87,807	79,014
Calculus BC	3,710	41,785	45,973	10	844	8,760	35,195	27,780	18,193
Chemistry.	5,680	61,584	65,698	7	3,595	33,139	27,119	35,732	29,966
Computer Science—A . .	2,082	15,660	14,674	-6	2,045	5,732	6,325	12,356	2,318
Computer Science—AB	1,374	7,799	7,071	-9	673	2,854	3,325	6,331	740
Economics-Macro	2,201	32,184	38,177	19	333	3,910	32,734	21,006	17,171
Economics-Micro	1,871	23,108	25,667	11	434	3,201	21,124	14,820	10,847
English Language/Composition	6,557	156,193	175,860	13	1,904	134,342	34,677	65,839	110,021
English Literature/Composition	10,871	215,313	229,367	7	295	14,773	208,371	83,492	145,875
Environmental Science . .	1,568	24,376	29,906	23	855	9,898	18,004	12,954	16,952
European History	3,643	68,876	73,807	7	36,403	10,852	24,045	34,957	38,850
French Language.	3,216	17,372	18,496	6	943	4,938	11,814	5,534	12,962
French Literature	412	1,697	1,862	10	68	410	1,337	587	1,275
German Language	1,128	4,171	3,973	-5	235	786	2,739	1,923	2,050
Government and Politics—Comparative . .	1,054	10,461	12,001	15	880	1,785	8,989	6,279	5,722
Government and Politics—U.S.	4,977	90,937	104,636	15	4,189	10,017	87,301	49,561	55,075
Human Geography. . . .	473	5,286	7,329	39	1,818	1,439	2,448	3,452	3,877
Latin—Literature	451	2,857	2,703	-5	136	1,082	1,421	1,313	1,390
Latin—Vergil	626	3,740	3,942	5	284	1,704	1,833	2,060	1,882
Music Theory	1,617	6,859	7,894	15	603	2,449	4,562	4,199	3,695
Physics B	3,534	37,447	40,926	9	819	13,985	24,885	26,945	13,981
Physics—Electricity and Magnetism	1,407	9,439	10,019	6	72	928	8,727	7,709	2,310
Physics—Mechanics. . . .	2,341	19,252	20,491	6	149	2,457	17,353	15,115	5,376
Psychology.	2,810	51,831	62,666	21	1,316	18,047	41,410	21,404	41,262
Spanish Language	5,544	74,240	83,811	13	8,787	28,955	40,391	29,574	54,237
Spanish Literature	1,117	10,895	10,848	-	764	3,301	6,299	3,400	7,448
Statistics	3,356	49,824	58,230	17	2,048	11,376	43,121	29,078	29,152
Studio Art, Drawing	2,372	9,972	10,642	7	181	1,853	8,166	3,581	7,061
Studio Art, 2D Design . . .	1,796	7,170	7,601	6	123	1,279	5,911	2,374	5,227
Studio Art, 3D Design . . .	687	1,358	1,491	-	26	214	1,187	568	923
U.S. History	9,202	227,757	242,699	7	15,265	203,629	16,370	110,385	132,314
World History	1,474	20,955	34,286	64	25,195	4,172	2,594	15,681	18,605
Candidates taking exams [1] .	(X)	937,951	1,017,396	8	110,178	385,543	481,818	447,906	569,490

- Represents or rounds to zero.   X Not applicable.   [1] Includes candidates and exams taken in other grades not shown separately. Source: The College Entrance Examination Board, New York, NY, *National Summary Report, 2003* (copyright). *All rights reserved.* See Internet site <http://www.collegeboard.com>

No. 252. Foreign Language Enrollment in Public High Schools: 1970 to 2000

[In thousands (13,301.9 represents 13,301,900), except percent. As of fall, for grades 9 through 12]

Language	1970	1974	1978	1982	1985	1990	1994	2000
Total enrollment.	13,301.9	13,648.9	13,941.4	12,879.3	12,466.5	11,099.6	11,847.5	13,457.8
Enrolled in all foreign languages . . .	3,779.3	3,294.5	3,200.1	2,909.8	4,028.9	4,256.9	5,001.9	5,899.4
Percent of all students.	28.4	24.1	23.0	22.6	32.3	38.4	42.2	43.8
Enrolled in modern foreign languages [1] . .	3,514.1	3,127.3	3,048.3	2,740.2	3,852.0	4,093.0	4,813.0	5,721.9
Spanish	1,810.8	1,678.1	1,631.4	1,562.8	2,334.4	2,611.4	3,219.8	4,057.6
French.	1,230.7	977.9	856.0	858.0	1,133.7	1,089.4	1,105.9	1,075.4
German	410.5	393.0	330.6	266.9	312.2	295.4	326.0	283.3
Italian	27.3	40.2	45.5	44.1	47.3	40.4	43.8	64.1
Japanese	(NA)	(NA)	(NA)	9.2	8.6	25.1	42.3	50.9
Russian	20.2	15.1	8.8	5.7	6.4	16.5	16.4	10.6
Percent of all students [1]	26.4	22.9	21.9	21.3	30.9	36.9	40.6	42.5
Spanish	13.6	12.3	11.7	12.1	18.7	23.5	27.2	30.2
French	9.3	7.2	6.1	6.7	9.1	9.8	9.3	8.0
German	3.1	2.9	2.4	2.1	2.5	2.7	2.8	2.1
Italian	0.2	0.3	0.3	0.3	0.4	0.4	0.4	0.5
Japanese	(NA)	(NA)	(NA)	0.1	0.1	0.2	0.4	0.4
Russian	0.2	0.1	0.1	(Z)	0.1	0.2	0.1	0.1

NA Not available.   Z Less than 0.05 percent.   [1] Includes other foreign languages, not shown separately.

Source: The American Council on the Teaching of Foreign Languages, Yonkers, NY, *Foreign Language Enrollments in Public Secondary Schools, fall 1994* and *fall 2000*.

No. 253. Public High School Graduates by State: 1980 to 2003

[In thousands (2,747.7 represents 2,747,700). For school year ending in year shown]

State	1980	1990	2000	2003, est.	State	1980	1990	2000	2003, est.
United States	2,747.7	2,320.3	2,553.8	2,684.9	Missouri	62.3	49.0	52.8	54.9
Alabama	45.2	40.5	37.8	36.9	Montana	12.1	9.4	10.9	10.7
Alaska	5.2	5.4	6.6	7.2	Nebraska	22.4	17.7	20.1	20.3
Arizona	28.6	32.1	38.3	47.6	Nevada	8.5	9.5	14.6	12.9
Arkansas	29.1	26.5	27.3	27.4	New Hampshire	11.7	10.8	11.8	13.0
California	249.2	236.3	309.9	331.7					
Colorado	36.8	33.0	38.9	41.7	New Jersey	94.6	69.8	74.4	82.3
Connecticut	37.7	27.9	31.6	33.0	New Mexico	18.4	14.9	18.0	17.7
Delaware	7.6	5.6	6.1	6.8	New York	204.1	143.3	141.7	146.0
District of Columbia	5.0	3.6	2.7	2.6	North Carolina	70.9	64.8	62.1	68.3
Florida	87.3	88.9	106.7	120.3	North Dakota	9.9	7.7	8.6	8.0
Georgia	61.6	56.6	62.6	67.1	Ohio	144.2	114.5	111.7	113.6
Hawaii	11.5	10.3	10.4	10.0	Oklahoma	39.3	35.6	37.6	36.3
Idaho	13.2	12.0	16.2	15.9	Oregon	29.9	25.5	30.2	31.6
Illinois	135.6	108.1	111.8	120.6	Pennsylvania	146.5	110.5	114.0	119.0
Indiana	73.1	60.0	57.0	56.5	Rhode Island	10.9	7.8	8.5	9.1
Iowa	43.4	31.8	33.9	34.3	South Carolina	38.7	32.5	31.6	33.1
Kansas	30.9	25.4	29.1	29.9	South Dakota	10.7	7.7	9.3	8.8
Kentucky	41.2	38.0	36.8	34.4	Tennessee	49.8	46.1	41.6	43.6
Louisiana	46.3	36.1	38.4	37.7	Texas	171.4	172.5	212.9	228.5
Maine	15.4	13.8	12.2	13.0	Utah	20.0	21.2	32.5	30.3
Maryland	54.3	41.6	47.8	51.5	Vermont	6.7	6.1	6.7	6.8
Massachusetts	73.8	55.9	53.0	55.3	Virginia	66.6	60.6	65.6	71.6
Michigan	124.3	93.8	97.7	110.6	Washington	50.4	45.9	57.6	58.5
Minnesota	64.9	49.1	57.4	60.0	West Virginia	23.4	21.9	19.4	17.2
Mississippi	27.6	25.2	24.2	23.4	Wisconsin	69.3	52.0	58.5	61.7
					Wyoming	6.1	5.8	6.5	6.0

Source: U.S. National Center for Education Statistics, *Digest of Education Statistics*, annual.

No. 254. High School Dropouts by Race and Hispanic Origin: 1975 to 2002

[In percent. As of October] Based on the Current Population Survey. See text, Section 1 and Appendix III)

Item	1975	1980	1985	1990 [1]	1995	1996	1997	1998	1999	2000	2001	2002
EVENT DROPOUTS [2]												
Total [3]	5.8	6.0	5.2	4.0	5.4	4.7	4.3	4.4	4.7	4.5	4.7	3.3
White	5.4	5.6	4.8	3.8	5.1	4.5	4.2	4.4	4.4	4.3	4.6	3.0
Male	5.0	6.4	4.9	4.1	5.4	4.8	4.9	4.4	4.1	4.7	5.3	3.0
Female	5.8	4.9	4.7	3.5	4.8	4.1	3.5	4.4	4.7	4.0	3.8	3.0
Black	8.7	8.3	7.7	5.1	6.1	6.3	4.8	5.0	6.0	5.6	5.7	4.4
Male	8.3	8.0	8.3	4.1	7.9	4.6	4.1	4.6	5.2	7.6	6.1	5.1
Female	9.0	8.5	7.2	6.0	4.4	7.8	5.7	5.5	6.8	3.8	5.4	3.8
Hispanic [4]	10.9	11.5	9.7	8.0	11.6	8.4	8.6	8.4	7.1	6.8	8.1	5.3
Male	10.1	16.9	9.3	8.7	10.9	9.2	10.4	8.6	6.9	7.1	7.6	6.2
Female	11.6	6.9	9.8	7.2	12.5	7.6	6.7	8.2	7.3	6.5	8.7	4.4
STATUS DROPOUTS [5]												
Total [3]	15.6	15.6	13.9	13.6	13.9	12.8	13.0	13.9	13.1	12.4	13.0	12.3
White	13.9	14.4	13.5	13.5	13.6	12.5	12.4	13.7	12.8	12.2	13.4	12.2
Male	13.5	15.7	14.7	14.2	14.3	12.9	13.8	15.7	13.9	13.5	15.3	13.7
Female	14.2	13.2	13.2	12.3	13.0	12.1	10.9	11.7	11.8	10.9	11.4	10.6
Black	27.3	23.5	17.6	15.1	14.4	16.0	16.7	17.1	16.0	15.3	13.8	14.6
Male	27.8	26.0	18.8	13.6	14.2	17.4	17.5	20.5	16.3	17.4	16.9	16.9
Female	26.9	21.5	16.6	16.2	14.6	14.7	16.1	14.3	15.7	13.5	11.0	12.5
Hispanic [4]	34.9	40.3	31.5	37.3	34.7	34.5	30.6	34.4	33.9	32.3	31.7	30.1
Male	32.6	42.6	35.8	39.8	34.2	36.2	33.2	39.7	36.4	36.8	37.1	33.8
Female	36.8	38.1	27.0	34.5	35.4	32.7	27.6	28.6	31.1	27.3	25.5	25.6

[1] Beginning 1990 reflects new editing procedures for cases with missing data on school enrollment. [2] Percent of students who drop out in a single year without completing high school. For grades 10 to 12. [3] Includes other races, not shown separately. [4] Persons of Hispanic origin may be of any race. [5] Percent of the population who have not completed high school and are not enrolled, regardless of when they dropped out. For persons 18 to 24 years old.

Source: U.S. Census Bureau, Current Population Reports, PPL-148; and earlier PPL and P-20 reports; and data published on the Internet. See Internet site <http://www.census.gov/population/www/socdemo/school.html>

Education 165

High School Dropouts by Age, Race, and Hispanic Origin: 1980 to 2002

[As of October (5,212 represents 5,212,000). For persons 14 to 24 years old. See Table 257 for definition of dropouts]

Age and race	Number of dropouts (1,000)					Percent of population				
	1980	1990	1995	2000	2002	1980	1990	1995	2000	2002
Total dropouts [1][2]...	5,212	3,854	3,963	3,883	3,840	12.0	10.1	9.9	9.1	8.8
16 to 17 years	709	418	406	460	346	8.8	6.3	5.4	5.8	4.3
18 to 21 years	2,578	1,921	1,980	2,005	1,849	15.8	13.4	14.2	12.9	11.8
22 to 24 years	1,798	1,458	1,491	1,310	1,526	15.2	13.8	13.6	11.8	13.0
White [2]	4,169	3,127	3,098	3,065	2,987	11.3	10.1	9.7	9.1	8.7
16 to 17 years	619	334	314	366	253	9.2	6.4	5.4	5.8	4.0
18 to 21 years	2,032	1,516	1,530	1,558	1,419	14.7	13.1	13.8	12.6	11.4
22 to 24 years	1,416	1,235	1,181	1,040	1,222	14.0	14.0	13.4	11.7	13.2
Black [2]	934	611	605	705	660	16.0	10.9	10.0	10.9	10.1
16 to 17 years	80	73	70	84	69	6.9	6.9	5.8	7.0	5.3
18 to 21 years	486	345	328	383	332	23.0	16.0	15.8	16.0	14.7
22 to 24 years	346	185	194	232	239	24.0	13.5	12.5	14.3	14.3
Hispanic [2][3]	919	1,122	1,355	1,499	1,597	29.5	26.8	24.7	23.5	21.5
16 to 17 years	92	89	94	121	93	16.6	12.9	10.7	11.0	7.7
18 to 21 years	470	502	652	733	725	40.3	32.9	29.9	30.0	27.2
22 to 24 years	323	523	598	602	755	40.6	42.8	37.4	35.5	33.5

[1] Includes other groups not shown separately.   [2] Includes persons 14 to 15 years, not shown separately.   [3] Persons of Hispanic origin may be of any race.
Source: U.S. Census Bureau, *Current Population Reports*, PPL-148; and earlier PPL and P-20 reports; and data published on the Internet. See Internet site <http://www.census.gov/population/www/socdemo/school.html>.

No. 256. Enrollment Status by Race, Hispanic Origin, and Sex: 1975 and 2002

[As of October (15,693 represents 15,693,000). For persons 18 to 21 years old. For the civilian noninstitutional population. Based on the Current Population Survey; see text, Section 1, and Appendix III]

Characteristic	Total persons 18 to 21 years old (1,000)		Percent distribution							
			Enrolled in high school		High school graduates				Not high school graduates	
					Total		In college			
	1975	2002	1975	2002	1975	2002	1975	2002	1975	2002
Total [1]	15,693	15,638	5.7	10.1	78.0	78.0	33.5	45.4	16.3	11.8
White	13,448	12,416	4.7	9.6	80.6	78.8	34.6	45.9	14.7	11.4
Black	1,997	2,255	12.5	13.3	60.4	72.0	24.9	37.6	27.0	14.7
Hispanic [2]	899	2,665	12.0	12.5	57.2	60.3	24.4	24.9	30.8	27.2
Male [1]	7,584	7,935	7.4	12	76.6	74.7	35.4	41.3	15.9	13.2
White	6,545	6,308	6.2	11.4	79.7	76.0	36.9	41.8	14.1	12.4
Black	911	1,112	15.9	16	55.0	65.7	23.9	31.8	29.0	18.2
Hispanic [2]	416	1,441	17.3	15.1	54.6	55.7	25.2	21.3	27.9	29.3
Female [1]	8,109	7,703	4.2	8.2	79.2	81.3	31.8	49.7	16.6	10.5
White	6,903	6,107	3.2	7.8	81.4	81.8	32.4	50.2	15.3	10.4
Black	1,085	1,144	9.7	10.5	65.0	77.9	25.8	43.2	25.4	11.5
Hispanic [2]	484	1,224	7.6	9.4	59.3	65.8	23.6	29.1	33.1	24.8

[1] Includes other races not shown separately.   [2] Persons of Hispanic origin may be of any race.
Source: U.S. Census Bureau, Current Population Reports, PPL-148; and earlier PPL and P-20 reports; and data published on the Internet. See Internet site <http://www.census.gov/population/www/socdemo/school.html>

No. 257. Employment Status of High School Graduates and School Dropouts: 1980 to 2003

[In thousands (11,622 represents 11,622,000), except percent. As of October. For civilian noninstitutional population 16 to 24 years old. Based on Current Population Survey; see text, Section 1, and Appendix III]

Employment status, sex, and race	Graduates [1]				Dropouts [3]			
	1980	1990	2000 [2]	2003 [2]	1980	1990	2000 [2]	2003 [2]
Civilian population	11,622	8,370	7,351	7,133	5,254	3,800	3,776	3,552
In labor force	9,795	7,107	6,195	5,831	3,549	2,506	2,612	2,385
Percent of population	84.3	84.9	84.3	81.8	67.5	66.0	69.2	67.1
Employed	8,567	6,279	5,632	5,012	2,651	1,993	2,150	1,899
Percent of labor force	87.5	88.3	90.9	86.0	74.7	79.5	82.3	79.6
Unemployed	1,228	828	563	819	898	513	463	486
Unemployment rate, total [4]	12.5	11.7	9.1	14.1	25.3	20.5	17.7	20.4
Male	13.5	11.1	9.3	13.5	23.5	18.8	16.3	18.3
Female	11.5	12.3	8.8	14.8	28.7	23.5	20.3	24.8
White [5]	10.8	9.0	7.2	11.0	21.6	17.0	15.0	17.5
Black [5]	26.1	26.0	18.1	28.3	43.9	43.3	33.2	35.1
Not in labor force	1,827	1,262	1,156	1,302	1,705	1,294	1,163	1,167
Percent of population	15.7	15.1	15.7	18.3	32.5	34.1	30.8	32.9

[1] For persons not enrolled in college who have completed 4 years of high school only.   [2] Data not strictly comparable with data for earlier years. See text, this section, and February 2000 and February 2003 issues of Employment and Earnings.   [3] For persons not in regular school and who have not completed the 12th grade nor received a general equivalency degree.   [4] Includes other races not shown separately.   [5] For 2003, for persons who selected this race group only. See footnote 2, Table 212.
Source: U.S. Bureau of Labor Statistics, Bulletin 2307; *News*, USDL 03-330, June 25, 2003 and 04-479, April 27, 2004; and unpublished data. See Internet site <http://www.bls.gov/news.release/hsgec.toc.htm>

No. 258. General Educational Development (GED) Credentials Issued: 1974 to 2001

[GEDs issued in thousands (294 represents 294,000). For the 50 states and DC]

Year	GEDs issued	Percent distribution by age of test taker				
		19 years old or under	20 to 24 years old	25 to 29 years old	30 to 34 years old	35 years old and over
1974	294	35	27	13	9	17
1975	340	33	26	14	9	18
1980	479	37	27	13	8	15
1985	413	32	26	15	10	16
1990	410	36	25	13	10	15
1995	504	38	25	13	9	15
1997	460	43	24	12	8	13
1998	481	44	24	11	7	13
1999	498	44	25	11	7	13
2000	487	45	25	11	7	13
2001	648	41	26	11	8	14

Source: U.S. National Center for Education Statistics, *Digest of Education Statistics*, 2002.

No. 259. College Enrollment of Recent High School Graduates: 1960 to 2002

[(1,679 represents 1,679,000). For persons 16 to 24 who graduated from high school in the preceeding 12 months. Includes persons receiving GEDs. Based on surveys and subject to sampling error]

Year	Number of high school graduates (1,000)					Percent enrolled in college [2]				
	Total [1]	Male	Female	White	Black	Total [1]	Male	Female	White	Black
1960	1,679	756	923	1,565	(NA)	45.1	54.0	37.9	45.8	(NA)
1965	2,659	1,254	1,405	2,417	(NA)	50.9	57.3	45.3	51.7	(NA)
1970	2,758	1,343	1,415	2,461	(NA)	51.7	55.2	48.5	52.0	(NA)
1975	3,185	1,513	1,672	2,701	302	50.7	52.6	49.0	51.1	41.7
1980	3,088	1,498	1,589	2,554	350	49.3	46.7	51.8	49.8	42.7
1985	2,668	1,287	1,381	2,104	332	57.7	58.6	56.8	60.1	42.2
1986	2,786	1,332	1,454	2,146	378	53.8	55.8	51.9	56.8	36.9
1987	2,647	1,278	1,369	2,040	333	56.8	58.3	55.3	58.6	52.2
1988	2,673	1,334	1,339	2,013	378	58.9	57.1	60.7	61.1	44.4
1989	2,450	1,204	1,246	1,889	332	59.6	57.6	61.6	60.7	53.4
1990	2,362	1,173	1,189	1,819	331	60.1	58.0	62.2	63.0	46.8
1991	2,276	1,140	1,136	1,727	310	62.5	57.9	67.1	65.4	46.4
1992	2,397	1,216	1,180	1,724	354	61.9	60.0	63.8	64.3	48.2
1993	2,342	1,120	1,223	1,719	304	62.6	59.9	65.2	62.9	55.6
1994	2,517	1,244	1,273	1,915	316	61.9	60.6	63.2	64.5	50.8
1995	2,599	1,238	1,361	1,861	349	61.9	62.6	61.3	64.3	51.2
1996	2,660	1,297	1,363	1,875	406	65.0	60.1	69.7	67.4	56.0
1997	2,769	1,354	1,415	1,909	384	67.0	63.6	70.3	68.2	58.5
1998	2,810	1,452	1,358	1,980	386	65.6	62.4	69.1	68.5	61.9
1999	2,897	1,474	1,423	1,978	436	62.9	61.4	64.4	66.3	58.9
2000	2,756	1,251	1,505	1,938	393	63.3	59.9	66.2	65.7	54.9
2001	2,545	1,275	1,270	1,832	379	61.7	59.7	63.6	64.2	54.6
2002	2,796	1,412	1,384	1,903	382	65.2	62.1	68.4	67.0	55.3

NA Not available. [1] Includes other races, not shown separately. [2] As of October.
Source: U.S. National Center for Education Statistics, *Digest of Education Statistics*, annual.

No. 260. College Enrollment by Sex and Attendance Status: 1983 to 2001

[As of fall. In thousands (12,465 represents 12,465,000)]

Sex and age	1983		1988		1993		1998 [1]		2001 [1]	
	Total	Part time	Total	Part time	Total	Part time	Total	Part time	Total	Part time
Total	12,465	5,204	13,055	5,619	14,305	6,177	14,507	5,944	15,930	6,481
Male	6,024	2,264	6,002	2,340	6,427	2,537	6,369	2,436	6,961	2,661
14 to 17 years old	102	16	55	5	83	10	45	5	215	157
18 to 19 years old	1,256	158	1,290	132	1,224	138	1,535	296	1,543	231
20 to 21 years old	1,241	205	1,243	216	1,294	209	1,374	245	1,468	278
22 to 24 years old	1,158	382	1,106	378	1,260	392	1,127	350	1,214	395
25 to 29 years old	1,115	624	875	485	950	564	908	485	948	473
30 to 34 years old	570	384	617	456	661	484	463	322	557	352
35 years old and over	583	494	816	668	955	739	917	733	1,017	773
Female	6,441	2,940	7,053	3,278	7,877	3,640	8,138	3,508	8,970	3,820
14 to 17 years old	142	16	115	17	93	6	74	21	287	206
18 to 19 years old	1,496	179	1,536	195	1,416	172	1,847	292	1,919	274
20 to 21 years old	1,125	204	1,278	218	1,414	279	1,437	295	1,773	349
22 to 24 years old	884	378	932	403	1,263	493	1,250	463	1,360	513
25 to 29 years old	947	658	932	633	1,058	689	1,083	617	1,148	641
30 to 34 years old	721	553	698	499	811	575	732	506	726	479
35 years old and over	1,126	953	1,563	1,313	1,824	1,427	1,715	1,315	1,757	1,358

[1] In this table, data beginning in 1998 reflect the new classification of institutions. See footnote 1, Table 261.
Source: U.S. National Center for Education Statistics, *Digest of Education Statistics*, annual.

U.S. Census Bureau, Statistical Abstract of the United States: 2004-2005

No. 261. Higher Education—Summary: 1980 to 2001

[Institutions, staff, and enrollment as of fall (686 represents 686,000). Finances for fiscal year ending in the following year. Covers universities, colleges, professional schools, junior and teachers colleges, both publicly and privately controlled, regular session. Includes estimates for institutions not reporting. See also Appendix III]

Item	Unit	1980	1985	1990	1995	1997	1998	1999	2000	2001
ALL INSTITUTIONS										
Number of institutions [1]	Number.	3,231	3,340	3,559	3,706	4,064	4,048	4,084	4,182	4,197
4-year	Number .	1,957	2,029	2,141	2,244	2,309	2,335	2,363	2,450	2,364
2-year	Number .	1,274	1,311	1,418	1,462	1,755	1,713	1,721	1,732	1,833
Instructional staff—										
(Lecturer or above) [2]	1,000. . .	686	715	817	932	990	999	1,028	(NA)	1,113
Percent full-time	Percent .	66	64	61	59	57	(NA)	58	(NA)	56
Total enrollment [3] [4]	1,000. . .	12,097	12,247	13,819	14,262	14,502	14,507	14,791	15,312	15,928
Male	1,000. . .	5,874	5,818	6,284	6,343	6,396	6,369	6,491	6,722	6,961
Female	1,000. . .	6,223	6,429	7,535	7,919	8,106	8,138	8,301	8,591	8,967
4-year institutions	1,000. . .	7,571	7,716	8,579	8,769	8,897	9,018	9,199	9,364	9,677
2-year institutions	1,000. . .	4,526	4,531	5,240	5,493	5,606	5,489	5,593	5,948	6,251
Full-time	1,000. . .	7,098	7,075	7,821	8,129	8,438	8,563	8,786	9,010	9,448
Part-time	1,000. . .	4,999	5,172	5,998	6,133	6,064	5,944	6,005	6,303	6,480
Public	1,000. . .	9,457	9,479	10,845	11,092	11,196	11,138	11,309	11,753	12,233
Private	1,000. . .	2,640	2,768	2,974	3,169	3,306	3,369	3,482	3,560	3,695
Undergraduate [4]	1,000. . .	10,475	10,597	11,959	12,232	12,451	12,437	12,681	13,155	13,716
Men	1,000. . .	5,000	4,962	5,380	5,401	5,469	5,446	5,559	5,778	6,004
Women	1,000. . .	5,475	5,635	6,579	6,831	6,982	6,991	7,122	7,377	7,711
First-time freshmen	1,000. . .	2,588	2,292	2,257	2,169	2,219	2,213	2,352	2,428	2,497
First professional	1,000. . .	278	274	273	298	298	302	303	307	309
Men	1,000. . .	199	180	167	174	170	169	165	164	161
Women	1,000. . .	78	94	107	124	129	134	138	143	148
Graduate [4]	1,000. . .	1,343	1,376	1,586	1,732	1,753	1,768	1,807	1,850	1,904
Men	1,000. . .	675	677	737	768	758	754	766	780	796
Women	1,000. . .	670	700	849	965	996	1,013	1,041	1,071	1,108
Public institutions:										
Current funds revenues [5]	Mil. dol .	43,196	65,005	94,905	123,501	137,571	144,970	157,314	174,503	174,503
Tuition and fees	Mil. dol.	5,570	9,439	15,258	23,257	26,058	27,428	29,126	31,464	31,464
Federal government	Mil. dol.	5,540	6,852	9,763	13,672	14,544	15,554	16,952	1,716	18,668
State government	Mil. dol.	19,676	29,221	38,240	44,243	49,115	52,132	56,370	55,949	62,543
Auxiliary enterprises	Mil. dol.	4,615	6,685	9,059	11,595	13,070	13,776	15,174	31,643	16,379
Public institutions:										
Current funds expenditures [5]	Mil. dol .	42,280	63,194	92,961	119,525	132,846	140,539	152,325	170,345	168,296
Educational and general	Mil. dol.	34,173	50,873	74,395	96,086	106,741	113,594	122,709	136,613	135,549
Auxiliary enterprises	Mil. dol.	4,658	6,830	9,050	11,309	12,819	13,567	14,448	16,377	16,245
2-YEAR INSTITUTIONS										
Number of institutions [1] [6]	Number.	1,274	1,311	1,418	1,462	1,755	1,713	1,721	1,732	1,833
Public	Number .	945	932	972	1,047	1,092	1,069	1,068	1,076	1,101
Private	Number .	329	379	446	415	663	644	653	656	732
Instructional staff—										
(Lecturer or above) [2]	1,000. . .	192	211	(NA)	285	307	(NA)	314	(NA)	349
Enrollment [3] [4]	1,000. . .	4,526	4,531	5,240	5,493	5,606	5,489	5,593	5,948	6,251
Public	1,000. . .	4,329	4,270	4,996	5,278	5,361	5,246	5,339	5,697	5,997
Private	1,000. . .	198	261	244	215	245	243	253	251	254
Male	1,000. . .	2,047	2,002	2,233	2,329	2,390	2,333	2,387	2,559	2,675
Female	1,000. . .	2,479	2,529	3,007	3,164	3,216	3,216	3,390	3,205	3,575

NA Not available.   [1] Number of institutions includes count of branch campuses. Due to revised survey procedures, data beginning 1990 are not comparable with previous years. Beginning 1997 data reflect a new classification of institutions; this classification includes some additional, primarily 2-year, colleges than before and excludes a few institutions that did not award degrees. Includes institutions that were eligible to participate in Title IV federal financial aid programs.   [2] Due to revised survey methods, data beginning 1990 not comparable with previous years.   [3] Branch campuses counted according to actual status, e.g., 2-year branch in 2-year category.   [4] Includes unclassified students. (Students taking courses for credit, but are not candidates for degrees.)   [5] Includes items not shown separately.   [6] Includes schools accredited by the National Association of Trade and Technical Schools. See footnote 1 for information pertaining to data beginning 1997.

Source: U.S. National Center for Education Statistics, *Digest of Education Statistics*, annual; and unpublished data.

No. 262. College Enrollment by Selected Characteristics: 1990 to 2001

[In thousands (13,818.6 represents 13,818,600). As of fall. Nonresident alien students are not distributed among racial/ethnic groups]

Characteristic	1990	1995	1996 [1]	1997 [1]	1998 [1]	1999 [1]	2000 [1]	2001 [1]
Total	13,818.6	14,261.8	14,367.5	14,502.3	14,507.0	14,791.2	15,312.3	15,928.0
Male.	6,283.9	6,342.5	6,352.8	6,396.0	6,369.3	6,490.6	6,721.8	6,960.8
Female	7,534.7	7,919.2	8,014.7	8,106.3	8,137.7	8,300.6	8,590.5	8,967.2
Public.	10,844.7	11,092.4	11,120.5	11,196.1	11,137.8	11,309.4	11,752.8	12,233.2
Private	2,973.9	3,169.4	3,247.0	3,306.2	3,369.2	3,481.8	3,559.5	3694.8
2-year.	5,240.1	5,492.5	5,563.3	5,605.6	5,489.3	5,592.7	5,948.4	6,250.6
4-year.	8,578.6	8,769.3	8,804.2	8,896.8	9,017.7	9,198.5	9,363.9	9,677.4
Undergraduate	11,959.2	12,232.0	12,326.9	12,450.6	12,436.9	12,681.2	13,155.4	13,715.6
Graduate.	1,586.2	1,732.0	1,742.3	1,753.5	1,767.6	1,806.8	1,850.3	1,903.7
First professional	273.4	297.6	298.3	298.3	302.5	303.2	306.6	308.6
White [2]	10,722.5	10,311.2	10,263.9	10,266.1	10,178.8	10,282.1	10,462.1	10,774.5
Male.	4,861.0	4,594.1	4,552.2	4,548.8	4,499.4	4,551.1	4,634.6	4,762.3
Female	5,861.5	5,717.2	5,711.7	5,717.4	5,679.4	5,731.0	5,827.5	6,012.2
Public.	8,385.4	7,945.4	7,871.9	7,857.8	7,750.6	7,803.2	7,963.4	8,214.0
Private	2,337.0	2,365.9	2,392.0	2,408.3	2,428.3	2,478.8	2,498.7	2560.5
2-year.	3,954.3	3,794.0	3,780.8	3,770.0	3,641.3	3,672.0	3,804.1	3,955.7
4-year.	6,768.1	6,517.2	6,483.1	6,496.1	6,537.5	6,610.1	6,658.0	6,818.8
Undergraduate	9,272.6	8,805.6	8,769.5	8,783.9	8,703.6	8,805.7	8,983.5	9,278.7
Graduate.	1,228.4	1,282.3	1,272.6	1,261.8	1,254.3	1,256.5	1,258.5	1,275.1
First professional	221.5	223.3	221.7	220.4	220.9	219.9	220.1	220.8
Black [2]	1,247.0	1,473.7	1,505.6	1,551.0	1,582.9	1,643.2	1,730.3	1,850.4
Male.	484.7	555.9	564.1	579.8	584.0	604.2	635.3	672.4
Female	762.3	917.8	941.4	971.3	999.0	1,038.9	1,095.0	1,178.0
Public.	976.4	1,160.6	1,177.4	1,205.3	1,218.6	1,253.4	1,319.2	1,397.1
Private	270.6	313.0	328.1	345.8	364.2	389.8	411.1	453.3
2-year.	524.3	621.5	636.0	654.6	655.4	679.1	734.9	795.7
4-year.	722.8	852.2	869.6	896.4	927.6	964.1	995.4	1,054.7
Undergraduate	1,147.2	1,333.6	1,358.6	1,398.1	1,421.7	1,471.9	1,548.9	1,657.1
Graduate.	83.9	118.6	125.5	131.6	138.7	148.7	157.9	169.4
First professional	15.9	21.4	21.5	21.4	22.5	22.5	23.5	23.9
Hispanic	782.4	1,093.8	1,166.1	1,218.5	1,257.1	1,319.1	1,461.8	1,560.6
Male.	353.9	480.2	506.6	525.8	538.6	563.6	627.1	664.2
Female	428.5	613.7	659.5	692.7	718.5	755.5	834.7	896.4
Public.	671.4	937.1	990.7	1,031.6	1,057.8	1,099.1	1,229.3	1,308.8
Private	111.0	156.8	175.4	186.9	199.3	220.0	232.5	251.8
2-year.	424.2	608.4	657.3	688.5	704.2	735.7	843.9	904.3
4-year.	358.2	485.5	508.8	530.0	552.9	583.4	617.9	656.3
Undergraduate	724.6	1,012.0	1,079.4	1,125.9	1,159.8	1,214.0	1,351.0	1,444.4
Graduate.	47.2	68.0	72.8	78.7	82.9	90.4	95.4	100.5
First professional	10.7	13.8	13.9	13.9	14.4	14.7	15.4	15.6
American Indian/Alaska Native [2] .	102.8	131.3	137.6	142.5	144.2	145.5	151.2	158.2
Male.	43.1	54.8	57.2	59.0	59.0	58.6	61.4	63.6
Female	59.7	76.5	80.4	83.4	85.1	86.8	89.7	94.5
Public.	90.4	113.8	118.8	123.6	122.6	124.2	127.3	133.6
Private	12.4	17.5	18.8	18.8	21.5	21.3	23.9	24.6
2-year.	54.9	65.6	70.2	71.0	71.5	72.1	74.7	78.2
4-year.	47.9	65.7	67.3	71.5	72.6	73.4	76.5	80.0
Undergraduate	95.5	120.7	126.5	130.8	132.2	133.4	138.5	144.8
Graduate.	6.2	8.5	8.9	9.4	9.8	10.0	10.3	11.2
First professional	1.1	2.1	2.2	2.3	2.2	2.1	2.3	2.1
Asian/Pacific Islander [2]	572.4	797.4	828.2	859.2	900.5	913.0	978.2	1,019.0
Male.	294.9	393.3	405.5	417.7	433.6	437.1	465.9	480.8
Female	277.5	404.1	422.6	441.5	466.9	475.8	512.3	538.3
Public.	461.0	638.0	657.9	680.4	713.2	716.1	770.5	806.1
Private	111.5	159.4	170.3	178.8	187.3	196.9	207.7	213.0
2-year.	215.2	314.9	327.0	340.7	361.9	356.2	401.9	417.5
4-year.	357.2	482.4	501.1	518.5	538.5	556.8	576.3	601.6
Undergraduate	500.5	692.2	717.6	743.7	778.3	786.0	845.5	883.9
Graduate.	53.2	75.6	79.1	82.6	87.0	90.7	95.8	97.4
First professional	18.7	29.6	31.4	32.9	35.1	36.3	36.8	37.7
Nonresident alien . .	391.5	454.4	466.3	465.0	443.5	488.5	528.7	565.3
Male.	246.3	264.3	267.2	264.9	254.6	276.0	297.3	317.4
Female	145.2	190.1	199.0	200.1	188.9	212.4	231.4	247.8
Public.	260.0	297.5	303.8	297.3	274.9	313.3	343.1	373.6
Private	131.4	156.9	162.5	167.7	168.7	175.1	185.6	191.6
2-year.	67.1	88.1	92.0	80.7	55.0	77.6	89.0	99.2
4-year.	324.3	366.2	374.3	384.3	388.5	410.8	439.7	466.1
Undergraduate	218.7	267.6	275.3	268.2	241.3	270.3	288.0	306.7
Graduate.	167.3	179.5	183.3	189.4	194.8	210.6	232.3	250.1
First professional	5.4	7.3	7.6	7.5	7.4	7.6	8.4	8.4

[1] Beginning 1996 data reflect a new classification of institutions; this classification includes some additional, primarily 2-year, colleges than before and excludes a few institutions that did not award degrees.   [2] Non-Hispanic.

Source: U.S. National Center for Education Statistics, *Digest of Education Statistics*, annual.

Education   169

No. 263. Degree-Granting Institutions, Number and Enrollment by State: 2000

[15,314 represents 15,314,000. Number of institutions beginning in academic year. Opening fall enrollment of resident and extension students attending full time or part time. Excludes students taking courses for credit by mail, radio, or TV, and students in branches of U.S. institutions operated in foreign countries. See Appendix III]

State	Num-ber of institu-tions [1]	Enrollment (1,000)							Minority enrollment			Non-resi-dent alien
		Total	Male	Female	Public	Private	Full time	White [2]	Total [3]	Black [2]	His-panic	
United States..	**4,182**	**15,314**	**6,722**	**8,591**	**11,753**	**3,560**	**9,010**	**10,462**	**4,323**	**1,730**	**1,462**	**529**
Alabama.	76	234	100	134	207	27	155	157	72	62	4	6
Alaska	9	28	11	17	27	1	11	21	6	1	1	1
Arizona.	75	343	156	187	285	58	163	237	96	14	56	10
Arkansas	47	115	48	67	102	13	78	90	22	18	1	3
California	419	2,257	1,010	1,247	1,928	329	1,054	1,052	1,133	170	528	72
Colorado.	74	264	121	143	218	46	145	207	51	10	27	6
Connecticut.	46	161	70	92	101	60	93	123	32	14	10	6
Delaware	10	44	17	26	34	10	28	33	10	7	1	1
District of Columbia .	17	73	31	42	5	67	51	35	29	21	3	8
Florida	164	708	304	404	557	151	365	429	252	113	112	27
Georgia	125	346	147	199	272	74	224	220	116	97	7	10
Hawaii	21	60	26	34	45	16	37	15	39	2	2	6
Idaho	14	66	29	36	54	12	44	59	5Z	(Z)	2	1
Illinois	181	744	326	417	534	210	398	495	226	98	80	23
Indiana.	98	314	145	169	240	74	213	265	37	23	8	12
Iowa	64	189	86	103	135	54	132	167	14	5	4	8
Kansas.	59	180	80	100	160	20	102	151	24	10	7	6
Kentucky	69	188	78	110	152	36	126	164	21	16	2	4
Louisiana	85	224	94	130	189	35	160	143	75	63	6	6
Maine.	33	58	23	35	41	18	34	54	3	1	1	1
Maryland	57	274	113	161	224	50	141	166	95	68	9	12
Massachusetts.	117	421	182	239	183	238	273	313	80	28	22	28
Michigan.	108	568	247	321	468	100	308	444	101	65	13	23
Minnesota.	113	293	134	160	219	75	183	254	30	12	4	9
Mississippi	42	137	56	81	125	12	101	85	50	48	1	2
Missouri	116	321	140	181	202	120	188	263	49	32	7	9
Montana.	24	42	20	23	37	5	32	36	5	(Z)	1	1
Nebraska	38	112	51	62	89	24	71	99	10	4	3	3
Nevada	15	88	38	49	83	5	33	61	24	6	9	2
New Hampshire	25	62	26	35	36	26	40	56	4	1	1	4
New Jersey	58	336	146	190	267	69	194	212	110	44	39	14
New Mexico	44	111	46	65	101	9	59	48	61	3	45	2
New York	325	1,044	441	602	583	460	698	660	329	141	108	54
North Carolina	120	405	170	234	329	75	252	286	110	89	7	9
North Dakota.	21	40	20	20	36	4	32	36	3	(Z)	(Z)	1
Ohio	175	550	242	308	411	138	356	453	79	56	9	18
Oklahoma.	50	178	81	97	154	24	114	130	41	14	6	8
Oregon.	56	183	83	100	155	28	102	151	26	4	8	6
Pennsylvania.	263	610	272	337	339	270	435	496	92	53	14	22
Rhode Island.	13	75	33	42	38	37	50	61	12	4	4	3
South Carolina.	62	186	77	109	156	30	120	129	53	47	2	4
South Dakota	25	43	19	24	35	8	30	38	4	(Z)	(Z)	1
Tennessee	87	264	113	151	203	61	179	200	58	49	4	6
Texas.	201	1,034	465	569	897	137	579	584	414	113	244	36
Utah	24	164	83	81	123	41	102	147	12	1	5	5
Vermont	25	35	16	20	20	15	25	33	2	(Z)	1	1
Virginia.	96	382	164	218	314	68	220	268	102	69	11	12
Washington.	79	321	143	178	274	47	192	249	62	13	14	10
West Virginia.	36	88	39	49	76	12	64	80	6	4	1	2
Wisconsin.	68	307	135	172	250	57	192	270	30	13	7	7
Wyoming	9	30	13	17	29	1	17	27	2	(Z)	1	(Z)
U.S. military [4] . .	4	13	11	2	13	-	13	11	2	1	1	(Z)

- Represents zero.   Z Fewer than 500.   [1] Branch campuses counted as separate institutions.   [2] Non-Hispanic.
[3] Includes other races not shown separately.   [4] Service schools.

Source: U.S. National Center for Education Statistics, *Digest of Education Statistics*, annual.

No. 264. College Enrollment by Sex, Age, Race, and Hispanic Origin: 1980 to 2002

[In thousands (11,387 represents 11,387,000). As of October for the civilian noninstitutional population, 14 years old and over. Based on the Current Population Survey; see text, Section 1, and Appendix III]

Characteristic	1980	1985	1990 [1]	1995	1996	1997	1998	1999	2000	2001	2002
Total [2]	11,387	12,524	13,621	14,715	15,226	15,436	15,546	15,203	15,314	15,873	16,497
Male [3]	5,430	5,906	6,192	6,703	6,820	6,843	6,905	6,956	6,682	6,875	7,240
18 to 24 years	3,604	3,749	3,922	4,089	4,187	4,374	4,403	4,397	4,342	4,437	4,629
25 to 34 years	1,325	1,464	1,412	1,561	1,523	1,509	1,500	1,458	1,361	1,476	1,460
35 years old and over . .	405	561	772	985	1,013	899	953	1,024	918	908	1,071
Female [3]	5,957	6,618	7,429	8,013	8,406	8,593	8,641	8,247	8,631	8,998	9,258
18 to 24 years	3,625	3,788	4,042	4,452	4,582	4,829	4,919	4,863	5,109	5,192	5,404
25 to 34 years	1,378	1,599	1,749	1,788	1,920	1,760	1,915	1,637	1,846	1,946	1,941
35 years old and over . .	802	1,100	1,546	1,684	1,765	1,892	1,732	1,675	1,589	1,776	1,797
White [3]	9,925	10,781	11,488	12,021	12,189	12,442	12,401	12,053	11,999	12,208	12,781
18 to 24 years	6,334	6,500	6,635	7,011	7,123	7,495	7,541	7,446	7,566	7,548	7,921
25 to 34 years	2,328	2,604	2,698	2,686	2,644	2,522	2,568	2,345	2,339	2,469	2,515
35 years old and over . .	1,051	1,448	2,023	2,208	2,254	2,297	2,199	2,174	1,978	2,103	2,236
Male	4,804	5,103	5,235	5,535	5,453	5,552	5,602	5,562	5,311	5,383	5,719
Female	5,121	5,679	6,253	6,486	6,735	6,890	6,799	6,491	6,689	6,826	7,062
Black [3]	1,163	1,263	1,393	1,772	1,901	1,903	2,016	1,998	2,164	2,230	2,278
18 to 24 years	688	734	894	988	983	1,085	1,115	1,146	1,216	1,206	1,227
25 to 34 years	289	295	258	426	519	423	539	453	567	562	542
35 years old and over . .	156	213	207	334	354	372	340	354	361	429	454
Male	476	552	587	710	764	723	770	833	815	781	802
Female	686	712	807	1,062	1,136	1,180	1,247	1,164	1,349	1,449	1,476
Hispanic origin [3][4]	443	580	748	1,207	1,223	1,260	1,363	1,307	1,426	1,700	1,656
18 to 24 years	315	375	435	745	706	806	820	740	899	1,035	979
25 to 34 years	118	189	168	250	310	254	336	334	309	392	414
35 years old and over . .	(NA)	(NA)	130	193	184	151	198	226	195	260	249
Male	222	279	364	568	529	555	550	568	619	731	705
Female	221	299	384	639	693	704	814	739	807	969	951

NA Not available.   [1] Beginning 1990, based on a revised edit and tabulation package.   [2] Includes other races not shown separately.   [3] Includes persons 14 to 17 years old, not shown separately.   [4] Persons of Hispanic origin may be of any race.

Source: U.S. Census Bureau, *Current Population Reports*, PPL-148; and earlier PPL and P-20 reports. See Internet site <http://www.census.gov/population/www/socdemo/school.html>.

No. 265. Foreign (Nonimmigrant) Student Enrollment in College: 1976 to 2003

[In thousands (179 represents 170,000). For fall of the previous year]

Region of origin	1976	1980	1985	1990	1993	1994	1995	1996	1997	1998	1999	2000	2001	2002	2003
All regions . . .	179	286	342	387	439	449	453	454	458	481	491	515	548	583	586
Africa	25	36	40	25	21	21	21	21	22	23	26	30	34	38	40
Nigeria	11	16	18	4	2	2	2	2	2	2	3	4	4	4	6
Asia [1]	97	165	200	245	291	294	292	290	291	308	308	315	339	363	367
China: Taiwan . . .	11	18	23	31	37	37	36	33	30	31	31	29	29	29	28
Hong Kong	12	10	10	11	14	14	13	12	11	10	9	8	8	8	8
India	10	9	15	26	36	35	34	32	31	34	37	42	55	67	75
Indonesia	1	2	7	9	11	11	12	13	12	13	12	11	12	12	10
Iran	20	51	17	7	4	4	3	3	2	2	2	2	2	2	2
Japan	7	12	13	30	43	44	45	46	46	47	46	47	46	47	46
Malaysia	2	4	22	14	13	14	14	14	15	15	12	9	8	7	7
Saudi Arabia	3	10	8	4	4	4	4	4	4	5	5	5	5	6	4
South Korea	3	5	16	22	29	31	34	36	37	43	39	41	46	49	52
Thailand	7	7	7	7	9	9	11	12	13	15	12	11	11	12	10
Europe	14	23	33	46	58	62	65	67	68	72	74	78	81	82	78
Latin America [2]	30	42	49	48	43	45	47	47	50	51	55	62	64	68	69
Mexico	5	6	6	7	8	8	9	9	9	10	10	11	11	13	13
Venezuela	5	10	10	3	3	4	4	4	5	5	5	5	5	6	5
North America	10	16	16	19	22	23	23	24	24	23	23	24	26	27	27
Canada	10	15	15	18	21	22	23	23	22	23	23	24	25	27	27
Oceania	3	4	4	4	4	4	4	4	4	4	4	4	5	5	5

[1] Includes countries not shown separately.   [2] Includes Central America, Caribbean, and South America.

Source: Institute of International Education, New York, NY, *Open Doors Report on International Educational Exchange*, annual (copyright).

Education 171

No. 266. College Enrollment—Summary by Sex, Race and Hispanic Origin: 2002

[In thousands (16,497 represents 16,497,000), except percent. As of October. Covers civilian noninstitutional population 15 years old and over enrolled in colleges and graduate schools. Based on Current Population Survey, see text, Section 1, Population and Appendix III]

Characteristic	Sex			Race and Hispanic origin				
				White			Asian and Pacific Islander	Hispanic [2]
	Total [1]	Male	Female	Total	Non-Hispanic	Black		
Total enrollment	**16,497**	**7,240**	**9,258**	**12,781**	**11,236**	**2,278**	**1,258**	**1,656**
15 to 17 years old.	195	80	116	109	97	56	28	15
18 to 19 years old.	3,581	1,635	1,946	2,891	2,549	430	236	360
20 to 21 years old.	3,525	1,640	1,885	2,810	2,525	418	269	303
22 to 24 years old.	2,927	1,354	1,573	2,220	1,931	379	299	316
25 to 29 years old.	2,093	918	1,175	1,582	1,317	301	182	274
30 to 34 years old.	1,308	542	766	933	812	241	105	140
35 years old and over	2,867	1,071	1,797	2,236	2,007	454	140	249
Type of school:								
2-year.	4,378	1,884	2,494	3,307	2,653	699	303	685
15 to 19 years old	1,227	570	657	948	791	188	86	163
20 to 24 years old	1,433	672	761	1,043	814	217	145	236
25 years old and over . .	1,718	643	1,076	1,316	1,048	294	72	286
4-year.	9,047	4,045	5,002	7,130	6,429	1,205	632	761
15 to 19 years old	2,516	1,125	1,391	2,029	1,832	289	177	212
20 to 24 years old	4,380	2,036	2,344	3,526	3,219	496	331	336
25 years old and over . .	2,151	884	1,267	1,575	1,378	420	124	213
Graduate school	3,072	1,311	1,761	2,344	2,155	375	324	210
15 to 24 years old	672	306	366	484	445	93	92	47
25 to 34 years old	1,296	548	748	970	881	144	163	99
35 years old and over . .	1,104	457	647	889	828	138	69	65
Public	12,833	5,609	7,225	9,774	8,488	1,868	1,040	1,374
2-year	3,948	1,677	2,271	2,949	2,341	655	279	635
4-year	6,882	3,096	3,787	5,355	4,793	955	506	609
Graduate	2,003	837	1,167	1,469	1,354	258	255	130
Percent of students:								
Employed full-time	31.8	32.1	31.6	32.0	31.5	35.9	20.0	36.1
Employed part-time	29.1	27.0	30.6	31.1	31.5	19.3	27.4	28.5

[1] Includes other races, not shown separately.   [2] Persons of Hispanic origin may be of any race.

Source: U.S. Census Bureau, unpublished data. See Internet site <http://www.census.gov/population/www/socdemo/school.html>

No. 267. Higher Education Enrollments in Foreign Languages: 1970 to 2002

[As of fall (1,111.5 represents 1,111,500). For credit enrollments]

Item	1970	1977	1980	1983	1986	1990	1995	1998	2002
Enrollment [1] (1,000)	1,111.5	933.5	924.8	966.0	1,003.2	1,184.1	1,138.8	1,193.8	1,397.3
Index (1960=100).	171.8	144.3	142.9	149.3	155.0	183.0	176.0	184.5	215.9
By selected language (1,000):									
Spanish	389.2	376.7	379.4	386.2	411.3	533.9	606.3	656.6	746.3
French	359.3	246.1	248.4	270.1	275.3	272.5	205.4	199.1	202.0
German	202.6	135.4	126.9	128.2	121.0	133.3	96.3	89.0	91.1
Italian	34.2	33.3	34.8	38.7	40.9	49.7	43.8	49.3	63.9
American Sign Language	(X)	(X)	(X)	(X)	(X)	1.6	4.3	11.4	60.8
Japanese	6.6	10.7	11.5	16.1	23.5	45.7	44.7	43.1	52.2
Chinese	6.2	9.8	11.4	13.2	16.9	19.5	26.5	28.5	34.2
Latin.	27.6	24.4	25.0	24.2	25.0	28.2	25.9	26.1	29.8
Russian	36.2	27.8	24.0	30.4	34.0	44.6	24.7	23.8	23.9
Hebrew.	16.6	19.4	19.4	18.2	15.6	13.0	13.1	15.8	22.8
Ancient Greek	16.7	25.8	22.1	19.4	17.6	16.4	16.3	16.4	20.4
Arabic.	1.3	3.1	3.5	3.4	3.4	3.5	4.4	5.5	10.6
Portuguese	5.1	5.0	4.9	4.4	5.1	6.2	6.5	6.9	8.4
Korean	0.1	(NA)	0.4	(NA)	(NA)	2.3	3.3	4.5	5.2

NA Not available. X Not applicable.   [1] Includes other foreign languages, not shown separately.

Source: Association of Departments of Foreign Languages, New York, NY, *ADFL Bulletin*, Vol. 35, No. 2, Winter 2004; and earlier issues (copyright).

No. 268. College Freshmen—Summary Characteristics: 1970 to 2003

[In percent, except as indicated (12.8 represents $12,800). **As of fall** for first-time full-time freshmen in 4-year colleges and universities. Based on sample survey and subject to sampling error; see source]

Characteristic	1970	1980	1985	1990	1995	2000	2001	2002	2003
Sex: Male	52.1	48.8	48.9	46.9	45.6	45.2	44.9	45.0	45.1
Female	47.9	51.2	51.1	53.1	54.4	54.8	55.1	55.0	55.0
Applied to three or more colleges	(NA)	31.5	35.4	42.9	44.4	50.5	51.3	50.8	54.2
Average grade in high school:									
A- to A+	19.6	26.6	28.7	29.4	36.1	42.9	44.1	45.7	46.6
B- to B+	62.5	58.2	57.1	57.0	54.2	50.5	49.5	49.0	48.3
C to C+	17.7	14.9	14.0	13.4	9.6	6.5	6.2	5.2	5.0
D	0.3	0.2	0.2	0.2	0.1	0.1	0.1	0.1	0.1
Political orientation:									
Liberal	35.7	21.0	22.4	24.6	22.9	24.8	26.9	25.3	24.2
Middle of the road	43.4	57.0	53.1	51.7	51.3	51.9	49.5	50.8	50.3
Conservative	17.3	19.0	21.3	20.6	21.8	18.9	19.1	20.0	21.1
Probable field of study:									
Arts and humanities	(NA)	10.5	10.1	10.5	11.2	12.1	12.6	12.6	12.3
Biological sciences	(NA)	4.5	4.5	4.9	8.3	6.6	6.9	7.2	7.3
Business	(NA)	21.2	24.6	21.1	15.4	16.7	16.6	16.2	15.9
Education	(NA)	8.4	6.9	10.3	10.1	11.0	10.1	10.6	10.1
Engineering	(NA)	11.2	11.0	9.7	8.1	8.7	9.1	9.5	9.3
Physical science	(NA)	3.2	3.2	2.8	3.1	2.6	2.6	2.7	2.7
Social science	(NA)	8.2	9.4	11.0	9.9	10.0	10.3	10.4	10.5
Professional	(NA)	15.5	13.1	13.0	16.5	11.6	12.0	12.3	14.3
Technical	(NA)	3.1	2.4	1.1	1.2	2.1	2.2	1.4	1.5
Data processing/computer programming	(NA)	1.7	1.7	0.7	0.8	1.5	1.4	0.9	0.7
Other [1]	(NA)	14.0	15.1	15.8	16.0	17.9	17.5	16.9	16.0
Communications	(NA)	2.4	2.8	2.9	1.8	2.7	2.6	2.5	2.4
Computer science	(NA)	2.6	2.4	1.7	2.2	3.7	3.3	2.2	1.7
Personal objectives—very important or essential:									
Being very well off financially	36.2	62.5	69.2	72.3	72.8	73.4	73.6	73.2	73.8
Developing a meaningful philosophy of life	79.1	62.5	46.9	45.9	45.4	42.4	43.1	40.6	39.3
Keeping up to date with political affairs	57.2	45.2	(NA)	46.6	32.3	28.1	31.4	32.9	33.9
Attitudes—agree or strongly agree:									
Capital punishment should be abolished	59.4	34.8	27.6	23.1	22.0	31.2	32.2	32.1	32.6
Legalize marijuana	40.6	37.1	21.4	18.8	33.4	34.2	36.5	39.7	38.8
There is too much concern for the rights of criminals	50.7	65.0	(NA)	65.1	73.2	66.5	64.4	64.0	61.1
Abortion should be legalized	85.7	53.7	56.4	65.5	59.9	53.9	55.0	53.6	54.5
Median family income ($1,000)	12.8	24.5	37.3	46.6	54.8	64.4	67.2	69.5	71.3

NA Not available.   [1] Includes other fields, not shown separately.

Source: The Higher Education Research Institute, University of California, Los Angeles, CA, *The American Freshman: National Norms*, annual.

No. 269. Undergraduates Reported Disability Status by Selected Characteristic: 1999-2000

[In percent. Based on the 1999-2000 National Postsecondary Student Aid Survey; see source and Appendix III for details]

Student characteristic	Any disability or difficulty reported [1]	None reported	Consider self with disability	Don't consider self with disability
Total	**9.3**	**90.7**	**3.6**	**96.4**
PERCENT DISTRIBUTION				
Total	100.0	100.0	100.0	100.0
Age: [1]				
18 years or younger	5.8	9.9	3.1	9.8
19 to 23 years old	36.3	49.3	24.5	49.1
24 to 29 years old	15.5	16.1	15.3	16.1
30 to 39 years old	19.2	13.5	23.7	13.7
40 years or older	23.3	11.1	33.4	11.5
Sex: Male	39.6	42.4	46.2	42.0
Female	60.4	57.6	53.8	58.0
Race:				
White, non-Hispanic	70.8	66.7	70.8	67.1
Black, non-Hispanic	10.9	11.8	13.0	11.7
Hispanic	9.9	11.6	8.0	11.4
Asian	2.1	4.9	1.1	4.8
American Indian/Alaska Native	1.9	0.7	2.5	0.8
Native Hawaiian/Other Pacific Islander	0.8	0.8	1.4	0.7
Other race	1.4	1.5	0.8	1.6
More than one race	2.3	1.9	2.5	1.9
Parents' highest education level:				
High school or less	40.7	36.4	45.1	36.4
Some postsecondary education	24.1	22.8	21.6	23.0
Bachelor's degree or equivalent	35.2	40.9	33.3	40.7

[1] Those who indicated they had a long lasting condition, such as blindness or deafness; or a condition substantially limiting a basic physical activity, such as walking or lifting; or a physical, emotional, or mental condition lasting six months or more which made it difficult to do any one of the following: get to school, get around campus, learn, dress, or work at a job.

Source: U.S. National Center for Education Statistics, *Profile of Undergraduates in U.S. Postsecondary Education Institutions, 1999-2000*, NCES 2002-168, July 2002.

Education 173

No. 270. Distance Education in Degree-Granting Postsecondary Institutions: 2000-01

[For the school year (3,077 represents 3,077,000). Distance education is education or training courses delivered to off campus sites via audio, video (live or prerecorded), or computer technologies (simultaneous) or not simultaneous). Based on the Postsecondary Education Quick Information System; see source for details]

Institution type and size	Institutions offering distance education courses			Enrollments in distance education course (1,000)			
				Total [1]	Enrollments in college-level courses		
	Number of institu- tions	Number	Percent		Total [2]	Under- graduate enroll- ments	Graduate enroll- ments [3]
All institutions [4]	4,130	2,320	56	3,077	2,876	2,350	510
Type:							
Public 2-year	1,070	960	90	1,472	1,436	1,435	(B)
Private 2-year.	640	100	16	(B)	(B)	(B)	(B)
Public 4-year.	620	550	89	945	888	566	308
Private 4-year.	1,800	710	40	589	480	278	202
Enrollment size:							
Less than 3,000	2,840	1,160	41	486	460	368	91
3,000 to 9,999	870	770	88	1,171	1,132	932	197
10,000 or more.	420	400	95	1,420	1,284	1,049	222

B Base figure too small to meet statistical standards of reliability for a derived figure. [1] Includes all levels and audiences (for example, adult education and continuing education). [2] Includes duplication for students enrolled in more than one course. [3] Includes first-professional. [4] Includes data for private 2-year institutions.

Source: U.S. National Center for Education Statistics, *Distance Education at Degree Granting Postsecondary Institutions: 2000-2001*, NCES 2003-017, July 2003.

No. 271. Average Total Price of Attendance of Undergraduate Education: 1999-2000

[In dollars. Excludes students attending more than one institution. Price of attendance includes tuition and fees, books and supplies, room and board, transportation, and personal and other expenses allowed for federal cost of attendance budgets. Based on the 1999-2000 National Postsecondary Student-Aid Study; see source for details. See also Appendix III]

Student characteristic	Type of institution						
	Total [1]	Public 2-year	Public 4-year		Private not-for-profit 4-year		Private for-profit
			Non- doctorate	Doctor- ate	Non- doctorate	Doctor- ate	
Total	9,283	4,997	8,839	10,915	16,242	22,212	14,294
Age: [2]							
18 years or younger.	11,077	5,674	9,127	12,006	19,170	25,991	14,289
19 to 23 years	11,150	5,688	9,461	11,563	19,551	24,529	14,112
24 to 29 years	7,962	5,038	8,397	9,571	12,474	14,190	14,517
30 to 39 years	6,696	4,555	7,817	8,624	10,327	11,050	14,452
40 years or older.	5,341	3,667	6,691	7,117	9,641	9,597	14,068
Sex:							
Male	9,298	4,943	8,852	10,895	16,288	22,196	14,972
Female	9,271	5,039	8,829	10,933	16,209	22,225	13,846
Race:							
One race:							
White.	9,410	4,940	8,834	10,878	16,855	22,361	14,585
Black or African American	8,559	5,041	8,826	10,655	13,647	19,489	13,270
Asian.	10,132	5,200	9,166	11,890	18,513	25,991	15,688
American Indian/Alaska Native	7,369	5,132	7,381	9,381	12,225	(B)	12,292
Native Hawaiian or other Pacific Islander . . .	8,345	5,431	9,698	9,645	(B)	(B)	13,691
Other race	8,897	5,309	8,505	10,825	12,827	20,746	14,310
More than one race	9,488	4,919	9,545	11,436	12,792	20,921	13,308
Hispanic or Latino (any race):							
Not Hispanic or Latino	9,428	5,001	8,961	10,989	17,053	22,678	14,468
Hispanic or Latino	8,235	4,974	7,922	10,119	11,090	18,279	13,639
Attendance pattern:							
Full-time, full-year	14,710	9,083	11,238	13,278	21,131	26,790	18,360
Full-time, part-year.	7,991	4,978	6,537	7,394	11,584	14,865	12,875
Part-time, full-year.	8,109	6,209	8,605	10,089	12,725	15,431	14,076
Part-time, part-year	2,968	2,325	3,414	4,323	5,492	5,691	7,842
Local residence:							
On campus	15,713	5,261	10,492	12,694	22,138	26,984	17,222
Off campus	8,180	4,828	8,802	10,626	12,740	18,212	14,373
With parents/other relatives.	7,915	5,347	7,758	9,361	14,312	19,722	13,676

B Base too small to meet statistical standards for reliability of a derived figure. [1] Includes public less-than-2-year and private not-for-profit less-than-4-year. [2] As of December 31, 1999.

Source: U.S. National Center for Education Statistics, *Student Financing of Undergraduate Education 1999-2000*, July 2002, NCES 2002-167.

No. 272. Higher Education Price Indexes: 1970 to 2003

[1983=100. For years ending June 30. Reflects prices paid by colleges and universities]

Year	Personnel compensation					Contracted services, supplies, and equipment					
	Index, total	Total	Profes-sional salaries	Nonpro-fessional salaries	Fringe benefits	Total	Serv-ices	Supplies and materials	Equip-ment	Library acquisi-tions	Utilities
1970 ..	39.5	42.1	47.7	38.8	24.7	31.9	42.8	37.6	41.9	25.7	16.3
1975 ..	54.3	56.3	60.3	54.6	42.9	48.5	56.8	58.0	58.3	46.7	31.8
1980 ..	77.5	78.4	79.4	80.2	72.6	75.0	77.0	84.6	81.6	77.8	64.1
1981 ..	85.8	85.8	86.3	87.7	81.8	85.9	85.2	95.6	89.6	85.9	79.7
1982 ..	93.9	93.5	93.7	94.6	91.5	94.9	94.2	100.4	96.4	93.5	92.4
1983 ..	100.0	100.0	100.0	100.0	100.0	100.0	100.0	100.0	100.0	100.0	100.0
1984 ..	104.8	105.4	104.7	105.1	108.3	103.0	104.9	99.7	102.3	105.3	102.5
1985 ..	110.8	112.0	111.4	109.2	117.7	107.1	110.8	103.0	104.8	111.3	105.3
1986 ..	116.3	118.8	118.2	112.8	127.7	109.0	115.1	102.6	107.2	121.2	103.1
1987 ..	120.9	125.4	125.0	116.3	137.4	107.4	119.7	99.0	108.9	132.9	91.0
1988 ..	126.2	131.7	130.9	120.6	147.2	109.8	123.0	101.1	120.5	140.5	87.7
1989 ..	132.8	139.6	138.8	125.3	158.8	112.8	128.8	108.3	115.1	153.5	85.3
1990 ..	140.8	148.3	147.6	130.3	171.4	118.7	134.0	114.3	119.6	167.0	90.1
1991 ..	148.2	156.5	155.6	135.4	184.3	123.3	139.8	116.4	123.3	179.8	92.4
1992 ..	153.5	162.4	160.8	140.2	194.3	126.9	145.7	115.2	126.3	193.9	93.3
1993 ..	158.0	167.6	165.0	144.2	204.3	129.4	149.5	113.2	128.6	203.4	94.7
1994 ..	163.3	173.3	170.3	148.2	213.6	133.6	154.8	114.3	130.8	213.6	98.7
1995 ..	168.1	179.1	176.1	152.5	221.4	135.3	158.0	115.7	133.5	220.2	96.8
1996 ..	173.0	184.1	181.7	157.3	224.5	139.9	163.8	130.1	137.0	230.9	93.3
1997 ..	178.4	189.0	187.2	162.1	226.7	147.2	167.3	128.6	139.3	253.4	106.1
1998 ..	184.7	195.8	193.5	168.0	236.7	151.6	172.8	126.2	141.3	266.5	111.1
1999 ..	189.1	202.0	200.7	174.1	239.2	150.8	177.0	123.2	143.3	282.1	100.5
2000 ..	196.9	210.8	208.4	180.4	254.8	155.8	182.9	123.1	145.0	298.6	104.9
2001 ..	206.5	218.1	215.8	187.9	261.7	172.2	189.2	130.5	147.3	317.4	140.7
2002 ..	214.9	(NA)	(NA)	(NA)	(NA)	(NA)	(NA)	(NA)	(NA)	(NA)	(NA)
2003 ..	221.1	(NA)	(NA)	(NA)	(NA)	(NA)	(NA)	(NA)	(NA)	(NA)	(NA)

NA Not available.

Source: Research Associates of Washington, Arlington, VA, *Inflation Measures for Schools, Colleges, and Libraries,* periodic (copyright).

No. 273. Federal Student Financial Assistance: 1995 to 2004

[For award years July 1 of year shown to the following June 30 (35,477 represents ($35,477,000,000). Funds utilized exclude operating costs, etc., and represent funds given to students]

Type of assistance	1995	1999	2000	2001	2002	2003	2004, est.
FUNDS UTILIZED (mil. dol.)							
Total	35,477	40,162	44,007	48,582	55,525	61,806	68,703
Federal Pell Grants	5,472	7,209	7,956	9,975	11,640	12,680	13,072
Federal Supplemental Educational Opportunity Grant	764	875	907	1,007	1,033	962	975
Federal Work-Study	764	917	939	1,032	1,097	1,203	1,196
Federal Perkins Loan	1,029	1,101	1,144	1,239	1,460	1,201	1,263
Federal Direct Student Loan (FDSL)	8,296	9,953	10,348	10,635	11,689	11,969	13,219
Federal Family Education Loans (FFEL)	19,152	20,107	22,712	24,694	28,606	33,791	38,978
NUMBER OF AWARDS (1,000)							
Total	13,667	14,566	15,043	16,154	17,976	19,246	20,822
Federal Pell Grants	3,612	3,764	3,899	4,341	4,953	5,141	5,344
Federal Supplemental Educational Opportunity Grant	1,083	1,170	1,175	1,295	1,354	1,236	1,254
Federal Work-Study	702	733	713	740	759	863	858
Federal Perkins Loan	688	655	639	660	728	640	673
Federal Direct Student Loan (FDSL)	2,339	2,891	2,739	2,763	2,908	2,937	3,129
Federal Family Education Loans (FFEL)	5,243	5,354	5,878	6,355	7,274	8,429	9,564
AVERAGE AWARD (dol.)							
Total	2,596	2,757	2,925	3,007	3,089	3,211	3,300
Federal Pell Grants	1,515	1,915	2,041	2,298	2,350	2,467	2,441
Federal Supplemental Educational Opportunity Grant	705	748	772	778	763	778	778
Federal Work-Study	1,088	1,252	1,318	1,395	1,446	1,394	1,394
Federal Perkins Loan	1,496	1,681	1,790	1,877	2,003	1,875	1,875
Federal Direct Student Loan (FDSL)	3,547	3,443	3,778	3,849	4,020	4,075	4,225
Federal Family Education Loans (FFEL)	3,653	3,756	3,864	3,886	3,933	4,009	4,075
COHORT DEFAULT RATE [1]							
Federal Perkins Loan	12.6	10.61	9.9	9.51	8.85	(NA)	(NA)
FFEL/FDSL Combined Rates	10.4	5.6	5.9	5.40	(NA)	(NA)	(NA)

NA Not available.   [1] As of June 30. Represents the percent of borrowers entering repayment status in year shown who defaulted in the following year.

Source: U.S. Dept. of Education, Office of Postsecondary Education, unpublished data.

Education   175

No. 274. State Appropriations for Higher Education, 2000 and 2001, and by State, 2002

[Preliminary. For academic year ending in year shown (8,596.8 represents 8,596,800). Data for the 50 states]

State	FTE enrollment [1] (1,000)	Educational appropriations per FTE [2] (dol.)	Higher ed. appropriations as a percent of state and local tax revenue [3]	State	FTE enrollment [1] (1,000)	Educational appropriations per FTE [2] (dol.)	Higher ed. appropriations as a percent of state and local tax revenue [3]
Total, 2000 . . .	8,596.8	5,941	7.4	MS	130.2	4,257	11.5
Total, 2001 . . .	8,824.4	6,182	7.3	MO	139.0	6,614	6.1
Total, 2002 .	**9,168.9**	**6,182**	**7.3**	MT	34.3	3,975	6.6
AL	173.8	4,697	11.2	NE	67.7	5,736	10.7
AK	16.2	11,239	9.0	NV	50.0	6,403	5.9
AZ	191.2	5,676	8.9	NH	27.5	3,314	3.0
AR	93.1	5,008	9.4	NJ	162.4	8,936	4.8
CA	1,535.2	6,669	9.4	NM	68.6	6,925	11.0
CO	147.7	4,340	5.6	NY	466.9	7,041	3.9
CT	64.1	9,780	4.4	NC	286.3	7,051	10.8
DE	26.8	6,637	6.7	ND	33.1	4,781	10.7
FL	443.8	5,169	5.9	OH	353.6	5,172	6.0
GA	188.4	7,807	7.5	OK	128.5	5,410	9.7
HI	32.9	6,849	6.6	OR	120.2	4,560	6.3
ID	46.2	6,801	10.2	PA	293.7	6,091	4.8
IL	339.0	7,984	7.6	RI	26.9	6,503	4.9
IN	203.6	4,761	6.6	SC	137.0	4,476	8.3
IA	110.8	5,887	9.0	SD	22.6	4,563	7.0
KS	104.3	6,438	10.3	TN	160.8	5,292	8.1
KY	131.3	6,966	9.9	TX	711.6	5,909	10.6
LA	172.1	4,285	8.5	UT	98.7	5,365	9.7
ME	30.6	6,804	5.0	VT	16.4	2,628	2.8
MD	175.1	6,063	7.6	VA	246.6	5,956	7.4
MA	123.6	7,943	4.1	WA	219.1	5,548	6.7
MI	350.3	6,660	7.7	WV	64.8	4,825	9.3
MN	176.5	6,841	7.3	WI	202.4	6,533	7.6
				WY	23.5	8,453	13.8

[1] Full-time equivalent. Credit and non-credit enrollment, including summer session. Excludes medical enrollments.   [2] State and local appropriations. Includes aid to students attending in-state public institutions. Excludes sums for research, agriculture experiment stations, and cooperative extension, and hospitals and medical schools.   [3] Includes state and local appropriations (including sums for research, agriculture experiment stations and cooperative extension, and hospitals and medical schools).

Source: State Higher Education Executive Officers, Denver, CO., (copyright). See Internet site <http://www.sheeo.org>.

No. 275. Average Amount of Aid Received by Undergraduates Receiving Aid: 1999-2000

[Average amount in dollars. Based on the Student Postsecondary Aid Study and subject to sampling error; see source for details. See also Appendix III]

Characteristic	Total aid [1]		Total grants		Total loans [2]	
	Percent receiving aid	Average amount	Percent receiving grants	Average amount	Percent receiving loans	Average amount
Total	**55.3**	**6,206**	**44.4**	**3,476**	**28.8**	**5,131**
Attendance pattern:						
Full-time, full-year	72.5	8,474	58.7	4,949	45.4	5,437
Part-time or part-year.	44.6	3,902	35.4	1,952	18.4	4,660
Institution type: [3]						
Public 2-year	37.8	2,311	32.7	1,571	7.4	3,319
Public 4-year	62.1	6,188	46.3	3,203	39.6	4,834
Private not-for-profit 4-year	76.1	11,577	66.4	7,008	49.8	6,226
Private for-profit	84.9	7,218	59.7	2,654	66.5	5,772
Price of attendance: [3]						
Less than $4,000	24.8	763	22.1	673	1.4	1,635
$4,000 to 7,999	50.6	2,581	42.1	1,843	14.8	2,762
$8,000 to 11,999	64.2	4,948	49.7	2,692	35.4	4,268
$12,000 or more	78.4	11,035	62.1	6,145	59.5	6,222
Dependency status: [4]						
Dependent.	58.9	7,367	46.1	4,574	34.9	4,612
Independent.	51.9	4,932	42.7	2,331	23.0	5,893
Dependent 1998 income: [5]						
Low (under $30,000)	74.8	7,005	71.4	4,383	38.1	4,427
Middle ($30,000-80,000)	57.4	7,508	42.5	4,648	37.3	4,575
High (over $80,000)	47.7	7,561	30.6	4,777	27.8	4,922
Independent 1998 income: [6]						
Low (under $12,000)	72.6	6,226	67.9	2,979	38.6	5,704
Middle ($12,000-45,000)	51.8	4,753	40.5	2,116	23.5	5,895
High (over $45,000)	34.3	3,051	24.9	1,410	8.9	6,583

[1] Includes other aid not shown separately.   [2] Includes only loans to students.   [3] Excludes students attending more than one institution.   [4] Dependent or independent for federal aid purposes.   [5] Dependent student parent's income.   [6] Independent student's income (including spouse).

Source: U.S. National Center for Education Statistics, *Student Financing of Undergraduate Education 1999-2000*, July 2002, NCES 2002-167.

No. 276. Institutions of Higher Education—Charges: 1985 to 2003

[In dollars. Estimated. **For the entire academic year ending in year shown.** Figures are average charges per full-time equivalent student. Room and board are based on full-time students]

Academic control and year	Tuition and required fees [1]				Board rates [2]				Dormitory charges			
	All institutions	2-yr. colleges	4-yr. colleges	Other 4-yr. schools	All institutions	2-yr. colleges	4-yr. colleges	Other 4-yr. schools	All institutions	2-yr. colleges	4-yr. colleges	Other 4-yr. schools
Public:												
1985.....	971	584	1,386	1,117	1,241	1,302	1,276	1,201	1,196	921	1,237	1,200
1990.....	1,356	756	2,035	1,608	1,635	1,581	1,728	1,561	1,513	962	1,561	1,554
1995.....	2,057	1,192	2,977	2,499	1,949	1,712	2,108	1,866	1,959	1,232	1,992	2,044
1998.....	2,360	1,314	3,486	2,877	2,228	1,795	2,438	2,130	2,225	1,401	2,285	2,312
1999.....	2,430	1,327	3,640	2,974	2,347	1,828	2,576	2,247	2,330	1,450	2,408	2,410
2000.....	2,506	1,338	3,768	3,091	2,364	1,834	2,628	2,239	2,440	1,549	2,516	2,521
2001.....	2,562	1,333	3,979	3,208	2,455	1,906	2,686	2,358	2,569	1,600	2,657	2,652
2002.....	2,727	1,379	4,281	3,419	2,597	2,036	2,835	2,498	2,721	1,722	2,837	2,793
2003.....	2,928	1,479	4,698	3,675	2,702	2,174	2,939	2,605	2,925	1,943	3,023	3,022
Private:												
1985.....	5,315	3,485	6,843	5,135	1,462	1,294	1,647	1,405	1,426	1,424	1,753	1,309
1990.....	8,174	5,196	10,348	7,778	1,948	1,811	2,339	1,823	1,923	1,663	2,411	1,774
1995.....	11,111	6,914	14,537	10,653	2,509	2,023	3,035	2,362	2,587	2,233	3,469	2,347
1998.....	12,801	7,464	17,229	12,338	2,762	2,785	3,132	2,648	2,954	2,672	3,756	2,731
1999.....	13,428	7,854	18,340	12,815	2,865	2,884	3,188	2,765	3,075	2,581	3,914	2,850
2000.....	14,081	8,235	19,307	13,361	2,882	2,922	3,157	2,790	3,224	2,808	4,070	2,976
2001.....	15,000	9,067	20,106	14,233	2,993	3,000	3,300	2,893	3,374	2,722	4,270	3,121
2002.....	15,851	10,010	21,183	14,995	3,106	2,664	3,465	2,996	3,564	3,204	4,471	3,294
2003.....	16,517	10,755	22,686	15,532	3,236	3,821	3,653	3,095	3,750	3,184	4,712	3,476

[1] For in-state students.   [2] Beginning 1990, rates reflect 20 meals per week, rather than meals served 7 days a week.

Source: U.S. National Center for Education Statistics, *Digest of Education Statistics,* annual.

No. 277. Voluntary Financial Support of Higher Education: 1990 to 2003

[For school years ending in years shown (9,800 represents $9,800,000,000); enrollment as of fall of preceding year. Voluntary support, as defined in Gift Reporting Standards, excludes income from endowment and other invested funds as well as all support received from Federal, state, and local governments and their agencies and contract research]

Item	Unit	1990	1995	1998	1999	2000	2001	2002	2003
Estimated support, total	Mil. dol.	9,800	12,750	18,400	20,400	23,200	24,200	23,900	23,900
Individuals	Mil. dol .	4,770	6,540	10,000	10,740	12,220	12,030	11,300	11,150
Alumni	Mil. dol .	2,540	3,600	5,500	5,930	6,800	6,830	5,900	6,600
Business corporations	Mil. dol .	2,170	2,560	3,250	3,610	4,150	4,350	4,370	4,250
Foundations	Mil. dol .	1,920	2,460	3,800	4,530	5,080	6,000	6,300	6,600
Fundraising consortia and other organizations	Mil. dol .	700	940	1,050	1,190	1,380	1,450	1,570	1,540
Religious organizations	Mil. dol .	240	250	300	330	370	370	360	360
Current operations	Mil. dol .	5,440	7,230	9,000	9,900	11,270	12,200	12,400	12,900
Capital purposes.	Mil. dol .	4,360	5,520	9,400	10,500	11,930	12,000	11,500	11,000
Enrollment, higher education [1] . .	1,000 . .	13,819	14,262	14,507	14,791	15,312	15,442	15,608	15,756
Support per student.	Dollars .	709	894	1,268	1,379	1,515	1,567	1,531	1,517
In 2002-2003 dollars	Dollars .	998	1,079	1,432	1,523	1,619	1,628	1,566	1,517
Expenditures, higher education .	Bil. dol .	164	211	249	267	284	291	299	306
Expenditures per student	Dollars .	11,848	14,819	17,198	18,049	18,534	18,851	19,130	19,438
In 2002-2003 dollars	Dollars .	16,679	17,892	19,414	19,935	19,805	19,586	19,566	19,438
Institutions reporting support	Number.	1,056	1,086	1,034	938	945	960	955	954
Total support reported	Mil. dol.	8,214	10,992	15,771	17,229	19,419	20,569	19,824	19,823
Private 4-year institutions	Mil. dol .	5,072	6,500	9,118	9,848	11,047	11,391	10,953	10,318
Public 4-year institutions.	Mil. dol .	3,056	4,382	6,556	7,252	8,254	9,026	8,754	9,400
2-year colleges	Mil. dol .	85	110	98	129	117	152	117	105

[1] Excludes proprietary schools.

Source: Council for Aid to Education, New York, NY, *Voluntary Support of Education,* annual.

No. 278. Average Salaries for College Faculty Members: 2002 to 2004

[In thousands of dollars (62.0 represents $62,000). **For academic year ending in year shown.** Figures are for 9 months teaching for full-time faculty members in 2-year and 4-year institutions with ranks. Fringe benefits averaged in 2002, $14,926 in public institutions and $18,356 in private institutions; in 2003, $16,208 in public institutions and $19,261 in private institutions and in 2004, $17,090 in public institutions and $20,565 in private institutions]

Type of control and academic rank	2002	2003	2004	Type of control and academic rank	2002	2003	2004
Public: All ranks.	62.0	64.0	65.0	Private: [1] All ranks	71.5	74.4	76.6
Professor	81.3	84.1	85.8	Professor	96.1	101.2	104.0
Associate professor	59.4	61.5	62.4	Associate professor	63.4	66.3	68.5
Assistant professor.	49.6	51.5	52.5	Assistant professor.	53.2	55.6	57.5
Instructor	36.2	37.2	37.9	Instructor	40.1	41.1	41.8

[1] Excludes church-related colleges and universities.

Source: American Association of University Professors, Washington, DC, *AAUP Annual Report on the Economic Status of the Profession.*

Education 177

No. 279. Employees in Higher Education Institutions by Sex and Occupation: 1976 to 2001

[In thousands (1,863.8 represents 1,863,800). As of fall. Based on survey and subject to sampling error; see source]

Year and status	Professional staff										Nonprofessional staff, total
	Total	Executive, administrative, and managerial		Faculty [1]		Research/instruction assistants		Other			
	Total	Total	Male	Female	Male	Female	Male	Female	Male	Female	total
1976, total	1,863.8	1,073.1	74.6	26.6	460.6	172.7	106.5	53.6	87.5	91.0	790.7
Full time	1,339.9	709.4	72.0	25.0	326.8	107.2	18.6	9.4	76.2	74.1	630.5
Part time	523.9	363.7	2.6	1.7	133.7	65.4	87.9	44.2	11.3	16.9	160.2
1991, total	2,545.2	1,595.5	85.4	59.3	525.6	300.7	119.1	78.6	165.4	261.3	949.8
Full time	1,812.9	1,031.8	82.9	56.2	366.2	169.4	(NA)	(NA)	142.2	214.8	781.1
Part time	732.3	563.7	2.5	3.1	159.4	131.2	119.1	78.6	23.2	46.4	168.7
2001, total [2]	3,134.0	2,170.2	81.1	75.0	657.2	481.5	142.2	119.1	241.5	372.7	963.8
Full time	2,077.9	1,308.8	78.8	71.6	387.3	244.6	-	-	210.9	315.7	769.1
Part time	1,056.1	861.4	2.4	3.3	269.9	237.0	142.2	119.1	30.6	57.0	194.7

- Represents zero. NA Not available. [1] Instruction and research. [2] In this table, 2001 data reflect the new classification of institutions. See footnote 1, Table 261.

Source: U.S. National Center for Education Statistics, *Fall Staff in Postsecondary Institutions, 2001*, NCES 2004-159, November 2003, and earlier issues; and *Digest of Education Statistics, 2001*.

No. 280. Faculty in Institutions of Higher Education: 1970 to 2001

[In thousands (474 represents 474,000), except percent. As of fall. Based on survey and subject to sampling error; see source]

Year	Employment status			Control		Level		Percent		
	Total	Full time	Part time	Public	Private	4-Year	2-Year or less	Part time	Public	2-Year or less
1970	474	369	104	314	160	382	92	22	66	19
1975	628	440	188	443	185	467	161	30	71	26
1980	686	450	236	495	191	494	192	34	72	28
1985	715	459	256	503	212	504	211	36	70	30
1991 [1]	826	536	291	581	245	591	235	35	70	28
1993	915	546	370	650	265	626	289	40	71	32
1995	932	551	381	657	275	647	285	41	70	31
1997 [2]	990	569	421	695	295	683	307	43	70	31
1999	1,028	591	437	713	315	714	314	43	69	31
2001	1,139	632	507	786	352	764	375	45	69	33

[1] Data beginning 1991 not comparable to prior years. [2] In this table, data beginning in 1997 reflect the new classification of institutions. See footnote 1, Table 261.

Source: U.S. National Center for Education Statistics, *Fall Staff in Postsecondary Institutions, 2001*, NCES 2004-159, November 2003, and earlier issues; and *Digest of Education Statistics, 2001*.

No. 281. Salary Offers to Candidates for Degrees: 2001 to 2003

[In dollars. Data are average beginning salaries based on offers made by business, industrial, government, nonprofit, and educational employers to graduating students. Data from representative colleges throughout the United States]

Field of study	Bachelor's			Master's [1]			Doctor's		
	2001	2002	2003	2001	2002	2003	2001	2002	2003
Accounting	39,720	39,494	40,647	43,196	43,625	42,241	(NA)	(NA)	(NA)
Business administration/ management [2]	37,844	36,378	36,012	50,679	52,241	[3]50,835	[3]82,167	[3]81,357	[3]87,000
Marketing	35,194	33,690	34,038	[3]48,833	[3]56,000	[3]35,000	(NA)	(NA)	(NA)
Engineering:									
Civil	40,979	41,193	41,669	44,234	47,756	47,245	[3]61,606	[3]56,228	[3]69,079
Chemical	51,255	51,137	52,384	57,317	[3]55,812	[3]57,857	74,153	75,552	[3]70,729
Computer	53,653	51,135	51,343	60,974	[3]64,268	[3]64,200	[3]71,720	[3]59,211	(NA)
Electrical	52,092	50,391	49,794	64,188	62,194	64,556	79,383	77,316	74,283
Mechanical	48,588	48,282	48,585	56,565	55,013	59,098	70,124	63,161	[3]69,904
Nuclear [4]	[3]47,914	[3]48,583	50,104	[3]55,496	[3]51,500	(NA)	(NA)	(NA)	(NA)
Petroleum	54,761	56,622	55,987	[3]58,500	(NA)	[3]67,500	(NA)	(NA)	(NA)
Engineering technology	45,458	45,059	44,930	(NA)	(NA)	(NA)	(NA)	(NA)	(NA)
Chemistry	38,744	34,566	37,733	[3]51,467	[3]59,836	[3]52,583	62,067	63,168	58,481
Mathematics	44,277	41,543	40,512	[3]55,482	[3]82,000	[3]42,348	[3]58,555	[3]54,219	[3]58,778
Physics	48,458	[3]47,471	[3]42,365	[3]61,000	[3]41,333	(NA)	[3]63,220	[3]51,936	55,485
Humanities	30,653	[3]31,087	[3]29,694	[3]32,650	[3]29,944	[3]32,465	(NA)	[3]41,750	[3]41,100
Social sciences [5]	31,634	28,835	29,098	[3]31,508	[3]38,109	[3]36,992	(NA)	[3]47,434	[3]43,603
Computer science	52,473	49,413	47,109	62,312	65,001	62,806	[3]84,033	[3]74,453	[3]64,640

NA Not available. [1] Candidates with 1 year or less of full-time nonmilitary employment. [2] For master's degree, offers are after nontechnical undergraduate degree. [3] Fewer than 50 offers reported. [4] Includes engineering physics. [5] Excludes economics.

Source: National Association of Colleges and Employers, Bethlehem, PA," "Salary Survey, *A Study of Beginning Offers*, annual (copyright).

No. 282. Earned Degrees Conferred by Level and Sex: 1960 to 2002

[In thousands (477 represents 477,000), except percent. Includes the 50 states and DC. Based on survey; see Appendix III]

Year ending	All degrees Total	Percent male	Associate's Male	Associate's Female	Bachelor's Male	Bachelor's Female	Master's Male	Master's Female	First professional Male	First professional Female	Doctor's Male	Doctor's Female
1960 [1]	477	65.8	(NA)	(NA)	254	138	51	24	(NA)	(NA)	9	1
1965 [1]	660	61.5	(NA)	(NA)	282	212	81	40	(NA)	(NA)	15	2
1970	1,271	59.2	117	89	451	341	126	83	34	1	26	4
1975	1,666	56.0	191	169	505	418	162	131	49	7	27	7
1980	1,731	51.1	184	217	474	456	151	147	53	17	23	10
1985	1,828	49.3	203	252	483	497	143	143	50	25	22	11
1986	1,830	49.0	196	250	486	502	144	145	49	25	22	12
1987	1,823	48.4	191	245	481	510	141	148	47	25	22	12
1988	1,835	48.0	190	245	477	518	145	154	45	25	23	12
1989	1,873	47.3	186	250	483	535	149	161	45	26	23	13
1990	1,940	46.6	191	264	492	560	154	171	44	27	24	14
1991	2,025	45.8	199	283	504	590	156	181	44	28	25	15
1992	2,108	45.6	207	297	521	616	162	191	45	29	26	15
1993	2,167	45.5	212	303	• 533	632	169	200	45	30	26	16
1994	2,206	45.1	215	315	532	637	176	211	45	31	27	17
1995	2,218	44.9	218	321	526	634	179	219	45	31	27	18
1996 [2]	2,248	44.2	220	336	522	642	179	227	45	32	27	18
1997 [2]	2,288	43.6	224	347	521	652	181	238	46	33	27	19
1998 [2]	2,298	43.2	218	341	520	664	184	246	45	34	27	19
1999 [2]	2,323	42.7	218	342	519	682	186	254	44	34	25	19
2000 [2]	2,385	42.6	225	340	530	708	192	265	44	34	25	20
2001 [2]	2,416	42.4	232	347	532	712	194	274	44	36	25	20
2002 [2]	2,494	42.2	238	357	550	742	199	283	43	38	24	20

NA Not available. [1] First-professional degrees are included with bachelor's degrees. See footnote 1, Table 261. [2] Data beginning in 1996 reflect the new classification of institutions.

Source: U.S. National Center for Education Statistics, *Digest of Education Statistics*, annual.

No. 283. Degrees Earned by Level and Race/Ethnicity: 1981 to 2002

[For school year ending in year shown. Based on survey; see Appendix III]

Level of degree and race/ethnicity	Total 1981 [1]	Total 1985 [1]	Total 1990	Total 1995	Total 2000 [2]	Total 2002 [2]	Percent distribution 1981	Percent distribution 2002 [2]
Associate's degrees, total	410,174	429,815	455,102	539,691	564,933	595,133	100.0	100.0
White, non-Hispanic	339,167	355,343	376,816	420,656	408,772	417,739	82.7	70.2
Black, non-Hispanic	35,330	35,791	34,326	47,067	60,221	67,337	8.6	11.3
Hispanic	17,800	19,407	21,504	35,962	51,573	60,003	4.3	10.1
Asian or Pacific Islander	8,650	9,914	13,066	20,677	27,782	30,947	2.1	5.2
American Indian/Alaskan Native	2,584	2,953	3,430	5,482	6,497	6,830	0.6	1.1
Nonresident alien	6,643	6,407	5,960	9,847	10,088	12,277	1.6	2.1
Bachelor's degrees, total	934,800	968,311	1,051,344	1,160,134	1,237,875	1,291,900	100.0	100.0
White, non-Hispanic	807,319	826,106	887,151	914,610	929,106	958,585	86.4	74.2
Black, non-Hispanic	60,673	57,473	61,046	87,236	108,013	116,624	6.5	9.0
Hispanic	21,832	25,874	32,829	54,230	75,059	82,969	2.3	6.4
Asian or Pacific Islander	18,794	25,395	39,230	60,502	77,912	83,101	2.0	6.4
American Indian/Alaskan Native	3,593	4,246	4,390	6,610	8,719	9,165	0.4	0.7
Nonresident alien	22,589	29,217	26,698	36,946	39,066	41,456	2.4	3.2
Master's degrees, total	294,183	280,421	324,301	397,629	457,056	482,118	100.0	100.0
White, non-Hispanic	241,216	223,628	254,299	293,345	320,485	327,635	82.0	68.0
Black, non-Hispanic	17,133	13,939	15,336	24,166	35,874	40,373	5.8	8.4
Hispanic	6,461	6,864	7,892	12,905	19,253	22,387	2.2	4.6
Asian or Pacific Islander	6,282	7,782	10,439	16,847	23,218	25,414	2.1	5.3
American Indian/Alaskan Native	1,034	1,256	1,090	1,621	2,246	2,626	0.4	0.5
Nonresident alien	22,057	26,952	35,245	48,745	55,980	63,683	7.5	13.2
Doctor's degrees, total	32,839	32,307	38,371	44,446	44,808	44,160	100.0	100.0
White, non-Hispanic	25,908	23,934	26,221	27,846	27,843	26,905	78.9	60.9
Black, non-Hispanic	1,265	1,154	1,149	1,667	2,246	2,397	3.9	5.4
Hispanic	456	677	780	984	1,305	1,432	1.4	3.2
Asian or Pacific Islander	877	1,106	1,225	2,689	2,420	2,317	2.7	5.2
American Indian/Alaskan Native	130	119	98	130	160	180	0.4	0.4
Nonresident alien	4,203	5,317	8,898	11,130	10,834	10,929	12.8	24.7
First-professional degrees, total	71,340	71,057	70,988	75,800	80,057	80,698	100.0	100.0
White, non-Hispanic	64,551	63,219	60,487	59,402	59,637	58,874	90.5	73.0
Black, non-Hispanic	2,931	3,029	3,409	4,747	5,555	5,811	4.1	7.2
Hispanic	1,541	1,884	2,425	3,231	3,865	3,965	2.2	4.9
Asian or Pacific Islander	1,456	1,816	3,362	6,396	8,584	9,584	2.0	11.9
American Indian/Alaskan Native	192	248	257	413	564	581	0.3	0.7
Nonresident alien	669	861	1,048	1,611	1,852	1,883	0.9	2.3

[1] Excludes some persons whose race/ethnicity was unknown and are slight undercounts of degrees awarded. [2] In this table, data beginning in 2000 reflect the new classification of institutions. See footnote 1, Table 261.

Source: U.S. National Center for Education Statistics, *Digest of Education Statistics*, annual.

U.S. Census Bureau, Statistical Abstract of the United States: 2004-2005

No. 284. Degrees and Awards Earned Below Bachelor's by Field: 2002

[Covers associate degrees and other awards based on postsecondary curriculums of less than 4 years in institutions of higher education. Based on survey; see Appendix III]

Field of study	Less than 1-year awards		1- to less than 4-year awards		Associate degrees	
	Total	Women	Total	Women	Total	Women
Total	**163,977**	**83,563**	**145,254**	**83,339**	**595,133**	**357,024**
Agriculture and natural resources	2,994	549	2,272	746	6,494	2,299
Architecture and related programs	31	20	114	99	443	342
Area, ethnic, and cultural studies	263	198	96	82	319	256
Biological/life sciences	82	38	29	17	1,517	1,039
Business management and administrative services [1]	34,339	21,134	25,094	18,409	98,796	67,585
Communications and communications technologies	785	392	683	284	4,840	2,198
Computer and information sciences	9,014	2,838	8,634	3,171	30,965	11,150
Construction trades	3,916	217	5,440	207	2,639	139
Consumer and personal services	5,881	4,514	8,945	6,624	10,115	4,808
Education	2,056	1,616	893	770	9,267	7,397
Engineering and engineering technologies	5,080	918	6,110	786	34,619	4,803
English language and literature/letters	324	212	121	80	864	569
Foreign languages and literatures	280	199	41	39	517	297
Health professions and related sciences	44,405	34,703	43,942	38,274	79,888	69,703
Home economics and vocational home economics	9,025	6,787	4,443	3,987	9,480	8,739
Law and legal studies	768	663	1,390	1,221	6,825	6,048
Liberal/general studies and humanities	268	182	3,408	2,246	207,163	130,987
Library science	150	136	49	39	96	84
Mathematics	2	-	5	3	685	240
Mechanics and repairers	9,419	944	15,180	824	12,086	767
Multi/interdisciplinary studies	436	224	193	143	13,204	7,434
Parks, recreation, leisure, and fitness	250	124	411	278	830	367
Physical sciences	167	76	130	63	2,308	1,062
Precision production trades	5,454	804	7,823	1,172	10,818	2,427
Protective services	13,740	3,182	4,104	987	16,689	6,397
Psychology	50	42	34	30	1,705	1,334
Public administration and services	489	410	376	309	3,323	2,855
R.O.T.C. and military technologies	-	-	-	-	62	8
Social sciences and history	291	135	48	25	5,593	3,747
Theological studies, religion and philosophy	81	49	470	226	548	300
Transportation and material moving	12,275	1,482	842	66	1,159	161
Visual and performing arts	1,659	774	3,854	2,073	20,911	11,298
Undistributed and unclassified	3	1	80	59	365	184

- Represents zero.   [1] Includes marketing.

Source: U.S. National Center for Education Statistics, *Digest of Education Statistics,* annual.

No. 285. Bachelor's Degrees Earned by Field: 1971 to 2002

[Based on survey; see Appendix III]

Field of study	1971	1980	1990	1995	2002 [1]	Percent female	
						1971	2002 [1]
Total	**839,730**	**929,417**	**1,051,344**	**1,160,134**	**1,291,900**	**43.4**	**57.4**
Agriculture and natural resources	12,672	22,802	12,900	19,841	23,353	4.2	45.9
Architecture and environmental design	5,570	9,132	9,364	8,756	8,808	11.9	40.7
Area, ethnic and cultural studies	2,582	2,840	4,613	5,706	6,557	52.4	68.9
Biological sciences/life sciences	35,743	46,370	37,204	55,984	60,256	29.1	60.8
Business and management	114,729	184,867	248,698	234,323	281,330	9.1	50.0
Communications [2]	10,802	28,616	51,308	48,803	63,901	35.3	63.0
Computer and information sciences	2,388	11,154	27,257	24,404	47,299	13.6	27.6
Education	176,307	118,038	105,112	106,079	106,383	74.5	77.4
Engineering [2]	50,046	68,893	81,322	78,154	73,598	0.8	19.0
English language and literature/letters	64,342	32,541	47,519	51,901	53,162	65.6	68.6
Foreign languages and literatures	20,536	12,089	12,386	13,775	15,318	74.0	71.2
Health sciences	25,226	63,902	58,302	79,855	70,517	77.1	85.5
Home economics	11,167	18,411	14,491	15,345	18,153	97.3	88.0
Law and legal studies	545	683	1,592	2,032	1,971	5.0	70.2
Liberal/general studies	7,481	23,196	27,985	33,356	39,333	33.6	67.2
Library and archival sciences	1,013	398	77	50	74	92.0	75.7
Mathematics	24,937	11,872	15,176	13,723	12,395	37.9	46.7
Multi/interdisciplinary studies	6,286	11,277	16,267	26,033	27,629	22.8	67.6
Parks and recreation	1,621	5,753	4,582	12,889	20,554	34.7	51.7
Philosophy, religion, and theology	11,890	13,276	12,068	12,854	9,306	25.5	38.9
Physical sciences [2]	21,412	23,410	16,066	19,177	17,851	13.8	42.2
Protective services	2,045	15,015	15,334	24,157	25,536	9.2	46.2
Psychology	38,187	42,093	53,952	72,083	76,671	44.4	77.5
Public administration and services	5,466	16,644	13,908	18,586	19,392	68.4	80.9
R.O.T.C. and military technologies	357	38	196	27	3	0.3	-
Social sciences [3]	155,324	103,662	118,083	128,154	132,874	36.8	51.7
Visual and performing arts	30,394	40,892	39,934	48,690	66,773	59.7	59.4
Unclassified [4]	662	1,535	5,628	5,397	12,903	0.9	25.5

- Represents zero.   [1] In this table, data for 2002 reflect the new classification of institutions. See footnote 1, Table 261.
[2] Includes technologies.   [3] Includes history.   [4] Includes precision production trades and transportation and materials moving.

Source: U.S. National Center for Education Statistics, *Digest of Education Statistics,* annual.

180   Education

No. 286. Master's and Doctorate's Degrees Earned by Field: 1971 to 2002

[Based on survey; see Appendix III]

Level and field of study	1971	1980	1990	1995	2002 [1]	Percent female 1971	Percent female 2002 [1]
MASTER'S DEGREES							
Total	230,509	298,081	324,301	397,629	482,118	40.1	58.7
Agriculture and natural resources	2,457	3,976	3,382	4,252	4,519	5.9	48.1
Architecture and related programs	1,705	3,139	3,499	3,923	4,566	13.8	42.9
Area, ethnic and cultural studies	1,032	852	1,212	1,639	1,578	38.3	61.3
Biological sciences/life sciences	5,728	6,510	4,869	5,393	6,205	33.6	57.8
Business management and administrative services	25,977	54,484	76,676	93,809	120,785	3.9	41.1
Communications and technologies	1,856	3,082	4,362	5,609	6,059	34.6	63.7
Computer and information sciences	1,588	3,647	9,677	10,326	16,038	10.3	33.4
Education	87,666	101,819	84,881	101,242	136,579	56.2	76.4
Engineering and engineering technologies .	16,443	16,243	24,772	29,670	26,920	1.1	21.4
English language and literature/letters	10,686	6,189	6,567	7,845	7,268	60.6	68.0
Foreign languages	5,217	2,854	2,760	3,136	2,861	64.2	69.2
Health sciences	5,749	15,704	20,321	31,243	43,644	55.3	77.6
Home economics	1,452	2,690	2,100	2,864	2,608	93.9	85.1
Law and legal studies	955	1,817	1,888	2,511	4,053	4.8	41.8
Liberal arts and sciences, general studies and humanities	885	2,646	1,999	2,565	2,754	44.6	62.6
Library science	7,001	5,374	4,341	5,057	5,113	81.3	81.8
Mathematics	5,695	3,382	4,146	4,181	3,487	27.1	42.4
Multi/interdisciplinary studies	821	2,306	2,834	2,457	3,211	25.0	61.5
Parks and recreation	218	647	529	1,755	2,754	29.8	50.7
Philosophy, religion, and theology	4,036	5,126	6,265	6,620	6,286	27.1	38.1
Physical sciences and science technologies	6,367	5,219	5,449	5,753	5,034	13.3	37.6
Protective services	194	1,805	1,151	1,706	2,935	10.3	45.0
Psychology	5,717	9,938	10,730	13,921	14,888	40.6	76.4
Public administration and services	7,785	17,560	17,399	23,501	25,448	50.0	74.4
R.O.T.C. and military technologies	2	46	-	124	-	-	-
Social sciences [2]	16,539	12,176	11,634	14,845	14,112	28.5	50.8
Visual and performing arts	6,675	8,708	8,481	10,277	11,595	47.4	57.6
Unclassified [3]	63	142	2,377	1,405	818	-	1.1
DOCTORATE'S DEGREES							
Total	32,107	32,615	38,371	44,446	44,160	14.3	46.3
Agriculture and natural resources	1,086	991	1,295	1,264	1,166	2.9	33.5
Architecture and related programs	36	79	103	141	183	8.3	36.1
Area, ethnic and cultural studies	144	151	131	186	216	16.7	50.5
Biological sciences/life sciences	3,645	3,636	3,844	4,645	4,489	16.3	44.3
Business management and administrative services	757	753	1,093	1,394	1,158	2.8	35.4
Communications and technologies	145	193	273	321	383	13.1	56.1
Computer and information sciences	128	240	627	884	750	2.3	22.8
Education	6,041	7,314	6,502	6,905	6,967	21.0	66.5
Engineering and engineering technology . .	3,638	2,507	4,981	6,128	5,210	0.6	17.3
English language and literature/letters	1,650	1,294	1,078	1,561	1,446	28.8	58.5
Foreign languages	988	755	724	905	843	34.6	59.0
Health sciences	466	786	1,536	2,069	3,523	16.5	63.3
Home economics	123	192	301	388	355	61.0	69.6
Law and legal studies	20	40	111	88	79	-	39.2
Liberal arts and sciences, general studies and humanities	32	192	63	90	113	31.3	64.6
Library science	39	73	42	55	45	28.2	62.2
Mathematics	1,249	763	966	1,226	958	7.6	29.0
Multi/interdisciplinary studies	59	209	272	238	384	6.8	45.6
Parks and recreation	2	21	35	149	151	50.0	43.0
Philosophy, religion, and theology	866	1,693	1,756	2,098	1,961	5.8	21.4
Physical sciences and science technologies	4,390	3,089	4,164	4,483	3,803	5.6	28.0
Protective services	1	18	38	26	49	-	53.1
Psychology	2,144	3,395	3,811	3,822	4,341	24.0	68.2
Public administration and services	174	342	508	556	571	24.1	56.2
Social sciences [2]	3,660	3,230	3,010	3,725	3,902	13.9	43.1
Visual and performing arts	621	655	849	1,080	1,114	22.2	56.0
Unclassified [3]	3	4	258	19	-	-	-

- Represents zero.   [1] Data for 2002 reflect the new classification of institutions. See footnote 1, Table 261.   [2] Includes history.   [3] Includes precision production trades and transportation and materials moving.

Source: U.S. National Center for Education Statistics, *Digest of Education Statistics,* annual.

Education   181

No. 287. First Professional Degrees Earned in Selected Professions: 1970 to 2001

[First professional degrees include degrees which require at least 6 years of college work for completion (including at least 2 years of preprofessional training). Based on survey; see Appendix III]

Type of degree and sex of recipient	1970	1975	1980	1985	1990	1995	1998	1999	2000	2001
Medicine (M.D.):										
Institutions conferring degrees. . . .	86	104	112	120	124	119	117	118	118	118
Degrees conferred, total.	8,314	12,447	14,902	16,041	15,075	15,537	15,424	15,562	15,286	15,403
Percent to women	8.4	13.1	23.4	30.4	34.2	38.8	41.6	42.5	42.7	43.3
Dentistry (D.D.S. or D.M.D.):										
Institutions conferring degrees. . . .	48	52	58	59	57	• 53	53	53	54	54
Degrees conferred, total.	3,718	4,773	5,258	5,339	4,100	3,897	4,032	4,144	4,250	4,391
Percent to women	0.9	3.1	13.3	20.7	30.9	36.4	38.2	35.5	40.1	38.6
Law (LL.B. or J.D.):										
Institutions conferring degrees. . . .	145	154	179	181	182	183	185	188	190	192
Degrees conferred, total.	14,916	29,296	35,647	37,491	36,485	39,349	39,331	39,167	38,152	37,904
Percent to women	5.4	15.1	30.2	38.5	42.2	42.6	44.4	44.8	45.9	47.3
Theological (B.D., M.Div., M.H.L.):										
Institutions conferring degrees. . . .	(NA)	(NA)	(NA)	(NA)	(NA)	192	190	193	198	191
Degrees conferred, total.	5,298	5,095	7,115	7,221	5,851	5,978	5,873	5,558	6,129	5,026
Percent to women	2.3	6.8	13.8	18.5	24.8	25.7	26.1	28.3	29.2	32.0

NA Not available.

Source: U.S. National Center for Education Statistics, *Digest of Education Statistics*, annual.

No. 288. Participation in Adult Education: 1994-95 to 2000-2001

[In thousands (189,543 represents 189,543,000), except percent. For the civilian noninstitutional population 17 years old and over not enrolled full time in elementary or secondary school at the time of the survey. Adult education is considered any enrollment in any educational activity at any time in the prior 12 months, except full-time enrollment in a higher education credential program. Based on the Adult Education Survey of the National Household Education Survey Program and subject to sampling error; see source and Appendix III for details]

Characteristic	Adult population (1,000)	Percent taking courses	Characteristic	Adult population (1,000)	Percent taking courses
Total, 1995	189,543	40	Educational attainment:		
Total, 1999 [1]	194,559	45	Up to 8th grade	12,582	19
Total, 2001	198,739	46	9th to 12th grade	18,697	24
			High school diploma or GED	64,606	34
Age:			Vocational school after high school . .	6,925	51
17 to 24	23,460	53	Some college	34,660	57
25 to 34	38,325	53	Associate's degree	10,974	62
35 to 44	43,355	54	Bachelor's or higher	50,295	66
45 to 54	38,109	53			
55 to 64	23,950	38	**Occupation:** [3]		
65 and over.	31,541	21	Professional	22,708	74
			Executive, administrative and		
Sex:			managerial	17,132	66
Male	94,898	43	Technical and related support.	8,037	75
Female.	103,841	49	Sales workers	16,948	51
			Administrative support and clerical. . .	22,030	59
Race/ethnicity:			Service.	19,793	49
? White, Non-Hispanic	144,094	47	Agriculture, forestry, and fishing	2,883	46
Black, Non-Hispanic	22,186	43	Precision production, craft		
Hispanic	21,526	42	and repair	14,063	34
Other Non-Hispanic races	10,932	49	Machine operators, assemblers [4] . . .	10,336	39
			Transportation and materials		
Region: [2]			moving	6,968	30
Northeast	38,300	45	Handlers, equipment cleaners,		
Midwest	45,577	46	helpers and laborers	3,472	18
South	70,499	45	Nonclassifiable, undetermined	835	65
West	44,363	51	**Household income:** [5]		
			Under $10,000.	7,357	39
Marital status:			$10,001 to $15,000.	5,764	34
Never married	41,765	50	$15,001 to $20,000.	8,572	36
Currently married	121,455	47	$20,001 to $25,000.	9,439	44
Other	35,519	38	$25,001 to $30,000.	8,683	46
			$30,001 to $40,000●	18,280	52
Children under 18 in household:			$40,001 to $50,000.	7,270	53
Yes	83,968	53	$50,001 to $75,000.	8,334	57
No	114,771	42	More than $75,000	14,890	60

[1] Revised from previous estimates. [2] For composition of regions, see map inside front cover. [3] For currently employed.
[4] Includes inspectors. [5] For those employed in the 12 months prior to the interview.

Source: National Center for Education Statistics, 1995, 1999, and 2001 National Household Education Surveys. See Internet site <http://nces.ed.gov/nhes/>.

Section 5

Law Enforcement, Courts, and Prisons

This section presents data on crimes committed, victims of crimes, arrests, and data related to criminal violations and the criminal justice system. The major sources of these data are the Bureau of Justice Statistics (BJS), the Federal Bureau of Investigation (FBI), and the Administrative Office of the U.S. Courts. BJS issues several reports, including *Sourcebook of Criminal Justice Statistics, Criminal Victimization in the United States, Prisoners in State and Federal Institutions, Census of State Correctional Facilities and Survey of Prison Inmates, Census of Jails and Survey of Jail Inmates, Parole in the United States, Capital Punishment,* and the annual *Expenditure and Employment Data for the Criminal Justice System.* The Federal Bureau of Investigation's major annual reports are *Crime in the United States, Law Enforcement Officers Killed and Assaulted,* annual, and *Hate Crimes,* annual. which presents data on reported crimes as gathered from state and local law enforcement agencies.

Legal jurisdiction and law enforcement—Law enforcement is, for the most part, a function of state and local officers and agencies. The U.S. Constitution reserves general police powers to the states. By act of Congress, federal offenses include only offenses against the U.S. government and against or by its employees while engaged in their official duties and offenses which involve the crossing of state lines or an interference with interstate commerce. Excluding the military, there are 52 separate criminal law jurisdictions in the United States: 1 in each of the 50 states, 1 in the District of Columbia, and the federal jurisdiction. Each of these has its own criminal law and procedure and its own law enforcement agencies. While the systems of law enforcement are quite similar among the states, there are often substantial differences in the penalties for like offenses.

Law enforcement can be divided into three parts: Investigation of crimes and

arrests of persons suspected of committing them; prosecution of those charged with crime; and the punishment or treatment of persons convicted of crime.

Crime—There are two major approaches taken in determining the extent of crime. One perspective is provided by the FBI through its Uniform Crime Reporting Program (UCR). The FBI receives monthly and annual reports from law enforcement agencies throughout the country, currently representing 94 percent of the national population. Each month, city police, sheriffs, and state police file reports on the number of index offenses, hate crimes and law enforcement assaults that become known to them. Additionally, data are collected for officers killed in the line of duty.

The FBI Crime Index offenses are as follows: *Murder and nonnegligent manslaughter* is based on police investigations, as opposed to the determination of a medical examiner or judicial body, includes willful felonious homicides and excludes attempts and assaults to kill, suicides, accidental deaths, justifiable homicides, and deaths caused by negligence; *forcible rape* includes forcible rapes and attempts; *robbery* includes stealing or taking anything of value by force or violence or threat of force or violence and includes attempted robbery; *aggravated assault* includes assault with intent to kill; *burglary* includes any unlawful entry to commit a felony or a theft and includes attempted burglary and burglary followed by larceny; *larceny* includes theft of property or articles of value without use of force and violence or fraud and excludes embezzlement, "con games," forgery, etc.; *motor vehicle theft* includes all cases where vehicles are driven away and abandoned but excludes vehicles taken for temporary use and returned by the taker. Arson was added as the eighth Index offense in April 1979 following a Congressional mandate. *Arson* includes any willful or malicious burning

Law Enforcement, Courts, and Prisons 183

or attempt to burn, with or without intent to defraud, a dwelling house, public building, motor vehicle or aircraft, personal property of another, etc.

The monthly Uniform Crime Reports also contain data on crimes cleared by arrest and on characteristics of persons arrested for all criminal offenses. In summarizing and publishing crime data, the FBI depends primarily on the adherence to the established standards of reporting for statistical accuracy, presenting the data as information useful to persons concerned with the problem of crime and criminal law enforcement.

National Crime Victimization Survey (NCVS)—A second perspective on crime is provided by this survey of the Bureau of Justice Statistics. Details about the crimes come directly from the victims. No attempt is made to validate the information against police records or any other source.

The NCVS measures rape, robbery, assault, household and personal larceny, burglary, and motor vehicle theft. The NCVS includes offenses reported to the police, as well as those not reported.

Police reporting rates (percent of victimizations) varied by type of crime. In 1994, for instance, 32 percent of the rapes/sexual assaults were reported; 55 percent of the robberies; 40 percent of assaults; 33 percent of personal thefts; 51 percent of the household burglaries; and 78 percent of motor vehicle thefts.

Murder and kidnaping are not covered. Commercial burglary and robbery were dropped from the program during 1977. The so-called victimless crimes, such as drunkenness, drug abuse, and prostitution, also are excluded, as are crimes for which it is difficult to identify knowledgeable respondents or to locate data records.

Crimes of which the victim may not be aware also cannot be measured effectively. Buying stolen property may fall into this category, as may some instances of embezzlement. Attempted crimes of many types probably are under recorded

for this reason. Events in which the victim has shown a willingness to participate in illegal activity also are excluded.

In any encounter involving a personal crime, more than one criminal act can be committed against an individual. For example, a rape may be associated with a robbery or a household offense, such as a burglary, can escalate into something more serious in the event of a personal confrontation. In classifying the survey-measured crimes, each criminal incident has been counted only once—by the most serious act that took place during the incident and ranked in accordance with the seriousness classification system used by the Federal Bureau of Investigation. The order of seriousness for crimes against persons is as follows: Rape, robbery, assault, and larceny. Personal crimes take precedence over household offenses.

A *victimization,* basic measure of the occurrence of crime, is a specific criminal act as it affects a single victim. The number of victimizations is determined by the number of victims of such acts. Victimization counts serve as key elements in computing rates of victimization. For crimes against persons, the rates are based on the total number of individuals age 12 and over or on a portion of that population sharing a particular characteristic or set of traits. As general indicators of the danger of having been victimized during the reference period, the rates are not sufficiently refined to represent true measures of risk for specific individuals or households.

An *incident* is a specific criminal act involving one or more victims; therefore the number of incidents of personal crimes is lower than that of victimizations.

Courts—Statistics on criminal offenses and the outcome of prosecutions are incomplete for the country as a whole, although data are available for many states individually. The only national compilations of such statistics were made by the Census Bureau for 1932 to 1945 covering a maximum of 32 states and by the Bureau of Justice Statistics for 1986, 1988, 1990, and 1992 based on a nationally representative sample survey.

The bulk of civil and criminal litigation in the country is commenced and determined in the various state courts. Only when the U.S. Constitution and acts of Congress specifically confer jurisdiction upon the federal courts may civil or criminal litigation be heard and decided by them. Generally, the federal courts have jurisdiction over the following types of cases: Suits or proceedings by or against the United States; civil actions between private parties arising under the Constitution, laws, or treaties of the United States; civil actions between private litigants who are citizens of different states; civil cases involving admiralty, maritime, or prize jurisdiction; and all matters in bankruptcy. The Administrative Office of the United States Courts has compiled statistics on the caseload of the federal courts annually since 1940.

There are several types of courts with varying degrees of legal jurisdiction. These jurisdictions include original, appellate, general, and limited or special. A court of original jurisdiction is one having the authority initially to try a case and pass judgment on the law and the facts; a court of appellate jurisdiction is one with the legal authority to review cases and hear appeals; a court of general jurisdiction is a trial court of unlimited original jurisdiction in civil and/or criminal cases, also called a "major trial court"; a court of limited or special jurisdiction is a trial court with legal authority over only a particular class of cases, such as probate, juvenile, or traffic cases.

The 94 federal courts of original jurisdiction are known as the U.S. district courts. One or more of these courts is established in every state and one each in the District of Columbia, Puerto Rico, the Virgin Islands, the Northern Mariana Islands, and Guam. Appeals from the district courts are taken to intermediate appellate courts of which there are 13, known as U.S. courts of appeals and the United States Court of Appeals for the Federal Circuit. The Supreme Court of the United States is the final and highest appellate court in the federal system of courts.

Juvenile offenders—For statistical purposes, the FBI and most states classify as juvenile offenders persons under the age of 18 years who have committed a crime or crimes.

Delinquency cases are all cases of youths referred to a juvenile court for violation of a law or ordinance or for seriously "antisocial" conduct. Several types of facilities are available for those adjudicated delinquent, ranging from the short-term physically unrestricted environment to the long-term very restrictive atmosphere.

Prisoners—Data on prisoners in federal and state prisons and reformatories were collected annually by the Census Bureau until 1950, by the Federal Bureau of Prisons until 1971, transferred then to the Law Enforcement Assistance Administration, and, in 1979, to the Bureau of Justice Statistics. Adults convicted of criminal activity may be given a prison or jail sentence. A *prison* is a confinement facility having custodial authority over adults sentenced to confinement of more than 1 year. A *jail* is a facility, usually operated by a local law enforcement agency, holding persons detained pending adjudication and/or persons committed after adjudication to 1 year or less. Nearly every state publishes annual data either for its whole prison system or for each separate state institution.

Statistical reliability—For discussion of statistical collection, estimation and sampling procedures, and measures of statistical reliability pertaining to the National Crime Victimization Survey and Uniform Crime Reporting Program, see Appendix III.

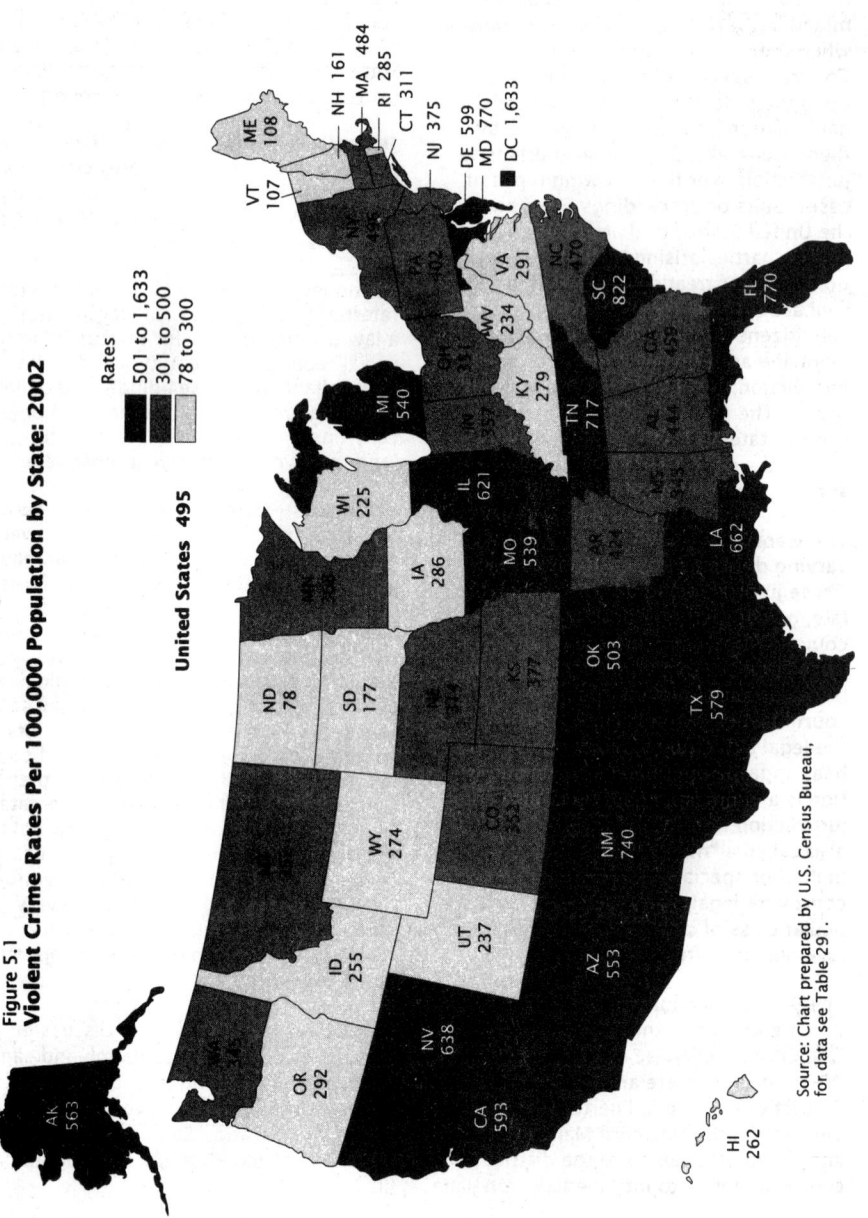

Figure 5.1
Violent Crime Rates Per 100,000 Population by State: 2002

Rates

501 to 1,633
301 to 500
78 to 300

United States 495

Source: Chart prepared by U.S. Census Bureau,
for data see Table 291.

No. 289. Crimes and Crime Rates by Type of Offense: 1980 to 2002

[13,408 represents 13,408,000. Data refer to offenses known to the police. Rates are based on Census Bureau estimated resident population as of July 1; 1980, 1990 and 2000, enumerated as of April 1. See source for details. For definitions of crimes, see text, this section.]

Item and year	Total	Violent crime					Property crime			
		Total	Murder [1][2]	Forcible rape	Robbery	Aggravated assault	Total	Burglary	Larceny/theft	Motor vehicle theft
Number of offenses (1,000):										
1980	13,408	1,345	23	83	566	673	12,064	3,795	7,137	1,132
1985	12,430	1,328	19	88	498	723	11,103	3,073	6,926	1,103
1987	13,509	1,484	20	91	518	855	12,025	3,236	7,500	1,289
1988	13,923	1,566	21	92	543	910	12,357	3,218	7,706	1,433
1989	14,251	1,646	22	95	578	952	12,605	3,168	7,872	1,565
1990	14,476	1,820	23	103	639	1,055	12,655	3,074	7,946	1,636
1991	14,873	1,912	25	107	688	1,093	12,961	3,157	8,142	1,662
1992	14,438	1,932	24	109	672	1,127	12,506	2,980	7,915	1,611
1993	14,145	1,926	25	106	660	1,136	12,219	2,835	7,821	1,563
1994	13,990	1,858	23	102	619	1,113	12,132	2,713	7,880	1,539
1995	13,863	1,799	22	97	581	1,099	12,064	2,594	7,998	1,472
1996	13,494	1,689	20	96	536	1,037	11,805	2,506	7,905	1,394
1997	13,195	1,636	18	96	499	1,023	11,558	2,461	7,744	1,354
1998	12,486	1,534	17	93	447	977	10,952	2,333	7,376	1,243
1999	11,634	1,426	16	89	409	912	10,208	2,101	6,956	1,152
2000	11,608	1,425	16	90	408	912	10,183	2,051	6,972	1,160
2001	11,877	1,439	16	91	424	909	10,437	2,117	7,092	1,228
2002	11,877	1,426	16	95	421	894	10,451	2,152	7,053	1,246
Rate per 100,000 population:										
1980	5,950.0	596.6	10.2	36.8	251.1	298.5	5,353.3	1,684.1	3,167.0	502.2
1985	5,224.5	558.1	8.0	36.8	209.3	304.0	4,666.4	1,291.7	2,911.2	463.5
1987	5,575.5	612.5	8.3	37.6	213.7	352.9	4,963.0	1,335.7	3,095.4	531.9
1988	5,694.5	640.6	8.5	37.8	222.1	372.2	5,054.0	1,316.2	3,151.7	586.1
1989	5,774.0	666.9	8.7	38.3	234.3	385.6	5,107.1	1,283.6	3,189.6	634.0
1990	5,802.7	729.6	9.4	41.1	256.3	422.9	5,073.1	1,232.2	3,185.1	655.8
1991	5,898.4	758.2	9.8	42.3	272.7	433.4	5,140.2	1,252.1	3,229.1	659.0
1992	5,661.4	757.7	9.3	42.8	263.7	441.9	4,903.7	1,168.4	3,103.6	631.6
1993	5,487.1	747.1	9.5	41.1	256.0	440.5	4,740.0	1,099.7	3,033.9	606.3
1994	5,373.8	713.6	9.0	39.3	237.8	427.6	4,660.2	1,042.1	3,026.9	591.3
1995	5,275.9	684.5	8.2	37.1	220.9	418.3	4,590.5	987.0	3,043.2	560.3
1996	5,086.6	636.6	7.4	36.3	201.9	391.0	4,451.0	945.0	2,980.3	525.7
1997	4,930.0	611.0	6.8	35.9	186.2	382.1	4,316.3	918.8	2,891.8	505.7
1998	4,619.3	567.6	6.3	34.5	165.5	361.4	4,052.5	863.2	2,729.5	459.9
1999	4,266.5	523.0	5.7	32.8	150.1	334.3	3,743.6	770.4	2,550.7	422.5
2000	4,124.8	506.5	5.5	32.0	145.0	324.0	3,618.3	728.8	2,477.3	412.2
2001	4,162.6	504.5	5.6	31.8	148.5	318.5	3,658.1	741.8	2,485.7	430.5
2002	4,118.8	494.6	5.6	33.0	145.9	310.1	3,624.1	746.2	2,445.8	432.1

[1] Includes nonnegligent manslaughter. [2] The murder and non-negligent homicides that occurred as a result of the events of September 11, 2001, were not included in this table.

Source: U.S. Federal Bureau of Investigation, *Crime in the United States*, annual. See also <http://www.fbi.gov/ucr/02cius.htm> (released 27 October 2003).

No. 290. Crimes and Crime Rates by Type and Area: 2002

[In thousands (11,877 represents 11,877,000), except rate. Rate per 100,000 population; see headnote, Table 289. Estimated totals based on reports from city and rural law enforcement agencies representing 96 percent of the national population. For definitions of crimes, see text, this section]

Type of crime	United States		Metropolitan areas [1]		Other cities		Rural areas	
	Total	Rate	Total	Rate	Total	Rate	Total	Rate
Total	11,877	4,119	10,202	4,409	1,017	4,524	659	1,909
Violent crime	1,426	495	1,262	546	91	403	73	213
Murder and nonnegligent manslaughter [2]	16	6	14	6	1	3	1	4
Forcible rape	95	33	78	34	9	39	8	24
Robbery	421	146	401	173	14	61	6	17
Aggravated assault	894	310	769	332	67	300	58	169
Property crime	10,451	3,624	8,939	3,864	926	4,121	585	1,696
Burglary	2,152	746	1,778	769	181	805	193	558
Larceny-theft	7,053	2,446	6,008	2,596	699	3,108	347	1,005
Motor vehicle theft	1,246	432	1,154	499	47	208	46	133

[1] Defined as a core area containing a substantial population nucleus, together with adjacent communities having a high degree of economic and social integration with that core, see Appendix II. [2] The murder and non-negligent homicides that occurred as a result of the events of September 11, 2001, were not included in this table.

Source: U.S. Federal Bureau of Investigation, <http://www.fbi.gov/ucr/02cius.htm> (released 27 October 2003).

U.S. Census Bureau, Statistical Abstract of the United States: 2004-2005

No. 291. Crime Rates by State, 2000 to 2002, and by Type, 2002

[Offenses known to the police per 100,000 population. Based on Census Bureau estimated resident population as of July 1; 2000 enumerated as of April 1. For definitions of crimes, see text, this section]

State	2000, total	2001, total	2002 Total	Violent crime Total	Mur-der[1]	Forc-ible rape	Rob-bery	Aggra-vated assault	Property crime Total	Bur-glary	Lar-ceny/ theft	Motor vehicle theft
United States.....	4,125	4,163	4,119	495	6	33	146	310	3,624	746	2,446	432
Alabama	4,546	4,319	4,465	444	7	37	133	268	4,021	949	2,762	310
Alaska............	4,249	4,236	4,310	563	5	79	76	403	3,746	607	2,755	384
Arizona	5,830	6,077	6,386	553	7	30	147	370	5,833	1,083	3,694	1,057
Arkansas	4,115	4,134	4,158	424	5	28	93	298	3,733	857	2,625	251
California.........	3,740	3,903	3,944	593	7	29	185	373	3,350	679	2,038	633
Colorado	3,983	4,219	4,348	352	4	46	79	223	3,995	703	2,778	514
Connecticut	3,233	3,118	2,997	311	2	21	117	170	2,686	494	1,858	334
Delaware [2].......	4,478	4,053	3,939	599	3	44	143	409	3,340	663	2,298	379
District of Columbia [3]..	7,277	7,710	8,022	1,633	46	46	672	869	6,389	906	3,802	1,681
Florida...........	5,695	5,570	5,421	770	6	40	195	529	4,650	1,061	3,060	530
Georgia...........	4,751	4,646	4,507	459	7	25	157	270	4,048	864	2,740	444
Hawaii............	5,199	5,386	6,044	262	2	30	97	133	5,782	1,022	3,964	796
Idaho	3,186	3,133	3,173	255	3	37	18	197	2,918	555	2,167	196
Illinois [4]........	4,239	4,098	4,016	621	8	34	201	379	3,396	644	2,396	356
Indiana	3,752	3,831	3,750	357	6	30	107	214	3,393	692	2,372	329
Iowa	3,234	3,301	3,448	286	2	27	40	217	3,163	635	2,330	198
Kansas[4]	4,409	4,321	4,087	377	3	38	80	256	3,710	725	2,720	266
Kentucky [4].......	2,960	2,938	2,903	279	5	27	75	173	2,624	681	1,729	214
Louisiana	5,423	5,338	5,098	662	13	34	159	456	4,436	1,012	2,974	450
Maine	2,620	2,688	2,656	108	1	29	21	57	2,548	538	1,900	110
Maryland	4,816	4,867	4,747	770	9	25	246	490	3,978	729	2,626	623
Massachusetts	3,026	3,099	3,094	484	3	28	112	343	2,610	517	1,679	414
Michigan	4,110	4,082	3,874	540	7	53	118	362	3,334	706	2,133	495
Minnesota	3,488	3,584	3,535	268	2	45	78	142	3,268	559	2,433	276
Mississippi	4,004	4,185	4,159	343	9	39	117	178	3,816	1,031	2,454	332
Missouri...........	4,528	4,776	4,602	539	6	26	124	383	4,064	753	2,819	492
Montana [4]	3,880	3,689	3,513	352	2	26	31	293	3,161	362	2,604	196
Nebraska..........	4,096	4,330	4,257	314	3	27	79	206	3,943	597	2,975	371
Nevada...........	4,269	4,266	4,498	638	8	43	236	351	3,860	872	2,184	805
New Hampshire	2,433	2,322	2,220	161	1	35	32	93	2,059	379	1,527	153
New Jersey	3,161	3,225	3,024	375	4	16	162	193	2,650	511	1,723	416
New Mexico........	5,519	5,324	5,078	740	8	55	119	557	4,338	1,058	2,879	401
New York..........	3,100	2,925	2,804	496	5	20	191	280	2,308	400	1,660	247
North Carolina	4,919	4,938	4,721	470	7	26	147	291	4,251	1,196	2,756	299
North Dakota	2,288	2,418	2,406	78	1	26	9	43	2,328	354	1,814	161
Ohio	4,042	4,178	4,107	351	5	42	157	148	3,756	868	2,513	375
Oklahoma	4,559	4,607	4,743	503	5	45	85	369	4,240	1,007	2,868	366
Oregon	4,845	5,044	4,868	292	2	35	78	177	4,576	730	3,377	469
Pennsylvania	2,995	2,961	2,841	402	5	30	139	228	2,439	451	1,722	266
Rhode Island	3,476	3,685	3,589	285	4	37	86	159	3,304	600	2,248	456
South Carolina	5,347	4,753	5,297	822	7	48	141	627	4,475	1,065	3,000	411
South Dakota	2,320	2,332	2,279	177	1	47	15	113	2,101	399	1,595	108
Tennessee.........	4,890	5,153	5,019	717	7	40	162	508	4,302	1,057	2,788	458
Texas	4,956	5,153	5,190	579	6	39	173	361	4,611	976	3,163	471
Utah	4,476	4,243	4,452	237	2	41	49	145	4,216	653	3,229	333
Vermont	2,987	2,769	2,530	107	2	20	13	72	2,423	566	1,733	125
Virginia	3,028	3,178	3,140	291	5	25	95	166	2,849	435	2,160	253
Washington	5,106	5,152	5,107	345	3	45	96	202	4,761	905	3,189	667
West Virginia	2,603	2,560	2,515	234	3	18	37	176	2,281	537	1,528	216
Wisconsin	3,209	3,321	3,253	225	3	23	87	113	3,028	513	2,267	247
Wyoming..........	3,298	3,518	3,581	274	3	30	19	222	3,307	491	2,668	149

[1] Includes nonnegligent manslaughter. [2] Forcible rape figures furnished by the state-level uniform crime reporting (UCR) program administered by the Delaware State Bureau of Investigation were not in accordance with the national UCR guidelines; therefore, it was necessary that the forcible rape count be estimated. [3] Includes offenses reported by the police at the National Zoo. [4] Complete data were not available; therefore, it was necessary for the crime counts to be estimated for Illinois, Kansas, Kentucky, and Montana for all years shown.

Source: U.S. Federal Bureau of Investigation, Crime in the United States, annual. See also <http://www.fbi.gov/ucr/02cius.htm> (released 27 October 2003).

188   Law Enforcement, Courts, and Prisons

No. 292. Crime Rates by Type—Selected Large Cities: 2002

[Offenses known to the police per 100,000 population. Based on U.S. Census Bureau estimated resident population as of July 1. For definitions of crimes, see text, this section]

City ranked by population size, 2002	Crime index, total	Violent crime Total	Murder	Forcible rape	Robbery	Aggravated assault	Property crime Total	Burglary	Larceny-theft	Motor vehicle theft
New York, NY	3,100.1	789.6	7.3	20.9	336.8	424.7	2,310.4	372.3	1,603.7	334.4
Los Angeles, CA	4,986.0	1,349.5	17.1	36.9	448.9	846.6	3,636.5	662.4	2,083.6	890.5
Chicago, IL [1]	(NA)	(NA)	22.1	(NA)	630.7	845.5	5,008.9	869.6	3,280.1	859.2
Houston, TX	7,313.9	1,223.1	12.5	43.7	549.5	617.4	6,090.9	1,318.5	3,599.2	1,173.1
Philadelphia, PA.	5,471.1	1,315.9	18.9	67.9	581.9	647.2	4,155.2	737.7	2,544.8	872.7
Phoenix, AZ	7,823.5	727.6	12.6	29.2	290.0	395.8	7,095.9	1,199.7	4,072.4	1,823.9
San Diego, CA.	3,951.9	567.1	3.7	26.0	128.3	409.1	3,384.8	602.3	1,937.7	844.8
Dallas, TX	9,024.7	1,370.8	15.8	52.8	647.7	654.5	7,653.9	1,639.3	4,535.4	1,479.3
San Antonio, TX	7,873.3	817.1	8.4	38.8	176.8	593.1	7,056.2	1,118.1	5,457.6	480.4
Las Vegas MPD Jurisidiction, NV [2]	4,924.8	778.6	11.9	42.8	327.3	396.5	4,146.3	965.4	2,098.2	1,082.7
Detroit, MI.	8,839.5	2,072.8	41.8	73.6	653.6	1,303.8	6,766.7	1,496.8	2,790.0	2,480.0
San Jose, CA	2,601.5	445.6	2.8	40.8	89.1	312.8	2,156.1	326.1	1,470.3	359.7
Honolulu, HI [2]	6,360.4	288.9	2.0	33.8	119.1	134.0	6,071.5	992.0	4,136.9	942.7
Indianapolis, IN [2]	6,032.5	935.0	13.9	54.8	365.3	501.0	5,097.4	1,201.7	3,087.1	808.7
San Francisco, CA	5,299.0	752.4	8.4	26.1	398.4	319.5	4,546.6	738.5	3,038.5	769.6
Jacksonville, FL	6,632.5	915.6	11.7	36.0	262.1	605.8	5,717.0	1,192.5	3,820.7	703.8
Columbus, OH.	9,257.7	908.0	11.3	94.0	489.4	313.2	8,349.7	2,244.7	5,038.6	1,066.5
Austin, TX	6,267.1	467.1	3.6	37.3	171.2	254.9	5,800.1	1,008.5	4,334.5	457.1
Baltimore, MD	8,318.6	2,054.9	37.7	26.5	702.5	1,288.2	6,263.7	1,305.3	3,981.4	977.0
Memphis, TN	9,947.2	1,572.4	22.5	78.0	640.7	831.2	8,374.8	2,469.7	4,513.5	1,391.7
Charlotte-Mecklenburg, NC.	7,512.7	1,172.3	10.4	44.7	447.2	670.0	6,340.4	1,625.7	3,997.7	717.0
Milwaukee, WI	7,647.8	954.8	18.3	53.8	527.9	354.7	6,693.0	1,143.0	4,363.3	1,186.8
Boston, MA	5,986.5	1,166.2	10.1	61.9	424.7	669.6	4,820.2	642.1	2,988.4	1,189.7
El Paso, TX	4,585.6	661.1	2.4	37.5	97.7	523.5	3,924.6	377.2	3,208.0	339.4
Seattle, WA	8,004.3	705.4	4.5	26.2	271.7	403.0	7,298.9	1,256.7	4,610.0	1,432.2
Washington, DC	7,767.9	1,595.6	45.9	45.9	653.5	850.2	6,172.4	905.1	3,661.4	1,605.9
Denver, CO	5,511.1	534.2	8.8	55.2	205.0	265.2	4,976.9	1,049.6	2,646.7	1,280.7
Nashville, TN	8,209.5	1,549.1	11.2	71.9	371.0	1,094.9	6,660.4	1,332.2	4,474.5	853.7
Fort Worth, TX	8,021.0	759.7	9.5	57.5	295.1	397.7	7,261.3	1,743.3	4,813.1	704.9
Portland, OR	7,955.7	828.5	3.7	65.0	237.6	522.2	7,127.2	1,047.0	5,129.0	951.1
Oklahoma City, OK.	9,743.2	822.3	7.4	86.8	228.1	500.0	8,920.9	1,622.4	6,573.5	725.0
Tucson, AZ	9,692.9	909.8	9.1	65.3	260.8	574.6	8,783.1	1,297.7	6,286.4	1,199.0
New Orleans, LA	6,418.9	937.1	53.1	33.3	410.2	440.6	5,481.8	978.9	2,946.6	1,556.3
Cleveland, OH	6,900.2	1,322.3	16.6	128.6	678.0	499.1	5,577.9	1,682.2	2,753.1	1,142.6
Long Beach, CA	4,034.3	757.8	14.0	30.1	314.5	399.2	3,276.4	711.6	1,782.7	782.1
Albuquerque, NM	7,817.0	1,068.7	11.1	64.0	283.1	710.4	6,748.4	1,191.7	4,671.4	885.3
Kansas City, MO	10,039.5	1,352.4	18.5	67.0	449.2	817.6	8,687.1	1,782.2	5,397.3	1,507.7
Fresno, CA	7,648.1	852.6	9.5	35.6	333.6	473.9	6,795.6	1,009.6	4,167.7	1,618.3
Virginia Beach, VA	3,671.4	219.1	0.7	31.5	101.1	85.8	3,452.3	522.6	2,736.6	193.1
Atlanta, GA	11,355.2	2,289.1	34.9	63.4	957.1	1,233.8	9,066.0	1,964.2	5,443.5	1,658.3
Sacramento, CA.	7,294.3	840.6	11.1	43.8	410.9	374.7	6,453.8	1,189.4	3,684.6	1,579.7
Mesa, AZ	7,907.8	684.9	5.2	30.6	140.0	509.1	7,222.9	1,175.9	4,840.5	1,206.5
Oakland, CA	7,213.4	1,366.9	26.1	60.1	592.0	688.6	5,846.5	1,026.7	3,308.6	1,511.2
Tulsa, OK	7,568.5	1,086.3	6.5	61.1	226.4	792.3	6,482.2	1,586.4	4,000.0	895.8
Omaha, NE.	7,303.2	717.9	6.6	43.9	253.2	414.1	6,585.3	817.1	4,691.8	1,076.4
Minneapolis, MN	6,820.9	1,056.1	12.0	92.7	459.5	491.8	5,764.9	1,135.5	3,750.1	879.3
Miami, FL	8,957.3	1,906.9	17.1	25.3	713.9	1,150.5	7,050.4	1,572.9	4,191.1	1,286.4
Colorado Springs, CO.	5,407.1	507.8	6.6	60.8	121.7	318.7	4,899.3	1,028.3	3,444.7	426.3
Saint Louis, MO	14,285.7	2,124.3	31.4	38.5	798.3	1,256.1	12,161.3	1,999.7	7,375.6	2,786.1
Wichita, KS	6,930.4	680.8	5.8	59.8	228.9	386.4	6,249.6	1,282.1	4,463.2	504.3
Santa Ana, CA.	3,435.6	550.8	6.6	18.8	248.6	276.8	2,884.8	349.6	1,850.8	684.4
Pittsburgh, PA	5,762.1	1,107.6	13.7	43.2	471.8	578.9	4,654.5	962.8	2,951.0	740.7
Arlington, TX	6,784.0	633.1	4.0	43.7	228.3	357.1	6,150.9	1,046.0	4,527.5	577.4
Anaheim, CA.	3,587.0	408.5	5.0	23.5	136.7	243.2	3,178.5	586.7	2,042.3	549.6
Cincinnati, OH	8,506.8	1,275.2	21.0	105.0	718.0	431.2	7,231.6	1,929.6	4,240.4	1,061.6
Toledo, OH	8,468.1	1,008.9	8.9	58.6	436.8	504.6	7,459.2	1,841.8	4,599.0	1,018.4
Tampa, FL	11,149.6	1,981.9	11.7	64.3	735.5	1,170.4	9,167.7	1,980.0	5,069.9	2,117.7
Buffalo, NY	6,436.8	1,271.7	14.6	62.6	550.7	643.8	5,165.2	1,305.5	3,085.2	774.4
Saint Paul, MN	6,076.1	805.1	4.4	65.5	332.1	403.1	5,271.0	1,103.1	3,426.9	741.0
Aurora, CO	6,222.4	630.9	5.5	83.6	188.5	353.3	5,591.5	749.4	3,632.8	1,209.3
Corpus Christi, TX	7,328.1	711.9	6.6	83.9	176.3	445.1	6,616.2	1,235.7	4,881.6	499.0
Raleigh, NC	6,248.8	688.9	6.7	37.1	244.2	400.9	5,559.9	1,344.2	3,746.5	469.2
Newark, NJ	6,378.8	1,143.3	23.3	31.5	561.1	527.4	5,235.5	806.7	2,160.3	2,268.4
Anchorage, AK	5,114.5	643.9	6.7	95.0	142.9	399.2	4,470.6	569.1	3,462.7	438.9
Lexington, KY	4,746.3	541.7	5.7	44.4	237.3	254.4	4,204.6	924.5	3,034.0	246.0
Riverside, CA	5,731.1	765.9	7.6	35.5	232.9	489.9	4,965.2	954.5	3,077.0	933.7
Louisville, KY.	5,950.2	785.1	13.5	18.9	383.5	369.2	5,165.1	1,356.2	2,971.4	837.5
Mobile, AL [3]	6,996.5	536.4	15.6	41.7	293.1	185.9	6,460.2	1,399.4	4,495.9	564.8
Saint Petersburg, FL.	8,056.8	1,703.9	8.9	47.8	395.6	1,251.6	6,352.9	1,397.6	4,064.2	891.0

NA Not available.   [1] The rates for forcible rape, violent crime, and crime index are not shown because the forcible rape figures were not in accordance with national Uniform Crime Reporting guidelines.   [2] Due to reporting changes or annexations, figures are not comparable to previous years.   [3] Beginning in 2002, Mobile, Alabama, population includes a redistribution of jurisdiction with the Mobile County Sheriff's Department.

Source: U.S. Federal Bureau of Investigation, *Crime in the United States*, annual. See also <http://www.fbi.gov/ucr/02Cius.htm> (released 27 October 2003).

Law Enforcement, Courts, and Prisons   189

No. 293. Murder Victims—Circumstances and Weapons Used or Cause of Death: 1990 to 2002

[Based solely on police investigation. For definition of murder, see text, this section]

Characteristic	1990	2000	2001	2002	Characteristic	1990	2000	2001	2002
Murders, total ..	20,273	13,230	14,061	14,274					
Percent distribution ...	100.0	100.0	100.0	100.0	Unknown	24.8	30.8	32.3	32.7
CIRCUMSTANCES					TYPE OF WEAPON				
					OR CAUSE OF DEATH				
Felonies, total	20.8	16.8	16.8	16.4					
Robbery	9.2	8.1	7.7	7.8	Guns	64.3	65.5	63.2	66.8
Narcotics	6.7	4.5	4.1	4.7	Handguns.	49.8	51.2	49.3	51.1
Sex offenses	1.1	0.6	0.5	0.4					
Other felonies	3.7	3.7	4.5	3.5	Cutting or stabbing . . .	17.4	13.5	13.0	12.5
Suspected felonies . . .	0.7	0.5	0.5	0.5	Blunt objects [1]	5.4	4.7	4.8	4.8
Argument, total	34.4	31.8	29.9	29.1	Personal weapons [2] . . .	5.5	7.0	6.8	6.7
Property or money . .	2.5	1.6	1.4	1.4	Strangulations,				
Romantic triangle. . .	2.0	0.9	0.8	0.9	asphyxiations	2.0	2.0	1.9	1.7
Other arguments . . .	29.8	29.3	27.7	26.7	Fire.	1.4	1.0	0.8	0.7
Other motives	19.4	20.2	20.4	21.4	All other [3]	4.0	6.4	9.4	6.8

[1] Refers to club, hammer, etc.   [2] Hands, fists, feet, etc.   [3] Includes poison, drowning, explosives, narcotics, and unknown.
Source: U.S. Federal Bureau of Investigation, *Crime in the United States*, annual. See also <http://www.fbi.gov/ucr/02cius.htm> (released 27 October 2003).

No. 294. Murder Victims by Age, Sex, and Race: 2002

Age		Sex				Race		
	Total	Male	Female	Unknown	White	Black	Other	Unknown
Total	14,274	10,932	3,316	26	6,857	6,834	385	198
Percent of total	100	77	23	-	48	48	3	1
Under 18 yrs. old	1,383	879	502	2	700	622	48	13
18 yrs. old and over	12,597	9,842	2,751	4	6,033	6,100	335	129
Infant (under 1 yr. old).	185	96	89	-	107	71	4	3
1 to 4 yrs. old	338	185	151	2	179	139	16	4
5 to 8 yrs. old	89	36	53	-	53	33	3	-
9 to 12 yrs. old	92	50	42	-	53	35	4	-
13 to 16 yrs. old	392	283	109	-	180	198	11	3
17 to 19 yrs. old	1,205	1,035	170	-	525	629	40	11
20 to 24 yrs. old	2,810	2,400	408	2	1,131	1,598	58	23
25 to 29 yrs. old	2,077	1,758	319	-	816	1,180	49	32
30 to 34 yrs. old	1,617	1,232	385	-	681	868	53	15
35 to 39 yrs. old	1,356	988	366	2	685	633	24	14
40 to 44 yrs. old	1,152	825	327	-	628	476	41	7
45 to 49 yrs. old	864	630	234	-	490	339	26	9
50 to 54 yrs. old	574	416	158	-	341	213	16	4
55 to 59 yrs. old	360	250	110	-	240	101	15	4
60 to 64 yrs. old	249	183	66	-	174	60	10	5
65 to 69 yrs. old	166	105	61	-	119	44	2	1
70 to 74 yrs. old.	156	96	60	-	115	35	4	2
75 yrs. old and over	298	153	145	-	216	70	7	5
Age unknown	294	211	63	20	124	112	2	56

- Represents zero.
Source: U.S. Federal Bureau of Investigation, *Crime in the United States*, annual. See also <http://www.fbi.gov/ucr/02cius.htm> (released 27 October 2003).

No. 295. Murder Victims of September 11, 2001, Terrorist Attacks by Race, Sex, and Location

Race		Sex			Race		Sex		
	Total	Male	Female	Un-known		Total	Male	Female	Un-known
ALL LOCATIONS					PENTAGON				
Total	2,973	2,256	712	5	Total	184	108	71	5
White	2,401	1,879	522	-	White	120	79	41	-
Black	265	162	103	-	Black	49	21	28	-
Other	173	117	56	-	Other	2	2	-	-
Unknown	134	98	31	5	Unknown	13	6	2	5
WORLD TRADE CENTER					SOMERSET COUNTY, PA				
Total	2,749	2,128	621	-	Total	40	20	20	-
White	2,245	1,782	463	-	White	36	18	18	-
Black	213	140	73	-	Black	3	1	2	-
Other	170	114	56	-	Other	1	1	-	-
Unknown	121	92	29	-	Unknown	-	-	-	-

- Represents zero.
Source: US Federal Bureau of Investigation, *Crime in the United States*, annual. See also<http://www.fbi.gov/ucr/02cius.htm> (Released 27 October 2002).

No. 296. Homicide Trends: 1976 to 2000

[Rate per 100,000 inhabitants. Not all agencies which report offence information to the FBI also submit supplemental data on homicides. To account for the total number of homicides.To account for the totalnumber of homicide victims, the data was weighted to matchnational and state estimtes prepared by the FBI; hence, columns may not equal total.]

Year	Esti-mated number of victims	Homicide Rate by gender of victim			Estimated number of homicide victims		Homicide Rate by race of victim			Estimated number of homicide victims		
		Rate	Male	Female	Male	Female	White	Black	Other	White	Black	Other
1976	18,780	8.8	13.6	4.2	14,171	4,590	5.1	37.1	7.9	9,585	8,745	387
1977	19,120	8.8	13.7	4.2	14,397	4,710	5.4	36.2	7.6	10,041	8,669	377
1978	19,560	9.0	14.0	4.1	14,895	4,642	5.6	35.1	7.1	10,568	8,572	367
1979	21,460	9.7	15.4	4.4	16,428	5,017	6.1	37.5	8.9	11,625	9,311	470
1980	23,040	10.2	16.2	4.5	17,788	5,232	6.3	37.7	5.7	12,275	9,767	327
1981	22,520	9.8	15.6	4.3	17,405	5,096	6.2	36.4	6.1	12,163	9,862	348
1982	21,010	9.1	14.1	4.3	15,902	5,093	5.9	32.3	6.5	11,643	8,880	399
1983	19,310	8.3	12.8	3.9	14,588	4,703	5.3	29.4	6.4	10,604	8,200	417
1984	18,690	7.9	12.1	3.9	13,910	4,741	5.2	27.2	5.4	10,490	7,678	377
1985	18,980	8.0	12.1	4.0	14,079	4,881	5.2	27.5	5.4	10,589	7,891	399
1986	20,610	8.6	13.2	4.1	15,471	5,109	5.3	31.3	6.2	10,916	9,107	484
1987	20,100	8.3	12.5	4.2	14,811	5,268	5.1	30.6	5.2	10,526	9,000	424
1988	20,680	8.5	12.9	4.2	15,414	5,238	4.9	33.3	4.0	10,184	9,959	344
1989	21,500	8.7	13.6	4.0	16,407	5,085	4.9	34.9	4.2	10,325	10,566	390
1990	23,440	9.4	15.1	4.0	18,304	5,115	5.4	37.7	4.2	11,279	11,488	400
1991	24,700	9.8	15.7	4.2	19,270	5,394	5.5	39.3	6.0	11,661	12,226	608
1992	23,760	9.3	14.9	4.0	18,513	5,217	5.3	37.2	5.4	11,229	11,777	573
1993	24,530	9.5	15.0	4.2	18,937	5,550	5.3	38.7	5.5	11,278	12,435	601
1994	23,330	9.0	14.4	3.8	18,294	5,007	5.0	36.4	4.6	10,773	11,856	526
1995	21,610	8.2	12.9	3.7	16,551	5,023	4.8	31.6	4.9	10,371	10,444	585
1996	19,650	7.4	11.7	3.3	15,152	4,470	4.3	28.3	4.1	9,482	9,477	512
1997	18,210	6.8	10.7	3.0	14,057	4,124	3.9	26.1	4.1	8,619	8,842	524
1998	16,910	6.3	9.7	3.0	12,753	4,139	3.8	23.0	2.9	8,389	7,931	393
1999	15,533	5.7	8.8	2.7	11,704	3,800	3.5	20.5	3.3	7,777	7,139	458
2000	15,517	5.5	8.5	2.6	11,766	3,717	3.3	20.5	2.7	7,526	7,393	398

Source: U.S. Bureau of Justice Statistics, *Homicide Trends in the United States, 1976-2000. See also:* <http://www.ojp.usdoj.gov/bjs/pub/pdf/htius.pdf>

No. 297. Homicide Victims by Race and Sex: 1980 to 2001

[Rates per 100,000 resident population in specified group. Excludes deaths to nonresidents of United States. Begining 1999, deaths classified according to the tenth revision of the *International Classification of Diseases;* see text, Section 2, and footnote 3]

Year	Homicide victims					Homicide rate [2]				
		White		Black			White		Black	
	Total [1]	Male	Female	Male	Female	Total [1]	Male	Female	Male	Female
1980	24,278	10,381	3,177	8,385	1,898	10.7	10.9	3.2	66.6	13.5
1985	19,893	8,122	3,041	6,616	1,666	8.3	8.2	2.9	48.4	11.0
1987	21,103	7,979	3,149	7,518	1,969	8.7	7.9	3.0	53.3	12.6
1988	22,032	7,994	3,072	8,314	2,089	9.0	7.9	2.9	58.0	13.2
1989	22,909	8,337	2,971	8,888	2,074	9.2	8.2	2.8	61.1	12.9
1990	24,932	9,147	3,006	9,981	2,163	10.0	9.0	2.8	69.2	13.5
1991	26,513	9,581	3,201	10,628	2,330	10.5	9.3	3.0	72.0	14.2
1992	25,488	9,456	3,012	10,131	2,187	10.0	9.1	2.8	67.5	13.1
1993	26,000	9,054	3,232	10,640	2,297	10.1	8.6	3.0	69.7	13.6
1994	24,926	9,055	2,921	10,083	2,124	9.6	8.5	2.6	65.1	12.4
1995	22,895	8,336	3,028	8,847	1,936	8.7	7.8	2.7	56.3	11.1
1996	20,971	7,570	2,747	8,183	1,800	7.9	7.0	2.5	51.5	10.2
1997	19,846	7,343	2,570	7,601	1,652	7.4	6.7	2.3	47.1	9.3
1998	18,272	6,707	2,534	6,873	1,547	6.8	6.1	2.2	42.1	8.6
1999 [3]	16,889	6,162	2,466	6,214	1,434	6.2	5.6	2.2	37.5	7.8
2000	16,765	5,925	2,414	6,482	1,385	6.1	5.3	2.1	38.6	7.5
2001	20,308	8,254	3,074	6,780	1,446	7.1	7.2	2.6	38.3	7.4

[1] Includes races not shown separately. [2] Rate based on enumerated population figures as of April 1 for 1980, 1990 and 2000; July 1 estimates for other years. [3] Effective with data for 1999, causes of death are classified by The Tenth Revision International Classification of Diseases (ICD-10), replacing the Ninth Revision (ICD-9) used for 1979-98 data. Breaks in the comparability of some cause of death statistics result from changes in category titles, changes in the structure and content of the classification, and changes in coding rules used to select the underlying cause of death. In ICD-9, the category Homicide also inludes death as a result of legal intervention. ICD-10 has two separate categories for these two causes of death. Some caution should be used in comparing data between 1998 and 1999.

Source: U.S. National Center for Health Statistics, *Vital Statistics of the United States,* annual; and *National Vital Statistics Reports (NVSR)* (formerly *Monthly Vital Statistics Report*); and unpublished data.

No. 298. Forcible Rape—Number and Rate: 1980 to 2002
[For definition of rape, see text, this section]

Item	1980	1990	1995	1996	1997	1998	1999	2000	2001	2002
NUMBER										
Total..................	82,990	102,560	97,460	96,250	96,153	93,144	89,411	90,186	90,863	95,136
By force	63,599	86,541	85,249	84,053	84,931	82,823	79,697	81,111	82,004	86,564
Attempt..................	19,391	16,019	12,211	12,197	11,222	10,321	9,714	9,075	8,859	8,572
RATE										
Per 100,000 population	36.8	41.1	37.1	36.3	35.9	34.5	32.8	32.0	31.8	33.0
Per 100,000 females	71.6	80.5	72.5	71.0	70.4	67.4	64.1	62.7	62.6	64.8
PERCENT CHANGE IN RATE [1]										
Per 100,000 population	6.1	8.1	-5.6	-2.2	-1.0	-4.1	-5.2	-2.4	-1.4	3.8

[1] From immediate prior year.
Source: U.S. Federal Bureau of Investigation, *Population-at-Risk Rates and Selected Crime Indicators*, annual.

No. 299. Rape and Sexual Assault—Reports to Police and Medical Attention: 1992 - 2000
[Rate per 100,000 inhabitants. Data is for the period 1992 to 2000].

Injury Status and Police Report	Completed rape		Attempted rape		Sexual assault	
	Number	Percent	Number	Percent	Number	Percent
Total victimizations	131,950	100	98,970	100	135,550	100
Not injured	-	-	60,010	61	112,520	83
Injured	131,950	100	38,960	39	23,020	17
Serious injury................	7,180	5	(B)	(B)	(B)	(B)
Minor injury.................	42,630	33	25,450	26	12,390	9
Undetermined injury	81,140	61	10,730	11	8,590	6
Reported to police	47,960	36	33,560	34	34,830	26
By victim..................	23,890	18	24,040	24	21,560	16
By other household member......	10,080	8	(B)	(B)	4,970	4
By someone else	13,990	11	6,010	6	8,310	6
Not reported	83,700	63	64,600	65	99,840	74
Medical treatment received:						
Total injured	131,950	100	38,960	100	23,020	100
Treated.....................	42,230	32	12,490	32	6,250	27

- Represents zero.   B Base figure too small to meet statistical standards for reliablity of a derived figure.
Source: U.S. Bureau of Justice Statistics, *Rape and Sexual Assault: Reporting to Police and Medical Attention, 1992-2000*, Serices NCJ 194530, August 2002.

No. 300. Violence by Intimate Partners by Sex, 1993 to 2001, and by Type of Crime, 2001
[Violent acts covered include murder, rape, sexual assault, robbery, and aggravated and simple assault. Intimate partners involve current spouses, former spouses, current boy/girlfriends, and former boy/girlfriends. Based on the National Criminal Victimization Survey; see text, this section, and Appendix III. See Appendix III]

Year and type of crime	All persons		Females		Males	
	Number	Rate[1]	Number	Rate per 100,000[1]	Number	Rate[1]
1993	1,228,760	580.9	1,072,090	982.0	156,670	153.1
1994	1,148,210	537.2	1,003,190	908.9	145,020	140.3
1995	1,063,520	493.0	953,700	855.8	109,820	105.3
1996	1,008,860	462.8	879,290	781.7	129,570	122.8
1997	953,780	432.7	848,480	747.3	105,300	98.5
1998	1,054,260	475.7	896,030	780.9	158,230	146.7
1999	783,120	347.7	672,330	578.4	110,790	101.6
2000	630,530	277.2	547,310	466.5	83,220	75.5
2001, total........................	691,710	293.6	588,490	496.7	103,220	77.8
Rape or sexual assault	41,740	18.2	41,740	35.2	(B)	(B)
Robbery	60,630	26.4	44,060	37.2	16,570	14.9
Aggravated assault......................	117,480	51.1	81,140	68.5	36,350	32.6
Simple assault.......................	471,860	205.2	421,550	355.8	50,310	45.1

B Base figure too small to meet statistical standards for reliability of derived figure. In this case, 10 or fewer sample cases.
[1] Rates are the number of victimizations per 100,000 persons.

Source: U.S. Bureau of Justice Statistics, *Intimate Partner Violence*, Series NCJ 197838, February 2003.

No. 301. Hate Crimes—Number of Incidents, Offenses, Victims, and Known Offenders by Bias Motivation: 2002

[The FBI collected statistics on hate crimes from 12,073 law enforcement agencies representing over 247 million inhabitants in 2002. Hate crime offenses cover incidents motivated by race, religion, sexual orientation, ethnicity/national origin, and disability]

Bias motivation	Incidents reported	Offenses	Victims [1]	Known offenders [2]
Total	7,462	8,832	9,222	7,314
Race, total	3,642	4,393	4,580	4,011
Anti-White	719	888	910	1,064
Anti-Black	2,486	2,967	3,076	2,510
Anti-American Indian/Alaskan native.	62	68	72	52
Anti-Asian/Pacific Islander	217	268	280	242
Anti-multi-racial group	158	202	242	143
Ethnicity/national origin, total	1,102	1,345	1,409	1,247
Anti-Hispanic	480	601	639	656
Anti-other ethnicity/national origin.	622	744	770	591
Religion, total	1,426	1,576	1,659	568
Anti-Jewish	931	1,039	1,084	317
Anti-Catholic	53	58	71	21
Anti-Protestant	55	57	58	34
Anti-Islamic	155	170	174	103
Anti-other religious group	198	217	237	73
Anti-multireligious group	31	32	32	18
Anti-atheism/agnosticism/etc	3	3	3	2
Sexual orientation, total	1,244	1,464	1,513	1,438
Anti-male homosexual	825	957	984	1,022
Anti-female homosexual.	172	207	221	172
Anti-homosexual.	222	259	267	225
Anti-heterosexual	10	26	26	6
Anti-bisexual	15	15	15	13
Disability, total	45	47	50	47
Anti-physical	20	20	20	21
Anti-mental	25	27	30	26
Multiple bias	3	7	11	3

[1] The term "victim" may refer to a person, business, institution, or a society as a whole. [2] The term "known offender" does not imply that the identity of the suspect is known, but only that an attribute of the suspect is identified which distinguishes him/her from an unknown offender.

Source: U.S. Federal Bureau of Investigation, *Hate Crime Statistics*, annual. See also <http://www.fbi.gov/ucr/02hate.pdf> released October 2003) and subsequent updates because of late data submissions.

No. 302. Hate Crimes Reported, by State: 2002

[See headnote, Table 301]

State	Number of participating agencies	Population covered (1,000)	Agencies submitting incidents reported	Incidents reported	State	Number of participating agencies	Population covered (1,000)	Agencies submitting incidents reported	Incidents reported
United States	12,073	247,247	1,868	7,462	Missouri	144	2,955	19	64
					Montana	93	881	6	13
Alabama	31	260	2	2	Nebraska	203	1,363	17	74
Alaska	1	267	1	7	Nevada	35	2,173	7	62
Arizona	88	5,024	29	238	New Hampshire	107	654	19	27
Arkansas.	7	388	-	-	New Jersey	557	8,590	220	570
California	726	35,057	243	1,648	New Mexico	49	1,181	3	15
Colorado	190	4,252	30	96					
Connecticut	84	2,839	50	129	New York	505	19,155	63	693
Delaware.	50	807	8	13	North Carolina	446	8,242	29	62
District of Columbia. . . .	2	571	2	14	North Dakota	74	563	7	18
Florida	489	16,660	93	257	Ohio.	400	8,245	63	363
					Oklahoma	301	3,494	19	44
Georgia	76	1,559	10	31	Oregon	172	3,509	24	61
Hawaii	(1)	(1)	(1)	(1)	Pennsylvania	849	11,086	26	92
Idaho	117	1,330	14	43	Rhode Island	48	1,070	7	38
Illinois	59	4,639	46	155	South Carolina	310	4,104	35	70
Indiana	163	4,476	25	77					
Iowa.	221	2,863	18	46	South Dakota.	130	735	4	4
Kansas.	339	2,367	13	55	Tennessee.	443	5,796	54	129
Kentucky.	341	3,663	38	76	Texas.	969	21,698	82	347
Louisiana	159	3,419	13	15	Utah.	59	1,790	17	54
Maine	180	1,291	14	36	Vermont	57	566	10	18
Maryland	148	5,458	26	211	Virginia	399	7,258	54	291
Massachusetts	305	5,822	90	430	Washington	246	6,037	47	174
Michigan	619	9,815	164	416	West Virginia	336	1,758	16	41
Minnesota	279	4,844	71	203	Wisconsin	370	5,438	13	32
Mississippi	66	943	3	3	Wyoming	31	291	4	5

- Represents or rounds to zero. [1] Did not report.

Source: U.S. Federal Bureau of Investigation, *Hate Crime Statistics*, annual. See also <http://www.fbi.gov/ucr/02hate.pdf> (released: October 2003) and subsequent updates because of late data submissions.

Law Enforcement, Courts, and Prisons 193

No. 303. Robbery and Property Crimes by Type and Selected Characteristic: 1990 to 2002

[For definition of crime, see text, this section]

Characteristic of offenses	Number of offenses (1,000)				Rate per 100,000 inhabitants				Average value lost (dol.)	
	1990	2000	2001	2002	1990	2000	2001	2002	2001	2002
Robbery, total [1]	639	408	424	421	256.3	144.9	148.5	145.9	1,208	1,281
Type of crime:										
Street or highway	359	188	188	180	144.2	66.7	65.7	62.4	914	1,045
Commercial house	73	57	61	61	29.5	20.1	21.4	21.3	1,888	1,676
Gas station	18	12	12	11	7.1	4.1	4.2	3.9	717	679
Convenience store	39	26	28	27	15.6	9.3	9.7	9.4	615	665
Residence	62	50	53	57	25.1	17.7	18.7	19.7	1,289	1,340
Bank	9	9	10	10	3.8	3.1	3.6	3.4	4,046	4,763
Weapon used:										
Firearm	234	161	170	173	94.1	57.0	59.5	60.1	(NA)	(NA)
Knife or cutting instrument	76	36	38	37	30.7	12.8	13.2	12.8	(NA)	(NA)
Other dangerous weapon	61	53	53	44	24.5	18.9	18.7	15.2	(NA)	(NA)
Strongarm	268	159	163	167	107.7	56.4	57.1	57.8	(NA)	(NA)
Burglary, total	3,074	2,050	2,117	2,152	1,232.2	728.4	741.8	746.2	1,533	1,549
Forcible entry	2,150	1,297	1,332	1,346	864.5	460.7	466.9	466.8	(NA)	(NA)
Unlawful entry	678	615	646	662	272.8	218.7	226.3	229.5	(NA)	(NA)
Attempted forcible entry	245	138	139	144	98.7	49.0	48.6	50.0	(NA)	(NA)
Residence	2,033	1,335	1,380	1,416	817.4	474.3	483.8	491.0	1,465	1,482
Nonresidence	1,041	715	736	736	418.5	254.1	225.1	233.7	1,659	1,678
Occurred during the night[1]	1,135	699	721	731	456.4	248.3	252.6	253.4	(NA)	(NA)
Occurred during the day[1]	1,151	836	867	903	462.8	297.2	303.8	313.1	(NA)	(NA)
Larceny-theft, total	7,946	6,972	7,092	7,053	3,185.1	2,477.3	2,484.6	2445.8	787	699
Pocket picking	81	36	33	32	32.4	12.7	11.7	11.3	453	328
Purse snatching	82	37	39	39	32.8	13.2	13.5	13.5	351	332
Shoplifting	1,291	959	979	986	519.1	340.7	343.1	341.8	183	187
From motor vehicles	1,744	1,754	1,833	1,866	701.3	623.3	642.4	647.0	708	692
Motor vehicle accessories	1,185	677	723	756	476.3	240.6	254.0	262.1	437	432
Bicycles	443	312	291	277	178.2	110.9	102.1	96.0	315	257
From buildings	1,118	914	944	883	449.4	324.6	330.7	306.3	1,055	1,013
From coin-operated machines	63	46	52	52	25.4	16.2	18.2	18.2	288	250
Other	1,940	2,232	2,198	2,162	780.0	793.0	770.1	749.7	1,193	984
Motor vehicles, total [2]	1,636	1,160	1,228	1,246	655.8	412.2	430.5	432.1	6,630	6,701
Automobiles	1,304	877	917	919	524.3	311.5	321.4	318.8	(NA)	(NA)
Trucks and buses	238	209	221	230	95.5	74.1	77.8	79.7	(NA)	(NA)

NA Not available. [1] Includes other crimes not shown separately. [2] Includes other types of motor vehicles not shown separately.

Source: U.S. Federal Bureau of Investigation, *Population-at-Risk Rates and Selected Crime Indicators*, annual.

No. 304. Violent Victimizations Reported to the Police: 1992 to 2000

[In percent. Data is for the period of 1992 to 2000. Offender characteristics are based on victim's perception. See source for details. For definitions of crimes, see text, this section]

Characteristic of offender	Percent of the victimizations reported to the police					
	Violent crimes					
	All	Forcible rape	Robbery	Aggravated assault	Simple assault	Serious violent crime [1]
Total	43	31	57	55	38	53
Gender						
Male	43	32	56	54	38	52
Female	40	[2]13	55	55	37	53
Both	63	[2]59	74	75	56	74
Race						
White	42	29	55	54	38	50
Black	47	39	59	59	38	58
Number of offenders						
One	42	31	55	53	38	50
Two	55	44	65	64	44	64
Three or more	51	28	57	62	42	59
Relationship to victim						
Nonstranger	41	27	59	55	37	51
Intimate	54	24	72	63	53	55
Other relative	50	48	53	61	47	57
Friend/acquanintance	36	27	55	52	31	48
Stranger	45	41	56	55	39	55
Don't know relationship	43	[2]39	62	53	32	55
Drug/alcohol use						
Using drugs/alcohol	51	32	58	60	48	55
Not using drugs/alcohol	33	23	50	47	30	43
Don't know	45	39	58	55	37	55

[1] Includes rape, sexual assault, robbery and aggravated assault. [2] Based on 10 or fewer sample cases.
Source: U.S. Bureau of Justice Statistics, *Reporting Crime to the Police: 1992-2000*, Series NCJ 195710, March 2003.

No. 305. Criminal Victimizations and Victimization Rates: 1995 to 2002

[Based on National Crime Victimization Survey; see text, this section and Appendix III]

Type of crime	Number of victimizations (1,000)				Victimization rates [1]			
	1995	2000	2001	2002	1995	2000	2001	2002
All crimes, total	39,926	25,893	24,216	23,036	(X)	(X)	(X)	(X)
Personal crimes [2]	10,436	6,597	5,932	5,497	46.2	29.1	25.9	23.7
Crimes of violence.	10,022	6,323	5,744	5,341	44.5	27.9	25.1	23.1
Completed violence	2,960	2,044	1,828	1,753	12.9	9.0	8.0	7.6
Attempted/threatened violence	7,061	4,279	3,916	3,588	31.6	18.9	17.1	15.5
Rape/sexual assault	363	261	248	248	1.6	1.2	1.1	1.1
Rape/attempted rape.	252	147	146	168	1.1	0.6	0.6	0.7
Rape	153	92	84	90	0.7	0.4	0.4	0.4
Attempted rape	99	55	63	78	0.4	0.2	0.3	0.3
Sexual assault	112	114	102	80	0.5	0.5	0.4	0.3
Robbery	1,171	732	631	513	5.3	3.2	2.8	2.2
Completed/property taken	753	520	427	386	3.5	2.3	1.9	1.7
With injury	224	160	174	170	1.0	0.7	0.8	0.7
Without injury	529	360	253	216	2.4	1.6	1.1	0.9
Attempted to take property	418	212	204	127	1.8	0.9	0.9	0.5
With injury	84	66	68	43	0.4	0.3	0.3	0.2
Without injury	335	146	136	84	1.4	0.6	0.6	0.4
Assault	8,487	5,330	4,865	4,581	37.6	23.5	21.2	19.8
Aggravated	2,050	1,293	1,222	990	8.8	5.7	5.3	4.3
With injury	533	346	392	316	2.4	1.5	1.7	1.4
Threatened with weapon	1,517	946	831	674	6.4	4.2	3.6	2.9
Simple	6,437	4,038	3,643	3,591	28.9	17.8	15.9	15.5
With minor injury.	1,426	989	845	907	6.0	4.4	3.7	3.9
Without injury	5,012	3,048	2,798	2,684	22.9	13.4	12.2	11.6
Personal theft [3]	414	274	188	155	1.7	1.2	0.8	0.7
Property crimes	29,490	19,297	18,284	17,539	279.5	178.1	166.9	159.0
Household burglary	5,004	3,444	3,140	3,056	47.4	31.8	28.7	27.7
Completed	4,232	2,909	2,687	2,597	40.0	26.9	24.5	23.5
Attempted forcible entry	773	534	453	458	7.4	4.9	4.1	4.2
Motor vehicle theft.	1,717	937	1,009	989	16.2	8.6	9.2	9.0
Completed	1,163	642	724	781	10.8	5.9	6.6	7.1
Attempted.	554	295	285	208	5.5	2.7	2.6	1.9
Theft.	22,769	14,916	14,135	13,495	215.9	137.7	129.0	122.3
Completed [4]	21,857	14,300	13,672	13,040	207.6	132.0	124.8	118.2
Attempted	911	616	463	455	8.4	5.7	4.2	4.1

X Not applicable. [1] Per 1,000 persons age 12 or older or per 1,000 households. [2] The victimization survey cannot measure murder because of the inability to question the victim. [3] Includes pocket picking, purse snatching, and attempted purse snatching. [4] Includes thefts in which the amount taken was not ascertained.

Source: U.S. Bureau of Justice Statistics, *Criminal Victimization*, annual; and *Criminal Victimization 2002, Changes 2001-02 with Trends 1993-2002*, Series NCJ-194610. See also <http://www.ojp.usdoj.gov/bjs/pub/pdf/cv02.pdf>.

No. 306. Victimization Rates by Type of Violent Crime and Characteristic of the Victim: 2002

[**Rate per 1,000 persons age 12 years or older**. Based on National Crime Victimization Survey; see text, this section, and Appendix III]

Characteristic of the victim	Crimes of violence							Personal theft
	All crime	Total	Rape/ sexual assault	Robbery	Assault			
					Total	Aggravated	Simple	
Total	23.7	23.1	1.1	2.2	19.8	4.3	15.5	0.7
Male.	26.1	25.5	0.3	2.9	22.3	5.2	17.1	0.6
Female	21.5	20.8	1.8	1.6	17.4	3.4	14.0	0.7
12 to 15 yrs. old	45.3	44.4	2.1	3.0	39.3	5.0	34.3	[1]0.9
16 to 19 yrs. old	58.8	58.2	5.5	4.0	48.6	11.9	36.7	[1]0.6
20 to 24 yrs. old	49.0	47.4	2.9	4.7	39.8	10.1	29.7	[1]1.6
25 to 34 yrs. old	26.8	26.3	0.6	[1]2.8	22.8	5.2	17.6	[1]0.5
35 to 49 yrs. old	18.8	18.1	0.5	[1]1.5	16.1	3.5	12.7	0.7
50 to 64 yrs. old	11.0	10.7	0.2	[1]1.6	8.9	1.7	7.2	[1]0.3
65 yrs. old and over.	4.0	3.4	0.1	[1]1.0	2.2	0.7	1.5	[1]0.6
White	23.5	22.8	0.8	1.9	20.0	4.1	15.9	0.7
Black	28.6	27.9	2.5	4.1	21.3	6.7	14.6	[1]0.7
Other	15.1	14.7	1.2	[1]2.4	[1]11.0	0.9	10.1	[1]0.4
Hispanic	24.0	23.6	0.7	[1]3.2	19.7	6.1	13.7	[1]0.4
Non-Hispanic	23.8	23.0	1.1	2.1	19.8	4.1	15.8	0.7
Household income:								
Less than $7,500.	47.2	45.5	2.5	[1]6.3	36.7	11.2	25.5	[1]1.7
$7,500-$14,999	32.0	31.5	3.2	4.1	24.2	5.8	18.4	[1]0.5
$15,000-$24,999	30.8	30.0	2.1	2.9	25.0	6.1	18.9	[1]0.8
$25,000-$34,999	27.4	27.0	1.2	[1]2.9	22.9	4.1	18.9	[1]0.3
$35,000-$49,999	26.0	25.6	0.9	[1]2.2	22.4	5.2	17.2	[1]0.4
$50,000-$74,999	19.3	18.7	0.2	[1]2.1	16.5	2.5	14.0	[1]0.6
$75,000 or more	19.7	19.0	0.4	[1]1.0	17.6	2.8	14.8	0.7

[1] Based on 10 or fewer sample cases.

Source: U.S. Bureau of Justice Statistics, *Criminal Victimization*, annual; and series NCJ-199994. See also <http://www.ojp.usdoj.gov/bjs/pub/pdf/cv02.pdf>.

Law Enforcement, Courts, and Prisons 195

No. 307. Victim-Offender Relationship in Crimes of Violence, by Characteristics of the Criminal Incident: 2002

[In percent. Covers only crimes of violence. Based on National Crime Victimization Survey; see text, this section, and Appendix III]

Characteristics of incident	Total	Rape/ sexual assault	Robbery	Assault Total	Assault Aggra-vated[1]	Assault Simple
Total	100	100	100	100	100	100
Victim/offender relationship: [2]						
Relatives	9	2	7	9	10	9
Well-known	29	40	20	30	23	31
Casual acquaintance	15	26	2	15	11	16
Stranger	47	32	70	46	55	43
Time of day: [3]						
6 a.m. to 6 p.m.	54	37	47	56	43	59
6 p.m. to midnight	33	34	37	33	39	31
Midnight to 6 a.m.	12	29	17	11	18	9
Location of crime:						
At or near victim's home or lodging.	32	31	34	32	34	31
Friend's/relative's/neighbor's home	9	17	6	9	9	9
Commercial places	11	17	4	12	11	12
Parking lots/garages	8	2	15	7	9	7
School.	15	4	4	17	7	20
Streets other than near victim's home	14	14	28	13	19	11
Other [4]	11	16	10	11	11	11
Victim's activity: [5]						
At work or traveling to or from work	19	12	11	20	20	20
School.	14	4	9	15	9	17
Activities at home	26	32	24	26	28	26
Shopping/errands	3	5	3	3	3	3
Leisure activities away from home	22	30	21	22	25	21
Traveling	8	8	20	7	8	7
Other [6]	7	8	11	7	7	7
Distance from victim's home: [7]						
Inside home or lodging.	17	31	22	15	16	15
Near victim's home	17	6	15	18	18	18
1 mile or less	20	13	29	19	18	19
5 miles or less	23	26	13	25	23	25
50 miles or less	20	19	19	20	21	20
More than 50 miles	3	4	2	3	4	3
Weapons:						
No weapons present	77	92	47	79	4	100
Weapons present	23	8	53	21	96	-
Firearm	8	5	29	6	27	-
Other type of weapon [8].	15	3	24	15	69	-

- Represents zero. [1] An aggravated assault is any assault in which an offender possesses or uses a weapon or inflicts serious injury. [2] Excludes "don't know" relationships. [3] Excludes "not known and not available" time of day. [4] Includes areas on public transportation or inside station, in apartment yard, park, field, playground, or other areas. [5] Excludes "don't know" and "not available" victim activity. [6] Includes sleeping. [7] Excludes "don't know" and "not available" distance from victim's home. [8] Includes knives, other sharp objects, blunt objects, and other types of weapons.

Source: U.S. Bureau of Justice Statistics, *Criminal Victimization*, annual; and series NCJ-199994, August 2003. See also <http://www.ojp.usdoj.gov/bjs/pub/pdf/cv02.pdf>.

No. 308. Property Victimization Rates by Selected Household Characteristic: 2002

[Victimizations per 1,000 households. Based on National Crime Victimization Survey; see text, this section, and Appendix III]

Characteristic	Total	Burglary	Motor vehicle theft	Theft
Total.	159.0	27.7	9.0	122.3
Race:				
White	157.6	26.0	7.5	124.1
Black	173.7	41.3	17.2	115.2
Other	139.8	19.4	12.5	107.9
Ethnicity:				
Hispanic	210.1	30.3	17.7	162.1
Non-Hispanic.	153.3	27.4	8.0	118.0
Household income:				
Less than $7,500	188.9	51.4	[1]3.2	134.3
$7,500-$14,999	166.7	31.8	8.1	126.8
$15,000-$24,999	172.1	33.8	9.9	128.5
$25,000-$34,999	161.7	27.8	12.6	121.2
$35,000-$49,999	175.4	27.3	11.3	136.9
$50,000-$74,999	158.3	24.6	9.2	124.5
$75,000 or more	169.8	21.0	5.9	142.9
Residence:				
Urban.	215.3	40.5	17.1	157.7
Suburban.	145.3	22.4	7.5	115.4
Rural	118.3	22.6	2.2	93.5
Form of tenure:				
Home owned.	136.4	23.9	6.5	105.9
Home rented.	207.0	35.7	14.2	157.1

[1] Based on 10 or fewer sample cases.

Source: U.S. Bureau of Justice Statistics, *Criminal Victimization*, annual; and series NCJ-199994. See also <http://www.ojp.usdoj.gov/bjs/pub/pdf/cv02.pdf>.

No. 309. Persons Arrested by Charge and Selected Characteristics: 2002

[10,452.2 represents 10,452,200. Represents arrests (not charges) reported by approximately 10,280 agencies with a total 2002 population of approximately 215 million as estimated by FBI. Age and sex data is mandatory, while race data is optional and not always reported with arrest data; hence, two different total number of arrests]

Offense charged	Total arrests (1,000)							
	Total	Male	Female	Total	White	Black	American Indian or Alaskan Native	Asian or Pacific Islander
Total.	10,452.2	8,047.3	2,404.8	10,428.3	7,279.8	2,890.3	135.1	123.0
Serious crimes [1]:	1,711.4	1,250.2	461.3	1,708.2	1,107.0	557.3	18.9	24.8
Murder and nonnegligent manslaugher	10.8	9.6	1.2	10.8	5.1	5.5	(Z)	(Z)
Forcible rape	21.5	21.2	0.3	21.5	13.4	7.5	(Z)	(Z)
Robbery	83.8	75.3	8.5	83.8	36.2	46.1	(Z)	0.9
Aggravated assault	357.6	285.0	72.6	357.0	224.4	124.3	4.0	4.2
Burglary	218.2	189.5	28.8	217.9	151.8	61.8	1.9	2.5
Larceny/theft	892.5	563.3	329.2	890.4	599.5	265.7	10.8	14.3
Motor vehicle theft	114.4	95.6	18.8	114.3	67.1	43.6	1.2	2.4
Arson	12.6	10.7	1.9	12.5	9.5	2.8	(Z)	(Z)
All other nonserious crimes:								
Other assaults	985.2	749.3	235.9	983.0	646.1	313.8	12.2	11.0
Forgery and counterfeiting	88.5	53.2	35.3	88.3	60.3	26.2	(Z)	1.3
Fraud	258.1	140.7	117.5	257.2	173.6	80.4	1.4	1.8
Stolen property—buying, receiving, possessing	96.6	79.4	17.3	96.5	56.5	38.3	0.6	1.0
Weapons; carrying, possessing etc. . . .	124.8	114.7	10.1	124.6	75.9	46.5	0.9	1.4
Prostitution and commercialized vice .	63.1	21.8	41.3	63.0	36.0	25.2	(Z)	1.4
Sex offenses (except forcible rape and prostitution)	71.2	65.4	5.9	71.2	52.7	16.8	0.7	1.0
Drug abuse violations	1,191.4	977.1	214.3	1,190.0	767.7	405.9	7.1	9.1
Offenses against family and children .	102.2	76.9	25.3	101.9	69.2	29.9	1.2	1.6
Driving under the influence	1,067.2	881.6	185.6	1,064.2	931.9	106.3	16.0	10.0

Z Less than 500.   [1] Includes arson.

Source: U.S. Federal Bureau of Investigation, *Crime in the United States*, annual.

No. 310. Percentage of Students in Grades 9-12 Who Reported Carrying a Weapon: 1993 to 2001

[Percentages are based on students who reported carrying a weapon at least one day during the previous thirty days]

Student Characteristics	Anywhere					On school property				
	1993	1995	1997	1999	2001	1993	1995	1997	1999	2001
Total	22.1	20.0	18.3	17.3	17.4	11.8	9.8	8.5	6.9	6.4
Sex										
Male	34.3	31.1	27.7	28.6	29.3	17.9	14.3	12.5	11.0	10.2
Female	9.2	8.3	7.0	6.0	6.2	5.1	4.9	3.7	2.8	2.9
Race/ethnicity [1]										
White	(2)	(2)	(2)	16.4	17.9	(2)	(2)	(2)	6.4	6.1
Black	(2)	(2)	(2)	17.2	15.2	(2)	(2)	(2)	5.0	6.3
Hispanic	(2)	(2)	(2)	18.7	16.5	(2)	(2)	(2)	7.9	6.4
Asian	(2)	(2)	(2)	13.0	10.6	(2)	(2)	(2)	6.5	7.2
American Indian	(2)	(2)	(2)	21.8	31.2	(2)	(2)	(2)	11.6	16.4
Pacific Islander	(2)	(2)	(2)	25.3	17.4	(2)	(2)	(2)	9.3	10.0
Grade										
9th	25.5	22.6	22.6	17.6	19.8	12.6	10.7	10.2	7.2	6.7
10th	21.4	21.1	17.4	18.7	16.7	11.5	10.4	7.7	6.6	6.7
11th	21.5	20.3	18.2	16.1	16.8	11.9	10.2	9.4	7.0	6.1
12th	19.9	16.1	15.4	15.9	15.1	10.8	7.6	7.0	6.2	6.1

[1] Includes other races not shown separately. [2] The response categories for race/ethnicity changed in 1999 making comparisons of some categories with earlier years problematic.

Source: National Center for Education Statistics, *Indicators of School Crime and Safety*, 2003.

No. 311. Number of School-Associated Violent Deaths Occuring at and Away From School: 1992 to 2002

[At school includes on school property, on the way to or from school, and while attending or traveling to or from a school sponsored event]

School year	Total student, staff, and nonstudent school-associated violent deaths [1]	Homicides of youth ages 5-19	
		Homicides at school	Homicides away from school
Total 1992-2000	390	234	24,406
1995-1996	53	32	3,303
1996-1997	48	28	2,950
1997-1998	57	34	2,728
1998-1999	47	33	2,366
1999-2000	[2]32	[2]16	2,124
2000-2001	[2]27	[2]10	2,045
2001-2002	[2]31	[2]14	(NA)

NA Not available.   [1] Includes other races not shown separately.   [2] Preliminary data.

Source: National Center for Education Statistics, *Indicators of School Crime and Safety*, 2003.

Law Enforcement, Courts, and Prisons   197

No. 312. Juvenile Arrests for Selected Offenses: 1980 to 2002

[169,439 represents 169,439,000. Juveniles are persons under 18 years of age]

Offense	1980	1990	1995	1996	1997	1998	1999	2000	2001	2002
Number of contributing agencies ..	8,178	10,765	10,037	10,026	9,472	9,589	9,502	9,904	10,281	10,946
Population covered (1,000)	169,439	204,543	206,762	195,805	194,925	194,612	195,324	204,965	215,380	220,157
NUMBER										
Violent crime, total.	77,220	97,103	123,131	104,455	100,273	90,201	81,715	78,450	78,443	71,059
Murder.	1,475	2,661	2,812	2,184	1,887	1,587	1,131	1,027	1,069	1,014
Forcible rape.	3,668	4,971	4,556	4,228	4,127	3,988	3,544	3,402	3,504	3,553
Robbery.	38,529	34,944	47,240	39,788	36,419	29,989	26,125	24,206	23,408	19,491
Aggravated assault	33,548	54,527	68,523	58,255	57,840	54,637	50,915	49,815	50,462	47,001
Weapon law violations	21,203	33,123	46,506	40,145	39,358	34,122	31,307	28,514	29,290	26,786
Drug abuse, total	86,685	66,300	149,236	148,783	155,444	148,066	138,774	146,594	146,758	133,557
Sale and manufacturing	13,004	24,575	34,077	32,558	30,761	29,312	26,134	26,432	24,649	22,086
Heroin/cocaine.	1,318	17,511	19,187	17,465	15,855	15,094	12,686	11,000	10,535	8,832
Marijuana.	8,876	4,372	10,682	11,489	11,208	10,800	10,770	11,792	10,552	9,962
Synthetic narcotics	465	346	701	614	671	813	722	945	911	974
Dangerous nonnarcotic drugs .	2,345	2,346	3,507	2,990	3,027	2,597	1,956	2,695	2,651	2,318
Possession.	73,681	41,725	115,159	116,225	124,683	118,754	112,640	120,162	122,109	111,471
Heroin/cocaine.	2,614	15,194	21,253	17,560	18,328	16,278	13,445	12,586	11,734	10,969
Marijuana.	64,465	20,940	82,015	87,712	94,046	91,467	89,523	95,962	97,088	85,769
Synthetic narcotics	1,524	1,155	2,047	1,713	1,987	1,916	1,581	2,052	2,237	2,805
Dangerous nonnarcotic drugs .	5,078	4,436	9,844	9,240	10,322	9,093	8,091	9,832	11,050	11,928

Source: U.S. Federal Bureau of Investigation, *Crime in the United States,* annual. See also <http://www.fbi.gov/ucr/02cius.htm> (released 27 October 2003).

No. 313. Immigration and Naturalization Service Enforcement Activities: 1990 to 2000

[For year ending September 30. See text, Section 8]

Item	Unit	1990	1994	1995	1996	1997	1998	1999	2000
Deportable aliens located.	1,000	1,169.9	1,094.7	1,394.6	1,650.0	1,536.5	1,679.4	1,714.0	1,814.7
Border Patrol	1,000	1,103.4	1,031.7	1,324.2	1,549.9	1,413.0	1,555.8	1,579.0	1,676.4
Southwestern border	1,000	(NA)	979.1	1,271.4	1,507.0	1,368.7	1,516.7	1,537.0	1,643.7
Mexican.	1,000	1,054.8	999.9	1,293.5	1,523.1	1,387.7	1,522.9	1,534.5	1,636.9
Canadian	1,000	5.7	3.4	3.5	2.7	2.9	2.3	2.7	2.2
Other	1,000	42.8	28.4	27.2	24.0	22.4	30.5	41.8	37.3
Number of seizures by									
Border Patrol	Number . .	17,275	9,134	9,327	11,129	11,792	14,401	16,803	17,269
Value of seizures by Border Patrol.	Mil. dol. . . .	843.6	1,622.0	2,011.8	1,256.0	1,094.6	1,405.0	2,004.0	1,945.0
Narcotics	Mil. dol. . . .	797.8	1,555.7	1,965.3	1,208.8	1,046.3	1,340.0	1,919.0	1,848.0
Aliens expelled:									
Formal removals [1]	1,000	30.0	45.7	45.2	69.7	114.4	173.0	180.3	184.8
Voluntary departures [2]	1,000	1,022.5	1,029.1	1,313.8	1,573.4	1,440.7	1,570.1	1,574.5	1,675.3

NA Not available. [1] Include deportations, exclusions, and removals. [2] Includes aliens under docket control required to depart and voluntary departures not under docket control.
Source: U.S. Bureau of Citizenship and Immigration Services, *Statistical Yearbook,* annual. See also <http://www.immigration.gov /graphics/shared/aboutus/statistics/index.htm>.

No. 314. Drug Use by Arrestees in Major U.S. Cities by Type of Drug and Sex: 2003

[Percent testing positive. Based on data from the Arrestee Drug Abuse Monitoring Program]

City	Male				Female			
	Any drug [1]	Mari- juana	Cocaine	Opiates	Any drug [1]	Mari- juana	Cocaine	Opiates
Albuquerque, NM	70.3	41.6	35.0	11.2	70.0	29.4	38.1	13.8
Atlanta, GA	73.5	41.8	49.8	3.0	(NA)	(NA)	(NA)	(NA)
Chicago, IL	86.0	53.2	50.6	24.9	66.7	38.9	33.3	22.2
Cleveland, OH	74.9	48.9	39.0	5.4	72.4	27.2	52.7	6.7
Dallas, TX	63.8	39.1	32.7	6.9	(NA)	(NA)	(NA)	(NA)
Denver, CO	72.6	42.3	38.3	6.8	75.1	34.3	52.5	6.1
Indianapolis, IN.	66.4	44.8	35.3	5.1	79.9	42.0	55.7	5.7
Las Vegas, NV	70.0	34.4	21.9	6.4	(NA)	(NA)	(NA)	(NA)
Los Angeles, CA	68.9	40.7	23.5	2.0	63.0	29.6	25.9	0.0
New Orleans, LA.	79.6	50.8	47.6	14.0	62.2	30.3	37.3	13.3
New York, NY.	72.7	43.1	35.7	15.0	73.3	36.7	50.0	23.3
Oklahoma City, OK	73.5	54.9	24.6	3.0	78.4	43.3	35.3	5.6
Philadelphia, PA	68.8	45.8	30.3	11.5	(NA)	(NA)	(NA)	(NA)
Phoenix, AZ	76.8	40.9	23.4	4.4	78.5	31.6	28.1	6.1
Portland, OR	72.7	38.4	29.7	15.0	84.4	35.2	39.6	22.0
Sacramento, CA	81.1	49.2	21.6	6.9	(NA)	(NA)	(NA)	(NA)
San Antonio, TX	65.2	41.9	30.5	9.1	(NA)	(NA)	(NA)	(NA)
San Diego, CA	71.2	41.0	10.3	5.1	72.6	29.1	15.2	8.7
San Jose, CA	63.7	35.4	12.9	3.1	72.8	29.1	10.1	3.4
Seattle, WA.	69.4	37.2	36.6	6.8	(NA)	(NA)	(NA)	(NA)
Tucson, AZ	76.4	44.1	42.5	4.2	73.2	29.0	40.0	9.7
Washington, DC	65.8	37.4	26.5	9.8	66.7	29.1	30.9	10.9

NA Not available. [1] Includes other drugs not shown separately.
Source: U.S. National Institute of Justice, *2003 Annual Report on Drug Use Among Adult and Juvenile Arrestees,* June 2004.

No. 315. Drug Arrest Rates for Drug Abuse Violations, 1990 to 2002, and by Region, 2002

[Rate per 100,000 inhabitants. Based on Census Bureau estimated resident population as of July 1, except 1990, enumerated as of April 1. For composition of regions, see map, inside front cover]

Offense	1990	1995	2000	2002 Total	North-east	Midwest	South	West
Drug arrest rate, total	435.3	564.7	587.1	505.8	474.1	371.6	524.4	604.9
Sale and/or manufacture	139.0	140.7	122.7	99.5	126.7	74.5	99.7	99.6
Heroin or cocaine [1]	93.7	83.7	60.8	48.7	87.2	23.2	49.9	37.3
Marijuana.	26.4	32.7	34.2	27.1	29.4	28.5	25.3	26.7
Synthetic or manufactured drugs	2.7	3.9	6.4	7.0	4.3	5.0	11.8	4.7
Other dangerous nonnarcotic drugs . .	16.2	20.3	21.2	16.7	5.9	17.8	10.0	31.0
Possession	296.3	423.9	464.4	406.3	347.4	297.1	424.7	505.3
Heroin or cocaine [1]	144.4	157.4	138.7	113.4	116.7	44.6	127.5	146.1
Marijuana.	104.9	192.7	244.4	200.5	198.1	190.3	239.0	165.2
Synthetic or manufactured drugs	6.6	8.5	12.0	14.7	8.0	10.3	20.5	15.5
Other dangerous nonnarcotic drugs . .	40.4	65.4	69.4	77.7	24.7	51.9	37.7	178.4

[1] Includes other derivatives such as morphine, heroin, and codeine.

Source: U.S. Federal Bureau of Investigation, *Crime in the United States,* annual. See also <http://www.fbi.gov/ucr/cius01/01crime.pdf> (released 27 October 2003).

No. 316. Federal Drug Seizures by Type of Drug: 1990 to 2003

[In pounds. For year ending September 30. Reflects the combined drug seizure effort of the Drug Enforcement Administration, the Federal Bureau of Investigation, the U.S. Customs Services, and beginning October 1993 the U.S. Border Patrol within the jurisdiction of the United States as well as maritime seizures by the U.S. Coast Guard. Based on reports to the Federal-wide Drug Seizure System, which eliminates duplicate reporting of a seizure involving more than one federal agency]

Drug	1990	1995	1997	1998	1999	2000	2001	2002	2003
Total	745,003	1,662,592	1,762,763	2,084,881	2,663,510	2,985,794	2,914,817	2,661,455	2,963,208
Heroin.	1,515	3,406	3,592	3,212	2,539	3,694	5,503	6,113	5,206
Cocaine.	211,828	244,888	221,491	259,896	288,952	235,059	232,748	226,431	257,804
Cannabis.	531,660	1,414,298	1,537,680	1,821,773	2,372,019	2,747,041	2,676,566	2,428,911	2,700,198
Marijuana	514,723	1,382,396	1,536,018	1,821,241	2,370,261	2,723,059	2,676,212	2,427,542	2,699,856
Hashish	16,937	31,902	1,662	532	1,758	23,982	354	1,369	342

Source: U.S. Drug Enforcement Administration, unpublished data from Federal-wide Drug Seizure System.

No. 317. Authorized Intercepts of Communication—Summary: 1980 to 2003

[Data for jurisdictions with statutes authorizing or approving interception of wire or oral communication]

Item	1980	1985	1990	1995	1996	1997	1998	1999	2000	2001	2002	2003
Jurisdictions: [1]												
With wiretap statutes	28	32	40	41	46	45	45	45	45	46	47	47
Reporting interceptions	22	22	25	19	24	24	26	28	26	25	20	24
Intercept applications autho- rized	564	784	872	1,156	1,254	1,279	1,482	1,489	1,266	1,561	1,358	1,442
Intercept installations	524	722	812	1,024	1,035	1,094	1,245	1,277	1,139	1,405	1,273	1,367
Federal	79	235	321	527	574	563	562	595	472	481	490	576
State	445	487	491	497	461	531	683	682	667	924	783	791
Intercepted communications, average [2]	1,058	1,320	1,487	2,028	1,969	2,081	1,858	1,921	1,769	1,565	1,708	3,004
Incriminating	315	275	321	459	422	418	350	390	402	333	403	993
Persons arrested [3]	1,871	2,469	2,057	2,577	2,464	3,086	3,450	4,372	3,411	3,683	3,060	3,674
Convictions [3]	259	660	420	494	502	542	911	654	736	732	493	843
Major offense specified:												
Gambling	199	206	116	95	114	98	93	60	49	82	82	49
Drugs	282	434	520	732	821	870	955	978	894	1,167	1,052	1,104
Homicide and assault	13	25	21	30	41	31	55	62	72	52	58	80
Racketeering	(NA)	(NA)	(NA)	98	105	93	153	139	76	70	72	96
Other	70	119	215	201	173	187	228	260	175	190	94	113

NA Not available. [1] Jurisdictions include federal government, states, and District of Columbia. [2] Average per authorized installation. [3] Based on information received from intercepts installed in year shown; additional arrests/convictions will occur in subsequent years but are not shown here.

Source: Administrative Office of the U.S. Courts, *Report on Applications for Orders Authorizing or Approving the Interception of Wire, Oral or Electronic Communications* (Wiretap Report), annual. See also <http://www.uscourts.gov/wiretap03/2003wttxt.pdf> (issued April 2004).

U.S. Census Bureau, Statistical Abstract of the United States: 2004-2005

No. 318. Background Checks for Firearm Transfers: 1994 to 2002

[In thousands (45,717 represents 45,717,000), except rates. For "Interim period" of 1994 to November 29, 1998, covered hand-gun purchases from licensed firearm dealers; beginning November 29, 1998 (effective date for the Brady Handgun Violence Prevention Act, P.L. 103-159,1993) covers the transfer of both handguns and long guns from a federal firearms licensee, as well as purchases from pawnshops and retail gun shops]

Inquiries and rejections	1994-2002, period [1]	Interim period					Permanent Brady		
		1994	1995	1996	1997	1998 [2]	1999 [3]	2000	2002
Applications and rejections:									
Applications received	45,717	2,483	2,706	2,593	2,574	3,277	8,621	7,699	7,806
Applications rejected	976	62	41	70	69	90	204	153	136
Rejection rate	2.1	2.5	1.5	2.7	2.7	2.9	2.4	2.0	1.7

[1] Represents from the Inception of the Brady Act on March 1, 1994 to 2002.   [2] For period January 1 to November 29, 1998. Counts are from the National Instant Criminal Background Check System and may include multiple transactions for the same application.   [3] For period November 30 to December 31, 1999. Counts are from the National Instant Criminal Background Check System and may include multiple transactions for the same application.

Source: U.S. Bureau of Justice Statistics, *Background Checks for Firearm Transfers, 2002,* Series NCJ 200116, September 2003.

No. 319. Firearm Use by Offenders: 1997

[In percent. Based on the Survey of Inmates in State and Federal Correctional Facilities]

Characteristic	Percent of prison inmates		Characteristic	Percent of prison inmates		Characteristic	Percent of prison inmates	
	State	Fed-eral		State	Fed-eral		State	Fed-eral
TYPE OF FIREARM[1] . .			Property	3.1	2.9	Criminal history		
			Drug	8.1	8.7	First-time offender . .	22.3	9.5
Total	18.4	14.8	Public order	19.1	27.3	Recidivist	17.2	18.4
Handgun	15.3	12.8						
Rifle	1.3	1.3	Gender			Use of firearm [2]	100.0	100.0
Shotgun	2.4	2.0	Male	19.1	15.5	Fired	49.1	12.8
			Female	7.3	6.2	Killed/injured victim. .	22.8	5.0
INMATES WHO CARRIED FIREARMS			Age			Other.	26.3	7.8
			24 or younger	29.4	19.1	Brandished to:. . . .	73.2	46.2
Offense:			25 to 34	16.5	15.5	Scare someone . .	48.6	29.3
Violent	30.2	35.4	35 or older	14.8	13.6	Defend self	41.1	24.9

[1] Percents of subtotals may not add to totals because inmates may have had more than one firearm.   [2] Percents of subtotals may not add to totals because inmates may have used a firearm in more than one way.

Source: U.S. Bureau of Justice Statistics, Firearm Use by Offenders, Series NCJ 189369, November 2001. See also <http://www.ojp.usdoj.gov/bjs/pub/pdf/fuo.pdf>.

No. 320. General Purpose Law Enforcement Agencies—Number and Employment: 2000

[Includes both full-time and part-time employees. State police data are based on the 49 primary law enforcement agencies; Excludes agencies that perform primarily court-related duties.]

Type of Agency	Number of agencies [1]	Number of employees					
		Full-time			Part-time		
		Total	Sworn	Civilian	Total	Sworn	Civilian
2000 Total.	**15,785**	**946,766**	**661,979**	**284,787**	**86,039**	**37,872**	**48,174**
Local police.	12,666	565,915	440,920	124,995	62,197	27,351	34,853
Sheriff	3,070	293,823	164,711	129,112	23,025	10,426	12,599
State police.	49	87,028	56,348	30,680	817	95	722

[1] The number of agencies reported here is the result of a weighted sample and not an exact enumeration.

Source: U.S. Bureau of Justice Statistics, *Law Enforcement Management and Administrative Statistics, 2000,* series NCJ 184481, November 2001.

No. 321. Casework Loads in DNA Laboratories: 1997 and 2000

[Based on the National Study of DNA (deoxyribonucleic acid) Laboratories' Survey, which obtained data from 110 of the approximately 120 known public forensic DNA laboratories]

Case status	1997	2000	Percent Change	Case status	1997	2000	Percent Change
Work received				Convicted offender[2] .	44,810	148,347	231
Casework [1]	20,793	31,394	51	Backlog of work			
Convicted offender [2].	115,681	177,184	53	Casework.	6,800	15,981	135
Work analyzed				Convicted offender. .	286,819	265,329	-7
Casework[1]	14,289	24,790	73	Full-time employees. . .	672	893	33

[1] Casework refers to cases received by forensic crime laboratories which involve criminal incident under investigation.   [2] Convicted offender samples are DNA samples collected from persons convicted of a crime, normally a violent crime or felony. The samples are to be analyzed, and the results are to be included in a DNA database.

Source: US Bureau of Justice Statistics, *Survey of DNA Crime Laboratories, 2001,* Series NCJ 191191, January 2002.

No. 322. Law Enforcement Officers Killed and Assaulted: 1990 to 2002

[Covers officers killed feloniously and accidentally in line of duty; includes federal officers. For composition of regions, see map, inside front cover]

Item	1990	1995	1996	1997	1998	1999	2000	2001 [1]	2002
OFFICERS KILLED									
Total killed	132	133	113	133	142	107	134	218	132
Northeast	13	16	17	16	6	11	13	79	10
Midwest	20	19	21	25	19	17	32	26	22
South.................	68	63	47	55	70	56	67	68	65
West	23	32	18	30	36	22	19	38	28
Puerto Rico............	8	2	10	7	9	1	3	7	7
Outlying areas, foreign countries............	-	1	-	-	2	-	-	-	-
Feloniously killed	65	74	61	70	61	42	51	142	56
Firearms	56	62	57	68	58	41	47	61	51
Handgun	47	43	50	50	40	25	33	46	38
Rifle	8	14	6	12	17	11	10	11	10
Shotgun.............	1	5	1	6	1	5	4	4	3
Knife	3	2	1	1	1	-	4	4	3
Bomb	-	8	-	-	1	-	-	-	1
Personal weapons	2	-	1	1	-	1	-	-	-
Other	4	2	2	-	-	-	-	1	-
Accidentally killed........	67	59	52	63	81	65	83	76	76
ASSAULTS									
Population (1,000) [2]	197,426	191,759	165,264	184,825	193,098	207,124	204,599	213,645	216,343
Number of—									
Agencies represented	9,343	8,503	7,803	8,120	8,153	9,832	8,940	9,773	9,987
Police officers..........	410,131	428,379	371,964	411,015	452,361	462,782	452,331	471,096	482,762
Total assaulted	72,091	57,762	46,608	52,149	60,673	55,971	58,398	57,463	58,066
Firearm	3,651	2,354	1,878	2,110	2,126	1,772	1,749	1,841	1,889
Knife or cutting instrument ...	1,647	1,356	871	971	1,098	999	1,015	1,168	1,056
Other dangerous weapon ...	7,423	6,414	5,069	5,800	7,415	7,560	8,132	8,233	8,326
Hands, fists, feet, etc	59,370	47,638	38,790	43,268	50,034	45,640	47,502	46,221	46,795

- Represents zero.   [1] The 72 officers feloniously slain during the events of September 11, 2001 are included in data for 2001.
[2] Represents the number of persons covered by agencies shown.

Source: U.S. Federal Bureau of Investigation, Law Enforcement Officers Killed and Assaulted, annual.

No. 323. U.S. Supreme Court—Cases Filed and Disposition: 1980 to 2002

[Statutory term of court begins first Monday in October]

Action	1980	1990	1995	1997	1998	1999	2000	2001	2002
Total cases on docket	5,144	6,316	7,565	7,692	8,083	8,445	8,965	9,176	9,406
Appellate cases on docket............	2,749	2,351	2,456	2,432	2,387	2,413	2,305	2,210	2,190
From prior term	527	365	361	347	326	321	351	324	321
Docketed during present term	2,222	1,986	2,095	2,085	2,061	2,092	1,954	1,886	1,869
Cases acted upon [1]............	2,324	2,042	2,130	2,142	2,092	2,096	2,024	1,932	1,899
Granted review	167	114	92	75	72	78	85	82	83
Denied, dismissed, or withdrawn	1,999	1,802	1,945	1,990	1,940	1,958	1,842	1,751	1,727
Summarily decided	90	81	62	36	44	34	63	57	46
Cases not acted upon	425	309	326	290	295	317	281	278	291
Pauper cases on docket	2,371	3,951	5,098	5,253	5,689	6,024	6,651	6,958	7,209
Cases acted upon	2,027	3,436	4,514	4,616	4,951	5,273	5,736	6,139	6,488
Granted review	17	27	13	14	9	14	14	6	8
Denied, dismissed, or withdrawn ...	1,968	3,369	4,439	4,581	4,926	5,239	5,658	6,114	6,459
Summarily decided	32	28	55	14	11	16	61	13	17
Cases not acted upon	344	515	584	637	738	751	915	819	721
Original cases on docket	24	14	11	7	7	8	9	8	7
Cases disposed of during term	7	3	5	1	2	-	2	1	1
Total cases available for argument	264	201	145	138	124	124	138	137	139
Cases disposed of	162	131	93	97	94	87	89	90	87
Cases argued	154	125	90	96	90	83	86	88	84
Cases dismissed or remanded without argument	8	6	3	1	4	4	3	2	3
Cases remaining	102	70	52	41	30	37	49	47	52
Cases decided by signed opinion	144	121	87	93	84	79	83	85	79
Cases decided by per curiam opinion.....	8	4	3	1	4	2	4	3	5
Number of signed opinions.	123	112	75	91	75	74	77	76	71

- Represents zero.   [1] Includes cases granted review and carried over to next term, not shown separately.

Source: Office of the Clerk, Supreme Court of the United States, unpublished data.

U.S. Census Bureau, Statistical Abstract of the United States: 2004-2005

No. 324. U.S. District Courts—Civil Cases Commenced and Pending: 2000 to 2003

[For years ending **June 30**]

Type of case	Cases commenced				Cases pending			
	2000	2001	2002	2003	2000	2001	2002	2003
Cases total [1]	**263,049**	**253,354**	**268,071**	**254,499**	**249,692**	**251,335**	**270,667**	**261,608**
Contract actions [1]	54,494	45,438	36,845	32,356	38,262	35,685	33,237	30,789
Recovery of overpayments [2]	25,636	16,116	6,737	3,466	12,107	8,987	5,342	2,713
Real property actions	6,481	7,296	7,731	7,503	4,249	5,458	6,485	6,302
Tort actions	40,877	34,071	56,565	46,295	63,116	60,320	76,907	65,562
Personal injury	36,867	30,194	52,654	42,233	59,232	56,459	72,962	61,496
Personal injury product liability [1]	15,349	12,569	35,074	24,255	31,772	29,953	46,264	34,655
Asbestos	7,893	5,656	24,844	3,718	4,949	6,247	21,045	5,606
Other personal injury	21,518	17,625	17,580	17,978	27,460	26,506	26,698	26,841
Personal property damage	4,010	3,877	3,911	4,062	3,884	3,861	3,945	4,066
Actions under statutes [1]	161,187	166,535	166,920	168,332	144,053	149,862	154,027	158,943
Civil rights [1]	41,226	40,979	40,172	40,567	44,259	43,703	43,589	43,981
Employment	21,404	21,121	20,881	20,777	24,456	23,803	23,778	23,618
Bankruptcy suits	3,378	3,012	3,792	3,342	2,555	2,216	2,921	2,522
Commerce (ICC rates, etc.)	1,007	554	578	574	444	459	453	455
Environmental matters	894	1,794	848	935	1,355	2,264	2,134	2,296
Prisoner petitions	57,706	59,159	55,596	55,112	43,560	46,157	44,210	44,306
Forfeiture and penalty	2,246	2,143	2,062	2,120	1,772	1,694	1,787	1,932
Labor laws	14,229	14,880	17,706	17,290	11,267	11,484	14,084	14,621
Protected property rights [3]	8,745	8,143	8,500	8,613	7,858	7,491	8,094	8,654
Securities commodities and exchanges	2,500	3,152	3,559	3,449	3,578	4,187	4,659	5,227
Social Security laws	14,365	17,530	17,868	17,483	13,667	16,182	17,489	17,526
Tax suits	938	961	1,147	1,232	1,068	971	1,115	1,106
Freedom of information	335	350	284	266	380	371	348	347

[1] Includes other types not shown separately. [2] Includes enforcement of judgments in student loan cases, and overpayments of veterans benefits. [3] Includes copyright, patent, and trademark rights.

Source: Administrative Office of the U.S. Courts, *Statistical Tables for the Federal Judiciary*, annual.

No. 325. U.S. District Courts—Offenders Convicted and Sentenced to Prison and Length of Sentence: 2001

Most serious offense of conviction	Offenders convicted	Convicted offenders sentenced to prison	Mean length of sentence (mo.)[1]	Most serious offense of conviction	Offenders convicted	Convicted offenders sentenced to prison	Mean length of sentence (mo.)[1]
Total [2]	**68,533**	**51,057**	**56.5**	Possession	1,840	1,652	79.0
Violent offenses	2,604	2,399	90.8	Trafficking and manufacturing	23,248	21,422	73.5
Property offenses	12,349	7,744	24.1	Public-order offenses	4,347	2,686	39.3
Fraudulent offenses [3]	10,359	6,537	22.2	Regulatory offenses	1,410	597	23.5
Embezzlement	780	463	16.5	Other offenses	2,937	2,089	43.8
Fraud [4]	8,328	5,318	22.9	Tax law violations [5]	492	276	21.8
Forgery	105	58	19.6	Weapons	4,925	4,541	86.9
Other offenses [3]	1,990	1,207	34.7	Immigration	10,050	9,065	29.2
Larceny [3]	1,393	755	28.3	Misdemeanors	9,100	1,515	10.0
Drug offenses [3]	25,088	23,074	73.8				

[1] Excludes sentences of life, death, and indeterminate sentences. [2] Total may include offenders for whom offense category could not be determined. [3] Includes offenses not shown separately. [4] Excludes tax fraud. [5] Includes tax fraud.

Source: U.S. Bureau of Justice Statistics, *Compendium of Federal Justice Statistics, 2000*, Series NCJ 194067, August 2002.

No. 326. Federal Prosecutions of Public Corruption: 1980 to 2002

[As of **Dec. 31.** Prosecution of persons who have corrupted public office in violation of Federal Criminal Statutes]

Prosecution Status	1980	1985	1990	1994	1995	1996	1997	1998	1999	2000	2001	2002
Total: [1] Indicted	727	1,157	1,176	1,165	1,051	984	1,057	1,174	1,134	1,000	1,087	1,136
Convicted	602	997	1,084	969	878	902	853	1,014	1,065	938	920	1,011
Awaiting trial	213	256	300	332	323	244	327	340	329	327	437	413
Federal officials: Indicted	123	563	615	571	527	456	459	442	480	441	502	478
Convicted	131	470	583	488	438	459	392	414	460	422	414	429
Awaiting trial	16	90	103	124	120	64	83	85	101	92	131	119
State officials: Indicted	72	79	96	99	61	109	51	91	115	92	95	110
Convicted	51	66	79	97	61	83	49	58	80	91	61	132
Awaiting trial	28	20	28	17	23	40	20	37	44	37	75	50
Local officials: Indicted	247	248	257	248	236	219	255	277	237	211	224	299
Convicted	168	221	225	202	191	190	169	264	219	183	184	262
Awaiting trial	82	49	98	96	89	60	118	90	95	89	110	118

[1] Includes individuals who are neither public officials nor employees but who were involved with public officials or employees in violating the law, not shown separately.

Source: U.S. Department of Justice, *Federal Prosecutions of Corrupt Public Officials, 1970-1980* and *Report to Congress on the Activities and Operations of the Public Integrity Section*, annual.

No. 327. Computer Related Crime Prosecuted by Prosecutors' Offices: 2001

[In percent]

Type of computer crime prosecuted	Percent of prosecutors' offices				
		Full-time offices (population served)			
	All offices	Large (1,000,000 or more)	Medium (250,000 to 999,999)	Small (under 250,000)	Part-time
Any computer-related crime	41.5	97.0	72.9	44.2	16.8
Credit card fraud	27.4	93.5	61.2	28.2	7.4
Bank card fraud [1]	22.3	83.3	50.9	22.6	6.9
Computer sabotage [2]	4.6	53.6	14.4	3.8	0.5
Theft of intellectual property	3.2	40.7	13.4	2.3	0.5
Transmitting child pornography	30.0	87.1	67.1	30.4	10.8
Identity theft	18.2	80.0	51.9	17.2	4.5

[1] ATM or debit. [2] To hinder the normal function of a computer system through the introduction of worms, viruses, or logic bombs.

Source: U.S. Bureau of Justice Statistics, *Prosecutors in State Courts*, 2001.

No. 328. Per Capita Justice Expenditure and Employment of State and Local Governments by State: 1999

[State and local expenditure and employment data per 10,000 population estimated as of July 1]

State	Expenditure per capita (dollars)				Full-time equivalent justice employment per 10,000 population [1]			
	Total justice system	Police protection	Judicial and legal	Corrections	Total justice system	Police protection	Judicial and legal	Corrections
United States	442.1	189.8	89.9	162.4	67.4	30.2	13.3	23.9
Alabama	295.0	145.3	57.9	91.7	55.2	28.1	11.1	15.9
Alaska	724.9	283.4	195.1	246.4	70.1	26.9	20.9	22.3
Arizona	472.4	201.8	105.0	165.6	73.0	30.8	17.7	24.6
Arkansas	279.7	126.2	48.4	105.1	54.9	28.5	6.8	19.5
California	602.9	240.9	169.2	192.8	65.1	28.0	14.7	22.4
Colorado	438.3	180.9	74.3	183.1	61.2	28.4	12.5	20.4
Connecticut	455.0	193.6	107.8	153.6	68.4	30.7	12.0	25.7
Delaware	561.1	194.0	109.8	257.3	79.7	29.8	20.1	29.8
District of Columbia	1,212.3	592.1	66.8	553.4	139.6	78.8	6.5	54.3
Florida	503.1	224.2	84.0	194.9	79.0	33.3	17.2	28.5
Georgia	364.8	144.6	63.1	157.2	70.7	28.2	10.9	31.5
Hawaii	429.7	182.5	136.4	110.8	70.6	28.9	22.8	18.9
Idaho	384.2	149.1	75.7	159.3	55.9	25.2	10.7	20.0
Illinois	418.2	224.4	70.6	123.3	69.7	36.4	13.2	20.1
Indiana	283.2	124.5	50.0	108.7	53.6	26.7	9.5	17.4
Iowa	314.7	135.8	82.7	96.2	48.6	23.7	10.9	14.1
Kansas	355.0	161.6	74.4	119.0	67.8	33.0	13.4	21.5
Kentucky	302.8	109.6	69.2	124.0	53.5	24.1	14.2	15.2
Louisiana	410.7	183.3	76.3	151.2	76.7	34.3	15.1	27.3
Maine	257.4	122.5	50.9	84.0	46.2	25.6	6.6	14.0
Maryland	451.1	191.2	87.8	172.1	73.3	33.2	13.1	27.0
Massachusetts	464.8	218.7	99.8	146.3	66.1	35.7	11.0	19.4
Michigan	439.3	172.3	83.2	183.7	59.6	24.9	11.5	23.2
Minnesota	363.6	166.8	85.2	111.6	48.5	21.5	11.5	15.6
Mississippi	281.7	135.7	53.6	92.5	59.7	30.0	10.2	19.4
Missouri	324.5	153.9	56.2	114.4	68.3	30.7	13.0	24.6
Montana	339.5	134.5	71.0	134.0	52.0	24.2	11.0	16.8
Nebraska	284.0	128.8	54.3	100.9	53.6	25.9	10.4	17.2
Nevada	542.7	231.7	107.8	203.2	70.4	30.7	16.2	23.5
New Hampshire	299.0	141.8	69.7	87.4	49.1	26.4	9.2	13.5
New Jersey	518.4	236.6	113.9	167.9	82.5	39.3	24.4	18.8
New Mexico	440.6	194.1	85.2	161.3	75.4	29.3	15.9	30.2
New York	630.1	292.4	113.4	224.2	92.6	44.7	15.6	32.4
North Carolina	350.9	155.4	58.1	137.5	64.4	27.6	8.2	28.5
North Dakota	243.3	102.9	66.2	74.3	46.2	22.3	11.6	12.3
Ohio	424.2	179.4	95.6	149.3	68.3	28.0	17.6	22.6
Oklahoma	301.6	119.9	51.1	130.6	63.1	31.6	11.1	20.4
Oregon	463.5	184.3	74.6	204.6	60.9	24.6	13.6	22.8
Pennsylvania	424.4	171.2	79.6	173.7	60.2	25.0	14.2	20.9
Rhode Island	408.1	179.2	94.7	134.2	58.1	29.2	11.8	17.2
South Carolina	330.9	147.0	43.9	140.0	69.4	33.3	8.8	27.3
South Dakota	268.0	115.3	49.2	103.5	49.4	22.1	9.8	17.5
Tennessee	323.3	151.0	70.2	102.1	58.9	29.6	9.6	19.8
Texas	387.6	148.5	60.0	179.2	71.1	27.8	10.5	32.8
Utah	400.4	161.4	80.7	158.4	53.3	24.2	11.7	17.5
Vermont	248.1	102.8	81.2	64.2	47.3	21.8	10.3	15.1
Virginia	388.3	156.6	67.9	163.8	66.1	25.4	9.6	31.0
Washington	418.3	162.0	83.8	172.5	55.8	23.3	12.5	20.0
West Virginia	228.0	87.3	55.7	85.0	40.0	20.2	11.3	8.5
Wisconsin	448.6	196.6	79.3	172.8	60.2	28.6	10.2	21.4
Wyoming	482.6	189.2	100.9	192.5	69.0	34.0	14.1	21.0

[1] Population based on Census Bureau, Current Population Reports, Series P-25, No. 1045, as of March 1999.

Source: U.S. Bureau of Justice Statistics, *Justice Expenditure and Employment in the United States, 1999*, Series NCJ 191746, February 2002.

Law Enforcement, Courts, and Prisons **203**

No. 329. Delinquency Cases Disposed by Juvenile Courts by Reason for Referral: 1990 to 2000

[In thousands (1,317 represents 1,317,000), except rate. A delinquency offense is an act committed by a juvenile for which an adult could be prosecuted in a criminal court. Disposition of a case involves taking a definite action such as waiving the case to criminal court, dismissing the case, placing the youth on probation, placing the youth in a facility for delinquents, or such actions as fines, restitution, and community service]

Reason for referral	1990	1991	1992	1993	1994	1995	1996	1997	1998	1999	2000
All delinquency offenses .	1,317	1,414	1,482	1,522	1,666	1,768	1,796	1,811	1,743	1,667	1,612
Case rate [1]	51.4	54.0	55.2	55.3	59.4	61.9	62.0	61.7	58.8	55.5	52.5
Violent offenses.	94	106	114	118	132	137	128	109	100	86	81
Criminal homicide.	2	2	2	3	3	3	3	2	2	2	2
Forcible rape	5	6	6	7	7	7	6	6	5	4	5
Robbery	28	32	33	35	38	40	38	34	29	25	22
Aggravated assault.	59	66	72	73	84	87	81	67	64	55	52
Property offenses.	773	849	862	834	868	888	874	846	779	703	661
Burglary	564	615	619	594	609	630	621	601	539	481	452
Larceny	145	155	160	151	146	142	145	142	131	113	109
Motor vehicle theft	341	382	382	372	392	424	413	398	355	321	299
Arson	70	71	70	62	62	54	54	52	45	38	37
Delinquency offenses	660	692	749	810	925	1001	1048	1101	1103	1100	1079
Simple assault.	132	143	162	177	198	219	223	248	254	255	248
Vandalism	99	113	119	119	130	127	123	118	117	111	107
Drug law violations	71	65	73	92	131	166	185	194	194	191	193
Obstruction of justice.	80	74	78	94	110	122	150	166	169	172	179
Other [2].	278	297	317	328	356	368	367	375	370	371	352

[1] Number of cases disposed per 1,000 youth (ages 10 to 17) at risk.   [2] Includes such offenses as stolen property offenses, trespassing, weapons offenses, other sex offenses, liquor law violations, disorderly conduct, and miscellaneous offenses.

Source: National Center for Juvenile Justice, Pittsburgh, PA, *Juvenile Court Statistics*, annual. See also <http://www.ojjdp.ncjrs.org/ojstatbb/index.html>.

No. 330. Delinquency Cases and Case Rates by Sex and Race: 1992 to 2000

[A delinquency offense is an act committed by a juvenile for which an adult could be prosecuted in a criminal court. Disposition of a case involves taking a definite action such as waiving the case to criminal court, dismissing the case, placing the youth on probation, placing the youth in a facility for delinquents, or such actions as fines, restitution, and community service.]

Sex, race, and offense	Number of cases disposed			Case rate [1]		
	1992	1999	2000	1992	1999	2000
Male, total	1,195,200	1,270,000	1,216,500	86.6	82.4	77.2
Person	243,800	281,600	267,700	17.7	18.3	17.0
Property	694,500	535,400	499,400	50.3	34.8	31.7
Drugs.	64,000	160,900	160,700	4.6	10.4	10.2
Public order.	193,000	292,100	288,700	14.0	19.0	18.3
Female, total	286,900	397,100	396,000	21.9	27.2	26.5
Person	64,900	103,800	101,300	5.0	7.1	6.8
Property	167,800	167,700	162,000	12.8	11.5	10.8
Drugs.	8,700	30,400	32,400	0.7	2.1	2.2
Public order.	45,600	95,300	100,300	3.5	6.5	6.7
White, total	975,600	1,137,400	1,111,100	45.3	47.9	46.0
Person	177,300	241,700	229,500	8.2	10.2	9.5
Property	607,000	492,800	462,700	28.2	20.8	19.2
Drugs.	37,500	135,600	145,800	1.7	5.7	6.0
Public order.	153,800	267,300	273,200	7.1	11.3	11.3
Black, total	453,500	473,600	445,000	112.1	102.2	92.5
Person	121,700	132,400	128,100	30.1	28.6	26.6
Property	221,300	181,400	171,200	54.7	39.2	35.6
Drugs.	33,500	51,300	42,600	8.3	11.1	8.9
Public order.	77,100	108,500	103,100	19.1	23.4	21.4
Other races, total.	53,000	56,100	56,400	40.5	33.9	32.3
Person	9,700	11,200	11,500	7.4	6.8	6.6
Property	34,000	28,900	27,500	26.0	17.4	15.8
Drugs.	1,600	4,400	4,800	1.2	2.6	2.7
Public order.	7,600	11,600	12,700	5.8	7.0	7.3

[1] Cases per 1,000 youth (ages 10 to 17) at risk.

Source: National Center for Juvenile Justice, Pittsburgh, PA, *Juvenile Court Statistics*, annual. See also <http://www.ojjdp.ncjrs.org/ojstatbb/index.html>.

No. 331. Child Abuse and Neglect Cases Substantiated and Indicated—Victim Characteristics: 1990 to 2002

[Based on reports alleging child abuse and neglect that were referred for investigation by the respective child protective services agency in each state. The reporting period may be either calendar or fiscal year. The majority of states provided duplicated counts. Children are counted each time they were subjects of an investigation report. In 2001, the data are from 51 States. Victims are children whose alleged maltreatments have been substantiated, indicated, or assessed as maltreatments. A substantiated case represents a type of investigation disposition that determines that there is sufficient evidence under State law to conclude that maltreatment occurred or that the child is at risk of maltreatment. An indicated case represents a type of disposition that concludes that there was a reason to suspect maltreatment had occurred, but the level of evidence does not reach the State standard. An alternative response-victim case represents a type of disposition that identifies child as a victim within the alternative response system.]

ITEM	1990 Number	1990 Percent	1999 Number	1999 Percent	2000 Number	2000 Percent	2002 Number	2002 Percent
TYPES OF SUBSTANTIATED MALTREATMENT								
Victims, total [1]	690,658	(X)	783,632	(X)	864,837	(X)	897,168	(X)
Neglect	338,770	49.1	439,094	56.0	517,118	59.8	525,131	58.5
Physical abuse	186,801	27.0	167,703	21.4	167,713	19.4	167,168	18.6
Sexual abuse	119,506	17.3	88,801	11.3	87,770	10.2	88,688	9.9
Emotional maltreatment	45,621	6.6	59,842	7.6	66,965	7.7	58,029	6.5
Medical neglect	(NA)	(NA)	18,809	2.4	25,498	3.0	18,128	2.0
SEX OF VICTIM								
Victims, total	742,519	100.0	779,787	100.0	864,837	100.0	897,168	100.0
Male	323,339	43.5	371,588	47.7	413,744	47.8	429,637	47.9
Female	369,919	49.8	402,051	51.6	446,230	51.6	463,675	51.7
AGE OF VICTIM								
Victims, total	731,282	100.0	780,145	100.0	864,837	100.0	897,168	100.0
1 year and younger	97,101	13.3	109,597	14.1	133,094	15.4	142,189	15.9
2 to 5 years old	172,791	23.6	186,178	23.9	205,790	23.8	218,000	24.3
6 to 9 years old	157,681	21.6	196,639	25.2	212,186	24.5	207,862	23.2
10 to 13 years old	135,130	18.5	157,879	20.2	176,071	20.4	188,492	21.0
14 to 17 years old	103,383	14.1	117,436	15.1	126,207	14.6	135,070	15.1
18 and over	4,880	0.7	4,101	0.5	992	0.1	994	0.1

NA Not available. X Not applicable. [1] A child may be a victim of more than one maltreatment. Therefore, the total for this item adds up to more than 100%.

No. 332. Child Abuse and Neglect Cases Reported and Investigated by State: 2002

[See headnote, Table 331]

State	Population under 18 years old	Number of reports [1]	Number of children subject of an investigation [2]	Number of child victims [3]	State	Population under 18 years old	Number of reports [1]	Number of children subject of an investigation [2]	Number of child victims [3]
U.S. [4]	72,894,483	1,811,974	3,136,751	897,168	MO	1,397,461	53,116	80,653	9,810
					MT	216,320	10,336	17,078	1,995
AL	1,107,108	20,544	32,682	9,903	NE	439,393	7,463	12,262	3,909
AK	192,428	10,002	10,002	7,950	NV	572,590	13,195	22,491	5,008
AZ	1,476,856	33,151	52,288	5,114	NH	308,371	7,509	10,564	962
AR	677,522	18,697	26,237	7,302	NJ	2,127,391	39,148	70,786	8,103
CA	9,452,391	260,924	512,880	132,181	NM	500,506	13,995	22,997	6,273
CO	1,151,118	27,889	40,552	7,570	NY	4,613,251	155,678	262,643	79,049
CT	872,853	34,513	53,414	12,818	NC	2,068,840	63,747	127,702	35,523
DE	189,698	5,163	8,042	1,304	ND	146,812	4,109	7,089	1,493
DC	112,128	5,049	8,243	3,032	OH	2,879,927	68,236	110,495	50,141
FL	3,882,271	142,547	254,856	122,131	OK	873,560	39,592	68,971	13,721
GA	2,268,477	69,108	126,677	41,206	OR	855,107	17,763	27,913	9,228
HI	295,514	3,619	7,318	3,744	PA	2,863,452	24,330	24,330	5,057
ID	370,439	6,475	9,412	1,947	RI	239,248	7,211	10,772	3,247
IL	3,254,523	58,704	137,321	28,160	SC	979,163	18,579	30,937	10,738
IN	1,594,857	33,336	50,163	20,416	SD	195,625	8,411	8,411	3,961
IA	698,045	23,215	34,793	12,202	TN	1,404,661	28,348	37,525	8,494
KS	696,519	17,504	26,696	6,425	TX	6,102,316	129,956	210,375	48,808
KY	931,588	41,218	62,738	16,945	UT	713,012	18,965	29,836	10,282
LA	1,185,674	23,493	37,825	10,971	VT	139,662	3,194	4,000	1,447
ME	279,058	4,474	8,121	3,746	VA	1,779,408	20,619	40,552	7,571
MD	1,379,925	(NA)	(NA)	15,843	WA	1,513,360	18,423	28,718	4,673
MA	1,463,340	38,445	64,343	34,995	WV	389,171	15,052	24,089	6,635
MI	2,570,264	72,999	190,164	28,830	WI	1,338,064	42,087	42,087	11,628
MN	1,252,125	17,770	26,344	9,982	WY	122,344	2,403	4,355	692
MS	760,747	11,670	18,009	4,003					

NA Not available. [1] The number of investigations includes assessments. The number of investigations is based on the total number of investigations that received a disposition in 2001. [2] The number of Children Subject of an Investigation of Assessment is based on the total number of children for whom an alleged maltreatment was substantiated, indicated, or assesed to have occurred or the child was at risk of occurrence. [3] Victims are defined as children subject of a substantiated, indicated, or alternative response-victim maltreatment. [4] Includes estimates for States that did not report.

Source of Tables 331 and 332: U.S. Department of Health and Human Services, Administration on Children, Youth and Families. *Child Maltreatment 2002* (Washington, DC: U. S. Government Printing Office, 2004).

U.S. Census Bureau, Statistical Abstract of the United States: 2004-2005

No. 333. Characteristics of Missing Children: 1999

Characteristic	Estimated number of children	Percent distribution	Characteristic	Estimated number of children	Percent distribution
RUNAWAY CHILDREN			FAMILY ABDUCTED CHILDREN		
Characteristic of Episode:					
Season:			Characteristic of child:		
Winter	335,400	20			
Spring	333,600	20	Age:		
Summer	655,100	39	0 to 3	43,400	21
Fall	343,300	20	3 to 5 years old	47,100	23
Number of miles traveled			6 to 11 years old	71,000	35
from home:			12 to 14 years old	35,200	17
2 or less	139,900	8	15 to 17 years old	7,200	4
3 to 10	503,100	30			
12 to 50	521,900	31	Gender:		
52 to 100	160,100	10	Male	100,300	49
More than 101	210,600	13	Female	103,500	51
No information	147,300	9			
Child left the State			Race/Ethnicity:		
Yes	147,600	9	White	119,400	59
No.	1,393,000	83	Black	23,900	12
No information	142,300	8	Hispanic	40,600	20
Duration			Other	16,200	8
8 hours to 23 hours	307,400	18			
25 hours to 6 days	975,700	58	Family Structure:		
1 week to less than 1			Single Parent.	85,500	42
month.	248,000	15	One parent and partner . .	35,300	17
Episode outcome:			Relative or foster parent .	30,300	15
Child returned	1,676,200	99			

Source: Office of Justice Programs, Office of Juvenile Justice and Delinquency Prevention, *National Incidence Studies of Missing, Abducted, Runaway and Thrownaway Children,* October 2002. See also <http://www.missingkids.com/enUS/documents/nismart2overview.pdf> (issued October 2002).

No. 334. Jail Inmates by Sex, Race, and Hispanic Origin: 1990 to 2001

[As of June 30. Excludes federal and state prisons or other correctional institutions; institutions exclusively for juveniles; state-operated jails in Alaska, Connecticut, Delaware, Hawaii, Rhode Island, and Vermont; and other facilities which retain persons for less than 48 hours. Data based on the Annual Survey of Jails, which is a sample survey and subject to sampling variability. Due to rounding, inmates may not add to total]

Characteristic	1990	1995	1996	1997	1998	1999	2000	2001
Total Inmates.	405,320	507,044	567,079	592,462	605,943	621,149	631,240	665,475
Male	365,821	448,000	498,678	520,581	528,998	543,120	551,007	581,411
Female.	37,198	51,300	59,296	63,791	67,487	70,414	72,621	76,817
Juveniles	2,301	7,800	9,105	8,090	9,458	7,613	7,613	7,248
White non-Hispanic.	169,600	203,300	230,300	244,900	249,900	260,500	271,700	291,800
Black non-Hispanic.	172,300	220,600	237,900	244,000	251,800	256,300	256,200	264,900
Hispanic.	58,100	74,400	88,900	91,800	93,800	94,100	93,000	9,800
Other [1]	5,400	8,800	10,000	11,800	10,400	10,200	10,300	10,800

[1] Includes American Indians, Alaska Natives, Asians, and Pacific Islanders.
Source: U.S. Bureau of Justice Statistics, through 1994, *Jail Inmates,* annual; beginning 1995, *Prison and Jail Inmates at Midyear,* annual.

No. 335. State and Federal Correctional Facilities—Inmates and Staff: 1990 to 2000

[Covers all state and Federal correctional institutions or places of confinement such as prisons, prison farms, boot camps, and community based halfway houses and work release centers. Excludes jails and other regional detention centers, private facilities, facilities for the military, Immigration and Naturalization Service, Bureau of Indian Affairs, U.S. Marshall Service, and correctional hospital wards not operated by correctional authorities]

Characteristic	1990	1995	2000	Characteristic	1990	1995	2000
FACILITIES				INMATES			
Total	1,287	1,464	1,668	Total	715,649	1,023,572	1,305,253
Type of facility:				Male	675,624	961,210	1,219,225
Confinement	1,037	1,160	1,208	Female	40,025	62,362	86,028
Community	250	304	460	Type of facility:			
Federal	80	77	84	Confinement	698,570	992,333	1,244,574
State	1,207	1,387	1,584	Community	17,079	31,239	60,679
Size of facility:				Federal	56,821	80,960	110,974
Fewer than 500	816	817	860	State	658,828	942,612	1,194,279
500-999	260	283	305	Custody level:			
1,000-2,499	185	309	438	Maximum/close/high. . .	150,205	202,174	244,797
2,500 or more	26	55	65	Medium	292,372	415,688	509,558
Age of facility:				Minimum/low.	219,907	366,227	474,353
Less than 10 years	314	497	444	Not classified	53,165	39,483	76,545
10-19 years old	163	273	398	STAFF			
20-49 years old	373	366	380				
50-99 years old	379	310	290	Total	264,201	347,320	430,033
100 years old or more. .	58	45	81	Federal	18,451	25,379	32,700
Not reported	-	9	75	State.	245,750	321,941	397,333

- Represents zero.
Source: U.S. Bureau of Justice Statistics, *Census of State and Federal Correctional Facilities,* 2000.

206 Law Enforcement, Courts, and Prisons

No. 336. Prisoners Under Jurisdiction of State and Federal Correctional Authorities—Summary by State: 1990 to 2002

[For years ending December 31]

State	1990	2000	2001	2002, advance Total	Percent change, 2001-2002	State	1990	2000	2001	2002, advance Total	Percent change, 2001-2002
U.S. [1]	773,919	1,391,261	1,404,032	1,440,655	2.6	MO	14,943	27,543	28,757	30,099	4.7
AL . . .	15,665	26,332	26,741	27,947	4.5	MT	1,425	3,105	3,328	3,290	-1.1
AK [2] . . .	2,622	4,173	4,571	4,398	-3.8	NE	2,403	3,895	3,937	4,058	3.1
AZ [3] . . .	14,261	26,510	27,710	29,359	6.0	NV	5,322	10,063	10,233	10,478	2.4
AR	7,322	11,915	12,594	13,090	3.9	NH	1,342	2,257	2,392	2,451	2.5
CA	97,309	163,001	159,444	162,317	1.8	NJ.	21,128	29,784	28,142	27,891	-0.9
CO [2] . . .	7,671	16,833	17,448	18,833	7.9	NM	3,187	5,342	5,668	5,989	5.7
CT [2] . . .	10,500	18,355	19,196	20,720	7.9	NY	54,895	70,199	67,533	67,065	-0.7
DE [2] . . .	3,471	6,921	7,003	6,778	-3.2	NC	18,411	31,266	32,253	32,803	1.7
DC [2] [4] . . .	9,947	7,456	(NA)	(NA)	(NA)	ND	483	1,076	1,111	1,112	0.1
FL [3] . . .	44,387	71,319	72,404	75,210	3.9	OH	31,822	45,833	45,281	45,646	0.8
GA [3] . . .	22,411	44,232	45,937	47,445	3.3	OK [4] . . .	12,285	23,181	22,780	23,385	2.7
HI [2] . . .	2,533	5,053	5,431	5,423	-0.1	OR	6,492	10,580	11,410	12,086	5.9
ID [3] . . .	1,961	5,535	5,984	6,204	3.7	PA	22,290	36,847	38,062	40,168	5.5
IL [3] . . .	27,516	45,281	44,348	42,693	-3.7	RI [2] . . .	2,392	3,286	3,241	3,520	8.6
IN	12,736	20,125	20,966	21,611	3.1	SC	17,319	21,778	22,576	23,715	5.0
IA [3] . . .	3,967	7,955	7,962	8,398	5.5	SD	1,341	2,616	2,790	2,898	3.9
KS	5,775	8,344	8,577	8,935	4.2	TN	10,388	22,166	23,671	24,989	5.6
KY	9,023	14,919	15,424	15,933	3.3	TX	50,042	166,719	162,070	162,003	0.0
LA	18,599	35,207	35,810	35,736	-0.2	UT	2,496	5,637	5,339	5,567	4.3
ME [5] . . .	1,523	1,679	1,704	1,900	11.5	VT [2] . . .	1,049	1,697	1,741	1,863	7.0
MD	17,848	23,538	23,752	24,162	1.7	VA	17,593	30,168	31,662	33,729	6.5
MA [3] [5] . . .	8,345	10,722	10,588	10,329	-2.4	WA	7,995	14,915	15,159	16,062	6.0
MI [3] [5] . . .	34,267	47,718	48,849	50,591	3.6	WV	1,565	3,856	4,215	4,544	7.8
MN	3,176	6,238	6,606	7,129	7.9	WI.	7,465	20,754	21,495	22,133	3.0
MS	8,375	20,241	21,460	22,705	5.8	WY	1,110	1,680	1,684	1,737	3.1

NA Not available. [1] State-level data excludes Federal inmates. [2] Includes both jail and prison inmates (State has combined jail and prison system). [3] Numbers are for custody rather than jurisdiction counts. [4] The transfer of responsibility for sentenced felons from the District of Columbia to the Federal System was completed by the year end 2001. Since June 30, 2000, the inmate population in the District of Columbia has dropped by 5,825 inmates. Approximately 58% of the growth in the Federal System in the last 6 months of 2001 was the result of this transfer of responsibility. [5] 1980 and 1990, data are for custody counts; thereafter, jurisdiction counts are reported.

Source: U.S. Bureau of Justice Statistics, *Prisoners in 2002*, Series NCJ 195189; and earlier reports.

No. 337. Adults on Probation, in Jail or Prison, or on Parole: 1980 to 2002

[As of December 31, except jail counts as of June 30]

Year	Total [1]	Percent of adult population	Probation	Jail	Prison	Parole	Male	Female
1980	1,840,400	(NA)	1,118,097	[2]182,288	319,598	220,438	(NA)	(NA)
1981	2,006,600	(NA)	1,225,934	[2]195,085	360,029	225,539	(NA)	(NA)
1982	2,192,600	(NA)	1,357,264	207,853	402,914	224,604	(NA)	(NA)
1983	2,475,100	(NA)	1,582,947	221,815	423,898	246,440	(NA)	(NA)
1984	2,689,200	(NA)	1,740,948	233,018	448,264	266,992	(NA)	(NA)
1985	3,011,500	1.7	1,968,712	254,986	487,593	300,203	2,606,000	405,500
1986	3,239,400	1.8	2,114,621	272,735	526,436	325,638	2,829,100	410,300
1987	3,459,600	1.9	2,247,158	294,092	562,814	355,505	3,021,000	438,600
1988	3,714,100	2.0	2,356,483	341,893	607,766	407,977	3,223,000	491,100
1989	4,055,600	2.2	2,522,125	393,303	683,367	456,803	3,501,600	554,000
1990	4,348,000	2.3	2,670,234	403,019	743,382	531,407	3,746,300	601,700
1991	4,535,600	2.4	2,728,472	424,129	792,535	590,442	3,913,000	622,600
1992	4,762,600	2.5	2,811,611	441,781	850,566	658,601	4,050,300	712,300
1993	4,944,000	2.6	2,903,061	455,500	909,381	676,100	4,215,800	728,200
1994	5,141,300	2.7	2,981,022	479,800	990,147	690,371	4,377,400	763,900
1995	5,335,100	2.8	3,077,861	499,300	1,078,542	679,421	4,513,000	822,100
1996	5,482,700	2.8	3,164,996	510,400	1,127,528	679,733	4,629,900	852,800
1997	5,725,800	2.9	3,296,513	557,974	1,176,564	694,787	4,825,300	900,500
1998	6,126,100	3.1	3,670,441	584,372	1,224,469	696,385	(NA)	(NA)
1999	6,331,400	3.1	3,779,922	596,485	1,287,172	714,457	(NA)	(NA)
2000	6,437,400	3.1	3,826,209	613,534	1,316,333	723,898	(NA)	(NA)
2001	6,574,100	3.1	3,931,731	623,628	1,330,007	732,333	(NA)	(NA)
2002, advance . . .	6,684,100	3.1	3,955,165	658,228	1,367,856	753,141	(NA)	(NA)

NA Not available. [1] Totals may not add due to individuals having multiple correctional statuses. [2] Estimated.

Source: U.S. Bureau of Justice Statistics, *Correctional Populations in the United States*, annual.

U.S. Census Bureau, Statistical Abstract of the United States: 2004-2005

No. 338. Federal and State Prisoners, by Sex: 1980 to 2002

[Prisoners, as of **December 31.** Includes all persons under jurisdiction of Federal and State authorities rather than those in the custody of such authorities. Represents inmates sentenced to maximum term of more than a year]

Year	Total	Rate [1]	State	Male	Female	Year	Total	Rate [1]	State	Male	Female
1980 .	315,974	139	295,363	303,643	12,331	1992 .	846,277	332	780,571	799,776	46,501
1981 .	353,673	154	331,504	339,375	14,298	1993 .	932,074	359	857,675	878,037	54,037
1982 .	395,516	171	371,864	379,075	16,441	1994 .	1,016,691	389	936,896	956,566	60,125
1983 .	419,346	179	393,015	401,870	17,476	1995 .	1,085,022	411	1,001,359	1,021,059	63,963
1984 .	443,398	188	415,796	424,193	19,205	1996 .	1,137,722	427	1,048,907	1,068,123	69,599
1985 .	480,568	202	447,873	459,223	21,345	1997 .	1,195,498	445	1,100,511	1,121,663	73,835
1986 .	522,084	217	485,553	497,540	24,544	1998 .	1,245,402	461	1,141,720	1,167,802	77,600
1987 .	560,812	231	521,289	533,990	26,822	1999 .	1,304,074	476	1,189,799	1,221,611	82,463
1988 .	603,732	247	560,994	573,587	30,145	2000 .	1,331,278	470	1,204,323	1,246,234	85,044
1989 .	680,907	276	633,739	643,643	37,264	2001 .	1,345,217	470	1,208,708	1,260,033	85,184
1990 .	739,980	297	689,577	699,416	40,564	2002 .	1,380,370	476	1,237,330	1,291,326	89,044
1991 .	789,610	313	732,914	745,808	43,802						

[1] Rate per 100,000 estimated population. Based on U.S. Census Bureau estimated resident population.

Source: U.S. Bureau of Justice Statistics, *Prisoners in State and Federal Institutions on December 31*, annual.

No. 339. Prisoners Under Sentence of Death by Characteristic: 1980 to 2002

[**As of December 31.** Excludes prisoners under sentence of death who remained within local correctional systems pending exhaustion of appellate process or who had not been committed to prison]

Characteristic	1980	1990	1993	1994	1995	1996	1997	1998	1999	2000	2001	2002
Total [1]	**688**	**2,346**	**2,727**	**2,905**	**3,064**	**3,242**	**3,328**	**3,465**	**3,540**	**3,601**	**3,577**	**3,557**
White	418	1,368	1,575	1,653	1,732	1,833	1,864	1,917	1,960	1,989	1,968	1,931
Black and other	270	978	1,152	1,252	1,332	1,409	1,464	1,548	1,580	1,612	1,609	1,626
Under 20 years.	11	8	13	19	20	17	16	16	16	11	4	4
20 to 24 years	173	168	211	231	264	288	275	273	251	237	192	153
25 to 34 years	334	1,110	1,066	1,088	1,068	1,088	1,077	1,108	1,108	1,103	1,099	1,058
35 to 54 years	186	1,006	1,330	1,449	1,583	1,711	1,809	1,897	1,958	2,019	2,043	2,069
55 years and over.	10	64	96	103	119	138	151	171	194	223	243	273
Years of school completed:												
7 years or less	68	178	185	186	191	196	205	208	201	214	212	215
8 years	74	186	183	198	195	201	206	218	221	233	236	234
9 to 11 years	204	775	885	930	979	1,040	1,069	1,122	1,142	1,157	1,145	1,130
12 years	162	729	887	939	995	1,037	1,084	1,128	1,157	1,184	1,183	1,173
More than 12 years	43	209	244	255	272	282	288	301	307	315	304	294
Unknown	163	279	332	382	422	486	476	488	499	490	501	511
Marital status:												
Never married	268	998	1,222	1,320	1,412	1,507	1,555	1,645	1,689	1,749	1,763	1,746
Married	229	632	671	707	718	739	740	752	731	739	716	709
Divorced [2]	217	726	823	863	924	996	1,033	1,068	1,107	1,105	1,102	1,102
Time elapsed since sentencing:												
Less than 12 months	185	231	262	280	287	306	262	293	259	208	151	147
12 to 47 months	389	753	716	755	784	816	844	816	800	786	734	609
48 to 71 months	102	438	422	379	423	447	456	482	499	507	476	468
72 months and over	38	934	1,316	1,476	1,560	1,673	1,766	1,874	1,969	2,092	2,220	2,333
Legal status at arrest:												
Not under sentence	384	1,345	1,562	1,662	1,764	1,881	1,957	2,036	2,088	2,202	2,189	2,165
Parole or probation [3]	115	578	754	800	866	894	880	879	886	921	918	909
Prison or escaped	45	128	102	103	110	112	116	127	125	126	135	141
Unknown	170	305	298	325	314	355	375	423	428	344	339	342

[1] Revisions to the total number of prisoners were not carried to the characteristics except for race.   [2] Includes persons married but separated, widows, widowers, and unknown.   [3] Includes prisoners on mandatory conditional release, work release, leave, AWOL, or bail: 28 in 1990, 33 in 1993 and 1995, 31 in 1994 and 1996, 30 in 1997, 26 in 1998, 21 in 1999 and 2000, and 17 in 2001 and 2002.

Source: U.S. Bureau of Justice Statistics, *Capital Punishment,* annual. See also <http://www.ojp.usdoj.gov/bjs/pub/pdf/cp02.pdf> (Released November 2003).

No. 340. Movement of Prisoners Under Sentence of Death: 1980 to 2002

[Prisoners reported under sentence of death by civil authorities. The term "under sentence of death" begins when the court pronounces the first sentence of death for a capital offense]

Status	1980	1990	1993	1994	1995	1996	1997	1998	1999	2000	2001	2002
Under sentence of death, Jan. 1	595	2,243	2,580	2,727	2,905	3,064	3,242	3,328	3,465	3,540	3,601	3,577
Received death sentence [1]	203	244	282	306	310	299	256	285	272	214	155	159
White	125	147	146	162	168	174	146	145	157	122	89	83
Black	77	94	130	136	138	119	106	132	104	86	61	73
Dispositions other than executions	101	108	108	112	105	99	89	93	112	76	109	108
Executions	-	23	38	31	56	45	74	68	98	85	66	71
Under sentence of death, Dec. 31 [1]	688	2,346	2,727	2,905	3,064	3,242	3,328	3,465	3,540	3,601	3,577	3,557
White	418	1,368	1,575	1,653	1,732	1,833	1,864	1,917	1,960	1,989	1,968	1,931
Black	268	940	1,111	1,197	1,275	1,358	1,406	1,486	1,514	1,535	1,538	1,554

- Represents zero.   [1] Includes races other than White or Black.
Source: U.S. Bureau of Justice Statistics, *Capital Punishment*, annual. See also <http://www.ojp.usdoj.gov/bjs/pub/pdf/cp02.pdf>.

No. 341. Prisoners Executed Under Civil Authority by Sex and Race: 1930 to 2003

[Excludes executions by military authorities. The Army (including the Air Force) carried out 160 (148 between 1942 and 1950; 3 each in 1954, 1955, and 1957; and 1 each in 1958, 1959, and 1961). Of the total, 106 were executed for murder (including 21 involving rape), 53 for rape, and 1 for desertion. The Navy carried out no executions during the period]

Year or period	Total [1]	Male	Female	White	Black	Executed for murder Total [1]	Executed for murder White	Executed for murder Black
All years, 1930-2003	**4,744**	**4,702**	**42**	**2,319**	**2,369**	**4,219**	**2,232**	**1,933**
1930 to 1939	1,667	1,656	11	827	816	1,514	803	687
1940 to 1949 [2]	1,284	1,272	12	490	781	1,064	458	595
1950 to 1959 [2]	717	709	8	336	376	601	316	280
1960 to 1967	191	190	1	98	93	155	87	68
1968 to 1976	-	-	-	-	-	-	-	-
1977 to 2003	885	875	10	568	303	885	568	303
1985	18	18	-	11	7	18	11	7
1986	18	18	-	11	7	18	11	7
1987	25	25	-	13	12	25	13	12
1988	11	11	-	6	5	11	6	5
1989	16	16	-	8	8	16	8	8
1990	23	23	-	16	7	23	16	7
1991	14	14	-	7	7	14	7	7
1992	31	31	-	19	11	31	19	11
1993	38	38	-	23	14	38	23	14
1994	31	31	-	20	11	31	20	11
1995	56	56	-	33	22	56	33	22
1996	45	45	-	31	14	45	31	14
1997	74	74	-	45	27	74	45	27
1998	68	66	2	48	18	68	48	18
1999	98	98	-	61	33	98	61	33
2000	85	83	2	49	35	85	49	35
2001	66	63	3	48	17	66	48	17
2002	71	69	2	53	18	71	53	18
2003	65	65	-	44	20	65	44	20

- Represents zero.   [1] Includes races other than White or Black.   [2] Includes 25 armed robbery, 20 kidnapping, 11 burglary, 8 espionage (6 in 1942 and 2 in 1953), and 6 aggravated assault.
Source: Through 1978, U.S. Law Enforcement Assistance Administration; thereafter, U.S. Bureau of Justice Statistics, *Correctional Populations in the United States*, annual; and *Capital Punishment*, annnual.

No. 342. Prisoners Under Sentence of Death and Executed Under Civil Authority by State: 1977 to 2003

[Alaska, District of Columbia, Hawaii, Iowa, Maine, Massachusetts, Michigan, Minnesota, New York, North Dakota, Rhode Island, Vermont, West Virginia, and Wisconsin are jurisdictions without a death penalty]

State	1977 to 2003	2000	2001	2002	2003	State	1977 to 2003	2000	2001	2002	2003	State	1977 to 2003	2000	2001	2002	2003
U.S.	885	85	66	71	65	IL	12	-	-	-	-	OK	69	11	18	7	14
AL	28	4	-	2	3	IN	11	-	2	-	2	OR	2	-	-	-	-
AZ	22	3	-	-	-	KY	2	-	-	-	-	PA	3	-	-	-	-
AR	25	2	1	-	1	LA	27	1	-	1	-	SC	28	1	-	3	-
CA	10	1	1	1	-	MD	3	-	-	-	-	TN	1	1	-	-	-
DE	13	1	2	-	-	MS	6	-	-	2	-	TX	313	40	17	33	24
FL	57	6	1	3	3	MO	61	5	7	6	2	UT	6	-	-	-	-
GA	34	-	4	4	3	NE	3	-	-	-	-	VA	89	8	2	4	2
ID	1	-	-	-	-	NV	9	-	1	-	-	WA	4	-	1	-	-
						NC	30	1	5	2	7	WY	1	-	-	-	-

- Represents zero.
Source: Through 1978, U.S. Law Enforcement Assistance Administration; thereafter, U.S. Bureau of Justice Statistics, *Capital Punishment*, annual.

Law Enforcement, Courts, and Prisons   209

No. 343. Fire Losses—Total and Percent Change: 1980 to 2002

[5,579 represents $5,579,000,000. Includes allowance for uninsured and unreported losses but excludes losses to government property and forests. Represents incurred losses]

Year	Total (mil. dol.)	Per capita[1] (dol.)	Year	Total (mil. dol.)	Per capita[1] (dol.)	Year	Total (mil. dol.)	Per capita[1] (dol.)
1980	5,579	24.56	1988	9,626	39.11	1996	12,544	47.29
1981	5,625	24.53	1989	9,514	38.33	1997	12,940	48.32
1982	5,894	25.61	1990	9,495	38.07	1998	11,510	45.59
1983	6,320	27.20	1991	11,302	44.82	1999	12,428	45.58
1984	7,602	32.35	1992	13,588	53.28			
1985	7,753	32.70	1993	11,331	43.96	2000	13,457	47.68
1986	8,488	35.21	1994	12,778	49.08	2001[2]	17,118	60.00
1987	8,504	34.96	1995	11,887	45.23	2002	15,540	53.89

[1] Based on U.S. Census Bureau resident population as of July 1. [2] Excludes fire losses related to 9/11 Terrorist attack.

Source: Insurance Information Institute, New York, NY, The Fact Book, Property/Casualty Insurance Facts, annual (copyright).

No. 344. Fires—Number and Loss, by Type and Property Use: 1999 to 2002

[Number of 1,823 represents 1,823,000 and property loss of 10,024 represents $10,024,000,000. Based on annual sample survey of fire departments. No adjustments were made for unreported fires and losses. Property loss includes direct property loss only]

Type and property use	Number (1,000)				Property loss (mil. dol.)			
	1999	2000	2001	2002	1999	2000	2001	2002
Fires, total	1,823	1,708	1,734	1,688	10,024	[1]11,207	[2]44,023	10,377
Structure	523	506	521	519	8,490	8,501	[2]42,314	8,742
Outside of structure[3]	64	69	75	71	123	214	86	121
Brush and rubbish	724	670	623	603	-	-	-	-
Vehicle	369	349	351	330	1,324	1,381	1,512	1,392
Other	143	114	164	165	87	111	111	82
Structure by property use:								
Public assembly	16	15	15	14	412	365	336	342
Educational	8	7	7	7	71	108	170	92
Institutional	8	7	7	7	23	20	27	26
Stores and offices	29	24	26	24	659	587	[2]34,155	604
Residential	383	380	396	401	5,092	5,674	5,643	6,055
1-2 family units[4]	283	284	295	301	4,123	4,639	4,652	5,005
Apartments	88	85	88	88	842	886	864	926
Other residential[5]	12	11	13	12	127	149	127	124
Storage[6]	36	33	34	32	[7]1,375	694	930	627
Industry, utility, defense[6]	18	15	13	12	671	778	858	658
Special structures	25	25	22	22	187	275	195	338

- Represents zero. [1] Includes $1 billion in property damage in the Cerro Grande, New Mexico Wildland Fire. Property loss by specific property type was not available. [2] Includes $33.4 billion in property loss that occured due to the events of September 11, 2001. [3] Includes outside storage, crops, timber, etc. [4] Includes mobile homes. [5] Includes hotels and motels, college dormitories, boarding houses, etc. [6] Data underreported as some incidents were handled by private fire brigades or fixed suppression systems which do not report. [7] Includes estimated losses of $515 million due to two power plant fires.

Source: National Fire Protection Association, Quincy, MA, "2002 U.S. Fire Loss", NFPA Journal, November 2003, and prior issues (copyright 2003).

No. 345. Fires and Property Loss for Incendiary and Suspicious Fires and Civilian Fire Deaths and Injuries, by Selected Property Type: 1999 to 2002

[523 represents 523,000. Based on sample survey of fire departments]

Characteristic	1999	2000	2001	2002	Characteristic	1999	2000	2001	2002
NUMBER (1,000)					CIVILIAN FIRE DEATHS				
Structure fires, total	523	506	521	519	**Deaths, total[1]**	3,570	4,045	[2]6,196	3,380
Structure fires of incendiary					Residential property	2,920	3,445	3,140	2,695
or suspicious origin	72	75	-	-	One- and two-family				
Fires of incendiary origin	44	46	46	45	dwellings	2,375	2,920	2,650	2,280
Fires of suspicious origin	28	29	-	-	Apartments	520	500	460	390
					Vehicles	470	465	485	565
PROPERTY LOSS[3] (mil. dol.)					CIVILIAN FIRE INJURIES				
Structure fires, total	8,490	8,501	[5]42,314	8,742	**Injuries, total[1]**	21,875	22,350	[4]21,100	18,425
Structure fires of incendiary					Residential property	16,425	17,400	15,575	14,050
or suspicious origin	1,281	1,340	-	-	One- and two-family				
Fires of incendiary origin	828	792	[5]34,453	919	dwellings	11,550	12,575	11,400	9,950
Fires of suspicious origin	453	548	-	-	Apartments	4,500	4,400	3,800	3,700
					Vehicles	1,850	1,600	1,875	1,125

- Represents zero. [1] Includes other not shown separately. [2] Includes 2,451 civilian deaths due to the events of September 11, 2001. [3] Direct property loss only. [4] Incluces 800 civilian injuries due to the events of September 11, 2001. [5] Includes $33.4 billion in property loss due to the events of September 11, 2001.

Source: National Fire Protection Association, Quincy, MA, "2002 U.S. Fire Loss", NFPA Journal, November 2003, and prior issues (copyright 2003).

Section 6
Geography and Environment

This section presents a variety of information on the physical environment of the United States, starting with basic area measurement data and ending with climatic data for selected weather stations around the country. The subjects covered between those points are mostly concerned with environmental trends but include related subjects such as land use, water consumption, air pollutant emissions, toxic releases, oil spills, hazardous waste sites, municipal waste and recycling, threatened and endangered wildlife, and the environmental industry.

The information in this section is selected from a wide range of federal agencies that compile the data for various administrative or regulatory purposes, such as the Environmental Protection Agency (EPA), U.S. Geological Survey (USGS), National Oceanic and Atmospheric Administration (NOAA), Natural Resources Conservation Service (NRCS), and General Services Administration (GSA). New information on pollution abatement expenditures may be found in Tables 370 and 371 produced by the U.S. Census Bureau.

Area—For the 2000 census, area measurements were calculated by computer based on the information contained in a single, consistent geographic database, the Topologically Integrated Geographic Encoding & Referencing system (TIGER) database, rather than relying on historical, local, and manually calculated information. Information from the 2000 census may be found in Table 346.

Geography—The USGS conducts investigations, surveys, and research in the fields of geography, geology, topography, geographic information systems, mineralogy, hydrology, and geothermal energy resources as well as natural hazards. The USGS provides United States cartographic data through the Earth Sciences Information Center, water resources data through the National Water Data Exchange (NAWDEX), and a variety of research and Open-File reports which are announced monthly in *New Publications of the USGS.*

In a joint project with the U.S. Census Bureau, during the 1980s, the USGS provided the basic information on geographic features for input into a national geographic and cartographic database prepared by the Census Bureau, called TIGER database. Since then, using a variety of sources, the Census Bureau has updated these features and their related attributes (names, descriptions, etc.) and inserted current information on the boundaries, names, and codes of legal and statistical geographic entities; very few of these updates added aerial water features. Maps prepared by the Census Bureau using the TIGER database show the names and boundaries of entities and are available on a current basis.

The U.S. Census Bureau uses the Boundary and Annexation Survey to maintain a current inventory of government units and their legal boundaries. The information is available to the public on line. There are also several series of maps for Census 2000: P.L. County Block Maps, Census Tract Outline Maps, and Voting District/State Legislative District Outline Maps. These maps can be obtained online via the American Fact-Finder.

An inventory of the nation's land resources by type of use/cover was conducted by the National Resources Inventory Conservation Service (formerly the Soil Conservation Service) every 5 years beginning in 1977. The most recent survey results, which were published in the 1997 National Resources Inventory, cover

U.S. Census Bureau, Statistical Abstract of the United States: 2004-2005

all nonfederal land in Puerto Rico, the Virgin Islands, and the United States except Alaska. Tables 361 and 362 provide results from the survey. Beginning with the release of the 2001 estimates (tentatively scheduled for fall 2003), this program will shift to become an annual release of land use data.

Environment —The principal federal agency responsible for pollution abatement and control activities is the Environmental Protection Agency (EPA). It is responsible for establishing and monitoring national air quality standards, water quality activities, solid and hazardous waste disposal, and control of toxic substances. Many of these series now appear in the Envirofacts portion of the EPA Web site at <http://www.epa.gov/enviro/>. In 2003, EPA released a major compilation of environmental indicators, entitled *Draft Report on the Environment: 2003,* found at <http://www.epa.govindicators/>.

National Ambient Air Quality Standards (NAAQS) for suspended particulate matter, sulfur dioxide, photochemical oxidants, carbon monoxide, and nitrogen dioxide were originally set by the EPA in April 1971. Every 5 years, each of the NAAQS is reviewed and revised to include any additional or new health or welfare data. The standard for photochemical oxidants, now called ozone, was revised in February 1979. Also, a new NAAQS for confining lead was promulgated in October 1978 and for suspended particulate matter in 1987. Table 359 gives some of the health related standards for the six air pollutants having NAAQS. Data gathered from state networks are periodically submitted to EPA's National Aerometric Information Retrieval System (AIRS) for summarization in annual reports on the nationwide status and trends in air quality. For details, see *National Air Quality and Emissions Trends Report.* More current information on emissions may be found on the EPA Web site at <http://www.epa.gov/ttn/chief/trends>.

The Toxics Release Inventory (TRI), published by the EPA, is a valuable source of information regarding toxic chemicals that are being used, manufactured, treated, transported, or released into the environment. Sections 313 of the Emergency Planning and Community Right-To-Know Act (EPCRA) and 6607 of the Pollution Prevention Act (PPA), mandate that a publicly accessible toxic chemical database be developed and maintained by EPA. This database, known as the TRI, contains information concerning waste management activities and the release of toxic chemicals by facilities that manufacture, process, or otherwise use said materials. Data on the release of these chemicals are collected from manufacturing facilities and facilities added in 1998 that have the equivalent of 10 or more full-time employees and meet the established thresholds for manufacturing, processing, or "other use" of listed chemicals. Facilities must report their releases and other waste management quantities. Since 1994 federal facilities have been required to report their data regardless of industry classification. In May 1997, EPA added seven new industry sectors that reported to the TRI for the first time in July 1999 for the 1998 reporting year.

Climate—NOAA, through the National Weather Service and the National Environmental Satellite, Data, and Information Service, is responsible for climate data. NOAA maintains about 11,600 weather stations, of which over 3,000 produce autographic precipitation records, about 600 take hourly readings of a series of weather elements, and the remainder record data once a day. These data are reported monthly in the Climatological Data and Storm Data, published monthly and annually in the Local Climatological Data (published by location for major cities).

The normal climatological temperatures, precipitation, and degree days listed in this publication are derived for comparative purposes and are averages for the 30-year period, 1971-2000. For stations that did not have continuous records for the entire 30 years from the same instrument site, the normals have been adjusted to provide representative values for the current location. The information in all other tables is based on data from the beginning of the record at that location through 2001.

212   Geography and Environment

No. 346. Land and Water Area of States and Other Entities: 2000

[One square mile=2.59 square kilometers. Area is calculatd from the specific boundary recorded for each entity in the U.S. Census Bureau's geographic TIGER database]

State and other area	Total area Sq. mi.	Total area Sq. km.	Land area Sq. mi.	Land area Sq. km.	Water area Total Sq. mi.	Water area Total Sq. km.	Water area Inland (sq. mi.)	Water area Coastal (sq. mi.)	Water area Great Lakes (sq. mi.)	Water area Territorial (sq. mi.)
Total.........	3,800,286	9,842,696	3,540,999	9,171,146	259,287	671,550	79,018	42,241	60,251	77,777
United States ...	3,794,083	9,826,630	3,537,439	9,161,923	256,645	664,707	78,797	42,225	60,251	75,372
Alabama.........	52,419	135,765	50,744	131,426	1,675	4,338	956	519	-	200
Alaska.........	663,267	1,717,854	571,951	1,481,347	91,316	236,507	17,243	27,049	-	47,024
Arizona.........	113,998	295,254	113,635	294,312	364	942	364	-	-	-
Arkansas	53,179	137,732	52,068	134,856	1,110	2,876	1,110	-	-	-
California	163,696	423,970	155,959	403,933	7,736	20,037	2,674	222	-	4,841
Colorado.........	104,094	269,601	103,718	268,627	376	974	376	-	-	-
Connecticut.......	5,543	14,357	4,845	12,548	699	1,809	161	538	-	-
Delaware	2,489	6,447	1,954	5,060	536	1,388	72	371	-	93
District of Columbia .	68	177	61	159	7	18	7	-	-	-
Florida	65,755	170,304	53,927	139,670	11,828	30,634	4,672	1,311	-	5,845
Georgia	59,425	153,909	57,906	149,976	1,519	3,933	1,016	48	-	455
Hawaii	10,931	28,311	6,423	16,635	4,508	11,677	38	-	-	4,470
Idaho.........	83,570	216,446	82,747	214,314	823	2,131	823	-	-	-
Illinois	57,914	149,998	55,584	143,961	2,331	6,037	756	-	1,575	-
Indiana.........	36,418	94,321	35,867	92,895	551	1,427	316	-	235	-
Iowa	56,272	145,743	55,869	144,701	402	1,042	402	-	-	-
Kansas.........	82,277	213,096	81,815	211,900	462	1,197	462	-	-	-
Kentucky	40,409	104,659	39,728	102,896	681	1,763	681	-	-	-
Louisiana	51,840	134,264	43,562	112,825	8,278	21,440	4,154	1,935	-	2,189
Maine...........	35,385	91,646	30,862	79,931	4,523	11,715	2,264	613	-	1,647
Maryland	12,407	32,133	9,774	25,314	2,633	6,819	680	1,843	-	110
Massachusetts.......	10,555	27,336	7,840	20,306	2,715	7,031	423	977	-	1,314
Michigan.........	96,716	250,494	56,804	147,121	39,912	103,372	1,611	-	38,301	-
Minnesota........	86,939	225,171	79,610	206,189	7,329	18,982	4,783	-	2,546	-
Mississippi	48,430	125,434	46,907	121,489	1,523	3,945	785	590	-	148
Missouri	69,704	180,533	68,886	178,414	818	2,120	818	-	-	-
Montana.........	147,042	380,838	145,552	376,979	1,490	3,859	1,490	-	-	-
Nebraska	77,354	200,345	76,872	199,099	481	1,247	481	-	-	-
Nevada	110,561	286,351	109,826	284,448	735	1,903	735	-	-	-
New Hampshire	9,350	24,216	8,968	23,227	382	989	314	-	-	68
New Jersey	8,721	22,588	7,417	19,211	1,304	3,377	396	401	-	507
New Mexico	121,590	314,915	121,356	314,309	234	606	234	-	-	-
New York	54,556	141,299	47,214	122,283	7,342	19,016	1,895	981	3,988	479
North Carolina.....	53,819	139,389	48,711	126,161	5,108	13,229	3,960	-	-	1,148
North Dakota......	70,700	183,112	68,976	178,647	1,724	4,465	1,724	-	-	-
Ohio	44,825	116,096	40,948	106,056	3,877	10,040	378	-	3,499	-
Oklahoma........	69,898	181,036	68,667	177,847	1,231	3,189	1,231	-	-	-
Oregon..........	98,381	254,805	95,997	248,631	2,384	6,174	1,050	80	-	1,254
Pennsylvania......	46,055	119,283	44,817	116,075	1,239	3,208	490	-	749	-
Rhode Island......	1,545	4,002	1,045	2,706	500	1,295	178	9	-	314
South Carolina.....	32,020	82,932	30,110	77,983	1,911	4,949	1,008	72	-	831
South Dakota	77,117	199,731	75,885	196,540	1,232	3,191	1,232	-	-	-
Tennessee	42,143	109,151	41,217	106,752	926	2,399	926	-	-	-
Texas...........	268,581	695,621	261,797	678,051	6,784	17,570	5,056	404	-	1,324
Utah	84,899	219,887	82,144	212,751	2,755	7,136	2,755	-	-	-
Vermont.........	9,614	24,901	9,250	23,956	365	945	365	-	-	-
Virginia..........	42,774	110,785	39,594	102,548	3,180	8,237	1,006	1,728	-	446
Washington.......	71,300	184,665	66,544	172,348	4,756	12,317	1,553	2,537	-	666
West Virginia......	24,230	62,755	24,078	62,361	152	394	152	-	-	-
Wisconsin........	65,498	169,639	54,310	140,663	11,188	28,976	1,830	-	9,358	-
Wyoming	97,814	253,336	97,100	251,489	713	1,847	713	-	-	-
Other areas:										
Puerto Rico	5,325	13,790	3,425	8,870	1,900	4,921	67	16	-	1,817
U.S. Minor Outlying Islands .	141	365	3	7	138	359	138	-	-	-
Virgin Islands of the U.S	737	1,910	134	346	604	1,564	16	-	-	588

- Represents or rounds to zero.

Source: U.S. Census Bureau, 2000 Census of Population and Housing, *Summary Population and Housing Characteristics*, Series PHC-1; and unpublished data from the Census TIGER ™ data base.

Geography and Environment 213

No. 347. Total and Federally Owned Land by State: 2003

[(2,271,343 represents 2,271,343,000). As of end of fiscal year; see text, Section 8. Total land area figures are not comparable with those in Table 346]

State	Total (1,000 acres)	Not owned by federal government (1,000 acres)	Owned by federal government [1] Acres (1,000)	Owned by federal government [1] Per-cent	State	Total (1,000 acres)	Not owned by federal government (1,000 acres)	Owned by federal government [1] Acres (1,000)	Owned by federal government [1] Per-cent
United States .	2,271,343	1,599,584	671,759	29.6	Missouri	44,248	42,010	2,238	5.1
					Montana	93,271	64,032	29,239	31.3
Alabama	32,678	31,476	1,203	3.7	Nebraska	49,032	47,573	1,459	3.0
Alaska	365,482	121,635	243,847	66.7	Nevada	70,264	5,675	64,589	91.9
Arizona	72,688	36,193	36,495	50.2	New Hampshire . . .	5,769	4,939	830	14.4
Arkansas	33,599	29,643	3,956	11.8	New Jersey	4,813	4,633	180	3.7
California	100,207	53,227	46,980	46.9	New Mexico	77,766	51,248	26,518	34.1
Colorado	66,486	43,311	23,174	34.9	New York	30,681	30,439	242	0.8
Connecticut	3,135	3,120	15	0.5	North Carolina	31,403	27,801	3,602	11.5
Delaware	1,266	1,236	29	2.3	North Dakota	44,452	43,119	1,333	3.0
District of Columbia .	39	29	10	26.3	Ohio	26,222	25,764	458	1.7
Florida	34,721	30,116	4,606	13.3	Oklahoma	44,088	42,756	1,331	3.0
Georgia	37,295	34,981	2,314	6.2	Oregon	61,599	30,960	30,639	49.7
Hawaii	4,106	3,434	672	16.4	Pennsylvania	28,804	28,080	725	2.5
Idaho	52,933	17,797	35,136	66.4	Rhode Island	677	672	5	0.8
Illinois	35,795	35,144	652	1.8	South Carolina	19,374	18,138	1,236	6.4
Indiana	23,158	22,624	534	2.3	South Dakota	48,882	46,568	2,314	4.7
Iowa	35,860	35,558	303	0.8	Tennessee	26,728	24,712	2,016	7.5
Kansas	52,511	51,869	642	1.2	Texas	168,218	165,046	3,172	1.9
Kentucky	25,512	23,806	1,707	6.7	Utah	52,697	17,672	35,025	66.5
Louisiana	28,868	27,366	1,502	5.2	Vermont	5,937	5,487	450	7.6
Maine	19,848	19,684	164	0.8	Virginia	25,496	22,879	2,617	10.3
Maryland	6,319	6,127	193	3.0	Washington	42,694	29,447	13,247	31.0
Massachusetts . . .	5,035	4,929	106	2.1	West Virginia	15,411	14,144	1,266	8.2
Michigan	36,492	32,854	3,639	10.0	Wisconsin	35,011	33,029	1,982	5.7
Minnesota	51,206	47,671	3,535	6.9	Wyoming	62,343	30,812	31,532	50.6
Mississippi	30,223	28,122	2,101	7.0					

[1] Excludes trust properties.

Source: U.S. General Services Administration, *Federal Real Property Profile* annual. See also <http://www. gsa.gov/cmattachments/GSAPUBLICATIONS/AnnualReport26R2AV1-z-c0Z5RDZ-i34K-pR.pdf> (released 11 March 2003).

No. 348. Land Cover/Use by Type: 1982 to 2002

[In millions of acres (1,937.7 represents 1,937,700,000), except percent. Excludes Alaska and District of Columbia]

Year	Total surface area	Nonfederal rural land Rural land, total [1]	Crop-land	Pasture land	Range-land	Forest land	Other rural land	Devel-oped land	Water areas	Fed-eral land
Total Land (mil. Acres)										
1982	1,937.7	1,417.2	420.4	131.4	414.5	402.6	48.3	72.8	48.6	399.1
1992	1,937.6	1,400.2	381.2	125.1	406.6	404.0	49.3	86.5	49.4	401.5
2002	1,937.7	1,378.1	368.4	117.3	405.3	404.9	50.6	107.3	50.4	401.9
Percent of total land										
1982	100.0	73.1	21.7	6.8	21.4	20.8	2.5	3.8	2.5	20.6
1992	100.0	72.3	19.7	6.5	21.0	20.9	2.5	4.5	2.5	20.7
2002	100.0	71.1	19.0	6.1	20.9	20.9	2.6	5.5	2.6	20.7

X Not applicable.   [1] Includes Conservation Reserve Program land not shown separately.

Source: U.S. Department of Agriculture, Natural Resources and Conservation Service, *National Resources Inventory 2002 Annual NRI, Land Use*, April 2004. See also <http://www.nrcs.usda.gov/technical/land/nri02/landuse.pdf>.

No. 349. Developed Land by Type: 1982 to 2001

[(1,937.7 represents 1,937,700,000). Excludes Alaska and District of Columbia]

Year	Total surface area	Developed land Developed land, total	Developed land Large urban and built-up areas	Developed land Small built-up areas	Developed land Rural trans-portation land
Land (mil. acres)					
1982	1,937.7	72.8	46.9	4.7	21.2
1992	1,937.7	86.5	59.6	5.4	21.5
2001	1,937.7	106.3	77.6	6.7	22.0
Percent of total land					
1982	100.0	3.8	2.4	0.2	1.1
1992	100.0	4.5	3.1	0.3	1.1
2001	100.0	5.5	4.0	0.3	1.1

Source: U.S. Department of Agriculture, Natural Resources and Conservation Service, *National Resources Inventory 2001 Annual NRI, Urbanization and Development of Rural Land*, July 2003. See also <http://www.nrcs.usda.gov/technical/land/nri01/urban.pdf> (released July 2003).

No. 350. Land Cover/Use by State: 1997

[In thousands of acres (1,944,130 represents 1,944,130,000), except percent. Excludes Alaska and District of Columbia]

State	Total surface area	Rural land, total	Percent of total	Nonfederal rural land Cropland	CRP land [1]	Pasture land	Rangeland	Forest land	Other rural land
Total	1,944,130	1,393,760	71.7	376,998	32,696	119,992	405,977	406,955	51,142
United States . . .	1,941,823	1,392,098	71.7	376,630	32,696	119,549	405,832	406,315	51,077
Alabama	33,424	28,950	86.6	2,954	522	3,528	74	21,261	612
Arizona	72,964	40,858	56.0	1,212	-	73	32,323	4,216	3,035
Arkansas	34,037	28,638	84.1	7,625	230	5,351	38	15,011	384
California	101,510	47,555	46.8	9,635	173	1,049	18,269	13,936	4,494
Colorado	66,625	40,850	61.3	8,770	1,890	1,211	24,574	3,442	964
Connecticut	3,195	2,178	68.2	204	-	112	-	1,759	103
Delaware	1,534	988	64.4	485	1	24	-	352	128
Florida	37,534	25,498	67.9	2,752	120	4,231	3,229	12,536	128
Georgia	37,741	30,648	81.2	4,757	595	2,865		21,560	2,630
Hawaii	4,158	3,565	85.7	246	-	36	1,009	1,635	639
Idaho	53,488	18,618	34.8	5,517	785	1,315	6,501	3,948	553
Illinois	36,059	31,675	87.8	24,011	726	2,502	-	3,784	652
Indiana	23,158	20,069	86.7	13,407	378	1,830	-	3,781	674
Iowa	36,017	33,673	93.5	25,310	1,739	3,572	-	2,182	870
Kansas	52,661	49,685	94.3	26,524	2,849	2,322	15,728	1,546	716
Kentucky	25,863	22,327	86.3	5,178	332	5,686	-	10,667	465
Louisiana	31,377	24,664	78.6	5,659	140	2,385	277	13,226	2,976
Maine	20,966	18,794	89.6	413	30	123	-	17,691	537
Maryland	7,870	4,808	61.1	1,616	19	478	-	2,373	321
Massachusetts	5,339	3,394	63.6	277	-	119	-	2,744	254
Michigan	37,349	29,426	78.8	8,540	321	2,032	-	16,354	2,178
Minnesota	54,010	45,356	84.0	21,414	1,544	3,434	-	16,248	2,716
Mississippi	30,527	26,429	86.6	5,352	799	3,679	-	16,209	389
Missouri	44,614	39,358	88.2	13,751	1,606	10,849	88	12,431	634
Montana	94,110	64,958	69.0	15,171	2,721	3,443	36,751	5,431	1,443
Nebraska	49,510	47,187	95.3	19,469	1,245	1,801	23,089	826	757
Nevada	70,763	10,079	14.2	701	2	279	8,372	305	420
New Hampshire	5,941	4,353	73.3	134	-	94	-	3,932	193
New Jersey	5,216	2,766	53.0	589	1	111	-	1,698	367
New Mexico	77,823	50,071	64.3	1,875	467	231	39,990	5,467	2,041
New York	31,361	26,702	85.1	5,417	54	2,722	-	17,702	808
North Carolina	33,709	24,592	73.0	5,639	131	2,039	-	15,959	824
North Dakota	45,251	41,442	91.6	25,004	2,802	1,129	10,689	454	1,363
Ohio	26,445	22,070	83.5	11,627	324	2,006	-	7,081	1,032
Oklahoma	44,738	40,610	90.8	9,737	1,138	7,963	14,033	7,281	459
Oregon	62,161	28,858	46.4	3,762	483	1,961	9,286	12,643	724
Pennsylvania	28,995	23,816	82.1	5,471	90	1,845	-	15,478	932
Rhode Island	813	458	56.3	22	-	25	-	387	24
South Carolina	19,939	16,018	80.3	2,574	263	1,197	-	11,188	797
South Dakota	49,358	44,411	90.0	16,738	1,686	2,108	21,876	518	1,484
Tennessee	26,974	22,597	83.8	4,644	374	4,990	-	12,042	547
Texas	171,052	155,530	90.9	26,938	3,906	15,914	95,745	10,816	2,211
Utah	54,339	17,599	32.4	1,679	216	695	10,733	1,883	2,392
Vermont	6,154	5,183	84.2	607	-	338	-	4,150	88
Virginia	27,087	19,886	73.4	2,918	71	2,995	-	13,316	587
Washington	44,035	28,508	64.7	6,656	1,017	1,193	5,857	12,835	951
West Virginia	15,508	13,252	85.5	864	-	1,527	-	10,582	279
Wisconsin	35,920	30,374	84.6	10,613	661	2,994	-	14,448	1,658
Wyoming	62,603	32,773	52.4	2,174	247	1,146	27,302	1,004	900
Caribbean	2,307	1,662	72.0	368	-	443	145	640	65

- Represents or rounds to zero. [1] Conservation Reserve Program (CRP). A federal program established under the Food Security Act of 1985 to assist private landowners to convert highly erodible cropland to vegetative cover for 10 years.

Source: U.S. Department of Agriculture, Natural Resources and Conservation Service, and Iowa State University, Statistical Laboratory, *Summary Report, 1997 National Resources Inventory*, revised December 2000. See also <http://www.nrcs.usda.gov/technical/NRI/1997/summaryreport/> (revised December 2000).

Geography and Environment 215

No. 351. Extreme and Mean Elevations by State and Other Area

[One foot=.305 meter]

State and other areas	Highest point Name	Highest Elevation Feet	Highest Elevation Meters	Lowest point Name	Lowest Elevation Feet	Lowest Elevation Meters	Approximate mean elevation Feet	Approximate mean elevation Meters
U.S	Mt. McKinley (AK)	20,320	6,198	Death Valley (CA).	-282	-86	2,500	763
AL	Cheaha Mountain	2,405	733	Gulf of Mexico	(1)	(1)	500	153
AK	Mount McKinley.	20,320	6,198	Pacific Ocean	(1)	(1)	1,900	580
AZ	Humphreys Peak	12,633	3,853	Colorado River	70	21	4,100	1,251
AR	Magazine Mountain	2,753	840	Ouachita River	55	17	650	198
CA	Mount Whitney	14,494	4,419	Death Valley.	-282	-86	2,900	885
CO	Mt. Elbert	14,433	4,402	Arkansas River	3,350	1,022	6,800	2,074
CT	Mt. Frissell on South slope.	2,380	726	Long Island Sound	(1)	(1)	500	153
DE	Ebright Road, [2] New Castle County. . . .	448	137	Atlantic Ocean	(1)	(1)	60	18
DC	Tenleytown at Reno Reservoir.	410	125	Potomac River	1	(Z)	150	46
FL	Sec. 30, T6N, R20W, Walton County.	345	105	Atlantic Ocean	(1)	(1)	100	31
GA	Brasstown Bald	4,784	1,459	Atlantic Ocean	(1)	(1)	600	183
HI	Puu Wekiu	13,796	4,208	Pacific Ocean	(1)	(1)	3,030	924
ID	Borah Peak	12,662	3,862	Snake River	710	217	5,000	1,525
IL	Charles Mound	1,235	377	Mississippi River	279	85	600	183
IN	Franklin Twp., Wayne Co .	1,257	383	Ohio River	320	98	700	214
IA	Sec. 29, T100N, R41W, Osceola County [3]	1,670	509	Mississippi River	480	146	1,100	336
KS	Mount Sunflower	4,039	1,232	Verdigris River	679	207	2,000	610
KY	Black Mountain	4,139	2,162	Mississippi River	257	78	750	229
LA	Driskill Mountain	535	163	New Orleans	-8	-2	100	31
ME	Mount Katahdin	5,267	1,606	Atlantic Ocean	(1)	(1)	600	183
MD	Backbone Mountain	3,360	1,025	Atlantic Ocean	(1)	(1)	350	107
MA	Mount Greylock	3,487	1,064	Atlantic Ocean	(1)	(1)	500	153
MI	Mount Arvon	1,979	604	Lake Erie.	571	174	900	275
MN	Eagle Mountain, Cook Co .	2,301	702	Lake Superior.	601	183	1,200	366
MS	Woodall Mountain	806	246	Gulf of Mexico	(1)	(1)	300	92
MO	Taum Sauk Mountain	1,772	540	St. Francis River	230	70	800	244
MT	Granite Peak	12,799	3,904	Kootenai River	1,800	549	3,400	1,037
NE	Johnson Twp., Kimball Co .	5,424	1,654	Missouri River.	840	256	2,600	793
NV	Boundary Peak	13,140	4,007	Colorado River	479	146	5,500	1,678
NH	Mount Washington	6,288	1,918	Atlantic Ocean	(1)	(1)	1,000	305
NJ	High Point	1,803	550	Atlantic Ocean	(1)	(1)	250	76
NM	Wheeler Peak	13,161	4,014	Red Bluff Reservoir	2,842	867	5,700	1,739
NY	Mount Marcy	5,344	1,630	Atlantic Ocean	(1)	(1)	1,000	305
NC	Mount Mitchell.	6,684	2,039	Atlantic Ocean	(1)	(1)	700	214
ND	White Butte, Slope Co . . .	3,506	1,069	Red River	750	229	1,900	580
OH	Campbell Hill	1,549	472	Ohio River	455	139	850	259
OK	Black Mesa.	4,973	1,517	Little River	289	88	1,300	397
OR	Mount Hood	11,239	3,428	Pacific Ocean.	(1)	(1)	3,300	1,007
PA	Mount Davis	3,213	980	Delaware River	(1)	(1)	1,100	336
RI	Jerimoth Hill	812	248	Atlantic Ocean	(1)	(1)	200	61
SC	Sassafras Mountain	3,560	1,086	Atlantic Ocean	(1)	(1)	350	107
SD	Harney Peak.	7,242	2,209	Big Stone Lake.	966	295	2,200	671
TN	Clingmans Dome	6,643	2,026	Mississippi River	178	54	900	275
TX	Guadalupe Peak	8,749	2,668	Gulf of Mexico	(1)	(1)	1,700	519
UT	Kings Peak	13,528	4,126	Beaver Dam Wash	2,000	610	6,100	1,861
VT	Mount Mansfield	4,393	1,340	Lake Champlain	95	29	1,000	305
VA	Mount Rogers	5,729	1,747	Atlantic Ocean	(1)	(1)	950	290
WA	Mount Rainier	14,410	4,395	Atlantic Ocean	(1)	(1)	1,700	519
WV	Spruce Knob.	4,861	1,483	Potomac River	240	73	1,500	458
WI	Timms Hill	1,951	595	Lake Michigan	579	177	1,050	320
WY	Gannett Peak	13,804	4,210	Belle Fourche River. . . .	3,099	945	6,700	2,044
Other areas:								
Puerto Rico	Cerro de Punta	4,390	1,339	Atlantic Ocean	(1)	(1)	1,800	549
American Samoa. . . .	Lata Mountain	3,160	964	Pacific Ocean.	(1)	(1)	1,300	397
Guam	Mount Lamlam	1,332	406	Pacific Ocean.	(1)	(1)	330	101
Virgin Is. . .	Crown Mountain	1,556	475	Atlantic Ocean	(1)	(1)	750	229

Z Less than 0.5 meter.   [1] Sea level.   [2] At DE-PA state line.   [3] "Sec." denotes section; "T," township; "R," range; "N," north; and "W," west.

Source: U.S. Geological Survey, for highest and lowest points, *Elevations and Distances in the United States, 1990*; for mean elevations, 1983 edition.

No. 352. U.S. Wetland Resources and Deepwater Habitats by Type: 1986 and 1997

[In thousands of acres (144,673.3 represents 144,677,300). Wetlands and deepwater habitats are defined separately because the term wetland does not included permanent water bodies. Deepwater habitats are permanently flooded land lying below the deepwater boundary of wetlands. Deepwater habitats include environments where surface water is permanent and often deep, so that water, rather than air, is the principal medium within which the dominant organisms live, whether or not they are attached to the substrate. As in wetlands, the dominant plants are hydrophytes; however, the substrates are considered nonsoil because the water is too deep to support emergent vegetation. In general terms, wetlands are lands where saturation with water is the dominant factor determining the nature of soil development and the types of plant and animal communities living in the soil and on its surface. The single feature that most wetlands share is soil or substrate that is at least periodically saturated with or covered by water. Wetlands are lands transitional between terrestrial and aquatic systems where the water table is usually at or near the surface or the land is covered by shallow water]

Wetland or deepwater category	1986	1997	Change, 1986 to 1997
All wetlands and deepwater habitats, total	144,673.3	144,136.8	-536.5
All deepwater habitats, total	38,537.6	38,645.1	107.5
Lacustrine [1]	14,608.9	14,725.3	116.4
Riverine [2]	6,291.1	6,255.9	-35.2
Estuarine Subtidal [3]	17,637.6	17,663.9	26.3
All wetlands, total	106,135.7	105,491.7	-644
Intertidal wetlands [4]	5,336.6	5,326.2	-10.4
Marine intertidal	133.1	130.9	-2.2
Estuarine intertidal non-vegetated	580.4	580.1	-0.3
Estuarine intertidal vegetated	4,623.1	4,615.2	-7.9
Freshwater wetlands	100,799.1	100,165.5	-633.6
Freshwater non-vegetated	5,251.0	5,914.3	663.3
Freshwater vegetated	95,548.1	94,251.2	-1,296.9
Freshwater emergent [5]	26,383.3	25,157.1	-1,226.2
Freshwater forested [6]	51,929.6	50,728.5	-1,201.1
Freshwater shrub [7]	17,235.2	18,365.6	1,130.4

[1] The lacustrine system includes deepwater habitats with all of the following characteristics: (1) situated in a topographic depression or a dammed river channel; (2) lacking trees, shrubs, persistent emergents, emergent mosses or lichens with greater than 30 percent coverage; (3) total area exceeds 20 acres. [2] The riverine system includes deepwater habitats contained within a channel, with the exception of habitats with water containing ocean derived salts in excess of 0.5 parts per thousand. [3] The estuarine system consists of deepwater tidal habitats and adjacent tidal wetland that are usually semi-enclosed by land but have open, partly obstructed, or sporadic access to the open ocean, and in which ocean water is at least occasionally diluted by freshwater runoff from the land. Subtidal is where the substrate is continuously submerged by marine or estuarine waters. [4] Intertidal is where the substrate is exposed and flooded by tides. Intertidal includes the splash zone of coastal waters. [5] Emergent wetlands are characterized by erect, rooted, herbaceous hydrophytes, excluding mosses and lichens. This vegetation is present for most of the growing season in most years. These wetlands are usually dominated by perennial plants. [6] Forested wetlands are characterized by woody vegetation that is 20 feet tall or taller. [7] Shrub wetlands include areas dominated by woody vegetation less than 20 feet tall. The species include true shrubs, young trees, and trees or shrubs that are small or stunted because of environmental conditions.

Source: U.S. Fish and Wildlife Service, *Status and Trends of Wetlands in the Conterminous United States, 1986 to 1997,* January 2001. See also <ftp://wetlands.fws.gov/status-trends/SandT2000Reportlowres.pdf>.

No. 353. Water Areas for Selected Major Bodies of Water: 2000

[Includes only that portion of body of water under the jurisdiction of the United States, excluding Hawaii. One square mile=2.59 square kilometers]

Body of water and State	Area Sq. mi.	Area Sq. km.	Body of water and State	Area Sq. mi.	Area Sq. km.
Atlantic Coast water bodies:			Willapa Bay (WA)	125	325
Chesapeake Bay (MD-VA)	2,747	7,115	Hood Canal (WA)	117	303
Pamlico Sound (NC)	1,622	4,200	**Interior water bodies:**		
Long Island Sound (CT-NY)	914	2,368	Lake Michigan (IL-IN-MI-WI)	22,342	57,866
Delaware Bay (DE-NJ)	614	1,591	Lake Superior (MI-MN-WI) [1]	20,557	53,243
Cape Cod Bay (MA)	598	1,548	Lake Huron (MI) [1]	8,800	22,792
Albemarle Sound (NC)	492	1,274	Lake Erie (MI-NY-OH-PA) [1]	5,033	13,036
Biscayne Bay (FL)	218	565	Lake Ontario (NY) [1]	3,446	8,926
Buzzards Bay (MA)	215	558	Great Salt Lake (UT)	1,836	4,756
Tangier Sound (MD-VA)	172	445	Green Bay (MI-WI)	1,396	3,617
Currituck Sound (NC)	116	301	Lake Okeechobee (FL)	663	1,717
Pocomoke Sound (MD-VA)	111	286	Lake Sakakawea (ND)	563	1,459
Chincoteague Bay (MD-VA)	105	272	Lake Oahe (ND-SD)	538	1,394
Gulf Coast water bodies:			Lake of the Woods (MN) [1]	462	1,196
Mississippi Sound (AL-LA-MS)	813	2,105	Lake Champlain (NY-VT) [1]	414	1,072
Laguna Madre (TX)	733	1,897			
Lake Pontchartrain (LA)	631	1,635	**Alaska water bodies:**		
Florida Bay (FL)	616	1,596	Chatham Strait	1,559	4,039
Breton Sound (LA)	511	1,323	Prince William Sound	1,382	3,579
Mobile Bay (AL)	310	802	Clarence Strait	1,199	3,107
Lake Borgne (LA-MS)	271	702	Iliamna Lake	1,022	2,646
Matagorda Bay (TX)	253	656	Frederick Sound	792	2,051
Atchafalaya Bay (LA)	245	635	Sumner Strait	791	2,048
Galveston Bay (TX)	236	611	Stephens Passage	702	1,819
Tampa Bay (FL)	212	549	Kvichak Bay	640	1,659
Pacific Coast water bodies:			Montague Strait	463	1,198
Puget Sound (WA)	808	2,092	Becharof Lake	447	1,158
San Francisco Bay (CA)	264	684	Icy Strait	436	1,130

[1] Area measurements for Lake Champlain, Lake Erie, Lake Huron, Lake Ontario, Lake St. Clair, Lake Superior, and Lake of the Woods include only those portions under the jurisdiction of the United States.

Source: U. S. Census Bureau, unpublished data from the Census TIGER™ data base.

Geography and Environment 217

No. 354. Flows of Largest U.S. Rivers—Length, Discharge, and Drainage Area

River	Location of mouth	Source stream (name and location)	Length (miles) [1]	Average discharge at mouth (1,000 cubic ft. per second)	Drainage area (1,000 sq. mi.)
Missouri	Missouri.	Red Rock Creek, MT	2,540	76.2	[2]529
Mississippi	Louisiana.	Mississippi River, MN.	[3]2,340	[4]593	[2][5]1,150
Yukon	Alaska.	McNeil River, Canada	1,980	225	[2]328
St. Lawrence	Canada.	North River, MN	1,900	348	[2]396
Rio Grande	Mexico-Texas	Rio Grande, CO	1,900	-	336
Arkansas	Arkansas	East Fork Arkansas River, CO . . .	1,460	41	161
Colorado.	Mexico	Colorado River, CO	1,450	-	246
Atchafalaya [6].	Louisiana.	Tierra Blanca Creek, NM	1,420	58	95.1
Ohio	Illinois-Kentucky . . .	Allegheny River, PA.	1,310	281	203
Red	Louisiana.	Tierra Blanca Creek, NM	1,290	56	93.2
Brazos	Texas	Blackwater Draw, NM.	1,280	-	45.6
Columbia	Oregon-Washington .	Columbia River, Canada.	1,240	265	[2]258
Snake	Washington	Snake River, WY.	1,040	56.9	108
Platte	Nebraska.	Grizzly Creek, CO	990	-	84.9
Pecos	Texas	Pecos River, NM.	926	-	44.3
Canadian	Oklahoma	Canadian River, CO.	906	-	46.9
Tennessee	Kentucky	Courthouse Creek, NC	886	68	40.9
Colorado (of Texas) . .	Texas	Colorado River, TX	862	-	42.3
North Canadian	Oklahoma	Corrumpa Creek, NM.	800	-	17.6
Mobile	Alabama	Tickanetley Creek, GA	774	67.2	44.6
Kansas.	Kansas.	Arikaree River, CO	743	-	59.5
Kuskokwim	Alaska.	South Fork Kuskokwim River, AK.	724	67	48
Yellowstone.	North Dakota	North Folk Yellowstone River, WY.	692	-	70
Tanana	Alaska.	Nabesna River, AK	659	41	44.5
Gila	Arizona	Middle Fork Gila River, NM	649	-	58.2
Porcupine	Alaska.	Porcupine River, Canada	569	23	45.1
Susquehanna	Maryland	Hayden Creek, NY	447	38.2	27.2

- Represents zero. [1] From source to mouth. [2] Drainage area includes both the United States and Canada. [3] The length from the source of the Missouri River to the Mississippi River and thence to the Gulf of Mexico is about 3,710 miles. [4] Includes about 167,000 cubic ft. per second diverted from the Mississippi into the Atchafalaya River but excludes the flow of the Red River. [5] Excludes the drainage areas of the Red and Atchafalaya Rivers. [6] In east-central Louisiana, the Red River flows into the Atchafalaya River, a distributary of the Mississippi River. Data on average discharge, length, and drainage area include the Red River, but exclude all water diverted into the Atchafalaya from the Mississippi River.

Source: U.S. Geological Survey, *Largest Rivers in the United States*, Open File Report 87-242, May 1990.

No. 355. U.S. Water Withdrawals and Consumptive Use Per Day by End Use: 1940 to 2000

[In billions of gallons, except as indicated. (140 represents 140,000,000,000). Includes Puerto Rico. Withdrawal signifies water physically withdrawn from a source. Includes fresh and saline water; excludes water used for hydroelectric power]

Year	Total	Per capita [1] (gal.)	Irrigation	Public sup- ply [2]	Rural [3]	Industrial and misc. [4]	Steam electric utilities
WITHDRAWALS							
1940	140	1,027	71	10	3.1	29	23
1950	180	1,185	89	14	3.6	37	40
1955	240	1,454	110	17	3.6	39	72
1960	270	1,500	110	21	3.6	38	100
1965	310	1,602	120	24	4.0	46	130
1970	370	1,815	130	27	4.5	47	170
1975	420	1,972	140	29	4.9	45	200
1980	440	1,953	150	34	5.6	45	210
1985	399	1,650	137	38	7.8	31	187
1990	408	1,620	137	41	7.9	30	195
1995	402	1,500	134	40	8.9	29	190
2000	408	1,430	137	43	9.2	23	196
CONSUMPTIVE USE							
1960	61	339	52	3.5	2.8	3.0	0.2
1965	77	403	66	5.2	3.2	3.4	0.4
1970	87	427	73	5.9	3.4	4.1	0.8
1975	96	451	80	6.7	3.4	4.2	1.9
1980	100	440	83	7.1	3.9	5.0	3.2
1985	92	380	74	[5]	9.2	6.1	6.2
1990	94	370	76	[5]	8.9	6.7	4.0
1995	100	374	81	[5]	9.9	4.8	3.7
2000	(NA)	(NA)	(NA)	(NA)	(NA)	(NA)	(NA)

NA Not available. [1] Based on U.S. Census Bureau resident population as of July 1. [2] Includes commercial water withdrawals. [3] Rural farm and nonfarm household and garden use, and water for farm stock and dairies. [4] For 1940 to 1960, includes manufacturing and mineral industries, rural commercial industries, air-conditioning, resorts, hotels, motels, military and other state and Federal agencies, and miscellaneous; thereafter, includes manufacturing, mining and mineral processing, ordnance, construction, and miscellaneous. [5] Public supply consumptive use included in end-use categories.

Source: 1940-1960, U.S. Bureau of Domestic Business Development, based principally on committee prints, *Water Resources Activities in the United States*, for the Senate Committee on National Water Resources, U.S. Senate, thereafter, U.S. Geological Survey, *Estimated Use of Water in the United States in 2000*, circular 1268.

No. 356. Water Withdrawals by Source, Type, and Use—State and Other Areas: 2000

[In millions of gallons per day(408,000 represents 408,000,000,000), except as noted. Figures may not add due to rounding. Withdrawal signifies water physically withdrawn from a source. Includes fresh and saline water. For information on methodology and differences with prior surveys, see <http://water.usgs.gov/pubs/circ/2004/circ1268/htdocs/text-intro.html>]

State and other area		Source		Type		Selected major uses				
	Total	Ground water	Surface water	Fresh water	Saline water	Public supply	Domestic	Irrigation	Industrial [1]	Thermo-electric [1]
Total [2]	408,000	84,500	323,000	345,000	62,300	43,300	3,590	137,000	19,780	195,500
Alabama	9,990	440	9,550	9,990	-	834	79	43	833	8,190
Alaska	305	141	164	161	144	80	11	1	12	34
Arizona	6,730	3,430	3,300	6,720	8	1,080	29	5,400	20	100
Arkansas	10,900	6,920	3,950	10,900	-	421	29	7,910	134	2,180
California	51,200	15,400	35,800	38,400	12,800	6,120	286	30,500	202	12,952
Colorado	12,600	2,320	10,300	12,600	-	899	67	11,400	120	138
Connecticut	4,150	143	4,010	708	3,440	424	56	30	11	3,627
Delaware	1,320	115	1,210	582	741	95	13	44	63	1,104
District of Columbia .	10	-	10	10	-	-	-	-	-	10
Florida	20,100	5,020	15,100	8,140	12,000	2,440	199	4,290	292	12,658
Georgia	6,500	1,450	5,060	6,410	92	1,250	110	1,140	652	3,312
Hawaii	641	434	208	640	1	250	12	364	15	-
Idaho	19,500	4,140	15,300	19,500	-	244	85	17,100	56	-
Illinois	13,700	813	12,900	13,700	-	1,760	135	154	391	11,300
Indiana	10,100	656	9,460	10,100	-	670	122	101	2,400	6,700
Iowa	3,360	679	2,680	3,360	-	383	33	22	237	2,540
Kansas	6,610	3,790	2,820	6,610	-	416	22	3,710	53	2,260
Kentucky	4,160	189	3,970	4,160	-	525	28	29	317	3,260
Louisiana	10,400	1,630	8,730	10,400	-	753	41	1,020	2,680	5,610
Maine	799	81	718	504	295	102	36	6	247	408
Maryland	7,910	225	7,690	1,430	6,490	824	77	42	293	6,639
Massachusetts	4,660	269	4,390	1,050	3,610	739	42	126	37	3,718
Michigan	10,000	734	9,260	10,000	-	1,140	239	201	698	7,710
Minnesota	3,870	720	3,150	3,870	-	500	81	227	154	2,270
Mississippi	2,960	2,180	781	2,810	148	359	69	1,410	242	510
Missouri	8,230	1,780	6,450	8,230	-	872	54	1,430	63	5,640
Montana	8,290	188	8,100	8,290	-	149	19	7,950	61	110
Nebraska	12,300	7,860	4,390	12,200	5	330	48	8,790	38	2,820
Nevada	2,810	757	2,050	2,810	-	629	22	2,110	10	37
New Hampshire	1,210	85	1,120	447	761	97	41	5	45	997
New Jersey	5,560	584	4,980	2,170	3,390	1,050	80	140	132	4,040
New Mexico	3,260	1,540	1,710	3,260	-	296	31	2,860	11	56
New York	12,100	893	11,200	7,080	5,010	2,570	142	36	297	9,050
North Carolina	11,400	580	10,800	9,730	1,620	945	189	287	293	9,470
North Dakota	1,140	123	1,020	1,140	-	64	12	145	18	902
Ohio	11,100	878	10,300	11,100	-	1,470	134	32	807	8,590
Oklahoma	2,020	1,030	990	1,760	256	675	26	718	26	146
Oregon	6,930	993	5,940	6,930	-	566	76	6,080	195	15
Pennsylvania	9,950	666	9,290	9,950	-	1,460	132	14	1,190	6,980
Rhode Island	429	29	400	138	290	119	9	3	4	292
South Carolina	7,170	330	6,840	7,170	-	566	64	267	565	5,710
South Dakota	528	222	306	528	-	93	10	373	5	5
Tennessee	10,800	417	10,400	10,800	-	890	33	22	842	9,040
Texas	29,600	8,970	20,700	24,800	4,850	4,230	131	8,630	2,357	13,260
Utah	4,970	1,050	3,920	4,760	203	638	16	3,860	48	62
Vermont	447	43	404	447	-	60	21	4	7	355
Virginia	8,830	314	8,520	5,200	3,640	720	133	26	523	7,430
Washington	5,310	1,470	3,840	5,270	40	1,020	125	3,040	617	519
West Virginia	5,150	91	5,060	5,150	-	190	40	-	968	3,950
Wisconsin	7,590	813	6,780	7,590	-	623	96	196	447	6,090
Wyoming	5,170	763	4,400	4,940	222	107	7	4,500	6	243
Puerto Rico	2,810	137	2,670	620	2,190	513	1	95	11	2,190
Virgin Islands	148	1	147	12	136	6	2	1	3	136

- Represents zero.   [1] Represents both fresh and saline water.   [2] Includes Puerto Rico and Virgin Islands.

Source: U.S. Geological Survey, *Estimated Use of Water in the United States in 2000*, circular 1268. See also <http://water.usgs.gov/pubs/circ/2004/circ1268/#availability> (released March 2004).

Geography and Environment   219

No. 357. U.S. Water Quality Conditions by Type of Waterbody: 2000

[Section 305(b) of the Clean Water Act requires states and other jurisdictions to assess the health of their waters and the extent to which their waters support water quality standards. Section 305(b) requires that states submit reports describing water quality conditions to the Environmental Protection Agency every two years. Water quality standards have three elements (designated uses, criteria developed to protect each use, and an antidegradation policy). For information on survey methodology and assessment criteria, see report]

Item	Rivers and streams (miles)	Lakes, reservoirs, and ponds (acres)	Esturaries (sq. miles)	Great Lakes shoreline (miles)	Ocean shoreline (miles)
Total size	3,692,830	40,603,893	87,369	5,521	58,618
Amount accessed [1]	699,946	17,339,080	31,072	5,066	3,221
Percent of total size	19	43	36	92	6
Amount accessed as—					
Good [2]	463,441	8,026,988	13,850	-	2,176
Good but threatened [3]	85,544	1,343,903	1,023	1,095	193
Polluted [4]	291,264	7,702,370	15,676	3,955	434
Percent of accessed as—					
Good [2]	53	47	45	-	79
Good but threatened [3]	8	8	4	22	7
Polluted [4]	39	45	51	78	14
Amount impaired by leading sources of pollution: [5]					
Agriculture	128,859	3,158,393	2,811	75	(NA)
Atmospheric deposition	(NA)	983,936	3,692	71	(NA)
Construction	(NA)	(NA)	(NA)	(NA)	29
Contaminated sediments	(NA)	(NA)	(NA)	519	(NA)
Forestry	28,156	(NA)	(NA)	(NA)	(NA)
Habitat modification	37,654	(NA)	(NA)	62	(NA)
Hydrologic modification	53,850	1,413,624	2,171	(NA)	(NA)
Industrial discharges/point sources . .	(NA)	(NA)	4,116	(NA)	76
Land disposal of wastes	(NA)	856,586	(NA)	61	123
Municipal point sources	27,988	943,715	5,779	(NA)	89
Nonpoint sources	(NA)	1,045,036	(NA)	(NA)	142
Resource extraction	27,695	(NA)	1,913	(NA)	(NA)
Septic tanks	(NA)	(NA)	(NA)	61	103
Urban runoff and storm sewers	34,871	13,699,327	5,045	152	241

- Represents zero.   NA Not available.   [1] Includes waterbodies accessed as not attainable for one or more uses. Most states do not assess all their waterbodies during the 2-year reporting cycle, but use a "rotating basin approach" whereby all waters are monitored over a set period of time.   [2] Based on assessment of available data, water quality supports all designated uses. Water quality meets narrative and/or numberic criteria adopted to protect and support a designated use.   [3] Although all assessed uses are currently met, data show a declining trend in water quality. Projections based on this trend indicate water quality will be impaired in the future, unless action is taken to prevent further degradation.   [4] Impaired or not attainable. The reporting state or jurisdiction has performed a "use-attainability analysis" and demonstrated that support of one or more designated beneficial uses is not attainable due to specific biological, chemical, physical, or economic/social conditions.   [5] Excludes unknown and natural sources.

Source: U.S. Environmental Protection Agency, *National Water Quality Inventory: 2000 Report*, EPA-841-R-02-001, August 2002. See also <http://www.epa.gov/305b/2000report>.

No. 358. Oil Spills in U.S. Water—Number and Volume: 1998 to 2001

[Based on reported discharges into U.S. navigable waters, including territorial waters (extending 3 to 12 miles from the coastline), tributaries, the contiguous zone, onto shoreline, or into other waters that threaten the marine environment. Data found in Marine Safety Management System]

Spill characteristic	Number of spills				Spill volume (gallons)			
	1998	1999	2000	2001	1998	1999	2000	2001
Total	8,315	8,539	8,354	7,559	885,303	1,172,449	1,431,370	854,520
Size of spill (gallons):								
1-100	7,962	8,212	8,058	7,256	38,093	39,119	39,355	33,276
101-1,000	259	240	219	216	86,606	86,530	78,779	86,955
1,001-3,000	54	42	37	45	96,743	74,582	67,529	77,447
3,001-5,000	15	18	12	16	64,609	73,798	45,512	67,241
5,001-10,000	15	10	16	11	108,148	66,274	112,415	89,224
10,001-50,000	8	12	6	14	216,335	301,510	108,400	376,057
50,001-100,000	-	4	4	-	-	245,406	266,380	-
100,001-1,000,000	2	1	2	1	274,769	285,230	713,000	124,320
1,000,000 and over	-	-	-	-	-	-	-	-
Waterbody:								
Atlantic ocean	109	148	150	83	6,674	29,440	135,010	7,168
Pacific ocean	644	758	623	493	192,775	150,694	36,301	53,295
Gulf of Mexico	2,190	1,756	1,838	1,728	181,372	45,786	112,069	133,872
Great Lakes	119	129	96	109	3,006	906	4,535	1,600
Lakes	25	31	32	35	63	624	349	244
Rivers and canals	1,944	1,924	1,816	1,682	280,651	504,264	663,404	237,980
Bays and sounds	891	1,299	1,248	1,140	24,234	136,650	49,783	139,300
Harbors	790	907	801	893	97,223	105,213	273,095	158,667
Other	1,603	1,587	1,750	1,396	99,305	198,872	156,824	122,394
Source:								
Tankship	104	92	111	95	56,673	8,414	608,176	125,217
Tankbarge	220	227	229	246	248,089	158,977	133,540	212,298
All other vessels	4,848	5,361	5,220	4,680	316,473	409,084	291,927	232,341
Facilities	937	1,019	1,054	995	166,269	367,537	311,604	201,025
Pipelines	45	25	25	34	47,863	36,140	17,021	13,577
All other non-vessels	571	571	566	436	32,584	147,704	45,136	55,921
Unknown	1,590	1,244	1,149	1,073	17,352	44,593	23,966	14,141

- Represents or rounds to zero.
Source: U.S. Coast Guard, <http://www.uscg.mil/hq/g-m/nmc/response/stats/Summary.htm> and <http://www.uscg.mil/hq/g-m/nmc/response/stats/chpt2001.pdf> (released August 2003).

No. 359. National Ambient Air Pollutant Concentrations: 1992 to 2001

[Data represent annual composite averages of pollutant based on daily 24-hour averages of monitoring stations, except carbon monoxide is based on the second-highest, non-overlapping, 8-hour average; ozone, the second-highest daily maximum 1-hour value or the fourth-highest maximum 8-hour value; and lead, the maximum quarterly average of ambient lead levels. Based on data from the Air Quality System. µg/m³=micrograms of pollutant per cubic meter of air; ppm=parts per million]

Pollutant	Unit	Monitoring stations, number	Air quality standard [1]	1992	1995	1997	1998	1999	2000	2001
Carbon monoxide .	ppm. . . .	387	[2]9	5.2	4.6	4.1	3.8	3.7	3.3	3.2
Ozone.	ppm. . . .	785	[3].12	0.104	0.111	0.104	0.110	0.107	0.1	0.101
Ozone.	ppm. . . .	785	[4]0.08	0.081	0.087	0.082	0.087	0.086	0.08	0.081
Sulfur dioxide	ppm. . . .	449	.03	0.0075	0.0057	0.0055	0.0055	0.0053	0.0051	0.0049
Particulates (PM-10).	µg/m³. . .	770	[5]50	27.7	25.7	24.6	24.3	24.8	24.4	23.9
Nitrogen dioxide . .	ppm. . .	250	.053	0.019	0.018	0.017	0.018	0.018	0.017	0.017
Lead.	µg/m³. . .	96	[6]1.5	0.08	0.06	0.05	0.05	0.05	0.05	0.06

[1] Refers to the primary National Ambient Air Quality Standard that protects the public health. [2] Based on 8-hour standard of 9 ppm. [3] Based on 1-hour standard of .12 ppm. [4] Based on 8-hour standard of .08 ppm. [5] The particulates (PM-10) standard replaced the previous standard for total suspended particulates in 1987. [6] Based on 3-month standard of 1.5 µg/m³.

No. 360. National Air Pollutant Emissions: 1970 to 2001

[In thousands of tons (13,042 represents 13,042,000), except as indicated. PM-10=Particulate matter of less than ten microns; PM-2.5=particulate matter of less than 2.5 microns effective diameter. Methodologies to estimate data for 1970 to 1980 period and 1985 to present emissions differ. Beginning with 1985, the methodology for more recent years is described in the document available at <http://www.epa.gov/ttn/chief/trends/trends99/neiproc99.pdf>]

Year	PM-10	PM-10, fugitive dust[1]	PM-2.5	Sulfur dioxide	Nitrogen dioxides	Volatile organic compounds	Carbon monoxide	Lead[2] (tons)
1970	13,042	(NA)	(NA)	31,161	20,928	30,982	129,444	220,869
1975	7,671	(NA)	(NA)	28,011	22,632	26,079	116,757	159,659
1980	7,013	(NA)	(NA)	25,925	27,079	31,106	185,407	74,153
1985	11,590	29,734	(NA)	23,307	25,757	27,404	176,844	22,890
1990	9,690	18,068	7,561	23,078	25,530	24,116	154,189	4,975
1991	9,270	18,075	7,320	22,375	25,179	23,577	147,128	4,169
1992	8,927	18,170	7,198	22,082	25,260	23,066	140,896	3,810
1993	8,411	18,953	7,150	21,772	25,357	22,730	135,901	3,916
1994	8,888	19,722	7,541	21,346	25,349	22,569	133,559	4,047
1995	8,807	17,012	6,929	18,619	24,956	22,041	126,777	3,929
1996	9,017	13,845	6,726	18,387	24,790	20,870	128,860	2,627
1997	8,396	14,516	6,257	18,841	24,712	19,534	117,913	(NA)
1998	8,345	14,555	6,263	18,947	24,349	18,783	115,382	(NA)
1999	9,185	12,447	6,813	17,651	23,671	19,378	117,229	(NA)
2000	10,385	14,314	8,175	16,317	23,199	19,704	123,568	(NA)
2001	9,442	14,662	7,380	15,790	22,349	17,963	120,759	(NA)

NA Not available. [1] Sources such as agricultural tilling, construction, mining and quarrying, paved roads, unpaved roads, and wind erosion. [2] Beginning 1996, lead and lead compounds are inventoried through the hazardous air pollutants (HAPs) portion of the National Emission Inventory (NEI) every three years; data for 1997 forward are currently not available.

No. 361. Air Pollutant Emissions by Pollutant and Source: 2001

[In thousands of tons, except as indicated. See headnote, Table 360]

Source	PM-10 [1]	PM-2.5	Sulfur dioxide	Nitrogen dioxides	Volatile organic compounds	Carbon monoxide
Total emissions	24,104	7,379	15,790	22,349	17,963	120,760
Fuel combustion, stationary sources.	1,504	1,319	13,632	8,599	1,184	4,592
Electric utilities	663	568	10,821	4,891	63	492
Industrial	330	258	2,262	2,640	168	1,181
Other fuel combustion	511	493	549	1,068	953	2,919
Residential	423	419	164	674	925	2,759
Industrial processes	667	483	1,405	847	1,249	2,519
Chemical and allied product manufacturing . . .	54	46	329	117	305	381
Metals processing	172	143	358	96	72	1,356
Petroleum and related industries	39	26	310	129	394	169
Other	402	268	408	505	478	613
Solvent utilization	5	-	1	4	5,053	50
Storage and transport	86	41	6	11	1,150	174
Waste disposal and recycling	504	475	35	169	541	3,229
Highway vehicles	219	162	261	8,249	4,874	74,826
Light-duty gas vehicles and motorcycles	51	27	103	2,386	2,620	41,231
Light-duty trucks	31	17	71	1,503	1,805	29,333
Heavy-duty gas vehicles.	10	7	14	456	224	3,133
Diesels	127	111	73	3,904	225	1,129
Off highway [2]	316	290	440	4,156	2,622	24,677
Miscellaneous [3]	20,803	4,609	10	314	1,290	10,693

- Represents or rounds to zero. [1] Represents both PM-10 and PM-10 fugitive dust; see Table 361. [2] Includes emissions from farm tractors and other farm machinery, construction equipment, industrial machinery, recreational marine vessels, and small general utility engines such as lawn mowers. [3] Includes emissions such as from forest fires and other kinds of burning, various agricultural activities, fugitive dust from paved and unpaved roads, and other construction and mining activities, and natural sources.

Source of Tables 359-361: U.S. Environmental Protection Agency, *Latest Findings on National Air Quality, 2002 Status and Trends*, EPA 454/K-02-001, September 2002. See also <http://www.epa.gov/ttn/chief/trends/index.html#tables>.

Geography and Environment 221

No. 362. Emissions of Greenhouse Gases by Type and Source: 1990 to 2002

[6,156.0 represents 6,156,000,000 tons. Emission estimates were mandated by Congress through Section 1605(a) of the Energy Policy Act of 1992 (Title XVI). Gases that contain carbon can be measured either in terms of the full molecular weight of the gas or just in terms of their carbon dioxide equivalent. Both measures are utilized below]

Type and source	Unit	1990	1995	1999	2000	2001	2002
CARBON DIOXIDE EQUIVALENT							
Total emissions	Mil. metric tons.	6,156.0	6,470.0	6,795.0	6,957.0	6,829.0	6,862.0
Carbon dioxide, total.	Mil. metric tons.	5,006.1	5,318.5	5,686.1	5,854.0	5,748.3	5,795.6
Energy sources	Mil. metric tons .	4,988.6	5,255.8	5,630.5	5,798.6	5,691.7	5,729.3
C02 in natural gas.	Mil. metric tons .	14.0	16.7	17.8	18.2	18.6	18.1
Cement production	Mil. metric tons .	33.3	36.9	40.1	41.3	41.4	43.3
Gas flaring.	Mil. metric tons .	9.1	17.2	6.7	5.5	5.2	5.1
Other industrial	Mil. metric tons .	26.8	28.4	29.3	29.6	27.7	27.4
Waste combustion.	Mil. metric tons .	17.0	22.2	25.2	19.9	19.8	19.8
Other, adjustments	Mil. metric tons .	-82.7	-58.6	-63.5	-59.1	-56.2	-47.3
Methane.	Mil. metric tons .	719.1	701.8	639.7	638.8	630.2	612.8
Nitrous oxide	Mil. metric tons .	333.8	355.3	347.2	341.2	336.8	333.1
HFCs, PFCs, and SF	Mil. metric tons .	96.8	94.6	122.1	123.2	113.6	120.6
GAS							
Carbon dioxide	Mil. metric tons .	5,006.1	5,318.5	5,686.1	5,854.0	5,748.3	5,795.6
Methane, total	Mil. metric tons .	31.27	30.51	27.81	27.77	27.40	26.65
Nitrous oxide, total	Mil. metric tons .	1.13	1.20	1.17	1.15	1.14	1.13
HFCs, PFCs, and SF	Mil. metric tons .	(¹)	(¹)	(¹)	(¹)	(¹)	(¹)

¹ Mixture of gases.

Source: U.S. Energy Information Administration, *Emissions of Greenhouse Gases in the United States*, Series DOE/EIA-0573(2001), annual. See also <ftp://ftp.eia.doe.gov/pub/oiaf/1605/cdrom/pdf/ggrpt/057301.pdf> (issued 20 December 2002).

No. 363. Municipal Solid Waste Generation, Recovery, and Disposal: 1980 to 2001

[In millions of tons (151.6 represents 151,600,000), except as indicated. Covers post-consumer residential and commercial solid wastes which comprise the major portion of typical municipal collections. Excludes mining, agricultural and industrial processing, demolition and construction wastes, sewage sludge, and junked autos and obsolete equipment wastes. Based on material-flows estimating procedure and wet weight as generated]

Item and material	1980	1990	1995	1998	1999	2000	2001
Waste generated	151.6	205.2	211.4	223.4	231.0	232.0	229.2
Per person per day (lb.)	3.7	4.5	4.4	4.5	4.6	4.5	4.4
Materials recovered	14.5	33.2	54.9	61.1	64.8	67.7	68.0
Per person per day (lb.)	0.35	0.7	1.1	1.2	1.3	1.3	1.3
Combustion for energy recovery	2.7	31.9	35.5	34.4	34.0	33.7	33.6
Per person per day (lb.)	0.06	0.7	0.7	0.7	0.7	0.7	0.7
Combustion without energy recovery	11.0	(¹)	(¹)	(¹)	(¹)	(¹)	(¹)
Per person per day (lb.)	0.27	(¹)	(¹)	(¹)	(¹)	(¹)	(¹)
Landfill, other disposal.	123.4	140.1	120.9	127.1	132.1	130.6	127.6
Per person per day (lb.)	3.0	3.1	2.5	2.6	2.7	2.5	2.5
Percent distribution of generation:							
Paper and paperboard	36.4	35.4	38.6	37.7	38.2	37.4	35.7
Glass	10.0	6.4	6.1	5.7	5.6	5.4	5.5
Metals.	10.2	8.1	7.5	7.5	7.7	7.8	7.9
Plastics	4.5	8.3	8.9	10.0	10.4	10.7	11.1
Rubber and leather	2.8	2.8	2.9	3.1	2.7	2.7	2.8
Textiles	1.7	2.8	3.5	3.9	3.9	4.0	4.3
Wood	4.6	6.0	4.9	5.4	5.4	5.6	5.7
Food wastes	8.6	10.1	10.3	11.2	10.9	11.2	11.4
Yard wastes	18.1	17.1	14.0	12.4	12.0	12.0	12.2
Other wastes	3.2	3.0	3.3	3.2	3.2	3.2	3.4

¹ Combustion without energy recovery is no longer available separately.

Source: Franklin Associates, a Division of ERG, Prairie Village, KS, *Municipal Solid Waste in the United States: 2001 Facts and Figures*. Prepared for the U.S. Environmental Protection Agency.

No. 364. Generation and Recovery of Selected Materials in Municipal Solid Waste: 1980 to 2001

[In millions of tons (151.6 represents 151,600,000), except as indicated. Covers post-consumer residential and commercial solid wastes which comprise the major portion of typical municipal collections. Excludes mining, agricultural and industrial processing, demolition and construction wastes, sewage sludge, and junked autos and obsolete equipment wastes. Based on material-flows estimating procedure and wet weight as generated]

Item and material	1980	1990	1995	1998	1999	2000	2001
Waste generated, total	151.6	205.2	211.4	223.4	230.9	232.0	229.2
Paper and paperboard	55.2	72.7	81.7	84.2	88.3	86.8	81.9
Ferrous metals	12.6	12.6	11.6	12.4	13.3	13.5	13.5
Aluminum	1.7	2.8	3.0	3.1	3.1	3.2	3.2
Other nonferrous metals	1.2	1.1	1.3	1.4	1.4	1.4	1.4
Glass	15.1	13.1	12.8	12.6	12.9	12.6	12.6
Plastics	6.8	17.1	18.9	22.4	24.1	24.7	25.4
Yard waste	27.5	35.0	29.7	27.7	27.7	27.7	28.0
Other wastes	31.5	50.7	52.4	59.6	60.1	62.1	63.3
Materials recovered, total	14.5	33.2	54.9	61.1	64.8	67.7	68.0
Paper and paperboard	11.9	20.2	32.7	34.4	36.1	36.7	36.7
Ferrous metals	0.4	2.2	4.1	4.3	4.5	4.6	4.6
Aluminum	0.3	1.0	0.9	0.9	0.9	0.9	0.8
Other nonferrous metals	0.5	0.7	0.8	0.9	0.9	0.9	0.9
Glass	0.8	2.6	3.1	2.9	3.0	2.7	2.4
Plastics	-	0.4	1.0	1.2	1.3	1.3	1.4
Yard waste	-	4.2	9.0	12.6	14.2	15.8	15.8
Other wastes	0.6	1.8	3.2	3.9	3.9	4.8	5.4
Percent of generation recovered, total	9.6	16.2	26.0	27.4	28.1	29.2	29.7
Paper and paperboard	21.6	27.8	40.0	40.9	40.9	42.3	44.9
Ferrous metals	3.2	17.5	35.3	34.7	33.8	34.0	33.8
Aluminum	17.6	35.7	30.0	29.0	29.0	27.4	24.5
Other nonferrous metals	41.7	63.6	61.5	64.3	64.3	66.9	64.8
Glass	5.3	19.8	24.2	23.0	23.3	21.1	19.1
Plastics	-	2.3	5.3	5.4	5.4	5.4	5.5
Yard waste	-	12.0	30.3	45.5	51.3	56.9	56.5
Other wastes	1.9	3.6	6.1	6.5	6.5	7.8	8.5

- Represents zero.

Source: Franklin Associates, a Division of ERG, Prairie Village, KS, *Municipal Solid Waste in the United States: 2001 Facts and Figures.* Prepared for the U.S. Environmental Protection Agency.

No. 365. Curbside Recycling Programs—Number and Population Served by Region: 1995 to 2001

[(121,335 represents 121,335,000). For composition of regions, see map, inside front cover]

Region	Number of programs					Population served [1] (1,000)				
	1995	1997	1999	2000	2001	1995	1997	1999	2000	2001
Total	7,375	8,969	9,349	9,247	9,704	121,335	136,229	139,826	133,165	139,366
Northeast	2,210	3,406	3,414	3,459	3,421	37,256	43,200	43,162	43,482	43,981
South	1,281	1,344	1,581	1,427	1,677	31,521	36,952	37,914	37,510	26,496
Midwest	2,985	3,357	3,477	3,582	3,572	25,487	26,970	30,106	22,618	25,851
West	899	862	877	779	1,034	27,071	29,107	28,644	29,555	43,038

[1] Calculated using population of states reporting data.

Source: Franklin Associates, a Division of ERG, Prairie Village, KS, *Municipal Solid Waste in the United States: 2001 Facts and Figures.* Prepared for the U.S. Environmental Protection Agency. Also in *Biocycle Magazine.*

Geography and Environment **223**

No. 366. Toxic Chemical Releases and Transfers by Media: 1988 to 2001

[In millions of pounds (3,153.7 represents 3,153,700,000), except as indicated. Based on reports filed as required by section 313 of the Emergency Planning and Community Right-to-Know Act (EPCRA, or Title III of the Superfund Amendments and Reauthorization Act of 1986), Public Law 99-499. Owners and operators of facilities that are classified within Standard Classification Code groups 20 through 39, have 10 or more full-time employees, and that manufacture, process, or otherwise uses any listed toxic chemical in quantities greater than the established threshold in the course of a calendar year are covered and required to report]

Media	Core chemicals [1]				
	1988	1998	1999	2000	2001
Total facilities reporting	19,610	19,294	18,881	18,692	17,773
Total releases.	**3,153.7**	**1,873.0**	**1,709.8**	**1,639.0**	**1,435.7**
On-site releases	2,760.5	1,481.8	1,307.2	1,212.7	995.8
Air emissions	2,177.8	1,017.5	863.2	802.5	649.5
Surface water	41.7	18.5	15.5	15.4	14.6
Underground injection	161.9	114.4	109.1	111.1	94.9
Releases to land	379.1	331.4	319.3	283.6	236.7
Off-site releases	393.2	391.2	402.6	426.4	439.9
Total transfers offsite for further waste management	598.0	2,482.8	2,605.6	2,613.6	2,401.4
Tranfers to recycling	(NA)	1,684.2	1,796.3	1,794.2	1,624.1
Transfers to energy recovery.	(NA)	437.0	472.2	485.3	447.1
Transfers to treatment.	323.8	212.9	193.8	187.8	196.9
Transfers to POTW's [2]	231.6	148.1	143.2	145.5	131.8
Other off-site transfers	42.6	0.7	0.1	0.9	1.5
Total production-related waste managed. . .	(NA)	17,043.4	17,557.1	21,999.7	16,316.6
Recycled on-site.	(NA)	5,820.3	5,672.6	6,643.9	5,676.7
Recycled off-site	(NA)	1,746.8	1,845.0	1,849.3	1,642.4
Energy recovery on-site	(NA)	2,467.5	2,476.2	2,521.9	2,317.6
Energy recovery off-site	(NA)	447.8	469.9	489.5	445.2
Treated on-site.	(NA)	4,431.5	5,068.7	8,566.2	4,499.4
Treated off-site.	(NA)	383.7	348.1	346.3	342.5
Quantity released on- and off-site	(NA)	1,745.8	1,676.5	1,582.5	1,392.9

NA Not available.   [1] Chemicals covered for all reporting years. Excludes chemicals removed from the list, those added in 1990, 1994, and 1995, and aluminum oxide, ammonia, hydrochloric acid, PBT chemicals, sulfuric acid, vanadium and vanadium compounds.   [2] POTW (Publicly Owned Treatment Work) is a wastewater treatment facility that is owned by a state or municipality.

No. 367. Toxic Chemical Releases by Industry: 2001

[In millions of pounds (6,158.8 represents 6,158,000,000), except as indicated. "Original Industries" include owners and operators. Covers facilities that are classified within Standard Classification Code groups 20 through 39,10,12,49, 5169, 5171, and 4953/7169 that have 10 or more full-time employees, and that manufacture, process, or otherwise uses any listed toxic chemical in quantities greater than the established threshold in the course of a calendar year are covered and required to report]

Industry	1987 SIC[1] code	Total facilities (number)	Total on and off-site releases	On-site release				Off-site releases/ transfers to disposal
				Total	Air emissions	Surface water discharges	Other [2]	
Total [3]	**(X)**	**24,896**	**6,158.0**	**5,580.3**	**1,679.4**	**220.8**	**3,680.1**	**577.7**
Metal mining	10	89	2,782.6	2,782.0	2.9	0.4	2,778.7	0.5
Coal mining	12	88	16.1	16.1	0.8	0.8	14.6	-
Food and kindred products	20	1,688	125.1	118.9	56.1	55.2	7.6	6.2
Tobacco products	21	31	3.6	3.2	2.5	0.5	0.2	0.3
Textile mill products	22	289	7.0	6.2	5.7	0.2	0.3	0.7
Apparel and other textile products	23	16	0.4	0.3	0.3	-	-	0.1
Lumber and wood products	24	1,006	31.4	30.9	30.5	-	0.4	0.5
Furniture and fixtures	25	282	8.0	7.8	7.8	-	-	0.2
Paper and allied products	26	507	195.7	189.9	157.2	16.5	16.2	5.8
Printing and publishing	27	231	19.7	19.3	19.3	-	-	0.4
Chemical and allied products.	28	3,618	582.6	501.3	227.8	57.6	215.9	81.3
Petroleum and coal products.	29	542	71.4	68.1	48.2	17.1	2.8	3.3
Rubber and misc. plastic products	30	1,822	88.5	78.1	77.1	0.1	0.9	10.5
Leather and leather products.	31	60	2.6	1.3	1.2	0.1	-	1.3
Stone, clay, glass products	32	1,027	40.5	35.4	31.3	0.2	4.0	5.1
Primary metal industries	33	1,941	558.6	286.8	57.6	44.7	184.5	271.8
Fabricated metals products	34	2,959	64.0	42.8	40.4	1.7	0.6	21.2
Industrial machinery and equipment	35	1,143	15.4	10.7	8.3	-	2.5	4.6
Electronic, electric equipment	36	1,831	23.9	16.4	12.7	2.9	0.7	7.6
Transportation equipment	37	1,348	80.6	67.7	66.7	0.2	0.8	13.0
Instruments and related products	38	375	9.4	8.6	7.2	1.4	-	0.8
Miscellaneous	39	312	8.4	6.8	6.8	-	-	1.6
Electric utilities	49	732	1,062.2	989.2	717.6	3.5	268.1	73.1
Chemical wholesalers	5169	475	1.5	1.3	1.3	-	-	0.2
Petroleum bulk terminals	5171	596	21.3	21.2	21.2	-	-	0.2
RCRA/solvent recovery	4953/7369	223	219.9	168.4	1.0	-	167.4	51.4

- Represents or rounds to zero.   X Not applicable.   [1] Standard Industrial Classification, see text, Section 12, Labor Force.   [2] Includes underground injection for Class I and Class II to V wells and land releases.   [3] Includes industries with no specific industry identified, not shown separately.

Source of Tables 366 and 367: U.S. Environmental Protection Agency, Toxics Release Inventory, annual.

224   Geography and Environment

No. 368. Toxic Chemical Releases by State: 1988 to 2001

[In millions of pounds (3,153.7 represents 3,153,700,000). Excludes delisted chemicals, chemicals added in 1990, 1994, and 1995, and aluminum oxide, ammonia, hydorchloric acid, PBT chemicals, sulfuric acid, vanadium, and vanadium compounds. See headnote, Table 366]

State and outlying area	Core chemicals 1988	1998	1999	2000	2001	State and outlying area	Core chemicals 1988	1998	1999	2000	2001
Total	3,153.7	1,873.0	1,709.8	1,639.0	1,435.7	Montana	33.5	44.2	45.7	46.6	18.2
						Nebraska.	16.7	9.9	8.6	10.3	12.2
United States.	3,138.3	1,865.5	1,704.2	1,633.3	1,430.1	Nevada	2.3	3.7	5.4	4.1	3.2
						New Hampshire .	13.8	2.3	2.4	2.3	1.2
Alabama	109.5	75.9	73.6	66.7	61.0	New Jersey	46.7	11.3	11.3	11.3	26.8
Alaska.	3.7	0.3	0.2	0.3	0.5	New Mexico. . . .	29.3	23.3	19.6	0.5	0.6
Arizona	61.5	50.9	47.7	38.7	52.7	New York.	98.5	21.7	18.8	17.5	13.6
Arkansas	40.8	38.6	38.8	44.8	33.5	North Carolina . .	124.0	49.2	46.7	40.8	35.8
California	107.9	23.9	23.2	23.4	16.7	North Dakota . . .	1.2	1.2	1.1	0.8	0.9
Colorado	15.4	3.1	3.0	2.8	2.5	Ohio	200.2	125.8	116.1	108.4	90.5
Connecticut . . .	37.9	6.0	4.5	4.5	3.6	Oklahoma	30.5	13.9	13.6	13.6	12.3
Delaware	8.7	5.8	5.2	5.6	5.2	Oregon	21.2	27.3	24.9	24.0	21.9
DC	-	(Z)	(Z)	(Z)	0.0	Pennsylvania . . .	133.7	82.6	81.3	88.0	97.5
Florida.	32.7	30.5	29.5	₋31.8	26.3	Rhode Island . . .	7.8	1.6	1.2	1.1	0.9
Georgia	85.2	47.5	46.4	44.8	35.3	South Carolina . .	65.8	50.2	55.8	51.6	52.0
Hawaii.	0.8	0.3	0.3	0.4	0.4	South Dakota . . .	2.4	1.4	1.1	1.2	1.1
Idaho	7.3	12.7	14.6	13.0	8.6	Tennessee	126.0	84.8	88.5	81.2	62.8
Illinois	137.6	82.4	79.3	77.2	67.8	Texas	317.8	172.8	169.0	150.9	130.2
Indiana	181.0	190.8	109.7	104.0	106.5	Utah	122.2	93.3	77.2	101.5	48.4
Iowa	42.3	24.4	25.0	24.8	19.2	Vermont	1.7	0.2	0.2	0.1	0.1
Kansas	30.2	17.5	20.1	16.8	12.8	Virginia	112.2	39.6	39.4	34.6	31.6
Kentucky	64.7	31.1	31.1	27.8	28.6	Washington	30.5	24.1	17.3	16.6	11.7
Louisiana	128.7	91.6	78.9	80.0	70.3	West Virginia . . .	39.3	16.3	11.8	10.2	9.0
Maine	15.5	6.6	5.9	6.3	5.0	Wisconsin	61.1	33.7	31.7	29.0	25.5
Maryland	19.6	8.7	9.2	10.6	7.7	Wyoming	2.0	1.2	1.3	1.2	0.8
Massachusetts . .	32.1	6.5	4.9	4.8	4.5						
Michigan	139.2	73.0	63.6	52.4	59.9	American Samoa.	-	-	-	-	-
Minnesota	55.3	14.6	14.3	15.3	13.5	Guam	-	-	-	-	-
Mississippi	58.5	42.7	41.5	43.1	36.3	Puerto Rico	12.9	6.6	5.2	5.3	4.8
Missouri.	82.2	44.3	43.4	46.0	43.0	Virgin Island . . .	2.6	0.9	0.5	0.4	0.8

- Represents zero. Z Less than 50,000.

Source: U.S. Environmental Protection Agency, *Toxics Release Inventory*, annual. See also <http://www.epa.gov/tri/tri00/pdr /2000pdr.pdf> (released May 2002).

No. 369. Hazardous Waste Sites on the National Priority List by State and Outlying Area: 2003

[As of December 31. Includes both proposed and final sites listed on the National Priorities List for the Superfund program as authorized by the Comprehensive Environmental Response, Compensation, and Liability Act of 1980 and the Superfund Amendments and Reauthorization Act of 1986]

State and outlying area	Total sites	Rank	Per-cent distri-bution	Fed-eral	Non-Fed-eral	State and outlying area	Total sites	Rank	Per-cent distri-bution	Fed-eral	Non-Fed-eral
Total	1,296	(X)	(X)	164	1,132	Montana	15	24	1.2	-	15
						Nebraska	11	38	0.9	1	10
United States . . .	1,283	(X)	100.0	163	1,120	Nevada	1	49	0.1	-	1
						New Hampshire	20	19	1.6	1	19
Alabama.	15	24	1.2	3	12	New Jersey.	116	1	9.0	8	108
Alaska.	6	44	0.5	5	1	New Mexico	12	34	0.9	1	11
Arizona.	9	40	0.7	2	7	New York	91	4	7.1	4	87
Arkansas	11	37	0.9	-	11	North Carolina	29	15	2.3	2	27
California	98	2	7.6	24	74	North Dakota	-	50	-	-	-
Colorado.	18	22	1.4	3	15	Ohio	35	11	2.7	5	30
Connecticut.	16	23	1.2	1	15	Oklahoma	11	39	0.9	1	10
Delaware	15	24	1.2	1	14	Oregon.	12	35	0.9	2	10
District of Columbia .	1	(X)	0.1	1	-	Pennsylvania.	95	3	7.4	6	89
Florida	52	6	4.1	6	46	Rhode Island.	12	36	0.9	2	10
Georgia	15	24	1.2	2	13	South Carolina. . . .	25	17	1.9	2	23
Hawaii	3	46	0.2	2	1	South Dakota	2	47	0.2	1	1
Idaho	9	41	0.7	2	7	Tennessee	13	31	1.0	4	9
Illinois	45	8	3.5	5	40	Texas.	45	9	3.5	4	41
Indiana.	29	14	2.3	-	29	Utah	19	21	1.5	4	15
Iowa	14	29	1.1	1	13	Vermont	9	42	0.7	-	9
Kansas.	12	32	0.9	2	10	Virginia.	30	13	2.3	11	19
Kentucky.	14	30	1.1	1	13	Washington.	47	7	3.7	14	33
Louisiana	15	24	1.2	1	14	West Virginia	9	43	0.7	2	7
Maine.	12	33	0.9	3	9	Wisconsin.	40	10	3.1	-	40
Maryland	19	20	1.5	9	10	Wyoming	2	47	0.2	1	1
Massachusetts. . . .	32	12	2.5	7	25						
Michigan.	69	5	5.4	1	68	Guam	2	(X)	(X)	1	1
Minnesota.	24	18	1.9	2	22	Puerto Rico.	9	(X)	(X)	-	9
Mississippi	4	45	0.3	-	4	Virgin Islands.	2	(X)	(X)	-	2
Missouri	25	16	1.9	3	22						

- Represents zero.

Source: U.S. Environmental Protection Agency, *Supplementary Materials: National Priorities List, Proposed Rule*, December 2003.

No. 370. Pollution Abatement Capital Expenditures and Operating Costs by Media and Industry: 1999

[In millions of dollars. (5,809.9 represents 5,809,900,000). Based on probability sample of about 21,000 manufacturing, mining, and electric utility plants. Pollution abatement is the reduction of elimination of pollution that is created by the production process and has the potential to produce undesirable environmental and/or health effects. Capital expenditures include installation and retrofit that occurred for separately identifiable methods, techniques, or process technologies installed exclusively for the purpose of removing pollutants. Operating costs include all costs for operating and maintaining all pollution abatement technology]

Industry	NAICS code [1]	Pollution abatement capital expenditures				Pollution abatement operating costs			
		Total [2]	Air	Water	Solid waste	Total [2]	Air	Water	Solid waste
All industries	(X)	5,809.9	3,463.7	1,801.9	361.9	11,864.4	5,069.1	4,586.5	2,013.3
Mining	21	277.3	79.0	157.8	36.9	458.9	180.7	208.8	67.1
Oil & gas extraction	211	116.2	20.6	63.5	32.1	146.9	58.2	72.1	16.0
Mining (except oil & gas)	212	159.5	57.6	93.6	4.7	305.1	121.8	131.5	50.2
Support activities for mining	213	1.6	0.8	0.7	0.1	6.9	0.7	5.3	0.8
Electric power generation	22111	1,145.1	1,071.1	55.1	17.1	1,163.8	910.1	99.9	127.1
Manufacturing	31-33	4,387.3	2,313.4	1,588.9	307.9	10,240.3	3,977.5	4,277.4	1,818.8
Food	311	369.9	70.1	281.0	18.5	924.3	105.2	699.3	113.9
Beverage and tobacco product	312	17.1	4.4	9.0	3.5	66.1	12.2	47.4	(D)
Textile mills	313	37.1	21.3	7.5	8.2	105.0	18.6	72.4	13.6
Textile product mills	314	7.2	(D)	(D)	(D)	4.9	(D)	2.4	(D)
Apparel	315	(Z)	(D)	(D)	(D)	1.8	(D)	1.3	(D)
Leather and allied product	316	7.3	(D)	6.4	(D)	19.6	(D)	14.5	3.5
Wood product	321	82.1	65.6	12.3	3.9	134.9	86.3	26.2	19.7
Paper	322	611.9	252.6	261.3	25.5	945.6	264.4	462.0	190.6
Printing and related support activities	323	35.2	31.4	2.4	1.3	80.3	56.0	8.2	15.2
Petroleum and coal products	324	488.1	349.0	104.1	23.8	1,697.9	1,206.2	344.1	136.1
Chemicals	325	990.9	488.2	335.4	133.9	2,808.0	829.3	1,289.7	633.2
Plastics and rubber products	326	102.6	92.0	5.7	4.7	164.7	86.0	30.3	46.8
Nonmetallic mineral product	327	232.6	195.1	16.2	20.1	281.5	154.6	50.2	61.7
Primary metal	331	605.7	481.2	93.6	22.8	1,543.9	755.5	571.8	205.0
Fabricated metal product	332	283.3	38.2	232.4	9.7	405.3	89.2	167.2	137.0
Machinery	333	163.3	26.3	92.5	3.0	97.7	25.6	41.2	28.8
Computer and electronic product	334	138.0	58.5	67.5	11.7	325.4	59.5	208.6	50.6
Elect. equip., appliance, & component	335	33.7	20.8	10.6	2.2	97.0	40.7	32.2	22.7
Transportation equipment	336	134.7	74.8	46.4	11.0	454.4	152.0	190.6	104.1
Furniture and related product	337	35.0	31.3	(D)	1.8	39.1	17.7	7.0	13.6
Miscellaneous	339	11.5	5.5	3.9	1.4	42.8	16.5	10.8	13.6

Z Less than $50,000. D Withheld to avoid disclosing data for individual companies. [1] North American Industry Classification System, 1997; see text, Section 15. [2] Includes expenditures and cost for multimedia, not shown separately.

No. 371. Pollution Abatement Capital Expenditures and Operating Costs by Media and State: 1999

[Represents based on probability sample of about 21,000 manufacturing, mining, and electric utility plants. Pollution abatement is the reduction of elimination of pollution that is created by the production process and has the potential to produce undesirable environmental and/or health effects. Capital expenditures include installation and retrofit that occurred for separately identifiable methods, techniques, or process technologies installed exclusively for the purpose of removing pollutants. Operating costs include all costs for operating and maintaining all pollution abatement technology]

State	Pollution abatement capital expenditures			Pollution abatement operating costs		State	Pollution abatement capital expenditures			Pollution abatement operating costs	
	Expenditures, total (mil. dol.)	Percent for air pollutants	Percent for hazardous materials	Expenditures, total (mil. dol.)	Percent for air pollutants		Expenditures, total (mil. dol.)	Percent for air pollutants	Percent for hazardous materials	Expenditures, total (mil. dol.)	Percent for air pollutants
US [1]	5,809.9	59.6	22.6	11,864.4	42.7	MT	4.6	87.0	-	21.3	55.4
AL	166.0	66.4	25.1	263.0	36.6	NE	18.5	53.0	20.0	39.5	17.2
AK	63.7	17.4	0.2	34.4	37.8	NV	11.0	57.3	52.7	44.9	47.9
AZ	58.4	67.8	68.0	70.9	61.4	NH	204.6	0.4	0.3	35.6	21.6
AR	91.9	31.1	12.3	183.8	36.5	NJ	57.0	78.4	24.6	165.1	32.1
CA	253.5	46.2	16.8	830.1	55.8	NM	29.4	44.2	25.5	100.7	60.3
CO	19.9	37.2	21.6	49.9	33.3	NY	160.6	76.6	78.3	310.0	51.3
CT	45.7	50.5	54.3	53.0	18.5	NC	58.4	66.1	45.2	267.7	32.4
DE	87.0	96.6	5.6	88.8	58.8	ND	17.2	79.7	1.2	64.4	70.0
FL	127.0	29.8	15.0	410.2	58.8	OH	271.5	57.3	11.6	947.9	57.2
GA	210.8	46.7	26.9	241.0	31.2	OK	34.0	90.6	44.1	78.8	42.3
HI	12.5	16.0	-	5.0	28.0	OR	61.3	45.2	8.6	80.0	44.3
ID	16.9	36.1	17.8	54.4	28.5	PA	422.2	87.1	7.2	534.0	39.6
IL	172.2	43.5	19.0	511.5	36.1	RI	3.1	22.6	74.2	9.4	(D)
IN	128.5	76.3	44.6	638.4	43.6						
IA	42.5	46.8	3.1	138.0	26.7	SC	382.7	92.7	6.3	224.9	38.3
KS	40.8	54.2	36.5	145.7	9.7	SD	3.0	36.7	3.3	8.0	27.5
KY	145.5	69.5	33.8	259.8	40.9	TN	156.6	63.5	11.0	331.6	30.4
LA	228.8	43.6	29.9	522.7	39.7	TX	617.6	58.0	38.3	1,679.2	45.9
ME	30.2	8.6	0.7	59.2	22.0	UT	21.0	79.0	19.5	55.5	48.5
MD	89.4	78.7	6.0	118.5	31.5	VT	28.5	54.7	22.5	10.9	(D)
MA	63.6	54.4	52.5	133.4	23.8	VA	114.1	51.5	8.9	318.5	46.0
MI	160.1	62.3	23.2	394.0	35.0	WA	144.5	71.5	13.4	254.9	42.4
MN	120.4	41.8	14.4	293.6	44.2	WV	107.9	76.8	26.4	205.6	28.6
MS	71.9	43.4	6.0	151.1	46.9	WI	163.1	18.4	5.5	196.0	18.8
MO	209.4	84.5	54.7	180.0	45.1	WY	60.8	98.2	-	41.6	66.8

- Represents zero. D Withheld to avoid disclosing data for individual companies. [1] Includes offshore, not shown separately.

Source of Tables 370 and 371: U.S. Census Bureau, Current Industrial Reports, *Pollution Abatement Costs and Expenditures: 1999,* Series MA200(99).

226 Geography and Environment

No. 372. Environmental Industry—Revenues and Employment, by Industry Segment: 1990 to 2003

[150.7 represents $150,700,000,000. Covers approximately 59,000 private and public companies engaged in environmental activities]

Industry segment	Revenue (bil. dol.)				Employment (1,000)			
	1990	1995	2000	2003	1990	1995	2000	2003
Industry total	150.7	183.7	211.0	227.3	1,215.2	1,382.8	1,471.3	1,491.6
Analytical services [1]	2.1	1.8	1.8	1.8	24.1	21.2	20.2	19.9
Wastewater treatment works [2]	19.8	23.4	27.8	30.4	88.8	101.5	114.8	120.4
Solid waste management [3] . . . ₁	26.1	32.5	39.4	43.2	205.5	243.4	266.3	276.0
Hazardous waste management [4]	6.3	6.2	5.1	4.5	53.8	52.5	41.8	38.3
Remediation/industrial services	11.1	11.0	11.5	12.4	133.5	125.2	113.9	112.0
Consulting and engineering.	12.5	15.5	17.4	19.1	147.1	180.3	184.0	190.4
Water equipment and chemicals	13.5	16.5	19.8	21.4	92.7	110.3	130.5	133.5
Instrument manufacturing . . . ₁.	2.0	3.0	3.6	4.0	18.0	26.2	29.4	30.5
Air pollution control equipment [5].	11.1	15.3	19.1	18.5	81.5	109.1	129.6	127.2
Waste management equipment [6]	8.7	9.8	9.9	9.8	69.6	75.5	74.6	70.4
Process and prevention technology	0.4	0.8	1.2	1.4	9.3	19.5	29.0	27.1
Water utilities [7] . . ₁	19.8	25.3	29.9	32.6	98.5	118.2	130.0	135.0
Resource recovery [8]	13.1	16.9	16.0	15.3	142.9	136.0	127.2	114.5
Clean energy systems and power.	4.3	5.6	8.6	13.0	49.9	63.9	80.0	96.4

[1] Covers environmental laboratory testing and services. [2] Mostly revenues collected by municipal entities. [3] Covers such activities as collection, transportation, transfer stations, disposal, landfill ownership and management for solid waste. [4] Transportation and disposal of hazardous, medical and nuclear waste. [5] Includes stationery and mobile sources. [6] Includes vehicles, containers, liners, processing and remediation equipment. [7] Revenues generated from the sale of water. [8] Revenues generated from the sale of recovered metals, paper, plastic, etc.

Source: Environmental Business International, Inc., San Diego, CA, *Environmental Business Journal*, monthly (copyright).

No. 373. Threatened and Endangered Wildlife and Plant Species— Number: 2004

[As of April. Endangered species: One in danger of becoming extinct throughout all or a significant part of its natural range. Threatened species: One likely to become endangered in the foreseeable future]

Item	Mammals	Birds	Reptiles	Amphibians	Fishes	Snails	Clams	Crustaceans	Insects	Arachnids	Plants
Total listings	346	272	115	30	125	33	72	21	48	12	747
Endangered species, total.	320	252	78	20	82	22	64	18	39	12	598
United States	69	77	14	12	71	21	62	18	35	12	597
Foreign	251	175	64	8	11	1	2	-	4	-	1
Threatened species, total.	26	20	37	10	43	11	8	3	9	-	149
United States	9	14	22	9	43	11	8	3	9	-	147
Foreign	17	6	15	1	-	-	-	-	-	-	2

- Represents zero.

Source: U.S. Fish and Wildlife Service, *Endangered Species Bulletin*, bimonthly; and <http://ecos.fws.gov/tesspublic/TESSBoxscore> (released 14 April 2004).

No. 374. Tornadoes, Floods, Tropical Storms, and Lightning: 1993 to 2003

Weather type	1993	1994	1995	1996	1997	1998	1999	2000	2001	2002	2003, prel.
Tornadoes:[1]											
Lives lost.	33	69	30	26	67	130	94	41	40	55	54
Injuries	(NA)	(NA)	650	705	1,033	1,868	1,842	882	743	968	1,087
Property loss (mil. dol.)	(NA)	(NA)	410.8	719.6	730.7	1,714.2	1,989.9	423.6	630.1	801.3	1,263.2
Floods and flash floods:											
Lives lost.	103	91	80	131	118	136	68	38	48	49	85
Injuries	(NA)	(NA)	57	95	525	6,440	301	47	277	88	65
Property loss (mil. dol.)	(NA)	(NA)	1,250.5	2,120.7	6,910.6	2,324.8	1,420.7	1,255.1	1,220.3	655.0	2,540.9
North Atlantic tropical storms and hurricanes [2]	8	7	19	13	7	14	12	15	15	12	(NA)
Number of hurricanes reaching U.S. mainland	1	-	2	2	1	3	3	-	-	1	(NA)
Direct deaths on U.S. mainland .	2	9	17	37	1	9	19		24	51	14
Property loss in U.S. (mil.dol.) . .	57.0	973.0	5,932.3	1,436.1	667.6	3,546.6	4,190.1	8.1	5,187.8	1,104.4	1,879.5
Lightning:											
Deaths	43	69	85	52	42	44	46	51	44	51	44
Injuries	295	577	433	309	306	283	243	364	371	256	237

- Represents zero. NA Not available. [1] Source: U.S. National Weather Service, Internet site <http://www.spc.noaa.gov /climo/torn/monthlytornstats.html> (accessed 14 April 2004). A violent, rotating column of air descending from a cumulonimbus cloud in the form of a tubular- or funnel-shaped cloud, usually characterized by movements along a narrow path and wind speeds from 100 to over 300 miles per hour. Also known as a "twister" or "waterspout." [2] Source: National Hurricane Center (NHC), Coral Gables, FL, unpublished data. For data on individual hurricanes, see the NHC web site at <http://www.nhc.noaa.gov/>. Tropical storms have winds of 39 to 73 miles per hour; hurricanes have winds of 74 miles per hour or higher.

Source: Except as noted, U.S. National Oceanic and Atmospheric Administration (NOAA), *Storm Data*, monthly. See also NOAA website at <http://www.noaa.gov/om/hazstats.shtml> and <http://www.nws.noaa.gov/om/severeweather/sum03.pdf> (released 03 March 2004).

Geography and Environment 227

No. 375. Major U.S. Weather Disasters: 1990 to 2003

[5.0 represents $5,000,000,000. Covers only weather related disasters costing $1 billion or more]

Event	Description	Time period	Esti-mated cost (bil. dol.)	Deaths
Southern California wildfires..........	Dry weather, high winds, and resulting wildfires in southern CA burned 743,000 acres & destroyed 3700 homes	Oct.-early Nov. 2003	2.5	22
Hurricane Isabel......	Category 2 hurricane makes landfall in eastern NC, causing damage along coasts of NC, VA, and MD with wind damage and flooding in NC, VA, MD, DE, WV, NJ, NY and PA....	September 2003	over 4	47
Midwest severe storms and tornadoes	Numerous tornadoes over the midwest, MS River valley, and OH/TN River valleys with record 400 tornadoes in one week	Early May 2003	over 3.1	41
Storms and hail	Sever storms and large hail over southern plains, lower MS River valley, and TX	Early April 2003	over 1.6	-
Widespread drought ...	Moderate to extreme drought over large portions of 30 states	Spring to fall 2002	over 10	-
Western fire season ...	Major fires over 11 western states from Rockies to west coast	Spring to fall 2002	over 2	21
Tropical Storm Allison ..	Tropical storm produced rainfall and severe flooding in coastal portions of TX & LA & damage in MS, FL, VA. and PA ..	June 2001	5.0	43
Midwest and Ohio Valley hail and tornadoes ...	Storms, tornadoes, and hail in TX, OK, KS, NE, IA, MO, IL, IN, WI, MI, OH, KY, and PA	April 2001	1.7	3
Southern drought/heat wave	Severe drought and heat over south-central and southeast states cause significant losses in agriculture and related industries	Spring-summer 2000	over 4.0	140
Western fire season ...	Severe fire season in western states	Spring-summer 2000	over 2.0	-
Hurricane Floyd	Category 2 hurricane in NC, causing severe flooding in NC and some flooding in SC, VA, MD, PA, NY, NJ, DE, RI, CT, MA, and VT.............................	September 1999	6.0	75
Drought/heat wave	Drought/heatwave over eastern U.S.	Summer 1999	1.0	256
Oklahoma-Kansas tornadoes	Category F4-F5 tornados hit OK, KS, TX, and TN	May 1999	1.0	55
Arkansas-Tennessee tornados	Two outbreaks of tornadoes in 6-day period	January 1999	1.3	31
Texas flooding	Severe flooding in southeast Texas from 2 heavy rain events with 10-20 in. totals............................	Oct.-Nov. 1998	1.0	31
Hurricane Georges	Category 2 hurricane in Puerto Rico, Florida Keys, and Gulf coasts of LA, MS, AL, and FL.	September 1998	3-4	16
Hurricane Bonnie	Category 3 hurricane in eastern NC and VA	August 1998	1.0	2
Southern drought/heat wave	Severe drought and heat wave from TX/OK to the Carolinas	Summer 1998	6.0	200
Minnesota severe storms/hail.........	Very damaging severe thunderstorms with large hail over wide areas of Minnesota........................	May 1998	1.5	1
Southeast severe weather..........	Tornadoes and flooding related to strong El Nino in the southeast	Winter/Spring 1998	1.0	Over 130
Northeast ice storm....	Intense ice storm hits ME, NH, VT, and NY	January 1998	1.4	16
Northern plains flooding.	Severe flooding in Dakotas and Minnesota due to heavy spring snowmelt	April-May 1997	2.0	11
MS and OH valleys flooding and tornadoes.	Tornadoes and severe flooding hit the states of AR, MO, MS, TN, IL, IN, KY, OH, and WV	March 1997	1.0	67
West Coast flooding ...	Flooding from rains and snowmelt in CA, WA, OR, ID, NV, & MT	Dec. 1996-Jan. 1997	2-3	36
Hurricane Fran	Category 3 hurricane in NC and VA................	Sept. 1996	5.0	37
Southern Plains severe drought	Drought in agricultural areas of TX & OK	Fall 1995-summer 1996	Over 4	(NA)
Pacific Northwest severe flooding...........	Flooding from heavy rain & snowmelt in OR, WA, ID, and MT.	Feb. 1996	1.0	9
Blizzard of '96 followed . by flooding.........	Heavy snowstorm followed by severe flooding in Appalachians, Mid-Atlantic, and Northeast.	Jan. 1996	3.0	187
Hurricane Opal.......	Category 3 hurricane in FL, AL, parts of GA, TN, & Carolinas.	Oct. 1995	Over 3	27
Hurricane Marilyn	Category 2 hurricane in Virgin Islands	Sept. 1995	2.1	13
TX/OK/LA/MS severe weather and flooding ..	Flooding, hail, & tornadoes across TX, OK, parts of LA, MS, Dallas & New Orleans hardest hit	May 1995	5-6	32
California flooding.....	Flooding from frequent winter storms across much of CA .	Jan.-Mar. 1995	3.0	27
Western Fire Season...	Severe fire season in western states due to dry weather ..	Summer-Fall 1994	1.0	(NA)
Texas flooding	Flooding from torrential rain & thunderstorms across southeast TX.	Oct. 1994	1.0	19
Tropical Storm Alberto ..	Flooding due to 10 to 25 inch rain across GA, AL, part of FL	July 1994	1.0	32
Southeast ice storm ...	Intense ice storm in pts of TX, OK, AR, LA, MS, AL, TN, GA, SC, NC, & VA	Feb. 1994	3.0	9
California wildfires.....	Out-of-control wildfires over southern CA	Fall 1993	1.0	4
Midwest flooding......	Extreme flooding across central U.S.	Summer 1993	15-20	48
Drought/heat wave	Extreme drought/heatwave across southeastern U.S.	Summer 1993	1.0	(NA)
Storm/blizzard	"Storm of the Century" hits entire eastern seaboard. ...	Mar. 1993	3-6	270
Nor'easter of 1992	Slow-moving storm batters northeast U.S. coast, New England.	Dec. 1992	1-2	19
Hurricane Iniki	Category 4 hurricane hit Hawaiian island of Kauai	Sept. 1992	1.8	7
Hurricane Andrew.....	Category 4 hurricane hit FL & LA	Aug. 1992	27.0	58
Oakland Firestorm	Oakland, CA firestorm due to low humidity & high winds .	Oct. 1991	1.5	25
Hurricane Bob	Category 2 hurricane—mainly coastal NC, Long Island, & New England	Aug. 1991	1.5	18
TX/OK/LA/AR Flooding .	Torrential rains cause flooding along Trinity, Red, and Arkansas rivers	May 1990	1.0	13

- Represents zero.   NA Not available or not reported. $del

Source: U.S. National Oceanic and Atmospheric Administration, National Climatic Data Center, *"Billion Dollar U.S. Weather Disasters, 1980-2003"* (release date: March 2, 2004). See also <http://www.ncdc.noaa.gov/oa/reports/billionz.html#TOP> (released 02 March 2004).

No. 376. Highest and Lowest Temperatures by State Through 2000

State	Highest temperatures			Lowest temperatures		
	Station	Tempera-ture (F)	Date	Station	Tempera-ture (F)	Date
U.S.	Greenland Ranch, CA. .	134	Jul. 10, 1913	Prospect Creek, AK . . .	-80	Jan. 23, 1971
AL.	Centerville	112	Sep. 5, 1925	New Market	-27	Jan. 30, 1966
AK.	Fort Yukon	100	[1]Jun. 27, 1915	Prospect Creek Camp . .	-80	Jan. 23, 1971
AZ.	Lake Havasu City	128	Jun. 29, 1994	Hawley Lake	-40	Jan. 7, 1971
AR.	Ozark	120	Aug. 10, 1936	Pond.	-29	Feb. 13, 1905
CA.	Greenland Ranch	134	Jul. 10, 1913	Boca.	-45	Jan. 20, 1937
CO	Bennett	118	Jul. 11, 1888	Maybell	-61	Feb. 1, 1985
CT.	Danbury	106	Jul. 15, 1995	Falls Village	-32	Feb. 16, 1943
DE.	Millsboro	110	Jul. 21, 1930	Millsboro	-17	Jan. 17, 1893
FL.	Monticello	109	Jun. 29, 1931	Tallahassee	-2	Feb. 13, 1899
GA	Greenville	112	Aug. 20, 1983	CCC Camp F-16.	-17	[1]Jan. 27, 1940
HI	Pahala	100	Apr. 27, 1931	Mauna Kea Obs. 111.2. .	12	May 17, 1979
ID	Orofino	118	Jul. 28, 1934	Island Park Dam	-60	Jan. 18, 1943
IL	East St. Louis.	117	Jul. 14, 1954	Congerville.	-36	Jan. 5, 1999
IN	Collegeville	116	Jul. 14, 1936	New Whiteland	-36	Jan. 19, 1994
IA	Keokuk	118	Jul. 20, 1934	Elkader	-47	[2]Feb. 3, 1996
KS.	Alton (near)	121	[2]Jul. 24, 1936	Lebanon	-40	Feb. 13, 1905
KY.	Greensburg	114	Jul. 28, 1930	Shelbyville	-37	Jan. 19, 1994
LA.	Plain Dealing	114	Aug. 10, 1936	Minden	-16	Feb. 13, 1899
ME	North Bridgton	105	[2]Jul. 10, 1911	Van Buren	-48	Jan. 19, 1925
MD	Cumberland & Frederick.	109	[2]Jul. 10, 1936	Oakland	-40	Jan. 13, 1912
MA	New Bedford & Chester .	107	Aug. 2, 1975	Chester.	-35	Jan. 12, 1981
MI	Mio.	112	Jul. 13, 1936	Vanderbilt	-51	Feb. 9, 1934
MN	Moorhead	114	[2]Jul. 6, 1936	Tower	-60	Feb. 2, 1996
MS	Holly Springs	115	Jul. 29, 1930	Corinth	-19	Jan. 30, 1966
MO	Warsaw & Union	118	[2]Jul. 14, 1954	Warsaw.	-40	Feb. 13, 1905
MT	Medicine Lake	117	Jul. 5, 1937	Rogers Pass	-70	Jan. 20, 1954
NE.	Minden	118	[2]Jul. 24, 1936	Camp Clarke	-47	Feb. 12, 1899
NV.	Laughlin	125	Jun. 29, 1994	San Jacinto	-50	Jan. 8, 1937
NH	Nashua	106	Jul. 4, 1911	Mt. Washington.	-47	Jan. 29, 1934
NJ.	Runyon	110	Jul. 10, 1936	River Vale	-34	Jan. 5, 1904
NM	Waste Isolat Pilot Plt . . .	122	Jun. 27, 1994	Gavilan	-50	Feb. 1, 1951
NY.	Troy	108	Jul. 22, 1926	Old Forge	-52	[2]Feb. 18, 1979
NC	Fayetteville.	110	Aug. 21, 1983	Mt. Mitchell	-34	Jan. 21, 1985
ND	Steele.	121	Jul. 6, 1936	Parshall	-60	Feb. 15, 1936
OH	Gallipolis (near).	113	[2]Jul. 21, 1934	Milligan	-39	Feb. 10, 1899
OK	Tipton	120	[2]Jun. 27, 1994	Watts	-27	Jan. 18, 1930
OR	Pendleton	119	Aug. 10, 1898	Seneca	-54	[2]Feb. 10, 1933
PA.	Phoenixville.	111	[2]Jul. 10, 1936	Smethport	-42	[1]Jan. 5, 1904
RI	Providence.	104	Aug. 2, 1975	Kingston	-23	Jan. 11, 1942
SC.	Camden	111	[2]Jun. 28, 1954	Caesars Head	-19	Jan. 21, 1985
SD.	Gannvalley.	120	Jul. 5, 1936	McIntosh	-58	Feb. 17, 1936
TN.	Perryville.	113	[2]Aug. 9, 1930	Mountain City	-32	Dec. 30, 1917
TX.	Seymour	120	Aug. 12, 1936	Seminole.	-23	[2]Feb. 8, 1933
UT.	Saint George	117	Jul. 5, 1985	Peter's Sink	-69	Feb. 1, 1985
VT.	Vernon	105	Jul. 4, 1911	Bloomfield	-50	Dec. 30, 1933
VA.	Balcony Falls	110	[2]Jul. 15, 1954	Mtn. Lake Bio. Stn.	-30	Jan. 22, 1985
WA	Ice Harbor Dam	118	[2]Aug. 5, 1961	Mazama & Winthrop . . .	-48	Dec. 30, 1968
WV	Martinsburg	112	[2]Jul. 10, 1936	Lewisburg	-37	Dec. 30, 1917
WI	Wisconsin Dells	114	Jul. 13, 1936	Couderay	-55	Feb. 4, 1996
WY	Basin	114	Jul. 12, 1900	Riverside R.S.	-66	Feb. 9, 1933

[1] Estimated.   [2] Also on earlier dates at the same or other places.

Source: U.S. National Oceanic and Atmospheric Administration, <http://www.lwf.ncdc.noaa.gov/oa/climate/severeweather/temperatures.html> (released 25 April 2002).

No. 377. Normal Daily Mean, Maximum, and Minimum Temperatures—Selected Cities

[In Fahrenheit degrees. Airport data except as noted. Based on standard 30-year period, 1971 through 2000]

State	Station	Daily mean temperature			Daily maximum temperature			Daily minimum temperature		
		Jan.	July	Annual average	Jan.	July	Annual average	Jan.	July	Annual average
AL	Mobile.	50.1	81.5	66.8	60.7	91.2	77.4	39.5	71.8	56.2
AK	Juneau	25.7	56.8	41.5	30.6	64.3	47.6	20.7	49.2	35.3
AZ	Phoenix.	54.2	92.8	72.9	65.0	104.2	84.5	43.4	81.4	61.1
AR	Little Rock	40.1	82.4	62.1	49.5	92.8	72.7	30.8	72.0	51.5
CA	Los Angeles	57.1	69.3	63.3	65.6	75.3	70.6	48.6	63.3	56.1
	Sacramento	46.3	75.4	61.1	53.8	92.4	73.7	38.8	58.3	48.4
	San Diego	57.8	70.9	64.4	65.8	75.8	70.8	49.7	65.9	58.1
	San Francisco	49.4	62.8	57.3	55.9	71.1	65.1	42.9	54.5	49.6
CO	Denver	29.2	73.4	50.1	43.2	88.0	64.2	15.2	58.7	35.8
CT	Hartford.	25.7	73.7	50.2	34.1	84.9	60.5	17.2	62.4	40.0
DE	Wilmington	31.5	76.6	54.4	39.3	86.0	63.6	23.7	67.3	45.1
DC	Washington	34.9	79.2	57.5	42.5	88.3	66.4	27.3	70.1	48.6
FL	Jacksonville	53.1	81.6	68.0	64.2	90.8	78.4	41.9	72.4	57.6
	Miami	68.1	83.7	76.7	76.5	90.9	84.2	59.6	76.5	69.1
GA	Atlanta	42.7	80.0	62.2	51.9	89.4	72.0	33.5	70.6	52.3
HI	Honolulu	73.0	80.8	77.5	80.4	87.8	84.7	65.7	73.8	70.2
ID	Boise	30.2	74.7	52.0	36.7	89.2	62.6	23.6	60.3	41.3
IL	Chicago.	22.0	73.3	49.1	29.6	83.5	58.3	14.3	63.2	39.8
	Peoria.	22.5	75.1	50.8	30.7	85.7	60.7	14.3	64.6	40.9
IN	Indianapolis	26.5	75.4	52.5	34.5	85.6	62.3	18.5	65.2	42.7
IA	Des Moines	20.4	76.1	50.0	29.1	86.0	59.8	11.7	66.1	40.2
KS	Wichita	30.2	81.0	56.4	40.1	92.9	67.4	20.3	69.1	45.2
KY	Louisville	33.0	78.4	57.0	41.0	87.0	66.0	24.9	69.8	47.9
LA	New Orleans	52.6	82.7	68.8	61.8	91.1	78.0	43.4	74.2	59.6
ME	Portland	21.7	68.7	45.8	30.9	78.8	55.2	12.5	58.6	36.3
MD	Baltimore	32.3	76.5	54.6	41.2	87.2	65.1	23.5	65.8	44.2
MA	Boston	29.3	73.9	51.6	36.5	82.2	59.3	22.1	65.5	43.9
MI	Detroit.	24.5	73.5	49.8	31.1	83.4	58.4	17.8	63.6	41.0
	Sault Ste. Marie . . .	13.2	63.9	40.1	21.5	75.7	49.6	4.9	52.0	30.5
MN	Duluth	8.4	65.5	39.1	17.9	76.3	48.7	-1.2	54.6	29.3
	Minneapolis-St. Paul.	13.1	73.2	45.4	21.9	83.3	54.7	4.3	63.0	35.9
MS	Jackson.	45.0	81.4	64.1	55.1	91.4	75.0	35.0	71.4	53.2
MO	Kansas City	26.9	78.5	54.2	36.0	88.8	64.3	17.8	68.2	44.0
	St. Louis	29.6	80.2	56.3	37.9	89.8	65.7	21.2	70.6	46.9
MT	Great Falls.	21.7	66.2	43.8	32.1	82.0	56.4	11.3	50.4	31.1
NE	Omaha	21.7	76.7	50.7	31.7	87.4	61.5	11.6	65.9	39.8
NV	Reno	33.6	71.3	51.3	45.5	91.2	67.4	21.8	51.4	35.2
NH	Concord	20.1	70.0	45.9	30.6	82.9	57.7	9.7	57.1	34.1
NJ	Atlantic City	32.1	75.3	53.5	41.4	85.1	63.6	22.8	65.4	43.3
NM	Albuquerque.	35.7	78.5	56.8	47.6	92.3	70.4	23.8	64.7	43.2
NY	Albany	22.2	71.1	47.6	31.1	82.2	57.6	13.3	60.0	37.5
	Buffalo	24.5	70.8	48.0	31.1	79.6	55.9	17.8	62.1	39.9
	New York [1]	32.1	76.5	54.6	38.0	84.2	61.7	26.2	68.8	47.5
NC	Charlotte	41.7	80.3	61.4	51.3	90.1	71.7	32.1	70.6	51.0
	Raleigh	39.7	78.8	59.6	49.8	89.1	70.6	29.6	68.5	48.6
ND	Bismarck	10.2	70.4	42.3	21.1	84.5	54.5	-0.6	56.4	30.1
OH	Cincinnati.	29.7	76.3	54.2	38.0	86.4	64.0	21.3	66.1	44.3
	Cleveland	25.7	71.9	49.7	32.6	81.4	58.1	18.8	62.3	41.2
	Columbus	28.3	75.1	52.9	36.2	85.3	62.6	20.3	64.9	43.2
OK	Oklahoma City	36.7	82.0	60.1	47.1	93.1	71.1	26.2	70.8	49.2
OR	Portland	39.9	68.1	53.5	45.6	79.3	62.1	34.2	56.9	44.8
PA	Philadelphia	32.3	77.6	55.3	39.0	85.5	63.2	25.5	69.7	47.4
	Pittsburgh	27.5	72.6	51.0	35.1	82.7	60.4	19.9	62.4	41.5
RI	Providence.	28.7	73.3	51.1	37.1	82.6	60.2	20.3	64.1	42.0
SC	Columbia.	44.6	82.0	63.6	55.1	92.1	74.8	34.0	71.8	52.5
SD	Sioux Falls.	14.0	73.0	45.1	25.2	85.6	57.2	2.9	60.3	33.0
TN	Memphis	39.9	82.5	62.4	48.6	92.1	72.1	31.3	72.9	52.5
	Nashville	36.8	79.1	58.9	45.6	88.7	69.0	27.9	69.5	48.8
TX	Dallas-Fort Worth . .	44.1	85.0	65.5	54.1	95.4	75.8	34.0	74.6	55.1
	El Paso	45.1	83.3	64.7	57.2	94.5	77.1	32.9	72.0	52.1
	Houston	51.8	83.6	68.8	62.3	93.6	79.4	41.2	73.5	58.2
UT	Salt Lake City.	29.2	77.0	52.0	37.0	90.6	62.9	21.3	63.4	41.2
VT	Burlington	18.0	70.6	45.2	26.7	81.4	54.5	9.3	59.8	35.8
VA	Norfolk	40.1	79.1	59.6	47.8	86.8	67.8	32.3	71.4	51.4
	Richmond	36.4	77.9	57.6	45.3	87.5	67.8	27.6	68.3	47.4
WA	Seattle-Tacoma. . . .	40.9	65.3	52.3	45.8	75.3	59.8	35.9	55.3	44.8
	Spokane	27.3	68.6	47.3	32.8	82.5	57.4	21.7	54.6	37.2
WV	Charleston	33.4	73.9	54.5	42.6	84.9	65.4	24.2	62.9	43.5
WI	Milwaukee	20.7	72.0	47.5	28.0	81.1	55.9	13.4	62.9	39.2
WY	Cheyenne	25.9	67.7	45.0	37.1	81.9	57.6	14.8	53.4	32.3
PR	San Juan.	76.6	82.2	79.9	82.4	87.4	85.5	70.8	76.9	74.2

[1] City office data.

Source: U.S. National Oceanic and Atmospheric Administration, *Climatography of the United States*, No. 81.

No. 378. Highest Temperature of Record—Selected Cities

[In **Fahrenheit degrees**. Airport data, except as noted. For period of record through 2002]

State	Station	Length of record (yr.)	Jan.	Feb.	Mar.	Apr.	May	June	July	Aug.	Sept.	Oct.	Nov.	Dec.	Annual
AL	Mobile	61	84	82	90	94	100	102	104	105	99	93	87	81	105
AK	Juneau	58	57	57	61	72	82	86	90	83	73	61	56	54	90
AZ	Phoenix	65	88	92	100	105	113	122	121	116	118	107	95	88	122
AR	Little Rock	61	83	85	91	95	98	105	112	109	106	97	86	80	112
CA	Los Angeles	67	88	92	95	102	97	104	97	98	110	106	101	94	110
	Sacramento	52	70	76	88	95	105	115	114	110	108	104	87	72	115
	San Diego	62	88	90	93	98	96	101	95	98	111	107	97	88	111
	San Francisco	75	72	78	85	92	97	106	105	100	103	99	85	75	106
CO	Denver	61	73	76	84	90	96	104	104	101	97	89	79	75	104
CT	Hartford	48	66	73	89	96	99	100	102	102	99	91	81	76	102
DE	Wilmington	55	75	78	86	94	96	100	102	101	100	91	85	75	102
DC	Washington	61	79	82	89	95	99	101	104	105	101	94	86	79	105
FL	Jacksonville	61	85	88	91	95	100	103	105	102	100	96	88	84	105
	Miami	60	88	89	92	96	96	98	98	98	97	95	91	87	98
GA	Atlanta	54	79	80	89	93	95	101	105	102	98	95	84	79	105
HI	Honolulu	33	88	88	88	91	93	92	94	93	95	94	93	89	95
ID	Boise	63	63	71	81	92	98	109	111	110	102	94	78	65	111
IL	Chicago	44	65	72	88	91	93	104	104	101	99	91	78	71	104
	Peoria	63	70	72	86	92	93	105	103	103	100	90	81	71	105
IN	Indianapolis	63	71	76	85	89	93	102	104	102	100	90	81	74	104
IA	Des Moines	63	65	73	91	93	98	103	105	108	101	95	81	69	108
KS	Wichita	50	75	87	89	96	100	110	113	110	108	95	85	83	113
KY	Louisville	55	77	77	86	91	95	102	106	101	104	92	84	76	106
LA	New Orleans	56	83	85	89	92	96	100	101	102	101	94	87	84	102
ME	Portland	62	64	64	88	85	94	98	99	103	95	88	74	71	103
MD	Baltimore	52	75	79	89	94	98	101	104	105	100	92	83	77	105
MA	Boston	51	66	70	89	94	95	100	102	102	100	90	79	76	102
MI	Detroit	44	62	70	81	89	93	104	102	100	98	91	77	69	104
	Sault Ste. Marie	62	45	49	75	85	89	93	97	98	95	80	67	62	98
MN	Duluth	61	52	55	78	88	90	94	97	97	95	86	71	55	97
	Minneapolis-St. Paul	64	58	61	83	95	96	102	105	102	98	90	77	68	105
MS	Jackson	39	83	85	89	94	99	105	106	107	104	95	88	84	107
MO	Kansas City	30	69	77	86	93	95	105	107	109	106	92	82	74	109
	St. Louis	45	76	85	89	93	94	102	107	107	104	94	85	76	107
MT	Great Falls	65	67	70	78	89	93	101	105	106	98	91	76	69	106
NE	Omaha	66	69	78	89	97	99	105	114	110	104	96	83	72	114
NV	Reno	61	70	75	83	89	96	103	108	105	101	91	77	70	108
NH	Concord	61	68	67	89	95	97	98	102	101	98	90	80	73	102
NJ	Atlantic City	59	78	75	87	94	99	106	104	103	99	90	84	77	106
NM	Albuquerque	63	69	76	85	89	98	107	105	101	100	91	77	72	107
NY	Albany	56	65	68	89	92	94	99	100	99	100	89	82	71	100
	Buffalo	59	72	71	81	94	90	96	97	99	98	87	80	74	99
	New York [1]	134	72	75	86	96	99	101	106	104	102	94	84	75	106
NC	Charlotte	63	79	81	90	93	100	103	103	103	104	98	85	78	104
	Raleigh	58	80	84	92	95	97	104	105	105	104	98	88	80	105
ND	Bismarck	63	63	69	81	93	98	111	109	109	105	95	79	65	111
OH	Cincinnati	41	69	75	84	89	93	102	103	102	98	88	81	75	103
	Cleveland	61	73	74	83	88	92	104	103	102	101	90	82	77	104
	Columbus	63	74	75	85	89	94	102	100	101	100	90	80	76	102
OK	Oklahoma City	49	80	92	93	100	104	105	110	110	108	96	87	86	110
OR	Portland	62	63	71	80	90	100	100	107	107	105	92	73	65	107
PA	Philadelphia	61	74	74	87	95	97	100	104	101	100	96	81	73	104
	Pittsburgh	50	72	76	82	89	91	98	103	100	97	87	82	74	103
RI	Providence	49	69	72	85	98	95	97	102	104	100	86	78	77	104
SC	Columbia	55	84	84	91	94	101	107	107	107	101	101	90	83	107
SD	Sioux Falls	57	66	70	87	94	100	110	108	108	104	94	81	63	110
TN	Memphis	61	79	81	85	94	99	104	108	107	103	95	86	81	108
	Nashville	63	78	84	86	91	97	106	107	104	105	94	84	79	107
TX	Dallas-Fort Worth	49	88	95	96	95	103	113	110	108	111	102	89	88	113
	El Paso	63	80	83	89	98	104	114	112	108	104	96	87	80	114
	Houston	33	84	91	91	95	99	103	104	107	109	96	89	85	109
UT	Salt Lake City	74	62	69	78	86	96	104	107	106	100	89	75	69	107
VT	Burlington	59	66	62	84	91	93	100	100	101	98	85	75	67	101
VA	Norfolk	54	80	82	88	97	100	101	103	104	99	95	86	80	104
	Richmond	73	81	83	93	96	100	104	105	102	103	99	86	81	105
WA	Seattle-Tacoma	58	64	70	75	85	93	96	100	99	98	89	74	64	100
	Spokane	55	59	63	71	90	96	101	103	108	98	86	67	56	108
WV	Charleston	55	79	79	89	94	93	98	104	101	102	92	85	80	104
WI	Milwaukee	62	62	68	82	91	93	101	103	103	98	89	77	68	103
WY	Cheyenne	67	66	71	74	83	91	100	100	96	95	83	75	69	100
PR	San Juan	48	92	96	96	97	96	97	95	97	97	98	96	94	98

[1] City office data.

Source: U.S. National Oceanic and Atmospheric Administration, *Comparative Climatic Data*, annual.

Geography and Environment   231

No. 379. Lowest Temperature of Record—Selected Cities

[In Fahrenheit degrees. Airport data, except as noted. For period of record through 2002]

State	Station	Length of record (years)	Jan.	Feb.	Mar.	Apr.	May	June	July	Aug.	Sept.	Oct.	Nov.	Dec.	Annual
AL	Mobile............	61	3	11	21	32	43	49	60	59	42	30	22	8	3
AK	Juneau	58	-22	-22	-15	6	25	31	36	27	23	11	-5	-21	-22
AZ	Phoenix..........	65	17	22	25	32	40	50	61	60	47	34	25	22	17
AR	Little Rock	61	-4	-5	11	28	40	46	54	52	37	29	17	-1	-5
CA	Los Angeles	67	23	32	34	39	43	48	49	51	47	41	34	32	23
	Sacramento	52	23	23	26	31	36	41	48	49	43	36	26	18	18
	San Diego	62	29	36	39	41	48	51	55	57	51	43	38	34	29
	San Francisco	75	24	25	30	31	36	41	43	42	38	34	25	20	20
CO	Denver [1]	61	-25	-30	-11	-2	22	30	43	41	17	3	-8	-25	-30
CT	Hartford..........	48	-26	-21	-6	9	28	35	44	36	30	17	1	-14	-26
DE	Wilmington........	55	-14	-6	2	18	30	41	48	43	36	24	14	-7	-14
DC	Washington	61	-5	4	11	24	34	47	54	49	39	29	16	1	-5
FL	Jacksonville	61	7	19	23	34	45	47	61	59	48	36	21	11	7
	Miami	60	30	32	32	46	53	60	69	68	68	51	39	30	30
GA	Atlanta	54	-8	5	10	26	37	46	53	55	36	28	3	-	-8
HI	Honolulu	33	53	53	55	57	60	65	66	67	66	61	57	54	53
ID	Boise	63	-17	-15	6	19	22	31	35	34	23	11	-3	-25	-25
IL	Chicago..........	44	-27	-19	-8	7	24	36	40	41	28	17	1	-25	-27
	Peoria...........	63	-25	-19	-10	14	25	39	47	41	26	19	-2	-23	-25
IN	Indianapolis	63	-27	-21	-7	16	28	37	44	41	28	17	-2	-23	-27
IA	Des Moines	63	-24	-26	-22	9	30	38	47	40	26	14	-4	-22	-26
KS	Wichita	50	-12	-21	-2	15	31	43	51	48	31	18	1	-16	-21
KY	Louisville	55	-22	-19	-1	22	31	42	50	46	33	23	-1	-15	-22
LA	New Orleans	56	14	16	25	32	41	50	60	60	42	35	24	11	11
ME	Portland	62	-26	-39	-21	8	23	33	40	33	23	15	3	-21	-39
MD	Baltimore........	52	-7	-3	6	20	32	40	50	45	35	25	13	-	-7
MA	Boston	51	-12	-4	6	16	34	45	50	47	38	28	15	-7	-12
MI	Detroit..........	44	-21	-15	-4	10	25	36	41	38	29	17	9	-10	-21
	Sault Ste. Marie ...	62	-36	-35	-24	-2	18	26	36	29	25	16	-10	-31	-36
MN	Duluth	61	-39	-39	-29	-5	17	27	35	32	22	8	-23	-34	-39
	Minneapolis-St. Paul.	64	-34	-32	-32	2	18	34	43	39	26	13	-17	-29	-34
MS	Jackson..........	39	2	10	15	27	38	47	51	55	35	26	17	4	2
MO	Kansas City	30	-17	-19	-10	12	30	42	51	43	31	17	1	-23	-23
	St. Louis	45	-18	-12	-5	22	31	43	51	47	36	23	1	-16	-18
MT	Great Falls.......	65	-37	-35	-29	-6	15	31	36	30	16	-11	-25	-43	-43
NE	Omaha	66	-23	-21	-16	5	27	38	44	43	25	13	-9	-23	-23
NV	Reno	61	-16	-16	-2	13	18	25	33	24	20	8	1	-16	-16
NH	Concord	61	-33	-37	-16	8	21	30	35	29	21	10	-5	-22	-37
NJ	Atlantic City	59	-10	-11	5	12	25	37	42	40	32	20	10	-7	-11
NM	Albuquerque......	63	-17	-5	8	19	16	40	52	50	37	21	-7	-7	-17
NY	Albany	56	-28	-21	-21	10	26	36	40	34	24	16	5	-22	-28
	Buffalo	59	-16	-20	-7	12	26	35	43	38	32	20	9	-10	-20
	New York [2]	134	-6	-15	3	12	32	44	52	50	39	28	5	-13	-15
NC	Charlotte	63	-5	5	4	24	32	45	53	53	39	24	11	2	-5
	Raleigh	58	-9	-	11	23	31	38	48	46	37	19	11	4	-9
ND	Bismarck	63	-44	-43	-31	-12	15	30	35	33	11	-10	-30	-43	-44
OH	Cincinnati........	41	-25	-11	-11	15	27	39	47	43	31	16	1	-20	-25
	Cleveland	61	-20	-15	-5	10	25	31	41	38	32	19	3	-15	-20
	Columbus	63	-22	-13	-6	14	25	35	43	39	31	20	5	-17	-22
OK	Oklahoma City	49	-4	-3	3	20	37	47	53	51	36	16	11	-8	-8
OR	Portland	62	-2	-3	19	29	29	39	43	44	34	26	13	6	-3
PA	Philadelphia	61	-7	-4	7	19	28	44	51	44	35	25	15	1	-7
	Pittsburgh	50	-22	-12	-1	14	26	34	42	39	31	16	-1	-12	-22
RI	Providence.......	49	-13	-7	1	14	29	41	48	40	33	20	6	-10	-13
SC	Columbia	55	-1	5	4	26	34	44	54	53	40	23	12	4	-1
SD	Sioux Falls.......	57	-36	-31	-23	5	17	33	38	34	22	9	-17	-28	-36
TN	Memphis	61	-4	-11	12	29	38	48	52	48	36	25	9	-13	-13
	Nashville	63	-17	-13	2	23	34	42	51	47	36	26	-1	-10	-17
TX	Dallas-Fort Worth ..	49	4	7	15	29	41	51	59	56	43	29	20	-1	-1
	El Paso..........	63	-8	8	14	23	31	46	57	56	41	25	1	5	-8
	Houston	33	12	20	22	31	44	52	62	60	48	29	19	7	7
UT	Salt Lake City.....	74	-22	-30	2	14	25	35	40	37	27	16	-14	-21	-30
VT	Burlington	59	-30	-30	-20	2	24	33	39	35	25	15	-2	-26	-30
VA	Norfolk	54	-3	8	18	28	36	45	54	49	45	27	20	7	-3
	Richmond	73	-12	-10	11	23	31	40	51	46	35	21	10	-1	-12
WA	Seattle-Tacoma....	58	-	1	11	29	28	38	43	44	35	28	6	6	-
	Spokane	55	-22	-24	-7	17	24	33	37	35	22	7	-21	-25	-25
WV	Charleston.......	55	-16	-12	-	19	26	33	46	41	34	17	6	-12	-16
WI	Milwaukee	62	-26	-26	-10	12	21	33	40	44	28	18	-5	-20	-26
WY	Cheyenne	67	-29	-34	-21	-8	16	25	38	36	8	-1	-16	-28	-34
PR	San Juan........	48	61	62	60	64	66	69	69	70	69	46	66	59	46

- Represents zero.   [1] Period of record through 2000.   [2] City office data.

Source: U.S. National Oceanic and Atmospheric Administration, *Comparative Climatic Data,* annual.

No. 380. Normal Monthly and Annual Precipitation—Selected Cities

[In inches. Airport data, except as noted. Based on standard 30-year period, 1971 through 2000]

State	Station	Jan.	Feb.	Mar.	Apr.	May	June	July	Aug.	Sept.	Oct.	Nov.	Dec.	Annual
AL	Mobile..........	5.75	5.10	7.20	5.06	6.10	5.01	6.54	6.20	6.01	3.25	5.41	4.66	66.29
AK	Juneau	4.81	4.02	3.51	2.96	3.48	3.36	4.14	5.37	7.54	8.30	5.43	5.41	58.33
AZ	Phoenix.........	0.83	0.77	1.07	0.25	0.16	0.09	0.99	0.94	0.75	0.79	0.73	0.92	8.29
AR	Little Rock	3.61	3.33	4.88	5.47	5.05	3.95	3.31	2.93	3.71	4.25	5.73	4.71	50.93
CA	Los Angeles.......	2.98	3.11	2.40	0.63	0.24	0.08	0.03	0.14	0.26	0.36	1.13	1.79	13.15
	Sacramento	3.84	3.54	2.80	1.02	0.53	0.20	0.05	0.06	0.36	0.89	2.19	2.45	17.93
	San Diego	2.28	2.04	2.26	0.75	0.20	0.09	0.03	0.09	0.21	0.44	1.07	1.31	10.77
	San Francisco	4.45	4.01	3.26	1.17	0.38	0.11	0.03	0.07	0.20	1.04	2.49	2.89	20.11
CO	Denver	0.51	0.49	1.28	1.93	2.32	1.56	2.16	1.82	1.14	0.99	0.98	0.63	15.81
CT	Hartford	3.84	2.96	3.88	3.86	4.39	3.85	3.67	3.98	4.13	3.94	4.06	3.60	46.16
DE	Wilmington.......	3.43	2.81	3.97	3.39	4.15	3.59	4.28	3.51	4.01	3.08	3.19	3.40	42.81
DC	Washington	3.21	2.63	3.60	2.77	3.82	3.13	3.66	3.44	3.79	3.22	3.03	3.05	39.35
FL	Jacksonville	3.69	3.15	3.93	3.14	3.48	5.37	5.97	6.87	7.90	3.86	2.34	2.64	52.34
	Miami	1.88	2.07	2.56	3.36	5.52	8.54	5.79	8.63	8.38	6.19	3.43	2.18	58.53
GA	Atlanta	5.02	4.68	5.38	3.62	3.95	3.63	5.12	3.67	4.09	3.11	4.10	3.82	50.20
HI	Honolulu	2.73	2.35	1.89	1.11	0.78	0.43	0.50	0.46	0.74	2.18	2.26	2.85	18.29
ID	Boise	1.39	1.14	1.41	1.27	1.27	0.74	0.39	0.30	0.76	0.76	1.38	1.38	12.19
IL	Chicago.........	1.75	1.63	2.65	3.68	3.38	3.63	3.51	4.62	3.27	2.71	3.01	2.43	36.27
	Peoria..........	1.50	1.67	2.83	3.56	4.17	3.84	4.02	3.16	3.12	2.76	2.99	2.40	36.03
IN	Indianapolis	2.48	2.41	3.44	3.61	4.35	4.13	4.42	3.82	2.88	2.76	3.61	3.03	40.95
IA	Des Moines	1.03	1.19	2.21	3.58	4.25	4.57	4.18	4.51	3.15	2.62	2.10	1.33	34.72
KS	Wichita	0.84	1.02	2.71	2.57	4.16	4.25	3.31	2.94	2.96	2.45	1.82	1.35	30.38
KY	Louisville........	3.28	3.25	4.41	3.91	4.88	3.76	4.30	3.41	3.05	2.79	3.80	3.69	44.54
LA	New Orleans	5.87	5.47	5.24	5.02	4.62	6.83	6.20	6.15	5.55	3.05	5.09	5.07	64.16
ME	Portland	4.09	3.14	4.14	4.26	3.82	3.28	3.32	3.05	3.37	4.40	4.72	4.24	45.83
MD	Baltimore........	3.47	3.02	3.93	3.00	3.89	3.43	3.85	3.74	3.98	3.16	3.12	3.35	41.94
MA	Boston	3.92	3.30	3.85	3.60	3.24	3.22	3.06	3.37	3.47	3.79	3.98	3.73	42.53
MI	Detroit..........	1.91	1.88	2.52	3.05	3.05	3.55	3.16	3.10	3.27	2.23	2.66	2.51	32.89
	Sault Ste. Marie ...	2.64	1.60	2.41	2.57	2.50	3.00	3.14	3.47	3.71	3.32	3.40	2.91	34.67
MN	Duluth..........	1.12	0.83	1.69	2.09	2.95	4.25	4.20	4.22	4.13	2.46	2.12	0.94	31.00
	Minneapolis-St. Paul.	1.04	0.79	1.86	2.31	3.24	4.34	4.04	4.05	2.69	2.11	1.94	1.00	29.41
MS	Jackson.........	5.67	4.50	5.74	5.98	4.86	3.82	4.69	3.66	3.23	3.42	5.04	5.34	55.95
MO	Kansas City	1.15	1.31	2.44	3.38	5.39	4.44	4.42	3.54	4.64	3.33	2.30	1.64	37.98
	St. Louis	2.14	2.28	3.60	3.69	4.11	3.76	3.90	2.98	2.96	2.76	3.71	2.86	38.75
MT	Great Falls.......	0.68	0.51	1.01	1.40	2.53	2.24	1.45	1.65	1.23	0.93	0.59	0.67	14.89
NE	Omaha	0.77	0.80	2.13	2.94	4.44	3.95	3.86	3.21	3.17	2.21	1.82	0.92	30.22
NV	Reno	1.06	1.06	0.86	0.35	0.62	0.47	0.24	0.27	0.45	0.42	0.80	0.88	7.48
NH	Concord	2.97	2.36	3.04	3.07	3.33	3.10	3.37	3.21	3.16	3.46	3.57	2.96	37.60
NJ	Atlantic City	3.60	2.85	4.06	3.45	3.38	2.66	3.86	4.32	3.14	2.86	3.26	3.15	40.59
NM	Albuquerque......	0.49	0.44	0.61	0.50	0.60	0.65	1.27	1.73	1.07	1.00	0.62	0.49	9.47
NY	Albany	2.71	2.27	3.17	3.25	3.67	3.74	3.50	3.68	3.31	3.23	3.31	2.76	38.60
	Buffalo	3.16	2.42	2.99	3.04	3.35	3.82	3.14	3.87	3.84	3.19	3.92	3.80	40.54
	New York [1]......	4.13	3.15	4.37	4.28	4.69	3.84	4.62	4.22	4.23	3.85	4.36	3.95	49.69
NC	Charlotte	4.00	3.55	4.39	2.95	3.66	3.42	3.79	3.72	3.83	3.66	3.36	3.18	43.51
	Raleigh	4.02	3.47	4.03	2.80	3.79	3.42	4.29	3.78	4.26	3.18	2.97	3.04	43.05
ND	Bismarck	0.45	0.51	0.85	1.46	2.22	2.59	2.58	2.15	1.61	1.28	0.70	0.44	16.84
OH	Cincinnati........	2.92	2.75	3.90	3.96	4.59	4.42	3.75	3.79	2.82	2.96	3.46	3.28	42.60
	Cleveland	2.48	2.29	2.94	3.37	3.50	3.89	3.52	3.69	3.77	2.73	3.38	3.14	38.71
	Columbus	2.53	2.20	2.89	3.25	3.88	4.07	4.61	3.72	2.92	2.31	3.19	2.93	38.52
OK	Oklahoma City	1.28	1.56	2.90	3.00	5.44	4.63	2.94	2.48	3.98	3.64	2.11	1.89	35.85
OR	Portland	5.07	4.18	3.71	2.64	2.38	1.59	0.72	0.93	1.65	2.88	5.61	5.71	37.07
PA	Philadelphia	3.52	2.74	3.81	3.49	3.88	3.29	4.39	3.82	3.88	2.75	3.16	3.31	42.05
	Pittsburgh	2.70	2.37	3.17	3.01	3.80	4.12	3.96	3.38	3.21	2.25	3.02	2.86	37.85
RI	Providence.......	4.37	3.45	4.43	4.16	3.66	3.38	3.17	3.90	3.70	3.69	4.40	4.14	46.45
SC	Columbia........	4.66	3.84	4.59	2.98	3.17	4.99	5.54	5.41	3.94	2.89	2.88	3.38	48.27
SD	Sioux Falls.......	0.51	0.51	1.81	2.65	3.39	3.49	2.93	3.01	2.58	1.93	1.36	0.52	24.69
TN	Memphis	4.24	4.31	5.58	5.79	5.15	4.30	4.22	3.00	3.31	3.31	5.76	5.68	54.65
	Nashville	3.97	3.69	4.87	3.93	5.07	4.08	3.77	3.28	3.59	2.87	4.45	4.54	48.11
TX	Dallas-Fort Worth ..	1.90	2.37	3.06	3.20	5.15	3.23	2.12	2.03	2.42	4.11	2.57	2.57	34.73
	El Paso.........	0.45	0.39	0.26	0.23	0.38	0.87	1.49	1.75	1.61	0.81	0.42	0.77	9.43
	Houston	3.68	2.98	3.36	3.60	5.15	5.35	3.18	3.83	4.33	4.50	4.19	3.69	47.84
UT	Salt Lake City.....	1.37	1.33	1.91	2.02	2.09	0.77	0.72	0.76	1.33	1.57	1.40	1.23	16.50
VT	Burlington	2.22	1.67	2.32	2.88	3.32	3.43	3.97	4.01	3.83	3.12	3.06	2.22	36.05
VA	Norfolk	3.93	3.34	4.08	3.38	3.74	3.77	5.17	4.79	4.06	3.47	2.98	3.03	45.74
	Richmond	3.55	2.98	4.09	3.18	3.95	3.54	4.67	4.18	3.98	3.60	3.06	3.12	43.91
WA	Seattle-Tacoma....	5.13	4.18	3.75	2.59	1.77	1.49	0.79	1.02	1.63	3.19	5.90	5.62	37.07
	Spokane	1.82	1.51	1.53	1.28	1.60	1.18	0.76	0.68	0.76	1.06	2.24	2.25	16.67
WV	Charleston.......	3.25	3.19	3.90	3.25	4.30	4.09	4.86	4.11	3.45	2.67	3.66	3.32	44.05
WI	Milwaukee	1.85	1.65	2.59	3.78	3.06	3.56	3.58	4.03	3.30	2.49	2.70	2.22	34.81
WY	Cheyenne	0.45	0.44	1.05	1.55	2.48	2.12	2.26	1.82	1.43	0.75	0.64	0.46	15.45
PR	San Juan........	3.02	2.30	2.14	3.71	5.29	3.52	4.16	5.22	5.60	5.06	6.17	4.57	50.76

[1] City office data.

Source: U.S. National Oceanic and Atmospheric Administration, *Climatography of the United States*, No. 81.

Geography and Environment   233

No. 381. Average Number of Days With Precipitation of 0.01 Inch or More— Selected Cities

[Airport data, except as noted. For period of record through 2002]

State	Station	Length of record (yr.)	Jan.	Feb.	Mar.	Apr.	May	June	July	Aug.	Sept.	Oct.	Nov.	Dec.	Annual
AL	Mobile.........	61	11	9	10	7	8	11	16	14	10	6	8	10	121
AK	Juneau.........	58	19	17	18	17	17	16	17	18	21	24	20	21	223
AZ	Phoenix........	63	4	4	4	2	1	1	4	5	3	3	2	4	36
AR	Little Rock.....	60	10	9	10	10	10	8	8	7	7	7	8	9	104
CA	Los Angeles.....	67	6	6	6	3	1	1	1	(Z)	1	2	3	5	35
	Sacramento.....	63	10	9	9	5	3	1	(Z)	(Z)	1	3	7	9	58
	San Diego.....	62	7	6	7	5	2	1	(Z)	-	1	2	4	6	42
	San Francisco	75	11	10	10	6	3	1	(Z)	(Z)	1	4	7	10	63
CO	Denver [1]	61	6	6	9	9	11	9	9	9	6	5	6	5	89
CT	Hartford........	48	11	10	12	11	12	11	10	10	10	9	11	12	127
DE	Wilmington.....	55	11	9	11	11	11	10	9	9	8	8	9	10	117
DC	Washington	61	10	9	11	10	11	10	10	9	8	7	8	9	112
FL	Jacksonville	61	8	8	8	6	8	13	14	15	13	9	6	8	116
	Miami.........	60	7	6	6	6	10	15	16	18	17	14	8	7	131
GA	Atlanta........	68	12	10	11	9	9	10	12	9	8	7	9	10	115
HI	Honolulu.......	53	9	9	9	9	7	6	7	6	7	8	9	10	96
ID	Boise.........	63	12	10	10	8	8	6	2	2	4	6	10	11	89
IL	Chicago.......	44	11	9	12	13	11	10	10	9	9	9	11	11	125
	Peoria........	63	9	8	11	12	12	10	9	8	8	8	9	10	114
IN	Indianapolis	63	12	10	13	12	12	10	10	9	8	8	10	12	126
IA	Des Moines	63	7	7	10	11	12	11	9	9	9	8	7	8	108
KS	Wichita........	49	5	5	8	8	11	9	8	7	8	6	5	6	86
KY	Louisville......	55	11	10	13	12	12	10	10	8	8	7	10	12	124
LA	New Orleans	54	10	9	9	7	8	11	14	13	10	6	8	10	114
ME	Portland	62	11	10	11	12	12	11	10	9	9	9	12	11	129
MD	Baltimore.......	52	10	9	11	11	11	10	9	9	8	7	9	9	114
MA	Boston........	51	12	10	12	11	12	11	9	10	9	9	11	12	126
MI	Detroit........	44	13	11	13	13	11	10	10	10	10	10	12	13	135
	Sault Ste. Marie ...	61	19	14	13	11	11	11	10	11	13	14	17	19	165
MN	Duluth........	61	12	9	11	11	12	13	12	11	12	10	11	11	134
	Minneapolis-St. Paul.	64	9	7	10	10	11	12	10	10	10	8	8	9	116
MS	Jackson........	39	11	9	10	8	9	9	11	10	8	7	9	10	110
MO	Kansas City	30	7	7	10	11	12	10	9	9	8	8	7	7	105
	St. Louis.......	45	9	8	11	11	11	9	9	8	8	8	9	9	111
MT	Great Falls......	65	9	8	9	9	11	12	8	8	7	6	7	7	100
NE	Omaha	66	6	7	8	10	12	10	9	9	8	6	6	6	99
NV	Reno	60	6	6	6	4	4	3	2	2	3	3	5	6	51
NH	Concord	61	11	9	11	11	12	11	10	10	9	9	11	11	127
NJ	Atlantic City	59	11	10	11	11	10	9	9	9	8	7	9	10	113
NM	Albuquerque......	63	4	4	5	3	4	4	9	10	6	5	4	4	61
NY	Albany	56	13	11	12	12	13	11	10	10	10	9	12	12	135
	Buffalo	59	20	17	16	14	13	11	10	10	11	12	16	19	168
	New York [2]	133	11	10	11	11	11	10	10	8	8	8	9	10	121
NC	Charlotte	63	10	9	11	9	9	10	11	9	7	7	8	10	111
	Raleigh........	58	10	10	10	9	10	10	11	10	8	7	8	9	113
ND	Bismarck........	63	8	7	8	8	10	12	9	8	7	6	6	7	96
OH	Cincinnati.......	55	12	11	13	13	12	11	10	9	8	8	11	12	130
	Cleveland	61	16	14	15	15	13	11	10	10	10	11	14	16	155
	Columbus	63	13	11	13	13	13	11	11	9	8	9	11	13	137
OK	Oklahoma City ...	63	5	6	7	8	10	9	6	6	7	7	5	6	83
OR	Portland	62	18	16	17	15	12	9	4	5	7	12	18	19	152
PA	Philadelphia.....	62	11	9	11	11	11	10	9	9	8	8	9	10	117
	Pittsburgh	50	16	14	15	14	13	12	11	10	10	10	13	16	152
RI	Providence......	49	11	10	12	11	11	11	9	9	9	9	10	12	124
SC	Columbia.......	55	10	9	10	8	8	10	12	11	8	6	7	9	109
SD	Sioux Falls......	57	6	7	9	10	11	11	10	9	8	6	7	6	98
TN	Memphis	52	10	9	11	10	9	9	9	7	7	6	9	10	107
	Nashville	61	11	10	12	11	11	10	10	9	8	7	9	11	119
TX	Dallas-Fort Worth ..	49	7	7	8	8	9	7	5	5	6	6	6	7	79
	El Paso........	63	4	3	2	2	2	3	8	8	5	4	3	4	49
	Houston	33	10	8	9	7	8	10	9	9	9	8	8	9	105
UT	Salt Lake City.....	74	10	9	10	10	8	5	4	6	5	6	8	9	91
VT	Burlington	59	15	11	13	12	14	13	12	12	12	12	14	15	154
VA	Norfolk	54	11	10	11	10	10	9	11	10	8	7	8	9	116
	Richmond	65	10	9	11	9	11	9	11	9	8	7	8	9	113
WA	Seattle-Tacoma....	58	19	16	17	14	11	9	5	6	9	13	18	19	155
	Spokane	55	14	11	11	9	9	8	5	5	6	8	13	14	112
WV	Charleston	55	15	14	15	14	13	12	13	11	9	9	12	14	151
WI	Milwaukee	62	11	10	12	12	12	11	10	9	9	9	10	11	125
WY	Cheyenne	67	6	6	9	10	12	11	11	10	8	6	6	6	100
PR	San Juan........	47	17	13	12	13	16	15	19	19	18	17	19	19	197

- Represents zero.   Z Less than 1/2 day.   [1] Period of record through 2000.   [2] City office data.

Source: U.S. National Oceanic and Atmospheric Administration, *Comparative Climatic Data*, annual.

No. 382. Snow and Ice Pellets—Selected Cities

[In inches. Airport data, except as noted. For period of record through 2001. T denotes trace]

State	Station	Length of record (yr)	Jan.	Feb.	Mar.	Apr.	May	June	July	Aug.	Sept.	Oct.	Nov.	Dec.	Annual
AL	Mobile	60	0.1	0.1	0.1	T	T	-	T	-	-	-	T	0.1	0.4
AK	Juneau	58	25.6	19.1	14.6	3.3	T	T	-	-	-	1	11.8	21.9	97.3
AZ	Phoenix[2]	62	T	-	T	T	T	T	-	-	-	-	T	-	T
AR	Little Rock[2]	56	2.4	1.5	0.5	T	T	T	-	-	-	T	0.2	0.6	5.2
CA	Los Angeles[2]	62	T	T	T	T	-	T	T	-	-	-	-	T	T
	Sacramento[2]	50	T	T	T	-	T	-	-	-	-	-	-	T	T
	San Diego[2]	60	T	-	T	T	-	-	-	-	-	-	T	T	T
	San Francisco[2]	69	-	T	T	T	-	-	-	-	-	-	T	T	T
CO	Denver[2]	61	8.1	7.5	12.5	8.9	1.6	-	T	T	1.6	3.7	9.1	7.3	60.3
CT	Hartford	45	12.9	12.2	10.1	1.5	-	T	-	-	-	0.1	2.1	10.1	49.0
DE	Wilmington	52	6.7	6.1	3.2	0.2	T	T	T	-	-	0.1	0.9	3.3	20.5
DC	Washington	59	5.5	5.1	2.3	T	T	T	T	T	-	-	0.8	2.9	16.6
FL	Jacksonville[2]	60	-	-	-	T	T	T	-	-	-	-	-	T	T
	Miami[2]	59	-	-	-	-	T	-	-	-	-	-	-	-	T
GA	Atlanta	65	1	0.5	0.4	T	-	-	T	-	-	T	T	0.2	2.1
HI	Honolulu[2]	52	-	-	-	-	-	-	-	-	-	-	-	-	0.0
ID	Boise	63	6.5	3.7	1.7	0.6	0.1	-	T	T	-	0.1	2.3	5.7	20.7
IL	Chicago	43	11.2	7.9	6.9	1.6	0.1	T	T	T	T	0.4	2	8.4	38.5
	Peoria	59	6.7	5	4.2	0.8	T	T	T	T	T	0.2	2	6.1	24.9
IN	Indianapolis	71	6.8	5.4	3.5	0.5	T	-	T	-	T	0.2	1.9	5.3	23.6
IA	Des Moines	59	8.3	7.1	6	1.8	-	T	T	T	T	0.3	3.1	6.5	33.1
KS	Wichita	49	4.2	3.9	2.8	0.2	T	T	T	T	T	-	1.3	3.3	15.7
KY	Louisville	55	5.4	4.3	3.1	0.1	T	T	T	T	-	0.1	1	2.4	16.4
LA	New Orleans[2]	51	T	0.1	T	T	T	-	-	-	-	-	T	0.1	0.2
ME	Portland	62	19.3	16.5	13.5	2.9	0.2	-	T	-	T	0.2	3.3	14.5	70.4
MD	Baltimore	52	6.3	6.5	3.8	0.1	T	T	-	T	-	-	1	3.1	20.8
MA	Boston	65	12.8	11.5	8.1	0.9	-	T	-	T	-	T	1.3	7.6	42.2
MI	Detroit	44	10.6	9	6.9	1.7	-	T	-	T	-	0.2	2.7	10	41.1
	Sault Ste. Marie[4]	57	29.2	18.2	14.6	5.8	0.5	T	-	T	T	2.4	15.6	31	117.4
MN	Duluth	59	17.7	11.9	13.8	6.8	0.7	T	T	T	0.1	1.6	12.9	15.2	80.7
	Minneapolis-St. Paul[2]	62	10.7	8.1	10.5	2.8	0.1	T	T	T	T	0.5	7.8	9.4	49.9
MS	Jackson	38	0.5	0.2	0.2	T	-	-	-	T	T	-	T	0.1	1.0
MO	Kansas City	68	5.6	4.4	3.4	0.8	T	T	T	-	-	T	1.2	4.4	19.9
	St. Louis	66	5.4	4.4	3.4	0.5	-	T	T	T	-	0.1	1.2	4.4	19.6
MT	Great Falls	65	9.5	8.5	10.6	7.1	1.9	0.3	T	0.1	1.5	3.4	7.3	8.1	58.3
NE	Omaha	67	7.2	6.7	6.3	1	0.1	-	T	T	T	0.3	2.6	5.7	29.9
NV	Reno[2]	54	5.8	5.2	4.3	1.2	0.8	-	-	-	T	0.3	2.4	4.3	24.3
NH	Concord	61	17.8	14.1	11.6	2.5	0.1	-	-	-	T	0.1	3.9	13.7	63.8
NJ	Atlantic City	53	4.9	5.3	2.5	0.3	T	T	-	-	-	T	0.4	2.3	15.7
NM	Albuquerque	63	2.5	2.1	1.8	0.6	T	T	T	T	T	0.1	1.2	2.7	11.0
NY	Albany	56	16.7	13.7	11.6	2.7	0.1	T	-	T	T	0.2	4.3	14.6	63.9
	Buffalo	59	24	17.7	12.5	3.2	0.2	T	-	T	T	0.3	11.4	24.3	93.6
	New York[1]	134	7.5	8.5	5.1	0.9	T	T	-	T	-	-	0.9	5.5	28.4
NC	Charlotte	63	2.1	1.6	1.2	T	T	T	T	-	-	-	0.1	0.5	5.5
	Raleigh	58	2.8	2.5	1.3	T	T	T	T	-	-	-	0.1	0.8	7.5
ND	Bismarck	63	7.8	7	8.5	4.1	0.9	T	T	T	0.2	1.9	7	6.9	44.3
OH	Cincinnati	55	7.2	5.4	4.3	0.5	-	T	T	T	-	0.3	2	3.7	23.4
	Cleveland	61	13.5	12	10.9	2.4	0.1	T	T	T	-	0.6	5.3	12.1	56.9
	Columbus	55	8.8	5.9	4.4	0.9	T	T	-	T	T	0.1	2.2	5.4	27.7
OK	Oklahoma City	63	3.2	2.4	1.5	T	T	T	-	T	T	T	0.5	1.9	9.5
OR	Portland[2]	55	3.2	1.1	0.4	T	-	T	-	-	T	T	0.4	1.4	6.5
PA	Philadelphia	60	6.1	6.6	3.5	0.3	-	T	-	-	T	-	0.7	3.3	20.5
	Pittsburgh	50	11.8	8.9	8.5	1.7	0.1	T	T	T	T	0.4	3.5	8.1	43.0
RI	Providence[2]	49	9.6	9.6	7.3	0.7	0.2	-	-	-	-	0.1	1.2	6.8	35.5
SC	Columbia	54	0.5	0.8	0.2	T	T	-	-	-	-	-	-	0.3	1.8
SD	Sioux Falls	57	6.9	8	9.3	2.9	T	T	T	T	T	0.9	6.1	7	41.1
TN	Memphis	49	2.2	1.4	0.8	T	T	T	-	T	-	-	0.1	0.6	5.1
	Nashville[2]	57	3.7	3	1.5	-	-	-	T	-	-	T	0.4	1.4	10.0
TX	Dallas-Fort Worth	44	1.1	1	0.2	T	T	-	-	-	-	-	T	0.2	2.6
	El Paso[2]	57	1.3	0.8	0.4	0.3	T	-	-	-	T	-	0.9	1.6	5.3
	Houston	68	0.2	0.2	T	T	T	T	T	-	-	-	T	T	0.4
UT	Salt Lake City	74	13.6	9.8	9.3	5	0.6	T	T	T	0.1	1.3	7	11.8	58.5
VT	Burlington	59	19.3	16.5	13.9	4.2	0.2	-	-	T	T	0.2	6.8	17.7	78.8
VA	Norfolk	52	3	2.9	1	T	-	T	-	-	-	-	0.4	2	7.8
	Richmond	63	3.9	3.9	2.4	0.1	T	-	-	-	-	T	1.1	2.4	13.8
WA	Seattle-Tacoma[2]	52	4.9	1.6	1.3	0.1	T	T	-	T	-	T	1.1	2.4	11.4
	Spokane	55	15.4	7.6	3.9	0.6	0.1	T	-	-	T	0.4	6.3	14.5	48.8
WV	Charleston[2]	49	11.1	8.7	5.4	0.9	-	T	T	-	T	0.4	2.4	5.3	34.0
WI	Milwaukee	62	13.9	9.3	8.3	1.9	0.1	T	-	T	T	0.2	2.4	5.3	47.3
WY	Cheyenne	67	6.4	6.4	11.8	9.3	3.4	0.2	T	T	1.1	3.8	7.1	6.1	55.6
PR	San Juan	47	-	-	-	-	-	-	-	-	-	-	-	-	-

- Represents zero or rounds to zero.   [1] City office data.   [2] Period of record through 2000.

Source: U.S. National Oceanic and Atmospheric Administration, *Comparative Climatic Data*, annual.

Geography and Environment 235

No. 383. Sunshine, Average Wind Speed, Heating and Cooling Degree Days, and Average Relative Humidity—Selected Cities

[Airport data, except as noted. For period of record through 2002, except heating and cooling normals for period 1971-2000. M=morning. A=afternoon]

State	Station	Average percentage of possible sunshine [1] Length of record (yr.)	An- nual	Average wind speed (m.p.h.) Length of record (yr.)	An- nual	Jan.	July	Heat- ing degree days	Cool- ing degree days	Length of record (yr.)	Annual M	Annual A	Jan. M	Jan. A	July M	July A
AL	Mobile	47	60	53	8.8	10.1	6.9	1,667	2,548	40	87	62	83	65	90	66
AK	Juneau	47	23	56	8.2	8.1	7.5	8,574	-	36	80	70	78	74	79	67
AZ	Phoenix	57	81	56	6.2	5.3	7.1	1,040	4,355	42	50	23	64	32	43	20
AR	Little Rock	35	60	59	7.8	8.4	6.7	3,084	2,086	38	83	60	80	65	86	58
CA	Los Angeles	60	72	53	7.5	6.7	7.9	1,286	682	43	79	65	71	61	86	69
	Sacramento	49	73	51	7.8	7.1	8.9	2,666	1,248	16	83	46	91	70	77	30
	San Diego	55	72	61	7.0	6.0	7.5	1,063	866	42	77	63	72	58	82	67
	San Francisco	68	71	74	10.6	7.2	13.6	2,862	142	43	84	62	86	68	86	60
CO	Denver	61	67	47	8.6	8.6	8.3	6,128	695	35	67	40	63	49	68	34
CT	Hartford	41	52	47	8.4	8.9	7.3	6,104	759	43	77	52	72	57	79	51
DE	Wilmington	47	55	53	9.0	9.8	7.8	4,887	1,125	55	78	55	76	60	79	54
DC	Washington	48	55	53	9.4	10.0	8.3	3,999	1,560	42	75	54	71	54	76	53
FL	Jacksonville	47	61	52	7.8	8.1	7.0	1,353	2,636	66	89	56	88	58	89	59
	Miami	46	68	52	9.2	9.5	7.9	155	4,383	38	83	61	84	60	83	63
GA	Atlanta	61	59	63	9.1	10.4	7.7	2,827	1,810	42	82	56	79	59	88	59
HI	Honolulu	47	74	52	11.3	9.4	13.1	-	4,561	33	72	56	81	61	68	52
ID	Boise	56	58	62	8.7	7.9	8.4	5,809	769	63	69	43	80	70	54	21
IL	Chicago	37	52	43	10.3	11.6	8.4	6,493	835	44	80	63	78	70	82	60
	Peoria	52	53	58	9.8	10.9	7.8	6,095	998	43	83	65	80	71	86	63
IN	Indianapolis	64	51	53	9.6	10.9	7.5	5,521	1,042	43	84	62	81	71	87	60
IA	Des Moines	46	55	52	10.7	11.4	8.9	6,432	1,052	41	80	63	77	70	83	61
KS	Wichita	46	58	48	12.2	12.0	11.3	4,765	1,658	49	80	58	79	65	79	53
KY	Louisville	47	53	54	8.3	9.5	6.8	4,352	1,443	42	81	59	78	65	85	58
LA	New Orleans	47	60	53	8.2	9.3	6.1	1,417	2,776	54	87	65	85	68	91	68
ME	Portland	54	55	61	8.7	9.0	7.6	7,325	347	62	79	59	76	61	80	59
MD	Baltimore	45	58	51	8.8	9.4	7.6	4,634	1,220	49	78	54	73	57	80	53
MA	Boston	60	55	44	12.4	13.7	11.0	5,630	777	38	73	58	69	58	74	57
MI	Detroit	37	49	43	10.3	11.9	8.5	6,449	727	44	81	60	80	70	82	54
	Sault Ste. Marie	54	43	60	9.2	9.6	7.8	9,230	145	61	85	66	81	74	88	62
MN	Duluth	47	49	52	11.0	11.6	9.4	9,742	189	41	81	66	78	72	85	63
	Minneapolis-St. Paul	57	54	63	10.5	10.5	9.4	7,882	699	43	78	63	76	69	81	59
MS	Jackson	30	59	38	7.0	8.2	5.2	2,368	2,290	39	90	62	86	68	93	64
MO	Kansas City	23	59	29	10.6	11.1	9.2	5,249	1,325	30	81	64	77	67	85	64
	St. Louis	47	55	52	9.6	10.6	8.0	4,757	1,561	42	82	62	81	68	83	60
MT	Great Falls	57	51	60	12.5	14.9	10.0	7,675	326	41	68	46	67	61	68	31
NE	Omaha	49	59	65	10.5	10.9	8.8	6,312	1,095	38	81	63	79	68	85	63
NV	Reno	53	69	59	6.6	5.6	7.2	5,601	493	39	68	31	79	50	60	18
NH	Concord	54	55	59	6.7	7.2	5.7	7,485	442	37	81	53	76	59	84	51
NJ	Atlantic City	37	56	43	9.8	10.7	8.3	5,113	935	38	82	56	79	59	83	57
NM	Albuquerque	56	76	62	8.9	8.0	8.9	4,281	1,290	42	59	29	68	39	59	27
NY	Albany	57	49	63	8.9	9.8	7.5	6,861	544	37	80	58	78	64	81	55
	Buffalo	52	43	62	11.8	14.0	10.2	6,693	548	42	80	63	79	73	79	55
	New York [2]	42	64	64	9.3	10.6	7.6	4,744	1,160	68	72	56	68	60	75	55
NC	Charlotte	49	59	52	7.4	7.8	6.6	3,208	1,644	42	82	53	78	55	86	56
	Raleigh	47	59	52	7.6	8.2	6.7	3,465	1,521	38	85	54	80	55	89	58
ND	Bismarck	56	55	62	10.2	10.0	9.2	8,809	471	43	81	61	76	71	84	53
OH	Cincinnati	44	49	54	9.0	10.4	7.2	5,200	1,053	40	82	60	80	69	86	58
	Cleveland	54	45	60	10.5	12.2	8.6	6,097	712	42	80	62	79	70	82	57
	Columbus	46	48	52	8.3	9.8	6.5	5,546	925	43	81	59	78	68	84	56
OK	Oklahoma City	44	64	53	12.2	12.5	10.9	3,663	1,907	37	80	59	78	62	80	55
OR	Portland	47	39	53	7.9	9.9	7.6	4,366	398	62	85	59	85	76	82	45
PA	Philadelphia	55	56	61	9.5	10.3	8.2	4,759	1,235	43	76	55	74	60	78	54
	Pittsburgh	43	44	49	9.0	10.4	7.3	5,829	726	42	79	58	77	66	83	54
RI	Providence	42	55	48	10.4	10.9	9.4	5,754	714	39	75	55	72	57	77	56
SC	Columbia	48	60	53	6.8	7.2	6.3	2,595	2,063	36	86	51	83	54	88	53
SD	Sioux Falls	50	57	53	11.0	10.9	9.8	7,746	757	39	82	64	78	71	84	60
TN	Memphis	43	59	53	8.8	10.0	7.5	3,033	2,190	63	80	59	78	65	84	60
	Nashville	54	57	60	8.0	9.1	6.5	3,658	1,656	37	83	61	79	66	88	61
TX	Dallas-Fort Worth	42	64	48	10.7	11.0	9.8	2,370	2,571	39	81	59	79	63	79	53
	El Paso	53	80	59	8.8	8.3	8.3	2,604	2,165	42	56	27	65	34	61	29
	Houston	26	56	32	7.6	8.1	6.7	1,525	2,893	33	89	65	85	68	92	63
UT	Salt Lake City	69	62	72	8.8	7.5	9.5	5,607	1,089	43	67	43	79	69	52	22
VT	Burlington	52	44	58	9.0	9.7	8.0	7,665	489	37	77	59	73	64	78	53
VA	Norfolk	47	58	53	10.5	11.4	8.9	3,342	1,630	54	78	57	75	59	81	59
	Richmond	50	56	53	7.7	8.1	6.9	3,878	1,466	68	83	53	80	57	85	56
WA	Seattle-Tacoma [3]	51	38	53	8.8	9.5	8.1	4,797	173	43	84	62	82	75	82	49
	Spokane	48	48	54	8.9	8.7	8.6	6,820	394	43	78	52	86	79	65	28
WV	Charleston	47	48	54	5.8	6.9	4.8	4,589	1,064	55	84	57	78	63	90	60
WI	Milwaukee	55	52	61	11.5	12.6	9.7	7,096	616	42	80	66	76	70	82	64
WY	Cheyenne	60	64	44	12.9	15.2	10.4	7,289	280	43	66	45	58	51	70	38
PR	San Juan	40	76	46	8.4	8.4	9.7	-	5,426	47	79	65	82	65	79	67

- Represents zero.   [1] Percent of days that are either clear or partly cloudy.   [2] Airport data for sunshine.   [3] Does not represent airport data.

Source: U.S. National Oceanic and Atmospheric Administration, *Comparative Climatic Data*, annual.

236 Geography and Environment

Elections

This section relates primarily to presidential, congressional, and gubernatorial elections. Also presented are summary tables on congressional legislation; state legislatures; Black, Hispanic, and female officeholders; population of voting age; voter participation; and campaign finances.

Official statistics on federal elections, collected by the Clerk of the House, are published biennially in *Statistics of the Presidential and Congressional Election* and *Statistics of the Congressional Election*. Federal and state elections data appear also in *America Votes*, a biennial volume published by CQ Press (a division of Congressional Quarterly, Inc.), Washington, DC. Federal elections data also appear in the U.S. Congress, *Congressional Directory*, and in official state documents. Data on reported registration and voting for social and economic groups are obtained by the U.S. Census Bureau as part of the Current Population Survey (CPS) and are published in Current Population Reports, Series P20 (see text, Section 1).

Almost all federal, state, and local governmental units in the United States conduct elections for political offices and other purposes. The conduct of elections is regulated by state laws or, in some cities and counties, by local charter. An exception is that the U.S. Constitution prescribes the basis of representation in Congress and the manner of electing the President and grants to Congress the right to regulate the times, places, and manner of electing federal officers. Amendments to the Constitution have prescribed national criteria for voting eligibility. The 15th Amendment, adopted in 1870, gave all citizens the right to vote regardless of race, color, or previous condition of servitude. The 19th Amendment, adopted in 1919, further extended the right to vote to all citizens regardless of sex. The payment of poll taxes as a prerequisite to voting in federal elections was banned by the 24th Amendment in 1964. In 1971, as a result of the 26th Amendment, eligibility to vote in national elections was extended to all citizens, 18 years old and over.

Presidential election—The Constitution specifies how the President and Vice President are selected. Each state elects, by popular vote, a group of electors equal in number to its total of members of Congress. The 23d Amendment, adopted in 1961, grants the District of Columbia three presidential electors, a number equal to that of the least populous state. Subsequent to the election, the electors meet in their respective states to vote for President and Vice President. Usually, each elector votes for the candidate receiving the most popular votes in his or her state. A majority vote of all electors is necessary to elect the President and Vice President. If no candidate receives a majority, the House of Representatives, with each state having one vote, is empowered to elect the President and Vice President, again, with a majority of votes required.

The 22nd Amendment to the Constitution, adopted in 1951, limits presidential tenure to two elective terms of 4 years each or to one elective term for any person who, upon succession to the Presidency, has held the office or acted as President for more than 2 years.

Congressional election—The Constitution provides that Representatives be apportioned among the states according to their population, that a census of population be taken every 10 years as a basis for apportionment, and that each state have at least one Representative. At the time of each apportionment, Congress decides what the total number of Representatives will be. Since 1912, the total has been 435, except during 1960 to 1962 when it increased to 437, adding one Representative each for Alaska and Hawaii. The total reverted to 435 after

U.S. Census Bureau, Statistical Abstract of the United States: 2004-2005

reapportionment following the 1960 census. Members are elected for 2-year terms, all terms covering the same period. The District of Columbia, American Samoa, Guam, and the Virgin Islands each elect one nonvoting Delegate, and Puerto Rico elects a nonvoting Resident Commissioner.

The Senate is composed of 100 members, 2 from each state, who are elected to serve for a term of 6 years. One-third of the Senate is elected every 2 years. Senators were originally chosen by the state legislatures. The 17th Amendment to the Constitution, adopted in 1913, prescribed that Senators be elected by popular vote.

Voter eligibility and participation— The Census Bureau publishes estimates of the population of voting age and the percent casting votes in each state for Presidential and congressional election years. These voting-age estimates include a number of persons who meet the age requirement but are not eligible to vote, (e.g. aliens and some institutionalized persons). In addition, since 1964, voter participation and voter characteristics data have been collected during November of election years as part of the CPS. These survey data include noncitizens in the voting age population estimates but exclude members of the Armed Forces and the institutional population.

Statistical reliability— For a discussion of statistical collection and estimation, sampling procedures, and measures of statistical reliability applicable to Census Bureau data, see Appendix III.

Figure 7.1
Vote Cast for President by Major Political Party: 1992 to 2000

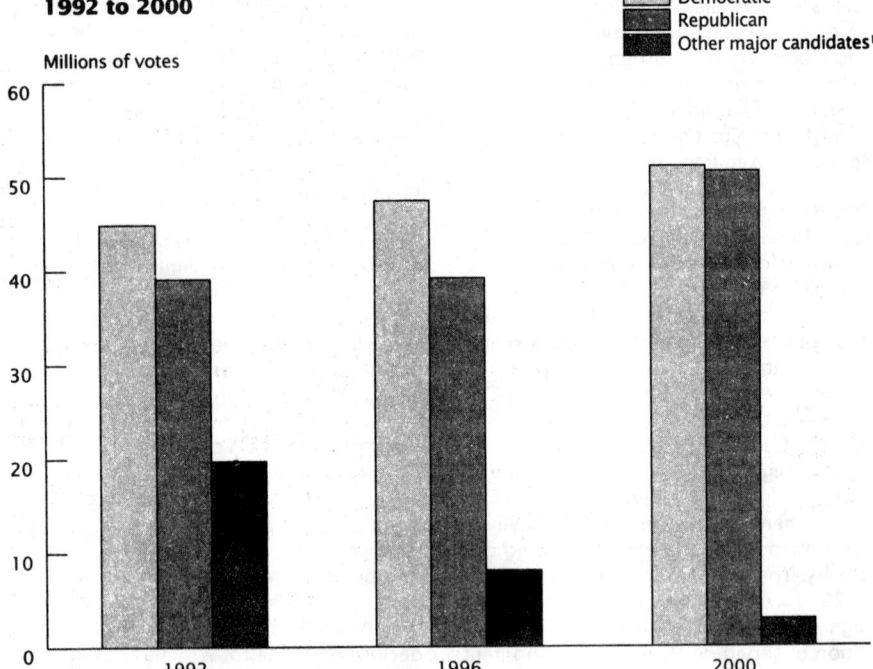

[1] Candidates with 1 million or more votes: 1992 - Independent, Ross Perot; 1996 - Reform, Ross Perot; 2000 - Green, Ralph Nader.

Source: Chart prepared by U.S. Census Bureau. For data, see Tables 384 and 385.

U.S. Census Bureau, Statistical Abstract of the United States: 2004-2005

No. 384. Vote Cast for President by Major Political Party: 1940 to 2000

[49,900 represents 49,900,000. Prior to 1960, excludes Alaska and Hawaii; prior to 1964, excludes DC. Vote cast for major party candidates include the votes of minor parties cast for those candidates]

Year	Candidates for President Democratic	Republican	Vote cast for President Total popular vote [1] (1,000)	Democratic Popular vote Number (1,000)	Per-cent	Elec-toral vote	Republican Popular vote Number (1,000)	Per-cent	Electoral vote
1940....	F. D. Roosevelt ..	Willkie	49,900	27,313	54.7	449	22,348	44.8	82
1944....	F. D. Roosevelt ..	Dewey........	47,977	25,613	53.4	432	22,018	45.9	99
1948....	Truman	Dewey........	48,794	24,179	49.6	303	21,991	45.1	189
1952....	Stevenson	Eisenhower.....	61,551	27,315	44.4	89	33,936	55.1	442
1956....	Stevenson	Eisenhower.....	62,027	26,023	42.0	73	35,590	57.4	457
1960....	Kennedy	Nixon........	68,838	34,227	49.7	303	34,108	49.5	219
1964....	Johnson.......	Goldwater......	70,645	43,130	61.1	486	27,178	38.5	52
1968....	Humphrey	Nixon........	73,212	31,275	42.7	191	31,785	43.4	301
1972....	McGovern	Nixon........	77,719	29,170	37.5	17	47,170	60.7	520
1976....	Carter	Ford	81,556	40,831	50.1	297	39,148	48.0	240
1980....	Carter	Reagan	86,515	35,484	41.0	49	43,904	50.7	489
1984....	Mondale	Reagan	92,653	37,577	40.6	13	54,455	58.8	525
1988....	Dukakis.......	Bush........	91,595	41,809	45.6	111	48,886	53.4	426
1992....	Clinton........	Bush........	104,425	44,909	43.0	370	39,104	37.4	168
1996....	Clinton........	Dole	96,278	47,402	49.2	379	39,199	40.7	159
2000....	Gore	Bush........	105,397	50,992	48.4	266	50,455	47.9	271

[1] Include votes for minor party candidates, independents, unpledged electors, and scattered write-in votes.
Source: CQ Press (a division of Congressional Quarterly, Inc), Washington, DC, *America at the Polls 2*, 1965, and *America Votes*, biennial, (copyright).

No. 385. Vote Cast for Leading Minority Party Candidates for President: 1940 to 2000

[116 represents 116,000. See headnote, Table 384]

Year	Candidate	Party	Popular vote (1,000)	Candidate	Party	Popular vote (1,000)
1940 ..	Norman Thomas ...	Socialist	116	Roger Babson	Prohibition.........	59
1944 ..	Norman Thomas ...	Socialist	79	Claude Watson	Prohibition.........	75
1948 ..	Strom Thurmond ...	States' Rights.......	1,176	Henry Wallace.....	Progressive	1,157
1952 ..	Vincent Hallinan....	Progressive	140	Stuart Hamblen	Prohibition.........	73
1956 ..	T. Coleman Andrews.	States' Rights.......	111	Eric Hass	Socialist Labor	44
1960 ..	Eric Hass	Socialist Labor	48	Rutherford Decker ..	Prohibition.........	46
1964 ..	Eric Hass	Socialist Labor	45	Clifton DeBerry	Socialist Workers ...	33
1968 ..	George Wallace....	American Independent.	9,906	Henning Blomen ...	Socialist Labor	53
1972 ..	John Schmitz......	American..........	1,099	Benjamin Spock....	People's	79
1976 ..	Eugene McCarthy ..	Independent	757	Roger McBride.....	Libertarian.........	173
1980 ..	John Anderson	Independent	5,720	Ed Clark..........	Libertarian.........	921
1984 ..	David Bergland	Libertarian........	228	Lyndon H. LaRouche.	Independent	79
1988 ..	Ron Paul	Libertarian........	432	Lenora B. Fulani ...	New Alliance	217
1992 ..	H. Ross Perot	Independent	19,742	Andre Marrou	Libertarian.........	292
1996 ..	H. Ross Perot	Reform Party	8,085	Ralph Nader	Green............	685
2000 ..	Ralph Nader	Green............	2,883	Pat Buchanan	Reform...........	449

Source: CQ Press (a division of Congressional Quarterly, Inc.), Washington, DC, *America at the Polls 1920-1996, 1997;* and *America Votes*, biennial (copyright).

No. 386. Democratic and Republican Percentages of Two-Party Presidential Vote by Selected Characteristics of Voters: 1996 and 2000

[In percent. Covers citizens of voting age living in private housing units in the contiguous United States. Percentages for Democratic Presidential vote are computed by subtracting the percentage Republican vote from 100 percent; third-party or independent votes are not included as valid data. Data are from the National Election Studies and are based on a sample and subject to sampling variability; for details, see source]

Characteristic	1996 Demo-cratic	Repub-lican	2000 Demo-cratic	Repub-lican	Characteristic	1996 Demo-cratic	Repub-lican	2000 Demo-cratic	Repub-lican
Total [1]	58	42	52	48	Race:				
Year of birth:					White...........	51	49	46	54
1975 or later......	61	39	63	37	Black...........	99	1	92	8
1959 to 1974	58	42	46	54					
1943 to 1958	58	42	53	47	Education:				
1927 to 1942	56	44	48	52	Grade school	88	12	74	26
1911 to 1926.....	64	36	64	36	High school.......	64	36	54	46
1895 to 1910	57	43	-	100	College	49	51	50	50
Sex:									
Male	51	49	47	53	Union household.....	75	25	61	39
Female	65	35	56	44	Non-union household. .	54	46	50	50

- Represents zero. [1] Includes other characteristics, not shown separately.
Source: Center for Political Studies, University of Michigan, Ann Arbor, MI, National Election Studies (NES); "The NES Guide to Public Opinion and Electoral Behavior;" accessed 26 April, 2003; <http://www.umich.edu/~nes/nesguide/nesguide.htm>. (copyright).

Elections 239

No. 387. Electoral Vote Cast for President, by Major Political Party—States: 1960 to 2000

[D=Democratic, R=Republican. For composition of regions, see map, inside front cover]

State	1960 [1]	1964	1968 [2]	1972 [3]	1976 [4]	1980	1984	1988 [5]	1992	1996	2000 [6]
Democratic	303	486	191	17	297	49	13	111	370	379	266
Republican	219	52	301	520	240	489	525	426	168	159	271
Northeast:											
Democratic.	121	126	102	14	86	4	-	53	106	106	102
Republican.	12	-	24	108	36	118	113	60	-	-	4
Midwest:											
Democratic.	71	149	31	-	58	10	10	29	100	100	68
Republican.	82	-	118	145	87	135	127	108	29	29	61
South:											
Democratic.	101	121	45	3	149	31	3	8	68	80	15
Republican.	50	47	77	165	20	138	174	168	116	104	168
West:											
Democratic.	10	90	13	-	4	4	-	21	96	93	81
Republican.	75	5	82	102	97	98	111	90	23	26	38
AL	[1]D-5	R-10	([2])	R-9	D-9	R-9	R-9	R-9	R-9	R-9	R-9
AK	R-3	D-3	R-3	R-3	R-3	R-3	R-3	R-3	R-3	R-3	R-3
AZ	R-4	R-5	R-5	R-6	R-6	R-6	R-7	R-7	R-8	D-8	R-8
AR	D-8	D-6	([2])	R-6	D-6	R-6	R-6	R-6	D-6	D-6	R-6
CA	R-32	D-40	R-40	R-45	R-45	R-45	R-47	R-47	D-54	D-54	D-54
CO	R-6	D-6	R-6	R-7	R-7	R-7	R-8	R-8	D-8	R-8	R-8
CT	D-8	D-8	D-8	R-8	R-8	R-8	R-8	R-8	D-8	D-8	D-8
DE	D-3	D-3	R-3	R-3	D-3	R-3	R-3	R-3	D-3	D-3	D-3
DC	(X)	D-3	D-3	D-3	D-3	D-3	D-3	D-3	D-3	D-3	[6]D-2
FL	R-10	D-14	R-14	R-17	D-17	R-17	R-21	R-21	R-25	D-25	R-25
GA	D-12	R-12	([2])	R-12	D-12	D-12	R-12	R-12	D-13	R-13	R-13
HI	D-3	D-4	D-4	R-4	D-4	D-4	D-4	D-4	D-4	D-4	D-4
ID	R-4	D-4	R-4	R-4	R-4	R-4	R-4	R-4	R-4	R-4	R-4
IL	D-27	D-26	R-26	R-26	R-26	R-26	R-24	R-24	D-22	D-22	D-22
IN	R-13	D-13	R-13	R-13	R-13	R-13	R-12	R-12	R-12	R-12	R-12
IA	R-10	D-9	R-9	R-8	R-8	R-8	R-8	D-8	D-7	D-7	D-7
KS	R-8	D-7	R-7	R-7	R-7	R-7	R-7	R-7	R-6	R-6	R-6
KY	R-10	D-9	R-9	R-9	D-9	R-9	R-9	R-9	D-8	D-8	R-8
LA	D-10	R-10	([2])	R-10	D-10	R-10	R-10	R-10	D-9	D-9	R-9
ME	R-5	D-4	D-4	R-4	R-4	R-4	R-4	R-4	D-4	D-4	D-4
MD	D-9	D-10	D-10	R-10	D-10	D-10	R-10	R-10	D-10	D-10	D-10
MA	D-16	D-14	D-14	D-14	D-14	D-14	D-13	D-13	D-12	D-12	D-12
MI	D-20	D-21	D-21	R-21	R-21	R-21	R-20	R-20	D-18	D-18	D-18
MN	D-11	D-10	D-10	R-10	D-10	D-10	D-10	D-10	D-10	D-10	D-10
MS	([1])	R-7	([2])	R-7	D-7	R-7	R-7	R-7	R-7	R-7	R-7
MO	D-13	D-12	R-12	R-12	D-12	R-12	R-11	R-11	D-11	D-11	R-11
MT	R-4	D-4	R-4	R-4	R-4	R-4	R-4	R-4	D-3	R-3	R-3
NE	R-6	D-5	R-5	R-5	R-5	R-5	R-5	R-5	R-5	R-5	R-5
NV	D-3	D-3	R-3	R-3	R-3	R-3	R-4	R-4	D-4	D-4	R-4
NH	R-4	D-4	R-4	R-4	R-4	R-4	R-4	R-4	D-4	D-4	R-4
NJ	D-16	D-17	R-17	R-17	R-17	R-17	R-16	R-16	D-15	D-15	D-15
NM	D-4	D-4	R-4	R-4	R-4	R-4	R-5	R-5	D-5	D-5	D-5
NY	D-45	D-43	D-43	R-41	D-41	R-41	R-36	D-36	D-33	D-33	D-33
NC	D-14	D-13	[2]R-12	R-13	D-13	R-13	R-13	R-13	R-14	R-14	R-14
ND	R-4	D-4	R-4	R-3	R-3	R-3	R-3	R-3	R-3	R-3	R-3
OH	R-25	D-26	R-26	R-25	D-25	R-25	R-23	R-23	D-21	D-21	R-21
OK	[1]R-7	D-8	R-8	R-8	R-8	R-8	R-8	R-8	R-8	R-8	R-8
OR	R-6	D-6	R-6	R-6	R-6	R-6	R-7	D-7	D-7	D-7	D-7
PA	D-32	D-29	D-29	R-27	D-27	R-27	R-25	R-25	D-23	D-23	D-23
RI	D-4	D-4	D-4	R-4	D-4	D-4	R-4	D-4	D-4	D-4	D-4
SC	D-8	R-8	R-8	R-8	D-8	R-8	R-8	R-8	R-8	R-8	R-8
SD	R-4	D-4	R-4	R-4	R-4	R-4	R-3	R-3	R-3	R-3	R-3
TN	R-11	D-11	R-11	R-10	D-10	R-10	R-11	R-11	D-11	D-11	R-11
TX	D-24	D-25	D-25	R-26	D-26	R-26	R-29	R-29	R-32	R-32	R-32
UT	R-4	D-4	R-4	R-4	R-4	R-4	R-5	R-5	R-5	R-5	R-5
VT	R-3	D-3	R-3	R-3	R-3	R-3	R-3	R-3	D-3	D-3	D-3
VA	R-12	D-12	R-12	[3]R-11	R-12	R-12	R-12	R-12	R-13	R-13	R-13
WA	R-9	D-9	D-9	R-9	[4]R-8	R-9	R-10	D-10	D-11	D-11	D-11
WV	D-8	D-7	D-7	R-6	D-6	D-6	R-6	[5]D-5	D-5	D-5	R-5
WI	R-12	D-12	R-12	R-11	D-11	R-11	R-11	R-11	D-11	D-11	D-11
WY	R-3	D-3	R-3	R-3	R-3	R-3	R-3	R-3	R-3	R-3	R-3

- Represents zero. X Not applicable. [1] Excludes 15 electoral votes cast for Harry F. Byrd as follows: AL 6, MS 8, and OK 1. [2] Excludes 46 electoral votes cast for American Independent George C. Wallace as follows: AL 10, AR 6, GA 12, LA 10, MS 7, and NC 1. [3] Excludes one electoral vote cast for Libertarian John Hospers in Virginia. [4] Excludes one electoral vote cast for Ronald Reagan in Washington. [5] Excludes one electoral vote cast for Lloyd Bentsen for President in West Virginia. [6] Excludes one electoral vote left blank by a Democratic elector in the District of Columbia.

Source: 1960-72, U.S. Congress, Clerk of the House, *Statistics of the Presidential and Congressional Election*, quadrennial; 1976-2000, CQ Press (a division of Congressional Quarterly, Inc.), Washington, DC *America Votes*, biennial (copyright).

No. 388. Popular Vote Cast for President by Political Party—States: 1996 and 2000

[In thousands (96,278 represents 96,278,000), except percent]

State	1996				2000				
								Percent of total vote	
	Total [1]	Democratic Party	Republican Party	Perot (Reform Party)	Total [1]	Democratic Party	Republican Party	Democratic Party	Republican Party
United States. .	96,278	47,402	39,199	8,085	105,397	50,992	50,455	48.4	47.9
Alabama.	1,534	662	769	92	1,666	693	941	41.6	56.5
Alaska	242	80	123	26	286	79	167	27.7	58.6
Arizona.	1,404	653	622	112	1,532	685	782	44.7	51.0
Arkansas	884	475	325	70	922	423	473	45.9	51.3
California	10,019	5,120	3,828	698	10,966	5,861	4,567	53.4	41.7
Colorado.	1,511	671	692	100	1,741	738	884	42.4	50.8
Connecticut.	1,393	736	483	140	1,460	816	561	55.9	38.4
Delaware	271	140	99	29	328	180	137	55.0	41.9
District of Columbia .	186	158	17	4	202	172	18	85.2	9.0
Florida.	5,304	2,547	2,245	484	5,963	2,912	2,913	48.8	48.8
Georgia	2,299	1,054	1,081	146	2,597	1,116	1,420	43.0	54.7
Hawaii	360	205	114	27	368	205	138	55.8	37.5
Idaho	492	165	257	63	502	139	337	27.6	67.2
Illinois	4,311	2,342	1,587	346	4,742	2,589	2,019	54.6	42.6
Indiana.	2,136	887	1,007	224	2,199	902	1,246	41.0	56.6
Iowa	1,234	620	493	105	1,316	639	634	48.5	48.2
Kansas.	1,074	388	583	93	1,072	399	622	37.2	58.0
Kentucky	1,389	637	623	120	1,544	639	872	41.4	56.5
Louisiana	1,784	928	713	123	1,766	792	928	44.9	52.6
Maine.	606	313	186	86	652	320	287	49.1	44.0
Maryland	1,781	966	682	116	2,020	1,141	814	56.5	40.3
Massachusetts.	2,557	1,572	718	227	2,703	1,616	879	59.8	32.5
Michigan.	3,849	1,990	1,481	337	4,233	2,170	1,953	51.3	46.1
Minnesota.	2,193	1,120	766	258	2,439	1,168	1,110	47.9	45.5
Mississippi	894	394	440	52	994	405	573	40.7	57.6
Missouri	2,158	1,026	890	217	2,360	1,111	1,190	47.1	50.4
Montana.	407	168	180	55	411	137	240	33.4	58.4
Nebraska	677	237	363	71	697	232	434	33.3	62.2
Nevada	464	204	199	44	609	280	302	46.0	49.5
New Hampshire. . . .	499	246	196	48	569	266	274	46.8	48.1
New Jersey.	3,076	1,652	1,103	262	3,187	1,789	1,284	56.1	40.3
New Mexico	556	273	233	32	599	287	286	47.9	47.8
New York	6,316	3,756	1,933	503	6,822	4,108	2,403	60.2	35.2
North Carolina.	2,516	1,108	1,226	168	2,911	1,258	1,631	43.2	56.0
North Dakota.	266	107	125	33	288	95	175	33.1	60.7
Ohio	4,534	2,148	1,860	483	4,702	2,184	2,350	46.4	50.0
Oklahoma.	1,207	488	582	131	1,234	474	744	38.4	60.3
Oregon.	1,378	650	538	121	1,534	720	714	47.0	46.5
Pennsylvania.	4,506	2,216	1,801	431	4,913	2,486	2,281	50.6	46.4
Rhode Island.	390	233	105	44	409	250	131	61.0	31.9
South Carolina.	1,152	506	573	64	1,383	566	786	40.9	56.8
South Dakota	324	139	151	31	316	119	191	37.6	60.3
Tennessee	1,894	909	864	106	2,076	982	1,062	47.3	51.1
Texas.	5,612	2,460	2,736	379	6,408	2,434	3,800	38.0	59.3
Utah	666	222	362	66	771	203	515	26.3	66.8
Vermont	258	138	80	31	294	149	120	50.6	40.7
Virginia.	2,417	1,091	1,138	160	2,739	1,217	1,437	44.4	52.5
Washington.	2,254	1,123	841	201	2,487	1,248	1,109	50.2	44.6
West Virginia.	636	328	234	72	648	295	336	45.6	51.9
Wisconsin	2,196	1,072	845	227	2,599	1,243	1,237	47.8	47.6
Wyoming	212	78	105	26	218	60	148	27.7	67.8

[1] Includes other parties.

Source: CQ Press (a division of Congressional Quarterly, Inc.), Washington, DC, *America Votes*, biennial (copyright).

Elections · 241

No. 389. Vote Cast for United States Senators, 2000 and 2002, and Incumbent Senators, 2002—States

[1,397 represents 1,397,000. D=Democrat; R=Republican]

State	2000 Total (1,000)[1]	2000 Percent for leading party	2002 Total (1,000)[1]	2002 Percent for leading party	Incumbent senators and year term expires — Name, party, and year	Incumbent senators and year term expires — Name, party, and year
Alabama........	(X)	(X)	1,353	R-58.6	Jeff Sessions (R) 2009	Richard C. Shelby (R) 2005
Alaska.........	(X)	(X)	230	R-78.2	Lisa Murkowski (R) 2005	Ted Stevens (R) 2009
Arizona........	1,397	R-79.3	(X)	(X)	John McCain (R) 2005	Jon Kyl (R) 2007
Arkansas	(X)	(X)	804	D-53.9	Blanche Lincoln (D) 2005	Mark Pryor (D) 2009
California	10,624	D-55.8	(X)	(X)	Barbara Boxer (D) 2005	Dianne Feinstein (D) 2007
Colorado.......	(X)	(X)	1,416	R-50.7	Ben N. Campbell (R) 2005	Wayne Allard (R) 2009
Connecticut....	1,311	D-63.2	(X)	(X)	Christopher J. Dodd (D) 2005	Joseph I. Lieberman (D) 2007
Delaware	327	D-55.5	232	D-58.2	Joseph R. Biden Jr. (D) 2009	Thomas R. Carper (D) 2007
Florida	5,857	D-51.0	(X)	(X)	Bob Graham (D) 2005	Bill Nelson (D) 2007
Georgia	2,429	D-58.2	2,032	R-52.7	Saxby Chambliss (R) 2009	Zell Miller (D) 2005
Hawaii	346	D-72.7	(X)	(X)	Daniel K. Akaka (D) 2007	Daniel K. Inouye (D) 2005
Idaho.........	(X)	(X)	409	R-65.2	Larry E. Craig (R) 2009	Michael D. Crapo (R) 2005
Illinois........	(X)	(X)	3,487	D-60.3	Peter Fitzgerald (R) 2005	Richard J. Durbin (D) 2009
Indiana........	2,145	R-66.6	(X)	(X)	Evan Bayh (D) 2005	Richard G. Lugar (R) 2007
Iowa	(X)	(X)	1,023	D-54.2	Tom Harkin (D) 2009	Charles E. Grassley (R) 2005
Kansas........	(X)	(X)	767	R-83.6	Sam Brownback (R) 2005	Pat Roberts (R) 2009
Kentucky[2]....	(X)	(X)	1,131	R-64.7	Jim Bunning (R) 2005	Mitch McConnell (R) 2009
Louisiana[2]	(X)	(X)	2,482	D-49.8	John B. Breaux (D) 2005	Mary Landrieu (D) 2009
Maine.........	635	R-68.9	505	R-58.4	Susan Collins (R) 2009	Olympia J. Snowe (R) 2007
Maryland	1,947	D-63.2	(X)	(X)	Barbara A. Mikulski (D) 2005	Paul S. Sarbanes (D) 2007
Massachusetts..	2,599	D-72.7	2,007	D-80.0	Edward M. Kennedy (D) 2007	John F. Kerry (D) 2009
Michigan......	4,168	D-49.5	3,129	D-60.6	Carl Levin (D) 2009	Debbie Stabenow (D) 2007
Minnesota.....	2,420	D-48.8	2,255	R-49.5	Norm Coleman (R) 2009	Mark Dayton (D) 2007
Mississippi....	994	R-65.9	630	R-84.6	Thad Cochran (R) 2009	Trent Lott (R) 2007
Missouri	2,362	D-50.5	1,878	R-49.8	Christopher S. Bond (R) 2005	James Talent (R) 2007
Montana......	412	R-50.6	327	D-62.7	Max Baucus (D) 2009	Conrad Burns (R) 2007
Nebraska	692	D-51.0	480	R-82.8	Chuck Hagel (R) 2009	Ben Nelson (D) 2007
Nevada	600	R-55.1	(X)	(X)	Harry Reid (D) 2005	John Ensign (R) 2007
New Hampshire..	(X)	(X)	447	R-50.8	Judd Gregg (R) 2005	John Sununu (R) 2009
New Jersey....	3,016	D-50.1	2,113	D-53.9	Frank Lautenberg (D) 2009	Jon Corzine (D) 2007
New Mexico ...	590	D-61.7	483	R-65.0	Jeff Bingaman (D) 2007	Pete V. Domenici (R) 2009
New York	6,780	D-55.3	(X)	(X)	Hillary Rodham Clinton (D) 2007	Charles E. Schumer (D) 2005
North Carolina..	(X)	(X)	2,331	R-53.6	John Edwards (D) 2005	Elizabeth Dole (R) 2009
North Dakota...	288	D-61.4	(X)	(X)	Byron L. Dorgan (D) 2005	Kent Conrad (D) 2007
Ohio	4,449	R-59.9	(X)	(X)	George V. Voinovich (R) 2005	Mike DeWine (R) 2007
Oklahoma.....	(X)	(X)	1,018	R-57.3	James Inhofe (R) 2009	Don Nickles (R) 2005
Oregon........	(X)	(X)	1,267	R-56.2	Gordon Smith (R) 2009	Ron Wyden (D) 2005
Pennsylvania...	4,736	R-52.4	(X)	(X)	Rick Santorum (R) 2007	Arlen Specter (R) 2005
Rhode Island...	392	R-56.8	324	D-78.4	Jack Reed (D) 2009	Lincoln Chafee (R) 2007
South Carolina..	(X)	(X)	1,103	R-54.4	Ernest F. Hollings (D) 2005	Lindsey Graham (R) 2009
South Dakota ..	(X)	(X)	338	D-49.6	Thomas A. Daschle (D) 2005	Tim Johnson (D) 2009
Tennessee	1,929	R-65.1	1,642	R-54.3	Lamar Alexander (R) 2009	Bill Frist (R) 2007
Texas........	6,277	R-65.0	4,514	R-55.3	Kay Bailey Hutchison (R) 2007	John Cornyn (R) 2009
Utah	770	R-65.6	(X)	(X)	Robert F. Bennett (R) 2007	Orrin G. Hatch (R) 2007
Vermont[3]	289	R-65.6	(X)	(X)	Patrick J. Leahy (D) 2005	[3]James M. Jeffords (I) 2007
Virginia.......	2,718	R-52.3	1,489	R-82.6	George F. Allen (R) 2007	John W. Warner (R) 2009
Washington....	2,461	D-48.7	(X)	(X)	Patty Murray (D) 2005	Maria Cantwell (D) 2007
West Virginia...	603	D-77.8	436	D-63.1	Robert C. Byrd (D) 2007	John D. Rockefeller IV (D) 2009
Wisconsin.....	2,540	D-61.5	(X)	(X)	Herb Kohl (D) 2007	Russell Feingold (D) 2005
Wyoming......	214	R-73.8	183	R-73.0	Mike Enzi (R) 2009	Craig Thomas (R) 2007

X Not applicable.   [1] Includes vote cast for minor parties.   [2] Louisiana holds an open-primary election with candidates from all parties running on the same ballot. Any candidate who receives a majority is elected.   [3] Jeffords was reelected in Vermont in 2000 as a Republican, but subsequently switched to Independent status in June 2001.

Source: CQ Press (a division of Congressional Quarterly, Inc.), Washington, DC, *America Votes*, biennial (copyright).

No. 390. Apportionment of Membership in House of Representatives by State: 1790 to 2000

[Total membership includes Representatives assigned to newly admitted states after the apportionment acts. Population figures used for apportionment purposes are those determined for states by each decennial census. No reapportionment based on 1920 population census. For method of calculating apportionment and a short history of apportionment, see House Report 91-1314, 91st Congress, 2d session, The Decennial Population Census and Congressional Apportionment]

State	1790	1800	1810	1820	1830	1840	1850	1860	1870	1880	1890	1900	1910	1930	1940	1950	1960	1970	1980	1990	2000
U.S.	106	142	186	213	242	232	237	243	293	332	357	391	435	435	435	437	435	435	435	435	435
AL	(X)	(X)	[1]1	3	5	7	7	6	8	8	9	9	10	9	9	9	8	7	7	7	7
AK	(X)	(X)	(X)	(X)	(X)	(X)	(X)	(X)	(X)	(X)	(X)	(X)	(X)	(X)	(X)	[1]1	1	1	1	1	1
AZ	(X)	(X)	(X)	(X)	(X)	(X)	(X)	(X)	(X)	(X)	(X)	(X)	[2]1	1	2	2	3	4	5	6	8
AR	(X)	(X)	(X)	(X)	[1]1	1	2	3	4	5	6	7	7	7	7	6	4	4	4	4	4
CA	(X)	(X)	(X)	(X)	(X)	[1]2	2	3	4	6	7	8	11	20	23	30	38	43	45	52	53
CO	(X)	(X)	(X)	(X)	(X)	(X)	(X)	(X)	[1]1	1	2	3	4	4	4	4	4	5	6	6	7
CT	7	7	7	6	6	4	4	4	4	4	4	5	5	6	6	6	6	6	6	6	5
DE	1	1	2	1	1	[1]1	1	1	1	1	1	1	1	1	1	1	1	1	1	1	1
FL	(X)	(X)	(X)	(X)	(X)	[1]1	1	1	1	2	2	3	4	5	6	8	12	15	19	23	25
GA	2	4	6	7	9	8	8	7	9	10	11	11	12	10	10	10	10	10	10	11	13
HI	(X)	(X)	(X)	(X)	(X)	(X)	(X)	(X)	(X)	(X)	(X)	(X)	(X)	(X)	(X)	[1]1	2	2	2	2	2
ID	(X)	(X)	(X)	(X)	(X)	(X)	(X)	(X)	(X)	[1]1	1	1	2	2	2	2	2	2	2	2	2
IL	(X)	(X)	[1]1	1	3	7	9	14	19	20	22	25	27	27	26	25	24	24	22	20	19
IN	(X)	(X)	[1]1	3	7	10	11	11	13	13	13	13	13	12	11	11	11	11	10	10	9
IA	(X)	(X)	(X)	(X)	(X)	[1]2	2	6	9	11	11	11	11	9	8	8	7	6	6	5	5
KS	(X)	(X)	(X)	(X)	(X)	(X)	(X)	1	3	7	8	8	8	7	6	6	5	5	5	4	4
KY	2	6	10	12	13	10	10	9	10	11	[1]11	11	11	9	9	8	7	7	7	6	6
LA	(X)	(X)	[1]1	3	3	4	4	5	6	6	6	7	8	8	8	8	8	8	8	7	7
ME	(X)	(X)	(X)	7	8	7	6	5	5	4	4	4	4	3	3	3	2	2	2	2	2
MD	8	9	9	9	8	6	6	5	6	6	6	6	6	6	6	7	8	8	8	8	8
MA	14	17	20	13	12	10	11	10	11	12	13	14	16	15	14	14	12	12	11	10	10
MI	(X)	(X)	(X)	(X)	[1]1	3	4	6	9	11	12	12	13	17	17	18	19	19	18	16	15
MN	(X)	(X)	(X)	(X)	(X)	(X)	[1]2	2	3	5	7	9	10	9	9	9	8	8	8	8	8
MS	(X)	(X)	[1]1	1	2	4	5	5	6	7	7	8	8	7	7	6	5	5	5	5	4
MO	(X)	(X)	(X)	1	2	5	7	9	13	14	15	16	16	13	13	11	10	10	9	9	9
MT	(X)	(X)	(X)	(X)	(X)	(X)	(X)	(X)	(X)	[1]1	1	1	2	2	2	2	2	2	2	1	1
NE	(X)	(X)	(X)	(X)	(X)	(X)	(X)	(X)	1	3	6	6	6	5	4	4	3	3	3	3	3
NV	(X)	(X)	(X)	(X)	(X)	(X)	(X)	(X)	[1]1	1	1	1	1	1	1	1	1	1	2	2	3
NH	4	5	6	6	5	4	3	3	3	2	2	2	2	2	2	2	2	2	2	2	2
NJ	5	6	6	6	6	5	5	5	7	7	8	10	12	14	14	14	15	15	14	13	13
NM	(X)	(X)	(X)	(X)	(X)	(X)	(X)	(X)	(X)	(X)	(X)	(X)	[2]1	1	2	2	2	2	3	3	3
NY	10	17	27	34	40	34	33	31	33	34	34	37	43	45	45	43	41	39	34	31	29
NC	10	12	13	13	13	9	8	7	8	9	9	10	10	11	12	12	11	11	11	12	13
ND	(X)	(X)	(X)	(X)	(X)	(X)	(X)	(X)	(X)	[1]1	1	2	3	2	2	2	2	1	1	1	1
OH	(X)	[1]1	6	14	19	21	21	19	20	21	21	21	22	24	23	23	24	23	21	19	18
OK	(X)	(X)	(X)	(X)	(X)	(X)	(X)	(X)	(X)	(X)	(X)	[1]5	8	9	8	6	6	6	6	6	5
OR	(X)	(X)	(X)	(X)	(X)	(X)	[1]1	1	1	1	2	2	3	3	4	4	4	4	5	5	5
PA	13	18	23	26	28	24	25	24	27	28	30	32	36	34	33	30	27	25	23	21	19
RI	2	2	2	2	2	2	2	2	2	2	2	2	3	2	2	2	2	2	2	2	2
SC	6	8	9	9	9	7	6	4	5	7	7	7	7	6	6	6	6	6	6	6	6
SD	(X)	(X)	(X)	(X)	(X)	(X)	(X)	(X)	(X)	[1]2	2	2	3	2	2	2	2	2	1	1	1
TN	[1]1	3	6	9	13	11	10	8	10	10	10	10	10	9	10	9	9	9	8	9	9
TX	(X)	(X)	(X)	(X)	(X)	[1]2	2	4	6	11	13	16	18	21	21	22	23	24	27	30	32
UT	(X)	(X)	(X)	(X)	(X)	(X)	(X)	(X)	(X)	(X)	[1]1	1	2	2	2	2	2	2	3	3	3
VT	2	4	6	5	5	4	3	3	3	2	2	2	2	1	1	1	1	1	1	1	1
VA	19	22	23	22	21	15	13	11	9	10	10	10	10	9	9	10	10	10	10	11	11
WA	(X)	(X)	(X)	(X)	(X)	(X)	(X)	(X)	(X)	[1]1	2	3	5	6	6	7	7	7	8	9	9
WV	(X)	(X)	(X)	(X)	(X)	(X)	(X)	(X)	3	4	4	5	6	6	6	6	5	4	4	3	3
WI	(X)	(X)	(X)	(X)	(X)	[1]2	3	6	8	9	10	11	11	10	10	10	10	9	9	9	8
WY	(X)	(X)	(X)	(X)	(X)	(X)	(X)	(X)	(X)	[1]1	1	1	1	1	1	1	1	1	1	1	1

X Not applicable.   [1] Assigned after apportionment.   [2] Included in apportionment in anticipation of statehood.

Source: U.S. Census Bureau, *Congressional Apportionment, Census 2000 Brief,* Series C2KBR/01-7, issued July 2001; and see also http://www.census.gov/population/www/censusdata/apportionment.html>.

U.S. Census Bureau, Statistical Abstract of the United States: 2004-2005

No. 391. Vote Cast for United States Representatives by Major Political Party—States: 1998 to 2002

[In thousands (65,897 represents 65,897,000), except percent. R=Republican, D=Democrat, and I=Independent. In each state, totals represent the sum of votes cast in each Congressional District or votes cast for Representative at Large in states where only one member is elected. In all years there are numerous districts within the state where either the Republican or Democratic party had no candidate. In some states the Republican and Democratic vote includes votes cast for the party candidate by endorsing parties]

State	1998				2000				2002			
	Total[1]	Demo-cratic	Repub-lican	Percent for leading party	Total[1]	Demo-cratic	Repub-lican	Percent for leading party	Total[1]	Demo-cratic	Repub-lican	Percent for leading party
U.S.	65,897	31,482	32,255	R-48.9	97,226	46,521	46,954	R-48.3	73,845	33,865	37,290	R-50.5
AL	1,215	545	666	R-54.8	1,439	486	849	R-59.0	1,269	507	695	R-54.7
AK	223	77	140	R-62.6	274	45	191	R-69.6	228	39	170	R-74.5
AZ [2]	1,004	407	574	R-57.1	1,466	558	855	R-58.3	1,194	472	682	R-57.1
AR [2]	525	169	320	R-60.9	633	355	277	D-56.2	688	392	284	D-57.0
CA	7,990	4,040	3,510	D-50.6	10,438	5,407	4,446	D-51.8	7,258	3,731	3,226	D-51.4
CO	1,274	533	716	R-56.2	1,624	496	969	R-59.7	1,397	589	753	R-53.9
CT	954	496	442	D-51.9	1,313	699	595	D-53.2	989	509	466	D-51.5
DE	181	57	120	R-66.4	313	96	212	R-67.6	228	61	165	R-72.1
FL [2]	1,213	581	558	D-47.9	5,011	1,976	2,852	R-56.9	3,767	1,537	2,161	R-57.4
GA	1,632	592	1,040	R-63.7	2,417	918	1,498	R-62.0	1,919	814	1,105	R-57.6
HI	397	261	119	D-65.7	340	221	111	D-65.0	360	232	117	D-64.5
ID	379	169	205	R-54.0	493	142	333	R-67.5	405	138	256	R-63.3
IL	3,215	1,566	1,625	R-50.5	4,393	2,454	1,907	D-55.8	3,429	1,741	1,657	D-50.8
IN	1,576	673	862	R-54.7	2,157	953	1,141	R-52.9	1,521	641	841	R-55.3
IA	901	338	552	R-61.3	1,276	532	717	R-56.2	1,013	454	546	R-54.0
KS	727	272	450	R-61.9	1,038	328	658	R-63.4	830	260	536	R-64.6
KY	1,099	456	637	R-58.0	1,435	562	825	R-57.5	1,094	351	694	R-63.4
LA [2]	310	213	97	D-68.7	1,202	360	747	R-62.1	1,325	448	794	R-59.9
ME	415	281	125	D-67.7	638	423	203	D-66.2	495	290	206	D-58.5
MD	1,482	792	690	D-53.5	1,927	1,061	856	D-55.1	1,662	904	753	D-54.4
MA	1,742	1,306	413	D-75.0	2,347	1,968	343	D-83.8	1,841	1,529	290	D-83.0
MI	2,985	1,469	1,438	D-49.2	4,070	2,178	1,787	D-53.5	3,056	1,507	1,474	D-49.3
MN	2,040	1,090	863	D-53.5	2,364	1,234	993	D-52.2	2,202	1,098	1,030	D-49.9
MS	551	263	232	D-47.7	986	496	468	D-50.3	678	320	339	R-50.0
MO	1,572	788	748	D-50.1	2,326	1,136	1,136	D-48.8	1,854	829	986	R-53.2
MT	332	147	176	R-53.0	411	190	211	R-51.5	331	108	214	R-64.6
NE	526	105	393	R-74.7	683	178	487	R-71.2	474	47	387	R-81.6
NV	410	79	275	R-67.1	585	225	331	R-56.5	500	171	301	R-60.2
NH	318	124	190	R-59.8	556	239	303	R-54.5	443	176	255	R-57.5
NJ	1,815	902	858	D-49.7	2,988	1,532	1,384	D-51.3	2,006	1,030	934	D-51.4
NM	498	228	246	R-49.5	588	300	274	D-51.0	438	262	175	D-59.9
NY	4,267	2,278	1,858	D-53.4	5,824	3,190	2,466	D-54.8	3,822	1,771	1,527	D-46.3
NC	1,904	827	1,014	R-53.3	2,780	1,194	1,515	R-54.5	2,244	971	1,209	R-53.9
ND	213	120	88	D-56.2	286	151	127	D-52.9	231	121	110	D-52.4
OH	3,375	1,594	1,752	R-51.9	4,518	2,067	2,203	R-48.8	3,158	1,332	1,776	R-56.2
OK	859	314	538	R-62.7	1,088	337	702	R-64.5	1,002	392	547	R-54.9
OR	1,090	631	402	D-57.9	1,440	790	607	D-54.9	1,240	677	529	D-54.6
PA	2,896	1,381	1,472	R-50.8	4,554	2,279	2,229	D-50.0	3,310	1,349	1,859	R-56.2
RI	293	204	77	D-69.5	384	247	89	D-64.4	329	225	97	D-68.3
SC	974	370	580	R-59.6	1,321	525	730	R-55.2	985	346	570	R-57.8
SD	259	64	194	R-75.1	315	78	231	R-73.4	337	154	180	R-53.4
TN	914	412	470	R-51.4	1,854	819	992	R-53.5	1,529	708	771	R-50.4
TX	3,462	1,531	1,787	R-51.6	5,986	2,799	2,932	R-49.0	4,295	1,885	2,291	R-53.3
UT	471	127	304	R-64.6	759	305	427	R-56.2	557	221	322	R-57.8
VT	215	(X)	71	I-67.1	283	15	52	I-76.4	225	(X)	73	I-67.7
VA	1,149	514	542	R-47.2	2,422	1,060	1,132	R-46.7	1,516	440	1,008	R-66.5
WA	1,858	980	819	D-52.8	2,382	1,246	998	D-52.3	1,739	907	779	D-52.2
WV	351	283	29	D-80.6	580	421	109	D-72.6	400	264	136	D-66.0
WI	1,673	762	880	R-52.6	2,506	1,188	1,311	R-52.3	1,638	677	889	R-54.3
WY	174	67	101	R-57.8	212	61	142	R-66.8	182	66	110	R-60.5

X Not applicable.   [1] Includes vote cast for minor parties.   [2] State law does not require tabulation of votes for unopposed candidates.

Source: CQ Press (a division of Congressional Quarterly, Inc.), Washington, DC, *America Votes*, biennial (copyright).

244   Elections

No. 392. Vote Cast for United States Representatives by Major Political Party—Congressional Districts: 2002

[In some states the Democratic and Republican vote includes votes cast for the party candidate by endorsing parties]

State and district	Democratic candidate Name	Percent of total	Republican candidate Name	Percent of total
AL	(X)........	(X)	(X).......	(X)
1st...	Belk.....	37.78	Bonner.....	60.50
2d...	Woods.....	29.52	Everett.....	68.75
3d...	Turnham....	48.20	Rogers.....	50.30
4th...	(1)		Aderholt....	86.72
5th...	Cramer.....	73.28	Engel.....	24.71
6th...	(1)		Bachus.....	89.83
7th...	Davis.....	92.44	(1)......	(1)
AK ...	Greene.....	17.28	Young.....	74.51
AZ ...	(X)........	(X)	(X).......	(X)
1st...	Cordova....	45.64	Renzi.....	49.21
2d...	Camacho...	36.55	Franks.....	59.92
3d...	Hill.....	30.29	Shadegg....	67.32
4th...	Pastor.....	67.38	Barnett....	27.82
5th...	Columbus..	36.25	Hayworth...	61.17
6th...	Thomas....	31.57	Flake.....	65.94
7th...	Grijalva....	59.00	Hieb.....	37.06
8th...	Ryan.....	33.59	Kolbe.....	63.33
AR [2] ...	(X)........	(X)	(X).......	(X)
1st...	Berry.....	66.84	Robinson..	33.16
2d...	Snyder.....	92.92	(1)	(1)
3d...	(1)	(1)	Boozman...	98.90
4th...	Ross.....	60.56	Dickey.....	39.44
CA	(X).....	(X)	(X).......	(X)
1st...	Thompson .	64.07	Wiesner....	32.40
2d...	Johnson...	29.31	Herger.....	65.79
3d...	Beeman....	34.44	Ose.....	62.45
4th...	Norberg....	31.89	Doolittle....	64.77
5th...	Matsui.....	70.47	Frankhuizen .	26.41
6th...	Woolsey...	66.69	Erickson....	29.61
7th...	Miller.....	70.71	Hargrave....	26.44
8th...	Pelosi.....	79.58	German.....	12.50
9th...	Lee.....	81.41	Udinsky.....	15.18
10th...	Tauscher...	75.59	(1)	(1)
11th...	Shaw.....	39.69	Pombo.....	60.31
12th...	Lantos.....	68.13	Moloney....	24.76
13th...	Stark.....	71.06	Mahmood ..	22.06
14th...	Eshoo.....	68.18	Nixon.....	28.16
15th...	Honda.....	65.77	Hermann..	31.01
16th...	Lofgren....	67.02	McNea.....	29.80
17th...	Farr.....	68.07	Engler.....	27.02
18th...	Cardoza...	51.26	Monteith...	43.37
19th...	Veen.....	30.04	Radanovich...	67.31
20th...	Dooley.....	63.70	Minuth.....	34.28
21st...	LaPere.....	26.24	Nunes.....	70.49
22d...	Corvera....	23.73	Thomas.....	73.33
23d...	Capps.....	59.03	Rogers.....	38.59
24th...	Rudin.....	31.76	Gallegly....	65.18
25th...	Conaway...	31.10	McKeon.....	64.97
26th...	Mikels.....	33.49	Dreier.....	63.77
27th...	Sherman...	61.96	Levy.....	38.04
28th...	Berman....	71.40	Hernandez..	23.16
29th...	Schiff.....	62.56	Scileppi....	33.42
30th...	Waxman....	70.37	Goss.....	29.63
31st...	Becerra....	81.15	Vega......	18.85
32d...	Solis.....	68.79	Fischbeck..	27.46
33d...	Watson.....	82.55	Kim.....	14.10
34th...	Roybal-Allard..	74.04	Miller......	25.96
35th...	Waters.....	77.51	Moen.....	19.37
36th...	Harman....	61.35	Johnson.....	35.01
37th...	Millender-McDonald ..	72.92	Velasco.....	23.16
38th...	Napolitano ..	71.11	Burrola.....	26.27
39th...	Sanchez....	54.81	Escobar....	40.82
40th...	Avalos.....	29.47	Royce.....	67.64
41st...	Johnson....	29.63	Lewis.....	67.38
42d...	Waldron....	28.98	Miller.....	67.80
43d...	Baca.....	66.39	Neighbor....	30.47
44th...	Vandenberg..	31.56	Calvert.....	63.66
45th...	Kurpiewski..	32.72	Bono.....	65.23
46th...	Schipske ...	34.54	Rohrabacher .	61.73
47th...	Sanchez....	60.56	Chavez	34.69
48th...	Graham	28.44	Cox......	68.44
49th...	(1)	(1)	Issa......	77.22
50th...	Stewart....	32.34	Cunningham .	64.33
51st...	Filner.....	57.93	Garcia.....	39.33
52d...	Kochlacs....	25.75	Hunter.....	70.15
53d...	Davis.....	62.19	VanDeWeghe..	37.78
CO	(X)........	(X)	(X)......	(X)
1st...	DeGette....	66.28	Chlouber....	29.59
2d...	Udall.....	60.09	Hume.....	36.77
3d...	Berckefeldt..	31.27	McInnis	65.80
4th...	Matsunaka .	41.68	Musgrave ..	54.94
5th...	Imrie.....	24.68	Hefley.....	69.37
6th...	Wright.....	30.03	Tancredo...	66.88
7th...	Feeley.....	47.24	Beauprez...	47.31
CT	(X)........	(X)	(X)......	(X)
1st...	Larson.....	66.79	Steele.....	33.20
2d...	Courtney...	45.91	Simmons ...	54.09
3d...	DeLauro....	65.58	Elser.....	29.54
4th...	Sanchez....	35.57	Shays.....	64.43
5th...	Maloney....	43.26	Johnson	54.25
DE [2] ...	Miller.....	26.71	Castle.....	72.07
FL [2] ...	(X)........	(X)	(X)......	(X)
1st...	Oram.....	25.40	Miller.....	74.59
2d...	Boyd.....	66.90	McGurk	33.10
3d...	Brown.....	59.29	Carroll.....	40.71
4th...	(1)	(1)	Crenshaw...	99.70
5th...	Thurman....	46.24	Brown-Waite .	47.90
6th...	Bruderly...	34.64	Stearns.....	65.36
7th...	Hogan.....	40.42	Mica.....	59.58
8th...	Diaz.....	34.86	Keller.....	65.14
9th...	Kalogianis..	28.53	Bilirakis...	71.46
10th...	(1)	(1)	Young.....	(1)
11th...	Davis.....	(1)	(1)	(1)
12th...	(1)	(1)	Putnam.....	(1)
13th...	Schneider..	45.21	Harris......	54.78
14th...	(1)	(1)	Goss......	(1)
15th...	Tso.....	36.85	Weldon.....	63.15
16th...	(1)	(1)	Foley.....	78.88
17th...	Meek.....	99.94	(1)	(1)
18th...	Chote.....	28.61	Ros-Lehtinen.	69.11
19th...	Wexler.....	72.16	Merkl.....	27.84
20th...	Deutsch....	34.28	(1)	(1)
21st...	(1)	(1)	Diaz-Balart ..	(1)
22d...	Roberts	38.35	Shaw......	60.77
23d...	Hastings ...	77.49	Laurie.....	22.51
24th...	Jacobs.....	38.16	Feeney.....	61.84
25th...	Betancourt..	35.35	Diaz-Balart..	64.65
GA	(X)........	(X)	(X)......	(X)
1st...	Smart.....	27.86	Kingston....	72.14
2d...	Bishop.....	100.00		
3d...	Marshall ..	50.51	Clay......	49.49
4th...	Majette ...	77.03	Van Auken ..	22.97
5th...	Lewis.....	100.00	(1)	(1)
6th...	Weisberger ..	20.13	Isakson	79.87
7th...	Berlon ...	21.08	Linder.....	78.92
8th...	Petrakopou-los	21.67	Collins	78.33
9th...	Irwin	27.16	Norwood....	72.84
10th...	(1)	(1)	Deal.....	100.00
11th...	Kahn.....	48.36	Gingrey	51.64
12th...	Walker.....	44.81	Burns.....	55.19
13th...	Scott	59.63	Cox.....	40.37
HI	(X)........	(X)	(X)......	(X)
1st...	Abercrombie	72.85	Terry	24.92
2d...	Mink ...	56.16	McDermott ..	39.98
ID	(X)........	(X)	(X)......	(X)
1st...	Richardson ..	38.94	Otter	58.57
2d...	Kinghorn....	29.05	Simpson....	68.18

See footnotes at end of table.

U.S. Census Bureau, Statistical Abstract of the United States: 2004-2005

[See headnote, p. 245]

State and district	Democratic candidate Name	Percent of total	Republican candidate Name	Percent of total
IL.....	(X).....	(X)	(X)......	(X)
1st...	Rush....	81.17	Wardingly..	16.21
2d...	Jackson....	82.30	Nelson....	17.70
3d...	Lipinski...	100.00	[1]......	[1]
4th...	Gutierrez..	79.68	Lopez-Cisneros...	15.12
5th...	Emanuel...	66.81	Augusti....	28.86
6th...	Berry....	34.91	Hyde.....	65.09
7th...	Davis....	83.21	Tunney....	15.25
8th...	Bean....	42.56	Crane....	57.42
9th...	Schakowsky...	70.27	Duric....	26.83
10th...	Perritt....	31.19	Kirk.....	68.81
11th...	Van Duyne.	35.68	Weller....	64.32
12th...	Costello...	69.25	Sadler....	30.75
13th...	Mason....	29.74	Biggert....	70.26
14th...	Quick....	25.86	Hastert...	74.14
15th...	Hartke..	31.04	Johnson...	65.17
16th...	Kutsch..	29.39	Manzullo..	70.61
17th...	Evans..	62.42	Calderone..	37.58
18th...	[1]...	[1]	LaHood...	100.00
19th...	Phelps...	45.21	Shimkus...	54.79
IN.....	(X).....	(X)	(X).....	(X)
1st...	Visclosky..	66.94	Leyva....	31.02
2d...	Thompson...	45.77	Chocola...	50.45
3d...	Rigdon...	34.45	Souder....	63.14
4th...	Abbott...	26.15	Buyer....	71.36
5th...	Carr...	25.18	Burton....	71.97
6th...	Fox...	34.40	Pence....	63.79
7th...	Carson...	53.13	McVey....	44.14
8th...	Hartke...	46.02	Hostettler..	51.31
9th...	Hill....	51.15	Sodrel.....	46.13
IA.....	(X).....	(X)	(X).....	(X)
1st...	Hutchinson..	42.65	Nussle....	57.15
2d...	Thomas...	45.74	Leach....	52.19
3d...	Boswell...	53.41	Thompson..	45.04
4th...	Norris...	43.07	Latham....	54.76
5th...	Shomshor.	37.78	King.....	62.15
KS.....	(X).....	(X)	(X).....	(X)
1st...	[1]......	[1]	Moran.....	91.09
2d...	Lykins...	37.52	Ryun.....	60.42
3d...	Moore...	50.18	Taff.....	46.89
4th...	Nolla...	37.00	Tiahrt....	60.58
KY....	(X).....	(X)	(X).....	(X)
1st...	Alexander...	34.75	Whitfield...	65.25
2d...	Williams...	29.17	Lewis.....	69.64
3d...	Conway...	48.39	Northup...	51.61
4th...	Lucas...	51.11	Davis.....	47.54
5th...	Bailey...	21.71	Rogers....	78.29
6th[3]...	[1]...	[1]	Fletcher....	71.95
LA[2][3]...	(X)...	(X)	(X).....	(X)
1st...	[1]......	[1]	Vitter....	81.47
2d...	Jefferson..	63.53	Sullivan...	10.86
3d...	[1]......	[1]	Tauzin....	86.68
4th...	Milkovich..	26.45	McCrery...	71.61
5th...	Alexander..	28.68	Fletcher...	24.52
6th...	[1]......	[1]	Baker.....	84.04
7th...	John.....	86.82	[1]......	(X)
ME....	(X)...	(X)	(X)......	(X)
1st...	Allen....	63.81	Joyce....	36.19
2d...	Michaud...	52.01	Raye....	47.99
MD....	(X)...	(X)	(X)......	(X)
1st...	Tamlyn...	23.16	Gilchrest...	76.67
2d...	Ruppersberger..	54.16	Bentley....	45.57
3d...	Cardin...	65.72	Conwell....	34.18
4th...	Wynn....	78.57	Kimble....	20.82
5th...	Hoyer....	69.27	Crawford...	30.52
6th...	DeArmon..	33.80	Bartlett....	66.11
7th...	Cummings..	73.53	Ward....	26.38
8th...	Van Hollen..	51.71	Morella....	47.49
MA....	(X)...	(X)	(X)......	(X)
1st...	Olver....	67.56	Kinnaman..	32.38
2d...	Neal....	99.13	[1]......	[1]
3d...	McGovern..	98.83	[1]......	[1]
4th...	Frank....	98.99	[1]......	[1]
5th...	Meehan..	60.15	McCarthy..	34.03
6th...	Tierney..	68.27	Smith.....	31.63
7th...	Markey...	98.24	[1]......	[1]
8th...	Capuano..	99.56	[1]......	[1]
9th...	Lynch...	99.45	[1]......	[1]
10th...	Delahunt...	69.20	[1]......	[1]
MI.....	(X)	(X)	(X)......	(X)
1st...	Stupak...	67.67	Hooper....	31.10
2d...	Wrisley...	27.70	Hoekstra...	70.40
3d...	Lynnes...	28.32	Ehlers....	69.97
4th...	Hollenbeck.	30.17	Camp.....	68.21
5th...	Kildee....	91.56	[1]......	[1]
6th...	Giguere...	29.31	Upton.....	69.17
7th...	Simpson...	38.61	Smith.....	59.66
8th...	McAlpine..	30.75	Rogers....	67.88
9th...	Fink....	39.88	Knollenberg.	58.10
10th...	Marlinga...	35.52	Miller....	63.31
11th...	Kelley...	39.66	McCotter...	57.19
12th...	Levin....	68.26	Dean.....	29.78
13th...	Kilpatrick..	91.61	[1]......	[1]
14th...	Conyers...	83.21	Stone....	15.20
15th...	Dingell...	72.21	Kaltenbach..	25.72
MN....	(X)...	(X)	(X)......	(X)
1st...	Andreasen..	34.65	Gutknecht..	61.50
2d...	Luther...	42.22	Kline....	53.33
3d...	Stanton...	27.88	Ramstad...	72.02
4th...	McCollum..	62.22	Billington...	33.91
5th...	Sabo....	67.03	Mathias...	25.89
6th...	Robert...	35.06	Kennedy...	57.34
7th...	Peterson..	65.27	Stevens...	34.64
8th...	Oberstar...	68.65	Lemen....	31.23
MS....	(X)...	(X)	(X)......	(X)
1st...	Weathers..	24.20	Wicker....	71.43
2d...	Thompson..	55.14	LeSueur...	42.75
3d...	Shows....	34.76	Pickering...	63.58
4th...	Taylor...	75.21	Mertz....	21.24
MO....	(X)...	(X)	(X)......	(X)
1st...	Clay....	70.11	Schwadron.	27.09
2d...	Hogan....	31.03	Akin.....	67.14
3d...	Gephardt...	59.06	Enz......	38.94
4th...	Skelton...	67.64	Noland....	30.66
5th...	McCarthy..	65.88	Gordon....	32.36
6th...	Rinehart...	35.18	Graves....	63.03
7th...	Lapham...	23.00	Blunt....	74.81
8th...	Curtis...	26.91	Emerson...	71.76
9th...	Deichman..	28.55	Hulshof...	68.20
MT...	Kelly....	32.67	Rehberg...	64.62
NE....	(X)...	(X)	(X)......	(X)
1st...	[1]......	[1]	Bereuter...	85.35
2d...	Simon....	32.98	Terry....	63.32
3d...	[1]......	[1]	Osborne...	93.17
NV....	(X)...	(X)	(X)......	(X)
1st...	Berkley...	53.72	Boggs-McDonald..	42.73
2d...	Souza....	19.97	Gibbons...	74.34
3d...	Herrera...	37.24	Porter....	56.08
NH....	(X)...	(X)	(X)......	(X)
1st...	Clark....	38.48	Bradley....	58.11
2d...	Swett....	40.86	Bass.....	56.81
NJ....	(X)...	(X)	(X)......	(X)
1st...	Andrews...	92.74	[1]......	[1]
2d...	Farkas....	28.28	LoBiondo...	69.21
3d...	Strada....	33.92	Saxton....	65.02
4th...	Brennan...	32.11	Smith.....	66.15
5th...	Sumers...	38.28	Garrett....	59.48
6th...	Pallone...	66.46	Medrow....	30.89
7th...	Carden...	40.92	Ferguson...	57.95
8th...	Pascrell...	66.83	Silverman..	30.59
9th...	Rothman...	69.76	Glass....	30.24
10th...	Payne....	84.45	Wirtz....	15.55
11th...	Pawar....	26.39	Frelinghuysen..	72.38
12th...	Holt....	61.04	Soaries....	36.65
13th...	Menendez.	78.30	Geron....	18.17

See footnotes at end of table.

246　Elections

[See headnote, p. 245]

State and district	Democratic candidate Name	Percent of total	Republican candidate Name	Percent of total
NM	(X)......	(X)	(X)......	(X)
1st...	Romero....	44.66	Wilson....	55.34
2d...	Smith.....	43.72	Pearce...	56.23
3d...	Udall.....	100.00	(¹)......	(¹)
NY....	(X)......	(X)	(X).....	(X)
1st...	Bishop....	50.23	Grucci....	48.59
2d...	Israel....	58.48	Finley....	40.46
3d...	Finz.....	27.22	King.....	71.88
4th...	McCarthy..	56.25	O'Grady...	43.24
5th...	Ackerman..	92.32	(¹).....	(¹)
6th...	Meeks....	96.51	(¹)......	(¹)
7th...	Crowley...	73.29	Brawley...	26.71
8th...	Nadler....	76.07	Farrin....	18.48
9th...	Weiner....	65.71	Donohue..	34.29
10th..	Towns.....	97.83	(¹)......	(¹)
11th..	Owens....	86.56	Cleary....	12.55
12th..	Valazquez..	95.81	(¹)......	(¹)
13th..	Mattsson...	28.32	Fossella..	69.63
14th..	Maloney...	75.25	Srdanovic.	24.75
15th..	Rangel....	88.46	Fields....	11.54
16th..	Serrano...	92.07	Dellavalle..	7.93
			Vander-	
17th..	Engel.....	62.61	hoef.....	34.43
18th..	Lowey....	92.04	(¹)......	(¹)
19th..	Selendy...	25.98	Kelly.....	69.97
			Stoppen-	
20th..	bach......	23.98	Sweeney..	73.32
21st..	McNulty...	75.09	Rosenstein.	24.91
22d...	Hinchey...	64.19	Hall......	32.87
23d...	(¹)......	(¹)	McHugh....	100.00
24th..	Boehlert...	70.70	(¹)......	(¹)
25th..	Aldersley..	26.64	Walsh....	72.29
26th..	Nariman...	22.42	Reynolds.	73.63
27th..	Crotty....	27.49	Quinn....	69.06
28th..	Slaughter..	62.46	Wojtaszek.	37.54
29th..	Peters....	21.26	Houghton.	73.10
NC....	(X)......	(X)	(X).....	(X)
1st...	Ballance...	63.74	Dority....	34.83
2d...	Etheridge..	65.36	Ellen.....	33.27
3d...	(¹)......	(¹)	Jones....	90.70
4th...	Price.....	61.18	Nguyen...	36.15
5th...	Crawford...	29.81	Burr.....	70.19
6th...	(¹)......	(¹)	Coble....	90.41
7th...	McIntyre...	71.13	Adams...	27.32
8th...	Kouri.....	44.62	Hayes....	53.63
9th...	McGuire...	25.83	Myrick...	72.42
10th..	Daugherty..	37.85	Ballenger.	59.30
11th..	Neill.....	42.85	Taylor....	55.54
12th..	Watt.....	65.34	Kish.....	32.79
13th..	Miller....	54.72	Grant....	42.39
ND....	Pomeroy...	52.41	Clayburgh.	47.59
OH....	(X)......	(X)	(X).....	(X)
1st...	Harris....	35.20	Chabot...	64.80
2d...	Sanders...	25.95	Portman..	74.05
3d...	Carne.....	41.22	Turner....	58.77
4th...	Clark.....	32.48	Oxley....	67.52
5th...	Anderson..	27.55	Gillmor..	67.08
6th...	Strickland..	59.48	Halleck...	40.52
7th...	Anastasio.	27.18	Hobson...	67.56
			Harden-	
8th...	brook.....	29.19	Boehner..	70.81
9th...	Kaptur....	73.99	Emery....	26.01
10th..	Kucinich...	74.06	Heben....	23.80
11th..	Jones.....	76.33	Pappano..	23.67
12th..	Brown.....	35.61	Tiberi....	64.39
13th..	Brown....	68.97	Oliveros...	31.03
14th..	Blanchard.	27.82	LaTourette.	72.12
15th..	Brown....	33.41	Pryce....	66.59
16th..	Rice.....	31.13	Regula...	68.87
17th..	Ryan.....	51.14	Benjamin..	33.67
18th..	(¹)......	(¹)	Ney.....	100.00
OK....	(X)......	(X)	(X).....	(X)
1st...	Dodd.....	42.17	Sullivan...	55.62
2d...	Carson....	74.12	Pharaoh..	25.88
3d...	(¹)......	(¹)	Lucas....	75.58
4th...	Roberts...	46.17	Cole.....	53.83
5th...	Barlow....	32.41	Istook....	62.23
OR....	(X)......	(X)	(X).....	(X)
1st...	Wu......	62.69	Greenfield.	33.99
2d...	Buckley...	25.76	Walden...	71.86
3d...	Blumenauer.	66.75	Seale....	26.73
			VanLeeu-	
4th...	DeFazio...	63.82	wen.....	34.36
5th...	Hooley...	54.75	Boquist...	45.10
PA....	(X)......	(X)	(X).....	(X)
1st...	Brady....	86.43	Delany...	12.45
2d...	Fattah....	87.77	Dougherty.	12.23
3d...	(¹)......	(¹)	English...	77.67
4th...	Drobac...	35.44	Hart.....	64.55
5th...	(¹)......	(¹)	Peterson..	87.24
6th...	Wofford...	48.63	Gerlach...	51.36
7th...	Lennon....	33.91	Weldon...	66.09
			Green-	
8th...	Reece....	37.40	wood....	62.58
9th...	Henry.....	28.92	Shuster...	71.02
10th..	(¹)......	(¹)	Sherwood.	92.60
11th..	Kanjorski..	55.60	Barletta...	42.43
12th..	Murtha....	73.48	Choby....	26.52
13th..	Hoeffel...	50.95	Brown....	47.34
14th..	Doyle....	99.93	(¹)......	(¹)
15th..	O'Brien....	42.64	Toomey...	57.36
16th..	(¹)......	(¹)	Pitts....	88.45
17th..	Holden....	51.41	Gekas....	48.59
18th..	Machek...	39.86	Murphy...	60.14
19th..	(¹)......	(¹)	Platts....	91.06
RI....	(X)......	(X)	(X).....	(X)
1st...	Kennedy..	59.88	Rogers...	37.31
2d...	Langevin...	76.29	Matson...	22.27
SC....	(X)......	(X)	(X).....	(X)
1st...	(¹)......	(¹)	Brown....	89.56
2d...	(¹)......	(¹)	Wilson....	84.12
3d...	Brightharp..	31.28	Barrett....	67.14
4th...	Ashy.....	29.67	DeMint...	69.00
5th...	Spratt....	85.87	(¹)......	(¹)
6th...	Clyburn...	66.98	McLeod...	32.03
SD....	Herseth...	45.62	Janklow...	53.45
TN....	(X)......	(X)	(X).....	(X)
1st...	(¹)......	(¹)	Jenkins...	98.77
2d...	Greene....	19.91	Duncan...	78.98
3d...	Wolfe.....	33.82	Wamp....	64.54
4th...	Davis.....	52.08	Bowling..	46.49
5th...	Cooper....	63.73	Duvall...	33.25
6th...	Gordon....	65.92	Garrison..	32.33
7th...	Barron....	26.48	Blackburn.	70.73
8th...	Tanner....	70.14	McClain...	27.30
9th...	Ford.....	83.81	(¹)......	(¹)

See footnotes at end of table.

Elections 247

No. 392. Vote Cast for United States Representatives by Major Political Party—Congressional Districts: 2002—Con.

[See headnote, p. 245]

State and district	Democratic candidate Name	Percent of total	Republican candidate Name	Percent of total	State and district	Democratic candidate Name	Percent of total	Republican candidate Name	Percent of total
TX	(X)	(X)	(X)	(X)	VA	(X)	(X)	(X)	(X)
1st...	Sandlin...	56.45	Lawrence..	43.55	1st...	(1)	(1)	Davis...	95.91
2d...	Turner....	60.85	Brookshire.	38.19	2d...	(1)	(1)	Schrock...	83.15
3d...	Molera..	24.33	Johnson ..	73.95	3d...	Scott...	96.10	(1)	(1)
4th...	Hall....	57.82	Graves...	40.37	4th...	Lucas....	(5)	Forbes...	97.92
5th...	Chapman...	40.26	Hensarling.	58.21	5th...	Richards...	36.48	Goode....	63.47
6th...	Alvarado...	27.68	Barton....	70.35	6th...	(1)	(1)	Goodlatte..	97.06
7th...	(1)	(1)	Culberson.	89.19	7th...	Jones.....	30.46	Cantor....	69.45
8th...	(1)	(1)	Brady....	93.14	8th...	Moran....	59.81	Tate.....	37.32
9th...	Lampson...	58.60	Williams...	40.31	9th...	Boucher...	65.76	Katzen...	34.22
10th..	Doggett..	84.37	(1)	(1)	10th...	Stevens...	28.13	Wolf.....	71.72
11th..	Edwards...	51.55	Farley....	47.11	11th...	(1)	(1)	Davis....	82.90
12th..	(1)	(1)	Granger...	91.87	WA	(X)	(X)	(X)	(X)
13th..	Reese....	20.73	Thornberry.	79.27	1st...	Inslee....	55.64	Marine...	41.31
14th..	Windham..	31.91	Paul.....	68.09	2d...	Larsen....	50.07	Smith....	45.77
15th..	Hinojosa..	100.00	(1)	(1)	3d...	Baird....	61.69	Zarelli...	38.31
16th..	Reyes....	100.00	(1)	(1)	4th...	Mason....	33.10	Hastings .	66.90
17th..	Stenholm..	51.36	Beckham..	47.39	5th...	Haggin....	32.21	Nethercutt.	62.66
18th..	Lee.....	76.91	Abbott....	21.70	6th...	Dicks.....	64.20	Lawrence..	31.35
19th..	(1)	(1)	Combest ..	91.64	7th...	McDermott..	74.07	Cassady ..	21.92
20th..	Gonzalez...	100.00	(1)	(1)				Behrens-	
21st..	Courage...	25.31	Smith....	72.87	8th...	Benedict...	37.34	Dunn....	59.82
22d..	Riley.....	35.02	DeLay....	63.17	9th...	Smith....	58.52	Casada...	38.57
23d..	Cuellar....	47.20	Bonilla...	51.53	WV	(X)	(X)	(X)	(X)
24th..	Frost.....	64.66	Ortega....	33.95	1st...	Mollohan..	99.71	(1)	(1)
25th..	Bell.....	54.76	Reiser....	43.09	2d...	Humphreys .	39.96	Capito....	60.04
26th..	LeBon....	22.76	Burgess...	74.81	3d...	Rahall....	70.22	Chapman..	29.78
27th..	Ortiz.....	61.10	Ahumada..	36.54	WI	(X)	(X)	(X)	(X)
28th..	Rodriguez ..	71.09	Perales...	26.86	1st...	Thomas....	30.63	Ryan....	67.19
29th..	Green.....	95.16	(1)	(1)	2d...	Baldwin....	66.01	Greer....	33.83
30th..	Johnson ...	74.26	Bush.....	24.19	3d...	Kind.....	62.82	Arndt....	33.54
31st..	Bagley....	27.36	Carter....	69.08	4th...	Kleczka...	86.32	(1)	(1)
32d..	Dixon....	30.35	Sessions...	67.77				Sensenbren-	
UT	(X)	(X)	(X)	(X)	5th...	(1)	(1)	ner.....	86.13
1st...	Thomas...	36.84	Bishop ...	60.90	6th...	(1)	(1)	Petri.....	99.22
2d...	Matheson ..	49.43	Swallow...	48.69	7th...	Obey.....	64.21	Rothbauer .	35.76
3d...	Woodside ..	28.98	Cannon...	67.43	8th...	Becker....	23.89	Green....	72.58
VT	(1)	(1)	Meub	32.29	WY	Akin.....	36.21	Cubin....	60.51

X Not applicable. [1] No candidate. [2] According to state law, it is not required to tabulate votes for unopposed candidates. [3] Louisiana holds an open-primary election with candidates from all parties running on the same ballot. Any candidate who receives a majority is elected; if no candidate receives 50 percent, there is a run off election in November between the top two finishers. [4] Sanders, an Independent, was elected with 64.26 percent of the vote. [5] Lucas withdrew after the primary election. Republican candidate, Forbes, took office in her place.

Source: Congressional Quarterly Inc., *Congressional Quarterly Weekly Report* (copyright).

No. 393. Composition of Congress by Political Party: 1973 to 2004

[D=Democratic, R=Republican. Data for beginning of first session of each Congress (as of January 3), except as noted. Excludes vacancies at beginning of session]

Year	Party and President	Congress	House Majority party	House Minority party	House Other	Senate Majority party	Senate Minority party	Senate Other
1973 [1][2]	R (Nixon)	93d.	D-239	R-192	1	D-56	R-42	2
1975 [3]	R (Ford)	94th	D-291	R-144	-	D-60	R-37	2
1977 [4]	D (Carter)	95th	D-292	R-143	-	D-61	R-38	1
1979 [4]	D (Carter)	96th	D-276	R-157	-	D-58	R-41	1
1981 [4]	R (Reagan)	97th	D-243	R-192	-	D-53	R-46	1
1983	R (Reagan)	98th	D-269	R-165	-	R-54	D-46	-
1985	R (Reagan)	99th	D-252	R-182	-	R-53	D-47	-
1987	R (Reagan)	100th	D-258	R-177	-	D-55	R-45	-
1989 [5]	R (Bush)	101st	D-259	R-174	-	D-55	R-45	-
1991 [5]	R (Bush)	102d.	D-267	R-167	1	D-56	R-44	-
1993 [5]	D (Clinton)	103d.	D-258	R-176	1	D-57	R-43	-
1995 [5]	D (Clinton)	104th	R-230	D-204	1	R-52	D-48	-
1997 [6]	D (Clinton)	105th	R-226	D-207	2	R-55	D-45	-
1999 [5]	D (Clinton)	106th	R-222	D-212	1	R-55	D-45	-
2001 [6]	R (Bush)	107th	R-221	D-211	2	D-50	R-50	-
2004 [7][8][9][10]	R (Bush)	108th	R-228	D-205	1	R-51	D-48	1

- Represents zero. [1] Senate had one Independent and one Conservative-Republican. [2] House had one Independent-Democrat. [3] Senate had one Independent, one Conservative-Republican, and one undecided (New Hampshire). [4] Senate had one Independent. [5] House had one Independent-Socialist. [6] House had one Independent-Socialist and one Independent. [7] As of beginning of second session. [8] House and Senate each had one Independent. [9] Vacancy due to the reservation of South Dakota's at large representative, William J. Janklow, January 20, 2004. [10] As of March 4, 2004.

Source: U.S. Congress, Joint Committee on Printing, *Congressional Directory*, annual through 1976; beginning 1977, biennial; thereafter, Office of the Clerk, *Official List of Members by State*, annual. Also see <http://clerk.house.gov/members/olm108.pdf>.

No. 394. Composition of Congress by Political Party Affiliation—States: 1997 to 2004

[Figures are for the beginning of the first session (as of January 3), except as noted. Dem.=Democratic; Rep.=Republican]

State	Representatives 105th Cong., 1997 [1][2] Dem.	Rep.	106th Cong., 1999 [1] Dem.	Rep.	107th Cong., 2001 [1][3] Dem.	Rep.	108th Cong., 2003 [1][4][5][6] Dem.	Rep.	Senators 105th Cong., 1997 Dem.	Rep.	106th Cong., 1999 Dem.	Rep.	107th Cong., 2001 [7][8] Dem.	Rep.	108th Cong., 2003 [4][6][7] Dem.	Rep.
U.S. ..	207	228	212	222	211	221	205	228	45	55	45	55	50	50	48	51
AL.	2	5	2	5	2	5	2	5	-	2	-	2	-	2	-	2
AK.	-	1	-	1	-	1	-	1	-	2	-	2	-	2	-	2
AZ.	1	5	1	5	1	5	2	6	-	2	-	2	-	2	-	2
AR.	2	2	2	2	3	1	3	1	1	1	1	1	1	1	2	-
CA.	29	23	28	24	31	20	33	20	2	-	2	-	2	-	2	-
CO	2	4	2	4	2	4	2	5	-	2	-	2	-	2	-	2
CT.	4	2	4	2	3	3	2	3	2	-	2	-	2	-	2	-
DE.	-	1	-	1	-	1	-	1	1	1	1	1	1	1	1	1
FL.	8	15	8	15	8	15	7	18	1	1	1	1	1	1	1	1
GA.	3	8	3	8	3	8	5	8	1	1	1	1	1	1	1	1
HI.	2	-	2	-	2	-	2	-	2	-	2	-	2	-	2	-
ID.	-	2	-	2	-	2	-	2	-	2	-	2	-	2	-	2
IL.	10	10	10	10	10	10	9	10	2	-	1	1	1	1	1	1
IN.	4	6	4	6	4	6	3	6	-	2	1	1	1	1	1	1
IA.	1	4	1	4	1	4	1	4	1	1	1	1	1	1	1	1
KS.	-	4	1	3	1	3	1	3	-	2	-	2	-	2	-	2
KY.	1	5	1	5	1	5	2	4	1	1	-	2	-	2	-	2
LA.	2	5	2	5	2	5	3	4	2	-	2	-	2	-	2	-
ME.	2	-	2	-	2	-	2	-	-	2	-	2	-	2	-	2
MD.	4	4	4	4	4	4	6	2	2	-	2	-	2	-	2	-
MA.	10	-	10	-	10	-	10	-	2	-	2	-	2	-	2	-
MI.	10	6	10	6	9	7	6	9	1	1	1	1	2	-	2	-
MN.	6	2	6	2	5	3	4	4	1	1	1	1	2	-	1	1
MS.	2	3	3	2	3	2	2	2	-	2	-	2	-	2	-	2
MO.	5	3	5	4	4	5	4	5	-	2	-	2	1	1	-	2
MT.	-	1	-	1	-	1	-	1	1	1	1	1	1	1	1	1
NE.	-	3	-	3	-	3	-	3	1	1	1	1	1	1	1	1
NV.	-	2	1	1	1	1	1	2	2	-	2	-	1	1	1	1
NH.	-	2	-	2	-	2	-	2	-	2	-	2	-	2	-	2
NJ.	6	7	7	6	7	6	7	6	2	-	2	-	2	-	2	-
NM.	1	2	1	2	1	2	1	2	1	1	1	1	1	1	1	1
NY.	18	13	19	12	19	12	19	10	1	1	2	-	2	-	2	-
NC.	6	6	5	7	5	7	6	7	-	2	1	1	1	1	1	1
ND.	1	-	1	-	1	-	1	-	2	-	2	-	2	-	2	-
OH.	8	11	8	11	8	11	6	12	1	1	-	2	-	2	-	2
OK.	-	6	-	6	1	5	1	4	-	2	-	2	-	2	-	2
OR.	4	1	4	1	4	1	4	1	1	1	1	1	1	1	1	1
PA.	11	10	11	10	10	11	7	12	-	2	-	2	-	2	-	2
RI.	2	-	2	-	2	-	2	-	1	1	1	1	1	1	1	1
SC.	2	4	2	4	2	4	2	4	1	1	1	1	1	1	1	1
SD.	-	1	-	1	-	1	-	-	2	-	2	-	2	-	2	-
TN.	4	5	4	5	4	5	5	4	-	2	-	2	-	2	-	2
TX.	17	13	17	13	17	13	16	16	-	2	-	2	-	2	-	2
UT.	-	3	-	3	1	2	1	2	-	2	-	2	-	2	-	2
VT.	-	-	-	-	-	-	-	-	1	1	1	1	1	-	1	-
VA.	6	5	6	5	4	6	3	8	1	1	1	1	1	1	1	1
WA.	3	6	5	4	6	3	6	3	1	1	1	1	1	1	2	-
WV.	3	-	3	-	2	1	2	1	2	-	2	-	2	-	2	-
WI.	5	4	5	4	5	4	4	4	2	-	2	-	2	-	2	-
WY.	-	1	-	1	-	1	-	1	-	2	-	2	-	2	-	2

- Represents zero. [1] Vermont had one Independent Representative. [2] Missouri had one Independent Representative. [3] Virginia had one Independent Representative. [4] As of beginning of second session. [5] Vacancy due to resignation of William J. Janklow, January 20, 2004. [6] As of March 4, 2004. [7] Vermont had one Independent Senator. [8] California had one vacancy.

Source: U.S. Congress, Joint Committee on Printing, *Congressional Directory*, annual through 1976; beginning 1977, biennial; thereafter, Office of the Clerk, *Official List of Members by State*, annual. See also <http://clerk.house.gov/members/olm108.pdf>.

Elections 249

No. 395. Members of Congress—Incumbents Reelected: 1964 to 2002

Year	Representatives Retirements[1]	Total	Re-elected Number	Re-elected Per-cent of candidates	Defeated in Primary	Defeated in General election	Senators Retirements[1]	Total	Re-elected Number	Re-elected Per-cent of candidates	Defeated in Primary	Defeated in General election
PRESIDENTIAL-YEAR ELECTIONS												
1964	33	397	344	86.6	8	45	2	33	28	84.8	1	4
1968	23	409	396	96.8	4	9	6	28	20	71.4	4	4
1972	40	390	365	93.6	12	13	6	27	20	74.1	2	5
1976	47	384	368	95.8	3	13	8	25	16	64.0	-	9
1980	34	398	361	90.7	6	31	5	29	16	55.2	4	9
1984	22	411	392	95.4	3	16	4	29	26	89.7	-	3
1988	23	409	402	98.3	1	6	6	27	23	85.2	-	4
1992	65	368	325	88.3	[2]19	[3]24	7	28	23	82.1	1	4
1996	49	384	361	94.0	2	21	13	21	19	90.5	1	1
2000	32	403	394	97.8	3	6	5	29	23	79.3	-	6
MIDTERM ELECTIONS												
1966	22	411	362	88.1	8	41	3	32	28	87.5	3	1
1970	29	401	379	94.5	10	12	4	31	24	77.4	1	6
1974	43	391	343	87.7	8	40	7	27	23	85.2	2	2
1978	49	382	358	93.7	5	19	10	25	15	60.0	3	7
1982	40	393	354	90.1	[2]10	[3]29	3	30	28	93.3	-	2
1986	40	394	385	97.7	3	6	6	28	21	75.0	-	7
1990	27	406	390	96.1	1	15	3	32	31	96.9	-	1
1994	48	387	349	90.2	4	34	9	26	24	92.3	-	2
1998	33	402	395	98.3	1	6	5	29	26	89.7	-	3
2002	35	398	382	96.0	[2]8	[3]8	5	28	24	85.7	1	3

- Represents zero. [1] Does not include persons who died or resigned before the election. [2] Number of incumbents defeated in primaries by other incumbents due to redistricting: six in 1982 and four each in 1992 and 2002. [3] Number of incumbents defeated in general election by other incumbents due to redistricting: six in 1982, five in 1992, and four in 2002.

Source: Ornstein, Norman J., Thomas E. Mann, and Michael J. Malbin, *Vital Statistics on Congress, 1999-2000* (The AEI Press, Washington, DC, 2000) Harold W. Stanley and Richard G. Niemi, *Vital Statistics on American Politics 2003-2004* (CQ Press, Washington, DC, 2003).

No. 396. Members of Congress—Selected Characteristics: 1985 to 2003

[As of beginning of first session of each Congress, (January 3). Figures for Representatives exclude vacancies]

Members of congress and year	Male	Fe-male	Black[1]	API[2]	His-panic[3]	Age[4] (in years) Under 40	40 to 49	50 to 59	60 to 69	70 and over	Seniority[5][6] Less than 2 yrs.	2 to 9 yrs.	10 to 19 yrs.	20 to 29 yrs.	30 yrs. or more
REPRESENTATIVES															
99th Cong., 1985	412	22[7]	21	5	10	71	154	131	59	19	49	237	104	34	10
100th Cong., 1987	412	23[7]	23	6	11	63	153	137	56	26	51	221	114	37	12
101st Cong., 1989	408	25[7]	24	6	10	41	163	133	74	22	39	207	139	35	13
102d Cong., 1991[8]	407	28[7]	26	5	11	39	152	134	86	24	55	178	147	44	11
103d Cong., 1993[8]	388	47[7]	38	7	17	47	151	128	89	15	118	141	132	32	12
104th Cong., 1995	388	47[9]	40	7	17	53	155	135	79	13	92	188	110	36	9
106th Cong., 1999	379	56[9]	39	6	19	23	116	173	87	35	41	236	104	46	7
107th Cong., 2001	376	59[9]	39	7	19	14	97	167	117	35	44	155	158	63	14
108th Cong., 2003	376	59[9]	39	5	22	19	86	174	121	32	54	178	140	48	13
SENATORS															
99th Cong., 1985	98	2	-	2	-	4	27	38	25	6	8	56	27	7	2
100th Cong., 1987	98	2	-	2	-	5	30	36	22	7	14	41	36	7	2
101st Cong., 1989	98	2	-	3	-	-	30	40	22	8	23	22	43	10	2
102d Cong., 1991	98	2	-	2	-	-	23	46	24	7	5	34	47	10	4
103d Cong., 1993[8]	93	7	1	2	-	1	16	48	22	12	15	30	39	11	5
104th Cong., 1995	92	8	1	2	-	1	14	41	27	17	12	38	30	15	5
106th Cong., 1999	91	9	-	2	-	-	14	38	35	13	8	39	33	14	6
107th Cong., 2001	87	13	-	2	-	-	8	39	33	18	11	34	30	14	9
108th Cong., 2003	86	14	-	2	-	1	12	29	34	24	9	42	29	13	7

- Represents zero. [1] Source: Joint Center for Political and Economic Studies, Washington, DC, *Black Elected Officials: Statistical Summary*, annual (copyright). [2] Asian and Pacific Islanders. Source: Library of Congress, Congressional Research Service, *Asian Pacific Americans in the United States Congress*, Report 94-767 GOV. [3] Source: National Association of Latino Elected and Appointed Officials, Washington, DC, *National Roster of Hispanic Elected Officials*, annual. [4] Some members do not provide date of birth. [5] Represents consecutive years of service. [6] Some members do not provide years of service. [7] Includes District of Columbia delegate but not Virgin Islands Delegate. [8] Includes members elected to fill vacant seats through June 14, 1993. [9] Includes District of Columbia and Virgin Islands delegate.

Source: Except as noted, compiled by U.S. Census Bureau from data published in *Congressional Directory*, biennial.

No. 397. U.S. Congress—Measures Introduced and Enacted and Time in Session: 1987 to 2003

[Excludes simple and concurrent resolutions]

Item	100th Cong., 1987-88	101st Cong., 1989-90	102d Cong., 1991-92	103d Cong., 1993-94	104th Cong., 1995-96	105th Cong., 1997-98	106th Cong., 1999-00	107th Cong., 2001-02	108th Cong., 2003
Measures introduced	9,588	6,664	6,775	8,544	6,808	7,732	9,158	9,130	5,812
Bills	8,515	5,977	6,212	7,883	6,545	7,532	8,968	8,953	5,703
Joint resolutions	1,073	687	563	661	263	200	190	177	109
Measures enacted	761	666	609	473	337	404	604	337	174
Public	713	650	589	465	333	394	580	331	174
Private	48	16	20	8	4	10	24	6	-
HOUSE OF REPRESENTATIVES									
Number of days	298	281	280	265	290	251	272	265	133
Number of hours	1,659	1,688	1,796	1,887	2,445	2,001	2,179	1,694	1,015
Number of hours per day	5.6	6.0	6.4	7.1	8.4	8.0	8.0	6.4	7.6
SENATE									
Number of days	307	274	287	291	343	296	303	322	167
Number of hours	2,341	2,254	2,292	2,514	2,876	2,188	2,200	2,279	1,454
Number of hours per day	7.6	8.2	8.0	8.6	8.4	7.4	7.3	7.1	8.7

- Represents zero.

Source: U.S. Congress, *Congressional Record* and *Daily Calendar*, selected issues. See also <http://thomas.loc.gov/home/resume/108-1res.pdf>.

No. 398. Congressional Bills Vetoed: 1961 to 2004

Period	President	Total vetoes	Regular vetoes	Pocket vetoes	Vetoes sus- tained	Bills passed over veto
1961-63	John F. Kennedy	21	12	9	21	-
1963-69	Lyndon B. Johnson	30	16	14	30	-
1969-74	Richard M. Nixon	43	26	17	36	7
1974-77	Gerald R. Ford	66	48	18	54	12
1977-81	Jimmy Carter	31	13	18	29	2
1981-89	Ronald W. Reagan	78	39	39	69	9
1989-93	George Bush	44	29	15	43	1
1993-2001	William J. Clinton	38	37	1	36	2
2001-2004 [1]	George W. Bush	-	-	-	-	-

- Represents zero. [1] Through April 15, 2004.

Source: U.S. Congress, Senate Library, *Presidential Vetoes ... 1789-1968*; U.S. Congress, *Calendars of the U.S. House of Representatives and History of Legislation*, annual. See also <http://clerk.house.gov/>.

No. 399. Number of Governors by Political Party Affiliation: 1975 to 2004

[Reflects figures after inaugurations for each year]

Year	Demo- cratic	Repub- lican	Indepen- dent/ other	Year	Demo- cratic	Repub- lican	Indepen- dent/ other	Year	Demo- cratic	Repub- lican	Indepen- dent/ other
1975	36	13	1	1993	30	18	2	1999	17	31	2
1980	31	19	-	1994	29	19	2	2000	17	31	2
1985	34	16	-	1995	19	30	1	2001	21	27	2
1990	29	21	-	1996	18	31	1	2002	21	27	2
1991 [1]	29	19	2	1997	17	32	1	2003	24	26	-
1992	28	20	2	1998	17	32	1	2004	22	28	-

- Represents zero. [1] Reflects result of runoff election in Arizona in February 1991.

Source: National Governors Association, Washington, DC, 1970-87 and 1991-2004, *Directory of Governors of the American States, Commonwealths & Territories*, annual; and 1988-90, *Directory of Governors*, annual. (copyright).

Elections 251

No. 400. Vote Cast for and Governor Elected by State: 1990 to 2003

[In thousands (1,216 represents 1,216,000), except percent. D=Democratic, R=Republican, I=Independent]

State	1990 Total vote [1]	1990 Percent leading party	1998 Total vote [1]	1998 Percent leading party	2000 Total vote [1]	2000 Percent leading party	2002 Total vote [1]	2002 Percent leading party	Candidate elected at most recent election
AL.	1,216	R-52.1	1,318	D-57.7	(X)	(X)	1,367	R-49.2	Bob Riley
AK.	195	I-38.9	220	D-51.3	(X)	(X)	231	R-55.8	Frank H. Murkowski
AZ.	[2]941	[2]R-52.4	1,018	R-60.9	(X)	(X)	1,226	D-46.2	Janet Napolitano
AR.	696	D-57.5	706	R-59.8	(X)	(X)	806	R-53.0	Mike Huckabee
CA.	7,699	R-49.2	8,385	D-58.0	(X)	(X)	7,476	D-47.3	[3]Gray Davis
CO	1,011	D-61.9	1,321	R-49.1	(X)	(X)	1,413	R-62.6	Bill Owens
CT.	1,141	I-40.4	1,000	R-62.9	(X)	(X)	1,023	R-56.1	John G. Rowland
DE.	(X)	(X)	(X)	(X)	324	D-59.2	(X)	(X)	Ruth Ann Minner
FL.	3,531	D-56.5	3,964	R-55.3	(X)	(X)	5,101	R-56.0	Jeb Bush
GA	1,450	D-52.9	1,793	D-52.5	(X)	(X)	2,027	R-51.4	Sonny Perdue
HI.	340	D-59.8	408	D-50.1	(X)	(X)	382	R-51.6	Linda Lingle
ID.	321	D-68.2	381	R-67.7	(X)	(X)	411	R-56.3	Dirk Kempthorne
IL.	3,257	R-50.7	3,359	R-51.0	(X)	(X)	3,539	D-52.2	Rod R. Blagojevich
IN.	(X)	(X)	(X)	(X)	2,179	D-56.6	(X)	(X)	Frank L. O'Bannon
IA.	976	R-60.6	956	D-52.3	(X)	(X)	1,026	D-52.7	Tom Vilsack
KS. [4]	783	D-48.6	743	R-73.4	(X)	(X)	836	D-52.9	Kathleen Sebelius
KY [4]	(X)	(X)	(X)	(X)	580	D-60.7	1,083	R-55.0	Ernie Fletcher
LA [4]	(X)	(X)	(X)	(X)	1,295	R-62.2	1,407	D-51.9	Kathleen Blanco
ME	522	R-46.7	421	R-18.9	(X)	(X)	505	D-47.1	John Baldacci
MD	1,111	D-59.8	1,536	D-55.1	(X)	(X)	1,706	R-51.6	Robert L. Erlich Jr.
MA	2,343	R-50.2	1,903	R-50.8	(X)	(X)	2,194	R-49.8	Mitt Romney
MI.	2,565	R-49.8	3,027	R-62.2	(X)	(X)	3,178	D-51.4	Jennifer M. Granholm
MN [4]	1,807	R-49.6	2,091	R-34.3	(X)	(X)	2,252	R-44.4	Tim Pawlenty
MS [4]	(X)	(X)	(X)	(X)	764	D-49.6	894	D-52.6	Haley Barbour
MO	(X)	(X)	(X)	(X)	2,347	D-49.1	(X)	(X)	Bob Holden
MT.	(X)	(X)	(X)	(X)	410	R-51.0	(X)	(X)	Judy Martz
NE.	587	D-49.9	545	R-53.9	(X)	(X)	481	R-68.7	Mike Johanns
NV.	321	D-64.8	434	R-51.6	(X)	(X)	504	R-68.2	Kenny Guinn
NH.	295	R-60.3	319	D-66.1	565	D-48.7	443	R-58.6	Craig Benson
NJ [5].	2,254	D-61.2	2,418	R-46.9	(X)	(X)	2,227	D-56.4	James E. McGreevey
NM	411	D-54.6	499	R-54.5	(X)	(X)	484	D-55.5	Bill Richardson
NY.	4,057	D-53.2	4,735	R-54.3	(X)	(X)	4,579	R-49.4	George E. Pataki
NC	(X)	(X)	(X)	(X)	2,942	D-52.0	(X)	(X)	Mike Easley
ND	(X)	(X)	(X)	(X)	289	R-55.0	(X)	(X)	John Hoeven
OH	3,478	R-55.7	3,354	R-50.0	(X)	(X)	3,229	R-57.8	Bob Taft
OK	911	D-57.4	874	R-57.9	(X)	(X)	1,036	D-43.3	Brad Henry
OR.	1,113	D-45.7	1,113	D-64.4	(X)	(X)	1,260	D-49.0	Theodore R. Kulongoski
PA.	3,053	D-67.7	3,025	R-57.4	(X)	(X)	3,583	D-53.4	Edward G. Rendell
RI.	357	D-74.1	306	R-51.0	(X)	(X)	333	R-54.7	Donald L. Carcieri
SC.	761	R-69.5	1,071	D-53.2	(X)	(X)	1,108	R-52.8	Mark Sanford
SD.	257	R-58.9	260	R-64.0	(X)	(X)	335	R-56.8	Mike Rounds
TN.	790	D-60.8	976	R-68.6	(X)	(X)	1,653	D-50.6	Phil Bredesen
TX.	3,893	D-49.5	3,738	R-68.2	(X)	(X)	4,554	R-57.8	Rick Perry
UT.	(X)	(X)	(X)	(X)	762	R-55.8	(X)	(X)	Michael O. Leavitt
VT.	211	R-51.8	218	D-55.7	293	D-50.5	230	R-44.9	Jim Douglas
VA [5].	1,789	D-50.1	1,736	R-55.8	(X)	(X)	1,887	D-52.2	Mark Warner
WA.	(X)	(X)	(X)	(X)	2,470	D-58.4	(X)	(X)	Gary Locke
WV.	(X)	(X)	(X)	(X)	648	D-50.1	(X)	(X)	Bob Wise
WI.	1,380	R-58.2	1,756	R-59.7	(X)	(X)	1,775	D-45.1	James E. Doyle
WY.	160	D-65.4	175	R-55.6	(X)	(X)	185	D-50.0	Dave Freudenthal

X Not applicable. [1] Includes minor party and scattered votes. [2] Runoff election in 1991. [3] Recall election in 2003; Arnold Schwarzenegger (Republican) was elected governor. [4] Voting years 1999 and 2003 [5] Voting years 1989, 1997, and 2001.

Source: CQ Press (a division of Congressional Quarterly, Inc.), Washington, DC, America Votes, biennial; and unpublished data (copyright).

No. 401. Composition of State Legislatures by Political Party Affiliation: 2002 and 2003

[Data reflect election results in year shown for most states; and except as noted, results in previous year for other states. Figures reflect immediate results of elections, including holdover members in state houses which do not have all of their members running for re-election. Dem.=Democrat, Rep.=Republican, Vac.=Vacancies. In general, Lower House refers to body consisting of state Representatives; Upper House, of state Senators]

State	Lower House 2002				Lower House 2003				Upper House 2002				Upper House 2003			
	Dem.	Rep.	Other	Vac.	Dem.	Rep.	Other	Vac.	Dem.	Rep.	Other	Vac.	Dem.	Rep.	Other	Vac.
U.S.	2,694	2,687	21	9	2,700	2,693	16	2	939	974	51	7	941	977	2	2
AL [1]	64	41	-	-	63	42	-	-	25	10	-	-	25	10	-	-
AK [2]	13	27	-	-	13	27	-	-	8	12	-	-	8	12	-	-
AZ [3]	21	39	-	-	21	39	-	-	13	17	-	-	13	17	-	-
AR [2]	72	28	-	-	70	30	-	-	27	8	-	-	27	8	-	-
CA [2]	48	32	-	-	48	32	-	-	25	15	-	-	25	15	-	-
CO [2]	28	37	-	-	28	37	-	-	17	18	-	-	17	18	-	-
CT [3]	94	57	-	-	95	56	-	-	21	15	-	-	21	15	-	-
DE [2]	12	29	-	-	12	29	-	-	13	8	-	-	13	8	-	-
FL [2]	39	81	-	-	39	81	-	-	14	25	-	1	14	26	-	-
GA [3]	107	72	1	-	107	72	1	-	26	30	-	-	26	30	-	-
HI [2]	36	15	-	-	36	15	-	-	20	5	-	-	20	5	-	-
ID [3]	16	54	-	-	16	54	-	-	7	28	-	-	7	28	-	-
IL [4]	66	52	-	-	66	52	-	-	26	32	1	-	26	32	1	-
IN [2]	51	49	-	-	51	49	-	-	18	32	-	-	18	32	-	-
IA [2]	45	54	-	1	47	53	-	-	21	29	-	-	21	29	-	-
KS [2]	45	80	-	-	45	80	-	-	10	30	-	-	10	30	-	-
KY [2]	65	35	-	-	63	36	-	1	16	22	-	-	16	22	-	-
LA [1]	70	34	1	-	68	37	-	-	23	15	-	1	24	15	-	-
ME [3]	80	67	4	-	80	67	4	-	18	17	-	-	18	17	-	-
MD [1]	98	43	-	-	98	43	-	-	33	14	-	-	33	14	-	-
MA [3]	135	23	1	1	136	23	1	-	34	6	-	-	34	6	-	-
MI [2]	62	47	-	1	63	47	-	-	16	22	-	-	16	22	-	-
MN [2]	53	80	-	1	53	81	-	-	35	31	1	-	35	31	1	-
MS [1]	81	38	3	-	80	42	-	-	31	21	-	-	30	22	-	-
MO [2]	73	90	-	-	73	90	-	-	14	20	-	-	14	20	-	-
MT [2]	47	53	-	-	47	53	-	-	21	29	-	-	21	29	-	-
NE [5]	(5)	(5)	(5)	(5)	(5)	(5)	(5)	(5)	(5)	(5)	49	-	(5)	(5)	(5)	(5)
NV [2]	23	19	-	-	23	19	-	-	8	13	-	-	8	13	-	-
NH [3]	117	282	-	1	119	281	-	-	6	18	-	-	6	18	-	-
NJ [2]	43	35	1	1	47	33	-	-	20	20	-	-	22	18	-	-
NM [2]	42	28	-	-	43	27	-	-	24	18	-	-	24	18	-	-
NY [3]	103	47	-	-	103	47	-	-	25	37	-	-	25	37	-	-
NC [3]	60	60	-	-	59	61	-	-	28	22	-	-	28	22	-	-
ND [1]	28	66	-	-	28	66	-	-	16	31	-	-	16	31	-	-
OH [2]	38	61	-	-	37	62	-	-	11	22	-	-	11	22	-	-
OK [2]	53	48	-	-	53	48	-	-	27	20	-	1	28	20	-	-
OR [2]	25	35	-	-	25	35	-	-	15	15	-	-	14	15	-	1
PA [3]	94	108	-	1	94	108	-	1	21	28	-	1	21	29	-	-
RI [3]	63	11	1	-	63	11	1	-	32	6	-	-	32	6	-	-
SC [2]	50	73	-	1	51	73	-	-	21	24	-	1	20	25	-	1
SD [3]	21	49	-	-	21	49	-	-	9	26	-	-	9	26	-	-
TN [2]	54	45	-	-	54	45	-	-	18	15	-	-	18	15	-	-
TX [2]	62	88	-	-	62	88	-	-	12	19	-	-	12	19	-	-
UT [2]	19	56	-	-	19	56	-	-	7	22	-	-	7	22	-	-
VT [3]	69	74	7	-	69	74	7	-	19	11	-	-	19	11	-	-
VA [2]	34	64	2	-	37	61	2	-	17	23	-	-	16	24	-	-
WA [2]	52	46	-	-	52	46	-	-	24	25	-	-	24	25	-	-
WV [2]	68	32	-	-	68	32	-	-	24	10	-	-	24	10	-	-
WI [2]	40	58	-	1	40	59	-	-	13	18	-	2	15	18	-	-
WY [2]	15	45	-	-	15	45	-	-	10	20	-	-	10	20	-	-

- Represents zero. [1] Members of both houses serve 4-year terms. [2] Upper House members serve 4-year terms and Lower House members serve 2-year terms. [3] Members of both houses serve 2-year terms. [4] Illinois—4 and 2 year term depending on district. [5] Nebraska—4 year term and only state to have a nonpartisan legislature.

Source: The Council of State Governments, Lexington, KY, *The Book of States 2004*, biennial (copyright).

Elections   253

No. 402. Political Party Control of State Legislatures by Party: 1981 to 2004

[As of beginning of year. Nebraska has a nonpartisan legislature]

Year	Legislatures under— Democratic control	Split control or tie	Republican control	Year	Legislatures under— Democratic control	Split control or tie	Republican control	Year	Legislatures under— Democratic control	Split control or tie	Republican control
1981...	28	6	15	1992...	29	14	6	1999...	20	12	17
1983[1].	34	4	11	1993...	25	16	8	2000...	16	15	18
1985...	27	11	11	1994...	24	17	8	2001...	16	15	18
1987...	28	12	9	1995...	18	12	19	2002...	17	15	17
1989[2].	28	13	8	1996...	16	15	18	2003...	16	12	21
1990...	29	11	9	1997...	20	11	18	2004...	17	11	21

[1] Two 1984 midterm recall elections resulted in a change in control of the Michigan State Senate. At the time of the 1984 election, therefore, Democrats controlled 33 legislatures. [2] A party change during the year by a Democratic representative broke the tie in the Indiana House of Representatives, giving the Republicans control of both chambers.

Source: National Conference of State Legislatures, Denver, CO, *State Legislatures*, periodic.

No. 403. Women Holding State Public Offices by Office and State: 2003

[As of January. For data on women in U.S. Congress, see Table 396]

State	State-wide elective executive office[1]	State legislature	State	State-wide elective executive office[1]	State legislature	State	State-wide elective executive office[1]	State legislature
United States .	**81**	**1,654**	Kentucky	-	15	North Dakota ...	2	22
Alabama	5	14	Louisiana......	2	23	Ohio	2	26
Alaska........	-	12	Maine	-	50	Oklahoma	4	18
Arizona	3	25	Maryland	-	63	Oregon	1	27
Arkansas	-	22	Massachusetts ..	1	52	Pennsylvania ...	2	35
California	-	36	Michigan	2	35	Rhode Island ...	-	23
Colorado	2	34	Minnesota	3	55	South Carolina ..	1	16
Connecticut	4	55	Mississippi	1	21	South Dakota ...	-	17
Delaware	3	18	Missouri.......	2	42	Tennessee	-	23
Florida........	3	39	Montana	2	37	Texas	2	35
Georgia.......	3	51	Nebraska......	3	9	Utah	1	23
Hawaii........	1	21	Nevada	2	18	Vermont.......	2	56
Idaho........	1	28	New Hampshire. .	-	116	Virginia.......	-	22
Illinois	2	50	New Jersey	-	20	Washington	2	54
Indiana	3	27	New Mexico	3	33	West Virginia ...	-	25
Iowa	2	32	New York	1	47	Wisconsin......	3	36
Kansas	3	45	North Carolina. .	3	35	Wyoming	1	16

- Represents zero. [1] Excludes women elected to the judiciary, women appointed to State cabinet-level positions, women elected to executive posts by the legislature, and elected members of university Board of Trustees or Board of Education.

Source: Center for the American Woman and Politics, Eagleton Institute of Politics, Rutgers University, New Brunswick, NJ, information releases, (copyright).

No. 404. Public Confidence Levels in Selected Public and Private Institutions: 2001

[Based on a sample survey of 4,216 persons 21 years old and over conducted during the spring and subject to sampling variability; see source]

Institution	Level of confidence A lot	Some	None	Don't Know
Organized labor...................................	9.9	46.3	39.6	4.2
Media (e.g. newspapers, TV, radio).................	5.1	48.2	45.3	1.4
Major corporations................................	6.2	49.2	41.9	2.8
State government	9.2	58.0	31.0	1.7
Political organizations, parties	2.8	36.7	58.6	1.9
Local government	12.6	58.7	27.1	1.6
Congress..	4.0	44.0	49.7	2.3

Source: Toppe, Chris, Arthur Kirsch, and Westat, Inc., *Giving and Volunteering in the United States:* 2001 Edition. (Copyright and published by INDEPENDENT SECTOR, Washington, DC 2002.)

No. 405. Black Elected Officials by Office, 1970 to 2001, and State, 2001

[As of January 2001, no Black elected officials had been identified in Hawaii, Montana, North Dakota, or South Dakota]

State	Total	U.S. and state legisla- tures [1]	City and county offices [2]	Law enforce- ment [3]	Educa- tion [4]	State	Total	U.S. and state legisla- tures [1]	City and county offices [2]	Law enforce- ment [3]	Educa- tion [4]
1970 (Feb.) .	1,469	179	715	213	362	MD	175	40	93	33	9
1980 (July). .	4,890	326	2,832	526	1,206	MA	60	6	44	2	8
1990 (Jan.). .	7,335	436	4,485	769	1,645	MI.	346	25	147	55	119
1995 (Jan.). .	8,385	604	4,954	987	1,840	MN	20	2	4	9	5
1998 (Jan.). .	8,830	614	5,210	998	2,008	MS	892	46	607	109	130
1999 (Jan.). .	8,896	618	5,354	997	1,927	MO	201	19	142	16	24
2000 (Jan.). .	9,001	621	5,420	1,037	1,923	NE	8	1	4	-	3
2001 (Jan.) .	**9,061**	**633**	**5,456**	**1,044**	**1,928**	NV	14	5	5	2	2
						NH	5	5	-	-	-
AL	756	36	569	57	94	NJ.	249	16	139	1	93
AK	3	1	2	-	-	NM	4	1	-	2	1
AZ	12	1	1	5	5	NY	325	34	83	83	125
AR	502	15	298	67	122	NC	491	28	349	29	85
CA	224	10	70	67	77	OH	313	20	217	28	48
CO	18	4	4	9	1	OK	105	6	75	3	21
CT	72	14	47	3	8	OR	6	3	1	2	-
DE	24	4	16	1	3	PA	185	19	74	65	27
DC	176	[5]2	171	-	3	RI	8	7	1	-	-
FL.	243	25	163	39	16	SC	534	32	335	9	158
GA	611	53	395	43	120	TN	180	18	108	27	27
ID	2	-	2	-	-	TX	460	19	302	44	95
IL.	624	28	318	55	223	UT	5	1	3	1	-
IN.	86	13	52	13	8	VT	1	1	-	-	-
IA.	13	1	8	1	3	VA	246	16	130	15	85
KS	17	7	4	3	3	WA	26	2	12	11	1
KY	60	5	44	5	6	WV	19	2	13	3	1
LA	705	32	388	122	163	WI.	33	8	15	5	5
ME	1	-	-	-	1	WY	1	-	1	-	-

- Represents zero. [1] Includes elected State administrators. [2] County commissioners and councilmen, mayors, vice mayors, aldermen, regional officials, and other. [3] Judges, magistrates, constables, marshals, sheriffs, justices of the peace, and other. [4] Members of State education agencies, college boards, school boards, and other. [5] Includes one shadow senator.

Source: Joint Center for Political and Economic Studies, Washington, DC, *Black Elected Officials: A Statistical Summary*, annual (copyright) and <http://www.jointcenter.org/databank/graphs/99beo.pdf> (accessed 17 April 2003).

No. 406. Hispanic Public Elected Officials by Office, 1985 to 2003, and State, 2003

State	Total	State execu- tives and legisla- tors [1]	County and munici- pal offi- cials	Judicial and law enforce- ment	Educa- tion and school boards	State	Total	State execu- tives and legisla- tors [1]	County and munici- pal offi- cials	Judicial and law enforce- ment	Educa- tion and school boards
1985 (Sept.) .	3,147	129	1,316	517	1,185	MD	4	4	-	-	-
1990 (Sept.) .	4,004	144	1,819	583	1,458	MA	17	4	9	-	4
1991 (Sept.) .	4,202	151	1,867	596	1,588	MI.	16	1	6	3	6
1992 (Sept.) .	4,994	150	1,908	628	2,308	MN	4	1	1	1	1
1993 (Sept.) .	5,170	182	2,023	633	2,332	MO	1	-	1	-	-
1994 (Sept.) .	5,459	199	2,197	651	2,412	MT	1	-	-	1	-
2000 (Sept.) .	5,205	223	1,846	454	2,682	NE	3	1	2	-	-
2001 (Sept.) .	5,205	223	1,846	454	2,682	NV	8	3	2	1	2
2002 (Jan.). .	4,303	208	1,960	532	1,603	NH	2	1	-	-	1
2003 (Jan.) .	**4,432**	**231**	**1,958**	**549**	**1,694**	NJ.	74	7	45	-	22
AZ	346	15	133	37	161	NM	603	50	309	86	158
CA	936	28	362	36	510	NY	85	15	24	8	38
CO	135	9	91	6	29	NC	4	2	2	-	-
CT	25	5	16	-	4	ND	1	-	1	-	-
DE	2	1	1	-	-	OH	8	-	6	2	-
FL.	87	16	57	9	5	OR	13	1	6	5	1
GA	6	3	2	1	-	PA	14	1	9	3	1
HI	1	1	-	-	-	RI	5	3	2	-	-
ID	3	1	2	-	-	TX	1,913	38	801	338	736
IL	65	11	42	5	7	UT	2	-	2	-	-
IN	10	1	7	1	1	VA	2	-	1	-	1
IA.	1	-	1	-	-	WA	8	3	3	-	2
KS	8	3	5	-	-	WI.	13	1	4	4	4
LA	3	-	1	2	-	WY	3	1	2	-	-

- Represents zero. [1] Includes U.S. Representatives, not shown separately.

Source: National Association of Latino Elected and Appointed Officials, Washington, DC, *National Roster of Hispanic Elected Officials*, annual.

Elections 255

No. 407. Voting-Age Population, Percent Reporting Registered, and Voted: 1980 to 2000

[157.1 represents 157,100,000. As of November. Covers civilian noninstitutional population 18 years old and over. Includes aliens. Figures are based on Current Population Survey (see text, Section 1, Population, and Appendix III) and differ from those in Table 421 based on population estimates and official vote counts]

Characteristic	Voting-age population (mil.)							Percent reporting they registered								Percent reporting they voted							
								Presidential election years				Congressional election years				Presidential election years				Congressional election years			
	1980	1988	1990	1994	1996	1998	2000	1980	1992	1996	2000	1986	1990	1994	1998	1980	1992	1996	2000	1986	1990	1994	1998
Total [1]	**157.1**	**178.1**	**182.1**	**190.3**	**193.7**	**198.2**	**202.6**	**66.9**	**68.2**	**65.9**	**63.9**	**64.3**	**62.2**	**62.0**	**62.1**	**59.2**	**61.3**	**54.2**	**54.7**	**46.0**	**45.0**	**44.6**	**41.9**
18 to 20 years old	12.3	10.7	10.8	10.3	10.8	11.4	11.9	44.7	48.3	45.6	40.5	35.4	35.4	37.2	32.1	35.7	38.5	31.2	28.4	18.6	18.4	16.5	13.5
21 to 24 years old	15.9	14.8	14.0	14.9	13.9	14.1	14.9	52.7	55.3	51.2	49.3	46.6	43.3	45.5	35.0	43.1	45.7	33.4	35.4	24.2	22.0	22.3	19.2
25 to 34 years old	35.7	42.7	42.7	41.1	40.1	38.6	37.3	62.0	60.6	56.9	54.7	55.8	52.0	51.5	52.4	54.6	53.2	43.1	43.7	35.1	33.8	32.2	28.0
35 to 44 years old	25.6	35.2	37.9	41.9	43.3	44.4	44.5	70.6	69.2	66.5	63.8	67.9	65.5	63.3	62.4	64.4	63.6	54.9	55.0	49.3	44.8	46.0	40.7
45 to 64 years old	43.6	45.9	46.9	50.9	53.7	57.4	61.4	75.8	75.3	73.5	71.2	74.8	71.4	71.0	71.1	69.3	70.0	64.4	64.1	58.7	55.8	56.0	53.6
65 years old and over	24.1	28.8	29.9	31.1	31.9	32.3	32.8	74.6	78.0	77.0	76.1	76.9	76.5	75.6	75.4	65.1	70.1	67.0	67.6	60.9	60.3	60.7	59.5
Male	74.1	84.5	86.6	90.0	92.6	95.2	97.1	66.6	66.9	64.4	62.2	63.4	61.2	60.8	60.6	59.1	60.2	52.8	53.1	45.8	44.6	44.4	41.4
Female	83.0	93.6	95.5	99.3	101.0	103.0	105.5	67.1	69.3	67.3	65.6	65.0	63.1	63.2	63.5	59.4	62.3	55.5	56.2	46.1	45.4	44.9	42.4
White	137.7	152.9	155.6	160.3	162.8	165.8	168.7	68.4	70.1	67.7	65.6	65.3	63.8	64.2	63.9	60.9	63.6	56.0	56.4	47.0	46.7	46.9	43.3
Black	16.4	19.7	20.4	21.8	22.5	23.3	24.1	60.0	63.9	63.5	63.6	64.0	58.8	58.3	60.2	50.5	54.0	50.6	53.5	43.2	39.2	37.0	39.6
Hispanic [2]	8.2	12.9	13.8	17.5	18.4	20.3	21.6	36.3	35.0	35.7	34.9	35.9	32.3	30.0	33.7	29.9	28.9	26.7	27.5	24.2	21.0	19.1	20.0
Region: [3]																							
Northeast	35.5	37.9	38.1	38.4	38.3	38.5	38.9	64.8	67.0	64.7	63.7	62.0	61.0	60.9	60.8	58.5	61.2	54.5	55.2	44.4	45.2	45.2	41.2
Midwest	41.5	43.3	43.9	44.5	45.2	45.9	46.4	73.8	74.6	71.6	70.2	70.7	68.2	68.7	68.2	65.8	67.2	59.3	60.9	49.5	48.6	48.8	47.3
South	50.6	60.7	62.4	66.4	68.1	70.1	71.8	64.8	67.2	65.9	64.5	63.0	61.3	60.7	62.7	65.6	59.0	52.2	53.5	43.0	42.4	40.5	38.6
West	29.5	36.2	37.7	41.0	42.1	43.7	45.5	63.3	63.6	60.8	56.9	60.8	57.7	58.1	56.0	57.2	58.5	51.8	49.9	48.4	45.0	46.4	42.3
School years completed:																							
High school:																							
8 years or less	22.7	19.1	17.7	14.7	14.1	13.3	12.9	53.0	43.9	40.7	36.1	50.5	44.0	40.1	40.2	42.6	35.1	28.1	26.8	32.7	27.7	23.2	24.6
1 to 3 years [4]	22.5	21.1	21.0	20.7	21.0	21.0	20.1	54.6	50.4	47.9	45.9	52.4	47.9	44.7	43.4	45.6	41.2	33.8	33.6	33.8	30.9	27.0	25.0
4 years [5]	61.2	70.0	71.5	64.9	65.2	65.6	66.3	66.4	64.9	62.2	60.1	62.9	60.0	58.9	58.6	58.9	57.5	49.1	49.4	44.1	42.2	40.5	37.1
College:																							
1 to 3 years [6]	26.7	34.3	36.3	50.4	50.9	52.9	55.3	74.4	75.4	72.9	70.0	70.0	68.7	68.4	68.3	67.2	68.7	60.5	60.3	49.9	50.0	49.1	46.2
4 years or more [7]	24.0	33.6	35.6	39.4	42.5	45.4	48.0	84.3	84.8	80.4	77.3	77.8	77.3	76.3	75.1	79.9	81.0	73.0	72.0	62.5	62.5	63.1	57.2
Employed	95.0	113.8	115.5	122.6	125.6	130.5	133.4	68.7	69.9	67.0	64.7	64.4	62.6	62.9	62.6	61.8	63.8	55.2	55.5	45.7	45.1	45.2	41.2
Unemployed	6.9	5.8	6.7	6.5	6.4	5.2	4.9	50.3	53.7	52.5	46.1	50.6	44.6	46.4	48.5	41.2	46.2	37.2	35.1	31.2	27.9	28.3	28.4
Not in labor force	55.2	58.5	59.9	61.2	61.6	62.5	64.2	65.8	66.8	65.1	63.8	65.4	63.4	61.9	62.1	57.0	58.7	54.1	54.5	48.2	46.7	45.8	44.5

[1] Includes other races not shown separately. [2] Hispanic persons may be of any race. [3] For composition of regions, see map, inside cover. [4] Beginning 1992, represents those who completed 9th to 12th grade, but have no high school diploma. [5] Beginning 1992, high school graduate. [6] Beginning 1992, some college or associate degree. [7] Beginning 1992, bachelor's or advanced degree.

Source: U.S. Census Bureau, Current Population Reports, P20-542 and earlier reports.

[202,609 represents 202,609,000. See headnote, Table 407]

State	Voting-age population (1,000)	Percent of voting-age population		State	Voting-age population (1,000)	Percent of voting-age population	
		Registered	Voted			Registered	Voted
U.S.	202,609	63.9	54.7	MO	4,066	74.3	65.4
AL	3,278	73.6	59.6	MT	658	70.0	62.2
AK	412	72.5	65.5	NE	1,205	71.8	58.9
AZ	3,524	53.3	46.7	NV	1,377	52.3	46.5
AR	1,893	59.4	49.4	NH	902	69.6	63.3
CA	24,749	52.8	46.4	NJ	6,109	63.2	55.2
CO	3,049	64.1	53.6	NM	1,261	59.5	51.3
CT	2,415	62.5	55.2	NY	13,725	58.6	51.0
DE	567	67.9	62.2	NC	5,629	66.1	53.2
DC	407	72.4	65.6	ND	449	91.1	69.8
FL	11,633	60.5	51.6	OH	8,301	67.0	58.1
GA	5,775	61.1	49.0	OK	2,457	68.3	58.3
HI	855	47.0	39.7	OR	2,515	68.2	60.8
ID	927	61.4	53.9	PA	8,950	65.3	55.7
IL	8,859	66.7	56.8	RI	729	69.7	60.1
IN	4,380	68.5*	58.5	SC	2,929	68.0	58.9
IA	2,110	72.2	64.1	SD	530	70.9	58.7
KS	1,908	67.7	60.2	TN	4,173	62.1	52.3
KY	2,996	69.7	54.9	TX	14,533	61.4	48.2
LA	3,143	75.4	64.6	UT	1,472	64.7	56.3
ME	979	80.3	69.2	VT	458	72.0	63.3
MD	3,812	65.6	57.1	VA	5,177	64.1	57.2
MA	4,614	70.3	60.1	WA	4,314	66.1	58.6
MI	7,231	69.1	60.1	WV	1,405	63.1	52.1
MN	3,506	76.7	67.8	WI	3,884	76.5	67.8
MS	2,029	72.2	59.8	WY	350	68.6	62.5

Source: U.S. Census Bureau, Current Population Reports, P20-466. See also <http://www.census.gov/population/www/socdemo/voting.html>.

No. 409. Participation in Elections for President and U.S. Representatives: 1932 to 2002

[75,768 represents 75,768,000. As of November. Estimated resident population 21 years old and over, 1932-70, except as noted, and 18 years old and over thereafter; includes Armed Forces. Prior to 1960, excludes Alaska and Hawaii. District of Columbia is included in votes cast for President beginning 1964 and in votes cast for Representative from 1972 to 1994]

Year	Resident population (incl. aliens) of voting age [1] (1,000)	Votes cast				Year	Resident population (incl. aliens) of voting age [1] (1,000)	Votes cast			
		For President [2] (1,000)	Percent of voting-age population	For U.S. Representatives (1,000)	Percent of voting-age population			For President [2] (1,000)	Percent of voting-age population	For U.S. Representatives (1,000)	Percent of voting-age population
1932	75,768	39,758	52.5	37,657	49.7	1968	120,285	73,212	60.9	66,288	55.1
1934	77,997	(X)	(X)	32,256	41.4	1970	124,498	(X)	(X)	54,173	43.5
1936	80,174	45,654	56.9	42,886	53.5	1972	140,777	77,719	55.2	71,430	50.7
1938	82,354	(X)	(X)	36,236	44.0	1974	146,338	(X)	(X)	52,495	35.9
1340	84,728	49,900	58.9	46,951	55.4	1976	152,308	81,556	53.5	74,422	48.9
1942	86,465	(X)	(X)	28,074	32.5	1978	158,369	(X)	(X)	55,332	34.9
1944	85,654	47,977	56.0	45,103	52.7	1980	163,945	86,515	52.8	77,995	47.6
1946	92,659	(X)	(X)	34,398	37.1	1982	169,643	(X)	(X)	64,514	38.0
1948	95,573	48,794	51.1	45,933	48.1	1984	173,995	92,653	53.3	83,231	47.8
1950	98,134	(X)	(X)	40,342	41.1	1986	177,922	(X)	(X)	59,619	33.5
1952	99,929	61,551	61.6	57,571	57.6	1988	181,956	91,595	50.3	81,786	44.9
1954	102,075	(X)	(X)	42,580	41.7	1990	185,812	(X)	(X)	61,513	33.1
1956	104,515	62,027	59.3	58,426	55.9	1992	189,493	104,425	55.1	96,239	50.8
1958	106,447	(X)	(X)	45,818	43.0	1994	193,010	(X)	(X)	70,781	36.7
1960	109,672	68,838	62.8	64,133	58.5	1996	196,789	96,278	48.9	89,863	45.7
1962	112,952	(X)	(X)	51,267	45.4	1998	201,270	(X)	(X)	65,897	32.7
1964	114,090	70,645	61.9	65,895	57.8	2000	205,813	105,397	51.2	97,226	47.2
1966	116,638	(X)	(X)	52,908	45.4	2002[3]	214,557	(X)	(X)	73,449	34.2

X Not applicable. [1] Population 18 and over in Georgia, 1944-70, and in Kentucky, 1956-70; 19 and over in Alaska and 20 and over in Hawaii, 1960-70. Source: U.S. Census Bureau, Current Population Reports, P25-1085; also see (released July 31, 2000). [2] Source: 1932-58, U.S. Congress, Clerk of the House, Statistics of the Presidential and Congressional Election, biennial. [3] Projection.

Source: Except as noted, CQ Press (a division of Congressional Quarterly, Inc.), Washington, DC, America Votes, biennial (copyright).

Elections 257

No. 410. Resident Population of Voting Age and Percent Casting Votes— States: 1996 to 2002

[196,789 represents 196,789,000. As of November. Estimated population, 18 years old and over. Voting-age population excluding states without registration (210,007,000). Includes Armed Forces stationed in each state, aliens, and institutional population]

State	Voting-age population (1,000)				Percent casting votes for—				
					Presidential electors		U.S. Representatives		
	1996	1998	2000	2002	1996	2000	1998	2000	2002
U.S.	196,789	201,270	205,813	214,557	48.9	51.2	32.8	47.3	34.2
AL	3,221	3,280	3,333	3,397	47.6	50.0	37.0	43.2	37.4
AK	419	425	430	438	57.7	66.4	52.5	63.8	52.0
AZ	3,245	3,421	3,625	3,960	43.3	42.3	29.3	40.4	30.2
AR	1,852	1,891	1,929	2,031	47.7	47.8	27.8	32.8	33.9
CA	23,002	23,902	24,873	25,849	43.6	44.1	33.4	42.0	28.1
CO	2,837	2,946	3,067	3,392	53.3	56.8	43.3	52.9	41.2
CT	2,475	2,489	2,499	2,534	56.3	58.4	38.3	52.6	39.0
DE	552	566	582	608	49.1	56.3	31.9	53.8	37.6
DC	428	421	411	(NA)	43.4	49.1	(NA)	(NA)	(NA)
FL	11,078	11,398	11,774	12,789	47.9	50.6	10.6	42.6	29.5
GA	5,420	5,647	5,893	6,354	42.4	44.1	28.9	41.0	30.2
HI	886	902	909	919	40.6	40.5	44.1	37.5	39.2
ID	845	883	921	986	58.2	54.5	42.9	53.5	41.1
IL	8,787	8,894	8,983	9,327	49.1	52.8	36.2	48.9	36.8
IN	4,340	4,399	4,448	4,576	49.2	49.4	35.8	48.5	33.2
IA	2,126	2,148	2,165	2,230	58.0	60.8	41.9	58.9	45.4
KS	1,902	1,940	1,983	2,013	56.5	54.1	37.5	52.4	41.2
KY	2,918	2,959	2,993	3,143	47.6	51.6	37.1	48.0	34.8
LA	3,129	3,195	3,255	3,299	57.0	54.2	9.7	36.9	34.6
ME	941	955	968	993	64.4	67.3	43.4	66.0	49.9
MD	3,799	3,862	3,925	4,004	46.9	51.5	38.4	49.1	41.5
MA	4,652	4,701	4,749	4,897	55.0	56.9	37.1	49.4	37.6
MI	7,207	7,294	7,358	7,424	53.4	57.5	40.9	55.3	41.2
MN	3,415	3,480	3,547	3,741	64.2	68.8	58.6	66.6	58.9
MS	1,960	2,005	2,047	2,126	45.6	48.6	27.5	48.2	31.9
MO	3,984	4,046	4,105	4,257	54.2	57.5	38.9	56.7	43.5
MT	648	659	668	686	62.8	61.5	50.3	61.5	48.3
NE	1,208	1,222	1,234	1,277	56.1	56.5	43.0	55.4	37.1
NV	1,199	1,285	1,390	1,614	38.7	43.8	31.9	42.1	31.0
NH	869	889	911	956	57.4	62.5	35.7	61.1	46.4
NJ	6,042	6,144	6,245	6,433	50.9	51.0	29.5	47.9	31.2
NM	1,214	1,241	1,263	1,339	45.8	47.4	40.1	46.5	32.7
NY	13,606	13,721	13,805	14,463	46.4	49.4	31.1	42.2	26.4
NC	5,501	5,645	5,797	6,298	45.7	50.2	33.7	48.0	35.6
ND	476	477	477	477	56.0	60.4	44.6	59.9	48.4
OH	8,332	8,394	8,433	8,521	54.4	55.8	40.2	53.6	37.1
OK	2,427	2,477	2,531	2,611	49.7	48.8	34.7	43.0	38.4
OR	2,404	2,466	2,530	2,654	57.3	60.6	44.2	56.9	46.7
PA	9,153	9,163	9,155	9,356	49.2	53.7	31.6	49.7	35.4
RI	751	752	753	798	52.0	54.3	39.0	51.0	41.2
SC	2,802	2,889	2,977	3,128	41.1	46.4	33.7	44.4	31.5
SD	535	540	542	565	60.5	58.4	47.9	58.1	59.6
TN	4,007	4,114	4,221	4,413	47.3	49.2	22.2	43.9	34.7
TX	13,643	14,223	14,850	15,708	41.1	43.1	24.3	40.3	27.3
UT	1,350	1,411	1,465	1,587	49.3	52.6	33.4	51.8	35.1
VT	442	451	460	475	58.5	64.0	47.7	61.6	47.5
VA	5,066	5,168	5,263	5,527	47.7	52.1	22.2	46.0	27.4
WA	4,109	4,237	4,368	4,531	54.9	56.9	43.9	54.5	38.4
WV	1,400	1,411	1,416	1,409	45.5	45.8	24.9	41.0	28.4
WI	3,838	3,888	3,930	4,073	57.2	66.1	43.0	63.8	40.2
WY	347	354	358	371	61.0	61.0	49.2	59.3	49.1

NA Not available.

Source: Compiled by U.S. Census Bureau. Population data from U.S. Census Bureau, *Current Population Reports*, P25-1132; votes cast from Elections Research Center, Chevy Chase, MD, *America Votes*, annual, (copyright); and CQ Press (a division of Congressional Quarterly, Inc.), Washington, DC (copyright).

No. 411. Political Action Committees—Number by Committee Type: 1980 to 2002

[As of December 31]

Committee type	1980	1985	1990	1995	1998	1999	2000	2001	2002
Total...................	2,551	3,992	4,172	4,016	3,798	3,835	3,706	3,907	4,027
Corporate................	1,206	1,710	1,795	1,674	1,567	1,548	1,523	1,545	1,528
Labor....................	297	388	346	334	321	318	316	317	320
Trade/membership/health........	576	695	774	815	821	844	812	860	975
Nonconnected..............	374	1,003	1,062	1,020	935	972	902	1,026	1,055
Cooperative...............	42	54	59	44	39	38	39	41	39
Corporation without stock........	56	142	136	129	115	115	114	118	110

Source: U.S. Federal Election Commission, press release of January 2003.

No. 412. Political Action Committees—Financial Activity Summary by Committee Type: 1997 to 2002

[In millions of dollars (502.6 represents $502,600,000). Covers financial activity during 2-year calendar period indicated]

Committee type	Receipts			Disbursements [1]			Contributions to candidates		
	1997-98	1999-00	2001-02	1997-98	1999-00	2001-02	1997-98	1999-00	2001-02
Total.............	502.6	604.9	685.3	470.8	579.4	656.5	219.9	259.8	282.0
Corporate...........	144.1	164.5	191.7	137.6	158.3	178.3	78.0	91.5	99.6
Labor...............	111.3	136.0	167.8	98.2	128.7	158.0	44.6	51.6	53.9
Trade/membership/health ..	119.6	142.9	166.7	114.4	137.2	165.7	62.3	71.8	46.3
Nonconnected.........	114.3	144.3	145.8	107.8	139.7	141.3	28.2	37.3	75.1
Cooperative...........	4.5	3.7	3.7	4.3	3.3	3.6	2.4	2.4	2.7
Corporation without stock ..	8.8	13.6	9.7	8.5	12.2	9.6	4.4	5.3	4.4

[1] Comprises contributions to candidates, independent expenditures, and other disbursements.

Source: U.S. Federal Election Commission, *FEC Reports on Financial Activity, Final Report, Party and Non-Party Political Committees*, biennial.

No. 413. Presidential Campaign Finances—Federal Funds for General Election: 1980 to 2000

[In millions of dollars (62.7 represents $62,700,000). Based on FEC certifications, audit reports, and Dept. of Treasury reports]

1980		1992		1996		2000	
Candidate	Amount	Candidate	Amount	Candidate	Amount	Candidate	Amount
Total .:.....	62.7	Total........	110.4	Total........	152.6	Total........	147.7
Anderson [1]....	4.2	Bush........	55.2	Clinton	61.8	Bush.........	67.6
Carter	29.4	Clinton	55.2	Dole	61.8	Gore........	67.6
Reagan	29.2	Perot	-	Perot	29.0	Buchanan	12.6

- Represents zero.   [1] John Anderson, as the candidate of a new party, was permitted to raise funds privately. Total receipts for the Anderson campaign, including Federal funds, were $17.6 million, and total expenditures were $15.6 million.

Source: U.S. Federal Election Commission, periodic press releases.

No. 414. Presidential Campaign Finances—Primary Campaign Receipts and Disbursements: 1991 to 2000

[In millions of dollars (125.2 represents $125,200,000). Covers campaign finance activity during 2-year calendar period indicated. Covers candidates who received Federal matching funds or who had significant financial activity]

Item	Total [1]			Democratic			Republican		
	1991-92	1995-96	1999-00	1991-92	1995-96	1999-00	1991-92	1995-96	1999-00
Receipts, total [2].............	125.2	243.9	351.6	70.0	46.2	96.6	49.7	187.0	236.7
Individual contributions..........	82.4	126.4	238.2	44.7	31.3	66.7	34.4	93.1	159.1
Federal matching funds	41.5	56.0	61.6	24.4	14.0	29.3	15.0	41.6	26.5
Disbursements	118.7	234.1	343.5	64.4	41.8	92.2	48.8	182.1	233.2

[1] Includes other parties, not shown separately.   [2] Includes other types of receipts, not shown separately.

Source: U.S. Federal Election Commission, *FEC Reports on Financial Activity, Final Report, Presidential Pre-Nomination Campaigns*, quadrennial.

Elections   259

No. 415. Congressional Campaign Finances—Receipts and Disbursements: 1995 to 2000

[505.4 represents 505,400,000. Covers all campaign finance activity during 2-year calendar period indicated for primary, general, run-off, and special elections, for 1999-2000 relates to 2,083 House of Representatives candidates and 333 Senate candidates. Data have been adjusted to eliminate transfers between all committees within a campaign. For further information on legal limits of contributions, see Federal Election campaign act of 1971, as amended]

Item	House of representatives						Senate					
	Amount (mil. dol.)			Percent distribution			Amount (mil. dol.)			Percent distribution		
	1995-96	1997-98	1999-00	1995-96	1997-98	1999-00	1995-96	1997-98	1999-00	1995-96	1997-98	1999-00
Total receipts [1]	505.4	493.7	610.4	100	100	100	285.1	287.5	437.0	100	100	100
Individual contributions.	272.9	253.2	315.6	55	52	52	166.9	166.5	252.1	59	58	58
Other committees	155.0	158.5	193.4	31	32	32	45.6	48.1	52.0	16	17	12
Candidate loans	42.0	46.8	61.9	8	10	10	40.3	52.2	89.0	14	18	20
Candidate contributions	7.0	5.3	6.3	1	1	1	16.4	1.3	18.7	6	(Z)	4
Democrats.	233.1	233.4	286.7	46	47	47	126.5	134.1	230.4	44	47	53
Republicans.	266.9	255.8	317.7	53	52	52	157.7	153.0	203.8	55	53	47
Others	5.4	4.5	6.0	1	1	1	0.9	0.4	2.8	(Z)	(Z)	1
Incumbents	279.8	293.6	361.8	56	60	59	81.8	135.5	130.6	29	47	30
Challengers₂	119.1	92.8	127.4	24	19	21	79.2	113.9	99.6	28	40	23
Open seats [2]	101.1	102.7	121.1	14	21	20	124.1	37.7	206.7	44	13	47
Total disbursements . . .	477.8	452.5	572.3	95	100	100	287.4	287.9	434.7	100	100	100
Democrats.	221.1	211.1	266.8	44	47	47	127.4	134.6	226.3	44	47	52
Republicans.	251.4	237.2	299.7	50	52	52	159.1	152.9	205.7	55	53	47
Others	5.3	4.2	5.7	1	1	1	0.9	0.4	2.7	(Z)	(Z)	1
Incumbents	258.1	257.2	327.0	51	57	57	85.4	137.3	130.2	30	48	30
Challengers₂	119.6	94.7	125.6	24	21	22	78.9	112.5	99.3	27	39	23
Open seats [2]	100.2	100.6	119.7	20	22	21	123.1	38.1	205.1	43	13	47

Z Less than 0.5 percent.   [1] Includes other types of receipts, not shown separately.   [2] Elections in which an incumbent did not seek re-election.

Source: U.S. Federal Election Commission, *FEC Reports on Financial Activity, Final Report, U.S. Senate and House Campaigns*, biennial.

No. 416. Contributions to Congressional Campaigns by Political Action Committees (PAC) by Type of Committee: 1993 to 2002

[In millions of dollars. (132.4 represents 132,400,000). Covers amounts given to candidates in primary, general, run-off, and special elections during the 2-year calendar period indicated. For number of political action committees, see Table 411]

Type of committee	Total [1]	Democrats	Republicans	Incumbents	Challengers	Open seats [2]
HOUSE OF REPRESENTATIVES						
1993-94	132.4	88.2	43.9	101.4	12.7	18.3
1995-96	155.8	77.3	77.7	113.9	21.4	20.5
1997-98	158.7	77.6	80.9	124.0	14.9	19.8
1999-00	193.4	98.2	94.7	150.5	19.9	23.0
2001-02, total [3]	**206.9**	**102.6**	**104.2**	**161.0**	**13.8**	**32.1**
Corporate	68.2	23.6	44.6	59.7	1.6	6.9
Trade association [4]	57.2	23.0	34.2	47.1	2.1	8.0
Labor	44.4	39.9	4.3	31.5	5.2	7.7
Nonconnected [5]	32.2	14.0	18.1	18.5	4.8	8.9
SENATE						
1993-94	47.2	24.0	23.2	26.3	5.7	15.1
1995-96	45.6	16.6	29.0	19.4	6.9	19.3
1997-98	48.1	20.7	27.3	34.3	6.6	7.2
1999-00	51.9	18.7	33.2	33.5	7.1	11.3
2001-02, total [3]	**59.2**	**25.4**	**33.8**	**37.0**	**14.2**	**8.1**
Corporate	23.4	7.0	16.4	15.8	4.3	3.4
Trade association [4]	14.3	4.9	9.3	9.5	3.1	1.7
Labor	7.5	7.0	0.5	4.1	2.4	1.1
Nonconnected [5]	12.5	5.8	6.6	6.6	4.1	1.8

[1] Includes other parties, not shown separately.   [2] Elections in which an incumbent did not seek re-election.   [3] Includes other types of political action committees not shown separately.   [4] Includes membership organizations and health organizations.   [5] Represents "ideological" groups as well as other issue groups not necessarily ideological in nature.

Source: U.S. Federal Election Commission, *FEC Reports on Financial Activity, Party and Non-Party Political Committees, Final Report*, biennial.

U.S. Census Bureau, Statistical Abstract of the United States: 2004-2005

State and Local Government Finances and Employment

This section presents data on revenues, expenditures, debt, and employment of state and local governments. Nationwide statistics relating to state and local governments, their numbers, finances, and employment are compiled primarily by the U.S. Census Bureau through a program of censuses and surveys. Every fifth year (for years ending in "2" and "7") the Census Bureau conducts a census of governments involving collection of data for all governmental units in the United States. In addition, the Census Bureau conducts annual surveys which cover all the state governments and a sample of local governments.

Annually, the Census Bureau releases information on the Internet which presents financial data for the federal government, nationwide totals for state and local governments, and state-local data by states. Also released annually is a series on state, city, county, and school finances and on state and local public employment. There is also a series of quarterly data releases covering tax revenue and finances of major public employee retirement systems.

Basic information for Census Bureau statistics on governments is obtained by mail canvass from state and local officials; however, financial data for each of the state governments and for many of the large local governments are compiled from their official records and reports by Census Bureau personnel. In over two-thirds of the states, all or part of local government financial data are obtained through central collection arrangements with state governments. Financial data on the federal government are primarily based on the *Budget* published by the Office of Management and Budget (see text, Section 9, Federal Government Finances and Employment).

Governmental units—The governmental structure of the United States includes, in addition to the federal government and

the states, thousands of local governments—counties, municipalities, townships, school districts, and many "special districts." In 2002, 87,525 local governments were identified by the census of governments (see Tables 417-419). As defined by the census, governmental units include all agencies or bodies having an organized existence, governmental character, and substantial autonomy. While most of these governments can impose taxes, many of the special districts—such as independent public housing authorities and numerous local irrigation, power, and other types of districts—are financed from rentals, charges for services, benefit assessments, grants from other governments, and other nontax sources. The count of governments excludes semi-autonomous agencies through which states, cities, and counties sometimes provide for certain functions—for example, "dependent" school systems, state institutions of higher education, and certain other "authorities" and special agencies which are under the administrative or fiscal control of an established governmental unit.

Finances—The financial statistics relate to government fiscal years ending June 30 or at some date within the 12 previous months. The following governments are exceptions and are included as though they were part of the June 30 group; ending September 30, the state governments of Alabama and Michigan, the District of Columbia, and Alabama school districts; and ending August 31, the state government of Texas and Texas school districts. New York State ends its fiscal year on March 31. The federal government ended the fiscal year June 30 until 1976 when its fiscal year, by an act of Congress, was revised to extend from Oct. 1 to Sept. 30. A 3-month quarter (July 1 to Sept. 30, 1976) bridged the transition.

Nationwide government finance statistics have been classified and presented in terms of uniform concepts and categories, rather than according to the highly diverse terminology, organization, and fund structure utilized by individual governments.

Statistics on governmental finances distinguish among general government, utilities, liquor stores, and insurance trusts. *General government* comprises all activities except utilities, liquor stores, and insurance trusts. Utilities include government water supply, electric light and power, gas supply, and transit systems. Liquor stores are operated by 17 states and by local governments in 6 states. Insurance trusts relate to employee retirement, unemployment compensation, and other social insurance systems administered by the federal, state, and local governments.

Data for cities or counties relate only to municipal or county and their dependent agencies and do not include amounts for other local governments in the same geographic location. Therefore, expenditure figures for "education" do not include spending by the separate school districts which administer public schools within most municipal or county areas. Variations in the assignment of governmental responsibility for public assistance, health, hospitals, public housing, and other functions to a lesser degree also have an important effect upon reported amounts of city or county expenditure, revenue, and debt.

Employment and payrolls—These data are based mainly on mail canvassing of state and local governments. Payroll includes all salaries, wages, and individual fee payments for the month specified, and employment relates to all persons on governmental payrolls during a pay period of the month covered— including paid officials, temporary help, and (unless otherwise specified) part-time as well as full-time personnel. Beginning 1986, statistics for full-time equivalent employment have been computed with a formula using hours worked by part-time employees. A payroll based formula was used prior to 1985. Full-time equivalent employment statistics were not computed for 1985. Figures shown for individual governments cover major dependent agencies such as institutions of higher education, as well as the basic central departments and agencies of the government.

Statistical reliability—For a discussion of statistical collection and estimation, sampling procedures, and measures of statistical reliability applicable to Census Bureau data, see Appendix III.

No. 417. Number of Governmental Units by Type: 1952 to 2002

Type of government	1952 [1]	1962	1967	1972	1977	1982	1987	1992	1997	2002
Total units	116,807	91,237	81,299	78,269	79,913	81,831	83,237	85,006	87,504	87,576
U.S. Government	1	1	1	1	1	1	1	1	1	1
State government	50	50	50	50	50	50	50	50	50	50
Local governments	116,756	91,186	81,248	78,218	79,862	81,780	83,186	84,955	87,453	87,525
County	3,052	3,043	3,049	3,044	3,042	3,041	3,042	3,043	3,043	3,034
Municipal	16,807	18,000	18,048	18,517	18,862	19,076	19,200	19,279	19,372	19,429
Township and town	17,202	17,142	17,105	16,991	16,822	16,734	16,691	16,656	16,629	16,504
School district	67,355	34,678	21,782	15,781	15,174	14,851	14,721	14,422	13,726	13,506
Special district	12,340	18,323	21,264	23,885	25,962	28,078	29,532	31,555	34,683	35,052

[1] Adjusted to include units in Alaska and Hawaii which adopted statehood in 1959.

Source: U.S. Census Bureau, *2002 Census of Governments, Volume 1, Number 1, Government Organization,* Series GC02(1)-1. See also <http://www.census.gov/prod/2003pubs/gc021x1.pdf>(issued December 2002).

No. 418. Number of Local Governments by Type—States: 2002

[Governments in existence in January. Limited to governments actually in existence. See Appendix III]

State	All govern-mental units [1]	County	Municipal	Town-ship [1]	School district	Special district [2] Total [3]	Special district [2] Natural resources	Special district [2] Fire protection	Special district [2] Housing & community develop-ment
United States..	87,525	3,034	19,429	16,504	13,506	35,052	6,979	5,725	3,399
Alabama	1,171	67	451	-	128	525	68	12	152
Alaska.	175	12	149	-	-	14	-	-	13
Arizona	638	15	87	-	231	305	83	151	-
Arkansas	1,588	75	499	-	310	704	258	80	122
California.	4,409	57	475	-	1,047	2,830	484	368	71
Colorado	1,928	62	270	-	182	1,414	178	250	91
Connecticut	580	-	30	149	17	384	1	64	93
Delaware.	339	3	57	-	19	260	239	-	3
District of Columbia	2	-	1	-	-	1	-	-	-
Florida.	1,191	66	404	-	95	626	124	57	105
Georgia.	1,448	156	531	-	180	581	38	2	201
Hawaii.	19	3	1	-	-	15	14	-	-
Idaho	1,158	44	200	-	116	798	176	142	10
Illinois	6,903	102	1,291	1,431	934	3,145	979	823	112
Indiana	3,085	91	567	1,008	294	1,125	141	1	63
Iowa	1,975	99	948	-	386	542	251	67	23
Kansas	3,887	104	627	1,299	324	1,533	261	-	199
Kentucky	1,439	119	424	-	176	720	166	163	17
Louisiana.	473	60	302	-	66	45	4	-	-
Maine	826	16	22	467	99	222	15	-	23
Maryland	265	23	157	-	-	85	44	-	21
Massachusetts . . .	841	5	45	306	82	403	16	16	250
Michigan	2,804	83	533	1,242	580	366	80	4	-
Minnesota	3,482	87	854	1,793	345	403	114	-	167
Mississippi	1,000	82	296	-	164	458	242	34	57
Missouri.	3,422	114	946	312	536	1,514	183	317	136
Montana	1,127	54	129	-	352	592	125	155	12
Nebraska.	2,791	93	531	446	575	1,146	80	421	125
Nevada	210	16	19	-	17	158	33	19	5
New Hampshire . .	559	10	13	221	167	148	10	14	21
New Jersey	1,412	21	324	242	549	276	16	196	2
New Mexico	858	33	101	-	96	628	583	-	6
New York.	3,420	57	616	929	683	1,135	3	911	-
North Carolina . . .	960	100	541	-	-	319	155	-	91
North Dakota	2,735	53	360	1,332	226	764	79	281	39
Ohio	3,636	88	942	1,308	667	631	98	73	77
Oklahoma	1,798	77	590	-	571	560	97	26	105
Oregon	1,439	36	240	-	236	927	179	256	20
Pennsylvania	5,031	66	1,018	1,546	516	1,885	7	-	90
Rhode Island	118	-	8	31	4	75	3	34	25
South Carolina . . .	701	46	269	-	85	301	48	86	46
South Dakota	1,866	66	308	940	176	376	102	72	40
Tennessee	930	92	349	-	14	475	108	-	98
Texas	4,784	254	1,196	-	1,089	2,245	442	141	398
Utah	605	29	236	-	40	300	81	19	16
Vermont	733	14	47	237	283	152	14	19	10
Virginia	521	95	229	-	1	196	47	-	-
Washington	1,787	39	279	-	296	1,173	170	387	41
West Virginia	686	55	234	-	55	342	15	-	39
Wisconsin	3,048	72	585	1,265	442	684	191	-	164
Wyoming	722	23	98	-	55	546	134	64	-

- Represents zero.   [1] Includes "town" governments in the six New England States and in Minnesota, New York, and Wisconsin.   [2] Single function districts.   [3] Includes other special districts not shown separately.

No. 419. County, Municipal, and Township Governments by Population Size: 2002

[Number of governments as of January 2002. Population enumerated as of April 1, 2000. (252,051 represents 252,051,000). Consolidated city-county governments are classified as municipal rather than county governments. Township governments include "towns" in the six New England States, Minnesota, New York, and Wisconsin. See Appendix III]

Population-size group	County governments Number, 2002	County governments Population, 2000 Number (1,000)	County governments Population, 2000 Percent	Municipal governments Number, 2002	Municipal governments Population, 2000 Number (1,000)	Municipal governments Population, 2000 Percent	Township governments Number, 2002	Township governments Population, 2000 Number (1,000)	Township governments Population, 2000 Percent
Total	3,034	252,051	100	19,429	174,882	100	16,504	57,365	100
300,000 or more	161	131,575	52	58	47,768	27	3	1,527	3
200,000 to 299,999	84	20,606	8	30	7,163	4	3	728	1
100,000 to 199,999	228	31,576	13	153	21,076	12	30	3,974	7
50,000 to 99,999	383	27,160	11	364	24,960	14	97	6,588	11
25,000 to 49,999	638	22,913	9	643	22,576	13	273	9,275	16
10,000 to 24,999	869	14,488	6	1,436	22,589	13	773	12,067	21
5,000 to 9,999	385	2,911	1	1,637	11,644	7	1,085	7,560	13
2,500 to 4,999	173	643	(Z)	2,070	7,352	4	1,909	6,732	12
1,000 to 2,499	84	158	(Z)	3,677	5,951	3	3,679	5,905	10
Less than 1,000	29	21	(Z)	9,361	3,803	2	8,652	3,008	5

Z Less than 0.5 percent.

Source of tables 418 and 419: U.S. Census Bureau, *Census of Governments, Government Organization*, Series GC02(1)-1), quinquennial. <http://www.census.gov/prod/www/abs/govern.html> (accessed 16 June 2003).

State and Local Government Finances and Employment   263

No. 420. Government Current Receipts and Expenditures by Type: 1990 to 2003

[In billions of dollars (1,707.8 represents $1,707,800,000,000). For explanation of national income, see text, Section 13. A comprehensive National Income and Product Accounts (NIPA) revision was released on December 10, 2003; for more information on this revision of NIPA, go to www.bea.doc.gov/bea/dn/2003benchmark/CR2003content.htm. Minus sign(-) indicates a deficit.]

Item	1990	1995	1998	1999	2000	2001	2002	2003
Current receipts	1,707.8	2,212.6	2,724.2	2,895.0	3,125.9	3,124.2	2,980.7	3,011.3
Current tax receipts	1,161.9	1,517.2	1,911.7	2,036.2	2,206.8	2,172.6	2,006.2	2,002.0
Personal current taxes	592.8	744.1	1,027.0	1,107.5	1,235.7	1,243.7	1,053.1	990.6
Taxes on production and imports	425.5	558.2	639.8	674.0	708.9	729.8	760.1	788.7
Taxes on corporate income	140.6	211.0	239.2	248.8	255.0	192.0	185.9	215.9
Taxes from the rest of the world	3.0	3.9	5.7	5.9	7.3	7.2	7.2	6.8
Contributions for government social insurance	410.1	532.8	624.2	661.4	702.7	728.5	750.3	776.2
Income receipts on assets	98.7	92.1	102.4	106.8	117.4	120.0	116.1	118.3
Interest and miscellaneous receipts. . .	98.4	91.1	100.7	105.0	115.6	118.0	114.0	116.1
Dividends	0.2	1.0	1.7	1.8	1.9	2.0	2.1	2.2
Current transfer receipts	35.6	59.1	75.5	80.6	93.7	101.9	105.3	109.8
From business (net)	17.2	26.5	35.0	35.9	43.7	47.3	46.8	46.8
From persons	18.4	32.6	40.6	44.7	50.0	54.6	58.6	63.1
Current surplus of government enterprises	1.6	11.4	10.3	10.1	5.3	1.2	2.8	5.0
Current expenditures	1,872.6	2,397.6	2,633.4	2,741.0	2,886.5	3,056.4	3,224.0	3,426.4
Consumption expenditures	964.4	1,136.5	1,256.0	1,334.0	1,417.1	1,497.7	1,595.4	1,708.6
Current transfer payments.	586.1	872.5	969.6	1,005.5	1,062.4	1,159.2	1,271.1	1,357.5
Government social benefits	574.8	860.3	954.9	990.4	1,044.1	1,145.3	1,252.3	1,334.4
To persons	573.1	858.4	952.6	988.0	1,041.6	1,142.6	1,249.5	1,331.6
To the rest of the world	1.8	1.9	2.3	2.4	2.5	2.7	2.7	2.8
Other current transfer payments to the rest of the world.	11.3	12.1	14.6	15.1	18.3	14.0	18.8	23.1
Interest payments	295.3	354.6	372.4	357.3	362.8	344.1	319.3	312.1
To persons and business.	254.6	300.8	293.2	282.7	279.8	263.4	245.4	245.7
To the rest of the world	40.8	53.8	79.3	74.5	83.0	80.7	73.9	66.4
Subsidies.	26.8	34.0	35.4	44.2	44.3	55.3	38.2	48.2
Less: Wage accruals less disbursements.	0.1	-	-	-	-	-	-	-
Net government saving	-164.8	-184.9	90.8	154.0	239.4	67.8	-243.3	-415.0
Social insurance funds	45.0	23.0	60.7	95.8	114.4	88.4	51.9	42.6
Other	-209.8	-208.0	30.1	58.2	125.1	-20.6	-295.1	-457.6

- Represents zero.

Source: U.S. Bureau of Economic Analysis, *Survey of Current Business*, May 2004. See also: <http://www.bea.doc.gov/bea /dn/nipaweb/selecttable.asp?selected=N> (released April 2004).

No. 421. Government Consumption Expenditures and Gross Investment by Level of Government and Type: 1990 to 2003

[In billions of dollars (1,180.2 represents $1,180,200,000,000). For explanation of national income, see text, Section 13. A comprehensive National Income and Product Accounts (NIPA) revision was released on December 10, 2003; for more information on this revision of NIPA, go to www:bea.doc.gov/bea/dn/2003benchmark/CR2003content.htm.]

Level of government and type	1990	1995	1998	1999	2000	2001	2002	2003
Consumption expenditures & gross investment, total	1,180.2	1,369.2	1,518.3	1,620.8	1,721.6	1,814.7	1,932.5	2,054.8
Consumption expenditures [1]	964.4	1,136.5	1,256.0	1,334.0	1,417.1	1,497.7	1,595.4	1,708.6
Gross investment [2]	215.7	232.7	262.4	286.8	304.5	317.0	337.1	346.3
Structures	112.6	134.4	159.3	175.3	189.3	198.8	212.4	216.8
Equipment and software	103.1	98.4	103.1	111.5	115.2	118.2	124.7	129.4
Federal	508.3	519.2	530.4	555.8	578.8	612.9	679.5	757.2
Consumption expenditures	419.8	440.5	454.6	475.1	499.3	531.7	590.8	662.9
Gross investment	88.5	78.8	75.8	80.7	79.5	81.2	88.7	94.3
Structures	14.1	17.1	15.7	15.6	13.3	13.0	14.3	15.1
Equipment and software	74.4	61.7	60.1	65.1	66.2	68.2	74.4	79.2
National defense	374.0	348.7	345.7	360.6	370.3	393.0	438.3	497.3
Consumption expenditures	308.1	297.3	300.7	312.9	321.5	342.8	382.7	437.3
Gross investment	65.9	51.4	45.0	47.7	48.8	50.2	55.7	60.0
Structures	6.1	6.3	5.1	5.0	5.0	4.6	4.4	4.9
Equipment and software	59.8	45.1	39.9	42.8	43.8	45.6	51.2	55.1
Nondefense	134.3	170.5	184.7	195.2	208.5	219.9	241.2	259.9
Consumption expenditures	111.7	143.2	153.9	162.2	177.8	188.8	208.1	225.6
Gross investment	22.6	27.3	30.8	33.0	30.7	31.0	33.0	34.3
Structures	8.0	10.8	10.6	10.6	8.3	8.4	9.9	10.2
Equipment and software	14.6	16.5	20.2	22.4	22.3	22.6	23.2	24.0
State and local	671.9	850.0	987.9	1,065.0	1,142.8	1,201.8	1,253.1	1,297.6
Consumption expenditures	544.6	696.1	801.4	858.9	917.8	966.1	1,004.6	1,045.6
Gross investment	127.2	154.0	186.5	206.0	225.0	235.8	248.4	252.0
Structures	98.5	117.3	143.6	159.7	176.0	185.8	198.1	201.8
Equipment and software	28.7	36.7	43.0	46.4	49.0	50.0	50.3	50.2

[1] Government consumption expenditures are services (such as education and national defense) produced by government that are valued at their cost of production. Excludes government sales to other sectors and government own-account investment (construction and software). [2] Gross government investment consists of general government and government enterprise expenditures for fixed assets; inventory investment is included in government consumption expenditures.

Source: U.S. Bureau of Economic Analysis, *Survey of Current Business*, May 2004. See also <http://www.bea.doc.gov/bea /dn/nipaweb/selecttable.asp?selected (released 29 April 2004).

No. 422. Real Government Consumption Expenditures and Gross Investment in Chained (2000) Dollars by Level of Government and Type: 1990 to 2003

[In billions dollars (1,530.0 represents $1,530,000,000,000). For explanation of national income. See text, Section 13. A comprehensive National Income and Product Accounts (NIPA) revision was released on December 10, 2003; for more information on this revision of NIPA, go to http://www.bea.doc.gov/bea/dn/2003benchmark/CR2003content.htm]

Item	1990	1995	1998	1999	2000	2001	2002	2003
Consumption expenditures and gross Investment, total	1,530.0	1,549.7	1,624.4	1,686.9	1,721.6	1,768.9	1,836.9	1,898.4
Consumption expenditures [1]	1,277.2	1,301.9	1,351.2	1,393.1	1,417.1	1,456.7	1,509.0	1,565.7
Gross investment [2]	253.0	248.8	273.6	294.0	304.5	312.2	328.0	332.6
Structures	151.2	159.5	172.7	183.3	189.3	192.2	199.4	198.3
Equipment and software	99.1	89.5	101.1	110.7	115.2	120.1	128.8	135.0
Federal	659.1	580.3	561.2	573.7	578.8	600.5	648.0	704.3
Consumption expenditures	562.5	502.9	484.7	492.8	499.3	519.0	558.5	609.1
Gross investment	95.4	77.6	76.8	81.0	79.5	81.4	89.5	95.2
Structures	19.0	20.0	17.0	16.3	13.3	12.5	13.5	13.8
Equipment and software	75.8	58.1	59.9	64.8	66.2	68.9	76.1	81.5
National defense	479.4	389.2	365.3	372.2	370.3	384.7	418.8	463.0
Consumption expenditures	404.9	338.1	319.8	324.6	321.5	334.0	362.2	401.9
Gross investment	72.9	50.9	45.6	47.6	48.8	50.7	56.6	61.0
Structures	8.6	7.4	5.5	5.2	5.0	4.4	4.2	4.5
Equipment and software	64.2	43.7	40.1	42.5	43.8	46.3	52.5	56.7
Nondefense	178.6	191.0	195.9	201.5	208.5	215.8	229.2	241.4
Consumption expenditures	156.5	164.7	164.8	168.1	177.8	185.0	196.3	207.1
Gross investment	23.1	26.7	31.2	33.4	30.7	30.8	32.9	34.3
Structures	10.6	12.6	11.5	11.1	8.3	8.1	9.3	9.4
Equipment and software	12.9	14.7	19.8	22.3	22.3	22.6	23.6	24.9
State and local	868.4	968.3	1,063.0	1,113.2	1,142.8	1,168.5	1,189.1	1,194.6
Consumption expenditures	714.2	798.4	866.4	900.3	917.9	937.7	950.5	956.9
Gross investment	154.6	170.4	196.7	212.9	225.0	230.8	238.6	237.8
Structures	132.1	139.5	155.6	167.0	176.0	179.7	186.0	184.5
Equipment and software	25.0	31.7	41.2	45.9	49.0	51.1	52.6	53.4
Residual	1.0	-1.1	-0.3	-0.1	0.1	-	-0.3	-0.9

- Represents zero. [1] Government consumption expenditures are services (such as education and national defense) produced by government that are valued at their cost of production. Excludes government sales to other sectors and government own-account investment (construction and software). [2] Gross government investment consists of general government and government enterprise expenditures for fixed assets; inventory investment is included in government consumption expenditures.

Source: U.S. Bureau of Economic Analysis, *Survey of Current Business*, May 2004. See also <http://www.bea.doc.gov/bea /dn/nipaweb/selecttable.asp?selected=N>; (released 30 May 2003).

No. 423. Federal Grants-in-Aid to State and Local Governments: 1980 to 2004

[91,385 represents $91,385,000,000, except as indicated. For year ending Sept. 30. Minus sign (-) indicates decrease]

Year	Total grants (mil. dol.)	Annual percent change [1]	Grants to individuals Total (mil. dol.)	Grants to individuals Percent of total grants	State /localgovt. expendi- tures [2]	Federal outlays	Gross domestic product	Total grants (bil. dol.)	Annual percent change [1]
	Current dollars				Grants as percent of—			Constant (2000) dollars	
1980	91,385	9.6	32,619	35.7	39.9	15.5	3.3	192.6	-1.6
1985	105,852	8.5	50,059	47.3	29.6	11.2	2.6	163.1	4.6
1990	135,325	11.0	77,264	57.1	25.2	10.8	2.4	172.1	6.3
1992	178,065	15.2	112,522	63.2	28.7	12.9	2.9	211.4	12.1
1993	193,612	8.7	124,155	64.1	29.6	13.7	3.0	223.9	5.9
1994	210,596	8.8	134,153	63.7	30.9	14.4	3.0	238.1	6.3
1995	224,991	6.8	144,427	64.2	31.5	14.8	3.1	247.9	4.1
1996	227,811	1.3	146,493	64.3	30.8	14.6	3.0	245.5	-1.0
1997	234,160	2.8	148,236	63.3	30.2	14.6	2.9	247.7	0.9
1998	246,128	5.1	160,305	65.1	30.3	14.9	2.8	257.3	3.9
1999	267,081	8.5	172,384	64.5	31.2	15.7	2.9	274.7	6.8
2000	284,659	6.6	182,592	64.1	28.3	15.9	2.9	284.7	3.6
2001	317,211	11.4	203,920	64.3	29.5	17.0	3.2	309.5	8.7
2002	351,550	10.8	227,373	64.7	31.5	17.5	3.4	337.4	9.0
2003	387,281	10.2	246,570	63.7	33.5	17.9	3.6	363.0	7.6
2004, est	418,091	8.0	266,057	63.6	(NA)	18.0	3.6	384.2	5.8

NA Not available.   [1] Percent change from immediate/prior year shown.   [2] Expenditures from own sources as defined in the national income and product accounts.

Source: U. S. Office of Management and Budget, based on *Historical Tables* and *Analytical Prospectives, Budget of the United States Government,* annual.

No. 424. Federal Aid to State and Local Governments: 1980 to 2004

[In millions of dollars (91,385 represents $91,385,000,000). For year ending Sept 30. Includes trust funds. Minus sign (-) indicates previously disbursed funds returned to the federal government.]

Program	1980	1990	1995	2000	2001	2002	2003	2004 est.
Grant-in-aid shared revenue [1]	91,385	135,325	224,991	284,659	317,211	351,550	387,281	418,091
National defense	93	241	68	2	47	91	(NA)	(NA)
Energy	499	461	492	433	492	528	589	613
Natural resources and environment	5,363	3,745	4,148	4,595	4,882	5,085	5,593	6,511
Environmental Protection Agency[2]	4,603	2,874	2,912	3,490	3,750	3,588	3,917	4,277
Agriculture	569	1,285	780	724	755	750	800	865
Commerce and Housing Credit	3	-	5	3	6	2	4	28
Transportation	13,022	19,174	25,787	32,222	36,647	40,998	41,029	43,460
Grants for Airports [2]	590	1,220	1,826	1,624	2,017	2,860	2,681	3,395
Federal-aid highways [3]	9,208	14,171	19,475	24,711	27,075	29,833	29,960	30,380
Urban mass transportation [2]	3,129	3,730	4,353	5,262	6,963	7,462	7,448	8,296
Community and regional development	6,486	4,965	7,230	8,665	9,485	10,501	15,082	14,759
Homeland Security	380	1,184	1,772	2,439	3,010	3,456	7,861	6,963
Appalachian regional development programs	335	124	182	125	86	101	74	88
Community development fund	3,902	2,818	4,333	4,955	4,939	5,429	5,569	5,990
Education, training, employment, social services	21,862	23,359	34,125	42,125	40,133	44,827	51,543	56,941
Compensatory education for the disadvantaged [4]	3,370	4,437	6,785	8,511	8,616	9,211	11,204	14,049
School improvement programs [4]	523	1,080	1,288	2,394	2,721	3,401	5,964	8,041
Impact aid	622	799	803	875	1,021	1,116	1,103	1,331
Vocational and adult education	854	1,287	1,449	1,448	1,651	1,742	1,908	1,870
Social services-block grant	2,763	2,749	2,797	1,827	1,852	1,780	1,740	1,767
Children and family services programs	1,548	2,618	4,463	5,843	6,614	7,749	8,161	8,253
Training and employment services	6,191	3,042	3,620	2,957	3,132	4,206	4,291	3,656
Office of libraries	158	127	109	152	189	202	239	251
Health	15,758	43,890	93,587	124,843	139,295	158,677	173,814	191,929
Substance abuse, and mental health services	679	1,241	2,444	1,931	2,094	2,193	2,171	2,268
Grants to States for Medicaid [4]	13,957	41,103	89,070	117,921	129,434	147,650	160,805	177,407
Income security	18,495	35,189	55,122	63,200	76,064	81,506	86,476	88,333
Food stamp program	412	2,130	2,740	3,508	3,664	3,949	4,162	4,381
Child nutrition programs [4]	3,388	4,871	7,387	9,060	9,416	10,100	10,664	11,295
Veterans benefits and services [4]	90	134	253	434	405	360	403	443
Administration of justice	529	574	1,222	5,120	6,612	5,826	4,498	4,266
General government [5]	8,616	2,309	2,172	2,287	2,388	2,398	7,449	9,929

NA Not available.   - Represents or rounds to zero.   [1] Includes items not shown separately.   [2] Grants includes trust funds.   [3] Trust funds.   [4] Includes grants for payments to individuals.   [5] Includes general purpose fiscal assistance.

Source: U.S. Office of Management and Budget, *Historical Tables, Budget of the United States Government,* annual.

No. 425. Federal Aid to State and Local Governments—Selected Programs by State: 2002

[In millions of dollars (362,389 represents $362,389,000,000). For fiscal year ending September 30]

State and island area	Department of Agriculture						Department of Education				
	Federal aid, total [1]	Food and nutrition service				Other	Total	Office of Special Education and Rehabilitative Services			Other
		Total	Child nutrition programs [2]	Food stamp program [3]	Special supplemental food program (WIC)			Adult education for the disadvantaged	Special education	Rehabilitation services & disability research	
Total	362,389	21,487	10,161	3,859	4,376	3,090	32,739	1,356	8,532	2,652	20,962
United States	355,690	19,669	9,949	2,487	4,206	3,028	32,032	1,335	8,439	2,554	20,458
Alabama	5,557	363	196	32	71	64	528	27	136	55	326
Alaska	2,250	117	29	8	20	61	274	9	27	11	235
Arizona	6,314	392	203	35	98	56	730	35	130	49	544
Arkansas	3,559	228	119	18	45	46	338	20	82	35	213
California	41,627	2,653	1,301	357	757	238	3,980	344	883	261	2,758
Colorado	3,951	209	97	27	43	41	407	24	112	27	262
Connecticut	4,492	158	79	25	36	18	337	9	100	20	210
Delaware	958	52	28	4	9	11	99	2	25	9	63
District of Columbia	4,025	57	28	10	11	8	140	2	22	12	104
Florida	15,044	981	560	92	248	81	1,553	96	456	119	942
Georgia	9,300	650	394	62	125	69	894	27	232	74	572
Hawaii	1,460	100	42	11	25	22	194	3	34	11	146
Idaho	1,560	111	41	10	17	43	150	9	40	15	94
Illinois	13,296	769	408	99	169	93	1,315	60	378	100	812
Indiana	5,997	334	164	44	72	52	562	14	190	61	301
Iowa	3,391	196	84	21	34	57	294	6	93	31	165
Kansas	2,889	176	101	9	33	34	344	18	89	27	223
Kentucky	5,719	336	172	30	67	67	484	16	127	48	285
Louisiana	6,820	451	260	39	78	73	573	13	136	46	381
Maine	2,049	81	35	10	10	26	156	8	44	15	94
Maryland	5,660	284	146	43	53	43	497	9	150	39	298
Massachusetts	9,202	312	170	40	65	37	686	29	214	48	410
Michigan	11,185	586	257	99	119	111	1,143	60	291	92	742
Minnesota	5,776	329	166	44	57	62	468	9	151	44	266
Mississippi	4,605	351	179	33	57	83	403	9	87	40	268
Missouri	7,137	370	184	52	67	68	564	12	170	58	325
Montana	1,654	106	32	11	13	49	186	3	31	13	141
Nebraska	2,028	128	65	11	22	30	201	8	59	17	123
Nevada	1,646	90	47	10	23	10	165	3	48	13	100
New Hampshire	1,326	59	20	7	10	23	111	2	38	11	60
New Jersey	10,239	390	199	84	76	32	807	17	269	51	469
New Mexico	3,418	203	114	18	35	35	467	16	154	23	290
New York	38,637	1,353	714	236	280	124	2,468	64	576	138	1,708
North Carolina	9,510	581	325	59	111	85	803	20	238	79	470
North Dakota	1,189	65	25	8	10	22	131	2	20	11	99
Ohio	13,262	633	288	126	139	79	1,085	22	321	111	631
Oklahoma	4,510	332	162	38	64	68	506	9	109	42	347
Oregon	4,457	416	107	54	59	196	377	20	111	37	224
Pennsylvania	15,603	639	293	129	132	85	1,186	61	315	115	730
Rhode Island	1,794	62	32	7	13	10	122	2	34	10	75
South Carolina	4,883	312	171	32	59	50	474	9	130	45	290
South Dakota	1,350	86	30	11	13	32	164	3	24	11	127
Tennessee	7,374	427	215	39	95	78	540	10	172	60	294
Texas	21,945	1,690	1,036	164	361	129	2,544	111	675	185	1,644
Utah	2,208	158	81	20	32	26	267	9	83	24	157
Vermont	1,087	60	16	11	10	23	94	3	20	11	62
Virginia	6,233	342	142	72	76	52	703	11	212	61	417
Washington	7,103	405	166	39	93	108	644	40	164	50	421
West Virginia	3,034	157	76	11	29	40	235	4	58	25	147
Wisconsin	6,173	287	133	34	58	63	542	10	159	53	321
Wyoming	1,192	44	15	4	7	17	96	2	21	8	66
Island areas:	5,683	1,801	213	1,373	170	45	682	21	93	72	504
American Samoa	113	23	12	4	6	1	1	-	-	1	-
Micronesia	114	2	-	-	-	1	8	-	4	1	4
Guam	212	19	5	3	6	4	5	-	1	2	2
Marshall Islands	53	-	-	-	-	-	-	-	-	-	-
Northern Marianas . . .	66	13	4	7	-	2	1	-	-	1	-
Palau	38	-	-	-	-	-	-	-	-	-	-
Puerto Rico	4,793	1,712	177	1,351	153	31	650	21	78	67	493
Virgin Islands	294	32	15	8	5	5	16	-	10	2	4
Undistributed amounts . .	1,015	17	-	-	-	17	26	-	-	26	-

See footnote at end of table.

[In millions of dollars (3,406 represents $3,406,000,000). For fiscal year ending September 30]

| State and island areas | FEMA total [4] | Department of Housing and Urban Development | | | | | | | Department of Labor | | |
| | | | | Public housing programs | | | | | State unemployment insurance and employment service | | Work-force invest-ment |
		Total	Commu-nity develop-ment block grants	Low rent hous-ing assis-tance	Neigh-borhood revital-ization	Hous-ing certi-ficate pro-gram	Capital pro-gram	Other	Total	service	
Total	3,406	36,965	5,437	3,709	467	18,499	3,767	5,177	8,376	3,607	3,431
United States	3,194	36,213	5,318	3,590	465	17,909	3,596	5,019	8,067	3,572	3,173
Alabama	27	509	68	113	2	183	86	47	130	45	59
Alaska	7	174	17	12	-	31	1	113	58	30	19
Arizona	14	489	75	30	6	157	12	205	139	48	60
Arkansas	21	236	32	27	1	121	29	25	69	31	27
California	546	4,203	685	121	25	2,690	134	534	1,207	517	564
Colorado	20	415	52	18	7	261	22	51	94	53	25
Connecticut	3	599	52	58	7	352	48	78	103	62	25
Delaware	3	104	9	10	3	54	8	19	24	11	8
District of Columbia	3	686	91	51	15	165	264	92	161	69	38
Florida	178	1,324	208	96	43	412	83	470	285	118	112
Georgia	31	884	130	123	11	412	127	71	167	76	63
Hawaii	4	144	18	11	-	87	6	21	53	18	20
Idaho	3	74	12	1	-	45	2	14	50	24	17
Illinois	16	2,016	236	266	19	1,020	250	201	388	171	169
Indiana	10	538	91	40	2	298	44	60	125	61	40
Iowa	15	215	48	6	-	124	9	28	61	31	16
Kansas	44	189	43	16	-	87	15	26	54	27	15
Kentucky	21	492	68	53	10	232	76	50	104	40	27
Louisiana	22	569	108	68	13	225	80	68	120	37	76
Maine	5	179	23	9	-	115	7	25	51	19	20
Maryland	10	701	85	77	24	377	41	90	152	71	54
Massachusetts	19	1,506	154	106	9	990	82	156	173	92	59
Michigan	7	912	170	51	1	471	65	149	307	148	99
Minnesota	43	571	85	42	-	314	56	70	151	66	42
Mississippi	23	288	52	28	1	144	29	30	106	36	58
Missouri	60	589	111	45	8	274	58	89	127	62	44
Montana	20	108	14	4	-	41	3	44	35	15	16
Nebraska	6	149	31	10	-	66	19	21	39	21	11
Nevada	2	187	20	16	-	106	15	29	57	34	16
New Hampshire	5	137	19	7	-	89	8	14	32	14	13
New Jersey	82	1,381	136	155	41	768	146	120	226	125	80
New Mexico	5	180	30	9	-	79	11	49	68	19	43
New York	1,232	5,196	769	924	16	2,011	888	542	544	244	231
North Carolina	123	757	78	101	31	374	72	91	216	88	64
North Dakota	37	86	10	3	-	39	3	30	27	14	7
Ohio	11	1,473	241	161	10	739	124	183	280	114	131
Oklahoma	122	457	56	25	3	176	21	169	69	31	29
Oregon	15	359	37	15	-	227	15	62	155	62	70
Pennsylvania	16	1,808	304	240	44	775	248	177	372	179	129
Rhode Island	2	242	27	21	-	142	16	33	34	18	8
South Carolina	7	352	58	30	5	189	26	39	97	44	37
South Dakota	7	108	15	3	-	45	3	40	26	11	8
Tennessee	18	628	67	101	33	281	78	58	118	52	20
Texas	184	1,732	317	119	40	925	134	182	504	191	249
Utah	8	135	31	4	-	77	4	18	57	37	11
Vermont	4	93	19	4	-	55	3	12	18	10	7
Virginia	28	697	84	91	15	366	50	84	134	60	45
Washington	25	611	75	36	8	333	36	118	235	107	98
West Virginia	49	234	56	16	4	103	15	38	77	21	47
Wisconsin	28	462	91	19	8	244	22	75	166	85	46
Wyoming	5	36	7	1	-	18	2	8	21	11	7
Island areas:	70	752	120	118	2	292	171	159	309	34	258
American Samoa	-	-	-	-	-	-	-	-	2	-	1
Micronesia	-	-	-	-	-	-	-	-	2	-	2
Guam	25	25	1	2	-	18	2	2	15	2	11
Marshall Islands	-	-	-	-	-	-	-	-	1	-	1
Northern Marianas	1	-	-	-	-	-	-	-	1	-	1
Palau	-	-	-	-	-	-	-	-	-	-	-
Puerto Rico	32	674	116	98	1	260	155	37	280	28	240
Virgin Islands	12	53	2	18	1	14	14	2	8	3	2
Undistributed amounts	141	-	-	-	-	-	-	-	-	-	-

See footnote at end of table.

U.S. Census Bureau, Statistical Abstract of the United States: 2004-2005

No. 425. Federal Aid to State and Local Governments—Selected Programs by State: 2002—Con.

[In millions of dollars (204,197 represents $204,197,000,000). For fiscal year ending September 30]

State and island areas	Department of Health and Human Services						Department of Transportation				Other federal aid
		Administration for children									
	Total	Temporary assistance to needy families	Children & family services (Head Start)	Foster care and adoption assistance	Centers for Medicare and Medicaid Services	Other	Total	Higway trust fund	Federal transit administration	Other	
Total	204,197	18,538	7,749	5,881	150,640	21,388	38,719	29,444	5,223	4,060	16,500
United States	203,343	18,471	7,494	5,881	150,351	21,146	37,618	28,539	5,024	4,053	15,554
Alabama.	2,931	130	125	34	2,300	342	840	673	25	141	230
Alaska.	780	75	50	16	519	120	509	328	12	168	332
Arizona.	3,476	297	166	62	2,597	354	639	481	61	97	435
Arkansas	2,090	60	84	44	1,721	180	476	395	10	71	102
California	23,482	3,416	936	1,318	15,503	2,308	3,975	2,628	1,008	339	1,581
Colorado.	1,976	232	125	62	1,238	318	537	342	91	103	293
Connecticut.	2,576	278	64	86	1,878	270	589	493	79	17	126
Delaware	489	30	18	13	361	67	131	120	3	8	57
District of Columbia	1,339	154	85	38	763	299	416	150	260	7	1,222
Florida.	8,355	735	286	184	6,076	1,074	1,811	1,496	135	180	557
Georgia	5,349	449	192	111	4,078	519	1,052	873	96	82	274
Hawaii	687	70	34	29	461	94	176	122	33	21	102
Idaho.	786	38	41	8	601	97	262	206	7	49	125
Illinois	7,064	600	341	389	4,783	952	1,324	889	259	177	404
Indiana.	3,593	258	113	66	2,798	357	646	560	29	56	190
Iowa	2,080	118	65	40	1,667	189	404	333	22	50	128
Kansas.	1,582	104	77	43	1,187	171	399	360	18	21	101
Kentucky	3,440	159	134	64	2,792	290	616	524	22	71	226
Louisiana	4,367	221	161	67	3,596	322	541	448	36	57	177
Maine.	1,271	80	35	40	1,011	104	187	162	8	17	118
Maryland	3,034	306	99	158	2,023	448	727	572	105	50	255
Massachusetts.	5,531	507	141	96	4,258	528	673	505	131	37	302
Michigan.	6,871	926	275	242	4,649	779	1,014	823	89	102	345
Minnesota.	3,375	334	109	104	2,419	409	595	384	108	104	243
Mississippi	2,803	149	179	18	2,243	214	459	385	5	69	173
Missouri	4,315	195	147	81	3,495	396	862	727	36	100	249
Montana.	654	69	40	13	440	91	342	295	5	42	203
Nebraska	1,152	53	47	35	866	152	233	193	10	29	120
Nevada	736	57	31	22	485	142	234	161	16	56	176
New Hampshire	678	39	20	13	519	87	195	141	8	45	110
New Jersey.	6,031	740	156	82	4,384	669	1,039	710	291	38	282
New Mexico	1,743	110	69	25	1,375	164	334	302	8	24	417
New York	24,769	2,783	515	652	19,187	1,632	2,173	1,274	773	126	901
North Carolina	5,615	361	192	84	4,395	584	1,087	959	42	86	329
North Dakota.	479	29	33	15	340	61	244	216	4	24	119
Ohio	8,274	773	296	361	5,931	913	1,167	901	137	129	340
Oklahoma.	2,347	150	123	44	1,751	279	432	347	20	65	246
Oregon.	2,235	175	111	53	1,661	234	595	272	122	200	305
Pennsylvania.	9,449	711	265	395	7,127	952	1,741	1,345	269	127	392
Rhode Island.	1,027	90	32	18	796	92	221	171	26	24	85
South Carolina.	2,988	131	103	51	2,415	289	482	411	14	58	170
South Dakota	539	22	44	7	391	75	241	199	5	37	178
Tennessee	4,651	248	138	39	3,813	413	617	521	39	57	375
Texas.	11,949	555	589	193	9,196	1,417	2,722	2,209	271	243	631
Utah	1,063	91	52	26	749	146	321	239	55	27	198
Vermont	605	51	21	20	452	60	146	134	3	9	68
Virginia.	3,002	178	181	93	2,138	412	1,036	882	66	87	290
Washington.	3,988	491	155	77	2,785	480	775	548	106	121	420
West Virginia.	1,686	182	57	34	1,248	165	437	318	8	111	159
Wisconsin	3,764	444	125	111	2,694	390	681	587	36	58	241
Wyoming	277	14	19	3	192	49	262	224	2	36	451
Island areas:	844	67	250	-	290	237	322	67	180	75	905
American Samoa	17	-	6	-	4	6	28	-	-	28	43
Micronesia.	1	-	-	-	-	1	-	-	-	-	-
Guam	27	3	5	-	8	11	21	20	-	1	76
Marshall Islands	-	-	-	-	-	-	-	-	-	-	-
Northern Marianas . . .	7	-	-	-	3	3	15	2	13	28	-
Palau	-	-	-	-	-	-	-	-	-	-	-
Puerto Rico	752	61	231	-	265	195	231	40	179	12	462
Virgin Islands	40	3	9	-	8	20	26	5	1	20	105
Undistributed amounts . .	10	-	5	-	-	5	780	828	20	-68	42

- Represents or rounds to zero. [1] Includes programs not shown separately. [2] Includes special milk program. [3] For Puerto Rico, amount shown is for nutritional assistance grant program, all other amounts are grant payments for food stamp administration. [4] FEMA = Federal Emergency Management Agency.

Source: U.S. Census Bureau, Federal Aid to States For Fiscal Year 2002 (Issued May 2003.) See also <http://www.census.gov/prod/2003pubs/fas02.pdf>

State and Local Government Finances and Employment 269

No. 426. State and Local Government Current Receipts and Expenditures in the National Income and Product Accounts: 1980 to 2003

[In billions of dollars (338.2 represents $338,200,000,000). For explanation of national income, see text, Section 13. A comprehensive National Income and Product Accounts (NIPA) revision released on December 10, 2003. For more information on this revision of the National Income and Product Accounts, go to <http://www.bea.doc.gov/bea/dn/2003benchmark/CR2003content.htm>]

Item	1980	1990	1995	1996	1997	1998	1999	2000	2001	2002	2003
Current receipts.......	338.2	737.8	990.2	1,043.3	1,097.4	1,163.2	1,236.7	1,319.5	1,382.7	1,424.7	1,500.9
Current tax receipts.........	230.0	519.1	672.1	709.6	749.9	794.9	840.4	893.2	917.7	925.5	964.2
Personal current taxes......	48.9	122.6	158.1	168.7	182.0	201.2	214.5	236.6	243.7	221.9	226.4
Income taxes..........	42.6	109.6	141.7	152.3	164.7	183.0	195.5	217.3	224.1	201.7	205.4
Other..............	6.3	13.0	16.4	16.3	17.3	18.2	19.0	19.4	19.6	20.2	21.0
Taxes on production and imports...............	166.7	374.1	482.4	507.9	533.8	558.8	590.2	621.1	643.8	672.5	700.6
Sales taxes...........	82.9	184.3	242.7	256.2	268.7	283.9	301.6	316.6	322.7	328.8	340.5
Property taxes.........	68.8	161.5	202.6	212.4	223.5	231.0	242.8	254.6	269.6	291.0	304.0
Other.............	15.0	28.3	37.0	39.4	41.6	43.9	45.8	49.9	51.6	52.6	56.1
Taxes on corporate income ..	14.5	22.5	31.7	33.0	34.1	34.9	35.8	35.5	30.2	31.1	37.2
Contributions for government social insurance...........	3.6	10.0	13.6	12.5	10.8	10.4	9.8	11.0	13.2	13.5	13.8
Income receipts on assets.....	26.3	68.4	68.4	73.3	77.8	80.9	85.3	92.2	95.6	95.5	94.1
Interest receipts.........	23.1	64.1	62.9	67.3	71.5	74.6	78.4	84.0	86.7	86.0	84.1
Dividends............	0.1	0.2	1.0	1.4	1.5	1.7	1.8	1.9	2.0	2.1	2.2
Rents and royalties........	3.1	4.2	4.5	4.6	4.8	4.6	5.1	6.3	7.0	7.4	7.8
Current transfer receipts......	79.5	133.5	224.1	234.1	246.6	266.8	290.8	315.4	350.8	384.2	422.3
Federal grants-in-aid........	72.3	111.4	184.1	191.2	198.6	212.8	232.9	247.3	276.3	304.6	339.0
From business (net).......	2.5	7.1	13.5	15.2	17.7	22.1	23.0	28.8	31.4	32.7	32.1
From persons..........	4.7	14.9	26.5	27.8	30.3	31.9	34.9	39.2	43.1	46.9	51.2
Current surplus of government enterprises...........	-1.2	6.7	12.0	13.9	12.3	10.2	10.4	7.7	5.4	5.9	6.5
Current expenditures ...	329.4	730.5	978.2	1,017.5	1,058.3	1,111.2	1,186.3	1,269.5	1,365.4	1,427.9	1,501.5
Consumption expenditures	258.4	544.6	696.1	724.8	758.9	801.4	858.9	917.8	966.1	1,004.6	1,045.6
Government social benefit payments to persons	51.2	127.7	217.6	224.3	227.6	235.8	252.4	271.7	305.1	332.3	362.3
Interest payments	19.4	57.9	64.2	68.1	71.4	73.6	74.6	79.5	86.6	89.9	93.2
Subsidies................	0.4	0.4	0.3	0.3	0.4	0.4	0.4	0.5	7.7	1.0	0.3
Net state and local government saving	8.8	7.2	12.0	25.8	39.1	52.0	50.4	50.0	17.3	-3.2	-0.6
Social insurance funds	1.3	2.0	4.0	2.8	1.2	1.7	1.7	2.0	3.4	3.4	3.4
Other.................	7.5	5.3	8.0	23.0	38.0	50.3	48.7	47.9	14.0	-6.6	-4.0

Source: U.S. Bureau of Economic Analysis, *Survey of Current Business*, May 2004. See also <http://www.bea.doc.gov/bea>/dn/nipaweb/selecttable.asp>.

No. 427. State and Local Government Consumption Expenditures and Social Benefits in the National Income and Product Accounts: 1980 to 2003

[In billions of dollars (322.4 represents $322,400,000,000). For explanation of national income, see text, Section 13. A comprehensive National Income and Product Accounts (NIPA) revision released on December 10, 2003. For more information on this revision of the National Income and Product Accounts, go to <http://www.bea.doc.gov/bea/dn/2003benchmark/CR2003content.htm>]

Expenditure	1980	1990	1995	1997	1998	1999	2000	2001	2002	2003
Consumption expenditures [1] ..	322.4	671.9	850.0	937.8	987.9	1,065.0	1,142.8	1,201.8	1,253.1	1,297.6
Consumption expenditures.........	258.4	544.6	696.1	758.9	801.4	858.9	917.8	966.1	1,004.6	1,045.6
Gross investment...............	64.0	127.2	154.0	178.9	186.5	206.0	225.0	235.8	248.4	252.0
Structures.................	55.1	98.5	117.3	139.5	143.6	159.7	176.0	185.8	198.1	201.8
Equipment and software.........	8.9	28.7	36.7	39.4	43.0	46.4	49.0	50.0	50.3	50.2
Transfers	51.2	127.7	217.6	227.6	235.8	252.4	271.7	305.1	332.3	(NA)
Benefits from social insurance funds ..	2.8	9.2	10.7	10.7	10.4	10.6	11.5	12.3	12.7	(NA)
Temporary disability insurance.....	0.8	2.2	2.1	2.0	2.1	2.2	2.8	3.3	3.6	(NA)
Workers' compensation	2.0	7.0	8.6	8.7	8.3	8.4	8.7	9.0	9.1	(NA)
Public assistance.............	44.0	111.1	195.8	205.2	212.9	228.3	245.4	276.5	302.5	(NA)
Medical care.............	24.9	78.2	155.0	168.3	175.3	189.3	205.0	234.6	258.7	(NA)
Medicaid.............	23.9	73.1	149.6	163.1	170.2	184.6	199.5	227.3	250.0	(NA)
Other medical care	1.1	5.0	5.4	5.2	5.1	4.7	5.5	7.4	8.6	(NA)
Family assistance [2]	12.5	19.2	22.6	17.9	17.4	17.9	18.4	18.6	19.7	(NA)
Supplemental security income .	2.0	3.8	3.8	3.7	3.9	4.2	4.4	4.5	4.8	(NA)
General assistance.........	1.4	2.9	3.6	3.3	3.5	3.6	3.6	3.1	3.7	(NA)
Energy assistance	1.3	1.6	1.4	1.4	1.2	1.4	1.7	2.5	1.9	(NA)
Other [3]................	1.7	5.4	9.4	10.6	11.4	11.9	12.3	13.1	13.7	(NA)
Education.................	2.4	5.3	8.7	9.1	9.8	10.5	11.6	12.7	13.4	(NA)
Employment and training	1.7	0.9	1.1	1.0	1.1	1.1	1.0	1.4	1.7	(NA)
Other [4]	0.3	1.1	1.3	1.5	1.6	1.8	2.1	2.1	2.1	(NA)

NA Not available. [1] Consumption expenditures for durable goods excludes expenditures classified as investment, except for goods transferred to foreign countries by the federal government. [2] Consists of aid to families with dependent children. Beginning with 1996, assistance programs operating under the Personal Responsibility and work opportunity Act of 1996. [3] Consists of expenditures for food under the supplemental program for women, infants, and children, foster care adoption assistance; and payments to nonprofit welfare institutions. [4] Consists largely of veterans benefits, Alaska dividends, and crime-victim payments.

Source: U.S. Bureau of Economic Analysis, *Survey of Current Business*, May 2004 <http://www.bea.gov/bea/dn/nipaweb/selecttable.asp?selected=N.> (accessed 30 May 2004).

No. 428. State and Local Governments—Summary of Finances: 1990 to 2001

[In millions of dollars (1,032,115 represents $1,032,115,000,000), except as indicated. For fiscal year ending in year shown; see text, this section. Local government amounts are estimates subject to sampling variation; see Appendix III and source]

Item	Total (mil. dol.)				Per capita [1] (dol.)			
	1990	1999	2000	2001	1990	1999	2000	2001
Revenue [2]	1,032,115	1,794,557	1,942,328	1,890,891	4,150	6,581	6,902	6,627
From federal government	136,802	270,628	291,950	324,033	550	992	1,037	1,136
Public welfare	59,961	136,571	148,549	167,823	241	501	528	588
Highways	14,368	21,492	24,414	28,702	58	79	87	101
Education	23,233	42,051	45,873	49,945	93	154	163	175
Health and hospitals	5,904	14,516	15,611	17,839	24	53	55	63
Housing and community development .	9,655	18,044	17,690	18,541	39	66	63	65
Other and unallocable	23,683	37,954	39,812	41,184	95	139	141	144
From state and local sources	895,313	1,523,929	1,650,379	1,566,858	3,600	5,588	5,864	5,492
General, net intergovernmental	712,700	1,163,836	1,249,373	1,323,128	2,865	4,268	4,439	4,637
Taxes	501,619	815,777	872,351	914,119	2,017	2,992	3,100	3,204
Property	155,613	240,107	249,178	263,689	626	881	885	924
Sales and gross receipts	177,885	290,993	309,290	320,217	715	1,067	1,099	1,122
Individual income	105,640	189,309	211,661	226,334	425	694	752	793
Corporation income	23,566	33,922	36,059	35,296	95	124	128	124
Other	38,915	61,446	66,164	68,583	156	225	235	240
Charges and miscellaneous	211,081	348,060	377,022	409,009	849	1,276	1,340	1,434
Utility and liquor stores	58,642	86,125	89,546	100,460	236	316	318	352
Water supply system	17,674	29,039	30,515	30,794	71	106	108	108
Electric power system	29,268	40,890	42,436	50,952	118	150	151	179
Gas supply system	5,216	7,708	8,049	8,764	21	28	29	31
Transit system	3,043	4,244	3,954	5,096	12	16	14	18
Liquor stores	3,441	4,245	4,592	4,854	14	16	16	17
Insurance trust revenue [3]	123,970	273,968	311,460	143,271	498	1,005	1,107	502
Employee retirement	94,268	236,527	273,881	102,692	379	867	973	360
Unemployment compensation	18,441	22,234	23,366	23,341	74	82	83	82
Direct expenditure	972,695	1,622,103	1,742,914	1,894,847	3,911	5,949	6,193	6,641
By function:								
Direct general expenditure [3]	831,573	1,398,533	1,502,768	1,621,760	3,356	5,129	5,340	5,684
Education [3]	288,148	483,259	521,612	563,575	1,159	1,772	1,853	1,975
Elementary and secondary	202,009	339,871	365,181	392,278	812	1,246	1,298	1,375
Higher education	73,418	122,716	134,352	146,158	295	450	477	512
Highways	61,057	93,018	101,336	107,235	245	341	360	376
Public welfare	107,287	215,190	233,350	257,380	444	789	829	902
Health	24,223	47,628	51,366	53,465	97	175	183	187
Hospitals	50,412	71,733	75,976	80,545	203	263	270	282
Police protection	30,577	53,367	56,798	59,584	123	196	202	209
Fire protection	13,186	21,262	23,102	24,970	53	78	82	88
Correction	24,635	45,598	48,805	52,370	100	167	173	184
Natural resources	12,330	18,232	20,235	22,163	50	67	72	78
Sanitation and sewerage	28,453	43,047	45,261	46,718	114	158	161	164
Housing and community development	15,479	25,234	26,590	27,402	62	93	94	96
Parks and recreation	14,326	23,417	25,038	27,920	58	86	89	98
Financial administration	16,217	27,593	29,300	30,007	65	101	104	105
Interest on general debt [4]	49,739	67,294	69,814	73,836	200	247	248	259
Utility and liquor stores [4]	77,801	108,398	114,916	133,544	313	398	408	468
Water supply system	22,101	34,089	35,789	36,757	89	125	127	129
Electric power system	30,997	38,132	39,719	54,921	125	140	141	192
Gas supply system	2,989	4,108	3,724	5,023	12	15	13	18
Transit system	18,788	28,522	31,883	32,875	76	105	113	115
Liquor stores	2,926	3,547	3,801	3,968	12	13	14	14
Insurance trust expenditure [3]	63,321	115,172	125,230	139,543	255	422	445	489
Employee retirement	38,355	85,318	95,679	104,414	154	313	340	366
Unemployment compensation	16,499	19,223	18,648	22,986	66	70	66	81
By character and object:								
Current operation	700,131	1,199,494	1,288,746	1,405,033	2,815	4,399	4,579	4,924
Capital outlay	123,102	198,483	217,063	233,258	495	728	771	818
Construction	89,144	147,181	161,694	177,094	358	540	575	621
Equipment, land, and existing structures	33,958	51,302	55,369	56,164	137	188	197	197
Assistance and subsidies	27,227	31,494	31,375	32,583	109	115	111	114
Interest on debt (general and utility) . .	58,914	77,459	80,499	84,431	237	284	286	296
Insurance benefits and repayments . . .	63,321	115,172	125,230	139,543	255	422	445	489
Expenditure for salaries and wages [5] . . .	340,654	522,528	548,796	587,124	1,372	1,916	1,950	2,058
Debt outstanding, year end	858,006	1,369,253	1,451,815	1,554,018	3,460	5,021	5,159	5,447
Long-term	838,700	1,351,408	1,427,524	1,531,897	3,382	4,956	5,073	5,369
Short-term	19,306	17,844	24,291	22,121	78	65	86	78
Long-term debt:								
Issued	108,468	229,374	184,831	199,576	436	841	657	699
Retired	64,831	153,100	121,897	130,574	261	561	433	458

[1] 1990 and 2000 based on enumerated resident population as of April 1. Other years based on estimated resident population as of July 1; see Table 17. [2] Aggregates exclude duplicative transactions between state and local governments; see source. [3] Includes amounts not shown separately. [4] Interest on utility debt included in utility expenditure. For total interest on debt, see Interest on debt (general and utility). [5] Included in items above.

Source: U.S. Census Bureau, Government Finances, 2000-2001. See also Government Finances, annual. See also <http://www.census.gov/govs/www/estimate01.html> (accessed February, 2004).

State and Local Government Finances and Employment **271**

No. 429. State and Local Governments—Revenue and Expenditures by Function: 2001

[In millions of dollars (1,890,891 represents $1,890,891,000,000) except as indicated. For fiscal year ending in year shown; see text, this section. Local government amounts are estimates subject to sampling variation; see Appendix III and source]

Item	Amount (mil. dol.)			Per capita [1] (dol.)		
	State and local	State	Local	State and local	State	Local
Revenue [2]	1,890,891	1,180,305	1,068,151	6,627	4,145	3,744
Intergovernmental revenue	324,033	305,621	375,977	1,136	1,073	1,318
Total revenue from own sources	1,566,858	874,684	692,174	5,492	3,072	2,426
General revenue from own sources	1,323,128	743,677	579,451	4,637	2,612	2,031
Taxes [3]	914,119	559,679	354,439	3,204	1,966	1,242
Property	263,689	10,430	253,259	924	37	888
Individual income	226,334	208,079	18,254	793	731	64
Corporation income	35,296	31,687	3,609	124	111	13
Sales and gross receipts	320,217	258,018	62,199	1,122	906	218
General	223,428	179,319	44,110	783	630	155
Selective [3]	96,789	78,699	18,089	339	276	63
Motor fuel	32,045	31,026	1,020	112	109	4
Alcoholic beverages	4,522	4,167	355	16	15	1
Tobacco products	8,833	8,644	190	31	30	1
Public utilities	18,360	8,966	9,394	64	31	33
Motor vehicle and operators' licenses	17,778	16,471	1,308	62	58	5
Death and gift	7,551	7,499	51	26	26	-
Charges and miscellaneous [3]	409,009	183,998	225,011	1,434	646	789
Current charges [3]	239,485	93,051	146,435	839	327	513
Education [3]	69,861	53,295	16,566	245	187	58
School lunch sales	5,741	15	5,727	20	-	20
Higher education	59,136	52,723	6,413	207	185	22
Natural resources	3,496	2,117	1,379	12	7	5
Hospitals	59,518	20,482	39,037	209	72	137
Sewerage	25,786	22	25,764	90	-	90
Solid waste management	11,009	376	10,634	39	1	37
Parks and recreation	6,456	1,169	5,287	23	4	19
Housing and community development	4,255	486	3,769	15	2	13
Airports	11,883	908	10,975	42	3	38
Sea and inland port facilities	2,707	722	1,985	9	3	7
Highways	7,934	5,083	2,851	28	18	10
Interest earnings	79,979	37,867	42,111	280	133	148
Special assessments	3,933	68	3,866	14	-	14
Sale of property	2,386	555	1,831	8	2	6
Utility and liquor store revenue	100,460	11,022	89,438	352	39	313
Insurance trust revenue	143,271	119,985	23,285	502	421	82
Expenditure [2]	1,899,153	1,186,108	1,070,084	6,656	4,166	3,750
Intergovernmental expenditure	4,306	350,327	11,019	15	1,230	39
Direct expenditure	1,894,847	835,782	1,059,065	6,641	2,935	3,712
General expenditure [3]	1,621,760	694,969	926,791	5,684	2,441	3,248
Education [3]	563,575	152,351	411,224	1,975	535	1,441
Elementary and secondary education	392,278	4,287	387,991	1,375	15	1,360
Higher education	146,158	122,925	23,233	512	432	81
Public welfare	257,380	220,419	36,961	902	774	130
Hospitals	80,545	34,117	46,428	282	120	163
Health	53,465	27,638	25,827	187	97	91
Highways	107,235	66,436	40,800	376	233	143
Police protection	59,584	8,868	50,716	209	31	178
Fire protection	24,970	-	24,970	88	-	88
Corrections	52,370	35,811	16,559	184	126	58
Natural resources	22,163	16,103	6,060	78	57	21
Sewerage	28,061	987	27,075	98	3	95
Solid waste management	18,657	2,601	16,055	65	9	56
Housing and community development	27,402	3,218	24,185	96	11	85
Governmental administration	85,910	36,916	48,993	301	130	172
Parks and recreation	27,920	4,530	23,390	98	16	82
Interest on general debt	73,836	30,452	43,384	259	107	152
Utility	129,576	18,632	110,944	454	65	389
Liquor store expenditure	3,968	3,347	621	14	12	2
Insurance trust expenditure	139,543	118,833	20,710	489	417	73
By character and object:						
Current operation	1,405,033	580,374	824,659	4,924	2,038	2,890
Capital outlay	233,258	81,881	151,377	818	288	531
Construction	177,094	64,668	112,426	621	227	394
Equip., land, and existing structures	56,164	17,213	38,951	197	60	137
Assistance and subsidies	32,583	23,496	9,088	114	83	32
Interest on debt (general and utility)	84,431	31,198	53,233	296	110	187
Insurance benefits and repayments	139,543	118,833	20,710	489	417	73
Expenditure for salaries and wages [4]	587,124	165,751	421,373	2,058	582	1,477

- Represents or rounds to zero.   [1] Based on estimated resident population as of July 1.   [2] Aggregates exclude duplicative transactions between levels of government; see source.   [3] Includes amounts not shown separately.   [4] Included in items shown above.

Source: U.S. Census Bureau, Governmental Finances, 2000-2001. See also <http://www.census.gov/govs/estimate/01.html> (accessed February 2004).

No. 430. State and Local Governments—Capital Outlays: 1990 to 2001

[In millions of dollars (123,102 represents $123,102,000,000), except percent. For fiscal year ending in year shown; see text, this section. Local government amounts are subject to sampling variation; see Appendix III and source]

Level and function	1990	1995	1996	1997	1998	1999	2000	2001
State & local governments: Total	123,102	151,440	158,911	171,414	181,871	198,483	217,063	233,258
Annual percent change [1]	4.9	1.2	10.1	4.9	6.1	9.1	9.4	7.5
Direct expenditure	972,695	1,347,763	1,393,714	1,456,698	1,525,762	1,622,103	1,742,914	1,894,847
Percent of direct expenditure	12.7	11.2	11.4	11.8	11.9	12.2	12.5	12.3
By function:								
Education [2]	25,997	35,708	40,302	44,077	49,332	54,418	60,968	65,116
Higher education	18,057	24,808	28,868	32,210	36,198	13,114	15,257	15,911
Elementary and secondary	7,441	10,461	11,006	11,279	12,590	40,768	45,150	48,404
Highways	33,867	42,561	43,453	44,962	48,067	51,906	56,439	60,108
Health and hospitals	3,848	4,883	5,166	5,065	5,692	5,699	5,502	5,630
Natural resources	2,545	2,891	3,042	3,041	3,206	3,359	4,347	4,908
Housing [3]	3,997	4,527	4,704	5,490	5,544	5,615	6,184	5,888
Air transportation	3,434	3,802	3,814	4,877	5,004	6,666	6,717	8,420
Water transportation [4]	924	1,101	1,246	1,376	1,252	1,487	1,618	4,306
Sewerage	8,356	8,894	9,326	9,589	9,061	9,718	10,093	9,224
Parks and recreation	3,877	4,085	4,869	5,577	6,154	6,486	6,916	8,540
Utilities	16,601	19,028	18,755	20,107	20,357	21,861	24,847	24,553
Water	6,873	7,466	7,381	8,721	8,644	10,325	10,542	10,742
Electric	3,976	3,715	3,522	3,459	3,026	3,613	4,177	4,812
Transit	310	340	318	390	986	7,533	9,728	8,545
Gas	5,443	7,507	7,533	7,528	7,701	389	400	453
Other	19,657	23,961	24,233	27,254	28,202	31,268	33,431	36,566
State governments: Total	45,524	57,829	58,927	59,599	64,441	68,509	76,233	81,881
Annual percent change [1]	8.2	9.3	1.9	1.1	8.1	6.3	11.3	7.4
Direct expenditure	397,291	596,325	607,594	629,049	651,098	693,432	757,027	835,782
Percent of direct expenditure	11.5	9.7	9.7	9.5	9.9	9.9	10.1	9.8
By function:								
Education [2]	7,253	10,042	10,445	10,915	11,970	12,294	14,077	14,936
Highways	24,850	31,687	32,198	32,726	35,008	37,986	41,651	44,761
Health and hospitals	1,531	2,402	2,375	2,253	2,274	2,276	2,228	2,390
Natural resources	1,593	1,956	2,044	2,058	2,199	2,349	2,758	3,105
Housing [3]	119	187	263	225	202	202	860	600
Air transportation	339	356	356	446	339	536	561	667
Water transportation [4]	202	223	305	269	305	270	310	362
Sewerage	333	853	913	474	639	627	403	393
Parks and recreation	601	650	706	938	1,293	1,023	1,044	1,185
Utilities	2,605	2,226	2,607	2,361	2,758	3,034	4,232	3,641
Other	6,098	7,246	6,716	6,934	7,454	7,912	8,108	9,840
Local governments: Total	77,578	93,611	99,984	111,814	117,430	129,974	140,830	151,377
Annual percent change [1]	4.5	10.6	6.8	11.8	5.0	10.7	8.4	7.5
Direct expenditure	575,404	751,438	786,120	827,648	874,664	928,671	985,886	1,059,065
Percent of direct expenditure	13.5	12.5	12.7	13.5	13.4	14.0	14.3	14.3
By function:								
Education [2]	18,744	25,667	29,858	33,162	37,362	42,124	46,890	50,180
Highways	9,017	10,874	11,255	12,235	13,059	13,920	14,789	15,347
Health and hospitals	2,316	2,481	2,790	2,811	3,418	3,423	3,274	3,239
Natural resources	952	935	998	983	1,007	1,010	1,589	1,803
Housing [3]	3,878	4,340	4,441	5,265	5,342	5,413	5,324	5,288
Air transportation	3,095	3,446	3,458	4,431	4,665	6,129	6,156	7,753
Water transportation [4]	722	877	941	1,107	947	1,217	1,308	3,944
Sewerage	8,023	8,040	8,413	9,116	8,422	9,091	9,690	8,831
Parks and recreation	3,276	3,435	4,163	4,639	4,861	5,463	5,872	7,355
Utilities	13,996	16,801	16,149	17,746	17,599	18,827	20,615	20,912
Other	13,559	16,715	17,518	20,320	20,748	23,356	25,323	26,726

[1] Change from immediate prior year except 1990, change from 1985.　[2] Includes other education.　[3] Includes community development.　[4] Includes terminals.

Source: U.S. Census Bureau, 1990, *Government Finances*, Series GF, No. 5, annual; thereafter, <http://www.census.gov/govs/www/estimate01.html> (accessed 8 April 2004).

No. 431. State and Local Governments—Expenditure for Public Works: 1995 to 2001

[In millions of dollars (180,148 represents $180,148,000,000); except as noted. Public works include expenditures on highways, airports, water transport terminals, and sewerage, solid waste management, water supply, and mass transit systems. Represents direct expenditures excluding intergovernmental grants]

Item	Total	Highways	Airport transportation	Water transport and terminals	Sewerage	Solid waste management	Water supply	Mass transit
1995, Total	180,148	77,109	8,397	2,309	23,583	14,990	28,041	25,719
State	56,392	46,893	783	604	1,462	1,658	178	4,814
Local	123,756	30,216	7,614	1,706	22,121	13,331	27,863	20,904
Capital expenditures (percent)	40.7	55.2	45.3	47.7	37.7	13.2	26.6	29.2
2000, Total	230,569	101,336	13,160	3,141	28,052	17,208	35,789	31,883
State	74,974	61,942	1,106	863	955	2,347	354	7,407
Local	155,595	39,394	12,054	2,277	27,098	14,861	35,435	24,476
Capital expenditures (percent)	41.9	55.7	51.0	51.5	36.0	8.9	29.5	30.5
2001, Total	245,112	107,235	15,532	5,995	28,061	18,657	36,757	32,875
State	79,517	66,436	1,321	951	987	2,601	347	6,874
Local	165,595	40,800	14,211	5,044	27,075	16,055	36,410	26,001
Capital expenditures (percent)	42.0	56.1	54.2	71.8	32.9	8.5	29.2	26.0

Source: U.S. Census Bureau; 1990-92, "Government Finances, Series GF, No. 5, annual; thereafter, <http://www.census.gov/govs/estimate/01.html>; (accessed 8 April 2004), State and Local Government Finance Estimates by State, annual, and unpublished data.

No. 432. State and Local Governments—Revenue by State: 2000

[In millions of dollars (1,942,328 represents $1,942,328,000,000). For fiscal year ending in year shown; see text, this section]

State	Total revenue [1]	General revenue — Total	Inter-governmental from Federal Government	General revenue own sources	Taxes — Total [1]	Property	Sales and gross receipts	Indi-vidual income [2]	Motor vehicle	Other taxes
United States..	1,942,328	1,541,322	291,950	1,249,372	872,351	249,178	309,290	247,720	16,401	49,763
Alabama.........	25,726	21,012	5,087	15,925	9,415	1,340	4,586	2,402	213	874
Alaska..........	10,525	9,042	1,411	7,631	2,312	761	284	438	46	782
Arizona.........	27,778	22,863	4,475	18,388	13,334	3,906	6,070	2,815	153	389
Arkansas	13,833	11,582	2,823	8,759	5,961	966	2,947	1,707	118	224
California	270,380	208,373	38,476	169,897	120,068	26,235	39,695	46,213	1,764	6,160
Colorado........	29,603	23,436	3,711	19,725	13,216	3,680	4,848	3,972	209	508
Connecticut......	25,828	23,108	3,674	19,434	15,651	5,407	5,054	4,400	233	556
Delaware	6,224	5,203	830	4,373	2,619	382	298	1,015	33	891
District of Columbia .	6,383	5,732	1,748	3,984	3,216	693	1,000	1,339	17	168
Florida	92,402	75,865	11,718	64,147	41,937	14,098	22,264	1,183	955	3,436
Georgia	49,310	39,690	7,070	32,620	23,254	5,932	9,298	7,077	236	711
Hawaii	8,488	7,092	1,294	5,798	4,102	603	2,141	1,140	127	91
Idaho..........	7,590	6,477	1,150	4,927	3,294	867	1,070	1,091	113	153
Illinois.........	80,695	64,420	10,791	53,629	40,256	14,511	13,376	9,898	1,115	1,355
Indiana.........	32,716	29,749	5,169	24,580	16,363	5,552	5,113	5,193	161	345
Iowa...........	17,220	15,134	2,885	12,249	8,091	2,599	2,698	2,143	349	302
Kansas	16,235	13,391	2,482	10,909	7,616	2,173	2,886	2,134	146	277
Kentucky	25,200	19,423	4,595	14,828	10,172	1,722	3,686	3,755	208	801
Louisiana	27,109	22,342	5,070	17,272	10,887	1,742	6,227	1,804	114	1,001
Maine..........	8,554	7,440	1,630	5,810	4,262	1,598	1,195	1,227	81	161
Maryland	33,949	29,076	4,609	24,467	18,290	4,809	4,622	7,586	179	1,094
Massachusetts.....	46,103	38,295	6,439	31,856	24,042	7,643	5,156	10,348	228	667
Michigan........	70,112	56,415	10,331	46,084	31,474	9,499	9,906	10,112	817	1,141
Minnesota........	38,785	30,957	4,769	26,188	18,173	4,565	5,909	6,351	646	702
Mississippi......	16,672	13,590	3,528	10,062	6,299	1,462	3,202	1,234	113	288
Missouri........	31,635	25,905	5,628	20,277	14,314	3,405	5,833	4,115	252	709
Montana........	5,643	4,856	1,306	3,550	2,132	908	346	616	68	194
Nebraska.......	11,650	9,021	1,710	7,311	4,973	1,549	1,690	1,314	103	317
Nevada	11,885	9,592	1,233	8,359	5,825	1,437	3,586	-	114	688
New Hampshire....	6,948	5,755	1,062	4,693	3,278	2,028	556	378	65	252
New Jersey.......	62,331	51,504	7,883	43,621	32,838	14,449	8,229	8,585	353	1,222
New Mexico	13,073	10,062	2,398	7,664	4,801	620	2,434	1,040	142	564
New York	188,907	143,901	29,249	114,652	86,868	25,202	22,465	34,687	784	3,731
North Carolina....	50,542	41,131	9,051	32,080	21,440	4,607	7,201	8,407	410	815
North Dakota.....	4,495	3,914	1,126	2,788	1,768	527	714	277	44	206
Ohio	80,074	59,017	10,933	48,084	34,239	9,544	10,353	12,082	714	1,545
Oklahoma.......	18,760	15,698	3,181	12,517	8,251	1,303	3,234	2,329	635	751
Oregon.........	28,644	20,969	5,233	15,736	9,412	2,789	912	4,505	375	832
Pennsylvania.....	80,546	64,615	12,498	52,117	36,581	10,067	10,837	10,981	791	3,905
Rhode Island.....	7,427	5,748	1,196	4,552	3,412	1,360	1,004	904	51	93
South Carolina....	23,467	19,727	4,377	15,350	9,543	2,680	3,480	2,673	124	587
South Dakota	4,277	3,491	869	2,622	1,736	632	874	45	58	127
Tennessee......	33,625	24,824	6,321	18,503	12,431	2,887	7,316	794	330	1,104
Texas..........	120,666	95,539	18,576	76,963	52,227	19,817	26,579	-	1,200	4,630
Utah	14,954	11,208	2,172	9,036	5,873	1,303	2,430	1,825	80	234
Vermont	4,019	3,497	903	2,594	1,876	782	485	476	35	97
Virginia.........	44,175	35,434	5,010	30,424	21,083	5,986	5,970	7,395	431	1,301
Washington.......	46,372	33,426	5,828	27,598	18,734	5,493	11,481	-	416	1,344
West Virginia.....	10,760	9,055	2,489	6,566	4,362	855	1,836	1,184	88	399
Wisconsin.......	43,003	30,572	5,059	25,513	18,547	5,689	5,331	6,530	304	691
Wyoming	7,030	3,554	891	2,663	1,505	513	583	-	62	347

See footnote at end of table.

U.S. Census Bureau, Statistical Abstract of the United States: 2004-2005

No. 432. State and Local Governments—Revenue by State: 2000—Con.

[In millions of dollars (372,022 represents $372,022,000,000). For fiscal year ending in year shown; see text, this section]

State	General revenue								Utility and liquor stores	Insurance trust revenue
	Current charges and miscellaneous revenue									
	Current charges					Miscellaneous revenue				
	Total	Total[1]	Education	Hospital	Sewerage	Total[1]	Interest earnings	Special assessment		
United States.....	377,022	223,480	65,562	54,619	24,311	153,542	70,490	3,815	89,546	311,460
Alabama.........	6,510	4,836	1,294	2,535	232	1,674	805	9	1,895	2,819
Alaska..........	5,320	725	136	52	47	4,595	2,275	3	230	1,254
Arizona..........	5,054	2,618	1,063	219	294	2,436	1,161	62	2,656	2,259
Arkansas........	2,798	1,757	574	645	152	1,041	490	11	535	1,716
California........	49,830	30,900	6,855	6,408	3,143	18,930	8,741	967	13,846	48,161
Colorado........	6,508	3,989	1,431	602	399	2,519	1,205	66	1,424	4,744
Connecticut......	3,784	1,610	544	231	191	2,174	902	28	497	2,223
Delaware........	1,754	835	346	38	108	919	347	28	156	865
District of Columbia...	769	331	21	53	101	438	196	-	448	202
Florida..........	22,209	12,871	2,414	2,926	1,458	9,338	3,491	1	5,062	11,476
Georgia.........	9,367	5,609	1,310	2,060	621	3,758	1,500	950	2,826	6,794
								19		
Hawaii..........	1,696	1,125	223	162	138	571	315	20	185	1,212
Idaho...........	1,632	1,073	266	349	86	559	301	11	190	1,323
Illinois..........	13,373	6,974	2,438	754	703	6,399	3,371	89	2,682	13,593
Indiana.........	8,217	5,289	2,280	1,711	495	2,928	1,216	19	1,307	1,660
Iowa...........	4,159	2,864	1,121	1,110	229	1,295	534	18	727	1,359
Kansas.........	3,292	1,898	718	426	179	1,394	698	75	802	2,042
Kentucky........	4,656	2,529	1,015	466	251	2,127	1,459	3	962	4,815
Louisiana........	6,385	4,235	1,029	2,191	200	2,150	1,038	9	724	4,043
Maine..........	1,547	724	266	54	114	823	336	3	171	943
Maryland........	6,176	3,454	1,477	92	542	2,722	1,044	108	652	4,222
Massachusetts......	7,814	3,437	1,139	178	636	4,377	1,907	64	2,006	5,802
Michigan........	14,610	8,650	3,876	1,368	1,239	5,960	2,598	94	1,981	11,716
Minnesota.......	8,015	4,241	1,320	833	581	3,774	1,470	252	1,383	6,445
Mississippi.......	3,763	2,707	633	1,521	135	1,056	458	5	702	2,381
Missouri.........	5,963	3,706	1,332	1,076	385	2,257	1,299	20	1,273	4,457
Montana........	1,418	666	287	57	55	752	313	42	121	666
Nebraska........	2,337	1,332	539	312	108	1,005	435	31	2,019	611
Nevada.........	2,534	1,725	320	485	209	809	471	40	514	1,780
New Hampshire.....	1,414	746	352	5	74	668	413	1	366	827
New Jersey.......	10,784	6,002	1,751	570	1,033	4,782	1,787	14	1,212	9,615
New Mexico.......	2,863	1,310	478	429	97	1,553	760	9	328	2,683
New York........	27,784	16,806	2,363	4,725	1,304	10,978	4,659	72	8,429	36,576
North Carolina.....	10,640	7,659	1,873	3,385	855	2,981	1,763	12	2,768	6,642
North Dakota......	1,020	624	252	7	28	396	169	33	70	512
Ohio...........	13,846	8,368	3,395	1,493	1,399	5,478	2,184	106	2,366	18,691
Oklahoma.......	4,265	2,844	1,097	810	199	1,421	650	5	951	2,111
Oregon.........	6,324	3,696	985	751	432	2,628	1,153	71	989	6,686
Pennsylvania......	15,536	8,848	3,034	1,935	991	6,688	3,488	95	2,702	13,228
Rhode Island......	1,139	487	229	4	54	652	319	3	115	1,565
South Carolina.....	5,807	4,270	1,018	2,144	216	1,537	884	19	1,901	1,839
South Dakota......	885	430	168	28	44	455	234	6	145	642
Tennessee.......	6,072	4,277	1,122	1,662	398	1,795	694	5	5,241	3,560
Texas..........	24,737	14,453	4,565	3,665	1,791	10,284	5,215	87	6,212	18,915
Utah...........	3,162	1,887	755	365	150	1,275	550	3	1,332	2,414
Vermont........	719	393	264	-	32	326	154	5	182	340
Virginia.........	9,341	5,725	1,843	1,311	681	3,616	1,687	42	1,442	7,299
Washington.......	8,865	5,827	1,634	1,163	843	3,038	1,258	93	3,648	9,297
West Virginia......	2,203	1,224	415	299	118	979	469	3	179	1,526
Wisconsin........	6,967	4,309	1,578	615	513	2,658	1,199	106	863	11,568
Wyoming........	1,159	584	124	338	31	575	424	8	133	3,343

- Represents or rounds to zero. [1] Includes items not shown separately. [2] Includes individual and corporate income taxes.

Source: U.S. Census Bureau; "Government Finances 1999-2000," issued January 2003, <http://www.census.gov/govs/estimate/00allpub.pdf>; (accessed 16 June 2003).

No. 433. State and Local Governments—Expenditures and Debt by State: 2000

[In millions of dollars (1,746,943 represents $1,746,943,000,000), except as indicated. For fiscal year ending in year shown; see text, this section]

State	Total expenditure [1]	Total Amount	Per capita [2] (dol.)	Direct general expenditures, total	Education	Public welfare	Health and hospitals	High-ways	Police protection	Fire protection	Corrections
United States	1,746,943	1,506,797	5,354	1,502,768	521,612	233,350	127,342	101,336	56,798	23,102	48,805
Alabama	25,319	22,062	4,961	22,062	7,768	3,525	3,635	1,492	656	252	404
Alaska	8,628	7,712	12,302	7,600	1,761	810	235	827	177	66	175
Arizona	27,293	23,262	4,534	23,262	7,871	2,945	1,374	1,959	1,096	682	955
Arkansas	12,245	11,059	4,137	11,057	4,198	1,999	970	870	352	122	328
California	236,645	198,296	5,854	195,767	63,559	29,214	18,055	8,604	8,704	3,588	7,170
Colorado	26,173	22,531	5,238	22,527	7,904	2,731	1,341	1,743	830	327	820
Connecticut	24,011	21,420	6,290	21,420	6,722	3,116	1,596	1,187	682	373	554
Delaware	5,153	4,692	5,987	4,691	1,715	548	279	427	166	19	228
District of Columbia	6,527	5,152	9,006	5,152	969	1,254	633	38	330	113	305
Florida	84,301	75,290	4,711	75,290	22,826	9,506	7,307	5,175	3,738	1,630	3,273
Georgia	43,517	38,078	4,651	38,078	14,768	5,568	3,554	2,496	1,279	553	1,375
Hawaii	8,254	7,306	6,030	7,291	1,854	1,040	600	353	222	101	155
Idaho	6,404	5,828	4,504	5,828	2,132	790	512	561	207	77	191
Illinois	74,727	64,406	5,186	64,403	22,728	8,853	4,382	4,077	3,053	1,300	1,763
Indiana	31,250	28,744	4,727	28,740	11,450	4,264	2,603	1,965	843	395	727
Iowa	17,275	15,599	5,330	15,563	5,964	2,259	1,678	1,836	427	127	298
Kansas	14,419	12,885	4,793	12,884	4,884	1,354	934	1,714	430	175	349
Kentucky	21,473	19,020	4,705	19,020	6,374	4,096	1,097	1,754	488	257	611
Louisiana	25,018	22,277	4,985	22,277	7,185	3,071	3,375	1,652	829	283	780
Maine	7,652	6,964	5,462	6,955	2,228	1,586	397	572	164	78	123
Maryland	30,598	27,446	5,182	27,446	10,055	4,009	1,295	1,487	1,120	475	1,104
Massachusetts	44,362	37,951	5,977	37,770	11,445	6,309	2,245	3,235	1,479	774	795
Michigan	61,506	54,812	5,515	54,750	22,484	8,242	4,179	3,085	1,793	616	1,853
Minnesota	35,424	31,166	6,335	31,166	10,283	5,970	1,826	2,388	874	256	591
Mississippi	15,379	13,932	4,898	13,932	4,818	2,320	2,113	1,231	404	155	292
Missouri	27,953	24,821	4,436	24,818	9,224	4,041	2,166	2,147	885	394	672
Montana	4,983	4,523	5,013	4,523	1,641	555	343	518	136	41	125
Nebraska	10,831	8,417	4,919	8,406	3,267	1,425	521	880	235	107	231
Nevada	11,230	9,762	4,885	9,755	3,020	886	737	1,127	539	223	471
New Hampshire	6,222	5,664	4,583	5,664	2,059	1,113	170	469	187	100	115
New Jersey	54,590	47,309	5,622	47,231	18,788	5,823	2,332	2,341	2,231	630	1,480
New Mexico	11,195	10,099	5,552	10,099	3,696	1,515	812	1,064	382	129	315
New York	171,858	140,646	7,412	140,020	40,630	29,185	11,568	6,835	5,717	2,200	4,392
North Carolina	46,135	40,434	5,023	40,434	14,164	6,299	5,536	2,637	1,381	480	1,159
North Dakota	4,041	3,674	5,720	3,674	1,255	580	91	450	68	45	40
Ohio	68,418	57,650	5,078	57,649	20,612	9,567	4,963	3,951	2,125	1,014	1,937
Oklahoma	15,962	13,808	4,002	13,767	5,836	885	1,324	1,404	518	266	511
Oregon	24,086	20,161	5,893	20,161	6,448	3,070	1,951	1,246	696	313	747
Pennsylvania	75,624	66,028	5,376	65,871	23,256	13,318	3,945	4,123	2,221	434	2,222
Rhode Island	6,432	5,586	5,329	5,560	1,857	1,144	278	286	211	152	139
South Carolina	23,436	20,260	5,050	20,260	7,126	3,458	3,016	1,328	653	190	559
South Dakota	3,760	3,444	4,562	3,444	1,218	488	150	540	88	29	81
Tennessee	32,010	25,272	4,442	25,272	8,369	4,872	2,739	1,839	940	400	604
Texas	109,634	95,762	4,593	95,762	39,217	11,460	8,854	7,201	3,204	1,373	3,756
Utah	13,044	11,013	4,932	11,013	4,233	1,473	741	1,033	381	127	351
Vermont	3,766	3,456	5,676	3,446	1,330	701	79	327	78	25	66
Virginia	38,092	34,728	4,906	34,727	13,132	4,487	2,634	2,627	1,176	549	1,246
Washington	41,794	33,483	5,681	33,475	11,565	5,100	3,317	2,212	1,007	551	1,053
West Virginia	9,990	8,711	4,817	8,711	3,171	1,763	552	888	171	55	184
Wisconsin	34,559	30,864	5,754	30,762	11,427	4,470	1,839	2,711	1,124	458	1,030
Wyoming	3,743	3,331	6,746	3,330	1,125	291	464	426	99	23	98

See footnote at end of table.

No. 433. State and Local Governments—Expenditures and Debt by State: 2000—Con.

[See page 276]

State	General expenditure							Utility and liquor store expenditures	Employee retirement expenditures	Debt outstanding
	Environment and housing				Governmental administration	Interest on general debt	Other general expenditures			
	Sewerage	Solid waste management	Parks and recreation	Housing [3]						
United States..	28,052	17,208	25,038	26,590	81,659	69,814	142,061	114,916	95,679	1,451,815
Alabama	452	221	278	304	908	768	1,399	1,861	1,209	16,799
Alaska.	79	55	79	185	504	418	2,229	327	473	7,257
Arizona	389	269	469	354	1,522	1,026	2,351	2,674	1,062	23,599
Arkansas.	147	122	137	128	552	351	782	545	474	7,829
California.	3,743	2,370	3,095	4,547	13,471	7,549	22,100	18,805	14,233	177,920
Colorado	408	111	732	377	1,262	1,165	2,776	2,000	1,473	23,199
Connecticut	272	390	231	481	1,352	1,345	3,119	679	1,476	23,495
Delaware.	94	30	68	79	376	283	380	189	206	4,585
District of Columbia.	303	37	172	58	320	236	383	1,303	7	5,062
Florida.	1,563	1,530	1,478	934	4,446	3,836	8,048	5,880	2,378	78,495
Georgia.	865	478	540	602	2,076	1,056	2,867	3,461	1,627	29,948
Hawaii.	124	134	217	266	456	587	1,182	319	519	7,909
Idaho	129	76	91	25	379	179	478	163	248	3,430
Illinois	1,105	409	1,965	1,483	3,716	3,644	5,927	4,041	5,146	67,573
Indiana	558	210	556	478	1,554	968	2,168	1,309	984	19,869
Iowa	250	128	246	132	734	357	1,127	805	680	7,310
Kansas	147	112	189	113	953	473	1,056	741	638	10,440
Kentucky.	348	197	237	143	850	1,293	1,274	943	1,152	23,420
Louisiana.	298	231	395	302	1,103	954	1,818	853	1,733	17,980
Maine	119	95	55	113	355	321	749	144	470	5,845
Maryland	560	430	681	632	1,568	1,442	2,587	983	1,684	23,830
Massachusetts . . .	924	351	295	1,210	1,711	2,545	4,452	3,060	2,540	55,163
Michigan	1,694	410	740	275	2,761	2,143	4,476	2,435	3,426	47,195
Minnesota	622	258	714	591	1,572	1,356	3,865	1,622	2,201	27,409
Mississippi	126	118	139	134	630	455	997	656	686	8,519
Missouri.	412	144	432	301	1,149	968	1,881	1,421	1,398	19,286
Montana	45	49	50	62	303	215	440	100	250	3,798
Nebraska.	117	65	126	112	351	212	756	2,095	270	6,648
Nevada	108	14	370	147	742	505	867	835	438	13,235
New Hampshire . .	69	81	55	91	320	377	457	325	206	7,041
New Jersey	981	961	692	752	2,561	2,196	5,464	2,535	3,234	50,315
New Mexico	127	104	207	91	568	375	713	381	643	7,652
New York.	1,786	2,152	1,783	2,979	6,466	9,259	15,067	15,133	12,988	177,550
North Carolina . . .	598	559	605	603	1,574	1,259	3,581	3,310	1,953	29,114
North Dakota	19	30	124	92	171	146	562	73	112	2,781
Ohio	1,488	416	1,182	981	3,574	2,098	3,740	2,518	6,017	42,087
Oklahoma	226	138	272	148	748	508	982	919	996	11,409
Oregon	584	122	321	469	1,381	855	1,957	1,388	1,564	15,607
Pennsylvania	1,274	551	816	1,256	3,174	3,916	5,366	3,796	4,340	73,325
Rhode Island	94	71	46	128	340	335	481	152	429	6,878
South Carolina . . .	245	239	270	202	906	734	1,334	1,928	963	18,671
South Dakota	44	21	91	31	186	165	311	134	168	3,289
Tennessee	466	309	449	461	1,152	785	1,888	5,418	1,013	18,377
Texas	1,591	891	1,215	1,809	4,058	4,594	6,540	7,344	5,510	100,175
Utah	182	102	238	115	780	384	873	1,483	374	12,394
Vermont	36	34	19	81	188	149	331	186	83	2,839
Virginia	752	488	592	615	2,033	1,732	2,664	1,600	1,598	31,546
Washington	722	462	633	647	1,596	1,398	3,213	4,539	1,732	38,697
West Virginia	120	50	102	104	536	406	608	245	416	7,094
Wisconsin	611	354	497	351	1,479	1,363	3,049	1,093	2,115	25,563
Wyoming	38	31	51	12	194	129	348	167	145	2,368

[1] Includes items not shown separately. [2] Based on enumerated resident population as of April 1; see Table 17. [3] Includes community development.

Source: U.S. Census Bureau, <http://www.census.gov/govs/www/estimate0000us.html> (accessed 27 July 2003) <http://www.census.gov/govs/estimate/00allpub.pdg>. (released January 2003).

State and Local Government Finances and Employment   277

No. 434. State and Local Governments—Summary of Finances by State: 2000

[In millions of dollars (1,942,328 represents $1,942,328,000,000), except as indicated. For fiscal year ending in year shown; see text, this section]

State	Revenue [1]						Expenditures		Debt outstanding	
	All revenue		General revenue		Taxes		Direct general expendi- tures	Per capita [2] (dol.)	Total	Per capita [2] (dol.)
	Total	Per capita [2] (dol.)	Total	Per capita [2] (dol.)	Total	Per capita [2] (dol.)				
U.S.	1,942,328	6,902	1,541,322	5,477	872,351	3,100	1,502,768	5,340	1,451,815	5,159
Alabama.	25,726	5,785	21,012	4,725	9,415	2,117	22,062	4,961	16,799	3,778
Alaska	10,525	16,787	9,042	14,421	2,312	3,687	7,600	12,121	7,257	11,573
Arizona.	27,778	5,414	22,863	4,456	13,334	2,599	23,262	4,534	23,599	4,599
Arkansas	13,833	5,175	11,582	4,333	5,961	2,230	11,057	4,137	7,829	2,929
California	270,380	7,982	208,373	6,152	120,068	3,545	195,767	5,780	177,920	5,253
Colorado.	29,603	6,883	23,436	5,449	13,216	3,073	22,527	5,238	23,199	5,394
Connecticut. . . .	25,828	7,583	23,108	6,785	15,651	4,596	21,420	6,289	23,495	6,898
Delaware	6,224	7,938	5,203	6,637	2,619	3,342	4,691	5,983	4,585	5,848
District of Columbia. . .	6,383	11,159	5,732	10,022	3,216	5,621	5,152	9,007	5,062	8,850
Florida	92,402	5,782	75,865	4,747	41,937	2,624	75,290	4,711	78,495	4,911
Georgia	49,310	6,024	39,690	4,849	23,254	2,840	38,078	4,652	29,948	3,658
Hawaii	8,488	7,004	7,092	5,851	4,102	3,385	7,291	6,016	7,909	6,526
Idaho	7,590	5,866	6,077	4,696	3,294	2,546	5,828	4,504	3,430	2,650
Illinois	80,695	6,498	64,420	5,187	40,256	3,241	64,403	5,186	67,573	5,441
Indiana.	32,716	5,381	29,749	4,893	16,363	2,691	28,740	4,727	19,869	3,268
Iowa	17,220	5,885	15,134	5,172	8,091	2,765	15,563	5,319	7,310	2,498
Kansas	16,235	6,040	13,391	4,982	7,616	2,833	12,884	4,793	10,440	3,884
Kentucky	25,200	6,235	19,423	4,805	10,172	2,517	19,020	4,706	23,420	5,794
Louisiana	27,109	6,066	22,342	4,999	10,887	2,436	22,277	4,985	17,980	4,023
Maine.	8,554	6,709	7,440	5,835	4,262	3,343	6,955	5,455	5,845	4,585
Maryland	33,949	6,410	29,076	5,490	18,290	3,453	27,446	5,182	23,830	4,500
Massachusetts. . .	46,103	7,261	38,295	6,032	24,042	3,787	37,770	5,949	55,163	8,689
Michigan.	70,112	7,055	56,415	5,677	31,474	3,167	54,750	5,509	47,195	4,749
Minnesota.	38,785	7,885	30,957	6,293	18,173	3,694	31,166	6,336	27,409	5,572
Mississippi	16,672	5,860	13,590	4,777	6,299	2,214	13,932	4,897	8,519	2,994
Missouri	31,635	5,654	25,905	4,630	14,314	2,558	24,818	4,436	19,286	3,447
Montana.	5,643	6,256	4,856	5,384	2,132	2,363	4,523	5,014	3,798	4,210
Nebraska	11,650	6,809	9,021	5,272	4,973	2,906	8,406	4,913	6,648	3,885
Nevada	11,885	5,948	9,592	4,801	5,825	2,915	9,755	4,883	13,235	6,624
New Hampshire .	6,948	5,621	5,755	4,656	3,278	2,653	5,664	4,582	7,041	5,696
New Jersey. . . .	62,331	7,408	51,504	6,121	32,838	3,903	47,231	5,613	50,315	5,980
New Mexico . . .	13,073	7,187	10,062	5,532	4,801	2,639	10,099	5,552	7,652	4,207
New York	188,907	9,955	143,901	7,583	86,868	4,578	140,020	7,379	177,550	9,357
North Carolina . .	50,542	6,279	41,131	5,110	21,440	2,664	40,434	5,024	29,114	3,617
North Dakota. . .	4,495	7,002	3,914	6,096	1,768	2,753	3,674	5,722	2,781	4,331
Ohio	80,074	7,053	59,017	5,198	34,239	3,016	57,649	5,078	42,087	3,707
Oklahoma.	18,760	5,436	15,698	4,549	8,251	2,391	13,767	3,989	11,409	3,306
Oregon.	28,644	8,373	20,969	6,130	9,412	2,751	20,161	5,893	15,607	4,562
Pennsylvania. . . .	80,546	6,559	64,615	5,261	36,581	2,979	65,871	5,364	73,325	5,971
Rhode Island. . .	7,427	7,087	5,748	5,484	3,412	3,255	5,560	5,305	6,878	6,563
South Carolina. .	23,467	5,849	19,727	4,917	9,543	2,379	20,260	5,050	18,671	4,654
South Dakota . .	4,277	5,666	3,491	4,623	1,736	2,299	3,444	4,561	3,289	4,356
Tennessee	33,625	5,910	24,824	4,363	12,431	2,185	25,272	4,442	18,377	3,230
Texas.	120,666	5,787	95,539	4,582	52,227	2,505	95,762	4,592	100,175	4,804
Utah	14,954	6,697	11,208	5,019	5,873	2,630	11,013	4,932	12,394	5,551
Vermont	4,019	6,599	3,497	5,742	1,876	3,081	3,446	5,659	2,839	4,662
Virginia.	44,175	6,240	35,434	5,005	21,083	2,978	34,727	4,906	31,546	4,456
Washington. . . .	46,372	7,868	33,426	5,671	18,734	3,178	33,475	5,680	38,697	6,566
West Virginia. . .	10,760	5,951	9,055	5,008	4,362	2,412	8,711	4,818	7,094	3,924
Wisconsin	43,003	8,017	30,572	5,699	18,547	3,458	30,762	5,735	25,563	4,766
Wyoming	7,030	14,231	3,554	7,195	1,505	3,047	3,330	6,740	2,368	4,793

[1] Includes items not shown separately. [2] Based on enumerated resident population as of April 1, see Table 17.

Source: U.S. Census Bureau; "Government Finances: 1999-2000"; issued January 2003, <http://www.census.gov/govs/estimate /00allpub.pdf>; (accessed 16 June 2003).

No. 435. State and Local Governments—Indebtedness: 1980 to 2001

[In billions of dollars (335.6 represents $335,600,000,000), except per capita. For fiscal year ending in year shown; see text, this section. Local government amounts are estimates subject to sampling variation; see Appendix III and source]

Item	Debt outstanding						Long-term		
			Long-term						
	Total	Per capita [1] (dol.)	Local schools [2]	Utilities	All other	Short-term	Net long term	Debt issued	Debt retired
1980: Total	**335.6**	**1,481**	**32.3**	**55.2**	**235.0**	**13.1**	**262.9**	**42.4**	**17.4**
State.	122.0	540	3.8	4.6	111.5	2.1	79.8	16.4	5.7
Local	213.6	943	28.5	50.6	123.5	11.0	183.1	25.9	11.7
1985: Total	**568.6**	**2,390**	**43.8**	**90.8**	**414.5**	**19.6**	**430.5**	**101.2**	**43.5**
State.	211.9	893	6.7	8.6	193.8	2.8	110.4	41.7	16.4
Local	356.7	1,499	37.1	82.2	220.6	16.8	320.1	59.5	27.2
1990: Total	**858.0**	**3,449**	**60.4**	**134.8**	**643.5**	**19.3**	**474.4**	**108.5**	**64.8**
State.	318.3	1,282	4.4	12.3	298.7	2.8	125.5	43.5	22.9
Local	539.8	2,169	56.0	122.4	344.8	16.5	348.9	65.0	42.0
1995: Total	**1,115.4**	**4,244**	**118.2**	**163.9**	**806.2**	**27.0**	**697.3**	**129.3**	**95.1**
State.	427.2	1,629	11.3	17.0	392.8	6.1	205.3	52.6	37.5
Local	688.1	2,618	107.0	146.9	413.4	20.9	491.9	76.8	57.6
1998: Total	**1,283.6**	**4,750**	**159.2**	**182.8**	**924.3**	**17.3**	**842.6**	**204.4**	**144.6**
State.	483.1	1,791	13.6	16.7	450.6	2.2	237.2	83.4	58.1
Local	800.4	2,962	145.5	166.1	473.8	15.1	605.4	120.9	86.5
1999: Total	**1,369.3**	**5,021**	**180.7**	**194.9**	**975.7**	**17.8**	**907.3**	**229.4**	**153.1**
State.	510.5	1,876	15.4	16.7	475.8	2.7	249.4	83.2	55.6
Local	858.8	3,149	165.3	178.3	500.0	15.2	657.9	146.2	97.5
2000: Total	**1,451.8**	**5,159**	**197.7**	**200.1**	**1,029.8**	**24.3**	**959.6**	**184.8**	**121.9**
State.	547.9	1,951	18.7	17.9	505.0	6.4	266.9	75.0	44.4
Local	903.9	3,212	179.0	182.2	524.8	17.9	692.7	109.8	77.5
2001: Total	**1,554.0**	**5,447**	**225.3**	**210.4**	**1,096.2**	**22.1**	**1,038.6**	**199.6**	**130.6**
State.	576.5	2,025	21.5	18.7	532.6	3.7	287.4	81.3	50.7
Local	977.5	3,426	203.8	191.7	563.5	18.5	751.2	118.3	79.9

[1] 1980,1990, and 2000 based on enumerated resident population as of April 1; other years based on estimated resident population as of July 1; see Tables 1 and 2.   [2] Includes debt for education activities other than higher education.

Source: U.S. Census Bureau, 1980-90, *State and Local Government Finance Estimates*, annual; thereafter, <http://www.census.gov/govs/www/estimate/01.html> (accessed 8 April 2004).

No. 436. Long Term Municipal Bonds New Issues for State and Local Governments: 1980 to 2002

[In billions of dollars (45.6 represents $45,600,000,000)]

Item	1980	1985	1990	1995	1997	1998	1999	2000	2001	2002
Long-Term Municipal New Issues [1]	**45.6**	**202.4**	**125.9**	**156.2**	**214.3**	**279.7**	**219.2**	**194.3**	**283.5**	**355.8**
General obligation	13.7	39.6	40.2	60.2	72.2	92.6	69.8	65.2	101.3	125.6
Revenue.	31.9	162.8	85.7	96.0	142.1	187.1	149.4	129.1	182.2	230.2
Competitive.	19.3	27.8	30.2	41.0	47.8	65.2	52.8	48.7	63.1	71.9
Negotiated	26.4	174.6	95.9	115.4	166.5	214.5	166.4	145.6	220.4	283.9
States with largest issuance: [2]										
New York	2.9	12.7	16.9	18.8	27.4	36.3	19.8	19.1	22.5	48.7
California.	3.6	25.3	15.7	20.2	27.7	33.9	26.5	22.9	31.7	48.5
Texas	3.8	21.2	6.5	10.4	15.3	18.1	17.7	14.7	24.6	26.6
Florida	2.2	13.2	5.9	9.1	10.5	14.7	10.8	10.1	14.1	18.7
Illinois	2.3	9.2	6.3	6.6	9.6	10.1	12.4	8.9	14.1	14.7
All others. . . . . [3]	30.8	120.8	74.6	91.1	123.8	166.6	132.0	118.6	176.5	198.5
Type of issuer: [3]										
City, town, or village	8.5	36.5	22.7	27.9	34.8	44.3	33.0	29.3	45.6	46.9
College or university	0.2	2.9	1.5	2.5	3.3	4.6	4.1	3.8	5.6	7.1
County/parish.	4.6	15.8	10.0	13.3	15.5	21.2	17.1	12.7	19.0	23.5
Direct issuer.	-	0.4	0.2	0.4	0.8	2.1	2.0	2.6	3.1	4.9
District	3.9	15.6	15.2	22.4	33.7	43.6	34.1	27.8	47.9	54.4
Indian Tribe	(NA)	(NA)	(NA)	(NA)	(NA)	(NA)	(NA)	0.2	0.2	0.2
Local authority	9.2	51.1	20.7	27.9	41.5	53.9	43.2	33.1	53.1	59.8
State authority	14.1	68.1	40.6	47.2	66.0	85.2	68.1	64.2	78.9	125.0
State	5.1	12.1	15.0	14.6	18.7	24.7	17.6	20.8	30.2	34.0
General use of proceeds:										
Airports.	0.4	3.0	5.2	4.7	6.4	10.2	5.5	7.4	12.3	10.0
Combined utilities	0.3	2.4	1.0	0.7	1.5	1.8	1.0	0.3	1.3	2.2
Economic development	0.2	2.5	2.5	2.5	2.9	3.5	3.6	2.9	3.9	4.4
Education	4.0	20.4	20.5	28.5	42.7	56.5	47.6	39.9	64.5	76.4
Health care	3.1	30.0	12.6	11.5	22.1	33.4	22.0	14.4	20.1	22.4
Industrial development	1.0	2.9	1.9	3.2	3.5	3.6	3.5	3.4	2.9	2.3
Multi family housing.	2.5	20.2	3.1	6.1	5.4	6.4	6.1	6.2	7.3	10.1
Nursing homes/life care retirement.	0.3	1.2	1.6	1.9	3.6	4.8	4.9	1.8	3.0	3.7
Other miscellaneous	11.1	37.3	36.2	44.2	57.0	71.5	58.4	52.8	81.2	102.4
Pollution control	2.3	10.0	2.5	5.0	5.6	9.7	8.9	4.8	4.5	5.5
Electric & public power.	4.4	23.2	5.2	4.8	6.5	15.6	4.9	5.7	11.5	23.1
Single family housing.	10.6	16.4	12.5	10.0	13.6	12.9	12.6	12.0	14.0	12.4
Solid waste/resource recovery.	0.4	3.8	3.0	3.3	3.6	2.4	1.2	0.5	2.1	1.9
Student loans.	0.2	4.0	0.4	4.4	3.9	4.9	5.3	7.6	8.2	11.7
Transportation	1.3	11.0	7.6	11.3	16.6	20.5	16.0	15.9	18.6	33.8
Water, sewer, and gas facilities	3.1	13.4	9.3	13.2	18.2	20.9	16.4	11.3	27.1	32.2
Waterfront/seaports	0.5	1.5	0.5	0.8	0.8	1.2	0.9	1.2	1.1	1.0

- Represents or rounds to zero.   NA Not available.   [1] Excludes issues with a final maturity of less than 13 months, private placements, and not-for-profit cooperative utilities.   [2] Ranked by 1997 Long Term Municipal New Issue Volume.   [3] Includes island areas.

Source: Thomson Financial Securities Data Company, Newark, NJ, Municipal New Issues Database (copyright).

State and Local Government Finances and Employment **279**

No. 437. Bond Ratings for State Governments by State: 2003

[As of fourth quarter. Key to investment grade ratings are in declining order of quality. The ratings from AA to CCC may be modified by the addition of a plus or minus sign to show relative standing within the major rating categories. *S&P:* AAA, AA, A, BBB, BB, B, CCC, CC, C; *Moody's:* Aaa, Aa, A, Baa, Ba, B, Caa, Ca, C; Numerical modifiers 1, 2, and 3 are added to letter-rating. *Fitch:* AAA, AA, A, BBB, BB, B, CCC, CC, C]

State	Standard & Poor's	Moody's	Fitch	State	Standard & Poor's	Moody's	Fitch
Alabama	AA	Aa3	AA	Montana	AA-	Aa3	(NA)
Alaska	(¹)	Aa2	AA	Nebraska	(¹)	(NA)	(NA)
Arizona	AA-	(NA)	(NA)	Nevada	AA	Aa2	AA+
Arkansas	AA	Aa2	(NA)	New Hampshire . . .	AA	Aa2	AA
California	BBB	Baa1	BBB	New Jersey	AA	²Aa2	AA
Colorado	AA-	(NA)	(NA)	New Mexico	AA+	Aa1	(NA)
Connecticut	AA	Aa3	AA	New York	AA	A2	AA-
Delaware	AAA	Aaa	AAA	North Carolina	AAA	Aa1	AAA
Florida	AA+	Aa2	AA	North Dakota	AA-	Aa3	(NA)
Georgia	AAA	Aaa	AAA	Ohio	AA+	Aa1	AA+
Hawaii	AA-	Aa3	AA-	Oklahoma	AA	Aa3	AA
Idaho	AA-	Aa3	(NA)	Oregon	AA-	Aa3	A+
Illinois	AA	Aa3	AA	Pennsylvania	AA	Aa2	AA
Indiana	AA	Aa1	(NA)	Rhode Island	AA	Aa3	AA
Iowa	AA+	Aa1	³AA	South Carolina	AAA	Aaa	AAA
Kansas	AA+	Aa1	(NA)	South Dakota	(¹)	(NA)	(NA)
Kentucky	AA-	²Aa2	(NA)	Tennessee	AA	Aa2	AA
Louisiana	A+	A1	A+	Texas	AA	Aa1	AA+
Maine	AA+	Aa2	AA+	Utah	AAA	Aaa	AAA
Maryland	AAA	Aaa	AAA	Vermont	AA+	Aa1	AA+
Massachusetts	AA-	Aa2	AA-	Virginia	AAA	²Aa2	AAA
Michigan	AA+	Aa1	AA+	Washington	AA	Aa1	AA
Minnesota	AAA	Aa1	AAA	West Virginia	AA-	Aa3	AA-
Mississippi	AA	Aa3	AA	Wisconsin	AA-	Aa3	AA
Missouri	AAA	Aaa	AAA	Wyoming	AA	(NA)	(NA)

NA Not Available   ¹ Not reviewed.   ² Rating watch negative.   ³ Implied.

Sources: Standard & Poor's, New York, NY; Moody's Investors Service, New York, NY (copyright); and Fitch Ratings, New York, NY (copyright).

No. 438. Bond Ratings for City Governments by Largest Cities: 2003

[As of fourth quarter. See headnote in table 437]

Cities ranked by 2000 population	Standard & Poor's	Moody's	Fitch	Cities ranked by 2000 population	Standard & Poor's	Moody's	Fitch
New York, NY	A	A2	A+	Oakland, CA	A+	A1	A+
Los Angeles, CA	AA	Aa2	AA	Mesa, AZ	AA-	A1	(NA)
Chicago, IL	A+	A1	AA-	Tulsa, OK	AA	Aa2	(NA)
Houston, TX	AA-	Aa3	AA	Omaha, NE	AAA	Aaa	(NA)
Philadelphia, PA	BBB	Baa1	(NA)	Minneapolis, MN.	AAA	Aa1	(NA)
Phoenix, AZ.	AA+	Aa1	(NA)	Honolulu, HI.	AA-	Aa2	AA
San Diego, CA	AA-	²Aa1	AA	Miami, FL	BBB+	A3	(NA)
Dallas, TX	AAA	Aa1	(NA)	Colorado Springs, CO . .	AA	Aa3	(NA)
San Antonio, TX	AA+	Aa2	AA+	St. Louis, MO.	A-	A3	A-
Detroit, MI	A-	Baa1	A	Wichita, KS	AA	Aa2	(NA)
San Jose, CA.	AA+	Aa1	AA+	Santa Ana, CA	(¹)	(NA)	(NA)
Indianapolis, IN	AAA	(NA)	(NA)	Pittsburgh, PA	BB	²Ba1	BB
San Francisco, CA	AA	Aa3	AA	Arlington, TX	AA	Aa2	(NA)
Jacksonville, FL	(¹)	Aa2	(NA)	Cincinnati, OH	AA+	Aa1	(NA)
Columbus, OH	AAA	Aaa	(NA)	Anaheim, CA	AA	Aa2	(NA)
Austin, TX	AA+	Aa2	(NA)	Toledo, OH	A	A3	(NA)
Baltimore, MD	A+	A1	A+	Tampa, FL.	(¹)	Aa3	(NA)
Memphis, TN	AA	Aa2	AA	Buffalo, NY	BBB-	Baa3	(NA)
Milwaukee, WI	AA	Aa2	AA+	St. Paul, MN	AAA	Aa2	AA+
Boston, MA	AA-	Aa2	AA-	Corpus Christi, TX	A+	A2	AA-
Washington, DC	BBB+	A2	BBB+	Aurora, CO	AA	Aa2	(NA)
El Paso, TX	AA	Aa3	(NA)	Raleigh, NC	AAA	Aaa	AAA
Seattle, WA	AAA	Aaa	(NA)	Newark, NJ	AA-	Baa1	(NA)
Denver, CO	AA+	Aa1	AA+	Lexington-Fayette, KY . .	AA+	(NA)	(NA)
Nashville-Davidson, TN .	AA	Aa2	AA+	Anchorage, AK.	(¹)	Aa3	(NA)
Charlotte, NC.	AAA	Aaa	AAA	Louisville, KY	AA	Aa3	(NA)
Fort Worth, TX	AA+	Aa1	(NA)	Riverside, CA.	AA-	(NA)	(NA)
Portland, OR	(¹)	Aaa	(NA)	St Petersburg, FL	(¹)	(NA)	(NA)
Oklahoma City, OK	AA	Aa2	(NA)	Bakersfield, CA	(¹)	Aa3	(NA)
Tucson, AZ	AA	Aa2	(NA)	Stockton CA	A+	(NA)	(NA)
New Orleans, LA	BBB+	Baa1	(NA)	Birmingham, AL	AA	Aa3	AA-
Las Vegas, NV	AA-	Aa3	(NA)	Jersey City, NJ	BBB	Baa3	BBB
Cleveland, OH	A	A2	A+	Norfolk, VA	AA	A1	AA
Long Beach, CA	AA-	Aa3	(NA)	Baton Rouge, LA	(¹)	(NA)	(NA)
Albuquerque, NM	AA	Aa3	AA	Hialeah, FL	(¹)	(NA)	(NA)
Kansas City, MO.	AA	Aa3	AAA	Lincoln, NE	AAA	Aaa	(NA)
Fresno, CA	AA-	A1	(NA)	Greensboro, NC	AAA	Aa1	AAA
Virginia Beach, VA	AA+	Aa1	AA+	Plano, TX	AAA	Aaa	AAA
Atlanta, GA	AA-	Aa3	AA-	Rochester, NY	AA	A2	(NA)
Sacramento, CA	AA	Aa2	(NA)				

Not available.   ¹Not reviewed.   ² Rating watch negative.

Sources: Standard & Poor's, New York, NY; Moody's Investors Service, New York, NY (copyright); and Fitch Ratings, New York, NY (copyright).

No. 439. State Resources, Expenditures, and Balances: 2002 and 2003

[In millions of dollars (1,073,816 represents $1,073,816,000,000). For fiscal year ending in year shown; see text; this section. **General funds** exclude special funds earmarked for particular purposes, such as highway trust funds and federal funds; they support most on-going broad-based state services and are available for appropriation to support any governmental activity. Minus sign (-) indicates deficit]

| State | Expenditures by fund source | | | | State general fund | | | | | |
| | Total, 2002 | Total [2] | General fund | Federal funds | Resources [3][4] | | Expenditures [4] | | Balance [5] | |
		2003 [1]			2002	2003 [1]	2002	2003 [1]	2002	2003 [1]
United States..	1,073,816	1,125,623	497,782	321,792	498,789	502,868	488,186	491,198	9,795	8,462
Alabama.........	16,745	20,342	5,476	6,906	5,344	5,585	5,325	5,513	[6]19	[6]113
Alaska.........	(NA)	(NA)	(NA)	(NA)	2,392	2,471	2,392	2,471	[6]-	[6]-
Arizona.........	18,983	19,531	6,031	5,565	6,340	6,031	6,339	6,014	[6]1	[6]18
Arkansas........	12,068	13,557	3,317	3,926	3,182	3,251	3,182	3,251	-	-
California	145,843	163,955	75,461	54,566	74,618	79,412	76,752	78,142	[6]-2,133	1,402
Colorado........	13,660	14,045	6,104	3,051	6,823	6,137	6,685	5,914	138	223
Connecticut......	20,429	20,941	12,092	3,637	10,845	12,016	11,663	12,345	-222	-104
Delaware	5,684	5,700	2,503	907	2,936	2,918	2,454	2,454	[6]482	[6]464
Florida	47,438	50,327	20,645	15,535	20,151	21,197	19,166	20,707	[6]984	[6]491
Georgia	27,336	28,648	15,481	11,398	16,607	16,383	14,053	15,271	[6]2,554	[6]1,112
Hawaii	7,858	8,630	3,806	1,351	3,790	3,923	3,656	3,806	[6]-134	[6]-117
Idaho..........	4,241	4,625	1,952	1,659	1,981	1,941	1,980	1,926	[6]1	16
Illinois.........	39,537	40,460	18,145	8,329	24,504	25,161	22,739	21,893	[6]256	[6]317
Indiana.........	18,314	19,296	10,316	6,164	9,788	10,446	9,737	10,309	[6]-	[6]137
Iowa	13,154	13,194	4,468	3,441	4,680	4,484	4,591	4,529	[6]89	[6]-46
Kansas.........	9,803	10,182	4,358	3,086	4,478	4,260	4,466	4,138	12	123
Kentucky........	17,223	17,621	7,179	5,897	7,212	7,444	7,082	7,179	24	[6]163
Louisiana	17,608	18,900	6,649	6,057	6,521	6,662	6,487	6,662	[6]18	[6]23
Maine..........	5,717	5,719	2,546	1,905	2,579	2,564	2,565	2,540	[6]14	24
Maryland	21,443	23,159	10,478	5,680	10,850	10,469	10,947	10,669	[6]309	[6]123
Massachusetts.....	26,778	26,593	22,411	1,106	24,188	23,363	22,800	22,390	[6]1,388	[6]973
Michigan........	39,740	39,801	8,800	11,276	9,240	8,895	9,126	8,821	[6]115	74
Minnesota.......	20,609	23,888	13,930	5,433	13,884	14,180	12,754	14,000	1,130	180
Mississippi	10,521	11,133	3,547	4,034	3,436	3,494	3,579	3,509	[6]8	[6]33
Missouri	16,813	17,881	6,640	5,947	7,808	7,669	7,643	7,548	[6]165	[6]121
Montana........	3,236	3,508	1,283	1,441	1,437	1,322	1,356	1,280	81	42
Nebraska	6,567	6,782	2,622	1,830	2,655	2,622	2,599	2,619	[6]56	[6]3
Nevada	4,134	5,892	1,899	1,501	1,980	2,139	1,889	2,036	[6]90	[6]100
New Hampshire....	3,751	3,942	1,211	1,177	1,136	1,336	1,174	1,336	38	[6]-
New Jersey......	34,943	35,810	22,913	8,357	22,289	23,223	21,997	22,927	292	250
New Mexico	8,981	8,957	3,920	2,955	4,395	4,339	4,049	4,051	320	245
New York	85,043	90,895	37,444	31,985	42,254	40,328	41,222	39,513	[6]1,032	[6]815
North Carolina	26,429	26,492	13,833	7,676	13,861	14,271	13,741	13,856	4	[6]251
North Dakota.....	2,439	2,731	893	1,027	857	870	862	855	[6]-5	[6]15
Ohio	45,198	48,480	22,805	7,825	21,669	22,558	21,627	22,653	[6]109	[6]53
Oklahoma........	13,053	13,812	4,647	4,385	5,090	4,687	5,016	4,656	[6]75	[6]31
Oregon.........	18,889	18,404	3,804	4,073	4,692	3,969	5,760	3,912	-1,068	57
Pennsylvania......	43,728	47,280	20,714	15,334	20,572	20,679	20,429	20,715	143	[6]209
Rhode Island.....	5,264	5,536	2,701	1,708	2,691	2,735	2,650	2,699	[6]41	[6]36
South Carolina.....	14,894	15,000	5,437	4,978	5,219	5,040	5,168	4,995	50	46
South Dakota	2,444	2,490	868	1,011	867	891	850	884	[6]-	[6]-
Tennessee	18,549	19,960	8,239	7,732	7,593	8,126	7,516	8,026	[6]12	[6]21
Texas.........	56,714	59,049	29,920	19,176	32,393	31,064	29,890	30,389	[6]2,426	[6]83
Utah	7,248	7,362	3,436	1,829	3,734	3,560	3,733	3,521	[6]1	[6]18
Vermont........	2,889	(NA)	(NA)	(NA)	860	884	872	890	[6]-	[6]-
Virginia........	26,575	26,848	11,043	5,100	12,176	12,204	12,043	12,118	[6]133	[6]86
Washington.......	24,372	24,482	11,198	4,935	11,662	11,666	11,214	11,368	[6]437	[6]298
West Virginia.....	8,150	8,549	3,111	2,881	3,030	3,139	2,817	2,933	[6]197	[6]196
Wisconsin.......	31,177	23,503	11,092	5,688	11,352	10,772	11,259	11,033	54	-282
Wyoming	1,604	1,671	414	332	732	768	722	694	[6]10	[6]4

- Represents zero.   NA Not available.   [1] Estimated.   [2] Includes bonds and other state funds not shown separately.
[3] Includes funds budgeted, adjustments, and balances from previous year.   [4] May or may not include budget stabilization fund transfers, depending on state accounting practices.   [5] Resources less expenditures.   [6] Ending balance includes the balance in a budget stabilization fund.

Source: National Association of State Budget Officers, Washington, DC, *2002 State Expenditure Report*, and *State General Fund from NASBO*, Fiscal Survey of the States, semi-annual (copyright).

No. 440. State Governments—Summary of Finances: 1990 to 2001

[In millions of dollars (673,119 represents $673,119,000,000). For fiscal year ending in year shown; see text; this section]

Item	Total (million dollars)				Per capita [1] (dollars)			
	1990	1999	2000	2001	1990	1999	2000	2001
Borrowing and revenue	673,119	1,228,816	1,336,798	1,257,148	2,712	4,515	4,760	4,415
Borrowing	40,948	75,946	75,968	76,843	165	279	270	270
Revenue	632,172	1,152,870	1,260,829	1,180,305	2,547	4,236	4,489	4,145
General revenue	517,429	906,076	984,783	1,049,298	2,085	3,329	3,506	3,685
Taxes	300,489	499,943	539,655	559,679	1,211	1,837	1,922	1,966
Sales and gross receipts	147,069	239,367	252,147	258,018	593	879	898	906
General	99,702	164,378	174,461	179,319	402	604	621	630
Motor fuels	19,379	29,169	29,968	31,026	78	107	107	109
Alcoholic beverages	3,191	3,900	4,104	4,167	13	14	15	15
Tobacco products	5,541	8,170	8,391	8,644	22	30	30	30
Other	19,256	33,751	35,222	34,863	78	124	125	122
Licenses	18,842	30,440	32,598	32,866	76	112	116	115
Motor vehicles	9,848	14,083	15,099	15,141	40	52	54	53
Corporations in general	3,099	6,359	6,460	6,384	12	23	23	22
Other	5,895	9,998	11,039	11,341	24	37	39	40
Individual income	96,076	172,764	194,573	208,079	387	635	693	731
Corporation net income	21,751	30,766	32,522	31,687	88	113	116	111
Property	5,848	11,654	10,996	10,430	24	43	39	37
Other	10,902	14,952	16,819	18,597	44	55	60	65
Charges and miscellaneous	90,612	152,441	170,747	183,998	365	560	608	646
Intergovernmental revenue	126,329	253,692	274,382	305,621	509	932	977	1,073
From Federal Government	118,353	238,941	259,114	288,309	477	878	923	1,013
Public welfare	59,397	135,274	147,150	165,800	239	497	524	582
Education	21,271	38,738	42,086	45,760	86	142	150	161
Highways	13,931	20,874	23,790	27,894	56	77	85	98
Health and hospitals	5,475	13,205	14,223	16,426	22	49	51	58
Other	18,279	30,849	31,865	32,428	74	113	113	114
From local governments	7,976	14,751	15,268	17,312	32	54	54	61
Utility revenue	3,305	4,356	4,513	6,930	13	16	16	24
Liquor store revenue	2,907	3,599	3,895	4,092	12	13	14	14
Insurance trust revenue [2]	108,530	238,838	267,639	119,985	437	878	953	421
Employee retirement	78,898	201,500	230,166	79,527	318	740	820	279
Unemployment compensation	18,370	22,131	23,260	23,221	74	81	83	82
Expenditure and debt redemption	592,213	1,046,234	1,125,828	1,235,568	2,386	3,844	4,009	4,339
Expenditure	572,318	998,365	1,084,097	1,186,108	2,306	3,668	3,860	4,166
General expenditure	508,284	889,475	964,723	1,045,296	2,048	3,268	3,435	3,671
Education	184,935	318,602	346,465	374,444	745	1,171	1,234	1,315
Public welfare	104,971	221,167	238,890	262,346	423	813	851	921
Health	20,029	38,008	42,066	43,732	81	140	150	154
Hospitals	22,637	29,994	32,578	34,538	91	110	116	121
Highways	44,249	68,317	74,415	78,786	178	251	265	277
Police protection	5,166	8,794	9,788	10,145	21	32	35	36
Corrections	17,266	32,843	35,129	38,165	70	121	125	134
Natural resources	9,909	14,482	15,967	17,309	40	53	57	61
Housing and community development	2,856	4,000	4,726	5,009	12	15	17	18
Other and unallocable	96,267	153,269	164,698	180,823	388	563	586	635
Utility expenditure	7,131	8,779	10,723	18,632	29	32	38	65
Liquor store expenditure	2,452	2,967	3,195	3,347	10	11	11	12
Insurance trust expenditure [2]	54,452	97,144	105,456	118,833	219	357	375	417
Employee retirement	29,562	67,353	75,971	83,770	119	247	271	294
Unemployment compensation	16,423	19,160	18,583	22,920	66	70	66	80
By character and object:								
Intergovernmental expenditure	175,028	304,933	327,070	350,327	705	1,120	1,165	1,230
Direct expenditure	397,291	693,432	757,027	835,782	1,601	2,548	2,695	2,935
Current operation	258,046	476,968	523,114	580,374	1,040	1,752	1,863	2,038
Capital outlay	45,524	68,509	76,233	81,881	183	252	271	288
Construction	34,803	53,857	59,681	64,668	140	198	213	227
Land and existing structure	3,471	3,953	4,681	4,643	14	15	17	16
Equipment	7,250	10,699	11,871	12,570	29	39	42	44
Assistance and subsidies	16,902	22,229	22,136	23,496	68	82	79	83
Interest on debt	22,367	28,582	30,089	31,198	90	105	107	110
Insurance benefits [3]	54,452	97,144	105,456	118,833	219	357	375	417
Debt redemption	19,895	47,869	41,730	49,460	80	176	149	174
Debt outstanding	318,254	510,486	547,876	576,494	1,282	1,876	1,951	2,025
Long-term	315,490	507,819	541,497	572,831	1,271	1,866	1,928	2,012
Full-faith and credit	74,972	129,326	138,525	147,130	302	475	493	517
Nonguaranteed	240,518	378,493	402,972	425,701	969	1,391	1,435	1,495
Short-term	2,764	2,667	6,379	3,663	11	10	23	13
Net long-term [4]	125,524	249,432	266,870	287,450	506	916	950	1,010
Full-faith and credit only	63,481	119,511	128,384	137,341	256	439	457	482

[1] 1990 and 2000 based on enumerated resident population as of April 1. Other years based on estimated resident population as of July 1. [2] Includes other items not shown separately. [3] Includes repayments. [4] Less cash and investment assets specifically held for redemption of long-term debt.

Source: U.S. Census Bureau, 1990, *State Government Finances*, series GF, No. 3 thereafter,<http://www.census.gov/govs/www/state01.html> (accessed February, 2004).

U.S. Census Bureau, Statistical Abstract of the United States: 2004-2005

No. 441. State Governments—Revenue by State: 2001

[In millions of dollars (1,180,305 represents $1,180,305,000,000), except as noted. For fiscal year ending in year shown; see text, this section. Includes local shares of state imposed taxes.]

State	General revenue									Insurance trust revenue
	Total revenue [1]	Per capita [2]			Intergovernmental revenue		Charges and miscellaneous			
		Total	Total (dol.)	Rank	Total	From Federal government	Total	Current charges	Miscellaneous general revenue	
United States ..	1,180,305	1,049,298	3,685	(X)	305,621	288,309	183,998	93,051	90,947	119,985
Alabama	17,860	15,732	3,520	31	5,716	5,244	3,268	2,216	1,053	1,973
Alaska.........	6,186	6,043	9,532	1	1,290	1,285	3,325	351	2,974	117
Arizona	15,489	15,166	2,858	47	4,450	4,121	2,355	1,065	1,290	303
Arkansas	10,330	9,804	3,638	24	3,057	3,026	1,760	1,042	718	526
California......	176,081	148,977	4,306	13	40,145	37,771	18,378	10,325	8,053	25,332
Colorado	19,774	13,868	3,130	43	3,471	3,440	2,830	1,415	1,415	5,906
Connecticut	17,750	16,284	4,740	8	3,730	3,643	2,658	1,010	1,647	1,444
Delaware	5,114	4,459	5,595	2	901	869	1,452	614	838	646
Florida........	46,371	44,198	2,699	50	11,839	11,737	7,420	2,411	5,009	2,166
Georgia........	25,250	25,411	3,023	45	7,392	7,309	3,651	1,744	1,907	-161
Hawaii.........	6,591	6,045	4,927	5	1,214	1,212	1,324	858	465	546
Idaho	5,286	4,559	3,451	33	1,232	1,226	768	383	385	666
Illinois	47,348	40,227	3,213	41	11,027	10,059	6,049	2,359	3,691	7,122
Indiana	20,767	19,738	3,221	40	5,596	5,442	4,026	2,407	1,619	1,029
Iowa	10,255	10,329	3,523	30	2,892	2,765	2,278	1,374	905	-186
Kansas	8,713	9,027	3,341	39	2,659	2,624	1,380	676	705	-313
Kentucky	18,550	15,176	3,730	23	4,563	4,546	2,762	1,522	1,240	3,375
Louisiana.......	17,811	16,810	3,761	21	5,280	5,225	4,333	2,258	2,075	998
Maine	5,207	5,400	4,205	14	1,626	1,619	1,105	403	702	-272
Maryland	20,939	19,042	3,535	29	4,764	4,618	3,493	1,813	1,680	1,801
Massachusetts ...	29,304	29,288	4,575	9	6,097	5,729	5,966	1,926	4,040	-90
Michigan	43,347	40,619	4,060	16	10,694	10,452	7,662	4,266	3,396	2,135
Minnesota	26,135	21,750	4,363	12	4,981	4,873	3,235	1,472	1,763	4,385
Mississippi......	11,693	10,320	3,608	25	3,856	3,727	1,714	1,082	633	1,204
Missouri........	20,134	17,528	3,109	44	5,612	5,563	3,078	1,448	1,630	2,606
Montana	4,224	3,602	3,981	19	1,318	1,297	788	356	432	581
Nebraska.......	5,944	5,875	3,415	34	1,627	1,602	1,210	567	643	69
Nevada.......	6,644	5,776	2,753	49	1,162	1,097	782	457	326	717
New Hampshire ..	4,575	4,000	3,177	42	1,258	1,081	986	470	515	269
New Jersey	42,788	34,373	4,039	18	8,595	8,170	6,525	3,363	3,162	7,890
New Mexico.....	9,099	8,753	4,780	7	2,453	2,395	2,298	762	1,536	346
New York.......	112,439	91,802	4,810	6	35,575	29,066	11,368	4,952	6,416	17,651
North Carolina ...	32,203	29,392	3,582	28	9,547	8,760	4,245	2,639	1,607	2,811
North Dakota	3,373	2,840	4,459	11	999	975	677	460	217	533
Ohio	52,803	38,196	3,353	38	11,770	11,526	6,807	3,844	2,963	14,100
Oklahoma	12,746	12,193	3,514	32	3,540	3,443	2,312	1,375	937	221
Oregon	18,219	14,196	4,088	15	5,044	4,983	3,260	1,726	1,534	3,781
Pennsylvania	45,887	44,181	3,591	26	12,597	12,249	9,011	5,249	3,762	796
Rhode Island	5,485	4,766	4,497	10	1,549	1,474	971	361	610	706
South Carolina ...	16,865	13,873	3,415	35	4,793	4,373	2,665	1,923	741	2,130
South Dakota	3,171	2,584	3,409	36	1,034	1,018	573	225	348	587
Tennessee......	17,344	17,041	2,964	46	6,807	6,594	2,191	1,476	715	303
Texas	65,525	60,596	2,835	48	18,734	18,074	12,440	5,865	6,575	4,929
Utah..........	9,132	8,171	3,585	27	2,065	2,052	2,034	1,305	728	838
Vermont	3,143	3,107	5,068	4	976	934	578	313	265	4
Virginia	22,760	24,194	3,362	37	4,857	4,718	6,251	3,523	2,727	-1,753
Washington	23,646	22,418	3,741	22	5,909	5,800	3,830	2,332	1,499	885
West Virginia	8,297	6,959	3,864	20	2,201	2,163	1,335	663	673	1,287
Wisconsin	18,826	21,884	4,048	17	6,118	5,363	3,997	2,290	1,707	-3,058
Wyoming.......	2,880	2,727	5,520	3	1,009	974	593	115	478	106

See footnotes at end of table.

State and Local Government Finances and Employment   283

No. 441. State Governments—Revenue by State: 2001—Con.

[See headnote, page 283]

State	All taxes				Sales and gross receipts taxes						
		Per capita [2]					Selective sales taxes [3]				
	Total [3]	Total (dol.)	Rank	Property taxes	Total [3]	General sales taxes, total	Total [3]	Alcoholic beverages and tobacco sales	Insurance premiums	Motor fuels sales	Public utilities
United States..	559,679	1,966	(X)	10,430	258,018	179,319	78,699	12,810	10,264	31,026	8,96...
Alabama	6,748	1,510	46	183	3,298	1,713	1,585	195	203	503	52...
Alaska.	1,429	2,253	11	45	135	-	135	59	32	38	:
Arizona	8,360	1,575	43	312	4,864	3,825	1,039	212	188	604	3:
Arkansas	4,987	1,850	23	434	2,471	1,810	661	126	83	401	
California	90,454	2,614	6	3,322	30,750	24,298	6,452	1,439	1,497	3,142	26.
Colorado	7,567	1,708	36	-	2,887	1,970	917	98	145	571	
Connecticut	9,896	2,881	1	-	4,555	3,159	1,396	160	180	409	18
Delaware	2,106	2,642	5	-	295	-	295	39	58	99	3.
Florida	24,939	1,523	45	499	19,004	14,716	4,288	988	388	1,732	65
Georgia	14,369	1,709	35	51	6,039	4,907	1,132	222	245	665	
Hawaii.	3,508	2,859	2	-	2,198	1,640	558	93	74	77	13...
Idaho	2,558	1,936	19	-	1,092	782	310	35	61	208	:
Illinois	23,150	1,849	24	59	10,955	6,320	4,635	613	257	1,367	1,52:
Indiana	10,116	1,651	40	5	5,031	3,606	1,425	118	148	665	
Iowa	5,159	1,759	33	-	2,510	1,756	754	108	127	354	
Kansas	4,987	1,846	25	52	2,327	1,745	582	131	77	362	:
Kentucky	7,851	1,929	20	413	3,612	2,259	1,353	87	244	449	
Louisiana.	7,197	1,610	41	25	4,104	2,400	1,704	149	247	539	:
Maine	2,669	2,079	17	48	1,177	818	359	115	46	189	
Maryland	10,786	2,003	18	262	4,592	2,647	1,945	230	191	687	14.
Massachusetts . . .	17,225	2,691	4	-	5,260	3,756	1,504	335	333	660	
Michigan	22,264	2,225	12	1,790	9,882	7,723	2,160	733	201	1,075	2:
Minnesota	13,535	2,715	3	10	5,863	3,771	2,092	244	186	608	
Mississippi	4,749	1,661	38	1	3,137	2,326	812	95	121	405	:
Missouri.	8,837	1,568	44	19	4,025	2,805	1,220	134	193	676	
Montana	1,496	1,653	39	204	352	-	352	31	46	183	3:
Nebraska.	3,037	1,766	32	5	1,447	1,032	415	62	34	291	
Nevada	3,832	1,827	29	99	3,287	2,049	1,238	83	147	249	:
New Hampshire . .	1,756	1,394	48	458	574	-	574	98	61	119	58
New Jersey	19,253	2,262	10	3	8,506	5,759	2,748	477	323	516	851
New Mexico	4,002	2,186	13	40	2,083	1,620	463	53	45	200	12
New York.	44,858	2,351	8	-	13,094	8,779	4,315	1,199	611	513	927
North Carolina . . .	15,600	1,901	21	-	6,215	3,456	2,759	242	312	1,183	422
North Dakota	1,164	1,828	27	3	621	340	281	27	22	112	39
Ohio	19,618	1,722	34	25	8,966	6,288	2,678	363	350	1,307	641
Oklahoma	6,342	1,828	28	-	2,272	1,536	737	136	154	401	20
Oregon	5,893	1,697	37	-	668	-	668	190	62	406	8
Pennsylvania	22,572	1,835	26	58	10,666	7,238	3,428	509	472	1,706	684
Rhode Island	2,247	2,119	15	1	1,119	696	423	69	37	130	81
South Carolina . . .	6,415	1,579	42	14	3,275	2,500	775	159	88	365	44
South Dakota	977	1,290	50	-	757	515	242	30	43	122	2
Tennessee	8,043	1,399	47	-	6,062	4,704	1,358	160	296	775	4
Texas	29,423	1,377	49	-	23,304	14,708	8,597	1,126	767	2,766	673
Utah	4,073	1,787	31	-	1,980	1,480	500	73	74	325	2
Vermont	1,553	2,533	7	367	529	214	315	42	21	66	10
Virginia	13,085	1,818	30	31	4,576	2,643	1,933	143	268	847	97
Washington	12,679	2,116	16	1,399	10,056	8,067	1,989	434	280	736	332
West Virginia	3,423	1,901	22	4	1,839	928	911	40	115	237	193
Wisconsin	11,768	2,177	14	80	5,209	3,610	1,599	300	99	920	274
Wyoming	1,124	2,276	9	110	494	406	88	6	13	66	2

See footnotes at end of table.

U.S. Census Bureau, Statistical Abstract of the United States: 2004-2005

No. 441. State Governments—Revenue by State: 2001—Con.

[See headnote, page 283]

State	License taxes					Income			Other taxes	
	Total [3]	Corpo- ration license	Hunt- ing and fishing license	Motor vehicle and opera- tors license	Occu- pancy and busi- ness license, n.e.c. [4]	Total	Indi- vidual income	Corpo- ration net income	Total [3]	Death and gift
United States............	32,866	6,384	1,139	16,471	7,511	239,767	208,079	31,687	18,597	7,499
Alabama.................	433	82	15	206	117	2,639	2,438	202	195	47
Alaska..................	73	1	25	34	12	400	-	400	775	3
Arizona.................	258	11	18	159	61	2,845	2,304	541	81	77
Arkansas................	252	10	21	127	77	1,766	1,564	202	63	26
California...............	3,909	45	76	1,943	1,727	51,514	44,614	6,899	959	935
Colorado................	301	6	53	190	46	4,233	3,893	340	145	83
Connecticut.............	353	13	3	248	79	4,617	4,230	388	370	258
Delaware................	832	587	1	35	183	879	720	159	101	41
Florida.................	1,549	124	13	1,083	255	1,591	-	1,591	2,296	708
Georgia.................	506	33	22	281	80	7,618	6,926	691	155	126
Hawaii..................	116	3	-	82	21	1,166	1,105	60	28	18
Idaho..................	248	1	29	138	43	1,173	1,031	142	45	43
Illinois................	1,832	152	24	1,363	283	9,886	7,669	2,217	419	361
Indiana................	311	6	14	213	64	4,605	3,780	825	164	164
Iowa...................	496	29	19	351	71	2,056	1,889	167	97	88
Kansas.................	227	28	16	154	22	2,225	1,988	237	155	41
Kentucky...............	552	204	20	196	117	3,011	2,650	361	263	85
Louisiana...............	478	253	33	114	72	2,043	1,750	293	547	83
Maine..................	138	3	11	81	36	1,258	1,162	96	49	31
Maryland...............	399	14	12	205	165	5,225	4,724	501	308	169
Massachusetts...........	496	23	5	313	94	11,114	9,903	1,212	355	203
Michigan...............	1,229	12	48	884	213	8,892	6,790	2,102	470	155
Minnesota..............	810	4	48	526	209	6,638	5,906	732	214	53
Mississippi.............	304	66	11	147	65	1,244	1,033	211	63	28
Missouri...............	587	77	28	284	160	4,051	3,815	236	154	154
Montana................	125	1	31	56	29	660	556	104	155	20
Nebraska...............	183	6	12	88	58	1,365	1,227	138	36	27
Nevada.................	373	23	6	125	122	-	-	-	73	40
New Hampshire..........	145	4	6	75	50	427	77	350	151	59
New Jersey.............	853	146	13	445	184	9,290	7,989	1,301	600	478
New Mexico.............	160	2	12	114	30	1,021	830	191	698	23
New York...............	865	66	22	603	105	29,642	26,443	3,199	1,257	759
North Carolina..........	956	398	14	461	72	8,250	7,526	724	179	143
North Dakota............	94	-	9	51	34	277	213	63	170	5
Ohio...................	1,483	297	27	628	500	8,969	8,306	663	174	166
Oklahoma...............	806	43	14	588	151	2,447	2,279	167	817	85
Oregon.................	416	5	36	237	120	4,707	4,384	323	103	42
Pennsylvania............	2,181	877	61	812	356	8,544	7,155	1,389	1,122	777
Rhode Island............	91	11	2	51	26	1,006	928	78	30	27
South Carolina..........	347	56	15	125	124	2,691	2,499	192	89	49
South Dakota............	140	2	21	50	58	43	-	43	37	35
Tennessee..............	878	480	25	263	97	872	198	673	232	84
Texas..................	3,751	2,031	65	1,063	510	-	-	-	2,367	322
Utah...................	143	3	22	91	24	1,868	1,705	163	82	30
Vermont................	78	1	6	41	28	528	484	45	50	13
Virginia................	536	29	19	344	131	7,590	7,226	364	353	127
Washington.............	627	15	35	342	181	-	-	-	597	106
West Virginia...........	153	6	16	81	29	1,235	1,021	214	192	18
Wisconsin..............	702	88	59	324	218	5,644	5,149	495	133	77
Wyoming................	91	7	25	53	5	-	-	-	429	8

- Represents or rounds to zero.   X Not applicable.   [1] Duplicate intergovernmental transactions are excluded.   [2] Based on population as of April 1.   [3] Includes categories not shown separately.   [4] n.e.c. means not elsewhere classified.

Source: U.S. Census Bureau, <http://www.census.gov/govs/www/state01.html> (accessed January 2004).

State and Local Government Finances and Employment   285

[In millions of dollars (1,186,108 represents $1,186,108,000,000) except as indicated. For fiscal year ending in year shown; see text, this section]

State	General expenditure									
	Total				Direct expenditures					
	Total expendi-ture [1]	Amount	Per capita [2] (dol.)	Inter-govern-mental	Total	Educa-tion	Public welfare	Health and hospitals	High-ways	Police protec-tion
United States..	1,186,108	1,045,296	3,671	350,327	694,969	152,351	220,419	61,754	66,436	8,868
Alabama	16,718	15,056	3,369	3,893	11,163	3,002	3,776	1,706	976	95
Alaska.	9,047	8,389	13,232	987	7,402	789	904	130	646	50
Arizona	17,143	15,528	2,926	6,439	9,089	2,191	2,646	684	1,056	146
Arkansas	10,597	9,848	3,654	2,942	6,906	1,777	2,215	650	776	77
California.	170,470	145,582	4,208	69,747	75,835	16,465	21,100	6,507	4,939	1,090
Colorado	15,686	13,702	3,092	3,909	9,793	2,802	2,504	427	1,070	92
Connecticut	18,189	16,098	4,686	3,253	12,845	2,061	3,271	1,520	723	156
Delaware.	4,312	3,952	4,959	788	3,164	669	607	293	333	63
Florida.	50,265	46,595	2,846	15,011	31,585	4,744	10,893	2,776	4,340	394
Georgia.	27,860	25,662	3,053	8,383	17,279	4,783	5,801	1,178	1,717	255
Hawaii.	6,792	6,145	5,008	124	6,020	2,192	1,024	552	233	5
Idaho	4,952	4,426	3,351	1,363	3,063	694	923	132	384	41
Illinois	45,170	40,245	3,214	12,770	27,475	5,143	9,257	3,085	2,553	355
Indiana	21,584	20,255	3,306	7,052	13,203	4,266	4,060	706	1,396	237
Iowa	12,271	11,199	3,819	3,284	7,914	1,988	2,549	859	931	84
Kansas	10,197	9,406	3,481	2,954	6,452	1,576	1,622	497	1,067	53
Kentucky	17,331	15,636	3,843	3,620	12,016	2,683	4,346	785	1,586	167
Louisiana.	16,410	14,470	3,237	3,801	10,669	2,570	2,720	1,806	827	188
Maine	5,738	5,212	4,059	976	4,236	631	1,636	360	422	51
Maryland	21,484	19,244	3,573	5,004	14,240	3,010	4,294	1,133	1,049	247
Massachusetts . . .	32,435	29,488	4,607	6,886	22,602	2,988	6,943	2,301	2,416	267
Michigan	46,658	42,252	4,223	18,145	24,107	6,706	8,663	1,879	1,490	284
Minnesota	24,612	21,959	4,405	8,197	13,762	3,375	5,303	558	960	149
Mississippi	11,727	10,610	3,710	3,354	7,256	1,533	2,662	915	669	70
Missouri.	18,888	17,123	3,038	4,802	12,321	2,412	4,575	1,299	1,301	142
Montana	4,048	3,619	3,999	864	2,756	616	580	264	411	26
Nebraska.	6,111	5,843	3,397	1,684	4,158	1,079	1,496	280	477	53
Nevada	6,747	5,871	2,798	2,272	3,600	876	815	255	563	62
New Hampshire . .	4,411	3,890	3,090	1,041	2,850	558	965	156	333	40
New Jersey	37,660	30,477	3,581	9,082	21,395	4,836	4,796	2,042	1,942	399
New Mexico	9,174	8,399	4,587	2,562	5,837	1,340	1,746	692	692	87
New York.	106,599	89,237	4,676	34,713	54,524	7,346	21,867	4,529	3,377	436
North Carolina . . .	31,627	28,860	3,517	9,310	19,551	4,580	6,002	1,791	2,451	334
North Dakota	2,898	2,673	4,197	569	2,104	538	598	78	258	10
Ohio	47,880	39,035	3,427	14,594	24,441	6,204	8,291	2,090	2,154	217
Oklahoma	13,468	11,849	3,415	3,486	8,363	2,237	2,700	488	1,028	81
Oregon	16,321	13,546	3,900	4,028	9,519	1,673	3,257	1,188	583	144
Pennsylvania	51,488	45,517	3,700	13,121	32,396	7,099	12,005	2,036	3,187	814
Rhode Island . . .	5,261	4,564	4,305	711	3,852	615	1,365	273	249	46
South Carolina . . .	18,079	15,675	3,859	4,168	11,506	2,576	3,851	1,444	1,152	202
South Dakota	2,690	2,492	3,287	481	2,011	341	554	111	429	19
Tennessee	18,385	17,136	2,981	4,583	12,553	2,858	5,598	1,070	1,170	120
Texas	64,686	58,183	2,723	17,204	40,979	9,997	12,590	4,149	4,794	331
Utah	9,253	8,489	3,725	2,101	6,388	2,073	1,426	653	745	78
Vermont	3,371	3,200	5,221	920	2,281	489	754	87	202	42
Virginia	26,787	24,869	3,456	7,869	17,000	4,284	3,904	2,144	2,386	224
Washington	27,824	23,597	3,938	6,577	17,021	4,532	5,479	2,015	1,127	162
West Virginia	7,300	6,165	3,423	988	5,177	1,020	1,565	211	1,187	38
Wisconsin	24,857	21,694	4,013	8,896	12,798	3,250	3,594	873	1,208	122
Wyoming	2,645	2,331	4,718	819	1,512	280	328	98	326	22

See footnotes at end of table.

U.S. Census Bureau, Statistical Abstract of the United States: 2004-2005

No. 442. State Governments—Expenditures and Debt by State: 2001—Con.

[See headnote, page 286]

State	General expenditure—Con. Direct expenditures—Con.					Utility expenditures	Liquor stores expenditures	Insurance trust expenditures	Debt outstanding		
	Corrections	Natural resources	Parks and recreation	Governmental administration	Interest on general debt				Cash and security holdings	Total	Per capita [2] (dol.)
United States..	35,811	16,103	4,530	36,916	30,452	18,632	3,347	118,833	2,537,722	576,494	2,025
Alabama	304	205	16	381	268	-	156	1,506	28,094	5,577	1,249
Alaska	173	254	9	353	264	59	-	599	43,846	4,507	7,124
Arizona	668	173	41	434	192	25	-	1,590	37,541	3,711	700
Arkansas	277	192	73	376	125	-	749	17,840	2,842	1,056	
California	5,055	2,508	406	5,901	2,759	7,919	-	16,969	324,516	62,343	1,805
Colorado	616	213	56	393	320	8	-	1,976	36,841	4,917	1,110
Connecticut	603	116	39	822	1,106	243	-	1,849	29,312	19,027	5,543
Delaware	248	80	49	312	189	68	-	292	11,287	3,889	4,888
Florida	2,248	1,536	164	1,895	1,062	49	-	3,620	103,314	18,613	1,138
Georgia	971	453	140	569	438	1	-	2,197	60,970	7,520	896
Hawaii	149	91	46	324	318	-	-	647	13,478	5,301	4,327
Idaho	157	148	28	205	140	-	48	477	11,468	2,342	1,772
Illinois	1,318	411	144	1,210	1,987	-	-	4,925	89,510	30,248	2,416
Indiana	594	223	71	599	408	-	-	1,328	33,417	8,518	1,390
Iowa	235	265	19	452	134	-	79	994	23,064	2,542	867
Kansas	285	155	5	625	120	-	-	791	12,416	2,184	809
Kentucky	439	305	151	506	454	-	-	1,695	34,512	8,348	2,052
Louisiana	442	332	198	461	455	4	-	1,936	36,100	7,977	1,786
Maine	95	136	10	263	238	-	55	471	11,775	4,211	3,278
Maryland	964	383	194	830	852	419	-	1,822	42,038	11,661	2,166
Massachusetts	861	264	105	1,262	2,372	298	-	2,649	63,254	42,149	6,586
Michigan	1,614	458	117	760	1,059	-	485	3,920	78,142	20,114	2,010
Minnesota	310	462	107	675	337	-	-	2,654	53,465	5,624	1,128
Mississippi	260	213	73	203	189	-	137	981	23,110	3,819	1,337
Missouri	592	286	38	502	583	-	-	1,765	44,991	11,373	2,018
Montana	107	217	11	204	146	-	35	393	9,757	2,740	3,024
Nebraska	176	143	25	165	116	-	-	269	9,285	1,800	1,047
Nevada	235	76	17	193	254	169	-	707	18,527	3,387	1,617
New Hampshire	83	38	6	181	252	-	263	258	9,255	5,608	4,454
New Jersey	1,128	313	419	1,240	1,189	1,886	-	5,297	85,791	29,728	3,496
New Mexico	223	130	45	336	190	-	-	775	33,072	4,305	2,353
New York	2,424	421	500	3,885	3,684	6,143	-	11,219	221,203	80,385	4,214
North Carolina	935	549	158	815	558	-	-	2,767	73,325	9,998	1,220
North Dakota	35	93	11	95	86	-	-	225	6,778	1,549	2,435
Ohio	1,436	340	78	1,156	1,039	-	322	8,524	156,986	18,748	1,647
Oklahoma	474	192	70	408	252	299	-	1,320	24,582	5,986	1,726
Oregon	471	291	52	830	409	4	121	2,649	35,097	6,418	1,848
Pennsylvania	1,500	623	152	1,324	1,107	-	840	5,131	104,571	19,249	1,565
Rhode Island	151	42	39	275	355	77	-	620	12,180	5,727	5,408
South Carolina	480	273	63	547	291	900	-	1,504	26,854	9,560	2,355
South Dakota	66	87	24	100	124	-	-	199	7,712	2,216	2,922
Tennessee	374	223	112	426	194	5	-	1,245	29,045	3,388	590
Texas	2,976	609	80	1,454	1,014	-	-	6,503	176,317	16,816	788
Utah	266	153	25	428	196	-	91	673	18,105	4,023	1,765
Vermont	72	78	13	203	125	4	31	135	4,679	2,326	3,794
Virginia	955	215	120	878	848	26	288	1,603	55,169	12,963	1,802
Washington	729	555	75	484	658	16	310	3,900	63,796	12,607	2,104
West Virginia	122	146	58	314	217	4	44	1,087	10,313	4,092	2,271
Wisconsin	839	324	58	578	706	-	-	3,163	71,507	12,172	2,252
Wyoming	80	108	19	81	73	7	41	267	9,516	1,346	2,727

- Represents or rounds to zero. [1] Includes amounts not shown separately. [2] Based on estimated resident population as of July 1.

Source: U.S. Census Bureau, <http://www.census.gov/govs/www/state01.html> (accessed January 2004).

State and Local Government Finances and Employment 287

No. 443. Local Governments—Revenue by State: 2000

[In millions of dollars (1,013,825 represents $1,013,825,000,000), except as noted. For fiscal year ending in year shown; see text, this section]

State	Total revenue [1]	General revenue Total	General revenue Per capita [2] (dol.)	Intergovernmental revenue Total	Intergovernmental revenue From federal government	Intergovernmental revenue From state governments	Taxes Total [1]	Taxes Property	Taxes Sales and gross receipts	Taxes Income [3]	Taxes Motor licenses
United States. .	**1,013,825**	**888,865**	**3,158**	**349,894**	**32,836**	**317,058**	**332,696**	**238,182**	**57,143**	**20,625**	**1,302**
Alabama	13,046	11,071	2,490	4,482	343	4,139	2,977	1,160	1,358	88	21
Alaska	2,835	2,606	4,156	1,103	213	890	889	717	146	-	11
Arizona	17,365	14,507	2,827	6,257	635	5,622	5,233	3,609	1,427	-	-
Arkansas.	5,718	5,138	1,922	2,763	116	2,647	1,091	484	584	-	-
California.	160,439	135,131	3,989	64,891	4,821	60,070	36,260	22,904	10,075	-	-
Colorado	15,789	13,756	3,198	3,656	431	3,224	6,141	3,680	2,139	-	34
Connecticut	11,190	10,245	3,008	3,648	286	3,361	5,480	5,407	-	-	-
Delaware.	1,921	1,729	2,206	863	42	821	486	382	8	41	-
District of Columbia.	6,383	5,732	10,022	1,748	1,748	-	3,216	693	1,000	1,339	17
Florida	55,505	48,923	3,061	16,171	1,813	14,358	17,119	13,336	3,133	-	28
Georgia	27,036	23,651	2,889	7,967	659	7,307	9,742	5,884	3,552	-	-
Hawaii	1,703	1,519	1,253	322	170	152	767	603	89	-	51
Idaho	3,294	3,155	2,438	1,357	80	1,276	917	867	15	-	4
Illinois.	45,243	38,734	3,119	13,649	1,516	12,134	17,467	14,457	2,517	-	95
Indiana	18,046	16,679	2,743	6,004	377	5,627	6,259	5,548	76	515	2
Iowa.	9,053	8,414	2,876	3,327	254	3,073	2,905	2,599	219	38	13
Kansas	8,705	7,694	2,862	2,945	117	2,828	2,768	2,125	582	-	2
Kentucky	8,723	7,749	1,917	3,229	276	2,953	2,478	1,333	174	747	17
Louisiana	12,153	11,302	2,529	4,117	340	3,776	4,375	1,717	2,508	-	4
Maine	3,197	3,103	2,433	1,011	83	928	1,601	1,568	4	-	13
Maryland.	16,866	15,401	2,908	4,727	587	4,140	7,935	4,553	261	2,541	-
Massachusetts . . .	21,422	18,206	2,868	7,982	1,011	6,971	7,889	7,642	96	-	-
Michigan	36,411	32,736	3,294	16,772	1,163	15,609	8,718	7,796	121	539	1
Minnesota	19,251	17,340	3,525	7,673	389	7,285	4,834	4,556	133	-	4
Mississippi.	7,401	6,864	2,413	2,968	179	2,790	1,588	1,461	55	-	-
Missouri	15,641	13,734	2,455	4,687	423	4,264	5,742	3,386	1,801	299	12
Montana	2,132	2,054	2,277	794	119	674	721	689	2	-	13
Nebraska	6,877	4,726	2,762	1,553	169	1,384	1,992	1,545	245	-	19
Nevada.	7,113	6,631	3,319	2,688	234	2,454	2,108	1,345	432	-	-
New Hampshire . .	3,205	3,129	2,531	1,155	68	1,087	1,582	1,554	-	-	-
New Jersey	29,133	28,409	3,376	9,281	572	8,709	14,690	14,446	30	33	-
New Mexico.	5,011	4,683	2,575	2,720	266	2,454	1,057	586	427	-	-
New York	115,278	96,904	5,107	34,497	3,043	31,454	45,132	25,202	9,158	8,721	151
North Carolina . . .	26,160	23,349	2,901	10,440	996	9,444	6,125	4,607	1,260	-	17
North Dakota	1,791	1,707	2,659	714	152	562	596	525	59	-	-
Ohio.	37,394	35,444	3,122	13,452	1,091	12,362	14,562	9,522	1,294	3,210	107
Oklahoma	8,524	7,795	2,259	3,014	219	2,795	2,411	1,303	1,054	-	2
Oregon	11,786	11,024	3,222	4,702	608	4,094	3,466	2,789	185	-	8
Pennsylvania	38,472	35,359	2,879	14,358	1,993	12,364	14,114	9,949	376	2,514	-
Rhode Island	2,486	2,290	2,185	681	106	575	1,377	1,359	2	-	-
South Carolina . . .	10,948	9,857	2,457	3,444	322	3,122	3,162	2,667	239	-	16
South Dakota	1,821	1,653	2,189	520	88	432	808	632	141	-	18
Tennessee.	18,778	13,018	2,288	4,323	355	3,968	4,692	2,887	1,511	-	94
Texas	65,510	57,393	2,752	18,591	2,014	16,578	24,802	19,817	4,366	-	275
Utah.	6,633	5,418	2,426	2,190	294	1,895	1,894	1,303	506	-	-
Vermont	1,580	1,406	2,309	838	26	812	392	377	1	-	-
Virginia	21,172	19,125	2,702	6,950	696	6,254	8,435	5,952	1,618	-	121
Washington	22,703	19,119	3,244	7,584	733	6,851	6,166	3,795	1,797	-	121
West Virginia	3,777	3,631	2,008	1,692	124	1,568	1,019	852	36	-	-
Wisconsin	19,137	17,642	3,289	8,578	426	8,152	5,971	5,602	226	-	1
Wyoming.	2,070	1,979	4,005	817	47	769	541	411	107	-	9

See footnotes at end of table.

[See headnote, page 288]

State	Current charges & miscellaneous general revenue	Current charges				Miscellaneous general revenue			Utility revenue	Liquor store revenue	Insurance trust revenue
		Total ¹	Education	Hospital	Sewerage	Total ¹	Interest earnings	Special assessment			
United States.....	206,275	137,013	15,630	36,036	24,273	69,262	35,482	3,734	80,441	697	43,822
Alabama.........	3,612	2,736	265	1,669	232	876	443	9	1,744	-	231
Alaska..........	614	398	37	52	47	216	155	3	204	-	25
Arizona.........	3,017	1,785	355	219	294	1,232	686	62	2,634	-	224
Arkansas........	1,284	862	135	313	152	422	241	11	535	-	45
California........	33,981	21,471	1,565	4,173	3,143	12,510	5,727	937	13,623	-	11,685
Colorado........	3,959	2,648	286	570	399	1,311	657	66	1,424	-	609
Connecticut......	1,117	648	77	15	191	469	235	28	474	-	471
Delaware........	381	245	13	-	108	136	74	-	147	-	45
District of Columbia...	769	331	21	53	101	438	196	-	448	-	202
Florida..........	15,632	10,506	1,255	2,806	1,458	5,126	2,639	950	5,056	-	1,526
Georgia.........	5,942	3,976	224	1,805	621	1,966	1,025	19	2,826	-	559
Hawaii..........	430	280	-	-	138	150	78	14	185	-	-
Idaho..........	881	709	52	336	86	172	76	11	137	-	3
Illinois..........	7,617	4,732	886	486	703	2,885	1,580	89	2,682	-	3,828
Indiana.........	4,416	3,008	287	1,705	495	1,408	480	19	1,307	-	60
Iowa...........	2,183	1,625	438	631	229	558	269	18	620	-	19
Kansas.........	1,981	1,253	230	413	179	728	455	62	802	-	210
Kentucky........	2,042	1,000	104	141	250	1,042	883	3	962	-	13
Louisiana........	2,810	1,975	66	1,199	200	835	565	9	720	-	131
Maine..........	490	358	42	51	114	132	66	3	94	-	-
Maryland........	2,739	1,768	471	-	540	971	481	108	409	142	913
Massachusetts......	2,335	1,681	192	159	636	654	310	64	1,911	-	1,305
Michigan........	7,247	4,467	747	568	1,239	2,780	1,087	94	1,414	94	2,262
Minnesota.......	4,832	2,909	226	766	581	1,923	845	252	1,181	202	528
Mississippi.......	2,308	1,801	201	1,237	135	507	245	5	537	-	-
Missouri.........	3,305	2,355	428	758	385	950	535	20	1,273	-	634
Montana........	539	329	53	52	55	210	103	42	78	-	-
Nebraska........	1,181	799	164	229	108	382	202	31	2,019	-	132
Nevada.........	1,835	1,346	83	478	209	489	305	29	482	-	-
New Hampshire	391	293	37	-	74	98	53	1	75	-	1
New Jersey.......	4,437	2,793	527	210	1,005	1,644	620	14	713	-	11
New Mexico.......	906	551	73	127	97	355	222	9	328	-	-
New York.........	17,275	12,235	726	3,052	1,301	5,040	2,133	72	6,069	-	12,305
North Carolina.....	6,784	5,274	461	2,677	855	1,510	840	12	2,425	343	43
North Dakota......	397	195	40	-	28	202	76	33	70	-	14
Ohio...........	7,430	4,765	907	789	1,396	2,665	1,438	106	1,886	-	63
Oklahoma........	2,369	1,719	243	772	199	650	341	5	664	-	65
Oregon.........	2,856	1,909	332	304	432	947	447	71	761	-	1
Pennsylvania......	6,888	3,886	549	20	990	3,002	2,055	95	1,837	-	1,276
Rhode Island......	231	153	18	-	52	78	38	3	103	-	93
South Carolina.....	3,251	2,529	192	1,470	216	722	467	19	1,087	-	4
South Dakota......	324	217	40	26	44	107	64	6	135	10	23
Tennessee........	4,004	2,910	182	1,541	398	1,094	485	5	5,241	-	518
Texas..........	13,999	9,350	1,372	2,376	1,791	4,649	3,084	87	6,212	-	1,905
Utah...........	1,334	738	66	36	150	596	270	3	1,216	-	-
Vermont	176	98	16	-	32	78	25	5	153	-	20
Virginia	3,741	2,509	255	251	681	1,232	707	42	1,143	-	904
Washington.......	5,369	3,681	251	807	843	1,688	663	93	3,321	-	263
West Virginia......	921	577	35	244	118	344	248	3	129	-	16
Wisconsin........	3,093	2,145	363	116	513	948	473	87	863	-	632
Wyoming........	621	484	44	334	31	137	91	8	87	-	4

- Represents or rounds to zero.   ¹ Includes items not shown separately.   ² Based on enumerated resident population as of April 1.   ³ Represents individual and corporate income taxes.

Source: U.S. Census Bureau; "Government Finances 1999-2000;" issued January 2003, <http://www.census.gov/govs/estimate /00allpub.pdf>;(accessed 16 June 2003).

No. 444. Local Governments—Expenditures and Debt by State: 2000

[In millions of dollars, (996,267 represents $996,267,000,000), except as indicated. For fiscal year ending in year shown; see text, this section]

State	Total expenditure [1]	Total amount	Per capita [2] (dol)	Direct general expenditures	Education	Public welfare	Health	Hospitals	Highways	Police protection	Fire protection
					General expenditure — Selected functions (direct expenditures)						
United States.....	996,267	875,495	3,540	865,114	383,282	34,666	23,991	43,822	39,394	48,217	23,102
Alabama..........	13,357	11,574	3,004	11,571	4,961	41	268	1,762	605	564	252
Alaska...........	2,931	2,655	4,675	2,655	1,115	7	58	58	197	127	66
Arizona..........	17,092	14,351	3,331	14,177	5,844	465	175	369	647	951	682
Arkansas.........	5,381	4,818	2,013	4,816	2,598	13	28	270	255	279	122
California........	150,813	128,033	4,452	126,953	48,542	10,704	5,275	5,823	4,373	7,653	3,588
Colorado........	15,943	13,745	3,707	13,745	5,287	520	200	721	780	753	327
Connecticut......	10,660	9,935	3,130	9,926	5,218	96	104	20	436	542	373
Delaware.........	1,800	1,637	2,296	1,634	1,005	1	13	-	103	103	19
District of Columbia ...	6,527	5,152	11,411	5,152	969	1,254	274	359	38	330	113
Florida..........	53,358	47,070	3,339	46,878	18,672	440	476	3,560	1,632	3,371	1,630
Georgia.........	25,931	22,214	3,168	22,166	10,595	99	717	1,826	918	1,086	553
Hawaii...........	1,792	1,474	1,479	1,474	-	21	28	-	127	218	101
Idaho..........	3,192	3,070	2,467	3,067	1,481	29	52	330	204	170	77
Illinois.........	45,624	39,590	3,674	39,558	18,078	387	454	1,114	2,248	2,718	1,300
Indiana.........	17,753	16,349	2,920	16,288	7,352	459	156	1,792	711	644	395
Iowa............	9,082	8,338	3,104	8,254	4,102	106	261	649	819	346	127
Kansas..........	8,158	7,371	3,035	7,361	3,528	39	142	425	518	377	175
Kentucky........	9,074	8,106	2,245	8,104	3,948	45	266	133	338	327	257
Louisiana........	12,187	11,227	2,727	11,216	4,724	57	79	1,447	596	635	283
Maine	3,108	3,017	2,438	3,017	1,661	32	14	61	181	118	78
Maryland........	15,743	14,680	2,973	14,521	7,401	88	239	-	609	886	475
Massachusetts	21,572	17,818	3,398	17,189	8,722	62	97	213	626	1,087	774
Michigan........	36,046	33,098	3,627	32,948	16,200	636	1,881	563	1,826	1,509	616
Minnesota	19,799	17,893	4,025	17,802	7,164	1,193	378	888	1,435	750	256
Mississippi.......	7,656	7,133	2,691	7,131	3,350	26	48	1,216	455	337	155
Missouri.........	15,188	13,511	2,715	13,510	6,941	129	228	784	889	761	394
Montana.........	2,029	1,962	2,249	1,959	1,056	25	46	53	100	111	41
Nebraska........	6,640	4,461	3,881	4,455	2,259	44	33	241	326	187	107
Nevada.........	7,430	6,640	3,719	6,637	2,309	95	69	474	601	481	223
New Hampshire	2,967	2,890	2,400	2,833	1,528	136	18	-	141	149	100
New Jersey	28,660	28,001	3,406	27,710	14,310	1,124	284	243	973	1,829	630
New Mexico.......	4,963	4,582	2,729	4,561	2,322	52	26	126	208	305	129
New York.........	111,562	96,658	5,879	90,676	34,406	8,487	2,171	4,878	3,688	5,295	2,200
North Carolina	26,145	22,818	3,248	22,494	9,960	1,141	1,229	2,576	381	1,030	480
North Dakota	1,786	1,706	2,782	1,695	742	35	18	-	156	56	45
Ohio............	36,946	34,664	3,254	34,437	14,898	1,908	1,919	979	1,817	1,900	1,014
Oklahoma	8,381	7,711	2,428	7,710	3,793	22	100	762	427	443	266
Oregon..........	12,233	10,929	3,576	10,926	4,833	89	510	328	595	566	313
Pennsylvania	39,166	35,316	3,189	35,304	16,848	1,877	1,790	154	1,108	1,445	434
Rhode Island	2,438	2,252	2,326	2,250	1,287	9	4	-	65	175	152
South Carolina	11,024	9,889	2,748	9,871	4,722	17	275	1,411	212	450	190
South Dakota	1,806	1,665	2,392	1,664	897	11	15	28	200	70	29
Tennessee........	19,561	13,855	3,438	13,815	5,699	105	209	1,531	655	828	400
Texas...........	65,970	58,071	3,164	57,541	30,335	255	1,300	3,597	2,433	2,866	1,373
Utah............	6,438	5,042	2,883	5,034	2,414	21	131	32	268	307	127
Vermont	1,470	1,312	2,413	1,310	882	1	4	-	123	41	25
Virginia.........	20,932	19,273	2,957	19,251	9,189	948	494	269	485	965	549
Washington	22,293	17,933	3,782	17,895	7,506	42	588	933	1,115	854	551
West Virginia	3,804	3,587	2,104	3,581	2,156	1	60	254	51	119	55
Wisconsin	19,829	18,515	3,697	18,480	8,609	1,266	756	219	1,612	1,025	458
Wyoming.........	2,029	1,915	4,107	1,914	864	6	31	348	91	80	23

See footnotes at end of table.

U.S. Census Bureau, Statistical Abstract of the United States: 2004-2005

[See headnote, page 290]

| State | General expenditure-Con. | | | | | | | | Utility expen-ditures | Insur-ance trust expen-ditures | Debt out-standing |
| | Selected functions (direct expenditures)-Con. | | | | | | | | | | |
	Correc-tions	Parks and recre-ation	Hous-ing	Sewer-age	Solid waste	Govern-mental admin-istration	Interest on general debt	Other			
United States..	15,766	20,989	23,427	27,098	14,861	47,160	40,626	78,713	100,393	19,774	903,939
Alabama	131	267	301	452	217	563	492	696	1,710	74	11,507
Alaska.	1	70	134	79	55	169	170	349	262	14	3,106
Arizona	295	432	352	389	235	1,092	866	1,383	2,648	93	20,498
Arkansas	61	62	124	136	110	227	231	300	545	18	5,083
California.	3,052	2,809	4,402	3,627	1,638	8,209	4,936	12,321	18,691	4,088	120,750
Colorado	221	673	330	408	85	896	914	1,629	1,989	209	18,768
Connecticut	-	189	426	272	218	461	256	1,316	474	251	5,039
Delaware	-	20	41	94	10	88	65	73	138	25	1,324
District of Columbia	305	172	58	303	37	320	236	383	1,303	72	5,062
Florida.	1,056	1,333	845	1,563	1,518	2,575	2,760	5,448	5,824	464	60,314
Georgia	407	412	592	865	456	1,511	669	1,461	3,461	256	22,862
Hawaii.	-	171	76	122	134	144	104	227	319	-	2,317
Idaho	42	70	21	103	76	175	54	182	121	1	1,150
Illinois	485	1,824	1,430	1,080	374	2,556	1,819	3,692	4,041	1,993	38,745
Indiana	190	495	418	555	170	953	596	1,401	1,309	95	11,974
Iowa	73	228	128	250	124	323	226	491	731	12	4,948
Kansas	76	182	113	147	112	418	427	683	741	46	8,528
Kentucky	216	125	124	331	124	321	932	614	943	24	15,668
Louisiana.	383	227	277	298	211	643	543	813	851	120	10,210
Maine	31	45	83	118	84	145	95	269	91	-	1,785
Maryland	210	508	536	510	412	771	641	1,235	476	464	12,464
Massachusetts . . .	189	168	958	574	318	652	417	2,331	2,754	1,000	16,202
Michigan	370	615	234	1,694	352	1,969	1,224	3,260	1,970	978	27,750
Minnesota	298	615	561	622	229	908	1,006	1,497	1,445	284	21,806
Mississippi	50	90	130	126	118	407	273	352	523	-	5,297
Missouri.	158	393	233	412	111	686	425	965	1,421	256	9,466
Montana	21	36	32	45	48	116	73	156	67	-	1,240
Nebraska.	59	101	110	117	65	213	106	489	2,095	84	4,967
Nevada	254	352	135	108	8	589	385	554	790	-	10,245
New Hampshire . .	30	48	42	65	71	151	67	287	76	1	1,542
New Jersey	430	375	554	962	846	1,362	1,043	2,746	649	9	21,376
New Mexico	99	164	82	117	102	241	196	391	381	-	4,027
New York.	2,094	1,289	2,804	1,766	1,969	2,997	5,596	11,037	8,755	6,149	98,934
North Carolina . . .	253	452	551	597	544	849	674	1,775	3,013	17	19,778
North Dakota	12	115	81	19	30	91	69	225	73	7	1,261
Ohio	451	1,050	853	1,302	391	2,437	1,100	2,420	2,213	69	24,000
Oklahoma	49	211	141	226	136	360	272	503	641	29	5,745
Oregon	279	281	391	584	95	584	394	1,084	1,248	56	9,372
Pennsylvania	808	676	1,230	1,273	455	1,892	2,648	2,665	2,995	855	54,730
Rhode Island	-	33	113	58	29	84	58	184	93	92	1,197
South Carolina . . .	122	215	168	245	235	581	475	553	1,131	3	11,613
South Dakota	19	68	20	44	21	88	45	108	125	7	984
Tennessee	253	332	451	466	289	723	594	1,279	5,414	292	15,085
Texas	1,078	1,159	1,166	1,591	703	2,691	3,562	3,431	7,344	555	80,947
Utah	106	208	99	182	90	372	199	479	1,396	-	8,509
Vermont	-	13	26	36	26	50	25	59	154	4	674
Virginia	387	517	513	678	451	1,215	940	1,651	1,330	329	19,535
Washington	322	569	501	722	405	1,092	791	1,905	4,232	127	26,963
West Virginia	28	48	91	120	46	205	200	147	193	25	3,364
Wisconsin	284	443	333	611	249	878	676	1,062	1,093	221	14,109
Wyoming	25	40	8	38	30	116	65	150	111	3	1,118

-Represents or rounds to zero. [1] Duplicate intergovernmental transactions are excluded. [2] Based on enumerated population as of April 1. [3] Includes community development.

Source: U.S. Census Bureau, Governmental Finances, annual. See also <http://www.census.gov/govs/estimate/00allpub.pdf>(released September 2003).

U.S. Census Bureau, Statistical Abstract of the United States: 2004-2005

No. 445. Estimated State and Local Taxes Paid by a Family of Four in Selected Cities: 2002

[Data based on average family of four (two wage earners and two school age children) owning their own home and living in a city where taxes apply. Comprises state and local sales, income, auto, and real estate taxes. For definition of median, see Guide to Tabular Presentation]

City	Total taxes paid by gross family income level (dollars)					Total taxes paid as percent of income				
	$25,000	$50,000	$75,000	$100,000	$150,000	$25,000	$50,000	$75,000	$100,000	$150,000
Albuquerque, NM . . .	1,482	3,721	6,389	8,934	14,183	5.9	7.4	8.5	8.9	9.5
Atlanta, GA	2,035	5,137	8,514	11,550	17,483	8.1	10.3	11.4	11.5	11.7
Baltimore, MD	1,776	5,615	8,962	11,904	17,682	7.1	11.2	11.9	11.9	11.8
Boston, MA	1,763	4,496	7,189	9,520	14,132	7.1	9.0	9.6	9.5	9.4
Charlotte, NC	1,836	4,457	7,413	10,279	15,494	7.3	8.9	9.9	10.3	10.3
Chicago, IL	2,320	4,734	7,489	9,655	13,938	9.3	9.5	10.0	9.7	9.3
Columbus, OH.	2,064	4,544	7,391	10,185	16,003	8.3	9.1	9.9	10.2	10.7
Denver, CO.	1,309	3,347	5,656	7,534	11,179	5.2	6.7	7.5	7.5	7.5
Detroit, MI.	2,114	4,656	7,362	11,036	16,248	8.5	9.3	9.8	11.0	10.8
Honolulu, HI	1,763	3,999	6,668	9,037	13,890	7.1	8.0	8.9	9.0	9.3
Houston, TX	1,562	3,020	4,698	5,937	8,277	6.2	6.0	6.3	5.9	5.5
Indianapolis, IN	1,798	3,786	5,896	7,753	11,436	7.2	7.6	7.9	7.8	7.6
Jacksonville, FL. . . .	1,070	2,309	3,758	4,817	6,882	4.3	4.6	5.0	4.8	4.6
Kansas City, MO . . .	1,791	4,275	6,808	9,125	14,057	7.2	8.6	9.1	9.1	9.4
Las Vegas, NV	1,487	2,595	3,928	4,911	6,818	5.9	5.2	5.2	4.9	4.5
Los Angeles, CA . . .	2,154	4,354	7,705	11,246	18,472	8.6	8.7	10.3	11.2	12.3
Memphis, TN.	1,699	3,063	4,656	5,847	8,247	6.8	6.1	6.2	5.8	5.5
Milwaukee, WI.	1,935	5,189	8,562	11,466	17,106	7.7	10.4	11.4	11.5	11.4
Minneapolis, MN . . .	1,412	4,249	6,767	9,756	15,171	5.6	8.5	9.0	9.8	10.1
New Orleans, LA . . .	1,138	3,578	6,148	8,205	12,718	4.6	7.2	8.2	8.2	8.5
New York City, NY . .	1,408	5,400	9,546	13,398	21,165	5.6	10.8	12.7	13.4	14.1
Oklahoma City, OK. .	1,825	4,129	6,858	8,891	13,810	7.3	8.3	9.1	8.9	9.2
Omaha, NE.	1,788	4,152	7,110	9,790	15,335	7.2	8.3	9.5	9.8	10.2
Philadelphia, PA. . . .	2,760	6,581	9,763	12,629	18,333	11.0	13.2	13.0	12.6	12.2
Phoenix, AZ	1,676	3,820	5,733	8,506	13,368	6.7	7.6	7.6	8.5	8.9
Portland, OR.	2,241	5,095	8,220	11,112	16,775	9.0	10.2	11.0	11.1	11.2
Seattle, WA.	1,841	3,355	5,077	6,366	8,897	7.4	6.7	6.8	6.4	5.9
Virginia Beach, VA . .	1,795	3,958	6,336	8,490	12,669	7.2	7.9	8.4	8.5	8.4
Washington, DC. . . .	1,632	4,631	7,797	10,702	16,598	6.5	9.3	10.4	10.7	11.1
Wichita, KS.	1,041	3,275	5,802	8,187	12,798	4.2	6.5	7.7	8.2	8.5
Average [1]	1,787	4,153	6,774	9,188	13,946	7.1	8.3	9.0	9.2	9.3
Median [1]	1,763	4,152	6,858	9,419	14,057	7.1	8.3	9.1	9.4	9.4

[1] Based on selected cities and District of Columbia. For complete list of cities, see Table 446.

Source: Government of the District of Columbia, Department of Finance and Revenue, *Tax Rates and Tax Burdens in the District of Columbia: A Nationwide Comparison*, annual. <http://www.cfo.dc.gov/main.asp>

No. 446. Residential Property Tax Rates for Largest City in Each State: 2002

[Effective tax rate is amount each jurisdiction considers based upon assessment level used. Assessment level is ratio of assessed value to assumed market value. Nominal rate is announced rates it levied at taxable value of house]

City	Effective tax rate per $100		Assessment level (percent)	Nominal rate per $100	City	Effective tax rate per $100		Assessment level (percent)	Nominal rate per $100
	Rank	Rate				Rank	Rate		
Bridgeport, CT.	1	3.86	70.0	5.52	Portland, OR.	28	1.46	72.2	2.02
Newark, NJ.	2	2.95	11.8	24.95	Columbia, SC	29	1.45	4.0	36.35
Providence, RI	3	2.73	80.0	3.41	Salt Lake City, UT . . .	30	1.43	99.0	1.45
Milwaukee, WI.	4	2.67	98.1	2.72	Little Rock, AR	31	1.38	20.0	6.90
Philadelphia, PA	5	2.64	32.0	8.26	Wilmington, DE	32	1.38	53.1	2.59
Houston, TX	6	2.62	100.0	2.62	Wichita, KS.	33	1.31	11.5	11.35
Manchester, NH.	7	2.38	100.0	2.38	Minneapolis, MN	34	1.27	86.4	1.47
Baltimore, MD	8	2.33	100.0	2.33	Charlotte, NC	35	1.22	87.6	1.40
Des Moines, IA	9	2.28	51.4	4.44	Louisville, KY	36	1.21	100.0	1.21
Fargo, ND	10	2.00	4.1	49.00	Albuquerque, NM. . . .	37	1.18	33.3	3.54
Jacksonville, FL.	11	1.96	100.0	1.96	Oklahoma City, OK . .	38	1.16	11.0	10.50
Omaha, NE	12	1.94	93.0	2.09	Kansas City, MO	39	1.14	19.0	6.02
Burlington, VT.	13	1.92	75.5	2.55	Las Vegas, NV	40	1.14	35.0	3.25
Portland, ME.	14	1.90	78.0	2.43	Virginia Beach, VA . . .	41	1.11	90.6	1.22
Atlanta, GA.	15	1.83	40.0	4.57	Boston, MA	42	1.10	100.0	1.10
Phoenix, AZ	16	1.82	10.0	18.20	Los Angeles, CA	43	1.08	100.0	1.08
Detroit, MI	17	1.79	26.5	6.77	Seattle, WA.	44	1.01	90.6	1.12
Memphis, TN	18	1.76	25.0	7.02	Washington, DC	45	0.96	100.0	0.96
Boise City, ID	19	1.72	96.3	1.78	New York City, NY . . .	46	0.93	8.0	11.63
New Orleans, LA	20	1.70	10.0	17.00	Charleston, WV.	47	0.74	60.0	1.24
Jackson, MS.	21	1.69	10.0	16.91	Birmingham, AL.	48	0.70	10.0	6.95
Chicago, IL.	22	1.69	22.1	7.63	Cheyenne, WY	49	0.61	9.5	6.47
Anchorage, AK	23	1.63	95.0	1.72	Denver, CO	50	0.56	9.2	6.15
Billings, MT.	24	1.59	82.0	1.94	Honolulu, HI	51	0.37	100.0	0.37
Sioux Falls, SD	25	1.55	85.0	1.82					
Columbus, OH	26	1.54	29.6	5.21	Unweighted average .	(X)	1.61	55.9	6.7
Indianapolis, IN	27	1.50	15.0	10.00	Median	(X)	1.54	(X)	(X)

X Not applicable.

Source: Government of the District of Columbia, Department of Finance and Revenue, *Tax Rates and Tax Burdens in the District of Columbia: A Nationwide Comparison*, annual. <http://www.cfo.dc.gov/services/studies/index.shtm>

U.S. Census Bureau, *Statistical Abstract of the United States: 2004-2005*

No. 447. Gross Revenue From Parimutuel and Amusement Taxes and Lotteries by State: 2001 and 2002

[In millions of dollars (40,004.8 represents $40,004,800,000) except as indicated. For fiscal years; see text, this section]

State	Gross revenue 2001	Gross revenue 2002	Percent change 2001-2002	Amusement taxes [1]	Pari-mutuel taxes	Total [2] (mil.dol.)	Prizes	Adminis-tration	Proceeds available from ticket sales
United States.....	40,004.8	43,828.5	9.6	4,079.4	308.4	39,440.7	23,988.9	2,756.9	12,694.9
Alabama............	3.6	3.7	2.7	0.1	3.6	(X)	(X)	(X)	(X)
Alaska.............	2.4	2.5	6.6	2.5	(X)	(X)	(X)	(X)	(X)
Arizona............	256.6	296.3	15.5	0.6	0.7	294.9	160.2	47.5	87.2
Arkansas..........	6.3	4.4	-30.1	-	4.4	(X)	(X)	(X)	(X)
California...........	2,742.8	2,743.4	-	(X)	44.6	2,698.8	1,503.0	176.9	1,018.9
Colorado...........	417.9	478.2	14.4	95.2	5.8	377.2	238.9	31.8	106.6
Connecticut........	1,177.4	1,282.8	9.0	365.0	7.3	910.5	546.1	88.4	275.9
Delaware..........	350.5	397.1	13.3	(X)	0.2	397.0	59.2	7.3	330.5
Florida............	2,187.2	2,232.9	2.1	(X)	29.8	2,203.1	1,165.8	120.9	916.3
Georgia...........	1,945.3	2,162.8	11.2	(X)	(X)	2,162.8	1,308.2	131.1	723.4
Hawaii.............	(X)	(X)	(X)	(X)	(X)	(X)	(X)	(X)	(X)
Idaho.............	81.7	92.7	13.4	(X)	(X)	92.7	53.1	18.3	21.3
Illinois............	1,882.2	2,064.4	9.7	591.1	12.6	1,460.7	866.7	60.6	533.5
Indiana............	973.8	1,094.8	12.4	521.1	5.3	568.3	371.2	32.1	165.0
Iowa..............	328.9	375.4	14.1	202.5	3.3	169.6	100.0	25.9	43.8
Kansas............	175.2	184.3	5.2	0.7	3.8	179.8	99.0	21.7	59.2
Kentucky..........	603.2	656.8	8.9	0.3	17.8	638.7	384.2	88.9	165.6
Louisiana..........	723.2	787.8	8.9	497.0	6.1	284.7	155.6	19.1	110.0
Maine.............	145.3	157.7	8.5	(X)	4.9	152.8	91.2	19.6	42.0
Maryland	1,223.9	1,314.5	7.4	4.8	3.1	1,306.5	733.2	133.1	440.3
Massachusetts.....	3,712.7	4,214.9	13.5	5.9	6.9	4,202.1	3,000.9	73.7	1,127.6
Michigan..........	1,577.1	1,662.9	5.4	91.9	12.5	1,558.5	873.7	54.6	630.1
Minnesota.........	400.3	410.0	2.4	55.9	1.3	352.8	223.0	72.6	57.2
Mississippi........	182.2	184.2	1.1	184.2	(X)	(X)	(X)	(X)	(X)
Missouri...........	669.0	769.2	15.0	220.5	(X)	548.7	353.1	39.9	155.7
Montana...........	70.3	75.5	7.3	43.7	0.1	31.7	17.1	6.5	8.1
Nebraska..........	73.6	81.2	10.3	6.3	0.9	74.0	39.5	16.6	17.9
Nevada............	729.4	720.7	-1.2	720.7	(X)	(X)	(X)	(X)	(X)
New Hampshire.....	204.0	221.0	8.3	1.8	4.4	214.9	142.5	7.0	65.3
New Jersey........	2,049.6	2,306.0	12.5	351.0	-	1,955.1	1,115.9	67.7	771.4
New Mexico........	141.6	162.6	14.8	32.4	1.2	129.1	72.9	26.7	29.5
New York..........	3,856.1	4,373.9	13.4	0.7	38.0	4,335.2	2,664.1	91.8	1,579.2
North Carolina.....	11.8	11.1	-6.0	11.1	(X)	(X)	(X)	(X)	(X)
North Dakota.......	17.7	16.6	-6.5	14.1	2.5	(X)	(X)	(X)	(X)
Ohio..............	1,942.4	2,000.5	3.0	(X)	17.4	1,983.1	1,148.1	299.2	535.8
Oklahoma..........	10.9	10.1	-7.3	7.0	3.1	(X)	(X)	(X)	(X)
Oregon............	1,308.1	1,421.8	8.7	0.0	1.9	1,419.9	1,009.1	261.0	149.8
Pennsylvania.......	1,693.2	1,847.9	9.1	0.7	29.0	1,818.1	1,406.7	95.9	315.5
Rhode Island.......	855.3	1,019.4	19.2	(X)	5.4	1,014.0	796.6	7.2	210.2
South Carolina.....	37.7	364.5	868.1	29.0	(X)	335.5	(X)	(X)	(X)
South Dakota......	123.6	132.7	7.3	-	1.3	131.3	14.1	7.8	109.4
Tennessee	(X)	(X)	(X)	(X)	(X)	(X)	(X)	(X)	(X)
Texas.............	2,858.4	3,000.4	5.0	21.2	12.7	2,966.4	1,715.4	318.0	933.1
Utah..............	(X)	(X)	(X)	(X)	(X)	(X)	(X)	(X)	(X)
Vermont...........	81.2	82.0	1.0	(X)	-	82.0	52.3	13.3	16.3
Virginia............	997.7	1,104.9	10.8	0.1	(X)	1,104.9	663.6	128.2	313.0
Washington........	485.8	440.7	-9.3	0.1	2.0	438.6	282.2	60.7	95.7
West Virginia.......	309.2	461.5	49.3	(X)	12.0	449.5	120.2	28.7	300.6
Wisconsin.........	378.3	399.9	5.7	0.4	2.1	397.5	242.1	33.5	121.9
Wyoming	0.2	0.2	-16.5	(X)	0.2	(X)	(X)	(X)	(X)

- Represents or rounds to zero.   X Not applicable.   [1] Represents nonlicense taxes.   2 Excludes commissions.
Source: U.S. Census Bureau, unpublished data.

No. 448. Lottery Sales—Type of Game: 1980 to 2003
[In millions of dollars (2,393 represents $2,393,000,000). For fiscal years]

Game	1980	1985	1990	1995	2000	2001	2002	2003
Total ticket sales	2,393	9,035	20,017	31,931	37,201	38,441	41,979	43,521
Instant [1]	527	1,296	5,204	11,511	15,459	16,420	18,509	20,387
Three-digit [2]	1,554	3,376	4,572	5,737	5,341	5,245	5,356	5,394
Four-digit [3]	55	693	1,302	1,941	2,711	2,776	2,916	3,059
Lotto [4]	52	3,583	8,563	10,594	9,160	8,865	9,564	9,655
Other [4]	206	88	376	2,148	4,530	5,134	5,633	5,026
State proceeds (net income) [5]	978	3,735	7,703	11,100	11,404	11,916	12,478	13,991

NA Not available.   [1] Player scratches a latex section on ticket which reveals instantly whether ticket is a winner.
[2] Players choose and bet on three or four digits, depending on game, with various payoffs for different straight order or mixed combination bets.   [3] Players typically select six digits out of a large field of numbers. Varying prizes are offered for matching three through six numbers drawn by lottery.   [4] Includes break-open tickets, spiel, keno, video lottery and passive before 1990. etc.
[5] Sales minus prizes and expenses equal net government income.
Source: TLF Publications, Inc., Boyds, MD, *2004 World Lottery Almanac* annual; *LaFleur's Fiscal 2003 Lottery Interim TVLT Book* (copyright)).

State and Local Government Finances and Employment   293

No. 449. City Governments—Revenue for Largest Cities: 2001

[In millions of dollars (58,523 represents $58,523,000,000). For fiscal years ending in year shown; see text, this section. Cities ranked by enumerated resident population as of April 1. Data reflect inclusion of fiscal activity of dependent school systems where applicable. Regarding intercity comparisons, see text, this section. See Appendix III]

Cities ranked by 2000 population	Total revenue	General revenue — Total	Intergovernmental — Total	— From federal government	— From state/ local government	— From local government	General revenue from own sources — Total	Taxes — Total	Taxes — Property	Sales and gross receipts — Total	Sales and gross receipts — General sales	Sales and gross receipts — Public utilities	Current charges — Total	Current charges — Parks and recreation	Current charges — Sewerage	Miscellaneous — Total	Miscellaneous — Interest earnings	Utility revenue[2]	Employee retirement revenue
New York, NY	58,523	51,262	19,841	2,806	16,947	88	31,421	23,579	8,276	4,832	3,679	431	5,103	55	971	2,740	887	2,869	4,392
Los Angeles, CA	11,287	6,056	1,035	297	596	142	5,021	2,519	753	1,210	483	610	1,688	83	492	814	483	3,630	1,602
Chicago, IL	6,389	4,884	1,337	464	873	-	3,547	2,033	664	1,146	196	483	888	26	284	627	320	310	1,196
Houston, TX	2,569	2,164	163	121	38	-	2,001	1,153	567	552	330	176	592	14	196	255	158	281	124
Philadelphia, PA [3]	5,405	4,673	1,933	510	1,295	128	2,740	2,044	364	196	111	-	537	26	157	159	117	658	74
Phoenix, AZ	2,312	2,044	704	264	385	56	1,340	732	174	511	368	92	447	48	183	160	146	220	48
San Diego, CA	2,574	2,080	351	109	167	75	1,729	959	228	646	413	44	324	38	206	445	145	240	254
Dallas, TX	2,308	1,687	114	63	50	-	1,574	728	375	336	217	82	639	27	154	206	126	200	421
San Antonio, TX	2,463	984	148	41	100	-	836	409	195	199	134	22	255	13	155	171	71	1,426	53
Detroit, MI	3,409	3,758	2,299	363	1,905	31	1,459	893	401	139	-	53	286	20	204	280	107	191	-540
San Jose, CA [3]	1,109	977	177	89	98	-	800	368	222	41	-	97	217	17	186	215	52	132	-
Honolulu, HI [3]	1,493	1,484	177	115	61	-	1,307	800	684	-	-	23	430	22	67	77	62	18	-9
Indianapolis, IN [3]	1,895	1,518	429	64	352	13	1,089	625	484	41	-	-	358	37	152	106	255	347	30
San Francisco, CA [3]	6,095	4,893	1,740	378	1,356	-	3,153	1,747	662	674	387	89	1,053	-	124	352	185	337	865
Jacksonville, FL [3]	2,230	1,217	254	130	123	-	964	510	283	214	124	81	235	-	138	219	46	887	126
Columbus, OH	1,100	958	140	45	85	10	818	500	34	15	-	-	234	21	146	84	52	75	67
Austin, TX	1,864	885	58	41	17	-	827	373	180	165	112	24	314	11	70	140	38	913	66
Baltimore, MD [3]	2,571	2,369	1,330	83	1,177	70	1,039	785	491	62	-	26	136	46	62	118	70	76	126
Memphis, TN	2,941	1,532	995	20	496	479	537	331	275	44	-	16	133	-	47	73	45	1,180	229
Milwaukee, WI	1,042	752	389	70	305	15	363	184	174	30	-	-	106	24	104	73	38	62	228
Boston, MA	2,763	2,479	1,183	109	1,071	-	1,296	997	925	30	-	-	186	-	111	113	44	67	217
Washington, DC	5,936	5,679	1,643	1,589	-	54	4,036	3,337	707	999	617	200	299	-	94	400	111	190	67
Nashville, TN [3]	2,409	1,520	310	10	300	-	1,210	1,041	475	271	237	-	109	46	59	60	119	800	89
El Paso, TX	550	441	65	46	11	-	375	206	107	108	-	22	59	25	-	110	28	61	47
Seattle, WA	1,981	1,300	117	31	79	-	1,182	656	225	272	68	99	298	27	218	228	50	691	-10
Denver, CO [3]	2,137	1,852	179	13	166	-	1,673	733	154	486	136	16	645	-	109	296	63	153	132
Charlotte, NC	1,024	982	254	62	71	122	728	296	218	78	-	-	239	-	78	193	53	-	42
Ft. Worth, TX	842	541	33	-	33	-	508	320	157	-	-	-	143	27	93	45	40	129	172
Portland, OR	811	738	115	30	49	35	623	310	186	39	-	39	220	10	93	93	57	51	22
Oklahoma City, OK	860	694	75	45	29	-	620	327	38	252	252	27	182	16	70	111	22	129	37
Tucson, AZ [3]	702	577	225	68	148	9	352	239	41	158	158	18	74	-	57	39	50	102	23
New Orleans, LA	974	886	191	60	131	-	694	392	155	140	140	48	193	-	70	109	27	61	27
Las Vegas, NV	544	543	208	-	172	31	335	143	70	-	-	-	123	-	57	69	50	-	1
Cleveland, OH	1,240	911	193	46	147	-	718	421	66	37	37	34	165	-	20	132	67	329	-
Long Beach, CA	971	832	145	57	76	13	686	215	67	108	-	57	397	-	73	75	31	138	1

- Represents or rounds to zero.   [1] Includes solid waste management.   [2] Includes water, electric, and transit.   [3] Represents, in effect, city-county consolidated government.

Source: U.S. Census Bureau, *Government Finances 2000-2001*. See also <http://www.census.gov/govs/estimate.html>.

No. 450. City Governments—Expenditures and Debt for Largest Cities: 2001

[In millions of dollars (62,971 represents $62,971,000,000). For fiscal year ending in year shown; see headnote, Table 449].

Columns 4 through 17 ("Total" through "Interest on general debt") fall under the heading **General expenditures**.

Cities ranked by 2000 population	Total expendi-tures	Total direct expendi-tures	Total	Educa-tion	Housing and community develop-ment	Public welfare	Health and hos-pitals	Police protec-tion	Fire protec-tion	Correc-tion	High-ways	Parks and recre-ation	Sewer-age	Solid waste man-age-ment	Govern-mental admin-istration[1]	Interest on general debt	Utility expendi-tures[2]	Employee retire-ment expendi-tures	Debt out-standing
New York, NY	62,971	58,891	51,062	13,667	2,677	8,345	5,134	3,436	1,153	1,313	1,135	631	1,084	1,059	1,026	3,124	5,683	6,226	57,518
Los Angeles, CA	10,153	10,107	5,514	-	202	-	48	956	364	-	272	264	384	155	359	479	3,516	1,123	11,605
Chicago, IL	6,491	6,399	5,279	-	202	139	169	1,064	316	-	578	71	152	179	160	553	330	882	11,196
Houston, TX	2,871	2,856	2,426	-	62	-	98	422	227	14	194	139	252	70	94	244	278	168	7,887
Philadelphia, PA[3]	5,743	5,664	4,560	21	150	400	-	483	156	303	86	89	199	91	330	181	734	448	4,673
Phoenix, AZ	2,208	2,201	1,752	16	77	-	-	262	137	-	76	183	134	130	105	172	395	61	3,742
San Diego, CA	2,378	2,377	1,808	-	122	-	-	276	102	9	52	167	294	93	64	162	411	158	2,337
Dallas, TX	2,073	2,041	1,727	-	34	-	23	208	112	-	94	174	132	46	47	237	182	164	4,963
San Antonio, TX	2,388	2,378	1,088	-	11	-	39	185	112	-	117	120	102	44	36	62	1,252	47	4,781
Detroit, MI	4,943	4,880	4,030	1,604	121	46	108	359	117	-	149	114	384	95	212	112	634	279	4,111
San Jose, CA	1,435	1,396	1,313	-	235	-	-	178	88	-	84	139	109	67	70	116	29	94	2,374
Honolulu, HI[3]	1,441	1,441	1,086	-	42	-	18	163	59	-	93	115	138	120	64	83	355	-	1,927
Indianapolis, IN[3]	2,016	2,005	1,619	-	161	68	327	123	49	39	93	130	128	21	155	165	357	40	3,159
San Francisco, CA[3]	6,596	6,454	5,533	104	178	490	893	355	197	101	242	294	84	286	286	368	667	396	7,668
Jacksonville, FL[3]	2,280	2,215	1,291	-	12	31	41	142	89	46	64	45	190	60	65	168	891	99	5,706
Columbus, OH	1,128	1,108	990	-	16	-	42	183	142	12	94	78	111	42	65	95	138	-	1,674
Austin, TX	1,843	1,843	879	-	14	-	82	110	72	-	39	81	50	55	52	97	884	81	4,295
Baltimore, MD	2,364	2,310	2,065	959	36	-	63	230	100	-	129	47	106	55	117	70	92	208	1,404
Memphis, TN[3]	3,007	3,001	1,652	946	18	-	-	186	104	-	58	78	34	43	24	48	1,196	159	1,011
Milwaukee, WI	983	957	798	-	89	-	34	159	76	-	54	-	70	31	37	44	43	142	598
Boston, MA	2,647	2,391	2,325	810	106	120	74	251	121	83	90	27	109	43	76	57	158	249	1,539
Washington, DC[3]	5,651	5,453	5,418	1,142	66	1,349	571	352	130	267	69	209	137	82	273	208	-	-	4,880
Nashville, TN[3]	2,458	2,458	1,497	521	-	16	139	105	67	43	31	47	54	35	82	130	859	102	3,643
El Paso, TX	547	547	403	-	22	-	22	77	40	-	25	20	57	14	19	26	106	39	718
Seattle, WA[3]	2,093	1,981	1,157	-	66	-	17	151	90	-	92	151	161	85	89	45	853	83	2,563
Denver, CO[3]	2,027	1,976	1,737	-	24	109	49	139	69	13	77	90	44	-	124	273	224	66	4,852
Charlotte, NC	1,023	1,020	734	-	34	-	-	127	56	60	76	43	36	36	18	69	274	14	1,982
Ft Worth, TX	811	811	546	-	10	-	-	111	57	-	73	53	77	23	37	32	206	59	1,095
Portland, OR[3]	1,134	1,123	948	-	38	-	-	101	68	-	117	98	225	-	50	62	126	59	2,052
Oklahoma City, OK	769	769	693	-	23	-	-	104	92	-	67	122	81	23	47	54	65	10	955
Tucson, AZ	700	700	512	-	47	-	-	99	40	-	62	53	-	27	69	29	170	18	743
New Orleans, LA	890	890	766	-	83	-	12	111	57	26	35	20	69	31	87	68	88	37	1,124
Las Vegas, NV	502	415	501	-	20	-	-	84	69	19	48	51	28	-	55	17	-	-	364
Cleveland, OH	1,251	1,245	927	-	62	-	34	179	78	-	84	123	19	40	62	53	323	-	2,048
Long Beach, CA	914	914	741	-	72	-	29	126	62	-	41	30	-	52	36	77	170	-	1,453

- Represents or rounds to zero.   [1] Excludes public buildings.   [2] Includes water, electric, and transit.   [3] Represents, in effect, city-county consolidated government.

Source: U.S. Census Bureau, "Government Finances 2000-2001;" See also <http://www.census.gov/govs/estimate.html>.

U.S. Census Bureau, Statistical Abstract of the United States: 2004-2005

No. 451. County Governments—Revenue for Largest Counties: 2001

[In millions of dollars (16,690 represents $16,690,000,000). For fiscal year ending in year shown; see text, this section. See Appendix III]

Counties ranked by 2000 population	Total revenue [1]	General revenue	Intergovernmental	From federal government		From state government			From local government	General revenue from own sources	Taxes		Sales and gross receipts		Current charges				Miscellaneous general revenue	
		Total	Total	Total	Housing [2]	Total	Public welfare	Health and hospitals		Total	Total [1]	Property	Total	General sales	Total [1]	Parks and recreation	Sewerage [3]	Hospitals	Total	Interest earnings
Los Angeles, CA	16,690	15,054	10,309	275	58	9,647	4,308	1,900	386	4,745	2,332	2,101	136	70	1,340	65	37	673	1,074	336
Cook, IL	2,663	2,373	491	43	40	444	172	119	-	1,882	1,349	802	532	335	388	42	-	202	145	83
Harris, TX	2,165	2,165	428	74	26	286	137	26	69	1,737	1,032	969	28	-	422	-	-	95	283	209
Maricopa, AZ	1,986	1,986	977	37	-	918	137	203	22	1,009	538	410	104	104	265	17	-	212	206	150
Orange, CA	3,730	2,761	1,559	119	10	1,331	385	26	108	1,202	412	352	50	48	412	-	94	-	377	159
San Diego, CA	2,796	2,756	2,024	65	55	1,855	683	378	104	732	456	383	26	19	137	25	-	-	139	69
Dade, FL	5,026	4,774	1,011	469	176	542	67	28	-	3,763	1,299	868	357	-	1,898	25	466	709	566	355
Dallas, TX	1,127	1,110	176	29	-	147	-	-	-	934	445	401	10	-	405	64	64	320	84	45
Wayne, MI	2,312	2,167	1,278	135	16	1,108	509	28	35	889	306	290	10	-	363	-	280	-	220	92
King, WA	1,849	1,757	459	108	27	305	67	26	46	1,298	789	365	366	290	393	10	35	-	116	79
San Bernardino, CA	3,003	2,742	1,665	508	22	1,139	755	108	18	1,077	260	218	25	19	676	-	35	391	140	63
Santa Clara, CA	2,521	2,521	1,480	93	27	1,392	486	127	-	1,041	694	456	197	195	232	14	137	139	116	75
Broward, FL	1,674	1,632	295	76	14	165	105	127	54	1,336	646	523	97	17	464	-	137	-	226	137
Riverside, CA	1,797	1,796	1,198	20	14	1,040	486	72	124	598	272	230	23	17	191	14	46	69	135	68
Tarrant, TX	467	467	142	19	-	105	12	62	17	325	189	160	10	-	39	-	-	-	97	83
Alameda, CA	2,190	2,081	1,090	22	14	997	562	230	74	991	455	287	143	135	137	-	17	49	399	86
Suffolk, NY	2,051	1,942	666	18	-	466	221	60	182	1,276	1,046	282	764	762	121	-	-	-	109	58
Cuyahoga, OH	1,713	1,713	779	69	17	757	458	163	-	934	465	252	176	161	301	17	-	269	168	139
Bexar, TX	780	777	124	25	-	70	-	44	-	653	295	259	20	-	248	-	-	224	89	76
Clark, NV	3,056	2,749	593	32	13	438	-	337	86	2,156	874	373	501	450	841	15	72	373	441	206
Nassau, NY	2,662	2,662	707	25	23	682	392	76	-	1,955	1,460	653	803	799	351	18	-	210	143	81
Allegheny, PA	1,447	1,319	785	32	22	750	202	337	-	534	280	234	44	36	192	-	206	-	62	31
Sacramento, CA	2,574	2,352	1,316	22	12	1,260	570	83	52	1,035	384	186	150	122	443	13	-	-	209	95
Oakland, MI	932	764	491	39	-	452	194	-	-	273	189	178	-	-	38	-	-	-	46	31
Palm Beach, FL	1,247	1,208	168	19	-	129	-	73	21	1,040	569	422	129	82	324	-	159	256	147	64
Hennepin, MN	1,495	1,495	587	44	12	516	166	119	27	908	425	262	91	82	371	-	48	-	112	67
Franklin, OH	982	980	430	19	18	395	166	73	16	551	367	80	303	264	49	-	-	-	135	125
St Louis, MO	574	533	59	18	-	37	-	-	-	474	394	378	15	-	45	-	-	-	35	18
Hillsborough, FL	1,386	1,261	249	19	18	225	36	60	16	1,013	530	378	140	82	281	-	64	-	202	121
Fairfax, VA	1,393	1,345	745	69	34	319	93	33	-	600	357	192	154	154	313	24	182	-	217	138
Erie, NY	1,648	1,420	541	29	-	512	191	108	-	879	530	162	357	357	206	-	18	-	143	39
Contra Costa, CA	1,251	1,062	573	134	-	428	264	33	11	489	234	176	56	56	181	39	-	258	84	45
Milwaukee, WI	1,515	1,515	913	29	11	872	119	141	12	602	348	176	56	56	204	24	26	54	50	20
Westchester, NY	1,958	1,947	432	134	11	410	119	69	-	1,515	780	462	316	306	664	24	-	477	71	57
Pinellas, FL	843	787	107	28	9	77	233	69	15	680	378	271	96	62	176	-	18	-	126	72

- Represents or rounds to zero.   [1] Includes revenue sources not shown separately.   [2] Includes urban development.   [3] Includes solid waste management.

Source: U.S. Census Bureau, Government Finances, 2000-2001. See also <http://www.census.gov/govs/estimate/.html>.

No. 452. County Governments—Expenditures and Debt for Largest Counties: 2001

[In millions of dollars (15,149 represents $15,149,000,000). For fiscal year ending in year shown; see text, this section. See headnote, Table 451. See Appendix III]

Columns under "General expenditure": Total[1], Education, Housing[2], Public welfare, Health, Hospitals, Police protection, Correction, Highways, Parks and recreation, Natural resources, Sewerage and solid waste management, Governmental administration, Interest on general debt.

Counties ranked by 2000 population	Total expenditure	Total direct expenditure	Total[1]	Education	Housing[2]	Public welfare	Health	Hospitals	Police protection	Correction	Highways	Parks and recreation	Natural resources	Sewerage and solid waste management	Governmental administration	Interest on general debt	Utility expenditure[3]	Employee retirement expenditure	Debt outstanding
Los Angeles, CA	15,149	14,074	13,938	540	87	4,264	1,803	1,677	885	926	338	248	191	53	1,462	449	56	1,156	6,152
Cook, IL	2,749	2,724	2,550	1	24	10	39	889	87	339	84	114	87	–	563	110	–	199	2,010
Harris, TX	2,346	2,346	2,346	–	34	18	147	560	155	189	227	119	79	5	279	338	–	–	4,742
Maricopa, AZ	1,883	1,681	1,883	15	8	540	71	234	47	252	117	6	34	77	304	100	–	159	1,669
Orange, CA	2,753	2,547	2,594	211	24	630	286	–	206	218	43	56	10	25	364	200	12	156	3,139
San Diego, CA	2,983	2,809	2,814	290	61	651	422	912	193	231	81	21	37	425	388	87	494	–	804
Dade, FL	5,105	5,097	4,611	–	220	93	58	631	388	184	51	201	–	–	267	450	–	–	7,829
Dallas, TX	1,240	1,234	1,219	–	–	12	68	60	34	150	33	–	–	–	129	30	–	21	571
Wayne, MI	2,601	2,491	2,508	257	43	201	419	22	24	198	179	179	115	95	328	101	429	94	2,169
King, WA	1,899	1,864	1,470	173	6	6	270	233	90	107	96	59	43	272	190	158	5	–	2,398
San Bernardino, CA	2,749	2,523	2,621	–	20	717	226	307	379	141	43	22	37	52	171	79	–	123	1,335
Santa Clara, CA	2,357	2,148	2,357	–	28	548	249	–	49	208	49	20	2	25	359	31	148	–	613
Broward, FL	1,606	1,563	1,459	–	4	40	95	169	202	144	49	51	17	137	134	148	–	–	2,621
Riverside, CA	1,973	1,777	1,973	272	39	504	122	–	140	121	50	10	91	46	215	69	–	–	1,125
Tarrant, TX	436	434	436	27	15	3	85	160	16	79	48	–	72	–	98	84	165	–	1,449
Alameda, CA	1,951	1,851	1,832	231	24	554	227	454	61	167	20	33	10	58	237	68	–	119	1,171
Suffolk, NY	2,050	1,790	1,884	–	5	379	149	360	335	92	44	–	–	14	99	60	–	–	1,661
Cuyahoga, OH	1,778	1,757	1,778	–	22	445	272	376	24	86	24	12	–	–	234	129	781	–	2,022
Bexar, TX	771	705	769	–	1	66	40	304	25	66	–	217	8	28	83	61	34	2	890
Clark, NV	3,277	3,253	2,496	223	10	60	128	27	289	171	353	65	93	92	271	226	–	–	4,659
Nassau, NY	2,696	2,309	2,662	33	23	523	295	–	526	155	68	61	1	–	125	151	22	–	3,880
Allegheny, PA	1,319	1,218	1,274	108	28	262	200	7	33	62	35	24	–	–	90	74	3	45	1,416
Sacramento, CA	2,365	2,292	2,234	9	–	689	241	–	206	158	164	17	18	139	272	111	105	109	2,128
Oakland, MI	800	786	773	–	8	6	38	7	53	77	100	63	51	58	109	13	–	24	236
Palm Beach, FL	1,261	1,232	1,156	–	19	32	233	332	142	67	87	64	5	112	152	91	3	–	1,649
Hennepin, MN	1,382	1,381	1,382	–	7	252	266	–	65	114	48	20	–	45	121	25	105	–	663
Franklin, OH	983	960	981	–	5	239	41	–	23	58	41	43	–	4	101	108	1	–	1,800
St Louis, MO	492	344	478	–	18	15	24	–	53	19	77	105	–	–	49	26	–	–	417
Hillsborough, FL	1,189	1,170	1,048	–	32	49	132	–	104	67	35	15	46	76	95	104	141	14	2,275
Fairfax, VA	3,506	3,411	3,156	1,585	61	180	54	–	131	29	52	–	3	234	97	132	160	–	2,686
Erie, NY	1,403	1,060	1,369	99	–	516	137	234	33	60	63	92	–	29	41	39	34	190	945
Contra Costa, CA	1,534	1,484	1,420	69	8	281	87	323	61	79	31	45	16	12	124	51	152	114	629
Milwaukee, WI	1,188	1,188	950	80	15	281	125	125	50	34	24	25	–	116	79	29	31	86	578
Westchester, NY	1,960	1,724	1,928	–	–	382	124	474	24	114	59	–	–	122	86	47	74	–	1,171
Pinellas, FL	829	791	755	–	15	30	65	–	83	64	–	–	33	–	103	47	–	–	688

- Represents or rounds to zero. [1] Includes expenditure categories not shown separately. [2] Includes community development. [3] Includes water, electric, and transit.

Source: U.S. Census Bureau, *Government Finances, 2000-2001*. See also <http://www.census.gov/govs/estimate.html> (issued January 2004).

State and Local Government Finances and Employment 297

No. 453. Governmental Employment and Payrolls: 1980 to 2002

[Employees in thousands (16,213 represents 16,213,000), payroll in millions of dollars (19,935 represents $19,935,000,000). For 1980 to 1995 as of October; later years as of March. Covers both full-time and part-time employees. Local government data are estimates subject to sampling variation; see appendix III and source]

Type of government	1980	1985	1990	1995	1997	1998	1999	2000	2001	2002
EMPLOYEES (1,000)										
Total	16,213	16,690	18,369	19,521	19,540	19,854	20,306	20,876	20,970	21,039
Federal (civilian) [1]	2,898	3,021	3,105	2,895	2,807	2,765	2,799	2,899	2,698	2,690
State and local	13,315	13,669	15,263	16,626	16,733	17,089	17,506	17,976	18,272	18,349
Percent of total	82	82	83	85	86	86	86	86	87	87
State	3,753	3,984	4,503	4,719	4,733	4,758	4,818	4,877	4,985	5,072
Local	9,562	9,685	10,760	11,906	12,000	12,271	12,689	13,099	13,288	13,277
Counties	1,853	1,891	2,167	(NA)	2,425	(NA)	(NA)	(NA)	(NA)	2,729
Municipalities	2,561	2,467	2,642	(NA)	2,755	(NA)	(NA)	(NA)	(NA)	2,972
School districts	4,270	4,416	4,950	(NA)	5,675	(NA)	(NA)	(NA)	(NA)	6,367
Townships	394	392	418	(NA)	455	(NA)	(NA)	(NA)	(NA)	488
Special districts	484	519	585	(NA)	691	(NA)	(NA)	(NA)	(NA)	721
PAYROLLS (mil. dol.)										
Total	19,935	28,945	39,228	(NA)	49,156	51,568	54,363	58,166	60,632	63,923
Federal (civilian) [1]	5,205	7,580	8,999	(NA)	9,744	10,115	10,748	11,485	11,370	11,599
State and local	14,730	21,365	30,229	37,714	39,412	41,453	43,886	46,681	49,262	52,323
Percent of total	74	74	77	(NA)	80	80	81	80	81	82
State	4,285	6,329	9,083	10,927	11,413	11,845	12,565	13,279	14,136	14,838
Local	10,445	15,036	21,146	26,787	27,999	29,608	31,321	33,402	35,126	37,486
Counties	1,936	2,819	4,192	(NA)	5,750	(NA)	(NA)	(NA)	(NA)	7,902
Municipalities	2,951	4,191	5,564	(NA)	7,146	(NA)	(NA)	(NA)	(NA)	9,714
School districts	4,683	6,746	9,551	(NA)	12,579	(NA)	(NA)	(NA)	(NA)	16,720
Townships	330	446	642	(NA)	869	(NA)	(NA)	(NA)	(NA)	1,124
Special districts	546	834	1,197	(NA)	1,654	(NA)	(NA)	(NA)	(NA)	2,026

NA Not available.   [1] Includes employees outside the United States.

Source: U.S. Census Bureau; "Government Employment, March 2002," issued October 2003, <http://www.census.gov/govs/www/apes.html> (accessed 13 April 2004)

No. 454. All Governments—Employment and Payroll by Function: 2002

[Employees in thousands (21,039 represents 21,039,000), payroll in millions of dollars (63,923 represents $63,923,000,000). See headnote, Table 453]

Function	Employees (1,000)				Payrolls (mil. dol.)			
	Total	Federal (civilian) [1]	State and local			Total	Federal (civilian) [1]	State and local	
			Total	State	Local			Total	State	Local
Total	21,039	2,690	18,349	5,072	13,277	63,923	11,599	52,323	14,838	37,486
National defense [2]	681	681	(X)	(X)	(X)	2,544	2,544	(X)	(X)	(X)
Postal Service	830	830	(X)	(X)	(X)	3,030	3,030	(X)	(X)	(X)
Space research and technology	19	19	(X)	(X)	(X)	127	127	(X)	(X)	(X)
Elem and secondary educ . . .	7,242	(X)	7,242	69	7,174	19,623	(X)	19,623	190	19,432
Higher education	2,787	(X)	2,787	2,238	549	6,592	(X)	6,592	5,469	1,124
Other education	119	11	108	108	(X)	395	58	338	338	(X)
Health	601	135	467	182	285	2,114	707	1,407	603	803
Hospitals	1,139	149	991	431	560	3,661	661	3,000	1,310	1,690
Public welfare	558	9	549	244	304	1,665	51	1,614	742	872
Social insurance administration	158	66	92	92	(X)	623	318	304	304	(X)
Police protection	1,061	109	951	107	845	4,278	628	3,651	429	3,222
Fire protection	388	(X)	388	(X)	388	1,367	(X)	1,367	(X)	1,367
Correction	749	34	714	465	249	2,465	148	2,316	1,494	822
Streets & highways	568	3	565	253	313	1,797	19	1,778	859	920
Air transportation	98	52	46	3	43	601	431	170	13	157
Water transport/terminals	17	5	12	5	8	62	14	48	17	31
Solid waste management	120	(X)	120	2	118	350	(X)	350	8	342
Sewerage	133	(X)	133	2	131	445	(X)	445	9	436
Parks & recreation	403	26	377	42	336	785	105	679	98	581
Natural resources	402	191	211	168	43	1,522	901	620	505	115
Housing & community development	142	17	125	-	125	482	91	391	-	391
Water supply	170	-	170	1	169	551	-	551	3	548
Electric power	78	-	78	4	74	352	-	352	21	331
Gas supply	11	-	11	-	11	34	-	34	-	34
Transit	238	(X)	238	33	204	928	(X)	928	149	780
Libraries	182	4	178	1	177	344	22	321	1	320
State liquor stores	9	(X)	9	9	(X)	18	(X)	18	18	(X)
Financial administration	558	141	417	173	244	1,890	604	1,285	580	705
Other government administration	447	22	425	61	363	1,041	102	939	200	739
Judicial and legal	488	60	429	164	265	1,900	348	1,552	664	888
Other & unallocable	642	127	515	215	300	2,337	688	1,649	812	837

- Represents or rounds to zero.   X Not applicable.   [1] Includes employees outside the United States.   [2] Includes international relations.

Source: U.S. Census Bureau; "Government Employment, March 2002," issued October 2003, <http://www.census.gov/govs/www/apes.html> (accessed 13 April 2004).

U.S. Census Bureau, Statistical Abstract of the United States: 2004-2005

No. 455. State and Local Government—Employer Costs per Hour Worked: 2003

[In dollars. As of March. Based on a sample; see source for details. For additional data, see Table 630]

Occupation and industry	Total compensation	Wages and salaries	Benefits						
			Total	Paid leave	Supplemental pay	Insurance	Retirement and savings	Legally required benefits	Other [1]
Total workers	32.62	22.85	9.77	2.51	0.3	3.12	1.85	1.93	0.06
White-collar occupations	36.20	26.02	10.18	2.60	0.19	3.28	2.00	2.05	0.07
Professional specialty and technical .	42.24	31.21	11.03	2.56	0.20	3.44	2.40	2.33	0.10
Professional specialty.	43.59	32.36	11.24	2.57	0.18	3.52	2.50	2.37	0.10
Teachers	45.97	34.57	11.41	2.40	0.12	3.62	2.73	2.43	0.12
Technical	27.74	18.93	8.81	2.45	0.49	2.54	1.40	1.89	0.05
Executive, admin, & managerial. . . .	40.88	28.35	12.53	4.10	0.20	3.61	2.26	2.32	0.04
Admin support including clerical. . . .	21.02	13.87	7.15	1.88	0.14	2.77	1.01	1.32	0.04
Blue-collar occupations	25.73	16.68	9.05	2.38	0.44	3.09	1.28	1.81	0.04
Service occupations	24.63	15.81	8.82	2.28	0.61	2.62	1.67	1.58	0.06
Industry group:									
Services	34.13	24.66	9.47	2.30	0.21	3.12	1.84	1.94	0.07
Health services	27.20	18.20	9.00	2.71	0.74	2.50	1.12	1.89	0.04
Hospitals	28.00	18.81	9.18	2.80	0.72	2.51	1.17	1.94	0.05
Educational services	35.52	25.99	9.53	2.22	0.14	3.19	1.97	1.95	0.07
Elementary and secondary education	34.73	25.58	9.15	1.95	0.12	3.34	1.79	1.85	0.10
Higher education	38.03	27.56	10.47	2.84	0.17	2.93	2.36	2.16	-
Public administration	29.95	19.66	10.29	2.92	0.46	3.09	1.91	1.85	0.06

- Represents zero   [1] Includes severance pay and supplemental unemployment benefits.

Source: U.S. Bureau of Labor Statistics, *Compensation and Working Conditions, Fall 2003.*

No. 456. State and Local Governments—Full-Time Employment and Salary by Sex and Race/Ethnic Group: 1980 to 2001

[As of June 30. (2,350 represents 2,350,000). Excludes school systems and educational institutions. Based on reports from state governments (42 in 1980; 47 in 1983; 49 in 1981 and 1984 through 1987; and 50 in 1989 through 1991) and a sample of county, municipal, township, and special district jurisdictions employing 15 or more nonelected, nonappointed full-time employees. Beginning 1993, only for state and local governments with 100 or more employees. Data for 1992, 1994, 1996, 1998 2000 and 2002 are not available. For definition of median, see Guide to Tabular Presentation]

Year and occupation	Employment (1,000)						Median annual salary ($1,000)					
				Minority						Minority		
	Male	Female	White [1]	Total [2]	Black [1]	His-panic [3]	Male	Female	White [1]	Total [2]	Black [1]	His-panic [3]
1980	2,350	1,637	3,146	842	619	163	15.2	11.4	13.8	11.8	11.5	12.3
1981	2,740	1,925	3,591	1,074	780	205	17.7	13.1	16.1	13.5	13.3	14.7
1983	2,674	1,818	3,423	1,069	768	219	20.1	15.3	18.5	15.9	15.6	17.3
1984	2,700	1,880	3,458	1,121	799	233	21.4	16.2	19.6	17.4	16.5	18.4
1985	2,789	1,952	3,563	1,179	835	248	22.3	17.3	20.6	18.4	17.5	19.2
1986	2,797	1,982	3,549	1,230	865	259	23.4	18.1	21.5	19.6	18.7	20.2
1987	2,818	2,031	3,600	1,249	872	268	24.2	18.9	22.4	20.9	19.3	21.1
1989	3,030	2,227	3,863	1,394	961	308	26.1	20.6	24.1	22.1	20.7	22.7
1990	3,071	2,302	3,918	1,456	994	327	27.3	21.8	25.2	23.3	22.0	23.8
1991	3,110	2,349	3,965	1,494	1,011	340	28.4	22.7	26.4	23.8	22.7	24.5
1993	2,820	2,204	3,588	1,436	948	341	30.6	24.3	28.5	25.9	24.2	26.8
1995	2,960	2,355	3,781	1,534	993	379	33.5	27.0	31.4	26.3	26.8	28.6
1997	2,898	2,307	3,676	1,529	973	392	34.6	27.9	32.2	30.2	27.4	29.5
1999	2,939	2,393	3,723	1,609	1,012	417	37.0	29.9	34.8	31.1	29.6	31.2
2001, total	3,080	2,554	3,888	1,746	1,077	471	39.8	32.1	37.5	34.0	31.5	33.8
Officials/administrators .	212	118	271	60	37	15	63.2	54.8	60.8	58.2	57.7	59.5
Professionals	649	790	1,052	387	222	89	49.2	41.7	45.6	43.2	40.5	42.3
Technicians	269	197	337	128	71	37	39.9	32.1	37.2	34.5	32.7	35.5
Protective service	889	196	770	315	198	96	40.5	32.9	39.8	37.1	35.0	42.1
Paraprofessionals	106	297	234	169	120	36	29.1	26.3	28.1	26.2	24.2	28.1
Admin. support	126	803	610	318	189	97	29.1	27.3	27.4	27.3	27.2	27.5
Skilled craft	397	23	308	112	65	35	36.2	30.4	36.1	34.5	33.6	35.3
Service/maintenance . .	432	130	306	256	175	66	29.3	22.9	28.5	27.2	26.3	28.1

[1] Non-Hispanic.   [2] Includes other minority groups not shown separately.   [3] Persons of Hispanic origin may be of any race.

Source: U.S. Equal Employment Opportunity Commission, 1980-1991, *State and Local Government Information Report,* annual; beginning 1993, biennial.

No. 457. State and Local Government Full-Time Equivalent Employment by Selected Function and State: 2002

[In thousands (1,659.0 represents 1,659,000). For March. Local government data are estimates subject to sampling variation; see Appendix III and source]

State	Education Total State [1]	Education Total Local	Education Elem. & secondary State	Education Elem. & secondary Local	Education Higher education State	Education Higher education Local	Public welfare State	Public welfare Local	Health State	Health Local	Hospitals State	Hospitals Local
United States..	1,659.0	6,552.0	55.3	6,232.8	1,505.7	319.3	241.0	284.2	176.3	252.2	409.2	507.8
Alabama	39.6	93.7	-	93.7	37.1	-	3.8	1.5	5.2	4.6	12.5	24.0
Alaska.	8.8	16.1	3.4	16.0	4.9	0.1	1.8	0.2	0.7	0.4	0.2	0.6
Arizona	28.7	113.2	-	101.9	25.8	11.3	5.9	2.0	2.5	2.4	0.8	4.0
Arkansas	21.3	64.3	-	64.3	18.5	-	4.1	0.1	4.6	0.3	4.3	2.4
California	139.9	745.7	-	667.4	135.0	78.3	4.1	66.7	12.3	43.8	36.6	60.3
Colorado	37.5	91.5	-	90.0	36.2	1.5	2.0	5.7	1.1	3.9	3.7	7.3
Connecticut	23.6	76.3	4.1	76.3	16.4	-	4.8	1.8	2.2	1.7	10.5	-
Delaware	7.7	15.4	-	15.4	7.3	-	1.7	-	2.1	0.2	2.0	-
District of Columbia	-	12.5	-	11.6	-	1.0	13.9	1.4	-	1.7	-	2.0
Florida.	55.8	305.9	-	281.3	52.4	24.5	13.9	6.3	19.5	5.2	5.0	39.5
Georgia	52.2	208.2	-	207.8	49.1	0.4	8.7	1.2	4.3	12.1	7.7	22.1
Hawaii.	34.5	-	26.1	-	8.2	-	0.8	0.1	2.5	0.2	3.8	-
Idaho	9.7	32.1	-	30.7	9.0	1.4	1.7	0.2	1.1	0.9	0.9	5.1
Illinois	58.4	281.8	-	258.4	55.7	23.4	14.7	7.1	3.1	7.6	13.7	12.8
Indiana	53.0	135.9	-	135.9	51.9	-	5.2	1.3	1.7	3.2	4.8	23.3
Iowa	25.4	76.1	-	70.3	24.3	5.8	2.7	1.3	0.4	2.3	7.0	9.5
Kansas	19.8	80.2	-	72.9	19.2	7.2	2.8	1.0	1.0	2.9	2.3	7.1
Kentucky	31.8	104.7	-	104.7	27.3	-	7.1	0.5	2.2	5.0	5.5	4.1
Louisiana	32.3	105.4	-	105.4	28.9	-	5.2	0.6	4.1	1.6	19.3	16.6
Maine	7.6	37.2	0.1	37.2	7.1	-	2.1	0.4	1.3	0.2	0.7	0.6
Maryland	28.9	121.9	-	111.8	26.7	10.0	7.5	3.5	6.9	4.1	5.6	-
Massachusetts . . .	28.3	145.2	0.1	145.1	27.1	0.1	7.4	2.3	8.4	3.0	7.6	2.7
Michigan	70.7	229.2	1.0	216.4	68.0	12.8	12.5	2.4	1.9	11.8	12.2	8.9
Minnesota	37.7	119.0	-	119.0	33.6	-	2.6	11.2	2.2	3.7	4.7	11.2
Mississippi	20.3	75.0	-	68.8	18.8	6.1	2.9	0.4	3.0	0.2	11.9	17.6
Missouri	29.9	135.3	-	129.2	27.8	6.1	8.4	2.7	3.5	4.3	13.3	9.7
Montana	6.7	22.3	-	22.0	6.2	0.3	1.5	0.6	0.9	0.8	0.6	0.6
Nebraska.	12.7	46.8	-	44.1	12.1	2.7	2.8	1.1	0.8	0.6	5.0	4.3
Nevada.	8.9	33.7	-	33.7	8.8	-	1.1	0.7	1.0	0.8	1.0	5.0
New Hampshire . .	7.5	31.1	-	31.1	7.2	-	1.4	2.4	1.0	0.2	0.8	-
New Jersey	54.7	206.3	20.0	196.0	30.8	10.3	6.4	11.5	2.8	4.2	16.1	2.0
New Mexico	18.3	47.1	-	44.2	17.4	2.9	1.5	0.9	2.5	0.4	6.4	0.8
New York.	52.7	474.1	-	450.7	47.9	23.4	6.9	51.7	9.7	18.8	46.0	49.4
North Carolina . . .	51.7	194.1	-	177.3	48.9	16.9	1.9	14.6	4.1	20.8	17.8	24.4
North Dakota	7.5	13.8	-	13.8	7.2	-	0.4	0.9	1.3	0.5	1.0	-
Ohio	69.4	249.6	-	243.5	66.9	6.1	2.7	26.5	3.7	16.6	11.5	11.4
Oklahoma	28.0	86.8	-	86.3	25.8	0.5	6.1	0.3	5.8	2.4	2.6	9.3
Oregon	15.8	75.0	-	66.5	14.7	8.5	6.1	1.1	2.7	5.0	5.1	2.1
Pennsylvania	58.2	232.4	-	223.4	54.6	8.9	12.7	21.5	1.5	5.6	13.2	-
Rhode Island	6.8	21.1	0.5	21.1	5.6	-	1.6	0.2	1.4	0.1	1.3	-
South Carolina . . .	30.4	96.3	-	96.3	27.7	-	5.0	0.3	7.2	2.2	8.3	17.7
South Dakota	5.0	19.4	-	18.9	4.6	0.5	1.0	0.3	0.6	0.2	0.9	0.5
Tennessee	38.7	116.9	-	116.9	36.6	-	5.6	1.7	3.0	3.7	9.4	20.3
Texas	99.1	634.6	-	599.2	94.1	35.4	21.0	3.5	12.4	24.0	30.8	44.4
Utah	24.5	46.0	-	46.0	22.9	-	3.3	0.5	1.9	1.4	5.7	0.4
Vermont	5.5	18.3	-	18.3	4.9	-	1.2	-	0.6	-	0.2	-
Virginia	51.6	180.0	-	178.7	48.6	1.3	2.2	7.6	5.1	6.3	13.4	3.7
Washington	50.8	96.3	-	96.3	47.3	-	9.0	1.3	5.3	3.5	9.1	12.1
West Virginia	12.5	40.6	-	40.6	11.1	-	3.2	-	0.7	1.2	1.7	2.3
Wisconsin	35.6	130.4	-	120.6	34.4	9.8	1.4	13.2	2.0	5.4	3.9	1.3
Wyoming	3.3	17.4	-	15.5	3.1	1.8	0.7	-	0.5	0.4	0.9	4.6

See footnote at end of table.

U.S. Census Bureau, Statistical Abstract of the United States: 2004-2005

No. 457. State and Local Government Full-Time Equivalent Employment, by Selected Function and State: 2002—Con.

[In thousands. For March. Local government amounts are estimates subject to sampling variation; see Appendix III and source]

State	Highways		Police protection		Fire protection		Corrections		Parks and recreation		Government administration	
	State	Local	State	Local	State	Local	State	Local	State	Local	State	Local
United States ...	248.2	296.9	104.4	782.7	(X)	306.7	460.8	241.5	36.2	226.0	383.5	674.3
Alabama........	4.0	7.2	1.4	11.7	(X)	5.1	4.6	3.0	0.7	3.4	6.7	7.9
Alaska	2.9	0.7	0.5	1.2	(X)	0.7	1.8	0.1	0.1	0.6	2.8	1.7
Arizona.........	3.1	4.5	1.9	15.3	(X)	5.7	9.5	5.0	0.4	4.8	5.8	17.2
Arkansas	3.6	3.8	1.2	6.5	(X)	2.5	4.2	1.9	0.8	1.0	3.9	5.5
California	22.7	21.7	13.4	86.9	(X)	32.1	45.1	32.3	3.2	35.1	30.6	101.3
Colorado........	3.1	6.1	1.1	11.6	(X)	4.7	6.7	3.4	0.3	6.2	6.4	10.6
Connecticut.......	3.6	3.6	1.9	9.6	(X)	4.7	8.0	-	0.1	2.2	8.1	4.8
Delaware	1.7	0.6	0.9	1.6	(X)	0.2	3.0	-	0.2	0.3	2.5	1.2
District of Columbia .	-	0.4	-	4.3	(X)	1.8	-	1.6	-	0.9	-	2.4
Florida	9.0	14.4	4.1	55.1	(×)	23.2	26.4	15.2	1.4	18.7	26.7	40.4
Georgia	6.0	8.2	2.4	21.9	(X)	10.3	19.7	7.8	2.9	5.5	8.1	20.5
Hawaii	0.9	0.8	-	3.6	(X)	1.8	2.5	-	0.2	2.0	3.5	2.6
Idaho..........	1.8	1.7	0.5	3.3	(X)	1.1	1.9	1.1	0.2	0.8	2.2	3.7
Illinois	8.7	12.6	4.2	40.7	(X)	16.1	16.8	10.1	0.8	16.4	11.6	32.0
Indiana.........	4.3	6.2	2.0	13.9	(X)	7.3	8.5	4.7	0.1	3.4	4.5	15.1
Iowa	2.6	5.8	0.9	6.2	(X)	1.9	3.2	1.2	0.1	2.1	4.3	5.9
Kansas.........	3.7	5.3	1.1	7.5	(X)	2.9	3.6	2.4	0.6	2.3	4.9	6.8
Kentucky	5.5	3.2	2.2	7.4	(X)	3.7	3.7	3.1	1.6	1.5	9.4	5.6
Louisiana	5.3	5.2	1.7	14.4	(X)	4.6	7.8	5.9	1.2	3.0	5.8	12.3
Maine..........	2.6	1.8	0.6	2.6	(X)	1.5	1.3	0.6	0.2	0.7	2.4	2.6
Maryland	4.8	4.9	2.4	14.9	(X)	6.0	11.9	2.9	0.6	6.7	9.2	8.8
Massachusetts.....	4.1	6.2	5.9	18.0	(X)	13.2	7.2	3.0	1.0	2.1	15.8	8.8
Michigan........	3.1	10.2	3.5	23.0	(X)	8.2	19.1	5.6	0.3	5.3	7.1	26.1
Minnesota.......	5.2	7.5	1.0	10.3	(X)	2.4	3.8	4.9	0.6	4.7	6.5	13.3
Mississippi	3.2	5.0	1.2	7.6	(X)	3.5	4.2	1.5	0.4	1.1	2.3	6.7
Missouri	6.3	7.0	2.2	15.9	(X)	6.1	11.6	2.8	0.6	4.4	7.5	11.4
Montana........	2.1	1.3	0.4	1.9	(X)	0.5	0.9	0.7	0.1	0.4	1.6	2.4
Nebraska	2.2	3.2	0.7	4.0	(X)	1.2	2.4	1.1	0.3	1.1	1.6	4.4
Nevada	1.7	1.4	0.8	5.9	(X)	2.2	3.3	2.4	0.2	2.8	2.8	5.7
New Hampshire....	1.9	1.6	0.4	3.1	(X)	1.6	1.5	0.5	0.2	0.4	1.8	2.1
New Jersey.......	7.4	10.3	4.1	31.2	(X)	7.9	10.2	7.0	2.2	5.8	21.0	19.7
New Mexico	2.4	1.8	0.6	5.1	(X)	2.0	4.1	1.5	0.7	2.0	5.0	4.3
New York	13.1	27.5	6.2	82.6	(X)	23.7	35.3	26.5	2.9	10.9	37.9	40.6
North Carolina.....	12.2	3.8	3.4	20.0	(X)	7.2	20.3	4.1	1.0	5.1	10.9	11.8
North Dakota......	0.9	1.1	0.2	1.2	(X)	0.3	0.6	0.2	0.1	0.8	1.4	1.3
Ohio	7.0	13.9	2.7	31.0	(X)	16.0	17.2	8.5	0.7	8.8	12.0	35.7
Oklahoma........	2.9	6.0	1.9	7.6	(X)	4.1	6.0	1.1	1.0	2.2	5.5	6.7
Oregon..........	3.5	4.0	1.7	7.2	(X)	3.5	4.9	4.0	0.4	2.5	8.4	7.4
Pennsylvania......	13.4	10.5	5.6	26.1	(X)	6.3	16.4	12.2	2.0	4.2	14.2	32.2
Rhode Island......	0.9	0.9	0.3	3.1	(X)	2.2	1.8	-	0.1	0.6	2.6	1.5
South Carolina.....	4.9	2.6	3.1	10.3	(X)	4.3	8.2	2.6	0.7	2.5	3.5	8.9
South Dakota	1.1	1.5	0.3	1.5	(X)	0.4	0.8	0.5	0.1	0.5	1.2	1.7
Tennessee	4.5	6.6	2.0	15.6	(X)	6.8	6.8	6.0	1.0	3.8	5.5	12.0
Texas...........	15.6	19.8	3.7	56.8	(X)	21.4	45.5	25.3	1.1	15.9	16.8	46.0
Utah	1.8	1.6	0.8	4.7	(X)	1.9	3.2	1.7	0.3	2.5	3.5	4.5
Vermont........	1.0	1.0	0.4	0.8	(X)	0.3	1.0	-	0.1	0.2	1.8	1.0
Virginia.........	10.6	3.9	2.6	16.8	(X)	7.9	15.2	7.1	0.9	7.5	8.9	15.7
Washington.......	6.9	6.9	2.3	11.9	(X)	7.8	8.8	4.5	0.6	5.5	6.1	16.2
West Virginia......	5.0	0.9	1.0	2.7	(X)	0.9	0.5	0.3	0.6	0.7	3.9	3.7
Wisconsin........	2.0	9.4	0.9	15.3	(X)	4.8	9.0	3.5	0.2	3.4	6.1	12.2
Wyoming	1.8	0.8	0.3	1.5	(X)	0.4	1.0	0.4	0.1	0.6	1.1	1.6

- Represents or rounds to zero.   X Not applicable.   [1] Includes other categories not shown separately.

Source: U.S. Census Bureau, <http://www.census.gov/pub/govs/www/apesstl02.html>; (accessed 15 April 2004).

State and Local Government Finances and Employment   301

No. 458. State and Local Government Employment and Average Monthly Earnings by State: 1992 and 2002

[3,836 represents 3,836,000. 1992, as of October; 2002, as of March]

State	Full-time equivalent employment (1,000) State		Local [1]		Full-time equivalent employment per 10,000 population [2] State		Local [1]		Average monthly earnings [3] (dol.) State		Local [1]	
	1992	2002	1992	2002	1992	2002	1992	2002	1992	2002	1992	2002
United States..	3,836	4,223	9,346	11,379	150	147	364	395	2,618	3,657	2,556	3,420
Alabama..........	81	86	157	182	195	191	379	405	2,243	3,311	1,822	2,589
Alaska	24	25	23	26	404	385	385	402	3,275	3,979	3,766	3,869
Arizona..........	54	66	140	194	138	122	357	355	2,361	3,261	2,564	3,274
Arkansas	47	53	82	97	193	196	338	357	2,195	2,940	1,741	2,323
California	322	378	1,064	1,397	104	108	343	398	3,420	4,742	3,336	4,390
Colorado..........	53	66	130	174	152	146	373	386	3,016	4,209	2,507	3,360
Connecticut.......	54	67	99	114	164	193	299	329	3,286	4,275	3,246	3,965
Delaware	20	25	17	22	290	308	251	270	2,463	3,525	2,803	3,429
District of Columbia .	(X)	(X)	55	44	(X)	(X)	914	771	(X)	(X)	3,175	4,313
Florida	164	185	493	604	121	111	361	361	2,202	3,206	2,298	3,159
Georgia	114	123	288	352	168	143	422	411	2,075	3,128	1,999	2,833
Hawaii	51	56	14	14	437	450	120	116	2,554	3,123	3,031	3,468
Idaho...........	20	24	40	54	189	178	378	399	2,264	3,270	1,936	2,731
Illinois	137	147	416	496	117	116	356	394	2,642	3,857	2,711	3,616
Indiana..........	95	90	202	235	168	147	356	381	2,506	3,202	2,205	2,977
Iowa	47	52	107	122	168	178	379	415	2,895	4,039	2,185	2,854
Kansas..........	48	44	115	129	189	163	453	477	2,191	3,390	2,198	2,781
Kentucky	76	78	121	152	203	191	321	371	2,349	3,220	2,006	2,462
Louisiana	89	92	162	188	207	205	376	419	2,227	3,028	1,768	2,486
Maine...........	22	22	42	52	177	169	337	400	2,438	3,364	2,125	2,686
Maryland	82	92	157	193	167	169	319	354	2,720	3,878	2,932	3,833
Massachusetts.....	85	95	189	232	141	148	313	361	2,645	4,034	2,842	3,725
Michigan.........	138	143	310	364	145	142	327	362	3,134	4,143	3,010	3,692
Minnesota........	67	76	172	203	150	151	383	405	3,101	4,318	2,647	3,474
Mississippi	47	57	106	126	181	198	406	440	2,000	2,824	1,583	2,245
Missouri	74	92	173	221	142	162	332	389	2,075	2,825	2,148	2,798
Montana.........	17	18	32	35	207	196	384	380	2,300	3,255	2,061	2,645
Nebraska	29	33	69	81	178	192	431	467	2,185	2,983	2,208	2,990
Nevada	19	24	47	68	142	113	346	314	2,738	3,678	2,775	4,066
New Hampshire....	16	20	34	46	146	157	300	360	2,416	3,369	2,501	2,996
New Jersey.......	117	148	287	337	148	172	364	392	3,122	4,433	3,165	4,246
New Mexico	42	45	60	73	264	245	375	392	2,253	2,950	1,830	2,702
New York	267	253	857	937	147	132	469	489	3,143	4,333	3,174	4,460
North Carolina.....	109	135	262	339	158	162	380	407	2,413	3,295	2,095	2,924
North Dakota......	16	17	22	22	258	262	342	349	2,231	2,991	2,237	2,991
Ohio............	140	138	392	471	127	121	355	412	2,691	3,639	2,456	3,287
Oklahoma........	67	66	118	138	208	190	366	395	2,044	3,098	1,883	2,512
Oregon..........	50	55	102	128	166	157	342	364	2,607	3,484	2,658	3,484
Pennsylvania......	123	157	348	396	102	127	288	321	2,586	3,717	2,640	3,530
Rhode Island......	20	20	28	32	196	188	272	302	2,817	4,041	2,829	3,968
South Carolina.....	78	78	124	162	215	191	342	395	2,098	2,963	1,956	2,724
South Dakota	14	13	25	29	190	173	345	382	2,166	3,038	1,855	2,523
Tennessee	76	84	174	223	150	145	344	384	2,153	2,994	2,025	2,760
Texas...........	239	270	744	979	135	124	419	450	2,357	3,286	2,087	2,811
Utah............	40	49	55	74	216	212	299	321	2,100	3,348	2,191	3,091
Vermont	13	14	17	23	226	222	301	373	2,514	3,444	2,280	2,794
Virginia.	116	121	232	290	181	166	362	398	2,309	3,418	2,268	3,068
Washington.......	98	114	179	204	190	188	347	336	2,717	3,780	2,729	4,130
West Virginia......	34	34	58	59	186	190	319	327	1,969	2,902	2,057	2,704
Wisconsin........	73	71	184	218	145	130	367	400	3,216	3,978	2,632	3,439
Wyoming	11	11	25	30	242	225	545	599	2,055	3,061	2,198	2,856

X Not applicable.   [1] Estimates subject to sampling variation; see Appendix III and source.   [2] Based on estimated resident population as of July 1.   [3] For full-time employees.

Source: U.S. Census Bureau, 1990, *Public Employment*, series GE, No. 1, annual; 2001, *Government Employment, March 2001*. See also <http://www.census.gov/govs/www/Apes.html\> (accessed 15 April 2004).

No. 459. City Government Employment and Payroll—Largest Cities: 1992 and 2002

[In thousands, (405.8 represents 405,800) For 1992 as of October; 2002 as of March. See footnote 3, Table 449, for those areas representing city-county consolidated governments]

Cities ranked by 2000 population [1]	Total employment (1,000)		Full-time equivalent employment				Payroll (mil. dol.)		Average monthly earnings for full-time employees (dol.)	
			Total (1,000)		Per 10,000 population [1]					
	1992	2002	1992	2002	1992	2002	1992	2002	1992	2002
New York, NY [2][3]	405.8	455.5	415.0	382.1	566.7	426.6	1,307.9	2,016.2	3,154	4,949
Los Angeles, CA	48.8	51.2	49.5	49.2	142.1	133.1	187.6	259.2	3,815	5,223
Chicago, IL	41.1	41.4	41.1	40.3	147.8	139.2	134.5	180.2	3,269	4,441
Houston, TX	21.0	26.0	21.0	25.4	129.0	129.8	50.6	81.4	2,404	3,188
Philadelphia, PA	29.1	31.2	30.0	29.8	189.4	196.3	91.5	121.4	3,092	4,024
Phoenix, AZ	10.1	13.8	10.8	13.0	109.9	98.1	32.5	58.0	3,104	4,385
San Diego, CA.	9.7	12.2	10.4	10.6	93.2	86.6	29.3	52.0	2,894	4,728
Dallas, TX.	13.7	15.5	13.8	14.9	136.7	125.2	36.3	59.5	2,642	3,961
San Antonio, TX.	12.8	17.8	13.1	15.5	139.8	135.3	32.0	53.9	2,472	3,369
Detroit, MI.	20.2	42.9	20.7	34.8	201.4	366.3	53.8	143.9	2,639	3,955
San Jose, CA	5.5	8.2	5.9	6.6	75.6	73.3	23.8	42.2	4,206	6,090
Honolulu, HI	9.0	10.0	9.3	8.9	111.0	102.1	28.7	32.0	3,139	3,520
Indianapolis, IN	11.3	13.5	12.6	11.5	172.2	144.9	26.2	42.2	2,164	3,392
San Francisco, CA	25.6	28.9	25.6	28.9	354.1	372.4	99.4	165.6	3,881	5,725
Jacksonville, FL	9.0	10.6	9.9	9.4	155.6	128.4	27.1	37.1	2,888	3,784
Columbus, OH.	7.6	9.1	7.9	8.4	124.9	118.7	20.3	34.6	2,607	4,029
Austin, TX.	10.6	11.6	11.5	10.8	246.0	164.6	27.5	40.4	2,496	3,687
Baltimore, MD [2]	26.5	29.4	27.4	26.7	371.8	410.5	70.4	101.5	2,613	3,674
Memphis, TN [2]	21.9	26.7	22.4	24.9	366.7	383.0	52.6	86.8	2,361	3,430
Milwaukee, WI.	8.1	8.1	8.3	7.8	132.7	130.8	22.9	31.1	2,782	3,960
Boston, MA [2].	20.6	22.6	20.8	20.7	361.8	350.5	60.9	89.2	2,949	4,208
Washington DC [2][3]	44.4	36.5	46.3	32.4	763.6	566.1	138.3	145.4	3,022	4,245
Nashville-Davidson, TN	16.3	20.6	17.1	18.7	349.5	327.5	36.2	66.8	2,150	3,477
El Paso, TX.	5.0	5.5	5.1	5.4	98.6	95.0	11.1	15.2	2,220	2,823
Seattle,WA	9.2	12.5	10.2	9.7	197.0	172.6	34.6	53.2	3,494	4,983
Denver, CO.	12.1	13.4	12.5	12.4	266.3	223.5	35.5	54.2	2,859	4,256
Charlotte, NC	4.5	5.7	4.6	5.4	115.0	100.3	11.0	20.5	2,436	3,723
Fort Worth, TX.	4.8	6.2	5.1	5.4	114.3	101.6	11.3	21.4	2,277	3,784
Portland, OR.	4.4	6.4	4.5	5.3	104.0	99.3	16.2	25.5	3,638	4,736
Oklahoma City, OK.	4.4	5.0	4.6	4.5	104.3	88.4	11.7	18.7	2,567	4,103
Tucson, AZ.	4.5	6.7	4.8	5.5	117.4	112.8	12.2	21.6	2,645	3,757
New Orleans, LA	10.3	9.9	10.4	9.3	210.1	192.9	18.3	24.9	1,758	2,619
Las Vegas, NV	1.9	2.7	1.9	2.5	73.2	52.3	6.1	12.9	3,212	5,089
Cleveland, OH.	8.2	9.6	8.5	8.9	167.1	186.2	23.0	32.8	2,742	3,622
Long Beach, CA.	4.9	6.5	5.3	5.4	123.3	116.2	18.4	28.8	3,627	5,098
Albuquerque, NM	5.4	6.8	5.7	6.1	147.5	6.5	11.7	20.1	2,100	3,195
Kansas City, MO	6.4	7.1	6.5	6.8	149.9	6.9	16.4	24.3	2,547	3,556
Fresno, CA.	2.6	3.6	2.6	3.2	72.6	3.5	7.8	14.7	3,043	4,412
Virginia Beach, VA [2]	12.9	21.0	14.0	15.8	355.7	18.1	30.4	48.5	2,275	2,862
Atlanta,GA.	7.7	8.7	7.8	8.0	198.0	8.3	18.5	26.6	2,373	3,226
Sacramento, CA.	3.6	5.0	3.9	3.8	106.6	4.3	12.8	18.6	3,384	4,660
Oakland, CA.	4.1	5.3	4.9	5.3	130.4	5.3	17.3	33.1	3,985	6,293
Mesa, AZ.	2.4	4.0	2.4	3.6	81.6	3.8	6.8	16.6	2,908	4,465
Tulsa, OK.	4.4	4.6	4.4	4.4	120.0	4.4	10.8	14.9	2,463	3,373
Omaha, NE.	2.6	3.2	2.7	2.7	81.5	2.8	8.3	11.1	3,138	4,050
Baton Rouge, LA	5.1	7.2	5.7	5.7	148.8	6.5	12.2	17.8	2,224	2,902
Minneapolis, MN	5.5	6.5	5.9	5.6	161.0	6.3	17.6	24.4	3,097	4,047
Miami, FL.	3.5	4.0	3.6	3.5	100.7	3.9	14.1	17.0	3,994	4,662
Colorado Springs, CO.	4.7	7.6	5.1	6.5	180.6	7.1	12.8	27.7	2,594	3,993
St Louis, MO.	7.3	7.4	7.5	7.2	188.1	7.3	17.8	27.2	2,405	3,737
Wichita, KS.	2.8	3.5	2.9	2.9	96.7	3.1	7.1	10.2	2,429	3,388
Santa Ana, CA.	1.7	2.4	1.9	1.7	63.7	2.0	8.9	10.8	5,162	6,007
Pittsburgh, PA.	4.9	4.3	5.4	4.1	144.7	4.2	14.2	15.7	2,758	3,787
Arlington, TX.	1.8	3.1	1.9	2.3	74.4	2.5	5.4	8.3	2,863	3,421
Cincinnati, OH.	6.2	7.1	7.0	6.1	191.8	6.8	20.0	24.5	3,092	3,815
Anaheim, CA.	2.1	3.4	2.6	2.0	98.1	2.8	9.5	13.6	4,235	6,001
Toledo, OH.	2.9	3.0	2.9	3.0	86.5	3.0	8.5	11.7	2,955	3,908
Tampa, FL [2]	3.8	4.4	3.9	4.3	140.5	4.3	11.1	15.8	2,861	3,676
Buffalo, NY [2]	11.3	12.8	12.8	10.8	390.3	11.7	35.5	47.3	2,986	4,179
St Paul, MN	2.9	3.4	3.2	2.8	118.8	3.1	10.7	13.4	3,429	4,538
Corpus Christi, TX	2.9	3.1	3.0	2.9	114.8	2.9	6.4	8.6	2,195	2,964
Aurora, CO	1.9	2.5	1.9	2.5	87.2	2.5	5.4	10.2	2,808	4,089
Raleigh,NC	2.4	3.5	2.6	2.9	125.4	3.2	5.2	9.6	2,058	3,116
Newark, NJ.	3.8	6.4	3.8	5.4	138.6	5.8	12.2	26.4	3,220	4,756
Lexington-Fayette, KY.	3.4	4.1	3.5	3.6	154.2	3.8	6.9	11.2	2,006	3,020
Anchorage, AK	7.6	10.4	8.2	8.7	364.0	9.3	32.9	37.1	4,139	4,124
Louisville, KY.	4.2	4.7	4.3	4.2	159.6	4.4	8.3	13.5	1,965	3,108
Riverside, CA	2.0	2.3	2.2	1.8	98.1	2.1	7.9	9.7	3,756	5,171
St Petersburg, FL.	2.7	3.7	2.9	2.9	121.0	3.3	7.6	10.7	2,715	3,462
Bakersfield, CA	1.1	1.3	1.2	1.3	65.9	1.3	3.8	5.8	3,350	4,572
Stockton,CA	1.5	2.4	1.7	1.8	79.2	2.1	5.2	8.6	3,359	4,570
Birmingham, AL	3.8	4.8	3.9	4.4	144.8	4.6	8.8	17.2	2,293	3,799
Jersey City, NJ	2.8	3.7	2.9	3.2	127.3	3.4	8.7	15.0	3,037	4,596
Norfolk, VA [2]	9.7	13.6	10.3	10.4	394.1	11.5	23.7	33.8	2,349	2,995
Hialeah, FL	1.3	1.7	1.3	1.4	71.1	1.6	4.5	5.2	3,341	3,546
Lincoln, NE.	2.8	2.9	3.2	2.4	167.1	2.6	8.3	10.2	2,676	4,029
Greensboro, NC	2.3	2.9	2.5	2.7	135.2	2.8	5.7	7.6	2,388	2,781

NA Not available. [1] 2000 based on enumerated resident population as of April 1. Other years based on estimated resident population as of July 1. [2] Includes city-operated elementary and secondary schools. [3] Includes city-operated university or college.

Source: U.S. Census Bureau, *Government Employment, March 2002*, and <http://www.census.gov/govs/www/apes.html>.

No. 460. County Government Employment and Payroll—Largest Counties: 1992 and 2002

[In thousands, (83.4 represents 83,400). 2002 for March; 1992 for October. See text, this section]

Counties ranked by 2000 population [1]	Total employment (1,000)		Full-time equivalent employment				Payroll (mil. dol).		Average earnings for full-time employees (dol.)	
			Total (1,000)		Per 10,000 population [1]					
	1992	2002	1992	2002	1992	2002	1992	2002	1992	2002
Los Angeles, CA	83.4	103.4	89.9	95.2	101	109	316.6	452.4	3,545	4,610
Cook, IL	26.5	28.5	26.6	28.4	52	53	68.3	110.9	2,569	3,898
Harris, TX	17.8	22.1	18.2	20.9	65	65	45.0	73.4	2,484	3,407
Maricopa, AZ	15.0	15.2	15.4	14.7	72	50	31.6	45.2	2,072	3,027
Orange, CA	15.6	26.3	16.5	22.4	68	92	49.5	96.8	3,056	3,995
San Diego, CA	15.7	21.4	16.7	19.1	67	76	48.0	80.2	2,919	4,016
Dade, FL	33.8	41.0	35.5	37.2	183	182	101.4	159.5	2,938	4,102
Dallas, TX	10.0	14.4	10.5	13.1	57	65	24.1	48.3	2,206	3,538
Wayne, MI	5.8	7.0	5.8	6.6	28	34	15.9	28.7	2,729	4,291
King, WA	6.5	14.9	7.5	12.7	50	86	23.4	57.5	3,141	4,306
San Bernardino, CA	12.5	20.6	13.3	18.2	94	121	38.4	74.9	2,955	3,962
Santa Clara, CA	15.5	17.2	16.5	15.7	110	102	57.5	85.7	3,540	5,259
Broward, FL	8.7	12.6	8.9	11.9	71	78	22.3	47.1	2,527	3,896
Riverside, CA	10.4	19.3	11.1	17.3	95	125	36.0	76.6	3,273	4,220
Tarrant, TX	5.5	9.0	5.9	8.4	50	62	12.9	28.1	2,224	3,245
Alameda, CA	9.2	12.1	10.5	10.2	82	84	36.9	54.6	3,463	4,877
Suffolk, NY	10.9	12.6	11.2	11.4	85	89	38.1	57.8	3,389	4,950
Cuyahoga, OH	16.2	16.3	16.2	14.7	115	117	38.7	54.1	2,386	3,375
Bexar, TX	5.9	10.2	6.3	9.0	53	73	14.6	27.7	2,328	2,922
Clark, NV	9.3	17.7	9.9	15.6	134	129	31.4	74.6	3,235	4,672
Nassau, NY	13.9	19.5	15.2	16.1	118	146	58.9	81.9	3,990	4,775
Allegheny, PA	7.9	7.2	8.6	6.9	64	56	21.9	19.4	2,664	2,789
Sacramento, CA	12.7	15.2	13.0	13.5	125	125	34.1	68.5	2,628	4,840
Oakland, MI	3.9	4.6	4.2	4.1	39	38	10.8	17.1	2,625	4,029
Palm Beach, FL	8.3	9.4	8.4	9.0	97	83	21.2	31.8	2,543	3,486
Hennepin, MN	8.1	12.2	9.9	9.5	96	109	29.1	45.3	2,941	4,035
Franklin, OH	5.1	6.9	5.7	6.2	59	64	12.3	20.3	2,253	3,142
St Louis, MO	3.6	4.3	3.7	4.0	37	42	9.7	14.1	2,645	3,436
Hillsborough, FL	11.3	15.8	12.2	10.0	146	158	27.9	37.2	2,288	3,420
Fairfax, VA	29.9	38.4	32.2	34.3	394	396	80.5	140.9	2,546	3,928
Erie, NY	8.9	11.2	9.9	8.8	102	117	33.4	38.1	3,533	3,980
Contra Costa, CA	7.2	10.2	7.8	8.4	98	107	27.3	46.1	3,538	5,071
Milwaukee, WI	10.6	8.2	10.7	7.5	111	87	25.5	28.2	2,392	3,606
Westchester, NY	9.3	7.0	9.9	6.1	113	75	34.8	30.2	3,523	4,794
Pinellas, FL	5.2	6.7	5.2	6.5	61	73	12.4	22.1	2,362	3,374
Du Page, IL	2.4	4.0	2.6	3.5	33	44	6.4	15.0	2,500	4,114
Salt Lake, UT	2.8	6.0	3.4	3.8	46	66	7.8	16.9	2,544	4,139
Shelby, TN	9.2	13.7	9.7	12.9	117	152	20.9	41.3	2,203	3,165
Orange, FL	7.3	10.3	7.5	9.3	110	115	18.1	32.3	2,439	3,365
Bergen, NJ	5.8	6.3	6.5	4.2	78	72	18.8	19.1	3,003	4,274
Montgomery, MD	19.0	39.7	24.5	25.8	324	455	84.2	149.6	3,766	4,951
Hamilton, OH	5.3	6.4	5.4	5.9	63	75	12.1	17.7	2,235	2,868
Pima, AZ	6.2	7.8	6.6	6.3	98	93	13.8	22.8	2,122	3,274
Fulton, GA	5.4	7.3	5.5	6.4	84	90	12.6	25.5	2,309	3,817
Travis, TX	2.7	4.5	2.8	4.3	48	55	6.1	14.6	2,214	3,315
Prince Georges, MD	20.5	31.3	21.7	25.5	297	391	64.9	96.6	3,052	3,558
Fresno, CA	7.7	9.2	7.9	8.1	118	115	20.2	30.0	2,570	3,519
Essex, NJ	7.7	6.5	7.9	5.5	102	82	19.0	24.5	2,427	4,303
Macomb, MI	2.3	3.0	2.5	2.6	35	39	6.1	10.3	2,525	3,726
Baltimore, MD	17.9	24.9	20.4	18.4	294	330	57.3	79.7	2,932	3,908
Ventura, CA	6.9	9.0	7.3	8.4	109	119	21.9	36.8	2,989	4,240
Middlesex, NJ	4.8	4.5	5.1	3.4	77	59	14.1	15.6	2,745	4,285
Montgomery, PA	2.9	3.8	3.1	3.4	46	51	5.8	10.3	1,916	2,981
Monroe, NY	5.6	7.1	6.1	5.7	86	97	17.1	22.8	2,870	3,761
San Mateo, CA	4.9	6.8	5.3	5.2	81	96	18.6	31.0	3,572	5,169
Pierce, WA	2.3	3.6	2.3	3.2	40	51	7.0	14.9	3,039	4,514
Mecklenburg, NC	13.6	25.3	14.2	21.2	279	364	28.9	71.4	2,049	3,192
Jefferson, KY	3.0	3.7	3.1	3.5	46	53	6.4	10.4	2,067	2,914
El Paso, TX	2.8	4.1	3.2	3.8	53	61	6.3	11.9	2,017	3,039
Dekalb, GA	5.3	6.8	5.4	6.5	99	103	13.2	23.6	2,443	3,604
Jefferson, AL	4.6	4.9	4.7	4.7	72	74	10.9	16.0	2,306	3,326
Kern, CA	7.6	10.2	7.9	8.9	145	154	21.4	39.6	2,731	4,201
Multnomah, OR	3.3	7.1	3.8	5.1	65	108	9.3	20.2	2,592	3,706
Oklahoma, OK	1.6	2.2	1.7	2.0	28	34	2.9	5.0	1,755	2,513
Jackson, MO	2.0	2.1	2.0	1.8	32	32	3.6	5.3	1,781	2,701
Norfolk, MA	0.7	0.5	0.7	0.5	12	8	1.8	2.0	2,500	3,886
Lake, IL	2.2	3.0	2.2	2.7	43	47	5.3	10.7	2,431	3,838
Wake, NC	11.4	18.7	12.2	15.5	288	298	25.6	51.6	2,127	3,077
Monmouth, NJ	4.5	6.0	4.8	4.7	88	97	11.5	19.6	2,416	3,892
Hudson, NJ	4.8	4.5	5.1	3.3	93	73	11.7	12.2	2,309	3,579
Cobb, GA	3.3	4.4	3.5	3.8	77	72	8.2	13.3	2,388	3,359
Snohomish, WA	2.0	2.6	2.0	2.5	42	43	5.7	10.6	2,899	4,189
Bucks, PA	2.0	2.7	2.1	2.3	39	45	4.8	8.1	2,271	3,360
Gwinnett, GA	2.8	4.2	2.9	3.7	84	71	7.2	14.1	2,496	3,643
Kent, MI	2.3	2.3	2.6	2.0	52	39	6.2	7.9	2,467	3,717
Hidalgo, TX	1.4	2.1	1.4	2.1	38	37	2.0	4.9	1,423	2,335
San Joaquin, CA	5.8	8.3	6.5	6.3	135	147	15.1	27.1	2,373	3,871

[1] 2000 based on enumerated resident population as of April 1. Other years based on estimated resident population as of July 1.

Source: U.S. Census Bureau; "Government Employment, March 2002;" issued October 2003, <http://www.census.gov/govs/www/apes.html> (accessed 15 April 2004).

Section 9
Federal Government Finances and Employment

This section presents statistics relating to the financial structure and the civilian employment of the federal government. The fiscal data cover taxes, other receipts, outlays, and debt. The principal sources of fiscal data are the *Budget of the United States Government* and related documents, published annually by the Office of Management and Budget (OMB), and the Department of the Treasury's *United States Government Annual Report* and its *Appendix*. Detailed data on tax returns and collections are published annually by the Internal Revenue Service. The personnel data relate to staffing and payrolls. They are published by the Office of Personnel Management and the Bureau of Labor Statistics. The primary source for data on public lands is *Public Land Statistics*, published annually by the Bureau of Land Management, Department of the Interior. Data on federally owned land and real property are collected by the General Services Administration and presented in its annual *Inventory Report on Real Property Owned by the United States Throughout the World.*

Budget concept—Under the unified budget concept, all federal monies are included in one comprehensive budget. These monies comprise both federal funds and trust funds. Federal funds are derived mainly from taxes and borrowing and are not restricted by law to any specific government purpose. Trust funds, such as the Unemployment Trust Fund, collect certain taxes and other receipts for use in carrying out specific purposes or programs in accordance with the terms of the trust agreement or statute. Fund balances include both cash balances with Treasury and investments in U.S. securities. Part of the balance is obligated, part unobligated. Prior to 1985, the budget totals, under provisions of law, excluded some federal activities—including the Federal Financing Bank, the Postal Service, the Synthetic Fuels Corporation, and the lending activities of the Rural Electrification Administration. The Balanced Budget and Emergency Deficit Control Act of 1985 (P.L.99-177) repealed the off-budget status of these entities and placed social security (federal old-age and survivors insurance and the federal disability insurance trust funds) off-budget. Though social security is now off-budget and, by law, excluded from coverage of the congressional budget resolutions, it continues to be a federal program.

Receipts arising from the government's sovereign powers are reported as governmental receipts; all other receipts; i.e., from business-type or market-oriented activities, are offset against outlays. Outlays are reported on a checks-issued (net) basis (i.e., outlays are recorded at the time the checks to pay bills are issued).

Debt concept—For most of U.S. history, the total debt consisted of debt borrowed by the Treasury (i.e., public debt). The present debt series, includes both public debt and agency debt. The *gross federal debt* includes money borrowed by the Treasury and by various federal agencies; it is the broadest generally used measure of the federal debt. *Total public debt* is covered by a statutory debt limitation and includes only borrowing by the Treasury.

Treasury receipts and outlays—All receipts of the government, with a few exceptions, are deposited to the credit of the U.S. Treasury regardless of ultimate disposition. Under the Constitution, no money may be withdrawn from the Treasury unless appropriated by the Congress.

The day-to-day cash operations of the federal government clearing through the accounts of the U.S. Treasury are reported in the *Daily Treasury Statement*. Extensive detail on the public debt is published in the *Monthly Statement of the Public Debt of the United States.*

Budget receipts such as taxes, customs duties, and miscellaneous receipts, which are collected by government agencies, and outlays represented by checks issued and cash payments made by disbursing officers as well as government agencies are reported in the *Daily Treasury Statement of Receipts and Outlays of the United States Government* and in the Treasury's *United States Government Annual Report* and its *Appendix*. These deposits in and payments from accounts maintained by government agencies are on the same basis as the unified budget.

The quarterly *Treasury Bulletin* contains data on fiscal operations and related Treasury activities, including financial statements of government corporations and other business-type activities.

Income tax returns and tax collections—Tax data are compiled by the Internal Revenue Service of the Treasury Department. The annual *Internal Revenue Service Data Book* gives a detailed account of tax collections by kind of tax and by regions, districts, and states. The agency's annual *Statistics of Income* reports present detailed data from individual income tax returns and corporation income tax returns. The quarterly *Statistics of Income Bulletin* has, in general, replaced the supplemental *Statistics of Income* publications which presented data on such diverse subjects as tax-exempt organizations, unincorporated businesses, fiduciary income tax and estate tax returns, sales of capital assets by individuals, international income and taxes reported by corporations and individuals, and estate tax wealth.

Employment and payrolls—The Office of Personnel Management collects employment and payroll data from all departments and agencies of the federal government, except the Central Intelligence Agency, the National Security Agency, and the Defense Intelligence Agency. Employment figures represent the number of persons who occupied civilian positions at the end of the report month shown and who are paid for personal services rendered for the federal government, regardless of the nature of appointment or method of payment. Federal payrolls include all payments for personal services rendered during the report month and payments for accumulated annual leave of employees who separate from the service. Since most federal employees are paid on a biweekly basis, the calendar month earnings are partially estimated on the basis of the number of work days in each month where payroll periods overlap.

Federal employment and payroll figures are published by the Office of Personnel Management in its *Federal Civilian Workforce Statistics—Employment and Trends*. It also publishes biennial employment data for minority groups, data on occupations of white- and blue-collar workers, and data on employment by geographic area; reports on salary and wage distribution of federal employees are published annually. General schedule is primarily white-collar; wage system primarily blue-collar. Data on federal employment are also issued by the Bureau of Labor Statistics in its *Monthly Labor Review* and in Employment and Earnings and by the U.S. Census Bureau in its annual *Public Employment*.

Public lands—The data on applications, entries, selections, patents, and certifications refer to transactions that involve the disposal, under the public land laws (including the homestead laws), of federal public lands to nonfederal owners. In general, original entries and selections are applications to secure title to public lands thar have been accepted as properly filed (i.e., allowed). Some types of applications, however, are not reported until issuance of the final certificate, which passes equitable title to the land to the applicant.

Figure 9.1
Federal Budget Summary: 1980 to 2004

Receipts, outlays, and surplus or deficit

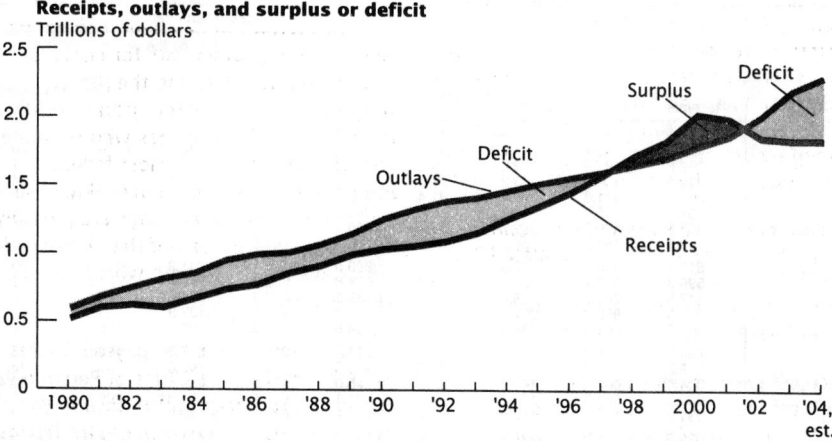

Outlays and federal debt as a percent of gross domestic product

Gross federal debt

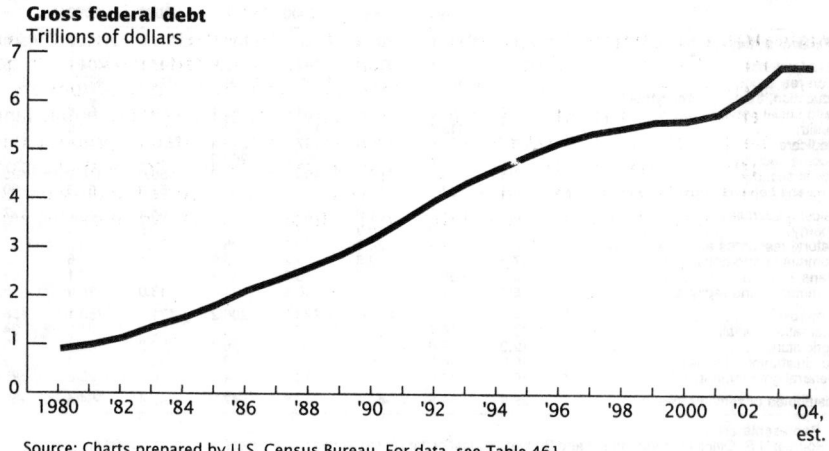

Source: Charts prepared by U.S. Census Bureau. For data, see Table 461.

Federal Government Finances and Employment   307

No. 461. Federal Budget—Receipts, Outlays, and Debt: 1960 to 2004

[In billions of dollars (92.5 represents $92,500,000,000), except percent. For fiscal years ending in year shown; see text, Section 8, State and Local Government Finances and Employment. The Balanced Budget and Emergency Deficit Control Act of 1985 put all the previously off-budget Federal entities into the budget and moved Social Security off-budget. Minus sign (-) indicates deficit]

Year					Gross federal debt [2]				
							Held by the public		
	Receipts	Outlays	Surplus or deficit(-)	Outlays as percent of GDP [1]	Total	Federal gov't account	Total	Federal Reserve System	As percent of GDP [1]
1960	92.5	92.2	0.3	17.8	290.5	53.7	236.8	26.5	56.0
1965	116.8	118.2	-1.4	17.2	322.3	61.5	260.8	39.1	46.9
1970	192.8	195.6	-2.8	19.3	380.9	97.7	283.2	57.7	37.6
1975	279.1	332.3	-53.2	21.3	541.9	147.2	394.7	85.0	34.7
1976	298.1	371.8	-73.7	21.4	629.0	151.6	477.4	94.7	36.2
TQ [3]	81.2	96.0	-14.7	20.9	643.6	148.1	495.5	96.7	35.0
1977	355.6	409.2	-53.7	20.7	706.4	157.3	549.1	105.0	35.8
1978	399.6	458.7	-59.2	20.7	776.6	169.5	607.1	115.5	35.0
1980	517.1	590.9	-73.8	21.7	909.0	197.1	711.9	120.8	33.4
1981	599.3	678.2	-79.0	22.2	994.8	205.4	789.4	124.5	32.5
1982	617.8	745.7	-128.0	23.1	1,137.3	212.7	924.6	134.5	35.3
1983	600.6	808.4	-207.8	23.5	1,371.7	234.4	1,137.3	155.5	39.8
1984	666.5	851.9	-185.4	22.1	1,564.6	257.6	1,307.0	155.1	40.7
1985	734.1	946.4	-212.3	22.8	1,817.4	310.2	1,507.3	169.8	43.8
1986	769.2	990.4	-221.2	22.5	2,120.5	379.9	1,740.6	190.9	48.1
1987	854.4	1,004.1	-149.7	21.6	2,346.0	456.2	1,889.8	212.0	50.4
1988	909.3	1,064.5	-155.2	21.2	2,601.1	549.5	2,051.6	229.2	51.9
1989	991.2	1,143.6	-152.5	21.2	2,867.8	677.1	2,190.7	220.1	53.1
1990	1,032.0	1,253.2	-221.2	21.8	3,206.3	794.7	2,411.6	234.4	55.9
1991	1,055.0	1,324.4	-269.3	22.3	3,598.2	909.2	2,689.0	258.6	60.6
1992	1,091.3	1,381.7	-290.4	22.1	4,001.8	1,002.1	2,999.7	296.4	64.1
1993	1,154.4	1,409.5	-255.1	21.4	4,351.0	1,102.6	3,248.4	325.7	66.1
1994	1,258.6	1,461.9	-203.3	21.0	4,643.3	1,210.2	3,433.1	355.2	66.7
1995	1,351.8	1,515.8	-164.0	20.7	4,920.6	1,316.2	3,604.4	374.1	67.2
1996	1,453.1	1,560.5	-107.5	20.3	5,181.5	1,447.4	3,734.1	390.9	67.3
1997	1,579.3	1,601.3	-22.0	19.6	5,369.2	1,596.9	3,772.3	424.5	65.6
1998	1,721.8	1,652.6	69.2	19.2	5,478.2	1,757.1	3,721.1	458.2	63.5
1999	1,827.5	1,701.9	125.6	18.6	5,605.5	1,973.2	3,632.4	496.6	61.4
2000	2,025.2	1,788.8	236.4	18.4	5,628.7	2,218.9	3,409.8	511.4	58.0
2001	1,991.2	1,863.9	127.4	18.6	5,769.9	2,450.3	3,319.6	534.1	57.5
2002	1,853.2	2,011.0	-157.8	19.4	6,198.4	2,658.0	3,540.4	656.1	59.8
2003	1,782.3	2,157.6	-375.3	19.9	6,760.0	2,846.4	3,913.6	(NA)	62.4
2004, estimate. .	1,798.1	2,318.8	-520.7	20.2	7,486.4	3,065.7	4,420.8	(NA)	65.3

NA Not available.   [1] Gross domestic product as of fiscal year; for calendar year GDP, see Section 13.   [2] See text, this section, for discussion of debt concept.   [3] Prior to fiscal year 1977 the federal fiscal years began on July 1 and ended on June 30. In calender year 1976 the July-September period was a separate accounting period (known as the transition quarter or TQ) to bridge the period required to shift to the new fiscal year.

Source: U.S. Office of Management and Budget, *Budget of the United States Government, Historical Tables*, annual. See also <http://www.whitehouse.gov/omb/budget/fy2005/pdf/hist.pdf>.

No. 462. Federal Budget Outlays—Defense, Human and Physical Resources, and Net Interest Payments: 1990 to 2004

[In billions of dollars (1,253.2 represents $1,253,200,000,000). For fiscal year ending in year shown. Minus sign (-) indicates offsets]

Outlays	1990	1995	1999	2000	2001	2002	2003	2004, est.
Federal outlays, total	1,253.2	1,515.8	1,701.9	1,788.8	1,863.9	2,011.0	2,157.6	2,318.8
National defense	299.3	272.1	274.9	294.5	305.5	348.6	404.9	453.7
Human resources	619.3	923.8	1,057.7	1,115.5	1,194.4	1,317.4	1,417.7	1,497.3
Education, training, employment and social services	37.2	51.0	50.6	53.8	57.1	70.5	82.6	87.2
Health	57.7	115.4	141.1	154.5	172.3	196.5	219.6	243.5
Medicare	98.1	159.9	190.4	197.1	217.4	230.9	249.4	270.5
Income security	148.7	223.7	242.4	253.6	269.6	312.5	334.4	339.5
Social security	243.6	335.8	390.0	409.4	433.0	456.0	474.7	496.2
Veterans benefits and services	29.1	37.9	43.2	47.1	45.0	51.0	57.0	60.5
Physical resources	126.0	59.1	81.9	84.7	97.9	104.4	113.2	127.2
Energy	3.3	4.9	0.9	-1.1	-	0.5	-0.8	1.0
Natural resources and environment . . .	17.1	21.9	24.0	25.0	25.6	29.5	29.7	31.7
Commerce and housing credit	67.6	-17.8	2.6	3.2	5.9	-0.4	-1.6	7.7
Transportation	29.5	39.4	42.5	46.9	54.4	61.8	67.1	68.1
Community and regional development .	8.5	10.7	11.9	10.6	11.9	13.0	18.9	18.8
Net interest	184.4	232.1	229.8	223.0	206.2	171.0	153.1	156.3
International affairs	13.8	16.4	15.2	17.2	16.5	22.4	21.2	34.2
Agriculture	12.0	9.8	23.0	36.6	26.4	22.0	22.6	20.1
Administration of justice	10.0	16.2	26.1	28.0	29.7	35.2	35.4	41.6
General government	10.6	14.0	15.6	13.3	14.6	16.8	23.0	25.4
Undistributed offsetting receipts	-36.6	-44.5	-40.4	-42.6	-47.0	-47.4	-54.4	-59.3

-Represents zero.

Source: U.S. Office of Management and Budget, *Budget of the United States Government, Historical Tables*, annual. See also <http://www.whitehouse.gov/omb/budget/fy2005/pdf/hist.pdf>.

No. 463. Federal Budget Outlays in Constant (1996) Dollars: 1990 to 2004

[Dollar amounts in billions of dollars (1,483.6 represents $1,483,600,000,000). For fiscal year ending in year shown; see text, Section 8. Given the inherent imprecision in deflating outlays, the data shown in constant dollars present a reasonable perspective—not precision. The deflators and the categories that are deflated are as comparable over time as feasible. Minus sign (-) indicates offset]

Type	1990	1995	1999	2000	2001	2002	2003	2004, est.
Constant (1996) dollar outlays, total.	1,483.6	1,551.5	1,620.7	1,660.6	1,692.3	1,932.1	2,030.9	2,143.1
National defense [1]	354.7	282.0	260.7	270.9	275.9	330.8	374.5	414.4
Nondefense, total	1,128.8	1,269.5	1,360.1	1,389.8	1,416.5	1,601.2	1,656.3	1,728.0
Payments for individuals [2]	688.5	895.7	955.7	982.3	1,027.6	1,200.5	1,279.0	1,307.3
Direct payments [2]	596.1	743.6	787.9	808.3	838.2	976.9	1,041.4	1,055.9
Grants to State and local gov'ts	92.5	152.1	167.8	174.0	189.5	223.7	237.7	251.5
All other grants	65.2	77.6	85.7	88.6	95.6	113.7	125.4	132.8
Net Interest [2]	214.3	236.8	219.3	208.8	188.5	164.1	144.6	145.7
All other [2]	209.2	106.3	136.6	147.9	145.6	167.3	156.6	196.0
Undistributed offsetting receipts [2]	-48.4	-46.8	-37.3	-37.8	-40.8	-44.3	-49.4	-53.2
Total nondefense	1,128.8	1,269.5	1,360.1	1,389.8	1,416.5	1,601.2	1,656.3	1,728.8
Total outlays as percent of GDP [3]	21.8	20.7	18.6	18.4	18.6	19.4	19.9	20.2
National defense [1]	5.2	3.7	3.0	3.0	3.0	3.4	3.7	4.0
Nondefense, total	16.6	17.0	15.6	15.4	15.6	16.0	16.2	16.3
Payments for individuals [2]	10.2	12.0	11.0	10.8	11.3	12.0	12.5	12.3
Direct payments [2]	8.8	9.9	9.0	8.9	9.2	9.7	10.1	9.9
Grants to State and local governments. . .	1.4	2.0	1.9	1.9	2.1	2.2	2.3	2.4
All other grants	1.0	1.0	1.0	1.0	1.1	1.2	1.3	1.3
Net Interest [2]	3.2	3.2	2.5	2.3	2.1	1.6	1.4	1.4
All other [2]	2.9	1.4	1.6	1.7	1.6	1.7	1.6	1.9
Total nondefense	16.6	17.0	15.6	15.4	15.6	16.0	16.2	16.3
Percent of outlays, total.	100.0	100.0	100.0	100.0	100.0	100.0	100.0	100.0
National defense [1]	23.9	17.9	16.2	16.5	16.4	17.3	18.8	19.6
Payments for individuals	46.7	57.9	58.8	58.9	60.5	61.8	62.5	60.7
Direct payments [2]	40.5	48.1	48.5	48.5	49.4	50.3	50.9	49.0
Grants to State and local governments. . .	6.3	9.8	10.3	10.4	11.2	11.5	11.6	11.7
All other grants	4.5	5.0	5.4	5.5	5.9	6.0	6.3	6.4
Net Interest [2]	14.7	15.3	13.5	12.5	11.1	8.5	7.1	6.7
All other [2]	13.1	6.8	8.5	9.0	8.7	8.8	7.8	9.2
Undistributed offsettingreceipts [2]	-2.9	-2.9	-2.4	-2.4	-2.5	-2.4	-2.5	-2.6

[1] Includes a small amount of grants to State and local governments and direct payments for individuals. [2] Includes some off-budget amounts; most of the off-budget amounts are direct payments for individuals (social security benefits). [3] Gross domestic product in chained (1996) dollars.

Source: U.S. Office of Management and Budget, *Budget of the United States Government, Historical Tables*, annual. See also <http://www.whitehouse.gov/omb/budget/fy2005/pdf/hist.pdf>.

No. 464. Federal Outlays by Agency: 1990 to 2004

[In billions of dollars (1,253.2 represents $1,253,200,000,000). See headnote, table 461]

Department or other unit	1990	1995	2000	2001	2002	2003	2004, est.
Outlays, total [1]	1,253.2	1,515.8	1,788.8	1,863.8	2,011.0	2,157.6	2,318.8
Legislative Branch	2.2	2.6	2.9	3.0	3.2	3.4	4.3
The Judiciary Branch	1.6	2.9	4.1	4.4	4.8	5.1	5.3
Agriculture	45.9	56.5	75.5	68.0	68.7	72.4	77.7
Commerce	3.7	3.4	7.8	5.0	5.3	5.7	6.2
Defense-Military	289.7	259.5	281.2	291.0	332.0	388.9	435.7
Education	23.0	31.2	33.9	35.7	46.3	57.4	62.8
Energy	12.1	17.6	15.0	16.3	17.7	19.4	20.6
Health and Human Services.	175.5	303.1	382.6	426.3	465.8	505.3	547.9
Homeland Security	7.2	9.4	13.1	15.0	17.6	32.0	30.7
Housing and Urban Development	20.2	29.0	30.8	33.9	31.9	37.5	46.2
Interior	5.8	7.5	8.0	7.9	9.7	9.2	10.0
Justice	5.9	10.1	17.3	18.7	21.1	21.5	23.5
Labor	26.1	32.8	31.9	39.8	64.7	69.6	59.9
State	4.8	6.3	6.9	7.4	9.5	9.3	11.3
Transportation	25.6	35.1	41.5	49.3	56.0	50.8	58.0
Treasury	253.9	346.9	388.6	386.9	370.6	367.0	369.0
Veterans Affairs	29.0	37.8	47.1	45.1	50.9	56.9	60.3
Corps of Engineers.	3.3	3.7	4.3	4.7	4.8	4.8	4.3
Other Defense-Civil Programs	21.7	28.0	32.9	34.2	35.2	39.9	41.9
Environmental Protection Agency	5.1	6.4	7.2	7.4	7.5	8.1	8.1
Executive Office of the President.	0.2	0.2	0.3	0.2	0.5	0.4	6.6
General Services Administration	-0.2	0.7	-0.2	-0.3	-0.7	0.6	0.8
International Assistance Programs.	10.1	11.1	12.1	11.8	13.3	13.5	17.4
National Aeronautics and Space Administration .	12.4	13.4	13.4	14.1	14.4	14.6	14.6
National Science Foundation	1.8	2.8	3.5	3.7	4.2	4.7	5.3
Office of Personnel Management	31.9	41.3	48.7	50.9	52.5	54.1	57.6
Social Security Administration (on-budget)	17.3	31.0	45.1	40.0	45.8	46.3	48.6
Social Security Administration (off-budget)	245.0	330.4	396.2	421.3	442.0	461.4	481.9
Undistributed offsetting receipts	-98.9	-137.6	-173.0	-191.1	-200.7	-210.5	-213.0

[1] Includes agencies and allowances not shown separately.

Source: U.S. Office of Management and Budget, *Budget of the United States Government, Historical Tables*, annual. See also <http://www.whitehouse.gov/omb/budget/fy2005/pdf/hist.pdf>.

Federal Government Finances and Employment 309

No. 465. Federal Outlays by Detailed Function: 1990 to 2004

[In billions of dollars (1,253.2 represents $1,253,200,000,000). For fiscal years ending in year shown; see text, Section 8]

Superfunction and function	1990	1995	1999	2000	2001	2002	2003	2004, est.
Outlays, total	1,253.2	1,515.8	1,701.9	1,788.8	1,863:9	2,011.0	2,157.6	2,318.8
National defense	299.3	272.1	274.9	294.5	305.5	348.6	404.9	453.7
Department of Defense-Military	289.7	259.4	261.3	281.2	291.0	332.0	[2]387.3	[2]434.8
Military personnel	75.6	70.8	69.5	76.0	74.0	86.8	106.7	117.4
Operation and maintenance.	88.3	91.0	96.3	105.8	112.0	130.0	151.4	165.7
Procurement.	81.0	55.0	48.8	51.7	55.0	62.5	67.9	77.7
Research, development, test, and evaluation	37.5	34.6	37.4	37.6	40.5	44.4	53.1	60.6
Military construction	5.1	6.8	5.5	5.1	5.0	5.1	5.9	6.2
Family housing	3.5	3.6	3.7	3.4	3.5	3.7	3.8	3.9
Atomic energy defense activities	9.0	11.8	12.2	12.1	12.9	14.8	16.0	16.6
International affairs.	13.8	16.4	15.2	17.2	16.5	22.4	21.2	34.2
International development and humanitarian assist. . .	5.5	7.6	5.7	6.5	7.2	7.8	10.3	17.9
International security assistance.	8.7	5.3	5.5	6.4	6.6	7.9	8.6	9.5
Conduct of foreign affairs	3.1	4.2	4.2	4.7	5.1	7.1	6.7	8.0
Foreign information and exchange activities.	1.1	1.4	1.2	0.8	0.8	0.9	1.0	1.0
International financial programs	-4.5	-2.0	-1.3	-1.2	-3.1	-1.3	-5.4	-2.2
General science, space and technology	14.4	16.7	18.1	18.6	19.8	20.8	21.0	22.3
General science and basic research	2.8	4.1	5.7	6.2	6.5	7.3	8.0	8.7
Space flight, research, and supporting activities	11.6	12.6	12.4	12.4	13.2	13.5	12.9	13.6
Energy	3.3	4.9	0.9	-1.1	-	0.5	0.8	1.0
Energy supply	2.0	3.6	-0.1	-2.1	-1.1	-0.8	-2.1	-0.4
Energy conservation	0.4	0.7	0.6	0.7	0.8	0.9	0.9	0.9
Emergency energy preparedness.	0.4	0.2	0.2	0.2	0.2	0.2	0.2	0.2
Energy information, policy, and regulation	0.6	0.5	0.2	0.2	0.2	0.2	0.2	0.3
Natural resources and environment [1]	17.1	21.9	24.0	25.0	25.6	29.5	30.0	31.7
Water resources	4.4	4.6	4.7	5.1	5.2	5.6	5.5	5.7
Conservation and land management.	4.0	6.0	6.4	6.8	7.1	9.8	9.7	10.4
Recreational resources.	1.4	2.0	2.7	2.6	2.3	2.8	2.9	3.0
Pollution control and abatement	5.2	6.5	6.9	7.4	7.6	7.6	8.2	8.3
Agriculture	11.9	9.7	22.9	36.5	26.2	22.0	22.6	20.1
Farm income stabilization	9.8	7.0	20.0	33.5	22.7	18.4	18.4	15.7
Agricultural research and services	2.1	2.6	2.8	3.0	3.5	3.6	4.2	4.4
Commerce and housing credit [1]	67.6	-17.8	2.6	3.2	5.9	-0.4	1.6	7.7
Mortgage credit.	3.8	-1.0	0.4	-3.3	-1.2	-7.0	-4.6	2.2
Postal Service	2.1	-1.8	1.1	2.1	2.4	0.2	-5.2	-4.9
Deposit insurance	57.9	-17.8	-5.3	-3.1	-1.4	-1.0	-1.4	-1.5
Transportation [1]	29.5	39.4	42.5	46.9	54.4	61.8	67.1	68.1
Ground transportation	19.0	25.3	28.1	31.7	35.8	40.2	37.5	42.8
Air transportation.	7.2	10.0	10.7	10.6	14.0	16.5	23.3	18.6
Water transportation	3.2	3.7	3.5	4.4	4.4	5.0	5.9	6.4
Community and regional development	8.5	10.7	11.9	10.6	11.8	13.0₀	18.9	18.8
Community development	3.5	4.7	5.1	5.5	5.3	6.0	6.3	6.9
Area and regional development	2.9	2.7	2.3	2.5	2.6	2.6	2.4	2.6
Disaster relief and insurance	2.1	3.3	4.4	2.6	3.8	4.4	10.1	9.2
Educ./training/employment/& soc. services [1]	37.2	51.0	50.6	53.8	57.1	70.5	83.0	87.2
Elementary, secondary, and vocational education . . .	9.9	14.7	17.6	20.6	22.9	25.9	31.5	37.6
Higher education.	11.1	14.2	10.7	10.1	9.6	17.0	22.7	21.6
Research and general education aids	1.6	2.1	2.3	2.5	2.8	2.9	3.0	3.2
Training and employment	5.6	7.4	6.8	6.8	7.2	8.3	8.4	7.3
Other labor services.	0.8	1.0	1.1	1.2	1.3	1.4	1.5	1.6
Social services	8.1	11.6	12.2	12.6	13.5	14.9	15.6	15.9
Health	57.7	115.4	141.1	154.5	172.3	196.5	219.6	243.5
Health care services	47.6	101.9	124.5	136.2	151.9	172.6	192.6	213.6
Health research and training	8.6	11.6	14.4	16.0	17.9	21.4	24.0	27.0
Consumer and occupational health and safety	1.5	1.9	2.2	2.3	2.4	2.6	2.9	2.9
Medicare	98.1	159.9	190.4	197.1	217.4	230.9	249.4	270.5
Income security [1]	148.7	223.7	242.4	253.6	269.6	312.5	334.4	339.5
Gen. retirement & disability ins. (exc. soc. sec.)	5.1	5.1	1.9	5.2	5.8	5.7	7.0	6.9
Federal employee retirement and disability.	52.0	65.9	75.1	77.2	81.0	83.4	85.2	89.3
Unemployment compensation	18.9	23.6	23.6	23.0	30.2	53.3	57.1	48.3
Housing assistance	15.9	27.5	27.7	28.8	30.1	33.1	35.3	37.3
Food and nutrition assistance	24.0	37.6	33.1	32.5	34.1	38.2	42.5	46.6
Social security.	248.6	335.8	390.0	409.4	433.0	456.0	474.7	496.2
Veterans benefits and services [1]	29.1	37.9	43.2	47.1	45.0	51.0	57.2	60.5
Income security for veterans	15.6	19.4	22.7	25.5	23.2	27.4	29.9	32.4
Veterans education, training and rehabilitation	0.4	1.3	1.4	1.4	1.4	1.9	2.3	2.6
Hospital and medical care for veterans	12.1	16.4	18.1	19.5	20.9	22.2	24.0	26.6
Veterans housing	0.6	0.4	0.6	0.4	-0.9	-1.0	0.5	-1.9
Administration of justice.	10.2	16.5	26.5	28.5	30.2	35.1	35.4	41.6
General government.	10.5	13.8	15.3	13.0	14.2	17.0	23.0	25.4
Net interest [1].	184.3	232.1	229.8	223.0	206.2	171.0	153.1	156.3
Interest on Treasury debt securities (gross)	264.7	332.4	353.5	361.9	359.5	332.5	318.1	319.2
Interest received by on-budget trust funds	-46.3	-59.9	-66.5	-69.3	-75.3	-76.5	-72.5	-67.4
Interest received by off-budget trust funds	-16.0	-33.3	-52.1	-59.8	-68.8	-76.8	-83.5	-86.3
Undistributed offsetting receipts	-36.6	-44.5	-40.4	-42.6	-47.0	-47.4	-54.4	-59.3

- Represents zero.   [1] Includes functions not shown separately.   [2] Department of Defense Military Outlay does not include monies allocated for rebuilding Iraq.

Source: U.S. Office of Management and Budget, *Budget of the United States Government, Historical Tables,* annual. See also <http://w3.access.gpo.gov/usbudget/fy2005/pdf/hist.pdf>.

No. 466. Department of Homeland Security—Budget: 2003 to 2005

[In millions of dollars (37,118.2 represents $37,118,200,000. For years ending Sept. 30]

Agency	2003		2004 Enacted	2005 Request
	Enacted	Supplemental		
Discretion budget authority, total	37,118.2	5,329.0	41,307.1	47,385.7
Intelligence and Warning	125.1	86.0	268.7	474.1
Border and Transportation Security	15,170.8	1,859.0	15,322.5	17,074.6
Domestic Counterterrorism	2,509.2	522.6	2,994.1	3,419.8
Protecting Critical Infrastructure and Key Assets . . .	12,893.1	388.3	12,571.0	14,060.0
Defending Against Catastrophic Threats	2,428.4	201.1	2,827.2	3,358.2
Emergency Preparedness and Response	3,873.2	2,272.0	7,132.5	8,802.4
Other	118.3	-	191.1	196.5

- Represents zero.

Source: U.S. Office of Management and Budget, *Budget of the United States Government, Fiscal Year 2005*. See also <http://www.whitehouse.gov/omb/budget/fy2005/budget/homeland.pdf>(released 04 February 2004).

No. 467. Federal Receipts by Source: 1990 to 2004

[In billions of dollars (1,032.0 represents $1,032,000,000,000). For fiscal years ending in year shown; see text, Section 8, State and Local Government Finances and Employment. Receipts reflect collections. Covers both Federal funds and trust funds; see text, this section. Excludes government-sponsored but privately-owned corporations, Federal Reserve System, District of Columbia government, and money held in suspense as deposit funds]

Source	1990	1995	1999	2000	2001	2002	2003	2004, est.
Total federal receipts [1]	1,032.0	1,351.8	1,827.5	2,025.2	1,991.2	1,853.2	1,782.3	1,798.1
Individual income taxes	466.9	590.2	879.5	1,004.5	994.3	858.3	793.7	765.4
Corporation income taxes	93.5	157.0	184.7	207.3	151.1	148.0	131.8	168.7
Social insurance and retirement receipts .	380.0	484.5	611.8	652.9	694.0	700.8	713.0	732.4
Excise taxes.	35.3	57.5	70.4	68.9	66.2	67.0	67.5	70.8
Social insurance and retirement receipts [1]	**380.0**	**484.5**	**611.8**	**652.9**	**694.0**	**700.8**	**713.0**	**732.4**
Employment and general retirement	353.9	451.0	580.9	620.5	661.4	668.5	675.0	688.4
Old-age & survivors ins.(Off-Budget) . .	255.0	284.1	383.6	411.7	434.1	440.5	447.8	456.5
Disability insurance (off-budget)	26.6	67.0	60.9	68.9	73.5	74.8	76.0	77.5
Hospital insurance	68.6	96.0	132.3	135.5	149.7	149.0	147.2	150.5
Railroad retirement/pension fund	2.3	2.4	2.6	2.7	2.7	2.5	2.3	2.2
Unemployment insurance	21.6	28.9	26.5	27.6	27.8	27.6	33.4	39.2
Other retirement	4.5	4.6	4.5	4.8	4.7	4.6	4.6	4.7
Federal employees retirement-employee share	4.4	4.5	4.4	4.7	4.6	4.5	4.6	4.7
Excise taxes, total [1]	**35.3**	**57.5**	**70.4**	**68.9**	**66.2**	**67.0**	**67.5**	**70.8**
Federal funds	15.6	26.9	19.3	22.7	24.1	24.0	23.8	24.1
Alcohol	5.7	7.2	7.4	8.1	7.6	7.8	7.9	8.0
Tobacco	4.1	5.9	5.4	7.2	7.4	8.3	7.9	8.0
Telephone	3.0	3.8	5.2	5.7	5.8	(X)	(X)	(X)
Ozone depleting chemicals/products . .	0.4	0.6	0.1	0.1	(Z)	(X)	(X)	(X)
Transportation fuels	-	8.5	0.8	0.8	1.2	0.8	0.9	0.3
Trust funds.	19.8	30.5	51.1	46.2	41.9	43.0	43.7	46.6
Highway.	13.9	22.6	39.3	35.0	31.5	32.6	33.7	35.5
Airport and airway	3.7	5.5	10.4	9.7	9.2	9.0	8.7	9.8
Black lung disability	0.7	0.6	0.6	0.5	0.5	0.6	0.5	0.5
Inland waterway	0.1	0.1	0.1	0.1	0.1	0.1	0.1	0.1
Hazardous substance superfund.	0.8	0.9	(Z)	(Z)	0.0	(X)	(X)	(X)
Oil spill liability.	0.1	0.2	-	0.2	-	(X)	(X)	(X)
Aquatic resources	0.2	0.3	0.4	0.3	0.4	0.4	0.4	0.4
Vaccine injury compensation	0.2	0.1	0.1	0.1	0.1	0.1	0.1	0.1

- Represents or rounds to zero.   X Not applicable.   Z $50 million or less.   [1] Totals reflect interfund and intragovernmental transactions and/or other functions, not shown separately.

Source: U.S. Office of Management and Budget, *Budget of the United States Government, Historical Tables*, annual. See also <http://www.whitehouse.gov/omb/budget/fy2005/pdf/hist.pdf>.

No. 468. Federal Trust Fund Receipts, Outlays, and Balances: 2001 to 2003

[In billions of dollars (1,125 represents $1,125,000,000,000). For fiscal years ending in year shown. Receipts deposited. Outlays on a checks-issued basis less refunds collected. Balances: That which have not been spent. See text, this section, for discussion of the budget concept and trust funds]

Description	Income			Outlays			Balances [1]		
	2001	2002	2003	2001	2002	2003	2001	2002	2003
Total [2]	1,125	1,164	1,185	897	962	1,006	2,340	2,542	2,723
Airport and airway trust fund..........	10	10	9	10	12	10	15	13	12
Federal employees health benefits fund ..	22	24	26	21	23	25	7	8	9
Fed./civ. employees retirement funds	79	81	80	48	50	51	554	586	615
Federal old-age, survivors and disability insurance trust funds........	597	615	630	434	456	475	1,170	1,329	1,485
Foreign military sales trust fund........	10	11	11	10	11	11	6	6	6
Highway trust fund	32	33	34	35	38	38	28	22	18
Health insurance trust funds:									
Medicare:									
Federal hospital insurance trust fund...	172	180	176	143	148	154	197	229	251
Federal supplemental medical insurance....................	99	107	110	103	110	124	42	39	25
Military retirement fund	41	43	42	34	35	36	165	173	179
Railroad retirement trust funds	10	12	31	9	10	29	17	18	24
Unemployment trust funds	34	34	38	32	55	59	89	69	48
Veterans life insurance trust funds	2	2	2	2	2	2	14	13	13
Other trust funds [3]	19	19	19	18	18	18	38	38	38

[1] Balances available on a cash basis (rather than an authorization basis) at the end of the year. Balances are primarily invested in Federal debt securities.   [2] Includes funds not shown separately.   [3] Effective August 9, 1989, the permanent insurance fund of the FDIC was classified under law as a Federal fund.

Source: U.S. Office of Management and Budget, *Budget of the United States Government, Analytical Perspectives*, annual. See also <http://www.whitehouse.gov/omb/budget/fy2005/spec.html>.

No. 469. United States Government Ledger Balance Sheet—Assets and Liabilities: 1995 to 2003

[In millions of dollars (89,349 represents $89,349,000,000). For fiscal year ending in year shown]

Item	1995	2000	2002	2003
Assets, total	89,349	181,729	265,951	267,473
Cash and monetary assets, total	84,080	98,401	141,061	114,443
U.S. Treasury operating cash:				
Federal Reserve account	8,620	8,459	7,879	7,224
Tax and loan note accounts	29,329	44,199	53,007	27,735
Special drawing rights (SDR):				
Total holdings	11,035	10,316	11,710	12,062
SDR's certificates issued to Federal Reserve banks	-10,168	-3,200	-2,200	-2,200
Monetary assets with IMF [1]	14,682	13,690	20,864	24,072
Other cash and monetary assets:				
Cash and other assets held outside the Treasury Account	29,697	24,937	49,802	45,549
U.S. Treasury monetary assets	356	-	1	-
U.S. Treasury time deposits	528	5,977	27,369	7,200
Loan financing accounts:				
Guaranteed loans	-12,714	-22,013	-16,293	-15,555
Direct loans	19,732	105,459	139,306	145,801
Miscellaneous asset accounts	-1,748	-119	376	-55
Liabilities, total	3,674,266	3,467,448	3,594,788	3,970,594
Federal securities, total.	4,920,944	5,629,009	6,198,129	6,759,792
Treasury debt securities, total	4,893,989	5,601,336	6,170,959	6,732,770
Agency securities outstanding	26,955	27,672	27,170	27,023
Deduct: Net Federal securities held as investments by government accounts	1,317,645	2,218,896	2,675,648	2,859,291
Equals: Borrowing from the public, total	3,603,299	3,410,113	3,540,155	3,914,555
Accrued interest payable.	50,611	44,211	32,869	31,806
Special drawing rights allocated by IMF [1]	7,380	6,359	6,481	7,005
Deposit fund liabilities.	8,186	2,625	7,186	9,945
Miscellaneous liability accounts (checks outstanding, etc.)	4,790	4,140	8,098	7,282

-Represents zero.   [1] IMF = International Monetary Funds.

Source: U.S. Dept of Treasury, *United States Government Annual Report*, 1995-2003; and beginning 2000, *Combined Statement of Receipts, Outlays, and Balances of the United States 2003*. See also <http://www.fms.treas.gov/annualreport/cs2003/sc1.pdf>. (released 11 December 2003).

No. 470. U.S. Savings Bonds: 1990 to 2003

[In billions of dollars (122.5 represents $122,500,000,000), except percent. As of end of fiscal year, see text, Section 8]

Item	1990	1994	1995	1996	1997	1998	1999	2000	2001	2002	2003
Amounts outstanding, total [1]	122.5	176.8	181.5	184.4	182.6	180.7	166.5	177.7	179.5	185.5	192.6
Sales	7.8	9.5	7.2	5.9	5.3	4.8	6.5	5.6	8.0	12.5	13.8
Accrued discounts	8.0	9.4	9.5	9.8	9.1	9.1	8.4	6.9	8.4	7.7	7.3
Redemptions [2]	7.5	9.4	11.8	2.5	2.1	14.3	16.6	14.5	13.8	12.5	12.1
Percent of total outstanding. . .	6.1	5.3	6.5	1.4	1.1	7.9	10.0	8.2	7.7	6.7	6.3

[1] Interest-bearing debt only for amounts end of year.   [2] Matured and unmatured bonds.
Source: U.S. Department of the Treasury, *Treasury Bulletin*, quarterly.

No. 471. Tax Expenditures Estimates Relating to Individual and Corporate Income Taxes by Selected Function: 2003 to 2005

[In millions of dollars (2,210 represents $2,210,000,000). For years ending Sept. 30. Tax expenditures are defined as *revenue losses* attributable to provisions of the Federal tax laws which allow a special exclusion, exemption, or deduction from gross income or which provide a special credit, a preferential rate of tax, or a deferral of liability]

Function and provision	2003	2004	2005	2005, rank
National defense:				
Exclusion of benefits and allowances to armed forces personnel	2,210	2,240	2,260	40
International affairs:				
Exclusion of income earned abroad by U.S. citizens	2,620	2,680	2,750	34
Exclusion of certain allowances for Federal employees abroad	770	800	840	60
Extraterritorial income exclusion	5,150	5,510	5,890	21
Inventory property sales source rules exception	1,540	1,620	1,700	47
Deferral of income from controlled foreign corporations (normal tax method)	7,450	7,900	8,400	17
Deferred taxes for financial firms on certain income earned overseas	2,050	2,130	2,190	41
General science, space, and technology:				
Expensing of research and experimentation expenditures (normal tax method)	-1,980	-2,350	4,500	24
Credit for increasing research activities	4,960	4,400	2,550	37
Agriculture:				
Capital gains treatment of certain income	1,050	1,100	1,160	50
Commerce and housing:				
Financial institutions and insurance:				
Exemption of credit union income	1,300	1,360	1,430	48
Exclusion of interest on life insurance savings	18,900	20,500	22,130	10
Housing:				
Exclusion of interest on owner-occupied mortgage subsidy bonds	910	990	1,080	55
Deductibility of mortgage interest on owner-occupied homes.	61,160	62,590	69,740	2
Deductibility of State and local property tax on owner-occupied homes	22,090	21,740	19,410	13
Deferral of income from post 1987 installment sales	1,080	1,100	1,120	51
Capital gains exclusion on home sales	20,260	20,860	21,490	11
Exception from passive loss rules for $25,000 of rental loss	5,710	4,570	4,390	25
Credit for low-income housing investments	6,210	6,550	6,860	19
Accelerated depreciation on rental housing (normal tax method)	1,220	620	-170	133
Commerce:				
Capital gains (except agriculture, timber, iron ore, and coal) [1]	25,730	27,300	30,190	6
Step-up basis of capital gains at death	14,880	16,280	18,240	15
Accelerated depreciation of buildings other than rental housing [1]	-2,290	-3,190	-4,060	135
Accelerated depreciation of machinery and equipment [1]	48,520	46,800	-10,920	136
Expensing of certain small investments [1]	1,030	1,590	4,850	23
Graduated corporation income tax rate [1]	3,030	3,090	3,910	27
Transportation:				
Exclusion of reimbursed employee parking expenses	2,130	2,240	2,360	39
Community and regional development:				
Empowerment zones, Enterprise communities, and renewal communities	1,070	1,080	1,120	51
Education, training, employment, and social services:				
Education:				
Exclusion of scholarship and fellowship income [1]	1,260	1,260	1,340	49
HOPE tax credit	3,290	3,420	3,510	32
Lifetime Learning tax credit	1,910	2,250	2,180	42
Deduction for higher education expenses.	1,730	1,810	2,580	36
Parental personal exemption for students age 19 or over	3,140	3,130	2,550	37
Deductibility of charitable contributions (education)	3,670	3,390	3,660	30
Training, employment, and social services:				
Exclusion of employee meals and lodging (other than military).	780	810	850	59
Child credit.	37,970	24,340	29,860	7
Credit for child and dependent care expenses	2,720	2,950	2,690	35
Deductibility of charitable contributions, other than education and health	30,020	27,370	29,670	8
Health:				
Exclusion of employer contributions for medical insurance premiums [2]	101,920	106,720	112,990	1
Self-employed medical insurance premiums.	2,550	3,740	3,780	28
Deductibility of medical expenses.	6,240	6,880	7,900	18
Exclusion of interest on hospital construction bonds	1,620	1,780	1,930	44
Deductibility of charitable contributions (health).	3,390	3,090	3,350	33
Income security:				
Exclusion of workers compensation benefits	6,100	6,460	6,850	20
Net exclusion of pension contributions and earnings:				
Employer plans.	59,480	59,380	61,740	3
401(k) plans.	51,560	56,740	58,910	4
Individual Retirement Accounts	20,060	19,810	20,090	12
Low and moderate income savers credit	880	960	1,100	53
Keogh plans.	6,020	8,730	9,260	16
Exclusion of other employee benefits:				
Premiums on group term life insurance	1,800	1,830	1,860	45
Special ESOP rules	1,780	1,920	2,060	43
Additional deduction for the elderly	1,840	1,710	1,800	46
Earned income tax credit	5,099	4,884	5,006	22
Social Security:				
Exclusion of social security benefits:				
Social Security benefits for retired workers.	18,600	19,620	19,040	14
Social Security benefits for disabled	3,230	3,570	3,720	29
Social Security benefits for dependents and survivors	4,060	4,380	4,310	26
Veterans benefits and services:				
Exclusion of veterans death benefits and disability compensation	3,320	3,330	3,600	31
General purpose fiscal assistance:				
Exclusion of interest on public purpose State and local bonds.	25,480	25,980	26,370	9
Deductibility of nonbusiness state and local taxes other than on owner-occupied	49,770	49,470	46,180	5
Tax credit for corporations receiving income from doing business in U.S. possessions.	1,200	1,150	1,100	53

[1] Normal tax method.   [2] Includes premiums and medial care.

Source: U.S. Office of Management and Budget, *Budget of the United States Government, Analytical Perspectives, Fiscal Year 2004.* See also <http://www.whitehouse.gov/omb/budget/fy2005/pdf/spec.pdf> (released 04 February 2004).

No. 472. Federal Funds—Summary Distribution by State and Outlying Area: 2002

[In millions of dollars (1,917,637 represents $1,917,637,000,000), except as indicated. For year ending Sept. 30. Data for grants, salaries and wages and direct payments to individuals are on an expenditures basis; procurement is on obligation basis]

State and outlying area	Federal funds Total	Per capita [1] (dol.)	Defense	Non-defense	Direct payments	Procure-ment	Grants	Salaries and wages
United States [2]	1,917,637	6,527	277,900	1,639,737	1,035,235	270,965	412,371	199,066
Alabama	34,291	7,643	7,026	27,265	18,803	6,035	6,344	3,109
Alaska	7,562	11,746	1,975	5,586	1,541	1,396	3,127	1,499
Arizona	34,761	6,371	8,605	26,157	17,664	7,291	6,664	3,142
Arkansas	18,372	6,779	1,682	16,690	11,979	1,095	4,047	1,251
California	206,401	5,878	36,152	170,250	104,422	34,753	48,084	19,143
Colorado	26,229	5,820	5,243	20,986	12,826	4,526	4,740	4,138
Connecticut	25,387	7,336	6,240	19,147	12,436	6,216	5,279	1,456
Delaware	4,766	5,903	518	4,248	2,972	207	1,121	465
District of Columbia	33,533	58,738	3,454	30,080	4,006	10,875	4,832	13,821
Florida	104,814	6,271	14,277	90,536	69,670	9,757	16,350	9,038
Georgia	51,336	5,997	10,991	40,345	26,105	7,364	10,500	7,366
Hawaii	10,474	8,414	3,964	6,510	4,334	1,621	1,835	2,684
Idaho	8,378	6,247	602	7,776	4,403	1,357	1,837	781
Illinois	70,275	5,577	4,324	65,951	44,291	4,664	14,975	6,344
Indiana	34,200	5,553	2,846	31,354	22,222	2,802	6,969	2,208
Iowa	18,839	6,415	914	17,926	12,739	955	4,060	1,084
Kansas	17,496	6,442	2,330	15,166	10,587	1,653	3,272	1,984
Kentucky	28,880	7,056	4,015	24,864	15,701	3,978	6,346	2,854
Louisiana	29,988	6,690	3,210	26,778	17,317	2,773	7,437	2,461
Maine	9,205	7,111	1,687	7,518	4,847	1,240	2,270	848
Maryland	49,537	9,076	10,220	39,318	20,074	13,488	6,312	9,664
Massachusetts	47,480	7,387	5,854	41,626	24,973	6,793	12,339	3,376
Michigan	55,909	5,563	3,134	52,775	35,805	3,539	13,279	3,286
Minnesota	27,056	5,390	1,971	25,084	16,314	2,228	6,492	2,022
Mississippi	21,308	7,420	3,658	17,651	11,688	2,734	5,046	1,840
Missouri	42,347	7,465	7,139	35,208	22,967	7,313	8,429	3,637
Montana	6,974	7,668	459	6,515	3,951	350	1,912	760
Nebraska	11,583	6,698	1,039	10,544	7,541	591	2,342	1,109
Nevada	10,737	4,940	1,244	9,493	6,551	1,250	1,840	1,096
New Hampshire	6,937	5,441	910	6,027	3,942	788	1,632	574
New Jersey	50,673	5,899	4,765	45,908	31,037	4,840	10,822	3,974
New Mexico	17,478	9,422	1,910	15,568	6,328	5,393	3,954	1,802
New York	128,994	6,733	6,288	122,707	70,590	7,417	42,461	8,526
North Carolina	48,180	5,791	6,546	41,633	28,340	2,923	10,939	5,978
North Dakota	6,437	10,151	627	5,810	4,027	329	1,425	655
Ohio	65,976	5,777	5,746	60,230	40,780	5,243	14,844	5,109
Oklahoma	24,355	6,971	3,897	20,459	13,580	2,515	5,108	3,152
Oregon	19,839	5,634	1,001	18,838	12,339	994	4,814	1,692
Pennsylvania	85,601	6,940	6,827	78,773	54,111	7,415	18,017	6,058
Rhode Island	7,503	7,014	916	6,587	4,129	495	2,094	786
South Carolina	26,103	6,355	3,765	22,339	14,771	3,105	5,592	2,636
South Dakota	6,315	8,297	471	5,844	3,801	378	1,506	631
Tennessee	39,276	6,775	2,551	36,724	21,505	5,912	8,658	3,200
Texas	123,431	5,667	22,267	101,164	64,972	20,581	24,858	13,019
Utah	12,302	5,311	2,508	9,794	5,592	2,084	2,697	1,929
Vermont	4,111	6,667	465	3,645	2,040	431	1,281	359
Virginia	74,537	10,220	29,632	44,904	27,149	26,170	7,714	13,504
Washington	40,218	6,627	6,500	33,717	21,057	5,586	8,296	5,278
West Virginia	13,361	7,415	474	12,887	8,240	602	3,298	1,221
Wisconsin	28,844	5,301	1,621	27,222	17,988	1,888	7,255	1,713
Wyoming	3,666	7,351	331	3,335	1,648	319	1,234	465
Outlying areas:								
American Samoa	154	2,691	6	148	41	13	93	6
Federated States of Micronesia	140	1,326	-	140	13	1	126	-
Guam	1,114	7,195	562	552	276	308	251	279
Marshall Islands	203	3,590	143	59	1	144	58	-
Northern Marianas	102	1,474	7	95	24	9	66	3
Palau	42	2,146	1	42	-	1	41	-
Puerto Rico	14,062	3,644	603	13,459	7,940	365	4,828	930
Virgin Islands	573	5,271	29	544	228	29	266	50
Undistributed	18,996	(X)	11,759	7,237	17	15,844	65	3,071

- Represents zero.   X Not applicable.   [1] Based on U.S. Census Bureau estimated resident population as of July 1.
[2] Includes outlying areas and undistributed.

Source: U.S. Census Bureau, *Consolidated Federal Funds Report, 2002.* See also <http://www.census.gov/prod/2003pubs/cffr02.pdf> (issued May 2003).

U.S. Census Bureau, Statistical Abstract of the United States: 2004-2005

No. 473. Tax Returns Filed—Examination Coverage: 1990 to 2003

[In thousands (109,868 represents 109,868,000, except as indicated. Return classification as Schedule C or C-EZ (nonfarm sole proprietorships) or Schedule F (farm proprietorships) for audit examination purposes was based on the largest source of income on the return and certain other characteristics. Therefore, some returns with business activity are reflected in the nonbusiness individual income tax return statistics in the table below (and vise versa), so that the statistics for the number of returns with Schedule C is not comparable to the number of nonfarm sole proprietorship returns in Table 719]

Year and type of return	Returns filed [1]	Returns examined					Average tax and penalty per return (dollars)		
		Total	Per-cent cover-age	By—			Revenue agents [3]	Tax audi-tors	Service centers
				Rev-enue agents	Tax audi-tors	Serv-ice cen-ters [2]			
INDIVIDUAL RETURNS									
1990	109,868	1,145	1.04	202	517	426	309,566	1,962	2,432
1991	112,305	1,313	1.17	200	500	613	664,440	2,398	2,738
1992	113,829	1,206	1.06	210	537	459	1,365,896	2,280	2,539
1993	114,719	1,059	0.92	251	506	303	103,250	2,625	2,974
1994	113,754	1,226	1.08	364	456	406	246,785	3,113	1,963
1995	114,683	1,919	1.67	339	459	1,122	204,616	3,497	1,404
1996	116,060	1,942	1.67	252	509	1,180	818,753	3,051	1,714
1997	118,363	1,519	1.28	210	506	804	802,549	3,460	2,963
1998	120,342	1,193	0.99	168	383	625	177,830	3,372	2,760
1999	122,547	1,100	0.90	124	236	716	322,230	3,265	2,085
2000	124,887	618	0.49	92	146	367	123,337	3,337	2,602
2001	127,097	732	0.58	78	116	529	99,990	3,396	2,517
2002	129,445	744	0.57	89	112	539	1,597,215	3,910	2,589
2003	130,341	849	0.65	94	110	643	358,917	4,591	3,338
ALL RETURNS 2003 [4]									
Individual, total	**130,341**	**849**	**0.65**	**94**	**110**	**643**	**359,917**	**4,591**	**3,338**
1040A, TPI under $25,000 [5]	35,631	182	0.51	4	7	170	16,307	4,322	2,906
Non 1040, TPI under $25,000 [5]	18,123	197	1.09	4	6	186	9,430	2,621	2,852
TPI $25,000 under $50,000 [5]	31,302	95	0.30	13	20	61	5,203	1,903	1,807
TPI $50,000 under $100,000 [5]	25,485	105	0.41	18	27	60	7,204	2,792	2,179
TPI $100,000 and over [5]	10,841	107	0.98	24	19	63	315,996	5,699	10,528
Sch C—TGR under $25,000 [6]	2,722	82	3.00	4	10	68	7,683	2,988	1,900
Sch C—TGR $25,000 under $100,000 [6]	3,534	47	1.33	8	14	25	11,393	6,413	2,052
Sch C—TGR $100,000 and over [6]	2,085	31	1.47	16	6	8	1,216,702	18,033	3,892
Sch F—TGR under $100,000 [6]	351	2	0.57	1	0.300	1	3,157	3,330	956
Sch F—TGR $100,000 and over [6]	267	2	0.78	1	0.200	1	157,829	8,417	1,779
Corporation (except S Corporation)	2,410	21	0.87	17	0.021	3	5,191,391	40,900	9,031
Fiduciary	3,658	6	0.17	4	0.001	2	30,512	-	8,302
Estate	114	7	6.38	7	(NA)	-	429,148	(NA)	-
Gift	283	2	0.66	2	(NA)	-	263,856	(NA)	-
Employment	29,514	16	0.06	12	1	0.4	372,570	10,350	644
Excise	836	9	1.05	9	-	-	27,327	-	-
Windfall profit	(NA)	(NA)	(NA)	(NA)	(NA)	(NA)	(NA)	(NA)	(NA)
Misc. taxable	(NA)	1	(NA)	1	-	0.013	300,568	-	8,222
Partnerships	2,272	8	0.35	6	0.003	1	(NA)	(NA)	(NA)
S Corporations (nontaxable)	3,191	10	0.30	9	0.008	1	(NA)	(NA)	(NA)
Miscellaneous nontaxable [7]	(NA)	-	(NA)	-	0.004	-	(NA)	(NA)	(NA)

- Represents zero.   NA Not available.   [1] Returns filed in previous calendar year.   [2] Includes taxpayer contacts by correspondence.   [3] Mostly reflects coordinated examination of large corporations and related returns.   [4] Includes activities to protect release of funds in Treasury in response to taxpayer efforts to recoup tax previously assessed and paid with penalty.   [5] Total positive income, i.e., excludes losses.   [6] TGR= Total gross receipts.   [7] Includes Domestic International Sales Corporations, Interest Charge Domestic International Sales Corporations, Real Estate Investment Mortgage Conduits, and other.

Source: U.S. Internal Revenue Service, *IRS Data Book*, annual, Publication 55B.

No. 474. Internal Revenue Gross Collections by Source: 1990 to 2003

[1,078 represents $1,078,000,000,000. For fiscal year ending in year shown; see text, Section 8]

Source of revenue	Collections (bil. dol.)					Percent distribution				
	1990	1995	2000	2002	2003	1990	1995	2000	2002	2003
All taxes	**1,078**	**1,389**	**2,097**	**2,017**	**1,952**	**100.0**	**100.0**	**100.0**	**100.0**	**100.0**
Individual income taxes	540	676	1,137	1,038	987	50.1	48.7	54.2	51.5	50.5
Withheld by employers	388	534	781	751	735	36.0	38.4	37.2	37.2	37.6
Employment taxes [1]	367	465	640	688	696	34.0	33.5	30.5	34.1	35.6
Old-age and disability insurance	358	455	628	677	685	33.2	32.8	29.9	33.6	35.1
Unemployment insurance	6	6	7	7	7	0.6	0.4	0.3	0.3	0.3
Corporation income taxes	110	174	236	211	194	10.2	12.5	11.2	10.5	9.9
Estate and gift taxes	12	15	30	27	23	1.1	1.1	1.4	1.4	1.2
Excise taxes	49	59	55	52	53	4.5	4.2	2.6	2.6	2.7

[1] Includes railroad retirement, not shown separately.

Source: U.S. Internal Revenue Service, *IRS Data Book*, annual. For most recent report, see <http://www.irs.gov/pub/irs-soi/03databk.pdf>.

Federal Government Finances and Employment   315

No. 475. Federal Individual Income Tax Returns With Adjusted Gross Income (AGI)—Summary: 2000 and 2001

[Includes Puerto Rico and Virgin Islands. Includes returns of resident aliens, based on a sample of unaudited returns as filed. Data are not comparable for all years because of tax changes and other changes, as indicated. See *Statistics of Income, Individual Income Tax Returns* publications for a detailed explanation. See Appendix III]

Item	Number of Returns (1,000) 2000	2001	Amount (mil. dol.) 2000	2001	Average amount (dollars) 2000	2001
Total returns	129,374	130,255	6,365,377	6,170,603	49,202	47,373
Adjusted gross income (AGI)	129,374	130,255	6,365,377	6,170,604	49,202	47,373
Salaries and wages	110,169	111,227	4,456,167	4,565,229	40,449	41,044
Taxable interest received	68,046	67,479	199,322	198,178	2,929	2,937
Tax-exempt interest	4,658	4,557	53,952	55,583	11,582	12,197
Dividends in AGI	34,141	32,621	146,988	119,534	4,305	3,664
Business or profession net income	13,313	13,611	244,598	249,508	18,373	18,331
Business or profession net loss	4,287	4,406	30,733	32,735	7,168	7,430
Net capital gain in AGI	22,646	12,630	644,285	348,133	28,451	27,564
Net capital loss in AGI	6,875	10,839	13,742	22,964	1,999	2,119
Sales of property other than capital assets, net gain	827	772	7,445	7,209	8,997	9,338
Sales of property other than capital assets, net loss	873	843	8,364	9,106	9,586	10,802
Pensions and annuities in AGI	21,765	22,262	325,828	338,745	14,970	15,216
Unemployment compensation in AGI	6,478	8,799	16,913	26,890	2,611	3,056
Social security benefits in AGI	10,609	10,779	89,964	93,560	8,480	8,680
Rent net income	4,201	4,226	45,099	47,307	10,736	11,194
Rent net loss	4,520	4,504	30,309	31,058	6,705	6,896
Royalty net income	1,104	1,133	7,998	10,630	7,245	9,382
Royalty net loss	36	46	101	90	2,800	1,957
Partnerships and S Corporations net income [1]	4,180	4,356	285,425	301,559	68,291	69,228
Partnerships and S Corporations net loss [1]	2,121	2,139	72,511	76,449	34,191	35,741
Estate or trust net income	557	493	12,134	12,378	21,803	25,108
Estate or trust net loss	39	44	1,128	2,159	28,900	49,068
Farm net income	703	649	8,270	7,656	11,763	11,797
Farm net loss	1,359	1,357	17,305	18,662	12,736	13,752
Statutory adjustments, total	23,197	23,497	58,610	60,573	2,527	2,578
Individual Retirement Arrangements	3,505	3,448	7,477	7,407	2,133	2,148
Student loan interest deduction	4,478	4,405	2,639	2,711	589	615
Medical savings accounts	65	69	120	124	1,839	1,797
Self-employed retirement plans	957	944	2,138	2,181	2,235	2,310
Deduction for self-employment tax	14,300	14,574	17,393	18,135	1,216	1,244
Self-employment health insurance	3,565	3,559	7,569	8,178	2,123	2,298
Exemptions, total [2]	252,332	256,186	690,109	727,555	2,735	2,840
Deductions, total	128,205	128,800	1,293,181	1,366,436	10,087	10,609
Standard deductions	85,671	84,238	470,821	466,971	5,496	5,543
Returns with additional standard deductions for age 65 or older or for blindness	11,331	11,116	14,736	14,936	1,301	1,344
Itemized deductions, total [3]	42,534	44,562	822,361	884,529	19,334	19,849
Medical and dental expenses	6,513	7,571	39,251	47,071	6,026	6,217
Taxes paid	41,824	43,797	294,712	307,974	7,047	7,032
Interest paid	35,405	38,800	322,932	349,901	9,121	9,018
Home mortgage interest paid	34,914	36,331	299,963	330,693	8,591	9,102
Charitable contributions	37,525	39,386	140,682	139,242	3,749	3,535
Taxable income	105,259	104,174	4,544,242	4,268,506	43,172	40,975
Income tax before credits	105,278	104,195	1,018,219	933,567	9,672	8,960
Tax credits, total [2]	37,736	49,792	37,722	45,631	1,000	916
Child care credit	6,368	6,184	2,794	2,721	439	440
Elderly and disabled credit	156	139	33	30	209	216
Child tax credit	26,405	26,452	19,689	22,427	746	848
Education credit	6,815	7,212	4,851	5,156	712	715
Foreign tax credit	3,936	3,942	5,990	6,255	1,522	1,587
General business credit	275	269	764	714	2,778	2,654
Income tax after credits	96,816	94,763	980,497	887,936	10,127	9,370
Income tax, total [4]	96,818	94,763	980,645	887,974	10,129	9,370
Alternative minimum tax	1,304	1,120	9,601	6,757	7,361	6,033
Earned income credit	19,277	19,593	32,296	33,376	1,675	1,703
Used to offset income tax before credits	5,416	4,412	1,969	1,470	363	333
Used to offset other taxes	3,148	3,506	2,524	2,863	802	817
Excess earned income credit (refundable)	16,126	16,631	27,804	29,043	1,724	1,746
Tax payments, total	122,244	123,451	1,084,868	1,076,501	8,875	8,720
Income tax withheld	113,733	114,798	763,901	773,326	6,717	6,736
Excess social security tax withheld	1,641	1,436	2,185	1,915	1,332	1,334
Estimated tax payments	13,327	13,167	221,622	220,196	16,630	16,723
Payments with requests for extension of filing time	1,611	1,448	63,397	42,495	39,354	29,347
Taxes due at time of filing	30,624	24,581	134,944	91,823	4,406	3,736
Tax overpayments, total	95,921	102,310	196,199	236,982	2,045	2,316
Overpayment refunds	93,000	99,011	167,577	202,274	1,802	2,043

[1] S Corporations are certain small corporations with up to 35 shareholders. [2] Includes items not shown separately. Beginning 1998, total exemptions amount is after limitation. [3] Beginning 1998, total itemized deductions are after limitation. [4] Includes minimum tax or alternative minimum tax.

Source: U.S. Internal Revenue Service, *Statistics of Income Bulletin*, and *Statistics of Income, Individual Income Tax Returns*, annual.

No. 476. Individual Income Tax Returns—Number, Income Tax, and Average Tax by Size of Adjusted Gross Income: 2000 and 2001

[In billions of dollars ($6,365 represents $6,365,000,000,000), except as indicated. See Appendix III]

Size of adjusted gross income	Number of returns (1,000)		Adjusted gross income (AGI)		Income tax total [1]		Tax as percent of AGI [2]		Average tax [2]	
	2000	2001	2000	2001	2000	2001	2000	2001	2000	2001
Total	129,374	130,255	6,365	6,170	981	888	16	15	10,129	9,370
Less than $1,000 [3]	2,966	3,276	-58	-70	-	-	2	1	648	11
$1,000 to $2,999	5,385	5,371	11	11	-	-	7	6	134	111
$3,000 to $4,999	5,599	5,383	22	21	-	-	4	3	179	106
$5,000 to $6,999	5,183	4,955	31	32	1	-	5	3	297	164
$7,000 to $8,999	4,972	4,975	40	40	1	-	4	3	331	225
$9,000 to $10,999	5,089	4,903	51	49	1	1	5	3	470	323
$11,000 to $12,999. . . .	4,859	4,667	58	56	2	1	6	5	704	560
$13,000 to $14,999	4,810	4,757	67	67	3	2	6	5	883	756
$15,000 to $16,999	4,785	4,656	76	74	3	3	7	6	1,052	929
$17,000 to $18,999	4,633	4,689	83	84	4	3	7	6	1,279	1,149
$19,000 to $21,999	6,502	6,380	133	131	7	6	8	7	1,565	1,464
$22,000 to $24,999	5,735	5,724	135	134	8	7	8	7	1,815	1,751
$25,000 to $29,999	8,369	8,563	229	235	16	16	8	8	2,248	2,205
$30,000 to $39,999	13,548	13,844	471	481	40	38	9	9	3,094	2,994
$40,000 to $49,999	10,412	10,613	466	475	46	44	10	10	4,462	4,314
$50,000 to $74,999	17,076	17,560	1,045	1,074	116	114	11	11	6,824	6,558
$75,000 to $99,999	8,597	8,904	738	764	100	100	14	13	11,631	11,124
$100,000 to $199,999. . .	8,083	8,469	1,066	1,114	184	185	17	17	22,783	21,896
$200,000 to $499,999. . .	2,136	2,018	614	579	146	135	24	23	68,628	66,764
$500,000 to $999,999. . .	396	356	269	241	76	68	28	28	192,092	190,893
$1,000,000 or more	240	193	817	579	226	164	28	29	945,172	851,009

- Represents zero.   [1] Consists of income after credits, and alternative minimum tax.   [2] Computed using taxable returns only.   [3] In addition to low income taxpayers, this size class (and others) includes taxpayers with "tax preferences," not reflected in adjusted gross income or taxable income which are subject to the "alternative minimum tax" (included in total income tax).

Source: U.S. Internal Revenue Service, *Statistics of Income Bulletin,* quarterly and *Statistics of Income, Individual Income Tax Returns,* annual.

No. 477. Individual Income Tax Returns—Itemized Deductions and Statutory Adjustments by Size of Adjusted Gross Income: 2001

[44,562 represents 44,562,000. Based on a sample of returns, see Appendix III]

Item	Unit	Adjusted gross income class							
		Total	Under $10,000	$10,000 to $19,999	$20,000 to $29,999	$30,000 to $39,999	$40,000 to $49,999	$50,000 to $99,999	$100,000 and over
Returns with itemized deductions:									
Number of returns [1]	1,000 .	44,562	808	2,286	3,509	4,522	4,762	18,544	10,131
Amount.	Mil. dol.	884,528	10,428	27,270	41,655	55,823	63,886	304,297	381,170
Medical and dental expenses:									
Returns	1,000 .	7,572	474	1,299	1,358	1,212	913	1,986	331
Amount.	Mil. dol.	47,071	3,686	8,895	7,213	6,481	5,217	11,081	4,502
Taxes paid:									
Returns	1,000 .	43,797	709	2,104	3,375	4,433	4,694	18,395	10,088
Amount, total	Mil. dol.	307,975	1,728	4,447	7,927	12,252	15,691	93,968	171,962
State and local income taxes:									
Returns	1,000 .	37,037	380	1,450	2,655	3,727	3,974	16,038	8,813
Amount	Mil. dol.	196,431	479	1,109	2,691	5,491	7,678	52,823	126,160
Real estate taxes:									
Returns	1,000 .	38,717	558	1,677	2,734	3,617	4,083	16,636	9,412
Amount	Mil. dol.	101,854	1,178	3,077	4,703	6,008	7,166	37,327	42,394
Interest paid:									
Returns	1,000 .	36,801	490	1,388	2,597	3,578	3,994	16,013	8,740
Amount.	Mil. dol.	349,901	3,892	8,849	16,852	23,915	27,699	134,313	134,380
Home mortgages interest:									
Returns	1,000 .	36,331	481	1,363	2,568	3,551	3,978	15,877	8,512
Amount.	Mil. dol.	330,692	3,781	8,720	16,629	23,575	27,317	132,090	118,581
Charitable contributions:									
Returns	1,000 .	39,386	505	1,714	2,803	3,740	4,083	16,887	9,655
Amount.	Mil. dol.	139,241	539	2,875	5,329	6,831	8,110	41,066	74,491
Returns with statutory adjustments: [2]									
Number of returns [2]	1,000 .	23,497	3,115	3,235	3,037	2,738	2,303	5,831	3,237
Amount of adjustments	Mil. dol.	60,573	2,679	3,683	4,320	4,517	4,158	14,898	26,318
Payments to IRA's: [3] Returns.	1,000 .	3,448	152	263	422	482	413	1,114	602
Amount.	Mil. dol.	7,407	245	490	821	892	886	2,508	1,564
Student loan interest deduction . . .	1,000 .	4,406	222	607	897	888	702	1,091	-
Amount.	Mil. dol.	2,712	127	319	598	652	465	550	-
Medical Savings Account deduction.	1,000 .	70	4	6	5	1	5	25	24
Amount.	Mil. dol.	123	7	8	4	2	9	39	55
Payments to Keogh plans	1,000 .	1,290	21	36	50	62	73	365	685
Amount.	Mil. dol.	13,114	42	91	127	239	340	2,122	10,154
Alimony paid.	1,000 .	657	32	34	60	69	52	243	167
Amount.	Mil. dol.	7,473	342	234	297	319	294	2,134	3,854

- Represents zero.   [1] After limitations.   [2] Includes disability income exclusion, employee business expenses, moving expenses, forfeited interest penalty, alimony paid, deduction for expense of living abroad, and other data not shown separately.   [3] Individual Retirement Account.

Source: U.S. Internal Revenue Service, *Statistics of Income, Individual Income Tax Returns,* annual.

Federal Government Finances and Employment   317

No. 478. Federal Individual Income Tax Returns—Adjusted Gross Income (AGI) by Source of Income and Income Class for Taxable Returns: 2001

[In millions of dollars (5,847,060 represents $5,847,060,000,000), except as indicated. Minus sign (-) indicates net loss was greater than net income. See headnote, Table 475. See Appendix III]

Item	Total [1]	Under $10,000	$10,000 to $19,999	$20,000 to $29,999	$30,000 to $39,999	$40,000 to $49,999	$50,000 to $99,999	$100,000 and over
Number of taxable returns (1,000).	94,764	6,465	13,791	14,060	12,845	10,308	26,269	11,025
Source of income:								
Adjusted gross income (AGI)	5,847,060	41,097	209,345	351,885	446,627	461,833	1,826,558	2,509,714
Salaries and wages	4,233,575	34,648	150,882	278,900	367,099	377,013	1,472,056	1,552,977
Percent of AGI for taxable returns	72	84	72	79	82	82	81	62
Interest received	181,316	2,602	11,654	12,095	11,645	10,952	42,684	89,685
Dividends in AGI	111,297	1,287	3,880	4,125	4,541	5,124	21,950	70,392
Business; profession, net profit less loss. .	190,165	1,027	6,587	8,256	11,653	11,131	50,140	101,370
Sales of property, [2] net gain less loss . . .	317,234	922	1,570	1,824	1,888	1,998	17,073	291,960
Pensions and annuities in AGI	318,191	2,279	26,229	35,091	32,373	33,178	117,965	71,076
Rents and royalties, net income less loss .	33,944	105	982	716	566	530	3,253	27,791
Other sources, [3] net	461,338	-1,772	7,562	10,878	16,864	21,907	101,437	304,463
Percent of all returns: [4]								
Number of returns	72.8	5.0	10.6	10.8	9.9	7.9	20.2	8.5
Adjusted gross income (AGI)	94.8	0.7	3.4	5.7	7.2	7.5	29.6	40.7
Salaries and wages	92.7	0.8	3.3	6.1	8.0	8.3	32.2	34.0
Interest received	91.5	1.3	5.9	6.1	5.9	5.5	21.5	45.3
Dividends in AGI	93.1	1.1	3.2	3.5	3.8	4.3	18.4	58.9
Business; profession, net profit less loss. .	87.7	0.5	3.0	3.8	5.4	5.1	23.1	46.8
Sales of property, [2] net gain less loss . . .	97.6	0.3	0.5	0.6	0.6	0.6	5.3	89.8
Pensions and annuities in AGI	93.9	0.7	7.7	10.4	9.6	9.8	34.8	21.0
Rents and royalties, net income less loss .	103.2	0.3	3.0	2.2	1.7	1.6	9.9	84.5

[1] Includes a small number of taxable returns with no adjusted gross income. [2] Includes sales of capital assets and other property; net gain less loss. [3] Excludes rental passive losses disallowed in the computation of AGI; net income less loss. [4] Without regard to taxability.

Source: U.S. Internal Revenue Service, *Statistics of Income, Individual Income Tax Returns*, annual.

No. 479. Federal Individual Income Tax Returns by State: 2001

[130,977 represents 130,977,000. See Appendix III]

State	Number of returns [1] (1,000)	Adjusted gross income (AGI) [2] (mil. dol.)	Income tax Total [3] (mil. dol.)	Income tax Per capita [4] (dol.)	State	Number of returns [1] (1,000)	Adjusted gross income (AGI) [2] (mil. dol.)	Income tax Total [3] (mil. dol.)	Income tax Per capita [4] (dol.)
U.S.	130,977	6,144,619	891,653	3,128	MT.	426	14,497	1,665	1,838
					NE.	806	32,538	4,115	2,394
AL	1,893	72,104	8,952	2,004	NV.	980	47,727	7,174	3,425
AK	333	14,164	2,026	3,203	NH.	632	32,414	4,871	3,870
AZ	2,201	97,892	13,023	2,458	NJ	4,089	247,502	40,998	4,821
AR	1,121	39,556	4,759	1,768	NM.	850	33,300	4,328	2,367
CA	15,067	797,785	119,291	3,454	NY.	8,668	484,814	81,726	4,285
CO	2,109	108,578	16,050	3,624	NC.	3,649	154,111	19,499	2,379
CT	1,679	114,473	21,357	6,222	ND.	301	10,680	1,279	2,011
DE	381	18,485	2,633	3,310	OH.	5,547	226,734	29,270	2,571
DC	282	15,914	2,677	4,674	OK.	1,473	55,606	6,992	2,017
FL	7,631	339,034	52,221	3,193	OR.	1,572	67,353	8,384	2,414
GA	3,655	166,756	22,789	2,715	PA	5,789	255,830	35,950	2,923
HI	577	23,883	2,928	2,391	RI	496	22,809	3,152	2,976
ID	563	21,448	2,493	1,887	SC	1,800	68,917	8,225	2,026
IL	5,775	290,608	44,668	3,569	SD	355	12,984	1,706	2,251
IN	2,824	117,977	15,222	2,484	TN	2,558	102,171	13,737	2,391
IA	1,338	52,696	6,348	2,165	TX	9,203	413,497	62,584	2,933
KS	1,226	52,117	6,794	2,516	UT	954	39,765	4,486	1,968
KY	1,759	67,345	8,202	2,016	VT	302	12,390	1,581	2,581
LA	1,881	70,034	8,996	2,014	VA	3,372	170,858	24,574	3,416
ME	610	23,878	2,898	2,256	WA	2,788	138,878	21,018	3,507
MD	2,583	138,921	19,834	3,684	WV	751	26,178	3,082	1,710
MA	3,106	185,543	30,516	4,768	WI	2,590	114,225	14,803	2,739
MI	4,586	208,988	28,403	2,839	WY	238	10,727	1,653	3,348
MN.	2,384	116,939	16,235	3,257					
MS.	1,165	39,227	4,481	1,568					
MO	2,567	107,032	14,155	2,511	Other [5]	1,483	46,741	6,848	(NA)

NA Not available. [1] Includes returns constructed by Internal Revenue Service for certain self-employment tax returns. [2] Less deficit. [3] Includes additional tax for tax preferences, self-employment tax, tax from investment credit recapture and other income-related taxes. Total is before earned income credit. [4] Based on resident population as of July 1. [5] Includes returns filed from Army Post Office and Fleet Post Office addresses by members of the armed forces stationed overseas; returns by other U.S. citizens abroad; and returns filed by residents of Puerto Rico with income from sources outside of Puerto Rico or with income earned as U.S. Government employees.

Source: U.S. Internal Revenue Service, *Statistics of Income Bulletin*, quarterly.

U.S. Census Bureau, Statistical Abstract of the United States: 2004-2005

No. 480. Federal Individual Income Tax—Tax Liability and Effective and Marginal Tax Rates for Selected Income Groups: 1990 to 2001

[Refers to income after exclusions. Effective rate represents tax liability divided by stated income. The marginal tax rate is the percentage of the first additional dollar of income which would be paid in income tax. Computations assume the low income allowance, standard deduction, zero bracket amount, or itemized deductions equal to 10 percent of adjusted gross income, whichever is greatest. Excludes self-employment tax]

Adjusted gross income	1990	1995	1997	1998	1999	2000	2001
TAX LIABILITY (dol.)							
Single person, no dependents:							
$5,000 [1]	-	-314	-332	-341	-347	-353	-364
$10,000 [2]	705	540	480	455	427	391	201
$20,000	2,205	2,040	1,980	1,958	1,943	1,920	1,283
$25,000	2,988	2,790	2,730	2,708	2,693	2,670	2,033
$35,000	5,718	4,973	4,692	4,559	4,479	4,372	3,595
$50,000	9,498	8,865	8,654	8,549	8,483	8,404	7,596
$75,000	16,718	15,418	15,107	14,951	14,852	14,738	13,784
Married couple, two dependents: [3] [4]							
$5,000 [5]	-700	-1,800	-2,000	-2,000	-2,000	-2,000	-2,000
$10,000 [5]	-953	-3,110	-3,556	-3,756	-3,816	-4,000	-4,000
$20,000 [5]	926	-832	-1,414	-1,811	-1,958	-2,553	-3,553
$25,000 [1]	1,703	929	389	-8	-155	-1,500	-2,120
$35,000	3,203	2,768	2,625	2,565	2,520	1,468	570
$50,000	5,960	5,018	4,875	4,815	4,770	3,718	2,820
$75,000	12,386	11,030	10,576	10,371	10,224	9,064	7,895
EFFECTIVE RATE (percent)							
Single person, no dependents:							
$5,000 [1]	-	-6.3	-6.6	-6.8	-6.9	-7.1	-7.3
$10,000 [2]	7.1	5.4	4.8	4.6	4.3	3.9	2.0
$20,000	11.0	10.2	9.9	9.8	9.7	9.6	6.4
$25,000	12.0	11.2	10.9	10.8	10.8	10.7	8.1
$35,000	16.3	14.2	13.4	13.0	12.8	12.5	10.3
$50,000	19.0	17.7	17.3	17.1	17.0	16.8	15.2
$75,000	22.3	20.6	20.1	19.9	19.8	19.7	18.4
Married couple, two dependents: [3]							
$5,000 [5]	-14.0	-36.0	-40	-40.0	-40.0	-40.0	-40.0
$10,000 [5]	-9.5	-31.1	-35.6	-37.6	38.2	-40.0	-40.0
$20,000 [5]	4.6	-4.2	-7.1	-9.1	-9.8	-12.8	-17.8
$25,000 [1]	6.8	3.7	1.6	0.0	-0.6	-6.0	-8.5
$35,000	9.2	7.9	7.5	7.3	7.2	4.2	1.6
$50,000	11.9	10.0	9.8	9.6	9.5	7.4	5.6
$75,000	16.5	14.7	14.1	13.8	13.6	12.1	10.5
MARGINAL TAX RATE (percent)							
Single person, no dependents:							
$5,000 [1]	-	-	-	-	-	-	-
$10,000 [2]	15	15	15	23	23	23	18
$20,000	15	15	15	15	15	15	15
$25,000	28	15	15	15	15	15	15
$35,000	28	28	28	28	28	28	28
$50,000	28	28	28	28	28	28	28
$75,000	33	31	31	31	31	31	28
Married couple, two dependents: [3] [4]							
$5,000 [5]	-14	-36	-40	-40	-40	-40	-40
$10,000 [5]	-	-	-	-	-	-40	-40
$20,000 [1]	25	35	36	36	36	21	11
$25,000	15	35	36	36	36	36	21
$35,000	15	15	15	15	15	15	15
$50,000	28	15	15	15	15	15	15
$75,000	28	28	28	28	28	28	28

- Represents zero.   [1] Beginning 1999, includes refundable earned income credit.   [2] Refundable earned income credit.   [3] Only one spouse is assumed to work.   [4] Beginning 1998, includes child tax credit.   [5] Beginning 1994, refundable earned income credit.

Source: U.S. Dept. of the Treasury, Office of Tax Analysis, unpublished data. See also <http://www.treas.gov/ota/index.html>.

Federal Government Finances and Employment   319

No. 481. Federal Individual Income Tax—Current Income Equivalent to 1996 Constant Income for Selected Income Groups: 1990 to 2001

[Constant 1996 dollar incomes calculated by using the NIPA Chain-Type Price Index for Personal Consumption Expenditures (1996 = 100), 1990, 85.63; 1995, 97.60; 1996, 100.0; 1997, 101.98; 1998, 102.93; 1999, 104.57; 2000, 109.60; and 2001, 111.10]

Adjusted gross income	1990	1995	1997	1998	1999	2000	2001
REAL INCOME EQUIVALENT (dol.)							
Single person, no dependents:							
$5,000	4,280	4,900	5,100	5,150	5,240	5,380	5,480
$10,000	8,560	9,790	10,200	10,290	10,470	10,750	10,950
$20,000	17,130	19,580	20,400	20,590	20,940	21,500	21,910
$25,000	21,410	24,480	25,500	25,730	26,180	26,880	27,380
$35,000	29,970	34,270	35,690	36,030	36,650	37,630	38,340
$50,000	42,820	48,950	50,990	51,470	52,360	53,760	54,770
$75,000	64,220	73,430	76,490	77,200	78,540	80,640	82,150
Married couple, two dependents: [1]							
$5,000	4,280	4,900	5,100	5,150	5,240	5,380	5,480
$10,000	8,560	9,790	10,200	10,290	10,470	10,750	10,950
$20,000	17,130	19,580	20,400	20,590	20,940	21,500	21,910
$25,000	21,410	24,480	25,500	25,730	26,180	26,880	27,380
$35,000	29,970	34,270	35,690	36,030	36,650	37,630	38,340
$50,000	42,820	48,950	50,990	51,470	52,360	53,760	54,770
$75,000	64,220	73,430	76,490	77,200	78,540	80,640	82,150
EFFECTIVE RATE (percent)							
Single person, no dependents:							
$5,000 [2]	-	-6.4	-6.5	-6.6	-6.6	-6.6	-6.6
$10,000	5.7	5.2	5.0	4.9	4.9	5.0	3.2
$20,000	10.4	10.1	10.0	9.9	9.9	10.0	7.2
$25,000	11.3	11.1	11.0	10.9	11.1	11.0	8.7
$35,000	14.6	13.9	13.7	13.5	13.5	13.6	11.8
$50,000	18.0	17.6	17.5	17.3	17.3	17.4	16.0
$75,000	21.0	20.4	20.3	20.2	20.2	20.2	19.1
Married couple, two dependents: [1]							
$5,000 [3]	-14.0	-36.0	-40.0	-40.0	-40.0	-40.0	-40.0
$10,000 [3]	-11.1	-31.8	-34.9	-36.5	-36.4	-37.3	-37.5
$20,000 [3]	1.2	-5.0	-6.2	-7.8	-9.7	-10.4	-14.1
$25,000	5.4	3.0	2.2	1.0	-2.8	-3.2	-5.0
$35,000	8.2	7.8	7.6	7.5	4.8	4.9	2.8
$50,000	10.2	9.9	9.9	9.8	7.9	8.0	6.4
$75,000	15.1	14.5	14.3	14.2	12.9	13.0	11.8
MARGINAL TAX RATE (percent)							
Single person, no dependents:							
$5,000	-	-	-	-	-	-	-
$10,000	15.0	15.0	15.0	15.0	15.0	15.0	10.0
$20,000	15.0	15.0	15.0	15.0	15.0	15.0	15.0
$25,000	15.0	15.0	15.0	15.0	15.0	15.0	15.0
$35,000	28.0	28.0	28.0	28.0	28.0	28.0	27.5
$50,000	28.0	28.0	28.0	28.0	28.0	28.0	27.5
$75,000	33.0	31.0	31.0	31.0	31.0	31.0	30.5
Married couple, two dependents: [1]							
$5,000 [3]	-14.0	-36.0	-40.0	-40.0	-40.0	-40.0	-40.0
$10,000 [3]	-	-	-	-	-	-	-10.0
$20,000 [3]	25.0	35.2	36.1	36.1	21.1	21.1	21.1
$25,000	15.0	35.2	36.1	36.1	36.1	36.1	21.1
$35,000	15.0	15.0	15.0	15.0	15.0	15.0	15.0
$50,000	15.0	15.0	15.0	15.0	15.0	15.0	15.0
$75,000	28.0	28.0	28.0	28.0	28.0	28.0	27.5

- Represents zero.   [1] Only one spouse is assumed to work.   [2] Beginning 1994, refundable earned income credit.
[3] Refundable earned income credit.

Source: U.S. Dept. of the Treasury, Office of Tax Analysis, unpublished data. â Includes income tax surcharge.

No. 482. Full-Time Federal Civilian Employment—Employees and Average Pay by Pay System: 1990 to 2003

[As of March 31. (2,036 represents 2,036,000). Excludes employees of Congress and Federal courts, maritime seamen of Dept. of Commerce, and small number for whom rates were not reported. See text, this section, for explanation of general schedule and wage system]

Pay system	Employees (1,000)				Average pay (dol.)			
	1990	2000	2002	2003	1990	2000	2002	2003
Total, excl. postal	2,036	1,671	1,681	1,755	31,174	50,429	55,715	57,480
General Schedule	1,506	1,216	1,238	1,243	31,239	49,428	54,329	56,874
Wage System	369	205	193	187	26,565	37,082	39,892	41,259
Other	161	250	250	325	41,149	66,248	74,771	69,138
Postal pay system [1]	753	788	753	729	29,264	37,627	40,434	42,119

[1] Source: Career employees—U.S. Postal Service, *Annual Report of the Postmaster General. See also* Average pay—U.S. Postal Service, *Comprehensive Statement of Postal Operations,* annual.

Source: Except as noted, U.S. Office of Personnel Management, *Pay Structure of the Federal Civil Service,* annual.

No. 483. Federal Civilian Employment and Annual Payroll by Branch: 1970 to 2003

[Employment in thousands (**2,997 represents 2,997,000**); payroll in millions of dollars (**$27,322 represents $27,322,000,000**). For fiscal year ending in year shown; see text, Section 8 State and Local Government Finances and Employment. Includes employees in U.S. territories and foreign countries. Data represent employees in active-duty status, including intermittent employees. Annual employment figures are averages of monthly figures. Excludes Central Intelligence Agency, National Security Agency, and, as of November 1984, the Defense Intelligence Agency, and as of October 1996, the National Imagery and Mapping Agency]

Year	Employment Total	Percent of U.S. em-ployed [1]	Executive Total	Defense	Legisla-tive	Judicial	Payroll Total	Executive Total	Defense	Legisla-tive	Judicial
1970....	2²,997	4	2,961	1,263	29	7	27,322	26,894	11,264	338	89
1971....	2,899	4	2,861	1,162	31	7	29,475	29,007	11,579	369	98
1972....	2,882	4	2,842	1,128	32	8	31,626	31,102	12,181	411	112
1973....	2,822	3	2,780	1,076	33	9	33,240	32,671	12,414	447	121
1974....	2,825	3	2,781	1,041	35	9	35,661	35,035	12,789	494	132
1975....	2,877	3	2,830	1,044	37	10	39,126	38,423	13,418	549	154
1976....	2,879	3	2,831	1,025	38	11	42,259	41,450	14,699	631	179
1977....	2,855	3	2,803	997	39	12	45,895	44,975	15,696	700	219
1978....	2,875	3	2,822	-987	40	13	49,921	48,899	16,995	771	251
1979....	2,897	3	2,844	974	40	13	53,590	52,513	18,065	817	260
1980....	2²,987	3	2,933	971	40	14	58,012	56,841	18,795	883	288
1981....	2,909	3	2,855	986	40	15	63,793	62,510	21,227	922	360
1982....	2,871	3	2,816	1,019	39	16	65,503	64,125	22,226	980	398
1983....	2,878	3	2,823	1,033	39	16	69,878	68,420	23,406	1,013	445
1984....	2,935	3	2,879	1,052	40	17	74,616	73,084	25,253	1,081	451
1985....	3,001	3	2,944	1,080	39	18	80,599	78,992	28,330	1,098	509
1986....	3,047	3	2,991	1,089	38	19	82,598	80,941	29,272	1,112	545
1987....	3,075	3	3,018	1,084	38	19	85,543	83,797	29,786	1,153	593
1988....	3,113	3	3,054	1,073	38	21	88,841	86,960	29,609	1,226	656
1989....	3,133	3	3,074	1,067	38	22	92,847	90,870	30,301	1,266	711
1990....	2³,233	3	3,173	1,060	38	23	99,138	97,022	31,990	1,329	787
1991....	3,101	3	3,038	1,015	38	25	104,273	101,965	32,956	1,434	874
1992....	3,106	3	3,040	1,004	39	27	108,054	105,402	31,486	1,569	1,083
1993....	3,043	3	2,976	952	39	28	114,323	111,523	32,755	1,609	1,191
1994....	2,993	2	2,928	900	37	28	116,138	113,264	32,144	1,613	1,260
1995....	2,920	2	2,880	852	34	28	118,304	115,328	31,753	1,598	1,379
1996....	2,881	2	2,819	811	32	29	119,321	116,385	31,569	1,519	1,417
1997....	2,816	2	2,755	768	31	30	119,603	116,693	31,431	1,515	1,396
1998....	2,783	2	2,721	730	31	31	121,964	118,800	30,315	1,517	1,647
1999....	2,789	2	2,726	703	30	32	124,990	121,732	30,141	1,560	1,699
2000....	2²,879	2	2,816	681	31	32	130,832	127,472	29,607	1,619	1,741
2001....	2,704	2	2,641	672	30	33	131,964	128,502	28,594	1,682	1,780
2002....	2,715	2	2,635	671	31	34	136,611	132,893	28,845	1,781	1,938
2003....	2,743	2	2,677	669	31	34	143,380	139,506	29,029	1,908	1,966

[1] Civilian only. See Table 571.   [2] Includes temporary census workers.

Source: U.S. Office of Personnel Management, *Federal Civilian Workforce Statistics—Employment and Trends*, bimonthly; and unpublished data.

No. 484. Paid Civilian Employment in the Federal Government by State: 2000 and 2002

[As of December 31. (**2,674 represents 2,674,000**). Excludes Central Intelligence Agency, Defense Intelligence Agency, seasonal and on-call employees, and National Security Agency]

State	Total 2000 (1,000)	Total 2002 (1,000)	Percent change, 2000-2002	State	Total 2000 (1,000)	Total 2002 (1,000)	Percent change, 2000-2002
United States [1]......	2,674	2,653	-0.8	Missouri.............	54	54	-
Alabama.............	48	48	-	Montana.............	11	12	9.1
Alaska..............	14	14	-	Nebraska............	15	15	-
Arizona.............	43	46	7.0	Nevada.............	13	15	15.4
Arkansas............	20	20	-	New Hampshire........	8	9	12.5
California...........	248	245	-1.2	New Jersey..........	62	63	1.6
Colorado............	51	52	2.0	New Mexico..........	25	26	4.0
Connecticut.........	21	20	-4.8	New York...........	134	133	-0.7
Delaware............	5	5	-	North Carolina.......	57	57	-
District of Columbia.......	181	189	4.4	North Dakota........	8	8	-
Florida.............	113	122	8.0	Ohio...............	84	80	-4.8
Georgia	89	91	2.2	Oklahoma...........	43	44	2.3
Hawaii	23	25	8.7	Oregon.............	29	29	-
Idaho..............	11	11	-	Pennsylvania.........	107	106	-0.9
Illinois.............	94	92	-2.1	Rhode Island	10	11	10.0
Indiana.............	37	36	-2.7	South Carolina.......	26	27	3.8
Iowa...............	18	18	-	South Dakota........	9	10	11.1
Kansas.............	25	25	-	Tennessee...........	50	49	-2.0
Kentucky............	30	31	3.3	Texas..............	162	166	2.5
Louisiana	33	33	-	Utah...............	30	33	10.0
Maine..............	13	14	7.7	Vermont............	6	6	-
Maryland............	130	133	2.3	Virginia	145	143	-1.4
Massachusetts.........	53	53	-	Washington	62	65	4.8
Michigan...........	58	57	-1.7	West Virginia	18	19	5.6
Minnesota...........	34	34	-	Wisconsin	30	29	-3.3
Mississippi...........	24	24	-	Wyoming............	6	6	-

- Represents zero.   [1] Includes employees outside the United States not shown separately.

Source: U.S. Office of Personnel Management, *Biennial Report of Employment by Geographic Area, 2002*.

Federal Government Finances and Employment   321

No. 485. Federal Civilian Employment by Branch and Agency: 1990 to 2003

[For fiscal year ending in year shown; excludes Central Intelligence Agency, National Security Agency; and, as of November 1984, the Defense Intelligence Agency; and, as of October 1996, the National Imagery and Mapping Agency]

Agency	1990	1995	2002	2003	Percent change 1990-1995	Percent change 2002-2003
Total, all agencies	3,128,267	2,920,277	2,715,487	2,743,063	-6.6	1.0
Legislative Branch, total	37,495	33,367	30,886	31,297	-11.0	1.3
Judicial Branch	23,605	28,993	34,699	34,472	22.8	-0.7
Executive Branch, total	3,067,167	2,857,917	2,649,902	2,677,294	-6.8	1.0
Executive Departments	2,065,542	1,782,834	1,645,361	1,687,158	-13.7	2.5
State	25,288	24,859	29,078	31,402	-1.7	8.0
Treasury	158,655	155,951	147,159	134,302	-1.7	-8.7
Defense	1,034,152	832,352	670,166	669,096	-19.5	-0.2
Justice	83,932	103,262	131,378	115,259	23.0	-12.3
Interior	77,679	76,439	72,929	74,818	-1.6	2.6
Agriculture	122,594	113,321	112,278	107,204	-7.6	-4.5
Commerce	69,920	36,803	37,744	37,330	-47.4	-1.1
Labor	17,727	16,204	16,302	16,296	-8.6	-
Health & Human Services	123,959	59,788	66,837	67,240	-51.8	0.6
Housing & Urban Development	13,596	11,822	10,470	10,660	-13.0	1.8
Transportation [1]	67,364	63,552	102,826	89,262	-5.7	-13.2
Energy	17,731	19,589	16,098	15,823	10.5	-1.7
Education	4,771	4,988	4,647	4,593	4.5	-1.2
Veterans Affairs	248,174	263,904	222,138	226,171	6.3	1.8
Homeland Security	(X)	(X)	(X)	146,963	(X)	(X)
Independent agencies	999,894	1,073,510	1,002,846	988,434	7.4	-1.4
Board of Governors Federal Reserve System	1,525	1,704	1,731	1,761	11.7	1.7
Commodity Futures Trading Commission	542	544	527	534	0.4	1.3
Consumer Product Safety Commission	520	486	473	482	-6.5	1.9
Environmental Protection Agency	17,123	17,910	18,169	18,126	4.6	-0.2
Equal Employment Opportunity Commission	2,880	2,796	2,774	2,669	-2.9	-3.8
Federal Communications Commission	1,778	2,116	2,060	2,058	19.0	-0.1
Federal Deposit Insurance Corporation	17,641	14,765	5,958	5,502	-16.3	-7.7
Federal Emergency Management Agency	3,137	5,256	5,601	6,191	67.5	10.5
Federal Trade Commission	988	996	1,082	1,076	0.8	-0.6
General Services Administration	20,277	16,500	14,359	13,615	-18.6	-5.2
National Archives & Records Administration	3,120	2,833	3,019	3,027	-9.2	0.3
National Aeronautics & Space Administration	24,872	21,635	18,826	18,908	-13.0	0.4
National Credit Union Administration	900	912	958	930	1.3	-2.9
National Labor Relations Board	2,263	2,050	1,959	1,932	-9.4	-1.4
National Science Foundation	1,318	1,292	1,332	1,327	-2.0	-0.4
Nuclear Regulatory Commission	3,353	3,212	2,974	3,034	-4.2	2.0
Office of Personnel Management	6,636	4,354	3,427	3,410	-34.4	-0.5
Peace Corps	1,178	1,179	1,072	1,118	0.1	4.3
Securities & Exchange Commission	2,302	2,852	3,027	3,132	23.9	3.5
Small Business Administration	5,128	5,085	3,823	3,824	-0.8	-
Smithsonian Institution	5,092	5,444	5,048	5,133	6.9	1.7
Social Security Administration	(X)	66,850	64,617	64,414	(X)	-0.3
Tennessee Valley Authority	28,392	16,545	13,444	13,379	-41.7	-0.5
U.S. Information Agency	8,555	7,480	(X)	2,362	-12.6	(X)
U.S. Postal Service	816,886	845,393	811,643	801,552	3.5	-1.2

-Represents or rounds to zero.   X Not applicable.   [1] Beginning in 2002, includes the Transportation Security Administration created within the Department of Transportation.

Source: U.S. Office of Personnel Management, *Federal Civilian Workforce Statistics— Employment and Trends,* bimonthly.

No. 486. Federal Employment Trends—Individual Characteristics: 1990 to 2002

[In percents, except as indicated. Covers only Federal civilian non-postal employees]

Characteristics	1990	1995	1996	1997	1998	1999	2000	2001	2002
Average age (years) [1]	42.3	44.3	44.8	45.2	45.6	45.9	46.3	46.5	46.5
Average length of service (years) [1]	13.4	15.5	15.9	16.3	16.6	16.9	17.1	17.1	16.8
Retirement eligible: [1]									
Civil Service Retirement System [2]	8	10	11	12	13	15	17	19	23
Federal Employees Retirement System	3	5	6	7	8	10	11	10	11
College-conferred [3]	35	39	39	40	40	40	41	41	41
Gender:									
Men	57	56	56	56	56	55	55	55	55
Women	43	44	44	44	44	45	45	45	45
Race and national origin:									
Total minorities	27.4	28.9	29.1	29.4	29.7	30.0	30.4	30.6	30.8
Black	16.7	16.8	16.7	16.7	16.7	17.0	17.1	17.1	17.0
Hispanic	5.4	5.9	6.1	6.2	6.4	6.5	6.6	6.7	6.9
Asian/Pacific Islander	3.5	4.2	4.3	4.4	4.5	4.5	4.5	4.6	4.7
American Indian/Alaska native	1.8	2.0	2.0	2.1	2.1	2.2	2.2	2.2	2.2
Disabled	7.0	7.0	7.0	7.0	7.0	7.0	7.0	7.0	7.0
Veterans preference	30.0	26.0	26.0	25.0	25.0	25.0	24.0	24.0	23.0
Vietnam Era veterans	17.0	17.0	17.0	15.0	14.0	14.0	14.0	13.0	13.0
Retired military	4.9	4.2	4.3	4.2	3.9	3.9	3.9	4.2	4.4
Retired officers	0.5	0.5	0.5	0.5	0.5	0.5	0.5	0.6	0.7

[1] Represents full-time permanent employees.   [2] Represents full-time permanent employees under the Civil Service Retirement System (excluding hires since January 1984), and the Federal Employees Retirement System (since January 1984).   [3] Bachelor's degree or higher.

Source: U.S. Office of Personnel Management, Office of Workforce Information, *The Fact Book, Federal Civilian Workforce Statistics,* annual. See also <http://www.opm.gov/feddata/02factbk.pdf> (released June 2002).

No. 487. Federal Executive Branch (Non-Postal) Employment by Race and National Origin: 1990 to 2003

[As of Sept. 30. Covers total employment for only Executive branch agencies participating in OPMs Central Personnel Data File (CPDF). For information on the CPDF, see <http://www.opm.gov/feddata/acpdf.pdf>]

Pay system	1990	1995	2000	2002	2003
All personnel	2,150,359	1,960,577	1,755,689	1,813,047	1,832,626
White, non-Hispanic	1,562,846	1,394,690	1,224,836	1,255,941	1,263,595
General schedule and related	1,218,188	1,101,108	961,261	973,957	972,094
Grades 1-4 ($13,870 - $24,833)	132,028	79,195	55,067	55,005	51,514
Grades 5-8 ($21,370 - $38,108)	337,453	288,755	239,128	237,807	234,637
Grades 9-12 ($32,380 - $61,040)	510,261	465,908	404,649	405,583	405,376
Grades 13-15 ($55,837 - $100,897)	238,446	267,250	262,417	275,562	280,567
Total executives/senior pay levels [1]	9,337	13,307	14,332	15,428	15,787
Wage pay system	244,220	186,184	146,075	138,785	133,334
Other pay systems	91,101	94,091	103,168	127,771	142,380
Black	356,867	327,302	298,701	306,128	310,622
General schedule and related	272,657	258,586	241,135	243,884	243,236
Grades 1-4 ($13,870 - $24,833)	65,077	41,381	26,895	23,841	21,857
Grades 5-8 ($21,370 - $38,108)	114,993	112,962	99,937	97,731	96,159
Grades 9-12 ($32,380 - $61,040)	74,985	79,795	82,809	86,619	87,633
Grades 13-15 ($55,837 - $100,897)	17,602	24,448	31,494	35,693	37,587
Total executives/senior pay levels [1]	479	942	1,180	1,207	1,247
Wage pay system	72,755	55,637	42,590	39,354	38,038
Other pay systems	10,976	12,137	13,796	21,683	28,101
Hispanic	115,170	115,964	115,247	124,868	130,492
General schedule and related	83,218	86,762	89,911	96,333	99,118
Grades 1-4 ($13,870 - $24,833)	15,738	11,081	8,526	8,314	8,053
Grades 5-8 ($21,370 - $38,108)	28,727	31,152	31,703	34,201	34,808
Grades 9-12 ($32,380 - $61,040)	31,615	34,056	36,813	39,310	40,998
Grades 13-15 ($55,837 - $100,897)	7,138	10,473	12,869	14,508	15,259
Total executives/senior pay levels [1]	154	382	547	594	631
Wage pay system	26,947	22,128	16,926	16,017	15,412
Other pay systems	4,851	6,692	7,863	11,924	15,331
American Indian, Alaska Natives, Asians, and Pacific	115,476	122,621	116,905	126,110	127,917
General schedule and related	81,499	86,768	86,074	92,402	92,828
Grades 1-4 ($13,870 - $24,833)	15,286	11,854	9,340	9,568	8,868
Grades 5-8 ($21,370 - $38,108)	24,960	26,580	25,691	27,479	27,000
Grades 9-12 ($32,380 - $61,040)	31,346	33,810	33,167	35,054	35,546
Grades 13-15 ($55,837 - $100,897)	9,907	14,524	17,876	20,301	21,354
Total executives/senior pay levels [1]	148	331	504	626	682
Wage pay system	24,927	21,553	17,613	17,439	16,379
Other pay systems	8,902	13,969	12,714	15,643	18,028

[1] General schedule pay rates and Senior Pay Levels effective as of January 1999.

Source: Office of Personnel Management, Central Personnel Data File.

No. 488. Federal General Schedule Employee Pay Increases: 1980 to 2003

[Percent change from prior year shown, except 1980, change from 1979. Represents legislated pay increases. For some years data based on range for details see source]

Date	Pay increase	Date	Pay increase	Date	Pay increase
1980	9.1	1989	4.1	1997	2.3
1981	4.8	1990	3.6	1998	2.3
1982	4.0	1991	4.1	1999	3.1
1984	4.0	1992	4.2	2000	3.8
1985	3.5	1993	3.7	2001	2.7
1986	-	1994	-	2002	3.6
1987	3.0	1995	2.0	2003	3.1
1988	2.0	1996	2.0		

- Represents zero.

Source: U.S. Office of Personnel Management, *Pay Structure of the Federal Civil Service*, annual.

No. 489. Turnover Data for The Executive Branch—All Areas: 1990 to 2003

[Turnover data exclude Legislative and Judicial branches, U.S. Postal Service, Postal Rate Commission]

Year	Accessions		Separations		Total employment		
	Total	New hires	Total	Quits	Average	Change from prior year	Percent change
1990 [1]	819,554	716,066	799,237	165,099	2,348,458	114,477	5.1
1992	430,021	290,883	446,126	129,167	2,238,635	14,246	0.6
1993	382,399	253,374	423,830	127,140	2,189,416	-49,219	-2.2
1994	317,509	219,026	398,134	111,096	2,114,387	-75,029	-3.4
1995	345,166	222,025	457,246	91,909	2,037,890	-76,542	-3.6
1996	266,473	199,463	356,566	80,922	1,960,892	-76,953	-3.8
1997	283,517	208,725	333,431	81,574	1,895,295	-65,597	-3.3
1998	320,830	242,637	321,292	84,124	1,855,112	-40,183	-2.1
1999	423,500	346,988	372,778	129,196	1,846,170	-8,942	-0.5
2000 [1]	1,168,783	1,092,888	1,027,653	801,684	1,946,684	100,514	5.4
2001	308,877	233,034	301,659	82,495	1,783,239	-163,445	-8.4
2002	316,941	242,410	280,714	55,167	1,805,627	22,388	1.3
2003	508,160	254,030	461,171	53,187	1,875,695	70,068	3.9

[1] Includes hiring for census enumerators.

Source: U.S. Office of Personnel Management, *Federal Civilian Workforce Statistics— Employment and Trends*, bimonthly. Also in *The Fact Book, Federal Civilian Workforce Statistics*, annual. See also <http://www.opm.gov/feddata/03factbk.pdf> (released April 2002).

Federal Government Finances and Employment 323

No. 490. Federal Land and Buildings Owned and Leased: 1990 to 2003

[For fiscal years ending in years shown; see text, section 8. (650,014 represents 650,014,000). Covers federal real property throughout the world, except as noted. Cost of land figures represent total cost of property owned in year shown. For further details see source. For data on Federal land by state, see Tables 347 and 491]

Item	Unit	1990	1995	1999	2000	2002	2003
Federally owned:							
Land, worldwide..........	1,000 acres .	650,014	549,670	630,648	635,824	675,864	673,207
United States............	1,000 acres .	649,802	549,474	630,266	635,355	674,100	671,759
Buildings [1]............	1,000	(NA)	(NA)	(NA)	435	446	437
United States...........	1,000	446	424	419	430	441	433
Buildings floor area [1]......	Mil. sq/ft. ...	(NA)	(NA)	(NA)	3,003	3,009	3,066
United States...........	Mil. sq/ft. ...	2,859	2,793	2,875	2,968	2,975	3,032
Costs..................	Mil. dol.....	187,865	199,387	238,327	260,069	334,708	312,415
Land	Mil. dol.....	(NA)	18,972	17,257	21,008	53,930	(NA)
Buildings	Mil. dol.....	(NA)	113,018	132,981	139,291	174,929	(NA)
Structures and facilities ...	Mil. dol.....	(NA)	67,398	88,090	99,770	105,849	(NA)
Federally leased:							
Land, worldwide..........	1,000 acres .	994	1,385	1,400	1,670	894	373
United States...........	1,000 acres .	938	1,351	1,342	1,611	842	309
Buildings [1]............	1,000	(NA)	(NA)	(NA)	84	57	54
United States...........	1,000	47	78	77	73	46	42
Buildings floor area [1]......	Mil. sq/ft. ...	(NA)	(NA)	(NA)	347	374	370
United States...........	Mil. sq/ft. ...	234	275	301	313	339	334
Annual rental	Mil. dol.....	2,590	3,633	3,998	3,394	5,111	6,135
United States...........	Mil. dol.....	2,125	3,174	3,590	2,931	4,588	5,656

NA Not available. [1] Excludes data for Dept. of Defense military functions outside of the United States.

Source: U.S. General Services Administration, *Summary Report on Real Property Owned by the United States Throughout the World*, annual; and *Summary Report of Real Property Leased by the United States Throughout the World, 2003.* See also <http://www.gsa.gov/>.

No. 491. Federally Owned Property in the United States by State: 2003

[As of September 30. For data on federal land by state, see Table 347]

State	Number of owned buildings [1]	Owned building area (mil. sq. ft)	Number of leased buildings	Leased building area (mil. sq. ft)	State	Number of owned buildings [1]	Owned building area (mil. sq. ft)	Number of leased buildings	Leased building area (mil. sq. ft)
U.S..	432,791	3,032.2	42,246	333.8	MO.....	6,720	43.2	746	3.1
AL	8,018	54.1	571	2.0	MT.....	6,934	15.5	532	2.4
AK	8,645	55.2	916	6.0	NE.....	540	4.4	227	1.1
AZ	5,664	24.2	514	2.0	NV.....	16,244	91.2	1,180	6.5
AR	14,228	54.0	468	4.6	NH.....	5,688	52.8	822	8.8
CA	60,475	380.1	2,139	23.0	NJ	14,790	67.3	440	3.0
CO	9,405	57.1	727	6.7	NM.....	11,196	104.7	1,981	15.8
CT	2,046	15.8	341	1.8	NY	4,705	26.6	443	1.1
DE	1,556	65.7	266	21.7	NC.....	3,245	18.9	625	2.3
DC	937	7.7	78	0.5	ND.....	7,744	31.9	217	1.9
FL	14,180	111.3	1,775	15.3	OH.....	5,048	70.9	1,341	7.6
GA	13,160	113.5	1,021	17.9	OK.....	8,813	56.1	791	4.7
HI	16,459	85.7	181	0.7	OR.....	7,072	23.0	671	4.4
ID	7,127	77.3	1,504	8.2	PA	7,509	81.9	1,930	11.5
IL	4,877	32.6	895	4.6	RI	1,333	12.5	113	0.7
IN	2,327	12.5	949	2.9	SC	9,828	63.0	557	3.1
IA	6,246	18.7	404	2.1	SD	3,187	17.6	630	1.4
KS	6,058	42.7	795	3.7	TN	8,402	73.3	798	5.0
KY	7,182	56.2	840	3.7	TX	24,200	214.2	2,472	18.8
LA	6,430	47.9	708	3.9	UT	8,359	50.8	342	3.3
ME	4,418	34.6	717	5.7	VT	476	2.5	266	1.3
MD....	10,364	108.7	1,063	22.2	VA	17,812	207.3	1,542	29.3
MA	2,135	13.5	421	1.3	WA.....	13,589	84.6	1,023	6.8
MI	6,321	32.9	1,203	6.8	WV.....	1,600	13.6	696	3.2
MN....	2,953	19.0	971	3.3	WI	5,096	22.1	962	4.4
MS....	6,605	50.3	1,177	10.7	WY.....	4,845	10.7	255	0.9

[1] Excludes data for Dept. of Defense military functions outside of the United States.

Source: U.S. General Services Administration, *Summary Report of Real Property Owned by the United States Throughout the World, 2003.* See also <http://www.gsa.gov/>.

Section 10
National Defense and Veterans Affairs

This section presents data on national defense and its human and financial costs; active and reserve military personnel; ships, equipment, and aircraft; and federally sponsored programs and benefits for veterans. The principal sources of these data are the annual *Selected Manpower Statistics* and the *Atlas/Data Abstract for the United States and Selected Areas* issued by the Office of the Secretary of Defense; *Annual Report of Secretary of Veterans Affairs, Department of Veterans Affairs,* and *The Budget of the United States Government,* Office of Management and Budget. For more data on expenditures and personnel, see Section 30.

Department of Defense (DOD)—The Department of Defense is responsible for providing the military forces of the United States. It includes the Office of the Secretary of Defense, the Joint Chiefs of Staff, the Army, the Navy, the Air Force, and the defense agencies. The President serves as Commander in Chief of the Armed Forces; from him, the authority flows to the Secretary of Defense and through the Joint Chiefs of Staff to the commanders of unified and specified commands (e.g., U.S. Strategic Command).

Reserve components—The Reserve Components of the Armed Forces consist of the Army National Guard of the United States, Army Reserve, Naval Reserve, Marine Corps Reserve, Air National Guard, Air Force Reserve, and Coast Guard Reserve. The National Guard has dual federal-state responsibilities and uses jointly provided equipment, facilities, and budget support. The President is empowered to mobilize the National Guard and to use such of the Armed Forces as he considers necessary to enforce federal authority in any state. There is in each Armed Force a Ready Reserve, a Standby Reserve, and a Retired Reserve. The Ready Reserve includes the Selected Reserve, which provides trained and ready units and individuals to augment the active forces during times of war or national emergency, or at other times when required; and the Individual Ready Reserves, which is a manpower pool, that can be called to active duty during times of war or national emergency and would normally be used as individual fillers for active, guard and reserve units, and as a source of combat replacements. Most of the Ready Reserve serves in an active status. The Standby Reserve cannot be called to active duty, other than for training, unless authorized by Congress under "full mobilization," and a determination is made that there are not enough qualified members in the Ready Reserve in the required categories who are readily available. The Retired Reserve represents a lower potential for involuntary mobilization.

Department of Veterans Affairs (VA)— The Department of Veterans Affairs administers laws authorizing benefits for eligible former and present members of the Armed Forces and for the beneficiaries of deceased members. Veterans benefits available under various acts of Congress include compensation for service-connected disability or death; pensions for nonservice-connected disability or death; vocational rehabilitation, education, and training; home loan insurance; life insurance; health care; special housing and automobiles or other conveyances for certain disabled veterans; burial and plot allowances; and educational assistance to families of deceased or totally disabled veterans, servicemen missing in action, or prisoners of war. Since these benefits are legislated by Congress, the dates they were enacted and the dates they apply to veterans may be different from the actual dates the conflicts occurred.

VA estimates of veterans cover all persons discharged from active U.S. military service under conditions other than dishonorable.

National Defense and Veterans Affairs   325

Figure 10.1
National Defense Outlays

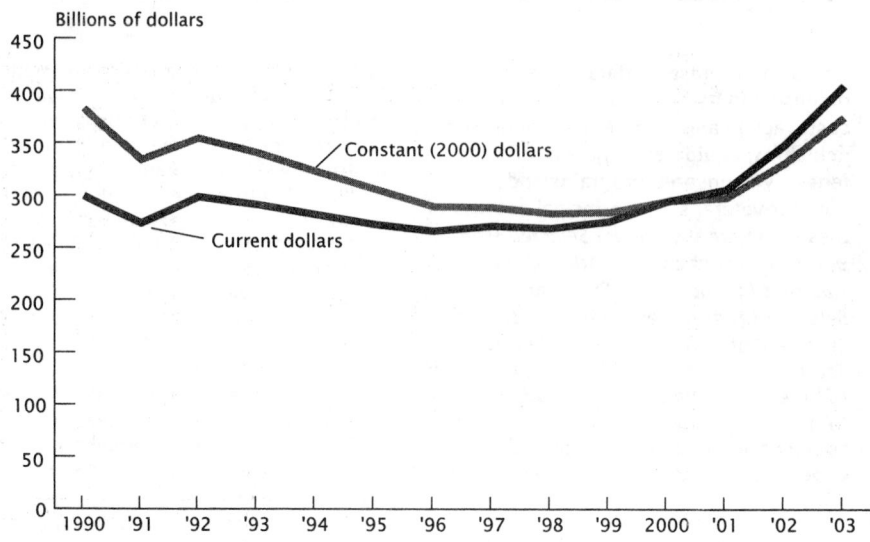

Billions of dollars

Source: Chart prepared by U.S. Census Bureau. For data, see Table 492.

Figure 10.2
Department of Defense Manpower: 2003
In thousands

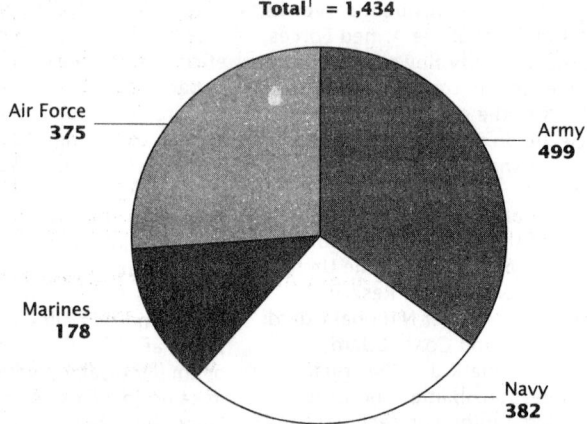

Total[1] = 1,434

Air Force
375

Army
499

Marines
178

Navy
382

[1]Includes National Guard, Reserve, and retired regular personnel on extended or continuous active duty. Excludes Coast Guard.

Source: Chart prepared by U.S. Census Bureau. For data, see Table 500.

U.S. Census Bureau, Statistical Abstract of the United States: 2004-2005

No. 492. National Defense Outlays and Veterans Benefits: 1960 to 2005

[(53.5 represents $53,500,000,000). For fiscal year ending in year shown, see text, section 8. Includes outlays of Department of Defense, Department of Veterans Affairs, and other agencies for activities primarily related to national defense and veterans programs. For explanation of average annual percent change, see Guide to Tabular Presentation. Minus sign (-) indicates decrease]

Year	National defense and veterans outlays				Annual percent change [1]			Defense outlays percent of—	
	Defense outlays								
	Total outlays (bil. dol.)	Current dollars (bil. dol.)	Constant (2000) dollars (bil. dol.)	Veterans outlays (bil. dol.)	Total outlays	Defense outlays	Veterans outlays	Federal outlays	Gross domestic product [2]
1960	53.5	48.1	300.2	5.4	2.5	2.4	3.1	52.2	9.3
1965	56.3	50.6	291.8	5.7	-6.8	-7.6	0.7	42.8	7.4
1970	90.4	81.7	375.1	8.7	0.3	-1.0	13.6	41.8	8.1
1975	103.1	86.5	262.7	16.6	11.2	9.0	24.0	26.0	5.5
1980	155.1	134.0	267.1	21.1	13.9	15.2	6.3	22.7	4.9
1985	279.0	252.7	356.5	26.3	10.3	11.1	2.7	26.7	6.1
1990	328.4	299.3	382.7	29.1	-1.6	-1.4	-3.2	23.9	5.2
1992	332.4	298.4	354.3	34.1	9.1	9.2	8.8	21.6	4.8
1993	326.8	291.1	340.3	35.7	-1.7	-2.4	4.7	20.7	4.4
1994	319.2	281.6	322.8	37.6	-2.3	-3.2	5.4	19.3	4.1
1995	310.0	272.1	305.9	37.9	-2.9	-3.4	0.8	17.9	3.7
1996	302.7	265.8	289.2	37.0	-2.3	-2.3	-2.4	17.0	3.5
1997	309.8	270.5	288.4	39.3	2.3	1.8	6.3	16.9	3.3
1998	310.2	268.5	282.6	41.8	0.1	-0.8	6.3	16.2	3.1
1999	320.2	274.9	283.7	43.2	3.2	2.4	3.4	16.1	3.0
2000	341.6	294.5	294.5	47.1	6.7	7.1	9.0	16.5	3.0
2001	350.5	305.5	297.5	45.0	2.6	3.7	-4.3	16.4	3.0
2002	399.5	348.6	330.8	51.0	14.0	14.1	13.2	17.3	3.4
2003	461.9	404.9	374.5	57.0	15.6	16.2	11.8	18.8	3.7
2004, est	514.1	453.7	414.4	60.5	11.3	12.0	6.0	19.6	4.0
2005, est	518.1	450.6	406.8	67.5	0.8	-0.7	11.6	18.8	3.7

[1] Change from immediate prior year for 1960, change from 1955.   [2] Represents fiscal year GDP; for definition, see text, Section 13.

No. 493. Federal Budget Outlays for Defense Functions: 1980 to 2004

[In billions of dollars (134.0 represents $134,000,000,000), except percent. For year ending September 30. Minus sign (-) indicates decrease]

Defense function	1980	1990	1995	1997	1998	1999	2000	2001	2002	2003	2004, est.
Total.	134.0	299.3	272.1	270.5	268.5	274.9	294.5	305.5	348.6	404.9	453.7
Percent change [1]	15.2	-1.4	-3.4	1.8	-0.8	2.4	7.1	3.7	14.1	16.2	12.0
Defense Dept., military	130.9	289.7	259.4	258.3	256.1	261.3	281.2	291.0	332.0	387.3	434.8
Military personnel	40.9	75.6	70.8	69.7	69.0	69.5	76.0	74.0	86.8	106.7	117.4
Operation, maintenance.	44.8	88.3	91.0	92.4	93.4	96.3	105.9	112.0	130.0	151.4	165.7
Procurement	29.0	81.0	55.0	47.7	48.2	48.8	51.7	55.0	62.5	67.9	77.7
Research and development . .	13.1	37.5	34.6	37.0	37.4	37.4	37.6	40.5	44.4	53.1	60.6
Military construction	2.5	5.1	6.8	6.2	6.0	5.5	5.1	5.0	5.1	5.9	6.2
Family housing.	1.7	3.5	3.6	4.0	3.9	3.7	3.4	3.5	3.7	3.8	3.9
Other [2]	-1.1	-1.2	-2.4	1.2	-1.9	0.1	1.6	1.1	-0.5	-1.5	3.4
Atomic energy activities [3]	2.9	9.0	11.8	11.3	11.3	12.2	12.1	12.9	14.8	16.0	16.6
Defense-related activities [4]	0.2	0.6	0.9	1.0	1.1	1.4	1.2	1.6	1.8	1.6	2.3

[1] Change from immediate prior year.   [2] Revolving and management funds, trust funds, special foreign currency program, allowances, and offsetting receipts.   [3] Defense activities only.   [4] Includes civil defense activities.

No. 494. National Defense—Budget Authority and Outlays: 1980 to 2004

[In billions of dollars (143.9 represents $143,900,000,000). For year ending September 30.]

Item	1980	1990	1995	1998	1999	2000	2001	2002	2003	2004, est.
Defense (Budget authority) [1]	143.9	303.3	266.4	271.3	292.3	304.1	335.5	362.1	456.2	460.5
Department of Defense-Military	140.7	293.0	255.7	258.5	278.5	290.4	319.4	345.0	437.9	441.7
Atomic energy defense activities . . .	3.0	9.7	10.1	11.7	12.4	12.4	14.3	15.2	16.4	16.8
Defense-related activities	0.2	0.6	0.6	1.1	1.4	1.3	1.7	1.9	2.0	2.1
Defense (Outlays) [1]	134.0	299.3	272.1	268.5	274.9	294.5	305.5	348.6	404.9	453.7
Department of Defense-Military	130.9	289.7	259.4	256.1	261.3	281.2	291.0	332.0	387.3	434.8
Atomic energy defense activities . . .	2.9	9.0	11.8	11.3	12.2	12.1	12.9	14.8	16.0	16.6
Defense-related activities	0.2	0.6	0.9	1.1	1.4	1.2	1.6	1.8	1.6	2.3

[1] Includes defense budget authority, balances, and outlays by other departments.

Source of Tables 492-494: U.S. Office of Management and Budget, Budget of the U.S. Government, *Historical Tables,* annual.

National Defense and Veterans Affairs   327

No. 495. Military Prime Contract Awards to All Businesses by Program: 1990 to 2003

[In billions of dollars (144.7 represents $144,700,000,000). Net values for year ending September 30. Includes all new prime contracts; debit or credit changes in contracts are also included. Actions cover official awards, amendments, or other changes in prime contracts to obtain military supplies, services, or construction. Excludes term contracts and contracts which do not obligate a firm total dollar amount or fixed quantity, but includes job orders, task orders, and delivery orders against such contracts]

DOD Procurement program	1990	1995	1997	1998	1999	2000	2001	2002	2003
Total	144.7	131.4	128.4	128.8	135.2	143.0	154.1	180.6	219.5
Intragovernmental [1]	10.0	12.3	11.5	9.9	11.6	14.8	13.4	17.0	19.5
For work outside the U.S.	7.1	5.6	6.4	5.6	7.4	7.5	7.1	9.3	16.2
Educ. and nonprofit institutions . . . . . . [2]	3.5	3.3	3.6	3.5	3.9	4.3	4.5	5.5	6.2
With business firms for work in the U.S. [2] . .	123.8	110.0	106.9	109.7	112.2	116.4	129.2	148.8	177.7
Major hard goods	79.1	56.0	52.5	56.0	57.5	59.8	67.9	76.1	90.6
Aircraft	24.0	18.8	18.4	20.8	23.3	28.8	30.5	30.6	41.1
Electronics and communication equip..	18.5	12.3	12.1	10.7	10.7	9.5	10.9	13.0	14.9
Missiles and space systems	17.1	10.6	9.5	9.9	9.5	8.2	8.2	11.2	13.3
Ships	10.3	9.1	6.8	8.6	7.8	8.3	12.0	11.4	10.2
Tanks, ammo. and weapons	9.2	5.3	5.7	6.0	6.2	5.0	6.3	9.8	11.0
Services	14.6	18.6	20.2	21.2	23.7	24.0	25.9	33.2	43.1

[1] Covers only purchases from other Federal agencies and reimbursable purchases on behalf of foreign governments.
[2] Includes Department of Defense. Includes other business not shown separately. Contracts awarded for work in U.S. possessions, and other areas subject to complete sovereignty of United States; contracts in a classified location; and any intragovernmental contracts entered into overseas.

Source: U.S. Dept. of Defense, *Prime Contract Awards*, semiannual.

No. 496. Department of Defense Contract Awards, Payroll, and Civilian and Military Personnel—States: 2002

[(In millions of dollars (158,737 represents $158,737,000,000). Awards and payroll for years ending September 30. Personnel as of September 30. Contracts refer to awards made in year specified; expenditures relating to awards may extend over several years. Civilian employees include United States citizen and foreign national direct hire civilians subject to Office of Management and Budget (OMB) ceiling controls and civilian personnel involved in civil functions in the United States. Excludes indirect hire civilians and those direct hire civilian not subject to OMB ceiling controls. Military personnel include active duty personnel based ashore. Excludes personnel temporarily shore-based in a transient status, or afloat. Payroll outlays include the gross earnings of civilian and active duty military personnel for services rendered to the government and for cash allowances for benefits. Excludes employer's share of employee benefits, accrued military retirement benefits and most permanent change of station costs]

State	Contract awards [1] (mil. dol.)	Payroll (mil. dol.)	Personnel (1,000) Civilian	Personnel (1,000) Military	State	Contract awards [1] (mil. dol.)	Payroll (mil. dol.)	Personnel (1,000) Civilian	Personnel (1,000) Military
U.S. . . .	158,737	114,950	628.0	1,045.1	MO	5,756	1,750	9.3	16.1
AL	4,672	2,714	20.5	11.4	MT	129	322	1.2	3.5
AK	911	1,044	4.2	15.9	NE	306	730	3.4	7.8
AZ	6,685	2,188	8.3	22.4	NV	359	905	2.1	8.5
AR	833	849	3.7	4.9	NH	606	292	1.1	0.3
CA	23,816	12,390	58.1	123.9	NJ	3,452	1,580	13.9	6.3
CO	2,624	2,686	10.2	29.7	NM	823	1,161	6.7	11.3
CT	5,639	581	2.5	4.2	NY	4,435	2,075	11.2	20.9
DE	135	371	1.4	3.9	NC	1,520	5,163	16.4	94.3
DC	2,420	1,676	15.6	12.8	ND	207	390	1.6	7.5
FL	7,073	7,546	27.1	55.8	OH	3,444	2,469	22.1	6.9
GA	5,814	5,495	31.2	64.4	OK	1,573	2,553	22.0	23.7
HI	1,433	2,842	16.5	34.6	OR	404	642	3.1	0.7
ID	161	425	1.5	4.3	PA	4,571	2,489	24.9	3.1
IL	2,006	2,438	12.8	25.0	RI	365	573	4.3	3.0
IN	1,860	1,052	8.7	1.0	SC	1,138	2,635	9.4	37.9
IA	552	331	1.5	0.4	SD	191	276	1.2	3.4
KS	1,223	1,244	5.6	15.8	TN	1,305	1,282	5.5	2.6
KY	2,268	2,034	8.3	34.1	TX	13,700	9,414	37.2	115.1
LA	1,683	1,531	7.4	16.5	UT	1,509	1,263	14.7	5.4
ME	1,108	659	5.8	2.7	VT	384	128	0.6	0.1
MD	6,505	4,220	32.1	30.9	VA	18,128	13,039	77.1	90.9
MA	4,929	942	6.8	2.4	WA	2,789	4,382	23.3	38.5
MI	2,180	1,012	8.0	1.2	WV	170	335	1.8	0.6
MN	1,529	526	2.6	0.7	WI	1,065	532	3.1	0.5
MS	2,272	1,518	9.3	14.0	WY	79	256	1.0	3.3

[1] Military awards for supplies, services, and construction. Net value of contracts of over $25,000 for work in each state and DC. Figures reflect impact of prime contracting on state distribution of defense work. Often the State in which a prime contractor is located in is not the State where the subcontracted work is done. See also headnote, Table 495. Undistributed civilians and military personnel, their payrolls, and prime contract awards for performance in classified locations are excluded.

Source: U.S. Dept. of Defense, *Atlas/Data Abstract for the United States and Selected Areas*, annual.

No. 497. U.S. Military Sales and Assistance to Foreign Governments: 1990 to 2002

[In millions of dollars (16,614 represents $16,614,000,000). For year ending September 30. Department of Defense (DOD) sales deliveries cover deliveries against sales orders authorized under Arms Export Control Act, as well as earlier and applicable legislation. For details regarding individual programs, see source]

Item	1990	1995	1996	1997	1998	1999	2000	2001	2002
Military sales agreements	16,614	8,183	9,304	8,328	8,938	11,594	11,324	13,056	12,483
Military construction sales agrmts .	636	24	139	29	428	288	285	124	76
Military sales deliveries [1]	8,065	11,793	11,466	15,471	12,861	16,719	10,382	11,907	10,479
Military sales financing	4,758	3,712	3,836	3,530	3,420	3,370	4,333	3,535	4,040
Military assistance programs [2] . .	137	117	330	92	95	268	86	41	46
Military assist. program delivery [3] .	27	17	27	113	92	13	10	15	20
IMET program/deliveries [4]	43	26	39	43	50	50	50	58	70

[1] Includes military construction sales deliveries.   [2] Also includes Military Assistance Service Funded (MASF) program data, Section 506(a) drawdown authority, and MAP Merger Funds.   [3] Includes Military Assistance Service Funded (MASF) program data and Section 506(a) drawdown authority.   [4] International Military Education and Training program/deliveries.

No. 498. U.S. Military Sales Deliveries by Selected Country: 1990 to 2002

[In millions of dollars (8,065 represents $8,065,000,000). For year ending September 30. Represents Department of Defense military sales]

Country	1990	1995	1996	1997	1998	1999	2000	2001	2002
Total [1]	8,065	11,793	11,466	15,471	12,861	16,719	10,382	11,907	10,479
Australia	384	303	228	196	207	269	330	245	156
Bahrain	(NA)	40	39	61	62	48	54	343	84
Belgium	150	8	157	107	194	250	58	170	69
Canada	119	127	154	83	111	96	84	111	88
China	455	1,335	831	2,372	1,424	2,520	789	1,166	1,470
Denmark	35	54	91	48	159	157	46	112	23
Egypt	368	1,479	1,083	897	551	448	805	867	1,977
France	109	65	52	57	35	248	217	142	207
Germany	366	257	377	208	190	251	131	330	222
Greece	114	220	210	691	398	463	315	451	465
Israel	146	327	386	456	1,195	1,216	565	748	597
Italy	61	54	77	51	43	106	41	98	104
Japan	272	693	753	492	409	443	489	494	497
Korea, South	328	442	340	478	836	588	1,446	736	554
Kuwait	52	472	745	1,213	323	316	348	567	133
Netherlands	397	153	391	168	344	321	161	413	243
Norway	117	25	135	98	119	220	64	192	89
Portugal	72	88	19	70	21	12	20	42	29
Saudi Arabia	874	3,568	2,838	4,640	3,800	4,695	2,052	1,953	1,353
Singapore	44	59	80	133	232	559	139	244	425
Spain	406	193	411	216	133	324	141	267	178
Thailand	175	356	270	151	145	133	116	119	170
Turkey	761	368	481	1,153	532	872	217	467	282
United Kingdom	205	106	147	214	105	151	102	343	252
United Arab Emirates	(NA)	345	112	93	26	95	71	9	40

NA Not available   [1] Includes other countries not shown separately.

Source of Tables 497 and 498: U.S. Defense Security Cooperation Agency, *Foreign Military Sales, Foreign Military Construction Sales,* and *Military Assistance Facts,* annual.

No. 499. Military and Civilian Personnel and Expenditures: 1990 to 2002

[(3,693 represents 3,693,000). For year ending September 30. For definitions, see headnote, table 496]

Item	1990	1995	1999	2000	2001	2002
Personnel, total [1] (1,000).	3,693	3,391	2,863	2,791	2,781	2,811
Active duty military	1,185	1,085	1,003	984	991	1,045
Civilian	931	768	634	634	628	628
Reserve and National Guard.	1,577	1,538	1,226	1,173	1,163	1,138
Expenditures, total (mil. dol.) [2]	209,904	209,695	218,861	229,072	243,778	276,281
Payroll outlays	88,650	98,396	101,811	103,447	106,013	114,950
Active duty military pay.	33,705	35,188	37,001	36,872	37,873	40,945
Civilian pay	28,230	29,932	29,128	29,935	29,879	32,805
Retired military pay	21,159	27,595	30,960	31,994	33,196	33,677
Reserve and National Guard pay	5,556	5,681	4,722	4,646	5,066	7,523
Prime contract awards [3] (mil. dol.)	121,254	109,005	114,875	123,295	135,225	158,737
Grants	6,329	7,543	7,733	(NA)	(NA)	(NA)

NA Not available.   [1] Includes those based ashore and excludes those temporarily shore-based, in a transient status, or afloat.   [2] Includes expenditures not shown separately.   [3] Represents contract awards over $25,000.

Source: U.S. Dept. of Defense, *Atlas/Data Abstract for the United States and selected areas,* annual.

No. 500. Department of Defense Manpower: 1950 to 2003

[In thousands (1,459 represents 1,459,000). As of end of fiscal year, see text, Section 8. Includes National Guard, Reserve, and retired regular personnel on extended or continuous active duty. Excludes Coast Guard. Other officer candidates are included under enlisted personnel]

Year	Total¹	Army					Navy²					Marine Corps					Air Force				
		Total¹	White	Black	Officers	Enlisted	Total¹	White	Black	Officers	Enlisted	Total¹	White	Black	Officers	Enlisted	Total¹	White	Black	Officers	Enlisted
1950	1,459	593	(NA)	(NA)	73	519	381	(NA)	(NA)	45	333	74	(NA)	(NA)	7	67	411	(NA)	(NA)	57	354
1955	2,935	1,109	(NA)	(NA)	122	986	661	(NA)	(NA)	75	583	205	(NA)	(NA)	18	187	960	(NA)	(NA)	137	823
1960	2,475	873	(NA)	(NA)	101	770	617	(NA)	(NA)	70	545	171	(NA)	(NA)	16	154	815	(NA)	(NA)	130	683
1965	2,654	969	(NA)	(NA)	112	855	670	(NA)	(NA)	78	588	190	(NA)	(NA)	17	173	825	(NA)	(NA)	132	690
1970	3,065	1,323	(NA)	(NA)	167	1,153	691	(NA)	(NA)	81	606	260	(NA)	(NA)	25	235	791	(NA)	(NA)	130	657
1972	2,322	811	(NA)	(NA)	121	687	587	(NA)	(NA)	73	511	198	(NA)	(NA)	20	178	726	(NA)	(NA)	122	600
1973	2,252	801	(NA)	(NA)	116	682	564	(NA)	(NA)	71	490	196	(NA)	(NA)	19	177	691	(NA)	(NA)	115	572
1974	2,162	783	(NA)	(NA)	106	674	546	(NA)	(NA)	67	475	189	(NA)	(NA)	19	170	644	(NA)	(NA)	110	529
1975	2,128	784	(NA)	(NA)	103	678	535	(NA)	(NA)	66	466	196	(NA)	(NA)	19	177	613	(NA)	(NA)	105	503
1976	2,082	779	(NA)	(NA)	99	678	525	(NA)	(NA)	64	458	192	(NA)	(NA)	19	174	585	(NA)	(NA)	100	481
1977	2,075	782	(NA)	(NA)	98	680	530	(NA)	(NA)	63	462	192	(NA)	(NA)	18	173	571	(NA)	(NA)	96	470
1978	2,062	772	(NA)	(NA)	98	670	530	(NA)	(NA)	63	463	191	(NA)	(NA)	18	172	570	(NA)	(NA)	95	470
1979	2,027	759	(NA)	(NA)	97	657	523	(NA)	(NA)	62	457	185	(NA)	(NA)	18	167	560	(NA)	(NA)	96	459
1980	2,051	777	503	229	99	674	527	436	55	63	460	189	142	39	18	170	558	460	80	98	456
1981	2,083	781	502	232	102	675	540	443	58	65	470	191	145	39	18	172	570	468	83	99	467
1982	2,109	780	504	230	103	673	553	450	62	67	481	192	149	38	19	174	583	476	87	102	476
1983	2,123	780	512	220	106	669	558	462	66	68	485	194	152	37	20	174	592	483	88	105	483
1984	2,138	780	520	215	108	668	565	455	67	69	491	196	153	36	20	176	597	486	89	106	486
1985	2,151	781	523	211	110	667	571	459	70	71	495	198	152	37	20	178	602	488	90	108	489
1986	2,169	781	524	210	110	667	581	464	75	72	504	200	151	38	20	179	608	491	92	109	495
1987	2,174	781	519	212	108	668	587	467	81	72	510	200	150	38	20	179	607	489	88	107	495
1988	2,138	772	507	213	107	660	593	466	85	72	516	197	147	38	20	177	576	462	87	105	467
1989	2,130	770	497	218	107	658	593	461	91	72	516	197	146	38	20	177	571	458		104	463
1990	2,044	732	466	213	104	624	579	446	93	72	503	197	145	38	20	177	535	428	82	100	431
1991	1,986	711	452	204	104	603	570	439	92	71	495	194	144	36	20	174	510	409	77	97	409
1992	1,807	610	388	173	95	511	542	415	88	69	468	185	138	32	19	165	470	377	70	90	376
1993	1,705	572	365	158	88	480	510	390	84	66	439	178	134	30	18	160	444	357	65	84	356
1994	1,610	541	344	147	85	453	469	355	78	62	403	174	131	28	18	156	426	341	62	81	341
1995	1,518	509	322	137	83	422	435	326	75	59	372	175	130	28	18	157	400	318	58	78	318
1996	1,472	491	(NA)	(NA)	81	407	417	(NA)	(NA)	57	355	175	(NA)	(NA)	18	157	389	(NA)	(NA)	76	309
1997	1,439	492	(NA)	(NA)	79	408	396	(NA)	(NA)	56	335	174	(NA)	(NA)	18	156	377	(NA)	(NA)	74	299
1998	1,407	484	(NA)	(NA)	78	401	382	(NA)	(NA)	55	323	173	(NA)	(NA)	18	155	368	(NA)	(NA)	72	292
1999	1,386	479	(NA)	(NA)	77	398	373	(NA)	(NA)	54	315	173	(NA)	(NA)	18	155	361	(NA)	(NA)	70	286
2000	1,384	482	(NA)	(NA)	77	401	373	(NA)	(NA)	54	315	173	(NA)	(NA)	18	155	356	(NA)	(NA)	69	282
2001	1,385	481	(NA)	(NA)	76	400	378	(NA)	(NA)	54	320	173	(NA)	(NA)	18	155	354	(NA)	(NA)	69	280
2002	1,414	487	(NA)	(NA)	78	404	385	(NA)	(NA)	55	326	174	(NA)	(NA)	18	155	368	(NA)	(NA)	72	292
2003	1,434	499	293	119	80	415	382	231	72	55	323	178	120	24	19	159	375	268	57	74	297

NA Not available. ¹ Includes cadets, midshipmen and other not shown separately ² Beginning 1980, excludes Navy Reserve personnel on active duty for Training and Administration of Reserves (TARS). Prior to 1980, includes Navy Reserve personnel on active duty for (TARS).

Source: U.S. Dept. of Defense, Selected Manpower Statistics, annual.

No. 501. Active Duty Military and Civilian Personnel in Installations: 2002

[As of September 30. See headnote, Table 496].

State	Military personnel				Civilian personnel			
	Total [1]	Army	Navy/Marine Corps	Air Force	Total [1]	Army	Navy/Marine Corps	Air Force
United States. . .	1,045,067	383,112	355,866	306,089	628,049	213,618	177,695	151,041
Alabama	11,354	6,259	643	4,452	20,414	16,607	33	2,357
Alaska	15,906	6,630	140	9,136	4,204	2,215	18	1,708
Arizona	22,448	5,174	5,415	11,859	8,290	3,627	453	3,289
Arkansas.	4,855	251	39	4,565	3,686	2,689	5	881
California.	123,948	7,932	96,047	19,969	58,076	6,738	33,163	9,934
Colorado.	29,733	14,951	908	13,874	10,183	2,682	48	4,965
Connecticut	4,239	22	4,179	38	2,497	460	1,082	263
Delaware.	3,899	8	17	3,874	1,429	248	-	1,107
District of Columbia.	12,767	5,239	4,425	3,103	15,640	4,566	9,905	876
Florida	55,815	3,098	27,570	25,147	27,144	3,019	12,661	8,632
Georgia	64,392	49,474	4,814	10,104	31,167	11,180	3,883	13,800
Hawaii	34,608	15,985	14,334	4,289	16,508	4,441	8,925	2,075
Idaho	4,251	40	68	4,143	1,472	695	51	681
Illinois.	25,036	688	18,627	5,721	12,780	6,400	1,745	3,129
Indiana	1,041	524	386	131	8,719	1,517	3,146	1,049
Iowa.	447	274	126	47	1,546	964	5	524
Kansas	15,819	12,665	154	3,000	5,603	4,176	3	1,039
Kentucky.	34,081	33,578	279	224	8,348	6,893	192	234
Louisiana	16,541	8,840	1,774	5,927	7,440	3,995	1,319	1,703
Maine	2,689	248	2,389	52	5,791	321	4,879	269
Maryland.	30,928	7,140	15,853	7,935	32,090	12,275	15,524	2,128
Massachusetts	2,427	255	515	1,657	6,829	2,381	264	2,986
Michigan.	1,173	489	551	133	8,038	5,042	25	1,164
Minnesota	702	308	301	93	2,576	1,494	22	807
Mississippi.	14,005	449	5,610	7,946	9,289	3,656	2,535	2,806
Missouri	16,119	9,807	2,254	4,058	9,330	5,828	250	1,208
Montana	3,512	22	19	3,471	1,187	475	-	667
Nebraska	7,793	78	535	7,180	3,365	1,391	17	1,574
Nevada.	8,461	93	1,054	7,314	2,072	351	317	1,220
New Hampshire . . .	326	8	261	57	1,051	569	39	284
New Jersey	6,306	821	740	4,745	13,943	9,466	2,105	1,513
New Mexico.	11,254	299	223	10,732	6,704	2,902	39	3,273
New York	20,882	17,630	2,819	433	11,220	6,994	154	2,470
North Carolina	94,296	41,120	43,522	9,654	16,444	5,994	7,281	1,225
North Dakota	7,465	19	8	7,438	1,621	452	2	1,081
Ohio	6,899	582	538	5,779	22,080	1,356	47	12,200
Oklahoma	23,664	13,365	1,422	8,877	21,972	4,265	92	16,129
Oregon.	705	229	401	75	3,121	2,229	22	839
Pennsylvania	3,098	1,214	1,617	267	24,920	8,186	8,124	1,532
Rhode Island	2,974	108	2,790	76	4,346	276	3,745	230
South Carolina	37,943	10,389	18,279	9,275	9,370	2,739	3,625	1,731
South Dakota	3,350	41	5	3,304	1,219	493	1	671
Tennessee.	2,554	370	1,946	238	5,496	2,655	1,077	915
Texas	115,100	61,083	7,800	46,217	37,238	17,289	1,569	14,347
Utah	5,447	320	162	4,965	14,725	2,151	29	11,270
Vermont	61	21	25	15	567	294	2	233
Virginia	90,851	24,916	52,120	13,815	77,119	19,815	34,492	4,082
Washington	38,521	19,555	11,692	7,274	23,259	5,641	14,699	1,866
West Virginia	558	202	309	47	1,783	1,264	70	427
Wisconsin	532	295	160	77	3,074	2,059	11	893
Wyoming.	3,292	4	1	3,287	1,004	203	⁀	755

- Represents zero. [1] Includes other DOD organizations not shown separately.
Source: U.S. Dept. of Defense, *Selected Manpower Statistics*, annual.

No. 502. Military Personnel on Active Duty by Location: 1980 to 2003

[In thousands (2,051 represents 2,051,000). As of September 30.]

Location	1980	1985	1990	1995	1998	1999	2000	2001	2002	2003
Total	2,051	2,151	2,044	1,518	1,407	1,386	1,384	1,385	1,412	1,434
Shore-based [1]	1,840	1,920	1,794	1,351	1,267	1,241	1,237	1,244	1,262	1,287
Afloat [2]	211	231	252	167	140	145	147	141	150	148
United States [3]	1,562	1,636	1,437	1,280	1,147	1,133	1,127	1,130	1,182	1,182
Foreign countries	488	516	609	238	260	253	258	255	230	253

[1] Includes Navy personnel temporarily on shore. [2] Includes Marine Corps. [3] Includes outlying areas.
Source: U.S. Dept. of Defense, *Selected Manpower Statistics*, annual.

National Defense and Veterans Affairs 331

No. 503. U.S. Military Personnel on Active Duty in Selected Foreign Countries: 1995 to 2002

[As of September 30]

Country	1995	1996	1997	1998	1999	2000	2001	2002
In foreign countries [1] .	238,064	240,421	227,258	259,871	252,763	257,817	254,788	230,484
Ashore	208,836	213,467	207,978	218,957	207,156	212,858	211,947	208,479
Afloat	29,228	26,954	19,280	40,914	45,607	44,959	42,841	22,005
Argentina	26	25	27	27	24	26	22	28
Australia	314	328	333	333	323	175	803	171
Austria	35	37	34	34	31	18	24	20
Bahamas, The	36	53	24	24	23	24	64	22
Bahrain.	618	598	748	748	1,511	949	2,065	1,560
Belgium	1,689	1,646	1,679	1,679	1,649	1,554	1,578	1,458
Bolivia	29	24	26	26	29	20	25	20
Bosnia and Herzegovina . . .	1	15,003	8,170	8,170	5,800	5,708	3,116	3,082
Brazil	50	47	45	45	43	38	39	27
Canada.	214	208	179	179	150	156	163	148
Chile	28	24	25	25	30	26	337	28
China	30	32	58	58	57	74	57	61
Colombia.	44	34	32	32	41	224	63	39
Cuba (Guantanamo)	5,129	1,886	1,527	1,527	1,030	688	557	549
Cyprus	24	50	25	25	38	41	30	28
Denmark.	37	38	39	39	32	26	28	22
Diego Garcia [2]	897	878	705	705	670	625	590	548
Dominican Republic	13	10	12	12	11	12	14	55
Ecuador	86	70	164	164	21	20	22	35
Egypt	1,123	1,066	5,846	5,846	892	499	500	433
El Salvador	25	26	28	28	30	27	26	23
France	67	73	74	74	73	67	71	74
Germany.	73,280	48,878	60,053	60,053	65,538	69,203	70,998	68,701
Greece	489	507	498	498	652	678	506	593
Greenland	131	141	131	131	129	125	153	88
Haiti	1,616	277	239	239	59	21	13	15
Honduras	193	865	427	427	513	351	394	402
Hungary	16	6,523	4,220	4,220	87	375	29	19
Iceland	1,982	1,893	1,960	1,960	1,681	1,636	1,743	1,665
India.	27	24	25	25	25	20	18	19
Indonesia	46	43	48	48	50	51	43	28
Israel	46	44	40	40	35	36	35	36
Italy	12,007	12,401	11,677	11,677	11,530	11,190	11,704	12,466
Japan.	39,134	42,962	41,257	41,257	40,338	40,159	40,217	41,848
Jordan	24	24	30	30	27	29	18	32
Kenya.	40	29	31	31	95	21	62	43
Korea, South	36,016	36,539	35,663	35,663	35,913	36,565	37,605	37,743
Kuwait	771	5,531	1,640	1,640	4,011	4,602	4,208	567
Macedonia, The Former Yugoslav, Republic of.	591	501	518	518	1,100	347	351	146
Mexico	36	35	27	27	33	29	27	31
Netherlands.	687	747	703	703	673	659	676	629
Norway.	57	104	107	107	95	81	83	123
Oman.	27	30	28	28	101	251	673	31
Pakistan	28	26	29	29	26	22	21	31
Peru.	26	26	29	29	50	425	43	41
Philippines.	126	138	35	35	84	79	35	86
Portugal	1,066	1,075	1,066	1,066	1,024	1,005	1,005	992
Qatar	2	43	26	26	39	52	116	71
Russia	60	74	68	68	88	101	20	78
Saudi Arabia	1,077	1,587	1,722	1,722	5,552	7,053	4,805	776
Serbia and Montenegro	13	8	13	13	6,410	5,427	5,679	2,804
Singapore	166	158	168	168	167	411	160	167
South Africa.	24	23	25	25	32	34	31	32
Spain	2,799	2,746	3,575	3,575	2,127	2,007	1,990	2,621
Switzerland	26	24	22	22	18	19	18	19
Thailand	99	242	126	126	120	526	113	125
Tunisia	20	19	193	193	13	12	15	17
Turkey	3,111	2,922	2,864	2,864	2,312	2,006	2,153	1,587
Ukraine.	5	8	10	10	18	16	10	13
United Arab Emirates.	30	23	22	22	679	402	204	21
United Kingdom	12,131	11,662	11,379	11,379	11,311	11,207	11,318	10,258
Venezuela	35	35	35	35	30	28	31	27

[1] Includes areas not shown separately.　[2] British Indian Ocean Territory.
Source: U.S. Dept. of Defense, *Selected Manpower Statistics*, annual.<http://www.dior.whs.mil/mmid/military/miltop.htm>.

No. 504. Coast Guard Personnel on Active Duty: 1970 to 2003

[As of end of fiscal year]

Year	Total	Officers	Cadets	Enlisted	Year	Total	Officers	Cadets	Enlisted
1970.	38,012	5,512	976	31,524	1996.	35,037	7,106	802	27,129
1975.	36,788	5,630	1,177	29,981	1997.	34,689	6,939	805	26,945
1980.	39,100	6,465	874	31,761	1998.	35,102	6,962	777	27,363
1985.	38,457	6,584	727	31,146	1999.	35,370	6,942	835	27,593
1990.	36,776	6,713	927	29,136	2000.	35,801	7,039	798	27,964
1993.	39,077	7,471	907	30,699	2001.	35,969	7,033	890	28,046
1994.	37,284	7,401	881	29,002	2002.	37,993	7,277	949	29,767
1995.	36,537	7,295	841	28,401	2003.	39,254	7,491	979	30,784

Source: U.S. Coast Guard Personnel Management Directorate Workforce Forecasting & Analysis Section (G-WP-1).

U.S. Census Bureau, *Statistical Abstract of the United States: 2004-2005*

No. 505. U.S. Active Duty Military Deaths by Manner of Death: 1980 to 2002

Manner of death	1980-2002	1980	1990	1994	1995	1996	1997	1998	1999	2000	2001	2002
Deaths, total	35,583	2,391	1,526	1,109	1,055	1,008	864	815	761	774	890	1,007
Accident	20,848	1,577	864	548	572	518	463	420	411	400	422	538
Illness.	6,451	401	275	217	167	180	177	156	126	124	175	178
Homicide.	1,922	161	71	86	59	65	43	28	34	31	42	46
Self-inflicted.	4,929	236	250	231	242	210	159	155	110	142	118	130
Pending/undetermined	781	15	42	8	9	14	22	53	80	60	78	98
Hostile deaths	652	1	24	19	6	21	-	3	-	17	55	17
Deaths per 100,000 of personnel strength	(X)	116.6	74.7	68.9	69.5	68.5	60.1	57.9	54.9	53.9	57.9	64.4
Nonhostile deaths [1]	(X)	116.5	73.5	67.7	69.1	67.1	60.1	57.7	54.9	52.7	54.3	63.3
Accidents	(X)	76.9	42.3	34.0	37.7	35.2	32.2	29.9	29.7	27.8	27.5	34.4
Illnesses	(X)	19.6	13.5	13.5	11.0	12.2	12.3	11.1	9.1	8.6	11.4	11.4
Homicides	(X)	7.9	3.5	5.3	3.9	4.4	3.0	2.0	2.5	2.2	2.7	2.9
Self-inflicted	(X)	11.5	12.2	14.3	15.9	14.3	11.1	11.0	7.9	9.9	7.7	8.3

- Represents zero.   X Not applicable.   [1] Includes other items not shown separately.

Source: U.S. Department of Defense, DOD Worldwide U.S. Active Duty Military Personnel. <www.diro.whs.mil/mmid/casualty/castop.htm>.

No. 506. Armed Forces Personnel—Summary of Major Conflicts

[For Revolutionary War, number of personnel serving not known, but estimates range from 184,000 to 250,000; for War of 1812, 286,730 served; for Mexican War, 78,718 served. Dates of the major conflicts may differ from those specified in various laws providing benefits for veterans]

Item	Unit	Civil War [1]	World War I	World War II	Korean conflict	Vietnam conflict	Persian Gulf War
Personnel serving [2]	1,000. . . .	2,213	4,735	[3]16,113	[4]5,720	[5]8,744	2,233
Average duration of service	Months. . .	20	12	33	19	23	(NA)
Service abroad: Personnel serving . . .	Percent . .	(NA)	53	73	[6]56	(NA)	(NA)
Average duration [7]	Months. . .	(NA)	6	16	13	(NA)	(NA)
Casualties: [8] Battle deaths [2]	1,000. . . .	140	53	292	34	[9]47	(Z)
Other deaths	1,000. . . .	224	63	114	3	11	(Z)
Wounds not mortal [2]	1,000. . . .	282	204	671	103	[9]153	(Z)
Draftees: Classified.	1,000. . . .	777	24,234	36,677	9,123	[5]75,717	(X)
Examined	1,000. . . .	522	3,764	17,955	3,685	[5]8,611	(X)
Rejected	1,000. . . .	160	803	6,420	1,189	[5]3,880	(X)
Inducted	1,000. . . .	46	2,820	10,022	1,560	[5]1,759	(X)

NA Not available.   X Not applicable.   Z Fewer than 500.   [1] Union forces only. Estimates of the number serving in Confederate forces range from 600,000 to 1.5 million.   [2] Source: U.S. Department of Defense, Selected Manpower Statistics, annual.   [3] Covers Dec. 1, 1941, to Dec. 31, 1946.   [4] Covers June 25, 1950, to July 27, 1953.   [5] Covers Aug. 4, 1964, to Jan. 27, 1973.   [6] Far East area only.   [7] During hostilities only.   [8] For periods covered, see footnotes 3, 4, and 5.   [9] Covers Jan. 1, 1961, to Jan. 27, 1973. Includes known military service personnel who have died from combat related wounds.

Source: Except as noted, the President's Commission on Veterans' Pensions, Veterans' Benefits in the United States, Vol. I, 1956; and U.S. Dept. of Defense, unpublished data.

No. 507. Military Personnel on Active Duty by Rank or Grade: 1990 to 2003

[In thousands (2,043.7 represents 2,043,700). As of Sept. 30]

Rank/grade	1990	1995	1999	2000	2001	2002	2003
Total [1].	2,043.7	1,518.2	1,385.7	1,384.3	1,385.1	1,411.6	1,434.4
Recruit—E-1	97.6	63.4	81.2	80.0	72.5	64.7	59.2
Private—E-2	140.3	99.7	93.9	99.0	92.4	91.8	85.1
Pvt. 1st class—E-3.	280.1	197.1	190.5	196.3	210.4	219.6	222.1
Corporal—E-4.	427.8	317.2	262.9	251.0	240.1	248.1	264.5
Sergeant—E-5.	361.5	261.4	229.5	229.5	239.7	242.5	250.7
Staff Sgt.—E-6.	239.1	180.5	162.9	164.9	164.9	170.0	172.4
Sgt. 1st class—E-7.	134.1	109.3	97.1	97.7	98.4	101.9	101.3
Master Sgt.—E-8	38.0	28.8	25.8	26.0	26.7	27.0	27.7
Sgt. Major—E-9	15.3	11.1	10.4	10.2	10.4	10.6	10.8
Warrant Officer—W-1	3.2	2.0	2.2	2.1	2.2	2.3	2.3
Chief Warrant—W-4	3.0	2.2	2.1	2.0	1.9	2.0	2.1
2d Lt.—O-1	31.9	25.6	24.9	26.4	28.1	29.0	29.1
1st Lt.—O-2	37.9	26.1	25.4	24.7	25.7	28.1	29.9
Captain—O-3	106.6	84.3	69.8	68.1	66.0	66.5	68.1
Major—O-4	53.2	43.9	43.5	43.2	43.1	43.6	44.1
Lt. Colonel—O-5.	32.3	28.7	28.0	27.5	27.2	28.2	28.5
Colonel—O-6	14.0	11.7	11.3	11.3	11.2	11.4	11.6
Brig. General—O-7	0.5	0.4	0.4	0.4	0.4	0.4	0.4
Major General—O-8	0.4	0.3	0.3	0.3	0.3	0.3	0.3
Lt. General—O-9	0.1	0.1	0.1	0.1	0.1	0.1	0.1
General—O-10	(Z)	(Z)	(Z)	(Z)	(Z)	(Z)	(Z)

Z Fewer than 50.   [1] Includes cadets and midshipmen and warrant officers, W-2 and W-3.

Source: U.S. Dept. of Defense, Selected Manpower Statistics, annual.

National Defense and Veterans Affairs   333

No. 508. Military Reserve Personnel: 1990 to 2003

[As of September 30. The Ready Reserve includes the Selected Reserve which is scheduled to augment active forces during times of war or national emergency, and the Individual Ready Reserve which, during times of war or national emergency, would be used to fill out Active, Guard and Reserve units, and which would also be a source for casualty replacements; Ready Reservists serve in an active status (except for the Inactive National Guard - a very small pool within the Army National Guard). The Standby Reserve cannot be called to active duty except in situations where those members are the only available assets with specific required specialties. The Retired Reseve is categorized into three groups, based on age and length of retirement, prioritized for mobilization purposes.]

Reserve status and branch of service	1990	1995	1999	2000	2001	2002	2003
Total reserves [1]	1,688,674	1,674,164	1,316,984	1,276,843	1,249,043	1,222,337	1,188,851
Ready reserve	1,658,707	1,648,388	1,288,844	1,251,452	1,224,121	1,199,321	1,167,101
Army[2]	1,049,579	999,462	752,790	725,771	713,251	699,548	682,522
Navy	240,228	267,356	192,634	184,080	168,454	159,098	152,855
Marine Corps	81,355	103,668	99,003	99,855	99,377	97,944	98,868
Air Force[3]	270,313	263,011	231,758	229,009	230,182	229,798	219,895
Coast Guard	17,232	14,891	12,654	12,737	12,857	12,933	12,961
Standby reserve	29,967	25,776	28,140	25,391	24,922	23,016	21,750
Army	788	1,128	673	701	753	726	744
Navy	11,791	12,707	9,777	7,213	5,650	4,051	2,520
Marine Corps	1,424	216	385	895	507	605	685
Air Force	15,369	11,453	17,129	16,429	17,826	17,430	17,578
Coast Guard	595	272	176	153	186	204	223
Retired reserve	462,371	505,905	564,358	573,305	580,785	590,018	601,611
Army	223,919	259,553	290,962	296,004	299,233	304,524	308,820
Navy	111,961	97,532	108,316	109,531	111,485	112,374	113,485
Marine Corps	9,101	11,319	12,635	12,937	13,352	13,672	13,926
Air Force	117,390	137,501	152,445	154,833	156,715	159,448	165,380

[1] Less retired reserves.　　[2] Includes Army National Guard.　　[3] Includes Air National Guard.

Source: U.S. Dept. of Defense, *Official Guard and Reserve Manpower Strengths and Statistics*, quarterly.

No. 509. Ready Reserve Personnel Profile—Race and Sex: 1990 to 2003

[In thousands (1,658.7 represents 1,658,700). As of September 30]

Year	Race						Sex			
	Total [1]	White	Black	Asian	American Indian	His-panic [2]	Officer		Enlisted	
							Male	Female	Male	Female
1990	1,658.7	1,304.6	272.3	14.9	7.8	83.1	226.8	40.5	1,204.7	186.7
1991	1,776.3	1,393.6	291.1	18.2	9.3	89.6	231.9	43.0	1,299.7	201.8
1992	1,876.4	1,459.5	309.7	20.2	9.3	95.4	232.7	44.7	1,382.4	216.6
1993	1,858.1	1,440.7	310.5	21.3	9.2	98.2	232.5	46.3	1,365.6	213.7
1994	1,795.8	1,380.9	298.3	22.4	9.0	99.1	223.9	46.2	1,315.8	210.0
1995	1,648.4	1,267.7	274.5	22.0	8.8	96.2	209.9	44.7	1,196.8	196.9
1996	1,536.6	1,179.0	249.8	21.5	8.6	93.1	196.9	43.6	1,108.8	187.4
1997	1,451.0	1,113.7	230.6	21.7	8.4	91.5	188.7	43.2	1,037.6	181.5
1998	1,353.4	1,033.9	210.4	21.7	7.8	88.2	175.9	40.3	964.1	173.1
1999	1,288.8	980.0	202.6	22.6	7.6	88.9	166.2	38.4	911.2	173.1
2000	1,251.5	942.2	199.6	26.7	8.4	91.8	159.4	36.9	879.9	175.3
2001	1,224.1	912.7	198.4	27.9	8.5	94.3	158.0	36.6	852.2	177.3
2002	1,199.3	891.3	193.2	27.9	8.8	96.0	152.1	35.6	835.2	176.4
2003	1,167.1	865.7	187.5	25.4	8.5	98.0	145.1	34.0	813.7	174.3

[1] Race subgroups do not sum to equal the Total. "Pacific Islanders, Other, and Unknowns" are not listed.　　[2] Persons of Hispanic origin may be of any race. Other/Unknowns are not listed.

Source: U.S. Dept. of Defense, *Official Guard and Reserve Manpower Strengths and Statistics*, annual.

No. 510. National Guard—Summary: 1980 to 2003

[As of September 30]

Item	Unit	1980	1985	1990	1995	1999	2000	2001	2002	2003
Army National Guard:										
Units	Number	3,379	4,353	4,055	5,872	5,360	5,300	5,200	5,150	5,100
Personnel [1]	1,000	368	438	444	375	357	353	352	352	351
Females	1,000	17	23	31	31	38	38	42	43	44
Funds obligated [2]	Bil. dol.	1.8	4.4	5.2	6.0	6.5	6.9	7.7	8.0	10.0
Value of equipment	Bil. dol.	7.6	18.8	29.0	33.0	34.0	35.0	35.0	35.0	36.0
Air National Guard:										
Units	Number	1,054	1,184	1,339	1,604	1,541	1,550	1,500	1,500	1,500
Personnel [1]	1,000	96	109	118	110	107	106	109	112	108
Females	1,000	8	12	(NA)	16	17	(NA)	(NA)	(NA)	(NA)
Funds obligated [2]	Bil. dol.	1.7	2.8	3.2	4.2	4.8	5.6	5.8	6.8	6.4
Value of equipment (est.) [3]	Bil. dol.	5.2	21.4	26.4	38.3	43.0	44.0	44.0	44.0	44.0

NA Not available.　　[1] Officers and enlisted personnel.　　[2] Federal funds; includes personnel, operations, maintenance, and military construction.　　[3] Beginning 1985, increase due to repricing of aircraft to current year dollars to reflect true replacement value. Beginning 1994 includes value of aircraft and support equipment.

Source: National Guard Bureau, *Annual Review of the Chief, National Guard Bureau*; and unpublished data.

No. 511. Summary of U.S. Military Force Structure: 1993 to 2001

Item	1993	1994	1995	1996	1997	1998	1999	2000	2001
DEPARTMENT OF DEFENSE (DOD) STRATEGIC FORCES [1]									
Land-based ICBMs: [2]									
Minuteman II (1 warhead each) plus									
Minuteman III (3 warheads each)	737	625	535	530	530	500	500	500	500
Peacekeeper (10 warheads each)	50	50	50	50	50	50	50	50	50
Heavy bombers (PAI): [3]									
B-52.	84	64	74	56	56	56	56	56	56
B-1 [4]	84	84	60	60	60	70	74	80	82
B-2.	-	3	6	9	10	12	13	16	16
Submarine-launched ballistic missiles: [2]									
Poseidon (C-3) and Trident (C-4)									
Missiles on pre-Ohio-class submarines .	96	48	-	-	-	-	-	-	-
Trident (C-4 and D-5) missiles									
on Ohio-class submarines.	312	336	360	384	408	432	432	432	432
DOD AIRLIFT AND SEALIFT FORCES									
Intertheater Airlift (PMAI): [5]									
C-5.	109	107	104	104	104	104	104	104	104
C-141	214	214	199	187	163	143	136	104	88
KC-10 [6]	57	54	54	54	54	54	54	54	54
C-17.	2	9	17	22	24	30	37	46	58
Intratheater Airlift (PMAI): [5]									
C-130 [7]	380	424	428	432	430	425	425	425	418
Sealift ships (Active): [8]									
Tankers.	20	18	18	12	13	10	10	10	10
Cargo.	40	51	51	49	48	43	49	52	57
Sealift ships, reserve:									
RRF [9]	97	93	77	82	87	88	87	87	72
SPECIAL OPERATIONS FORCES									
Army:									
Special forces groups, (Active)	5	5	5	5	5	5	5	5	5
Special forces groups, (National Guard) .	2	2	2	2	2	2	2	2	2
Special forces groups, (Reserve)	2	-	-	-	-	-	-	-	(NA)
Psychological operations groups (Active).	1	1	1	1	1	1	1	1	1
Special operations aviation regiments . . .	1	1	1	1	1	1	1	1	1
Ranger regiments	1	1	1	1	1	1	1	1	1
Civil affairs battalions (Active)	1	1	1	1	1	1	1	1	1
Civil affairs brigades (Reserve)	9	9	9	9	9	8	8	8	8
Civil affairs commands (Reserve).	3	3	3	3	3	4	4	4	4
Air Force:									
Special operations wings/groups:									
Active	3	3	3	3	3	3	3	3	3
National Guard	1	1	1	1	1	1	1	1	1
Special operations wing (Reserve)	1	1	1	1	1	1	1	1	1
Special tactics groups	1	1	1	1	1	1	1	1	1
Naval:									
Special boat squadrons	2	2	2	2	2	2	2	2	2

- Represents or rounds to zero.   NA Not available.   [1] Force levels shown are for the ends of the fiscal years in question. The actual force levels for FY 2000 and FY 2001 will depend on future decisions.   [2] Number of operational missiles. Not in maintenance or overhaul status.   [3] PAI=Primary aircraft inventory. PAI excludes backup and attrition reserve aircrafts as well as aircraft in depot maintenance. Total inventory counts will be higher than the PAI figures given here.   [4] B-1 are accountable under START I but will not be accountable under START II.   [5] PMAI = Primary mission aircraft inventory for active and reserve components. The numbers shown reflect only combat support and industrial funded PMAI aircraft and not developments/test or training aircraft.   [6] Includes 37 KC-10s allocated to an airlift code.   [7] Does not include Department of the Navy aircraft. [8] Includes fast sea lift (FSS), afloat prepositioning, and common-user (charter) ships, plus (through FY 1998) aviation support ships. For FY 1999 on, includes large medium-speed roll-on/roll-off (LMSR) and ready reserve force (RRF) ships tendered to the Military sealift command (MSC). FSS and LMSR vessels are maintained in a reserve, four-day ready status.

Source: U.S. Dept. of Defense, *Annual Report to the President and the Congress.*

No. 512. Veterans by Sex, Period of Service, and State: 2003

[In thousands (24,909 represents 24,909,000). As of September 30. Estimated starting with veteran's place of residence as of April 1, 2000, based on 2000 census of population data, extended to later years on the basis of estimates of veteran interstate migration, separations from the Armed Forces, and mortality; not directly comparable with earlier estimates previously published by the VA. Also excludes a small number of National Guard personnel or reservists who incurred service-connected disabilities while on an initial tour of active duty for training only. Veterans who served both in wartime and peacetime are only counted as serving in wartime.]

State	Total veterans [1] Both sexes	Male	Female	World War II	Korean conflict	Vietnam era	Gulf War	Peacetime
United States	24,909	23,250	1,659	4,335	3,530	8,125	3,751	6,313
Alabama	431	400	31	63	63	143	80	108
Alaska.	67	60	7	4	5	27	15	19
Arizona.	562	521	42	105	89	180	83	140
Arkansas.	274	256	18	45	38	90	46	70
California	2,326	2,167	159	435	349	785	294	590
Colorado	433	398	35	56	52	157	83	110
Connecticut	280	265	15	62	44	88	25	70
Delaware	81	76	6	13	12	27	11	23
District of Columbia	39	36	3	8	6	12	6	10
Florida.	1,830	1,700	130	405	301	543	260	443
Georgia.	746	682	63	84	85	254	162	201
Hawaii.	115	106	9	18	16	41	18	29
Idaho	136	127	9	21	17	44	27	33
Illinois	922	870	52	175	132	286	127	225
Indiana	555	524	31	89	74	177	77	153
Iowa	277	263	14	51	42	89	36	65
Kansas	253	237	16	45	34	84	41	60
Kentucky	366	345	22	57	50	121	59	93
Louisiana.	374	347	27	61	50	118	72	91
Maine	145	136	9	24	21	49	19	38
Maryland	484	444	40	74	62	159	78	135
Massachusetts	510	481	29	113	81	154	46	132
Michigan	846	799	47	148	115	270	113	218
Minnesota	439	416	23	73	62	148	50	117
Mississippi	244	226	18	38	35	77	48	61
Missouri.	562	528	34	95	81	183	82	143
Montana	105	98	7	17	14	36	18	25
Nebraska.	165	154	11	27	25	54	28	38
Nevada.	242	224	18	35	36	87	34	66
New Hampshire	131	123	8	20	18	45	16	37
New Jersey	610	580	30	138	98	183	54	154
New Mexico	185	170	15	28	26	66	30	46
New York.	1,212	1,144	68	258	187	354	133	307
North Carolina	773	713	59	111	102	253	148	199
North Dakota	58	54	4	9	8	19	10	14
Ohio	1,063	1,001	62	190	144	331	147	278
Oklahoma	361	338	23	57	50	127	62	84
Oregon	370	345	25	64	49	126	52	94
Pennsylvania	1,180	1,117	64	257	180	353	130	295
Rhode Island	94	89	5	21	15	29	9	24
South Carolina	412	381	31	56	55	142	82	104
South Dakota	77	72	5	12	12	25	14	18
Tennessee.	545	509	36	77	72	187	91	143
Texas	1,679	1,553	126	244	214	587	329	404
Utah	158	149	9	28	22	51	27	37
Vermont	59	56	4	10	8	20	7	17
Virginia.	755	685	70	97	94	274	165	189
Washington	641	592	49	91	79	233	107	169
West Virginia	192	182	10	33	28	64	28	46
Wisconsin	487	459	28	84	68	152	62	133
Wyoming	57	53	4	8	7	20	11	13

[1] Veterans serving in more than one period of service are counted only once in the total. The table total does not reflect the current situation in Iraq and Afghanistan.

No. 513. Veterans Living by Age and Period of Service: 2003

[In thousands (25,179 represents 25,179,000). As of September 30. Includes those living outside U.S. See headnote, Table 512]

Age	Total veterans	Wartime veterans Total [1]	Gulf War	Vietnam era	Korean conflict	World War II	Peacetime veterans
Total	25,179	18,791	3,783	8,211	3,580	4,370	6,389
Under 35 years old . . .	2,116	2,032	2,032	-	-	-	280
35-39 years old	1,405	672	672	-	-	-	733
40-44 years old	1,794	415	415	-	-	-	1,379
45-49 years old	2,021	951	307	705	-	-	1,071
50-54 years old	2,344	2,173	223	2,111	-	-	171
55-59 years old	3,435	3,314	101	3,301	-	-	121
60-64 years old	2,406	1,394	28	1,390	-	-	1,012
65 years old and over .	9,659	7,840	6	703	3,580	4,370	1,819
Female, total	1,675	1,106	594	265	84	197	568

- Represents or rounds to zero.   [1] Veterans who served in more than one wartime period are counted only once. The table total does not reflect the current situation in Iraq and Afghanistan.

Source of Tables 512 and 513. U.S. Dept. of Veterans Affairs, Office of Policy, Planning and Preparedness. <http://www.va.gov/vetdata/demographics>

No. 514. Veterans by Sex, Race, and Hispanic or Latino Origin: 2000

[(In thousands (26,404 represents 26,404,000). As of April 1. Data are based on a sample from the census. See Appendix III.]

Characteristics	Total number	18 to 64 years	65 years and over
Total	26,404	16,740	9,664
Sex:			
Male	24,810	15,495	9,316
Female	1,593	1,246	348
White alone.	22,573	13,711	8,863
Male	21,373	12,830	8,544
Female	1,200	881	319
Black or African American alone	2,572	2,022	550
Male	2,298	1,766	532
Female	274	256	18
American Indian/Alaska Native alone	196	160	36
Male	178	144	34
Female	18	16	2
Asian alone	284	198	86
Male	261	178	83
Female	23	20	3
Native Hawaiian, other Pacific Islander alone. . . .	29	24	5
Male	26	21	4
Female	3	3	-
Some other race alone	368	321	47
Male	333	288	45
Female	35	33	2
Two or more races	382	304	78
Male	342	267	74
Female	40	36	4
Hispanic or Latino origin [1]	1,139	905	234
Male	1,046	820	226
Female	93	85	8

- Represents or rounds to zero.   [1]Persons of Hispanic or Latino origin may be of any race.

Source: U.S. Census Bureau, American FactFinder, 2000 Census of Population and Housing, Summary File 3, tables P39, PCT66A, PCT 66B, PCT66C, PCT66D, PCT 66E, PCT 66F, PCT66G, PCT 66H and P66 (accessed 30 March 2004).

Figure 10.3
Living Veterans by Age: 2003
In thousands

Source: Chart prepared by U.S. Census Bureau. For data, see Table 513.

No. 515. Disabled Veterans Receiving Compensation by Period of Service: 1980 to 2003

[In thousands (2,274 represents 2,274,000), except as indicated. **For year ending September 30.** Represents veterans receiving compensation for service-connected disabilities]

Period of service	1980	1990	1995	1997	1998	1999	2000	2001	2002	2003
Disabled, all periods	2,274	2,184	2,236	2,263	2,277	2,294	2,308	2,321	2,398	2,485
Peace-time	262	444	514	539	550	561	567	569	575	583
World War I [1]	30	3	1	(Z)	(Z)	(Z)	(Z)	(Z)	(Z)	(Z)
World War II	1,193	876	692	616	578	541	505	470	440	414
Korea	236	209	191	182	179	175	171	166	165	164
Vietnam	553	652	705	724	729	736	741	750	799	848
Gulf [2]	(X)	(X)	134	202	241	282	325	366	419	476
Compensation (mil. dol.) . . .	6,104	9,284	11,644	13,004	13,791	14,542	15,489	16,529	18,547	20,796

X Not applicable.   Z Less than 500.   [1] Includes Spanish-American War and Mexican Border service.   [2] Service from August 2, 1990 to the present.

Source: U.S. Dept. of Veterans Affairs, *Annual Report of the Secretary of Veterans Affairs through 1998; Program Statistics 1999-2002,* and unpublished data. See also <www.va.gov/vetdata/programstatistics/index.htm>

No. 516. Veterans Benefits—Expenditures by Program: 1980 to 2003

[In millions of dollars (23,187 represents $23,187,000,000). **For year ending September 30.** Beginning with fiscal year 1990, data are for outlays]

Program	1980	1990	1995	1998	1999	2000	2001	2002	2003
Total	23,187	28,998	37,775	41,775	43,166	47,086	45,037	50,882	56,892
Medical programs	6,042	11,582	16,255	17,575	18,223	19,637	21,330	23,049	25,188
Construction	300	661	641	523	521	466	421	449	411
General operating expenses	605	811	954	877	989	1,016	1,222	1,318	1,399
Compensation and pension	11,044	14,674	17,765	20,165	21,024	21,963	23,198	25,408	27,904
Vocational rehabilitation and education .	2,350	452	1,127	1,438	1,605	2,053	1,786	2,170	2,348
All other [1]	2,846	818	1,034	1,196	804	1,952	-2,921	-1,511	-358

[1] Includes insurance, indemnities and miscellaneous funds and expenditures. (Excludes expenditures from personal funds of patients.)

Source: U.S. Dept. of Veterans Affairs, *Expenditure and Workload Data,* annual.

No. 517. Veterans Compensation and Pension Benefits—Number on Rolls by Period of Service and Status: 1980 to 2003

[In thousands (4,646 represents 4,646,000), except as indicated. **As of Sept. 30.** Living refers to veterans receiving compensation for disability incurred or aggravated while on active duty and war veterans receiving pension and benefits for nonservice connected disabilities. Deceased refers to deceased veterans whose dependents were receiving pensions and compensation benefits]

Period of service and veteran status	1980	1990	1995	1999	2000	2001	2002	2003
Total	4,646	3,584	3,330	3,252	3,236	3,218	3,285	3,369
Living veterans	3,195	2,746	2,669	2,673	2,672	2,669	2,745	2,832
Service connected	2,273	2,184	2,236	2,294	2,308	2,321	2,398	2,485
Nonservice connected	922	562	433	379	364	348	347	347
Deceased veterans	1,451	838	662	579	564	549	540	538
Service connected	358	320	307	304	307	307	310	314
Nonservice connected	1,093	518	355	274	257	241	230	224
Prior to World War I	14	4	2	1	1	1	1	1
Living	(Z)	(Z)	(Z)	(Z)	(Z)	(Z)	(Z)	(Z)
World War I	692	198	89	42	34	28	23	19
Living	198	18	3	(Z)	(Z)	(Z)	(Z)	(Z)
World War II	2,520	1,723	1,307	1,031	968	906	856	813
Living	1,849	1,294	961	730	676	624	583	546
Korean conflict [1]	446	390	368	333	323	313	308	306
Living	317	305	290	264	255	246	243	241
Peacetime	312	495	559	602	607	608	613	620
Living	262	444	514	561	567	569	575	583
Vietnam era [2]	662	774	868	953	969	987	1,052	1,120
Living	569	685	766	835	848	862	922	983
Gulf War [3]	(X)	(X)	138	290	334	376	431	490
Living	(X)	(X)	134	283	326	368	421	479

X Not applicable.   Z Fewer than 500.   [1] Service during period June 27, 1950, to Jan. 31, 1955.   [2] Service from Aug. 5, 1964, to May 7, 1975.   [3] Service from August 2, 1990 to the present.

Source: U.S. Dept. of Veterans Affairs, *Annual Report of the Secretary of Veterans Affairs to 1998; Program Statistics 1999-2002,* and unpublished data. See also <http://www.va.gov/vetdata/index.htm/>.

Section 11
Social Insurance and Human Services

This section presents data related to governmental expenditures for social insurance and human services; governmental programs for old-age, survivors, disability, and health insurance (OASDHI); governmental employee retirement; private pension plans; government unemployment and temporary disability insurance; federal supplemental security income payments and aid to the needy; child and other welfare services; and federal food programs. Also included here are selected data on workers compensation and vocational rehabilitation, child support, child care, charity contributions, and philanthropic trusts and foundations.

The principal source for these data is the Social Security Administration's *Annual Statistical Supplement to the Social Security Bulletin* which presents current data on many of the programs.

Social insurance under the Social Security Act—Programs established by the Social Security Act provide protection against wage loss resulting from retirement, prolonged disability, death, or unemployment, and protection against the cost of medical care during old age and disability. The federal OASDI program provides monthly benefits to retired or disabled insured workers and their dependents and to survivors of insured workers. To be eligible, a worker must have had a specified period of employment in which OASDI taxes were paid. The age of eligibility for full retirement benefits has been 65 years old for many years. However, for persons born in 1938 or later that age will gradually increase until it reaches age 67 for those born after 1959. Reduced benefits may be obtained as early as age 62. The worker's spouse is under the same limitations. Survivor benefits are payable to dependents of deceased insured workers. Disability benefits are payable to an insured worker under full retirement age with a prolonged disability and to the disabled worker's dependents on the same basis as

dependents of retired workers. Disability benefits are provided at age 50 to the disabled widow or widower of a deceased worker who was fully insured at the time of death. Disabled children, aged 18 or older, of retired, disabled, or deceased workers are also eligible for benefits. A lump sum benefit is generally payable on the death of an insured worker to a spouse or minor children. For information on the medicare program, see Section 3, Health and Nutrition.

Retirement, survivors, disability, and hospital insurance benefits are funded by a payroll tax on annual earnings (up to a maximum of earnings set by law) of workers, employers, and the self-employed. The maximum taxable earnings are adjusted annually to reflect increasing wage levels (see Table 525). Effective January 1994, there is no dollar limit on wages and self-employment income subject to the hospital insurance tax. Tax receipts and benefit payments are administered through federal trust funds. Special benefits for uninsured persons; hospital benefits for persons aged 65 and over with specified amounts of social security coverage less than that required for cash benefit eligibility; and that part of the cost of supplementary medical insurance not financed by contributions from participants are financed from federal general revenues.

Unemployment insurance is presently administered by the U.S. Employment and Training Administration and each state's employment security agency. By agreement with the U.S. Secretary of Labor, state agencies also administer unemployment compensation for eligible ex-military personnel and federal employees. Under state unemployment insurance laws, benefits related to the individual's past earnings are paid to unemployed eligible workers. State laws vary concerning the length of time benefits are paid and their amount. In most states, benefits are payable for 26 weeks and, during periods

U.S. Census Bureau, Statistical Abstract of the United States: 2004-2005

of high unemployment, extended benefits are payable under a federal-state program to those who have exhausted their regular state benefits. Some states also supplement the basic benefit with allowances for dependents.

Unemployment insurance is funded by a federal unemployment tax levied on the taxable payrolls of most employers. Taxable payroll under the federal act and 12 state laws is the first $7,000 in wages paid each worker during a year. Forty-one states have taxable payrolls above $7,000. Employers are allowed a percentage credit of taxable payroll for contributions paid to states under state unemployment insurance laws. The remaining percent of the federal tax finances administrative costs, the federal share of extended benefits, and advances to states. About 97 percent of wage and salary workers are covered by unemployment insurance.

Retirement programs for government employees—The Civil Service Retirement System (CSRS) and the Federal Employees' Retirement System (FERS) are the two major programs providing age and service, disability, and survivor annuities for federal civilian employees. In general, employees hired after December 31, 1983, are covered under FERS and the social security program (OASDHI), and employees on staff prior to that date are members of CSRS and are covered under medicare. CSRS employees were offered the option of transferring to FERS during 1987 and 1998. There are separate retirement systems for the uniformed services (supplementing OASDHI) and for certain special groups of federal employees. State and local government employees are covered for the most part by state and local retirement systems similar to the federal CSRS. In many jurisdictions these benefits supplement OASDHI coverage.

Workers' compensation—All states provide protection against work-connected injuries and deaths, although some states exclude certain workers (e.g., domestic workers). Federal laws cover federal employees, private employees in the District of Columbia, and longshoremen and harbor workers. In addition, the Department of Labor administers "black lung"

benefits programs for coal miners disabled by pneumoconiosis and for specified dependents and survivors. Specified occupational diseases are compensable to some extent. In most states, benefits are related to the worker's salary. The benefits may or may not be augmented by dependents' allowances or automatically adjusted to prevailing wage levels.

Income support—Income support programs are designed to provide benefits for persons with limited income and resources. The Supplemental Security Income (SSI) program and Temporary Assistance for Needy Families (TANF) program are the major programs providing monthly payments. In addition, a number of programs provide money payments or in-kind benefits for special needs or purposes. Several programs offer food and nutritional services. Also, various federal-state programs provide energy assistance, public housing, and subsidized housing to individuals and families with low incomes. General assistance may also be available at the state or local level.

The SSI program, administered by the Social Security Administration, provides income support to persons aged 65 or older and blind or disabled adults and children. Eligibility requirements and federal payment standards are nationally uniform. Most states supplement the basic SSI payment for all or selected categories of persons.

The Personal Responsibility and Work Opportunity Reconciliation Act of 1996 contained provisions that replaced the Aid to Families With Dependent Children (AFDC), Job Opportunities and Basic Skills (JOBS), and Emergency Assistance programs with the Temporary Assistance for Needy Families block grant program. This law contains strong work requirements, comprehensive child support enforcement, support for families moving from welfare to work, and other features. The TANF became effective as soon as each state submitted a complete plan implementing TANF, but no later than July 1, 1997. The AFDC program provided cash assistance based on need, income, resources, and family size.

Federal food stamp program—Under the food stamp program, single persons and those living in households meeting nationwide standards for income and assets may receive coupons redeemable for food at most retail food stores or provides benefits through electronic benefit transfer. The monthly amount of benefits or allotments a unit receives is determined by household size and income. Households without income receive the determined monthly cost of a nutritionally adequate diet for their household size. This amount is updated to account for food price increases. Households with income receive the difference between the amount of a nutritionally adequate diet and 30 percent of their income, after certain allowable deductions.

To qualify for the program, a household must have less than $2,000 in disposable assets ($3,000 if one member is aged 60 or older), gross income below 130 percent of the official poverty guidelines for the household size, and net income below 100 percent of the poverty guidelines. Households with a person aged 60 or older or a disabled person receiving SSI, social security, state general assistance, or veterans' disability benefits may have gross income exceeding 130 percent of the poverty guidelines. All households in which all members receive TANF or SSI are categorically eligible for food stamps without meeting these income or resource criteria. Households are certified for varying lengths of time, depending on their income sources and individual circumstances.

Health and welfare services—Programs providing health and welfare services are aided through federal grants to states for child welfare services, vocational rehabilitation, activities for the aged, maternal and child health services, maternity and infant care projects, comprehensive health services, and a variety of public health activities. For information about the medicaid program, see Section 3, Health and Nutrition.

Noncash benefits—The U.S. Census Bureau annually collects data on the characteristics of recipients of noncash (in-kind) benefits to supplement the collection of annual money income data in the Current Population Survey (see text, Section 1, Population, and Section 14, Prices). Noncash benefits are those benefits received in a form other than money which serve to enhance or improve the economic well-being of the recipient. As for money income, the data for noncash benefits are for the calendar year prior to the date of the interview. The major categories of noncash benefits covered are public transfers (e.g., food stamps, school lunch, public housing, and medicaid) and employer or union-provided benefits to employees.

Statistical reliability—For discussion of statistical collection, estimation, and sampling procedures and measures of statistical reliability applicable to HHS and Census Bureau data, see Appendix III.

U.S. Census Bureau, Statistical Abstract of the United States: 2004-2005

No. 518. Government Transfer Payments to Individuals—Summary: 1970 to 2002

[In billions of dollars (69.5 represents $69,500,000,000)]

Year	Total	Retirement & disability insurance benefits	Medical payments	Income mainte- nance benefits	Unemploy- ment insurance benefits	Veterans benefits	Federal education & training assistance payments [1]	Other [2]
1970	69.5	34.3	13.2	9.9	4.2	7.5	0.4	0.1
1980	263.4	128.8	62.6	34.3	18.7	14.7	4.1	0.2
1990	561.5	264.2	188.8	63.5	18.2	17.7	7.3	1.8
1991	635.3	286.0	222.8	72.5	26.9	18.1	7.3	1.8
1992	715.5	305.0	257.7	84.6	39.7	18.6	8.0	2.0
1993	759.9	321.2	283.6	90.3	34.9	19.4	9.1	1.5
1994	795.2	335.1	310.7	95.6	24.0	19.7	8.6	1.5
1995	840.0	350.3	336.5	100.4	21.8	20.5	9.0	1.4
1996	883.1	364.9	361.7	102.6	22.4	21.4	8.6	1.6
1997	912.8	379.3	377.3	100.5	20.3	22.2	11.5	1.6
1998	932.6	391.8	383.7	101.1	19.9	23.2	11.2	1.8
1999	966.5	402.5	401.1	104.8	20.8	24.1	11.4	1.9
2000	1,018.1	424.8	427.7	106.6	20.7	24.9	11.0	2.4
2001	1,116.2	449.7	481.5	110.0	32.2	26.5	13.1	3.2
2002	1,220.9	472.6	526.3	121.9	54.0	29.6	13.8	2.7

[1] See footnote 9, Table 519.   [2] See footnote 10, Table 519.

No. 519. Government Transfer Payments to Individuals by Type: 1990 to 2002

[In millions of dollars (561,484 represents $561,484,000,000)]

Item	1990	1995	1998	1999	2000	2001	2002
Total	**561,484**	**840,034**	**932,552**	**966,502**	**1,018,106**	**1,116,212**	**1,220,858**
Retirement & disability insurance benefit payments	264,230	350,310	391,758	402,507	424,810	449,650	472,564
Old age, survivors, & disability insurance.	244,135	327,667	369,242	379,763	401,218	424,985	446,559
Railroad retirement and disability	7,221	8,028	8,225	8,203	8,265	8,412	8,698
Worker's compensation payments (federal & state)	8,618	10,530	10,344	10,429	10,845	11,191	11,457
Other government disability insurance & retirement [1]	4,256	4,085	3,947	4,112	4,482	5,062	5,850
Medical payments.	188,808	336,506	383,687	401,097	427,689	481,483	526,310
Medicare	107,638	179,147	205,839	209,110	219,612	243,372	263,750
Public assistance medical care [2]	78,176	155,007	175,278	189,252	205,021	234,648	258,658
Military medical insurance [3]	2,994	2,352	2,570	2,735	3,056	3,463	3,902
Income maintenance benefit payments.	63,481	100,443	101,102	104,777	106,616	110,047	121,884
Supplemental Security Income (SSI).	16,670	27,726	30,322	31,023	31,675	33,162	34,664
Family assistance [4]	19,187	22,637	17,429	17,920	18,440	18,630	19,729
Food stamps	14,741	22,447	16,462	15,473	14,896	15,998	18,642
Other income maintenance [5]	12,883	27,633	36,889	40,361	41,605	42,257	48,849
Unemployment insurance benefit payments. .	18,208	21,838	19,879	20,756	20,680	32,195	53,974
State unemployment insurance compensation	17,644	20,937	19,178	20,015	19,913	31,352	52,939
Unemployment compensation for federal civilian employees	215	339	235	207	226	246	327
Unemployment compensation for railroad employees	89	62	61	65	81	98	96
Unemployment compensation for veterans.	144	320	210	201	182	217	325
Other unemployment compensation [6]	116	180	195	268	278	282	287
Veterans benefit payments	17,687	20,546	23,168	24,053	24,935	26,488	29,579
Veterans pension and disability	15,550	17,565	20,049	20,904	21,895	23,283	25,940
Veterans readjustment [7]	257	1,086	1,220	1,323	1,323	1,504	1,906
Veterans life insurance benefits	1,868	1,884	1,891	1,817	1,707	1,691	1,722
Other assistance to veterans [8]	12	11	8	9	10	10	11
Federal education & training assistance payments [9]	7,300	9,007	11,189	11,367	10,985	13,130	13,844
Other payments to individuals [10]	1,770	1,384	1,769	1,945	2,391	3,219	2,703

[1] Consists largely of temporary disability payments, pension benefit guaranty payments, and black lung payments. [2] Consists of medicaid and other medical vendor payments. [3] Consists of payments made under the TriCare Management Program (formerly called CHAMPUS) for the medical care of dependents of active duty military personnel and of retired military personnel and their dependents at nonmilitary medical facilities. [4] Through 1995, consists of emergency assistance and aid to families with dependent children. Beginning with 1998, consists of benefits— generally known as temporary assistance for needy families— provided under the Personal Responsibility and Work Opportunity Reconciliation Act of 1996. [5] Consists largely of general assistance, expenditures for food under the supplemental program for women, infants, and children; refugee assistance; foster home care and adoption assistance; earned income tax credits; and energy assistance. [6] Consists of trade readjustment allowance payments, Redwood Park benefit payments, public service employment benefit payments, and transitional benefit payments. [7] Consists largely of veterans' readjustment benefit payments, educational assistance to spouses and children of disabled or deceased veterans, payments to paraplegics, and payments for autos and conveyances for disabled veterans. [8] Consists largely of State and local government payments to veterans. [9] Excludes veterans. Consists largely of federal fellowship payments (National Science Foundation fellowships and traineeships, subsistence payments to state maritime academy cadets, and other federal fellowships), interest subsidy on higher education loans, basic educational opportunity grants, and Job Corps payments. [10] Consists largely of Bureau of Indian Affairs payments, education exchange payments, Alaska Permanent Fund dividend payments, compensation of survivors of public safety officers, compensation of victims of crime, disaster relief payments, compensation for Japanese internment, and other special payments to individuals.

Source of Tables 518 and 519: U.S. Bureau of Economic Analysis, "Regional Accounts Data, Annual State Personal Income"; <http://www.bea.doc.gov/bea/regional/spi/>; (accessed 29 April 2004).

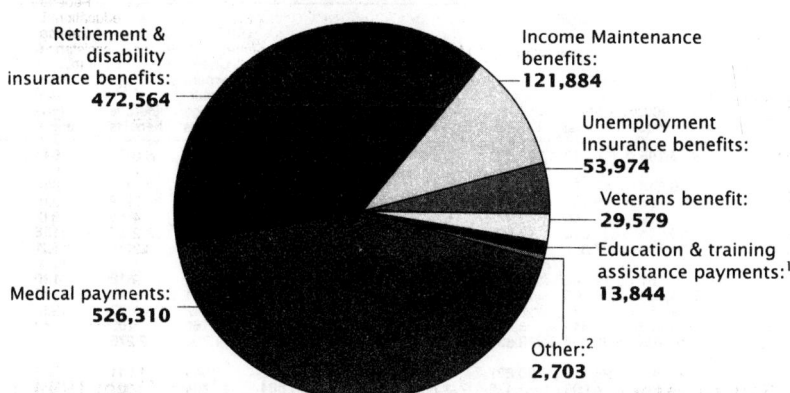

Figure 11.1
Government Transfer Payments to Individuals by State: 2002
In millions of dollars

Total =1,220,858

Retirement &
disability
insurance benefits:
472,564

Income Maintenance
benefits:
121,884

Unemployment
Insurance benefits:
53,974

Veterans benefit:
29,579

Education & training
assistance payments:[1]
13,844

Medical payments:
526,310

Other:[2]
2,703

[1]Excludes veterans. Consists largely of federal fellowship payments (National Science Foundation, fellowships and traineeships, subsistence payments to State maritime academy cadets, and other federal fellowships), interest subsidy on higher education loans, basic educational opportunity grants, and Job Corps payments.

[2]Consists largely of Bureau of Indian Affairs payments, education exchange payments, Alaska Permanent Fund dividend payments, compensation of survivors of public safety officers, compensation of victims of crime, disaster relief payments, compensation for Japanese internment, and other special payments to individuals.

Source: Chart prepared by U.S. Census Bureau. For data, see Table 520.

Figure 11.2
Old-age and Survivors Insurance (OASI) Benefits and Assets: 1990 to 2003

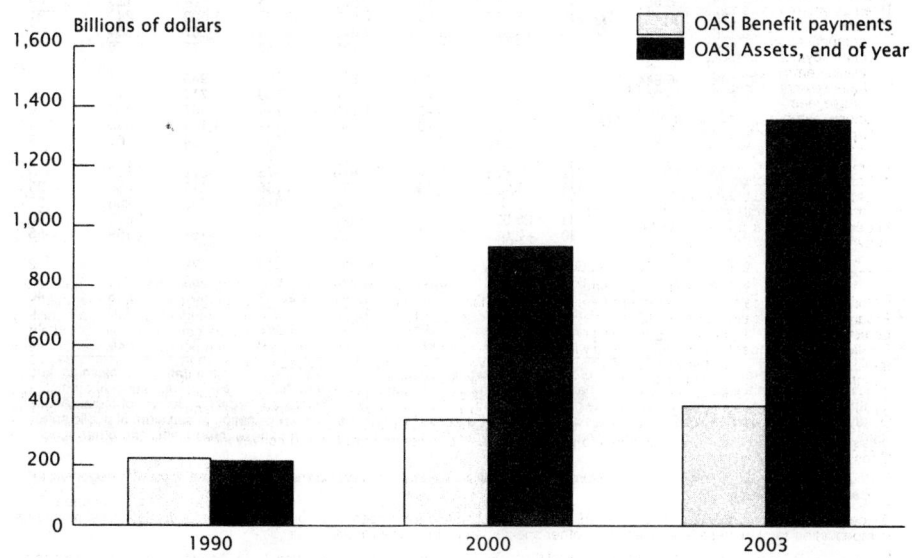

Billions of dollars

☐ OASI Benefit payments
■ OASI Assets, end of year

Source: Chart prepared by U.S. Census Bureau. For data, see Table 526.

Social Insurance and Human Services   343

No. 520. Government Transfer Payments to Individuals by State: 2000 to 2002

[In millions of dollars (1,018,106 represents $1,018,106,000,000)]

State	2000, total	2001, total	2002 Total	Retirement & disability insurance benefits	Medical payments	Income maintenance benefits	Unemployment insurance benefits	Veterans benefits [1]	Federal education & training assistance payments	Other [2]
U.S.	1,018,106	1,116,212	1,220,858	472,564	526,310	121,884	53,974	29,579	13,844	2,703
AL	16,643	17,993	19,560	8,135	7,791	2,227	422	683	284	18
AK	2,966	3,101	3,231	564	1,096	324	160	109	15	964
AZ	15,959	18,146	20,471	8,662	8,276	1,861	506	685	311	170
AR	10,006	11,042	12,093	4,936	4,861	1,237	406	487	156	10
CA	114,559	127,547	138,609	47,273	59,417	20,106	7,224	2,484	1,831	274
CO	11,169	12,242	13,675	5,475	5,509	1,236	701	518	190	45
CT	14,086	14,905	16,279	6,441	7,479	1,159	851	243	95	10
DE	2,857	3,113	3,413	1,489	1,417	257	142	77	26	4
DC	2,709	2,844	3,217	657	1,742	496	160	103	49	10
FL	64,208	70,069	76,636	32,906	32,764	6,171	1,700	2,275	760	59
GA	23,696	26,173	30,327	11,152	13,455	3,282	1,044	1,011	362	21
HI	3,844	4,098	4,478	1,886	1,599	584	204	157	44	4
ID	3,804	4,247	4,676	2,118	1,711	345	250	163	80	9
IL	41,726	44,943	49,265	19,972	20,018	4,944	3,051	693	531	57
IN	20,081	22,078	23,762	10,730	9,450	1,980	876	447	264	14
IA	10,046	10,821	12,180	5,522	5,024	781	442	240	162	10
KS	8,908	9,682	10,521	4,686	4,289	710	414	271	142	11
KY	15,778	17,049	18,474	7,418	7,626	2,053	648	496	223	9
LA	16,582	19,154	20,537	6,750	9,891	2,661	398	534	292	11
ME	5,307	5,731	6,268	2,386	2,779	614	157	273	56	4
MD	16,981	18,471	20,212	7,865	9,180	1,707	724	513	204	19
MA	26,471	29,020	32,105	10,740	15,492	2,396	2,536	655	267	19
MI	36,675	40,837	43,001	18,000	17,271	4,279	2,364	649	416	23
MN	15,748	17,614	19,405	7,796	8,403	1,478	1,043	452	215	19
MS	10,803	12,085	13,224	4,762	5,845	1,724	273	389	219	14
MO	20,904	23,016	24,999	10,272	10,959	2,159	734	583	273	20
MT	3,127	3,358	3,560	1,702	1,250	300	96	143	59	11
NE	5,694	6,230	6,666	2,951	2,740	504	148	233	86	4
NV	5,588	6,330	7,221	3,206	2,703	553	435	251	51	22
NH	3,918	4,247	4,717	2,114	1,977	265	153	162	42	3
NJ	33,092	36,429	40,179	15,744	18,214	2,423	2,879	557	304	57
NM	6,014	6,688	7,448	2,692	3,182	857	175	334	123	84
NY	95,735	102,448	112,900	33,685	59,531	12,660	4,290	1,302	1,241	191
NC	28,108	31,252	34,132	13,557	13,930	3,679	1,515	1,087	354	31
ND	2,322	2,394	2,572	1,199	1,002	172	60	73	48	19
OH	43,149	46,944	50,637	21,841	20,880	4,619	1,826	943	486	42
OK	11,999	13,245	14,367	5,970	5,718	1,394	336	717	213	20
OR	12,243	13,768	15,158	6,582	5,434	1,243	1,249	467	163	20
PA	54,928	58,882	63,602	25,726	27,903	4,791	3,484	1,128	540	30
RI	4,748	5,283	5,623	2,065	2,612	495	259	124	61	6
SC	14,340	15,872	17,312	7,024	7,046	1,878	575	572	197	20
SD	2,490	2,684	2,923	1,270	1,190	221	36	116	50	39
TN	21,864	23,786	25,725	9,948	11,266	2,704	818	699	263	27
TX	59,911	65,556	73,288	26,571	31,853	8,298	2,950	2,493	1,023	100
UT	4,962	5,456	6,130	2,694	2,109	639	316	157	159	55
VT	2,245	2,458	2,688	1,043	1,168	255	112	79	30	2
VA	19,916	22,141	23,883	10,752	8,865	2,070	927	953	296	21
WA	20,817	23,456	25,358	10,491	9,029	2,201	2,439	903	255	40
WV	8,894	9,498	10,301	4,771	3,796	1,027	232	360	110	6
WI	17,902	19,997	21,983	9,464	8,899	1,743	1,183	477	198	19
WY	1,583	1,707	1,863	926	669	126	50	61	26	5

[1] Excludes veterans. Consists largely of federal fellowship payments (National Science Foundation, fellowships and traineeships, subsistence payments to State maritime academy cadets, and other federal fellowships), interest subsidy on higher education loans, basic educational opportunity grants, and Job Corps payments.   [2] Consists largely of Bureau of Indian Affairs payments, education exchange payments, Alaska Permanent Fund dividend payments, compensation of survivors of public safety officers, compensation of victims of crime, disaster relief payments, compensation for Japanese internment, and other special payments to individuals.

Source: U.S. Bureau of Economic Analysis, Regional Accounts Data, Annual State Personal Income; <http://www.bea.doc.gov/bea/regional/spi/>; (accessed 29 April 2004).

No. 521. Number of Persons With Income by Specified Sources of Income: 2002

[In thousands (202,275 represents 202,275,000). Persons 15 years old and over as of March of the following year. Based on Current Population Survey; see text, Sections 1 and 13, and Appendix III]

Source of income	Total persons with income	Under 65 years old	65 years old and over	White [1]	Black [1]	Hispanic origin [2]
Total...................	202,275	168,941	33,334	167,914	22,113	22,643
Earnings................	151,911	146,231	5,680	125,669	16,615	18,730
Wages and salary.............	142,973	138,138	4,835	117,788	16,097	17,902
Nonfarm self-employment.........	12,337	11,549	788	10,788	830	1,073
Farm self-employment..........	2,247	2,000	247	2,034	121	135
Unemployment compensation......	8,351	8,153	198	6,762	988	985
Workers compensation..........	2,062	1,920	143	1,697	239	285
Social security, railroad retirement...	39,851	9,459	30,392	34,653	3,813	2,380
Supplemental security income (SSI)...	4,896	3,703	1,192	3,251	1,248	703
Public assistance.............	2,164	2,063	100	1,376	618	505
TANF/Welfare (AFDC) only [3].....	1,535	1,485	50	954	480	368
Other assistance only.........	555	510	45	383	112	122
Both...................	74	69	4	39	26	15
Veterans payments............	2,591	1,465	1,127	2,151	333	123
Survivors benefits............	2,633	967	1,666	2,367	173	95
Company or union..........	1,222	276	947	1,110	79	35
Disability benefits.............	1,646	1,455	191	1,306	262	175
Company or union..........	507	460	47	420	63	51
Pensions................	15,275	4,881	10,394	13,568	1,254	480
Company or union..........	11,149	3,418	7,731	9,996	825	377
Federal Government..........	1,690	533	1,157	1,384	229	76
Military retirement...........	1,138	664	474	964	120	56
State or local government.......	3,597	1,376	2,221	3,192	317	103
Property income.............	104,211	85,079	19,132	92,265	6,280	5,873
Interest................	98,935	80,796	18,138	87,741	5,870	5,443
Dividends...............	31,541	25,358	6,183	28,682	1,283	970
Rents, royalties, estates or trusts..	11,212	8,464	2,749	10,108	526	650
Education................	7,815	7,797	17	6,029	1,158	745
Pell grant only...........	1,512	1,510	2	1,030	350	211
Other government only........	1,095	1,091	4	841	184	101
Scholarships only..........	2,249	2,247	3	1,849	222	206
Child support..............	5,399	5,375	24	4,221	973	522
Alimony.................	414	359	55	373	28	18
Financial assistance...........	2,339	2,210	129	1,775	266	203
Other income..............	1,049	823	226	834	127	67
Combinations of income types:						
Government transfer payments....	58,999	27,394	31,604	49,181	7,086	4,767
Public assistance or SSI........	6,778	5,511	1,267	4,434	1,796	1,162

- Represents or rounds to zero. [1] The 2003 CPS asked respondents to choose one or more races. For example, "White Alone" refers to people who reported White and did not report any other race category. The use of this single-race population does not imply that it is the preferred method of presenting or analyzing data. Information on people who reported more than one race, such as "Asian and Black or African American," is available from Census 2000 through American Factfinder. [2] Persons of Hispanic origin may be of any race. [3] TANF-Temporary assistance for needy families program; AFDC=Aid to Families with Dependent Children program. [4] Includes estates and trusts reported as survivor benefits.

Source: U.S. Census Bureau, Table PINC-09. Source of Income in 2002—Number With Income and Mean Income of Specified Type in 2002 of People 15 Years Old and Over, by Race, Hispanic Origin and Sex"; published 26 February 2004; see also <http://ferret.bls.census.gov/macro/032003/perinc/toc.htm>.

No. 522. Households Receiving Means-Tested Noncash Benefits: 1980 to 2002

[In thousands (82,368 represents 82,368,000), except percent. Households as of March of following year. Covers civilian noninstitutional population, including persons in the Armed Forces living off post or with their families on post. A means-tested benefit program requires that the household's income and/or assets fall below specified guidelines in order to qualify for benefits. There are general trends toward underestimation of noncash beneficiaries. Households are classified according to poverty status of family or nonfamily householder; for explanation of poverty level, see text, Section 13. Data for 1980 and 1990 based on 1980 census population controls; 1995 and 2000, based on 1990 census population controls; 2002, based on 2000 census population controls and a 28,000 household sample expansion to 78,000 households. Based on Current Population Survey; see text, Section 1 and Appendix III]

Type of benefit received	1980	1990	1995	2000	2002 Total	2002 Below poverty level Number	2002 Below poverty level Percent of total	2002 Above poverty level
Total households	82,368	94,312	99,627	106,418	111,278	13,505	100	97,773
Receiving at least one noncash benefit..	14,266	16,098	21,148	20,131	22,478	7,806	58	14,672
Not receiving cash public assistance..	7,860	8,819	13,335	14,465	16,890	5,003	37	11,887
Receiving cash public assistance [1]...	6,407	7,279	7,813	5,667	5,588	2,803	21	2,785
Total households receiving—								
Food stamps.................	6,769	7,163	8,388	5,563	6,245	3,834	28	2,411
School lunch................	5,532	6,252	8,607	7,185	7,930	3,092	23	4,838
Public housing...............	2,777	4,339	4,846	4,689	5,125	2,593	19	2,532
Medicaid.................	8,287	10,321	14,111	14,328	16,765	6,182	46	10,583

[1] Households receiving money from aid to families with dependent children program (beginning 2000, temporary assistance for needy families program), supplemental security income program or other public assistance programs.

Source: U.S. Census Bureau, Table NC1. Means-Tested Noncash Benefits Received by Households, by Selected Household Characteristics, Race and Hispanic Origin, and Poverty Status: 2002"; May 2004; <http://ferret.bls.census.gov/macro/032002/noncash/toc.htm and Current Population Reports, P-60 reports.

No. 523. Government Expenditures for Income-Tested Benefits by Type of Benefit: 1980 to 2002

[In millions of dollars (106,036 represents $106,036,000,000). For years ending September 30. Programs covered provide cash, goods, or services to persons who make no payment and render no service in return. In case of many programs, including family cash welfare, food and housing programs, job and training programs, some educational programs, some recipients must work or study. Most of the programs base eligibility on individual, household, or family income, but some use group or area income tests; and a few offer help on the basis of presumed need. Constant dollar figures are based on the Consumer Price Index for all Urban Consumers]

Level of government and year	Total spending		Constant (2002) dollars							
	Current dollars	Constant (2002) dollars	Medical benefits	Cash aid	Food benefits	Housing benefits	Education benefits	Jobs/training	Services	Energy aid
TOTAL										
1980	106,036	237,093	72,890	64,226	30,288	24,520	11,573	19,466	10,281	3,848
1985	145,497	244,087	82,941	63,138	34,208	27,372	16,726	6,670	9,187	3,845
1990	214,738	298,497	120,687	75,417	34,899	27,394	20,003	5,897	11,799	2,402
1995	371,115	438,553	206,362	108,243	45,654	37,477	19,016	6,425	13,388	1,988
1996	376,036	432,261	204,539	106,279	44,936	38,188	18,827	5,384	12,669	1,439
1997	385,292	431,398	208,325	104,221	41,825	38,181	19,633	4,450	13,190	1,574
1998	395,519	437,997	214,412	101,403	38,890	37,432	20,068	5,416	18,896	1,479
1999	409,187	442,318	223,812	101,182	37,437	32,094	19,967	6,109	20,211	1,507
2000	428,556	448,985	235,591	98,907	35,776	32,651	17,085	7,897	18,915	2,162
2001	476,863	484,005	253,410	103,367	36,022	33,312	26,408	8,323	21,006	2,159
2002	522,156	522,156	282,468	102,157	39,306	35,566	30,484	7,808	22,215	2,152
FEDERAL										
1980	81,403	182,015	43,376	42,434	29,267	24,520	10,934	19,285	8,351	3,848
1985	107,267	179,952	46,772	41,078	32,482	27,372	15,964	6,534	5,957	3,793
1990	153,673	213,614	69,817	50,661	33,182	27,394	19,129	5,525	5,677	2,230
1995	262,905	310,679	119,841	80,266	43,492	34,729	17,888	5,467	7,104	1,892
1996	268,823	309,018	119,464	80,479	42,729	35,362	17,729	4,644	7,256	1,355
1997	274,980	307,885	120,685	80,446	39,615	35,431	18,485	4,250	7,472	1,503
1998	280,965	311,140	122,824	80,777	36,743	34,544	18,809	4,624	11,426	1,392
1999	291,798	315,424	129,364	80,385	35,237	32,094	18,680	5,164	13,085	1,415
2000	305,659	320,230	136,680	78,548	33,508	32,117	15,648	6,697	14,959	2,073
2001	342,877	348,013	147,249	83,837	33,674	32,550	24,766	7,083	16,814	2,039
2002	373,152	373,152	163,760	82,476	36,824	34,861	28,783	6,893	17,525	2,030
STATE AND LOCAL										
1980	24,633	55,079	29,515	21,792	1,022	-	639	181	1,930	52
1985	38,230	64,135	36,169	22,061	1,726	-	762	136	3,229	172
1990	61,065	84,884	50,870	24,757	1,717	-	874	371	6,122	96
1995	108,210	127,873	86,521	27,977	2,163	2,747	1,129	958	6,283	84
1996	107,213	123,243	85,075	25,800	2,207	2,827	1,098	740	5,413	72
1997	110,312	123,512	87,640	23,775	2,210	2,750	1,149	199	5,718	87
1998	114,554	126,857	91,588	20,626	2,146	2,888	1,259	792	7,469	92
1999	117,389	126,894	94,448	20,797	2,200	533	1,286	945	7,126	92
2000	122,897	128,755	98,912	20,359	2,268	533	1,437	1,201	3,956	89
2001	133,986	135,993	106,161	19,530	2,348	761	1,641	1,240	4,192	120
2002	149,004	149,004	118,708	19,681	2,482	705	1,701	915	4,690	122

- Represents or rounds to zero.

Source: Library of Congress, Congressional Research Service, "Cash and Noncash Benefits for Persons With Limited Income: Eligibility Rules, Recipient and Expenditure Data, FY2000-FY2002"; CRS Report RL 32233; November 25, 2003.

No. 524. Cash and Noncash Benefits for Persons With Limited Income: 2001 and 2002

[For years ending September 30, except as noted (476,863 represents $476,863,000,000). Programs covered provide cash, goods, or services to persons who make no payment and render no service in return. In case of many programs, including family cash welfare, food and housing programs, job and training programs and some educational programs, some recipients must work or study. Most of the programs base eligibility on individual, household, or family income, but some use group or area income tests; and a few offer help on the basis of presumed need]

Program	Average monthly recipients (1,000)		Expenditures (mil. dol.)					
			Total		Federal		State and local	
	2001	2002	2001	2002	2001	2002	2001	2002
Total	(X)	(X)	476,863	522,156	342,877	373,152	133,986	149,004
Medical care [1]	(X)	(X)	249,670	282,468	145,076	163,760	104,594	118,708
Medicaid [2][3]	44,600	50,900	228,039	258,216	129,840	146,643	98,199	111,573
Veterans [4][5]	1,479	1,640	7,731	8,185	7,731	8,185	-	-
General assistance [5]	(NA)	(NA)	4,705	4,956	-	-	4,705	4,956
State children's health insurance program	4,601	5,315	3,826	5,407	2,672	3,776	1,154	1,631
Indian health services [2][3]	1,600	1,600	2,629	2,758	2,629	2,758	-	-
Maternal and child health services	8,707	9,038	1,250	1,279	714	731	536	548
Consolidated health centers [2]	10,500	11,550	1,164	1,328	1,164	1,328	-	-
Cash aid [1]	(X)	(X)	101,842	102,157	82,600	82,476	19,242	19,681
Supplemental security income [3][6]	6,751	6,887	37,080	38,522	32,584	33,871	4,496	4,651
Temporary assistance for needy families (TANF) [7]	5,420	5,147	13,596	13,035	6,731	6,481	6,865	6,554
Earned income tax credit (refunded portion) [8]	16,827	(NA)	29,428	27,830	29,428	27,830	-	-
Foster care	265	254	8,311	8,618	4,395	4,523	3,916	4,095
Child tax credit (refunded portion)	8,634	(NA)	5,015	5,060	5,015	5,060	-	-
General assistance [8]	(NA)	(NA)	2,956	3,251	-	-	2,956	3,251
Pensions for needy veterans [9][10]	602	581	3,018	3,177	3,018	3,177	-	-
Food benefits [1]	(X)	(X)	35,490	39,306	33,177	36,824	2,313	2,482
Food stamps [3][11]	18,400	20,150	21,046	24,054	18,813	21,657	2,233	2,397
School lunch program [12][13]	15,500	16,000	5,659	6,064	5,659	6,064	(NA)	(NA)
Women, infants and children [3][14]	7,300	7,500	4,123	4,350	4,123	4,350	-	-
Child and adult care food program [15]	1,900	2,000	1,533	1,638	1,533	1,638	-	-
School breakfast [12]	6,400	6,700	1,402	1,515	1,402	1,515	-	-
Housing benefits [1]	(X)	(X)	32,820	35,566	32,070	34,861	750	705
Low-income housing asst. (Sec. 8) [16]	3,310	3,326	16,720	18,499	16,720	18,499	-	-
Low-rent public housing [16][17]	1,219	1,209	7,504	8,213	7,504	8,213	(NA)	(NA)
Rural housing loans [18][19]	46	43	3,406	3,499	3,406	3,499	-	-
Home investment partnerships [3][19][20]	82	84	2,541	2,500	1,796	1,796	745	704
Housing for special populations (elderly and disabled)	8	12	3,406	3,499	3,406	3,499	-	-
Education [1]	3,696	4,812	26,018	30,484	24,401	28,783	1,617	1,701
Pell grants [21][22]	3,696	4,182	11,314	11,364	11,314	11,364	-	-
Head Start	905	912	7,750	8,172	6,200	6,538	1,550	1,634
Stafford loans [21]	5,040	5,564	3,590	7,523	3,590	7,523	-	-
Federal Work-Study Program [21][22]	970	1,073	1,000	1,000	1,000	1,000	-	-
Federal Trio Programs	742	865	803	827	803	827	-	-
Services [1]	(X)	(NA)	20,696	22,215	16,566	17,525	4,130	4,690
Social services (Title 20)	12,826	(NA)	2,645	2,743	2,645	2,743	(NA)	(NA)
Child care for TANF recipients and ex-recipients [23]	(NA)	(NA)	2,346	2,322	1,583	1,572	763	750
Child care and development block grant [24]	1,814	(NA)	7,911	8,589	5,872	6,383	2,039	2,206
TANF services	(NA)	(NA)	5,528	6,147	4,200	4,413	1,328	1,734
Homeless assistance grants	(X)	(X)	967	1,044	967	1,044	-	-
Jobs and training [1]	(X)	(X)	8,200	7,808	6,978	6,893	1,222	915
TANF work activities	(NA)	(NA)	2,696	2,727	1,983	2,121	713	606
Training for disadvantaged adults and youth [25]	1,136	839	2,078	1,950	2,078	1,950	-	-
Job Corps	68	68	1,459	1,532	1,459	1,532	-	-
Energy assistance [1]	(X)	(X)	2,127	2,152	2,009	2,030	118	122
Low-income energy assistance [3][26]	4,832	4,672	1,856	1,800	1,856	1,800	(NA)	(NA)

- Represents zero. NA Not available. X Not applicable. [1] Includes other programs not shown separately. [2] Recipient data represent unduplicated annual number. [3] Expenditures include administrative expenses. [4] Medical care for veterans with a nonservice-connected disability. [5] Estimated expenditures. [6] Includes state-administered SSI supplements. [7] Excludes data for child support operations. [8] Estimated families. (In previous years, individual recipients were estimated.) [9] Estimated recipients as of September. [10] Includes dependents and survivors. [11] Includes Puerto Rico's nutritional assistance program. [12] Free and reduced-price segments. [13] Includes estimate of commodity assistance. [14] Special supplemental food program for women, infants and children. [15] Recipient data are numbers of children receiving free or reduced price meals and snacks in child care centers and estimates of children in family day care homes with incomes below 185 percent of poverty. [16] Recipient data represent units eligible for payment at end of year. [17] Includes operating subsidies, capital grants, and HUD-administered Indian housing. [18] Recipient data represent total families or dwelling units during year. [19] Expenditure data represent amounts obligated. [20] Recipient data are housing units provided or rehabilitated. [21] Recipient data are total numbers for the school year ending in year shown. [22] Expenditure data are appropriations available for school year ending the fiscal year named. [23] P.L. 104-193, which created TANF, established a mandatory block grant for TANF-related child care. [24] Recipient data are estimated number of children served. [25] Recipient data are total number of participants. [26] Households served during the year with heating and winter crisis aid. Federal funds include amounts transferred to other programs serving the needy.

Source: Library of Congress, Congressional Research Service, Cash and Noncash Benefits for Persons With Limited Income: Eligibility Rules, Recipient and Expenditure Data, FY2000-FY2002"; CRS Report RL32233; November 25, 2003.

Social Insurance and Human Services 347

No. 525. Social Security—Covered Employment, Earnings, and Contribution Rates: 1980 to 2003

[140.5 represents 140,500,000. Includes Puerto Rico, Virgin Islands, American Samoa, and Guam. Represents all reported employment. Data are estimated. OASDHI=Old-age, survivors, disability, and health insurance; SMI=Supplementary medical insurance]

Item	Unit	1980	1990	1995	1997	1998	1999	2000	2001	2002	2003
Workers with insured status [1]	Million . . .	140.5	164.1	173.3	178.0	180.2	182.6	185.2	187.8	190.1	192.4
Male.	Million . . .	76.6	86.5	90.1	92.1	93.1	94.0	95.2	96.5	97.6	98.8
Female	Million . . .	63.8	77.7	83.1	86.0	87.1	88.5	90.0	91.2	92.4	93.7
Under 25 years old	Million . . .	25.7	21.3	18.8	19.1	19.6	20.2	20.8	21.1	21.4	21.7
25 to 34 years old	Million . . .	36.5	41.6	39.4	38.2	37.6	37.0	36.6	36.5	36.5	36.5
35 to 44 years old	Million . . .	23.0	36.4	40.5	41.8	42.2	42.3	42.3	42.2	41.9	41.5
45 to 54 years old	Million . . .	18.6	22.8	29.5	31.9	33.2	34.4	35.6	36.6	37.6	38.5
55 to 59 years old	Million . . .	9.3	8.8	9.8	10.7	11.2	11.8	12.4	13.1	13.8	14.6
60 to 64 years old	Million . . .	8.2	8.8	8.5	8.8	9.1	9.1	9.6	10.1	10.3	10.8
65 to 69 years old	Million . . .	7.0	8.2	8.2	8.1	8.0	8.0	8.0	8.2	8.3	8.5
70 years old and over	Million . . .	12.2	16.3	18.6	19.3	19.4	19.6	19.9	20.1	20.3	20.4
Workers reported with—											
Taxable earnings [2]	Million . . .	113	134	141	146	149	151	154	154	154	154
Maximum earnings [2]	Million . . .	10	8	8	9	9	9	10	9	8	8
Earnings in covered employment [2]	Bil. dol . . .	1,329	2,704	3,402	3,859	4,172	4,458	4,812	4,913	4,940	5,059
Reported taxable [2]	Bil. dol . . .	1,181	2,358	2,919	3,285	3,527	3,750	4,008	4,170	4,243	4,352
Percent of total	Percent . .	88.9	87.2	85.8	85.1	84.5	84.1	83.3	84.9	85.9	86.0
Average per worker:											
Total earnings [2]	Dollars . . .	11,759	20,238	24,126	26,403	28,019	29,460	31,312	31,961	32,111	32,783
Taxable earnings [2]	Dollars . . .	10,449	17,650	20,703	22,478	23,684	24,777	26,081	27,129	27,582	28,203
Annual maximum taxable earnings [3]	Dollars . . .	25,900	51,300	61,200	65,400	68,400	72,600	76,200	80,400	84,900	87,000
Contribution rates for OASDHI: [4]											
Each employer and employee . .	Percent . .	6.13	7.65	7.65	7.65	7.65	7.65	7.65	7.65	7.65	7.65
Self-employed [5]	Percent . .	8.10	15.30	15.30	15.30	15.30	15.30	15.30	15.30	15.30	15.30
SMI, monthly premium [6]	Dollars . . .	9.60	28.60	46.10	43.80	43.80	45.50	45.50	50.00	54.00	58.70

[1] Estimated number fully insured for retirement and/or survivor benefits as of end of year. [2] Includes self-employment. [3] Beginning 1995 upper limit on earnings subject to HI taxes was repealed. [4] As of January 1, 2004, each employee and employer pays 7.65 percent and the self-employed pay 15.3 percent. [5] Beginning 1990, self-employed pays 15.3 percent, and half of the tax is deductible for income tax purposes and for computing self-employment income subject to social security tax. [6] 1980, as of July 1; beginning 1990, as of January 1. As of January 1, 2002, the monthly premium is $54.00.

Source: U.S. Social Security Administration, *Annual Statistical Supplement* to the *Social Security Bulletin;* and unpublished data.

No. 526. Social Security Trust Funds: 1990 to 2003

[In billions of dollars (272.4 represents $272,400,000,000)]

Type of trust fund	1990	1995	1997	1998	1999	2000	2001	2002	2003
Old-age and survivors insurance (OASI):									
Net contribution income [1]	272.4	310.1	357.4	380.4	407.3	433.0	453.4	468.1	456.1
Interest received [2]	16.4	32.8	39.8	44.5	49.8	57.5	64.7	71.2	75.2
Benefit payments [3]	223.0	291.6	316.3	326.8	334.4	352.7	372.3	388.1	399.8
Assets, end of year	214.2	458.5	589.1	681.6	798.8	931.0	1,071.5	1,217.5	1,355.3
Disability insurance (DI):									
Net contribution income [1]	28.7	54.7	56.5	59.5	63.9	71.8	75.7	78.2	77.4
Interest received [2]	0.9	2.2	4.0	4.8	5.7	6.9	8.2	9.2	9.7
Benefit payments [3]	24.8	40.9	45.7	48.2	51.4	55.0	59.6	65.7	70.9
Assets, end of year	11.1	37.6	66.4	80.8	97.3	118.5	141.0	160.5	175.4

[1] Includes deposits by states and deductions for refund of estimated employee-tax overpayment. Includes government contributions on deemed wage credits for military service in 1957 and later. Includes taxation of benefits. [2] In 1990, includes interest on advance tax transfers. Includes interest on reimbursement for unnegotiated checks. [3] Includes payments for vocational rehabilitation services furnished to disabled persons receiving benefits because of their disabilities. Amounts reflect deductions for unnegotiated benefit checks.

Source: U.S. Social Security Administration, *Annual Report of Board of Trustees, OASI, DI, HI, and SMI Trust Funds.* Also published in *Social Security Bulletin,* quarterly.

No. 527. Social Security (OASDI)—Benefits by Type of Beneficiary: 1980 to 2003

[35,585 represents 35,585,000. A person eligible to receive more than one type of benefit is generally classified or counted only once as a retired-worker beneficiary. OASDI=Old-age, survivors, and disability insurance. See also headnote, Table 525 and Appendix III]

Type of beneficiary	1980	1990	1995	1997	1998	1999	2000	2001	2002	2003
Number of benefits [1] (1,000) .	35,585	39,832	43,387	43,971	44,246	44,596	45,415	45,878	46,444	47,038
Retired workers [2] (1,000) .	19,562	24,838	26,673	27,275	27,511	27,775	28,499	28,837	29,190	29,532
Disabled workers [3] (1,000)	2,859	3,011	4,185	4,508	4,698	4,879	5,042	5,274	5,544	5,874
Wives and husbands [2][4] (1,000) . .	3,477	3,367	3,290	3,129	3,054	2,987	2,963	2,899	2,833	2,773
Children (1,000)	4,607	3,187	3,734	3,772	3,769	3,795	3,803	3,839	3,910	3,961
Under age 18	3,423	2,497	2,956	2,970	2,963	2,970	2,976	2,994	3,043	3,080
Disabled children [5]	450	600	686	705	713	721	729	737	745	753
Students [6]	733	89	92	97	93	104	98	109	123	128
Of retired workers	639	422	442	441	439	442	459	467	477	480
Of deceased workers	2,610	1,776	1,884	1,893	1,884	1,885	1,878	1,890	1,908	1,910
Of disabled workers	1,358	989	1,409	1,438	1,446	1,468	1,466	1,482	1,526	1,571
Widowed mothers [7] (1,000)	562	304	275	230	221	212	203	197	194	190
Widows and widowers [2][8] (1,000) . .	4,411	5,111	5,226	5,053	4,990	4,944	4,901	4,828	4,771	4,707
Parents [2] (1,000)	15	6	4	4	3	3	3	3	2	2
Special benefits [9] (1,000)	93	7	1	(Z)	(Z)	(Z)	(Z)	(Z)	(Z)	(Z)
AVERAGE MONTHLY BENEFIT, CURRENT DOLLARS										
Retired workers [2]	341	603	720	765	780	804	844	874	895	922
Retired worker and wife [2]	567	1,027	1,221	1,295	1,318	1,357	1,420	1,466	1,494	1,535
Disabled workers [3]	371	587	682	722	733	754	786	814	834	862
Wives and husbands [2][4]	164	298	354	379	386	398	416	430	439	450
Children of retired workers	140	259	322	349	358	373	395	413	426	444
Children of deceased workers	240	406	469	500	510	526	550	571	585	603
Children of disabled workers	110	164	183	201	208	216	228	238	245	254
Widowed mothers [7]	246	409	478	532	545	566	595	621	640	664
Widows and widowers, nondisabled [2]	311	556	680	731	749	775	810	841	861	888
Parents [2]	276	482	591	636	651	674	704	729	753	779
Special benefits [9]	105	167	192	201	204	209	217	224	227	232
AVERAGE MONTHLY BENEFIT, CONSTANT (2002) DOLLARS [10]										
Retired workers [2]	715	815	849	858	861	864	877	895	895	905
Retired worker and wife [2]	1,189	1,389	1,439	1,452	1,455	1,459	1,476	1,500	1,434	1,507
Disabled workers [3]	778	794	804	810	809	810	817	834	834	846
Wives and husbands [2][4]	344	403	417	425	426	428	432	440	439	442
Children of deceased workers	293	350	379	391	396	401	411	422	585	592
Widowed mothers [7]	503	549	553	561	562	565	572	584	640	652
Widows and widowers, nondisabled [2]	231	222	216	225	229	232	237	244	861	872
Number of benefits awarded (1,000)	4,215	3,717	3,882	3,866	3,800	3,917	4,290	4,162	4,336	4,322
Retired workers [2]	1,620	1,665	1,609	1,719	1,631	1,690	1,961	1,779	1,813	1,791
Disabled workers [3]	389	468	646	587	608	620	622	691	750	777
Wives and husbands [2][4]	469	379	322	319	311	322	385	358	363	353
Children	1,174	695	809	757	763	773	777	796	846	852
Widowed mothers [7]	108	58	52	44	42	42	40	41	41	39
Widows and widowers [2][8]	452	452	445	440	444	470	505	496	523	508
Parents [2]	1	(Z)	(Z)	(Z)	(Z)	(Z)	(Z)	(Z)	(Z)	(Z)
Special benefits [9]	1	(Z)	(Z)	(Z)	(Z)	(Z)	(Z)	(Z)	(Z)	(Z)
BENEFIT PAYMENTS DURING YEAR (bil. dol.)										
Total [11]	120.5	247.8	332.6	362.0	375.0	385.8	407.6	431.9	453.8	470.8
Monthly benefits [12]	120.1	247.6	332.4	361.8	374.8	385.6	407.4	431.7	453.6	470.6
Retired workers [2]	70.4	156.8	205.3	223.6	232.3	238.5	253.5	269.0	281.6	291.5
Disabled workers [3]	12.8	22.1	36.6	41.1	43.5	46.5	49.8	54.2	59.9	64.8
Wives and husbands [2][4]	7.0	14.5	17.9	18.6	18.9	18.8	19.4	19.9	20.3	20.4
Children	10.5	12.0	16.1	17.6	18.1	18.6	19.3	20.4	21.5	22.3
Under age 18	7.4	9.0	11.9	13.0	13.3	13.6	14.1	14.8	15.7	16.2
Disabled children [5]	1.0	2.5	3.6	4.0	4.2	4.4	4.6	4.8	5.1	5.2
Students [6]	2.1	0.5	0.6	0.6	0.7	0.7	0.7	0.7	0.8	0.8
Of retired workers	1.1	1.3	1.7	1.9	1.9	2.0	2.1	2.3	2.5	2.6
Of deceased workers	7.4	8.6	10.7	11.7	11.9	12.1	12.5	13.1	13.7	14.1
Of disabled workers	2.0	2.2	3.7	4.1	4.2	4.4	4.7	4.9	5.3	5.7
Widowed mothers [7]	1.6	1.4	1.6	1.5	1.4	1.4	1.4	1.4	1.5	1.5
Widows and widowers [2][8]	17.6	40.7	54.8	59.3	60.5	61.8	63.9	66.8	68.8	70.1
Parents [2]	0.1	(Z)	(Z)	(Z)	(Z)	(Z)	(Z)	(Z)	(Z)	(Z)
Special benefits [9]	0.1	(Z)	(Z)	(Z)	(Z)	(Z)	(Z)	(Z)	(Z)	(Z)
Lump sum	0.4	0.2	0.2	0.2	0.2	0.2	0.2	0.2	0.2	0.2

Z Fewer than 500 or less than $50 million.   [1] Number of benefit payments in current-payment status, i.e., actually being made at a specified time with no deductions or with deductions amounting to less than a month's benefit.   [2] 62 years and over.   [3] Disabled workers under age 65.   [4] Includes wife beneficiaries with entitled children in their care and entitled divorced wives.   [5] 18 years old and over. Disability began before age 18.   [6] Full-time students aged 18-21 through 1980 and aged 18 and 19 beginning 1990.   [7] Includes surviving divorced mothers with entitled children in their care and widowed fathers with entitled children in their care.   [8] Includes widows aged 60-61, surviving divorced wives aged 60 and over, disabled widows and widowers aged 50 and over; and widowers aged 60-61.   [9] Benefits for persons aged 72 and over not insured under regular or transitional provisions of Social Security Act.   [10] Constant dollar figures are based on the consumer price index (CPI-U) for December as published by the U.S. Bureau of Labor Statistics.   [11] Represents total disbursements of benefit checks by the U.S. Dept. of the Treasury during the years specified.   [12] Distribution by type estimated.

Source: U.S. Social Security Administration, *Annual Statistical Supplement* to the *Social Security Bulletin;* and unpublished data.

Social Insurance and Human Services   349

No. 528. Social Security—Beneficiaries, Annual Payments, and Average Monthly Benefit, 1990 to 2003 and by State and Other Areas, 2003

[Number of beneficiaries in current-payment status (39,832 represents 39,832,000) and average monthly benefit as of December. Data based on 10-percent sample of administrative records. See also headnote, Table 527, and Appendix III]

Year, state, and other area	Number of beneficiaries (1,000)				Annual payments[2] (mil. dol.)				Average monthly benefit (dol.)		
	Total	Retired workers and dependents[1]	Survivors	Disabled workers and dependents	Total	Retired workers and dependents[1]	Survivors	Disabled workers and dependents	Retired workers[3]	Disabled workers[4]	Widows and widowers[4]
1990.	39,832	28,369	7,197	4,266	247,796	172,042	50,951	24,803	603	587	557
1995.	43,380	30,139	7,379	5,862	332,581	224,381	67,302	40,898	720	682	680
2000.	45,417	31,761	6,981	6,675	407,431	274,645	77,848	54,938	845	787	810
2001.	45,874	32,046	6,915	6,913	431,737	290,799	81,359	59,579	875	815	841
2002.	46,453	32,362	6,870	7,220	453,601	303,983	83,973	65,645	895	834	861
2003, total[5]	46,448	32,360	6,870	7,220	470,546	314,024	85,621	70,899	922	862	888
United States	45,312	31,652	6,653	7,010	463,006	309,918	83,792	69,292	(NA)	(NA)	(NA)
Alabama	857	528	144	185	8,237	4,860	1,638	1,740	877	832	816
Alaska	59	38	10	11	574	364	107	104	892	844	836
Arizona	835	600	107	127	8,682	5,999	1,373	1,310	939	890	922
Arkansas.	529	335	83	111	4,951	3,018	906	1,026	855	815	795
California.	4,304	3,110	588	606	43,857	30,115	7,576	6,166	926	876	919
Colorado	550	389	78	82	5,507	3,717	989	801	902	855	894
Connecticut	581	437	71	74	6,418	4,686	981	751	1,010	894	983
Delaware.	141	100	19	22	1,518	1,037	250	231	967	901	951
District of Columbia. . . .	73	51	12	10	633	423	113	96	786	796	729
Florida	3,278	2,433	413	432	33,305	23,685	5,290	4,330	918	863	915
Georgia.	1,147	740	184	224	11,315	7,075	2,103	2,136	895	845	830
Hawaii	193	150	23	21	1,938	1,450	281	207	912	878	863
Idaho	205	146	28	30	2,060	1,404	357	299	900	844	902
Illinois	1,862	1,330	285	248	19,741	13,456	3,763	2,522	961	894	950
Indiana	1,012	704	151	157	10,768	7,219	2,002	1,547	967	868	947
Iowa	542	395	80	68	5,490	3,803	1,041	646	920	828	909
Kansas	442	318	65	59	4,560	3,151	853	557	944	832	941
Kentucky	754	448	126	181	7,242	4,057	1,459	1,726	870	848	805
Louisiana	725	436	152	138	6,801	3,814	1,715	1,273	858	855	816
Maine	258	173	34	51	2,427	1,556	413	458	851	787	842
Maryland	744	531	115	98	7,712	5,243	1,447	1,023	928	897	904
Massachusetts	1,063	754	135	174	10,807	7,363	1,770	1,674	927	849	922
Michigan	1,677	1,152	257	268	18,236	12,010	3,442	2,784	993	919	955
Minnesota	755	556	105	95	7,708	5,399	1,372	937	920	847	903
Mississippi	531	311	91	129	4,825	2,757	944	1,124	842	806	764
Missouri	1,022	693	150	179	10,209	6,657	1,846	1,706	910	841	887
Montana	162	114	24	24	1,583	1,069	294	220	885	832	880
Nebraska	287	210	41	36	2,847	1,979	524	344	904	819	909
Nevada	314	232	36	46	3,349	2,349	485	514	929	931	931
New Hampshire	208	148	26	34	2,185	1,502	342	341	944	863	940
New Jersey	1,363	1,007	182	175	15,223	10,860	2,488	1,875	1,018	938	980
New Mexico.	290	197	45	47	2,708	1,765	497	445	861	826	823
New York.	3,024	2,156	402	466	32,187	22,188	5,273	4,726	977	911	940
North Carolina	1,406	941	194	271	13,953	9,071	2,232	2,649	899	842	828
North Dakota	114	82	20	13	1,082	719	244	118	859	814	855
Ohio	1,930	1,340	320	270	19,853	13,046	4,200	2,607	938	849	920
Oklahoma	606	413	99	94	5,945	3,839	1,177	928	883	846	860
Oregon	588	429	77	81	6,093	4,243	1,030	819	931	857	933
Pennsylvania	2,377	1,703	359	314	24,919	16,941	4,804	3,174	948	876	933
Rhode Island	191	137	22	32	1,945	1,346	288	310	923	847	929
South Carolina	719	467	107	145	7,091	4,496	1,193	1,401	896	850	821
South Dakota	138	98	22	17	1,282	873	260	149	845	798	842
Tennessee.	1,028	664	164	200	10,097	6,290	1,905	1,902	894	829	839
Texas	2,731	1,865	477	389	27,068	17,506	5,738	3,824	898	854	863
Utah	251	183	35	33	2,561	1,791	460	311	926	853	951
Vermont	107	74	14	18	1,066	723	174	170	912	825	887
Virginia	1,072	732	158	182	10,759	7,033	1,930	1,796	904	864	849
Washington	874	634	114	126	9,305	6,457	1,541	1,307	960	877	949
West Virginia	399	236	74	89	4,012	2,197	894	921	910	901	849
Wisconsin	915	674	125	117	9,563	6,751	1,653	1,159	945	860	934
Wyoming	79	58	10	11	809	566	135	108	921	869	919
Puerto Rico	688	380	120	188	4,711	2,339	936	1,436	611	738	544
Guam	12	8	2	2	83	49	21	13	634	794	636
American Samoa.	5	2	1	2	34	11	11	12	551	653	516
Virgin Islands	15	11	2	2	127	91	21	16	804	860	690
Northern Mariana Islands	2	1	(Z)	(Z)	10	6	4	1	501	418	394
Abroad	414	306	92	16	2,575	1,610	836	129	532	738	589

NA Not available.   Z Fewer than 500.   [1] Includes special benefits for persons aged 72 and over not insured under regular or transitional provisions of Social Security Act.   [2] Unnegotiated checks not deducted. 1990 and 1995 include lump-sum payments to survivors of deceased workers.   [3] Excludes persons with special benefits.   [4] Nondisabled only.   [5] Includes those with state or area unknown.

Source: U.S. Social Security Administration, Annual Statistical Supplement to the Social Security Bulletin.

No. 529. Public Employee Retirement Systems—Participants and Finances: 1980 to 2002

[For fiscal year of retirement system, except data for the Thrift Savings Plan are for calendar year (4,629 represents 4,629,000)]

Retirement plan	Unit	1980	1990	1995	1997	1998	1999	2000	2001	2002, proj.
TOTAL PARTICIPANTS [1]										
Federal retirement systems:										
Defined benefit:										
Civil Service Retirement System	1,000	4,629	4,167	3,731	3,518	3,423	3,362	(NA)	(NA)	(NA)
Federal Employees Retirement System [2]	1,000	(X)	1,180	1,512	1,679	1,757	1,879	(NA)	(NA)	(NA)
Military Service Retirement System [3]	1,000	3,380	3,763	3,387	3,367	3,368	3,374	3,397	3,418	3,453
Thrift Savings Plan [4]	1,000	(X)	1,625	2,195	2,303	2,300	2,400	(NA)	2,600	3,000
State and local retirement systems [5][6]	1,000	(NA)	16,858	14,734	15,194	16,215	16,195	16,834	17,021	17,264
ACTIVE PARTICIPANTS										
Federal retirement systems:										
Defined benefit:										
Civil Service Retirement System	1,000	2,700	1,826	1,525	1,189	1,099	1,042	(NA)	(NA)	(NA)
Federal Employees Retirement System [2]	1,000	(X)	1,136	1,318	1,497	1,547	1,640	(NA)	(NA)	(NA)
Military Service Retirement System [3]	1,000	2,050	2,130	1,572	1,491	1,459	1,438	1,437	1,438	1,465
Thrift Savings Plan [4]	1,000	(X)	1,419	1,930	2,011	1,800	1,900	(NA)	1,900	2,300
State and local retirement systems [5][6]	1,000	(NA)	11,345	12,524	12,817	13,059	13,472	13,917	13,977	14,123
ASSETS										
Total	Bil. dol.	258	1,047	1,655	2,110	2,403	2,644	2,943	2,803	2,831
Federal retirement systems	Bil. dol.	73	326	537	631	686	738	774	645	673
Defined benefit	Bil. dol.	73	318	502	570	608	643	679	544	571
Civil Service Retirement System	Bil. dol.	73	220	311	344	361	376	390	414	414
Federal Employees Retirement System [2]	Bil. dol.	(X)	18	60	83	97	111	126	157	157
Military Service Retirement System [3]	Bil. dol.	(7)	80	131	143	150	156	163	174	174
Thrift Savings Plan [4]	Bil. dol.	(X)	8	35	61	77	95	98	102	102
State and local retirement systems [5]	Bil. dol.	185	721	1,118	1,479	1,717	1,906	2,169	2,158	2,158
CONTRIBUTIONS										
Total	Bil. dol.	83	103	127	139	137	142	143	145	151
Federal retirement systems	Bil. dol.	19	61	67	73	73	75	78	80	85
Defined benefit	Bil. dol.	19	59	61	66	65	67	69	70	73
Civil Service Retirement System	Bil. dol.	19	28	31	33	33	33	33	33	34
Federal Employees Retirement System [2]	Bil. dol.	(X)	4	6	7	6	8	8	9	10
Military Service Retirement System [3]	Bil. dol.	(7)	27	24	26	26	26	28	28	29
Thrift Savings Plan [4]	Bil. dol.	(X)	2	6	7	8	8	9	10	12
State and local retirement systems [5]	Bil. dol.	64	42	60	66	64	67	65	65	66
BENEFITS										
Total	Bil. dol.	39	89	125	142	152	160	172	185	197
Federal retirement systems	Bil. dol.	27	53	66	73	76	78	81	84	87
Defined benefit	Bil. dol.	27	53	65	72	74	76	78	81	85
Civil Service Retirement System	Bil. dol.	15	31	37	41	42	43	44	46	48
Federal Employees Retirement System [2]	Bil. dol.	(X)	(Z)	1	1	1	1	1	1	2
Military Service Retirement System [3]	Bil. dol.	12	22	28	30	31	32	33	34	35
Thrift Savings Plan [4]	Bil. dol.	(X)	(Z)	1	1	2	2	3	3	2
State and local retirement systems [5]	Bil. dol.	12	36	59	69	76	82	91	101	110

NA Not available. X Not applicable. Z Less than $500 million. [1] Includes active, separated vested, retired employees, and survivors. [2] The Federal Employees Retirement System was established June 6, 1986. [3] Includes nondisability and disability retirees, surviving families, and all active personnel with the exception of active reserves. [4] The Thrift Savings Plan (a defined contribution plan) was established April 1, 1987. [5] Excludes state and local plans that are fully supported by employee contributions. [6] Not adjusted for double counting of individuals participating in more than one plan. [7] The Military Retirement System was unfunded until October 1, 1984.

Source: Employee Benefit Research Institute, Washington, DC, *EBRI Databook on Employee Benefits, Twelfth Edition,* and unpublished data (copyright). See also <http://www.ebri.org/>.

No. 530. Federal Civil Service Retirement: 1980 to 2002

[As of Sept. 30 or for year ending Sept. 30 (2,720 represents 2,720,000). Covers both Civil Service Retirement System and Federal Employees Retirement System]

Item	Unit	1980	1990	1995	1997	1998	1999	2000	2001	2002
Employees covered [1]	1,000	2,720	2,945	2,668	2,681	2,658	2,668	2,764	2,655	2,654
Annuitants, total	1,000	1,675	2,143	2,311	2,352	2,369	2,368	2,376	2,383	2,383
Age and service	1,000	905	1,288	1,441	1,474	1,488	1,491	1,501	1,509	1,513
Disability	1,000	343	297	263	257	253	246	242	239	236
Survivors	1,000	427	558	607	621	628	631	633	635	634
Receipts, total [2]	Mil. dol	24,389	52,689	65,684	70,227	72,156	74,522	75,967	77,949	80,069
Employee contributions	Mil. dol	3,686	4,501	4,498	4,358	4,274	4,381	4,637	4,593	4,475
Federal government contributions	Mil. dol	15,562	27,368	33,130	35,386	36,188	36,561	37,722	38,442	39,692
Disbursements, total [3]	Mil. dol	14,977	31,416	38,435	41,722	43,058	43,932	45,194	47,356	48,970
Age and service annuitants [4]	Mil. dol	12,639	26,495	32,070	34,697	35,806	36,492	37,546	39,397	40,758
Survivors	Mil. dol	1,912	4,366	5,864	6,518	6,763	6,978	7,210	7,533	7,790
Average monthly benefit:										
Age and service	Dollars	992	1,369	1,643	1,749	1,796	1,830	1,885	1,967	2,031
Disability	Dollars	723	1,008	1,164	1,204	1,216	1,221	1,240	1,269	1,286
Survivors	Dollars	392	653	819	881	905	923	952	992	1,024
Cash and security holdings	Bil. dol	73.7	238.0	366.2	422.2	451.3	481.3	508.1	542.6	573.7

[1] Excludes employees in leave without pay status. [2] Includes interest on investments. [3] Includes refunds, death claims, and administration. [4] Includes disability annuitants.

Source: U.S. Office of Personnel Management, *Civil Service Retirement and Disability Trust Fund Annual Report.*

Social Insurance and Human Services **351**

No. 531. State and Local Government Retirement Systems—Beneficiaries and Finances: 1990 to 2002

[In billions of dollars, except as indicated (111.3 represents 111,300,000,000). For fiscal years closed during the 12 months ending June 30]

Year and level of government	Number of beneficiaries (1,000)	Receipts					Benefits and withdrawals			Cash and security holdings
		Total	Employee contributions	Government contributions		Earnings on investments	Total	Benefits	Withdrawals	
				State	Local					
1990: All systems	4,026	111.3	13.9	14.0	18.6	64.9	38.4	36.0	2.4	721
State-administered	3,232	89.2	11.6	14.0	11.5	52.0	29.6	27.6	2.0	575
Locally administered	794	22.2	2.2	(Z)	7.0	12.9	8.8	8.4	0.4	145
1995: All systems	4,979	148.8	18.6	16.6	24.4	89.2	61.5	58.8	2.7	1,118
State-administered	4,025	123.3	15.7	16.2	15.4	76.0	48.0	45.8	2.2	914
Locally administered	954	25.5	2.9	0.4	9.0	13.3	13.5	13.0	0.5	204
2001: All systems	7,322	123.3	26.4	17.5	21.2	57.9	112.2	100.9	4.1	2,157
State-administered	4,931	94.3	21.8	17.1	15.4	39.7	90.1	80.9	3.4	1,782
Locally administered	2,391	28.9	4.5	0.4	5.7	18.2	22.1	19.9	0.7	375
2002: All systems	6,198	-6.1	27.5	17.1	21.6	-72.4	121.9	110.1	4.0	2,157
State-administered	5,180	-8.4	23.0	16.7	15.2	-63.5	98.2	88.7	3.2	1,774
Locally administered	1,018	2.3	4.5	0.4	6.3	-8.9	23.7	21.4	0.8	375

Z Less than $50 million.

Source: U.S. Census Bureau, Through 1995, *Finances of Employee-Retirement Systems of State and Local Governments*, Series GF, No. 2, annual; beginning 2001, Federal, State, and Local Governments, State and Local Government Public Employee Retirement Systems"; <http://www.census.gov/govs/www/retire.html>.

No. 532. Private Pension Plans—Summary by Type of Plan: 1990 to 1999

[712.3 represents 712,300. "Pension plan" is defined by the Employee Retirement Income Security Act (ERISA) as "any plan, fund, or program which was heretofore or is hereafter established or maintained by an employer or an employee organization, or by both, to the extent that such plan (a) provides retirement income to employees, or (b) results in a deferral of income by employees for periods extending to the termination of covered employment or beyond, regardless of the method of calculating the contributions made to the plan, the method of calculating the benefits under the plan, or the method of distributing benefits from the plan." A defined benefit plan provides a definite benefit formula for calculating benefit amounts - such as a flat amount per year of service or a percentage of salary times years of service. A defined contribution plan is a pension plan in which the contributions are made to an individual account for each employee. The retirement benefit is dependent upon the account balance at retirement. The balance depends upon amounts contributed, investment experience, and, in the case of profit sharing plans, amounts which may be allocated to the account due to forfeitures by terminating employees. Employee Stock Ownership Plans (ESOP) and 401(k) plans are included among defined contribution plans. Data are based on Form 5500 series reports filed with the Internal Revenue Service]

Item	Unit	Total				Defined contribution plan				Defined benefit plan			
		1990	1995	1998	1999	1990	1995	1998	1999	1990	1995	1998	1999
Number of plans [1]	1,000...	712.3	693.4	730.0	733.0	599.2	623.9	673.6	683.1	113.1	69.5	56.4	49.9
Total participants [2 3]	Million	76.9	87.5	99.5	101.8	38.1	47.7	57.9	60.4	38.8	39.7	41.6	41.4
Active participants [2 4]	Million	61.8	66.2	73.3	73.0	35.5	42.7	50.3	50.4	26.3	23.5	23.0	22.6
Assets [5]	Million	1,674	2,724	4,022	4,408	712	1,322	2,085	2,350	962	1,402	1,937	2,058
Contributions [6]	Bil. dol.	98.8	158.8	201.9	215.8	75.8	117.4	166.9	185.9	23.0	41.4	35.0	30.0
Benefits [7]	Bil. dol.	129.4	183.0	273.1	314.5	63.0	97.9	161.9	195.1	66.4	85.1	111.2	119.4

[1] Excludes all plans covering only one participant. [2] Includes double counting of workers in more than one plan. [3] Total participants include active participants, vested separated workers, and retirees. [4] Any workers currently in employment covered by a plan and who are earning or retaining credited service under a plan. Includes any nonvested former employees who have not yet incurred breaks in service. [5] Asset amounts shown exclude funds held by life insurance companies under allocated group insurance contracts for payment of retirement benefits. These excluded funds make up roughly 10 to 15 percent of total private fund assets. [6] Includes both employer and employee contributions. [7] Benefits paid directly from trust and premium payments made from plan to insurance carriers. Excludes benefits paid directly by insurance carriers.

Source: U.S. Dept. of Labor, Pension and Welfare Benefits Administration, *Private Pension Plan Bulletin*, winter 2003, and unpublished data.

No. 533. Percent Of Workers Participating In Retirement Benefits by Worker Characteristics: 2003

[Based on National Compensation Survey, a sample survey of 3,168 private industry establishments of all sizes, representing over 107 million workers; see Appendix III. Survey covers all 50 States and the District of Columbia. See also Table 630]

Characteristic	Total [1]	Defined benefit	Defined contribution	Characteristic	Total [1]	Defined benefit	Defined contribution
Total	49	20	40	Full time [2]	58	24	48
White-collar occupations	59	22	51	Part time [2]	18	8	14
Blue-collar occupations	50	24	38	Union [3]	83	72	39
Service occupations	21	7	16	Nonunion [3]	45	15	40

[1] Total is less than the sum of the individual retirement items because many employees participated in both types of plans. [2] Employees are classified as working either a full-time or part-time schedule based on the definition used by each establishment. [3] Union workers are those whose wages are determined through collective bargaining.

Source: U.S. Bureau of Labor Statistics, *News*, USDL 03-489, September 17, 2003. See also <http://www.bls.gov/news.release/pdf/ebs2.pdf>.

No. 534. Defined Benefit Retirement Plans—Selected Features: 2000

[In percent, except as indicated (19,225 represents 19,225,000). Covers full-time employees in private industry. Based on National Compensation Survey, a sample survey of 1,436 private industry establishments of all sizes, representing over 107 million workers; see Appendix III. See also Table 630]

Feature	All employees	Professional, technical, and related	Clerical and sales	Blue-collar and service
Full-time employees with defined benefit plan (1,000)	19,225	5,794	5,179	8,252
Plan provisions:				
Benefits based on earnings	61	59	67	60
Early retirement benefits available	77	69	78	81
Availability of lump sum benefits at retirement	43	44	51	37
Benefit formula:				
Percent of terminal earnings	48	47	48	50
Percent of career earnings	13	12	19	10
Dollar amount formula	14	9	9	21
Percent of contribution formula	(Z)	-	-	1
Cash account [1]	23	31	23	18
Other	1	1	2	1
Requirements for normal retirement [2]				
No age requirement	11	15	10	8
Less than 20 years of service	5	11	3	1
30 years of service	6	4	7	7
At age 55	4	5	7	2
At age 60	10	16	7	8
At age 62	21	18	16	26
At age 65	49	41	55	51
Sum of age plus service [3]	3	4	5	2

- Represents no employees in this category or data do not meet publication criteria.   Z Less than 0.5 percent.   [1] Cash balance retirement plans are a defined benefit plan in which an account is maintained for each participant, with employer contributions based on employee earnings, plus interest, being credited to that account. Cash balance plans generally do not have provisions for many of the features found in traditional defined benefit plans. Due to the increase in the incidence of cash balance plans, the prevalence of some defined benefit plan provisions has declined from earlier surveys.   [2] Normal retirement is defined as the point at which the participant could retire and immediately receive all accrued benefits by virtue of service and earnings, without reduction due to age. If a plan had alternative age and service requirements, the earliest age and associated service level was tabulated; if one alternative did not specify an age, it was the requirement tabulated. Some age and service requirements are not shown separately.   [3] In some plans, participants must also satisfy a minimum age or service requirement.

Source: U.S. Bureau of Labor Statistics, *National Compensation Survey: Employee Benefits in Private Industry in the United States, 2000. U.S. Department of Labor Bulletin 2555*, January 2003.

No. 535. Pension Plan Coverage of Workers by Selected Characteristics: 2002

[63,767 represents 63,767,000. Covers workers as of March 2003 who had earnings in 2002. Based on Current Population Survey; see text, Section 1, Population and Appendix III]

Sex and age	Number with coverage (1,000)				Percent of total workers			
	Total [1]	White [2]	Black [2]	Hispanic [3]	Total [1]	White [2]	Black [2]	Hispanic [3]
Total	63,767	53,514	6,648	4,803	41.9	42.5	40.0	25.6
Male	34,602	29,637	3,046	2,757	43.0	43.7	40.0	43.7
Under 65 years old	33,808	28,942	2,999	2,726	43.7	44.6	40.4	24.9
15 to 24 years old	1,630	1,363	190	224	13.2	13.2	15.0	10.1
25 to 44 years old	17,251	14,593	1,589	1,643	45.6	46.7	41.3	25.2
45 to 64 years old	14,926	12,986	1,220	859	55.0	55.6	52.9	38.3
65 years old and over	794	694	46	32	24.9	24.4	24.2	17.6
Female	29,165	23,878	3,602	2,046	40.8	41.2	40.0	26.9
Under 65 years old	28,509	23,312	3,548	2,019	41.3	41.8	40.3	26.9
15 to 24 years old	1,377	1,115	184	149	12.1	12.0	13.2	10.3
25 to 44 years old	14,282	11,414	1,930	1,241	43.7	44.3	41.6	29.2
45 to 64 years old	12,850	10,783	1,433	629	51.7	52.0	51.9	35.1
65 years old and over	656	565	55	27	26.2	25.6	27.9	25.2

[1] Includes other races, not shown separately.   [2] The 2003 CPS asked respondents to choose one or more races. White alone refers to people who reported White and did not report any other race category. Black alone refers to people who reported Black and did not report any other race category. The use of this single-race population does not imply that it is the preferred method of presenting or analyzing data. The Census Bureau uses a variety of approaches. Information on people who reported more than one race, such as "White and American Indian and Alaska Native" or "Asian and Black or African American," is available from Census 2000 through American FactFinder. About 2.6 percent of people reported more than one race in Census 2001.   [3] Hispanic persons may be of any race.

Source: U.S. Census Bureau, Table NC8. Pension Plan Coverage of Workers by Selected Characteristics, Gender, Race and Hispanic Origin, and Poverty Status: 2002"; published May 2004; <http://ferret.bls.census.gov/macro/032003/noncash/toc.htm>.

Social Insurance and Human Services   353

No. 536. U.S. Households Owning IRAs: 2001 to 2003

[In millions (43.0 represents 43.000,000). Incidence of IRA ownership is based on an annual tracking survey of 3,000 randomly selected, representative U.S. households conducted in July 2003]

Type of IRA	Number (mil.)			Percent of U.S. households		
	2001 [1]	2002 [2]	2003 [3]	2001 [1]	2002 [2]	2003 [3]
Any type of IRA [4]	43.0	43.2	45.2	39.7	39.5	41.4
Traditional IRA	35.1	35.7	36.4	32.4	32.7	33.3
Roth IRA	12.2	13.2	16.0	11.3	12.1	14.6
SIMPLE IRA, SEP-IRA, or SAR-SEP IRA	8.3	8.5	8.2	7.7	7.8	7.5

[1] The number of U.S. households owning IRAs in 2001 is based on the U.S. Census Bureau's revised estimate of 108.2 million total U.S. households in 2001. [2] The number of U.S. households owning IRAs in 2002 is based on the U.S. Census Bureau's revised estimate of 109.3 million total U.S. households in 2002. [3] The number of U.S. households owning IRAs in 2003 is based on the U.S. Census Bureau's most recent estimate of 109.3 million total U.S. households. [4] Excludes ownership of Coverdell Education Savings Accounts, which were referred to as Education IRAs before July 2001.

Source: Investment Company Institute, Washington, DC, *Fundamentals, Investment Company Institute Research in Brief*, "IRA Ownership in 2002"; Vol 12, No. 3, September 2003 (copyright). See also <http://www.nasi.org/publications2763/publications_list.htm?cat=Reports>.

No. 537. 401(k) Plans—Selected Features: 2000

[In percent, except as indicated (30,178 represents 30,178,000). Covers full-time employees in private industry. Based on National Compensation Survey, a sample survey of private industry establishments of all sizes, representing millions of workers; see Appendix III. See also Table 630]

Feature	All employees	Professional, technical, and related	Clerical and sales	Blue-collar and service
Full-time employees with 401(k) plan (1,000)	30,178	9,969	9,061	11,147
Transfers/rollovers allowed [1]	70	73	68	69
MAXIMUM PRETAX EMPLOYEE CONTRIBUTIONS [2]				
Percent of employee earnings	84	85	83	85
Specified dollar amount	1	1	1	1
Up to the Internal Revenue Code limit	15	14	16	14
Average maximum pretax contribution as percent of earnings [3]	15.3	15.0	15.1	15.7
INVESTMENT CHOICES				
Employee permitted to choose investments for employee contributions	88	89	88	89
Employee permitted to choose investments for employer contributions	64	65	62	63

[1] Participants are allowed to transfer/rollover contributions and earnings from a previous employer's plan. [2] Includes contributions that are not matched by the employer. If maximum contributions vary, such as by length of service, the highest possible contribution was tabulated. [3] The average is presented for all covered workers; averages exclude workers without the plan provision.

Source: U.S. Bureau of Labor Statistics, *National Compensation Survey: Employee Benefits in Private Industry in the United States*, 2000. See also <http://stats.bls.gov/ncs/home.htm>.

No. 538. State Unemployment Insurance—Summary: 1980 to 2003

[3,356 represents 3,356,000. Includes unemployment compensation for state and local government employees where covered by state law]

Item	Unit	1980	1990	1995	1997	1998	1999	2000	2001	2002	2003
Insured unemployment, avg. weekly	1,000	3,356	2,522	2,572	2,323	2,222	2,188	2,110	2,974	3,585	3,531
Percent of covered employment [1]	Percent	3.9	2.4	2.3	2.0	1.9	1.8	1.7	2.3	2.8	(NA)
Percent of civilian unemployed	Percent	43.9	35.8	34.7	34.5	35.8	38.0	38.0	45.0	44.0	40.2
Unemployment benefits, avg. weekly	Dollars	100	161	187	193	200	212	221	238	257	262
Percent of weekly wage	Percent	36.6	36.0	35.5	33.5	32.9	33.1	32.9	34.6	36.8	(NA)
Weeks compensated	Million	149.0	116.2	118.3	106.6	101.4	100.6	96.0	136.3	166.3	163.2
Beneficiaries, first payments	1,000	9,992	8,629	8,035	7,325	7,332	6,951	7,033	9,877	10,088	9,935
Average duration of benefits [2]	Weeks	14.9	13.4	14.7	14.6	13.8	14.5	13.7	13.8	16.5	16.4
Claimants exhausting benefits	1,000	3,072	2,323	2,662	2,485	2,266	2,300	2,144	2,827	4,416	4,417
Percent of first payment [3]	Percent	33.2	29.4	34.3	32.8	31.8	31.4	31.8	34.1	42.5	43.4
Contributions collected [4]	Bil. dol.	11.4	15.2	22.0	21.2	19.8	19.2	19.9	19.7	19.7	25.3
Benefits paid	Bil. dol.	14.2	18.1	21.2	19.7	19.4	20.3	20.5	31.6	42.0	41.4
Funds available for benefits [5]	Bil. dol.	6.6	37.9	35.4	43.8	48.0	50.3	54.1	46.6	35.7	24.2
Average employer contribution rate [6]	Percent	2.4	2.0	2.4	2.1	1.9	1.8	1.8	1.7	1.8	(NA)

NA Not available. [1] Insured unemployment as percent of average covered employment in preceding year. [2] Weeks compensated divided by first payment. [3] Based on first payments for 12-month period ending June 30. [4] Contributions from employers; also employees in states which tax workers. [5] End of year. Sum of balances in state clearing accounts, benefit-payment accounts, and state accounts in Federal unemployment trust funds. [6] As percent of taxable wages.

Source: U.S. Employment and Training Administration, *Unemployment Insurance Financial Data Handbook*.

No. 539. State Unemployment Insurance by State and Other Area: 2003

[9,935 represents 9,935,000. See headnote, Table 538. For state data on insured unemployment, see Table 610]

State or other area	Beneficiaries, first payments (1,000)	Benefits paid (mil. dol.)	Avg. weekly unemploy- ment benefits * (dol.)	State or other area	Beneficiaries, first payments (1,000)	Benefits paid (mil. dol.)	Avg. weekly unemploy- ment benefits (dol.)
Total	9,935	41,359	262	MT	27	81	202
AL........	141	301	176	NE	46	137	216
AK........	49	136	193	NV	78	305	236
AZ........	116	367	173	NH	23	117	259
AR........	103	301	229	NJ........	367	2,098	334
CA........	1,380	6,115	246	NM	37	136	211
CO........	115	536	308	NY	599	3,124	272
CT........	155	736	286	NC	348	955	258
DE........	33	130	235	ND	16	47	222
DC........	21	113	258	OH	353	1,452	252
FL........	326	1,159	225	OK	77	287	229
GA........	255	758	243	OR	186	856	258
HI........	30	135	312	PA........	566	2,678	292
ID........	60	184	232	RI........	43	208	309
IL........	455	2,455	281	SC	149	419	210
IN........	213	769	263	SD	12	33	202
IA........	114	377	260	TN........	201	580	210
KS........	89	372	276	TX........	533	2,204	261
KY........	136	470	250	UT........	57	214	269
LA........	100	297	195	VT........	28	101	255
ME........	33	128	231	VA........	166	606	276
MD........	130	527	252	WA	268	1,456	324
MA........	280	1,794	357	WV	55	184	220
MI........	502	1,988	291	WI........	315	973	252
MN........	170	850	322	WY	16	49	238
MS........	72	192	173	PR	106	228	107
MO........	183	627	206	VI	2	17	277

Source: U.S. Employment and Training Administration, *Unemployment Insurance Financial Data Handbook.*

No. 540. Persons With Work Disability by Selected Characteristics: 2003

[In thousands, except percent (18,058 represents 18,058,000). As of March. Covers civilian noninstitutional population and members of Armed Forces living off post or with their families on post. Persons are classified as having a work disability if they (1) have a health problem or disability which prevents them from working or which limits the kind or amount of work they can do; (2) have a service-connected disability or ever retired or left a job for health reasons; (3) did not work in survey reference week or previous year because of long-term illness or disability; or (4) are under age 65, and are covered by medicare or receive supplemental security income. Based on Current Population Survey; see text, Section 1, and Appendix III]

Age and participation status in assistance programs	Total [1]	Male	Female	White [2]	Black [2]	Hispanic [3]
Persons with work disability	18,058	8,751	9,308	13,541	3,515	1,998
16 to 24 years old......................	1,395	724	671	962	344	185
25 to 34 years old......................	2,173	992	1,181	1,516	515	334
35 to 44 years old......................	3,708	1,791	1,917	2,752	736	408
45 to 54 years old......................	5,010	2,480	2,530	3,739	1,007	515
55 to 64 years old......................	5,772	2,764	3,009	4,572	913	557
Percent work disabled of total population ...						
16 to 24 years old......................	3.9	4.0	3.8	3.4	6.7	3.1
25 to 34 years old......................	5.6	5.1	6.0	4.9	10.4	4.5
35 to 44 years old......................	8.5	8.3	8.6	7.8	13.7	6.9
45 to 54 years old......................	12.5	12.7	12.3	11.3	22.0	14.1
55 to 64 years old......................	21.1	21.0	21.1	19.6	34.8	26.5
Percent of work disabled—						
Receiving social security income............	33.4	33.6	33.2	34.7	30.3	27.2
Receiving food stamps	17.1	13.0	21.0	14.5	26.1	21.8
Covered by medicaid...................	65.7	69.0	62.5	69.1	53.5	56.6
Residing in public housing	6.9	5.0	8.7	4.9	14.6	8.9
Residing in subsidized housing	3.9	3.3	4.5	3.1	6.6	4.5

[1] Includes other races not shown separately. [2] The 2003 Current Population Survey asked respondents to choose one or more races. White alone refers to people who reported White and did not report any other race category. The use of this single-race population does not imply that it is the preferred method of presenting or analyzing data. The Census Bureau uses a variety of approaches. Information on people who reported more than one race, such as "White and American Indian and Alaska Native" or "Asian and Black or African American," is available from Census 2001 through American FactFinder. About 2.6 percent of people reported more than one race in 2000. [3] Hispanic persons may be of any race.

Source: U.S. Census Bureau, unpublished data.

Social Insurance and Human Services   355

No. 541. Workers' Compensation Payments: 1980 to 2001

[In billions of dollars, except as indicated (22.3 represents 22,300,000). See headnote, Table 542]

Item	1980	1990	1994	1995	1996	1997	1998	1999	2000	2001
Workers covered [1] (mil.)	79	106	109	113	115	118	122	124	127	127
Premium amounts paid [2]	22.3	53.1	60.5	57.1	55.3	51.6	51.7	54.0	58.2	62.8
Private carriers [2]	15.7	35.1	34.0	31.6	30.5	30.0	30.4	32.0	35.3	36.8
State funds	3.0	8.0	11.2	10.5	10.2	8.0	7.9	8.0	8.6	11
Federal programs [3]	1.1	2.2	2.5	2.6	2.6	2.0	2.1	2.9	2.2	2.3
Self-insurers	2.4	7.9	12.8	12.5	12.0	11.8	11.3	11.8	12.0	12.7
Annual benefits paid [2]	13.6	38.2	44.6	43.4	41.8	41.4	42.5	44.5	47.0	48.7
By private carriers [2]	7.0	22.2	22.3	21.1	20.4	21.6	23.1	24.6	26.4	26.9
From state funds [4]	4.3	8.8	10.8	11.0	10.6	7.3	7.2	7.3	7.6	8.1
Employers' self-insurance [5]	2.3	7.2	11.5	11.2	10.8	10.6	10.2	10.6	10.8	11.5
Type of benefit:										
Medical/hospitalization	3.9	15.2	17.2	16.7	16.5	17.2	17.9	19.1	20.6	21.9
Compensation payments	9.7	23.1	27.5	26.7	25.3	24.2	24.6	25.4	26.4	26.8
Percent of covered payroll: [1]										
Workers' compensation costs [6][7] .	1.96	2.18	2.05	1.83	1.66	1.49	1.37	1.34	1.34	1.41
Benefits [7]	1.07	1.57	1.51	1.39	1.26	1.14	1.08	1.06	1.03	1.04

[1] Data for year 1980 not comparable with later years. [2] Premium and benefit amounts include estimated payments under insurance policy deductible provisions. Deductible benefits are allocated to private carriers and state funds. [3] Years 1980-1996 includes federal employer compensation program and that portion of federal black lung benefits program financed from employer contributions. Years 1997-2001 includes federal employer compensation program only due to changes in reporting methods. [4] Net cash and medical benefits paid by competitive and exclusive state funds and by federal workers' compensation programs. [5] Cash and medical benefits paid by self-insurers, plus value of medical benefits paid by employers carrying workers' compensation policies that exclude standard medical coverage. [6] Premiums written by private carriers and state funds, and benefits paid by self-insurers increased by 5-10 percent from 1980 to 1990 and by 11 percent for 1994-2000 for administrative costs. Also includes benefits paid and administrative costs of federal system for government employees. [7] Excludes programs financed from general revenue—black lung benefits and supplemental pensions in some states.

Source: 1980-1990, U.S. Social Security Administration, *Annual Statistical Supplement* to the *Social Security Bulletin.* Beginning 1994, National Academy of Social Insurance, Washington, DC, *Workers' Compensation: Benefits, Coverage, and Costs,* annual.

No. 542. Workers' Compensation Payments by State: 1997 to 2001

[In millions of dollars (42,313 represents $42,313,000,000). Calendar-year data. Payments represent compensation and medical benefits and include insurance losses paid by private insurance carriers (compiled from state workers' compensation agencies and A.M. Best Co); disbursements of state funds (compiled from the A.M. Best Co. and state workers' compensation agencies); and self-insurance payments (compiled from state workers' compensation agencies and authors estimates)]

State	1997	1998	1999	2000	2001	State	1997	1998	1999	2000	2001
Total	42,313	43,355	45,197	47,684	49,354	Montana	143	137	146	170	173
						Nebraska	217	164	198	211	237
Alabama	530	602	551	529	563	Nevada	324	331	384	361	381
Alaska	128	127	130	146	171	New Hampshire	174	170	190	182	215
Arizona	450	433	466	515	393	New Jersey	1,080	1,097	1,152	1,198	1,198
Arkansas	170	171	173	194	201	New Mexico	136	128	136	146	162
California	7,074	7,366	7,852	8,968	9,604	New York	2,620	2,601	2,796	2,909	2,978
Colorado	820	811	739	835	581	North Carolina	687	810	814	853	868
Connecticut	732	715	737	667	661	North Dakota	68	69	70	74	80
Delaware	143	147	133	146	145	Ohio	2,036	2,077	2,039	2,099	2,249
District of Columbia .	88	90	90	89	92	Oklahoma	578	536	497	485	497
Florida	2,443	2,538	2,768	2,545	2,639						
Georgia	861	889	896	996	1,067	Oregon	417	431	384	412	456
Hawaii	255	233	222	231	252	Pennsylvania	2,492	2,418	2,467	2,403	2,440
Idaho	153	164	169	179	197	Rhode Island	113	109	111	109	115
Illinois	1,764	1,838	1,953	2,049	2,116	South Carolina	459	467	512	597	532
Indiana	446	481	511	546	528	South Dakota	70	67	73	67	75
Iowa	286	304	309	352	396	Tennessee	473	551	586	642	683
Kansas	314	319	326	342	340	Texas	1,477	1,592	1,875	2,005	2,043
Kentucky	451	421	478	479	525	Utah	170	189	196	188	209
						Vermont	86	91	106	112	105
Louisiana	440	442	465	494	502	Virginia	562	658	629	681	665
Maine	282	254	266	267	264	Washington	1,218	1,287	1,395	1,528	1,638
Maryland	717	691	714	730	787	West Virginia	614	644	687	690	712
Massachusetts	747	729	733	828	764	Wisconsin	670	704	724	768	922
Michigan	1,332	1,367	1,393	1,474	1,478	Wyoming	70	73	75	83	98
Minnesota	739	737	745	798	908						
Mississippi	231	235	254	269	271	Federal total [1]	2,780	2,868	2,862	2,957	3,069
Missouri	980	980	1,021	1,085	1,108	Federal employees .	1,901	2,010	2,000	2,119	2,223

[1] Federal benefits include: those paid under the Federal Employees Compensation Act for civilian employees; the portion of the Black Lung benefit program that is financed by employers; and a portion of benefits under the Longshore and Harbor Workers' Compensation Act that are not reflected in state data, namely, benefits paid by self-insured employers and by special funds under the LHWCA. See Appendix H of source for more information about federal programs.

Source: National Academy of Social Insurance, Washington, DC, *Workers' Compensation: Benefits, Coverage, and Costs,* annual. Also see <http://www.nasi.org/>

356   Social Insurance and Human Services

No. 543. Supplemental Security Income—Recipients and Payments: 1980 to 2002

[As of December, except total payments, calendar year (4,142 represents 4,142,000). See also Appendix III]

Program	Unit	1980	1990	1995	1997	1998	1999	2000	2001	2002
Recipients, total [1]	1,000	4,142	4,817	6,514	6,495	6,566	6,557	6,602	6,688	6,787
Aged	1,000	1,808	1,454	1,446	1,363	1,332	1,308	1,289	1,264	1,251
Blind	1,000	78	84	84	81	80	79	79	78	77
Disabled	1,000	2,256	3,279	4,984	5,052	5,154	5,169	5,234	5,345	5,459
Payments, total [2]	Mil. dol	7,941	16,599	27,628	29,052	30,216	30,923	31,564	32,165	33,718
Aged	Mil. dol	2,734	3,736	4,467	4,532	4,425	4,712	4,811	4,664	4,803
Blind	Mil. dol	190	334	376	375	366	391	394	398	416
Disabled	Mil. dol	5,014	12,521	22,779	24,006	25,305	25,719	26,198	27,103	28,499
Average monthly payment, total [1]	Dollars	168	299	358	351	359	368	378	393	407
Aged	Dollars	128	213	251	268	277	289	299	314	330
Blind	Dollars	213	342	370	382	390	401	413	428	445
Disabled	Dollars	198	337	389	373	380	388	397	412	425

[1] Persons with a federal SSI payment and/or federally administered state supplementation. [2] Includes payments not distributed by reason for eligibility.

Source: U.S. Social Security Administration, Social Security Bulletin, quarterly and Annual Statistical Supplement to the Social Security Bulletin.

No. 544. Supplemental Security Income (SSI)—Recipients and Payments by State and Other Area: 1995 to 2002

[Recipients as of December; payments for calendar year (6,514 represents 6,514,000). Data cover federal SSI payments and/or federally-administered state supplementation. For explanation of methodology, see Appendix III]

State and other area	Recipients (1,000)		Payments for year (mil. dol.)			State and other area	Recipients (1,000)		Payments for year (mil. dol.)		
	1995	2002	1995	2001	2002		1995	2002	1995	2001	2002
Total	6,514	6,789	27,037	32,166	33,722	MO	114	114	431	495	515
U.S.	6,513	6,788	27,035	32,163	33,719	MT	14	14	53	61	63
AL	165	164	600	698	730	NE	21	22	76	90	93
AK	7	10	27	40	44	NV	21	29	79	120	133
AZ	73	88	288	382	406	NH	11	12	39	52	56
AR	94	85	326	341	354	NJ	144	148	594	700	721
CA	1,032	1,136	5,391	6,685	7,230	NM	45	49	166	205	217
CO	57	54	217	237	243	NY	589	625	2,724	3,320	3,408
CT	45	50	181	227	236	NC	191	193	639	769	798
DE	11	13	40	53	56	ND	9	8	29	31	32
DC	20	20	83	98	102	OH	248	241	1,044	1,162	1,190
FL	338	397	1,300	1,724	1,814	OK	74	74	266	316	328
GA	199	199	692	826	854	OR	47	56	183	246	263
HI	19	22	82	107	111	PA	265	302	1,159	1,464	1,551
ID	17	19	63	81	87	RI	24	29	100	141	146
IL	267	252	1,160	1,208	1,247	SC	111	106	384	446	454
IN	89	91	348	399	424	SD	14	13	47	51	52
IA	42	42	148	167	175	TN	180	162	648	689	705
KS	38	37	141	158	164	TX	404	436	1,391	1,683	1,797
KY	165	177	635	779	803	UT	20	21	80	93	98
LA	182	167	717	741	761	VT	13	13	50	54	55
ME	31	31	96	123	131	VA	130	132	471	555	575
MD	82	90	332	420	435	WA	92	106	398	521	540
MA	164	167	700	833	849	WV	68	74	276	335	349
MI	210	214	896	1,021	1,065	WI	112	87	487	371	386
MN	62	67	235	289	303	WY	6	6	21	25	25
MS	141	127	504	530	543	N. Mariana	1	1	2	3	3

Source: U.S. Social Security Administration, Annual Statistical Supplement to the Social Security Bulletin.

No. 545. Temporary Assistance for Needy Families (TANF)—Families and Recipients: 1980 to 2003

[In thousands (3,712 represents 3,712,000). Average monthly families and recipients for calendar year. Prior to TANF, the cash assistance program to families was called Aid to Families with Dependent Children (1980-1996). Under the new welfare law (Personal Responsibility and Work Opportunity Reconciliation Act of 1996), the program became TANF. See text, this section. Includes Puerto Rico, Guam, and Virgin Islands]

Year	Families	Recipients	Year	Families	Recipients	Year	Families	Recipients
1980	3,712	10,774	1988	3,749	10,915	1996	4,434	12,321
1981	3,835	11,079	1989	3,799	10,993	1997	3,740	10,376
1982	3,542	10,258	1990	4,057	11,695	1998	3,050	8,347
1983	3,686	10,761	1991	4,467	12,930	1999	2,554	6,824
1984	3,714	10,831	1992	4,829	13,773	2000	2,215	5,778
1985	3,701	10,855	1993	5,012	14,205	2001	2,104	5,359
1986	3,763	11,038	1994	5,033	14,161	2002	2,048	5,069
1987	3,776	11,027	1995	4,791	13,418	2003	2,025	4,932

Source: U.S. Administration for Children and Families, unpublished data.

Social Insurance and Human Services 357

No. 546. Temporary Assistance for Needy Families (TANF)—Recipients by State and Other Areas: 2001 to 2003

[In thousands (2,104 represents 2,104,000). Average monthly families and recipients for calendar year, except as noted. See headnote, Table 545]

State or other area	Families 2001	2002	2003	Recipients 2001	2002	2003	State or other area	Families 2001	2002	2003	Recipients 2001	2002	2003
Total .	2,104	2,048	2,025	5,359	5,069	4,932	MT......	5	6	6	15	17	17
U.S....	2,075	2,023	2,002	5,273	4,994	4,867	NE......	10	11	11	24	26	27
AL......	18	18	19	44	42	46	NV......	8	12	10	21	28	24
AK......	6	6	5	17	17	15	NH......	6	6	6	14	14	14
AZ......	35	42	49	85	99	116	NJ......	44	42	43	110	102	104
AR......	12	12	11	28	27	25	NM......	18	17	17	51	46	45
CA......	465	459	450	1,177	1,146	1,107	NY......	218	158	148	580	369	336
CO......	11	12	14	28	32	37	NC......	43	42	40	93	89	83
CT......	26	23	21	59	51	43	ND......	3	3	3	8	8	9
DE......	5	6	6	12	12	13	OH......	84	84	84	195	189	187
DC......	16	16	17	43	42	43	OK......	14	15	15	35	37	37
FL......	58	59	58	123	122	120	OR......	17	18	19	38	42	43
GA......	51	54	56	121	130	134	PA......	82	80	82	214	209	214
HI	13	11	10	39	29	25	RI......	15	14	13	41	38	35
ID	1	1	2	2	2	3	SC......	20	22	21	48	54	51
IL......	58	45	36	169	123	92	SD......	3	3	3	6	7	6
IN	43	51	52	121	141	138	TN......	60	64	70	158	168	185
IA	20	20	20	55	53	52	TX......	130	131	129	344	333	318
KS	13	14	16	34	37	41	UT......	7	8	9	19	20	22
KY	36	35	35	81	77	77	VT......	5	5	5	14	13	13
LA	25	23	23	64	60	57	VA......	29	30	20	65	68	47
ME.....	10	10	10	26	26	26	WA	54	54	55	141	136	135
MD.....	28	27	26	68	63	62	WV	15	16	16	41	41	41
MA	43	48	50	101	109	109	WI	18	19	21	41	46	50
MI	72	73	77	198	198	206	WY	1	-	-	1	1	1
MN.....	38	36	36	108	95	94	PR......	26	22	19	73	63	53
MS.....	16	18	20	37	42	45	GU.....	3	3	3	10	11	11
MO.....	45	44	41	121	115	101	VI.....	1	1	-	2	2	1

- Represents or rounds to zero.

Source: U.S. Administration for Children and Families, unpublished data.

No. 547. Temporary Assistance for Needy Families (TANF)—Expenditures by State: 2000 to 2002

[In millions of dollars (24,781 represents $24,781,000,000). Represents federal and state funds expended in fiscal year]

State	2000, total	2001, total	2002 Total [1]	2002 Expenditures on assistance	State	2000, total	2001, total	2002 Total [1]	2002 Expenditures on assistance
U.S....	24,781	25,667	25,414	11,222	MO	321	342	326	205
AL......	96	105	135	35	MT......	44	51	61	34
AK......	93	86	93	67	NE......	79	63	77	52
AZ......	261	274	309	131	NV......	69	61	89	54
AR......	139	90	70	26	NH......	73	64	72	37
CA......	6,481	6,466	5,477	3,428	NJ	321	555	952	239
CO......	205	189	233	55	NM......	149	153	123	83
CT......	436	413	436	154	NY......	3,512	3,805	3,852	1,899
DE......	55	56	56	36	NC......	440	475	471	138
DC......	157	167	209	67	ND......	33	37	33	17
FL......	781	926	993	304	OH......	995	1,158	901	351
GA......	386	474	511	69	OK......	130	124	148	113
HI	162	150	137	85	OR......	169	291	258	108
ID......	43	46	39	5	PA......	1,327	975	1,063	358
IL......	879	956	971	151	RI......	172	162	174	98
IN	342	352	328	160	SC......	245	128	134	38
IA	163	159	150	78	SD......	21	21	23	15
KS	151	150	137	85	TN......	293	283	311	161
KY.....	203	211	207	113	TX......	727	753	741	267
LA	118	128	240	68	UT......	100	80	110	53
ME.....	108	100	104	87	VT......	62	61	69	45
MD.....	336	395	428	227	VA	418	255	264	101
MA	690	681	670	298	WA	535	659	628	295
MI	1,264	1,249	1,267	239	WV	134	205	214	106
MN.....	381	430	466	184	WI	382	494	489	126
MS.....	62	131	144	65	WY	34	29	22	8

[1] Includes other items not shown separately.

Source: U.S. Administration for Children and Families, *Temporary Assistance for Needy Families (TANF) Program, Annual Report to Congress.*

No. 548. Child Support—Award and Recipiency Status of Custodial Parent: 2001

[In thousands except as noted (13,383 represents 13,383,000). Custodial parents 15 years and older with own children under 21 years of age present from absent parents as of spring 2002. Covers civilian noninstitutional population. Based on Current Population Survey; see text, section 1, and Appendix III. For definition of mean, see Guide to Tabular Presentation]

Award and recipiency status	All custodial parents				Custodial parents below the poverty level			
	Total				Total			
	Number	Percent distribu- tion	Mothers	Fathers	Number	Percent distribu- tion	Mothers	Fathers
Total.....................	13,383	(X)	11,291	2,092	3,131	(X)	2,823	308
With child support agreement or award ...	7,916	(X)	7,110	807	1,706	(X)	1,571	135
Supposed to receive payments in 2001..	6,924	100.0	6,212	712	1,469	100.0	1,339	130
Actually received payments in 2001..	5,119	73.9	4,639	480	963	65.6	885	77
Received full amount	3,099	44.8	2,821	278	453	30.8	423	30
Received partial payments.......	2,020	29.2	1,818	202	510	34.7	463	47
Did not receive payments in 2001....	1,804	26.1	1,573	232	507	34.5	454	53
Child support not awarded............	5,466	(X)	4,181	1,285	1,425	(X)	1,253	172
MEAN INCOME AND CHILD SUPPORT								
Received child support payments in 2001:								
Mean total money income (dol.).......	29,008	(X)	28,258	36,255	7,571	(X)	7,604	7,189
Mean child support received (dol.).....	4,274	(X)	4,274	4,273	3,041	(X)	3,078	2,622
Received the full amount due:								
Mean total money income (dol.)...	32,338	(X)	31,734	38,479	7,963	(X)	7,958	8,032
Mean child support received (dol.)..	5,665	(X)	5,655	5,768	4,576	(X)	4,701	2,831
Received partial payments:								
Mean total money income (dol.)...	23,899	(X)	22,865	33,199	7,223	(X)	7,281	6,647
Mean child support received (dol.)..	2,141	(X)	2,132	2,219	1,677	(X)	1,595	2,487
Received no payments in 2001:								
Mean total money income (dol.).......	23,571	(X)	21,835	35,348	6,832	(X)	6,755	7,492
Without child support agreement or award:								
Mean total money income (dol.).......	24,055	(X)	19,339	39,396	6,113	(X)	6,089	6,287

X Not applicable.

Source: U.S. Census Bureau, unpublished data.

No. 549. Child Support Enforcement Program—Caseload and Collections: 1990 to 2003

[For years ending Sept. 30 (12,796 represents 12,796,000). Includes Puerto Rico, Guam, and the Virgin Islands. The child support enforcement program locates absent parents, establishes paternity of children born out-of-wedlock, and establishes and enforces support orders. By law, these services are available to all families that need them. The program is operated at the state and local government level but 68 percent of administrative costs are paid by the federal government. Child support collected for families not receiving Temporary Assistance for Needy Families (TANF) goes to the family to help it remain self-sufficient. Most of the child support collected on behalf of TANF families goes to federal and state governments to offset TANF payments. Some states pass-through a portion of the CS collections to help families become self-sufficient. Based on data reported by state agencies. Minus sign (-) indicates net outlay]

Item	Unit	1990	1995	1998	1999	2000	2001	2002	2003, prel.
Total cases [1].................	1,000...	12,796	19,162	19,419	17,330	17,334	17,061	16,066	15,923
Paternities established, total [2]......	1,000...	393	659	848	845	867	777	697	663
Support orders established, total [3]....	1,000...	1,022	1,051	1,148	1,220	1,175	1,181	1,220	1,161
FINANCES									
Collections, total	Mil. dol .	6,010	10,827	14,348	15,901	17,854	18,958	20,137	21,176
TANF/FC collections [4]............	Mil. dol .	1,750	2,689	2,650	2,482	2,593	2,592	2,893	2,972
State share	Mil. dol .	620	939	1,089	1,048	1,080	1,004	947	948
Incentive payments to states......	Mil. dol .	264	400	396	377	353	337	338	356
Federal share [5]	Mil. dol .	533	822	961	922	968	895	1,183	1,167
Non-TANF collections	Mil. dol .	4,260	8,138	11,698	13,419	15,261	16,366	17,244	18,204
Administrative expenditures, total .	Mil. dol .	1,606	3,012	3,585	4,039	4,526	4,835	5,183	5,213
State share	Mil. dol .	545	918	1,200	1,359	1,519	1,613	1,752	1,764
Federal share	Mil. dol .	1,061	2,095	2,385	2,680	3,006	3,222	3,432	3,448
Program savings, total	Mil. dol .	-190	-852	-1,139	-1,692	-2,125	-2,599	-3,053	-3,098
State share	Mil. dol .	338	421	286	66	-87	-272	-463	-461
Federal share	Mil. dol .	-528	-1,273	-1,424	-1,758	-2,038	-2,327	-2,590	-2,637

[1] Passage of The Personal Responsibilty and Work Opportunity Reconciliation Act mandated new categories in 1999 and cases were no longer double counted resulting in a 2 million case reduction.   [2] Does not include in-hospital paternities. [3] Through 1990 includes modifications to orders.   [4] Collections for current assistance cases where the children are: (1) recipients of TANF under title IV-A of the Social Security Act or (2) entitled to Foster Care (FC) maintenance under title IV-E of the Social Security Act plus collections distributed as assistance reimbursements. Includes medical support and payments to families of current assistance not shown separately. Assistance reimbursements are collections that will be divided between the state and federal govenrments to reimburse their respective shares of either Title IV-A assistance payments or Title IV-E Foster Care maintenance payments.   [5] Prior to fiscal year 2000, incentives were paid out of the federal share of collections and the net federal share was reported.

Source: U.S. Department of Health and Human Services, Office of Child Support Enforcement, Annual Report to Congress.

Social Insurance and Human Services   359

No. 550. Federal Food Programs: 1990 to 2003

[20.1 represents 20,100,000. For years ending Sept. 30. Program data include Puerto Rico, Virgin Islands, Guam, American Samoa, Northern Marianas, and the former Trust Territory when a federal food program was operated in these areas. Participation data are average monthly figures except as noted. Participants are not reported for the commodity distribution programs. Cost data are direct federal benefits to recipients; they exclude Federal administrative payments and applicable state and local contributions. Federal costs for commodities and cash-in-lieu of commodities are shown separately from direct cash benefits for those programs receiving both]

Program	Unit	1990	1995	1998	1999	2000	2001	2002	2003
Food Stamp:									
Participants	Million . .	20.1	26.6	19.8	18.2	17.1	17.3	19.1	21.3
Federal cost.	Mil. dol. .	14,187	22,765	16,889	15,755	14,952	15,547	18,257	21,407
Monthly average coupon value per recipient .	Dollars . .	58.92	71.26	71.12	72.21	72.70	74.83	79.68	83.90
Nutrition assistance program for Puerto Rico:									
Federal cost.	Mil. dol. .	937	1,131	1,204	1,236	1,268	1,296	1,351	1,377
National school lunch program (NSLP):									
Free lunches served	Million . .	1,662	2,090	2,198	2,207	2,205	2,182	2,278	2,334
Reduced-price lunches served	Million . .	273	309	362	392	409	425	441	453
Children participating [1]	Million . .	24.1	25.7	26.6	26.9	27.2	27.5	28.0	28.4
Federal cost.	Mil. dol. .	3,214	4,466	5,102	5,314	5,493	5,612	6,051	6,339
School breakfast (SB):									
Children participating [1]	Million . .	4.1	6.3	7.1	7.4	7.6	7.8	8.1	8.4
Federal cost.	Mil. dol. .	596	1,049	1,272	1,345	1,393	1,450	1,567	1,651
Special supplemental food program (WIC): [2]									
Participants	Million . .	4.5	6.9	7.4	7.3	7.2	7.3	7.5	7.6
Federal cost.	Mil. dol. .	1,637	2,517	2,808	2,853	2,852	3,008	3,131	3,224
Child and adult care food program (CACFP): [3]									
Participants [4]	Million . .	1.5	2.4	2.6	2.7	2.7	2.7	2.9	2.9
Federal cost.	Mil. dol. .	720	1,296	1,372	1,438	1,501	1,548	1,658	1,728
Federal cost of commodities donated to— [5]									
Child nutrition (NSLP, CACFP, SFS, and SBP)	Mil. dol. .	646	733	774	754	704	917	862	908
Emergency feeding [6]	Mil. dol. .	286	100	190	234	182	333	380	396

[1] Average monthly participation (excluding summer months of June through August). Includes children in public and private elementary and secondary schools and in residential child care institutes. [2] WIC serves pregnant and postpartum women, infants, and children up to age five. [3] CACFP provides year-round subsidies to feed preschool children in child care centers and family day care homes. Certain care centers serving disabled or elderly adults also receive meal subsidies. [4] Average quarterly daily attendance at participating institutions. [5] Includes the Federal cost of commodity entitlements, cash-in-lieu of commodities, and bonus foods. [6] Provides free commodities to needy persons for home consumption through food banks, hunger centers, soup kitchens, and similar nonprofit agencies. Includes the Emergency Food Assistance Program, the commodity purchases for soup kitchens/food banks program (FY 1989-96), and commodity disaster relief.

Source: U.S. Dept. of Agriculture, Food and Nutrition Service, Food and Nutrition Service, Program Data; <http://www.fns.usda.gov/pd/>; updated monthly.

No. 551. Federal Food Stamp Program by State: 2001 to 2003

[Participation data are average monthly number (17,313 represents 17,313,000). For years ending Sept. 30. Food stamp costs are for benefits only and exclude administrative expenditures]

State	Persons (1,000)			Benefits (mil. dol.)			State	Persons (1,000)			Benefits (mil. dol.)		
	2001	2002	2003	2001	2002	2003		2001	2002	2003	2001	2002	2003
Total [1] . .	17,313	19,094	21,262	15,547	18,257	21,407	MS	298	325	356	254	298	335
U.S.	17,277	19,057	21,225	15,492	18,188	21,335	MO	454	515	592	395	477	568
							MT	62	63	71	54	58	69
AL.	411	444	472	365	417	466	NE	81	88	99	63	74	89
AK.	38	46	51	46	59	66	NV.	69	97	111	65	96	113
AZ.	291	379	466	280	386	498	NH	36	41	45	28	35	40
AR.	256	284	310	223	265	304							
CA.	1,668	1,710	1,708	1,583	1,707	1,808	NJ.	318	320	339	292	314	339
CO	154	178	208	131	165	203	NM	163	170	195	136	154	184
CT.	157	169	181	136	146	165	NY.	1,354	1,347	1,435	1,365	1,479	1,677
DE.	32	40	46	32	39	48	NC	494	574	649	425	536	645
DC	73	74	82	70	76	90	ND	38	37	40	27	31	37
FL.	887	985	1,041	771	878	988	OH	641	735	855	573	726	879
							OK	271	317	380	236	288	362
GA	574	646	750	515	621	782	OR	284	359	398	240	319	381
HI	108	106	100	150	152	156	PA.	748	767	823	639	700	785
ID	60	70	82	47	62	77	RI	71	72	74	59	64	69
IL	825	886	954	810	923	1,053							
IN	347	411	470	317	408	484	SC.	316	379	451	269	352	443
IA	126	141	154	107	129	149	SD.	45	48	51	39	45	51
KS.	124	140	161	92	113	140	TN.	522	598	728	454	552	722
KY.	413	450	503	350	410	486	TX.	1,361	1,554	1,875	1,270	1,522	1,881
LA.	518	588	655	483	587	685	UT.	80	90	106	67	80	102
ME	104	111	133	86	97	124	VT.	39	40	41	31	34	38
							VA.	332	352	394	263	305	366
MD	208	228	252	191	215	257	WA	309	350	404	261	318	394
MA	219	243	292	173	209	254	WV	221	236	247	178	198	216
MI	641	750	838	504	645	783	WI	216	262	297	152	197	233
MN	198	217	235	172	201	227	WY	23	24	25	19	22	24

[1] Includes Guam and the Virgin Islands. Several outlying areas receive nutrition assistance grants in lieu of food stamp assistance (e.g., Puerto Rico, American Samoa and the Northern Marianas).

Source: U.S. Dept. of Agriculture, Food and Nutrition Service. Food and Nutrition Service, Program Data; <http://www.fns.usda.gov/pd/>; updated monthly.

360 Social Insurance and Human Services

No. 552. Selected Characteristics of Food Stamp Households and Participants: 1990 to 2002

[7,803 represents 7,803,000. For years ending September 30. Data for 1990 exclude Guam and the Virgin Islands. Based on a sample of households from the Food Stamp Quality Control System]

Year	Households				Participants		
	Total (1,000)	Percent of total			Total (1,000)	Percent of total	
		With children	With elderly [1]	With disabled [2]		Children	Elderly [1]
1990......	7,803	60.3	18.1	8.9	20,411	49.6	7.7
1993......	10,791	62.1	15.5	10.7	27,595	51.5	6.8
1994......	11,091	61.1	15.8	12.5	28,009	51.4	7.0
1995......	10,883	59.7	16.0	18.9	26,955	51.5	7.1
1996......	10,552	59.5	16.2	20.2	25,926	51.0	7.3
1997......	9,452	58.3	17.6	22.3	23,117	51.4	7.9
1998......	8,246	58.3	18.2	24.4	19,969	52.8	8.2
1999......	7,670	55.7	20.1	26.5	18,149	51.5	9.4
2000......	7,335	53.9	21.0	27.5	17,091	51.3	10.0
2001......	7,450	53.6	20.4	27.7	17,297	51.1	9.6
2002......	8,201	54.1	18.7	27.0	19,041	51.0	8.9

[1] Persons 60 years old and over. [2] Beginning 1995, disabled households are defined as households with at least one member under age 65 who received SSI, or at least one member age 18 to 61 who received Social Security, veterans benefits, or other government benefits as a result of a disability. For years prior to 1995, disabled households are defined as households with SSI but no members over age 59. The substantial increase in the percentage of households with a disabled member between 1994 and 1995 is due in part to the change in the definition of disabled households. Using the previous definition, 13.3 percent of households included a disabled person in fiscal year 1995.

No. 553. Food Stamp Households and Participants—Summary: 2002

[8,201 represents 8,201,000. For year ending September 30. Based on a sample of 46,963 households from the Food Stamp Quality Control System]

Household type and income source	Households		Age, sex, race, and Hispanic origin	Participants	
	Number (1,000)	Percent		Number (1,000)	Percent
Total........................	8,201	100.0	Total..................	19,041	100.0
With children....................	4,437	54.1	Children...................	9,712	51.0
Single-parent households..........	2,825	34.5	Under 5 years old...........	3,224	16.9
Married-couple households.........	778	9.5	5 to 17 years old	6,488	34.1
Other	834	18.8	Adults	7,636	40.1
With elderly.....................	1,537	18.7	18 to 35 years old	3,994	21.0
Living alone....................	1,233	15.0	36 to 59 years old	3,642	19.1
Not living alone.................	303	3.7	60 years old and over........	1,687	8.9
Disabled........................	2,213	27.0			
Living alone....................	1,300	15.8	Male	7,769	40.8
Not living alone.................	914	11.1	Female	11,269	59.2
Earned income....................	2,299	28.0	White, non-Hispanic..........	7,925	41.6
Wages and salaries..............	1,919	23.4	Black, non-Hispanic..........	6,650	34.9
Unearned income.................	6,177	75.3	Hispanic...................	3,467	18.2
TANF [1]	1,716	20.9	Asian.....................	537	2.8
Supplemental Security Income........	2,417	29.5	Native American	303	1.6
Social Security.................	1,995	24.3	Other.....................	159	0.8
No income	865	10.5			

[1] Temporary Assistance for Needy Families (TANF) program.

Source of Tables 552 and 553: U.S. Dept. of Agriculture, Food and Nutrition Service, *Characteristics of Food Stamp Households: Fiscal Year 2002*, December 2003.

No. 554. Head Start—Summary: 1980 to 2003

[For years ending September 30 (376 represents 376,000)]

Year	Enrollment (1,000)	Appropriation (mil. dol.)	Age and race	Enrollment, 2003 (percent)	Item	Number
1980 ...	376	735	Under 3 years old	8	Average cost per child:	
1985 ...	452	1075	3 years old..........	34	1995	$4,534
1990 ...	541	1,552	4 years old..........	53	2000	$5,951
1994 ...	740	3,326	5 years old and over ...	5	2003	$7,092
1995 ...	751	3,534				
1996 ...	752	3,569			Paid staff (1,000):	
1997 ...	794	3,981	White	28	1995	147
1998 ...	822	4,347	Black	32	2000	180
1999 ...	826	4,658	Hispanic	31	2003	206
2000 ...	858	5,267	American Indian	3	Volunteers (1,000):	
2001 ...	905	6,200	Asian	2	1995	1,235
2002 ...	912	6,537	Hawaiian/		2000	1,252
2003 ...	910	6,668	Pacific Islander	1	2003	1,372

Source: U.S. Administration for Children and Families, Head Start Statistical Fact Sheet; <http://www2.acf.dhhs.gov/programs/hsb/research /index.htm>.

Social Insurance and Human Services 361

No. 555. Social Assistance—Taxable Establishments, Receipts, Payroll, and Employees by Kind of Business: 1997

[18,051 represents $18,051,000,000. For combined social assistance taxable and tax-exempt data, see T. 728]

Kind of business	NAICS code [1]	All firms		Employer firms			
		Establish-ments (number)	Receipts (mil. dol.)	Establish-ments (number)	Receipts (mil. dol.)	Annual payroll (mil. dol.)	Paid employ-ees [2] (1,000)
Social assistance	624	583,203	18,051	56,691	12,599	5,766	491.1
Individual & family services	6241	43,070	3,228	9,843	2,636	1,113	68.8
Child & youth services	62411	(NA)	(NA)	1,648	539	210	11.5
Services for elderly & disabled persons . . .	62412	(NA)	(NA)	2,976	807	394	32.2
Other individual & family services	62419	(NA)	(NA)	5,219	1,290	508	25.1
Community/emergency & other relief services	6242	1,682	136	344	112	29	1.6
Community food services	62421	(NA)	(NA)	95	18	4	0.4
Community housing services	62422	(NA)	(NA)	167	74	21	1.0
Emergency & other relief services	62423	(NA)	(NA)	82	20	4	0.2
Vocational rehabilitation services	6243	5,762	1,514	2,549	1,432	676	32.0
Child day care services	6244	532,689	13,172	43,955	8,419	3,948	388.7

NA Not available. [1] North American Industry Classification System, 1997; see text, Section 15. [2] For pay period including March 12.

No. 556. Social Assistance—Tax-Exempt Establishments, Receipts, Payroll, and Employees by Kind of Business: 1997

[44,756 represents $44,756,000,000. Covers establishments with payroll only. For combined social assistance taxable and tax-exempt data, see T. 728]

Kind of business	NAICS code [1]	Establishments (number)	Receipts (mil. dol.)	Annual payroll (mil. dol.)	Paid employees [2] (1,000)
Social assistance	624	69,737	44,756	18,628	1,253.1
Individual & family services	6241	36,364	26,453	10,781	642.6
Child & youth services	62411	11,086	7,719	3,171	172.0
Services for elderly & disabled persons	62412	9,960	8,217	3,260	226.7
Other individual & family services	62419	15,318	10,516	4,350	243.9
Community/emergency & other relief services . .	6242	9,606	6,085	1,739	100.8
Community food services	62421	2,988	1,598	324	23.0
Community housing services	62422	4,737	2,954	1,079	60.2
Emergency & other relief services	62423	1,881	1,534	336	17.7
Vocational rehabilitation services	6243	5,668	6,462	3,093	269.7
Child day care services	6244	18,099	5,757	3,015	240.0

[1] North American Industry Classification System, 1997; see text, Section 15. [2] For pay period including March 12.

Source of Tables 555 and 556: U.S. Census Bureau, *1997 Economic Census, Health Care and Social Assistance*, Series EC97S62A-US, issued October 1999 and *Nonemployer Statistics*.

No. 557. Social Assistance Services—Revenue for Employer Firms: 2000 to 2002

[In millions of dollars (74,158 represents $74,158,000,000). Based on the North American Industry Classification System 1997 (NAICS), see text, Section 15. See Appendix III]

Kind of business	NAICS code	2000, total	2001, total	2002		
				Total	Taxable firms	Tax-exempt firms
Social assistance	624	74,158	82,628	88,347	19,910	68,436
Individual and family services	6241	37,318	41,958	44,571	4,557	40,014
Child and youth services	62411	9,993	11,316	11,868	894	10,974
Services for elderly and disabled persons . . .	62412	11,311	12,468	13,418	1,465	11,954
Other individual and family services	62419	16,014	18,175	19,284	2,198	17,086
Community, emergency and other relief services	6242	7,736	8,476	9,055	490	8,565
Community food services	62421	2,194	2,371	2,512	(S)	2,267
Community housing services	62422	3,855	4,312	4,651	215	4,436
Emergency and other relief services	62423	1,688	1,793	1,893	(S)	1,863
Vocational rehabilitation services	6243	10,919	11,879	12,733	2,295	10,438
Child day care services	6244	18,184	20,314	21,988	12,569	9,419

S Figure does not meet publication standards.

Source: U.S. Census Bureau, *Service Annual Survey, 2002*. See also <http://www.census.gov/svsd/www/sas62.html>.

No. 558. Social Assistance—Nonemployer Establishments and Receipts: 1999 to 2001

[Receipts in millions of dollars (6,793 represents $6,793,000,000). Includes only firms subject to federal income tax. Nonemployers are businesses with no paid employees. Based on the North American Industry Classification System 1997 (NAICS), see text, Section 15]

Kind of business	NAICS code	Establishments			Receipts		
		1999	2000	2001	1999	2000	2001
Social assistance, total	624	605,113	642,946	675,764	6,793	7,539	8,228
Individual & family services	6241	63,775	72,433	79,250	949	1,106	1,276
Community/emergency & other relief services . .	6242	3,333	3,560	3,976	45	54	63
Vocational rehabilitation services.	6243	6,731	7,314	8,115	134	151	164
Child day care services	6244	531,274	559,639	584,423	5,665	6,228	6,725

Source: U.S. Census Bureau, Nonemployer Statistics; published September 2003; <http://www.census.gov/epcd/nonemployer/>.

No. 559. Child Care Arrangements of Preschool Children by Type of Arrangement: 1991 to 2001

[In percent, except as indicated (8,428 represents 8,428,000). Estimates are based on children 3 to 5 years old who have not entered kindergarten. Based on interviews from a sample survey of the civilian, noninstitutional population in households with telephones; see source for details. See also Appendix III]

Characteristic	Children		Type of nonparental arrangement [1]			
	Number (1,000)	Percent distribution	In relative care	In nonrelative care	In center-based program [2]	With parental care only
1991, total.	8,428	100.0	16.9	14.8	52.8	31.0
1995, total	9,232	100.0	19.4	16.9	55.1	25.9
2001, total	8,551	100.0	22.8	14.1	56.4	26.1
Age:						
3 years old	3,795	44.4	23.6	14.7	42.8	33.8
4 years old	3,861	45.1	22.5	13.6	65.9	20.4
5 years old	896	10.5	20.9	13.1	73.0	18.0
Race-ethnicity:						
White, non-Hispanic	5,313	62.1	19.6	16.5	59.1	25.3
Black, non-Hispanic.	1,251	14.6	36.7	8.5	63.1	15.1
Hispanic	1,506	17.6	22.8	11.3	39.9	39.0
Other	482	5.6	22.8	10.8	61.8	23.7
Household income:						
Less than $10,001	951	11.1	37.1	6.2	45.6	30.5
$10,001 to $20,000.	1,156	13.5	23.5	10.8	50.6	32.3
$20,001 to $30,000	1,134	13.3	24.3	10.4	49.3	32.4
$30,001 to $40,000	978	11.4	24.5	12.6	48.9	32.2
$40,001 to $50,000	822	9.6	21.9	15.2	42.9	36.4
$50,001 to $75,000	1,724	20.2	20.7	18.6	62.3	20.9
$75,001 or more.	1,788	20.9	15.3	18.6	75.1	12.8

[1] Columns do not add to 100 because some children participated in more than one type of nonparental arrangement.
[2] Center-based programs include day care centers, head start programs, preschools, prekindergarten, and nursery schools.

Source: U.S. Department of Education, National Center for Education Statistics, Early Childhood Program Participation Survey of the National Household Education Surveys Program (NHES), 2001.

No. 560. Licensed Child Care Centers and Family Child Care Providers by State and Other Area: 2003

[Centers as of February; family child care providers as of August]

State	Licensed child care centers	Licensed family child care providers	State	Licensed child care centers	Licensed family child care providers	State	Licensed child care centers	Licensed family child care providers
US, total. .	115,473	299,923	KY	2,173	9,184	OH	3,499	14,487
AL	1,340	1,951	LA	1,920	7,894	OK	1,974	4,558
AK	230	1,371	ME	835	1,834	OR	1,013	5,457
AZ	2,084	4,275	MD	2,547	10,421	PA	3,948	4,796
AR	2,574	1,192	MA	3,242	9,863	RI	436	1,288
CA	14,331	47,049	MI	4,835	14,721	SC	2,288	1,890
CO	2,844	4,735	MN	1,625	13,879	SD	271	1,029
CT	1,622	3,277	MS	1,792	589	TN	3,404	2,089
DE	320	1,671	MO	1,798	2,114	TX	10,870	14,386
DC	371	230	MT	268	1,164	UT	336	2,115
FL	6,641	8,190	NE	839	3,227	VT	623	1,320
GA	2,600	6,564	NV	458	597	VA	2,573	3,632
HI	521	429	NH	822	368	WA	2,219	7,259
ID	790	1,235	NJ	4,100	5,100	WV	606	5,023
IL	3,125	10,900	NM	618	9,279	WI.	2,410	8,293
IN	659	3,659	NY	3,705	14,553	WY	257	514
IA	1,497	5,845	NC	4,151	4,966	PR	702	41
KS	1,338	7,307	ND	131	2,154	VI	234	67

Source: Children's Foundation, Washington, DC, Child Care Center Licensing Study and Family Child Care Licensing Study, annual (copyright).

U.S. Census Bureau, Statistical Abstract of the United States: 2004-2005

No. 561. Charity Contributions—Average Dollar Amount: 1991 to 2000

[Estimates cover households' contribution activity (both cash and in-kind) for the year and are based on respondents' replies as to contribution and volunteer activity of household. For 2000, based on a sample survey of 4,216 persons 21 years old and over conducted during the spring of the following year and subject to sampling variability; see source]

Year and age	All contributing households Average amount (dol.)	All contributing households Percent of household income	Contributors and volunteers Average amount (dol.)	Contributors and volunteers Percent of household income	Household income	All contributing households Average amount (dol.)	All contributing households Percent of household income	Contributors and volunteers Average amount (dol.)	Contributors and volunteers Percent of household income
1991	899	2.2	1,155	2.6	**2000—**				
1995	1,017	2.2	1,279	2.6	Under $10,000 . . .	296	5.5	382	6.7
					$10,000-$19,999 . .	465	3.3	624	4.4
2000, total . . .	1,623	3.2	2,295	4.0	$20,000-$29,999 . .	916	3.9	1,299	5.5
21-24 years	958	2.3	1,635	3.1	$30,000-$39,999 . .	1,036	3.1	1,408	4.2
25-34 years	1,002	2.3	1,411	3.1	$40,000-$49,999 . .	1,147	2.7	1,638	3.8
35-44 years	1,831	2.8	2,471	3.5	$50,000-$59,999 . .	1,566	3.0	1,989	3.8
45-54 years	1,818	2.9	2,632	3.8	$60,000-$74,999 . .	1,935	3.0	2,483	3.8
55-64 years	1,888	3.3	2,626	4.3	$75,000-$99,999 . .	2,119	2.6	2,530	3.1
65-74 years	1,798	4.5	2,307	5.5	$100,000 and over .	3,976	2.7	4,894	3.3
75 years and over. .	1,628	5.1	2,498	6.5					
					Itemizers [1]	2,288	3.6	2,903	4.3
White	1,693	3.2	2,359	4.0	Claimed charitable				
Black	1,488	3.3	2,300	4.3	deduction	2,733	4.0	3,262	4.6
					Didn't claim chari-				
Hispanic [2]	1,276	2.5	2,285	3.6	table deduction . .	868	2.4	1,207	2.9
					Non-itemizers	954	2.7	1,464	3.6

[1] Persons who itemized their deductions on their 2000 federal tax returns. [2] Hispanic persons may be of any race.

No. 562. Charity Contributions—Percent of Households Contributing by Dollar Amount, 1991 to 2000, and Type of Charity, 2000

[In percent, except as noted. See headnote, Table 561]

Annual amount of household contributions	All households 1991	All households 1995	All households 2000	Givers 1991	Givers 1995	Givers 2000	Type of charity	2000 Percentage of households	2000 Average contribution (dol.)
None	27.8	31.5	11.7	(X)	(X)	(X)	Arts, culture, humanities .	16.6	234
Givers	72.2	68.5	88.3	100.0	100.0	100.0	Education	29.9	508
$1 to $100. . .	14.9	15.2	14.2	24.9	24.3	17.6	Environment	19.0	195
$101 to $200 . . .	8.1	7.2	8.6	13.5	11.6	10.6	Health	38.0	224
$201 to $300 . .	7.3	5.7	5.7	12.2	9.2	7.1	Human services	34.7	338
$301 to $400 . .	3.3	4.7	3.8	5.6	7.5	4.7	International	6.3	254
$401 to $500 . .	3.2	5.2	4.3	5.4	8.3	5.3	Private, community		
$501 to $600 . .	2.6	3.0	3.2	4.4	4.7	4.0	foundations	7.3	238
$601 to $700 . .	2.5	2.6	3.1	4.2	4.1	3.8	Public, societal benefit . .	11.1	251
$701 to $999 . .	3.4	3.7	6.2	5.7	6.0	7.7	Recreation - adults	5.9	371
$1,000 or more. .	14.5	15.2	31.9	24.2	24.3	39.4	Religion	60.6	1,358
Not reported . .	12.4	5.9	7.3	(X)	(X)	(X)	Youth development	33.8	254

X Not applicable. [1] Average contribution per household making a contribution to the specified type of charity.
Source of Tables 561 and 562: Toppe, Chris, Arthur Kirsch, and Westat, Inc., *Giving and Volunteering in the United States: 2001 Edition.* (Copyright and published by INDEPENDENT SECTOR, Washington, DC, 2002).

No. 563. Private Philanthropy Funds by Source and Allocation: 1990 to 2002

[In billions of dollars (101.4 represents $101,400,000,000). Estimates for sources of funds based on U.S. Internal Revenue Service reports of individual charitable deductions and household surveys of giving by Independent Sector and the Center on Philanthropy at Indiana University. For corporate giving, data are corporate charitable deductions from the US Internal Revenue Service and the contributions made by corporate foundations as reported by the Foundation Center. Data about foundation donations are based upon surveys of foundations and data provided by the Foundation Center. Estimates of the allocation of funds were derived from surveys of nonprofits conducted by various sources]

Source and allocation	1990	1992	1993	1994	1995	1996	1997	1998	1999	2000	2001	2002
Total funds	101.4	110.4	116.5	119.2	124.0	138.6	159.4	177.4	201.6	228.3	238.5	240.9
Individuals	81.0	87.7	92.0	92.5	95.4	107.6	124.2	138.4	155.2	175.1	182.5	183.7
Foundations [1]	7.2	8.6	9.5	9.7	10.6	12.0	13.9	17.0	20.5	24.6	27.2	26.9
Corporations	5.5	5.9	6.5	7.0	7.3	7.5	8.6	8.5	10.2	10.7	11.0	12.2
Charitable bequests	7.6	8.2	8.5	10.0	10.7	11.5	12.6	13.6	15.6	17.8	17.7	18.1
Allocation:												
Religion	49.8	51.0	52.9	56.4	58.1	61.9	64.7	68.2	71.2	77.0	80.3	84.3
Health	9.9	10.2	10.8	11.5	12.6	13.9	14.0	16.9	18.0	18.8	19.3	18.9
Education	12.4	14.3	15.4	16.6	17.6	19.2	22.0	25.3	27.5	31.7	31.9	31.6
Human service	11.8	11.6	12.5	11.7	11.7	12.2	12.7	16.1	17.4	18.0	20.7	18.7
Arts, culture and humanities . .	7.9	9.3	9.6	9.7	10.0	10.9	10.6	10.5	11.1	11.5	12.1	12.2
Public/societal benefit.	4.9	5.0	5.4	6.1	7.1	7.6	8.4	10.9	11.0	11.6	11.8	11.6
Environment/wildlife	2.5	2.9	3.0	3.3	3.8	3.8	4.1	5.3	5.8	6.2	6.4	6.6
International . . . . . [1] [2]	1.3	2.2	2.2	2.4	2.9	2.8	2.6	2.9	3.6	3.7	4.1	4.6
Gifts to foundations [1] [2]	3.8	5.0	6.3	6.3	8.5	12.6	14.0	19.9	28.8	24.7	25.7	22.0
Unallocated [3]	-3.0	-1.2	-1.5	-4.9	-8.2	-6.2	6.3	1.5	7.4	25.2	25.9	30.5

[1] Data are from the Foundation Center. [2] Estimate for gifts to foundations in 2002 is from Giving USA. [3] Money deducted as a charitable contribution by donors but not allocated to sources. May include gifts to governmental entities, in-kind giving, gifts to new charities.
Source: AAFRC Trust for Philanthropy, Indianapolis, IN, researched and written by the Center on Philanthropy at Indiana University, *Giving USA*, annual (copyright).

No. 564. Foundations—Number and Finances: 1980 to 2002

[48.2 represents $48,200,000,000. Covers nongovernmental nonprofit organizations with funds and programs managed by their own trustees or directors, whose goals were to maintain or aid social, educational, religious, or other activities deemed to serve the common good. Excludes organizations that make general appeals to the public for funds, act as trade associations for industrial or other special groups, or do not award grants. Constant dollar figures based on Consumer Price Index, all urban consumers, supplied by US Bureau of Labor Statistics. Minus sign (-) indicates decrease]

| Year | Number of foundations | Assets | | | | Total giving [2] | | | | Gifts received | | | |
| | | Current dollars | | Constant (1975) dollars | | Current dollars | | Constant (1975) dollars | | Current dollars | | Constant (1978) dollars | |
		Amount (bil. dol)	Percent change[1]	Amount (bil. dol)	Percent change[1]	Amount (bil. dol)	Percent change[1]	Amount (bil. dol)	Percent change[1]	Amount (bil. dol)	Percent change[1]	Amount (bil. dol)	Percent change[1]
1980.	22,088	48.2	15.8	31.5	2.0	3.4	20.4	2.2	6.3	2.0	-10.4	1.6	-21.0
1985.	25,639	102.1	37.8	51.1	33.1	6.0	19.6	3.0	15.4	5.2	54.2	3.1	48.9
1990.	32,401	142.5	3.6	58.7	-1.7	8.7	9.7	3.6	4.1	5.0	-10.0	2.5	-14.6
1993.	37,571	189.2	7.0	70.5	3.9	11.1	8.8	4.1	5.7	7.8	25.5	3.5	22.0
1994.	38,807	195.8	3.5	71.1	0.9	11.3	1.6	4.1	-0.9	8.1	4.2	3.6	1.5
1995.	40,140	226.7	15.8	80.1	12.6	12.3	8.6	4.3	5.6	10.3	26.9	4.4	23.5
1996.	41,588	267.6	18.0	92.2	14.6	13.8	12.9	4.7	9.6	16.0	56.1	6.7	51.7
1997.	44,146	329.9	23.3	110.6	19.9	16.0	15.5	5.4	12.9	15.8	-1.2	6.4	-3.4
1998.	46,832	385.1	16.7	127.1	14.9	19.5	21.7	6.4	19.8	22.6	42.6	9.0	40.4
1999.	50,201	448.6	16.5	144.9	14.0	23.3	19.9	7.5	17.3	32.1	42.1	12.6	39.0
2000.	56,582	495.6	10.5	154.9	6.9	27.6	18.2	8.6	14.3	27.6	-13.9	10.5	-16.7
2001.	61,810	476.8	-3.8	144.8	-6.5	30.5	10.7	9.3	7.6	28.7	4.0	10.6	1.1
2002.	64,843	435.2	-8.7	130.1	-10.1	30.4	-0.2	9.1	-1.8	22.2	-22.8	8.0	-24.0

[1] Percent change from immediate preceding year. [2] Includes grants, scholarships, and employee matching gifts.

Source: The Foundation Center, New York, NY, FC Stats; <http://fdncenter.org/fcstats/index.html>; (copyright).

No. 565. Foundations—Number and Finances by Asset Size: 2002

[Figures are for latest year reported by foundations (435,190 represents $435,190,000,000). See headnote, Table 564]

| Asset size | Number | Assets (mil. dol.) | Gifts received (mil. dol.) | Expenditures (mil. dol.) | Grants (mil. dol.) | Percent distribution | | | | |
						Number	Assets	Gifts received	Expenditures	Grants
Total	**64,843**	**435,190**	**22,163**	**37,420**	**30,432**	**100.0**	**100.0**	**100.0**	**100.0**	**100.0**
Under $50,000.	11,369	191	544	796	710	17.5	(Z)	2.4	2.1	2.3
$50,000-$99,999	5,004	369	163	215	186	7.7	0.1	0.7	0.6	0.6
$100,000-$249,999.	9,352	1,562	455	596	502	14.4	0.4	2.1	1.6	1.6
$250,000-$499,999.	8,530	3,092	441	617	530	13.2	0.7	2.0	1.6	1.7
$500,000-$999,999.	8,957	6,456	794	1,056	902	13.8	1.5	3.6	2.8	3.0
$1,000,000-$4,999,999	14,004	31,551	3,476	4,380	3,725	21.6	7.2	15.7	11.7	12.2
$5,000,000-$9,999,999 . . .	3,199	22,398	1,865	2,406	1,945	4.9	5.1	8.4	6.4	6.4
$10,000,000-$49,999,999 . . .	3,361	71,547	5,265	6,892	5,487	5.2	16.4	23.8	18.4	18.0
$50,000,000-$99,999,999 . . .	532	37,013	2,501	3,471	2,746	0.8	8.5	11.3	9.3	9.0
$100,000,000-$249,999,999. .	333	50,237	2,910	3,886	3,107	0.5	11.5	13.1	10.4	10.2
$250,000,000 or more.	202	210,772	3,749	13,106	10,592	0.3	48.4	16.9	35.0	34.8

Z Less than 0.05 percent.

Source: The Foundation Center, New York, NY, Foundation Yearbook, annual (copyright).

No. 566. Foundations—Grants Reported by Subject Field and Recipient Organization: 2002

[15,925 represents $15,925,000,000. Covers grants of $10,000 or more in size. Based on reports of 1,015 larger U.S.foundations. Grant sample dollar value represented half of all grant dollars awarded by private, corporate, and community foundations. For definition of foundations, see headnote, Table 564]

| Subject field | Number of grants | | Dollar value | | Recipient organization | Number of grants | | Dollar value | |
	Number	Percent distribution	Amount (mil. dol.)	Percent distribution		Number	Percent distribution	Amount (mil. dol.)	Percent distribution
Total	**127,728**	**100.0**	**15,925**	**100.0**	Community improvement				
Arts and culture	18,674	14.6	1,946	12.2	organizations	6,605	5.2	828	5.2
Education	26,490	20.7	4,209	26.4	Educational institutions .	32,442	25.4	5,910	37.1
Environment & animals .	7,830	6.1	943	5.9	Colleges & universities .	14,831	11.6	3,234	20.3
Health	15,188	11.9	2,920	18.3	Educational support				
Human services.	33,250	26.0	2,350	14.8	agencies	4,747	4.5	888	5.6
International affairs,					Schools	8,050	6.3	792	5.0
development & peace . .	3,025	2.4	413	2.6	Environmental agencies .	5,136	4.0	609	3.8
Public/societalbenefit . . .	15,480	12.1	1,821	11.4	Hospitals/medical care				
Science and technology .	2,200	1.7	568	3.6	facilities	4,542	3.6	656	4.1
Social sciences	1,567	1.2	310	1.9	Human service agencies .	25,214	19.7	1,675	10.5
					Museums/historical				
Religion	3,912	3.1	429	2.7	societies	5,130	4.0	669	4.2
Other.	112.0	0.1	15.0	0.1	Public/general health				
					organizations	3,188	2.5	628	3.9

Source: The Foundation Center, New York, NY, Foundation Giving Trends, annual (copyright). See also <http://www.fdncenter.org/>

No. 567. Volunteers by Selected Characteristics: 2002 and 2003

[59,783 represents 59,783,000. Data on volunteers relate to persons who performed unpaid volunteer activities for an organization at any point from September 1, through the survey period in September of the following year.]

Characteristic	2002			2003		
	Total volunteers (1,000)	Percent of population	Median annual hours [1]	Total volunteers (1,000)	Percent of population	Median annual hours [1]
Total, 16 years and over	59,783	27.4	52	63,791	28.8	52
AGE						
17 to 24 years	7,742	21.9	40	8,671	24.1	40
26 to 34 years	9,574	24.8	33	10,337	26.5	36
36 to 44 years	14,971	34.1	52	15,165	34.7	50
46 to 54 years	12,477	31.3	52	13,302	32.7	52
56 to 64 years	7,331	27.5	60	8,170	29.2	60
66 years and over	7,687	22.7	96	8,146	23.7	88
SEX						
Men.	24,706	23.6	52	26,805	25.1	52
Women	35,076	31.0	50	36,987	32.2	52
RACE AND HISPANIC ORIGIN						
White [3]	52,591	29.2	52	55,572	30.6	52
Black [3]	4,896	19.1	52	5,145	20.0	52
Hispanic origin [4]	4,059	15.5	40	4,364	15.7	40
EDUCATIONAL ATTAINMENT [5]						
Less than a high school diploma . [6]	2,806	10.1	48	2,793	9.9	48
High school graduate, no college [6] . . .	12,542	21.2	49	12,882	21.7	48
Less than a bachelor's degree [7]	15,066	32.8	52	15,966	34.1	52
College graduates	21,627	43.3	60	23,481	45.6	60
EMPLOYMENT STATUS						
Civilian labor force	42,773	29.3	48	45,499	30.9	48
Employed . [8]	40,742	29.5	48	43,138	31.2	48
Full time [8]	32,210	28.3	46	33,599	29.6	48
Part time [9]	8,532	35.4	52	9,539	38.4	52
Unemployed	2,031	25.1	50	2,361	26.7	48
Not in the labor force	17,010	23.7	72	18,293	24.6	66

[1] For those reporting annual hours. [2] Includes other races not shown separately. [3] Beginning in 2003, persons who selected this race group only; persons who selected more than one race group are not included. Prior to 2003, persons who reported more than one race group were included in the group they identified as the main race. [4] Persons of Hispanic origin may be of any race. [5] Data refer to persons 25 years and over. [6] Includes high school diploma or equivalent. [7] Includes the categories, some college, no degree; and associate degree. [8] Usually work 35 hours or more a week at all jobs. [9] Usually work less than 35 hours a week at all jobs.

Source: U.S. Bureau of Labor Statistics, *News*, USDL 03-888, December 17, 2003. See also <http://www.bls.gov/news.release /pdf/volun.pdf>.

No. 568. Volunteers by Type of Main Organization: 2003

[Data represents the percent of the population involved in the activity. See headnote, T. 567]

Type of main organization [1]	Total, both sexes	Sex		Age		Race and Hispanic or Latino origin		
		Men	Women	Total, 16 years and over	25 years and over	White	Black	Hispanic or Latino
Civic and political [2]	6.4	8.1	5.2	6.4	6.7	6.5	5.0	5.8
Educational or youth service.	27.4	24.7	29.3	27.4	26.7	27.3	27.4	38.5
Environmental or animal care.	1.7	1.9	1.5	1.7	1.6	1.7	0.4	0.7
Hospital or other health	8.2	6.3	9.6	8.2	8.1	8.4	5.9	5.5
Public safety	1.2	2.1	0.5	1.2	1.2	1.3	0.5	0.6
Religious	34.6	33.9	35.1	34.6	35.4	33.7	44.7	32.4
Social or community service	11.8	12.6	11.2	11.8	11.5	11.9	10.5	9.6
Sport and hobby [3]	4.1	5.5	3.2	4.1	4.2	4.3	1.7	1.9
Other.	3.1	3.4	3.0	3.1	3.2	3.3	1.8	3.5
Not determined	1.5	1.5	1.5	1.5	1.5	1.5	2.1	1.7

[1] Main organization is defined as the organization for which the volunteer worked the most hours during the year. See headnote for more details. [2] Includes professional and/or international. [3] Includes cultural and/or arts.

Source: U.S. Bureau of Labor Statistics, *News*, USDL 03-888, December 17, 2003. See also <http://www.bls.gov/news.release /pdf/volun.pdf>.

Labor Force, Employment, and Earnings

This section presents statistics on the labor force; its distribution by occupation and industry affiliation; and the supply of, demand for, and conditions of labor. The chief source of these data is the Current Population Survey (CPS) conducted by the U.S. Census Bureau for the Bureau of Labor Statistics (BLS). Comprehensive historical and current data are available from the BLS Internet site <http://www .bls.gov/cps/>. These data are published on a current basis in the BLS monthly publication *Employment and Earnings*. Detailed data on the labor force are also available from the Census Bureau's decennial census of population.

Types of data—Most statistics in this section are obtained by two methods: household interviews or questionnaires and reports of establishment payroll records. Each method provides data that the other cannot suitably supply. Population characteristics, for example, are readily obtainable only from the household survey, while detailed industrial classifications can be readily derived only from establishment records.

Household data are obtained from a monthly sample survey of the population. The CPS is used to gather data for the calendar week including the 12th of the month and provides current comprehensive data on the labor force (see text, Section 1, Population). The CPS provides information on the work status of the population without duplication since each person is classified as employed, unemployed, or not in the labor force. Employed persons holding more than one job are counted only once, according to the job at which they worked the most hours during the survey week.

Monthly, quarterly, and annual data from the CPS are published by the Bureau of Labor Statistics in *Employment and Earnings*. Data presented include national totals of the number of persons in the civilian labor force by sex, race, Hispanic or Latino origin, and age; the number employed; hours of work; industry and occupational groups; and the number unemployed, reasons for, and duration of unemployment. Annual data shown in this section are averages of monthly figures for each calendar year, unless otherwise specified. Historical national CPS data are available on the site <http://www.bls .gov/cps/>.

The CPS also produces annual estimates of employment and unemployment for each state, 50 large metropolitan statistical areas, and selected cities. These estimates are published by BLS in its annual *Geographic Profile of Employment and Unemployment* available at <http://www .bls.gov/opub/gp/laugp.htm>. More detailed geographic data (e.g., for counties and cities) are provided by the decennial population censuses.

Data based on establishment records are compiled by BLS and cooperating state agencies as part of an ongoing Current Employment Statistics program. Survey data, gathered monthly from a sample of employers through electronic interviewing (including electronic data interchange, touchtone data entry, and computer-assisted telephone interviewing) or by mail, fax, on magnetic tape or computer diskette, are supplemented by data from other government agencies and adjusted at intervals to data from government social insurance program reports. The estimates exclude self-employed persons, private household workers, unpaid family workers, agricultural workers, and the Armed Forces. In March 2003, reporting establishments employed 5 million manufacturing workers (34 percent of the total manufacturing employment at the time), 21 million workers in private nonmanufacturing industries (23 percent of the total in private nonmanufacturing), and 16 million federal, state, and local government employees (71 percent of total government).

The establishment survey counts workers each time they appear on a payroll during the reference period (the payroll period that includes the 12th of the month). Thus, unlike the CPS, a person with two jobs is counted twice. The establishment survey is designed to provide detailed industry information for the nation, states, and metropolitan areas on non-farm wage and salary employment, average weekly hours, and average hourly and weekly earnings. Establishment survey data also are published in *Employment and Earnings*. Historical national data are available on the site <http://www.bls.gov/ces/>. Historical data for states and metropolitan areas are available on the site <http://www.bls.gov/sae/>.

In June 2003, BLS completed a comprehensive sample redesign of the establishment survey begun in June 2000, changing from a quota-based sample to a probability-based sample. Also in June 2003, all establishment survey employment, hours, and earnings series were converted from being classified by the 1987 Standard Industrial Classification (SIC) system to being classified by the 2002 North American Industry Classification System (NAICS). The NAICS conversion resulted in major definitional changes to many of the previously published SIC-based series. All establishment survey historical time series were reconstructed as part of the NAICS conversion process and all published series have a NAICS-based history extending back to at least 1990. For total nonfarm industries and other high-level aggregates, NAICS history was reconstructed back to the previously existing start date for the series, 1939 in most cases. More information on the sample redesign, the conversion to NAICS, and other changes to the establishment survey implemented in June 2003 appears in "Revisions to the Current Employment Statistics National Estimates Effective May 2003" in the June 2003 issue of *Employment and Earnings,* as well as the Establishment Data portion of the Explanatory Notes and Estimates of Error section of *Employment and Earnings.*

The completion of the sample redesign and the conversion to NAICS for state and metropolitan area establishment survey data was implemented in March 2003 with the release of January 2003 estimates. For a discussion of the changes to the state and area establishment survey data, see "Revisions to the Current Employment Statistics State and Area Estimates Effective January 2003" in the March 2003 issue of *Employment and Earnings.*

Labor force—According to the CPS definitions, the civilian labor force comprises all civilians in the noninstitutional population 16 years and over classified as "employed" or "unemployed" according to the following criteria: Employed civilians comprise (a) all civilians, who, during the reference week, did any work for pay or profit (minimum of an hour's work) or worked 15 hours or more as unpaid workers in a family enterprise and (b) all civilians who were not working but who had jobs or businesses from which they were temporarily absent for noneconomic reasons (illness, weather conditions, vacation, labor-management dispute, etc.) whether they were paid for the time off or were seeking other jobs. Unemployed persons comprise all civilians who had no employment during the reference week, who made specific efforts to find a job within the previous 4 weeks (such as applying directly to an employer or to a public employment service or checking with friends) and who were available for work during that week, except for temporary illness. Persons on layoff from a job and expecting recall also are classified as unemployed. All other civilian persons, 16 years old and over, are classified as "not in the labor force."

Various breaks in the CPS data series have occurred over time due to the introduction of population adjustments and other changes. For details on these breaks in series and the effect that they had on the CPS data, see the section on noncomparability of labor force levels in the Household Data portion of the Explanatory Notes and Estimates of Error section of *Employment and Earnings* available on the site <http://www.bls.gov/cps/eetech_methods.pdf>.

Beginning in January 2003, the CPS reflects the introduction of Census 2000-based population controls. These new population controls substantially increased the size of the civilian noninstitutional population and the civilian labor force. Data from January 2000 through December 2002 were revised to reflect the higher population estimates from Census 2000 and the higher rates of population growth since the census. At the start of the revision period (January 2000), the new population controls raised the civilian noninstitutional population and the civilian labor force by 2.6 and 1.6 million, respectively. By December 2002, the civilian population and labor force were 3.8 and 2.5 million, respectively, higher than originally estimated. An additional population control adjustment, introduced with data for January 2003, had the effect of increasing the civilian population and labor force by about 950,000 and 600,000 respectively. The unemployment rate and other ratios were not substantially affected by either of these population control adjustments. An explanation of the changes and their effects on labor force estimates appears in "Revisions to the Current Population Survey Effective in January 2003" in the February 2003 issue of *Employment and Earnings,* available on the site <http://www.bls.gov/cps/rvcps03.pdf>.

Hours and earnings—Average hourly earnings, based on establishment data, are gross earnings (i.e., earnings before payroll deductions) and include overtime premiums; they exclude irregular bonuses and value of payments in kind. Hours are those for which pay was received. Wages and salaries from the CPS consist of total monies received for work performed by an employee during the income year. It includes wages, salaries, commissions, tips, piece-rate payments, and cash bonuses earned before deductions were made for taxes, bonds, union dues, etc. Persons who worked 35 hours or more are classified as working full time.

Industry and occupational groups— Industry data derived from the CPS for 1983-91 utilize the 1980 census industrial classification developed from the 1972 SIC. CPS data from 1971 to 1982 were based on the 1970 census classification system, which was developed from the 1967 SIC. Most of the industry categories were not affected by the change in classification.

The occupational classification system used in the 1980 census and in the CPS for 1983-91, evolved from the 1980 Standard Occupational Classification (SOC) system, first introduced in 1977. Occupational categories used in the 1980 census classification system are so radically different from the 1970 census system used in the CPS through 1982, that their implementation represented a break in historical data series. In cases where data have not yet been converted to the 1980 classifications and still reflect the 1970 classifications (e.g., Table 643), comparisons between the two systems should not be made.

Beginning in January 1992, the occupational and industrial classification systems used in the 1990 census were introduced into the CPS. (These systems were largely based on the 1980 Standard Occupational Classification and the 1987 Standard Industrial Classification Systems, respectively.)

Beginning in 2003, the 2002 Census Bureau occupational and industrial classification systems were introduced into the CPS. These systems were derived from the 2000 Standard Occupational Classification (SOC) and the 2002 North American Industry Classification System (NAICS). The composition of detailed occupational and and industrial classifications in the new classification systems was substantially changed from the previous systems in use, as was the structure for aggregating them into broad groups. Consequently, the use if the new classification systems created breaks in existing data series at all levels of aggregation. CPS data using the new classification systems are available beginning 2000. Additional information on the 2002 Census Bureau occupational and industrial classifications systems appears in "Revisions to the Current Population Survey Effective in January 2003" in the February 2003 issue of *Employment and Earnings*, available on the BLS web site <http://www.bls.gov /cps/rvcps03.pdf>.

For details on the changes over time in the industrial and occupational classification systems used in the CPS, see the section on changes in the occupational and industrial classification systems in the

Household Data portion of the Explanatory Notes and Estimates of Error section of *Employment and Earnings* available on the site <http://www.bls.gov/cps/eetech_methods.pdf>.

Establishments responding to the establishment survey are classified according to the 2002 North American Industrial Classification System (NAICS). Previously they were classified according to the Standard Industrial Classification Manual (SIC). See text, Section 15, Business Enterprise, for information about the SIC manual and NAICS.

Productivity—BLS publishes data on productivity as measured by output per hour (labor productivity), output per combined unit of labor and capital input (multifactor productivity), and, for manufacturing industries, output per combined unit of capital, labor, energy, materials, and purchased service inputs. Labor productivity and related indexes are published for the business sector as a whole and its major subsectors: nonfarm business, manufacturing, and nonfinancial corporations, and for over 200 industries at the NAICS 2; 3-, and 4-digit levels. Labor productivity data were converted to a NAICS classification for the SIC classification in September 2003. Data for the business and nonfarm business sectors were reconstructed back to 1947; data for nonfinancial corporations back to 1958, and data for the specific industry measures and the manufacturing sectors were reconstructed back to 1987. Multifactor productivity and related measures (currently SIC-based) are published for the private business sector and its major subsectors. Productivity indexes that take into account capital, labor, energy, materials, and service inputs are published for the 18 major industry groups that comprise most of the manufacturing sector, the utility services industry group, for 141 three-digit SIC manufacturing industries, and railroad transportation and air transportation. The major sector data are published in the BLS quarterly news release, *Productivity and Costs* and in the annual *Multifactor Productivity Trends* release. Industry productivity measures are updated and published annually in the news releases *Productivity and Costs by Industry*. The latest data are available at the BLS productivity and costs Web site <http://www.bls.gov/lpc/home.htm> Detailed information on methods, limitations, and data sources appears in the BLS *Handbook of Methods,* BLS Bulletin 2490 (1997), Chapters 10 and 11.

Unions—As defined here, unions include traditional labor unions and employee associations similar to labor unions. Data on union membership status provided by BLS are for employed wage and salary workers and relate to their principal job. Earnings by union membership status are usual weekly earnings of full-time wage and salary workers. The information is collected through the Current Population Survey.

Work stoppages—Work stoppages include all strikes and lockouts known to BLS that last for at least 1 full day or shift and involve 1,000 or more workers. All stoppages, whether or not authorized by a union, legal or illegal, are counted. Excluded are work slowdowns and instances where employees report to work late or leave early to attend mass meetings or mass rallies.

Seasonal adjustment—Many economic statistics reflect a regularly recurring seasonal movement that can be estimated on the basis of past experience. By eliminating that part of the change which can be ascribed to usual seasonal variation (e.g., climate or school openings and closings), it is possible to observe the cyclical and other nonseasonal movements in the series. However, in evaluating deviations from the seasonal pattern—that is, changes in a seasonally adjusted series—it is important to note that seasonal adjustment is merely an approximation based on past experience. Seasonally adjusted estimates have a broader margin of possible error than the original data on which they are based, since they are subject not only to sampling and other errors, but also are affected by the uncertainties of the adjustment process itself.

Statistical reliability—For discussion of statistical collection, estimation, sampling procedures, and measures of statistical reliability applicable to Census Bureau and BLS data, see Appendix III.

No. 569. Employment Status of the Civilian Population: 1970 to 2003

[In thousands (137,085 represents 137,085,000), except as indicated. Annual averages of monthly figures. For the civilian noninstitutional population 16 years old and over. Based on Current Population Survey; see text, Section 1, and Appendix III]

Year	Civilian noninsti-tutional population	Civilian labor force						Not in labor force	
		Total	Percent of population	Employed	Employ-ment/ population ratio [1]	Unemployed			
						Number	Percent of labor force	Number	Percent of population
1970	137,085	82,771	60.4	78,678	57.4	4,093	4.9	54,315	39.6
1980	167,745	106,940	63.8	99,303	59.2	7,637	7.1	60,806	36.2
1985	178,206	115,461	64.8	107,150	60.1	8,312	7.2	62,744	35.2
1986	180,587	117,834	65.3	109,597	60.7	8,237	7.0	62,752	34.7
1987	182,753	119,865	65.6	112,440	61.5	7,425	6.2	62,888	34.4
1988	184,613	121,669	65.9	114,968	62.3	6,701	5.5	62,944	34.1
1989	186,393	123,869	66.5	117,342	63.0	6,528	5.3	62,523	33.5
1990 [2]	189,164	125,840	66.5	118,793	62.8	7,047	5.6	63,324	33.5
1991	190,925	126,346	66.2	117,718	61.7	8,628	6.8	64,578	33.8
1992	192,805	128,105	66.4	118,492	61.5	9,613	7.5	64,700	33.6
1993 [2]	194,838	129,200	66.3	120,259	61.7	8,940	6.9	65,638	33.7
1994 [2]	196,814	131,056	66.6	123,060	62.5	7,996	6.1	65,758	33.4
1995	198,584	132,304	66.6	124,900	62.9	7,404	5.6	66,280	33.4
1996 [2]	200,591	133,943	66.8	126,708	63.2	7,236	5.4	66,647	33.2
1997 [2]	203,133	136,297	67.1	129,558	63.8	6,739	4.9	66,837	32.9
1998 [2]	205,220	137,673	67.1	131,463	64.1	6,210	4.5	67,547	32.9
1999 [2]	207,753	139,368	67.1	133,488	64.3	5,880	4.2	68,385	32.9
2000 [2]	212,577	142,583	67.1	136,891	64.4	5,692	4.0	69,994	32.9
2001	215,092	143,734	66.8	136,933	63.7	6,801	4.7	71,359	33.2
2002 [2]	217,570	144,863	66.6	136,485	62.7	8,378	5.8	72,707	33.4
2003 [2]	221,168	146,510	66.2	137,736	62.3	8,774	6.0	74,658	33.8

[1] Civilian employed as a percent of the civilian noninstitutional population.   [2] Data not strictly comparable with data for earlier years, see text, this section, and February 1994, March 1996, February 1997-99, and February 2003 issues of *Employment and Earnings*.

Source: U.S. Bureau of Labor Statistics, Bulletin 2307; and *Employment and Earnings*, monthly, January 2004 issue. See Internet site <http://www.bls.gov/cps/home.htm>.

No. 570. Civilian Labor Force and Participation Rates With Projections: 1980 to 2012

[106.9 represents 106,900,000. For civilian noninstitutional population 16 years old and over. Annual averages of monthly figures. Rates are based on annual average civilian noninstitutional population of each specified group and represent proportion of each specified group in the civilian labor force. Based on Current Population Survey; see text, Section 1, and Appendix III]

Race, Hispanic origin sex, and age	Civilian labor force (millions)						Participation rate (percent)					
	1980	1990 [1]	2000 [1]	2002	2003 [1]	2012, proj.	1980	1990 [1]	2000 [1]	2002	2003 [1]	2012, proj.
Total [2]	106.9	125.8	142.6	144.9	146.5	162.3	63.8	66.5	67.1	66.6	66.2	67.2
White [3]	93.6	107.4	118.5	120.2	120.5	130.4	64.1	66.9	67.3	66.8	66.5	66.2
Male	54.5	59.6	64.5	65.3	65.5	70.6	78.2	77.1	75.5	74.8	74.2	73.5
Female	39.1	47.8	54.1	54.8	55.0	59.8	51.2	57.4	59.5	59.3	59.2	59.2
Black [3]	10.9	13.7	16.4	16.6	16.5	19.8	61.0	64.0	65.8	64.8	64.3	66.3
Male	5.6	6.8	7.7	7.8	7.7	9.3	70.3	71.0	69.2	68.4	67.3	69.1
Female	5.3	6.9	8.7	8.8	8.8	10.4	53.1	58.3	63.1	61.8	61.9	64.0
Asian [3][4]	(NA)	(NA)	6.3	6.6	6.1	9.0	(NA)	(NA)	67.2	67.2	66.4	68.7
Male	(NA)	(NA)	3.4	3.6	3.3	4.9	(NA)	(NA)	76.1	75.9	75.6	77.3
Female	(NA)	(NA)	2.9	3.0	2.8	4.0	(NA)	(NA)	59.2	59.1	58.3	61.3
Hispanic or Latino [5] ...	6.1	10.7	16.7	17.9	18.8	23.8	64.0	67.4	69.7	69.1	68.3	68.8
Male	3.8	6.5	9.9	10.6	11.3	13.7	81.4	81.4	81.5	80.2	80.1	79.0
Female	2.3	4.2	6.8	7.3	7.5	10.1	47.4	53.1	57.5	57.6	55.9	58.6
Male	61.5	69.0	76.3	77.5	78.2	85.3	77.4	76.4	74.8	74.1	73.5	73.1
16 to 19 years.....	5.0	4.1	4.3	3.9	3.6	3.8	60.5	55.7	52.8	47.5	44.3	45.6
20 to 24 years.....	8.6	7.9	7.5	7.8	7.9	8.7	85.9	84.4	82.6	80.7	80.0	81.4
25 to 34 years.....	17.0	19.9	17.8	17.6	17.8	19.1	95.2	94.1	93.4	92.4	91.8	92.5
35 to 44 years.....	11.8	17.5	20.1	19.8	19.8	18.2	95.5	94.3	92.7	92.1	92.1	92.3
45 to 54 years.....	9.9	11.1	16.3	17.1	17.4	19.1	91.2	90.7	88.6	88.5	87.7	88.6
55 to 64 years.....	7.2	6.6	7.8	8.8	9.1	12.7	72.1	67.8	67.3	69.2	68.7	69.9
65 years and over ..	1.9	2.0	2.5	2.5	2.7	3.6	19.0	16.3	17.7	17.9	18.6	20.8
Female	45.5	56.8	66.3	67.4	68.3	77.0	51.5	57.5	59.9	59.6	59.5	61.6
16 to 19 years.....	4.4	3.7	4.0	3.7	3.6	3.8	52.9	51.6	51.2	47.3	44.8	47.4
20 to 24 years.....	7.3	6.8	6.7	7.0	7.0	8.1	68.9	71.3	73.1	72.1	70.8	75.1
25 to 34 years.....	12.3	16.1	14.9	14.6	14.6	16.3	65.5	73.5	76.1	75.1	74.1	78.2
35 to 44 years.....	8.6	14.7	17.5	17.1	16.9	16.2	65.5	76.4	77.2	76.4	76.0	79.9
45 to 54 years.....	7.0	9.1	14.8	15.5	15.9	17.9	59.9	71.2	76.8	76.0	76.8	79.8
55 to 64 years.....	4.7	4.9	6.6	7.6	8.1	11.9	41.3	45.2	51.9	55.2	56.6	60.6
65 years and over ..	1.2	1.5	1.8	1.9	2.1	2.8	8.1	8.6	9.4	9.8	10.6	12.1

NA Not available.   [1] See footnote 2, Table 569.   [2] Includes other races, not shown separately.   [3] The 2003 Current Population Survey (CPS) allowed respondents to choose more than one race. Data represent persons who selected this race group only and exclude persons reporting more than one race. The CPS in prior years only allowed respondents to report one race group. See also comments on race in the text for Section 1.   [4] Prior to 2003, includes Pacific Islanders.   [5] Persons of Hispanic or Latino origin may be of any race.

Source: U.S. Bureau of Labor Statistics, *Employment and Earnings*, monthly, January 2004 issue; *Monthly Labor Review*, February 2004; and unpublished data. See Internet site <http://www.bls.gov/cps/home.htm>.

Labor Force, Employment, and Earnings **371**

No. 571. Employment Status of the Civilian Population, by Sex, Race, and Ethnicity: 1970 to 2003

[In thousands (64,304 represents 64,304,000), except as indicated. Annual averages of monthly figures. See table 569 for U.S. totals and coverage.]

Year, sex, race, and Hispanic origin	Civilian noninstitutional population	Civilian labor force			Employment/population ratio[1]	Unemployed		Not in labor force	
		Total	Percent of population	Employed		Number	Percent of labor force	Number	Percent of population
Male: 1970	64,304	51,228	79.7	48,990	76.2	2,238	4.4	13,076	20.3
1980	79,398	61,453	77.4	57,186	72.0	4,267	6.9	17,945	22.6
1990[2]	90,377	69,011	76.4	65,104	72.0	3,906	5.7	21,367	23.6
1995	95,178	71,360	75.0	67,377	70.8	3,983	5.6	23,818	25.0
2000[2]	101,964	76,280	74.8	73,305	71.9	2,975	3.9	25,684	25.2
2001	103,282	76,886	74.4	73,196	70.9	3,690	4.8	26,396	25.6
2002	104,585	77,500	74.1	72,903	69.7	4,597	5.9	27,085	25.9
2003[2]	106,435	78,238	73.5	73,332	68.9	4,906	6.3	28,197	26.5
Female: 1970	72,782	31,543	43.3	29,688	40.8	1,855	5.9	41,239	56.7
1980	88,348	45,487	51.5	42,117	47.7	3,370	7.4	42,861	48.5
1990[2]	98,787	56,829	57.5	53,689	54.3	3,140	5.5	41,957	42.5
1995	103,406	60,944	58.9	57,523	55.6	3,421	5.6	42,462	41.1
2000[2]	110,613	66,303	59.9	63,586	57.5	2,717	4.1	44,310	40.1
2001	111,811	66,848	59.8	63,737	57.0	3,111	4.7	44,962	40.2
2002	112,985	67,363	59.6	63,582	56.3	3,781	5.6	45,621	40.4
2003[2]	114,733	68,272	59.5	64,404	56.1	3,868	5.7	46,461	40.5
White:[3]									
1970	122,174	73,556	60.2	70,217	57.5	3,339	4.5	48,618	39.8
1980	146,122	93,600	64.1	87,715	60.0	5,884	6.3	52,523	35.9
1990[2]	160,625	107,447	66.9	102,261	63.7	5,186	4.8	53,178	33.1
1995	166,914	111,950	67.1	106,490	63.8	5,459	4.9	54,965	32.9
2000[2]	176,220	118,545	67.3	114,424	64.9	4,121	3.5	57,675	32.7
2001	178,111	119,399	67.0	114,430	64.2	4,969	4.2	58,713	33.0
2002	179,783	120,150	66.8	114,013	63.4	6,137	5.1	59,633	33.2
2003[2]	181,292	120,546	66.5	114,235	63.0	6,311	5.2	60,746	33.5
Black:[3]									
1973	14,917	8,976	60.2	8,128	54.5	846	9.4	5,941	39.8
1980	17,824	10,865	61.0	9,313	52.2	1,553	14.3	6,959	39.0
1985	19,664	12,364	62.9	10,501	53.4	1,864	15.1	7,299	37.1
1990[2]	21,477	13,740	64.0	12,175	56.7	1,565	11.4	7,737	36.0
1995	23,246	14,817	63.7	13,279	57.1	1,538	10.4	8,505	34.2
2000[2]	24,902	16,397	65.8	15,156	60.9	1,241	7.6	8,505	34.2
2001	25,138	16,421	65.3	15,006	59.7	1,416	8.6	8,717	34.7
2002	25,578	16,565	64.8	14,872	58.1	1,693	10.2	9,013	35.2
2003[2]	25,686	16,526	64.3	14,739	57.4	1,787	10.8	9,161	35.7
Asian:[3][4]									
2000	9,330	6,270	67.2	6,043	64.8	227	3.6	3,060	32.8
2001	9,626	6,469	67.2	6,180	64.2	288	4.5	3,158	32.8
2002	9,833	6,604	67.2	6,215	63.2	389	5.9	3,229	32.8
2003[2]	9,220	6,122	66.4	5,756	62.4	366	6.0	3,098	33.6
Hispanic:[5]									
1980	9,598	6,146	64.0	5,527	57.6	620	10.1	3,451	36.0
1985	11,915	7,698	64.6	6,888	57.8	811	10.5	4,217	35.4
1986	12,344	8,076	65.4	7,219	58.5	857	10.6	4,268	34.6
1990[2]	15,904	10,720	67.4	9,845	61.9	876	8.2	5,184	32.6
1995	18,629	12,267	65.8	11,127	59.7	1,140	9.3	6,362	34.2
2000[2]	23,938	16,689	69.7	15,735	65.7	954	5.7	7,249	30.3
2001	24,942	17,328	69.5	16,190	64.9	1,138	6.6	7,614	30.5
2002	25,963	17,943	69.1	16,590	63.9	1,353	7.5	8,020	30.9
2003[2]	27,551	18,813	68.3	17,372	63.1	1,441	7.7	8,738	31.7
Mexican:									
1986	7,377	4,941	67.0	4,387	59.5	555	11.2	2,436	33.0
1990[2]	9,752	6,707	68.8	6,146	63.0	561	8.4	3,045	31.2
1995	11,609	7,765	66.9	7,016	60.4	750	9.7	3,844	33.1
2000[2]	15,333	10,783	70.3	10,144	66.2	639	5.9	4,550	29.7
2001	15,909	11,218	70.5	10,471	65.8	747	6.7	4,691	29.5
2002	16,420	11,542	70.3	10,673	65.0	869	7.5	4,878	29.7
2003[2]	17,464	12,081	69.2	11,151	63.9	930	7.7	5,383	30.8
Puerto Rican:									
1986	1,494	804	53.8	691	46.3	113	14.0	690	46.2
1990[2]	1,718	960	55.9	870	50.6	91	9.5	758	44.1
1995	1,896	1,098	57.9	974	51.4	123	11.2	798	42.1
2000[2]	2,193	1,411	64.3	1,318	60.1	92	6.6	783	35.7
2001	2,367	1,454	61.4	1,341	56.6	114	7.8	913	38.6
2002	2,484	1,546	62.2	1,401	56.4	145	9.4	938	37.8
2003[2]	2,652	1,649	62.2	1,495	56.4	154	9.3	1,003	37.8
Cuban:									
1986	842	570	67.7	533	63.3	36	6.4	272	32.3
1990[2]	918	603	65.7	559	60.9	44	7.2	315	34.3
1995	1,019	613	60.2	568	55.7	45	7.4	406	39.8
2000[2]	1,174	740	63.1	707	60.3	33	4.5	434	37.0
2001	1,118	671	60.0	628	56.1	44	6.5	447	40.0
2002	1,141	635	55.6	592	51.9	43	6.7	507	44.4
2003[2]	1,191	679	57.0	638	53.6	41	6.0	512	43.0

[1] Civilian employed as a percent of the civilian noninstitutional population. [2] See footnote 2, Table 569. [3] Beginning 2003, for persons in this race group only. See footnote 3, Table 570. [4] Prior to 2003, includes Pacific Islanders. [5] Persons of Hispanic or Latino ethnicity may be of any race. Includes persons of other Hispanic or Latino ethnicity, not shown separately.

Source: U.S. Bureau of Labor Statistics, Bulletin 2307; and Employment and Earnings, monthly. January 2004 issue. See Internet site <http://www.bls.gov/cps/home.htm>.

No. 572. Civilian Labor Force—Percent Distribution by Sex and Age: 1980 to 2003

[106,940 represents 106,940,000. For civilian noninstitutional population 16 years old and over. Annual averages of monthly figures. Based on Current Population Survey; see text, Section 1, Population, and Appendix III]

Year and sex	Civilian labor force (1,000)	Percent distribution						
		16 to 19 years	20 to 24 years	25 to 34 years	35 to 44 years	45 to 54 years	55 to 64 years	65 yrs. and over
Total: 1980	106,940	8.8	14.9	27.3	19.1	15.8	11.2	2.9
1990 [1]	125,840	6.2	11.7	28.6	25.5	16.1	9.2	2.7
1995	132,304	5.9	10.3	25.8	27.0	19.1	9.0	2.9
2000 [1]	142,583	5.8	10.0	23.0	26.3	21.8	10.1	3.0
2003 [1]	146,510	4.9	10.2	22.1	25.0	22.7	11.8	3.3
Male: 1980	61,453	8.1	14.0	27.6	19.3	16.1	11.8	3.1
1990 [1]	69,011	5.9	11.4	28.8	25.3	16.1	9.6	2.9
1995	71,360	5.7	10.3	26.2	26.9	18.8	9.1	3.1
2000 [1]	76,280	5.6	9.9	23.4	26.3	21.3	10.2	3.3
2003 [1]	78,238	4.6	10.1	22.7	25.3	22.2	11.7	3.4
Female: 1980	45,487	9.6	16.1	26.9	19.0	15.4	10.4	2.6
1990 [1]	56,829	6.5	12.0	28.3	25.8	16.1	8.7	2.6
1995	60,944	6.1	10.4	25.5	27.2	19.4	8.8	2.7
2000 [1]	66,303	6.0	10.2	22.5	26.4	22.3	9.9	2.7
2003 [1]	68,272	5.2	10.3	21.3	24.8	23.3	12.0	3.1

[1] See footnote 2, Table 569.

Source: U.S. Bureau of Labor Statistics, Bulletin 2307, and *Employment and Earnings*, monthly, January 2004 issue. See Internet site <http://www.bls.gov/cps/home.htm>.

No. 573. Civilian Labor Force and Participation Rates by Educational Attainment, Sex, Race, and Hispanic Origin: 1992 to 2003

[106,490 represents 106,490,000 Annual averages of monthly figures For the civilian noninstitutional population 25 years of age and older. See Table 608 for unemployment data. Based on Current Population Survey; see text, Section 1, and Appendix III]

Year, sex, and race	Civilian labor force					Participation rate [1]				
		Percent distribution								
	Total (1,000)	Less than high school diploma	High school graduate, no degree	Less than a bachelor's degree	College graduate	Total	Less than high school diploma	High school gradu-ates, no degree	Less than a bach-elor's degree	College graduate
Total: [2]										
1992	106,490	12.6	35.6	25.4	26.4	66.5	41.2	66.4	75.3	81.3
1995	110,851	10.8	33.1	27.9	28.1	66.7	39.9	65.4	74.5	81.0
2000 [3]	120,061	10.4	31.4	27.7	30.5	67.3	43.5	64.4	73.9	79.4
2002 [3]	122,497	10.3	30.8	27.4	31.4	67.2	44.4	64.2	73.1	78.6
2003 [3]	124,412	10.2	30.5	27.4	32.0	67.2	44.9	63.8	72.8	78.2
Male:										
1992	58,439	14.1	34.0	24.0	27.9	77.0	54.7	78.3	83.9	86.9
1995	59,986	12.2	32.3	26.1	29.4	76.0	52.1	76.5	82.1	85.8
2000 [3]	64,490	11.8	31.1	25.9	31.2	76.1	56.0	75.1	80.9	84.4
2002 [3]	65,861	11.9	30.7	25.5	31.9	75.9	57.2	74.5	80.2	84.0
2003 [3]	66,717	11.9	30.5	25.4	32.2	75.5	57.7	74.0	79.5	83.2
Female:										
1992	48,051	10.7	37.5	27.1	24.7	57.1	29.5	56.8	67.8	74.8
1995	50,865	9.2	34.2	30.0	26.6	58.3	29.2	56.4	68.1	75.4
2000 [3]	55,572	8.8	31.8	29.7	29.7	59.4	32.3	55.5	68.0	74.0
2002 [3]	56,636	8.4	30.9	29.7	31.0	59.4	32.5	55.3	67.2	73.0
2003 [3]	57,695	8.2	30.4	29.6	31.8	59.6	32.7	55.0	67.2	73.1
White: [4]										
1992	90,627	11.8	35.5	25.5	27.2	66.3	41.1	65.4	74.6	81.0
1995	94,139	10.1	33.0	27.8	29.1	66.7	40.0	64.8	73.8	80.6
2000 [3]	99,964	10.1	31.4	27.5	31.0	67.0	44.1	63.6	73.1	79.0
2002 [3]	101,711	10.0	30.8	27.3	31.9	67.0	44.9	63.4	72.5	78.2
2003 [3]	102,509	10.0	30.4	27.2	32.5	66.9	45.7	62.9	72.2	77.8
Black: [4]										
1992	11,583	18.2	39.5	26.4	15.9	66.7	40.6	72.9	80.9	86.2
1995	12,152	13.9	37.1	30.7	18.3	66.0	36.2	69.7	79.8	85.6
2000 [3]	13,582	12.4	36.0	31.2	20.5	68.2	39.3	69.9	79.3	84.4
2002 [3]	13,787	12.5	35.4	31.5	20.5	67.6	40.8	68.4	77.8	82.8
2003 [3]	13,863	11.5	35.5	31.2	21.8	67.5	39.8	68.1	77.0	82.3
Asian: [4][5]										
2000 [3]	5,402	9.1	20.7	20.2	50.1	70.9	46.0	65.6	76.4	79.1
2003 [3]	5,420	8.7	19.4	17.3	54.5	69.8	46.3	65.0	71.9	77.4
Hispanic: [6]										
1992	8,728	38.9	29.6	20.0	11.5	68.3	56.3	75.5	82.2	83.2
1995	9,599	37.2	29.3	21.7	11.7	67.5	55.3	74.3	79.7	83.1
2000 [3]	12,975	36.7	29.3	20.6	13.4	71.5	61.9	75.0	80.8	83.5
2002 [3]	14,162	36.3	29.4	20.3	13.9	71.0	61.3	74.1	80.7	83.2
2003 [3]	15,181	36.4	29.2	20.4	14.0	70.7	61.6	73.9	79.2	81.8

[1] See headnote, Table 570.   [2] Includes other races, not shown separately.   [3] See footnote 2, Table 569.   [4] Beginning 2003, for persons in this race group only. See footnote 3, Table 570.   [5] Prior to 2003, includes Pacific Islanders.   [6] Persons of Hispanic or Latino origin may be of any race.

Source: U.S. Bureau of Labor Statistics, *Employment and Earnings*, monthly, January 2004 issue. See Internet site <http://www.bls.gov/cps/home.htm>.

No. 574. Characteristics of the Civilian Labor Force by State: 2003

[In thousands (146,510 represents 146,510,000), except ratio and rate. For civilian noninstitutional population, 16 years old and over. Annual averages of monthly figures. Because of separate processing and weighting procedures, the totals for the United States may differ from results obtained by aggregrating totals for states]

State	Total Number	Total Female	Employed Total	Employed Female	Employed population ratio [1]	Unemployed Total Number	Unemployed Total Female	Rate [2] Total	Rate [2] Male	Rate [2] Female	Participation rate [3] Male	Participation rate [3] Female
United States..	146,510	68,272	137,736	64,404	62.3	8,774	3,868	6.0	6.3	5.7	73.5	59.5
Alabama.........	2,147	1,023	2,023	958	58.8	125	64	5.8	5.4	6.3	69.3	56.2
Alaska..........	332	155	305	145	66.5	27	10	8.0	9.3	6.6	76.4	68.3
Arizona..........	2,690	1,198	2,539	1,128	61.5	151	70	5.6	5.4	5.8	73.8	56.8
Arkansas	1,265	574	1,186	540	57.3	78	34	6.2	6.4	5.9	69.7	53.2
California	17,460	7,859	16,283	7,354	61.5	1,177	505	6.7	7.0	6.4	74.0	58.1
Colorado........	2,478	1,119	2,328	1,055	67.7	150	64	6.0	6.3	5.8	79.7	64.5
Connecticut......	1,803	861	1,704	820	63.6	99	41	5.5	6.1	4.8	73.9	61.3
Delaware	417	203	399	194	63.8	18	9	4.4	4.2	4.5	72.2	61.9
District of Columbia .	302	153	281	143	61.9	21	10	7.0	7.2	6.7	71.8	62.1
Florida	8,164	3,816	7,744	3,608	58.6	420	208	5.1	4.9	5.5	68.9	55.3
Georgia	4,414	2,043	4,207	1,954	65.4	207	89	4.7	5.0	4.4	76.8	61.1
Hawaii	618	296	592	284	62.7	27	12	4.3	4.6	3.9	71.2	60.3
Idaho..........	693	314	655	299	64.6	37	15	5.4	5.8	4.9	75.8	61.1
Illinois	6,330	2,951	5,908	2,783	61.6	422	168	6.7	7.5	5.7	73.2	59.4
Indiana.........	3,188	1,474	3,024	1,409	64.6	163	65	5.1	5.7	4.4	75.6	61.1
Iowa	1,612	763	1,540	732	67.4	72	31	4.5	4.8	4.1	76.5	64.9
Kansas	1,434	681	1,357	645	66.2	77	36	5.4	5.5	5.3	75.6	64.7
Kentucky	1,956	916	1,836	863	58.2	120	52	6.2	6.5	5.7	68.9	55.7
Louisiana	2,037	975	1,904	916	56.9	134	59	6.6	7.0	6.1	67.6	54.9
Maine..........	693	334	658	320	63.3	35	14	5.1	5.9	4.1	72.0	61.8
Maryland	2,904	1,414	2,773	1,350	66.3	131	63	4.5	4.5	4.5	75.9	63.8
Massachusetts.....	3,416	1,629	3,217	1,545	64.0	198	84	5.8	6.4	5.2	74.8	61.7
Michigan........	5,042	2,362	4,674	2,212	60.7	368	150	7.3	8.1	6.4	72.2	59.1
Minnesota........	2,923	1,387	2,778	1,330	71.3	145	57	5.0	5.7	4.1	80.4	69.9
Mississippi	1,312	621	1,229	580	57.5	83	41	6.3	6.0	6.7	68.9	54.7
Missouri	3,021	1,443	2,850	1,363	65.5	170	80	5.6	5.7	5.5	76.0	63.4
Montana........	475	224	452	214	63.3	22	10	4.7	5.1	4.3	71.4	61.7
Nebraska	976	464	937	446	71.1	39	17	4.0	4.3	3.8	79.8	68.7
Nevada	1,141	503	1082	475	64.2	59	28	5.2	5.0	5.5	75.3	60.0
New Hampshire	719	334	688	321	68.5	31	14	4.3	4.5	4.1	78.5	64.9
New Jersey.......	4,375	2,049	4,118	1,935	62.2	257	114	5.9	6.1	5.6	73.7	59.2
New Mexico	897	430	840	403	59.9	57	27	6.4	6.5	6.2	69.2	59.2
New York	9,315	4,426	8,726	4,157	58.6	589	270	6.3	6.5	6.1	69.4	56.4
North Carolina.....	4,230	1,984	3,957	1,854	62.5	273	130	6.5	6.4	6.5	74.3	60.0
North Dakota......	346	163	333	159	67.9	14	4	4.0	5.1	2.7	76.2	65.5
Ohio	5,915	2,788	5,552	2,627	63.3	363	162	6.1	6.5	5.8	74.5	61.0
Oklahoma........	1,696	784	1,600	741	60.5	96	43	5.7	5.8	5.5	71.7	57.1
Oregon..........	1,859	848	1,707	790	61.6	152	58	8.2	9.3	6.8	74.4	60.1
Pennsylvania......	6,170	2,914	5,826	2,766	60.3	344	148	5.6	6.0	5.1	70.9	57.5
Rhode Island......	573	280	543	266	64.3	30	14	5.3	5.7	4.9	73.3	63.0
South Carolina.....	2,003	961	1,866	895	59.4	136	66	6.8	6.8	6.9	70.4	57.8
South Dakota.....	425	203	410	197	71.1	15	7	3.6	3.9	3.2	78.9	68.9
Tennessee	2,909	1,362	2,740	1,278	60.9	169	84	5.8	5.5	6.2	72.1	57.9
Texas...........	10,910	4,897	10,173	4,573	63.4	738	323	6.8	6.9	6.6	77.2	59.3
Utah	1,184	534	1,118	505	67.3	67	29	5.6	5.8	5.4	79.5	63.4
Vermont	351	167	335	160	67.7	16	7	4.6	4.9	4.2	76.6	65.6
Virginia.........	3,773	1,822	3,619	1,749	65.4	154	73	4.1	4.1	4.0	74.6	62.5
Washington.......	3,140	1,458	2,903	1,358	61.8	237	100	7.5	8.2	6.8	73.3	60.7
West Virginia......	787	366	739	337	51.3	48	20	6.1	6.5	5.7	62.0	47.7
Wisconsin........	3,078	1,470	2,905	1,399	68.8	174	71	5.6	6.4	4.8	78.0	68.0
Wyoming	278	128	266	123	68.8	12	5	4.4	4.8	3.9	78.2	65.8

[1] Civilian employment as a percent of civilian noninstitutional population.   [2] Percent unemployed of the civilian labor force.
[3] Percent of civilian noninstitutional population of each specified group in the civilian labor force.

Source: U.S. Bureau of Labor Statistics, Local Area Unemployment Statistics, *Geographic Profile of Employment and Unemployment, 2003*. See Internet site (accessed July 2004)

No. 575. Civilian Labor Force by Selected Metropolitan Area: 2003

[146,510 represents 146,510,000. For the civilian noninstitutional population 16 years old and over. Annual averages of monthly figures. Data are derived from the Local Area Unemployment Statistics Program. For definition of metropolitan areas, see Appendix II. Metropolitan areas defined as of June 1999.]

Metropolitan areas ranked by labor force size, 2003	Civilian labor force (1,000)	Unem- ploy- ment rate [1]	Metropolitan areas ranked by labor force size, 2003	Civilian labor force (1,000)	Unem- ploy- ment rate [1]
U.S. total, 2003	146,510	6.0	Las Vegas, NV-AZ MSA	907	5.3
Los Angeles-Long Beach, CA PMSA . . .	4,789	7.0	Indianapolis, IN MSA	907	4.7
New York, NY PMSA	4,369	7.7	San Francisco, CA PMSA	903	5.7
Chicago, IL PMSA	4,235	6.8	San Jose, CA PMSA	895	8.2
Washington, DC-MD-VA-WV PMSA. . . .	2,848	3.5	Columbus, OH MSA.	895	4.9
Philadelphia, PA-NJ PMSA	2,627	5.5	Cincinnati, OH-KY-IN PMSA	878	5.1
Atlanta, GA MSA	2,435	4.9	Fort Lauderdale, FL PMSA	877	5.5
Houston, TX PMSA	2,320	6.9	Sacramento, CA PMSA.	874	5.4
Detroit, MI PMSA.	2,238	7.3	Charlotte-Gastonia-Rock Hill,		
Dallas, TX PMSA.	2,035	7.1	NC-SC MSA	872	6.7
Boston, MA-NH PMSA	1,871	5.2	San Antonio, TX MSA.	827	5.5
Minneapolis-St. Paul, MN-WI MSA	1,834	4.8	Milwaukee-Waukesha, WI PMSA	824	6.1
Phoenix-Mesa, AZ MSA	1,807	5.0	Norfolk-Virginia Beach-Newport News,		
Riverside-San Bernardino, CA PMSA . .	1,688	5.9	VA-NC MSA	794	4.4
Orange County, CA PMSA.	1,576	3.8	Austin-San Marcos, TX MSA	771	5.7
Nassau-Suffolk, NY PMSA	1,486	4.2	Salt Lake City-Ogden, UT MSA	747	5.8
San Diego, CA MSA.	1,482	4.3	Raleigh-Durham-Chapel Hill, NC MSA . .	715	4.7
St. Louis, MO-IL MSA.	1,397	5.9	Greensboro—Winston-Salem—High		
Seattle-Bellevue-Everett, WA PMSA . . .	1,394	7.1	Point, NC MSA	687	6.2
Baltimore, MD PMSA	1,345	5.1	Nashville, TN MSA.	687	4.4
Tampa-St. Petersburg-Clearwater,			Bergen-Passaic, NJ PMSA	680	5.9
FL MSA	1,331	4.4	Middlesex-Somerset-Hunterdon,		
Oakland, CA PMSA	1,268	6.3	NJ PMSA	661	4.9
Denver, CO PMSA.	1,252	6.3	Providence-Fall River-Warwick,		
Pittsburgh, PA MSA	1,185	5.6	RI-MA MSA.	644	5.7
Cleveland-Lorain-Elyria, OH PMSA	1,127	6.7	Hartford, CT MSA	611	5.9
Miami, FL PMSA	1,104	7.2	Grand Rapids-Muskegon-Holland,		
Portland-Vancouver, OR-WA PMSA. . . .	1,096	8.5	MI MSA	608	7.7
Newark, NJ PMSA	1,070	6.1	New Orleans, LA MSA	605	5.8
Kansas City, MO-KS MSA.	1,024	6.0	Jacksonville, FL MSA	592	5.2
Orlando, FL MSA.	974	4.9	West Palm Beach-Boca Raton, FL MSA.	585	5.6
Fort Worth-Arlington, TX PMSA	963	6.4	Memphis, TN-AR-MS MSA	581	6.2

[1] Percent unemployed of the civilian labor force.

Source: U.S. Bureau of Labor Statistics, Local Area Unemployment Statistics program. See Internet site <http://www.bls.gov/lau/>.

No. 576. School Enrollment and Labor Force Status: 1990 and 2003

[In thousands (31,421 represents 31,421,000), except percent. As of October. For the civilian noninstitutional population 16 to 24 years old. Based on Current Population Survey; see text, Section 1, and Appendix III]

Characteristic	Population		Civilian labor force		Employed		Unemployed		
							1990, total	2003	
	1990	2003	1990	2003	1990	2003		Total	Rate [1]
Total, 16 to 24 years [2]	31,421	36,017	20,679	21,858	18,317	19,304	2,363	2,555	11.7
Enrolled in school [2]	15,210	20,114	7,301	8,932	6,527	8,069	774	863	9.7
16 to 19 years	10,118	13,033	4,244	4,662	3,645	4,026	599	635	13.6
20 to 24 years	5,092	7,081	3,057	4,271	2,882	4,042	174	228	5.3
Sex: Male	7,704	9,783	3,635	4,211	3,215	3,777	420	434	10.3
Female	7,507	10,331	3,666	4,721	3,312	4,292	353	429	9.1
College level.	8,139	10,503	4,542	5,914	4,231	5,538	311	376	6.4
Full-time	6,810	8,809	3,376	4,496	3,117	4,198	259	298	6.6
Race:									
White [3].	12,308	15,573	6,294	7,309	5,705	6,712	588	597	8.2
Below college.	5,535	7,333	2,374	2,510	2,021	2,185	354	326	13.0
College level	6,772	8,239	3,919	4,798	3,685	4,527	234	271	5.7
Black [3]	2,129	2,835	718	951	576	758	142	193	20.3
Below college.	1,207	1,582	306	351	212	234	94	116	33.2
College level	922	1,253	411	600	364	524	47	77	12.8
Asian [3]	(NA)	1,048	(NA)	365	(NA)	329	(NA)	36	10.0
Below college.	(NA)	339	(NA)	55	(NA)	39	(NA)	16	[4]
College level	(NA)	709	(NA)	310	(NA)	290	(NA)	21	6.6
Not enrolled [2].	16,210	15,903	13,379	12,926	11,789	11,235	1,589	1,691	13.1
White [3]	13,317	12,570	11,226	10,449	10,193	9,350	1,083	1,100	10.5
Black [3]	2,441	2,345	1,752	1,742	1,298	1,288	454	454	26.1
Asian [3]	(NA)	400	(NA)	311	(NA)	255	(NA)	55	17.8

NA Not available.   [1] Percent unemployed of civilian labor force in each category.   [2] Includes other races, not shown separately.   [3] Beginning 2003, for persons in this race group only. See footnote 3, Table 570.   [4] Data not shown where base is less than 75,000.

Source: U.S. Bureau of Labor Statistics, Bulletin 2307; College Enrollment and Work Activity of High School Graduates, News, USDL 04-749, April 27, 2004; and unpublished data. See Internet site <http://www.bls.gov/bls/newsrels.htm#OEUS>.

Labor Force, Employment, and Earnings **375**

No. 577. Labor Force Participation Rates by Marital Status, Sex, and Age: 1970 to 2003

[Annual averages of monthly figures. See Table 574 for definition of participation rate. Based on Current Population Survey; see text, Section 1, and Appendix III]

Marital status and year	Male participation rate							Female participation rate						
	Total	16-19 years	20-24 years	25-34 years	35-44 years	45-64 years	65 and over	Total	16-19 years	20-24 years	25-34 years	35-44 years	45-64 years	65 and over
Single:														
1970 ..	65.5	54.6	73.8	87.9	86.2	75.7	25.2	56.8	44.7	73.0	81.4	78.6	73.0	19.7
1980 ..	72.6	59.9	81.3	89.2	82.2	66.9	16.8	64.4	53.6	75.2	83.3	76.9	65.6	13.9
1990 [1] .	74.8	55.1	81.6	89.9	84.5	67.3	15.7	66.7	51.7	74.5	80.9	80.8	66.2	12.1
1995 ..	73.7	54.4	80.3	88.7	81.4	67.0	17.9	66.8	52.2	72.9	80.2	79.5	67.3	11.6
1998 [1] .	73.3	52.9	79.7	89.1	82.5	70.2	15.2	68.5	52.4	75.3	83.0	80.9	69.9	9.7
1999 [1] .	73.4	52.5	79.7	89.5	83.5	70.6	17.3	68.7	51.1	76.1	84.2	80.8	69.6	9.9
2000 [1] .	73.6	52.5	80.5	89.4	82.9	69.7	17.3	68.9	51.1	76.1	83.9	80.9	69.9	10.8
2001 ..	72.7	50.0	79.6	89.0	83.2	69.8	15.4	68.1	49.1	75.3	83.2	81.3	69.9	12.1
2002 ..	71.7	47.2	78.7	88.7	83.1	69.6	16.9	67.4	47.3	74.5	83.3	79.9	69.6	14.3
2003 [1] .	70.4	44.0	77.9	87.7	82.9	67.6	19.4	66.2	44.8	72.9	82.2	79.8	69.9	15.2
Married: [2]														
1970 ..	86.1	92.3	94.7	98.0	98.1	91.2	29.9	40.5	37.8	47.9	38.8	46.8	44.0	7.3
1980 ..	80.9	91.3	96.9	97.5	97.2	84.3	20.5	49.8	49.3	61.4	58.8	61.8	46.9	7.3
1990 [1] .	78.6	92.1	95.6	96.9	96.7	82.6	17.5	58.4	49.5	66.1	69.6	74.0	56.5	8.5
1995 ..	77.5	89.2	94.9	96.3	95.4	82.4	18.0	61.0	51.6	64.7	72.0	75.7	62.7	9.1
1998 [1] .	77.6	83.8	95.0	96.4	95.8	83.7	17.5	61.2	49.8	66.1	71.6	74.5	64.9	8.9
1999 [1] .	77.5	83.2	93.7	96.5	95.9	83.4	18.3	61.2	49.8	64.5	70.9	74.6	65.3	9.6
2000 [1] .	77.3	79.5	94.1	96.7	95.8	83.0	19.2	61.1	53.2	63.8	70.3	74.8	65.4	10.1
2001 ..	77.4	77.7	94.2	95.9	95.6	83.7	19.1	61.2	45.1	63.9	69.9	74.5	66.1	10.3
2002 ..	77.4	81.1	93.3	95.7	95.1	83.8	19.4	61.0	49.6	63.4	69.3	73.8	66.5	10.7
2003 [1] .	77.3	76.6	93.2	95.3	95.1	83.5	19.9	61.0	46.7	62.6	68.5	73.3	67.4	11.3
Other: [3]														
1970 ..	60.7	(B)	90.4	93.7	91.1	78.5	19.3	40.3	48.6	60.3	64.6	68.8	61.9	10.0
1980 ..	67.5	(B)	92.6	94.1	91.9	73.3	13.7	43.6	50.0	68.4	76.5	77.1	60.2	8.2
1990 [1] .	68.9	(B)	93.1	93.0	90.7	74.9	12.0	47.2	53.9	65.4	77.0	82.1	65.0	8.4
1995 ..	66.2	(B)	92.7	90.9	88.2	72.4	12.1	47.4	55.8	67.2	77.1	80.7	67.2	8.4
1998 [1] .	66.9	66.2	89.1	93.0	89.1	73.7	13.1	48.8	50.4	73.7	81.0	82.8	68.6	8.4
1999 [1] .	65.9	(B)	90.2	92.3	88.7	73.4	12.3	49.1	45.3	73.6	82.4	83.4	69.1	8.4
2000 [1] .	66.8	60.5	88.1	93.2	89.9	73.9	12.9	49.0	46.0	74.0	83.1	82.9	69.8	8.7
2001 ..	66.0	57.3	85.4	92.4	89.4	73.5	13.9	49.0	47.2	75.5	81.6	82.6	69.3	8.9
2002 ..	65.5	57.5	87.4	91.2	89.6	74.1	13.2	49.2	46.2	74.7	80.7	82.7	69.7	8.9
2003 [1] .	65.0	45.6	88.0	91.4	89.3	72.4	14.3	49.6	44.1	71.4	79.1	81.9	70.7	9.8

B Percentage not shown where base is less than 35,000.   [1] See footnote 2, Table 569.   [2] Spouse present.   [3] Widowed, divorced, and married (spouse absent).

Source: U.S. Bureau of Labor Statistics, Bulletins 2217 and 2340; and unpublished data.

No. 578. Marital Status of Women in the Civilian Labor Force: 1970 to 2003

[Annual averages of monthly figures (31,543 represents 31,543,000). For civilian noninstitutional population 16 years old and over. Based on the Current Population Survey; see text, Section 1, and Appendix III]

Year	Female civilian labor force (1,000)				Female participation rate [3]			
	Total	Single	Married [1]	Other [2]	Total	Single	Married [1]	Other [2]
1970	31,543	7,265	18,475	5,804	43.3	56.8	40.5	40.3
1975	37,475	9,125	21,484	6,866	46.3	59.8	44.3	40.1
1980	45,487	11,865	24,980	8,643	51.5	64.4	49.8	43.6
1985	51,050	13,163	27,894	9,993	54.5	66.6	53.8	45.1
1986	52,413	13,512	28,623	10,277	55.3	67.2	54.9	45.6
1987	53,658	13,885	29,381	10,393	56.0	67.4	55.9	45.7
1988	54,742	14,194	29,921	10,627	56.6	67.7	56.7	46.2
1989	56,030	14,377	30,548	11,104	57.4	68.0	57.8	47.0
1990 [4]	56,829	14,612	30,901	11,315	57.5	66.7	58.4	47.2
1991	57,178	14,681	31,112	11,385	57.4	66.2	58.5	46.8
1992	58,141	14,872	31,700	11,570	57.8	66.2	59.3	47.1
1993	58,795	15,031	31,980	11,784	57.9	66.2	59.4	47.2
1994 [4]	60,239	15,333	32,888	12,018	58.8	66.7	60.7	47.5
1995	60,944	15,467	33,359	12,118	58.9	66.8	61.0	47.4
1996	61,857	15,842	33,618	12,397	59.3	67.1	61.2	48.1
1997 [4]	63,036	16,492	33,802	12,742	59.8	67.9	61.6	48.6
1998 [4]	63,714	17,087	33,857	12,771	59.8	68.5	61.2	48.8
1999 [4]	64,855	17,575	34,372	12,909	60.0	68.7	61.2	49.1
2000 [4]	66,303	17,849	35,146	13,308	59.9	68.9	61.1	49.0
2001	66,848	18,021	35,236	13,592	59.8	68.1	61.2	49.0
2002	67,363	18,203	35,477	13,683	59.6	67.4	61.0	49.2
2003 [4]	68,272	18,397	36,046	13,828	59.5	66.2	61.0	49.6

[1] Husband present.   [2] Widowed, divorced, or separated.   [3] See footnote 3, Table 574 for definition of participation rate.   [4] See footnote 2, Table 569.

Source: U.S. Bureau of Labor Statistics, Bulletin 2307; and unpublished data.

No. 579. Employment Status of Women by Marital Status and Presence and Age of Children: 1970 to 2003

[As of March (7.0 represents 7,000,000). For the civilian noninstitutional persons 16 years and over. Based on the Current Population Survey; see text, Section 1, and Appendix III]

Item	Total Single	Total Mar-ried[1]	Total Other[2]	With any children — Total Single	With any children — Total Mar-ried[1]	With any children — Total Other[2]	Children 6 to 17 only Single	Children 6 to 17 only Mar-ried[1]	Children 6 to 17 only Other[2]	Children under 6 Single	Children under 6 Mar-ried[1]	Children under 6 Other[2]
IN LABOR FORCE (mil.)												
1970	7.0	18.4	5.9	(NA)	10.2	1.9	(NA)	6.3	1.3	(NA)	3.9	0.6
1980	11.2	24.9	8.8	0.6	13.7	3.6	0.2	8.4	2.6	0.3	5.2	1.0
1990	14.0	31.0	11.2	1.5	16.5	4.2	0.6	9.3	3.0	0.9	7.2	1.2
1995	15.0	33.6	12.0	2.1	18.0	4.6	0.8	10.2	3.3	1.3	7.8	1.3
2000[3]	17.8	35.0	13.2	3.1	18.2	4.5	1.2	10.8	3.4	1.8	7.3	1.1
2001[3]	17.8	35.7	13.8	3.1	18.7	4.5	1.2	11.2	3.4	1.8	7.4	1.2
2002	18.1	35.6	13.7	3.2	18.3	4.6	1.4	11.1	3.4	1.8	7.2	1.2
2003[3]	17.9	36.2	14.2	3.2	18.3	4.7	1.3	11.1	3.6	1.9	7.2	1.1
PARTICIPATION RATE[4]												
1970	53.0	40.8	39.1	(NA)	39.7	60.7	(NA)	49.2	66.9	(NA)	30.3	52.2
1980	61.5	50.1	44.0	52.0	54.1	69.4	67.6	61.7	74.6	44.1	45.1	60.3
1990	66.4	58.2	46.8	55.2	66.3	74.2	69.7	73.6	79.7	48.7	58.9	63.6
1995	65.5	61.1	47.3	57.5	70.2	75.3	67.0	76.2	79.5	53.0	63.5	66.3
2000[3]	68.6	62.0	50.2	73.9	70.6	82.7	79.7	77.2	85.0	70.5	62.8	76.6
2001[3]	68.2	61.8	50.0	73.5	70.4	83.1	80.8	77.5	85.9	69.2	61.9	75.8
2002	67.1	61.5	49.3	75.3	69.6	82.1	81.7	76.8	83.6	71.0	60.8	77.9
2003[3]	65.0	61.8	50.1	73.1	69.2	82.0	77.6	77.0	84.8	70.2	59.8	74.3
EMPLOYMENT (mil.)												
1970	6.5	17.5	5.6	(NA)	9.6	1.8	(NA)	6.0	1.2	(NA)	3.6	0.6
1980	10.1	23.6	8.2	0.4	12.8	3.3	0.2	8.1	2.4	0.2	4.8	0.9
1990	12.9	29.9	10.5	1.2	15.8	3.8	0.5	8.9	2.7	0.7	6.9	1.1
1995	13.7	32.3	11.3	1.8	17.2	4.2	0.7	9.8	3.1	1.1	7.3	1.2
2000[3]	16.4	34.0	12.7	2.7	17.6	4.3	1.1	10.6	3.2	1.6	7.1	1.1
2001[3]	16.6	34.7	13.2	2.7	18.0	4.3	1.1	10.9	3.2	1.6	7.2	1.1
2002	16.5	34.3	12.9	2.8	17.5	4.3	1.2	10.7	3.2	1.6	6.8	1.1
2003[3]	16.2	34.8	13.2	2.8	17.5	4.3	1.2	10.7	3.3	1.6	6.8	1.0
UNEMPLOYMENT RATE[5]												
1970	7.1	4.8	4.8	(NA)	6.0	7.2	(NA)	4.8	5.9	(NA)	7.9	9.8
1980	10.3	5.3	6.4	23.2	5.9	9.2	15.6	4.4	7.9	29.2	8.3	12.8
1990	8.2	3.5	5.7	18.4	4.2	8.5	14.5	3.8	7.7	20.8	4.8	10.2
1995	8.7	3.9	5.8	16.6	4.3	8.1	11.8	3.6	7.1	19.5	5.3	10.8
2000[3]	7.3	2.7	4.3	11.0	2.9	5.1	8.7	2.6	4.8	12.6	3.5	5.9
2001[3]	7.1	2.9	4.3	12.1	3.4	5.3	10.7	3.0	4.6	13.1	3.9	7.6
2002	8.7	3.7	6.3	12.6	4.1	7.9	11.1	3.5	6.7	13.8	5.1	11.4
2003[3]	9.4	3.8	6.5	13.4	4.1	8.9	11.6	3.6	7.7	14.7	4.9	13.0

NA Not available. [1] Husband present. [2] Widowed, divorced, or separated. [3] See footnote 2, Table 568. [4] Percent of women in each specific category in the labor force. [5] Unemployed as a percent of civilian labor force in specified group.

Source: U.S. Bureau of Labor Statistics, Bulletin 2307; and unpublished data.

No. 580. Labor Force Participation Rates for Wives, Husband Present by Age of Own Youngest Child: 1975 to 2003

[As of March. For civilian noninstitutional population, 16 years old and over. For definition of participation rate, see Table 579. Based on Current Population Survey; see text, Section 1, and Appendix III]

Presence and age of child	Total 1975	Total 1990	Total 2003	White[1] 1975	White[1] 1990	White[1] 2003	Black[1] 1975	Black[1] 1990	Black[1] 2003
Wives, total	44.4	58.2	61.8	43.6	57.6	61.3	54.1	64.7	68.7
No children under 18	43.8	51.1	55.7	43.6	50.8	55.5	47.6	52.9	58.5
With children under 18	44.9	66.3	69.2	43.6	65.6	68.7	58.4	75.6	79.2
Under 6, total	36.7	58.9	59.8	34.7	57.8	59.4	54.9	73.1	70.5
Under 3	32.7	55.5	56.5	30.7	54.9	56.1	50.1	67.5	66.4
1 year or under	30.8	53.9	54.7	29.2	53.3	54.6	50.0	64.4	63.6
2 years	37.1	60.9	61.3	35.1	60.3	60.5	56.4	75.4	77.7
3 to 5 years	42.2	64.1	64.8	40.1	62.5	64.3	61.2	80.4	75.2
3 years	41.2	63.1	63.6	39.0	62.3	63.2	62.7	74.5	75.0
4 years	41.2	65.1	64.1	38.7	63.2	63.9	64.9	80.6	72.3
5 years	44.4	64.5	66.9	43.8	62.0	65.7	56.3	86.2	75.9
6 to 13 years	51.8	73.0	75.1	50.7	72.6	74.4	65.7	77.6	85.5
14 to 17 years	53.5	75.1	81.2	53.4	74.9	80.9	52.3	78.8	86.3

[1] Beginning 2003, for persons in this race group only. See footnote 3, Table 570.
Source: U.S. Bureau of Labor Statistics, Bulletin 2340; and unpublished data.

Labor Force, Employment, and Earnings 377

No. 581. Families With Own Children—Employment Status of Parents: 1995 and 2003

[In thousands, except percent distribution. Annual average of monthly figures (33,544 represents 33,544,000. For families with own children. Based on the Current Population Survey, see text, Section 1, and Appendix III]

Characteristic	Number 1995	Number 2003	Percent 1995	Percent 2003	Characteristic	Number 1995	Number 2003	Percent 1995	Percent 2003
WITH OWN CHILDREN UNDER 18 YEARS OLD					Father employed, not mother	2,921	3,261	22.5	23.4
Total families	33,544	35,428	100.0	100.0	Neither parent employed . .	517	443	4.0	3.2
Parent(s) employed	29,659	32,002	88.4	90.3	Families maintained by women [1]	4,360	5,009	100.0	100.0
No parent employed.	3,886	3,426	11.6	9.7	Mother employed	3,142	3,851	72.1	76.9
Married-couple families.	24,604	25,383	100.0	100.0	Mother not employed	1,219	1,157	27.9	23.1
Parent(s) employed	23,643	24,553	96.1	96.7	Families maintained by men [1]	908	1,199	100.0	100.0
Mother employed	16,629	16,820	67.6	66.3	Father employed	766	985	84.3	82.2
Both parents employed	15,491	15,420	63.0	60.7	Father not employed.	143	214	15.7	17.8
Mother employed, not father.	1,137	1,400	4.6	5.5	**WITH OWN CHILDREN UNDER 6 YEARS OLD**				
Father employed, not mother	7,014	7,733	28.5	30.5	Total families	15,275	15,302	100.0	100.0
Neither parent employed . .	962	830	3.9	3.3	Parent(s) employed	13,267	13,692	86.9	89.5
Families maintained by women [1]	7,433	8,069	100.0	100.0	No parent employed.	2,007	1,608	13.1	10.5
Mother employed	4,755	5,804	64.0	71.9	Married-couple families.	11,604	11,466	100.0	100.0
Mother not employed	2,678	2,265	36.0	28.1	Parent(s) employed	11,159	11,080	96.2	96.6
Families maintained by men [1]	1,507	1,975	100.0	100.0	Mother employed	7,066	6,607	60.9	57.6
Father employed	1,261	1,645	83.7	83.3	Both parents employed	6,646	6,097	57.3	53.2
Father not employed.	245	331	16.3	16.8	Mother employed, not father.	421	510	3.6	4.4
WITH OWN CHILDREN 6 to 17 YEARS OLD					Father employed, not mother	4,092	4,474	35.3	39.0
Total families	18,270	20,125	100.0	100.0	Neither parent employed . .	445	385	3.8	3.4
Parent(s) employed	16,391	18,309	89.7	91.0	Families maintained by women [1]	3,073	3,061	100.0	100.0
No parent employed.	1,878	1,814	10.3	9.0	Mother employed	1,613	1,953	52.5	63.8
Married-couple families.	13,001	13,917	100.0	100.0	Mother not employed	1,460	1,107	47.5	36.2
Parent(s) employed	12,484	13,473	96.0	96.8	Families maintained by men [1]	598	776	100.0	100.0
Mother employed	9,562	10,214	73.6	73.4	Father employed	496	659	82.8	84.9
Both parents employed	8,846	9,323	68.0	67.0	Father not employed.	102	116	17.1	14.9
Mother employed, not father.	717	890	5.5	6.4					

[1] No spouse present.

Source: U.S. Bureau of Labor Statistics, *Employmemt Characteristics of Families in 2003, News,* USDL 04-719, April 20, 2004, and earlier issues. See Internet site <http://www.bls.gov/bls/newsrels.htm#OEUS>.

No. 582. Employed Civilians and Weekly Hours: 1980 to 2003

[In thousands (99,303 represents 99,303,000), except as indicated. For civilian noninstitutional population 16 years old and over. Annual averages of monthly figures. Based on Current Population Survey; see text, Section 1, and Appendix III]

Item	1980	1990 [1]	1995	1999 [1]	2000 [1]	2001	2002	2003 [1]
Total employed	99,303	118,793	124,900	133,488	136,891	136,933	136,485	137,736
Age:								
16 to 19 years old	7,710	6,581	6,419	7,172	7,189	6,740	6,332	5,919
20 to 24 years old	14,087	13,401	12,443	12,891	13,229	13,348	13,351	13,443
25 to 34 years old	27,201	33,935	32,356	30,865	31,549	30,863	30,306	30,383
35 to 44 years old	19,523	30,817	34,202	36,728	36,433	36,049	35,235	34,881
45 to 54 years old	16,234	19,525	24,378	28,635	30,310	31,036	31,281	31,914
55 to 64 years old	11,586	11,189	11,435	13,315	14,002	14,645	15,674	16,598
65 years old and over.	2,960	3,346	3,666	3,882	4,179	4,253	4,306	4,608
Class of worker:								
Nonagriculture.	95,938	115,570	121,460	130,207	134,427	134,635	134,174	135,461
Wage and salary worker . .	88,525	106,598	112,448	121,323	125,114	125,407	125,156	126,015
Self-employed	7,000	8,719	8,902	8,790	9,205	9,121	8,923	9,344
Unpaid family workers	413	253	110	95	108	107	95	101
Agriculture	3,364	3,223	3,440	3,281	2,464	2,299	2,311	2,275
Wage and salary worker . .	1,425	1,740	1,814	1,944	1,421	1,283	1,282	1,299
Self-employed	1,642	1,378	1,580	1,297	1,010	988	1,003	951
Unpaid family workers	297	105	45	40	33	28	26	25
Weekly hours:								
Nonagriculture:								
Wage and salary workers. .	38.1	39.2	39.2	39.5	39.6	39.2	39.1	39.0
Self-employed	41.2	40.8	39.4	40.1	39.7	39.1	38.7	38.4
Unpaid family workers	34.7	34.0	33.5	33.4	32.5	30.2	31.5	31.7
Agriculture:								
Wage and salary workers. .	41.6	41.2	41.1	41.1	43.2	42.6	42.4	42.6
Self-employed	49.3	46.8	43.5	43.3	45.3	45.6	44.9	45.1
Unpaid family workers	38.6	38.5	42.0	36.6	38.3	42.1	38.7	33.4

[1] See footnote 2, Table 569.

Source: U.S. Bureau of Labor Statistics, *Employment and Earnings,* monthly, January 2004 issue; and unpublished data. See Internet site <http://www.bls.gov/cps/home.htm>.

No. 583. Employed Workers Actively Seeking a New Job: 2001

[In thousands (121,334 represents 121,334,000), except rate. As of February. For employed wage and salary workers 16 old and over (except as indicated) responding to the question on actively seeking work in the prior 3 months. Based on the Current Population Survey; see text, Section 1, and Appendix III. See headnote Table 587 regarding occupations.]

Characteristic	Total employed	Persons responding to search question Actively seeking Total work	Actively seeking work	Percent	Characteristic	Total employed	Persons responding to search question Actively seeking Total work	Actively seeking work	Percent
Total.............	121,334	118,163	4,937	4.2	Technicians and related				
Age:					support	4,440	4,332	258	6.0
16 to 19 years old	6,544	6,373	313	4.9	Sales	13,908	13,545	680	5.0
20 to 24 years old	12,997	12,632	902	7.1	Administrative support,				
25 to 34 years old	28,285	27,472	1,517	5.5	including clerical	18,391	17,920	608	3.4
35 to 44 years old	32,887	32,018	1,233	3.9	Private household	592	401	44	11.0
45 to 54 years old	26,052	25,515	749	2.9	Protective service	2,436	2,376	79	3.3
55 to 64 years old	11,743	11,426	213	1.9	Service, except private				
65 years old and over ...	2,826	2,728	10	0.4	households and				
Sex: Male	62,753	61,106	2,606	4.3	protective	13,493	13,007	556	4.3
Female ....,	58,581	57,058	2,332	4.1	Precision production, craft,				
Educational attainment: [1]					and repair	12,770	12,426	395	3.2
Less than high school					Machine operators,				
diploma	9,515	9,172	233	2.5	assemblers, and				
High school diploma, no					inspectors..........	6,730	6,613	242	3.7
college............	31,280	30,297	846	2.8	Transportation and				
Some college or associate					material moving				
degree............	28,984	28,320	1,175	4.1	occupations	5,266	5,109	191	3.7
Bachelor's degree or					Handlers, equipment				
more	32,014	31,370	1,469	4.7	cleaners, helpers, and				
Occupation:					laborers	4,846	4,675	241	5.2
Executive, administra-					Farming, forestry, and				
tive, and managerial....	17,390	17,091	750	4.4	fishing	1,402	1,330	41	3.1
Professional specialty....	19,670	19,337	852	4.4					

[1] Persons 25 years old and over.

Source: U.S. Bureau of Labor Statistics, unpublished data.

No. 584. Persons at Work by Hours Worked: 2003

[132,267 represents 132,267,000. For civilian noninstitutional population 16 years old and over. Annual averages of monthly figures. Based on Current Population Survey; see text, Section 1, and Appendix III]

Hours of work	Persons at work (1,000) Total	Agriculture industries	Non-agriculture industries	Percent distribution Total	Agriculture industries	Non-agriculture industries
Total.....................	132,267	2,170	130,096	100.0	100.0	100.0
1 to 34 hours...................	31,869	583	31,286	24.1	26.9	24.0
1 to 4 hours.................	1,323	48	1,275	1.0	2.2	1.0
5 to 14 hours................	5,030	139	4,891	3.8	6.4	3.8
15 to 29 hours...............	15,802	258	15,544	11.9	11.9	11.9
30 to 34 hours	9,715	139	9,576	7.3	6.4	7.4
35 hours and over	100,398	1,587	98,810	75.9	73.1	76.0
35 to 39 hours	8,989	99	8,889	6.8	4.6	6.8
40 hours....................	54,607	555	54,052	41.3	25.6	41.5
41 hours and over.............	36,802	933	35,869	27.8	43.0	27.6
41 to 48 hours	12,998	148	12,850	9.8	6.8	9.9
49 to 58 hours	13,816	260	13,557	10.4	12.0	10.4
60 hours and over	9,988	525	9,462	7.6	24.2	7.3
Average weekly hours: persons at work	39.0	43.5	39.0	(X)	(X)	(X)
Persons usually working full time	42.9	49.4	42.7	(X)	(X)	(X)

X Not applicable.
Source: U.S. Bureau of Labor Statistics, *Employment and Earnings,* monthly, January 2004 issue. See Inrenet site <http://www.bls.gov/cps/home.htm>.

No. 585. Persons With a Job But Not at Work: 1980 to 2003

[In thousands (5,881 represents 5,881,000), except percent. For civilian noninstitutional population 16 years old and over. Annual averages of monthly figures. Based on Current Population Survey; see text, Section 1 and Appendix III]

Reason for not working	1980	1990 [1]	1995	1996	1997 [1]	1998 [1]	1999 [1]	2000 [1]	2001	2002	2003 [1]
All industries, number	5,881	6,160	5,582	5,768	5,555	5,586	5,407	5,681	5,631	5,394	5,469
Percent of employed	5.9	5.2	4.5	4.6	4.3	4.2	4.1	4.2	4.1	4.0	4.0
Reason for not working:											
Vacation	3,320	3,529	2,982	3,085	2,942	3,033	2,899	3,109	3,039	2,929	2,922
Illness	1,426	1,341	1,084	1,090	1,114	1,095	1,096	1,156	1,095	1,072	1,090
Bad weather	155	90	122	256	146	130	104	89	100	97	123
Industrial dispute	105	24	21	11	20	10	7	14	9	7	18
All other	876	1,177	1,373	1,325	1,334	1,318	1,300	1,313	1,388	1,289	1,316

[1] See footnote 2, Table 569.
Source: U.S. Bureau of Labor Statistics, *Employment and Earnings,* monthly, January 2004 issue; and unpublished data. See Internet site <http://www.bls.gov/cps/home.htm>.

Labor Force, Employment, and Earnings **379**

No. 586. Self-Employed Workers by Industry and Occupation: 2000 to 2003

[In thousands (10,214 represents 10,214,000). For civilian noninstitutional population 16 years old and over. Annual averages of monthly figures. Based on occupational and industrial classifications derived from those used in the 2000 census and are not comparable to those used in the 1990 census. See text in this section. Based on the Current Population Survey; see text, Section 1, and Appendix III]

Item	2000	2001	2002	2003 [1]
Total self-employed	10,214	10,109	9,926	10,295
Industry:				
Agriculture and related industries	1,010	988	1,003	951
Mining	12	21	13	9
Construction	1,728	1,675	1,598	1,717
Manufacturing	334	354	312	325
Wholesale and retail trade [2]	1,221	1,195	1,163	1,247
Transportation and utilities [2]	348	375	369	357
Information	139	132	145	152
Financial activities [2]	735	697	675	736
Professional and business services [2]	1,927	2,001	1,863	1,908
Education and health services [2]	1,107	1,090	1,119	1,138
Leisure and hospitality [2]	660	631	627	686
Other services [3]	993	951	1,041	1,071
Occupation:				
Management, professional, and related occupations	4,169	4,085	4,064	4,176
Service occupations	1,775	1,775	1,786	1,690
Sales and office occupations	1,982	1,927	1,883	1,945
Natural resources, construction, and maintenance occupations	1,591	1,602	1,503	1,795
Production, transportation, and material moving occupations	698	720	690	689

[1] See footnote 2 Table 569.   [2] For composition of industries see Table 606.   [3] Includes private households.
Source: U.S. Bureau of Labor Statistics, *Employment and Earnings*, monthly, January 2004. See Internet site <http://www.bls.gov/cps/home.htm>.

No. 587. Persons Doing Job-Related Work at Home: 2001

[19,759 represents 19,759,000. As of May. For persons at work 16 years and over in non-agricultural industries doing job-related work at home at least once a week as part of their primary job. Based on the Current Population Survey; see text, Section 1, and Appendix III. Industry and occupational classifications not comparable to those in tables based on the 2000 census. See text this section.]

Characteristic		Percent distribution				Wage and salary workers paid to work at home			
		Wage and salary workers			Self-em-ployed [4]	Total [5] (1,000)	Percent distribution		
	Total [1] (1,000)	Rate [2]	Paid [3]	Unpaid			Hours vary	Usually less than 8 hours	Usually 35 hours or more
Total [6]	19,759	15.0	17.4	52.0	29.7	3,436	27.4	24.5	15.7
SEX									
Male	10,291	14.8	16.0	50.5	32.6	1,642	30.9	23.3	14.8
Female	9,468	15.2	18.9	53.7	26.5	1,794	24.2	25.7	16.5
RACE AND HISPANIC ORIGIN									
White	17,947	16.3	17.5	51.6	30.0	3,138	27.2	24.4	15.0
Black	1,152	7.6	14.9	57.9	26.0	172	29.7	22.1	28.9
Hispanic origin [7]	937	6.7	20.4	49.2	28.4	191	32.3	15.9	27.6
OCCUPATION									
Managerial and professional	12,628	29.8	14.2	62.8	22.4	1,798	28.0	24.1	13.9
Exec., admin., and managerial	5,262	25.7	16.7	52.5	30.0	880	25.8	24.3	12.9
Professional specialty	7,366	33.5	12.5	70.1	17.0	918	30.1	23.9	14.9
Technical, sales and admin. support	4,669	12.2	24.7	40.2	33.9	1,155	27.3	22.1	16.7
Technicians and related support	305	6.9	36.0	48.4	14.3	110	40.2	24.6	21.2
Sales	3,133	20.0	20.3	40.3	38.9	635	27.8	18.9	13.0
Admin support, inc. clerical	1,231	6.8	33.4	37.8	25.8	411	23.3	26.5	21.0
Service	972	5.3	24.1	18.4	55.1	234	25.6	19.6	33.1
Precision production, craft, and repair	1,050	7.1	15.7	19.4	64.4	165	29.1	47.2	2.7
Operators, fabricators, and laborers	381	2.2	19.4	24.3	49.3	74	(B)	(B)	(B)
Farming, forestry, and fishing	59	8.7	(B)	(B)	(B)	10	(B)	(B)	(B)
INDUSTRY									
Mining	65	11.1	(B)	(B)	(B)	9	(B)	(B)	(B)
Construction	1,134	12.4	11.6	20.5	65.2	131	31.8	36.5	5.1
Manufacturing	1,806	9.3	28.7	54.9	15.7	518	27.0	21.5	12.5
Transportation and public utilities	898	8.9	22.8	49.4	26.0	205	14.1	29.7	25.3
Wholesale trade	1,009	19.4	24.4	47.9	25.6	247	28.1	15.0	12.9
Retail trade	1,529	7.0	12.8	36.4	49.8	196	23.7	32.5	10.3
Finance, insurance, and real estate	1,810	20.8	18.8	48.2	33.0	340	30.7	24.0	9.5
Services	10,926	21.7	14.8	57.2	27.1	1,618	28.0	24.3	19.0
Public administration	581	9.2	29.6	69.8	-	172	33.7	27.1	12.8

- Represents zero.   B Base figure too small to meet statistical standards for reliability of a derived figure.   [1] Includes unpaid family workers and persons who did not report pay status.   [2] Persons working at home as a percent of the total employed.   [3] Persons with formal arrangements with their employers to be paid for the work done at home.   [4] Includes incorporated and unincorporated self-employed.   [5] Includes those not reporting usual number of hours worked.   [6] Includes other races, not shown separately.   [7] Persons of Hispanic origin may be of any race.
Source: U.S. Bureau of Labor Statistics, *Work at Home in 2001*, News, USDL 02-107, March 1, 2002. See Internet site <http://www.bls.gov/bls/newsrels.htm#OEUS>.

380   Labor Force, Employment, and Earnings

No. 588. Persons on Flexible Schedules: 2001

[In thousands, except percent. (99,631 represents 99,631,000) As of May. For employed full-time wage and salary workers 16 years old and over. Excludes the self-employed. Data relate to the primary job. Based on the Current Population Survey; see text, Section 1, and Appendix III. Occupational classifications not comparable to those based on the 2000 Census. See text this section.]

Item	Total	Total With flexible schedules		Male	Male With flexible schedules		Female	Female With flexible schedules	
	Total [1]	Number	Percent	Total [1]	Number	Percent	Total [1]	Number	Percent
Total	**99,631**	**28,724**	**28.8**	**56,066**	**16,792**	**30.0**	**43,566**	**11,931**	**27.4**
AGE									
16 to 19 years old	1,761	339	19.2	988	167	16.9	773	171	22.2
20 to 24 years old	9,343	2,327	24.9	5,219	1,203	23.0	4,124	1,124	27.2
25 to 34 years old	24,552	7,434	30.3	14,058	4,370	31.1	10,494	3,064	29.2
35 to 44 years old	28,702	8,578	29.9	16,522	5,120	31.0	12,180	3,458	28.4
45 to 54 years old	23,946	6,990	29.2	12,902	4,032	31.2	11,044	2,958	26.8
55 to 64 years old	9,971	2,633	26.4	5,531	1,590	28.8	4,440	1,043	23.5
65 years old and over	1,357	423	31.2	847	311	36.7	510	112	22.0
RACE AND HISPANIC ORIGIN									
White	82,205	24,647	30.0	47,498	14,734	31.0	34,707	9,913	28.6
Black	12,390	2,629	21.2	5,776	1,209	20.9	6,614	1,420	21.5
Hispanic origin [2]	11,919	2,356	19.8	7,305	1,344	18.4	4,614	1,011	21.9
OCCUPATION									
Executive, administrative, and managerial	16,279	7,404	45.5	8,748	4,277	48.9	7,531	3,128	41.5
Professional specialty	16,681	5,922	35.5	8,037	3,678	45.8	8,644	2,244	26.0
Technicians and related support	3,757	1,181	31.4	1,863	683	36.7	1,894	498	26.3
Sales	9,852	4,011	40.7	5,424	2,404	44.3	4,428	1,607	36.3
Administrative support, including clerical	13,997	3,426	24.5	3,206	753	23.5	10,791	2,672	24.8
Private household	377	132	35.0	5	3	(B)	371	129	34.8
Protective service	2,144	343	16.0	1,773	291	16.4	371	52	14.0
Service, exc. private household and protective	8,207	1,755	21.4	3,324	698	21.0	4,883	1,057	21.6
Precision production, craft, and repair	12,061	2,209	18.3	11,000	2,026	18.4	1,061	183	17.3
Operators, fabricators, and laborers	14,621	1,999	13.7	11,324	1,689	14.9	3,297	310	9.4
Farming, forestry, fishing	1,653	342	20.7	1,360	291	21.4	293	51	17.5

B Percent not shown where base is less than 75,000.   [1] Includes persons who did not provide information on flexible schedules.   [2] Persons of Hispanic origin may be of any race.

Source: U.S. Bureau of Labor Statistics, *Workers on Flexible and Shift Schedules, News,* USDL 02-225, April 18, 2002. See Internet site <http://www.bls.gov/bls/newsrels.htm#OEUS>.

No. 589. Persons on Shift Schedules: 2001

[In percent, except as indicated. (99,631 represents 99,631,000). As of May. For employed full-time wage and salary workers 16 years old and over. Excludes the self-employed. Data relate to the primary job. Based on the Current Population Survey; see text, Section 1, and Appendix III. See headnote Table 588 regarding occupations.]

Item	Total workers [1] (1,000)	Regular day-time schedules	Shift workers Total	Evening shift	Night shift	Rotating shift	Split shift	Irregular shift [2]	Other shift
Total	**99,631**	**84.8**	**14.5**	**4.8**	**3.3**	**2.3**	**0.4**	**2.8**	**0.7**
AGE									
16 to 19 years old	1,761	70.2	28.8	13.5	5.4	3.4	0.3	5.3	1.0
20 to 24 years old	9,343	77.8	21.3	8.7	4.7	3.3	0.4	3.5	0.8
25 to 34 years old	24,552	84.9	14.4	4.9	3.3	2.3	0.6	2.4	0.8
35 to 44 years old	28,702	86.2	13.2	3.7	3.3	2.3	0.4	2.8	0.6
45 to 54 years old	23,946	86.3	13.1	4.1	2.9	2.3	0.3	2.6	0.8
55 to 64 years old	9,971	86.3	13.2	4.5	3.1	1.7	0.4	2.8	0.6
65 years old and over	1,357	84.9	15.0	3.9	2.1	1.7	1.3	5.5	0.5
SEX									
Male	56,066	82.9	16.4	5.2	3.6	2.8	0.5	3.3	0.9
Female	43,566	87.3	12.1	4.3	3.0	1.8	0.4	2.1	0.5
RACE AND HISPANIC ORIGIN									
White	82,205	85.8	13.6	4.4	3.0	2.2	0.4	2.8	0.7
Black	12,390	79.3	19.7	7.0	5.0	3.3	0.5	3.2	0.6
Hispanic origin [3]	11,919	84.3	14.8	5.8	3.4	2.0	0.5	2.5	0.5
OCCUPATION									
Executive, administrative, and managerial	16,279	93.9	5.6	1.6	0.7	1.0	0.2	1.8	0.3
Professional specialty	16,681	91.7	7.8	1.7	1.7	1.1	0.3	2.5	0.4
Technicians and related support	3,757	83.9	15.6	3.8	4.2	2.4	0.1	3.8	1.4
Sales	9,852	84.3	15.2	4.1	1.3	3.6	0.3	5.2	0.5
Administrative support, including clerical	13,997	91.1	8.4	3.6	2.4	0.7	0.4	0.9	0.4
Private household	377	82.8	15.6	1.0	0.5	0.7	0.7	9.4	3.3
Protective service	2,144	49.8	49.0	12.4	9.7	12.3	1.1	8.1	5.4
Service, exc. private household and protective	8,207	66.9	32.0	14.5	5.9	3.9	1.3	4.7	1.5
Precision production, craft, and repair	12,061	87.4	12.0	4.0	3.6	2.3	0.3	1.3	0.5
Operators, fabricators, and laborers	14,621	73.6	25.4	8.4	8.0	3.7	0.6	3.8	0.8
Farming, forestry, fishing	1,653	93.5	5.6	2.3	0.8	0.7	0.5	1.0	0.3

[1] Includes persons who did not provide information on usual shift worked.   [2] Employer arranged schedule.   [3] Persons of Hispanic origin may be of any race.

Source: U.S. Bureau of Labor Statistics, *Workers on Flexible and Shift Schedules, News,* USDL 02-225, April 18, 2002. See Internet site <http://www.bls.gov/bls/newsrels.htm#OEUS>.

Labor Force, Employment, and Earnings   381

No. 590. Multiple Jobholders: 2003

[Annual average of monthly figures (7,315 represents 7,315,000). For the civilian noninstitutional population 16 years old and over. Multiple jobholders are employed persons who, either 1) had jobs as wage or salary workers with two employers or more; 2) were self-employed and also held a wage and salary job; or 3) were unpaid family workers on their primary jobs but also held a wage and salary job. Based on the Current Population Survey; see text, Section 1, Population, and Appendix III]

Characteristic	Total		Male		Female	
	Number (1,000)	Percent of employed	Number (1,000)	Percent of employed	Number (1,000)	Percent of employed
Total [1]	7,315	5.3	3,716	5.1	3,599	5.6
Age:						
16 to 19 years old	280	4.7	107	3.7	173	5.7
20 to 24 years old	778	5.8	350	5.0	428	6.7
25 to 54 years old	5,266	5.4	2,742	5.3	2,525	5.6
55 to 64 years old	837	5.0	430	4.9	407	5.2
65 years old and over	154	3.3	87	3.4	67	3.3
Race and Hispanic origin:						
White [2]	6,273	5.5	3,190	5.2	3,083	5.9
Black [2]	645	4.4	328	4.8	317	4.0
Asian [2]	196	3.4	96	3.1	100	3.7
Hispanic	[3]554	3.2	325	3.1	229	3.3
Marital status:						
Married, spouse present	4,067	5.1	2,398	5.4	1,669	4.8
Widowed, divorced, or separated	1,270	5.8	410	4.6	860	6.6
Single, never married	1,978	5.4	907	4.6	1,070	6.4
Full- or part-time status:						
Primary job full time, secondary job part time . .	3,825	(X)	2,164	(X)	1,661	(X)
Both jobs part time	1,651	(X)	510	(X)	1,141	(X)
Both jobs full time	273	(X)	187	(X)	86	(X)
Hours vary on primary or secondary job	1,523	(X)	831	(X)	692	(X)

X Not applicable.   [1] Includes a small number of persons who work part time on their primary job and full time on their secondary job(s), not shown separately. Includes other races, not shown separately.   [2] For persons who selected only one race. Excludes persons who selected more than one race.   [3] Persons of Hispanic or Latino origin may be of any race.

Source: U.S. Bureau of Labor Statistics, *Employment and Earnings*, January 2004. See Internet site <http://www.bls.gov/cps/home.htm>.

No. 591. Average Number of Jobs Held from Ages 18 to 36: 1978 to 2000

[For persons 35 to 43 in 2000. A job is an uninterrupted period of work with a particular employer. Educational attainment as of 2000. Based on the National Longitudinal Survey of Youth 1979; see source for details]

Sex and educational attainment	Number of jobs held by age—				
	Total [1]	Age 18 to 22 years old	Age 22 to 27 years old	Age 28 to 32 years old	Age 33 to 36 years old
Total [2]	9.6	4.4	3.2	2.6	2.0
Less than a high school diploma	9.7	4.0	3.1	2.6	2.0
High school graduates, no college	9.2	4.1	3.0	2.6	2.0
Less than a bachelor's degree	10.0	4.5	3.0	2.7	2.1
Bachelor's degree or more	10.0	5.0	3.5	2.6	1.9
Male	9.9	4.5	3.4	2.8	2.1
Less than a high school diploma	11.1	4.7	3.7	3.0	2.1
High school graduates, no college	9.6	4.4	3.4	2.8	2.0
Less than a bachelor's degree	10.5	4.7	3.5	2.9	2.2
Bachelor's degree or more	9.5	4.6	3.4	2.5	2.0
Female	9.3	4.3	3.0	2.4	1.9
Less than a high school diploma	7.8	3.0	2.3	2.1	1.7
High school graduates, no college	8.7	3.9	3.0	2.4	2.0
Less than a bachelor's degree	9.5	4.4	3.2	2.5	2.0
Bachelor's degree or more	10.6	5.4	3.7	2.6	1.8
White, non-Hispanic	9.8	4.6	3.3	2.6	2.0
Less than a high school diploma	10.3	4.3	3.3	2.7	2.1
High school graduates, no college	9.2	4.3	3.1	2.6	2.0
Less than a bachelor's degree	10.3	4.7	3.5	2.7	2.1
Bachelor's degree or more	10.0	5.1	3.5	2.6	1.9
Black, non-Hispanic	9.1	3.6	3.1	2.7	2.0
Less than a high school diploma	8.3	2.8	2.7	2.5	1.7
High school graduates, no college	9.2	3.5	3.0	2.7	2.1
Less than a bachelor's degree	9.0	3.8	3.1	2.6	2.1
Bachelor's degree or more	10.0	4.4	3.7	2.8	2.2
Hispanic origin	8.9	4.0	3.0	2.5	1.9
Less than a high school diploma	9.2	3.8	2.9	2.4	1.9
High school graduates, no college	8.7	3.9	2.9	2.5	1.9
Less than a bachelor's degree	8.8	4.1	3.0	2.4	1.8
Bachelor's degree or more	9.4	4.3	3.2	2.7	2.0

[1] Jobs held in more than one age category were counted in each category, but only once in the total.   [2] Includes other races, not shown separately.

Source: U.S. Bureau of Labor Statistics, Number of Jobs Held, Labor Market Activity, and *Earnings Growth Among Younger Baby Boomers: Results from More Than Two Decades of a Longitudinal Survey*, USDL 02-497, August 27, 2002. See Internet site <http://www.bls.gov/nls/home.htm>.

No. 592. Distribution of Workers by Tenure With Current Employer by Selected Characteristic: 2002

[118,424 represents 118,424,000. As of February. For employed wage and salary workers 16 years old and over. Based on the Current Population Survey and subject to sampling error; see source and Appendix III]

Characteristic	Num-ber em-ployed (1,000)	Percent distribution by tenure with current employer								Median years [1]
		12 months or less	13 to 23 months	2 years	3 to 4 years	5 to 9 years	10 to 14 years	15 to 19 years	20 years or more	
Total [2]	118,424	24.5	8.4	5.8	17.3	17.7	10.4	6.0	9.8	3.7
AGE AND SEX										
16 to 19 years old............	5,904	71.5	12.6	7.8	7.5	0.5	-	-	-	0.7
20 years old and over	112,520	22.1	8.2	5.7	17.9	18.6	10.9	6.3	10.3	4.0
20 to 24 years old	12,414	51.4	14.6	9.2	19.2	5.6	(Z)	-	-	1.2
25 to 34 years old	26,959	28.9	11.0	7.5	23.3	22.0	6.5	0.8	(Z)	2.7
35 to 44 years old	31,648	17.9	7.3	5.3	18.4	21.3	14.7	9.3	5.8	4.6
45 to 54 years old	26,422	12.9	5.5	3.7	14.2	18.8	13.8	9.5	21.6	7.6
55 to 64 years old	12,104	10.7	4.6	3.3	12.0	17.1	15.2	9.7	27.4	9.9
65 years old and over........	2,973	9.9	4.1	4.5	13.4	19.8	13.9	8.6	25.6	8.7
Male........................	61,023	23.5	8.1	5.6	17.0	17.7	10.4	6.3	11.3	3.9
16 to 19 years old	2,879	72.2	12.9	7.0	7.4	0.4	-	-	-	0.8
20 years old and over......	58,144	21.1	7.9	5.6	17.5	18.6	10.9	6.6	11.8	4.2
20 to 24 years old	6,368	49.4	13.9	9.2	21.0	6.4	0.1	-	-	1.3
25 to 34 years old	14,408	27.2	10.5	7.4	23.2	23.5	7.2	0.9	(Z)	2.9
35 to 44 years old	16,491	16.9	6.8	5.1	17.3	21.4	15.6	10.3	6.6	5.1
45 to 54 years old	13,201	12.1	5.4	3.5	12.7	17.0	13.0	10.1	26.2	9.1
55 to 64 years old	6,118	10.9	4.8	3.3	12.0	15.3	13.4	9.0	31.4	10.2
65 years old and over	1,558	10.0	4.1	5.2	14.1	20.2	12.3	8.3	25.8	8.1
Female......................	57,401	25.6	8.7	5.9	17.7	17.7	10.4	5.7	8.3	3.4
16 to 19 years old	3,025	71.0	12.3	8.6	7.6	0.5	-	-	-	0.7
20 years old and over.....	54,376	23.1	8.5	5.8	18.3	18.7	10.9	6.0	8.7	3.7
20 to 24 years old	6,045	53.4	15.4	9.2	17.4	4.6	(Z)	-	-	1.1
25 to 34 years old	12,551	30.8	11.6	7.7	23.4	20.3	5.6	0.6	-	2.5
35 to 44 years old	15,157	19.0	7.8	5.6	19.6	21.2	13.7	8.2	4.8	4.3
45 to 54 years old	13,221	13.8	5.5	4.0	15.7	20.5	14.6	8.9	17.0	6.5
55 to 64 years old	5,986	10.5	4.5	3.3	11.9	19.0	17.0	10.4	23.4	9.6
65 years old and over	1,415	9.8	4.2	3.8	12.6	19.5	15.7	8.9	25.4	9.5
RACE AND HISPANIC ORIGIN										
White	98,670	24.4	8.4	5.6	17.1	17.8	10.5	6.2	10.1	3.7
Male	51,473	23.3	8.0	5.4	16.8	17.8	10.4	6.5	11.9	4.0
Female	47,197	25.5	9.0	5.9	17.3	17.8	10.5	5.9	8.2	3.4
Black	14,143	25.4	7.5	6.6	18.0	17.9	9.6	5.6	9.5	3.5
Male	6,567	24.5	8.2	7.0	16.5	18.2	9.8	6.3	9.4	3.5
Female	7,577	26.3	6.8	6.2	19.2	17.7	9.4	4.9	9.5	3.5
Hispanic origin [3]............	13,776	29.4	8.5	7.7	19.2	17.7	8.4	4.0	5.1	2.9
Male	7,807	28.5	7.6	8.2	19.7	17.9	8.6	4.1	5.5	3.0
Female	5,968	30.5	9.7	7.1	18.6	17.5	8.2	3.8	4.5	2.7

- Represents zero.   Z Less than 0.05 percent.   [1] For definition of median, see Guide to Tabular Presentation.   [2] Includes other races, not shown separately.   [3] Persons of Hispanic origin may be of any race.
Source: U. S. Bureau of Labor Statistics, News, *Employee Tenure in 2002*, USDL 02-531, September 19, 2002; and unpublished data. See Internet site <http://www.bls.gov/bls/newsrels.htm#OEUS>.

No. 593. Part-Time Workers by Reason: 2003

[In thousands (31,869 represents 31,869,000), except hours. For persons working 1 to 34 hours per week. For civilian noninstitutional population 16 years old and over. Annual average of monthly figures. Based on the Current Population Survey and subject to sampling error; see text, Section 1, and Appendix III]

Reason	All industries			Nonagriculture industries		
		Usually work—			Usually work—	
	Total	Full time	Part time	Total	Full time	Part time
Total working fewer than 35 hours	31,869	9,841	22,028	31,286	9,653	21,633
Economic reasons	4,701	1,687	3,013	4,596	1,621	2,975
Slack work or business conditions	3,118	1,434	1,684	3,052	1,388	1,664
Could find only part-time work	1,279	-	1,279	1,264	-	1,264
Seasonal work	169	119	51	147	101	47
Job started or ended during the week	134	134	-	132	132	-
Noneconomic reasons	27,169	8,154	19,014	26,690	8,031	18,658
Child-care problems..................	742	73	669	737	73	665
Other family or personal obligations	5,715	726	4,989	5,617	714	4,902
Health or medical limitations	753	-	753	734	-	734
In school or training..................	6,109	95	6,014	6,049	94	5,955
Retired or Social Security limit on earnings ...	1,951	-	1,951	1,854	-	1,854
Vacation or personal day	3,456	3,456	-	3,419	3,419	-
Holiday, legal, or religious	731	731	-	724	724	-
Weather related curtailment.............	470	470	-	440	440	-
Other	7,241	2,603	4,638	7,117	2,568	4,549
Average hours per week:						
Economic reasons....................	23.0	24.0	22.5	23.0	24.0	22.5
Noneconomic reasons	21.4	25.3	19.7	21.4	25.4	19.7

- Represents or rounds to zero.
Source: U.S. Bureau of Labor Statistics, *Employment and Earnings*, monthly, January 2004. See Internet site <http://www.bls.gov/cps/home.htm>.

Labor Force, Employment, and Earnings   383

No. 594. Displaced Workers by Selected Characteristics: 2002

[In percent, except total (3,969 represents 3,969,000). As of January. For persons 20 years old and over with tenure of 3 years or more who lost or left a job between January 1999 and December 2001 because of plant closings or moves, slack work, or the abolishment of their positions. Data revised since originally published. Based on Current Population Survey and subject to sampling error; see source and Appendix III]

Characteristic	Employment status				Reason for job loss		
	Total (1,000)	Employed	Unem-ployed	Not in the labor force	Plant or company closed down or moved	Slack/ insufficient work	Position or shift abolished
Total [1]	3,969	63.6	21.2	15.2	47.2	25.4	27.3
20 to 24 years old	132	68.7	15.4	15.8	45.4	49.8	4.8
25 to 54 years old	3,117	67.5	21.7	10.8	46.5	25.3	28.2
55 to 64 years old	593	50.9	20.3	28.8	50.7	20.1	29.2
65 years old and over . . .	127	19.8	20.7	59.5	50.9	28.1	21.0
Males	2,186	65.2	22.8	12.0	44.5	27.8	27.7
20 to 24 years old	55	[2]	[2]	[2]	[2]	[2]	[2]
25 to 54 years old	1,740	69.0	22.9	8.1	42.3	28.9	28.7
55 to 64 years old	326	55.0	22.7	22.3	55.6	16.5	27.9
65 years old and over . . .	65	[2]	[2]	[2]	[2]	[2]	[2]
Females	1,783	61.6	19.3	19.1	50.6	22.5	26.9
20 to 24 years old	77	65.8	17.9	16.3	46.2	47.9	5.9
25 to 54 years old	1,377	65.7	20.2	14.2	51.8	20.7	27.5
55 to 64 years old	266	45.8	17.3	36.8	44.8	24.5	30.7
65 years old and over . . .	62	[2]	[2]	[2]	[2]	[2]	[2]
White	3,351	64.7	20.8	14.5	46.9	24.7	28.4
Black	474	57.7	22.3	20.0	49.2	29.5	21.3
Hispanic origin [3]	335	55.0	31.0	14.0	50.1	33.9	16.0

[1] Includes other races, not shown separately. [2] Data not shown where base is less than 75,000. [3] Persons of Hispanic origin may be of any race.

Source: U.S. Bureau of Labor Statistics, *Worker Displacement, 1999-2001*,News USDL 02-483, August 21, 2002. See Internet site <http://www.bls.gov/bls/newsrels.htm#OEUS>.

No. 595. Labor Force Status of Persons With a Work Disability by Age: 2003

[In percent, except as indicated (22,224 represents 22,224,000). As of March. For civilians 16 to 74 who have a condition which prevents them from working or limits the amount of work they can do. Data from the Current Population Survey and subject to sampling error; see text, Section 1, and Appendix III]

Labor force status	Total	Age						
		16 to 24 years old	25 to 34 years old	35 to 44 years old	45 to 54 years old	55 to 64 years old	65 to 69 years old	70 to 74 years old
Number (1,000)	22,224	1,395	2,173	3,708	5,010	5,772	2,113	2,053
In labor force	23.5	31.5	37.3	32.2	28.3	17.8	9.6	5.9
Employed	19.8	23.6	29.0	27.2	24.5	15.8	8.2	5.5
Full-time.	12.5	11.7	18.3	18.4	17.2	10.1	1.8	2.0
Not in labor force	76.5	68.5	62.7	67.8	71.7	82.2	90.4	94.1
Unemployment rate	15.7	25.1	22.5	15.5	13.2	11.1	15.2	7.1

Source: U.S. Census Bureau, "Disability Data from the March Current Population Survey"; <http://www.census.gov/hhes/www/disable/disabcps.html>; (accessed 16 July 2004).

No. 596. Persons Not in the Labor Force: 2003

[In thousands (74,658 represents 74,658,000). Annual average of monthly figures. For the civilian noninstitutional population 16 years old and over. Based on the Current Population Survey; see text, Section 1, and Appendix III]

Status and reason	Total	Age			Sex	
		16 to 24 years old	25 to 54 years old	55 years old and over	Male	Female
Total not in the labor force	74,658	13,800	20,980	39,878	28,197	46,461
Do not want a job now [1]	69,932	12,079	18,857	38,996	26,073	43,859
Want a job now	4,726	1,721	2,124	882	2,124	2,603
In the previous year—						
Did not search for a job.	2,631	882	1,129	620	1,127	1,503
Did search for a job [2]	2,096	838	995	262	996	1,099
Not available for work now	564	274	248	43	231	333
Available for work now, not looking for work. . .	1,531	565	747	220	765	766
Reason for not currently looking for work:						
Discouraged over job prospects [3]	457	134	248	75	266	190
Family responsibilities.	153	37	94	22	35	118
In school or training	239	194	42	3	125	114
Ill health or disability.	113	15	72	26	51	62
Other [4]	570	184	292	94	288	282

[1] Includes some persons who are not asked if they want a job. [2] Persons who had a job in the prior 12 months must have searched since the end of that job. [3] Includes such things as believes no work available, could not find work, lacks necessary schooling or training, employer thinks too young or old, and other types of discrimination. [4] Includes such things as child care and transportation problems.

Source: U.S. Bureau of Labor Statistics, *Employment and Earnings*, monthly, January 2004 issue. See Internet site <http://www.bls.gov/cps/home.htm>.

No. 597. Employed Civilians by Occupation, Sex, Race, and Hispanic Origin: 2003

[For civilian noninstitutional population 16 years old and over (137,736 represents 137,736,000). Annual average of monthly figures. Based on Current Population Survey; see text, Section 1, and Appendix III. Occupational classifications are those used in the 2000 Census and are not comparable to those used in the 1990 Census]

Occupation	Total employed (1,000)	Percent of total			
		Female	Black [1]	Asian [1]	His-panic [2]
Total	137,736	46.8	10.7	4.2	12.6
Management, professional, and related occupations.	**47,929**	**50.5**	**8.2**	**5.4**	**6.1**
Management, business, and financial operations occupations	19,934	42.1	6.9	4.2	5.9
Management occupations [3]	14,468	37.1	5.9	3.7	5.8
Chief executives.	1,617	23.5	3.2	3.1	3.3
General and operations managers	702	28.2	6.0	2.8	7.6
Marketing and sales managers	888	39.7	4.0	3.3	5.6
Administrative services managers	81	34.6	11.1	5.0	4.0
Computer and information systems managers	347	30.5	4.4	8.3	3.8
Financial managers.	1,041	52.7	6.9	3.4	6.1
Human resources managers	263	68.6	7.4	1.0	6.6
Industrial production managers	276	17.3	3.3	3.0	6.1
Purchasing managers	169	39.1	5.1	2.8	6.0
Transportation, storage, and distribution managers	225	15.9	5.9	2.4	8.0
Farm, ranch, and other agricultural managers	206	18.2	1.0	0.9	6.2
Farmers and ranchers	825	24.7	0.6	0.7	2.1
Construction managers	680	5.9	3.6	1.5	6.2
Education administrators	748	65.2	12.2	2.4	4.4
Engineering managers.	77	10.4	1.3	8.5	0.2
Food service managers	875	41.0	7.1	10.8	10.1
Lodging managers	160	59.1	7.4	8.1	6.0
Medical and health services managers	480	70.9	11.3	1.7	4.6
Property, real estate, and community association managers	540	50.2	5.0	2.8	9.6
Social and community service managers. . . . ., ...	307	64.5	11.0	2.9	7.1
Business and financial operations occupations [3]	5,465	55.4	9.3	5.6	6.2
Wholesale and retail buyers, except farm products	213	48.0	4.2	6.9	7.3
Purchasing agents, except wholesale, retail, and farm products .	235	52.6	7.7	2.3	7.5
Claims adjusters, appraisers, examiners, and investigators.	284	63.4	12.2	3.2	6.1
Compliance officers, except agriculture, construction, health, and safety, and transportation	126	47.7	13.4	2.3	9.6
Cost estimators	100	14.6	3.3	1.2	5.7
Human resources, training, and labor relations specialists	687	70.8	11.1	3.5	8.7
Management analysts	547	42.9	7.0	5.6	3.3
Accountants and auditors.	1,639	58.6	9.6	8.8	5.6
Appraisers and assessors of real estate	119	30.8	4.2	1.0	5.6
Personal financial advisors	315	28.3	4.8	5.5	4.6
Insurance underwriters	101	73.2	9.8	5.7	6.8
Loan counselors and officers	417	59.8	9.9	3.9	8.2
Tax examiners, collectors, and revenue agents	74	61.6	18.9	6.2	6.9
Tax preparers.	91	68.6	9.3	3.4	8.6
Professional and related occupations . . . . . [3]	27,995	56.4	9.1	6.3	6.2
Computer and mathematical occupations [3]	3,122	28.8	8.1	12.9	5.5
Computer scientists and systems analysts.	722	30.4	9.7	10.8	5.4
Computer programmers	563	28.1	7.1	11.5	5.1
Computer software engineers	758	24.4	6.1	22.7	4.8
Computer support specialists	330	37.4	11.7	5.9	6.8
Network and computer systems administrators	176	21.7	8.1	5.9	9.2
Network systems and data communications analysts.	359	23.6	7.3	9.0	5.7
Operations research analysts . . . . [3]	95	50.6	7.8	11.0	5.8
Architecture and engineering occupations [3]	2,727	14.1	4.4	8.7	5.2
Architects, except naval.	180	22.1	0.3	6.3	6.2
Aerospace engineers.	82	11.0	0.8	9.5	4.2
Chemical engineers	75	14.9	3.1	8.9	4.5
Civil engineers	278	8.7	4.6	11.7	5.3
Computer hardware engineers	99	10.4	5.8	18.9	1.9
Electrical and electronics engineers	363	7.1	4.4	13.6	2.4
Industrial engineers, including health and safety.	180	19.2	3.6	8.9	4.3
Mechanical engineers	285	5.5	2.2	8.3	3.7
Drafters	224	21.7	5.6	3.7	8.6
Engineering technicians, except drafters	419	21.8	10.3	4.9	8.4
Surveying and mapping technicians . . . . . . [3]	75	16.9	2.0	0.9	2.3
Life, physical, and social science occupations [3]	1,375	43.0	6.3	10.3	5.9
Biological scientists	112	46.1	5.1	13.3	2.3
Medical scientists	101	50.5	4.8	21.0	4.9
Chemists and materials scientists	140	36.4	5.9	19.8	6.4
Environmental scientists and geoscientists	85	29.8	3.1	1.0	3.2
Market and survey researchers	124	56.6	7.7	7.0	5.5
Psychologists.	185	65.8	4.0	2.3	5.9
Chemical technicians	86	28.8	14.8	8.9	7.7
Community and social services occupations [3]	2,184	60.6	18.7	3.2	8.4
Counselors	640	67.0	21.5	2.6	9.7
Social workers	673	79.5	19.7	4.0	9.2
Miscellaneous community and social service specialists.	307	68.8	26.2	1.7	10.6
Clergy	410	13.9	10.2	4.7	4.6
Religious workers, all other.	96	55.6	7.5	2.3	5.1
Legal occupations [3]	1,508	46.2	6.0	2.4	6.0
Lawyers	952	27.6	3.6	2.8	4.0
Paralegals and legal assistants	286	84.2	10.7	1.8	9.4
Miscellaneous legal support workers . . . . . ., ...	211	76.1	8.1	2.0	11.0
Education, training, and library occupations [3]	7,768	73.8	9.8	3.3	7.1
Postsecondary teachers.	1,121	44.9	5.0	10.5	4.5
Preschool and kindergarten teachers	665	97.8	13.9	2.3	8.4

See footnotes at end of table.

U.S. Census Bureau, Statistical Abstract of the United States: 2004-2005

No. 597. Employed Civilians by Occupation, Sex, Race, and Hispanic Origin: 2003—Con.

[For civilian noninstitutional population 16 years old and over (137,736 represents 137,736,000). Annual average of monthly figures. Based on Current Population Survey; see text, Section 1, and Appendix III. Occupational classifications are those used in the 2000 Census and are not comparable to those used in the 1990 Census]

Occupation	Total employed (1,000)	Percent of total			
		Female	Black [1]	Asian [1]	His-panic [2]
Elementary and middle school teachers	2,557	81.7	10.4	1.9	5.9
Secondary school teachers	1,124	55.2	8.5	1.7	6.1
Special education teachers	370	82.4	8.3	0.5	4.9
Other teachers and instructors	662	67.5	8.7	3.9	7.6
Librarians	194	84.4	5.6	2.7	5.0
Teacher assistants	932	91.6	14.8	2.0	15.2
Arts, design, entertainment, sports, and media occupations [3]	2,663	47.6	6.4	4.6	7.7
Artists and related workers	212	50.0	2.2	3.6	5.1
Designers	793	55.7	5.0	6.6	8.7
Producers and directors	133	31.8	9.0	4.0	8.0
Athletes, coaches, umpires, and related workers	215	38.2	6.9	1.6	5.5
Musicians, singers, and related workers	179	34.6	13.8	3.5	8.0
News analysts, reporters and correspondents	80	44.4	5.9	2.4	6.3
Public relations specialists	128	66.5	7.5	3.7	4.1
Editors	163	53.8	2.4	3.1	5.1
Writers and authors	190	54.5	5.0	2.4	1.7
Miscellaneous media and communication workers	79	68.8	2.6	16.4	37.6
Broadcast and sound engineering technicians and radio operators	94	8.1	12.5	0.9	8.9
Photographers	146	38.6	4.7	6.0	8.2
Healthcare practitioner and technical occupations [3]	6,648	73.7	10.1	7.4	4.9
Dentists	188	23.7	4.7	8.7	5.6
Dietitians and nutritionists	85	91.1	13.1	9.0	5.6
Pharmacists	232	51.5	5.4	9.7	2.8
Physicians and surgeons	819	29.9	5.0	16.1	4.7
Registered nurses	2,449	92.1	9.9	7.0	3.9
Occupational therapists	77	87.3	6.5	3.7	6.2
Physical therapists	182	69.8	2.6	9.3	4.1
Respiratory therapists	94	54.4	18.7	5.4	2.2
Speech-language pathologists	93	94.5	5.1	1.2	1.6
Clinical laboratory technologists and technicians	294	75.2	12.3	10.6	5.9
Dental hygienists	126	98.9	0.6	1.4	2.0
Diagnostic related technologists and technicians	268	69.1	11.6	4.1	6.4
Emergency medical technicians and paramedics	121	32.0	7.1	1.3	7.7
Health diagnosing and treating practitioner support technicians	388	81.6	16.8	4.0	8.1
Licensed practical and licensed vocational nurses	531	94.8	22.3	3.6	6.6
Medical records and health information technicians	107	92.6	13.4	4.4	14.1
Service occupations [3]	**22,086**	**57.2**	**15.4**	**4.2**	**18.9**
Healthcare support occupations [3]	2,926	89.4	25.2	3.9	12.5
Nursing, psychiatric, and home health aides	1,811	89.6	34.4	4.2	12.0
Massage therapists	108	82.1	2.3	3.8	4.2
Dental assistants	251	95.0	7.8	5.5	14.7
Protective service occupations [3]	2,727	20.7	18.7	1.5	10.1
First-line supervisors/managers of police and detectives	127	20.9	11.7	0.2	3.8
Fire fighters	258	3.6	8.2	0.4	6.2
Bailiffs, correctional officers, and jailers	371	26.2	25.8	0.5	9.4
Detectives and criminal investigators	112	23.6	11.7	0.9	8.2
Police and sheriffs patrol officers	612	12.4	13.2	1.2	11.0
Security guards and gaming surveillance officers	781	21.1	28.4	2.9	12.7
Food preparation and serving related occupations	7,254	56.6	11.6	5.6	19.9
Chefs and head cooks	281	20.1	12.1	14.1	19.9
First-line supervisors/managers of food preparation and serving workers	667	56.3	16.1	3.2	13.4
Cooks	1,814	42.1	17.1	6.5	27.2
Food preparation workers	612	57.3	11.8	7.9	28.3
Bartenders	349	57.7	2.5	2.3	7.7
Combined food preparation and serving workers, including fast food	259	72.4	13.3	5.1	13.3
Counter attendants, cafeteria, food concession, and coffee shop	349	66.7	11.0	4.8	14.1
Waiters and waitresses	1,842	74.3	6.9	4.6	12.6
Food servers, nonrestaurant	180	66.3	18.3	7.6	18.8
Dining room and cafeteria attendants and bartender helpers	374	46.6	9.7	5.6	31.2
Dishwashers	294	23.9	9.7	4.8	37.3
Hosts and hostesses, restaurant, lounge, and coffee shop	230	86.8	3.6	2.8	11.0
Building and grounds cleaning and maintenance occupations	4,947	41.0	15.0	2.7	31.2
First-line supervisors/managers of housekeeping and janitorial workers	166	46.0	24.0	4.0	21.8
First-line supervisors/managers of landscaping, lawn service, and groundskeeping workers	223	5.5	5.4	1.7	17.6
Janitors and building cleaners	1,973	32.7	16.7	2.8	25.8
Maids and housekeeping cleaners	1,370	88.4	18.1	4.1	38.7
Pest control workers	81	6.1	5.0	0.8	7.4
Grounds maintenance workers	1,135	6.9	9.3	1.1	37.1
Personal care and service occupations [3]	4,232	78.4	13.7	5.4	13.0
First-line supervisors/managers of gaming workers	131	40.6	5.8	1.3	6.4
First-line supervisors/managers of personal service workers	162	71.5	6.0	10.3	7.5
Nonfarm animal caretakers	114	68.9	3.9	0.3	11.6
Gaming services workers	85	50.7	10.2	15.9	13.8
Barbers	95	17.7	29.7	2.3	12.2
Hairdressers, hairstylists, and cosmetologists	718	93.7	12.3	3.7	11.6
Miscellaneous personal appearance workers	174	82.2	3.7	43.4	6.6
Baggage porters, bellhops, and concierges	85	20.3	21.6	9.6	20.7

See footnotes at end of table.

U.S. Census Bureau, Statistical Abstract of the United States: 2004-2005

[For civilian noninstitutional population 16 years old and over (137,736 represents 137,736,000). Annual average of monthly figures. Based on Current Population Survey; see text, Section 1, and Appendix III. Occupational classifications are those used in the 2000 Census and are not comparable to those used in the 1990 Census]

Occupation	Total employed (1,000)	Percent of total			
		Female	Black [1]	Asian [1]	His-panic [2]
Transportation attendants	120	77.6	11.0	5.6	7.8
Child care workers	1,284	95.1	15.1	2.4	17.2
Personal and home care aides	512	88.4	20.8	3.7	14.8
Recreation and fitness workers	299	69.6	10.6	4.2	8.8
Sales and office occupations	**35,496**	**63.8**	**10.9**	**3.7**	**10.8**
Sales and related occupations [3]	15,960	49.0	8.9	4.1	10.4
First-line supervisors/managers of retail sales workers	3,389	41.8	7.0	5.0	9.3
First-line supervisors/managers of non-retail sales workers	1,388	27.5	6.9	3.7	9.6
Cashiers	2,903	76.4	15.9	5.0	15.0
Counter and rental clerks	206	58.9	11.0	3.0	11.4
Parts salespersons	137	14.1	2.7	4.0	10.3
Retail salespersons	3,113	50.4	9.7	4.1	11.8
Advertising sales agents	192	59.7	5.1	2.9	6.0
Insurance sales agents	552	44.3	5.9	2.1	5.2
Securities, commodities, and financial services sales agents	389	32.0	7.1	5.1	7.8
Travel agents	88	83.4	3.7	5.8	9.6
Sales representatives, services, all other	485	39.4	8.2	3.9	5.8
Sales representatives, wholesale and manufacturing	1,399	25.6	3.7	2.5	7.1
Models, demonstrators, and product promoters	73	87.2	5.3	1.3	15.1
Real estate brokers and sales agents	850	57.2	5.2	3.3	6.7
Telemarketers	187	63.2	19.9	1.3	16.0
Door-to-door sales workers, news and street vendors, and related workers	297	66.8	8.1	2.9	11.8
Sales and related workers, all other [3]	264	45.4	6.9	3.8	9.3
Office and administrative support occupations [3]	19,536	75.9	12.6	3.3	11.1
First-line supervisors/managers of office and administrative support workers	1,623	70.3	9.8	2.7	9.6
Bill and account collectors	225	69.8	21.3	2.8	14.0
Billing and posting clerks and machine operators	454	90.5	13.3	3.7	13.0
Bookkeeping, accounting, and auditing clerks	1,545	92.3	7.3	3.4	7.1
Payroll and timekeeping clerks	170	92.3	10.6	4.2	11.6
Tellers	397	88.9	8.4	6.6	12.2
Court, municipal, and license clerks	89	83.6	15.1	2.7	5.9
Customer service representatives	1,747	69.3	18.1	2.6	12.6
Eligibility interviewers, government programs	78	76.2	19.7	4.3	17.0
File clerks	399	82.5	13.2	4.2	11.2
Hotel, motel, and resort desk clerks	113	70.9	12.4	1.7	17.8
Interviewers, except eligibility and loan	141	80.9	15.3	1.4	12.3
Library assistants, clerical	116	83.6	6.6	6.2	5.2
Loan interviewers and clerks	204	84.0	11.5	3.5	11.1
Order clerks	108	72.1	12.1	4.6	14.9
Receptionists and information clerks	1,376	93.2	9.4	2.6	13.4
Reservation and transportation ticket agents and travel clerks	179	67.8	17.8	7.3	14.9
Couriers and messengers	244	17.9	15.4	1.3	13.1
Dispatchers	249	52.8	14.3	1.2	8.7
Postal service clerks	189	44.7	23.7	7.2	9.8
Postal service mail carriers	323	34.6	15.3	4.8	5.4
Postal service mail sorters, processors, and processing machine operators	112	46.7	27.7	11.6	14.1
Production, planning, and expediting clerks	275	54.1	6.1	2.4	9.0
Shipping, receiving, and traffic clerks	557	28.9	11.8	3.2	21.5
Stock clerks and order fillers	1,360	37.6	14.6	3.5	15.9
Weighers, measurers, checkers, and samplers, recordkeeping	78	46.3	17.4	3.4	13.8
Secretaries and administrative assistants	3,632	96.6	9.2	2.2	8.0
Computer operators	191	48.2	18.1	3.9	8.3
Data entry keyers	581	80.3	17.8	4.5	10.9
Word processors and typists	362	93.6	16.7	5.6	10.8
Insurance claims and policy processing clerks	265	85.5	15.2	2.0	11.7
Mail clerks and mail machine operators, except postal service	147	53.6	24.5	3.7	10.5
Office clerks, general	885	84.1	14.8	4.8	13.1
Natural resources, construction, and maintenance occupations	**14,205**	**4.7**	**7.2**	**1.6**	**21.3**
Farming, fishing, and forestry occupations [3]	1,050	22.0	4.7	1.8	40.3
Graders and sorters, agricultural products	73	68.0	9.8	8.4	43.8
Logging workers	79	2.2	10.2	-	12.3
Construction and extraction occupations [3]	8,114	2.8	7.1	1.0	23.7
First-line supervisors/managers of construction trades and extraction workers	897	2.5	4.1	0.5	12.6
Brickmasons, blockmasons, and stonemasons	218	0.9	11.3	1.0	33.6
Carpenters	1,595	1.6	5.8	0.8	24.5
Carpet, floor, and tile installers and finishers	271	2.6	5.1	0.4	32.6
Cement masons, concrete finishers, and terrazzo workers	120	2.5	8.2	0.3	38.4
Construction laborers	1,151	3.0	9.9	1.0	35.0
Operating engineers and other construction equipment operators	376	1.5	7.8	0.1	11.7
Drywall installers, ceiling tile installers, and tapers	205	2.0	5.1	0.2	46.8
Electricians	774	2.1	7.0	1.5	10.8
Painters, construction and maintenance	660	6.7	7.3	1.8	33.0
Pipelayers, plumbers, pipefitters, and steamfitters	595	1.0	7.1	1.2	14.2
Roofers	233	1.3	7.0	1.6	33.1
Sheet metal workers	147	4.6	6.5	1.8	12.5
Helpers, construction trades	114	3.7	8.6	1.5	37.0

See footnotes at end of table.

U.S. Census Bureau, Statistical Abstract of the United States: 2004-2005

[For civilian noninstitutional population 16 years old and over (137,736 represents 137,736,000). Annual average of monthly figures. Based on Current Population Survey; see text, Section 1, and Appendix III. Occupational classifications are those used in the 2000 Census and are not comparable to those used in the 1990 Census]

Occupation	Total employed (1,000)	Percent of total			
		Female	Black [1]	Asian [1]	His-panic [2]
Construction and building inspectors	95	9.8	9.0	3.1	9.8
Highway maintenance workers	79	4.1	13.1	-	15.5
Installation, maintenance, and repair occupations [3]	5,041	4.2	7.8	2.5	13.4
First-line supervisors/managers of mechanics, installers, and repairers	340	8.2	8.6	0.8	10.0
Computer, automated teller, and office machine repairers	296	12.0	9.2	4.3	8.8
Radio and telecommunications equipment installers and repairers	251	13.9	13.3	2.9	12.8
Aircraft mechanics and service technicians	128	2.6	6.0	6.3	11.4
Automotive body and related repairers	203	2.4	4.0	5.0	23.8
Automotive service technicians and mechanics	884	1.3	6.9	3.4	16.5
Bus and truck mechanics and diesel engine specialists	339	0.8	6.6	1.4	11.6
Heavy vehicle and mobile equipment service technicians and mechanics	200	0.9	5.3	0.2	10.7
Heating, air conditioning, and refrigeration mechanics and installers	350	0.7	5.9	1.9	15.4
Industrial and refractory machinery mechanics	460	2.3	7.5	2.0	10.1
Maintenance and repair workers, general	309	2.7	7.2	1.6	14.8
Millwrights	73	3.7	2.1	-	1.8
Electrical power-line installers and repairers	111	0.9	6.1	1.1	8.7
Telecommunications line installers and repairers	138	6.6	17.2	0.3	10.5
Production, transportation, and material occupations	**18,020**	**23.7**	**13.9**	**3.9**	**19.0**
Production occupations [3]	9,700	31.0	12.4	5.3	20.0
First-line supervisors/managers of production and operating workers	939	20.1	10.1	4.1	11.5
Electrical, electronics, and electromechanical assemblers	240	59.6	9.9	20.5	19.4
Bakers	183	48.5	14.2	6.5	28.0
Butchers and other meat, poultry, and fish processing workers	311	26.6	12.7	4.1	41.5
Food batchmakers	111	39.7	7.9	1.6	34.2
Cutting, punching, and press machine setters, operators, and tenders, metal and plastic	152	26.5	8.8	1.0	15.1
Grinding, lapping, polishing, and buffing machine tool setters, operators, and tenders, metal and plastic	79	17.0	13.4	1.7	18.7
Machinists	454	4.8	7.1	4.9	12.9
Tool and die makers	88	4.1	2.1	-	3.6
Welding, soldering, and brazing workers	528	6.9	10.6	1.7	18.1
Job printers	83	20.2	15.3	5.7	14.5
Printing machine operators	191	18.0	6.0	4.0	12.3
Laundry and dry-cleaning workers	193	59.6	21.3	4.9	29.9
Pressers, textile, garment, and related materials	81	74.9	17.9	6.1	46.4
Sewing machine operators	341	78.6	14.2	13.9	38.5
Tailors, dressmakers, and sewers	118	71.0	9.9	22.3	21.4
Stationary engineers and boiler operators	113	2.1	9.2	2.6	9.7
Crushing, grinding, polishing, mixing, and blending workers	107	10.1	14.7	0.7	19.8
Cutting workers	95	21.2	9.7	4.3	32.7
Inspectors, testers, sorters, samplers, and weighers	692	39.7	14.4	4.7	14.0
Medical, dental, and ophthalmic laboratory technicians	100	49.4	10.8	7.4	14.3
Packaging and filling machine operators and tenders	294	56.5	16.6	4.6	37.3
Painting workers	177	15.4	7.0	3.8	25.3
Photographic process workers and processing machine operators	76	59.9	14.4	3.7	10.4
Helpers—production workers	89	35.2	9.9	5.2	31.7
Transportation and material moving occupations [3]	8,320	15.3	15.6	2.4	17.9
Supervisors, transportation and material moving workers	216	16.3	13.2	4.6	16.3
Aircraft pilots and flight engineers	116	3.4	0.7	1.5	4.3
Bus drivers	558	48.4	28.8	1.5	10.1
Driver/sales workers and truck drivers	3,214	4.6	12.8	1.6	15.0
Taxi drivers and chauffeurs	286	13.8	28.1	7.3	16.5
Parking lot attendants	74	9.8	19.0	5.9	23.7
Service station attendants	96	15.7	7.6	6.1	12.1
Dredge, excavating, and loading machine operators	88	1.6	3.6	-	11.3
Industrial truck and tractor operators	534	8.6	19.8	1.2	28.7
Cleaners of vehicles and equipment	326	14.1	18.6	2.1	29.8
Laborers and freight, stock, and material movers, hand	1,748	18.3	16.3	2.5	18.1
Packers and packagers, hand	419	61.1	12.1	6.1	39.8

- Represents or rounds to zero.   [1] For persons in this race group only. See footnote 3, table 570.   [2] Persons of Hispanic or Latino ethnicity may be of any race.   [3] Includes other occupations, not shown separately.

Source: U.S. Bureau of Labor Statistics, *Employment and Earnings*, monthy, January 2004 issue. See Internet site <http://www.bls.gov/cps/home.htm>.

No. 598. Employed Civilians by Occupation—States: 2002

[In thousands (1,978 represents 1,978,000). Based on the Current Population Survey and subject to sampling error; see text, Section 1, and Appendix III. Occupational classifications are those used in the 1990 Census and are not comparable to those in other tables using the 2000 Census classifications]

State	Total [1]	Managerial and professional specialty		Technical, sales, and administrative support					Operators, fabricators, and laborers		
		Executive, administrative, and managerial	Professional specialty	Technicians and related support	Sales	Administrative support [2]	Service occupations	Precision production, craft, and repair	Machine operators, assemblers [3]	Transportation and material moving	Handlers, equipment cleaners, helpers [4]
AL	1,978	287	299	79	216	252	266	221	161	90	68
AK	298	48	48	10	27	42	46	35	6	12	17
AZ	2,507	408	389	87	320	361	351	270	72	87	100
AR	1,216	148	167	28	152	145	162	148	89	67	57
CA	16,242	2,513	2,694	505	1,955	2,155	2,279	1,678	681	612	656
CO	2,298	404	396	82	277	294	305	265	62	75	84
CT	1,696	303	303	68	209	232	217	180	66	49	46
DE	405	63	69	15	39	67	58	42	14	16	15
DC	285	60	81	12	17	37	43	13	4	8	7
FL	7,642	1,175	1,111	275	1,059	1,018	1,195	822	211	291	291
GA	4,071	621	615	148	477	536	487	482	235	223	158
HI	557	85	86	16	65	79	102	52	(B)	22	21
ID	645	77	93	22	69	86	100	75	27	31	27
IL	5,963	899	894	179	729	818	817	631	341	290	255
IN	3,012	439	421	91	344	377	372	360	252	137	143
IA	1,601	197	250	48	195	225	207	168	101	70	68
KS	1,342	197	222	43	143	188	182	144	60	52	55
KY	1,857	257	297	60	212	249	244	185	107	103	85
LA	1,883	243	295	73	225	246	271	238	78	91	75
ME	656	93	109	19	79	82	93	80	29	29	23
MD	2,772	542	578	86	306	351	353	243	60	102	96
MA	3,301	576	673	104	392	407	459	312	130	104	100
MI	4,691	643	786	165	529	600	652	503	338	189	197
MN	2,790	436	457	101	332	389	372	290	118	102	91
MS	1,210	154	163	37	137	146	150	149	89	78	59
MO	2,825	389	446	88	339	387	388	321	140	120	129
MT	442	61	64	13	48	53	70	53	13	18	15
NE	925	125	129	30	105	131	126	100	41	37	37
NV	1,060	155	125	31	132	130	234	130	22	41	42
NH	672	103	116	21	87	88	82	81	34	27	21
NJ	4,113	731	725	155	496	588	552	351	134	178	158
NM	830	108	124	34	94	105	139	109	19	36	35
NY	8,790	1,370	1,557	255	986	1,242	1,494	767	340	383	275
NC	3,890	501	581	108	484	465	529	484	282	171	179
ND	332	41	47	11	37	42	54	34	10	17	13
OH	5,497	789	856	177	657	733	799	557	341	251	240
OK	1,617	218	250	46	186	228	220	203	71	77	64
OR	1,695	263	268	51	196	225	236	181	78	69	65
PA	5,934	850	974	229	695	850	817	595	298	274	243
RI	528	78	95	16	59	74	77	53	35	16	20
SC	1,851	257	295	59	213	216	250	240	131	93	56
SD	408	52	55	11	44	58	63	40	17	16	16
TN	2,776	404	361	89	341	401	328	326	205	129	126
TX	10,070	1,433	1,506	348	1,266	1,308	1,483	1,152	379	456	443
UT	1,108	159	162	41	135	173	137	133	54	41	48
VT	336	51	60	10	37	41	44	39	19	12	11
VA	3,583	650	677	121	406	426	452	396	142	128	120
WA	2,871	448	475	103	337	378	402	310	98	123	103
WV	755	92	109	31	84	99	118	94	33	51	31
WI	2,861	399	409	84	317	385	373	344	219	121	119
WY	259	35	34	7	26	33	36	37	6	19	10

B Base figure too small to meet statistical standards for reliability of a derived figure. [1] Includes farming, forestry, and fishing not shown separately. [2] Including clerical. [3] Including inspectors. [4] Including laborers.

Source: U.S. Bureau of Labor Statistics, Local Area Unemployment Statistics, *Geographic Profile of Employment and Unemployment, 2002* (published February 2004). See Internet site <http://www.bls.gov/gps/>.

Labor Force, Employment, and Earnings 389

No. 599. Employment Projections by Occupation: 2002 and 2012

[In thousands (365 represents 365,000), **except percent and rank**. Estimates based on the Current Employment Statistics Program; the Occupational Employment Statistics Survey; and the Current Population Survey. See source for methodological assumptions. Occupations based on the 2000 Standard Occupational Classification system]

Occupation	Employment (1,000) 2002	Employment (1,000) 2012	Change 2002-2012 Number (1,000)	Change 2002-2012 Per-cent	Quartile rank by 2002 median annual earnings [1]	Most significant source of postsecondary education or training
FASTEST GROWING						
Medical assistants.	365	579	215	59	3	Moderate-term on-the-job training
Network systems and data communications analysts	186	292	106	57	1	Bachelor's degree
Physician assistants	63	94	31	49	1	Bachelor's degree
Social and human service assistants	305	454	149	49	3	Moderate-term on-the-job training
Home health aides	580	859	279	48	4	Short-term on-the-job training
Medical records and health information technicians	147	216	69	47	3	Associate degree
Physical therapist aides	37	54	17	46	3	Short-term on-the-job training
Computer software engineers, applications . .	394	573	179	46	1	Bachelor's degree
Computer software engineers, systems software	281	409	128	45	1	Bachelor's degree
Physical therapist assistants	50	73	22	45	2	Associate degree
Fitness trainers and aerobics instructors	183	264	81	44	3	Postsecondary vocational award
Database administrators.	110	159	49	44	1	Bachelor's degree
Veterinary technologists and technicians	53	76	23	44	3	Associate degree
Hazardous materials removal workers	38	54	16	43	2	Moderate-term on-the-job training
Dental hygienists	148	212	64	43	1	Associate degree
Occupational therapist aides	8	12	4	43	3	Short-term on-the-job training
Dental assistants	266	379	113	42	3	Moderate-term on-the-job training
Personal and home care aides	608	854	246	40	4	Short-term on-the-job training
Self-enrichment education teachers	200	281	80	40	2	Work experience in a related occupation
Computer systems analysts	468	653	184	39	1	Bachelor's degree
Occupational therapist assistants	18	26	7	39	2	Associate degree
Environmental engineers	47	65	18	38	1	Bachelor's degree
Postsecondary teachers.	1,581	2,184	603	38	1	Doctoral degree
Network and computer systems administrators	251	345	94	37	1	Bachelor's degree
Environmental science and protection technicians, including health	28	38	10	37	2	Associate degree
Preschool teachers, except special education	424	577	153	36	4	Postsecondary vocational award
Computer and information systems managers	284	387	103	36	1	Bachelor's or higher degree, plus work experience
LARGEST JOB GROWTH						
Registered nurses.	2,284	2,908	623	27	1	Associate degree
Postsecondary teachers.	1,581	2,184	603	38	1	Doctoral degree
Retail salespersons.	4,076	4,672	596	15	4	Short-term on-the-job training
Customer service representatives	1,894	2,354	460	24	3	Moderate-term on-the-job training
Combined food preparation and serving workers, including fast food.	1,990	2,444	454	23	4	Short-term on-the-job training
Cashiers, except gaming	3,432	3,886	454	13	4	Short-term on-the-job training
Janitors and cleaners, except maids and housekeeping cleaners	2,267	2,681	414	18	4	Short-term on-the-job training
General and operations managers	2,049	2,425	376	18	1	Bachelor's or higher degree, plus work experience
Waiters and waitresses	2,097	2,464	367	18	4	Short-term on-the-job training
Nursing aides, orderlies, and attendants	1,375	1,718	343	25	3	Short-term on-the-job training
Truck drivers, heavy and tractor-trailer	1,767	2,104	337	19	2	Moderate-term on-the-job training
Receptionists and information clerks.	1,100	1,425	325	29	3	Short-term on-the-job training
Security guards	995	1,313	317	32	3	Short-term on-the-job training
Office clerks, general.	2,991	3,301	310	10	3	Short-term on-the-job training
Teacher assistants	1,277	1,571	294	23	4	Short-term on-the-job training
Sales representatives, wholesale and manufacturing, except technical and scientific products	1,459	1,738	279	19	1	Moderate-term on-the-job training
Home health aides	580	859	279	48	4	Short-term on-the-job training
Personal and home care aides	608	854	246	40	4	Short-term on-the-job training
Truck drivers, light or delivery services	1,022	1,259	237	23	3	Short-term on-the-job training
Landscaping and groundskeeping workers . .	1,074	1,311	237	22	3	Short-term on-the-job training
Elementary school teachers, except special education	1,467	1,690	223	15	2	Bachelor's degree
Medical assistants.	365	579	215	59	3	Moderate-term on-the-job training
Maintenance and repair workers, general . . .	1,266	1,472	207	16	2	Moderate-term on-the-job training
Accountants and auditors	1,055	1,261	205	19	1	Bachelor's degree
Computer systems analysts	468	653	184	39	1	Bachelor's degree
Secondary school teachers, except special and vocational education	988	1,167	180	18	1	Bachelor's degree
Computer software engineers, applications . .	394	573	179	46	1	Bachelor's degree

[1] Quartile ranks based on the Occupational Employment Statistics annual earnings. 1 = very high ($41,820 and over), 2 = high ($27,500 to $41,780), 3 = low ($19,710 to $27,380), and 4 = very low (up to $19,600). The rankings were based on quartiles using one-fourth of total employment to define each quartile. Earnings are for wage and salary workers.

Source: U.S. Bureau of Labor Statistics "Occupational employment projections to 2012", *Monthly Labor Review*, February 2004. See Internet site <http://www.bls.gov/emp/home.htm>.

No. 600. Occupations of the Employed by Selected Characteristics: 2003

[In thousands (118,385 represents 118,385,000). Annual averages of monthly figures. For civilian noninstitutional population 25 years old and over. Based on Current Population Survey; see text, Section 1, and Appendix III. See headnote, Table 586 regarding occupations.]

Sex, race, and educational attainment	Total employed	Managerial, professional, and related	Service	Sales and office	Natural resources, construction, and maintenance	Production, transportation, and material moving
Total [1]	118,385	44,951	16,479	29,079	12,193	15,683
Less than a high school diploma	11,537	750	3,268	1,468	2,675	3,377
High school graduates, no college	35,857	5,810	6,627	10,431	5,389	7,601
Less than a bachelor's degree	32,420	10,620	4,631	10,350	3,282	3,537
College graduates	38,570	27,772	1,953	6,830	847	1,168
White [2]	98,120	38,064	12,431	24,426	10,758	12,441
Less than a high school diploma	9,437	643	2,448	1,223	2,388	2,734
High school graduates, no college	29,645	5,046	4,812	8,953	4,779	6,055
Less than a bachelor's degree	26,703	8,989	3,622	8,490	2,854	2,747
College graduates	32,335	23,385	1,549	5,760	736	905
Black [2]	12,706	3,670	2,821	3,047	932	2,237
Less than a high school diploma	1,376	68	565	160	186	397
High school graduates, no college	4,465	516	1,326	1,060	423	1,139
Less than a bachelor's degree	3,979	1,088	725	1,326	266	574
College graduates	2,887	1,997	205	501	57	127
Asian [2]	5,132	2,440	788	1,048	202	654
Less than a high school diploma	427	17	170	47	33	160
High school graduates, no college	995	136	308	235	65	251
Less than a bachelor's degree	884	263	148	284	65	124
College graduates	2,825	2,024	163	481	38	120
Hispanic [3]	14,205	2,635	3,282	2,856	2,503	2,929
Less than a high school diploma	5,073	188	1,555	468	1,361	1,501
High school graduates, no college	4,169	452	1,007	1,067	720	922
Less than a bachelor's degree	2,925	759	527	936	318	385
College graduates	2,039	1,236	193	385	104	121

[1] Includes other races, not shown separately.   [2] Persons in this race group only. See footnote 3, Table 570.   [3] Persons of Hispanic or Latino ethnicity may be of any race.
Source: U.S. Bureau of Labor Statistics, unpublished data.

No. 601. Employment by Industry: 2000 to 2003

[In thousands (136,891 represents 136,891,000), except percent. Annual averages of monthly figures. Based on the Current Population Survey; see text, Section 1, and Appendix III. See headnote, Table 586 regarding industries.]

Industry	2000	2001	2002	2003, total [1]	2003, percent [1] Female	Black [2]	Asian [2]	Hispanic [3]
Total employed	136,891	136,933	136,485	137,736	46.8	10.7	4.2	12.6
Agriculture and related industries	2,464	2,299	2,311	2,275	25.5	2.7	1.0	19.6
Mining	475	538	502	525	13.9	3.9	0.6	10.8
Construction	9,931	10,155	9,981	10,138	9.6	6.2	1.1	20.3
Manufacturing	19,644	18,434	17,233	16,902	30.6	9.4	5.1	14.2
Durable goods	12,519	11,703	10,833	10,520	27.1	8.2	5.4	11.7
Nondurable goods	7,125	6,730	6,400	6,382	36.2	11.5	4.7	18.3
Wholesale trade	4,216	4,020	4,144	4,486	30.0	6.8	3.7	13.0
Retail trade	15,763	15,786	15,663	16,220	48.9	9.7	4.2	12.3
Transportation and utilities	7,380	7,261	7,244	6,950	24.5	15.7	3.4	11.8
Transportation and warehousing	6,096	6,017	5,971	5,758	24.7	16.7	3.6	12.8
Utilities	1,284	1,244	1,273	1,193	23.5	10.7	2.2	7.0
Information	4,059	4,005	3,691	3,687	43.5	11.6	4.5	8.4
Telecommunications	1,546	1,640	1,444	1,421	41.8	16.2	5.0	8.6
Financial activities	9,374	9,444	9,565	9,748	55.7	9.8	4.1	9.0
Finance and insurance	6,641	6,664	6,749	6,834	59.4	10.3	4.6	7.9
Real estate and rental and leasing	2,734	2,780	2,816	2,914	47.1	8.6	2.8	11.7
Professional and business services	13,649	14,068	14,015	13,879	43.0	8.9	4.8	12.7
Professional and technical services	8,266	8,489	8,408	8,243	44.9	5.7	6.1	6.5
Management, administrative, and waste services	5,383	5,579	5,607	5,636	40.2	13.6	2.9	21.7
Education and health services	26,188	26,848	27,624	28,260	75.3	13.7	4.3	8.7
Educational services	11,255	11,535	11,724	11,826	69.5	10.6	3.6	7.8
Health care and social assistance	14,933	15,313	15,900	16,434	79.4	15.9	4.9	9.3
Hospitals	5,202	5,256	5,330	5,652	77.7	15.2	6.0	7.7
Health services, except hospitals	7,009	7,304	7,738	7,964	78.4	15.5	4.8	9.0
Social assistance	2,722	2,753	2,832	2,818	85.9	18.7	3.1	13.4
Leisure and hospitality	11,186	11,370	11,541	11,607	51.4	10.8	5.7	17.9
Arts, entertainment, and recreation	2,539	2,590	2,639	2,587	45.3	8.7	3.0	10.0
Accommodation and food services	8,647	8,781	8,902	9,021	53.1	11.4	6.5	20.2
Other services	6,450	6,477	6,665	6,815	51.4	10.0	4.8	15.0
Other services, except private households	5,731	5,783	5,908	6,050	46.3	9.9	5.0	12.8
Private households	718	694	757	764	92.3	11.0	2.9	31.8
Government workers	6,113	6,228	6,307	6,243	46.4	16.4	3.3	8.2

[1] See footnote 2, Table 569   [2] Persons in this race group only. See footnote 3, Table 570.   [3] Persons of Hispanic or Latino origin may be of any race.
Source: U.S. Bureau of Labor Statistics, Employment and Earnings, monthly, January 2004 issue. See Internet site <http://www.bls.gov/cps/home.htm>.

Labor Force, Employment, and Earnings   **391**

No. 602. Employment Projections by Industry: 2002 to 2012

[15,047.2 represents 15,047,200. Estimates based on the Current Employment Statistics estimates. See source for methodological assumptions. Minus sign (-) indicates decline]

Industry	2002 NAICS code [1]	Employment (1,000) 2002	Employment (1,000) 2012	Change, 2002-2012 (1,000)	Average annual rate of change, 2002-2012
LARGEST GROWTH					
Retail trade	44-45	15,047.2	17,129.2	2,082.0	1.3
Employment services.	5613	3,248.8	5,012.3	1,763.5	4.4
State and local government education	(X)	9,876.0	11,606.0	1,730.0	1.6
Food services and drinking places	722	8,411.7	9,749.0	1,337.3	1.5
Offices of health practitioners	6211-3	3,189.9	4,418.8	1,228.9	3.3
Construction	23	6,731.7	7,745.4	1,013.7	1.4
Educational services	61	2,650.6	3,409.8	759.2	2.6
Ambulatory health care services except offices of health practitioners	6214-6,6219	1,443.6	2,113.4	669.8	3.9
State and local general government, n.e.c. [2]	(X)	6,838.4	7,508.1	669.7	0.9
Wholesale trade	42	5,641.1	6,279.3	638.2	1.1
Computer systems design and related services . . .	5415	1,162.7	1,797.7	635.0	4.5
Hospitals.	622	4,153.1	4,785.0	631.9	1.4
Individual, family, community, and vocational rehabilitation services.	6241-3	1,269.3	1,866.6	597.3	3.9
Nursing care and residential mental health facilities.	6231-2	2,047.8	2,607.1	559.3	2.4
Truck transportation and couriers and messengers .	484,492	1,897.1	2,404.3	507.2	2.4
Business support and investigation and security services, n.e.c. [2]	5614,5616,5619	1,772.3	2,260.8	488.5	2.5
Religious, grantmaking and giving services, and social advocacy organizations	8131-3	1,944.2	2,372.0	427.8	2.0
Amusement, gambling, and recreation industries . .	713	1,307.6	1,717.3	409.7	2.8
MOST RAPID GROWTH					
Software publishers.	5112	256.0	429.7	173.7	5.3
Management, scientific, and technical consulting services.	5416	731.8	1,137.4	405.6	4.5
Community care facilities for the elderly and residential care facilities, n.e.c. [2]	6233,6239	695.3	1,077.6	382.3	4.5
Computer systems design and related services . . .	5415	1,162.7	1,797.7	635.0	4.5
Employment services.	5613	3,248.8	5,012.3	1,763.5	4.4
Individual, family, community, and vocational rehabilitation services.	6241-3	1,269.3	1,866.6	597.3	3.9
Ambulatory health care services except offices of health practitioners.	6214-6,6219	1,443.6	2,113.4	669.8	3.9
Water, sewage, and other systems.	2213	48.5	71.0	22.5	3.9
Internet services, data processing, and other information services.	516,518,519	528.8	773.1	244.3	3.9
Child day care services	6244	734.2	1,050.3	316.1	3.6
Commercial and industrial machinery and equipment rental and leasing	5324	102.2	142.8	40.6	3.4
Offices of health practitioners	6211-3	3,189.9	4,418.8	1,228.9	3.3
Consumer goods rental and general rental centers .	5322,5323	352.9	484.2	131.3	3.2
Cable and other subscription programming and program distribution.	5152,5175	220.9	299.8	78.9	3.1
Amusement, gambling, and recreation industries . .	713	1,307.6	1,717.3	409.7	2.8
Transit and ground passenger transportation	485	371.5	487.7	116.2	2.8
Specialized design services	5414	122.9	160.8	37.9	2.7
Office administrative and facilities support services .	5611,2	390.3	507.6	117.3	2.7
MOST RAPID DECLINE					
Cut and sew apparel manufacturing	3152	281.8	77.1	-204.7	-12.2
Apparel knitting mills	3151	49.6	20.0	-29.6	-8.7
Textile and fabric finishing and fabric coating mills .	3133	82.4	40.1	-42.3	-6.9
Leather and hide tanning and finishing	3161	8.6	4.5	-4.1	-6.3
Textile mills	313	293.2	156.9	-136.3	-6.1
Other leather and allied product manufacturing . . .	3169	19.9	10.8	-9.1	-5.9
Fabric mills	3132	146.6	79.6	-67.0	-5.9
Apparel accessories and other apparel manufacturing	3159	26.2	15.1	-11.1	-5.4
Fiber, yarn, and thread mills	3131	64.2	37.2	-27.0	-5.3
Tobacco manufacturing	3122	33.2	20.2	-13.0	-4.8
Metal ore mining.	2122	29.4	18.0	-11.4	-4.8
Federal Government enterprises, n.e.c. [2]	(NA)	51.9	32.4	-19.5	-4.6
Coal mining.	2121	74.9	52.3	-22.6	-3.5
Other chemical product and preparation manufacturing	3259	112.4	79.4	-33.0	-3.4
Iron and steel mills and ferroalloy manufacturing . .	3311	107.1	76.0	-31.1	-3.4
Oil and gas extraction	211	122.5	88.4	-34.1	-3.2
Computer and peripheral equipment manufacturing.	3341	249.8	182.1	-67.7	-3.1
Forestry, fishing, hunting, and trapping	1131-2,114	67.6	50.4	-17.2	-2.9

NA Not available. X Not applicable. [1] Based on the North American Industry Classification System, 2002; see text, this section. [2] N.e.c. means not elsewhere classified.

Source: U.S. Bureau of Labor Statistics, "Industry Output and Employment Projections to 2002", Monthly Labor Review, February 2004. See Internet site <http://www.bls.gov/emp/home.htm>.

No. 603. Unemployed Workers—Summary: 1980 to 2003

[In thousands (7,637 represents 7,637,000), except as indicated. For civilian noninstitutional population 16 years old and over. Annual averages of monthly figures. For data on unemployment insurance, see Table 538]

Age, sex, race, Hispanic origin	1980	1985	1990 [1]	1995	2000 [1]	2001	2002	2003 [1]
UNEMPLOYED								
Total [2]	7,637	8,312	7,047	7,404	5,692	6,801	8,378	8,774
16 to 19 years old	1,669	1,468	1,212	1,346	1,081	1,162	1,253	1,251
20 to 24 years old	1,835	1,738	1,299	1,244	1,022	1,209	1,430	1,495
25 to 44 years old	2,964	3,681	3,323	3,390	2,340	2,853	3,581	3,775
45 to 64 years old	1,075	1,331	1,109	1,269	1,117	1,447	1,950	2,069
65 years and over	94	93	105	153	132	129	163	183
Male	4,267	4,521	3,906	3,983	2,975	3,690	4,597	4,906
16 to 19 years old	913	806	667	744	599	650	700	697
20 to 24 years old	1,076	944	715	673	547	688	792	841
25 to 44 years old	1,619	1,950	1,803	1,776	1,159	1,470	1,920	2,085
45 to 64 years old	600	766	662	697	587	808	1,098	1,176
65 years and over	58	55	59	94	83	74	87	107
Female	3,370	3,791	3,140	3,421	2,717	3,111	3,781	3,868
16 to 19 years old	755	661	544	602	483	512	553	554
20 to 24 years old	760	794	584	571	475	521	638	654
25 to 44 years old	1,345	1,732	1,519	1,615	1,181	1,383	1,661	1,690
45 to 64 years old	473	566	447	574	529	640	854	894
65 years and over	36	39	46	60	50	55	76	76
White [3]	5,884	6,191	5,186	5,459	4,121	4,969	6,137	6,311
16 to 19 years old	1,291	1,074	903	952	795	845	925	909
20 to 24 years old	1,364	1,235	899	866	682	829	977	1,012
Black [3]	1,553	1,864	1,565	1,538	1,241	1,416	1,693	1,787
16 to 19 years old	343	357	268	325	230	260	260	255
20 to 24 years old	426	455	349	311	281	307	365	375
Asian [3][4]	(NA)	(NA)	(NA)	(NA)	227	288	389	366
16 to 19 years old	(NA)	(NA)	(NA)	(NA)	40	31	41	31
20 to 24 years old	(NA)	(NA)	(NA)	(NA)	41	50	63	47
Hispanic [3][5]	620	811	876	1,140	954	1,138	1,353	1,441
16 to 19 years old	145	141	161	205	194	208	221	192
20 to 24 years old	138	171	167	209	190	212	265	273
Full-time workers	6,269	6,793	5,677	5,909	4,538	5,546	7,063	7,361
Part-time workers	1,369	1,519	1,369	1,495	1,154	1,254	1,314	1,413
UNEMPLOYMENT RATE (percent) [6]								
Total [2]	7.1	7.2	5.6	5.6	4.0	4.7	5.8	6.0
16 to 19 years old	17.8	18.6	15.5	17.3	13.1	14.7	16.5	17.5
20 to 24 years old	11.5	11.1	8.8	9.1	7.2	8.3	9.7	10.0
25 to 44 years old	6.0	6.2	4.9	4.8	3.3	4.1	5.2	5.5
45 to 64 years old	3.7	4.5	3.5	3.4	2.5	3.1	4.0	4.1
65 years and over	3.1	3.2	3.0	4.0	3.1	2.9	3.7	3.8
Male	6.9	7.0	5.7	5.6	3.9	4.8	5.9	6.3
16 to 19 years old	18.3	19.5	16.3	18.4	14.0	16.0	18.1	19.3
20 to 24 years old	12.5	11.4	9.1	9.2	7.3	9.0	10.2	10.6
25 to 44 years old	5.6	5.9	4.8	4.7	3.1	3.9	5.1	5.6
45 to 64 years old	3.5	4.5	3.7	3.5	2.4	3.2	4.2	4.4
65 years and over	3.1	3.1	3.0	4.3	3.3	3.0	3.4	4.0
Female	7.4	7.4	5.5	5.6	4.1	4.7	5.6	5.7
16 to 19 years old	17.2	17.6	14.7	16.1	12.1	13.4	14.9	15.6
20 to 24 years old	10.4	10.7	8.5	9.0	7.1	7.5	9.1	9.3
25 to 44 years old	6.4	6.6	4.9	5.0	3.6	4.3	5.2	5.4
45 to 64 years old	4.0	4.6	3.2	3.3	2.5	2.9	3.7	3.7
65 years and over	3.1	3.3	3.1	3.7	2.7	2.9	3.9	3.6
White [3]	6.3	6.2	4.8	4.9	3.5	4.2	5.1	5.2
16 to 19 years old	15.5	15.7	13.5	14.5	11.4	12.7	14.5	15.2
20 to 24 years old	9.9	9.2	7.3	7.7	5.9	7.0	8.1	8.4
Black [3]	14.3	15.1	11.4	10.4	7.6	8.6	10.2	10.8
16 to 19 years old	38.5	40.2	30.9	35.7	24.5	29.0	29.8	33.0
20 to 24 years old	23.6	24.5	19.9	17.7	15.0	16.3	19.1	19.8
Asian [3][4]	(NA)	(NA)	(NA)	(NA)	3.6	4.5	5.9	6.0
16 to 19 years old	(NA)	(NA)	(NA)	(NA)	14.2	12.6	16.2	17.5
20 to 24 years old	(NA)	(NA)	(NA)	(NA)	6.9	8.2	10.2	9.0
Hispanic [3][5]	10.1	10.5	8.2	9.3	5.7	6.6	7.5	7.7
16 to 19 years old	22.5	24.3	19.5	24.1	16.6	17.7	20.1	20.0
20 to 24 years old	12.1	12.6	9.1	11.5	7.5	8.1	9.9	10.2
Experienced workers [7]	6.9	6.8	5.3	5.4	3.8	4.6	5.7	5.8
Women maintaining families	9.2	10.4	8.3	8.0	5.9	6.6	8.0	8.5
Married men, wife present	4.2	4.3	3.4	3.3	2.0	2.7	3.6	3.8
Percent without work for—								
Fewer than 5 weeks	43.2	42.1	46.3	36.5	44.9	42.0	34.5	31.7
5 to 10 weeks	23.4	22.2	23.5	22.0	23.0	22.4	20.7	19.8
11 to 14 weeks	9.0	8.0	8.5	9.6	8.9	9.9	10.1	10.0
15 to 26 weeks	13.8	12.3	11.7	14.6	11.8	14.0	16.3	16.4
27 weeks and over	10.7	15.4	10.0	17.3	11.4	11.8	18.3	22.1
Unemployment duration, average (weeks)	11.9	15.6	12.0	16.6	12.6	13.1	16.6	19.2

NA Not available. [1] See footnote 2, Table 569. [2] Includes other races, not shown separately. [3] Includes other ages, not shown separately. Also beginning 2003, for this race group only. See footnote 3, Table 570. [4] Prior to 2003, includes Pacific Islanders. [5] Persons of Hispanic or Latino origin may be of any race. [6] Unemployed as percent of civilian labor force in specified group. [7] Wage and salary workers.

Source: U.S. Bureau of Labor Statistics, *Employment and Earnings*, monthly, January 2004 issue; and unpublished data. See Internet site <http://www.bls.gov/cps/>.

Labor Force, Employment, and Earnings 393

No. 604. Job Search Activity Using the Internet: 2001

[For the civilian non-institutional population 16 years old and over, except as noted. As of September. Refers to use of Internet from any location to search for a job from January to September 2001. Based on the Current Population Survey and subject to sampling error; see text, Section 1 and Appendix III]

Characteristic	Total who used Internet for job-searching[1] Total (1,000)	Percent of total	Read on-line ads or searched on-the-job listings	Research-ed infor-mation on potential employers	Submit-ted a resume or applica-tion	Posted a resume on a site or with a service	Posted a resume on own Web site
Total, 16 years and over [2]	212,357	19,616	9.2	92.0	67.4	49.5	36.7	4.8
Age:								
16 to 24 years old	35,195	4,415	12.5	92.3	63.2	45.9	35.6	4.8
16 to 19 years old	16,206	1,108	6.8	91.5	54.1	34.0	26.3	3.0
20 to 24 years old	18,990	3,308	17.4	92.5	66.2	49.9	38.7	5.4
25 years old and over	177,162	15,201	8.6	91.9	68.7	50.5	37.0	4.8
25 to 34 years old	37,032	6,238	16.8	92.3	70.7	52.9	42.2	5.5
35 to 44 years old	44,318	4,890	11.0	91.9	68.6	50.4	35.4	4.4
45 to 54 years old	38,642	3,051	7.9	91.3	66.2	48.9	32.5	4.3
55 to 64 years old	24,328	877	3.6	89.9	67.4	41.3	26.9	2.7
65 years old and over	32,842	145	0.4	94.1	46.5	43.2	24.6	6.6
Sex:								
Male	102,110	9,700	9.5	91.5	71.5	53.4	40.5	5.9
Female.	110,247	9,916	9.0	92.5	63.4	45.6	33.0	3.6
Race and Hispanic origin:								
White	176,220	16,018	9.1	91.9	67.1	48.2	35.1	4.5
Black	25,644	2,396	9.3	92.3	67.1	52.9	41.5	5.5
Hispanic origin [3]	23,288	1,377	5.9	89.2	67.7	47.0	36.6	5.8
Educational attainment:								
Total 25 years old and over	177,162	15,201	8.6	91.9	68.7	50.5	37.0	4.8
Less than high school diploma. . . .	27,484	402	1.5	88.8	58.2	38.9	30.3	4.6
High school graduate, no college . .	57,386	2,812	4.9	90.9	59.2	42.0	31.7	3.3
Some college, no degree	30,641	3,029	9.9	92.2	63.1	48.2	34.7	3.8
Associate degree	14,779	1,667	11.3	93.7	65.4	48.3	34.7	4.7
College degree	46,872	7,291	15.6	91.9	76.0	55.9	40.8	5.7
Advanced degree.	16,283	2,390	14.7	91.6	77.8	55.6	39.3	6.4
Occupation [4]	141,447	17,235	12.2	92.2	68.5	50.7	37.4	4.8
Managerial and professional	43,058	7,258	16.9	92.8	74.3	56.0	40.1	5.9
Executive, administrative, managerial	20,851	3,484	16.7	93.4	75.3	58.3	42.1	4.8
Professional specialty	22,206	3,775	17.0	92.4	73.3	53.9	38.2	6.9
Technical, sales, and administrative . .	40,521	5,809	14.3	92.7	65.7	50.8	38.1	4.3
Technical and related support	4,784	868	18.1	90.1	72.6	54.8	42.4	6.0
Sales	16,709	2,151	12.9	94.5	71.2	54.0	40.5	4.8
Administrative support, inc. clerical .	19,028	2,790	14.7	92.1	59.3	47.0	34.9	3.3
Service occupations	19,541	1,477	7.6	90.1	59.4	37.9	29.7	4.0
Precision production, craft, and repair	15,528	1,172	7.5	89.7	65.5	45.3	35.4	2.9
Operators, fabricators, and laborers . .	19,082	1,361	7.1	91.0	62.6	42.0	32.9	4.4
Farming, forestry, and fishing	3,705	152	4.1	87.5	62.8	37.1	19.9	2.2

[1] Includes other job search activities, not shown separately   [2] Includes other races, not shown separately   [3] Persons of Hispanic origin may be of any race   [4] Data for occupation are for the experienced labor force—the sum of the employed and unemployed whose last job was in one of these occupations.

Source: U.S. Bureau of Labor Statistics, *Computer and Internet Use at Work in 2001, News*, USDL 02-601, October 23, 2002. See Internet site site <http://www.bls.gov/bls/newsrels.htm#OEUS>.

No. 605. Unemployed Persons by Sex and Reason: 1980 to 2003

[In thousands (4,267 represents 4,267,000). For civilian noninstitutional population 16 years old and over. Annual averages of monthly figures. Based on Current Population Survey; see text, Section 1, and Appendix III]

Sex and reason	1980	1985	1990 [1]	1995	1996	1997 [1]	1998 [1]	1999 [1]	2000 [1]	2001	2002	2003 [1]
Male, total.	4,267	4,521	3,906	3,983	3,880	3,577	3,266	3,066	2,975	3,690	4,597	4,906
Job losers [2]	2,649	2,749	2,257	2,190	2,158	1,902	1,703	1,563	1,516	2,119	2,820	3,024
Job leavers	438	409	528	407	372	414	368	389	387	422	434	422
Reentrants	776	876	806	1,113	1,076	1,004	931	895	854	925	1,068	1,141
New entrants.	405	487	315	273	273	257	264	219	217	223	274	320
Female, total.	3,370	3,791	3,140	3,421	3,356	3,162	2,944	2,814	2,717	3,111	3,781	3,868
Job losers [2]	1,297	1,390	1,130	1,286	1,212	1,135	1,119	1,059	1,001	1,356	1,787	1,814
Job leavers	453	468	513	417	402	381	366	394	393	413	432	397
Reentrants	1,152	1,380	1,124	1,412	1,435	1,334	1,201	1,111	1,107	1,105	1,300	1,336
New entrants.	468	552	373	306	307	312	257	250	217	237	262	321

[1] See footnote 2, Table 569.   [2] Beginning 1995, persons who completed temporary jobs are identified separately and are included as job losers.

Source: U.S. Bureau of Labor Statistics, *Employment and Earnings*, monthly, January issues; and Bulletin 2307; and unpublished data. See Internet site <http://www.bls.gov/cps/home.htm>.

No. 606. Unemployment Rates by Industry, 2000 to 2003, and by Sex, 2000 and 2003

[In percent. For civilian noninstitutional population 16 years old and over. Annual averages of monthly figures. Rate represents unemployment as a percent of labor force in each specified group. Based on Current Population Survey; see text, Section 1, and Appendix III. See headnote, Table 586 regarding industries.]

Industry	2000	2001	2002	2003 [1]	Male 2000	Male 2003 [1]	Female 2000	Female 2003 [1]
All unemployed [2]	4.0	4.7	5.8	6.0	3.9	6.3	4.1	5.7
Industry: [3]								
Agriculture and related industries	9.0	11.2	10.1	10.2	8.3	9.3	11.5	13.0
Mining	4.4	4.2	6.3	6.7	4.6	6.3	2.8	9.1
Construction	6.2	7.1	9.2	9.3	6.4	9.6	5.1	6.7
Manufacturing	3.5	5.2	6.7	6.6	3.0	6.1	4.5	7.7
Wholesale trade	3.3	4.2	5.0	5.1	2.8	4.3	4.4	6.8
Retail trade	4.6	5.0	6.4	6.3	4.0	6.1	5.1	6.4
Transportation and utilities	3.4	4.3	4.9	5.3	3.2	5.3	4.2	5.1
Transportation and warehousing	3.8	4.6	5.4	5.7	1.9	5.9	4.6	5.2
Utilities	1.9	2.6	2.5	3.1	2.8	2.6	2.1	4.6
Information	3.2	4.9	6.9	6.8	2.7	6.6	3.7	7.1
Telecommunications	2.3	3.9	7.9	7.5	1.5	6.7	3.3	8.6
Financial activities	2.4	2.9	3.5	3.5	2.1	3.6	2.6	3.4
Finance and insurance	2.2	2.8	3.3	3.3	1.7	3.3	2.5	3.2
Real estate and rental and leasing	3.1	3.1	4.3	4.1	2.9	4.1	3.2	4.1
Professional and business services	4.8	6.1	7.9	8.2	4.4	7.9	5.2	8.7
Professional and technical services	2.5	3.9	5.5	5.4	2.2	5.1	2.9	5.8
Management, administrative, and waste services	8.1	9.4	11.2	12.1	7.6	11.5	8.8	12.9
Education and health services	2.5	2.8	3.4	3.6	2.2	3.8	2.5	3.6
Educational services	2.4	2.9	3.9	4.5	2.1	4.5	2.5	4.5
Health care and social assistance	2.5	2.8	3.2	3.4	2.3	3.5	2.5	3.4
Leisure and hospitality	6.6	7.5	8.4	8.7	6.2	8.6	7.0	8.8
Arts, entertainment, and recreation	5.9	6.6	8.2	7.8	6.1	8.2	5.7	7.4
Accommodation and food services	6.8	7.7	8.4	8.9	6.2	8.7	7.3	9.1
Other services [4]	3.9	4.0	5.1	5.7	3.7	6.4	4.0	5.1
Government workers	2.1	2.2	2.5	2.8	2.1	3.0	2.2	2.7

[1] See footnote 2, Table 569. [2] Includes the self-employed, unpaid family workers, and persons with no previous work experience, not shown separately. [3] Covers unemployed wage and salary workers. [4] Includes private household workers.

Source: U.S. Bureau of Labor Statistics, *Employment and Earnings*, monthly, January 2004 issue; and unpublished data. See Internet site <http://www.bls.gov/cps/home.htm>.

No. 607. Unemployment by Occupation, 2000 to 2003, and by Sex, 2003

[5,692 represents 5,692,000. For civilian noninstitutional population 16 years old and over. Annual averages of monthly data. Rate represents unemployment as a percent of the labor force for each specified group. Based on Current Population Survey; see text, Section 1, and Appendix III. See also headnote, Table 586 regarding occupations.]

Occupation	Number (1,000) 2000	Number (1,000) 2002	Number (1,000) 2003 [1]	Unemployment rate 2000	Unemployment rate 2002	2003 [1] Total	2003 [1] Male	2003 [1] Female
Total [2]	5,692	8,378	8,774	4.0	5.8	6.0	6.3	5.7
Management, professional, and related occupations	827	1,482	1,556	1.8	3.0	3.1	3.3	3.0
Management, business, and financial operations	320	622	627	1.6	3.0	3.1	2.9	3.3
Management	214	447	430	1.5	3.0	2.9	2.8	3.1
Business and financial operations	106	175	198	2.0	3.2	3.5	3.2	3.7
Professional and related occupations	507	859	929	1.9	3.0	3.2	3.7	2.9
Computer and mathematical	74	160	181	2.2	4.9	5.5	5.8	4.6
Architecture and engineering	51	122	124	1.7	4.3	4.4	4.0	6.6
Life, physical, and social science	18	42	48	1.4	3.1	3.3	3.3	3.4
Community and social services	40	49	57	2.0	2.2	2.5	2.2	2.7
Legal	18	37	35	1.2	2.4	2.3	1.6	3.1
Education, training, and library	136	203	225	1.8	2.6	2.8	2.5	2.9
Arts, design, entertainment, sports, and media	97	160	171	3.5	5.7	6.0	6.5	5.6
Healthcare practitioner and technical	73	87	88	1.2	1.3	1.3	1.2	1.4
Service occupations	1,132	1,544	1,681	5.2	6.6	7.1	7.5	6.7
Healthcare support	101	144	171	4.0	5.1	5.5	6.0	5.5
Protective service	70	111	129	2.7	3.9	4.5	4.1	6.3
Food preparation and serving related	469	622	683	6.6	8.2	8.6	9.2	8.1
Building and grounds cleaning and maintenance	301	405	447	5.8	7.4	8.3	8.6	7.9
Personal care and service	190	261	250	4.4	5.7	5.6	6.5	5.3
Sales and office occupations	1,446	2,110	2,070	3.8	5.6	5.5	5.4	5.6
Sales and related	673	998	995	4.1	5.9	5.9	4.8	7.0
Office and administrative support	773	1,112	1,076	3.6	5.4	5.2	6.4	4.8
Natural resources, construction, and maintenance	758	1,155	1,244	5.3	7.8	8.1	7.8	12.9
Farming, fishing, and forestry	133	142	136	10.2	12.0	11.4	9.1	18.7
Construction and extraction	507	788	814	6.2	9.1	9.1	9.1	10.9
Installation, maintenance, and repair	119	225	295	2.4	4.6	5.5	5.4	7.8
Production, transportation, and material moving	1,081	1,530	1,555	5.1	7.6	7.9	7.5	9.3
Production	575	848	807	4.8	7.8	7.7	7.0	9.2
Transportation and material moving	505	682	748	5.6	7.4	8.2	8.0	9.4

[1] See footnote 2, Table 569. [2] Includes persons with no previous work experience and those whose last job was in the Armed Forces.

Source: U.S. Bureau of Labor Statistics, *Employment and Earnings*, monthly, January 2004 issue; and unpublished data. See Internet site<http://www.bls.gov/cps/home.htm>.

Labor Force, Employment, and Earnings   395

No. 608. Unemployed and Unemployment Rates by Educational Attainment, Sex, Race, and Hispanic Origin: 1992 to 2003

[6,543 represents 6,543,000. Annual averages of monthly figures. For the civilian noninstitutional population 25 years old and over. See Table 573 for civilian labor force and participation rate data. Based on Current Population Survey; see text, Section 1, and Appendix III]

Year, sex, and race	Unemployed (1,000)					Unemployment rate [1]				
	Total	Less than high school diploma	High school graduates, no degree	Less than a bachelor's degree	College graduate	Total	Less than high school diploma	High school graduate, no degree	Less than a bachelor's degree	College graduate
Total: [2]										
1992	6,543	1,533	2,590	1,527	893	6.1	11.5	6.8	5.6	3.2
2000 [3]	3,589	791	1,298	890	610	3.0	6.3	3.4	2.7	1.7
2003 [3]	6,028	1,109	2,069	1,629	1,221	4.8	8.8	5.5	4.8	3.1
Male:										
1992	3,767	942	1,462	829	533	6.4	11.4	7.4	5.9	3.3
2000 [3]	1,829	411	682	427	309	2.8	5.4	3.4	2.6	1.5
2003 [3]	3,368	648	1,161	863	696	5.0	8.2	5.7	5.1	3.2
Female:										
1992	2,776	591	1,128	697	361	5.8	11.5	6.3	5.4	3.0
2000 [3]	1,760	380	616	463	301	3.2	7.8	3.5	2.8	1.8
2003 [3]	2,660	461	908	766	525	4.6	9.8	5.2	4.5	2.9
White: [4]										
1992	4,978	1,145	1,928	1,162	743	5.5	10.7	6.0	5.0	3.0
2000 [3]	2,644	564	924	667	489	2.6	5.6	2.9	2.4	1.6
2003 [3]	4,389	800	1,490	1,166	933	4.3	7.8	4.8	4.2	2.8
Black: [4]										
1992	1,269	322	565	301	81	11.0	15.3	12.3	9.8	4.4
2000 [3]	731	179	315	169	68	5.4	10.7	6.4	4.0	2.5
2003 [3]	1,157	222	459	340	137	8.3	13.9	9.3	7.9	4.5
Asian: [4][5]										
2000 [3]	146	28	34	35	49	2.7	5.7	3.0	3.2	1.8
2003 [3]	288	45	59	55	129	5.3	9.5	5.6	5.9	4.4
Hispanic: [6]										
1992	853	434	235	134	50	9.8	12.8	9.1	7.7	5.0
2000 [3]	569	297	150	85	38	4.4	6.2	3.9	3.2	2.2
2003 [3]	975	451	261	176	87	6.4	8.2	5.9	5.7	4.1

[1] Percent unemployed of the civilian labor force. [2] Includes other races, not shown separately. [3] See footnote 2, Table 569. [4] Beginning 2003, for persons in this race group only. See footnote 3, table 570. [5] Prior to 2003, includes Pacific Islanders. [6] Persons of Hispanic or Latino origin may be of any race.

Source: U.S. Bureau of Labor Statistics, *Employment and Earnings*, monthly, January 2004 issue. See Internet site <http://www.bls.gov/cps/home.htm>.

No. 609. Unemployed Persons by Reason of Unemployment: 2003

[8,774 represents 8,774,000. Annual averages of monthly data. Based on Current Population Survey; see text, Section 1, and Appendix III]

Age, sex, and reason	Total unemployed (1,000)	Percent distribution by duration				
		Less than 5 weeks	5 to 14 weeks	15 weeks and over		
				Total	15 to 26 weeks	27 weeks or longer
Total 16 years old and over	8,774	31.7	29.8	38.5	16.4	22.1
16 to 19 years old	1,251	44.6	31.9	23.5	13.3	10.1
Total 20 years old and over	**7,523**	**29.6**	**29.4**	**41.0**	**16.9**	**24.0**
Males	**4,209**	**28.7**	**29.2**	**42.1**	**16.9**	**25.2**
Job losers and persons who completed temporary jobs	2,899	29.1	29.6	41.3	17.0	24.3
On temporary layoff	686	46.9	34.7	18.3	12.1	6.3
Not on temporary layoff	2,213	23.6	28.0	48.5	18.5	30.0
Permanent job losers	1,667	21.3	26.8	51.9	19.4	32.5
Persons who completed temporary jobs	546	30.5	31.5	38.1	15.8	22.3
Job leavers	376	31.8	29.0	39.2	17.5	21.7
Reentrants	846	26.6	28.4	45.0	16.4	28.6
New entrants	88	24.3	24.1	51.6	15.9	35.7
Females	**3,314**	**30.7**	**29.7**	**39.6**	**17.0**	**22.6**
Job losers and persons who completed temporary jobs	1,751	30.2	28.8	40.9	18.3	22.7
On temporary layoff	367	53.8	29.9	16.3	9.3	7.0
Not on temporary layoff	1,384	24.0	28.6	47.5	20.6	26.8
Permanent job losers	1,102	21.7	27.6	50.7	21.5	29.2
Persons who completed temporary jobs	282	33.1	32.2	34.8	17.3	17.4
Job leavers	357	35.6	33.8	30.6	16.2	14.5
Reentrants	1,076	30.4	30.2	39.4	15.4	24.1
New entrants	130	25.9	27.0	47.1	15.4	31.7

Source: U.S. Bureau of Labor Statistics, *Employment and Earnings*, January 2004 issue. See Internet site <http://www.bls.gov/cps/home.htm>

No. 610. Total Unemployed and Insured Unemployed by State: 1980 to 2003

[7,637 represents 7,637,000. For civilian noninstitutional population 16 years old and over. Annual averages of monthly figures. Total unemployment estimates based on the Current Population Survey; see text, Section 1, and Appendix III. U.S. totals derived by independent population controls; therefore state data may not add to U.S. totals]

State	Total unemployed Number (1,000) 1980	1990 [2]	2000 [2]	2003 [2]	Total unemployed Percent [1] 1980	1990 [2]	2000 [2]	2003 [2]	Insured unemployed [3] Number (1,000) 2000	2002	Insured unemployed [3] Percent [4] 2000	2002
United States	7,637	7,047	5,692	8,774	7.1	5.6	4.0	6.0	[5]2,110	[5]3,585	[5]1.7	[5]2.8
Alabama.	147	130	97	125	8.8	6.9	4.5	5.8	29.0	41.3	1.6	2.3
Alaska	18	19	21	27	9.7	7.0	6.7	8.0	12.3	14.1	4.9	5.3
Arizona.	83	99	98	151	6.7	5.5	4.0	5.6	20.5	44.7	1.0	2.0
Arkansas	76	78	55	78	7.6	7.0	4.4	6.2	23.9	36.6	2.2	3.3
California	790	874	835	1,177	6.8	5.8	4.9	6.7	338.5	534.7	2.4	3.6
Colorado.	88	89	65	150	5.9	5.0	2.8	6.0	15.0	41.4	0.7	1.9
Connecticut.	94	95	40	99	5.9	5.2	2.2	5.5	28.3	51.4	1.7	3.1
Delaware	22	19	16	18	7.7	5.2	3.9	4.4	5.9	8.6	1.5	2.2
District of Columbia .	24	22	18	21	7.3	6.6	5.7	7.0	5.7	7.5	1.3	1.6
Florida	251	390	281	420	5.9	6.0	3.6	5.1	70.8	126.8	1.1	1.8
Georgia	163	182	156	207	6.4	5.5	3.7	4.7	34.5	73.3	0.9	1.9
Hawaii	21	16	25	27	4.9	2.9	4.3	4.3	8.4	12.1	1.7	2.3
Idaho	34	29	32	37	7.9	5.9	4.9	5.4	12.1	18.8	2.3	3.4
Illinois	459	369	281	422	8.3	6.2	4.3	6.7	103.8	187.1	1.8	3.2
Indiana.	252	149	100	163	9.6	5.3	3.2	5.1	31.8	62.7	1.1	2.2
Iowa	82	62	41	72	5.8	4.3	2.6	4.5	19.4	31.4	1.4	2.2
Kansas.	53	57	52	77	4.5	4.5	3.7	5.4	15.6	28.4	1.2	2.2
Kentucky	133	104	81	120	8.0	5.9	4.1	6.2	25.4	41.2	1.5	2.4
Louisiana	121	117	111	134	6.7	6.3	5.4	6.6	24.0	36.5	1.3	2.0
Maine.	39	33	24	35	7.8	5.2	3.5	5.1	8.9	12.9	1.6	2.2
Maryland	140	122	107	131	6.5	4.7	3.8	4.5	28.9	48.3	0.3	2.1
Massachusetts.	162	195	88	198	5.6	6.0	2.6	5.8	60.1	116.3	1.9	3.6
Michigan.	534	350	183	368	12.4	7.6	3.5	7.3	81.6	150.8	1.8	3.4
Minnesota.	125	117	91	145	5.9	4.9	3.3	5.0	31.4	61.6	1.2	2.4
Mississippi	79	90	74	83	7.5	7.6	5.6	6.3	19.7	27.8	1.8	2.6
Missouri	167	151	102	170	7.2	5.8	3.4	5.6	41.8	65.8	1.6	2.5
Montana	23	24	24	22	6.1	6.0	5.0	4.7	7.8	9.4	2.2	2.5
Nebraska	31	18	28	39	4.1	2.2	3.0	4.0	7.3	13.1	0.9	1.5
Nevada	27	33	42	59	6.2	4.9	4.0	5.2	19.5	31.5	2.0	3.1
New Hampshire	22	36	19	31	4.7	5.7	2.8	4.3	3.1	10.0	0.5	1.7
New Jersey.	260	206	160	257	7.2	5.1	3.7	5.9	84.8	134.6	2.3	3.5
New Mexico	42	46	42	57	7.5	6.5	5.0	6.4	9.5	14.9	1.4	2.1
New York	597	467	419	589	7.5	5.3	4.6	6.3	146.2	251.0	1.8	3.0
North Carolina	187	144	150	273	6.6	4.2	3.6	6.5	54.3	108.6	1.5	2.9
North Dakota	15	13	11	14	5.0	4.0	3.0	4.0	3.9	4.6	1.3	1.5
Ohio	426	310	233	363	8.4	5.7	4.0	6.1	71.6	132.4	1.3	2.5
Oklahoma.	66	86	51	96	4.8	5.7	3.1	5.7	12.2	25.4	0.9	1.8
Oregon.	107	83	88	152	8.3	5.6	4.9	8.2	41.2	68.3	2.7	4.4
Pennsylvania.	425	315	251	344	7.8	5.4	4.1	5.6	132.4	208.5	2.5	3.8
Rhode Island.	34	35	22	30	7.2	6.8	4.1	5.3	12.2	14.5	2.7	3.2
South Carolina.	96	83	75	136	6.9	4.8	3.8	6.8	27.1	49.9	1.5	2.8
South Dakota	16	13	9	15	4.9	3.9	2.3	3.6	2.0	3.5	0.6	1.0
Tennessee	152	126	110	169	7.3	5.3	3.9	5.8	42.2	61.2	1.6	2.4
Texas	352	544	441	738	5.2	6.3	4.2	6.8	107.9	201.0	1.2	2.2
Utah	40	35	37	67	6.3	4.3	3.3	5.6	10.5	20.5	1.1	2.0
Vermont	16	15	10	16	6.4	5.0	2.9	4.6	4.8	8.2	1.7	2.8
Virginia.	128	141	79	154	5.0	4.3	2.2	4.1	22.2	52.6	0.7	1.6
Washington	156	125	159	237	7.9	4.9	5.2	7.5	70.6	112.9	2.7	4.3
West Virginia	74	64	45	48	9.4	8.4	5.5	6.1	14.1	18.1	2.1	2.7
Wisconsin	167	114	105	174	7.2	4.4	3.6	5.6	53.1	90.8	2.0	3.4
Wyoming	9	13	10	13	4.0	5.5	4.4	4.4	2.9	3.4	1.3	1.5

[1] Total unemployment as percent of civilian labor force.   [2] See footnote 2, Table 569.   [3] Source: U.S. Employment and Training Administration, Unemployment Insurance, Financial Handbook, annual updates.   [4] Insured unemployment as percent of average covered employment in the previous year.   [5] Includes 49,800 in Puerto Rico and the Virgin Islands in 2000; and 54,400 in 2002.

Source: Except as noted, U.S. Bureau of Labor Statistics, Geographic Profile of Employment and Unemployment, annual. See Internet site <http://www.bls.gov/gps/>.

No. 611. Nonfarm Establishments—Employees, Hours, and Earnings by Industry: 1990 to 2003

[Annual averages of monthly data. (109,487 represents 109,487,000). Based on data from establishment reports. Includes all full- and part-time employees who worked during, or received pay for, any part of the pay period reported. Excludes proprietors, the self-employed, farm workers, unpaid family workers, private household workers, and Armed Forces. Establishment data shown here conform to industry definitions in the 2002 North American Industry Classification System (NAICS) and are adjusted to March 2003 employment benchmarks. Based on the Current Employment Statistics Program; see Appendix III]

Item and year	Total nonfarm	Private industry Total [1]	Construction	Manufacturing	Wholesale trade	Retail trade	Transportation and warehousing	Utilities	Information	Finance and insurance	Real estate and rental and leasing	Professional and technical services	Administration and waste management	Educational services	Health care and social insurance	Arts, entertainment, and recreation	Accommodations and food services	Government
EMPLOYEES (1,000)																		
1990	109,487	91,072	5,263	17,695	5,268	13,182	3,476	740	2,688	4,979	1,635	4,557	4,624	1,688	9,296	1,132	8,156	18,415
1995	117,298	97,866	5,274	17,241	5,433	13,897	3,838	666	2,843	5,072	1,755	5,101	6,057	2,010	11,278	1,459	9,042	19,432
1999	128,993	108,686	6,545	17,322	5,892	14,970	4,300	609	3,419	5,668	1,979	6,375	7,807	2,320	12,477	1,709	9,834	20,307
2000	131,785	110,996	6,787	17,263	5,933	15,280	4,410	601	3,631	5,680	2,007	6,734	8,136	2,390	12,718	1,788	10,074	20,790
2001	131,826	110,707	6,826	16,441	5,773	15,239	4,372	599	3,629	5,773	2,035	6,902	7,795	2,511	13,134	1,824	10,211	21,118
2002	130,341	108,828	6,716	15,259	5,652	15,025	4,224	596	3,395	5,817	2,030	6,676	7,595	2,643	13,556	1,783	10,203	21,513
2003	129,931	108,356	6,722	14,525	5,606	14,912	4,177	581	3,198	5,921	2,054	6,624	7,698	2,689	13,888	1,801	10,324	21,575
WEEKLY EARNINGS [2] (dol.)																		
1990	(NA)	349.29	513.43	436.16	444.81	235.62	471.72	670.40	479.50	378.21	286.81	504.87	272.70	(NA)	319.80	219.02	143.52	(NA)
1995	(NA)	399.53	571.57	509.26	515.14	272.56	513.37	811.52	564.98	477.39	321.69	583.41	306.54	(NA)	379.66	240.57	160.46	(NA)
1999	(NA)	462.49	655.11	573.17	602.77	321.63	547.97	924.59	675.32	567.75	379.66	714.68	368.31	(NA)	431.14	267.95	191.90	(NA)
2000	(NA)	480.41	685.78	590.65	631.40	333.38	562.70	955.66	700.89	589.64	395.85	745.83	386.33	(NA)	449.27	273.79	201.09	(NA)
2001	(NA)	493.20	685.89	595.19	643.45	346.16	562.70	977.18	731.11	612.36	409.75	769.63	400.95	(NA)	473.04	283.17	203.35	(NA)
2002	(NA)	506.07	711.82	618.75	644.38	360.81	579.75	979.09	738.17	632.34	419.76	784.51	417.44	(NA)	495.17	301.84	207.67	(NA)
2003	(NA)	517.36	727.11	636.07	657.12	367.28	597.79	1,016.94	761.13	670.58	437.25	801.61	427.15	(NA)	516.08	306.08	210.31	(NA)
WEEKLY HOURS [2]																		
1990	34.3	34.3	38.3	40.5	38.4	30.6	37.7	41.5	35.8	36.4	33.1	36.1	32.3	(NA)	31.8	26.1	25.9	(NA)
1995	34.3	34.3	38.8	41.3	38.6	30.8	38.9	42.3	36.0	36.5	32.7	35.8	32.5	(NA)	31.9	26.3	25.8	(NA)
1999	34.3	34.3	39.0	41.4	38.6	30.8	37.6	42.0	36.7	36.9	32.6	36.1	33.0	(NA)	32.0	26.0	26.2	(NA)
2000	34.3	34.3	39.2	41.3	38.8	30.7	37.4	42.0	36.8	37.1	32.6	36.2	33.1	(NA)	32.1	25.6	26.2	(NA)
2001	34.0	34.0	38.7	40.3	38.4	30.7	36.7	41.4	36.9	36.9	32.7	35.9	32.8	(NA)	32.3	25.5	25.8	(NA)
2002	33.9	33.9	38.4	40.5	38.0	30.9	36.8	40.9	36.5	36.6	32.8	35.6	33.0	(NA)	32.3	25.7	25.8	(NA)
2003	33.7	33.7	38.4	40.4	37.8	30.9	36.8	41.1	36.2	36.5	32.8	35.6	32.9	(NA)	32.5	25.5	25.6	(NA)
HOURLY EARNINGS [2] (dol.)																		
1990	10.19	10.19	13.42	10.78	11.58	7.71	12.50	16.14	13.40	10.40	8.66	13.99	8.45	(NA)	10.05	8.41	5.53	(NA)
1995	11.64	11.64	14.73	12.34	13.34	8.85	13.18	19.19	15.68	13.07	9.85	16.32	9.43	(NA)	11.89	9.14	6.22	(NA)
1999	13.47	13.47	16.80	13.85	15.62	10.45	14.55	22.03	18.40	15.38	11.66	19.78	11.15	(NA)	13.48	10.30	7.33	(NA)
2000	14.00	14.00	17.48	14.32	16.28	10.86	15.05	22.75	19.07	15.90	12.14	20.61	11.66	(NA)	13.98	10.68	7.68	(NA)
2001	14.53	14.53	18.00	14.76	16.77	11.29	15.33	23.58	19.80	16.59	12.53	21.42	12.21	(NA)	14.67	11.10	7.88	(NA)
2002	14.95	14.95	18.52	15.29	16.98	11.67	15.76	23.96	20.20	17.28	12.79	22.02	12.66	(NA)	15.32	11.75	8.04	(NA)
2003	15.35	15.35	18.95	15.74	17.36	11.90	16.25	24.76	21.01	18.36	13.32	22.53	13.00	(NA)	15.88	12.00	8.22	(NA)

NA Not available. [1] Includes other industries, not shown separately. [2] Average hours and earnings of production workers for natural resources and mining, manufacturing, and construction; average hours and earnings of nonsupervisory workers for the service-providing industries.

Source: U.S. Bureau of Labor Statistics, Employment and Earnings, monthly, March 2004 issue; and the Current Employment Statistics program Internet site <http://www.bls.gov/ces/home.htm>.

No. 612. Employees in Nonfarm Establishments—States: 2003

[In thousands (129,931 represents 129,931,000). For coverage, see headnote, Table 611. National totals differ from the sum of the state figures because of differing benchmarks among states and differing industrial and geographic stratification. Based on North American Industry Classification System, 2002; see text, this section]

State	Total [1]	Construction	Manufacturing	Trade, transportation, and utilities	Information	Financial activities [2]	Professional and business services [3]	Education and health services [4]	Leisure and hospitality [5]	Other services	Government
U.S. . . .	129,931	6,722	14,525	25,275	3,198	7,974	15,997	16,577	12,125	5,393	21,575
AL.	1,875	99	294	371	32	97	186	187	154	84	359
AK.	300	17	12	61	7	14	23	33	30	11	82
AZ.	2,289	177	174	445	49	159	320	246	232	86	394
AR.	1,144	51	206	240	20	50	103	140	88	41	198
CA.	14,410	789	1,545	2,722	471	887	2,108	1,536	1,398	506	2,427
CO	2,150	150	156	404	85	154	287	214	246	86	357
CT.	1,643	61	200	305	40	143	196	263	125	62	246
DE.	414	[6]24	36	78	7	46	59	50	38	18	57
DC	665	[6]13	3	28	25	31	141	88	49	56	231
FL.	7,286	446	389	1,462	172	484	1,258	886	809	318	1,056
GA	3,860	195	452	823	127	217	494	387	350	172	633
HI	567	[6]28	15	108	10	28	70	65	100	24	119
ID	572	37	62	116	9	27	70	63	54	18	113
IL	5,818	277	718	1,187	135	403	766	718	499	251	856
IN	2,897	145	573	573	41	141	255	362	273	106	423
IA	1,440	65	220	303	34	95	105	190	126	56	245
KS.	1,312	63	172	262	47	70	124	157	109	53	250
KY.	1,783	83	266	371	30	86	154	228	157	77	312
LA.	1,906	119	156	381	29	101	179	245	198	71	380
ME	606	30	64	123	11	35	51	107	58	21	104
MD	2,483	[6]168	148	462	50	156	361	339	219	116	463
MA	3,186	137	326	573	92	224	437	575	288	117	417
MI	4,412	190	727	815	71	219	587	544	398	171	681
MN	2,651	125	344	522	63	176	295	367	233	119	402
MS	1,117	51	178	219	15	46	79	115	123	37	244
MO	2,676	134	313	533	67	163	304	352	262	118	428
MT	400	23	19	84	8	20	33	53	52	16	86
NE.	904	46	102	194	22	62	91	113	78	35	160
NV.	1,087	100	44	195	16	59	121	76	304	30	135
NH	617	29	80	139	12	37	54	93	62	20	90
NJ	3,980	159	352	878	102	277	574	539	321	152	624
NM	776	47	36	136	16	34	89	99	81	29	195
NY.	8,404	319	615	1,473	277	697	1,041	1,496	645	349	1,486
NC	3,803	212	604	721	76	192	421	428	335	162	645
ND	333	16	23	72	8	18	24	48	30	15	76
OH	5,391	230	844	1,045	97	312	607	727	488	227	802
OK	1,451	63	143	277	32	83	156	175	126	74	292
OR	1,562	77	196	314	34	98	170	188	151	57	268
PA	5,602	245	716	1,115	123	338	598	978	469	260	743
RI	484	21	59	81	11	34	49	91	49	23	67
SC.	1,813	112	277	347	27	91	187	178	194	65	329
SD.	378	19	38	77	7	28	24	55	40	16	74
TN.	2,668	116	414	580	52	139	287	313	247	103	412
TX.	9,373	551	901	1,928	235	585	1,044	1,119	858	358	1,648
UT.	1,074	67	112	214	30	65	132	118	100	33	197
VT.	299	15	38	58	7	13	20	52	33	10	52
VA.	3,500	218	305	635	101	187	549	369	307	181	639
WA	2,659	156	267	510	92	153	292	312	248	99	521
WV.	726	33	65	135	13	31	56	108	66	55	142
WI	2,779	124	506	538	50	158	245	367	245	131	412
WY.	250	20	9	48	4	10	16	21	31	10	64

[1] Includes natural resources and mining, not shown separately. [2] Finance and insurance; real estate and rental and leasing. [3] Professional, scientific and technical services; management of companies and enterprises; administrative and support and waste management and remediation services. [4] Education services; health care and social assistance. [5] Arts, entertainment and recreation; accommodations and food services. [6] Natural resources and mining included with construction.

Source: U.S. Bureau of Labor Statistics, Employment and Earnings, monthly, May (state estimates) and March (national estimates) 2004 issues. See also Internet site <http://www.bls.gov/sae/home.htm>. Compiled from data supplied by cooperating state agencies.

Labor Force, Employment and Earnings   399

No. 613. Nonfarm Industries—Employees and Earnings: 1990 to 2003

[Annual averages of monthly figures (109,487 represents 109,487,000). Covers all full- and part-time employees who worked during, or received pay for, any part of the pay period including the 12th of the month. See also headnote, Table 611]

Industry	2002 NAICS[1] code	All employees (1,000)					Average hourly earnings [2] (dollars)		
		1990	2000	2001	2002	2003	2000	2002	2003
Total nonfarm	(X)	109,487	131,785	131,826	130,341	129,931	(NA)	(NA)	(NA)
Goods-producing [3]	(X)	23,723	24,649	23,873	22,557	21,817	15.27	16.33	16.80
Service-providing [4]	(X)	85,764	107,136	107,952	107,784	108,114	(NA)	(NA)	(NA)
Total private	(X)	91,072	110,996	110,707	108,828	108,356	14.00	14.95	15.35
Natural resources and mining	(X)	765	599	606	583	571	16.55	17.19	17.58
Mining	21	680	520	533	512	502	16.94	17.53	17.92
Oil and gas extraction	211	190	125	124	122	123	19.43	19.27	18.95
Mining, except oil and gas	212	302	225	219	211	203	18.07	18.61	19.15
Support activities for mining	213	188	171	190	180	177	14.55	15.58	16.06
Construction	23	5,263	6,787	6,826	6,716	6,722	17.48	18.52	18.95
Construction of buildings	236	1,413	1,633	1,589	1,575	1,576	16.74	17.73	18.35
Residential building	2361	673	823	781	804	834	15.18	16.23	16.85
Nonresidential building	2362	741	809	808	771	742	18.18	19.16	19.84
Heavy and civil engineering construction	237	813	937	953	931	911	16.80	18.00	18.73
Highway, street, and bridge construction	2373	289	340	346	346	341	18.17	19.15	19.46
Specialty trade contractors [5]	238	3,037	4,217	4,284	4,210	4,236	17.91	18.92	19.20
Building foundation and exterior contractors	2381	703	919	926	920	946	16.93	17.81	18.05
Building equipment contractors	2382	1,282	1,897	1,908	1,835	1,818	19.52	20.50	20.66
Building finishing contractors	2383	665	857	875	876	876	16.44	17.71	18.40
Manufacturing	31-33	17,695	17,263	16,441	15,259	14,525	14.32	15.29	15.74
Durable goods	(X)	10,736	10,876	10,335	9,483	8,970	14.93	16.02	16.46
Wood products	321	541	613	574	555	536	11.63	12.33	12.71
Nonmetallic mineral products	327	528	554	545	516	493	14.53	15.40	15.77
Cement and concrete products	3273	195	234	236	230	223	14.64	15.72	16.06
Primary metals	331	689	622	571	509	477	16.64	17.68	18.13
Foundries	3315	214	217	200	178	165	14.72	15.91	16.51
Fabricated metal products [5]	332	1,610	1,753	1,676	1,549	1,478	13.77	14.68	15.01
Architectural and structural metals	3323	357	428	422	399	379	13.43	14.21	14.54
Machine shops and threaded products	3327	309	365	348	318	308	14.53	15.62	15.78
Machinery [5]	333	1,408	1,455	1,368	1,230	1,154	15.22	15.92	16.30
Agricultural, construction, and mining machinery	3331	229	222	217	200	189	14.21	14.51	14.65
HVAC and commercial refrigeration equip.	3334	165	194	184	167	158	13.10	13.71	14.23
Metalworking machinery	3335	267	274	249	217	205	16.66	17.39	17.81
Computer and electronic products [5]	334	1,903	1,820	1,749	1,507	1,361	14.73	16.20	16.68
Computer and peripheral equipment	3341	367	302	286	250	226	18.39	19.64	20.19
Communications equipment	3342	232	248	234	186	157	14.39	15.68	16.84
Semiconductors and electronic components	3344	574	676	645	525	462	13.46	15.32	15.38
Electronic instruments	3345	626	479	475	450	429	15.83	16.64	17.06
Electrical equipment and appliances	335	633	591	557	497	460	13.23	13.98	14.35
Electrical equipment	3353	244	210	197	175	160	13.28	14.18	14.40
Transportation equipment [5]	336	2,133	2,056	1,938	1,829	1,775	18.89	20.64	21.25
Motor vehicles	3361	271	291	279	265	268	24.45	27.25	28.03
Motor vehicle parts	3363	653	840	775	734	707	17.95	19.80	20.42
Aerospace products and parts	3364	841	517	511	470	440	20.52	22.08	22.92
Furniture and related products	337	601	680	642	604	574	11.72	12.61	12.98
Household and institutional furniture	3371	398	440	416	400	382	11.39	12.29	12.69
Miscellaneous manufacturing	339	690	733	715	688	663	11.93	12.91	13.30
Medical equipment and supplies	3391	288	310	311	308	305	12.70	13.65	13.82
Nondurable goods	(X)	6,959	6,388	6,107	5,775	5,555	13.31	14.15	14.63
Food manufacturing [5]	311	1,507	1,553	1,551	1,526	1,519	11.77	12.55	12.80
Fruit and vegetable preserving and specialty	3114	218	197	193	183	184	11.90	12.81	12.79
Animal slaughtering and processing	3116	427	507	516	517	515	10.27	10.91	11.29
Bakeries and tortilla manufacturing	3118	292	306	303	297	293	11.45	12.30	12.62
Beverages and tobacco products	312	218	207	209	207	201	17.40	17.73	17.96
Beverages	3121	173	175	177	174	170	17.19	17.44	17.44
Textile mills	313	492	378	333	291	260	11.23	11.73	12.00
Textile product mills	314	209	216	206	195	180	10.43	10.96	11.24
Apparel	315	929	497	427	360	313	8.60	9.10	9.56
Cut and sew apparel	3152	776	394	335	283	245	8.40	8.89	9.39
Leather and allied products	316	133	69	58	50	45	10.35	11.00	11.67
Paper and paper products	322	647	605	578	547	519	15.91	16.85	17.32
Pulp, paper, and paperboard mills	3221	238	191	179	165	150	20.62	21.95	22.63
Converted paper products	3222	409	413	398	382	369	13.58	14.52	14.95
Printing and related support activities	323	809	807	768	707	680	14.09	14.93	15.37
Petroleum and coal products	324	153	123	121	118	115	22.80	23.04	23.64
Chemicals [5]	325	1,036	980	959	928	908	17.09	17.97	18.52
Basic chemicals	3251	249	188	181	170	163	21.06	21.84	22.11
Pharmaceuticals and medicines	3254	207	274	283	291	294	17.27	18.12	19.79
Plastics and rubber products	326	826	952	897	848	816	12.69	13.55	14.18
Plastics products	3261	619	738	699	664	639	12.04	12.84	13.41
Rubber products	3262	207	214	199	184	177	14.82	16.04	16.81

See footnotes at end of table.

U.S. Census Bureau, Statistical Abstract of the United States: 2004-2005

No. 613. Nonfarm Industries—Employees and Earnings: 1990 to 2003—Con.

[Annual averages of monthly figures (109,487 represents 109,487,000). Covers all full- and part-time employees who worked during, or received pay for, any part of the pay period including the 12th of the month. See also headnote, Table 611]

Industry	2002 NAICS [1] code	All employees (1,000)					Average hourly earnings [2] (dollars)		
		1990	2000	2001	2002	2003	2000	2002	2003
Trade, transportation, and utilities	(X)	22,666	26,225	25,983	25,497	25,275	13.31	14.02	14.34
Wholesale trade.	42	5,268	5,933	5,773	5,652	5,606	16.28	16.98	17.36
Durable goods [5]	423	2,834	3,251	3,130	3,008	2,949	16.71	17.61	17.91
Motor vehicles and parts	4231	309	356	347	346	344	14.27	15.55	15.74
Lumber and construction supplies . . .	4233	181	227	221	225	231	13.61	15.06	15.59
Commercial equipment	4234	597	722	696	665	657	20.29	21.65	22.18
Electric goods	4236	357	425	405	366	345	19.43	18.87	20.03
Hardware and plumbing	4237	216	247	241	233	231	15.07	16.02	16.37
Machinery and supplies	4238	690	725	703	673	646	16.47	17.40	17.47
Nondurable goods [5]	424	1,900	2,065	2,031	2,015	2,002	14.33	15.04	15.66
Paper and paper products	4241	162	177	169	159	150	15.65	15.66	16.20
Druggists' goods.	4242	136	192	202	211	211	18.98	18.07	19.08
Grocery and related products	4244	623	689	684	680	681	13.57	14.60	15.08
Electronic markets and agents and brokers.	425	535	618	611	629	654	20.79	20.48	20.41
Retail trade	44,45	13,182	15,280	15,239	15,025	14,912	10.86	11.67	11.90
Motor vehicle and parts dealers [5]	441	1,494	1,847	1,855	1,879	1,884	14.94	15.83	16.08
Automobile dealers	4411	983	1,217	1,225	1,253	1,255	16.95	17.74	17.86
Auto parts, accessories, and tire stores.	4413	418	499	493	485	480	11.04	11.78	11.97
Furniture and home furnishings stores . . .	442	432	544	541	539	543	12.33	13.08	13.29
Furniture stores	4421	244	289	282	281	282	13.37	14.23	14.41
Home furnishings stores	4422	188	254	259	258	261	11.06	11.75	12.02
Electronics and appliance stores.	443	382	564	555	525	512	13.67	16.19	16.14
Building material and garden supply stores.	444	891	1,142	1,152	1,177	1,191	11.25	12.23	12.67
Building material and supplies dealers .	4441	753	982	997	1,025	1,042	11.30	12.35	12.86
Food and beverage stores.	445	2,779	2,993	2,951	2,882	2,841	9.76	10.55	10.82
Grocery stores	4451	2,406	2,582	2,549	2,487	2,453	9.71	10.49	10.76
Specialty food stores	4452	232	270	261	256	250	9.97	10.92	10.99
Beer, wine, and liquor stores.	4453	141	141	140	139	139	10.40	11.11	11.60
Health and personal care stores	446	792	928	952	939	943	11.68	12.50	13.12
Gasoline stations	447	910	936	925	896	880	8.05	8.56	8.72
Clothing & clothing accessories stores . .	448	1,313	1,322	1,321	1,313	1,297	9.96	10.40	10.48
Clothing stores.	4481	930	954	955	960	947	9.88	10.20	10.30
Shoe stores.	4482	216	193	191	183	180	8.96	9.19	9.22
Jewelry, luggage, and leather goods stores.	4483	167	175	175	170	170	11.48	12.34	12.30
Sporting goods, hobby, book, and music stores.	451	532	686	679	661	645	9.33	10.05	10.23
Sporting goods and musical instrument stores	4511	352	437	438	435	427	9.55	10.45	10.57
Book, periodical, and music stores. . . .	4512	180	249	242	227	218	8.91	9.19	9.49
General merchandise stores	452	2,500	2,820	2,842	2,812	2,815	9.22	9.87	10.10
Department stores	4521	1,494	1,755	1,768	1,684	1,619	9.59	10.19	10.42
Miscellaneous store retailers [5]	453	738	1,007	993	960	934	10.20	10.73	10.93
Florists	4531	121	130	125	122	113	8.95	9.36	9.53
Office supplies, stationery, and gift stores.	4532	358	471	459	435	419	10.46	11.23	11.61
Nonstore retailers.	454	419	492	474	444	428	13.22	14.14	13.79
Electronic shopping and mail-order houses	4541	157	257	240	224	220	13.38	14.79	13.54
Transportation and warehousing.	48,49	3,476	4,410	4,372	4,224	4,177	15.05	15.76	16.25
Air transportation	481	529	614	615	564	527	13.57	15.45	16.01
Scheduled air transportation	4811	503	570	570	520	483	13.25	14.94	15.48
Rail transportation	482	272	232	227	218	215	(NA)	(NA)	(NA)
Water transportation	483	57	56	54	53	53	(NA)	(NA)	(NA)
Truck transportation	484	1,122	1,406	1,387	1,339	1,328	15.86	15.78	16.29
General freight trucking	4841	807	1,013	992	952	936	16.37	16.19	16.69
Specialized freight trucking	4842	315	393	395	388	392	14.51	14.68	15.24
Transit and ground passenger transportation	485	274	372	375	381	380	11.88	12.70	12.77
Pipeline transportation	486	60	46	45	42	40	19.86	21.50	23.03
Scenic and sightseeing transportation . .	487	16	28	29	26	28	12.49	13.59	14.02
Support activities for transportation	488	364	537	539	525	516	14.57	16.66	17.67
Freight transportation arrangement . . .	4885	111	178	179	168	167	13.46	15.62	16.50
Couriers and messengers	491,2	375	605	587	561	567	13.51	14.66	16.58
Couriers	4921	340	546	530	507	515	13.92	15.29	16.58
Warehousing and storage	493	407	514	514	517	522	14.46	14.36	14.80
Utilities.	22	740	601	599	596	581	22.75	23.96	24.76
Power generation and supply	2211	550	434	434	434	420	23.13	24.58	25.64
Natural gas distribution	2212	155	121	118	115	114	23.41	23.58	23.85
Water, sewage and other systems.	2213	35	46	48	48	47	16.93	18.67	18.61

See footnotes at end of table.

Labor Force, Employment, and Earnings 401

[Annual averages of monthly figures (109,487 represents 109,487,000). Covers all full- and part-time employees who worked during, or received pay for, any part of the pay period including the 12th of the month. See also headnote, Table 611]

Industry	2002 NAICS code	All employees (1,000)					Average hourly earnings [2] (dollars)		
		1990	2000	2001	2002	2003	2000	2002	2003
Information	51	2,688	3,631	3,629	3,395	3,198	19.07	20.20	21.01
Publishing industries, except Internet	511	871	1,035	1,021	964	926	20.18	21.59	21.95
Newspaper, book, and directory publishers	5111	773	774	752	711	687	15.06	15.77	16.48
Software publishers	5112	98	261	269	253	239	28.48	31.14	33.78
Motion picture and sound recording industries	512	255	383	377	388	376	21.25	21.20	21.38
Motion picture and video industries	5121	232	352	347	361	351	21.33	21.39	21.41
Broadcasting, except Internet	515	284	344	345	334	327	16.74	18.57	19.38
Radio and television broadcasting	5151	232	253	249	241	240	17.13	19.02	20.24
Cable and other subscription programming	5152	52	91	96	93	87	15.45	17.43	17.21
Internet publishing and broadcasting	516	17	51	46	34	30	(NA)	(NA)	(NA)
Telecommunications [5]	517	980	1,263	1,302	1,187	1,083	17.81	19.34	20.65
Wired telecommunications carriers	5171	673	719	732	651	579	18.52	20.81	22.21
Wireless telecommunications carriers	5172	36	186	201	197	194	14.41	15.75	17.92
Telecommunications resellers	5173	180	214	214	180	151	19.99	20.86	21.65
Cable and other program distribution	5175	70	123	129	130	133	14.67	15.72	16.61
ISPs, search portals, and data processing	518	252	510	494	441	408	20.57	20.62	21.25
ISPs and web search portals	5181	41	194	177	137	124	25.60	25.83	24.21
Data processing and related services	5182	211	316	317	304	284	16.97	18.29	19.90
Other information services	519	30	46	46	47	48	10.68	12.62	14.67
Financial activities	(X)	6,614	7,687	7,807	7,847	7,974	14.98	16.17	17.13
Finance and insurance [5]	52	4,979	5,680	5,773	5,817	5,921	15.90	17.28	18.36
Credit intermediation and related activities	522	2,425	2,548	2,598	2,686	2,786	13.14	14.34	15.62
Depository credit intermediation	5221	1,909	1,681	1,701	1,733	1,752	11.97	12.75	13.55
Commercial banking	52211	1,362	1,251	1,258	1,278	1,281	11.83	12.54	13.30
Nondepository credit intermediation	5222	398	644	661	695	741	15.30	17.59	19.78
Activities related to credit intermediation	5223	119	222	236	258	292	15.39	16.07	17.10
Securities, commodity contracts, investments	523	458	805	831	789	764	20.20	22.49	23.69
Securities and commodity contracts brokerage and exchanges	5232	338	566	577	528	496	20.07	22.09	23.42
Other financial investment activities	5239	120	239	254	261	269	20.48	23.28	24.18
Insurance carriers and related activities	524	2,016	2,221	2,234	2,233	2,266	17.37	18.87	19.88
Insurance carriers	5241	1,338	1,433	1,430	1,413	1,429	17.92	19.54	20.50
Insurance agencies, brokerages, and related services	5242	678	788	803	820	837	16.28	17.61	18.75
Funds, trusts, and other financial vehicles	525	56	85	88	85	82	17.66	19.91	21.71
Real estate and rental and leasing [5]	53	1,635	2,007	2,035	2,030	2,054	12.14	12.79	13.32
Real estate	531	1,107	1,312	1,340	1,353	1,384	12.24	12.87	13.54
Lessors of real estate	5311	564	607	611	606	607	11.16	12.05	12.68
Offices of real estate agents and brokers	5312	217	281	291	298	309	12.57	12.67	13.39
Activities related to real estate	5313	327	424	438	449	469	13.60	14.17	14.87
Rental and leasing services [5]	532	514	667	666	649	641	11.69	12.33	12.58
Automotive equipment rental and leasing	5321	163	208	208	195	195	10.70	11.44	11.96
Consumer goods rental	5322	220	292	290	288	286	9.53	10.30	10.14
Professional and business services	(X)	10,848	16,666	16,476	15,976	15,997	15.52	16.81	17.20
Professional and technical services	54	4,557	6,734	6,902	6,676	6,624	20.61	22.02	22.53
Legal services	5411	944	1,066	1,091	1,115	1,137	21.38	22.51	22.27
Accounting and bookkeeping services	5412	664	866	872	837	816	14.42	16.00	16.50
Architectural and engineering services	5413	942	1,238	1,275	1,246	1,228	20.49	21.59	22.50
Computer systems design and related services	5415	410	1,254	1,298	1,153	1,109	27.13	28.99	29.48
Management and technical consulting services	5416	324	705	746	734	747	20.86	22.89	23.59
Scientific research and development services	5417	494	515	532	538	542	21.39	23.51	25.24
Advertising and related services	5418	382	497	482	441	430	16.99	17.59	17.82
Other professional and technical services	5419	317	462	476	487	493	13.55	14.47	15.22
Management of companies and enterprises	55	1,667	1,796	1,779	1,705	1,676	15.28	16.33	16.76
Administrative and waste services	56	4,624	8,136	7,795	7,595	7,698	11.46	12.66	13.00
Administrative and support services [5]	561	4,395	7,823	7,478	7,277	7,376	11.49	12.43	12.77
Office administrative services	5611	211	264	269	289	304	14.68	15.70	16.59
Employment services	5613	1,494	3,817	3,437	3,247	3,336	11.83	13.04	13.36
Temporary help services	56132	1,156	2,636	2,338	2,194	2,243	11.79	12.73	12.63
Business support services	5614	505	787	780	757	747	11.08	11.90	12.21
Travel arrangement and reservation services	5615	250	299	285	252	240	12.72	13.89	14.47
Investigation and security services	5616	507	689	710	724	710	9.78	10.58	10.90
Services to buildings and dwellings	5617	1,175	1,571	1,606	1,606	1,632	10.02	10.70	11.00
Waste management and remediation services	562	229	313	317	318	322	15.29	16.90	17.32

See footnotes at end of table.

U.S. Census Bureau, Statistical Abstract of the United States: 2004-2005

No. 613. Nonfarm Industries—Employees and Earnings: 1990 to 2003—Con.

[Annual averages of monthly figures (109,487 represents 109,487,000). Cove⸱ ₃ all full- and part-time employees who worked during, or received pay for, any part of the pay period including the 12th of the month. See also headnite, Table 6.1]

Industry	2002 NAICS[1] code	All employees (1,000)					Average hourly earnings[2] (dollars)		
		1990	2000	2001	2002	2003	2000	2002	2003
Education and health services	(X)	10,984	15,109	15,645	16,199	16,577	13.95	15.21	15.64
Educational services	61	1,688	2,390	2,511	2,643	2,689	(NA)	(NA)	(NA)
Elementary and secondary schools	6111	461	716	753	786	795	(NA)	(NA)	(NA)
Junior colleges	6112	44	79	84	84	80	(NA)	(NA)	(NA)
Colleges and universities	6113	939	1,196	1,258	1,339	1,364	(NA)	(NA)	(NA)
Business, computer, and management training	6114	60	86	87	82	83	(NA)	(NA)	(NA)
Technical and trade schools	6115	72	91	93	95	95	(NA)	(NA)	(NA)
Other schools and instruction	6116	96	184	194	207	218	(NA)	(NA)	(NA)
Educational support services	6117	17	39	43	50	54	(NA)	(NA)	(NA)
Health care and social assistance	62	9,296	12,718	13,134	13,556	13,888	13.98	15.32	15.88
Ambulatory health care services [5]	621	2,842	4,320	4,462	4,633	4,776	14.99	16.26	16.87
Offices of physicians	6211	1,278	1,840	1,911	1,968	2,004	15.65	17.05	17.91
Offices of dentists	6212	513	688	705	725	745	15.96	17.79	18.38
Offices of other health practitioners	6213	276	438	457	486	501	14.24	15.49	15.51
Outpatient care centers	6214	261	386	400	413	423	15.29	16.50	17.67
Medical and diagnostic laboratories	6215	129	162	170	175	180	15.74	17.11	17.56
Home health care services	6216	288	633	639	680	727	12.86	13.37	13.69
Hospitals [5]	622	3,513	3,954	4,051	4,160	4,253	16.71	18.63	19.37
General medical and surgical hospitals . . .	6221	3,305	3,745	3,833	3,930	4,013	16.75	18.70	19.48
Psychiatric and substance abuse hospitals	6222	113	86	87	90	91	14.97	16.19	16.55
Nursing and residential care facilities [5] . . .	623	1,856	2,583	2,676	2,743	2,784	10.67	11.60	11.86
Nursing care facilities	6231	1,170	1,514	1,547	1,573	1,583	11.08	12.13	12.52
Residential mental health facilities	6232	269	437	461	473	485	9.96	10.72	10.83
Community care facilities for the elderly	6233	330	478	505	532	552	9.83	10.69	10.83
Social assistance	624	1,085	1,860	1,946	2,020	2,075	9.78	10.54	10.81
Individual and family services	6241	389	678	728	773	805	10.57	11.43	11.84
Emergency and other relief services. . . .	6242	67	117	124	127	128	10.95	11.76	12.01
Vocational rehabilitation services	6243	242	370	380	376	381	9.57	10.34	10.79
Child day care services	6244	388	696	715	744	761	8.88	9.50	9.54
Leisure and hospitality	(X)	9,288	11,862	12,036	11,986	12,125	8.11	8.58	8.76
Arts, entertainment, and recreation [5]	71	1,132	1,788	1,824	1,783	1,801	10.68	11.75	12.00
Performing arts and spectator sports	711	273	382	382	364	370	13.11	15.64	16.70
Museums, historical sites, zoos, and parks	712	68	110	115	114	114	12.21	12.72	12.64
Amusements, gambling, and recreation	713	791	1,296	1,327	1,305	1,317	9.86	10.57	10.60
Accommodations and food services	72	8,156	10,074	10,211	10,203	10,324	7.68	8.04	8.22
Accommodations	721	1,616	1,884	1,852	1,779	1,765	9.48	10.01	10.27
Traveler and other longer-term accommodations	7211	1,582	1,837	1,805	1,738	1,714	9.49	10.01	10.30
RV parks and recreational camps	7212	34	47	48	41	51	9.03	9.76	9.42
Food services and drinking places	722	6,540	8,189	8,359	8,425	8,559	7.18	7.57	7.73
Full-service restaurants	7221	3,070	3,845	3,933	3,992	4,084	7.15	7.57	7.77
Limited-service eating places	7222	2,765	3,462	3,529	3,537	3,584	6.85	7.21	7.31
Special food services	7223	392	491	501	513	511	9.45	9.90	10.29
Drinking places, alcoholic beverages	7224	312	391	396	382	381	7.24	7.52	7.61
Other services	81	4,261	5,168	5,258	5,372	5,393	12.73	13.72	13.84
Repair and maintenance	811	1,009	1,242	1,257	1,247	1,236	13.28	14.14	14.31
Automotive repair and maintenance.	8111	659	888	904	900	897	12.45	13.31	13.51
Personal and laundry services	812	1,120	1,243	1,255	1,257	1,258	10.18	11.04	11.44
Personal care services	8121	430	490	508	529	539	10.18	11.18	11.64
Death care services	8122	123	136	138	140	140	13.04	13.70	14.32
Dry-cleaning and laundry services.	8123	371	388	380	368	356	9.17	9.86	9.86
Dry-cleaning and laundry services, except coin-operated	81232	215	211	205	197	189	8.14	8.59	8.75
Other personal services	8129	196	229	229	221	222	10.52	11.41	12.07
Pet care services, except veterinary	81291	23	31	33	36	37	(NA)	(NA)	(NA)
Membership associations and organizations [5] . .	813	2,132	2,683	2,746	2,868	2,898	13.66	14.69	14.67
Social advocacy organizations	8133	126	143	155	171	176	12.08	13.02	13.97
Civic and social organizations	8134	377	404	413	412	415	9.85	10.59	10.67
Professional and similar organizations	8139	379	473	488	501	499	15.98	17.54	18.24
Government	92	18,415	20,790	21,118	21,513	21,575	(NA)	(NA)	(NA)
Federal	(X)	3,196	2,865	2,764	2,766	2,756	(NA)	(NA)	(NA)
State government	(X)	4,305	4,786	4,905	5,029	5,017	(NA)	(NA)	(NA)
Local government	(X)	10,914	13,139	13,449	13,718	13,802	(NA)	(NA)	(NA)

NA Not available.   X Not applicable.   [1] Based on the North American Industry Classification System, 2002 (NAICS). See text, this section.   [2] Production workers in the goods-producing industries and non-supervisory workers in service-producing industries. See footnotes 3 and 4.   [3] Natural resources and mining, construction, and manufacturing.   [4] Trade, transportation and utilities, information, financial activities, professional and business services, education and health services, leisure and hospitality, other services, and government.   [5] Includes other industries not shown separately.

Source: U.S. Bureau of Labor Statistics, *Employment and Earnings*, monthly, March 2004 issue; and the Current Employment Statistics program Internet site <http://www.bls.gov/ces/home.htm>.

No. 614. Private Sector Job Gains and Losses: 1992 to 2003

[In thousands (455 represents 455,000). For the three months ending in month shown. Based on the Quarterly Census of Employment and Wages; for details see source. Minus sign (-) indicates loss]

Year and month ending	Net change [1]	Gross job gains			Gross job losses		
		Total	Expand-ing establish-ments	Opening establish-ments	Total	Contract-ing establish-ments	Closing establish-ments
1992:							
September.	455	7,377	5,632	1,745	6,922	5,351	1,571
December.	216	7,101	5,465	1,636	6,885	5,487	1,398
1993:							
March.	313	7,309	5,410	1,899	6,996	5,354	1,642
June.	786	7,330	5,794	1,536	6,544	5,136	1,408
September.	874	7,523	5,881	1,642	6,649	5,316	1,333
December.	641	7,436	5,840	1,596	6,795	5,420	1,375
1994:							
March.	517	7,400	5,807	1,593	6,883	5,435	1,448
June.	1,021	7,807	6,060	1,747	6,786	5,295	1,491
September.	1,175	7,972	6,227	1,745	6,797	5,493	1,304
December.	507	7,630	5,998	1,632	7,123	5,647	1,476
1995:							
March.	746	7,782	6,129	1,653	7,036	5,660	1,376
June.	402	7,714	6,017	1,697	7,312	5,839	1,473
September.	771	7,970	6,291	1,679	7,199	5,680	1,519
December.	407	7,877	6,153	1,724	7,470	5,934	1,536
1996:							
March.	460	7,943	6,190	1,753	7,483	5,957	1,526
June.	642	8,080	6,302	1,778	7,438	5,894	1,544
September.	632	8,189	6,326	1,863	7,557	5,998	1,559
December.	861	8,278	6,409	1,869	7,417	5,889	1,528
1997:							
March.	799	8,292	6,448	1,844	7,493	5,900	1,593
June.	594	8,098	6,342	1,756	7,504	5,925	1,579
September.	854	8,593	6,680	1,913	7,739	5,981	1,758
December.	702	8,731	6,727	2,004	8,029	6,068	1,961
1998:							
March.	747	8,788	6,633	2,155	8,041	6,107	1,934
June.	666	8,722	6,569	2,153	8,056	6,218	1,838
September.	659	8,539	6,574	1,965	7,880	6,161	1,719
December.	759	8,576	6,778	1,798	7,817	6,060	1,757
1999:							
March.	380	8,744	6,733	2,011	8,364	6,466	1,898
June.	569	8,800	6,788	2,012	8,231	6,419	1,812
September.	548	8,817	6,871	1,946	8,269	6,397	1,872
December.	1,105	9,144	7,112	2,032	8,039	6,264	1,775
2000:							
March.	818	8,906	6,988	1,918	8,088	6,361	1,727
June.	541	8,764	6,975	1,789	8,223	6,509	1,714
September.	146	8,724	6,834	1,890	8,578	6,719	1,859
December.	336	8,690	6,862	1,828	8,354	6,582	1,772
2001:							
March.	-101	8,555	6,768	1,787	8,656	6,756	1,900
June.	-771	8,254	6,439	1,815	9,025	7,149	1,876
September.	-1,380	7,749	5,990	1,759	9,129	7,174	1,955
December.	-871	7,893	6,055	1,838	8,764	6,995	1,769
2002:							
March.	-1	8,128	6,324	1,804	8,129	6,400	1,729
June.	-80	8,050	6,246	1,804	8,130	6,411	1,719
September.	-211	7,763	6,083	1,680	7,974	6,345	1,629
December.	-175	7,702	6,059	1,643	7,877	6,267	1,610
2003							
March.	-404	7,472	5,932	1,540	7,876	6,321	1,555
June.	-142	7,560	6,033	1,527	7,702	6,138	1,564
September.	72	7,396	5,897	1,499	7,324	5,893	1,431
December.	344	7,646	6,063	1,583	7,302	5,816	1,486

[1] Difference between the total gross job gains and total gross job losses.

Source: U.S. Bureau of Labor Statistics, *Business Employment Dynamics: Fourth Quarter 2003*, USDL 04-1458, August 3, 2004. See Internet site: <http://www.bls.gov/bdm/home.htm>.

No. 615. Annual Indexes of Output Per Hour for Selected NAICS Industries: 1987 to 2002

[For a discussion of productivity measures, see text, this section. Minus sign (-) indicates decrease]

Industry	2002 NAICS code [1]	Indexes (1997=100)						Average annual percent change [2]
		1987	1990	1995	2000	2001	2002	
Mining	21	85.3	86.0	101.8	109.5	107.7	112.3	1.8
Oil and gas extraction	211	80.7	78.4	95.5	115.2	117.4	119.3	2.6
Mining, except oil and gas	212	69.5	79.3	94.0	106.8	109.0	111.7	3.2
Utilities:								
Power generation and supply	2211	64.7	71.2	88.6	107.0	106.4	102.4	3.1
Natural gas distribution	2212	66.8	71.4	89.0	113.1	110.0	114.9	3.7
Manufacturing:								
Sugar and confectionery products	3113	81.5	91.0	94.3	111.9	109.9	(NA)	2.2
Fruit and vegetable preserving and specialty	3114	90.1	86.4	97.1	109.8	117.0	(NA)	1.9
Dairy products	3115	82.4	90.8	98.7	96.0	96.2	(NA)	1.1
Animal slaughtering and processing	3116	97.6	94.5	98.5	101.9	102.7	(NA)	0.4
Bakeries and tortilla manufacturing	3118	98.8	92.6	99.7	105.3	106.3	(NA)	0.5
Other food products	3119	94.6	91.9	101.3	110.2	103.2	(NA)	0.6
Beverages	3121	75.0	86.5	99.6	90.6	91.7	(NA)	1.4
Fabric mills	3132	67.6	75.0	95.8	110.2	109.1	(NA)	3.5
Textile furnishings mills	3141	91.1	88.2	92.5	106.8	106.9	(NA)	1.1
Cut and sew apparel	3152	69.7	70.1	85.5	127.7	131.7	(NA)	4.6
Sawmills and wood preservation	3211	77.4	79.2	91.0	106.5	109.0	(NA)	2.5
Plywood and engineered wood products	3212	100.0	102.3	101.8	100.5	105.0	(NA)	0.3
Other wood products	3219	104.1	105.4	100.4	104.0	104.6	(NA)	-
Pulp, paper, and paperboard mills	3221	85.7	88.5	102.0	115.7	117.5	(NA)	2.3
Converted paper products	3222	88.5	90.5	97.2	101.9	101.0	(NA)	0.9
Printing and related support activities	3231	96.2	96.6	98.8	104.9	105.6	(NA)	0.7
Petroleum and coal products	3241	72.5	76.7	90.1	113.2	112.2	(NA)	3.2
Basic chemicals	3251	92.0	91.4	92.3	118.4	111.0	(NA)	1.4
Resin, rubber, and artificial fibers	3252	76.5	75.8	95.9	108.1	103.8	(NA)	2.2
Pharmaceuticals and medicines	3254	86.1	91.4	96.3	93.4	97.4	(NA)	0.9
Soap, cleaning compounds, and toiletries	3256	81.9	83.2	93.9	99.2	102.7	(NA)	1.6
Other chemical products and preparations	3259	75.5	76.6	94.4	120.0	111.3	(NA)	2.8
Plastics products	3261	82.5	84.7	94.5	111.2	113.3	(NA)	2.3
Rubber products	3262	75.8	83.0	92.8	103.9	104.2	(NA)	2.3
Glass and glass products	3272	83.0	80.0	88.8	109.7	105.2	(NA)	1.7
Cement and concrete products	3273	91.3	94.8	98.2	100.4	97.1	(NA)	0.4
Iron and steel mills and ferroalloy production	3311	63.8	69.6	89.7	108.5	106.7	(NA)	3.7
Foundries	3315	80.7	85.3	93.1	104.0	109.3	(NA)	2.2
Forging and stamping	3321	85.1	88.6	94.2	121.3	121.8	(NA)	2.6
Architectural and structural metals	3323	88.6	87.8	93.9	101.0	100.7	(NA)	0.9
Boilers, tanks, and shipping containers	3324	81.3	90.4	97.8	97.7	98.2	(NA)	1.4
Machine shops and threaded products	3327	76.6	78.8	98.7	107.2	107.2	(NA)	2.4
Coating, engraving, and heat treating metals	3328	76.0	81.6	102.8	105.9	105.1	(NA)	2.3
Other fabricated metal products	3329	91.7	86.7	97.1	100.8	98.2	(NA)	0.5
Agriculture, construction, and mining machinery	3331	74.9	82.8	95.6	101.0	99.5	(NA)	2.0
Industrial machinery	3332	74.6	80.6	97.9	129.7	104.6	(NA)	2.4
Commercial and service industry machinery	3333	83.8	91.4	103.0	101.4	94.4	(NA)	0.8
HVAC and commercial refrigeration equipment	3334	83.7	88.8	96.6	108.3	110.8	(NA)	2.0
Metalworking machinery	3335	84.6	85.3	99.1	106.4	102.0	(NA)	1.3
Turbine and power transmission equipment	3336	80.1	85.1	92.1	117.1	130.2	(NA)	3.5
Other general purpose machinery	3339	83.4	85.9	94.6	113.0	109.4	(NA)	2.0
Computer and peripheral equipment	3341	10.5	14.3	51.3	225.4	237.0	(NA)	24.9
Communications equipment	3342	38.4	47.3	74.6	165.5	155.2	(NA)	10.5
Semiconductors and electronic components	3344	16.5	21.4	63.4	233.3	231.6	(NA)	20.7
Electronic instruments	3345	67.7	76.0	96.8	114.3	116.1	(NA)	3.9
Household appliances	3352	70.5	76.4	92.7	117.5	122.6	(NA)	4.0
Electrical equipment	3353	68.4	73.6	98.1	100.6	101.0	(NA)	2.8
Other electrical equipment and components	3359	77.8	75.3	92.0	120.5	113.5	(NA)	2.7
Motor vehicles	3361	76.1	86.0	88.6	110.4	108.7	(NA)	2.6
Motor vehicle bodies and trailers	3362	85.1	75.8	97.3	98.4	99.4	(NA)	1.1
Motor vehicle parts	3363	78.4	75.7	92.3	112.7	114.8	(NA)	2.8
Aerospace products and parts	3364	84.9	87.7	93.7	101.0	114.7	(NA)	2.2
Ship and boat building	3366	95.3	99.6	93.1	120.1	119.8	(NA)	1.6
Household and institutional furniture	3371	86.0	87.6	97.1	102.5	106.1	(NA)	1.5
Office furniture and fixtures	3372	85.8	80.8	84.3	100.2	97.1	(NA)	0.9
Medical equipment and supplies	3391	74.9	81.2	95.0	114.2	119.0	(NA)	3.4
Other miscellaneous manufacturing	3399	88.1	90.1	96.0	112.9	110.9	(NA)	1.7
Wholesale trade	42	73.4	77.8	93.3	114.1	117.1	123.6	3.5
Durable goods	423	61.8	65.7	88.9	119.6	120.3	127.7	5.0
Nondurable goods	424	94.3	98.4	99.7	103.5	106.9	112.6	1.2
Electronic markets and agents and brokers	425	63.7	70.7	91.1	124.1	131.3	132.6	5.0
Retail trade	44-45	80.9	83.2	94.7	114.2	117.4	122.7	2.8
Motor vehicle and parts dealers	441	85.3	89.7	97.0	107.2	110.0	109.7	1.7
Automobile dealers	4411	87.1	92.1	97.2	106.6	109.1	106.0	1.3
Other motor vehicle dealers	4412	72.7	69.0	91.0	108.6	112.6	116.4	3.2
Auto parts, accessories, and tire stores	4413	77.5	85.0	97.9	112.0	109.3	115.8	2.7
Furniture and home furnishings stores	442	76.6	80.7	94.1	115.7	118.5	125.1	3.3
Furniture stores	4421	74.7	82.1	92.5	114.8	121.1	128.6	3.7
Home furnishings stores	4422	78.9	78.5	95.9	116.8	115.6	121.4	2.9
Electronics and appliance stores	443	37.0	46.0	89.2	177.7	199.1	240.0	13.3
Building material and garden supply stores	444	80.5	81.8	93.7	113.1	115.8	119.9	2.7

See footnotes at end of table.

U.S. Census Bureau, Statistical Abstract of the United States: 2004-2005

No. 615. Annual Indexes of Output Per Hour for Selected NAICS Industries: 1987 to 2002—Con.

[For a discussion of productivity measures, see text, this section. Minus sign (-) indicates decrease]

Industry	2002 NAICS code [1]	Indexes (1997=100)						Average annual percent change [2]
		1987	1990	1995	2000	2001	2002	
Building material and supplies dealers	4441	81.7	83.2	94.8	113.8	115.3	119.8	2.6
Lawn and garden equipment and supplies stores .	4442	74.0	74.5	87.0	108.2	119.4	121.2	3.3
Food and beverage stores	445	109.0	107.1	102.5	105.1	107.6	110.3	0.1
Grocery stores	4451	110.0	106.5	103.0	104.9	107.5	110.3	-
Specialty food stores	4452	125.4	122.9	101.1	105.6	110.8	114.2	-0.6
Beer, wine and liquor stores.	4453	96.3	100.1	96.2	111.1	110.4	111.8	1.0
Health and personal care stores.	446	85.6	92.0	93.0	111.4	112.7	118.8	2.2
Gasoline stations.	447	84.2	84.8	99.7	106.5	109.8	117.5	2.2
Clothing and clothing accessories stores	448	67.0	69.5	91.2	120.3	123.5	129.0	4.5
Clothing stores	4481	66.5	68.9	90.1	120.9	125.2	132.7	4.7
Shoe stores	4482	67.1	73.7	93.7	109.6	115.8	120.0	4.0
Jewelry, luggage, and leather goods stores	4483	69.7	68.6	94.1	118.0	122.5	121.5	3.8
Sporting goods, hobby, book, and music stores. . . .	451	73.6	80.8	93.0	121.1	125.4	132.9	4.0
Sporting goods and musical instrument stores . . .	4511	68.5	77.1	92.3	128.3	130.4	137.9	4.8
Book, periodical, and music stores	4512	86.6	89.0	94.5	108.0	116.0	123.8	2.4
General merchandise stores	452	73.4	75.3	92.2	119.9	124.2	130.5	3.9
Department stores	4521	87.0	84.0	94.7	106.3	104.0	104.7	1.2
Other general merchandise stores	4529	54.7	61.4	87.6	145.9	162.1	177.5	8.2
Miscellaneous store retailers	453	66.1	70.6	89.5	111.3	108.4	115.6	3.8
Florists.	4531	79.2	75.1	83.5	116.0	108.6	120.7	2.9
Office supplies, stationery and gift stores	4532	58.7	64.6	90.9	124.1	125.1	140.3	6.0
Used merchandise stores	4533	83.9	84.9	90.2	115.7	115.0	121.4	2.5
Other miscellaneous store retailers	4539	71.9	79.6	90.5	99.6	93.2	92.8	1.7
Nonstore retailers	454	49.2	54.4	80.9	142.8	146.9	169.6	8.6
Electronic shopping and mail-order houses.	4541	36.3	43.5	71.9	159.8	177.5	209.8	12.4
Vending machine operators	4542	98.7	97.1	89.3	127.1	110.4	113.3	0.9
Direct selling establishments	4543	65.7	70.0	94.7	104.3	98.7	110.2	3.5
Transportation and warehousing:								
Air transportation.	481	81.1	77.5	95.3	98.2	91.9	103.2	1.6
Line-haul railroads.	482111	58.9	69.8	92.0	114.3	121.9	131.9	5.5
General freight trucking, long-distance.	48412	79.4	88.5	95.4	105.5	104.2	109.4	2.2
Postal service.	491	92.4	96.1	98.3	104.9	106.1	107.0	1.0
Information:								
Newspaper, book, and directory publishers	5111	104.6	97.4	93.5	110.1	106.4	108.1	0.2
Software publishers	5112	9.9	28.6	73.0	103.9	101.9	106.7	17.2
Motion picture and video exhibition	51213	90.3	109.4	99.9	106.5	104.7	104.4	1.0
Radio and television broadcasting	5151	97.2	96.1	106.1	98.4	94.3	100.4	0.2
Cable and other subscription programming.	5152	102.1	98.8	94.4	135.7	125.3	131.4	1.7
Wired telecommunications carriers	5171	56.1	64.8	90.6	119.9	121.0	130.6	5.8
Wireless telecommunications carriers	5172	77.7	76.3	98.3	139.0	172.7	192.0	6.2
Cable and other program distribution.	5175	102.6	99.1	94.2	90.4	87.6	93.5	-0.6
Finance and insurance:								
Commercial banking	52211	73.3	80.5	96.0	104.2	101.6	103.8	2.3
Real estate and rental leasing:								
Passenger car rental	532111	91.3	89.8	101.1	112.0	112.1	113.3	1.5
Truck, trailer and RV rental and leasing.	53212	63.0	70.7	90.3	95.9	93.6	91.4	2.5
Professional and technical services:								
Tax preparation services	541213	95.7	92.4	96.2	91.8	78.2	92.1	-0.3
Advertising agencies	54181	96.5	105.0	101.4	116.6	116.7	123.9	1.7
Accommodation and food services:								
Traveler accommodations.	7211	86.4	82.9	99.2	107.7	102.0	104.1	1.3
Food services and drinking places	722	95.5	102.9	100.6	103.5	103.7	104.9	0.6
Full-service restaurants.	7221	90.4	99.1	96.6	100.8	100.8	102.0	0.8
Limited-service eating places.	7222	94.8	103.3	104.7	105.1	106.6	107.1	0.8
Special food services	7223	105.1	107.2	99.3	111.7	108.4	108.1	0.2
Drinking places, alcoholic beverages	7224	133.3	125.7	104.4	100.4	98.2	107.2	-1.4
Other services:								
Automotive repair and maintenance	8111	87.8	92.8	102.9	108.6	109.3	103.7	1.1
Hair, nail and skin care services.	81211	83.0	81.6	92.4	103.0	109.5	104.2	1.5
Funeral homes and funeral services	81221	104.1	96.1	100.4	94.5	93.9	90.9	-0.9
Drycleaning and laundry services	8123	97.5	95.6	98.8	113.7	121.1	120.2	1.4
Photofinishing.	81292	102.4	117.3	114.7	107.6	115.0	133.6	1.8

- Represents or rounds to zero.   NA Not available.   [1] North American Industry Classification System, 2002 (NAICS); see text, this section. [2] Average annual percent change, 1987 to 2002 (1987 to 2001 for manufacturing industries), based on compound rate formula.

Source: U.S. Bureau of Labor Statistics, Internet site <http://www.bls.gov/lpc/home.htm>

No. 616. Productivity and Related Measures: 1980 to 2003

[See text, this section. Minus sign (-) indicates decrease]

Item	1980	1985	1990	1995	1999	2000	2001	2002	2003
INDEXES (1992=100)									
Output per hour, business sector.	79.0	87.3	94.4	101.7	112.4	115.7	118.3	124.0	129.6
Nonfarm business	80.3	87.7	94.4	102.1	112.2	115.3	117.8	123.6	129.1
Manufacturing	(NA)	(NA)	92.9	110.1	128.2	134.2	137.1	147.1	154.6
Output,[1] business sector.	68.8	82.2	96.9	111.4	135.2	140.5	140.6	143.8	149.1
Nonfarm business	69.2	82.2	97.1	111.8	135.6	140.8	141.0	144.2	149.5
Manufacturing	(NA)	(NA)	97.6	115.0	134.6	138.6	132.3	131.5	131.6
Hours,[2] business sector	87.2	94.1	102.6	109.5	120.2	121.4	118.9	116.0	115.1
Nonfarm business	86.2	93.7	102.8	109.5	120.8	122.1	119.7	116.6	115.9
Manufacturing	(NA)	(NA)	105.0	104.4	105.0	103.3	96.5	89.4	85.1
Compensation per hour,[3] business sector	54.0	72.5	90.5	106.0	125.4	134.2	139.7	142.8	148.0
Nonfarm business	54.2	72.7	90.3	106.0	124.9	133.7	138.9	142.1	147.1
Manufacturing	(NA)	(NA)	90.1	107.7	123.8	135.0	138.3	143.8	152.3
Real hourly compensation,[3] business sector.	88.9	92.0	96.1	98.9	107.8	111.6	113.0	113.7	115.2
Nonfarm business	89.2	92.3	95.9	98.9	107.3	111.2	112.4	113.2	114.5
Manufacturing	(NA)	(NA)	95.7	100.5	106.3	112.3	111.8	114.5	118.5
Unit labor costs,[4] business sector.	68.4	83.0	95.9	104.3	111.6	116.0	118.1	115.2	114.2
Nonfarm business	67.5	82.9	95.6	103.8	111.3	116.0	118.0	115.0	114.0
Manufacturing	(NA)	(NA)	97.0	97.8	96.6	100.6	100.8	97.8	98.5
ANNUAL PERCENT CHANGE[5]									
Output per hour, business sector.	-0.2	2.4	1.9	0.3	2.9	2.9	2.2	4.9	4.5
Nonfarm business	-0.2	1.7	1.7	0.6	2.8	2.8	2.1	5.0	4.4
Manufacturing	(NA)	(NA)	2.9	3.9	3.8	4.7	2.2	7.2	5.1
Output,[1] business sector.	-1.1	4.6	1.5	2.9	5.1	3.9	0.1	2.3	3.7
Nonfarm business	-1.0	4.2	1.5	3.2	5.2	3.8	0.1	2.3	3.7
Manufacturing	(NA)	(NA)	0.3	4.5	2.9	3.0	-4.6	-0.6	0.1
Hours,[2] business sector	-0.9	2.2	-0.3	2.6	2.1	1.0	-2.1	-2.5	-0.8
Nonfarm business	-0.8	2.5	-0.3	2.6	2.3	1.0	-2.0	-2.6	-0.7
Manufacturing	(NA)	(NA)	-2.5	0.6	-0.8	-1.6	-6.6	-7.3	-4.8
Compensation per hour,[3] business sector	10.8	4.9	6.0	2.2	4.8	7.0	4.1	2.2	3.6
Nonfarm business	10.8	4.7	5.9	2.2	4.7	7.0	3.9	2.3	3.5
Manufacturing	(NA)	(NA)	4.7	2.0	4.2	9.1	2.4	4.0	5.9
Real hourly compensation,[3] business sector.	-0.2	1.5	1.0	-0.3	2.7	3.6	1.3	0.6	1.3
Nonfarm business	-0.2	1.3	0.9	-0.2	2.5	3.6	1.1	0.7	1.2
Manufacturing	(NA)	(NA)	-0.3	-0.4	2.0	5.6	-0.4	2.4	3.5
Unit labor costs,[4] business sector.	11.0	2.5	4.1	1.9	1.8	4.0	1.8	-2.5	-0.8
Nonfarm business	11.0	2.9	4.1	1.6	1.8	4.2	1.7	-2.5	-0.9
Manufacturing	(NA)	(NA)	1.7	-1.8	0.3	4.2	0.2	-3.0	0.7

NA Not available.   [1] Refers to gross sectoral product, annual weighted.   [2] Hours at work of all persons engaged in the business and nonfarm business sectors (employees, proprietors, and unpaid family workers); employees' and proprietors' hours in manufacturing.   [3] Wages and salaries of employees plus employers and contributions for social insurance and private benefit plans. Also includes an estimate of same for self-employed. Real compensation deflated by the consumer price index for all urban consumers, see text, Section 14.   [4] Hourly compensation divided by output per hour.   [5] All changes are from the immediate prior year.

Source: U.S. Bureau of Labor Statistics, *Productivity and Costs*, News USDL 04-995, June 3, 2004; and Internet site <http://www.bls.gov/lpc/home.htm>.

No. 617. Employed Persons Using Computers at Work by Sex and Occupation: 2001

[In percent, except as indicated (135,089 represents 135,089,000). As of September. For persons 16 years old and over, except as indicated. Based on the Current Population Survey and subject to sampling error; see Appendix III and source]

Characteristic	Total employed (1,000)	Total using a computer at work (1,000)	Percent of employed	Percent who used a computer at work for—					
				Word processing[1]	Internet or e-mail	Calendar or scheduling	Spreadsheets or databases	Graphics or design	Programming
Total, 16 years and over	**135,089**	**72,277**	**53.5**	**67.0**	**71.8**	**52.9**	**62.3**	**28.8**	**15.2**
Sex: Male	72,306	34,663	47.9	64.3	75.1	55.2	64.9	32.0	20.4
Women	62,784	37,614	59.9	69.4	68.8	50.9	59.9	25.8	10.5
Occupation:									
Managerial and professional	41,936	33,374	79.6	78.3	82.7	60.8	70.3	37.2	18.6
Executive, admin., and									
managerial	20,279	16,297	80.4	79.0	83.5	65.3	76.9	34.4	16.6
Professional specialty	21,657	17,077	78.9	77.6	81.9	56.5	63.9	39.9	20.5
Technical, sales, and admin.									
support	38,761	26,056	67.2	62.6	67.3	48.4	59.7	22.5	12.4
Technicians and related support .	4,617	3,462	75.0	58.5	70.4	52.3	59.3	29.5	27.0
Sales occupations	15,905	9,173	57.7	59.9	69.3	48.6	60.1	25.6	11.1
Administrative support, inc.									
clerical	18,238	13,421	73.6	65.6	65.1	47.2	59.6	18.5	9.6
Service occupations	18,279	4,259	23.3	52.6	51.1	45.7	43.8	17.2	8.9
Precision production, craft,									
and repair.	14,850	4,447	29.9	46.5	59.9	45.4	51.7	23.7	17.4
Operators, fabricators, and									
laborers	17,737	3,465	19.5	35.7	43.1	32.4	41.2	17.1	9.5
Farming, forestry, and fishing.	3,527	675	19.1	60.9	67.1	43.7	61.3	21.7	10.6

[1] Or desktop publishing.
Source: U.S. Bureau of Labor Statistics, *Computer and Internet Use at Work, 2001*, News, USDL 02-601, October 23, 2002. See Internet site <http://www.bls.gov/bls/newsrels.htm#OEUS>

Labor Force, Employment, and Earnings   **407**

No. 618. Annual Total Compensation and Wages and Salary Accruals Per Full-Time Equivalent Employee by Industry: 1999 to 2002

[In dollars. Wage and salary accruals include executives' compensation, bonuses, tips, and payments-in-kind; total compensation includes in addition to wages and salaries, employer contributions for social insurance, employer contributions to private and welfare funds, director's fees, jury and witness fees, etc. Based on the 1997 North American Industry Classification System (NAICS); see text, this section]

Industry	Annual total compensation				Annual wages and salary			
	1999	2000	2001	2002	1999	2000	2001	2002
Domestic industries	43,918	46,407	47,542	48,652	36,664	38,762	39,565	40,216
Private industries	42,684	45,240	46,201	47,085	36,294	38,446	39,106	39,603
Agriculture, forestry, fishing, and hunting	28,075	29,332	26,253	26,244	24,767	25,847	23,137	23,064
Mining.	65,576	70,413	73,258	74,425	54,451	58,291	60,599	61,041
Utilities	71,405	78,147	81,237	83,978	58,731	64,271	66,473	68,311
Construction.	42,598	44,764	47,822	48,966	35,375	37,196	39,646	40,373
Manufacturing.	50,114	54,219	54,134	56,154	40,930	44,216	43,786	44,873
Wholesale trade	54,448	56,264	59,885	61,061	46,601	48,017	50,973	51,549
Retail trade	28,747	30,225	30,038	31,005	25,013	26,307	26,027	26,687
Transportation and warehousing.	46,058	48,336	48,625	49,963	37,612	39,463	39,439	40,138
Information.	68,102	74,196	71,948	71,279	57,920	63,217	60,902	59,716
Finance and insurance	67,626	74,821	77,969	77,446	57,822	64,049	66,566	65,664
Real estate and rental and leasing . . .	38,892	41,906	42,124	43,661	33,579	36,178	36,229	37,392
Professional, scientific, and technical services	62,100	68,436	72,075	72,832	53,242	58,886	61,756	61,984
Management of companies and enterprises [1]	83,932	89,496	85,947	86,033	71,330	75,984	72,238	71,744
Administrative and waste management services	30,505	28,540	30,424	31,396	27,216	25,181	26,785	27,597
Educational services	31,130	32,736	34,119	35,507	27,579	28,974	30,081	31,166
Health care and social assistance. . . .	39,044	40,897	42,072	43,848	33,520	35,127	36,009	37,399
Arts, entertainment, and recreation . . .	34,107	35,898	35,842	37,143	29,682	31,259	31,098	32,079
Accommodation and food services . . .	18,234	19,092	20,449	21,041	16,065	16,830	17,951	18,375
Other services, except government. . .	27,470	28,630	29,449	31,085	24,492	25,495	26,121	27,510
Government.	50,682	52,845	54,852	56,886	38,692	40,501	42,071	43,436
Federal	66,566	70,004	73,493	77,076	44,225	46,646	48,672	50,895
State and local	46,174	48,020	49,822	51,465	37,122	38,773	40,290	41,433

[1] Consists of offices of bank and other holding companies and of corporate, subsidiary, and regional managing offices.

Source: U.S. Bureau of Economic Analysis, *Survey of Current Business*, March and April 2004. See also <http://www.bea.gov/bea/dn/nipaweb/selecttable.asp>.

No. 619. Average Hourly Earnings by Private Industry Group: 1990 to 2003

[In dollars. Average earnings include overtime. Data are for production workers in natural resources and mining, manufacturing, and construction, and nonsupervisory employees in other industries. See headnote, Table 611]

Private industry group	Current dollars					Constant (1982) dollars [1]				
	1990	2000	2001	2002	2003	1990	2000	2001	2002	2003
AVERAGE HOURLY EARNINGS										
Total private.	10.19	14.00	14.53	14.95	15.35	7.66	8.03	8.11	8.24	8.27
Natural resources and mining	13.40	16.55	17.00	17.19	17.58	10.07	9.50	9.49	9.47	9.47
Construction	13.42	17.48	18.00	18.52	18.95	10.08	10.03	10.05	10.20	10.21
Manufacturing	10.78	14.32	14.76	15.29	15.74	8.10	8.22	8.24	8.42	8.48
Trade, transportation and utilities	9.83	13.31	13.70	14.02	14.34	7.39	7.64	7.65	7.72	7.73
Information	13.40	19.07	19.80	20.20	21.01	10.07	10.94	11.06	11.13	11.32
Financial activities [2]	9.99	14.98	15.59	16.17	17.13	7.51	8.59	8.70	8.91	9.23
Professional and business services [2] . . .	11.14	15.52	16.33	16.81	17.20	8.37	8.90	9.12	9.26	9.27
Education and health services [2]	10.00	13.95	14.64	15.21	15.64	7.51	8.00	8.17	8.38	8.43
Leisure and hospitality [2].	5.88	8.11	8.35	8.58	8.76	4.42	4.65	4.66	4.73	4.72
Other services	9.08	12.73	13.27	13.72	13.84	6.82	7.30	7.41	7.56	7.46
AVERAGE WEEKLY EARNINGS										
Total private.	349.29	480.41	493.20	506.07	517.36	262.43	275.62	275.38	278.83	278.75
Natural resources and mining	602.54	734.92	757.92	741.97	766.83	452.70	421.64	423.18	408.80	413.16
Construction	513.43	685.78	695.89	711.82	727.11	385.75	393.45	388.55	392.19	391.76
Manufacturing	436.16	590.65	595.19	618.75	636.07	327.69	338.87	332.32	340.91	342.71
Trade, transportation and utilities	331.55	449.88	459.53	471.27	481.10	249.10	258.11	256.58	259.65	259.21
Information	479.50	700.89	731.11	738.17	761.13	360.26	402.12	408.21	406.71	410.09
Financial activities [2]	354.65	537.37	558.02	575.51	608.87	266.45	308.30	311.57	317.09	328.05
Professional and business services [2] . . .	380.61	535.07	557.84	574.66	586.68	285.96	306.98	311.47	316.62	316.10
Education and health services [2]	319.27	449.29	473.39	492.74	505.76	239.87	257.77	264.32	271.48	272.50
Leisure and hospitality [2].	152.47	211.79	215.19	221.26	224.35	114.55	121.51	120.15	121.91	120.88
Other services	297.91	413.41	428.64	439.76	434.49	223.82	237.18	239.33	242.29	234.10

[1] Earnings in current dollars divided by the Consumer Price Index (CPI-W) on a 1982 base; see text, Section 14, Prices.
[2] For composition of industries, see Table 612.

Source: U.S. Bureau of Labor Statistics, *Employment and Earnings,* monthly, March 2004 issue; and the Current Employment Statistics program. See Internet site <http://www.bls.gov/ces/home.htm>

No. 620. Mean Hourly Earnings and Weekly Hours for Metro and Nonmetro Areas by Selected Characteristics: 2002

[Covers civilian workers in private industry establishments and state and local governments in the 50 states and DC. Excludes private households, federal government and agriculture. Based on establishment survey; see source and Apendix III for details]

Item	Mean hourly earnings (dol.) [1]			Mean weekly hours		
	Total	Metro areas [2]	Nonmetro areas	Total	Metro areas [2]	Nonmetro areas
Total	**17.18**	**17.56**	**14.20**	**35.8**	**35.7**	**36.4**
Private industry	16.40	16.79	12.91	35.6	35.6	36.3
State and local government	21.54	22.37	18.02	36.7	36.7	36.8
WORKER CHARACTERISTIC						
White-collar occupations	21.09	21.43	17.75	36.1	36.1	36.4
Professional specialty and technical	27.18	27.71	22.73	36.1	36.2	36.0
Professional	29.34	29.80	25.34	36.2	36.2	36.1
Technical	19.89	20.54	15.08	35.9	35.9	35.8
Executive, administrative, and managerial	31.16	31.56	25.94	40.0	40.0	40.0
Sales	14.50	14.75	11.38	32.6	32.6	33.5
Administrative support	13.41	13.60	11.61	36.4	36.3	36.9
Blue-collar occupations	14.51	14.71	13.25	38.2	38.1	38.5
Precision production, craft, and repair	18.20	18.46	16.25	39.6	39.6	40.0
Machine operators, assemblers, and inspectors	12.94	13.07	12.38	39.2	39.1	39.6
Transportation and material moving	14.25	14.22	14.53	37.5	37.5	37.7
Handlers, equipment cleaners, helpers and laborer	10.98	11.14	10.02	35.6	35.6	35.9
Service occupations	10.32	10.49	9.31	31.6	31.3	33.4
Protective service	16.83	17.23	14.26	37.0	36.7	38.6
Food service	7.41	7.41	7.37	28.4	28.2	29.5
Health service	10.54	10.73	9.54	34.1	34.2	33.7
Cleaning and building service	10.23	10.41	9.10	34.7	34.6	35.2
Personal service	10.28	10.74	8.46	29.2	28.0	35.2
Full time	18.14	18.59	14.78	39.6	39.6	39.6
Part time	9.66	9.76	8.80	20.5	20.5	20.7
Union [3]	20.65	21.01	17.59	36.9	36.8	37.8
Nonunion	16.42	16.80	13.52	35.6	35.5	36.1
Time [4]	16.89	17.25	14.11	35.7	35.6	36.2
Incentive [4]	22.52	23.41	15.79	38.3	37.9	41.1
ESTABLISHMENT CHARACTERISTIC						
Goods producing [5]	17.74	(NA)	(NA)	39.5	(NA)	(NA)
Service producing [5]	15.88	(NA)	(NA)	34.3	(NA)	(NA)
1 to 99 workers [6]	14.43	14.59	12.60	34.6	34.7	34.3
100 to 499 workers	16.73	17.24	14.21	36.3	36.2	36.7
500 to 999 workers	18.80	19.55	15.77	37.2	37.1	37.9
1,000 to 2,499 workers	20.75	21.55	16.27	36.5	36.2	38.0
2,500 workers or more	23.30	23.66	14.33	37.4	37.3	39.5
GEOGRAPHIC REGION [7]						
New England	18.61	18.99	14.66	34.4	34.4	34.5
Middle Atlantic	19.79	19.97	15.83	34.8	34.8	34.9
East North Central	17.42	17.73	15.11	35.7	35.6	36.3
West North Central	16.11	16.82	13.38	35.3	35.3	35.3
South Atlantic	15.97	16.26	13.83	36.4	36.3	37.1
East South Central	14.19	15.06	12.37	37.1	36.5	38.5
West South Central	15.39	15.49	14.45	36.6	36.7	36.3
Mountain	15.67	15.67	15.70	35.5	35.5	35.7
Pacific	19.08	19.22	16.10	35.8	35.9	34.8

NA Not available. [1] Earnings are straight time hourly wages or salary, including incentive pay, cost-of-living adjustments, and hazard pay. Excludes premium pay for overtime, vacations and holidays, nonproduction bonuses and tips. [2] Metropolitan areas defined as of 1994. [3] Workers whose wages are determined through collective bargaining. [4] Time worker wages are based solely on an hourly rate or salary. Incentive workers wages are based at least in part on productivity payments such as piece rates or commissions. [5] For private industry only. [6] Private establishments employing 1 to 99 workers and state and local government establishments employing 50 or more workers. [7] Composition of regions: NEW ENGLAND: Maine, New Hampshire, Vermont, Massachusetts, Rhode Island, Connecticut. MIDDLE ATLANTIC: New York, New Jersey, and Pennsylvania. EAST NORTH CENTRAL: Ohio, Indiana, Illinois, Michigan, Wisconsin. WEST NORTH CENTRAL: Minnesota, Iowa, Missouri, North Dakota, South Dakota, Nebraska, and Kansas. SOUTH ATLANTIC: Delaware, Maryland, District of Columbia, Virginia, West Virginia, North Carolina, South Carolina, Georgia, Florida. EAST SOUTH CENTRAL: Kentucky, Tennessee, Alabama, Mississippi. WEST SOUTH CENTRAL: Arkansas, Louisiana, Oklahoma, and Texas. MOUNTAIN: Montana, Idaho, Wyoming, Colorado, New Mexico, Arizona, Utah, Nevada. PACIFIC: Washington, Oregon, California, Alaska, and Hawaii.

Source: U.S. Bureau of Labor Statistics, *National Compensation Survey: Occupational Wages in the United States, July 2002*, Bulletin 2561, September 2003. See Internet site <http://www.bls.gov/ncs/home.htm>.

No. 621. Average Annual Pay by State: 2001 and 2002

[In dollars, except percent change. For workers covered by state unemployment insurance laws and for federal civilian workers covered by unemployment compensation for federal employees, approximately 99 percent of wage and salary civilian employment in 2002. Excludes most agricultural workers on small farms, all Armed Forces, elected officials in most states, railroad employees, most domestic workers, most student workers at school, employees of certain nonprofit organizations, and most self-employed individuals. Pay includes bonuses, cash value of meals and lodging, and tips and other gratuities. Minus sign (-) indicates decrease]

State	Average annual pay 2001	Average annual pay 2002	Percent change, 2001-02	State	Average annual pay 2001	Average annual pay 2002	Percent change, 2001-02
United States......	36,219	36,764	1.5	Missouri...........	32,421	33,118	2.1
Alabama...........	30,102	31,163	3.5	Montana...........	25,195	26,001	3.2
Alaska............	36,170	37,134	2.7	Nebraska..........	28,377	29,448	3.8
Arizona............	33,411	34,036	1.9	Nevada............	33,121	33,993	2.6
Arkansas..........	27,260	28,074	3.0	New Hampshire.....	35,481	36,176	2.0
California..........	41,327	41,419	0.2	New Jersey........	44,320	45,182	1.9
Colorado...........	37,952	38,005	0.1	New Mexico........	28,702	29,431	2.5
Connecticut........	46,993	46,852	-0.3	New York..........	46,727	46,328	-0.9
Delaware..........	38,427	39,684	3.3	North Carolina......	32,024	32,689	2.1
District of Columbia....	55,908	57,914	3.6	North Dakota.......	25,707	26,550	3.3
Florida............	31,553	32,426	2.8	Ohio..............	33,283	34,214	2.8
Georgia...........	35,136	35,734	1.7	Oklahoma..........	28,016	28,654	2.3
Hawaii............	31,253	32,671	4.5	Oregon............	33,204	33,684	1.4
Idaho.............	27,768	28,163	1.4	Pennsylvania.......	34,978	35,808	2.4
Illinois............	39,083	39,688	1.5	Rhode Island.......	33,603	34,810	3.6
Indiana............	31,779	32,603	2.6	South Carolina......	29,255	30,003	2.6
Iowa..............	28,837	29,668	2.9	South Dakota.......	25,601	26,360	3.0
Kansas............	30,153	30,825	2.2	Tennessee.........	31,520	32,531	3.2
Kentucky..........	30,021	30,904	2.9	Texas.............	36,045	36,248	0.6
Louisiana..........	29,131	30,115	3.4	Utah..............	30,077	30,585	1.7
Maine.............	28,815	29,736	3.2	Vermont...........	30,238	31,041	2.7
Maryland..........	38,253	39,382	3.0	Virginia...........	36,733	37,222	1.3
Massachusetts......	44,975	44,954	(Z)	Washington........	37,459	38,242	2.1
Michigan...........	37,391	38,135	2.0	West Virginia.......	27,981	28,612	2.3
Minnesota..........	36,587	37,458	2.4	Wisconsin..........	31,540	32,464	2.9
Mississippi.........	25,923	26,665	2.9	Wyoming...........	28,043	28,975	3.3

Z Less than 0.5.

Source: U.S. Bureau of Labor Statistics. "Annual Wages for All Covered Workers by State". See Internet site <http://www.bls.gov/cew/home.htm>.

No. 622. Average Annual Pay by Selected Metropolitan Area: 2001 and 2002

[In dollars. Metropolitan areas ranked by average pay 2002. Includes data for Metropolitan Statistical Areas and Primary Metropolitan Statistical Areas defined as of June 1999; see Appendix II. In New England areas, the New England County Metropolitan Area (NECMA) definitions were used. See source for details. See also headnote, Table 621]

Metropolitan area	2001	2002	Metropolitan area	2001	2002
Metropolitan areas.........	37,908	38,423	Rochester, MN...........	37,753	39,036
San Jose, CA..............	65,931	63,056	Baltimore, MD............	37,495	38,718
New York, NY.............	59,097	57,708	New London-Norwich, CT....	38,505	38,650
San Francisco, CA..........	59,654	56,602	Huntsville, AL............	36,727	38,571
New Haven-Bridgeport-Stamford-			Charlotte-Gastonia-Rock Hill, NC-SC.	37,267	38,413
Waterbury-Danbury, CT.....	52,198	51,170	Dutchess County, NY.......	38,748	38,221
Middlesex-Somerset-Hunterdon, NJ..	49,950	50,457	Ventura, CA..............	37,783	38,195
Jersey City, NJ............	47,638	49,562	Monmouth-Ocean, NJ.......	37,056	37,710
Newark, NJ...............	47,715	48,781	Portland-Vancouver, OR-WA......	37,285	37,650
Washington, DC-MD-VA-WV.......	47,589	48,430	Springfield, IL...........	36,061	37,336
Trenton, NJ...............	46,831	47,969	Fort Worth-Arlington, TX......	36,379	37,195
Oakland, CA..............	45,920	46,877	Cincinnati, OH-KY-IN.......	36,050	37,168
Seattle-Bellevue-Everett, WA.....	45,299	46,093	Corvallis, OR............	35,525	36,766
Boston-Worcester-Lawrence-Lowell-			Richmond-Petersburg, VA......	35,879	36,751
Brockton, MA-NH..........	45,766	45,685	Kansas City, MO-KS........	35,794	36,731
Bergen-Passaic, NJ..........	44,701	45,185	Saint Louis, MO-IL........	35,928	36,712
Hartford, CT..............	43,880	44,387	Indianapolis, IN..........	35,989	36,608
Boulder-Longmont, CO.......	44,310	44,037	West Palm Beach-Boca Raton, FL....	35,957	36,550
Wilmington-Newark, DE-MD......	42,177	43,401	Milwaukee-Waukesha, WI........	35,617	36,523
Chicago, IL..............	42,685	43,239	Flint, MI...............	35,995	36,507
Detroit, MI...............	42,704	43,224	Santa Rosa, CA..........	36,145	36,494
Dallas, TX...............	42,706	43,000	Brazoria, TX............	35,655	36,253
Houston, TX..............	42,784	42,712	Columbus, OH...........	35,028	36,144
Denver, CO..............	42,351	42,133	Bloomington-Normal, IL......	35,111	36,133
Minneapolis-St. Paul, MN-WI......	40,868	41,722	Cleveland-Lorain-Elyria, OH.....	35,514	36,102
Los Angeles-Long Beach, CA......	40,891	41,709	Phoenix-Mesa, AZ........	35,514	36,045
Orange County, CA..........	40,252	41,219	Albany-Schenectady-Troy, NY......	35,355	35,994
Atlanta, GA..............	40,559	41,123	Birmingham, AL..........	34,519	35,940
Philadelphia, PA-NJ..........	40,231	41,121	Memphis, TN-AR-MS.......	34,603	35,922
Kokomo, IN..............	39,599	40,778	Lansing-East Lansing, MI......	34,724	35,785
Nassau-Suffolk, NY..........	39,662	40,396	Santa Cruz-Watsonville, CA......	35,022	35,721
Austin-San Marcos, TX........	40,831	39,540	Miami, FL..............	34,524	35,694
Sacramento, CA............	38,016	39,354	Des Moines, IA..........	34,303	35,641
San Diego, CA.............	38,418	39,305	Pittsburgh, PA..........	35,024	35,625
Ann Arbor, MI.............	37,582	39,220	Yolo, CA...............	35,352	35,591
Anchorage, AK............	37,998	39,112	Saginaw-Bay City-Midland, MI.....	35,429	35,444
Raleigh-Durham-Chapel Hill, NC....	38,691	39,056	Madison, WI............	34,097	35,410

Source: U.S. Bureau of Labor Statistics. "Annual Wages for All Covered Workers by Metropolitan Area". See Internet site <http://www.bls.gov/cew/home.htm>.

No. 623. Full-Time Wage and Salary Workers—Number and Earnings: 2000 to 2003

[In current dollars of usual weekly earnings. **Data represent annual averages (101,210 represents 101,210,000).** Occupational classifications are those used in the 2000 census; see text this section. Based on the Current Population Survey; see text, Section 1, Population, and Appendix III. For definition of median, see Guide to Tabular Presentation]

Characteristic	Number of workers (1,000)			Median weekly earnings (dol.)		
	2000	2002	2003 [1]	2000	2002	2003 [1]
All workers [2]	101,210	100,081	100,302	576	608	620
SEX						
Male	57,107	56,345	56,227	641	679	695
16 to 24 years old	6,770	6,317	6,158	375	391	398
25 years old and over	50,337	50,027	50,069	693	732	744
Female	44,103	43,737	44,076	493	529	552
16 to 24 years old	5,094	4,804	4,632	344	367	371
25 years old and over	39,009	38,933	39,444	516	568	584
RACE/ETHNICITY						
White [3]	83,228	82,324	81,916	590	623	636
Male	48,085	47,417	47,001	662	702	715
Female	35,143	34,908	34,916	502	547	567
Black [3]	12,410	12,109	11,887	474	498	514
Male	5,911	5,789	5,585	510	524	555
Female	6,500	6,319	6,301	429	473	491
Asian [3] [4]	4,598	4,613	4,314	615	658	693
Male	2,538	2,556	2,442	685	756	772
Female	2,060	2,058	1,872	547	566	598
Hispanic origin [5]	12,761	13,137	13,634	399	424	440
Male	8,077	8,272	8,677	417	451	464
Female	4,684	4,865	4,957	366	397	410
OCCUPATION						
Management, professional, and related occupations	34,831	35,441	35,680	810	859	887
Management, business, and financial operations	14,240	14,537	14,493	877	922	961
Management occupations	9,952	10,180	10,115	937	982	1,023
Business and financial operations occupations	4,288	4,357	4,378	760	797	842
Professional and related occupations	20,590	20,904	21,186	770	823	845
Computer and mathematical occupations	3,051	2,778	2,790	938	1,026	1,049
Architecture and engineering occupations	2,781	2,465	2,487	949	1,009	1,053
Life, physical, and social science occupations	989	1,041	1,085	811	873	891
Community and social services occupations	1,641	1,824	1,814	629	658	686
Legal occupations	1,039	1,068	1,024	919	996	1,051
Education, training, and library occupations	5,467	5,708	5,884	704	740	754
Arts, design, entertainment, sports, and media	1,488	1,504	1,473	724	740	745
Healthcare practitioner and technical occupations	4,134	4,517	4,630	727	794	816
Service occupations	12,595	13,136	13,333	365	396	403
Healthcare support occupations	1,731	1,878	2,023	358	393	400
Protective service occupations	2,281	2,390	2,405	591	659	630
Food preparation and serving related occupations	3,483	3,598	3,819	317	334	349
Building and grounds cleaning and maintenance	3,354	3,360	3,280	351	378	390
Personal care and service occupations	1,746	1,909	1,806	351	383	391
Sales and office occupations	25,606	24,983	25,108	492	527	545
Sales and related occupations	9,650	9,772	9,924	525	592	598
Office and administrative support occupations	15,956	15,211	15,184	480	511	523
Natural resources, construction, and maintenance occupations	10,958	10,780	11,082	582	597	608
Farming, fishing, and forestry occupations	842	819	778	310	340	369
Construction and extraction occupations	5,852	5,974	5,973	580	589	599
Installation, maintenance, and repair occupations	4,263	3,987	4,331	628	663	673
Production, transportation, and material moving occupations	17,221	15,741	15,100	475	511	519
Production occupations	10,378	9,055	8,599	471	508	519
Transportation and material moving occupations	6,843	6,685	6,501	481	514	520

[1] See footnote 2, Table 569. See footnote 3, table 570. [2] Includes other races, not shown separately. [3] Beginning 2003, for persons in this race group only. [4] Prior to 2003, includes Pacific Islanders. [5] Persons of Hispanic or Latino origin may be of any race.

Source: U.S. Bureau of Labor Statistics, Bulletin 2307, and *Employment and Earnings*, monthly, January 2004 issue. See Internet site <http://www.bls.gov/cps/home.htm>.

Labor Force, Employment, and Earnings   411

No. 624. Workers With Earnings by Occupation of Longest Held Job and Sex: 2002

[Covers persons 15 years old and over as of March 2003. (71,411 represents 71,411,000). Based on Current Population Survey; see text, Section 1, Population, and Appendix III. For definition of median, see Guide to Tabular Presentation]

Major occupation of longest job held in 2002	All workers				Full-time, year-round			
	Women		Men		Women		Men	
	Number (1,000)	Median earnings (dol.)	Number (1,000)	Median earnings (dol.)	Number (1,000)	Median earnings (dol.)	Number (1,000)	Median earnings (dol.)
Total [1]	71,411	21,429	80,500	31,647	41,876	30,203	58,761	39,429
Management, business, and financial occupations	9,053	36,861	12,101	53,044	6,896	41,276	10,402	59,716
Professional and related occupations	16,556	31,791	12,493	50,966	10,106	40,080	9,848	56,438
Service occupations	14,665	11,883	10,936	16,752	6,575	20,008	6,303	26,105
Sales and office occupations	25,382	20,362	14,169	30,684	14,836	26,950	10,156	37,400
Natural resources, construction, and maintenance	806	16,489	14,915	27,758	411	25,901	10,559	32,618
Production, transportation, and material moving occupations	4,880	17,953	15,214	26,202	2,993	21,907	10,893	31,144

[1] Includes people whose longest job in 2002 was in the Armed Forces.

Source: U.S. Census Bureau, *Current Population Reports*, P60-221. See Internet site <http://www.census.gov/hhes/www/income02.html>.

No. 625. Employment Cost Index (ECI)—Total Compensation by Occupation and Industry: 1985 to 2003

[As of December. The ECI is a measure of the rate of change in employee compensation (wages, salaries, and employer costs for employee benefits). Data are not seasonally adjusted: 1985 based on fixed employment counts from 1970 Census of Population; 1990 based on fixed employment counts from the 1980 Census of Population; beginning 1995 based primarily on 1990 Occupational Employment Survey]

Item	Indexes (June 1989=100)						Percent change for 12 months ending Dec.—				
	1985	1990	1995	2000	2002	2003	1985	1990	1995	2000	2003
Civilian workers [1]	86.8	107.6	127.2	150.6	162.2	168.4	4.3	4.9	2.7	4.1	3.8
Workers, by occupational group:											
White-collar occupations	85.8	108.3	128.0	152.5	164.3	170.7	4.9	5.2	2.9	4.2	3.9
Blue-collar occupations	88.4	106.5	125.8	146.5	157.5	163.7	3.3	4.4	2.5	4.2	3.9
Service occupations	87.2	108.0	127.4	150.0	162.2	167.9	3.9	5.1	2.5	3.6	3.5
Workers, by industry division:											
Manufacturing	87.8	107.2	128.3	149.3	160.5	167.1	3.3	5.1	2.6	4.0	4.1
Nonmanufacturing [2]	86.4	107.8	126.8	150.7	162.4	168.6	4.7	4.9	2.8	4.1	3.8
Service industries	84.1	110.2	129.4	152.4	163.9	169.5	4.7	6.3	2.4	4.0	3.4
Public administration [3]	85.4	108.7	128.3	148.3	161.7	168.1	4.9	5.3	3.3	2.7	4.0
State and local government. ...	84.6	110.4	130.4	148.9	161.5	166.8	5.6	5.8	2.9	3.0	3.3
Workers, by occupational group:											
White-collar occupations	84.2	110.9	129.1	148.3	160.7	165.7	5.8	6.0	2.9	3.0	3.1
Blue-collar workers	86.7	108.7	128.0	147.2	159.8	165.2	5.3	4.8	2.6	3.3	3.4
Workers, by industry division:											
Service industries	84.0	111.3	129.6	148.9	160.9	165.7	5.9	6.3	2.8	3.0	3.0
Schools..................	83.6	111.6	129.8	149.0	160.7	165.3	6.2	6.0	2.8	3.0	2.9
Elementary and secondary	83.6	112.1	130.1	148.1	158.8	163.7	6.4	6.3	2.8	2.8	3.1
Colleges and universities ...	(NA)	110.2	128.7	151.7	165.8	170.0	(NA)	5.3	2.5	3.5	2.5
Services, excluding schools [4]	85.2	110.2	129.4	148.8	162.8	168.2	4.7	6.8	3.0	3.5	3.3
Public administration [3]	85.4	108.7	128.3	148.3	161.7	168.1	4.9	5.3	3.3	2.7	4.0
Private industry workers [5]	87.3	107.0	126.7	150.9	162.3	168.8	3.9	4.6	2.6	4.4	4.0
Workers, by occupational group:											
White-collar occupations	86.4	107.4	127.6	153.6	165.2	172.0	4.9	4.9	2.8	4.6	4.1
Blue-collar occupations	88.5	106.4	125.6	146.4	157.3	163.6	3.1	4.4	2.4	4.2	4.0
Service occupations	88.4	107.3	125.2	148.1	159.8	164.9	3.0	4.7	1.9	3.9	3.2
Workers, by industry division:											
Manufacturing	87.8	107.2	128.3	149.3	160.5	167.1	3.3	5.1	2.6	4.0	4.1
Nonmanufacturing [2]	87.0	106.9	125.9	151.1	162.5	169.0	4.3	4.5	2.7	4.6	4.0
Service industries [2]	84.1	109.3	129.4	154.1	165.4	171.4	(NA)	6.2	2.2	4.4	3.6
Business services	(NA)	107.4	126.3	158.4	167.5	172.6	(NA)	6.0	2.7	4.3	3.0
Health services	83.7	110.8	132.2	150.6	164.4	170.8	(NA)	6.8	2.7	4.4	3.9
Hospitals	(NA)	110.7	131.3	151.1	168.1	175.9	(NA)	7.0	2.1	4.5	4.6
Workers, by bargaining status:											
Union....................	90.1	106.2	127.7	146.9	159.5	166.8	2.6	4.3	2.8	4.0	4.6
Nonunion	86.3	107.3	126.5	151.6	162.8	169.1	4.6	4.8	2.7	4.4	3.9

NA Not available. [1] Includes private industry and state and local government workers and excludes farm, household, and federal government workers. [2] Includes other industries, not shown separately. [3] Consists of executive, legislative, judicial, administrative, and regulatory activities. [4] Includes library, social, and health services. Formerly called hospitals and other services. [5] Excludes farm and household workers.

Source: U.S. Bureau of Labor Statistics, *News, Employment Cost Index*, quarterly; and Internet site <http://www.bls.gov/ncs/ect/home.htm>.

U.S. Census Bureau, Statistical Abstract of the United States: 2004-2005

No. 626. Federal Minimum Wage Rates: 1950 to 2000

Year	Current dollars	Year	Current dollars
1950		1976	2.30
1951	0.75	1977	2.30
1952	0.75	1978	2.65
1953	0.75	1979	2.90
1954	0.75		
1955	0.75	1980	3.10
1956	0.75	1981	3.35
1957	1.00	1982	3.35
1958	1.00	1983	3.35
1959	1.00	1984	3.35
1960	1.00	1985	3.35
1961	1.00	1986	3.35
1962	1.15	1987	3.35
1963	1.15	1988	3.35
1964	1.25	1989	3.35
1965	1.25		
1966	1.25	1990	3.80
1967	1.25	1991	4.25
1968	1.40	1992	4.25
1969	1.60	1993	4.25
1970	1.60	1994	4.25
1971	1.60	1995	4.25
1972	1.60	1996	4.75
1973	1.60	1997	5.15
1974	2.00	1998	5.15
1975	2.10	1999	5.15
		2000	5.15

Source: U.S. Employment Standards Administration, Internet site: <http://www.dol.gov/esa/whd/flsa/>.

No. 627. Workers Paid Hourly Rates by Selected Characteristics: 2003

[Data are annual averages (72,946 represents 72,946,000). For employed wage and salary workers. Based on Current Population Survey; see text, Section 1, and Appendix III]

Characteristic	Number of workers [1] (1,000)				Percent of all workers paid hourly rates			Median hourly earnings of workers paid hourly rates [2]
	Total paid hourly rates	At or below $5.15			At or below $5.15			
		Total	At $5.15	Below $5.15	Total	At $5.15	Below $5.15	
Total, 16 years and over [3]	72,946	2,100	545	1,555	2.9	.7	2.1	10.85
16 to 24 years	15,871	1,106	330	776	7.0	2.1	4.9	7.90
16 to 19 years	5,412	534	212	322	9.9	3.9	5.9	6.93
25 years and over	57,075	995	215	780	1.7	.4	1.4	12.05
Male, 16 years and over	35,853	706	213	493	2.0	.6	1.4	11.89
16 to 24 years	8,031	391	154	237	4.9	1.9	3.0	8.14
16 to 19 years........	2,608	205	109	96	7.9	4.2	3.7	7.02
25 years and over	27,823	314	58	256	1.1	.2	.9	13.25
Women, 16 years and over....	37,093	1,394	332	1,062	3.8	.9	2.9	10.08
16 to 24 years	7,841	713	175	538	9.1	2.2	6.9	7.59
16 to 19 years........	2,804	329	103	226	11.7	3.7	8.1	6.85
25 years and over	29,252	681	157	524	2.3	.5	1.8	11.01
White [4]	59,109	1,746	421	1,325	3.0	.7	2.2	10.97
Black [4]	9,419	250	105	145	2.7	1.1	1.5	7.89
Asian [4]	2,528	51	5	46	2.0	.2	1.8	11.12
Hispanic origin [5]	11,462	308	94	214	2.7	.8	1.9	9.76
Full-time workers	54,887	796	156	639	1.5	.3	1.2	11.96
Part-time workers [6]	17,932	1,299	388	910	7.2	2.2	5.1	8.03
Private sector industries......	63,945	1,986	492	1,494	3.1	.8	2.3	10.53
Goods-producing [7]	16,702	112	32	80	.7	.2	.5	(NA)
Service-producing [8]	47,243	1,874	460	1,413	4.0	1.0	3.0	(NA)
Public sector	9,001	114	52	62	1.3	.6	.7	12.97

NA Not available. [1] Excludes the incorporated self-employed. [2] For definition of median, see Guide to Tabular Presentation. [3] Includes races not shown separately. Also includes a small number of multiple jobholders whose full- part- time status can not be determined for their principal job. [4] For persons in this race group only. See footnote 3, Table 570. [5] Persons of Hispanic or Latino origin may be of any race. [6] Working fewer than 35 hours per week. [7] Includes agriculture, mining, construction, and manufacturing. [8] Includes wholesale and retail trade; transportation and utilities; information; finance and insurance; real estate and rental and leasing; professional and technical services; management, administrative and waste services; education services; health care and social assistance; arts, entertainment, and recreation; accommodations and food services; and other services.

Source: U.S. Bureau of Labor Statistics, Employment and Earnings, January 2004 and unpublished data. See Internet site <http://www.bls.gov/cps/home.htm>.

No. 628. Employer Costs for Employee Compensation Per Hour Worked: 2004

[In dollars. As of March, for private industry workers. Based on a sample of establishments from the National Compensation Survey; see source for details. See also Appendix III]

Compensation component	Total	Goods producing [1]	Service producing [2]	Metropolitan areas [3]	Non-metropolitan areas [3]	Union members	Non-union members	Full-time workers	Part-time workers
Total compensation . . .	23.29	27.19	22.33	23.66	19.00	31.94	22.28	26.50	12.63
Wages and salaries	16.64	18.12	16.28	16.93	13.30	20.32	16.21	18.62	10.07
Total benefits.	6.65	9.06	6.05	6.73	5.70	11.61	6.06	7.88	2.56
Paid leave	1.50	1.68	1.45	1.53	1.16	2.22	1.41	1.84	0.37
Vacation.	0.74	0.86	0.71	0.75	0.61	1.12	0.69	(NA)	(NA)
Holiday	0.52	0.61	0.49	0.53	0.39	0.72	0.49	(NA)	(NA)
Sick	0.18	0.13	0.19	0.19	0.11	0.27	0.17	(NA)	(NA)
Other	0.06	0.07	0.06	0.06	0.05	0.10	0.06	(NA)	(NA)
Supplemental pay.	0.66	1.12	0.54	0.67	0.56	1.07	0.61	0.81	0.17
Premium pay	0.24	0.56	0.16	0.23	0.30	0.65	0.19	(NA)	(NA)
Shift pay	0.06	0.08	0.05	0.06	0.07	0.17	0.04	(NA)	(NA)
Nonproduction bonuses .	0.36	0.48	0.33	0.38	0.18	0.24	0.38	(NA)	(NA)
Insurance	1.65	2.26	1.50	1.65	1.63	3.27	1.46	2.01	0.47
Health insurance	1.53	2.11	1.39	1.53	1.52	3.08	1.35	(NA)	(NA)
Retirement and savings . . .	0.80	1.32	0.67	0.81	0.61	2.15	0.64	0.98	0.18
Defined benefit	0.37	0.82	0.26	0.38	0.28	1.67	0.22	(NA)	(NA)
Defined contributions . . .	0.43	0.49	0.41	0.44	0.33	0.48	0.42	(NA)	(NA)
Legally required	2.01	2.59	1.86	2.03	1.73	2.79	1.92	2.20	1.38
Social Security and Medicare	1.39	1.56	1.35	1.42	1.15	1.76	1.35	(NA)	(NA)
Social Security.	1.12	1.26	1.09	1.14	0.93	1.42	1.08	(NA)	(NA)
Medicare	0.27	0.30	0.27	0.28	0.22	0.34	0.27	(NA)	(NA)
Federal unemployment. .	0.03	0.03	0.03	0.03	0.03	0.03	0.03	(NA)	(NA)
State unemployment . . .	0.13	0.17	0.12	0.13	0.13	0.18	0.13	(NA)	(NA)
Workers compensation . .	0.45	0.84	0.35	0.45	0.42	0.82	0.40	(NA)	(NA)
Other benefits [4]	0.04	0.08	0.02	0.04	-	0.10	0.03	0.05	-

- Represents or rounds to zero. NA Not available. [1] Based on the North American Industry Classification System, 2002 (NAICS). See text, this section. Includes mining, construction, and manufacturing. The agriculture, forestry, farming and hunting sector is excluded. [2] Based on the 2002 NAICS. Includes utilities; wholesale and retail trade; transportation and warehousing; information; finance and insurance; real estate and rental and leasing; professional and technical services; management of companies and enterprises, administrative and waste services; education services; health care and social assistance; arts, entertainment, and recreation; accommodations and food services; and other services, except public administration. [3] Based on Office of Management and Budget definitions as of June 1994; see Appendix II. [4] Includes severance pay, and supplemental unemployment benefits.

Source: U.S. Bureau of Labor Statistics, *Employer Costs for Employee Compensation, News*, USDL 04-1105, June 24, 2004. See Intenet site <http://www.bls.gov/ncs/ect/home.htm>.

No. 629. Employees With Employer- or Union-Provided Pension Plans or Group Health Plans: 2001

[Total in thousands (151,608 represents 151,608,000). For wage and salary workers 15 years old and over as of March 2002. Based on Current Population Survey, Annual Demographic Survey, March Supplement; see text, Section 1, and Appendix III. Data based on 1990 population controls]

Occupation	Total (1,000)	Percent— Included in pension plan	Percent— With group health plan	Characteristic	Total (1,000)	Percent— Included in pension plan	Percent— With group health plan
Total	151,608	43.2	53.7	AGE			
Executive, admin., managerial . . .	21,951	58.5	68.9	Total	151,608	43.2	53.7
Professional specialty	23,078	60.8	67.3	15 to 24 years	24,593	12.7	21.9
				25 to 44 years old	71,281	47.0	58.5
Technical/related support	4,894	55.3	65.4	45 to 64 years	50,230	54.7	63.7
Sales workers	18,236	32.7	43.8	65 years and over	5,504	23.6	42.6
Admin. support, inc. clerical	20,449	47.3	56.2	WORK EXPERIENCE			
				Worked.	151,608	43.2	53.7
Precision prod., craft/repair	16,040	41.9	56.1	Full time	122,001	50.1	62.4
				50 weeks or more	100,379	54.5	67.1
Mach. operators, assemblers [1] . . .	7,601	44.3	60.5	27 to 49 weeks	13,171	36.7	49.8
Transportation/material moving. . .	6,397	40.3	55.8	26 weeks or fewer	8,445	19.0	26.2
Handlers, equipment cleaners [2] . .	6,516	25.5	38.8	Part time	29,607	14.4	17.9
				50 weeks or more	14,094	19.1	22.9
Service workers	21,941	22.8	33.4	27 to 49 weeks	6,187	15.8	19.2
Private households	860	3.5	9.6	26 weeks or fewer	9,326	6.4	9.6
Other	21,080	23.5	34.4	EMPLOYER SIZE			
				Under 25 persons	44,717	17.2	29.6
Farming, forestry and fishing	3,853	11.9	22.2	25 to 99 persons	19,311	37.4	54.1
				100 to 499 persons	19,777	50.2	62.9
Armed Forces	653	70.2	36.2	500 to 999 persons	8,467	56.4	65.9
				Over 1,000 persons	59,336	60.4	67.0

[1] Includes inspectors. [2] Includes helpers and laborers.

Source: U.S. Census Bureau, "Pension Plan Coverage of Workers by Selected Characteristics, Sex, Race and Hispanic Origin and Proverty Status: 2001" and "All Workers and Poor Workers With Their Own Employment-Based Health Insurance Policy, by Employer Contribution and Selected Characteristics: 2001". See Internet site <http://ferret.bls.census.gov /macro/032002/noncash/toc.htm>.

No. 630. Percent of Workers With Access to Selected Employee Benefits in Private Industry: 2003

[Based on National Compensation Survey, a sample survey of 2,924 private industry establishments of all sizes, representing over 103 million workers; see Appendix III. See also Tables 142 and 144]

Characteristic	Paid holidays	Paid vacation	Paid jury duty	Paid military leave	Employer assistance for child care				Adoption assistance	Long-term care insurance	Flexible work plans[1]	Employer provided home personal computer	Subsidized commuting[2]
					Total	Employer provided funds	On-site and off-site child care	Child care resource and referral services					
Total	79	79	70	50	18	3	5	10	9	11	4	2	5
WORKER CHARACTERISTICS													
White-collar occupations	86	84	79	59	26	5	7	15	13	16	6	3	7
Blue-collar occupations	85	84	69	46	10	1	2	6	6	7	1	1	4
Service occupations	54	61	46	34	10	2	4	5	2	4	1	1	2
Full time[3]	91	91	77	56	21	4	5	12	10	13	4	3	6
Part time[3]	43	40	45	33	11	2	4	5	5	4	3	1	2
Union[4]	91	90	85	56	25	3	7	15	13	16	3	2	8
Nonunion[4]	78	78	68	50	18	3	5	10	9	11	4	2	5
Average wage less than $15 per hour	72	73	60	42	11	2	3	5	5	6	2	1	3
Average wage $15 per hour or more	91	90	84	64	31	5	8	18	16	19	7	4	9
ESTABLISHMENT CHARACTERISTICS													
Goods producing	90	87	76	56	16	3	2	11	9	11	3	3	5
Service producing	76	73	68	48	19	3	6	10	9	11	4	2	5
1 to 99 workers	74	73	57	38	7	2	2	3	3	3	2	1	2
100 or more workers	86	87	84	64	32	5	8	19	16	20	5	3	9
GEOGRAPHIC AREAS[5]													
Metropolitan areas	79	79	71	51	21	4	5	12	10	12	4	2	6
Nonmetropolitan areas	80	79	61	44	5	2	2	2	2	4	1	1	1
New England division	77	79	69	54	22	2	8	12	11	11	4	2	8
Middle Atlantic division	83	85	72	54	24	4	6	14	12	12	5	3	8
East North Central division	83	81	73	53	21	3	6	11	10	10	2	2	2
West North Central division	74	71	70	50	17	3	6	8	7	7	2	2	3
South Atlantic division	79	80	71	50	15	3	3	8	9	14	4	1	5
East South Central division	81	79	72	45	16	4	4	9	4	7	2	1	2
West South Central division	77	79	68	53	14	2	3	7	8	10	4	2	6
Mountain division	75	73	71	51	19	2	5	12	7	7	5	1	6
Pacific division	80	79	62	41	17	4	3	10	8	14	5	3	10

[1] Arrangements permitting employees to work at home several days of the workweek. [2] Employers subsidize employees' cost of commuting to and from work via public transportation, company sponsored van pool, discounted subway fares, etc. [3] Employees are classified as working either a full-time or part-time schedule based on the definition used by each establishment. [4] Union workers are those whose wages are determined through collective bargaining. [5] Metropolitan areas as defined by the U.S. Office of Management and Budget in 1994; see Appendix II. For composition of divisions, see map, inside front cover.

Source: U.S. Bureau of Labor Statistics, Employee Benefits in Private Industry, 2003, News, USDL 03-489, September 17, 2003. See Internet site <http://www.bls.gov/ncs/ebs/home.htm>

Labor Force, Employment, and Earnings 415

No. 631. Workers Killed or Disabled on the Job: 1970 to 2002

[Data for 2002 are preliminary estimates (13.8 represents 13,800). Excludes homicides and suicides. Estimates based on data from the U.S. National Center for Health Statistics, state vital statistics departments, state industrial commissions and beginning 1995, Bureau of Labor Statistics, Census of Occupational Fatalities. Numbers of workers based on data from the U.S. Bureau of Labor Statistics]

	Deaths						Deaths, 2001		
Year	Total		Manufacturing		Non-manufacturing		Dis-abling injur-ies [2]	Year and industry group		Dis-abling injur-ies 2001 [2]
	Num-ber (1,000)	Rate [1]	Num-ber (1,000)	Rate [1]	Num-ber (1,000)	Rate [1]	(mil.)		Num-ber (1,000)	Rate [1]	(1,000)
1970 . . .	13.8	18	1.7	9	12.1	21	2.2	Total [3]	4,900	3.6	3,700
1975 . . .	13.0	15	1.6	9	11.4	17	2.2	Agriculture [4]	730	21.0	150
1980 . . .	13.2	13	1.7	8	11.5	15	2.2	Mining and quarrying [5] .	150	29.1	10
1985 . . .	11.5	11	1.2	6	10.3	12	2.0	Construction.	1,150	12.6	460
1990 . . .	10.1	9	1.0	5	9.1	9	3.9	Manufacturing.	510	2.8	520
1995 . . .	5.0	4	0.6	3	4.4	4	3.6	Transportation and			
1998 . . .	5.1	4	0.6	3	4.5	4	3.8	utilities	810	10.1	390
1999 . . .	5.2	4	0.6	3	4.6	4	3.8	Trade [6]	420	1.5	710
2000 . . .	5.0	4	0.6	3	4.4	4	3.9	Services [7]	630	1.3	900
2001 . . .	5.0	4	0.5	3	4.5	4	3.9	Government	500	2.4	560
2002 . . .	4.9	4	0.5	3	4.4	4	3.7				

[1] Per 100,000 workers. [2] Disabling injury defined as one which results in death, some degree of physical impairment, or renders the person unable to perform regular activities for a full day beyond the day of the injury. Due to change in methodology, data beginning 1990 not comparable with prior years. [3] Includes deaths where industry is not known. [4] Includes forestry and fishing. [5] Includes oil and gas extraction. [6] Includes wholesale and retail trade. [7] Includes finance, insurance, and real estate.

Source: National Safety Council, Itasca, IL, *Accident Facts*, annual through 1998 edition; thereafter, *Injury Facts*, annual-(copyright).

No. 632. Worker Deaths, Injuries, and Production Time Lost: 1995 to 2002

[45.7 represents 45,700. Data may not agree with Table 631 because data here are not revised]

Item	Deaths (1,000)			Disabling injuries [1] (mil.)			Production time lost (mil. days)					
							In the current year			In future years [2]		
	1995	2000	2002	1995	2000	2002	1995	2000	2002	1995	2000	2002
All accidents	45.7	47.0	49.6	9.9	10.5	10.8	225	240	250	455	460	495
On the job	5.3	5.2	4.9	3.6	3.9	3.7	75	80	80	65	60	65
Off the job.	40.4	41.8	44.7	6.3	6.6	7.1	150	160	170	390	400	430
Motor vehicle	22.9	22.8	23.1	1.2	1.2	1.2	(NA)	(NA)	(NA)	(NA)	(NA)	(NA)
Public nonmotor vehicle . . .	7.5	8.3	7.8	2.3	2.8	2.6	(NA)	(NA)	(NA)	(NA)	(NA)	(NA)
Home	10.0	10.7	13.8	2.8	2.6	3.3	(NA)	(NA)	(NA)	(NA)	(NA)	(NA)

NA Not available. [1] See footnote 2, Table 631 for a definition of disabling injuries. [2] Based on an average of 5,850 days lost in future years per fatality and 565 days lost in future years per permanent injury.

Source: National Safety Council, Itasca, IL, *Accident Facts*, annual through 1998 edition; thereafter, *Injury Facts*, annual-(copyright).

No. 633. Industries With the Highest Total Case Incidence Rates for Nonfatal Injuries and Illnesses: 2002

[4,700.6 represents 4,700,600. Rates per 100 full-time employees. Industries shown are those with the highest rates for 2002. Rates refer to any OSHA-recordable occupational injury or illness, whether or not it resulted in days away from work, job transfer, or restriction. Incidence rates were calculated as: Number of injuries and illnesses divided by total hours worked by all employees during the year multiplied by 200,000 as base for 100 full-time equivalent workers (working 40 hours per week, 50 weeks per year)]

Industry	1987 SIC [1] code	Num-ber (1,000)	Rate	Industry	1987 SIC [1] code	Num-ber (1,000)	Rate
Private industry [2]	(X)	4,700.6	5.3	Aluminum foundries . . . . [3]	3365	2.8	12.8
Malleable iron foundries	3322	0.4	18.3	Transportation equipment, n.e.c. [3] .	3799	3.9	12.6
Gray and ductile iron foundries . . .	3321	11.8	17.4	Nursing and personal care facili-			
Mobile homes.	2451	8.5	17.0	ties	805	187.0	12.6
Ship building and repairing	3731	16.6	16.6	Electron tubes	3671	2.0	12.5
Aluminum die-castings	3363	5.4	15.9	Heating equipment, except electric .	3433	2.2	12.3
Truck trailers	3715	4.2	15.6	Air transportation, scheduled	451	97.0	12.3
Meat packing plants.	2011	23.4	14.9	Bottled and canned soft drinks. . . .	2086	12.5	12.0
Motor vehicles and car bodies . . [3] .	3711	48.5	14.8	Automotive stampings	3465	13.2	12.0
Structural wood member, n.e.c. [3] . .	2439	7.0	14.1	Steel pipe and tubes	3317	3.2	11.9
Steel foundries, n.e.c.	3325	2.9	14.1	Livestock, except dairy and poultry .	021	5.1	11.8
Partitions and fixtures, except				Miscellaneous metal work	3449	1.9	11.8
wood.	2542	4.3	13.9	Vitreous china table and kitchen-			
Fabricated structural metal	3441	11.7	13.7	ware	3262	0.5	11.7
Metal sanitary ware	3431	1.8	13.6	Motorcycles, bicycles, and parts. . .	375	2.1	11.6
Public building and related furni-				Concrete products, n.e.c. [3]	3272	9.8	11.4
ture.	253	6.6	13.5	Steel wire and related products . . .	3315	1.7	11.4
Truck and bus bodies.	3713	5.9	13.4	Machine tools, metal forming types.	3542	1.4	11.4
Prefabricated wood buldings	2452	3.4	13.3	Travel trailers and campers	3792	2.7	11.4

X Not applicable. [1] 1987 Standard Industrial Classification; see text, this section. [2] Includes other industries not shown separately. [3] N.e.c. means not elsewhere classified.

Source: U.S. Bureau of Labor Statistics, *Workplace Injuries and Illnesses in 2002*. See Internet site <http://www.bls.gov/iif/>

No. 634. Nonfatal Occupational Injury and Illness Incidence Rates: 2002

[Rates per 100 full-time employees. Except as noted, rates refer to any Occupational Safety and Health Administration (OSHA) recordable occupational injury or illness, whether or not it resulted in days away from work, job transfer, or restriction. Incidence rates were calculated as: Number of injuries and illnesses divided by total hours worked by all employees during the year multiplied by 200,000 as base for 100 full-time equivalent workers (working 40 hours, per week, 50 weeks per year)]

Industry	1987 SIC [1]	Number (1,000)	Rate	Industry	1987 SIC [1]	Number (1,000)	Rate
Private sector [2]	(X)	4,701	5.3	Local passenger transit	41	29	7.9
Agriculture, forestry, fishing [2]	A	96	6.4	Trucking and warehousing	42	125	7.0
Mining [3]	B	23	4.0	Water transportation	44	12	6.8
Metal mining [3]	10	1	4.1	Transportation by air	45	112	11.8
Coal mining [3]	12	6	6.8	Transportation services	47	11	2.9
Oil and gas extraction	13	12	3.4	Communications	48	45	3.0
Nonmetallic minerals, exc. fuels [3]	14	5	3.8	Electric, gas, sanitary services	49	42	5.0
Construction	C	418	7.1	Wholesale and retail trade	F, G	1,228	5.3
General building contractors	15	80	6.2	Wholesale trade	F	322	5.2
Heavy construction, except building	16	54	6.4	Retail trade	G	906	5.3
Special trade contractors	17	285	7.5	Finance, insurance, real estate	H	115	1.7
Manufacturing	D	1,160	7.2	Depository institutions	60	28	1.5
Durable goods	(X)	758	7.9	Nondepository institutions	61	7	1.0
Lumber and wood products	24	74	10.1	Security and commodity brokers	62	3	.5
Furniture and fixtures	25	45	9.9	Insurance carriers	63	21	1.6
Stone, clay, and glass products	32	51	9.4	Insurance agents, brokers, and service	64	6	.9
Primary metal industries	33	60	10.3	Real estate	65	46	3.5
Fabricated metal products	34	131	9.8	Holding and other investment offices	67	4	1.8
Industrial machinery and equip.	35	119	6.7	Services [5]	I	1,278	4.6
Electronic/other electric equip.	36	61	4.5	Hotels and other lodging places	70	88	6.6
Transportation equipment	37	170	10.1	Personal services	72	29	3.0
Instruments/related products	38	26	3.3	Business services	73	149	2.7
Miscellaneous manufacturing industries	39	21	6.2	Auto repair, services, and parking	75	50	4.5
Nondurable goods	(X)	402	6.2	Miscellaneous repair services	76	16	4.9
Food and kindred products	20	156	9.3	Motion pictures	78	8	2.2
Tobacco products	21	1	4.0	Amusement and recreation services	79	69	6.3
Textile mill products	22	21	5.2	Health services	80	624	7.4
Apparel and other textile products	23	21	4.6	Legal services	81	7	.8
Paper and allied products	26	34	5.6	Educational services	82	38	2.8
Printing and publishing	27	50	4.0	Social services	83	131	5.5
Chemicals and allied products	28	33	3.3	Museums, botanical, zoological gardens	84	4	4.9
Petroleum and coal products	29	5	3.6	Membership organizations	86	18	2.6
Rubber and misc. plastics products	30	78	8.8	Engineering and management services	87	48	1.5
Leather and leather products	31	4	7.3				
Transportation/public utilities [4]	E	383	6.1				
Railroad transportation [4]	40	7	3.0				

X Not applicable. [1] 1987 Standard Industrial Classification; see text, this section. [2] Excludes farms with fewer than 11 employees. [3] Data for mining operators in coal, metal, and nonmetal mining are provided to BLS by the Mine Safety and Health Administration (MHSA), U.S. Department of Labor. Independent mining contractors are excluded. Data provided by MSHA do not reflect 2002 OSHA recordkeeping requirements; therefore, estimates for these industries are not comparable with estimates for other industries. [4] Data for employers in railroad transportation are provided to BLS by the Federal Railroad Administration, U.S. Department of Transportation. Data do not reflect the 2002 OSHA recordkeeping requirements; therefore, estimates for these industries are not comparable with estimates for other industries. [5] Includes industries not shown seperately.

Source: U.S. Bureau of Labor Statistics, Workplace Injuries and Illnesses in 2002. See Internet site <http://www.bls.gov/iif/>.

No. 635. Fatal Work Injuries by Event or Exposure: 2002

[See headnote, Table 636]

Cause	Number of fatalities	Percent distribution	Cause	Number of fatalities	Percent distribution
Total	5,534	100	Struck by object [1]	505	9
			Struck by falling objects	302	5
Transportation accidents [1]	2,385	43	Struck by flying object	38	1
Highway accidents [1]	1,373	25	Caught in or compressed by—		
Collision between vehicles, mobile equipment	636	11	Equipment or objects	231	4
Noncollision accidents	373	7	Collapsing materials		
Nonhighway accident (farm, industrial premises)	323	6	Falls	719	13
Aircraft accidents	194	4			
Workers struck by a vehicle	356	6	Exposure to harmful substances or environments [1]	539	10
Water vehicle accidents	71	1	Contact with electric current	289	5
Railway accidents	64	1	Exposure to caustic, noxious or allergenic substances	99	2
Assaults and violent acts [1]	840	15	Oxygen deficiency	90	2
Homicides [1]	609	11	Drowning, submersion	60	1
Shooting	469	8			
Stabbing	58	1	Fires and explosions	165	3
Self-inflicted injury	199	4	Other events and exposures	14	(Z)
Contacts with objects and equipment [1]	872	16			

Z Less than 0.5 percent. [1] Includes other causes, not shown separately.

Source: U.S. Bureau of Labor Statistics, "Census of Fatal Occupational Injuries (CFOI)—Revised Data". See Internet site <http://www.bls.gov/iif/oshcfoil.htm>.

Labor Force, Employment, and Earnings 417

No. 636. Fatal Occupational Injuries by Industry and Event or Exposure: 2002

[For the 50 states and DC. Based on the Census of Fatal Occupational Injuries. For details, see source. Due to methodological differences, data differ from those in Table 631]

Industry	1987 SIC [1] code	Fatalities [2]	Event or exposure—Percent distribution				
			Trans-portation incidents	Assaults/ violent acts	Contact with objects [3]	Falls	Expo-sure [4]	Rate [5]
Total.	(X)	5,534	43	15	16	13	10	4
Private industry	(X)	4,978	42	14	17	14	10	4
Agriculture, forestry, fishing	A	790	49	8	23	8	10	23
Mining [6]	B	122	31	-	34	8	14	24
Coal mining.	12	25	-	-	60	-	-	29
Oil and gas extraction	13	72	35	-	25	10	13	23
Construction	C	1,125	26	3	18	33	17	12
General building contractors	15	189	25	4	16	42	11	-
Heavy construction, except building.	16	246	45	-	25	13	14	-
Special trade contractors	17	665	19	3	16	38	21	-
Manufacturing [6]	D	564	30	7	36	12	8	3
Food and kindred products.	20	64	30	13	23	16	9	4
Lumber and wood products	24	142	34	-	58	-	-	20
Transportation and public utilities [6] . .	E	910	72	7	8	5	7	11
Local passenger transit	41	60	43	52	-	-	-	9
Trucking and warehousing	42	584	77	5	10	4	4	21
Transportation by air	45	71	96	-	-	-	-	9
Electric, gas, sanitary services	49	81	48	-	10	-	26	-
Wholesale trade	F	205	54	14	20	4	5	4
Retail trade [6]	G	488	27	58	5	6	3	2
Food stores.	54	100	-	82	5	-	-	-
Automotive dealer and service stations	55	68	50	43	-	-	-	-
Eating and drinking places	58	126	17	71	-	6	6	2
Finance, insurance, real estate.	H	88	35	40	-	14	-	1
Services [6]	I	682	39	25	10	12	12	2
Business services.	73	165	40	25	7	18	10	2
Auto repair, services, and parking.	75	114	42	20	21	-	9	7
Government.	J	556	54	22	6	6	5	3

- No data reported or data do not meet publication standards.   X Not applicable.   [1] 1987 Standard Industrial Classification code, see text this section.   [2] Includes 4 fatalities in private industry in 2002 for which there was insufficient information to determine industry classification. Includes fatalities caused by other events and exposures, not shown separately.   [3] Includes equipment.   [4] Exposure to harmful substances or environments.   [5] Rate per 100,000 employed civilians 16 years old and over.   [6] Includes other industries, not shown separately.

Source: U.S. Bureau of Labor Statistics, "Census of Fatal Occupational Injuries (CFOI)—Revised Data". See Internet site <http://www.bls.gov/iif/oshcfoi1.htm>.

No. 637. Work Stoppages: 1960 to 2003

[896 represents 896,000. Excludes work stoppages involving fewer than 1,000 workers and lasting less than 1 day. Information is based on reports of labor disputes appearing in daily newspapers, trade journals, and other public sources. The parties to the disputes are contacted by telephone, when necessary, to clarify details of the stoppages]

Year	Number of stoppages [1]	Workers involved [2] (1,000)	Days idle		Year	Number of stoppages [1]	Workers involved [2] (1,000)	Days idle	
			Number [3] (1,000)	Percent estimated working time [4]				Number [3] (1,000)	Percent estimated working time [4]
1960	222	896	13,260	0.09	1986	69	533	11,861	0.05
1965	268	999	15,140	0.10	1987	46	174	[5]4,481	0.02
1970	381	2,468	52,761	0.29	1988	40	118	[5]4,381	0.02
1971	298	2,516	35,538	0.19	1989	51	452	16,996	0.07
1972	250	975	16,764	0.09	1990	44	185	5,926	0.02
1973	317	1,400	16,260	0.08	1991	40	392	4,584	0.02
1974	424	1,796	31,809	0.16	1992	35	364	3,989	0.01
1975	235	965	17,563	0.09	1993	35	182	3,981	0.01
1976	231	1,519	23,962	0.12	1994	45	322	5,020	0.02
1977	298	1,212	21,258	0.10	1995	31	192	5,771	0.02
1978	219	1,006	23,774	0.11	1996	37	273	4,889	0.02
1979	235	1,021	20,409	0.09	1997	29	339	4,497	0.01
1980	187	795	20,844	0.09	1998	34	387	5,116	0.02
1981	145	729	16,908	0.07	1999	17	73	1,996	0.01
1982	96	656	9,061	0.04	2000	39	394	20,419	0.06
1983	81	909	17,461	0.08	2001	29	99	1,151	(Z)
1984	62	376	8,499	0.04	2002	19	46	660	(Z)
1985	54	324	7,079	0.03	2003	14	129	4,091	0.01

Z Less than 0.005 percent.   [1] Beginning in year indicated.   [2] Workers counted more than once if involved in more than one stoppage during the year.   [3] Resulting from all stoppages in effect in a year, including those that began in an earlier year.   [4] Agricultural and government employees are included in the total working time; private household and forestry and fishery employees are excluded.   [5] Revised since originally published.

Source: U.S. Bureau of Labor Statistics, Major Work Stoppages in 2003, News, USDL 04-418, March 19, 2004. See Internet site <http://www.bls.gov/cba/>.

No. 638. Labor Union Membership by Sector: 1983 to 2003

[See headnote, Table 640. (17,717.4 represents 17,717,400)]

Sector	1983	1985	1990	1995	1999	2000	2001	2002	2003
TOTAL (1,000)									
Wage and salary workers:									
Union members	17,717.4	16,996.1	16,739.8	16,359.6	16,476.7	16,258.2	16,288.8	15,978.7	15,776.0
Covered by unions	20,532.1	19,358.1	19,057.8	18,346.3	18,182.3	17,944.1	17,878.1	17,501.6	17,448.4
Public sector workers:									
Union members.	5,737.2	5,743.1	6,485.0	6,927.4	7,058.1	7,110.5	7,147.5	7,327.2	7,324.1
Covered by unions.	7,112.2	6,920.6	7,691.4	7,986.6	7,966.3	7,975.6	7,975.4	8,131.9	8,184.7
Private sector workers:									
Union members.	11,980.2	11,253.0	10,254.8	9,432.1	9,418.6	9,147.7	9,141.3	8,651.5	8,451.8
Covered by unions.	13,419.9	12,437.5	11,366.4	10,359.8	10,216.0	9,968.5	9,902.7	9,369.7	9,263.7
PERCENT									
Wage and salary workers:									
Union members	20.1	18.0	16.1	14.9	13.9	13.5	13.5	13.3	12.9
Covered by unions	23.3	20.5	18.3	16.7	15.3	14.9	14.8	14.6	14.3
Public sector workers:									
Union members.	36.7	35.7	36.5	37.7	37.3	37.5	37.4	37.8	37.2
Covered by unions.	45.5	43.1	43.3	43.5	42.1	42.0	41.7	41.9	41.5
Private sector workers:									
Union members.	16.5	14.3	11.9	10.3	9.4	9.0	9.0	8.6	8.2
Covered by unions.	18.5	15.9	13.2	11.3	10.2	9.8	9.7	9.3	9.0

Source: The Bureau of National Affairs, Inc., Washington, DC, *Union Membership and Earnings Data Book: Compilations from the Current Population Survey (2004 edition)*, (copyright by BNA PLUS); authored by Barry Hirsch of Trinity University, San Antonio, TX and David Macpherson of Florida State University. Internet site <http://www.bna.com/bnaplus/labor/laborrpts.html>.

No. 639. Union Members by Selected Characteristics: 2003

[Annual averages of monthly data (122,358 represents 122,358,000). Covers employed wage and salary workers 16 years old and over. Excludes self-employed workers whose businesses are incorporated although they technically qualify as wage and salary workers. Based on Current Population Survey, see text, Section 1, and Appendix III]

Characteristic	Employed wage and salary workers			Median usual weekly earnings [3] (dol.)			
	Total (1,000)	Percent					
		Union members [1]	Repre-sented by unions [2]	Total	Union members [1]	Repre-sented by unions [2]	Not repre-sented by unions
Total [4].	122,358	12.9	14.3	620	760	755	599
16 to 24 years old	18,904	5.1	5.9	387	497	494	381
25 to 34 years old	28,179	11.0	12.3	594	707	701	580
35 to 44 years old	30,714	14.0	15.4	687	787	783	665
45 to 54 years old	27,567	17.6	19.3	723	812	807	695
55 to 64 years old	13,633	16.9	18.7	708	797	798	678
65 years and over	3,361	7.7	8.8	516	619	624	504
Men	63,236	14.3	15.6	695	805	802	667
Women	59,122	11.4	12.9	552	696	691	523
White [5].	100,589	12.5	13.8	636	779	774	612
Men	52,827	14.0	15.2	715	827	825	688
Women	47,762	10.8	12.2	567	711	707	539
Black [5].	13,928	16.5	18.2	514	665	654	491
Men	6,302	18.3	19.8	555	693	687	518
Women	7,626	15.0	16.9	491	633	622	467
Asian [5].	5,096	11.4	12.9	693	759	760	681
Men	2,699	11.0	12.8	772	783	775	771
Women	2,397	11.9	13.1	598	710	723	587
Hispanic [6].	16,068	10.7	11.9	440	632	622	419
Men	9,567	11.0	12.1	464	664	652	437
Women	6,501	10.2	11.6	410	586	584	394
Private sector industry [7]	102,648	8.2	9.0	603	717	713	592
Agriculture and related industries.	1,089	1.6	2.1	397	(B)	(B)	396
Mining.	504	9.1	10.5	797	(B)	783	799
Construction	7,126	16.0	16.7	615	884	873	580
Manufacturing	16,130	13.5	14.3	637	689	689	626
Wholesale and retail trade	18,343	6.2	6.6	533	590	586	528
Transportation and utilities	4,942	26.2	27.3	704	817	816	653
Information	3,297	13.6	14.6	776	868	862	758
Financial activities.	8,360	2.1	2.8	691	618	625	694
Professional and business services	10,588	2.3	2.9	692	699	691	692
Education and health services.	16,635	8.0	9.4	598	670	684	590
Leisure and hospitality	10,207	2.8	3.3	400	497	485	395
Other services	5,425	3.3	3.7	515	726	709	510
Public sector	19,710	37.2	41.5	728	801	795	656

B Data not shown where base is less than 50,000.   [1] Members of a labor union or an employee association similar to a labor union.   [2] Members of a labor union or an employee association similar to a union as well as workers who report no union affiliation but whose jobs are covered by a union or an employee association contract.   [3] For full-time employed wage and salary workers.   [4] Includes races not shown separately. Also includes a small number of multiple jobholders whose full- and part- time status can not be determined for their principal job.   [5] For persons in this race group only. See footnote 3, Table 570.   [6] Persons of Hispanic or Latino ethnicity may be of any race.   [7] See headnote, Table 586.

Source: U.S. Bureau of Labor Statistics, *Employment and Earnings*, January 2004. See Internet site <http://www.bls.gov/cps/home.htm>.

Labor Force, Employment, and Earnings 419

No. 640. Labor Union Membership by State: 1983 and 2003

[Annual averages of monthly figures (17,717.4 represents 17,717,400). For wage and salary workers in agriculture and non-agriculture. Data represent union members by place of residence. Based on the Current Population Survey and subject to sampling error. For methodological details, see source]

State	Union members (1,000)		Workers covered by unions (1,000)		Percent of workers—					
					Union members		Covered by unions		Private sector union members	
	1983	2003	1983	2003	1983	2003	1983	2003	1983	2003
United States. .	17,717.4	15,776.0	20,532.1	17,448.4	20.1	12.9	23.3	14.3	16.5	8.2
Alabama [1]	228.2	147.0	268.2	172.4	16.9	8.1	19.8	9.5	15.3	5.2
Alaska . , ...	41.7	59.1	49.2	65.0	24.9	22.3	29.3	24.6	17.3	11.4
Arizona [1]	125.0	113.1	156.4	139.7	11.4	5.2	14.3	6.4	8.6	3.4
Arkansas [1]	82.2	49.8	103.2	60.6	11.0	4.8	13.8	5.9	10.2	3.4
California	2,118.9	2,414.2	2,505.2	2,646.9	21.9	16.8	25.9	18.4	17.7	9.6
Colorado.	177.9	155.9	209.6	180.2	13.6	7.8	16.0	9.0	11.2	5.2
Connecticut.	314.0	228.7	345.1	244.0	22.7	15.4	25.0	16.4	16.7	8.3
Delaware	49.2	41.9	54.1	45.7	20.1	11.4	22.1	12.5	15.9	6.6
District of Columbia .	52.4	39.0	69.4	46.0	19.5	14.6	25.9	17.2	15.2	9.8
Florida [1]	393.7	407.2	532.9	557.0	10.2	6.1	13.8	8.4	7.1	3.3
Georgia [1]	267.0	249.2	345.1	298.0	11.9	6.7	15.3	8.0	11.1	4.5
Hawaii	112.6	121.7	124.9	126.7	29.2	23.8	32.4	24.8	21.9	16.1
Idaho [1]	41.3	38.6	53.7	47.0	12.5	7.0	16.2	8.6	10.3	4.5
Illinois	1,063.8	966.9	1,205.1	1,003.4	24.2	17.9	27.4	18.6	21.5	12.9
Indiana.	503.3	327.4	544.5	352.0	24.9	11.8	27.0	12.7	25.0	9.3
Iowa [1] . , ...	185.9	156.8	231.3	196.3	17.2	11.5	21.5	14.4	14.6	7.8
Kansas [1]	125.2	95.5	170.4	123.9	13.7	7.9	18.7	10.3	12.2	6.2
Kentucky [1]	223.7	175.0	259.8	215.9	17.9	10.4	20.8	12.8	18.2	8.7
Louisiana [1]	204.2	109.2	267.8	132.4	13.8	6.5	18.1	7.9	11.0	4.4
Maine.	88.0	72.5	100.4	81.1	21.0	12.8	24.0	14.3	14.2	6.7
Maryland	346.5	354.1	423.1	410.0	18.5	14.3	22.6	16.5	14.4	9.2
Massachusetts.	603.2	415.5	661.4	454.4	23.7	14.2	26.0	15.5	17.6	7.9
Michigan	1,005.4	919.0	1,084.6	968.2	30.4	21.9	32.8	23.1	25.3	16.6
Minnesota. , ...	393.9	414.0	439.4	440.7	23.2	17.0	25.9	18.1	17.1	10.1
Mississippi [1]	79.4	55.4	99.7	73.1	9.9	5.0	12.5	6.6	9.0	4.5
Missouri	374.4	336.5	416.7	362.7	20.8	13.2	23.2	14.2	21.5	10.8
Montana . , ...	49.5	50.3	55.5	53.7	18.3	14.0	20.5	14.9	14.8	7.7
Nebraska [1]	80.6	64.4	94.8	87.2	13.6	7.9	16.0	10.6	9.7	4.4
Nevada [1]	90.0	136.1	106.7	148.5	22.4	14.4	26.6	15.8	19.6	11.9
New Hampshire	48.5	56.5	60.8	68.8	11.5	9.3	14.4	11.3	7.5	4.7
New Jersey.	822.1	737.1	918.2	800.7	26.9	19.5	30.0	21.2	21.1	11.7
New Mexico	52.6	56.7	70.6	70.5	11.8	7.6	15.8	9.5	10.1	4.8
New York . . . , . . .	2,155.6	1,935.8	2,385.9	2,017.2	32.5	24.6	36.0	25.6	24.0	14.8
North Carolina [1]	178.7	111.4	238.1	134.6	7.6	3.1	10.2	3.8	5.4	2.1
North Dakota [1]	28.4	20.9	35.1	25.7	13.2	7.3	16.3	9.0	9.5	3.5
Ohio . . . , ...	1,011.0	850.3	1,125.0	922.8	25.1	16.7	27.9	18.1	22.5	11.2
Oklahoma [2]	131.5	96.2	168.2	111.1	11.5	6.8	14.7	7.9	9.1	3.9
Oregon.	222.9	229.9	261.9	240.1	22.3	15.7	26.2	16.4	16.4	8.9
Pennsylvania.	1,195.7	794.3	1,350.0	847.3	27.5	15.1	31.1	16.1	23.2	9.4
Rhode Island.	85.8	84.0	93.7	86.5	21.5	17.0	23.5	17.5	13.7	9.0
South Carolina [1]	69.6	71.3	100.6	89.7	5.9	4.2	8.6	5.3	3.9	2.7
South Dakota [1]	26.8	19.1	34.8	22.7	11.5	5.4	14.9	6.4	8.0	3.1
Tennessee [1]	252.4	178.8	300.9	218.4	15.1	7.5	18.0	9.2	12.4	5.2
Texas [1]	583.7	508.2	712.8	620.9	9.7	5.6	11.9	6.8	8.1	3.4
Utah [1]	81.6	53.0	100.9	68.7	15.2	5.2	18.9	6.8	11.3	2.2
Vermont	25.9	27.2	31.5	32.9	12.6	9.7	15.3	11.7	6.7	4.7
Virginia [1]	268.3	209.9	346.1	251.0	11.7	6.5	15.1	7.7	10.2	4.1
Washington.	419.9	501.5	499.7	530.7	27.1	19.7	32.3	20.9	22.0	13.1
West Virginia.	142.7	87.8	160.6	95.3	25.3	13.1	28.5	14.2	26.1	10.3
Wisconsin , ...	465.5	414.4	526.7	437.9	23.8	15.9	26.9	16.8	19.8	10.0
Wyoming [1]	27.1	17.8	31.8	22.0	13.9	8.0	16.2	9.8	10.4	5.1

[1] Right to work state.   [2] Passed right to work law in 2001.

Source: The Bureau of National Affairs, Inc., Washington, DC, *Union Membership and Earnings Data Book: Compilations from the Current Population Survey (2004 edition)*, (copyright by BNA PLUS); authored by Barry Hirsch of Trinity University, San Antonio, TX, and David Macpherson of Florida State University. Internet site <http://www.bna.com/bnaplus/labor/laborrpts.html>.

Section 13
Income, Expenditures, and Wealth

This section presents data on gross domestic product (GDP), gross national product (GNP), national and personal income, saving and investment, money income, poverty, and national and personal wealth. The data on income and expenditures measure two aspects of the U.S. economy. One aspect relates to the national income and product accounts (NIPAs), a summation reflecting the entire complex of the nation's economic income and output and the interaction of its major components; the other relates to the distribution of money income to families and individuals or consumer income.

The primary source for data on GDP, GNP, national and personal income, gross saving and investment, and fixed reproducible tangible wealth is the *Survey of Current Business*, published monthly by the Bureau of Economic Analysis (BEA). A comprehensive revision to the NIPAs was released beginning in October 1999. Discussions of the revision appeared in the January, June, August, September and the December 2003 issues of the *Survey of Current Business*. Summary historical estimates appeared in the February 2004 issue of the *Survey of Current Business*. Detailed historical data will appear in forthcoming *National Income and Product Accounts of the United States, 1929-2000* report.

Sources of income distribution data are the decennial censuses of population and the Current Population Survey (CPS), both products of the U.S. Census Bureau (see text, Section 1 and Section 4). Annual data on income of families, individuals, and households are presented in *Current Population Reports, Consumer Income,* P60 Series, in print, and many data series found on the Census Web site at <http://www.census.gov/hhes/www/income.html>. Data from the 2000 census may be found in Tables 663, 676, and 682. Data on the household sector's saving and assets are published by the Board

of Governors of the Federal Reserve System in the quarterly *Flow of Funds Accounts*. The Board also periodically conducts the *Survey of Consumer Finances*, which presents financial information on family assets and net worth. There are also two new tables (691 and 692) on household assets and net worth based on the Census Bureau's Survey of Income and Program Participation. Detailed information on personal wealth is published periodically by the Internal Revenue Service (IRS) in *SOI Bulletin*.

National income and product—Gross domestic product is the total output of goods and services produced by labor and property located in the United States, valued at market prices. GDP can be viewed in terms of the expenditure categories that comprise its major components purchases of goods and services by consumers and government, gross private domestic investment, and net exports of goods and services. The goods and services included are largely those bought for final use (excluding illegal transactions) in the market economy. A number of inclusions, however, represent imputed values, the most important of which is rental value of owner-occupied housing. GDP, in this broad context, measures the output attributable to the factors of production located in the United States. Gross state product (GSP) is the gross market value of the goods and services attributable to labor and property located in a state. It is the state counterpart of the nation's gross domestic product.

In January 1996, BEA replaced its fixed weighted index as the featured measure of real GDP with an index based on chain type annual weights. Changes in this measure of real output and prices are calculated as the average of changes based on weights for the current and preceding years. (Components of real output are weighted by price, and components of prices are weighted by output.) These annual changes are "chained" (multiplied) together to form a time series that allows for the effects of changes in relative prices and changes in the composition of output over time. Quarterly and monthly changes are also based on annual weights. The new output indexes are expressed as 2000=100, and for recent years, in 2000 dollars; the new price indexes are based to 2000=100. For more information on chain-dollar indexes, see the article on this subject in the November 2003 issue of the *Survey of Current Business.*

Chained (2000) dollar estimates of most components of GDP are not published for periods prior to 1990, because during periods far from the base period, the levels of the components may provide misleading information about their contributions to an aggregate. Values are published in index form (2000=100) for 1929 to the present to allow users to calculate the percent changes for all components, changes that are accurate for all periods.

Gross national product measures the output attributable to all labor and property supplied by United States residents. GNP differs from "national income" mainly in that GNP includes allowances for depreciation consumption of fixed capital.

National Income includes all net incomes (net of CFC) earned in production. National income is the sum of compensation of employees, proprietors' income with inventory valuation adjustment (IVA) and capital consumption adjustment (CCAdj), rental income of persons with CCAdj, corporate profits with IVA and CCAdj, net interest and miscellaneous payments, taxes on production and imports, business current transfer payments, current surplus of government enterprises, less subsidies.

Capital consumption adjustment for corporations and for nonfarm sole proprietorships and partnerships is the difference between capital consumption based on income tax returns and capital consumption measured using empirical evidence on prices of used equipment and structures in resale markets, which have shown that depreciation for most types of assets approximates a geometric pattern.

The tax return data are valued at historical costs and reflect changes over time in service lives and depreciation patterns as permitted by tax regulations. *Inventory valuation adjustment* represents the difference between the book value of inventories used up in production and the cost of replacing them.

Personal income is the current income received by persons from all sources minus their personal contributions for government social insurance. Classified as "persons" are individuals (including owners of unincorporated firms), nonprofit institutions that primarily serve individuals, private trust funds, and private noninsured welfare funds. Personal income includes personal current transfer receipts (payments not resulting from current production) from government and business such as social security benefits, public assistance, etc., but excludes transfers among persons. Also included are certain nonmonetary types of income chiefly, estimated net rental value to owner-occupants of their homes and the value of services furnished without payment by financial intermediaries. Capital gains (net losses) are excluded.

Disposable personal income is personal income less personal current taxes. It is the income available to persons for spending or saving. Personal current taxes are tax payments (net of refunds) by persons (except personal contributions for government social insurance) that are not chargeable to business expense and certain personal payments to general government that are treated like taxes. Personal taxes include income, estate and gift, and personal property taxes andmotor vehicle licenses. Nontax payments include passport fees, fines and forfeitures, and donations.

Gross domestic product by industry—The BEA also prepares estimates of value added by industry. Value added is a measure of the contribution of each private industry and of government to the Nation's GDP. It is defined as an industry's gross output (which consists of sales or receipts and other operating income, commodity taxes, and inventory change) minus its intermediate inputs (which consists of energy, raw materials, semi-finished goods, and services that are purchased from domestic industries or from foreign sources). These estimates of value added are produced for 61 private industries and for 4 government classifications—federal general government and government enterprises and state and local general government and government enterprises.

The estimates by industry are available in current dollars and are derived from the estimates of gross domestic income, which consists of three components the compensation of employees, gross operating surplus, and taxes on production and imports, less subsidies. Real, or inflation-adjusted, estimates are also prepared.

Regional Economic Accounts—These accounts consist of estimates of state and local area personal income and of gross state product and are consistent with estimates of personal income and gross domestic product in the Bureau's national economic accounts. BEA's estimates of state and local area personal income provide a framework for analyzing individual state and local economies, and they show how the economies compare with each other. The *personal income* of a state and/or local area is the income received by, or on behalf of, the residents of that state or area. Estimates of labor and proprietors' earnings by place of work indicate the economic activity of business and government within that area, and estimates of personal income by place of residence indicate the income within the area that is available for spending. BEA prepares estimates for all states, 3,110 counties, 335 metropolitan areas, and 172 BEA economic areas.

Gross state product estimates measure the value added to the Nation's production by the labor and property in each state. GSP is often considered the state counterpart of the Nation's GDP. The GSP estimates provide the basis for analyzing the regional impacts of national economic trends. GSP is measured as the sum of the distributions by industry and state of the components of gross domestic income that is, the sum of the costs incurred and

incomes earned in the production of GDP. The GSP estimates are presented in current dollars and in real (chained dollars) for 63 industries.

Consumer Expenditure Survey—The Consumer Expenditure Survey program was begun in late 1979. The principal objective of the survey is to collect current consumer expenditure data, which provide a continuous flow of data on the buying habits of American consumers. The data are necessary for future revisions of the Consumer Price Index.

The survey conducted by the Census Bureau for the Bureau of Labor Statistics consists of two components: (1) an interview panel survey in which the expenditures of consumer units are obtained in five interviews conducted every 3 months, and (2) a diary or recordkeeping survey completed by participating households for two consecutive 1-week period.

Each component of the survey queries an independent sample of consumer units representative of the U.S. total population.

Over 52 weeks of the year, 5,000 consumer units are sampled for the diary survey. Each consumer unit keeps a diary for two 1-week periods yielding approximately 10,000 diaries a year. The interview sample is selected on a rotating panel basis, targeted at 5,000 consumer units per quarter. Data are collected in 88 urban and 16 rural areas of the country that are representative of the U.S. total population. The survey includes students in student housing. Data from the two surveys are combined; integration is necessary to permit analysis of total family expenditures because neither the diary nor quarterly interview survey was designed to collect a complete account of consumer spending.

Distribution of money income to families and individuals—Money income statistics are based on data collected in various field surveys of income conducted since 1936. Since 1947, the Census Bureau has collected the data on an annual basis and published them in *Current Population Reports*, P60 Series. In each of the surveys, field representatives

U.S. Census Bureau, Statistical Abstract of the United States: 2004-2005

interview samples of the population with respect to income received during the previous year. *Money income* as defined by the Census Bureau differs from the BEA concept of "personal income." Data on consumer income collected in the CPS by the Census Bureau cover money income received (exclusive of certain money receipts such as capital gains) before payments for personal income taxes, social security, union dues, medicare deductions, etc. Therefore, money income does not reflect the fact that some families receive part of their income in the form of noncash benefits (see Section 11) such as food stamps, health benefits, and subsidized housing; that some farm families receive noncash benefits in the form of rent-free housing and goods produced and consumed on the farm; or that noncash benefits are also received by some nonfarm residents which often take the form of the use of business transportation and facilities, full or partial payments by business for retirement programs, medical and educational expenses, etc. These elements should be considered when comparing income levels. None of the aggregate income concepts (GDP, national income, or personal income) is exactly comparable with money income, although personal income is the closest.

In October 1983, the Census Bureau began to collect data under the new Survey of Income and Program Participation-(SIPP). The data collected in SIPP will be used to study federal and state aid programs (such as food stamps, welfare, medicaid, and subsidized housing), to estimate program costs and coverage, and to assess the effects of proposed changes in program eligibility rules or benefit levels. The core questions are repeated at each interview and cover labor force activity, the types and amounts of income received, and participation status in various programs. The core also contains questions covering attendance in postsecondary schools and private health insurance coverage. Various supplements or topical modules covering areas such as educational attainment, assets and liabilities (see new tables 691 and 692), and pension plan coverage are periodically included.

Poverty—Families and unrelated individuals are classified as being above or below the poverty level using the poverty index originated at the Social Security Administration in 1964 and revised by Federal Interagency Committees in 1969 and 1980.

The poverty index is based solely on money income and does not reflect the fact that many low-income persons receive noncash benefits such as food stamps, medicaid, and public housing. The index is based on the Department of Agriculture's 1961 Economy Food Plan and reflects the different consumption requirements of families based on their size and composition. The poverty thresholds are updated every year to reflect changes in the Consumer Price Index. The following technical changes to the thresholds were made in 1981: (1) distinctions based on sex of householder have been eliminated, (2) separate thresholds for farm families have been dropped, and (3) the matrix has been expanded to families of nine or more persons from the old cutoff of seven or more persons. These changes have been incorporated in the calculation of poverty data beginning with 1981. Besides the Census Bureau Web site at <http://www.census.gov/hhes/www/poverty.html>, information on poverty guidelines and research may be found at the U.S. Department of Human Services Web site at <http://aspe.hhs.gov/poverty/poverty.shtml>.In the recent past, the Census Bureau has published a number of technical papers that presented experimental poverty estimates based on income definitions that counted the value of selected government noncash benefits. The Census Bureau has also published annual reports on aftertax income. In addition, in July 1999, the Census Bureau released a report (P60-205) that showed the effect of using experimental poverty following the recommendations of a National Academy of Sciences panel on redefining our nation's poverty measure.

Statistical reliability—For a discussion of statistical collection and estimation, sampling procedures, and measures of statistical reliability pertaining to Census Bureau data, see Appendix III.

No. 641. Gross Domestic Product in Current and Real (2000) Dollars: 1960 to 2003

[In billions of dollars (526.4 represents $526,400,000,000). For explanation of gross domestic product and chained dollars, see text, this section]

Item	1960	1970	1980	1990	1991	1992	1993	1994	1995	1996	1997	1998	1999	2000	2001	2002	2003
CURRENT DOLLARS																	
Gross domestic product	526.4	1,038.5	2,789.5	5,803.1	5,995.9	6,337.7	6,657.4	7,072.2	7,397.7	7,816.9	8,304.3	8,747.0	9,268.4	9,817.0	10,100.8	10,480.8	10,987.9
Personal consumption expenditures	331.7	648.5	1,757.1	3,839.9	3,986.1	4,235.3	4,477.9	4,743.3	4,975.8	5,256.8	5,547.4	5,879.5	6,282.5	6,739.4	7,045.4	7,385.3	7,757.4
Durable goods	43.3	85.0	214.2	474.2	453.9	483.6	526.7	582.2	611.6	652.6	692.7	750.2	817.6	863.3	881.9	911.3	941.6
Nondurable goods	152.8	272.0	696.1	1,249.9	1,284.8	1,330.6	1,379.4	1,437.2	1,485.1	1,555.5	1,619.0	1,683.6	1,804.8	1,947.2	2,013.6	2,086.0	2,209.7
Services	135.6	291.5	846.9	2,115.9	2,247.4	2,421.2	2,571.8	2,723.9	2,879.1	3,048.7	3,235.8	3,445.7	3,660.0	3,928.8	4,149.8	4,388.0	4,606.2
Gross private domestic investment	78.9	152.4	479.3	861.0	802.9	864.8	953.4	1,097.1	1,144.0	1,240.3	1,389.8	1,509.1	1,625.7	1,735.5	1,607.2	1,589.2	1,670.6
Fixed investment	75.7	150.4	485.6	846.4	803.3	848.5	932.5	1,033.3	1,112.9	1,209.5	1,317.8	1,438.4	1,558.8	1,679.0	1,643.4	1,583.9	1,673.0
Change in business inventories	3.2	2.0	-6.3	14.5	-0.4	16.3	20.8	63.8	31.1	30.8	72.0	70.8	66.9	56.5	-36.1	5.4	-2.4
Net exports of goods and services	4.2	4.0	-13.1	-78.0	-27.5	-33.2	-65.0	-93.6	-91.4	-96.2	-101.6	-159.9	-260.5	-379.5	-366.5	-426.3	-495.0
Exports	27.0	59.7	280.8	552.4	596.8	635.3	655.8	720.9	812.2	868.6	955.3	955.9	991.2	1,096.3	1,035.1	1,006.8	1,048.9
Imports	22.8	55.8	293.8	630.3	624.3	668.6	720.9	814.5	903.6	964.8	1,056.9	1,115.9	1,251.7	1,475.8	1,401.7	1,433.1	1,543.8
Government consumption expenditures and gross investment	111.6	233.8	566.2	1,180.2	1,234.4	1,271.0	1,291.2	1,325.5	1,369.2	1,416.0	1,468.7	1,518.3	1,620.8	1,721.6	1,814.7	1,932.5	2,054.8
Federal	64.1	113.5	243.8	508.3	527.7	533.9	525.2	519.1	519.2	527.4	530.9	530.4	555.8	578.8	612.9	679.5	757.2
National defense	53.4	87.6	168.0	374.0	383.2	376.9	362.9	353.7	348.7	354.6	349.6	345.7	360.6	370.3	393.0	438.3	497.3
Nondefense	10.7	25.8	75.8	134.3	144.5	157.0	162.4	165.5	170.5	172.8	181.3	184.7	195.2	208.5	219.9	241.2	259.9
State and local	47.5	120.3	322.4	671.9	706.7	737.0	766.0	806.3	850.0	888.6	937.8	987.9	1,065.0	1,142.8	1,201.8	1,253.1	1,297.6
CHAINED (2000) DOLLARS																	
Gross domestic product	2,501.8	3,771.9	5,161.7	7,112.5	7,100.5	7,336.6	7,532.7	7,835.5	8,031.7	8,328.9	8,703.5	9,066.9	9,470.3	9,817.0	9,866.6	10,083.0	10,398.0
Personal consumption expenditures	1,597.4	2,451.9	3,374.1	4,770.3	4,778.4	4,934.8	5,099.8	5,290.7	5,433.5	5,619.4	5,831.8	6,125.8	6,438.6	6,739.4	6,904.6	7,140.4	7,365.2
Durable goods	(NA)	(NA)	(NA)	453.5	427.9	453.0	488.4	529.4	552.6	595.9	646.9	720.3	804.6	863.3	899.1	957.2	1,027.5
Nondurable goods	(NA)	(NA)	(NA)	1,484.0	1,480.5	1,510.1	1,550.4	1,603.9	1,638.6	1,680.4	1,725.3	1,794.4	1,876.6	1,947.2	1,983.3	2,043.6	2,121.0
Services	(NA)	(NA)	(NA)	2,851.7	2,900.0	3,000.8	3,085.7	3,176.6	3,259.9	3,356.0	3,468.0	3,615.0	3,758.0	3,928.8	4,022.4	4,141.8	4,225.7
Gross private domestic investment	266.6	427.1	645.3	895.1	822.2	889.0	968.3	1,099.6	1,134.0	1,234.3	1,387.7	1,524.1	1,642.6	1,735.5	1,590.6	1,572.0	1,638.0
Fixed investment	(NA)	(NA)	(NA)	886.6	829.1	878.3	953.5	1,042.3	1,109.6	1,209.2	1,320.6	1,455.0	1,576.3	1,679.0	1,625.7	1,565.8	1,635.2
Change in business inventories	(NA)	(NA)	(NA)	15.4	-0.5	16.5	20.6	63.6	29.9	28.7	71.2	72.6	68.9	56.5	-36.0	5.7	-0.7
Net exports of goods and services	(NA)	(NA)	(NA)	-54.7	-14.6	-15.9	-52.1	-79.4	-71.0	-79.6	-104.6	-203.7	-296.2	-379.5	-398.1	-470.6	-509.1
Exports	90.6	161.4	323.5	552.5	589.1	629.7	650.0	706.5	778.2	843.4	943.7	966.5	1,008.2	1,096.3	1,039.0	1,014.2	1,034.7
Imports	103.3	213.4	310.9	607.1	603.7	645.6	702.1	785.9	849.1	923.0	1,048.3	1,170.3	1,304.4	1,475.8	1,437.1	1,484.7	1,543.8
Government consumption expenditures and gross investment	715.4	1,012.9	1,115.4	1,530.0	1,547.2	1,555.3	1,541.1	1,541.3	1,549.7	1,564.9	1,594.0	1,624.4	1,686.9	1,721.6	1,768.9	1,836.9	1,898.4
Federal	(NA)	(NA)	(NA)	659.1	658.0	646.6	619.6	596.4	580.3	573.5	567.6	561.2	573.7	578.8	600.5	648.0	704.3
National defense	(NA)	(NA)	(NA)	479.4	474.2	450.7	425.3	404.6	389.2	383.8	373.0	365.3	372.2	370.3	384.7	418.8	463.0
Nondefense	(NA)	(NA)	(NA)	178.6	182.8	195.4	194.1	191.7	191.0	189.6	194.5	195.9	201.5	208.5	215.8	229.2	241.4
State and local	(NA)	(NA)	(NA)	868.4	886.8	906.5	919.5	943.3	968.3	990.5	1,025.9	1,063.0	1,113.2	1,142.8	1,168.5	1,189.1	1,194.6
Residual	-64.9	-68.0	14.3	-91.1	-96.0	-89.1	-78.6	-63.7	-51.1	-38.5	-23.8	-14.6	-5.8	0.2	1.8	2.4	-0.4

NA Not available.

Source: U.S. Bureau of Economic Analysis, *National Income and Product Accounts, 1929-2000*, and *Survey of Current Business*, June 2004. See also <http://www.bea.doc.gov/bea/dn/nipaweb/SelectTable.asp?Selected=N> (released 27 May 2004).

No. 642. Gross Domestic Product in Current and Real (2000) Dollars by Industry: 2000 to 2003

[In billions of dollars (9817.0 represents $9,817,000,000,000). Data are based on the 1997 NAICS. Data include nonfactor charges (capital consumption allowances, indirect business taxes, etc.) as well as factor charges against gross product; corporate profits and capital consumption allowances have been shifted from a company to an establishment basis]

Industry	Current dollars				Chained (2000) dollars			
	2000	2001	2002	2003	2000	2001	2002	2003
Gross domestic product [1]	9,817.0	10,100.8	10,480.8	10,987.9	9,817.0	9,866.6	10,083.0	10,398.0
Private industries	8,614.3	8,841.1	9,154.1	9,597.9	8,614.3	8,664.2	8,859.1	9,129.3
Agriculture, forestry, and fishing	98.0	103.0	98.6	112.0	98.0	97.8	100.0	101.8
Farms	71.5	75.5	70.7	(NA)	71.5	68.5	69.8	(NA)
Agricultural services	26.5	27.4	27.9	(NA)	26.5	29.6	30.5	(NA)
Mining	121.3	118.7	105.6	124.9	121.3	114.9	114.6	112.1
Metal mining	81.0	73.9	64.1	(NA)	81.0	79.1	80.3	(NA)
Coal mining	27.0	27.0	26.1	(NA)	27.0	25.6	24.1	(NA)
Oil and gas extraction	13.4	17.8	15.3	(NA)	13.4	10.6	10.8	(NA)
Utilities	189.3	195.1	201.6	212.7	189.3	173.3	182.3	187.4
Construction	435.9	459.5	464.9	481.8	435.9	426.6	413.3	413.9
Manufacturing	1,426.2	1,346.0	1,351.6	1,392.8	1,426.2	1,349.1	1,380.9	1,404.9
Durable goods	865.3	788.0	786.1	810.1	865.3	820.7	836.9	865.7
Wood products	31.4	31.1	32.1	(NA)	31.4	30.6	31.9	(NA)
Nonmetallic mineral products	45.7	44.7	44.5	(NA)	45.7	44.9	43.9	(NA)
Primary metals	48.2	42.0	40.8	(NA)	48.2	44.2	42.6	(NA)
Fabricated metal products	121.7	113.5	112.2	(NA)	121.7	110.8	108.8	(NA)
Machinery	109.3	103.5	98.1	(NA)	109.3	100.4	94.5	(NA)
Computer and electronic products	185.6	141.6	139.9	(NA)	185.6	186.4	207.8	(NA)
Elect. equip., appliances, & components	50.6	48.7	46.1	(NA)	50.6	47.9	46.2	(NA)
Motor vehicles, bodies & trailers, & pts.	118.1	108.0	119.3	(NA)	118.1	108.2	125.0	(NA)
Other transportation equipment	64.4	67.2	64.2	(NA)	64.4	63.2	59.0	(NA)
Furniture and related products	32.7	30.8	30.6	(NA)	32.7	29.6	28.7	(NA)
Miscellaneous manufacturing	57.5	56.9	58.5	(NA)	57.5	54.8	54.9	(NA)
Nondurable goods	560.9	558.0	565.5	582.7	561.0	528.5	543.9	540.6
Food & beverage & tobacco	154.8	161.6	168.8	(NA)	154.8	151.0	150.4	(NA)
Textile mills and textile product mills	26.5	23.1	22.7	(NA)	26.5	21.9	22.0	(NA)
Apparel and leather and allied products	25.1	22.9	23.3	(NA)	25.1	22.8	23.5	(NA)
Paper products	55.6	50.0	48.9	(NA)	55.6	49.7	49.2	(NA)
Printing and related support activities	49.0	47.4	47.1	(NA)	49.0	45.8	45.2	(NA)
Petroleum and coal products	26.2	32.3	24.2	(NA)	26.2	22.9	30.1	(NA)
Chemical products	157.1	157.2	167.9	(NA)	157.1	152.9	163.8	(NA)
Plastics and rubber products	66.7	63.5	62.8	(NA)	66.7	61.3	60.1	(NA)
Wholesale trade	591.7	603.0	622.9	642.9	591.7	626.6	640.5	656.3
Retail trade	662.4	687.7	765.8	792.2	662.4	708.3	764.4	803.0
Transportation and warehousing	301.6	295.1	294.9	310.6	301.6	291.4	289.8	298.4
Air transportation	57.7	50.6	47.9	(NA)	57.7	57.3	58.7	(NA)
Rail transportation	25.5	25.3	24.3	(NA)	25.5	24.5	22.8	(NA)
Water transportation	7.2	7.3	6.9	(NA)	7.2	7.0	6.4	(NA)
Truck transportation	92.8	92.5	94.1	(NA)	92.8	87.0	86.5	(NA)
Transit & ground passenger transport	14.5	15.7	16.3	(NA)	14.5	15.1	15.3	(NA)
Pipeline transportation	8.7	9.1	9.2	(NA)	8.7	8.3	7.7	(NA)
Other transportation & support	70.2	69.3	70.7	(NA)	70.2	67.2	67.8	(NA)
Warehousing and storage	25.0	25.2	25.3	(NA)	25.0	24.5	24.2	(NA)
Information	458.3	474.8	484.0	536.1	458.3	474.5	489.3	534.7
Publishing industries (includes software)	116.7	118.6	120.1	(NA)	116.7	115.3	117.1	(NA)
Motion picture and sound recording	32.5	33.7	34.6	(NA)	32.5	32.0	31.6	(NA)
Broadcasting and telecommunications	271.3	281.3	283.9	(NA)	271.3	287.5	297.7	(NA)
Information and data processing services	37.7	41.2	45.4	(NA)	37.7	39.8	43.0	(NA)
Finance and insurance [2]	740.5	770.1	804.0	863.6	740.5	762.0	773.9	829.7
Real estate and rental and leasing	1,190.5	1,257.8	1,321.7	1,364.9	1,190.5	1,214.7	1,235.7	1,257.5
Professional, scientific, and technical services	675.1	710.9	723.5	753.3	675.1	682.5	685.9	699.3
Legal services	136.1	143.3	149.7	(NA)	136.1	135.5	136.2	(NA)
Computer systems design, related services	125.7	137.1	129.4	(NA)	125.7	134.3	127.4	(NA)
Miscellaneous services	413.3	430.6	444.3	(NA)	413.3	412.8	422.1	(NA)
Management of companies & enterprises	183.4	187.7	202.0	216.2	183.4	191.1	206.3	215.5
Administrative and waste management	282.4	289.2	294.7	303.9	282.4	273.6	283.2	283.7
Educational services	79.2	85.8	91.5	96.8	79.2	80.2	80.6	80.9
Health care and social assistance	599.2	646.9	701.6	745.9	599.2	613.0	640.0	661.9
Ambulatory health care services	307.6	333.4	364.0	(NA)	307.6	320.8	344.7	(NA)
Hospitals, nursing, residential care	238.6	256.0	276.0	(NA)	238.6	237.9	240.8	(NA)
Social assistance	53.0	57.5	61.7	(NA)	53.0	54.4	55.1	(NA)
Arts, entertainment, and recreation	88.7	94.8	99.6	104.9	88.7	90.7	92.1	94.2
Performing arts, spectator sports, museums, and related activities	40.0	42.6	45.0	(NA)	40.0	40.4	41.1	(NA)
Amusements, gambling, & recreation	48.7	52.2	54.6	(NA)	48.7	50.3	51.0	(NA)
Accommodation and food services	261.4	264.2	272.0	280.3	261.4	262.0	267.4	272.3
Accommodation	90.7	88.3	89.8	(NA)	90.7	86.6	88.4	(NA)
Food services and drinking places	170.8	175.9	182.1	(NA)	170.8	175.5	179.1	(NA)
Government	1,202.7	1,259.6	1,326.7	1,390.0	1,202.7	1,213.6	1,228.5	1,245.0
Federal	378.7	386.9	408.9	(NA)	378.7	373.3	377.5	(NA)
State and local	823.9	872.7	917.8	(NA)	823.9	840.3	851.0	(NA)

NA Not available. [1] Includes industries, not shown separately.

Source: U.S. Bureau of Economic Analysis, *Survey of Current Business*, June 2004. See also <http://www.bea.gov/bea/industry/gpotables/gpolist.cfm?anon=591&registered=> (released 17 June 2004).

No. 643. Gross Domestic Product in Current and Real (2000) Dollars by Type of Product and Sector: 1990 to 2003

[In billions of dollars (5,803.1 represents $5,803,100,000,000). For explanation of chained dollars, see text, this section]

Type of product and sector	1990	1995	1997	1998	1999	2000	2001	2002	2003
CURRENT DOLLARS									
Gross domestic product	5,803.1	7,397.7	8,304.3	8,747.0	9,268.4	9,817.0	10,100.8	10,480.8	10,987.9
PRODUCT									
Goods	2,155.8	2,661.1	3,007.7	3,143.4	3,311.3	3,449.3	3,400.5	3,456.2	3,579.8
Durable goods	957.9	1,235.7	1,449.0	1,530.5	1,616.5	1,689.4	1,581.8	1,582.8	1,633.6
Nondurable goods	1,198.0	1,425.4	1,558.7	1,612.8	1,694.8	1,760.0	1,818.7	1,873.4	1,946.2
Services	3,113.7	4,098.4	4,548.4	4,789.8	5,081.8	5,425.6	5,717.6	6,049.8	6,377.7
Structures	533.5	638.1	748.2	813.8	875.3	942.1	982.7	974.8	1,030.4
SECTOR									
Business	4,462.6	5,700.6	6,471.9	6,827.1	7,243.4	7,666.7	7,822.5	8,065.6	8,476.9
Nonfarm	4,386.0	5,632.0	6,383.8	6,748.2	7,174.7	7,595.1	7,747.0	7,994.9	8,393.4
Farm	76.6	68.5	88.1	78.9	68.8	71.5	75.5	70.7	83.5
Households and institutions	618.9	815.5	895.8	949.7	1,012.3	1,080.7	1,153.1	1,226.4	1,265.2
General government	721.6	881.6	936.7	970.3	1,012.7	1,069.6	1,125.1	1,188.8	1,245.8
Federal	258.9	284.7	290.9	293.1	300.9	315.4	325.2	345.3	367.9
State and local	462.6	596.9	645.8	677.2	711.8	754.2	799.9	843.5	877.9
CHAINED (2000) DOLLARS									
Gross domestic product	7,112.5	8,031.7	8,703.5	9,066.9	9,470.3	9,817.0	9,866.6	10,083.0	10,398.0
PRODUCT									
Goods	2,252.7	2,639.0	2,971.3	3,132.7	3,312.6	3,449.3	3,378.7	3,450.5	3,599.1
Durable goods	877.2	1,124.5	1,354.0	1,473.1	1,594.1	1,689.4	1,605.5	1,638.1	1,735.3
Nondurable goods	1,407.1	1,531.6	1,623.7	1,661.8	1,718.9	1,760.0	1,772.2	1,811.3	1,865.0
Services	4,170.0	4,654.7	4,901.1	5,057.5	5,245.1	5,425.6	5,548.5	5,721.3	5,869.3
Structures	718.3	753.5	835.7	879.1	913.0	942.1	938.5	910.8	932.8
SECTOR									
Business	5,287.0	6,076.8	6,693.8	7,017.1	7,376.8	7,666.7	7,673.6	7,848.7	8,138.3
Nonfarm	5,237.9	6,030.2	6,627.2	6,955.3	7,314.2	7,595.1	7,605.2	7,779.0	8,066.5
Farm	49.3	49.6	64.4	61.6	62.9	71.5	68.5	69.8	72.0
Households and institutions	841.2	945.1	983.5	1,010.4	1,042.3	1,080.7	1,104.8	1,128.8	1,141.2
General government	1,003.9	1,020.6	1,030.0	1,041.0	1,051.4	1,069.6	1,088.0	1,105.4	1,120.8
Federal	371.6	334.1	318.8	315.2	312.7	315.4	316.1	321.4	332.1
State and local	633.6	686.5	711.2	725.8	738.7	754.2	771.9	783.9	788.8

Source: U.S. Bureau of Economic Analysis, *National Income and Product Accounts, 1929-2000*; and *Survey of Current Business*, June 2004. See also <http://www.bea.doc.gov/bea/dn/nipaweb/SelectTable.asp?Selected=N> (released as 27 May 2004).

No. 644. GDP Components in Real (2000) Dollars—Annual Percent Change: 1990 to 2003

[Change from previous year; for 1990, change from 1989 and for 1995, change from 1994. Minus sign (-) indicates decrease]

Component	1990	1995	1996	1997	1998	1999	2000	2001	2002	2003
Gross domestic product (GDP)	1.9	2.5	3.7	4.5	4.2	4.4	3.7	0.5	2.2	3.1
Personal consumption expenditures	2.0	2.7	3.4	3.8	5.0	5.1	4.7	2.5	3.4	3.1
Durable goods	(NA)	4.4	7.8	8.6	11.3	11.7	7.3	4.1	6.5	7.3
Nondurable goods	(NA)	2.2	2.6	2.7	4.0	4.6	3.8	1.9	3.0	3.8
Services	(NA)	2.6	2.9	3.3	4.2	4.0	4.5	2.4	3.0	2.0
Gross private domestic investment	-3.4	3.1	8.8	12.4	9.8	7.8	5.7	-8.3	-1.2	4.2
Fixed investment	(NA)	6.5	9.0	9.2	10.2	8.3	6.5	-3.2	-3.7	4.4
Nonresidential	(NA)	10.5	9.3	12.1	11.1	9.2	8.7	-4.5	-7.2	3.0
Structures	(NA)	6.4	5.7	7.3	5.1	-0.4	6.8	-2.6	-18.4	-4.6
Equipment and software	(NA)	12.0	10.6	13.8	13.3	12.7	9.4	-5.2	-2.8	5.5
Residential	(NA)	-3.2	8.0	1.9	7.6	6.0	0.7	0.4	4.9	7.4
Exports	9.0	10.1	8.4	11.9	2.4	4.3	8.7	-5.2	-2.4	2.0
Goods	(NA)	11.7	8.8	14.4	2.2	3.8	11.2	-6.1	-4.0	1.9
Services	(NA)	6.4	7.2	6.0	2.9	5.6	2.9	-3.0	1.5	2.3
Imports	3.6	8.0	8.7	13.6	11.6	11.5	13.1	-2.6	3.3	4.0
Goods	(NA)	9.0	9.3	14.4	11.7	12.4	13.5	-3.2	3.7	4.8
Services	(NA)	3.3	5.5	9.4	11.4	6.9	11.1	0.4	1.4	-0.0
Government consumption expenditures and gross investment	3.2	0.5	1.0	1.9	1.9	3.8	2.1	2.7	3.8	3.3
Federal	(NA)	-2.7	-1.2	-1.0	-1.1	2.2	0.9	3.7	7.9	8.7
National defense	(NA)	-3.8	-1.2	-2.8	-2.1	1.9	-0.5	3.9	8.9	10.6
Nondefense	(NA)	-0.4	-0.7	2.6	0.7	2.9	3.5	3.5	6.2	5.3
State and local	(NA)	2.7	2.3	3.6	3.6	4.7	2.7	2.2	1.8	0.5

NA Not available.

Source: U.S. Bureau of Economic Analysis, *Survey of Current Business*, June 2004. See also <http://www.bea.doc.gov/bea/dn/nipaweb/SelectTable.asp?Selected=N> (released as 27 May 2004).

U.S. Census Bureau, Statistical Abstract of the United States: 2004-2005

No. 645. Gross State Product in Current and Real (1996) Dollars by State: 1990 to 2001

[In billions of dollars (5,706.7 represents 5,706,700,000,000). For definition of gross state product or chained dollars, see text, this section]

State	Current dollars					Chained (1996) dollars [1]				
	1990	1995	1999	2000	2001	1990	1995	1999	2000	2001
United States	5,706.7	7,309.5	9,251.5	9,891.2	10,137.2	6,630.7	7,434.0	8,882.6	9,298.2	9,335.4
Alabama.	71.6	95.5	115.1	119.3	121.5	83.2	96.6	110.4	112.3	112.0
Alaska	24.8	24.8	25.6	28.1	28.6	27.8	26.4	25.1	24.7	24.5
Arizona.	68.9	104.6	144.6	153.5	160.7	79.0	105.4	141.4	148.8	153.7
Arkansas	38.4	53.8	65.0	66.8	67.9	44.1	54.7	63.2	64.0	63.7
California	798.9	925.9	1,213.4	1,330.0	1,359.3	927.6	941.9	1,169.8	1,258.4	1,260.0
Colorado.	74.7	109.0	152.3	169.3	173.8	87.0	111.2	145.5	158.2	159.3
Connecticut.	98.9	118.6	149.0	161.9	166.2	117.3	120.8	142.7	152.0	153.0
Delaware	20.3	27.6	34.7	37.2	40.5	25.0	28.2	32.0	33.4	35.7
District of Columbia	40.4	48.4	55.4	60.0	64.5	50.9	49.7	51.3	54.1	56.1
Florida	258.3	344.8	442.6	471.6	491.5	303.7	350.6	420.2	438.6	446.5
Georgia	141.4	203.5	276.5	295.5	299.9	164.8	206.4	261.5	274.9	273.9
Hawaii	32.3	37.2	40.7	42.5	43.7	38.1	37.9	38.0	38.9	38.8
Idaho	17.7	27.2	34.6	36.8	36.9	20.0	27.4	34.7	37.1	36.8
Illinois	275.8	359.5	440.9	466.3	475.5	317.9	364.1	424.9	441.9	441.8
Indiana.	110.8	148.4	181.3	189.8	189.9	127.0	150.0	175.4	181.5	178.2
Iowa	55.8	71.7	85.5	89.7	90.9	63.4	73.1	84.4	87.5	87.0
Kansas	51.5	64.1	80.2	84.5	87.2	59.8	65.6	77.5	79.9	80.7
Kentucky	67.9	91.5	112.4	117.2	120.3	77.5	92.8	106.6	109.5	110.1
Louisiana	94.9	112.2	133.9	145.0	148.7	108.0	116.5	129.5	125.7	125.3
Maine.	23.5	28.0	34.1	36.3	37.4	27.8	28.3	32.4	33.7	34.0
Maryland	115.0	139.5	173.8	185.0	195.0	137.1	142.1	164.0	170.7	175.3
Massachusetts.	160.0	197.5	257.8	283.1	287.8	187.2	200.5	247.4	266.8	265.7
Michigan.	190.8	254.2	312.1	323.7	320.5	225.1	258.3	299.5	306.4	297.5
Minnesota.	100.4	131.8	171.5	186.1	188.1	116.6	133.8	165.6	176.8	175.4
Mississippi.	39.2	54.6	64.2	66.2	67.1	44.9	55.4	61.8	62.3	61.5
Missouri	104.8	139.5	168.9	177.1	181.5	122.8	141.9	161.4	166.7	167.4
Montana.	13.4	17.5	20.6	21.7	22.6	15.5	17.9	19.9	20.5	20.7
Nebraska	33.5	44.1	53.5	55.6	57.0	38.6	45.2	52.0	53.5	53.6
Nevada	31.6	49.4	69.5	75.5	79.2	37.1	50.1	64.4	68.2	69.5
New Hampshire	23.9	32.4	43.4	47.4	47.2	27.3	32.6	42.5	46.1	45.3
New Jersey.	217.0	271.4	332.2	357.5	365.4	253.6	275.0	316.0	332.9	332.9
New Mexico	27.2	42.2	49.2	52.6	55.4	29.4	42.7	50.3	52.4	54.9
New York	502.2	597.6	743.9	798.4	826.5	593.4	609.1	717.7	756.6	766.5
North Carolina	141.1	194.6	260.6	272.9	275.6	162.6	197.5	242.9	249.8	246.3
North Dakota	11.5	14.5	17.1	18.6	19.0	13.2	15.0	16.8	17.8	17.8
Ohio	230.0	295.7	357.4	370.6	373.7	265.9	299.2	345.0	352.7	349.3
Oklahoma.	57.8	70.0	85.4	90.9	93.9	66.1	71.8	83.0	85.1	85.9
Oregon.	57.8	81.1	110.4	121.4	120.1	66.5	81.3	111.4	124.8	124.8
Pennsylvania.	249.9	318.8	380.2	399.5	408.4	291.5	322.9	362.5	374.0	374.5
Rhode Island.	21.6	25.7	31.9	36.1	36.9	25.5	26.2	30.1	33.3	33.5
South Carolina	66.1	86.9	106.8	112.2	115.2	76.0	87.8	102.4	106.1	106.5
South Dakota	13.0	18.3	21.7	23.5	24.3	15.1	18.7	21.5	22.9	23.2
Tennessee	95.0	136.8	170.8	177.4	182.5	110.5	138.6	162.7	166.6	168.4
Texas.	388.1	513.9	678.8	738.3	763.9	439.5	527.7	660.5	688.5	698.5
Utah	31.4	46.3	62.6	68.4	70.4	36.3	47.0	59.7	63.6	63.9
Vermont	11.8	14.0	17.2	18.1	19.1	13.4	14.1	16.6	17.4	18.0
Virginia.	148.2	189.0	241.5	260.8	273.1	174.5	192.5	224.5	236.9	241.5
Washington.	115.5	151.3	208.5	218.1	223.0	136.6	154.0	198.3	202.8	202.5
West Virginia.	28.3	36.3	40.5	40.9	42.4	31.8	36.6	39.1	38.7	39.0
Wisconsin	100.4	133.7	164.9	173.0	177.4	115.3	135.2	160.2	166.0	167.3
Wyoming	13.4	14.9	17.0	19.1	20.4	14.3	15.6	16.9	17.5	18.3

[1] For chained (1996) dollar estimates, states will not add to U.S. total.

Source: U.S. Bureau of Economic Analysis, *Survey of Current Business*, June 2003; and Internet site at <http://www.bea.doc.gov/bea /regional/gsp/> and <http://www.bea.doc.gov/bea/newsrel/gsp0503.pdf> (released 22 May 2003). Next update scheduled for December 2004.

No. 646. Gross State Product in Chained (1996) Dollars by Industry and State: 2001

[In billions of dollars (9,335.4 represents $9,335,400,000,000). For definition of gross state product or chained dollars, see text, this section. Industries based on 1987 Standard Industrial Classification]

State	Total [1]	Farms, forestry, fisheries [2]	Construction	Manufacturing	Transportation, public utilities	Wholesale trade	Retail trade	Finance, insurance, real estate	Services	Government [3]
United States.....	9,335.4	163.9	371.9	1,490.3	780.5	748.7	951.2	1,843.6	1,843.3	1,047.4
Alabama............	112.0	2.9	4.6	21.9	9.6	8.7	12.8	15.4	18.3	16.6
Alaska.............	24.5	0.4	1.1	0.9	4.3	0.9	2.0	2.8	3.2	4.8
Arizona............	153.7	2.9	7.5	29.4	10.6	11.6	18.0	27.3	28.5	17.4
Arkansas...........	63.7	2.9	2.6	13.3	6.6	5.0	8.3	7.2	9.6	7.6
California.........	1,260.0	27.5	44.7	184.0	89.1	98.3	129.7	279.9	270.5	130.6
Colorado...........	159.3	3.2	9.2	15.3	19.5	11.8	17.3	28.3	34.6	17.7
Connecticut........	153.0	1.1	4.6	25.4	9.4	11.0	13.2	46.0	29.6	12.8
Delaware...........	35.7	0.5	1.2	4.8	1.8	1.7	2.7	14.9	5.2	2.9
District of Columbia	56.1	-	0.4	0.7	3.2	0.8	1.8	9.9	19.7	19.7
Florida............	446.5	8.5	20.9	30.3	37.9	41.1	57.2	95.3	104.0	51.4
Georgia	273.9	5.0	11.9	39.9	32.9	29.3	29.0	42.8	50.7	32.0
Hawaii.............	38.8	0.6	1.5	1.0	3.9	1.8	5.0	8.9	8.1	8.1
Idaho..............	36.8	2.7	2.0	9.1	2.7	2.5	4.0	3.9	5.5	4.5
Illinois	441.8	4.9	18.3	73.7	38.1	40.8	39.8	93.8	89.6	41.6
Indiana............	178.2	3.0	7.7	53.7	13.0	12.8	17.9	23.6	28.4	17.2
Iowa	87.0	4.6	3.1	20.8	7.0	6.9	8.4	12.6	13.4	9.7
Kansas.............	80.7	3.1	3.1	13.3	10.9	7.2	8.7	10.1	12.9	10.3
Kentucky...........	110.1	3.1	4.4	27.9	9.2	8.2	11.6	12.2	16.7	14.3
Louisiana..........	125.3	1.5	5.0	15.3	11.8	8.7	12.8	17.0	20.6	15.0
Maine..............	34.0	0.7	1.3	5.2	2.3	2.4	4.6	6.2	6.6	4.6
Maryland...........	175.3	1.9	8.8	14.1	13.6	12.9	17.3	37.1	40.2	29.6
Massachusetts.......	265.7	1.5	10.5	38.5	15.4	21.4	23.2	66.6	66.3	22.3
Michigan...........	297.5	3.3	12.4	75.5	19.3	24.9	32.0	43.7	55.2	30.1
Minnesota..........	175.4	4.0	7.7	31.1	12.7	16.9	18.7	32.1	33.7	17.4
Mississippi........	61.5	2.3	2.4	12.0	5.9	4.3	7.5	7.0	9.9	9.9
Missouri...........	167.4	3.0	7.5	30.2	17.0	14.6	17.9	26.2	32.0	18.5
Montana............	20.7	1.1	1.0	1.4	2.3	1.5	2.4	2.8	4.0	3.3
Nebraska...........	53.6	3.7	2.1	7.4	5.9	4.8	5.1	7.7	9.6	7.0
Nevada	69.5	0.6	5.8	3.0	5.5	4.0	8.7	12.9	19.9	7.1
New Hampshire	45.3	0.4	1.8	9.5	2.6	3.7	5.0	10.3	8.4	3.3
New Jersey.........	332.9	2.0	12.2	40.3	31.7	37.2	29.6	80.7	69.1	30.8
New Mexico	54.9	1.6	1.9	13.9	3.9	2.4	5.1	6.4	8.4	8.6
New York	766.5	3.9	21.2	76.6	58.2	51.7	57.6	272.0	157.3	69.6
North Carolina.....	246.3	6.3	10.9	51.6	17.6	18.4	25.6	45.4	39.8	30.9
North Dakota.......	17.8	1.4	0.7	1.8	1.8	1.8	1.9	2.4	3.0	2.6
Ohio	349.3	4.0	12.8	83.8	24.3	29.2	38.0	57.6	60.9	36.7
Oklahoma...........	85.9	2.5	3.0	13.6	8.4	6.2	10.0	10.3	14.6	13.6
Oregon.............	124.8	3.5	4.6	48.0	7.2	9.3	10.3	15.3	14.6	13.6
Pennsylvania.......	374.5	4.5	14.3	71.2	32.7	27.9	37.8	68.1	80.0	35.6
Rhode Island.......	33.5	0.2	1.5	4.3	2.2	2.0	3.4	9.5	6.6	3.7
South Carolina.....	106.5	1.7	5.3	24.0	9.4	7.7	12.5	14.4	16.1	15.4
South Dakota	23.2	2.3	0.7	3.1	1.6	1.9	2.5	4.6	3.5	2.8
Tennessee	168.4	2.2	6.3	34.7	14.3	14.5	20.7	23.9	32.9	18.6
Texas..............	698.5	11.1	29.3	102.9	79.2	63.4	75.7	101.5	129.9	73.4
Utah...............	63.9	1.1	3.4	8.0	5.2	4.7	7.1	12.3	12.0	8.9
Vermont	18.0	0.5	0.7	3.7	1.3	1.2	2.0	3.1	3.6	2.2
Virginia...........	241.5	2.7	10.3	26.0	22.1	16.0	23.2	45.4	53.5	41.7
Washington.........	202.5	5.4	8.5	26.4	17.4	16.7	22.5	35.8	43.3	26.5
West Virginia......	39.0	0.4	1.7	5.1	4.2	2.5	4.4	4.3	6.9	6.1
Wisconsin..........	167.3	4.4	6.7	45.3	11.3	12.5	16.9	25.3	27.3	17.5
Wyoming............	18.3	0.6	0.8	1.4	2.4	0.9	1.5	2.0	2.0	2.4

- Represents zero.   [1] Includes mining not shown separately.   [2] Includes agricultural services.   [3] Includes Federal civilian and military and state and local government.   [4] States will not add to U.S. total as chained-dollar estimates are usually not additive.

Source: U.S. Bureau of Economic Analysis, *Survey of Current Business*, June 2003; and Internet site at <http://www.bea.doc.gov/bea /regional/gsp/> and <http://www.bea.doc.gov/bea/newsrel/gsp0503.pdf> (released 22 May 2003). Next update scheduled for December 2004.

No. 647. Relation of GDP, GNP, Net National Product, National Income, Personal Income, Disposable Personal Income, and Personal Saving: 1990 to 2003

[In billions of dollars (5,803.1 represents $5,803,100,000,000). For definitions, see text, this section]

Item	1990	1995	1998	1999	2000	2001	2002	2003
Gross domestic product	5,803.1	7,397.7	8,747.0	9,268.4	9,817.0	10,100.8	10,480.8	10,987.9
Plus: Income receipts from the rest of the world [1]	189.1	233.9	287.1	320.8	382.7	319.0	299.1	317.3
Less: Income payments to the rest of the world [2]	154.3	198.1	265.8	287.0	343.7	283.8	277.6	273.6
Equals: Gross national product.	5,837.9	7,433.4	8,768.3	9,302.2	9,855.9	10,135.9	10,502.3	11,031.6
Less: Consumption of fixed capital	682.5	878.4	1,030.2	1,101.3	1,187.8	1,266.9	1,288.6	1,310.9
Equals: Net national product	5,155.4	6,555.1	7,738.2	8,200.9	8,668.1	8,869.0	9,213.7	9,720.7
Less: Statistical discrepancy	66.2	101.2	-14.6	-35.7	-127.2	-112.2	-77.2	12.9
Equals: National income.	5,089.1	6,453.9	7,752.8	8,236.7	8,795.2	8,981.2	9,290.8	9,707.8
Less: Corporate profits [3]	437.8	696.7	801.6	851.3	817.9	770.4	904.2	1,069.9
Taxes on production and imports less subsidies	398.7	524.2	604.4	629.8	664.6	674.5	721.8	740.4
Contributions for government social insurance	410.1	532.8	624.2	661.4	702.7	728.5	750.3	776.8
Net interest and miscellaneous payments on assets	442.2	367.1	487.1	495.4	559.0	568.4	582.4	583.2
Business current transfer payments (net)	39.4	46.9	64.7	67.4	87.1	92.5	89.8	95.2
Current surplus of government enterprises	1.6	11.4	10.3	10.1	5.3	1.2	2.8	5.0
Wage accruals less disbursements . . .	0.1	16.4	-0.7	5.2	-	-	-	-
Plus: Personal income receipts on assets	924.0	1,016.4	1,283.2	1,264.2	1,387.0	1,374.9	1,378.5	1,393.3
Personal current transfer receipts	595.2	877.4	978.6	1,022.1	1,084.0	1,192.6	1,292.2	1,377.5
Equals: Personal income	4,878.6	6,152.3	7,423.0	7,802.4	8,429.7	8,713.1	8,910.3	9,208.0
Less: Personal current taxes	592.8	744.1	1,027.0	1,107.5	1,235.7	1,243.7	1,053.1	991.4
Equals: Disposable personal income. .	4,285.8	5,408.2	6,395.9	6,695.0	7,194.0	7,469.4	7,857.2	8,216.5
Less: Personal outlays	3,986.4	5,157.3	6,119.1	6,536.4	7,025.6	7,342.2	7,674.0	8,043.0
Equals: Personal saving	299.4	250.9	276.8	158.6	168.5	127.2	183.2	173.5

- Represents zero or rounds to zero. [1] Consists largely of receipts by U.S. residents of interest and dividends and reinvested earnings of foreign affiliates of U.S. corporations. [2] Consists largely of payments to foreign residents of interest and dividends and reinvested earnings of U.S. affiliates of foreign corporations. [3] With inventory valuation and capital consumption adjustments.

Source: U.S. Bureau of Economic Analysis, *National Income and Product Accounts, 1929-2000*; and *Survey of Current Business*, June 2004. See also <http://www.bea.doc.gov/bea/dn/nipaweb/SelectTable.asp?Selected=N> (released as 27 May 2004).

No. 648. Selected Per Capita Income and Product Measures in Current and Real (2000) Dollars: 1960 to 2003

[In dollars. Based on U.S. Census Bureau estimated population including Armed Forces abroad; based on quarterly averages. For explanation of chained dollars, see text, this section]

Year	Current dollars					Chained (2000) dollars				
	Gross domestic product	Gross national product	Personal income	Disposable personal income	Personal consumption expenditures	Gross domestic product	Gross national product	Disposable personal income	Personal consumption expenditures
1960	2,912	2,929	2,277	2,022	1,835	13,840	13,938	9,735	8,837
1965	3,700	3,727	2,860	2,563	2,283	16,420	16,554	11,594	10,331
1970	5,064	5,095	4,090	3,587	3,162	18,391	18,520	13,563	11,955
1975	7,586	7,646	6,181	5,498	4,789	19,961	20,133	15,291	13,320
1980	12,249	12,400	10,134	8,822	7,716	22,666	22,956	16,940	14,816
1981	13,601	13,745	11,266	9,765	8,439	23,007	23,259	17,217	14,879
1982	14,017	14,174	11,951	10,426	8,945	22,346	22,607	17,418	14,944
1983	15,092	15,251	12,635	11,131	9,775	23,146	23,396	17,828	15,656
1984	16,638	16,792	13,915	12,319	10,589	24,593	24,828	19,011	16,343
1985	17,695	17,806	14,787	13,037	11,406	25,382	25,544	19,476	17,040
1986	18,542	18,616	15,466	13,649	12,048	26,024	26,137	19,906	17,570
1987	19,517	19,590	16,255	14,241	12,766	26,664	26,770	20,072	17,994
1988	20,827	20,923	17,358	15,297	13,685	27,514	27,647	20,740	18,554
1989	22,169	22,275	18,545	16,257	14,546	28,221	28,358	21,120	18,898
1990	23,195	23,335	19,500	17,131	15,349	28,429	28,600	21,281	19,067
1991	23,650	23,770	19,923	17,609	15,722	28,007	28,150	21,109	18,848
1992	24,668	24,783	20,870	18,494	16,485	28,556	28,693	21,548	19,208
1993	25,578	25,700	21,356	18,872	17,204	28,940	29,079	21,493	19,593
1994	26,844	26,944	22,176	19,555	18,004	29,741	29,850	21,812	20,082
1995	27,749	27,884	23,078	20,287	18,665	30,128	30,271	22,153	20,382
1996	28,982	29,112	24,176	21,091	19,490	30,881	31,015	22,546	20,835
1997	30,424	30,544	25,334	21,940	20,323	31,886	32,010	23,065	21,365
1998	31,674	31,752	26,880	23,161	21,291	32,912	32,912	24,131	22,183
1999	33,181	33,302	27,933	23,968	22,491	33,904	34,027	24,564	23,050
2000	34,760	34,897	29,848	25,472	23,863	34,760	34,897	25,472	23,863
2001	35,397	35,520	30,534	26,115	24,690	34,576	34,698	25,653	24,196
2002	36,361	36,436	30,913	27,259	25,622	34,981	35,057	26,355	24,773
2003	37,748	37,898	31,633	28,227	26,650	35,721	35,864	26,800	25,303

Source: U.S. Bureau of Economic Analysis, *National Income and Product Accounts, 1929-2000*; and *Survey of Current Business*, May 2004. See also <http://www.bea.doc.gov/bea/dn/nipaweb/SelectTable.asp?Selected=N> (released as 30 April 2004).

No. 649. Personal Consumption Expenditures in Current and Real (2000) Dollars by Type: 1990 to 2002

[In billions of dollars (3,839.9 represents $3,839,900,000,000). For definition of "chained" dollars, see text, this section]

Expenditure	Current dollars				Chained (2000) dollars			
	1990	2000	2001	2002	1990	2000	2001	2002
Total expenditures [1]	3,839.9	6,739.4	7,045.4	7,385.3	4,770.3	6,739.4	6,904.6	7,140.4
Food and tobacco [1]	677.8	1,003.7	1,047.8	1,094.8	867.1	1,003.7	1,014.3	1,034.4
Food purchased for off-premise consumption	401.6	566.7	592.7	614.8	485.7	566.7	576.2	589.1
Purchased meals and beverages [2]	227.7	348.8	362.0	380.5	289.6	348.8	351.0	359.1
Tobacco products	41.0	78.5	83.2	89.3	87.7	78.5	77.3	76.4
Clothing, accessories, and jewelry [1]	261.5	397.0	396.8	405.5	247.7	397.0	400.6	418.0
Shoes	31.5	47.0	47.6	49.1	30.4	47.0	47.9	50.1
Clothing	172.4	250.4	249.5	255.0	157.7	250.4	255.2	268.7
Jewelry and watches	30.3	50.6	49.1	51.0	26.5	50.6	49.1	52.4
Personal care	56.9	93.4	94.3	97.2	68.5	93.4	92.4	94.5
Housing [1]	597.9	1,006.5	1,073.7	1,144.6	802.2	1,006.5	1,033.9	1,061.9
Owner-occupied nonfarm dwellings-space rent	412.8	712.2	768.9	821.7	551.6	712.2	740.4	760.2
Tenant-occupied nonfarm dwellings-space rent	150.7	227.5	241.1	259.0	199.9	227.5	231.0	239.1
Household operation [1]	433.3	719.3	738.4	748.3	485.0	719.3	722.7	742.1
Furniture [3]	38.4	67.6	67.2	69.8	41.8	67.6	68.4	72.4
Semidurable house furnishings [4]	22.5	36.5	36.5	37.4	20.1	36.5	37.3	39.4
Cleaning and polishing preparations	38.9	61.6	64.3	66.8	46.2	61.6	62.0	64.0
Household utilities	141.1	209.9	223.8	220.3	174.5	209.9	207.1	211.4
Electricity	74.2	102.3	107.3	111.3	81.1	102.3	100.2	105.0
Gas	26.8	41.0	48.9	41.0	36.6	41.0	40.9	40.3
Water and other sanitary services	27.1	50.8	52.2	53.4	41.1	50.8	50.7	50.3
Fuel oil and coal	12.9	15.8	15.4	14.6	16.7	15.8	15.2	15.9
Telephone and telegraph	60.5	125.1	128.7	129.9	58.3	125.1	131.4	132.4
Medical care [1]	635.1	1,218.3	1,322.8	1,436.6	905.9	1,218.3	1,274.8	1,347.7
Drug preparations and sundries [5]	65.4	169.4	192.6	213.1	90.1	169.4	184.2	195.6
Physicians	138.6	236.8	256.8	275.9	194.7	236.8	249.7	268.3
Dentists	32.4	61.8	66.8	72.6	53.5	61.8	64.2	66.8
Hospitals and nursing homes [6]	270.9	482.6	521.7	568.0	386.4	482.6	500.5	525.4
Health insurance	43.4	84.0	89.3	95.1	70.1	84.0	86.5	90.9
Medical care [7]	31.8	68.4	73.0	78.5	52.8	68.4	70.4	73.6
Personal business [1]	250.9	539.1	539.0	564.0	330.0	539.1	539.8	549.5
Expense of handling life insurance [8]	53.2	96.1	94.6	94.6	86.2	96.1	91.7	87.9
Legal services	40.9	63.9	68.0	70.7	62.2	63.9	64.6	63.4
Funeral and burial expenses	9.5	14.0	14.6	14.2	15.0	14.0	14.1	13.1
Transportation [1]	471.7	853.4	874.0	876.7	590.1	853.4	874.6	891.1
User-operated transportation [1]	434.7	793.8	819.0	823.0	546.6	793.8	816.9	832.1
New autos	89.7	103.6	103.3	101.1	102.5	103.6	103.8	102.8
Net purchases of used autos	29.3	60.7	59.3	56.1	42.4	60.7	58.6	57.2
Tires, tubes, accessories, etc.	29.9	49.0	49.1	49.7	29.3	49.0	47.9	47.7
Repair, greasing, washing, parking, storage, rental, and leasing	84.9	183.5	189.1	187.1	109.4	183.5	183.0	176.5
Gasoline and oil	111.2	175.7	173.1	165.8	141.8	175.7	179.6	183.3
Purchased local transportation [1]	8.4	12.2	12.7	12.9	10.9	12.2	12.3	12.3
Mass transit systems	5.8	9.1	9.5	9.6	7.5	9.1	9.2	9.1
Taxicab	2.6	3.1	3.2	3.3	3.4	3.1	3.1	3.2
Purchased intercity transportation [1]	28.6	47.4	42.3	40.8	32.5	47.4	45.2	46.8
Railway (commutation)	0.6	0.5	0.6	0.6	0.8	0.5	0.5	0.5
Bus	1.3	2.4	2.4	2.3	1.5	2.4	2.3	2.2
Airline	22.7	36.7	32.1	30.5	24.8	36.7	35.2	36.7
Recreation [1][9]	290.2	585.7	603.4	633.9	276.5	585.7	611.2	651.3
Magazines, newspapers, and sheet music	21.6	35.0	34.5	34.2	29.3	35.0	33.9	32.9
Nondurable toys and sport supplies	32.8	56.6	58.0	59.7	28.3	56.6	60.4	65.9
Video and audio products, including musical instruments and computer goods	53.0	116.6	115.5	120.8	18.6	116.6	132.1	156.2
Computers, peripherals, and software	8.9	43.8	42.0	44.2				
Education and research	83.7	163.8	176.3	187.9	125.6	163.8	168.4	172.0
Higher education	43.8	86.4	93.2	99.7	69.6	86.4	88.9	90.5
Religious and welfare activities	88.7	172.3	186.1	202.0	121.2	172.3	179.2	188.3
Foreign travel and other, net [1]	-7.7	-13.0	-7.2	-6.3	-13.1	-13.0	-7.4	-10.1
Foreign travel by U.S. residents	42.7	84.4	80.7	77.4	53.3	84.4	79.6	72.8
Expenditures abroad by U.S. residents	3.6	4.6	5.1	5.7	3.6	4.6	5.1	5.4
Less: Expenditures in the United States by nonresidents	53.0	100.7	91.5	87.9	68.8	100.7	90.6	86.8

[1] Includes other expenditures not shown separately. [2] Consists of purchases (including tips) of meals and beverages from retail, service, and amusement establishments; hotels; dining and buffet cars; schools; school fraternities; institutions; clubs; and industrial lunch rooms. Includes meals and beverages consumed both on and off-premise. [3] Includes mattresses and bedsprings. [4] Consists largely of textile house furnishings including piece goods allocated to house furnishing use. Also includes lamp shades, brooms, and brushes. [5] Excludes drug preparations and related products dispensed by physicians, hospitals, and other medical services. [6] Consists of (1) current expenditures (including consumption of fixed capital) of nonprofit hospitals and nursing homes and (2) payments by patients to proprietary and government hospitals and nursing homes. [7] Consists of (1) commercial insurance carriers and (2) administrative expenses (including consumption of fixed capital) of Blue Cross and Blue Shield plans and of other independent prepaid and self-insured health plans. [8] Consists of (1) operating expenses of life insurance carriers and private noninsured pension plans and (2) premiums less benefits and dividends of fraternal benefit societies. Excludes expenses allocated by commercial carriers to accident and health insurance. [9] For additional details, see Table 1228.

Source: U.S. Bureau of Economic Analysis, *Survey of Current Business*, January 2004. See also <http://www.bea.doc.gov/bea/dn/nipaweb/SelectTable.asp?Selected=N> (released as 16 December 2003).

No. 650. Personal Income and Its Disposition: 1990 to 2003

[In billions of dollars (4,878.6 represents $4,878,600,000,000), except as indicated. For definition of personal income and chained dollars, see text, this section]

Item	1990	1995	1998	1999	2000	2001	2002	2003
Personal income	**4,878.6**	**6,152.3**	**7,423.0**	**7,802.4**	**8,429.7**	**8,713.1**	**8,910.3**	**9,208.0**
Compensation of employees, received.	3,338.2	4,177.0	5,020.1	5,352.0	5,782.7	5,940.4	6,019.1	6,203.0
Wage and salary disbursements . . .	2,754.0	3,419.3	4,183.4	4,466.3	4,829.2	4,942.9	4,974.6	5,100.2
Supplements to wages and salaries .	584.2	757.7	836.7	885.7	953.4	997.6	1,044.5	1,102.8
Proprietors' income [1]	380.6	492.1	627.8	678.3	728.4	770.6	797.7	846.9
Farm	31.9	22.7	29.4	28.6	22.7	25.0	14.3	19.5
Nonfarm . . . . [1] . .	348.7	469.5	598.4	649.7	705.7	745.6	783.4	827.4
Rental income of persons [1]	50.7	122.1	137.5	147.3	150.3	163.1	173.0	164.2
Personal income receipts on assets . .	924.0	1,016.4	1,283.2	1,264.2	1,387.0	1,374.9	1,378.5	1,393.3
Personal interest income	755.2	763.2	933.2	928.6	1,011.0	1,003.7	982.4	964.6
Personal dividend income	168.8	253.2	349.9	335.6	376.1	371.2	396.2	428.7
Personal current transfer receipts	595.2	877.4	978.6	1,022.1	1,084.0	1,192.6	1,292.2	1,377.5
Government social benefits to persons.	573.1	858.4	952.6	988.0	1,041.6	1,142.6	1,249.5	1,331.6
Old-age, survivors, disability, and health insurance benefits	351.8	506.8	575.1	588.9	620.8	668.4	710.3	743.7
Other current transfer receipts, from business (net)	22.2	19.0	26.0	34.1	42.4	49.9	42.6	45.9
Less: Contributions for government social insurance.	410.1	532.8	624.2	661.4	702.7	728.5	750.3	776.8
Less: Personal current taxes	*592.8*	*744.1*	*1,027.0*	*1,107.5*	*1,235.7*	*1,243.7*	*1,053.1*	*991.4*
Equals: Disposable personal income. .	**4,285.8**	**5,408.2**	**6,395.9**	**6,695.0**	**7,194.0**	**7,469.4**	**7,857.2**	**8,216.5**
Less: Personal outlays	*3,986.4*	*5,157.3*	*6,119.1*	*6,536.4*	*7,025.6*	*7,342.2*	*7,674.0*	*8,043.0*
Personal consumption expenditures . .	3,839.9	4,975.8	5,879.5	6,282.5	6,739.4	7,045.4	7,385.3	7,757.4
Personal interest payments	116.1	132.7	174.5	181.0	204.7	209.1	194.7	185.4
Personal current transfer payments. . .	30.4	48.9	65.2	73.0	81.5	87.7	94.0	100.2
Equals: Personal saving.	**299.4**	**250.9**	**276.8**	**158.6**	**168.5**	**127.2**	**183.2**	**173.5**
Personal saving as a percentage of disposable personal income	7.0	4.6	4.3	2.4	2.3	1.7	2.3	2.1
Addenda: Disposable personal income: Total, billions of chained (2000) dollars.	5,324.2	5,905.7	6,663.9	6,861.3	7,194.0	7,320.2	7,596.7	7,801.1
Per capita: Current dollars.	17,131	20,287	23,161	23,968	25,472	26,175	27,259	28,227
Chained (2000) dollars	21,281	22,153	24,131	24,564	25,472	25,653	26,355	26,800

[1] With inventory valuation adjustments and capital consumption adjustment.

Source: U.S. Bureau of Economic Analysis, *National Income and Product Accounts, 1929-2000*; and *Survey of Current Business,* June 2004. See also <http://www.bea.doc.gov/bea/dn/nipaweb/SelectTable.asp?Selected=N> (released as 27 May 2004).

No. 651. Gross Saving and Investment: 1990 to 2003

[In billions of dollars (940.4 represents $940,400,000,000)]

Item	1990	1995	1998	1999	2000	2001	2002	2003
Gross saving.	**940.4**	**1,184.5**	**1,598.7**	**1,674.3**	**1,770.5**	**1,658.0**	**1,539.4**	**1,484.9**
Net saving	258.0	306.2	568.6	573.0	582.7	391.1	250.8	174.0
Net private saving.	422.7	491.1	477.8	419.0	343.3	323.2	494.0	587.6
Personal saving	299.4	250.9	276.8	158.6	168.5	127.2	183.2	173.5
Undistributed corporate profits with IVA and CCA [1]	123.3	223.8	201.7	255.3	174.8	196.0	310.8	414.1
Wage accruals less disbursements	0.0	16.4	-0.7	5.2	-	-	-	-
Net government saving	-164.8	-184.9	90.8	154.0	239.4	67.8	-243.3	-413.6
Federal	-172.0	-197.0	38.8	103.6	189.5	50.5	-240.0	-413.0
State and local	7.2	12.0	52.0	50.4	50.0	17.3	-3.2	-0.6
Consumption of fixed capital.	682.5	878.4	1,030.2	1,101.3	1,187.8	1,266.9	1,288.6	1,310.9
Private	551.6	713.4	851.2	914.3	990.8	1,061.0	1,077.8	1,092.7
Domestic business.	466.4	600.2	718.3	769.8	836.1	893.6	902.6	908.2
Households and institutions	85.1	113.2	132.9	144.5	154.8	167.4	175.2	184.5
Government.	130.9	165.0	179.0	187.0	197.0	205.9	210.8	218.2
Federal	67.9	81.9	82.8	84.8	87.2	88.2	89.1	90.9
State and local	63.0	83.1	96.2	102.1	109.8	117.7	121.7	127.3
Gross domestic investment, capital account transactions, and net lending .	**1,006.7**	**1,285.7**	**1,584.1**	**1,638.5**	**1,643.3**	**1,545.8**	**1,462.2**	**1,497.8**
Gross domestic investment	1,076.7	1,376.7	1,771.5	1,912.4	2,040.0	1,924.2	1,926.3	2,016.8
Gross private domestic investment.	861.0	1,144.0	1,509.1	1,625.7	1,735.5	1,607.2	1,589.2	1,670.6
Gross government investment	215.7	232.7	262.4	286.8	304.5	317.0	337.1	346.3
Capital account transactions (net)	6.6	0.9	0.7	4.8	0.8	1.1	1.3	1.5
Net lending or net borrowing	-76.6	-91.9	-188.1	-278.7	-397.4	-379.5	-465.4	-520.5
Statistical discrepancy	66.2	101.2	-14.6	-35.7	-127.2	-112.2	-77.2	12.9
Addenda:								
Gross private saving	974.3	1,204.5	1,328.9	1,333.3	1,334.1	1,384.3	1,571.8	1,680.2
Gross government saving.	-33.8	-19.9	269.8	341.0	436.4	273.7	-32.4	-195.4
Federal	-104.1	-115.1	121.6	188.5	276.6	138.8	-150.9	-322.1
State and local	70.3	95.2	148.2	152.5	159.8	135.0	118.5	126.8
Net domestic investment	394.2	498.4	741.3	811.2	852.1	657.3	637.7	705.9
Gross saving as a percentage of gross national income	16.3	16.2	18.2	17.9	17.7	16.2	14.6	13.5
Net saving as a percentage of gross national income	4.5	4.2	6.5	6.1	5.8	3.8	2.4	1.6

- Represents or rounds to zero. [1] Inventory valuation adjustment and capital consumption adjustment.

Source: U.S. Bureau of Economic Analysis, *National Income and Product Accounts, 1929-2000*; and *Survey of Current Business,* June 2004. See also <http://www.bea.doc.gov/bea/dn/nipaweb/SelectTable.asp?Selected=N> (released as 27 May 2004).

No. 652. Personal Income in Current and Constant (2000) Dollars by State: 1990 to 2003

[In billions of dollars (4,861.9 represents $4,861,900,000,000). Represents a measure of income received from all sources during the calendar year by residents of each state. Data exclude federal employees overseas and U.S. residents employed by private U.S. firms on temporary foreign assignment. Totals may differ from those in Tables 647, 648, and 650]

State	Current dollars					Constant (2000) dollars [1]				
	1990	2000	2001	2002	2003, prel.	1990	2000	2001	2002	2003, prel.
United States ..	4,861.9	8,422.1	8,703.0	8,900.0	9,199.0	6,039.9	8,422.1	8,529.2	8,604.9	8,894.0
Alabama	63.7	105.8	111.0	114.4	118.5	79.1	105.8	108.8	110.6	114.6
Alaska	12.6	18.7	20.1	21.0	21.8	15.7	18.7	19.7	20.3	21.1
Arizona	62.6	132.6	138.0	143.4	149.8	77.8	132.6	135.3	138.7	144.8
Arkansas	34.1	58.7	62.1	63.7	66.2	42.3	58.7	60.9	61.6	64.0
California	648.3	1,103.8	1,135.8	1,154.7	1,197.6	805.3	1,103.8	1,113.2	1,116.4	1,157.8
Colorado	64.7	144.4	150.6	151.8	156.0	80.4	144.4	147.6	146.8	150.8
Connecticut	87.3	141.6	146.1	146.9	150.4	108.4	141.6	143.1	142.0	145.4
Delaware	14.3	24.3	25.1	25.9	26.8	17.8	24.3	24.6	25.0	25.9
District of Columbia ...	16.0	23.1	25.9	26.6	27.2	19.9	23.1	25.4	25.8	26.3
Florida	255.0	457.5	478.3	496.7	518.2	316.8	457.5	468.8	480.2	501.0
Georgia	114.6	230.4	239.7	246.2	255.7	142.4	230.4	234.9	238.1	247.2
Hawaii	24.7	34.5	35.1	37.1	38.9	30.7	34.5	34.4	35.8	37.6
Idaho	15.9	31.3	33.0	34.2	35.4	19.8	31.3	32.3	33.1	34.2
Illinois	238.5	400.4	410.3	416.0	426.3	296.3	400.4	402.1	402.2	412.2
Indiana	97.2	165.3	169.2	172.6	178.3	120.8	165.3	165.8	166.9	172.4
Iowa	48.4	77.8	80.2	82.5	85.5	60.1	77.8	78.6	79.7	82.7
Kansas	44.9	74.6	76.9	78.4	81.5	55.7	74.6	75.4	75.8	78.8
Kentucky	57.0	98.8	101.5	104.3	108.1	70.8	98.8	99.5	100.8	104.5
Louisiana	64.1	103.2	109.5	113.2	117.4	79.6	103.2	107.3	109.5	113.5
Maine	21.4	33.2	34.9	36.3	37.6	26.6	33.2	34.2	35.1	36.4
Maryland	109.7	182.0	190.3	197.9	205.7	136.3	182.0	186.5	191.3	198.8
Massachusetts	138.8	240.2	249.2	251.0	256.1	172.4	240.2	244.3	242.7	247.7
Michigan	176.2	294.2	295.1	299.4	306.8	218.9	294.2	289.3	289.5	296.6
Minnesota	87.3	158.0	163.1	167.4	174.3	108.5	158.0	159.9	161.9	168.5
Mississippi	33.8	59.8	62.8	64.6	67.6	41.9	59.8	61.5	62.5	65.3
Missouri	90.4	152.7	157.4	161.6	166.9	112.3	152.7	154.3	156.3	161.3
Montana	12.4	20.7	21.8	22.6	23.8	15.4	20.7	21.3	21.9	23.0
Nebraska	28.4	47.3	49.4	50.4	53.5	35.3	47.3	48.4	48.7	51.7
Nevada	24.8	61.4	63.6	66.2	70.1	30.9	61.4	62.3	64.0	67.7
New Hampshire	22.8	41.4	42.5	43.3	44.7	28.3	41.4	41.7	41.9	43.2
New Jersey	190.8	323.6	332.3	338.4	349.2	237.0	323.6	325.7	327.2	337.6
New Mexico	22.7	40.3	43.8	46.0	47.9	28.2	40.3	42.9	44.4	46.3
New York	423.9	663.0	679.6	685.1	701.9	526.6	663.0	666.0	662.4	678.6
North Carolina	114.9	218.7	225.4	230.8	237.4	142.8	218.7	220.9	223.1	229.5
North Dakota	10.2	16.1	16.4	17.0	18.5	12.6	16.1	16.1	16.5	17.9
Ohio	203.6	320.5	325.9	333.1	342.4	253.0	320.5	319.4	322.0	331.1
Oklahoma	51.0	84.3	88.2	90.5	93.6	63.3	84.3	86.5	87.5	90.5
Oregon	51.5	96.4	99.0	101.4	104.4	64.0	96.4	97.0	98.0	101.0
Pennsylvania	234.3	364.8	372.9	383.6	395.7	291.1	364.8	365.4	370.9	382.6
Rhode Island	20.1	30.7	31.9	33.0	34.3	25.0	30.7	31.2	31.9	33.2
South Carolina	55.6	98.3	101.8	104.7	108.4	69.1	98.3	99.7	101.2	104.8
South Dakota	11.3	19.4	20.4	20.5	22.3	14.0	19.4	20.0	19.8	21.6
Tennessee	81.7	148.8	154.7	159.9	166.2	101.5	148.8	151.6	154.6	160.7
Texas	297.1	593.1	617.7	631.2	649.7	369.1	593.1	605.3	610.3	628.1
Utah	25.8	53.6	55.6	57.1	58.7	32.1	53.6	54.5	55.2	56.8
Vermont	10.1	16.9	17.8	18.3	19.0	12.5	16.9	17.4	17.7	18.4
Virginia	127.1	220.8	232.5	239.0	248.7	157.9	220.8	227.9	231.1	240.5
Washington	97.4	187.9	193.4	198.0	204.4	121.0	187.9	189.5	191.5	197.6
West Virginia	26.0	39.6	41.6	42.9	44.1	32.3	39.6	40.7	41.5	42.7
Wisconsin	88.6	153.5	158.7	163.5	169.1	110.1	153.5	155.5	158.0	163.5
Wyoming	8.2	14.1	14.9	15.5	16.4	10.1	14.1	14.6	15.0	15.9

[1] Constant dollar estimates are computed by the U.S. Census Bureau using the national implicit price deflator for personal consumption expenditures from the Bureau of Economic Analysis. Any regional differences in the rate of inflation are not reflected in these constant dollar estimates.

Source: Except as noted, U.S. Bureau of Economic Analysis, *Survey of Current Business*, May 2004, and unpublished data. See also <http://www.bea.doc.gov/bea/regional/spi/> (released 27 April 2004).

No. 653. Personal Income Per Capita in Current and Constant (2000) Dollars by State: 1990 to 2003

[In dollars, except as indicated. 2003 preliminary. See headnote, Table 652]

State	Current dollars				Constant (2000) dollars [1]				Income rank	
	1990	2000	2002	2003	1990	2000	2002	2003	1990	2003
United States	19,477	29,847	30,906	31,632	24,196	29,847	29,881	30,033	(X)	(X)
Alabama	15,723	23,768	25,548	26,338	19,532	23,768	24,701	25,006	42	40
Alaska.	22,804	29,863	32,799	33,568	28,329	29,863	31,712	31,871	6	12
Arizona	17,005	25,661	26,360	26,838	21,125	25,661	25,486	25,481	35	38
Arkansas	14,460	21,926	23,556	24,289	17,963	21,926	22,775	23,061	49	49
California	21,638	32,466	32,989	33,749	26,881	32,466	31,895	32,043	8	9
Colorado	19,575	33,371	33,723	34,283	24,318	33,371	32,605	32,550	18	8
Connecticut	26,504	41,495	42,468	43,173	32,925	41,495	41,060	40,990	1	1
Delaware	21,422	30,871	32,090	32,810	26,612	30,871	31,026	31,151	9	14
District of Columbia	26,473	40,428	46,800	48,342	32,887	40,428	45,248	45,898	(X)	(X)
Florida	19,564	28,511	29,758	30,446	24,304	28,511	28,771	28,907	19	23
Georgia	17,603	27,989	28,821	29,442	21,868	27,989	27,865	27,953	29	27
Hawaii.	22,186	28,417	29,875	30,913	27,561	28,417	28,885	29,350	7	19
Idaho	15,724	24,076	25,476	25,911	19,534	24,076	24,631	24,601	41	45
Illinois	20,824	32,187	33,053	33,690	25,869	32,187	31,957	31,987	10	10
Indiana	17,491	27,134	28,032	28,783	21,729	27,134	27,103	27,328	30	35
Iowa	17,389	26,554	28,089	29,043	21,602	26,554	27,158	27,575	32	33
Kansas	18,085	27,694	28,905	29,935	22,467	27,694	27,947	28,422	22	26
Kentucky	15,437	24,414	25,494	26,252	19,177	24,414	24,649	24,925	44	41
Louisiana	15,173	23,080	25,296	26,100	18,849	23,080	24,457	24,780	45	43
Maine	17,376	25,972	28,038	28,831	21,586	25,972	27,108	27,373	33	34
Maryland	22,852	34,257	36,303	37,331	28,389	34,257	35,099	35,444	5	4
Massachusetts	23,043	37,756	39,085	39,815	28,626	37,756	37,789	37,802	4	3
Michigan	18,922	29,553	29,816	30,439	23,506	29,553	28,828	28,900	20	24
Minnesota	19,891	32,018	33,322	34,443	24,710	32,018	32,217	32,702	15	7
Mississippi	13,089	21,007	22,550	23,448	16,260	21,007	21,802	22,263	50	50
Missouri	17,627	27,243	28,512	29,252	21,898	27,243	27,567	27,773	28	30
Montana	15,448	22,932	24,831	25,920	19,191	22,932	24,008	24,610	43	44
Nebraska	17,983	27,627	29,182	30,758	22,340	27,627	28,215	29,203	26	21
Nevada	20,346	30,438	30,559	31,266	25,275	30,438	29,546	29,685	13	18
New Hampshire	20,512	33,398	33,985	34,702	25,482	33,398	32,858	32,948	11	6
New Jersey	24,572	38,372	39,461	40,427	30,525	38,372	38,153	38,383	2	2
New Mexico.............	14,924	22,134	24,823	25,541	18,540	22,134	24,000	24,250	46	46
New York.	23,523	34,900	35,805	36,574	29,222	34,900	34,618	34,725	3	5
North Carolina	17,246	27,071	27,785	28,235	21,423	27,071	26,864	26,808	34	37
North Dakota	15,943	25,109	26,852	29,204	19,806	25,109	25,962	27,728	39	32
Ohio	18,743	28,208	29,195	29,944	23,284	28,208	28,227	28,430	21	25
Oklahoma	16,187	24,410	25,936	26,656	20,109	24,410	25,076	25,308	37	39
Oregon	18,010	28,100	28,792	29,340	22,374	28,100	27,837	27,857	24	29
Pennsylvania	19,687	29,697	31,116	31,998	24,457	29,697	30,084	30,380	17	16
Rhode Island	20,006	29,216	30,859	31,916	24,853	29,216	29,836	30,302	14	17
South Carolina	15,894	24,426	25,502	26,132	19,745	24,426	24,657	24,811	40	42
South Dakota.	16,172	25,722	26,967	29,234	20,090	25,722	26,073	27,756	38	31
Tennessee..............	16,692	26,099	27,611	28,455	20,736	26,099	26,696	27,016	36	36
Texas	17,421	28,313	29,039	29,372	21,642	28,313	28,076	27,887	31	28
Utah	14,913	23,878	24,639	24,977	18,526	23,878	23,822	23,714	47	47
Vermont	17,876	27,680	29,764	30,740	22,207	27,680	28,777	29,186	27	22
Virginia	20,449	31,084	32,793	33,671	25,403	31,084	31,706	31,969	12	11
Washington	19,865	31,780	32,638	33,332	24,678	31,780	31,556	31,647	16	13
West Virginia	14,493	21,901	23,794	24,379	18,004	21,901	23,005	23,146	48	48
Wisconsin	18,072	28,573	30,050	30,898	22,451	28,573	29,054	29,336	23	20
Wyoming	18,002	28,463	31,021	32,808	22,364	28,463	29,993	31,149	25	15

X Not applicable.   [1] Constant dollar estimates are computed by the U.S. Census Bureau using the national implicit price deflator for personal consumption expenditures from the Bureau of Economic Analysis. Any regional differences in the rate of inflation are not reflected in these constant dollar estimates.

Source: U.S. Bureau of Economic Analysis, *Survey of Current Business,* May 2004, and unpublished data. See also <http://www.bea.doc.gov/bea/regional/spi/> (released 27 April 2004).

No. 654. Disposable Personal Income Per Capita in Current and Constant (2000) Dollars by State: 1990 to 2003

[In dollars, except percent. 2003 preliminary. Disposable personal income is the income available to persons for spending or saving; it is calculated as personal income less personal tax and nontax payments. See headnote, Table 652.]

State	Current dollars				Constant (2000) dollars [1]				Percent of U.S. average	
	1990	2000	2002	2003	1990	2000	2002	2003	1990	2003
United States	17,108	25,472	27,253	28,230	21,253	25,472	26,349	26,803	100.0	100.0
Alabama	14,047	21,050	23,086	24,028	17,450	21,050	22,321	22,813	82.1	85.1
Alaska.	20,147	26,422	29,641	30,641	25,028	26,422	28,658	29,092	117.8	108.5
Arizona	15,131	22,327	23,607	24,293	18,797	22,327	22,824	23,065	88.4	86.1
Arkansas	12,987	19,377	21,252	22,123	16,134	19,377	20,547	21,005	75.9	78.4
California	18,871	26,718	28,806	29,798	23,443	26,718	27,851	28,291	110.3	105.6
Colorado	17,201	28,236	29,577	30,507	21,368	28,236	28,596	28,965	100.5	108.1
Connecticut	23,121	33,388	35,541	36,726	28,723	33,388	34,363	34,869	135.1	130.1
Delaware.	18,474	26,279	27,972	28,960	22,950	26,279	27,045	27,496	108.0	102.6
District of Columbia	22,858	33,385	40,512	42,345	28,396	33,385	39,169	40,204	133.6	150.0
Florida	17,525	24,812	25,474	27,610	21,771	24,812	25,790	26,214	102.4	97.8
Georgia	15,464	24,054	25,474	26,356	19,211	24,054	24,629	25,023	90.4	93.4
Hawaii.	19,269	24,837	26,643	27,837	23,938	24,837	25,760	26,430	112.6	98.6
Idaho	13,988	20,960	22,989	23,584	17,377	20,960	22,227	22,392	81.8	83.5
Illinois	18,168	27,414	29,114	30,063	22,570	27,414	28,149	28,543	106.2	106.5
Indiana	15,368	23,649	24,979	25,929	19,091	23,649	24,151	24,618	89.8	91.8
Iowa	15,369	23,389	25,299	26,409	19,093	23,389	24,460	25,074	89.8	93.5
Kansas	15,971	24,048	25,761	27,033	19,840	24,048	24,907	25,666	93.4	95.8
Kentucky	13,621	21,346	22,668	23,567	16,921	21,346	21,916	22,376	79.6	83.5
Louisiana	13,689	20,576	22,952	23,889	17,006	20,576	22,191	22,681	80.0	84.6
Maine	15,387	22,491	24,931	25,900	19,115	22,491	24,104	24,591	89.9	91.7
Maryland	19,591	28,800	31,333	32,637	24,338	28,800	30,294	30,987	114.5	115.6
Massachusetts	19,795	30,311	33,435	34,570	24,591	30,311	32,327	32,822	115.7	122.5
Michigan	16,571	25,436	26,413	27,275	20,586	25,436	25,537	25,896	96.9	96.6
Minnesota	17,304	27,187	29,026	30,397	21,496	27,187	28,064	28,860	101.1	107.7
Mississippi	11,910	18,937	20,653	21,677	14,796	18,937	19,968	20,581	69.6	76.8
Missouri	15,536	23,677	25,365	26,317	19,300	23,677	24,524	24,986	90.8	93.2
Montana	13,795	20,236	22,351	23,528	17,137	20,236	21,610	22,338	80.6	83.3
Nebraska	16,031	24,091	26,104	27,865	19,915	24,091	25,239	26,456	93.7	98.7
Nevada	17,866	26,323	27,251	28,188	22,195	26,323	26,348	26,763	104.4	99.9
New Hampshire	18,292	28,568	30,220	31,251	22,724	28,568	29,218	29,671	106.9	110.7
New Jersey	21,381	32,015	34,075	35,411	26,561	32,015	32,945	33,621	125.0	125.4
New Mexico	13,413	19,577	22,443	23,301	16,663	19,577	21,699	22,123	78.4	82.5
New York	20,183	28,883	30,398	31,527	25,073	28,883	29,390	29,933	118.0	111.7
North Carolina	15,196	23,398	24,609	25,307	18,878	23,398	23,793	24,028	88.8	89.6
North Dakota	14,457	22,598	24,509	26,902	17,960	22,598	23,696	25,542	84.5	95.3
Ohio	16,446	24,264	25,660	26,684	20,431	24,264	24,809	25,335	96.1	94.5
Oklahoma	14,280	21,519	23,274	24,169	17,740	21,519	22,502	22,947	83.5	85.6
Oregon	15,823	23,907	25,365	26,102	19,657	23,907	24,524	24,782	92.5	92.5
Pennsylvania	17,344	25,575	27,497	28,557	21,546	25,575	26,585	27,113	101.4	101.2
Rhode Island	17,639	25,060	27,120	28,365	21,913	25,060	26,221	26,931	103.1	100.5
South Carolina	14,095	21,503	22,946	23,753	17,510	21,503	22,185	22,552	82.4	84.1
South Dakota	14,822	23,164	24,721	27,149	18,413	23,164	23,901	25,776	86.6	96.2
Tennessee	15,122	23,410	25,279	26,314	18,786	23,410	24,441	24,984	88.4	93.2
Texas	15,623	24,964	26,308	26,922	19,408	24,964	25,436	25,561	91.3	95.4
Utah	13,197	20,802	22,061	22,581	16,394	20,802	21,330	21,439	77.1	80.0
Vermont	15,759	24,010	26,558	27,750	19,577	24,010	25,678	26,347	92.1	98.3
Virginia	17,872	26,212	28,629	29,683	22,202	26,212	27,680	28,186	104.5	105.1
Washington	17,676	27,310	29,311	30,288	21,959	27,310	28,339	28,757	103.3	107.3
West Virginia	12,965	19,536	21,518	22,252	16,106	19,536	20,805	21,127	75.8	78.8
Wisconsin	15,801	24,500	26,478	27,508	19,629	24,500	25,600	26,117	92.4	97.4
Wyoming	16,149	24,500	27,589	29,600	20,062	24,500	26,674	28,103	94.4	104.9

[1] Constant dollar estimates are computed by the U.S. Census Bureau using the national implicit price deflator for personal consumption expenditures from the Bureau of Economic Analysis. Any regional differences in the rate of inflation are not reflected in these constant dollar estimates.

Source: U.S. Bureau of Economic Analysis, *Survey of Current Business*, May 2004, and unpublished data. See also <http://www.bea.doc.gov/bea/regional/spi/> (released 27 April 2004).

Income, Expenditures, and Wealth **435**

No. 655. Personal Income by Selected Large Metropolitan Area: 2000 to 2002

[8,422,074 represents $8,422,074,000,000. Metropolitan areas as defined December 2003. See Appendix II]

Metropolitan area ranked by 2002 population	Personal income				Per capita personal income			
	2000 (mil. dol.)	2001 (mil. dol.)	2002 (mil. dol.)	Annual percent change, 2001-2002	2000 (dol.)	2001 (dol.)	2002 (dol.)	Percent of national average, 2002
United States	8,422,074	8,703,023	8,900,007	2.3	29,847	30,527	30,906	100.0
New York-Northern New Jersey-Long Island, NY-NJ-PA	732,799	751,488	755,390	0.5	39,920	40,664	40,680	131.6
Los Angeles-Long Beach-Santa Ana, CA	385,053	402,424	413,165	2.7	31,049	32,066	32,547	105.3
Chicago-Naperville-Joliet, IL-IN-WI	318,439	325,965	329,814	1.2	34,921	35,430	35,583	115.1
Philadelphia-Camden-Wilmington, PA-NJ-DE-MD	193,919	199,176	205,346	3.1	34,062	34,856	35,753	115.7
Dallas-Fort Worth-Arlington, TX	176,530	182,207	185,167	1.6	33,973	34,063	33,816	109.4
Miami-Fort Lauderdale-Miami Beach, FL	157,015	163,369	168,639	3.2	31,226	31,923	32,373	104.7
Washington-Arlington-Alexandria, DC-VA-MD-WV	196,093	208,098	214,441	3.0	40,665	42,241	42,773	138.4
Houston-Baytown-Sugar Land, TX	161,398	170,558	173,757	1.9	34,041	35,200	34,969	113.1
Atlanta-Sandy Springs-Marietta, GA	141,817	147,307	149,974	1.8	33,120	33,439	33,257	107.6
Detroit-Warren-Livonia, MI	151,793	151,682	152,800	0.7	34,048	33,913	34,129	110.4
Boston-Cambridge-Quincy, MA-NH	182,380	188,380	188,418	-	41,435	42,501	42,436	137.3
San Francisco-Oakland-Fremont, CA	199,989	200,185	195,396	-2.4	48,347	47,906	46,920	151.8
Riverside-San Bernardino-Ontario, CA	74,787	80,077	84,301	5.3	22,810	23,668	24,073	77.9
Phoenix-Mesa-Scottsdale, AZ	92,975	96,477	99,387	3.0	28,365	28,516	28,481	92.2
Seattle-Tacoma-Bellevue, WA	115,203	117,090	118,739	1.4	37,746	37,832	38,037	123.1
Minneapolis-St. Paul-Bloomington, MN-WI	109,818	113,143	115,502	2.1	36,840	37,407	37,787	122.3
San Diego-Carlsbad-San Marcos, CA	92,654	97,141	101,293	4.3	32,797	33,926	34,872	112.8
St. Louis, MO-IL.	84,222	86,138	88,410	2.6	31,174	31,748	32,462	105.0
Baltimore-Towson, MD.	85,144	89,050	92,410	3.8	33,294	34,519	35,556	115.0
Tampa-St. Petersburg-Clearwater, FL	68,891	71,522	73,986	3.4	28,655	29,263	29,728	96.2
Pittsburgh, PA	74,361	76,386	78,241	2.4	30,610	31,539	32,381	104.8
Denver-Aurora, CO	82,196	85,894	86,526	0.7	37,852	38,651	38,008	123.0
Cleveland-Elyria-Mentor, OH.	67,935	68,364	69,060	1.0	31,626	31,885	32,244	104.3
Cincinnati-Middletown, OH-KY-IN.	61,393	62,996	64,769	2.8	30,477	31,080	31,804	102.9
Portland-Vancouver-Beaverton, OR-WA	62,190	63,892	64,755	1.4	32,127	32,326	32,167	104.1
Sacramento-Arden-Arcade-Roseville, CA	54,234	57,497	59,829	4.1	29,993	30,793	31,069	100.5
Kansas City, MO-KS	58,247	59,737	61,255	2.5	31,612	32,055	32,467	105.1
San Antonio, TX	45,997	47,317	48,884	3.3	26,752	27,368	27,368	88.6
Orlando, FL.	44,751	46,354	48,431	4.5	27,018	27,146	27,587	89.3
San Jose-Sunnyvale-Santa Clara, CA.	92,947	85,586	79,596	-7.0	53,408	48,981	45,925	148.6
Columbus, OH.	49,770	51,420	53,061	3.2	30,740	31,359	32,043	103.7
Virginia Beach-Norfolk-Newport News, VA-NC . . .	41,659	43,856	45,773	4.4	26,355	27,557	28,365	91.8
Providence-New Bedford-Fall River, RI-MA . . .	45,976	48,076	49,645	3.3	28,976	30,089	30,796	99.6
Indianapolis, IN	48,862	50,763	51,841	2.1	31,920	32,672	32,916	106.5
Las Vegas-Paradise, NV	41,239	42,457	44,572	5.0	29,601	29,152	29,396	95.1
Milwaukee-Waukesha-West Allis, WI	49,151	50,691	51,798	2.2	32,722	33,673	34,308	111.0
Charlotte-Gastonia-Concord, NC-SC	43,120	44,965	46,512	3.4	32,187	32,716	33,083	107.0
Nashville-Davidson-Murfreesboro, TN.	40,309	42,030	43,317	3.1	30,605	31,447	32,026	103.6
Austin-Round Rock, TX.	41,157	43,152	42,671	-1.1	32,546	32,678	31,677	102.5
New Orleans-Metairie-Kenner, LA	34,606	36,767	38,085	3.6	26,304	28,023	28,995	93.8
Memphis, TN-MS-AR.	34,459	36,299	37,496	3.3	28,520	29,839	30,557	98.9
Louisville, KY-IN.	34,250	35,463	36,195	2.1	29,398	30,251	30,666	99.2
Jacksonville, FL	33,151	33,974	35,338	4.0	29,439	29,549	30,037	97.2

- Represent zero.

Source: U.S. Bureau of Economic Analysis, *Survey of Current Business*, June 2004. See also <http://www.bea.doc.gov/bea/regional/reis/> (released 25 May 2004).

No. 656. Flow of Funds Accounts—Composition of Individuals' Savings: 1990 to 2003

[In billions of dollars (540.6 represents $540,600,000,000). Combined statement for households, farm business, and nonfarm noncorporate business. Minus sign (-) indicates decrease]

Composition of savings	1990	1995	1997	1998	1999	2000	2001	2002	2003
Increase in financial assets	540.6	536.0	601.3	929.5	709.6	677.9	880.4	719.6	909.9
Foreign deposits	1.4	4.6	6.5	0.1	5.2	15.0	-5.0	10.7	3.5
Checkable deposits and currency	-9.8	-27.1	-11.3	18.7	-35.8	-63.8	90.8	-23.0	-53.4
Time and savings deposits	33.6	131.4	142.6	175.6	101.3	308.7	257.8	295.8	342.6
Money market fund shares	27.8	99.6	83.5	139.4	118.3	154.2	158.2	-37.9	-98.4
Securities	191.8	21.1	2.7	133.4	107.0	-347.1	-57.1	91.4	188.9
Open market paper	6.2	1.3	1.5	7.5	4.1	4.8	-30.8	5.8	-1.6
U.S. government securities	109.3	5.6	-112.4	-7.7	164.5	-129.5	-161.6	-232.5	134.6
Municipal securities	27.6	-52.4	37.3	5.8	23.5	10.2	52.3	106.6	62.5
Corporate and foreign bonds	74.8	93.9	67.7	127.1	51.9	65.8	117.8	165.3	-116.6
Corporate equities [1]	-48.6	-102.8	-257.4	-247.1	-308.1	-470.0	-231.7	-72.5	-183.1
Mutual fund shares	22.5	75.5	266.0	247.8	171.2	171.6	196.8	118.8	293.1
Life insurance reserves	26.5	45.8	59.3	48.0	50.8	50.2	77.2	60.1	56.7
Pension fund reserves	207.7	158.9	201.3	217.4	181.8	209.1	210.9	215.2	232.7
Investment in bank personal trusts	32.9	6.4	-53.0	-46.1	-8.1	56.6	-59.9	-2.4	-26.3
Miscellaneous assets	28.7	95.4	169.5	242.9	189.1	295.1	207.4	109.6	263.5
Gross investment in tangible assets	829.5	1,033.3	1,148.7	1,253.5	1,380.5	1,489.2	1,554.6	1,558.2	1,655.7
Minus: Consumption of fixed capital	567.4	696.5	753.9	791.1	837.0	890.7	936.8	974.3	991.0
Equals: Net investment in tangible assets	262.1	336.8	394.8	462.4	543.5	598.6	617.8	584.0	664.7
Net increase in liabilities	234.5	419.0	561.0	801.1	887.1	927.0	828.7	942.9	1,151.2
Mortgage debt on nonfarm homes	207.1	176.9	258.1	383.2	422.2	416.2	531.1	723.3	818.2
Other mortgage debt [2]	-0.3	5.7	31.8	105.6	101.2	114.9	107.4	102.0	109.2
Consumer credit	15.1	147.0	62.1	96.8	112.1	165.2	137.7	81.4	100.2
Policy loans	4.1	10.5	3.2	0.1	-5.1	2.8	2.2	1.1	-0.2
Security credit	-3.7	3.5	36.8	21.6	75.2	7.2	-38.8	-48.2	32.6
Other liabilities [2]	12.2	75.4	169.0	193.8	181.4	220.6	89.1	83.3	91.4
Personal saving with consumer durables [3]	583.4	474.5	462.8	623.8	403.4	385.9	706.3	394.9	453.8
Personal saving, without consumer durable [3]	495.2	337.6	298.3	417.2	182.3	143.6	436.1	146.7	181.7
Personal saving (NIPA, excludes consumer durables) [4]	299.4	250.9	218.3	276.8	158.6	168.4	127.2	183.2	165.6

[1] Only directly held and those in closed-end funds. Other equities are included in mutual funds, life insurance and pension reserves, and bank personal trusts. [2] Includes corporate farms. [3] Flow of Funds measure. [4] National Income and Product Accounts measure.

Source: Board of Governors of the Federal Reserve System, *Flow of Funds Accounts*, quarterly. See also <http://www.federalreserve.gov/releases/Z1/20030306/z1.pdf> (released 04 March 2004).

No. 657. Annual Expenditure Per Child by Husband-Wife Families by Family Income and Expenditure Type: 2003

[In dollars. Expenditures based on data from the 1990-92 Consumer Expenditure Survey updated to 2003 dollars using the Consumer Price Index. Excludes expenses for college. For more on the methodology, see report cited below]

Family income and age of child	Expenditure type							
	Total	Housing	Food	Trans-por-tation	Clothing	Health care	Child care and educa-tion	Miscel-lan-eous [1]
INCOME: LESS THAN $40,700								
Less than 2 yrs. old	6,820	2,620	950	800	350	500	950	650
3 to 5 yrs. old	6,970	2,580	1,050	770	340	480	1,080	670
6 to 8 yrs. old	7,040	2,500	1,360	900	380	550	640	710
9 to 11 yrs. old	6,990	2,250	1,620	970	420	600	390	740
12 to 14 yrs. old	7,840	2,510	1,710	1,100	710	610	270	930
15 to 17 yrs. old	7,770	2,030	1,850	1,480	630	650	450	680
INCOME: $40,700-$68,400								
Less than 2 yrs. old	9,510	3,540	1,130	1,190	410	660	1,570	1,010
3 to 5 yrs. old	9,780	3,510	1,310	1,160	400	630	1,740	1,030
6 to 8 yrs. old	9,730	3,420	1,670	1,290	450	720	1,110	1,070
9 to 11 yrs. old	9,600	3,180	1,960	1,360	490	780	730	1,100
12 to 14 yrs. old	10,350	3,440	1,980	1,490	830	790	530	1,290
15 to 17 yrs. old	10,560	2,950	2,200	1,880	740	830	920	1,040
INCOME: MORE THAN $68,400								
Less than 2 yrs. old	14,140	5,620	1,500	1,660	540	760	2,370	1,690
3 to 5 yrs. old	14,470	5,590	1,700	1,630	530	730	2,580	1,710
6 to 8 yrs. old	14,240	5,500	2,050	1,760	580	830	1,770	1,750
9 to 11 yrs. old	14,040	5,260	2,380	1,840	630	900	1,240	1,790
12 to 14 yrs. old	14,850	5,520	2,500	1,960	1,050	900	950	1,970
15 to 17 yrs. old	15,350	5,040	2,630	2,380	950	950	1,670	1,730

[1] Expenses include personal care items, entertainment, and reading materials.

Source: Dept. of Agriculture, Center for Nutrition Policy and Promotion, *Expenditures on Children by Families, 2003 Annual Report.* See also <http://www.cnpp.usda.gov/Crc/crc2003.pdf> (released May 2004).

No. 658. Average Annual Expenditures of All Consumer Units by Selected Major Types of Expenditure: 1990 to 2002

[In dollars, except as indicated (96,968 represents 96,968,000). Based on Consumer Expenditure Survey. Data are averages for the noninstitutional population. Expenditures reported here are out-of-pocket]

Type	1990	1995	1997	1998	1999	2000	2001	2002
Number of consumer units (1,000)	96,968	103,123	105,576	107,182	108,465	109,367	110,339	112,108
Expenditures, total	28,381	32,264	34,819	35,535	36,995	38,045	39,518	40,677
Food.	4,296	4,505	4,801	4,810	5,031	5,158	5,321	5,375
Food at home	2,485	2,803	2,880	2,780	2,915	3,021	3,086	3,099
Meats, poultry, fish, and eggs	668	752	743	723	749	795	828	798
Dairy products	295	297	314	301	322	325	332	328
Fruits and vegetables	408	457	476	472	500	521	522	552
Other food at home.	746	856	895	858	896	927	952	970
Food away from home	1,811	1,702	1,921	2,030	2,116	2,137	2,235	2,276
Alcoholic beverages.	293	277	309	309	318	372	349	376
Housing [1]	8,703	10,458	11,272	11,713	12,057	12,319	13,011	13,283
Shelter.	4,836	5,928	6,344	6,680	7,016	7,114	7,602	7,829
Fuels, utilities, public services . . .	1,890	2,191	2,412	2,405	2,377	2,489	2,767	2,684
Apparel and services	1,618	1,704	1,729	1,674	1,743	1,856	1,743	1,749
Transportation	5,120	6,014	6,457	6,616	7,011	7,417	7,633	7,759
Vehicle purchases	2,129	2,638	2,736	2,964	3,305	3,418	3,579	3,665
Gasoline and motor oil	1,047	1,006	1,098	1,017	1,055	1,291	1,279	1,235
Other vehicles expenses	1,642	2,015	2,230	2,206	2,254	2,281	2,375	2,471
Health care	1,480	1,732	1,841	1,903	1,959	2,066	2,182	2,350
Entertainment	1,422	1,612	1,813	1,746	1,891	1,863	1,953	2,079
Reading	153	162	164	161	159	146	141	139
Tobacco products, smoking supplies . . .	274	269	264	273	300	319	308	320
Personal insurance and pensions.	2,592	2,964	3,223	3,381	3,436	3,365	3,737	3,899
Life and other personal insurance	345	373	379	398	394	399	410	406
Pensions and Social Security	2,248	2,591	2,844	2,982	3,042	2,966	3,326	3,493

[1] Includes expenditures not shown separately.

Source: U.S. Bureau of Labor Statistics, *Consumer Expenditures in 2002; and* earlier reports. See also <http://www.bls.gov/cex/csxann02.pdf> (released February 2004).

No. 659. Average Annual Expenditures of All Consumer Units by Metropolitan Area: 2001-2002

[In dollars. Metropolitan areas defined June 30, 1983, CMSA=Consolidated Metropolitan Statistical Area; MSA=Metropolitan Statistical Area; PMSA=Primary Metropolitan Statistical Area. See text, Section 1, Population, and Appendix II. See headnote, Table 658]

Metropolitan area	Total expendi- tures [1]	Food	Housing				Transportation			Health care
			Total [1]	Shel- ter	Utility, fuels [2]		Total [1]	Vehicle pur- chases	Gaso- line and motor oil	
Anchorage, AK MSA	56,169	6,993	17,299	10,628	2,656		10,860	5,242	1,455	2,484
Atlanta, GA MSA	40,492	4,986	14,965	8,998	3,420		7,458	3,504	1,276	2,010
Baltimore, MD MSA.	38,628	5,737	13,440	8,202	2,671		5,108	1,643	1,182	1,840
Boston-Lawrence-Salem, MA-NH CMSA	40,246	5,659	14,693	9,685	2,668		6,953	3,021	1,134	2,056
Chicago-Gary-Lake County, IL-IN-WI CMSA.	47,861	5,934	17,239	10,668	3,206		8,571	4,061	1,327	2,255
Cincinnati-Hamilton, OH-KY-IN CMSA.	40,421	5,547	12,912	7,665	2,609		8,009	3,932	1,183	2,034
Cleveland-Akron-Lorain, OH CMSA .	38,125	4,700	12,698	7,421	3,024		7,655	3,470	1,177	1,929
Dallas-Fort Worth, TX CMSA	50,281	7,374	15,754	9,047	3,456		10,051	5,160	1,506	2,432
Denver-Boulder-Greeley, CO CMSA. .	49,014	5,819	16,862	10,590	2,626		10,077	4,676	1,297	2,393
Detroit-Ann Arbor, MI CMSA	44,491	5,422	14,663	8,748	2,904		8,870	3,376	1,380	2,155
Honolulu, HI MSA	43,458	6,418	14,207	9,470	2,200		7,230	3,040	1,124	2,365
Houston-Galveston-Brazoria, TX CMSA.	47,523	6,373	15,049	8,127	3,262		9,536	4,473	1,525	2,449
Kansas City, MO-Kansas City, KS CMSA.	43,201	5,736	13,962	7,801	3,406		8,087	3,579	1,551	2,528
Los Angeles-Long Beach, CA PMSA .	47,459	5,883	17,602	11,675	2,576		8,861	3,923	1,475	2,031
Miami-Fort Lauderdale, FL CMSA . . .	41,850	5,885	15,622	9,823	3,038		7,617	3,097	1,315	1,969
Milwaukee, WI PMSA	40,341	5,280	13,968	8,530	2,462		6,796	3,007	1,207	2,175
Minneapolis-St. Paul, MN-WI MSA. . .	52,581	6,270	16,668	10,141	2,648		9,266	4,104	1,425	2,297
New York-Northern New Jersey- Long Island, NY-NJ-CT CMSA.	49,931	6,859	18,668	12,203	3,004		7,658	2,917	1,051	2,277
Philadelphia-Wilmington-Trenton, PA-NJ-DE-MD CMSA.	40,346	5,168	14,583	8,713	3,114		6,466	2,341	1,146	2,068
Phoenix-Mesa, AZ MSA	41,615	5,252	13,897	8,116	2,695		8,197	3,632	1,253	2,241
Pittsburgh-Beaver Valley, PA CMSA .	41,626	5,575	12,018	6,363	2,844		8,086	3,857	1,117	2,339
Portland-Vancouver, OR-WA CMSA . .	43,358	5,203	15,095	9,476	2,631		6,989	2,673	1,235	2,353
San Diego, CA MSA	42,588	5,036	17,050	11,465	2,454		7,806	3,424	1,335	1,884
San Francisco-Oakland-San Jose, CA CMSA.	55,346	6,453	21,127	14,592	2,645		9,223	3,962	1,472	2,349
Seattle-Tacoma, WA CMSA	48,348	6,019	16,621	10,685	2,753		9,680	4,424	1,392	2,326
St. Louis-East St. Louis-Alton, MO-IL CMSA	43,034	5,951	13,220	7,479	2,948		8,077	4,023	1,241	2,184
Tampa-St. Petersburg-Clearwater, FL MSA	38,167	3,888	13,112	7,752	2,946		8,850	4,886	1,219	2,282
Washington, DC-MD-VA MSA	47,775	5,867	18,105	11,545	2,954		7,543	3,256	1,242	2,201

[1] Includes expenditures not shown separately. [2] Includes public services.

Source: U.S. Bureau of Labor Statistics, *Consumer Expenditures in 2002.* See also <http://www.bls.gov/cex/csxann02.pdf> (released February 2004).

U.S. Census Bureau, Statistical Abstract of the United States: 2004-2005

No. 660. Average Annual Expenditures of All Consumer Units by Race, Hispanic Origin, and Age of Householder: 2002

[In dollars. Based on Consumer Expenditure Survey. Data are averages for the noninstitutional population. Expenditures reported here are out-of-pocket]

Item	All consumer units	Black	His-panic	Age of householder Under 25 yrs.	25 to 34 yrs.	35 to 44 yrs.	45 to 54 yrs.	55 to 64 yrs.	65 yrs. and over
Expenditures, total	**40,677**	**30,136**	**34,742**	**24,229**	**40,318**	**48,330**	**48,748**	**44,330**	**28,105**
Food	5,375	4,186	5,666	3,621	5,471	6,314	6,228	5,559	3,910
Food at home	3,099	2,669	3,643	1,926	3,093	3,601	3,528	3,114	2,548
Cereals and bakery products	450	390	498	287	442	542	500	423	386
Cereals and cereal products	154	152	191	113	163	191	169	133	120
Bakery products	296	238	308	174	279	351	332	290	266
Meats, poultry, fish, and eggs	798	862	1,057	460	817	918	929	807	641
Beef	231	220	334	131	253	271	273	216	174
Pork	167	208	216	95	162	198	188	169	144
Other meats	101	96	110	52	96	122	117	103	84
Poultry	144	168	202	96	159	164	168	134	110
Fish and seafood	121	133	137	61	113	126	146	154	98
Eggs	34	37	58	24	34	38	37	32	30
Dairy products	328	232	385	200	324	392	367	325	274
Fresh milk and cream	127	96	168	87	130	153	136	121	107
Other dairy products	201	135	217	113	195	238	232	204	167
Fruits and vegetables	552	460	720	338	522	597	627	591	510
Fresh fruits	178	136	242	105	154	191	204	207	169
Fresh vegetables	175	128	247	100	162	185	205	191	163
Processed fruits	116	114	138	81	118	128	127	113	103
Processed vegetables	83	82	92	53	88	93	91	81	75
Other food at home	970	725	982	640	988	1,153	1,106	967	738
Nonalcoholic beverages	254	199	279	160	260	303	296	265	178
Food away from home	2,276	1,517	2,023	1,696	2,378	2,712	2,700	2,445	1,362
Alcoholic beverages	376	190	301	394	395	367	465	420	237
Housing	13,283	10,756	11,841	7,436	13,727	16,350	15,476	13,831	9,176
Shelter	7,829	6,279	7,372	4,851	8,470	9,902	9,223	7,667	4,834
Owned dwellings	5,165	3,223	3,567	830	4,701	7,105	6,787	5,595	3,162
Mortgage interest and charges	2,962	2,000	2,232	443	3,286	4,608	4,061	2,712	897
Property taxes	1,242	669	696	281	823	1,473	1,557	1,540	1,199
Rented dwellings	2,160	2,852	3,645	3,644	3,476	2,351	1,733	1,303	1,259
Other lodging	505	204	161	377	293	446	704	770	413
Utilities, fuels, and public services	2,684	2,768	2,413	1,348	2,503	3,026	3,106	2,953	2,371
Natural gas	330	380	245	108	288	369	383	355	338
Electricity	981	1,034	808	471	864	1,105	1,138	1,112	894
Fuel oil and other fuels	88	30	46	21	55	86	90	127	119
Telephone	957	1,050	1,021	641	1,032	1,096	1,109	981	689
Water and other public services	328	274	292	108	263	369	387	378	331
Household operations	706	509	407	198	895	1,010	613	561	602
Personal services	331	287	212	99	650	580	165	79	218
Other household expenses	375	222	195	99	245	430	448	481	384
Housekeeping supplies	545	313	471	226	389	589	633	838	466
Household furnishings and equipment	1,518	887	1,179	812	1,469	1,823	1,900	1,811	903
Household textiles	136	68	141	93	128	137	152	183	106
Furniture	401	293	345	170	472	524	453	484	186
Floor coverings	40	27	13	8	30	44	59	53	30
Major appliances	188	173	148	88	148	252	219	220	139
Miscellaneous household equipment	652	276	441	377	583	776	893	738	374
Apparel and services	1,749	1,704	2,097	1,365	1,989	2,101	2,029	1,791	972
Men and boys	409	363	551	266	486	562	477	337	208
Women and girls	704	649	638	609	647	787	850	840	450
Children under 2 years old	83	81	142	102	188	97	51	49	21
Footwear	313	404	521	246	385	382	365	290	160
Other apparel products and services	240	207	245	142	283	273	286	276	133
Transportation	7,759	5,447	6,769	5,102	8,423	9,400	9,173	8,449	4,481
Vehicle purchases (net outlay)	3,665	2,420	3,130	2,635	4,269	4,592	4,203	3,882	1,818
Cars and trucks, new	1,753	1,000	1,149	664	1,739	2,394	1,966	2,080	1,038
Cars and trucks, used	1,842	1,410	1,900	1,917	2,454	2,115	2,109	1,763	761
Gasoline and motor oil	1,235	925	1,261	903	1,257	1,473	1,495	1,292	777
Other vehicle expenses	2,471	1,875	2,062	1,339	2,505	2,935	3,055	2,735	1,586
Vehicle finance charges	397	335	407	217	516	529	479	370	153
Maintenance and repair	697	499	529	394	609	843	848	832	482
Vehicle insurance	894	692	799	479	872	987	1,125	991	666
Public transportation	389	228	317	225	392	400	421	540	300
Health care [1]	2,350	1,339	1,366	640	1,417	1,980	2,550	3,007	3,586
Entertainment [2]	2,079	1,124	1,409	1,212	2,027	2,685	2,565	2,297	1,139
Personal care products and services	526	488	492	329	488	615	588	557	451
Reading	139	67	60	57	103	135	167	181	147
Education	752	463	488	1,664	571	738	1,208	589	202
Tobacco products and smoking supplies	320	210	186	286	315	376	415	361	152
Miscellaneous	792	606	628	422	678	841	989	930	686
Cash contributions	1,277	917	612	319	743	1,247	1,571	1,520	1,679
Personal insurance and pensions	3,899	2,640	2,827	1,382	3,972	5,183	5,323	4,838	1,286
Life and other personal insurance	406	312	196	51	230	409	559	595	407
Pensions and Social Security	3,493	2,328	2,631	1,331	3,742	4,774	4,764	4,243	880
Personal taxes [1]	**2,496**	**1,136**	**878**	**567**	**2,259**	**3,075**	**4,051**	**2,856**	**1,037**

[1] For additional health care expenditures, see Table 125.   [2] For additional recreation expenditures, see Section 26.

Source: U.S. Bureau of Labor Statistics, Consumer Expenditures in 2002. See also <http://www.bls.gov/cex/csxann02.pdf> (released February 2004).

No. 661. Average Annual Expenditures of All Consumer Units by Region and Size of Unit: 2002

[In dollars. For composition of regions, see map, inside front cover. See headnote, Table 658]

Item	Region				Size of consumer unit				
	North-east	Mid-west	South	West	One person	Two per-sons	Three per-sons	Four per-sons	Five or more
Expenditures, total	42,390	40,601	37,281	44,728	24,190	41,797	48,098	54,033	55,501
Food	5,813	5,180	5,102	5,630	2,913	5,318	6,361	7,445	8,302
Food at home	3,296	2,932	2,961	3,317	1,558	2,943	3,733	4,431	5,247
Cereals and bakery products	498	435	421	469	225	413	523	660	821
Cereals and cereal products	168	146	145	166	74	133	180	229	310
Bakery products	330	289	277	304	151	279	344	431	511
Meats, poultry, fish, and eggs	878	706	809	807	359	767	986	1,148	1,400
Beef	232	209	242	237	93	219	289	342	429
Pork	164	157	182	157	73	169	203	245	274
Other meats	120	100	96	94	48	93	128	147	178
Poultry.	168	125	140	150	65	131	183	206	271
Fish and seafood.	158	91	117	126	64	122	144	164	188
Eggs	35	26	33	42	18	32	39	44	60
Dairy products	348	320	300	365	166	307	398	480	552
Fresh milk and cream.	128	129	119	138	64	112	152	191	235
Other dairy products.	221	191	181	227	102	195	246	289	317
Fruits and vegetables.	605	490	511	635	292	547	650	754	893
Fresh fruits.	198	157	161	210	97	182	200	244	278
Fresh vegetables	196	145	159	213	90	181	204	234	276
Processed fruits	132	108	103	129	62	105	139	163	204
Processed vegetables	80	79	88	83	43	79	107	114	135
Other food at home	967	981	919	1,041	515	910	1,176	1,389	1,580
Nonalcoholic beverages	261	264	233	270	136	246	306	357	397
Food away from home	2,517	2,247	2,141	2,314	1,356	2,375	2,628	3,014	3,055
Alcoholic beverages	458	410	282	420	285	453	399	389	334
Housing	14,558	12,641	11,766	15,297	8,619	13,380	15,183	17,636	17,660
Shelter	8,962	7,097	6,478	9,792	5,465	7,728	8,847	10,299	10,088
Owned dwellings.	5,793	4,944	4,322	6,211	2,605	5,225	6,121	7,809	7,344
Mortgage interest and charges.	2,844	2,644	2,530	4,088	1,260	2,682	3,723	5,049	4,754
Property taxes.	1,946	1,316	906	1,103	755	1,373	1,346	1,597	1,617
Maintenance, repair, insurance, other .	1,003	983	886	1,019	590	1,170	1,053	1,164	974
Rented dwellings.	2,567	1,657	1,744	3,003	2,538	1,839	2,234	1,957	2,214
Other lodging	602	496	412	578	322	664	492	532	529
Utilities, fuels, and public services	2,750	2,682	2,775	2,485	1,712	2,736	3,114	3,418	3,702
Natural gas	450	458	203	298	225	321	368	425	476
Electricity.	861	905	1,203	806	600	1,022	1,125	1,245	1,388
Fuel oil and other fuels.	238	77	47	38	63	98	92	99	116
Telephone	952	934	987	936	624	955	1,160	1,219	1,262
Water and other public services	250	308	335	406	201	341	369	431	461
Household operations	804	570	690	787	400	513	977	1,267	998
Personal services	432	260	337	310	134	99	578	806	584
Other household expenses	372	310	354	478	266	415	399	461	413
Housekeeping supplies	498	709	489	506	270	677	551	676	722
Household furnishings and equipment. . .	1,544	1,583	1,333	1,727	772	1,725	1,695	1,976	2,151
Household textiles	122	129	115	186	81	161	131	149	201
Furniture	461	362	358	460	179	487	407	548	576
Floor coverings	48	45	37	34	15	59	45	47	41
Major appliances.	189	196	163	222	94	220	196	243	280
Small appliances, misc. housewares. . .	91	101	89	127	57	118	128	97	137
Miscellaneous household equipment. . .	633	749	571	698	346	680	787	892	916
Apparel and services.	1,965	1,728	1,592	1,836	921	1,559	2,247	2,380	3,150
Men and boys	433	427	363	445	176	341	522	635	829
Women and girls.	785	732	637	712	413	673	887	882	1,124
Children under 2 years old	79	88	80	84	15	41	159	157	191
Footwear.	378	274	303	313	149	250	390	436	718
Other apparel products and services . . .	289	207	209	282	168	254	290	269	288
Transportation	7,185	8,133	7,393	8,449	3,890	8,110	10,003	10,685	10,510
Vehicle purchases (net outlay).	3,036	4,034	3,591	3,937	1,662	3,805	4,994	5,177	4,966
Cars and trucks, new	1,603	1,612	1,796	1,959	791	2,066	2,274	2,356	1,961
Cars and trucks, used	1,372	2,314	1,742	1,917	846	1,679	2,579	2,708	2,942
Gasoline and motor oil	1,081	1,269	1,238	1,325	646	1,257	1,512	1,713	1,809
Other vehicle expenses	2,456	2,487	2,299	2,742	1,306	2,591	3,099	3,318	3,366
Vehicle finance charges	298	396	452	393	143	416	515	603	616
Maintenance and repair	593	687	644	883	437	721	837	909	872
Vehicle insurance	921	876	861	940	486	951	1,090	1,156	1,246
Public transportation	612	342	265	445	276	458	397	476	369
Health care [1]	2,207	2,383	2,431	2,310	1,522	3,010	2,496	2,472	2,340
Entertainment [2]	2,287	2,143	1,705	2,436	1,193	2,115	2,308	2,928	3,038
Personal care products and services	518	517	509	569	310	557	611	682	706
Reading	165	149	103	162	108	162	143	150	132
Education	1,062	718	487	947	562	491	935	1,156	1,279
Tobacco products and smoking supplies . .	315	396	321	247	210	327	418	352	434
Miscellaneous	733	776	764	905	602	797	859	926	1,049
Cash contributions	1,199	1,363	1,193	1,389	998	1,516	1,203	1,242	1,523
Personal insurance and pensions	3,924	4,065	3,632	4,132	2,055	4,002	4,932	5,590	5,043
Life and other personal insurance	460	448	389	345	183	492	499	520	493
Pensions and Social Security	3,464	3,617	3,243	3,787	1,872	3,510	4,433	5,071	4,550
Personal taxes.	**2,405**	**2,827**	**2,024**	**3,008**	**1,815**	**2,753**	**2,847**	**3,152**	**2,287**

[1] For additional health care expenditures, see Table 125.   [2] For additional recreation expenditures, see Section 26.

Source: U.S. Bureau of Labor Statistics, Consumer Expenditures in 2002. See also <http://www.bls.gov/cex/csxann02.pdf> (released February 2004).

No. 662. Average Annual Expenditures of All Consumer Units by Income Level: 2001-2002

[In dollars. Based on Consumer Expenditure Survey. Data are averages for the noninstitutional population. Expenditures reported here are out-of-pocket]

| Income level | Total expenditures [1] | Food | Housing | | | | Transportation | | | Health care |
			Total [1]	Shelter	Utility fuels [2]	Total [1]	Vehicle purchases	Gasoline and motor oil	
All consumer units	40,102	5,348	13,148	7,716	2,725	7,697	3,622	1,257	2,267
Consumer units with complete reporting	41,988	5,637	13,304	7,721	2,710	7,953	3,778	1,271	2,318
Less than $5,000............	20,117	3,490	7,047	4,226	1,527	3,202	1,489	626	1,110
$5,000 to $9,999	16,562	2,963	6,049	3,409	1,605	2,656	1,249	510	1,207
$10,000 to $14,999	20,780	3,323	7,287	4,081	1,946	3,744	1,867	647	1,823
$15,000 to $19,999	25,033	3,765	8,421	4,851	2,120	4,693	2,292	829	2,133
$20,000 to $29,999	28,733	4,423	9,562	5,375	2,386	5,457	2,512	1,017	2,190
$30,000 to $39,999	35,262	4,976	11,124	6,346	2,593	7,293	3,606	1,249	2,291
$40,000 to $49,999	41,351	5,703	12,706	7,327	2,794	8,662	4,224	1,380	2,420
$50,000 to $59,999	47,668	6,395	14,674	8,298	3,016	9,955	4,910	1,535	2,557
$60,000 to $69,999	53,567	7,087	16,107	9,355	3,239	10,589	4,923	1,690	2,644
$70,000 to $89,999	60,740	7,736	18,454	10,853	3,395	12,104	5,681	1,872	2,731
$90,000 and over...........	87,292	9,805	27,290	16,320	4,100	14,780	6,808	2,046	3,319

[1] Includes expenditures not shown separately.   [2] Includes public services.

Source: U.S. Bureau of Labor Statistics, *Consumer Expenditures in 2002.* See also <http://www.bls.gov/cex/csxann02.pdf> (released February 2004).

No. 663. Money Income of Households—Distribution of Income and Median Income by Race and Hispanic Origin: 1999

[In thousands, except as indicated (105,539 represents 105,539,000). Households as of April 2000. Based on sample data from the 2000 Census of Population and Housing; see text, Section 1, Population, and Appendix III]

| Income Interval | All households | Race of householder | | | | | | | Hispanic or Latino [1] |
		White alone	Black or African American alone	American Indian and Alaska Native alone	Asian alone	Native Hawaiian and other Pacific Islander alone	Some other race alone	Two or more races	
All households	105,539	83,698	12,024	770	3,129	100	3,834	1,984	9,273
Under $10,000	10,067	6,584	2,294	128	314	9	469	268	1,150
$10,000 to $14,999	6,657	4,955	1,038	68	143	5	300	148	723
$15,000 to $19,999	6,601	4,974	960	63	143	6	315	141	739
$20,000 to $24,999	6,936	5,303	935	63	153	7	331	145	768
$25,000 to $29,999	6,801	5,259	874	56	146	7	319	140	727
$30,000 to $34,999	6,718	5,281	787	54	157	6	299	134	682
$35,000 to $39,999	6,236	4,953	697	47	149	6	261	122	605
$40,000 to $44,999	5,966	4,794	624	42	154	6	235	111	546
$45,000 to $49,999	5,244	4,249	522	35	136	5	202	95	466
$50,000 to $59,999	9,537	7,834	879	60	267	9	323	165	773
$60,000 to $74,999	11,003	9,161	918	62	349	12	323	180	796
$75,000 to $99,999	10,799	9,121	797	51	396	11	258	164	683
$100,000 to $124,999......	5,492	4,695	343	21	247	5	102	78	296
$125,000 to $149,999......	2,656	2,285	148	9	136	2	40	36	127
$150,000 to $199,999......	2,322	2,023	106	6	128	2	28	29	97
$200,000 and over........	2,503	2,227	102	6	111	1	27	28	96
Median income (dollars)	41,994	44,687	29,423	30,599	51,908	42,717	32,694	35,587	33,676
Aggregate household income (mil. dol).............	5,978,107	4,996,446	479,476	30,917	211,949	5,318	159,556	94,444	410,310

[1] Persons of Hispanic origin or Latino may be of any race.

Source: U.S. Census Bureau, *2000 Census of Population and Housing, Summary File 3,* using American FactFinder, tables P52, P53, P54, P151A-H, P152A-H, and P153A-H (accessed 05 September 2003).

Income, Expenditures, and Wealth   441

No. 664. Median Income of Households in Constant (2001) Dollars by State: 3-Year Averages for 1989 to 2001

[Constant dollars based on the CPI-U-RS deflator. Data based on the Current Population Survey; see text, this section and Section 1 and Appendix III. The CPS is designed to collect reliable data on income primarily at the national level and secondarily at the regional level. When the income data are tabulated by state, the estimates are considered less reliable and, therefore, particular caution should be used when trying to interpret the results]

State	1989-1991	1993-1995	1994-1996	1995-1997	1996-1998	1997-1999	1998-2000	1999-2001
United States	**39,119**	**38,371**	**39,098**	**39,958**	**40,914**	**42,076**	**42,908**	**42,873**
Alabama	30,291	30,790	32,050	33,049	36,166	37,642	37,244	36,693
Alaska	50,907	53,568	56,067	55,795	55,684	54,159	53,914	55,426
Arizona	38,900	36,459	36,037	35,715	37,258	38,554	40,748	40,965
Arkansas	29,725	29,258	30,149	29,672	29,749	30,131	30,880	31,798
California	43,965	41,845	42,677	43,314	43,883	44,839	46,255	47,243
Colorado	39,080	44,419	45,884	46,834	48,029	49,814	50,521	50,053
Connecticut	54,273	47,548	47,429	47,369	48,710	50,925	51,984	52,887
Delaware	41,988	42,059	42,276	43,925	45,483	47,349	48,719	50,301
District of Columbia	36,911	34,662	35,652	35,472	35,736	37,465	39,010	41,539
Florida	35,182	34,454	34,447	34,808	35,992	37,221	38,323	38,141
Georgia	36,218	38,236	37,671	38,719	39,587	41,381	42,627	42,508
Hawaii	48,874	50,272	48,758	47,124	45,408	45,478	46,924	49,232
Idaho	33,441	37,453	37,980	37,806	38,503	38,220	38,745	38,310
Illinois	42,100	41,666	43,264	44,583	45,555	47,171	47,924	47,578
Indiana	35,134	35,660	36,968	40,254	41,781	43,112	42,354	41,921
Iowa	36,079	38,210	39,119	38,477	38,203	40,370	42,641	42,255
Kansas	37,817	34,791	35,021	37,237	38,843	39,912	39,400	41,097
Kentucky	31,587	31,738	34,072	35,862	37,506	37,373	37,814	37,184
Louisiana	31,002	31,439	32,189	34,271	34,998	35,243	33,370	33,194
Maine	36,765	35,991	37,949	38,024	37,891	38,684	40,931	38,733
Maryland	49,173	47,277	47,690	49,368	51,670	53,718	54,247	55,013
Massachusetts	47,539	45,686	45,569	45,025	45,503	46,362	46,955	49,018
Michigan	40,817	41,035	42,589	42,896	44,010	45,694	47,268	46,929
Minnesota	40,100	41,379	43,183	45,538	48,279	49,657	51,406	52,804
Mississippi	26,214	29,130	30,196	30,640	30,964	32,497	32,846	33,305
Missouri	35,940	36,813	38,110	39,621	40,764	42,616	45,453	43,884
Montana	31,609	32,198	32,294	32,122	32,865	33,188	33,413	32,929
Nebraska	36,609	37,651	37,918	38,115	38,619	39,616	40,030	42,518
Nevada	41,417	42,402	42,432	42,549	43,048	43,375	44,420	45,493
New Hampshire	50,333	44,207	43,697	44,847	46,039	47,630	49,315	50,866
New Jersey	51,854	49,825	51,313	52,267	53,392	53,297	53,129	52,137
New Mexico	32,560	31,349	29,982	30,416	31,826	33,932	34,983	34,599
New York	41,735	38,008	38,520	39,082	39,901	40,826	41,915	42,157
North Carolina	35,005	35,744	37,486	38,765	39,426	39,317	39,435	39,040
North Dakota	33,592	33,628	34,105	34,575	34,346	34,204	34,611	35,830
Ohio	39,061	38,560	38,737	39,439	40,076	41,347	43,101	42,631
Oklahoma	32,308	31,306	31,020	31,883	33,960	35,342	34,932	34,554
Oregon	38,683	39,699	39,663	40,930	41,068	42,194	43,076	42,701
Pennsylvania	38,711	38,366	38,970	40,096	40,926	41,312	42,441	42,320
Rhode Island	40,865	39,644	40,018	40,201	41,315	42,668	44,541	44,825
South Carolina	35,118	33,408	35,912	36,718	37,567	37,533	37,675	38,362
South Dakota	32,244	34,236	34,138	33,314	33,795	35,479	36,907	38,407
Tennessee	30,612	32,529	33,964	33,916	35,085	36,492	36,879	36,542
Texas	35,970	35,983	36,814	37,561	38,178	39,596	40,325	40,547
Utah	39,147	42,482	41,961	43,576	45,565	48,017	47,776	48,378
Vermont	40,312	39,597	39,221	37,972	39,201	41,825	42,014	41,888
Virginia	46,300	43,404	43,435	44,357	46,104	47,621	48,932	49,085
Washington	43,097	41,219	40,615	43,745	47,213	49,640	47,649	44,835
West Virginia	29,431	27,862	28,300	29,097	29,185	30,153	30,003	30,342
Wisconsin	39,981	42,457	44,661	45,241	44,434	45,682	46,638	46,734
Wyoming	38,736	37,013	36,764	35,966	36,587	38,237	39,307	40,007

Source: U.S. Census Bureau, *Current Population Reports*, P60-221; and <http://www.census.gov/hhes/income/histinc/h08b.html> (released 13 May 2004).

No. 665. Money Income of Households—Percent Distribution by Income Level, Race, and Hispanic Origin, in Constant (2002) Dollars: 1980 to 2002

[Constant dollars based on CPI-U-RS deflator. Households as of March of following year. (82,368 represents 82,368,000). Based on Current Population Survey; see text, Sections 1 and 13, and Appendix III. For data collection changes over time, see <http://www.census.gov/hhes/income/histinc/hstchg.html>. For definition of median, see Guide to Tabular Presentation]

Year	Number of house-holds (1,000)	Under $15,000	$15,000-$24,999	$25,000-$34,999	$35,000-$49,999	$50,000-$74,999	$75,000-$99,999	$100,000 and over	Median income (dollars)
ALL HOUSEHOLDS [1]									
1980	82,368	19.4	15.0	13.6	18.5	19.6	8.1	5.9	36,608
1990 [2]	94,312	17.6	13.6	13.3	17.1	19.0	9.5	9.7	39,949
2000 [2]	108,209	15.3	12.6	12.6	15.2	18.7	11.0	14.5	43,848
2001	109,297	15.6	13.2	12.4	15.3	18.3	11.0	14.3	42,900
2002	111,278	16.1	13.2	12.3	15.1	18.3	11.0	14.1	42,409
WHITE									
1980	71,872	17.3	15.3	13.6	19.0	20.6	8.6	6.4	38,621
1990 [2]	80,968	15.4	14.1	13.4	17.5	19.8	10.1	10.4	41,668
2000 [2]	90,030	13.8	12.3	12.5	15.2	19.2	11.5	15.4	45,860
2001	90,682	14.1	12.8	12.2	15.4	18.7	11.6	15.2	45,225
2002 [3]	91,645	14.5	12.8	12.0	15.2	18.9	11.6	15.0	45,086
BLACK									
1980	8,847	36.5	18.6	13.3	14.7	11.5	3.8	1.5	22,250
1990 [2]	10,671	34.6	15.5	13.6	14.5	13.3	4.7	3.8	24,917
2000 [2]	13,174	25.2	16.1	14.1	15.7	15.3	7.0	6.7	30,980
2001	13,315	26.3	16.3	14.3	14.9	15.4	7.0	5.9	29,939
2002 [3]	13,465	27.4	16.4	14.5	14.8	13.9	6.7	6.4	29,026
ASIAN AND PACIFIC ISLANDER									
1990	1,958	13.3	10.8	9.8	14.7	21.4	13.4	16.6	51,299
2000 [2]	3,963	11.2	8.9	10.0	13.6	19.0	13.7	23.5	58,225
2001	4,071	12.3	10.0	9.7	14.3	18.9	12.6	22.3	54,488
2002 [3 4]	3,917	11.9	10.5	10.5	13.6	18.8	12.6	22.1	52,626
HISPANIC [5]									
1980	3,906	24.7	20.2	15.6	17.1	15.2	4.5	2.5	28,218
1990 [2]	6,220	25.1	17.8	15.2	17.2	14.8	5.6	4.3	29,792
2000 [2]	10,034	18.2	16.8	15.5	17.3	17.3	8.1	6.7	34,636
2001	10,499	18.7	17.4	15.4	17.3	16.1	7.8	7.2	34,099
2002	11,339	19.1	17.2	15.7	16.4	16.9	7.5	7.2	33,103

[1] Includes other races not shown separately. [2] Data reflect implementation of Census 2000-based population controls and a 28,000 household sample expansion to 78,000 households. [3] The 2003 Current Population Survey (CPS) allowed respondents to choose more than one race. For 2002, data represent persons who selected this race group only and excludes persons reporting more than one race. The CPS in prior years only allowed respondents to report one race group. See also comments on race in the text for Section 1, Population. [4] See footnote 5, Table 666. [5] People of Hispanic origin may be of any race.

No. 666. Money Income of Households—Median Income by Race and Hispanic Origin, in Current and Constant (2002) Dollars: 1980 to 2002

[In dollars. See headnote, Table 665]

Year	Median income in current dollars					Median income in constant (2002) dollars				
	All house-holds [1]	White	Black	Asian, Pacific Islander	His-panic [2]	All house-holds [1]	White	Black	Asian, Pacific Islander	His-panic [2]
1980	17,710	18,684	10,764	(NA)	13,651	36,608	38,621	22,250	(NA)	28,218
1985	23,618	24,908	14,819	(NA)	17,465	37,648	39,704	23,622	(NA)	27,840
1990	29,943	31,231	18,676	38,450	22,330	39,949	41,668	24,917	51,299	29,792
1991	30,126	31,569	18,807	36,449	22,691	38,791	40,649	24,216	46,932	29,217
1992	30,636	32,209	18,755	37,801	22,597	38,482	40,458	23,558	47,482	28,384
1993	31,241	32,960	19,533	38,347	22,886	38,287	40,394	23,939	46,996	28,048
1994	32,264	34,028	21,027	40,482	23,421	38,726	40,843	25,238	48,590	28,112
1995	34,076	35,766	22,393	40,614	22,860	39,931	41,911	26,240	47,592	26,788
1996	35,492	37,161	23,482	43,276	24,906	40,503	42,407	26,797	49,386	28,422
1997	37,005	38,972	25,050	45,249	26,628	41,346	43,544	27,989	50,558	29,752
1998	38,885	40,912	25,351	46,637	28,330	42,844	45,077	27,932	51,385	31,214
1999	40,816	42,504	27,910	51,205	30,735	43,915	45,673	30,118	54,991	33,178
2000 [3]	41,990	43,916	29,667	55,757	33,168	43,848	45,860	30,980	58,225	34,636
2001	42,228	44,517	29,470	53,635	33,565	42,900	45,225	29,939	54,488	34,099
2002	42,409	45,086	29,026	[5]52,626	33,103	42,409	45,086	29,026	[5]52,626	33,103

NA Not available. [1] Includes other races not shown separately. [2] People of Hispanic origin may be of any race. [3] Implementation of Census 2000 based population controls and sample expanded by 28,000 households. [4] The 2003 Current Population Survey (CPS) allowed respondents to choose more than one race. For 2002, data represent persons who selected this race group only and excludes persons reporting more than one race. The CPS in prior years only allowed respondents to report one race group. See also comments on race in the text for Section 1, Population. [5] Data represent Asian alone, which refers to people who reported Asian and did not report any other race category.

Source of Tables 665 and 666: U.S. Census Bureau, Current Population Reports, P60-221; and Internet sites <http://www.census.gov/prod/2003pubs/p60-221.pdf> (released 26 September 2003) and <http://www.census.gov/hhes/income/histinc/h05.html>.

No. 667. Money Income of Households—Distribution by Income Level and Selected Characteristics: 2002

[111,278 represents 111,278,000. Households as of March of the following year. Based on Current Population Survey (CPS); see text, Sections 1 and 13, and Appendix III. The 2003 CPS allowed respondents to choose more than one race. For 2002, data represents persons who selected this race group only and excludes persons reporting more than one race. The CPS in prior years allowed respondents to report only one race group. See also comments on race in the text for Section 1, Population]

Characteristic	Number of house-holds (1,000)	Number (1,000)							Median income (dollars)
		Under $15,000	$15,000-$24,999	$25,000-$34,999	$35,000-$49,999	$50,000-$74,999	$75,000-$99,999	$100,000 and over	
Total [1]	111,278	17,926	14,646	13,672	16,809	20,315	12,230	15,676	42,409
Age of householder:									
15 to 24 years	6,611	1,696	1,262	1,096	1,142	861	341	214	27,828
25 to 34 years	19,055	2,251	2,227	2,598	3,404	4,322	2,197	2,057	45,330
35 to 44 years	24,069	2,292	2,375	2,599	3,790	5,239	3,428	4,346	53,521
45 to 54 years	22,623	2,234	1,830	2,113	3,272	4,617	3,491	5,069	59,021
55 to 64 years	16,260	2,495	1,792	1,877	2,330	3,036	1,856	2,875	47,203
65 years and over	22,659	6,957	5,161	3,390	2,872	2,241	920	1,116	23,152
White	91,645	13,319	11,724	10,989	13,898	17,333	10,667	13,714	45,086
Black	13,465	3,678	2,206	1,954	1,988	1,874	900	866	29,026
Hispanic [2]	11,339	2,166	1,955	1,783	1,854	1,910	854	815	33,103
Region: [3]									
Northeast	21,229	3,403	2,601	2,391	2,992	3,738	2,495	3,609	45,862
Midwest	25,630	3,960	3,276	3,114	3,975	5,049	2,917	3,337	43,622
South	40,107	7,087	5,705	5,186	6,170	7,096	4,006	4,858	39,522
West	24,313	3,474	3,066	2,983	3,670	4,434	2,813	3,872	45,143
Size of household:									
One person	29,431	10,672	5,815	4,040	3,939	2,848	1,077	1,041	21,523
Two people	37,078	3,852	4,985	5,093	6,189	7,415	4,261	5,283	45,556
Three people	17,889	1,532	1,742	1,920	2,818	4,010	2,632	3,234	54,783
Four people	15,967	1,128	1,131	1,490	2,268	3,639	2,662	3,652	62,467
Five people	7,029	460	591	692	1,013	1,514	1,074	1,681	61,623
Six people	2,521	201	230	273	389	557	338	533	56,097
Seven or more people	1,364	81	153	163	195	335	188	252	56,352
Type of household:									
Family households	75,596	6,776	8,196	8,855	11,669	15,961	10,396	13,742	52,704
Married-couple	57,320	3,002	4,972	5,899	8,449	13,034	9,235	12,731	61,254
Male householder, wife absent	4,656	483	655	724	922	1,031	441	403	41,711
Female householder, husband absent	13,620	3,289	2,568	2,232	2,299	1,900	723	609	29,001
Nonfamily households	35,682	11,150	6,452	4,817	5,140	4,355	1,837	1,934	25,406
Male householder	16,020	3,743	2,699	2,250	2,606	2,433	1,113	1,175	31,404
Female householder	19,662	7,407	3,751	2,569	2,533	1,919	722	759	20,913
Educational attainment of householder: [4]									
Total	104,667	16,229	13,385	12,576	15,669	19,453	11,892	15,463	44,039
Less than 9th grade	6,715	2,763	1,447	920	770	493	188	134	18,380
9th to 12th grade (no diploma)	9,282	2,983	1,923	1,407	1,340	984	370	277	23,267
High school graduate	31,857	5,729	5,230	4,697	5,176	6,005	2,910	2,111	35,646
Some college, no degree	18,822	2,293	2,303	2,496	3,232	3,984	2,196	2,317	45,333
Associate degree	8,508	823	881	1,000	1,431	1,976	1,223	1,172	51,058
Bachelor's degree or more	29,484	1,638	1,604	2,057	3,720	6,011	5,002	9,452	73,600
Bachelor's degree	19,013	1,152	1,141	1,487	2,559	4,062	3,227	5,384	69,156
Master's degree	7,238	338	329	437	894	1,500	1,295	2,442	76,470
Professional degree	1,746	74	75	88	156	218	242	896	100,000
Doctorate degree	1,486	73	56	46	111	232	239	730	98,632
Work experience of householder:									
Total	111,278	17,926	14,646	13,672	16,809	20,315	12,230	15,676	42,409
Worked	77,866	5,670	7,795	9,216	12,854	17,305	10,852	14,173	53,782
Worked at full-time jobs	66,652	3,408	6,147	7,733	11,220	15,432	9,852	12,862	56,548
50 weeks or more	56,307	1,764	4,571	6,411	9,476	13,515	8,839	11,730	60,010
27 to 49 weeks	6,548	647	950	826	1,206	1,359	738	820	45,185
26 weeks or less	3,797	997	626	495	538	555	275	312	30,384
Worked at part-time jobs	11,214	2,262	1,651	1,484	1,633	1,873	1,000	1,310	36,605
50 weeks or more	6,047	917	873	813	970	1,107	596	772	41,216
27 to 49 weeks	2,445	498	353	321	326	399	230	321	37,314
26 weeks or less	2,722	848	425	350	340	367	177	218	27,790
Did not work	33,412	12,256	6,851	4,457	3,955	3,009	1,380	1,504	20,991
Tenure:									
Owner occupied	75,909	8,377	8,252	8,250	11,235	15,538	10,254	14,002	52,113
Renter occupied	33,798	9,042	6,080	5,216	5,340	4,588	1,924	1,608	27,880
Occupier paid no cash rent	1,571	507	314	207	234	190	53	66	23,728

[1] Includes other races not shown separately.   [2] People of Hispanic origin may be of any race.   [3] For composition of regions, see map inside front cover.   [4] People 25 years old and over.

Source: U.S. Census Bureau, *Current Population Reports*, P60-221; and Internet site <http://ferret.bls.census.gov/macro/032003/hhinc/new01000.htm> (released 28 October 2003).

No. 668. Money Income of Households—Number and Distribution by Race and Hispanic Origin: 2002

[Households as of **March of the following year. (111,278 represents 111,278,000).** Based on Current Population Survey (CPS); see text, Sections 1 and 13, and Appendix III]. The 2003 CPS allowed respondents to choose more than one race. For 2002, data represent persons who selected this race group only and excludes persons reporting more than one race. The CPS in prior years allowed respondents to report only one race group. See also comments on race in the text for Section 1, Population]

Income interval	Number (1,000)					Percent distribution				
	All races	White	Black	Asian	His-panic [1]	All races	White	Black	Asian	His-panic [1]
All households [1]	**111,278**	**91,645**	**13,465**	**3,917**	**11,339**	**100.0**	**100.0**	**100.0**	**100.0**	**100.0**
Under $10,000	10,090	7,106	2,387	311	1,247	9.1	7.8	17.7	7.9	11.0
$10,000 to $14,999	7,836	6,213	1,291	157	919	7.0	6.8	9.6	4.0	8.1
$15,000 to $19,999	7,227	5,724	1,146	212	960	6.5	6.2	8.5	5.4	8.5
$20,000 to $24,999	7,419	6,000	1,060	200	995	6.7	6.5	7.9	5.1	8.8
$25,000 to $29,999	6,943	5,592	1,011	191	954	6.2	6.1	7.5	4.9	8.4
$30,000 to $34,999	6,729	5,397	943	219	829	6.0	5.9	7.0	5.6	7.3
$35,000 to $39,999	6,066	4,885	829	200	745	5.5	5.3	6.2	5.1	6.6
$40,000 to $44,999	5,713	4,825	585	163	614	5.1	5.3	4.3	4.2	5.4
$45,000 to $49,999	5,030	4,188	574	169	495	4.5	4.6	4.3	4.3	4.4
$50,000 to $59,999	9,226	7,817	886	341	945	8.3	8.5	6.6	8.7	8.3
$60,000 to $74,999	11,089	9,516	988	398	965	10.0	10.4	7.3	10.2	8.5
$75,000 to $84,999	6,076	5,272	477	249	434	5.5	5.8	3.5	6.4	3.8
$85,000 to $99,999	6,154	5,395	423	244	420	5.5	5.9	3.1	6.2	3.7
$100,000 to $149,999	10,073	8,763	605	539	560	9.1	9.6	4.5	13.8	4.9
$150,000 to $199,999	2,977	2,622	151	169	149	2.7	2.9	1.1	4.3	1.3
$200,000 to $249,999	1,154	1,010	52	81	47	1.0	1.1	0.4	2.1	0.4
$250,000 and above	1,472	1,319	59	77	59	1.3	1.4	0.4	2.0	0.5

[1] Persons of Hispanic origin may be of any race.

Source: U.S. Census Bureau, *Current Population Reports*, P60-221; and Internet site at <http://ferret.bls.census.gov/macro/032003 /hhinc/new06000.htm> (revised 13 November 2003).

No. 669. Money Income of Families—Number and Distribution by Race and Hispanic Origin: 2002

[Households as of **March of the following year. (75,616 represents 75,616,000).** Based on Current Population Survey (CPS); see text, Sections 1 and 13, and Appendix III. The 2003 CPS allowed respondents to choose more than one race. For 2002, data represent persons who selected this race group only and excludes persons reporting more than one race. The CPS in prior years only allowed respondents to report one race group. See also comments on race in the text for Section 1, Popu-lation]

Income interval	Number (1,000)					Percent distribution				
	All races	White	Black	Asian	His-panic [1]	All races	White	Black	Asian	His-panic [1]
All families [1]	**75,616**	**62,313**	**8,932**	**2,845**	**9,094**	**100.0**	**100.0**	**100.0**	**100.0**	**100.0**
Under $10,000	4,048	2,673	1,129	108	810	5.4	4.3	12.6	3.8	8.9
$10,000 to $14,999	3,276	2,364	723	90	704	4.3	3.8	8.1	3.2	7.7
$15,000 to $19,999	4,046	3,041	793	119	808	5.4	4.9	8.9	4.2	8.9
$20,000 to $24,999	4,465	3,563	669	127	852	5.9	5.7	7.5	4.5	9.4
$25,000 to $29,999	4,457	3,539	680	134	778	5.9	5.7	7.6	4.7	8.6
$30,000 to $34,999	4,447	3,552	636	149	676	5.9	5.7	7.1	5.2	7.4
$35,000 to $39,999	4,001	3,190	549	139	626	5.3	5.1	6.1	4.9	6.9
$40,000 to $44,999	3,985	3,359	398	128	500	5.3	5.4	4.5	4.5	5.5
$45,000 to $49,999	3,629	2,994	453	122	394	4.8	4.8	5.1	4.3	4.3
$50,000 to $59,999	6,822	5,796	645	271	748	9.0	9.3	7.2	9.5	8.2
$60,000 to $74,999	8,742	7,500	766	324	811	11.6	12.0	8.6	11.4	8.9
$75,000 to $84,999	5,005	4,345	407	191	360	6.6	7.0	4.6	6.7	4.0
$85,000 to $99,999	5,197	4,560	364	198	341	6.9	7.3	4.1	7.0	3.7
$100,000 to $149,999	8,592	7,491	508	451	467	11.4	12.0	5.7	15.9	5.1
$150,000 to $199,999	2,627	2,314	127	154	122	3.5	3.7	1.4	5.4	1.3
$200,000 to $249,999	1,003	886	36	72	44	1.3	1.4	0.4	2.5	0.5
$250,000 and above	1,275	1,146	49	68	51	1.7	1.8	0.5	2.4	0.6

[1] Persons of Hispanic origin may be of any race.

Source: U.S. Census Bureau, *Current Population Reports*, P60-221; and Internet site at <http://ferret.bls.census.gov/macro/032003 /faminc/new07000.htm> (revised 13 November 2003).

Income, Expenditures, and Wealth 445

No. 670. Money Income of Families—Percent Distribution by Income Level, Race, and Hispanic Origin, in Constant (2002) Dollars: 1980 to 2002

[Constant dollars based on CPI-U-RS deflator. Families as of March of following year (60,309,000). Beginning with 1980, based on householder concept and restricted to primary families. Based on Current Population Survey; see text, Sections 1 and 13, and Appendix III. For data collection changes over time, see <http://www.census.gov/hhes/income/histinc/hstchg.html>. For definition of median, see Guide to Tabular Presentation]

Year	Number of families (1,000)	Percent distribution Under $15,000	$15,000- $24,999	$25,000- $34,999	$35,000- $49,999	$50,000- $74,999	$75,000- $99,999	$100,000 and over	Median income (dollars)
ALL FAMILIES [1]									
1980	60,309	11.5	13.5	13.2	20.3	23.6	10.1	7.4	43,456
1990	66,322	11.4	11.8	11.6	17.9	22.3	11.9	12.3	47,167
1995	69,597	11.7	12.3	12.3	17.3	21.5	12.3	13.5	47,588
2000 [2]	73,778	9.1	10.9	10.6	15.6	21.1	13.4	18.3	52,977
2001	74,340	9.4	11.3	11.1	15.6	20.6	13.4	18.2	52,225
2002	75,616	9.7	11.3	11.3	15.4	20.6	13.5	17.8	51,680
WHITE									
1980	52,710	9.7	12.5	13.5	20.8	24.8	10.7	8.0	45,277
1990	56,803	9.1	11.1	12.5	18.3	23.3	12.6	13.2	49,251
2000 [2]	61,330	7.6	9.9	11.6	15.6	21.8	14.1	19.4	55,376
2001	61,647	7.8	10.4	11.4	15.7	21.2	14.0	19.5	54,927
2002 [3]	62,313	8.1	10.6	11.4	15.3	21.3	14.3	19.0	54,633
BLACK									
1980	6,317	29.1	19.2	14.1	16.5	14.2	4.9	2.0	26,198
1990	7,471	29.5	15.2	13.8	15.4	15.4	6.0	4.8	28,582
2000 [2]	8,731	19.4	16.0	14.6	16.2	17.2	8.4	8.3	35,166
2001	8,847	20.7	16.4	14.0	15.1	17.4	8.8	7.6	34,132
2002 [3]	8,932	20.8	16.4	14.7	15.7	15.8	8.6	8.0	33,525
ASIAN AND PACIFIC ISLANDER [5]									
1990	1,536	9.8	10.0	9.4	14.3	21.7	15.7	19.2	56,364
2000 [2]	2,982	7.5	7.9	9.0	13.4	19.7	15.3	27.2	65,388
2001	2,980	7.5	9.8	9.4	13.7	19.6	14.1	25.9	61,115
2002 [3]	2,845	6.9	8.7	10.0	13.7	20.9	13.6	26.2	60,984
HISPANIC ORIGIN [4]									
1980	3,235	20.7	20.3	16.3	18.6	16.6	4.8	2.8	30,419
1990	4,981	22.6	18.1	15.1	17.7	15.7	6.2	4.8	31,261
2000 [2]	8,017	16.1	17.1	15.8	17.4	17.9	8.5	7.2	35,966
2001	8,516	16.6	17.5	16.1	17.4	16.3	8.4	7.6	35,039
2002	9,094	16.7	18.3	16.0	16.7	17.2	7.7	7.5	34,185

[1] Includes other races not shown separately. [2] Data reflect implementation of Census 2000-based population controls and a 28,000 household sample expansion to 78,000 households. [3] The 2003 Current Population Survey (CPS) allowed respondents to choose more than one race. For 2002, data represent persons who selected this race group only and excludes persons reporting more than one race. The CPS in prior years only allowed respondents to report one race group. See also comments on race in the text for Section 1, Population. [4] Persons of Hispanic origin may be of any race. [5] Data represent Asian alone, which refers to people who reported Asian and did not report any other race category.

Source: U.S. Census Bureau, *Current Population Reports*, P60-221; and Internet sites <http://www.census.gov/prod/2003pubs/p60-221.pdf> (released 26 September 2003) and <http://ferret.bls.census.gov/macro/032003/faminc/new01000.htm> (released 28 October 2003).

No. 671. Money Income of Families—Median Income by Race and Hispanic Origin in Current and Constant (2002) Dollars: 1980 to 2002

[See headnote, Table 670]

Year	Median income in current dollars All families [1]	White	Black [2]	Asian, Pacific Islander	His- panic [3]	Median income in constant (2002) dollars All families [1]	White	Black [2]	Asian, Pacific Islander	His- panic [3]
1980	21,023	21,904	12,674	(NA)	14,716	43,456	45,277	26,198	(NA)	30,419
1985	27,735	29,152	16,786	(NA)	19,027	44,211	46,469	26,757	(NA)	30,330
1986	29,458	30,809	17,604	(NA)	19,995	46,115	48,230	27,558	(NA)	31,301
1987	30,970	32,385	18,406	(NA)	20,300	46,885	49,027	27,864	(NA)	30,732
1988	32,191	33,915	19,329	36,560	21,769	47,021	49,539	28,233	53,402	31,798
1989	34,213	35,975	20,209	40,351	23,446	47,916	50,384	28,303	56,513	32,837
1990	35,353	36,915	21,423	42,246	23,431	47,167	49,251	28,582	56,364	31,261
1991	35,939	37,783	21,548	40,974	23,895	46,275	48,650	27,745	52,759	30,767
1992	36,573	38,670	21,103	42,255	23,555	45,940	48,574	26,508	53,077	29,588
1993	36,959	39,300	21,542	44,456	23,654	45,295	48,164	26,401	54,483	28,989
1994	38,782	40,884	24,698	46,122	24,318	46,549	49,072	29,644	55,359	29,188
1995	40,611	42,646	25,970	46,356	24,570	47,588	49,973	30,432	54,321	28,791
1996	42,300	44,756	26,522	49,105	26,179	48,272	51,074	30,266	56,037	29,875
1997	44,568	46,754	28,602	51,850	28,142	49,797	52,239	31,958	57,933	31,444
1998	46,737	49,023	29,404	52,826	29,608	51,495	54,014	32,398	58,204	32,622
1999	48,831	51,079	31,850	56,127	31,523	52,694	55,120	34,370	60,567	34,017
2000	50,732	53,029	33,676	62,617	34,442	52,977	55,376	35,166	65,388	35,966
2001	51,407	54,067	33,598	60,158	34,490	52,225	54,927	34,132	61,115	35,039
2002 [4]	51,680	54,633	33,525	[5]60,984	34,185	51,680	54,633	33,525	[5]60,984	34,185

NA Not available. [1] Includes other races not shown separately. [2] Prior to 1967 data are for Black and Other Races. [3] People of Hispanic origin may be of any race. [4] The 2003 Current Population Survey (CPS) allowed respondents to choose more than one race. For 2002, data represent persons who selected this race group only and excludes persons reporting more than one race. The CPS in prior years only allowed respondents to report one race group. See also comments on race in the text for Section 1, Population. [5] See footnote 5, Table 670.

Source: U.S. Census Bureau, Current Population Reports, P60-221; and Internet site P60-221; and Internet site <http://www.census.gov/prod/2003pubs/p60-221.pdf> (released 26 September 2003)

No. 672. Share of Aggregate Income Received by Each Fifth and Top 5 Percent of Families: 1980 to 2002

[Families as of March of the following year (60,309 represents 60,309,000). Income in constant 2002 CPI-U-RS adjusted dollars. Based on the Current Population Survey; see text, Sections 1 and 13, and Appendix III. For data collection changes over time, see <http://www.census.gov/hhes/income/histinc/hstchg.html>

Year	Number of families (1,000)	Income at selected positions (dollars)					Percent distribution of aggregate income					
		Upper limit of each fifth				Top 5 percent	Lowest 5th	Second 5th	Third 5th	Fourth 5th	Highest 5th	Top 5 percent
		Lowest	Second	Third	Fourth							
1980	60,309	10,400	17,510	24,800	34,800	55,000	5.3	11.6	17.6	24.4	41.1	14.6
1985	63,558	13,285	22,886	33,152	48,229	78,965	4.8	11.0	16.9	24.3	43.1	16.1
1986	64,491	14,000	24,100	35,120	50,570	83,400	4.7	10.9	16.9	24.1	43.4	16.5
1987	65,204	14,598	25,182	36,801	53,330	86,949	4.6	10.7	16.8	24.0	43.8	17.2
1988	65,837	15,102	26,182	38,500	55,906	92,001	4.6	10.7	16.7	24.0	44.0	17.2
1989	66,090	16,003	28,000	40,800	59,550	98,963	4.6	10.6	16.5	23.7	44.6	17.9
1990	66,322	16,846	29,044	42,040	61,490	102,358	4.6	10.8	16.6	23.8	44.3	17.4
1991	67,173	17,000	29,111	43,000	62,991	102,824	4.5	10.7	16.6	24.1	44.2	17.1
1992	68,216	16,713	29,674	44,000	64,050	106,012	4.3	10.5	16.5	24.0	44.7	17.6
1993	68,506	16,970	30,000	45,030	66,794	113,182	4.1	9.9	15.7	23.3	47.0	20.3
1994	69,313	17,940	31,300	47,000	69,998	120,043	4.2	10.0	15.7	23.3	46.9	20.1
1995	69,597	19,070	32,985	48,985	72,260	123,656	4.4	10.1	15.8	23.2	46.5	20.0
1996	70,241	19,680	34,315	51,086	75,316	128,000	4.2	10.0	15.8	23.1	46.8	20.3
1997	70,884	20,586	36,000	53,616	80,000	137,080	4.2	9.9	15.7	23.0	47.2	20.7
1998	71,551	21,600	37,692	56,020	83,693	145,199	4.2	9.9	15.7	23.0	47.3	20.7
1999	73,206	22,796	39,492	59,270	88,033	155,020	4.3	9.9	15.6	23.0	47.2	20.4
2000	73,778	24,000	40,840	61,325	91,374	160,120	4.3	9.8	15.4	22.7	47.7	21.1
2001	74,340	24,000	41,127	62,500	94,150	164,104	4.2	9.7	15.4	22.9	47.8	21.0
2002	75,616	24,000	41,440	63,000	94,469	164,323	4.2	9.7	15.5	23.0	47.6	20.8

Source: U.S. Census Bureau, Current Population Reports, P60-221, *Income in the United States: 2002*; and Internet sites at <http://www.census.gov/prod/2003pubs/p60-221.pdf> (released 26 September 2003) and <http://www.census.gov/hhes/income/histinc/f01.html> and <http://www.census.gov/hhes/income/histinc/f02.html>.

No. 673. Money Income of Families—Distribution by Family Characteristics and Income Level: 2001

[74,340 represents 74,340,000]. See headnote, Table 670. For composition of regions, see map inside front cover]

Characteristic	Number of families (1,000)	Income level (1,000)							Median income (dollars)
		Under $15,000	$15,000 to $24,999	$25,000 to $34,999	$35,000 to $49,999	$50,000 to $74,999	$75,000 to $99,999	$100,000 and over	
All families	74,340	7,164	8,403	8,809	11,660	15,429	9,774	13,102	$51,407
Age of householder:									
15 to 24 years old	3,618	949	718	545	607	485	164	151	26,900
25 to 34 years old	13,220	1,685	1,575	1,664	2,158	3,066	1,588	1,483	46,272
35 to 44 years old	18,820	1,461	1,646	1,949	2,904	4,221	2,973	3,666	57,492
45 to 54 years old	16,540	912	1,110	1,282	2,175	3,757	2,890	4,413	68,114
55 to 64 years old	10,501	899	874	1,035	1,694	2,252	1,395	2,352	57,457
65 years old and over	11,641	1,258	2,477	2,334	2,124	1,651	759	1,037	33,816
White	61,647	4,916	6,489	7,167	9,755	13,181	8,507	11,633	54,067
Black	8,847	1,858	1,463	1,242	1,343	1,536	764	639	33,598
Hispanic origin [1]	8,516	1,430	1,502	1,380	1,471	1,427	687	618	34,490
Northeast	14,131	1,288	1,350	1,492	2,018	2,920	1,944	3,121	57,000
Midwest	17,447	1,305	1,861	1,994	2,805	4,036	2,526	2,919	54,096
South	27,021	3,143	3,466	3,373	4,387	5,296	3,257	4,103	46,688
West	15,740	1,430	1,725	1,952	2,453	3,181	2,044	2,959	51,966
Type of family:									
Married-couple families	56,755	2,904	4,989	5,855	8,833	13,116	8,781	12,275	60,335
Male householder, wife absent .	4,440	639	648	793	831	796	382	351	36,590
Female householder, husband . .	13,146	3,623	2,764	2,161	1,997	1,517	607	476	25,745
Unrelated subfamilies	474	185	125	77	50	26	5	5	17,707
Education attainment of householder: [2]									
Total	70,722	6,215	7,683	8,265	11,054	14,944	9,609	12,951	52,864
Less than 9th grade	4,306	1,057	1,089	767	696	410	169	118	25,077
9th to 12th grade (no diploma) . . .	6,176	1,214	1,271	1,149	1,108	901	294	241	29,512
High school graduate (includes equivalency)	21,769	2,225	2,985	3,114	4,084	4,987	2,432	1,941	43,870
Some college, no degree	12,627	833	1,213	1,580	2,149	3,099	1,884	1,871	53,809
Associate degree	5,956	312	392	620	1,025	1,517	1,088	1,000	60,033
Bachelor's degree or more	19,887	575	735	1,036	1,992	4,030	3,745	7,780	84,836
Bachelor's degree	12,665	394	516	740	1,443	2,840	2,411	4,321	78,518
Master's degree	4,888	120	144	190	402	917	977	2,138	90,811
Professional degree	1,255	32	41	54	83	132	180	734	100,000
Doctorate degree	1,079	27	33	50	62	144	107	587	100,000

[1] Persons of Hispanic origin may be of any race.   [2] Persons 25 years old and over.

Source: U.S. Census Bureau, *Current Population Reports, Income in the United States, 2001*, P60-218. See also <http://www.census.gov/prod/2002pubs/p60-218.pdf> (released September 2002) and <http://ferret.bls.census.gov/macro/032002/faminc/new01000.htm> (released 23 September 2002).

Income, Expenditures, and Wealth   447

No. 674. Median Income of Families by Type of Family in Current and Constant (2002) Dollars: 1980 to 2002

[In dollars. See headnote, Table 670. See Appendix III]

Year	Current dollars						Constant (2002) dollars					
	Married-couple families				Male house-holder, no wife present	Female house-holder, no hus-band present	Married-couple families				Male house-holder, no wife present	Female house-holder, no husband present
	Total	Total	Wife in paid labor force	Wife not in paid labor force			Total	Total	Wife in paid labor force	Wife not in paid labor force		
1980	21,023	23,141	26,879	18,972	17,519	10,408	43,456	47,834	55,561	39,217	36,213	21,514
1990	35,353	39,895	46,777	30,265	29,046	16,932	47,167	53,227	62,409	40,379	38,753	22,590
1995	40,611	47,062	55,823	32,375	30,358	19,691	47,588	55,148	65,414	37,937	35,574	23,074
1996	42,300	49,707	58,381	33,748	31,600	19,911	48,272	56,724	66,623	38,512	36,061	22,722
1997	44,568	51,591	60,669	36,027	32,960	21,023	49,797	57,644	67,787	40,254	36,827	23,489
1998	46,737	54,180	63,751	37,161	35,681	22,163	51,495	59,696	70,241	40,944	39,314	24,419
1999	48,831	56,501	66,478	38,480	37,339	23,762	52,694	60,971	71,737	41,524	40,293	25,642
2000 [1]	50,732	59,099	69,235	39,982	37,727	25,716	52,977	61,715	72,299	41,752	39,397	26,854
2001	51,407	60,335	70,834	40,782	36,590	25,745	52,225	61,295	71,961	41,431	37,172	26,154
2002	51,680	61,130	72,806	40,102	37,739	26,423	51,680	61,130	72,806	40,102	37,739	26,423

[1] Data reflect implementation of Census 2000-based population controls and a 28,000 household sample expansion to 78,000 households.

No. 675. Married-Couple Families—Number and Median Income by Work Experience of Husbands and Wives and Presence of Children: 2002

Work experience of husband or wife	Number (1,000)					Median income (dollars)				
	All married-couple families	No related chil-dren	One or more related children under 18 years old			All married-couple families	No related chil-dren	One or more related children under 18 years old		
			Total	One child	Two or more			Total	One child	Two or more
All married-couple families.	57,327	30,275	27,052	10,375	16,677	61,130	56,895	65,399	68,013	63,645
Husband worked.............	45,476	20,004	25,471	9,658	15,813	70,264	73,066	67,419	70,958	65,658
Wife worked..............	33,606	15,225	18,381	7,541	10,840	75,637	78,561	73,071	75,876	71,277
Wife did not work.....	11,869	4,779	7,090	2,117	4,973	51,236	52,645	50,176	49,076	50,449
Husband year-round, full-time worker.............	37,485	15,613	21,872	8,195	13,677	74,176	77,878	71,240	74,433	69,248
Wife worked..........	27,997	12,270	15,727	6,400	9,327	78,807	82,576	76,028	78,930	74,160
Wife did not work..........	9,488	3,342	6,145	1,795	4,350	55,708	59,812	53,060	52,178	53,658
Husband did not work	11,852	10,271	1,581	718	863	30,326	30,477	29,059	31,821	26,764
Wife worked..........	3,369	2,426	943	426	517	41,522	43,959	35,624	38,172	33,172
Wife did not work..........	8,482	7,844	638	292	346	27,069	27,590	19,109	21,123	18,051

Source of Tables 674 and 675: U.S. Census Bureau, Current Population Reports, P60-221; and <http://www.census.gov/prod/2003pubs/p60-221.pdf> (released September 2003) and <http://ferret.bls.census.gov/macro/032002/faminc/new04000.htm> (released 28 October 2003).

No. 676. Money Income of Families—Distribution of Income and Median Income by Race and Hispanic Origin: 1999

[In thousands, except as indicated. Families as of April 2000. Based on sample data from the 2000 Census of Population and Housing; see text, Section 1, Population, and Appendix III]

Income Interval	Race of householder								
	All fami-lies	White alone	Black or African American alone	American Indian and Alaska Native alone	Asian alone	Native Hawaiian and other Pacific Islander alone	Some other race alone	Two or more races	Hispanic or Latino [1]
All families	72,262	56,470	8,209	564	2,350	79	3,207	1,382	7,483
Under $10,000....	4,155	2,241	1,203	75	134	6	359	137	781
$10,000 to $19,999	6,756	4,448	1,296	91	189	8	537	187	1,200
$20,000 to $29,999	8,404	6,105	1,229	89	211	10	566	196	1,253
$30,000 to $39,999	8,664	6,678	1,022	75	224	10	476	180	1,066
$40,000 to $49,999	8,110	6,477	828	60	219	9	366	150	832
$50,000 to $59,999	7,300	5,976	666	48	209	8	268	125	633
$60,000 to $74,999	8,831	7,355	726	50	284	10	266	139	653
$75,000 to $99,999	9,009	7,619	660	42	336	10	212	131	561
$100,000 to $124,999...	4,662	3,992	289	17	214	4	81	63	242
$125,000 to $149,999...	2,274	1,960	125	7	119	2	32	28	104
$150,000 to $199,999...	1,984	1,732	88	5	112	1	22	23	78
$200,000 and over	2,113	1,887	78	5	98	1	22	22	80
Median income (dollars)	50,046	53,356	33,255	33,144	59,324	45,915	32,398	39,432	34,397

NA Not available.   [1] Persons of Hispanic origin or Latino may be of any race.

Source: U.S. Census Bureau, 2000 Census of Population and Housing, Summary File 3, using American FactFinder, tables P76, P77, P78, P154A-H, and P155A-H (accessed 05 September 2003).

No. 677. Money Income of People—Selected Characteristics by Income Level: 2002

[Covers people 15 years old and over (108,814 represents 108,814,000). For definition of median, see Guide to Tabular Presentation. For composition of regions, see map, inside front cover. See Appendix III]

Characteristic	All people (1,000)	People with income — Number (1,000)									Median income (dollars)
		Total (1,000)	Under $5,000 [1]	$5,000 to $9,999	$10,000 to $14,999	$15,000 to $24,999	$25,000 to $34,999	$35,000 to $49,999	$50,000 to $74,999	$75,000 and over	
MALE											
Total	108,814	99,788	7,760	8,301	9,473	17,769	14,788	15,725	13,738	12,237	$29,238
15 to 24 years old	20,216	14,120	4,659	2,543	1,934	2,714	1,229	747	199	98	9,642
25 to 34 years old . . .	19,564	18,695	715	1,130	1,497	3,744	3,768	3,751	2,663	1,429	30,677
35 to 44 years old . . .	21,733	20,979	658	1,020	1,120	3,212	3,383	4,021	3,945	3,619	37,892
45 to 54 years old . . .	19,606	18,971	649	899	1,087	2,458	2,678	3,607	3,738	3,856	40,969
55 to 64 years old . . .	13,166	12,750	590	822	1,065	1,846	1,803	2,116	2,128	2,377	36,277
65 yr. old and over . . .	14,528	14,273	490	1,887	2,771	3,793	1,929	1,485	1,066	852	19,436
Northeast.	20,809	19,040	1,447	1,490	1,757	3,154	2,724	2,955	2,803	2,712	30,649
Midwest.	24,600	22,931	1,927	1,816	1,881	3,973	3,529	3,853	3,340	2,612	30,238
South	38,471	35,035	2,594	3,134	3,567	6,533	5,392	5,409	4,541	3,864	27,524
West.	24,934	22,782	1,793	1,860	2,267	4,108	3,144	3,509	3,054	3,047	29,094
Education attainment of householder: [2]											
Total	88,597	85,668	3,101	5,757	7,540	15,055	13,560	14,981	13,537	12,138	32,471
Less than 9th grade. .	6,049	5,705	332	1,246	1,248	1,696	630	348	144	64	15,130
9th to 12th grade [3] . .	8,026	7,488	432	1,042	1,208	2,123	1,325	840	361	156	19,802
High school graduate [4].	27,356	26,298	1,060	1,916	2,693	5,846	5,295	4,809	3,336	1,345	27,526
Some college, no degree.	15,175	14,747	583	710	1,057	2,358	2,660	3,257	2,617	1,507	35,023
Associate degree	6,394	6,274	181	229	431	863	1,058	1,493	1,353	667	37,970
Bachelor's degree or more	25,598	25,155	514	614	904	2,170	2,592	4,233	5,728	8,399	55,188
Bachelor's degree . .	16,351	16,057	371	430	624	1,573	1,926	2,924	3,771	4,441	50,600
Master's degree. . . .	5,882	5,768	97	121	165	411	460	949	1,442	2,122	60,830
Professional degree .	1,837	1,816	19	30	62	122	103	179	244	1,058	88,216
Doctorate degree. . .	1,528	1,514	27	33	51	67	107	182	272	780	76,147
Tenure:											
Owner occupied . . .	78,794	72,894	5,645	5,033	6,030	11,497	10,344	12,046	11,488	10,812	32,203
Renter occupied . . .	28,618	25,642	1,984	3,148	3,256	5,960	4,256	3,522	2,138	1,378	21,855
Occupier paid no cash rent	1,401	1,252	133	121	187	311	189	158	109	46	20,704
FEMALE											
Total	116,436	102,487	16,621	16,405	13,658	19,770	13,917	11,534	6,964	3,617	16,812
15 to 24 years old	19,850	13,584	5,162	2,658	2,059	2,341	857	382	94	34	7,582
25 to 34 years old . . .	19,679	17,336	2,563	1,726	1,806	3,649	3,262	2,566	1,278	489	21,649
35 to 44 years old . . .	22,341	20,487	2,924	1,949	2,070	4,177	3,327	3,110	1,857	1,077	22,322
45 to 54 years old . . .	20,627	19,094	2,214	1,797	1,859	3,607	3,258	3,082	2,158	1,119	25,165
55 to 64 years old . . .	14,233	12,926	1,990	1,931	1,508	2,302	1,845	1,576	1,125	645	19,165
65 yr. old and over . . .	19,706	19,061	1,768	6,344	4,358	3,694	1,371	820	455	254	11,406
Northeast.	22,617	20,251	3,088	3,191	2,749	3,748	2,605	2,401	1,571	898	17,243
Midwest.	26,337	23,933	3,941	3,724	3,176	4,865	3,395	2,654	1,476	697	16,921
South	41,738	36,278	5,967	6,213	4,859	7,042	4,960	4,019	2,115	1,103	16,223
West.	25,744	22,024	3,624	3,278	2,875	4,114	2,958	2,461	1,800	914	17,283
Education attainment of householder: [2]											
Total	96,586	88,903	11,460	13,747	11,600	17,429	13,060	11,153	6,870	3,582	18,965
Less than 9th grade. .	6,228	5,015	933	1,939	1,134	724	189	65	20	8	8,965
9th to 12th grade [3] . .	8,297	7,103	1,121	2,210	1,493	1,453	516	217	58	35	10,613
High school graduate [4].	31,936	29,161	3,781	5,190	4,710	7,288	4,437	2,448	980	327	15,972
Some college, no degree.	16,588	15,616	1,993	1,991	1,865	3,490	2,813	2,055	1,008	398	20,602
Associate degree	8,754	8,323	895	847	847	1,739	1,685	1,393	716	201	23,766
Bachelor's degree or more	24,784	23,686	2,734	1,570	1,551	2,734	3,418	4,976	4,087	2,614	34,292
Bachelor's degree . .	16,862	16,003	2,104	1,178	1,157	2,094	2,526	3,261	2,330	1,354	30,788
Master's degree. . . .	6,275	6,073	517	296	312	512	774	1,441	1,412	809	40,939
Professional degree .	967	946	73	66	49	78	86	158	184	249	44,748
Doctorate degree. . .	680	663	41	30	34	50	33	114	157	202	52,336
Tenure:											
Owner occupied . . .	83,391	74,447	12,461	11,032	9,167	13,711	10,190	8,994	5,773	3,121	17,721
Renter occupied . . .	31,580	26,815	3,877	5,105	4,292	5,845	3,602	2,466	1,141	487	15,173
Occupier paid no cash rent	1,465	1,225	283	268	199	214	124	74	51	10	11,315

[1] Includes persons with income deficit. [2] Persons 25 years and over. [3] No diploma attained. [4] Includes high school equivalency.

Source: U.S. Census Bureau, Current Population Reports, *Income in the United States, 2002*, series P60-221. See also <http://www.census.gov/prod/2003pubs/p60-221.pdf> (released 26 September 2003). and <http://ferret.bls.census.gov/macro/032003/perinc/toc.htm> (17 October 2003).

Income, Expenditures, and Wealth **449**

No. 678. Median Income of People With Income in Constant (2001) Dollars by Sex, Race, and Hispanic Origin: 1980 to 2001

[People as of March of following year (78,661 represents 78,661,000). People 15 years old and over. Constant dollars based on CPI-U-RS deflator. Based on the Current Population Survey; see text, Sections 1 and 13, and Appendix III. For data collection changes over time, see <http://www.census.gov/hhes/income/histinc/hstchg.html>

Race and Hispanic origin	Male					Female				
	1980	1990	1995	2000[1]	2001	1980	1990	1995	2000[1]	2001
NUMBER WITH INCOME (1,000)										
All races	78,661	88,220	92,066	98,504	98,873	80,826	92,245	96,007	101,704	101,941
White	69,420	76,480	79,022	83,372	83,750	70,573	78,566	80,608	84,123	84,207
Black	7,387	8,820	9,339	9,905	9,944	8,596	10,687	11,607	12,461	12,414
Asian and Pacific Islander	(NA)	2,235	3,095	4,303	4,165	(NA)	2,333	3,025	4,192	4,164
Hispanic[2]	3,996	6,767	8,577	11,343	11,766	3,617	5,903	7,478	9,431	9,691
White non-hispanic	65,564	69,987	70,754	72,530	72,649	67,084	72,939	73,506	75,206	75,117
MEDIAN INCOME IN CONSTANT (2001) DOLLARS										
All races	12,530	20,293	22,562	28,343	29,101	4,920	10,070	12,130	16,063	16,614
White	13,328	21,170	23,895	29,797	30,240	4,947	10,317	12,316	16,079	16,652
Black	8,009	12,868	16,006	21,343	21,466	4,580	8,328	10,961	15,881	16,282
Asian and Pacific Islander	(NA)	19,394	22,162	30,833	31,096	(NA)	7,532	8,928	12,248	12,583
Hispanic[2]	9,659	13,470	14,840	19,498	20,189	4,405	7,532	8,928	12,248	12,583
White non-hispanic	13,681	21,958	25,481	32,387	31,791	4,980	10,581	12,807	17,130	17,229

NA Not available.   [1] Data reflect implementation of Census 2000-based population controls and a 28,000 household sample expansion to 78,000 households.   [2] People of Hispanic origin may be of any race.

No. 679. Average Earnings of Year-Round, Full-Time Workers by Educational Attainment: 2002

[In dollars. For people 18 years old and over as of March 2003. See headnote, Table 678]

Sex and Age	All workers	Less than 9th grade	High school		College		Bachelor's degree or more
			9th to 12th grade (no diploma)	High school graduate (includes equivalency)	Some college, no degree	Associate degree	
Male, total	52,435	24,134	29,608	37,680	46,252	48,342	80,144
18 to 24 years old	24,521	17,322	21,759	23,942	24,454	28,666	33,956
25 to 34 years old	41,629	21,512	25,862	34,611	39,148	40,726	57,790
35 to 44 years old	57,179	25,114	34,050	40,301	51,105	52,679	86,431
45 to 54 years old	62,176	24,481	29,312	41,221	54,437	55,148	91,856
55 to 64 years old	60,451	30,611	37,271	42,875	51,880	50,033	86,824
65 years old and over	52,424	27,875	36,284	39,555	50,279	(B)	72,940
Female, total	35,863	19,271	20,091	27,184	31,430	33,902	51,656
18 to 24 years old	21,389	(B)	14,461	19,279	19,934	23,197	29,486
25 to 34 years old	33,624	16,137	19,361	25,034	28,019	30,327	45,536
35 to 44 years old	37,244	16,943	20,015	27,528	33,437	34,785	54,276
45 to 54 years old	39,435	18,621	21,699	28,881	35,539	36,454	56,765
55 to 64 years old	38,888	19,623	23,973	31,114	35,609	36,034	57,264
65 years old and over	32,970	(B)	(B)	26,562	34,487	(B)	45,933

B Base too small to meet statistical standards for reliability of derived figure.

No. 680. Per Capita Money Income in Current and Constant (2001) Dollars by Race and Hispanic Origin: 1980 to 2001

[In dollars. Constant dollars based on CPI-U-RS deflator. People as of March of following year. Based on the Current Population Survey; see text, Sections 1 and 13, and Appendix III. For data collection changes over time, see <http://www.census.gov/hhes/income/histinc/hstchg.html]

Year	Current dollars					Constant (2001) dollars				
	All races[1]	White	Black	Asian, Pacific Islander	His-panic[2]	All races[1]	White	Black	Asian, Pacific Islander	His-panic[2]
1980	7,787	8,233	4,804	(NA)	4,865	15,844	16,752	9,775	(NA)	9,899
1985	11,013	11,671	6,840	(NA)	6,613	17,280	18,313	10,733	(NA)	10,376
1990	14,387	15,265	9,017	(NA)	8,424	18,894	20,047	11,842	(NA)	11,063
1991	14,617	15,510	9,170	(NA)	8,662	18,626	19,658	11,623	(NA)	10,979
1992[3]	14,847	15,785	9,239	(NA)	8,591	18,358	19,517	11,424	(NA)	10,622
1993	15,777	16,800	9,863	15,691	8,830	19,033	20,267	11,898	18,929	10,652
1994	16,555	17,611	10,650	16,902	9,435	19,559	20,807	12,583	19,969	11,147
1995	17,227	18,304	10,982	16,567	9,300	19,871	21,113	12,667	19,109	10,727
1996	18,136	19,181	11,899	17,921	10,048	20,372	21,546	13,366	20,131	11,287
1997	19,241	20,425	12,351	18,226	10,772	21,162	22,464	13,584	20,045	11,847
1998	20,120	21,394	12,957	18,709	11,434	21,821	23,203	14,053	20,291	12,401
1999	21,181	22,375	14,397	21,134	11,621	22,499	23,767	15,293	22,449	12,344
2000[4]	22,346	23,582	14,796	23,350	12,651	22,970	24,240	15,209	24,002	13,004
2001	22,851	24,127	14,953	24,277	13,003	22,851	24,127	14,953	24,277	13,003

NA Not available.   [1] Includes other races not shown separately.   [2] Persons of Hispanic origin may be of any race.   [3] Data based on Census 1990-based population controls and a sample of approximately 50,000 households.   [4] Data reflect implementation of Census 2000-based population controls and a 28,000 household sample expansion to 78,000 households.

Source of Tables 678-680: U.S. Census Bureau, *Current Population Reports*, P60-218, and <http://www.census.gov/hhes/income/histinc/incperdet.html(released 01 October 2002).

No. 681. Money Income of People—Number by Income Level and by Sex, Race, and Hispanic Origin: 2002

[In thousands. People as of March of the following year. (108,814 represents 108,814,000). Based on Current Population Survey (CPS); see text, Sections 1 and 13, and Appendix III. The 2003 CPS allowed respondents to choose more than one race. For 2002, data represent persons who selected this race group only and excludes persons reporting more than one race. The CPS in prior years only allowed respondents to report one race group. See also comments on race in the text for Section 1, Population]

Income interval	Male					Female				
	All races	White	Black	Asian	His-panic [1]	All races	White	Black	Asian	His-panic [1]
All households [1]	108,814	90,080	11,821	4,419	14,353	116,436	94,418	14,461	4,910	13,607
Under $10,000	25,087	18,754	4,356	1,160	4,124	46,975	37,373	6,066	2,264	7,411
$10,000 to $14,999	9,473	7,819	1,101	346	1,816	13,658	11,291	1,658	405	1,625
$15,000 to $19,999	9,063	7,431	1,087	319	1,813	10,631	8,627	1,424	359	1,196
$20,000 to $24,999	8,706	7,181	983	316	1,537	9,139	7,504	1,099	353	884
$25,000 to $29,999	7,500	6,305	781	239	1,178	7,487	6,016	1,059	270	718
$30,000 to $34,999	7,288	6,106	739	276	866	6,430	5,253	827	220	499
$35,000 to $39,999	6,240	5,263	601	226	660	4,750	3,933	567	152	340
$40,000 to $44,999	5,406	4,636	493	188	496	4,116	3,432	468	147	276
$45,000 to $49,999	4,079	3,524	315	155	373	2,668	2,198	285	126	168
$50,000 to $59,999	7,048	6,194	509	224	566	3,886	3,213	399	205	215
$60,000 to $74,999	6,690	5,928	370	299	396	3,078	2,523	345	170	148
$75,000 to $84,999	3,260	2,865	167	181	177	1,118	948	89	59	44
$85,000 to $99,999	2421	2138	108	140	99	841	689	80	60	22
$100,000 to $149,999	3,940	3,542	135	229	157	1,147	981	54	96	48
$150,000 to $199,999	1,124	1,036	24	54	37	281	255	11	9	7
$200,000 to $249,999	538	488	21	21	17	114	83	17	12	1
$250,000 and above	954	870	29	47	39	116	98	12	5	6

[1] Persons of Hispanic origin may be of any race.

Source: U.S. Census Bureau, Current Population Reports, P60-221; and Internet site at <http://ferret.bls.census.gov/macro/032003/hhinc/new06000.htm> (revised 13 November 2003).

No. 682. People Below Poverty Level by Race, Sex, and Age: 1999

[Persons as of April 2000. Covers persons for whom poverty status was determined. Based on sample data from the 2000 Census of Population and Housing; see text, Section 1, Population, and Appendix III]

Income Interval	Race of householder								
	All races	White alone	Black or African American alone	American Indian and Alaska Native alone	Asian alone	Native Hawaiian and other Pacific Islander alone	Some other race alone	Two or more races	His-panic or Latino [1]
NUMBER BELOW POVERTY LEVEL (1,000)									
Total	33,900	18,848	8,146	608	1,257	65	3,688	1,289	7,798
Male	14,925	8,203	3,447	279	598	31	1,766	602	3,699
Female	18,975	10,645	4,699	329	659	34	1,922	687	4,099
Under 5 years old	3,412	1,579	982	69	81	8	489	204	1,030
5 years old	690	317	205	14	18	2	98	35	204
6 to 11 years old	4,149	1,904	1,271	88	120	9	564	192	1,172
12 to 17 years old	3,497	1,669	1,009	79	125	9	461	146	932
18 to 64 years old	18,865	11,007	4,051	327	818	36	1,976	651	4,133
65 years and over	3,288	2,371	628	31	95	2	100	61	326
65 to 74 years old	1,551	1,040	339	19	56	1	63	34	194
75 years old and over	1,737	1,331	289	12	39	1	37	27	132
PERCENT BELOW POVERTY LEVEL									
Total	12.4	9.1	24.9	25.7	12.6	17.7	24.4	18.2	22.6
Male	11.2	8.1	22.8	24.0	12.5	16.7	22.7	17.1	21.1
Female	13.5	10.1	26.7	27.2	12.7	18.7	26.2	19.3	24.2
Under 5 years old	18.2	12.5	36.7	34.5	12.5	24.7	30.8	21.5	28.8
5 years old	17.6	12.0	35.2	33.6	13.6	24.4	30.6	19.9	28.5
6 to 11 years old	16.9	11.3	33.5	31.7	14.8	23.1	30.3	19.8	28.2
12 to 17 years old	14.8	10.0	29.4	29.0	15.2	20.6	28.2	18.3	26.2
18 to 64 years old	11.1	8.6	20.7	22.6	12.0	15.6	21.3	17.0	19.9
65 years and over	9.9	8.2	23.5	23.5	12.3	11.5	22.8	16.9	19.6
65 to 74 years old	8.5	6.7	21.4	21.9	11.6	11.7	21.9	15.5	18.4
75 years old and over	11.5	10.0	26.6	26.3	13.7	11.0	24.5	18.9	21.8

[1] Persons of Hispanic origin or Latino may be of any race.

Source: U.S. Census Bureau, 2000 Census of Population and Housing, Summary File 3, using American FactFinder, tables P52, P53, P54, P151A-H, P152A-H, and P153A-H (accessed 05 September 2003).

Income, Expenditures, and Wealth   451

No. 683. People Below Poverty Level and Below 125 Percent of Poverty Level by Race and Hispanic Origin: 1980 to 2002

[People as of March of the following year (29,272 represents 29,272,000). Based on Current Population Survey; See text, this section 1, and Appendix III. For data collection changes over time, see <http://www.census.gov/hhes/income/histinc/hstchg.html>.

Year	Number below poverty level (1,000)					Percent below poverty level					Below 125 percent of poverty level	
	All races [1]	White	Black	Asian and Pacific Islander	His-panic [2]	All races sup1	White	Black	Asian and Pacific Islander	His-panic [2]	Num-ber (1,000)	Percent of total popula-tion
1980	29,272	19,699	8,579	(NA)	3,491	13.0	10.2	32.5	(NA)	25.7	40,658	18.1
1985	33,064	22,860	8,926	(NA)	5,236	14.0	11.4	31.3	(NA)	29.0	44,166	18.7
1986	32,370	22,183	8,983	(NA)	5,117	13.6	11.0	31.1	(NA)	27.3	43,486	18.2
1987	32,221	21,195	9,520	1,021	5,422	13.4	10.4	32.4	16.1	28.0	43,032	17.9
1988	31,745	20,715	9,356	1,117	5,357	13.0	10.1	31.3	17.3	26.7	42,551	17.5
1989	31,528	20,785	9,302	939	5,430	12.8	10.0	30.7	14.1	26.2	42,653	17.3
1990	33,585	22,326	9,837	858	6,006	13.5	10.7	31.9	12.2	28.1	44,837	18.0
1991	35,708	23,747	10,242	996	6,339	14.2	11.3	32.7	13.8	28.7	47,527	18.9
1992	38,014	25,259	10,827	985	7,592	14.8	11.9	33.4	12.7	29.6	50,592	19.7
1993	39,265	26,226	10,877	1,134	8,126	15.1	12.2	33.1	15.3	30.6	51,801	20.0
1994	38,059	25,379	10,196	974	8,416	14.5	11.7	30.6	14.6	30.7	50,401	19.3
1995	36,425	24,423	9,872	1,411	8,574	13.8	11.2	29.3	14.6	30.3	48,761	18.5
1996	36,529	24,650	9,694	1,454	8,697	13.7	11.2	28.4	14.5	29.4	49,310	18.5
1997	35,574	24,396	9,116	1,468	8,308	13.3	11.0	26.5	14.0	27.1	47,853	17.8
1998	34,476	23,454	9,091	1,360	8,070	12.7	10.5	26.1	12.5	25.6	46,036	17.0
1999	32,258	21,922	8,360	1,163	7,439	11.8	9.8	23.6	10.7	22.8	44,286	16.2
2000 [3]	31,581	21,645	7,982	1,258	7,747	11.3	9.5	22.5	9.9	21.5	43,612	15.6
2001	32,907	22,739	8,136	1,275	7,997	11.7	9.9	22.7	10.2	21.4	45,320	16.1
2002 [4]	34,570	23,466	8,602	[5]1,161	8,555	12.1	10.2	24.1	[5]10.1	21.8	47,084	16.5

NA Not available. [1] Includes other races not shown separately. [2] Persons of Hispanic origin may be of any race. [3] Implementation of Census 2000 based population controls and sample expanded by 28,000 households. [4] The 2003 Current Population Survey (CPS) allowed respondents to choose more than one race. For 2002, data represent persons who selected this race group only and excludes persons reporting more than one race. The CPS in prior years only allowed respondents to report one race group. See also comments on race in the text for Section 1, Population. [5] Data represent Asian alone, which refers to people who reported Asian and did not report any other race category.

Source: U.S. Census Bureau, Current Population Reports, *Poverty in the United States, 2001*,P60-219. See also <http://www.census.gov/prod/2002pubs/p60-219.pdf> (released September 2002).

No. 684. Children Below Poverty Level by Race and Hispanic Origin: 1980 to 2002

[Persons as of March of the following year. (11,114 represents 11,114,000). Covers only related children in families under 18 years old. Based on Current Population Survey; see text, this section and Section 1, and Appendix III] For data collection changes over time, see <http://www.census.gov/hhes/income/histinc/hstchg.html]

Year	Number below poverty level (1,000)					Percent below poverty level				
	All races [1]	White	Black	Asian and Pacific Islander	His-panic [2]	All races [1]	White	Black	Asian and Pacific Islander	His-panic [2]
1980	11,114	6,817	3,906	(NA)	1,718	17.9	13.4	42.1	(NA)	33.0
1985	12,483	7,838	4,057	(NA)	2,512	20.1	15.6	43.1	(NA)	39.6
1986	12,257	7,714	4,037	(NA)	2,413	19.8	15.3	42.7	(NA)	37.1
1987	12,275	7,398	4,234	432	2,606	19.7	14.7	44.4	22.7	38.9
1988	11,935	7,095	4,148	458	2,576	19.0	14.0	42.8	23.5	37.3
1989	12,001	7,164	4,257	368	2,496	19.0	14.1	43.2	18.9	35.5
1990	12,715	7,696	4,412	356	2,750	19.9	15.1	44.2	17.0	37.7
1991	13,658	8,316	4,637	348	2,977	21.1	16.1	45.6	17.1	39.8
1992	14,521	8,752	5,015	352	3,440	21.6	16.5	46.3	16.0	39.0
1993	14,961	9,123	5,030	358	3,666	22.0	17.0	45.9	17.6	39.9
1994	14,610	8,826	4,787	308	3,956	21.2	16.3	43.3	17.9	41.1
1995	13,999	8,474	4,644	532	3,938	20.2	15.5	41.5	18.6	39.3
1996	13,764	8,488	4,411	553	4,090	19.8	15.5	39.5	19.1	39.9
1997	13,422	8,441	4,116	608	3,865	19.2	15.4	36.8	19.9	36.4
1998	12,845	7,935	4,073	542	3,670	18.3	14.4	36.4	17.5	33.6
1999	11,510	7,123	3,644	348	3,382	16.3	12.9	32.7	11.5	29.9
2000 [3]	11,005	6,834	3,495	407	3,342	15.6	12.4	30.9	12.5	27.6
2001	11,175	7,086	3,423	353	3,433	15.6	12.8	30.0	[5]11.1	27.4
2002 [4]	11,646	7,203	3,570	[5]302	3,653	16.3	13.1	32.1	[5]11.4	28.2

NA Not available. [1] Includes other races not shown separately. [2] Persons of Hispanic origin may be of any race. [3] Implementation of Census 2000 based population controls and sample expanded by 28,000 households. [4] The 2003 Current Population Survey (CPS) allowed respondents to choose more than one race. For 2002, data represent persons who selected this race group only and excludes persons reporting more than one race. The CPS in prior years only allowed respondents to report one race group. See also comments on race in the text for Section 1, Population. [5] Data represent Asian alone, which refers to people who reported Asian and did not report any other race category.

Source: U.S. Census Bureau, Current Population Reports, *Poverty in the United States, 2002*, P60-222. See also <http://www.census.gov/prod/2003pubs/p60-222.pdf> (released September 2003).

No. 685. Weighted Average Poverty Thresholds by Size of Unit: 1980 to 2002

[In dollars. For information on the official poverty thresholds; see text, this section]

Size of family unit	1980[1]	1990	1995	1997	1998	1999	2000	2001	2002
One person (unrelated individual) . . .	4,190	6,652	7,763	8,183	8,316	8,501	8,794	9,044	9,183
Under 65 years	4,290	6,800	7,929	8,350	8,480	8,667	8,959	9,214	9,359
65 years and over	3,949	6,268	7,309	7,698	7,818	7,990	8,259	8,494	8,628
Two persons	5,363	8,509	9,933	10,473	10,634	10,869	11,239	11,559	11,756
Householder under 65 years	5,537	8,794	10,259	10,805	10,972	11,214	11,590	11,920	12,110
Householder 65 years and over . . .	4,983	7,905	9,219	9,712	9,862	10,075	10,419	10,715	10,885
Three persons	6,565	10,419	12,158	12,802	13,003	13,290	13,738	14,129	14,348
Four persons	8,414	13,359	15,569	16,400	16,660	17,029	17,603	18,104	18,392
Five persons	9,966	15,792	18,408	19,380	19,680	20,127	20,819	21,411	21,744
Six persons	11,269	17,839	20,804	21,886	22,228	22,727	23,528	24,197	24,576
Seven persons	12,761	20,241	23,552	24,802	25,257	25,912	26,754	27,514	28,001
Eight persons	14,199	22,582	26,237	27,593	28,166	28,967	29,701	30,546	30,907
Nine or more persons	16,896	26,848	31,280	32,566	33,339	34,417	35,060	36,058	37,062

[1] Poverty levels for nonfarm families.

Source: U.S. Census Bureau, Current Population Reports, *Poverty in the United States, 2002*, P60-222. See also <http://www.census.gov/prod/2003pubs/p60-222.pdf> (released September 2003).

No. 686. Persons Below Poverty Level by Selected Characteristics: 2002

[People as of March 2003 (34,570 represents 34,570,000). Based on Current Population Survey (CPS); see text, this section and Section 1, and Appendix III. The 2003 CPS allowed respondents to choose more than one race. For 2002, data represent persons who selected this race group only and excludes persons reporting more than one race. The CPS in prior years allowed respondents to report only one race group. See also comments on race in the text for Section 1, Population. For composition of regions, see map, inside front cover]

Characteristic	Number below poverty level (1,000)					Percent below poverty level				
	All races [1]	White	Black	Asian	His-panic [2]	All races [1]	White	Black	Asian	His-panic [2]
Total	34,570	23,466	8,602	1,161	8,555	12.1	10.2	24.1	10.1	21.8
Male	15,162	10,381	3,632	535	3,954	10.9	9.1	22.0	9.7	19.7
Female	19,408	13,085	4,969	626	4,601	13.3	11.2	26.0	10.4	24.1
Under 18 years old	12,133	7,549	3,645	315	3,782	16.7	13.6	32.3	11.7	28.6
18 to 24 years old	4,536	3,099	1,084	196	1,014	16.5	14.4	28.0	16.8	21.1
25 to 34 years old	4,674	3,300	989	201	1,410	11.9	10.7	19.7	9.1	19.0
35 to 44 years old	4,087	2,778	944	199	1,016	9.3	7.8	17.4	10.1	17.2
45 to 54 years old	2,999	2,012	818	101	559	7.5	6.0	17.8	6.4	15.2
55 to 59 years old	1,302	994	233	38	169	8.4	7.5	15.7	7.1	14.2
60 to 64 years old	1,263	995	209	29	165	10.6	9.8	18.2	6.9	18.1
65 years old and over . . .	3,576	2,739	680	82	439	10.4	9.1	23.8	8.4	21.4
65 to 74 years old	1,696	1,224	387	43	247	9.4	7.9	23.3	6.9	20.2
75 years old and over .	1,880	1,515	292	39	192	11.7	10.5	24.4	10.9	23.1
Northeast	5,871	3,930	1,575	188	1,405	10.9	8.9	23.6	8.2	25.3
Midwest	6,616	4,473	1,731	187	662	10.3	8.1	26.6	13.5	19.4
South	14,019	8,631	4,697	276	3,014	13.8	11.1	24.4	11.2	22.3
West	8,064	6,432	599	511	3,474	12.4	12.1	18.5	9.5	20.8
Native	29,012	19,339	8,079	373	4,983	11.5	9.3	24.7	8.9	21.3
Foreign born	5,558	4,127	522	788	3,572	16.6	18.6	19.4	10.7	22.6
Naturalized citizen. . . .	1,285	848	151	248	602	10.0	11.1	12.6	6.9	15.3
Not a citizen.	4,273	3,279	371	540	2,970	20.7	22.5	20.6	14.4	25.1

[1] Includes other races not shown separately.   [2] Persons of Hispanic origin may be of any race.

Source: U.S. Census Bureau, Current Population Reports, *Poverty in the United States, 2002*, P60-222. See also <http://www.census.gov/prod/2003pubs/p60-222.pdf> (released September 2003) and <http://ferret.bls.census.gov/macro/032003/pov/toc.htm> (released September 2003).

Income, Expenditures, and Wealth   453

No. 687. Work Experience During 2002 by Poverty Status, Sex, and Age: 2002

[Number in thousands (100,659 represents 100,659,000). Covers only persons 16 years old and over. Based on Current Population Survey; see text, this section and Section 1, and Appendix III]

Sex and age	Worked full-time year-round			Did not work full-time year-round			Did not work		
		Below poverty level			Below poverty level			Below poverty level	
	Number (1,000)	Number (1,000)	Percent	Number (1,000)	Number (1,000)	Percent	Number (1,000)	Number (1,000)	Percent
BOTH SEXES									
Total	100,659	2,635	2.6	50,887	6,318	12.4	69,595	14,647	21.0
16 to 17 years old	95	6	5.9	2,845	196	6.9	5,579	962	17.2
18 to 64 years old	98,272	2,588	2.6	44,646	6,020	13.5	35,470	10,253	28.9
18 to 24 years old. . . .	7,946	380	4.8	12,411	1,963	15.8	7,082	2,193	31.0
25 to 34 years old. . . .	23,594	845	3.6	9,519	1,639	17.2	6,129	2,189	35.7
35 to 54 years old. . . .	53,971	1,196	2.2	17,152	1,971	11.5	13,184	3,919	29.7
55 to 64 years old. . . .	12,762	167	1.3	5,563	447	8.0	9,075	1,951	21.5
65 years old and over . . .	2,291	42	1.8	3,397	103	3.0	28,546	3,432	12.0
MALE									
Total	58,765	1,486	2.5	21,517	2,585	12.0	26,455	5,410	20.5
16 to 17 years old	63	6	(B)	1,432	85	5.9	2,811	462	16.4
18 to 64 years old	57,266	1,458	2.5	18,337	2,457	13.4	12,300	3,889	31.6
18 to 24 years old. . . .	4,595	190	4.1	6,023	800	13.3	3,217	887	27.6
25 to 34 years old. . . .	14,075	468	3.3	3,848	630	16.4	1,641	686	41.8
35 to 54 years old. . . .	31,247	707	2.3	6,125	840	13.7	3,967	1,510	38.1
55 to 64 years old. . . .	7,349	92	1.2	2,341	188	8.0	3,475	806	23.2
65 years old and over . . .	1,436	23	1.6	1,748	42	2.4	11,343	1,060	9.3
FEMALE									
Total	41,893	1,149	2.7	29,370	3,734	12.7	43,140	9,237	21.4
16 to 17 years old	32	-	(B)	1,413	110	7.8	2,768	501	18.1
18 to 64 years old	41,006	1,130	2.8	26,308	3,563	13.5	23,170	6,364	27.5
18 to 24 years old. . . .	3,351	189	5.7	6,388	1,163	18.2	3,865	1,307	33.8
25 to 34 years old. . . .	9,519	377	4.0	5,671	1,009	17.8	4,488	1,503	33.5
35 to 54 years old. . . .	22,723	488	2.1	11,027	1,131	10.3	9,217	2,410	26.1
55 to 64 years old. . . .	5,412	75	1.4	3,221	260	8.1	5,600	1,145	20.4
65 years old and over . . .	855	19	2.2	1,649	60	3.7	17,203	2,372	13.8

B Base figure too small to meet statistical standards for reliability of a derived figure. - Represents zero.

Source: U.S. Census Bureau, <http://ferret.bls.census.gov/macro/032003/pov/new22100.htm> (released September 2003).

No. 688. Persons Below Poverty Level—Number and Rate by State: 2000 to 2002 Average

[33,019 represents 33,019,000. Based on the Current Population survey; see text Sections 1 and 13, and Appendix III. The CPS is designed to collect reliable data on income primarily at the national level and secondarily at the regional level. When the income data are tabulated by state, the estimates are considered less reliable and, therefore, particular caution should be used when trying to interpret the results; for additional detail, see source]

State	Number below poverty level (1,000)	Percent below poverty level	State	Number below poverty level (1,000)	Percent below poverty level
United States	33,019	11.7	Missouri	531	9.6
Alabama	640	14.6	Montana	122	13.7
Alaska	52	8.3	Nebraska	161	9.5
Arizona	707	13.3	Nevada	173	8.3
Arkansas	480	18.0	New Hampshire	70	5.6
California	4,406	12.8			
			New Jersey	659	7.8
Colorado	415	9.4	New Mexico	321	17.8
Connecticut	262	7.8	New York	2,653	14.0
Delaware	64	8.1	North Carolina	1,059	13.1
District of Columbia	94	16.8	North Dakota	74	11.9
Florida	1,963	12.1			
			Ohio	1,130	10.1
Georgia	997	12.1	Oklahoma	500	14.7
Hawaii	127	10.6	Oregon	386	11.2
Idaho.	153	11.8	Pennsylvania	1,114	9.2
Illinois	1,383	11.2	Rhode Island	107	10.3
Indiana	525	8.7			
			South Carolina	537	13.5
Iowa	239	8.3	South Dakota	75	10.2
Kansas	250	9.4	Tennessee	800	14.2
Kentucky	525	13.1	Texas	3,231	15.3
Louisiana	745	17.0	Utah	212	9.3
Maine	143	11.3			
			Vermont	60	9.9
Maryland	391	7.3	Virginia	614	8.7
Massachusetts	609	9.6	Washington	642	10.8
Michigan	1,015	10.3	West Virginia	282	16.0
Minnesota	321	6.5	Wisconsin	461	8.6
Mississippi	490	17.6	Wyoming	46	9.5

Source: U.S. Census Bureau, Current Population Reports, *Poverty in the United States, 2002*, P60-222. See also <http://www.census.gov/prod/2003pubs/p60-222.pdf> (released September 2003).

No. 689. Families Below Poverty Level and Below 125 Percent of Poverty by Race and Hispanic Origin: 1980 to 2002

[Families as of March of the following year (6,217 represents 6,217,000). Based on Current Population Survey; See text, this section 1, and Appendix III. For data collection changes over time, see <http://www.census.gov/hhes/income/histinc/hstchg.html>]

Year	Number below poverty level (1,000)					Percent below poverty level					Below 125 percent of poverty level	
	All races [1]	White	Black	Asian and Pacific Islander	His-panic [2]	All races [1]	White	Black	Asian and Pacific Islander	His-panic [2]	Num-ber (1,000)	Percent
1980	6,217	4,195	1,826	(NA)	751	10.3	8.0	28.9	(NA)	23.2	8,764	14.5
1981	6,851	4,670	1,972	(NA)	792	11.2	8.8	30.8	(NA)	24.0	9,568	15.7
1982	7,512	5,118	2,158	(NA)	916	12.2	9.6	33.0	(NA)	27.2	10,279	16.7
1983	7,647	5,220	2,161	(NA)	981	12.3	9.7	32.3	(NA)	25.9	10,358	16.7
1984	7,277	4,925	2,094	(NA)	991	11.6	9.1	30.9	(NA)	25.2	9,901	15.8
1985	7,223	4,983	1,983	(NA)	1,074	11.4	9.1	28.7	(NA)	25.5	9,753	15.3
1986	7,023	4,811	1,987	(NA)	1,085	10.9	8.6	28.0	(NA)	24.7	9,476	14.7
1987	7,005	4,567	2,117	199	1,168	10.7	8.1	29.4	13.5	25.5	9,338	14.3
1988	6,874	4,471	2,089	201	1,141	10.4	7.9	28.2	13.6	23.7	9,284	14.1
1989	6,784	4,409	2,077	182	1,133	10.3	7.8	27.8	11.9	23.4	9,267	14.0
1990	7,098	4,622	2,193	169	1,244	10.7	8.1	29.3	11.0	25.0	9,564	14.4
1991	7,712	5,022	2,343	210	1,372	11.5	8.8	30.4	13.0	26.5	10,244	15.3
1992	8,144	5,255	2,484	215	1,529	11.9	9.1	31.1	12.2	26.7	10,959	16.1
1993	8,393	5,452	2,499	235	1,625	12.3	9.4	31.3	13.5	27.3	11,203	16.4
1994	8,053	5,312	2,212	208	1,724	11.6	9.1	27.3	13.1	27.8	10,771	15.5
1995	7,532	4,994	2,127	264	1,695	10.8	8.5	26.4	12.4	27.0	10,223	14.7
1996	7,708	5,059	2,206	284	1,748	11.0	8.6	26.1	12.7	26.4	10,476	14.9
1997	7,324	4,990	1,985	244	1,721	10.3	8.4	23.6	10.2	24.7	10,032	14.2
1998	7,186	4,829	1,981	270	1,648	10.0	8.0	23.4	11.0	22.7	9,714	13.6
1999	6,676	4,377	1,898	258	1,525	9.3	7.3	21.9	10.3	20.2	9,320	12.9
2000 [3]	6,400	4,333	1,686	233	1,540	8.7	7.1	19.3	7.8	19.2	9,032	12.2
2001 [4]	6,813	4,579	1,829	234	1,649	9.2	7.4	20.7	7.8	19.4	9,525	12.8
2002 [4]	7,229	4,862	1,923	[5]210	1,792	9.6	7.8	21.5	[5]7.4	19.7	9,998	13.2

NA Not available.   [1] Includes other races not shown separately.   [2] Persons of Hispanic origin may be of any race.   [3] Implementation of Census 2000 based population controls and sample expanded by 28,000 households.   [4] The 2003 Current Population Survey (CPS) allowed respondents to choose more than one race. For 2002, data represent persons who selected this race group only and excludes persons reporting more than one race. The CPS in prior years only allowed respondents to report one race group. See also comments on race in the text for Section 1, Population.   [5] Data represent Asian alone, which refers to people who reported Asian and did not report any other race category.

Source: U.S. Census Bureau, Current Population Reports, *Poverty in the United States*, 2002, P60-222. See also <http://www.census.gov/prod/2002pubs/p60-222.pdf> (released September 2003).

No. 690. Families Below Poverty Level by Selected Characteristics: 2002

[Families as of March 2003. (7,229 represents 7,229,000). Based on Current Population Survey; see text, this section and Section 1, and Appendix III]

Characteristic	Number below poverty level (1,000)					Percent below poverty level				
	All races [1]	White	Black	Asian and Pacific Islander	His-panic [2]	All races [1]	White	Black	Asian and Pacific Islander	His-panic [2]
Total	7,229	4,862	1,923	210	1,792	9.6	7.8	21.5	7.4	19.7
Age of householder:										
15 to 24 years old	933	568	322	16	233	27.7	23.5	43.8	14.6	30.2
25 to 34 years old	1,933	1,312	513	37	579	14.4	12.4	26.7	6.3	23.8
35 to 44 years old	1,828	1,191	486	76	497	9.8	7.9	20.6	9.3	18.6
45 to 54 years old	973	636	280	37	236	5.8	4.5	15.0	5.8	15.2
55 to 64 years old	743	579	129	19	104	6.6	6.0	12.6	4.9	11.8
65 years old and over	766	544	180	23	123	6.5	5.3	18.3	8.2	16.8
Region:										
Northeast	1,156	773	324	30	317	8.1	6.5	20.2	5.1	23.3
Midwest	1,317	898	359	27	133	7.7	6.0	23.1	8.4	17.4
South	3,165	1,911	1,129	53	639	11.4	8.8	22.6	8.8	19.9
West	1,591	1,280	111	100	703	9.6	9.3	14.4	7.5	18.8
Type of family:										
Married couple	3,052	2,510	331	135	927	5.3	5.0	7.9	5.9	15.0
Female householder, no husband present	3,613	2,004	1,433	48	717	26.5	22.6	36.8	14.2	35.3
Male household, no wife present	564	349	160	27	148	12.1	9.9	20.9	12.4	17.0
Education of householder: [3]										
No high school diploma	2,255	1,598	532	54	963	21.6	19.1	35.0	19.5	27.3
High school diploma, no college	2,181	1,413	657	40	358	10.0	7.8	23.9	8.4	15.9
Some college, less than bachelor's degree	1,273	836	355	38	163	6.6	5.3	14.1	7.9	10.3
Bachelor's degree or more	535	415	43	61	55	2.6	2.4	3.1	4.1	6.1

[1] Includes other races not shown separately.   [2] Hispanic persons may be of any race.   [3] Householder 25 years old and over.

Source: U.S. Census Bureau, Current Population Reports, *Poverty in the United States*, 2002, P60-222. See also <http://www.census.gov/prod/2003pubs/p60-222.pdf> (released September 2003) and <http://ferret.bls.census.gov/macro/032001/pov/new16a000.htm> (released 23 September 2002).

No. 691. Asset Ownership Rates for Households by Type of Asset and Household Characteristic: 2000

[In percent. Excludes group quarters. Based on the Survey of Income and Program Participation and subject to sampling variability. Data are similar but not comparable to those found in tables 693 and 694, which are based on the Survey of Consumer Finances]

Household characteristic	Interest earning assets at financial institutions	Stocks and mutual fund shares	Own business or profession	Motor vehicles	Own home	Rental property	IRA or Keogh accounts	401K or thrift savings plans
Total households	65.0	27.1	10.8	85.8	67.2	4.9	23.1	29.9
White	68.6	29.7	11.6	88.3	70.7	5.2	25.7	31.4
White not of Hispanic origin. . . .	71.1	31.9	12.0	89.2	73.0	5.4	27.5	32.9
Black	41.6	10.2	4.7	70.2	46.8	2.2	6.5	19.6
Hispanic origin	44.6	9.2	8.1	77.5	47.8	3.0	8.1	17.4
Not of Hispanic origin.	67.0	28.9	11.0	86.6	69.1	5.0	24.6	31.1
Age of householder:								
Less than 35 years	55.7	18.4	7.7	85.5	42.2	1.6	12.0	30.4
35 to 44 years.	64.6	26.9	14.0	88.8	67.0	4.1	20.7	41.1
45 to 54 years.	67.6	31.3	14.7	89.5	74.5	5.8	28.0	40.5
55 to 64 years.	67.7	32.3	13.5	87.8	78.8	7.9	33.9	30.5
65 years and over	70.5	29.0	4.8	78.0	78.4	6.1	25.4	6.3
65 to 69 years	69.1	29.8	7.5	84.9	81.3	6.7	33.7	12.1
70 to 74 years	70.4	29.9	6.0	83.3	80.7	7.2	33.4	7.2
75 and over.	71.4	28.1	2.8	71.6	75.6	5.3	16.7	2.8
Educational attainment:								
No high school diploma. . . .	42.8	6.9	5.5	71.1	56.1	2.3	6.7	8.4
High school graduate only . . .	59.6	19.5	9.5	85.7	67.3	3.9	16.4	23.8
Some college, no degree . . .	66.7	27.3	11.2	88.7	65.0	4.8	22.9	32.1
Associate's degree.	72.0	29.9	11.1	91.8	70.7	5.1	24.6	38.8
Bachelor's degree or higher. .	82.6	49.3	15.7	91.4	74.9	7.7	42.3	46.8
Type of household:								
Married-couple households . .	73.4	33.2	15.1	94.1	81.0	6.6	29.2	37.5
Male householder	55.7	21.6	9.4	82.5	49.1	3.1	17.1	25.4
Female householder.	54.6	19.0	3.5	72.1	52.1	2.6	15.2	18.3
Household net worth:								
Negative or zero	31.6	5.2	5.6	60.8	19.7	0.5	3.9	11.2
$1 to $4,999	38.4	3.3	2.0	78.6	12.8	0.1	2.2	9.8
$5,000 to $9,999	47.2	6.6	4.6	91.4	30.3	0.3	5.4	20.1
$10,000 to $24,999	56.9	12.4	6.2	88.6	58.8	0.7	9.0	28.1
$25,000 to $49,999	63.8	17.6	7.2	89.6	80.0	1.3	12.5	32.2
$50,000 to $99,999	71.7	21.9	9.6	91.0	90.2	3.0	17.7	32.9
$100,000 to $249,999.	82.7	37.1	13.8	92.4	93.3	6.0	33.1	39.5
$250,000 to $499,999.	89.4	61.5	18.3	94.0	95.7	12.6	53.4	43.7
$500,000 and over.	93.4	77.8	29.4	94.0	95.1	21.0	69.8	47.2
Region:								
Northeast	71.8	30.1	10.4	77.5	64.1	4.2	26.2	32.2
Midwest	70.3	30.0	11.0	87.4	72.5	4.6	26.4	33.8
South	57.0	23.1	10.3	86.9	69.3	4.5	17.9	26.2
West	65.7	28.0	11.7	89.3	60.7	6.4	25.1	29.5
Tenure:								
Owner.	74.4	34.4	13.3	92.0	100.0	6.7	29.8	35.2
Renter.	45.5	12.3	5.6	73.2	-	1.2	9.4	19.1

- Represents zero.

No. 692. Asset Ownership Rates for Households and Median Value by Type of Asset: 1998 and 2000

[In percent. Excludes group quarters. Based on the Survey of Income and Program Participation and subject to sampling variability. Data are similar but not comparable to those found in tables 693 and 694, which are based on the Survey of Consumer Finances]

Asset type	1998 (in constant (2000) dollars)			2000		
	Percent of households that own asset type	Median value of asset for asset owners (dol.)	Percent distribution of worth	Percent of households that own asset type	Median value of asset for asset owners (dol.)	Percent distribution of worth
All assets.	(X)	49,932	100	(X)	55,000	100
Interest-earning assets at financial institutions	63.9	3,854	8.1	65.0	4,000	8.9
Other interest-earning assets . .	3.9	31,281	2.7	3.3	29,013	1.7
Regular checking accounts . . .	38.9	521	0.4	37.5	600	0.3
Stocks and mutual fund shares .	27.1	17,517	18.8	27.1	19,268	15.6
Own home	66.4	55,263	33.7	67.2	59,000	32.3
Rental property	5.4	59,434	4.5	4.9	70,000	3.7
Other real estate	6.5	31,281	3.2	6.6	40,000	3.6
Vehicles	85.3	6,073	4.4	85.8	5,875	3.7
Business or profession	11.5	7,299	7.3	10.8	10,000	7.7
U.S. savings bonds	16.3	834	0.6	14.7	1,000	0.5
IRA or Keogh accounts	21.3	19,811	7.9	23.1	24,000	8.6
401K and thrift savings plans . .	26.8	15,641	8.6	29.9	20,000	9.7
Other financial investments[1] . .	4.7	24,367	2.6	3.9	22,000	1.6
Unsecured liabilities[2]	54.7	3,649	3.4	52.7	4,000	3.0

X Not applicable. [1] Includes mortgages held for sale of real estate, amount due from sale of business or property, and other financial assets. [2] Because net worth is assets less liabilities, unsecured liabilities are subtracted from the distribution of net worth and are shown as negative.

Source of Tables 691 and 692: U.S. Census Bureau, Asset Ownership of Households: 1998 and 2000, P70-88, May 2003. See also <http://www.census.gov/prod/2003pubs/p70-88.pdf> (released May 2003).

No. 693. Nonfinancial Assets Held by Families by Type of Asset: 2001

[Median value in thousands of dollars (147.4 represents $147,400). Constant dollar figures are based on consumer price index for all urban consumers published by U.S. Bureau of Labor Statistics. Families include one-person units and, as used in this table, are comparable to the U.S. Census Bureau household concept. For definition of family, see text, Section 1, Population. Based on Survey of Consumer Finance; see Appendix III. For data on financial assets, see Table 1167. For definition of median, see Guide to Tabular Presentation]

Age of family head, and family income	Total	Vehicles	Primary residence	Other residential property	Equity in nonresidential property	Business equity	Other	Any nonfinancial asset
PERCENT OF FAMILIES HOLDING ASSET								
All families, total	96.7	84.8	67.7	11.3	8.3	11.8	7.6	90.7
Age of family head:								
Under 35 years old	93.1	78.8	39.9	3.4	2.8	7.0	6.9	83.0
35 to 44 years old	97.4	88.9	67.8	9.2	7.6	14.2	8.0	93.2
45 to 54 years old	98.1	90.5	76.2	14.7	10.0	17.1	7.2	95.2
55 to 64 years old	98.2	90.7	83.2	18.3	12.3	15.6	7.9	95.4
65 to 74 years old	97.1	81.3	82.5	13.7	12.9	11.6	9.7	91.6
75 years old and over	97.8	73.9	76.2	15.2	8.3	2.4	6.2	86.4
Race or ethnicity of respondent:								
White non-Hispanic	99.0	89.1	74.1	12.9	9.6	13.9	9.0	94.7
Non white or Hispanic	89.4	70.9	47.0	6.4	4.1	5.1	2.9	77.9
Tenure:								
Owner occupied	100.0	92.2	100.0	14.9	11.0	15.5	8.7	100.0
Renter occupied or other	89.7	69.3	(X)	3.9	2.6	4.2	5.1	71.3
MEDIAN VALUE [1] ($1,000)								
All families, total	147.4	13.5	122.0	80.0	49.0	100.0	12.0	113.2
Age of family head:								
Under 35 years old	39.4	11.3	95.0	75.0	33.3	50.0	10.0	30.5
35 to 44 years old	157.6	14.8	125.0	75.0	39.5	100.0	9.0	117.8
45 to 54 years old	211.6	15.7	135.0	65.0	56.4	102.0	11.0	140.3
55 to 64 years old	226.3	15.1	130.0	80.0	78.5	100.0	30.0	147.9
65 to 74 years old	214.6	13.6	129.0	145.0	50.0	100.0	20.0	149.2
75 years old and over	169.6	8.8	111.0	80.0	28.0	510.9	15.0	122.6
Race or ethnicity of respondent:								
White non-Hispanic	183.9	14.6	130.0	80.0	50.0	100.0	15.0	131.4
Non white or Hispanic	56.8	10.0	92.0	60.0	22.5	50.0	5.0	58.2
Tenure:								
Owner occupied	240.1	16.2	122.0	80.0	50.0	105.0	15.0	156.9
Renter occupied or other	13.4	7.6	(X)	60.0	32.5	35.0	6.0	8.9

X Not applicable.   [1] Median value of financial asset for families holding such assets.

No. 694. Family Net Worth—Mean and Median Net Worth in Constant (2001) Dollars by Selected Family Characteristics: 1992 to 2001

[Net worth in thousands of constant (2001) dollars (230.5 represents $230,500). Constant dollar figures are based on consumer price index for all urban consumers published by U.S. Bureau of Labor Statistics. Families include one-person units and as used in this table are comparable to the Census Bureau household concept. Based on Survey of Consumer Finance; see Appendix III. For definition of median, see Guide to Tabular Presentation]

Family characteristic	1992		1995		1998		2001	
	Mean	Median	Mean	Median	Mean	Median	Mean	Median
All families	230.5	61.3	244.8	66.4	307.4	78.0	395.5	86.1
Age of family head:								
Under 35 years old	56.2	11.4	49.9	13.9	69.5	9.9	90.7	11.6
35 to 44 years old	164.8	55.1	165.9	60.3	213.6	69.0	259.5	77.6
45 to 54 years old	331.7	96.8	342.4	107.5	394.1	114.8	485.8	133.0
55 to 64 years old	418.0	141.1	442.3	133.2	579.3	139.2	727.0	181.5
65 to 74 years old	354.6	121.7	402.9	128.0	507.9	159.5	673.8	176.3
75 years old and over	264.0	107.5	298.5	107.5	338.3	136.7	465.9	151.4
Race or ethnicity or respondent:								
White non-Hispanic	274.8	86.2	289.8	88.5	363.9	103.4	482.9	120.9
Non white or Hispanic	95.8	14.8	89.1	18.3	109.9	17.9	115.3	17.1
Tenure:								
Owner occupied	333.7	122.3	350.8	120.2	439.9	143.8	558.2	171.7
Renter occupied or other	47.8	4.0	50.5	5.6	47.3	4.6	55.0	4.8

Source of Tables 693 and 694: Board of Governors of the Federal Reserve System, *Federal Reserve Bulletin*, January 2003, and unpublished data found at <http://www.federalreserve.gov/pubs/oss/oss2/2001/scf2001home.html>.

No. 695. Household and Nonprofit Organization Sector Balance Sheet: 1980 to 2003

[In billions of dollars (11,016 represents $11,016,000,000,000). As of December 31. For details of financial assets and liabilities, see Table 1161]

Item	1980	1990	1995	1997	1998	1999	2000	2001	2002	2003
Assets . . . . [1]	11,016	24,120	32,699	39,726	43,652	49,166	49,425	49,358	48,575	54,168
Tangible assets [1]	4,378	9,259	11,054	12,151	13,132	14,176	15,475	16,705	18,165	19,827
Real estate	3,421	7,386	8,795	9,732	10,607	11,521	12,657	13,755	15,045	16,547
Equipment owned by nonprofit organizations	26	58	83	91	97	104	113	120	123	127
Consumer durable goods	931	1,815	2,176	2,329	2,427	2,551	2,704	2,830	2,997	3,153
Financial assets [1]	6,638	14,861	21,646	27,574	30,521	34,990	33,950	32,653	30,410	34,341
Deposits	1,521	3,259	3,298	3,622	3,900	4,023	4,352	4,835	5,063	5,253
Checkable deposits and currency	220	412	544	437	421	346	226	315	279	215
Time and savings deposits. . . .	1,239	2,465	2,281	2,566	2,729	2,811	3,100	3,350	3,644	3,985
Money market fund shares. . . .	62	369	450	582	712	822	968	1,116	1,076	986
Credit market instruments [1]	425	1,556	1,940	2,132	2,253	2,558	2,473	2,433	2,433	2,510
U.S. government securities . . .	165	538	843	902	880	1,108	935	757	478	688
Treasury	160	471	783	736	698	807	586	487	382	418
Savings bonds	73	126	185	187	187	186	185	190	195	204
Corporate equities	875	1,781	4,141	6,242	7,074	9,052	7,474	6,184	4,601	5,709
Mutual fund shares.	46	457	1,153	1,961	2,394	3,115	3,036	2,870	2,539	3,292
Pension fund reserves	970	3,376	5,671	7,323	8,210	9,068	9,071	8,681	8,003	9,304
Equity in noncorporate business	2,219	3,183	3,629	4,131	4,343	4,571	4,847	4,965	5,178	5,414
Liabilities.	1,453	3,720	5,082	5,819	6,303	6,877	7,466	8,077	8,812	9,757
Credit market instruments.	1,402	3,598	4,885	5,552	6,006	6,499	7,077	7,722	8,498	9,401
Home mortgages.	932	2,505	3,353	3,818	4,148	4,524	4,900	5,389	6,063	6,821
Consumer credit	358	824	1,168	1,334	1,431	1,543	1,719	1,857	1,938	2,040
Net worth.	9,563	20,400	27,618	33,906	37,350	42,288	41,959	41,281	39,763	44,411

[1] Includes types of assets and/or liabilities not shown separately.

Source: Board of Governors of the Federal Reserve System, *"Federal Reserve Statistical Release, Z.1, Flow of Funds Accounts of the United States"*; published: 4 March 2004; <http://www.federalreserve.gov/releases/Z1/20040304/data.htm>.

No. 696. Net Stock of Fixed Reproducible Tangible Wealth in Current and Real (2000) Dollars: 1980 to 2002

[In billions of dollars (10,108 represents $10,108,000,000,000). As of December 31]

Item	1980	1990	1995	1997	1998	1999	2000	2001	2002
CURRENT DOLLARS									
Net stock, total.	10,108	18,154	22,678	25,034	26,438	28,135	29,988	31,732	32,827
Fixed assets	9,198	16,318	20,382	22,548	23,830	25,374	27,047	28,662	29,632
Private.	7,049	12,717	15,878	17,646	18,729	19,975	21,335	22,685	23,413
Nonresidential	3,545	6,606	8,037	8,913	9,425	9,983	10,654	11,192	11,425
Equipment and software. . . .	1,396	2,606	3,161	3,490	3,682	3,932	4,198	4,337	4,412
Information processing equipment and software . .	(NA)	(NA)	823	934	996	1,097	1,220	1,277	1,312
Structures	2,149	4,000	4,876	5,423	5,743	6,052	6,456	6,855	7,012
Residential	3,505	6,111	7,841	8,734	9,304	9,992	10,680	11,493	11,988
Housing units.	(NA)	(NA)	6,354	7,072	7,545	8,106	8,661	9,338	9,738
Government	2,149	3,601	4,505	4,901	5,101	5,399	5,713	5,978	6,219
Nonresidential	2,071	3,452	4,317	4,704	4,894	5,179	5,481	5,731	5,978
Equipment and software. . . .	252	551	675	671	677	698	703	709	726
Structures	1,820	2,900	3,642	4,033	4,217	4,481	4,778	5,022	5,252
Residential	78	149	188	197	207	220	232	247	241
Federal	648	1,079	1,291	1,335	1,356	1,399	1,425	1,446	1,470
Defense	439	735	865	868	872	891	896	902	914
State and local	1,501	2,522	3,213	3,567	3,745	4,000	4,288	4,532	4,749
Consumer durable goods	910	1,837	2,296	2,487	2,608	2,761	2,941	3,070	3,196
Motor vehicles and parts.	(NA)	(NA)	768	824	876	947	1,018	1,082	1,138
Furniture, household equipment . . .	(NA)	(NA)	1,011	1,101	1,147	1,196	1,260	1,293	1,337
Other	(NA)	(NA)	518	561	586	618	662	695	722
CHAINED (2000) DOLLARS									
Net stock, total.	(NA)	(NA)	25,143	26,685	27,582	28,568	29,583	30,456	31,254
Fixed assets.	(NA)	(NA)	23,011	24,309	25,042	25,828	26,637	27,318	27,919
Private.	(NA)	(NA)	17,879	18,994	19,636	20,318	21,020	21,593	22,074
Nonresidential	(NA)	(NA)	8,713	9,342	9,714	10,109	10,527	10,817	10,996
Equipment and software . . .	(NA)	(NA)	3,053	3,432	3,667	3,932	4,207	4,370	4,479
Structures	(NA)	(NA)	5,697	5,922	6,052	6,177	6,320	6,449	6,523
Residential	(NA)	(NA)	9,175	9,656	9,924	10,209	10,492	10,776	11,076
Government	(NA)	(NA)	5,158	5,341	5,423	5,518	5,618	5,718	5,832
Nonresidential	(NA)	(NA)	4,927	5,101	5,187	5,287	5,390	5,494	5,609
Equipment and software . . .	(NA)	(NA)	686	687	690	699	706	714	727
Structures	(NA)	(NA)	4,234	4,411	4,494	4,587	4,684	4,781	4,884
Residential	(NA)	(NA)	220	215	219	224	227	231	235
Consumer durable goods	(NA)	(NA)	2,186	2,398	2,548	2,740	2,946	3,147	3,367

NA Not available.

Source: U.S. Bureau of Economic Analysis, *Survey of Current Business*, May 2004, and <http://www.bea.doc.gov/bea/dn/FA2004/SelectTable.asp> (released 17 May 2004).

Prices

This section presents indexes of producer and consumer prices, actual prices for selected commodities, and energy prices. The primary sources of these data are monthly publications of the Department of Labor, Bureau of Labor Statistics (BLS), which include *Monthly Labor Review, Consumer Price Index, Detailed Report, Producer Price Indexes,* and *U.S. Import and Export Price Indexes.* The Department of Commerce, Bureau of Economic Analysis is the source for gross domestic product measures.

Producer price index (PPI)—This index, dating from 1890, is the oldest continuous statistical series published by BLS. It is designed to measure average changes in prices received by producers of all commodities, at all stages of processing, produced in the United States.

The index has undergone several revisions (see *Monthly Labor Review,* February 1962, April 1978, and August 1988). It is now based on approximately 10,000 individual products and groups of products along with about 100,000 quotations per month. Indexes for the net output of manufacturing and mining industries have been added in recent years. Prices used in constructing the index are collected from sellers and generally apply to the first significant large-volume commercial transaction for each commodity—i.e., the manufacturer's or other producer's selling price or the selling price on an organized exchange or at a central market.

The weights used in the index represent the total net selling value of commodities produced or processed in this country. Values are f.o.b. (free on board) production point and are exclusive of excise taxes. Effective with the release of data for January 1988, many important producer price indexes were changed to a new reference base year, 1982=100, from 1967=100. The reference year of the PPI shipment weights has been taken

primarily from the 1987 Census of Manufactures. For further detail regarding the PPI, see the BLS *Handbook of Methods,* Bulletin 2490 (April 1997), Chapter 16. The PPI Web page is <http://stats.bls.gov/ppihome.htm>.

Consumer price indexes (CPI)—The CPI is a measure of the average change in prices over time in a "market basket" of goods and services purchased either by urban wage earners and clerical workers or by all urban consumers. In 1919, BLS began to publish complete indexes at semiannual intervals, using a weighting structure based on data collected in the expenditure survey of wage-earner and clerical-worker families in 1917-19 (BLS Bulletin 357, 1924). The first major revision of the CPI occurred in 1940, with subsequent revisions in 1953, 1964, 1978, 1987, and 1998.

Beginning with the release of data for January 1988 in February 1988, most consumer price indexes shifted to a new reference base year. All indexes previously expressed on a base of 1967=100, or any other base through December 1981, have been rebased to 1982-84=100. The expenditure weights are based upon data tabulated from the Consumer Expenditure Surveys for 1993, 1994, and 1995.

BLS publishes CPIs for two population groups: (1) a CPI for all urban consumers (CPI-U), which covers approximately 80 percent of the total population; and (2) a CPI for urban wage earners and clerical workers (CPI-W), which covers 32 percent of the total population. The CPI-U includes, in addition to wage earners and clerical workers, groups which historically have been excluded from CPI coverage, such as professional, managerial, and technical workers; the self-employed; short-term workers; the unemployed; and retirees and others not in the labor force.

The current CPI is based on prices of food, clothing, shelter, fuels, transportation fares, charges for doctors' and dentists' services, drugs, etc. purchased for day-to-day living. Prices are collected in 87 areas across the country from over 50,000 housing units and 23,000 establishments. Area selection was based on the 1990 census. All taxes directly associated with the purchase and use of items are included in the index. Prices of food, fuels, and a few other items are obtained every month in all 87 locations. Prices of most other commodities and services are collected monthly in the three largest geographic areas and every other month in other areas.

In calculating the index, each item is assigned a weight to account for its relative importance in consumers' budgets. Price changes for the various items in each location are then averaged. Local data are then combined to obtain a U.S. city average. Separate indexes are also published for regions, area size-classes, cross-classifications of regions and size-classes, and for 26 local areas, usually consisting of the Metropolitan Statistical Area (MSA); see Appendix II. Area definitions are those established by the Office of Management and Budget in 1983. Definitions do not include revisions made since 1992. Area indexes do not measure differences in the level of prices among cities; they only measure the average change in prices for each area since the base period. For further detail regarding the CPI, see the BLS *Handbook of Methods,* Bulletin 2490, Chapter 17; the *Consumer Price Index,* and the CPI home page: <http://stats.bls.gov/cpihome.htm>. In January 1983, the method of measuring homeownership costs in the CPI-U was changed to a rental equivalence approach. This treatment calculates homeowner costs of shelter based on the implicit rent owners would pay to rent the homes they own. The rental equivalence approach was introduced into the CPI-W in 1985. The CPI-U was used to prepare the consumer price tables in this section.

Other price indexes—Chain-weighted price indexes, produced by the Bureau of Economic Analysis (BEA), are weighted averages of the detailed price indexes used in the deflation of the goods and services that make up the gross domestic product (GDP) and its major components. Growth rates are constructed for years and quarters using quantity weights for

the current and preceding year or quarter; these growth rates are used to move the index for the preceding period forward a year or quarter at a time. The gross domestic purchases chained price index measures the average price of goods and services purchased in the United States. It differs from the GDP chained price index, which measures the average price of goods produced in the United States, by excluding net exports. All chain-weighted price indexes are expressed in terms of the reference year value 1996=100.

Measures of inflation—Inflation is defined as a time of generally rising prices for goods and factors of production. The Bureau of Labor Statistics samples prices of items in a representative market basket and publishes the result as the CPI. The media invariably announce the inflation rate as the percent change in the CPI from month to month. A much more meaningful indicator of inflation is the percent change from the same month of the prior year. The producer price index measures prices at the producer level only. The PPI shows the same general pattern of inflation as does the CPI but is more volatile. The PPI can be roughly viewed as a leading indicator. It often tends to foreshadow trends that later occur in the CPI.

Other measures of inflation include the gross domestic purchases chain-weighted price index, the index of industrial materials prices; the Dow Jones Commodity Spot Price Index; Futures Price Index; the Employment Cost Index, the Hourly Compensation Index, or the Unit Labor Cost Index as a measure of the change in cost of the labor factor-of production; and changes in long-term interest rates that are often used to measure changes in the cost of the capital factor of production.

International price indexes—The BLS International Price Program produces export and import price indexes for nonmilitary goods traded between the United States and the rest of the world.

The export price index provides a measure of price change for all products sold by U.S. residents to foreign buyers. The import price index provides a measure of price change for goods purchased from other countries by U.S. residents. The reference period for the indexes is 2000=100, unless otherwise indicated. The product universe for both the import and export indexes includes raw materials, agricultural products, semifinished manufactures, and finished manufactures, including both capital and consumer goods. Price data for these items are collected primarily by mail questionnaire. In nearly all cases, the data are collected directly from the exporter or importer, although in a few cases, prices are obtained from other sources.

To the extent possible, the data gathered refer to prices at the U.S. border for exports and at either the foreign border or the U.S. border for imports. For nearly all products, the prices refer to transactions completed during the first week of the month. Survey respondents are asked to indicate all discounts, allowances, and rebates applicable to the reported prices, so that the price used in the calculation of the indexes is the actual price for which the product was bought or sold.

In addition to general indexes for U.S. exports and imports, indexes are also published for detailed product categories of exports and imports. These categories are defined according to the five-digit level of detail for the Bureau of Economic Analysis End-Use Classification, the three-digit level of detail for the Standard International Trade Classification (SITC), and the four-digit level of detail for the Harmonized System. Aggregate import indexes by country or region of origin are also available.

No. 697. Purchasing Power of the Dollar: 1950 to 2003

[Indexes:PPI, 1982=$1.00; CPI, 1982-84=$1.00. Producer prices prior to 1961, and consumer prices prior to 1964, exclude Alaska and Hawaii. Producer prices based on finished goods index. Obtained by dividing the average price index for the 1982=100, PPI; 1982-84=100, CPI base periods (100.0) by the price index for a given period and expressing the result in dollars and cents. Annual figures are based on average of monthly data]

Year	Annual average as measured by—		Year	Annual average as measured by—	
	Producer prices	Consumer prices		Producer prices	Consumer prices
1950	3.546	4.151	1977	1.546	1.649
1951	3.247	3.846	1978	1.433	1.532
1952	3.268	3.765	1979	1.289	1.380
1953	3.300	3.735	1980	1.136	1.215
1954	3.289	3.717	1981	1.041	1.098
1955	3.279	3.732	1982	1.000	1.035
1956	3.195	3.678	1983	0.984	1.003
1957	3.077	3.549	1984	0.964	0.961
1958	3.012	3.457	1985	0.955	0.928
1959	3.021	3.427	1986	0.969	0.913
1960	2.994	3.373	1987	0.949	0.880
1961	2.994	3.340	1988	0.926	0.846
1962	2.985	3.304	1989	0.880	0.807
1963	2.994	3.265	1990	0.839	0.766
1964	2.985	3.220	1991	0.822	0.734
1965	2.933	3.166	1992	0.812	0.713
1966	2.841	3.080	1993	0.802	0.692
1967	2.809	2.993	1994	0.797	0.675
1968	2.732	2.873	1995	0.782	0.656
1969	2.632	2.726	1996	0.762	0.638
1970	2.545	2.574	1997	0.759	0.623
1971	2.469	2.466	1998	0.765	0.614
1972	2.392	2.391	1999	0.752	0.600
1973	2.193	2.251	2000	0.725	0.581
1974	1.901	2.029	2001	0.711	0.565
1975	1.718	1.859	2002	0.720	0.556
1976	1.645	1.757	2003	0.698	0.544

Source: U.S. Bureau of Labor Statistics. Monthly data in U.S. Bureau of Economic Analysis, *Survey of Current Business.*

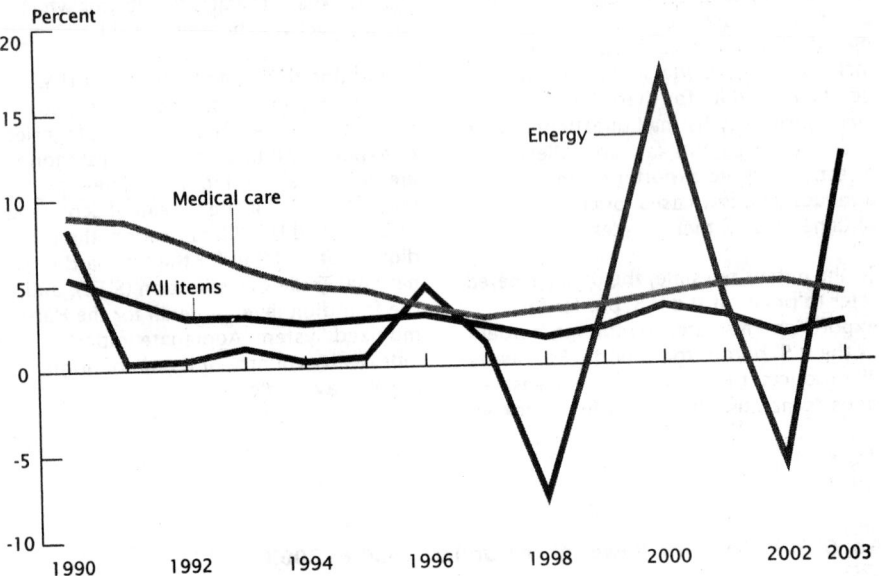

Figure 14.1
**Annual Percent Change in Consumer
Price Indexes: 1990 to 2003**

Source: Chart prepared by U.S. Census Bureau. For data, see Table 698.

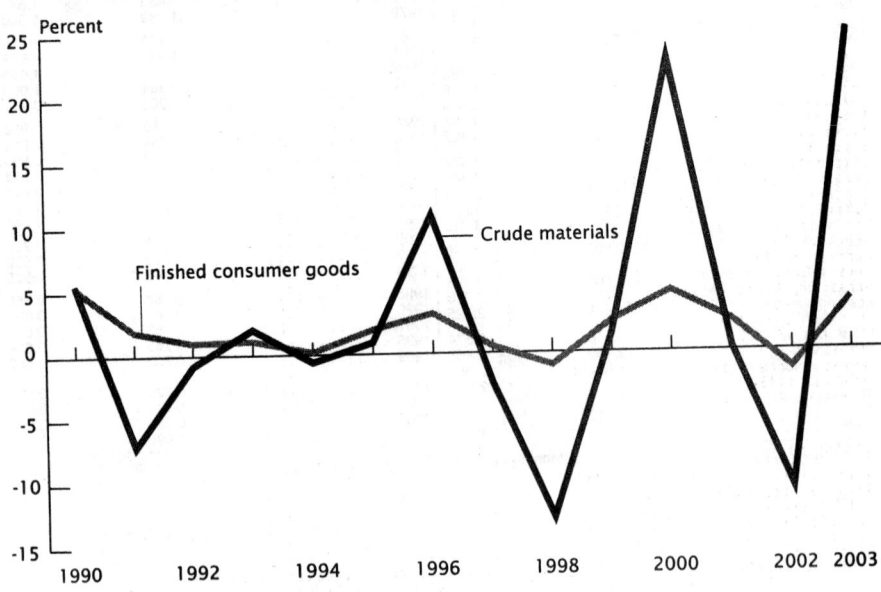

Figure 14.2
**Annual Percent Change in Producer Price Indexes
by Stage of Processing: 1990 to 2003**

Source: Chart prepared by U.S. Census Bureau. For data, see Table 703.

No. 698. Consumer Price Indexes (CPI-U) by Major Groups: 1980 to 2003

[1982-84=100. except as indicated. Represents annual averages of monthly figures. Reflects buying patterns of all urban consumers. Minus sign (-) indicates decrease. See text, this section]

Year	All items	Commodities	Services	Food	Energy	All items less food and energy	Food and beverages	Shelter	Transportation	Medical care	Apparel	Education and communication [1]
1980	82.4	86.0	77.9	86.8	86.0	80.8	86.7	81.0	83.1	74.9	90.9	(NA)
1988	118.3	111.5	125.7	118.2	89.3	123.4	118.2	127.1	108.7	138.6	115.4	(NA)
1989	124.0	116.7	131.9	125.1	94.3	129.0	124.9	132.8	114.1	149.3	118.6	(NA)
1990	130.7	122.8	139.2	132.4	102.1	135.5	132.1	140.0	120.5	162.8	124.1	(NA)
1991	136.2	126.6	146.3	136.3	102.5	142.1	136.8	146.3	123.8	177.0	128.7	(NA)
1992	140.3	129.1	152.0	137.9	103.0	147.3	138.7	151.2	126.5	190.1	131.9	(NA)
1993	144.5	131.5	157.9	140.9	104.2	152.2	141.6	155.7	130.4	201.4	133.7	85.5
1994	148.2	133.8	163.1	144.3	104.6	156.5	144.9	160.5	134.3	211.0	133.4	88.8
1995	152.4	136.4	168.7	148.4	105.2	161.2	148.9	165.7	139.1	220.5	132.0	92.2
1996	156.9	139.9	174.1	153.3	110.1	165.6	153.7	171.0	143.0	228.2	131.7	95.3
1997	160.5	141.8	179.4	157.3	111.5	169.5	157.7	176.3	144.3	234.6	132.9	98.4
1998	163.0	141.9	184.2	160.7	102.9	173.4	161.1	182.1	141.6	242.1	133.0	100.3
1999	166.6	144.4	188.8	164.1	106.6	177.0	164.6	187.3	144.4	250.6	131.3	101.2
2000	172.2	149.2	195.3	167.8	124.6	181.3	168.4	193.4	153.3	260.8	129.6	102.5
2001	177.1	150.7	203.4	173.1	129.3	186.1	173.6	200.6	154.3	272.8	127.3	105.2
2002	179.9	149.7	209.8	176.2	121.7	190.5	176.8	208.1	152.9	285.6	124.0	107.9
2003	184.0	151.2	216.5	180.0	136.5	193.2	180.5	213.1	157.6	297.1	120.9	109.8
PERCENT CHANGE [2]												
1980	13.5	12.3	15.4	8.6	30.9	12.4	8.5	17.6	17.9	11.0	7.1	(NA)
1988	4.1	3.5	4.6	4.1	0.8	4.4	4.1	4.8	3.1	6.5	4.3	(NA)
1989	4.8	4.7	4.9	5.8	5.6	4.5	5.7	4.5	5.0	7.7	2.8	(NA)
1990	5.4	5.2	5.5	5.8	8.3	5.0	5.8	5.4	5.6	9.0	4.6	(NA)
1991	4.2	3.1	5.1	2.9	0.4	4.9	3.6	4.5	2.7	8.7	3.7	(NA)
1992	3.0	2.0	3.9	1.2	0.5	3.7	1.4	3.3	2.2	7.4	2.5	(NA)
1993	3.0	1.9	3.9	2.2	1.2	3.3	2.1	3.0	3.1	5.9	1.4	(NA)
1994	2.6	1.7	3.3	2.4	0.4	2.8	2.3	3.1	3.0	4.8	-0.2	3.9
1995	2.8	1.9	3.4	2.8	0.6	3.0	2.8	3.2	3.6	4.5	-1.0	3.8
1996	3.0	2.6	3.2	3.3	4.7	2.7	3.2	3.2	2.8	3.5	-0.2	3.4
1997	2.3	1.4	3.0	2.6	1.3	2.4	2.6	3.1	0.9	2.8	0.9	3.3
1998	1.6	0.1	2.7	2.2	-7.7	2.3	2.2	3.3	-1.9	3.2	0.1	1.9
1999	2.2	1.8	2.5	2.1	3.6	2.1	2.2	2.9	2.0	3.5	-1.3	0.9
2000	3.4	3.3	3.4	2.3	16.9	2.4	2.3	3.3	6.2	4.1	-1.3	1.3
2001	2.8	1.0	4.1	3.2	3.8	2.6	3.1	3.7	0.7	4.6	-1.8	2.6
2002	1.6	-0.7	3.1	1.8	-5.9	2.4	1.8	3.7	-0.9	4.7	-2.6	2.6
2003	2.3	1.0	3.2	2.2	12.2	1.4	2.1	2.4	3.1	4.0	-2.5	1.8

NA Not available. [1] Dec. 1997=100. [2] Change from immediate prior year. 1980 change from 1979; 1988 change from 1987.
Source: U.S. Bureau of Labor Statistics, *Monthly Labor Review* and *Handbook of Labor Statistics*, periodic.

No. 699. Consumer Price Indexes (CPI-U)—Selected Areas: 2003

[1982-84=100, except as indicated. Represents annual averages of monthly figures. Local area CPI indexes are byproducts of the national CPI program. Each local index has a smaller sample size than the national index and is therefore, subject to substantially more sampling and other measurement error. As a result, local area indexes show greater volatility than the national index, although their long-term trends are similar. Area definitions are those established by the Office of Management and Budget in 1983. For further detail see the U.S. Bureau of Labor Statistics Handbook of Methods, Bulletin 2285, Chapter 19, the Consumer Price Index, and Report 736, the CPI: 1987 Revision. See also text, this section and Appendix III]

Area	All items	Food and beverages	Food	Housing	Apparel	Transportation	Medical care	Fuel and other utilities
U.S. city average	184.0	180.5	180.0	184.8	120.9	157.6	297.1	154.5
Anchorage, AK MSA	162.5	161.8	161.6	146.8	123.2	158.3	(NA)	160.4
Atlanta, GA MSA	180.8	186.8	192.8	181.6	125.7	144.1	311.2	178.0
Boston, MA MSA	203.9	189.1	189.4	209.1	141.2	154.1	397.9	155.0
Chicago-Gary, IL-IN CMSA	184.5	181.0	180.0	191.9	92.7	151.5	291.9	140.9
Cincinnati-Hamilton, OH-KY-IN CMSA	173.4	164.6	162.8	165.8	121.6	152.7	295.8	140.8
Cleveland-Akron-Lorain, OH CMSA	176.2	183.6	186.2	174.1	112.6	158.1	(NA)	155.7
Dallas-Fort Worth, TX CMSA	176.2	179.3	175.9	165.4	130.4	159.9	277.1	167.2
Denver-Boulder-Greeley, CO CMSA	186.8	174.8	177.0	185.2	83.5	194.8	333.3	162.2
Detroit-Ann Arbor-Flint, MI CMSA	182.5	175.0	174.5	173.8	125.1	173.3	292.3	156.1
Honolulu, HI MSA	184.5	174.9	174.1	186.2	98.5	176.4	(NA)	154.1
Houston-Galveston-Brazoria, TX CMSA	163.7	167.9	167.5	151.2	147.4	143.2	272.5	133.5
Kansas City, MO-KS CMSA	177.0	176.4	177.7	174.2	106.7	152.4	271.0	158.7
Los Angeles-Anaheim-Riverside, CA CMSA	187.0	190.2	188.4	193.2	106.4	160.3	290.1	186.9
Miami-Fort Lauderdale, FL CMSA	180.6	188.7	189.4	172.9	148.9	163.4	281.2	129.7
Milwaukee, WI PMSA	177.7	179.7	180.8	181.2	112.9	147.9	293.4	148.0
Minneapolis-St. Paul, MN-WI MSA	182.7	192.8	188.4	171.9	126.1	164.1	292.3	147.3
New York-Northern New Jersey-Long Island, NY-NJ-CT CMSA	197.8	184.1	182.8	208.0	111.0	166.4	308.4	136.4
Philadelphia-Wilmington-Trenton, PA-NJ-DE-MD CMSA	188.8	175.4	175.1	191.7	97.0	160.6	341.3	151.3
Pittsburgh, PA MSA	177.5	173.1	171.8	177.9	145.0	140.2	280.3	174.3
Portland, OR MSA	186.3	167.5	168.2	185.4	117.4	171.6	293.1	175.0
San Diego, CA MSA	205.3	190.1	188.3	225.7	123.7	168.0	292.8	160.7
San Francisco-Oakland-San Jose, CA CMSA	196.4	190.7	190.6	223.7	109.7	144.9	273.6	193.3
Seattle-Tacoma, WA CMSA	192.3	190.3	191.6	200.3	123.7	167.4	282.1	157.7
St. Louis-East St. Louis, MO-IL CMSA	173.4	173.3	171.6	167.4	121.9	153.3	(NA)	145.5
Tampa-St. Petersburg-Clearwater, FL MSA [1]	158.1	156.5	155.1	152.9	142.9	147.6	223.4	137.6
Washington-Baltimore, DC-MD-VA-WV CMSA [2]	116.2	114.5	114.7	121.6	90.0	108.7	118.5	123.9

NA Not available. [1] 1987=100. [2] 1997=100; except "Apparel and upkeep" and "Transportation," 1996=100.
Source: U.S. Bureau of Labor Statistics, *Monthly Labor Review* and *CPI Detailed Report*, January issues.

No. 700. Consumer Price Indexes for All Urban Consumers (CPI-U) for Selected Items and Groups: 1990 to 2003

[1982-84 = 100 except as noted. Annual averages of monthly figures. See headnote, Table 698]

Item	1990	1995	1999	2000	2001	2002	2003	Annual percent change 2002-2003
All Items	**130.7**	**152.4**	**166.6**	**172.2**	**177.1**	**179.9**	**184.0**	**2.3**
Food and beverages	132.1	148.9	164.6	168.4	173.6	176.8	180.5	2.1
Food	132.4	148.4	164.1	167.8	173.1	176.2	180.0	2.2
Food at home	132.3	148.8	164.2	167.9	173.4	175.6	179.4	2.2
Cereals and bakery products	140.0	167.5	185.0	188.3	193.8	198.0	202.8	2.4
Cereals and cereal products	141.1	167.1	175.0	175.9	178.7	181.8	185.2	1.9
Cereal	158.6	192.5	195.2	198.0	199.7	203.0	204.3	0.6
Rice, pasta, and cornmeal	122.0	140.2	151.9	150.7	154.6	155.8	160.3	2.9
Bakery products	139.2	167.4	189.4	194.1	201.3	206.1	211.7	2.7
White bread	136.4	165.5	192.5	199.1	208.3	213.4	218.6	2.4
Cookies, cakes, and cupcakes	142.7	169.1	185.0	187.9	192.0	196.7	202.8	3.1
Meats, poultry, fish and eggs	130.0	138.8	147.9	154.5	161.3	162.1	169.3	4.4
Meats	128.5	135.5	142.3	150.7	159.3	160.3	169.0	5.4
Beef and veal	128.8	134.9	139.2	148.1	160.5	160.6	175.1	9.0
Uncooked ground beef and related products	118.1	116.1	118.4	125.2	135.5	138.1	149.2	8.0
Pork	129.8	134.8	145.9	156.5	162.4	161.8	164.9	1.9
Bacon	113.4	120.0	151.5	177.5	184.6	186.2	196.6	5.6
Chops	140.2	144.2	143.5	152.2	159.0	156.0	160.9	3.1
Ham	132.4	139.6	147.0	152.7	157.3	160.0	161.9	1.2
Poultry	132.5	143.5	157.9	159.8	164.9	167.0	169.1	1.3
Fish and seafood	146.7	171.6	185.3	190.4	191.1	188.1	190.0	1.0
Canned fish and seafood	119.5	125.5	131.5	127.4	127.3	130.0	128.9	-0.8
Eggs	124.1	120.5	128.1	131.9	136.4	138.2	157.3	13.8
Dairy and related products	126.5	132.8	159.6	160.7	167.1	168.1	167.9	-0.1
Fruits and vegetables	149.0	177.7	203.1	204.6	212.2	220.9	225.9	2.3
Fresh fruits and vegetables	(NA)	206.0	237.2	238.8	247.9	258.4	265.3	2.7
Fresh fruits	170.9	219.0	266.3	258.3	265.1	270.2	279.1	3.3
Apples	147.5	183.5	200.1	212.6	213.9	230.7	244.4	5.9
Bananas	138.2	153.8	159.4	162.5	166.6	166.5	164.8	-1.0
Oranges, tangerines	160.6	224.5	337.0	257.0	271.7	294.6	302.0	2.5
Fresh vegetables	151.1	193.1	209.3	219.4	230.6	245.4	250.5	2.1
Potatoes	162.6	174.7	193.1	196.3	202.3	238.5	228.1	-4.4
Lettuce	150.3	221.2	208.3	228.1	233.8	252.1	246.2	-2.3
Tomatoes	160.8	188.3	224.1	234.7	250.0	251.0	271.0	8.0
Processed fruits and vegetables [1]	(NA)	(NA)	(NA)	105.6	109.0	113.1	114.1	0.9
Nonalcoholic beverages and beverage materials [1]	113.5	131.7	134.3	137.8	139.2	139.2	139.8	0.4
Carbonated drinks	112.1	119.5	118.8	123.4	125.4	125.6	125.6	-
Coffee	117.5	163.1	154.8	154.0	146.7	142.6	144.9	1.6
Food away from home	(NA)	149.0	165.1	169.0	173.9	178.3	182.1	2.1
Alcoholic beverages	129.3	153.9	169.7	174.7	179.3	183.6	187.2	2.0
Alcoholic beverages at home	123.0	143.1	153.7	158.1	161.1	164.0	166.5	1.5
Beer and ale, and other malt beverages	123.6	143.9	151.9	156.8	160.7	164.7	168.5	2.3
Distilled spirits	125.7	145.7	156.2	162.3	168.0	171.4	173.1	1.0
Wine	114.4	133.6	149.4	151.6	151.5	152.3	153.1	0.5
Alcoholic beverages away from home	144.4	176.5	201.0	207.1	215.2	222.5	228.6	2.7
Housing	128.5	148.5	163.9	169.6	176.4	180.3	184.8	2.5
Shelter	140.0	165.7	187.3	193.4	200.6	208.1	213.1	2.4
Owners' equivalent rent of primary residence [2]	144.8	171.3	192.9	198.7	206.3	214.7	219.9	2.4
Fuels and utilities	111.6	123.7	128.8	137.9	150.2	143.6	154.5	7.6
Fuels	104.5	111.5	113.5	122.8	135.4	127.2	138.2	8.6
Fuel oil and other	99.3	88.1	91.4	129.7	129.3	115.5	139.5	20.8
Gas (piped) and electricity	109.3	119.2	120.9	128.0	142.4	134.4	145.0	7.9
Electricity	117.4	129.6	126.5	128.5	137.8	136.2	139.5	2.4
Utility natural gas service	97.3	102.9	113.0	132.0	158.3	135.3	166.3	22.9
Water and sewerage maintenance	150.2	196.5	222.0	227.5	234.6	242.5	251.7	3.8
Garbage and trash collection [3]	171.2	241.2	263.8	269.8	275.5	283.0	291.9	3.1

See footnotes at end of table.

U.S. Census Bureau, Statistical Abstract of the United States: 2004-2005

No. 700. Consumer Price Indexes for All Urban Consumers (CPI-U) for Selected Items and Groups: 1990 to 2003—Con.

[1982-84 = 100 except as noted. Annual averages of monthly figures. See headnote, Table 698]

Item	1990	1995	1999	2000	2001	2002	2003	Annual percent change 2002-2003
Household furnishings and operations.......	113.3	123.0	126.7	128.2	129.1	128.3	126.1	-1.7
Furniture and bedding.................	115.7	130.9	134.9	134.4	132.2	129.4	127.7	-1.3
Bedroom furniture.................	118.5	136.4	141.0	138.4	136.6	135.3	133.9	-1.0
Housekeeping supplies..............	125.2	137.1	148.1	153.4	158.4	159.8	157.5	-1.4
Apparel..............................	124.1	132.0	131.3	129.6	127.3	124.0	120.9	-2.5
Men's and boy's apparel.............	120.4	126.2	131.1	129.7	125.7	121.7	118.0	-3.0
Women's and girl's apparel..........	122.6	126.9	123.3	121.5	119.3	115.8	113.1	-2.3
Infants' and toddlers'...............	125.8	127.2	129.0	130.6	129.2	126.4	122.1	-3.4
Footwear..........................	117.4	125.4	125.7	123.8	123.0	121.4	119.6	-1.5
Transportation.......................	120.5	139.1	144.4	153.3	154.3	152.9	157.6	3.1
Private transportation...............	118.8	136.3	140.5	149.1	150.0	148.8	153.6	3.2
New vehicles.....................	121.4	141.0	142.9	142.8	142.1	140.0	137.9	-1.5
New cars ₃.....................	121.0	139.0	139.6	139.6	138.9	137.3	134.7	-1.9
New trucks [3]....................	121.6	145.9	152.0	151.7	150.7	147.8	146.1	-1.2
Used cars and trucks	117.6	156.5	152.0	155.8	158.7	152.0	142.9	-6.0
Motor fuel........................	101.2	100.0	100.7	129.3	124.7	116.1	135.8	17.0
Motor vehicle maintenance and repair	130.1	154.0	171.9	177.3	183.5	190.2	195.6	2.8
Motor vechicle insurance.............	177.9	234.3	253.8	256.7	268.1	291.6	314.4	7.8
Motor vehicle fees [1].................	(NA)	(NA)	103.8	107.3	109.3	112.5	116.5	3.6
Public transportation	142.6	175.9	197.7	209.6	210.6	207.4	209.3	0.9
Airline fares......................	148.4	189.7	218.8	239.4	239.4	231.6	231.3	-0.1
Medical care	162.8	220.5	250.6	260.8	272.8	285.6	297.1	4.0
Medical care commodities............	163.4	204.5	230.7	238.1	247.6	256.4	262.8	2.5
Prescription drugs and medical supplies....	181.7	235.0	273.4	285.4	300.9	316.5	326.3	3.1
Nonprescription drugs, and medical supplies [4]	120.6	140.5	176.7	149.5	150.6	150.4	152.0	1.1
Medical care services................	162.7	224.2	255.1	266.0	278.8	292.9	306.0	4.5
Professional services	156.1	201.0	229.2	237.7	246.5	253.9	261.2	2.9
Hospital and related services	178.0	257.8	299.5	317.3	338.3	367.8	394.8	7.3
Recreation [1].......................	(NA)	(NA)	102.0	103.3	104.9	106.2	107.5	1.2
Video and audio	80.8	73.9	100.7	101.0	101.5	102.8	103.6	0.8
Cable television [3]...............	158.4	200.7	254.6	266.8	278.4	295.0	309.5	4.9
Photography [1]..................	(NA)	(NA)	99.4	99.2	99.0	97.9	96.0	-1.9
Sporting goods	114.9	123.5	120.3	119.0	118.5	116.4	115.3	-0.9
Other recreational goods [1]	(NA)	(NA)	92.3	87.8	84.6	80.5	76.1	-5.5
Pets, pet products and services [1]........	(NA)	(NA)	103.4	106.1	109.7	113.2	115.7	2.2
Recreation services [1]..............	(NA)	(NA)	106.9	111.7	116.1	119.6	124.5	4.1
Recreational reading materials...........	(NA)	(NA)	186.1	188.3	191.4	195.8	197.5	0.9
Tobacco and smoking products	181.5	225.7	355.8	394.9	425.2	461.5	469.0	1.6
Personal care.......................	130.4	147.1	161.1	165.6	170.5	174.7	178.0	1.9
Personal care services................	132.8	151.5	171.4	178.1	184.3	188.4	193.2	2.5
Education and communication [1]	(NA)	92.2	101.2	102.5	105.2	107.9	109.8	2.8
Education [1].......................	(NA)	(NA)	107.0	112.5	118.5	126.0	134.4	6.7
Educational books and supplies	171.3	214.4	261.7	279.9	295.9	317.6	335.4	5.6
Tuition/and child care fees and other school fees	175.7	253.8	308.4	324.0	341.1	362.1	386.7	6.8
College tuition	175.0	264.8	318.7	331.9	348.8	372.6	403.9	8.4
Communication [1]...................	(NA)	99.0	95.9	93.0	93.3	92.3	89.7	-2.8
Postage	125.1	160.3	165.1	165.1	171.5	181.8	190.9	5.0
Delivery services [1]..............	(NA)	(NA)	110.0	114.5	123.0	127.9	134.9	5.5
Information and information processing [1] ...	(NA)	98.9	95.4	92.8	92.3	90.8	87.8	-3.3
Telephone services [1]..............	(NA)	(NA)	100.1	98.5	99.3	99.7	98.3	-1.4
Telephone services, local charges	149.3	160.4	168.7	175.6	184.8	193.2	201.1	4.1
Telephone services, long distance charges [1]	(NA)	(NA)	98.6	97.8	88.8	84.9	77.8	-8.4
Cellular telephone services [1]	(NA)	(NA)	81.1	76.0	68.1	67.4	66.8	-0.9
Information and information processing other than telephone services [5].......	(NA)	63.8	30.5	25.9	21.3	18.3	16.1	-12.0
Personal computers and peripheral equipment [1]	(NA)	(NA)	47.2	41.1	29.5	22.2	17.6	-20.7
Computer software and accessories [1] ..	(NA)	(NA)	88.2	85.4	79.1	74.0	67.4	-8.9
Computer information processing services [1]	(NA)	(NA)	96.0	96.4	98.1	98.9	99.8	0.9
All commodities	122.8	136.4	144.4	149.2	150.7	149.7	151.2	1.0
All commodities less food................	117.4	129.8	134.0	139.2	138.9	136.0	136.5	0.4
Energy	102.1	105.2	106.6	124.6	129.3	121.7	136.5	12.2

- Represents zero. NA Not available. [1] December 1997=100. [2] December 1982=100. [3] December 1983=100.
[4] December 1986=100. [5] December 1988=100.

Source: U.S. Bureau of Labor Statistics, *Monthly Labor Review* and *CPI Detailed Report*, January issues.

No. 701. Cost of Living Index—Selected Metropolitan Areas: Fourth Quarter 2003

[Measures relative price levels for consumer goods and services in participating areas for a mid-management standard of living. The nationwide average equals 100, and each index is read as a percent of the national average. The index does not measure inflation, but compares prices at a single point in time. Excludes taxes. Metropolitan areas as defined by the Office of Management and Budget. For definitions and components of MSAs, see source for details]

Metropolitan areas (MA)	Composite index (100%)	Grocery items (14%)	Housing (29%)	Utilities (10%)	Transportation (10%)	Health care (4%)	Misc. goods and services (33%)
Birmingham-Hoover, AL Metro	96.1	101.6	85.1	104.0	95.3	84.8	102.7
Decatur, AL Metro	88.0	89.7	74.5	93.6	97.2	84.1	95.1
Florence, AL Metro	87.9	91.8	72.1	94.7	86.6	78.9	99.6
Huntsville, AL Metro	91.8	100.4	74.1	93.4	103.3	87.0	100.4
Mobile, AL Metro	89.9	94.2	80.4	96.8	88.8	80.4	95.9
Montgomery, AL Metro	96.1	95.4	92.8	100.9	98.5	86.1	98.2
Tuscaloosa, AL Metro	97.2	98.0	92.2	93.0	104.2	83.3	102.2
Fairbanks, AK Metro	124.7	117.4	132.4	127.9	117.8	164.9	117.4
Flagstaff, AZ Metro................	108.7	105.8	120.3	101.7	109.9	122.5	99.8
Phoenix-Mesa-Scottsdale, AZ Metro:							
Phoenix, AZ....................	98.5	100.8	88.9	91.5	111.2	112.3	102.6
Tucson, AZ Metro.................	97.3	119.3	79.9	98.7	111.8	113.0	96.4
Fayetteville-Springdale-Rogers, AR-MO Metro	96.5	91.2	89.1	111.5	98.0	93.2	100.7
Fort Smith, AR-OK Metro............	89.1	88.2	70.8	112.7	87.0	90.3	99.0
Jonesboro, AR Metro	85.9	88.9	74.7	93.2	85.0	80.3	93.2
Fresno, CA Metro.................	115.6	120.9	129.3	111.5	111.7	110.6	104.2
Los Angeles-Long Beach-Glendale, CA Metro Div.:.................	148.8	121.9	228.6	140.0	115.3	105.5	108.3
Riverside-San Bernardino-Ontario, CA Metro:							
Hemet-San Jacinto, CA	107.8	114.2	105.3	123.1	115.8	103.4	100.6
Palm Springs, CA	118.7	117.6	122.9	115.0	116.5	148.1	113.7
Riverside City, CA...............	114.2	112.2	133.5	93.2	120.9	130.8	100.4
San Diego-Carlsbad-San Marcos, CA Metro	139.8	127.8	200.6	92.8	130.1	131.0	109.8
San Francisco-San Mateo-Redwood City, CA Metro Div.:	169.8	124.7	292.5	110.7	125.1	152.2	114.6
Colorado Springs, CO Metro	98.2	105.8	100.1	79.9	102.2	111.6	96.0
Denver-Aurora, CO Metro	104.8	105.1	110.6	90.6	106.9	118.4	101.6
Fort Collins-Loveland, CO Metro:							
Fort Collins, CO	102.2	106.5	105.1	93.0	106.5	110.4	98.5
Grand Junction, CO Metro............	100.1	117.9	96.0	90.1	107.1	103.8	96.7
Pueblo, CO Metro	90.3	101.8	80.4	97.6	88.1	86.8	92.9
New Haven-Milford, CT Metro:							
Hew Haven, CT	117.0	104.3	126.8	123.7	111.9	155.3	108.7
Washington-Arlington-Alexandria, DC-VA-MD-WV Metro Div.:..........	138.8	111.2	206.8	104.4	120.6	124.9	108.4
Fort Walton Beach-Crestview-Destin, FL Metro:							
Fort Walton Beach, FL.............	95.7	106.0	84.5	90.6	98.3	90.5	102.5
Jacksonville, FL Metro..............	92.0	103.6	85.0	79.8	101.3	74.1	96.2
Orlando, FL Metro	97.2	97.9	91.9	97.3	95.5	94.8	102.3
Panama City-Lynn Haven, FL Metro:							
Panama City, FL................	96.8	107.2	76.3	99.3	111.6	99.8	104.8
Pensacola-Ferry Pass-Brent, FL Metro:							
Pensacola, FL	95.6	108.4	83.4	94.5	102.9	88.6	100.0
Sarasota-Bradenton-Venice, FL Metro:							
Sarasota, FL	104.5	102.3	114.6	90.7	106.1	104.8	100.2
Tallahassee, FL Metro..............	100.0	102.4	95.4	105.9	105.4	95.8	100.0
Tampa-St. Petersburg-Clearwater, FL Metro:							
St. Petersburg-Clearwater, FL	91.8	95.6	86.4	94.5	100.6	88.5	91.7
Tampa, FL....................	96.5	97.7	97.8	94.8	96.3	98.8	95.0
West Palm Beach-Boca Raton-Boynton Beach, FL Metro Div.:	108.3	106.7	113.7	100.2	105.4	103.1	108.3
Albany, GA Metro	87.8	97.2	72.8	92.7	87.9	80.6	96.4
Atlanta-Sandy Springs-Marietta, GA Metro:							
Atlanta, GA	97.6	103.3	91.8	90.3	99.0	106.3	100.9
Augusta-Richmond County, GA-SC Metro:							
Augusta-Aiken, GA-SC	91.8	105.8	76.7	91.3	94.3	86.7	99.3
Boise City-Nampa, ID Metro:							
Boise, ID.....................	98.8	91.2	95.6	97.0	108.5	106.4	101.6
Peoria, IL Metro	95.1	88.7	92.3	110.3	102.1	94.4	93.5
Springfield, IL Metro	93.3	93.0	86.2	110.4	96.7	96.4	93.0
Lafayette, IN Metro................	94.0	93.8	82.6	110.1	97.5	94.6	98.2

See footnotes at end of table.

U.S. Census Bureau, Statistical Abstract of the United States: 2004-2005

[See headnote, page 466]

Metropolitan areas (MA)	Composite index (100%)	Grocery items (14%)	Housing (29%)	Utilities (10%)	Transportation (10%)	Health care (4%)	Misc. goods and services (33%)
South Bend-Mishawaka, IN-MI Metro.....	96.2	85.4	98.1	102.9	92.3	95.1	98.3
Cedar Rapids, IA Metro	94.0	91.6	83.2	101.7	96.6	92.4	101.5
Waterloo-Cedar Falls, IA Metro	92.5	91.8	86.0	82.9	97.4	88.2	100.6
Lawrence, KS Metro	97.8	93.9	96.4	101.5	94.9	86.1	102.0
Clarksville, TN-KY Metro:							
Hopkinsville, KY	91.4	91.3	79.6	106.0	92.9	83.4	97.9
Lexington-Fayette, KY Metro	94.8	88.4	91.1	105.7	91.7	89.9	94.7
Louisville, KY-IN Metro	91.1	85.2	82.7	97.8	105.9	79.0	96.0
Baton Rouge, LA Metro	100.6	106.0	96.3	114.3	96.4	104.9	98.6
Lake Charles, LA Metro	96.5	89.4	101.9	97.0	92.3	89.6	96.7
Monroe, LA Metro	95.6	94.6	88.9	96.1	100.7	86.8	101.4
New Orleans-Metairie-Kenner, LA Metro:							
New Orleans, LA	97.0	90.3	93.5	112.4	101.2	88.1	98.0
Shreveport-Bossier City, LA Metro	93.0	86.5	94.2	92.4	94.1	76.1	96.7
Baltimore-Towson, MD Metro:							
Baltimore, MD	93.7	95.1	85.6	97.5	96.4	95.6	98.0
Bethesda-Frederick-Gaithersburg, MD Metro Div.:							
Bethesda-Frederick-Gaithersburg, MD Metro Div.	124.1	117.5	157.9	104.6	123.5	109.4	105.0
Boston-Quincy, MA Metro Div.	136.9	119.2	180.1	148.3	114.1	111.9	113.0
Grand Rapids-Wyoming, MI Metro	98.1	107.5	89.1	97.7	99.9	108.0	100.3
Minneapolis-St. Paul-Bloomington, MN-WI Metro	111.0	101.9	120.4	111.7	110.0	123.9	105.2
Rochester, MN Metro	98.4	93.1	92.9	106.1	93.3	113.7	102.7
St. Cloud, MN Metro	99.2	100.1	95.3	103.9	96.4	102.1	101.3
Hattiesburg, MS Metro	92.3	94.2	83.3	101.3	97.4	90.6	95.2
Jackson, MS Metro	91.6	86.8	86.7	103.5	95.0	84.6	94.2
Columbia, MO Metro	95.7	92.0	95.9	95.2	95.2	91.1	98.0
Joplin, MO Metro	88.3	83.1	83.5	89.5	82.6	90.2	95.9
St. Louis, MO-IL Metro	101.3	105.5	99.1	90.9	97.8	96.7	106.2
Springfield, MO Metro	88.6	99.7	78.2	73.1	93.1	94.5	95.7
Billings, MT Metro	98.5	104.4	87.8	101.2	96.5	104.2	104.4
Great Falls, MT Metro	94.8	102.5	83.1	109.0	97.9	107.9	94.9
Missoula, MT Metro	101.7	111.7	98.5	94.9	100.3	113.6	101.4
Lincoln, NE Metro	97.1	90.2	103.0	93.6	97.1	94.5	96.3
Omaha-Council Bluffs, NE-IA Metro:	91.4	90.6	84.7	104.5	96.8	96.2	91.4
Las Vegas-Paradise, NV Metro:							
Las Vegas, NV	103.0	113.6	96.6	83.2	111.8	126.7	104.4
Reno-Sparks, NV Metro	102.0	99.7	99.5	100.1	121.2	103.4	99.7
Albuquerque, NM Metro:							
Albuquerque, NM	102.4	99.5	106.9	112.4	106.9	110.7	94.4
Santa Fe, NM Metro:							
Santa Fe, NM.	118.3	103.2	146.4	108.5	107.1	122.1	106.1
Buffalo-Cheektowaga-Tonawanda, NY Metro:							
Buffalo, NY	101.3	109.2	94.0	129.8	104.4	95.4	95.5
Glens Falls, NY Metro	102.9	108.3	83.5	125.5	115.5	110.3	106.2
New York-Wayne-White Plains, NY-NJ Metro Div.:							
New York (Manhattan), NY	217.1	141.7	403.6	142.9	130.6	179.2	138.4
New York (Queens), NY	136.7	131.2	162.1	143.7	123.1	129.7	119.6
Asheville, NC Metro	100.8	91.3	110.0	97.9	98.6	94.5	98.9
Fayetteville, NC Metro	93.1	102.7	82.6	93.9	88.8	95.5	99.1
Jacksonville, NC Metro	92.0	99.7	80.2	93.1	85.9	100.0	99.1
Wilmington, NC Metro	99.3	97.4	107.6	91.5	95.4	95.2	96.7
Bismarck, ND Metro:							
Bismarck-Mandan, ND	93.5	98.5	83.3	93.1	104.2	78.5	99.1
Akron, OH Metro	94.8	110.2	83.5	107.6	103.2	91.5	92.2
Cincinnati-Middletown, OH-KY-IN Metro:							
Cincinnati, OH	94.8	92.4	85.2	110.6	97.7	95.0	98.7
Cleveland-Elyria-Mentor, OH Metro:							
Cleveland, OH	102.8	106.4	100.1	109.4	107.4	107.5	99.8
Dayton, OH Metro	92.6	85.5	82.3	96.9	100.0	100.2	100.1
Lima, OH Metro	93.8	110.8	85.6	98.4	97.4	90.8	91.6
Mansfield, OH Metro.	94.3	102.0	78.5	114.4	102.6	84.2	97.6
Toledo, OH Metro.	98.6	103.2	84.7	116.8	110.0	96.3	100.1
Youngstown-Warren-Boardman, OH-PA Metro:							
Youngstown-Warren, OH	93.2	98.4	89.5	113.4	86.0	74.5	92.4

See footnotes at end of table.

[See headnote, page 466]

Metropolitan areas (MA)	Composite index (100%)	Grocery items (14%)	Housing (29%)	Utilities (10%)	Transportation (10%)	Health care (4%)	Misc. goods and services (33%)
Tulsa, OK Metro.	93.0	91.7	81.5	94.4	104.9	89.5	100.2
Corvallis, OR Metro	109.7	108.9	110.4	95.1	114.8	129.5	109.7
Philadelphia, PA Metro Div.	120.8	110.5	129.3	123.1	122.9	120.7	116.2
Pittsburgh, PA Metro.	96.9	103.3	89.9	95.5	115.9	84.4	96.5
Williamsport, PA Metro:							
Williamsport-Lycoming County, PA	100.9	97.7	110.8	101.7	95.1	78.4	97.9
York-Hanover, PA Metro:							
York County, PA	97.1	91.6	95.4	105.8	96.2	75.5	101.1
Charleston-North Charleston, SC Metro . . .	98.3	99.2	90.2	103.4	99.4	101.0	102.7
Columbia, SC Metro	97.5	100.4	94.6	109.5	92.7	101.4	96.1
Myrtle Beach-Conway-North Myrtle Beach, SC Metro:							
Myrtle Beach, SC	97.3	99.4	100.3	90.8	93.3	94.8	97.2
Sumter, SC Metro.	94.3	95.7	88.9	92.0	96.4	88.4	99.3
Sioux Falls, SD Metro	93.8	90.5	83.2	110.9	92.5	95.4	99.6
Chattanooga, TN-GA Metro	93.1	95.9	83.5	88.3	100.2	94.4	99.6
Jackson, TN Metro	87.6	87.4	78.1	84.6	99.1	81.2	94.3
Johnson City, TN Metro.	89.2	89.1	86.9	103.9	83.0	78.2	90.2
Kingsport-Bristol TN-VA Metro	87.2	95.8	78.0	92.0	85.1	86.6	90.7
Knoxville, TN Metro	89.8	96.1	78.7	95.0	89.6	87.6	95.6
Memphis, TN-MS-AR Metro	90.7	95.4	80.4	88.0	93.7	90.7	97.5
Abilene, TX Metro	89.4	87.8	83.5	98.2	96.5	89.0	90.6
Amarillo, TX Metro	88.2	86.2	87.2	89.5	88.0	84.2	90.2
Beaumont-Port Arthur, TX Metro	91.3	92.6	81.5	92.6	90.7	90.3	99.2
El Paso, TX Metro	92.0	98.6	80.4	99.5	95.7	113.1	93.4
Fort Worth-Arlington, TX Metro Div.:							
Arlington, TX	94.4	92.1	90.8	93.4	96.1	93.3	98.6
Fort Worth, TX	94.3	101.5	81.0	96.0	96.8	103.1	100.4
Weatherford, TX	89.6	82.2	79.6	87.5	90.9	89.7	101.6
Houston-Baytown-Sugar Land, TX Metro:							
Brazoria, TX.	90.5	83.4	89.0	89.4	93.4	93.5	94.1
Conroe, TX.	90.5	89.0	82.4	86.7	101.3	100.5	95.1
Houston, TX.	91.6	87.1	79.2	104.3	102.9	103.3	95.8
Killeen-Temple-Fort Hood, TX Metro:							
Temple, TX	90.3	82.9	80.7	96.8	94.0	87.7	99.2
Longview, TX Metro	87.9	87.1	81.7	79.5	91.2	97.1	94.0
Lubbock, TX Metro	86.6	85.7	77.1	80.4	84.8	102.0	95.8
Odessa, TX Metro	88.3	87.4	76.9	88.3	94.6	91.9	96.4
San Antonio, TX Metro:							
San Antonio, TX	92.9	75.6	94.3	91.6	86.6	97.3	100.8
Seguin, TX	84.6	75.4	81.2	92.9	84.3	87.1	88.8
Sherman-Denison, TX Metro	92.3	96.7	77.2	109.3	88.6	103.0	98.5
Tyler, TX Metro.	94.8	91.4	89.6	111.3	89.6	105.0	96.2
Waco, TX Metro.	89.7	89.4	81.4	95.9	83.7	98.5	96.0
Salt Lake City, UT Metro	99.8	100.0	94.4	95.8	107.8	98.9	103.3
Burlington-South Burlington, VT Metro:							
Burlington-Chittenden County, VT	116.2	105.8	133.3	116.5	111.4	104.4	108.4
Richmond, VA Metro.	100.7	108.5	96.2	102.1	99.9	82.5	103.4
Roanoke, VA Metro.	92.6	93.5	87.9	91.0	91.8	88.1	97.7
Virginia Beach-Norfolk-Newport News, VA-NC Metro:							
Hampton Roads-SE Virginia, VA	97.0	98.0	98.2	117.3	99.8	95.8	88.7
Bellingham, WA Metro.	109.7	119.0	114.0	97.4	103.0	120.1	106.4
Olympia, WA Metro	100.9	107.8	91.4	88.8	108.6	133.0	103.8
Spokane, WA Metro	100.4	110.2	90.2	86.8	106.7	118.4	105.4
Yakima, WA Metro	98.9	103.8	94.3	80.0	107.7	132.9	99.8
Huntington-Ashland WV-KY-OH Metro: . . .							
Huntington, WV	93.5	99.3	88.7	97.9	92.1	87.8	95.1
Appleton, WI Metro.	96.0	97.0	85.7	91.9	114.8	96.7	100.2
Eau Claire, WI Metro	101.1	97.8	103.8	87.6	100.9	105.3	103.7
Green Bay, WI Metro	96.1	85.6	97.9	89.5	103.7	103.2	98.0
Wausau, WI Metro	95.5	91.9	90.1	107.0	100.3	97.5	96.5
Cheyenne, WY Metro	106.8	116.4	109.2	115.7	97.9	98.0	101.7

Source: ACCRA, 4232 King St., Alexandria, VA 22302-1507, *ACCRA Cost of Living Index*, Fourth Quarter 2002 (copyright).

No. 702. Annual Percent Changes From Prior Year in Consumer Prices—United States and OECD Countries: 1990 to 2003

[Covers member countries of Organization for Economic Cooperation (OECD). For consumer price indexes for OECD countries, see Section 30. 1990 change from1989; 1995 change from 1994; 1998 change from 1997]

Country	1990	1995	1998	1999	2000	2001	2002	2003
United States	5.4	2.8	1.6	2.2	3.4	2.8	1.5	2.3
OECD	7.0	5.7	4.0	3.4	4.0	3.0	(NA)	(NA)
Australia	7.3	4.6	0.9	1.5	4.5	3.0	3.0	2.8
Canada	4.8	2.2	1.0	1.7	2.7	4.6	2.2	2.8
Japan	3.1	-0.1	0.7	-0.3	-0.7	-0.2	-2.0	0.8
New Zealand	6.1	3.8	1.3	-0.1	2.6	2.7	2.7	1.8
Austria	3.3	2.2	0.9	0.6	2.4	1.7	1.8	1.3
Belgium	3.4	1.5	1.0	1.1	2.5	1.8	1.6	1.6
Denmark	2.6	2.1	1.8	2.5	2.9	2.9	2.4	2.1
Finland	6.1	0.8	1.4	1.2	3.4	1.9	1.5	0.9
France	3.6	1.8	0.8	0.5	1.7	2.6	1.9	2.1
Greece	20.4	8.9	4.8	2.6	3.2	4.4	3.6	3.6
Ireland	3.3	2.5	2.4	1.6	5.6	5.1	4.7	3.5
Italy [1]	6.5	5.2	2.0	1.7	2.5	2.7	2.5	2.7
Luxembourg	3.3	1.9	1.0	1.0	3.2	2.5	2.1	2.0
Netherlands	2.5	1.9	2.0	2.2	2.5	2.7	3.3	2.2
Norway	4.1	2.4	2.3	2.3	3.1	4.8	1.3	2.5
Portugal [2]	13.4	4.2	2.8	2.3	2.9	4.1	3.5	3.3
Spain	6.7	4.7	1.8	2.3	3.4	3.8	3.1	3.0
Sweden	10.4	2.9	0.4	0.3	1.3	3.3	2.3	2.1
Switzerland	5.4	1.8	0.0	0.8	1.6	1.3	0.7	0.6
Turkey [2]	60.3	89.1	84.6	64.9	54.9	27.0	45.0	25.3
United Kingdom	9.5	3.4	3.4	1.6	2.9	3.2	1.6	2.9
Germany	2.7	1.7	0.9	0.6	1.9	1.3	1.4	1.0

[1] Households of wage and salary earners.　[2] Excludes rent.

Source: Organization for Economic Cooperation and Development, Paris, France, *Main Economic Indicators*, monthly (copyright).

No. 703. Producer Price Indexes by Stage of Processing: 1980 to 2003

[1982=100, except as indicated. See Appendix III]

Year	Crude materials				Interme-diate materials, supplies, and components	Finished goods		Finished consumer foods		Finished consumer goods excl. food
	Total	Food-stuffs and feed-stuffs	Fuel	Crude nonfood materials except fuel		Con-sumer goods	Capital equip-ment	Crude	Pro-cessed	
1980	95.3	104.6	69.4	91.8	90.3	88.6	85.8	93.9	92.3	87.1
1985	95.8	94.8	102.7	94.3	102.7	103.8	107.5	102.9	104.8	103.3
1988	96.0	106.1	82.1	85.9	107.1	106.2	114.3	109.8	112.7	103.1
1989	103.1	111.2	85.3	95.8	112.0	112.1	118.8	119.6	118.6	108.9
1990	108.9	113.1	84.8	107.3	114.5	118.2	122.9	123.0	124.4	115.3
1991	101.2	105.5	82.9	97.5	114.4	120.5	126.7	119.3	124.4	118.7
1992	100.4	105.1	84.0	94.2	114.7	121.7	129.1	107.6	124.4	120.8
1993	102.4	108.4	87.1	94.1	116.2	123.0	131.4	114.4	126.5	121.7
1994	101.8	106.5	82.4	97.0	118.5	123.3	134.1	111.3	127.9	121.6
1995	102.7	105.8	72.1	105.8	124.9	125.6	136.7	118.8	129.8	124.0
1996	113.8	121.5	92.6	105.7	125.7	129.5	138.3	129.2	133.8	127.6
1997	111.1	112.2	101.3	103.5	125.6	130.2	138.2	126.6	135.1	128.2
1998	96.8	103.9	86.7	84.5	123.0	128.9	137.6	127.2	134.8	126.4
1999	98.2	98.7	91.2	91.1	123.2	132.0	137.6	125.5	135.9	130.5
2000	120.6	100.2	136.9	118.0	129.2	138.2	138.8	123.5	138.3	138.4
2001	121.0	106.1	151.4	101.5	129.7	141.5	139.7	127.7	142.4	141.4
2002	108.1	99.5	117.3	101.0	127.8	139.4	139.1	128.5	141.0	138.8
2003 prel.	135.3	113.5	186.1	116.8	133.7	145.2	139.6	130.1	147.3	144.6
PERCENT CHANGE [1]										
1980	10.9	4.6	21.1	22.0	15.2	14.3	10.7	1.7	6.3	18.5
1985	-7.4	-9.5	-2.3	2.2	-0.4	0.5	2.2	-7.6	-0.1	1.1
1988	2.5	10.3	-2.4	16.4	5.5	2.5	2.3	2.5	2.8	2.4
1989	7.4	4.8	3.9	-2.9	4.6	5.6	3.9	8.9	5.2	5.6
1990	5.6	1.7	-0.6	12.0	2.2	5.4	3.5	2.8	4.9	5.9
1991	-7.1	-6.7	-2.2	-9.1	-0.1	1.9	3.1	-3.0	-	2.9
1992	-0.8	-0.4	1.3	-3.4	0.3	1.0	1.9	-9.8	-	1.8
1993	2.0	3.1	3.7	-0.1	1.3	1.1	1.8	6.3	1.7	0.7
1994	-0.6	-1.8	-5.4	3.1	2.0	0.2	2.1	-2.7	1.1	-0.1
1995	0.9	-0.7	-12.5	9.1	5.4	1.9	1.9	6.7	1.5	2.0
1996	10.8	14.8	28.4	-0.1	0.6	3.1	1.2	8.8	3.1	2.9
1997	-2.4	-7.7	9.4	-2.1	-0.1	0.5	-0.1	-2.0	1.0	0.5
1998	-12.9	-7.4	-14.4	-18.4	-2.1	-1.0	-0.4	0.5	-0.2	-1.4
1999	1.4	-5.0	5.2	7.8	0.2	2.4	0.6	-1.3	0.8	3.2
2000	22.8	1.5	50.1	29.5	4.9	4.7	0.9	-1.6	1.8	6.1
2001	0.3	5.9	10.6	-14.0	0.4	2.4	0.6	3.4	3.0	2.2
2002	-10.7	-6.2	-22.5	-0.5	-1.5	-1.5	-0.4	0.6	-1.0	-1.8
2003 prel.	25.2	14.1	58.7	15.6	4.6	4.2	0.4	1.2	4.5	4.2

- Represents or rounds to zero.　[1] Change from immediate prior year.

Source: U.S. Bureau of Labor Statistics, *Producer Price Indexes*, monthly and annual.

Prices　469

No. 704. Producer Price Indexes by Stage of Processing: 1990 to 2003

[1982=100, except as indicated. See Appendix III]

Stage of processing	1990	1995	1998	1999	2000	2001	2002	2003 [1]
Finished goods	119.2	127.9	130.7	133.0	138.0	140.7	138.9	143.3
Finished consumer goods	118.2	125.6	128.9	132.0	138.2	141.5	139.4	145.2
Finished consumer foods	124.4	129.0	134.3	135.1	137.2	141.3	140.1	146.0
Fresh fruits and melons	118.1	85.8	90.5	103.6	91.4	97.7	91.5	83.7
Fresh and dry vegetables	118.1	144.4	139.5	118.0	126.7	124.7	136.5	136.3
Eggs for fresh use (Dec. 1991=100)	(NA)	86.3	90.1	77.9	84.9	81.8	82.9	106.6
Bakery products	141.0	164.3	175.8	178.0	182.3	187.7	189.9	195.1
Milled rice	102.5	113.1	124.9	121.3	101.2	87.3	80.3	102.3
Pasta products (June 1985=100)	114.1	125.0	122.6	122.1	121.6	122.1	121.7	126.4
Beef and veal	116.0	100.9	99.4	106.3	113.7	120.6	114.7	138.2
Pork	119.8	101.5	96.6	96.0	113.4	120.3	109.0	115.5
Processed young chickens	111.0	113.5	125.2	113.4	110.4	117.2	109.7	119.8
Processed turkeys	107.6	104.9	95.2	94.8	98.7	98.9	95.3	92.3
Finfish and shellfish	147.2	170.8	183.2	190.9	198.1	190.8	191.2	195.1
Dairy products	117.2	119.7	138.2	139.2	133.7	145.2	136.2	139.4
Processed fruits and vegetables	124.7	122.4	125.7	128.1	128.6	129.6	132.6	133.6
Confectionery end products	140.0	160.7	168.7	170.4	170.6	171.4	175.6	183.7
Soft drinks	122.3	133.1	134.8	137.9	144.1	148.2	151.3	152.8
Roasted coffee	113.0	146.5	143.9	134.7	133.5	124.2	121.5	127.4
Shortening and cooking oils	123.2	142.5	143.4	140.4	132.4	132.9	140.8	160.6
Finished consumer goods excluding foods	115.3	124.0	126.4	130.5	138.4	141.4	138.8	144.6
Alcoholic beverages	117.2	128.5	135.2	136.7	140.6	145.4	147.0	148.5
Women's apparel	116.1	119.6	122.3	123.9	124.6	123.7	122.7	123.7
Men's and boy's apparel	120.2	130.3	133.2	133.1	133.2	132.4	129.0	127.1
Girls', children's, and infants' apparel	115.3	121.6	121.8	118.2	117.4	116.6	118.4	119.6
Textile house furnishings	109.5	119.5	123.1	122.7	122.0	122.5	122.3	122.4
Footwear	125.6	139.2	144.7	144.5	144.9	145.8	146.0	147.5
Residential electric power (Dec. 1990=100)	(NA)	111.8	110.7	109.5	110.8	116.6	115.4	118.9
Residential gas (Dec. 1990=100)	(NA)	104.4	114.0	114.3	135.5	158.7	131.9	167.5
Gasoline	78.7	63.7	53.4	64.7	94.6	90.5	83.3	102.7
Fuel oil No. 2	73.3	56.6	48.1	56.1	93.5	84.3	75.0	95.2
Pharmaceutical preps, ethical (prescription)	200.8	257.0	322.9	335.0	344.4	(NA)	(NA)	(NA)
Pharmaceutical preps, proprietary (over-counter)	156.8	186.5	184.5	186.0	187.7	(NA)	(NA)	(NA)
Soaps and synthetic detergents	117.7	122.9	126.1	126.3	128.2	130.6	130.0	130.6
Cosmetics and other toilet preparations	121.6	129.0	132.9	135.4	137.4	138.5	139.4	140.4
Tires, tubes, and tread	96.8	100.2	94.0	92.9	93.0	94.1	95.2	98.0
Sanitary papers and health products	135.3	144.4	145.1	144.3	146.7	147.3	149.3	150.4
Newspaper circulation	144.1	185.6	202.9	207.1	210.0	219.5	225.6	230.5
Periodical circulation	150.3	176.6	193.8	196.9	198.9	200.7	210.0	220.2
Book publishing	153.4	185.0	205.9	213.0	218.2	225.5	234.8	243.2
Household furniture	125.1	141.8	148.4	150.5	152.7	154.9	157.1 •	158.2
Floor coverings	119.0	123.7	128.3	127.2	129.6	130.2	130.5	133.2
Household appliances	110.8	112.4	108.0	108.5	107.3	105.3	104.6	102.4
Home electronic equipment	82.7	78.9	75.9	73.7	71.8	70.4	69.0	67.6
Household glassware	132.5	153.2	162.7	163.9	166.0	169.6	169.9	168.8
Household flatware	122.1	138.3	139.2	139.7	142.6	142.8	144.7	145.2
Lawn and garden equipment, except tractors	123.0	130.4	131.7	132.0	132.0	132.8	133.9	133.4
Passenger cars	118.3	134.1	131.9	131.3	132.8	132.0	129.5	129.5
Toys, games, and children's vehicles	118.1	124.3	124.4	124.1	123.7	121.9	123.4	124.9
Sporting and athletic goods	112.6	122.0	126.2	126.2	126.1	126.3	125.5	124.3
Tobacco products	221.4	231.3	283.6	374.0	397.2	441.9	459.4	431.5
Mobile homes	117.5	145.6	154.3	158.4	161.3	164.1	166.6	169.5
Jewelry, platinum, and karat gold	122.8	127.8	128.1	127.1	127.2	128.5	130.0	132.3
Costume jewelry and novelties	125.3	135.1	139.6	140.1	141.6	144.0	144.2	144.8
Capital Equipment	122.9	136.7	137.6	137.6	138.8	139.7	139.1	139.6
Agricultural machinery and equipment	121.7	142.9	150.4	152.1	153.7	156.1	158.5	160.7
Construction machinery and equipment	121.6	136.7	145.2	147.2	148.6	149.1	151.1	153.3
Metal cutting machine tools	129.8	148.0	159.2	160.7	161.9	158.8	152.4	150.4
Metal forming machine tools	128.7	145.7	157.6	159.7	161.8	164.8	166.8	167.6
Tools, dies, jigs, fixtures, and industrial molds	117.2	133.8	138.8	139.8	141.1	141.3	140.6	139.5
Pumps, compressors, and equipment	119.2	139.4	149.0	151.7	154.1	157.6	161.0	163.0
Industrial material handling equipment	115.0	125.3	131.3	132.9	134.7	136.8	136.9	137.9

See footnote at end of table.

U.S. Census Bureau, Statistical Abstract of the United States: 2004-2005

[1982=100, except as indicated]

Stage of processing	1990	1995	1998	1999	2000	2001	2002	2003[1]
Capital Equipment—Continued								
Electronic computers (Dec. 1990=100)	(NA)	51.8	24.7	87.2	73.0	56.7	42.8	34.1
Textile machinery	128.8	146.7	152.7	154.2	156.2	158.0	157.0	157.6
Paper industries machinery (June 1982=100)	134.8	151.0	160.3	162.6	164.7	166.8	168.9	170.3
Printing trades machinery	124.9	133.6	141.5	141.0	142.1	143.3	143.7	142.9
Transformers and power regulators	120.9	128.9	131.0	132.6	135.8	134.4	131.7	131.9
Communication/related equip.(Dec. 1985=100)	106.1	112.1	114.0	112.7	110.6	109.5	107.6	105.5
X-ray and electromedical equipment	109.8	111.8	106.7	104.3	101.5	100.2	100.9	100.4
Oil field and gas field machinery	102.4	114.1	125.8	126.5	128.2	134.3	135.8	139.6
Mining machinery and equipment	121.0	135.6	142.2	144.2	146.1	148.5	151.8	155.0
Office and store machines and equipment	109.5	111.5	112.3	112.3	112.7	112.7	112.5	112.5
Commercial furniture	133.4	148.2	155.2	156.6	158.4	160.3	160.9	162.5
Light motor trucks	130.0	159.0	155.1	157.5	157.6	155.0	150.5	150.1
Heavy motor trucks	120.3	144.1	142.1	146.5	148.0	147.7	152.2	154.7
Truck trailers	110.8	131.7	135.0	136.3	139.4	138.8	138.1	139.4
Civilian aircraft (Dec. 1985=100)	115.3	141.8	150.1	151.7	159.6	168.5	171.3	179.9
Ships (Dec. 1985=100)	110.1	132.8	145.7	145.8	146.9	148.9	150.6	158.5
Railroad equipment	118.6	134.8	134.9	135.2	135.7	135.2	134.9	136.3
Intermediate materials, supplies, and components	114.5	124.9	123.0	123.2	129.2	129.7	127.8	133.7
Intermediate foods and feeds	113.3	114.8	116.1	111.7	111.7	115.9	115.5	125.8
Flour	103.6	123.0	109.2	104.3	103.8	109.9	116.2	123.8
Refined sugar	122.7	119.3	119.8	121.0	110.6	109.9	117.7	121.9
Confectionery materials	101.2	109.1	93.8	94.0	94.2	105.8	117.4	125.1
Crude vegetable oils	115.8	130.0	131.1	90.2	73.6	70.1	87.6	128.1
Prepared animal feeds	107.4	109.1	107.9	98.3	102.9	105.1	105.7	112.6
Intermediate materials less foods and feeds	120.9	135.2	133.5	123.9	130.1	130.5	128.5	134.2
Synthetic fibers	106.7	109.4	109.8	103.8	107.2	108.6	106.2	106.4
Processed yarns and threads	112.6	112.8	112.7	108.6	107.9	105.6	102.6	103.6
Gray fabrics	117.2	121.2	121.6	114.4	113.2	114.0	112.6	110.9
Leather	177.5	191.4	178.5	176.3	182.2	200.9	202.5	213.4
Liquefied petroleum gas	77.4	65.1	60.1	73.7	127.1	119.0	104.5	150.6
Commercial electric power	115.3	131.7	130.5	129.1	131.5	139.6	137.5	140.9
Industrial electric power	119.6	130.8	130.0	128.9	131.5	141.1	139.9	146.1
Commercial natural gas (Dec. 1990=100)	(NA)	96.5	106.6	108.1	134.7	168.3	135.0	173.1
Industrial natural gas (Dec. 1990=100)	(NA)	90.9	104.2	103.3	139.0	177.3	136.5	180.0
Natural gas to electric utilities (Dec. 1990=100)	(NA)	87.7	80.5	81.6	120.7	146.5	103.9	157.5
Jet fuels	76.0	55.0	46.0	52.5	88.5	77.4	71.6	86.6
No. 2 Diesel fuel	74.1	57.0	47.3	57.3	93.3	83.4	77.9	100.5
Residual fuel	57.7	52.6	43.8	51.5	84.7	74.6	75.4	101.4
Industrial chemicals	113.2	128.4	121.6	118.9	129.1	128.4	127.3	141.8
Prepared paint	124.8	142.1	155.0	157.4	160.8	164.4	166.9	170.7
Paint materials	136.3	139.4	143.8	144.1	148.5	149.8	165.9	173.1
Medicinal and botanical chemicals	102.2	128.3	135.0	142.2	146.2	141.2	132.6	135.4
Fats and oils, inedible	88.1	126.9	116.9	88.4	70.1	77.6	90.3	123.2
Mixed fertilizers	103.3	111.1	115.3	113.7	112.4	116.6	113.9	119.1
Nitrogenates	92.3	129.4	108.2	94.6	118.2	143.0	106.0	146.8
Phosphates	96.5	109.1	112.5	112.0	96.9	95.2	99.8	109.5
Other agricultural chemicals	119.9	144.3	149.7	144.5	146.1	148.3	148.5	148.8
Plastic resins and materials	124.1	143.5	125.6	125.8	141.6	134.2	130.7	146.1
Synthetic rubber	111.9	126.3	117.2	113.9	119.1	122.9	119.3	126.0
Plastic construction products	117.2	133.8	126.2	128.0	135.8	132.9	136.1	138.6
Unsupported plastic film, sheet, and shapes	119.0	135.6	128.1	127.5	133.2	138.0	136.5	142.9
Plastic parts and components for manufacturing	112.9	115.9	117.1	117.4	117.3	116.9	116.2	116.1
Softwood lumber	123.8	178.5	182.4	196.0	178.6	170.1	170.8	171.1
Hardwood lumber	131.0	167.0	178.7	177.3	185.9	181.3	178.3	189.7
Millwork	130.4	163.8	171.1	174.7	176.4	179.2	179.8	181.8
Plywood	114.2	165.3	157.6	176.4	157.6	154.3	151.7	166.9
Woodpile	151.3	183.2	122.0	119.7	125.8	125.8	116.2	121.4
Paper	128.8	159.0	146.0	141.8	149.8	150.6	144.7	146.1
Paperboard	135.7	183.1	151.7	153.2	176.7	172.1	164.3	162.7
Paper boxes and containers	129.9	163.8	154.7	158.0	172.6	175.2	172.8	172.9
Building paper and board	112.2	144.9	132.8	141.6	138.8	129.3	129.3	159.7

See footnotes at end of table.

U.S. Census Bureau, Statistical Abstract of the United States: 2004-2005

[1982=100, except as indicated]

Stage of processing	1990	1995	1998	1999	2000	2001	2002	2003 [1]
Intermediate materials less foods and feeds—Continued								
Commercial printing (June 1982=100)	128.0	144.5	152.1	152.2	155.2	157.6	157.0	158.3
Foundry and forge shop products	117.2	129.3	135.0	135.1	136.5	136.9	136.8	137.4
Steel mill products	112.1	120.1	113.9	105.3	108.4	101.3	104.8	109.6
Primary nonferrous metals	133.4	146.8	106.7	101.5	113.6	105.2	100.8	105.1
Aluminum mill shapes	127.9	160.4	142.1	138.1	149.0	148.7	143.3	143.2
Copper and brass mill shapes	174.6	195.2	153.4	151.2	162.3	155.0	149.6	152.6
Nonferrous wire and cable	142.6	151.5	140.9	135.6	143.7	140.4	134.3	134.6
Metal containers	114.0	117.2	108.7	106.4	106.8	106.3	107.8	109.1
Hardware	125.9	141.1	147.0	148.7	151.2	154.4	156.0	156.4
Plumbing fixtures and brass fittings	144.3	166.0	175.1	176.7	180.4	180.8	181.9	183.4
Heating equipment	131.6	147.5	153.2	154.0	155.6	157.1	157.9	163.3
Fabricated structural metal products	121.8	135.1	142.5	143.3	144.9	144.6	145.0	145.6
Fabricated ferrous wire products (June 1982=100)	114.6	125.7	130.1	130.6	130.0	129.8	129.7	131.4
Other miscellaneous metal products	120.7	124.9	126.2	125.5	126.0	127.0	126.8	127.5
Mechanical power transmission equipment	125.3	146.9	157.7	161.1	163.9	167.0	169.5	171.3
Air conditioning and refrigeration equipment	122.1	130.2	134.6	135.5	135.3	136.0	136.9	137.2
Metal valves, excluding fluid power (Dec. 1982=100).	125.3	145.3	156.6	160.2	162.1	164.7	167.2	169.4
Ball and roller bearings	130.6	152.0	165.2	166.8	168.8	169.5	170.0	171.2
Wiring devices	132.2	147.2	154.2	152.5	152.9	153.5	153.8	152.7
Motors, generators, motor generator sets	132.9	143.9	145.8	145.9	146.2	146.8	146.8	147.4
Switchgear and switchboard equipment	124.4	140.3	148.3	151.0	153.0	156.9	158.4	159.7
Electronic components and accessories	118.4	113.6	100.1	98.2	97.1	93.9	92.4	90.9
Internal combustion engines	120.2	135.6	140.7	143.0	143.8	143.9	144.4	144.6
Machine shop products	124.3	131.3	136.3	136.8	138.0	140.1	140.0	140.7
Flat glass	107.5	113.2	107.2	106.4	109.7	112.0	111.2	110.9
Cement	103.7	128.1	145.7	150.6	150.1	150.2	152.6	152.2
Concrete products	113.5	129.4	140.1	143.7	147.8	151.7	152.7	153.5
Asphalt felts and coatings	97.1	100.0	99.6	99.2	104.1	107.5	110.9	116.4
Gypsum products	105.2	154.5	177.2	208.0	201.4	156.4	168.9	171.4
Glass containers	120.4	130.5	125.9	125.9	127.4	132.9	135.6	140.2
Motor vehicle parts	111.2	116.0	114.6	114.0	113.6	113.3	112.9	111.7
Aircraft engines and engine parts (Dec. 1985=100)	113.5	132.8	136.9	138.5	141.0	145.1	145.7	153.5
Aircraft parts and auxiliary equipment, N.e.c. [2] (June 1985=100)	117.7	135.7	142.6	143.7	145.7	149.2	151.1	150.2
Photographic supplies	127.6	126.8	128.9	128.3	125.2	128.5	121.6	117.7
Medical/surgical/personal aid devices	127.3	141.3	143.3	144.6	146.0	148.3	150.9	154.7
Crude materials for further processing	108.9	102.7	96.7	98.2	120.6	121.0	108.1	135.3
Crude foodstuffs and feedstuffs	113.1	105.8	103.8	98.7	100.2	106.1	99.5	113.5
Wheat	87.6	118.6	87.8	79.5	80.3	85.5	97.9	98.5
Corn	100.9	109.0	91.7	78.2	76.4	78.8	89.4	93.8
Slaughter cattle	122.5	99.5	92.5	97.6	104.1	108.4	100.8	124.3
Slaughter hogs	94.1	70.2	52.2	53.8	72.7	73.4	55.4	66.1
Slaughter broilers/fryers	119.5	129.1	151.8	134.5	127.6	138.4	125.9	149.3
Slaughter turkeys	116.9	120.3	110.4	120.0	120.7	110.3	104.3	102.8
Fluid milk	100.8	93.6	112.6	106.3	92.0	111.8	90.8	93.6
Soybeans	100.8	102.2	103.4	80.1	83.4	78.6	87.7	108.8
Cane sugar, raw	119.2	119.7	117.2	113.7	101.8	111.4	110.9	114.1
Crude nonfood materials	101.5	96.8	88.3	94.3	130.4	126.8	111.4	148.2
Raw cotton	118.2	156.2	111.0	87.4	95.2	67.2	61.5	92.9
Leaf tobacco	95.8	102.5	104.6	101.6	(NA)	105.2	(NA)	102.0
Cattle hides	217.8	209.9	153.3	141.9	169.4	(NA)	(NA)	(NA)
Coal	97.5	95.0	93.1	90.7	87.9	96.2	99.8	100.0
Natural gas	80.4	66.6	83.7	91.2	155.5	171.8	122.5	215.0
Crude petroleum	71.0	51.1	35.7	50.3	85.2	69.2	67.9	82.9
Logs and timber	142.8	220.4	208.2	202.0	196.4	182.8	180.1	181.8
Wastepaper	138.9	371.1	146.0	183.6	282.5	148.6	173.1	197.2
Iron ore	83.3	91.8	95.5	94.9	94.8	96.2	95.2	95.9
Iron and steel scrap	166.0	202.7	164.9	139.2	142.1	120.0	141.4	182.3
Nonferrous metal ores (Dec. 1983=100)	98.3	101.6	66.9	63.1	68.0	63.7	68.1	77.5
Copper base scrap	181.3	193.5	116.3	108.2	123.7	114.8	111.4	127.8
Aluminum base scrap	172.6	209.4	162.8	161.7	177.0	156.5	158.0	168.7
Construction sand, gravel, and crushed stone	125.4	142.3	152.7	157.2	163.1	168.8	173.0	177.1

NA Not available. [1] Preliminary data. [2] N.e.c. Not elsewhere classified.

Source: U.S. Bureau of Labor Statistics, *Producer Price Indexes*, monthly and annual.

[Indexes are based on selling prices reported by establishments of all sizes by probability sampling. Manufacturing industries selected by shipment value. N.e.c.= not elsewhere classified. See text, Section 22, and Appendix III]

Industry	SIC code [1]	Index base [2]	1999	2000	2001	2002	2003[3]
Iron ores	1011	12/84	94.0	93.9	95.2	94.2	95.0
Copper ores	1021	06/88	71.3	88.7	81.7	80.1	88.0
Lead and zinc ores	1031	12/85	111.8	118.8	89.2	(X)	(X)
Gold ores	1041	06/85	85.6	84.2	81.5	92.4	107.6
Metal mining services	1081	12/85	120.2	109.0	117.6	115.9	116.1
Metal ores, n.e.c.	1099	12/85	82.9	85.8	77.9	91.6	112.5
Bituminous coal and lignite	1211	12/81	90.6	(X)	(X)	(X)	(X)
Anthracite mining	1231	12/79	158.7	157.3	161.0	163.0	168.5
Coal mining services	1241	06/85	107.7	108.4	117.0	118.6	124.8
Crude petroleum and natural gas liquids	1331	06/96	102.6	174.3	(X)	(X)	(X)
Drilling oil and gas wells	1381	12/85	133.1	138.2	173.9	153.5	153.5
Oil and gas exploration services	1382	12/85	92.7	80.4	72.7	71.8	74.1
Oil and gas field services, n.e.c.	1389	12/85	112.9	123.3	142.4	137.4	135.9
Dimension stone	1411	06/85	145.9	153.4	156.9	164.0	169.9
Crushed and broken limestone	1422	12/83	140.6	145.6	150.9	154.7	159.2
Crushed and broken granite	1423	12/83	172.5	182.3	188.3	193.2	197.5
Crushed and broken stone, n.e.c.	1429	12/83	149.9	153.1	156.8	160.8	164.0
Construction sand and gravel	1442	06/82	169.0	175.5	181.6	185.8	189.0
Industrial sand	1446	06/82	145.2	148.0	154.3	157.1	162.1
Kaolin and ball clay	1455	06/84	113.3	113.3	119.6	118.8	121.0
Clay and related minerals, n.e.c.	1459	06/84	133.5	135.7	140.3	140.9	142.5
Potash, soda, and borate minerals	1474	12/84	113.6	111.6	110.0	107.7	106.2
Chemicals and fertilizer mineral mining, n.e.c.	1479	12/89	90.0	90.1	85.8	92.1	92.2
Non-metallic minerals (except fuels) services	1481	06/85	106.5	107.2	109.3	110.5	114.8
Miscellaneous nonmetallic minerals	1499	06/85	138.0	138.7	143.1	143.2	146.4
Meat packing plants	2011	12/80	104.2	113.4	120.3	113.1	130.3
Sausage and other prepared meats	2013	12/82	113.8	121.3	125.8	121.1	129.9
Poultry slaughtering and processing	2015	12/81	119.8	118.3	121.5	115.9	122.0
Natural and processed cheese	2022	06/81	124.3	117.8	129.6	121.5	126.9
Dry, condensed, and evaporated milk products	2023	12/83	142.4	140.9	150.3	139.9	139.1
Ice cream and frozen desserts	2024	06/83	150.0	150.4	157.1	158.8	160.4
Fluid milk	2026	12/82	145.9	141.8	153.6	146.4	147.8
Canned specialties	2032	12/82	168.6	171.5	173.8	174.6	176.1
Canned fruits, vegetables, preserves, jams, and jellies	2033	06/81	138.2	139.1	142.2	143.7	144.8
Pickled fruits/veg./veg. sauces/seasonings/salad dressings	2035	06/81	163.2	163.6	163.1	165.3	169.0
Frozen fruits and vegetables	2037	06/81	141.8	141.0	140.2	144.1	147.5
Frozen specialties	2038	12/82	137.4	136.1	138.8	139.0	139.2
Flour and other grain mill products	2041	06/83	97.1	97.2	101.9	107.6	113.9
Cereal breakfast foods	2043	12/83	159.5	159.6	161.7	163.3	166.3
Wet corn milling	2046	06/85	101.3	102.6	112.3	112.7	122.5
Dog and cat food	2047	12/85	132.2	131.3	134.7	135.7	136.1
Prepared animal feeds, n.e.c.	2048	12/80	86.7	89.0	92.2	95.3	101.8
Bread and other bakery products, except cookies and crackers	2051	06/80	204.5	211.3	221.5	236.3	228.1
Cookies and crackers	2052	06/83	171.0	172.0	173.3	175.0	181.5
Candy and other confectionery products, and chewing gum	2064	06/83	149.4	150.9	152.4	154.4	160.6
Soybean oil mill products	2075	12/79	68.0	69.1	67.3	72.1	87.2
Malt beverages	2082	06/82	131.4	136.1	140.5	142.7	145.6
Bottled and canned soft drinks	2086	06/81	145.7	152.0	156.5	159.5	161.3
Flavoring extracts and syrups, n.e.c.	2087	12/85	133.6	137.3	140.7	142.7	145.4
Fresh or frozen packaged fish	2092	12/82	160.9	171.5	161.7	157.2	161.7
Coffee	2095	06/81	145.8	144.3	136.4	133.8	139.4
Potato and corn chips, and similar snacks	2096	06/91	112.7	116.7	121.8	123.7	124.5
Macaroni, spaghetti, and noodles	2098	06/85	122.3	121.9	122.4	122.0	126.3
Food preparations, n.e.c.	2099	12/85	128.9	129.1	131.0	134.2	137.8
Cigarettes	2111	12/82	356.7	379.2	425.8	442.8	411.7
Cigars	2121	12/82	259.6	268.8	279.1	289.8	304.6
Cotton broadwoven fabric	2211	12/80	114.1	110.6	111.7	108.9	108.8
Manmade fiber and silk broadwoven fabric	2221	06/81	108.6	108.6	108.9	106.4	105.7
Narrow fabric mills	2241	06/84	124.3	125.3	126.2	126.0	125.0
Knit outerwear	2253	12/84	116.4	117.0	116.6	113.6	105.2
Carpet and rugs	2273	06/90	105.6	107.8	108.8	108.9	111.0
Spun yarn	2281	12/82	96.9	95.5	94.0	90.8	92.7
Men's and boys' separate trousers and slacks	2325	12/81	137.0	134.8	135.1	132.2	128.4
Women's, misses', and juniors' dresses	2335	12/80	126.3	125.8	123.6	122.1	122.9
Women's, misses', and juniors' outerwear, n.e.c.	2339	06/83	112.6	113.3	112.1	111.5	112.8
House furnishings, n.e.c.	2392	06/83	118.8	117.7	117.2	116.5	116.5
Automotive trimmings, apparel findings, and related products	2396	12/83	122.6	123.9	124.5	124.4	124.3
Logging camps and logging contractors	2411	12/81	182.8	177.6	167.6	165.1	168.7
Sawmills and planing mills	2421	12/80	157.4	148.0	141.2	139.1	141.2
Millwork	2431	06/83	160.0	161.3	164.8	165.4	166.1
Wood kitchen cabinets	2434	06/84	155.7	159.8	162.6	164.5	167.8
Softwood plywood	2436	12/80	164.7	140.4	135.8	131.8	154.5
Mobile homes	2451	06/81	164.2	167.1	170.0	172.6	175.6
Wood household furniture, except upholstered	2511	12/79	200.5	204.1	207.6	211.4	212.6
Upholstered wood household furniture	2512	06/82	142.0	144.4	146.2	147.8	149.0
Nonwood office furniture	2522	12/79	191.8	193.4	195.3	198.3	202.1
Public building and related furniture	2531	12/84	136.8	138.6	139.1	138.9	138.9

See footnotes at end of table

[See headnote, page 473]

Industry	SIC code [1]	index base [2]	1999	2000	2001	2002	2003[3]
Paper mills	2621	06/81	139.7	148.7	150.5	144.1	145.4
Paperboard mills	2631	12/82	167.0	192.4	187.4	179.7	180.4
Corrugated and solid fiber boxes	2653	03/80	175.5	196.8	198.0	193.2	192.9
Folding paperboard boxes	2657	12/83	142.3	145.4	146.9	146.6	146.3
Paper coated and laminated, n.e.c.	2672	06/93	109.8	111.7	112.8	111.9	111.2
Plastics, foil and coated paper bags	2673	12/83	159.0	168.6	169.2	166.1	176.1
Sanitary paper products	2676	06/83	145.1	148.3	148.0	149.8	150.5
Newspaper publishing	2711	12/79	339.3	351.2	367.9	381.8	395.5
Periodical publishing	2721	12/79	284.9	292.6	305.9	320.4	332.9
Book publishing	2731	12/80	247.6	255.0	263.3	273.0	283.0
Miscellaneous publishing	2741	06/84	194.5	201.3	210.0	217.7	225.9
Commercial printing, lithographic	2752	06/82	153.2	156.0	158.1	157.0	157.1
Commercial printing, n.e.c.	2759	06/82	162.6	166.2	168.4	169.9	171.9
Manifold business forms	2761	12/83	170.5	185.7	193.1	199.7	201.8
Industrial inorganic chemicals, n.e.c.	2819	12/82	129.2	132.7	142.6	141.1	145.1
Plastic materials and resins	2821	12/80	142.8	164.3	159.9	148.9	167.7
Noncellulosic manmade fibers	2824	06/81	98.9	101.5	102.8	101.2	101.6
Medicinal chemicals and botanical products (in bulk)	2833	06/82	143.2	147.8	143.3	135.9	138.9
Pharmaceutical preparations	2834	06/81	298.5	306.6	314.5	326.7	343.1
In vivo and In vitro diagnostics	2835	03/80	184.5	189.9	192.0	196.2	200.8
Biological products, except diagnostics	2836	06/91	126.1	127.5	137.5	140.5	137.3
Soap and other detergents	2841	06/83	125.9	127.4	129.6	129.0	129.7
Specialty cleaning, polishing and sanitation preparations	2842	06/83	135.1	138.1	139.9	139.3	139.3
Toilet preparations	2844	03/80	174.8	177.7	179.2	180.4	181.7
Paints and allied products	2851	06/83	157.3	160.5	163.9	165.8	169.1
Cyclic (coal tar) crudes and intermediates, organic dyes and pigments	2865	12/82	110.1	124.3	114.1	114.4	123.9
Industrial organic chemicals, n.e.c.	2869	12/82	169.1	185.5	182.9	179.2	192.1
Agricultural chemicals, n.e.c.	2879	06/82	135.4	136.6	138.0	138.2	138.0
Adhesives and sealants	2891	12/83	151.7	153.6	158.0	158.5	159.7
Chemicals and chemical preparations, n.e.c.	2899	06/85	134.8	135.8	138.0	139.1	141.7
Petroleum refining	2911	06/85	73.6	111.6	103.1	96.3	121.2
Tires and inner tubes	3011	06/81	100.4	100.4	101.5	102.7	105.7
Fabricated rubber products, n.e.c.	3069	06/83	132.2	133.1	134.6	134.8	135.3
Unsupported plastic film and sheet	3081	06/93	103.2	109.0	113.8	112.3	118.9
Plastic bottles	3085	06/93	106.1	110.4	111.3	108.2	114.0
Plastic foam products	3086	06/93	108.6	110.1	110.3	110.4	115.0
Custom compounding of purchased plastic resins	3087	06/93	104.2	111.1	113.5	107.0	109.9
Plastic products, n.e.c.	3089	06/93	106.7	108.0	109.3	108.9	110.3
Products of purchased glass	3231	06/83	128.4	131.6	133.7	133.8	133.4
Concrete products	3272	12/79	161.0	166.4	172.3	175.7	177.1
Ready-mixed concrete	3273	06/82	145.6	150.2	153.4	153.0	153.9
Blast furnaces and steel mills	3312	06/82	102.0	104.1	96.9	100.1	103.8
Cold finishing of steel shapes - mfpm [4]	3316	06/82	110.3	113.6	107.5	114.5	118.1
Steel pipe and tubes - mfpm [4]	3317	06/82	127.1	132.1	129.4	132.9	141.5
Gray iron foundries	3321	12/80	144.5	147.1	148.0	148.6	149.7
Primary copper	3331	06/80	102.2	111.6	(NA)	103.9	113.2
Secondary nonferrous metals	3341	06/80	84.8	88.4	85.9	85.1	87.3
Rolling, drawing and extruding of copper	3351	12/82	130.0	137.6	132.2	127.4	129.8
Aluminum sheet, plate, foil and welded tube products	3353	06/81	139.5	150.4	148.2	140.9	141.0
Nonferrous wire drawing and insulating	3357	12/82	143.7	153.2	149.0	143.7	144.7
Metal cans	3411	06/81	107.8	108.1	108.0	109.4	110.5
Hardware, n.e.c.	3429	06/85	127.4	129.7	132.0	133.2	133.7
Fabricated structural metal	3441	06/82	139.1	142.0	140.9	138.6	136.0
Metal doors, sash and trim	3442	06/83	153.6	156.1	158.1	159.2	161.0
Fabricated plate work (boiler shops)	3443	03/80	167.2	168.9	170.4	171.4	171.9
Sheet metal work	3444	12/82	140.1	141.8	141.5	142.9	144.4
Bolts, nuts, screws, rivets, and washers	3452	06/82	126.4	126.5	126.5	127.4	127.4
Automotive stampings	3465	12/82	110.4	110.6	110.1	110.3	113.0
Metal stampings, n.e.c.	3469	06/84	128.6	128.7	129.9	130.6	131.5
Metal coating and allied services	3479	12/84	118.8	119.1	122.5	122.7	122.8
Industrial valves	3491	06/91	122.4	123.9	126.4	128.0	129.8
Fabricated metal products, n.e.c.	3499	06/82	131.8	133.0	133.7	132.5	133.8
Turbines and turbine generator sets	3511	06/82	148.7	149.6	150.8	152.8	154.0
Internal combustion engines, n.e.c.	3519	12/82	138.1	139.0	140.2	141.1	141.1
Farm machinery and equipment	3523	12/82	142.2	143.9	146.4	149.0	151.2
Lawn and garden equipment	3524	12/82	124.5	124.6	125.2	125.9	125.8
Construction machinery	3531	12/80	170.8	172.7	173.5	175.9	178.4
Special tools, dies, jigs, fixtures and industrial molds	3544	06/81	145.8	147.0	146.9	145.7	145.4
Special industry machinery, n.e.c.	3559	12/81	168.2	169.4	170.1	168.6	169.5
Pumps and pumping equipment	3561	12/83	156.2	158.6	162.4	167.1	174.7
General industrial machinery, n.e.c.	3569	12/84	153.8	156.8	159.1	161.4	162.2
Electronic computers	3571	12/90	91.1	80.8	71.3	61.1	49.2
Computer storage devices	3572	12/92	95.0	85.2	78.2	64.2	55.7
Computer peripheral equipment, n.e.c.	3577	12/93	80.1	78.8	78.3	78.6	78.2
Refrigeration and heating equipment	3585	12/82	131.5	130.6	130.6	131.4	131.7
Service industry machinery, n.e.c.	3589	06/82	164.0	165.9	168.5	171.3	174.2
Machinery, except electrical, n.e.c.	3599	06/84	127.6	129.8	132.2	132.6	132.1
Switchgear and switchboard apparatus	3613	06/85	141.0	143.3	147.6	149.8	151.1
Electric motors and generators	3621	06/83	139.9	140.4	141.6	142.0	142.3
Relays and industrial controls	3625	06/85	142.8	144.4	148.2	150.0	152.2

See footnotes at end of table

Industry	SIC code [1]	Index base [2]	1999	2000	2001	2002	2003 [3]
Household audio & video equipment	3651	03/80	77.8	76.1	74.6	74.0	72.7
Telephone & telegraph apparatus	3661	12/85	115.8	113.1	108.8	104.6	101.0
Radio and television broadcast and communication equipment	3663	12/91	104.1	101.5	101.7	98.2	95.1
Printed circuit boards	3672	06/91	92.2	91.7	91.8	90.5	89.5
Semiconductors and related devices	3674	06/81	97.4	91.1	86.8	83.8	76.8
Electronic components, n.e.c.	3679	06/82	113.8	114.5	109.4	110.2	111.4
Electrical equipment for internal combustion engines	3694	12/82	127.4	127.6	128.1	127.9	128.1
Electrical equipment and supplies, not elsewhere classified	3699	12/85	118.6	118.3	119.0	119.1	120.2
Motor vehicles and passenger car bodies	3711	06/82	137.6	138.7	137.6	134.9	135.0
Truck and bus bodies	3713	12/82	157.0	160.3	163.3	165.6	167.4
Motor vehicle parts and accessories	3714	12/82	112.0	111.6	111.5	111.1	110.0
Aircraft	3721	12/85	144.1	150.5	155.7	158.8	164.2
Aircraft engines and engine parts	3724	12/85	136.8	139.7	144.0	145.7	152.7
Aircraft parts and auxiliary equipment, n.e.c.	3728	06/85	142.2	143.3	146.6	148.1	147.7
Ship building and repairing	3731	12/85	135.4	137.6	140.1	144.1	151.1
Railroad equipment	3743	06/84	128.1	128.6	128.2	127.7	128.9
Search, detection, navigation, and guidance systems aeronautical and nautical nav syst	3812	12/91	109.0	108.7	108.3	110.7	113.3
Industrial process control instruments	3823	06/83	151.0	152.3	154.3	156.8	160.2
Electrical measuring and integrating instruments	3825	12/83	135.5	137.3	138.9	140.4	140.5
Laboratory analytical instruments	3826	12/85	116.9	119.2	121.6	124.0	126.2
Surgical and medical instruments and apparatus	3841	06/82	127.4	127.2	128.7	130.8	133.1
Surgical, orthopedic and prosthetic appliances and supplies	3842	06/83	163.0	166.4	169.8	173.3	176.4
Electromedical equipment	3845	06/85	101.4	98.5	96.6	96.1	95.1
Photographic equipment and supplies	3861	12/83	106.7	106.3	107.5	104.3	102.3
Sporting and athletic goods, n.e.c.	3949	12/85	128.8	127.9	127.8	126.5	125.5
Signs and advertising displays	3993	12/85	139.1	140.7	145.0	146.1	145.7
Manufacturing industries, n.e.c.	3999	12/85	126.1	127.3	128.6	130.0	131.6
Railroads, line haul operations	4011	12/84	113.0	114.5	116.6	118.9	121.4
Local trucking without storage	4212	06/93	106.3	110.0	113.3	115.0	117.5
Trucking, except local	4213	06/92	118.0	123.5	127.0	127.9	131.4
Local trucking with storage	4214	06/93	113.2	114.1	115.7	117.5	118.9
Courier services, except by air	4215	12/92	126.0	130.6	135.4	138.5	145.0
Farm product warehousing and storage	4221	12/92	107.1	110.6	114.2	115.6	116.1
Refrigerated warehousing and storage	4222	12/91	106.4	108.1	109.8	109.8	109.7
General warehousing and storage	4225	06/93	111.5	113.6	117.1	119.2	121.2
United States Postal Service	4311	06/89	135.3	135.2	143.4	150.2	155.0
Deep sea foreign transportation of freight	4412	06/88	134.0	155.8	172.2	185.8	219.9
Domestic deep sea transportation of freight	4424	06/88	124.3	129.8	134.2	139.5	145.3
Freight transportation on the Great Lakes-St Lawrence Seaway	4432	12/91	107.4	107.4	108.2	106.6	106.3
Water transportation of freight, n.e.c.	4449	12/90	111.2	117.9	123.4	120.6	124.0
Marine cargo handling	4491	12/91	106.7	109.1	111.4	110.9	111.3
Tugging and towing services	4492	12/92	119.7	124.2	125.4	127.4	129.3
Air transportation, scheduled	4512	12/89	161.2	186.5	200.6	200.4	206.3
Air courier services	4513	12/89	117.3	128.0	133.6	136.3	141.1
Air transportation, nonscheduled	4522	06/92	109.2	114.7	120.3	122.4	125.6
Airports, flying fields, and airport services	4581	06/92	116.2	122.1	125.6	129.9	134.4
Crude petroleum pipelines	4612	06/86	95.5	101.0	111.1	112.3	111.2
Refined petroleum pipelines	4613	06/86	104.9	105.3	108.5	111.0	112.5
Travel agencies	4724	12/89	112.0	121.8	123.3	114.0	112.6
Freight transportation arrangement	4731	12/94	99.2	100.3	100.3	99.5	99.9
Telephone communications, except radiotelephone	4813	06/95	96.0	93.9	91.3	87.3	85.6
Radio broadcasting	4832	06/88	162.3	170.6	172.3	171.9	178.8
Cable and other pay television services	4841	06/93	116.2	120.9	124.9	129.0	134.2
Electric power and natural gas utilities	4981	12/90	109.5	114.4	123.9	118.5	131.9
Scrap and waste materials	5093	12/86	127.9	152.8	123.9	129.3	151.4
Life insurance carriers	6311	12/98	100.4	99.2	100.1	101.6	103.3
Property and casualty insurance	6331	06/98	100.8	102.0	104.4	108.8	115.0
Operators and lessors of nonresidential buildings	6512	12/95	105.9	109.0	111.6	114.4	115.5
Real estate agents and managers	6531	12/95	104.4	107.8	111.4	113.3	115.3
Hotels and motels	7011	06/93	124.9	128.8	134.6	134.5	135.2
Advertising agencies	7311	06/95	107.4	110.2	116.2	118.9	121.0
Building cleaning and maintenance services, n.e.c.	7349	12/94	108.0	111.3	116.3	117.8	118.0
Employment agencies	7361	06/94	109.9	111.9	114.0	115.7	117.4
Help supply services	7363	06/94	111.1	113.4	114.1	114.7	117.5
Prepackaged software	7372	12/97	100.1	100.8	101.4	98.0	97.1
Truck rental and leasing, without drivers	7513	06/91	104.2	108.2	108.0	107.2	111.3
Passenger car rental, without drivers	7514	12/91	129.4	134.9	133.8	141.8	144.7
Offices and clinics of doctors of medicine	8011	12/93	113.8	115.8	119.1	119.1	120.8
Skilled and intermediate care facilities	8053	12/94	124.1	131.0	139.3	144.6	149.2
General medical and surgical hospitals	8062	12/92	116.6	119.8	123.4	127.9	135.2
Psychiatric hospitals	8063	12/92	109.2	109.1	110.5	113.1	116.4
Specialty hospitals, except psychiatric	8069	12/92	120.0	123.9	126.5	134.3	146.1
Medical laboratories	8071	06/94	105.9	108.0	112.0	113.9	115.7
Home health care services	8082	12/96	107.1	111.1	114.0	116.6	116.8
Legal services	8111	12/96	108.7	112.5	117.9	121.7	125.6
Engineering design, analysis, and consulting services	8711	12/96	107.9	111.1	115.5	121.4	125.0
Architectural design, analysis, and consulting services	8712	12/96	111.8	115.8	117.7	119.5	120.6
Accounting, auditing, and bookkeeping services	8721	06/95	111.9	115.4	117.5	120.1	123.6

NA Not available.   [1] Standard Industrial Classification code.   [2] Index base month/year equals 100.   [3] Preliminary data.
[4] MFPM Manufactured from purchased materials.

Source: U.S. Bureau of Labor Statistics, *Producer Price Indexes*, monthly.

[2000=100. For explanation of "chain-type," see text, Section 13]

Item	1980	1985	1990	1995	2000	2001	2002
Personal consumption expenditures	52.1	66.9	80.5	91.6	100.0	102.0	103.4
Durable goods [1]	83.3	96.6	104.6	110.7	100.0	98.1	95.2
Motor vehicles and parts	60.4	73.8	83.1	98.0	100.0	100.4	98.8
Furniture and household equipment	133.8	146.3	143.2	131.9	100.0	94.1	88.8
Other	70.3	81.1	96.9	104.6	100.0	100.3	99.5
Nondurable goods [1]	60.4	71.5	84.2	90.6	100.0	101.5	102.1
Food	56.0	67.2	81.2	89.6	100.0	102.9	104.9
Clothing and shoes	90.7	97.8	108.5	106.3	100.0	98.0	95.4
Gasoline, fuel oil, and other energy goods	74.5	76.7	78.3	77.1	100.0	96.8	90.5
Gasoline and oil	75.5	76.6	78.4	77.8	100.0	96.3	90.4
Fuel oil and coal	68.2	76.1	76.9	69.9	100.0	101.7	91.8
Other	46.9	63.2	78.9	89.2	100.0	102.8	105.0
Services [1]	42.3	59.3	74.2	88.3	100.0	103.2	105.9
Housing	41.8	59.0	74.5	86.1	100.0	103.9	107.8
Household operation	54.9	79.8	85.3	95.5	100.0	104.4	103.5
Electricity	59.1	84.9	91.5	100.9	100.0	107.1	106.0
Gas	49.5	78.9	73.2	77.3	100.0	119.5	101.7
Other	43.8	60.8	71.0	86.7	100.0	104.9	109.5
Transportation	46.8	61.4	75.5	89.6	100.0	101.5	102.8
Medical care	34.0	51.5	69.7	88.0	100.0	103.6	106.2
Recreation	47.7	60.2	73.8	85.7	100.0	103.4	106.5
Other	45.7	59.6	74.1	88.4	100.0	101.8	105.4

[1] Includes other items not shown separately.

Source: U.S. Bureau of Economic Analysis, *The National Income and Product Accounts of the United States, 1929-2003, Vol. 2*; and *Survey of Current Business*, April 2004. See also <http://www.bea.gov/bea/dn/nipaweb/SelectTable.asp?Selected=N#S2>.

No. 707. Chain-Type Price Indexes for Gross Domestic Product: 1980 to 2003

[2000=100. For explanation of "chain-type," see text Section 13]

Item	1980	1985	1990	1995	2000	2002	2003
Gross domestic product	54.1	69.7	81.6	92.1	100.0	103.9	105.7
Personal consumption expenditures	52.1	66.9	80.5	91.6	100.0	103.4	105.3
Durable goods	83.3	96.6	104.6	110.7	100.0	95.2	91.7
Nondurable goods	60.4	71.5	84.2	90.6	100.0	102.1	104.2
Services	42.3	59.3	74.2	88.3	100.0	105.9	109.0
Gross private domestic investment	74.4	86.7	96.4	100.9	100.0	101.1	102.1
Fixed investment	72.9	85.5	95.5	100.3	100.0	101.2	102.3
Nonresidential	83.2	95.9	104.7	106.2	100.0	98.9	98.7
Structures	51.7	63.9	74.0	83.9	100.0	107.0	109.2
Equipment and software	100.9	111.4	118.2	115.2	100.0	96.1	95.3
Residential	51.4	63.2	74.9	85.8	100.0	107.1	111.3
Exports	86.8	92.0	100.0	104.4	100.0	99.3	101.4
Goods	101.3	102.0	108.0	109.2	100.0	98.7	100.7
Services	57.0	70.9	82.5	93.1	100.0	100.7	103.0
Imports	94.5	88.8	103.8	106.4	100.0	96.5	100.0
Goods	101.7	94.2	108.2	108.6	100.0	95.3	98.1
Services	67.1	67.6	85.7	96.1	100.0	102.7	110.2
Government consumption expenditures and gross investment	50.8	67.0	77.1	88.4	100.0	105.2	108.2
Federal	53.3	70.0	77.1	89.5	100.0	104.9	107.5
National defense	53.9	71.6	78.0	89.6	100.0	104.7	107.4
Nondefense	51.7	65.7	75.3	89.4	100.0	105.2	107.7
State and local	48.9	64.7	77.4	87.8	100.0	105.4	108.6

Source: U.S. Bureau of Economic Analysis, *The National Income and Product Accounts of the United States, 1929-2003*, and *Survey of Current Business*, April 2004. See also <http://www.bea.gov/bea/dn/nipaweb/SelectTable.asp?Selected=N#S2>.

No. 708. Commodity Research Bureau Futures Price Index: 1980 to 2002

[1967=100. Index computed daily. Represents unweighted geometric average of commodity futures prices (through 6 months forward) of 17 major commodity futures markets. Represents end of year index]

Item	1980	1985	1990	1994	1995	1996	1997	1998	1999	2000	2001	2002
All commodities	308.5	229.2	222.6	236.6	243.2	239.6	229.1	191.2	205.1	227.8	190.6	234.5
Softs [1]	426.0	398.2	276.0	352.3	354.4	322.2	408.7	344.8	280.9	254.4	252.8	303.7
Industrials	324.6	211.7	245.5	263.6	272.5	266.3	210.9	185.3	192.9	211.0	141.8	176.6
Grains and oilseeds [2]	312.1	198.5	171.2	191.2	218.6	284.7	210.7	172.8	156.6	174.9	159.0	188.2
Energy [3]	(NA)	96.5	246.0	173.8	180.0	224.0	180.4	135.0	221.0	355.8	204.9	320.7
Oilseeds [3]	314.6	245.4	223.6	259.9	277.5	307.9	(3)	(3)	(3)	(3)	(3)	(3)
Livestock and meats	217.4	206.9	226.2	192.3	192.4	241.7	238.1	186.7	239.6	253.6	247.4	251
Metals (precious)	531.4	256.6	257.8	273.9	276.0	271.3	249.3	234.3	253.4	265.7	246.8	289.1

NA Not available. [1] Prior to 1997, reported as Imported. Softs include commodities that are grown and not mined such as coffee, cocoa, lumber, cotton and sugar. [2] Prior to 1997, reported as Grains. [3] Incorporated into Grains and Oilseeds beginning 1997.

Source: Commodity Research Bureau (CRB), Chicago, IL, *CRB Commodity Index Report*, weekly (copyright).

No. 709. Indexes of Spot Primary Market Prices: 1980 to 2002

[1967=100. Computed weekly for 1980; daily thereafter. Represents unweighted geometric average of price quotations of 23 commodities; much more sensitive to changes in market conditions than is a monthly producer price index]

Items and number of commodities	1980	1985	1990	1995	1996	1997	1998	1999	2000	2001	2002
All commodities (23)	283.5	236.7	258.1	289.1	288.2	271.8	235.2	227.3	224.0	212.1	244.3
Foodstuffs (10).	269.5	235.2	206.4	236.4	231.8	227.3	197.5	178.1	184.7	201.6	238.1
Raw industrials (13)	293.5	237.6	301.2	332.2	334.9	307.5	265.3	268.9	255.8	217.3	248.6
Livestock and products (5)	281.0	271.1	292.7	307.4	363.0	306.1	232.3	265.7	265.5	257.2	317.8
Metals (5)	288.3	207.7	283.2	300.6	289.9	269.8	218.5	261.6	214.0	172.5	184.5
Textiles and fibers (4)	240.4	206.7	257.6	274.3	267.4	261.5	237.5	223.8	245.7	217.4	230.2
Fats and oils (4)	255.9	220.2	188.7	226.7	246.4	257.1	236.0	174.8	163.6	175.8	234.0

Source: Commodity Research Bureau, Chicago, IL, *CRB Commodity Index Report*, weekly (copyright).

No. 710. Average Prices of Selected Fuels and Electricity: 1990 to 2003

[In dollars per unit, except electricity, in cents per kWh. Represents price to end-users, except as noted]

Type	Unit [1]	1990	1995	1996	1997	1998	1999	2000	2001	2002	2003
Crude oil, composite [2]. . .	Barrel	22.22	17.23	20.71	19.04	12.52	17.51	28.26	22.95	24.10	28.50
Motor gasoline: [3]											
Unleaded regular	Gallon	1.16	1.15	1.23	1.23	1.06	1.17	1.51	1.46	1.36	1.59
Unleaded premium . . .	Gallon	1.35	1.34	1.41	1.42	1.25	1.36	1.69	1.66	1.56	1.78
No. 2 heating oil.	Gallon	1.06	0.87	0.99	0.98	0.85	0.88	1.31	1.25	1.13	(NA)
No. 2 diesel fuel.	Gallon	0.73	0.56	0.68	0.64	0.49	0.58	0.94	0.84	0.76	0.94
Residual fuel oil	Gallon	0.44	0.39	0.46	0.42	0.31	0.37	0.60	0.53	0.57	0.70
Natural gas, residential . .	1,000 cu/ft . .	5.80	6.06	6.34	6.94	6.82	6.69	7.76	9.63	7.91	9.52
Electricity, residential. . . .	kWh	7.83	8.40	8.36	8.43	8.26	8.16	8.24	8.62	8.46	8.74

NA Not available.   [1] See headnote.   [2] Refiner acquisition cost.   [3] Average, all service.

Source: U.S. Energy Information Administration, *Monthly Energy Review*.

No. 711. Weekly Food Cost by Type of Family: 1990 and 2003

[In dollars. Assumes that food for all meals and snacks is purchased at the store and prepared at home. See source for details on estimation procedures]

Family type	December 1990				December 2003			
	Thrifty plan	Low-cost plan	Moderate-cost plan	Liberal-plan	Thrifty-plan	Low-cost plan	Moderate-cost plan	Liberal-plan
FAMILIES								
Family of two:								
20-50 years.	48.10	60.60	74.70	92.70	67.00	85.10	105.40	132.10
51 years and over	45.60	58.30	71.80	85.80	63.70	82.20	101.80	122.40
Family of four:								
Couple, 20-50 years and children—								
1-2 and 3-5 years	70.10	87.30	106.60	131.00	97.30	122.30	150.40	186.10
6-8 and 9-11 years	80.10	102.60	128.30	154.40	112.50	144.50	180.20	218.40
INDIVIDUALS [1]								
Child:								
1-2 years	12.70	15.40	18.00	21.80	17.50	21.80	25.50	31.40
3-5 years	13.70	16.80	20.70	24.90	17.40	21.40	25.50	30.80
6-8 years	16.60	22.20	27.90	32.50	19.00	23.50	29.10	35.20
9-11 years	19.80	25.30	32.50	37.60	23.80	31.60	39.00	45.40
Male:								
12-14 years.	20.60	28.60	35.70	42.00	28.90	40.00	49.60	58.50
15-19 years.	21.40	29.60	36.80	42.60	29.80	41.20	51.60	60.10
20-50 years.	22.90	29.30	36.60	44.30	31.90	41.30	51.60	63.00
51 years and over	20.90	27.90	34.30	41.10	29.30	39.60	48.70	58.60
Female:								
12-19 years.	20.80	24.80	30.10	36.30	28.90	34.70	42.10	50.90
20-50 years.	20.80	25.80	31.30	40.00	29.00	36.10	44.20	57.10
51 years and over	20.60	25.10	31.00	36.90	28.60	35.10	43.80	52.70

[1] The costs given are for individuals in four-person families. For individuals in other size families, the following adjustments are suggested: one-person, add 20 percent; two-person, add 10 percent; three-person, add 5 percent; five- or six-person, subtract 5 percent; seven- (or more) person, subtract 10 percent.

Source: U.S. Dept. of Agriculture, *Official USDA Food Plans: Cost of Food at Home at Four Levels*, monthly. See also http://www.usda.gov/cnpp/FoodPlans/updates/fooddec02.pdf>.

No. 712. Food—Retail Prices of Selected Items: 1990 to 2003

[In dollars per pound, except as indicated. As of December. See Appendix III]

Food	1990	1995	1997	1998	1999	2000	2001	2002	2003
Cereals and bakery products:									
Flour, white, all purpose	0.24	0.24	0.28	0.28	0.27	0.28	0.28	0.29	0.29
Rice, white, lg. grain, raw	0.49	0.55	0.58	0.54	0.50	(NA)	(NA)	0.46	0.48
Spaghetti and macaroni	0.85	0.88	0.88	0.88	0.88	0.88	0.91	0.93	0.93
Bread, whole wheat	(NA)	1.15	1.30	1.32	1.36	1.36	1.46	1.44	(NA)
Meats, poultry, fish and eggs:									
Ground beef, 100% beef	1.63	1.40	1.39	1.39	1.53	1.63	1.71	1.69	2.23
Ground beef, lean and extra lean	(NA)	2.04	2.06	2.08	2.15	2.33	2.51	2.62	2.93
Sirloin steak, boneless	(NA)	4.01	4.17	4.24	4.60	4.81	5.20	5.45	6.93
T-bone steak	5.45	5.92	6.07	6.40	6.71	6.82	7.31	(NA)	(NA)
Pork:									
Bacon, sliced	2.28	2.17	2.61	2.58	2.75	3.03	3.30	3.24	3.18
Chops, center cut, bone-in	3.32	3.29	3.39	3.03	3.21	3.46	3.53	3.32	2.91
Sausage	2.42	1.92	2.08	2.43	2.50	2.75	2.87	(NA)	(NA)
Poultry:									
Chicken, fresh, whole	0.86	0.94	1.00	1.06	1.05	1.08	1.11	1.05	1.05
Chicken breast, bone-in	2.00	1.95	1.99	2.11	2.08	2.14	2.11	2.33	(NA)
Turkey, frozen, whole	0.96	0.99	0.98	0.95	0.98	0.99	1.00	0.99	1.05
Tuna, light, chunk, canned	2.11	2.00	2.03	2.22	2.03	1.92	1.96	2.03	1.83
Eggs, Grade A, large, (dozen)	1.00	1.16	1.17	1.09	0.92	0.96	0.93	1.18	1.56
Dairy products:									
Milk, fresh, whole, fortified (per gal.)	(NA)	2.52	2.67	2.86	2.88	2.79	2.90	2.68	2.95
Butter, salted, grade AA, stick	1.92	1.73	2.46	3.18	2.27	2.80	3.31	2.84	2.80
Ice cream, prepack., bulk,reg.(1/2 gal.)	2.54	2.68	3.02	3.30	3.40	3.66	3.84	3.76	3.90
Fresh fruits and vegetables:									
Apples, red Delicious	0.77	0.83	0.90	0.85	0.92	0.82	0.89	0.99	0.96
Bananas	0.43	0.45	0.46	0.51	0.49	0.49	0.51	0.50	0.50
Oranges, navel	0.56	0.64	0.58	0.61	0.64	0.62	0.71	0.74	0.86
Grapefruit	0.56	0.49	0.53	0.55	0.58	0.58	0.60	0.62	0.68
Grapes, thompson seedless	(NA)	1.86	2.19	(NA)	2.40	2.36	(NA)	2.27	2.25
Lemons	0.97	1.12	1.06	1.37	1.41	1.11	1.40	1.44	1.26
Pears, Anjou	0.79	(NA)	0.85	0.98	1.03	(NA)	0.98	(NA)	(NA)
Potatoes, white	0.32	0.38	0.37	0.38	0.40	0.35	0.41	0.48	0.44

NA Not available.

Source: U.S. Bureau of Labor Statistics, *Monthly Labor Review* and *CPI Detailed Report*, January issues.

No. 713. Import Price Indexes—Selected Commodities: 1990 to 2003

[2000 = 100. Indexes are weighted by the 2000 Tariff Schedule of the United States Annotated, a scheme for describing and reporting product composition and value of U.S. imports. Import prices are based on U.S. dollar prices paid by importer]

Commodity	1990	1995 [1]	1998	1999	2000 [1]	2001	2002	2003
All commodities	90.8	101.4	93.1	92.9	100.2	97.6	94.1	96.2
Food and live animals	92.1	108.6	106.3	101.2	99.0	96.0	94.5	99.4
Meat	118.4	100.8	100.0	96.1	100.8	106.2	104.0	102.9
Fish	70.9	92.5	99.6	94.9	99.3	90.0	79.8	81.3
Crustaceans; fresh, chilled, frozen, salted or dried	65.2	91.9	94.6	88.0	100.9	83.6	70.0	69.9
Beverages and tobacco	76.5	88.6	97.4	98.1	100.4	101.7	103.0	103.9
Crude materials	90.4	109.5	96.2	99.1	99.4	102.8	96.4	99.5
Mineral fuels and related products	54.7	61.9	45.7	54.6	101.3	90.4	86.1	101.7
Crude petroleum and petroleum products	54.8	63.0	43.9	54.6	102.2	89.3	85.9	97.6
Natural gas	54.9	49.3	54.5	51.8	99.8	100.5	97.0	130.1
Chemicals and related products	93.7	106.8	99.3	96.2	94.6	100.4	98.0	94.4
Intermediate manufactured products	91.3	102.7	96.7	94.6	100.1	98.5	97.1	95.8
Machinery and transport equipment	100.8	112.4	102.6	100.9	100.1	98.5	97.1	95.8
Computer equipment and office machines	198.5	167.2	117.2	105.1	99.9	93.6	87.8	81.8
Computer equipment	284.6	198.4	132.3	108.9	100.4	89.3	80.3	71.9
Telecommunications [2]	120.9	119.1	105.9	103.8	100.2	97.2	94.4	89.3
Electrical machinery and equipment	111.3	122.9	102.2	100.1	100.7	98.8	97.1	95.4
Road vehicles	82.0	97.3	98.4	99.4	100.1	99.8	100.2	100.7
Miscellaneous manufactured articles	94.7	103.2	101.4	100.5	99.7	99.8	98.6	99.7
Plumbing, heating & lighting fixtures	102.0	107.4	102.7	99.5	99.2	99.2	98.5	94.8
Furniture and parts	96.0	103.1	102.6	101.1	99.6	98.5	98.8	100.2
Articles of apparel and clothing	96.5	99.0	101.5	100.6	99.6	100.6	99.7	100.6
Footwear	96.5	99.3	100.0	100.0	99.6	100.1	99.2	100.0

[1] June 1995 and 2000 may not equal 100 because indexes were reweighted to an "average" trade value in 1995 and 2000.
[2] Includes sound recording and reproducing equipment.

Source: U.S. Bureau of Labor Statistics, *U.S. Import and Export Price Indexes*, monthly.

No. 714. Export Price Indexes—Selected Commodities: 1990 to 2003

[2000=100. Indexes are weighted by 2000 export values according to the Schedule B classification system of the U.S. Census Bureau. Prices used in these indexes were collected from a sample of U.S. manufacturers of exports and are factory transaction prices, except as noted. N.e.s. = not elsewhere specified.]

Commodities	1990	1995	1998	1999	2000 [1]	2001	2002	2003
All commodities	**95.1**	**104.5**	**99.9**	**98.2**	**100.1**	**99.4**	**98.0**	**99.5**
Food and live animals	102.4	112.1	104.6	102.6	100.6	101.1	99.8	107.5
Meat	81.4	95.7	93.7	87.6	104.8	106.1	90.0	102.9
Fish	86.8	107.1	83.8	123.0	100.6	90.8	97.9	108.2
Cereals and cereal preparations	126.5	133.2	115.4	106.0	100.0	102.6	106.5	118.5
Wheat	116.9	132.5	109.6	101.4	99.4	111.3	113.5	121.4
Maize	144.0	144.6	119.5	108.3	101.0	95.9	104.8	121.3
Fruits and vegetables	93.2	107.2	109.8	109.9	97.9	98.6	99.0	99.6
Feeding stuff for animals	99.5	104.9	101.3	92.5	100.4	101.1	101.2	108.8
Miscellaneous food products	94.0	94.8	98.3	100.1	100.0	100.1	100.7	101.5
Beverages and tobacco	84.9	98.2	98.2	99.4	100.0	98.4	98.2	98.2
Tobacco and tobacco manufactures	85.0	98.1	97.8	99.2	99.9	98.2	97.6	96.6
Crude materials	96.7	125.4	98.7	90.2	101.6	92.6	95.3	103.9
Oil seeds and oleaginous fruits	116.1	115.6	122.8	94.8	103.3	95.6	102.9	122.7
Cork and wood	76.5	117.5	94.5	94.4	99.8	92.8	87.1	90.4
Pulp and waste paper	70.9	122.2	70.1	72.3	106.9	80.6	89.3	90.1
Textile fibers	118.2	154.3	114.4	99.1	100.5	90.9	88.6	103.2
Metalliferous ores and metal scrap	105.9	132.2	97.2	89.7	99.2	91.0	99.8	109.0
Mineral fuels and related materials	67.2	68.5	69.3	68.5	97.4	103.2	93.9	107.6
Coal, coke and briquettes	109.5	106.4	106.2	104.3	99.5	106.9	110.9	(NA)
Crude petroleum and petroleum products	57.5	59.6	61.4	61.9	96.8	101.8	87.9	102.7
Chemicals and related products	90.4	108.4	97.9	96.4	100.9	96.2	95.8	100.8
Organic chemicals	93.9	122.8	88.7	86.4	102.1	90.6	90.8	103.1
Chemical materials and products, n.e.s.	86.4	100.7	101.2	100.3	99.7	99.1	97.5	101.6
Intermediate manufactured products	86.8	100.6	97.7	96.7	100.2	99.5	98.1	100.0
Rubber manufactures	81.4	95.7	97.7	101.2	100.1	99.8	102.7	110.1
Paper and paperboard products	90.8	115.6	93.7	93.3	100.5	97.4	94.8	98.3
Textiles	91.2	102.8	104.9	100.8	100.2	98.5	100.0	102.7
Nonmetallic mineral manufactures	85.8	94.3	100.6	100.2	100.4	100.8	100.2	100.4
Nonferrous metals	87.1	98.2	86.7	83.7	98.5	98.0	85.3	80.3
Manufactures of metals, n.e.s.	81.2	92.3	98.6	100.2	100.9	101.5	102.5	104.8
Machinery and transport equipment [2]	97.9	102.8	101.4	100.3	100.0	100.3	98.9	97.8
Power generating machinery [3]	77.0	88.5	95.3	97.6	99.7	102.3	104.5	107.2
Rotating electric plant and parts thereof, n.e.s.	87.0	97.9	100.4	100.1	100.1	99.8	107.8	106.9
Machinery specialized for particular industries	82.7	94.0	99.0	99.8	100.2	100.3	101.8	102.6
Agricultural machinery and parts [4]	86.0	95.6	98.3	98.9	99.9	98.9	99.8	98.9
Civil engineering and contractors, plant and equip.	81.8	93.6	98.8	100.4	100.3	100.4	101.6	104.9
Metalworking machinery	82.1	92.3	100.0	100.4	99.3	101.0	99.9	101.0
General industrial machines, parts, n.e.s.	82.5	92.0	98.1	99.2	100.1	101.3	102.3	102.4
Computer equipment and office machines	193.2	147.5	112.0	104.8	99.9	95.6	90.4	88.1
Computer equipment [5]	234.5	160.7	116.9	106.1	99.7	96.0	92.1	88.1
Telecommunications	97.3	103.8	102.1	100.2	100.3	99.8	97.7	93.8
Electrical machinery and equipment	112.7	117.2	107.2	103.1	99.8	98.3	93.9	89.7
Electronic valves, diodes, transistors & integr. cir.	135.0	135.1	112.1	105.0	99.5	95.4	87.5	80.7
Road vehicles	88.7	96.1	98.1	98.6	100.0	100.2	100.3	101.1
Miscellaneous manufactured articles	90.5	98.6	99.4	99.6	99.7	100.1	100.4	101.2

NA Not available. [1] June 2000 may not equal 100 because indexes were reweighted to an "average" trade value in 2000. [2] Excludes military and commercial aircraft. [3] Includes equipment. [4] Excludes tractors. [5] Includes sound recording and reproducing equipment.

Source: U.S. Bureau of Labor Statistics, U.S. Import and Export Price Indexes, monthly.

No. 715. Refiner/Reseller Sales Price of Gasoline by State: 2001 to 2003

[In cents per gallon. As of March. Represents all refinery and gas plant operators' sales through company-operated retail outlets. Gasoline prices exclude excise taxes]

State	Gasoline excise taxes 2003	Average, all grades			Midgrade			Premium		
		2001	2002	2003	2001	2002	2003	2001	2002	2003
United States	(NA)	102.6	87.5	126.7	109.2	93.2	132.9	117.3	101.1	142.5
Alabama	18.0	100.7	85.0	119.4	107.3	89.0	125.7	116.6	99.1	133.3
Alaska	8.0	137.1	115.2	(NA)	144.6	122.2	(NA)	155.8	127.2	178.5
Arizona	18.0	113.9	88.9	151.8	121.4	96.8	160.8	132.2	102.6	169.9
Arkansas	21.5	96.9	85.5	120.3	102.1	90.4	128.0	110.5	99.7	133.2
California	18.0	120.1	100.3	159.8	123.9	106.7	168.6	133.4	115.2	174.7
Colorado	22.0	107.7	93.2	129.6	115.5	99.8	135.8	123.1	108.9	145.6
Conn.e.c.ticut	25.0	107.0	84.7	125.6	115.0	89.9	131.5	123.8	98.4	140.2
Delaware	23.0	100.5	82.8	121.2	107.8	88.8	128.0	116.3	97.2	137.3
District of Columbia . .	20.0	(D)	(D)	(D)	(D)	(D)	(D)	(D)	(D)	(D)
Florida	13.6	98.2	84.1	125.2	104.8	89.7	131.3	112.0	97.6	139.9
Georgia	7.5	95.5	83.9	120.7	100.8	89.2	128.1	109.5	98.4	135.3
Hawaii	16.0	146.3	114.1	156.0	149.9	118.7	151.7	153.8	120.4	169.1
Idaho	25.0	103.4	84.0	127.9	109.8	91.2	135.8	117.8	97.8	141.4
Illinois	19.0	102.4	94.3	126.5	108.8	100.4	134.0	119.3	107.4	142.8
Indiana	18.0	100.5	88.8	123.8	107.2	95.7	131.8	115.3	103.8	139.6
Iowa	20.0	99.0	89.5	120.1	101.9	90.2	123.0	108.7	97.8	132.7
Kansas	23.0	97.1	86.6	119.3	103.6	92.3	126.5	110.7	100.1	135.8
Kentucky	16.4	101.5	88.3	125.2	107.8	94.5	132.3	116.1	104.2	142.3
Louisiana	20.0	98.4	82.8	119.5	105.7	89.1	126.6	115.2	98.3	135.8
Maine	22.0	105.5	87.6	126.8	113.1	94.9	134.9	120.4	102.1	140.2
Maryland	23.5	100.5	84.9	121.8	107.1	89.3	128.1	111.2	95.9	134.9
Massachusetts	21.0	109.0	87.7	128.2	115.8	93.2	134.8	123.2	101.5	143.7
Michigan	19.0	96.6	87.3	124.1	101.6	92.4	129.1	111.4	99.4	136.0
Minnesota	20.0	108.9	97.7	124.4	110.8	98.8	126.2	119.9	108.5	137.0
Mississippi	18.4	104.7	87.1	124.4	110.7	93.7	130.1	119.9	102.6	140.6
Missouri	17.0	99.7	87.9	120.6	106.6	95.0	129.9	115.6	103.5	137.3
Montana	27.0	101.8	91.8	123.4	106.8	97.6	129.6	117.2	102.5	138.4
Nebraska	24.6	100.6	87.7	118.7	105.2	89.5	120.8	109.5	95.4	129.6
Nevada	23.0	126.8	96.4	151.8	138.2	104.9	163.6	141.0	109.6	163.9
New Hampshire	19.5	107.0	88.0	126.7	114.3	96.0	135.3	121.7	102.7	141.7
New Jersey	10.5	106.7	85.0	127.0	112.7	90.5	132.7	120.0	98.6	141.0
New Mexico	18.9	102.6	90.0	126.1	110.2	(NA)	135.9	117.7	105.8	140.3
New York	22.0	101.8	81.5	124.0	108.4	87.6	130.6	115.6	93.9	137.2
North Carolina	23.4	98.1	81.8	120.7	103.7	87.9	127.8	112.1	96.2	136.2
North Dakota	21.0	109.8	94.7	128.3	114.4	97.1	129.0	115.0	98.5	135.3
Ohio	22.0	100.4	90.1	124.1	107.8	97.7	132.4	115.2	107.1	140.9
Oklahoma	17.0	92.0	83.4	115.6	96.9	88.3	121.6	104.3	96.6	128.8
Oregon	24.0	109.4	90.3	144.2	119.7	99.6	154.2	126.2	107.8	162.3
Pennsylvania	25.9	96.1	80.1	118.9	101.6	85.3	125.0	110.6	93.0	133.4
Rhode Island	30.0	102.8	84.3	123.4	110.0	90.6	130.5	116.8	98.2	138.2
South Carolina	16.0	95.4	83.8	120.8	101.7	89.6	127.8	110.7	99.7	137.3
South Dakota	22.0	109.2	94.6	123.0	115.2	96.7	125.8	118.1	107.3	135.1
Tennessee	20.0	96.2	80.8	119.2	102.0	86.7	126.2	108.6	93.9	134.6
Texas	20.0	94.4	83.2	118.4	102.1	89.1	124.9	108.7	97.4	132.3
Utah	24.5	100.0	82.8	124.7	104.2	87.1	129.6	112.9	95.4	138.0
Vermont	20.0	106.8	90.5	128.4	112.8	95.9	134.6	118.2	104.1	141.4
Virginia	17.5	102.0	84.3	122.5	107.7	88.9	128.2	116.2	97.3	137.2
Washington	23.0	111.3	88.8	142.1	119.9	96.9	152.2	129.6	105.2	161.1
West Virginia	25.4	98.5	85.0	125.6	105.0	90.6	132.0	113.0	97.2	139.2
Wisconsin	28.1	100.7	91.0	124.1	103.2	94.5	125.0	113.8	103.0	137.3
Wyoming	14.0	108.4	93.5	131.1	114.8	100.5	138.6	119.7	104.6	144.3

D Withheld to avoid disclosure of individual company data.   NA Not available.

Source: U.S. Energy Information Administration, Petroleum Marketing Monthly.

Section 15
Business Enterprise

This section relates to the place and behavior of the business firm and to business initiative in the American economy. It includes data on the number, type, and size of businesses; financial data of domestic and multinational U.S. corporations; business investments, expenditures, and profits; and sales and inventories.

The principal sources of these data are the *Survey of Current Business*, published by the Bureau of Economic Analysis (BEA), the *Statistical Supplement to the Federal Reserve Bulletin*, issued by the Board of Governors of the Federal Reserve System, the annual *Statistics of Income (SOI)* reports of the Internal Revenue Service (IRS), and the Census Bureau's *Economic Census, County Business Patterns, Quarterly Financial Report for Manufacturing, Mining, and Trade Corporations (QFR), Surveys of Minority- and Women-Owned Business Enterprises*, and *Annual Capital Expenditures Survey*.

Business firms—A firm is generally defined as a business organization under a single management and may include one or more establishments. The terms firm, business, company, and enterprise are used interchangeably throughout this section. A firm doing business in more than one industry is classified by industry according to the major activity of the firm as a whole.

The IRS concept of a business firm relates primarily to the legal entity used for tax reporting purposes. A sole proprietorship is an unincorporated business owned by one person and may include large enterprises with many employees and hired managers and part-time operators. A partnership is an unincorporated business owned by two or more persons, each of whom has a financial interest in the business. A corporation is a business that is legally incorporated under state laws. While many corporations file consolidated tax returns, most corporate tax returns

represent individual corporations, some of which are affiliated through common ownership or control with other corporations filing separate returns.

Economic census—The economic census is the major source of facts about the structure and functioning of the nation's economy. It provides essential information for government, business, industry, and the general public. It furnishes an important part of the framework for such composite measures as the gross domestic product estimates, input/output measures, production and price indexes, and other statistical series that measure short-term changes in economic conditions. The Census Bureau takes the economic census every 5 years, covering years ending in "2" and "7." The economic census forms an integrated program at 5-year intervals since 1967, and before that for 1963, 1958, and 1954. Prior to that time, the individual censuses were taken separately at varying intervals.

The economic census is collected on an establishment basis. A company operating at more than one location is required to file a separate report for each store, factory, shop, or other location. Each establishment is assigned a separate industry classification based on its primary activity and not that of its parent company. Establishments responding to the establishment survey are classified into industries on the basis of their principal product or activity (determined by annual sales volume) in accordance with the *North American Industry Classification System—United States, 1997 manual* (see below).

More detailed information about the scope, coverage, classification system, data items, and publications for each of the economic censuses and related surveys is published in the *Guide to the 1997 Economic Census* at <http://www.census.gov/epcd/www/guide.html>. More information on the methodology, procedures,

U.S. Census Bureau, Statistical Abstract of the United States: 2004-2005

and history of the censuses is available in the *History of the 1997 Economic Census* found on the Census Bureau Web site at <http://www.census.gov/prod/ec97/pol00-hec.pdf>.

Data from the 1997 Economic Census were released through the Census Bureau's American FactFinder service, on CD-ROM, in Adobe Acrobat PDF reports and in hypertext "drill-down" tables available on the Census Bureau Web site. For more information on these various media of release, see the following page on the Census Bureau Web site <http://www.census.gov/epcd/www/econ97.html>.

North American Industry Classification System (NAICS)—The 1997 Economic Census is the first census to present data based on the new NAICS. Previous census data were based on the Standard Industrial Classification (SIC) system. This new system of industrial classification was developed by experts on classification in the United States, Canada, and Mexico.

There are 20 NAICS sectors, which are subdivided into 96 subsectors (three-digit codes), 313 industry groups (four-digit codes), and, as implemented in the United States, 1,170 industries (five- and six-digit codes). While many of the individual NAICS industries correspond directly to industries as defined under the SIC system, most of the higher level groupings do not.

Most of the 1997 Economic Census data are issued on a NAICS basis as seen in the industry and geographic series from the census. Other related census reports remain on an SIC basis due to use of administrative records and other methodological and data processing issues. Current survey data from the Census Bureau as well as other statistical agencies are converting over time to NAICS after benchmarking to the 1997 Economic Census where appropriate or implementation of data collection on a NAICS basis.

Quarterly Financial Report—The Quarterly Financial Report (QFR) program publishes quarterly aggregate statistics on the financial conditions of U.S. corporations. The QFR requests companies to report estimates from their statements of income and retained earnings, balance sheets, and related financial and operating ratios for domestic operations. The statistical data are classified and aggregated by type of industry and asset size. The QFR sample includes large manufacturing companies, mostly with $250 million or more in assets. It also includes a small sample of manufacturing companies, mostly with assets between $250 thousand and $250 million, and a sample of mining, wholesale, and retail companies, mostly with assets of $50 million or more. The data are published quarterly in the *Quarterly Financial Report for Manufacturing, Mining, and Trade Corporations* and on the Internet at <http://www.census.gov/csd/qfr/>.

No. 716. Number of Returns, Receipts, and Net Income by Type of Business: 1980 to 2001

[8,932 represents 8,932,000. Covers active enterprises only. Figures are estimates based on sample of unaudited tax returns; see Appendix III. Minus sign (-) indicates net loss]

Item	Number of returns (1,000)			Business receipts [2] (bil. dol.)			Net income (less loss) [3] (bil. dol.)		
	Nonfarm propri-etor-ships [1]	Partner-ships	Corpora-tions	Nonfarm propri-etor-ships [1]	Partner-ships	Corpora-tions	Nonfarm propri-etor-ships [1]	Partner-ships	Corpora-tions
1980	8,932	1,380	2,711	411	286	6,172	55	8	239
1985	11,929	1,714	3,277	540	349	8,050	79	-9	240
1990	14,783	1,554	3,717	731	541	10,914	141	17	371
1991	15,181	1,515	3,803	713	539	10,963	142	21	345
1992	15,495	1,485	3,869	737	571	11,272	154	43	402
1993	15,848	1,468	3,965	757	627	11,814	156	67	498
1994	16,154	1,494	4,342	791	732	12,858	167	82	577
1995	16,424	1,581	4,474	807	854	13,969	169	107	714
1996	16,955	1,654	4,631	843	1,042	14,890	177	145	806
1997	17,176	1,759	4,710	870	1,297	15,890	187	168	915
1998	17,409	1,855	4,849	918	1,534	16,543	202	187	838
1999	17,576	1,937	4,936	969	1,829	18,009	208	228	929
2000	17,905	2,058	5,045	1,021	2,316	19,593	215	269	928
2001	18,338	2,132	5,136	1,017	2,569	19,308	217	276	604

[1] In 1980, represents individually owned businesses, including farms; thereafter, represents only nonfarm proprietors, i.e., business owners. [2] Excludes investment income except for partnerships and corporations in finance, insurance, and real estate before 1998. Beginning 1998 finance and insurance, real estate, and management of companies included investment income for partnerships and corporations. Starting 1985, investment income no longer included for S corporations. [3] Net income (less loss) is defined differently by form of organization, basically as follows: (a) Proprietorships: Total taxable receipts less total business deductions, including cost of sales and operations, depletion, and certain capital expensing, excluding charitable contributions and owners' salaries; (b) Partnerships: Total taxable receipts (including investment income except capital gains) less deductions, including cost of sales and operations and certain payments to partners, excluding charitable contributions, oil and gas depletion, and certain capital expensing; (c) Corporations: Total taxable receipts (including investment income, capital gains, and income from foreign subsidiaries deemed received for tax purposes, except for S corporations beginning 1985) less business deductions, including cost of sales and operations, depletion, certain capital expensing, and officers' compensation excluding S corporation charitable contributions and investment expenses starting 1985; net income is before income tax.

Source: U.S. Internal Revenue Service, *Statistics of Income*, various publications.

No. 717. Number of Returns and Business Receipts by Size of Receipts: 1990 to 2001

[3,717 represents 3,717,000. Covers active enterprises only. Figures are estimates based on sample of unaudited tax returns; see Appendix III]

Size-class of receipts	Returns (1,000)					Business receipts [1] (bil. dol.)				
	1990	1995	1999	2000	2001	1990	1995	1999	2000	2001
Corporations	3,717	4,474	4,936	5,045	5,136	10,914	13,969	18,009	19,593	19,308
Under $25,000 [2]	879	1,030	1,189	1,220	1,248	5	4	4	4	3
$25,000 to $49,999	252	288	297	302	296	9	11	11	10	11
$50,000 to $99,999	359	447	487	477	485	26	33	36	35	36
$100,000 to $499,999	1,162	1,393	1,500	1,515	1,550	291	350	379	397	388
$500,000 to $999,999	416	513	546	582	601	294	361	388	407	428
$1,000,000 or more	649	803	918	946	956	10,289	13,210	17,191	18,738	18,442
Partnerships	1,554	1,581	1,937	2,058	2,132	541	854	1,829	2,316	2,569
Under $25,000 [2]	963	931	1,036	1,105	1,130	4	4	4	5	5
$25,000 to $49,999	126	133	170	183	183	4	5	6	7	7
$50,000 to $99,999	222	245	338	353	373	10	10	14	13	14
$100,000 to $499,999	133	142	187	187	192	51	56	79	82	88
$500,000 to $999,999	52	59	84	92	103	36	42	59	66	73
$1,000,000 or more	57	69	122	137	151	435	738	1,667	2,143	2,383
Nonfarm proprietorships	14,783	16,424	17,576	17,905	18,338	731	807	969	1,021	1,017
Under $25,000 [2]	10,196	11,317	11,821	11,997	12,345	69	76	80	(NA)	(NA)
$25,000 to $49,999	1,660	1,983	2,227	2,247	2,239	58	71	79	(NA)	(NA)
$50,000 to $99,999	1,282	1,393	1,558	1,645	1,704	91	99	110	(NA)	(NA)
$100,000 to $499,999	1,444	1,514	1,702	1,733	1,759	296	310	349	(NA)	(NA)
$500,000 to $999,999	143	147	182	190	197	97	100	123	(NA)	(NA)
$1,000,000 or more	57	70	86	92	93	119	151	227	(NA)	(NA)

NA Not available. [1] Excludes investment income except for partnerships and corporations in finance, insurance, and real estate before 1998. Beginning 1998 finance and insurance, real estate, and management of companies included investment income for partnerships and corporations. [2] Includes firms with no receipts.

Source: U.S. Internal Revenue Service, *Statistics of Income Bulletin*; and unpublished data.

Business Enterprise   483

No. 718. Number of Returns, Receipts, and Net Income by Type of Business and Industry: 2001

[18,338 represents 18,338,000. Covers active enterprises only. Figures are estimates based on sample of unaudited tax returns; see Appendix III. Based on the North American Industry Classification System (NAICS), 1997; see text, this section. Minus sign (-) indicates net loss]

Industry	NAICS code	Number of returns (1,000)			Business receipts [1] (bil. dol.)			Net income (less loss) (bil. dol.)		
		Non-farm propri-etor-ships	Partner-ships	Corpo-rations	Non-farm propri-etor-ships	Partner-ships	Corpo-rations	Non-farm propri-etor-ships	Partner-ships	Corpo-rations
Total [2]	(X)	18,338	2,132	5,136	1,017	2,569	19,308	217	276	604
Agriculture, forestry, fishing, and hunting [3]	11	270	117	141	16	19	103	1	1	1
Mining	21	115	27	32	7	61	151	1	14	9
Utilities	22	9	3	8	(Z)	139	1,004	(Z)	4	17
Construction	23	2,373	127	624	164	157	1,085	29	11	33
Special trade contractors	235	1,854	44	368	108	24	445	22	2	14
Manufacturing	31-33	347	37	279	25	462	4,862	3	22	129
Wholesale and retail trade [4]	(X)	2,564	146	963	224	491	5,183	13	5	75
Wholesale trade	42	310	37	362	39	222	2,433	4	6	30
Retail trade [5]	44-45	2,254	109	598	185	269	2,749	10	(-Z)	45
Motor vehicle and parts dealers	441	127	13	92	35	74	740	1	1	8
Food and beverage stores	445	106	13	84	32	25	447	1	(-Z)	8
Gasoline stations	447	25	5	37	22	23	137	(Z)	(Z)	(Z)
Transportation and warehousing	48-49	940	25	164	53	47	494	8	2	-7
Information	51	285	26	115	8	159	816	2	-11	-38
Broadcasting and telecommunications	513	45	8	29	2	115	456	(Z)	-11	-30
Finance and insurance	52	577	262	221	83	344	2,622	14	100	268
Real estate and rental and leasing	53	968	948	540	49	171	207	20	59	5
Professional, scientific, and technical services [5]	54	2,592	143	710	119	215	632	49	50	-6
Legal services	5411	351	33	90	32	91	65	14	32	6
Accounting, tax preparation, bookkeeping, and payroll services	5412	359	13	55	10	36	28	4	6	2
Management, scientific, and technical consulting services	5416	630	32	188	27	30	126	14	5	4
Management of companies and enterprises	55	(NA)	15	48	(NA)	23	788	(NA)	6	83
Administrative and support and waste management and remediation services	56	1,567	39	224	39	44	339	11	3	8
Educational services	61	378	5	38	5	2	25	2	(Z)	(Z)
Health care and social assistance	62	1,679	45	327	94	86	429	40	11	12
Arts, entertainment and recreation	71	1,037	35	103	21	44	69	5	-2	(Z)
Accommodation and food services	72	361	70	259	37	90	329	1	(Z)	8
Accommodation	721	62	23	33	6	47	82	(Z)	(Z)	(Z)
Food services and drinking places	722	299	47	226	32	43	246	16	1	8
Other services [5]	81	2,085	58	326	72	17	169	3	4	4
Auto repair and maintenance	8111	346	21	103	25	7	62	3	(Z)	1
Personal and laundry services	812	1,143	30	128	30	7	68	9	(Z)	2
Religious, grantmaking, civic, professional, and similar organizations	813	231	(Z)	43	3	(Z)	9	1	(Z)	(Z)
Unclassified	(X)	190	3	12	2	(Z)	1	1	(Z)	(Z)

NA Not applicable. Z Less than 500 or $500 million. [1] Includes investment income for partnerships and corporations in finance and insurance, real estate, and management of companies industries. Excludes investment income for S corporations. [2] For corporations, includes businesses not allocable to individual industries. [3] For corporations, represents agricultural services only. [4] For corporations, includes trade business not identified as wholesale or retail. [5] Includes other industries not shown separately.

Source: U.S. Internal Revenue Service, Statistics of Income, various publications.

No. 719. Nonfarm Sole Proprietorships—Selected Income and Deduction Items: 1990 to 2001

[In billions of dollars (731 represents $731,000,000,000) except as indicated. All figures are estimates based on sample. Tax law changes have affected the comparability of the data over time; see *Statistics of Income* reports for a description. See Appendix III]

Item	1990	1994	1995	1996	1997	1998	1999	2000	2001
Number of returns (1,000)	14,783	16,154	16,424	16,955	17,176	17,409	17,576	17,905	18,338
Businesses with net income (1,000)	11,222	12,187	12,213	12,524	12,703	13,080	13,159	13,308	13,603
Business receipts	731	791	807	843	870	918	969	1,021	1,017
Income from sales and operations	719	778	797	832	858	905	955	1,008	1,002
Business deductions [1]	589	624	638	666	684	716	761	806	800
Cost of goods sold/operations [1]	291	301	307	316	320	341	370	387	363
Purchases	210	216	219	220	224	231	256	269	265
Labor costs	23	23	24	26	25	27	29	29	28
Materials and supplies	30	34	34	40	38	42	42	43	44
Advertising	(NA)	(NA)	(NA)	(NA)	9	9	9	10	11
Car and truck expenses	22	31	33	37	39	40	41	46	47
Commissions	9	9	10	11	11	11	11	12	12
Depreciation	24	26	27	28	29	29	31	32	33
Pension and profit sharing plans	1	1	1	1	1	1	1	1	1
Insurance	13	13	13	13	13	13	13	14	14
Interest paid	13	9	10	11	11	11	11	12	13
Office expenses	(NA)	(NA)	(NA)	(NA)	9	10	10	10	11
Rent paid	23	27	28	29	29	30	31	33	34
Repairs	9	10	10	11	11	11	12	12	12
Salaries and wages (net)	47	54	54	56	58	59	61	63	64
Supplies	(NA)	(NA)	(NA)	(NA)	20	20	22	22	23
Taxes paid	10	14	13	14	14	14	14	14	14
Travel	(NA)	(NA)	(NA)	(NA)	7	8	8	8	9
Utilities	14	17	17	18	19	18	18	19	20
Business use of home	(NA)	(NA)	(NA)	(NA)	4	4	5	6	6
Net income (less loss) [2]	141	167	169	177	187	202	208	215	217
Net income [2]	162	188	192	200	210	226	233	245	250

NA Not available. [1] Includes other amounts not shown separately. [2] After adjustment for the passive loss carryover from prior years. Therefore, "business receipts" minus "total deductions" do not equal "net income".

Source: U.S. Internal Revenue Service, *Statistics of Income Bulletin.*

No. 720. Partnerships—Selected Income and Balance Sheet Items: 1990 to 2001

[In billions of dollars (1,735 represents $1,735,000,000,000), except as indicated. Covers active partnerships only. All figures are estimates based on samples. See Appendix III]

Item	1990	1994	1995	1996	1997	1998	1999	2000	2001
Number of returns (1,000)	1,554	1,494	1,581	1,654	1,759	1,855	1,937	2,058	2,132
Number with net income (1,000)	854	890	955	1,010	1,092	1,171	1,226	1,261	1,301
Number of partners (1,000)	17,095	14,990	15,606	15,662	16,184	15,663	15,924	13,660	14,232
Assets [1][2]	1,735	2,295	2,719	3,368	4,171	5,127	5,999	6,694	8,428
Depreciable assets (net)	681	712	767	848	980	1,153	1,314	1,487	1,646
Inventories, end of year	57	76	88	137	147	176	174	150	208
Land	215	208	221	232	257	291	326	359	392
Liabilities [1][2]	1,415	1,662	1,886	2,235	2,658	3,151	3,453	3,696	4,835
Accounts payable	67	81	91	121	159	191	244	230	362
Short-term debt [3]	88	126	124	126	127	230	232	252	289
Long-term debt [4]	498	508	544	607	706	884	989	1,132	1,286
Nonrecourse loans	470	463	466	474	492	523	582	639	700
Partners' capital accounts [2]	320	633	832	1,133	1,513	1,976	2,546	2,999	3,593
Receipts [1]	566	762	890	1,089	1,354	1,603	1,907	2,405	2,665
Business receipts [5]	483	732	854	1,042	1,297	1,534	1,829	2,316	2,569
Interest received	21	19	31	33	41	51	62	82	85
Deductions [1]	550	680	784	943	1,186	1,416	1,679	2,136	2,389
Cost of goods sold/operations	243	335	395	486	625	737	902	1,226	1,338
Salaries and wages	56	70	80	94	115	143	170	201	231
Taxes paid	9	12	13	15	18	24	27	31	35
Interest paid	30	36	43	49	60	73	74	93	97
Depreciation	60	22	23	29	38	43	52	59	72
Net income (less loss)	17	82	107	145	168	187	228	269	276
Net income	116	151	179	228	262	298	348	410	446

[1] Includes items not shown separately. [2] Assets, liabilities, and partners' capital accounts are understated because not all partnerships file complete balance sheets. [3] Mortgages, notes, and bonds payable in less than 1 year. [4] Mortgages, notes, and bonds payable in 1 year or more. [5] Excludes investment income except for partnerships in finance, insurance, and real estate from 1994 to 1997. Beginning 1998 finance and insurance, real estate, and management of companies included investment income for partnerships.

Source: U.S. Internal Revenue Service, *Statistics of Income,* various issues.

No. 721. Partnerships—Selected Items by Industry: 2001

[In billions of dollars (8,428 represents $8,428,000,000,000), except as indicated. Covers active partnerships only. Figures are estimates based on samples. Based on the North American Industry Classification System (NAICS), 1997; see text, this section. See Appendix III]

Industry	NAICS code	Number of partnerships (1,000)			Total assets [1]	Business receipts [2]	Total deductions	Net income less loss	Net income	Net loss
		Total	With net income	With net loss						
Total [3]	(X)	2,132	1,301	831	8,428	2,569	2,389	276.3	446.1	169.7
Agriculture, forestry, fishing and hunting	11	117	64	53	81	19	23	0.7	5.3	4.6
Mining	21	27	20	7	125	61	54	14.0	20.6	6.6
Utilities	22	3	2	1	121	139	138	4.4	7.1	2.7
Construction	23	127	77	51	141	157	151	10.5	15.1	4.6
Manufacturing	31-33	37	19	18	337	462	459	22.2	35.5	13.3
Wholesale trade	42	37	17	20	67	222	220	5.7	8.6	2.8
Retail trade	44-45	109	56	53	83	269	275	-0.3	6.2	6.5
Transportation and warehousing	48-49	25	13	12	85	47	48	1.9	5.5	3.6
Information	51	26	10	16	396	159	180	-10.9	20.0	30.9
Finance & insurance	52	262	200	62	4,274	344	244	99.6	119.9	20.3
Real estate & rental & leasing	53	948	582	366	2,069	171	120	59.0	102.4	43.3
Professional, scientific, and technical services	54	143	90	53	103	215	174	49.9	57.2	7.3
Management of companies & enterprises	55	15	9	6	261	23	17	6.2	12.7	6.5
Admin/support waste mgt/remediation services	56	39	23	15	29	44	43	2.7	3.8	1.2
Educational services	61	5	4	2	3	2	2	0.1	0.3	0.2
Health care and social assistance	62	45	29	16	54	86	80	11.3	14.4	3.1
Arts, entertainment & recreation	71	35	14	21	55	44	51	-1.9	3.8	5.7
Accommodation & food services	72	70	36	34	129	90	93	0.3	6.0	5.7
Other services	81	58	35	23	13	17	17	0.9	1.7	0.8

X Not applicable.   [1] Total assets are understated because not all partnerships file complete balance sheets.   [2] Finance and insurance, real estate, and management of companies includes investment income for partnerships.   [3] Includes businesses not allocable to individual industries.

Source: U.S. Internal Revenue Service, Statistics of Income, various issues.

No. 722. Nonfarm Noncorporate Business-Sector Balance Sheet: 1990 to 2003

[In billions of dollars (3,823 represents $3,823,000,000,000), except as noted. Represents yearend outstandings]

Item	1990	1995	1997	1998	1999	2000	2001	2002	2003
Assets	3,823	4,228	4,942	5,454	5,964	6,558	6,870	7,290	7,904
Tangible assets	3,466	3,680	4,168	4,461	4,788	5,135	5,292	5,570	6,025
Real estate [1]	3,085	3,230	3,668	3,924	4,187	4,574	4,685	4,908	5,293
Residential	2,175	2,405	2,762	2,948	3,191	3,488	3,630	3,829	4,162
Nonresidential	909	825	906	976	996	1,086	1,055	1,080	1,130
Equipment and software [2]	335	394	441	476	534	491	540	594	663
Residential [3]	50	61	65	68	69	73	76	77	76
Nonresidential	284	333	375	409	465	418	464	517	587
Inventories [2]	47	56	59	61	66	70	67	68	70
Financial assets	356	548	774	993	1,177	1,423	1,578	1,720	1,879
Checkable deposits and currency	71	105	146	179	218	274	275	287	298
Time and savings deposits	51	71	86	98	118	138	145	147	149
Money market fund shares	7	17	23	33	41	49	59	61	53
Treasury securities	13	24	32	38	37	40	43	45	48
Municipal securities	-	2	3	3	3	2	4	4	4
Mortgages	31	22	19	27	25	23	27	28	27
Trade receivables	98	140	205	233	273	342	344	367	417
Miscellaneous assets	86	167	260	382	464	554	683	781	884
Insurance receivables	39	44	45	46	46	46	48	52	58
Equity investment in GSEs [4]	1	1	2	2	2	2	2	2	2
Other	47	122	213	335	416	506	634	727	825
Liabilities	1,349	1,396	1,713	2,022	2,328	2,665	2,879	3,077	3,301
Credit market instruments	1,093	1,062	1,224	1,406	1,595	1,788	1,948	2,097	2,227
Bank loans n.e.c. [5]	136	165	237	262	309	353	391	404	379
Other loans and advances	94	92	96	109	117	128	128	131	137
Mortgages	863	805	891	1,035	1,170	1,308	1,429	1,561	1,712
Trade payables	60	86	148	179	213	260	255	276	323
Taxes payable	32	33	40	44	53	65	69	77	87
Miscellaneous liabilities	164	215	301	393	467	553	608	628	665
Net worth	2,474	2,832	3,229	3,432	3,636	3,892	3,991	4,213	4,603
Debt/net worth (percent)	44.2	37.5	37.9	41.0	43.9	45.9	48.8	49.8	48.4

- Represents or rounds to zero.   [1] At market value.   [2] At replacement (current) cost.   [3] Durable goods in rental properties.   [4] GSEs=government sponsored enterprises. Equity in the Farm Credit System.   [5] Not elsewhere classified.

Source: Board of Governors of the Federal Reserve System, "Federal Reserve Statistical Release, Z.1, Flow of Funds Accounts of the United States"; published: 4 March 2004; <http://www.federalreserve.gov/releases/Z1/20040304/data.htm>.

No. 723. Nonfinancial Corporate Business-Sector Balance Sheet: 1990 to 2003

[In billions of dollars (9,807 represents $9,807,000,000,000). Represents yearend outstandings]

Item	1990	1995	1997	1998	1999	2000	2001	2002	2003
Assets.	9,807	11,627	13,357	14,997	16,709	19,080	19,133	19,519	20,495
Tangible assets [1]	6,232	6,669	7,548	8,181	8,615	9,307	9,224	9,461	9,747
Real estate [1]	3,438	3,210	3,777	4,245	4,439	4,849	4,745	4,950	5,237
Equipment and software [2]	1,892	2,390	2,641	2,771	2,924	3,124	3,214	3,214	3,187
Inventories [2, 3]	901	1,070	1,130	1,165	1,252	1,334	1,265	1,297	1,324
Financial assets [3]	3,575	4,959	5,809	6,816	8,094	9,772	9,909	10,059	10,748
Checkable deposits and currency . . .	166	205	252	275	331	381	335	364	480
Time and savings deposits	75	100	119	113	137	137	132	124	117
Money market fund shares	20	60	88	126	155	191	302	329	276
Commercial paper	14	20	36	39	48	58	60	67	74
U.S. government securities	41	81	35	34	32	34	34	49	68
Consumer credit	67	85	79	76	79	83	82	82	75
Trade receivables [1]	967	1,185	1,367	1,452	1,655	1,938	1,822	1,850	2,052
Mutual fund shares [1]	10	46	69	95	134	123	106	91	128
Liabilities [3]	4,729	6,010	6,629	7,458	8,407	9,611	9,777	10,006	10,422
Credit market instruments.	2,533	2,910	3,382	3,775	4,181	4,543	4,767	4,806	4,971
Commercial paper.	117	157	169	193	230	278	190	126	86
Municipal securities [4]	115	135	142	148	153	154	158	161	164
Corporate bonds [5]	1,008	1,344	1,611	1,846	2,068	2,230	2,579	2,711	2,873
Bank loans n.e.c.	545	602	693	769	813	861	758	662	612
Other loans and advances	473	454	508	562	585	656	661	675	670
Mortgages	274	218	260	257	331	363	421	471	566
Trade payables	626	878	992	1,050	1,228	1,541	1,431	1,453	1,666
Taxes payable	38	40	59	64	71	78	81	93	107
Net worth (market value).	5,078	5,618	6,728	7,540	8,302	9,468	9,356	9,514	10,073
Debt/net worth (percent).	49.9	51.8	50.3	50.1	50.4	48.0	51.0	50.5	49.4

[1] At market value. [2] At replacement (current) cost. [3] Includes items not shown separately. [4] Industrial revenue bonds. Issued by state and local governments to finance private investment and secured in interest and principal by the industrial user of the funds. [5] Through 1992, corporate bonds include net issues by Netherlands Antillian financial subsidiaries.

Source: Board of Governors of the Federal Reserve System, "Federal Reserve Statistical Release, Z.1, Flow of Funds Accounts of the United States"; published: 4 March 2004; <http://www.federalreserve.gov/releases/Z1/20040304/data.htm>.

No. 724. Corporate Funds—Sources and Uses: 1990 to 2003

[In billions of dollars (238 represents $238,000,000,000). Covers nonfarm nonfinancial corporate business]

Item	1990	1995	1996	1997	1998	1999	2000	2001	2002	2003
Profits before tax (book)	238	419	457	493	449	457	422	308	334	417
-Taxes on corporate income	98	141	153	161	158	171	170	108	334	125
-Net dividends	117	177	196	214	240	223	250	247	256	268
+Capital consumption allowance [1]	365	462	494	528	557	597	629	681	769	824
=U.S. internal funds, book	388	563	602	645	609	660	629	681	769	849
+Foreign earnings retained abroad.	51	60	62	60	60	80	116	126	747	107
+Inventory valuation adjustment (IVA) . . .	-13	-18	3	14	20	1	-14	9	-2	-11
=Internal funds + IVA	426	605	667	719	689	741	734	770	859	944
Gross investment	372	664	702	737	745	849	899	925	820	915
Capital expenditures [2]	431	628	646	748	791	867	927	800	783	797
Fixed investment [3]	419	580	620	674	721	799	871	834	774	795
Net financial investment	-59	36	56	-11	-46	-18	-28	834	774	795
Net acquisition of financial assets [2] . . .	124	426	454	272	570	970	1,209	187	237	118
Foreign deposits	(Z)	2	11	-5	7	1	-7	-8	5	605
Checkable deposits and currency . .	6	4	39	8	23	56	50	-46	28	11
Money market fund shares.	9	23	8	20	39	28	37	111	27	116
Commercial paper	(-Z)	1	11	5	3	8	10	3	6	-53
U.S. government securities	-20	10	-5	-41	-1	-2	2	(Z)	15	7
Consumer credit	3	-2	-7	1	-3	2	4	(-Z)	(-Z)	20
Trade receivables.	29	78	88	94	85	203	283	-116	28	-9
Mutual fund shares.	-1	5	3	-8	10	17	5	-2	9	203
Miscellaneous assets [2]	114	320	314	157	427	657	818	253	123	9
U.S. direct investment abroad [4] . . .	35	90	77	84	129	194	657	818	253	299
Insurance receivables	13	8	3	2	2	1	128	97	117	127
Net increase in liabilities [2]	184	391	398	283	616	988	1,237	10	17	22
Net funds raised in markets	71	169	135	214	177	261	244	63	200	486
Net new equity issues	-63	-58	-47	-77	-216	-110	-118	176	-2	93
Credit market instruments [2]	134	227	183	292	392	372	362	-47	-42	-49
Commercial paper.	10	18	-1	14	24	37	48	224	39	142
Corporate bonds [4]	47	91	116	151	235	222	163	-88	-64	-40
Bank loans n.e.c [5]	3	75	40	51	76	44	48	348	132	162
Mortgages	19	8	10	32	-3	40	31	-103	-96	-49
Trade payables	28	81	50	65	58	178	313	59	50	71
Taxes payable	(Z)	(-Z)	10	9	5	7	7	-110	22	212
Miscellaneous liabilities [2]	84	141	204	-5	377	541	673	3	12	13
Foreign direct investment in U.S. . .	59	54	72	100	144	247	181	-6	168	168
								71	23	49

Z Less than $500 million. [1] Consumption of fixed capital plus capital consumption adjustment. [2] Includes other items not shown separately. [3] Nonresidential fixed investment plus residential fixed investment. [4] 1990, corporate bonds include net issues by Netherlands Antillean financial subsidiaries, and U.S. direct investment abroad excludes net inflows from those bond issues. [5] Not elsewhere classified.

Source: Board of Governors of the Federal Reserve System, "Federal Reserve Statistical Release, Z.1, Flow of Funds Accounts of the United States"; published: 4 March 2004; <http://www.federalreserve.gov/releases/Z1/20040304/data.htm>.

No. 725. Corporations—Selected Financial Items: 1990 to 2001

[In billions of dollars (18,190 represents $18,190,000,000,000), except as noted. Covers active corporations only. All corporations are required to file returns except those specifically exempt. See source for changes in law affecting comparability of historical data. Based on samples; see Appendix III]

Item	1990	1994	1995	1996	1997	1998	1999	2000	2001
Number of returns (1,000)	3,717	4,342	4,474	4,631	4,710	4,849	4,936	5,045	5,136
Number with net income (1,000)	1,911	2,392	2,455	2,588	2,647	2,761	2,812	2,819	2,822
S Corporation returns [1] (1,000)	1,575	2,024	2,153	2,304	2,452	2,588	2,726	2,860	2,986
Assets [2]	18,190	23,446	26,014	28,642	33,030	37,347	41,464	47,027	49,154
Cash	771	853	962	1,097	1,299	1,336	1,597	1,820	1,926
Notes and accounts receivable	4,198	4,768	5,307	5,783	6,632	7,062	7,745	8,754	8,756
Inventories	894	1,126	1,045	1,079	1,114	1,139	1,198	1,272	1,208
Investments in Govt. obligations	921	1,309	1,363	1,339	1,343	1,366	1,340	1,236	1,392
Mortgage and real estate	1,538	1,661	1,713	1,825	2,029	2,414	2,555	2,822	3,229
Other investments	4,137	6,265	7,429	8,657	10,756	13,201	15,799	17,874	18,344
Depreciable assets	4,318	5,284	5,571	5,923	6,208	6,541	6,936	7,292	7,614
Depletable assets	129	148	154	169	177	193	184	191	199
Land	210	239	242	254	262	271	286	303	320
Liabilities [2]	18,190	23,446	26,014	28,642	33,030	37,347	41,464	47,027	49,154
Accounts payable	1,094	1,606	1,750	1,905	2,111	2,501	2,792	3,758	3,927
Short-term debt [3]	1,803	1,831	2,034	2,328	2,582	3,216	3,658	4,020	4,132
Long-term debt [4]	2,665	3,100	3,335	3,651	4,072	4,813	5,448	6,184	6,782
Net worth	4,739	7,031	8,132	9,495	11,353	13,108	15,363	17,349	17,615
Capital stock	1,585	2,132	2,194	2,278	2,951	3,244	3,522	3,966	4,253
Paid-in or capital surplus	2,814	4,790	5,446	6,427	7,253	8,610	10,186	12,265	13,920
Retained earnings [5]	1,410	1,698	2,191	2,519	3,113	3,373	3,970	3,627	2,131
Receipts [2 6]	11,410	13,360	14,539	15,526	16,610	17,324	18,892	20,606	20,273
Business receipts [6 7]	9,860	11,884	12,786	13,659	14,461	15,010	16,314	17,637	17,504
Interest [8]	977	882	1,039	1,082	1,140	1,277	1,354	1,628	1,549
Rents and royalties	133	132	145	156	176	200	223	254	251
Deductions [2 6]	11,033	12,775	13,821	14,728	15,704	16,489	17,967	19,692	19,683
Cost of sales and operations [7]	6,611	7,625	8,206	8,707	9,114	9,362	10,284	11,135	11,042
Compensation of officers	205	282	304	319	336	357	374	401	383
Rent paid on business property	185	223	232	248	265	308	347	380	398
Taxes paid	251	322	326	341	350	355	371	390	392
Interest paid	825	611	744	771	866	967	1,019	1,272	1,203
Depreciation	333	403	437	474	513	542	584	614	650
Advertising	126	157	163	177	188	198	216	234	220
Net income (less loss) [6 9]	371	577	714	806	915	838	929	928	604
Net income	553	740	881	987	1,118	1,091	1,229	1,337	1,112
Deficit	182	162	166	180	202	253	300	409	508
Income subject to tax	366	494	565	640	684	663	694	760	635
Income tax before credits [10]	119	168	194	220	235	231	242	266	221
Tax credits	32	37	42	53	55	50	49	62	54
Foreign tax credit	25	25	30	40	42	37	38	49	41
Income tax after credits [11]	96	136	156	171	184	182	193	204	167

[1] Represents certain small corporations with up to 75 shareholders (35 for 1990-1996), mostly individuals, electing to be taxed at the shareholder level. [2] Includes items not shown separately. [3] Payable in less than 1 year. [4] Payable in 1 year or more. [5] Appropriated and unappropriated and "adjustments to shareholders' equity" which was formerly included in "retained earnings, appropriated." [6] Receipts, deductions and net income of S corporations are limited to those from trade or business. Those from investments are excluded. [7] Includes gross sales and cost of sales of securities, commodities, and real estate by exchanges, brokers, or dealers selling on their own accounts. Excludes investment income. [8] Includes tax-exempt interest in state and local government obligations. [9] Excludes regulated investment companies. [10] Consists of regular (and alternative tax) only. [11] Includes minimum tax, alternative minimum tax, adjustments for prior year credits, and other income-related taxes.

Source: U.S. Internal Revenue Service, Statistics of Income, Corporation Income Tax Returns, annual.

No. 726. Corporations by Receipt-Size Class and Industry: 2000 and 2001

[Number of returns in thousands (5,045 represents 5,045,000); receipts and net income in billions of dollars (19,593 represents $19,593,000,000,000). Covers active enterprises only. Figures are estimates based on a sample of unaudited tax returns; see Appendix III. Numbers in parentheses represent North American Industry Classification System 1997 codes, see text, this section]

Industry	2000, total	2001 Total	Under $1 mil. [1]	$1 mil.- $4.9 mil.	$5 mil.- $9.9 mil.	$10 mil.- $49.9 mil.	$50 mil. or more
Total: [2]							
Number of returns [3]	5,045	5,136	4,180	715	114	101	26
Business receipts [3]	19,593	19,308	866	1,517	799	2,068	14,058
Net income (less loss)	928	604	-14	21	12	51	534
Agriculture, forestry, fishing, and hunting (11):							
Number	141	141	126	12	2	1	(Z)
Business receipts [3]	106	103	20	24	11	20	27
Mining (21):							
Number	33	32	26	4	(Z)	1	(Z)
Business receipts [3]	141	151	4	9	3	14	121
Utilities (22):							
Number	8	8	7	(Z)	(Z)	(Z)	(Z)
Business receipts [3]	708	1,004	1	1	1	3	999
Construction (23):							
Number	598	624	475	116	19	13	2
Business receipts [3]	1,034	1,085	118	247	129	251	340
Manufacturing (31-33):							
Number	289	279	169	71	17	17	6
Business receipts [3]	5,259	4,862	47	162	116	354	4,183
Wholesale and retail trade (42,44-45):							
Number	960	963	656	217	39	42	10
Business receipts [3]	5,268	5,183	180	478	270	876	3,378
Transportation and warehousing (48-49):							
Number	160	164	132	25	4	3	1
Business receipts [3]	506	494	26	54	25	54	335
Information (51):							
Number	118	115	98	11	2	2	1
Business receipts [3]	817	816	16	23	14	47	715
Finance and insurance (52):							
Number	221	221	184	23	5	6	3
Business receipts [3]	2,916	2,622	30	52	33	123	2,383
Real estate and rental and leasing (53):							
Number	532	540	517	20	2	1	(Z)
Business receipts [3]	205	207	45	39	13	27	84
Professional, scientific, and technical services (54):							
Number	689	710	633	61	9	5	1
Business receipts [3]	623	632	109	124	64	108	226
Management of companies & enterprises (55):							
Number	48	48	42	2	1	2	1
Business receipts [3]	693	788	1	7	10	38	732
Administrative and support and waste management and remediation services (56):							
Number	212	224	187	31	3	2	1
Business receipts [3]	314	339	40	62	23	42	173
Educational services (61):							
Number	37	38	35	3	(Z)	(Z)	(Z)
Business receipts [3]	22	25	5	6	2	5	8
Health care and social services (62):							
Number	306	327	270	48	6	3	1
Business receipts [3]	404	429	81	94	45	56	152
Arts, entertainment, and recreation (71):							
Number	98	103	93	8	1	(Z)	(Z)
Business receipts [3]	64	69	17	17	4	9	23
Accommodation and food services (72):							
Number	258	259	219	36	3	1	(Z)
Business receipts [3]	347	329	62	70	19	27	151
Other services (81):							
Number	316	326	297	25	2	(Z)	(Z)
Business receipts [3]	164	169	48	48	16	13	27

Z Less than 500 returns.   [1] Includes businesses without receipts.   [2] Includes businesses not allocable to individual industries.   [3] Includes investment income for corporations in finance and insurance and management of companies industries. Excludes investment income for S corporations (certain small corporations with up to 75 shareholders, mostly individuals, electing to be taxed at the shareholder level).

Source: U.S. Internal Revenue Service, *Statistics of Income*, various publications; and unpublished data.

[In millions of dollars (115,434 represents $115,434,000,000), except number of returns. Covers active corporations only. Excludes corporations not allocable by industry. Numbers in parentheses represent North American Industry Classification System 1997 codes, see text, this section]

Industry	Total	Under $10 mil.¹	$10-$24.9 mil.	$25-$49.9 mil.	$50-$99.9 mil.	$100-$249.9 mil.	$250 mil. and over
Agriculture, forestry, fishing, and hunting (11):							
Returns	140,806	139,926	567	163	86	41	21
Total receipts	115,434	76,558	8,913	6,154	6,868	6,128	10,813
Mining (21):							
Returns	31,776	30,680	501	214	101	112	168
Total receipts	169,540	23,175	6,385	5,489	4,150	10,715	119,625
Utilities (22):							
Returns	7,802	7,425	102	53	33	36	154
Total receipts	1,051,655	9,820	2,332	845	3,842	2,595	1,032,222
Construction (23):							
Returns	624,478	618,924	3,893	952	400	177	134
Total receipts	1,102,724	672,570	115,117	61,676	49,650	41,092	162,619
Manufacturing (31-33):							
Returns	278,995	264,317	7,241	2,893	1,689	1,306	1,546
Total receipts	5,315,599	561,128	188,205	147,524	157,421	243,639	4,017,682
Wholesale and retail trade (42, 44-45):							
Returns	963,403	948,725	9,473	2,615	1,179	723	689
Total receipts	5,312,290	1,806,222	476,575	260,450	212,396	252,109	2,304,538
Transportation and warehousing (48-49):							
Returns	164,492	162,911	903	269	146	138	126
Total receipts	516,416	146,559	26,295	13,899	13,455	23,901	292,306
Information (51):							
Returns	115,435	112,414	1,366	585	359	267	444
Total receipts	946,598	81,572	20,443	14,968	17,642	28,268	783,705
Finance and insurance (52):							
Returns	220,895	202,321	3,637	2,792	2,914	3,466	5,766
Total receipts	2,621,772	188,318	22,969	21,961	30,322	62,304	2,295,897
Real estate and rental and leasing (53):							
Returns	539,965	535,036	3,224	953	399	206	147
Total receipts	239,599	118,212	13,512	9,416	7,411	9,389	81,659
Professional, scientific, and technical services (54):							
Returns	709,837	706,475	1,842	653	384	294	190
Total receipts	665,085	393,506	43,189	28,674	26,474	38,871	134,371
Management of companies & enterprises (55):							
Returns	47,866	41,410	1,149	1,123	1,363	1,555	1,267
Total receipts	788,062	16,944	1,611	3,148	7,464	19,567	739,328
Administrative and support and waste management and remediation services (56):							
Returns	223,999	223,017	506	202	104	77	93
Total receipts	352,935	175,757	18,596	14,215	13,865	21,209	109,293
Educational services (61):							
Returns	38,480	38,332	80	25	17	14	11
Total receipts	26,923	16,196	1,874	1,151	1,536	2,091	4,076
Health care and social assistance (62):							
Returns	327,338	326,385	507	193	106	75	72
Total receipts	443,352	288,694	15,196	12,166	10,345	14,587	102,363
Arts, entertainment, and recreation (71):							
Returns	102,631	101,995	364	128	63	55	25
Total receipts	75,491	43,106	4,141	2,855	3,989	6,823	14,577
Accommodation and food services (72):							
Returns	259,465	258,204	712	218	119	100	113
Total receipts	353,715	166,042	13,224	9,942	9,835	21,866	132,807
Other services (81):							
Returns	325,602	325,147	287	73	42	30	23
Total receipts	174,836	139,673	5,799	2,969	4,592	5,728	16,074

¹ Includes returns with zero assets.

Source: U.S. Internal Revenue Service, *Statistics of Income, Corporation Income Tax Returns*, annual.

No. 728. Economic Census Summary (NAICS 1997 Basis): 1997 and 2002

[25 represents 25,000. Data for 2002 are preliminary. Data are based on the 1997 and 2002 economic censuses which are subject to nonsampling error. Data for the construction sector are also subject to samping errors. For details on survey methodology and nonsampling and sampling errors, see Appendix III]

Kind of business	NAICS code [1]	Establishments (1,000)		Sales, receipts or shipments (bil. dol.)		Annual payroll (bil. dol.)		Paid employees [2] (1,000)	
		1997	2002	1997	2002	1997	2002	1997	2002
Mining	21	25	(S)	174	(S)	20.8	(S)	509	(S)
Oil & gas extraction	211	8	8	103	107	5.5	5.4	111	100
Mining (except oil & gas)	212	7	7	51	54	9.4	8.9	229	200
Mining support activities	213	9	(S)	20	(S)	5.9	(S)	169	(S)
Utilities	22	16	19	412	478	36.6	45.1	703	739
Construction [3]	23	656	698	859	1,140	174.2	235.5	5,665	6,944
Manufacturing	31-33	363	344	3,835	3,833	569.8	568.4	16,805	14,543
Wholesale trade	42	453	442	4,060	4,379	214.9	255.6	5,797	6,035
Wholesale trade, durable goods	421	291	288	2,180	2,354	133.2	159.0	3,398	3,565
Wholesale trade, nondurable goods	422	163	154	1,880	2,025	81.7	96.6	2,398	2,470
Retail trade	44-45	1,118	1,112	2,461	3,171	237.2	306.0	13,991	15,029
Motor vehicle & parts dealers	441	123	123	645	812	50.2	64.3	1,719	1,884
Furniture & home furnishings stores	442	65	65	72	94	10.0	13.0	483	554
Electronics & appliance stores	443	43	47	69	88	7.1	10.0	345	418
Bldg material & garden equip & supp dealers	444	93	(S)	228	(S)	25.6	(S)	1,118	(S)
Food & beverage stores	445	149	150	402	488	40.6	49.1	2,893	2,896
Health & personal care stores	446	83	79	118	183	15.2	20.6	904	1,043
Gasoline stations	447	127	(S)	198	(S)	11.5	(S)	922	(S)
Clothing & clothing accessories stores	448	157	149	136	170	16.6	21.2	1,280	1,425
Sporting goods, hobby, book, & music stores	451	69	63	62	78	7.1	9.0	561	633
General merchandise stores	452	36	40	330	451	30.9	42.6	2,508	2,549
Miscellaneous store retailers	453	130	129	78	95	10.2	13.7	753	849
Nonstore retailers	454	44	56	123	171	12.3	17.6	506	587
Transportation & warehousing [4][5]	48-49	178	201	318	(S)	82.3	116.8	2,921	3,751
Information [4]	51	114	137	623	905	129.5	189.7	3,066	3,846
Publishing industries	511	34	32	179	235	43.4	64.1	1,006	1,132
Motion picture & sound recording industries	512	22	23	56	77	9.4	11.7	276	334
Broadcasting & telecommunications	513	43	57	346	499	63.5	83.7	1,434	1,740
Information & data processing services [4]	514	15	25	42	94	13.3	30.2	350	638
Finance & insurance [6]	52	395	449	2,198	2,616	264.6	343.5	5,835	6,664
Real estate & rental & leasing [6]	53	288	326	241	348	41.6	61.8	1,702	2,136
Professional, scientific, & technical services [4]	54	621	747	595	896	231.4	374.5	5,361	7,509
Management of companies & enterprises	55	47	(S)	92	(S)	154.2	(S)	2,618	(S)
Admin/support waste mgt/remediation services [4]	56	276	276	296	414	137.3	193.5	7,347	8,345
Administrative & support services [4]	561	260	258	257	362	128.4	181.4	7,067	8,003
Waste management & remediation services [4]	562	16	18	39	51	8.9	12.1	281	342
Educational services [4]	61	41	50	20	32	6.4	10.2	321	452
Health care and social assistance	62	646	712	885	1,234	378.2	497.8	13,562	15,347
Ambulatory health care services	621	455	492	355	500	155.9	204.3	4,414	5,071
Hospitals	622	7	7	379	511	155.8	196.2	4,933	5,165
Nursing & residential care facilities	623	57	70	93	130	42.2	59.8	2,471	2,878
Social assistance	624	126	144	57	93	24.4	37.6	1,744	2,233
Arts, entertainment, & recreation	71	99	111	105	138	32.8	43.1	1,588	1,896
Perform arts, spectator sports, & related ind	711	31	39	38	55	14.5	19.6	327	438
Museums, historical sites, & like institutions	712	6	9	7	9	1.8	2.9	92	124
Amusement, gambling, & recreation industries	713	63	66	60	74	16.5	20.6	1,169	1,334
Accommodation & food services	72	545	562	350	463	97.0	128.7	9,451	10,836
Accommodation	721	58	(S)	98	(S)	26.7	(S)	1,697	(S)
Food services & drinking places	722	487	(S)	252	(S)	70.3	(S)	7,755	(S)
Other services (except public administration) [4]	81	520	528	266	315	65.5	82.7	3,256	3,528
Repair & maintenance [4]	811	235	233	105	120	29.9	35.5	1,276	1,367
Personal and laundry services [4]	812	185	192	58	73	18.6	22.6	1,217	1,311
Religious/grantmaking/prof/like organizations	813	99	102	103	122	17.1	24.6	763	849

S Estimates did not meet publication standards. [1] Based on North American Industry Classification System, 1997; see text this section. [2] For pay period including March 12. [3] For detailed industries, see Table 919. [4] Enterprise support establishments are included in the 2002 data but not in the 1997 data affecting comparability for this industry. [5] For detailed industries, see Table 1050. [6] For detailed industries, see Table 1155.

Source: U.S. Census Bureau, 2002 Economic Census Advance Report, published 29 March 2004; <http://www.census.gov/econ/census02/>.

No. 729. Nonemployer Establishments and Receipts by Industry: 1997 to 2002

[Establishments: 15,440 represents 15,440,000. Includes only firms subject to federal income tax. Nonemployers are businesses with no paid employees. Data originate chiefly from administrative records of the Internal Revenue Service; see Appendix III. Based on the North American Industry Classification System (NAICS), 1997; see text, this section]

Kind of business	NAICS code	Establishments (1,000)			Receipts (mil. dol)		
		1997	2000	2002	1997	2000	2002
All Industries	(X)	15,440	16,530	17,646	586,316	709,379	770,032
Forestry, fishing & hunting, & ag support services	113-115	240	223	220	8,533	9,196	8,994
Mining	21	92	86	83	4,964	5,227	4,924
Utilities	22	16	14	13	515	504	549
Construction	23	1,890	2,014	2,071	87,101	107,538	115,269
Manufacturing	31-33	303	285	290	12,319	13,022	13,402
Wholesale trade	42	406	388	364	30,759	31,684	30,022
Retail trade	44-45	1,831	1,743	1,839	69,418	73,810	77,896
Transportation & warehousing	48-49	646	747	809	29,428	37,824	40,698
Information	51	174	238	233	5,767	7,620	7,550
Finance & insurance	52	679	692	660	36,966	49,058	44,139
Real estate & rental & leasing	53	1,397	1,696	1,880	101,704	133,398	161,790
Professional, scientific, & technical services	54	2,650	2,420	2,553	81,165	90,272	96,395
Admin/support waste mgt/ remediation services	56	892	1,032	1,263	16,975	23,754	26,910
Educational services	61	235	283	345	2,798	3,736	4,581
Health care & social assistance	62	1,168	1,317	1,457	31,203	36,550	42,268
Arts, entertainment, & recreation	71	693	782	866	14,366	17,713	20,000
Accommodation & food services	72	191	218	242	9,035	13,418	14,178
Other services (except public administration)	81	1,936	2,350	2,459	43,299	55,056	60,468

Source: U.S. Census Bureau, "Nonemployer Statistics"; <http://www.census.gov/epcd/nonemployer/> and 2002 Economic Census: Advance Nonemployer Statistics; published 21 May 2004; <http://www.census.gov/epcd/nonemployer/2002/us/US000.HTM>.

No. 730. Establishments, Employees, and Payroll by Employment-Size Class: 1990 to 2001

[6,176 represents 6,176,000. Excludes most government employees, railroad employees, self-employed persons. Employees are for the week including March 12. Covers establishments with payroll. An establishment is a single physical location where business is conducted or where services or industrial operations are performed. For statement on methodology, see Appendix III]

Employment-size class	Unit	1990	1994	1995	1996	1997	1998	1999	2000	2001
Establishments, total	1,000	6,176	6,509	6,613	6,739	6,895	6,942	7,008	7,070	7,095
Under 20 employees	1,000	5,354	5,662	5,733	5,843	5,968	5,991	6,036	6,069	6,083
20 to 99 employees	1,000	684	704	730	741	767	786	802	826	836
100 to 499 employees	1,000	122	128	135	138	143	147	152	157	157
500 to 999 employees	1,000	10	10	10	11	11	11	12	12	12
1,000 or more employees	1,000	6	6	6	6	6	6	7	7	7
Employees, total	1,000	93,476	96,733	100,335	102,199	105,299	108,118	110,706	114,065	115,061
Under 20 employees	1,000	24,373	25,373	25,785	26,115	26,883	27,131	27,289	27,569	27,681
20 to 99 employees	1,000	27,414	28,138	29,202	29,697	30,631	31,464	32,193	33,147	33,555
100 to 499 employees	1,000	22,926	24,048	25,364	26,086	26,993	27,842	28,707	29,736	29,692
500 to 999 employees	1,000	6,551	6,663	7,021	7,274	7,422	7,689	7,923	8,291	8,357
1,000 or more employees	1,000	12,212	12,513	12,962	13,026	13,370	13,991	14,594	15,322	15,776
Annual payroll, total	Bil. dol	2,104	2,488	2,666	2,849	3,048	3,309	3,555	3,879	3,989
Under 20 employees	Bil. dol	485	579	608	647	688	734	773	818	839
20 to 99 employees	Bil. dol	547	650	696	747	796	866	925	1,006	1,037
100 to 499 employees	Bil. dol	518	621	675	730	786	858	931	1,031	1,052
500 to 999 employees	Bil. dol	174	202	219	240	254	277	298	336	342
1,000 or more employees	Bil. dol	381	436	467	485	524	575	628	690	719

Source: U.S. Census Bureau, "County Business Patterns"; published 2 June 2003; <http://www.census.gov/epcd/cbp/view/cbpview.html>.

No. 731. Establishments, Employees, and Payroll by Employment-Size Class and Industry: 1999 to 2001

[Establishments and employees in thousands (7,008.4 represents 7,008,400); payroll in billions of dollars. See headnote, Table 730. Based on the North American Industry Classification System (NAICS), 1997; see text, this section]

Industry	NAICS code	1999, total	2000, total	2001 Total	2001 Under 20 employees	2001 20 to 99 employees	2001 100 to 499 employees	2001 500 to 999 employees	2001 1,000 or more employees
Establishments, total	(X)	7,008.4	7,070.0	7,095.3	6,083.0	835.8	157.1	12.3	7.0
Agriculture, forestry, fishing & hunting	11	26.9	26.1	26.4	24.8	1.5	0.2	(Z)	(Z)
Mining	21	23.7	23.7	24.3	19.8	3.6	0.7	0.1	(Z)
Utilities	22	16.6	17.3	17.7	12.5	3.8	1.2	0.1	0.1
Construction	23	698.5	709.6	698.9	634.8	56.5	7.2	0.4	0.2
Manufacturing	31-33	360.2	354.5	352.6	236.3	82.7	29.2	3.0	1.4
Wholesale trade	42	450.0	446.2	438.9	373.0	57.1	8.2	0.4	0.1
Retail trade	44-45	1,111.3	1,113.6	1,120.0	971.9	122.7	24.8	0.6	0.1
Transportation and warehousing	48-49	187.3	190.0	190.7	159.7	25.5	4.9	0.3	0.3
Information	51	126.5	133.6	137.3	107.7	22.5	6.1	0.7	0.3
Finance and insurance	52	418.3	423.7	425.0	378.7	38.2	6.6	0.9	0.5
Real estate and rental and leasing	53	298.1	300.2	307.0	291.2	13.9	1.8	0.1	(Z)
Professional, scientific, and technical services	54	704.8	722.7	736.5	677.1	49.7	8.7	0.7	0.3
Management of companies and enterprises	55	46.5	47.4	47.6	31.4	10.8	4.2	0.7	0.4
Admin/support waste mgt/remediation services	56	350.4	351.5	362.7	300.6	45.1	15.0	1.3	0.7
Educational services	61	66.5	68.0	70.9	53.6	13.8	2.8	0.4	0.3
Health care and social assistance	62	649.8	658.6	671.4	570.6	78.5	18.8	1.7	1.8
Arts, entertainment, and recreation	71	102.8	103.8	106.0	88.0	15.2	2.5	0.2	0.1
Accommodation and food services	72	539.6	542.4	548.6	393.8	145.3	8.9	0.3	0.2
Other services [1]	81	717.9	723.3	719.4	670.0	45.2	4.0	0.1	(Z)
Auxiliaries [2]	95	14.6	14.8	14.9	9.3	3.7	1.5	0.3	0.1
Unclassified establishments	99	98.0	99.0	78.6	78.3	0.3	-	-	-
Employees, total	(X)	110,706	114,065	115,061	27,681	33,555	29,692	8,357	15,776
Agriculture, forestry, fishing & hunting	11	192	184	183	(D)	(D)	30	(D)	(D)
Mining	21	457	456	486	92	(D)	149	45	(D)
Utilities	22	667	655	654	66	171	227	92	98
Construction	23	6,202	6,573	6,492	2,478	2,173	1,301	236	304
Manufacturing	31-33	16,660	16,474	15,950	1,382	3,659	5,915	2,045	2,950
Wholesale trade	42	5,972	6,112	6,142	1,846	2,225	1,501	290	281
Retail trade	44-45	14,477	14,841	14,890	5,184	4,905	4,329	368	104
Transportation and warehousing	48-49	3,627	3,790	3,751	667	1,049	899	207	929
Information	51	3,235	3,546	3,755	494	961	1,203	481	615
Finance and insurance	52	5,965	5,963	6,248	1,703	1,489	1,332	625	1,099
Real estate and rental and leasing	53	1,874	1,942	2,014	1,037	521	324	(D)	(D)
Professional, scientific, and technical services	54	6,432	6,816	7,157	2,357	1,954	1,668	440	738
Management of companies and enterprises	55	2,788	2,874	2,879	171	486	912	479	830
Admin/support waste mgt/remediation services	56	8,367	9,138	9,062	1,198	1,977	2,958	879	2,049
Educational services	61	2,432	2,532	2,612	257	582	546	257	971
Health care and social assistance	62	13,865	14,109	14,535	2,961	3,154	3,488	1,192	3,739
Arts, entertainment, and recreation	71	1,640	1,741	1,780	342	636	455	112	235
Accommodation and food services	72	9,638	9,881	9,972	2,370	5,582	1,434	237	349
Other services [1]	81	5,151	5,293	5,370	2,831	1,656	691	87	105
Auxiliaries [2]	95	959	1,001	1,022	59	164	329	200	271
Unclassified establishments	99	106	144	105	(D)	(D)	-	-	-
Annual payroll, total	(X)	3,555	3,879	3,989	839	1,037	1,052	342	719
Agriculture, forestry, fishing & hunting	11	5	5	5	(D)	(D)	1	(D)	(D)
Mining	21	21	22	25	4	(D)	9	2	(D)
Utilities	22	39	41	42	3	10	15	7	7
Construction	23	219	240	247	80	87	57	10	12
Manufacturing	31-33	626	644	618	42	124	217	81	154
Wholesale trade	42	250	270	276	75	96	71	16	16
Retail trade	44-45	282	303	315	101	110	92	8	4
Transportation and warehousing	48-49	117	126	130	20	33	30	7	39
Information	51	170	209	207	25	45	66	27	45
Finance and insurance	52	313	347	374	80	87	86	37	84
Real estate and rental and leasing	53	54	59	64	30	18	12	(D)	(D)
Professional, scientific, and technical services	54	311	362	374	106	110	98	28	33
Management of companies and enterprises	55	192	211	213	14	34	62	34	69
Admin/support waste mgt/remediation services	56	183	210	221	37	52	65	18	49
Educational services	61	57	62	67	6	13	14	5	30
Health care and social assistance	62	409	431	466	109	92	89	38	138
Arts, entertainment, and recreation	71	39	43	46	11	12	15	3	5
Accommodation and food services	72	117	126	129	30	63	22	5	9
Other services [1]	81	102	110	115	57	36	18	2	9
Auxiliaries [2]	95	45	55	53	3	7	16	9	17
Unclassified establishments	99	3	4	2	(D)	(D)	-	-	-

- Represents zero.   D Data withheld to avoid disclosure.   X Not applicable.   Z Less than 50 establishments.   [1] Except public administration.   [2] Excludes corporate, subsidiary and regional management.

Source: U.S. Census Bureau, "County Business Patterns"; published 2 June 2003; <http://www.census.gov/epcd/cbp/view/cbpview.html>.

Business Enterprise   493

No. 732. Employer Firms, Employment, and Annual Payroll by Enterprise Size and Industry: 2001

[5,658 represents 5,658,000. A firm is an aggregation of all establishments owned by a parent company (within a geographic location and/or industry) with some annual payroll. A firm may be a single location or it can include multiple locations. Employment is measured in March and payroll is annual leading to some firms with zero employment. Numbers in parentheses represent North American Industry Classification System codes, 1997; see text, this section]

Industry and data type	Unit	All industries—employment size of enterprise								
		Total	0	1 to 4	5 to 9	10 to 19	20 to 99	100 to 499	Less than 500	More than 500
Total [1]:										
Firms	1,000 . .	5,658	704	2,698	1,019	616	518	85	5,640	17
Employment	1,000 . .	115,061	-	5,630	6,698	8,275	20,370	16,410	57,383	57,678
Annual payroll	Bil. dol .	3,989	34	154	179	237	624	539	1,768	2,222
Construction (23):										
Firms	1,000 . .	691	99	340	121	70	53	6	690	1
Employment	1,000 . .	6,492	-	711	792	942	2,007	1,075	5,527	965
Annual payroll	Bil. dol .	247	4	19	23	32	79	46	203	44
Manufacturing (31-33):										
Firms	1,000 . .	305	21	96	57	48	63	16	301	5
Employment	1,000 . .	15,950	-	216	379	661	2,601	2,781	6,638	9,312
Annual payroll	Bil. dol .	618	2	6	10	20	85	97	220	398
Wholesale trade (42):										
Firms	1,000 . .	346	33	154	63	44	41	8	343	3
Employment	1,000 . .	6,142	-	325	417	589	1,496	1,037	3,865	2,277
Annual payroll	Bil. dol .	276	2	12	15	22	59	43	154	122
Retail trade (44-45):										
Firms	1,000 . .	735	80	342	153	88	61	9	733	2
Employment	1,000 . .	14,890	-	754	1,006	1,154	2,264	1,284	6,462	8,428
Annual payroll	Bil. dol .	315	3	13	19	24	61	37	156	159
Transportation & warehousing (48-49):										
Firms	1,000 . .	157	22	77	24	16	15	3	156	1
Employment	1,000 . .	3,751	-	149	154	216	578	461	1,558	2,193
Annual payroll	Bil. dol .	130	1	4	4	6	16	14	45	85
Information (51):										
Firms	1,000 . .	77	11	33	12	9	9	2	76	1
Employment	1,000 . .	3,755	-	66	81	122	358	367	995	2,760
Annual payroll	Bil. dol .	207	1	3	3	5	16	19	46	161
Finance & insurance (52):										
Firms	1,000 . .	231	26	135	33	16	15	4	229	2
Employment	1,000 . .	6,248	-	275	213	214	609	630	1,941	4,307
Annual payroll	Bil. dol .	374	2	9	9	11	32	34	98	276
Real estate & rental & leasing (53):										
Firms	1,000 . .	248	35	150	33	15	11	2	246	1
Employment	1,000 . .	2,014	-	283	211	200	388	298	1,381	633
Annual payroll	Bil. dol .	64	1	7	6	6	12	10	42	22
Professional, scientific & technical services (54):										
Firms	1,000 . .	682	99	382	100	55	38	6	680	2
Employment	1,000 . .	7,157	-	734	650	727	1,445	1,034	4,589	2,568
Annual payroll	Bil. dol .	374	6	28	26	33	77	61	230	145
Management of companies & enterprises (55):										
Firms	1,000 . .	27	1	4	1	1	5	8	20	7
Employment	1,000 . .	2,879	-	6	5	8	69	238	325	2,554
Annual payroll	Bil. dol .	213	(Z)	(Z)	(Z)	(Z)	4	13	18	195
Admin/support waste mgt/remediation services (56):										
Firms	1,000 . .	309	49	142	49	30	28	8	305	3
Employment	1,000 . .	9,062	-	291	321	399	1,103	1,411	3,526	5,536
Annual payroll	Bil. dol .	221	3	8	8	10	28	32	89	133
Health care and social assistance (62):										
Firms	1,000 . .	541	46	231	127	70	51	14	537	4
Employment	1,000 . .	14,535	-	517	838	925	2,010	2,616	6,906	7,629
Annual payroll	Bil. dol .	466	3	20	29	34	65	67	218	247
Accommodation & food services (72):										
Firms	1,000 . .	416	57	129	79	68	74	8	415	2
Employment	1,000 . .	9,972	-	299	527	936	2,795	1,442	5,999	3,973
Annual payroll	Bil. dol .	129	2	4	6	10	32	17	71	58
Other services (except public administration) (81):										
Firms	1,000 . .	658	54	360	133	65	41	4	657	1
Employment	1,000 . .	5,370	-	763	865	855	1,464	646	4,594	777
Annual payroll	Bil. dol .	115	1	14	16	17	30	16	95	20

- Represents zero.   Z Less than $500 million.   [1] Includes other industries not shown separately.

Source: U.S. Small Business Administration, Office of Advocacy, "Statistics of U.S. Businesses: Firm Size Data provided by U.S. Census Bureau"; published 12 March 2004; <http://www.sba.gov/advo/stats/data.html>.

494   Business Enterprise

No. 733. Employer Firms, Establishments, Employment, and Annual Payroll by Enterprise Size: 1990 to 2001

[In thousands except as noted (5,074 represents 5,074,000). Firms are an aggregation of all establishments owned by a parent company with some annual payroll. Establishments are locations with active payroll in any quarter. Employment is measured in March and payroll is annual leading to some enterprises with zero employment. This table illustrates the changing importance of enterprise sizes over time, not job growth as enterprises can grow or decline and change enterprise size cells over time]

Item	All industries—employment size of enterprise							
	Total	0-4 [1]	5-9	10-19	20-99	100-499	Less than 500	More than 500
Firms:								
1990	5,074	3,021	952	563	454	70	5,060	14
1994	5,277	3,208	965	563	452	73	5,262	15
1995	5,369	3,250	981	577	470	76	5,354	15
1996	5,478	3,328	996	586	476	76	5,462	16
1997	5,542	3,358	1,007	594	487	80	5,526	16
1998	5,579	3,376	1,012	600	494	80	5,563	16
1999	5,608	3,389	1,013	606	502	81	5,591	17
2000	5,653	3,397	1,021	617	516	84	5,635	17
2001	5,658	3,402	1,019	616	518	85	5,640	17
Establishments:								
1990	6,176	3,032	971	600	590	255	5,448	728
1994	6,509	3,218	983	609	631	284	5,725	784
1995	6,613	3,260	998	618	639	284	5,799	814
1996	6,738	3,338	1,013	625	636	281	5,893	846
1997	6,895	3,364	1,023	639	683	309	6,018	877
1998	6,942	3,383	1,026	640	675	307	6,030	911
1999	7,008	3,398	1,027	643	671	309	6,048	960
2000	7,070	3,406	1,035	652	674	312	6,080	990
2001	7,095	3,410	1,034	650	670	316	6,080	1,015
Employment:								
1990	93,469	5,117	6,252	7,543	17,710	13,545	50,167	43,302
1994	96,722	5,319	6,333	7,544	17,694	14,118	51,008	45,714
1995	100,315	5,395	6,440	7,734	18,422	14,660	52,653	47,662
1996	102,187	5,486	6,541	7,855	18,643	14,650	53,175	49,013
1997	105,299	5,546	6,610	7,962	19,110	15,317	54,545	50,754
1998	108,118	5,584	6,643	8,048	19,378	15,411	55,064	53,053
1999	110,706	5,606	6,652	8,130	19,703	15,638	55,729	54,977
2000	114,065	5,593	6,709	8,286	20,277	16,260	57,124	56,941
2001	115,061	5,630	6,698	8,275	20,370	16,410	57,383	57,678
Annual payroll (bil. dol.):								
1990	2,104	117	114	144	352	279	1,007	1,097
1994	2,488	135	132	166	408	336	1,176	1,312
1995	2,666	142	137	175	437	361	1,252	1,414
1996	2,849	151	145	185	465	384	1,330	1,518
1997	3,048	158	151	194	495	418	1,416	1,632
1998	3,309	168	160	207	531	446	1,513	1,797
1999	3,555	177	167	218	565	475	1,601	1,954
2000	3,879	186	174	231	608	528	1,727	2,152
2001	3,989	188	179	237	624	539	1,768	2,222

[1] Employment is measured in March, thus some firms (start-ups after March, closures before March, and seasonal firms) will have zero employment and some annual payroll.

No. 734. Firm Births and Deaths by Employment Size of Enterprise: 1990 to 2001

[In thousands (541.1 represents 541,100). Data represent activity from March of the beginning year to March of the ending year. Establishments with no employment in the first quarter of the beginning year were excluded. This table provides the number of births and deaths of initial establishments (based on plant number) as an approximation of firm births and deaths]

Item	Births (initial locations)				Deaths (initial locations)			
	Total	Less than 20	Less than 500	More than 500	Total	Less than 20	Less than 500	More than 500
Firms:								
1990 to 1991	541.1	515.9	540.9	0.3	546.5	517.0	546.1	0.4
1993 to 1994	570.6	546.4	570.3	0.3	503.6	476.7	503.1	0.4
1994 to 1995	594.4	568.9	594.1	0.3	497.2	472.4	496.9	0.4
1995 to 1996	597.8	572.4	597.5	0.3	512.4	485.5	512.0	0.4
1996 to 1997	590.6	564.2	590.3	0.3	530.0	500.0	529.5	0.5
1997 to 1998	590.0	564.8	589.7	0.3	540.6	511.6	540.1	0.5
1998 to 1999	579.6	554.3	579.3	0.3	544.5	514.3	544.0	0.4
1999 to 2000	574.3	548.0	574.0	0.3	542.8	514.2	542.4	0.5
2000 to 2001	585.1	558.0	584.8	0.3	553.3	524.0	552.8	0.5
Employment:								
1990 to 1991	3,105	1,713	2,907	198	3,208	1,723	3,044	164
1993 to 1994	3,106	1,760	2,890	216	3,077	1,549	2,801	276
1994 to 1995	3,322	1,836	3,049	273	2,823	1,517	2,634	189
1995 to 1996	3,256	1,845	3,056	200	3,100	1,560	2,808	291
1996 to 1997	3,228	1,814	3,030	198	3,275	1,621	2,961	314
1997 to 1998	3,205	1,812	3,002	203	3,233	1,662	2,992	242
1998 to 1999	3,225	1,670	2,991	235	3,180	1,645	2,969	210
1999 to 2000	3,229	1,793	3,031	198	3,177	1,654	2,946	230
2000 to 2001	3,418	1,821	3,109	310	3,262	1,701	3,050	212

Source of Tables 733 and 734: U.S. Small Business Administration, Office of Advocacy, "Statistics of U.S. Businesses: Firm Size Data provided by U.S. Census Bureau"; published 12 March 2004; <http://www.sba.gov/advo/stats/data.html>.

No. 735. Employer Firms, Employment, and Payroll by Employment Size of Enterprise and State: 1990 and 2001

[5,073.8 represents 5,073,800. A firm is an aggregation of all establishments owned by a parent company (within a state) with some annual payroll. A firm may be a single location or it can include multiple locations. Employment is measured in March and payroll is annual leading to some firms with zero employment]

State	Employer firms (1,000)					Employment, 2001 (mil.)			Annual payroll, 2001 (bil. dol.)		
	1990		2001								
	Total	Less than 20 employees	Total	Less than 20 employees	Less than 500 employees	Total	Less than 20 employees	Less than 500 employees	Total	Less than 20 employees	Less than 500 employees
U.S. . . .	5,073.8	4,535.6	5,657.8	5,036.8	5,640.4	115.1	20.6	57.4	3,989.1	603.8	1,767.5
AL.	71.5	61.7	78.8	67.3	76.6	1.6	0.3	0.8	45.2	6.9	20.1
AK.	12.8	11.3	16.0	14.1	15.5	0.2	0.1	0.1	8.3	1.8	4.4
AZ.	71.6	61.8	93.9	80.0	91.2	1.9	0.3	0.9	60.0	9.2	26.4
AR.	46.0	40.2	51.6	44.7	50.1	1.0	0.2	0.5	25.8	4.1	10.8
CA.	628.5	552.8	668.1	582.8	662.3	13.2	2.4	7.0	521.8	80.9	245.5
CO	82.7	72.4	117.4	102.6	114.6	2.0	0.4	1.0	71.5	11.9	32.4
CT.	81.1	70.4	77.9	66.5	75.8	1.6	0.3	0.8	68.9	10.3	30.4
DE.	16.3	13.6	20.3	16.8	19.0	0.4	0.1	0.2	15.0	1.9	5.4
DC	16.5	12.6	16.3	12.3	15.1	0.4	0.1	0.2	20.8	2.7	9.6
FL.	302.8	271.3	358.4	323.7	354.2	6.4	1.2	2.9	189.6	33.5	83.5
GA	128.1	110.5	161.5	139.2	157.5	3.5	0.6	1.5	115.9	16.3	46.1
HI	24.4	20.9	24.6	20.9	23.8	0.4	0.1	0.3	12.7	2.4	6.8
ID	23.0	20.1	32.4	28.2	31.4	0.5	0.1	0.3	12.4	2.5	6.2
IL	230.8	198.8	252.9	217.1	248.5	5.4	0.9	2.7	204.3	29.1	89.2
IN	105.9	90.7	115.3	97.5	112.4	2.6	0.4	1.3	79.3	10.8	34.3
IA	61.4	53.5	64.9	55.7	63.3	1.3	0.2	0.7	34.5	5.2	16.1
KS.	55.9	48.3	61.0	51.9	59.1	1.1	0.2	0.6	33.3	5.2	15.5
KY.	66.6	57.2	71.8	60.7	69.7	1.5	0.3	0.8	42.6	6.2	18.7
LA.	73.2	63.1	81.3	69.2	79.2	1.6	0.3	0.9	45.2	7.4	21.4
ME	30.7	27.2	34.2	30.2	33.3	0.5	0.1	0.3	14.2	2.9	7.7
MD	95.9	81.8	106.7	91.0	104.1	2.1	0.4	1.1	74.2	11.9	35.7
MA	135.6	116.8	149.0	128.4	146.0	3.1	0.5	1.6	134.7	18.3	59.5
MI	175.9	153.0	192.7	166.6	189.6	4.0	0.7	2.0	142.9	21.2	63.4
MN	95.5	82.1	117.0	100.2	114.5	2.4	0.4	1.2	84.9	11.6	37.2
MS	44.5	39.0	47.6	40.7	46.0	0.9	0.2	0.5	22.7	3.7	10.0
MO	109.4	94.8	116.8	99.9	114.0	2.4	0.4	1.2	74.4	10.8	32.7
MT.	22.2	19.9	28.4	25.3	27.7	0.3	0.1	0.2	7.2	2.0	4.6
NE.	37.6	32.7	41.3	35.5	40.0	0.7	0.1	0.4	20.8	3.3	9.6
NV.	26.0	21.8	40.7	33.8	39.0	0.9	0.1	0.4	27.5	4.3	12.2
NH	29.4	25.5	31.9	27.1	30.8	0.6	0.1	0.3	18.5	3.6	9.9
NJ.	188.0	165.5	202.2	178.1	199.0	3.6	0.7	1.8	154.2	24.4	67.5
NM	30.7	26.6	35.3	30.0	33.9	0.6	0.1	0.3	14.8	2.9	7.8
NY.	412.5	368.1	426.5	380.8	422.2	7.4	1.4	3.8	343.5	49.9	143.6
NC	135.9	119.0	163.6	141.7	160.2	3.4	0.6	1.6	103.0	15.3	43.1
ND	16.6	14.6	17.1	14.6	16.6	0.3	0.1	0.2	6.4	1.3	3.7
OH	200.7	172.7	211.2	179.6	207.4	4.9	0.8	2.4	156.9	21.6	68.0
OK	63.2	55.5	70.0	60.7	68.2	1.2	0.2	0.6	33.4	5.8	15.9
OR	69.9	61.0	85.0	74.0	83.0	1.4	0.3	0.8	44.1	7.6	21.2
PA.	233.5	202.8	236.8	204.0	232.9	5.1	0.9	2.5	169.9	23.9	74.5
RI	25.1	21.6	25.2	21.5	24.3	0.4	0.1	0.2	13.2	2.5	7.1
SC.	66.1	57.4	78.0	66.9	75.8	1.6	0.3	0.7	43.8	6.9	18.3
SD.	18.3	16.0	20.7	17.9	20.1	0.3	0.1	0.2	7.6	1.5	4.2
TN.	92.8	79.9	100.9	85.3	97.9	2.4	0.4	1.1	70.7	9.6	29.1
TX.	316.9	280.0	369.3	321.0	364.3	8.2	1.3	3.8	282.3	40.3	114.2
UT.	30.9	26.2	47.7	40.7	46.0	0.9	0.2	0.4	26.1	4.1	11.8
VT.	18.0	16.0	18.9	16.5	18.3	0.3	0.1	0.2	7.3	1.6	4.3
VA.	121.3	105.2	140.5	120.8	137.3	2.9	0.5	1.4	102.5	14.5	43.9
WA	113.2	99.3	137.7	120.4	135.1	2.3	0.5	1.3	86.5	13.4	38.9
WV	31.8	27.6	32.9	28.2	31.8	0.6	0.1	0.3	14.5	2.5	6.8
WI	104.3	89.7	115.5	98.3	113.1	2.4	0.4	1.3	74.3	11.2	35.4
WY	13.0	11.4	16.3	14.2	15.7	0.2	0.1	0.1	4.9	1.3	3.0

Source: U.S. Small Business Administration, Office of Advocacy, "Statistics of U.S. Businesses: Firm Size Data provided by U.S. Census Bureau"; published 12 March 2004; <http://www.sba.gov/advo/stats/data.html>.

No. 736. Small Business Administration Loans to Small Businesses: 1990 to 2003

[576 represents $576,000,000. For year ending September 30. A small business must be independently owned and operated, must not be dominant in its particular industry, and must meet standards set by the Small Business Administration as to its annual receipts or number of employees]

Minority group	Number of loans					Amount (mil. dol.)				
	1990	1995	2000	2002	2003	1990	1995	2000	2002	2003
Total minority loans	2,367	10,877	11,999	14,300	20,180	576	1,838	3,661	4,250	4,213
Percent of all loans	12.0	18.1	24.8	25.0	28.0	(NA)	(NA)	(NA)	(NA)	(NA)
African American	513	2,770	2,120	2,146	3,769	96	293	393	422	399
Asian American	1,075	3,767	5,838	7,249	9,505	317	945	2,397	2,810	2,755
Hispanic American	694	3,940	3,500	4,270	6,112	149	539	768	891	941
Native American	85	400	541	635	794	14	61	102	127	118

NA Not available.

Source: U.S. Small Business Administration, Management Information Summary, unpublished data.

No. 737. U.S. Firms—Ownership by Race and Hispanic Origin: 1997

[20,822 represents 20,822,000. A Hispanic firm may be of any race and, therefore may be included in more than one minority group. See Appendix III]

Group	All firms		Firms with paid employees			
	Firms (1,000)	Sales and receipts (mil. dol.)	Firms (1,000)	Sales and receipts (mil. dol.)	Employees (1,000)	Annual payroll (mil. dol.)
All firms	20,822	18,553,243	5,295	17,907,940	103,360	2,936,493
Black	823	71,215	93	56,378	718	14,322
Hispanic	1,200	186,275	212	158,675	1,389	29,830
Cuban	125	26,492	30	23,873	176	4,163
Mexican, Mexican American, Chicano	472	73,707	91	62,271	695	13,015
Puerto Rican	70	7,461	11	5,814	62	1,497
Spaniard	57	16,923	13	15,264	76	2,046
Hispanic Latin American	287	40,998	43	34,798	239	5,863
Other Spanish/Hispanic/Latino	188	20,694	24	16,654	140	3,247
American Indian and Alaska Native . . .	197	34,344	33	29,226	299	6,624
Asian and Pacific Islander . . .	913	306,933	290	278,294	2,203	46,180
Asian Indian	167	67,503	67	61,760	491	12,586
Chinese	253	106,197	91	98,233	692	12,945
Filipino	85	11,078	15	8,966	110	2,667
Japanese	86	43,741	23	41,295	262	7,107
Korean	136	45,936	50	40,746	334	5,789
Vietnamese	98	9,323	19	6,768	79	1,166
Other Asian	71	19,016	22	16,801	202	3,136
Native Hawaiian	16	2,250	2	1,957	21	498
Other Pacific Islander	4	1,888	1	1,768	13	286
White non-Hispanic	17,317	7,763,011	4,373	7,252,270	54,084	1,395,150
Fifty-percent minority/fifty-percent nonminority	85	37,732	39	34,632	302	8,619
Other [1]	382	10,161,242	(S)	10,104,058	44,458	1,437,195

S Does not meet publication standards.   [1] Includes publicly-held corporations, foreign-owned companies, and not-for-profit companies.

Source: U.S. Census Bureau, 1997 Economic Census, Company Statistics Series, Company Summary 1997, EC97CS-1; and Survey of Minority-Owned Business Enterprises—Asians and Pacific Islanders 1997, EC97CS-5; and Hispanic 1997, EC97CS-4.

No. 738. Women-Owned Firms by Industry Division: 1997

[818,669,084 represents $818,669,084,000. Based on the 1987 Standard Industrial Classification code; see text, this section. See Appendix III]

Industry division	All firms		Firms with paid employees			
	Firms [1] (number)	Sales and receipts ($1,000)	Firms [1] (number)	Sales and receipts ($1,000)	Employees (number)	Annual payroll ($1,000)
All Industries	5,417,034	818,669,084	846,780	717,763,965	7,076,081	149,115,699
Agric. services, forestry, and fishing . . .	74,444	5,852,901	16,652	4,599,852	77,370	1,442,618
Mining	20,030	7,186,113	2,180	6,491,900	25,982	873,455
Construction [2]	157,173	67,632,059	65,707	63,738,665	518,142	15,302,000
Manufacturing	121,108	113,722,304	41,141	111,658,770	901,434	24,674,596
Transportation and public utilities	128,999	32,944,160	35,623	30,063,926	321,759	7,803,912
Wholesale trade	125,645	188,488,639	50,459	184,574,784	468,276	14,086,123
Retail trade	919,990	152,041,311	211,583	137,296,015	1,574,747	19,520,353
Finance, insurance, and real estate . . .	479,469	56,021,358	66,375	38,920,419	276,045	7,549,811
Services	2,981,266	186,161,274	355,768	140,255,817	2,908,080	57,808,228
Industries not classified	411,596	8,618,965	3,979	163,817	4,246	54,604

[1] Firms may be classified in more than one industry division.   [2] Includes SIC 6552, Subdividers and developers.

Source: U.S. Census Bureau, 1997 Economic Census, Company Statistics Series, Survey of Women-Owned Business Enterprises, Women-Owned Businesses 1997, Series EC97CS-2.

[For years ending June 30. Covers only bankruptcy cases filed under the Bankruptcy Reform Act of 1978. *Bankruptcy*: legal recognition that a company or individual is insolvent and must restructure or liquidate. Petitions "filed" means the commencement of a proceeding through the presentation of a petition to the clerk of the court; "pending" is a proceeding in which the administration has not been completed]

Item	1990	1995	1997	1998	1999	2000	2001	2002	2003
Total filed	725,484	858,104	1,316,999	1,429,451	1,391,964	1,276,922	1,386,606	1,505,306	1,650,279
Business [1]	64,688	51,288	53,993	50,202	39,934	36,910	37,135	39,201	37,182
Nonbusiness [2]	660,796	806,816	1,263,006	1,379,249	1,352,030	1,240,012	1,349,471	1,466,105	1,613,097
Voluntary	723,886	856,991	1,315,782	1,428,550	1,391,130	1,276,146	1,385,840	1,504,500	1,649,543
Involuntary	1,598	1,113	1,217	901	834	776	766	806	736
Chapter 7 [3]	505,337	581,390	917,274	1,015,453	993,414	885,447	972,659	1,053,230	1,165,993
Chapter 9 [4]	7	12	9	5	3	8	10	8	7
Chapter 11 [5]	19,591	13,221	11,159	9,613	8,684	9,947	10,272	11,401	10,602
Chapter 12 [6]	1,351	904	1,006	845	732	206	367	775	
Chapter 13 [7]	199,186	262,551	387,521	403,501	389,004	380,770	403,418	440,231	472,811
Section 304 [8]	12	26	29	34	30	18	41	69	91
Total pending	961,919	1,090,446	1,331,290	1,389,917	1,394,794	1,400,416	1,535,903	1,613,742	1,729,354

[1] Business bankruptcies include those filed under chapters 7, 9, 11, or 12.   [2] Bankruptcies include those filed under chapters 7, 11, or 13.   [3] Chapter 7, liquidation of nonexempt assets of businesses or individuals.   [4] Chapter 9, adjustment of debts of a municipality.   [5] Chapter 11, individual or business reorganization.   [6] Chapter 12, adjustment of debts of a family farmer with regular income, effective November 26, 1986.   [7] Chapter 13, adjustment of debts of an individual with regular income.   [8] Chapter 11 U.S.C., Section 304, cases ancillary to foreign proceedings.

Source: Administrative Office of the U.S. Courts, *Statistical Tables for the Federal Judiciary.*

No. 740. Bankruptcy Cases Filed by State: 1995 to 2003

[In thousands (858.1 represents 858,100). For years ending June 30. Covers only bankruptcy cases filed under the Bankruptcy Reform Act of 1978. *Bankruptcy*: legal recognition that a company or individual is insolvent and must restructure or liquidate. Petitions "filed" means the commencement of a proceeding through the presentation of a petition to the clerk of the court]

State	1995	2000	2002	2003	State	1995	2000	2002	2003
Total [1]	858.1	1,276.9	1,505.3	1,650.3	Missouri	15.1	26.3	31.5	37.3
					Montana	2.1	3.3	4.1	4.3
Alabama	24.3	31.4	39.6	42.0	Nebraska	3.4	5.6	7.3	8.3
Alaska	0.9	1.4	1.4	1.6	Nevada	7.3	14.3	18.6	20.7
Arizona	14.8	21.7	27.3	31.7	New Hampshire ...	3.1	3.9	3.7	4.3
Arkansas	7.9	16.3	21.8	24.5					
California	140.4	160.6	148.4	148.6	New Jersey	25.5	38.7	40.5	42.0
					New Mexico......	3.7	7.1	8.7	10.0
Colorado........	13.1	15.6	19.2	24.2	New York	48.8	61.7	67.9	75.0
Connecticut	8.5	11.4	11.2	12.2	North Carolina	14.0	25.8	34.9	38.6
Delaware	1.4	4.9	4.0	3.9	North Dakota	1.2	2.0	2.0	2.3
District of Columbia	1.4	2.6	2.5	2.5					
Florida	43.4	74.0	88.0	94.9	Ohio	32.4	53.6	73.2	85.4
					Oklahoma	13.2	19.3	23.3	26.1
Georgia	42.1	57.9	72.6	80.2	Oregon	13.2	18.1	23.5	25.5
Hawaii	1.8	5.0	4.7	4.1	Pennsylvania	22.0	43.8	52.0	57.9
Idaho	3.7	7.3	8.5	9.3	Rhode Island	3.0	4.8	4.7	4.8
Illinois	39.2	62.3	77.3	86.9					
Indiana	22.3	37.5	50.6	55.3	South Carolina	6.9	11.7	15.1	15.9
					South Dakota.....	1.3	2.1	2.7	2.8
Iowa........	5.9	8.2	11.2	12.4	Tennessee	35.5	47.1	61.5	65.9
Kansas........	8.5	11.4	14.0	16.0	Texas	43.8	62.9	77.0	88.4
Kentucky........	13.0	20.8	26.3	28.7	Utah	6.9	14.4	20.7	22.8
Louisiana	13.4	23.1	26.5	28.4					
Maine	1.9	4.1	4.4	4.6	Vermont	0.9	1.6	1.7	1.9
					Virginia	25.5	37.1	41.9	44.1
Maryland........	16.3	31.1	34.5	35.8	Washington	18.6	31.2	37.3	40.7
Massachusetts....	14.3	16.7	16.9	18.0	West Virginia	3.8	8.2	9.7	11.0
Michigan........	22.7	36.4	50.2	60.8	Wisconsin	11.8	18.0	23.2	27.7
Minnesota.......	14.1	15.4	19.1	20.6	Wyoming........	1.2	2.0	2.2	2.5
Mississippi.......	10.6	17.9	22.0	23.0					

[1] Includes outlying areas not shown separately.

Source: Administrative Office of the U.S. Courts, *Statistical Tables for the Federal Judiciary.*

No. 741. Mergers and Acquisitions—Summary: 1990 to 2003

[206 represents $206,000,000,000. Covers transactions valued at $5 million or more. Values based on transactions for which price data revealed. All activity includes mergers, acquisitions, acquisitions of partial interest that involve a 40 percent stake in the target or an investment of at least $100 million, divestitures, and leveraged transactions that result in a change in ownership. Divestiture: sale of a business, division, or subsidiary by corporate owner to another party. Leveraged buyout: acquisition of a business in which buyers use mostly borrowed money to finance purchase price and incorporate debt into capital structure of business after change in ownership]

Item	Unit	1990	1995	1997	1998	1999	2000	2001	2002	2003
All activity: Number	Number	4,239	4,981	8,770	9,634	9,599	11,169	7,713	7,032	7,743
Value	Bil. dol.	206	896	1,610	2,480	3,402	3,440	1,688	1,185	1,318
Divestitures: Number	Number	1,907	2,227	3,189	3,304	3,184	3,497	2,816	2,631	3,090
Value	Bil. dol.	91	365	616	555	678	892	644	473	501
Leveraged buyouts: Number	Number	177	206	198	238	344	476	329	303	366
Value	Bil. dol.	18	24	24	27	58	86	60	83	86
Foreign acquisitions of U.S. companies:										
Number	Number	773	80	441	483	560	741	448	336	321
Value	Bil. dol.	56	4	65	233	297	335	125	68	58
U.S. acquisitions overseas:										
Number	Number	392	317	539	746	698	746	470	378	398
Value	Bil. dol.	21	63	88	128	158	136	108	56	106
US companies acquiring US companies:										
Number	Number	(NA)	2,250	3,753	3,882	3,353	3,119	2,079	1,994	2,070
Value	Bil. dol.	(NA)	462	834	1,379	1,259	1,400	638	370	463

NA Not available.

No. 742. Mergers and Acquisitions by Industry: 2003

[462,808 represents $462,808,000,000. See headnote Table 741]

Industry	U.S. company acquiring U.S. company		Foreign company acquiring U.S. company		U.S. company acquiring foreign company	
	Number	Value (mil. dol.)	Number	Value (mil. dol.)	Number	Value (mil. dol.)
Total activity [1]	2,070	462,808	321	58,371	398	106,423
Aerospace and aircraft	7	2,038	1	14	2	1,820
Agriculture, forestry, and fishing	10	628	3	322	3	1,136
Amusement and recreation services	15	1,070	-	-	5	304
Business services	209	33,417	33	1,562	56	5,391
Chemicals and allied products	31	9,192	15	1,739	13	4,409
Commercial banks, bank holding companies	130	65,995	3	227	13	7,154
Communications equipment	35	2,093	7	427	2	13
Computer and office equipment	25	2,407	3	72	4	300
Construction firms	27	3,028	3	149	3	757
Credit institutions	23	11,423	7	961	6	720
Drugs	70	15,914	14	7,502	19	11,548
Educational services	12	1,815	1	30	3	109
Electric, gas, water distribution	75	26,240	16	1,386	4	246
Electronic and electrical equipment	72	9,577	16	1,827	17	932
Food and kindred products	36	7,033	10	1,339	8	5,999
Health services	54	10,935	2	217	1	10
Hotels and casinos	44	5,819	10	286	6	994
Insurance	56	54,893	4	13,366	5	3,095
Investment & commodity firms, dealers, exchanges						
Machinery	59	18,522	10	910	28	3,563
Measuring, medical, photo equip; clocks	24	896	6	296	10	1,391
Metal and metal products	69	12,239	11	997	21	5,394
Mining	46	6,542	8	669	8	856
Motion picture production and distribution	16	1,112	6	233	5	1,357
Oil and gas; petroleum refining	15	14,584	3	335	-	-
Other financial	111	20,742	19	1,585	12	3,827
Paper and allied products	7	7,615	1	11	2	292
Prepackaged software	12	1,384	4	451	3	327
Printing, publishing, and allied services	134	11,884	19	1,261	38	982
Radio & television broadcasting stations	17	2,612	7	1,650	3	4,099
Real estate, mortgage bankers and brokers	71	13,132	-	-	11	5,420
Retail trade-food stores	123	26,559	21	3,005	13	16,378
Retail trade—general merchandise and apparel	19	2,115	3	889	2	19
Rubber & misc plastic products	18	1,960	-	-	5	348
Savings and loans, mutual savings banks	17	1,159	2	106	5	488
Soaps, cosmetics, & personal-care products	40	7,430	-	-	1	24
Telecommunications	7	425	2	3,089	3	6,951
Textile and apparel products	49	5,973	5	8,237	11	2,789
Tobacco products	27	7,416	2	27	3	94
Transportation and shipping (except air)	4	3,103	-	-	-	-
Transportation equipment	31	5,129	5	469	8	2,188
Wholesale trade—durable goods	17	2,471	5	162	4	227
Wholesale trade-nondurable goods	31	2,405	5	115	10	558
Wood products, furniture, and fixtures	26	2,864	2	23	3	2,622
	18	5,607	4	545	2	84

- Represents zero. [1] Includes other industries not shown separately.

Source of Tables 741 and 742: Thomson Financial, Newark, NJ, Merger & Corporate Transactions Database (copyright).

No. 743. Venture Capital Commitments by Source: 1990 to 2003

[In billions of dollars (3.4 represents $3,400,000,000). Venture capital commitment: investment in venture capital partnerships]

Source	1990	1995	1996	1997	1998	1999	2000	2001	2002	2003
Capital commitments, total	3.4	10.0	11.6	18.2	30.4	58.2	105.4	37.3	9.1	11.0
Corporations	0.2	0.5	2.3	4.6	3.6	8.3	3.9	1.0	0.2	0.2
Endowments & foundations	0.5	2.0	1.4	3.0	1.9	10.0	22.2	8.1	1.9	2.2
Individuals & families	0.4	1.7	0.8	2.3	3.4	5.6	12.4	3.5	0.8	1.1
Financial & insurance	0.3	2.0	0.4	1.1	3.2	9.0	24.6	9.1	2.3	2.7
Pension funds	1.9	3.8	6.8	7.2	18.3	25.3	42.3	15.6	3.8	4.7

Source: Venture Economics Investor Services, Boston, MA, *Venture Capital Journal*, monthly.

No. 744. Patents and Trademarks: 1980 to 2003

[In thousands (113.0 represents 113,000). Calendar year data. Covers U.S. patents issued to citizens of the United States and residents of foreign countries. For data on foreign countries, see Table 1348]

Type	1980	1990	1995	1998	1999	2000	2001	2002	2003
Patent applications filed	113.0	176.7	228.8	261.4	289.5	315.8	346.6	357.5	367.0
Inventions	104.3	164.6	212.4	243.0	270.2	295.9	326.5	334.4	342.4
Designs	7.8	11.3	15.4	17.1	17.8	18.3	18.3	20.9	22.6
Botanical plants	0.2	0.4	0.5	0.7	0.9	0.8	0.9	1.1	1.0
Reissues	0.6	0.5	0.6	0.6	0.7	0.8	0.8	1.0	0.9
Patents issued	66.2	99.2	113.8	163.1	169.1	176.0	184.0	184.4	187.0
Inventions	61.8	90.4	101.4	147.5	153.5	157.5	166.0	167.3	169.0
Individuals	13.8	17.3	17.4	22.5	22.8	22.4	21.7	20.5	19.6
Corporations:									
United States	27.7	36.1	44.0	66.1	69.4	70.9	74.3	74.2	75.3
Foreign [1]	19.1	36.0	39.1	57.9	60.3	63.3	69.0	71.8	73.2
U.S. Government	1.2	1.0	1.0	1.0	1.0	0.9	1.0	0.9	0.9
Designs	3.9	8.0	11.7	14.8	14.7	17.4	16.9	15.5	16.6
Botanical plants	0.1	0.3	0.4	0.6	0.4	0.5	0.6	1.1	1.0
Reissues	0.3	0.4	0.3	0.3	0.4	0.5	0.5	0.5	0.4
U.S. residents [2]	40.8	52.8	64.4	90.6	94.0	96.9	98.6	97.1	98.6
Foreign country residents [2]	25.4	46.2	49.4	72.5	75.1	79.1	85.4	87.3	88.5
Percent of total	38.4	46.7	43.4	44.4	44.4	44.9	46.4	47.3	47.3
Other published documents [3]	(Z)	0.1	0.1	0.1	0.1	0.1	0.1	(Z)	(Z)
Trademarks:									
Applications filed	46.8	127.3	181.0	238.0	328.6	361.8	277.3	264.1	273.6
Issued	24.7	60.8	92.5	136.1	191.9	115.2	142.9	176.0	166.6
Trademarks	18.9	53.6	85.6	129.9	184.9	106.4	109.6	146.9	130.9
Trademark renewals	5.9	7.2	6.9	6.2	7.0	8.8	33.3	29.2	35.6

Z Less than 50. [1] Includes patents to foreign governments. [2] Includes patents for inventions, designs, botanical plants, and reissues. [3] Includes Defensive Publications, a practice which began in November 1968 and ended in July 1986; and Statutory Invention Registrations, the current practice, which began May 1985. These documents are patent applications, which are published to provide the defensive properties of a patent, but do not have the enforceable rights of a patent.

Source: U.S. Patent and Trademark Office, "Statistical Reports Available For Viewing, Calendar Year Patent Statistics"; <http://www.uspto.gov/web/offices/ac/ido/oeip/taf/reports.htm> and unpublished data.

No. 745. Patents by Industry: 1980 to 2002

[Based on the 1972 Standard Industrial Classification (SIC); see text, this section. Includes all U.S. patents for inventions granted to residents of the United States, its territories, and foreign citizens. Individual industries may not add to total since a patent may be recorded in more than one industry category. Data for all years have been revised to reflect the U.S. Patent Classification System as of December 2002]

Industry	SIC code	1980	1990	1995	2000	2001	2002
Total	(X)	61,819	90,365	101,419	157,495	166,037	167,334
Durable goods:							
Stone, clay, and glass products	32	1,222	1,639	1,574	2,119	2,414	2,435
Primary metals	33, 3462-3	706	913	901	980	1,200	1,282
Fabricated metal products [1]	34	5,013	6,786	5,930	8,550	8,380	8,225
Machinery, except electrical	35	14,321	19,256	21,408	35,507	36,994	35,986
Electronic and other electric equipment	36, 3825	10,724	19,002	25,154	44,175	48,295	50,736
Transportation equipment	37, 348	3,115	4,734	4,472	6,729	7,783	7,596
Instruments and related products [2]	38	7,452	12,254	14,383	20,651	20,983	21,632
Nondurable goods:							
Food and kindred products	20	484	730	601	925	882	757
Textile mill products	22	420	502	609	743	718	594
Chemicals and allied products	28	9,880	12,499	13,564	19,435	20,867	20,948
Oil and gas extraction, petroleum products	13, 29	595	664	643	752	793	730
Rubber and miscellaneous plastics products	30	2,607	3,801	3,934	5,036	5,074	5,161
Other industries	(X)	5,281	7,585	8,247	11,892	11,654	11,252

X Not applicable. [1] Excludes SIC groups 3462, 3463, and 348. [2] Excludes SIC group 3825.

Source: U.S. Patent and Trademark Office, *Patenting Trends in the United States, State Country Report, 1963-2002.*

No. 746. Patents by State: 2003

[Includes only U.S. patents granted to residents of the United States and territories]

State	Total	Inventions	Designs	Botanical plants	Re-issues	State	Total	Inventions	Designs	Botanical plants	Re-issues
U.S.[1]	98,563	87,901	10,045	395	222	Missouri	945	823	117	5	-
Alabama	459	397	55	5	2	Montana	125	121	4	-	-
Alaska	43	37	6	-	-	Nebraska	240	184	43	13	-
Arizona	1,714	1,582	127	-	5	Nevada	455	388	66	-	1
Arkansas	176	152	23	1	-	New Hampshire	730	677	53	-	-
California	22,075	19,692	2,138	197	48	New Jersey	3,920	3,522	381	4	13
Colorado	2,301	2,068	227	2	4	New Mexico	404	390	14	-	-
Connecticut	1,844	1,667	169	1	7	New York	6,921	6,237	664	3	17
Delaware	372	346	25	-	1	North Carolina	2,174	1,874	291	6	3
Dist. of Columbia	50	49	1	-	-	North Dakota	62	55	7	-	-
Florida	3,119	2,561	490	64	4	Ohio	3,892	3,184	699	1	8
Georgia	1,535	1,336	190	5	4	Oklahoma	563	516	44	1	2
Hawaii	96	75	20	1	-	Oregon	1,867	1,665	181	18	3
Idaho	1,850	1,803	43	-	4	Pennsylvania	3,555	3,177	370	4	4
Illinois	3,964	3,299	645	15	5	Rhode Island	325	266	58	-	1
Indiana	1,676	1,385	282	4	5	South Carolina	649	570	78	-	1
Iowa	711	665	41	-	5	South Dakota	89	80	9	-	-
Kansas	491	428	63	-	-	Tennessee	973	799	168	4	2
Kentucky	494	438	55	-	1	Texas	6,376	6,027	331	7	11
Louisiana	438	390	41	-	2	Utah	724	637	86	-	1
Maine	165	151	14	5	-	Vermont	465	428	36	-	1
Maryland	1,577	1,453	114	3	7	Virginia	1,249	1,114	129	-	6
Massachusetts	4,191	3,909	273	1	8	Washington	2,516	2,285	217	6	8
Michigan	4,218	3,855	344	7	12	West Virginia	141	139	2	-	-
Minnesota	3,260	2,955	285	6	14	Wisconsin	2,082	1,786	290	4	2
Mississippi	184	162	20	2	-	Wyoming	84	71	13	-	-

- Represents zero.   [1] Includes U.S. territories not shown separately.

Source: U.S. Patent and Trademark Office, unpublished data.

No. 747. Copyright Registration by Subject Matter: 1990 to 2003

[In thousands (590.7 represents 590,700). For years ending September 30. Comprises claims to copyrights registered for both U.S. and foreign works. Semiconductor chips and renewals are not considered copyright registration claims]

Subject matter	1990	2000	2002	2003	Subject matter	1990	2000	2002	2003
Total copyright claims	590.7	497.6	501.0	514.1	Works of the visual arts [3]	76.7	85.8	79.9	93.4
Monographs [1]	179.7	169.7	199.2	188.0					
Serials	111.5	69.0	60.8	56.3	Semiconductor chip products	1.0	0.7	0.5	0.4
Sound recordings	37.5	34.2	37.1	47.0	Renewals	51.8	16.8	19.1	19.5
Musical works [2]	185.3	138.9	124.0	129.4					

[1] Includes computer software and machine readable works.   [2] Includes dramatic works, accompanying music, choreography, pantomimes, motion pictures, and filmstrips.   [3] Two-dimensional works of fine and graphic art, including prints and art reproductions; sculptural works; technical drawings and models; photographs; commercial prints and labels; works of applied arts, cartographic works, and multimedia works.

Source: The Library of Congress, Copyright Office, *Annual Report*.

No. 748. Net Stock of Private Fixed Assets by Industry: 1990 to 2001

[In billions of dollars (12,760 represents $12,760,000,000,000). Estimates as of Dec. 31. Net stock estimates are presented in terms of current cost and cover equipment, software, and structures. Based on the 1987 Standard Industrial Classification]

Industry	1990	1995	1998	1999	2000	2001
Private fixed assets	12,760	15,908	18,650	19,880	21,215	22,190
Agriculture, forestry, and fishing	481	551	620	647	674	696
Mining	431	455	530	531	581	610
Construction	82	101	126	137	144	146
Manufacturing	1,217	1,457	1,654	1,714	1,777	1,810
Durable goods	636	747	860	893	932	953
Nondurable goods	581	711	794	821	846	858
Transportation and public utilities	1,855	2,232	2,471	2,578	2,764	2,869
Transportation	582	692	766	777	817	831
Communications	436	549	653	712	806	860
Electric, gas, and sanitary services	837	991	1,052	1,089	1,141	1,178
Wholesale trade	286	379	464	501	541	561
Retail trade	391	514	618	658	704	734
Finance, insurance, and real estate [1]	7,466	9,481	11,242	12,091	12,906	13,571
Real estate	6,944	8,779	10,362	11,123	11,855	12,481
Owner-occupied housing	4,337	5,718	6,827	7,377	7,900	8,372
Tenant-occupied housing	1,640	1,880	2,153	2,264	2,382	2,469
Other	967	1,182	1,383	1,482	1,573	1,640
Services	552	739	925	1,024	1,125	1,193

[1] Includes other industries not shown separately.

Source: U.S. Bureau of Economic Analysis, *Survey of Current Business*, September 2002.

No. 749. Gross Private Domestic Investment in Current and Real (2000) Dollars: 1990 to 2002

[In billions of dollars (861 represents $861,000,000,000). Covers equipment, software, and structures]

Item	1990	1995	1997	1998	1999	2000	2001	2002
CURRENT DOLLARS								
Gross private domestic investment . . .	861	1,144	1,390	1,509	1,626	1,736	1,607	1,589
Less: Consumption of fixed capital	552	713	800	851	914	991	1,061	1,078
Equals: Net private domestic investment	309	431	590	658	711	745	546	511
Fixed investment	846	1,113	1,318	1,438	1,559	1,679	1,643	1,584
Less: Consumption of fixed capital . . .	552	713	800	851	914	991	1,061	1,078
Equals: Net fixed investment	295	400	518	587	644	688	582	506
Nonresidential	622	810	969	1,053	1,134	1,232	1,174	1,080
Residential	224	303	349	386	425	447	469	504
Change in private inventories	15	31	72	71	67	57	-36	5
CHAINED (2000) DOLLARS								
Gross private domestic investment . . .	895	1,134	1,388	1,524	1,643	1,736	1,591	1,572
Less: Consumption of fixed capital	572	707	797	856	922	991	1,055	1,079
Equals: Net private domestic investment	323	427	591	669	721	745	536	494
Fixed investment	887	1,110	1,321	1,455	1,576	1,679	1,626	1,566
Nonresidential	595	763	934	1,038	1,133	1,232	1,177	1,093
Residential	299	353	389	418	444	447	449	470
Change in private inventories	15	30	71	73	69	57	-36	6

Source: U.S. Bureau of Economic Analysis, *National Income and Product Accounts, Volume 1, 1929-2000*, and *Survey of Current Business*, April 2004. See also <http://www.bea.gov/bea/dn/nipaweb/selecttable.asp>.

No. 750. Capital Expenditures: 1999 to 2002

[In billions of dollars (1,047 represents $1,047,000,000,000). Based on a sample survey and subject to sampling error; see source for details]

Item	All companies				Companies with employees				Companies without employees			
	1999	2000	2001	2002	1999	2000	2001	2002	1999	2000	2001	2002
Capital expenditures, total	1,047	1,161	1,109	1,009	975	1,090	1,052	928	72	71	57	80
Structures	320	364	364	349	294	338	346	316	26	26	18	33
New	296	329	336	308	276	309	324	287	20	20	12	21
Used	24	35	28	41	18	29	22	29	6	6	6	12
Equipment and software.	727	797	745	660	681	752	706	612	46	45	39	47
New	690	751	706	619	656	718	679	584	33	32	27	34
Used	37	46	39	41	24	34	27	28	13	12	12	13
Capital leases	17	20	16	16	17	19	16	15	1	(Z)	(Z)	(Z)

Z Less than $500 million.

Source: U.S. Census Bureau, *Annual Capital Expenditures, 2002*, Series ACE.

No. 751. Capital Expenditures by Industry: 2000 and 2002

[In billions of dollars (1,090 represents $1,090,000,000,000). Covers only companies with employees. Based on the North American Industry Classification System (NAICS), 1997; see text, this section. Based on a sample survey and subject to sampling error; see source for details]

Industry	NAICS code	2000	2002	Industry	NAICS code	2000	2002
Total expenditures. . . .	(X)	1,090	928	Professional, scientific, and technical services.	54	34	27
Forestry, fishing, and agricultural services.	113-115	1	2	Management of companies and enterprises	55	5	3
Mining.	21	43	42	Admin/support waste mgt/remediation services. . .	56	18	15
Utilities.	22	61	67	Educational services.	61	18	19
Construction	23	25	25	Health care and social assistance.	62	52	59
Manufacturing	31-33	215	163	Arts, entertainment, and recreation	71	19	14
Durable goods	321, 327, 33	134	90	Accommodation and food services	72	26	23
Nondurable goods	31, 322-326	81	73	Other services (except public administration)	81	21	21
Wholesale trade	42	34	28	Structure and equipment expenditures serving multiple industry categories. . . .	(X)	2	1
Retail trade.	44-45	70	59				
Transportation and warehousing	48-49	60	48				
Information.	51	160	89				
Finance and insurance	52	134	126				
Real estate and rental and leasing.	53	92	97				

X Not applicable.

Source: U.S. Census Bureau, *Annual Capital Expenditures, 2002* Series ACE.

No. 752. Composite Indexes of Leading, Coincident, and Lagging Economic Indicators: 1990 to 2003

Item	Unit	1990	1995	2000	2001	2002	2003
Leading index, composite	1996=100	95.0	98.2	109.4	108.5	110.9	112.3
Average weekly hours, manufacturing	Hours	40.5	41.3	41.2	40.4	40.5	40.4
Average weekly initial claims for unemployment insurance	1,000	385.4	359.1	299.4	406.8	404.5	402.4
Manufacturers' new orders, consumer goods and materials (1982 dol.)	Mil. dol.	112,431	133,038	152,072	142,732	142,633	141,484
Vendor performance, slower deliveries diffusion index [1]	Percent	47.9	52.8	53.3	48.0	53.2	53.0
Manufacturers' new orders, nondefense capital goods (1982 dol.)	Mil. dol.	31,882	37,329	49,878	41,859	39,010	40,885
Building permits, new private housing units	1,000	1,155	1,336	1,598	1,637	1,750	1,829
Stock prices, 500 common stocks [1]	1941-43=10	334.6	541.6	1,426.8	1,192.1	995.6	963.7
Money supply, M2 (2000 dol.)	Bil. dol.	4,010	3,893	4,802	5,118	5,433	5,706
Interest rate spread, 10-year Treasury bonds less federal funds	Percent	0.45	0.74	-0.21	1.13	2.94	2.89
Index of consumer expectations [1]	1966:1=100	70.2	83.2	102.7	82.3	84.6	81.4
Coincident index, composite	1996=100	88.5	97.1	115.4	114.8	114.3	114.7
Employees on nonagricultural payrolls	1,000	109,489	117,306	131,790	131,830	130,376	130,055
Personal income less transfer payments (2000 dol.)	Bil. dol.	5,321	5,760	7,345	7,370	7,366	7,412
Industrial production	1997=100	77.2	89.3	115.4	111.5	110.9	111.3
Manufacturing and trade sales (2000 dol.)	Mil. dol.	592,717	698,196	843,871	836,407	850,168	868,209
Lagging index, composite	1996=100	101.5	99.1	106.5	105.0	102.1	100.0
Average duration of unemployment	Weeks	12.0	16.6	12.6	13.1	16.7	19.2
Inventories to sales ratio, manufacturing and trade (2000 dol.)	Ratio	1.43	1.37	1.38	1.40	1.34	1.33
Change in labor cost per unit of output, manufacturing	Percent	1.1	-2.1	2.1	-11.2	-1.8	-
Average prime rate	Percent	10.0	8.8	9.2	6.9	4.7	4.1
Commercial and industrial loans outstanding (2000 dol.)	Mil. dol.	664,764	618,215	934,354	828,325	671,306	577,296
Consumer installment credit to personal income ratio	Percent	16.5	17.5	19.1	20.3	21.0	21.2
Change in consumer price index for services	Percent	5.8	3.5	3.8	3.9	3.2	3.1

- Represents zero.   [1] Data are from private sources and provided through the courtesy of the compilers and are subject to their copyrights: stock prices, Standard & Poors Corporation; index of consumer expectations, University of Michigan's Survey Research Center; vendor perfomance, Institute for Supply Management.

Source: The Conference Board, New York, NY 10022-6601, *Business Cycle Indicators*, monthly, <http://www.globalindicators.org/> (copyright).

No. 753. Business Cycle Expansions and Contractions—Months of Duration: 1918 to 2001

[A trough is the low point of a business cycle; a peak is the high point. Contraction, or recession, is the period from peak to subsequent trough; expansion is the period from trough to subsequent peak. Business cycle reference dates are determined by the National Bureau of Economic Research, Inc.]

Business cycle reference date				Contraction (peak to trough)	Expansion (previous trough to this peak)	Length of cycle	
Peak		Trough				Trough from previous trough	Peak from previous peak
Month	Year	Month	Year				
August	1918	March	1919	7	[1]44	[1]51	[2]67
January	1920	July	1921	18	10	28	17
May	1923	July	1924	14	22	36	40
October	1926	November	1927	13	27	40	41
August	1929	March	1933	43	21	64	34
May	1937	June	1938	13	50	63	93
February	1945	October	1945	8	80	88	93
November	1948	October	1949	11	37	48	45
July	1953	May	1954	10	45	55	56
August	1957	April	1958	8	39	47	49
April	1960	February	1961	10	24	34	32
December	1969	November	1970	11	106	117	116
November	1973	March	1975	16	36	52	47
January	1980	July	1980	6	58	64	74
July	1981	November	1982	16	12	28	18
July	1990	March	1991	8	92	100	108
March	2001	November	2001	8	120	128	128
Average, all cycles:							
1854 to 2001 (32 cycles)				17	38	55	[3]56
1854 to 1919 (16 cycles)				22	27	48	[4]49
1919 to 1945 (6 cycles)				18	35	53	53
1945 to 2001 (10 cycles)				10	57	67	67
Average, peacetime cycles:							
1854 to 2001 (27 cycles)				18	33	51	[5]52
1854 to 1919 (14 cycles)				22	24	46	[6]47
1919 to 1945 (5 cycles)				20	26	46	45
1945 to 2001 (8 cycles)				10	52	63	63

[1] Previous trough: December 1914.   [2] Previous peak: January 1913.   [3] 31 cycles.   [4] 15 cycles.   [5] 26 cycles.   [6] 13 cycles.

Source: National Bureau of Economic Research, Inc., Cambridge, MA, "Business Cycle Expansions and Contractions"; <http://www.nber.org/cycles.html>; (accessed: 26 April 2004).

No. 754. Industrial Production Indexes by Industry: 1980 to 2003

[Except as noted, based on the North American Industry Classification System (NAICS); 1997; see text, this section. Minus sign (-) indicates decrease]

Industry	NAICS code	1980	1985	1990	1992	1993	1994	1995	1996	1997	1998	1999	2000	2001	2002	2003	2000-2001	2001-2002	2002-2003
		Index (1997=100)															Percent change		
Total index	(X)	62.5	68.1	77.2	78.2	80.8	85.2	89.3	93.1	100.0	105.9	110.6	115.4	111.5	110.9	111.1	-3.4	-0.6	0.2
Manufacturing (SIC) [1]	(X)	58.2	65.1	74.9	76.1	78.8	83.6	88.0	92.1	100.0	106.8	112.1	117.4	112.7	111.8	112.2	-4.0	-0.7	0.3
Manufacturing (NAICS)	31-33	57.1	63.8	73.8	75.3	78.1	83.1	87.8	92.1	100.0	106.8	112.3	117.7	113.1	112.5	112.6	-3.9	-0.5	0.1
Durable goods	(X)	48.7	55.3	64.4	65.6	69.3	75.4	81.9	89.0	100.0	110.7	119.9	129.5	123.5	122.9	125.4	-4.6	-0.5	2.0
Wood products	321	68.4	75.3	86.8	85.7	86.7	91.8	94.0	97.1	100.0	105.0	108.8	107.2	106.0	100.6	99.2	-6.2	-0.1	-1.4
Nonmetallic mineral products	327	77.6	77.7	85.1	81.9	83.6	88.3	90.9	96.7	100.0	104.7	106.1	106.0	101.4	99.9	100.8	-4.4	-1.5	0.9
Primary metals	331	102.3	75.2	85.5	82.2	86.2	92.6	93.7	95.9	100.0	102.3	101.7	98.5	89.0	86.5	84.6	-9.6	-2.8	-2.3
Fabricated metal products	332	75.9	75.2	78.3	77.1	80.0	87.0	92.3	95.8	100.0	103.0	103.8	107.9	100.1	97.4	94.5	-7.3	-2.7	-2.9
Machinery	333	79.2	69.5	77.6	72.6	78.1	85.5	91.5	94.9	100.0	102.6	100.4	105.8	93.8	86.9	86.7	-11.4	-7.4	-0.2
Computers and electronic products	334	10.1	20.0	28.7	33.6	37.1	44.2	57.5	73.8	100.0	129.1	169.0	224.0	226.1	234.7	266.5	-1.0	3.8	13.6
Electrical equip, appliances, and components	335	75.3	76.8	79.7	80.2	85.2	91.4	93.5	96.4	100.0	104.1	105.9	111.6	100.9	96.4	93.9	-9.6	-4.5	-2.6
Motor vehicles and parts	3361-3	45.0	62.9	64.7	70.4	77.8	89.4	92.0	92.7	100.0	105.2	116.4	116.2	105.6	114.5	117.5	-9.1	8.4	2.6
Aerospace and other misc transportation equipment	3364-9	104.2	101.1	121.6	108.3	101.0	90.7	86.4	89.6	100.0	115.9	111.8	98.3	106.3	97.5	94.5	8.2	-8.3	-3.0
Furniture and related products	337	65.8	76.1	82.0	81.7	85.2	88.1	89.6	90.3	100.0	107.1	110.7	113.0	106.2	103.4	101.1	-6.0	-2.6	-2.3
Miscellaneous products	339	53.4	61.5	79.1	84.1	88.9	89.5	92.8	97.5	100.0	106.0	108.2	114.8	114.1	116.0	116.6	-0.6	1.7	0.5
Nondurable goods	(X)	70.3	77.0	88.2	90.1	91.4	94.6	96.2	96.5	100.0	101.5	102.2	102.8	99.8	99.2	97.0	-2.9	-0.6	-2.2
Food, beverage and tobacco products	311,2	77.0	84.0	91.2	93.1	92.8	96.0	98.7	98.0	100.0	102.8	100.9	102.2	102.1	101.3	99.7	-0.1	-0.7	-3.6
Textile and product mills	313,4	76.1	77.7	81.2	89.3	92.8	97.9	96.9	94.7	100.0	98.8	99.0	97.2	87.5	83.9	77.6	-10.0	-4.2	-7.5
Apparel and leather	315,6	109.6	106.8	98.4	100.3	102.4	103.6	102.8	100.4	100.0	94.6	90.5	87.3	77.9	70.8	63.2	-10.8	-9.0	-10.7
Paper	322	74.5	81.4	92.0	94.5	95.6	99.7	101.1	98.0	100.0	101.1	101.9	105.8	99.9	99.1	97.9	-5.6	-0.8	-1.2
Printing and related support	323	56.8	76.3	92.5	94.6	94.9	95.9	97.3	98.0	100.0	101.0	101.9	102.3	96.9	93.7	89.4	-5.3	-3.3	-4.6
Petroleum and coal products	324	92.1	85.9	91.4	89.7	90.3	94.5	94.5	96.7	100.0	99.9	104.0	105.9	103.9	104.6	105.5	-1.9	0.7	0.8
Chemical	325	65.6	70.1	87.0	88.0	89.0	91.3	92.7	94.6	100.0	99.8	103.8	105.5	103.9	105.3	105.8	-1.4	1.3	0.2
Plastics and rubber products	326	41.4	56.3	72.0	76.7	82.2	89.0	91.1	94.3	100.0	101.8	103.8	109.6	103.1	103.3	102.0	-5.9	0.2	-1.1
Other manufacturing (non-NAICS) [2]	1133, 5111	81.8	94.6	99.0	90.8	93.5	94.9	92.9	92.1	100.0	106.5	109.9	112.2	105.6	102.0	105.8	-5.9	-3.4	3.7
Mining	21	106.4	102.6	98.8	94.4	94.4	96.6	96.4	98.1	100.0	98.2	94.0	96.3	96.8	93.0	93.1	0.5	-3.9	0.1
Utilities		69.3	74.0	86.8	88.9	92.0	93.9	97.2	100.0	100.0	102.5	105.5	108.6	108.1	111.3	110.7	-0.5	3.0	-0.5
Electric pwr generation, transmsn & distribution	2211,2	64.3	72.6	86.9	88.5	91.7	93.7	97.1	99.7	100.0	104.1	107.1	110.2	109.9	113.3	113.5	-0.3	3.1	0.2
Natural gas distribution	2212	93.0	81.4	86.0	90.8	94.2	94.9	97.3	102.0	100.0	93.4	96.1	99.1	97.7	99.9	101.6	-1.4	2.2	1.7

X Not applicable. [1] Standard Industrial Classification (SIC); see text, this section. [2] Those industries—logging and newspaper, periodical, book, and directory publishing— that have traditionally been considered to be manufacturing.

Source: Board of Governors of the Federal Reserve System, *Statistical Supplement to the Federal Reserve Bulletin,* monthly; and *Industrial Production and Capacity Utilization,* Statistical Release G.17, monthly.

[1997 output=100. Annual figures are averages of monthly data. Capacity represents estimated quantity of output relative to output in 1997 which the current stock of plant and equipment was capable of producing]

Year	Index of capacity		Relation of output to capacity (percent)				
				Stage of process			
	Total industry	Manufacturing	Total industry	Crude [1]	Primary and semifinished [2]	Finished [3]	Manufacturing
1980	77.3	73.8	80.9	89.2	78.9	79.7	78.8
1985	85.7	82.9	79.5	83.4	80.1	77.3	78.5
1990	93.7	91.7	82.4	88.8	82.3	80.7	81.6
1991	95.6	93.8	79.6	86.0	79.4	77.9	78.3
1992	97.4	95.8	80.3	85.7	80.9	78.2	79.4
1993	99.4	98.2	81.3	85.5	83.0	78.2	80.3
1994	102.1	101.2	83.4	87.2	86.3	79.1	82.6
1995	106.8	106.4	83.6	87.9	86.4	79.2	82.7
1996	113.0	113.5	82.4	87.6	85.1	78.0	81.1
1997	119.6	121.0	83.6	89.0	85.7	79.8	82.6
1998	127.7	130.3	83.0	86.1	84.4	80.6	82.0
1999	134.2	137.8	82.4	85.9	84.8	78.8	81.4
2000	139.8	144.6	82.6	87.4	85.3	78.2	81.1
2001	144.1	149.4	77.4	85.1	78.6	74.3	75.4
2002	146.7	151.4	75.6	82.9	77.5	71.9	73.9
2003	148.6	153.0	74.8	83.5	76.7	71.0	73.4

[1] Crude processing, covers a relatively small portion of total industrial capacity and consists of logging (NAICS 1133), much of mining (excluding stone, sand, and gravel mining and oil and gas drilling, which are NAICS 21231, 21221-2, and 213111) and some basic manufacturing industries, including basic chemicals (NAICS 3251); fertilizers, pesticides, and other agricultural chemicals (NAICS 32531,2); pulp, paper, and paperboard mills (NAICS 3221); and alumina, aluminum, and other nonferrous production and processing mills (NAICS 3313,4). [2] Primary and semifinished processing loosely corresponds to the previously published aggregate, primary processing. Includes utilities and portions of several 2-digit SIC industries included in the former advanced processing group. These include printing and related support activities (NAICS 3231); paints and adhesives (NAICS 3255); and newspaper, periodical, book, and directory publishers (NAICS 5111). [3] Finished processing generally corresponds to the previously published aggregate, advanced processing. Includes oil and gas well drilling and carpet and rug mills.

Source: Board of Governors of the Federal Reserve System, *Industrial Production and Capacity Utilization*, Statistical Release G.17, monthly. (Based on data from Federal Reserve Board, U.S. Dept. of Commerce, U.S. Bureau of Labor Statistics, and McGraw-Hill Information Systems Company, New York, NY; and other sources.)

No. 756. Manufacturing and Trade—Sales and Inventories: 1992 to 2003

[In billions of dollars (541 represents $541,000,000,000), except ratios. Based on North American Industry Classification System (NAICS) 1997; see text, this section]

Year	Sales, average monthly [1]				Inventories [2]				Inventory-sales ratios [3]			
	Total	Manufacturing	Retail trade	Merchant wholesalers	Total	Manufacturing	Retail trade	Merchant wholesalers	Total	Manufacturing	Retail trade	Merchant wholesalers
1992	541	242	155	144	840	379	268	193	1.53	1.57	1.67	1.31
1993	568	252	166	151	867	380	286	201	1.50	1.51	1.68	1.31
1994	611	270	180	161	931	400	312	218	1.47	1.44	1.66	1.29
1995	655	290	189	176	989	425	330	234	1.48	1.44	1.72	1.30
1996	687	300	201	187	1,009	431	341	237	1.46	1.43	1.67	1.28
1997	724	320	210	195	1,050	444	351	255	1.42	1.37	1.64	1.27
1998	744	325	220	198	1,082	449	365	268	1.44	1.39	1.62	1.32
1999	788	336	240	212	1,142	464	394	284	1.41	1.35	1.59	1.30
2000	835	351	256	229	1,201	481	418	302	1.41	1.35	1.59	1.29
2001	819	331	263	225	1,146	452	406	288	1.44	1.42	1.58	1.32
2002	822	324	269	229	1,164	444	431	289	1.40	1.37	1.56	1.25
2003	857	333	283	240	1,185	439	451	295	1.37	1.33	1.56	1.21

[1] Averages of monthly not seasonally adjusted figures. [2] Seasonally adjusted end-of-year data. [3] Averages of seasonally adjusted monthly ratios.

Source: U.S. Council of Economic Advisors, *Economic Indicators*, March 2004.

No. 757. Corporate Profits, Taxes, and Dividends: 1990 to 2003

[In billions of dollars (438 represents $438,000,000,000). Covers corporations organized for profit and other entities treated as corporations. Represents profits to U.S. residents, without deduction of depletion charges and exclusive of capital gains and losses; intercorporate dividends from profits of domestic corporations are eliminated; net receipts of dividends, reinvested earnings of incorporated foreign affiliates and earnings of unincorporated foreign affiliates are added. CCA=capital consumption adjustment]

Item	1990	1995	1999	2000	2001	2002	2003
Corporate profits with IVA and CCA.	438	697	851	818	770	904	1,070
Taxes on corporate income	145	219	259	265	201	195	225
Profits after tax with IVA and CCA	292	478	593	553	569	709	845
Net dividends	169	254	337	378	373	398	431
Undistributed profits with IVA and CCA .	123	224	255	175	196	311	414
Cash flow:							
Net cash flow with IVA and CCA	491	711	887	865	937	1,058	1,164
Undistributed profits with IVA and CCA .	123	224	255	175	196	311	414
Consumption of fixed capital	368	487	632	690	741	747	750
Less: Inventory valuation adjustment (IVA)	-13	-18	1	-14	9	-2	-13
Equals: Net cash flow	504	729	886	879	928	1,060	1,177

Source: U.S. Bureau of Economic Analysis, *National Income and Product Accounts, Volume 1, 1929-2000*, and *Survey of Current Business*, monthly. See also <http://www.bea.gov/bea/dn/nipaweb/selecttable.asp>.

No. 758. Corporate Profits Before Taxes by Industry: 1998 to 2002

[In millions of dollars (718,270 represents $718,270,000,000). Profits are without inventory valuation and capital consumption adjustments. Minus sign (-) indicates loss. See headnote, Table 757]

Industry	NAICS code [1]	1998	1999	2000	2001	2002
Corporate profits before tax.	(X)	718,270	775,876	773,398	696,766	744,971
Domestic industries.	(X)	615,320	654,363	627,695	535,293	591,591
Agriculture, forestry, fishing, and hunting	11	709	1,934	1,621	1,297	997
Mining.	21	4,561	3,509	14,733	16,198	6,161
Utilities	221	32,543	33,237	24,896	23,489	22,372
Construction.	23	35,238	41,051	41,867	44,106	40,776
Manufacturing.	31-33	146,593	148,151	153,317	51,106	72,223
Wholesale trade	42	45,882	55,080	61,693	47,732	52,187
Retail trade	44-45	64,905	66,267	61,297	70,031	76,320
Transportation and warehousing	48-49	20,736	16,482	15,164	-591	-1,910
Information.	51	19,980	10,214	-17,748	-27,601	-20,818
Finance and insurance.	52	106,975	126,704	113,371	131,415	152,760
Real estate and rental and leasing	53	10,245	9,807	9,407	9,674	4,792
Professional, scientific, and technical services.	54	24,855	20,686	1,416	8,847	13,941
Management of companies and enterprises [2].	551111,551112	58,442	67,550	86,801	94,230	102,340
Admin/support waste mgt/remediation services.	56	8,530	9,438	8,534	10,033	10,673
Educational services	61	1,820	1,588	1,885	1,894	1,688
Health care and social assistance	62	15,415	20,550	24,913	31,363	34,287
Arts, entertainment, and recreation.	71	2,360	2,738	2,170	2,994	3,417
Accommodation and food services	72	8,757	11,737	13,934	10,935	11,426
Other services, except public administration . .	81	6,774	7,640	8,424	8,141	7,959
Rest of the world [3]	(X)	102,950	121,513	145,703	161,473	153,380

X Not applicable. [1] Based on North American Industry Classification System, 1997; see text, this section. [2] Consists of bank and other holding companies. [3] Consists of receipts by all U.S. residents, including both corporations and persons, of dividends from foreign corporations, and, for U.S. corporations, their share of reinvested earnings of their incorporated foreign affiliates, and earnings of unincorporated foreign affiliates, net of corresponding payments.

Source: U.S. Bureau of Economic Analysis, *National Income and Product Accounts, Volume 1, 1929-2000*, and *Survey of Current Business*, February 2004. See also <http://www.bea.gov/bea/dn/nipaweb/selecttable.asp>.

No. 759. Corporate Profits With Inventory Valuation and Capital Consumption Adjustments—Financial and Nonfinancial Industries: 1998 to 2003

[In billions of dollars (802 represents $802,000,000,000). Based on the North American Industry Classification System 1997 ; see text, this section. See headnote, Table 757]

Item	1998	1999	2000	2001	2002	2003
Corporate profits with IVA/CCA [1] . .	802	851	818	770	904	1,070
Domestic industries	699	730	672	609	751	905
Rest of the world	103	122	146	162	153	165
Corporate profits with IVA [1]	739	777	759	706	743	844
Domestic industries	636	655	614	544	589	679
Financial [2]	165	194	200	226	255	269
Nonfinancial	470	461	413	319	334	410
Utilities	33	33	24	24	22	24
Manufacturing	157	151	144	54	73	97
Wholesale trade	53	56	60	52	49	45
Retail trade	66	65	60	71	77	80
Transportation and warehousing	21	16	15	(Z)	-2	12
Information	20	11	-18	-27	-20	-5
Other nonfinancial [3]	120	130	128	145	136	157
Rest of the world	103	122	146	162	153	165

Z Less than $500 million. [1] Inventory valuation adjustment and capital consumption adjustment. [2] Consists of finance and insurance and bank and other holding companies. [3] Consists of agriculture, forestry, fishing, and hunting; mining; construction; real estate and rental and leasing; professional, scientific, and technical services; administrative and waste management services; educational services; health care and social assistance; arts, entertainment, and recreation; accommodation and food services; and other services, except government.

Source: U.S. Bureau of Economic Analysis, *National Income and Product Accounts, Volume 1, 1929-2000*, and *Survey of Current Business*, monthly. See also <http://www.bea.gov/bea/dn/nipaweb/selecttable.asp>.

506   Business Enterprise

No. 760. Manufacturing, Mining, and Trade Corporations—Profits and Stockholders' Equity by Industry: 2002 and 2003

[Averages of quarterly figures at annual rates. Manufacturing data exclude estimates for corporations with less than $250,000 in assets at time of sample selection. Based on sample; see source for discussion of methodology. Based on North American Industry Classification System (NAICS), 1997; see text, this section. Minus sign (-) indicates loss]

Industry	NAICS code	Ratio of profits after taxes to stockholders' equity (percent)		Profits after taxes per dollar of sales (cents)		Ratio of stockholders' equity to debt	
		2002	2003	2002	2003	2002	2003
Manufacturing	31-33	**7.4**	**12.5**	**3.2**	**5.3**	**1.4**	**1.5**
Nondurable manufacturing	(X)	14.5	17.7	5.8	7.0	1.1	1.2
Food	311	16.9	16.6	4.3	4.5	0.9	1.0
Beverage and tobacco products	312	34.0	23.5	15.3	11.6	0.9	0.8
Textile mills and textile product mills	313, 314	2.9	6.9	0.8	2.0	1.0	1.1
Apparel and leather products	315, 316	13.2	26.5	3.4	8.4	1.3	1.5
Paper	322	3.6	3.7	1.5	1.4	0.8	0.7
Printing and related support activities	323	18.5	15.4	3.5	3.0	0.8	0.8
Petroleum and coal products	324	6.4	16.9	4.2	7.2	2.2	2.6
Chemicals	325	19.2	21.0	9.2	10.4	1.1	1.1
Plastics and rubber products	326	2.1	10.0	0.8	2.5	0.9	0.8
Durable manufacturing	(X)	2.1	8.3	1.0	3.8	1.7	1.8
Wood products	321	7.9	13.9	1.8	3.2	0.9	1.0
Nonmetallic mineral products	327	-2.6	5.0	-1.1	1.8	1.0	1.0
Primary metals	331	-4.8	-0.6	-1.6	-0.2	1.0	1.1
Fabricated metal products	332	9.4	9.3	3.2	3.2	1.2	1.3
Machinery	333	-3.0	5.7	-1.6	2.7	1.3	1.5
Computer and electronic products	334	-6.4	4.9	-5.7	4.2	3.0	3.2
Electrical equipment, appliances, and components	335	19.5	17.2	10.5	10.7	2.6	2.8
Transportation equipment	336	8.3	11.8	2.0	2.8	1.3	1.2
Furniture and related products	337	14.3	10.8	3.9	3.1	1.5	1.7
Miscellaneous manufacturing	339	16.2	15.1	8.6	8.5	1.6	1.6
All mining	21	2.5	10.7	3.7	13.2	1.6	1.7
All wholesale trade	42	9.7	8.9	1.5	1.4	1.3	1.5
Durable goods	421	7.3	7.3	1.4	1.5	1.4	1.6
Nondurable goods	422	13.0	11.3	1.6	1.3	1.3	1.4
All retail trade	44-45	13.1	14.9	2.4	2.8	1.3	1.4
Food and beverage stores	445	13.4	9.8	1.7	1.2	0.8	0.8
Clothing and general merchandise stores	448, 452	12.3	15.6	2.6	3.5	1.3	1.4
All other retail trade	(X)	14.0	15.7	2.6	3.0	1.7	1.8

X Not applicable.

Source: U.S. Census Bureau, *Quarterly Financial Report for Manufacturing, Mining, and Trade Corporations.*

No. 761. Gross Product, Employment, and Capital Expenditures of Nonbank U.S. MNCs, U.S. Parents, and Foreign Affiliates: 1989 to 2001

[Gross product and capital expenditures in billions of dollars (1,365 represents $1,365,000,000,000); employees in thousands. See headnote, table 762. MNC=Multinational company. MOFA=Majority-owned foreign affiliate. Minus sign (-) indicates decrease]

Item	1989	1990	1994	1995	1999 [1]	2000 [1]	2001 [1]	Percent change at annual rates	
								1994-2000	2000-2001
GROSS PRODUCT									
MNCs worldwide:									
Parents and all affiliates	(NA)	(NA)	(NA)	(NA)	(NA)	(NA)	(NA)	(NA)	(NA)
Parents and MOFAs	1,365	(NA)	1,717	1,831	2,481	2,748	2,536	8.3	-7.7
Parents	1,045	(NA)	1,314	1,365	1,914	2,141	1,952	8.7	-8.8
Affiliates, total	(NA)	(NA)	(NA)	(NA)	(NA)	(NA)	(NA)	(NA)	(NA)
MOFAs	320	356	404	466	566	607	583	7.2	-3.8
Other	(NA)	(NA)	(NA)	(NA)	(NA)	(NA)	(NA)	(NA)	(NA)
EMPLOYEES									
MNCs worldwide:									
Parents and all affiliates	25,388	25,264	25,670	25,921	32,227	33,598	33,226	4.7	-1.1
Parents and MOFAs	23,879	23,786	24,273	24,500	30,773	32,057	31,644	4.8	-1.3
Parents	18,765	18,430	18,565	18,576	23,007	23,885	23,450	4.4	-1.8
Affiliates, total	6,622	6,834	7,105	7,345	9,220	9,713	9,776	5.5	0.6
MOFAs	5,114	5,356	5,707	5,924	7,766	8,171	8,193	6.3	0.3
Other	1,508	1,478	1,398	1,421	1,454	1,542	1,582	1.7	2.6
CAPITAL EXPENDITURES									
MNCs worldwide:									
Parents and all affiliates	277	(NA)	328	(NA)	514	(NA)	(NA)	(NA)	(NA)
Parents and MOFAs	260	275	303	324	483	507	529	9.1	4.3
Parents	202	213	232	248	370	396	417	9.5	5.2
Affiliates, total	75	(NA)	96	(NA)	144	(NA)	(NA)	(NA)	(NA)
MOFAs	59	62	71	76	113	111	111	7.7	0.7
Other	16	(NA)	25	(NA)	31	(NA)	(NA)	(NA)	(NA)

NA Not available. [1] Data for 1999 through 2001 are not strictly comparable with data prior to 1999; see source.

Source: U.S. Bureau of Economic Analysis, *Survey of Current Business,* December 2002 and unpublished data.

No. 762. U.S. Multinational Companies—Selected Characteristics: 2001

[Preliminary. In billions of dollars (13,902 represents $13,902,000,000,000), except as indicated. Consists of nonbank U.S. parent companies and their nonbank foreign affiliates. U.S. parent comprises the domestic operations of a multinational and is a U.S. person that owns or controls directly or indirectly, 10 percent or more of the voting securities of an incorporated foreign business enterprise, or an equivalent interest in an unincorporated foreign business enterprise. A U.S. person can be an incorporated business enterprise. A majority-owned foreign affiliate (MOFA) is a foreign business enterprise in which a U.S. parent company owns or controls more than 50 percent of the voting securities]

Industry [1]	NAICS code	U.S. parents				MOFAs		
		Total assets	Capital expenditures	Gross product	Employment (1,000)	Capital expenditures	Gross product	Employment (1,000)
All Industries	(X)	13,902	417.1	1,952	23,450	111.4	583	8,193
Mining	21	154	13.7	35	130	22.7	55	60
Utilities	22	705	39.8	100	410	4.8	11	88
Manufacturing [2]	31-33	4,133	157.5	855	8,779	47.2	301	4,710
Food	311	181	6.2	51	722	2.9	19	321
Beverages and tobacco products	312	150	4.3	43	223	1.5	26	214
Petroleum and coal products	324	359	20.2	94	235	3.2	46	138
Chemicals [2]	325	637	21.2	139	999	10.3	58	755
Pharmaceuticals and medicines	3254	285	10.7	66	388	4.3	27	326
Machinery	333	535	17.3	76	887	1.4	17	438
Computers and electronic products	334	501	25.9	89	1,040	8.0	36	725
Transportation equipment [2]	336	1,015	33.2	161	1,844	10.0	45	1,082
Motor vehicles, bodies and trailers, and parts	3361-3363	817	27.9	99	1,080	9.7	42	924
Wholesale trade	42	456	21.2	93	872	7.2	93	471
Information [2]	51	1,549	90.7	253	1,967	7.4	19	324
Broadcasting and telecommunications [2]	513	1,049	81.3	175	1,243	5.7	3	119
Telecommunications	5133	755	74.7	150	868	(D)	3	58
Finance (except depository institutions) and insurance [2]	52 exc. 521, 522	5,639	19.5	123	1,446	6.0	24	323
Securities, commodity contracts, and other intermediation	5231	2,246	4.6	61	459	1.6	14	111
Insurance carriers and related activities	524	3,064	12.9	57	879	0.8	9	178
Professional, scientific, and technical services [2]	54	261	11.5	102	1,045	3.5	31	500
Computer systems design and related services	5415	121	7.9	37	380	2.3	16	310
Other industries [2]	(X)	1,004	63.1	391	8,802	12.7	50	1,718
Retail trade	44-45	353	27.0	153	3,888	2.4	20	551
Transportation and warehousing	48-49	189	12.4	85	1,143	1.1	7	131

D Data withheld to avoid disclosure.   X Not applicable.   [1] Represents North American Industry Classification System, 1997 based industry of U.S. parent or industry of foreign affiliate.   [2] Includes other industries not shown separately.

Source: U.S. Bureau of Economic Analysis, unpublished data.

No. 763. U.S. Multinational Companies—Gross Product: 2000 and 2001

[In billions of dollars (2,748.1 represents $2,748,100,000,000). Gross product measures value added by a firm. See headnote, Table 762. Data are by industry of U.S. parent. Based on the North American Industry Classification System, 1997 (NAICS); see text this section]

Industry	NAICS code	U.S. multinationals		U.S. parents		Majority-owned foreign affiliates	
		2000	2001	2000	2001	2000	2001
All Industries	(X)	2,748.1	2,535.6	2,141.5	1,952.1	606.6	583.4
Mining	21	39.0	47.0	27.7	35.3	11.3	11.6
Utilities	22	85.7	110.2	80.5	100.3	5.1	9.9
Manufacturing [1]	31-33	1,410.5	1,249.4	995.1	854.5	415.3	394.8
Food	311	59.3	65.4	47.2	50.9	12.1	14.5
Beverages and tobacco products	312	74.7	73.1	48.2	42.9	26.5	30.2
Petroleum and coal products	324	232.0	207.6	111.9	94.3	120.1	113.3
Chemicals [1]	325	212.0	208.8	141.3	138.9	70.7	69.9
Pharmaceuticals and medicines	3254	96.0	100.1	63.2	65.5	32.8	34.5
Machinery	333	98.8	100.2	75.2	76.3	23.6	23.9
Computers and electronic products	334	188.0	124.8	142.1	88.6	45.9	36.1
Transportation equipment [1]	336	270.8	216.1	208.6	161.1	62.2	55.1
Motor vehicles, bodies and trailers, and parts	3361-3363	187.4	146.1	136.0	98.5	51.4	47.6
Wholesale trade	42	132.7	123.1	99.0	92.9	33.8	30.1
Information [1]	51	324.7	273.3	302.3	252.7	22.4	21.6
Broadcasting and telecommunications [1]	513	226.3	180.9	218.3	175.4	8.0	5.5
Telecommunications	5133	186.2	153.0	181.2	149.6	5.0	3.4
Finance (except depository institutions) and insurance [1]	52 exc. 521, 522	181.1	147.2	156.7	123.1	24.4	24.1
Securities, commodity contracts, and other intermediation	5231	90.4	74.4	79.3	61.1	11.1	13.3
Insurance carriers and related activities	524	80.2	66.3	70.5	57.3	9.7	9.0
Professional, scientific, and technical services [1]	54	141.4	141.6	100.7	102.4	40.8	39.1
Computer systems design and related services	5415	69.0	65.1	39.1	37.3	29.9	27.7
Other industries [1]	(X)	433.0	442.8	379.5	390.7	53.5	52.1
Retail trade	44-45	166.2	173.6	148.7	153.4	17.5	20.2
Transportation and warehousing	48-49	90.8	91.1	85.3	85.4	5.5	5.7

X Not applicable.   [1] Includes other industries not shown separately.

Source: U.S. Bureau of Economic Analysis, unpublished data.

Section 16
Science and Technology

This section presents statistics on scientific, engineering, and technological resources, with emphasis on patterns of research and development (R&D) funding and on scientific, engineering, and technical personnel; education; and employment. Also included are statistics on space program outlays and accomplishments. Principal sources of these data are the National Science Foundation (NSF) and the National Aeronautics and Space Administration (NASA).

NSF gathers data chiefly through recurring surveys. Current NSF publications containing data on funds for research and development and on scientific and engineering personnel include detailed statistical tables; issue briefs; and annual, biennial, triennial, and special reports. Titles or the areas of coverage of these reports include the following: *Science and Engineering Indicators*; *National Patterns of R&D Resources*; *Women, Minorities, and Persons with Disabilities in Science and Engineering*—science and technology data presented in chart and tabular form in a pocket-sized publication—*Federal Funds for Research and Development*; *Federal R&D Funding by Budget Function*; *Federal Support to Universities, Colleges, and Selected Nonprofit Institutions*; *Research and Development in Industry*; R&D expenditures and graduate enrollment and support in academic science and engineering; and characteristics of doctoral scientists and engineers and of recent graduates in the United States. Statistical surveys in these areas pose problems of concept and definition and the data should therefore be regarded as broad estimates rather than precise, quantitative statements. See sources for methodological and technical details.

The National Science Board's biennial *Science and Engineering Indicators* contains data and analysis of international and domestic science and technology, including measures of inputs and outputs.

The *Budget of the United States Government*, published by the U.S. Office of Management and Budget, contains summary financial data on federal R&D programs.

Research and development outlays— NSF defines research as "systematic study directed toward fuller scientific knowledge of the subject studied" and development as "the systematic use of scientific knowledge directed toward the production of useful materials, devices, systems, or methods, including design and development of prototypes and processes."

National coverage of R&D expenditures is developed primarily from periodic surveys in four principal economic sectors: (1) *Government*, made up primarily of federal executive agencies; (2) *industry*, consisting of manufacturing and nonmanufacturing firms and the federally funded research and development centers (FFRDCs) they administer; (3) *universities and colleges*, composed of universities, colleges, and their affiliated institutions, agricultural experiment stations, and associated schools of agriculture and of medicine, and FFRDCs administered by educational institutions; and (4) *other nonprofit institutions*, consisting of such organizations as private philanthropic foundations, nonprofit research institutes, voluntary health agencies, and FFRDCs administered by nonprofit organizations.

The R&D funds reported consist of current operating costs, including planning and administration costs, except as otherwise noted. They exclude funds for routine testing, mapping and surveying, collection of general-purpose data, dissemination of scientific information, and training of scientific personnel.

Scientists, engineers, and technicians—Scientists and engineers are defined as persons engaged in scientific and engineering work at a level requiring a knowledge of sciences equivalent at least to that acquired through completion of a 4-year college course. Technicians are defined as persons engaged in technical work at a level requiring knowledge acquired through a technical institute, junior college, or other type of training less extensive than 4-year college training. Craftsmen and skilled workers are excluded.

No. 764. Research and Development (R&D) Expenditures by Source and Objective: 1970 to 2003

[In millions of dollars (26,271 represents $26,271,000,000) except as indicated. For calendar years]

Year	Sources of funds						Objective (percent of total)			Character of work		
	Total	Federal government	Industry	Universities/ colleges	Non-profit	Non-federal government[1]	Defense related[2]	Space related[3]	Other	Basic research	Applied research	Development
1970	26,271	14,984	10,449	259	343	237	33	10	56	3,594	5,752	16,925
1971	26,952	15,210	10,824	290	366	262	33	10	58	3,720	5,833	17,399
1972	28,740	16,039	11,715	312	393	282	33	8	59	3,850	6,147	18,743
1973	30,952	16,587	13,299	343	422	302	32	7	61	4,099	6,655	20,197
1974	33,359	17,287	14,885	393	474	320	29	7	64	4,511	7,344	21,504
1975	35,671	18,533	15,824	432	534	348	28	8	65	4,875	8,091	22,706
1976	39,435	20,292	17,702	480	592	369	27	8	65	5,373	8,976	25,085
1977	43,338	22,071	19,642	569	662	394	27	7	66	6,008	9,662	27,667
1978	48,719	24,414	22,457	679	727	443	26	6	68	6,959	10,704	31,056
1979	55,379	27,225	26,097	785	791	482	25	6	70	7,836	12,097	35,445
1980	63,213	29,975	30,929	920	871	519	24	5	70	8,790	13,745	40,678
1981	72,269	33,715	35,948	1,058	967	581	24	5	70	9,830	16,391	46,047
1982	80,783	37,168	40,692	1,207	1,095	621	26	5	69	10,824	18,280	51,679
1983	89,971	41,472	45,264	1,357	1,220	658	28	4	68	12,059	20,373	57,540
1984	102,251	46,477	52,187	1,514	1,351	721	29	3	68	13,484	22,505	66,261
1985	114,685	52,655	57,962	1,743	1,491	834	30	3	67	14,857	25,410	74,417
1986	120,259	54,633	60,991	2,019	1,647	969	31	3	66	17,247	27,259	75,754
1987	126,217	58,466	62,576	2,262	1,849	1,065	32	3	65	18,498	27,915	79,804
1988	133,880	60,130	67,977	2,527	2,081	1,165	30	4	66	19,786	29,528	84,566
1989	141,889	60,463	74,966	2,852	2,333	1,274	28	4	69	21,889	32,277	87,723
1990	151,990	61,607	83,208	3,187	2,589	1,399	25	4	71	23,028	34,896	94,067
1991	160,872	60,780	92,300	3,457	2,852	1,483	22	4	73	27,139	38,629	95,104
1992	165,342	60,912	96,229	3,568	3,113	1,525	22	4	74	27,604	37,933	99,810
1993	165,723	60,522	96,549	3,708	3,387	1,557	21	4	74	28,739	37,280	99,704
1994	169,195	60,769	99,203	3,937	3,664	1,622	20	5	76	29,644	36,615	102,936
1995	183,611	62,959	110,870	4,109	3,924	1,750	19	4	77	29,602	40,932	113,077
1996	197,330	63,383	123,416	4,434	4,238	1,860	18	4	78	32,790	43,165	121,375
1997	212,134	64,561	136,227	4,836	4,589	1,921	17	4	79	35,256	46,542	128,674
1998	226,321	66,356	147,843	5,168	4,984	1,970	16	4	80	38,710	46,353	144,712
1999	243,517	67,015	163,229	5,630	5,549	2,095	15	3	82	40,077	51,865	152,941
2000[4]	264,634	66,327	183,688	6,211	6,170	2,238	13	2	84	42,321	56,481	165,827
2001[4]	274,211	73,341	184,892	6,778	6,818	2,382	14	2	84	47,112	64,401	162,698
2002[4]	276,434	80,490	178,514	7,332	7,550	2,548	15	3	82	50,807	65,559	160,068
2003[4]	283,795	85,279	179,615	7,944	8,247	2,710	16	3	81	54,103	67,780	161,911

[1] Nonfederal R&D expenditures to university and college performers, including space activities, and a portion of the Department of Energy funds. [2] R&D spending by the Department of Defense, [3] For the National Aeronautics and Space Administration only. [4] Preliminary.

Source: U.S. National Science Foundation, *National Patterns of R&D Resources*, annual. See also <http://www.nsf.gov/sbe/srs/nprdr/start.htm>.

No. 765. Performance Sector of R&D Expenditures: 1995 to 2003

[In millions of dollars {183,617 represents $183,617,000,000}. For calendar year. FFRDCs are federally funded research and development centers. For most academic institutions and the Federal Government before 1997, began on July 1 instead of October 1]

Year	Total	Federal government	Industry — Total	Industry — Funded by Federal government	Industry — Funded by Industry [1]	Industry FFRDC's	Universities and colleges — Total	Universities and colleges — Federal government	Universities and colleges — Funded by Non-federal government [2]	Universities and colleges — Funded by Industry	Universities and colleges — Funded by Universities & colleges	Universities and colleges — Funded by Nonprofits	Universities & colleges FFRDC's [3]	Other nonprofit institutions — Total	Other nonprofit institutions — Federal government	Other nonprofit institutions — Funded by Industry	Nonprofits FFRDC's
RESEARCH AND DEVELOPMENT TOTAL																	
1995	183,611	16,904	129,830	21,178	108,652	2,273	22,603	13,582	1,750	1,547	4,109	1,616	5,367	5,827	2,847	671	2,308
1999	243,517	17,851	180,672	20,496	160,176	2,039	28,135	16,223	2,095	2,077	5,630	2,110	5,652	8,175	3,761	975	3,440
2000	264,634	17,917	197,539	17,118	180,421	2,000	30,566	17,637	2,238	2,165	6,211	2,316	5,742	9,404	4,447	1,103	3,854
2001	274,211	21,048	198,505	16,899	181,606	2,020	33,518	19,654	2,382	2,177	6,778	2,528	6,225	10,702	5,302	1,110	4,290
2002, prel.	276,434	23,788	192,379	17,085	175,294	2,235	36,846	22,052	2,548	2,150	7,332	2,764	7,132	11,766	5,910	1,070	4,786
2003, prel.	283,795	24,959	193,729	17,314	176,415	2,383	40,262	24,499	2,710	2,123	7,944	2,986	7,421	12,661	6,323	1,077	5,261
BASIC RESEARCH																	
1995	29,602	2,689	5,569	190	5,379	530	15,139	9,629	1,069	945	2,509	987	2,702	2,899	1,170	390	1,338
1999	38,710	3,347	6,560	1,198	5,362	557	20,900	12,773	1,429	1,417	3,841	1,439	2,765	4,185	1,734	541	1,910
2000	42,321	3,765	6,942	925	6,017	547	22,726	13,836	1,539	1,488	4,271	1,592	2,873	4,852	2,099	612	2,140
2001	47,112	4,317	7,911	754	7,157	552	24,862	15,299	1,643	1,501	4,675	1,744	3,041	5,518	2,520	616	2,382
2002, prel.	50,807	4,617	7,671	762	6,908	611	27,369	17,122	1,765	1,489	5,079	1,915	3,484	6,105	2,854	594	2,657
2003, prel.	54,103	4,463	7,725	773	6,952	651	29,940	19,022	1,877	1,470	5,503	2,069	3,625	6,709	3,190	598	2,921
APPLIED RESEARCH																	
1995	40,932	4,952	26,919	3,164	23,755	535	5,655	2,775	559	494	1,311	516	1,050	1,692	934	170	589
1999	51,865	5,530	36,418	3,109	33,309	274	5,843	2,740	546	542	1,467	550	1,251	2,419	1,300	247	872
2000	56,481	6,105	38,812	2,682	36,130	269	6,661	3,349	573	554	1,591	593	1,330	3,087	1,831	279	977
2001	64,401	7,164	43,486	3,603	39,883	916	7,366	3,839	606	554	1,724	643	1,548	3,570	2,202	281	1,087
2002, prel.	65,559	8,083	42,140	3,643	38,497	955	8,146	4,418	642	542	1,848	697	1,938	3,933	2,448	271	1,213
2003, prel.	67,780	8,837	42,434	3,691	38,743	1,040	8,927	4,954	683	535	2,002	753	1,968	4,215	2,609	273	1,333
DEVELOPMENT																	
1995	113,077	9,262	97,342	17,824	79,518	1,208	1,810	1,178	123	108	288	113	1,616	1,236	744	111	381
1999	152,941	8,974	137,694	16,189	121,505	1,208	1,392	711	120	119	322	121	1,636	1,570	726	187	658
2000	165,827	8,047	151,784	13,510	138,274	1,185	1,179	452	126	122	349	130	1,540	1,461	513	211	737
2001	162,698	9,567	147,108	12,542	134,566	552	1,290	516	133	122	378	141	1,636	1,614	581	212	821
2002, prel.	160,068	11,088	142,569	12,680	129,889	669	1,331	512	141	119	406	153	1,710	1,728	608	205	916
2003, prel.	161,911	11,658	143,569	12,850	130,719	692	1,395	523	150	117	439	165	1,828	1,736	524	206	1,006

[1] For R&D funded by the federal government. [2] Includes all non-federal sources. [3] Includes all R&D expenditures of FFRDC's administered by academic institutions and funded by the federal government.

Source: National Science Foundation. Data derived from: *Research and Development in Industry*, annual; *Academic Research and Development Expenditures*, annual; and *Federal Funds For Research and Development*, annual. Also see <http://www.nsf.gov/sbe/srs/nprdr/start.htm>.

No. 766. National R&D Expenditures as a Percent of Gross Domestic Product by Country: 1985 to 2001

Year	Total R&D						Nondefense R&D [1]					
	United States	Japan	Unified Germany	France	United Kingdom	Italy	United States	Japan	Unified Germany	France	United Kingdom	Italy
1985 ..	2.76	2.54	2.68	2.22	2.24	1.12	1.9	2.5	2.6	1.8	1.8	1.1
1990 ..	2.65	2.78	2.67	2.37	2.15	1.29	2.0	2.8	2.5	1.9	1.7	1.3
1995 ..	2.51	2.69	2.26	2.31	1.95	1.00	2.1	2.7	2.2	2.0	1.6	1.0
1996 ..	2.55	2.77	2.26	2.30	1.88	1.01	2.1	2.8	2.2	2.0	1.5	1.1
1997 ..	2.58	2.83	2.29	2.22	1.81	1.05	2.2	2.9	2.3	2.0	1.5	1.1
1998 ..	2.60	2.94	2.31	2.17	1.80	1.07	2.3	2.9	2.4	2.0	1.6	1.0
1999 ..	2.65	2.94	2.44	2.18	1.88	1.04	2.4	3.0	2.4	2.0	1.6	1.1
2000 ..	2.72	2.98	2.49	2.18	1.85	1.10	2.4	(NA)	2.5	2.0	(NA)	(NA)
2001 ..	2.82	(NA)	2.53	2.20	(NA)	(NA)						

NA Not available.   [1] Estimated.
Source: National Science Foundation, National Patterns of R&D Resources, annual; and Organization for Economic Cooperation and Development.

No. 767. Federal Obligations for R&D in Current and Constant (1996) Dollars, by Agency: 1980 to 2003

[In millions of dollars (29,830 represents $29,830,000,000). For fiscal years ending in year shown; see text, Section 8. Includes those agencies with obligations of $1 billion or more in 2000]

Agency	Current dollars				Constant (1996) dollars [1]			
	1980	1990	2002, prel.	2003, prel.	1980	1990	2002, prel.	2003, prel.
Obligations, total [2]	29,830	63,559	92,979	98,608	53,278	73,863	83,916	87,878
Dept. of Defense	13,981	37,268	43,164	45,012	24,971	43,310	38,957	40,114
Dept. of Health and Human Services . . .	3,780	8,406	24,189	27,551	6,752	9,769	21,831	24,553
National Aeronautics and Space Administration [3]	3,234	6,533	8,095	8,598	5,776	7,592	7,306	7,663
Dept. of Energy	4,754	5,631	7,484	7,541	8,490	6,544	6,754	6,720
National Science Foundation	882	1,690	3,250	3,404	1,575	1,964	2,933	3,033
Dept. of Agriculture	688	1,108	2,050	1,984	1,228	1,288	1,850	1,768

[1] Based on gross domestic product implicit price deflator.   [2] Includes other agencies, not shown separately.   [3] Beginning in fiscal year 2001, the National Aeronautics and Space Administration reclassified Space Station as a physical asset and Space Station research as equipment and transferred funding for the program from R&D to R&D plant.
Source: U.S. National Science Foundation, Federal Funds for Research and Development, annual. See also <http://www.nsf.gov/sbe/srs/nsf04310/pdf/nsf04310.pdf> (released March 2004).

No. 768. Federal Obligations for Research in Current and Constant (1996) Dollars by Field of Science: 1980 to 2003

[In millions of dollars (11,597 represents $11,597,000,000). For fiscal years ending in year shown; see text, Section 8. Excludes R&D plant]

Field of science	1980	1985	1990	1995	1999	2000	2001	2002, prel.	2003, prel.
CURRENT DOLLARS									
Research, total	11,597	16,133	21,622	28,434	33,528	38,471	44,714	49,809	53,377
Basic	4,674	7,819	11,286	13,877	17,444	19,570	21,958	24,174	25,977
Applied	6,923	8,315	10,337	14,557	16,084	18,901	22,756	25,635	27,400
Life sciences	4,192	6,363	8,830	11,811	15,422	17,965	23,057	25,868	28,673
Psychology	199	327	449	623	633	1,627	742	839	955
Physical sciences	2,001	3,046	3,809	4,278	4,066	4,788	4,601	5,145	5,200
Environmental sciences	1,261	1,404	2,174	2,854	3,095	3,329	3,252	3,668	3,879
Mathematics and computer sciences . . .	241	575	841	1,579	1,981	2,206	2,611	2,752	2,866
Engineering	2,830	3,618	4,227	5,708	6,263	6,346	8,197	8,951	9,161
Social sciences	524	460	630	679	855	1,050	1,009	1,027	1,050
Other sciences, n.e.c.	350	342	664	902	1,212	1,160	1,246	1,559	1,593
CONSTANT (1996) DOLLARS [2]									
Research, total	20,713	21,953	25,127	29,002	32,011	35,988	40,872	44,954	47,569
Basic	8,348	10,640	13,116	14,154	16,655	18,307	20,071	21,817	23,150
Applied	12,365	11,314	12,013	14,848	15,356	17,681	20,800	23,136	24,419
Life sciences	7,487	8,658	10,261	12,047	14,724	16,805	21,076	23,347	25,553
Psychology	355	445	522	635	604	1,522	678	757	851
Physical sciences	3,574	4,145	4,426	4,364	3,882	4,479	4,205	4,644	4,635
Environmental sciences	2,252	1,910	2,526	2,911	2,955	3,114	2,972	3,310	3,457
Mathematics and computer sciences . . .	430	782	977	1,611	1,891	2,064	2,386	2,484	2,554
Engineering	5,054	4,923	4,912	5,822	5,980	5,936	7,493	8,079	8,164
Social sciences	936	626	732	693	816	982	922	927	936
Other sciences, n.e.c.	625	465	772	920	1,157	1,085	1,139	1,407	1,419

[1] N.e.c. = Not elsewhere classified.   [2] Based on gross domestic product implicit price deflator.
Source: U.S. National Science Foundation, Federal Funds for Research and Development, annual. See also <http://128.150.4.107:80/sbe/srs/pubdata.htm>.

No. 769. Federal Budget Authority for R&D in Current and Constant (1996) Dollars by Selected Budget Functions: 1980 to 2004

[In millions of dollars (29,739 represents $29,739,000,000). For fiscal years ending in year shown; see text, Section 8. Excludes R&D plant. Represents budget authority. Functions shown are those for which $1 billion or more was authorized since 1995]

Function	1980	1985	1990	1995	2000	2001	2002	2003, prel.	2004, prel.
CURRENT DOLLARS									
Total [1]	29,739	49,887	63,781	68,791	78,664	86,756	97,624	111,593	117,967
Eight functions, percent of total	96	98	98	98	98	98	98	98	98
National defense	14,946	33,698	39,925	37,204	42,580	45,713	53,016	62,463	66,835
Health	3,694	5,418	8,308	11,407	17,869	20,758	23,560	26,358	28,059
Space research and technology [2]	2,738	2,725	5,765	7,916	5,363	6,126	6,270	7,215	7,550
Energy [3]	3,603	2,389	2,726	2,844	996	1,314	1,327	1,359	1,358
General science [3]	1,233	1,862	2,410	2,794	4,977	5,468	5,753	6,165	6,441
Natural resources and environment	999	1,059	1,386	1,988	1,999	2,096	2,160	2,234	2,195
Transportation	887	1,030	1,045	1,833	1,636	1,640	1,838	1,867	1,860
Agriculture	585	836	950	1,194	1,426	1,657	1,606	1,710	1,564
CONSTANT (1996) DOLLARS [4]									
Total [1]	53,115	67,883	74,121	70,166	73,662	79,302	88,108	99,450	103,616
National defense	26,694	45,854	46,397	37,948	39,873	41,785	47,848	55,666	58,704
Health	6,598	7,372	9,655	11,635	16,733	18,974	21,264	23,490	24,646
Space research and technology [2]	4,890	3,708	6,700	8,074	5,022	5,600	5,659	6,430	6,632
Energy [3]	6,435	3,251	3,168	2,901	933	1,201	1,198	1,211	1,193
General science [3]	2,202	2,534	2,801	2,850	4,661	4,998	5,192	5,494	5,657
Natural resources and environment	1,784	1,441	1,611	2,028	1,872	1,916	1,949	1,991	1,928
Transportation	1,584	1,402	1,214	1,870	1,532	1,499	1,659	1,664	1,634
Agriculture	1,045	1,138	1,104	1,218	1,335	1,515	1,449	1,524	1,374

[1] Includes other functions, not shown separately. [2] In FY 2000, the National Aeronautics and Space Administration reclassified Space Station as a physical asset and Space Station research as equipment and transferred funding for the Space Station program from R&D to R&D plant. [3] Beginning in FY 2000, a number of DOE programs were reclassified from energy. [4] Based on gross domestic product implicit price deflator.

Source: U.S. National Science Foundation, Federal R&D Funding by Budget Function, annual. See also <http://www.nsf.gov/>.

No. 770. R&D Expenditures in Science and Engineering at Universities and Colleges in Current and Constant (1996) Dollars: 1990 to 2002

In millions of dollars (16,286 represents $16,286,000,000). Due to rounding, detail may not add to totals]

Characteristic	Current dollars				Constant (1996) dollars [1]			
	1990	1995	2001	2002	1990	1995	2001	2002
Total [2]	16,286	22,170	32,767	36,333	18,926	22,613	29,932	32,943
Basic research [2]	10,643	14,808	24,273	26,959	12,368	15,104	22,173	24,443
Applied R&D [2]	5,643	7,362	8,494	9,374	6,558	7,509	7,759	8,499
Source of funds:								
All governments	9,638	13,331	19,213	21,834	11,200	13,598	17,551	19,797
Institutions' own funds	1,324	1,689	2,316	2,501	1,539	1,723	2,116	2,268
Industry	3,006	4,047	6,587	7,109	3,493	4,128	6,017	6,446
Other	1,127	1,489	2,214	2,188	1,310	1,519	2,022	1,984
Fields:								
Physical sciences	1,807	2,256	2,805	3,008	2,100	2,301	2,562	2,727
Environmental sciences	1,069	1,434	1,830	2,022	1,242	1,463	1,672	1,833
Mathematical sciences	222	279	359	387	258	285	328	351
Computer sciences	515	682	954	1,126	598	696	871	1,021
Life sciences	8,726	12,188	19,213	21,404	10,141	12,432	17,551	19,407
Psychology	253	371	583	671	294	378	533	608
Social sciences	703	1,019	1,440	1,583	817	1,039	1,315	1,435
Other sciences	336	427	577	627	390	436	527	568
Engineering	2,656	3,515	5,007	5,504	3,087	3,585	4,574	4,990

[1] Based on gross domestic product implicit price deflator. [2] Basic research and applied R&D statistics were re-estimated for FY 2001 and forward. These data are not directly comparable to those from earlier years.

Source: U.S. National Science Foundation, Survey of Research and Development Expenditures at Universities and Colleges, annual. See also <http://www.nsf.gov/sbe/srs/rdexp/start.htm>.

No. 771. Federal Obligations for Science and Engineering to Universities and Colleges in Current and Constant (1996) Dollars: 1990 to 2002

[In millions of dollars (10,471 represents $10,471,000,000) except percent. For fiscal years ending in year shown; see text, Section 8.]

Item	Current dollars				Constant (1996) dollars [1]			
	1990	1995	2001	2002	1990	1995	2001	2002
Academic science/engineering obligations	10,471	14,461	22,492	24,394	12,887	15,688	21,977	23,422
Research and development	9,017	12,181	19,390	21,118	11,097	13,214	18,947	20,276
Research and development plant	142	341	399	301	174	370	390	289
Other science/engineering activities	1,312	1,939	2,702	2,975	1,615	2,103	2,641	2,856

[1] Based on gross domestic product implicit price deflator.

Source: U.S. National Science Foundation, Survey of Federal S&E Support to Universities, Colleges, and Nonprofit Institutions, annual. Also see <http://www.nsf.gov/>.

No. 772. Federal R&D Obligations to Selected Universities and Colleges: 2001 and 2002

[In millions of dollars (19,390.2 represents $19,390,200,000), except rank. For fiscal years ending in year shown; see text, Section 8. For the top 51 institutions receiving Federal R&D funds in 2002. Awards to the administrative offices of university systems are excluded from totals for individual institutions because that allocation of funds is unknown, but those awards are included in "total all institutions"]

Major institution ranked by total 2002 Federal R&D obligations	2001	2002	Major institution ranked by total 2002 Federal R&D obligations	2001	2002
Total, all institutions [1]	19,390.2	21,117.9	Case Western Reserve University	200.0	213.4
Johns Hopkins University	838.0	974.7	University of Illinois—Urbana Champaign	186.9	194.0
University of Washington	474.5	525.6	The Scripps Research Institute	157.4	193.6
University of Pennsylvania	412.0	447.2	University of Rochester	171.2	189.2
University of Michigan	403.4	419.7	University of California—Berkeley	210.6	187.3
University of California—Los Angeles	363.9	415.7	University of California—Davis	166.2	185.3
Stanford University	351.1	381.0	Boston University	154.4	182.9
University of California—San Diego	333.9	373.6	Emory University	161.9	180.6
University of California—San Francisco	344.9	361.0	Ohio State University	156.6	174.7
Washington University	314.7	348.0	Northwestern University	164.0	174.0
University of Pittsburgh	300.8	335.8	University of Iowa	163.9	172.7
Columbia University—Main Division	305.8	330.2	University of Arizona	166.9	168.5
University of Wisconsin—Madison	290.2	327.9	University of Florida	157.4	167.1
Duke University	274.1	327.5	University of Texas SW Medical Ctr Dallas	146.9	162.3
Harvard University	321.7	313.4	University of Chicago	160.1	161.5
University of Colorado	290.7	308.3	University of Virginia	153.0	159.1
Yale University	276.2	306.9	University of Utah	149.7	157.9
University of North Carolina at Chapel Hill	275.9	297.9	Oregon Health & Science University	138.4	154.4
University of Minnesota	273.1	291.9	California Institute of Technology	127.6	152.2
Pennsylvania State University	253.6	287.1	Mt. Sinai School of Medicine	133.1	146.3
Cornell University	271.9	283.1	University of Texas at Austin	164.5	146.0
Massachusetts Institute of Technology	252.5	268.8	Indiana University	143.7	143.1
Baylor College of Medicine	231.7	266.8	New York University	134.4	142.5
University Southern California	232.5	254.3	Carnegie Mellon University	95.7	131.4
University of Alabama—Birmingham	201.6	224.2	University of Miami	111.2	127.0
Vanderbilt University	166.1	215.5	University of Maryland— College Park	133.9	126.7

[1] Includes other institutions, not shown separately.

Source: U.S. National Science Foundation, *Federal S&E Support to Universities and Colleges and Nonprofit Institutions*, annual.

No. 773. Science and Engineering Degree Recipients: 1999 to 2001

[In thousands (758.3 represents 758,300). FT represents full-time. Based on a survey and subject to sampling error; see source for details]

Degree and field	Graduates 1999 and 2000 (1,000)	2001 [1] In school [2]	Employed In S&E [3]	Employed In other	Not employed or not FT students	Median salary [4] ($1,000)
Bachelor's recipients	758.3	168.4	171.5	373.8	44.6	34
All science fields	649.0	154.5	94.7	358.4	41.4	31
Computer and information sciences	61.5	(B)	35.6	19.5	4.4	51
Mathematical sciences	24.4	4.3	3.8	14.6	(B)	33
Life and related sciences	159.4	52.9	17.8	81.6	7.1	29
Physical and related sciences	32.2	10.1	10.6	9.9	1.6	34
Psychology	152.9	41.0	11.1	91.2	9.6	28
Social and related sciences	218.7	44.2	15.9	141.7	17.0	30
All engineering fields	109.2	13.8	76.8	15.3	3.3	49
Aerospace and related engineering	2.2	0.4	1.3	0.4	(B)	44
Chemical engineering	10.8	2.2	6.4	1.7	(B)	50
Civil and architectural engineering	16.8	1.5	12.5	2.2	(B)	42
Electrical, electronics, computer and communications engineering	34.2	4.3	25.8	3.3	(B)	54
Industrial engineering	6.9	(B)	4.6	1.7	(B)	49
Mechanical engineering	25.8	2.7	18.8	3.6	(B)	48
Other engineering	12.6	2.3	7.5	2.2	(B)	45
Master's recipients	160.1	29.5	77.3	45.9	7.4	51
All science fields	115.3	23.9	44.1	41.4	5.8	45
Computer and mathematical sciences	24.3	1.6	17.1	4.4	(B)	65
Mathematical sciences	6.2	1.6	2.5	2.0	(B)	45
Life and related sciences	16.2	4.7	5.9	5.0	(B)	37
Physical and related sciences	8.6	3.2	3.9	1.1	(B)	45
Psychology	33.0	5.8	9.1	16.1	2.0	35
Social and related sciences	27.1	7.1	5.6	12.8	1.5	43
All engineering fields	44.8	5.6	33.2	4.5	1.5	60
Aerospace and related engineering	1.2	0.2	0.8	(B)	(B)	62
Chemical engineering	2.0	0.6	1.2	(B)	(B)	58
Civil and architectural engineering	6.3	(B)	5.1	(B)	(B)	50
Electrical, electronics, computer and communications engineering	16.4	1.7	13.0	1.0	(B)	66
Industrial engineering	3.2	(B)	2.4	(B)	(B)	62
Mechanical engineering	6.1	1.0	4.5	(B)	(B)	60
Other engineering	9.5	1.6	6.3	1.2	(B)	61

B Base figure too small to meet statistical standards of reliability of a derived figure. [1] As of April. [2] Full-time students. [3] In science and engineering. [4] For the principal job. Excludes full-time students, the self-employed, and persons whose principal job is less than 35 hours per week. For Definition of Median, see Guide to Tabular Presentation.

Source: National Science Foundation, *National Survey of Recent College Graduates: 2001*.

No. 774. Graduate Science/Engineering Students in Doctorate-Granting Colleges by Characteristic and Field: 1990 to 2002

[In thousands (397.8 represents 397,800). As of fall. Includes outlying areas]

Field of science or engineering	Total			Characteristic							
				Female			Foreign		Part-time		
	1990	2001	2002	1990	2001	2002	2001	2002	1990	2001	2002
Total, all surveyed fields .	397.8	452.3	482.2	149.7	204.8	219.6	134.2	145.6	123.2	122.6	129.4
Science/engineering	350.6	384.3	409.3	113.4	154.0	165.3	128.2	138.7	100.7	98.5	103.0
Engineering, total.	99.9	103.4	112.5	13.6	21.0	23.3	51.1	56.6	35.9	27.9	29.4
Sciences, total.	250.7	280.9	296.9	99.8	133.0	142.0	77.1	82.1	64.8	70.7	73.7
Physical sciences	32.5	30.0	31.3	7.6	9.0	9.7	12.1	12.9	3.6	3.3	3.1
Environmental	12.9	12.6	13.1	3.8	5.3	5.7	2.7	2.7	3.0	2.6	2.5
Mathematical sciences . . .	17.3	15.1	16.4	5.3	5.5	6.0	6.3	6.8	4.0	3.1	3.3
Computer sciences	27.7	43.9	47.6	6.4	12.5	13.4	22.6	23.8	12.9	16.9	17.8
Agricultural sciences	10.9	11.3	11.8	3.2	4.9	5.2	2.5	2.5	2.0	2.5	2.6
Biological sciences	46.0	53.9	57.2	21.0	28.8	31.0	12.2	13.5	6.8	7.4	7.5
Psychology	35.8	39.3	40.8	23.6	28.6	29.8	2.3	2.6	10.3	10.9	11.9
Social sciences	67.7	74.7	78.8	29.0	38.4	41.2	16.5	17.3	22.1	24.0	24.9
Health fields, total	47.2	68.0	72.9	36.3	50.8	54.4	6.0	6.8	22.5	24.1	26.4

Source: U.S. National Science Foundation, *Survey of Graduate Science Engineering Students and Postdoctorates*, annual.

No. 775. Doctorates Conferred by Recipients' Characteristics: 1990 and 2002

[In percent, except as indicated. Based on the Survey of Earned Doctorate Awards; for description of methodology, see <http://www.nsf.gov/sbe/srs/ssed/sedmeth.htm>.]

Characteristic	1990, total	2002									
		All fields [1]	Engin- eer- ing	Physi- cal sci- ences [2]	Earth sci- ences	Math- ematics	Com- puter sci- ences	Biologi- cal sci- ences [3]	Agri- cul- tural	Social sci- ences [4]	Psychol- ogy
Total conferred (number).	36,068	39,955	5,073	3,190	797	917	811	5,680	1,011	3,412	3,199
Male.	63.7	54.5	82.3	73.2	68.4	70.9	78.9	55.3	69.0	55.3	33.1
Female.	36.3	45.4	17.5	26.7	31.4	28.8	20.7	44.7	30.7	44.4	66.7
Median age [5]	33.9	33.3	31.4	29.8	33.1	30.3	32.1	20.6	34.3	34.6	32.1
CITIZENSHIP [6]											
Total conferred (number).	34,697	37,289	4,806	3,048	742	881	772	5,388	820	3,756	2,942
U.S. citizen	71.8	74.0	39.3	58.2	61.5	46.7	46.2	70.3	47.4	67.4	92.4
Foreign citizen	28.2	26.0	60.7	41.8	38.5	53.3	53.4	29.7	52.6	32.6	7.6
RACE/ETHNICITY [7]											
Total conferred (number).	26,604	27,585	2,164	1,940	493	443	421	4,122	424	2,703	2,796
White [8]	86.5	77.4	68.1	79.6	85.8	83.3	69.1	75.5	84.2	77.5	79.6
Black [8]	3.8	6.3	4.0	3.3	1.2	3.2	4.0	3.0	2.8	7.0	6.2
Asian/Pacific [8]	4.9	7.6	19.0	10.4	6.3	6.5	20.4	14.1	5.7	6.3	4.5
Indian/Alaskan [8]. . . .	0.4	0.5	0.3	0.4	-	0.7	0.5	0.3	0.5	0.8	0.5
Hispanic . . . . . [9] . .	3.1	4.9	4.4	3.3	3.2	2.7	3.3	4.3	4.0	5.0	6.6
Other/unknown [9] . . .	1.4	3.2	4.1	3.1	3.4	3.6	2.6	2.8	2.8	3.5	2.6

- Represents zero. [1] Includes other fields, not shown separately. [2] Astronomy, physics, and chemistry. [3] Biochemistry, botany, microbiology, physiology, zoology, and related fields. [4] Anthropology, sociology, political science, economics, international relations and related fields. [5] For definition of median, see Guide to Tabular Presentation. [6] For those with known citizenship. Includes those with temporary visas. [7] Excludes those with temporary visas. [8] Non-Hispanic. [9] For the year 2002, includes Native Hawaiians and other Pacific Islanders, respondents choosing multiple races (excluding those selecting an Hispanic ethnicity), and respondents with unknown race/ethnicity.

Source: U.S. National Science Foundation, *Science and Engineering Doctorate Awards*, annual. See also <http://www.nsf.gov/sbe/srs/nsf03300/pdf/nsf03300.pdf> (released October 2003).

No. 776. Funds for Performance of Industrial R&D in Current and Constant (1996) Dollars by Source of Funds and Selected Industries: 1999 to 2002

[In millions of dollars (182,823 represents $182,823,000,000). For calendar years. Covers basic research, applied research, and development. Based on the Survey of Industry Research and Development]

Source of funds and industry	NAICS[1] code	1999	2000	2001	2002
CURRENT DOLLARS					
Total funds	(X)	182,823	199,539	198,505	190,809
Petroleum and coal products	324	615	(D)	(D)	(D)
Chemicals and allied products	325	20,246	20,918	17,892	20,641
Machinery	333	6,057	6,580	6,404	6,429
Navigational, measuring, electromedical, and control instruments	3345	14,337	15,116	12,947	13,729
Electrical equipment, appliances, and components	335	(D)	(D)	4,980	2,039
Motor vehicles, trailers, and parts	3361-3363	(D)	(D)	(D)	(D)
Aerospace products and parts	3364	14,425	10,319	7,868	9,654
All other[2]	(X)	(D)	(D)	(D)	(D)
Company funds	(X)	160,288	180,421	181,606	174,408
Petroleum and coal products	324	(D)	1,172	1,057	1,233
Chemicals	325	20,051	20,768	17,713	20,395
Machinery	333	5,658	6,539	6,337	6,366
Navigational, measuring, electromedical, and control instruments	3345	8,632	10,114	7,565	8,549
Electrical equipment, appliances, and components	335	3,820	3,390	4,680	1,978
Motor vehicles, trailers, and parts	3361-3363	17,987	18,306	16,089	15,199
Aerospace products and parts	3364	5,309	3,895	4,083	5,349
All other[2]	(X)	(D)	116,237	124,082	115,339
CONSTANT (1996) DOLLARS[3]					
Total funds	(X)	174,699	186,677	181,416	172,491
Petroleum and coal products	324	588	(D)	(D)	(D)
Chemicals	325	19,346	19,570	16,352	18,659
Machinery	333	5,788	6,156	5,853	5,812
Navigational, measuring, electromedical, and control instruments	3345	13,700	14,142	11,832	12,411
Electrical equipment, appliances, and components	335	(D)	(D)	4,551	1,843
Motor vehicles, trailers, and parts	3361-3363	(D)	(D)	(D)	(D)
Aerospace products and parts	3364	13,784	9,654	7,191	8,727
All other[2]	(X)	(D)	(D)	(D)	(D)
Company funds	(X)	153,166	168,791	165,971	157,664
Petroleum and coal products	324	(D)	1,096	966	1,115
Chemicals	325	19,160	19,429	16,188	18,437
Machinery	333	5,407	6,118	5,791	5,755
Navigational, measuring, electromedical, and control instruments	3345	8,248	9,462	6,914	7,728
Electrical equipment, appliances, and components	335	3,650	3,171	4,277	1,788
Motor vehicles, trailers, and parts	3361-3363	17,188	17,126	14,704	13,740
Aerospace products and parts	3364	5,073	3,644	3,731	4,835
All other[2]	(X)	(D)	108,745	113,400	104,266

D Figure withheld to avoid disclosure of information pertaining to a specific organization or individual.   X Not applicable.
[1] North American Industry Classification System, 1997; see text, Section 15.   [2] All other manufacturing and nonmanufacturing.
[3] Based on gross domestic product implicit price deflator.

Source: U.S. National Science Foundation, *Research and Development in Industry*, annual.

No. 777. R&D Funds in R&D-Performing Manufacturing and Nonmanufacturing Companies by Industry: 2000 to 2002

Industry	NAICS[1] code	Total R&D funds as a percent of net sales			Company R&D funds as a percent of net sales		
		2000	2001	2002	2000	2001	2002
All industries, total	(X)	3.8	4.1	3.9	3.4	3.8	3.6
All manufacturing industries, total	(X)	3.6	4.0	3.6	3.3	3.6	3.2
Food	311	(D)	0.5	(D)	0.4	0.5	0.6
Paper, printing, and support activities	322, 326	(D)	(D)	(D)	1.6	2.1	1.3
Petroleum and coal products	324	(D)	(D)	(D)	0.3	0.3	0.4
Chemicals	325	5.9	4.9	6.0	5.9	4.8	5.9
Plastic and rubber products	326	(D)	2.4	(D)	1.8	2.9	1.8
Nonmetallic mineral products	327	1.8	2.4	(D)	1.8	2.3	1.2
Primary metals	331	0.5	0.7	0.7	0.5	0.7	0.7
Fabricated metal products	332	1.4	1.7	1.5	1.4	1.6	1.4
Machinery	333	3.9	4.3	4.4	3.8	4.2	4.3
Navigational, measuring, electromedical, and control instruments	3345	12.0	12.6	8.7	8.0	7.3	5.4
Electrical equipment, appliances, and components	335	(D)	3.1	2.8	2.1	2.9	2.7
Motor vehicles, trailers, and parts	3361-3363	(D)	(D)	(D)	3.2	3.5	3.1
Aerospace products and parts	3364	7.3	5.7	4.1	2.8	3.0	2.3
All nonmanufacturing industries, total	(X)	4.1	4.3	4.4	3.3	4.0	4.1
Transportation and warehousing services	48, 49	(D)	2.5	(D)	0.4	2.4	0.5
Software publishing	5112	20.5	19.4	21.5	1.6	19.3	21.4
Architectural, engineering, and related services	5413	10.8	7.5	7.8	0.3	5.2	5.3
Computer systems design and related services	5415	12.3	17.4	16.5	5.9	16.5	14.3
Scientific R&D services	5417	42.9	47.7	21.3	1.8	36.5	17.6
Management of companies and enterprises	55	4.4	7.8	7.6	1.8	7.8	7.6

D Figure withheld to avoid disclosure of information pertaining to a specific organization or individual.   X Not applicable.
[1] North American Industry Classification System 1997 (NAICS); see text, Section 15.

Source: U.S. National Science Foundation, *Research and Development in Industry*, annual. See also <http://www.nsf.gov/sbe/srs/sird/sirdmeth.htm>.

No. 778. R&D Scientists and Engineers— Employment and Cost, by Industry: 2000 to 2002

[1,037.5 represents 1,037,500. Data are estimates; on average full-time-equivalent (FTE) basis]

Industry	NAICS[1] code	2000	2001	2002
EMPLOYED SCIENTISTS (1,000)				
Average FTE of scientists and engineers[2][3]	(X)	1,037.5	1,050.8	1,063.2
Chemicals	325	82.0	81.4	84.2
Machinery	333	51.9	53.8	56.2
Electrical equipment, appliances, and components	335	23.3	11.4	7.0
Motor vehicles, trailers, and parts	3361-3363	75.4	74.4	78.4
Aerospace products and parts	3364	40.2	22.1	25.8
Transportation and warehousing services	48, 49	1.5	1.3	0.4
Software publishing	5112	79.7	82.2	81.0
Architectural, engineering, and related services	5413	33.0	28.9	28.0
Computer systems design and related services	5415	41.6	54.6	76.8
Scientific R&D services	5417	52.4	58.4	55.0
Management of companies and enterprises	55	0.4	0.9	1.5
CONSTANT (1996) DOLLARS[4] ($1,000)				
Cost per scientist or engineer[3][5]	(X)	179.9	172.7	170.9
Chemicals	325	238.6	200.9	225.3
Machinery	333	118.7	108.8	108.7
Electrical equipment, appliances, and components	335	(D)	(D)	(D)
Motor vehicles, trailers, and parts	3361-3363	(D)	(D)	(D)
Aerospace products and parts	3364	(D)	325.9	(D)
Transportation and warehousing services	48, 49	(D)	(D)	(D)
Software publishing	5112	148.3	145.8	153.6
Architectural, engineering, and related services	5413	95.9	107.3	143.8
Computer systems design and related services	5415	116.2	153.2	125.5
Scientific R&D services	5417	230.3	223.1	245.1
Management of companies and enterprises	55	124.4	386.1	157.9

D Withheld to avoid disclosure. X Not applicable. [1] North American Industry Classification System 1997 (NAICS); see text, Section 15. [2] The mean number of FTE R&D scientists and engineers employed in January of the year shown and the following January. [3] Includes industries not shown separately. [4] Based on gross domestic product implicit price deflator. [5] Represents the arithmetic mean of the numbers of R&D scientists and engineers reported in each industry for January in 2 consecutive years divided into total R&D expenditures in each industry.
Source: U.S. National Science Foundation, Research and Development in Industry, annual.

No. 779. Civilian Employment of Scientists, Engineers, and Technicians by Occupation and Industry: 2002

[In thousands (6,703.1 represents 6,703,100). Based on sample and subject to sampling error. For details, see source]

Occupation	Wage and salary workers								Self-employed[3]
	Total[1]	Mining[2]	Construction	Manufacturing	Information	Professional, scientific and technical services	Government	Other service-providing industries	
Scientists, engineers, and technicians, total	6,703.1	42.2	86.8	1,301.9	529.8	1,799.2	1,075.1	1,544.9	304.7
Scientists	998.6	7.0	1.4	99.3	29.4	210.0	323.6	224.9	93.5
Physical scientists	251.1	6.8	(NA)	47.7	1.3	77.4	84.3	22.8	10.2
Life scientists	214.0	(NA)	(NA)	23.5	0.1	43.4	90.1	39.0	9.6
Mathematical science occupations	107.0	(NA)	0.2	9.7	7.4	24.0	20.7	39.9	5.1
Social scientists and related occupations	426.4	0.2	1.2	18.3	20.6	65.2	128.4	123.3	68.6
Computer specialists	2,911.2	5.0	11.9	269.6	407.9	853.4	313.8	916.9	131.5
Engineers[4]	1,478.3	16.0	42.5	565.6	59.8	354.5	191.6	192.9	54.8
Civil engineers	228.1	0.7	19.8	4.1	0.8	106.2	72.0	9.1	15.3
Electrical/electronics engineers	291.9	0.5	5.5	106.7	34.1	62.3	31.6	41.9	9.3
Mechanical engineers	215.1	0.7	5.2	116.2	2.4	44.8	12.8	26.4	6.6
Drafters, engineering, and mapping technicians[5]	904.8	5.0	27.6	297.7	31.3	268.9	119.5	133.9	20.2
Electrical/electronics engineering technicians	203.6	0.9	3.5	82.9	22.0	26.3	17.0	49.9	0.9
Other engineering technicians	274.7	1.3	5.4	105.6	3.5	70.7	51.4	35.6	1.1
Drafters	216.1	0.6	14.3	60.5	1.9	105.4	6.7	18.6	8.1
Surveying and mapping technicians	60.1	0.7	1.0	(NA)	0.4	38.7	11.0	4.8	3.3
Life, physical, and social science technicians	345.9	8.3	0.3	69.6	0.9	66.3	118.0	73.3	2.4
Surveyors, cartographers, and photogrammetrists	64.3	0.8	3.1	0.1	0.4	46.1	8.6	2.9	2.2

NA Not available. [1] Includes agriculture, forestry, and fishing not shown separately. [2] Includes oil and gas extraction. [3] Includes secondary jobs. [4] Includes kinds of engineers and technicians not shown separately. [5] Includes other drafters, technicians, and mapping technicians not shown separately.
Source: U.S. Bureau of Labor Statistics, National Industry-Occupation Employment Matrix, February 2004. (Data collected biennially.)

No. 780. Space Vehicle Systems—Net Sales and Backlog Orders: 1970 to 2002

[In millions of dollars (1,956 represents $1,956,000,000). Backlog orders as of Dec. 31. Based on data from major companies engaged in manufacture of aerospace products. Includes parts but excludes engines and propulsion units]

Year	Net sales			Backlog orders			Year	Net sales			Backlog orders		
	Total	Military	Non-military	Total	Military	Non-military		Total	Military	Non-military	Total	Military	Non-military
1970...	1,956	1,025	931	1,184	786	398	1997...	13,410	4,916	8,494	23,357	8,790	14,567
1975...	2,119	1,096	1,023	1,304	1,019	285	1998...	9,490	4,227	5,264	20,371	7,970	12,402
1980...	3,483	1,461	2,022	1,814	951	863	1999...	9,022	5,107	3,915	22,356	10,666	11,690
1985...	6,300	4,241	2,059	6,707	4,941	1,766	2000...	8,164	3,723	4,441	21,395	8,942	12,453
1990...	9,691	6,556	3,135	12,462	8,130	4,332	2001 [1]...	5,112	3,605	1,507	18,893	8,039	10,854
1995...	11,314	4,782	6,532	15,650	5,872	9,778	2002 [1]...	5,983	3,092	2,891	22,562	12,677	9,886

[1] Includes engines and/or propulsion units for space vehicles, including parts.

Source: U.S. Census Bureau, Current Industrial Reports, M336G, Civil Aircraft and Aircraft Engines, annual and, beginning 1995, Internet site <http://www.census.gov/industry/1/m336g0213.pdf>.

No. 781. Federal Outlays for General Science, Space, and Other Technology, 1970 to 2003, and Projections, 2004 to 2009 in Current and Constant (2000) Dollars

[In billions of dollars (4.5 represents $4,500,000,000). For fiscal years ending in year shown; see text, Section 8.]

Year	Current dollars			Constant (2000) dollars		
	Total	General science/basic research	Space and other technologies	Total	General science/basic research	Space and other technologies
1970	4.5	0.9	3.6	19.3	4.0	15.2
1980	5.8	1.4	4.5	12.0	2.8	9.1
1985	8.6	2.0	6.6	13.7	3.2	10.5
1990	14.4	2.8	11.6	20.0	3.9	16.1
1995	16.7	4.1	12.6	18.7	4.6	14.1
1996	16.7	4.0	12.7	18.0	4.3	13.7
1997	17.1	4.1	13.1	18.2	4.4	13.9
1998	18.2	5.3	12.9	19.2	5.6	13.6
1999	18.1	5.6	12.4	18.7	5.8	12.9
2000	18.6	6.2	12.4	18.6	6.2	12.4
2001	19.7	6.5	13.2	19.3	6.4	12.9
2002	20.7	7.2	13.5	19.7	6.9	12.8
2003	20.8	7.9	12.9	20.3	7.4	12.0
2004, proj.	22.1	8.6	13.6	22.0	7.8	12.4
2005, proj.	24.3	8.9	15.4	22.0	8.0	13.9
2006, proj.	24.6	9.0	15.6	21.4	7.8	13.6
2007, proj.	25.6	8.9	16.7	22.0	7.7	14.3
2008, proj.	26.0	9.0	17.0	21.9	7.6	14.3
2009, proj.	26.0	9.0	17.0	21.5	7.4	14.0

Source: U.S. Office of Management and Budget, Budget of the United States, Historical Tables, Fiscal Year 2005, annual. Also see <http://www.whitehouse.gov/omb/budget/fy2005/hist.html>.

No. 782. U.S. and Worldwide Commercial Space Industry Revenue by Type: 2000 to 2002

[In billions of dollars (35.4 represents $35,400,000,000). For calendar years]

Industry	U.S.			World		
	2000	2001	2002	2000	2001	2002
Revenue, total	35.4	20.8	22.7	73.7	78.6	86.8
Satellite manufacturing [1]	6.0	3.8	4.4	11.5	9.5	12.1
Launch industry	2.7	1.1	1.0	5.3	3.0	3.7
Satellite services [2]	11.8	15.9	17.3	39.2	46.5	49.8
Ground equipment manufacturing [3]	14.9	(NA)	(NA)	17.7	19.6	21.2

NA Not available. [1] Includes revenues from the construction and sale of satellites to both commercial and government. [2] Includes revenues derived from transponder leasing and subscription/retail services such as direct-to-home television and satellite mobile and data communications. [3] Includes revenues from the manufacture of gateways and satellite control stations, satellite news-gathering trucks, very small aperture terminals, direct-to-home television equipment and mobile satellite phones.

Source: Satellite Industry Association/Futron Corporation, Bethesda, MD, 2002-2003 Satellite Industry Indicators Survey (copyright). Also see <http://www.sia.org/>.

No. 783. National Aeronautics and Space Administration—Budget Appropriations: 2004 and Projections, 2005 to 2009

[In millions of dollars (15,378 represents $15,378,000,000). Figures may not add due to rounding]

Item	2004	2005	2006	2007	2008	2009
Appropriation, total............	15,378	16,244	17,002	17,815	18,001	18,034
Exploration, science & aeronautics..........	7,831	7,760	7,869	8,320	8,900	9,091
Space science...........	3,943	4,138	4,404	4,906	5,520	5,561
Solar system exploration.............	1,302	1,187	1,202	1,300	1,392	1,438
Mars exploration..................	595	691	724	944	1,188	1,268
Lunar exploration	(NA)	70	135	280	375	420
Astronomical search for origins	894	1,067	1,196	1,212	1,182	927
Structure & evolution of the universe........	404	378	365	382	425	457
Sun-Earth connections	749	746	781	788	958	1,051
Earth science......................	1,526	1,485	1,390	1,368	1,343	1,474
Earth system science.............	1,451	1,409	1,313	1,290	1,266	1,397
Earth science applications.............	74	77	77	77	77	77
Biological & physical research............	965	1,049	950	938	941	944
Biological sciences research	356	492	499	496	500	502
Physical sciences research	350	300	220	210	210	210
Research partnerships & flight support	259	257	232	232	231	232
Aeronautics technology	946	919	957	938	926	942
Education	164	169	169	171	170	170
Earmarks [1]	287	(NA)	(NA)	(NA)	(NA)	(NA)
Exploration capabilities	7,521	8,456	9,104	9,465	9,070	8,911
Exploration systems	1,563	1,782	2,579	2,941	2,809	3,313
Human & robotic technology	655	1,094	1,318	1,317	1,386	1,450
Transporation systems	909	689	1,261	1,624	1,423	1,863
Space flight......................	5,857	6,674	6,525	6,524	6,261	5,598
Space station......................	1,497	1,863	1,764	1,780	1,779	2,115
Space shuttle.....................	3,928	4,319	4,326	4,314	4,027	3,030
Space flight support................	432	492	435	430	456	453
Earmarks........................	101	(NA)	(NA)	(NA)	(NA)	(NA)
Inspector General....................	27	28	29	30	31	32

NA Not available.   [1] FY 2004 budget column does not allocate earmarks across budget functions/categories.

Source: U.S. National Aeronautics and Space Administration, <http://ifmp.nasa.gov/codeb/budget2005, (released February 2004).

No. 784. World-Wide Successful Space Launches: 1957 to 2003

[Criterion of success is attainment of Earth orbit or Earth escape]

Country	Total, 1957-03	1957-64	1965-69	1970-74	1975-79	1980-84	1985-89	1990-94	1995-01	2002	2003
Total..........	4,305	289	586	555	607	605	550	466	524	62	61
Soviet Union/Russia [1] .	2,701	82	302	405	461	483	447	283	193	24	21
United States	1,277	207	279	139	126	93	61	122	210	17	23
Japan..............	60	-	-	5	10	12	11	9	8	3	2
ESA [2]	152	-	-	-	1	8	21	33	74	11	4
China	75	-	-	2	6	6	9	15	27	4	6
France	10	-	4	3	3	-	-	-	-	-	-
India...............	14	-	-	-	-	3	-	3	5	1	2
Israel	4	-	-	-	-	-	1	1	1	1	-
Ukraine [1]...........	10	-	-	-	-	-	-	-	6	1	3
Australia	1	-	1	-	-	-	-	-	-	-	-
United Kingdom	1	-	-	1	-	-	-	-	-	-	-

- Represents zero.   NA Not available.   [1] Launches conducted by the former Soviet Union are listed separately as Russia or Ukraine.
[2] European Space Agency. Includes launches by Arianespace.

Source: Library of Congress, Congressional Research Service, Science Policy Research Division, *Space Activities of the United States, CIS, and Other Launching Countries/Organizations 1957-1999;* thereafter, Resources, Science, and Industry Division, 2003.

Science and Technology   519

No. 785. Space Shuttle Launches—Summary: 1981 to January 2003

Flight number	Mission date	Orbiter name	Crew size (up/down)[1]	Days/hours duration	Flight number	Mission date	Orbiter name	Crew size (up/down)[1]	Days/hours duration
1	04/12/81	Columbia	2	2	58	10/18/93	Columbia	7	14
2	11/12/81	Columbia	2	2	61	12/02/93	Endeavour	7	11
3	03/22/82	Columbia	2	8	60	02/03/94	Discovery	6	8
4	06/27/82	Columbia	2	7	62	03/04/94	Columbia	5	14
5	11/11/82	Columbia	4	5	59	04/09/94	Endeavour	6	11
6	04/04/83	Challenger	4	5	65	07/08/94	Columbia	7	15
7	06/18/83	Challenger	5	6	64	09/09/94	Discovery	6	11
8	08/30/83	Challenger	5	6	68	09/30/94	Endeavour	6	11
9	11/28/83	Columbia	6	10	66	11/03/94	Atlantis	6	11
10	02/03/84	Challenger	5	8	63	02/03/95	Discovery	6	8
11	04/06/84	Challenger	5	7	67	03/02/95	Endeavour	7	17
12	08/30/84	Discovery	6	7	71	06/27/95	Atlantis	7/8	10
13	10/05/84	Challenger	7	8	70	07/13/95	Discovery	5	9
14	11/08/84	Discovery	5	8	69	09/07/95	Endeavour	5	11
15	01/24/85	Discovery	5	4	73	10/20/95	Columbia	7	16
16	04/12/85	Discovery	7	7	74	11/08/95	Atlantis	5	8
17	04/29/85	Challenger	7	7	72	01/11/96	Endeavour	6	08/22
18	06/17/85	Discovery	7	7	75	02/22/96	Columbia	7	15/18
19	07/29/85	Challenger	7	8	76	03/22/96	Atlantis	6/5	09/05
20	08/27/85	Discovery	5	7	77	05/19/96	Endeavour	6	10/01
21	10/03/85	Atlantis	5	4	78	06/20/96	Columbia	7	16/22
22	10/30/85	Challenger	8	7	79	09/16/96	Atlantis	6/7	10/03
23	11/26/85	Atlantis	7	7	80	11/19/96	Columbia	5	17/16
24	01/12/86	Columbia	7	6	81	01/12/97	Atlantis	6/6	10/05
25	01/28/86	Challenger[2]	7	-	82	02/11/97	Discovery	7	10/00
26	09/29/88	Discovery	5	4	83	04/04/97	Columbia	7	03/23
27	12/02/88	Atlantis	5	4	84	05/15/97	Atlantis	7/7	09/05
29	03/13/89	Discovery	5	5	94	07/01/97	Columbia	7	15/17
30	05/04/89	Atlantis	5	4	85	08/07/97	Discovery	6	11/20
28	08/08/89	Columbia	5	5	86	09/25/97	Atlantis	7/8	10/19
34	10/18/89	Atlantis	5	5	87	11/19/97	Columbia	6	15/17
33	11/22/89	Discovery	5	5	89	01/22/98	Endeavor	7/7	08/20
32	01/09/90	Columbia	5	11	90	04/17/98	Columbia	7	15/22
36	02/28/90	Atlantis	5	4	91	06/02/98	Discovery	6/7	09/20
31	04/24/90	Discovery	5	5	95	10/29/98	Discovery	7	08/22
41	10/06/90	Discovery	5	4	88	12/04/98	Endeavor	6	11/19
38	11/15/90	Atlantis	5	5	96	05/27/99	Discovery	7	09/19
35	12/02/90	Columbia	7	9	93	07/23/99	Columbia	5	04/23
37	04/05/91	Atlantis	5	6	103	12/19/99	Discovery	7	07/23
39	04/28/91	Discovery	7	8	99	02/11/00	Endeavor	6	11/06
40	06/05/91	Columbia	7	9	101	05/19/00	Atlantis	7	09/21
43	08/02/91	Atlantis	5	9	106	09/08/00	Atlantis	7	11/19
48	09/12/91	Discovery	5	5	92	10/11/00	Discovery	7	12/22
44	11/24/91	Atlantis	6	7	97	11/30/00	Endeavor	5	10/20
42	01/22/92	Discovery	7	8	98	02/07/01	Atlantis	5	12/21
45	03/24/92	Atlantis	7	9	102	03/08/01	Discovery	7/7	12/20
49	05/07/92	Endeavour	7	9	100	04/19/01	Endeavor	7	11/20
50	06/25/92	Columbia	7	14	104	07/12/01	Atlantis	7	12/19
46	07/31/92	Atlantis	7	8	105	08/10/01	Discovery	7/7	11/21
47	09/12/92	Endeavour	7	8	108	12/05/01	Endeavor	8/7	10/20
52	10/22/92	Columbia	6	10	109	03/01/02	Columbia	7	10/22
53	12/02/92	Discovery	5	7	110	04/08/02	Atlantis	7	10/20
54	01/13/93	Endeavour	5	6	111	06/05/02	Endeavour	7/7	13/25
56	04/08/93	Discovery	5	9	112	10/07/02	Atlantis	6	10/20
55	04/26/93	Columbia	7	10	113	11/23/02	Endeavour	7/7	13/19
57	06/21/93	Endeavour	6	10	107	01/16/03	Columbia[2]	7	15/22
51	09/12/93	Discovery	5	10					

- Represents zero. [1] Differences in crew size due to docking with the Mir Space Station. [2] Loss of vehicle and crew.

Source: U.S. National Aeronautics and Space Administration, Internet site <http://science.ksc.nasa.gov/shuttle/missions/missions.html> (Accessed 24 May 2004).

No. 786. Nobel Prize Laureates in Selected Sciences: 1901 to 2003

[Presented by location of award-winning research and by date of award]

Country	1901-2003 Total	Physics	Chemistry	Physiology/ Medicine	1901-1930	1931-1945	1946-1960	1961-1975	1976-1990	1991-2002	2003
Total	494	171	143	180	93	49	74	92	98	82	7
United States	219	74	51	90	6	14	38	41	63	54	5
United Kingdom	76	21	27	28	15	11	14	20	9	5	1
Germany[1]	63	19	29	15	27	11	4	8	7	4	-
France	25	11	7	7	13	2	-	5	2	3	-
Soviet Union	12	9	1	2	2	-	4	3	1	1	1
Japan	8	4	4	-	-	-	1	2	1	4	-
Other countries	91	30	22	39	30	11	13	13	15	4	-

- Represents zero. [1] Between 1946 and 1991, data are for the former West Germany only.

Source: U.S. National Science Foundation, unpublished data.

Agriculture

This section presents statistics on farms and farm operators; land use; farm income, expenditures, and debt; farm output, productivity, and marketings; foreign trade in agricultural products; specific crops; and livestock, poultry, and their products.

The principal sources are the reports issued by the National Agricultural Statistics Service (NASS) and the Economic Research Service (ERS) of the U.S. Department of Agriculture. The information from the 2002 Census of Agriculture is available in printed form in the Volume 1, Geographic Area Series; in electronic format on CD-ROM; and on the Internet site <http://www.nass.usda.gov/census/>. The Department of Agriculture publishes annually *Agricultural Statistics*, a general reference book on agricultural production, supplies, consumption, facilities, costs, and returns. The ERS publishes data on farm assets, debt, and income on the Internet site <http://www.ers.usda .gov/briefing/farmincome/>. Sources of current data on agricultural exports and imports include *Outlook for U.S. Agricultural Trade*, published by the ERS; the ERS Internet site <http://www.ers.usda.gov /briefing/AgTrade>; and the reports of the U.S. Census Bureau, particularly *U.S. Imports of Merchandise on CD-ROM*, and *U.S. Exports of Merchandise on CD-ROM*.

The 45 field offices of the NASS collect data on crops, livestock and products, agricultural prices, farm employment, and other related subjects mainly through sample surveys. Information is obtained on some 75 crops and 50 livestock items as well as scores of items pertaining to agricultural production and marketing. State estimates and supporting information are sent to the Agricultural Statistics Board of NASS, which reviews the estimates and issues reports containing state and national data. Among these reports are annual summaries such as *Crop Production, Crop Values, Agricultural Prices*, and *Livestock Production, Disposition and*

Income. For more information about concepts and methods underlying USDA's statistical series, see *Major Statistical Series of the U.S. Department of Agriculture* (Agricultural Handbook No. 671), a 12-volume set of publications.

Farms and farmland—The definitions of a farm have varied through time. Since 1850, when minimum criteria defining a farm for census purposes first were established, the farm definition has changed nine times. The current definition, first used for the 1974 census, is any place from which $1,000 or more of agricultural products were produced and sold, or normally would have been sold, during the census year.

Acreage designated as "land in farms" consists primarily of agricultural land used for crops, pasture, or grazing. It also includes woodland and wasteland not actually under cultivation or used for pasture or grazing, provided it was part of the farm operator's total operation. Land in farms includes acres set aside under annual commodity acreage programs as well as acres in the Conservation Reserve and Wetlands Reserve Programs for places meeting the farm definition. Land in farms is an operating unit concept and includes land owned and operated as well as land rented from others. All grazing land, except land used under government permits on a per-head basis, was included as "land in farms" provided it was part of a farm or ranch.

An evaluation of coverage has been conducted for each census of agriculture since 1945 to provide estimates of the completeness of census farm counts. The 2002 coverage evaluation shows the census covered 96 percent of the farms with $50,000 or more in sales, but only 78 percent of farms with less than $50,000 in sales. The overall coverage of all farms was 82 percent. The census covered nearly 98 percent of all land in farms and

Agriculture   521

97 percent of the market value of agricultural products sold. In 2002, census farm counts and totals were statistically adjusted for coverage and reported at the county level. The size of the adjustments varies considerably by state. In general, farms not on the census mail list tended to be small in acreage, production, and sales of farm products. For more explanation about census mail list compilation, collection methods, coverage measurement, and adjustments, see Appendices A and C, 2002 Census of Agriculture, Volume 1 reports.

Farm income—The final agricultural sector output comprises cash receipts from farm marketings of crops and livestock, federal government payments made directly to farmers for farm-related activities, rental value of farm homes, value of farm products consumed in farm homes, and other farm-related income such as machine hire and custom work. Farm marketings represent quantities of agricultural products sold by farmers multiplied by prices received per unit of production at the local market. Information on prices received for farm products is generally obtained by the NASS Agricultural Statistics Board from surveys of firms (such as grain elevators, packers, and processors) purchasing agricultural commodities directly from producers. In some cases, the price information is obtained directly from the producers.

Crops—Estimates of crop acreage and production by the NASS are based on current sample survey data obtained from individual producers and objective yield counts, reports of carlot shipments, market records, personal field observations by field statisticians, and reports from other sources. Prices received by farmers are marketing year averages. These averages are based on U.S. monthly prices weighted by monthly marketings during specific periods. U.S. monthly prices are state average prices weighted by marketings during the month. Marketing year average prices do not include allowances for outstanding loans, government purchases, deficiency payments or disaster payments.

All state prices are based on individual state marketing years, while U.S. marketing year averages are based on standard marketing years for each crop. For a listing of the crop marketing years and the participating states in the monthly program, see *Crop Values*. Value of production is computed by multiplying state prices by each state's production. The U.S. value of production is the sum of state values for all states. Value of production figures shown in Tables 822-825, 829, and 830 should not be confused with cash receipts from farm marketings which relate to sales during a calendar year, irrespective of the year of production.

Livestock—Annual inventory numbers of livestock and estimates of livestock, dairy, and poultry production prepared by the Department of Agriculture are based on information from farmers and ranchers obtained by probability survey sampling methods.

Statistical reliability—For a discussion of statistical collection and estimation, sampling procedures, and measures of statistical reliability pertaining to Department of Agriculture data, see Appendix III.

Figure 17.1
Farms by Size, 1997 and 2002

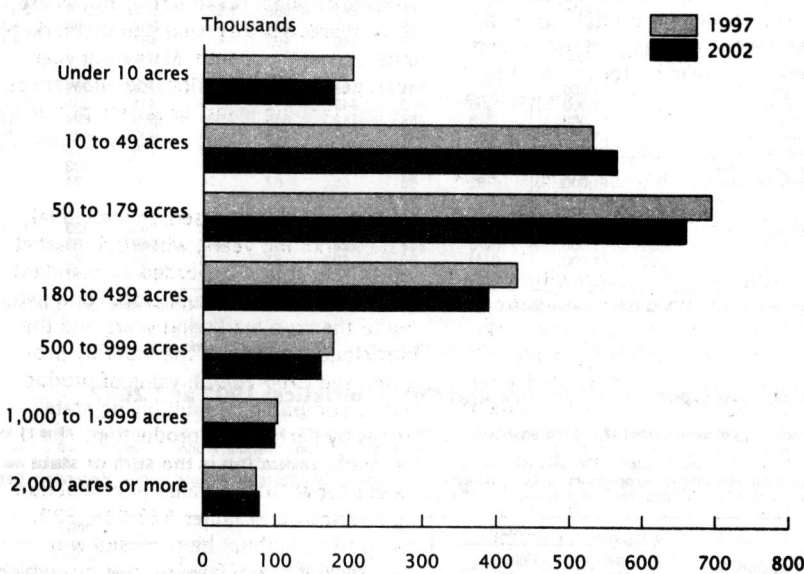

Source: Chart prepared by U.S. Census Bureau. For data, see Table 787.

Figure 17.2
Age of Principal Operator: 2002

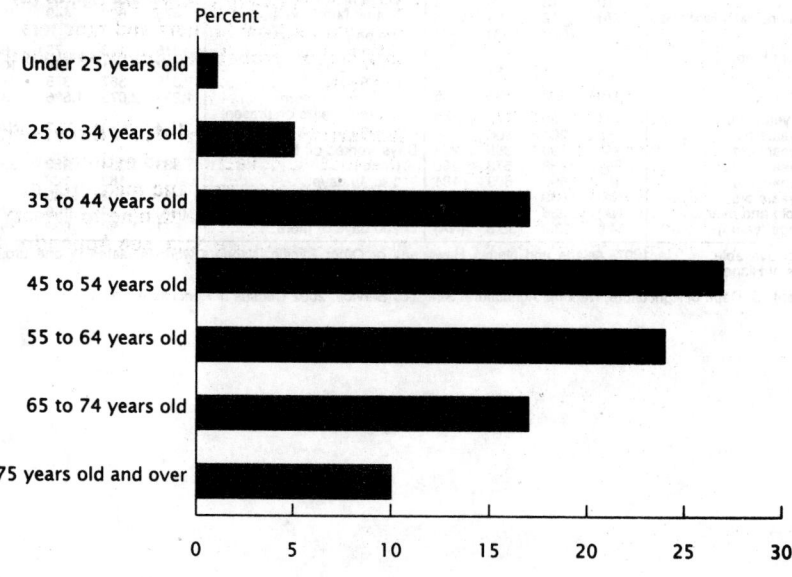

Source: Chart prepared by U.S. Census Bureau. For data, see Table 788.

Agriculture 523

[2,314 represents 2,314,000. For comments on adjustment, see text, this section. See also Appendix III]

Size and type of organization	Unit	Not adjusted for coverage						1997 [1]	2002 [1]
		1974	1978	1982	1987	1992	1997		
Farms	1,000...	2,314	2,258	2,241	2,088	1,925	1,912	2,216	2,129
Land in farms	Mil. acres.	1,017	1,015	987	964	946	932	955	938
Average size of farm	Acres...	440	449	440	462	491	487	431	441
Farms by size:									
Under 10 acres	1,000...	128	151	188	183	166	154	205	179
10 to 49 acres	1,000...	380	392	449	412	388	411	531	564
50 to 179 acres	1,000...	828	759	712	645	584	593	694	659
180 to 499 acres	1,000...	616	582	527	478	428	403	428	389
500 to 999 acres	1,000...	207	213	204	200	186	176	179	162
1,000 to 1,999 acres	1,000...	93	98	97	102	102	101	103	99
2,000 acres or more	1,000...	62	63	65	67	71	75	74	78
Farms by type of organization:									
Family or individual	1,000...	(NA)	1,966	1,946	1,809	1,653	1,643	1,923	1,910
Partnership	1,000...	(NA)	233	223	200	187	169	186	130
Corporation	1,000...	(NA)	50	60	67	73	84	90	74
Other [2]	1,000...	(NA)	9	12	12	12	15	17	16

NA Not available.   [1] Data have been adjusted for coverage; see text, this section.   [2] Cooperative, estate or trust, institutional, etc.

Source: U.S. Dept. of Agriculture, National Agricultural Statistics Service. *2002 Census of Agriculture*, Vol. 1.

[In thousands, except as indicated (2,216 represents 2,216,000). An "operator" is a person who operates a farm, either doing the work or making day-to-day decisions. A farm operation may have more than one operator. A principal operator is the person primarily responsible for the on-site, day-to-day operation of the farm or ranch business. Data on operator characteristics were collected up to a maximum of three operators per farm, though operations were asked to report the total number of operators. Data have been adjusted for coverage; see text, this section and Appendix III]

Characteristic	Principal operators, 1997	2002			Characteristic	Principal operators, 1997	2002		
		Total operators	Principal operators	Other operators			Total operators	Principal operators	Other operators
Total	2,216	3,054	2,129	925	Full owner	1,385	(NA)	1,428	(NA)
					Part owner	616	(NA)	551	(NA)
White	2,154	2,966	2,067	899	Tenant	215	(NA)	150	(NA)
Black or African American	27	36	29	7					
American Indian or Alaska Native	13	24	15	9	Principal occupation:				
					Farming	1,044	1,658	1,224	434
Native Hawaiian or Other Pacific Islander [1]	(NA)	2	1	1	Other	1,171	1,396	905	491
Asian [1]	10	13	8	5	Place of residence: [3]				
More than one race reported	(NA)	12	8	4	On farm operated	1,577	2,391	1,680	711
Other	12	(NA)	(NA)	(NA)	Not on farm operated	475	662	449	214
Operators of Hispanic origin [2]	33	72	51	22	Years on present farm: [3]				
					2 years or less	115	143	75	68
Female	210	822	238	585	3 to 4 years	157	251	144	108
Under 25 years old	24	60	17	43	5 to 9 years	318	587	375	212
25 to 34 years old	155	201	106	95	10 years or more	1,253	2,073	1,536	537
35 to 44 years old	444	590	366	224	Average years on present farm	19.4	(NA)	20.7	(NA)
45 to 54 years old	552	838	573	265					
55 to 64 years old	481	690	509	181	Days worked off farm: [3]				
65 to 74 years old	(NA)	439	354	85	None	833	1,354	962	392
75 years old and over	(NA)	236	203	32	1 to 49 days	121	183	122	61
Average age (years)	54.0	53.2	55.3	(NA)	50 to 99 days	65	102	66	36
					100 to 199 days	(NA)	224	146	78
					200 days or more	871	1,190	832	358

NA Not available.   [1] In 1997, Asians and Native Hawaiians or Other Pacific Islanders were tabulated in one group.   [2] Operators of Hispanic origin may be of any race.   [3] Data for 1997 exclude not reported.

Source: U.S. Dept. of Agriculture, National Agricultural Statistics Service, *2002 Census of Agriculture*, Vol. 1.

No. 789. Farms—Number and Acreage by Size of Farm: 1997 and 2002

[2,216 represents 2,216,000. Data have been adjusted for coverage; see text, this section and Appendix III]

Size of farm	Number of farms (1,000)		Land in farms (mil. acres)		Cropland harvested (mil. acres)		Percent distribution, 2002		
	1997	2002	1997	2002	1997	2002	Number of farms	All land in farms	Cropland harvested
Total	2,216	2,129	954.8	938.3	318.9	302.7	100.0	100.0	100.0
Under 10 acres.	205	179	0.9	0.8	0.3	0.2	8.4	0.1	0.1
10 to 49 acres	531	564	14.0	14.7	4.3	4.1	26.5	1.6	1.4
50 to 69 acres	154	152	9.0	8.8	2.7	2.5	7.1	0.9	0.8
70 to 99 acres	200	191	16.5	15.7	5.2	4.7	9.0	1.7	1.5
100 to 139 acres.	187	175	21.7	20.2	7.0	6.1	8.2	2.2	2.0
140 to 179 acres.	153	142	24.1	22.3	8.4	7.3	6.7	2.4	2.4
180 to 219 acres.	100	91	19.8	18.0	7.2	6.2	4.3	1.9	2.1
220 to 259 acres.	79	72	18.8	17.1	7.5	6.5	3.4	1.8	2.1
260 to 499 acres.	249	226	89.2	80.6	40.1	34.1	10.6	8.6	11.3
500 to 999 acres.	179	162	124.6	112.4	66.5	56.7	7.6	12.0	18.7
1,000 to 1,999 acres . .	103	99	140.7	135.7	75.9	72.8	4.7	14.5	24.0
2,000 acres or more . .	74	78	475.6	491.9	94.1	101.6	3.7	52.4	33.6

Source: U.S. Dept. of Agriculture, National Agricultural Statistics Service. *2002 Census of Agriculture*, Vol. 1.

No. 790. Farms—Number and Acreage by Tenure of Principal Operator: 1997 and 2002

[2,216 represents 2,216,000. Full owners own all the land they operate. Part owners own a part and rent from others the rest of the land they operate. A principal operator is the person primarily responsible for the on-site, day-to-day operation of the farm or ranch business. Data have been adjusted for coverage; see text, this section and Appendix III]

Item and year	Unit	Total	Full owner	Part owner	Tenant	Percent distribution			
						Total	Full owner	Part owner	Tenant
NUMBER OF FARMS									
1997	1,000	2,216	1,385	616	215	100	63	28	10
2002, total	1,000	2,129	1,428	551	150	100	67	26	7
Under 50 acres	1,000	743	639	64	41	100	86	9	5
50 to 179 acres	1,000	659	487	131	41	100	74	20	6
180 to 499 acres	1,000	389	203	153	33	100	52	39	8
500 to 999 acres	1,000	162	54	91	17	100	33	56	10
1,000 acres or more	1,000	177	46	112	18	100	26	64	10
LAND IN FARMS									
1997	Mil. acres. .	955	332	512	111	100	35	54	12
2002	Mil. acres. .	938	357	495	87	100	38	53	9

Source: U.S. Dept. of Agriculture, National Agricultural Statistics Service, *2002 Census of Agriculture*, Vol. 1.

No. 791. Farms—Number, Acreage, and Value by Type of Organization: 1997 and 2002

[2,216 represents 2,216,000. Data have been adjusted for coverage; see text, this section and Appendix III]

Item and year	Unit	Total [1]	Individual or family	Part- nership	Corpor- ation	Percent distribution			
						Total	Individual or family	Part- nership	Corpor- ation
NUMBER OF FARMS									
1997	1,000	2,216	1,923	186	90	100	87	8	4
2002	1,000	2,129	1,910	130	74	100	90	6	4
LAND IN FARMS									
1997	Mil. acres. .	955	605	151	133	100	63	16	14
2002	Mil. acres. .	938	622	146	108	100	66	16	12
Value of land and buildings, 2002 [2]	Bil. dol. . . .	1,145	836	158	129	100	73	14	11
Value of farm products sold, 2002 . .	Bil. dol. . . .	201	104	37	57	100	52	18	28

[1] Includes other types, not shown separately.   [2] Based on a sample of farms.

Source: U.S. Dept. of Agriculture, National Agricultural Statistics Service, *2002 Census of Agriculture*, Vol. 1.

Agriculture   525

[108.3 represents 108,300,000. Data have been adjusted for coverage; see text, this section and Appendix III]

Item	Unit	All corporations	Family held corporations			Other corporations		
			Total	1-10 stock-holders	11 or more stock-holders	Total	1-10 stock-holders	11 or more stock-holders
Farms	Number...	73,752	66,667	65,017	1,650	7,085	6,010	1,075
Percent distribution	Percent...	100	90	88	2	10	8	1
Land in farms	Mil. acres..	108.3	99.0	92.0	7.0	9.3	6.3	3.0
Average per farm	Acres	1,469	1,485	1,416	4,226	1,315	1,050	2,799
Value of—								
Land and buildings [1]	Bil. dol. ...	128.9	114.1	105.9	8.2	14.7	9.5	5.3
Average per farm.	$1,000 ...	1,759	1,720	1,642	4,446	2,142	1,646	4,684
Farm products sold	Bil. dol. ...	57.0	44.0	38.0	6.0	13.0	7.5	5.4
Average per farm.	$1,000 ...	773	660	585	3,625	1,828	1,255	5,032

[1] Based on a sample of farms.

Source: U.S. Dept. of Agriculture, National Agricultural Statistics Service, *2002 Census of Agriculture*, Vol. 1.

[2,129 represents 2,129,000. Data have been adjusted for coverage; see text, this section and Appendix III]

Market value of agricultural products sold	Farms (1,000)	Acreage		Value of sales		Percent distribution		
		Total (mil.)	Average per farm	Total (mil. dol.)	Average per farm (dol.)	Farms	Acreage	Value of sales
Total	2,129	938.3	441	200,646	94,244	100.0	100.0	100.0
Less than $2,500	827	107.0	129	485	586	38.8	11.4	0.2
$2,500 to $4,999	213	23.1	108	763	3,582	10.0	2.5	0.4
$5,000 to $9,999	223	34.8	156	1,577	7,072	10.5	3.7	0.8
$10,000 to $24,999	256	69.5	271	4,068	15,891	12.0	7.4	2.0
$25,000 to $49,999	158	77.9	494	5,594	35,405	7.4	8.3	2.8
$50,000 to $99,999	140	110.1	784	10,024	71,600	6.6	11.7	5.0
$100,000 to $249,999.....	159	189.4	1,191	25,401	159,755	7.5	20.2	12.7
$250,000 to $499,999.....	82	140.8	1,723	28,530	347,927	3.9	15.0	14.2
$500,000 to $999,999.....	42	94.0	2,241	28,944	689,143	2.0	10.0	14.4
$1,000,000 or more	29	91.7	3,198	95,259	3,284,793	1.4	9.8	47.5

Source: U.S. Dept. of Agriculture, National Agricultural Statistics Service, *2002 Census of Agriculture*, Vol. 1.

[2,129 represents 2,129,000. Economic class of farm is a combination of value of agricultural products sold and federal farm program payments. Full owners own all the land they operate. Part owners own a part and rent from others the rest of the land they operate. Data have been adjusted for coverage; see text, this section and Appendix III]

Economic class of farm	Tenure of principal operator [2]				Type of organization		
	Total [1]	Full owner	Part owner	Tenant	Individual or family	Partner-ship	Corpora-tion
NUMBER OF FARMS (1,000)							
Total	2,129	1,428	551	150	1,910	130	74
Less than $1,000	431	372	42	17	410	13	6
$1,000 to $2,499	307	260	34	13	293	9	3
$2,500 to $4,999	243	193	38	12	229	9	3
$5,000 to $9,999	247	180	51	16	230	11	3
$10,000 to $24,999	272	175	76	22	248	16	6
$25,000 to $49,999	164	86	60	17	145	12	5
$50,000 to $99,999	143	59	67	17	122	12	7
$100,000 to $249,999.................	163	49	94	20	132	17	12
$250,000 to $499,999.................	86	26	51	9	61	13	11
$500,000 to $999,999.................	44	16	24	4	27	9	8
$1,000,000 to $2,499,999	22	9	11	2	10	5	6
$2,500,000 to $4,999,999	5	3	2	1	2	1	2
$5 million or more	3	2	1	(Z)	1	1	2
Market value of agricultural products sold and government payments (mil. dol.)..	207,192	89,718	94,808	22,666	108,863	38,221	57,668

Z Less than 500.   [1] Includes other types, not shown separately.   [2] A principal operator is the person primarily responsible for the on-site, day-to-day operation of the farm or ranch business.

Source: U.S. Department of Agriculture, National Agricultural Statistics Service. *2002 Census of Agriculture*, Vol. 1.

No. 795. Farms—Number, Acreage, and Value by State: 1997 and 2002

[2,216 represents 2,216,000. Data have been adjusted for coverage; see text, this section and Appendix III]

State	Number of farms (1,000) 1997	Number of farms (1,000) 2002	Land in farms (mil. acres) 1997	Land in farms (mil. acres) 2002	Average size of farm (acres) 1997	Average size of farm (acres) 2002	Total value of land and buildings [1] (bil. dol.) 1997	Total value of land and buildings [1] (bil. dol.) 2002	Market value of agricultural products sold and government payments, 2002 (mil. dol.)	Total number of operators, 2002 (1,000)
United States........	2,216	2,129	954.8	938.3	431	441	921.6	1,144.9	207,192	3,115
Alabama.............	50	45	9.5	8.9	191	197	14.1	15.1	3,343	63
Alaska..............	1	1	0.9	0.9	1,608	1,479	0.3	0.3	48	1
Arizona.............	9	7	27.2	26.6	3,194	3,645	11.0	10.6	2,427	12
Arkansas............	49	47	14.8	14.5	300	305	17.5	21.2	5,189	70
California...........	88	80	28.8	27.6	327	346	73.8	96.1	25,906	125
Colorado...........	30	31	32.4	31.1	1,071	991	20.3	23.8	4,651	50
Connecticut.........	5	4	0.4	0.4	83	85	2.5	3.5	474	7
Delaware...........	3	2	0.6	0.5	221	226	1.5	2.3	627	4
Florida	46	44	10.7	10.4	233	236	24.8	29.3	6,264	64
Georgia	49	49	11.3	10.7	228	218	17.9	22.6	5,030	67
Hawaii	5	5	1.4	1.3	263	241	3.5	4.6	534	8
Idaho	26	25	12.1	11.8	470	470	12.5	15.3	4,002	39
Illinois.............	79	73	27.7	27.3	350	374	58.2	66.7	8,089	102
Indiana.............	67	60	15.5	15.1	233	250	32.4	38.4	5,008	86
Iowa...............	97	91	32.3	31.7	334	350	54.1	64.2	12,813	127
Kansas.............	65	64	46.7	47.2	712	733	27.3	32.6	9,074	90
Kentucky...........	91	87	13.9	13.8	153	160	20.3	25.5	3,174	123
Louisiana	30	27	8.4	7.8	275	286	10.3	12.2	1,939	39
Maine..............	7	7	1.3	1.4	177	190	1.7	2.3	472	11
Maryland...........	13	12	2.2	2.1	165	170	7.1	8.5	1,326	19
Massachusetts........	7	6	0.6	0.5	79	85	3.1	4.6	389	10
Michigan...........	54	53	10.4	10.1	195	190	18.0	27.1	3,917	80
Minnesota	79	81	27.6	27.5	350	340	31.4	41.8	8,926	114
Mississippi..........	42	42	11.4	11.1	271	263	12.6	15.6	3,262	58
Missouri	111	107	30.2	29.9	272	280	32.7	45.3	5,248	158
Montana	28	28	58.4	59.6	2,115	2,139	18.0	23.3	2,093	43
Nebraska	55	49	45.9	45.9	841	930	30.0	35.7	10,051	71
Nevada.............	3	3	6.4	6.3	2,000	2,118	2.5	2.8	451	5
New Hampshire	4	3	0.5	0.4	118	132	1.2	1.4	149	6
New Jersey..........	10	10	0.9	0.8	85	81	5.7	7.4	754	15
New Mexico..........	18	15	46.2	44.8	2,583	2,954	9.7	10.6	1,750	23
New York	38	37	7.8	7.7	204	206	10.4	12.9	3,228	58
North Carolina	59	54	9.4	9.1	160	168	20.7	28.0	7,059	76
North Dakota	32	31	39.7	39.3	1,227	1,283	16.0	15.8	3,526	42
Ohio...............	79	78	14.7	14.6	187	187	30.3	39.6	4,461	114
Oklahoma	84	83	34.1	33.7	405	404	21.6	23.8	4,606	121
Oregon.............	40	40	17.7	17.1	442	427	17.7	20.4	3,248	66
Pennsylvania	60	58	7.8	7.7	130	133	19.9	26.3	4,343	87
Rhode Island	1	1	0.1	0.1	65	71	0.4	0.6	56	1
South Carolina	26	25	5.0	4.8	193	197	7.6	10.1	1,528	34
South Dakota........	33	32	44.1	43.8	1,330	1,380	15.7	19.6	4,050	46
Tennessee..........	92	88	12.0	11.7	131	133	22.4	28.5	2,259	123
Texas..............	228	229	134.0	129.9	587	567	82.5	100.5	14,664	335
Utah...............	16	15	12.0	11.7	760	768	7.2	9.0	1,143	24
Vermont	7	7	1.3	1.2	186	189	2.1	2.5	497	11
Virginia............	49	48	8.8	8.6	177	181	17.6	23.3	2,416	70
Washington	40	36	15.8	15.3	393	426	20.9	22.4	5,465	56
West Virginia	22	21	3.7	3.6	172	172	4.2	4.8	488	30
Wisconsin	80	77	16.2	15.7	204	204	20.6	35.8	5,871	118
Wyoming...........	9	9	34.3	34.4	3,633	3,651	7.6	10.2	902	16

[1] Based on reports for a sample of farms.

Source: U.S. Dept. of Agriculture, National Agricultural Statistics Service, *2002 Census of Agriculture*, Vol. 1.

Agriculture 527

No. 796. Farms—Number and Acreage: 1980 to 2003

[As of June 1 (2,440 represents 2,440,000). Based on 1974 census definition; for definition of farms and farmland, see text of this section. Activities included as agriculture have undergone changes in recent years. Data for period 1995 to 2003 are not directly comparable with data for 1980 to 1990. Data for census years (indicated by italics) have been adjusted for underenumeration and are used as reference points along with data from acreage and livestock surveys in estimating data for other years. Minus sign (-) indicates decrease]

Year	Farms		Land in farms		Year	Farms		Land in farms	
	Number (1,000)	Annual change [1] (1,000)	Total (mil. acres)	Average per farm (acres)		Number (1,000)	Annual change [1] (1,000)	Total (mil. acres)	Average per farm (acres)
1980......	2,440	3	1,039	426	1998......	2,192	2	952	434
1985......	2,293	-41	1,012	441	1999......	2,187	-5	948	434
1990......	2,146	-29	987	460	2000......	2,167	-21	945	436
1995......	2,196	-1	963	438	2001......	2,149	-18	942	438
1996......	2,191	-6	959	438	*2002......*	*2,135*	*-13*	*940*	*440*
1997......	*2,191*	-	*956*	*436*	2003......	2,127	-9	939	441

- Represents or rounds to zero.   [1] Annual change from immediate preceding year.

No. 797. Farms—Number and Acreage by State: 2000 and 2003

[2,167 represents 2,167,000. See headnote, Table 796]

State	Farms (1,000)		Acreage (mil.)		Acreage per farm		State	Farms (1,000)		Acreage (mil.)		Acreage per farm	
	2000	2003	2000	2003	2000	2003		2000	2003	2000	2003	2000	2003
U.S.......	2,167	2,127	945	939	436	441	Montana.....	28	28	59	60	2,133	2,146
Alabama....	47	45	9	9	191	198	Nebraska....	52	49	46	46	887	946
Alaska.....	1	1	1	1	1,569	1,475	Nevada......	3	3	6	6	2,065	2,100
Arizona.....	11	10	27	27	2,514	2,573	New						
Arkansas.....	48	48	15	14	304	303	Hampshire...	3	3	(Z)	(Z)	133	132
California....	83	79	28	27	337	345	New Jersey...	10	10	1	1	86	83
Colorado....	30	31	32	31	1,053	987	New Mexico...	18	18	45	45	2,494	2,554
Connecticut...	4	4	(Z)	(Z)	86	86	New York....	38	37	8	8	205	207
Delaware.....	3	2	1	1	215	230	North Carolina.	56	54	9	9	166	170
Florida	44	44	10	10	236	232	North Dakota..	31	30	39	39	1,279	1,300
Georgia	49	49	11	11	222	219	Ohio........	79	78	15	15	187	188
Hawaii	6	6	1	1	251	236	Oklahoma....	85	84	34	34	400	404
Idaho.......	25	25	12	12	486	472	Oregon......	40	40	17	17	433	430
Illinois......	77	73	28	28	357	377	Pennsylvania...	59	58	8	8	130	132
Indiana	63	60	15	15	240	253	Rhode Island..	1	1	(Z)	(Z)	75	71
Iowa.......	94	90	33	32	346	352	South Carolina.	24	24	5	5	203	199
Kansas.....	65	65	48	47	736	732	South Dakota..	32	32	44	44	1,358	1,386
Kentucky.....	90	87	14	14	152	159	Tennessee....	88	87	12	12	134	133
Louisiana	29	27	8	8	277	289	Texas.......	228	229	131	131	573	570
Maine.......	7	7	1	1	190	190	Utah........	16	15	12	12	748	758
Maryland.....	12	12	2	2	172	170	Vermont.....	7	7	1	1	192	192
Massachusetts.	6	6	1	1	89	85	Virginia	49	48	9	9	180	181
Michigan	53	53	10	10	192	189	Washington ...	37	36	16	15	420	431
Minnesota....	81	80	28	28	344	346	West Virginia ..	21	21	4	4	173	173
Mississippi....	42	43	11	11	266	260	Wisconsin	78	77	16	16	206	204
Missouri	109	106	30	30	277	285	Wyoming	9	9	35	34	3,750	3,743

Z Less than 500,000 acres.

Source of Tables 796 and 797: U.S. Dept. of Agriculture, National Agricultural Statistics Service, *Farm Numbers; Farms and Land in Farms, Final Estimates by States, 1979-1987; Farms and Land in Farms, Final Estimates, 1988-1992; Farms and Land in Farms, Final Estimates, 1993-1997; Farm Numbers and Land in Farms, Final Estimates, 1998-2002;* and *Farms and Land In Farms,* February releases.

No. 798. Certified Organic Farmland Acreage and Livestock: 1997 to 2001

Item	Unit	1997	2000	2001	Crop	Certified organic acreage (1,000)	
						1997	2001
Certified growers.........	Number .	5,021	6,592	6,949	Corn.................	43	94
					Wheat...............	126	195
Certified organic acreage,					Oats................	30	33
total.................	1,000...	1,347	2,029	2,344	Barley...............	30	31
Pastureland and rangeland.	1,000...	496	810	1,040	Rice	11	32
Cropland	1,000...	850	1,219	1,305	Millet...............	12	23
					Buckwheat...........	8	14
Certified animals:					Soybeans............	82	174
Beef cows	Number .	4,429	13,829	15,197	Dry beans	5	15
Milk cows	Number .	12,897	38,196	48,677	Hay and silage........	127	254
Hogs and pigs	Number .	482	1,724	3,135	Sunflowers...........	11	15
Sheep and lambs	Number .	705	2,279	4,207	Lettuce	6	16
Layer hens	1,000...	538	1,114	1,612	Apples	9	12
Broilers.............	1,000...	38	1,925	2,204	Grapes	19	15
Turkeys.............	Number .	(NA)	9,138	98,653	Cotton..............	10	11
Unclassified/other	Number .	226,105	111,359	17,244	Trees for maple syrup	14	12

NA Not available.
Source: U.S. Dept. of Agriculture, Economic Research Service, *U.S. Organic Farming Emerges in the 1990s: Adoption of Certified Systems,* AIB No. 770, June 2001; *U.S. Organic Farming in 2000-2001: Adoption of Certified Systems,* AIB No. 780, February 2003; and "U.S. Organic Agriculture Data Tables"; <http://www.ers.usda.gov/data/organic>. February 2003; and "U.S. Organic Agriculture Data Tables"; <http://www.ers.usda.gov/data/organic>.

528   Agriculture

No. 799. Farm Sector Output and Value Added: 1990 to 2002

[In billions of dollars (180.1 represents $180,100,000,000). For definition of value added, see text, Section 13. Minus sign (-) indicates decrease]

Item	1990	1993	1994	1995	1996	1997	1998	1999	2000	2001	2002
CURRENT DOLLARS											
Farm output, total	180.1	182.2	197.6	192.0	215.9	222.0	208.9	198.5	203.6	213.3	202.2
Cash receipts from farm marketings	172.1	182.3	181.1	194.3	201.6	211.2	199.0	190.2	196.6	202.5	195.6
Farm products consumed on farms	0.7	0.6	0.6	0.5	0.5	0.5	0.5	0.5	0.6	0.6	0.5
Other farm income	4.9	5.1	5.1	6.3	6.1	7.4	8.5	9.4	8.4	9.5	9.3
Change in farm finished goods inventories	2.4	-5.9	10.8	-9.2	7.8	2.8	0.8	-1.6	-2.0	0.7	-3.2
Less: Intermediate goods and services consumed [1]	103.5	111.6	115.9	123.5	125.2	133.9	130.0	129.8	132.1	137.8	131.5
Equals: Gross farm value added	**76.6**	**70.6**	**81.6**	**68.5**	**90.7**	**88.1**	**78.9**	**68.8**	**71.5**	**75.5**	**70.7**
Less: Consumption of fixed capital	18.6	18.9	19.2	19.6	19.9	20.3	20.9	21.2	21.3	21.7	22.1
Equals: Net farm value added	58.0	51.7	62.4	48.9	70.8	67.8	58.0	47.6	50.2	53.8	48.7
Compensation of employees	13.4	14.2	14.4	15.4	16.0	17.1	18.2	18.9	19.7	20.9	20.5
Taxes on production and imports	3.8	3.8	4.0	4.2	4.2	4.4	4.3	4.9	4.7	4.8	5.1
Less: Subsidies to operators	7.6	11.3	6.6	6.1	6.2	6.4	10.5	18.6	19.6	18.3	9.5
Net operating surplus	48.5	45.0	50.6	35.4	56.7	52.6	46.0	42.4	45.4	46.4	32.5
CHAINED (2000) DOLLARS [2]											
Farm output, total	164.5	171.5	187.4	179.6	183.3	198.4	198.4	200.5	203.6	203.2	200.8
Cash receipts from farm marketings	159.0	173.3	173.3	183.5	172.1	189.2	189.2	192.0	196.6	192.4	194.3
Farm products consumed on farms	0.7	0.6	0.6	0.5	0.5	0.5	0.6	0.6	0.6	0.6	0.6
Other farm income	4.8	5.0	4.9	5.8	5.2	6.5	7.9	9.5	8.4	9.4	8.8
Change in farm finished goods inventories	2.1	-5.8	10.0	-8.8	6.0	2.5	0.9	-1.8	-2.0	0.8	-3.2
Less: Intermediate goods and services consumed [1]	117.5	123.5	126.7	134.4	128.5	133.7	137.5	138.1	132.1	134.8	131.0
Equals: Gross farm value added	49.3	50.6	60.9	49.6	56.1	64.4	61.6	62.9	71.5	68.5	69.8
Less: Consumption of fixed capital	23.0	21.6	21.4	21.3	21.1	21.3	21.6	21.6	21.3	21.3	21.4
Equals: Net farm value added	29.4	31.2	40.1	30.4	36.0	42.9	40.2	41.5	50.2	47.2	48.4

[1] Includes rent paid to nonoperator landlords.   [2] See text, Section 13.

Source: U.S. Bureau of Economic Analysis, *National Income and Product Accounts, Volume 1, 1929-2000*, and *Survey of Current Business*, February 2004. See also <http://www.bea.gov/bea/dn/nipaweb/selecttable.asp>.

No. 800. Value Added to Economy by Agricultural Sector: 1990 to 2002

[In billions of dollars (188.8 represents $188,800,000,000). Data are consistent with the net farm income accounts and include income and expenses related to the farm operator dwellings. The concept presented is consistent with that employed by the Organization for Economic Co-operation and Development]

Item	1990	1993	1994	1995	1996	1997	1998	1999	2000	2001	2002
Final agricultural sector output	**188.8**	**191.6**	**208.2**	**203.5**	**228.4**	**230.6**	**219.7**	**213.0**	**218.5**	**227.7**	**217.2**
Final crop output (sales) [1]	83.3	82.6	100.3	95.7	115.5	112.4	101.7	92.6	94.8	95.1	97.2
Final animal output (sales) [1]	90.2	92.1	89.8	87.8	92.1	96.5	94.2	95.3	99.3	106.4	93.2
Services and forestry	15.3	17.0	18.1	19.9	20.8	21.8	23.8	25.1	24.4	26.2	26.8
Machine hire and customwork	1.8	1.9	2.1	1.9	2.2	2.4	2.2	2.0	2.2	2.1	2.2
Forest products sold	1.9	2.5	2.6	2.8	2.7	2.9	3.1	2.7	2.9	2.7	2.6
Other farm income	4.5	4.6	4.3	5.8	6.2	6.9	8.7	10.1	8.7	10.1	10.6
Gross imputed rental value of farm dwellings	7.2	8.1	9.0	9.4	9.8	9.7	9.9	10.2	10.7	11.4	11.3
Less: Intermediate consumption outlays	92.9	100.7	104.9	109.7	113.2	119.8	117.6	118.6	121.7	126.0	122.4
Farm origin	39.5	41.3	41.3	41.8	42.7	46.9	44.8	45.6	47.9	48.7	47.8
Feed purchased	20.4	21.4	22.6	23.8	25.2	26.3	25.0	24.5	24.5	24.8	24.5
Livestock and poultry purchased	14.6	14.7	13.3	12.5	11.3	13.8	12.6	13.8	15.8	15.6	14.9
Seed purchased	4.5	5.2	5.4	5.5	6.2	6.7	7.2	7.2	7.5	8.2	8.4
Manufactured inputs [2]	22.0	23.1	24.4	26.1	28.6	29.2	28.1	27.1	28.7	29.4	27.5
Fertilizers and lime	8.2	8.4	9.2	10.0	10.9	10.6	9.9	9.8	10.0	10.3	9.9
Other intermediate expenses [2]	31.4	36.2	39.2	41.7	41.9	43.7	44.6	45.9	45.1	47.9	47.1
Repair and maintenance of capital items	8.6	9.2	9.1	9.5	10.3	10.4	10.4	10.5	10.8	11.1	10.7
Plus: Net government transactions [3]	3.1	6.9	1.0	0.1	0.1	0.1	4.9	14.3	15.5	13.3	3.6
Direct Government payments	9.3	13.4	7.9	7.3	7.3	7.5	12.4	21.5	22.9	20.7	11.0
Property taxes	5.9	6.2	6.5	6.7	6.8	6.9	7.0	6.8	6.9	6.9	6.9
Equals: Gross value added	**98.9**	**97.8**	**104.3**	**93.9**	**115.3**	**110.9**	**107.0**	**108.6**	**112.4**	**115.0**	**98.4**
Less: Capital consumption	18.1	18.3	18.6	19.2	19.4	19.5	19.9	20.0	20.3	20.8	21.5
Equals: Net value added	**80.8**	**79.5**	**85.7**	**74.8**	**95.9**	**91.4**	**87.2**	**88.7**	**92.0**	**94.2**	**76.9**
Less: Employee compensation	12.5	13.2	13.5	14.3	15.2	15.9	16.8	17.4	17.9	18.8	18.9
Less: Net rent received by nonoperator landlords	10.2	10.9	11.8	10.9	13.0	11.9	11.4	10.6	11.4	11.2	9.7
Less: Real estate and nonreal estate interest	13.4	10.7	11.6	12.6	13.0	13.1	13.4	13.8	14.9	13.6	13.0
Equals: Net farm income	**44.6**	**44.7**	**48.9**	**36.9**	**54.8**	**50.5**	**45.6**	**46.8**	**47.8**	**50.6**	**35.3**

[1] Includes home consumption and value of inventory adjustment.   [2] Includes other outlays not shown separately.   [3] Direct Government payments minus motor vehicle registration and licensing fees and property taxes.

Source: U.S. Dept. of Agriculture, Economic Research Service, "United States and State Farm Income Data"; <http://www.ers.usda.gov/Data/farmincome/finfidmu.htm>; accessed 9 January 2004.

Agriculture 529

No. 801. Farm Income—Cash Receipts From Farm Marketings: 1995 to 2002

[In millions of dollars (188,244 represents $188,244,000,000). Represents gross receipts from commercial market sales as well as net Commodity Credit Corporation loans. The source estimates and publishes individual cash receipt values only for major commodities and major producing states. The U.S. receipts for individual commodities, computed as the sum of the reported states, may understate the value of sales for some commodities. The degree of underestimation in some of the minor commodities can be substantial]

Commodity	1995	2000	2001	2002	Commodity	1995	2000	2001	2002
Total	188,244	191,977	199,779	192,948	Carrots	545	438	576	579
Livestock and					Corn, sweet	647	708	759	741
products [1]	87,217	99,545	106,413	93,480	Cucumbers	302	384	380	386
Cattle and calves	34,044	40,711	40,442	37,968	Lettuce [1]	2,004	1,863	1,881	2,265
Hogs	10,255	11,803	12,427	9,626	Head.	1,447	1,202	1,250	1,447
Sheep and lambs	566	465	393	423	Onions	706	740	790	764
Dairy products	19,880	20,608	24,710	20,547	Peppers, green. . . .	446	527	459	499
Broilers.	11,762	13,989	16,694	13,435	Tomatoes	1,584	1,809	1,628	1,854
Chicken eggs	3,893	4,348	4,446	4,263	Fresh	871	1,160	1,080	1,171
Turkeys	2,769	2,765	2,729	2,643	Processing.	713	650	547	683
Horses/mules	662	1,239	1,014	982	Cantaloups	347	367	431	406
Aquaculture [1] [2]	797	876	752	670					
Catfish	400	469	444	410	Fruits/nuts [1]	11,075	12,527	12,022	13,042
					Lemons.	266	283	273	340
					Oranges	1,749	1,783	1,626	1,714
Crops [1]	101,027	92,432	93,366	99,468	Apples	1,558	1,524	1,358	1,538
Rice.	1,282	837	1,029	842	Avocados	242	353	335	373
Wheat	9,054	5,654	5,360	5,541	Grapes [1]	2,045	3,100	2,935	2,853
Barley	825	557	550	529	Wine	965	1,909	1,820	1,683
Corn	18,893	15,162	15,346	17,489	Table.	367	437	435	457
Hay	3,288	3,844	4,547	4,635	Raisins	528	487	404	439
Sorghum grain.	1,377	864	902	900	Peaches	401	482	493	504
Cotton	6,851	2,949	3,637	3,855	Strawberries.	812	1,047	1,071	1,221
Tobacco	2,548	2,316	1,893	1,744	Almonds	881	666	740	1,190
Peanuts	1,014	897	1,001	594	Pistachios	161	245	163	336
Soybeans	13,868	12,047	11,779	13,473					
Sunflower	470	305	303	324	Sugarbeets	1,071	1,113	1,025	1,099
Vegetables [1]	14,983	15,647	15,641	16,862	Cane for sugar.	893	881	947	1,008
Beans, dry	567	436	415	497	Greenhouse/nursery [1]	10,775	13,610	14,189	14,275
Potatoes	2,490	2,375	2,593	3,035	Floriculture.	3,329	4,576	4,803	4,879
Beans, snap	285	394	390	409	Christmas trees . . .	415	471	453	466
Broccoli.	443	637	501	551	Mushrooms.	758	867	864	888

[1] Includes other commodities not shown separately.   [2] See also Table 855.

Source: U.S. Dept. of Agriculture, Economic Research Service, "United States and State Farm Income Data"; <http://www.ers.usda.gov /Data/farmincome/finfidmu.htm>; accessed 9 January 2004.

No. 802. Balance Sheet of the Farming Sector: 1990 to 2002

[In billions of dollars, except as indicated (841 represents $841,000,000,000). As of December 31]

Item	1990	1993	1994	1995	1996	1997	1998	1999	2000	2001	2002
Assets	841	909	935	966	1,003	1,051	1,083	1,139	1,203	1,256	1,304
Real estate	619	678	704	740	770	808	840	887	946	996	1,046
Livestock and poultry [1] . .	71	73	68	58	60	67	63	73	77	79	76
Machinery, motor vehicles [2]	86	85	87	88	88	89	90	90	90	93	94
Crops [3]	23	23	23	27	32	33	30	28	28	25	23
Purchased inputs	3	4	5	3	4	5	5	4	5	4	6
Financial assets	38	46	48	49	49	50	55	57	57	59	60
Claims.	841	909	935	966	1,003	1,051	1,083	1,139	1,203	1,256	1,304
Debt [4]	131	134	139	143	149	157	165	168	178	186	193
Real estate debt	68	68	70	72	74	79	83	87	91	96	103
Non-real estate debt	63	66	69	71	74	78	82	80	87	90	90
Equity	709	775	796	823	854	894	919	971	1,026	1,070	1,111
FINANCIAL RATIOS (percent)											
Farm debt/equity ratio	18.5	17.3	17.5	17.4	17.4	17.5	17.9	17.3	17.3	17.4	17.4
Farm debt/asset ratio	15.6	14.8	14.9	14.8	14.8	14.9	15.2	14.7	14.8	14.8	14.8
Rate of return on assets from:											
Total	3.5	6.1	5.3	4.3	5.9	5.8	5.2	5.3	5.1	4.8	3.2
Current income [5]	4.1	3.2	3.8	2.2	4.2	3.0	2.4	1.8	2.0	2.1	0.6
Real capital gains [6]	-0.7	2.9	1.5	2.1	1.7	2.8	2.8	3.5	3.2	2.6	2.5
Rate of return on equity from:											
Total	3.0	6.1	5.0	3.9	5.7	5.5	4.8	5.1	5.0	4.6	2.7
Current income [7]	3.0	2.3	3.0	1.1	3.3	2.0	1.4	0.7	0.9	1.2	-0.4
Real capital gains [8]	0.1	3.8	2.0	2.8	2.3	3.5	3.4	4.3	4.1	3.4	3.2

[1] Excludes horses, mules, and broilers.   [2] Includes only farm share value for trucks and autos.   [3] All non-CCC crops held on farms plus the value above loan rate for crops held under Commodity Credit Corporation.   [4] Excludes debt for nonfarm purposes.   [5] Returns to farm assets from current income/farm business assets. Measures how efficiently the farm business uses its assets; the per dollar return on farm assets from current income only.   [6] Real capital gains on farm business assets/farm business assets. The per dollar return on farm assets from real capital gains.   [7] Returns to farm assets from current income minus interest/Farm business equity. Measures the returns to equity capital employed in farm business from current income less interest.   [8] Real capital gains on farm business assets/farm business equity. The per dollar return on farm equity from real capital gains.

Source: U.S. Dept. of Agriculture, Economic Research Service, "Farm Business Balance Sheet and Financial Ratios"; published 7 November 2003; <http://www.ers.usda.gov/Data/FarmBalanceSheet/fbsdmu.htm>.

No. 803. Farm Assets, Debt, and Income by State: 2000 and 2002

[Assets and debt, as of December 31 (1,203,215 represents $1,203,215,000,000). Farm income data are after inventory adjustment and include income and expenses related to the farm operator's dwelling]

State	Assets (mil. dol.)		Debt (mil. dol.)		Debt/asset ratio (percent)		Final agricultural sector output (mil. dol.)		Net farm income (mil. dol.)	
	2000	2002	2000	2002	2000	2002	2000	2002	2000	2002
United States [1] ..	1,203,215	1,304,039	177,637	193,312	14.8	14.8	218,543	217,195	47,809	35,323
Alabama.........	16,521	17,919	2,054	2,288	12.4	12.8	3,842	3,746	1,151	1,200
Alaska.........	624	655	24	25	3.8	3.9	58	55	21	20
Arizona.........	35,823	41,723	1,448	1,550	4.0	3.7	2,622	3,340	777	1,462
Arkansas.......	22,372	24,664	4,315	4,746	19.3	19.2	5,250	5,148	1,522	816
California.......	88,124	92,970	17,837	19,477	20.2	21.0	27,232	27,632	5,499	5,197
Colorado........	25,108	25,687	3,686	4,039	14.7	15.7	5,062	5,069	644	711
Connecticut......	2,318	2,642	284	328	12.3	12.4	584	527	185	100
Delaware	1,795	1,813	378	421	21.0	23.2	833	808	135	82
Florida.........	28,959	32,711	4,771	5,215	16.5	15.9	7,030	7,207	2,529	2,667
Georgia........	24,535	28,185	3,600	3,988	14.7	14.2	5,780	5,270	1,998	1,699
Hawaii.........	3,808	4,175	254	277	6.7	6.6	545	544	102	98
Idaho.........	16,874	17,925	3,012	3,244	17.9	18.1	3,824	4,428	917	1,256
Illinois	76,078	81,893	9,383	10,195	12.3	12.5	7,938	7,897	1,569	642
Indiana.........	40,218	43,078	5,655	6,199	14.1	14.4	5,255	5,032	808	108
Iowa	73,326	77,600	13,117	14,097	17.9	18.2	11,643	12,475	2,357	1,767
Kansas.........	36,983	36,901	7,141	7,664	19.3	20.8	8,639	8,362	933	376
Kentucky	25,704	28,553	3,433	3,785	13.4	13.3	4,610	3,808	1,730	744
Louisiana	11,798	12,327	1,777	1,932	15.1	15.7	1,953	2,019	485	232
Maine..........	1,923	2,106	395	421	20.5	20.0	556	504	114	47
Maryland	7,887	8,609	1,087	1,238	13.8	14.4	1,739	1,640	381	195
Massachusetts.....	3,490	4,012	387	435	11.1	10.8	461	464	54	37
Michigan........	24,548	28,171	3,074	3,423	12.5	12.2	3,793	3,991	294	167
Minnesota.......	46,958	51,633	8,969	9,754	19.1	18.9	8,360	8,818	1,282	462
Mississippi	15,197	16,281	2,887	3,124	19.0	19.2	3,312	3,383	781	401
Missouri........	45,005	50,575	6,015	6,539	13.4	12.9	5,469	5,257	976	451
Montana........	24,516	25,786	2,685	2,850	11.0	11.1	1,984	2,107	277	216
Nebraska.......	44,121	45,461	9,325	9,910	21.1	21.8	9,488	9,787	1,370	980
Nevada	3,311	3,432	259	294	7.8	8.6	456	436	100	93
New Hampshire....	988	1,097	104	120	10.5	10.9	173	173	14	5
New Jersey.......	5,972	6,774	465	523	7.8	7.7	963	961	256	198
New Mexico	11,441	11,963	1,419	1,569	12.4	13.1	2,197	2,122	531	678
New York	13,967	14,943	2,509	2,755	18.0	18.4	3,375	3,517	589	568
North Carolina.....	26,880	29,022	3,688	4,119	13.7	14.2	9,483	8,095	3,184	1,661
North Dakota......	22,485	24,810	3,981	4,292	17.7	17.3	3,385	3,734	964	605
Ohio	38,537	41,737	4,239	4,739	11.0	11.4	5,414	4,831	1,155	268
Oklahoma........	26,587	29,073	4,413	4,656	16.6	16.0	4,641	4,434	1,021	758
Oregon.........	18,659	20,234	2,519	2,710	13.5	13.4	3,697	3,691	422	360
Pennsylvania......	23,442	25,125	2,828	3,129	12.1	12.5	4,834	4,593	1,118	611
Rhode Island......	377	418	39	45	10.2	10.7	55	55	8	6
South Carolina.....	8,338	9,232	1,143	1,298	13.7	14.1	1,774	1,543	574	178
South Dakota	24,696	26,551	4,198	4,434	17.0	16.7	4,363	3,807	1,445	559
Tennessee	26,990	29,756	2,605	2,917	9.7	9.8	2,666	2,677	574	339
Texas..........	98,539	107,480	11,970	13,000	12.2	12.1	14,907	15,076	3,873	3,686
Utah	11,424	12,687	857	933	7.5	7.4	1,200	1,250	243	291
Vermont........	2,699	3,034	378	424	14.0	14.0	591	563	152	105
Virginia.........	21,619	23,696	2,069	2,356	9.6	9.9	2,889	2,667	704	508
Washington.......	20,786	21,774	3,504	3,727	16.9	17.1	5,981	5,869	1,073	969
West Virginia......	4,567	5,121	408	444	8.9	8.7	511	489	50	7
Wisconsin........	36,065	40,780	5,983	6,532	16.6	16.0	6,075	6,374	730	640
Wyoming	10,217	11,244	1,067	1,132	10.5	10.1	1,055	919	135	100

[1] The U.S. total will exceed the sum of the states because data for some states are not included in the state's statistics due to disclosure issues.

Source: U.S. Dept. of Agriculture, Economic Research Service, "Farm Income Summary Totals for 50 States;" published 24 November 2003; <http://www.ers.usda.gov/Data/FarmIncome/50State/50stmenu.htm>; and "Farm Business Balance Sheet and Financial Ratios"; published 7 November 2003; <http://www.ers.usda.gov/Data/FarmBalanceSheet/fbsdmu.htm>.

Agriculture 531

No. 804. Cash Receipts for Selected Commodities—Leading States: 2002

[37,968 represents $37,968,000,000. See headnote, Table 801]

State	Value of receipts (mil. dol.)	Percent of total receipts	Rank	State	Value of receipts (mil. dol.)	Percent of total receipts	Rank
Cattle and calves	**37,968**	**100.0**	**(X)**	**Corn**	**17,489**	**100.0**	**(X)**
Texas	5,863	15.4	1	Iowa	3,259	18.6	1
Nebraska	4,959	13.1	2	Illinois	3,106	17.8	2
Kansas	4,810	12.7	3	Nebraska	2,252	12.9	3
Colorado	2,805	7.4	4	Indiana	1,506	8.6	4
Oklahoma	1,872	4.9	5	Minnesota	1,349	7.7	5
Dairy products	**20,547**	**100.0**	**(X)**	**Vegetables**	**16,862**	**100.0**	**(X)**
California	3,812	18.6	1	California	6,458	38.3	1
Wisconsin	2,663	13.0	2	Florida	1,570	9.3	2
New York	1,556	7.6	3	Arizona	1,351	8.0	3
Pennsylvania	1,482	7.2	4	Washington	833	4.9	4
Minnesota	1,011	4.9	5	Idaho	814	4.8	5

X Not applicable.

No. 805. Farm Income—Farm Marketings, 2001 and 2002, and Principal Commodities, 2002 by State

[In millions of dollars (199,779 represents $199,779,000,000). Cattle include calves and greenhouse includes nursery]

State	2001 Total	2001 Crops	2001 Livestock and products	2002 Total	2002 Crops	2002 Livestock and products	State rank for total farm marketings and four principal commodities in order of marketing receipts
U.S.	199,779	93,366	106,413	192,948	99,468	93,480	Cattle, dairy products, corn, greenhouse
AL	3,448	632	2,816	2,962	584	2,378	29-Broilers, cattle, chicken eggs, greenhouse
AK	52	23	29	51	23	28	49-Greenhouse, dairy products, hay, potatoes
AZ	2,601	1,409	1,192	2,997	1,903	1,094	27-Lettuce, cattle, dairy products, cotton
AR	4,966	1,450	3,516	4,527	1,575	2,952	14-Broilers, soybeans, cattle, rice
CA	26,378	19,035	7,343	26,107	19,865	6,242	1-Dairy products, greenhouse, grapes, lettuce
CO	4,719	1,346	3,373	4,881	1,379	3,502	12-Cattle, corn, dairy products, greenhouse
CT	483	307	175	468	314	154	43-Greenhouse, dairy products, chicken eggs, aquaculture
DE	845	187	659	724	177	546	40-Broilers, greenhouse, corn, soybeans
FL	6,690	5,288	1,402	6,848	5,609	1,239	8-Greenhouse, oranges, sugar cane, tomatoes
GA	5,274	1,735	3,539	4,472	1,582	2,890	15-Broilers, chicken eggs, cotton, cattle
HI	513	425	88	509	424	85	41-Pineapples, greenhouse, sugar cane, macadamia nuts
ID	3,714	1,652	2,062	3,934	1,935	1,999	19-Cattle, dairy products, potatoes, wheat
IL	7,308	5,461	1,846	7,486	5,924	1,562	6-Corn, soybeans, hogs, cattle
IN	5,157	3,290	1,868	4,800	3,249	1,551	13-Corn, soybeans, hogs, dairy products
IA	10,653	4,728	5,505	10,834	5,759	5,075	3-Corn, hogs, soybeans, cattle
KS	7,979	2,474	5,505	7,862	2,536	5,325	5-Cattle, wheat, corn, soybeans
KY	3,528	1,265	2,263	3,112	1,151	1,961	24-Horses/mules, tobacco, broilers, cattle
LA	1,786	1,084	701	1,773	1,159	614	33-Sugar cane, cotton, cattle, corn
ME	490	217	273	442	212	230	44-Potatoes, dairy products, chicken eggs, aquaculture
MD	1,596	647	949	1,432	621	810	36-Broilers, greenhouse, dairy products, corn
MA	367	273	94	380	297	83	45-Greenhouse, cranberries, dairy products, sweet corn
MI	3,507	2,015	1,492	3,390	2,130	1,260	22-Dairy products, greenhouse, soybeans, corn
MN	7,537	3,255	4,283	7,478	3,833	3,645	7-Corn, soybeans, hogs, dairy products
MS	3,141	865	2,276	2,962	1,013	1,950	28-Broilers, cotton, soybeans, aquaculture
MO	4,723	2,039	2,684	4,402	2,100	2,302	16-Soybeans, cattle, corn, hogs
MT	1,760	635	1,124	1,687	702	985	34-Cattle, wheat, hay, barley
NE	9,221	3,126	6,095	9,589	3,764	5,824	4-Cattle, corn, soybeans, hogs
NV	428	157	271	366	155	211	47-Cattle, hay, dairy products, onions
NH	157	90	67	148	91	56	48-Greenhouse, dairy products, apples, cattle
NJ	837	634	203	856	663	193	39-Greenhouse, horses/mules, blueberries, dairy products
NM	2,213	543	1,670	1,957	575	1,382	32-Dairy products, cattle, hay, greenhouse
NY	3,391	1,169	2,222	3,104	1,234	1,870	25-Dairy products, greenhouse, hay, apples
NC	7,585	2,931	4,654	6,603	2,659	3,944	9-Broilers, greenhouse, tobacco
ND	2,938	2,211	727	3,223	2,499	724	23-Wheat, cattle, soybeans, sugar beets
OH	4,529	2,669	1,860	4,276	2,646	1,630	17-Soybeans, corn, greenhouse, dairy products
OK	3,937	796	3,142	3,731	837	2,893	21-Cattle, hogs, broilers, wheat
OR	3,127	2,302	825	3,102	2,294	808	26-Greenhouse, cattle, dairy products, hay
PA	4,514	1,366	3,148	4,042	1,360	2,682	18-Dairy products, cattle, agaricus mushrooms, greenhouse
RI	48	40	8	46	40	6	50-Greenhouse, dairy products, sweet corn, potatoes
SC	1,595	713	883	1,452	692	760	35-Broilers, greenhouse, turkeys, tobacco
SD	3,897	1,640	2,257	3,779	1,720	2,060	20-Cattle, corn, soybeans, hogs
TN	2,118	989	1,130	2,000	1,087	913	31-Cattle, broilers, greenhouse, soybeans
TX	13,509	4,165	9,345	12,665	4,577	8,088	2-Cattle, greenhouse, cotton, broilers
UT	1,113	257	855	1,057	249	808	37-Cattle, dairy products, hay, hogs
VT	558	67	490	476	76	400	42-Dairy products, cattle, greenhouse, maple products
VA	2,457	756	1,702	2,173	722	1,451	30-Broilers, cattle, dairy products, greenhouse
WA	5,200	3,479	1,721	5,209	3,714	1,495	11-Apples, dairy products, cattle, potatoes
WV	437	89	348	378	78	300	46-Broilers, cattle, dairy products, chicken eggs
WI	5,761	1,290	4,471	5,319	1,551	3,768	10-Dairy products, cattle, corn, soybeans
WY	995	153	842	876	126	750	38-Cattle, hay, sugar beets, sheep/lambs

Source of Tables 804 and 805: U.S. Dept. of Agriculture, Economic Research Service, "Farm Income"; published 28 August 2003; <http://www.ers.usda.gov/Data/farmincome/finfidmu.htm>.

Indexes of Prices Received and Paid by Farmers: 2000 to 2003

[1990-92=100, except as noted]

Item	2000	2001	2002	2003	Item	2000	2001	2002	2003
Prices received, all products	96	102	98	107	**Prices paid, total** [2]	118	122	121	126
Crops	96	99	106	111	Production	116	120	119	124
Food grains	85	91	104	108	Feed	102	109	112	115
Feed grains and hay	86	91	100	104	Livestock & poultry	110	111	102	109
Cotton	82	64	56	85	Seed	124	132	142	154
Tobacco	107	107	108	106	Fertilizer	110	123	108	124
Oil-bearing crops	85	80	88	107	Agricultural chemicals	120	121	119	121
Fruits and nuts	98	109	105	88	Fuels	134	119	112	144
Commercial vegetables [1]	121	130	142	140	Supplies & repairs	124	128	131	134
Potatoes & dry beans	93	98	129	104	Autos and trucks	119	118	116	115
All other crops	110	112	114	114	Farm machinery	139	144	148	149
					Building materials	121	121	122	124
Livestock and products	97	106	90	103	Farm services	119	121	120	123
Meat animals	94	97	87	103	Rent	110	117	119	120
Dairy products	94	115	93	96	Interest	113	109	104	104
Poultry and eggs	106	116	94	110	Taxes	123	124	126	128
					Wage rates	140	146	153	157
					Parity ratio (1910-14=100) [3]	38	40	38	40

[1] Excludes potatoes and dry beans. [2] Includes production items, interest, taxes, wage rates, and a family living component. The family living component is the Consumer Price Index for all urban consumers from the Bureau of Labor Statistics. See text, Section 14, and Table 698. [3] Ratio of prices received by farmers to prices paid.

Source: U.S. Dept. of Agriculture, National Agricultural Statistics Service, *Agricultural Prices: Annual Summary*.

Value of Selected Commodities Produced Under Contracts: 2002

[67,510 represents $67,510,000,000. Marketing contracts refer to verbal or written agreements between a buyer and a grower that set a price and determine an outlet for a specified quantity of a commodity before harvest or before the farmer markets the commodity. Production contracts involve paying the farmer a fee for providing management, labor, facilities, and equipment, while assigning ownership of the product to the contractor. Survey based estimates (see source) exclude Alaska and Hawaii and do not represent official U.S. Dept. of Agriculture estimates of farm sector activity]

Commodity	Value of production under contract (mil. dol.)	Percent of total production [1]	Commodity	Value of production under contract (mil. dol.)	Percent of total production [1]
Total	**67,510**	**37**	Sugar beets	[4]900	97
Marketing contracts [2]	37,736	21	Vegetables	3,448	[4]29
Cattle	[3]612	[3]2	**Production contracts** [2]	**29,774**	**16**
Corn	2,771	16	Poultry and eggs [5]	15,451	90
Cotton	1,457	50	Cattle	4,597	15
Fruits	[4]7,045	67	Hogs	5,358	51
Hogs	[4]610	6	Vegetables	1,542	[4]13
Soybeans	1,378	10			

[1] Represents percent of value of production under contract as percent of total value of commodity production. [2] Includes other commodities not shown separately. [3] Data have relative standard error above 75 percent. [4] Data have relative standard error between 25 and 50 percent. [5] Data not available to estimate value of production for broilers.

Source: U.S. Dept. of Agriculture, Economic Research Service, Agricultural Resource Management Survey, annual.

Civilian Consumer Expenditures for Farm Foods: 1990 to 2002

[In billions of dollars, except percent (449.8 represents $449,800,000,000). Excludes imported and nonfarm foods, such as coffee and seafood, as well as food consumed by the military, or exported]

Item	1990	1993	1994	1995	1996	1997	1998	1999	2000	2001	2002
Consumer expenditures, total	449.8	489.2	512.2	529.5	546.7	566.5	585.0	625.3	661.1	687.5	709.4
Farm value, total	106.2	109.6	109.6	113.8	122.2	121.9	119.6	122.2	123.3	130.0	132.5
Marketing bill, total [1]	343.6	379.6	402.6	415.7	424.5	444.6	465.4	503.1	537.8	557.5	576.9
Percent of total consumer expenditures	76.4	77.6	78.6	78.5	77.6	78.5	79.6	80.5	81.3	81.1	81.3
At-home expenditures [2]	276.2	294.9	308.7	316.9	328.0	339.2	346.8	370.7	390.2	403.9	416.8
Farm value	80.2	76.4	75.3	76.1	81.6	79.0	77.0	78.7	79.6	83.9	85.7
Marketing bill [1]	196.0	218.5	233.4	240.8	246.4	260.2	269.8	292.0	310.6	320.0	331.1
Away-from-home expenditures	173.6	194.3	203.5	212.6	218.7	227.3	238.2	254.6	270.9	283.6	292.6
Farm value	26.0	33.2	34.3	37.7	40.6	42.9	42.6	43.5	43.7	46.1	46.8
Marketing bill [1]	147.6	161.1	169.2	174.9	178.1	184.4	195.6	211.1	227.2	237.5	245.8
Marketing bill cost components:											
Labor cost	154.0	178.0	186.1	196.6	204.6	216.9	229.9	241.5	252.9	263.8	273.1
Packaging materials	36.5	40.9	43.3	48.2	47.7	48.7	50.4	50.9	53.5	55.0	56.8
Rail and truck transport	19.8	21.2	21.8	22.3	22.9	23.6	24.4	25.2	26.4	27.5	28.4
Corporate profits before taxes	13.2	18.1	20.9	19.5	20.7	22.3	25.5	29.2	31.1	32.0	33.0
Fuels and electricity	15.2	17.2	17.9	18.6	19.6	20.2	20.7	22.0	23.1	24.1	24.9
Advertising	17.1	18.6	19.3	19.8	20.9	22.1	23.4	24.8	26.1	27.5	28.1
Depreciation	16.3	17.2	18.1	18.9	20.1	21.0	21.6	23.0	24.2	24.5	25.3
Net interest	13.5	10.1	11.0	11.6	11.4	12.5	12.9	14.4	16.9	18.6	19.2
Net rent	13.9	17.9	18.9	19.8	21.0	21.8	23.7	25.3	26.7	29.4	30.3
Repairs	6.2	7.2	7.8	7.9	8.5	8.8	9.0	9.6	10.1	10.6	10.9
Taxes	15.7	18.2	18.7	19.1	19.4	19.8	20.9	22.2	23.5	24.1	24.9
Other	22.2	15.0	18.8	13.4	7.7	6.9	3.0	15.0	23.3	20.4	22.0

[1] The difference between expenditures for domestic farm-originated food products and the farm value or payment farmers received for the equivalent farm products. [2] Food primarily purchased from retail food stores for use at home.

Source: U.S. Dept. of Agriculture, Economic Research Service, *Food Cost Review, 1950-97*, ERS Agricultural Economic Report No. AER780, June 1999; and "ERS/USDA Briefing Room - Food marketing and price spreads: USDA marketing bill"; <http://www.ers.usda.gov/Briefing/FoodPriceSpreads/bill/>.

Agriculture 533

No. 809. Hired Farmworkers—Selected Characteristics: 1990 to 2003

[Annual averages (886 represents 886,000). Data for 1990 and 2003 are not directly comparable with data for period 1995 to 2002. Data are calculated by source using data from the Census Bureau's Current Population Survey earnings microdata file]

Characteristic	1990	1995	1999	2000	2001	2002	2003, prel.
Number of workers (1,000)	886	849	840	878	745	793	753
PERCENT DISTRIBUTION							
Total	100.0	100.0	100.0	100.0	100.0	100.0	100.0
Age:							
Less than 25 years old	31.5	30.1	30.4	26.0	26.2	29.4	23.6
25 to 44 years old	47.6	44.2	44.0	46.9	48.4	43.2	49.8
45 to 59 years old	14.4	18.2	18.8	19.6	19.9	20.4	20.2
60 years old and over	6.5	7.5	6.8	7.5	5.5	7.0	6.4
Median age	28.0	32.0	33.0	35.0	35.0	36.0	34.0
Sex:							
Male	82.9	84.5	80.7	82.1	80.7	78.7	82.4
Female	17.1	15.5	19.3	17.9	19.3	21.3	17.6
Racial/ethnic group:							
White	61.0	53.5	50.1	47.2	49.1	52.2	52.3
Hispanic	29.4	41.1	43.0	46.4	45.7	42.0	42.8
Black and other	9.6	5.3	6.4	6.4	5.2	5.8	4.9
Years of school completed:							
0 to 4 years	11.1	14.2	11.3	13.4	10.6	11.1	8.6
5 to 8 years	21.6	22.5	22.6	21.0	21.2	19.9	22.2
9 to 11 years	22.8	22.7	20.7	21.2	23.3	21.2	21.4
12 years [1]	31.4	25.9	27.1	25.7	27.3	27.6	28.9
13 years or more	13.1	14.7	18.3	18.7	17.6	20.2	18.9
Employment status:							
Part-time	21.8	18.3	20.5	19.3	19.3	17.5	17.3
Full-time [2]	78.2	81.7	79.5	80.7	80.7	82.5	82.7
Median weekly earnings (dol.): [3]							
Full-time workers [2]	338	314	353	341	358	342	373
All workers	282	290	309	299	312	307	350

[1] A person received a high school diploma, GED, or equivalent degree.   [2] Full-time workers usually work 35 or more hours per week.   [3] Median earnings are in 2003 dollars.

Source: U.S. Dept. of Agriculture, Economic Research Service, "Briefing Room: Farm Labor"; published 10 November 2003; <http://www.ers.usda.gov/Briefing/FarmLabor/> and unpublished data.

No. 810. Agricultural Exports and Imports—Volume by Principal Commodities: 1990 to 2003

[In thousands of metric tons, except fruit juices, wine and malt beverages in thousands of hectoliters (7,703 represents 7,703,000). Includes Puerto Rico, U.S. territories, and shipments under foreign aid programs]

Commodity	1990	1995	1999	2000	2001	2002	2003
EXPORTS							
Fruit juices and wine	7,703	10,688	15,385	14,356	13,503	15,118	13,802
Beef, pork, and poultry meats	1,451	3,723	4,670	4,935	5,369	5,074	5,144
Wheat, unmilled	27,384	32,317	28,486	27,568	25,585	24,159	25,281
Wheat products	37	47	49	47	44	44	44
Rice, paddy, milled	2,534	3,275	2,932	3,241	2,889	3,808	4,477
Feed grains	61,066	66,795	58,309	54,946	54,702	53,218	48,637
Feed grain products	1,430	2,018	2,045	2,062	2,234	3,153	4,372
Feeds and fodders [1]	10,974	13,338	11,920	13,065	12,587	12,677	11,881
Fresh fruits and nuts	2,648	3,323	2,900	3,450	3,432	3,493	3,471
Fruit products	390	462	460	471	474	475	503
Vegetables, fresh	1,297	1,708	1,862	2,029	2,002	2,059	1,995
Vegetables, frozen and canned	529	892	1,078	1,112	1,087	1,065	1,011
Oilcake and meal	5,079	6,404	6,839	6,462	7,426	6,672	5,647
Oilseeds	15,820	23,596	24,217	28,017	29,974	29,139	32,487
Vegetable oils	1,226	2,532	2,408	2,043	2,193	2,682	2,256
Tobacco, unmanufactured	223	209	192	180	186	153	155
Cotton, excluding linters	1,696	2,039	699	1,485	1,868	2,108	2,561
IMPORTS							
Fruit juices	33,116	21,922	32,570	31,154	29,615	29,047	35,440
Wine	2,510	2,781	4,162	4,584	4,888	5,655	6,213
Malt beverages	10,382	13,251	20,878	23,464	25,533	27,087	27,605
Bananas and plantains	3,270	3,869	4,558	4,288	4,107	4,193	4,175
Coffee, including products	1,214	989	1,307	1,370	1,229	1,238	1,302
Rubber and allied gums, crude	840	1,044	1,144	1,232	1,002	1,213	1,120
Beef, pork, lamb, and poultry meats	1,169	1,050	1,444	1,579	1,635	1,704	1,665
Grains	2,071	4,553	5,164	4,622	5,234	4,472	3,592
Biscuits, pasta, and noodles	300	489	662	711	761	834	904
Feeds and fodders [1]	959	1,247	1,187	1,224	1,219	1,266	1,155
Fruits, nuts, and preparations	2,131	2,660	3,871	4,066	4,031	4,518	4,855
Vegetables, fresh or frozen	1,898	2,777	3,782	3,763	4,064	4,457	4,765
Tobacco, unmanufactured	173	190	220	216	233	260	288
Oilseeds and oilnuts	509	713	932	1,056	964	825	622
Vegetable oils and waxes	1,204	1,509	1,613	1,846	1,898	1,931	1,834
Oilcake and meal	316	805	1,103	1,254	1,070	1,008	1,314

[1] Excluding oil meal.

Source: U.S. Dept. of Agriculture, Economic Research Service, "foreign agricultural trade of the united states (fatus)"; <http://www.ers.usda.gov/data/fatus/> and U.S. Dept. of Agriculture, Foreign Agricultural Service, "U.S. Trade Internet System"; <http://www.fas.usda.gov/ustrade>.

No. 811. Agricultural Exports and Imports—Value: 1990 to 2003

[In billions of dollars, except percent (16.6 represents $16,600,000,000). Includes Puerto Rico, U.S. territories, and shipments under foreign aid programs. Excludes fish, forest products, distilled liquors, manufactured tobacco, and products made from cotton; but includes raw tobacco, raw cotton, rubber, beer and wine, and processed agricultural products]

Year	Trade balance	Exports, domestic products	Percent of all exports	Imports for consumption	Percent of all imports	Year	Trade balance	Exports, domestic products	Percent of all exports	Imports for consumption	Percent of all imports
1990...	16.6	39.5	11	22.9	5	1997...	21.0	57.2	9	36.1	4
1991...	16.5	39.3	10	22.9	5	1998...	14.9	51.8	8	36.9	4
1992...	18.3	43.1	10	24.8	5	1999...	10.7	48.4	8	37.7	4
1993...	17.7	42.9	10	25.1	4	2000...	12.3	51.2	7	39.0	3
1994...	19.2	46.2	10	27.0	4	2001...	14.3	53.7	8	39.4	3
1995...	26.0	56.3	10	30.3	4	2002...	11.2	53.1	8	41.9	4
1996...	26.8	60.3	10	33.5	4	2003...	12.2	59.6	8	47.3	4

Source: U.S. Dept. of Agriculture, Economic Research Service, *U.S. Agricultural Trade Update*, February 13, 2004; and "foreign agricultural trade of the united states (fatus)"; <http://www.ers.usda.gov/data/fatus/> and U.S. Dept. of Agriculture, Foreign Agricultural Service, "U.S. Trade Internet System"; <http://www.fas.usda.gov/ustrade>.

No. 812. Agricultural Imports—Value by Selected Commodity: 1990 to 2003

[In millions of dollars (22,918 represents $22,918,000,000). See headnote, Table 811]

Commodity	1990	1995	1997	1998	1999	2000	2001	2002	2003
Total	22,918	30,255	36,149	36,896	37,673	38,974	39,366	41,909	47,342
Competitive products.....	17,344	21,792	26,796	27,912	29,714	31,213	32,744	34,892	37,996
Cattle, live	978	1,413	1,124	1,144	1,001	1,152	1,461	1,446	867
Beef and veal	1,872	1,447	1,609	1,842	2,136	2,399	2,712	2,741	2,623
Pork	938	686	754	682	753	997	1,048	1,001	1,189
Dairy products	891	1,118	1,225	1,465	1,557	1,671	1,789	1,783	1,978
Grains and feeds......	1,188	2,312	2,963	2,878	2,989	3,076	3,320	3,666	3,921
Fruits and preparations..	1,228	1,618	2,018	2,185	2,757	2,716	2,799	3,177	3,553
Vegetables and preparations	2,317	3,189	3,706	4,374	4,583	4,740	5,252	5,614	6,393
Sugar and related products..........	1,213	1,335	1,852	1,682	1,589	1,555	1,600	1,854	2,129
Wine.............	917	1,153	1,711	1,876	2,187	2,207	2,250	2,671	3,264
Malt beverages.......	923	1,166	1,495	1,712	1,893	2,179	2,348	2,581	2,680
Oilseeds and products ..	952	1,746	2,122	2,067	1,818	1,847	1,630	1,789	2,064
Noncompetitive products..	5,574	8,464	9,353	8,984	7,959	7,761	6,622	7,017	9,346
Bananas and plantains..	939	1,140	1,220	1,202	1,209	1,130	1,179	1,175	1,146
Coffee and products....	1,915	3,263	3,886	3,431	2,893	2,700	1,677	1,693	1,958
Cocoa and products....	1,072	1,106	1,471	1,666	1,522	1,404	1,536	1,761	2,432
Rubber, crude natural...	707	1,629	1,229	977	704	842	613	751	1,047

Source: U.S. Dept. of Agriculture, Economic Research Service, "foreign agricultural trade of the united states (fatus)"; <http://www.ers.usda.gov/data/fatus/> and U.S. Dept. of Agriculture, Foreign Agricultural Service, "U.S. Trade Internet System"; <http://www.fas.usda.gov/ustrade>.

No. 813. Imports' Share of Food Consumption by Selected Commodity: 1990 to 2002

[In percent. Import share is the total quantity imported divided by the quantity available for domestic human food consumption. Calculated from supply and utilization balance sheets. A portion of the imports of some commodities is exported plus, some is diverted to such nonfood uses as feed, seed, alcohol and fuel production, and industrial uses. These can overstate the importance of imports]

Commodity	1990	2000	2002	Commodity	1990	2000	2002
Total food consumption [1]	10.1	12.0	13.0	Vegetables................	5.7	8.1	9.6
Red meat................	8.1	8.9	9.5	Vegetables—fresh, frozen	7.3	10.5	11.8
Beef.................	9.7	11.0	11.9	Broccoli	57.8	76.9	82.8
Pork	5.6	5.2	5.1	Cucumbers	33.7	42.4	42.5
Fish and shellfish	56.3	68.3	78.6	Onions	10.1	9.3	11.3
Dairy products	1.9	2.7	3.5	Peppers, bell & chili	19.7	22.2	22.9
Cheese	4.8	4.8	4.8	Potatoes	5.8	6.0	5.9
Fruits—fresh and frozen	10.5	17.7	19.3	Tomatoes	20.5	32.4	33.5
Citrus................	3.6	11.8	13.9	Vegetables—processed.......	1.9	1.8	2.5
Non-citrus.............	12.0	19.0	20.4	Beans, dry	5.0	6.1	11.5
Apples	4.3	7.3	8.1	Mushrooms	23.5	35.1	30.9
Grapes.............	40.5	45.0	50.8	Olives.............	46.9	78.8	62.7
Melons	14.2	22.9	22.1	Tomatoes	1.8	0.6	1.9
Strawberries	13.0	11.4	14.3	Vegetable oils	16.5	18.3	15.5
Fruits—processed	2.8	3.0	3.6	Spices................	7.7	14.3	18.3
Fruit juices...............	49.6	32.5	31.3	Wheat................	4.1	8.7	8.4
Orange juice	56.0	20.8	12.7	Oats................	18.0	45.4	49.3
Apple juice	57.9	61.6	68.6	Rice................	5.1	9.4	10.5
Grape juice.........	33.6	39.3	56.7	Flour and cereals	1.5	2.7	3.1
Tree nuts..............	30.4	39.9	40.7	Cane and beet sugar........	29.9	16.4	15.4
Wine................	13.9	21.3	25.0	Confectionery products........	5.6	11.1	13.3
				Malt beverages	4.5	9.9	11.2

[1] Calculated from units of weight, weight equivalents; or content weight.

Source: U.S. Dept. of Agriculture, Economic Research Service, "The Import Share of U.S.-Consumed Food Continues to Rise," *Electronic Outlook Report*, FAU-66-01, July 2002 and online at <http://www.ers.usda.gov/data/foodconsumption>.

Agriculture 535

No. 814. Selected Farm Products—United States and World Production and Exports: 2000 to 2003

[In metric tons, except as indicated (61 represents 61,000,000). Metric ton=1.102 short tons or .984 long tons]

Commodity	Unit	United States 2000	United States 2002	United States 2003	World 2000	World 2002	World 2003	United States as percent of world 2000	United States as percent of world 2002	United States as percent of world 2003
PRODUCTION [1]										
Wheat	Million.	61	44	64	581	566	549	10.5	7.8	11.7
Corn for grain	Million.	252	228	257	588	602	613	42.9	37.9	41.9
Soybeans.	Million.	75	75	66	175	197	190	42.8	38.0	34.6
Rice, milled.	Million.	5.9	6.5	6.3	398	378	390	1.5	1.7	1.6
Cotton [2]	Million bales [3].	17.0	20.3	17.2	87.5	98.5	88.2	19.4	20.6	19.5
EXPORTS [4]										
Wheat [5]	Million.	28.0	23.0	32.5	103.6	109.2	101.9	27.0	21.0	31.9
Corn	Million.	48.3	41.2	51.0	76.5	78.0	77.9	63.1	52.8	65.5
Soybeans	Million.	27.1	28.4	24.5	55.5	62.1	61.9	48.8	45.8	39.6
Rice, milled basis.	Million.	2.5	3.8	3.3	24.4	27.7	25.1	10.2	13.7	13.1
Cotton [2]	Million bales [3].	6.8	11.0	11.9	27.2	29.0	30.6	24.8	38.0	38.9

[1] Production years vary by commodity. In most cases, includes harvests from July 1 of the year shown through June 30 of the following year. [2] For production and trade years ending in year shown. [3] Bales of 480 lb. net weight. [4] Trade years may vary by commodity. Wheat, corn and soybean data are for trade year beginning in year shown. Rice data are for calendar year shown. [5] Includes wheat flour on a grain equivalent.

Source: U.S. Dept. of Agriculture, Foreign Agricultural Service, *Foreign Agricultural Commodity Circular Series*, periodic.

No. 815. Percent of U.S. Agricultural Commodity Output Exported: 1980 to 2003

Commodity group	1980-84, average	1985-89, average	1990-94, average	1995-99, average	2000	2001	2002	2003, prel.
Total agriculture	30.2	24.7	23.7	23.3	22.8	22.9	22.5	21.3
Livestock [1].	2.7	3.5	5.4	9.7	10.4	11.0	10.2	10.5
Red meat	1.3	2.0	4.1	7.1	8.2	8.4	8.6	9.2
Poultry meat	3.9	3.6	7.4	14.8	15.1	16.5	14.0	14.2
Dairy products [2].	8.3	10.4	5.0	4.6	4.1	3.1	3.6	4.0
Crops	31.9	26.0	24.9	24.3	23.7	23.8	23.5	22.2
Wheat and rice	62.8	53.3	52.1	48.1	47.1	45.9	46.7	46.1
Coarse grains [3]	28.3	22.7	22.3	22.0	21.2	21.0	20.5	17.7
Oilseeds/meal/oil	34.6	28.7	25.0	26.8	27.1	27.2	27.4	27.7
Fruits and nuts [4]	9.5	9.5	13.4	14.2	13.7	15.2	15.4	14.5
Vegetables [5]	5.1	4.0	5.7	6.4	6.6	6.8	6.7	6.4
Cotton and tobacco	49.0	41.7	40.7	38.1	43.7	57.1	60.3	66.3

[1] Excludes hides, animal fats, and live animals. [2] Includes butter, cheese, and nonfat dried milk. [3] Includes corn, barley, sorghum, and oats. [4] Includes fruit juices and wine, whose exports are converted from volume to weight measure using 8.3454 pounds per gallon. [5] Total vegetable production is estimated from U.S. per capita use of major fresh and processing vegetables; includes olives.

Source: U.S. Dept. of Agriculture, Economic Research Service, USDA's commodity yearbooks, "Foreign Agricultural Trade of the U.S." <http://www.ers.usda.gov/data/Fatus/>, and "Production, Supply, and Distribution database" <http://www.Fas.usda.gov/psd/>.

No. 816. Top 10 U.S. Export Markets for Selected Commodities: 2003

[In thousands of metric tons (43,153 represents 43,153,000)]

Corn Country	Corn Amount	Wheat [1] Country	Wheat [1] Amount	Soybeans Country	Soybeans Amount	Cotton [2] Country	Cotton [2] Amount
World, total.	43,153	World, total .	25,281	World, total .	31,219	World, total .	2,561
Japan	14,439	Japan	2,975	China [3]	11,112	China [3]	551
Mexico	5,577	Egypt	2,889	European Union.	4,346	Turkey.	358
Taiwan [3].	4,490	Mexico	2,599	Mexico	4,200	Mexico	356
Canada	3,479	Nigeria	1,787	Japan	3,535	Indonesia.	186
Egypt.	3,373	European Union.	1,436	Taiwan [3]	1,591	Thailand	119
Colombia	1,606	Korea, South . .	1,321	Indonesia.	1,274	Pakistan	118
Turkey	981	Philippines	1,307	Korea, South . .	1,070	India	106
Algeria	976	Taiwan [3]	830	Thailand	720	Taiwan [3]	101
Dominican Republic .	916	Colombia	740	Canada.	658	Korea, South . .	84
Israel	736	Venezuela	690	Turkey.	381	Canada	72
Rest of world.	6,580	Rest of world . .	8,706	Rest of world . .	2,332	Rest of world . .	510

[1] Unmilled. [2] Excluding linters. [3] See footnote 2, Table 1321.

Source: U.S. Dept. of Agriculture, Foreign Agricultural Service, "FAS Online, U.S.Trade Exports - FATUS Commodity Aggregations"; <http://www.fas.usda.gov/ustrade/USTExFatus.asp>; accessed 27 February 2004.

No. 817. Agricultural Exports—Value by Principal Commodities: 1990 to 2003

[(39,492 represents $39,492,000,000)].

Commodity	Value (mil. dol.)							Percent		
	1990	1995	1999	2000	2001	2002	2003	1990	2000	2003
Total agricultural exports [1]	39,492	56,251	48,378	51,246	53,659	53,115	59,552	100.0	100.0	100.0
Animals and animal products [1]	6,648	10,889	10,360	11,600	12,431	11,087	12,385	16.8	22.6	20.8
Meat and meat products	2,558	4,522	4,816	5,276	5,284	5,042	5,750	6.5	10.3	9.7
Beef and veal	1,580	2,647	2,724	2,986	2,632	2,585	3,150	4.0	5.8	5.3
Poultry and poultry products	910	2,348	2,123	2,235	2,636	2,064	2,289	2.3	4.4	3.8
Dairy products	353	795	958	1,018	1,130	993	1,052	0.9	2.0	1.8
Fats, oils, and greases	424	827	507	383	334	461	539	1.1	0.7	0.9
Hides and skins, including furskins	1,751	1,748	1,139	1,562	1,963	1,745	1,792	4.4	3.0	3.0
Bovine hides, whole	1,337	1,388	877	1,193	1,471	1,042	1,070	3.4	2.3	1.8
Grains and feeds [1]	14,409	18,644	13,995	13,687	13,923	14,459	15,181	36.5	26.7	25.5
Wheat and products	4,035	5,734	3,810	3,578	3,560	3,845	4,116	10.2	7.0	6.9
Rice	801	996	942	855	692	769	1,027	2.0	1.7	1.7
Feed grains and products	7,150	8,341	5,747	5,372	5,503	5,875	5,839	18.1	10.5	9.8
Corn	6,026	7,304	4,924	4,469	4,502	4,845	4,747	15.3	8.7	8.0
Fruits and preparations	2,009	2,660	2,516	2,742	2,768	2,775	2,965	5.1	5.4	5.0
Fresh fruits	1,486	1,973	1,820	2,080	2,125	2,134	2,269	3.8	4.1	3.8
Nuts and preparations	976	1,410	1,190	1,319	1,292	1,525	1,766	2.5	2.6	3.0
Vegetables and preparations	2,225	3,637	4,295	4,457	4,483	4,554	4,820	5.6	8.7	8.1
Fresh vegetables	696	1,017	1,053	1,207	1,180	1,232	1,292	1.8	2.4	2.2
Oilseeds and products [1]	5,728	8,953	8,143	8,586	9,219	9,632	11,680	14.5	16.8	19.6
Soybean meal	979	986	1,069	1,169	1,386	1,216	1,177	2.5	2.3	2.0
Soybeans	3,548	5,400	4,532	5,258	5,403	5,677	7,980	9.0	10.3	13.4
Vegetable oils and waxes	832	1,852	1,599	1,259	1,250	1,050	1,035	2.1	2.5	1.7
Tobacco, unmanufactured	1,441	1,400	1,312	1,204	1,269	1,634	1,697	3.6	2.3	2.8
Cotton, excluding linters	2,783	3,681	954	1,873	2,162	2,015	3,203	7.0	3.7	5.4
Other	3,273	4,977	5,614	5,777	6,112	6,017	6,518	8.3	11.3	10.9

[1] Includes commodities not shown separately.

Source: U.S. Dept. of Agriculture, Economic Research Service, U.S. Agricultural Trade Update, February 13, 2004; and "foreign agricultural trade of the united states (fatus)"; <http://www.ers.usda.gov/data/fatus/> and U.S. Dept. of Agriculture, Foreign Agricultural Service, "U.S. Trade Internet System"; <http://www.fas.usda.gov/ustrade>.

No. 818. Agricultural Exports—Value by Selected Countries of Destination: 1990 to 2003

[(39,492 represents $39,492,000,000). See headnote, Table 817].

Country	Value (mil. dol.)							Percent		
	1990	1995	1999	2000	2001	2002	2003	1990	2000	2003
Total agricultural exports [1]	39,492	56,251	48,378	51,246	53,659	53,115	59,552	100.0	100.0	100.0
Canada	4,217	5,791	7,058	7,640	8,121	8,660	9,300	10.7	14.9	15.6
Mexico	2,561	3,538	5,624	6,410	7,404	7,226	7,917	6.5	12.5	13.3
Caribbean	1,016	1,282	1,492	1,408	1,399	1,518	1,589	2.6	2.7	2.7
Central America	482	873	1,099	1,120	1,233	1,250	1,339	1.2	2.2	2.2
South America [2]	1,063	2,348	1,834	1,701	1,703	1,788	1,899	2.7	3.3	3.2
Colombia	119	465	440	415	452	520	512	0.3	0.8	0.9
Asia [2]	15,862	25,704	18,049	19,872	20,312	19,724	23,630	40.2	38.8	39.7
Japan	8,146	11,161	8,892	9,290	8,883	8,382	8,935	20.6	18.1	15.0
Korea, South	2,650	3,754	2,448	2,546	2,588	2,672	2,853	6.7	5.0	4.8
Taiwan [3]	1,663	2,597	1,945	1,996	2,009	1,966	2,036	4.2	3.9	3.4
China [3][4]	818	2,634	855	1,717	1,940	2,069	4,995	2.1	3.4	8.4
Hong Kong	704	1,502	1,209	1,262	1,227	1,091	1,114	1.8	2.5	1.9
Indonesia	274	816	531	668	907	810	984	0.7	1.3	1.7
Philippines	381	765	783	901	794	776	628	1.0	1.8	1.1
Western Europe [2]	7,359	9,015	6,941	6,685	7,042	6,718	6,789	18.6	13.0	11.4
European Union [5]	7,076	8,655	6,413	6,244	6,404	6,145	6,454	17.9	12.2	10.8
Netherlands	1,586	2,144	1,533	1,442	1,364	1,173	1,123	4.0	2.8	1.9
Germany	1,131	1,226	923	905	923	970	1,018	2.9	1.8	1.7
Spain	939	1,270	681	609	644	674	848	2.4	1.2	1.4
United Kingdom	813	1,050	1,079	1,035	1,062	1,004	1,039	2.1	2.0	1.7
Italy	715	720	493	551	567	543	489	1.8	1.1	0.8
Russia	(X)	1,046	728	580	917	551	579	(X)	1.1	1.0
Eastern Europe	537	292	170	170	232	213	206	1.4	0.3	0.3
Middle East [2]	1,855	2,482	2,058	2,341	2,244	2,281	2,547	4.7	4.6	4.3
Israel	304	484	422	482	427	464	426	0.8	0.9	0.7
Turkey	226	536	502	658	571	675	901	0.6	1.3	1.5
Africa [2]	1,935	2,073	2,073	2,308	2,105	2,297	2,528	4.9	4.5	4.2
Egypt	692	1,448	966	1,050	1,022	862	1,001	1.8	2.0	1.7
Oceania	343	507	486	489	471	511	821	0.9	1.0	1.4

X Not applicable. [1] Totals include transshipments through Canada, but transshipments are not distributed by country after 1998. [2] Includes areas not shown separately. [3] See footnote 2, Table 1321. [4] China includes Macao. However Hong Kong remains separate economically until 2050 and is not included. [5] Includes Belgium, Denmark, France, Greece, Ireland, Luxembourg, and Portugal. Beginning 1995, also includes Austria, Finland, and Sweden. For consistency, data for all years are shown on the basis of 15 countries in the European Union.

Source: U.S. Dept. of Agriculture, Economic Research Service, U.S. Agricultural Trade Update, February 13, 2004; and "foreign agricultural trade of the united states (fatus)"; <http://www.ers.usda.gov/data/fatus/> and U.S. Dept. of Agriculture, Foreign Agricultural Service, "U.S. Trade Internet System"; <http://www.fas.usda.gov/ustrade>.

[In millions of acres, except as indicated (341 represents 341,000,000)]

Item	1990	1995	1996	1997	1998	1999	2000	2001	2002	2003
Cropland used for crops.....	341	332	346	349	345	344	345	340	341	344
Index (1977=100).........	90	88	92	92	91	91	91	90	90	91
Cropland harvested [1]........	310	302	314	321	315	316	314	311	307	314
Crop failure..............	6	8	10	7	10	8	11	10	15	8
Cultivated summer fallow......	25	22	22	21	20	20	20	19	19	21
Cropland idled by all Federal programs..............	62	55	34	33	30	30	31	32	34	34
Acres of crops harvested [2]...	322	314	326	332	326	327	325	321	317	324

[1] Land supporting one or more harvested crops. [2] Area in principal crops harvested as reported by Crop Reporting Board plus acreages in fruits, vegetables for sale, tree nuts, and other minor crops.

Source: U.S. Dept. of Agriculture, Economic Research Service, *Major Uses of Land in the United States, 1997*, SB-973, 2001. Also in *Agricultural Statistics*, annual. Beginning 1995 *Agricultural Resources and Environmental Indicators*, periodic, and *AREI Updates: Cropland Use.* See also ERS Briefing Room at <http://www.ers.usda.gov/Briefing/LandUse/majorlandusechapter.htm#trends>.

No. 820. Percent of Corn, Soybean, and Cotton Acreage Planted With Genetically Modified Seed: 2000 and 2003

[In percent. Based on the June Agricultural Survey. Randomly selected farmers across the United States were asked if they planted corn, soybeans, or upland cotton seed that, through biotechnology, is resistant to herbicides, insects, or both. The states published individually below represent 81 percent of all corn planted acres, 89 percent of all soybean planted acres, and 82 percent of all upland cotton planted acres. Conventionally bred herbicide resistant varieties were excluded. Insect resistant varieties include only those containing bacillus thuringiensis (Bt). The acreage estimates are subject to sampling variability because all operations planting biotech varieties are not included in the sample]

State	Corn 2000	Corn 2003	State	Soybeans 2000	Soybeans 2003	State	Cotton 2000	Cotton 2003
US, total............	25	40	US, total.........	54	75	US, total.........	61	73
IL...................	17	28	AR.................	43	84	AR.................	70	95
IN...................	11	16	IL.................	44	77	CA.................	24	39
IA...................	30	45	IN.................	63	88	GA.................	82	93
KS...................	33	47	IA.................	59	84	LA.................	80	91
MI...................	12	35	KS.................	66	87	MS.................	78	92
MN...................	37	53	MI.................	50	73	NC.................	76	93
MO...................	28	42	MN.................	46	79	TX.................	46	53
NE...................	34	52	MS.................	48	89	Other states [1].....	74	88
OH...................	9	9	MO.................	62	83			
SD...................	48	75	NE.................	72	86			
WI...................	18	32	ND.................	22	74			
Other states [1]........	17	36	OH.................	48	74			
			SD.................	68	91			
			WI.................	51	84			
			Other states [1].....	54	76			

[1] Includes all other states in the specified commodity estimating program.

Source: U.S. Dept. of Agriculture, National Agricultural Statistics Service, *Acreage*, annual.

No. 821. Quantity of Pesticides Applied to Selected Crops: 1990 to 2002

[In million pounds of active ingredients, except as indicated (497.7 represents 497,700,000)]

Type of pesticide and commodity	1990	1995	1997	1998	1999	2000	2001	2002
Total......................	497.7	543.3	579.3	544.4	553.7	539.4	511.1	483.3
Herbicides.................	344.6	324.9	362.6	340.3	316.8	308.6	307.6	282.0
Insecticides...............	57.4	69.9	60.2	52.0	75.4	77.4	62.0	55.8
Fungicides.................	27.8	47.5	48.5	45.7	42.3	36.6	33.3	33.7
Other......................	67.9	101.0	108.0	106.4	119.1	116.8	108.3	111.8
Corn......................	240.7	201.3	227.3	212.4	186.0	176.1	187.3	153.5
Cotton.....................	50.9	83.7	68.4	55.4	90.6	94.5	72.8	64.5
Wheat.....................	17.8	21.5	25.5	23.9	21.4	19.2	18.3	10.4
Soybeans..................	74.4	68.7	83.5	78.8	77.3	79.1	72.2	90.7
Potatoes..................	43.8	53.1	59.4	63.6	64.6	61.8	60.5	55.3
Other vegetables..........	39.8	78.0	73.3	67.8	70.5	70.1	66.5	76.1
Citrus fruit...............	11.0	14.0	15.0	14.1	13.3	13.0	12.8	12.4
Apples....................	8.3	9.0	10.6	9.3	7.9	7.6	7.6	7.3
Other deciduous fruit......	10.9	14.1	16.4	19.2	22.2	18.1	13.1	13.2
POUNDS OF ACTIVE INGREDIENT PER PLANTED ACRE								
Total......................	2.2	2.4	2.4	2.3	2.3	2.2	2.2	2.1
Herbicides.................	1.5	1.4	1.5	1.4	1.3	1.3	1.3	1.2
Insecticides...............	0.3	0.3	0.2	0.2	0.3	0.3	0.3	0.2
Fungicides.................	0.1	0.2	0.2	0.2	0.2	0.2	0.1	0.1
Other......................	0.3	0.4	0.4	0.4	0.5	0.5	0.5	0.5

Source: U.S. Dept. of Agriculture, Economic Research Service, *Production Practices for Major Crops in U.S. Agriculture, 1990-97*, Statistical Bulletin No. 969, August 2000 and unpublished data.

No. 822. Principal Crops—Production, Supply, and Disappearance: 1990 to 2003

[67.0 represents 67,000,000. Marketing year beginning January 1 for potatoes, May 1 for hay, June 1 for wheat, August 1 for cotton, September 1 for soybeans and corn. Acreage, production, and yield of all crops periodically revised on basis of census data]

Item	Unit	1990	1995	1999	2000	2001	2002	2003
CORN FOR GRAIN								
Acreage harvested	Million	67.0	65.2	70.5	72.4	68.8	69.3	71.1
Yield per acre	Bushel	119	114	134	137	138	129	142
Production	Mil. bu.	7,934	7,400	9,431	9,915	9,503	8,967	10,114
Farm price [1]	Dol./bu.	2.28	3.24	1.82	1.85	1.97	2.32	2.45
Farm value	Mil. dol.	18,192	24,118	17,104	18,499	18,888	20,975	24,804
Total supply [2]	Mil. bu.	9,282	8,974	11,232	11,639	11,412	10,578	11,211
Total disappearance [3]	Mil. bu.	7,761	8,548	9,515	9,740	9,815	9,491	10,355
Exports	Mil. bu.	1,725	2,228	1,937	1,941	1,905	1,592	2,000
Ending stocks	Mil. bu.	1,521	426	1,718	1,899	1,596	1,087	856
SOYBEANS								
Acreage harvested	Million	56.5	61.5	72.4	72.4	73.0	72.5	72.3
Yield per acre	Bushel	34.1	35.3	36.6	38.1	39.6	38.0	33.4
Production	Mil. bu.	1,926	2,174	2,654	2,758	2,891	2,756	2,418
Farm price [1]	Dol./bu.	5.74	6.72	4.63	4.54	4.38	5.53	7.25
Farm value	Mil. dol.	11,042	14,617	12,205	12,467	12,606	15,215	17,465
Total supply [2]	Mil. bu.	2,169	2,514	3,006	3,052	3,141	2,969	2,604
Total disappearance [3]	Mil. bu.	1,840	2,330	2,716	2,804	2,933	2,791	2,489
Exports	Mil. bu.	557	849	975	996	1,064	1,045	900
Ending stocks	Mil. bu.	329	183	290	248	208	178	115
HAY								
Acreage harvested	Million	61.0	59.8	63.2	59.9	63.5	63.9	63.3
Yield per acre	Sh. tons	2.40	2.58	2.53	2.54	2.46	2.34	2.48
Production	Mil. sh. tons	146	154	160	152	156	149	157
Farm price [4] [5]	Dol./ton	80.60	82.20	76.90	84.60	96.50	92.40	92.90
Farm value	Mil. dol.	10,462	11,042	11,014	11,417	12,597	12,450	12,331
WHEAT								
Acreage harvested	Million	69.1	61.0	53.8	53.1	48.5	45.8	52.8
Yield per acre	Bushel	39.5	35.8	42.7	42.0	40.2	35.0	44.2
Production	Mil. bu.	2,730	2,183	2,296	2,228	1,947	1,606	2,337
Farm price [1]	Dol./bu.	2.61	4.55	2.48	2.62	2.78	3.56	3.35
Farm value	Mil. dol.	7,184	9,787	5,594	5,782	5,440	5,679	7,955
Total supply [2]	Mil. bu.	3,303	2,757	3,336	3,268	2,931	2,460	2,903
Total disappearance [3]	Mil. bu.	2,435	2,381	2,386	2,392	2,154	1,969	2,372
Exports	Mil. bu.	1,069	1,241	1,086	1,062	962	854	1,165
Ending stocks	Mil. bu.	868	376	950	876	777	491	531
COTTON								
Acreage harvested	Million	11.7	16.0	13.4	13.1	13.8	12.4	12.1
Yield per acre	Pounds	634	537	607	632	705	665	725
Production	Mil. bales [7]	15.5	17.9	17.0	17.2	20.3	17.2	18.2
Farm price [1]	Cents/lb.	68.2	76.5	46.8	51.6	32.0	45.7	63.8
Farm value	Mil. dol.	5,076	6,575	3,810	4,260	3,122	3,777	5,582
Total supply [2]	Mil. bales [7]	18.5	21.0	21.0	21.1	24.7	24.7	23.7
Total disappearance [3]	Mil. bales [7]	16.5	18.3	16.9	15.6	18.7	19.2	20.1
Exports [8]	Mil. bales [7]	7.8	7.7	6.8	6.7	11.0	11.9	13.8
Ending stocks	Mil. bales [7]	2.3	2.6	3.9	6.0	7.4	5.4	3.6
POTATOES								
Acreage harvested	Million	1.4	1.4	1.3	1.3	1.2	1.3	1.3
Yield per acre	Cwt.	293	323	359	381	358	362	367
Production	Mil. cwt.	402	445	478	514	438	458	459
Farm price [1]	Dol./cwt.	6.08	6.77	5.77	5.08	6.99	6.69	5.85
Farm value	Mil. dol.	2,431	2,992	2,746	2,591	3,058	3,064	2,680

[1] Marketing year average price. U.S. prices are computed by weighting U.S. monthly prices by estimated monthly marketings and do not include an allowance for outstanding loans and government purchases and payments. [2] Comprises production, imports, and beginning stocks. [3] Includes feed, residual, and other domestic uses not shown separately. [4] Prices are for hay sold baled. [5] Season average prices received by farmers. U.S. prices are computed by weighting state prices by estimated sales. [6] State production figures, which conform with annual ginning enumeration with allowance for cross-state ginnings, rounded to thousands and added for U.S. totals. [7] Bales of 480 pounds, net weight. [8] Stock estimates based on Census Bureau data which results in an unaccounted difference between supply and use estimates and changes in ending stocks.

Source: Production—U.S. Dept. of Agriculture, National Agricultural Statistics Service. In *Crop Production*, annual; and *Crop Values*, annual. Supply and disappearance—U.S. Dept. of Agriculture, Economic Research Service, *Feed Situation*, quarterly; *Wheat Situation*, quarterly; *Cotton and Wool Outlook Statistics*, periodic; and *Fats and Oils Situation*, quarterly; *Cotton and Wool Outlook Statistics*, periodic; and *Agricultural Supply and Demand Estimates*, periodic. Data are also in *Agricultural Statistics*, annual; and "Agricultural Outlook: Statistical Indicators"; <http://www.ers.usda.gov/publications/agoutlook/aotables/>.

No. 823. Corn—Acreage, Production, and Value by Leading States: 2001 to 2003

[68,768 represents 68,768,000. One bushel of corn=56 pounds]

State	Acreage harvested (1,000 acres)			Yield per acre (bu.)			Production (mil. bu.)			Price ($/bu.)			Farm value (mil. dol.)		
	2001	2002	2003	2001	2002	2003	2001	2002	2003	2001	2002	2003	2001	2002	2003
U.S.[1]	68,768	69,330	71,139	138	129	142	9,503	8,967	10,114	1.97	2.32	2.45	18,888	20,975	24,804
IA	11,400	11,850	12,000	146	163	157	1,664	1,932	1,884	1.90	2.22	2.40	3,162	4,359	4,522
IL	10,850	10,900	11,050	152	135	164	1,649	1,472	1,812	2.04	2.35	2.50	3,364	3,516	4,531
NE	7,750	7,350	7,700	147	128	146	1,139	941	1,124	1.94	2.32	2.45	2,210	2,183	2,754
MN	6,200	6,700	6,650	130	157	146	806	1,052	971	1.90	2.15	2.35	1,531	2,262	2,282
IN	5,670	5,220	5,390	156	121	146	885	632	787	1.98	2.41	2.50	1,751	1,522	1,967
OH	3,170	2,970	3,070	138	89	156	437	264	479	2.00	2.48	2.45	875	626	1,173
SD	3,400	3,250	3,850	109	95	111	371	309	427	1.75	2.17	2.25	649	660	962
WI	2,600	2,900	2,850	127	135	129	330	392	368	1.97	2.22	2.40	650	869	882
MO	2,600	2,700	2,800	133	105	108	346	284	302	1.96	2.45	2.50	678	695	756
KS	3,050	2,600	2,500	127	116	120	387	302	300	2.03	2.48	2.55	786	719	765
MI	1,900	2,000	2,090	105	117	126	200	234	263	1.97	2.34	2.40	393	544	632
TX	1,420	1,790	1,650	118	113	118	168	202	195	2.29	2.57	2.60	384	529	506
KY	1,100	1,070	1,080	142	104	137	156	111	148	2.08	2.58	2.55	325	274	377
ND	705	995	1,170	115	114	112	81	113	131	1.87	2.16	2.35	152	247	308
CO	1,070	720	890	140	150	135	150	108	120	2.13	2.53	2.55	319	284	306
PA	960	840	890	98	68	115	94	57	102	2.33	2.97	2.90	226	176	297
TN	610	610	630	132	107	131	81	65	83	2.06	2.58	2.35	169	171	194
MS	385	530	530	130	120	135	50	64	72	1.99	2.33	2.25	100	154	161
NC	625	680	680	125	83	106	78	56	72	2.36	2.89	2.70	184	168	195
LA	307	540	500	148	121	134	45	65	67	2.20	2.40	2.40	100	164	161
NY	540	460	440	105	97	121	57	45	53	2.51	2.87	2.80	142	125	149

[1] Includes other states, not shown separately.

Source: U.S. Dept. of Agriculture, National Agricultural Statistics Service, Crop Production, annual; and Crop Values, annual.

No. 824. Soybeans—Acreage, Production, and Value by Leading States: 2001 to 2003

[72,975 represents 72,975,000. One bushel of soybeans=60 pounds]

State	Acreage harvested (1,000 acres)			Yield per acre (bu.)			Production (mil. bu.)			Price ($/bu.)			Farm value (mil. dol.)		
	2001	2002	2003	2001	2002	2003	2001	2002	2003	2001	2002	2003	2001	2002	2003
U.S.[1]	72,975	72,497	72,321	40	38	33	2,891	2,756	2,418	4.38	5.53	7.25	12,606	15,215	17,465
IL	10,620	10,550	10,250	45	43	37	478	454	374	4.55	5.66	7.35	2,174	2,568	2,750
IA	10,920	10,400	10,550	44	48	32	480	499	338	4.35	5.54	7.30	2,090	2,766	2,464
MN	7,200	7,100	7,400	37	44	31	266	309	229	4.32	5.42	7.00	1,211	1,674	1,606
IN	5,590	5,770	5,350	49	42	38	274	239	203	4.42	5.55	7.35	1,211	1,329	1,494
NE	4,900	4,580	4,490	46	39	40	223	176	180	4.19	5.43	7.10	934	957	1,275
OH	4,580	4,280	4,280	41	32	38	188	151	163	4.46	5.59	7.20	837	818	1,171
MO	4,900	5,000	4,940	38	34	29	186	170	143	4.32	5.54	7.55	804	942	1,082
SD	4,470	4,090	4,190	32	31	27	143	127	113	4.13	5.33	6.95	591	676	786
AR	2,850	2,880	2,890	32	34	38	91	96	110	4.37	5.65	7.25	399	545	796
ND	2,110	2,630	3,030	34	33	29	71	87	88	4.05	5.32	6.85	286	462	602
KS	2,730	2,540	2,480	34	23	23	87	58	57	4.16	5.49	7.60	363	321	434
MS	1,120	1,370	1,430	33	32	39	37	44	56	4.39	5.52	6.85	162	242	382
MI	2,130	2,040	1,990	30	39	27	64	79	54	4.47	5.62	7.20	286	441	387
KY	1,220	1,290	1,240	40	33	43	49	43	53	4.47	5.74	7.60	218	239	405

[1] Includes other states, not shown separately.

Source: U.S. Dept. of Agriculture, National Agricultural Statistics Service, Crop Production, annual; and Crop Values, annual.

No. 825. Wheat—Acreage, Production, and Value by Leading States: 2001 to 2003

[48,473 represents 48,473,000. One bushel of wheat= 60 pounds]

State	Acreage harvested (1,000 acres)			Yield per acre (bu.)			Production (mil. bu.)			Price ($/bu.)			Farm value (mil. dol.)		
	2001	2002	2003	2001	2002	2003	2001	2002	2003	2001	2002	2003	2001	2002	2003
U.S.[1]	48,473	45,824	52,839	40.2	35.0	44.2	1,947	1,606	2,337	2.78	3.56	3.35	5,440	5,679	7,955
KS	8,200	8,200	10,000	40.0	33.0	48.0	328	271	480	2.69	3.41	3.15	882	911	1,512
ND	9,080	7,915	8,500	32.2	27.3	37.3	292	216	317	2.79	3.80	3.70	813	823	1,178
OK	3,700	3,700	4,600	33.0	28.0	39.0	122	104	179	2.74	3.37	3.25	335	340	583
WA	2,350	2,390	2,345	55.9	54.3	59.4	131	130	139	3.23	3.83	3.80	428	497	528
MT	4,215	4,795	5,050	22.9	23.1	27.2	97	111	138	3.14	4.04	3.85	304	446	526
SD	2,044	1,677	2,747	37.6	26.4	42.3	77	44	116	2.78	3.83	3.70	214	161	404
MN	1,815	1,834	1,825	43.9	34.0	57.8	80	62	105	2.93	3.86	3.70	233	240	390
TX	3,200	2,700	3,450	34.0	29.0	28.0	109	78	97	2.78	3.02	3.05	302	236	295

[1] Includes other states, not shown separately.

Source: U.S. Dept. of Agriculture, National Agricultural Statistics Service, Crop Production, annual; and Crop Values, annual.

No. 826. Floriculture and Nursery Crops—Value of Production, Trade, and Consumption: 1990 to 2002

[In millions of dollars, except as noted (8,677 represents $8,677,000,000). Includes all floriculture and nursery crops except cut Christmas trees, seeds, and food crops grown under cover. Domestic production based on grower wholesale receipts. Domestic consumption equals supply minus exports. Supply equals domestic production plus imports]

Year	Production and trade				Consumption			
	Domestic production	Imports	Supply	Exports	Domestic consumption	Per household (dol.)	Per capita (dol.)	Import share (percent)
1990	8,677	538	9,215	204	9,011	98	36	6.0
1991	9,035	547	9,582	216	9,366	101	37	5.8
1992	9,294	604	9,898	222	9,677	102	38	6.2
1993	9,398	654	10,052	242	9,810	103	38	6.7
1994	9,853	712	10,566	252	10,314	107	39	6.9
1995	10,336	859	11,195	241	10,954	113	41	7.8
1996	10,830	952	11,782	242	11,539	117	43	8.2
1997	11,861	1,004	12,865	283	12,582	126	46	8.0
1998	12,043	1,080	13,124	306	12,818	127	46	8.4
1999	13,042	1,101	14,143	299	13,844	134	50	8.0
2000	13,741	1,160	14,901	279	14,622	139	52	7.9
2001	13,795	1,151	14,946	264	14,681	137	51	7.8
2002	13,829	1,133	14,962	249	14,713	136	51	7.7

Source: U.S. Dept. of Agriculture, Economic Research Service, *Floriculture and Nursery Crops Yearbook.*

No. 827. Fresh Fruits and Vegetables—Supply and Use: 1990 to 2003

[In millions of pounds, except per capita in pounds (7,327 represents 7,327,000,000)]

Year	Utilized production[1]	Imports[2]	Supply, total[1]	Consumption		Exports[2]
				Total	Per capita	
FRUITS						
Citrus:						
1990	7,327	184	7,510	5,331	21.4	2,179
2000	8,355	684	9,040	6,602	23.4	2,438
2001	8,331	871	9,202	6,787	23.8	2,415
2002	8,254	762	9,016	6,456	22.4	2,560
2003	8,547	1,024	9,571	6,942	23.9	2,629
Noncitrus:[3]						
1990	12,122	7,852	19,974	17,978	70.4	1,995
2000	13,850	11,225	25,074	21,685	76.6	3,389
2001	12,759	10,979	23,738	20,636	72.1	3,102
2002	12,853	11,598	24,452	21,546	74.5	2,906
VEGETABLES & MELONS						
1990	35,341	3,458	39,679	35,364	141.5	2,690
2000	47,270	6,720	55,334	48,928	173.3	4,197
2001	46,742	7,342	55,350	49,011	171.8	4,128
2002	46,822	7,704	55,858	49,501	171.8	4,269
2003	46,656	7,984	55,890	49,717	170.8	4,209
POTATOES						
1990	11,335	684	12,019	11,691	46.8	327
2000	13,239	806	14,045	13,368	47.3	677
2001	13,206	671	13,877	13,241	46.4	636
2002	12,664	883	13,547	12,854	44.5	693
2003	13,390	872	14,262	13,673	46.9	590

[1] Crop-year basis for fruits. [2] Fiscal year for fruits; calendar year for vegetables and potatoes. [3] Includes bananas.

No. 828. Nuts—Supply and Use: 1990 to 2002

[In millions of pounds (shelled) (326.2 represents 326,200,000)]

Year	Beginning stocks	Marketable production[1]	Imports	Supply, total	Consumption	Exports	Ending stocks
1990	326.2	961.5	198.4	1,486.1	609.6	522.6	354.0
1995	334.1	770.1	204.0	1,308.2	512.5	543.8	251.9
1999	223.9	1,295.7	283.4	1,803.0	706.7	730.7	365.6
2000	365.6	1,110.1	297.0	1,772.7	647.0	851.1	274.5
2001	274.5	1,325.0	322.5	1,921.9	796.6	843.4	281.9
2002	281.9	1,536.5	353.7	2,172.1	887.5	924.0	360.6

[1] Utilized production minus inedibles and noncommercial usage.

Source of Tables 827 and 828: U.S. Dept. of Agriculture, Economic Research Service, *Fruit and Tree Nuts Situation and Outlook Yearbook* and *Vegetables and Specialties Situation and Outlook Yearbook.*

No. 829. Commercial Vegetable and Other Specified Crops—Area, Production, and Value, 2001 to 2003, and Leading Producing States, 2003

[290 represents 290,000. Except as noted, relates to commercial production for fresh market and processing combined. Includes market garden areas but excludes minor producing acreage in minor producing states. Excludes production for home use in farm and nonfarm gardens. Value is for season or crop year and should not be confused with calendar-year income]

Crop	Area [1] (1,000 acres)			Production [2] (1,000 short tons)			Value [3] (mil. dol.)			Leading states in order of production, 2003 [4]
	2001	2002	2003	2001	2002	2003	2001	2002	2003	
Beans, snap	290	300	284	998	1,092	1,015	390	404	385	WI, OR, NY [4]
Beans, dry edible . .	1,250	1,739	1,347	981	1,516	1,126	426	514	412	ND, NE, MI
Broccoli	133	130	137	935	919	1,010	484	568	644	CA, AZ
Cabbage [5]	77	76	74	1,273	1,211	1,118	333	308	277	CA, NY, TX
Cantaloups [5]	95	90	86	1,131	1,122	1,105	429	398	372	CA, AZ, TX
Carrots	108	102	102	1,844	1,695	1,800	511	521	554	CA, MI, CO [5]
Celery	28	27	28	943	937	944	272	240	257	CA, MI
Corn, sweet	692	663	674	4,488	4,392	4,715	753	718	790	(NA)
Fresh market . . .	245	246	248	1,341	1,324	1,449	524	509	560	FL, CA, NY
Processed	447	417	427	3,148	3,068	3,266	230	209	230	MN, WA, WI
Cucumbers	161	173	174	1,101	1,166	1,127	375	377	368	(NA)
Fresh market . . .	53	55	55	520	547	478	206	208	189	FL, GA, CA
Processed [5] . . .	108	118	119	582	619	648	169	169	178	MI, NC, FL
Lettuce, head [5] . . .	184	185	186	3,446	3,407	3,300	1,235	1,435	1,188	CA, AZ
Lettuce, leaf [5] . . .	51	54	56	570	671	619	314	452	387	CA, AZ
Lettuce, Romaine [5] .	53	58	66	753	928	962	291	467	524	CA, AZ
Mushrooms [6]	34	31	29	423	416	416	826	871	852	PA, CA, FL
Onions	165	163	159	3,498	3,492	3,485	680	765	919	CA, WA, OR
Peas, green [4]	212	212	232	391	350	468	103	88	117	MN, WA, WI
Peppers, bell	58	54	55	825	783	824	474	464	505	CA, FL
Potatoes	1,221	1,266	1,250	21,884	22,909	22,952	3,058	3,064	2,687	ID, WA, WI
Spinach	40	43	48	300	337	392	127	171	217	CA, AZ [5]
Strawberries	46	48	48	825	942	1,041	1,069	1,162	1,321	CA, FL
Sweet potatoes . . .	94	82	92	726	640	796	225	215	331	NC, LA, CA
Tomatoes	406	441	418	11,134	13,650	11,577	1,679	1,933	1,865	(NA)
Fresh market . . .	131	129	124	1,885	1,979	1,757	1,131	1,253	1,289	FL, CA
Processed	275	312	294	9,249	11,671	9,820	547	680	576	CA, IN
Watermelons	161	153	150	2,024	1,979	1,928	273	328	347	TX, FL, CA

NA Not available. [1] Area of crops for harvest for fresh market, including any partially harvested or not harvested because of low prices or other factors, plus area harvested for processing. [2] Excludes some quantities not marketed. [3] Fresh market vegetables valued at f.o.b. shipping point. Processing vegetables are equivalent returns at packinghouse door. [4] Processed only. [5] Fresh market only. [6] Area is shown in million square feet. All data are for marketing year ending June 30.

Source: U.S. Dept. of Agriculture, National Agricultural Statistics Service, *Vegetables Final Estimates 1998-2003*, May 2004. Also in *Agricultural Statistics*, annual.

No. 830. Fruits and Nuts—Utilized Production and Value, 2001 to 2003, and Leading Producing States, 2003

[4,607 represents 4,607,000]

Fruit or nut	Unit	Utilized production [1]			Farm value (mil. dol.)			Leading states in order of production, 2003
		2001	2002	2003	2001	2002	2003	
Apples [2]	1,000 tons . .	4,607	4,203	4,449	1,452	1,572	1,730	WA, NY, MI
Apricots	1,000 tons . .	75	80	98	27	29	35	CA
Avocados	1,000 tons . .	223	218	(NA)	374	382	(NA)	CA
Cherries, sweet	1,000 tons . .	220	177	235	271	274	327	WA, CA, OR
Cherries, tart	1,000 tons . .	154	31	113	57	28	84	MI, UT, WA
Cranberries	1,000 tons . .	239	284	306	114	171	194	WI, MA, NJ
Grapefruit	1,000 tons . .	2,462	2,424	2,063	285	292	258	FL, TX
Grapes (13 states)	1,000 tons . .	6,568	7,362	6,324	2,948	2,842	2,534	CA, WA, NY
Lemons	1,000 tons . .	996	801	1,026	237	328	293	CA, AZ
Nectarines (CA)	1,000 tons . .	275	299	278	128	115	121	CA
Olives (CA)	1,000 tons . .	134	103	118	90	59	50	CA
Oranges	1,000 tons . .	12,221	12,374	11,526	1,683	1,846	1,612	FL, CA
Peaches	1,000 tons . .	1,168	1,236	1,207	483	488	467	CA, GA, SC
Pears	1,000 tons . .	964	867	921	263	264	282	WA, CA, OR
Pineapples	1,000 tons . .	323	320	315	96	101	103	HI
Plums (CA)	1,000 tons . .	210	201	212	64	78	89	CA
Prunes (dried basis) (CA)	1,000 tons . .	135	149	161	98	132	118	CA
Tangelos	1,000 tons . .	95	97	106	8	11	13	FL
Tangerines	1,000 tons . .	373	420	371	97	125	114	FL, CA
Temples	1,000 tons . .	56	70	59	5	7	6	FL
Almonds (shelled basis) (CA) . .	Mil. lb	830	1,060	1,020	740	1,201	1,419	CA
Hazelnuts (in the shell)	1,000 tons . .	50	18	35	35	20	37	OR
Macadamia nuts	Mil. lb	56	52	51	33	30	30	HI
Pecans (in the shell) (11 states) . .	Mil. lb	339	178	262	201	165	263	TX, GA, NM
Pistachios	Mil. lb	161	300	116	163	333	133	CA
Walnuts, English (in the shell) . .	1,000 tons . .	305	282	325	342	305	(NA)	CA

NA Not available. [1] Excludes quantities not harvested or not marketed. [2] Production in commercial orchards with 100 or more bearing age trees.

Source: U.S. Dept. of Agriculture, National Agricultural Statistics Service, *Noncitrus Fruits and Nuts Final Estimates 1997-2002*, May 2004; *Noncitrus Fruits and Nuts*, annual; and *Citrus Fruits*, annual.

No. 831. Meat Supply and Use: 1990 to 2003

[In millions of pounds (carcass weight equivalent) (62,255 represents 62,255,000,000). Carcass weight equivalent is the weight of the animal minus entrails, head, hide, and internal organs; includes fat and bone. Covers federal and state inspected, and farm slaughter]

Year and type of meat	Production	Imports	Supply,[1] total	Consumption[2]	Exports	Ending stocks
RED MEAT AND POULTRY						
1990	62,255	3,295	66,673	62,937	2,472	1,263
1995	74,068	2,838	78,636	69,911	6,956	1,768
2000	82,372	4,137	88,481	77,069	9,344	2,069
2001	82,746	4,278	89,093	76,912	10,060	2,120
2002	85,384	4,466	91,971	80,187	9,445	2,339
2003	85,234	4,374	91,948	80,164	9,758	2,025
ALL RED MEATS						
1990	38,787	3,295	42,742	40,784	1,250	707
1995	43,675	2,832	47,511	43,967	2,614	929
2000	46,299	4,128	51,341	46,560	3,760	1,021
2001	45,804	4,260	51,085	46,089	3,836	1,160
2002	47,305	4,450	52,915	47,612	4,065	1,238
2003	46,757	4,358	52,353	47,046	4,247	1,060
Beef:						
1990	22,743	2,356	25,434	24,031	1,006	397
1995	25,222	2,104	27,874	25,534	1,821	519
2000	26,888	3,032	30,332	27,338	2,468	525
2001	26,212	3,164	29,901	27,026	2,269	606
2002	27,192	3,218	31,016	27,878	2,447	691
2003	26,349	3,006	30,046	27,004	2,523	519
Pork:						
1990	15,354	898	16,565	16,031	238	296
1995	17,849	664	18,952	17,768	787	396
2000	18,952	967	20,407	18,643	1,287	478
2001	19,160	951	20,588	18,492	1,560	536
2002	19,685	1,070	21,291	19,147	1,611	533
2003	20,003	1,185	21,721	19,472	1,717	532
Veal:						
1990	327	(NA)	331	325	(NA)	6
1995	319	(NA)	326	319	(NA)	7
2000	225	(NA)	230	225	(NA)	5
2001	205	(NA)	210	204	(NA)	6
2002	205	(NA)	211	204	(NA)	7
2003	202	(NA)	209	204	(NA)	5
Lamb and mutton:						
1990	363	41	412	397	6	8
1995	285	64	359	346	6	8
2000	234	130	372	354	5	13
2001	227	146	386	368	7	12
2002	223	162	397	383	7	7
2003	203	167	377	366	7	4
POULTRY, TOTAL						
1990	23,468	-	23,931	22,153	1,222	556
1995	30,393	6	31,125	25,944	4,342	839
2000	36,073	9	37,140	30,508	5,584	1,048
2001	36,942	18	38,008	30,823	6,224	960
2002	38,079	16	39,056	32,575	5,380	1,101
2003	38,477	16	39,595	33,118	5,511	965
Broilers:						
1990	18,430	-	18,651	17,266	1,143	242
1995	24,827	1	25,286	20,832	3,894	560
2000	30,209	6	31,011	25,295	4,918	798
2001	30,938	14	31,749	25,482	5,555	712
2002	31,895	12	32,619	27,049	4,807	763
2003	32,399	12	33,173	27,633	4,932	608
Mature chicken:						
1990	523	-	530	496	25	9
1995	496	3	513	406	99	7
2000	531	2	540	311	220	9
2001	515	3	527	337	182	8
2002	547	3	557	418	134	5
2003	502	3	511	412	96	3
Turkeys:						
1990	4,514	-	4,750	4,390	54	306
1995	5,069	2	5,326	4,706	348	271
2000	5,333	1	5,589	4,902	445	241
2001	5,489	1	5,731	5,004	487	241
2002	5,638	1	5,879	5,108	439	333
2003	5,576	1	5,911	5,074	482	354

- Represents zero.   NA Not available.   [1] Total supply equals production plus imports plus ending stocks of previous year.
[2] Includes shipments to territories.

Source: U.S. Department of Agriculture, Economic Research Service, *Food Consumption, Prices, and Expenditures, 1970-2000*; and "Agricultural Outlook: Statistical Indicators"; <http://www.ers.usda.gov/publications/agoutlook/aotables/>.

Agriculture   543

No. 832. Livestock Inventory and Production: 1990 to 2004

[95.8 represents 95,800,000. **Production in live weight**; includes animals for slaughter market, younger animals shipped to other states for feeding or breeding purposes, farm slaughter and custom slaughter consumed on farms where produced, minus livestock shipped into states for feeding or breeding with an adjustment for changes in inventory]

Type of livestock	Unit	1990	1995	1997	1998	1999	2000	2001	2002	2003	2004
ALL CATTLE [1]											
Inventory:[2] Number on farms	Mil	95.8	102.8	101.7	99.7	99.1	98.2	97.3	96.7	96.1	94.9
Total value	Bil. dol.	59.0	63.2	53.4	60.2	58.8	67.1	70.5	72.3	69.9	77.7
Value per head	Dol	616	615	525	603	594	683	725	747	728	819
Production: Quantity	Bil. lb	39.2	42.5	40.9	41.7	42.6	43.0	42.6	42.4	42.2	(NA)
Beef, price per 100 lb	Dol	74.60	61.80	63.10	59.60	63.40	68.60	71.30	66.50	79.70	(NA)
Calves, price per 100 lb	Dol	95.60	73.10	78.90	78.80	87.70	104.00	106.00	96.40	102.00	(NA)
Value of production	Bil. dol.	29.3	24.7	24.8	24.2	26.1	28.5	29.4	27.1	32.2	(NA)
HOGS AND PIGS											
Inventory:[3] Number on farms	Mil	53.8	59.7	56.1	61.2	62.2	59.3	59.1	59.7	59.6	60.4
Total value	Bil. dol.	4.3	3.2	5.3	5.0	2.8	4.3	4.5	4.6	4.2	4.0
Value per head	Dol	79	53	94	82	44	72	77	77	71	66
Production: Quantity	Bil. lb	21.3	24.4	24.0	25.8	25.9	25.7	25.9	26.3	26.3	(NA)
Price per 100 lb	Dol	53.70	40.50	52.90	34.40	30.30	42.30	44.40	33.40	37.20	(NA)
Value of production	Bil. dol.	11.3	9.8	12.6	8.7	7.8	10.8	11.4	8.7	9.7	(NA)
SHEEP AND LAMBS											
Inventory:[2] Number on farms	Mil	11.4	9.0	8.0	7.8	7.2	7.0	6.9	6.6	6.3	6.1
Total value	Mil. dol.	901	663	762	798	641	670	690	614	657	721
Value per head	Dol	79	75	96	102	88	95	100	92	104	118
Production: Quantity	Mil. lb	781	602	603	554	512	501	485	468		(NA)
Sheep, price per 100 lb	Dol	23.20	28.00	37.90	30.60	31.10	34.30	34.60	28.20	34.90	(NA)
Lambs, price per 100 lb	Dol	55.50	78.20	90.30	72.30	74.50	79.80	66.90	74.10	94.40	(NA)
Value of production	Mil. dol	374	414	490	355	352	365	303	314	390	(NA)

NA Not available. [1] Includes milk cows. [2] As of Jan. 1. [3] As of Dec. 1 of preceding year.

Source: U.S. Dept. of Agriculture, National Agricultural Statistics Service, *Meat Animals—Production, Disposition, and Income Final Estimates 1998-2002*, May 2004; *Meat Animals Production, Disposition, and Income*, annual; and annual livestock summaries. Also in *Agricultural Statistics*, annual.

No. 833. Livestock Operations by Size of Herd: 1995 to 2003

[In thousands (1,191 represents 1,191,000). An operation is any place having one or more head on hand at any time during the year]

Size of herd	1995	2000	2003	Size of herd	1995	2000	2003
CATTLE [1]				**MILK COWS** [2]			
Total operations	1,191	1,076	1,014	Total operations	140	105	86
1 to 49 head	746	671	633	1 to 49 head	79	53	42
50 to 99 head	208	186	171	50 to 99 head	39	31	26
100 to 499 head	210	192	182	100 or more head	21	21	19
500 to 999 head	18	19	18	**HOGS AND PIGS**			
1,000 head or more	9	10	10	Total operations	168	87	74
BEEF COWS [2]				1 to 99 head	97	50	44
Total operations	898	831	792	100 to 499 head	44	17	12
1 to 49 head	716	655	621	500 to 999 head	15	8	6
50 to 99 head	105	100	96	1,000 to 1,999 head	7	6	5
100 to 499 head	70	71	70	2,000 to 4,999 head	4	5	5
500 head or more	6	6	5	5,000 head or more	1	2	2

[1] Includes calves.   [2] Included in operations with cattle.

Source: U.S. Dept. of Agriculture, National Agricultural Statistics Service, *Cattle Final Estimates, 1994-1998*, January 1999; *Milk Cows and Production Final Estimates 1993-1997*, January 1999; *Hogs and Pigs Final Estimates 1993-1997*, December 1998; *Livestock Operations Final Estimates 1998-2002*, April 2004; *Agricultural Statistics*, annual and unpublished data.

No. 834. Hogs and Pigs—Number, Production, and Value by State: 2001 to 2003

[59,722 represents 59,722,000. See headnote, Table 832]

State	Number on farms [1] (1,000)			Quantity produced (mil. lb.)			Value of production (mil. dol.)			Commercial slaughter [2] (mil. lb.)	
	2001	2002	2003	2001	2002	2003	2001	2002	2003	2002	2003
U.S. [3]	59,722	59,554	60,389	25,866	26,274	26,334	11,416	8,691	9,729	26,561	26,876
IA	15,400	15,500	15,900	6,400	6,701	6,831	2,746	2,030	2,247	7,639	7,788
NC	9,800	9,700	10,000	3,700	3,875	3,768	1,734	1,393	1,531	2,597	2,765
MN	5,800	6,100	6,500	2,774	2,786	3,016	1,231	937	1,127	2,312	2,357
IL	4,250	4,150	4,000	1,826	1,811	1,828	843	651	752	2,495	2,278
IN	3,200	3,250	3,100	1,446	1,466	1,568	614	462	560	1,796	1,847
NE	2,900	3,000	2,900	1,451	1,508	1,427	666	560	583	1,827	1,824
OK	2,480	2,240	2,380	1,142	1,102	1,169	481	342	415	1,274	1,295

[1] As of December 1.   [2] Includes slaughter in federally inspected and other slaughter plants; excludes animals slaughtered on farms.   [3] Includes other states not shown separately.

Source: U.S. Dept. of Agriculture, National Agricultural Statistics Service, *Meat Animals-Production, Disposition and Income*, annual; and *Livestock Slaughter*, annual.

No. 835. Cattle and Calves—Number, Production, and Value by State: 2001 to 2004

[96,723 represents 96,723,000. Includes milk cows. See headnote, Table 832]

State	Number on farms [1] (1,000)			Quantity produced (mil. lb.)			Value of production (mil. dol.)			Commercial slaughter [2] (mil. lb.)	
	2002	2003	2004	2001	2002	2003	2001	2002	2003	2002	2003
U.S. [3]	96,723	96,100	94,882	42,581	42,409	42,244	29,403	27,098	32,168	44,688	43,705
TX	13,600	14,000	13,900	7,734	7,183	7,767	5,462	4,658	6,029	7,675	7,671
NE	6,400	6,200	6,250	4,335	4,493	4,401	2,711	2,630	3,380	10,144	9,648
KS	6,600	6,350	6,650	3,942	4,067	4,025	2,463	2,364	3,033	9,112	8,926
OK	5,200	5,400	5,100	1,825	2,006	2,044	1,475	1,499	1,671	41	34
CA	5,200	5,250	5,200	1,993	1,833	1,987	946	848	1,148	1,667	1,759
CO	3,050	2,650	2,400	2,109	2,015	1,865	1,463	1,454	1,522	3,310	3,063
IA	3,550	3,550	3,450	1,616	1,840	1,797	1,132	1,152	1,420	870	1,002
SD	3,950	3,700	3,650	1,554	1,557	1,473	1,240	1,142	1,212	234	(4)
MO	4,350	4,500	4,350	1,186	1,186	1,155	999	909	991	113	120
MN	2,500	2,450	2,400	1,134	1,150	1,096	743	683	789	1,058	1,082
ID	1,990	2,000	2,010	1,044	1,143	1,095	702	705	809	1,023	949

[1] As of January 1. [2] Data cover cattle only. Includes slaughter in federally inspected and other slaughter plants; excludes animals slaughtered on farms. [3] Includes other states not shown separately. [4] Included in U.S. total. Not printed to avoid disclosing individual operation.

Source: U.S. Dept. of Agriculture, National Agricultural Statistics Service, Meat Animals-Production, Disposition and Income, annual; and Livestock Slaughter, annual.

No. 836. Milk Cows—Number, Production, and Value by State: 2001 to 2003

[9,103 represents 9,103,000]

State	Number on farms [1] (1,000)			Milk produced on farms (mil. lb.)			Value of production [2] (mil. dol.)		
	2001	2002	2003	2001	2002	2003	2001	2002	2003
United States [3] ..	9,103	9,139	9,084	165,332	170,063	170,312	24,869	20,720	21,370
California	1,589	1,648	1,688	33,217	35,065	35,437	4,630	3,836	4,033
Wisconsin	1,292	1,271	1,256	22,199	22,074	22,266	3,285	2,693	2,872
New York	672	675	671	11,780	12,218	11,952	1,861	1,564	1,566
Pennsylvania	599	585	575	10,849	10,775	10,338	1,801	1,487	1,447
Idaho	366	388	404	7,757	8,155	8,774	1,047	922	1,009
Minnesota	510	487	473	8,812	8,458	8,258	1,313	1,023	1,057
New Mexico	268	301	317	5,561	6,316	6,666	823	752	800
Michigan	303	301	302	5,870	6,120	6,360	892	741	801
Texas	326	317	319	5,107	5,300	5,630	807	684	732

[1] Average number during year. Represents cows and heifers that have calved, kept for milk; excluding heifers not yet fresh. [2] Valued at average returns per 100 pounds of milk in combined marketings of milk and cream. Includes value of milk fed to calves. [3] Includes other states not shown separately.

Source: U.S. Dept. of Agriculture, National Agricultural Statistics Service, Dairy Products, annual; and Milk: Production, Disposition, and Income, annual.

No. 837. Milk Production and Manufactured Dairy Products: 1990 to 2003

[193 represents 193,000]

Item	Unit	1990	1995	1997	1998	1999	2000	2001	2002	2003
Number of farms with milk cows	1,000	193	140	124	117	111	105	97	91	86
Cows and heifers that have calved, kept for milk.	Mil. head ..	10.0	9.5	9.3	9.2	9.2	9.2	9.1	9.1	9.1
Milk produced on farms	Bil. lb ..	148	155	156	157	163	167	165	170	170
Production per cow	1,000 lb. ..	14.8	16.4	16.9	17.2	17.8	18.2	18.2	18.6	18.7
Milk marketed by producers [1]	Bil. lb ..	146	154	155	156	161	166	164	169	169
Value of milk produced	Bil. dol. ..	20.4	20.1	21.1	24.3	23.4	20.8	24.9	20.7	21.4
Cash receipts from marketing of milk and cream	Bil. dol. ..	20.1	19.9	20.9	24.1	23.2	20.6	24.7	20.6	21.2
Number of dairy manufacturing plants	Number ..	1,723	1,495	1,384	1,323	1,192	1,163	1,179	1,149	1,126
Manufactured dairy products:										
Butter (incl. whey butter)	Mil. lb	1,302	1,264	1,151	1,168	1,277	1,256	1,232	1,355	1,242
Cheese, total [2]	Mil. lb	6,059	6,917	7,330	7,492	7,941	8,258	8,261	8,547	8,598
American (excl. full-skim American)...	Mil. lb	2,894	3,131	3,286	3,315	3,568	3,642	3,544	3,691	3,670
Cream and Neufchatel	Mil. lb	431	544	615	621	639	687	645	686	677
All Italian varieties	Mil. lb	2,207	2,674	2,881	3,005	3,152	3,289	3,426	3,470	3,522
Cottage cheese: Creamed [3]	Mil. lb	832	711	706	728	720	735	742	748	765
Curd, pot, and bakers	Mil. lb	493	459	458	466	465	461	453	437	448
Condensed bulk milk	Mil. lb	1,426	1,372	1,275	1,263	1,365	1,202	1,110	1,191	1,046
Nonfat dry milk [4]	Mil. lb	902	1,243	1,223	1,140	1,364	1,457	1,419	1,596	1,589
Dry whey	Mil. lb	1,143	1,147	1,137	1,178	1,188	1,147	1,115	1,086	1,126
Yogurt, plain and fruit flavored	Mil. lb	(NA)	1,646	1,574	1,639	1,717	1,837	2,003	2,311	2,388
Ice cream, regular	Mil. gal	824	862	914	935	972	980	970	1,005	1,015
Ice cream, lowfat [6]	Mil. gal	352	357	386	407	381	373	380	339	353

NA Not available. [1] Comprises sales to plants and dealers, and retail sales by farmers direct to consumers. [2] Includes varieties not shown separately. [3] Includes partially creamed (low fat). [4] Includes dry skim milk for animal feed. [5] Includes animal but excludes modified whey production. [6] Includes freezer-made milkshake in most states.

Source: U.S. Dept. of Agriculture, National Agricultural Statistics Service, Dairy Products, annual; and Milk: Production, Disposition, and Income, annual.

No. 838. Milk Production and Commercial Use: 1990 to 2003

[In billions of pounds milkfat basis (147.7 represents 147,700,000,000) except as noted]

Year	Production	Farm use	Commercial Farm marketings	Beginning stock	Imports	Commercial supply, total	CCC net removals[1]	Commercial Ending stock	Commercial Disappearance	Milk price per 100 lb.[2] (dol.)
1990	147.7	2.0	145.7	4.1	2.7	152.5	8.5	5.1	138.8	13.68
1995	155.3	1.6	153.7	4.3	2.9	160.9	2.1	4.1	154.7	12.78
1998	157.4	1.4	156.1	4.9	4.6	165.5	0.4	5.3	159.9	15.42
1999	162.7	1.4	161.3	5.3	4.7	171.4	0.3	6.1	164.9	14.36
2000	167.6	1.3	166.2	6.1	4.4	176.8	0.8	6.9	169.1	12.40
2001	165.5	1.2	164.3	6.8	5.7	176.8	0.1	7.0	169.7	15.04
2002	169.8	1.1	168.6	7.0	5.1	180.8	0.3	9.9	170.5	12.19
2003	170.3	1.1	169.2	9.9	5.0	184.2	1.2	8.3	174.7	12.60

[1] Removals from commercial supply by Commodity Credit Corporation (CCC). [2] Wholesale price received by farmers for all milk delivered to plants and dealers.

Source: U.S. Dept. of Agriculture, Economic Research Service, "Agricultural Outlook: Statistical Indicators"; <http://www.ers.usda.gov/publications/agoutlook/aotables/>.

No. 839. Broiler, Turkey, and Egg Production: 1990 to 2003

[For year ending November 30 (353 represents 353,000,000)]

Item	Unit	1990	1995	1996	1997	1998	1999	2000	2001	2002	2003
Chickens:[1]											
Number[2]	Million	353	388	393	410	425	437	437	444	444	449
Value per head[2]	Dollars	2.29	2.41	2.65	2.72	2.69	2.64	2.44	2.41	2.38	2.47
Value, total[2]	Mil. dol.	808	935	1,039	1,113	1,143	1,156	1,064	1,069	1,055	1,108
Number sold	Million	208	180	174	191	200	214	218	202	200	188
Price per lb.	Cents	9.6	6.5	6.6	7.7	8.1	7.1	5.7	4.5	4.8	4.8
Value of sales	Mil. dol.	94	60	59	71	80	75	64	47	50	48
PRODUCTION											
Broilers:[3]											
Number	Million	5,864	7,326	7,597	7,764	7,934	8,146	8,284	8,390	8,591	8,493
Weight	Bil. lb.	25.6	34.2	36.5	37.5	38.6	40.8	41.6	42.5	44.1	44.0
Price per lb	Cents	32.6	34.4	38.1	37.7	39.3	37.1	33.6	39.3	30.5	34.6
Production value	Mil. dol.	8,366	11,762	13,903	14,159	15,147	15,129	13,989	16,696	13,437	15,215
Turkeys:											
Number	Million	282	292	303	301	286	270	270	273	275	274
Weight	Bil. lb.	6.0	6.8	7.2	7.2	7.1	6.9	7.0	7.2	7.5	7.5
Price per lb	Cents	39.6	41.0	43.3	39.9	38.0	40.8	40.6	39.0	36.5	36.0
Production value	Mil. dol.	2,393	2,769	3,124	2,884	2,683	2,807	2,828	2,797	2,732	2,720
Eggs:											
Number	Billion	68.1	74.8	76.4	77.5	79.8	82.9	84.7	86.1	87.3	87.2
Price per dozen	Cents	70.8	62.5	75.0	70.3	66.8	62.0	61.6	62.0	58.9	73.1
Production value	Mil. dol.	4,021	3,893	4,776	4,540	4,439	4,287	4,346	4,446	4,281	5,315

[1] Excludes commercial broilers. [2] As of December 1. [3] Young chickens of the heavy breeds and other meat-type birds, to be marketed at 2-5 lbs. live weight and from which no pullets are kept for egg production.

Source: U.S. Dept. of Agriculture, National Agricultural Statistics Service, *Poultry Production and Value Final Estimates 1998-2002*, April 2004; *Turkeys Final Estimates 1998-2002*, April 2004; *Chickens and Eggs Final Estimates 1998-2002*, April 2004; *Poultry—Production and Value*, annual; *Turkeys*, annual; and *Chickens and Eggs*, annual.

No. 840. Broiler and Turkey Production by State: 2001 to 2003

[In millions of pounds, liveweight production (42,452 represents 42,452,000,000)]

State	Broilers 2001	Broilers 2002	Broilers 2003	Turkeys 2001	Turkeys 2002	Turkeys 2003	State	Broilers 2001	Broilers 2002	Broilers 2003	Turkeys 2001	Turkeys 2002	Turkeys 2003
U.S.[1]	42,452	44,059	43,958	7,173	7,495	7,549	MS	3,827	4,078	4,189	(NA)	(NA)	(NA)
AL	5,139	5,362	5,405	(NA)	(NA)	(NA)	MO	(NA)	(NA)	(NA)	660	783	816
AR	5,737	5,813	5,843	473	522	477	NC	4,203	4,411	4,320	1,131	1,160	1,105
CA	(NA)	(NA)	(NA)	451	439	419	ND	(NA)	(NA)	(NA)	42	50	29
DE	1,495	1,544	1,507	(Z)	(Z)	(NA)	OH	213	215	226	181	219	212
FL	634	631	511	(NA)	(NA)	(NA)	OK	1,111	1,141	1,115	(NA)	(NA)	(NA)
GA	6,237	6,453	6,303	(NA)	(NA)	(NA)	PA	701	706	687	214	234	216
IL	(NA)	(NA)	(NA)	83	90	90	SC	1,049	1,080	1,145	326	369	494
IN	(NA)	(NA)	(NA)	399	403	397	SD	(NA)	(NA)	(NA)	166	159	153
IA	(NA)	(NA)	(NA)	235	261	268	TN	932	895	948	(NA)	(NA)	(NA)
KY	1,292	1,404	1,490	(NA)	(NA)	(NA)	TX	2,714	2,882	2,947	(NA)	(NA)	(NA)
MD	1,381	1,377	1,374	15	16	15	VA	1,330	1,301	1,299	530	446	492
MI	(NA)	(NA)	(NA)	162	180	191	WV	368	359	358	91	89	92
MN	220	230	229	1,100	1,148	1,215	WI	138	145	155	(NA)	(NA)	(NA)

NA Not available. Z Less than 500,000 pounds. [1] Includes other states not shown separately.

Source: U.S. Dept. of Agriculture, National Agricultural Statistics Service, *Poultry—Production and Value Final Estimates 1998-2002*, April 2004 and *Poultry—Production and Value*, annual.

This section presents data on the area, ownership, production, trade, reserves, and disposition of natural resources. Natural resources is defined here as including forestry, fisheries, and mining and mineral products.

Forestry—Presents data on the area, ownership, and timber resource of commercial timberland; forestry statistics covering the National Forests and Forest Service cooperative programs; product data for lumber, pulpwood, woodpulp, paper and paperboard, and similar data.

The principal sources of data relating to forests and forest products are *Forest Resources of the United States, 1991; Timber Demand and Technology Assessment, 2001; U.S. Timber Production, Trade, Consumption, and Price Statistics; Land Areas of the National Forest System,* issued annually by the Forest Service of the Department of Agriculture; *Agricultural Statistics* issued by the Department of Agriculture; and reports of the annual survey of manufactures, and the annual *Current Industrial Reports,* issued by the Census Bureau on the Internet and in print in the annual *Manufacturing Profiles.* Additional information is published in the monthly *Survey of Current Business* of the Bureau of Economic Analysis, and the annual *Wood Pulp* and *Fiber Statistics* and *The Statistics of Paper, Paperboard, and Wood Pulp* of the American Forest and Paper Association, Washington, DC.

The completeness and reliability of statistics on forests and forest products vary considerably. The data for forest land area and stand volumes are much more reliable for areas that have been recently surveyed than for those for which only estimates are available. In general, more data are available for lumber and other manufactured products such as particle board and softwood panels, etc., than for the primary forest products such as poles and piling and fuelwood.

Fisheries—The principal source of data relating to fisheries is *Fisheries of the United States,* issued annually by the National Marine Fisheries Service (NMFS), National Oceanic and Atmospheric Administration (NOAA). The NMFS collects and disseminates data on commercial landings of fish and shellfish. Annual reports include quantity and value of commercial landings of fish and shellfish disposition of landings and number and kinds of fishing vessels and fishing gear. Reports for the fish-processing industry include annual output for the wholesaling and fish processing establishments, annual and seasonal employment. The principal source for these data is the annual *Fisheries of the United States.*

Mining and mineral products—Presents data relating to mineral industries and their products, general summary measures of production and employment, and more detailed data on production, prices, imports and exports, consumption, and distribution for specific industries and products. Data on mining and mineral products may also be found in Sections 19, 21, and 28 of this *Abstract;* data on mining employment may be found in Section 12.

Mining comprises the extraction of minerals occurring naturally (coal, ores, crude petroleum, natural gas) and quarrying, well operation, milling, refining and processing, and other preparation customarily done at the mine or well site or as a part of extraction activity. (Mineral preparation plants are usually operated together with mines or quarries.) Exploration for minerals is included as is the development of mineral properties.

The principal governmental sources of these data are the *Minerals Yearbook* and *Mineral Commodity Summaries,* published by the U.S. Geological Survey, Department of the Interior, and various monthly and annual publications of the Energy Information Administration, Department of

Energy. See text, Section 19, for a list of Department of Energy publications. In addition, the Census Bureau conducts a census of mineral industries every 5 years.

Nongovernment sources include the *Annual Statistical Report* of the American Iron and Steel Institute, Washington, DC; *Metals Week* and the monthly *Engineering and Mining Journal,* issued by the McGraw-Hill Publishing Co., New York, NY; *The Iron Age,* issued weekly by the Chilton Co., Philadelphia, PA; and the *Joint Association Survey of the U.S. Oil and Gas Industry,* conducted jointly by the American Petroleum Institute, Independent Petroleum Association of America, and Mid-Continent Oil and Gas Association.

Mineral statistics, with principal emphasis on commodity detail, have been collected by the U.S. Geological Survey and the former Bureau of Mines since 1880. Current data in U.S. Geological Survey publications include quantity and value of nonfuel minerals produced, sold or used by producers, or shipped; quantity of minerals stocked; crude materials treated and prepared minerals recovered; and consumption of mineral raw materials.

Censuses of mineral industries have been conducted by the Census Bureau at various intervals since 1840. Beginning with the 1967 census, legislation provides for a census to be conducted every 5 years for years ending in "2" and "7." The most recent results, published for 2002, are based on the North American Industry Classification System (NAICS). The censuses provide, for the various types of mineral establishments, information on operating costs, capital expenditures, labor, equipment, and energy requirements in relation to their value of shipments and other receipts. Commodity statistics on many manufactured mineral products are also collected by the Census Bureau at monthly, quarterly, or annual intervals and issued in its *Current Industrial Reports* series.

In general, figures shown in the individual commodity tables include data for outlying areas and may therefore not agree with summary tables. Except for crude petroleum and refined products, the export and import figures include foreign trade passing through the customs districts of United States and Puerto Rico but exclude shipments between U.S. territories and the customs districts.

No. 841. Natural Resource-Related Industries—Employees, Annual Payroll, and Establishments by Industry: 1999 to 2001

[Excludes government employees, railroad employees, self-employed persons, etc. See "General Explanation" in source for definitions and statement on reliability of data. An establishment is a single physical location where business is conducted or where services or industrial operations are performed]

Industry	NAICS code [1]	1999 Number of employees [2] (1,000)	1999 Annual payroll (bil. dol.)	1999 Average payroll per employee (dol.)	2000 Number of employees [2] (1,000)	2000 Annual payroll (bil. dol.)	2000 Average payroll per employee (dol.)	2001 Number of employees [2] (1,000)	2001 Annual payroll (bil. dol.)	2001 Average payroll per employee (dol.)	2001 Establishment Total	2001 Under 20 employees	2001 20 to 99 employees	2001 100 to 499 employees	2001 500 and over employees
Natural resource-related industries, total	(X)	1,803.0	65.39	36,266	1,791.3	66.58	37,166	1,759.8	69.10	38,718	73,794	47,980	10,973	3,640	289
Percent of all industries	(X)	1.63	1.19	112.95	1.57	1.72	109.28	1.53	1.73	111.68	1.04	0.79	1.31	2.32	1.50
Forestry, fishing, hunting and agriculture support	11	192.2	4.81	25,046	183.6	4.68	25,509	183.5	4.79	26,117	26,447	24,813	1,467	159	8
Forestry and logging	113	83.8	2.26	26,916	83.1	2.26	27,137	78.0	2.16	27,722	12,795	12,095	626	73	1
Timber tract operations	1131	3.3	0.12	37,422	3.3	0.13	39,563	3.2	0.13	38,399	441	368	28	45	-
Forest nurseries & gathering forest products	1132	1.4	0.05	35,954	1.7	0.07	39,933	2.0	0.07	34,196	256	227	29	-	-
Logging	1133	79.2	2.08	26,326	78.1	2.06	26,331	72.7	1.96	27,069	12,098	11,500	569	28	1
Fishing, hunting & trapping	114	10.0	0.33	33,302	10.0	0.34	34,287	9.9	0.34	34,249	2,636	2,551	72	12	1
Fishing	1141	7.6	0.26	34,645	7.5	0.27	35,669	7.3	0.26	35,179	2,252	2,183	59	10	-
Hunting & trapping	1142	2.4	0.07	28,998	2.5	0.08	30,173	2.6	0.08	31,625	384	368	13	2	-
Agriculture & forestry support activities	115	98.3	2.22	22,613	90.4	2.08	23,043	95.5	2.29	23,960	11,016	10,119	769	121	7
Crop production support activities	1151	67.4	1.58	23,386	57.6	1.35	23,400	59.6	1.46	24,553	5,464	4,880	491	89	4
Animal production support activities	1152	16.7	0.33	19,507	18.2	0.38	21,086	20.1	0.45	21,798	3,999	3,820	165	13	1
Forestry support activities	1153	14.1	0.32	22,603	14.7	0.35	24,067	15.2	0.37	24,587	1,553	1,419	113	19	2
Mining	21	456.6	20.98	45,935	456.1	22.09	48,432	485.6	25.01	51,516	24,319	9,823	3,628	748	95
Oil & gas extraction	211	90.0	5.38	59,742	83.0	5.39	64,967	87.9	6.21	70,673	7,691	6,862	687	130	12
Oil & gas extraction	2111	90.0	5.38	59,742	83.0	5.39	64,967	87.9	6.21	70,673	7,691	6,862	687	130	12
Mining (except oil & gas)	212	215.9	9.63	44,572	204.3	9.34	45,731	200.7	9.58	47,743	7,323	5,276	1,680	326	41
Coal mining	2121	76.4	3.70	48,413	70.7	3.54	50,125	71.9	3.78	53,327	1,266	692	392	164	18
Metal ore mining	2122	39.9	1.84	46,206	34.8	1.72	49,353	32.8	1.65	50,290	484	375	84	6	19
Nonmetallic mineral mining & quarrying	2123	99.6	4.08	40,972	98.8	4.08	41,313	97.9	4.14	42,791	5,572	4,209	1,204	115	4
Mining support activities	213	150.7	5.97	39,641	168.8	7.35	43,570	196.8	9.21	46,802	9,305	7,710	1,244	342	42
Mining support activities	2131	150.7	5.97	39,641	168.8	7.35	43,570	196.8	9.21	46,802	9,305	7,710	1,244	342	42
Timber-related manufacturing	(X)	1,154.2	39.60	34,309	1,151.6	39.80	34,562	1,090.7	39.30	35,141	23,028	13,344	5,878	2,733	186
Wood product manufacturing	321	595.2	16.37	27,509	597.7	16.51	27,626	557.5	16.82	28,393	17,289	11,483	4,481	1,311	27
Sawmills & wood preservation	3211	131.9	3.75	28,431	131.4	3.78	28,798	122.1	3.52	28,811	4,594	3,099	1,203	291	1
Veneer, plywood & engineered wood product manufacturing	3212	117.5	3.63	30,846	120.6	3.75	31,098	116.4	3.70	31,744	1,944	811	774	348	11
Other wood product manufacturing	3219	345.7	9.00	26,023	345.8	8.95	25,882	318.8	8.61	27,009	10,751	7,531	2,504	672	15
Paper manufacturing	322	559.0	23.23	41,549	553.9	23.29	42,046	533.2	22.50	42,196	5,739	1,861	2,297	1,422	159
Pulp, paper & paperboard mills	3221	185.2	9.74	52,607	177.1	9.48	53,490	170.0	9.20	54,080	606	91	166	234	115
Converted paper product manufacturing	3222	373.8	13.48	36,071	376.8	13.82	36,666	363.2	13.30	36,632	5,133	1,770	2,131	1,188	44

- Represents zero. X Not applicable. [1] North American Industry Classification System, 1997. [2] Covers full- and part-time employees who are on the payroll in the pay period including March 12.

Source: U.S. Census Bureau, *County Business Patterns: 2000*, Series CBP/00-1. See also <http://www.census.gov/prod/2003pubs/01cbp/cbp01-1.pdf> (issued April 2003).

Natural Resources 549

No. 842. Natural Resource-Related Industries—Establishments, Sales, Payroll and Employees by Industry: 1997 and 2002

[174 represents $174,000,000,000. Includes only establishments of firms with payroll. See Appendix III]

Industry	NAICS code[1]	1997				2002[2]			
		Establishments	Sales, receipts, revenue, or shipments (bil. dol.)	Annual payroll (bil. dol.)	Paid employees (1,000)	Establishments	Sales, receipts, revenue, or shipments (bil. dol.)	Annual payroll (bil. dol.)	Paid employees (1,000)
Mining	21	25,000	174	21	509	(S)	(S)	(S)	(S)
Oil & gas extraction	211	8,312	103	6	111	7,514	107	5	100
Mining (except oil & gas) . .	212	7,348	51	9	229	7,173	54	9	200
Support activities	213	9,340	20	6	169	S	S	S	S
Manufacturing[3]	31-33	362,829	3,835	570	16,805	344,259	3,833	568	14,543
Wood product manufacturing.	321	17,367	88	14	570	16,912	89	16	535
Paper manufacturing	322	5,868	150	22	574	5,463	151	21	476
Petroleum & coal products manufacturing	324	2,146	177	6	108	2,278	212	6	106

S Figure does not meet publication standards. [1] North American Industry Classification System, 1997. [2] Preliminary data. [3] Includes industry not shown separately.
Source: U.S. Census Bureau, 2002 Economic Census, *Advance Comparative Statistics for the United States 1997 NAICS Basis.* See also <http://www.census.gov/econ/census02/>.

No. 843. Gross Domestic Product of Natural Resource-Related Industries in Current and Real (1996) Dollars by Industry: 1990 to 2001

[In billions of dollars (5,803.2 represents $5,803,200,000,000). Data are based on the 1987 SIC. Data include nonfactor charges (capital consumption allowances, indirect business taxes, etc.) as well as factor charges against gross product; corporate profits and capital consumption allowances have been shifted from a company to an establishment basis]

Industry	Current dollars				Chained (1996) dollars			
	1990	1995	2000	2001	1990	1995	2000	2001
All industries, total	5,803.2	7,400.5	9,824.6	10,082.2	6,707.9	7,543.8	9,191.4	9,214.5
Industries covered	297.3	306.7	369.7	374.8	321.9	329.9	363.6	359.4
Percent of all industries	5.12	4.14	3.76	3.72	4.80	4.37	3.96	3.90
Agriculture, forestry, and fishing	108.3		134.3	140.7	118.5	123.1	166.7	163.9
Farms	79.6	73.2	77.8	80.6	84.2	85.5	120.5	114.3
Agricultural services	28.7	36.7	56.5	60.1	34.6	37.6	47.6	49.1
Mining	111.9	95.7	133.1	139.0	105.8	113.0	101.9	106.8
Metal mining	5.2	6.5	5.2	5.7	4.4	5.5	8.0	9.6
Coal mining	11.8	10.7	9.2	10.5	7.5	10.1	11.9	13.9
Oil and gas extraction	87.1	69.3	106.5	110.3	87.5	88.6	70.5	72.9
Nonmetallic minerals, except fuels . . .	7.8	9.1	-12.2	12.6	8.1	9.1	12.2	12.4
Timber-related manufacturing	77.2	101.3	102.3	95.1	97.6	93.8	94.9	88.7
Lumber and wood products	32.2	42.3	42.1	39.2	45.1	41.6	41.8	39.0
Paper and allied products	45.0	58.9	60.2	55.9	52.5	52.2	53.1	49.7

Source: U.S. Bureau of Economic Analysis, *National Income and Product Accounts, 1929-97;* and *Survey of Current Business,* November 2002. See also <http://www.bea.doc.gov/bea/ARTICLES/2002/11November/1102GDPbyIndustry.pdf> (released 28 October 2002).

No. 844. National Forest System Land—State and Other Areas: 2003

[In thousands of acres (232,332 represents 232,332,000). As of Sept. 30.]

State and other area	Gross area within unit boundaries[1]	National Forest System Land[2]	State and other area	Gross area within unit boundaries[1]	National Forest System Land[2]	State and other area	Gross area within unit boundaries[1]	National Forest System Land[2]
Total ..	232,332	192,511	KS	116	108	OH.	834	236
U.S.	232,277	192,483	KY	2,208	809	OK.	772	400
AL	1,288	666	LA	1,025	605	OR.	17,503	15,666
AK	24,356	21,981	ME	93	53	PA	743	513
AZ	11,891	11,262	MD	-	-	RI	1,379	617
AR	3,451	2,592	MA	-	-	SC	2,369	2,013
CA	24,430	20,741	MI	4,894	2,865	SD	1,276	701
CO	16,015	14,487	MN	5,467	2,840	TN	1,994	755
CT			MS	2,317	1,171	TX	9,196	8,180
DE			MO	3,060	1,487	UT	817	389
DC			MT	19,117	16,923	VT	3,223	1,662
FL	1,434	1,153	NE	442	352	VA	10,113	9,273
GA	1,857	865	NV	6,275	5,835	WA	1,869	1,034
HI			NH	828	732	WV	2,023	1,526
ID	21,652	20,465	NJ	-	-	WI	9,703	9,238
IL	857	293	NM	10,455	9,418	WY		
IN	644	200	NY	16	16	PR	56	28
IA			NC	3,165	1,252	VI	-	-
			ND	1,106	1,106			

- Represents zero or rounds to zero. [1] Comprises all publicly and privately owned land within authorized boundaries of national forests, purchase units, national grasslands, land utilization projects, research and experimental areas, and other areas. [2] Federally owned land within the "gross area within unit boundaries."
Source: U.S. Forest Service, *Land Areas of the National Forest System,* annual.

No. 845. Timber-Based Manufacturing Industries—Employees, Payroll, and Shipments: 2001

Selected industries	1997 NAICS code [1]	All employees			Value added by manufactures			
			Payroll		Produc-tion workers, total (1,000)	Total (mil. dol.)	Per produc-tion worker (dol.)	Value of ship-ments (mil. dol.)
		Number (1,000)	Total (mil. dol.)	Per employee (dol.)				
Manufacturing, all industries	31-33	**15,879**	**593,051**	**37,347**	**11,235**	**1,853,929**	**165,012**	**3,970,500**
Timber-based manufacturing, total	321-322	**1,086**	**37,619**	**34,636**	**867**	**106,166**	**122,495**	**243,096**
Percent of total manfacturing	(X)	6.84	6.34	(X)	7.71	5.73	(X)	6.12
Wood product manufacturing	321	556	15,431	27,759	459	33,130	72,191	87,250
Sawmills & wood preservation	3211	124	3,481	27,978	106	7,484	70,853	25,924
Sawmills	321113	114	3,169	27,899	97	6,781	69,814	21,694
Wood preservation	321114	11	313	28,805	9	704	82,724	4,231
Veneer, plywood, & engineered wood product	3212	115	3,515	30,463	95	7,586	79,638	19,636
Other wood product	3219	316	8,435	26,685	258	18,060	69,990	41,689
Millwork	32191	146	4,167	28,559	119	9,166	76,752	22,149
Wood container & pallet	32192	49	1,097	22,324	41	2,169	52,756	4,687
All other wood product	32199	121	3,171	26,197	97	6,724	68,974	14,854
Paper	322	530	22,188	41,845	408	73,036	179,108	155,846
Pulp, paper, & paperboard mills	3221	171	9,179	53,783	134	37,279	277,782	71,987
Pulp mills	32211	7	414	57,419	6	1,413	253,647	3,239
Paper mills	32212	115	6,163	53,745	91	24,837	273,804	46,853
Paperboard mills	32213	49	2,601	53,335	38	11,029	290,842	21,896
Converted paper product	3222	360	13,010	36,180	274	35,757	130,703	83,859
Paperboard container	32221	205	7,483	36,502	157	17,534	111,575	45,817
Paper bag & coated & treated paper	32222	71	2,665	37,741	51	8,443	164,924	18,390
Stationery product	32223	45	1,452	32,175	35	3,485	100,021	8,075
Other converted paper product	32229	39	1,410	36,296	30	6,295	207,137	11,576

X Not applicable. [1] North American Industry Classification System, 1997; see text, Section 15.

Source: U.S. Census Bureau, *Annual Survey of Manufactures, 2001*, Series M01(AS)-1. See also <http://www.census.gov/prod/2003pubs /m01-as1.pdf> (issued January 2003).

No. 846. Timber Products—Production, Foreign Trade, and Consumption by Type of Product: 1990 to 2003

[In millions of cubic feet, roundwood equivalent (15,577 represents 15,577,000,000)]

Type of product	1990	1994	1995	1996	1997	1998	1999	2000	2001	2002	2003
Industrial roundwood:											
Domestic production [1]	15,577	15,306	15,537	15,413	15,703	15,620	15,632	15,436	14,634	14,902	14,819
Softwoods	10,968	10,268	10,191	10,153	10,180	10,097	10,381	10,201	9,859	10,124	10,001
Hardwoods	4,609	5,038	5,347	5,260	5,523	5,523	5,251	5,235	4,775	4,778	4,817
Imports	3,091	3,632	3,907	3,885	4,008	4,157	4,370	4,529	4,605	4,505	4,954
Exports	2,307	2,139	2,282	2,264	2,290	1,951	1,964	1,996	1,759	1,769	1,698
Consumption [2]	16,361	16,800	17,161	17,034	17,421	17,827	18,038	17,969	17,481	17,637	18,075
Softwoods	11,779	11,906	11,961	11,996	12,072	12,339	12,754	12,659	12,552	12,790	12,944
Hardwoods	4,582	4,894	5,200	5,038	5,349	5,488	5,284	5,310	4,929	4,847	5,131
Lumber:											
Domestic production	7,317	7,052	6,815	6,886	7,103	7,093	7,379	7,199	6,820	7,060	7,240
Imports	1,909	2,395	2,522	2,616	2,619	2,721	2,807	2,845	2,903	3,036	3,193
Exports	589	512	460	449	452	350	404	428	354	353	360
Consumption	8,637	8,935	8,877	9,053	9,270	9,463	9,782	9,616	9,369	9,744	10,073
Plywood and veneer:											
Domestic production	1,423	1,320	1,303	1,281	1,213	1,201	1,208	1,187	1,067	1,074	1,044
Imports	97	94	107	97	114	131	160	155	173	205	240
Exports	109	86	89	87	103	55	45	42	32	31	35
Consumption	1,410	1,328	1,321	1,291	1,224	1,277	1,323	1,300	1,208	1,249	1,249
Pulp products:											
Domestic production	5,313	5,576	6,079	5,908	6,097	6,114	5,813	5,881	5,691	5,708	5,706
Imports	1,038	1,102	1,248	1,144	1,249	1,269	1,355	1,459	1,458	1,180	1,437
Exports	646	758	905	891	929	818	768	842	801	810	793
Consumption	5,704	5,920	6,422	6,161	6,417	6,565	6,400	6,498	6,348	6,078	6,351
Logs:											
Imports	4	18	13	18	20	30	47	68	70	81	80
Exports	674	429	451	422	384	316	326	331	307	309	356
Pulpwood chips, exports	288	354	377	416	422	412	422	353	265	265	155
Fuelwood consumption	3,019	3,134	2,937	2,739	2,542	2,523	2,542	2,561	2,571	2,581	2,591

[1] Includes log exports. [2] Includes log imports.

Source: U.S. Forest Service, *U.S. Timber Production, Trade, Consumption, and Price Statistics, 1965-1999*, Research Paper FPL-RP-595; and unpublished data. See also <http://www.fpl.fs.fed.us/documnts/fplrp/fplrp595.pdf>.

Natural Resources 551

No. 847. Selected Timber Products—Imports and Exports: 1990 to 2003

Product	Unit	1990	1995	1997	1998	1999	2000	2001	2002	2003
IMPORTS [1]										
Lumber, total [2]	Mil. bd. ft . .	13,063	17,524	18,237	19,012	19,576	19,906	20,443	21,434	21,981
From Canada	Percent . . .	91.3	97.1	96.3	96.0	93.0	92.0	93.0	90.4	90.0
Logs, total	Mil. bd. ft.[3]	23	80	128	185	294	435	452	525	497
From Canada	Percent . . .	84	70	83	91	95	96	97	97	98
Paper and board [4]	1,000 tons .	12,195	14,292	14,525	14,538	16,917	17,555	18,513	19,433	20,034
Woodpulp	1,000 tons .	4,893	5,969	6,398	5,984	6,660	7,227	7,348	7,247	6,691
Plywood	Mil. sq. ft.[5]	1,687	1,951	2,111	2,429	2,987	2,917	3,246	3,868	4,489
EXPORTS										
Lumber, total [2]	Mil. bd. ft . .	4,614	2,958	2,933	2,189	2,549	2,700	2,190	2,186	2,193
To: Canada	Percent . . .	14	22	24	26	26	26	26	27	29
Japan	Percent . . .	28	33	27	16	14	12	10	7	7
Europe	Percent . . .	15	17	20	26	21	19	18	16	16
Logs, total	Mil. bd. ft.[3]	4,213	2,820	2,398	1,978	2,038	2,068	1,918	1,934	2,224
To: Canada	Percent . . .	9	25	30	39	39	41	46	50	54
Japan	Percent . . .	62	61	56	51	49	45	39	34	29
China:	Percent . . .	9	1	1	1	-	-	1	2	2
Paper and board [4]	1,000 tons .	5,163	7,621	10,368	9,103	9,477	10,003	11,504	11,564	11,868
Woodpulp	1,000 tons .	5,905	8,261	6,990	6,025	5,936	6,409	6,167	6,254	5,847
Plywood	Mil. sq. ft.[5]	1,766	1,517	1,802	970	797	754	580	563	640

- Represents zero. [1] Customs value of imports; see text, Section 28. [2] Includes railroad ties. [3] Log scale. [4] Includes paper and board products. Excludes hardboard. [5] 3/8 inch basis.

Source: U.S. Forest Service, *U.S. Timber Production, Trade, Consumption, and Price Statistics, 1965-1999*, Research Paper FPL-RP-595; and unpublished data. See also <http://www.fpl.fs.fed.us/documnts/fplrp/fplrp595.pdf>.

No. 848. Lumber Consumption by Species Group and End Use: 1995 to 2003

[In million board feet (59.3 represents 59,300,000), except per capita in board feet. Per capita consumption based on estimated resident population as of **July 1**]

Item	1995	2000	2001	2002	2003	End-use	1995	2000	2001	2002	2003
Total	59.3	66.1	64.6	67.5	67.5	New housing	15.9	20.6	20.1	20.0	20.0
						Residential upkeep and					
Per capita	225	240	227	235	232	improvements	14.3	16.4	17.0	17.3	17.5
						New nonresidential					
Species group:						construction [1]	5.8	7.7	5.6	5.5	5.5
Softwoods . . .	47.6	54.0	53.7	56.4	56.2	Manufacturing.	5.5	(NA)	(NA)	(NA)	8.1
Hardwoods . .	11.7	12.2	11.0	11.1	11.3	Shipping	8.5	7.7	8.1	8	7.5
						Other [2]	10.2	6.7	7.3	7.5	6.9

NA Not available. [1] In addition to new construction, includes railroad ties laid as replacements in existing track and lumber used by railroads for railcar repair. [2] Includes upkeep and improvement of nonresidential buildings and structures; made-at-home projects, such as furniture, boats, and picnic tables; made-on-the-job items such as advertising and display structures; and miscellaneous products and uses.

Source: U.S. Forest Service, *U.S. Timber Production, Trade Consumption, and Price Statistics, 1965-1999, Research Paper FPL-RP-595*. See also <http://www.fpl.fs.fed.us/documnts/fplrp/fplrp595.pdf>.

No. 849. Selected Timber Products—Producer Price Indexes: 1990 to 2003

[1982=100. For information about producer prices, see text, Section 14, Prices]

Product	1990	1995	1997	1998	1999	2000	2001	2002	2003
INDEX									
Lumber and wood products	129.7	178.1	183.8	179.1	183.6	178.2	174.4	173.3	177.5
Lumber	124.6	173.4	194.5	179.5	188.2	178.8	171.6	170.6	174.8
Softwood lumber.	123.8	178.5	206.5	182.7	196.0	178.6	170.1	170.8	171.1
Hardwood lumber	131.0	167.0	174.1	176.7	177.3	185.9	181.3	178.3	189.7
Millwork	130.4	163.8	170.9	171.1	174.7	176.4	179.2	179.8	181.8
General millwork.	132.0	165.4	171.1	172.4	175.6	178.0	181.8	183.3	185.4
Prefabricated structural members. . .	122.3	163.5	177.8	170.1	178.1	175.1	173.5	168.5	171.1
Plywood	114.2	165.3	159.3	157.3	176.4	157.6	154.3	151.7	166.9
Softwood plywood.	119.6	188.1	175.5	174.9	207.0	173.3	167.8	164.1	195.6
Hardwood plywood and related products. . .	102.7	122.2	127.1	126.9	128.6	130.2	130.4	131.5	129.0
Other wood products	114.7	143.7	128.4	128.5	135.2	131.1	130.5	130.5	127.2	129.9
Boxes	119.1	145.0	149.2	150.7	152.3	155.2	154.5	154.3	157.6
Pulp, paper, and allied products. . . .	141.2	172.2	167.9	171.7	174.1	183.7	184.8	185.9	190.0
Pulp, paper, and prod, ex bldg paper	132.9	163.4	144.7	147.0	147.9	161.4	157.7	155.3	157.1
Woodpulp	151.3	183.2	128.6	122.6	119.7	145.3	125.8	116.2	121.4
Wastepaper	138.9	371.1	163.3	145.4	183.6	282.5	148.6	173.1	197.2
Paper	128.8	159.0	143.9	145.4	141.8	149.8	150.6	144.7	146.1
Writing and printing papers	129.1	158.4	140.0	139.0	137.8	146.6	146.4	143.8	144.7
Newsprint	119.6	161.8	133.9	143.4	(NA)	127.5	138.6	105.7	111.8
Paperboard	135.7	183.1	144.4	151.6	153.2	176.7	172.1	164.3	162.7
Converted paper and paperboard products .	135.2	157.0	148.4	152.2	153.5	162.7	164.5	163.8	165.3
Office supplies and accessories	121.4	134.9	131.0	131.2	129.5	133.8	136.9	135.7	137.5
Building paper & building board mill prods . . .	112.2	144.9	129.6	132.9	141.6	138.8	129.3	129.3	159.7

NA Not available. [1] Includes other products not shown separately.

Source: U.S. Bureau of Labor Statistics, *Producer Price Indexes*, monthly.

No. 850. Selected Species—Stumpage Prices In Current and Constant (1996) Dollars: 1990 to 2003

[In dollars per 1,000 board feet. Stumpage prices are based on sales of sawtimber from National Forests]

Species	1990	1994	1995	1996	1997	1998	1999	2000	2001	2002	2003
CURRENT DOLLARS											
Softwoods:											
Douglas fir [1] [2]	466	652	454	436	331	254	315	433	258	185	305
Southern pine [2]	127	266	248	241	307	288	269	258	168	166	162
Sugar pine [3] [4]	285	625	397	318	234	200	229	187	192	209	54
Ponderosa pine [3] [4]	218	291	150	274	270	205	181	155	143	118	35
Western hemlock [5]	203	335	297	248	211	161	96	46	34	73	104
Hardwoods:											
All eastern hardwoods [6]	146	352	309	259	287	241	195	341	264	384	279
Oak, white, red, and black [6] [7]	188	317	297	237	265	270	317	258	153	207	236
Maple, sugar [7]	135	313	286	238	357	395	448	314	271	485	586
CONSTANT (1996) DOLLARS [8]											
Softwoods:											
Douglas fir [1] [2]	428	598	417	436	304	233	289	397	237	170	279
Southern pine [2]	117	244	228	241	282	264	247	237	154	153	148
Sugar pine [3] [4]	262	574	364	318	215	183	210	172	176	191	49
Ponderosa pine [3] [4]	200	267	138	274	248	188	166	142	131	108	32
Western hemlock [5]	186	307	272	248	194	148	88	42	31	67	95
Hardwoods:											
All eastern hardwoods [6]	134	323	283	259	263	221	179	313	242	353	256
Oak, white, red, and black [6] [7]	172	291	272	237	243	248	291	237	140	190	216
Maple, sugar [7]	124	287	262	238	328	362	411	237	288	445	538

[1] Western Washington and western Oregon. [2] Southern region. [3] Pacific Southwest region (formerly California region). [4] Includes Jeffrey pine. [5] Pacific Northwest region. [6] Eastern and Southern regions. [7] Eastern region. [8] Deflated by the producer price index, all commodities.

Source: U.S. Forest Service, *Timber Demand and Technolgy Assessment*, RWU-4851. Also in *Agricultural Statistics*, annual.

No. 851. Paper and Paperboard—Production and New Supply: 1990 to 2002

[In millions of short tons (80.45 represents 80,450,000)]

Item	1990	1995	1996	1997	1998	1999	2000	2001	2002, prel.
Production, total	80.45	91.33	92.25	96.92	96.40	98.65	96.05	90.38	91.14
Paper, total	39.36	42.87	42.48	44.70	44.76	45.98	45.52	42.10	41.54
Paperboard, total	39.32	46.64	47.95	50.40	49.83	51.04	48.97	46.81	48.13
Unbleached kraft	20.36	22.70	22.23	23.22	23.20	23.11	21.80	20.44	21.09
Semichemical	5.64	5.66	5.62	6.05	5.89	6.01	5.95	5.58	5.84
Bleached kraft	4.40	5.30	5.24	5.55	5.49	5.71	5.44	5.30	5.30
Recycled	8.92	12.98	14.87	15.58	15.25	16.21	15.79	15.50	15.91
Wet machine board E.	0.15	0.15	0.10	0.10	0.10	0.06	0.06	0.05	0.05
Building paper E.	0.81	0.81	0.79	0.79	0.79	0.66	0.64	0.58	0.58
Insulating board E.	0.86	0.86	0.93	0.93	0.93	0.91	0.86	0.85	0.85
New supply, all grades, excluding products	87.68	98.16	98.34	101.27	103.01	106.90	105.12	99.17	100.81
Paper, total	49.49	52.77	50.69	54.15	55.13	57.30	57.22	53.29	53.85
Newsprint	13.41	12.76	11.77	12.61	12.80	13.09	13.01	11.52	11.52
Printing/writing papers	25.46	29.55	28.30	30.75	31.38	32.53	32.99	30.38	30.95
Packaging and ind. conv. papers	4.72	4.24	4.33	4.27	4.29	4.71	4.27	4.31	4.20
Tissue	5.90	6.22	6.29	6.52	6.66	6.98	6.95	7.07	7.18
Paperboard, total	36.30	43.45	43.67	45.13	45.67	47.59	46.02	44.09	45.29
Construction and other	1.90	1.95	1.99	1.99	2.20	2.00	1.88	1.80	1.66

Source: American Forest and Paper Association, Washington, DC, *Monthly Statistical Summary of Paper, Paperboard and Woodpulp.*

Natural Resources 553

No. 852. Fishery Products—Domestic Catch, Imports, and Disposition: 1990 to 2002

[Live weight, in millions of pounds (16,349 represents 16,349,000,000). For data on commercial catch for selected countries, see Table 1356, Section 30]

Item	1990	1995	1996	1997	1998	1999	2000	2001	2002
Total...........	16,349	16,484	16,474	17,131	16,897	17,378	17,338	18,118	19,028
For human food.......	12,662	13,584	13,625	13,739	14,175	14,462	14,738	15,306	16,007
For industrial use......	3,687	2,900	2,848	3,392	2,722	2,916	2,599	2,812	3,021
Domestic catch......	9,404	9,788	9,565	9,845	9,194	9,339	9,069	9,492	9,397
For human food.....	7,041	7,667	7,474	7,248	7,174	6,832	6,912	7,314	7,205
For industrial use....	2,363	2,121	2,091	2,597	2,020	2,507	2,157	2,178	2,192
Imports...........	6,945	6,696	6,909	7,286	7,703	8,039	8,269	8,826	9,631
For human food . , ..	5,621	5,917	6,150	6,491	7,001	7,630	7,827	7,992	8,802
For industrial use [2]...	1,324	779	759	795	702	409	442	634	829
Exports...........	4,627	5,166	5,220	5,537	4,889	5,208	5,757	7,107	6,979
For human food.......	3,832	4,175	4,176	4,326	3,709	4,130	4,586	5,774	5,587
For industrial use	795	991	1,044	1,211	1,180	1,078	1,171	1,333	1,392
Disposition of domestic catch....	9,404	9,788	9,565	9,846	9,194	9,339	9,069	9,492	9,397
Fresh and frozen......	6,501	7,099	7,054	6,877	6,870	6,416	6,657	7,085	6,826
Canned............	751	769	678	648	516	712	530	536	652
Cured.............	126	90	93	108	129	133	119	123	117
Reduced to meal, oil, etc.	2,026	1,830	1,740	2,213	1,679	2,078	1,763	1,748	1,802

[1] Excludes imports of edible fishery products consumed in Puerto Rico; includes landings of tuna caught by foreign vessels in American Samoa. [2] Fish meal and sea herring.

No. 853. Fisheries—Quantity and Value of Domestic Catch: 1980 to 2002

Year	Quantity (mil. lb. [1])			Value (mil. dol.)	Average price per lb. (cents)	Year	Quantity (mil. lb. [1])			Value (mil. dol.)	Average price per lb. (cents)
	Total	For human food	For indus- trial prod- ucts [2]				Total	For human food	For indus- trial prod- ucts [2]		
1980	6,482	3,654	2,828	2,237	34.5	1992	9,637	7,618	2,019	3,678	38.2
1981	5,977	3,547	2,430	2,388	40.0	1993	[3]10,467	8,214	2,253	3,471	33.2
1982	6,367	3,285	3,082	2,390	37.5	1994	10,461	7,936	2,525	3,807	36.8
1983	6,439	3,238	3,201	2,355	36.6	1995	9,788	7,667	2,121	3,770	38.5
1984	6,438	3,320	3,118	2,350	36.5	1996	9,565	7,474	2,091	3,487	36.5
1985	6,258	3,294	2,964	2,326	37.2	1997	9,845	7,248	2,597	3,448	35.0
1986	6,031	3,393	2,638	2,763	45.8	1998	9,194	7,174	2,020	3,128	34.0
1987	6,896	3,946	2,950	3,115	45.2	1999	9,339	6,832	2,507	3,467	37.1
1988	7,192	4,588	2,604	3,520	48.9	2000	9,069	6,912	2,157	3,549	39.1
1989	8,463	6,204	2,259	3,238	38.3	2001	9,492	7,314	2,178	3,228	34.0
1990	9,404	7,041	2,363	3,522	37.5	2002	9,397	7,205	2,192	3,092	32.9
1991	9,484	7,031	2,453	3,308	34.9						

[1] Live weight. [2] Meal, oil, fish solubles, homogenized condensed fish, shell products, bait, and animal food. [3] Represents record year.

No. 854. Domestic Fish and Shellfish Catch and Value by Major Species Caught: 1990 to 2002

Species	Quantity (1,000 lb.)				Value ($1,000)			
	1990	2000	2001	2002	1990	2000	2001	2002
Total.............	9,403,571	9,068,985	9,491,836	9,397,164	3,521,995	3,549,481	3,228,285	3,092,318
Fish, total [1]...........	8,091,068	7,689,661	8,242,490	8,089,987	1,900,097	1,594,815	1,479,988	1,359,392
Cod: Atlantic...........	95,881	25,060	33,211	29,841	61,329	26,384	32,086	30,715
Pacific............	526,396	530,505	471,711	512,827	91,384	142,330	118,071	96,206
Flounder............	254,519	412,723	352,363	372,697	112,921	109,910	105,240	102,370
Halibut............	70,454	75,190	77,978	82,044	96,700	143,826	115,169	135,603
Herring, sea; Atlantic......	113,095	160,269	209,191	135,871	5,746	9,972	12,717	9,106
Herring, sea; Pacific......	108,120	74,835	91,297	78,408	32,178	12,043	13,213	11,534
Menhaden	1,962,160	1,760,498	1,741,430	1,750,609	93,896	112,403	102,690	105,102
Pollock, Alaska	3,108,031	2,606,802	3,179,407	3,341,105	268,344	160,525	230,723	203,696
Salmon..............	733,146	628,638	722,832	567,179	612,367	270,213	208,926	155,010
Tuna	62,393	50,779	51,854	49,358	105,040	95,176	93,497	84,116
Whiting (Atlantic, silver).....	44,500	26,855	28,479	17,622	11,281	11,370	13,232	7,454
Whiting (Pacific, hake).....	21,232	452,718	379,304	285,714	1,229	18,809	16,147	13,584
Shellfish, total [1]	1,312,503	1,379,324	1,138,512	1,178,590	1,621,898	1,954,666	1,711,391	1,706,426
Clams	139,198	118,482	122,764	130,076	130,194	153,973	161,992	167,215
Crabs...............	499,416	299,006	272,246	307,601	483,837	405,006	381,667	397,695
Lobsters: American........	61,017	83,180	73,637	82,252	154,677	301,300	254,334	293,329
Oysters	29,193	41,146	32,673	34,397	93,718	90,667	80,946	89,071
Scallops, sea..........	39,917	32,747	46,958	53,056	153,696	164,609	175,349	203,707
Shrimp..............	346,494	332,486	324,481	316,727	491,433	690,453	568,547	460,878
Squid, Pacific	36,082	259,508	191,532	160,677	2,636	27,077	17,834	18,262

[1] Includes other types of fish and shellfish, not shown separately.

Source of Tables 852-854: U.S. National Oceanic and Atmospheric Administration, National Marine Fisheries Service, *Fisheries of the United States*, annual. See also <http://www.st.nmfs.gov/st1/fus/fus01/2002-fus.pdf> (released September 2003).

No. 855. U.S. Private Aquaculture—Trout and Catfish Production and Value: 1990 to 2002

[67.8 represents 67,800,000. Periods are from Sept. 1 of the previous year to Aug. 31 of stated year. Data are for foodsize fish, those over 12 inches long]

Item	Unit	1990	1995	1997	1998	1999	2000	2001	2002
TROUT FOODSIZE									
Number sold	Millions .	67.8	60.2	59.3	57.6	61.0	58.5	54.5	50.2
Total weight	Mil. lb . .	56.8	55.6	56.9	57.9	60.2	59.2	56.9	54.5
Total value of sales	Mil. dol. .	64.6	60.8	60.7	60.3	64.7	63.7	64.4	58.3
Average price received	Dol./lb . .	1.14	1.09	1.07	1.04	1.07	1.08	1.13	1.07
Percent sold to processors	Percent .	58	68	63	62	68	70	68	69
CATFISH FOODSIZE									
Number sold	Millions .	272.9	321.8	391.8	409.8	424.5	420.1	406.9	405.8
Total weight	Mil. lb . .	392.4	481.5	569.6	601.4	635.2	633.8	647.5	673.7
Total value of sales	Mil. dol. .	305.1	378.1	406.8	445.4	464.7	468.8	410.7	378.5
Average price received	Dol./lb . .	0.78	0.79	0.71	0.74	0.73	0.74	0.63	0.56
Fish sold to processors	Mil. lb . .	360.4	446.9	524.9	564.4	596.6	593.6	597.1	630.6
Avg. price paid by processors	Cents/lb .	75.8	78.6	71.2	74.3	73.7	75.1	64.7	56.8
Processor sales	Mil. lb . .	183.1	227.0	261.8	281.4	292.7	297.2	296.4	317.6
Avg. price received by processors . . .	Cents/lb .	224.1	240.3	226.0	229.0	234.0	236.0	226.0	207.0
Inventory (Jan. 1)	Mil. lb . .	9.4	10.9	11.9	10.8	12.6	13.6	15.0	12.3

Source: U.S. Dept. of Agriculture, National Agricultural Statistics Service, *Trout Production* released February; *Catfish Production* released February; and *Catfish Processing* released February. Also in annual.

No. 856. Supply of Selected Fishery Items: 1990 to 2002

[In millions of pounds (734 represents 734,000,000). Totals available for U.S. consumption are supply minus exports plus imports. Round weight is the complete or full weight as caught]

Species	Unit •	1990	1995	1996	1997	1998	1999	2000	2001	2002
Shrimp	Heads-off weight. .	734	832	842	923	1,002	1,084	1,172	1,312	1,430
Tuna, canned	Canned weight. . .	856	875	859	829	912	1,020	980	796	922
Snow crab	Round weight. . . .	37	42	46	110	254	216	122	171	172
Clams	Meat weight.	152	144	134	124	119	125	133	139	144
Salmon, canned	Canned weight. . .	148	147	104	82	83	123	95	108	135
American lobster	Round weight. . . .	95	94	97	112	110	122	124	125	135
Spiny lobster	Round weight. . . .	89	89	81	76	100	91	99	79	87
Scallops	Meat weight.	74	62	71	66	58	64	78	76	91
Sardines, canned	Canned weight. . .	61	44	46	49	50	57	(NA)	(NA)	(NA)
Oysters	Meat weight.	56	63	58	58	61	55	71	58	62
King crab	Round weight. . . .	19	21	30	45	62	52	41	38	47
Crab meat, canned	Canned weight. . .	9	12	13	15	22	26	29	35	44

NA Not available.

Source: U.S. National Oceanic and Atmospheric Administration, National Marine Fisheries Service, *Fisheries of the United States*, annual. See also <http://www.st.nmfs.gov/st1/fus/fus01/2001-fus.pdf>. (released September 2002).

No. 857. Canned, Fresh, and Frozen Fishery Products—Production and Value: 1990 to 2002

[Fresh fishery products exclude Alaska and Hawaii. Canned fishery products data are for natural pack only]

Product	Production (mil. lb.)					Value (mil. dol.)				
	1990	1995	2000	2001	2002	1990	1995	2000	2001	2002
Canned, total [1]	1,178	1,927	1,747	1,634	1,315	1,562	1,887	1,626	1,400	1,288
Tuna	581	667	671	507	547	902	939	856	658	675
Salmon	196	244	171	185	224	366	419	288	259	296
Clam products	110	129	127	126	139	76	110	120	125	117
Sardines, Maine	13	14	(Z)	(Z)	(Z)	17	24	(Z)	(Z)	(Z)
Shrimp	1	1	2	2	2	3	7	11	10	9
Crabs	1	(Z)	(Z)	(Z)	(Z)	4	(Z)	(Z)	(Z)	(Z)
Oysters [2]	1	(Z)	(Z)	1	(Z)	1	(Z)	1	1	(Z)
Fish fillets and steaks [3] . .	441	385	368	480	519	843	841	823	914	984
Cod	65	65	56	40	51	132	152	167	123	155
Flounder	54	35	27	30	29	154	86	71	74	77
Haddock	7	7	6	6	7	24	11	24	27	29
Ocean perch, Atlantic	1	(Z)	(Z)	(Z)	(Z)	1	1	1	1	1
Rockfish	33	25	11	7	8	53	38	25	17	18
Pollock, Atlantic	12	4	2	2	5	21	10	4	8	15
Pollock, Alaska	164	135	160	271	304	174	184	178	296	327
Other	105	118	106	124	115	284	359	353	368	362

Z Less than 500,000 pounds or $500,000.   [1] Includes other products, not shown separately.   [2] Includes oyster specialties.   [3] Fresh and frozen.

Source: U.S. National Oceanic and Atmospheric Administration, National Marine Fisheries Service, *Fisheries of the United States*, annual. See also <http://www.st.nmfs.gov/st1>. (Released September 2003).

Natural Resources   555

No. 858. Mining and Primary Metal Production Indexes: 1990 to 2002
[Index 1997=100]

Industry group	1990	1994	1995	1996	1997	1998	1999	2000	2001	2002
Mining	98.7	96.6	96.4	98.1	100.0	98.2	94.0	96.0	96.6	93.8
Coal	96.4	95.0	94.6	96.9	100.0	101.2	99.4	98.2	100.7	96.3
Oil and gas extraction	102.9	100.8	99.8	99.9	100.0	98.3	96.3	96.5	97.6	97.3
Crude oil and natural gas	104.4	101.4	100.1	99.9	100.0	98.5	96.1	95.9	97.3	97.0
Oil and gas drilling	92.9	83.5	81.3	87.2	100.0	98.3	82.0	110.3	125.0	91.0
Metal mining	84.8	91.9	92.8	94.9	100.0	99.2	90.7	90.3	82.0	74.0
Iron ore	89.2	91.9	98.9	98.1	100.0	99.3	91.3	99.2	72.7	81.8
Nonferrous ores	91.9	100.0	100.4	103.4	100.0	107.5	99.4	94.5	89.3	(NA)
Copper ore	89.4	104.7	104.7	108.7	100.0	105.4	90.7	81.4	76.9	(NA)
Primary metals, manufacturing	85.5	92.6	93.7	95.9	100.0	102.3	101.7	98.8	88.2	85.6
Nonferrous metals	89.4	98.8	98.7	100.8	100.0	109.1	101.4	88.2	90.0	77.3
Copper	60.6	102.6	112.0	95.1	100.0	122.6	107.8	46.7	63.4	50.5
Aluminum	97.6	97.6	93.4	94.9	100.0	104.5	105.0	99.4	86.0	87.3
Iron and steel	85.3	93.3	94.8	97.1	100.0	100.0	100.4	100.3	86.7	88.7

NA Not available.
Source: Board of Governors of the Federal Reserve System, *Federal Reserve Bulletin*, monthly; and *Industrial Production and Capacity Utilization*, Statistical Release G.17, monthly.

No. 859. Mineral Industries—Employment, Hours, and Earnings: 1990 to 2003

[Based on the Current Employment Statistics Program, see Appendix III]

Industry and item	Unit	1990	2000	2003	Industry and item	Unit	1990	2000	2003
All mining:					Avg. weekly hours	Number.	44.4	41.3	41.1
All employees	1,000...	765	599	571	Avg. weekly earnings	Dollars..	591	802	778
Production workers	1,000...	538	446	419	Metal mining:				
Avg. weekly hours	Number.	45.0	44.4	43.6	All employees	1,000...	53	38	27
Avg. weekly earnings	Dollars..	603	735	767	Production workers	1,000...	43	29	20
Coal mining:					Avg. weekly hours	Number.	42.5	43.4	43.7
All employees	1,000...	136	72	70	Avg. weekly earnings	Dollars..	646	871	957
Production workers	1,000...	110	59	59	Nonmetallic minerals, except fuels:				
Avg. weekly hours	Number.	44.7	45.6	46.2	All employees	1,000...	113	115	105
Avg. weekly earnings	Dollars..	822	945	964	Production workers	1,000...	85	87	78
Oil and gas extraction:					Avg. weekly hours	Number.	45.0	46.1	45.1
All employees	1,000...	190	125	123	Avg. weekly earnings	Dollars..	532	722	773
Production workers	1,000...	84	67	68					

Source: U.S. Bureau of Labor Statistics, *Bulletin 2370* and *Employment and Earnings*, March and June issues.

No. 860. Selected Mineral Products—Average Prices: 1980 to 2003
[Excludes Alaska and Hawaii, except as noted]

Year	Copper, electrolytic (cents per lb.)	Plati-num [1] (dol./ troy oz.)	Gold (dol./ fine oz.)	Silver (dol./ fine oz.)	Lead (cents per lb.)	Tin (New York) (cents per lb.)	Zinc (cents per lb.)	Sulfur, crude [2] (dol./ metric ton)	Bitumi-nous coal [3][4] (dol./ short ton)	Crude petro-leum [3] (dol./ bbl.)	Natural gas [3] (dol./ 1,000 cu. ft.)
1980	101	677	613	20.63	43	846	37	89.06	29.17	21.59	1.59
1981	84	446	460	10.52	37	733	45	111.48	31.51	31.77	1.98
1982	73	327	376	7.95	26	654	39	108.27	32.15	28.52	2.46
1983	77	424	424	11.44	22	655	41	87.24	31.11	26.19	2.59
1984	67	357	361	8.14	26	624	49	94.31	30.63	25.88	2.66
1985	67	291	318	6.14	19	596	40	106.46	30.78	24.09	2.51
1986	66	461	368	5.47	22	383	38	105.22	28.84	12.51	1.94
1987	83	553	478	7.01	36	419	42	89.78	28.19	15.40	1.67
1988	121	523	438	6.53	37	441	60	85.95	27.66	12.58	1.69
1989	131	507	383	5.50	39	520	82	86.62	27.40	15.86	1.69
1990	123	467	385	4.82	46	386	75	80.14	27.43	20.03	1.71
1991	109	371	363	4.04	34	363	53	71.45	27.49	16.54	1.64
1992	107	360	345	3.94	35	402	58	48.14	26.78	15.99	1.74
1993	92	375	361	4.30	32	350	46	31.86	26.15	14.25	2.04
1994	111	411	385	5.29	37	369	49	28.60	25.68	13.19	1.85
1995	138	425	386	5.15	42	416	56	44.46	25.56	14.62	1.55
1996	109	398	389	5.19	49	412	51	34.11	25.17	18.46	2.17
1997	107	397	332	4.89	47	381	65	36.06	24.64	17.23	2.32
1998	79	375	295	5.54	45	373	51	29.14	24.87	10.87	1.96
1999	76	379	280	5.25	44	366	54	37.81	23.92	15.56	2.19
2000	88	549	280	5.00	44	370	56	24.73	24.15	26.72	3.69
2001	77	533	272	4.39	44	315	44	10.01	25.36	21.84	4.02
2002	76	543	311	4.62	44	292	39	11.84	26.35	22.51	2.95
2003	82	590	350	4.66	44	357	39	25.00	(NA)	27.56	4.98

NA Not available. [1] Average annual dealer prices. [2] F.o.b. works. [3] Average value at the point of production or domestic first purchase price. [4] Includes lignite.
Source: Nonfuels, through 1994, U.S. Bureau of Mines, thereafter, U.S. Geological Survey, *Minerals Yearbook* and *Mineral Commodities Summaries*, annual; fuels, U.S. Energy Information Administration, *Annual Energy Review* and most recent year from the *Monthly Energy Review*.

556   Natural Resources

No. 861. Mineral Production: 1990 to 2003

[Data represent production as measured by mine shipments, mine sales or marketable production]

Minerals and Metals	Unit	1990	1995	2000	2002	2003, est.
FUEL MINERALS						
Coal, total	Mil. sh. tons	1,029.1	1,033.0	1,073.6	1,094.3	1,069.5
Bituminous	Mil. sh. tons	693.2	613.8	574.3	565.7	(NA)
Subbituminous	Mil. sh. tons	244.3	328.0	409.2	444.7	(NA)
Lignite	Mil. sh. tons	88.1	86.5	85.6	82.1	(NA)
Anthracite	Mil. sh. tons	3.5	4.7	4.6	1.3	(NA)
Natural gas (marketed production)	Tril. cu. ft.	18.59	19.51	20.20	19.92	20.07
Petroleum (crude)	Mil. bbl. [1]	2,686	2,394	2,125	5,746	5,737
Uranium (recoverable content)	Mil. lb.	8.9	6.0	4.0	(NA)	(NA)
NONFUEL MINERALS						
Asbestos (sales)	1,000 metric tons . .	(D)	9	5	3	-
Barite, primary, sold/used by producers . .	1,000 metric tons . .	430	543	392	420	480
Boron minerals, sold or used by producers	1,000 metric tons . .	1,090	1,190	1,070	(NA)	(NA)
Bromine, sold or used by producers	1,000 metric tons . .	177	218	228	222	216
Cement:						
Portland	Mil. metric tons	67	73	84	(NA)	(NA)
Masonry	Mil. metric tons	3	4	4	(NA)	(NA)
Clays	1,000 metric tons . .	42,900	43,100	40,800	39,300	39,300
Diatomite [2]	1,000 metric tons . .	631	722	677	624	625
Feldspar [2]	1,000 metric tons . .	630	880	790	790	800
Fluorspar, finished shipments	1,000 metric tons . .	64	51	(NA)	(NA)	(NA)
Garnet (industrial)	1,000 metric tons . .	47	46	60	39	39
Gypsum, crude	Mil. metric tons . . .	15	17	20	16	16
Helium [3]	Mil. cu. meters	85	101	98	87	87
Lime, sold or used by producers	Mil. metric tons	16	19	20	18	18
Mica, scrap & flake, sold/used by producers	1,000 metric tons . .	109	108	101	81	98
Peat, sales by producers	1,000 metric tons . .	721	660	792	642	618
Perlite, processed, sold or used	1,000 metric tons . .	576	700	672	521	512
Phosphate rock (marketable)	Mil. metric tons . . .	46	44	39	36	33
Potash (K_2O equivalent) sales	1,000 metric tons . .	1,710	1,480	1,300	1,200	1,100
Pumice & pumicite, producer sales	1,000 metric tons . .	443	529	1,050	956	914
Salt, common, sold/used by producers . .	Mil. metric tons . . .	37	41	43	38	39
Sand & gravel, sold/used by producer . .	Mil. metric tons . . .	855	935	1,148	1,157	1,158
Construction	Mil. metric tons . . .	829	907	1,120	1,130	1,130
Industrial	Mil. metric tons . . .	26	28	28	27	28
Sodium carbonate (natural) (soda ash) . .	1,000 metric tons . .	9,100	10,100	10,200	10,500	10,600
Sodium sulfate (natural)	1,000 metric tons . .	349	327	462	500	500
Stone [4]	Mil. metric tons	1,110	2,420	2,870	2,780	2,840
Crushed and broken	Mil. metric tons	1,110	1,260	1,550	1,520	1,490
Dimension [5]	1,000 metric tons . .	1,120	1,160	1,320	1,260	1,350
Sulfur: Total shipments	1,000 metric tons . .	11,500	12,100	10,700	9,260	9,500
Sulfur: Frasch mines (shipments)	1,000 metric tons . .	3,680	(D)	900	-	-
Talc, and pyrophyllite, crude	1,000 metric tons . .	1,270	1,060	851	775	817
Vermiculite concentrate	1,000 metric tons . .	209	171	150	(D)	100
METALS						
Antimony ore and concentrate	Metric tons	(D)	262	(D)	-	-
Aluminum	1,000 metric tons . .	4,048	3,375	3,668	2,707	2,700
Bauxite (dried)	1,000 metric tons . .	(D)	(D)	(NA)	(NA)	(NA)
Copper (recoverable content)	1,000 metric tons . .	1,590	1,850	1,450	1,140	1,120
Gold (recoverable content)	Metric tons	294	317	353	298	266
Iron ore (gross weight) [6]	Mil. metric tons	57	61	63	52	50
Lead (recoverable content)	1,000 metric tons . .	484	394	465	451	450
Magnesium metal	1,000 metric tons . .	139	142	82	74	75
Manganiferous ore (gross weight) [7] . . .	1,000 metric ton . . .	(D)	(D)	(NA)	(NA)	-
Mercury [8]	Metric tons	562	(D)	(NA)	(NA)	(NA)
Molybdenum (concentrate)	1,000 metric tons . .	62	61	41	33	34
Nickel	1,000 metric tons . .	-	2	-	-	-
Palladium metal	Kilograms	5,930	5,260	10,300	14,800	14,600
Platinum metal	Kilograms	1,810	1,590	3,110	4,390	4,100
Silicon (silicon content)	1,000 metric tons . .	418	396	367	261	250
Silver (recoverable content)	Metric tons	2,120	1,560	1,860	1,420	1,300
Titanium concentrate: Ilmenite (gross weight)	1,000 metric tons . .	(D)	(D)	(NA)	(NA)	(NA)
Tungsten ore and concentrate [9]	Metric tons	(D)	(D)	(NA)	(NA)	(NA)
Zinc (recoverable content)	1,000 metric tons . .	515	614	852	780	770

- Represents zero. D Withheld to avoid disclosing individual company data. NA Not available. [1] 42 gal. bbl.
[2] Beginning 1995, includes aplite. [3] Refined. [4] Excludes abrasive stone, bituminous limestone and sandstone, and ground soapstone, all included elsewhere in table. Includes calcareous marl and slate. [5] Includes Puerto Rico. [6] Represents shipments; includes byproduct ores. [7] 5 to 35 percent manganiferous ore. [8] Covers mercury recovered as a by product of gold ores only. [9] Content of ore and concentrate.

Source: Nonfuels, through 1995, U.S. Bureau of Mines, thereafter, U.S. Geological Survey, *Minerals Yearbook* and *Mineral Commodities Summaries*, annual; fuels, U.S. Energy Information Administration, *Annual Energy Review* and *Uranium Industry Annual*.

Natural Resources **557**

No. 862. Nonfuel Mineral Commodities—Summary: 2003

[Preliminary estimates. Average price in dollars per metric tons except as noted]

Mineral	Unit	Mineral disposition		Net import reliance[1] (percent)	Consumption, apparent	Average price per unit (dollars)	Employment (number)
		Production	Exports				
Aluminum	1,000 metric tons.	2,700	1,500	41	6,500	[2]67.00	60,000
Antimony (contained)	Metric tons	[3]4,200	3,300	(D)	(D)	[2]110.00	30
Asbestos	1,000 metric tons.	-	4	100	(NA)	220.00	-
Barite	1,000 metric tons.	480	50	81	2,470	[4]28.90	340
Bauxite and alumina	1,000 metric tons.	(NA)	1,140	100	3,000	[4]20.00	(NA)
Beryllium (contained)	Metric tons	100	120	47	190	[2][6](NA)	(NA)
Bismuth (contained)	Metric tons	-	110	95	(NA)	[2]2.90	-
Boron (B$_2$O$_3$ content)	1,000 metric tons.	536	244	[5]	488	[4][7](NA)	1,300
Bromine (contained)	1,000 metric tons.	216	12	[5]	211	[8][9]72.00	1,700
Cadmium (contained)	Metric tons	[3]640	250	[5]	530	[2][10]0.30	(NA)
Cement	1,000 metric tons.	91,000	900	20	112,000	[4]76.00	18,100
Chromium	1,000 metric tons.	[11]129	16	74	492	[4][12](NA)	(NA)
Clays	1,000 metric tons.	39,300	4,980	[5]	34,600	(NA)	6,400
Cobalt (contained)	Metric tons	[11]2,200	2,500	78	10,000	[2]9.40	(NA)
Copper (Mine, contained)	1,000 metric tons.	1,120	774	38	2,370	82.00	7
Diamond (industrial)	Million carats	241	66	80	398	[14]2.46	(NA)
Diatomite	1,000 metric tons.	625	39	[5]	588	[4]254.00	1,000
Feldspar	1,000 metric tons.	800	10	[5]	799	[4]55.00	400
Fluorspar	1,000 metric tons.	92	30	100	590	(NA)	-
Garnet (industrial)	Metric tons	38,700	10,900	56	58,900	[4](NA)	180
Germanium (contained)	Kilograms	12,000	(NA)	(NA)	(NA)	(NA)	65
Gold (contained)	Metric tons	266	320	[5]	(NA)	[17]350.00	8,140
Gypsum (crude)	1,000 metric tons.	16,000	165	23	33,000	[4]6.90	5,900
Iodine	Metric tons	1,750	1,150	74	6,650	[8][21]11.79	30
Iron ore (usable)	Million metric tons.	50	6.4	11	56.1	[4][22]18.00	4,500
Iron and steel slag (metal)	1,000 metric tons.	19,000	400	6	18,600	[4]15.50	2,700
Lead (contained)	1,000 metric tons.	1,750	160	11	1,460	[2]44.00	2,750
Lime	1,000 metric tons.	18,200	103	(Z)	18,200	91.50	5,350
Magnesium compounds	1,000 metric tons.	285	50	51	585	(NA)	370
Magnesium metal	1,000 metric tons.	[11](NA)	22	47	120	(NA)	375
Mercury	Metric tons	[11](NA)	200	(NA)	(NA)	[26]170.00	(NA)
Mica, scrap and flake	1,000 metric tons.	205	7	7	105	[4]120.00	510
Molybdenum (contained)	Metric tons	34,100	32,300	[5]	13,900	[8]11.57	
Nickel (contained)	Metric tons	-	54,730	48	126,000	[2][27]4.29	-
Nitrogen (fixed)-ammonia	1,000 metric tons.	9,300	500	42	16,000	[4][28]240.00	1,550
Peat	1,000 metric tons.	618	30	55	1,390	[4]25.75	800
Perlite	1,000 metric tons.	512	40	28	712	[4]37.36	140
Phosphate rock	1,000 metric tons.	33,300	5	10	(NA)	[4]26.93	5,500
Platinum-group metals	Kilograms	18,700	33,190	170	(NA)	[17][29]155.00	1,400
Potash (K$_2$O equivalent)	1,000 metric tons.	1,100	370	80	5,300	[4][30]23.56	1,140
Pumice and pumicite	1,000 metric tons.	914	30	29	1,280	[4]122.00	100
Salt	1,000 metric tons.	41,200	500	23	50,100	[4][31]49.00	4,100
Silicon (contained)	1,000 metric tons.	250	23	54	530	[17]4.66	980
Silver (contained)	Metric tons	1,300	320	56	5,430	[33]105.00	2,600
Sodium carbonate (soda ash)	1,000 metric tons.	10,600	4,400	[5]	6,200	[34]114.00	225
Sodium sulfate	1,000 metric tons.	500	140	[5]	405	[4]5.78	78,000
Stone (crushed)	Million metric tons.	1,490	3	(Z)	1,500	[4]25.00	2,700
Sulfur (all forms)	1,000 metric tons.	9,550	890	20	11,900	[4][35]25.00	
Talc	1,000 metric tons.	817	180	8	887	[4]114.00	500
Thallium (contained)	Kilograms	(NA)	(NA)	100	(NA)	[8]1,300.00	(NA)
Tin (contained)	Metric tons	[11]11,000	4,020	91	44,980	[2]224.00	(NA)
Titanium dioxide	1,000 metric tons.	1,110	590	[5]	1,070	[2][36]0.90	4,500
Tungsten (contained)	Metric tons	4,300	5,010	69	11,700	[37]50.00	(NA)
Vermiculite	1,000 metric tons.	(D)	10	28	138	[4]143.00	90
Zinc (contained)	1,000 metric tons.	1,100	831	57	1,370	[2]0.39	2,000
Zirconium (ZrO$_2$) content	Metric tons	100,000	44,800	(NA)	(D)	[4][39]293.00	(NA)

- Represents or rounds to zero. D Withheld to avoid disclosure. NA Not available. Z Less than half the unit of measure. [1] Calculated as a percent of apparent consumption. [2] Dollars per pound. [3] Refinery production. [4] Dollars per metric ton. [5] Net exporter. [6] Metal, vacuum-cast ingot. [7] Granulated pentahydrate borax in bulk, f.o.b. mine. [8] Dollars per kilogram. [9] Bulk, purified bromine. [10] 1- to 5-short ton lots. [11] Secondary production. [12] Turkish, chromite price. [13] Columbite. [14] Value of imports, dollars per carat. [15] Reported consumption. [16] Zone refined. [17] Dollars per troy ounce. [18] Price of flake imports. [19] Includes employment at calcining plants. [20] 99.97% indium. [21] C.i.f. value, crude, per kilogram. [22] Price of eastern Canadian ore. [23] Delivered, No. 1 Heavy Melting composite price. [24] Year-end price. [25] 46%-48% Mn metallurgical ore, per unit contained Mn, c.i.f. U.S. ports. [26] Dollars per 76-pound flask. [27] London Metal Exchange cash price. [28] F.o.b. gulf coast. [29] Dealer price of platinum. [30] Price of K2O, muriate. [31] Vacuum and open pan, bulk, pellets and packaged, f.o.b. mine and plant. [32] Ferrosilicon, 50% Si. [33] Quoted year-end price, dense, bulk, f.o.b. Green River, WY, dollars per short ton. [34] Quoted price, bulk, f.o.b. works, East, dollars per short ton. [35] Elemental sulfur, f.o.b. mine and/or plant. [36] Rutile, list, year-end. [37] Dollars per unit W03 (7.93 kilograms of contained tungsten per unit). [38] All forms. [39] Price for imported zircon, f.o.b. U.S. east coast.

Source: U.S. Geological Survey, *Mineral Commodity Summaries*, annual.

No. 863. Value of Domestic Nonfuel Mineral Production by State: 1990 to 2003

[In millions of dollars (33,445 represents $33,445,000,000), except as indicated. For similar data on fuels, see table 881]

State	1990	1995	2000	2001	2002	2003 Total	2003 Rank	2003 Percent of U.S.
United States.....	[1]33,445	38,506	40,100	38,900	38,000	38,000	(X)	100.00
Alabama..........	559	706	1,070	938	968	863	17	2.29
Alaska...........	577	538	1,140	1,060	1,030	1,060	12	2.82
Arizona..........	3,085	4,190	2,550	2,110	1,920	2,100	3	5.58
Arkansas.........	381	492	506	491	543	445	30	1.18
California.........	2,771	2,760	3,350	3,250	3,440	3,170	1	8.42
Colorado.........	377	570	566	676	619	672	22	1.79
Connecticut.......	122	93	[2]100	104	142	142	42	0.38
Delaware.........	10	9	[2]12	13	17,500	16	50	0.04
Florida...........	1,574	1,540	1,920	1,750	2,020	2,000	5	5.33
Georgia..........	1,504	1,690	1,660	1,610	1,450	1,670	6	4.45
Hawaii...........	106	114	91	70	75	74	45	0.20
Idaho	375	510	398	344	307	294	36	0.78
Illinois...........	667	828	907	911	950	911	16	2.42
Indiana..........	428	589	729	718	740	734	18	1.95
Iowa............	310	456	510	487	487	477	29	1.27
Kansas	349	498	624	640	661	688	20	1.83
Kentucky.........	359	432	497	531	372	559	24	1.49
Louisiana.........	368	434	404	274	294	331	34	0.88
Maine...........	55	68	[2]102	91	106	100	43	0.27
Maryland.........	368	324	357	356	375	382	33	1.01
Massachusetts	128	190	210	209	235	186	39	0.49
Michigan	1,440	1,520	1,670	1,620	1,580	1,350	7	3.60
Minnesota........	1,482	1,530	1,570	1,440	1,090	1,230	11	3.28
Mississippi........	111	131	157	177	176	174	40	0.46
Missouri..........	1,105	1,140	1,320	1,340	1,290	1,290	8	3.43
Montana	573	574	582	514	442	492	26	1.31
Nebraska.........	90	146	170	163	89	94	44	0.25
Nevada..........	2,621	3,060	[2]2,800	2,930	2,900	2,940	2	7.81
New Hampshire	36	50	[2]59	60	68	64	47	0.17
New Jersey	229	243	286	348	285	272	37	0.72
New Mexico.......	1,103	1,130	812	615	571	533	25	1.42
New York.........	773	886	970	1,050	1,010	978	14	2.60
North Carolina	586	735	779	744	708	676	21	1.80
North Dakota	25	31	42	39	39	38	48	0.10
Ohio............	733	891	1,060	1,070	1,060	968	15	2.57
Oklahoma	259	357	453	530	462	479	28	1.27
Oregon	205	239	[2]439	326	320	311	35	0.83
Pennsylvania	1,031	1,080	[2]1,250	1,270	1,270	1,260	10	3.35
Rhode Island	18	31	24	28	17	26	49	0.07
South Carolina	450	447	560	531	460	484	27	1.29
South Dakota	319	332	260	255	186	206	38	0.55
Tennessee........	663	665	770	708	629	606	23	1.61
Texas	1,459	1,680	2,050	2,210	2,180	2,030	4	5.39
Utah............	1,335	1,850	[2]1,420	1,310	1,240	1,260	9	3.36
Vermont	87	60	43	69	71	73	46	0.19
Virginia	507	515	692	751	697	727	19	1.93
Washington	483	582	691	545	450	430	31	1.14
West Virginia	133	181	[2]182	185	173	168	41	0.45
Wisconsin	215	416	349	368	340	404	32	1.07
Wyoming..........	911	973	922	986	1,010	1,010	13	2.68

X Not applicable.   [1] Includes undistributed not shown separately.   [2] Partial data only; excludes values withheld to avoid disclosing individual company data.

Source: U.S. Geological Survey, *Minerals Yearbook,* annual, and *Mineral Commodities Summaries,* annual. See also <http://minerals.er.usgs.gov/minerals/pubs/mcs/2003/mcs2003.pdf> (released 31 January 2003).

Natural Resources   559

No. 864. Principal Fuels, Nonmetals, and Metals—World Production and the U.S. Share: 1980 to 2003

Mineral	Unit	World production 1980	1990	1995	2003 [1]	Percent U.S. of world 1980	1990	1995	2003 [1]
Fuels: [2]									
Coal	Mil. sh. ton	4,193	5,386	5,218	(NA)	19.8	19.1	20.0	(NA)
Petroleum (crude)	Bil. bbl	21.8	22.1	22.8	(NA)	14.4	12.2	10.5	(NA)
Natural gas (dry, marketable)	Tril. cu. ft	53.5	73.6	78.0	(NA)	36.3	24.2	23.9	(NA)
Natural gas plant liquids	Bil. bbl	1.3	1.7	2.0	(NA)	45.7	33.7	32.1	(NA)
Nonmetals:									
Asbestos	1,000 metric tons	4,699	4,003	2,420	2,060	2	(D)	(Z)	(Z)
Barite	1,000 metric tons	7,495	5,633	4,300	6,700	27	8	13	7
Feldspar	1,000 metric tons	3,202	5,456	6,780	10,400	20	12	13	8
Fluorspar	1,000 metric tons	5,006	5,131	4,050	4,540	2	1	1	-
Gypsum	Mil. metric tons	78	100	97	102	14	15	17	16
Mica (incl. scrap)	1,000 metric tons	228	215	253	300	46	51	43	33
Nitrogen, (fixed) - ammonia	Mil. metric tons	74	97	96	108	20	13	14	8
Phosphate rock, gross wt.	Mil. metric tons	144	162	130	138	38	29	33	27
Potash (k_2O equivalent)	Mil. metric tons	28	28	25	27	8	6	6	4
Sulfur, elemental	Mil. metric tons	55	58	53	59	22	20	22	16
Metals, mine basis:									
Bauxite	Mil. metric tons	89	109	107	144	2	(D)	(D)	(NA)
Columbian concentrates (Nb content)	1,000 metric tons	15	15	18	30	-	-	-	-
Copper	1,000 metric tons	7,405	9,017	10,100	13,900	16	18	18	8
Gold	Metric tons	1,219	2,133	2,220	2,600	2	14	14	10
Iron ore [3]	Mil. metric tons	891	982	1,027	1,120	8	6	6	4
Lead [3]	1,000 metric tons	3,470	3,353	2,780	2,840	17	15	14	16
Mercury	Metric tons	6,806	4,523	3,160	1,600	16	12	(D)	(NA)
Molybdenum	1,000 metric tons	111	128	141	127	62	48	43	27
Nickel [3]	1,000 metric tons	779	965	1,030	1,400	2	(Z)	(Z)	(Z)
Silver	1,000 metric tons	11	16	15	19	9	13	10	7
Tantalum concentrates	Metric tons	544	400	362	1,230	-	-	-	-
Titanium concentrates:									
Ilmenite	1,000 metric tons	3,726	4,072	3,970	4,300	14	(D)	(D)	(D)
Rutile	1,000 metric tons	436	481	416	420	(D)	(D)	(D)	(D)
Tungsten [3]	1,000 metric tons	52	43	39	60	5	14	-	-
Vanadium [3]	1,000 metric tons	37	31	35	60	12	(D)	(D)	(D)
Zinc [3]	1,000 metric tons	5,954	7,184	7,240	8,500	6	8	9	9
Metals, smelter basis:									
Aluminum	1,000 metric tons	15,383	19,292	19,900	27,300	30	21	17	10
Cadmium	1,000 metric tons	18	20	19	15	9	8	7	4
Copper	1,000 metric tons	7,649	9,472	10,200	(NA)	14	15	16	8
Iron, pig	Mil. metric tons	514	532	533	634	12	9	10	6
Lead [4]	1,000 metric tons	5,430	5,763	5,590	(NA)	23	23	25	22
Magnesium [5]	1,000 metric tons	316	354	389	447	49	39	37	(NA)
Raw steel	Mil. metric tons	717	771	755	924	14	12	13	10
Tin [6]	1,000 metric tons	251	223	201	265	1	-	-	(NA)
Zinc	1,000 metric tons	6,049	7,060	7,550	(NA)	6	5	5	(NA)

- Represents or rounds to zero. NA Not available. D Withheld to avoid disclosing company data. Z Less than half the unit of measure. [1] Preliminary data. [2] Source: Energy Information Administration, *International Energy Annual.* [3] Content of ore and concentrate. [4] Refinery production. [5] Primary production; no smelter processing necessary. [6] Production from primary sources only.
Source: Nonfuels, through 1990, U.S. Bureau of Mines, thereafter, U.S. Geological Survey, *Minerals Yearbook,* annual, and *Mineral Commodities Summaries,* annual; fuels, U.S. Energy Information Administration, *International Energy Annual.* See also <http://minerals.er.usgs.gov/minerals/pubs/mcs/2004/mcs2004.pdf>.

No. 865. Federal Strategic and Critical Materials Inventory: 1990 to 2002

[As of Dec. 31. Covers strategic and critical materials essential to military and industrial requirements in time of national emergency]

Mineral	Unit	Quantity [1] 1990	1995	2000	2002	Value (mil.dol.) [2] 1990	1995	2000	2002
Bauxite [3]	1,000 lg. ton	18,033	16,032	6,267	1,722	888	203	49	13
Chromium [4]	1,000 sh. ton	1,074	1,192	937	849	917	839	606	556
Cobalt	Mil. lb.	53	44	23	14	443	1,121	313	139
Diamonds: Stones	Carat 1,000	7,777	5,135	1,509	796	267	52	15	8
Industrial, bort	Carat 1,000	17,353	1,967	-	-	16	9	-	-
Lead	1,000 sh. ton	(NA)	465	226	170	(NA)	263	103	72
Manganese [5]	1,000 sh. ton	4,017	2,817	2,146	1,743	962	464	255	215
Palladium	1,000 troy oz	(NA)	1,265	842	189	(NA)	143	326	64
Platinum	1,000 troy oz	453	453	217	21	186	154	84	10
Silver	1,000 troy oz	92,151	46,667	15,942	664	374	158	61	2
Tantalum Group	1,000 lb	(NA)	3,031	2,282	2,124	(NA)	127	94	73
Tin	1,000 metric ton	169	130	60	44	962	908	323	211
Titanium [6]	1,000 sh. ton	37	37	30	15	402	221	96	44
Tungsten [6]	Mil. lb.	82	82	74	65	253	253	156	154
Zinc	1,000 sh. ton	379	301	151	120	483	281	152	105

- Represents or rounds to zero. NA Not available. [1] Consists of stockpile and nonstockpile grades and reflects uncommitted balances. [2] Market values are estimated trade values of similar materials and not necessarily amounts that would be realized at time of sale. [3] Consists of abrasive grade, metallic grade Jamaica, metallic grade Suriname, and refractory. [4] Consists of ferro-high carbon, ferro-low carbon, ferro-silicon, and metal. [5] Consists of chemical grade, dioxide battery natural, dioxide battery synthetic, electrolytic, ferro-high carbon, ferro-med. carbon, ferro-silicon, and metal. [6] Consists of carbide powder, ferro, metal powder, and ores and concentrates.
Source: U.S. Defense Logistics Agency, *Statistical Supplement, Stockpile Report to the Congress* (AP-3).

No. 866. Net U.S. Imports of Selected Minerals and Metals as Percent of Apparent Consumption: 1980 to 2003

[In percent. Based on net imports which equal the difference between imports and exports plus or minus Government stockpile and industry stock changes]

Minerals in rank of net imports	1980	1990	1995	1998	1999	2000	2001	2002	2003
Bauxite [1]	94	98	99	100	100	100	100	100	100
Columbium	100	100	100	100	100	100	100	100	100
Manganese. . . .	98	100	100	100	100	100	100	100	100
Mica (sheet) . . .	100	100	100	100	100	100	100	100	100
Strontium	100	100	100	100	100	100	100	100	100
Vanadium	35	(D)	84	78	80	(NA)	100	100	100
Tin.	79	71	84	85	85	86	88	79	91
Barite.	44	71	65	80	67	71	87	76	81
Potash	65	68	75	80	80	70	80	80	80
Tantalum	90	71	80	80	80	80	80	80	80
Chromium.	91	84	80	80	80	78	78	63	74
Cobalt	93	86	79	73	73	74	78	75	78
Zinc [2]	60	41	35	35	30	60	60	60	57
Tungsten	53	81	90	77	81	68	59	70	69
Nickel.	76	64	60	64	63	58	56	43	48
Silver.	7	(NA)	(NA)	14	14	52	44	61	56
Aluminum	(3)	36	23	27	30	33	35	39	41
Copper.	16	15	27	14	27	37	31	37	38
Gypsum	35	46	30	28	29	22	25	25	23
Iron and steel . .	13	13	21	27	22	17	15	14	9
Iron ore	25	3	14	12	17	19	15	11	11
Sulfur.	14	21	21	18	17	22	12	15	20
Cadmium	55	(3)	23	20	19	6	3	(3)	(3)
Mercury	27	(D)	(NA)	(NA)	(NA)	(NA)	(NA)	(NA)	(3)
Platinum group .	87	88	(NA)	(NA)	(NA)	(NA)	(NA)	(NA)	(NA)
Selenium	59	46	31	(D)	(D)	(D)	(D)	(D)	(D)

D Withheld to avoid disclosure. NA Not available. [1] Includes alumina. [2] Beginning 1990, effect of sharp rise in exports of concentrates. If calculated on a refined zinc-only basis, reliance would be about the same as pre-1990 level; 1990, 64%; 1995,71%; 1998, 69%; and 1999, 71%. [3] Net exports.

Source: Through 1994, U.S. Bureau of Mines; thereafter, U.S. Geological Survey, *Mineral Commodity Summaries;* import and export data from U.S. Census Bureau.

No. 867. Federal Offshore Leasing, Exploration, Production, and Revenue: 1990 to 2002

[See source for explanation of terms and for reliability statement]

Item	Unit	1990	1995	1997	1998	1999	2000	2001	2002
Tracts offered	Number. .	10,459	10,995	9,870	8,205	7,453	7,992	8,790	8,548
Tracts leased.	Number. .	825	835	1,780	1,157	333	553	942	804
Acres offered.	Millions . .	56.79	59.70	26.24	44.10	40.22	42.89	49.15	45.69
Acres leased	Millions . .	4.30	4.34	9.62	6.34	1.77	2.92	5.00	4.20
Bonus paid for leased tracts	Bil. dol. . .	0.6	0.4	(NA)	1.3	0.3	0.3	1.0	0.1
New wells being drilled:									
Active	Number. .	120	124	186	173	219	224	213	119
Suspended	Number. .	266	247	244	122	110	146	97	72
Cumulative wells (since 1953):									
Wells completed	Number. .	13,167	13,475	13,546	13,702	13,676	13,718	13,921	13,282
Wells plugged and abandoned .	Number. .	14,677	18,008	18,728	21,050	22,115	22,814	24,218	25,232
Revenue, total [1]	Bil. dol. . .	3.4	2.7	5.3	4.3	3.2	5.2	[4]5.8	[5]5.0
Bonuses	Bil. dol. . .	0.8	0.4	1.4	1.3	0.2	0.4	[4]0.5	[5]0.1
Oil and gas royalties [1]	Bil. dol. . .	2.6	2.1	3.4	2.7	2.6	4.1	[4]4.8	[5]4.7
Rentals	Bil. dol. . .	0.09	0.09	0.23	0.26	0.21	0.21	[4]0.13	[5]0.44
Sales value [2]	Bil. dol. . .	17.0	13.8	22.3	17.6	17.4	27.4	[4]31.4	[5]31.0
Oil	Bil. dol. . .	7.0	6.3	9.0	6.2	6.5	11.5	[4]11.3	[5]12.1
Natural gas	Bil. dol. . .	9.5	7.5	13.3	11.4	10.9	15.9	[4]20.1	[5]18.9
Sales volume: [3]									
Oil	Mil. bbls. .	324	409	479	477	513	566	[4]463	[5]612
Natural gas	Bil. cu. ft .	5,093	4,692	5,077	4,836	4,992	4,723	[4]3,470	[5]4,971

NA Not available. [1] Includes condensate royalties. [2] Production value is value at time of production, not current value. [3] Excludes sales volumes for gas lost, gas plant products or sulfur. [4] Covers January through September 2001 only. [5] Estimated.

Source: U.S. Dept. of the Interior, Minerals Management Service, *Federal Offshore Statistics,* annual.

No. 868. Petroleum Industry—Summary: 1980 to 2002

[Includes all costs incurred for drilling and equipping wells to point of completion as productive wells or abandonment after drilling becomes unproductive. Based on sample of operators of different size drilling establishments]

Item	Unit	1980	1990	1995	1997	1998	1999	2000	2001	2002
Crude oil producing wells (Dec. 31).	1,000. . .	548	602	574	573	562	546	534	530	519
Daily output per well	Bbl. . . .	15.9	12.2	11.4	11.3	11.1	10.8	10.9	10.9	11.2
Completed wells drilled, total	1,000. . .	57.73	26.50	17.75	24.39	20.61	16.53	25.68	31.46	22.43
Crude oil.	1,000. . .	30.88	11.54	7.09	10.01	6.77	4.02	7.09	7.75	4.78
Gas.	1,000. . .	15.25	10.36	7.78	10.79	10.64	10.34	15.85	21.12	15.26
Dry	1,000. . .	11.60	4.60	2.88	3.59	3.19	2.17	2.74	2.59	2.39
Average depth per well [1]	Feet . .	4,172	4,649	5,500	5,535	6,057	5,253	4,894	5,387	5,580
Average cost per well [1]	$1,000. .	368	384	513	604	769	856	755	943	1,054
Average cost per foot [1]	Dollars. .	77.02	76.07	87.22	107.83	128.97	152.02	142.16	181.94	195.31
Crude oil production, total	Mil. bbl. .	3,138	2,685	2,394	2,355	2,282	2,147	2,125	2,117	2,097
Value at wells	Bil. dol. .	67.9	53.8	35.0	40.6	24.8	33.4	56.9	46.3	47.8
Average price per barrel	Dollars. .	21.59	20.03	14.62	17.23	10.87	15.56	26.72	21.84	22.51
Lower 48 states	Mil. bbl. .	2,548	2,037	1,853	1,882	1,853	1,764	1,771	1,766	1,738
Alaska	Mil. bbl. .	590	647	542	473	429	383	354	351	359
Onshore	Mil. bbl. .	2,760	2,290	1,838	1,753	1,664	1,508	1,478	1,416	1,371
Offshore	Mil. bbl. .	377	395	557	602	618	639	647	702	724
Imports: Crude oil	Mil. bbl. .	1,921	2,151	2,639	3,002	3,178	3,187	3,311	3,405	3,302
Refined petroleum products	Mil. bbl. .	601	775	586	707	731	775	872	928	844
Exports: Crude oil	Mil. bbl. .	104.8	39.8	34.7	39.4	40.2	43.1	18.3	7.3	3.3
Proved reserves	Bil. bbl . .	29.8	26.3	22.4	22.5	21.0	21.8	22.0	22.4	22.7
Operable refineries.	Number . .	319	205	175	164	163	159	158	(NA)	(NA)
Capacity (Jan. 1)	Mil. bbl. .	6,566	5,683	5,632	5,639	5,734	5,935	6,026	(NA)	(NA)
Refinery input, total.	Mil. bbl. .	5,119	5,325	5,555	5,807	5,893	5,878	5,948	5,979	5,948
Crude oil	Mil. bbl. .	4,921	4,894	5,100	5,352	5,434	5,403	5,499	5,522	5,448
Natural gas plant liquids.	Mil. bbl. .	169	170	172	152	147	136	139	157	162
Other liquids	Mil. bbl. .	30	260	775	304	311	338	310	301	338
Refinery output, total.	Mil. bbl. .	5,337	5,574	5,838	6,117	6,216	6,201	6,294	6,309	6,297
Motor gasoline	Mil. bbl. .	2,370	2,540	2,723	2,826	2,881	2,896	2,902	2,928	2,983
Jet fuel	Mil. bbl. .	365	543	517	567	557	571	586	558	552
Distillate fuel oil	Mil. bbl. .	971	1,068	1,152	1,238	1,250	1,241	1,307	1,349	1,310
Residual fuel oil	Mil. bbl. .	577	347	288	258	278	255	254	263	219
Liquefied petroleum gases . . .	Mil. bbl. .	120	182	239	252	246	250	257	243	246
Utilization rate	Percent . .	75.4	87.1	92.0	95.2	95.6	92.6	92.6	92.6	90.3

NA Not available. [1] Source: American Petroleum Institute, *Joint Association Survey on Drilling Costs,* annual.

Source: Except as noted, U.S. Energy Information Administration, *Annual Energy Review, Petroleum Supply Annual; U.S. Crude Oil, Natural Gas,* and *Natural Gas Liquids Reserves;* and *Monthly Energy Review.*

No. 869. U.S. Petroleum Balance: 1980 to 2002

[In millions of barrels (6,242 represents 6,242,000,000)]

Item	1980	1990	1995	1997	1998	1999	2000	2001	2002
Petroleum products supplied for domestic use	**6,242**	**6,201**	**6,470**	**6,796**	**6,905**	**7,125**	**7,211**	**7,172**	**7,213**
Production of products	5,765	5,934	6,322	6,671	6,733	6,774	6,903	6,942	6,925
Crude input to refineries	4,934	4,894	5,100	5,351	5,434	5,403	5,514	5,522	5,456
Oil, field production.	3,138	2,685	2,394	2,355	2,282	2,147	2,125	2,117	2,097
Alaska.	590	647	542	473	429	383	354	351	359
Lower 48 States	2,548	2,037	1,853	1,882	1,853	1,764	1,771	1,766	1,738
Net imports	1,821	2,112	2,604	2,963	3,137	3,144	3,301	3,398	3,333
Imports (gross excluding SPR) [1]	1,910	2,142	2,639	3,002	3,178	3,184	3,317	3,401	3,330
SPR [1] imports	16	10	-	-	-	3	3	4	6
Exports	-105	40	35	39	40	43	18	7	3
Other sources	33	98	102	34	15	113	82	7	26
Natural gas liquids (NGL), supply	577	574	708	721	717	757	799	801	798
Other liquids	253	465	514	599	582	614	589	619	671
Net imports of refined products	484	326	101	154	225	252	305	303	249
Imports	578	598	407	469	508	537	648	636	581
Exports	94	272	307	315	283	284	343	333	332
Stock withdrawal, refined products	-7	-59	46	-29	-53	98	2	-73	39
TYPE OF PRODUCT SUPPLIED									
Total products supplied	**6,242**	**6,201**	**6,469**	**6,796**	**6,905**	**7,125**	**7,211**	**7,172**	**7,213**
Finished motor gasoline	2,407	2,641	2,843	2,926	3,012	3,077	3,101	3,143	3,229
Distillate fuel oil.	1,049	1,103	1,170	1,254	1,263	1,304	1,362	1,404	1,378
Residual fuel oil	918	449	311	291	324	303	333	296	255
Liquified petroleum gases [2]	414	568	693	744	713	801	816	746	789
Other	1,454	1,440	1,452	1,582	1,593	1,639	1,598	1,583	1,561
ENDING STOCKS									
Ending stocks, all oils	**1,392**	**1,621**	**1,563**	**1,560**	**1,647**	**1,493**	**1,468**	**1,586**	**1,548**
Crude oil and lease condensate. . . [1]	358	323	303	305	324	284	286	312	278
Strategic Petroleum Reserve (SPR) [1]	108	586	592	563	571	567	541	550	599
Other	926	712	668	692	752	641	641	724	671

- Represents zero. [1] SPR=Strategic petroleum reserve. For more information, see Table 911. [2] Includes ethane.

Source: U.S. Energy Information Administration, *Petroleum Supply Annual,* volume 1. See also <http://www.eia.doe.gov/pub/oilgas /petroleum/datapublications/petroleumsupplyannual/psavolume1/current/pdf/volume1all.pdf> (released June 2003).

No. 870. Crude Petroleum and Natural Gas—Production and Value by Major Producing States: 1990 to 2002

[2,685 mil. bbl. represents 2,685,000,000 bbl. or 18,594 bil. cu. ft. represents 18,594,000,000,000 cu. ft.]

State	Crude petroleum Quantity (mil. bbl.)			Value (mil. dol.)			Natural gas marketed production Quantity (bil. cu. ft.)			Value (mil. dol.)		
	1990	2000	2002	1990	2000	2002	1990	2000	2002	1990	2000	2002
Total [2]	2,685	2,131	2,097	53,772	56,932	47,206	18,594	20,198	19,921	31,658	74,339	58,723
AL	18	10	9	387	289	202	135	523	356	373	2,087	1,238
AK	658	355	359	10,086	8,439	7,018	403	459	463	554	807	989
AR	10	7	7	222	193	158	175	172	162	360	898	718
CA	322	271	258	5,732	6,729	5,643	363	377	360	857	1,812	1,052
CO	31	18	18	722	533	448	243	753	842	377	2,765	2,030
FL	6	5	4	(NA)	(NA)	(NA)	6	6	3	15	(NA)	(NA)
IL	20	12	12	467	343	287	1	(Z)	(Z)	1	(NA)	(NA)
IN	3	2	2	73	59	46	(Z)	1	1	1	3	4
KS	59	34	33	1,359	970	773	574	526	455	893	1,690	1,187
KY	5	3	3	124	92	60	75	82	88	169	258	265
LA	148	105	93	3,409	3,060	2,322	5,242	5,069	1,362	9,587	18,642	4,363
MI	20	8	7	458	222	171	140	297	274	420	724	594
MS	30	20	18	630	520	398	95	89	113	167	293	346
MT	20	15	17	429	429	384	50	70	86	90	198	206
NE	5	3	3	119	83	66	1	1	2	2	3	3
NM	66	67	67	1,472	1,935	1,616	965	1,687	1,632	1,629	5,790	4,380
NY	(Z)	-	-	9	6	4	25	18	37	55	67	112
ND	39	33	31	849	922	748	52	52	57	93	206	170
OH	8	7	6	196	181	136	155	105	103	393	426	466
OK	117	70	67	2,690	2,035	1,632	2,258	1,613	1,551	3,548	5,857	4,568
PA	2	2	2	54	43	56	178	201	158	417	(NA)	(NA)
TX	674	443	412	15,060	12,681	9,793	6,343	6,205	5,141	9,939	24,384	16,258
UT	23	16	14	524	446	326	146	269	275	249	883	547
WV	2	1	1	43	38	31	178	264	190	568	(NA)	(NA)
WY	103	61	55	2,169	1,633	1,202	736	1,088	1,454	856	3,640	3,923
Federal offshore	296	558	598	6,468	28,420	25,410	(NA)	(NA)	(NA)	(NA)	(NA)	(NA)

NA Not available. Z Less than 500,000 barrels, 500 million cubic feet, or less than $500,000. [1] Excludes nonhydrocarbon gases. [2] Includes other states not shown separately. State production does not include state offshore production. U.S. level totals shown in Tables 868 and 869 may contain revisions not carried to state level.
Source: U.S. Energy Information Administration, *Petroleum Supply Annual*, Vol. 2, and *Petroleum Marketing Annual*; and *Natural Gas Annual*, and *Natural Gas Monthly.*

No. 871. Crude Oil, Natural Gas, and Natural Gas Liquids—Reserves by State: 1990 to 2002

[26,254 mil. bbl. represents 26,254,000,000 bbl. As of December 31. Proved reserves are estimated quantities of the mineral, which geological and engineering data demonstrate with reasonable certainty, to be recoverable in future years from known reservoirs under existing economic and operating conditions. Based on a sample of operators of oil and gas wells]

Area	1990 Crude oil proved (mil.bbl.)	Natural gas (bil. cu. ft.)	Natural gas liquids (mil. bbl.)	2001 Crude oil proved (mil.bbl.)	Natural gas (bil. cu. ft.)	Natural gas liquids (mil. bbl.)	2002 Crude oil proved (mil.bbl.)	Natural gas (bil. cu. ft.)	Natural gas liquids (mil. bbl.)
United States [1]	26,254	169,346	7,586	22,446	183,460	7,993	22,677	186,946	7,994
Lower 48 States	19,730	160,046	7,246	17,595	174,660	7,588	17,999	178,478	7,589
Alabama	44	4,125	170	42	3,915	64	51	3,884	57
Alaska	6,524	9,300	340	4,851	8,800	405	4,678	8,468	405
Arkansas	60	1,731	9	43	1,616	5	49	1,650	4
California	[1]4,658	[1]3,185	[1]105	3,627	2,681	76	3,633	2,951	95
Colorado	305	4,555	169	196	12,527	345	214	13,888	396
Florida	(NA)	(NA)	(NA)	75	84	12	73	91	14
Illinois	(NA)	(NA)	(NA)	92	(NA)	(NA)	107	(NA)	(NA)
Indiana	131	(NA)	(NA)	12	(NA)	(NA)	15	(NA)	(NA)
Kansas	(NA)	(NA)	(NA)	216	5,101	302	237	4,983	263
Kentucky	321	9,614	313	17	1,860	72	27	1,907	66
Louisiana	33	1,016	25	564	9,811	391	501	8,960	323
Michigan	(NA)	(NA)	(NA)	46	2,976	43	61	3,254	47
Mississippi	(NA)	(NA)	(NA)	167	661	10	179	744	8
Montana	(NA)	(NA)	(NA)	260	898	6	288	906	6
Nebraska	221	899	15	15	(NA)	(NA)	18	(NA)	(NA)
New Mexico	(NA)	(NA)	(NA)	715	17,414	873	710	17,320	838
New York	687	17,260	990	(NA)	318	(NA)	(NA)	315	(NA)
North Dakota	285	586	60	328	443	57	342	471	47
Ohio	65	1,214	(NA)	46	970	(NA)	67	1,117	(NA)
Oklahoma	734	16,151	657	556	13,558	694	598	14,886	695
Pennsylvania	22	1,720	(NA)	10	1,775	(NA)	12	2,216	(NA)
Texas	[1]7,106	[1]38,192	[1]2,575	4,944	43,527	2,653	5,015	44,297	2,711
Utah	249	1,510	(2)	271	4,579	(2)	241	4,135	(2)
Virginia	(NA)	138	(NA)	(NA)	1,752	(NA)	(NA)	1,673	(NA)
West Virginia	31	2,207	86	8	2,678	106	13	3,360	99
Wyoming	794	9,944	[3]812	489	18,398	[3]947	524	20,527	[3]938
Federal offshore	2,805	31,433	619	4,835	27,036	1078	5,009	25,204	973

NA Not available. [1] Excludes Federal offshore. [2] Included with Wyoming. [3] Includes Utah.
Source: Energy Information Administration, *U.S. Crude Oil, Natural Gas, and Natural Gas Liquids Reserves, 2002 Annual Report*, December 2003.

Natural Resources 563

No. 872. World Daily Crude Oil Production by Major Producing Country: 1980 to 2001

[In thousands of barrels per day (59,600 barrels represents 59,600,000 barrels)]

Country	1980	1990	1995	1996	1997	1998	1999	2000	2001
World, total [1]	59,600	60,566	62,335	63,711	65,690	66,921	65,848	68,342	68,057
Algeria	1,106	1,175	1,202	1,242	1,277	1,246	1,202	1,254	1,270
Angola	150	475	646	709	714	735	745	746	742
Argentina	491	483	715	756	834	847	802	761	781
Australia	380	575	562	570	588	544	539	722	657
Brazil	182	631	695	795	841	969	1,132	1,269	1,295
Canada	1,435	1,553	1,805	1,837	1,922	1,981	1,907	1,977	2,029
China	2,114	2,774	2,990	3,131	3,200	3,198	3,195	3,249	3,300
Colombia	126	440	585	623	652	733	816	691	602
Egypt	595	873	920	922	856	834	852	748	698
India	182	660	703	651	675	661	653	646	642
Indonesia	1,577	1,462	1,503	1,547	1,520	1,518	1,472	1,423	1,369
Iran	1,662	3,088	3,643	3,686	3,664	3,634	3,557	3,696	3,724
Iraq	2,514	2,040	560	579	1,155	2,150	2,508	2,571	2,432
Kazakhstan	(X)	(X)	362	403	466	476	530	610	704
Kuwait	1,656	1,175	2,057	2,062	2,007	2,085	1,898	2,079	1,998
Libya	1,787	1,375	1,390	1,401	1,446	1,390	1,319	1,410	1,367
Malaysia	283	619	682	695	700	720	693	690	659
Mexico	1,936	2,553	2,618	2,855	3,023	3,070	2,906	3,012	3,157
Nigeria	2,055	1,810	1,993	2,001	2,132	2,153	2,130	2,165	2,256
Norway	528	1,704	2,768	3,104	3,143	3,017	3,018	3,197	3,117
Oman	282	685	851	883	904	900	910	970	960
Qatar	472	406	442	510	550	696	665	737	714
Russia	(X)	(X)	5,995	5,850	5,920	5,854	6,079	6,479	7,049
Saudi Arabia	9,900	6,410	8,231	8,218	8,362	8,389	7,833	8,404	8,031
Syria	164	388	575	582	561	553	538	523	518
United Arab Emirates	1,709	2,117	2,233	2,278	2,316	2,345	2,169	2,368	2,276
United Kingdom	1,622	1,820	2,489	2,568	2,518	2,616	2,684	2,275	2,282
United States	8,597	7,355	6,560	6,465	6,452	6,252	5,881	5,822	5,801
Venezuela	2,168	2,137	2,750	2,938	3,280	3,167	2,826	3,155	2,880
Yemen	(X)	193	345	340	362	388	409	440	438

X Not applicable.   [1] Includes countries not shown separately.

Source: U.S. Energy Information Administration, *International Energy Annual, 2001*. See also <http://tonto.eia.doe.gov /FTPROOT/international/021901.pdf> (issued March 2003).

No. 873. Liquefied Petroleum Gases—Summary: 1980 to 2003

[In millions of 42-gallon barrels (561 barrels represents 561,000,000 barrels). Includes ethane]

Item	1980	1990	1995	1998	1999	2000	2001	2002	2003
Production	561	638	760	775	814	845	813	813	822
At natural gas plants	441	456	521	529	564	587	570	568	577
At refineries	121	182	234	246	250	258	243	245	245
Imports	79	68	53	71	66	79	75	67	67
Refinery input	85	107	105	92	87	87	88	90	90
Exports	9	14	21	15	18	27	16	24	24
Stocks, Dec. 31	116	98	93	115	89	83	121	106	106

Source: U.S. Energy Information Administration, *Petroleum Supply Annual*, volume 1.

No. 874. Natural Gas Plant Liquids—Production and Value: 1980 to 2003

[Barrels of 42 gallons (576 barrels represents 576,000,000 barrels)]

Item	Unit	1980	1990	1995	1998	1999	2000	2001	2002	2003
Field production [1]	Mil. bbl ...	576	566	643	642	675	699	682	686	686
Pentanes plus	Mil. bbl ...	126	112	122	113	111	112	112	109	109
Liquefied petroleum gases	Mil. bbl ...	441	454	521	529	564	587	570	577	577
Natural gas processed	Tril. cu. ft. .	15	15	17	17	17	17	17	(NA)	(NA)

NA Not available.   [1] Includes other finished petroleum products, not shown separately.

Source: U.S. Energy Information Administration, *Petroleum Supply Annual* and *Natural Gas Annual*.

564   Natural Resources

No. 875. Natural Gas—Supply, Consumption, Reserves, and Marketed Production: 1980 to 2002

[182 represents 182,000 wells]

Item	Unit	1980	1990	1995	1997	1998	1999	2000	2001	2002
Producing wells (year-end)......	1,000.....	182	269	299	311	317	302	342	367	386
Production value at wells.......	Bil. dol	32.1	31.8	30.2	46.1	38.2	43.4	74.3	82.5	58.9
Avg. per 1,000 cu. ft........	Dollars	1.59	1.71	1.55	2.32	1.96	2.19	3.68	4.00	2.95
Proved reserves [1]	Tril. cu. ft ..	199	169	165	167	164	167	177	183	187
**Marketed production [2]...... **	**Bil. cu. ft .. **	**20,180**	**18,594**	**19,506**	**19,866**	**19,961**	**19,805**	**20,198**	**20,630**	**19,969**
Minus: Extraction losses [3]	Bil. cu. ft ...	777	784	908	964	938	973	1,016	954	922
Equals: Dry production	Bil. cu. ft...	19,403	17,810	18,599	18,902	19,024	18,832	19,182	19,676	19,047
Plus: Supplemental gas supplies..	Bil. cu. ft...	155	123	110	103	102	98	90	86	80
Equals: Dry production with supplemental gas..........	Bil. cu. ft...	19,558	17,932	18,709	19,005	19,126	18,930	19,272	19,762	19,127
Plus: Withdrawals from storage...	Bil. cu. ft...	1,972	1,986	3,025	2,894	2,432	2,808	3,550	2,344	3,126
Plus: Imports [4].............	Bil. cu. ft...	985	1,532	2,841	2,994	3,152	3,586	3,782	3,977	4,008
Plus: Balancing item..........	Bil. cu. ft...	-640	307	396	871	657	-119	-271	45	-610
Equals: Total supply	Bil. cu. ft...	21,875	21,758	24,971	25,764	25,367	25,205	26,333	26,128	25,651
Minus: Exports.............	Bil. cu. ft...	49	86	154	157	159	163	244	373	516
Minus: Additions to storage [5]	Bil. cu. ft...	1,949	2,499	2,610	2,870	2,961	2,636	2,721	3,509	2,679
**Equals: Consumption, total .... **	**Bil. cu. ft .. **	**19,877**	**19,174**	**22,207**	**22,737**	**22,246**	**22,405**	**23,368**	**22,246**	**22,455**
Lease and plant fuel	Bil. cu. ft...	1,026	1,236	1,220	1,203	1,173	1,079	1,151	1,089	1,053
Pipeline fuel..............	Bil. cu. ft...	635	660	700	751	635	645	642	624	630
Residential................	Bil. cu. ft...	4,752	4,391	4,850	4,984	4,520	4,726	4,996	4,776	4,914
Commercial [6].............	Bil. cu. ft...	2,611	2,623	3,031	3,215	2,999	3,045	3,218	3,037	3,114
Industrial	Bil. cu. ft...	7,172	7,018	8,164	8,511	8,320	8,079	8,142	7,363	7,177
Vehicle fuel	Bil. cu. ft...	(NA)	-	5	8	9	12	13	15	15
Electric utilities	Bil. cu. ft...	3,682	2,794	3,288	3,039	3,544	3,729	4,093	4,164	4,209
World production (dry)........	Tril. cu. ft ..	53.4	73.6	78.0	81.5	83.0	84.9	88.3	90.5	92.3
U.S. production (dry)........	Tril. cu. ft ..	19.4	17.8	18.6	18.9	19.0	18.8	19.2	19.7	19.1
Percent U.S. of world........	Percent ...	36.4	24.2	23.9	23.2	22.9	22.2	21.7	21.7	20.6

- Represents zero. NA Not available. [1] Estimated, end of year. Source: U.S. Energy Information Administration, *U.S. Crude Oil, Natural Gas, and Natural Gas Liquids Reserves, annual.* [2] Marketed production includes gross withdrawals from reservoirs less quantities used for reservoir repressuring and quantities vented or flared. Excludes nonhydrocarbon gases subsequently removed. [3] Volumetric reduction in natural gas resulting from the extraction of natural gas constituents at natural gas processing plants. [4] Includes imports of liquefied natural gas. [5] Includes liquefied natural gas (LNG) storage in above ground tanks. [6] Includes deliveries to municipalities and public authorities for institutional heating and other purposes.
Source: Except as noted, U.S. Energy Information Administration, *Annual Energy Review, International Energy Annual, Natural Gas Annual,* Volume I and II, and *Monthly Energy Review.*

No. 876. World Natural Gas Production by Major Producing Country: 1980 to 2002

[In trillion cubic feet (53.35 represents 53,350,000,000,000)]

Country	1980	1990	1995	1997	1998	1999	2000	2001	2002
**World Total [1] .... **	**53.35**	**73.57**	**77.96**	**81.52**	**83.03**	**84.93**	**88.29**	**90.51**	**92.29**
Russia	(X)	(X)	21.01	20.17	20.87	20.83	20.63	20.51	21.03
United States	**19.40**	**17.81**	**18.60**	**18.90**	**19.02**	**18.83**	**19.18**	**19.68**	**19.05**
Canada.................	2.76	3.85	5.60	5.76	5.98	6.26	6.47	6.60	6.63
Algeria	0.41	1.79	2.05	2.43	2.60	2.88	2.94	2.79	2.80
Netherlands..............	3.40	2.69	2.98	2.99	2.84	2.67	2.56	2.75	2.66
Indonesia...............	0.63	1.53	2.24	2.27	2.27	2.51	2.36	2.34	2.48
Uzbekistan	(X)	(X)	1.70	1.74	1.94	1.96	1.99	2.23	2.04
Iran	0.25	0.84	1.25	1.66	1.77	2.04	2.13	2.33	2.65
Norway.................	0.92	0.98	1.08	1.62	1.63	1.76	1.87	1.95	2.41
Malaysia................	0.06	0.65	1.02	1.36	1.37	1.42	1.50	1.66	1.71
Saudi Arabia.............	0.33	1.08	1.34	1.60	1.65	1.63	1.76	1.90	2.00
Turkmenistan.............	(X)	(X)	1.14	0.90	0.47	0.79	1.64	1.70	1.89
United Arab Emirates........	0.20	0.78	1.11	1.28	1.31	1.34	1.36	1.39	1.53
Argentina...............	0.28	0.63	0.88	0.97	1.04	1.22	1.32	1.31	1.28
Mexico	0.90	0.90	0.96	1.17	1.27	1.29	1.31	1.30	1.33
Australia...............	0.31	0.72	1.03	1.06	1.10	1.10	1.16	1.19	1.26
Qatar	0.18	0.28	0.48	0.61	0.69	0.78	1.03	0.95	1.04
Venezuela...............	0.52	0.76	0.89	0.99	1.11	0.95	0.96	1.12	1.05
China	0.51	0.51	0.60	0.75	0.78	0.85	0.96	1.07	1.15
Pakistan................	0.29	0.48	0.65	0.70	0.71	0.78	0.86	0.77	0.81
India..................	0.05	0.40	0.63	0.72	0.76	0.75	0.79	0.85	0.88
Germany................	0.93	0.72	0.74	0.79	0.77	0.82	0.78	0.79	0.79
Egypt	0.03	0.29	0.44	0.48	0.49	0.52	0.65	0.87	0.94
Thailand	(X)	0.21	0.37	0.54	0.57	0.63	0.66	0.66	0.69
Ukraine................	(X)	(X)	0.62	0.64	0.64	0.63	0.64	0.64	0.65
Nigeria	0.04	0.13	0.18	0.21	0.21	0.25	0.44	0.53	0.50
Italy	0.44	0.61	0.72	0.68	0.67	0.62	0.59	0.54	0.51
Trinidad and Tobago	0.08	0.18	0.27	0.33	0.33	0.41	0.49	0.54	0.61
Romania	1.20	1.00	0.68	0.61	0.52	0.50	0.48	0.51	0.47
Oman	0.03	0.10	0.15	0.18	0.25	0.20	0.32	0.49	0.53
Brunei.................	0.32	0.32	0.33	0.32	0.32	0.33	0.35	0.37	0.38
Kazakhstan	(X)	(X)	0.17	0.22	0.19	0.16	0.31	0.36	0.46
Bangladesh..............	0.05	0.16	0.26	0.27	0.29	0.32	0.34	0.36	0.38
Kuwait	0.24	0.19	0.21	0.33	0.32	0.31	0.34	0.30	0.29
Bahrain................	0.10	0.21	0.23	0.28	0.29	0.30	0.30	0.31	0.33

X Not applicable. [1] Includes countries not shown separately.
Source: U. S. Energy Information Administration, *International Energy Annual.* See also <http://www.eia.doe.gov>.

No. 877. Coal Supply, Disposition, and Prices: 1997 to 2003

[In millions of short tons (1,089.9 represents 1,089,900,000)]

Item	1997	1998	1999	2000	2001	2002	2003
United States, total	**1,089.9**	**1,117.5**	**1,100.4**	**1,073.6**	**1,127.7**	**1,094.3**	**1,069.5**
Consumption by sector							
Total	1,030.1	1,038.3	1,045.3	1,084.1	1,060.1	1,066.4	1,090.5
Electric power	922.0	937.8	946.8	985.8	964.4	977.5	1,000.6
Coke plants	30.2	28.2	28.1	28.9	26.1	23.7	24.2
Other industrial plants	71.5	67.4	65.5	65.2	65.3	60.7	61.2
Residential/commercial users	6.5	4.9	4.9	4.1	4.4	4.4	4.4
Year-end coal stocks							
Total	140.4	164.6	183.0	140.0	181.9	192.1	164.0
Electric power	98.8	120.5	136.0	102.0	138.5	141.7	121.6
Coke plants	2.0	2.0	1.9	1.5	1.5	1.4	0.9
Other industrial plants	5.6	5.5	5.6	4.6	6.0	5.8	4.7
Producers/distributors	34.0	36.5	39.5	31.9	35.9	43.3	36.8
U.S. coal trade							
Net exports	76.1	69.3	49.4	46.0	28.9	22.7	18.0
Exports	83.5	78.0	58.5	58.5	48.7	39.6	43.0
Steam coal	31.4	31.0	26.3	25.7	23.3	18.1	20.9
Metallurgical coal	52.2	47.1	32.1	32.8	25.4	21.5	22.1
Imports	7.5	8.7	9.1	12.5	19.8	16.9	25.0
Average delivered price (dollars per short ton)							
Electric utilities	26.16	25.64	24.72	24.28	24.68	24.74	25.39
Coke plants	47.61	46.06	45.85	44.38	46.42	50.67	50.63
Other industrial plants	32.41	32.26	31.59	31.46	32.26	35.49	34.17
Average free alongside ship (f.a.s.):							
Exports	40.55	38.89	36.50	34.90	36.97	40.44	35.98
Steam coal	32.42	30.24	29.91	29.67	31.88	34.51	26.94
Metallurgical coal	45.45	44.58	41.91	38.99	41.63	45.41	44.55
Imports	34.32	32.18	30.77	30.10	34.00	35.51	31.45

Source: U.S. Energy Information Administration, *U.S. Coal Supply and Demand: 2002 Review*, annual. See also <http://tonto.eia.doe.gov/FTPROOT/coal/coalpubs.htm>.

No. 878. Coal and Coke—Summary: 1980 to 2003

[830 short tons represents 830,000,000 short tons. Includes coal consumed at mines. Recoverability varies between 40 and 90 percent for individual deposits; 50 percent or more of overall U.S. coal reserve base is believed to be recoverable]

Item	Unit	1980	1990	1995	1999	2000	2001	2002	2003
COAL									
Coal production, total [1]	Mil. sh. tons	830	1,029	1,033	1,100	1,074	1,128	1,094	1,069
Value	Bil. dol.	20.45	22.39	19.45	19.42	18.02	19.60	19.48	(NA)
Anthracite production	Mil. sh. tons	6.1	3.5	4.7	4.8	4.6	1.9	1.3	(NA)
Bituminous coal and lignite	Mil. sh. tons	824	1,026	1,028	1,096	1,069	1,126	1,093	(NA)
Underground	Mil. sh. tons	337	425	396	392	374	(NA)	357	(NA)
Surface	Mil. sh. tons	487	605	637	709	700	(NA)	736	(NA)
Exports	Mil. sh. tons	92	106	89	59	58.5	48.7	39.6	43.0
Imports	Mil. sh. tons	1	3	9	9	12.5	19.8	16.9	25.0
Consumption [2]	Mil. sh. tons	703	896	941	1,045	1,081	1,060	1,065	(NA)
Electric power utilities	Mil. sh. tons	569	774	829	894	859	(NA)	976	(NA)
Industrial	Mil. sh. tons	126	115	106	94	94	(NA)	84	(NA)
Number of mines	Number	5,598	3,243	2,104	1,591	707	(NA)	(NA)	(NA)
Daily employment	1,000	225	131	90	79	72	77	75	(NA)
Production, by state:									
Alabama	Mil. sh. tons	26	29	25	20	19	19	19	20
Illinois	Mil. sh. tons	63	60	48	40	33	34	33	32
Indiana	Mil. sh. tons	31	36	26	34	28	37	35	35
Kentucky	Mil. sh. tons	150	173	154	140	131	134	124	113
Montana	Mil. sh. tons	30	38	39	41	38	39	37	37
Ohio	Mil. sh. tons	39	35	26	22	22	25	21	22
Pennsylvania	Mil. sh. tons	93	71	62	76	75	74	68	64
Virginia	Mil. sh. tons	41	47	34	32	33	(NA)	30	32
West Virginia	Mil. sh. tons	122	169	163	158	158	(NA)	150	138
Wyoming	Mil. sh. tons	95	184	264	337	339	(NA)	373	376
Other States	Mil. sh. tons	140	187	192	200	197	(NA)	202	201
World production	Mil. sh. tons	4,200	5,441	5,157	4,988	4,995	5,266	(NA)	(NA)
Percent U.S. of world	Percent	19.8	18.9	20.0	22.1	21.5	21.3	(NA)	(NA)
COKE									
Coke production [3]	Mil. sh. tons	46.13	27.62	23.75	20.02	20.81	18.95	16.78	17.17
Imports	Mil. sh. tons	0.66	0.77	3.82	3.22	3.78	2.53	3.24	2.76
Exports	Mil. sh. tons	2.07	0.57	1.36	0.90	1.15	1.35	0.79	0.72
Consumption	Mil. sh. tons	41.28	27.82	25.85	22.42	23.24	20.20	19.60	19.44

NA Not available. [1] Includes bituminous coal, subbituminous coal, lignite, and anthracite. [2] Includes some categories not shown separately. [3] Includes beehive coke.

Source: U.S. Energy Information Administration, *Coal Industry*, annual; *Annual Energy Review, International Energy Annual*, and *Quarterly Coal Report*. See also <ftp://ftp.eia.doe.gov/pub/pdf/coal.nuclear/05842000.pdf> (issued June 2002).

No. 879. World Coal Production by Major Producing Country: 1980 to 2001

[In millions of short tons (4,188.6 represents 4,188,600,000)]

Country	1980	1990	1995	1996	1997	1998	1999	2000	2001
World, total	4,188.6	5,440.9	5,156.9	5,193.5	5,196.2	5,093.3	4,987.9	4,995.2	5,266.0
China	683.6	1,190.4	1,537.0	1,545.3	1,507.1	1,429.0	1,364.9	1,314.4	1,459.0
United States	829.7	1,029.1	1,033.0	1,063.9	1,089.9	1,117.5	1,100.4	1,073.6	1,121.3
India	125.9	233.4	297.8	314.9	326.1	322.2	326.8	342.7	338.6
Australia	116.1	225.8	266.6	272.4	292.1	316.8	320.8	338.2	356.9
South Africa	132.0	247.6	227.3	227.3	244.3	246.9	243.0	248.4	250.3
Russia	(X)	(X)	296.4	304.0	257.9	241.0	259.2	279.2	299.5
Germany [1]	532.2	513.7	274.2	265.0	251.7	233.0	226.0	225.3	225.7
Poland	253.5	237.1	220.2	193.1	221.5	196.2	187.6	178.3	178.9
Korea, North	39.7	99.2	106.9	105.7	104.7	99.5	100.5	105.7	105.3
Ukraine	(X)	(X)	94.6	83.5	84.8	85.1	90.9	90.2	90.1
Kazakhstan	(X)	(X)	91.9	84.7	80.1	76.9	64.4	79.7	88.5
Canada	40.4	75.4	82.6	83.5	86.8	82.9	79.9	76.2	77.7
Turkey	20.2	52.6	60.7	62.1	66.1	74.3	73.9	69.6	72.6
Indonesia	0.6	11.6	45.7	55.5	60.2	66.5	79.4	84.4	99.6
Czech Republic	(X)	(X)	81.9	84.0	81.0	74.4	65.2	71.8	72.9
Greece	25.6	57.2	63.6	65.9	64.9	67.1	68.4	70.4	74.5
Colombia	4.5	22.6	28.4	33.1	35.9	37.2	36.1	42.0	47.9
Serbia and Montenegro	(X)	(X)	44.1	42.4	44.8	48.6	36.7	37.9	39.5
United Kingdom	143.8	104.1	52.5	53.5	51.8	44.1	39.9	33.7	34.7
Romania	38.8	42.1	45.3	46.2	37.3	28.9	25.2	32.3	33.1
Bulgaria	39.6	39.0	33.9	33.7	32.8	34.1	31.2	32.7	31.5
Spain	40.9	39.6	31.3	30.8	29.2	28.7	26.8	25.9	25.0
Thailand	1.6	13.7	20.3	23.9	25.8	22.0	20.1	19.6	21.6
Hungary	28.3	19.7	16.1	16.7	17.2	17.1	16.8	16.2	16.0
Mexico	4.0	8.6	10.3	11.1	11.5	12.4	11.4	12.5	12.8

X Not applicable.   [1] For 1980 and 1990, represents East and West Germany combined.

Source: U.S. Energy Information Administration, *International Energy Annual, 2001*. See also (issued March 2003).

No. 880. Demonstrated Coal Reserves by Major Producing State: 2001 and 2002

[In millions of short tons. As of January 1. The demonstrated reserve base represents the sum of coal in both measured and indicated resource categories of reliability. Measured resources of coal are estimates that have a high degree of geologic assurance from sample analyes and measurements from closely spaced and geological well known sample sites. Indicated resources are estimates based partly from sample and analyses and measurements and partly from reasonable geologic projections. For more information on the classification of coal resources and related terminology, see report cited below]

State	2001			2002		
	Total reserves	Method of mining		Total reserves	Method of mining	
		Under ground	Surface		Under ground	Surface
United States	501,059	338,525	162,534	497,708	336,928	160,780
Alabama	4,389	1,157	3,232	4,318	1,097	3,221
Alaska	6,118	5,423	695	6,115	5,423	692
Colorado	16,552	11,780	4,772	16,430	11,661	4,769
Illinois	104,773	88,188	16,586	104,648	88,077	16,570
Indiana	9,738	8,831	907	9,637	8,801	835
Iowa	2,189	1,732	457	2,189	1,732	457
Kentucky	31,053	17,797	13,257	30,614	17,484	13,130
Kentucky, Eastern	11,326	1,727	9,598	10,977	1,491	9,486
Kentucky, Western	19,728	16,069	3,658	19,637	15,993	3,644
Missouri	5,992	1,479	4,513	5,991	1,479	4,512
Montana	119,472	70,958	48,514	119,377	70,958	48,418
New Mexico	12,324	6,203	6,121	12,249	6,199	6,051
North Dakota	9,243	-	9,243	9,166	-	9,166
Ohio	23,495	17,679	5,816	23,419	17,631	5,788
Oklahoma	1,566	1,235	331	1,562	1,233	328
Pennsylvania	28,101	23,769	4,332	27,838	23,541	4,297
Anthracite	7,208	3,847	3,361	7,204	3,845	3,359
Bituminous	20,893	19,922	971	20,634	19,696	938
Texas	12,672	-	12,672	12,559	-	12,559
Utah	5,639	5,371	268	5,534	5,267	268
Virginia	1,960	1,332	628	1,850	1,247	603
Washington	1,368	1,332	36	1,356	1,332	23
West Virginia	34,244	30,097	4,147	33,713	29,722	3,991
Wyoming	66,219	42,501	23,718	65,291	42,501	22,790
East of the MS River	239,379	190,116	49,262	(NA)	(NA)	(NA)
West of the MS River	261,680	148,409	113,271	(NA)	(NA)	(NA)

- Represents or rounds to zero.   NA Not available.

Source: U.S. Energy Information Administration, unpublished data from the Coal Reserves Database.

Natural Resources 567

No. 881. Uranium Concentrate (U₃O₈) Industry—Summary: 1990 to 2002

[See also Table 920 in Section 19]

Item	Unit	1990	1991	1992	1993	1994	1995	1996	1997	1998	1999	2000	2001	2002
Exploration and development, surface drilling	Mil. ft.	1.7	1.8	1.1	1.1	0.7	1.3	3.0	4.9	4.6	2.5	1.0	0.7	(D)
Expenditures	Mil. dol.	17.1	17.8	14.5	11.3	3.7	6.0	10.1	30.4	21.7	9.0	6.7	4.8	0.4
Number of mines operated	Number	39	15	17	12	12	12	13	14	15	14	10	7	6
Underground	Number	27	6	4	-	-	-	1	1	4	3	1	-	-
Openpit	Number	2	2	1	-	-	-	-	-	-	-	-	-	-
In situ leaching	Number	7	6	4	5	5	5	6	7	6	6	4	3	3
Other sources	Number	3	1	8	7	7	7	6	6	5	5	5	4	3
Mine production	1,000 pounds	5,876	5,182	986	2,050	2,526	3,528	4,705	4,710	4,782	4,548	3,123	2,647	2,405
Underground	1,000 pounds	(D)	(D)	(D)	-	-	-	(D)	(D)	(D)	(D)	(D)	-	-
Openpit	1,000 pounds	1,881	2,528	(D)	-	-	-	-	-	-	-	-	-	-
In situ leaching	1,000 pounds	(D)	(D)	(D)	(D)	2,448	3,372	4,379	4,084	3,721	3,830	2,995	(D)	(D)
Other sources	1,000 pounds	3,995	2,654	986	2,050	78	156	326	626	1,062	718	128	(D)	(D)
Uranium concentrate production [1]	1,000 pounds	8,886	7,952	5,645	3,063	3,352	6,043	6,321	5,643	4,705	4,611	3,958	2,639	2,344
Concentrate shipments from mills and plants	1,000 pounds	12,957	8,437	6,853	3,374	6,319	5,500	5,982	5,817	4,863	5,527	3,187	2,203	3,810
Employment	Person-years	1,335	1,016	682	871	980	1,107	1,118	1,097	1,120	848	627	423	426

- Represents zero. D Data withheld to avoid disclosing figures for individual companies. [1] U₃O₈.

Source: U.S. Department of Energy, *Uranium Industry*, annual. See also <http://www.eia.doe.gov/cneaf/nuclear/uia/uia.pdf> (released May 2003) and <http://www.eia.doe.gov/cneaf/nuclear/uia/contents.html> (released May 2003).

568   Natural Resources

Section 19
Energy and Utilities

This section presents statistics on fuel resources, energy production and consumption, electric energy, hydroelectric power, nuclear power, solar energy, wood energy, and the electric and gas utility industries. The principal sources are the U.S. Department of Energy's Energy Information Administration (EIA), the Edison Electric Institute, Washington, DC, and the American Gas Association, Arlington, VA. The Department of Energy was created in October 1977 and assumed and centralized the responsibilities of all or part of several agencies including the Federal Power Commission (FPC), the U.S. Bureau of Mines, the Federal Energy Administration, and the U.S. Energy Research and Development Administration. For additional data on transportation, see Section 23; on fuels, see Section 18; and on energy-related housing characteristics, see Section 20.

The EIA, in its *Annual Energy Review*, provides statistics and trend data on energy supply, demand, and prices. Information is included on petroleum and natural gas, coal, electricity, hydroelectric power, nuclear power, solar, wood, and geothermal energy. Among its annual reports are *Annual Energy Review, Electric Power Annual, Natural Gas Annual, Petroleum Supply Annual, State Energy Data Report, State Energy Price and Expenditure Report, Performance Profiles of Major Energy Producers, Annual Energy Outlook,* and *International Energy Annual*. These various publications contain state, national, and international data on production of electricity, net summer capability of generating plants, fuels used in energy production, energy sales and consumption, and hydroelectric power. The EIA also issues the *Monthly Energy Review*, which presents current supply, disposition, and price data and monthly publications on petroleum, coal, natural

gas, and electric power. Data on residential energy consumption, expenditures, and conservation activities are available from EIA's Residential Energy Consumption Survey and are published every 4 years.

The Edison Electric Institute's monthly bulletin and annual *Statistical Year Book of the Electric Utility Industry for the Year* contain data on the distribution of electric energy by public utilities; information on the electric power supply, expansion of electric generating facilities, and the manufacture of heavy electric power equipment is presented in the annual *Year-End Summary of the Electric Power Situation in the United States*. The American Gas Association, in its monthly and quarterly bulletins and its yearbook, *Gas Facts*, presents data on gas utilities and financial and operating statistics.

Btu conversion factors—Various energy sources are converted from original units to the thermal equivalent using British thermal units (Btu). A Btu is the amount of energy required to raise the temperature of 1 pound of water 1 degree Fahrenheit (F) at or near 39.2 degrees F. Factors are calculated annually from the latest final annual data available; some are revised as a result. The following list provides conversion factors used in 2002 for production and consumption, in that order, for various fuels: Petroleum, 5.800 and 5.324 mil. Btu per barrel; total coal, 20.620 and 20.814 mil. Btu per short ton; and natural gas (dry), 1,027 Btu per cubic foot for both. The factors for the production of nuclear power and geothermal power were 10,442 and 21,017 Btu per kilowatt-hour, respectively. The fossil fuel steam-electric power plant generation factor of 10,119 Btu per kilowatt-hour was used for hydroelectric power generation and for wood and waste, wind, photovoltaic, and solar thermal energy consumed at electric utilities.

U.S. Census Bureau, Statistical Abstract of the United States: 2004-2005

In the past few years, EIA has restructured the industry categories it once used to gather and report electricity statistics. The electric power industry, previously divided into electric utilities and non-utilities, now consists of electricity only and combined-heat-and-power (CHP) plants that sell electricity, or electric heat, to the public.

Electricity-only plants are composed of traditional electric utilities, and nontraditional participants, including energy service providers, power marketers, independent power producers (IPPs), and the portion of combined-heat-and-power plants (CHPs) that produce only electricity.

A utility is defined as a corporation, person, agency, authority, or other legal entity or instrumentality aligned with distribution facilities for delivery of electric energy for use primarily by the public. Electric utilities include investor-owned electric utilities, municipal and State utilities, Federal electric utilities, and rural electric cooperatives. In total, there are more than 3,100 electric utilities in the United States.

An independent power producer is an entity defined as a corporation, person, agency, authority, or other legal entity or instrumentality that owns or operates facilities whose primary business is to produce electricity for use by the public. They are not generally aligned with distribution facilities and are not considered electric utilities.

Combined-heat-and-power producers are plants designed to produce both heat and electricity from a single heat source. These types of electricity producers can be independent power producers or industrial or commercial establishments. As some independent power producers are combined-heat-and-power producers, their information is included in the data for the combined-heat-and-power sector. There are approximately 2,800 unregulated independent power producers and combined-heat-and-power plants in the United States. For more information, please refer to the Electric Power Annual 2002 website located at <htp://www.eia.doe.gov/cneaf/electricity/epa/review.html>.

No. 882. Utilities—Establishments, Revenue, Payroll, and Employees by Kind of Business (NAICS Basis): 1997 and 2002

[411,713 represents $411,713,000,000. See headnote, Table 728 and Appendix III]

Kind of business	NAICS code [1]	Establishments (number)	Revenue Total (mil. dol.)	Revenue Per paid employee (dol.)	Annual payroll Total (mil. dol.)	Annual payroll Per paid employee (dol.)	Paid employee for pay period including March 12 (number)
1997							
Utilities	22	15,513	411,713	585,899	36,595	52,077	702,703
Electric power generation, transmission, & distribution	2211	7,935	269,095	476,676	30,440	53,921	564,525
Electric power generation	22111	1,745	73,375	493,492	8,369	56,289	148,686
Fossil fuel electric power generation	221112	1,009	48,324	515,374	5,049	53,843	93,765
Nuclear electric power generation	221113	67	13,967	406,231	2,202	64,045	34,381
Other electric power generation	221119	316	8,011	608,723	725	55,069	13,160
Electric power transmission, control & distribution	22112	6,190	195,720	470,663	22,070	53,074	415,839
Electric bulk power transmission & control	221121	120	956	395,361	116	47,852	2,418
Electric power distribution	221122	6,070	194,764	471,103	21,955	53,105	413,421
Other combination utilities	2211223	30	428	630,811	52	76,771	678
Natural gas distribution	2212	2,747	136,995	1,331,629	5,110	49,666	102,878
Natural gas transmission & distribution..	2212101	713	18,267	629,034	1,534	52,838	29,039
Natural gas distribution	2212102	1,682	87,105	1,387,135	2,955	47,059	62,795
Mixed, manu., or LP gas pro &/or dist. ..	2212103	86	(D)	(D)	(D)	(D)	(²)
Electric & other serv. combined (natural gas distribution)	2212104	145	28,110	4,193,063	413	61,565	6,704
Gas & other serv. combined (natural gas distribution)	2212105	119	2,853	915,151	149	47,705	3,117
Water, sewage, & other systems	2213	4,831	5,623	159,284	1,045	29,614	35,300
Water supply & irrigation systems	22131	4,052	4,454	159,447	825	29,550	27,933
Sewage treatment facilities	22132	696	596	106,399	139	24,816	5,600
Steam & air-conditioning supply	22133	83	573	324,314	81	45,838	1,767
2002							
Utilities	22	18,594	478,268	647,524	45,111	61,076	738,611

D Withheld to avoid disclosing data of individual companies; data are included in higher level totals.   [1] North American Industry Classification System, 1997; see text, Section 15.   [2] 1,000 to 2,499 employees.

Source: U.S. Census Bureau, *1997 Economic Census*, Series EC97T22A-US, issued December 1999; *2002 Economic Census Advance Report*, published 29 March 2004; <http://www.census.gov/econ/census02/>.

No. 883. Private Utilities—Employees, Annual Payroll, and Establishments by Industry: 2001

[41,942 represents $41,942,000,000. Excludes government employees, railroad employees, self-employed persons, etc. See "General Explanation" in source for definitions and statement on reliability of data. An *establishment* is a single physical location where business is conducted or where services or industrial operations are performed. See Appendix III]

Year and industry	NAICS code [1]	Number of employees [2]	Annual payroll (mil. dol.)	Average payroll per employee (dol.)	Establishment by employment size-class Total	Under 20 employees	20 to 99 employees	100 to 499 employees	500 and over employees
Utilities, total	22	654,484	41,942	64,085	17,702	12,505	3,837	1,168	192
Electric power generation, transmission and distribution	2211	515,988	34,338	66,548	9,207	5,202	2,902	933	170
Electric power generation	22111	139,254	10,188	66,548	2,208	1,305	582	263	58
Hydroelectric power generation	221111	11,650	793	68,028	462	363	71	25	3
Fossil fuel electric power generation.	221112	80,674	5,683	70,445	1,301	664	412	211	14
Nuclear electric power generation ..	221113	33,064	2,791	84,424	72	18	9	11	34
Other electric power generation ..	221119	13,866	921	66,426	373	260	90	16	7
Electric pwr transmsn, control & distribution	22112	376,734	24,150	64,103	6,999	3,897	2,320	670	112
Electric bulk power transmission & control	221121	6,233	366	58,683	161	103	45	12	1
Electric power distribution.	221122	370,501	23,784	64,194	6,838	3,794	2,275	658	111
Natural gas distribution.	2212	95,348	6,001	62,939	2,831	2,001	616	194	20
Water, sewage & other systems	2213	43,148	1,603	37,162	5,664	5,302	319	41	2
Water supply & irrigation systems	22131	35,206	1,325	37,634	4,832	4,562	234	34	2
Sewage treatment facilities	22132	6,312	198	31,340	748	688	54	6	-
Steam & air-conditioning supply	22133	1,630	81	49,506	84	52	31	1	-

- Represents zero.   [1] North American Industry Classification System, 1997; see text, section 15.   [2] Covers full-and part-time employees who are on the payroll in the pay period including March 12.

Source: U.S. Census Bureau, *County Business Patterns*, annual. See also <http://www.census.gov/epcd/cbp/view/us01.txt> (issued April 2003).

Energy and Utilities 571

No. 884. Energy Supply and Disposition by Type of Fuel: 1960 to 2002

[In quadrillion British thermal units (Btu). (42.80 represents 42,800,000,000,000,000 Btu). For Btu conversion factors, see source and text, this section]

Year	Production Total[1]	Crude oil[2]	Natural gas	Coal	Nuclear power[3]	Renewable energy[4] Total[1]	Hydro-electric power	Biofuel[5]	Solar energy	Net imports total[6]	Consumption Total[1]	Petro-leum[7]	Natural gas[8]	Coal	Nuclear power	Renewable energy[4] total
1960	42.80	14.94	12.66	10.82	(Z)	2.93	1.61	1.32	(NA)	2.71	45.09	19.92	12.39	9.84	(Z)	2.93
1970	63.50	20.40	21.67	14.61	0.24	4.08	2.63	1.43	(NA)	5.71	67.84	29.52	21.80	12.27	0.24	4.08
1972	63.92	20.04	22.21	14.09	0.58	4.40	2.86	1.50	(NA)	9.27	72.70	32.95	22.70	12.08	0.58	4.40
1973	63.59	19.49	22.19	13.99	0.91	4.43	2.86	1.53	(NA)	12.58	75.71	34.84	22.51	12.97	0.91	4.43
1974	62.37	18.58	21.21	14.07	1.27	4.77	3.18	1.54	(NA)	12.10	73.99	33.46	21.73	12.66	1.27	4.77
1975	61.36	17.73	19.64	14.99	1.90	4.72	3.16	1.50	(NA)	11.71	72.00	32.73	19.95	12.66	1.90	4.72
1976	61.60	17.26	19.48	15.65	2.11	4.77	2.98	1.71	(NA)	14.59	76.01	35.12	20.35	13.58	2.11	4.77
1977	62.05	17.45	19.57	15.76	2.70	4.25	2.33	1.84	(NA)	17.90	78.00	37.12	19.93	13.92	2.70	4.25
1978	63.14	18.43	19.49	14.91	3.02	5.04	2.94	2.04	(NA)	17.19	79.99	37.97	20.00	13.77	3.02	5.04
1979	65.95	18.10	20.08	17.54	2.78	5.17	2.93	2.15	(NA)	16.60	80.90	37.12	20.67	15.04	2.78	5.17
1980	67.24	18.25	19.91	18.60	2.74	5.49	2.90	2.49	(NA)	12.10	78.29	34.20	20.39	15.42	2.74	5.49
1981	67.01	18.15	19.70	18.38	3.01	5.47	2.76	2.59	(NA)	9.41	76.34	31.93	19.93	15.91	3.01	5.47
1982	66.57	18.31	18.32	18.64	3.13	5.99	3.27	2.62	(NA)	7.25	73.23	30.23	18.51	15.32	3.13	5.99
1983	64.11	18.39	16.59	17.25	3.20	6.49	3.53	2.83	(Z)	8.06	73.07	30.05	17.36	15.89	3.20	6.49
1984	68.83	18.85	18.01	19.72	3.55	6.43	3.39	2.88	(Z)	8.68	76.69	31.05	18.51	17.07	3.55	6.43
1985	67.65	18.99	16.98	19.33	4.08	6.03	2.97	2.86	(Z)	7.58	76.42	30.92	17.83	17.48	4.08	6.03
1986	67.09	18.38	16.54	19.51	4.38	6.13	3.07	2.84	(Z)	10.13	76.72	32.20	16.71	17.26	4.38	6.13
1987	67.61	17.68	17.14	20.14	4.75	5.69	2.64	2.82	(Z)	11.59	79.16	32.87	17.74	18.01	4.75	5.69
1988	68.95	17.28	17.60	20.74	5.59	5.49	2.33	2.94	(Z)	12.93	82.77	34.22	18.55	18.85	5.59	5.49
1989 [9]	69.36	16.12	17.85	21.35	5.60	6.29	2.84	3.06	0.06	14.11	84.89	34.21	19.71	19.07	5.60	6.29
1990	70.73	15.57	18.33	22.46	6.10	6.13	3.05	2.66	0.06	14.06	84.61	33.55	19.73	19.17	6.10	6.13
1991	70.36	15.70	18.23	21.59	6.42	6.16	3.02	2.70	0.06	13.19	84.52	32.85	20.15	18.99	6.42	6.16
1992	69.93	15.22	18.38	21.63	6.48	5.91	2.62	2.85	0.07	14.44	85.87	33.53	20.84	19.12	6.48	5.91
1993	68.26	14.49	18.58	20.25	6.41	6.16	2.89	2.80	0.07	17.01	87.58	33.84	21.35	19.84	6.41	6.16
1994	70.68	14.10	19.35	22.11	6.69	6.07	2.68	2.94	0.07	18.33	89.25	34.67	21.84	19.91	6.69	6.07
1995	71.16	13.89	19.08	22.03	7.08	6.67	3.21	3.07	0.07	17.75	91.22	34.55	22.78	20.09	7.08	6.67
1996	72.47	13.72	19.34	22.68	7.09	7.14	3.59	3.13	0.07	19.07	94.22	35.76	23.20	21.45	7.09	7.14
1997	72.39	13.66	19.39	23.21	6.60	7.08	3.64	3.01	0.07	20.70	94.73	36.27	23.33	21.66	6.60	7.08
1998	72.79	13.24	19.61	23.94	7.07	6.56	3.30	2.84	0.07	22.28	95.15	36.93	22.94	21.62	7.07	6.56
1999	71.65	12.45	19.34	23.19	7.61	6.60	3.27	2.89	0.07	23.54	96.77	37.96	22.01	22.58	7.61	6.60
2000	71.22	12.36	19.66	22.62	7.86	6.16	2.81	2.91	0.07	24.97	98.94	38.40	23.95	21.90	7.86	6.16
2001	71.37	12.28	20.23	23.05	8.03	5.32	2.20	2.68	0.07	26.39	96.32	38.33	22.87	22.18	8.03	5.32
2002 [10]	70.95	12.31	19.56	22.55	8.15	5.90	2.67	2.76	0.06	25.38	97.35	38.18	23.06	22.18	8.15	5.90

NA Not available. Z Less than 50 trillion. [1] Includes types of fuel not shown separately. [2] Includes lease condensate. [3] Data on the generation of electricity in the United States represent net generation, which is gross output of electricity (measured at the generator terminals) minus power plant use. [4] End-use consumption and electricity net generation. [5] Wood, waste, and alcohol (ethanol blended into motor gasoline). [6] Imports minus exports. [7] Petroleum products supplied, including natural gas plant liquids and crude oil burned as fuel. [8] Includes supplemental gaseous fuels. [9] There is a discontinuity in this time series between 1989 and 1990 due to the expanded coverage of nonelectric utility use of renewable energy beginning in 1990. [10] Preliminary.

Source: U.S. Energy Information Administration, Annual Energy Review and Internet site <http://www.eia.doe.gov/emeu/aer/overview.html>

Figure 19.1
Energy Production, Trade, and Consumption: 1980 to 2002

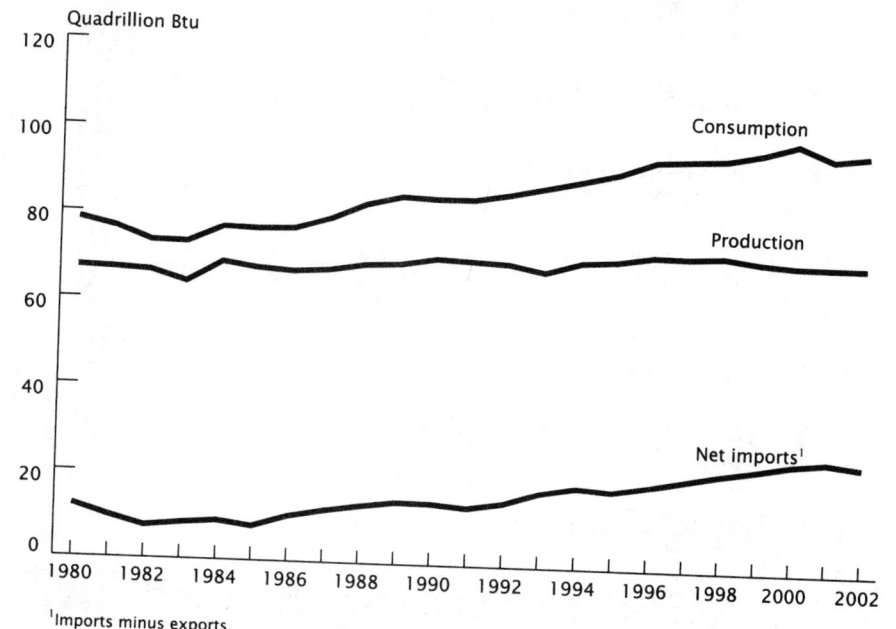

Quadrillion Btu

[1]Imports minus exports.
Source: Chart prepared by U.S. Census Bureau. For data, see Table 884.

Figure 19.2
Top Suppliers of U.S. Crude Oil Imports: 2003
(In millions of barrels)

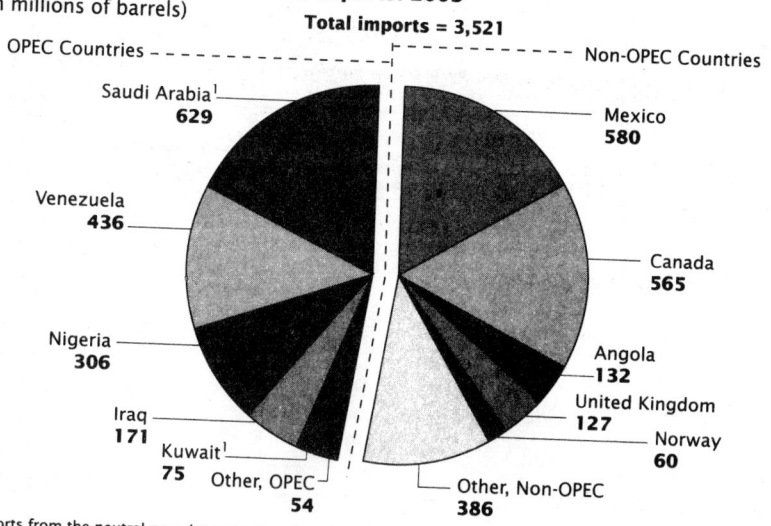

Total imports = 3,521

OPEC Countries -------------------- Non-OPEC Countries

Saudi Arabia[1]
629

Mexico
580

Venezuela
436

Canada
565

Nigeria
306

Angola
132

United Kingdom
127

Iraq
171

Norway
60

Kuwait[1]
75

Other, OPEC
54

Other, Non-OPEC
386

[1]Imports from the neutral zone between Kuwait and Saudi Arabia are included in Saudi Arabia.

Source: Chart prepared by U.S. Census Bureau. For data, see Table 897.

Energy and Utilities   573

[Quadrillion Btu (72.72 represents 72,720,000,000,000,000) per year. Btu=British thermal unit. Projections are "reference" or mid-level forecasts. See report for methodology and assumptions used in generating projections]

Type of fuel	2001	2002	Projections			
			2005	2010	2015	2020
Production, total	72.72	71.85	74.57	78.30	80.36	84.09
Crude oil and lease condensate	12.16	11.91	12.41	12.56	11.71	10.49
Natural gas plant liquids	2.55	2.56	2.98	3.10	3.20	3.47
Natural gas, dry	20.23	19.56	20.11	21.05	22.20	24.43
Coal	23.97	22.70	23.51	25.25	26.14	27.92
Nuclear power	8.03	8.15	8.26	8.29	8.48	8.53
Renewable energy [1]	5.25	5.84	6.54	7.18	7.84	8.45
Other [2]	0.53	1.13	0.76	0.88	0.79	0.81
Imports, total	29.95	29.21	32.29	37.76	43.72	48.06
Crude oil [3]	20.26	19.84	21.35	24.51	29.37	31.55
Petroleum products [4]	5.04	4.75	5.39	5.76	6.00	7.83
Natural gas	4.06	4.10	4.78	6.54	7.29	7.56
Other imports [5]	0.59	0.52	0.77	0.95	1.06	1.12
Exports, total	3.65	3.58	3.90	3.95	3.88	3.75
Petroleum [6]	2.01	2.03	2.07	2.15	2.18	2.13
Natural gas	0.38	0.52	0.82	0.91	0.90	0.93
Coal	1.26	1.03	1.02	0.89	0.80	0.69
Consumption, total	96.94	97.72	102.75	111.77	119.75	127.92
Petroleum products [7]	38.49	38.11	40.52	44.15	48.26	51.35
Natural gas	23.05	23.37	24.14	26.82	28.74	31.21
Coal	22.04	22.18	23.18	25.23	26.32	28.30
Nuclear power	8.03	8.15	8.26	8.29	8.48	8.53
Renewable energy [1], other [8]	5.33	5.91	6.65	7.29	7.95	8.53
Net imports of petroleum	23.29	22.56	24.68	28.13	33.20	37.25
Prices (1999 dollars per unit)[9]:						
World oil price (dol per bbl)	22.25	23.68	23.30	24.17	25.07	26.02
Gas wellhead price (dol. per mcf) [10] . .	4.14	2.95	3.54	3.40	4.19	4.28
Coal minemouth price (dol per ton)	17.79	17.90	17.24	16.88	16.47	16.32
Average electric price (cents per kWh) . .	7.40	7.20	6.80	6.60	6.80	6.90

[1] Includes grid-connected electricity from conventional hydroelectric; wood and wood waste; landfill gas; municipal solid waste; other biomass; wind; photovoltaic and solar thermal sources; non-electric energy from renewable sources, such as active and passive solar systems, and wood; and both the ethanol and gasoline components of E85, but not the ethanol components of blends less than 85 percent. Excludes electricity imports using renewable sources and nonmarketed renewable energy. See Table A18 of source for selected nonmarketed residential and commercial renewable energy. [2] Includes liquid hydrogen, methanol, supplemental natural gas, and some domestic inputs to refineries. [3] Includes imports of crude oil for the Strategic Petroleum Reserve. [4] Includes imports of finished petroleum products, imports of unfinished oils, alcohols, ethers, and blending components. [5] Includes coal, coal coke (net), and electricity (net). [6] Includes crude oil and petroleum products. [7] Includes natural gas plant liquids, crude oil consumed as a fuel, and nonpetroleum based liquids for blending, such as ethanol. [8] Includes net electricity imports, methanol, and liquid hydrogen. [9] Average refiner acquisition cost for imported crude oil. [10] Represents lower 48 onshore and offshore supplies.

Source: U.S. Energy Information Administration, *Annual Energy Outlook, 2004*, DOE/EIA-0383(2004). See also <http://www.eia.doe.gov/oiaf/aeo/pdf/appa.pdf>.

No. 886. Energy Consumption by End-Use Sector: 1970 to 2002

[67.84 represents 67,840,000,000,000,000 Btu. Btu=British thermal units. For Btu conversion factors, see source and text, this section. See Appendix III]

Year	Total (quad. Btu)	Residential and commercial [1] (quad. Btu)	Industrial [2] (quad. Btu)	Transportation (quad. Btu)	Percent of total		
					Residential and commercial [1]	Industrial [2]	Transportation
1970	67.84	22.11	29.64	16.10	32.6	43.7	23.7
1975	72.00	24.31	29.45	18.24	33.8	40.9	25.3
1980	78.29	26.44	32.15	19.70	33.8	41.1	25.2
1985	76.42	27.49	28.89	20.04	36.0	37.8	26.2
1990	84.60	30.36	31.89	22.36	35.9	37.7	26.4
1993	87.58	32.13	32.69	22.77	36.7	37.3	26.0
1994	89.25	32.32	33.57	23.37	36.2	37.6	26.2
1995	91.22	33.37	34.00	23.85	36.6	37.3	26.1
1996	94.22	34.81	34.97	24.44	36.9	37.1	25.9
1997	94.73	34.73	35.24	24.75	36.7	37.2	26.1
1998	95.15	35.02	34.88	25.26	36.8	36.7	26.5
1999	96.77	36.03	34.79	25.95	37.2	36.0	26.8
2000	98.94	37.71	34.68	26.55	38.1	35.1	26.8
2001	96.32	37.56	32.48	26.28	39.0	33.7	27.3
2002 [3]	97.35	38.33	32.49	26.52	39.4	33.4	27.2

[1] Commercial sector fuel use, including that at commercial combined-heat-and-power (CHP) and commercial electricity-only plants. [2] Industrial sector fuel use, including that at industrial combined-heat-and-power (CHP) and industrial electricity-only plants. [3] Preliminary.

Source: U.S. Energy Information Administration, *Annual Energy Review 2002*, DOE/EIA-0384(2003). See also <http://www.eia.doe.gov/emeu/aer/pdf/pages/sec24.pdf>.

No. 887. Energy Consumption—End-Use Sector and Selected Source by State: 2000

[In trillions of Btu (98,216 represents 98,216,000,000,000,000), except as indicated]

State	Total [1]	Per capita [2] (mil. Btu)	End-use sector [3]				Source				
			Residential	Commercial	Industrial [1]	Transportation	Petroleum	Natural gas (dry) [4]	Coal	Hydro electric power [5]	Nuclear electric power
United States	98,216	349	18,178	14,931	38,217	26,889	38,402	23,003	22,580	3,020	7,862
Alabama	1,977	445	339	219	936	483	581	351	900	59	327
Alaska	627	1,001	42	63	310	212	260	334	22	10	-
Arizona	1,216	237	283	263	206	463	506	207	433	89	317
Arkansas	1,084	405	194	126	466	298	394	259	268	24	122
California	8,519	252	1,318	1,189	2,950	3,063	3,558	2,273	70	436	367
Colorado	1,200	279	267	247	316	370	455	349	388	15	-
Connecticut	863	253	243	191	200	230	376	130	36	16	171
Delaware	303	386	54	48	128	73	139	54	50	-	-
District of Columbia	166	291	33	102	3	27	34	34	(Z)	-	-
Florida	3,944	247	989	795	736	1,425	1,971	561	761	1	337
Georgia	2,770	338	589	429	883	869	1,040	408	820	24	339
Hawaii	265	219	24	26	89	127	222	3	18	1	-
Idaho	511	395	95	88	201	127	175	73	14	113	-
Illinois	4,418	356	885	719	1,839	975	1,327	1,043	1,027	2	933
Indiana	2,778	457	463	306	1,342	667	910	591	1,595	6	-
Iowa	1,099	376	213	154	458	274	417	234	446	9	46
Kansas	1,036	385	201	168	384	282	407	324	363	(Z)	95
Kentucky	1,868	462	306	214	903	446	713	234	1,002	24	-
Louisiana	3,965	887	322	238	2,505	900	1,681	1,605	253	5	165
Maine	561	440	92	61	287	122	251	9	10	78	-
Maryland	1,520	287	353	325	436	407	553	217	312	18	144
Massachusetts	1,723	271	418	329	521	455	677	349	115	15	58
Michigan	3,122	314	734	553	1,013	822	1,062	950	779	13	197
Minnesota	1,688	343	346	221	604	517	680	360	374	64	135
Mississippi	1,144	402	206	141	432	365	469	294	148	-	112
Missouri	1,659	297	425	330	343	561	693	290	689	4	104
Montana	595	659	63	54	369	108	168	68	177	98	-
Nebraska	584	341	129	114	166	175	226	125	207	15	90
Nevada	633	317	125	96	207	206	230	188	199	25	-
New Hampshire	329	266	79	59	90	102	181	22	44	25	83
New Jersey	2,707	322	530	506	744	927	1,262	614	115	-1	298
New Mexico	621	341	92	108	192	229	251	227	306	2	-
New York	4,620	244	1,132	1,253	1,252	984	1,699	1,292	331	315	329
North Carolina	2,502	311	567	434	792	709	976	236	786	33	408
North Dakota	365	569	54	43	187	81	120	59	425	23	-
Ohio	4,002	353	844	622	1,541	994	1,331	917	1,438	6	175
Oklahoma	1,401	406	262	195	514	429	522	539	381	22	-
Oregon	1,080	316	225	182	354	319	378	231	39	390	-
Pennsylvania	4,780	389	854	609	2,305	1,012	1,416	728	1,507	19	769
Rhode Island	250	239	66	51	68	66	97	81	(Z)	10	-
South Carolina	1,477	368	285	201	608	383	481	160	432	5	531
South Dakota	246	326	54	40	67	86	119	40	51	59	-
Tennessee	2,026	356	434	316	687	589	720	276	705	58	269
Texas	11,589	556	1,333	1,161	6,483	2,611	5,501	4,253	1,548	12	392
Utah	718	322	125	119	251	223	275	173	403	8	-
Vermont	165	270	44	29	40	52	88	11	(Z)	38	47
Virginia	2,304	325	497	455	658	694	904	282	505	-6	295
Washington	2,174	369	410	321	815	627	868	297	106	795	90
West Virginia	744	411	136	100	321	187	218	154	980	12	-
Wisconsin	1,800	336	369	277	731	423	666	396	499	23	120
Wyoming	417	845	36	44	223	114	158	102	506	10	-

- Represents zero. Z Less than .5 trillion Btu. [1] U.S. total energy and U.S. industrial sector include 65.4 trillion Btu of net imports of coal coke that is not allocated to the States. State and U.S. totals include 81.8 trillion Btu of net imports of electricity generated from nonrenewable energy sources. [2] Based on estimated resident population as of July 1. [3] End-use sector data include electricity sales and associated electrical system energy losses. [4] Includes supplemental gaseous fuels. [5] Includes net imports of hydroelectricity. A negative number in this column results from pumped storage for which, overall, more electricity is expended than created to provide electricity during peak demand periods.

Source: U.S. Energy Information Administration, *State Energy Data Report, 2000* annual. See also <http://www.eia.doe.gov/emeu/states/sep_sum/html/pdf/sum_use_all.pdf> (released May 2003).

No. 888. Renewable Energy Consumption Estimates by Source : 1995 to 2002

[In quadrillion Btu (6.66 represents 6,660,000,000,000,000. Renewable energy is obtained from sources that are essentially inexhaustible unlike fossil fuels of which there is a finite supply]

Source and sector	1995	1997	1998	1999	2000	2001	2002 [1]
Consumption, total	6.66	7.07	6.55	6.59	6.15	5.31	5.88
Conventional hydroelectric power [2]	3.21	3.64	3.30	3.27	2.81	2.20	2.67
Geothermal energy [3]	0.29	0.33	0.33	0.33	0.32	0.31	0.30
Biomass [4]	3.06	3.00	2.82	2.87	2.89	2.66	2.74
Solar energy [5]	0.07	0.07	0.07	0.07	0.07	0.07	0.06
Wind energy [6]	0.03	0.03	0.03	0.05	0.06	0.07	0.11
Residential [7]	0.67	0.51	0.46	0.49	0.50	0.48	0.42
Biomass [4]	0.60	0.43	0.39	0.41	0.43	0.41	0.35
Geothermal [3]	0.01	0.01	0.01	0.01	0.01	0.01	0.01
Solar [5] [8]	0.07	0.07	0.07	0.06	0.06	0.06	0.06
Commercial [9]	0.09	0.11	0.11	0.11	0.11	0.09	0.10
Biomass [4]	0.09	0.11	0.10	0.11	0.10	0.08	0.09
Geothermal [3]	0.01	0.01	0.01	0.01	0.01	0.01	0.01
Hydroelectric [2]	(Z)	(Z)	(Z)	(Z)	(Z)	(Z)	(Z)
Industrial [10]	1.91	1.98	1.84	1.84	1.83	1.63	1.72
Biomass [4]	1.85	1.92	1.78	1.79	1.78	1.59	1.68
Geothermal [3]	(Z)	(Z)	(Z)	(Z)	(Z)	0.01	0.01
Hydroelectric [2]	0.06	0.06	0.06	0.05	0.04	0.03	0.04
Transportation:							
Alcohol fuels [11]	0.11	0.10	0.11	0.11	0.13	0.13	0.16
Electric power [12]	3.89	4.38	4.03	4.03	3.58	2.98	3.49
Electric utilities [13]	3.17	3.62	3.28	3.12	2.61	2.03	2.46
Biomass [4]	0.02	0.02	0.02	0.02	0.02	0.02	0.03
Geothermal [3]	0.10	0.12	0.11	0.04	(Z)	(Z)	(Z)
Hydroelectric [2]	3.06	3.49	3.15	3.07	2.58	2.01	2.43
Solar [5]	(Z)	(Z)	(Z)	(Z)	(Z)	(Z)	(Z)
Wind [6]	(Z)	(Z)	(Z)	(Z)	(Z)	(Z)	(Z)

Z Less than 5 trillion Btu. [1] Preliminary. [2] Power produced from natural streamflow as regulated by available storage. [3] As used at electric power plants, hot water or steam extracted from geothermal reservoirs in the Earth's crust that is supplied to steam turbines at electric power plants that drive generators to produce electricity. [4] Organic nonfossil material of biological origin constituting a renewable energy source. [5] Includes small amounts of distributed solar thermal and photovoltaic energy. [6] Energy present in wind motion that can be converted to mechanical energy for driving pumps, mills, and electric power generators. Wind pushes against sails, vanes, or blades radiating from a central rotating shaft. [7] Consists of living quarters for private households, but excludes institutional living quarters. [8] The radiant energy of the sun, which can be converted into other forms of energy, such as heat or electricity. [9] Consists of service-providing facilities and equipment of businesses, governments, and other private and public organizations. Includes institutional living quarters and sewage treatment facilities. [10] Consists of all facilities and equipment used for producing, processing, or assembling goods. [11] Ethanol primarily derived from corn. [12] A corporation or Consists of electricity only and combined heat and power plants who sell electricity and heat to the public. [13] other legal entity aligned with distribution facilities for delivery of electric energy, primarily for public use.

Source: U.S. Energy Information Administration, *Renewable Energy Annual 2002*, Series DOE/EIA-0603(2002). See also <http://www.eia.doe.gov/cneaf/solar.renewables/page/readata/appendixb.html> (accessed November 2003).

No. 889. Energy Expenditures and Average Fuel Prices by Source and Sector: 1970 to 2000

[82,898 represents $82,898,000,000. For definition of Btu, see text, this section. End-use sector and electric utilities exclude expenditures and prices on energy sources such as hydropower, solar, wind, and geothermal. Also excludes expenditures for reported amounts of energy consumed by the energy industry for production, transportation, and processing operations]

Source and sector	1970	1975	1980	1985	1990	1995	1996	1997	1998	1999	2000
EXPENDITURES											
(mil. dol.)											
Total [1]	82,898	171,802	374,319	437,271	472,214	516,207	562,600	569,011	527,028	560,161	703,188
Natural gas	10,891	20,061	51,061	72,938	64,102	74,150	85,634	91,736	81,628	83,559	115,910
Petroleum products	47,942	103,372	237,628	223,597	235,328	237,110	268,447	267,621	232,367	262,912	362,026
Motor gasoline	31,596	59,446	124,408	118,048	126,558	136,647	148,344	149,668	132,730	149,260	193,999
Coal	4,630	13,021	22,607	29,673	28,637	27,632	28,168	28,276	28,139	27,621	28,728
Electricity sales	23,345	50,680	98,095	124,408	176,737	205,932	211,011	213,645	216,928	216,737	231,653
Residential sector [2]	20,213	36,932	69,438	98,899	109,954	128,330	137,931	138,848	134,977	137,300	155,625
Commercial sector [2]	10,628	22,869	46,932	70,349	78,942	91,644	95,959	100,362	98,298	98,099	113,030
Industrial sector [1]	16,678	41,068	94,268	106,835	102,650	108,484	120,549	120,852	109,104	115,755	152,582
Transportation sector	35,379	70,933	163,680	161,188	180,668	187,749	208,161	208,950	184,649	209,017	(NA)
Motor gasoline	30,525	57,992	121,809	115,205	123,845	134,641	146,106	147,164	130,709	147,592	(NA)
Electric utilities [3]	4,316	16,396	37,435	42,507	38,287	34,765	36,635	37,765	37,527	36,490	41,375
AVERAGE FUEL PRICES											
(dol. per mil. Btu)											
All sectors [1]	1.65	3.33	6.89	8.36	8.25	8.24	8.72	8.78	8.15	8.34	9.85
Residential sector [2]	2.10	3.81	7.46	10.96	11.94	12.60	12.71	13.28	13.46	13.17	14.28
Commercial sector [2]	1.98	4.08	7.85	11.65	11.95	12.69	12.82	13.09	13.08	12.78	13.93
Industrial sector [1]	0.98	2.12	5.15	6.27	5.18	4.32	5.11	4.83	4.24	4.38	5.18
Transportation sector	2.31	4.02	8.61	8.26	8.28	8.09	8.76	8.70	7.48	8.19	(NA)
Electric utilities [1] [3]	0.32	0.96	1.75	1.85	1.46	1.23	1.28	1.30	1.24	1.22	1.43

NA Not available. [1] There are no direct fuel costs for hydroelectric, geothermal, wind, photovoltaic, or solar thermal energy. [2] There are no direct fuel costs for geothermal, photovoltaic, or solar thermal energy. [3] Net imports of electricity generated from nonrenewable energy sources are included in this total but not in any other columns.

Source: U.S. Energy Information Administration, *State Energy Price and Expenditure Report*, annual. See also <http://www.eia.doe.gov/emeu/states/sep_prices/total/pdf/pr_us.pdf> (accessed May 2003).

No. 890. Energy Expenditures—End-Use Sector and Selected Source by State: 2000

[In millions of dollars (703,188 represents $703,188,000,000). End-use sector and electric utilities exclude expenditures on energy sources such as hydroelectric, photovoltaic, solar thermal, wind, and geothermal. Also excludes expenditures for reported amounts of energy consumed by the energy industry for production, transportation, and processing operations]

State	Total [1]	End-use sector				Source			
		Residential	Commercial	Industrial	Transportation	Petroleum products	Natural gas	Coal	Electricity sales
U.S.	703,188	155,625	113,030	152,582	281,952	362,026	115,910	28,728	231,653
AL.........	12,094	2,739	1,574	2,863	4,919	5,787	1,550	1,291	4,592
AK.........	2,722	354	368	239	1,759	1,992	247	47	532
AZ.........	10,562	2,520	1,961	1,094	4,987	5,439	1,100	546	4,431
AR.........	7,326	1,571	784	1,939	3,032	3,809	1,254	383	2,349
CA.........	71,058	13,305	11,886	13,084	32,784	35,101	13,512	115	22,915
CO	8,690	1,894	1,472	1,189	4,135	4,820	1,458	361	2,508
CT.	8,275	2,631	1,699	1,012	2,933	4,314	997	83	2,852
DE.	2,072	494	311	454	811	1,121	294	74	682
DC	1,530	312	853	18	347	400	338	(Z)	798
FL.........	31,178	8,220	5,448	3,098	14,412	17,476	2,803	1,240	13,526
GA	19,782	4,876	3,047	3,412	8,447	9,827	2,479	1,269	7,368
HI	2,634	512	500	525	1,097	1,614	47	31	1,341
ID	3,158	599	427	674	1,457	1,838	324	16	953
IL	30,122	7,248	5,257	6,671	10,947	13,259	6,682	1,226	9,293
IN	17,033	3,321	1,898	4,830	6,984	8,426	3,067	1,889	5,022
IA	8,314	1,807	1,052	2,438	3,017	4,457	1,454	408	2,319
KS.........	7,392	1,607	1,149	1,983	2,653	3,941	1,359	359	2,242
KY.........	11,356	1,961	1,201	3,466	4,729	6,495	1,220	1,242	3,248
LA.........	20,726	2,680	1,856	8,999	7,191	11,753	4,986	327	5,117
ME	3,772	1,029	579	732	1,433	2,426	43	22	1,179
MD	11,796	3,134	2,356	1,437	4,869	5,940	1,731	405	4,089
MA	15,459	4,242	3,032	2,677	5,508	7,439	2,829	244	4,914
MI.........	22,704	5,194	3,988	4,462	9,061	11,283	3,975	1,049	7,400
MN	12,224	2,684	1,447	2,543	5,549	6,723	1,954	434	3,477
MS	7,462	1,628	990	1,545	3,299	4,091	1,148	225	2,606
MO	13,277	3,271	2,121	1,850	6,035	7,142	1,870	644	4,370
MT	2,852	429	310	901	1,213	1,481	366	279	717
NE.	4,323	886	679	861	1,897	2,376	668	123	1,292
NV.	4,834	932	631	907	2,364	2,567	951	253	1,692
NH	3,227	919	594	459	1,255	1,906	174	66	1,143
NJ.	21,639	4,902	4,247	3,307	9,183	11,403	3,565	161	6,599
NM	4,109	741	731	587	2,050	2,460	571	421	1,219
NY.........	42,563	12,818	12,854	5,321	11,571	17,030	9,695	487	16,167
NC	19,351	5,009	3,023	3,608	7,712	9,884	1,539	1,142	7,767
ND	2,077	388	263	615	810	1,187	189	430	509
OH	29,645	7,173	4,754	6,675	11,043	13,359	5,544	2,110	10,499
OK	9,337	1,990	1,272	1,916	4,159	4,788	2,344	384	2,897
OR	7,644	1,488	1,033	1,422	3,701	4,129	1,135	41	2,460
PA.	30,484	8,076	4,796	6,579	11,033	14,115	4,545	2,001	10,175
RI.	2,381	690	480	413	798	1,088	544	(Z)	743
SC.........	10,176	2,387	1,398	2,318	4,074	4,810	934	613	4,332
SD.........	1,952	429	264	336	923	1,233	198	54	524
TN.........	13,792	3,059	2,156	2,618	5,959	6,858	1,505	798	5,313
TX.........	74,045	11,356	8,257	29,809	24,623	43,536	15,373	1,902	20,328
UT.........	4,561	799	630	690	2,442	2,725	679	429	1,111
VT.........	1,629	501	287	186	655	996	57	(Z)	579
VA.........	16,791	4,237	2,813	2,305	7,437	9,041	1,867	715	5,722
WA	13,180	2,439	1,688	2,378	6,675	7,548	1,476	235	4,131
WV	4,434	947	584	1,063	1,841	2,305	595	1,207	1,395
WI.	13,059	2,962	1,795	3,269	5,032	6,878	2,415	537	3,691
WY	2,242	237	235	663	1,107	1,413	260	413	526

Z Less than $500,000.   [1] Includes sources not shown separately. Total expenditures are the sum of purchases for each source (including electricity sales) less electric utility purchases of fuel.

Source: U.S. Energy Information Administration, *State Energy Price and Expenditure Report, 2000*, series DOE/EIA-0376(00). See also <http://www.eia.doe.gov/emeu/states/sepfuel/html/pdf/fuelte.pdf> and <http://www.eia.doe.gov/emeu/states/sepprices/total/pdf/prall.pdf> (accessed May 2003).

No. 891. Residential Energy Consumption, Expenditures, and Average Price: 1980 to 2001

[9.32 represents 9,320,000,000,000,000 Btu. For period April to March for 1980; January to December for 1987 to 2001. Excludes Alaska and Hawaii in 1980. Covers occupied units only. Excludes household usage of gasoline for transportation and the use of wood or coal. Based on Residential Energy Consumption Survey; see source. Btu=British thermal unit; see text, this section]

Type of fuel	Unit	1980	1987	1990	1993	1997	2001
CONSUMPTION							
Total	Quad. Btu	9.32	9.13	9.22	10.01	10.25	9.86
Avg. per household	Mil. Btu	114	101	98	104	101	92
Natural gas	Quad. Btu . .	4.97	4.83	4.86	5.27	5.28	4.84
Electricity, site	Quad. Btu . .	2.48	2.76	3.03	3.28	3.54	3.89
Fuel oil, kerosene	Quad. Btu . .	1.52	1.22	1.04	1.07	1.07	0.76
Liquid petroleum gas	Quad. Btu . .	0.35	0.32	0.28	0.38	0.36	0.38
EXPENDITURES							
Total	Bil. dol.	75.61	97.75	110.18	123.91	135.79	159.74
Avg. per household	Dollars	926	1,080	1,172	1,282	1,338	1,493
Natural gas	Bil. dol.	19.77	26.15	27.26	32.04	35.81	46.98
Electricity	Bil. dol.	40.81	61.58	71.54	81.08	88.33	100.34
Fuel oil, kerosene	Bil. dol.	12.24	7.21	8.25	6.98	7.61	6.83
Liquid petroleum gas	Bil. dol.	2.80	2.81	3.14	3.81	4.04	5.60
AVERAGE PRICE							
Total	Dol./mil. Btu.	8.12	10.71	11.95	12.38	13.25	16.19
Natural gas	Dol./mil. Btu .	3.98	5.41	5.61	6.07	6.78	9.70
Electricity	Dol./mil. Btu .	16.46	22.34	23.60	24.69	24.97	25.80
Fuel oil, kerosene	Dol./mil. Btu .	8.03	5.89	7.92	6.53	7.13	9.05
Liquid petroleum gas	Dol./mil. Btu .	8.00	8.91	11.18	10.04	11.23	14.87

NA Not available.

Source: U.S. Energy Information Administration, *Residential Energy Consumption Survey: Household Energy Consumption and Expenditures*, 1980, 1987, 1990, 1993, 1997, and 2001. See also <http://www.eia.gov/emeu/recs/recs2001/detailcetbls .html#total>.

No. 892. Residential Energy Consumption and Expenditures, by Type of Fuel and Selected Household Characteristic: 2001

[For period January through December. Quad.=quadrillion. (9.86 represents 9,860,000,000,000,000 Btu). See headnote, Table 891]

Characteristic	Consumption (Btu's)					Expenditures				
	Total [1] (quad.)	Avg. per house-hold [1] [2] (mil.)	Natural gas (quad.)	Electric-ity (quad.)	Fuel oil [3] (quad.)	Total [1] (bil. dol.)	Avg. per house-hold [1] [2] (dol.)	Natural gas (bil. dol.)	Electric-ity (bil. dol.)	Fuel oil [3] (bil. dol.)
Total households . .	9.86	92.2	4.84	3.89	0.71	159.74	1,493	46.98	100.34	6.83
Single family	7.91	107.3	3.98	3.01	0.59	125.02	1,697	38.04	76.69	5.32
Two-to-four unit building . . .	0.74	78.1	0.45	0.23	0.06	11.97	1,261	4.70	6.68	0.54
Five-or-more unit building . .	0.70	41.0	0.28	0.36	0.05	13.66	803	2.98	10.29	0.37
Mobile home	0.52	75.9	0.14	0.29	0.01	9.09	1,336	1.26	6.68	0.08
Year house built:										
1949 or earlier	2.92	109.8	1.68	0.76	0.34	42.18	1,586	16.47	20.65	3.04
1950 to 1959	1.39	97.9	0.75	0.46	0.14	21.25	1,500	7.15	12.34	1.29
1960 to 1969	1.19	86.5	0.61	0.45	0.09	19.48	1,414	6.00	12.09	0.77
1970 to 1979	1.48	79.0	0.57	0.77	0.07	26.03	1,388	5.28	18.99	0.61
1980 to 1989	1.45	79.7	0.57	0.78	0.04	26.22	1,438	5.53	19.37	0.40
1990 to 2001 [4]	1.43	92.5	0.66	0.68	0.02	24.59	1,591	6.54	16.90	0.21
2001 family income:										
Less than $10,000	0.72	65.2	0.38	0.27	0.04	11.47	1,039	3.75	6.93	0.32
$10,000 to $29,999	2.42	79.1	1.19	0.93	0.16	38.49	1,260	11.56	23.57	1.45
$30,000 to $49,999	2.43	89.8	1.15	0.97	0.19	39.46	1,456	11.10	24.97	1.70
$50,000 or more	4.30	112.1	2.13	1.72	0.31	70.32	1,836	20.57	44.87	2.84

B Base figure too small to meet statistical standards for reliability of a derived figure.   [1] Includes liquid petroleum gas, not shown separately.   [2] The averages are over the set of all households; otherwise the averages are over the set of households using a given fuel end use.   [3] Includes kerosene.   [4] New construction for 2001 includes only those housing units built and occupied between January and the April-August period when the household interviews were conducted.

Source: U.S. Energy Information Administration, *Residential Energy Consumption Survey: Household Energy Consumption and Expenditures*, 2001. Also see <http://www.eia.doe.gov/emeu/recs/contents.html>.

No. 893. Commercial Buildings—Energy Consumption and Expenditures: 1999

[4,657 represents 4,657,000. Covers buildings using one or more major fuel. Excludes industrial buildings, predominantly residential buildings, and buildings of less than 1,000 sq. ft. Based on a sample survey of building representatives and energy suppliers; therefore, subject to sampling variability. For characteristics of commercial buildings, see table 970 in Section 20. For composition of regions, see inside front cover]

Building characteristic	All buildings using any major fuel — Number (1,000)	All buildings using any major fuel — Square feet (mil.)	Consumption (tril. Btu) — Major fuel, total [1]	Consumption (tril. Btu) — Electricity	Consumption (tril. Btu) — Natural gas	Expenditures (mil. dol.) — Major fuel, total [1]	Expenditures (mil. dol.) — Electricity	Expenditures (mil. dol.) — Natural gas
All buildings	4,657	67,338	5,733	3,098	2,023	81,552	66,424	10,609
Region:								
Northeast	686	12,360	1,116	543	299	18,996	15,133	1,895
Midwest	1,188	16,761	1,509	662	709	17,258	12,933	3,277
South	1,762	23,485	1,961	1,247	618	27,303	23,275	3,294
West	1,021	14,731	1,147	645	396	17,995	15,083	2,144
Year constructed:								
1919 or before	419	4,034	275	91	120	3,271	2,170	684
1920 to 1945	499	6,445	461	184	195	5,797	4,174	968
1946 to 1959	763	9,127	674	310	256	9,216	6,989	1,390
1960 to 1969	665	10,866	975	468	372	13,237	10,250	1,986
1970 to 1979	774	11,840	1,044	621	326	15,858	13,461	1,726
1980 to 1989	846	13,931	1,214	755	391	18,342	15,777	2,033
1990 to 1999	690	11,094	1,090	669	364	15,832	13,604	1,820
Principal activity within building:								
Education	327	8,651	649	257	227	8,018	5,820	1,111
Food sales	174	994	201	165	31	3,587	3,359	195
Food service	349	1,851	447	216	216	6,380	5,082	1,185
Health care	127	2,918	515	232	217	5,653	4,268	881
Inpatient	11	1,865	427	172	195	4,151	2,948	757
Outpatient	116	1,053	88	60	22	1,503	1,320	124
Lodging	153	4,521	450	196	181	5,716	4,266	943
Mercantile	667	10,398	724	521	186	13,085	11,851	1,126
Retail (other than mall)	534	4,766	344	221	110	5,922	5,166	670
Enclosed and strip malls	133	5,631	380	301	76	7,164	6,685	456
Office	739	12,044	1,089	767	219	17,775	15,683	1,215
Public assembly	305	4,393	359	191	96	5,096	3,983	560
Public order and safety	72	1,168	102	40	33	1,222	805	176
Religious worship	307	3,405	110	42	62	1,494	1,041	409
Service	478	3,388	421	138	260	4,639	3,108	1,371
Warehouse and storage	603	10,477	461	220	230	6,029	4,829	1,124
Other	102	1,222	176	101	45	2,498	2,063	224
Vacant	253	1,908	31	10	19	361	265	89
Square footage:								
1,001 to 5,000	2,348	6,774	772	415	312	12,355	10,262	1,802
5,001 to 10,000	1,110	8,238	608	283	292	9,228	7,146	1,810
10,001 to 25,000	708	11,153	743	370	319	10,873	8,663	1,813
25,001 to 50,000	257	9,311	692	371	234	10,090	8,188	1,274
50,001 to 100,000	145	10,112	865	494	250	12,057	10,023	1,253
100,001 to 200,000	59	8,271	772	451	230	10,344	8,555	1,104
200,001 to 500,000	23	6,851	660	340	237	8,015	6,432	958
500,001 and over	7	6,628	621	373	149	8,592	7,155	594

[1] Includes fuel oil, propane, and purchased steam not shown separately.

Source: U.S. Energy Information Administration, *Commercial Buildings Energy Survey: Consumption and Expenditures, 1999.* See also <http://www.eia.doe.gov/emeu/cbecs/pdf/alltables.pdf> (accessed May 2003).

No. 894. Fossil Fuel Prices in Current and Constant (1996) Dollars by Type of Fuel: 1980 to 2002

[In cents per million British thermal units (Btu), except as indicated. All fuel prices taken as close to the point of production as possible. See text, this section, for explanation of Btu conversions from mineral fuels]

Fuel	1980	1985	1990	1995	1996	1997	1998	1999	2000	2001	2002 [1]
CURRENT DOLLARS											
Composite [2]	2.04	2.51	1.84	1.47	1.82	1.81	1.41	1.65	2.61	2.56	2.22
Crude oil [3]	3.72	4.15	3.45	2.52	3.18	2.97	1.87	2.68	4.61	3.77	3.88
Natural gas [4]	1.45	2.26	1.55	1.40	1.96	2.10	1.77	1.98	3.33	3.64	2.67
Bituminous coal [5]	1.10	1.15	1.00	0.88	0.87	0.85	0.83	0.79	0.80	0.85	0.86
CONSTANT (1996) DOLLARS											
Composite [2]	3.58	3.41	2.13	1.50	1.82	1.77	1.37	1.58	2.44	2.34	2.00
Crude oil [3]	6.53	5.64	3.99	2.57	3.18	2.91	1.82	2.56	4.31	3.44	3.51
Natural gas [4]	2.54	3.06	1.79	1.43	1.96	2.06	1.71	1.89	3.12	3.33	2.41
Bituminous coal [5]	1.93	1.56	1.15	0.90	0.87	0.84	0.80	0.75	0.75	0.78	0.78

[1] Preliminary. [2] Derived by multiplying the price per Btu of each fossil fuel by the total Btu content of the production of each fossil fuel and dividing this accumulated value of total fossil fuel production by the accumulated Btu content of total fossil fuel production. [3] Domestic first purchase prices. [4] Wellhead prices. [5] Includes bituminous coal, subbituminous coal, and lignite.

Source: U.S. Energy Information Administration, *Annual Energy Review.* See also <http://www.eia.doe.gov/emeu/aer/finan.html>.

No. 895. Energy Imports and Exports by Type of Fuel: 1980 to 2002

[In quadrillion of Btu. (12.10 represents 12,100,000,000,000,000 Btu). For definition of Btu, see text, this section]

Type of fuel	1980	1985	1990	1995	1996	1997	1998	1999	2000	2001	2002[1]
Net imports, total [2]	12.10	7.58	14.06	17.75	19.07	20.70	22.28	23.54	24.97	26.39	25.38
Coal	-2.39	-2.39	-2.70	-2.08	-2.17	-2.01	-1.87	-1.30	-1.21	-0.77	-0.61
Natural gas (dry)	0.96	0.90	1.46	2.74	2.85	2.90	3.06	3.50	3.62	3.69	3.58
Petroleum [3]	13.50	8.95	15.29	16.89	18.23	19.64	20.94	21.18	22.38	23.36	22.28
Other [4]	0.04	0.13	0.01	0.19	0.16	0.16	0.16	0.16	0.18	0.11	0.14
Imports, total	15.80	11.78	18.82	22.26	23.70	25.22	26.58	27.25	28.97	30.15	29.04
Coal	0.03	0.05	0.07	0.24	0.20	0.19	0.22	0.23	0.31	0.49	0.42
Natural gas (dry)	1.01	0.95	1.55	2.90	3.00	3.06	3.22	3.66	3.87	4.07	4.10
Petroleum [3]	14.66	10.61	17.12	18.88	20.29	21.74	22.91	23.13	24.53	25.40	24.31
Other [4]	0.10	0.17	0.08	0.24	0.21	0.22	0.23	0.23	0.26	0.19	0.20
Exports, total	3.69	4.20	4.75	4.51	4.63	4.51	4.30	3.71	4.01	3.76	3.65
Coal	2.42	2.44	2.77	2.32	2.37	2.19	2.09	1.53	1.53	1.27	1.03
Natural gas (dry)	0.05	0.06	0.09	0.16	0.16	0.16	0.16	0.16	0.25	0.38	0.52
Petroleum [3]	1.16	1.66	1.82	1.99	2.06	2.10	1.97	1.95	2.15	2.04	2.04
Other [4]	0.07	0.04	0.07	0.05	0.05	0.05	0.06	0.07	0.07	0.08	0.06

[1] Preliminary.　[2] Net imports equals imports minus exports.　Minus sign (-) denotes an excess of exports over imports. [3] Includes imports into the Strategic Petroleum Reserve, which began in 1977.　[4] Coal coke and small amounts of electricity transmitted across U.S. borders with Canada and Mexico.

Source: U.S. Energy Information Administration, *Annual Energy Review.* See also <http://www.eia.doe.gov/emeu/aer/pdf/pages/sec111.pdf> (released October 2003).

No. 896. U.S. Foreign Trade in Selected Mineral Fuels: 1980 to 2002

[985 represents 985,000,000,000 cu. ft. Minus sign (-) indicates an excess of imports over exports]

Mineral fuel	Unit	1980	1985	1990	1995	1998	1999	2000	2001	2002[1]
Natural gas:										
Imports [2]	Bil. cu. ft.	985	950	1,532	2,841	3,152	3,586	3,782	3,977	4,008
Exports	Bil. cu. ft.	49	55	86	154	159	163	244	373	516
Net trade	Bil. cu. ft.	-936	-894	-1,447	-2,687	-2,993	-3,422	-3,538	-3,604	-3,491
Crude oil:										
Imports [3]	Mil. bbl.	1,926	1,168	2,151	2,639	3,178	3,187	3,320	3,405	3,302
Exports	Mil. bbl.	105	75	40	35	40	43	18	7	3
Net trade	Mil. bbl.	-1,821	-1,094	-2,112	-2,604	-3,137	-3,144	-3,301	-3,398	-3,299
Petroleum products:										
Imports	Mil. bbl.	603	681	775	586	731	774	874	928	843
Exports	Mil. bbl.	94	211	273	312	305	300	362	347	354
Net trade	Mil. bbl.	-508	-471	-502	-274	-426	-474	-512	-581	-489
Coal:										
Imports	Mil. sh. tons	1.2	2.0	2.7	9.5	8.7	9.1	12.5	19.8	16.9
Exports	Mil. sh. tons	91.7	92.7	105.8	88.5	78.0	58.5	58.5	48.7	39.6
Net trade	Mil. sh. tons	90.5	90.7	103.1	79.1	69.3	49.4	46.0	28.9	22.7

[1] Preliminary.　[2] Includes strategic petroleum reserve imports.

Source: U.S. Energy Information Administration, *Annual Energy Review.* See also <http://www.eia.doe.gov/emeu/aer/contents.html> (issued October 2003).

No. 897. Crude Oil Imports Into the U.S. by Country of Origin: 1980 to 2003

[In millions of barrels (1,921 represents 1,921,000,000). Barrels contain 42 gallons. Total OPEC excludes, and Non-OPEC, includes, petroleum imported into the United States indirectly from members of OPEC, primarily from Caribbean and West European areas, as petroleum products that were refined from crude oil produced by OPEC]

Country of origin	1980	1985	1990	1995	1997	1998	1999	2000	2001	2002	2003
Total imports	1,921	1,168	2,151	2,639	3,002	3,178	3,187	3,311	3,405	3,336	3,521
OPEC, [1] [2] [3] total	1,410	479	1,283	1,219	1,378	1,522	1,543	1,659	1,770	1,490	1,671
Algeria	166	31	23	10	2	4	9	(Z)	4	11	41
Iraq	10	17	188	-	32	123	265	226	290	168	171
Kuwait [4]	10	1	29	78	92	110	90	96	87	79	75
Saudi Arabia [4]	456	48	436	460	472	512	506	556	588	554	629
United Arab Emirates	63	13	3	2	-	1	-	1	8	4	4
Indonesia	115	107	36	23	19	18	26	13	15	18	10
Nigeria	307	102	286	227	251	251	227	319	307	215	306
Venezuela	57	112	243	420	509	503	420	446	471	438	436
Non-OPEC, total	511	689	869	1,419	1,624	1,656	1,643	1,652	1,635	1,846	1,850
Angola	(NA)	(NA)	86	131	155	170	130	108	117	117	132
Canada	73	171	235	380	437	462	430	492	495	527	565
Colombia [2]	(NA)	(NA)	51	76	99	127	165	116	95	86	59
Ecuador [2]	6	20	(NA)	35	42	36	42	46	41	37	50
Gabon [3]	9	19	(NA)	84	84	76	61	52	51	52	48
Mexico	185	261	251	375	496	482	458	479	509	548	580
Norway	53	11	35	94	105	81	96	110	103	-	60
Russia	(NA)	(NA)	(Z)	5	1	3	8	3	-	31	54
United Kingdom	63	101	57	124	62	59	104	106	89	148	127

- Represents zero.　NA Not available.　Z Less than 500,000 barrels.　[1] OPEC (Organization of Petroleum Exporting Countries) includes the Persian Gulf nations shown below, except Bahrain, which is not a member of OPEC, and also includes nations not shown.　[2] Ecuador withdrew from OPEC on Dec. 31, 1992; therefore, it is included under OPEC for the period 1973 to 1992.　[3] Gabon withdrew from OPEC on Dec. 31, 1994; therefore, it is included under OPEC for the period 1973 to 1994.　[4] Imports from the Neutral Zone between Kuwait and Saudi Arabia are included in Saudi Arabia.

Source: U.S. Energy Information Administration, *Petroleum Supply Monthly,* See also <http://www.eia.doe.gov/pub/oilgas/petroleum/datapublications/petroleumsupplymonthly/current/pdf/table40.pdf>.

No. 898. Crude Oil and Refined Products—Summary: 1980 to 2003

[13,481 represents 13,481,000 bbl. Barrels (bbl.) of 42 gallons. Data are averages]

Year	Crude oil (1,000 bbl. per day)					Refined oil products (1,000 bbl. per day)			Total oil imports[2] (1,000 bbl. per day)	Crude oil stocks[3] (mil. bbl.)	
	Input to refineries	Domestic production	Imports Total[1]	Imports Strategic reserve	Exports	Domestic demand	Imports	Exports		Total	Strategic reserve[4]
1980	13,481	8,597	5,263	44	287	17,056	1,646	258	6,909	[5]466	108
1985	12,002	8,971	3,201	118	204	15,726	1,866	577	5,067	814	493
1990	13,409	7,355	5,894	27	109	16,988	2,123	748	8,018	908	586
1993	13,613	6,847	6,787	15	98	17,237	1,833	904	8,620	922	587
1994	13,866	6,662	7,063	12	99	17,718	1,933	843	8,996	929	592
1995	13,973	6,560	7,230	-	95	17,725	1,605	855	8,835	895	592
1996	14,195	6,465	7,508	-	110	18,309	1,971	871	9,478	850	566
1997	14,662	6,452	8,225	-	108	18,620	1,936	896	10,162	868	563
1998	14,889	6,252	8,706	-	110	18,917	2,002	835	10,708	895	571
1999	14,804	5,881	8,731	8	118	19,519	2,122	822	10,852	852	567
2000	15,067	5,822	9,071	8	50	19,701	2,389	990	11,459	826	541
2001	15,128	5,801	9,328	11	20	19,649	2,543	951	11,871	862	550
2002	14,947	5,746	9,140	16	9	19,761	2,390	975	11,530	877	599
2003	15,303	5,737	9,646		12	20,044	2,608	1,005	12,254	906	638

- Represents zero. [1] Includes Strategic Petroleum Reserve. [2] Crude oil (including Strategic Petroleum Reserve imports) plus refined products. [3] End of year. [4] Crude oil stocks in the Strategic Petroleum Reserve include non-U.S. stocks held under foreign or commercial storage agreements. [5] Stocks of Alaskan crude oil in transit are included from January 1985 forward.

Source: U.S. Energy Information Administration, *Monthly Energy Review*, March 2004 issue.

No. 899. Petroleum and Coal Products Corporations—Sales, Net Profit, and Profit Per Dollar of Sales: 1990 to 2003

[318.5 represents $318,500,000,000. Represents SIC group 29 (NAICS group 324). Through 2000 based on Standard Industrial Classification code; beginning 2001 based on North American Industry Classification System, 1997 (NAICS). Profit rates are averages of quarterly figures at annual rates. Beginning 1990, excludes estimates for corporations with less than $250,000 in assets]

Item	Unit	1990	1994	1995	1996	1997	1998	1999	2000	2001	2002	2003
Sales	Bil. dol..	318.5	268.2	283.1	323.5	320.0	250.4	277.0	455.2	472.5	474.9	590.8
Net profit:												
Before income taxes	Bil. dol..	23.1	17.2	16.5	32.6	36.8	9.7	20.3	55.5	47.2	22.4	51.4
After income taxes	Bil. dol..	17.8	14.9	13.9	26.6	29.4	8.3	17.2	42.6	35.8	19.5	42.5
Depreciation[1]	Bil. dol..	18.7	17.1	16.7	15.9	15.6	14.7	13.5	15.5	17.2	17.8	20.0
Profits per dollar of sales:												
Before income taxes	Cents ..	7.3	6.3	5.8	10.1	11.5	3.5	7.1	12.2	9.7	4.6	8.5
After income taxes	Cents ..	5.6	5.5	4.9	8.2	9.2	3.1	6.0	9.4	7.4	4.2	7.2
Profits on stockholders' equity:												
Before income taxes	Percent .	16.4	13.2	12.6	23.2	23.5	6.0	13.0	29.4	21.8	9.7	20.6
After income taxes	Percent .	12.7	11.4	10.6	18.9	18.9	5.2	11.0	22.6	16.5	8.4	1.7

[1] Includes depletion and accelerated amortization of emergency facilities.

Source: U.S. Census Bureau, *Quarterly Financial Report for Manufacturing, Mining and Trade Corporations*.

No. 900. Major Petroleum Companies—Financial Summary: 1980 to 2003

[32.9 represents $32,900,000,000. Data represent a composite of approximately 42 major worldwide petroleum companies aggregated on a consolidated total company basis]

Item	1980	1985	1990	1995	1998	1999	2000	2001	2002	2003
FINANCIAL DATA (bil. dol.)										
Net income	32.9	19.4	26.8	24.3	14.5	35.3	76.4	62.0	44.3	85.5
Depreciation, depletion, etc	32.5	53.0	38.7	43.1	61.0	45.0	53.3	63.4	61.2	68.0
Cash flow[1]	65.4	72.4	65.5	67.4	75.5	75.3	129.7	140.0	118.0	157.7
Dividends paid	9.3	12.0	15.9	17.6	20.9	21.7	23.0	29.7	27.3	27.5
Net internal funds available for investment or debt repayment[2]	56.1	60.4	49.6	49.8	54.6	54.1	106.7	110.4	90.7	130.3
Capital and exploratory expenditures	62.1	58.3	59.6	59.8	83.9	67.7	72.8	99.9	88.7	90.7
Long-term capitalization	211.4	272.1	300.0	304.3	382.0	456.2	516.9	543.8	548.1	606.1
Long-term debt	49.8	93.5	90.4	85.4	103.9	105.4	112.8	143.2	153.5	142.1
Preferred stock	2.0	3.3	5.2	5.7	3.9	4.8	5.4	6.7	2.5	2.2
Common stock and retained earnings[3]	159.6	175.3	204.4	213.2	274.2	346.0	398.7	393.9	392.1	461.8
Excess of expenditures over cash income[4]	6.0	-2.1	10.0	10.0	29.3	13.6	-33.9	-10.5	-2.0	-39.5
RATIOS[5] (percent)										
Long-term debt to long-term capitalization	23.6	34.4	30.1	28.1	27.2	23.1	21.8	26.7	28.3	26.5
Net income to total average capital	17.0	7.0	9.1	8.1	3.8	8.9	15.7	12.3	8.7	15.2
Net income to average common equity	22.5	10.8	13.5	11.6	5.2	12.4	20.5	16.3	11.5	20.1

[1] Generally represents internally-generated funds from operations. Sum of net income and noncash charges such as depreciation, depletion, and amortization. [2] Cash flow minus dividends paid. [3] Includes common stock, capital surplus, and earned surplus accounts after adjustments. [4] Capital and exploratory expenditures plus dividends paid minus cash flow. [5] Represents approximate year-to-year comparisons because of changes in the makeup of the group due to mergers and other corporate changes.

Source: Carl H. Pforzheimer & Co., New York, NY, *Comparative Oil Company Statements*, annual.

[2,826.6 represents 2,826,600,000,000 kWh. Net generation for calendar years; capacity as of December 31]

Item	Unit	1990	1995	1999	2000	2001	2002
ELECTRIC POWER INDUSTRY, ALL SECTORS							
Consumption, total	Bil. kWh	2,826.6	3,157.3	3,494.6	3,604.7	3,553.8	3,660.0
Net generation, total	Bil. kWh	3,038.0	3,353.5	3,694.8	3,802.1	3,736.6	3,838.6
Electric power sector	Bil. kWh	2,901.3	3,194.2	3,530.0	3,637.5	3,580.1	3,675.4
Commercial sector	Bil. kWh	5.8	8.2	8.6	7.9	7.4	8.7
Industrial sector	Bil. kWh	130.8	151.0	156.3	156.7	149.2	154.4
Electricity imports	Bil. kWh	18.4	42.9	43.2	48.9	38.5	36.2
Electricity exports	Bil. kWh	16.1	3.6	14.2	14.8	16.5	13.4
Electricity losses and unaccounted for	Bil. kWh	213.7	235.4	229.2	231.5	204.9	201.4
Retail sales of electricity	Bil. kWh	2,712.6	3,013.3	3,312.1	3,421.4	3,369.8	3,475.2
Direct use of electricity	Bil. kWh	114.0	144.1	182.5	183.3	184.0	184.8
Electricity retail prices per kWh:							
All sectors, current dollars	Cents	6.57	6.89	6.64	6.81	7.32	7.19
All sectors, real (1996) dollars	Cents	7.59	7.02	6.34	6.37	6.69	6.50
Residential, current dollars	Cents	7.83	8.40	8.16	8.24	8.62	8.45
Residential, real (1996) dollars	Cents	9.05	8.56	7.79	7.71	7.88	7.64
Commercial, current dollars	Cents	7.34	7.69	7.26	7.43	7.93	7.89
Commercial, real (1996) dollars	Cents	8.48	7.84	6.93	6.95	7.25	7.13
Industrial, current dollars	Cents	4.74	4.66	4.43	4.64	5.04	4.83
Industrial, real (1996) dollars	Cents	5.48	4.75	4.23	4.34	4.61	4.36
Other users, current dollars	Cents	6.40	6.88	6.35	6.56	7.03	6.78
Other users, real (1996) dollars	Cents	7.40	7.01	6.07	6.14	6.42	6.13
Net generation, total [1]	Bil. kWh	3,038.0	3,353.5	3,694.8	3,802.1	3,736.6	3,838.6
Coal	Bil. kWh	1,594.0	1,709.4	1,881.1	1,966.3	1,904.0	1,926.4
Petroleum	Bil. kWh	126.6	74.6	118.1	111.2	124.9	89.9
Natural gas	Bil. kWh	372.8	496.1	556.4	601.0	639.1	685.8
Nuclear	Bil. kWh	576.9	673.4	728.3	753.9	768.8	780.1
Hydroelectric pumped storage plants	Bil. kWh	-3.5	-2.7	-6.1	-5.5	-8.8	-8.8
Conventional hydroelectric power plants	Bil. kWh	292.9	310.8	319.5	275.6	217.0	263.6
Geothermal	Bil. kWh	15.4	13.4	14.8	14.1	13.7	13.4
Wood	Bil. kWh	32.5	36.5	37.0	37.6	35.2	36.5
Waste	Bil. kWh	13.3	20.4	22.6	23.1	21.8	22.9
Wind	Bil. kWh	2.8	3.2	4.5	5.6	6.7	10.5
Solar	Bil. kWh	0.4	0.5	0.5	0.5	0.5	0.5
Net summer capacity, total [1]	Mil. kW	734.1	769.5	785.9	812.7	848.3	902.7
Coal-fired plants	Mil. kW	307.4	311.4	315.5	316.0	314.2	313.8
Petroleum-fired plants	Mil. kW	49.0	43.7	35.6	36.0	39.7	40.1
Natural gas-fired plants	Mil. kW	56.2	75.4	73.6	95.7	125.8	171.1
Dual-fired plants	Mil. kW	113.6	122.0	146.0	149.8	153.5	161.7
Nuclear electric power plants	Mil. kW	99.6	99.5	97.4	97.9	98.2	98.6
Hydroelectric pumped storage plants	Mil. kW	19.5	21.4	19.6	19.5	19.1	19.1
Conventional hydroelectric power plants	Mil. kW	73.9	78.6	79.4	79.4	79.5	79.8
Geothermal energy plants	Mil. kW	2.7	3.0	2.8	2.8	2.2	2.2
Wood energy plants	Mil. kW	5.5	6.7	6.8	6.1	5.9	5.9
Waste energy plants	Mil. kW	2.5	3.5	3.7	3.9	3.8	3.8
Wind energy plants	Mil. kW	1.8	1.7	2.3	2.4	3.9	4.0
Solar energy plants	Mil. kW	0.3	0.3	0.4	0.4	0.4	0.4
Fuel consumption:							
Coal	Mil. sh. tons	792.5	860.6	949.8	994.9	972.7	985.4
Distillate fuel and kerosene	Mil. bbl	18.1	19.6	26.0	31.7	31.1	19.8
Residual fuel	Mil. bbl	190.8	95.5	158.2	143.4	165.3	110.5
Petroleum coke	Mil. sh. tons	1.9	3.4	4.6	3.7	3.9	5.0
Natural gas	Bil. cu. ft.	3,691.6	4,737.9	5,322.0	5,691.5	5,832.3	6,065.0
ELECTRIC POWER SECTOR, ELECTRICITY-ONLY PLANTS							
Net generation, total [1]	Bil. kWh	2,840.0	3,052.8	3,374.6	3,472.9	3,410.5	3,483.7
Coal	Bil. kWh	1,560.2	1,658.0	1,832.1	1,910.6	1,851.8	1,873.3
Petroleum	Bil. kWh	117.6	62.0	104.8	98.0	113.2	78.6
Natural gas	Bil. kWh	264.7	317.4	356.6	399.4	427.0	452.6
Nuclear	Bil. kWh	576.9	673.4	728.3	753.9	768.8	780.1
Hydroelectric pumped storage plants	Bil. kWh	-3.5	-2.7	-6.1	-5.5	-8.8	-8.8
Conventional hydroelectric power plants	Bil. kWh	289.8	305.4	314.7	271.3	213.7	259.5
Net summer capacity, total [1]	Mil. kW	698.6	719.1	730.0	755.2	791.4	841.3
Coal-fired plants	Mil. kW	299.9	301.3	305.5	305.8	305.2	304.8
Petroleum-fired plants	Mil. kW	47.8	42.4	34.2	34.5	38.1	38.5
Natural Gas-fired plants	Mil. kW	44.1	55.5	49.8	67.6	93.5	134.3
Dual-fired plants	Mil. kW	106.4	112.1	135.2	141.8	148.3	156.4
Nuclear electric power plants	Mil. kW	99.6	99.5	97.4	97.9	98.2	98.6
Hydroelectric Pumped Storage plants	Mil. kW	19.5	21.4	19.6	19.5	19.1	19.1
Conventional Hydroelectric Power plants	Mil. kW	73.3	77.4	78.3	78.2	78.4	78.8
COMBINED-HEAT-AND-POWER PLANTS							
Net generation, total [1]	Bil. kWh	61.3	141.5	155.4	164.6	169.5	191.7
Coal	Bil. kWh	11.9	28.1	26.6	32.5	31.0	31.4
Petroleum	Bil. kWh	1.3	6.1	6.7	7.2	6.0	6.0
Natural gas	Bil. kWh	44.8	101.7	116.4	118.6	128.0	147.9
Net summer capacity, total [1]	Mil. kW	11.2	22.7	26.5	27.9	27.4	30.7
Coal-fired plants	Mil. kW	2.4	4.8	5.2	5.2	4.6	4.6
Petroleum-fired plants	Mil. kW	0.1	0.3	0.2	0.4	0.4	0.4
Natural Gas-fired plants	Mil. kW	3.9	10.0	11.8	15.1	17.5	20.9
Dual-fired plants	Mil. kW	4.4	7.0	8.4	6.1	3.7	3.7

[1] Includes types not shown separately.

Source: U.S. Energy Information Administration, *Annual Energy Review.* See also <http://www.eia.doe.gov/emeu/aer/elect.html>

No. 902. Electric Power Industry—Net Generation and Net Summer Capacity by State: 1995 to 2002

[Capacity as of Dec. 31. (3,353.5 represents 3,353,500,000,000) Covers utilities for public use]

State	Net generation (bil. kWh)					Net summer capacity (mil. kW)			
	1995	2000	2001	2002 Total	2002 Percent from coal	1995	2000	2001	2002
United States	3,353.5	3,802.1	3,736.6	3,858.5	50.1	767.8	809.4	846.6	905.3
Alabama	105.2	124.4	125.3	132.9	54.2	21.3	23.5	23.8	26.6
Alaska	6.0	6.2	6.7	6.8	8.5	2.0	2.1	2.1	2.0
Arizona	69.8	88.9	89.9	94.1	40.6	15.4	15.3	16.7	19.4
Arkansas	42.0	43.9	47.2	47.6	48.5	10.1	9.7	10.1	11.3
California	181.5	208.1	198.6	184.2	1.3	53.3	51.9	54.2	56.7
Colorado	35.6	44.2	46.9	45.6	77.6	7.3	8.4	8.9	9.4
Connecticut	31.5	33.0	30.5	31.3	10.3	7.4	6.4	7.9	7.4
Delaware	9.0	6.0	6.8	6.0	57.7	2.4	2.1	2.7	3.4
District of Columbia	0.2	0.1	0.1	0.3	-	0.8	0.8	0.8	0.8
Florida	167.4	191.8	190.9	203.4	32.4	39.7	41.5	42.8	47.1
Georgia	107.9	123.9	118.3	126.5	62.3	23.7	27.8	29.5	34.6
Hawaii	10.3	10.6	10.6	11.7	13.3	2.4	2.4	2.3	2.3
Idaho	11.8	11.9	9.3	9.8	0.9	3.0	3.0	3.2	3.3
Illinois	148.7	178.5	179.2	188.1	46.1	33.8	36.3	40.0	44.7
Indiana	109.2	127.8	122.6	125.6	93.7	21.0	23.3	23.6	25.3
Iowa	34.8	41.5	40.7	42.5	83.2	8.6	9.1	9.2	9.3
Kansas	38.4	44.8	44.7	47.2	75.0	9.7	10.1	10.4	10.4
Kentucky	86.2	93.0	95.4	92.1	90.4	15.4	16.8	17.6	19.1
Louisiana	84.6	92.9	87.9	95.0	23.2	19.7	21.0	21.7	25.6
Maine	9.8	14.0	19.6	22.5	2.7	3.8	4.2	4.2	4.3
Maryland	46.4	51.1	49.1	48.3	59.5	11.3	10.4	11.8	11.9
Massachusetts	37.7	38.7	38.5	42.0	27.4	11.0	12.4	11.8	12.2
Michigan	107.4	104.2	111.8	117.9	56.6	24.9	25.8	26.9	29.3
Minnesota	45.2	51.4	48.5	52.8	64.3	9.6	10.3	11.1	11.3
Mississippi	29.0	37.6	53.4	42.9	34.6	7.5	9.0	11.1	13.7
Missouri	65.7	76.6	79.5	81.2	83.1	15.8	17.3	18.9	19.8
Montana	26.0	26.5	24.2	25.5	60.2	5.1	5.2	5.1	5.2
Nebraska	25.3	29.1	30.5	31.6	63.1	5.5	6.0	6.0	6.1
Nevada	24.0	35.5	33.9	32.1	51.1	6.3	6.7	6.9	6.9
New Hampshire	15.4	15.0	15.1	16.0	23.3	2.8	2.9	2.8	3.4
New Jersey	45.1	58.1	59.4	61.6	15.6	16.9	16.5	16.1	18.4
New Mexico	29.8	34.0	33.6	30.7	87.7	5.3	5.6	5.9	5.9
New York	133.4	138.1	143.9	139.6	16.6	37.5	35.6	35.7	36.0
North Carolina	106.3	122.3	117.5	124.5	60.4	22.4	24.5	26.1	26.7
North Dakota	29.0	31.3	30.3	31.3	94.6	4.5	4.7	4.7	4.7
Ohio	139.3	149.1	142.3	147.1	90.4	27.6	28.4	29.5	31.5
Oklahoma	52.7	55.6	55.2	59.2	60.8	13.6	14.1	14.9	16.2
Oregon	45.3	51.8	45.1	47.1	8.0	10.8	11.3	11.8	12.5
Pennsylvania	185.5	201.7	196.6	204.3	55.7	36.2	36.7	37.6	39.8
Rhode Island	4.5	6.0	7.5	7.1	-	1.0	1.2	1.2	1.7
South Carolina	80.9	93.3	89.2	96.6	38.3	17.1	18.7	19.4	20.4
South Dakota	8.8	9.7	7.4	7.7	42.4	2.9	2.8	2.8	2.9
Tennessee	85.7	95.8	96.2	96.1	62.1	16.8	19.5	20.2	20.7
Texas	317.6	377.7	372.6	385.6	36.8	72.5	81.7	87.8	94.5
Utah	32.8	36.6	35.9	36.6	94.2	5.0	5.2	5.3	5.8
Vermont	5.2	6.3	5.5	5.5	-	1.2	1.0	1.0	1.0
Virginia	63.0	77.2	74.1	75.0	50.8	17.7	19.4	20.1	20.2
Washington	102.2	108.2	83.0	102.8	8.4	25.3	26.1	26.6	27.1
West Virginia	80.5	92.9	81.8	94.8	98.1	15.0	15.0	15.7	16.2
Wisconsin	53.9	59.6	58.8	58.4	68.1	12.1	13.6	14.1	14.2
Wyoming	40.3	45.5	44.8	43.8	95.8	6.1	6.2	6.3	6.3

- Represents zero.

Source: U.S. Energy Information Administration, *Electric Power Annual 2002* and *Inventory of Electric Utility Power Plants in the United States 2000.* Also see <http://www.eia.doe.gov/fuelelectric.html> (accessed August 4, 2003).

Energy and Utilities 583

No. 903. Electric Utility Industry—Capability, Peak Load, and Capacity Margin: 1980 to 2002

[558,237 represents 558,237,000 kW. Excludes Alaska and Hawaii. Capability represents the maximum kilowatt output with all power sources available and with hydraulic equipment under actual water conditions, allowing for maintenance, emergency outages, and system operating requirements. Capacity margin is the difference between capability and peak load]

Year	Capability at the time of— Summer peak load (1,000 kW) Amount	Change from prior year	Winter peak load (1,000 kW) Amount	Change from prior year	Noncoincident peak load Summer (1,000 kW)	Winter (1,000 kW)	Capacity margin Summer Amount (1,000 kW)	Percent of capability	Winter Amount (1,000 kW)	Percent of capability
1980	558,237	13,731	572,195	17,670	427,058	384,567	131,179	23.5	187,628	32.8
1982	586,142	13,923	598,066	11,497	415,618	373,985	170,524	29.1	224,081	37.5
1983	596,449	10,307	612,453	14,387	447,526	410,779	148,923	25.0	201,674	32.9
1984	604,240	7,791	622,125	9,672	451,150	436,374	153,090	25.3	185,751	29.9
1985	621,597	17,357	636,475	14,350	460,503	423,660	161,094	25.9	212,815	33.4
1986	633,291	11,694	646,721	10,246	476,320	422,857	156,971	24.8	223,864	34.6
1987	648,118	14,827	662,977	16,256	496,185	448,277	151,933	23.4	214,700	32.4
1988	661,580	13,462	676,940	13,963	529,460	466,533	132,120	20.0	210,407	31.1
1989	673,316	11,736	685,249	8,309	523,432	496,378	149,884	22.3	188,871	27.6
1990	685,091	11,775	696,757	11,508	545,537	484,014	139,554	20.4	212,743	30.5
1991	690,915	5,824	703,212	6,455	551,320	485,435	139,595	20.2	217,777	31.0
1992	695,436	4,521	707,752	4,540	548,707	492,983	146,729	21.1	214,769	30.3
1993	694,250	-1,186	711,957	4,205	575,356	521,733	118,894	17.1	190,224	26.7
1994	702,985	8,735	715,090	3,133	585,320	518,253	117,665	16.7	196,837	27.5
1995	714,222	11,237	727,679	12,589	620,249	544,684	93,973	13.2	182,995	25.1
1996	723,571	9,349	740,526	12,847	615,529	545,061	108,042	14.9	195,465	26.4
1997	729,079	5,508	743,774	3,248	631,355	560,228	97,724	13.4	183,546	24.7
1998	724,193	-4,886	735,090	-8,684	660,293	567,558	63,900	8.8	167,532	22.8
1999	733,481	9,288	748,036	12,946	681,449	570,915	52,032	7.1	177,121	23.7
2000	750,771	17,290	767,505	19,469	678,413	588,426	72,358	9.6	179,079	23.3
2001	783,737	32,966	806,598	39,093	687,812	576,312	95,925	12.2	230,286	28.6
2002 [1]	825,145	41,408	850,984	44,386	714,565	604,986	110,580	13.4	245,998	28.9

[1] Preliminary.

Source: Edison Electric Institute, Washington, DC, *Statistical Yearbook of the Electric Utility Industry*, annual.

No. 904. Electric Energy Retail Sales by Class of Service and State: 2001

[In billions of kilowatt-hours (3,369.8 represents 3,369,800,000,000)]

State	Total [1]	Residential	Commercial	Industrial	State	Total [1]	Residential	Commercial	Industrial
United States	3,369.8	1,202.6	1,089.2	964.2	Missouri	73.2	30.2	26.0	15.8
Alabama	79.2	27.8	18.9	31.8	Montana	11.2	3.9	3.6	3.3
Alaska	5.4	1.9	2.3	1.1	Nebraska	24.7	8.6	7.2	7.3
Arizona	62.3	26.2	22.1	11.4	Nevada	28.2	9.6	6.7	11.2
Arkansas	41.7	15.1	9.2	16.7	New Hampshire	10.3	3.8	3.9	2.5
California	235.4	77.3	100.2	46.5	New Jersey	72.3	25.4	34.0	12.4
Colorado	44.2	14.5	17.9	10.9	New Mexico	18.7	5.0	6.8	5.3
Connecticut	30.5	12.0	12.4	5.6	New York	141.4	44.0	59.4	24.7
Delaware	10.7	3.7	3.6	3.2	North Carolina	117.6	46.2	37.7	31.5
District of Columbia	9.4	1.7	7.3	0.3	North Dakota	9.8	3.5	3.1	2.8
Florida	199.7	101.4	74.0	18.8	Ohio	154.5	47.3	39.5	63.8
Georgia	117.8	44.4	37.8	33.9	Oklahoma	49.7	19.8	13.6	13.4
Hawaii	9.8	2.8	3.1	3.8	Oregon	45.9	17.5	14.8	13.1
Idaho	21.1	6.9	6.5	7.3	Pennsylvania	137.9	46.3	44.0	46.4
Illinois	135.7	41.8	43.8	37.9	Rhode Island	7.8	2.7	3.7	1.3
Indiana	97.7	29.4	25.6	42.1	South Carolina	74.8	24.9	17.5	31.5
Iowa	39.2	12.4	8.5	16.2	South Dakota	8.6	3.6	2.9	1.7
Kansas	35.8	12.1	12.8	10.6	Tennessee	95.3	36.9	26.0	31.3
Kentucky	80.0	23.7	14.3	38.7	Texas	316.1	117.3	88.2	95.8
Louisiana	74.7	25.8	17.7	28.6	Utah	23.2	6.7	8.3	7.4
Maine	11.8	4.7	4.5	2.6	Vermont	5.6	2.0	2.0	1.6
Maryland	59.8	24.0	25.4	9.7	Virginia	96.1	37.3	29.0	19.5
Massachusetts	52.7	18.0	25.0	9.0	Washington	79.7	31.6	23.8	20.5
Michigan	102.0	32.3	34.9	33.9	West Virginia	27.7	9.8	6.8	11.0
Minnesota	60.3	19.4	19.8	20.4	Wisconsin	65.2	20.4	18.7	25.3
Mississippi	44.3	16.9	11.4	15.3	Wyoming	13.0	2.1	2.9	7.7

[1] Includes "other service" not shown separately.

Source: U.S. Energy Information Administration, *Electric Sales and Revenue 2002*. Also see <http://www.eia.doe.gov/cneaf/electricity/esr/esrsum.html> (issued January 2003).

No. 905. Electric Energy Price by Class of Service and State: 2002

[Revenue (in cents) per kilowatthour. Data include both bundled and unbundled consumers]

State	Total [1]	Residential	Commercial	Industrial	State	Total [1]	Residential	Commercial	Industrial
United States	7.21	8.46	7.86	4.88	Montana	5.75	7.23	6.53	3.70
Alabama	5.71	7.12	6.63	3.82	Nebraska	5.55	6.73	5.62	3.89
Alaska	10.46	12.05	10.13	7.65	Nevada	8.42	9.43	9.06	7.25
Arizona	7.21	8.27	7.28	5.20	New Hampshire	10.49	11.77	10.09	8.83
Arkansas	5.61	7.25	5.68	4.01					
California	12.50	12.90	13.22	10.83	New Jersey	9.31	10.38	8.87	7.83
					New Mexico	6.73	8.50	7.22	4.48
Colorado	6.00	7.37	5.67	4.52	New York	11.29	13.58	12.46	5.16
Connecticut	9.73	10.96	9.35	7.68	North Carolina	6.74	8.19	6.51	4.70
Delaware	7.05	8.70	6.98	5.11	North Dakota	5.45	6.39	5.85	3.98
District of Columbia....	7.37	7.82	7.38	4.95					
Florida	7.31	8.16	6.64	5.23	Ohio..............	6.66	8.29	7.68	4.68
					Oklahoma	5.59	6.73	5.75	3.81
Georgia	6.24	7.63	6.46	3.95	Oregon............	6.32	7.12	6.59	4.72
Hawaii	13.39	15.63	14.11	11.02	Pennsylvania	8.01	9.71	8.03	6.06
Idaho	5.58	6.59	5.71	4.34	Rhode Island	9.19	10.21	8.84	8.04
Illinois	6.97	8.39	7.49	5.01					
Indiana	5.34	6.91	5.98	3.95	South Carolina	5.83	7.72	6.48	3.85
					South Dakota	6.26	7.40	6.24	4.54
Iowa..............	6.01	8.35	6.56	4.06	Tennessee	5.72	6.41	6.45	4.15
Kansas	6.31	7.67	6.28	4.53	Texas	6.62	8.05	6.95	4.66
Kentucky	4.26	5.65	5.30	3.09	Utah	5.39	6.79	5.60	3.84
Louisiana	5.99	7.10	6.64	4.42					
Maine	11.36	11.98	10.47	11.24	Vermont	10.87	12.78	11.10	7.90
Maryland	6.21	7.71	6.09	3.88	Virginia	6.23	7.79	5.87	4.13
Massachusetts	10.18	10.97	10.14	8.77	Washington	5.80	6.29	6.11	4.56
Michigan	6.92	8.28	7.36	4.95	West Virginia	5.11	6.23	5.41	3.81
Minnesota	5.84	7.49	5.88	4.19	Wisconsin	6.28	8.18	6.54	4.43
Mississippi	6.24	7.28	6.83	4.40	Wyoming	4.68	6.97	5.71	3.55
Missouri	6.09	7.06	5.88	4.42					

[1] Includes "other service" not shown separately.

Source: U.S. Energy Information Administration, *Electric Sales and Revenue 2002.* Also see <http://www.eia.doe.gov/cneaf/electricity/esr/esrsum.html>

No. 906. Electric Utilities—Generation, Sales, Revenue, and Customers: 1980 to 2003

[2,286 represents 2,286,000,000,000 kWh. Sales and revenue are to and from ultimate customers]

Class	Unit....	1980	1990	1995	1998	1999	2000	2001	2002	2003
Generation [1]	Bil. kWh.	2,286	2,808	2,995	3,212	3,174	3,015	2,630	2,549	2,527
Sales [2]	Bil. kWh.	2,094	2,713	3,013	3,264	3,312	3,421	3,370	3,463	3,500
Residential or domestic.....	Bil. kWh.	717	924	1,043	1,130	1,145	1,192	1,203	1,267	1,280
Percent of total.........	Percent	34.2	34.1	34.6	34.6	34.6	34.9	35.7	36.6	36.6
Commercial [3]	Bil. kWh.	488	751	863	979	1,002	1,055	1,089	1,116	1,119
Industrial [4]	Bil. kWh.	815	946	1,013	1,051	1,058	1,064	964	972	991
Revenue [2]	Bil. dol .	98.4	178.2	207.7	219.8	219.9	233.2	246.6	249.6	259.1
Residential or domestic.....	Bil. dol .	38.7	72.4	87.6	93.4	93.5	98.2	103.7	107.2	111.4
Percent of total.........	Percent	39.3	40.6	42.2	42.5	42.5	42.1	42.0	43.0	43.0
Commercial [3]	Bil. dol .	26.8	55.1	66.4	72.6	72.8	78.4	86.4	87.7	91.0
Industrial [4]	Bil. dol .	30.2	44.9	47.2	47.0	46.8	49.4	48.6	47.5	49.1
Ultimate customers, Dec. 31 [2].	Million .	92.7	110.1	118.3	124.4	125.9	127.6	130.8	133.4	(NA)
Residential or domestic.....	Million	82.2	97.0	103.9	109.0	110.4	111.7	114.3	116.4	(NA)
Commercial [3]	Million	9.7	12.1	12.9	13.9	14.1	14.3	14.9	15.3	(NA)
Industrial [4]	Million	0.5	0.5	0.6	0.6	0.6	0.5	0.6	0.6	(NA)
Avg. kWh used per customer.										
Residential	1,000...	22.6	24.6	25.5	26.2	26.3	26.8	25.8	26.0	(NA)
Commercial [3]	1,000...	8.7	9.5	10.0	10.4	10.4	10.7	10.5	10.9	(NA)
Industrial [4]	1,000...	50.3	62.0	66.6	70.5	71.2	73.5	72.9	73.1	(NA)
Avg. annual bill per customer.										
Residential	Dollar .	1,062	1,619	1,756	1,767	1,746	1,828	1,885	1,872	(NA)
Commercial [3]	Dollar .	471	746	843	856	847	879	907	921	(NA)
Industrial [4]	Dollar .	2,767	4,553	5,124	5,226	5,171	5,464	5,780	5,741	(NA)
Avg. revenue per kWh sold...	Cents ..	4.70	6.57	6.89	6.74	6.64	6.81	7.32	7.21	7.40
Residential	Cents ..	5.40	7.83	8.40	8.26	8.26	8.24	8.62	8.46	8.71
Commercial [3]	Cents ..	5.50	7.34	7.69	7.41	7.26	7.43	7.93	7.86	8.13
Industrial [4]	Cents ..	3.70	4.74	4.66	4.48	4.43	4.64	5.04	4.88	4.95

NA Not available. [1] "Generation" includes batteries, chemicals, hydrogen, pitch, sulfur, and purchased steam. [2] Includes other types not shown separately. [3] Small light and power. [4] Large light and power.

Source: Edison Electric Institute, Washington, DC, *Statistical Yearbook of the Electric Utility Industry,* annual.

[In millions of nominal dollars (199,967 represents $199,967,000,000). Covers approximately 180 investor-owned electric utilities that during each of the last 3 years met any one or more of the following conditions—1 mil. megawatt-hours of total sales; 100 megawatt-hours of sales for resale, 500 megawatt-hours of gross interchange out, and 500 megawatt-hours of wheeling for other]

Item	1995	1997	1998	1999	2000	2001	2002
Utility operating revenues	199,967	215,083	218,175	214,160	235,336	267,525	219,389
Electric utility	183,655	195,898	201,970	197,578	214,707	244,219	200,135
Other utility	16,312	19,185	16,205	16,583	20,630	23,306	19,254
Utility operating expenses	165,321	182,796	186,498	182,258	210,324	235,198	188,745
Electric utility	150,599	165,443	171,689	167,266	191,329	213,733	171,291
Operation	91,881	104,337	110,759	108,461	132,662	159,929	116,374
Production	68,983	80,153	85,956	83,555	107,352	136,08⁷	90,649
Cost of fuel	29,122	31,861	31,252	29,826	32,555	29,490	24,132
Purchased power	29,981	37,991	42,612	43,258	61,969	98,231	58,828
Other	9,880	10,301	12,092	10,470	12,828	8,368	7,688
Transmission	1,425	1,915	2,197	2,423	2,699	2,365	3,494
Distribution	2,561	2,700	2,804	2,956	3,115	3,217	3,113
Customer accounts	3,613	3,767	4,021	4,195	4,246	4,434	4,165
Customer service	1,922	1,197	1,955	1,889	1,839	1,856	1,821
Sales	348	501	514	492	403	282	261
Administrative and general	13,028	13,384	13,311	12,951	13,009	11,686	12,872
Maintenance	11,767	12,368	12,486	12,276	12,185	11,167	10,843
Depreciation	19,885	23,072	24,122	23,968	22,761	20,845	17,319
Taxes and other	27,065	25,667	24,322	22,561	23,721	21,792	26,755
Other utility	14,722	17,353	14,809	14,992	18,995	21,465	17,454
Net utility operating income	34,646	32,286	31,677	31,902	25,012	32,327	30,644

Source: U.S. Energy Information Administration, *Electric Power Annual*, 2002. Also see <http://www.eia.doe.gov/cneaf/electricity /epa/epat8p1.html> (released November 2003).

No. 908. Uranium Concentrate—Supply, Inventories, and Average Prices: 1980 to 2002

[43.70 represents 43,700,000 pounds. Years ending Dec. 31. For additional data on uranium, see Section 18]

Item	Unit	1980	1990	1995	1997	1998	1999	2000	2001	2002
Production	Mil. lb.	43.70	8.89	6.04	5.64	4.71	4.61	3.96	2.64	2.34
Exports	Mil. lb.	5.8	2.0	9.8	17.0	15.1	8.5	13.6	11.7	15.4
Imports	Mil. lb.	3.6	23.7	41.3	43.0	43.7	47.6	44.9	46.7	52.7
Utility purchases from domestic suppliers	Mil. lb.	(NA)	20.5	22.3	19.4	21.6	21.4	24.3	27.5	22.7
Loaded into U.S. nuclear reactors [1]	Mil. lb.	(NA)	(NA)	51.1	48.2	38.2	58.8	51.5	52.7	57.3
Inventories, total	Mil. lb.	(NA)	129.1	72.5	106.2	136.5	127.1	111.3	103.6	101.1
At domestic suppliers	Mil. lb.	(NA)	26.4	13.7	40.4	70.7	68.8	56.5	48.1	47.9
At electric utilities	Mil. lb.	(NA)	102.7	58.7	65.9	65.8	58.3	54.8	55.6	53.3
Average price per pound:										
Purchased imports	Dollars	(NA)	12.55	10.20	11.81	11.19	10.55	9.84	9.51	10.05
Domestic purchases	Dollars	(NA)	15.70	11.11	12.87	12.31	11.88	11.45	10.45	10.35

NA Not available. [1] Does not include any fuel rods removed from reactors and later reloaded into the reactor.

Source: Through 2000, U.S. Energy Information Administration, *Annual Energy Review 2001*, thereafter, U.S. Energy Information Administration, *Uranium Industry Annual 2002*. Also see <http://www.eia.doe.gov/emeu/aer/nuclear.html>.

No. 909. Nuclear Power Plants—Number, Capacity, and Generation: 1980 to 2003

[51.8 represents 51,800,000 kW]

Item	1980	1985	1990	1995	1996	1997	1998	1999	2000	2001	2002	2003
Operable generating units [1][2]	71	96	112	109	109	107	104	104	104	104	104	104
Net summer capacity [2][3] (mil. kW)	51.8	79.4	99.6	99.5	100.8	99.7	97.1	97.4	97.9	98.2	98.6	98.7
Net generation (bil. kWh)	251.1	383.7	576.9	673.4	674.7	628.6	673.7	728.3	753.9	768.8	780.1	763.7
Percent of total electricity net generation	11.0	15.5	19.0	20.1	19.6	18.0	18.6	19.7	19.8	20.6	20.2	19.8
Capacity factor [4] (percent)	56.3	58.0	66.0	77.4	76.2	71.1	78.2	85.3	88.1	89.4	90.4	88.4

[1] Total of nuclear generating units holding full-power licenses, or equivalent permission to operate, at the end of the year. Although Browns Ferry 1 was shut down in 1985, the unit has remained fully licensed and thus has continued to be counted as operable during the shutdown. [2] As of year-end. [3] Net summer capacity is the peak steady hourly output that generating equipment is expected to supply to system load, exclusive of auxiliary and other power plant, as demonstrated by test at the time of summer peak demand. [4] Weighted average of monthly capacity factors. Monthly factors are derived by dividing actual monthly generation by the maximum possible generation for the month (number of hours in the month multiplied by the net summer capacity at the end of the month).

Source: U.S. Energy Information Administration, *Monthly Energy Review, 2004.* See also <http://www.eia.doe.gov/emeu/mer/nuclear.html> (accessed June 14, 2004).

No. 910. Nuclear Power Plants—Number of Units, Net Generation, and Net Summer Capacity by State: 2002

[780,064 represents 780,064,000,000 kWh]

State	Number of units	Net generation Total (mil. kWh)	Net generation Percent of total[1]	Net summer capacity Total (mil. kW)	Net summer capacity Percent of total[1]	State	Number of units	Net generation Total (mil. kWh)	Net generation Percent of total[1]	Net summer capacity Total (mil. kW)	Net summer capacity Percent of total[1]
U.S.	104	780,064	20.2	98.66	10.9	MS	1	10,059	23.4	1.23	9.0
AL	5	31,857	24.0	4.97	18.7	MO	1	8,390	10.3	1.14	5.8
AZ	3	30,862	32.8	3.73	19.2	NE	2	10,122	32.0	1.23	20.3
AR	2	14,559	30.6	1.78	15.7	NH	1	9,295	58.3	1.16	33.9
CA	4	34,352	18.6	4.32	7.6	NJ	4	30,866	50.1	3.88	21.1
CT	2	14,918	47.6	2.01	27.1	NY	6	39,617	28.4	5.05	14.0
FL	5	33,704	16.6	3.91	8.3	NC	5	39,627	31.8	4.73	17.7
GA	4	31,108	24.6	4.02	11.6	OH	2	10,865	7.4	2.11	6.7
IL	11	90,860	48.3	11.31	25.3	PA	9	76,089	37.2	9.13	22.9
IA	1	4,574	10.8	0.57	6.1	SC	7	53,326	55.2	6.49	31.9
KS	1	9,042	19.2	1.17	11.3	TN	3	27,574	28.7	3.39	16.4
LA	2	17,305	18.2	2.07	8.1	TX	4	35,618	9.2	4.74	5.0
MD	2	12,128	25.1	1.69	14.2	VT	1	3,963	72.6	0.51	50.9
MA	1	5,769	13.7	0.67	5.5	VA	4	27,346	36.5	3.47	17.2
MI	4	31,087	26.4	3.94	13.4	WA	1	9,048	8.8	1.11	4.1
MN	3	13,685	25.9	1.65	14.6	WI	3	12,449	21.3	1.51	10.6

[1] For total generation and capacity, see Table 902.
Source: U.S. Energy Information Administration, *Electric Power Annual 2002.* See also <http://www.eia.doe.gov/cneaf/electricity /epa/epa_sprdshts.html>.

No. 911. Solar Collector Shipments by Type, End Use, and Market Sector: 1980 to 2002

[Shipments in thousands of square feet (19,398 represents 19,398,000). Solar collector is a device for intercepting sunlight, converting the light to heat, and carrying the heat to where it will be either used or stored. 1985 data are not available. Based on the Annual Solar Thermal Collector Manufacturers Survey]

Year	Number of manufac-turers	Total ship-ments[1][2][3]	Collector type Low tempera-ture[1][2]	Collector type Medium tempera-ture, spe-cial, other[2]	End use Pool heating	End use Hot water	End use Space heating	Market sector Resi-dential	Market sector Com-mercial	Market sector Industrial
1980	233	19,398	12,233	7,165	12,029	4,790	1,688	16,077	2,417	488
1986 [4]	98	9,360	3,751	1,111	3,494	1,181	127	4,131	703	13
1990 [4]	51	11,409	3,645	2,527	5,016	1,091	2	5,835	294	22
1995	36	7,666	6,813	840	6,763	755	132	6,966	604	82
1999	29	8,583	8,152	427	8,141	373	42	7,774	785	18
2000	26	8,354	7,948	400	7,863	367	99	7,473	810	57
2001	26	11,189	10,919	268	10,797	274	70	10,125	1,012	17
2002	27	11,663	11,046	615	11,073	423	146	11,000	595	62

[1] Includes shipments of high temperature collectors to the government, including some military, but excluding space applications. Also includes end uses such as process heating, utility, and other market sectors not shown separately. [2] Includes imputation of shipment data to account for nonrespondents. [3] Total shipments include all domestic and export shipments and may include imported collectors that subsequently were shipped to domestic or foreign customers. [4] Declines between 1986 and 1990 are primarily due to the expiration of the Federal energy tax credit and industry consolidation.

Source: U.S. Energy Information Administration, 1980-1990, *Solar Collector Manufacturing Activity,* annual reports; thereafter, *Renewable Energy Annual.* See also <http://www.eia.doe.gov/cneaf/solar.renewables/page/readata/rea.pdf> (released November 2003).

No. 912. Total Renewable Net Generation by Source and State: 2001

[In millions of kilowatthours (294,946 represents 294,946,000,000) MSW=municipal solid waste]

State	Total [1]	Hydro-electric	MSW/landfill gas	Other Bio-mass [2]	Wood/Wood Waste	State	Total [1]	Hydro-electric	MSW/landfill gas	Other Bio-mass [2]	Wood/Wood Waste
U.S..	294,946	216,961	19,931	1,834	35,200	MO	1,167	1,104	(X)	62	(X)
AL	12,553	8,356	3	21	4,172	MT	6,679	6,613	(X)	(X)	65
AK	1,347	1,346	(X)	(X)	(X)	NE	1,143	1,124	(X)	17	(X)
AZ	7,663	7,624	34	5	(X)	NV	3,714	2,514	(X)	(X)	(X)
AR	4,060	2,548	(X)	7	1,505	NH	2,075	991	226	(X)	859
CA	47,359	25,542	1,861	410	3,324	NJ	1,321	18	1,290	13	(X)
CO	1,608	1,495	(X)	64	(X)	NM	256	237	(X)	19	(X)
CT	2,064	286	1,567	211	(X)	NY	25,694	23,084	2,087	(X)	503
DE	(X)	(X)	(X)	(X)	(X)	NC	4,376	2,596	129	9	1,642
DC	(X)	(X)	(X)	(X)	(X)	ND	1,340	1,332	(X)	8	(X)
FL	5,191	148	2,990	225	1,828	OH	942	511	28	(X)	403
GA	5,606	2,596	29	6	2,974	OK	2,575	2,345	(X)	(X)	231
HI	767	101	402	56	(X)	OR	29,522	28,645	87	34	701
ID	7,756	7,223	(X)	(X)	533	PA	4,312	1,650	2,020	34	597
IL	872	144	641	87	(X)	RI	107	3	104	(X)	(X)
IN	701	571	126	4	(X)	SC	2,141	1,225	49	1	866
IA	1,445	845	97	15	(X)	SD	3,433	3,432	(X)	(X)	(X)
KS	65	26	(X)	(X)	(X)	TN	7,775	6,947	49	(X)	779
KY	3,865	3,856	(X)	(X)	(X)	TX	3,395	1,200	51	59	898
LA	3,480	732	(X)	107	2,641	UT	671	508	10	(X)	(X)
ME	6,734	2,645	400	158	3,530	VT	1,267	884	(X)	(X)	370
MD	1,804	1,184	609	-	12	VA	3,158	1,014	991	5	1,148
MA	2,786	703	1,929	24	130	WA	56,021	54,734	175	47	1,065
MI	4,069	1,562	743	64	1,700	WV	978	952	25	(X)	1
MN	3,090	832	780	7	575	WI	3,321	2,056	401	86	705
MS	1,432	(X)	(X)	-	1,432	WY	1,244	879	(X)	(X)	(X)

X Not applicable.   - Represents zero.   [1] Includes types not shown separately.   [2] Agriculture byproducts/crops, sludge waste, tires and other biomass solids, liquids and gases.

Source: Energy Information Administration, *Renewable Energy Annual 2002*. Also see <http://www.eia.doe.gov/cneaf/solar .renewables/page/readata/tablec6.html> (released November 2003).

No. 913. Privately Owned Gas Utility Industry—Balance Sheet and Income Account: 1980 to 2002

[In millions of dollars (75,851 represents $75,851,000,000). The gas utility industry consists of pipeline and distribution companies. Excludes operations of companies distributing gas in bottles or tanks]

Item	1980	1990	1995	1997	1998	1999	2000	2001	2002
COMPOSITE BALANCE SHEET									
Assets, total	75,851	121,686	141,965	134,715	119,715	155,413	165,709	171,681	185,064
Total utility plant	67,071	112,863	143,636	140,268	135,092	166,134	162,206	175,530	197,717
Depreciation and amortization. ...	26,162	49,483	62,723	62,554	61,226	73,823	69,366	73,753	85,038
Utility plant (net).	40,909	63,380	80,912	77,714	73,866	92,311	92,839	101,777	112,679
Investment and fund accounts	15,530	23,872	26,489	22,812	12,337	17,344	10,846	10,237	13,000
Current and accrued assets	17,243	23,268	18,564	19,084	17,348	22,443	35,691	29,345	25,786
Deferred debits [1]	2,169	9,576	13,923	12,884	13,721	13,721	20,922	24,279	31,928
Liabilities, total	75,851	121,686	141,965	134,775	119,715	155,413	165,709	171,681	185,064
Capitalization, total	51,382	74,958	90,581	78,887	71,718	95,244	96,079	107,310	117,362
Capital stock	29,315	43,810	54,402	42,530	37,977	[2]859	760	701	333
Long-term debts	22,067	31,148	35,548	35,971	33,386	46,906	48,267	49,739	58,962
Current and accrued liabilities. ...	18,119	29,550	28,272	33,507	26,953	32,683	42,312	34,962	30,856
Deferred income taxes [3]	4,149	11,360	14,393	13,636	13,239	17,120	17,157	20,445	24,612
Other liabilities and credits	2,201	5,818	8,715	8,745	7,806	10,365	10,161	8,964	12,135
COMPOSITE INCOME ACCOUNT									
Operating revenues, total ..	85,918	66,027	58,390	62,617	57,117	59,142	72,042	79,231	68,544
Minus: Operating expenses [4]	81,789	60,137	50,760	59,375	50,896	38,752	64,988	57,151	47,002
Operation and maintenance ...	74,508	51,627	37,966	46,070	41,026	41,415	54,602	58,873	48,638
Federal, state, and local taxes. .	4,847	4,957	6,182	7,182	5,429	5,605	6,163	7,394	6,302
Equals: Operating income	4,129	5,890	7,630	3,242	6,220	20,390	7,053	8,064	8,312
Utility operating income	4,471	6,077	7,848	3,337	6,361	16,614	7,166	8,192	8,573
Income before interest charges. ...	6,929	8,081	9,484	4,193	7,779	17,531	7,589	8,266	9,319
Net income	4,194	4,410	5,139	48	4,379	10,420	4,245	4,038	4,776
Dividends	2,564	3,191	4,037	6,258	2,263	5,595	3,239	3,560	3,933

[1] Includes capital stock discount and expense and reacquired securities.   [2] Data not comparable to prior years.   [3] Includes reserves for deferred income taxes.   [4] Includes expenses not shown separately.

Source: American Gas Association, Arlington, VA, *Gas Facts*, annual (copyright).

No. 914. Gas Utility Industry—Summary: 1980 to 2002

[47,223 represents 47,223,000. Covers natural, manufactured, mixed, and liquid petroleum gas. Based on a questionnaire mailed to all privately and municipally owned gas utilities in United States, except those with annual revenues less than $25,000]

Item	Unit	1980	1990	1995	1998	1999	2000	2001	2002
End users [1]	1,000	47,223	54,261	58,728	61,528	60,778	61,262	61,385	62,034
Residential .	1,000	43,489	49,802	53,955	56,517	56,017	56,494	56,680	57,293
Commercial .	1,000	3,498	4,246	4,530	4,825	4,599	4,610	4,546	4,590
Industrial and other .	1,000	187	166	181	183	159	157	156	149
Sales [2] .	Tril. Btu [3] .	15,413	9,842	9,221	8,781	8,975	9,232	8,667	8,864
Residential .	Tril. Btu ...	4,826	4,468	4,803	4,534	4,622	4,741	4,525	4,589
Percent of total .	Percent ...	31	45	52	52	51	51	52	52
Commercial .	Tril. Btu .	2,453	2,192	2,281	2,063	2,067	2,077	2,053	2,055
Industrial .	Tril. Btu .	7,957	3,010	1,919	1,370	1,553	1,698	1,461	1,748
Other. .	Tril. Btu ...	177	171	218	814	734	715	627	472
Revenues [2] .	Mil. dol ...	48,303	45,153	46,436	47,084	47,202	59,243	69,150	57,112
Residential .	Mil. dol ...	17,432	25,000	28,742	30,130	30,095	35,828	42,454	35,062
Percent of total .	Percent ...	36	55	62	64	64	60	61	61
Commercial .	Mil. dol .	8,183	10,604	11,573	11,020	10,731	13,339	16,848	13,512
Industrial .	Mil. dol .	22,215	8,996	5,571	4,189	4,715	7,432	7,513	6,841
Other. .	Mil. dol .	473	553	549	1,745	1,662	2,645	2,335	1,698
Prices per mil. Btu [3] .	Dollars ...	3.13	4.59	5.05	5.36	5.26	6.42	7.98	6.44
Residential .	Dollars ...	3.61	5.60	6.00	6.64	6.51	7.56	9.38	7.64
Commercial .	Dollars ...	3.34	4.84	5.07	5.34	5.19	6.42	8.20	6.57
Industrial .	Dollars ...	2.79	2.99	2.98	3.06	3.04	4.38	5.14	3.91
Gas mains mileage .	1,000	1,052	1,189	1,278	1,351	1,340	1,369	1,374	1,411
Field and gathering .	1,000	84	32	31	29	32	27	20	22
Transmission. .	1,000	266	292	297	300	301	297	287	310
Distribution .	1,000	702	865	950	1,022	1,008	1,046	1,066	1,080
Construction expenditures [4] .	Mil. dol .	5,350	7,899	10,760	10,978	8,320	8,624	9,516	11,674
Transmission. .	Mil. dol .	1,583	2,886	3,380	3,656	1,785	1,590	3,212	5,281
Distribution .	Mil. dol .	1,869	3,714	5,394	5,035	4,180	5,437	4,546	4,897
Production and storage. .	Mil. dol .	1,150	309	367	598	161	138	113	74
General .	Mil. dol .	352	770	1,441	1,389	1,974	1,273	1,457	1,667
Underground storage .	Mil. dol .	396	219	177	299	220	185	187	254

[1] Annual average. [2] Excludes sales for resale. [3] For definition of Btu, see text, this section. [4] Includes general.

Source: American Gas Association, Arlington, VA, *Gas Facts,* annual (copyright).

No. 915. Gas Utility Industry—Customers, Sales, and Revenues by State: 2002

[62,034 represents 62,034,000. See headnote, Table 914. For definition of Btu, see text, this section]

State	Customers [1] (1,000)		Sales [2] (tril. Btu)		Revenues [2] (mil. dol.)		State	Customers [1] (1,000)		Sales [2] (tril. Btu)		Revenues [2] (mil. dol.)	
	Total	Resi-dential	Total	Resi-dential	Total	Resi-dential		Total	Resi-dential	Total	Resi-dential	Total	Resi-dential
U.S..	62,034	57,293	8,864	4,589	57,112	35,062	MO .	1,481	1,341	180	117	1,345	913
							MT .	259	229	34	22	176	115
AL .	869	801	104	48	849	487	NE .	450	413	64	37	348	222
AK .	110	97	113	17	260	71	NV .	614	580	82	33	574	310
AZ .	981	925	88	36	770	426	NH .	102	87	15	7	137	70
AR .	626	553	74	40	571	350							
CA .	10,149	9,701	757	521	4,924	3,610	NJ .	2,523	2,323	363	209	2,261	1,469
							NM .	533	488	61	35	418	265
CO .	1,550	1,413	213	132	1,076	724	NY .	4,307	3,983	513	328	4,544	3,251
CT .	509	462	86	41	727	444	NC .	1,011	906	139	60	1,013	552
DE .	138	126	19	10	173	101	ND .	125	109	25	12	116	60
DC .	125	117	15	11	161	117	OH .	2,346	2,164	286	210	2,051	1,544
FL .	647	604	45	15	425	204							
							OK .	957	875	115	69	786	522
GA .	347	316	57	18	380	167	OR .	634	564	78	40	696	410
HI .	34	31	3	1	48	12	PA .	2,527	2,321	319	218	2,816	2,014
ID .	293	261	34	21	266	172	RI .	242	220	27	18	289	207
IL .	3,801	3,567	545	426	3,442	2,662	SC .	566	509	143	28	840	269
IN .	1,756	1,606	248	158	1,747	1,185							
							SD .	167	147	24	13	143	89
IA .	922	824	121	73	760	507	TN .	1,132	1,009	165	71	1,153	565
KS .	928	843	109	73	705	513	TX .	4,130	3,806	1,497	216	6,164	1,529
KY .	793	714	104	57	698	414	UT .	712	661	94	61	543	380
LA .	1,021	957	197	50	999	396	VT .	35	30	8	3	59	29
ME .	25	18	5	1	46	12							
							VA .	987	905	121	69	991	661
MD .	867	812	86	64	788	607	WA .	951	862	139	75	1,129	685
MA .	1,414	1,296	169	112	1,557	1,098	WV .	1,672	1,515	250	141	1,608	1,009
MI .	3,244	3,000	501	361	3,007	2,224	WI .	395	361	52	32	389	260
MN .	1,406	1,283	280	139	1,583	893	WY .	137	122	19	10	103	59
MS .	487	435	75	27	456	205							

[1] Averages for the year. [2] Excludes sales for resale.

Source: American Gas Association, Arlington, VA, *Gas Facts,* annual (copyright).

Energy and Utilities 589

No. 916. Public Drinking Water Systems by Size of Community Served and Source of Water: 2003

[As of September. Covers systems that provide water for human consumption through pipes and other constructed conveyances to a least 15 service connections or serve an average of at least 25 persons for at least 60 days a year. Based on reported data in the Safe Drinking Water Information System maintained by the Environmental Protection Agency]

Type of system	Total	Size of community served					Water source	
		500 or fewer persons	501 to 3,300 persons	3,301 to 10,000 persons	10,001 to 100,000	100,000 persons or more	Ground water	Surface water
Total systems	161,201	132,568	19,837	4,879	3,550	367	146,468	14,733
COMMUNITY WATER SYSTEMS [1]								
Number of systems	53,363	30,417	14,394	4,686	3,505	361	41,499	11,864
Percent of systems	100	57	27	9	7	1	78	22
Population served (1,000)	273,329	5,011	20,262	27,201	98,706	122,149	86,348	186,981
Percent of population	100	2	7	10	36	45	32	68
NON-TRANSIENT NON-COMMUNITY WATER SYSTEM [2]								
Number of systems	19,686	16,785	2,786	97	16	2	18,908	778
Percent of systems	100	85	14	-	-	-	96	4
Population served (1,000)	6,298	2,328	2,772	506	412	280	5,568	730
Percent of population	100	37	44	8	7	4	88	12
TRANSIENT NON-COMMUNITY WATER SYSTEM [3]								
Number of systems	88,152	85,366	2,657	96	29	4	86,061	2,091
Percent of systems	100	97	3	-	-	-	98	2
Population served (1,000)	23,335	7,316	2,603	529	619	12,269	10,527	12,808
Percent of population	100	31	11	2	3	53	45	55

- Represents zero.   [1] A public water system that supplies water to the same population year-round.   [2] A public water system that regularly supplies water to at least 25 of the same people at least 6 months per year, but not year-round. Some examples are schools, factories, and office buildings which have their own water systems.   [3] A public water system that provides water in a place such as a gas station or campground where people do not remain for long periods of time.

Source: U.S. Environmental Protection Agency, *Factoids: Drinking Water and Ground Water Statistics for 2003*, annual reports. See also <http://www.epa.gov/safewater/data/pdfs/factoids2003.pdf> (accessed January 2004).

No. 917. Water and Sewage Treatment Facilities: 1997

[Based on the North American Industry Classification System (NAICS), 1997; see text, Section 15]

State	Water Supply (NAICS 2213101)		Sewage Treatment Facilities (NAICS 22132)		State	Water Supply (NAICS 2213101)		Sewage Treatment Facilities (NAICS 22132)	
	Number of establish-ments	Paid employees	Number of establish-ments	Paid employ-ees		Number of establish-ments	Paid employees	Number of establish-ments	Paid employ-ees
U.S. ...	3,721	26,597	696	5,600	MO	57	(4)	15	(5)
AL......	96	(1)	13	(2)	MT.....	35	113	6	(3)
AK......	6	(3)	(NA)	(NA)	NE.....	(NA)	(NA)	(NA)	(NA)
AZ......	129	1,131	8	40	NV.....	23	(5)	(NA)	(NA)
AR......	140	(4)	9	(5)	NH.....	10	(2)	(NA)	(NA)
CA......	374	2,848	27	116	NJ.....	49	(6)	24	(4)
CO......	71	314	14	51	NM.....	90	323	(NA)	(NA)
CT......	32	(6)	9	(5)	NY.....	41	(4)	28	(2)
DE......	9	(1)	(NA)	(NA)	NC.....	81	577	18	(5)
DC......	(NA)	(NA)	(NA)	(NA)	ND.....	24	(5)	(NA)	(NA)
FL......	129	1,393	88	(4)	OH.....	60	686	19	(2)
GA......	34	130	10	(2)	OK.....	105	(1)	9	(5)
HI	9	24	13	(2)	OR.....	63	(2)	7	(5)
ID	35	(2)	6	20	PA.....	125	2,568	59	(1)
IL	82	(4)	27	(2)	RI	(NA)	(NA)	(NA)	(NA)
IN	114	(6)	30	(2)	SC.....	48	(1)	12	(5)
IA	25	(2)	7	(5)	SD.....	29	(2)	(NA)	(NA)
KS.....	38	(1)	(NA)	(NA)	TN.....	30	(1)	11	(4)
KY.....	42	(4)	13	116	TX.....	601	2,514	38	(4)
LA.....	192	(2)	21	(2)	UT.....	23	71	(NA)	(NA)
ME.....	22	(5)	(NA)	(NA)	VT.....	7	(5)	(NA)	(NA)
MD.....	8	(2)	9	107	VA.....	48	(1)	12	(5)
MA.....	18	(2)	21	(1)	WA	148	(1)	8	(5)
MI	12	66	10	24	WV.....	40	523	20	94
MN.....	6	(5)	13	(5)	WI	(NA)	(NA)	13	47
MS.....	332	1,001	14	(5)	WY.....	16	(5)	(NA)	(NA)

NA Not available.   [1] 250-499 employees.   [2] 100-249 employees.   [3] 1-19 employees.   [4] 500-999 employees.   [5] 20-99 employees.   [6] 1000-2499 employees.

Source: U.S. Census Bureau, *1997 Economic Census, Utilities*. See also <http://www.census.gov/epcd/www/97EC22.htm> (accessed May 2002).

Construction and Housing

This section presents data on the construction industry and on various indicators of its activity and costs; on housing units and their characteristics and occupants; and on the characteristics and vacancy rates for commercial buildings. This edition contains data from the 2003 American Housing Survey.

The principal source of these data is the U.S. Census Bureau, which issues a variety of current publications, as well as data from the decennial census. Current construction statistics compiled by the Census Bureau appear in its *New Residential Construction* and *New Residential Sales* press releases and Web sites <http://www.census.gov/const/www/>. Statistics on expenditures by owners of residential properties are issued quarterly and annually in *Expenditures for Residential Upkeep and Improvements. Value of New Construction Put in Place* presents data on all types of construction. Reports of the censuses of construction industries (see below) are also issued on various topics.

Other Census Bureau publications include the *Current Housing Reports* series, which comprises the quarterly *Housing Vacancies*, the quarterly *Market Absorption of Apartments*, the biennial *American Housing Survey* (formerly *Annual Housing Survey)*, and reports of the censuses of housing and of construction industries.

Other sources include the monthly *Dodge Construction Potentials* of F. W. Dodge Division, McGraw-Hill Information Systems Company, New York, NY, which presents national and state data on construction contracts; the National Association of Home Builders with state-level data on housing starts; the NATIONAL ASSOCIATION OF REALTORS®, which presents data on existing home sales; the Society of Industrial and Office Realtors and Oncor

International on commercial office and industrial space; the Bureau of Economic Analysis, which presents data on residential capital and gross housing product; and the U.S. Energy Information Administration, which provides data on commercial buildings through its periodic sample surveys.

Censuses and surveys—Censuses of the construction industry were first conducted by the Census Bureau for 1929, 1935, and 1939; beginning in 1967, a census has been taken every 5 years (through 2002, for years ending in "2" and "7"). The latest reports are part of the 2002 Economic Census. See text, Section 15, Business Enterprise.

The construction sector of the economic census, covers all employer establishments primarily engaged in (1) building construction by general contractors or operative builders; (2) heavy (nonbuilding) construction by general contractors; and (3) construction by special trade contractors. This sector includes construction management and land subdividers and developers. The 2002 census was conducted in accordance with the 2002 North American Industrial Classification System (NAICS). See text, Section 15, Business Enterprise, for general information on the SIC and NAICS.

From 1850 through 1930, the Census Bureau collected some housing data as part of its censuses of population and agriculture. Beginning in 1940, separate censuses of housing have been taken at 10-year intervals. For the 1970 and 1980 censuses, data on year-round housing units were collected and issued on occupancy and structural characteristics, plumbing facilities, value, and rent; for 1990 such characteristics were presented for all housing units.

The American Housing Survey (*Current Housing Reports* Series H-150 and H-170), which began in 1973, provided an annual and ongoing series of data on selected housing and demographic characteristics until 1983. In 1984, the name of the survey was changed from the Annual Housing Survey. Currently, national data are collected every other year, and data for selected metropolitan areas are collected on a rotating basis. All samples represent a cross section of the housing stock in their respective areas. Estimates are subject to both sampling and nonsampling errors; caution should therefore be used in making comparisons between years.

Data on residential mortgages were collected continuously from 1890 to 1970, except 1930, as part of the decennial census by the Census Bureau. Since 1973, mortgage status data, limited to single family homes on less than 10 acres with no business on the property, have been presented in the American Housing Survey. Data on mortgage activity are covered in Section 25, Banking and Finance.

Housing units—In general, a housing unit is a house, an apartment, a group of rooms or a single room occupied or intended for occupancy as separate living quarters; that is, the occupants live separately from any other individual in the building, and there is direct access from the outside or through a common hall. Transient accommodations, barracks for workers, and institutional-type quarters are not counted as housing units.

Statistical reliability—For a discussion of statistical collection and estimation, sampling procedures, and measures of statistical reliability applicable to Census Bureau data, see Appendix III.

U.S. Census Bureau, Statistical Abstract of the United States: 2004-2005

[For establishments with payroll. (6,572.8 represents 6,572,800). See Appendix III]

Industry	1997 NAICS code [1]	Establishments		Paid employees [2] (1,000)		Annual payroll (mil. dol.)	
		2000	2001	2000	2001	2000	2001
Construction	23	709,590	698,898	6,572.8	6,491.9	239,910.1	247,211.1
Building, developing, & general contracting	233	216,354	215,806	1,604.9	1,616.9	60,798.1	64,956.9
Land subdivision & land development	2331	13,111	13,358	77.9	88.9	3,269.2	3,990.1
Residential building construction	2332	159,550	155,437	781.0	735.3	25,519.7	25,985.7
Single-family housing construction	23321	151,296	146,670	713.3	661.4	23,058.3	23,160.0
Multifamily housing construction	23322	8,254	8,767	67.7	73.9	2,461.3	2,825.8
Nonresidential building construction	2333	43,693	47,011	746.0	792.5	32,009.3	34,980.9
Mfg & industrial building construction	23331	7,039	5,887	164.9	114.0	6,797.3	4,565.6
Commercial & institutional building construction	23332	36,654	41,124	581.2	678.5	25,212.0	30,415.3
Heavy construction	234	39,516	40,476	901.0	901.2	38,628.0	39,801.6
Highway, street, bridge, & tunnel construction	2341	11,795	12,133	304.9	311.0	14,316.1	15,697.5
Highway & street construction	23411	10,889	11,314	265.7	275.1	12,328.6	13,758.5
Bridge & tunnel construction	23412	906	819	39.3	35.8	1,987.5	1,938.9
Other heavy construction	2349	27,721	28,343	596.1	590.1	24,311.9	24,104.0
Water, sewer, & pipeline construction	23491	7,483	9,090	165.8	193.3	7,033.0	8,484.8
Power & communication transmission line construction	23492	3,644	4,065	97.5	114.9	3,815.8	4,382.0
Industrial nonbuilding structure construction	23493	689	647	101.7	105.3	4,137.8	4,036.4
All other heavy construction	23499	15,905	14,541	231.0	176.4	9,325.3	7,200.6
Special trade contractors	235	453,720	442,616	4,066.9	3,973.8	140,484.1	142,452.8
Plumbing, heating, & air-conditioning contractors	2351	90,487	89,550	897.9	898.4	33,406.0	34,507.9
Painting & wall covering contractors	2352	40,973	40,364	221.8	220.4	6,121.4	6,300.6
Electrical contractors	2353	66,802	65,860	815.1	831.8	32,698.0	33,480.1
Masonry, drywall, insulation, & tile contractors	2354	53,625	50,885	565.0	529.5	17,389.8	17,188.6
Masonry & stone contractors	23541	25,030	23,664	197.9	178.8	5,667.8	5,605.9
Drywall, plastering, acoustical, & insulation contractors	23542	21,774	20,337	319.3	300.9	10,224.4	9,973.1
Tile, marble, terrazzo, & mosaic contractors	23543	6,821	6,884	47.8	49.7	1,497.7	1,609.4
Carpentry & floor contractors	2355	58,525	57,441	347.3	337.5	9,963.6	9,951.5
Carpentry contractors	23551	45,028	44,391	269.8	262.9	7,533.3	7,507.0
Floor laying & other floor contractors	23552	13,497	13,050	77.5	74.6	2,430.3	2,444.4
Roofing, siding, & sheet metal contractors	2356	30,966	30,247	260.8	247.4	7,928.8	7,833.9
Concrete contractors	2357	30,238	30,743	292.6	295.2	9,501.2	10,419.0
Water well drilling contractors	2358	3,797	3,722	21.6	22.2	688.5	758.9
Other special trade contractors	2359	78,307	73,804	644.9	590.9	22,786.6	22,012.3
Structural steel erection contractors	23591	5,382	4,782	93.6	81.9	3,585.8	3,260.9
Glass & glazing contractors	23592	5,772	5,531	45.8	47.1	1,570.1	1,756.1
Excavation contractors	23593	27,005	25,409	152.5	144.4	5,253.6	5,482.1
Wrecking & demolition contractors	23594	1,752	1,923	21.9	27.1	808.7	953.0
Building equip & other machinery installation contractors	23595	4,820	4,600	80.9	72.6	3,859.6	3,543.1
All other special trade contractors	23599	33,576	31,559	250.1	217.7	7,708.7	7,016.5

[1] North American Industry Classification System code, 1997; see text, Section 15. [2] Employees on the payroll for the pay period including March 12.

Source: U.S. Census Bureau, "County Business Patterns"; 2001 data published 10 April 2003; <http://www.census.gov/epcd/cbp/view/cbpview.html>

No. 919. Construction—Establishments, Value of Work Done, Payroll, and Employees by Kind of Business (NAICS Basis): 1997 and 2002

[(858,581 represents $858,581,000,000) 2002 preliminary. For establishments with payroll. Based on the 1997 and 2002 Economic Censuses; See Appendix III]

Kind of business	NAICS code [1]	Number of establishments	Value of work done (mil. dol.)	Annual payroll (mil. dol.)	Paid employees (1,000)
1997 NAICS [1]					
Construction:					
1997	23	656,448	858,581	174,185	5,665
2002	23	697,747	1,140,368	235,530	6,944
Building, developing, and general contracting:					
1997	233	199,289	386,926	42,546	1,343
2002	233	223,114	531,162	61,882	1,753
Heavy construction:					
1997	234	42,557	130,795	30,292	880
2002	234	36,647	155,468	35,949	925
Special trade contractors:					
1997	235	414,602	340,861	101,347	3,442
2002	235	437,986	453,737	137,699	4,265
2002 NAICS [1]					
Construction	23	697,514	1,141,199	235,810	6,953
Construction of buildings	236	216,279	520,459	61,480	1,731
Heavy and civil engineering construction	237	36,566	153,210	32,957	841
Specialty trade contractors	238	444,669	467,529	141,373	4,381

[1] North American Industry Classification System; see text, Section 15.

Source: U.S. Census Bureau, 2002 Economic Census, *Advance Report,* issued March 2004. See Internet site: <http://www.census.gov/econ/census02/>

No. 920. Construction Materials—Producer Price Indexes: 1990 to 2003

[1982=100, except as noted. Data for 2003 are preliminary. For discussion of producer price indexes, see text, Section 14. This index, more formally known as the special commodity grouping index for construction materials, covers materials incorporated as integral part of a building or normally installed during construction and not readily removable. Excludes consumer durables such as kitchen ranges, refrigerators, etc. This index is not the same as the stage-of-processing index of intermediate materials and components for construction]

Commodity	1990	1995	1997	1998	1999	2000	2001	2002	2003
Construction materials	**119.6**	**138.8**	**142.1**	**141.4**	**142.8**	**144.1**	**142.8**	**144.0**	**147.1**
Interior solvent based paint	133.0	164.5	180.5	185.7	188.0	191.1	190.2	190.5	199.1
Construction products from plastics	117.2	133.8	128.2	126.2	128.0	135.8	132.9	136.1	138.6
Douglas fir, dressed	138.4	198.8	221.3	186.1	212.1	185.2	178.1	178.5	176.9
Southern pine, dressed	111.2	166.9	201.2	177.3	185.7	161.0	152.5	145.2	145.8
Millwork	130.4	163.8	170.9	171.1	174.7	176.4	179.2	179.8	181.8
Softwood plywood	119.6	188.1	175.5	174.9	207.0	173.3	167.8	164.1	195.6
Hardwood plywood and related products	102.7	122.2	127.1	126.9	128.6	130.2	130.4	131.5	129.0
Softwood plywood veneer, ex. reinforced/backed	142.3	203.5	201.7	180.1	197.4	182.2	175.8	172.8	183.9
Building paper and building board mill products	112.2	144.9	129.6	132.9	141.6	138.8	129.3	129.3	159.7
Steel pipe and tubes [1]	102.6	104.4	106.9	109.4	102.5	106.6	104.0	106.7	113.5
Builders hardware	133.0	153.2	158.4	160.8	161.9	163.8	166.4	169.3	170.2
Plumbing fixtures and brass fittings	144.3	166.0	174.5	175.1	176.7	180.4	180.8	181.9	183.4
Heating equipment	131.6	147.5	152.4	153.3	154.0	155.6	157.1	157.9	163.3
Metal doors, sash, and trim	131.4	156.5	161.0	161.3	162.2	165.1	167.1	168.0	169.9
Siding, aluminum [2]	(NA)	132.4	132.1	134.5	135.4	142.2	141.5	141.0	(NA)
Outdoor lighting equipment, including parts [3]	113.0	120.8	123.2	122.8	122.3	124.7	125.7	126.2	126.9
Commercial fluorescent fixtures [4]	113.0	121.0	122.8	119.0	118.7	117.7	114.0	114.0	115.5
Architectural and ornamental metalwork [5]	118.7	128.0	133.5	135.4	136.2	139.8	141.7	144.2	147.2
Fabricated ferrous wire products [1]	114.6	125.7	128.0	130.1	130.6	130.0	129.8	129.7	131.4
Elevators, escalators, and other lifts	110.1	113.0	114.8	116.0	117.5	118.7	119.4	120.0	118.6
Stamped metal switch and receptacle box	158.0	183.5	189.0	191.5	192.8	183.0	195.4	195.4	196.1
Concrete ingredients and related products	115.3	134.7	142.5	147.6	152.1	155.6	159.1	162.6	164.9
Concrete products	113.5	129.4	136.0	140.0	143.7	147.8	151.7	152.7	153.5
Clay construction products exc. refractories	129.9	141.3	143.5	144.9	148.3	152.8	155.7	152.8	154.2
Prep. asphalt and tar roofing and siding products	95.8	97.8	96.5	95.7	95.2	100.0	103.3	106.6	110.6
Gypsum products	105.2	154.5	170.8	177.6	208.0	201.4	156.4	168.9	171.4
Insulation materials	108.4	118.8	117.7	119.7	131.7	128.6	127.6	128.3	128.7
Paving mixtures and blocks	101.2	105.8	113.2	112.5	112.9	130.4	134.6	136.2	142.7

NA Not available. [1] June 1982=100. [2] December 1982=100. [3] June 1985=100. [4] Recessed nonair. [5] December 1983=100.

Source: U.S. Bureau of Labor Statistics, *Producer Price Indexes,* monthly and annual. See Internet site <http://www.bls.gov/ppi/home.htm>.

No. 921. Price and Cost Indexes for Construction: 1980 to 2003

[1996=100. Excludes Alaska and Hawaii. Indexes of certain of these sources are published on bases different from those shown here]

Name of index	1980	1985	1990	1995	1999	2000	2001	2002	2003
U.S. Census Bureau Composite:									
Fixed-weighted [1]	59.3	71.8	85.5	97.7	110.3	115.3	120.2	122.7	(NA)
Implicit price deflator [2]	59.0	71.1	85.0	97.8	110.4	115.4	119.6	122.6	(NA)
U.S. Census Bureau houses under construction: [3]									
Fixed-weighted	58.0	69.8	84.6	98.1	110.4	115.4	121.2	124.5	130.3
Price deflator	57.0	68.3	83.4	98.1	110.4	115.5	121.3	124.7	130.8
Federal Highway Administration, composite [4]	79.7	83.6	88.9	99.8	111.9	119.3	118.7	121.2	(NA)
Bureau of Reclamation composite [5]	62	75	85	98	107	111	112	114	(NA)
Turner Construction Co.: Building construction [6]	54	74	87	97	113	118	121	123	(NA)
Engineering News-Record: [7]									
Buildings	60.6	75.8	84.4	97.1	107.9	110.5	111.6	113.1	(NA)
Construction	57.6	74.6	84.2	97.3	107.8	110.7	112.7	116.3	(NA)
Handy-Whitman public utility: [8]									
Buildings	66	76	85	97	107	110	114	116	(NA)
Electric [9]	60	74	86	98	105	109	113	116	(NA)
Gas	60	75	86	99	107	111	114	116	(NA)
Water [10]	64	76	85	98	107	112	116	120	(NA)
C. A. Turner Telephone Plant [11]	79	77	87	96	101	103	106	108	(NA)

NA Not available. [1] Weighted average of the various indexes used to deflate the Construction Put in Place series. In calculating the index, the weights (i.e., the composition of current dollar estimates in 1996 by category) are held constant. [2] Derived ratio of total current to constant dollar Construction Put in Place (multiplied by 100). [3] Excludes value of site. [4] Based on average contract unit bid prices for composite mile (involving specific average amounts of excavation, paving, reinforcing steel, structural steel, and structural concrete). [5] Derived from the four quarterly indexes which are weighted averages of costs of labor, materials, and equipment for the construction of dams and reclamation projects. [6] Based on firm's cost experience with respect to labor rates, materials prices, competitive conditions, efficiency of plant and management, and productivity. [7] Building construction index computed on the basis of a hypothetical unit of construction requiring 6 bbl. of portland cement, 1,088 M bd. ft. of 2" x 4" lumber, 2,500 lb. of structural steel, and 68.38 hours of skilled labor. General construction index based on same materials components combined with 200 hours of common labor. [8] Based on data covering public utility construction costs in six geographic regions. Covers skilled and common labor. [9] As derived by U.S. Census Bureau. Covers steam generation plants only. [10] As derived by U.S. Census Bureau. Reflects costs for structures and improvements at water pumping and treatment plants. [11] Computed by the Census Bureau by averaging the weighted component indexes published for six geographic regions.

Source: U.S. Census Bureau, "Construction Spending", Internet site <http://www.census.gov/const/www/c30index.html>.

No. 922. Value of New Construction Put in Place: 1980 to 2003

[In millions of dollars (273,936 represents $273,936,000,000). Represents value of construction put in place during year; differs from building permit and construction contract data in timing and coverage. Includes installed cost of normal building service equipment and selected types of industrial production equipment (largely site fabricated). Excludes cost of shipbuilding, land, and most types of machinery and equipment. For methodology, see Appendix III]

Year		Private			Public		
	Total	Total	Residential buildings	Nonresiden-tial	Total	Federal	State and local
1980	273,936	210,290	100,381	109,909	63,646	9,642	54,004
1981	289,070	224,378	99,241	125,137	64,691	10,413	54,278
1982	279,332	216,268	84,676	131,592	63,064	10,008	53,056
1983	311,887	248,437	125,833	122,604	63,450	10,557	52,893
1984	370,190	299,952	155,015	144,937	70,238	11,240	58,998
1985	403,416	325,601	160,520	165,081	77,815	12,004	65,811
1986	433,454	348,872	190,677	158,195	84,582	12,412	72,170
1987	446,643	355,994	199,652	156,342	90,648	14,052	76,596
1988	462,012	367,277	204,496	162,781	94,735	12,264	82,471
1989	477,502	379,328	204,255	175,073	98,174	12,155	86,018
1990	476,778	369,300	191,103	178,197	107,478	12,099	95,379
1991	432,592	322,483	166,251	156,232	110,109	12,845	97,264
1992	463,661	347,814	199,393	148,421	115,847	14,376	101,471
1993	491,033	375,073	225,067	150,006	115,960	14,424	101,535
1994	539,193	418,999	258,561	160,438	120,193	14,440	105,753
1995	557,818	427,885	247,351	180,534	129,933	15,751	114,181
1996	615,900	476,638	281,115	195,523	139,263	15,325	123,938
1997	653,059	502,734	289,014	213,720	150,695	14,087	136,608
1998	705,685	551,383	314,607	236,776	154,302	14,318	139,984
1999	766,065	596,331	350,562	245,769	169,732	14,025	155,706
2000	828,160	642,633	374,457	268,176	185,529	14,166	171,362
2001	858,291	652,496	388,324	264,172	205,797	15,081	190,715
2002	871,342	651,706	421,912	229,794	219,636	16,578	203,057
2003	915,742	690,019	476,143	213,876	225,724	17,561	208,163

Source: U.S. Census Bureau, "Construction Spending", Internet site <http://www.census.gov/const/www/c30index.html>.

Construction and Housing   595

No. 923. Value of Private Construction Put in Place: 1995 to 2003

[In millions of dollars (427,885 represents $427,885,000,000). Represents value of construction put in place during year; differs from building permit and construction contract data in timing and coverage. See Appendix III]

Type of construction	1995	1996	1997	1998	1999	2000	2001	2002	2003
Total construction [1]	**427,885**	**476,638**	**502,734**	**551,383**	**596,331**	**642,633**	**652,496**	**651,706**	**690,019**
Residential	247,351	281,115	289,014	314,607	350,562	374,457	388,324	421,912	476,143
New single family	153,515	170,790	175,179	199,409	223,837	236,788	249,086	265,889	310,575
New multi-family	17,889	20,324	22,883	24,574	27,434	28,259	30,305	32,952	35,318
Improvements	75,947	90,002	90,951	90,624	99,290	109,410	108,933	123,071	130,250
Nonresidential	180,534	195,523	213,720	236,776	245,769	268,176	264,172	229,794	213,876
Lodging	7,131	10,914	12,898	14,818	15,955	16,304	14,519	10,467	9,946
Office [1]	22,996	26,530	32,813	40,394	45,052	52,407	49,745	35,296	30,413
General	20,569	23,216	29,301	37,615	41,745	49,637	47,136	32,356	27,205
Financial	2,339	3,231	3,157	2,636	3,125	2,689	2,586	2,857	3,184
Commercial [1]	44,096	49,381	53,088	55,681	59,376	64,055	63,606	59,183	57,680
Automotive [1]	4,191	5,251	5,736	5,270	5,904	5,967	5,650	5,807	5,017
Sales	883	1,250	1,743	1,542	1,573	1,629	2,014	2,235	2,065
Service/parts	2,448	2,993	3,213	2,527	3,270	3,009	2,394	2,308	1,854
Parking	860	1,008	781	1,200	1,062	1,330	1,242	1,265	1,099
Food/beverage [1]	7,169	7,478	8,566	9,118	8,277	8,786	8,765	7,914	8,392
Food	3,062	3,776	4,658	4,665	4,610	4,792	4,300	4,207	4,138
Dining/drinking	3,408	2,958	3,058	3,817	2,874	2,935	3,441	2,916	3,416
Fast food	699	744	850	636	793	1,058	1,024	792	837
Multiretail [1]	11,976	13,331	12,157	13,254	15,234	14,911	16,373	15,581	15,496
General merchandise	5,339	5,159	4,083	3,778	4,668	5,100	5,066	6,009	5,495
Shopping center	4,086	5,496	5,694	6,045	7,187	6,803	7,769	6,605	6,756
Shopping mall	2,175	2,189	1,949	2,917	2,873	2,523	2,701	2,108	2,264
Other commercial [1]	8,432	8,202	10,203	11,050	11,179	13,537	11,945	12,083	11,174
Drug store	536	750	1,007	1,409	1,645	1,682	1,185	1,644	1,786
Building supply store	1,372	1,201	1,323	1,742	1,588	2,592	3,016	2,471	2,310
Other stores	5,653	5,327	7,090	7,025	6,849	8,136	6,995	7,145	6,119
Warehouse	9,299	11,458	12,563	12,698	13,702	14,822	15,691	11,908	12,305
General commercial	8,944	10,849	11,501	11,732	12,756	13,511	14,440	10,934	10,993
Farm	3,014	3,658	3,815	4,284	5,059	5,988	5,135	5,786	5,284
Health care	15,259	15,420	17,390	17,737	18,388	19,455	19,506	22,438	23,648
Hospital	8,807	8,348	9,968	9,469	9,491	10,183	11,313	13,925	14,797
Medical building	4,064	3,728	4,001	4,070	4,910	5,066	4,638	4,924	5,864
Special care	2,388	3,344	3,421	4,197	3,987	4,206	3,555	3,538	2,957
Educational [1]	5,699	6,985	8,802	9,829	9,756	11,683	12,846	13,109	13,384
Preschool	326	398	531	619	663	770	874	593	714
Primary/secondary	1,245	1,560	2,032	2,174	2,420	2,948	3,536	3,605	3,265
Higher education [1]	3,055	3,619	4,327	4,945	5,204	6,333	6,597	6,875	7,169
Instructional	1,712	2,028	1,991	2,469	2,258	3,058	3,210	3,619	3,597
Dormitory	483	573	789	955	1,274	1,356	1,555	1,528	1,769
Sports/recreation	192	260	475	403	515	645	755	772	665
Other educational	817	1,042	1,714	1,798	1,232	1,318	1,421	1,651	1,791
Gallery/museum	571	662	1,107	1,127	778	920	990	1,312	1,371
Religious [1]	4,348	4,537	5,782	6,604	7,371	8,030	8,393	8,335	8,481
House of worship	2,951	3,211	3,844	4,549	5,057	5,656	6,040	6,021	6,169
Other religious	1,389	1,318	1,935	2,054	2,314	2,347	2,330	2,312	2,312
Auxiliary building	619	620	874	992	1,252	1,280	1,247	1,358	1,264
Public safety	185	321	569	586	465	423	274	217	191
Amusement and recreation [1]	5,886	7,016	8,537	8,589	9,550	8,768	7,828	7,478	7,892
Theme/amusement park	563	727	723	866	919	747	462	230	252
Sports	910	1,193	1,333	1,136	1,495	1,068	1,067	1,427	1,364
Fitness	637	622	801	889	1,137	1,152	1,294	1,286	1,266
Performance/meeting center	365	539	628	603	546	732	977	900	862
Social center	1,558	1,597	1,979	2,093	2,006	2,368	2,337	2,285	2,044
Movie theater/studio	848	1,271	2,199	2,441	2,376	1,461	792	568	832
Transportation [1]	4,759	5,820	6,208	7,290	6,525	6,879	7,058	6,855	6,515
Air	666	871	901	1,093	1,106	1,804	1,993	1,281	1,032
Land	4,008	4,794	5,183	6,112	5,164	4,907	4,883	5,406	5,389
Railroad	3,509	4,398	4,922	5,736	4,670	4,263	4,456	4,665	4,750
Communication	11,112	11,824	12,452	12,473	18,405	18,799	19,596	18,059	12,412
Power [1]	22,006	17,413	16,362	21,078	21,136	28,008	30,032	31,073	27,930
Electricity	14,274	11,256	11,325	12,381	14,585	22,038	23,803	23,400	19,721
Gas	6,279	4,722	4,006	7,372	4,918	4,891	5,078	6,144	6,508
Oil	929	1,015	969	1,265	1,489	1,003	943	1,193	1,117
Sewage and waste disposal	576	637	468	339	516	508	402	246	298
Water supply	670	468	448	563	413	714	563	397	394
Manufacturing [1]	35,364	38,101	37,624	40,482	32,631	31,800	29,529	16,403	14,231
Food/beverage/tobacco	4,525	4,294	3,957	3,538	3,383	3,374	3,193	2,026	1,774
Textile/apparel/leather & allied	824	743	584	712	456	350	240	204	153
Wood	616	689	522	492	427	412	266	344	260
Paper	1,448	1,711	1,548	1,232	838	628	990	422	558
Print/publishing	1,197	993	930	1,104	856	719	959	480	431
Petroleum/coal	4,741	2,348	1,186	1,064	927	1,069	907	640	443
Chemical	5,531	5,445	6,034	8,264	6,181	3,223	3,800	4,052	3,315
Plastic/rubber	1,475	1,632	1,959	2,137	2,222	1,398	1,077	559	420
Nonmetallic mineral	856	1,220	1,004	1,481	1,188	1,603	1,734	387	618
Primary metal	2,533	2,244	2,802	2,603	1,992	1,677	611	173	301
Fabricated metal	808	1,585	2,162	2,036	1,891	1,823	1,128	602	429
Machinery	1,275	1,169	1,106	1,257	966	731	674	572	506
Computer/electronic/electrical	6,332	8,945	7,537	7,557	4,415	5,386	4,734	1,386	1,006
Transportation equipment	2,382	2,948	3,453	3,497	3,418	5,347	5,385	2,770	2,291
Furniture	213	308	167	296	282	348	182	105	196

[1] Includes other types of construction, not shown separately.

Source: U.S. Census Bureau, "Construction Spending", Internet site <http://www.census.gov/const/www/c30index.html>.

No. 924. Value of State and Local Government Construction Put in Place: 1995 to 2003

[In millions of dollars (114,181 represents $114,181,000,000). See headnote, Table 923]

Type of construction	1995	1996	1997	1998	1999	2000	2001	2002	2003
Total construction [1]	114,181	123,938	136,608	139,984	155,706	171,362	190,715	203,057	208,163
Residential	4,043	4,220	4,336	4,340	4,603	4,200	5,025	5,183	5,281
Multifamily	3,976	4,144	4,238	4,242	4,584	4,175	4,950	5,070	5,093
Nonresidential	110,138	119,718	132,272	135,644	151,103	167,163	185,690	197,875	202,882
Office	3,914	4,404	4,619	4,605	4,521	6,256	7,214	7,980	8,258
Commercial [1]	1,329	1,724	2,227	1,993	2,519	2,543	3,197	3,081	3,058
Automotive	965	1,257	1,553	1,603	1,915	1,719	2,492	2,178	2,215
Parking	794	1,020	1,425	1,549	1,703	1,596	2,473	2,152	2,163
Warehouse	231	280	295	258	342	464	395	375	448
Health care	3,156	3,442	3,501	2,884	3,166	3,944	3,815	4,442	5,228
Hospital	1,960	2,108	2,498	1,980	2,220	2,716	2,756	3,230	3,561
Medical building	801	937	657	515	494	684	631	649	1,092
Special care	395	396	345	389	452	545	428	562	576
Educational [1]	25,743	28,603	33,758	35,015	41,117	45,616	50,974	57,549	59,286
Primary/secondary [1]	17,545	20,009	23,853	26,064	30,494	32,888	35,399	40,611	40,247
Elementary	5,242	6,301	8,015	9,492	10,314	11,939	13,612	14,660	13,275
Middle/junior high	3,745	3,685	3,988	3,930	5,992	5,676	6,685	8,140	7,993
High	4,833	6,130	6,687	7,627	11,053	12,988	13,587	16,588	18,122
Higher education [1]	6,883	7,311	8,198	7,721	8,914	10,483	12,897	13,827	15,473
Instructional	4,277	4,746	4,459	4,307	5,272	6,163	7,601	7,728	9,120
Parking	158	169	262	331	369	498	542	419	464
Administration	128	91	189	179	270	287	192	441	235
Dormitory	324	396	388	548	802	1,051	1,378	1,569	2,035
Library	300	439	695	368	327	300	360	425	549
Student union/cafeteria	238	231	405	318	298	314	597	999	678
Sports/recreation	625	538	873	795	767	942	1,243	1,498	1,357
Infrastructure	788	585	654	780	701	814	804	527	623
Other educational	1,110	1,121	1,250	1,128	1,372	1,602	2,088	2,546	2,699
Library/archive	704	853	779	566	945	948	1,616	2,050	1,805
Public safety [1]	5,928	6,718	6,668	7,575	7,858	8,146	7,865	7,582	7,753
Correctional	4,854	5,586	5,701	6,588	6,575	6,611	6,358	5,786	5,577
Detention	4,049	4,749	4,786	5,618	5,338	5,431	4,989	4,346	4,163
Police/sheriff	804	837	916	970	1,237	1,180	1,369	1,440	1,414
Other public safety	1,025	1,126	967	988	1,284	1,534	1,507	1,796	2,176
Fire/rescue	652	831	773	795	1,095	1,387	1,287	1,569	1,811
Amusement and recreation [1]	6,142	6,056	6,857	7,666	9,159	10,563	11,863	11,722	11,262
Sports	1,637	1,477	2,311	3,173	3,402	3,181	3,525	3,268	2,775
Performance/meeting center	1,751	2,127	1,629	1,343	1,572	2,905	3,788	3,703	3,037
Convention center	1,224	1,318	938	835	1,099	1,957	2,941	2,703	2,068
Social center	772	911	961	947	1,399	1,605	1,852	1,840	2,153
Neighborhood center	581	612	673	622	1,059	1,234	1,379	1,189	1,648
Park/camp	1,696	1,430	1,874	2,020	2,584	2,681	2,392	2,456	2,718
Transportation	8,967	9,998	9,708	10,197	11,296	14,231	16,117	17,291	17,288
Air [1]	3,855	4,666	4,852	5,594	5,960	7,347	7,961	8,121	8,457
Passenger terminal	1,209	1,656	2,086	2,196	2,217	3,198	2,822	3,042	3,883
Runway	2,176	2,593	2,260	2,563	3,100	3,520	4,403	4,304	3,925
Land [1]	4,009	4,067	3,642	3,823	4,275	5,649	6,356	7,284	7,664
Passenger terminal	1,147	1,362	1,237	1,222	1,249	1,366	1,584	1,861	2,255
Mass transit	1,734	1,787	1,607	1,548	1,347	1,624	2,526	3,368	3,366
Railroad	462	402	401	564	1,033	1,607	1,124	670	477
Water [1]	1,103	1,264	1,214	780	1,061	1,236	1,800	1,886	1,164
Dock/marina	690	898	729	421	657	940	1,289	1,197	911
Dry dock/marine terminal	204	308	477	352	404	257	485	689	252
Power	2,879	2,503	3,101	2,495	3,228	3,891	4,128	3,237	3,913
Electrical	2,231	2,225	2,893	2,052	2,538	3,714	3,874	2,787	3,348
Distribution	733	656	1,650	1,511	1,494	1,479	1,064	992	1,227
Highway and street [1]	37,616	39,500	43,017	44,782	49,174	53,081	58,861	60,625	61,991
Pavement	29,164	30,472	32,416	33,180	36,464	39,048	42,897	43,831	43,070
Lighting	659	796	812	1,180	910	878	1,280	951	1,321
Retaining wall	187	176	493	711	816	1,133	651	793	646
Tunnel	346	430	539	862	926	919	1,116	701	696
Bridge	6,615	6,682	7,299	7,229	8,479	9,568	11,382	12,567	14,436
Toll/weigh	152	138	219	247	277	331	109	231	205
Maintenance building	53	159	307	362	354	302	424	317	273
Rest facility/streetscape	167	464	722	838	940	901	1,004	1,236	1,340
Sewage and waste disposal [1]	8,419	9,801	10,515	9,943	10,524	10,249	11,100	12,711	12,782
Sewage/dry waste [1]	4,825	6,420	6,830	6,589	7,082	6,836	7,089	8,254	7,994
Plant	1,641	2,173	1,969	1,925	2,178	2,025	1,882	2,221	2,231
Line/pump station	2,960	4,001	4,639	4,422	4,612	4,629	5,003	5,872	5,644
Waste water	3,522	3,346	3,664	3,317	3,436	3,413	4,011	4,457	4,788
Plant	2,467	2,211	2,680	2,276	2,613	2,363	2,991	3,504	3,635
Line/drain	1,055	1,135	984	1,041	823	1,050	1,020	954	1,153
Water supply [1]	4,713	5,618	6,493	6,678	6,967	6,972	8,984	9,674	9,599
Plant	1,204	1,372	1,664	1,912	2,154	2,246	3,189	3,170	3,493
Well	212	260	179	247	254	277	309	460	296
Line	2,516	2,841	3,353	3,106	3,089	3,395	4,162	4,305	4,082
Pump station	286	437	349	418	571	458	537	705	636
Reservoir	208	409	514	429	409	195	325	383	367
Tank/tower	246	298	433	565	491	462	462	651	725
Conservation and development [1]	1,265	1,191	1,503	1,444	1,346	1,304	1,400	1,288	1,267
Dam/levee	329	349	631	597	525	425	317	355	313
Breakwater/jetty	358	472	360	456	382	377	637	500	597

[1] Includes other types of construction, not shown separately.
Source: U.S. Census Bureau, "Construction Spending", Internet site <http://www.census.gov/const/www/c30index.html>.

[151.8 reresents $151,800,000,000. Building construction includes new structures and additions; nonbuilding construction includes major alterations to existing structures which affect only valuation, since no additional floor area is created by "alteration"]

Year	Total	Resi-dential build-ings	Nonresidential buildings Total	Com-mer-cial[1]	Manu-fac-turing	Educa-tional[2]	Health	Public build-ings	Reli-gious	Social and recrea-tional	Mis-cella-neous	Non-build-ing con-struc-tion
VALUE (bil. dol.)												
1980	151.8	60.4	56.9	27.7	9.2	7.4	5.4	1.6	1.2	2.7	1.7	34.5
1985	235.6	102.1	92.1	54.6	8.1	10.0	7.8	3.1	2.0	4.0	2.5	41.4
1990	246.0	100.9	95.4	44.8	8.4	16.6	9.2	5.7	2.2	5.3	3.1	49.7
1994	296.7	133.6	101.5	40.8	11.2	21.0	10.5	6.1	2.5	6.5	3.0	61.6
1995	306.5	127.9	114.2	46.6	13.8	22.9	10.8	6.3	2.8	7.1	3.8	64.4
1996	332.0	146.5	120.5	51.9	13.1	23.0	11.1	6.3	2.9	8.1	4.1	65.1
1997	362.4	153.6	138.9	59.8	14.0	28.4	11.9	7.0	3.8	10.0	4.0	69.8
1998	405.6	179.8	154.5	74.0	12.1	30.1	12.9	6.6	4.3	10.8	3.6	71.3
1999	447.2	195.0	168.7	77.2	11.3	37.1	13.6	8.2	4.5	11.6	5.1	83.5
2000	473.0	208.3	173.3	80.9	8.9	40.9	12.4	7.5	4.6	13.8	4.4	91.3
2001	496.6	219.6	169.1	70.3	8.1	47.0	14.4	7.8	4.8	12.0	4.8	107.9
2002	503.0	248.3	154.8	59.5	5.4	45.3	16.1	7.3	5.1	11.5	4.6	99.9
2003	527.0	282.0	153.5	58.0	6.2	47.4	15.4	6.9	4.5	10.7	4.3	91.5
FLOOR SPACE (mil. sq. ft.)												
1980	3,102	1,839	1,263	738	220	103	55	18	28	49	52	(X)
1985	3,853	2,324	1,529	1,039	165	111	73	28	32	44	38	(X)
1990	3,020	1,817	1,203	694	128	152	69	47	29	51	32	(X)
1994	3,411	2,267	1,144	600	143	172	72	45	30	51	31	(X)
1995	3,454	2,172	1,281	700	163	186	70	40	33	56	33	(X)
1996	3,776	2,479	1,297	723	155	177	77	41	32	60	33	(X)
1997	4,126	2,586	1,540	855	191	204	89	48	42	77	35	(X)
1998	4,812	3,015	1,797	1,107	166	219	96	42	47	85	39	(X)
1999	5,091	3,253	1,838	1,115	141	261	98	49	48	87	29	(X)
2000	4,982	3,113	1,869	1,180	111	273	88	44	49	94	27	(X)
2001	4,829	3,158	1,672	989	93	295	92	44	50	80	25	(X)
2002	4,787	3,352	1,436	810	67	277	97	37	52	71	25	(X)
2003	5,052	3,672	1,380	781	68	269	92	35	45	66	25	(X)

X Not applicable.   [1] Includes nonindustrial warehouses.   [2] Includes science.

Source: McGraw-Hill Construction Dodge, a Division of the McGraw-Hill Companies, New York, NY (copyright).

No. 926. Construction Contracts—Value by State: 2000 to 2003

[In millions of dollars (472,965 represents $472,965,000,000). Represents value of construction in states in which work was actually done. See headnote, Table 925]

State	2000	2002	2003 Total[1]	2003 Resi-den-tial	2003 Non-resi-den-tial	State	2000	2002	2003 Total[1]	2003 Resi-den-tial	2003 Non-resi-den-tial
U.S.	472,965	503,036	526,996	282,037	153,476	MO	7,499	8,714	9,358	4,834	2,509
AL	7,225	6,979	7,522	3,231	2,322	MT	1,004	950	974	405	243
AK	1,327	1,971	1,830	542	638	NE	2,646	3,356	3,457	1,563	1,085
AZ	13,966	14,427	17,729	11,507	4,688	NV	6,978	8,106	9,536	5,519	2,225
AR	3,740	3,592	3,974	1,960	1,105	NH	2,514	2,419	2,170	1,222	691
CA	52,880	57,777	59,781	33,907	17,320	NJ	10,940	11,418	11,739	4,344	5,135
CO	12,491	12,227	11,574	7,142	2,699	NM	3,140	2,896	3,096	1,514	1,124
CT	5,181	4,779	4,826	2,118	2,294	NY	20,757	24,014	20,556	11,676	4,891
DE	1,350	1,436	1,504	798	446	NC	17,258	17,755	18,853	7,407	4,445
DC	1,763	2,491	1,837	311	1,222	ND	854	1,102	746	413	246
FL	35,086	42,442	48,876	32,217	9,941	OH	16,270	17,182	16,792	8,193	5,521
GA	20,422	19,620	20,084	12,027	5,254	OK	5,330	4,656	5,099	2,537	1,675
HI	1,409	1,808	2,245	1,363	467	OR	6,020	6,321	7,356	4,309	1,890
ID	2,521	2,619	3,050	2,130	621	PA	14,861	16,345	14,655	6,216	5,793
IL	17,167	20,813	19,034	9,921	5,916	RI	1,063	1,330	1,183	558	323
IN	11,011	11,261	12,673	6,472	4,307	SC	7,759	8,845	9,707	5,621	2,419
IA	3,776	4,776	6,517	2,097	1,706	SD	1,221	1,279	1,188	564	221
KS	4,463	4,954	4,529	2,306	1,224	TN	10,108	9,347	10,127	5,882	2,878
KY	6,625	6,745	7,157	3,250	2,139	TX	41,129	41,912	44,683	23,583	12,942
LA	5,528	5,251	6,541	2,895	2,080	UT	4,421	5,177	4,950	3,276	1,146
ME	1,711	1,842	2,058	1,068	598	VT	602	946	890	435	317
MD	7,836	8,857	8,972	4,287	3,086	VA	13,634	14,114	14,970	8,176	4,495
MA	11,983	9,873	8,751	3,983	3,659	WA	10,317	10,794	12,788	6,629	3,369
MI	14,741	13,034	13,918	7,199	4,400	WV	1,859	1,871	1,697	703	485
MN	8,838	9,227	10,446	6,059	2,408	WI	8,045	8,976	9,966	5,368	2,491
MS	2,917	3,445	3,654	1,700	1,146	WY	778	1,071	1,028	421	272

[1] Includes nonbuilding construction, not shown separately.

Source: McGraw-Hill Construction Dodge, a Division of the McGraw-Hill Companies, New York, NY, (copyright).

[1,592.3 represents 1,592,300. Based on about 19,000 places in United States having building permit systems]

State	Housing units (1,000)			Valuation (mil. dol.)			State	Housing units (1,000)			Valuation (mil. dol.)		
	2000	2003 Total	1 unit	2000	2003 Total	1 unit		2000	2003 Total	1 unit	2000	2003 Total	1 unit
U.S.	1,592.3	1,889.2	1,460.9	185,744	249,693	218,229	MT...	2.6	3.8	2.3	235	412	324
AL...	17.4	22.3	17.7	1,718	2,464	2,169	NE...	9.1	10.3	8.7	830	1,250	1,146
AK...	2.1	3.5	1.7	333	560	335	NV...	32.3	43.4	33.1	3,312	4,879	4,313
AZ...	61.5	75.0	65.8	7,158	10,519	9,922	NH...	6.7	8.6	6.6	937	1,208	1,062
AR...	9.2	14.8	10.1	859	1,541	1,328	NJ...	34.6	33.0	22.2	3,376	3,782	3,073
CA...	145.6	191.9	139.9	23,344	31,778	27,194	NM...	8.9	13.8	11.9	1,073	1,703	1,621
CO...	54.6	39.6	33.8	6,822	6,258	5,767	NY...	44.1	49.7	24.2	4,992	6,194	4,070
CT...	9.4	10.4	8.2	1,425	1,665	1,519	NC...	78.4	79.2	66.9	8,643	10,268	9,514
DE...	4.6	7.8	6.7	414	791	756	ND...	2.1	3.7	2.3	190	398	319
DC...	0.8	1.4	0.2	54	96	19	OH...	49.7	53.0	42.7	6,154	7,503	6,884
FL...	155.3	213.6	156.9	17,462	28,352	23,121	OK...	11.1	15.0	12.7	1,204	1,861	1,736
GA...	91.8	96.7	80.7	8,722	10,837	9,894	OR...	19.9	25.0	17.9	2,533	3,771	3,219
HI...	4.9	7.3	6.2	823	1,316	1,167	PA...	41.1	47.4	38.6	4,616	6,052	5,466
ID...	10.9	15.1	12.6	1,359	1,943	1,811	RI...	2.6	2.3	1.9	296	338	314
IL...	51.9	62.2	45.4	6,528	9,106	7,806	SC...	32.8	38.2	31.6	3,533	4,616	4,177
IN...	37.9	39.4	31.9	4,414	5,393	4,859	SD...	4.2	5.0	4.1	369	541	476
IA...	12.5	16.1	11.8	1,333	2,063	1,729	TN...	32.2	37.5	32.2	3,378	4,479	4,172
KS...	12.5	15.0	11.5	1,397	1,895	1,698	TX...	141.2	177.2	134.2	15,418	19,552	17,283
KY...	18.5	20.4	17.4	1,767	2,347	2,200	UT...	17.6	22.5	18.4	2,138	3,082	2,765
LA...	14.7	22.2	18.5	1,553	2,596	2,220	VT...	2.5	2.8	2.4	319	406	367
ME...	6.2	7.9	7.3	723	1,067	1,012	VA...	48.4	55.9	46.3	5,052	6,877	6,403
MD...	30.4	29.9	23.4	3,232	3,724	3,312	WA...	39.0	42.8	33.1	4,426	6,346	5,565
MA...	18.0	20.3	13.0	2,741	3,141	2,506	WV...	3.8	5.1	4.7	360	646	619
MI...	52.5	53.9	44.7	6,256	7,053	6,434	WI...	34.2	40.9	28.7	3,917	5,505	4,584
MN...	32.8	42.0	32.7	4,204	6,269	5,337	WY...	1.6	2.8	2.3	314	389	351
MS...	11.3	12.0	10.1	918	1,268	1,142							
MO...	24.3	29.3	22.7	2,569	3,597	3,148							

Source: U.S. Census Bureau, Construction Reports, Series C40, *Building Permits*, monthly; publication discontinued in 2001. See Internet site <http://www.census.gov/const/www/newresconstindex.html> and *New Residential Construction*, monthly.

[In thousands (1,434 represents 1,434,000). For composition of regions, see map inside front cover]

Year	Total units	Structures with—			Region				Units for sale		
		One unit	2 to 4 units	5 or more units	North-east	Mid-west	South	West	Total	Single-family	Multi-family
1970	1,434	813	85	536	218	294	612	311	(NA)	(NA)	(NA)
1975	1,160	892	64	204	149	294	442	275	576	531	45
1977	1,987	1,451	122	414	202	465	783	538	994	904	90
1978	2,020	1,433	125	462	200	451	824	545	1,032	901	131
1979	1,745	1,194	122	429	178	349	748	470	915	742	173
1980	1,292	852	110	331	125	218	643	306	689	526	163
1981	1,084	705	91	288	117	165	562	240	584	426	158
1982	1,062	663	80	320	117	149	591	205	549	409	140
1983	1,703	1,068	113	522	168	218	935	382	923	713	210
1984	1,750	1,084	121	544	204	243	866	436	934	728	206
1985	1,742	1,072	93	576	252	240	782	468	867	713	154
1986	1,805	1,179	84	542	294	296	733	483	925	782	143
1987	1,621	1,146	65	409	269	298	634	420	862	732	130
1988	1,488	1,081	59	348	235	274	575	404	808	709	99
1989	1,376	1,003	55	318	179	266	536	396	735	648	87
1990	1,193	895	37	260	131	253	479	329	585	529	56
1991	1,014	840	36	138	113	233	414	254	531	490	41
1992	1,200	1,030	31	139	127	288	497	288	659	618	41
1993	1,288	1,126	29	133	126	298	562	302	760	716	44
1994	1,457	1,198	35	224	138	329	639	351	815	763	52
1995	1,354	1,076	34	244	118	290	615	331	763	712	51
1996	1,477	1,161	45	271	132	322	662	361	833	774	59
1997	1,474	1,134	44	296	137	304	670	363	843	784	59
1998	1,617	1,271	43	303	149	331	743	395	941	882	59
1999	1,641	1,302	32	307	156	347	746	392	981	912	69
2000	1,569	1,231	39	299	155	318	714	383	946	871	75
2001	1,603	1,273	37	293	149	330	732	391	990	919	71
2002	1,705	1,359	39	308	158	350	782	416	1,070	999	71
2003	1,848	1,499	34	315	163	374	839	472	1,207	1,120	87

NA Not available.

Source: U.S. Census Bureau, Current Construction Reports, Series C20, *Housing Starts*, monthly; publication discontinued in 2001. See Internet site <http://www.census.gov/const/www/newresconstindex.html> and *New Residential Construction*, monthly.

[In thousands of units (1,535 represents 1,535,000)]

State	2000	2003, est.	2004, est.	2005, est. Total units	2005, est. Single-family units	State	2000	2003, est.	2004, est.	2005, est. Total units	2005, est. Single-family units
U.S.	1,535	1,840	1,774	1,708	1,398	MO	26.0	29.0	27.9	27.6	24.6
AL	21.2	21.0	20.2	20.1	16.8	MT	2.2	3.1	2.9	2.7	2.1
AK	2.1	2.3	2.2	2.0	1.5	NE	8.4	10.7	10.6	10.0	8.9
AZ	60.0	70.9	66.7	64.1	57.3	NV	34.5	42.1	39.6	38.0	29.7
AR	12.5	13.6	13.4	13.0	9.5	NH	6.0	8.1	7.7	7.1	6.0
CA	128.2	182.4	184.7	178.4	137.0	NJ	31.2	29.0	28.7	27.7	21.2
CO	45.9	37.9	36.7	37.6	30.8	NM	8.1	11.6	10.9	10.5	9.3
CT	10.0	9.5	9.1	8.8	7.9	NY	34.9	44.1	41.2	38.9	22.8
DE	5.2	6.8	6.6	6.2	6.1	NC	74.8	79.6	76.2	74.4	63.2
DC	0.4	1.7	1.4	1.1	0.2	ND	2.7	3.9	3.8	3.4	2.4
FL	148.1	205.1	194.4	181.9	139.9	OH	45.3	55.0	52.6	51.0	44.4
GA	81.5	96.4	92.5	89.2	76.0	OK	15.5	14.8	13.9	13.6	12.0
HI	3.8	6.9	7.0	6.7	5.6	OR	22.2	22.1	19.8	20.0	15.7
ID	11.5	13.9	13.4	12.9	11.4	PA	37.5	42.7	41.4	40.3	35.6
IL	48.1	65.2	63.3	60.2	47.6	RI	2.7	2.4	2.5	2.3	2.1
IN	37.6	42.5	41.0	39.9	34.6	SC	33.9	38.3	36.7	34.9	29.7
IA	13.0	16.1	15.6	14.8	12.2	SD	3.5	5.3	5.2	4.9	4.2
KS	15.2	14.1	14.0	13.7	12.0	TN	33.9	35.4	34.7	34.6	30.8
KY	21.4	20.4	19.8	19.7	16.8	TX	148.4	177.3	168.0	159.4	125.4
LA	15.8	19.2	18.9	18.2	15.8	UT	19.5	21.8	20.5	20.1	16.8
ME	5.8	7.7	7.7	7.1	6.9	VT	2.4	3.0	2.9	2.6	2.6
MD	27.9	29.3	29.5	29.2	24.0	VA	50.2	57.3	55.9	54.1	47.1
MA	17.7	17.1	16.6	16.3	12.6	WA	40.9	42.3	39.8	39.2	31.1
MI	50.9	57.4	55.5	53.6	47.7	WV	5.3	4.9	4.9	4.8	4.6
MN	30.7	44.1	42.5	39.7	33.9	WI	32.0	40.1	39.1	37.6	29.5
MS	12.8	12.5	12.2	12.1	9.8	WY	1.8	2.2	2.1	2.1	2.1

Source: National Association of Home Builders, Economics Division, Washington, DC. Data provided by the Econometric Forecasting Service.

[Percent distribution, except total houses. (966 represents 966,000). Data are percent distribution of characteristics for all houses completed (includes new houses completed, houses built for sale completed, contractor-built and owner-built houses completed, and houses completed for rent). Percents exclude houses for which characteristics specified were not reported]

Characteristic	1990	1995	2000	2002	2003	Characteristic	1990	1995	2000	2002	2003
Total houses (1,000)	966	1,066	1,242	1,325	1,386	Bedrooms	100	100	100	100	100
						2 or less	15	13	11	11	12
Construction type	100	100	100	100	100	3	57	57	54	52	51
Site built	(NA)	94	94	94	95	4 or more	29	30	35	36	37
Modular	(NA)	3	3	3	3						
Other	(NA)	3	3	3	2	Bathrooms	100	100	100	100	100
						1 1/2 or less	13	11	7	6	5
Exterior wall material	100	100	100	100	100	2	42	41	39	39	38
Brick	18	20	20	20	20	2 1/2 or more	45	48	54	55	56
Wood	39	25	14	10	8						
Stucco	18	16	17	19	21	Heating fuel	100	100	100	100	100
Vinyl siding [1]	(NA)	30	39	40	38	Gas	59	67	70	68	70
Aluminum siding	5	3	1	1	1	Electricity	33	28	27	28	27
Other [1]	20	6	7	11	13	Oil	5	3	3	3	2
						Other	3	1	1	1	1
Floor area	100	100	100	100	100						
Under 1,200 sq. ft.	11	10	6	5	5	Heating system	100	100	100	100	100
1,200 to 1,599 sq. ft.	22	22	18	19	17	Warm air furnace	65	67	71	71	71
1,600 to 1,999 sq. ft.	22	23	23	21	21	Electric heat pump	23	25	23	23	24
2,000 to 2,399 sq. ft.	17	17	18	18	19	Other	12	9	6	6	5
2,400 sq. ft. and over	29	28	35	37	38						
Average (sq. ft.)	2,080	2,095	2,266	2,320	2,330	Central air-conditioning	100	100	100	100	100
Median (sq. ft.)	1,905	1,920	2,057	2,114	2,137	With	76	80	85	87	88
						Without	24	20	15	13	12
Number of stories	100	100	100	100	100						
1	46	49	47	47	46	Fireplaces	100	100	100	100	100
2 or more	49	48	52	52	53	No fireplace	34	37	40	42	42
Split level	4	3	1	1	1	1 or more	66	63	60	58	58
Foundation	100	100	100	100	100	Parking facilities	100	100	100	100	100
Full or partial basement	38	39	37	34	32	Garage	82	84	89	88	88
Slab	40	42	46	50	52	Carport	2	2	1	1	1
Crawl space	21	19	17	16	15	No garage or carport	16	14	11	10	10

NA Not available.   [1] Prior to 1995 "other" includes vinyl siding.

Source: U.S. Census Bureau and U.S. Dept. of Housing and Urban Development, Current Construction Reports, Series C25, New One-Family Houses Sold, monthly, and Characteristics of New Housing, annual; publication discontinued in 2001, see Internet site <http://www.census.gov/const/www/charindex.html>.

No. 931. Average Length of Time From Start to Completion of New Privately Owned 1 Unit Residential Buildings: 1971 to 2003

[In months. For buildings started in permit issuing places]

Year	Total [1]	Purpose of construction			Region [2]			
		Built for sale	Contractor built	Owner built	Northeast	Midwest	South	West
1971	4.8	4.4	4.0	7.2	5.9	5.2	4.4	4.4
1972	5.2	4.8	4.4	7.8	6.0	5.6	4.9	5.0
1973	6.0	5.7	4.9	7.9	6.5	6.0	5.8	5.9
1974	6.2	6.1	4.9	8.0	6.6	6.5	6.0	6.2
1975	6.1	5.7	4.6	8.5	6.3	6.6	5.8	6.1
1976	5.5	5.2	4.6	7.4	6.1	6.0	5.0	5.5
1977	5.7	5.4	4.7	7.6	5.8	5.8	5.4	6.0
1978	6.2	5.9	5.3	8.5	6.5	6.6	5.7	6.7
1979	6.7	6.2	5.8	9.0	7.0	7.1	6.1	7.0
1980	6.9	6.2	5.5	10.1	7.7	8.0	6.1	7.4
1981	6.6	5.8	5.2	9.6	7.7	7.4	5.7	7.4
1982	6.6	5.6	5.5	10.4	8.0	7.5	5.9	7.2
1983	5.8	4.8	4.8	10.0	7.2	6.5	5.1	6.2
1984	6.1	5.2	4.8	10.7	7.0	6.7	5.4	6.7
1985	6.2	5.4	4.9	10.6	7.2	6.0	5.7	6.7
1986	6.2	5.4	4.9	11.1	7.3	6.5	5.6	6.4
1987	6.2	5.6	5.1	10.3	7.6	5.9	5.7	6.4
1988	6.5	5.8	5.3	10.4	8.8	5.8	5.7	6.6
1989	6.4	5.9	5.3	10.2	9.3	5.8	5.6	6.5
1990	6.4	5.9	5.3	10.3	9.3	5.6	5.7	6.9
1991	6.3	5.6	5.1	10.2	8.9	5.6	5.5	6.9
1992	5.8	5.0	5.0	9.5	7.6	5.6	5.1	6.1
1993	5.6	4.9	5.4	9.0	7.2	5.5	5.2	6.0
1994	5.6	4.9	5.3	9.1	7.1	5.7	5.3	5.6
1995	5.9	5.2	5.8	9.5	7.4	6.0	5.4	6.0
1996	6.0	5.2	5.8	9.9	8.2	6.1	5.6	5.6
1997	6.0	5.2	5.9	9.8	7.3	6.2	5.6	5.8
1998	6.0	5.4	6.0	9.5	7.1	6.2	5.5	6.1
1999	6.1	5.5	6.4	9.2	7.0	6.4	5.7	6.3
2000	6.2	5.6	6.5	9.2	7.5	6.4	5.9	6.0
2001	6.2	5.6	7.0	9.2	7.6	6.5	5.8	6.3
2002	6.1	5.5	6.6	9.6	7.3	6.4	5.6	6.2
2003	6.2	5.5	6.8	9.9	7.5	6.7	5.7	6.2

[1] Includes units built for rent, not shown separately. [2] For composition of regions, see map inside front cover.

Source: U.S. Census Bureau, *New Residential Construction.* See Internet site <http://www.census.gov/const/www/newresconstindex.html> (accessed 03 June 2004)

No. 932. Price Indexes of New One-Family Houses Sold by Region: 1979 to 2003

[1996=100. Based on kinds of homes sold in 1996. Includes the value of lot. For composition of regions, see map, inside front cover]

Year	Total	Northeast	Midwest	South	West
1979	54.0	43.7	54.3	56.6	52.1
1980	59.5	48.0	56.8	63.2	58.4
1981	64.2	52.1	62.1	68.7	62.0
1982	65.7	54.0	63.9	70.9	62.8
1983	67.1	57.3	63.7	72.8	64.0
1984	69.8	62.2	67.5	75.2	66.3
1985	70.7	68.5	66.4	76.7	66.7
1986	73.4	78.6	70.2	79.0	68.4
1987	77.4	89.2	74.9	81.9	72.0
1988	80.3	91.5	78.2	83.7	75.9
1989	83.5	94.1	80.0	86.1	80.7
1990	85.1	92.2	80.7	86.3	84.6
1991	86.2	89.2	82.8	87.9	85.1
1992	87.3	96.1	84.3	88.8	85.6
1993	91.1	93.3	90.0	93.0	88.7
1994	95.5	94.5	94.4	96.4	94.9
1995	98.2	96.7	98.1	99.4	96.5
1996	100.0	100.0	100.0	100.0	100.0
1997	102.9	102.8	103.3	102.8	102.9
1998	105.5	104.5	105.3	106.0	105.1
1999	110.7	108.8	110.3	110.5	111.7
2000	115.4	114.6	114.4	114.7	117.3
2001	119.5	122.6	115.8	117.8	123.9
2002	124.8	127.5	120.7	121.2	132.5
2003	131.9	137.5	124.7	126.5	144.3

Source: U.S. Census Bureau, *New Residential Sales.* See Internet site <http://www.census.gov/const/www/newressalesindex.html> (accessed 03 June 2003)

No. 933. New Privately Owned One-Family Houses Sold by Region and Type of Financing, 1980 to 2003, and by Sales-Price Group, 2003

[In thousands (545 represents 545,000). Based on a national probability sample of monthly interviews with builders or owners of one-family houses for which building permits have been issued or, for nonpermit areas, on which construction has started. For details, see source and Appendix III. For composition of regions, see map inside front cover]

Year and sales-price group	Total sales	Region				Financing type			
		Northeast	Midwest	South	West	Conventional[1]	FHA and VA	Rural Housing Service[2]	Cash
1980	545	50	81	267	145	302	196	14	32
1985	688	112	82	323	170	403	208	11	64
1990	534	71	89	225	149	337	138	10	50
1995	667	55	125	300	187	490	129	9	39
1996	757	74	137	337	209	570	140	9	38
1997	804	78	140	363	223	616	137	6	46
1998	886	81	164	398	243	693	136	9	48
1999	880	76	168	395	242	689	143	6	41
2000	877	71	155	406	244	695	138	4	40
2001	908	66	164	439	239	726	141	2	39
2002	973	65	185	450	273	788	140	4	42
2003	**1,086**	**79**	**189**	**511**	**307**	**911**	**130**	**4**	**41**
Under $100,000	54	(Z)	9	40	4	(NA)	(NA)	(NA)	(NA)
$100,000 to $149,999	242	8	45	152	37	(NA)	(NA)	(NA)	(NA)
$150,000 to $199,999	264	13	53	133	64	(NA)	(NA)	(NA)	(NA)
$200,000 to $299,999	260	25	48	108	80	(NA)	(NA)	(NA)	(NA)
$300,000 and over	265	33	34	77	121	(NA)	(NA)	(NA)	(NA)

NA Not available.   Z Represents or rounds to zero.   [1] Includes all other types of financing.   [2] Prior to 1996, the Farmers Home Administration.

Source: U.S. Census Bureau and U.S. Dept. of Housing and Urban Development, Current Construction Reports, Series C25, Characteristics of New Housing, annual; and New One-Family Houses Sold, monthly; publications discontinued in 2001. See Internet site <http://www.census.gov/const/www/newressalesindex.html> and New Residential Sales, monthly.

No. 934. Median Sales Price of New Privately Owned One-Family Houses Sold by Region: 1980 to 2003

[In dollars. For definition of median, see Guide to Tabular Presentation. For composition of regions, see map inside front cover. See Appendix III. See also headnote, table 933]

Year	U.S.	Northeast	Midwest	South	West	Year	U.S.	Northeast	Midwest	South	West
1980	64,600	69,500	63,400	59,600	72,300	1997	146,000	190,000	149,900	129,600	160,000
1985	84,300	103,300	80,300	75,000	92,600	1998	152,500	200,000	157,500	135,800	163,500
1990	122,900	159,000	107,900	99,000	147,500	1999	161,000	210,500	164,000	145,900	173,700
1993	126,500	162,600	125,000	115,000	135,000	2000	169,000	227,400	169,700	148,000	196,400
1994	130,000	169,000	132,900	116,900	140,400	2001	175,200	246,400	172,600	155,400	213,600
1995	133,900	180,000	134,000	124,500	141,400	2002	187,600	264,300	178,000	163,400	238,500
1996	140,000	186,000	138,000	126,200	153,900	2003	195,000	264,500	184,300	168,100	260,900

Source: U.S. Census Bureau and U.S. Dept. of Housing and Urban Development, Current Construction Reports, Series C25, Characteristics of New Housing, annual; and New One-Family Houses Sold, monthly; publications discontinued in 2001. See Internet site <http://www.census.gov/const/www/newressalesindex.html> and New Residential Sales, monthly.

No. 935. New Manufactured (Mobile) Homes Placed for Residential Use and Average Sales Price by Region: 1980 to 2003

[233.7 represents 233,700. A mobile home is a moveable dwelling, 8 feet or more wide and 40 feet or more long, designed to be towed on its own chassis, with transportation gear integral to the unit when it leaves the factory, and without need of permanent foundation. Excluded are travel trailers, motor homes, and modular housing. Data are based on a probability sample and subject to sampling variability; see source. For composition of regions, see map inside front cover]

Year	Units placed (1,000)					Average sales price (dol.)				
	Total	Northeast	Midwest	South	West	U.S.	Northeast	Midwest	South	West
1980	233.7	12.3	32.3	140.3	48.7	19,800	18,500	18,600	18,200	25,400
1985	283.4	20.2	38.6	187.6	36.9	21,800	22,700	21,500	20,400	28,700
1990	195.4	18.8	37.7	108.4	30.6	27,800	30,000	27,000	24,500	39,300
1992	212.0	15.0	42.2	124.4	30.4	28,400	30,900	28,800	25,400	39,000
1993	242.5	15.4	44.5	146.7	35.9	30,500	32,000	31,400	27,700	40,500
1994	290.9	16.3	53.3	177.7	43.6	32,800	32,900	34,000	30,200	41,900
1995	319.4	15.0	57.5	203.2	43.7	35,300	35,800	35,700	33,300	44,100
1996	337.7	16.2	58.8	218.2	44.4	37,200	37,300	38,000	35,500	45,000
1997	336.3	14.3	55.3	219.4	47.3	39,800	41,300	40,300	38,000	47,300
1998	373.7	14.7	58.3	250.3	50.4	41,600	42,200	42,400	40,100	48,400
1999	338.3	14.1	53.6	227.2	43.5	43,300	44,000	44,400	40,300	49,600
2000	280.9	14.9	48.7	178.7	38.6	46,400	47,000	47,900	44,300	54,100
2001	196.2	12.2	37.6	116.4	30.0	48,900	50,000	49,100	46,500	58,000
2002	174.3	11.8	34.2	101.0	27.2	51,300	53,200	51,700	48,000	62,600
2003	137.7	11.0	25.1	76.1	25.5	54,900	57,500	55,200	50,300	68,000

Source: U.S. Census Bureau, Manufactured Housing Statistics. See <http://www.census.gov/const/www/mhsindex.html>.

No. 936. Existing One-Family Homes Sold and Price by Region: 1970 to 2003

[1,612 represents 1,612,000. Includes existing detached single-family homes and townhomes. Based on data (adjusted and aggregated to regional and national totals) reported by participating real estate multiple listing services. For definition of median, see Guide to Tabular Presentation. For composition of regions, see map inside front cover]

Year	Homes sold (1,000)					Median sales price (dol.)				
	Total	North-east	Mid-west	South	West	Total	North-east	Mid-west	South	West
1970	1,612	251	501	568	292	23,000	25,700	20,100	22,200	24,300
1975	2,476	370	701	862	543	35,300	39,300	30,100	34,800	39,600
1980	2,973	403	806	1,092	672	62,200	60,800	51,900	58,300	89,300
1985	3,134	561	806	1,063	704	75,500	88,900	58,900	75,200	95,400
1987	3,436	618	892	1,163	763	85,600	133,300	66,000	75,200	95,400
1988 [1]	3,513	606	865	1,224	817	89,300	143,000	68,400	80,400	113,200
1989	3,325	490	832	1,185	818	89,500	127,700	71,800	82,200	124,900
1990	3,219	458	809	1,193	759	92,000	126,400	75,300	84,400	127,100
1991	3,186	463	812	1,173	737	97,100	129,100	79,500	85,100	129,600
1992	3,479	521	913	1,242	802	99,700	128,900	83,000	88,500	135,300
1993	3,786	550	967	1,386	882	103,100	129,100	86,000	91,500	131,500
1994	3,916	552	365	1,436	962	107,200	129,100	89,300	94,300	132,500
1995	3,888	547	945	1,433	964	110,500	126,700	94,800	95,700	139,400
1996	4,196	584	986	1,511	1,116	115,800	127,800	101,000	97,700	141,000
1997	4,382	607	1,005	1,595	1,174	121,800	131,800	107,000	103,400	147,100
1998	4,970	662	1,130	1,868	1,309	128,400	135,900	114,300	109,600	155,200
1999	5,205	656	1,148	2,015	1,386	133,300	139,000	119,600	116,200	164,800
2000	5,152	643	1,119	2,015	1,376	139,000	139,400	123,600	120,300	173,900
2001	5,296	638	1,158	2,114	1,386	147,800	146,500	130,200	128,300	183,000
2002	5,566	656	1,217	2,203	1,490	158,100	164,300	136,000	137,400	194,500
2003	6,100	692	1,322	2,436	1,651	170,000	190,500	141,300	147,300	215,400

[1] Beginning 1989 data not comparable to earlier years due to rebenchmarking.

Source: NATIONAL ASSOCIATION OF REALTORS®, Washington, DC, prior to 1990, *Home Sales*, monthly, and *Home Sales Yearbook: 1990*; (copyright); thereafter, *Real Estate Outlook; Market Trends & Insights*, monthly, (copyright). See Internet site <http://www.realtor.org/research>.

No. 937. Median Sales Price of Existing One-Family Homes by Selected Metropolitan Area: 2001 to 2003

[In thousands of dollars (147.8 represents $147,800). Includes existing detached single family homes and townhouses. Areas are metropolitan statistical areas defined by Office of Management and Budget as of 1992, except as noted]

Metropolitan area	2001	2002	2003
United States, total	147.8	158.1	170.0
Albany-Schenectady-Troy, NY	121.6	126.0	141.9
Anaheim-Santa Ana MSA (Orange Cty), CA [1]	355.6	412.7	487.0
Atlanta, GA	138.8	146.5	152.4
Atlantic City, NJ	125.7	143.6	174.4
Aurora-Elgin, IL	178.2	193.3	208.1
Austin-San Marcos, TX	152.0	156.5	156.7
Baltimore, MD	158.2	179.6	208.9
Boston, MA [2]	(NA)	(NA)	354.8
Bradenton, FL [2]	137.8	150.0	172.7
Charleston, SC.	150.8	159.4	168.9
Charlotte-Gastonia-Rock Hill, NC-SC	145.3	149.1	151.5
Chicago, IL	198.5	220.9	238.9
Colorado Springs, CO	173.3	176.9	184.5
Columbus, OH	135.7	140.3	146.3
Denver, CO	218.3	228.1	238.2
Eugene-Springfield, OR	134.6	143.7	151.7
Ft. Lauderdale-Hollywood-Pompano Beach, FL	168.1	197.0	227.6
Ft. Myers-Cape Coral, FL	(NA)	133.6	147.6
Gainesville, FL	118.0	130.0	145.0
Hartford, CT.	167.3	175.9	202.3
Honolulu, HI.	299.9	335.0	383.7
Kansas City, MO-KS	135.7	137.4	144.2
Lake County, IL	178.9	240.0	257.9
Las Vegas, NV	149.1	159.8	179.2
Los Angeles Area, CA [1]	241.4	290.0	354.7
Madison, WI	162.5	177.0	188.7
Miami-Hialeah, FL.	162.7	189.8	226.8
Milwaukee, WI	149.4	173.8	182.1
Minneapolis-St. Paul, MN-WI	167.4	185.0	199.6
New Haven-Meriden, CT	168.0	192.3	225.3
New York-North N.J.-Long Island,NY-NJ-CT	258.2	309.8	353.0
NY: Bergen-Passaic, NJ.	288.8	337.9	370.7
NY: Middlesex-Somerset-Hunterdon, NJ	244.3	284.1	314.0
NY: Monmouth-Ocean, NJ	208.6	251.7	288.3
NY: Nassau-Suffolk, NY	248.4	312.9	364.5
NY: Newark, NJ	263.1	300.5	331.2
Orlando, FL.	124.1	136.6	145.1
Philadelphia, PA-NJ.	134.8	146.1	168.0
Phoenix, AZ.	139.4	143.8	152.5
Portland, ME	158.0	180.0	199.1
Portland, OR	172.3	180.4	192.0
Providence, RI	158.0	193.2	233.4
Raleigh-Durham, NC	168.2	172.2	174.7
Reno, NV	165.1	183.2	204.9
Richland-Kennewick-Pasco, WA.	(NA)	140.8	145.3
Richmond-Petersburg, VA	133.3	142.3	155.1
Riverside-San Bernardino, CA [1]	156.7	176.5	221.0
Sacramento, CA [1]	173.2	210.2	247.6
Salt Lake City-Ogden, UT.	147.6	148.8	148.0
San Diego, CA [1]	298.6	364.2	424.9
San Francisco Bay Area, CA [1]	475.9	517.1	558.1
Sarasota, FL [2]	(NA)	176.2	207.9
Seattle, WA	245.4	254.0	268.8
Springfield, MA.	127.4	139.8	153.4
Tacoma, WA	159.5	170.4	178.1
Trenton, NJ	165.3	179.5	212.4
Tucson, AZ	128.8	146.4	156.3
Washington, DC-MD-VA.	213.9	250.2	286.2
Wilmington, DE-NJ-MD	136.5	150.1	166.2
Worcester, MA	152.6	225.6	252.6

NA Not available. [1] California data supplied by the California Association of REALTORS. [2] In 1992, Bradenton and Sarasota were merged and Aurora/Elgin was incorporated into Chicago. The source still collects price data on the previous jurisdictions.

Source: NATIONAL ASSOCIATION OF REALTORS®, Washington, DC, *Real Estate Outlook: Market Trends & Insights*, monthly, (copyright). See Internet site <http://www.realtor.org/research>.

Construction and Housing   603

No. 938. Existing Home Sales by State: 1990 to 2003

[In thousands (3,599 represents 3,599,000). Includes condos and co-ops as well as single-family homes]

State	1990	2000	2002	2003	State	1990	2000	2002	2003
United States ..	**3,599**	**5,814**	**6,387**	**6,998**	Missouri	77.1	119.9	125.4	148.6
Alabama	52.0	79.8	97.9	114.5	Montana	13.5	18.5	24.0	26.6
Alaska	12.3	17.7	21.2	25.3	Nebraska	23.6	32.4	34.3	39.1
Arizona	71.8	167.0	204.3	239.3	Nevada	26.9	52.4	74.5	97.5
Arkansas	33.7	57.7	67.0	70.6	New Hampshire	13.5	40.3	33.9	41.6
California	413.1	677.8	667.9	698.8	New Jersey	85.7	135.3	140.3	145.5
Colorado	77.7	147.0	144.3	151.7	New Mexico	24.7	28.7	37.4	42.4
Connecticut	37.4	49.4	51.5	52.5	New York	135.9	179.8	191.1	194.7
Delaware	7.9	8.0	9.0	10.6	North Carolina	98.9	233.5	247.2	283.4
District of Columbia ..	7.2	13.4	14.1	15.6	North Dakota	8.5	10.4	11.8	13.1
Florida	281.1	529.9	578.1	652.8	Ohio	146.9	192.2	210.6	232.1
Georgia	91.2	152.2	184.3	197.3	Oklahoma	62.2	96.5	114.0	125.5
Hawaii	19.0	21.3	27.1	33.0	Oregon	56.6	59.9	69.0	76.6
Idaho	22.3	28.5	30.4	34.4	Pennsylvania	143.2	169.3	178.5	191.6
Illinois	163.3	241.1	262.8	282.0	Rhode Island	9.6	19.5	19.5	20.2
Indiana	83.6	129.5	146.1	145.3	South Carolina	54.3	107.6	121.5	143.0
Iowa	42.8	54.4	59.5	66.1	South Dakota	10.8	15.4	18.2	20.4
Kansas	36.8	65.8	75.0	85.5	Tennessee	66.2	148.4	165.4	196.5
Kentucky	47.9	75.6	84.3	94.3	Texas	311.8	549.0	593.1	631.4
Louisiana	57.1	89.0	95.5	102.4	Utah	29.4	47.7	55.0	61.5
Maine	17.0	37.6	39.3	41.1	Vermont	7.2	6.7	7.2	7.5
Maryland	67.0	106.7	124.8	134.6	Virginia	89.3	138.9	160.4	177.4
Massachusetts	47.9	88.6	91.4	97.7	Washington	85.9	173.7	179.7	208.2
Michigan	137.6	153.3	168.6	179.4	West Virginia	22.6	22.6	27.7	30.2
Minnesota	68.1	108.0	137.5	149.8	Wisconsin	62.1	97.0	111.7	118.7
Mississippi	28.2	47.6	59.1	64.2	Wyoming	8.5	12.6	13.9	15.2

Source: NATIONAL ASSOCIATION OF REALTORS®, Washington, DC, *Real Estate Outlook: Market Trends & Insights,* monthly (copyright). See Internet site <http://www.realtor.org/research>.

No. 939. Existing Apartment Condos and Co-Ops—Units Sold and Median Sales Price by Region: 1990 to 2003

[348 represents 348,000. For definition of median, see Guide to Tabular Presentation. For composition of regions, see map inside front cover]

Year	Units sold (1,000)					Median sales price (dol.)				
	Total	North-east	Mid-west	South	West	U.S.	North-east	Mid-west	South	West
1990	348	45	42	151	110	85,200	110,200	70,200	66,800	105,200
1994	439	69	54	196	119	87,200	99,500	86,200	69,500	108,800
1995	428	70	53	188	116	87,400	94,800	90,700	70,600	105,300
1996	476	78	58	206	134	90,900	97,500	95,200	73,500	109,900
1997	524	88	64	220	152	95,500	101,100	99,100	76,300	118,300
1998	607	104	75	252	176	100,600	103,400	106,400	80,000	126,400
1999	681	118	81	295	190	108,000	112,500	114,600	84,100	132,100
2000	706	116	82	311	197	111,800	111,200	121,700	87,700	136,800
2001	746	121	88	339	198	123,200	124,200	134,900	97,100	141,900
2002	820	132	97	376	215	142,200	147,000	148,600	114,500	171,600
2003	898	148	109	409	233	164,100	176,800	163,900	131,600	203,400

Source: NATIONAL ASSOCIATION OF REALTORS®, Washington, DC, *Real Estate Outlook: Market Trends & Insights,* monthly (copyright). See Internet site <http://www.realtor.org/research>.

No. 940. New Apartments Completed and Rented in 3 Months by Region: 2000 to 2003

[226.2 represents 226,200. Structures with five or more units, privately financed, nonsubsidized, unfurnished rental apartments. Based on sample and subject to sampling variability; see source for details. For composition of regions, see map, inside front cover]

Year and rent	Number (1,000)					Percent rented in 3 months				
	U.S.	North-east	Mid-west	South	West	U.S.	North-east	Mid-west	South	West
2000	226.2	14.8	39.5	125.9	45.9	72	85	76	67	77
2001	193.1	16.5	31.6	97.4	47.6	64	83	67	64	64
2002	204.1	19.4	34.5	96.2	54.0	59	51	69	57	58
2003, prel.	167.8	21.5	35.5	71.4	39.4	62	82	62	57	63
Less than $550	25.2	0.6	8.2	13.1	3.3	73	48	73	73	74
$550 to $749	46.2	0.4	16.2	22.3	7.3	61	78	64	56	69
$550 to $649	23.2	0.3	9.8	10.5	2.6	63	84	63	59	75
$650 to $749	23.0	0.1	6.4	11.8	4.7	59	60	65	53	66
$750 to $949	29.3	3.0	4.0	14.8	7.5	57	66	64	51	64
$750 to $849	15.1	0.7	2.4	8.1	3.9	58	94	71	50	61
$850 to $949	14.2	2.3	1.6	6.7	3.6	56	57	54	52	69
$950 or more	67.1	17.5	7.1	21.2	21.3	62	86	44	41	58
Median monthly asking rent (dol.) ..	$932	(¹)	$747	$853	(¹)	(X)	(X)	(X)	(X)	(X)

X Not applicable. ¹ Over $1,050.
Source: U.S. Census Bureau, *Current Housing Reports,* Series H130, *Market Absorption of Apartments,* and unpublished data. See Internet site: <http://www.census.gov/prod/www/abs/apart.html>.

No. 941. Total Housing Inventory for the United States: 1980 to 2003

[In thousands (87,739 represents 87,739,000), except percent. Based on the Current Population Survey and the Housing Vacancy Survey and subject to sampling error; see source and Appendix III for details]

Item	1980	1985	1990	1995	1998	1999	2000	2001	2002 [1]	2003
All housing units	87,739	97,333	106,283	112,655	117,282	119,044	119,628	121,480	119,297	120,834
Vacant	8,101	9,446	12,059	12,669	13,748	14,116	13,908	14,470	14,332	15,274
Year-round vacant.	5,996	7,400	9,128	9,570	10,516	10,848	10,439	10,916	10,771	11,631
For rent	1,575	2,221	2,662	2,946	3,046	3,119	3,024	3,203	3,347	3,676
For sale only	734	1,006	1,064	1,022	1,205	1,184	1,148	1,301	1,220	1,308
Rented or sold	623	664	660	810	927	956	856	882	842	976
Held off market	3,064	3,510	4,742	4,793	5,338	5,589	5,411	5,530	5,362	5,671
Occasional use	814	977	1,485	1,667	1,792	1,948	1,892	1,887	1,819	1,989
Usual residence elsewhere	568	659	1,068	801	910	965	1,037	1,064	995	994
Other	1,683	1,875	2,189	2,325	2,636	2,676	2,482	2,579	2,548	2,688
Seasonal [2]	2,106	2,046	2,931	3,099	3,232	3,268	3,469	3,554	3,561	3,643
Total occupied	79,638	87,887	94,224	99,985	103,534	104,928	105,720	107,010	104,965	105,560
Owner	52,223	56,152	60,248	64,739	68,638	70,097	71,250	72,593	71,278	72,054
Renter	27,415	31,736	33,976	35,246	34,896	34,831	34,470	34,417	33,687	33,506
PERCENT DISTRIBUTION										
All housing units	100.0	100.0	100.0	100.0	100.0	100.0	100.0	100.0	100.0	100.0
Vacant	9.2	9.7	11.3	11.2	11.7	11.9	11.6	11.9	12.0	12.6
Total occupied	90.8	90.3	88.7	88.8	88.3	88.1	88.4	88.1	88.0	87.4
Owner	59.5	57.7	56.7	57.5	58.5	58.9	59.6	59.8	59.7	59.6
Renter	31.2	32.6	32.0	31.3	29.8	29.3	28.8	28.3	28.2	27.7

[1] Revised. Based on 2000 census controls. [2] Beginning 1990 includes vacant seasonal mobile homes. For years shown, seasonal vacant housing units were underreported prior to 1990.
Source: U.S. Census Bureau, "Housing Vacancies and Home Ownership". See Internet site <http://www.census.gov/hhes /www/hvs.html>.

No. 942. Occupied Housing Inventory by Age of Householder: 1985 to 2003

[In thousands (87,887 represents 87,887,000). Based on the Current Population Survey/Housing Vacancy Survey; See source for details]

Age of householder	1985	1990	1995	1997	1998	1999	2000	2001	2002 [1]	2003
Total [2]	87,887	94,224	99,986	102,201	103,534	104,929	105,719	107,009	104,965	105,560
Less than 25 years old	5,483	5,143	5,502	5,517	5,750	6,000	6,221	6,460	6,372	6,441
25 to 29 years old	9,543	9,508	8,662	8,755	8,666	8,661	8,482	8,358	8,231	8,213
30 to 34 years old	10,288	11,213	11,206	10,622	10,494	10,400	10,219	10,301	10,176	10,084
35 to 39 years old	9,615	10,914	11,993	12,166	12,026	11,950	11,834	11,587	10,924	10,777
40 to 44 years old	7,919	9,893	11,151	11,869	12,141	12,206	12,377	12,504	11,839	11,748
45 to 49 years old	6,517	8,038	10,080	10,532	10,744	10,973	11,164	11,529	11,204	11,341
50 to 54 years old	6,157	6,532	7,882	8,650	9,040	9,412	9,834	10,288	10,123	10,194
55 to 59 years old	6,558	6,182	6,355	6,731	7,051	7,389	7,602	7,827	8,261	8,550
60 to 64 years old	6,567	6,446	5,860	5,947	6,055	6,183	6,215	6,345	6,422	6,776
65 to 69 years old	5,976	6,407	6,088	5,926	5,852	5,845	5,816	5,749	5,644	5,570
70 to 74 years old	5,003	5,397	5,693	5,574	5,583	5,621	5,567	5,496	5,137	5,163
75 years old and over . . .	7,517	8,546	9,514	9,912	10,131	10,289	10,388	10,565	10,632	10,703

[1] Revised. Based on 2000 census controls. [2] 1985 total includes ages not reported. Thereafter cases allocated by age.
Source: U.S. Census Bureau, "Housing Vacancies and Home Ownership". See Internet site <http://www.census.gov/hhes /www/hvs.html>.

No. 943. Vacancy Rates for Housing Units—Characteristics: 2000 to 2003

[In percent. Rate is relationship between vacant housing for rent or for sale and the total rental and homeowner supply, which comprises occupied units, units rented or sold and awaiting occupancy, and vacant units available for rent or sale. Based on the Current Population/ Housing Vacancy Survey; see source for details. For composition of regions, see map, inside front cover]

Characteristic	Rental units				Homeowner units			
	2000	2001	2002 [1]	2003	2000	2001	2002 [1]	2003
Total units	8.0	8.4	8.9	9.8	1.6	1.8	1.7	1.8
Northeast	5.6	5.3	5.8	6.6	1.2	1.2	1.2	1.2
Midwest	8.8	9.7	10.1	10.8	1.3	1.7	1.8	1.7
South	10.5	11.1	11.6	12.5	1.9	2.1	1.9	2.1
West	5.8	6.2	6.9	7.7	1.5	1.6	1.6	1.6
Units in structure:								
1 unit	7.0	7.9	8.0	8.4	1.5	1.6	1.5	1.6
2 units or more	8.7	8.9	9.7	10.7	4.7	5.7	4.8	5.5
5 units or more	9.2	9.6	10.4	11.4	5.8	6.0	4.7	5.3
Units with—								
3 rooms or less	10.3	10.5	11.3	12.2	10.4	8.7	8.9	8.1
4 rooms	8.2	8.8	9.0	10.0	2.9	3.0	2.8	3.4
5 rooms	6.9	7.5	8.3	8.9	2.0	2.1	2.0	2.1
6 rooms or more	5.2	5.6	6.2	7.0	1.1	1.2	1.2	1.3

[1] Revised. Based on 2000 census controls.
Source: U.S. Census Bureau, "Housing Vacancies and Home Ownership". See Internet site <http://www.census.gov/hhes /www/hvs.html>.

No. 944. Housing Units and Tenure—States: 2000

[115,905 represents 115,905,000. As of April 1. Based on the 2000 Census of Population and Housing; see text, Section 1, and Appendix III]

State	Housing units Total (1,000)	Occupied (1,000)	Vacant (1,000) Total	For seasonal use [1]	Vacancy rate Homeowner [2]	Renter [3]	Owner occupied units Total (1,000)	Average household size	Renter occupied units Total (1,000)	Average household size
United States.....	115,905	105,480	10,425	3,579	1.7	6.8	69,816	2.69	35,664	2.40
Alabama............	1,964	1,737	227	47	2.0	11.8	1,259	2.57	478	2.30
Alaska.............	261	222	39	21	1.9	7.8	139	2.89	83	2.49
Arizona............	2,189	1,901	288	142	2.1	9.2	1,294	2.69	608	2.53
Arkansas..........	1,173	1,043	130	29	2.5	9.6	724	2.54	319	2.40
California..........	12,215	11,503	712	237	1.4	3.7	6,546	2.93	4,957	2.79
Colorado...........	1,808	1,658	150	72	1.4	5.5	1,116	2.64	542	2.30
Connecticut........	1,386	1,302	84	23	1.1	5.6	870	2.67	432	2.25
Delaware..........	343	299	44	26	1.5	8.2	216	2.61	83	2.37
District of Columbia	275	248	27	2	2.9	5.9	101	2.31	147	2.06
Florida	7,303	6,338	965	483	2.2	9.3	4,442	2.49	1,896	2.39
Georgia	3,282	3,006	275	50	1.9	8.2	2,029	2.71	977	2.51
Hawaii	461	403	57	26	1.6	8.2	228	3.07	175	2.71
Idaho..............	528	470	58	27	2.2	7.6	340	2.75	130	2.52
Illinois............	4,886	4,592	294	30	1.5	6.2	3,089	2.76	1,503	2.37
Indiana............	2,532	2,336	196	34	1.8	8.8	1,669	2.64	667	2.24
Iowa	1,233	1,149	83	16	1.7	6.8	831	2.57	318	2.15
Kansas............	1,131	1,038	93	10	2.0	8.8	719	2.63	319	2.25
Kentucky	1,751	1,591	160	30	1.8	8.7	1,125	2.55	465	2.27
Louisiana	1,847	1,656	191	40	1.6	9.3	1,125	2.70	531	2.44
Maine..............	652	518	134	101	1.7	7.0	371	2.54	147	2.03
Maryland	2,145	1,981	164	39	1.6	6.1	1,342	2.73	639	2.35
Massachusetts......	2,622	2,444	178	94	0.7	3.5	1,508	2.72	936	2.17
Michigan...........	4,234	3,786	449	234	1.6	6.8	2,793	2.67	993	2.24
Minnesota..........	2,066	1,895	171	106	0.9	4.1	1,413	2.69	482	2.03
Mississippi	1,162	1,046	116	22	1.6	9.2	757	2.67	289	2.52
Missouri	2,442	2,195	247	66	2.1	9.0	1,542	2.59	652	2.20
Montana	413	359	54	24	2.2	7.6	248	2.55	111	2.22
Nebraska	723	666	56	12	1.8	7.6	449	2.63	217	2.20
Nevada	827	751	76	17	2.6	9.7	457	2.71	294	2.47
New Hampshire	547	475	72	56	1.0	3.5	331	2.70	144	2.14
New Jersey.........	3,310	3,065	246	109	1.2	4.5	2,011	2.81	1,053	2.43
New Mexico	781	678	103	32	2.2	11.6	474	2.72	204	2.41
New York	7,679	7,057	622	235	1.6	4.6	3,739	2.78	3,318	2.41
North Carolina.......	3,524	3,132	392	135	2.0	8.8	2,172	2.54	960	2.37
North Dakota........	290	257	33	8	2.7	8.2	171	2.60	86	2.02
Ohio...............	4,783	4,446	337	47	1.6	8.3	3,073	2.62	1,373	2.19
Oklahoma..........	1,514	1,342	172	32	2.5	10.6	918	2.55	424	2.36
Oregon............	1,453	1,334	119	37	2.3	7.3	857	2.59	477	2.36
Pennsylvania.......	5,250	4,777	473	148	1.6	7.2	3,406	2.62	1,371	2.12
Rhode Island	440	408	31	13	1.0	5.0	245	2.66	163	2.19
South Carolina.......	1,754	1,534	220	70	1.9	12.0	1,108	2.59	426	2.37
South Dakota	323	290	33	10	1.8	8.0	198	2.64	92	2.22
Tennessee	2,439	2,233	207	37	2.0	8.8	1,561	2.57	672	2.29
Texas	8,158	7,393	764	173	1.8	8.5	4,717	2.87	2,676	2.53
Utah	769	701	67	30	2.1	6.5	502	3.28	200	2.75
Vermont	294	241	54	43	1.4	4.2	170	2.58	71	2.11
Virginia	2,904	2,699	205	55	1.5	5.2	1,838	2.62	861	2.36
Washington.........	2,451	2,271	180	60	1.8	5.9	1,467	2.65	804	2.32
West Virginia.......	845	736	108	33	2.2	9.1	554	2.47	183	2.17
Wisconsin..........	2,321	2,085	237	142	1.2	5.6	1,426	2.66	658	2.15
Wyoming	224	194	30	12	2.1	9.7	136	2.58	58	2.25

[1] For seasonal, recreational or occasional use. [2] Proportion of the homeowner housing inventory which is vacant for sale.
[3] Proportion of the rental inventory which is vacant for rent.

Source: U.S. Census Bureau, "2000 Census of Population and Housing, Profiles of General Demographic Characteristics"; <http://www.census.gov/Press-Release/www/2002/demoprofiles.html>.

No. 945. Housing Units and Tenure for Large Cities: 2000

[115,905 represents 115,905,000. As of April 1. For cities with 200,000 or more inhabitants in 2000. Based on the 2000 Census of Population and Housing; see text, Section 1, and Appendix III]

City	Housing units Total (1,000)	Occupied (1,000)	Vacant (1,000) Total	For seasonal use [1]	Vacancy rate Homeowner [2]	Renter [3]	Owner occupied units Total (1,000)	Average household size	Renter occupied units Total (1,000)	Average household size
United States	115,905	105,480	10,425	3,579	1.7	6.8	69,816	2.69	35,664	2.40
Albuquerque, NM	198.5	183.2	15.2	0.8	1.9	11.8	110.6	2.55	72.6	2.16
Anaheim, CA	99.7	97.0	2.8	0.2	0.9	3.2	48.5	3.24	48.5	3.45
Anchorage, AK	100.4	94.8	5.5	1.1	1.4	5.3	57.0	2.81	37.9	2.46
Arlington, TX	130.6	124.7	5.9	0.4	1.4	6.1	68.3	2.87	56.4	2.38
Atlanta, GA	186.9	168.1	18.8	1.1	4.1	7.2	73.5	2.37	94.7	2.25
Aurora, CO	109.3	105.6	3.6	0.2	1.1	3.5	67.5	2.65	38.1	2.50
Austin, TX	276.8	265.6	11.2	1.4	1.0	3.5	119.1	2.65	146.5	2.19
Baltimore, MD	300.5	258.0	42.5	1.4	3.6	7.6	129.9	2.57	128.1	2.27
Boston, MA	251.9	239.5	12.4	1.6	1.0	3.0	77.2	2.51	162.3	2.22
Buffalo, NY	145.6	122.7	22.9	0.3	4.2	11.1	53.3	2.47	69.4	2.16
Charlotte, NC	230.4	215.4	15.0	0.7	2.2	8.4	123.9	2.56	91.6	2.30
Chicago, IL	1,152.9	1,061.9	90.9	4.5	1.7	5.7	464.9	2.90	597.1	2.49
Cincinnati, OH	166.0	148.1	17.9	0.6	2.2	9.9	57.7	2.43	90.4	1.97
Cleveland, OH	215.9	190.6	25.2	0.8	2.1	10.8	92.5	2.56	98.1	2.32
Colorado Springs, CO	148.7	141.5	7.2	0.7	1.2	6.2	86.0	2.65	55.5	2.27
Columbus, OH	327.2	301.5	25.6	1.1	2.0	8.3	148.0	2.48	153.5	2.13
Corpus Christi, TX	107.8	98.8	9.0	1.1	2.0	9.5	58.9	2.89	39.9	2.56
Dallas, TX	484.1	451.8	32.3	1.5	1.4	7.0	195.3	2.78	256.5	2.44
Denver, CO	251.4	239.2	12.2	1.4	1.7	4.5	125.5	2.41	113.7	2.10
Detroit, MI	375.1	336.4	38.7	0.6	1.6	8.3	184.6	2.84	151.8	2.68
El Paso, TX	193.7	182.1	11.6	0.7	1.6	7.9	111.8	3.20	70.3	2.86
Fort Worth, TX	211.0	195.1	16.0	0.6	1.9	9.1	109.1	2.84	86.0	2.44
Fresno, CA	149.0	140.1	8.9	0.4	1.9	6.4	70.9	2.94	69.2	3.05
Honolulu, HI [4]	158.7	140.3	18.3	5.2	1.7	10.2	65.9	2.75	74.5	2.40
Houston, TX	782.0	717.9	64.1	4.2	1.6	8.7	328.7	2.84	389.2	2.54
Indianapolis, IN [5]	352.4	320.1	32.3	1.2	2.0	10.9	187.6	2.53	132.5	2.18
Jacksonville, FL	308.8	284.5	24.3	0.9	1.8	9.0	179.7	2.64	104.8	2.34
Kansas City, MO	202.3	184.0	18.4	0.7	1.9	9.6	106.1	2.52	77.9	2.11
Las Vegas, NV	190.7	176.8	14.0	1.8	2.5	8.4	104.5	2.76	72.3	2.52
Lexington-Fayette, KY [4]	116.2	108.3	7.9	0.9	1.1	8.4	59.9	2.47	48.4	2.07
Long Beach, CA	171.6	163.1	8.5	0.8	2.2	4.2	66.9	2.81	96.2	2.74
Los Angeles, CA	1,337.7	1,275.4	62.3	4.9	1.8	3.5	491.9	2.99	783.5	2.73
Louisville, KY	121.3	111.4	9.9	0.4	1.8	7.5	58.5	2.33	52.9	2.10
Memphis, TN	271.6	250.7	20.8	0.7	2.0	8.4	140.0	2.62	110.7	2.40
Mesa, AZ	175.7	146.6	29.1	18.1	2.4	10.7	97.3	2.74	49.3	2.54
Miami, FL	148.4	134.2	14.2	2.9	2.9	6.6	46.8	2.79	87.4	2.52
Milwaukee, WI	249.2	232.2	17.0	0.5	1.3	6.0	105.2	2.60	127.0	2.42
Minneapolis, MN	168.6	162.4	6.3	0.8	0.7	2.8	83.4	2.43	78.9	2.05
Nashville-Davidson, TN [5]	242.5	227.4	15.0	1.1	2.0	6.5	124.0	2.43	103.4	2.13
New Orleans, LA	215.1	188.3	26.8	2.4	2.2	7.9	87.6	2.60	100.7	2.37
New York, NY	3,200.9	3,021.6	179.3	28.2	1.7	3.2	912.3	2.81	2,109.3	2.50
Newark, NJ	100.1	91.4	8.8	0.1	2.0	5.6	21.7	3.22	69.6	2.74
Oakland, CA	157.5	150.8	6.7	0.4	1.0	2.7	62.5	2.76	88.3	2.49
Oklahoma City, OK	228.1	204.4	23.7	1.1	2.2	12.3	121.5	2.51	82.9	2.27
Omaha, NE	165.7	156.7	9.0	0.5	1.0	7.2	93.4	2.64	63.3	2.10
Philadelphia, PA	662.0	590.1	71.9	1.8	1.9	7.0	349.6	2.65	240.4	2.23
Phoenix, AZ	495.8	465.8	30.0	4.5	1.4	7.9	282.7	2.89	183.2	2.63
Pittsburgh, PA	163.4	143.7	19.6	0.9	2.8	8.8	74.9	2.37	68.8	1.95
Portland, OR	237.3	223.7	13.6	1.0	2.3	6.2	124.8	2.47	99.0	2.08
Raleigh, NC	120.7	112.6	8.1	0.4	2.1	8.3	58.1	2.43	54.5	2.15
Riverside, CA	86.0	82.0	4.0	0.2	1.9	4.8	46.5	3.18	35.6	2.81
Sacramento, CA	164.0	154.6	9.4	0.6	2.0	5.4	77.5	2.65	77.1	2.50
San Antonio, TX	433.1	405.5	27.6	2.3	1.4	6.9	235.7	2.95	169.8	2.51
San Diego, CA	469.7	450.7	19.0	5.1	0.8	3.2	223.3	2.71	227.4	2.52
San Francisco, CA	346.5	329.7	16.8	3.8	0.8	2.5	115.4	2.73	214.3	2.06
San Jose, CA	281.8	276.6	5.2	0.8	0.4	1.8	171.0	3.22	105.6	3.16
Santa Ana, CA	74.6	73.0	1.6	0.1	0.8	1.9	36.0	4.54	37.0	4.57
Seattle, WA	270.5	258.5	12.0	0.8	1.2	3.5	125.2	2.32	133.3	1.84
St. Louis, MO	176.4	147.1	29.3	0.5	3.5	11.8	68.9	2.49	78.1	2.12
St. Paul, MN	115.7	112.1	3.6	0.4	0.7	2.8	61.5	2.72	50.6	2.15
Tampa, FL	135.8	124.8	11.0	0.8	2.1	7.8	68.6	2.49	56.2	2.20
Toledo, OH	139.9	128.9	10.9	0.4	1.5	8.8	77.1	2.50	51.9	2.19
Tucson, AZ	209.6	192.9	16.7	3.5	1.6	8.1	103.1	2.58	89.8	2.24
Tulsa, OK	179.4	165.7	13.7	0.9	1.6	8.7	92.2	2.41	73.5	2.18
Virginia Beach, VA	162.3	154.5	7.8	2.3	1.5	4.0	101.3	2.79	53.1	2.54
Washington, DC	274.8	248.3	26.5	2.2	2.9	5.9	101.2	2.31	147.1	2.06
Wichita, KS	152.1	139.1	13.0	0.4	2.0	12.0	85.7	2.61	53.4	2.17

[1] For seasonal, recreational or occasional use. [2] Proportion of the homeowner housing inventory which is vacant for sale. [3] Proportion of the rental inventory which is vacant for rent. [4] The population shown in this table is for the census designated place (CDP). [5] Represents the portion of a consolidated city that is not within one or more separately incorporated places.

Source: U.S. Census Bureau, "2000 Census of Population and Housing, Profiles of General Demographic Characteristics"; <http://www.census.gov/Press-Release/www/2002/demoprofiles.html>.

No. 946. Housing Inventory for Selected Metropolitan Areas— Summary Characteristics: 1995 to 2002

[539.4 represents 539,400. Based on the American Housing Survey and subject to sampling error; see Appendix III and source for details. For definition of median, see Guide to Tabular Presentation]

Year and metropolitan area	Total units (1,000)	Percent Owner occu-pied	Percent Renter occu-pied	Percent Vacant and sea-sonal	Percent Single-family	Percent Multi-family	Percent Mobile homes	Owner occupied Median monthly housing costs (dol.)	Median value (dol.)	Renter occu-pied, median monthly housing costs (dol.)
1995										
Charlotte, NC-SC MSA.	539.4	62.7	30.6	6.7	68.4	20.8	10.8	532	86,763	489
Chicago, IL Area PMSA	2,987.1	59.6	33.8	6.6	54.7	44.5	0.7	850	136,362	584
Columbus, OH MSA	604.9	57.9	34.0	8.1	75.8	21.4	2.8	654	92,664	484
Denver, CO PMSA	773.9	61.2	32.5	6.2	68.9	28.8	2.2	763	119,694	539
Detroit, MI PMSA	1,802.7	66.3	26.9	6.7	75.0	22.9	2.1	551	89,648	508
Kansas City, MO-KS MSA	715.5	61.9	30.2	7.9	76.2	21.0	2.8	565	78,542	481
Los Angeles-Long Beach, CA PMSA	3,276.0	42.0	48.0	10.0	54.7	44.0	1.3	943	192,803	654
Miami-Fort Lauderdale, FL CMSA	1,483.8	52.1	31.8	16.1	49.9	46.5	3.5	729	97,058	609
New Orleans, LA MSA	547.7	54.6	33.9	11.5	65.2	30.2	4.7	404	75,768	441
New York-Nassau-Suffolk-Orange County, NY PMSA	4,577.3	41.0	50.9	8.1	32.3	67.4	0.3	931	172,651	650
Northern New Jersey PMSA	2,442.2	56.0	34.2	9.8	59.2	40.0	0.8	976	176,713	669
Philadelphia, PA-NJ PMSA	1,986.6	63.7	28.0	8.4	73.1	25.8	1.0	673	112,769	578
Pittsburgh, PA MSA	1,051.7	66.5	25.7	7.8	73.9	21.5	4.7	416	73,383	417
Portland, OR-WA PMSA	702.6	60.3	32.9	6.8	70.2	23.9	5.9	704	127,731	566
San Antonio, TX MSA	538.7	55.4	34.6	10.0	67.0	27.3	5.6	507	62,577	475
1996										
Atlanta, GA MSA.	1,421.1	58.6	33.4	8.1	66.9	28.6	4.5	803	105,037	651
Cleveland, OH PMSA	829.6	62.4	30.7	6.9	67.0	31.5	1.5	552	99,283	492
Hartford, CT MSA	480.2	60.5	31.1	8.4	63.0	36.5	0.5	888	139,641	616
Indianapolis, IN MSA	640.8	62.2	30.2	7.6	73.4	22.5	4.0	603	91,213	507
Memphis, TN-AR-MS MSA	442.0	59.3	31.5	9.2	70.0	26.1	3.9	592	76,175	477
Oklahoma City, OK MSA	446.4	57.8	28.7	13.5	72.0	22.1	6.0	461	65,638	434
Sacramento, CA PMSA	625.4	55.1	34.1	10.8	71.2	24.0	4.8	874	140,758	590
St. Louis, MO-IL MSA	1,107.0	64.3	26.5	9.2	71.2	23.6	5.2	557	82,111	462
Seattle-Everett, WA MSA	965.3	58.3	35.1	6.5	60.4	33.9	5.7	897	164,554	630
1998										
Baltimore, MD MSA.	1,028.2	61.7	27.8	10.5	78.8	19.6	1.6	739	127,557	589
Birmingham, AL MSA.	394.0	64.1	26.9	9.0	75.9	15.6	8.5	385	87,670	480
Boston, MA-NH CMSA.	1,345.9	56.5	37.4	6.1	59.2	39.8	1.0	933	191,179	748
Cincinnati, OH-KY-IN, PMSA.	647.5	61.2	30.3	8.5	68.1	28.6	3.3	611	103,553	484
Houston, TX, PMSAs.	1,547.3	53.0	36.6	10.4	68.7	26.9	4.4	678	82,543	557
Minneapolis-St. Paul, MN-WI MSA.	1,150.3	70.6	26.0	3.3	72.0	25.6	2.4	786	122,624	583
Norfolk-Virginia Beach-Newport News, VA MSA.	632.1	55.9	33.3	10.8	73.8	22.2	4.0	729	101,935	582
Oakland, CA PMSA.	895.0	56.8	38.8	4.4	71.8	26.4	1.9	1,086	226,173	775
Providence-Pawtucket-Warwick, RI-MA PMSA.	415.4	57.8	33.6	8.6	62.0	36.6	1.4	768	124,005	540
Rochester, NY MSA.	448.5	63.8	27.6	8.6	71.0	24.4	4.6	724	94,468	572
Salt Lake City, UT MSA.	444.0	67.9	24.5	7.5	75.0	21.7	3.3	713	141,888	594
San Francisco, CA PMSA.	700.2	46.2	48.5	5.3	57.7	41.4	0.9	1,229	[1]	899
San Jose, CA PMSA.	591.0	58.2	37.6	4.2	72.7	23.2	4.1	1,186	[1]	1,038
Tampa-St. Petersburg, FL MSA.	1,138.3	58.6	23.6	17.8	62.8	19.6	17.6	541	81,510	565
Washington, DC-MD-VA, MSA.	1,817.4	59.3	32.7	8.0	72.4	26.7	0.9	1,104	170,022	746
1999										
Chicago, IL, PMSA	3,060.7	60.7	32.4	7.0	58.5	40.8	0.7	855	147,742	637
Detroit, MI, PMSA	1,876.7	68.0	24.8	7.2	77.8	20.1	2.1	583	124,157	557
Los Angeles-Long Beach, CA PMSA	3,278.5	44.0	49.4	6.6	60.9	37.8	1.3	1,033	199,011	663
New York-Nassau-Suffolk-Orange County, NY PMSA	4,615.9	41.7	52.1	6.2	39.0	60.6	0.4	910	186,164	684
Northern NJ, PMSA.	2,502.1	59.7	32.9	7.4	65.4	33.8	0.7	983	181,898	732
Philadelphia, PA, PMSA	2,025.2	65.9	26.7	7.4	80.6	18.7	0.7	660	116,478	642
2002										
Anaheim-Santa Ana, CA PMSA	995.6	60.0	34.2	5.8	74.8	21.6	3.6	1,394	[1]	1,030
Buffalo, NY CMSA.	515.5	61.0	28.5	10.5	63.9	34.3	1.7	684	92,434	522
Charlotte, NC-SC MSA.	667.8	63.5	25.4	11.1	77.4	13.9	8.8	782	125,551	634
Columbus, OH MSA.	682.6	58.8	31.0	10.2	79.2	18.0	2.8	769	135,208	607
New Orleans, LA MSA.	1,365.4	57.4	33.0	9.5	72.6	23.2	4.1	1,011	126,492	692
Fort Worth-Arlington, TX PMSA	639.4	61.4	30.2	8.4	77.6	17.9	4.5	809	99,230	642
Kansas City, MO-KS MSA	766.5	63.5	27.4	9.0	83.5	13.8	2.6	745	116,778	605
Miami-Fort Lauderdale, FL CMSA	1,638.7	56.6	31.0	12.5	65.7	31.1	3.2	860	136,773	711
Milwaukee, WI PMSA	626.5	59.3	34.0	6.7	62.9	36.6	0.6	879	143,281	604
Phoenix, AZ MSA	1,340.4	60.5	26.5	13.0	71.7	20.7	7.6	913	140,490	673
Portland, OR-WA MSA	811.7	61.3	30.8	7.9	71.4	23.8	4.8	1,017	179,311	684
Riverside-San Bernardino-Ontario, CA PMSA	1,229.5	62.3	25.8	11.9	79.8	10.1	10.0	964	164,853	676
San Diego, CA MSA	1,072.0	54.6	38.5	6.8	66.9	28.3	4.7	1,210	297,453	886

[1] More than $300,000.

Source: U.S. Census Bureau, *American Housing Survey for the* (name) *Metropolitan Area (year)*, series H-170. See Internet site <http://www.census.gov/hhes/www/housing/ahs/metropolitandata.html>

No. 947. Housing Units—Characteristics by Tenure and Region: 2003

[In thousands of units (120,777 represents 120,777,000), except as indicated. Preliminary as of fall. Based on the American Housing Survey; see Appendix III. For composition of regions, see map, inside front cover]

Characteristic	Total housing units	Sea-sonal	Year-round Total	Occupied Owner	Occupied Renter	Occupied North-east	Occupied Mid-west	Occupied South	Occupied West	Vacant
Total units	**120,777**	**3,558**	**105,867**	**72,254**	**33,614**	**20,171**	**24,487**	**38,140**	**23,070**	**11,352**
Percent distribution	100.0	2.9	87.7	59.8	27.8	16.7	20.3	31.6	19.1	9.4
Units in structure:										
Single family detached	74,813	2,022	67,746	59,650	8,095	11,016	17,326	24,981	14,423	5,045
Single family attached	7,255	202	6,274	3,683	2,592	1,829	1,018	2,121	1,307	779
2 to 4 units	9,975	104	8,491	1,426	7,065	2,599	1,926	2,134	1,831	1,380
5 to 9 units	6,036	76	5,139	502	4,637	996	1,046	1,763	1,335	821
10 to 19 units	5,460	82	4,474	486	3,988	752	861	1,736	1,125	904
20 to 49 units	3,981	117	3,300	388	2,912	920	551	840	989	565
50 or more units	4,299	126	3,595	601	2,994	1,487	619	722	766	578
Mobile home or trailer	8,958	829	6,849	5,518	1,331	571	1,140	3,843	1,295	1,280
Stories in structure: [1]										
One story	39,197	1,380	34,240	25,774	8,466	1,220	3,992	18,764	10,263	3,577
2 stories	39,353	863	34,930	22,722	12,208	6,195	9,849	10,436	8,450	3,560
3 stories	25,148	283	22,861	15,572	7,289	8,190	8,211	4,067	2,393	2,004
4 to 6 stories	5,794	95	5,125	2,243	2,882	2,959	982	688	497	573
7 or more stories	2,327	107	1,862	425	1,437	1,036	313	341	172	358
Foundation: [2]										
Full or partial basement	35,419	467	33,067	29,614	3,453	10,882	14,040	5,215	2,929	1,885
Crawlspace	21,786	867	18,815	15,471	3,344	781	2,599	9,845	5,591	2,104
Concrete slab	24,153	678	21,721	17,949	3,772	1,136	1,618	11,847	7,121	1,754
Other	709	212	416	298	118	46	88	194	89	81
Year structure built:										
Median year	1971	1972	1971	1972	1968	1956	1965	1976	1974	1970
1980 or later	38,804	1,098	34,173	25,397	8,775	3,658	6,471	15,765	8,279	3,532
1970 to 1979	23,517	848	20,455	13,352	7,103	2,780	4,324	8,287	5,074	2,214
1960 to 1969	15,484	481	13,769	9,180	4,589	2,482	3,185	4,908	3,195	1,234
1950 to 1959	13,410	403	11,920	8,684	3,236	2,606	3,054	3,673	2,587	1,087
1940 to 1949	8,123	238	7,088	4,638	2,450	1,653	1,643	2,265	1,526	797
1939 and earlier	21,437	489	18,461	11,002	7,460	6,991	5,809	3,242	2,419	2,487
Main heating equipment:										
Warm-air furnace	73,449	1,566	65,429	48,145	17,284	8,155	19,788	22,595	14,891	6,454
Electric heat pump	13,278	512	11,355	8,280	3,075	284	587	9,198	1,287	1,410
Steam or hot water system	14,425	101	13,252	7,798	5,453	9,649	2,151	648	803	1,072
Floor, wall, or pipeless furnace	6,039	171	5,299	2,285	3,015	430	420	1,417	3,032	568
Built-in electric units	5,739	355	4,772	2,191	2,580	1,190	1,065	870	1,647	612
Room heaters with flue	1,719	99	1,419	807	613	177	208	719	316	201
Room heaters without flue	1,867	59	1,496	983	512	29	33	1,378	56	312
Stoves	1,350	217	1,047	872	175	159	162	375	351	86
Fireplaces	250	54	192	166	25	10	31	65	86	5
Cooking stoves	174	14	147	57	90	46	-	62	39	13
None	1,117	282	441	201	241	2	6	134	299	394
Portable electric heaters	899	73	734	346	388	13	18	507	196	91
Other	471	54	284	122	162	28	19	171	66	132
Kitchen equipment:										
Lacking complete facilities	5,676	563	1,556	303	1,253	318	353	452	433	3,557
With complete facilities	115,101	2,994	104,312	71,951	32,361	19,852	24,134	37,688	22,637	7,795
Kitchen sink	119,774	3,366	105,661	72,215	33,446	20,135	24,441	38,096	22,989	10,747
Refrigerator	117,632	3,201	105,693	72,182	33,511	20,149	24,443	38,080	23,021	8,738
Cooking stove or range	116,785	3,016	105,073	71,932	33,140	20,022	24,330	37,839	22,882	8,696
Burners only, no stove or range	160	-	144	63	81	40	22	52	30	16
Microwave oven only	476	49	343	147	196	45	86	140	71	84
Dishwasher	69,771	1,216	63,810	50,312	13,498	10,551	13,464	24,254	15,541	4,745
Washing machine	91,380	1,499	86,044	69,219	16,825	14,949	20,385	32,579	18,131	3,837
Clothes dryer	89,120	1,780	82,566	67,290	15,275	13,887	20,143	31,117	17,478	4,774
Disposal in kitchen sink	54,530	928	49,646	35,568	14,078	4,803	11,666	16,953	16,225	3,955
Trash compactor	4,285	110	3,911	3,246	665	572	606	1,550	1,183	264
Air conditioning: Central	72,649	1,258	66,068	50,667	15,401	5,844	16,041	33,279	10,904	5,324
Percent of total units	60.2	35.4	62.4	70.1	45.8	29.0	65.5	87.3	47.3	46.9
One or more room units	29,685	749	26,345	15,198	11,147	10,383	6,297	6,331	3,335	2,591
Source of water:										
Public system or private company	104,639	2,230	92,382	60,361	32,021	16,978	20,551	33,229	21,624	10,026
Percent of total units	86.6	62.7	87.3	83.5	95.3	84.2	83.9	87.1	93.7	88.3
Well serving 1 to 5 units	15,347	1,098	13,063	11,547	1,516	3,102	3,864	4,703	1,394	1,186
Other	792	229	423	346	77	90	73	208	52	140
Means of sewage disposal:										
Public sewer	94,762	1,718	84,113	53,093	31,019	15,984	19,737	28,023	20,369	8,931
Percent of total units	78.5	48.3	79.5	73.5	92.3	79.2	80.6	73.5	88.3	78.7
Septic tank, cesspool, chemical toilet	25,591	1,637	21,673	19,120	2,553	4,181	4,734	10,075	2,684	2,281
Other	424	203	81	40	41	6	16	43	16	140

- Represents or rounds to zero. NA Not available. [1] Excludes mobile homes. [2] Limited to single-family units.

Source: U.S. Census Bureau, Current Housing Reports, Series H150/03, *American Housing Survey for the United States.* See Internet site <http://www.census.gov/hhes/www/housing/ahs/nationaldata.html>

No. 948. Housing Units by Units in Structure by State: 2000

[In percent, except as indicated (115,905 represents 115,905,000. As of April 1. Based on the 2000 Census of Population and Housing; see text, Section 1, and Appendix III]

State	Total housing units (1,000)	Percent of units by units in structure—								
		1-unit detached	1-unit attached	2 units	3 or 4 units	5 to 9 units	10 to 19 units	20 or more units	Mobile homes	Boat, RV, van, etc.
U.S.	115,905	60.3	5.6	4.3	4.7	4.7	4.0	8.6	7.6	0.2
AL............	1,964	66.2	2.0	2.2	3.3	3.8	2.4	3.6	16.3	0.3
AK............	261	58.5	7.0	5.5	7.4	5.7	3.0	5.4	6.8	0.7
AZ............	2,189	56.8	6.0	1.5	3.4	3.8	3.7	9.7	13.8	1.3
AR............	1,173	69.0	1.8	3.2	3.0	2.7	2.3	2.8	14.9	0.4
CA............	12,215	56.4	7.6	2.7	5.7	5.9	5.1	12.0	4.4	0.3
CO............	1,808	62.1	6.3	2.1	3.8	4.6	5.6	9.7	5.7	0.2
CT............	1,386	58.9	5.1	8.6	9.2	5.5	3.8	7.9	0.8	(Z)
DE............	343	55.9	14.1	2.0	2.6	3.7	5.5	4.9	11.2	0.2
DC............	275	13.2	26.4	3.0	8.0	7.9	10.3	30.9	0.1	0.1
FL............	7,303	52.3	5.9	2.7	4.3	5.0	5.0	12.9	11.6	0.4
GA	3,282	64.2	2.9	2.8	4.0	5.3	3.9	4.7	12.0	0.1
HI	461	52.0	8.3	2.3	4.6	6.7	5.0	20.8	0.2	0.1
ID	528	70.1	2.9	2.8	4.1	2.7	1.8	3.0	12.2	0.5
IL	4,886	57.9	4.8	6.9	6.5	6.2	4.3	10.1	3.2	(Z)
IN	2,532	71.2	2.9	3.4	4.0	4.6	3.2	4.1	6.6	0.1
IA............	1,233	74.0	2.3	3.2	3.9	3.7	3.1	4.6	5.3	0.1
KS............	1,131	72.4	3.5	3.0	3.6	3.5	3.1	4.4	6.4	0.1
KY............	1,751	66.0	2.1	3.2	4.1	4.3	3.1	4.9	13.0	0.3
LA	1,847	64.1	3.8	4.0	4.5	5.8	4.3	2.9	9.8	0.3
ME	652	67.4	2.2	5.6	5.8	5.6	7.9	7.2	1.9	(Z)
MD	2,145	51.2	21.0	2.1	2.9	6.0	4.3	9.3	0.9	(Z)
MA	2,622	52.4	4.0	11.6	11.4	4.0	3.4	5.1	6.5	0.2
MI	4,234	70.6	3.9	3.5	2.8	2.4	3.8	10.7	4.5	0.3
MN	2,066	67.8	5.2	3.0	2.3	3.3	3.4	2.7	16.6	0.2
MS	1,162	68.1	1.7	2.4	3.3	3.8	3.2	4.1	8.2	0.3
MO	2,442	68.8	2.7	3.9	5.1	2.9	1.8	3.1	14.3	0.3
MT	413	67.0	2.7	3.3	4.6	3.8	4.5	6.1	5.1	0.1
NE............	723	71.9	2.9	2.6	3.0	8.0	5.4	10.0	9.7	0.5
NV............	827	52.3	5.4	1.5	7.3	6.0	3.2	5.8	6.5	0.1
NH	547	62.4	4.4	6.5	6.0	4.8	4.9	9.6	1.0	(Z)
NJ............	3,310	54.2	8.6	10.0	6.8	3.5	2.5	2.3	5.1	18.6	0.6
NM............	781	61.0	4.5	2.0	3.5	5.3	4.3	22.9	2.7	0.1
NY............	7,679	41.7	4.9	10.9	2.5	3.2	3.2	2.9	16.4	0.2
NC............	3,524	64.4	3.0	2.5	4.3	4.2	5.3	8.6	9.0	0.1
ND............	290	62.1	4.1	2.5	4.8	4.8	3.9	5.5	4.6	0.1
OH	4,783	67.4	3.8	5.2	1.9	2.8	3.6	2.7	4.2	10.7	0.4
OK	1,514	71.4	2.4	3.0	4.2	4.3	3.8	7.8	10.3	0.6
OR	1,453	62.8	3.3	5.2	4.6	3.4	2.5	5.4	4.9	0.1
PA	5,250	55.9	17.9	2.9	12.3	12.8	5.2	3.4	7.5	1.0	(Z)
RI	440	54.8	2.9	2.5	3.3	4.4	2.4	3.2	20.3	0.1
SC............	1,754	61.5	2.3	2.7	3.7	3.5	3.4	5.6	11.4	0.1
SD............	323	67.4	2.3	3.4	3.4	4.4	3.1	4.3	11.0	0.2
TN............	2,439	67.3	2.8	2.1	3.3	4.4	4.3	10.0	9.0	0.4
TX............	8,158	63.4	3.1	3.8	4.8	3.6	3.9	5.8	5.1	0.3
UT............	769	67.7	4.9	7.2	6.4	5.1	1.5	2.8	7.7	0.2
VT............	294	65.6	3.4	2.1	3.3	5.0	5.3	5.9	6.4	0.1
VA............	2,904	62.3	9.6	2.8	3.8	2.6	5.1	9.3	8.5	0.5
WA............	2,451	62.3	3.1	1.6	2.6	2.9	2.6	2.4	16.9	0.4
WV............	845	69.1	1.6	3.4	8.2	3.9	4.6	3.3	6.2	4.4	0.1
WI............	2,321	66.0	3.4	2.5	4.6	3.0	1.9	3.2	15.9	0.4
WY	224	64.9	3.6							

Z Less than .05 percent.

Source: U.S. Census Bureau, "2000 Census of Population and Housing, Profiles of General Demographic Characteristics";
<http://www.census.gov/Press-Release/www/2002/demoprofiles.html>.

No. 949. Housing Units—Size of Units and Lot: 2003

[In thousands (120,777 represents 120,777,000), except as indicated. Preliminary. As of fall. Based on the American Housing Survey; see Appendix III. For composition of regions, see map inside front cover]

Item	Total housing units	Seasonal	Year-round units							Vacant
			Occupied							
			Total	Owner	Renter	Northeast	Midwest	South	West	
Total units	120,777	3,558	105,867	72,254	33,614	20,171	24,487	38,140	23,070	11,352
Rooms:										
1 room	520	57	347	13	334	131	54	33	129	117
2 rooms	1,425	133	984	58	926	320	158	211	295	308
3 rooms	10,943	616	8,621	987	7,634	2,224	1,692	2,478	2,227	1,706
4 rooms	23,363	1,306	18,562	6,974	11,588	3,385	4,074	6,611	4,492	3,495
5 rooms	27,976	789	24,431	16,814	7,617	3,944	5,760	9,688	5,040	2,756
6 rooms	24,646	409	22,554	19,055	3,499	4,325	5,374	8,398	4,457	1,683
7 rooms	14,670	149	13,842	12,647	1,195	2,554	3,352	5,033	2,903	679
8 rooms or more	17,234	101	16,526	15,705	820	3,288	4,025	5,688	3,525	608
Complete bathrooms:										
No bathrooms	2,243	518	644	272	372	168	131	216	130	1,081
1 bathroom	48,162	1,670	40,791	17,606	23,185	10,003	10,288	12,394	8,107	5,701
1 and one-half bathrooms	17,645	304	16,253	12,722	3,531	3,944	5,203	4,372	2,733	1,088
2 or more bathrooms	52,727	1,066	48,179	41,654	6,526	6,055	8,866	21,158	12,100	3,482
Square footage of unit:										
Single detached and mobile homes [1]	83,771	2,851	74,595	65,168	9,427	11,587	18,466	28,824	15,718	6,325
Less than 500	1,228	342	691	429	262	99	99	317	175	195
500 to 749	3,035	487	2,045	1,266	779	270	455	929	391	504
750 to 999	6,675	531	5,243	3,808	1,435	640	1,392	2,187	1,024	900
1,000 to 1,499	20,331	525	18,069	15,131	2,938	2,057	4,205	7,576	4,231	1,737
1,500 to 1,999	18,773	306	17,452	15,719	1,734	2,411	4,019	6,790	4,233	1,014
2,000 to 2,499	12,616	195	11,834	11,136	699	1,983	3,101	4,370	2,380	587
2,500 to 2,999	6,440	92	6,051	5,802	249	1,155	1,516	2,246	1,134	297
3,000 to 3,999	5,783	76	5,440	5,241	198	1,106	1,431	1,851	1,051	267
4,000 or more	3,375	29	3,142	2,966	177	743	825	1,069	505	204
Other [2]	5,516	267	4,627	3,670	957	1,121	1,424	1,489	594	622
Median square footage	1,709	968	1,756	1,822	1,299	1,949	1,795	1,696	1,706	1,361
Lot size:										
Single detached and attached units and mobile homes	88,678	2,856	78,995	67,305	11,690	13,030	19,110	30,399	16,455	6,828
Less than one-eighth acre	12,609	599	10,602	8,057	2,545	2,185	2,549	2,837	3,030	1,407
One-eighth to one-quarter acre	24,997	725	22,171	18,199	3,973	2,723	5,606	7,251	6,591	2,101
One-quarter to one-half acre	16,813	496	15,309	13,516	1,794	2,418	3,761	5,969	3,161	1,008
One-half up to one acre	11,363	288	10,449	9,345	1,104	2,035	2,223	4,911	1,280	626
1 to 5 acres	15,925	449	14,390	12,696	1,694	2,772	3,063	6,974	1,581	1,086
5 to 10 acres	2,574	96	2,338	2,193	145	320	657	1,017	344	140
10 acres or more	4,396	202	3,735	3,300	435	576	1,251	1,440	467	459
Median acreage	0.35	0.30	0.36	0.39	0.23	0.42	0.34	0.46	0.22	0.24

[1] Does not include selected vacant units. [2] Represents units not reported or size unknown.

Source: U.S. Census Bureau, Current Housing Reports, Series H150/03, *American Housing Survey for the United States.* See Internet site <http://www.census.gov/hhes/www/housing/ahs/nationaldata.html>.

No. 950. Occupied Housing Units—Tenure by Race of Householder: 1991 to 2003

[In thousands (93,147 represents 93,147,000), except percent. 2003 preliminary. As of fall. Based on the American Housing Survey; see Appendix III]

Race of householder and tenure	1991	1993	1995	1997	1999	2001	2003 [1]
ALL RACES [2]							
Occupied units, total	93,147	94,724	97,693	99,487	102,803	106,261	105,867
Owner occupied	59,796	61,252	63,544	65,487	68,796	72,265	72,254
Percent of occupied	64.2	64.7	65.0	65.8	66.9	68.0	68.2
Renter occupied	33,351	33,472	34,150	34,000	34,007	33,996	33,614
WHITE [3]							
Occupied units, total	79,140	80,029	81,611	82,154	83,624	85,292	87,512
Owner occupied	53,749	54,878	56,507	57,781	60,041	62,465	63,141
Percent of occupied	67.9	68.6	69.2	70.3	71.8	73.2	72.2
Renter occupied	25,391	25,151	25,104	24,372	23,583	22,826	24,370
BLACK [3]							
Occupied units, total	10,832	11,128	11,773	12,085	12,936	13,292	13,005
Owner occupied	4,635	4,788	5,137	5,457	6,013	6,318	6,192
Percent of occupied	42.8	43.0	43.6	45.2	46.5	47.5	47.6
Renter occupied	6,197	6,340	6,637	6,628	6,923	6,974	6,813
HISPANIC ORIGIN [4]							
Occupied units, total	6,239	6,614	7,757	8,513	9,041	9,814	11,039
Owner occupied	2,423	2,788	3,245	3,646	4,087	4,731	5,106
Percent of occupied	38.8	42.2	41.8	42.8	45.2	48.2	46.3
Renter occupied	3,816	3,826	4,512	4,867	4,955	5,083	5,933

[1] Based on 2000 census controls. [2] Includes other races, not shown separately. [3] The 2003 Current Population Survey (CPS) allowed respondents to choose more than one race. Beginning 2003 data represent persons who selected this race group only and exclude persons reporting more than one race. The CPS in prior years only allowed respondents to report one race group. See also comments on race in the text for Section 1, Population. [4] Persons of Hispanic origin may be of any race.

Source: U.S. Census Bureau, Current Housing Reports, Series H150/91, H150/93, H150/95RV, H150/97, H150/99, H150/01, and H150/03, *American Housing Survey for the United States.* See Internet site <http://www.census.gov/hhes/www/housing/ahs/nationaldata.html>.

Construction and Housing 611

No. 951. Homeownership Rates by Age of Householder and Household Status: 1985 to 2003

[In percent. Represents the proportion of owner households to the total number of occupied households. Based on the Current Population Survey/Housing Vacancy Survey; see source and Appendix III for details]

Age of householder and household type	1985	1990	1995	1997	1998	1999	2000	2001	2002	2003
United States	63.9	63.9	64.7	65.7	66.3	66.8	67.4	67.8	67.9	68.3
AGE OF HOUSEHOLDER										
Less than 25 years old	17.2	15.7	15.9	17.7	18.2	19.9	21.7	22.5	22.9	22.8
25 to 29 years old	37.7	35.2	34.4	35.0	36.2	36.5	38.1	38.9	38.8	39.8
30 to 34 years old	54.0	51.8	53.1	52.6	53.6	53.8	54.6	54.8	54.9	56.5
35 to 39 years old	65.4	63.0	62.1	62.6	63.7	64.4	65.0	65.5	65.2	65.1
40 to 44 years old	71.4	69.8	68.6	69.7	70.0	69.9	70.6	70.8	71.7	71.3
45 to 49 years old	74.3	73.9	73.7	74.2	73.9	74.5	74.7	75.4	74.8	75.4
50 to 54 years old	77.5	76.8	77.0	77.7	77.8	77.8	78.5	78.2	77.9	77.9
55 to 59 years old	79.2	78.8	78.8	79.7	79.8	80.7	80.4	81.0	80.8	80.9
60 to 64 years old	79.9	79.8	80.3	80.5	82.1	81.3	80.3	81.8	81.6	81.9
65 to 69 years old	79.5	80.0	81.0	81.9	81.9	82.9	83.0	82.4	82.9	82.5
70 to 74 years old	76.8	78.4	80.9	82.0	82.2	82.8	82.6	82.5	82.5	82.0
75 years old and over	69.8	72.3	74.6	75.8	76.2	77.1	77.7	78.1	78.4	78.7
Less than 35 years old	39.9	38.5	38.6	38.7	39.3	39.7	40.8	41.2	41.3	42.2
35 to 44 years old	68.1	66.3	65.2	66.1	66.9	67.2	67.9	68.2	68.6	68.3
45 to 54 years old	75.9	75.2	75.2	75.8	75.7	76.0	76.5	76.7	76.3	76.6
55 to 64 years old	79.5	79.3	79.5	80.1	80.9	81.0	80.3	81.3	81.1	81.4
65 years and over	74.8	76.3	78.1	79.1	79.3	80.1	80.4	80.3	80.6	80.5
TYPE OF HOUSEHOLD										
Family households:										
Married-couple families	78.2	78.1	79.6	80.8	81.5	81.8	82.4	82.9	82.9	83.3
Male householder, no spouse present	57.8	55.2	55.3	54.0	55.7	56.1	57.5	57.9	57.3	57.9
Female householder, no spouse present	45.8	44.0	45.1	46.1	47.0	48.2	49.1	49.9	49.2	49.6
Nonfamily households:										
One-person	45.8	49.0	50.5	51.8	52.1	52.7	53.6	54.4	54.9	55.2
Male householder	38.8	42.4	43.8	45.2	45.7	46.3	47.4	48.2	48.6	50.0
Female householder	51.3	53.6	55.4	56.7	56.9	57.6	58.1	59.0	59.6	59.1
Other:										
Male householder	30.1	31.7	34.2	35.9	36.7	37.2	38.0	38.6	38.7	40.0
Female householder	30.6	32.5	33.0	39.5	40.3	41.5	40.6	41.0	41.9	43.1

Source: U.S. Census Bureau, "Housing Vacancies and Home Ownership". See Internet site <http://www.census.gov/hhes/www/hvs.html>.

No. 952. Homeownership Rates by State: 1985 to 2003

[In percent. See headnote, Table 951]

State	1985	1990	1995	2000	2002	2003	State	1985	1990	1995	2000	2002	2003
United States	63.9	63.9	64.7	67.4	67.9	68.3	Missouri	69.2	64.0	69.4	74.2	74.8	74.0
Alabama	70.4	68.4	70.1	73.2	73.7	76.2	Montana	66.5	69.1	68.7	70.2	69.4	71.5
Alaska	61.2	58.4	60.9	66.4	67.1	70.0	Nebraska	68.5	67.3	67.1	70.2	68.5	69.5
Arizona	64.7	64.5	62.9	68.0	65.6	67.0	Nevada	57.0	55.8	58.6	64.0	65.3	64.8
Arkansas	66.6	67.8	67.2	68.9	70.3	69.6	New Hampshire	65.5	65.0	66.0	69.2	69.5	74.4
California	54.2	53.8	55.4	57.1	57.7	58.9	New Jersey	62.3	65.0	64.9	66.2	66.9	66.9
Colorado	63.6	59.0	64.6	68.3	68.9	71.3	New Mexico	68.2	68.6	67.0	73.7	70.0	70.3
Connecticut	69.0	67.9	68.2	70.0	71.5	73.0	New York	50.3	53.3	52.7	53.4	54.8	54.3
Delaware	70.3	67.7	71.7	72.0	75.6	77.2	North Carolina	68.0	69.0	70.1	71.1	70.0	70.0
Dist. of Columbia	37.4	36.4	39.2	41.9	44.1	43.0	North Dakota	69.9	67.2	67.3	70.7	69.4	68.7
Florida	67.2	65.1	66.6	68.4	68.7	69.5	Ohio	67.9	68.7	67.9	71.3	72.1	72.8
Georgia	62.7	64.3	66.6	69.8	71.8	71.4	Oklahoma	70.5	70.3	69.8	72.7	69.6	69.1
Hawaii	51.0	55.5	50.2	55.2	57.9	58.3	Oregon	61.5	64.4	63.2	65.3	66.2	68.0
Idaho	71.0	69.4	72.0	70.5	73.0	74.4	Pennsylvania	71.6	73.8	71.5	74.7	74.0	73.7
Illinois	60.6	63.0	66.4	67.9	70.1	70.7	Rhode Island	61.4	58.5	57.9	61.5	59.4	59.9
Indiana	67.6	67.0	71.0	74.9	75.1	74.4	South Carolina	72.0	71.4	71.3	76.5	77.5	75.0
Iowa	69.9	70.7	71.4	75.2	73.9	73.4	South Dakota	67.6	66.2	67.5	71.2	71.5	70.9
Kansas	68.3	69.0	67.5	69.3	70.3	70.3	Tennessee	67.6	68.3	67.0	70.9	70.3	70.8
Kentucky	68.5	65.8	71.2	73.4	73.7	74.4	Texas	60.5	59.7	61.4	63.8	63.4	64.5
Louisiana	70.2	67.8	65.3	68.1	67.0	67.5	Utah	71.5	70.1	71.5	72.7	72.8	73.4
Maine	73.7	74.2	76.7	76.5	74.0	73.7	Vermont	69.5	72.6	70.4	68.7	70.3	71.4
Maryland	65.6	64.9	65.8	69.9	72.0	71.6	Virginia	66.8	61.8	61.6	63.6	66.9	65.9
Massachusetts	60.5	58.6	60.2	59.9	62.6	64.3	Washington	68.5	69.8	68.1	73.9	74.4	75.0
Michigan	70.7	72.3	72.2	77.2	76.0	75.6	West Virginia	75.9	72.0	73.1	75.9	77.2	78.1
Minnesota	70.0	68.0	73.3	76.1	77.3	77.2	Wisconsin	63.8	68.3	67.5	71.8	72.2	72.8
Mississippi	69.6	69.4	71.1	75.2	74.9	73.4	Wyoming	73.2	68.9	69.0	71.0	73.0	72.9

Source: U.S. Census Bureau, "Housing Vacancies and Home Ownership". See Internet site <http://www.census.gov/hhes/www/hvs.html>.

No. 953. Occupied Housing Units—Costs by Region: 2003

[(72,254 represents 72,254,000). Preliminary. As of fall. Specified owner-occupied units are limited to one-unit structures on less than 10 acres and no business on property. Specified renter-occupied units exclude one-unit structures on 10 acres or more. See headnote Table 954 for an explanation of housing costs. Based on the American Housing Survey; See Appendix III. For composition of regions, see map inside front cover]

Category	Number (1,000)					Percent distribution				
	Total units	North-east	Mid-west	South	West	Total units	North-east	Mid-west	South	West
OWNER OCCUPIED UNITS										
Total	72,254	12,988	17,888	26,695	14,682	100.0	100.0	100.0	100.0	100.0
Monthly housing costs:										
Less than $300	15,044	1,372	3,463	7,871	2,336	20.8	10.6	19.4	29.5	15.9
$300 to $399	6,497	1,131	1,979	2,297	1,089	9.0	8.7	11.1	8.6	7.4
$400 to $499	5,193	1,131	1,454	1,756	853	7.2	8.7	8.1	6.6	5.8
$500 to $599	4,428	932	1,231	1,592	673	6.1	7.2	6.9	6.0	4.6
$600 to $699	4,224	811	1,241	1,617	556	5.8	6.2	6.9	6.1	3.8
$700 to $799	4,120	790	1,098	1,629	604	5.7	6.1	6.1	6.1	4.1
$800 to $999	7,386	1,375	2,049	2,621	1,342	10.2	10.6	11.5	9.8	9.1
$1,000 to $1,249	7,390	1,304	1,893	2,514	1,679	10.2	10.0	10.6	9.4	11.4
$1,250 to $1,499	5,473	1,079	1,383	1,603	1,408	7.6	8.3	7.7	6.0	9.6
$1,500 or more	12,499	3,064	2,097	3,195	4,142	17.3	23.6	11.7	12.0	28.2
Median (dol.) [1]	738	848	666	589	983	(X)	(X)	(X)	(X)	(X)
RENTER OCCUPIED UNITS										
Total	33,614	7,182	6,599	11,444	8,388	100.0	100.0	100.0	100.0	100.0
Monthly housing costs:										
Less than $300	3,412	886	696	1,209	621	10.2	12.3	10.5	10.6	7.4
$300 to $399	2,296	380	607	953	356	6.8	5.3	9.2	8.3	4.2
$400 to $499	3,694	689	923	1,443	640	11.0	9.6	14.0	12.6	7.6
$500 to $599	4,316	792	1,068	1,594	862	12.8	11.0	16.2	13.9	10.3
$600 to $699	4,174	810	873	1,503	988	12.4	11.3	13.2	13.1	11.8
$700 to $799	3,704	810	708	1,256	930	11.0	11.3	10.7	11.0	11.1
$800 to $999	4,563	1,040	707	1,353	1,463	13.6	14.5	10.7	11.8	17.4
$1,000 to $1,249	2,744	685	328	662	1,069	8.2	9.5	5.0	5.8	12.7
$1,250 to $1,499	1,153	298	112	243	500	3.4	4.1	1.7	2.1	6.0
$1,500 or more	1,283	393	84	251	556	3.8	5.5	1.3	2.2	6.6
No cash rent	2,276	400	494	978	403	6.8	5.6	7.5	8.5	4.8
Median (dol.) [1]	647	679	577	602	756	(X)	(X)	(X)	(X)	(X)

X Not applicable. [1] For explanation of median, see Guide to Tabular Presentation.

No. 954. Occupied Housing Units—Financial Summary by Selected Characteristics of the Householder: 2003

[In thousands of units (105,867 represents 105,867,000), except as indicated. Preliminary. As of fall. Housing costs include real estate taxes, property insurance, utilities, fuel, water, garbage collection, and mortgage. Based on the American Housing Survey; see Appendix III]

Characteristic	Total occupied units	Tenure		Black [1]		Hispanic origin [2]		Elderly [3]		Households below poverty level	
		Owner	Renter	Owner	Renter	Owner	Renter	Owner	Renter	Owner	Renter
Total units [4]	105,867	72,254	33,614	6,192	6,813	5,106	5,933	17,355	4,276	6,062	7,908
Monthly housing costs:											
Less than $300	18,456	15,044	3,412	1,593	1,066	937	485	7,047	905	2,727	2,002
$300-$399	8,792	6,497	2,296	491	479	394	335	2,882	405	708	767
$400-$499	8,888	5,193	3,694	434	864	272	634	1,876	454	504	1,024
$500-$599	8,744	4,428	4,316	378	901	292	820	1,250	445	373	918
$600-$699	8,398	4,224	4,174	445	847	295	820	1,250	445	373	918
$700-$799	7,824	4,120	3,704	376	753	310	732	852	444	355	739
$800-$999	11,949	7,386	4,563	753	856	601	890	677	289	234	577
$1,000 or more	30,542	25,362	5,180	1,723	605	2,006	968	891	372	373	564
Median amount (dollars) [5]	682	718	647	645	586	818	669	1,880	471	788	1,316
								351	529	341	480
Monthly housing costs as percent of income: [6]											
Less than 5 percent	5,296	5,011	285	386	49	249	38	1,130	32	31	36
5 to 9 percent	12,323	11,222	1,101	731	191	612	144	2,904	84	119	32
10 to 14 percent	14,475	11,908	2,568	958	484	695	324	2,893	188	244	93
15 to 19 percent	14,717	11,176	3,541	895	663	693	446	2,396	277	321	122
20 to 24 percent	12,567	8,479	4,088	702	731	640	668	1,701	290	311	265
25 to 29 percent	9,717	6,137	3,580	520	788	517	648	1,256	439	307	461
30 to 34 percent	7,101	4,234	2,868	415	636	415	555	944	363	280	386
35 to 39 percent	4,900	2,791	2,109	290	431	282	474	622	218	231	341
40 percent or more	19,393	9,988	9,943	1,143	2,052	933	2,173	3,031	1,747	2,994	4,259
Median amount (percent) [5]	21	18	30	20	31	22	34	18	38	57	65
Median monthly costs (dol.): [5]											
Electricity	62	68	49	70	53	64	47	61	43	62	48
Piped gas	49	54	38	60	43	41	29	55	39	50	40
Fuel oil	79	81	65	78	62	78	78	77	61	69	63

[1] For persons who selected this race group only. See footnote 3 Table 950. [2] Persons of Hispanic origin may be of any race. [3] Householders 65 years old and over. [4] Includes units with mortgage payment not reported and no cash rent not shown separately. [5] For explanation of median, see Guide to Tabular Presentation. [6] Money income before taxes.

Source of Tables 953 and 954: U.S. Census Bureau, Current Housing Reports, Series H150/03, *American Housing Survey for the United States.* See Internet site <http://www.census.gov/hhes/www/housing/ahs/nationaldata.html>

Construction and Housing 613

No. 955. Specified Owner-Occupied Housing Units—Value and Costs by State: 2000

[In percent, except as indicated (55,212 represents 55,212,000. As of April 1. Specified owner-occupied units are owner-occupied, one-family, attached and detached houses on less than 10 acres without a business or medical office on the property. Based on sample data from the 2000 Census of Population and Housing; see text, Section 1, and Appendix III. For definition of median, see Guide to Tabular Presentation]

State	Total (1,000)	Percent of units with value of—			Median value (dol.)	Median selected monthly owner costs [1] (dol.)	Selected monthly owner costs as a percent of household income, 1999			
		$99,999 or less	$100,000 to $199,999	$200,000 or more			Less than 15 percent	15 to 24 percent	25 to 34 percent	35 percent or more
U.S.	55,212	40.3	38.4	21.4	119,600	1,088	36.5	31.4	15.5	15.8
AL...........	919	61.9	28.8	9.3	85,100	816	43.5	29.1	12.1	13.9
AK...........	106	22.5	57.9	19.7	144,200	1,315	32.6	33.3	17.4	16.2
AZ...........	1,032	35.6	45.9	18.5	121,300	1,039	34.8	31.8	16.3	16.2
AR...........	513	72.3	22.0	5.7	72,800	737	45.3	29.0	11.8	12.7
CA...........	5,528	11.6	35.5	52.9	211,500	1,478	28.0	28.7	19.3	23.2
CO	903	13.3	52.4	34.3	166,600	1,197	32.2	32.5	18.2	16.6
CT...........	728	12.5	50.6	36.9	166,900	1,426	31.8	32.9	17.7	17.1
DE...........	177	28.1	54.0	17.9	130,400	1,101	38.5	32.2	14.8	13.8
DC...........	76	18.6	43.5	37.8	157,200	1,291	38.2	27.0	14.6	18.6
FL...........	3,242	46.9	38.5	14.7	105,500	1,004	34.2	30.5	15.8	18.5
GA	1,596	43.7	39.1	17.2	111,200	1,039	36.4	32.5	15.0	15.2
HI	174	6.7	21.7	71.5	272,700	1,571	35.7	23.7	17.9	22.1
ID	255	45.2	43.9	10.9	106,300	887	36.6	32.6	15.6	14.5
IL	2,470	35.7	41.0	23.3	130,800	1,198	36.1	32.4	15.9	14.9
IN...........	1,379	55.3	36.4	8.3	94,300	869	42.7	32.5	12.9	11.2
IA...........	665	65.7	28.2	6.1	82,500	829	45.2	32.4	12.2	9.6
KS...........	582	61.6	29.9	8.4	83,500	888	43.5	32.8	12.5	10.5
KY...........	806	61.8	30.2	8.1	86,700	816	44.3	30.1	12.3	12.3
LA...........	865	62.3	29.2	8.5	85,000	816	45.7	27.0	11.4	14.2
ME	255	51.3	38.1	10.7	98,700	923	35.8	33.8	15.2	14.7
MD	1,179	23.1	50.3	26.6	146,000	1,296	32.1	33.7	17.6	16.1
MA	1,188	9.5	46.4	44.1	185,700	1,353	33.4	33.1	16.7	16.2
MI	2,269	41.3	41.6	17.2	115,600	972	41.8	31.5	13.2	12.7
MN	1,117	35.1	49.4	15.5	122,400	1,044	38.7	34.9	14.9	11.1
MS	532	72.5	21.8	5.7	71,400	752	42.4	27.5	12.3	16.0
MO	1,188	58.1	32.0	9.9	89,900	861	43.4	31.6	12.6	11.6
MT	165	50.5	40.2	9.3	99,500	863	38.0	30.9	15.1	15.3
NE	370	61.4	31.7	6.9	88,000	895	42.1	33.1	13.6	10.6
NV	363	15.7	63.7	20.6	142,000	1,190	28.0	32.1	19.2	19.8
NH	249	26.7	54.2	19.1	133,300	1,226	28.8	36.7	18.7	15.3
NJ...........	1,702	15.2	46.7	38.0	170,800	1,534	27.0	32.6	19.3	20.5
NM...........	340	45.2	40.3	14.6	108,100	929	40.3	27.9	14.6	16.0
NY...........	2,690	32.2	35.7	32.1	148,700	1,357	31.5	31.4	16.8	19.6
NC...........	1,616	45.3	39.7	15.0	108,300	985	37.7	31.5	14.8	15.0
ND	122	73.3	23.5	3.3	74,400	818	44.9	32.5	12.1	9.7
OH	2,613	47.7	40.8	11.4	103,700	963	38.6	33.1	14.5	13.2
OK	699	73.8	21.4	4.9	70,700	764	45.3	29.6	11.9	12.1
OR	654	17.0	56.4	26.6	152,100	1,125	32.2	32.0	17.8	17.5
PA...........	2,889	52.4	36.2	11.3	97,000	1,010	37.8	31.5	14.8	15.1
RI...........	202	20.5	61.1	18.3	133,000	1,205	30.2	33.6	18.5	17.1
SC...........	784	54.1	33.2	12.7	94,900	894	40.9	30.2	13.5	14.3
SD...........	138	68.9	26.0	5.1	79,600	828	43.4	32.5	13.0	10.4
TN...........	1,206	55.9	33.0	11.1	93,000	882	40.4	30.4	13.8	14.4
TX...........	3,850	63.3	26.9	9.8	82,500	986	40.7	31.5	13.2	13.6
UT...........	427	16.1	60.8	23.1	146,100	1,102	34.9	30.4	18.1	16.2
VT...........	106	41.0	48.2	10.8	111,500	1,021	30.1	35.6	17.7	16.2
VA...........	1,511	36.7	40.2	23.1	125,400	1,144	35.5	33.5	16.3	14.1
WA...........	1,157	15.1	48.5	36.4	168,300	1,268	30.3	31.9	19.1	18.1
WV...........	393	73.8	21.7	4.6	72,800	713	50.8	25.7	10.4	11.9
WI...........	1,122	41.9	46.1	12.0	112,200	1,024	36.8	35.1	15.6	12.0
WY...........	96	53.6	37.2	9.2	96,600	825	45.1	30.3	12.7	11.3

[1] For homes with a mortgage. Includes mortgages, deeds of trust, taxes, utilities, etc.

Source: U.S. Census Bureau, "2000 Census of Population and Housing, Profiles of General Demographic Characteristics"; <http://www.census.gov/Press-Release/www/2002/demoprofiles.html>.

[In percent, except as indicated (884.3 represents 884,300). As of April 1. Specified owner-occupied units are owner-occupied, one-family, attached and detached houses on less than 10 acres without a business or medical office on the property. Based on sample data from the 2000 Census of Population and Housing; see text Section 1, and Appendix III. See headnote Table 959 for information regarding metropolitan areas]

Metropolitan area	Total (1,000)	Percent of units with value of— $99,999 or less	Percent of units with value of— $200,000 or more	Median value (dol.)	Median selected monthly owner costs [1] (dol.)	Selected monthly owner costs as a percent of household income, 1999 Less than 15 percent	15 to 24 percent	25 to 34 percent	35 percent or more
Atlanta, GA MSA	884.3	27.9	24.3	135,300	1,165	32.8	34.9	16.3	15.4
Boston-Worcester-Lawrence, MA-NH-ME-CT CMSA	1,067.8	7.4	46.8	192,500	1,415	32.0	34.0	17.3	16.2
Chicago-Gary-Kenosha, IL-IN-WI CMSA	1,717.3	18.4	32.0	159,000	1,347	31.5	33.1	17.8	17.0
Cincinnati-Hamilton, OH-KY-IN CMSA	439.2	38.8	15.5	116,500	1,064	36.3	35.3	15.5	12.4
Cleveland-Akron, OH CMSA	711.1	37.7	15.3	117,900	1,049	35.5	33.2	15.6	15.1
Dallas-Fort Worth, TX CMSA	1,003.7	50.0	14.6	100,000	1,148	35.7	34.9	14.9	13.7
Denver-Boulder-Greeley, CO CMSA	565.3	6.1	39.7	179,500	1,271	30.7	33.4	18.8	16.6
Detroit-Ann Arbor-Flint, MI CMSA	1,305.3	32.4	22.7	132,600	1,076	40.1	31.6	13.7	13.8
Houston-Galveston-Brazoria, TX CMSA	863.4	57.4	12.2	89,700	1,072	39.4	32.6	13.1	13.8
Kansas City, MO-KS MSA	418.0	47.3	12.4	104,700	986	39.5	34.4	13.7	11.8
Los Angeles-Riverside-Orange County, CA CMSA	2,498.4	9.6	51.0	203,300	1,494	26.4	28.3	19.5	25.0
Miami-Fort Lauderdale, FL CMSA	634.5	33.1	18.3	126,100	1,225	24.2	30.0	18.8	25.9
Minneapolis-St. Paul, MN-WI MSA	704.0	18.3	21.2	141,200	1,157	34.2	37.1	16.7	11.8
New York-Northern New Jersey-Long Island, NY-NJ-CT-PA CMSA	3,088.9	7.0	51.0	203,100	1,679	27.8	30.7	18.5	22.3
Philadelphia-Wilmington-Atlantic City, PA-NJ-DE-MD CMSA	1,456.0	37.3	18.2	122,300	1,224	32.3	32.2	16.8	17.8
Phoenix-Mesa, AZ MSA	689.5	30.5	20.5	127,900	1,088	32.3	33.1	16.8	17.8
Pittsburgh, PA MSA	601.3	62.0	8.2	86,100	937	33.0	33.1	17.0	16.2
Portland-Salem, OR-WA CMSA	453.7	8.3	31.8	165,400	1,232	40.2	30.8	13.7	14.4
Sacramento-Yolo, CA CMSA	359.8	14.2	31.2	159,700	1,298	29.0	32.9	19.4	18.2
St. Louis, MO-IL MSA	624.4	50.4	13.5	99,400	953	28.7	31.6	19.4	19.7
San Diego, CA MSA	457.3	3.5	59.8	227,200	1,541	42.0	32.8	12.9	11.6
San Francisco-Oakland-San Jose, CA CMSA	1,258.0	2.7	82.5	353,500	1,822	27.7	28.4	19.9	23.2
Seattle-Tacoma-Bremerton, WA CMSA	719.2	6.2	47.8	195,400	1,399	29.4	28.2	19.5	22.2
Tampa-St. Petersburg-Clearwater, FL MSA	540.9	55.5	11.0	93,800	938	27.8	32.3	20.3	19.0
Washington-Baltimore, DC-MD-VA-WV CMSA	1,621.6	17.4	34.2	161,600	1,382	35.1	31.6	15.5	16.9

[1] For homes with a mortgage. Includes mortgages, deeds of trust, taxes, utilities, etc.

[In percent, except as indicated (104.8 represents 104,800). As of April 1. See headnote, Table 956 for coverage]

City	Total (1,000)	Percent of units with value of— $99,999 or less	$100,000 to $199,999	$200,000 or more	Median value (dol.)	Median selected monthly owner costs [1] (dol.)	Selected monthly owner costs as a percent of household income, 1999 Less than 15 percent	15 to 24 percent	25 to 34 percent	35 percent or more
Austin, TX	104.8	35.5	40.9	23.6	124,700	1,181	34.3	34.3	16.0	14.8
Baltimore, MD	116.6	83.3	12.5	4.3	69,100	853	35.0	28.0	14.8	20.5
Boston, MA	30.5	5.8	49.5	44.7	190,600	1,370	33.1	30.9	15.0	20.0
Chicago, IL	263.9	31.3	48.3	20.5	132,400	1,216	32.6	28.7	16.2	21.2
Columbus, OH	134.0	49.0	45.3	5.7	101,400	987	30.9	36.3	17.2	15.0
Dallas, TX	173.6	55.2	25.0	19.7	89,800	1,054	38.9	29.3	13.6	16.9
Denver, CO	104.3	10.7	55.6	33.7	165,800	1,134	33.2	29.7	17.2	19.2
Detroit, MI	164.2	84.8	12.9	2.3	63,600	769	41.1	23.9	12.0	20.4
El Paso, TX	102.0	79.9	16.4	3.7	71,300	810	38.4	30.3	14.4	15.7
Houston, TX	295.5	64.4	22.6	13.0	79,300	965	41.7	28.8	12.3	15.6
Indianapolis, IN [2]	172.7	51.7	39.6	8.7	98,200	928	37.6	33.6	14.5	13.5
Jacksonville, FL	157.7	61.3	30.4	8.4	87,800	902	37.2	32.4	14.2	15.2
Los Angeles, CA	412.8	4.6	39.7	55.7	221,600	1,556	27.2	24.8	17.4	29.4
Memphis, TN	130.7	73.2	19.3	7.5	72,800	838	34.0	29.4	15.1	19.8
Milwaukee, WI	82.3	73.0	24.8	2.2	80,400	863	36.7	32.5	15.0	15.0
Nashville-Davidson, TN [2]	109.1	41.2	43.3	15.5	113,300	1,006	35.6	32.1	16.2	15.3
New York, NY	391.4	4.2	40.8	55.0	211,900	1,535	30.4	25.3	15.8	26.8
Philadelphia, PA	315.4	84.9	12.6	2.5	59,700	800	39.2	26.3	12.8	19.4
Phoenix, AZ	250.1	41.9	41.0	17.1	112,600	1,021	30.7	33.6	17.0	17.8
San Antonio, TX	217.3	74.9	20.4	4.7	68,800	881	40.4	30.9	13.8	13.9
San Diego, CA	188.0	4.0	34.6	61.4	233,100	1,526	29.2	28.1	19.1	22.8
San Francisco, CA	79.5	5.6	3.6	90.8	396,400	1,693	36.9	23.7	15.6	22.9
San Jose, CA	146.9	2.1	3.4	94.5	394,000	1,717	27.5	30.1	20.0	21.8
Seattle, WA	102.7	2.5	25.9	71.6	259,600	1,497	32.0	29.0	18.7	19.7
Washington, DC	76.3	18.6	43.5	37.8	157,200	1,291	38.2	27.0	14.6	18.6

[1] Includes mortgages, deeds of trust, taxes, utilities, etc. [2] Represents the portion of a consolidated city that is not within one or more separately incorporated places.

Source of Tables 956 and 957: U.S. Census Bureau, "2000 Census of Population and Housing, Profiles of General Demographic Characteristics"; <http://www.census.gov/Press-Release/www/2002/demoprofiles.html>.

Construction and Housing 615

No. 958. Specified Renter-Occupied Housing Units—Gross Rent by State: 2000

[In percent, except as indicated (35,200 represents 35,200,000. As of April 1. Specified renter-occupied units include all renter-occupied units except 1-unit attached or detached houses on 10 acres or more. Based on the 2000 Census of Population and Housing; see text, Section 1, and Appendix III. For definition of median, see Guide to Tabular Presentation]

State	Total [1] (1,000)	Percent of units with gross rent of—					Median gross rent (dol.)	Gross rent as a percent of household income, 1999			
		$299 or less	$300 to $499	$500 to $749	$750 to $999	$1,000 or more		Less than 15 percent	15 to 24 percent	25 to 34 percent	35 percent or more
U.S.	35,200	10.4	22.0	33.7	17.2	11.6	602	18.1	27.1	17.8	29.5
AL	469	20.3	34.1	26.3	6.4	2.5	447	19.6	24.0	15.1	27.4
AK	82	4.0	11.7	31.7	22.4	16.9	720	17.3	26.1	17.2	25.4
AZ	605	6.8	20.6	38.8	18.3	10.1	619	15.8	26.9	18.8	30.9
AR	310	16.6	37.1	27.5	5.8	2.0	453	19.4	25.1	15.3	26.7
CA	4,922	4.9	12.6	31.3	23.6	24.5	747	14.6	26.7	19.2	34.1
CO	534	7.2	16.3	35.2	21.4	16.4	671	15.2	28.8	20.4	30.4
CT	429	9.6	12.8	35.6	22.7	15.0	681	18.4	27.5	18.5	29.0
DE	82	10.1	14.3	41.6	19.4	8.8	639	19.5	28.6	17.8	26.7
DC	147	12.8	17.6	34.5	16.8	15.4	618	20.0	26.9	17.8	28.2
FL	1,889	7.2	18.4	38.3	20.8	10.7	641	14.6	26.3	18.6	33.0
GA	964	11.9	20.9	31.2	20.8	9.2	613	18.4	27.4	17.5	28.1
HI	174	6.7	8.6	24.8	22.8	23.8	779	14.2	23.6	17.2	29.1
ID	126	12.7	30.4	34.0	10.9	3.7	515	17.5	27.1	17.6	28.1
IL	1,488	10.6	21.2	36.1	17.5	10.8	605	20.0	28.3	17.1	28.3
IN	654	11.9	31.2	38.4	9.7	3.4	521	21.0	28.3	17.0	26.4
IA	302	17.1	35.8	31.2	7.1	2.6	470	22.4	28.2	16.8	24.8
KS	310	13.9	33.4	31.4	10.3	4.8	498	21.1	29.3	16.7	25.0
KY	449	18.9	36.8	26.2	6.1	2.1	445	20.8	25.5	16.0	25.6
LA	526	17.3	34.4	28.7	7.0	2.9	466	18.6	23.3	14.8	29.8
ME	144	16.2	30.7	32.5	10.0	3.3	497	16.9	28.1	19.2	27.4
MD	632	8.7	14.2	33.6	24.3	14.9	689	18.2	29.3	19.1	27.0
MA	932	13.0	14.1	28.7	21.8	18.8	684	18.9	26.8	19.5	28.6
MI	976	10.8	28.3	38.3	12.5	5.7	546	20.9	27.2	16.8	28.4
MN	471	14.4	23.3	35.6	15.5	7.5	566	18.7	29.5	19.6	27.1
MS	283	21.1	33.3	25.9	6.0	1.9	439	18.9	23.4	14.8	27.6
MO	633	15.1	34.9	31.8	8.6	3.3	484	20.3	28.2	16.8	26.3
MT	105	18.6	36.9	26.4	6.1	2.4	447	18.2	30.2	16.9	28.2
NE	207	14.2	34.6	32.9	8.3	3.8	491	21.4	28.5	17.2	23.5
NV	293	4.1	12.2	40.7	26.7	13.0	699	15.2	28.5	20.2	30.5
NH	141	9.0	15.8	39.9	21.5	9.8	646	18.0	31.7	19.2	25.6
NJ	1,049	7.9	8.6	31.8	29.9	18.6	751	18.5	27.6	18.3	29.9
NM	201	13.4	31.3	32.5	10.8	5.8	503	16.6	24.5	16.8	30.5
NY	3,302	10.2	15.7	32.5	21.2	17.3	672	19.1	24.2	16.9	33.4
NC	944	11.2	26.8	34.7	13.7	5.3	548	19.3	27.2	16.3	26.7
ND	83	22.9	40.7	21.9	3.9	1.7	412	22.7	28.9	15.4	22.6
OH	1,353	12.7	32.0	36.1	10.3	4.0	515	20.5	28.1	17.0	27.4
OK	414	15.2	39.6	27.5	6.4	2.6	456	19.8	26.4	16.0	26.7
OR	468	7.4	18.9	42.4	18.0	9.4	620	14.7	28.0	19.6	32.2
PA	1,349	13.0	28.9	33.7	12.4	6.3	531	19.2	26.6	17.3	28.6
RI	163	15.6	22.6	38.5	12.9	6.5	553	18.7	26.5	19.4	28.9
SC	421	14.1	29.1	33.0	9.7	4.1	510	19.1	26.1	15.4	26.8
SD	88	22.9	35.7	25.3	4.7	2.0	426	20.9	29.2	16.3	22.7
TN	657	15.3	30.0	33.3	10.1	3.7	505	18.9	26.7	17.3	27.2
TX	2,649	9.1	25.1	37.1	15.4	7.9	574	18.8	28.8	17.4	27.1
UT	199	7.7	21.0	42.2	15.3	8.5	597	18.1	28.7	18.8	27.7
VT	67	11.6	25.2	38.1	14.0	5.4	553	15.9	27.7	20.1	29.5
VA	843	9.3	18.9	30.7	20.3	15.0	650	18.2	29.3	18.5	26.3
WA	796	7.3	16.4	36.4	21.6	14.0	663	15.1	28.4	19.8	30.8
WV	176	22.8	38.8	19.7	3.3	1.2	401	18.9	21.3	14.6	28.3
WI	642	10.5	29.5	39.7	12.3	4.3	540	21.1	30.8	17.5	25.4
WY	56	16.4	42.0	23.6	5.5	2.7	437	24.1	26.3	15.2	23.3

[1] Includes units with no cash rent.

Source: U.S. Census Bureau, "2000 Census of Population and Housing, Profiles of General Demographic Characteristics"; <http://www.census.gov/Press-Release/www/2002/demoprofiles.html>.

No. 959. Specified Renter-Occupied Housing Units—Gross Rent by the 25 Largest Metropolitan Areas: 2000

[In percent, except as indicated (501.9 represents 501,900). As of April 1. Specified renter-occupied units include all renter-occupied units except 1-unit attached or detached houses on 10 acres or more. Based on sample data from the 2000 Census of Population and Housing; see text Section 1, and Appendix III. Covers metropolitan statistical areas (MSA's) and consolidated metropolitan statistical areas (CMSAs) as defined by the U.S. Office of Management and Budget as of June 30, 1999. For definitions and components of metropolitan areas see Appendix II. For definition of median, see Guide to Tabular Presentation]

Metropolitan area	Total [1] (1,000)	Percent of units with gross rent of—			Median gross rent (dol.)	Gross rent as a percent of household income, 1999			
		$499 or less	$500 to $749	$750 or more		Less than 15 percent	15 to 24 percent	25 to 34 percent	35 percent or more
Atlanta, GA MSA	501.9	16.3	33.0	48.0	746	17.1	29.9	19.4	28.5
Boston-Worcester-Lawrence, MA-NH-ME-CT CMSA	847.2	23.6	28.3	44.9	720	18.7	27.6	19.6	28.3
Chicago-Gary-Kenosha, IL-IN-WI CMSA	1,145.5	23.5	39.0	34.8	659	19.2	28.7	17.5	29.1
Cincinnati-Hamilton, OH-KY-IN CMSA	250.3	45.4	34.4	16.7	516	21.2	28.9	16.9	27.4
Cleveland-Akron, OH CMSA	360.8	38.9	39.5	17.6	545	18.9	27.6	17.6	29.3
Dallas-Fort Worth, TX CMSA	750.9	21.7	42.9	32.8	649	18.9	32.0	19.0	25.4
Denver-Boulder-Greeley, CO CMSA	334.3	19.2	35.8	42.7	706	15.1	29.3	21.0	30.5
Detroit-Ann Arbor-Flint, MI CMSA	574.0	33.0	39.9	23.4	584	21.2	26.9	16.5	29.0
Houston-Galveston-Brazoria, TX CMSA	643.0	30.6	41.5	24.7	589	20.3	30.0	17.4	26.2
Kansas City, MO-KS MSA	219.9	34.2	39.8	21.9	575	20.2	31.2	17.6	24.7
Los Angeles-Riverside-Orange County, CA CMSA	2,412.5	16.2	35.0	46.4	733	14.2	26.3	19.1	35.2
Miami-Fort Lauderdale, FL CMSA	526.4	20.8	36.9	39.3	689	12.3	24.1	18.9	37.7
Minneapolis-St. Paul, MN-WI MSA	310.9	24.7	41.7	31.5	641	17.3	30.9	20.3	28.0
New York-Northern New Jersey-Long Island, NY-NJ-CT-PA CMSA	3,627.1	19.8	30.4	47.2	740	19.5	24.9	17.2	32.5
Philadelphia-Wilmington-Atlantic City, PA-NJ-DE-MD CMSA	695.1	24.0	38.9	33.0	651	17.3	26.8	17.7	31.2
Phoenix-Mesa, AZ MSA	381.2	20.4	41.6	34.3	661	15.3	28.2	19.7	30.9
Pittsburgh, PA MSA	275.0	50.3	31.3	12.3	482	20.2	25.7	17.2	28.5
Portland-Salem, OR-WA CMSA	317.1	18.8	45.0	33.4	660	14.8	29.7	20.2	30.9
Sacramento-Yolo, CA CMSA	255.9	20.6	40.6	36.2	673	14.9	27.6	19.1	33.8
St. Louis, MO-IL MSA	287.5	42.7	37.1	15.5	525	20.6	28.4	16.5	27.6
San Diego, CA MSA	441.6	13.0	33.4	49.4	761	12.6	27.0	20.3	34.1
San Francisco-Oakland-San Jose, CA CMSA	1,072.2	11.0	17.2	69.2	968	16.4	28.5	19.7	31.0
Seattle-Tacoma-Bremerton, WA CMSA	514.8	16.9	35.7	44.1	723	14.9	29.8	20.6	29.8
Tampa-St. Petersburg-Clearwater, FL MSA	294.3	27.8	42.6	25.5	608	15.7	28.3	19.0	30.7
Washington-Baltimore, DC-MD-VA-WV CMSA	996.7	19.1	29.9	47.5	744	18.6	30.3	19.2	26.2

[1] Includes units with no cash rent.

No. 960. Specified Renter-Occupied Housing Units—Gross Rent by the 25 Largest Cities: 2000

[In percent, except as indicated (146.1 represents 146,100). As of April 1. See headnote, Table 959 for coverage]

City	Total [1] (1,000)	Percent of units with gross rent of—					Median gross rent (dol.)	Gross rent as a percent of household income, 1999			
		$299 or less	$300 to $499	$500 to $749	$750 to $999	$1,000 or more		Less than 15 percent	15 to 24 percent	25 to 34 percent	35 percent or more
Austin, TX	146.1	3.2	9.0	41.0	28.9	16.1	724	14.4	28.3	19.4	33.5
Baltimore, MD	127.6	19.3	29.8	34.3	9.7	4.3	498	18.8	23.7	17.9	33.0
Boston, MA	162.1	15.6	8.8	19.2	24.0	30.5	803	17.2	24.2	20.0	32.1
Chicago, IL	596.1	10.1	18.8	39.6	17.4	12.1	616	19.3	27.4	16.9	30.8
Columbus, OH	153.3	8.1	23.5	46.5	14.9	5.3	586	18.3	30.3	18.0	29.0
Dallas, TX	256.1	5.4	19.2	45.3	18.4	10.0	623	18.8	30.6	19.2	26.8
Denver, CO	113.4	9.5	18.1	37.6	19.8	13.0	631	16.5	28.4	20.3	30.6
Detroit, MI	150.8	13.5	37.4	33.8	8.5	2.8	486	21.1	21.2	14.8	33.9
El Paso, TX	70.3	17.3	35.3	30.7	8.3	3.3	474	15.9	25.1	18.9	32.0
Houston, TX	388.6	5.1	27.9	42.0	14.9	7.8	575	19.9	29.5	17.7	27.0
Indianapolis, IN [2]	132.1	7.3	26.9	45.5	13.8	4.2	567	18.6	30.3	17.9	28.5
Jacksonville, FL	104.5	10.3	21.0	40.3	18.5	5.8	598	17.5	30.1	18.8	26.8
Los Angeles, CA	782.2	5.7	15.8	38.4	20.7	17.5	672	14.1	24.4	18.8	37.1
Memphis, TN	110.4	12.9	26.5	40.5	13.0	3.8	548	17.7	26.2	17.7	31.8
Milwaukee, WI	126.7	10.3	32.5	42.4	9.2	3.7	527	18.8	27.6	17.0	32.0
Nashville-Davidson, TN [2]	103.1	11.0	16.6	44.8	17.4	7.3	614	17.1	29.9	20.1	27.8
New York, NY	2,108.5	11.0	12.0	32.2	23.5	19.4	705	20.5	23.5	16.4	33.7
Philadelphia, PA	240.0	10.9	24.8	38.3	14.7	7.5	569	16.1	22.9	15.9	36.0
Phoenix, AZ	183.0	5.3	19.2	44.3	19.5	9.2	622	15.6	28.3	20.3	30.9
San Antonio, TX	169.7	10.7	28.1	37.9	13.3	6.0	549	17.5	29.7	18.3	28.0
San Diego, CA	227.2	4.1	11.0	31.4	23.6	25.9	763	12.8	26.6	20.0	34.4
San Francisco, CA	214.2	7.6	9.1	18.1	19.6	43.6	928	20.9	28.2	18.6	28.2
San Jose, CA	105.4	3.5	4.2	9.2	21.3	59.9	1,123	14.3	28.6	20.9	32.3
Seattle, WA	133.3	8.6	9.7	35.3	24.3	20.2	721	14.6	29.4	21.5	30.6
Washington, DC	146.9	12.8	17.6	34.5	16.8	15.4	618	20.0	26.9	17.8	28.2

[1] Includes units with no cash rent. [2] Represents the portion of a consolidated city that is not within one or more separately incorporated places.

Source of Tables 959 and 960: U.S. Census Bureau, "2000 Census of Population and Housing, Profiles of General Demographic Characteristics"; <http://www.census.gov/Press-Release/www/2002/demoprofiles.html>.

Construction and Housing   617

U.S. Census Bureau, Statistical Abstract of the United States: 2004-2005

No. 961. Mortgage Characteristics—Owner Occupied Units: 2003

[In thousands (72,254 represents 72,254,000). Preliminary. As of fall. Based on the American Housing Survey; see Appendix III]

Mortgage characteristic	Total owner-occupied units	Housing unit characteristics — New construction [1]	Housing unit characteristics — Mobile homes	Household characteristics — Black [2]	Household characteristics — Hispanic [3]	Household characteristics — Elderly [4]	Household characteristics — Moved in past year	Household characteristics — Below poverty level
ALL OWNERS								
Total	72,254	4,688	5,518	6,192	5,106	17,355	5,627	6,062
Mortgages currently on property:								
None, owned free and clear.	25,012	798	3,109	2,026	1,454	12,475	1,088	3,613
Regular and home equity mortgages . .	45,495	3,787	2,313	3,976	3,537	4,451	4,410	2,219
Regular mortgage only	42,282	3,694	2,218	3,796	3,445	3,602	4,314	2,074
Home equity lump sum mortage . . .	3,795	187	88	263	171	457	172	127
Home equity line-of-credit.	7,212	415	87	307	295	985	341	194
Not reproted	1,699	103	96	189	111	385	129	214
Number of regular and home equity mortgages: [5]								
1 mortgage.	33,449	2,949	2,072	3,076	2,865	3,309	3,514	1,609
2 mortgages	8,126	601	119	473	457	544	585	201
3 mortgages or more	853	50	4	58	40	85	53	43
Type of home equity mortgage:								
Regular and home equity lump sum [5] .	2,375	136	23	145	120	158	123	68
With home equity line of credit	449	22	-	26	16	50	23	15
No home equity line of credit	1,905	114	23	119	100	105	98	52
Regular no home equity lump sum [5] . .	39,908	3,558	2,195	3,651	3,325	3,445	4,191	2,007
With home equity line of credit	4,699	346	54	200	233	327	265	94
No home equity line of credit . . .	32,221	3,032	2,023	3,084	2,921	2,617	3,676	1,560
Home equity lump sum no regular [5] . .	1,420	51	65	117	51	300	49	60
With home equity line of credit	271	5	3	19	6	58	6	-
No home equity line of credit	1,126	42	61	97	45	242	39	55
No regular or home equity lump sum [5]	28,551	944	3,235	2,279	1,610	13,453	1,264	3,928
With home equity line of credit	1,793	42	30	63	41	549	47	85
No home equity line of credit	25,060	798	3,109	2,027	1,459	12,518	1,088	3,629
OWNERS WITH ONE OR MORE REGULAR OR LUMP SUM HOME EQUITY MORTGAGES, 2003								
Total [5]	43,703	3,745	2,283	3,914	3,496	3,902	4,363	2,134
Type of primary mortgage:								
FHA	5,329	490	103	924	751	283	615	298
VA.	1,985	227	53	272	142	155	231	76
RHS/RD [6].	394	28	7	47	47	48	58	41
Other types.	32,557	2,801	1,956	2,246	2,346	2,799	3,170	1,321
Mortgage origination:								
Placed new mortgage(s)	43,340	3,738	2,258	3,847	3,443	3,871	4,329	2,094
Primary obtained when property acquired	26,299	2,896	1,921	2,901	2,438	2,114	4,179	1,532
Obtained later	17,041	842	338	947	1,005	1,757	159	562
Assumed	278	7	22	49	41	27	27	32
Wrap-around.	8	-	-	2	6	-	3	-
Combination of the above	76	-	3	15	6	4	5	9
Payment plan of primary mortgage:								
Fixed payment, self amortizing	36,246	3,205	1,951	3,140	2,981	2,936	3,554	1,515
Adjustable rate mortgage	1,696	128	49	147	137	136	179	57
Adjustable term mortgage	114	3	3	15	2	30	11	12
Graduated payment mortgage	287	37	11	21	16	2	76	25
Balloon	408	35	59	23	21	37	62	16
Combination of the above	291	35	2	13	22	25	45	7
Payment plan of secondary mortgage:								
Units with two or more mortgages [5] . . .	4,235	317	68	323	272	255	384	153
Fixed payment, self amortizing	3,374	233	55	267	214	197	291	119
Adjustable rate mortgage	183	26	2	2	16	1	26	5
Adjustable term mortgage	129	13	11	6	21	11	7	-
Graduated payment mortgage.	18	-	-	-	-	-	3	3
Balloon.	104	6	1	15	4	18	3	-
Other.	5	-	-	-	-	-	-	-
Combination of the above	79	5	-	2	5	5	9	-
Reason primary refinanced:								
Units with a refinanced primary mortgage [7]	16,601	940	292	862	1,050	1,224	195	419
To get a lower interest rate.	14,924	906	214	732	915	958	184	347
To increase payment period	377	24	8	15	22	40	5	12
To reduce payment period	1,931	97	20	73	124	100	7	55
To renew or extend a loan that has fallen due	145	6	7	29	10	19	-	7
To receive cash	1,925	35	34	100	161	228	13	71
Other reason	1,372	45	61	91	122	145	17	38
Cash received in primary mortgage refinance:								
Units receiving refinance cash	1,915	35	34	100	161	228	13	71
Median amount received (dol.)	25,041	-	-	16,383	22,954	20,953	-	18,426

- Represents or rounds to zero. [1] Constructed in the past 4 years. [2] For persons who selected this race group only. See footnote 3 Table 950. [3] Persons of Hispanic origin may be of any race. [4] 65 years old and over. [5] Includes don't know and not reported. [6] Rural Housing Service/Rural Development Mortgage, formerly Farmers Home Adminsitration. [7] Persons reporting more than one reason are counted once in the total.

Source: U.S. Census Bureau, *Current Housing Reports*, Series H150/03, *American Housing Survey for the United States*. See Internet site <http://www.census.gov/hhes/www/housing/ahs/nationaldata.html>.

No. 962. Occupied Housing Units—Neighborhood Indicators by Selected Characteristics of the Householder: 2003

[In thousands (105,867 represents 105,867,000). Preliminary. As of fall. Based on the American Housing Survey; see Appendix III]

Characteristic	Total occupied units	Tenure		Black [1]		Hispanic origin [2]		Elderly [3]		Households below poverty level	
		Owner	Renter	Owner	Renter	Owner	Renter	Owner	Renter	Owner	Renter
Total units	**105,867**	**72,254**	**33,614**	**6,192**	**6,813**	**5,106**	**5,933**	**17,355**	**4,276**	**6,062**	**7,908**
Street noise or traffic present . . .	27,878	16,461	11,416	1,747	2,615	1,196	1,889	4,081	1,362	1,583	2,927
Condition not bothersome . . .	16,544	9,720	6,824	1,034	1,601	632	1,064	2,771	968	948	1,740
Condition bothersome	11,236	6,712	4,524	711	993	564	815	1,303	384	629	1,161
So bothersome they want to move	4,142	2,154	1,988	277	540	205	396	289	121	221	557
Neighborhood crime present . . .	15,489	8,404	7,084	1,228	2,063	710	1,378	1,634	618	880	1,906
Condition not bothersome . . .	6,394	3,614	2,780	460	792	272	447	876	311	386	723
Condition bothersome	9,021	4,771	4,250	765	1,252	438	919	756	295	493	1,165
So bothersome they want to move	3,721	1,503	2,218	305	749	182	511	192	95	210	723
Odors present	5,639	3,208	2,431	393	663	318	545	641	207	387	744
Condition not bothersome . . .	2,059	1,235	824	134	191	127	163	275	88	145	245
Condition bothersome	3,556	1,961	1,595	254	471	185	378	365	111	241	498
So bothersome they want to move	1,407	558	849	99	265	62	241	65	29	93	290
Other problems:											
Noise	2,486	1,391	1,095	150	228	145	200	296	93	85	281
Litter or housing deterioration .	1,903	1,185	718	213	193	100	147	265	51	91	214
Poor city or county services . .	780	494	286	120	102	51	66	101	23	52	82
People	4,015	2,363	1,652	295	390	202	324	476	133	235	467
With public transportation	57,900	34,188	23,712	3,839	5,462	3,265	4,733	8,077	3,087	2,567	5,682
Household uses it at least weekly	11,346	4,007	7,339	892	2,235	625	2,030	750	951	425	2,330
Household uses it less than weekly	8,748	5,164	3,584	677	894	458	658	1,068	538	372	869
Household does not use	36,640	24,431	12,210	2,207	2,182	2,150	1,985	6,104	1,536	1,703	2,348
Not reported	1,166	587	579	63	151	32	60	155	62	66	135
No public transportation	44,232	35,579	8,653	2,173	1,128	1,673	1,077	8,713	1,078	3,239	1,982
Not reported	3,736	2,487	1,249	181	223	168	123	565	111	256	244
Police protection:											
Satisfactory	93,971	64,484	29,487	5,263	5,721	4,474	5,101	15,647	3,924	4,991	6,673
Unsatisfacory	7,731	5,240	2,491	659	706	475	596	1,096	176	740	762
Not reported	4,165	2,530	1,635	271	386	158	236	611	176	331	473
Secured communities [4]:											
Community access secured withwalls or fences	6,993	3,039	3,954	232	890	322	1,007	926	505	216	806
Community access not secured.	97,861	68,560	29,301	5,890	5,822	4,745	4,884	16,242	3,715	5,759	6,998
Secured multiunits [4]:											
Multiunit access secured	5,288	910	4,377	88	989	82	744	361	1,007	72	1,061
Multiunit access not secured. .	19,261	2,427	16,834	231	3,599	277	3,194	674	1,944	225	4,019
Not reported	450	66	384	10	112	7	57	15	51	6	92
Senior citizen communities:											
Households with persons 55 years old and over	40,358	32,523	7,836	2,658	1,405	1,802	1,059	17,355	4,276	3,883	2,217
Community age restricted [5].	2,051	1,024	1,026	27	150	38	89	786	884	158	366
Community quality:											
Some or all activities present .	38,249	24,878	13,371	2,073	2,748	1,614	2,139	6,364	2,172	1,832	2,966
Community center or clubhouse	23,347	14,215	9,132	1,140	1,964	882	1,333	4,151	1,653	1,057	1,889
Golf in the community	10,992	8,452	2,540	375	288	377	299	2,305	330	563	473
Trails in the community . . .	18,329	13,010	5,319	871	801	791	764	2,936	708	846	904
Shuttle bus	10,006	6,197	3,809	483	567	398	651	2,085	989	521	967
Daycare	15,562	10,430	5,132	1,206	1,321	706	991	2,317	628	834	1,317
Private or restricted beach, park or shoreline	6,608	4,769	1,840	311	353	220	297	1,069	235	330	398
Trash, litter or junk on street: [6]											
None	93,860	65,784	28,076	5,238	5,240	4,404	4,773	16,003	3,770	5,237	6,165
Minor accumulation.	6,677	3,176	3,501	517	919	378	729	645	292	447	1,071
Major accumulation.	2,628	1,367	1,261	214	401	176	306	293	85	157	455
Not reported	2,702	1,926	776	223	254	148	125	413	130	222	216

[1] For persons who selected this race group only. See footnote 3 Table 950. [2] Persons of Hispanic origin may be of any race. [3] Householders 65 years old and over. [4] Public access is restricted (walls, gates, private security). Includes high rise apartments, retirement comminitites, resorts, etc. [5] At least one family member must be aged 55 years old or older. [6] Or on any properties within 300 feet. $del

Source: U.S. Census Bureau, Current Housing Reports, Series H150/03, American Housing Survey for the United States. See Internet site <http://www.census.gov/hhes/www/housing/ahs/nationaldata.html>

Construction and Housing   **619**

No. 963. Heating Equipment and Fuels for Occupied Units: 1995 to 2003

[(97,692 represents 97,692,000) 2003 preliminary. As of fall. Based on American Housing Survey. See Appendix III]

Type of equipment or fuel	Number (1,000)					Percent distribution	
	1995	1997	1999	2001	2003	1995	2003 [1]
Occupied units, total.	**97,692**	**99,487**	**102,803**	**106,261**	**105,867**	**100.0**	**100.0**
Heating equipment:							
Warm air furnace.	53,165	58,603	62,018	65,262	65,429	54.4	61.8
Heat pumps	9,406	11,101	10,992	11,080	11,355	9.6	10.7
Steam or hot water	13,669	12,929	13,153	13,441	13,252	14.0	12.5
Floor, wall, or pipeless furnace. . .	4,963	5,588	5,310	5,343	5,299	5.1	5.0
Built-in electric units.	7,035	4,531	4,939	5,063	4,772	7.2	4.5
Room heaters with flue.	1,620	1,584	1,624	1,542	1,419	1.7	1.3
Room heaters without flue.	1,642	1,754	1,790	1,558	1,496	1.7	1.4
Fireplaces, stoves, portable heaters or other.	5,150	2,780	2,434	2,571	2,404	5.3	2.3
None.	1,043	617	544	401	441	1.1	0.4
House main heating fuel:							
Utility gas.	49,203	51,052	52,366	54,689	54,907	50.4	51.9
Fuel oil, kerosene, etc.	12,029	10,855	10,750	10,473	10,142	12.3	9.6
Electricity	26,771	29,202	31,142	32,590	32,391	27.4	30.6
Bottled, tank, or LP gas	4,251	5,398	5,905	6,079	6,111	4.4	5.8
Coal or coke.	210	183	168	128	127	0.2	0.1
Wood and other fuel	4,186	2,177	1,927	1,902	1,746	4.3	1.6
None.	1,043	620	544	401	443	1.1	0.4
Cooking fuel:							
Electricity.	57,621	58,818	61,315	63,685	62,882	59.0	59.4
Gas [2]	39,218	40,083	41,051	42,161	42,612	40.1	40.3
Other fuel	566	113	69	66	61	0.6	(Z)
None.	287	474	367	349	313	0.3	0.3

Z Less than .05 percent. [1] Based on 2000 census controls. [2] Includes utility, bottled, tank, and LP gas.

Source: U.S. Census Bureau, Current Housing Reports, Series H150/95RV, H150/97, H150/99, H150/01, and H150/03 *American Housing Survey for the United States.* See Internet site <http://www.census.gov/hhes/www/housing/ahs/nationaldata.html>

No. 964. Occupied Housing Units—Housing Indicators by Selected Characteristics of the Householder: 2003

[In thousands of units (105,867 represents 105,867,000). Preliminary. As of fall. Based on the American Housing Survey; see Appendix III]

Characteristic	Total occupied units	Tenure		Black [1]		Hispanic origin [2]		Elderly [3]		Households below poverty level	
		Owner	Renter	Owner	Renter	Owner	Renter	Owner	Renter	Owner	Renter
Total units	**105,867**	**72,254**	**33,614**	**6,192**	**6,813**	**5,106**	**5,933**	**17,355**	**4,276**	**6,062**	**7,908**
Amenities:											
Porch, deck, balcony or patio.	89,581	66,029	23,552	5,318	4,539	4,580	3,863	15,627	2,645	5,286	5,123
Usable fireplace.	35,449	31,585	3,864	1,852	537	1,647	547	6,445	294	1,580	520
Separate dining room	50,708	41,326	9,382	3,775	2,030	2,567	1,529	9,284	900	2,959	1,869
With 2 or more living rooms or recreation rooms	30,236	28,137	2,099	1,988	341	1,351	194	5,864	209	1,327	328
Garage or carport with home .	65,274	54,684	10,590	3,527	1,292	3,797	1,870	13,342	1,263	3,721	1,729
Cars and trucks available:											
No cars, trucks, or vans	9,078	2,413	6,665	491	2,083	176	1,302	1,534	1,879	710	2,995
Other households without cars.	12,785	9,021	3,763	526	445	783	860	1,456	233	831	760
1 car with or without trucks or van	50,929	33,986	16,943	2,952	3,444	2,295	2,693	10,245	1,895	3,273	3,439
2 cars	25,178	19,887	5,290	1,702	705	1,290	904	3,458	227	997	606
3 or more cars	7,898	6,946	952	522	136	562	174	661	42	251	109
Selected deficiencies:											
Signs of rats in last 3 months.	830	410	419	61	126	73	154	86	38	77	148
Holes in floors	976	420	556	67	162	47	138	81	35	67	213
Open cracks or holes	5,228	2,664	2,564	371	740	215	464	443	165	363	764
Broken plaster or peeling paint (interior of unit).	2,339	1,102	1,236	213	352	90	272	216	78	174	423
No electrical wiring.	73	44	29	2	-	-	11	8	10	16	12
Exposed wiring	640	388	252	27	39	49	42	86	17	50	82
Rooms without electric outlet .	1,487	838	649	117	147	61	123	170	45	88	215
Water leakage [4].	8,480	4,824	3,656	494	895	350	614	714	253	392	922

- Represents or rounds to zero. [1] For persons who selected this race group only. See footnote 3 Table 950. [2] Persons of Hispanic origin may be of any race. [3] Householders 65 years old and over. [4] During the 12 months prior to the survey.

Source: U.S. Census Bureau, Current Housing Reports, Series H150/03, *American Housing Survey for the United States.* See Internet site <http://www.census.gov/hhes/www/housing/ahs/nationaldata.html>

No. 965. Appliances and Office Equipment Used by Households by Region and Household Income: 2001

[In millions (107.0 represents 107,000,000). Represents appliances possessed and generally used by the household. Based on Residential Energy Consumption Survey; see source. For composition of regions, see map, inside front cover]

Type of appliance	House-holds using appli-ance	Region				Household income in 2001			
		North-east	Midwest	South	West	Under $15,000	$15,000 -$29,999	$30,000 -$49,999	$50,000 and over
Total households.........	107.0	20.3	24.5	38.9	23.3	18.7	22.9	27.1	38.3
Oven [1].................	101.7	19.6	23.8	36.2	22.1	18.0	22.0	26.1	35.6
Electric...............	63.0	9.9	14.0	26.0	13.1	10.1	12.9	16.2	23.8
Natural gas............	34.3	8.6	8.7	8.8	8.2	7.1	7.8	8.6	10.9
Self cleaning oven	48.2	10.2	12.3	16.1	9.6	4.1	8.5	12.4	23.2
Range [1]	105.7	20.1	24.1	38.6	22.9	18.5	22.5	26.9	37.7
Electric.................	64.2	10.0	13.9	27.2	13.2	10.4	13.2	16.5	24.2
Natural gas.............	36.7	8.9	9.1	9.8	8.9	7.3	8.0	9.1	12.4
Refrigerator...............	106.8	20.2	24.5	38.9	23.2	18.6	22.8	27.1	38.3
Frost free	96.9	18.3	21.7	36.3	20.7	15.5	19.9	25.0	36.5
Freezer	34.2	4.9	9.6	13.6	6.2	4.4	6.9	9.2	13.7
1	30.8	4.5	8.6	12.2	5.6	3.9	6.1	8.4	12.4
2 or more	3.4	0.4	1.0	1.4	0.6	0.4	0.9	0.8	1.3
Most used defrost method:									
Frost free	12.2	1.8	2.8	5.7	1.8	1.3	2.0	3.2	5.7
Manual	22.0	3.1	6.7	7.9	4.4	3.0	4.9	6.0	8.1
Dishwasher...............	56.7	9.2	12.1	22.1	13.2	3.3	9.1	14.9	29.3
Electric coffee maker	65.5	12.4	16.1	23.0	14.0	8.7	12.8	16.7	27.3
Electric toaster oven	36.1	8.5	5.5	14.7	7.4	5.1	7.7	8.9	14.3
Microwave oven	92.1	15.2	22.3	34.7	19.9	14.0	19.4	23.8	35.0
Air conditioning	80.8	14.2	20.2	36.9	9.6	11.9	16.7	21.0	31.2
Central system.............	57.5	5.7	14.3	30.4	7.1	6.2	10.7	15.2	25.3
Room	23.3	8.5	5.8	6.4	2.5	5.7	6.0	5.8	5.9
Color TV.................	105.8	20.0	24.4	38.4	22.9	18.1	22.7	26.9	38.0
One	29.3	5.8	6.4	9.8	7.3	8.5	8.6	6.5	5.7
Two	38.4	8.1	8.2	13.7	8.4	6.4	8.5	10.7	12.8
Three	23.3	3.8	5.9	9.2	4.3	2.5	3.8	6.1	10.9
Four....................	10.2	1.6	2.7	3.9	2.0	0.6	1.4	2.6	5.7
Five or more	4.5	0.7	1.1	1.8	0.9	(S)	0.4	1.1	2.9
Large screen TV [2]	36.6	7.1	8.1	13.3	8.0	4.7	6.7	9.8	15.3
One	27.3	5.3	5.9	9.7	6.5	3.7	5.1	7.0	11.4
Two	7.9	1.4	1.8	3.3	1.4	0.9	1.5	2.2	3.2
Three or more	1.4	(S)	(S)	0.4	(S)	(S)	(S)	0.5	0.7
Cable/Satellite dish-antenna.....	82.2	16.3	19.1	30.2	16.6	12.1	16.2	20.9	33.0
VCR and DVD players	96.1	18.0	22.5	34.6	21.0	13.9	19.8	25.3	37.0
Stereo equipment...........	80.3	15.1	18.2	28.5	18.5	10.2	15.4	20.9	33.8
Clothes washer	84.1	14.7	19.8	32.7	16.9	10.7	16.4	22.1	34.9
Clothes dryer [1]	78.8	13.3	19.2	30.3	16.0	8.4	15.0	21.3	34.1
Electric.................	61.1	9.2	13.4	26.6	11.9	6.9	12.2	16.8	25.1
Natural gas.............	16.9	4.0	5.4	3.4	4.1	1.4	2.6	4.2	8.7
Water heater [1].............	107.0	20.3	24.5	38.9	23.3	18.7	22.9	27.1	38.3
Electric.................	40.8	4.7	6.3	22.4	7.3	8.3	9.5	10.6	12.4
Natural gas.............	58.0	10.8	16.9	15.4	14.9	9.3	11.7	14.1	23.0
Personal computers	60.0	10.9	14.1	20.7	14.3	3.7	8.7	16.0	31.6
Access to Internet	50.7	9.7	11.8	16.9	12.2	2.8	6.6	13.1	28.3
Cell/mobile telephone	56.8	10.3	12.8	21.4	12.3	4.4	8.6	14.7	29.1

S Figure does not meet publication standards.   [1] Includes other types, not shown separately.   [2] Determined by respondent.

Source: U.S. Energy Information Administration, "Residential Energy Consumption Survey—Detailed Tables"; <http://www.eia .doe.gov/emeu/recs/recs2001/detailtables.html> (accessed 04 May 2004).

No. 966. Net Stock of Residential Fixed Assets: 1992 to 2002

[In billions of dollars (6,758.9 represents $6,758,900,000,000). End of year estimates]

Item	1992	1995	1996	1997	1998	1999	2000	2001	2002
Total residential fixed assets ..	6,758.9	8,029.4	8,469.4	8,930.8	9,511.3	10,211.8	10,911.9	11,739.8	12,229.0
By type of owner and legal form of organization:									
Private..................	6,599.9	7,841.2	8,272.9	8,734.0	9,304.4	9,991.8	10,680.2	11,493.0	11,988.1
Corporate	69.7	76.7	80.1	84.9	90.3	94.9	100.0	105.7	109.5
Noncorporate	6,530.3	7,764.5	8,192.8	8,649.1	9,214.1	9,896.9	10,580.2	11,387.4	11,878.7
Government	159.0	188.2	196.5	196.8	206.9	219.9	231.7	246.7	240.9
Federal	52.8	61.6	63.7	65.9	68.7	72.2	75.4	79.5	81.8
State and local	106.2	126.6	132.7	130.9	138.2	147.7	156.4	167.2	159.1
By tenure group: [1]									
Owner occupied	4,928.6	5,988.0	6,344.3	6,712.5	7,174.7	7,752.3	8,327.3	9,012.9	9,437.4
Farm	50.4	51.3	52.2	57.9	62.0	67.0	72.2	77.3	79.6
Nonfarm	4,878.2	5,936.7	6,292.2	6,654.6	7,112.7	7,685.3	8,255.1	8,935.6	9,357.8
Tenant-occupied	1,804.1	2,012.6	2,095.5	2,187.9	2,304.8	2,425.7	2,548.8	2,688.5	2,752.2

[1] Excludes stocks of other nonfarm residential assets, which consists primarily of dormitories, and of fraternity and sorority houses.

Source: U.S. Bureau of Economic Analysis, Survey of Current Business, May 2004 issue, and <http://www.bea.gov/bea /dn/FA2004/index.asp> (accessed 03 June 2004)

Construction and Housing   621

No. 967. Expenditures by Residential Property Owners for Improvements and Maintenance and Repairs by Type of Property and Activity: 1990 to 2003

[In millions of dollars (115,432 represents $115,432,000,000) Based on personal interviews and mail surveys' see source for details]

Year and type of expenditure	Total	1-unit properties with owner occupant	Other properties	Additions and alterations					Maintenance and repairs
				Total	To structures		To property outside of structures	Major replacements	
					Additions	Alterations			
1990	115,432	63,441	51,991	39,929	9,160	23,510	7,261	19,700	55,800
1993	121,899	77,626	44,273	53,512	16,381	27,657	9,472	22,604	45,785
1994	130,625	85,903	44,722	56,835	12,906	30,395	13,534	26,606	47,185
1995	124,971	79,003	45,968	51,011	11,197	29,288	10,526	26,928	47,032
1996	131,362	84,462	46,900	64,513	17,388	32,889	14,235	26,738	40,108
1997	133,577	90,677	42,900	65,222	14,575	37,126	13,523	27,210	41,145
1998	133,693	96,159	37,534	62,971	11,897	38,787	12,287	28,741	41,980
1999	142,900	95,778	47,122	72,056	16,164	42,058	13,833	28,493	42,352
2000	152,975	100,161	52,814	77,979	18,189	40,384	19,407	32,760	42,236
2001	157,765	105,997	51,768	77,560	14,133	47,208	16,218	32,714	47,491
2002, total [1]	173,324	116,192	57,132	88,708	20,624	49,566	18,518	37,238	47,379
Heating and air conditioning [2]	11,232	7,163	4,069	2,369	(NA)	2,369	(NA)	6,305	2,558
Plumbing	14,062	5,857	8,205	3,982	(NA)	2,572	1,411	4,470	5,610
Roofing	12,236	7,715	4,521	(NA)	(NA)	(NA)	(NA)	8,936	3,300
Painting	14,685	6,802	7,884	(NA)	(NA)	(NA)	(NA)	(NA)	14,685
2003, total [1]	176,899	115,876	61,023	93,458	20,994	55,028	17,435	39,347	44,094
Heating and air conditioning [2]	13,026	7,344	5,682	2,429	(NA)	2,429	(NA)	8,220	2,377
Plumbing	10,332	4,597	5,811	1,797	(NA)	1,326	471	4,480	4,055
Roofing	12,259	6,976	5,283	(NA)	(NA)	(NA)	(NA)	7,525	4,734
Painting	14,965	6,513	8,452	(NA)	(NA)	(NA)	(NA)	(NA)	14,965

NA Not available. [1] Includes types of expenditures not separately specified. [2] Central air-conditioning.
Source: U.S. Census Bureau, "Resiential Improvement and Repair Statistics", Internet site <http://www.census.gov/const/www/c50index.html>.

No. 968. Home Remodeling—Work Done and Amount Spent: 2003

[In thousands, except percent (3,785 representrs 3,785,000). As of fall 2003. For work done in the prior 12 months. Based on household survey and subject to sampling error; see source]

Remodeling project	Households with work done [1]		Work done by—		Amount spent (dol.)		
	Number	Percent of house- holds	House- hold member	Outside contractor	Under $1,000	$1,000 to $2,999	Over $3,000
Conversion of garage/attic/basement into living space	3,785	1.8	2,302	836	793	931	1,322
Remodel bathroom	13,893	6.6	9,005	3,120	6,206	3,132	1,969
Remodel kitchen	9,387	4.5	5,115	2,816	2,866	1,427	3,050
Remodel bedroom	8,656	4.1	6,585	1,105	5,188	1,296	756
Remodel/convert room to home office	2,115	1.0	1,708	[2]117	1,140	[2]276	[2]178
Remodel other rooms	8,143	3.9	5,663	1,325	3,587	1,496	1,344
Add bathroom	1,606	0.8	836	443	[2]433	[2]329	523
Add/extend garage	1,095	0.5	559	[2]427	[2]155	[2]179	542
Add other rooms—exterior addition	1,814	0.9	743	735	[2]181	[2]202	1,201
Add deck/porch/patio	5,568	2.7	3,075	1,661	1,308	2,022	1,248
Roofing	10,408	5.0	2,894	5,984	2,462	2,257	3,750
Siding - vinyl/metal	3,533	1.7	1,099	1,680	660	687	1,348
Aluminum windows	1,384	0.7	[2]380	728	[2]301	390	[2]267
Clad-wood/Wood windows	1,007	0.5	374	344	[2]208	[2]154	327
Vinyl windows	4,202	2.0	1,530	2,044	969	1,359	1,114
Ceramic tile floors	7,115	3.4	3,671	2,501	3,734	1,156	837
Hardwood floors	4,539	2.2	2,042	1,619	1,322	1,233	962
Laminate flooring	3,697	1.8	2,025	1,311	1,790	1,100	[2]253
Vinyl flooring	4,665	2.2	2,385	1,716	2,967	668	[2]102
Carpeting	9,999	4.8	2,574	6,143	4,114	3,188	1,179
Kitchen cabinets	4,911	2.3	2,126	1,622	1,307	888	1,240
Kitchen counter tops	5,130	2.5	1,871	2,016	1,765	971	1,038
Skylights	788	0.4	[2]232	421	415	[2]117	[2]115
Exterior doors	6,083	2.9	3,049	2,239	3,522	923	355
Interior doors	3,694	1.8	2,043	967	2,104	419	[2]222
Garage doors	4,412	2.1	1,036	2,637	2,322	957	[2]237
Concrete or masonry work	4,959	2.4	2,125	2,205	2,136	960	1,052
Swimming pool—in ground	463	0.2	[2]39	[2]352	[2]54	[2]45	[2]310
Wall paneling	1,340	0.6	822	[2]186	696	[2]148	[2]15
Ceramic wall tile	2,354	1.1	1,296	736	1,420	367	[2]98

[1] Includes no response and amount unknown. [2] Figure does not meet standards of reliability or precision.
Source: Mediamark Research Inc., New York, NY, Top-Line Reports, (copyright) Internet site <http://www.mediamark.com/>.

U.S. Census Bureau, Statistical Abstract of the United States: 2004-2005

No. 969. Commercial Office Space—Overview for Selected Market Areas: 2003

[As of mid-October (4,180,727 represents 4,180,727,000). For the 76 market areas with the highest vacancy rates in 2003. Data based on responses from individuals knowledgeable in the local markets]

Market area	Inventory (1,000 sq. ft.)	Vacant space (1,000 sq. ft.)	Vacancy rate (percent)	Construction (1,000 sq. ft.)	Net absorption [1] (1,000 sq. ft.)
United States, all market areas [2] ...	4,180,727	674,367	16.13	56,456	22,791
Akron	4,102	707	17.24	46	-104
Allentown	5,882	1,969	33.48	-	-1,008
Atlanta	149,902	32,906	21.95	881	-1,018
Austin	33,548	6,467	19.28	525	221
Baltimore	51,243	8,732	17.04	881	1,538
Batavia	482	80	16.66	22	2
Binghamton	4,788	676	14.11	18	-
Boston	140,535	29,505	20.99	2,472	-1,162
Bridgeport/Stratford	6,472	1,208	18.67	-	-42
Charleston	5,405	773	14.31	409	120
Charlotte	33,575	4,746	14.14	781	655
Chicago	237,109	44,678	18.84	2,572	-1,230
Cincinnati	30,158	6,305	20.91	189	-560
Cleveland	37,296	6,787	18.20	-	-1,007
Columbia	5,400	749	13.87	360	121
Columbus	39,459	6,014	15.24	284	138
Corpus Christi	2,702	401	14.86	30	50
Dallas	208,546	45,697	21.91	2,047	-3,916
Dayton	13,730	1,972	14.36	-	98
Denver	113,098	18,966	16.77	-	256
Detroit	92,878	13,357	14.38	285	-
El Paso	8,090	1,999	24.71	258	-140
Fort Worth	20,237	3,836	18.95	-	-1,268
Grand Rapids	11,893	1,694	14.25	244	26
Greensboro, High-Point, Winston-Salem	16,254	3,043	18.72	-	70
Greenville	6,985	1,765	25.26	-	-1,045
Hartford	22,595	4,733	20.95	-	-233
Indianapolis	26,745	4,988	18.65	191	367
Jacksonville	19,983	3,521	17.62	248	2,167
Kansas City	43,571	7,945	18.23	1,270	818
Lake Charles	646	161	24.89	-	-26
Lansing	9,127	1,382	15.15	69	-124.975
Las Vegas	15,810	2,261	14.30	826	1,308
Los Angeles-Central	32,192	6,403	19.89	-	-198
Los Angeles-San Fernando Valley	33,772	4,728	14.00	175	486
Los Angeles-South Bay	28,114	5,754	20.47	80	-788
Los Angeles-West	42,643	7,493	17.57	-	8
Louisville	17,426	3,515	20.17	70	-43
Madison	9,807	1,463	14.92	286	317
Marin County	6,303	893	14.17	-	160
Milwaukee	29,275	4,292	14.66	455	527
Minneapolis/St. Paul	61,714	10,151	16.45	160	480
Mobile	3,235	749	23.16	850	70
Nashua	2,296	629	27.41	14	-111
Nashville	26,082	4,187	16.05	365	69
New Haven	14,760	2,750	18.63	-	-134
New Jersey Central	81,325	14,279	17.56	400	-3,746
New Jersey Northern	94,364	17,127	18.15	2,645	-1,821
Oakland	29,254	4,740	16.20	-	-318
Oklahoma City	15,275	3,730	24.42	-	-1,475
Omaha	11,806	1,945	16.48	1,160	135
Orange County	86,541	13,889	16.05	616	1,545
Orlando	22,933	3,238	14.12	455	489
Peoria	2,053	460	22.39	-	-
Philadelphia	112,257	23,133	20.61	746	-2,318
Phoenix	30,701	6,463	21.05	347	48
Pittsburgh	70,392	11,314	16.07	554	151
Raleigh	31,373	5,489	17.49	594	-1,467
Richmond	23,719	4,402	18.56	1,095	73
Salt Lake City	20,234	3,988	19.71	-	91
San Antonio	18,447	3,123	16.93	76	-99
San Francisco	83,279	14,730	17.69	1,077	-
San Jose	18,153	2,611	14.38	-	-331
Savannah	1,550	251	16.18	25	-33
Seattle	104,662	14,507	13.86	362	1,274
Shreveport	3,513	524	14.92	-	-
South Bend	3,020	473	15.66	-	72
St. Louis	42,458	9,054	21.32	218	2,424
Tacoma	3,999	934	23.34	50	-414
Tampa	42,612	7,354	17.26	432	-412
Toledo	9,771	1,557	15.93	196	312
Tulsa	15,656	2,699	17.24	-	-548
Washington DC/Suburban MD	59,600	8,288	13.91	1,430	746
West Palm Beach	24,984	3,524	14.11	339	303
Wichita	7,909	1,706	21.57	-	437
Wilmington	12,604	1,978	15.69	-	421

- Represents zero. [1] Net change in occupied stock. [2] Includes other market areas, not shown separately.

Source: Society of Industrial and Office REALTORS, Washington DC, *2002 Comparative Statistics of Industrial and Office Real Estate Markets* (copyright).

Construction and Housing 623

No. 970. Commercial Buildings—Summary: 1999

[4,675 represents 4,675,000. Excludes buildings 1,000 square feet or smaller. Building type based on predominant activity in which the occupants were engaged. Based on a sample survey of building representatives conducted in 1999, therefore subject to sampling variability]

Characteristic	All build-ings (1,000)	Floor-space (mil. sq.ft.)	Mean sq. ft. per build-ing (1,000)	Characteristic	All build-ings (1,000)	Floor-space (mil. sq.ft.)	Mean sq. ft. per build-ing (1,000)
All buildings	**4,657**	**67,338**	**14.5**	1980 to 1989.	846	13,931	16.5
Building floorspace (sq. ft.):				1990 to 1999.	690	11,094	16.1
1,001 to 5,000.	2,348	6,774	2.9	Workers (main shift):			
5,001 to 10,000.	1,110	8,238	7.4	Fewer than 5.	2,376	14,321	6.0
10,001 to 25,000	708	11,153	15.7	5 to 9.	807	6,325	7.8
25,001 to 50,000	257	9,311	36.2	10 to 19	683	8,028	11.8
50,001 to 100,000	145	10,112	69.9	20 to 49	487	10,814	22.2
100,001 to 200,000.	59	8,271	139.4	50 to 99	174	8,898	51.1
200,001 to 500,000.	23	6,851	296.3	100 to 249	90	8,356	92.4
Over 500,000	7	6,628	929.0	250 or more	39	10,595	270.0
Principal activity within building:				Energy sources: [1]			
Education	327	8,651	26.4	Electricity	4,395	65,716	15.0
Food sales	174	994	5.7	Natural gas	2,670	45,525	17.1
Food service	349	1,851	5.3	Fuel oil.	434	13,285	30.6
Health care	127	2,918	22.9	District heat.	117	5,891	50.2
Inpatient	11	1,865	168.2	District chilled water	50	2,750	55.4
Outpatient	116	1,053	9.1	Propane	451	6,290	14.0
Lodging	153	4,521	29.5	Wood.	79	570	7.2
Mercantile.	667	10,398	15.6	Heating equipment: [1]			
Retail (other than mall). . . .	534	4,766	8.9	Heat pumps	492	8,923	18.1
Enclosed mall and strip				Furnaces	1,460	14,449	9.9
cent	133	5,631	42.2	Individual space heaters	894	17,349	19.4
Office.	739	12,044	16.3	District heat.	96	5,534	57.7
Public assembly	305	4,393	14.4	Boilers	581	19,522	33.6
Public order and safety	72	1,168	16.2	Packaged heating units	1,347	25,743	19.1
Religious worship.	307	3,405	11.1	Other.	185	4,073	22.1
Service.	478	3,388	7.1	Cooling equipment: [1]			
Warehouse and storage	603	10,477	17.4	Residential-type central A/C . . .	676	8,329	12.3
Other.	102	1,222	12.0	Heat pumps	485	9,147	18.8
Vacant.	253	1,908	7.6	Individual A/C	799	14,276	17.9
Year constructed:				District chilled water	50	2,750	55.4
1919 or before.	419	4,034	9.6	Central chillers.	130	12,909	99.7
1920 to 1945.	499	6,445	12.9	Packaged A/C units	1,953	36,527	18.7
1946 to 1959.	763	9,127	12.0	Swamp coolers	136	2,219	16.3
1960 to 1969.	665	10,866	16.3	Other.	49	1,312	26.7
1970 to 1979.	774	11,840	15.3				

[1] More than one type may apply.

Source: U.S. Energy Information Administration, "1999 Commercial Buildings Energy Consumption Buildings (CBECS) Detailed Tables"; <http://www.eia.doe.gov/emeu/cbecs/detailedtables1999.html> (released August 2002).

No. 971. Office Building Markets—Summary: 2003

[As of end-of-year. In thousands of square feet, except as indicated. (159,907 represents 159,907,000). For top 27 areas in market size. Excludes government owned, and occupied, owner-occupied, and medical office buildings. CBD means central business district]

Market area	Total mar-ket size	Total mar-ket vacancy rate (per-cent)	CBD mar-ket size	Suburban market size	CBD mar-ket con-struction	Suburban market con-struction	CBD rental rate [1] (dol)
Atlanta	159,907	21.74	50,558	109,349	1,424	309	21.50
Boston	142,295	20.27	55,366	86,929	1,582	605	34.01
Charlotte	38,735	15.20	14,293	24,443	(NA)	645	19.19
Chicago	206,328	21.79	127,789	78,539	3,544	(NA)	28.22
Dallas.	203,970	25.80	42,880	161,090	(NA)	863	16.89
Denver.	84,366	22.65	23,349	61,017	(NA)	658	17.50
Detroit	76,390	20.66	15,991	60,399	(NA)	783	(NA)
Houston	260,337	17.14	43,410	216,927	(NA)	380	19.73
Kansas City.	64,068	20.64	12,009	52,059	(NA)	654	15.61
Los Angeles.	391,596	13.65	63,404	328,192	(NA)	1,292	22.93
Miami	59,177	13.27	14,334	44,843	423	639	24.05
Minneapolis	54,333	20.95	26,111	28,221	(NA)	77	21.03
New Jersey Central.	77,323	26.44	(X)	77,323	(NA)	646	(NA)
New Jersey North	113,301	20.90	14,820	98,481	30	139	25.32
New York City (Manhattan). . . .	480,955	12.72	480,955	(X)	(NA)	(NA)	40.91
Orlando	53,633	14.29	8,861	44,771	(NA)	403	21.75
Palm Beach.	33,417	13.85	3,356	30,061	(NA)	228	24.56
Philadelphia.	43,661	15.46	43,661	(X)	(NA)	(NA)	22.60
Pleasanton	30,782	16.40	(X)	30,782	(NA)	(NA)	(NA)
Raliegh/Durham	36,094	20.32	4,774	31,320	783	927	16.23
Sacramento	56,660	16.11	5,366	51,294	(NA)	1,213	30.60
San Diego.	56,951	11.71	9,128	47,823	410	987	25.80
San Francisco	89,503	17.56	53,261	36,242	(NA)	133	(NA)
Seattle	35,479	15.78	19,208	16,271	(NA)	(NA)	25.99
St. Louis	40,647	21.02	10,144	30,503	(NA)	(NA)	(NA)
Tampa	63,141	14.42	11,876	51,265	(NA)	1,181	18.42
Washington, D.C	114,031	7.39	114,031	(X)	6,321	(NA)	39

NA Not available.   X Not applicable.   [1] Per square foot. Direct asking rental rate (not including sublease).

Source: ONCOR International, Houston, TX, Year-End 2002 Market Data Book (copyright).

Section 21
Manufactures

This section presents summary data for manufacturing as a whole and more detailed information for major industry groups and selected products. The types of measures shown at the different levels include data for establishments, employment and wages, plant and equipment expenditures, value and quantity of production and shipments, value added by manufacture, inventories, and various indicators of financial status.

The principal sources of these data are U.S. Census Bureau reports of the censuses of manufactures conducted every 5 years, the *Annual Survey of Manufactures*, and *Current Industrial Reports*. Reports on current activities of industries or current movements of individual commodities are compiled by such government agencies as the Bureau of Labor Statistics; the Economic Research Service of the Department of Agriculture; the International Trade Administration; and by private research or trade associations.

Data on financial aspects of manufacturing industries are collected by the U.S. Census Bureau (see especially tables 989-991 as part of the Quarterly Financial Report. Industry aggregates in the form of balance sheets, profit and loss statements, analyses of sales and expenses, lists of subsidiaries, and types and amounts of security issues are published for leading manufacturing corporations registered with the Securities and Exchange Commission. The BEA issues data on capital in manufacturing industries and capacity utilization rates in manufacturing. See also Section 15, Business Enterprise.

Several private trade associations provide industry coverage for certain sections of the economy. They include the Aluminum Association (Table 998), American Iron and Steel Institute (Tables 999 and 1000), Consumer Electronics Association (Tables 1006 and 1007), and the Aerospace Industries Association (Tables 1012 and 1014). Machine tool consumption data

(Table 1002) is produced jointly by the Association for Manufacturing Technology and American Machine Tool Distributors Association.

Censuses and annual surveys—The first census of manufactures covered the year 1809. Between 1809 and 1963, a census was conducted at periodic intervals. Since 1967, it has been taken every 5 years (for years ending in "2" and "7"). Results from the 1997 census are presented in this section utilizing the new NAICS (North American Industry Classification System). Data from the 2002 census are being released on a flow basis and will mostly appear in the next edition of the *Statistical Abstract*. For additional information see text, Section 15, Business Enterprise, and the Census Bureau Web site at <http://www.census.gov/econ/census02/>. Census data either direct reports or estimates from administrative records, are obtained for every manufacturing plant with one paid employee or more.

The *Annual Survey of Manufactures* (ASM), conducted for the first time in 1949, collects data for the years between censuses for the more general measure of manufacturing activity covered in detail by the censuses. The annual survey data are estimates derived from a scientifically selected sample of establishments. The 2001 annual survey is based on a sample of about 55,000 establishments of an approximate total of 230,000. These establishments represent all manufacturing establishments of multiunit companies and all single-establishment manufacturing companies mailed schedules in the 1997 Census of Manufactures. For the current panel of the ASM sample, all establishments of companies with 1997 shipments in manufacturing in excess of $500 million were included in the survey with certainty. For the remaining portion of the mail survey, the establishment was defined as the sampling unit. For this portion, all establishments with 250 employees or more and establishments with a

Manufactures   625

very large value of shipments also were included. Therefore, of the 58,000 establishments included in the ASM panel, approximately 33,000 are selected with certainty. These establishments account for approximately 80 percent of total value of shipments in the 1992 census. Smaller establishments in the remaining portion of the mail survey were selected by sample.

Establishments and classification— Each of the establishments covered in the 1997 Economic Census—Manufacturing was classified in 1 of 480 industries (473 manufacturing industries and 7 former manufacturing industries) in accordance with the industry definitions in the 1997 NAICS Manual. In the NAICS system, an industry is generally defined as a group of establishments that have similar production processes. To the extent practical, the system uses supply based or production-oriented concepts in defining industries. The resulting group of establishments must be significant in terms of number, value added by manufacture, value of shipments, and number of employees.

Establishments frequently make products classified both in their industry (primary products) and other industries (secondary products). Industry statistics (employment, payroll, value added by manufacture, value of shipments, etc.) reflect the activities of the establishments, which may make both primary and secondary products. Product statistics, however, represent the output of all establishments without regard for the classification of the producing establishment. For this reason, when relating the industry statistics, especially the value of shipments, to the product statistics, the composition of the industry's output should be considered.

The censuses of manufactures for 1947 through 1992 cover operating manufacturing establishments as defined in the Standard Industrial Classification Manual (SIC), issued by the U.S. Office of Management and Budget (see text, Section 12). The Manual is also used for classifying establishments in the annual surveys. The comparability of manufactures data over time is affected by changes in the official definitions of industries as presented in the Manual. It is important to note, therefore, that the 1987 edition of the Manual was used for the 1987 and 1992 censuses; and the 1972 edition of the Manual and the 1977 Supplement were used for the 1972 through 1982 censuses.

Establishment—Establishment signifies a single physical plant site or factory. It is not necessarily identical to the business unit or company, which may consist of one or more establishments. A company operating establishments at more than one location is required to submit a separate report for each location. An establishment engaged in distinctly different lines of activity and maintaining separate payroll and inventory records is also required to submit separate reports.

Durable goods—Items with a normal life expectancy of 3 years or more. Automobiles, furniture, household appliances, and mobile homes are common examples.

Nondurable goods—Items which generally last for only a short time (3 years or less). Food, beverages, clothing, shoes, and gasoline are common examples.

Statistical reliability—For a discussion of statistical collection and estimation, sampling procedures, and measures of statistical reliability applicable to Census Bureau data, see Appendix III.

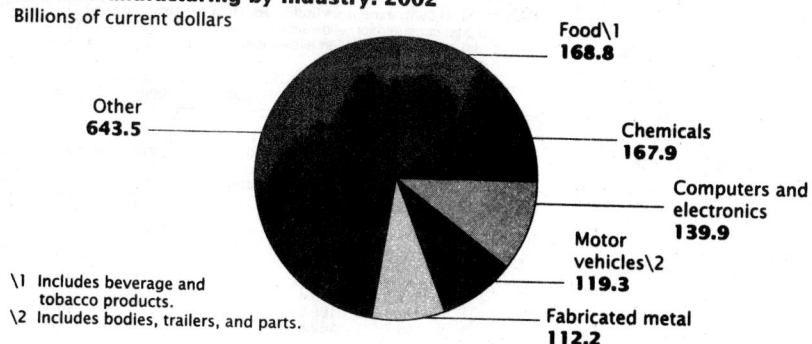

Figure 21.1
GDP in Manufacturing by Industry: 2002
Billions of current dollars

Food\1 **168.8**

Other **643.5**

Chemicals **167.9**

Computers and electronics **139.9**

Motor vehicles\2 **119.3**

Fabricated metal **112.2**

\1 Includes beverage and tobacco products.
\2 Includes bodies, trailers, and parts.

Figure 21.2
Manufacturing as a Percent of Total Gross Domestic Product (GDP): 1998 to 2003

Percent of Total GDP

Source: Figure 21.1 and 21.2 prepared by U.S. Census Bureau. For data, see Table 972.

Figure 21.3
Employment in Top Five Manufacturing Industries: 1990 to 2003

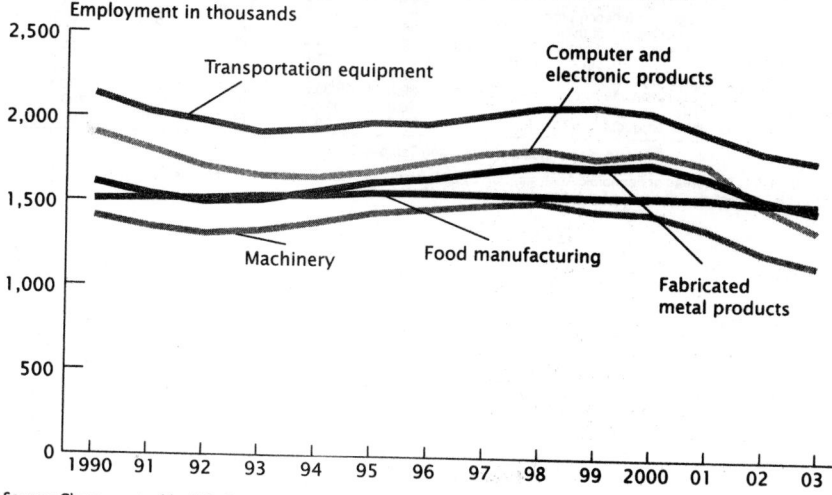

Employment in thousands

Transportation equipment

Computer and electronic products

Machinery

Food manufacturing

Fabricated metal products

Source: Chart prepared by U.S. Census Bureau. For data, see Table 982.

Manufactures 627

U.S. Census Bureau, Statistical Abstract of the United States: 2004-2005

No. 972. Gross Domestic Product in Manufacturing in Current and Real (2000) Dollars by Industry: 1998 to 2003

[In billions of dollars (8,747.0 represents $8,747,000,000,000), except as indicated. Data are based on the 1997 NAICS; see text, Section 15. Data include nonfactor charges (capital consumption allowances, indirect business taxes, etc.) as well as factor charges against gross product; corporate profits and capital consumption allowances have been shifted from a company to an establishment basis]

Industry	1998	1999	2000	2001	2002	2003
CURRENT DOLLARS						
Gross domestic product, total [1]	8,747.0	9,268.4	9,817.0	10,100.8	10,480.8	10,987.9
Manufacturing, total	1,343.9	1,373.1	1,426.2	1,346.0	1,351.6	1,392.8
Percent of total.	15.36	14.81	14.53	13.33	12.90	12.68
Durable goods	806.9	820.4	865.3	788.0	786.1	810.1
Wood products	29.4	31.9	31.4	31.1	32.1	(NA)
Nonmetallic mineral products.	42.3	45.1	45.7	44.7	44.5	(NA)
Primary metals	49.4	47.3	48.2	42.0	40.8	(NA)
Fabricated metal products.	112.7	116.4	121.7	113.5	112.2	(NA)
Machinery	111.5	105.6	109.3	103.5	98.1	(NA)
Computer and electronic products	165.7	162.8	185.6	141.6	139.9	(NA)
Electrical equipment, appliances, and components	44.7	48.2	50.6	48.7	46.1	(NA)
Motor vehicles, bodies and trailers, and parts . .	108.8	115.4	118.1	108.0	119.3	(NA)
Other transportation equipment	63.3	64.3	64.4	67.2	64.2	(NA)
Furniture and related products	29.1	31.0	32.7	30.8	30.6	(NA)
Miscellaneous manufacturing	49.9	52.5	57.5	56.9	58.5	(NA)
Nondurable goods.	537.0	552.7	560.9	558.0	565.5	582.7
Food and beverage and tobacco products	137.5	153.6	154.8	161.6	168.8	(NA)
Textile mills and textile product mills	27.1	26.4	26.5	23.1	22.7	(NA)
Apparel and leather and allied products.	26.0	24.7	25.1	22.9	23.3	(NA)
Paper products	52.2	54.2	55.6	50.0	48.9	(NA)
Printing and related support activities	46.5	48.2	49.0	47.4	47.1	(NA)
Petroleum and coal products	30.6	22.4	26.2	32.3	24.2	(NA)
Chemical products.	153.4	157.1	157.1	157.2	167.9	(NA)
Plastics and rubber products	63.6	66.1	66.7	63.5	62.8	(NA)
CHAINED (2000) DOLLARS						
Gross domestic product, total [1]	9,066.9	9,470.3	9,817.0	9,866.6	10,083.0	10,398.0
Manufacturing, total	1,286.2	1,342.1	1,426.2	1,349.1	1,380.9	1,404.9
Percent of total.	14.19	14.17	14.53	13.67	13.70	13.51
Durable goods	729.9	775.5	865.3	820.7	836.9	865.7
Wood products	29.9	30.4	31.4	30.6	31.9	(NA)
Nonmetallic mineral products.	44.1	45.1	45.7	44.9	43.9	(NA)
Primary metals	45.9	48.1	48.2	44.2	42.6	(NA)
Fabricated metal products.	114.4	114.9	121.7	110.8	108.8	(NA)
Machinery	113.8	105.0	109.3	100.4	94.5	**(NA)**
Computer and electronic products	96.3	125.4	185.6	186.4	207.8	(NA)
Electrical equipment, appliances, and components	44.6	48.0	50.6	47.9	46.2	(NA)
Motor vehicles, bodies and trailers, and parts . .	111.8	114.6	118.1	108.2	125.0	(NA)
Other transportation equipment	68.3	67.4	64.4	63.2	59.0	(NA)
Furniture and related products	30.2	31.5	32.7	29.6	28.7	(NA)
Miscellaneous manufacturing	50.4	52.1	57.5	54.8	54.9	(NA)
Nondurable goods.	559.6	568.2	561.0	528.5	543.9	540.6
Food and beverage and tobacco products	153.1	155.1	154.8	151.0	150.4	(NA)
Textile mills and textile product mills	26.3	25.6	26.5	21.9	22.0	(NA)
Apparel and leather and allied products.	26.4	24.4	25.1	22.8	23.5	(NA)
Paper products	60.0	61.0	55.6	49.7	49.2	(NA)
Printing and related support activities	47.7	48.5	49.0	45.8	45.2	(NA)
Petroleum and coal products	36.5	33.5	26.2	22.9	30.1	(NA)
Chemical products.	149.8	157.1	157.1	152.9	163.8	(NA)
Plastics and rubber products	62.4	64.7	66.7	61.3	60.1	(NA)

NA Not available.   [1] For additional industry detail, see Table 642.

Source: U.S. Bureau of Economic Analysis, *Survey of Current Business*, July 2004. See also <http://www.bea.gov/bea/industry /gpotables/gpolist.cfm?anon=591&registered=> (released 17 June 2004).

628   Manufactures

[114,065 represents 114,065,000. Excludes government employees, railroad employees, self-employed persons, etc. See "General Explanation" in source for definitions and statement on reliability of data. An *establishment* is a single physical location where business is conducted or where services or industrial operations are performed. See Appendix III]

Industry	NAICS code [1]	2000			2001		
		Estab-lish-ments, number	Number of employ-ees [2] (1,000)	Annual payroll (mil. dol.)	Estab-lish-ments, number	Number of employ-ees [2] (1,000)	Annual payroll (mil. dol.)
All industries, total	(X)	7,070,048	114,065	3,879,430	7,095,302	115,061	3,989,086
Manufacturing, total	31-33	354,498	16,474	643,954	352,619	15,950	617,699
Percent of all industries	(X)	5.01	14.44	16.60	4.97	13.86	15.48
Food	311	26,401	1,468	43,773	26,785	1,470	44,085
Beverage & tobacco product	312	2,869	169	7,318	3,212	171	7,258
Textile mills	313	4,449	339	9,491	4,452	308	8,403
Textile product mills	314	6,881	216	5,364	6,966	202	5,059
Apparel manufacturing	315	16,505	510	10,426	16,152	442	9,262
Leather & allied product	316	1,783	69	1,711	1,763	61	1,496
Wood product	321	17,328	598	16,511	17,289	558	15,829
Paper	322	5,790	554	23,291	5,739	533	22,501
Printing & related support activities	323	39,035	813	28,319	37,895	785	27,051
Petroleum & coal products	324	2,210	109	6,386	2,253	104	6,336
Chemical	325	13,426	886	45,610	13,361	870	46,395
Plastics & rubber products	326	16,292	1,057	34,110	15,981	1,003	32,641
Nonmetallic mineral product	327	16,537	524	19,123	16,732	524	19,350
Primary metal	331	6,300	602	25,545	6,684	573	23,642
Fabricated metal product	332	61,144	1,791	64,244	60,791	1,761	61,803
Machinery	333	29,442	1,378	58,387	28,922	1,333	54,714
Computer & electronic product	334	17,148	1,557	90,397	16,764	1,593	84,522
Electrical equip, appliance & component	335	7,041	589	21,853	6,940	575	20,873
Transportation equipment	336	12,766	1,873	88,632	12,627	1,753	83,440
Furniture & related product	337	19,848	640	17,964	20,593	619	17,434
Miscellaneous	339	31,303	732	25,500	30,718	713	25,605

X Not applicable. [1] North American Industry Classification System, 1997; see text, Section 15. [2] Covers full- and part-time employees who are on the payroll in the pay period including March 12.

Source: U.S. Census Bureau, *County Business Patterns*, annual. See also <http://www.census.gov/prod/2003pubs/01cbp/cbp01-1.pdf> (issued April 2003).

[15,950 represents 15,950,000. Excludes government employees, railroad employees, self-employed persons, etc. See "General Explanation" in source for definitions and statement on reliability of data. An *establishment* is a single physical location where business is conducted or where services or industrial operations are performed]

State	Establish-ments	Number of employ-ees [1] (1,000)	Annual payroll (mil. dol.)	State	Establish-ments	Number of employ-ees [2] (1,000)	Annual payroll (mil. dol.)
United States	352,619	15,950	617,699	Missouri	7,261	335	11,318
				Montana	1,226	21	646
Alabama	5,200	312	10,202	Nebraska	1,934	109	3,361
Alaska	503	11	367	Nevada	1,722	40	1,464
Arizona	4,937	194	7,917	New Hampshire	2,249	96	3,819
Arkansas	3,226	229	6,462	New Jersey	10,872	380	17,283
California	49,022	1,741	75,803	New Mexico	1,585	37	1,299
Colorado	5,449	162	6,569	New York	21,499	689	27,241
Connecticut	5,413	233	11,202	North Carolina	10,844	691	21,583
Delaware	694	42	1,745	North Dakota	681	24	762
District of Columbia	162	3	92	Ohio	17,597	936	37,463
Florida	15,392	413	14,578	Oklahoma	4,025	163	5,509
Georgia	8,688	492	16,141	Oregon	5,587	198	7,981
Hawaii	940	15	463	Pennsylvania	16,796	780	29,312
Idaho	1,729	67	2,138	Rhode Island	2,185	67	2,333
Illinois	17,134	820	32,832	South Carolina	4,430	326	11,289
Indiana	9,131	604	23,471	South Dakota	922	47	1,401
Iowa	3,721	238	8,355	Tennessee	7,013	449	15,237
Kansas	3,240	191	7,302	Texas	21,370	948	37,288
Kentucky	4,210	280	10,182	Utah	3,001	120	4,241
Louisiana	3,436	159	6,539	Vermont	1,180	48	1,825
Maine	1,866	77	2,705	Virginia	5,804	344	12,574
Maryland	3,936	157	6,792	Washington	7,565	316	14,458
Massachusetts	9,015	390	18,907	West Virginia	1,471	72	2,628
Michigan	15,431	756	33,634	Wisconsin	9,846	544	20,145
Minnesota	8,146	374	14,846	Wyoming	563	9	321
Mississippi	2,815	201	5,674				

[1] Covers full- and part-time employees who are on the payroll in the pay period including March 12.

Source: U.S. Census Bureau, *County Business Patterns*, annual. See also<http://www.census.gov/prod/2003pubs/01cbp/cbp01-1.pdf>

No. 975. Manufactures—Establishments, Employees, Payroll, and Value of Shipments by Industry (NAICS 1997 Basis): 1997 and 2002

[2002 preliminary. For establishments with payroll. (16,805.1 represents 16,805,100). Based on the 1997 and 2002 Economic Censuses; see Appendix III]

Industry	NAICS code[1]	1997 Number of establishments	1997 Paid employees (1,000)	1997 Annual payroll (mil. dol.)	1997 Value of shipments (mil. dol.)	2002 Number of establishments	2002 Paid employees (1,000)	2002 Annual payroll (mil. dol.)	2002 Value of shipments (mil. dol.)
Manufacturing, total	31-33	362,829	16,805.1	569,809	3,834,701	344,259	14,543.3	568,400	3,832,566
Food	311	26,302	1,467.0	38,366	421,737	26,374	1,507.9	45,456	457,333
Beverage and tobacco products	312	2,727	175.7	6,735	96,971	2,997	157.3	6,798	104,028
Textile mills	313	4,694	391.9	10,058	58,707	3,937	266.7	7,693	47,028
Textile products	314	7,899	235.4	5,089	31,052	7,333	190.3	4,989	32,527
Apparel	315	16,989	710.8	12,582	68,018	12,516	352.2	7,774	45,606
Leather and allied products	316	1,861	85.1	1,832	10,877	1,515	45.7	1,231	7,208
Wood products	321	17,367	570.0	14,319	88,470	16,912	535.2	15,910	89,168
Paper	322	5,868	574.3	22,312	150,296	5,463	475.8	20,678	151,371
Printing and related support activities	323	42,863	834.4	26,023	97,485	37,168	718.1	25,717	95,554
Petroleum and coal products	324	2,146	107.6	5,546	177,393	2,278	105.9	6,314	212,421
Chemicals	325	13,474	882.6	39,836	415,617	13,107	790.2	40,770	427,728
Plastics and rubber products	326	16,821	1,023.1	29,805	159,161	15,305	939.9	31,196	167,929
Nonmetallic mineral products	327	16,310	501.5	16,172	86,465	16,579	481.2	17,838	95,247
Primary metals	331	5,059	605.1	23,811	168,118	5,952	489.0	21,177	135,825
Fabricated metal products	332	62,384	1,763.8	56,632	242,813	60,602	1,557.1	56,994	245,288
Machinery	333	30,599	1,420.5	53,012	270,687	28,129	1,163.9	49,549	241,723
Computers and electronic products	334	17,435	1,691.1	72,484	439,381	15,698	1,302.0	65,808	353,566
Electrical equipment, appliances, and components	335	6,930	593.8	18,973	112,116	6,420	500.6	18,422	105,731
Transportation equipment	336	12,887	1,842.3	79,617	575,307	12,264	1,646.4	80,769	619,564
Furniture and related products	337	20,738	603.7	14,986	64,299	21,824	571.0	16,491	73,215
Miscellaneous products	339	31,476	725.4	21,618	99,730	31,886	746.8	26,823	124,508

[1] North American Industry Classification System, 1997; see text, Section 15.
Source: U.S. Census Bureau, 2002 Economic Census, *Advance Report*, issued March 2004. See Internet site: <http://www.census.gov/econ/census02/>

No. 976. Manufactures—Summary by Selected Industry: 2001

[15,879.5 represents 15,879,500. Based on the Annual Survey of Manufactures; see Appendix III]

Industry based on shipments	NAICS code[1]	All employees[2] Number (1,000)	All employees[2] Payroll Total (mil. dol.)	All employees[2] Payroll Per employee (dol.)	Production workers[2] (1,000)	Value added by manufactures[4] (mil. dol.)	Value of shipments[3] (mil. dol.)
Manufacturing, total	31-33	15,879.5	593,051	37,347	11,235.1	1,853,929	3,970,500
Food	311	1,504.7	43,586	28,967	1,145.1	193,224	451,386
Beverage and tobacco product	312	177.5	7,023	39,562	95.9	77,735	118,786
Textile mills	313	293.9	8,040	27,353	247.5	18,842	45,681
Textile product mills	314	209.7	5,051	24,091	170.1	12,852	31,971
Apparel	315	456.5	9,205	20,165	369.3	24,809	54,598
Wood product	321	555.9	15,431	27,759	458.9	33,130	87,250
Paper	322	530.2	22,188	41,845	407.8	73,036	155,846
Pulp, paper, and paperboard mills	3221	170.7	9,179	53,783	134.2	37,279	71,987
Printing and related support activities	323	799.2	27,158	33,980	574.2	60,483	100,792
Petroleum and coal products	324	101.5	5,830	57,465	67.5	47,346	219,075
Chemical[5]	325	875.0	43,800	50,060	499.2	226,615	438,410
Pharmaceutical and medicine	3254	251.3	13,396	53,308	120.4	91,697	130,021
Plastics and rubber products	326	1,028.1	32,539	31,651	810.9	86,558	170,717
Plastics	3261	834.5	25,588	30,664	657.8	69,475	137,276
Nonmetallic mineral product	327	507.3	18,147	35,771	394.6	53,195	94,861
Primary metal[5]	331	532.8	22,199	41,664	420.2	53,111	138,245
Iron and steel mills and ferroalloy	3311	130.3	6,700	51,421	102.0	14,749	44,896
Fabricated metal product	332	1,724.7	59,569	34,539	1,296.0	138,793	253,113
Machinery[5]	333	1,314.7	52,844	40,194	844.1	131,103	266,553
Industrial machinery	3332	190.5	8,533	44,786	105.1	17,448	35,211
Metalworking machinery	3335	217.7	9,055	41,601	153.0	16,030	26,684
Computer and electronic product[5]	334	1,598.8	77,137	48,248	779.9	223,718	429,471
Computer and peripheral equipment	3341	193.1	9,165	47,461	65.2	34,394	89,528
Communications equipment	3342	301.7	17,089	56,636	120.3	50,757	102,004
Semiconductor and other electronic components	3344	566.9	23,944	42,240	355.3	71,289	124,215
Navigational, measuring, medical, control instruments	3345	468.1	24,461	52,254	192.8	60,035	97,169
Electrical equipment, appliance, and component[5]	335	556.6	19,466	34,970	395.7	56,304	114,067
Electrical equipment[5]	3353	186.8	6,660	35,662	124.7	17,340	33,934
Transportation equipment[5]	336	1,717.6	80,416	46,818	1,246.5	227,675	602,496
Motor vehicle	3361	214.0	12,647	59,102	186.2	54,173	216,128
Motor vehicle parts	3363	736.0	31,501	42,800	584.6	74,532	186,839
Aerospace product and parts	3364	433.1	24,542	56,660	220.8	71,839	134,867
Furniture and related product	337	608.0	16,950	27,880	481.5	39,849	72,147

[1] North American Industry Classification System, 1997; see text, Section 15. [2] See footnote 1, Table 977. [3] See footnote 2, Table 977. [4] See footnote 3, Table 977. [5] Includes industries not shown separately.
Source: U.S. Census Bureau, *Annual Survey of Manufactures, Statistics for Industry Groups and Industries*, Series M01(AS)-1. See also <http://www.census.gov/prod/2003pubs/m01as-1.pdf> (issued January 2003).

No. 977. Manufactures—Summary by State: 2001

[15,879.5 represents 15,879,500. Sum of state totals may not add to U.S. total because U.S. and state figures were independently derived. See Appendix III]

State	All employees [1] Number (1,000)	All employees [1] Payroll Total (mil. dol.)	All employees [1] Payroll Per employee (dol.)	Production workers [1] Total (1,000)	Production workers [1] Wages (mil. dol.)	Value added by manufactures [2] Total (mil. dol.)	Value added by manufactures [2] Per production worker (dol.)	Value of shipments [3] (mil. dol.)
United States	15,879.5	593,051	37,347	11,235.1	342,990	1,853,929	165,012	3,970,500
Alabama.............	315.1	9,890	31,391	247.2	6,708	27,844	112,653	67,172
Alaska	12.6	409	32,426	10.1	297	1,182	116,523	3,987
Arizona.............	186.4	7,367	39,527	114.6	3,146	28,430	248,027	42,168
Arkansas	227.0	6,363	28,037	184.6	4,538	19,868	107,611	46,530
California	1,792.2	72,189	40,279	1,147.6	33,383	219,584	191,347	414,762
Colorado............	163.1	6,541	40,112	108.1	3,317	17,799	164,582	35,627
Connecticut..........	229.8	10,557	45,936	137.2	4,807	27,595	201,099	47,055
Delaware	38.0	1,458	38,402	28.4	928	6,621	232,937	16,664
District of Columbia	1.8	90	50,984	1.3	51	93	69,147	178
Florida	401.3	13,591	33,868	268.1	6,757	39,974	149,095	76,541
Georgia	484.0	15,721	32,483	371.8	10,281	57,578	154,882	127,624
Hawaii	14.4	447	31,108	9.1	225	907	100,159	3,196
Idaho..............	63.9	2,126	33,281	47.6	1,424	3,670	77,084	15,076
Illinois.............	811.3	31,498	38,826	559.5	17,577	94,124	168,233	196,449
Indiana.............	597.7	23,155	38,739	448.7	15,195	72,122	160,749	154,264
Iowa	235.9	8,221	34,854	176.7	5,221	29,636	167,718	65,428
Kansas.............	193.8	7,093	36,600	140.0	4,366	21,008	150,069	53,031
Kentucky	276.3	10,002	36,196	214.1	6,734	31,722	148,156	84,180
Louisiana	156.9	6,335	40,376	115.9	4,191	22,545	194,532	85,488
Maine..............	77.7	2,832	36,466	57.7	1,822	7,880	136,654	15,066
Maryland	162.4	6,917	42,601	103.9	3,324	18,757	180,611	36,038
Massachusetts........	376.7	16,623	44,128	226.7	7,535	44,447	196,045	79,851
Michigan............	749.5	33,028	44,068	563.8	22,179	86,262	153,010	209,003
Minnesota...........	376.7	14,519	38,549	249.2	7,709	38,545	154,675	82,304
Mississippi	197.8	5,559	28,110	158.3	3,838	15,573	98,400	38,560
Missouri	346.6	12,226	35,269	252.3	7,432	40,284	159,688	89,682
Montana	20.4	619	30,384	15.0	417	2,091	139,673	5,423
Nebraska	105.0	3,348	31,889	82.9	2,282	11,962	144,213	31,133
Nevada	40.4	1,518	37,629	27.6	791	3,844	139,224	7,581
New Hampshire.......	96.7	3,795	39,234	67.1	2,218	8,621	128,506	16,975
New Jersey..........	379.5	15,534	40,931	253.5	8,167	50,754	200,228	98,230
New Mexico	32.7	1,147	35,068	23.4	735	6,632	282,930	11,464
New York	707.2	26,380	37,300	482.1	14,217	78,484	162,782	146,455
North Carolina.......	693.7	21,436	30,902	531.7	13,622	91,184	171,497	167,124
North Dakota........	23.4	726	31,063	16.7	439	2,669	159,523	6,517
Ohio	923.5	36,190	39,186	682.1	23,431	107,440	157,514	241,902
Oklahoma...........	161.7	5,350	33,093	117.7	3,341	18,059	153,390	40,063
Oregon.............	199.2	7,200	36,148	142.4	4,369	22,027	154,646	43,271
Pennsylvania........	768.7	28,512	37,093	544.5	16,896	87,984	161,581	178,613
Rhode Island........	70.0	2,396	34,216	46.3	1,260	5,877	126,922	10,958
South Carolina.......	312.4	10,694	34,236	240.5	6,951	35,017	145,574	78,738
South Dakota	39.6	1,115	28,191	29.4	729	4,558	154,839	11,093
Tennessee	441.4	14,531	32,923	335.0	9,387	46,349	138,337	104,109
Texas..............	950.4	35,377	37,222	647.8	19,410	120,086	185,381	321,361
Utah	121.8	4,174	34,263	82.2	2,341	11,783	143,270	25,908
Vermont	45.8	1,740	37,963	30.1	849	5,078	168,881	8,926
Virginia............	327.4	11,268	34,418	245.9	7,076	53,043	215,686	92,874
Washington..........	309.2	12,603	40,759	194.6	6,922	38,193	196,236	89,280
West Virginia........	67.7	2,519	37,207	50.4	1,643	7,202	142,804	16,201
Wisconsin...........	544.3	19,817	36,406	396.6	12,302	59,585	150,257	126,542
Wyoming	9.0	305	33,958	6.9	213	1,358	197,002	3,835

[1] Includes employment and payroll at administrative offices and auxiliary units. All employees represents the average of production workers plus all other employees for the payroll period ended nearest the 12th of March. Production workers represents the average of the employment for the payroll periods ended nearest the 12th of March, May, August, and November. [2] Adjusted value added; takes into account (a) value added by merchandising operations (that is, difference between the sales value and cost of merchandise sold without further manufacture, processing, or assembly), plus (b) net change in finished goods and work-inprocess inventories between beginning and end of year. [3] Includes extensive and unmeasurable duplication from shipments between establishments in the same industry classification.

Source: U.S. Census Bureau, *Annual Survey of Manufactures, Geographic Area Statistics*, Series M01(AS)-3. See also <http://www.census.gov/prod/2003pubs/m01as-3.pdf> (issued January 2003).

Manufactures 631

No. 978. Manufacturing Industries—Export-Related Shipments and Employment by Industry: 2000

[(4,208,582 represents $4,208,582,000,000). Exports include both "direct" exports (exports manufactured in the U.S. and consumed in foreign markets and "indirect" exports (intermediate goods and services required to manufacture export goods). For methodology, see report]

Industry	NAICS code [1]	Value of manfac-turers' shipments (mil. dol.)	Export related ship-ments (mil. dol.)	All manufac-turing employ-ment (1,000)	Export related manufac-turing employ-ment (1,000)	Export related as percent of all manufacturers — Ship-ments	Export related as percent of all manufacturers — Employ-ment
Manufacturing, total	31-33	4,208,582	879,198	16,652	3,451	20.9	20.7
Food	311	435,230	29,897	1,506	101	6.9	6.7
Beverage and tobacco products	312	111,692	5,587	175	10	5.0	5.5
Textile mills	313	52,112	13,262	337	88	25.4	26.2
Textile products	314	33,654	2,799	230	23	8.3	10.1
Apparel.	315	60,339	8,231	520	74	13.6	14.1
Leather and allied products	316	9,647	2,511	69	17	26.0	24.1
Wood products.	321	93,669	8,002	587	48	8.5	8.1
Paper.	322	165,297	29,842	548	93	18.1	16.9
Printing and related support activities	323	104,396	11,293	830	89	10.8	10.7
Petroleum and coal products	324	235,134	19,726	101	10	8.4	10.3
Chemicals	325	449,159	115,362	890	235	25.7	26.4
Plastics and rubber products	326	178,236	31,786	1,080	193	17.8	17.9
Nonmetallic mineral products	327	97,329	12,261	522	71	12.6	13.5
Primary metals.	331	156,598	64,610	578	222	41.3	38.4
Fabricated metal products	332	268,212	59,470	1,815	420	22.2	23.1
Machinery	333	291,548	84,345	1,396	395	28.9	28.3
Computers and electronic products	334	510,640	185,534	1,653	612	36.3	37.0
Electrical equipment, appliances, and components.	335	125,443	32,300	591	157	25.7	26.6
Transportation equipment	336	639,861	140,940	1,838	448	22.0	24.4
Furniture and related products	337	75,107	3,315	641	30	4.4	4.7
Miscellaneous products	339	115,280	18,127	745	118	15.7	15.8

[1] North American Industry Classification System, 1997; see text, Section 15.

Source: U.S. Census Bureau, Exports from Manufacturing Establishments: 2000, series AR(00)-1. See also <http://www.census.gov/mcd/exports/ar00.pdf> (released March 2004).

No. 979. Manufacturing Industries—Export-Related Shipments and Employment by State: 2000

[(879,198 represents $879,178,000,000). Exports include both "direct" exports (exports manufactured in the U.S. and consumed in foreign markets and "indirect" exports (intermediate goods and services required to manufacture export goods). For methodology, see report]

State	Export related shipments (mil. dol.)	Export related manufac-turing employ-ment (1,000)	Export related as percent of all manufacturers — Ship-ments	Export related as percent of all manufacturers — Employ-ment	State	Export related shipments (mil. dol.)	Export related manufac-turing employ-ment (1,000)	Export related as percent of all manufacturers — Ship-ments	Export related as percent of all manufacturers — Employ-ment
U.S.	879,198	3,451	20.9	20.7	Nevada	852	6	11.9	16.0
Alabama . . .	13,437	50	19.1	14.8	New Hampshire .	5,307	25	27.1	24.7
Alaska	380	1	9.4	10.3	New Jersey .	15,730	65	15.5	16.7
Arizona	13,873	55	29.5	27.4	New Mexico .	7,488	13	49.1	35.7
Arkansas . . .	7,170	32	15.0	13.4	New York . . .	32,963	147	21.2	20.0
California . .	115,949	464	26.3	25.2	North Carolina . . .	32,612	143	18.5	19.2
Colorado . . .	10,044	44	25.6	26.4	North Dakota	700	4	11.8	15.4
Connecticut .	12,928	66	27.8	27.7	Ohio	57,777	228	22.4	23.3
Delaware . . .	1,455	6	8.5	15.8	Oklahoma . . .	5,752	27	12.9	15.7
District of Columbia . .	6	(D)	2.9	(D)	Oregon	15,541	54	31.2	26.5
Florida	12,231	60	15.2	14.1	Pennsylvania	32,030	134	17.1	16.9
Georgia . . .	21,631	73	16.0	14.3	Rhode Island	2,221	16	19.1	21.1
Hawaii	318	2	8.5	16.4	South Carolina . . .	18,872	79	24.0	23.9
Idaho	6,334	16	28.4	25.5	South Dakota	2,013	8	16.5	19.6
Illinois	40,984	164	19.3	19.0	Tennessee . .	18,348	81	17.6	17.2
Indiana	35,379	135	21.8	21.2	Texas	79,671	236	23.0	23.8
Iowa	10,944	45	16.5	18.0	Utah	5,569	23	20.1	18.6
Kansas	7,768	31	14.2	16.0	Vermont	5,514	20	58.6	46.6
Kentucky . . .	16,299	54	18.1	18.3	Virginia	14,503	58	15.1	16.6
Louisiana . . .	11,574	22	12.2	13.8	Washington .	38,043	119	42.1	36.8
Maine	2,693	13	15.9	16.6	West Virginia. . . .	3,109	13	18.4	18.7
Maryland . . .	4,173	23	11.4	14.0	Wisconsin. . .	20,013	93	15.4	16.3
Massachusetts	26,894	116	31.3	30.1	Wyoming . . .	320	1	8.4	9.3
Michigan . . .	51,877	204	22.6	25.2					
Minnesota . .	13,897	73	16.0	18.6					
Mississippi . .	6,075	24	14.8	11.3					
Missouri . . .	14,885	61	16.5	17.0					
Montana . . .	497	2	8.8	8.6					
Nebraska . . .	4,560	19	14.8	16.9					

D Data withheld to avoid disclosure of individual companies.

Source: U.S. Census Bureau, Exports from Manufacturing Establishments: 2000, series AR(00)-1. See also <http://www.census.gov/mcd/exports/ar00.pdf> (released March 2004).

No. 980. Manufacturers' E-Commerce Shipments by Industry: 2001 and 2002

[(3,970,500 represents $3,970,500,000,000). Based on the Annual Survey of Manufactures; subject to sampling variability. E-commerce is the value of goods and services sold over computer-mediated networks (open or proprietary)]

Industry	NAICS code [1]	2001				2002			
				E-commerce				E-commerce	
		Ship-ments, total (mil. dol)	Ship-ments, total (mil.dol)	Percent of total ship-ments	Percent distri-bution	Ship-ments, total (mil.dol)	Ship-ments, total (mil.dol)	Percent of total ship-ments	Percent distri-bution
Manufacturing, total	31-33	3,970,500	724,228	18.2	100.0	3,840,319	751,985	19.6	100.0
Food products	311	451,386	53,556	11.9	7.4	469,031	51,094	10.9	6.8
Beverage and tobacco..........	312	118,786	45,665	38.4	6.3	103,869	45,419	43.7	6.0
Textile mills	313	45,681	4,435	9.7	0.6	46,847	3,977	8.5	0.5
Textile product mills.........	314	31,971	7,409	23.2	1.0	31,642	7,491	23.7	1.0
Apparel.....................	315	54,598	10,652	19.5	1.5	45,848	9,726	21.2	1.3
Leather and allied products	316	8,834	1,438	16.3	0.2	7,349	783	10.7	0.1
Wood products................	321	87,250	4,919	5.6	0.7	88,492	4,567	5.2	0.6
Paper.......................	322	155,846	20,208	13.0	2.8	152,378	18,385	12.1	2.4
Printing and related support activities .	323	100,792	5,885	5.8	0.8	95,735	4,725	4.9	0.6
Petroleum and coal products	324	219,075	16,312	7.4	2.3	215,663	25,523	11.8	3.4
Chemicals...................	325	438,410	54,041	12.3	7.5	427,754	68,674	16.1	9.1
Plastics and rubber products.......	326	170,717	27,324	16.0	3.8	166,089	23,953	14.4	3.2
Nonmetallic mineral products	327	94,861	7,887	8.3	1.1	94,391	7,144	7.6	1.0
Primary metals	331	138,245	14,274	10.3	2.0	136,971	12,828	9.4	1.7
Fabricated metal products	332	253,113	24,168	9.5	3.3	242,204	21,427	8.8	2.8
Machinery...................	333	266,553	35,670	13.4	4.9	241,406	30,390	12.6	4.0
Computer and electronic products . .	334	429,471	73,221	17.0	10.1	353,529	73,406	20.8	9.8
Electrical equipment, appliances, and components...........	335	114,067	27,845	24.4	3.8	103,599	23,043	22.2	3.1
Transportation equipment........	336	602,496	264,326	43.9	36.5	620,649	297,280	47.9	39.5
Furniture and related products	337	72,147	9,348	13.0	1.3	73,112	8,082	11.1	1.1
Miscellaneous	339	116,201	15,644	13.5	2.2	123,761	14,068	11.4	1.9

[1] North American Industry Classification System, 1997; see text, Section 15.

Source: U.S. Census Bureau, Internet site <http://www.census.gov/eos/www/papers/2002/2002finaltext.pdf> (released 15 April 2004) and <http://www.census.gov/eos/www/historical/2002ht.pdf>.

No. 981. Manufacturing Employer Costs for Employee Compensation Per Hour Worked: 1990 to 2003

[As of March, for private industry workers. Based on a sample of establishments in the National Compensation Survey; see Appendix III and source for details. See also Table 628, Section 12]

Compensation component	Cost (dol.)					Percent distribution				
	1990	2000	2001	2002	2003	1990	2000	2001	2002	2003
Total compensation ...	17.33	23.41	24.30	25.20	26.02	100.0	100.0	100.0	100.0	100.0
Wages and salaries	11.86	16.01	16.66	17.19	17.43	68.4	68.4	68.6	68.2	67.0
Total benefits............	5.47	7.40	7.64	8.01	8.59	31.6	31.6	31.4	31.8	33.0
Paid leave	1.31	1.74	1.85	1.91	1.97	7.6	7.4	7.6	7.6	7.6
Vacation..........	0.67	0.86	0.92	0.97	1.00	3.9	3.7	3.8	3.8	3.8
Holiday	0.48	0.65	0.68	0.70	0.73	2.8	2.8	2.8	2.8	2.8
Sick	0.12	0.15	0.15	0.14	0.16	0.7	0.6	0.6	0.6	0.6
Other	0.05	0.10	0.10	0.10	0.10	0.3	0.4	0.4	0.4	0.4
Supplemental pay	0.65	1.04	1.09	1.13	1.23	3.8	4.4	4.5	4.5	4.7
Premium pay	0.34	0.58	0.58	0.56	0.60	2.0	2.5	2.4	2.2	2.3
Nonproduction bonuses .	0.22	0.36	0.41	0.46	0.51	1.3	1.5	1.7	1.8	2.0
Shift pay	0.09	0.10	0.11	0.11	0.11	0.5	0.4	0.5	0.4	0.4
Insurance	1.37	1.85	1.93	2.11	2.27	7.9	7.9	7.9	8.4	8.7
Health insurance	(NA)	1.69	1.75	1.92	2.08	(NA)	7.2	7.2	7.6	8.0
Retirement and savings ...	0.56	0.75	0.75	0.74	0.86	3.2	3.2	3.1	2.9	3.3
Defined benefit	(NA)	0.34	0.29	0.30	0.41	(NA)	1.5	1.2	1.2	1.6
Defined contributions ...	(NA)	0.41	0.46	0.44	0.45	(NA)	1.8	1.9	1.7	1.7
Legally required	1.54	1.92	1.95	2.05	2.18	8.9	8.2	8.0	8.1	8.4
Social Security	1.02	1.38	1.42	1.48	1.51	5.9	5.9	5.8	5.9	5.8
Federal unemployment . .	0.03	0.03	0.03	0.03	0.03	0.2	0.1	0.1	0.1	0.1
State unemployment ...	0.12	0.11	0.10	0.11	0.13	0.7	0.5	0.4	0.4	0.5
Workers compensation..	0.36	0.40	0.40	0.43	0.51	2.1	1.7	1.6	1.7	2.0
Other benefits [1]	0.04	0.09	0.07	0.07	0.08	0.2	0.4	0.3	0.3	0.3

NA Not available. [1] Includes severance pay, and supplemental unemployment benefits.

Source: U.S. Bureau of Labor Statistics, *Employer Costs for Employee Compensation Historical Listing, annual, 1986-2001,* and *Employer Costs for Employee Compensation, March 2003.* See also <ftp://ftp.bls.gov/pub/special.requests/ocwc/ect/ecechist.pdf> (issued 19 June 2002) and <http://www.bls.gov/news.release/pdf/ecec.pdf> (issued 19 June 2002 <http://www.bls.gov/news.release/pdf/ecec.pdf> (issued 11 June 2003).

[Annual averages of monthly figures (109,487 represents 109,487,000). Covers all full- and part-time employees who worked during, or received pay for, any part of the pay period including the 12th of the month. See also headnote, Table 611]

Industry	2002 NAICS code [1]	All employees (1,000)						Pecent change	
		1990	1995	2000	2001	2002	2003	1990-2000	2000-2003
All industries	(X)	109,487	117,298	131,785	131,826	130,341	129,931	20.4	-1.4
Manufacturing	31-33	17,695	17,241	17,263	16,441	15,259	14,525	-2.4	-15.9
Percent of all industries	(X)	16.16	14.70	13.10	12.47	11.71	11.18	(X)	(X)
Durable goods	(X)	10,736	10,372	10,876	10,335	9,483	8,970	1.3	-17.5
Wood products	321	541	574	613	574	555	536	13.4	-12.5
Sawmills and wood preservation	3211	148	137	134	127	121	117	-9.6	-13.0
Plywood and engineered wood products	3212	96	107	122	116	116	114	28.2	-7.1
Other wood products	3219	297	330	357	331	318	306	20.1	-14.2
Nonmetallic mineral products	327	528	513	554	545	516	493	4.9	-11.1
Clay products and refractories	3271	84	85	82	77	72	66	-1.9	-19.3
Glass and glass products	3272	152	144	141	136	124	117	-7.6	-17.3
Cement and concrete products	3273	195	194	234	236	230	223	20.1	-4.7
Lime, gypsum, and other nonmetallic mineral products	3279	98	91	97	95	91	87	-0.3	-10.7
Primary metals	331	689	642	622	571	509	477	-9.7	-23.3
Iron and steel mills and ferroalloy production	3311	187	154	135	122	107	102	-27.7	-24.4
Steel products from purchased steel	3312	70	70	73	68	63	60	4.0	-17.6
Alumina and aluminum production	3313	108	98	101	92	80	75	-7.3	-25.3
Other nonferrous metal production	3314	109	103	96	90	81	74	-11.7	-22.7
Foundries	3315	214	216	217	200	178	165	1.4	-23.9
Fabricated metal products	332	1,610	1,623	1,753	1,676	1,549	1,478	8.9	-15.6
Forging and stamping	3321	128	139	138	125	113	109	7.9	-21.1
Cutlery and hand tools	3322	79	78	79	72	64	62	0.3	-22.0
Architectural and structural metals	3323	357	359	428	422	399	379	20.0	-11.4
Boilers, tanks, and shipping containers	3324	117	108	107	103	96	91	-9.1	-14.7
Hardware	3325	57	55	50	46	42	40	-12.8	-20.4
Spring and wire products	3326	78	82	81	76	70	64	4.3	-21.2
Machine shops and threaded products	3327	309	330	365	348	318	308	18.4	-15.6
Coating, engraving, and heat treating metals	3328	143	155	175	163	149	143	22.7	-18.2
Other fabricated metal products	3329	344	317	330	321	296	283	-4.0	-14.2
Machinery	333	1,408	1,440	1,455	1,368	1,230	1,154	3.3	-20.7
Agricultural, construction, and mining machinery	3331	229	215	222	217	200	189	-2.8	-14.9
Industrial machinery	3332	152	164	163	149	131	124	7.5	-24.1
Commercial and service industry machinery	3333	147	144	147	143	130	119	0.3	-19.1
HVAC and commercial refrigeration equipment	3334	165	182	194	184	167	158	17.8	-18.6
Metalworking machinery	3335	267	273	274	249	217	205	2.5	-24.9
Turbine and power transmission equipment	3336	114	115	111	106	101	94	-2.4	-15.5
Other general purpose machinery	3339	335	347	343	321	285	264	2.4	-23.0
Computer and electronic products	334	1,903	1,688	1,820	1,749	1,507	1,361	-4.3	-25.2
Computer and peripheral equipment	3341	367	296	302	286	250	226	-17.8	-25.2
Communications equipment	3342	232	233	248	234	186	157	7.0	-36.6
Audio and video equipment	3343	60	54	52	47	42	39	-13.3	-26.1
Semiconductors and electronic components	3344	574	571	676	645	525	462	17.8	-31.7
Electronic instruments	3345	626	482	479	475	450	429	-23.6	-10.3
Magnetic media manufacturing and reproduction	3346	43	53	63	61	55	49	46.4	-23.5
Electrical equipment and appliances	335	633	593	591	557	497	460	-6.7	-22.2
Electric lighting equipment	3351	81	81	85	79	72	68	5.0	-19.8
Household appliances	3352	114	112	106	102	98	93	-7.0	-12.2
Electrical equipment	3353	244	219	210	197	175	160	-13.9	-23.7
Other electrical equipment and components	3359	195	181	191	180	152	139	-2.3	-26.9
Transportation equipment	336	2,133	1,977	2,056	1,938	1,829	1,775	-3.6	-13.6
Motor vehicles	3361	271	295	291	279	265	268	7.4	-8.2
Motor vehicle bodies and trailers	3362	130	160	183	159	152	151	40.8	-17.2
Motor vehicle parts	3363	653	787	840	775	734	707	28.6	-15.7
Aerospace products and parts	3364	841	514	517	511	470	440	-38.5	-14.9
Ship and boat building	3366	173	146	153	147	146	149	-11.4	-2.9
Other transportation equipment	3369	35	40	40	39	39	39	14.0	-2.5

See footnotes at end of table.

U.S. Census Bureau, Statistical Abstract of the United States: 2004-2005

[Annual averages of monthly figures (109,487 represents 109,487,000). Covers all full- and part-time employees who worked during, or received pay for, any part of the pay period including the 12th of the month. See also headnote, Table 611]

Industry	2002 NAICS code [1]	All employees (1,000)						Pecent change	
		1990	1995	2000	2001	2002	2003	1990-2000	2000-2003
Furniture and related products.........	337	601	607	680	642	604	574	13.0	-15.6
Household and institutional furniture ..	3371	398	399	440	416	400	382	10.6	-13.2
Office furniture and fixtures.........	3372	156	160	181	171	151	140	16.0	-23.1
Other furniture-related products	3379	47	49	58	56	54	52	23.1	-11.0
Miscellaneous manufacturing	339	690	715	733	715	688	663	6.2	-9.6
Medical equipment and supplies.....	3391	288	294	310	311	308	305	7.7	-1.7
Other miscellaneous manufacturing ..	3399	403	421	423	403	380	358	5.1	-15.3
Nondurable goods	(X)	6,959	6,869	6,388	6,107	5,775	5,555	-8.2	-13.0
Food manufacturing	311	1,507	1,560	1,553	1,551	1,526	1,519	3.0	-2.2
Animal food	3111	57	56	55	53	51	50	-4.2	-9.0
Grain and oilseed milling.........	3112	71	70	65	63	62	62	-9.1	-4.6
Sugar and confectionery products....	3113	99	100	92	89	84	84	-7.3	-9.0
Fruit and vegetable preserving and specialty................	3114	218	216	197	193	183	184	-9.5	-6.8
Fruit and vegetable canning and drying...............	31142	127	116	96	97	90	91	-24.2	-6.1
Dairy products	3115	145	137	136	137	137	136	-5.9	0.2
Animal slaughtering and processing ..	3116	427	476	507	516	517	515	18.6	1.7
Seafood product preparation and packaging................	3117	54	52	45	47	44	43	-17.2	-5.1
Bakeries and tortilla manufacturing ...	3118	292	304	306	303	297	293	4.9	-4.5
Other food products.............	3119	143	149	150	152	151	153	5.0	1.7
Beverages and tobacco products.....	312	218	203	207	209	207	201	-4.9	-3.1
Beverages	3121	173	164	175	177	174	170	1.2	-2.9
Textile mills	313	492	469	378	333	291	260	-23.1	-31.2
Fiber, yarn, and thread mills	3131	102	94	81	71	63	56	-20.5	-30.5
Fabric mills.................	3132	270	246	192	168	145	130	-29.0	-32.5
Textile and fabric finishing mills	3133	120	129	105	95	83	75	-12.1	-29.3
Textile product mills.............	314	209	219	216	206	195	180	3.3	-16.9
Textile furnishings mills..........	3141	127	128	129	121	116	105	1.3	-18.1
Other textile product mills	3149	82	91	88	84	78	75	6.4	-14.8
Apparel....................	315	929	814	497	427	360	313	-46.5	-37.1
Apparel knitting mills	3151	112	106	69	61	50	45	-38.4	-34.8
Cut and sew apparel	3152	776	666	394	335	283	245	-49.3	-37.8
Accessories and other apparel.....	3159	41	43	34	31	27	23	-16.9	-32.3
Leather and allied products..........	316	133	105	69	58	50	45	-48.3	-34.3
Footwear..................	3162	83	57	31	26	22	20	-62.8	-35.2
Leather and hide tanning and finishing and other leather prod..........	3169	51	48	38	32	28	25	-25.0	-33.4
Paper and paper products	322	647	640	605	578	547	519	-6.6	-14.2
Pulp, paper, and paperboard mills ..	3221	238	220	191	179	165	150	-19.7	-21.4
Converted paper products........	3222	409	419	413	398	382	369	1.1	-10.8
Printing and related support activities ...	323	809	817	807	768	707	680	-0.2	-15.7
Petroleum and coal products........	324	153	140	123	121	118	115	-19.4	-7.0
Chemicals...................	325	1,036	988	980	959	928	908	-5.3	-7.4
Basic chemicals	3251	249	228	188	181	170	163	-24.4	-13.4
Resin, rubber, and artificial fibers	3252	158	140	136	126	115	112	-14.2	-17.4
Agricultural chemicals..........	3253	52	50	48	46	45	40	-8.8	-15.5
Pharmaceuticals and medicines.....	3254	207	228	274	283	291	294	32.4	7.2
Paints, coatings, and adhesives	3255	85	79	79	75	72	69	-6.6	-12.8
Soaps, cleaning compounds, and toiletries.................	3256	132	126	129	127	121	118	-2.4	-7.9
Other chemical products and preparations	3259	153	137	127	120	114	111	-17.1	-12.2
Plastics and rubber products........	326	826	915	952	897	848	816	15.3	-14.3
Plastics products.............	3261	619	703	738	699	664	639	19.3	-13.4
Rubber products	3262	207	212	214	199	184	177	3.5	-17.4

X Not applicable. [1] Based on the North American Industry Classification System, 2002 (NAICS). See text, Section 13.

Source: U.S. Bureau of Labor Statistics, *Employment and Earnings*, monthly, March 2004 issue; and the Current Employment Statistics program Internet site <http://www.bls.gov/ces/home.htm>

No. 983. Average Hourly Earnings of Production Workers in Manufacturing Industries by State: 2001 and 2002

[In dollars. These data are now on a NAICS (North American Industry Classification System) basis and not comparable to previous data, which were based on the Standard Industrial Classification system]

State	2001	2002	State	2001	2002
United States	14.76	15.29	Missouri	16.11	16.79
			Montana	14.03	14.43
Alabama	12.76	13.10	Nebraska	13.64	14.05
Alaska	11.70	13.24	Nevada	13.79	14.62
Arizona	13.80	14.16	New Hampshire	13.98	14.20
Arkansas	12.90	13.30	New Jersey	14.74	15.20
California	14.69	14.89	New Mexico	13.27	13.43
Colorado	14.72	15.85	New York	16.24	16.74
Connecticut	16.42	17.25	North Carolina	12.81	13.18
Delaware	16.56	16.62	North Dakota	12.77	13.17
District of Columbia [1]	15.14	15.39	Ohio	16.79	17.49
Florida	12.68	13.30	Oklahoma	13.66	14.12
Georgia	12.50	13.39	Oregon	14.74	15.06
Hawaii	13.18	13.07			
			Pennsylvania	14.37	14.75
Idaho	13.85	13.80	Rhode Island	12.68	12.75
Illinois	14.66	14.99	South Carolina	13.79	14.00
Indiana	16.42	17.16	South Dakota	12.11	12.60
Iowa	14.67	15.31	Tennessee	12.88	13.15
Kansas	15.48	15.98	Texas	14.04	13.93
Kentucky	15.44	15.73	Utah	13.76	14.12
Louisiana	16.18	17.03	Vermont	14.18	14.33
Maine	14.71	15.55	Virginia	14.49	15.25
Maryland	14.56	15.21	Washington	17.96	18.15
Massachusetts	15.75	16.25	West Virginia	14.80	15.40
Michigan	19.45	20.48	Wisconsin	15.44	15.86
Minnesota	14.76	15.06	Wyoming	17.26	17.73
Mississippi	11.93	12.32			

[1] Washington PMSA (primary metropolitan statistical area).

Source: U.S. Bureau of Labor Statistics, *Employment and Earnings,* May 2003 issue and earlier issues.

No. 984. Manufacturing Full-Time Equivalent Employees and Wages by Industry: 1999 to 2002

[121,656 represents 121,656,000]

Industry	NAICS code [1]	Full-time equivalent (FTE) employees (1,000)				Wage and salary accruals per FTE worker (dol.)			
		1999	2000	2001	2002	1999	2000	2001	2002
All industries, total	(X)	121,656	124,319	124,632	123,382	36,754	38,846	39,660	40,318
Manufacturing	31-33	17,045	16,947	16,194	15,059	40,930	44,216	43,786	44,873
Durable goods	(X)	10,704	10,713	10,194	9,368	43,240	47,007	46,063	47,040
Wood products	321	618	606	576	567	28,858	30,360	30,652	31,078
Nonmetallic mineral products	327	535	545	535	511	36,641	38,879	39,226	40,417
Primary metals	331	609	611	560	499	44,464	45,745	45,801	46,591
Fabricated metal products	332	1,729	1,738	1,645	1,524	35,487	37,688	38,169	39,156
Machinery	333	1,433	1,420	1,348	1,212	43,846	46,882	46,021	47,150
Computer and electronic products	334	1,786	1,813	1,728	1,482	59,829	71,372	65,527	66,300
Electrical equipment, appliances, and components	335	552	568	548	490	40,204	42,732	40,864	42,080
Motor vehicles, bodies and trailers, and parts	3361-3363	1,289	1,283	1,198	1,141	47,838	49,727	48,741	51,445
Other transportation equipment	3364-3365	769	736	714	666	50,723	52,612	55,166	57,821
Furniture and related products	337	657	664	630	592	27,631	29,660	29,911	30,826
Miscellaneous manufacturing	339	727	728	712	685	36,135	38,504	39,634	40,552
Nondurable goods	(X)	6,341	6,235	6,000	5,691	37,030	39,420	39,917	41,307
Food and beverage and tobacco products	311-312	1,716	1,719	1,718	1,698	31,933	34,110	34,695	35,466
Textile mills and textile product mills	313-314	620	584	521	476	26,671	29,018	29,542	30,689
Apparel and leather and allied products	315	596	538	487	408	23,115	24,769	24,571	26,346
Paper products	322	607	596	564	530	43,652	45,578	46,909	48,608
Printing and related support activities	323	775	767	764	707	37,138	38,966	37,476	38,368
Petroleum and coal products	324	126	120	118	117	59,769	62,310	64,942	66,063
Chemical products	325	967	968	946	915	57,284	60,928	61,394	62,937
Plastics and rubber products	326	935	942	884	839	33,718	35,375	35,968	37,269

[1] North American Industry Classification System, 1997; see text, Section 15.

Source: U.S. Bureau of Economic Analysis, *Survey of Current Business,* March 2004. See also <http://www.bea.doc.gov /bea/dn/nipaweb/SelectTable.asp?Selected=N> (released 13 February 2004).

No. 985. Manufacturers' Shipments, Inventories, and New Orders: 1992 to 2003

[In billions of dollars (2,904 represents 2,904,000,000,000), except ratio. Based on a sample survey; for methodology, see publication cited below. These data are now on a NAICS (North American Industry Classification System) basis and not comparable to previous data, which were based on the Standard Industrial Classification system]

Year	Shipments	Inventories (Dec. 31)[1]	Ratio of inventories to shipments [2]	New orders (Dec. 31)	Unfilled orders (Dec. 31)
1992	2,904	370	1.57	(NA)	448
1993	3,020	371	1.51	2,960	422
1994	3,238	391	1.48	3,200	431
1995	3,480	415	1.47	3,427	443
1996	3,597	421	1.44	3,567	485
1997	3,835	433	1.39	3,780	508
1998	3,900	439	1.38	3,808	492
1999	4,032	453	1.38	3,957	501
2000	4,209	470	1.37	4,161	545
2001	3,970	442	1.37	3,875	513
2002	3,892	434	1.37	3,801	481
2003	3,999	428	1.32	3,950	502

NA Not available.   [1] Inventories are stated at current cost.   [2] Ratio based on December seasonally adjusted data.

Source: U.S. Census Bureau, *Current Industrial Reports, Manufacturers' Shipments, Inventories, and Orders: 1992-2002*, Series M3-1(02). See also <http://www.census.gov/prod/2003pubs/m3-02.pdf> (released August 2003) and <http://www.census.gov/indicator/www/m3/>.

No. 986. Ratios of Manufacturers' Inventories to Shipments and Unfilled Orders to Shipments by Industry Group: 1997 to 2003

[Based on a sample survey; for methodology, see publication cited below. These data are on a NAICS (North American Industry Classification System) basis and not comparable to previous data, which were based on the Standard Industrial Classification system]

Industry	1997	1998	1999	2000	2001	2002	2003
INVENTORIES TO SHIPMENTS RATIO							
All manufacturing industries	1.39	1.38	1.38	1.37	1.37	1.37	1.32
Durable goods	1.57	1.56	1.53	1.55	1.57	1.53	1.47
Wood products	1.26	1.26	1.26	1.32	1.34	1.33	1.24
Nonmetallic mineral products	1.25	1.17	1.17	1.23	1.21	1.29	1.27
Primary metals	1.60	1.59	1.69	1.68	1.67	1.67	1.58
Fabricated metals	1.60	1.55	1.56	1.55	1.55	1.51	1.52
Machinery	2.04	2.01	2.05	2.08	2.06	2.04	1.97
Computers and electronic products	1.51	1.41	1.42	1.55	1.59	1.57	1.37
Electrical equipment, appliances, and components	1.51	1.45	1.42	1.44	1.47	1.47	1.47
Transportation equipment	1.44	1.57	1.42	1.34	1.39	1.31	1.31
Furniture and related products	1.43	1.34	1.35	1.35	1.32	1.34	1.30
Miscellaneous products	1.92	1.85	1.89	1.90	1.87	1.83	1.74
Nondurable goods	1.16	1.14	1.18	1.14	1.13	1.18	1.14
Food products	0.85	0.82	0.86	0.88	0.85	0.87	0.86
Beverages and tobacco products	1.71	1.63	1.55	1.51	1.47	1.58	1.65
Textile mills	1.41	1.45	1.52	1.49	1.48	1.38	1.51
Textile product mills	1.76	1.63	1.62	1.76	1.83	1.72	1.76
Apparel	1.71	1.75	1.89	1.89	1.68	1.58	1.62
Leather and allied products	1.99	2.05	2.18	2.13	2.10	1.91	1.92
Paper products	1.21	1.15	1.16	1.11	1.16	1.17	1.09
Printing	0.88	0.80	0.81	0.79	0.77	0.78	0.78
Petroleum and coal products	0.82	0.84	0.90	0.71	0.74	0.90	0.75
Basic chemicals	1.31	1.31	1.38	1.40	1.39	1.44	1.38
Plastics and rubber products	1.22	1.19	1.20	1.21	1.18	1.30	1.33
UNFILLED ORDERS TO SHIPMENTS RATIO							
All manufacturing industries	1.61	1.53	1.51	1.57	1.56	1.50	1.52
Durable goods	2.87	2.67	2.61	2.78	2.86	2.74	2.83
Primary metals	1.94	1.56	1.69	1.45	1.47	1.33	1.51
Fabricated metals	2.08	2.00	2.02	2.02	1.93	1.80	1.90
Machinery	2.60	2.40	2.50	2.51	2.46	2.04	2.08
Computers and electronic products	2.49	2.57	2.93	3.07	3.56	3.66	3.71
Electrical equipment, appliances, and components	1.65	1.56	1.78	1.75	1.54	1.62	1.61
Transportation equipment	5.59	5.00	4.24	4.93	5.03	4.72	4.89
Furniture and related products	1.38	1.19	1.27	1.14	1.09	0.94	0.96
Miscellaneous products	0.37	0.46	0.49	0.62	0.44	0.45	0.58

Source: U.S. Census Bureau, *Current Industrial Reports, Manufacturers' Shipments, Inventories, and Orders: 1992-2002*, Series M3-1(02). See also <http://www.census.gov/prod/2003pubs/m3-02.pdf> (released August 2003) and <http://www.census.gov/indicator/www/m3/>.

[In millions of dollars (3,834,699 represents $3,834,699,000,000). Based on a sample survey; for methodology, see publication cited below. These data are on a NAICS (North American Industry Classification System) basis and not comparable to previous data, which were based on the Standard Industrial Classification system]

Industry	1997	1998	1999	2000	2001	2002	2003
SHIPMENTS							
All manufacturing industries	3,834,699	3,899,813	4,031,887	4,208,584	3,970,499	3,891,753	3,999,124
Durable goods	2,147,384	2,231,588	2,326,736	2,373,688	2,174,406	2,131,404	2,150,638
Wood products	88,470	91,175	97,311	93,669	87,250	87,652	93,238
Nonmetallic mineral products.	86,465	92,501	96,153	97,329	94,861	88,222	87,500
Primary metals	168,118	166,109	156,648	156,598	138,246	135,930	131,307
Fabricated metals	242,812	253,720	257,071	268,213	253,113	252,232	245,469
Machinery	270,687	280,651	276,904	291,548	266,554	255,561	253,516
Computers and electronic products.	439,380	443,768	467,059	510,639	429,471	392,026	418,651
Electrical equipment, appliances, and components	112,116	116,024	118,313	125,443	114,068	103,673	101,415
Transportation equipment	575,307	612,882	676,328	639,861	602,495	624,129	618,670
Furniture and related products	64,299	69,616	72,659	75,107	72,147	69,999	69,870
Miscellaneous products	99,730	105,142	108,290	115,281	116,201	121,890	131,002
Nondurable goods	1,687,315	1,668,225	1,705,151	1,834,896	1,796,093	1,760,349	1,848,486
Food products	421,737	428,479	426,001	435,229	451,385	450,183	461,064
Beverages and tobacco products	96,971	102,359	106,920	111,692	118,786	109,832	105,310
Textile mills	58,707	57,416	54,306	52,112	45,681	43,170	39,775
Textile product mills	31,052	31,137	32,689	33,654	31,971	34,232	35,247
Apparel	68,018	64,932	62,305	60,339	54,598	53,621	52,970
Leather and allied products.	10,877	10,186	9,653	9,647	8,834	10,408	10,903
Paper products	150,296	154,984	156,915	165,298	155,845	151,530	159,611
Printing	97,485	100,297	101,536	104,396	100,792	97,968	95,036
Petroleum and coal products.	177,394	137,957	162,620	235,134	219,074	206,879	244,097
Basic chemicals	415,617	416,742	420,321	449,159	438,410	424,143	459,110
Plastics and rubber products	159,161	163,736	171,885	178,236	170,717	178,383	185,363
INVENTORIES (Dec. 31)							
All manufacturing industries	433,451	438,845	452,803	470,084	441,527	433,756	428,176
Durable goods	273,330	282,698	288,362	298,232	275,855	264,446	255,969
Wood products	9,441	9,684	10,289	10,329	9,664	9,566	9,598
Nonmetallic mineral products.	8,840	8,877	9,279	9,799	9,440	9,306	9,051
Primary metals	22,728	22,305	22,309	22,199	19,502	19,144	17,420
Fabricated metals	31,776	32,215	32,800	34,085	32,145	31,227	30,504
Machinery	44,490	45,728	46,050	49,151	44,532	42,296	40,512
Computers and electronic products.	53,045	50,066	52,838	63,024	54,598	49,287	45,945
Electrical equipment, appliances, and components	13,530	13,503	13,510	14,505	13,488	12,234	11,949
Transportation equipment	66,414	77,014	76,781	69,199	67,188	65,769	65,146
Furniture and related products	7,527	7,599	7,983	8,261	7,765	7,632	7,375
Miscellaneous products	15,539	15,707	16,523	17,680	17,533	17,985	18,469
Nondurable goods	160,121	156,147	164,441	171,852	165,672	169,310	172,207
Food products	30,152	29,419	30,650	31,882	31,865	32,534	33,082
Beverages and tobacco products	14,188	14,294	14,167	14,331	14,855	14,717	14,725
Textile mills	6,640	6,684	6,648	6,243	5,411	4,759	4,817
Textile product mills	4,331	4,024	4,219	4,698	4,648	4,691	4,951
Apparel	9,267	9,114	9,454	9,170	7,363	6,784	6,901
Leather and allied products.	1,718	1,667	1,675	1,634	1,479	1,580	1,673
Paper products	15,042	14,688	15,034	15,205	14,950	14,621	14,352
Printing	6,621	6,212	6,394	6,445	6,046	5,985	5,754
Petroleum and coal products.	11,492	9,102	11,375	12,840	12,479	14,302	13,973
Basic chemicals	44,691	44,943	47,806	51,623	50,052	50,363	51,917
Plastics and rubber products	15,979	16,000	17,019	17,781	16,524	18,974	20,062
NEW ORDERS							
All manufacturing industries	3,779,835	3,808,143	3,957,242	4,161,472	3,875,329	3,800,930	3,949,998
Durable goods	2,092,520	2,139,918	2,252,091	2,326,576	2,079,236	2,040,581	2,101,512
Wood products	88,470	91,175	97,311	93,669	87,250	87,652	93,238
Nonmetallic mineral products.	86,465	92,501	96,153	97,329	94,861	88,222	87,500
Primary metals	171,407	160,743	156,968	153,625	136,291	134,089	132,850
Fabricated metals	247,839	253,847	258,116	270,021	248,872	249,408	246,590
Machinery	272,998	278,100	278,277	294,608	260,392	244,559	253,978
Computers and electronic products.	363,635	372,433	402,216	436,415	363,049	325,378	358,127
Electrical equipment, appliances, and components	113,411	115,711	120,774	126,196	110,628	103,013	101,038
Transportation equipment	581,780	600,205	660,215	663,326	591,756	617,098	625,535
Furniture and related products	66,256	69,098	73,393	74,532	71,614	68,959	69,972
Miscellaneous products	100,259	106,105	108,668	116,855	114,523	122,203	132,684
Nondurable goods	1,687,315	1,668,225	1,705,151	1,834,896	1,796,093	1,760,349	1,848,486

Source: U.S. Census Bureau, Current Industrial Reports, Manufacturers' Shipments, Inventories, and Orders: 1992-2002, Series M3-1(02). See also <http://www.census.gov/prod/2003pubs/m3-02.pdf> (released August 2003) and <http://www.census.gov /indicator/www/m3/>.

No. 988. Value of Manufacturers' Shipments, Inventories, and New Orders by Market Grouping: 1997 to 2003

[In millions of dollars (3,834,699 represents 3,834,699,000,000). Based on a sample survey; for methodology, see publication cited below. These data are on a NAICS (North American Industry Classification System) basis and not comparable to previous data, which were based on the Standard Industrial Classification system]

Market grouping	1997	1998	1999	2000	2001	2002	2003
SHIPMENTS							
All manufacturing industries	3,834,699	3,899,813	4,031,887	4,208,584	3,970,499	3,891,753	3,999,124
Consumer goods	1,369,992	1,364,326	1,438,519	1,514,377	1,493,707	1,472,647	1,529,699
Consumer durable goods	371,669	385,918	426,337	405,308	380,734	396,590	400,023
Consumer nondurable goods	998,323	978,408	1,012,182	1,109,069	1,112,973	1,076,057	1,129,676
Aircraft and parts	100,126	116,812	120,242	111,658	118,226	111,726	107,161
Defense aircraft and parts	27,472	26,938	27,719	24,560	27,928	35,127	39,856
Nondefense aircraft and parts	72,654	89,874	92,523	87,098	90,298	76,599	67,305
Construction materials and supplies	399,880	418,756	434,138	444,812	424,517	419,040	421,903
Motor vehicles and parts	421,573	439,590	498,716	471,180	427,175	450,136	442,840
Computers and related products	110,055	114,482	113,162	110,242	89,529	81,449	93,449
Information technology industries	349,846	362,564	374,384	399,751	353,237	319,391	337,316
Nondefense capital goods	702,971	747,046	768,799	808,345	727,980	673,223	683,195
Excluding aircraft	665,074	695,717	713,042	757,617	677,991	634,549	652,339
Defense capital goods	76,261	74,690	70,955	67,051	74,019	79,825	91,883
Durables excluding capital goods	1,368,152	1,409,852	1,486,982	1,498,292	1,372,407	1,378,356	1,375,560
INVENTORIES (Dec. 31)							
All manufacturing industries	433,451	438,845	452,803	470,084	441,527	433,756	428,176
Consumer goods	118,980	116,715	123,218	129,478	126,855	129,445	131,660
Consumer durable goods	25,251	25,137	26,307	27,438	25,704	26,289	25,932
Consumer nondurable goods	93,729	91,578	96,911	102,040	101,151	103,156	105,728
Aircraft and parts	37,509	46,921	42,599	36,091	36,393	34,978	34,293
Defense aircraft and parts	8,380	11,376	11,052	9,423	9,384	9,610	11,296
Nondefense aircraft and parts	29,129	35,545	31,547	26,668	27,009	25,368	22,997
Construction materials and supplies	44,877	45,617	47,510	49,389	46,344	46,196	45,350
Motor vehicles and parts	20,298	20,764	22,102	22,283	19,653	20,256	19,604
Computers and related products	10,289	8,017	7,963	8,350	6,341	5,975	5,639
Information technology industries	46,117	43,592	44,375	50,795	46,650	41,802	38,432
Nondefense capital goods	117,932	122,415	121,653	127,162	119,258	109,106	102,129
Excluding aircraft	95,226	94,045	96,254	106,669	98,483	90,539	85,879
Defense capital goods	14,814	17,775	19,754	17,153	17,677	17,705	19,270
Durables excluding capital goods	140,584	142,508	146,955	153,917	138,920	137,635	134,570
NEW ORDERS							
All manufacturing industries	3,779,835	3,808,143	3,957,242	4,161,472	3,875,329	3,800,930	3,949,998
Consumer goods	1,372,919	1,364,268	1,440,903	1,515,799	1,491,143	1,471,270	1,530,443
Consumer durable goods	374,596	385,860	428,721	406,730	378,170	395,213	400,767
Consumer nondurable goods	998,323	978,408	1,012,182	1,109,069	1,112,973	1,076,057	1,129,676
Aircraft and parts	109,077	108,004	107,336	130,575	111,432	105,382	105,544
Defense aircraft and parts	23,280	23,854	25,717	31,326	37,311	40,087	44,662
Nondefense aircraft and parts	85,797	84,150	81,619	99,249	74,121	65,295	60,882
Construction materials and supplies	403,860	419,330	435,034	446,792	420,300	418,315	422,639
Motor vehicles and parts	422,427	440,934	499,527	468,470	425,580	450,183	444,327
Computers and related products	107,564	115,806	114,481	107,656	89,320	82,398	94,130
Information technology industries	352,700	365,723	389,160	409,500	350,726	314,473	349,234
Nondefense capital goods	728,362	745,600	772,703	831,335	700,027	647,894	689,340
Excluding aircraft	676,119	698,279	728,089	767,754	665,899	617,878	663,352
Defense capital goods	64,497	64,127	67,900	79,598	83,033	79,264	104,824
Durables excluding capital goods	1,299,661	1,330,191	1,411,488	1,415,643	1,296,176	1,313,423	1,307,348

Source: U.S. Census Bureau, *Current Industrial Reports, Manufacturers' Shipments, Inventories, and Orders: 1992-2002,* Series M3-1(02). See also <http://www.census.gov/prod/2003pubs/m3-02.pdf> (released August 2003) and <http://www.census.gov /indicator/www/m3/>.

No. 989. Finances and Profits of Manufacturing Corporations: 1990 to 2003

[In billions of dollars (2,811 represents $2,811,000,000,000). Data exclude estimates for corporations with less than $250,000 in assets at time of sample selection. For 1990-2001, based on Standard Industrial Classification system; thereafter, based on North American Industry Classification Sytem. See Table 760 for individual industry data]

Item	1990	1995	1997	1998	1999	2000	2001 [1]	2001 [2]	2002 [2]	2003 [2]
Net sales	2,811	3,528	3,920	3,949	4,149	4,548	4,308	4,295	4,217	4,382
Net operating profit	173	268	298	298	317	348	185	186	225	232
Net profit										
Before taxes	160	274	331	315	355	381	82	83	196	307
After taxes	112	198	245	234	258	275	36	36	135	234
Cash dividends	62	81	108	121	104	132	102	103	106	106
Net income retained in business	49	117	136	114	154	143	-67	-66	28	128

[1] Based on Standard Industrial Classification system. [2] Based on the North American Industry Classification System; see Text, Section 15.

Source: U.S. Census Bureau, *Quarterly Financial Report for Manufacturing, Mining, and Trade Corporations.* See also <http://www.census.gov/prod/2004pubs/qfr02-q4.pdf> (released April 2004).

[Corporations and assets as of end of 4th quarter; profits for entire year (2,629,458 represents $2,629,458,000,000). Through 2000 based on Standard Industrial Classification code; beginning 2001 based on North American Industry Classification System. For corporations above a certain asset value based on complete canvass. The asset value for complete canvass was raised in 1988 to $50 million and in 1995 to $250 million. Asset sizes less than these values are sampled, except as noted. For details regarding methodology, see source for first quarter, 1988. Minus sign (-) indicates loss]

Year	Unit	Total	Asset-size class						
			Under $10 mil. [1]	$10-$25 mil. [1]	$25-$50 mil. [1]	$50-$100 mil. [1]	$100-$250 mil. [1]	$250-$1 bil. [1]	$1 bil. and over [1]
Assets:									
1990	Mil. dol.	2,629,458	142,498	74,477	55,914	72,554	123,967	287,512	1,872,536
1991	Mil. dol.	2,688,422	140,056	70,567	58,549	72,694	127,748	295,743	1,923,066
1992	Mil. dol.	2,798,625	143,766	70,446	65,718	75,967	132,742	302,287	2,007,698
1993	Mil. dol.	2,904,869	149,763	72,854	61,243	81,389	134,388	317,774	2,087,457
1994	Mil. dol.	3,080,231	148,751	81,505	66,405	82,116	138,950	358,100	2,204,404
1995	Mil. dol.	3,345,229	155,618	87,011	68,538	87,262	159,133	370,263	2,417,403
1996	Mil. dol.	3,574,407	163,928	87,096	69,722	93,205	156,702	398,651	2,605,102
1997	Mil. dol.	3,746,797	167,921	87,398	76,034	85,186	157,130	397,559	2,775,573
1998	Mil. dol.	3,967,309	170,068	87,937	69,627	86,816	148,060	419,153	2,985,647
1999	Mil. dol.	4,382,814	170,058	85,200	67,352	97,810	138,143	398,881	3,425,370
2000	Mil. dol.	4,852,106	171,666	85,482	72,122	90,866	149,714	389,537	3,892,720
2001	Mil. dol.	4,747,789	169,701	84,664	67,493	88,088	131,617	393,752	3,812,474
2002	Mil. dol.	4,823,219	166,191	82,369	62,654	81,667	134,821	407,423	3,888,095
2003	Mil. dol.	4,978,403	161,720	81,454	61,575	75,314	129,529	395,977	4,072,834
Net profit: [2]									
1990	Mil. dol.	110,128	8,527	5,160	2,769	2,661	3,525	7,110	80,377
1991	Mil. dol.	66,407	6,820	4,271	2,564	1,704	1,707	5,027	44,316
1992	Mil. dol.	22,085	9,567	4,748	3,245	3,034	4,553	5,919	-8,979
1993	Mil. dol.	83,156	11,195	5,415	3,439	3,218	3,584	4,555	51,750
1994	Mil. dol.	174,874	14,131	7,057	4,072	4,996	6,745	14,626	123,250
1995	Mil. dol.	198,151	13,224	5,668	3,767	5,771	7,000	16,549	146,172
1996	Mil. dol.	224,869	15,802	6,872	4,266	5,664	7,935	16,059	168,271
1997	Mil. dol.	244,505	17,948	8,383	4,153	4,675	7,074	18,433	183,836
1998	Mil. dol.	234,386	18,350	6,421	3,790	4,681	5,610	14,364	181,170
1999	Mil. dol.	257,805	17,398	7,618	3,504	4,798	4,795	12,756	206,934
2000	Mil. dol.	275,313	16,578	6,820	3,403	2,742	3,510	15,121	227,137
2001	Mil. dol.	36,168	8,387	3,366	-408	403	-543	-6,732	31,746
2002	Mil. dol.	134,686	10,003	2,784	807	1,699	3,356	-1,227	117,262
2003	Mil. dol.	233,578	9,408	3,330	1,967	2,868	3,238	5,433	206,778

NA Not available.   [1] Excludes estimates for corporations with less than $250,000 in assets at time of sample selection.
[2] After taxes.

Source: U.S. Census Bureau, *Quarterly Financial Report for Manufacturing, Mining and Trade Corporations.* See also <http://www.census.gov/prod/2004pubs/qfr02-q4.pdf>(released April 2004).

No. 991. Manufacturing Corporations—Selected Finances: 1990 to 2003

[In billions of dollars (2,811 represents $2,811,000,000,000). Data are not necessarily comparable from year to year due to changes in accounting procedures, industry classifications, sampling procedures, etc.; for detail, see source. Through 2000 based on Standard Industrial Classification code; beginning 2001 based on North American Industry Classification System (NAICS). See text, Section 15]

Year	All manufacturing corporations			Durable goods industries			Nondurable goods industries		
		Profits [1]			Profits [1]			Profits [1]	
	Sales	Before taxes	After taxes	Sales	Before taxes	After taxes	Sales	Before taxes	After taxes
1990	2,811	158	110	1,357	57	41	1,454	101	69
1991	2,761	99	66	1,304	14	7	1,457	85	59
1992 [2]	2,890	31	22	1,390	-34	-24	1,500	65	46
1993	3,015	118	83	1,490	39	27	1,525	79	56
1994	3,256	244	175	1,658	121	87	1,598	123	88
1995	3,528	275	198	1,808	131	94	1,721	144	104
1996	3,758	307	225	1,942	147	106	1,816	160	119
1997	3,922	331	244	2,076	167	121	1,847	164	123
1998	3,949	315	234	2,169	175	128	1,781	140	107
1999	4,149	355	258	2,314	199	140	1,835	157	117
2000	4,548	381	275	2,457	191	132	2,091	190	144
2001	4,295	83	36	2,321	-69	-76	1,974	152	112
2002	4,217	196	135	1,826	45	21	1,956	149	113
2003	4,382	307	234	2,268	114	86	2,114	193	147

[1] Beginning 1998, profits before and after income taxes reflect inclusion of minority stockholders' interest in net income before and after income taxes.   [2] Data for 1992 (most significantly 1992:I qtr.) reflect the early adoption of Financial Accounting Standards Board Statement 106 (Employer's Accounting for Post-Retirement Benefits Other Than Pensions) by a large number of companies during the fourth quarter of 1992. Data for 1993: I qtr. also reflect adoption of Statement 106. Corporations must show the cumulative effect of a change in accounting principle in the first quarter of the year in which the change is adopted.

Source: U.S. Census Bureau, *Quarterly Financial Report for Manufacturing, Mining and Trade Corporations.* See also <http://www.census.gov/prod/2004pubs/qfr02-q4.pdf> (released April 2004).

No. 992. Tobacco Products—Summary: 1990 to 2003

[Production data are for calendar years. Excludes cigars produced in customs bonded manufacturing warehouses]

Item	Unit	1990	1995	1997	1998	1999	2000	2001	2002	2003
PRODUCTION										
Cigarettes, total	Billions	710.0	747.0	720.0	680.0	607.0	565.0	562.4	532.0	497.0
Nonfilter tip	Billions	23.0	15.0	11.9	11.5	8.0	7.3	6.1	5.4	5.1
Filter tip	Billions	687.0	732.0	707.7	669.0	599.0	557.7	556.3	526.6	491.9
Cigars	Billions	1.9	2.1	2.3	2.8	2.9	2.8	3.7	3.8	3.8
Tobacco [1]	Mil. lb.	142.0	131.0	134.0	131.0	133.0	133.0	129.9	132.6	135.3
Smoking	Mil. lb.	16.4	12.2	11.4	12.5	15.0	14.0	12.8	15.5	18.9
Chewing tobacco	Mil. lb.	72.9	62.9	58.1	53.3	51.0	49.0	47.0	44.5	41.7
Snuff	Mil. lb.	53.1	60.2	64.3	65.5	67.0	70.0	70.1	72.6	74.7
EXPORTS										
Cigarettes	Bil. pieces	164.3	231.1	217.0	201.3	151.4	147.9	133.9	127.4	121.4
Cigars	Bil. cigars	72.0	94.0	86.0	93.0	84.0	113.0	124.0	122.7	155.0
Smoking tobacco	Bil. lb.	0.8	0.3	0.8	1.1	1.6	0.5	11.0	7.9	0.7
IMPORTS										
Cigarettes	Bil. pieces	1.4	3.0	3.2	4.3	8.7	11.3	14.7	20.8	23.1
Cigars	Bil. cigars	111.0	195.0	448.1	582.3	463.4	497.0	543.4	413.5	401.1
Smoking tobacco	Bil. lb.	2.9	4.2	4.3	4.3	4.3	4.2	1.9	2.1	2.0
CONSUMPTION										
Consumption per person [2]	Lb. [3]	5.6	4.7	4.5	4.5	4.3	4.2	4.1	4.2	4.1
Cigarettes	1,000	2.8	3.0	2.4	2.3	2.1	2.0	2.0	2.0	1.9
EXPENDITURES										
Consumer expenditures, total	Bil. dol.	43.8	48.7	52.2	57.3	72.1	77.5	82.9	88.2	86.6
Cigarettes	Bil. dol.	41.6	45.8	48.7	53.2	68.3	72.9	77.8	82.8	81.1
Cigars	Bil. dol.	0.7	1.0	1.2	1.6	1.8	1.8	2.1	2.2	2.3
Other	Bil. dol.	1.5	2.5	2.2	2.4	2.7	2.7	3.0	3.1	3.2

[1] Smoking and chewing tobaccos and snuff output. [2] Based on estimated population 18 years old and over, as of July 1, including Armed Forces abroad. [3] Unstemmed processing weight equivalent.

Source: U.S. Dept. of Agriculture, Economic Research Service, *Tobacco Situation and Outlook*, quarterly. See also <http://usda.mannlib.cornell.edu/reports/erssor/specialty/tbs-bb/2004/tbs256.pdf> (released 22 April 2004).

No. 993. Cotton, Wool, and Manmade Fibers—Consumption by End-Use: 1990 to 2002

[14,011 represents 14,011,000,000. Represents products manufactured by U.S. mills. Excludes glass fiber]

Year	Cotton Total (mil. lb.)	Cotton Total (mil. lb.)	Cotton Percent of end-use	Wool Total (mil. lb.)	Wool Percent of end-use	Mfg. fibers Total (mil. lb.)	Mfg. fibers Percent of end-use	Artificial [1] Total (mil. lb.)	Artificial [1] Percent of end-use	Synthetic [2] Total (mil. lb.)	Synthetic [2] Percent of end-use
Total:											
1990	14,011	4,699	33.5	185	1.3	9,127	65.1	599	4.3	8,528	60.9
1995	16,815	5,508	32.8	184	1.1	11,123	66.1	540	3.2	10,583	62.9
1999	18,036	5,332	29.6	141	0.8	12,563	69.7	330	1.8	11,902	66.0
2000	17,989	5,128	28.5	131	0.7	12,730	70.8	303	1.7	11,776	65.5
2001	16,237	4,618	28.4	116	0.7	11,503	70.8	265	1.6	10,874	67.0
2002	15,595	4,103	26.3	96	0.6	11,397	73.1	(NA)	(NA)	(NA)	(NA)
Apparel:											
1990	5,204	2,897	55.7	118	2.3	2,189	42.1	287	5.5	1,902	36.5
1995	6,877	3,640	52.9	132	1.9	3,106	45.2	306	4.4	2,800	40.7
1999	6,445	3,278	50.9	89	1.4	3,077	47.7	172	2.7	2,894	44.9
2000	6,153	3,089	50.2	79	1.3	2,985	48.5	150	2.4	2,822	45.9
2001	5,436	2,648	48.7	73	1.3	2,715	49.9	135	2.5	2,571	47.3
2002	4,773	2,232	46.8	63	1.3	2,478	51.9	(NA)	(NA)	(NA)	(NA)
Home textiles:											
1990	2,235	1,325	59.3	14	0.6	896	40.1	104	4.7	792	35.4
1995	2,530	1,487	58.8	12	0.5	1,030	40.7	93	3.7	937	37.0
1999	2,831	1,656	58.5	15	0.5	1,160	41.0	66	2.3	1,080	38.1
2000	2,866	1,644	57.4	15	0.5	1,207	42.1	65	2.3	1,122	39.1
2001	2,669	1,587	59.5	13	0.5	1,070	40.1	53	2.0	972	36.4
2002	2,521	1,515	60.1	10	0.4	996	39.5	(NA)	(NA)	(NA)	(NA)
Floor coverings:											
1990	3,075	18	0.6	21	0.7	3,036	98.7	-	0.0	3,036	98.7
1995	3,731	25	0.7	25	0.7	3,681	98.7	-	0.0	3,681	98.7
1999	4,469	27	0.6	25	0.6	4,417	98.8	-	0.0	4,180	93.5
2000	4,518	31	0.7	24	0.5	4,464	98.8	-	0.0	4,048	89.6
2001	4,048	30	0.7	20	0.5	3,998	98.8	-	0.0	3,801	93.9
2002	4,228	29	0.7	14	0.3	4,185	99.0	(NA)	(NA)	(NA)	(NA)
Industrial: [3]											
1990	2,965	313	10.6	10	0.3	2,642	89.1	179	6.0	2,463	83.1
1995	3,677	355	9.7	15	0.4	3,307	89.9	141	3.8	3,165	86.1
1999	4,292	372	8.7	13	0.3	3,908	91.1	93	2.2	3,750	87.4
2000	4,452	364	8.2	13	0.3	4,076	91.6	89	2.0	3,785	85.0
2001	4,084	354	8.7	10	0.2	3,721	91.6	89	2.0	3,785	85.0
2002	4,073	326	8.0	8	0.2	3,738	91.8	(NA)	(NA)	(NA)	(NA)

- Represents or rounds to zero. NA Not available. [1] Rayon and acetate. [2] Nylon, polyester, acrylic, and olefin. [3] Includes consumer-type products.

Source: Fiber Economics Bureau, Inc., Arlington, VA, *Fiber Organon*, monthly (copyright).

No. 994. Broadwoven and Knit Fabrics—Shipments and Foreign Trade: 2002

[2,946,508 represents 2,946,508,000. Fabric blends as shown in the report are reported based on the chief weight of the fiber; whereas, fabrics blends as shown for imports are based on the chief value of the fiber.]

Product description	Manufac-turers' ship-ments (quantity)	Imports for consumption		Percent imports to manufac-turers' ship-ments	Exports of domestic merchandise		Percent exports to manufac-turers' ship-ments
		Quantity	Value [1] ($1,000)		Quantity	Value ($1,000)	
BROADWOVEN FABRICS (quantity 1,000 sq. meters)							
Cotton fabrics [2]	2,946,508	1,877,612	1,839,632	63.7	753,161	1,328,474	25.6
Manmade fiber fabrics	7,536,164	1,673,022	1,314,539	22.2	559,220	1,274,352	7.4
Silk fabrics	(D)	31,417	240,871	(D)	2,780	19,506	(D)
Wool fabrics	23,224	23,283	184,223	100.3	10,324	62,095	44.5
KNIT FABRICS (quantity in 1,000 kilograms)							
Total	529,266	169,998	1,082,208	32.1	187,967	1,221,455	35.5
Pile fabrics	40,122	24,348	174,556	60.7	38,944	225,151	97.1
Elastic fabric	30,632	41,951	389,191	(S)	39,413	403,704	128.7
Other warp knit fabrics	49,710	7,324	56,717	14.7	16,018	124,114	32.2
Other narrow knit fabrics	11,807	3,267	23,692	27.7	1,370	12,923	11.6
Other knit fabrics	396,994	93,108	438,052	23.5	92,222	455,563	23.2

NA Not available. D Data withheld to avoid disclosing figures for individual companies. S Does not meet publication standards. [1] Dollar value represents the c.i.f. (cost, insurance, and freight) at the first port of entry in the United States plus calculated import duty. [2] Includes all cotton and chiefly cotton mixed with manmade fiber.
Source: U.S. Census Bureau, *Current Industrial Reports*, Series MQ313 and MA313K, annual. See also <http://www.census.gov/industry/1/mq313t025.pdf> (issued June 2003) and <http://www.census.gov/industry/1/ma313k02.pdf> (issued July 2003).

No. 995. Footwear—Production, Foreign Trade, and Apparent Consumption: 2002

[Quantity in thousands of pairs (60,327 represents 60,327,000 pairs), value in thousands of dollars (315,587 represents $315,587,000)]

Product description	Manufac-turers' ship-ments (quantity)	Exports of domestic merchandise		Percent exports to domestic produc-tion	Imports for consumption		Apparent consump-tion (quantity)	Percent imports to apparent consump-tion
		Quantity	Value		Quantity	Value		
Total	60,327	26,291	315,587	43.6	1,508,305	13,215,517	1,542,341	97.8
Rubber or plastic uppers and rubber or plastic	2,712	10,170	108,197	375.0	521,015	2,968,166	513,557	101.5
Waterproof	2,464	824	8,686	33.4	11,037	63,139	12,677	87.1
Not waterproof	248	9,346	99,511	3,768.5	509,978	2,905,027	500,880	101.8
Leather uppers	18,248	7,861	157,752	43.1	666,889	9,023,999	677,276	98.5
Athletic	1,576	4,557	82,239	289.1	507,097	5,910,167	504,116	100.6
Leather soles	5,442	1,686	45,288	31.0	43,128	1,139,015	46,884	92.0
Other soles	11,230	1,618	30,225	14.4	116,664	1,974,817	126,276	92.4
Fabric uppers	36,163	8,260	49,638	174.3	320,401	1,223,352	348,304	92.0

Source: U.S. Census Bureau, *Current Industrial Reports*, Series MA316A, annual. See also <http://www.census.gov/industry/1/ma316a02.pdf> (released June 2003).

No. 996. Pharmaceutical Preparations—Value of Shipments: 1990 to 2002

[In millions of dollars (33,954 represents 33,954,000,000]

Product description	Product code	1990	1995	1999	2000	2001	2002
Pharmaceutical preparations, except biologicals	(X)	33,954	48,864	70,417	79,262	90,182	100,636
Affecting neoplasms, endocrine systems, and metabolic disease	3254121100	2,743	4,076	7,988	9,784	14,819	17,480
Acting on the central nervous system and sense organs	3254124100	7,219	9,228	14,881	18,508	18,975	24,322
Acting on the cardiovascular system	3254127100	4,815	5,988	9,601	8,993	9,798	10,318
Acting on the respiratory system	325412A100	3,724	5,196	8,155	10,179	11,692	12,514
Acting on the digestive system	325412D100	4,840	8,593	8,741	10,046	12,616	13,334
Acting on the skin.	325412G100	1,558	2,171	2,798	2,941	2,708	2,817
Vitamin, nutrient, and hematinic preps. . . .	325412L100	2,588	4,812	6,161	5,676	5,884	6,000
Affecting parasitic and infective disease . . .	325412P100	5,411	7,196	9,778	11,037	11,193	11,336
Pharmaceutical preps. for veterinary use . .	325412T100	1,057	1,605	2,314	2,096	2,497	2,515

X Not applicable.
Source: U.S. Census Bureau, 1990, *Current Industrial Reports*, Series MA28G; thereafter, MA325G(01)-1. See also <http://www.census.gov/industry/1/ma325g02.pdf> (released July 2003).

No. 997. Inorganic Chemicals and Fertilizers—Production: 1995 to 2002

[17,402 represents 17,402,000]

Product description	Unit	1995	1998	1999	2000	2001	2002
INORGANIC FERTILIZERS							
Ammonia, synthetic anhydrous	1,000 sh. tons....	17,402	18,475	17,337	15,809	12,227	13,598
Ammonium nitrate, original solution	1,000 sh. tons....	8,489	9,079	7,630	7,979	6,431	6,973
Ammonium sulfate	1,000 sh. tons....	2,647	2,787	2,875	2,808	2,588	2,848
Urea (100%)	1,000 sh. tons....	8,117	8,865	8,907	7,682	6,702	7,758
Nitric acid (100%)...............	1,000 sh. tons....	8,839	9,285	8,945	8,708	7,074	7,651
Phosphoric acid (100% P2O5)	1,000 sh. tons....	13,134	13,891	13,708	12,492	11,546	11,846
Sulfuric acid, gross (100%)	1,000 sh. tons....	47,519	48,513	44,756	43,643	40,064	39,196
Superphosphates and other fertilizer materials (100% P2O5)	1,000 sh. tons....	10,364	10,260	9,133	8,899	8,109	8,545
INORGANIC CHEMICALS							
Chlorine gas	1,000 metric tons..	12,395	11,650	12,114	14,000	11,489	11,684
Sodium hydroxide, total liquid	1,000 metric tons..	11,408	11,896	11,974	11,523	9,813	9,461
Potassium hydroxide liquid	1,000 metric tons..	(D)	450	430	539	465	470
Finished sodium bicarbonate	1,000 metric tons..	520	493	505	536	513	535
Titanium dioxide, composite and pure	1,000 metric tons..	1,382	1,323	1,355	1,547	1,327	1,409
Hydrochloric acid	1,000 metric tons..	3,904	4,226	4,191	4,717	3,970	4,038
Aluminum oxide	1,000 metric tons..	4,764	4,537	4,016	(D)	2,863	(D)
Aluminum sulfate (commercial)	1,000 metric tons..	1,144	1,058	1,052	1,076	1,020	1,054
Sodium chlorate	1,000 metric tons..	617	707	742	940	792	721
Sodium phosphate tripoly	1,000 metric tons..	(D)	205	(D)	(D)	(D)	(D)
Sodium silicats [1]	1,000 metric tons..	1,203	1,097	992	1,136	1,070	1,054
Sodium metasilicates	1,000 metric tons..	93	70	63	72	63	58
Sodium sulfate	1,000 metric tons..	(D)	571	599	509	76	74
Carbon activated [2]	1,000 metric tons..	156	150	151	166	(S)	(D)
Hydrogen peroxide	1,000 metric tons..	355	324	342	1,083	(S)	(S)
Phosphorous, oxychloride and trichlorde ...	1,000 metric tons..	226	(D)	163	(D)	(S)	(D)

D Withheld to avoid disclosing data for individual companies. NA Not available. S Does not meet publication standards.
[1] Other than metasilicates. [2] Granular and pulverized.

Source: U.S. Census Bureau, *Current Industrial Reports*, Series MAQ325A, and MA325B, annual. See also <http://www.census.gov/cir/www/325/mq325a.html> (released August 2002) and <http://www.census.gov/industry/1/mq325a025.pdf> (issued August 2003)

No. 998. Aluminum—Supply, Shipments, and Foreign Trade: 1990 to 2003

[In millions of pounds (17,334 represents 17,334,000,000)]

Item	1990	1995	1998	1999	2000	2001	2002	2003
SUPPLY								
Aluminum supply, total	17,334	20,425	22,970	24,590	23,586	20,071	21,118	21,147
Primary production	8,925	7,441	8,185	8,330	8,087	5,812	5,964	5,962
Recovery from scrap	5,276	7,028	7,589	8,146	7,606	6,572	6,452	6,216
Imports of ingot and mill products......	3,133	5,956	7,196	8,113	7,893	7,687	8,702	8,969
Aluminum net shipments, total [1] .	17,188	21,019	23,189	24,673	24,496	22,519	23,601	23,280
PRODUCT								
Mill products, total	13,013	15,716	17,019	17,989	17,676	15,467	15,715	15,667
Sheet, plate, and foil	9,297	11,168	11,801	12,437	12,116	10,376	10,573	10,561
Rod, bar, and wire	370	534	657	670	690	571	172	139
Electrical conductor	542	566	631	676	681	676	705	698
Extruded shapes and tube.........	2,546	3,102	3,559	3,817	3,792	3,482	3,903	3,909
Powder and paste	106	108	123	130	142	142	142	146
Forgings and impacts	152	238	248	259	255	220	220	214
Ingot for castings and other [2]	4,175	5,303	6,170	6,684	6,820	7,052	7,886	7,613
MARKET								
Domestic, total	14,637	18,152	20,358	21,707	21,680	20,531	21,245	21,390
Building and construction	2,663	2,679	3,070	3,237	3,204	3,297	3,447	3,442
Transportation	3,205	5,749	7,162	7,938	7,947	7,035	7,516	7,761
Consumer durables	1,122	1,369	1,599	1,675	1,692	1,502	1,592	1,586
Electrical	1,309	1,395	1,527	1,646	1,704	1,513	1,493	1,444
Machinery and equipment	992	1,257	1,386	1,458	1,496	1,414	1,359	1,368
Containers and packaging	4,772	5,088	5,012	5,106	4,992	4,961	4,979	4,941
Other...................	2,551	2,867	2,831	2,967	2,816	809	859	848
Exports	574	615	602	647	645	1,988	2,356	1,890
FOREIGN TRADE [3]								
Exports	3,753	3,846	3,743	3,865	4,097	3,712	3,729	3,662
Imports	3,718	6,910	8,342	9,506	9,357	8,853	9,680	9,885

[1] Data presented on this report have been adjusted to represent total U.S. producer's shipments and inventories plus imports by consumers. [2] Net ingot for foundry castings, export and destructive uses. [3] U.S. imports and exports of aluminum ingot, mill products and scrap.

Source: The Aluminum Association, Inc., Washington, DC, *Aluminum Statistical Review*, annual.

No. 999. Iron and Steel Industry—Summary: 1990 to 2002

[95.5 represents 95,500,000 tons. For financial data, the universe in 1992 consists of the companies that produced 68 percent of the total reported raw steel production. The financial data represent the operations of the steel segment of the companies. Minus sign (-) indicates net loss]

Item	Unit	1990	1995	1997	1998	1999	2000	2001	2002, prel.
Steel mill products, apparent supply . . .	Mil. tons [1] . .	95.5	109.6	124.6	131.6	127.9	131.9	116.4	117.0
Net shipments.	Mil. tons [1] . .	85.0	97.5	105.9	102.4	106.2	109.1	98.9	99.2
Exports	Mil. tons [1] . .	4.3	7.1	6.0	5.5	5.4	6.5	6.1	6.0
Imports	Mil. tons [1] . .	17.2	24.4	31.2	41.5	31.2	29.4	30.1	32.6
Scrap consumed	Mil. tons [1] . .	50.1	62.0	64.0	64.0	62.0	65.0	63.0	(NA)
Scrap inventory.	Mil. tons [1] . .	3.6	4.1	5.5	4.5	5.3	5.3	4.9	(NA)
Iron and steel products: Exports.	Mil. tons [1] . .	5.3	8.2	7.4	6.9	6.7	7.7	7.2	7.0
Imports	Mil. tons [1] . .	21.9	27.3	34.4	45.4	40.2	42.6	34.4	37.3
Capacity by steelmaking process	Mil. net ton .	116.7	112.4	121.4	125.3	128.2	130.3	125.5	113.7
Revenue	Bil. dol.. . . .	30.9	35.1	36.6	38.1	36.3	38.8	31.0	(NA)
Net income	Bil. dol.. . . .	0.1	1.5	1.0	1.1	-0.5	-1.1	-3.9	(NA)
Stockholders' equity.	Bil. dol.. . . .	4.3	8.6	9.8	12.5	11.8	9.9	5.5	(NA)
Total assets	Bil. dol.. . . .	28.3	35.1	38.3	42.2	43.7	43.9	38.1	(NA)
Capital expenditures [2]	Bil. dol.. . . .	2.6	2.5	2.7	3.1	2.8	2.1	1.1	(NA)
Working capital ratio [2]	Ratio	1.6	1.5	1.6	1.6	1.7	1.7	1.6	(NA)
Inventories	Bil. dol.. . . .	4.7	5.1	5.8	6.8	6.5	6.8	5.7	(NA)
Average employment.	1,000	169.0	122.6	111.8	109.6	102.2	99.5	88.0	(NA)
Hours worked	Million . . .	350.0	269.2	247.2	240.0	222.7	219.7	186.4	(NA)
Index of output, all employees [3]	1997=100 . .	106.5	89.7	100.0	101.7	106.5	108.5	106.7	(NA)

NA Not available.   [1] In millions of short tons.   [2] Current assets to current liabilities.   [3] NAICS code 3311. Output per hour.
Source: U.S. Bureau of Labor Statistics, Internet site <http://stats.bls.gov/iprhome.htm>.
Source: Except as noted, American Iron and Steel Institute, Washington, DC, *Annual Statistical Report* (copyright).

No. 1000. Steel Products—Net Shipments by Market Classes: 1990 to 2002

[In thousands of short tons (84,981 represents 84,981,000). Comprises carbon, alloy, and stainless steel]

Market class	1990	1995	1997	1998	1999	2000	2001	2002
Net shipments, total [1]	84,981	97,494	105,858	102,420	106,201	109,050	99,448	99,191
Automotive.	11,100	14,622	15,251	15,842	16,771	16,063	14,059	12,562
Steel service centers, distributors	21,111	23,751	27,800	27,751	28,089	30,108	27,072	22,828
Construction, incl. maintenance [2]	9,245	14,892	15,885	15,289	18,428	20,290	21,543	15,729
Containers, packaging, shipping.	4,474	4,139	4,163	3,829	3,842	3,708	3,232	3,251
Machinery, industrial equipment, tools . . .	2,388	2,310	2,355	2,147	1,722	1,784	1,456	1,137
Steel for converting and processing . . .	9,441	10,440	11,263	9,975	11,309	12,708	10,311	7,201
Rail transportation	1,080	1,373	1,410	1,657	1,031	1,307	981	751
Contractors' products	2,870	(2)	(2)	(2)	(2)	(2)	(2)	(2)
Oil and gas industries	1,892	2,643	3,811	2,649	2,151	2,885	2,953	1,658
Electrical equipment.	2,453	2,397	2,434	2,255	2,267	2,055	1,684	1,336
Appliances, utensils, and cutlery	1,540	1,589	1,635	1,729	1,789	1,907	1,820	1,734

[1] Includes nonclassified shipments and other classes not shown separately.   [2] Beginning 1994, contractors' products included with construction.
Source: American Iron and Steel Institute, Washington, DC, *Annual Statistical Report* (copyright).

No. 1001. Metalworking Machinery—Value of Shipments: 1990 to 2002

[In millions of dollars (3,426.1 represents $3,426,100,000)]

Product	NAICS product code	1990	1995	1998	1999	2000	2001	2002
Metalworking machinery	(X)	3,426.1	4,547.1	4,817.1	3,783.3	3,632.4	2,987.6	2,002.1
Metal cutting type [1]	(X)	2,371.3	3,036.6	3,481.8	2,512.6	2,552.4	2,163.7	1,418.7
Boring machines [2]	333512A1	(2)	172.4	73.6	53.8	87.2	124.8	128.3
Drilling machines [2]	333512A1	184.1	78.9	102.9	50.6	23.7	22.6	17.1
Gear cutting machines	33351211	102.7	137.1	197.7	132.0	180.6	137.2	111.0
Grinding and polishing machines . . .	33351220	433.6	549.6	535.5	477.1	454.3	367.7	210.7
Lathes [3]	33351230	355.6	478.0	472.9	297.4	287.0	262.0	132.4
Milling machines [4]	33351240	214.3	194.8	281.1	200.5	150.5	137.8	56.1
Machining centers [5]	33351270	437.0	698.8	897.3	597.9	629.7	435.5	273.6
Station type machines	33351280	502.1	477.0	571.0	407.1	401.8	347.9	169.9
Other metal cutting machine tools [6] . . .	33351290	141.9	246.2	344.6	291.7	333.2	276.4	238.3
Metal forming type	(X)	1,080.2	1,510.5	1,335.3	1,270.7	1,080.0	823.9	583.4
Punching and shearing machines . . .	33351310 pt.	200.1	326.3	254.3	220.0	230.8	155.3	105.9
Bending and forming machines	33351310 pt.	222.9	256.9	262.7	265.8	262.4	202.6	141.3
Presses, except forging	33351330	308.3	379.2	399.5	433.7	303.3	180.3	140.1
Forging machines [7]	33351350 pt.	73.9	(D)	(D)	(D)	(D)	(D)	(D)
Other metal forming [7]	33351350 pt.	275.0	548.1	418.8	351.2	310.7	275.8	187.4

D Data withheld to avoid disclosure.   X Not applicable.   [1] Beginning 1995, data for "All lathes (turning machines)" and "All milling machines," valued at under $3,025 each are included in total "Metal cutting type" for 1995 through 2000.   [2] For 1990, data for "Boring machines" were combined with "Drilling machines" to avoid disclosing individual company data.   [3] Beginning 1995, product code 33351230, "Lathes," excludes the value for product code 3335123031, All lathes valued under $3,025 each.   [4] Beginning 1995, product code 33351240, "Milling machines," excludes the value for product code 3335124001, "All milling machines valued under $3,025 each."   [5] Multi-function numerically controlled machines.   [6] Excludes those designed primarily for home workshops, labs, etc.   [7] For 1995 through 2002, data for "Forging machines" have been combined with "Other metal forming machines" to avoid disclosing individual company data.
Source: U.S. Census Bureau, 1990, *Current Industrial Reports*, Series MQ35W; and thereafter, MQ333W. See also <http://www.census.gov/industry/1/mq333w025.pdf> (released July 2003).

No. 1002. U.S. Machine Tool Consumption—Gross New Orders and Exports: 2002 and 2003

[Value in millions of dollars (2,495 represents $2,495,000,000)]

Item	2002				2003			
	Total	Metal cutting machines	Metal forming machines	Other manufac-turing technol-ogy	Total	Metal cutting machines	Metal forming machines	Other manufac-turing technol-ogy
New order units, total	17,899	14,626	1,695	1,577	15,738	13,177	1,300	1,261
Northeast [1]	2,844	2,349	267	228	2,610	2,151	217	241
South [2]	3,198	2,522	346	329	2,844	2,347	250	247
Midwest [3]	5,544	4,393	555	596	5,107	4,148	433	526
Central [4]	3,724	3,094	371	259	3,148	2,691	297	160
West [5]	2,589	2,268	156	165	2,029	1,839	103	87
New order value, total	2,495	1,927	237	331	2,289	1,804	189	296
Northeast [1]	350	279	32	39	286	244	17	25
South [2]	426	319	47	60	426	332	41	53
Midwest [3]	1,008	731	103	175	960	709	89	163
Central [4]	449	372	38	39	398	328	30	41
West [5]	262	226	18	18	218	192	12	15
Export order units [6]	1,208	951	138	119	1,176	866	112	198
Export order value [6]	274	209	27	38	330	221	31	78

[1] Covers Maine, New Hampshire, Vermont, New York, Massachusetts, Connecticut, Rhode Island, New Jersey, and Pennsylvania. [2] Covers Delaware, Maryland, Virginia, West Virginia, Kentucky, North Carolina, South Carolina, Tennessee, Mississippi, Alabama, Georgia, and Florida. [3] Covers Wisconsin, Michigan, Ohio, Illinois, and Indiana. [4] Covers Minnesota, North Dakota, South Dakota, Montana, Wyoming, Idaho, Iowa, Nebraska, Kansas, Missouri, Oklahoma, Arkansas, Louisiana, Texas, New Mexico, Colorado, and Utah. [5] Covers Washington, Oregon, California, Nevada, and Arizona. [6] Represents orders placed with U.S. builders.

Source: The Association for Manufacturing Technology, McLean, VA, (copyright); and American Machine Tool Distributors Association, Rockville, MD, U.S. Machine Tool Consumption Report, monthly.

No. 1003. Semiconductors, Printed Circuit Boards, and Other Electronic Components—Value of Shipments by Class of Product: 1990 to 2002

[In millions of dollars (56,301 represents $56,301,000,000). N.e.c.=not elsewhere classified]

Class of product	NAICS product code [1]	1990	1995	1999	2000	2001	2002
Total	(X)	56,301	118,906	141,660	164,853	118,868	111,407
Transmittal, industrial, and special-purpose electron tubes (except x-ray)	3344111	1,097	855	673	703	700	594
Electron tubes, receiving type	(X)	24	([2])	([2])	([2])	([2])	([2])
Receiving type electron tubes and cathode ray picture tubes	3344114	1,344	[2] 2,907	[2] 3,579	[2] 3,458	[2] 2,847	[2] 2,043
Electron tube parts	3344118	143	120	136	144	125	69
Printed circuit boards	3344120	7,175	8,367	9,150	11,892	8,910	6,045
Integrated microcircuits (semiconductor networks)	3344131	16,623	48,438	62,868	73,664	46,337	55,772
Transistors	3344134	682	943	994	1,569	913	747
Diodes and rectifiers	3344137	668	1,067	1,038	621	403	281
Other semiconductor devices	334413A	5,741	12,639	11,745	9,757	7,632	6,805
Capacitors for electronic applications	3344140	1,392	1,785	2,035	2,786	1,734	1,300
Resistors	3344150	800	953	971	982	776	683
Coils, transformers, reactors, and chokes for electronic applications	3344160	976	1,412	1,423	1,719	1,362	1,130
Coaxial connectors	3344171	420	732	631	805	506	366
Cylindrical connectors	3344174	514	553	550	725	688	672
Rack and panel connectors	3344177	500	541	391	532	359	234
Printed circuit connectors	334417A	805	1,026	1,376	1,811	1,147	744
Other connectors including parts	334417D	1,085	1,402	2,041	2,059	2,052	1,288
Filters (except microwave) and piezoelectric devices	3344191	457	729	858	1,168	984	718
Transducers, electrical/electronic input or output	3344194	741	1,111	1,331	1,519	1,331	1,154
Switches, mechanical types for electronic circuitry	3344197	579	666	883	903	828	840
Printed circuit assemblies	334418A	8,269	24,448	30,091	37,273	31,214	23,259
Microwave components and devices	334419A	1,369	1,233	1,622	2,435	1,848	1,599
All other electronic components n.e.c	334419D	4,898	6,978	7,276	8,332	6,173	5,067

X Not applicable. [1] North American Industry Classification System, 1997; see text, Section 15. [2] Product codes combined to avoid disclosing figures for individual companies.

Source: U.S. Census Bureau, 1990, Current Industrial Reports, Series MA36Q; thereafter, MA334Q. See also <http://www.census.gov/industry/1/ma334q02.pdf> (revised 07 August 2003).

Manufactures 645

No. 1004. Computers and Office and Accounting Machines—Value of Shipments: 1990 to 2002

[In millions of dollars (25,630 represents $25,630,000,000)]

Selected products	1990	1995	1998	1999	2000	2001	2002
Electronic computers [1]	25,630	49,038	56,892	64,696	62,857	48,541	41,818
Host computers (multi-users)	(NA)	(NA)	15,010	21,089	22,877	16,469	14,207
Single user computers	(NA)	(NA)	41,002	42,765	38,981	31,492	26,749
Other computers	(NA)	(NA)	48	(D)	998	581	862
Loaded computer processor boards and board subassemblies [2]	2,247	24,448	26,047	30,091	37,273	31,214	23,259
Computer storage devices & equipment	7,488	7,903	9,319	9,827	8,995	7,319	5,661
Parts for computer storage devices & subassemblies	955	2,236	2,310	2,254	1,692	1,699	1,560
Computer terminals	2,067	1,086	529	541	415	361	286
Computer peripheral equipment, n.e.c.	7,697	12,331	12,145	12,889	12,434	10,637	10,364
Parts for input/output equipment	3,706	2,391	2,630	2,388	2,766	2,360	2,217
Calculating and accounting machines	(D)	1,279	1,061	1,196	1,210	1,191	828
Magnetic and optical recording media	3,695	5,106	4,736	3,907	3,206	2,228	2,325

NA Not available. D Withheld to avoid disclosing data for individual companies. [1] Beginning 1998, computer industry data are not entirely comparable to previous years. [2] These data are collected on two Current Industrial Report forms, MA35R, Computers and Office and Accounting Machines (Shipments) and MA36Q, Semiconductors, Printed Circuit Boards, And Other Electronic Components.

Source: U.S. Census Bureau, *Current Industrial Reports*, Series MA334R. See also <http://www.census.gov/industry/1/ma334r02.pdf> (released August 2003).

No. 1005. Computers and Office and Accounting Machines—Shipments: 2001 and 2002

[Quantity in thousands of units (22,209 represents 22,209,000, value in millions of dollars (48,541 represents $48,541,000,000)]

Product	Number of companies, 2002	Quantity (1,000)		Value (mil. dol.)	
		2001	2002	2001	2002
Electronic computers (automatic data processors)	125	22,209	19,647	48,541	41,818
Host computers (multi-users):					
Large scale systems and unix servers	13	309	106	4,701	4,036
Medium-scale systems and unix servers	22	323	279	8,301	6,704
PC servers	24	(D)	(D)	(D)	(D)
Other host computers	9	(D)	(D)	(D)	(D)
Single user computers:					
Personal computers	34	14,591	12,920	18,870	16,186
Workstations	38	1,316	1,132	3,381	2,380
Laptops (AC/DC)	9	7	8	21	23
Notebooks, subnotebooks (battery operated)	16	4,249	4,126	8,682	7,850
Personal digital assistants	6	(D)	(D)	(D)	(D)
Other portable computers	7	(D)	(D)	(D)	(D)
Other single user computers	6	184	102	94	55
Other computers	31	106	120	581	862
Computer storage devices and equipment	58	(X)	(X)	7,319	5,661
Parts for computer storage devices and subassemblies	18	(X)	(X)	1,699	1,560
Computer terminals	31	(X)	(X)	361	286
Computer peripheral equipment, n.e.c. [1]	202	(X)	(X)	10,637	10,364
Keyboards	24	(D)	(D)	(D)	(D)
Computer printers:					
Laser	25	3,475	1,270	2,011	1,803
Inkjet	11	7,986	(D)	615	(D)
Calculating and accounting machines	33	(X)	(X)	1,191	828
Printed circuit assemblies	654	(X)	(X)	31,214	23,259
Magnetic and optical recording media	36	(X)	(X)	2,228	2,325

D Withheld to avoid disclosure of individual companies. X Not applicable. [1] N.e.c. = Not elsewhere classsified.

Source: U.S. Census Bureau, *Current Industrial Reports*, Series MA334R. See also <http://www.census.gov/industry/1/ma334r02.pdf> (released August 2003).

No. 1006. Computers and Industrial Electronics—Factory Shipments: 1990 to 2001

[In millions of dollars (50,793.2 represents 50,793,200,000]

Item	1990	1995	1998	1999	2000	2001
Computer and peripheral equipment, total	50,793.2	73,555.0	78,355.5	87,412.0	84,286.7	68,035.9
Computers	25,973.1	49,038.0	56,891.5	64,696.1	62,856.9	49,289.0
Peripheral equipment	24,820.1	24,517.0	21,464.0	22,715.9	21,429.8	18,746.9
Industrial electronics, total	26,182.6	33,732.0	36,887.2	37,733.9	41,525.8	34,108.6
Controlling, processing equipment	12,728.0	16,450.0	18,081.7	18,220.5	19,219.7	17,513.9
Testing, measuring equipment	6,859.1	10,109.0	11,212.7	11,563.5	14,635.7	11,072.1
Nuclear electronic equipment	566.8	501.0	560.2	538.0	568.2	544.1
Robots, accessories, and components	275.0	(NA)	(NA)	(NA)	(NA)	(NA)
Other electronic equipment	5,753.7	6,672.0	7,032.5	7,411.9	7,102.2	4,978.5

NA Not available.

Source: Consumer Electronics Association, Washington, DC, *Electronic Market Data Book*, annual (copyright).

646 Manufactures

No. 1007. Consumer Electronics and Electronic Components— Factory Sales by Product Category: 1990 to 2003

[In millions of dollars (43,033 representes $43,033,000,000). Factory sales include imports]

Product category	1990	1995	1999	2000	2001	2002	2003
Total [1]	43,033	67,905	85,553	96,369	93,711	94,175	96,351
Video products	12,440	15,376	16,307	17,920	16,607	18,765	19,095
Analog direct-view color TV	6,197	6,798	6,199	6,503	5,130	5,782	4,769
Analog projection TV	626	1,417	1,632	1,481	1,060	733	315
Monochrome TV	99	34	20	15	15	12	9
Digital direct-view and projection TV	(NA)	(NA)	295	1,355	2,485	3,574	4,009
LCD TV	83	75	61	107	101	246	651
Plasma TV	(NA)	(NA)	(NA)	(NA)	116	515	1,457
TV Combinations	178	723	1,014	969	790	993	718
Videocassette players	65	59	15	14	5	4	2
VCR decks	2,439	2,767	2,333	1,861	1,058	826	374
Camcorders	2,260	2,130	2,444	2,838	2,236	2,361	2,105
Direct-to-home satellite	421	1,265	957	790	1,175	1,116	1,380
Personal video recorders	(NA)	(NA)	46	77	144	57	193
Digital versatile disc players (DVD)	(NA)	(NA)	1,099	1,717	2,097	2,427	3,050
Home and portable products	5,210	6,378	6,037	6,323	5,726	5,111	4,619
Compact audio systems	1,270	1,162	1,695	1,776	1,357	965	656
Separate audio components	1,935	1,911	1,530	1,545	1,261	1,202	960
Home radios	360	284	348	351	326	300	289
Portable audio equipment	1,645	2,506	1,987	2,156	1,846	1,526	1,289
Portable MP3 players	(NA)	(NA)	100	80	100	205	556
Mobile electronics	5,733	11,422	12,957	16,958	16,656	16,031	16,840
Aftermarket autosound equipment	1,192	1,931	2,070	2,169	2,098	2,211	1,904
Mobile video and navigation	(NA)	(NA)	(NA)	(NA)	293	429	422
Factory installed autosound	3,100	3,100	2,610	2,700	2,850	2,950	3,245
Wireless (cellular) telephones	1,133	2,574	6,066	8,995	8,651	8,106	9,163
Pagers	118	300	660	750	790	810	729
Family Radio Services (FRS)	(NA)	(NA)	205	218	461	251	235
Vehicle security	190	142	(NA)	(NA)	266	265	260
PDAs	(NA)	(NA)	(NA)	(NA)	1,077	875	759
Home office products	11,021	24,140	34,526	36,856	34,923	32,418	33,313
Cordless telephones	842	1,141	1,808	1,562	1,960	1,261	1,139
Corded telephones	638	557	483	386	294	266	251
Telephone answering devices	827	1,077	1,044	984	1,062	1,060	1,181
Caller ID devices	(NA)	(NA)	(NA)	(NA)	35	20	11
Home computers	4,187	12,600	16,390	16,400	12,960	11,523	12,458
Computer printers	(NA)	2,430	4,500	5,116	5,245	4,829	4,196
Modems/fax modems	(NA)	770	1,460	1,564	1,564	1,445	1,419
Computer peripherals	1,980	816	1,950	1,950	2,150	2,256	2,425
Computer software (incl. CDROM)	971	2,500	4,480	4,480	5,062	4,961	5,060
Home fax machines	920	919	455	387	349	297	242
Digital cameras	(NA)	(NA)	1,209	1,825	1,972	2,794	3,421
Electronic gaming:							
Electronic gaming hardware	975	1,500	2,250	2,700	3,250	3,750	3,188
Electronic gaming software	2,400	3,000	5,100	5,850	6,725	7,375	7,744
Blank media:							
Blank audio cassettes	376	334	208	162	129	98	87
Blank videocassettes	948	708	590	351	357	602	569
Blank computer media	314	373	900	1,200	1,550	1,600	1,800
Accessories and batteries:							
Electronic accessories	793	944	1,398	1,356	1,378	1,500	1,635
Total primary batteries	1,383	2,600	3,620	4,943	4,590	4,960	5,406

NA Not available. [1] Includes categories, not shown separately.

Source: Consumer Electronics Association, Washington, DC, *Electronic Market Data Book*, annual (copyright).

No. 1008. Communication Equipment—Value of Shipments: 1990 to 2002

[In millions of dollars (36,990 represents $36,990,000,000]

Product description	NAICS product code [1]	1990	1995	1999	2000	2001	2002
Total	(X)	36,990	56,362	89,557	104,389	93,803	66,523
Telephone switching and switchboard equipment	3342101	7,537	8,178	13,742	15,174	12,188	7,366
Carrier line equipment and modems	3342104	5,014	5,869	9,263	13,112	10,943	4,730
Other telephone and telegraph equipment and components	3342107	3,181	10,510	23,258	28,971	22,841	17,648
Communication systems and equipment (except broadcast)	3342201	14,768	23,032	33,281	36,357	36,501	25,600
Broadcast, studio, and related electronic equipment	3342203	1,856	2,845	4,000	4,029	3,490	3,300
Intercommunications systems, including inductive paging systems (selective calling)	3342903	346	296	401	447	451	367
Alarm systems	3342901	1,027	1,662	2,218	2,755	2,374	2,993
Vehicular and pedestrian traffic control equipment and electrical railway signals and attachments	3342902	471	711	952	838	806	808
Electronic teaching machines, teaching aids, trainers and simulators	3333197	1,209	913	701	782	1,172	728
Laser sources [2]	3359997	(NA)	788	(S)	(S)	1,051	938
Ultrasonic equipment	335999A	109	172	226	272	233	174
Other electronic systems and equipment, n.e.c.	335999C	1,473	1,387	1,515	1,652	1,752	1,870

NA Not available.   S Does not meet publication standards.   [1] North American Industry Classification System, 1997; see text, Section 15.   [2] Beginning in 1995, data for laser equipment, instrumentation, and components were eliminated from this survey. Only laser sources are being collected.

Source: U.S. Census Bureau, *Current Industrial Reports*, Series MA334P. See also <http://www.census.gov/industry/1/ma334p02.pdf> (released September 2003)

No. 1009. Motor Vehicle Manufactures—Summary by Selected Industry: 2001

[Payroll of 47,955 represents $47,955,000,000. Based on the Annual Survey of Manufactures; see Appendix III]

Industry	NAICS code[1]	All employees[2] Number	Payroll Total (mil. dol.)	Payroll Per employee (dol.)	Production workers[2]	Value of shipments[3] (mil. dol.)
Motor vehicle manufacturing, total	3361-3363	1,073,104	47,955	44,688	867,975	427,176
Motor vehicle, total	3361	213,981	12,647	59,102	186,209	216,128
Automobile & light duty motor vehicle	33611	186,527	11,435	61,304	165,090	203,514
Automobile	336111	91,062	5,388	59,166	78,607	87,046
Light truck & utility vehicle	336112	95,465	6,047	63,343	86,483	116,468
Heavy duty truck	33612	27,454	1,212	44,142	21,119	12,613
Motor vehicle body & trailer	3362	123,120	3,807	30,924	97,153	24,209
Motor vehicle body & trailer	33621	123,120	3,807	30,924	97,153	24,209
Motor vehicle body	336211	41,771	1,325	31,725	30,934	10,535
Truck trailer	336212	26,360	825	31,286	20,830	4,296
Motor home	336213	16,102	502	31,169	13,064	3,345
Travel trailer & camper	336214	38,887	1,156	29,716	32,325	6,034
Motor vehicle parts	3363	736,003	31,501	42,800	584,613	186,839
Motor vehicle gasoline engine & engine parts	33631	88,635	4,288	48,377	73,021	28,202
Carburetor, piston, piston ring, & valve	336311	16,656	745	44,749	13,944	2,907
Gasoline engine & engine parts	336312	71,979	3,543	49,217	59,077	25,294
Motor vehicle electrical & electronic equip.	33632	109,477	4,312	39,391	80,650	23,310
Vehicular lighting equipment	336321	14,665	640	43,665	10,913	2,780
Other motor vehicle electrical & electronic equipment	336322	94,812	3,672	38,730	69,737	20,530
Motor vehicle steering & suspension components, ex. spring	33633	47,015	2,207	46,948	38,239	10,044
Motor vehicle brake system	33634	38,736	1,420	36,660	29,542	10,636
Motor vehicle transmission & power train parts	33635	98,753	5,178	52,435	79,306	31,466
Motor vehicle seating & interior trim	33636	52,670	1,675	31,793	42,269	14,814
Motor vehicle metal stamping	33637	112,488	5,392	47,932	94,033	21,858
Other motor vehicle parts	33639	188,229	7,029	37,341	147,553	46,510

[1] North American Industry Classification System, 1997; see text, Section 15. [2] Includes employment and payroll at administrative offices and auxiliary units. All employees represents the average of production workers plus all other employees for the payroll period ended nearest the 12th of March. Production workers represents the average of the employment for the payroll periods ended nearest the 12th of March, May, August, and November. [3] Includes extensive and unmeasurable duplication from shipments between establishments in the same industry classification.

Source: U.S. Census Bureau, Annual Survey of Manufactures, Statistics for Industry Groups and Industries, Series M01(AS)-1. See also <http://www.census.gov/prod/2003pubs/m01-as1.pdf> (issued January 2003).

No. 1010. Motor Vehicle Manufactures—Employees, Payroll, and Shipments by Major State: 2001

[Payroll of 12,647 represents 12,647,000,000. Industry based on the North American Industry Classification System (NAICS), 1997; see text, Section 15]

Major State based on employment	Motor vehicle manufacturing (NAICS 3361) Employees, total	Payroll (mil. dol.)	Shipments (mil. dol.)	Motor vehicle body and trailer manufacturing (NAICS 3362) Employees, total	Payroll (mil. dol.)	Shipments (mil. dol.)	Motor vehicle parts manufacturing (NAICS 3363) Employees, total	Payroll (mil. dol.)	Shipments (mil. dol.)
United States..	213,981	12,647	216,128	123,120	3,807	24,209	736,003	31,501	186,839
Alabama	(D)	(D)	(D)	3,158	94	754	11,531	565	3,315
Arkansas	(NA)	(NA)	(NA)	1,549	35	281	7,522	173	873
California	7,429	416	2,965	11,287	341	4,693	25,824	771	3,849
Florida	(NA)	(NA)	(NA)	3,793	134	806	4,409	124	625
Georgia	7,620	386	8,130	2,977	80	(S)	28,464	930	5,271
Illinois	8,083	481	7,863	3,719	127	649	93,497	4,226	22,712
Indiana	11,867	618	10,811	24,414	867	4,845	9,169	307	1,693
Iowa	(NA)	(NA)	(NA)	8,000	247	1,403	27,764	934	7,240
Kentucky	18,810	1,287	22,470	(NA)	(NA)	(NA)	178,681	9,230	52,242
Michigan	42,260	2,722	51,873	3,925	113	599	9,718	296	1,673
Mississippi	(NA)	(NA)	(NA)	780	22	109	19,520	569	4,030
Missouri	(D)	(D)	(D)	2,049	52	227	3,609	123	668
Nebraska	(NA)	(NA)	(NA)	1,109	29	190	30,232	1,737	8,703
New York	(NA)	(NA)	(NA)	1,088	32	768	18,661	619	4,512
North Carolina	(D)	(D)	(D)	3,714	141	961	96,775	4,881	29,924
Ohio	29,972	1,784	32,648	4,387	142	809	5,531	165	1,031
Oklahoma	(D)	(D)	(D)	4,086	105	691	2,525	98	500
Oregon	1,749	60	781	4,635	113	552	15,328	581	3,328
Pennsylvania	(D)	(D)	(D)	7,243	191	1,118	16,109	557	4,570
South Carolina	6,210	298	4,501	(S)	(S)	(S)	32,130	1,065	8,098
Tennessee	14,241	840	7,552	1,818	52	381	16,186	468	3,389
Texas	(D)	(D)	(D)	5,963	169	800	5,341	223	2,387
Utah	(NA)	(NA)	(NA)	1,085	27	177	6,747	253	1,718
Virginia	(D)	(D)	(D)	(D)	(D)	(D)	23,387	970	5,412
Wisconsin	(D)	(D)	(D)	5,258	188	909			

D Withheld to avoid disclosing data on individual companies. NA Not available. S Does not meet publication standards.

Source: U.S. Census Bureau, Annual Survey of Manufactures, Geographic Area Statistics, Series M01(AS)-3. See also <http://www.census.gov/prod/2003pubs/m01as-3.pdf> (issued January 2003).

No. 1011. Aerospace—Sales, New Orders, and Backlog: 1990 to 2002

[In billions of dollars (136.6 represents $136,600,000,000), except as indicated. Reported by establishments in which the principal business is the development and/or production of aerospace products]

Item	1990	1995	1998	1999	2000	2001	2002
Net sales	136.6	102.8	119.3	124.2	109.3	117.1	111.3
Percent U.S. Government	53.8	50.5	33.5	36.3	37.5	38.6	46.5
Complete aircraft and parts [1]	49.9	42.5	63.6	68.0	57.2	58.7	51.9
Aircraft engines and parts	16.4	12.5	12.8	14.4	12.5	15.9	14.8
Missiles and space vehicles, parts . . .	22.0	18.4	16.1	15.7	15.6	15.5	15.0
Other products, services	48.3	29.4	26.7	26.1	24.0	26.9	29.6
Net, new orders	146.0	109.1	110.0	115.3	140.1	122.2	114.6
Backlog, Dec. 31	250.1	202.6	200.3	188.4	215.0	220.1	222.8

[1] Except engines sold separately.

Source: U.S. Census Bureau, 1990-1995, *Current Industrial Reports*, Series M37G; thereafter M336G. See also <http://www.census.gov/industry/1/m336g0213.pdf> (released August 2003).

No. 1012. Net Orders for U.S. Civil Jet Transport Aircraft: 1990 to 2003

[1990 data are net new firm orders; beginning 1995, net announced orders. Minus sign (-) indicates net cancellations. In 1997 Boeing acquired McDonnell Douglas]

Type of aircraft and customer	1990	1995	1998	1999	2000	2001	2002	2003
Total number [1]	670	421	601	346	585	271	174	237
U.S. customers	259	138	392	192	412	49	89	84
Foreign customers	411	283	209	70	193	130	172	185
Boeing 737, total	189	189	350	258	378	184	117	204
U.S. customers	38	85	207	155	302	51	64	74
Foreign customers	151	104	143	45	86	73	127	145
Boeing 747, total	153	35	-4	22	24	16	17	4
U.S. customers	24	2	1	1	1	7	-	-
Foreign customers	129	33	-5	19	18	13	13	9
Boeing 757, total	66	-7	47	18	43	23	13	-
U.S. customers	33	-6	34	7	38	15	2	-1
Foreign customers	33	-1	13	2	14	6	-	-7
Boeing 767, total	60	26	40	32	6	32	-2	6
U.S. customers	23	4	31	21	6	6	-2	10
Foreign customers	37	22	9	1	14	9	12	15
Boeing 777, total	34	83	65	21	14	9	12	15
U.S. customers	34	-	42	8	60	30	26	12
Foreign customers	-	83	23	8	53	20	-1	11
McDonnell Douglas MD-11, total . . .	52	-6	12	-20	-	-	-	8
U.S. customers	16	3	3	-	-	-	-	-
Foreign customers	36	-9	9	-20	-	-	-	-
McDonnell Douglas MD-80/90, total . . .	116	51	26	-	-	-	-	-
U.S. customers	91	-	24	-20	-	-	-	-
Foreign customers	25	51	2	-20	-	-	-	-
McDonnell Douglas MD-95, total . . .	-	50	65	15	21	13	16	8
U.S. customers	-	50	50	15	-14	-23	23	6
Foreign customers	-	-	15	-	8	9	-7	2

- Represents zero. [1] Includes types of aircraft not shown separately. Beginning 1999, includes unidentified customers.

Source: Aerospace Industries Association of America, Washington, DC, Research Center, Statistical Series 23, Internet site at <http://www.aia-aerospace.org/stats/aerostats/aerostats.cfm>.

No. 1013. U.S. Aircraft Shipments, 1980 to 2003, and Projections, 2004

[Value in millions of dollars (18,929 represents $18,929,000,000)]

Year	Total Units	Total Value	Large transports Units	Large transports Value	General aviation [1] Units	General aviation [1] Value	Helicopters Units	Helicopters Value	Military Units	Military Value
1980	14,677	18,929	387	9,895	11,877	2,486	1,366	656	1,047	5,892
1985	3,610	27,269	278	8,448	2,029	1,431	384	506	919	16,884
1990	3,321	38,585	521	22,215	1,144	2,007	603	254	1,053	14,109
1991	3,092	44,657	589	26,856	1,021	1,968	571	211	911	15,622
1992	2,585	47,397	567	28,750	941	1,840	324	142	753	16,665
1993	2,585	41,166	408	24,133	964	2,144	258	113	955	14,776
1994	2,309	36,568	309	18,124	928	2,357	308	185	764	15,902
1995	2,436	33,658	256	15,263	1,077	2,842	292	194	811	15,359
1996	2,220	55,583	269	18,915	1,115	3,048	278	193	558	33,427
1997	2,757	65,129	374	26,929	1,549	4,593	346	231	488	33,376
1998	3,533	75,724	559	35,663	2,193	5,534	363	252	418	34,275
1999	3,799	80,974	620	38,171	2,475	6,803	345	200	359	35,800
2000	4,113	72,669	485	30,327	2,802	8,040	493	270	333	34,032
2001	3,902	77,586	526	34,155	2,616	7,991	415	247	345	35,193
2002	3,248	72,850	379	27,547	2,196	7,261	318	157	355	37,885
2003	3,238	66,571	281	20,500	2,080	6,205	517	366	360	39,500
2004, proj.	(NA)	(NA)	285	20,000	2,050	6,180	545	400	(NA)	(NA)

NA Not available. [1] Excludes off-the-shelf military aircraft.

Source: U.S. Department of Commerce, International Trade Administration, Internet site <http://www.ita.doc.gov/td/aerospace/inform/information.htm>

No. 1014. Aerospace Industry Sales by Product Group and Customer: 1990 to 2004

[In billions of dollars (134.4 represents $134,400,000,000). Due to reporting practices and tabulating methods, figures may differ from those in Table 1011]

Product group and customer	1990	1995	1997	1998	1999	2000	2001	2002[1]	2003[2]	2004[2]
CURRENT DOLLARS										
Total sales	134.4	107.8	131.6	148.0	153.7	144.7	154.2	153.4	147.1	148.1
Product group:										
Aircraft, total	71.4	55.0	70.8	84.0	88.7	81.6	86.4	80.2	73.2	72.6
Civil[4]	31.3	24.0	37.4	49.7	52.9	47.6	51.3	42.3	33.7	32.0
Military	40.1	31.1	33.4	34.3	35.8	34.0	35.2	37.9	39.5	40.6
Missiles	14.2	7.4	8.0	7.7	8.8	9.3	10.4	12.7	12.9	13.2
Space	26.4	27.4	30.8	31.6	30.5	29.7	31.7	35.0	35.1	36.0
Related products and services[5]	22.4	18.0	21.9	24.7	25.6	24.1	25.7	25.6	25.9	26.3
Customer group:										
Aerospace, total	112.0	89.8	109.7	123.3	128.1	120.6	128.5	127.8	121.2	121.8
DOD[6]	60.5	42.4	43.7	42.9	45.7	47.5	50.1	57.0	59.1	61.0
NASA[7] and other agencies	11.1	11.4	12.8	13.3	13.4	13.4	14.5	16.4	16.5	17.1
Other customers[8]	40.4	36.0	53.2	67.0	69.0	59.7	63.9	54.5	45.6	43.7
Related products and services[5]	22.4	18.0	21.9	24.7	25.6	24.1	25.7	25.6	25.9	26.3
CONSTANT (1987) DOLLARS[3]										
Total sales	123.7	86.6	103.0	115.2	118.8	108.6	112.6	110.7	104.2	103.0
Product group:										
Aircraft, total	65.7	44.2	55.4	65.3	68.6	61.2	63.1	57.8	51.8	50.5
Civil[4]	28.8	19.2	29.3	38.7	40.9	35.7	37.4	30.5	23.9	22.3
Military	36.9	25.0	26.1	26.7	27.7	25.5	25.7	27.3	27.8	28.2
Missiles	13.1	5.9	6.3	6.0	6.8	7.0	7.6	9.1	9.1	9.2
Space	24.4	22.0	24.1	24.6	23.6	22.3	23.1	25.2	24.9	25.0
Related products and services[5]	20.6	14.4	17.2	19.2	19.8	18.1	18.8	18.4	18.34	18.3
Customer group:										
Aerospace, total	103.1	72.1	85.8	96.0	99.0	90.5	93.9	92.2	85.8	84.7
DOD[6]	55.7	34.1	34.2	33.4	35.3	35.6	36.6	41.1	41.9	42.4
NASA[7] and other agencies	10.0	9.2	10.0	10.4	10.4	10.0	10.6	11.8	11.7	11.9
Other customers[8]	36.5	28.9	41.6	52.2	53.3	44.8	46.7	39.3	32.3	30.4
Related products and services[5]	20.6	14.4	17.2	19.2	19.8	18.1	18.8	18.4	18.3	18.3

[1] Preliminary. [2] Estimate. [3] Based on AIA's aerospace composite price deflator. [4] All civil sales of aircraft (domestic and export sales of jet transports, commuters, business, and personal aircraft and helicopters). [5] Electronics, software, and ground support equipment, plus sales of non-aerospace products which are produced by aerospace-manufacturing use technology, processes, and materials derived from aerospace products. [6] Department of Defense. [7] National Aeronautics and Space Administration. [8] Includes civil aircraft sales (see footnote 4), commercial space sales, all exports of military aircraft and missiles and related propulsion and parts.

Source: Aerospace Industries Association of America, Inc., Washington, DC, 2004 Year-end Review and Forecast; and Internet site <http://www.aia-aerospace.org>

No. 1015. Major Household Appliances—Value of Shipments: 1990 to 2002

[In millions of dollars (11,670.0 represents $11,670,000,000)]

Product	Product code	1990	1995	1998	1999	2000	2001	2002
Total	33522	11,670.0	13,966.2	15,551.4	16,622.3	17,041.0	16,710.6	17,672.8
Electric household ranges, ovens, and surface cooking units, equipment and parts	3352211110	1,659.8	1,791.8	2,242.9	2,197.1	2,170.3	2,004.5	1,918.4
Gas household ranges, ovens, and surface cooking units, equipment and parts	3352213000	739.4	654.1	696.7	786.3	779.1	902.0	937.1
Other household ranges, cooking equipment, outdoor cooking equipment incl. parts and accessories	3352215000	581.1	911.6	1,029.0	1,218.6	1,251.1	1,027.0	1,054.0
Household refrigerators[1][2]	3352221000	3,208.1	4,739.4	5,035.6	4,968.8	5,395.8	5,227.1	5,164.3
Food freezers, complete units, for freezing and/or storing frozen food- (household type)[2]	3352222000	226.6	(D)	(D)	(D)	(D)	(D)	(D)
Parts and attachments for household refrigerators and freezers	3352223000	134.0	111.8	89.7	92.4	99.4	63.7	77.9
Household laundry machines and parts	3352240000	2,924.5	3,095.4	3,327.3	4,029.7	4,046.6	4,162.0	4,296.4
Water heaters, electric	3352281000	433.8	513.0	541.3	580.0	572.7	555.7	576.0
Water heaters, except electric	3352283000	577.2	681.8	810.7	842.8	843.6	799.3	842.9
Household appliances, n.e.c. and parts	3352285000	1,185.5	1,579.2	1,867.9	1,998.8	2,066.1	2,033.1	2,255.0

D Withheld to avoid disclosing data for individual companies. [1] Includes combination refrigerator-freezers. [2] Product code 33522210000 and 3352222000 are combined to avoid disclosing data for individual companies.

Source: U.S. Census Bureau, 1990, Current Industrial Reports, Series MA36F; thereafter Series MA335F. See also <http://www.census.gov/industry/1/ma335f02.pdf> (released July 2003).

Section 22
Domestic Trade

This section presents statistics relating to the distributive trades, specifically whole-sale trade and retail trade. Data shown for the trades are classified by kind of business and cover sales or receipts, establishments, employees, payrolls, and other items. The principal sources of these data are from the Census Bureau and include the *1997 Economic Census* reports, annual survey reports, and the *County Business Patterns* program. These data are supplemented by several tables from trade associations, such as the National Automobile Dealers Association (Table 1027). Several notable research groups are also represented, such as Claritas (Table 1025), National Research Bureau and the International Council of Shopping Centers (Tables 1040 and 1041), Jupiter Media Matrix (Table 1037), and Forrester Research, Inc. (Table 1036).

Data on retail and wholesale trade appear in several other sections. For instance, labor force employment and earnings data appear in Section 12, Labor Force, Employment, and Earnings; gross domestic product of the industry (Table 642) appear in the Section 13, Income, Expenditures, and Wealth; financial data (several tables) from the quarterly *Statistics of Income Bulletin*, published by the Internal Revenue Service, appear in Section 15, Business Enterprise.

Censuses—Censuses of retail trade and wholesale trade have been taken at various intervals since 1929. Beginning with the 1967 census, legislation provides for a census of each area to be conducted every 5 years (for years ending in "2" and "7"). For more information on these censuses, see the *History of the 1997 Economic Census* found at <http://www.census.gov/prod/ec97/pol00-hec.pdf>. The industries covered in the censuses and surveys of business are those classified in 13 sectors defined in the *North American Industry Classification System*, called NAICS (see below). *Retail trade* refers to places of business primarily

engaged in retailing merchandise generally in small quantities to the general public; and *wholesale trade*, to establishments primarily engaged in selling goods to other businesses and normally operate from a warehouse or office that have little or no display of merchandise. All Census Bureau tables in this section are utilizing the new NAICS codes, which replaced the Standard Industrial Classification (SIC) system. NAICS makes substantial structural improvements and identifies over 350 new industries. At the same time, it causes breaks in time series far more profound than any prior revision of the previously used SIC system. For information on this system and how it affects the comparability of retail and wholesale statistics historically, see text, Section 15, Business Enterprise, and especially the Census Bureau Web site at <http://www.census.gov/epcd/www/naics.html>. In general, the 2002 Economic Census has two series of publications and documents for these two sectors subject series with reports on such as commodity line sales and establishment and firm sizes and geographic reports with individual reports for each state. For information on these series, see the Census Bureau Web site at <http://www.census.gov/econ/census02/>.

Current surveys—Current sample surveys conducted by the Census Bureau cover various aspects of the retail and wholesale trade. Its *Monthly Retail Trade and Food Services* contains monthly estimates of sales, inventories, and inventory/sales ratios, purchases, and accounts receivable for the United States, by kind of business. Annual figures on sales, year-end inventories, and inventory/sales ratios, purchases, and accounts receivable, by kind of business, appear in the *Annual Benchmark Report for Retail Trade and Food Services*. Statistics from the Bureau's monthly wholesale trade survey include national estimates of merchant wholesalers' sales, inventories,

U.S. Census Bureau, Statistical Abstract of the United States: 2004-2005

and inventory/sales ratios by major summary groups "durable and nondurable," and four-digit NAICS industry groups. Merchant wholesalers are those wholesalers who take title to the goods they sell (e.g., jobbers, exporters, importers, industrial distributors). These data, based on reports submitted by a sample of firms, appear in the *Monthly Wholesale Trade Report*. Annual figures on sales, inventory/sales ratios, year-end inventories, and purchases appear in the *Annual Benchmark Report for Wholesale Trade*. The reports just mentioned may appear in print in some cases, but principally are available as documents on the Census Bureau Web site at <http://www.census.gov/econ/www/retmenu.html>.

E-commerce—Electronic commerce (or e-commerce) are sales of goods and services over the Internet and extranet, electronic data interchange (EDI), or other online systems. Payment may or may not be made online. This edition has several tables on e-commerce sales, such as

Tables 1036 to 1039 in this section, 980 in Section 21, Manufactures, and 1267 in Section 27, Accommodation, Food Services, and Other Services. Also, there are several private sources for similar data such as Forrester Research Inc., Cambridge MA; BizRate.com, Los Angeles, CA; and Jupiter Media Matrix, New York, NY. These sources show estimated and projected online retail sales by key categories from business to consumers or to other businesses. Their methods of collecting the data vary widely between the sources and consequently these estimates of this activity vary also. Users of these estimates may want to contact the sources for descriptions of their methodology. Methodology for Census Bureau estimates can be found at <www.census.gov/estats>.

Statistical reliability—For a discussion of statistical collection and estimation, sampling procedures, and measures of statistical reliability applicable to Census Bureau data, see Appendix III.

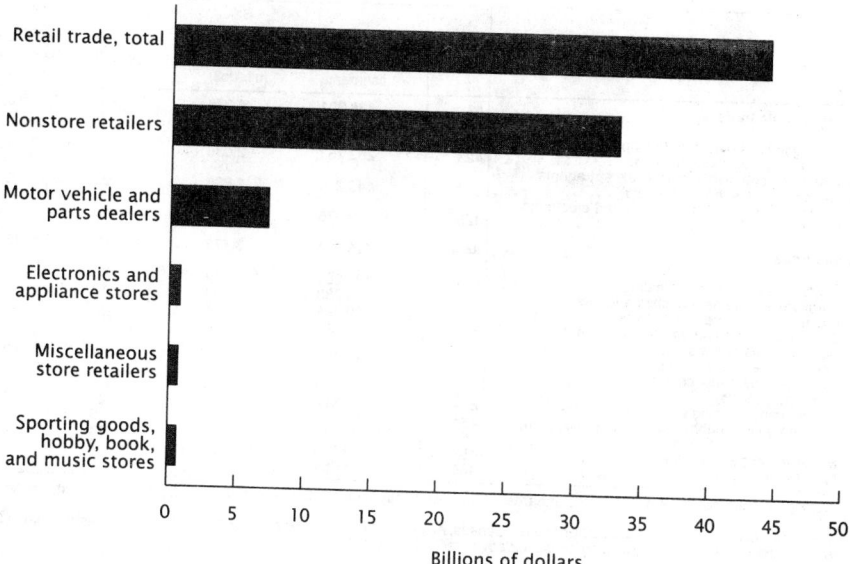

Figure 22.1
Retail E-Commerce Sales: 2002

Retail trade, total

Nonstore retailers

Motor vehicle and parts dealers

Electronics and appliance stores

Miscellaneous store retailers

Sporting goods, hobby, book, and music stores

Billions of dollars

Source: Chart prepared by U.S. Census Bureau. For data, see Table 1039.

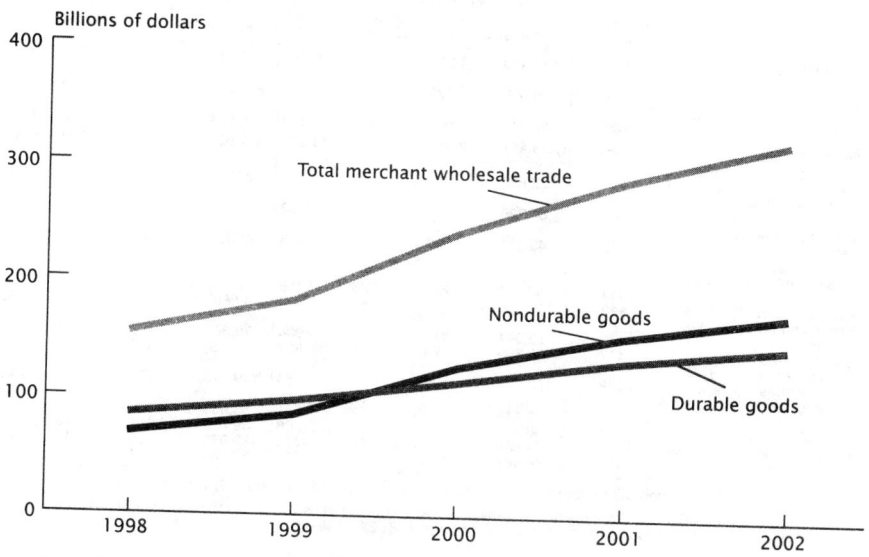

Figure 22.2
Merchant Wholesale E-Commerce Trade Sales: 1998 to 2002

Billions of dollars

Total merchant wholesale trade

Nondurable goods

Durable goods

Source: Chart prepared by U.S. Census Bureau. For data, see Table 1043.

U.S. Census Bureau, Statistical Abstract of the United States: 2004-2005

[4,376 represents 4,376,000,000,000 except as indicated. Covers establishments with payroll. These data are preliminary and are subject to change. For statement on methodology, see Appendix III]

Kind of business	NAICS code [1]	Establishments	Sales, receipts, revenue, or shipments (bil. dol.)	Annual payroll (bil. dol.)	Paid employees (1,000)
Wholesale trade	42	438,301	4,376	255	6,011
Durable goods wholesalers (except agents, broker, and electronic markets	423	262,751	2,086	153	3,404
Nondurable goods wholesalers (except agents, brokers, and electronic markets)	424	143,274	1,838	93	2,382
Wholesale trade, agents, brokers, and electronic markets	425	32,276	452	9	225
Retail trade	44-45	1,115,092	3,173	307	15,053
Motor vehicle and parts dealers	441	126,201	814	65	1,907
Furniture and home furnishings stores	442	65,088	94	13	554
Electronics and appliance stores	443	46,724	88	10	418
Building material and garden equipment and supplies dealers	444	(S)	(S)	(S)	(S)
Food and beverage stores	445	149,802	488	49	2,896
Health and personal care stores	446	79,360	183	21	1,043
Gasoline stations	447	(S)	(S)	(S)	(S)
Clothing and clothing accessories stores	448	149,318	170	21	1,425
Sporting goods, hobby, book, and music stores	451	63,033	78	9	633
General merchandise stores	452	39,846	451	43	2,549
Miscellaneous store retailers	453	129,070	95	14	849
Nonstore retailers	454	55,764	171	18	587

S Figure does not meet publication standards. [1] North American Industry Classification System, 2002; see text, Section 15.

Source: U.S. Census Bureau, 2002 Economic Census, Advance Summary Statistics for the United States, issued March 2004 See also: <http://www.census.gov/econ/census02/advance/TABLE1.HTM>

No. 1017. Wholesale and Retail Trade—Establishments, Sales, Payroll and Employees: 1997 and 2002

[4,060 represents $4,060,000,000,000 except as indicated. Covers establishments with payroll. The 2002 data are preliminary and are subject to change. For statement on methodology, see Appendix III]

Kind of business	NAICS code [1]	1997				2002			
		Establishments	Sales, receipts, revenue, or shipments (bil. dol.)	Annual payroll (bil. dol.)	Paid employees (1,000)	Establishments	Sales, receipts, revenue, or shipments (bil. dol.)	Annual payroll (bil. dol.)	Paid employees (1,000)
Wholesale trade	42	453,470	4,060	215	5,797	441,810	4,379	256	6,035
Wholesale trade, durable goods	421	290,629	2,180	133	3,398	288,286	2,354	159	3,565
Wholesale trade, nondurable goods	422	162,841	1,880	82	2,398	153,524	2,025	97	2,470
Retail trade	44-45	1,118,447	2,461	237	13,991	1,111,583	3,171	306	15,029
Motor vehicle and parts dealers	441	122,633	645	50	1,719	122,692	812	64	1,884
Furniture and home furnishings stores	442	64,725	72	10	483	65,088	94	13	554
Electronics and appliance stores	443	43,373	69	7	345	46,724	88	10	418
Building material and garden equipment and supplies dealers	444	93,117	228	26	1,118	(S)	(S)	(S)	(S)
Food and beverage stores	445	148,528	402	41	2,893	149,802	488	49	2,896
Health and personal care stores	446	82,941	118	15	904	79,360	183	21	1,043
Gasoline stations	447	126,889	198	11	922	(S)	(S)	(S)	(S)
Clothing and clothing accessories stores	448	156,601	136	17	1,280	149,318	170	21	1,425
Sporting goods, hobby, book, and music store	451	69,149	62	7	561	63,033	78	9	633
General merchandise stores	452	36,171	330	31	2,508	39,846	451	43	2,549
Miscellaneous store retailers	453	129,838	78	10	753	129,070	95	14	849
Nonstore retailers	454	44,482	123	12	506	55,764	171	18	587

S Figure does not meet publication standards [1] North American Industry Classification System, 1997; see text, Section 15.

Source: U.S. Census Bureau, 2002 Economic Census, Advance Comparative Statistics for the United States, issued March 2004. See also: <http://www.census.gov/econ/census02/advance/TABLE2.HTM>.

No. 1018. Wholesale and Retail Trade—Establishments, Employees, and Payroll by State: 2000 and 2001

[6,112 represents 6,112,000. Covers establishments with payroll. Employees are for the week including March 12. Excludes most government employees, railroad employees, and self-employed persons. Kind-of-business classification based on North American Industry Classification System (NAICS) 1997; see text, Section 15. For statement on methodology, see Appendix III]

State	Wholesale establishments (NAICS 42)						Retail establishments (NAICS 44,45)					
	Number of establishments		Number of employees (1,000)		Annual payroll (mil. dol)		Number of establishments		Number of employees (1,000)		Annual payroll (mil. dol)	
	2000	2001	2000	2001	2000	2001	2000	2001	2000	2001	2000	2001
U.S. . . .	446,237	438,924	6,112	6,142	270,122	275,899	1,113,573	1,119,950	14,841	14,890	302,553	314,757
AL	6,132	5,984	82	80	2,892	2,866	19,723	19,654	230	227	4,074	4,193
AK	752	716	7	7	281	292	2,733	2,696	33	33	790	825
AZ	6,731	6,620	86	88	3,627	3,824	16,911	17,182	255	266	5,694	6,080
AR	3,505	3,479	45	44	1,402	1,443	12,211	12,250	135	137	2,268	2,373
CA	58,326	57,975	808	830	40,011	41,903	107,987	109,405	1,491	1,532	36,073	37,999
CO	7,452	7,352	97	99	4,906	5,014	18,748	19,046	252	261	5,883	5,993
CT	5,076	4,979	77	79	4,481	4,493	14,111	14,053	191	187	4,540	4,775
DE	1,009	989	19	24	1,117	1,433	3,742	3,778	52	52	1,048	1,116
DC	372	345	5	6	282	289	1,945	1,903	19	18	431	417
FL	30,671	29,958	315	311	12,536	12,493	67,396	69,077	903	915	18,044	18,942
GA	13,892	13,629	199	202	9,064	9,447	33,788	34,179	464	465	9,365	9,583
HI	1,809	1,803	19	20	627	652	4,924	5,012	63	65	1,313	1,342
ID	2,012	1,958	24	25	845	854	5,871	5,897	70	72	1,347	1,399
IL	21,509	20,975	344	343	16,683	16,482	43,800	43,716	637	609	12,992	13,119
IN	8,642	8,573	120	120	4,607	4,605	24,261	24,274	354	351	6,332	6,468
IA	5,155	5,020	65	65	2,173	2,171	14,382	14,239	184	182	3,169	3,288
KS	4,876	4,811	62	59	2,333	2,283	12,261	12,206	153	152	2,747	2,813
KY	4,939	4,803	74	74	2,536	2,616	16,988	16,852	221	221	3,804	3,934
LA	6,192	6,035	79	78	2,723	2,839	17,755	17,862	232	229	4,032	4,162
ME	1,740	1,723	22	22	744	776	7,015	7,040	77	80	1,436	1,540
MD	6,098	5,967	95	95	4,526	4,543	19,539	19,659	285	285	6,062	6,397
MA	9,735	9,627	156	162	9,114	9,220	25,813	25,539	353	352	7,729	8,408
MI	13,576	13,226	191	189	8,887	8,888	38,862	39,097	545	544	10,667	11,094
MN	9,294	9,159	137	140	6,399	6,705	20,862	21,196	304	316	5,980	6,711
MS	3,116	3,054	40	37	1,222	1,145	12,794	12,649	141	140	2,384	2,467
MO	9,072	8,841	146	141	5,458	5,088	23,911	23,812	318	317	6,258	6,453
MT	1,537	1,523	15	15	433	453	5,101	5,179	52	53	920	969
NE	3,061	2,981	41	39	1,346	1,320	8,248	8,256	110	109	1,895	1,979
NV	2,556	2,512	31	32	1,238	1,311	6,940	7,065	108	109	1,895	1,979
NH	2,105	2,069	25	24	1,184	1,161	6,545	6,570	93	93	1,930	2,054
NJ	17,157	16,791	279	281	14,724	15,163	34,841	35,071	439	434	9,897	10,461
NM	2,162	2,088	22	22	753	750	7,249	7,256	91	89	1,745	1,789
NY	36,606	36,019	422	427	20,941	21,246	75,500	75,910	844	841	18,116	18,937
NC	12,364	12,187	173	172	7,153	7,235	35,785	35,889	450	441	8,739	8,768
ND	1,543	1,518	18	17	532	534	3,435	3,460	42	41	719	754
OH	16,646	16,502	261	263	10,437	10,707	42,708	42,868	644	638	11,903	12,299
OK	5,005	4,868	62	62	2,126	2,194	14,147	14,087	168	169	2,913	3,027
OR	5,836	5,840	79	81	3,266	3,535	14,256	14,246	193	194	4,126	4,165
PA	16,796	16,447	243	244	10,287	10,679	48,518	48,597	668	670	12,556	13,155
RI	1,530	1,504	21	19	768	727	4,342	4,288	53	54	1,149	1,226
SC	5,091	4,991	65	62	2,353	2,266	18,619	18,629	224	219	4,083	4,025
SD	1,390	1,324	16	16	472	478	4,181	4,231	50	50	879	924
TN	8,006	7,823	127	130	4,848	5,173	24,624	24,337	311	310	5,908	6,025
TX	32,631	32,174	458	457	20,176	20,538	74,758	75,834	1,021	1,049	21,846	22,758
UT	3,294	3,310	44	44	1,583	1,670	7,952	8,189	124	126	2,455	2,474
VT	889	876	11	11	401	414	3,974	3,989	38	39	750	801
VA	7,893	7,756	110	111	4,651	4,799	28,794	28,998	399	399	7,949	8,252
WA	9,869	9,771	125	125	5,412	5,518	22,700	22,711	313	317	7,181	7,246
WV	1,869	1,800	22	22	698	698	7,788	7,713	92	88	1,493	1,497
WI	7,928	7,832	119	120	4,636	4,707	21,354	21,465	322	316	5,891	6,078
WY	790	817	7	7	229	260	2,881	2,839	28	29	515	543

Source: U.S. Census Bureau, *County Business Patterns*, annual. See also <http://www.census.gov/prod/2003pubs/01cbp/cbp01-1.pdf> (issued April 2003).

Domestic Trade 655

No. 1019. Retail Trade—Establishments, Employees, and Payroll: 2000 and 2001

[1,113.6 represents 1,113,600 except as indicated. Covers establishments with payroll. Employees are for the week including March 12.] Most government employees are excluded. For statement on methodology, see Appendix III]

Kind of business	NAICS code [1]	Establishments (1,000)		Employees (1,000)		Payroll (bil. dol.)	
		2000	2001	2000	2001	2000	2001
Retail trade, total	44,45	1,113.6	1,120.0	14,841	14,890	302.6	314.8
Motor vehicle & parts dealers [2]	441	124.5	125.7	1,866	1,850	63.9	66.6
Automobile dealers	4411	50.9	51.6	1,225	1,225	47.8	50.1
New car dealers	44111	26.2	26.4	1,112	1,112	44.8	46.9
Used car dealers	44112	24.7	25.1	110	113	3.1	3.2
Automotive parts, accessories & tire stores	4413	59.1	59.1	517	493	12.2	12.4
Furniture & home furnishing stores	442	64.8	65.7	549	567	13.4	13.6
Electronics & appliance stores	443	45.6	47.7	407	425	11.2	11.5
Appliance, TV & all other electronics stores	44311	29.6	31.6	279	295	6.6	7.2
Computer & software stores	44312	12.9	13.0	106	109	4.2	3.8
Camera & photographic supplies stores	44313	3.1	3.0	22	22	0.4	0.4
Bldg material & garden equip & supp dealers	444	91.9	94.1	1,235	1,249	32.5	34.7
Building material & supplies dealers	4441	70.9	71.8	1,055	1,062	28.4	30.3
Lawn & garden equip & supplies stores	4442	21.0	22.2	180	186	4.0	4.3
Food & beverage stores . . . •	445	154.5	156.2	3,004	2,963	48.4	49.3
Grocery stores	4451	98.3	99.3	2,717	2,665	44.0	44.6
Grocery (except convenience) stores	44511	68.8	68.7	2,544	2,487	41.8	42.3
Convenience stores	44512	29.5	30.5	173	178	2.2	2.3
Specialty food stores	4452	27.8	28.2	154	161	2.4	2.5
Meat markets	44521	6.5	6.6	41	42	0.6	0.7
Fish & seafood markets	44522	1.9	1.9	8	9	0.1	0.1
Fruit & vegetable markets	44523	3.2	3.3	18	21	0.3	0.4
Other specialty food stores	44529	16.2	16.2	86	90	1.3	1.3
Beer, wine & liquor stores [3]	4453	28.5	28.6	134	136	2.1	2.1
Health & personal care stores.	446	81.2	81.9	914	958	19.3	20.6
Pharmacies & drug stores	44611	40.6	40.0	680	699	14.5	15.4
Cosmetics, beauty supplies & perfume stores. . .	44612	9.6	10.6	61	76	0.8	1.0
Optical goods stores	44613	14.3	14.0	74	75	1.7	1.7
Other health & personal care stores	44619	16.7	17.2	98	109	2.2	2.4
Food (health) supplement stores.	446191	8.7	9.0	49	59	0.7	0.8
All other health & personal care stores.	446199	8.0	8.2	49	50	1.5	1.6
Gasoline stations	447	119.6	118.8	937	927	13.3	13.4
Gasoline stations with convenience stores	44711	80.5	81.1	653	655	8.9	9.0
Other gasoline stations.	44719	39.1	37.7	284	271	4.4	4.4
Clothing & clothing accessories stores	448	150.9	151.7	1,369	1,393	20.2	21.1
Clothing stores.	4481	90.0	92.7	1,015	1,033	13.7	14.5
Men's clothing stores	44811	10.7	10.7	85	86	1.6	1.6
Women's clothing stores.	44812	35.6	35.5	302	305	3.9	4.0
Children's & infants' clothing stores.	44813	5.6	5.7	59	57	0.7	0.7
Family clothing stores.	44814	20.6	21.8	453	470	5.9	6.4
Clothing accessories stores	44815	5.7	5.9	28	29	0.4	0.4
Other clothing stores	44819	11.8	12.0	88	87	1.2	1.3
Shoe stores	4482	29.7	28.2	185	188	2.6	2.7
Jewelry, luggage & leather goods stores	4483	31.3	31.8	168	172	3.9	3.9
Jewelry stores.	44831	29.3	29.8	156	159	3.6	3.7
Luggage & leather goods stores	44832	2.0	2.0	12	12	0.2	0.2
Sporting goods, hobby, book & music stores	451	65.0	64.5	616	622	8.8	9.2
Sporting goods, hobby, musical instrument stores. .	4511	43.6	43.2	389	408	6.0	6.3
Book, periodical & music stores.	4512	21.4	21.3	228	214	2.8	2.9
Prerecorded tape, CD & record stores.	45122	7.7	7.7	76	70	0.9	0.9
General merchandise stores.	452	39.6	41.2	2,526	2,526	39.8	42.2
Department stores	4521	10.4	10.4	1,766	1,727	27.2	28.6
Other general merchandise stores	4529	29.2	30.8	760	799	12.6	13.6
Warehouse clubs & superstores	45291	2.0	2.1	478	495	8.7	9.3
All other general merchandise stores.	45299	27.2	28.7	283	303	3.8	4.3
Miscellaneous store retailers [2]	453	131.0	129.3	850	842	13.8	13.9
Used merchandise stores.	4533	17.5	17.4	114	116	1.6	1.7
Other miscellaneous store retailers.	4539	46.4	45.5	264	262	5.4	5.3
Nonstore retailers.	454	44.8	42.9	567	566	18.1	18.3
Electronic shopping & mail-order houses.	4541	11.8	11.0	277	281	10.4	10.4
Vending machine operators	4542	6.2	6.0	67	64	1.5	1.5
Direct selling establishments	4543	26.8	26.0	223	221	6.1	6.4
Fuel dealers	45431	11.8	11.6	106	105	3.1	3.3
Other direct selling establishments	45439	15.0	14.2	117	116	3.0	3.1

[1] North American Industry Classification System 1997; see text, Section 15. [2] Includes other kinds of business not shown separately. [3] Includes government employees.

Source: U.S. Census Bureau, County Business Patterns, annual. See also <http://www.census.gov/prod/2003pubs/01cbp/cbp01-1.pdf> (issued April 2003).

[In billions of dollars (2,062.5 represents $2,062,500,000,000)]

Kind of business	NAICS code [1]	1992	1995	1998	1999	2000	2001	2002	2003
Retail and food services sales, total	44, 45, 72	2,062.5	2,502.0	2,917.4	3,164.8	3,376.6	3,476.0	3,563.6	3,756.7
Retail sales, total	44, 45	1,859.1	2,268.3	2,644.8	2,878.9	3,070.2	3,156.8	3,230.1	3,399.5
GAFO, total [2]		536.9	653.0	762.5	823.0	872.4	894.0	926.8	961.1
Motor vehicle and parts dealers	441	427.6	588.0	699.5	779.8	816.6	841.1	846.2	895.7
Automobile and other motor vehicle dealers	4411, 4412	377.2	528.7	631.9	707.9	742.0	767.4	769.2	814.5
Automobile dealers	4411	359.1	502.5	597.5	669.5	699.3	723.9	724.3	758.5
New car dealers	44111	333.8	464.6	545.1	611.5	638.8	662.3	659.5	685.9
Used cars dealers	44112	25.3	37.8	52.3	57.9	60.5	61.7	64.8	72.7
Auto parts, access., and tire stores	4413	50.4	59.3	67.6	71.9	74.6	73.7	77.1	81.2
Furniture, home furnishings, electronics and appliance stores	442, 443	97.8	130.4	154.6	167.1	178.0	176.6	183.6	192.5
Furniture and home furnishings stores	442	55.0	65.5	78.6	85.2	91.7	91.4	93.7	98.0
Furniture stores	4421	31.6	37.0	44.1	47.0	50.5	50.4	51.1	52.1
Home furnishings stores	4422	23.4	28.5	34.4	38.2	41.1	41.0	42.6	45.8
Electronics and appliance stores [3]	443	42.8	64.9	76.0	81.9	86.4	85.2	89.9	94.6
Appl. T.V., and other elect. stores	44311	29.0	42.1	46.3	51.4	56.9	58.5	61.3	64.7
Computer and software stores	44312	11.5	20.5	27.2	27.7	26.4	24.0	26.1	27.3
Building mat. garden equip. & supply stores	444	160.2	199.1	243.5	263.2	276.0	287.2	299.9	321.1
Building mat. & supply dealers	4441	135.5	172.3	210.0	229.6	241.3	251.5	265.4	283.4
Food and beverage stores [3]	445	371.5	391.3	421.6	443.2	459.2	481.4	489.4	505.9
Grocery stores	4451	337.9	356.9	382.4	402.5	415.3	434.9	441.7	455.5
Beer, wine and liquor stores	4453	21.8	22.1	25.7	27.0	29.2	30.5	31.1	32.1
Health and personal care stores	446	90.8	102.5	130.2	143.6	156.9	168.1	181.1	192.2
Pharmacies and drug stores	44611	77.8	85.9	108.3	121.1	130.9	141.8	153.5	163.9
Gasoline stations	447	156.6	181.3	191.7	211.3	247.2	247.0	244.8	268.5
Clothing and clothing access, stores [3]	448	120.3	131.6	149.4	160.1	167.9	167.3	171.8	178.4
Clothing stores [3]	4481	85.9	91.4	104.9	112.4	118.6	119.5	122.6	127.1
Men's clothing stores	44811	10.2	9.3	10.6	10.5	10.8	10.3	10.2	10.5
Women's clothing stores	44812	31.8	28.7	28.7	30.3	32.5	32.9	33.0	33.8
Family clothing stores	44814	33.2	40.0	49.5	53.8	56.4	56.8	59.9	62.7
Shoe stores	4482	18.1	19.8	21.5	22.0	22.1	22.1	22.3	22.6
Jewelry stores	44831	15.2	19.2	21.5	24.1	25.3	24.2	25.3	27.1
Sporting goods, hobby, book & music stores [3]	451	49.3	60.9	69.5	74.0	78.1	79.8	80.2	79.4
Sporting goods stores	45111	15.7	20.0	22.6	24.2	26.0	27.1	27.2	26.8
Book stores	451211	8.3	11.2	13.4	14.5	15.4	15.7	16.3	16.8
General merchandise stores	452	248.0	300.6	351.7	381.4	406.2	430.1	451.4	471.1
Department stores (excl. L.D.) [4]	4521	177.1	205.9	223.7	231.0	233.6	229.9	222.6	214.1
Department stores (incl. L.D.) [4]	4521	181.3	210.9	228.5	236.1	238.7	234.0	225.9	216.8
Other general merchandise stores	4529	70.9	94.7	128.1	150.4	172.6	200.2	228.7	256.9
Warehouse clubs and superstores	45291	40.0	65.1	98.6	119.1	140.2	165.6	192.6	217.5
Miscellaneous stores retail	453	55.8	77.2	99.8	105.8	108.5	105.1	104.4	104.9
Nonstore retailers	454	81.3	105.4	133.3	149.5	175.7	173.0	177.3	189.7
Electronic shopping and mail order	4541	35.3	52.7	79.5	92.4	110.1	109.2	114.5	121.2
Fuel dealers	45431	19.3	21.6	19.7	20.7	27.8	27.1	24.8	29.8
Food services and drinking places [3]	722	203.4	233.6	272.6	285.9	306.4	319.2	333.5	357.1
Full service restaurants	7221	86.5	99.4	119.7	124.9	132.9	138.9	145.9	158.4
Limited service eating places	7222	87.4	103.1	116.8	122.2	131.4	137.7	144.6	155.3
Drinking places	7224	12.4	12.5	14.1	14.8	15.8	16.1	16.8	17.1

[1] North American Industry Classification System, 1997; see text, Section 15, Business Enterprise. [2] GAFO represents store classified in the following NAICS codes: 442,443,448,451,452, and 4532. [3] Includes other kinds of business not shown separately. [4] L.D. represents leased departments.

Source: U.S. Census Bureau, Current Business Reports, Annual Benchmark Report for Retail Trade and Food Services, January 1992 Through March 2003, Series BR/01-A.

No. 1021. Retail Trade Corporations—Sales, Net Profit, and Profit Per Dollar of Sales: 2002

[Represents North American Industry Classification System, 1997 (NAICS) groups 44 and 45. Profit rates are averages of quarterly figures at annual rates. Covers corporations with assets of $50,000,000 or more.

Item	Unit	Total retail trade	Food and beverage stores (NAICS) 445	Clothing and general merchandise stores NAICS 448 and 452	All other retail stores
Sales	Bil. dol	1,415.5	311.9	586.1	517.5
Net profit:					
Before income taxes	Bil. dol	58.7	10.3	25.8	22.6
After income taxes	Bil. dol	37.0	6.6	16.2	14.3
Profits per dollar of sales:					
Before income taxes	Cents	4.2	3.3	4.3	4.4
After income taxes	Cents	2.6	2.1	2.7	2.8
Profits on stockholders' equity:					
Before income taxes	Percent	22.5	26.4	20.2	23.8
After income taxes	Percent	14.2	16.9	12.6	15.1

Source: U.S. Census Bureau, Quarterly Financial Report for Manufacturing, Mining and Trade Corporations. annual.

No. 1022. Retail Trade and Food Services—Estimated Per Capita Sales by Selected Kinds of Business: 1992 to 2002

[As of Dec. 31. In dollars. Based on estimated resident population estimates as of July 1] For statement on methodology, see Appendix III.]

Kind of business	NAICS code [1]	1992	1994	1995	1996	1997	1998	1999	2000	2001	2002
Retail sales, total	44-45	7,290	8,283	8,631	9,097	9,412	9,787	10,556	11,264	11,052	11,254
Total(Excluding motor vehicle and parts dealers)	44-45 ex 441	5,613	6,170	6,394	6,702	6,945	7,199	7,696	8,270	8,106	8,297
Motor vehicle and parts dealers	441	1,677	2,113	2,237	2,395	2,467	2,588	2,860	2,995	2,946	2,957
Furniture, home furnishings	442	216	241	249	262	277	291	313	336	320	329
Electronics and appliance stores	443	168	221	247	258	262	281	300	317	299	312
Building material and garden equipment and supply stores	444	628	733	757	802	857	901	964	1,013	1,007	1,042
Food and beverage stores	445	1,456	1,480	1,489	1,516	1,532	1,560	1,623	1,689	1,684	1,702
Health and personal care stores	446	356	374	390	415	445	482	527	576	587	625
Gasoline stations	447	614	658	690	734	746	710	775	905	860	835
Clothing and clothing accessories stores	448	472	497	501	516	525	553	587	616	586	596
Sporting goods, hobby, book, and music stores	451	193	221	232	242	245	257	272	286	278	284
General merchandise stores.	452	972	1,096	1,144	1,189	1,238	1,302	1,399	1,490	1,508	1,580
Miscellaneous store retailers	453	219	271	294	317	342	369	388	398	368	362
Nonstore retailers.	454	319	378	401	451	476	493	549	646	607	627
Food services and drinking places.	722	798	867	889	916	964	1,009	1,049	1,123	1,116	1,160

[1] North American Industry Classification System, 1997; see text, Section 15.

Source: U.S. Census Bureau, *Current Business Reports, Annual Benchmark Report for Retail Trade and Food Services: January 1992 Through March 2003, Drinking Places Series (BR/01-A)* and Population Division, Population Estimates Program.

No. 1023. Retail Trade—Estimated Purchases by Kind of Business: 1992 to 2002

[In billions of dollars. (1,351.1 represents $1,351,100,000,000)]

Kind of business	NAICS code [1]	1992	1995	1997	1998	1999	2000	2001	2002
Total.	44,45	1,351.1	1,650.0	1,834.9	1,923.0	2,102.0	2,242.1	2,301.2	2,349.5
Total(excl. motor vehicle and parts dealers)	44,45	1,008.4	1,178.6	1,300.1	1,353.4	1,464.6	1,571.0	1,610.9	1,658.3
Motor vehicle and parts dealers	441	342.6	471.4	534.8	569.6	637.5	671.2	690.3	691.2
Furniture and home furnishings stores	442	32.1	38.3	43.0	45.2	48.8	52.2	51.4	52.8
Electronics and appliance stores	443	30.8	49.0	52.1	56.6	61.0	63.3	62.2	65.9
Building material, garden equipment and supplies dealers	444	115.9	145.2	169.8	177.9	192.5	197.0	203.1	214.1
Food and beverage stores	445	279.2	290.3	303.6	309.9	323.6	334.6	345.9	349.9
Health and personal care stores	446	63.7	72.3	83.0	90.6	101.9	110.3	119.3	127.3
Gasoline stations	447	125.4	140.1	155.7	149.6	166.4	198.6	198.1	197.7
Clothing and clothing accessories stores . . .	448	71.7	78.3	83.5	87.2	92.7	98.6	96.6	98.9
Sporting goods, hobby, book, and music stores	451	31.1	39.2	41.1	44.4	47.2	49.7	49.3	48.5
General merchandise stores	452	182.0	223.1	243.4	256.8	280.2	299.0	322.1	341.8
Miscellaneous store retailers	453	31.5	44.8	53.1	58.7	62.7	63.4	61.2	60.0
Nonstore retailers.	454	45.1	58.0	71.8	76.4	87.7	104.3	101.8	101.5
Electronic shopping and mail order.	4541	19.3	30.1	41.2	47.7	57.2	67.8	66.9	68.8

[1] North American Industry Classification System, 1997; see text, Section 15.

Source: U.S. Census Bureau, *Current Business Reports, Annual Benchmark Report for Retail Trade and Food Services, January 1992 Through March 2003* Series (BR/01-A) and unpublished data.

No. 1024. Retail Trade—Merchandise Inventories and Inventory/Sales Ratio by Kind of Business: 2000 to 2003

[Inventories in billions of dollars (417.7 represents $417,700,000,000. As of Dec. 31. Estimates exclude food services. Includes warehouses. Adjusted for seasonal variations. Sales data also adjusted for holiday and trading-day differences]

Kind of business	NAICS code [1]	Inventories				Inventory/Sales Ratio			
		2000	2001	2002	2003	2000	2001	2002	2003
Total	44,45	417.7	406.0	436.3	451.5	1.62	1.53	1.57	1.55
Excluding motor vehicle and parts dealers	44,45 ex 441	285.9	282.8	289.9	299.1	1.49	1.46	1.44	1.39
Motor vehicle and parts dealers	441	131.8	123.2	146.5	152.4	2.00	1.74	1.91	1.98
Furniture, home furnishings, electronics, and appliance stores	442,443	25.5	24.1	26.5	27.2	1.79	1.57	1.64	1.63
Building material and garden equipment and supplies dealers	444	40.6	40.6	43.3	47.5	1.73	1.72	1.77	1.70
Food and beverage stores	445	33.0	34.3	34.3	34.7	0.84	0.84	0.84	0.82
Clothing and clothing accessories stores . .	448	36.5	35.2	36.1	37.2	2.58	2.49	2.51	2.42
General merchandise stores.	452	65.3	65.3	66.3	67.7	1.87	1.74	1.76	1.68
Department stores	4521	43.0	40.9	37.6	37.4	2.17	2.13	2.18	2.10

[1] North American Industry Classification System, 1997; see text, Section 15.

Source: U.S. Census Bureau, *Current Business Reports, Annual Benchmark Report for Retail Trade and Food Services: January 1992 Through December 2003* Series BR/01-A, and unpublished data.

No. 1025. Retail Trade and Food Services—Sales by Type of Store and State: 2002

[In millions of dollars (3,367,086 represents $3,367,086,000,000) except as indicated. Kind-of-business classification based on North American Industry Classification System (NAICS), 1997; see text, Section 15. Data are estimates]

State	All retail stores [1] (NAICS 44, 45)	Total retail sales + food and drink	Motor vehicle and parts dealers (NAICS 441)	Furniture and home furnishings (NAICS 442)	Electronics and appliances (NAICS 443)	Building material & garden equip. & supp. dealers (NAICS 444)	Food and beverage stores (NAICS 445)	Health and personal care (NAICS 446)
U.S...	3,367,086	3,724,992	889,259	98,993	98,775	330,901	489,332	198,080
AL	43,234	47,715	11,724	1,093	704	4,311	5,761	2,454
AK	7,389	8,348	1,592	112	151	930	1,294	118
AZ	65,581	72,096	18,535	2,105	1,985	5,604	8,560	3,591
AR	27,531	29,921	7,845	593	470	2,742	3,065	1,196
CA	413,238	462,002	109,959	12,647	20,537	38,764	64,889	24,860
CO	59,450	65,964	15,874	2,393	1,905	6,711	8,921	1,825
CT	46,651	51,264	11,423	1,410	1,353	4,760	7,982	3,063
DE	11,149	12,399	2,914	522	369	1,259	1,324	805
DC	2,657	4,431	110	125	87	236	625	372
FL.....	200,009	218,991	61,063	5,938	5,686	16,280	31,331	13,271
GA	100,254	111,249	28,449	3,313	2,401	12,549	14,867	4,230
HI.....	13,680	15,952	2,116	233	210	848	2,569	1,154
ID.....	16,137	17,416	4,275	447	410	2,128	2,183	461
IL.....	137,124	153,674	34,848	3,918	4,052	13,157	21,035	9,880
IN.....	69,538	76,635	18,699	1,688	1,510	7,526	8,454	4,119
IA.....	35,870	38,721	9,502	884	896	5,001	4,935	1,794
KS	33,664	36,512	8,726	954	1,042	3,296	4,760	1,411
KY	39,519	44,343	9,874	812	642	4,468	5,340	2,532
LA	44,995	50,074	12,140	979	680	4,460	6,190	2,806
ME	18,127	19,559	4,074	351	233	1,833	3,520	688
MD	64,219	70,943	16,394	1,961	2,204	5,735	11,966	3,988
MA	80,287	91,025	19,887	2,139	1,821	7,108	13,896	5,351
MI.....	119,825	131,501	33,013	3,414	2,881	10,663	14,597	9,254
MN	71,046	77,438	17,059	2,381	2,183	9,022	8,983	3,157
MS	26,897	29,355	7,439	748	402	3,057	3,729	1,376
MO	64,900	71,787	17,765	1,601	1,442	6,358	7,833	3,207
MT	8,851	9,921	2,174	207	176	1,215	1,551	275
NE	20,459	22,420	4,773	1,036	450	2,598	2,887	941
NV	27,602	31,338	6,477	890	781	2,702	3,953	1,320
NH	23,743	25,535	6,967	628	815	1,919	3,330	915
NJ.....	109,105	118,760	27,829	3,892	3,539	8,365	17,201	9,213
NM	19,795	21,818	4,733	605	394	1,639	2,515	1,022
NY	195,874	218,324	42,587	6,055	5,780	16,897	31,131	16,921
NC	91,712	101,778	25,456	3,378	2,154	11,368	12,447	4,885
ND	8,085	8,759	1,865	204	187	1,604	801	452
OH	133,507	147,920	35,401	3,868	3,982	13,213	17,310	9,851
OK	36,828	40,657	10,971	873	995	2,902	4,276	1,929
OR	42,625	47,148	11,073	1,130	1,016	4,767	6,202	1,317
PA	135,599	149,811	35,624	3,349	2,781	12,338	21,544	10,216
RI.....	9,932	11,687	2,397	276	219	692	1,712	1,061
SC	43,237	48,208	11,431	1,161	726	5,834	6,290	2,011
SD	14,724	15,579	2,466	208	179	1,434	1,352	393
TN	70,166	77,277	19,075	1,875	1,247	6,545	11,472	3,514
TX	274,981	303,468	81,868	8,141	9,036	22,842	33,264	11,452
UT	26,134	28,368	6,882	987	834	3,292	4,201	426
VT	7,712	8,394	2,050	173	177	964	1,338	375
VA	86,194	94,674	21,741	3,067	3,060	9,160	11,878	4,084
WA	71,587	80,394	16,180	1,983	1,911	8,167	10,474	3,591
WV	17,288	18,930	4,419	315	201	1,677	2,422	1,563
WI	71,360	77,365	17,940	1,803	1,787	9,327	10,137	3,257
WY	6,585	7,141	1,578	126	89	634	1,035	134

See footnotes at end of table.

U.S. Census Bureau, Statistical Abstract of the United States: 2004-2005

No. 1025. Retail Trade and Food Services—Sales by Type of Store and State: 2002—Con.

[See headnote, page 659]

State	Gasoline stations (NAICS 447)	Clothing and clothing accessories (NAICS 448)	Sporting goods, hobby, book & music stores (NAICS 451)	General merchandise (NAICS 452)	Miscellaneous stores (NAICS 453)	Nonstore retailers (NAICS 454)	Food services & drinking places (NAICS 722)
U.S...	228,063	179,674	93,052	483,234	113,481	164,242	357,906
AL	3,859	1,986	836	8,231	1,452	823	4,480
AK	451	348	212	1,672	212	298	959
AZ	5,048	2,368	1,773	9,792	3,019	3,202	6,514
AR	2,659	1,079	566	5,827	924	564	2,390
CA	23,963	24,650	13,897	53,823	13,954	11,294	48,764
CO	3,801	2,568	2,532	8,354	2,375	2,190	6,514
CT	2,277	2,877	1,373	3,783	1,403	4,947	4,613
DE	531	643	407	1,550	404	420	1,250
DC	216	364	210	95	169	47	1,774
FL.....	11,499	11,415	4,712	24,786	6,616	7,412	18,982
GA	8,310	4,860	2,016	13,901	3,139	2,220	10,995
HI.....	918	1,629	412	2,806	681	105	2,272
ID.....	1,087	477	530	2,561	604	974	1,279
IL.....	7,829	8,792	3,419	17,190	4,004	9,001	16,550
IN.....	5,608	2,416	1,384	11,845	1,982	4,308	7,097
IA....	3,689	1,239	754	5,202	876	1,099	2,850
KS ...	2,751	1,579	852	6,567	1,055	669	2,848
KY ...	3,953	1,438	769	7,388	1,531	771	4,824
LA ...	4,298	2,101	837	8,440	1,321	745	5,079
ME ...	1,380	790	429	2,099	528	2,203	1,432
MD	3,606	4,314	2,218	7,874	2,061	1,898	6,724
MA....	4,295	5,688	2,677	8,859	2,759	5,809	10,738
MI.....	6,855	5,139	4,272	21,583	5,041	3,113	11,676
MN ...	5,489	2,815	2,508	9,253	2,279	5,916	6,392
MS ...	2,781	954	385	4,738	829	459	2,458
MO	6,277	2,314	1,497	10,836	2,165	3,604	6,887
MT	686	258	314	1,530	281	184	1,070
NE	1,630	857	450	2,907	472	1,459	1,961
NV	1,608	2,148	719	3,330	1,494	2,180	3,736
NH	1,270	1,049	731	3,219	663	2,237	1,793
NJ.	4,920	7,180	3,934	12,283	3,550	7,199	9,655
NM ...	1,749	794	575	3,389	1,261	1,118	2,022
NY ...	9,526	19,450	6,788	22,260	8,279	10,199	22,450
NC ...	6,733	4,336	1,839	12,527	3,788	2,801	10,066
ND ...	626	233	274	1,266	238	334	674
OH	8,731	5,964	3,008	22,346	3,718	6,545	13,983
OK	3,592	1,046	862	7,314	1,251	817	3,830
OR	2,350	1,661	1,450	7,641	1,752	2,264	4,524
PA	8,449	7,454	3,244	15,798	3,554	11,247	14,212
RI	614	636	303	1,002	297	723	1,755
SC	3,857	2,153	702	6,643	1,767	662	4,972
SD	874	304	242	1,315	298	5,658	856
TN	5,718	3,564	1,454	12,049	2,293	1,360	7,111
TX	20,070	13,651	6,658	42,052	8,836	17,110	28,487
UT	1,843	1,098	906	4,089	538	1,040	2,234
VT	633	301	229	543	222	709	681
VA	7,137	4,679	2,238	12,925	2,270	3,955	8,480
WA....	3,808	2,998	2,660	12,725	2,916	4,173	8,807
WV....	1,714	676	304	3,158	520	318	1,642
WI.....	5,499	2,175	1,539	10,702	1,609	5,584	6,005
WY....	999	167	152	1,165	234	274	556

[1] Includes other types of stores, not shown separately.

Source: Market Statistics, a division of Claritas Inc., Arlington, VA, *The Survey of Buying Power Data Service*, annual (copyright).

U.S. Census Bureau, Statistical Abstract of the United States: 2004-2005

[1,761 represents 1,761,000. Includes only firms subject to federal income tax. Nonemployers are businesses with no paid employees. Based on the North American Industry Classification System (NAICS), 1997, see text, Section 15]

Kind of business	NAICS code	Establishments (1,000)			Receipts (mil. dol.)		
		1999	2000	2001	1999	2000	2001
Retail trade, total	44-45	1,761	1,743	1,739	73,314	73,810	73,675
Motor vehicle & parts dealers [1]	441	121	122	127	17,184	17,355	17,404
Used car dealers	44112	74	74	76	13,212	13,255	13,197
Motorcycle & boat & other MV dealers	44122	20	21	23	1,874	1,969	2,062
Automotive parts, accessories, & tire stores. .	4413	24	25	25	1,839	1,872	1,885
Furniture & home furnishings stores.	442	37	37	37	2,542	2,574	2,592
Furniture stores	4421	14	14	14	1,026	1,034	1,054
Home furnishings stores.	4422	23	23	23	1,516	1,540	1,538
Electronics & appliance stores	443	30	29	28	1,741	1,688	1,658
Bldg material & garden equip & supp dealers [1]	444	28	28	28	2,165	2,182	2,196
Building material & supplies dealers	4441	20	20	20	1,685	1,677	1,691
Food & beverage stores	445	84	82	82	8,465	8,493	8,505
Grocery stores	4451	40	39	39	4,597	4,609	4,591
Specialty food stores	4452	34	33	33	2,141	2,135	2,149
Beer, wine, & liquor stores	4453	10	10	10	1,727	1,749	1,765
Health & personal care stores.	446	89	92	97	1,813	1,915	2,012
Gasoline stations	447	10	10	10	1,713	1,721	1,665
Clothing & clothing accessories stores [1]	448	88	89	91	4,389	4,464	4,472
Clothing stores	4481	60	60	61	2,647	2,718	2,724
Jewelry stores	44831	23	23	24	1,406	1,416	1,419
Sporting goods, hobby, book, & music stores [1] .	451	98	96	94	3,775	3,761	3,733
Sporting goods stores	45111	24	23	23	1,330	1,340	1,337
Book, periodical, & music stores	4512	33	32	31	1,025	1,007	982
General merchandise stores.	452	26	28	28	1,250	1,291	1,318
Miscellaneous store retailers [1]	453	350	339	329	13,169	12,963	12,617
Gift, novelty, & souvenir stores	45322	72	73	72	2,130	2,104	2,097
Used merchandise stores	4533	80	76	72	2,243	2,115	1,927
Nonstore retailers [1]	454	799	792	787	15,109	15,401	15,504
Electronic shopping & mail-order houses. . . .	4541	45	49	50	1,260	1,391	1,531
Direct selling establishments	4543	717	708	704	12,860	13,047	13,019

[1] Includes other kinds of business not shown separately.

Source: U.S. Census Bureau, "Nonemployer Statistics"; published 28 March 2003; <http://www.census.gov/epcd/nonemployer/>.

No. 1027. Franchised New Car Dealerships—Summary: 1980 to 2003

[130.5 represents $130,500,000,000]

Item	Unit	1980	1985	1990	1995	1998	1999	2000	2001	2002	2003
Dealerships [1]	Number .	27,900	24,725	24,825	22,800	22,600	22,400	22,250	21,800	21,725	21,650
Sales	Bil. dol .	130.5	251.6	316.0	456.2	546.3	606.5	650.3	690.4	679.5	699.2
New cars sold [2]	1,000 . .	8,979	11,042	9,300	8,635	8,137	8,699	8,847	8,423	8,103	7,609
Used vehicles sold	Millions .	9.72	13.30	14.18	18.48	19.33	20.07	20.45	21.39	19.42	19.5
Employment	1,000 . .	745	856	924	996	1,048	1,081	1,114	1,130	1,130	1,130
Annual payroll	Bil. dol . .	11.0	20.1	24.0	33.1	39.8	42.5	46.1	48.0	48.8	50.0
Advertising expenses	Bil. dol . .	1.2	2.8	3.7	4.6	5.3	5.6	6.4	6.6	7.5	8.5
Dealer pretax profits as a percentage of sales	Percent .	0.6	2.2	1.0	1.4	1.7	1.8	1.6	2.0	1.9	1.7
Inventory: [3]											
Domestic: [4]											
Total	1,000 . .	2,112	2,339	2,537	2,974	2,732	2,901	3,183	2,824	2,727	3,085
Days' supply.	Days . . .	57	60	73	71	63	62	68	63	63	63
Imported: [4]											
Total	1,000 . .	269	345	707	445	350	378	468	508	521	618
Days' supply.	Days . . .	31	30	72	72	54	47	50	51	49	49

[1] At beginning of year. [2] Data provided by "Ward's Automotive Reports". [3] Annual average. Includes light trucks. [4] Classification based on where automobiles are produced (i.e., automobiles manufactured by foreign companies but produced in the U.S. are classified as domestic).

Source: National Automobile Dealers Association, McLean, VA, NADA Data, annual.

No. 1028. Retail Sales—New Passenger Cars: 1990 to 2001

[In thousands, except as indicated (9,300 represents 9,300,000)].

Item	1990	1994	1995	1996	1997	1998	1999	2000	2001
Total retail new passenger car sales [1]	9,300	8,991	8,635	8,527	8,272	8,142	8,698	8,847	8,423
Domestic [2].	6,897	7,255	7,129	7,254	6,917	6,762	6,979	6,831	6,325
Imports	2,403	1,735	1,506	1,273	1,355	1,380	1,719	2,016	2,098
Japan	1,719	1,239	982	727	726	691	758	863	837
Germany	265	192	207	238	297	367	467	517	523
Other	419	303	317	308	332	322	494	637	738

[1] Retail new car sales include both sales to individuals and to corporate fleets. It also includes leased cars. [2] Includes cars produced in Canada and Mexico.

Source: U.S. Bureau of Transportation Statistics, National Transportation Statistics 2003. Data supplied by following sources: 1970: American Automobile Manufacturers Association, Motor Vehicle Facts & Figures, 1992 and 1997, Southfield, MI; Ward's Motor Vehicle Facts & Figures, 2002, Southfield, MI: 2002. See also: <http://www.bts.gov>.

No. 1029. Retail Sales of New Cars by Sector: 1990 to 2002

[In thousands (9,300 represents 9,300,000), except as indicated)]

Item [1]	1990	1995	1996	1997	1998	1999	2000	2001	2002
Total, Sales of new cars [2]	9,300	8,687	8,527	8,265	8,142	8,697	8,852	8,422	8,082
Consumer	5,677	4,351	4,079	3,905	3,980	4,389	4,696	4,640	4,486
Business	3,477	4,186	4,273	4,213	3,991	4,135	3,989	3,617	3,434
Government	147	151	176	147	170	173	167	166	163
Percentage of total sales	61.0	50.1	47.8	47.3	48.9	50.5	53.0	55.1	55.5
Consumer	37.4	48.2	50.1	51.0	49.0	47.5	45.1	42.9	42.5
Business	1.6	1.7	2.1	1.8	2.1	2.0	1.9	2.0	2.0
Government									

[1] Includes imported cars, but not vans, trucks, or sport utility vehicles.   [2] Numbers may not add to totals due to rounding.

Source: U.S. Bureau of Transportation Statistics, *National Transportation Statistics 2003*. Data supplied by following source: U.S. Department of Commerce, Bureau of Economic Analysis, National Income and Wealth Division, unpublished data. See also <http://www.bts.gov>.

No. 1030. New and Used Car Sales and Leases: 1990 to 2002

[In thousands, except as indicated (46,830 represents 46,830,000)]

Item	1990	1995	1996	1997	1998	1999	2000	2001	2002
Total car sales	46,830	50,393	49,327	49,509	48,983	49,437	50,467	51,047	(NA)
New passenger car sales [1]	9,300	8,635	8,526	8,272	8,142	8,698	9,847	8,423	(NA)
Used passenger car sales [2]	37,530	41,758	40,801	41,237	40,841	40,739	41,620	42,624	43,025
Value of transactions (bil. dol.)	220	319	329	336	335	350	356	376	372
Average price (dol.)	5,857	7,644	8,073	8,139	8,211	8,587	8,547	8,618	8,655
New passenger car leases [3]	534	1,795	1,806	2,062	2,174	2,301	2,272	2,015	1,732

NA Not available.   [1] Includes leased cars.   [2] Used car sales include sales from franchised dealers, independent dealers, and casual sales.   [3] Consumer leases only.

Source: U.S. Bureau of Transportation Statistics, *National Transportation Statistics 2003*. Data supplied by following sources: New passenger car sales: 1994-98, American Automobile Manufacturers Association, *Motor Vehicle Facts & Figures, 2002*, Southfield, MI; *Ward's Motor Vehicle Facts & Figures, 2002*, Southfield, MI; Used passenger car sales: ADT Automotive, *2003 Used Car Market Report* Nashville, TN; Leased passenger cars: CNW Marketing/Research, Bandon, OR, personal communication.

No. 1031. New Motor Vehicle Sales and Expenditures by Model Year: 1990 to 2002

[In thousands of units (14,169 represents 14,169,000), except as indicated. A model year begins on Oct. 1 and ends on Sept. 30. It covers the fourth quarter of one calendar year and the first three quarters of the next calendar year]

Sales and expenditures	1990	1995	1997	1998	1999	2000	2001	2002
New motor vehicle sales	14,169	15,204	15,498	15,963	17,414	17,817	17,472	17,118
New-car sales	9,436	8,687	8,273	8,142	8,697	8,852	8,422	8,082
Domestic	6,790	7,178	6,906	6,764	6,982	6,833	6,323	5,854
Import	2,645	1,510	1,366	1,378	1,715	2,019	2,100	2,228
New-truck sales	4,733	6,517	7,226	7,821	8,717	8,965	9,050	9,036
Light	4,428	6,089	6,797	7,297	8,072	8,387	8,607	8,633
Domestic	3,996	5,694	6,226	6,651	7,310	7,546	7,629	7,572
Import	432	395	571	646	763	841	978	1,061
Other	306	429	429	524	645	578	443	402
Domestic-car production	6,231	6,351	5,927	5,547	5,637	5,540	4,879	5,016
Avg. expenditure per new car [1] (dollar)	14,371	17,959	19,531	20,370	20,673	20,909	21,258	21,440
Domestic (dollar)	13,936	16,864	17,907	18,485	18,639	18,884	19,039	19,126
Import (dollar)	15,510	23,202	27,722	29,615	28,951	27,766	27,941	27,524

[1] BEA estimate based on the manufacturer's suggested retail price.

Source: U.S. Bureau of Economic Analysis, *Survey of Current Business*, February 2002 and unpublished data. Data on unit sales and production are mainly from "Ward's Automotive Reports" published by Ward's Communications, Southfield, MI.

No. 1032. Annual U.S. Mothor Vehicle Production and Factory (Wholesale) Sales: 1990 to 2001

[In thousands, except as indicated (9,783 represents 9,783,000)]

Item	1990	1994	1995	1996	1997	1998	1999	2000	2001
Production, total [1]	9,783	12,263	11,985	11,833	12,119	12,003	13,025	12,774	11,425
Passenger cars	6,077	6,614	6,351	6,083	5,927	5,554	5,638	5,542	4,879
Commercial vehicles [2]	3,706	5,649	5,635	5,749	6,192	6,448	7,387	7,231	6,546
Factory (wholesale) sales, total	9,775	12,189	12,023	11,916	12,223	12,112	12,127	12,527	11,108
Passenger cars	6,050	6,549	6,310	6,140	6,070	5,677	5,428	5,504	4,884
Commercial vehicles [2]	3,725	5,640	5,713	5,776	6,153	6,435	6,699	7,022	6,224

[1] Factory sales can be greater than production total because of sales from previous year's inventory.   [2] Includes trucks under 10,000 pounds gross vehicle weight rating (GVWR), such as compact and conventional pickups, sport utility vehicles, minivans and vans, and trucks and buses.

Source: U.S. Bureau of Transportation Statistics, *National Transportation Statistics 2003*. Data supplied by following sources: *Motor Vehicle Facts & Figures, 2002*, Southfield, MI; *Ward's Motor Vehicle Facts & Figures, 2002*, Southfield, MI: 2002; See also: <http://www.bts.gov>.

No. 1033. Retail Foodstores—Number and Sales by Type: 1990 to 2002

[282.6 represents 282,600. Beginning with 2001 data based on North American Industry Classification System (NAICS), 1997. All other years based on Standard Industrial Classification (SIC) codes]

Type of foodstore	Number [1] (1,000)					Sales [2] (bil. dol.)					Percent distribution			
											Number		Sales	
	1990	1995	2000	2001	2002	1990	1999	2000	2001	2002	1990	2002	1990	2002
Total............	282.6	264.4	243.8	219.5	224.6	368.3	402.5	483.7	442.0	458.4	100.0	100.0	100.0	100.0
Grocery stores........	190.3	176.9	163.2	145.4	146.4	348.2	382.2	458.3	425.4	441.7	67.3	65.2	94.5	96.4
Supermarkets [3]......	24.5	25.3	24.6	23.9	24.1	261.7	300.4	337.3	354.5	359.1	8.7	10.7	71.1	78.3
Conventional........	13.2	12.3	9.9	8.9	8.3	92.3	76.4	63.4	65.8	74.0	4.7	3.7	25.1	16.1
Superstore [4]........	5.8	6.8	7.9	7.9	7.9	87.6	116.7	142.4	152.1	147.1	2.1	3.5	23.8	32.1
Warehouse [5].......	3.4	2.7	2.4	2.7	2.7	33.1	20.7	22.0	24.2	24.0	1.2	1.2	9.0	5.2
Combination food and drug [6]......	1.6	2.7	3.7	3.9	4.5	29.3	59.3	81.8	83.8	85.7	0.6	2.0	8.0	18.7
Superwarehouse [7]....	0.3	0.6	0.5	0.5	0.5	12.6	17.8	17.4	17.7	17.1	0.1	0.2	3.4	3.7
Hypermarket [8]......	0.1	0.2	0.2	0.2	0.3	6.8	9.5	10.3	11.0	11.2	(Z)	0.1	1.8	2.4
Convenience stores [9]...	93.0	86.9	81.9	56.2	66.1	37.0	42.4	48.5	19.5	24.3	32.9	29.4	10.0	5.3
Superette [10]........	72.8	64.7	56.7	65.2	56.2	49.5	39.4	72.5	51.4	58.3	25.8	25.0	13.4	12.7
Specialized food stores [11].	92.3	87.5	80.6	74.1	78.2	20.1	20.3	25.4	16.6	16.7	32.7	34.8	5.5	3.6

Z Less than 0.05 percent. [1] Estimated. [2] Includes nonfood items. [3] A grocery store, primarily self-service in operation, providing a full range of departments, and having at least $2.5 million in annual sales in 1985 dollars. [4] Contains greater variety of products than conventional supermarkets, including specialty and service departments, and considerable nonfood (general merchandise) products. [5] Contains limited product variety and fewer services provided, incorporating case lot stocking and shelving practices. [6] Contains a pharmacy, a nonprescription drug department, and a greater variety of health and beauty aids than that carried by conventional supermarkets. [7] A larger warehouse store that offers expanded product variety and often service meat, deli, or seafood departments. [8] A very large store offering a greater variety of general merchandise—like clothes, hardware, and seasonal goods—and personal care products than other grocery stores. [9] A small grocery store selling a limited variety of food and nonfood products, typically open extended hours. [10] A grocery store, primarily self-service in operation, selling a wide variety of food and nonfood products with annual sales below $2.5 million (1985 dollars). [11] Primarily engaged in the retail sale of a single food category such as meat and seafood stores and retail bakeries.

Source: U.S. Dept. of Agriculture, Economic Research Service, *Food Marketing Review*, annual.

No. 1034. Percent of Supermarkets Offering Selected Services and Product Lines: 1990 to 2002

[In percent. Based on a sample survey of chain and independent supermarkets and subject to sampling variability; for details, see source]

Service or product line offered	1990	1993	1996	1997	1998	1999	2000	2001	2002
Service delicatessen............	73	79	80	81	81	81	81	80	80
Service bakery................	60	62	69	69	69	69	71	72	72
Service meat.................	42	47	74	60	59	60	62	66	66
Service seafood.............	33	37	46	43	43	45	45	51	43
Specialty cheese department......	33	34	31	30	31	32	33	42	36
Salad bar..................	18	19	27	24	24	24	25	22	22
Automated teller machines (ATM's) ..	20	38	60	62	62	63	64	65	68
Banking in store..............	(NA)	(NA)	14	22	21	22	21	20	22
Pharmacy.................	15	20	26	26	26	32	30	32	34
Warehouse aisle..............	(NA)	(NA)	10	16	17	17	16	14	14

NA Not available.

Source: Progressive Grocer, New York, NY, *Progressive Grocer 70th Annual Report* (copyright). Used by permission of Progressive Grocer magazine(A VNU company).

No. 1035. Food and Alcoholic Beverage Sales by Sales Outlet: 1990 to 2002

[In billions of dollars (556.6 represents $556,600,000,000)]

Sales outlet	1990	1994	1995	1996	1997	1998	1999	2000	2001	2002
Food sales, total [1]........	556.6	635.3	654.7	679.9	705.3	737.2	779.7	825.5	861.7	900.1
Food at home............	308.1	344.1	352.7	367.8	377.3	391.6	417.6	439.8	463.6	485.2
Food stores [2]............	256.4	274.0	276.1	285.6	289.6	296.1	309.3	326.8	347.1	356.3
Other stores [3]........	32.3	47.8	53.1	57.3	61.8	69.7	80.7	84.2	87.7	99.4
Home-delivered, mail order	5.3	8.0	8.6	10.0	10.6	10.6	11.4	12.2	11.8	12.4
Farmers, manufacturers, wholesalers..............	6.3	7.2	7.8	8.1	8.8	8.6	9.0	9.4	9.6	9.8
Home production and donations .	7.7	7.1	7.0	6.8	6.4	6.6	7.2	7.2	7.3	7.3
Food away from home [4]........	248.5	291.2	302.0	312.1	328.0	345.6	362.0	385.7	398.1	415.0
Alcoholic beverage sales, total................	72.6	78.3	80.5	83.9	86.9	92.5	98.1	102.8	105.9	112.3
Packaged alcoholic beverages....	38.0	40.4	41.6	43.7	44.9	48.6	52.1	54.1	55.6	59.2
Liquor stores.............	18.6	19.0	19.0	20.1	20.9	22.3	23.4	25.3	26.4	27.2
Food stores.............	10.8	11.8	12.3	13.0	12.8	13.8	14.5	14.9	15.3	16.2
All other.............	8.6	9.7	10.3	10.6	11.2	12.5	14.2	13.9	13.9	15.8
Alcoholic drinks............	34.5	37.9	38.9	40.2	42.0	43.9	46.0	48.8	50.3	53.2
Eating and drinking places [5] ...	26.6	29.4	30.3	31.6	33.7	35.2	36.8	39.2	40.4	43.2
Hotels and motels [5].......	3.8	3.9	3.9	3.9	4.1	4.1	4.4	4.6	4.7	4.7
All other..............	4.1	4.7	4.7	4.7	4.3	4.5	4.8	5.0	5.2	5.3

[1] Includes taxes and tips. [2] Excludes sales to restaurants and institutions. [3] Includes eating and drinking establishments, trailer parks, commissary stores, and military exchanges. [4] Includes food furnished and donations. [5] Includes tips.

Source: U.S. Department of Agriculture, Economic Research Service, "food cpi, prices, and expenditures: food expenditure tables"; published 2 June 2003; <http://www.ers.usda.gov/briefing/CPIFoodAndExpenditures/Data/>.

No. 1036. U.S. Online Retail E-Commerce Projections: 2002 to 2004

[In millions of dollars (110.7 represents $110,700,000,000), except as indicated]

Online product or service	Projected online sales			Percent change	
	2002	2003	2004	2002-2003	2003-2004
Retail trade, total [1]	110.7	95.7	122.6	-13.6	28.1
Event tickets	2.0	3.3	5.2	66.2	57.6
Flowers	1.8	0.8	1.2	-55.8	50.0
Apparel	14.5	8.6	10.7	-40.5	24.4
Leisure travel	21.0	27.3	33.6	30.0	23.1
Automobiles	9.4	7.2	8.1	-23.1	12.5
Home products	8.3	10.6	16.7	28.4	57.5
Pet supplies	2.5	0.3	0.4	-88.1	33.3
Health and beauty	4.5	1.5	2.4	-66.4	60.0
Food and beverage	5.1	3.7	5.2	-26.9	40.5

[1] Includes items sold to consumers in product categories not shown separately.

Source: Forrester Research, Inc., Cambridge, MA, *Online Retail Ripple Effect* (copyright).

No. 1037. Online Consumer Spending Forecast by Kind of Business: 2002 to 2004

[Forecast data: October 2003. (41.2 represents $41,200,000,000). Figures below reflect a partial revision of the Jupiter Internet Shopping Model]

Category	Online retail spending (bil.dol.)			Percentage of spending online			Number of online buyers (mil.)		
	2002	2003	2004	2002	2003	2004	2002	2003	2004
Total	41.2	52.6	65.1	(X)	(X)	(X)	(X)	(X)	(X)
PCs	7.6	8.9	9.8	32.1	36.6	39.1	6.9	8.7	10.2
Peripherals	2.3	2.6	2.7	23.7	25.5	26.3	13.5	16.0	18.1
Software	2.6	3.0	3.3	32.0	35.9	38.3	25.5	29.3	32.5
Consumer electronics	2.1	2.6	3.3	4.6	5.6	7.1	7.9	10.3	13.9
Books	2.8	3.2	3.5	11.9	13.1	14.2	41.5	50.2	57.8
Music	0.8	0.8	1.1	5.9	7.0	9.7	29.6	34.8	39.5
Videos	0.9	1.2	1.5	6.2	7.3	8.3	18.6	23.4	29.4
Movie tickets	0.3	0.4	0.5	3.3	4.3	5.2	9.0	13.2	17.8
Event tickets	2.2	2.7	3.3	12.0	14.5	16.5	18.7	22.1	25.2
Over-the-counter drugs	0.1	0.2	0.3	0.6	0.9	1.5	6.7	9.7	13.1
Nutraceuticals	0.1	0.2	0.4	0.8	1.2	2.2	11.4	13.9	16.5
Medical supplies and contact lenses	0.2	0.3	0.4	1.2	2.0	3.0	6.6	9.0	11.6
Personal care	0.2	0.4	0.8	0.5	1.0	1.7	12.2	15.2	18.2
Apparel	4.8	6.2	7.5	2.4	3.0	3.5	36.3	45.7	54.7
Footwear	0.8	1.0	1.3	1.4	1.7	2.2	10.5	14.7	20.9
Jewelry	1.2	1.4	1.6	3.6	4.2	4.8	6.9	9.0	10.9
Grocery	1.1	1.7	2.4	0.2	0.3	0.4	1.6	2.4	3.3
Pets	0.2	0.4	0.5	1.1	1.6	2.3	3.9	5.2	6.8
Toys	0.7	0.8	0.8	3.6	3.7	3.8	16.0	18.7	21.0
Sporting goods	0.9	1.3	1.6	4.0	5.3	6.4	11.3	15.4	19.0
Flowers	0.8	1.0	1.2	5.0	6.2	7.1	16.9	21.4	25.9
Specialty gifts	0.8	1.1	1.4	2.2	2.8	3.6	14.3	17.5	20.6
Furniture	0.3	0.5	0.6	0.4	0.7	0.9	1.2	2.5	4.1
Large appliances	0.5	0.7	0.9	2.3	3.0	3.9	0.9	1.2	1.7
Housewares/small appliances	1.1	1.9	2.9	1.6	2.7	4.0	8.7	14.1	20.1
Art and collectibles	0.5	0.6	0.8	1.6	2.2	2.8	2.1	3.0	4.0
Home improvement	0.6	1.0	1.5	0.4	0.6	0.9	6.3	9.3	12.5
Garden supplies	0.2	0.3	0.5	0.5	0.8	1.1	3.7	5.9	8.5
Office products	1.2	1.8	2.6	3.6	5.2	7.3	13.0	17.7	25.5
Auto parts	0.1	0.3	0.6	0.3	0.8	1.4	1.0	2.7	4.3
Other	2.7	3.7	4.6	(NA)	(NA)	(NA)	(NA)	(NA)	(NA)

NA not available.   X Not applicable.

Source: Jupiter Research, Inc., New York, NY Unpublished data.

No. 1038. Electronic Shopping and Mail-Order Houses—Total and E-commerce Sales by Merchandise Line: 2002

[114,480 represents $114,480,000,000 in sales. Represents NAICS code 454110. Covers establishments with payroll. Based on 2002 Annual Retail Trade Survey.]

Merchandise line	Value of sales		E-commerce as percent of total sales	Percent distribution of total sales	Percent distribution of E-commerce sales
	Total (mil.dol.)	E-commerce (mil.dol.)			
Electronic shopping and mail-order houses, total [1]	114,480	32,191	28.1	100	100
Books and magazines	4,017	1,848	46.0	3.5	5.7
Clothing and clothing accessories (includes footwear)	14,020	4,272	30.5	12.2	13.3
Computer hardware	21,203	5,873	27.7	18.5	18.2
Computer software	4,433	1,456	32.8	3.9	4.5
Drugs, health aids, beauty aids	20,709	1,446	7.0	18.1	4.5
Electronics and appliances	4,419	2,030	45.9	3.9	6.3
Food, beer and wine	1,869	639	34.2	1.6	2.0
Furniture and home furnishings	7,116	2,447	34.4	6.2	7.6
Music and videos	3,862	1,454	37.6	3.4	4.5
Office equipment and supplies	6,114	2,450	40.1	5.3	7.6
Sporting Goods	2,687	910	33.9	2.3	2.8
Toys, hobby goods, and games	3,458	1,250	36.1	3.0	3.9
Other merchandise [2]	15,651	3,858	24.7	13.7	12.0
Nonmerchandise receipts [3]	4,922	2,258	45.9	4.3	7.0

[1] This industry comprises businesses primarily engaged in retailing all types of merchandise through catalogs, television, and the internet. Data are preliminary and, therefore, subject to revision. [2] Includes other merchandise such as jewelry, collectibles, souvenirs, auto parts and accessories, hardware, and lawn and garden equipment and supplies. [3] Includes nonmerchandise receipts such as auction commissions, shipping and handling, customer training, customer support, and online advertising.

Source: U.S. Census Bureau, *2002 Annual Retail Trade Survey,* "2002 E-Commerce Multi-Sector Report"; published April 2004. See also: <http://www.census.gov/eos/www/ebusiness614.htm>

No. 1039. Retail Trade Sales-Total and E-Commerce by Kind of Business: 2002

[3,230,122 represents $3,230,122,000,000. Covers retailers with and without payroll. Based on 2001 Annual Retail Trade Survey, See Appendix III.]

Kind of business	NAICS code [1]	Value of sales (mil. dol.)		E-commerce as percent of total sales	Percent distribution of E-commerce sales
		Total	E-commerce		
Retail trade, total	44,45	3,230,122	44,287	1.4	100
Motor vehicle and parts dealers	441	846,248	7,231	0.9	16.3
Furniture and home furnishings stores	442	93,689	(S)	(S)	(S)
Electronics and appliance stores	443	89,930	778	0.9	1.8
Building material and garden equipment supplies stores	444	299,893	603	0.2	1.4
Food and beverage stores	445	489,445	(S)	(S)	(S)
Health and personal care stores	446	181,111	(S)	(S)	(S)
Gasoline stations	447	244,796	(Z)	(Z)	(Z)
Clothing and clothing acces. stores	448	171,759	487	0.3	1.1
Sporting goods, hobby, book and music stores	451	80,222	662	0.8	1.5
General merchandise stores	452	451,365	(S)	(S)	(S)
Miscellaneous store retailers	453	104,400	684	0.7	1.5
Nonstore retailers	454	177,264	33,117	18.7	74.8
Electronic shopping and mail-order houses	454110	114,480	32,191	28.1	72.7

S Data do not meet publication standards because of high sampling variability or poor response quality. Unpublished estimates derived from this table by subtraction should be used with caution and not be attributed to the U.S. Census Bureau. For more information on methodology visit <www.census.gov/estats>. Z Less than $500,000 or 0.05 percent. [1] North American Industry Classification System, 1997; see text, Section 15.

Source: U.S. Census Bureau, *2002 Annual Retail Trade Survey,* "2002 E-Commerce Multi-Sector Report"; published April 2004. See also <http://www.census.gov/eos/www/ebusiness614.htm>.

No. 1040. Shopping Centers—Number, Gross Leasable Area, and Retail Sales by Gross Leasable Area: 1990 to 2003

[4,390 represents 4,390,000,000. As of December 31. A shopping center is a group of architecturally unified commercial establishments built on a site that is planned, developed, owned, and managed as an operating unit related in its location, size, and type of shops to the trade area that the unit serves. The unit provides on-site parking in definite relationship to the types and total size of the stores. The data base attempts to include all centers with three or more stores. Estimates are based on a sample of data available on shopping center properties; for details, contact source]

Year	Total	Gross leasable area (sq. ft.)					
		Less than 100,001	100,001-200,000	200,001-400,000	400,001-800,000	800,001-1,000,000	More than 1 million
NUMBER							
1990	36,515	23,231	8,756	2,781	1,102	288	357
1995	41,235	26,001	9,974	3,345	1,234	301	380
2000	45,115	28,062	10,958	3,935	1,424	326	410
2001	45,827	28,474	11,100	4,038	1,466	329	420
2002	46,438	28,819	11,220	4,137	1,507	332	424
2003	47,104	29,234	11,336	4,233	1,540	334	427
Percent distribution	100.0	62.1	24.1	9.0	3.3	0.7	0.9
Percent change, 2002-2003	1.4	1.4	1.0	2.3	2.2	0.6	0.7
GROSS LEASABLE AREA							
1990 (mil. sq. ft.)	4,390	1,125	1,197	734	618	259	457
1995 (mil. sq. ft.)	4,967	1,267	1,368	886	689	271	486
2000 (mil. sq. ft.)	5,566	1,383	1,514	1,059	790	294	526
2001 (mil. sq. ft.)	5,679	1,406	1,534	1,091	812	296	539
2002 (mil. sq. ft.)	5,774	1,424	1,552	1,119	836	299	544
2003 (mil. sq. ft.)	5,865	1,446	1,569	1,147	854	301	548
Percent distribution	100.0	24.6	26.8	19.6	14.6	5.1	9.3
Percent change, 2002-2003	1.6	1.5	1.1	2.5	2.2	0.6	0.6
RETAIL SALES							
1990 (bil. dol.)	706.4	205.1	179.5	108.0	91.7	45.1	77.0
1995 (bil. dol.)	893.8	259.6	227.1	136.4	115.8	57.0	97.8
2000 (bil. dol.)	1,181.1	342.8	300.0	180.5	152.8	75.2	129.8
2001 (bil. dol.)	1,221.7	354.5	310.3	186.8	158.0	77.8	134.4
2002 (bil. dol.)	1,277.2	370.6	324.4	195.3	165.1	81.3	140.6
2003 (bil. dol.)	1,339.2	388.5	340.1	204.8	173.1	85.2	147.5
Percent distribution	100.0	29.0	25.4	15.3	12.9	6.4	11.0
Percent change, 2001-02	4.5	4.5	4.5	4.6	4.5	4.5	4.6
Percent change, 2002-03	4.9	4.8	4.8	4.9	4.8	4.8	4.9

No. 1041. Shopping Centers—Gross Leasable Area and Retail Sales, by State: 2003

[5,865 represents 5,865,000,000. See headnote, Table 1040.]

State	Gross leasable area, (mil. sq. ft.)	Retail sales, (bil. dol.)	Retail sales per sq. ft, (dol.)	Percent change, 2001-2002 Gross leasable area	Retail sales	State	Gross leasable area, (mil. sq. ft.)	Retail sales, (bil. dol.)	Retail sales per sq. ft. (dol.)	Percent change, 2001-2002 Gross leasable area	Retail sales
U.S. ...	5,865	1,339.2	228	1.6	4.9	MO	125	29.1	232	2.8	4.6
						MT......	10	2.6	256		4.8
AL.....	82	19.4	237	1.0	4.1	NE......	38	7.3	194	0.3	4.5
AK.....	8	2.8	364	0.3	6.1	NV......	61	8.8	146	6.5	5.3
AZ.....	144	32.1	223	3.2	5.0	NH.....	27	6.3	236	4.9	7.0
AR.....	38	9.2	245	1.0	3.8						
CA.....	736	160.4	218	1.4	4.8	NJ......	185	37.8	205	1.8	5.5
						NM.....	32	8.1	252	0.3	4.3
CO.....	116	30.5	262	3.7	5.4	NY......	261	57.3	220	1.7	4.7
CT.....	99	25.4	257	0.4	5.9	NC.....	194	37.1	191	2.8	4.6
DE.....	23	5.9	259	0.1	5.8	ND.....	10	2.7	275		4.8
DC.....	10	2.2	221	0.7	4.8						
FL.....	469	124.6	266	1.8	5.4	OH.....	263	52.9	202	1.3	4.5
						OK.....	61	16.1	262	0.2	3.6
GA.....	199	40.2	202	1.9	4.5	OR.....	61	12.4	203	0.5	5.2
HI.....	21	6.1	297	0.9	7.2	PA.....	262	52.3	199	1.3	4.9
ID	20	4.1	204	1.3	4.0	RI	22	4.9	227	5.2	4.9
IL.....	275	55.1	201	1.4	5.1						
IN	129	27.2	211	1.5	4.4	SC.....	91	19.8	217	1.8	4.4
						SD.....	7	1.6	235	-	4.5
IA	47	9.6	203	1.5	4.5	TN.....	139	29.5	212	0.5	4.7
KS.....	60	14.8	245	0.6	4.5	TX.....	396	111.9	283	1.5	4.6
KY.....	70	17.5	251	0.7	4.4	UT.....	39	8.1	205	2.0	4.0
LA.....	89	23.8	268	0.6	4.5						
ME.....	19	5.7	307	-	6.1	VT.....	9	2.4	271	-	5.8
						VA.....	183	41.6	227	1.9	5.1
MD.....	133	32.2	242	0.5	4.8	WA.....	105	23.2	221	0.9	5.1
MA.....	119	30.9	260	0.5	5.3	WV.....	23	4.6	195	2.8	3.7
MI.....	152	32.5	214	1.1	4.7	WI.....	80	19.0	238	0.6	4.9
MN.....	75	18.1	243	2.9	4.9	WY.....	6	1.7	275		4.2
MS.....	45	10.0	221	-	3.5						

- Represents zero.

Source of Tables 1040 and 1041: National Research Bureau, Chicago, IL (copyright, 2004).

No. 1042. Merchant Wholesalers—Summary: 1992 to 2003

[In billions of dollars (1,731.6 represents $1,731,600,000,000) except ratios. Inventories and stock/sales ratios, as of December. Data reflect latest revision. Based on Annual Trade Survey; see Appendix III]

SALES

Kind of business	NAICS code [1]	1992	1994	1996	1998	2000	2002	2003
Merchant wholesalers	(X)	1,731.6	1,933.6	2,239.8	2,379.8	2,743.6	2,742.3	2,885.0
Durable goods	(X)	832.8	1,004.2	1,156.6	1,265.8	1,421.5	1,334.1	1,369.3
Motor vehicles, parts, and supplies	4211	149.6	163.4	165.7	173.2	199.5	215.4	222.0
Furniture and homefurnishings	4212	28.5	31.3	36.5	40.4	46.7	43.6	45.0
Lumber and construction materials	4213	45.8	56.0	59.1	63.7	70.9	77.9	87.5
Professional and commercial equipment	4214	133.5	165.4	220.2	254.1	269.9	249.4	252.9
computer, peripheral equipment and software	42143	(NA)	(NA)	(NA)	150.8			
Metals and minerals, except petroleum	4215	76.7	89.1	94.5	97.1	102.7	89.8	89.7
Electrical goods	4216	98.2	141.3	171.5	186.7	240.4	204.4	209.4
Hardware, plumbing and heating equipment	4217	41.3	49.2	54.3	60.4	67.1	66.1	66.4
Machinery, equipment and supplies	4218	147.5	174.4	206.6	242.5	252.1	223.3	230.4
Miscellaneous durable goods	4219	111.5	134.0	148.2	147.7	172.1	164.2	165.9
Nondurable goods	(X)	898.8	929.4	1,083.2	1,114.1	1,322.1	1,408.2	1,515.7
Paper and paper products	4221	48.1	55.4	64.8	69.9	80.6	76.7	77.1
Drugs, proprietaries, and sundries	4222	67.1	76.4	94.3	124.6	168.5	233.2	260.9
Apparel, piece goods, and notions	4223	62.7	68.5	73.1	84.2	88.3	91.1	86.0
Groceries and related products	4224	274.8	289.9	317.8	344.4	383.9	402.7	417.9
Farm-product raw materials	4225	106.2	99.1	137.5	108.0	107.0	111.3	125.2
Chemicals and allied products	4226	39.2	43.3	53.6	55.1	59.0	60.4	62.9
Petroleum and petroleum products	4227	137.5	125.4	143.5	116.4	187.7	181.1	226.9
Beer, wine, and distilled beverages	4228	50.4	52.0	55.9	61.8	71.6	79.8	84.4
Miscellaneous nondurable goods	4229	112.8	119.4	142.5	149.7	175.6	171.9	174.5

INVENTORIES

Kind of business	NAICS code [1]	1992	1994	1996	1998	2000	2002	2003
Merchant wholesalers	(X)	194.5	219.8	238.8	268.5	302.9	291.4	298.2
Durable goods	(X)	119.8	138.4	153.2	171.5	190.9	171.1	173.8
Motor vehicles, parts, and supplies	4211	21.4	21.5	21.6	22.2	25.7	25.0	26.0
Furniture and homefurnishings	4212	4.2	4.4	4.8	4.9	5.7	5.3	5.7
Lumber and construction materials	4213	4.8	5.4	5.7	5.8	6.8	7.1	7.9
Professional and commercial equipment	4214	16.9	21.0	24.6	26.2	27.1	23.3	23.8
computer, peripheral equipment and software	42143	(NA)	(NA)	(NA)	12.3	10.6	7.1	7.1
Metals and minerals, except petroleum	4215	10.3	12.6	12.7	14.3	14.8	13.9	14.2
Electrical goods	4216	14.9	18.5	21.3	22.5	28.8	22.4	21.6
Hardware, plumbing and heating equipment	4217	6.4	7.8	8.6	9.4	10.6	10.1	10.1
Machinery, equipment and supplies	4218	28.0	31.6	37.7	47.8	50.0	45.0	43.4
Miscellaneous durable goods	4219	12.9	15.5	16.3	18.5	21.3	19.2	21.2
Nondurable goods	(X)	74.6	81.4	85.6	97.0	112.0	120.0	124.4
Paper and paper products	4221	4.5	4.9	5.3	6.0	7.1	6.4	6.7
Drugs, proprietaries, and sundries	4222	9.3	10.8	11.9	15.7	23.3	31.0	31.6
Apparel, piece goods, and notions	4223	10.5	12.0	12.0	13.6	12.7	12.4	11.8
Groceries and related products	4224	18.0	17.9	18.2	19.4	22.1	22.4	23.0
Farm-product raw materials	4225	8.1	9.9	9.5	11.7	12.6	12.4	14.9
Chemicals and allied products	4226	3.8	4.6	5.3	5.7	5.8	6.0	6.1
Petroleum and petroleum products	4227	3.9	4.2	4.5	3.7	4.7	5.1	5.7
Beer, wine, and distilled beverages	4228	4.3	4.6	5.1	5.6	6.4	6.9	7.1
Miscellaneous nondurable goods	4229	12.2	12.5	13.9	15.7	17.4	17.5	17.6

STOCK/SALES RATIO

Kind of business	NAICS code [1]	1992	1994	1996	1998	2000	2002	2003
Merchant wholesalers	(X)	1.34	1.29	1.26	1.31	1.35	1.26	1.16
Durable goods	(X)	1.68	1.55	1.57	1.59	1.72	1.59	1.43
Motor vehicles, parts, and supplies	4211	1.72	1.57	1.56	1.44	1.55	1.35	1.27
Furniture and homefurnishings	4212	1.70	1.55	1.50	1.46	1.61	1.61	1.51
Lumber and construction materials	4213	1.28	1.10	1.13	1.18	1.40	1.37	1.16
Professional and commercial equipment	4214	1.44	1.37	1.33	1.12	1.25	1.05	0.99
computer, peripheral equipment and software	42143	(NA)	(NA)	(NA)	0.93	0.91	0.70	0.64
Metals and minerals, except petroleum	4215	1.58	1.58	1.59	1.93	1.99	2.23	1.94
Electrical goods	4216	1.72	1.44	1.57	1.45	1.51	1.39	1.21
Hardware, plumbing and heating equipment	4217	1.84	1.76	1.84	1.95	2.19	2.12	1.96
Machinery, equipment and supplies	4218	2.23	2.04	2.09	2.33	2.54	2.43	2.06
Miscellaneous durable goods	4219	1.32	1.30	1.25	1.51	1.58	1.48	1.43
Nondurable goods	(X)	1.01	1.01	0.94	0.99	0.99	0.97	0.92
Paper and paper products	4221	1.11	0.94	0.98	1.02	1.11	1.01	1.01
Drugs, proprietaries, and sundries	4222	1.63	1.66	1.43	1.30	1.53	1.47	1.28
Apparel, piece goods, and notions	4223	1.94	2.16	1.79	2.43	2.18	2.14	1.82
Groceries and related products	4224	0.78	0.71	0.70	0.65	0.68	0.66	0.65
Farm-product raw materials	4225	0.94	1.12	0.86	1.11	1.25	1.02	1.08
Chemicals and allied products	4226	1.13	1.16	1.20	1.31	1.25	1.33	1.21
Petroleum and petroleum products	4227	0.36	0.40	0.35	0.39	0.27	0.30	0.28
Beer, wine, and distilled beverages	4228	1.04	1.03	1.09	0.89	0.95	0.85	0.82
Miscellaneous nondurable goods	4229	1.39	1.19	1.19	1.14	1.20	1.24	1.15

NA Not available.   X Not applicable.   [1] North American Industry Classification System, 1997; see text, Section 15, Business Enterprise.

Source: U.S. Census Bureau, *Current Business Reports, Annual Benchmark Report for Wholesale Trade, January 1992 through January 2004*, Series BW/01-A.

U.S. Census Bureau, Statistical Abstract of the United States: 2004-2005

No. 1043. Merchant Wholesale Trade Sales-Total and E-Commerce: 2002

[2,742,285 represents $2,742,285,000,000. Covers only businesses with paid employees. Based on 2002 Annual Trade Survey, see Appendix III.]

Kind of business	NAICS code [1]	Value of sales (mil. dol.) Total	Value of sales (mil. dol.) E-commerce	E-commerce as percent of total sales	Percent distribution of E-commerce sales
Merchant wholesale trade, total.	42	2,742,285	319,755	11.7	100.0
Durable goods [2]	421	1,334,066	146,287	11.0	45.7
Motor vehicles, parts and supplies	4211	215,437	53,348	24.8	16.7
Furniture and home furnishings	4212	43,611	4,690	10.8	1.5
Professional & commercial equipment & supplies	4214	249,419	32,897	13.2	10.3
Computer, peripheral equipment and software	42143	113,541	15,032	13.2	4.7
Electrical goods	4216	204,350	19,263	9.4	6.0
Hardware, and plumbing and heating equipment and supplies.	4217	66,088	7,706	11.7	2.4
Machinery, equipment and supplies	4218	223,295	8,645	3.9	2.7
Miscellaneous durable goods	4219	164,176	15,752	9.6	4.9
Nondurable goods [2]	422	1,408,219	173,468	12.3	54.3
Drugs and druggists' sundries.	4222	233,188	110,745	47.5	34.6
Apparel, piece goods and notions	4223	91,071	13,664	15.0	4.3
Groceries and related products	4224	402,691	21,357	5.3	6.7
Farm product raw materials	4225	111,302	3,697	3.3	1.2

[1] North American Industry Classification System, 1997; see text, Section 15, Business Enterprise. [2] Includes kinds of business not shown separately.

Source: U.S. Census Bureau, 2002 E-Commerce Multi-Sector Report; published April 2004; <http://www.census.gov/eos/www /ebusiness614.htm>.

No. 1044. Wholesale Trade—Establishments, Employees, and Payroll: 2000 and 2001

[446.2 represents 446,200. Covers establishments with payroll. Employees are for the week including March 12. Excludes most government employees, railroad employees, and self-employed persons. Kind-of-business classification based on North American Industry Classification System (NAICS) 1997; see text, Section 15, Business Enterprise. For statement on methodology, see Appendix III]

Kind of business	NAICS code	Establishments (1,000) 2000	Establishments (1,000) 2001	Employees (1,000) 2000	Employees (1,000) 2001	Payroll (bil. dol.) 2000	Payroll (bil. dol.) 2001
Wholesale trade	42	446.2	438.9	6,112	6,142	270.1	275.9
Wholesale trade, durable goods	421	288.6	283.4	3,625	3,633	171.8	173.2
Motor vehicle/motor vehicle pt & supply whsle .	4211	28.4	27.6	402	387	14.1	14.1
Furniture & home furnishing whsle	4212	14.9	14.5	167	166	6.6	6.6
Lumber & other construction materials whsle . .	4213	15.1	15.5	184	185	7.2	7.5
Professional & commercial equip & supp whsle.	4214	44.4	43.1	763	777	44.9	45.1
Metal & mineral (except petroleum) whsle	4215	12.1	11.9	173	166	7.6	7.2
Electrical goods whsle	4216	38.3	37.8	535	559	33.9	34.8
Hardware, & plumb & heating equip & sup whsle	4217	21.4	21.3	249	248	10.4	10.7
Machinery, equipment, & supplies whsle	4218	73.7	72.1	796	797	34.2	34.3
Miscellaneous durable goods whsle	4219	40.2	39.6	355	347	12.9	12.9
Wholesale trade, nondurable goods	422	157.7	155.5	2,487	2,509	98.4	103.3
Paper & paper product whsle	4221	14.9	14.4	232	226	8.9	8.9
Drugs & druggists' sundries whsle	4222	7.4	7.2	210	235	12.0	13.7
Apparel, piece goods & notions whsle.	4223	20.0	19.5	214	212	8.9	9.0
Grocery & related product whsle	4224	39.7	39.2	875	871	31.6	33.0
Farm product raw material whsle	4225	9.5	9.3	92	91	2.5	2.6
Chemical & allied products whsle	4226	15.3	15.8	166	164	8.3	8.3
Petroleum & petroleum products whsle	4227	10.7	10.4	132	129	5.2	5.6
Beer/wine/distilled alcoholic beverage whsle. . .	4228	4.6	4.6	157	161	6.8	7.1
Miscellaneous nondurable goods whsle.	4229	35.4	35.1	409	420	14.3	14.6

Source: U.S. Census Bureau, County Business Patterns, annual. See also <http://www.census.gov/prod/2003pubs/01cbp/cbp01-1.pdf> (issued April 2002).

Section 23

Transportation

This section presents data on civil air transportation, both passenger and cargo, and on water transportation, including inland waterways, oceanborne commerce, the merchant marine, cargo, and vessel tonnages.

This section also presents statistics on revenues, passenger and freight traffic volume, and employment in various revenue-producing modes of the transportation industry, including motor vehicles, trains, and pipelines. Data are also presented on highway mileage and finances, motor vehicle travel, accidents, and registrations; and characteristics of public transit, railroads, and pipelines. Data from the 2001 National Household Travel Survey are now included in Section 26.

Principal sources of air and water transportation data are the annual *National Transportation Statistics*, issued by the U.S. Bureau of Transportation Statistics; the *Annual Report* issued by the Air Transport Association of America, Washington, DC; and the annual *Waterborne Commerce of the United States* issued by the Corps of Engineers of the Department of the Army. In addition, the U.S. Census Bureau in its commodity flow survey (part of the census of transportation, taken every 5 years through 2002, for years ending in "2" and "7") provides data on the type, weight, and value of commodities shipped by manufacturing establishments in the United States, by means of transportation, origin, and destination. The latest reports for 2002 are part of the 2002 Economic Census. This census was conducted in accordance with the 2002 North American Industry Classification System (NAICS). See text, Section 15, Business Enterprise, for a discussion of the 2002 Economic Census and NAICS.

Additional sources of data on water transportation include *Merchant Fleets of the World*, issued periodically by the U.S. Maritime Administration; *The Bulletin,*

issued monthly by the American Bureau of Shipping, New York, NY; and the annual *World Fleet Statistics.*

The principal compiler of data on public roads and on operation of motor vehicles is the U.S. Department of Transportation's (DOT) Federal Highway Administration (FHWA). These data appear in FHWA's annual *Highway Statistics* and other publications.

The U.S. National Highway Traffic Safety Administration issues data on traffic accident deaths and death rates in two annual reports: the *Fact Book* and the *Fatal Accident Reporting System Annual Report.* DOT's Federal Railroad Administration presents data on accidents involving railroads in its annual *Accident/Incident Bulletin,* and the *Rail-Highway Crossing Accident/Incident and Inventory Bulletin.*

Data are also presented in many nongovernment publications. Among them are the weekly and annual *Cars of Revenue Freight Loaded* and the annual *Yearbook of Railroad Facts,* both published by the Association of American Railroads, Washington, DC; *Transit Fact Book,* containing electric railway and motorbus statistics, published annually by the American Public Transit Association, Washington, DC.; *Injury Facts,* issued by the National Safety Council, Chicago, IL; and *Transportation in America,* issued by the Eno Foundation for Transportation, Washington, DC.

Civil aviation—Federal promotion and regulation of civil aviation have been carried out by the FAA and the Civil Aeronautics Board (CAB). The CAB promoted and regulated the civil air transportation industry within the United States and between the United States and foreign countries. The Board granted licenses to provide air transportation service, approved or disapproved proposed rates and fares, and approved or disapproved proposed agreements and corporate relationships involving air carriers. In December 1984, the CAB ceased to exist as an agency. Some of its functions were transferred to the Department of Transportation (DOT), as outlined below. The responsibility for investigation of aviation accidents resides with the National Transportation Safety Board.

The Office of the Secretary, DOT aviation activities include: negotiation of international air transportation rights, selection of U.S. air carriers to serve capacity controlled international markets, oversight of international rates and fares, maintenance of essential air service to small communities, and consumer affairs. DOT's Bureau of Transportation Statistics (BTS) handles aviation information functions formerly assigned to CAB. Prior to BTS, the Research and Special Programs Administration handled these functions.

The principal activities of the FAA include: the promotion of air safety; controlling the use of navigable airspace; prescribing regulations dealing with the competency of airmen, airworthiness of aircraft and air traffic control; operation of air route traffic control centers, airport traffic control towers, and flight service stations; the design, construction, maintenance, and inspection of navigation, traffic control, and communications equipment; and the development of general aviation.

The CAB published monthly and quarterly financial and traffic statistical data for the certificated route air carriers. BTS continues these publications, including both certificated and noncertificated (commuter) air carriers. The FAA annually publishes data on the use of airway facilities; data related to the location of airmen, aircraft, and airports; the volume of activity in the field of nonair carrier (general aviation) flying; and aircraft production and registration.

General aviation comprises all civil flying (including such commercial operations as small demand air taxis, agriculture application, powerline patrol, etc.) but excludes certificated route air carriers, supplemental operators, large-aircraft commercial operators, and commuter airlines.

Air carriers and service—The CAB previously issued "certificates of public convenience and necessity" under Section 401 of the Federal Aviation Act of 1958 for scheduled and nonscheduled (charter) passenger services and cargo services. It also issued certificates under Section 418 of the Act to cargo air carriers for domestic all-cargo service only. The DOT Office of the Secretary now issues the certificates under a "fit, willing, and able" test of air carrier operations. Carriers operating only a 60-seat-or-less aircraft are given exemption authority to carry passengers, cargo, and mail in scheduled and nonscheduled service under Part 298 of the DOT (formerly CAB) regulations. Exemption authority carriers who offer scheduled passenger service to an essential air service point must meet the "fit, willing, and able" test.

Vessel shipments, entrances, and clearances—Shipments by dry cargo vessels comprise shipments on all types of watercraft, except tanker vessels; shipments by tanker vessels comprise all types of cargo, liquid and dry, carried by tanker vessels.

A vessel is reported as entered only at the first port which it enters in the United States, whether or not cargo is unloaded at that port. A vessel is reported as cleared only at the last port at which clearance is made to a foreign port, whether or not it takes on cargo. Army and Navy vessels entering or clearing without commercial cargo are not included in the figures.

Units of measurement—Cargo (or freight) tonnage and shipping weight both represent the gross weight of the cargo including the weight of containers, wrappings, crates, etc. However, shipping weight excludes lift and cargo vans and similar substantial outer containers. Other tonnage figures generally refer to stowing capacity of vessels, 100 cubic feet being called 1 ton. Gross tonnage comprises the space within the frames and the ceiling of the hull, together with those closed-in spaces above deck available for cargo, stores, passengers, or crew, with certain minor exceptions. Net or registered tonnage is the gross tonnage less the spaces occupied by the propelling machinery, fuel, crew quarters, master's cabin, and navigation spaces. Substantially, it represents space available for cargo and passengers. The net tonnage capacity of a ship may bear little relation to weight of cargo. Deadweight tonnage is the weight in long tons required to depress a vessel from light water line (that is, with only the machinery and equipment on board) to load line. It is, therefore, the weight of the cargo, fuel, etc., which a vessel is designed to carry with safety.

Federal-aid highway systems—The Intermodal Surface Transportation Efficiency Act (ISTEA) of 1991 eliminated the historical Federal-Aid Highway Systems and created the National Highway System (NHS) and other federal-aid highway categories. The final NHS was approved by Congress in December of 1995 under the National Highway System Designation Act.

Functional systems—Roads and streets are assigned to groups according to the character of service intended. The functional systems are (1) arterial highways that generally handle the long trips, (2) collector facilities that collect and disperse traffic between the arterials and the lower systems, and (3) local roads and streets that primarily serve direct access to residential areas, farms, and other local areas.

Regulatory bodies—The ICC, created by the U.S. Congress to regulate transportation in interstate commerce, has jurisdiction over railroads, trucking companies, bus lines, freight forwarders, water carriers, coal slurry pipelines, and transportation brokers. The Federal Energy Regulatory Commission is responsible for setting rates and charges for transportation and sale of natural gas and for establishing rates or charges for transportation.

Motor carriers—For 1960-73, Class I for-hire motor carriers of freight were classified by the ICC as those with $1 million or more of gross annual operating revenue; 1974-79, the class minimum was $3 million. Effective January 1, 1980, Class I carriers are those with $5 million or more in revenue. For 1960-68, Class I motor carriers of passengers were classified by the ICC as those with $200,000 or more of

gross annual operating revenue; for 1969-76, as those with revenues of $1 million or more; and since 1977, as those with $3 million or more. Effective January 1, 1988, Class I motor carriers of passengers are those with $5 million or more in operating revenues; Class II less than $5 million in operating revenues.

Railroads—Railroad companies reporting to the ICC are divided into specific groups as follows: (1) regular line-haul (interstate) railroads (and their nonoperating subsidiaries), (2) switching and terminal railroads, (3) private railroads prior to 1964 (identified by ICC as "circular" because they reported on brief circulars), and (4) unofficial railroads, so designated when their reports are received too late for tabulation. For the most part, the last three groups are not included in the statistics shown here.

For years prior to 1978, Class I railroads were those with annual revenues of $1 million or more for 1950-55; $3 million or more for 1956-64; $5 million or more for 1965-75; and $10 million or more for 1976-77. In 1978, the classification became Class I, those having more than $50 million gross annual operating revenue; Class II, from $10 million to $50 million; and Class III, less than $10 million. Effective January 1, 1982, the ICC adopted a procedure to adjust the threshold for inflation by restating current revenues in constant 1978 dollars. In 1988, the criteria for Class I and Class II railroads were $92.0 million and $18.4 million, respectively. Also effective January 1, 1982, the ICC adopted a Carrier Classification Index Survey Form for carriers not filing annual report Form R-1 with the commission. Class II and Class III railroads are currently exempted from filing any financial report with the Commission. The form is used for reclassifying carriers.

The Surface Transportation Board (STB) was established pursuant to the ICC Termination Act of 1995, Pub. L. No. 104-88, 109 Stat. 803 (1995) (ICCTA), to assume certain of the regulatory functions that had been administered by the Interstate Commerce Commission. The Board has broad economic regulatory oversight of railroads, addressing such matters as rate

U.S. Census Bureau, Statistical Abstract of the United States: 2004-2005

reasonableness, car service and interchange, mergers and line acquisitions, line construction, and line abandonments (49 U.S.C. 10101-11908). Other ICC regulatory functions were either eliminated or transferred to the Federal Highway Administration or the Bureau of Transportation Statistics within DOT.

Class I Railroads are regulated by the STB and subject to the Uniform System of Accounts and required to file annual and periodic reports. Railroads are classified based on their annual operating revenues. The class to which a carrier belongs is determined by comparing its adjusted operating revenues for 3 consecutive years to the following scale: Class I, $250 million or more; Class II, $20 million to $250 million; and Class III, $0 to $20 million.

Postal Service—The Postal Service provides mail processing and delivery services within the United States. The Postal Reorganization Act of 1970 created the Postal Service, effective July 1971, as an independent establishment of the Federal Executive Branch.

Revenue and cost analysis describes the Postal Service's system of attributing revenues and costs to classes of mail and service. This system draws primarily upon probability sampling techniques to develop estimates of revenues, volumes, and weights, as well as costs by class of mail and special service. The costs attributed to classes of mail and special services are primarily incremental costs which vary in response to changes in volume; they account for roughly 60 percent of the total costs of the Postal Service. The balance represents "institutional costs." Statistics on revenues, volume of mail, and distribution of expenditures are presented in the Postal Service's annual report, *Cost and Revenue Analysis*, and its *Annual Report of the Postmaster General* and its annual *Comprehensive Statement on Postal Operations*.

Statistical reliability—For a discussion of statistical collection and estimation, sampling procedures, and measures of statistical reliability applicable to Census Bureau data, see Appendix III.

No. 1045. Transportation-Related Components of U.S. Gross Domestic Product: 1990 to 2002

[In billions dollars (627.3 represents $627,300,000,000), except percent]

Item	1990	1995	1999	2000	2001	2002
CURRENT DOLLARS						
Total transportation-related final demand...	627.3	805.1	1,044.1	1,088.7	1,103.9	1,099.4
Total gross domestic product (GDP)...	5,803.1	7,397.7	9,268.4	9,817.0	10,100.8	10,480.8
Transportation-related final demand as a percent...	10.8	10.9	11.3	11.1	10.9	10.5
Personal consumption of transportation...	471.7	594.6	785.1	853.5	874.0	876.7
Motor vehicles and parts...	212.8	266.7	370.8	386.5	406.9	418.1
Gasoline and oil...	111.2	120.2	137.9	175.7	173.1	165.8
Transportation services...	147.7	207.7	276.4	291.3	294.0	292.8
Gross private domestic investment...	72.6	119.6	173.9	167.4	148.1	134.7
Transportation structures...	2.6	3.5	6.3	6.6	6.8	6.7
Transportation equipment...	70.0	116.1	167.6	160.8	141.3	128.0
Net exports of transportation-related goods and service [1]	-28.8	-43.6	-83.3	-109.0	-108.2	-112.1
Exports (+)...	105.6	132.4	174.9	179.0	174.3	175.6
Civilian aircraft, engines, and parts...	32.2	26.1	52.9	48.1	52.6	50.5
Automotive vehicles, engines, and parts...	36.1	61.3	75.3	80.4	75.4	78.9
Passenger fares...	15.3	18.9	19.8	20.7	75.4 [sic] 17.9	17.0
Other transportation...	22.0	26.1	26.9	29.8	28.4	29.2
Imports (-)...	134.4	176.0	258.2	288.0	282.5	287.7
Civilian aircraft, engines,and parts...	10.5	10.7	23.8	26.4	31.4	25.5
Automotive vehicles, engines, and parts...	88.4	123.6	179.0	195.9	189.8	203.7
Passenger fares...	10.5	14.7	21.3	24.3	22.6	20.0
Other transportation...	25.0	27.0	34.1	41.4	38.7	38.5
Government transportation-related purchases...	111.8	134.5	168.4	176.8	190.0	200.1
Federal purchases [2]	12.9	16.3	18.7	19.4	20.9	22.9
State and local purchases [2]	90.1	109.8	140.7	148.4	159.4	166.2
Defense-related purchases [3]	8.8	8.4	9.0	9.0	9.7	11.0
Total domestic transportation-related final demand [4]	656.1	848.7	1,127.4	1,197.7	1,212.1	1,211.5
Total gross domestic demand (GDD)...	5,881.1	7,489.0	9,529.0	10,196.5	10,467.3	10,907.0
Transportation-related final demand as a percent...	11.2	11.3	11.8	11.7	11.6	11.1
CHAINED (2000) DOLLARS						
Total transportation-related final demand...	789.1	889.3	1,098.6	1,088.7	1,098.8	1,098.7
Total gross domestic product (GDP)...	7,112.5	8,031.7	9,470.3	9,817.0	9,866.6	10,083.0
Transportation-related final demand as a percent...	11.1	11.1	11.6	11.1	11.1	10.9
Personal consumption of transportation...	593.6	658.6	832.1	853.5	873.3	888.8
Motor vehicles and parts...	256.1	272.3	372.4	386.5	405.4	423.3
Gasoline and oil...	141.8	154.5	176.3	175.7	178.3	180.7
Transportation services...	195.7	231.8	283.4	291.3	289.6	284.8
Gross private domestic investment...	84.4	124.6	174.2	167.4	149.2	134.6
Transportation structures...	3.4	4.0	6.5	6.6	6.6	6.4
Transportation equipment...	81.0	120.6	167.7	160.8	142.6	128.2
Net exports of transportation-related goods and service [1]	-33.7	-46.9	-83.5	-109.0	-108.5	-114.5
Exports (+)...	131.5	142.1	181.0	179.0	171.6	170.8
Civilian aircraft, engines, and parts...	45.7	30.3	55.1	48.1	49.9	46.6
Automotive vehicles, engines, and parts...	40.3	63.4	75.9	80.4	75.2	78.3
Passenger fares...	19.8	19.6	20.3	20.7	17.8	16.4
Other transportation...	25.7	28.8	29.7	29.8	28.7	29.5
Imports (-)...	165.2	189.0	264.5	288.0	280.1	285.3
Civilian aircraft, engines, and parts...	15.0	12.4	24.5	26.4	30.2	24.2
Automotive vehicles, engines, and parts...	103.3	126.6	180.2	195.9	189.9	203.3
Passenger fares...	14.9	17.3	22.5	24.3	20.7	17.4
Other transportation...	32.0	32.7	37.3	41.4	39.3	40.4
Government transportation-related purchases...	144.8	153.0	175.8	176.8	184.8	189.8
Federal purchases [2]	17.1	18.2	19.3	19.4	20.5	21.8
State and local purchases [2]	116.5	125.1	147.1	148.4	155.0	157.7
Defense-related purchases [3]	11.2	9.7	9.4	9.0	9.3	10.3
Total domestic transportation-related final demand [4]	822.8	936.2	1,182.1	1,197.7	1,207.3	1,213.2
Total gross domestic demand (GDD)...	7,195.4	8,117.2	9,768.1	10,196.5	10,264.1	10,549.3
Transportation-related final demand as a percent...	11.4	11.5	12.1	11.7	11.8	11.5

[1] Sum of exports and imports. [2] Federal purchases and state and local purchases are the sum of consumption expenditures and gross investment. [3] Defense-related purchases are the sum of transportation of material and travel. [4] Sum of total personal consumption of transportation, total gross private domestic investment, net exports of transportation-related goods and services, and total government.

Source: U.S. Bureau of Transportation Statistics, calculations based on data from U.S. Bureau of Economic Analysis, "National Income and Product Accounts Tables," Internet site <http://www.bea.gov/bea/dn/nipaweb/SelectTable.asp?Selected=N> as of April 2004.

System	1980	1990	1995	1996	1997	1998	1999	2000	2001
Highway (1,000)	3,860	3,867	3,912	3,920	3,946	3,906	3,917	3,936	3,948
Class 1 rail	164,822	119,758	108,264	105,779	102,128	100,570	99,430	99,250	97,817
Amtrak	24,000	24,000	24,000	25,000	25,000	22,000	23,000	23,000	23,000
Transit:									
Commuter rail [1]	(X)	4,132	4,160	3,682	4,417	5,172	5,191	5,209	5,209
Heavy rail [2]	(X)	1,351	1,458	1,478	1,527	1,527	1,540	1,558	1,572
Light rail [3]	(X)	483	568	638	659	676	802	834	897
Navigable channels	26,000	26,000	26,000	26,000	26,000	26,000	26,000	26,000	26,000
Oil pipeline [4]	218,393	208,752	181,912	177,535	179,873	178,648	177,463	176,996	(NA)
Gas pipeline (1,000) [5]	1,052	1,207	1,262	1,276	1,251	1,294	1,389	1,380	1,433

NA Not available. X Not appplicable. [1] Also called metropolitan rail or regional rail. [2] Also called metro, subway, rapid transit, or rapid rail. [3] Also called streetcar, tramway, or trolley. [4] Includes trunk and gathering lines for crude-oil pipeline. [5] Excludes service pipelines.

Source: U.S. Bureau of Transportation Statistics, *National Transportation Statistics, 2003.* See Internet site <http://www.bts.gov/publications/nationaltransportationstatistics/2003/>.

No. 1047. U.S. Aircraft, Vehicles, and Other Conveyances: 1980 to 2001

System	1980	1990	1995	1996	1997	1998	1999	2000	2001
Air:									
Air carrier [1]	3,808	6,083	7,411	7,478	7,616	8,111	8,228	8,055	8,497
General aviation [2] (active fleet)	211,045	198,000	188,089	191,129	192,414	204,710	219,464	217,533	211,446
Highway, registered vehicles (1,000):									
Passenger car	121,601	133,700	128,387	129,728	129,749	131,839	132,432	133,621	137,633
Motorcycle	5,694	4,259	3,897	3,872	3,826	3,879	4,152	4,346	4,903
Vans, pick-ups, SUVs	27,876	48,275	65,738	69,134	70,224	71,330	75,356	79,085	84,188
Trucks	5,791	6,196	6,719	7,013	7,083	7,732	7,791	8,023	7,858
Bus	529	627	686	695	698	716	729	746	750
Transit: [3]									
Motor bus	59,411	58,714	67,107	71,678	72,770	72,142	74,228	75,013	76,075
Light rail cars [4]	1,013	913	999	1,140	1,229	1,220	1,297	1,577	1,366
Heavy rail cars [5]	9,641	10,419	10,157	10,201	10,242	10,301	10,306	10,591	10,718
Trolley bus	823	832	885	871	859	880	859	951	600
Commuter rail cars and locomotives	4,500	4,415	4,565	4,665	4,943	4,963	4,883	5,073	5,124
Demand response	(X)	16,471	29,352	30,804	32,509	29,646	31,884	33,080	34,661
Other [6]	(X)	1,197	2,809	3,003	3,808	4,703	5,059	5,208	5,727
Rail:									
Class I, Freight cars (1,000)	1,168	659	583	571	568	576	579	560	500
Class I, Locomotive	28,094	18,835	18,812	19,269	19,684	20,261	20,256	20,028	19,745
Nonclass I freight cars	102,161	103,527	84,724	87,364	116,108	121,659	126,762	132,448	125,470
Car companies and shippers freight cars	440,552	449,832	550,717	582,344	585,818	618,404	662,934	688,194	688,806
Amtrak, Passenger train car	2,128	1,863	1,722	1,730	1,728	1,962	1,992	1,894	2,084
Amtrak, Locomotive	419	318	313	299	332	345	329	378	401
Water:									
Nonself-propelled vessels [7]	31,662	31,209	31,360	32,811	33,011	33,509	33,387	33,152	33,042
Self-propelled vessels [8]	7,126	8,236	8,281	8,293	8,408	8,523	8,379	8,202	8,546
Oceangoing steam and motor ships (1,000 gross tons and over)	864	636	509	495	477	470	463	454	443
Recreational boats (1,000)	8,578	10,996	11,735	11,878	12,313	12,566	12,738	12,782	12,876

X Not applicable. [1] Air carrier aircraft are those carrying passengers or cargo for hire under 14 CFR 121 and 14 CFR 135. [2] Includes air taxi aircraft. [3] 2001 data are preliminary. [4] Fixed rail streetcar or trolley, for example. [5] Metro, subway, or rapid transit, for example. [6] Includes aerial tramway, automated guideway transit, cablecar, ferry boat, inclined plane, monorail, and vanpool. [7] Includes dry-cargo barges, tank barges, and railroad-car floats. [8] Includes dry-cargo and/or passenger, offshore supply vessels, railroad-car ferries, tankers, and towboats.

Source: U.S. Bureau of Transportation Statistics, *National Transportation Statistics, 2003.* See Internet site <http://www.bts.gov/publications/nationaltransportationstatistics/2003/>.

No. 1048. Transportation Outlays by Type of Transport: 1970 to 2001

[In billions of dollars (97.0 represents $97,000,000,000)]

Type of transport	1970	1980	1985	1990	1995	2000	2001
Private transportation	**97.0**	**305.2**	**434.7**	**517.2**	**629.8**	**831.3**	**862.1**
Automobiles	95.0	297.1	426.8	507.3	619.4	809.4	835.6
New and used cars	32.0	71.5	137.1	148.1	169.6	205.4	200.6
Other motor vehicles [1]	2.7	11.8	40.8	57.5	80.2	125.9	149.0
Tires, tubes, accessories	7.0	20.6	27.9	32.9	40.6	45.9	45.8
Gasoline and oil	27.4	99.7	111.8	118.0	124.6	164.4	162.1
Tolls	0.8	1.3	1.7	2.5	3.7	4.6	4.9
Insurance less claims	4.4	10.8	11.5	19.9	32.7	30.7	32.1
Interest on debt	4.7	39.1	21.0	28.2	38.0	48.7	51.0
Auto registration fees	1.7	2.9	4.8	6.1	7.0	7.6	7.7
Operators' permit fees	0.2	0.4	0.5	0.6	0.8	0.7	0.8
Repair, greasing, washing, parking, leasing, rentals	14.1	39.1	69.6	93.4	122.2	175.5	181.6
Air	2.0	8.1	7.9	9.9	10.4	21.9	26.5
Aircraft	0.3	2.9	2.3	3.4	4.3	14.3	18.5
Operating costs	1.7	5.2	5.6	6.5	6.1	7.6	8.0
For-hire transportation	**14.9**	**51.0**	**71.9**	**99.6**	**117.6**	**159.9**	**148.1**
Local	5.0	17.3	25.3	31.6	41.0	52.5	53.4
Bus and transit [2]	1.8	9.3	13.5	16.7	21.6	30.6	30.6
Taxi	1.7	2.8	3.8	4.0	5.0	5.6	5.7
Railroad commutation [2]	0.2	1.5	2.2	2.8	4.5	4.2	4.5
School bus	1.2	3.8	5.7	8.0	9.9	12.1	12.6
Intercity	7.7	28.4	39.5	53.1	57.8	79.9	70.2
Air [3]	6.6	25.1	35.9	49.5	54.0	75.1	64.9
Bus	0.8	1.7	2.0	1.8	1.5	2.0	2.2
Rail [4]	0.3	1.5	1.6	1.7	2.2	2.7	2.9
Water	(Z)	(Z)	0.1	0.1	0.1	0.2	0.1
International	2.2	5.3	7.1	14.9	18.8	27.5	24.5
Air [3]	1.9	5.0	6.6	13.6	16.8	23.0	20.4
Water	0.3	0.3	0.5	1.3	2.0	4.5	4.0
Freight, total	**84.0**	**213.7**	**273.6**	**351.0**	**442.6**	**575.8**	**579.6**
Highway	62.5	155.3	205.6	270.8	348.1	460.8	467.3
Truck, intercity [5]	33.6	94.6	123.2	162.3	219.6	305.2	309.4
Truck, local [6]	28.8	60.5	82.2	108.4	128.4	155.5	157.7
Bus, intercity	0.1	0.2	0.2	0.1	0.1	0.1	0.1
Rail	11.9	27.9	29.2	30.1	34.6	36.5	36.7
Water	5.3	15.5	18.4	20.1	22.7	28.7	27.6
Oil pipeline	1.4	7.5	8.9	8.5	9.1	9.0	9.1
Air carrier	1.2	4.0	6.8	13.7	18.8	27.6	25.8
Other carriers	0.4	1.1	1.7	4.0	5.0	7.8	7.7
Other shipper costs	1.4	2.4	3.0	3.7	4.4	5.4	5.4

Z Less than $50,000,000. [1] Includes small pickup trucks, vans, recreational vehicles, and mobile homes. [2] Includes federal, state, and local government operating subsidies and capital grants, except 1970 data for railroad commutations. [3] Includes domestic and international air passenger federal excise taxes. [4] Includes federal operating subsidies and capital grants for Amtrak and the Northeast Corridor. [5] Includes freight, mail, express, and where applicable, subsidies and user fees. [6] Excludes use of small trucks/vans used almost exclusively for personal travel.

Source: Eno Transportation Foundation, Inc., Washington, D.C. *Transportation in America,* annual (copyright).

No. 1049. Volume of Domestic Intercity Freight and Passenger Traffic by Type of Transport: 1980 to 2001

[Freight traffic in billions ton-miles (2,487 represents 2,487,000,000,000); passenger traffic in billions passenger-miles. A ton-mile is the movement of 1 ton (2,000 pounds) of freight for the distance of 1 mile. A passenger-mile is the movement of one passenger for the distance of 1 mile. Comprises public and private traffic, both revenue and nonrevenue. ICC = Interstate Commerce Commission]

Type of transport	1980	1985	1990	1994	1995	1996	1997	1998	1999	2000	2001, est.
Freight traffic, total [1]	**2,487**	**2,458**	**2,896**	**3,261**	**3,407**	**3,516**	**3,534**	**3,591**	**3,686**	**3,746**	**3,733**
Railroads	932	895	1,091	1,275	1,375	1,426	1,421	1,442	1,499	1,534	1,558
Truck:											
ICC truck	242	250	311	391	401	428	436	459	474	483	471
Non-ICC truck	313	360	424	517	520	544	560	568	585	591	580
Water:											
Rivers/canals	311	306	390	388	406	392	392	392	403	409	400
Great Lakes	96	76	85	87	91	93	95	96	92	97	94
Oil pipelines	588	564	584	591	601	619	617	620	618	617	616
Domestic airways [2]	5	7	10	12	13	14	14	14	15	16	15
Passenger traffic, total [3]	**1,468**	**1,636**	**1,847**	**2,065**	**2,098**	**2,182**	**2,247**	**2,328**	**2,424**	**2,494**	**2,498**
Private automobiles [3]	1,210	1,310	1,452	1,625	1,641	1,693	1,740	1,806	1,873	1,911	1,938
Air, private carrier [4]	15	12	13	10	11	12	13	13	14	15	16
Air, public carrier	204	278	346	388	404	435	451	463	488	515	488
Bus	27	24	23	28	28	29	31	32	35	38	42
Railroads [5]	11	11	13	14	14	13	14	14	14	15	15

[1] Includes both for-hire and private carrier freight, mail and express. [2] Includes both scheduled and nonscheduled carriers. [3] Includes small trucks used for travel purposes. [4] General aviation including air taxi and small air commuter. [5] Traffic by other than Amtrak and classified as noncommutation.

Source: Eno Transportation Foundation, Inc., Washington, DC, *Transportation in America,* annual (copyright).

No. 1050. Transportation and Warehousing—Establishments, Revenue, Payroll, and Employees by Kind of Business (NAICS Basis): 1997 and 2002

[318,245 represents $318,245. 2002 preliminary. For establishments with payroll. (318,245 represents $318,245,000,000). Based on the 1997 and 2002 Economic Censuses; See Appendix III]

Kind of business	1997 NAICS code [1]	Number of establishments	Revenue (mil. dol.)	Annual payroll (mil. dol.)	Paid employees (1,000)
Transportation and warehousing: [2]					
1997.	48-49	178,025	318,245	82,346	2,920.8
2002.	48-49	200,706	(B)	116,767	3,751.0
Air transportation:					
1997.	481	3,598	20,249	2,748	89.1
2002.	481	4,014	22,374	3,816	96.2
Water transportation:					
1997.	483	1,921	24,019	2,834	72.9
2002.	483	1,954	26,651	3,110	69.0
Truck transportation: [2]					
1997.	484	103,798	141,225	38,471	1,293.8
2002.	484	113,237	167,151	47,466	1,464.9
Transit and ground passenger transportation:					
1997.	485	16,013	13,792	5,549	339.6
2002.	485	17,390	19,144	7,691	407.6
Pipeline transportation:					
1997.	486	2,311	26,837	2,661	49.3
2002.	486	2,410	27,845	3,390	51.1
Scenic and sightseeing transportation:					
1997.	487	2,325	1,893	492	23.9
2002.	487	2,580	1,737	483	23.2
Support activities for transportation:					
1997.	488	30,675	39,758	12,592	411.6
2002.	488	34,458	62,525	17,837	519.3
Couriers and messengers:					
1997.	492	10,887	39,812	14,072	530.8
2002.	492	12,540	54,735	17,083	584.9
Warehousing and storage: [2]					
1997.	493	6,497	10,658	2,926	109.8
2002.	493	12,123	(B)	15,891	534.8

B Data do not meet publication standards. [1] North American Industry Classification System, 1997; see text, Section 15. [2] 2002 data include enterprise support establishments, not included in 1997.

Source: U.S. Census Bureau, 2002 Economic Census, *Advance Report*, issued March 2004. See Internet site: <http://www.census.gov/econ/census02/>

No. 1051. Employment and Earnings in Transportation and Warehousing by Industry: 1990 to 2003

[3,476 represents 3,476,000. Annual average of monthly figures. Earnings data for rail and water transportation are not available. Based on Current Employment Statistics program; see Appendix III]

Industry	2002 NAICS code [1]	1990	1995	1999	2000	2001	2002	2003
EMPLOYEES (1,000)								
Transportation and warehousing.	48,49	3,476	3,838	4,300	4,410	4,372	4,224	4,177
Air transportation.	481	529	511	586	614	615	564	527
Rail transportation.	482	272	233	229	232	227	218	215
Water transportation.	483	57	51	52	56	54	53	53
Truck transportation.	484	1,122	1,249	1,392	1,406	1,387	1,339	1,328
Transit and ground.	485	274	328	371	372	375	381	380
Pipeline transportation.	486	60	54	47	46	45	42	40
Scenic and sightseeing.	487	16	22	26	28	29	26	28
Support activities.	488	364	430	518	537	539	525	516
Couriers and messengers.	491,2	375	517	586	605	587	561	567
Warehousing and storage.	493	407	444	494	514	514	517	522
AVG. WEEKLY EARNINGS [2] (dol.)								
Transportation and warehousing.	48,49	471.72	513.37	547.97	562.31	562.70	579.75	597.79
Air transportation.	481	496.75	485.42	456.91	496.14	536.48	560.55	580.43
Truck transportation.	484	489.65	554.10	625.57	635.18	603.79	626.32	651.81
Transit and ground.	485	315.91	355.78	390.96	399.59	400.17	421.93	425.32
Pipeline transportation.	486	610.40	750.77	805.88	826.00	860.35	936.68	1,077.68
Scenic and sightseeing.	487	288.86	303.32	340.42	360.05	371.80	361.05	369.53
Support activities.	488	437.09	490.92	530.00	549.04	577.97	616.04	659.20
Couriers and messengers.	491,2	235.75	342.66	382.18	384.31	390.42	398.07	403.83
Warehousing and storage.	493	404.59	462.91	536.46	558.49	564.78	571.73	567.38

[1] North American Industry Classification System 2002, see text, sections 12 and 15. [2] For nonsupervisory workers.

Source: U.S. Bureau of Labor Statistics, *Employment and Earnings*, monthly, March 2004 issue. See also Internet site: <http://www.bls.gov/ceshome.htm/>.

[3,790.0 represents 3,790,000. For establishments with payroll. See Appendix III. County Business Patterns excludes rail transportation (NAICS 482) and the National Postal Service (NAICS 491)]

Industry	1997 NAICS code [1]	Establishments		Paid employees [2] (1,000)		Annual payroll (mil. dol.)	
		2000	2001	2000	2001	2000	2001
Transportation & warehousing.	48-49	190,044	190,683	3,790.0	3,750.7	125,592.4	129,506.2
Air transportation	481	5,429	5,451	615.6	609.0	26,569.3	28,780.7
Scheduled air transportation	4811	3,324	3,331	570.9	562.1	24,484.5	26,589.7
Scheduled passenger air transportation .	481111	2,740	2,825	536.2	533.5	23,470.7	25,672.1
Scheduled freight air transportation. . . .	481112	584	506	34.7	28.6	1,013.8	917.6
Nonscheduled air transportation.	4812	2,105	2,120	44.7	46.9	2,084.8	2,190.9
Water transportation	483	1,900	1,871	67.6	70.5	3,003.2	3,342.1
Deep sea, coastal, & Great Lakes water transportation	4831	1,254	1,227	47.8	50.7	2,214.2	2,491.1
Inland water transportation	4832	646	644	19.7	19.7	789.0	850.9
Inland water freight transportation.	483211	402	395	16.3	16.0	673.9	729.3
Inland water passenger transportation . .	483212	244	249	3.5	3.8	115.1	121.6
Truck transportation	484	110,416	109,814	1,415.8	1,397.9	46,451.5	46,080.9
General freight trucking.	4841	55,874	56,378	922.7	915.0	31,614.0	31,223.9
General freight trucking, local.	48411	20,329	20,726	153.3	149.8	4,529.8	4,434.0
General freight trucking, long distance. .	48412	35,545	35,652	769.5	765.2	27,084.2	26,789.8
Specialized freight trucking	4842	54,542	53,436	493.1	482.9	14,837.5	14,857.1
Used household & office goods moving .	48421	9,147	8,913	128.9	128.2	3,661.4	3,657.9
Specialized freight (except used goods) trucking, local	48422	32,493	32,099	200.4	196.2	5,692.4	5,800.4
Specialized freight (except used goods) trucking, long-distance	48423	12,902	12,424	163.7	158.5	5,483.7	5,398.7
Transit & ground passenger transportation . .	485	16,383	16,466	386.9	391.6	7,214.7	7,558.7
Urban transit systems	4851	705	715	43.1	42.2	1,295.8	1,345.6
Mixed mode systems	485111	152	164	6.2	5.5	146.9	137.4
Commuter rail.	485112	15	15	(D)	(D)	(D)	(D)
Bus and other motor vehicle mode systems	485113	505	496	31.4	31.6	925.1	952.6
Other.	485119	33	40	(D)	(D)	(D)	(D)
Interurban & rural bus transportation. . . .	4852	444	460	26.8	24.7	709.7	811.0
Taxi & limousine service	4853	6,806	6,842	67.8	69.4	1,244.3	1,257.7
Taxi service	48531	3,116	3,086	30.4	30.3	485.2	488.7
Limousine service	48532	3,690	3,756	37.5	39.2	759.1	769.0
School & employee bus transportation . .	4854	4,217	4,287	162.9	168.9	2,322.6	2,471.8
Charter bus industry	4855	1,451	1,395	34.1	33.4	668.7	659.5
Other transit & ground passenger transportation	4859	2,760	2,767	52.2	52.9	973.6	1,013.2
Special needs transpiration	485991	1,914	1,887	34.8	35.9	648.9	697.4
Pipeline transportation.	486	2,802	2,785	53.0	50.9	3,828.6	3,880.3
Pipeline transportation of crude oil	4861	307	229	6.7	6.0	425.6	430.9
Pipeline transportation of natural gas	4862	1,938	2,017	39.2	38.2	2,961.1	2,981.3
Other pipeline transportation	4869	557	539	7.0	6.7	441.9	468.1
Scenic & sightseeing transportation	487	2,254	2,380	23.6	23.4	583.5	556.8
Scenic & sightseeing transportation, land. .	4871	454	521	8.7	8.6	192.8	188.1
Scenic & sightseeing transportation, water. .	4872	1,642	1,699	13.0	12.9	331.2	313.3
Scenic & sightseeing transportation, other .	4879	158	160	2.0	1.9	59.5	55.4
Support activities for transportation	488	31,440	31,876	472.4	484.6	16,507.0	17,098.2
Support activities for air transportation . . .	4881	4,368	4,417	126.7	127.6	3,634.0	3,713.4
Airport operations	48811	1,834	1,811	67.9	65.9	1,569.5	1,515.3
Air traffic control.	488111	137	151	0.8	0.8	29.9	35.9
Other support activities for air transportation	48819	2,534	2,606	58.8	61.7	2,064.6	2,198.1
Support activities for rail transportation . . .	4882	821	831	21.4	23.0	714.4	739.0
Support activities for water transportation . .	4883	2,543	2,496	81.6	78.7	3,250.7	3,350.0
Port and harbor operations	48831	196	201	7.4	7.3	265.8	254.9
Marine cargo handling	48832	607	612	53.5	50.3	2,194.7	2,249.5
Navigational services to shipping	48833	863	830	11.8	12.0	478.7	507.8
Other.	48839	877	853	8.9	9.2	311.5	337.8
Support activities for road transportation . .	4884	7,010	7,325	56.2	61.3	1,308.8	1,483.3
Motor vehicle towing	48841	6,078	6,294	41.8	43.7	961.7	1,030.8
Freight transportation arrangement.	4885	15,177	15,334	161.7	168.2	6,620.3	6,829.4
Other support activities for transportation. .	4889	1,521	1,473	24.7	25.9	978.6	983.1
Couriers & messengers	492	12,297	12,855	619.3	577.6	17,399.4	17,815.3
Couriers	4921	6,667	7,105	548.9	513.6	15,890.5	16,455.5
Local messengers & local delivery	4922	5,630	5,750	70.5	64.0	1,508.9	1,359.8
Warehousing & storage	493	7,123	7,185	135.9	145.3	4,035.3	4,393.1

D Figure withheld to avoid disclosure pertaining to individual companies. [1] North American Industry Classification System, 1997; see text, Section 15. [2] For employees on the payroll for the pay period including March 12.

Source: U.S. Census Bureau, "County Business Patterns"; 2001 published 10 April 2003; <http://www.census.gov/epcd/cbp/view/cbpview.html>.

[6,216 represents 6,216,000]

Year and casualty	Motor ve-hicle [1] (1,000)	Rail-road [2]	Air Air-lines [3]	Air Commuter air carriers [4]	Air On demand air carriers [5]	Air General aviation	Recre-ational boat-ing [6]	Pipeline [7] Gas	Pipeline [7] Hazard-ous liquid	Water-borne [8]	Rail Rapid Tran-sit [9]	Hazard-ous materi-als [10]
Accidents:												
1980....	6,216	8,205	19	38	171	3,590	5,513	1,524	246	4,624	6,789	15,719
1990....	6,471	2,879	24	15	107	2,241	6,411	198	180	3,613	12,178	8,879
1995....	6,699	2,459	36	12	75	2,056	8,019	161	188	4,298	14,327	14,852
2000....	6,394	2,983	56	12	80	1,837	7,740	234	147	3,887	12,782	17,625
2002....	6,570	2,701	41	8	59	1,714	5,705	183	140	4,110	(NA)	15,111
Deaths:												
1980....	51.1	584	1	37	105	1,239	1,360	15	4	206	83	19
1990....	44.6	599	39	6	51	767	865	6	3	85	117	8
1995....	41.8	567	168	9	52	735	829	18	3	51	79	7
2000....	41.9	512	92	5	71	585	701	37	1	49	80	16
2002....	42.8	596	-	-	33	576	(NA)	10	1	28	(NA)	7
Injuries:												
1980....	2,848	58,696	19	14	43	681	2,650	177	15	180	6,801	626
1990....	3,231	22,736	29	11	36	409	3,822	69	7	175	10,036	423
1995....	3,465	12,546	25	17	14	396	4,141	53	11	145	11,238	400
2000....	3,189	10,424	27	7	12	310	4,355	77	4	130	10,848	251
2002....	2,926	10,067	20	-	13	312	4,062	50	-	157	(NA)	126

- Represents zero. NA Not available. [1] Data on deaths are from U.S. National Highway Traffic Safety Administration and are based on 30 day definition. Includes only police reported crashes. For more detail, see Table 1077. [2] Accidents which result in damages to railroad property. Grade crossing accidents are also included when classified as a train accident. Deaths exclude fatalities in railroad-highway grade crossing accidents. [3] Includes scheduled and nonscheduled (charter) air carriers. Represents serious injuries. [4] All scheduled service. Represents serious injuries. [5] All nonscheduled service. Represents serious injuries. [6] Accidents resulting in death; injury or requiring medical treatment beyond first aid; damages exceeding $500; or a person's disappearance. [7] Beginning 1990, pipeline accidents/incidents are credited to year of occurrence; prior data are credited to the year filed. [8] Covers accidents involving commercial vessels which must be reported to U.S. Coast Guard if there is property damage exceeding $25,000; material damage affecting the seaworthiness or efficiency of a vessel; stranding or grounding; loss of life; or injury causing a person's incapacity for more than 3 days. [9] Reporting criteria and source of data changed between 1989 and 1990; these data from 1990 to present are not comparable to earlier years. [10] Accidents, deaths, and injuries involving hazardous materials cover all types of transport.

Source: U.S. Bureau of Transportation Statistics, *National Transportation Statistics*, annual. See Internet site <http://www.bts.gov/publications/nts/index.html>.

[For calendar years or Dec. 31 (547.8 represents 547,800,000). For domestic and international operations. Covers carriers certificated under Section 401 of the Federal Aviation Act. Minus sign (-) indicates loss]

Item	Unit	1995	1997	1998	1999	2000	2001 [1]	2002 [1]	2003 [2]
SCHEDULED SERVICE									
Revenue passengers enplaned..	Mil.	547.8	594.7	612.9	636.0	666.2	622.1	612.9	646.5
Revenue passenger miles	Bil......	540.7	603.4	618.1	652.0	692.8	651.7	641.1	655.8
Available seat miles	Bil......	807.1	857.2	874.1	918.4	957.0	930.5	892.6	893.9
Revenue passenger load factor [3]	Percent	67.0	70.4	70.7	71.0	72.4	70.0	71.8	73.4
Mean passenger trip length [3]	Miles ...	987	1,015	1,008	1,025	1,040	1,048	1,046	1,014
Cargo ton miles	Mil.	16,921	20,513	20,496	21,613	23,888	22,003	24,591	25,980
Aircraft departures	1,000 ..	8,062	8,127	8,292	8,627	9,035	8,788	9,187	10,840
FINANCES									
Total operating revenue [4] ..	Mil. dol..	95,117	109,917	113,810	119,455	130,839	115,526	106,985	115,906
Passenger revenue	Mil. dol..	69,835	79,540	81,052	84,383	93,622	80,947	73,577	77,016
Freight and express revenue ...	Mil. dol..	8,616	10,477	10,697	11,415	12,486	12,066	12,865	13,210
Mail revenue	Mil. dol..	1,266	1,362	1,708	1,739	1,970	1,063	660	900
Charter revenue..........	Mil. dol..	3,742	3,748	4,059	4,284	4,913	4,449	4,225	5,140
Total operating expense	Mil. dol..	89,266	101,375	104,528	111,119	123,840	125,852	115,552	118,107
Operating profit (or loss) ...	Mil. dol..	5,852	8,542	9,283	8,337	6,999	-10,326	-8,566	-2,200
Interest income (or expense) ..	Mil. dol..	-2,426	-1,738	-1,753	-1,833	-2,193	-2,506	-3,263	-3,334
Net profit (or loss)	Mil. dol..	2,283	5,119	4,847	5,277	2,486	-8,275	-11,312	-3,625
Revenue per passenger mile ...	Cents...	12.9	13.2	13.1	12.9	13.5	12.4	11.5	11.7
Rate of return on investment ..	Percent	11.9	14.7	12.0	11.1	6.4	-6.5	-9.6	-0.3
Operating profit margin	Percent	6.2	7.8	8.2	7.0	5.3	-8.9	-8.0	-1.9
Net profit margin	Percent	2.4	4.7	4.3	4.4	1.9	-7.2	-10.6	-3.1
EMPLOYEES [5]									
Total	1,000...	547.0	586.5	621.1	646.4	680.0	672.0	601.4	570.9
Pilots and copilots	1,000...	55.4	60.4	64.1	67.2	72.4	73.8	68.8	68.0
Other flight personnel	1,000...	8.6	10.7	11.1	12.4	10.8	9.6	7.5	8.2
Flight attendants	1,000...	86.7	96.2	97.6	105.6	112.6	111.0	97.7	89.9
Mechanics	1,000...	50.5	65.5	69.9	70.3	72.1	70.8	61.7	57.4
Aircraft and traffic servicing personnel........	1,000...	251.1	269.6	290.1	295.6	311.7	303.9	280.9	267.8
All other	1,000...	94.8	84.1	88.3	95.3	100.3	102.9	84.9	79.6

[1] Includes cash compensation remitted to carriers under the Air Transportation Safety and System Stabilization Act (P.L. 107-42). [2] Includes security costs reimbursements remitted to carriers under the Emergency Wartime Supplemental Appropriations Act (P.L. 108-11). [3] For definition of mean, see Guide to Tabular Presentation. [4] Includes other types of revenues, not shown separately. [5] Average number of full time equivalents.

Source: Air Transport Association of America, Washington, DC, *Air Transport Annual Report*.

No. 1055. Airline Cost Indexes: 1980 to 2002

[1982 = 100. Covers U.S. major and national passenger carriers. Major carriers have operating revenues of $1 billion or more; nationals have operating revenues from $100 million to $1 billion]

Index	1980	1985	1990	1995	1996	1997	1998	1999	2000	2001	2002
Composite index [1]	87.2	108.8	142.2	161.1	162.5	168.4	171.4	173.8	176.5	182.3	186.9
Labor costs............	84.7	109.6	121.1	152.2	155.2	159.1	160.0	162.0	169.9	182.0	192.5
Fuel	92.0	91.0	77.4	54.9	65.0	63.4	50.4	52.2	77.2	76.7	71.6
Aircraft ownership [2]	91.7	138.6	207.3	247.2	260.5	254.1	259.6	277.5	296.8	298.6	307.6
Non-aircraft ownership	79.9	111.7	184.0	212.3	190.4	191.0	195.5	202.4	206.4	230.2	226.0
Professional services	83.2	134.9	196.8	248.0	247.3	258.8	281.1	282.6	285.6	290.9	279.4
Food and beverage	93.4	99.5	128.8	109.7	102.9	101.7	103.7	104.8	102.4	102.5	89.0
Landing fees.............	90.1	98.7	141.2	171.1	173.7	176.6	170.2	178.3	174.3	180.6	201.6
Maintenance material	108.3	127.3	191.5	147.2	154.8	179.4	176.2	163.3	168.8	148.2	126.2
Aircraft insurance.........	93.4	150.7	56.8	119.5	110.1	99.4	53.6	36.0	36.0	50.9	94.0
Non-aircraft insurance.......	91.6	160.4	84.0	266.0	276.8	242.5	179.9	124.7	120.7	218.0	683.0
Passenger commissions	77.1	112.5	163.9	134.8	127.0	122.9	109.1	95.2	77.2	61.5	38.5
Communication	70.3	98.4	114.2	115.0	113.3	110.0	116.2	134.8	131.4	144.5	133.2
Advertising and promotion	69.8	95.1	96.8	64.0	58.4	56.3	60.6	61.0	59.7	55.1	44.5
Utilities and office supplies	88.8	113.2	128.4	115.4	123.6	128.7	127.8	128.1	137.8	143.2	119.5
Other operating expenses	86.1	111.2	130.6	148.1	150.9	153.9	155.8	158.0	161.3	165.2	167.0
Interest [3]	87.9	98.5	97.9	94.7	86.7	71.2	60.2	53.8	54.4	50.6	53.6

[1] Weighted average of all components, including interest. less depreciation and amortization. [2] Includes lease, aircraft and engine rentals, depreciation and amortization. [3] Interest on long-term debt and capital and other interest expense.

Source: Air Transport Association of America, Washington, DC, *Airline Cost Index, Major and National Carriers, Second Quarter 2003.* See Internet site <http://www.airlines.org/econ/econ.aspx> (accessed 02 June 2004).

No. 1056. Top 40 Airports in 2003—Passengers Enplaned: 1993 and 2003

[In thousands (466,677 represents 466,677,000), except rank. For calendar year. Airports ranked by total passengers enplaned by large certificated air carriers, 2003]

Airport	1993 Total	1993 Rank	2003 Total	2003 Rank	Airport	1993 Total	1993 Rank	2003 Total	2003 Rank
All airports.	466,677	(X)	593,974	(X)	St. Louis, (Lambert-St.				
Total top 40	355,936	(X)	458,846	(X)	Louis Muni.), MO	9,902	14	9,302	23
Atlanta, GA (Hartsfield Intl.) .	22,295	3	38,229	1	Salt Lake City Intl, UT	7,147	25	8,874	24
Chicago, IL (O'Hare Intl.) . .	28,459	1	30,798	2	Chicago, (Midway) IL.	2,978	45	8,656	25
Dallas / Ft. Worth Intl., TX .	24,654	2	24,502	3	Ft. Lauderdale-Hollywood				
Los Angeles Intl., CA......	18,445	4	20,913	4	Intl., FL	3,879	36	8,046	26
Denver Intl., CO	14,210	5	17,272	5	Honolulu Intl., HI.	8,484	19	7,485	27
Phoenix Sky Harbor Intl., AZ.	11,295	7	17,176	6	San Diego Intl. (Lindbergh),				
Las Vegas (McCarran Intl.),					CA	5,699	26	7,428	28
NV	10,118	13	16,702	7	Tampa Intl., FL.	4,577	28	7,328	29
Houston Intercontinental, TX.	8,697	18	15,495	8	Washington, (Dulles Intl.),				
Minneapolis-St. Paul Intl.,					DC.	3,982	33	6,926	30
MN.	10,377	10	15,362	9	Oakland Metropolitan Intl.,				
Detroit (Wayne County), MI .	11,045	8	14,656	10	CA	3,578	39	6,543	31
Newark, NJ (Newark)	10,970	9	13,088	11	Washington, (Reagan				
Seattle-Tacoma Intl., WA . . .	9,010	16	12,788	12	National), DC	7,186	24	6,068	32
San Francisco Intl., CA	14,004	6	12,228	13	Portland Intl., OR	4,188	30	5,950	33
Orlando Intl., FL	8,725	17	12,049	14	Greater Pittsburgh, PA.	8,384	20	5,853	34
Miami Intl., FL	10,138	12	11,050	15	Norman Y. Mineta San Jose				
New York, (JFK Intl.), NY . .	8,258	21	10,746	16	Intl., CA.	3,186	43	5,027	35
Greater Cincinnati, OH.	5,128	27	10,257	17	Kansas City Intl., MO.	3,779	38	4,806	36
Philadelphia Intl., PA	7,294	23	10,185	18	Cleveland, (Hopkins Intl.),				
New York, (La Guardia), NY .	9,340	15	10,136	19	OH	3,890	35	4,803	37
Charlotte (Douglas Muni.),					New Orleans Intl., LA	3,282	40	4,554	38
NC.	7,805	22	9,573	20	San Juan (Luis Munoz				
Boston,(Logan Intl.), MA . . .	10,207	11	9,536	21	Marin Intl.), PR.	4,150	31	4,544	39
Baltimore, (BWI), MD.	3,952	34	9,409	22	Memphis Intl., TN	3,239	41	4,505	40

X Not applicable.

Source: U.S. Bureau of Transportation Statisics, Office of Airline Information, BTS Form 41, Schedule T-3, unpublished data.

No. 1057. Domestic Airline Markets: 2003

[In thousands (3,506 represents 3,506,000). For calendar year. Data are for the 25 top markets and include all commercial airports in each metro area. Data do not include connecting passengers]

Market	Passengers	Market	Passengers
New York to—from Ft. Lauderdale	3,506	Dallas/Ft. Worth to—from Houston.	1,477
New York to—from Orlando	2,908	New York to—from San Francisco.	1,455
New York to—from Chicago	2,686	New York to—from Tampa	1,417
New York to—from Atlanta	2,270	New York to—from Miami	1,339
New York to—from Los Angeles	2,196	Los Angeles to—from Oakland	1,269
Honolulu to—from Kahului, Maui	1,791	Chicago to—from Phoenix	1,230
New York to—from Las Vegas.	1,694	Los Angeles to—from Las Vegas.	1,225
New York to—from West Palm Beach. . . .	1,654	Honolulu to—from Lihue, Kauai	1,220
New York to—from Washington	1,648	Chicago to—from Orlando	1,210
Chicago to—from Los Angeles	1,616	New York to—from Dallas/Ft. Worth	1,206
New York to—from Boston	1,601	Honolulu to—from Kona, Hawaii	1,165
New York to—from San Juan	1,568	Chicago to—from Atlanta	1,133
Chicago to—from Las Vegas	1,524		

Source: Air Transport Association of America, Washington, DC, *Annual Report.*

No. 1058. Worldwide Airline Fatalities: 1986 to 2003

[For scheduled air transport operations]

Year	Fatal accidents	Passenger deaths	Death rate [1]	Death rate [2]	Year	Fatal accidents	Passenger deaths	Death rate [1]	Death rate [2]
1986	24	641	0.07	0.04	1995	25	711	0.05	0.03
1987	25	900	0.09	0.06	1996	24	1,146	0.07	0.05
1988	29	742	0.07	0.04	1997	26	929	0.06	0.04
1989	29	879	0.08	0.05	1998	20	904	0.05	0.03
1990	27	544	0.05	0.03	1999	21	499	0.03	0.02
1991	29	638	0.06	0.03	2000	18	755	0.04	0.03
1992	28	1,076	0.09	0.06	2001	13	577	0.03	0.02
1993	33	864	0.07	0.04	2002	13	791	0.04	0.03
1994	27	1,171	0.09	0.06	2003	6	334	0.02	0.01

[1] Rate per 100 million passenger miles flown.   [2] Rate per 100 million passenger kilometers flown.

Source: International Civil Aviation Organization, Montreal, Canada, *Civil Aviation Statistics of the World*, annual.

No. 1059. Airline Passenger Screening Results: 1980 to 2001

[Calendar year data (585 represents 585,000,000)]

Item	1980	1985	1990	1995	1997	1998	1999	2000	2001
Persons screened (mil.)	585	993	1,145	1,263	1,660	1,667	1,767	1,812	1,320
WEAPONS DETECTED									
Firearms, total	1,914	2,913	2,549	2,390	2,067	1,515	1,552	1,937	1,071
Handguns	1,878	2,823	2,490	2,230	1,905	1,401	1,421	1,643	1,008
Long guns	36	90	59	160	162	114	131	294	63
Other/other dangerous articles	108	74	304	(X)	(X)	(X)	(X)	(X)	(X)
Explosive/incendiary devices......	8	12	15	(X)	(X)	(X)	(X)	(X)	(X)
Persons arrested:									
Carrying firearms/explosives	1,031	1,310	1,336	1,194	924	660	633	600	362
Giving false information	32	42	18	68	72	86	58	61	90
Bomb threats received:									
Against airports..............	1,179	477	448	346	(NA)	(NA)	(NA)	(NA)	(NA)
Against aircraft	268	153	338	327	(NA)	(NA)	(NA)	(NA)	(NA)

NA Not available.   X Not applicable.

Source: U.S. Bureau or Transportation Statistics, *National Transportation Statistics, 2002*, and *Pocket Guide to Transportation, 2004*. See Internet site <https://www.bts.gov:443/pdc/index.xml>

No. 1060. Aircraft Accidents: 1985 to 2003

[For years ending December 31]

Item	Unit	1985	1990	1995	2000	2001	2002	2003, prel.
Air carrier accidents, all services [1]	Number...	21	24	36	56	46	41	54
Fatal accidents..................	Number...	7	6	3	3	6	-	2
Fatalities [2]	Number...	526	39	168	92	531	-	22
Aboard.......................	Number...	525	12	162	92	525	-	21
Rates per 100,000 flight hours:								
Accidents..................	Rate.....	0.241	0.198	0.267	0.306	0.236	0.241	0.315
Fatal accidents	Rate.....	0.080	0.049	0.022	0.016	0.011	-	0.012
Commuter air carrier accidents [3]........	Number...	18	15	12	12	7	8	2
Fatal accidents..................	Number...	7	3	2	1	2	-	1
Fatalities	Number...	37	6	9	5	13	-	2
Aboard.......................	Number...	36	4	9	5	13	-	2
Rates per 100,000 flight hours:								
Accidents..................	Rate.....	1.036	0.641	0.457	3.247	2.33	3.181	0.720
Fatal accidents	Rate.....	0.403	0.128	0.076	0.271	0.666	-	0.360
On-demand air taxi accidents [4]........	Number...	157	107	75	80	72	59	77
Fatal accidents..................	Number...	35	29	24	22	18	18	19
Fatalities	Number...	76	51	52	71	60	35	45
Aboard.......................	Number...	75	49	52	68	59	35	43
Rates per 100,000 flight hours:								
Accidents..................	Rate.....	6.11	4.76	3.02	2.04	2.40	2.03	2.61
Fatal accidents	Rate.....	1.36	1.29	0.97	0.66	0.60	0.62	0.64
General aviation accidents [5]...........	Number...	2,739	2,242	2,056	1,837	1,726	1,713	1,732
Fatal accidents..................	Number...	498	444	413	345	325	345	351
Fatalities	Number...	956	770	735	596	562	581	626
Aboard.......................	Number...	945	765	728	585	558	575	622
Rates per 100,000 flight hours:								
Accidents..................	Rate.....	9.63	7.85	8.21	6.57	6.78	6.69	6.71
Fatal accidents	Rate.....	1.74	1.55	1.63	1.21	1.27	1.33	1.36

- Represents zero.   [1] U.S. air carriers operating under 14 CFR 121. Beginning 1999, includes aircraft with 10 or more seats, previously operating under 14 CFR 135.   [2] Other than persons aboard aircraft who were killed, fatalities resulting from the September 11, 2001 terrorist acts are excluded.   [3] All scheduled service of U.S. air carriers operating under 14 CFR 135. Beginning 1999, only aircraft with fewer than 10 seats.   [4] All nonscheduled service of U.S. air carriers operating under 14 CFR 121 or 135.   [5] U.S. civil registered aircraft not operated under 14 CFR 121 or 135.

Source: U.S. National Transportation Safety Board, "Aviation Accident Statistics", Internet site <http://www.ntsb.gov/aviation/stats.htm> (accessed 10 May 2004).

No. 1061. On-Time Flight Arrivals and Departures at Major U.S. Airports: 2003

[In percent. Quarterly, based on gate arrival and departure times for domestic scheduled operations of U.S. major airlines. All U.S. airlines with 1 percent or more of total U.S. domestic scheduled airline passenger revenues are required to report on-time data. A flight is considered on time if it operated less than 15 minutes after the scheduled time shown in the carrier's computerized reservation system. Cancelled and diverted flights are considered late. See source for data on individual airlines]

Airport	On-time arrivals				On-time departures			
	1st qtr.	2d qtr.	3d qtr.	4th qtr.	1st qtr.	2d qtr.	3d qtr.	4th qtr.
Total, all airports	81.0	84.7	81.4	80.9	84.5	87.8	85.1	84.9
Total major airports.	81.0	84.7	81.3	80.5	84.0	87.2	84.1	84.4
Atlanta, Hartsfield International	76.5	81.5	77.8	80.5	79.3	83.1	79.9	83.5
Baltimore/Washington International	80.4	86.4	80.5	83.9	80.9	87.0	82.1	83.4
Boston, Logan International	78.9	84.1	79.0	79.8	80.8	86.8	83.2	82.6
Charlotte Douglas.	80.9	82.4	80.1	87.1	81.8	84.3	81.3	89.2
Chicago Midway.	80.0	86.8	83.5	82.9	78.2	84.2	80.7	81.9
Chicago, O'Hare	76.7	82.0	76.9	67.0	80.1	84.4	79.2	73.4
Cincinnati International	77.5	83.6	81.8	83.4	82.4	86.6	84.8	86.0
Dallas/Ft. Worth Regional	84.8	84.7	83.0	86.6	85.5	83.6	81.8	86.0
Denver International	85.1	87.9	88.1	84.6	87.0	89.7	89.1	87.4
Detroit, Metro Wayne	83.1	87.9	83.3	85.4	84.0	87.4	83.9	86.9
Fort Lauderdale	77.6	82.7	78.5	82.9	82.6	87.1	86.5	87.0
Houston George Bush.	81.7	87.2	83.6	84.2	89.3	92.2	89.9	90.4
Las Vegas, McCarran International	82.6	87.0	85.3	79.5	83.4	88.5	85.2	82.9
Los Angeles International.	87.2	87.7	88.2	81.3	89.7	91.2	90.2	86.0
Miami International	80.7	80.4	75.8	82.3	85.5	83.2	78.9	86.1
Minneapolis/St. Paul International	83.3	86.4	85.2	81.4	86.7	88.8	86.6	87.2
Newark International	77.0	76.8	66.0	71.7	83.4	87.1	79.7	81.7
New York, Kennedy International.	78.1	84.7	77.7	82.7	80.4	86.9	82.2	83.7
New York, LaGuardia	77.0	82.4	72.7	72.8	83.2	88.9	82.2	82.8
Orlando International	80.7	85.4	79.5	84.9	86.4	89.4	84.8	89.3
Philadelphia International	76.2	80.1	73.3	78.2	79.1	81.5	76.1	80.4
Phoenix, Sky Harbor International	81.0	88.5	87.3	84.2	81.4	87.8	84.7	83.5
Pittsburgh, Greater International	82.5	85.6	78.2	84.5	86.0	88.4	82.5	88.1
Portland International	85.0	89.0	86.7	80.7	89.3	92.2	90.2	86.8
Ronald Reagan National	81.4	85.0	77.0	83.1	86.6	90.2	85.3	89.2
St. Louis, Lambert	82.9	85.3	83.0	86.4	87.7	90.2	87.6	89.3
Salt Lake City International	87.4	91.4	89.8	81.9	88.8	93.4	91.7	84.7
San Diego International, Lindbergh	85.9	86.9	86.2	80.2	88.2	90.7	89.1	84.5
San Francisco International	82.2	83.0	84.2	74.1	89.8	90.5	90.9	84.5
Seattle-Tacoma International	81.1	87.3	84.0	77.4	85.7	88.5	86.6	83.9
Tampa International	81.9	84.4	81.5	84.7	87.3	89.1	86.7	89.9
Washington/Dulles	77.6	83.4	80.2	82.2	77.0	84.6	82.8	85.5

Source: U.S. Department of Transportation, Aviation Consumer Protection Division , Air Travel Consumer Report, monthly. See Internet site <http://airconsumer.ost.dot.gov>.

No. 1062. Consumer Complaints Against U.S. Airlines: 1990 to 2003

[Calendar year data. Represents complaints filed by consumers to the U.S. Department of Transportation, Aviation Consumer Proection Division, regarding service problems with air carrier personnel. See source for data on individual airlines]

Complaint category	1990	1995	1997	1998	1999	2000	2001	2002	2003
Total	7,703	4,629	6,394	7,980	17,345	20,564	14,076	7,697	4,600
Flight problems [1]	3,034	1,133	1,699	2,270	6,449	8,698	5,048	1,808	1,049
Customer service [2]	758	667	1,418	1,716	3,657	4,074	2,531	1,808	1,049
Baggage	1,329	628	826	1,105	2,351	2,753	1,965	1,082	801
Ticketing/boarding [3]	624	666	904	805	1,329	1,405	1,310	898	643
Refunds	701	576	531	601	935	803	942	737	428
Fares [4]	312	185	195	276	584	708	568	436	243
Disability [5]	(NA)	(NA)	(NA)	331	520	612	457	420	323
Oversales [6]	399	263	414	387	673	759	539	364	223
Discrimination [7]	(NA)	(NA)	(NA)	(NA)	(NA)	(NA)	164	176	73
Advertising	96	66	57	39	57	42	42	43	13
Tours	29	18	13	23	28	25	11	[8]	[8]
Animals	(NA)	(NA)	(NA)	(NA)	(NA)	1	6	-	[9]
Smoking	74	15	5	[9]	[9]	[9]	[9]	[9]	[9]
Credit.	5	4	1	[9]	[9]	[9]	[9]	[9]	[9]
Other	342	408	331	427	762	684	493	255	218

- Represents zero. NA Not available. [1] Cancellations, delays, etc. from schedule. [2] Unhelpful employees, inadequate meals or cabin service, treatment of delayed passengers. [3] Errors in reservations and ticketing; problems in making reservations and obtaining tickets. [4] Incorrect or incomplete information about fares, discount fare conditions, and availability, etc. [5] Prior to 1998, included in ticketing/boarding. [6] All bumping problems, whether or not airline complied with DOT regulations. [7] Allegations of discrimination by airlines due to factors other than disability, such as race, religion, national origin or sex. [8] Included in "Other" beginning 2002. [9] Included in "Other" beginning 1998.

Source: U.S. Department of Transportation, Aviation Consumer Protection Division, Air Travel Consumer Report, monthly. See Internet site <http://airconsumer.ost.dot.gov>.

No. 1063. Commuter/Regional Airline Operations—Summary: 1980 to 2002

[Calendar year data (14.8 represents 14,800,000). Commuter/regional airlines operate primarily aircraft of predominately 75 passengers or less and 18,000 pounds of payload capacity serving short haul and small community markets. Represents operations within all North America by U.S. Regional Carriers. Averages are means. For definition of mean, see Guide to Tabular Presentation]

Item	Unit	1980	1985	1990	1995	2000	2001	2002
Passenger carriers operating	Number.	214	179	150	124	94	91	91
Passengers enplaned	Millions .	14.8	[1]26.0	42.1	57.2	84.6	82.8	98.4
Average passengers enplaned per carrier. .	1,000 .	69.2	[1]52.4	277.5	461.4	830.4	910.2	1,080.9
Revenue passenger miles (RPM)	Billions .	1.92	[1]4.41	7.61	12.75	25.27	25.74	32.77
Average RPMs per carrier	Millions .	8.97	[1]24.64	50.75	102.80	268.83	282.83	360.11
Airports served	Number .	732	854	811	780	729	726	707
Average trip length	Miles. . .	129	173	183	223	299	311	333
Passenger aircraft operated	Number .	1,339	1,745	1,917	2,138	2,271	2,323	2,385
Average seating capacity (seats).	Number .	13.9	19.2	22.1	24.6	31.7	33.5	35.1
Fleet flying hours	1,000 . .	1,740	2,854	3,447	4,659	5,362	5,161	5,248
Average annual utilization per aircraft.	Hours . .	1,299	1,635	1,798	2,179	2,368	2,222	2,201

[1] Adjusted to exclude a merger in 1986.   [2] Prior to 1995, utilization results reflected airborne rather than block hours.

Source: Regional Airline Association and AvStat Associates, Washington, DC, *Annual Report of the Regional Airline Industry* (copyright).

No. 1064. Airports, Aircraft, and Airmen: 1980 to 2002

[As of Dec. 31 or for years ending Dec. 31]

Item	1980	1985	1990	1995	1999	2000	2001	2002
Airports, total [1]	15,161	16,319	17,490	18,224	19,098	19,281	19,356	19,572
Public	4,814	5,858	5,589	5,415	5,324	5,317	5,294	5,286
Percent—With lighted runways	66.2	68.1	71.4	74.3	76.1	75.9	76.2	76
With paved runways	72.3	66.7	70.7	73.3	74.2	74.3	74.6	75
Private	10,347	10,461	11,901	12,809	13,774	13,964	14,062	14,286
Percent—With lighted runways	15.2	9.1	7.0	6.4	6.7	7.2	8.0	8
With paved runways	13.3	17.4	31.5	33.0	31.8	32.0	32.4	32
Certificated [2]	730	700	680	667	655	651	635	633
Civil	(X)	(X)	(X)	572	565	563	560	558
Civil military.	(X)	(X)	(X)	95	90	88	75	75
General aviation	14,431	15,619	16,810	17,557	18,443	18,630	18,721	18,939
Active air carrier fleet [3].	3,808	4,678	6,083	7,411	8,228	8,055	8,497	(NA)
Fixed wing	3,803	4,673	6,072	7,293	8,106	8,016	8,370	(NA)
Helicopter	2	5	11	118	122	39	127	(NA)
General aviation fleet [4].	211,043	196,500	198,000	188,089	219,464	217,533	211,446	(NA)
Fixed-wing	200,097	184,700	184,500	162,342	184,723	183,276	177,697	(NA)
Turbojet	2,992	4,100	4,100	4,559	7,120	7,001	7,787	(NA)
Turboprop	4,090	5,000	5,300	4,995	5,679	5,762	6,596	(NA)
Piston.	193,014	175,600	175,200	152,788	171,923	170,513	163,314	(NA)
Rotocraft	6,001	6,000	6,900	5,830	7,448	7,150	6,783	(NA)
Other.	4,945	5,800	6,600	4,741	6,765	6,700	6,545	(NA)
Gliders	(NA)	(NA)	(NA)	2,182	2,041	2,041	1,904	(NA)
Lighter than air.	(NA)	(NA)	(NA)	2,559	4,725	4,660	4,641	(NA)
Experimental.	(NA)	(NA)	(NA)	15,176	20,528	20,407	20,421	(NA)
Airman certificates held: [5]								
Pilot.	827,071	709,540	702,659	639,184	635,472	625,581	612,274	631,762
Women	52,902	43,082	40,515	38,032	37,373	36,757	36,757	38,257
Student.	199,833	146,652	128,663	101,279	97,359	93,064	86,731	85,991
Recreational	(NA)	(NA)	87	232	343	340	316	317
Airplane:								
Private	357,479	311,086	299,111	261,399	258,749	251,561	243,823	245,230
Commercial	183,442	151,632	149,666	133,980	124,261	121,858	120,502	125,920
Air transport.	69,569	82,740	107,732	123,877	137,642	141,596	144,702	144,708
Rotocraft only [6]	6,030	8,123	9,567	7,183	7,728	7,775	7,727	7,770
Glider only.	7,039	8,168	7,833	11,234	9,390	9,387	8,473	21,826
Flight instructor certificates	60,440	58,940	63,775	77,613	79,694	80,931	82,875	86,089
Instrument ratings	260,462	258,559	297,073	298,798	308,951	311,944	315,276	317,389
Nonpilot [7].	368,356	395,139	492,237	651,341	538,264	547,453	513,100	515,570
Mechanic	250,157	274,100	344,282	405,294	340,402	344,434	310,850	315,928
Repairmen	(NA)	(NA)	(NA)	61,233	35,989	38,208	40,085	37,114
Parachute rigger.	9,547	9,395	10,094	11,824	10,447	10,477	7,927	8,063
Ground instructor	61,550	58,214	66,882	96,165	71,238	72,326	72,261	73,658
Dispatcher.	6,799	8,511	11,002	15,642	15,655	16,340	16,070	16,695
Flight navigator	1,936	1,542	1,290	916	642	570	509	431
Flight engineer	38,367	43,377	58,687	60,267	63,891	65,098	65,398	63,681

NA Not available.   X Not applicable.   [1] Existing airports, heliports, seaplane bases, etc. recorded with FAA. Includes military airports with joint civil and military use. Includes U.S. outlying areas. Airport-type definitions: Public—publicly owned and under control of a public agency; private—owned by a private individual or corporation. May or may not be open for public use. [2] Certificated airports serve air-carriers with aircraft seating more that 30 passengers.   [3] Air-carrier aircraft are aircraft carrying passengers or cargo for hire under 14 CFR 121 (large aircraft—more than 30 seats) and 14 CFR 135 (small aircraft— 30 seats or fewer).   [4] Beginning 1995 excludes commuters.   [5] Source: U.S. Federal Aviation Administration. See Internet site <http://apo.faa.gov/pubs.asp>. Prior years in the *Statistical Handbook of Aviation*, annual.   [6] Data for 1980 and 1985 are for helicopters only.   [7] All certificates on record. No medical examination required

Source: Except as noted, U.S. Bureau of Transportation Statistics, *National Transportation Statistics, 2002.* See Internet site <http://www.bts.gov/publications/nts/index.html>.

No. 1065. Freight Carried on Major U.S. Waterways: 1980 to 2002

[In millions of tons (4.0 represents 4,000,000)]

Item	1980	1985	1990	1995	1998	1999	2000	2001	2002
Atlantic intracoastal waterway	4.0	3.1	4.2	3.5	3.8	3.4	3.1	2.5	1.9
Great Lakes	183.5	148.1	167.1	177.8	192.2	182.9	187.5	171.4	167.2
Gulf intracoastal waterway	94.5	102.5	115.4	118.0	113.6	109.6	113.8	112.2	107.7
Mississippi River system [1]	584.2	527.8	659.1	707.2	707.4	716.9	715.5	714.8	712.8
Mississippi River mainstem	441.5	384.0	475.3	520.3	503.9	512.3	515.6	504.2	501.7
Ohio River system [2]	179.3	203.9	260.0	267.6	277.9	277.9	274.4	281.8	280.9
Columbia River	49.2	42.4	51.4	57.1	49.1	50.7	55.2	50.3	45.0
Snake River	5.1	3.5	4.8	6.8	5.8	5.8	6.7	5.6	4.3

[1] Main channels and all tributaries of the Mississippi, Illinois, Missouri and Ohio Rivers. [2] Main channels and all navigable tributaries and embayments of the Ohio, Tennessee, and Cumberland Rivers.

Source: U.S. Army Corps of Engineers, *Waterborne Commerce of the United States*, annual.

No. 1066. Waterborne Commerce by Type of Commodity: 1995 to 2002

[In millions of short tons (2,240.4 represents 2,240,400,000). Domestic trade includes all commercial movements between United States ports and on inland rivers, Great Lakes, canals, and connecting channels of the United States, Puerto Rico, and Virgin Islands]

Commodity	1995	2000	2001	2002 Total	2002 Domestic	2002 Foreign imports	2002 Foreign exports
Total	2,240.4	2,424.6	[1]2,393.3	2,340.3	1,021.0	934.9	384.4
Coal	324.5	297.0	303.3	286.9	227.0	16.7	43.3
Petroleum and petroleum products	907.1	1,044.0	1,048.6	1,017.9	348.7	609.3	59.9
Crude petroleum [2]	504.6	571.4	573.6	566.0	85.5	479.3	1.2
Petroleum products [2]	402.5	472.4	475.0	451.9	263.2	130.0	58.7
Gasoline	114.4	125.2	127.7	122.6	86.6	29.3	6.7
Distillate fuel oil	76.7	91.7	91.1	88.4	62.7	19.9	5.9
Residual fuel oil	111.9	131.6	133.7	117.0	69.4	35.4	12.1
Chemicals and related products	153.7	172.4	169.7	167.6	73.1	39.6	55.0
Fertilizers	35.7	35.1	39.0	32.4	13.0	6.1	13.2
Other chemicals and related products	118.0	137.3	130.6	135.2	60.0	33.4	41.7
Crude material, inedible	381.7	380.3	354.0	352.0	214.7	92.2	45.0
Forest products, wood and chips	47.2	33.1	27.1	25.1	9.2	7.0	8.9
Pulp and waste paper	14.9	13.6	13.8	14.0	0.1	1.2	12.7
Soil, sand, gravel, rock, and stone [2]	152.5	165.0	162.6	166.1	128.8	33.7	3.7
Limestone	54.0	67.4	68.9	68.8	54.4	11.7	2.7
Phosphate rock	10.7	3.4	1.7	6.2	3.5	2.7	0.0
Sand & gravel	77.0	79.0	77.5	76.0	67.5	7.9	0.6
Iron ore and scrap	104.9	97.9	76.8	85.8	58.5	15.5	11.8
Marine shells	0.5	0.3	0.3	0.3	0.3	0.0	0.0
Non-ferrous ores and scrap	27.9	29.2	25.7	24.3	6.6	15.5	2.2
Sulphur, clay and salt	23.4	11.3	10.3	9.8	1.3	3.8	4.7
Slag	1.9	4.0	4.4	3.1	1.2	1.9	0.0
Other nonmetal minerals	8.4	25.9	33.1	23.3	8.7	13.5	1.1
Primary manufactured goods	106.3	153.0	137.1	140.8	42.4	83.9	14.5
Papers products	13.1	12.1	11.9	11.0	0.3	4.8	6.0
Lime, cement and glass	33.9	55.9	52.1	51.2	18.9	31.0	1.2
Primary iron and steel products	44.1	57.1	46.6	46.3	14.4	30.8	1.0
Primary nonferrous metal products	12.3	25.5	23.8	29.3	8.7	14.6	6.0
Primary wood products	2.9	2.5	2.7	3.1	0.1	2.7	0.3
Food and farm products	303.2	283.3	281.9	280.0	97.6	32.2	150.3
Fish [2]	3.6	2.4	2.4	2.7	0.1	1.4	1.2
Grain [2]	167.9	145.2	140.7	139.3	55.3	1.6	82.3
Wheat	48.5	43.4	40.3	36.0	9.7	0.2	26.1
Corn	105.0	88.2	87.9	89.8	41.7	0.1	47.9
Oilseeds	46.1	57.6	61.5	60.5	26.0	0.6	33.9
Soybeans	42.0	47.3	49.4	49.8	21.5	0.0	28.2
Vegetables products	9.0	8.9	8.8	8.5	1.2	3.4	3.9
Processed grain and animal feed	33.0	23.1	22.4	21.9	7.7	0.9	13.3
Other agricultural products	43.5	46.1	46.1	47.2	7.3	24.2	15.7
All manufactured equip, machinery and products	57.0	83.6	80.3	81.9	14.6	54.9	12.4
Waste and scrap, nec. [3]	5.4	4.3	3.5	2.7	2.7	-	-
Unknown or not elsewhere classified	1.6	6.8	8.2	10.4	0.2	6.2	4.0

- Represents or rounds to zero. [1] U.S. total revised. Revisions not available by commodity group. [2] Includes commodities not shown separately. [3] N.e.c. means not elsewhere classified.

Source: U.S. Army Corps of Engineers, *Waterborne Commerce of the United States*, annual.

Transportation 683

No. 1067. Cargo-Carrying U.S.-Flag Fleet by Area of Operation: 2002

[Tons in thousands of metric tons (30,495 represents 30,495,000. As of July 1. One ton equals 100 cubic feet of space. Represents active vessels]

Area of operation	Total fleet		Liquid carriers		Dry bulk carriers		Containerships		Other freighters [1]	
	Number	Tons	Number	Tons	Number	Tons	Number	Tons	Number	Tons
VESSELS OF 1,000 GROSS TONS AND OVER										
Grand total	3,869	30,495	2,196	15,714	759	5,889	123	3,108	791	5,784
Foreign waterborne trade [2]	268	5,319	53	946	116	1,115	61	2,510	38	748
Domestic trade	3,430	21,921	2,116	13,887	643	4,774	57	512	614	2,748
Coastal	1,344	13,299	567	8,770	355	2,146	57	512	365	1,871
Inland waterway	2,000	6,454	1,542	5,075	227	576	-	-	231	803
Great Lakes	86	2,168	7	42	61	2,052	-	-	18	74
Government	171	3,255	27	881	-	-	5	86	139	2,288
Total self-propelled	462	14,914	114	6,230	69	2,600	90	2,898	189	3,186
Foreign waterborne trade [2]	127	4,588	17	771	12	579	61	2,510	37	728
Domestic trade	164	7,071	70	4,578	57	2,021	24	302	13	170
Coastal	105	5,063	68	4,559	2	71	24	302	11	131
Inland waterway	-	-	-	-	-	-	-	-	-	-
Great Lakes	59	2,008	2	19	55	1,950	-	-	2	39
Government	171	3,255	27	881	-	-	5	86	139	2,288
Total non-self-propelled [3]	3,407	15,581	2,082	9,484	690	3,289	33	210	602	2,598
Foreign waterborne trade [2]	141	731	36	175	104	536	-	-	1	20
Domestic trade	3,266	14,850	2,046	9,309	586	2,753	33	210	601	2,578
Coastal	1,239	8,236	499	4,211	353	2,075	33	210	354	1,740
Inland waterway	2,000	6,454	1,542	5,075	227	576	-	-	231	803
Great Lakes	27	160	5	23	6	102	-	-	16	35
VESSELS LESS THAN 1,000 GROSS TONS										
Grand total	32,229	46,381	2,214	3,965	23,010	36,438	4	2	7,001	5,976
Foreign waterborne trade [2]	109	50	3	1	106	49	-	-	-	-
Domestic trade	32,120	46,331	2,211	3,964	22,904	36,389	4	2	7,001	5,976
Coastal	3,930	3,562	241	982	573	741	1	1	3,115	1,838
Inland waterway	27,890	42,394	1,961	2,975	22,211	35,478	3	1	3,715	3,940
Great Lakes	300	375	9	7	120	170	-	-	171	198
Total self-propelled	384	948	77	797	4	2	-	-	303	149
Domestic trade	384	948	77	797	4	2	-	-	303	149
Coastal	256	902	71	795	-	-	-	-	185	107
Inland waterway	109	27	2	-	-	-	-	-	107	27
Great Lakes	19	19	4	2	4	2	-	-	11	15
Total non-self-propelled	31,845	45,433	2,137	3,168	23,006	36,436	4	2	6,698	5,827
Foreign waterborne trade [2]	109	50	3	1	106	49	-	-	-	-
Domestic trade	31,736	45,383	2,134	3,167	22,900	36,387	4	2	6,698	5,827
Coastal	3,674	2,660	170	187	573	741	1	1	2,930	1,731
Inland waterway	27,781	42,367	1,959	2,975	22,211	35,478	3	1	3,608	3,913
Great Lakes	281	356	5	5	116	168	-	-	160	183

- Represents zero. [1] Includes general cargo, ro-ro (roll-on roll-off), multi-purpose, LASH (lighter aboard ship) vessels and deck barges. Excludes offshore supply vessels. [2] Includes U.S./Canada TransLakes.
[3] Includes Integrated Tug Barge (ITB) Units.

Source: U.S. Maritime Administration, Office of Statistical & Economic Analysis; adapted from Corps of Engineers, Lloyds Maritime Information Service, U.S. Coast Guard and Customs Service data.

No. 1068. Selected U.S. Ports by Tons of Traffic: 2002

[In thousands of short tons, except rank (6,836 represents 6,836,000). For calendar year for the top 70 ports. Represents tons of cargo shipped from or received by the specified port. Excludes cargo carried on general ferries; coal and petroleum products loaded from shore facilities directly onto bunkers of vessels for fuel; and amounts of less than 100 tons of government owned equipment in support of Corps projects]

Port name	Rank	Total	Foreign Total	Foreign Inbound	Foreign Outbound	Domestic
Albany, NY	66	6,836	1,304	713	591	5,531
Anacortes, WA	42	15,363	2,572	1,712	860	12,791
Ashtabula, OH	55	9,838	5,368	1,066	4,302	4,469
Baltimore, MD	19	38,823	23,634	18,256	5,378	15,189
Baton Rouge, LA	9	60,583	20,938	16,808	4,129	39,645
Beaumont, TX	4	85,911	67,729	62,626	5,104	18,182
Boston, MA	36	20,354	13,244	12,471	772	7,110
Burns Waterway Harbor, IN	60	8,621	1,985	1,696	289	6,636
Calcite, MI	61	8,575	1,402	104	1,298	7,173
Charleston, SC	29	24,993	18,998	13,461	5,537	5,995
Chicago, IL	35	20,403	1,625	1,059	566	18,777
Cincinnati, OH	45	13,007	-	-	-	13,007
Cleveland, OH	48	11,412	2,328	2,271	57	9,084
Conneaut, OH	52	10,474	5,094	759	4,335	5,380
Corpus Christi, TX	7	72,000	50,580	41,714	8,866	21,420
Detroit, MI	39	17,306	4,409	4,202	207	12,897
Duluth-Superior, MN and WI	18	44,161	14,461	624	13,837	29,700
Freeport, TX	24	27,164	22,084	19,778	2,306	5,080
Galveston, TX	58	9,136	5,248	1,216	4,033	3,887
Gary, IN	57	9,482	420	251	169	9,062
Honolulu, HI	40	16,636	4,855	4,269	586	11,781
Houston, TX	2	177,561	115,188	80,027	35,161	62,373
Huntington - Tristate	6	81,064	-	-	-	81,064
Indiana Harbor, IN	44	13,839	513	472	42	13,326
Jacksonville, FL	38	17,906	9,677	8,689	988	8,229
Kalama, WA	70	6,386	5,582	342	5,241	804
Lake Charles, LA	16	47,522	27,431	23,105	4,326	20,091
Long Beach, CA	8	67,872	52,292	37,907	14,385	15,580
Lorain, OH	67	6,672	354	354	-	6,318
Los Angeles, CA	12	52,216	45,408	31,628	13,780	6,808
Louisville, KY	63	7,894	-	-	-	7,894
Marcus Hook, PA	28	25,207	15,581	15,562	19	9,627
Matagorda Ship Channel, TX	56	9,590	6,678	4,640	2,038	2,912
Memphis, TN	41	16,401	-	-	-	16,401
Miami, FL	59	8,927	7,705	4,463	3,243	1,222
Mobile, AL	17	46,022	24,150	15,662	8,489	21,871
New Castle, DE	53	10,387	3,171	3,170	1	7,216
New Haven, CT	54	10,142	3,590	3,280	310	6,552
New Orleans, LA	5	85,000	51,762	21,926	29,836	33,238
New York, NY and NJ	3	134,505	69,572	59,419	10,153	64,933
Newport News, VA	49	11,301	5,108	1,143	3,965	6,193
Nikishka, AK	65	7,235	3,537	225	3,313	3,698
Norfolk Harbor, VA	23	27,901	21,073	8,704	12,369	6,828
Oakland, CA	46	12,455	9,460	4,021	5,439	2,995
Pascagoula, MS	22	31,858	20,486	17,497	2,990	11,371
Paulsboro, NJ	27	26,383	18,098	17,776	323	8,284
Philadelphia, PA	20	34,101	20,381	20,073	307	13,720
Pittsburgh, PA	13	52,051	-	-	-	52,051
Plaquemines, LA, Port of	10	59,111	23,284	13,725	9,559	35,827
Port Arthur, TX	30	22,676	15,218	11,687	3,531	7,458
Port Everglades, FL	32	21,280	8,697	6,708	1,990	12,582
Portland, ME	25	27,132	25,145	24,971	174	1,987
Portland, OR	26	26,635	15,431	4,066	11,365	11,204
Presque Isle, MI	51	10,592	1,957	103	1,855	8,635
Providence, RI	62	8,244	2,949	2,552	397	5,295
Richmond, CA	31	21,901	10,313	8,692	1,621	11,588
San Juan, PR	47	12,378	5,308	4,885	423	7,071
Savannah, GA	33	20,664	18,728	10,905	7,823	1,936
Seattle, WA	37	19,591	13,470	7,435	6,036	6,121
South Louisiana, LA, Port of	1	216,396	91,488	34,577	56,911	124,908
St. Louis, MO and IL	21	32,601	-	-	-	32,601
Stoneport, MI	64	7,455	204	106	98	7,250
Tacoma, WA	34	20,587	13,170	4,994	8,176	7,417
Tampa, FL	15	48,385	16,570	8,343	8,226	31,815
Texas City, TX	11	55,233	39,171	36,397	2,773	16,062
Toledo, OH	50	11,115	5,562	1,790	3,772	5,553
Two Harbors, MN	43	14,895	91	-	91	14,804
Valdez, AK	14	50,513	4	-	4	50,509
Vancouver, WA	68	6,610	4,577	711	3,866	2,033
Wilmington, NC	69	6,504	3,111	2,233	878	3,393

- Represents zero.

Source: U.S. Army Corps of Engineers, *Waterborne Commerce of the United States, 2002*. See Internet site <http://www.iwr.usace.army.mil/ndc/>.

U.S. Census Bureau, Statistical Abstract of the United States: 2004-2005

No. 1069. Highway Mileage—Urban and Rural by Ownership: 1980 to 2002

[In thousands (3,955 represents 3,955,000). As of Dec. 31. Includes Puerto Rico beginning 1998]

Type and control	1980	1985	1990	1995	1998	1999	2000	2001	2002
Total mileage [1]	[2]3,955	3,862	3,880	3,912	3,920	3,932	3,951	3,963	3,982
Urban mileage [3]	624	691	757	819	849	853	859	884	902
Under state control	79	111	96	112	111	111	112	110	112
Under local control	543	578	661	706	736	740	746	771	787
Rural mileage	[2]3,331	3,171	3,123	3,093	3,072	3,079	3,092	3,079	3,080
Under state control	702	773	703	691	663	663	664	665	665
Under local control	2,270	2,173	2,242	2,231	2,291	2,299	2,311	2,295	2,297
Under federal control	262	225	178	170	118	117	117	119	118

[1] Beginning 1985, includes only public road mileage as defined 23 USC 402. [2] Includes 98,000 miles of nonpublic road mileage previously contained in other rural categories. [3] Includes a small amount of road owned by the federal government, such as roads in federal parks that are not part of a state or local highway system.

Source: U.S. Federal Highway Administration, *Highway Statistics*, annual. See Internet site <http://www.fhwa.dot.gov/policy/ohpi/hss/hsspubs.htm>

No. 1070. Highway Mileage—Functional Systems and Urban/Rural: 2002

[As of Dec. 31. Excludes Puerto Rico. For definition of fuctional systems see text, this section]

State	Total	Functional systems					Urban	Rural
		Interstate	Other freeways and expressways	Arterial	Collector	Local		
U.S	3,966,485	46,483	9,323	380,271	790,893	2,739,515	894,724	3,071,761
AL.	94,434	905	21	8,796	20,529	64,183	20,968	73,466
AK.	14,118	1,083	-	1,513	2,734	8,788	1,845	12,273
AZ.	57,162	1,168	153	4,716	8,487	42,638	19,588	37,574
AR.	98,483	656	86	6,838	20,071	70,832	10,801	87,682
CA.	167,898	2,454	1,428	27,126	32,040	104,850	85,083	82,815
CO	86,310	954	228	8,208	16,603	60,317	15,045	71,265
CT	21,043	346	233	2,774	3,041	14,649	14,933	6,110
DE.	5,846	41	14	624	939	4,228	2,018	3,828
DC	1,535	13	22	264	152	1,084	1,535	-
FL.	119,785	1,471	470	12,161	14,219	91,464	68,852	50,933
GA.	115,777	1,245	120	13,143	23,269	78,000	28,318	87,459
HI.	4,300	55	34	752	831	2,628	2,120	2,180
ID	46,732	611	-	3,836	9,919	32,366	4,301	42,431
IL	138,338	2,170	88	13,998	21,646	100,436	36,834	101,504
IN	94,287	1,169	136	7,961	22,654	62,367	20,395	73,892
IA	113,450	782	-	9,563	31,559	71,546	9,915	103,535
KS.	135,038	874	136	9,195	33,358	91,475	10,510	124,528
KY.	78,372	762	87	5,500	17,564	54,459	11,889	66,483
LA	60,913	904	34	5,245	10,114	44,616	13,950	46,963
ME	22,692	367	18	2,288	5,974	14,045	2,632	20,060
MD	30,815	481	236	3,564	5,039	21,495	14,639	16,176
MA	35,460	566	211	5,618	5,488	23,577	23,179	12,281
MI	122,029	1,240	220	12,271	25,715	82,583	29,937	92,092
MN	132,121	913	150	12,730	29,437	88,891	16,107	116,014
MS	73,900	685	41	7,121	15,264	50,789	8,204	65,696
MO	124,685	1,181	326	9,414	24,976	88,788	17,576	107,109
MT	69,502	1,191	-	6,011	16,378	45,922	2,603	66,899
NE.	93,171	482	17	7,887	20,784	64,001	5,593	87,578
NV.	34,855	560	52	2,874	5,210	26,159	5,667	29,188
NH	15,502	224	41	1,546	2,721	10,970	2,998	12,504
NJ	36,556	431	315	5,361	4,556	25,893	24,252	12,304
NM	61,385	1,000	11	4,579	6,952	48,843	6,843	54,542
NY.	114,020	1,674	798	13,501	20,555	77,492	41,460	72,560
NC	101,743	1,020	291	8,909	17,733	73,790	24,115	77,628
ND	86,587	572	-	5,876	11,659	68,480	1,835	84,752
OH	124,885	1,573	394	10,649	22,105	90,164	39,916	84,969
OK	112,534	931	164	7,877	25,375	78,187	13,411	99,123
OR	66,641	728	53	6,722	17,383	41,755	11,172	55,469
PA	120,298	1,757	503	13,182	19,812	85,044	34,712	85,586
RI	6,051	70	69	845	856	4,211	4,718	1,333
SC.	66,194	842	71	6,875	13,379	45,027	10,674	55,520
SD.	83,610	678	-	6,300	19,281	57,351	2,135	81,475
TN.	88,286	1,073	121	8,753	18,081	60,258	18,083	70,203
TX.	301,776	3,234	1,150	28,573	63,340	205,479	83,205	218,571
UT.	42,610	940	7	3,342	7,840	30,481	7,973	34,637
VT.	14,289	320	19	1,299	3,122	9,529	1,382	12,907
VA.	70,950	1,117	234	8,182	14,121	47,296	19,191	51,759
WA	82,179	764	314	7,305	16,802	56,994	19,173	63,006
WV	36,996	549	9	3,237	8,785	24,416	3,085	33,911
WI	112,920	744	195	11,694	21,539	78,748	16,873	96,047
WY	27,422	913	3	3,673	10,902	11,931	2,481	24,941

- Represents zero.

Source: U.S. Federal Highway Administration, *Highway Statistics*, annual. See Internet site <http://www.fhwa.dot.gov/policy/ohpi/hss/hsspubs.htm>.

No. 1071. Commodity Shipments—Value, Tons, and Ton-Miles: 1997 and 2002

[2002 preliminary. 6,943,988 represents 6,943,988,000,000. For business establishments in mining, manufacturing, wholesale trade, and selected retail industries. Selected auxiliary establishments are also included. 2002 industries classified by the 1997 North American Classification System (NAICS); 1997 classified by the Standard Industrial Classification (SIC) Manual. See source for details. Based on the Economic Census: see Appendix III]

Mode of transportation	Value (mil. dol.)		Tons (1,000)		Ton-miles (mil.)	
	1997	2002	1997	2002	1997	2002
All modes	6,943,988	8,483,123	11,089,733	11,572,780	2,661,363	3,204,410
Single modes	5,719,558	7,052,924	10,436,538	10,878,148	2,383,473	2,913,015
Truck [1]	4,981,531	6,200,469	7,700,675	7,622,257	1,023,506	1,311,085
For-hire truck	2,901,345	3,838,514	3,402,605	3,665,982	741,117	1,001,463
Private truck.	2,036,528	2,340,328	4,137,294	3,920,474	268,592	302,026
Rail	319,629	320,469	1,549,817	1,816,528	1,022,547	1,199,407
Water.	75,840	90,895	563,369	713,884	261,747	323,085
Shallow draft	53,897	56,480	414,758	499,699	189,284	236,619
Great Lakes.	1,504	787	38,421	39,485	13,415	19,544
Deep draft	20,439	33,628	110,191	174,700	59,047	66,922
Air (includes truck and air)	229,062	279,489	4,475	3,891	6,233	5,560
Pipeline [2]	113,497	161,601	618,202	721,588	(S)	(S)
Multiple modes	945,874	1,110,975	216,673	198,454	204,514	214,833
Parcel, U.S. Postal Service or courier .	855,897	1,022,033	23,689	26,447	17,994	20,536
Truck and rail	75,695	(S)	54,246	(S)	55,561	(S)
Truck and water.	8,241	17,053	33,215	31,814	34,767	59,147
Rail and water	1,771	(S)	79,275	(S)	77,590	(S)
Other multiple modes	4,269	5,528	26,248	28,047	18,603	19,600
Other and unknown modes	278,555	319,224	436,521	496,178	73,376	76,563

S Data do not meet publication standards due to high sampling variability or other reasons.   [1] Truck as a single mode includes shipments that went by private truck only, for hire truck only, or a combination of private truck and for-hire truck.   [2] Commodity Flow Survey data exclude shipments of crude oil.

Source: U.S. Bureau of Transportation Statistics and U.S. Census Bureau, 2002 Economic Census, *Transportation, 2002 Commodity Flow Survey,* Series EC02TCF-US(P), issued December 2003. See Internet site <http://www.census.gov/econ/www/cfsnew.html>.

No. 1072. Shipment Characteristics, by Distance and Weight Shipped: 1997 and 2002

[6,943,988 represents $6,943,988,000,000. 2002 preliminary. Based on the Economic Census; see Appendix III. See also headnote Table 1071]

Item	Value (mil. dol.)		Tons (1,000)		Ton-miles (mil.)	
	1997	2002	1997	2002	1997	2002
Total	6,943,988	8,483,123	11,089,733	11,572,780	2,661,363	3,204,410
Distance shipped: [1]						
Less than 50 miles	2,168,057	2,447,018	6,444,454	6,028,724	135,926	121,093
50 to 99 miles	597,587	753,019	1,079,841	1,242,433	102,983	116,044
100 to 249 miles.	1,062,579	1,345,926	1,311,278	1,553,406	296,032	343,922
250 to 499 miles.	975,367	1,258,978	905,504	1,097,835	437,463	539,271
500 to 749 miles.	656,846	862,741	541,782	647,884	467,800	541,309
750 to 999 miles.	436,491	568,002	383,327	437,698	440,999	508,330
1,000 to 1,499 miles	469,777	545,968	302,918	386,657	487,859	619,659
1,500 to 1,999 miles	293,654	360,651	77,130	122,649	169,651	260,455
2,000 miles or more	283,628	340,820	43,499	55,493	122,651	154,327
Weight:						
Less than 50 pounds	853,289	1,009,779	21,348	19,140	9,950	10,869
50 to 99 pounds	249,541	298,263	14,200	13,855	4,450	5,308
100 to 499 pounds	727,368	829,694	82,166	81,940	19,601	22,757
500 to 749 pounds	219,136	250,562	38,955	39,364	8,852	9,907
750 to 999 pounds	154,348	181,610	32,484	33,991	7,260	8,128
1,000 to 9,999 pounds	1,536,448	1,797,380	579,490	584,664	131,388	154,612
10,000 to 49,999 pounds	2,286,364	3,111,754	4,073,970	4,358,037	734,805	906,343
50,000 to 99,999 pounds	360,091	351,127	2,229,997	1,948,882	188,735	211,709
100,000 pounds or more	557,404	652,955	4,017,124	4,492,907	1,556,321	1,874,776

[1] Based in Great Circle Distance (GCD) GCD is the shortest distance between 2 points on the surface of a sphere over the surface of that sphere.

Source: U.S. Bureau of Transportation Statistics and U.S. Census Bureau, 2002 Economic Census, *Transportation, Commodity Flow Survey,* Series EC02TCF-US(P) issued December 2003. See Internet site <http://www.census.gov/econ/www/cfsnew.html>.

No. 1073. Bridge Inventory—Total and Deficient, 1996 to 2003, and by State, 2003

[Based on the National Bridge Inventory program]

State and year	Number of bridges	Deficient and obsolete					
		Total number	Percent	Structurally deficient [1]		Functionally obsolete [2]	
				Number	Percent	Number	Percent
1996, total	581,862	182,726	31.4	101,518	17.4	81,208	14.0
1997, total	582,751	175,885	30.2	98,475	16.9	77,410	13.3
1998, total	582,984	172,582	29.6	93,076	16.0	79,506	13.6
1999, total	585,542	170,050	29.0	88,150	15.1	81,900	14.0
2000, total	587,755	167,993	28.6	87,106	14.8	80,887	13.8
2001, total	590,066	165,099	28.0	83,630	14.2	81,469	13.8
2002, total	591,220	163,010	27.6	81,437	13.8	81,573	13.8
U.S. total, 2003	**592,246**	**160,819**	**27.2**	**79,811**	**13.5**	**81,008**	**13.7**
Alabama	15,715	4,890	31.1	2,588	16.5	2,302	14.6
Alaska	1,174	349	29.7	144	12.3	205	17.5
Arizona	6,955	710	10.2	170	2.4	540	7.8
Arkansas	12,451	3,322	26.7	1,363	10.9	1,959	15.7
California	23,764	6,722	28.3	2,907	12.2	3,815	16.1
Colorado	8,097	1,334	16.5	399	4.9	935	11.5
Connecticut	4,172	1,340	32.1	339	8.1	1,001	24.0
Delaware	841	124	14.7	42	5.0	82	9.8
District of Columbia	247	160	64.8	19	7.7	141	57.1
Florida	11,451	2,115	18.5	316	2.8	1,799	15.7
Georgia	14,456	3,052	21.1	1,299	9.0	1,753	12.1
Hawaii	1,097	512	46.7	155	14.1	357	32.5
Idaho	4,053	732	18.1	307	7.6	425	10.5
Illinois	25,661	4,443	17.3	2,442	9.5	2,001	7.8
Indiana	18,138	4,128	22.8	2,111	11.6	2,017	11.1
Iowa	24,992	7,165	28.7	5,329	21.3	1,836	7.3
Kansas	25,620	6,018	23.5	3,304	12.9	2,714	10.6
Kentucky	13,523	4,047	29.9	1,175	8.7	2,872	21.2
Louisiana	13,394	4,446	33.2	2,220	16.6	2,226	16.6
Maine	2,364	845	35.7	365	15.4	480	20.3
Maryland	4,994	1,432	28.7	417	8.4	1,015	20.3
Massachusetts	4,999	2,555	51.1	624	12.5	1,931	38.6
Michigan	10,654	3,122	29.3	1,811	17.0	1,311	12.3
Minnesota	12,975	1,685	13.0	1,172	9.0	513	4.0
Mississippi	16,830	5,034	29.9	3,701	22.0	1,333	7.9
Missouri	23,787	8,383	35.2	5,275	22.2	3,108	13.1
Montana	5,098	1,090	21.4	583	11.4	507	9.9
Nebraska	15,455	4,082	26.4	2,608	16.9	1,474	9.5
Nevada	1,612	206	12.8	62	3.8	144	8.9
New Hampshire	2,352	795	33.8	367	15.6	428	18.2
New Jersey	6,377	2,295	36.0	854	13.4	1,441	22.6
New Mexico	3,835	729	19.0	388	10.1	341	8.9
New York	17,382	6,643	38.2	2,234	12.9	4,409	25.4
North Carolina	17,193	5,199	30.2	2,365	13.8	2,834	16.5
North Dakota	4,518	1,088	24.1	829	18.3	259	5.7
Ohio	27,901	7,150	25.6	3,109	11.1	4,041	14.5
Oklahoma	23,249	9,071	39.0	7,568	32.6	1,503	6.5
Oregon	7,202	1,764	24.5	561	7.8	1,203	16.7
Pennsylvania	22,176	9,352	42.2	5,474	24.7	3,878	17.5
Rhode Island	748	399	53.3	191	25.5	208	27.8
South Carolina	9,149	2,058	22.5	1,240	13.6	818	8.9
South Dakota	5,966	1,533	25.7	1,047	17.5	486	8.1
Tennessee	19,490	4,603	23.6	1,653	8.5	2,950	15.1
Texas	48,492	10,320	21.3	2,777	5.7	7,543	15.6
Utah	2,793	517	18.5	270	9.7	247	8.8
Vermont	2,686	960	35.7	491	18.3	469	17.5
Virginia	13,055	3,405	26.1	1,161	8.9	2,244	17.2
Washington	7,427	1,963	26.4	436	5.9	1,527	20.6
West Virginia	6,862	2,578	37.6	1,081	15.8	1,497	21.8
Wisconsin	13,651	2,650	19.4	1,762	12.9	888	6.5
Wyoming	3,038	643	21.2	421	13.9	222	7.3
Puerto Rico	2,135	1,061	49.7	285	13.3	776	36.3

[1] Bridges are structurally deficient if they have been restricted to light vehicles, require immediate rehabilitation to remain open, or are closed. [2] Bridges are functionally obsolete if they have deck geometry, load caring capacity, clearance or approach roadway alignment that no longer meet the criteria for the system of which the bridge is a part.

Source: U.S. Federal Highway Administration, Office of Bridge Technology, Internet site <http://www.fhwa.dot.gov/bridge/britab.htm>.

No. 1074. Funding for Highways and Disposition of Highway-User Revenue: 1990 to 2002

[In millions of dollars (75,444 represents $75,444,000,0000. Data compiled from reports of state and local authorities]

Type	1990	1995	1997	1998	1999	2000	2001	2002
Total receipts	75,444	96,269	107,421	111,581	121,650	131,115	132,324	134,765
Current income	69,880	87,620	98,667	102,533	110,376	119,815	119,659	122,018
Highway user revenues	44,346	59,331	66,266	68,951	74,222	81,335	77,719	79,587
Other taxes and fees	19,827	21,732	25,424	25,395	29,380	31,137	34,190	34,353
Investment income, other receipts	5,707	6,557	6,977	8,187	6,774	7,342	7,749	8,078
Bond issue proceeds [1]	5,564	8,649	8,754	9,048	11,274	11,301	12,665	12,747
Funds from (+) or to (-) reserves	-36	-2,791	-5,468	-3,606	-5,639	-8,418	-2,423	1,154
Total funds available	75,408	93,478	101,953	107,975	116,011	122,697	129,900	135,919
Total disbursements	75,408	93,478	101,953	107,975	116,011	122,697	129,900	135,919
Current disbursements	72,457	88,994	97,320	102,828	111,097	117,592	124,815	129,137
Capital outlay	35,151	44,228	48,360	52,308	57,227	61,323	65,968	68,175
Maintenance and traffic services	20,365	24,319	26,777	28,173	29,997	30,636	31,677	33,180
Administration and research	6,501	8,419	8,256	8,523	9,130	10,020	10,423	10,695
Law enforcement and safety	7,235	8,218	9,761	9,445	10,393	11,031	11,977	11,672
Interest on debt	3,205	3,810	4,166	4,379	4,350	4,583	4,770	5,416
Bond retirement [1]	2,951	4,484	4,633	5,147	4,914	5,105	5,086	6,782

[1] Excludes issue and redemption of short-term notes or refunding bonds.
Source: U.S. Federal Highway Administration, Highway Statistics, annual. See Internet site <http://www.fhwa.dot.gov/policy/ohpi/hss/hsspubs.htm>.

No. 1075. Federal Aid to State and Local Governments for Highway Trust Fund and Federal Transit Administration (FTA) by State: 2002

[Year ending Sept. 30. (29,444 represents $29,444,000,000]

State	Highway trust fund Total (mil. dol.)	Per capita (dol.)[1]	FTA Total (mil. dol.)	Per capita (dol.)[1]	State	Highway trust fund Total (mil. dol.)	Per capita (dol.)[1]	FTA Total (mil. dol.)	Per capita (dol.)[1]	State	Highway trust fund Total (mil. dol.)	Per capita (dol.)[1]	FTA Total (mil. dol.)	Per capita (dol.)[1]
U.S. [2]	29,444	100.6	5,223	17.8	IA	333	113.3	22	7.5	NC	959	115.2	42	5.0
U.S. [3]	28,539	99.0	5,024	17.4	KS	360	132.5	18	6.7	ND	216	340.4	4	6.6
					KY	524	127.9	22	5.3	OH	901	78.9	137	12.0
AL	673	150.1	25	5.7	LA	448	99.9	36	8.1	OK	347	99.3	20	5.8
AK	328	509.5	12	18.9	ME	162	125.0	8	6.0	OR	272	77.4	122	34.8
AZ	481	88.1	61	11.1	MD	572	104.8	105	19.3	PA	1,345	109.1	269	21.8
AR	395	145.7	10	3.5	MA	505	78.6	131	20.3	RI	171	160.2	26	24.5
CA	2,628	74.8	1,008	28.7	MI	823	81.9	89	8.9	SC	411	100.0	14	3.3
CO	342	76.0	91	20.3	MN	384	76.4	108	21.5	SD	199	261.1	5	6.2
CT	493	142.6	79	22.8	MS	385	134.2	5	1.9	TN	521	89.9	39	6.6
DE	120	148.5	3	3.8	MO	727	128.1	36	6.3	TX	2,209	101.4	271	12.4
DC	150	262.6	260	454.7	MT	295	324.2	5	5.6	UT	239	103.2	55	23.8
FL	1,496	89.5	135	8.0	NE	193	111.9	10	5.8	VT	134	216.8	3	5.6
GA	873	102.0	96	11.3	NV	161	74.3	16	7.3	VA	882	121.0	66	9.1
HI	122	98.2	33	26.7	NH	141	110.8	8	6.2	WA	548	90.4	106	17.5
ID	206	153.5	7	4.9	NJ	710	82.7	291	33.8	WV	318	176.5	8	4.5
IL	889	70.5	259	20.5	NM	302	162.8	8	4.3	WI	587	107.8	36	6.7
IN	560	90.9	29	4.8	NY	1,274	66.5	773	40.3	WY	224	448.4	2	4.1

[1] Based on estimated population as of July 1. [2] Includes outlying areas and undistributed funds, not shown separately.
[3] For the 50 states and D.C.
Source: U.S. Census Bureau, Federal Aid to States for Fiscal Year, 2002. See Inernet site <http://www.census.gov/prod/2003pubs/fas02.pdf>.

No. 1076. State Motor Fuel Tax Receipts, 2001 and 2002, and Gasoline Tax Rates, 2002

[559 represents $559,000,000]

State	Net receipts (mil.dol) 2001	2002	Tax rate[1] 2002	State	Net receipts (mil.dol) 2001	2002	Tax rate[1] 2002	State	Net receipts (mil.dol) 2001	2002	Tax rate[1] 2002
AL	559	571	18.00	KY	465	498	16.40	ND	98	100	21.00
AK	28	23	8.00	LA	545	554	20.00	OH	1,490	1,410	22.00
AZ	585	608	18.00	ME	167	171	22.00	OK	401	410	17.00
AR	412	427	21.70	MD	683	707	23.50	OR	394	395	24.00
CA	3,147	3,237	18.00	MA	661	667	21.00	PA	1,726	1,677	26.60
CO	542	539	22.00	MI	1,068	1,083	19.00	RI	134	131	30.00
CT	407	420	25.00	MN	619	619	20.00	SC	456	447	16.00
DE	99	111	23.00	MS	375	386	18.40	SD	125	128	22.00
DC	29	27	20.00	MO	661	669	17.00	TN	705	723	20.00
FL	1,682	1,750	13.90	MT	176	183	27.00	TX	2,784	2,836	20.00
GA	446	423	7.50	NE	297	299	24.50	UT	311	334	24.50
HI	71	72	16.00	NV	375	387	24.70	VT	87	86	20.00
ID	226	212	25.00	NH	142	143	19.50	VA	814	818	17.50
IL	1,217	1,294	19.00	NJ	534	489	10.50	WA	739	736	23.00
IN	740	759	15.00	NM	236	229	18.50	WV	297	301	25.35
IA	396	408	20.10	NY	1,454	1,519	22.60	WI	827	865	28.10
KS	357	393	23.00	NC	1,185	1,212	22.10	WY	96	99	14.00

[1] Cents per gallon. In effect Dec. 31.
Source: U.S. Federal Highway Administration, Highway Statistics, annual. See Internet site <http://www.fhwa.dot.gov/policy/ohpi/hss/hsspubs.htm>.

Transportation 689

No. 1077. Public Highway Debt—State and Local Governments: 1980 to 2002

[In millions of dollars (2,381 represents $2,381,000,000). Long-term obligations. Data are for varying calendar and fiscal years. Excludes duplicated and interunit obligations]

Item	1980	1985	1990	1995	1998	1999	2000	2001	2002
Total debt issued.........	2,381	8,194	5,708	11,305	16,412	12,822	14,513	15,697	(NA)
State	1,160	5,397	3,147	4,718	9,789	9,554	9,067	11,012	13,250
Local [1]	1,221	2,797	2,561	6,587	6,623	3,268	5,446	4,685	(NA)
Total debt redeemed.......	1,987	5,294	3,120	5,634	11,735	5,808	8,623	7,230	(NA)
State	1,114	3,835	1,648	2,939	6,466	3,609	3,897	4,660	9,988
Local [1]	873	1,459	1,472	2,695	5,269	2,199	4,726	2,570	(NA)
Total debt outstanding [2]	27,616	32,690	46,586	68,733	82,599	89,778	96,383	103,342	(NA)
State	20,210	21,277	28,362	39,228	49,182	55,646	61,434	66,256	70,826
Local [1]	7,406	11,413	18,224	29,505	33,417	34,132	34,949	37,086	(NA)

NA Not available. [1] Local data estimated. [2] End-of-year.
Source: U.S. Federal Highway Administration, *Highway Statistics*, annual. See Internet site <http://www.fhwa.dot.gov/policy/ohpi /hss/hsspubs.htm>.

No. 1078. State Disbursements for Highways by State: 1995 to 2002

[In millions of dollars (67,615 represents $67,615,000,000). Comprises disbursements from current revenues or loans for construction, maintenance, interest and principal payments on highway bonds, transfers to local units, and miscellaneous. Includes transactions by state toll authorities. Excludes amounts allocated for collection expenses and nonhighway purposes, and bonds redeemed by refunding]

State	1995	1997	1998	1999	2000	2001	2002
United States................	67,615	73,994	80,518	83,675	89,832	94,513	104,919
Alabama.......................	1,002	1,019	1,053	1,085	1,246	1,433	1,575
Alaska........................	438	435	404	416	501	482	541
Arizona.......................	1,199	1,359	1,430	1,860	2,040	2,149	2,445
Arkansas......................	666	832	815	736	817	976	1,161
California....................	5,966	6,219	6,574	6,876	6,750	6,795	8,570
Colorado......................	922	887	1,166	1,260	1,392	1,616	2,195
Connecticut...................	1,153	1,173	1,427	1,094	1,304	1,236	1,848
Delaware......................	441	449	647	507	595	647	738
District of Columbia..........	140	151	259	242	244	406	336
Florida.......................	3,421	3,734	4,024	3,992	4,208	4,348	4,985
Georgia.......................	1,437	1,372	1,613	1,763	1,567	1,748	1,945
Hawaii........................	360	387	326	355	272	263	275
Idaho.........................	350	403	414	445	492	480	508
Illinois......................	3,006	2,992	3,306	2,957	3,447	3,788	4,286
Indiana.......................	1,433	1,636	1,652	1,522	1,932	3,202	1,975
Iowa..........................	1,078	1,173	1,177	1,253	1,494	1,388	1,405
Kansas........................	1,019	1,087	1,306	1,155	1,206	1,271	1,951
Kentucky......................	1,397	1,331	1,481	1,578	1,651	1,612	1,776
Louisiana.....................	1,198	1,189	1,400	1,237	1,301	1,154	1,287
Maine.........................	379	474	485	458	488	505	744
Maryland......................	1,289	1,489	1,492	1,554	1,599	1,673	1,803
Massachusetts.................	2,501	3,287	3,351	4,407	3,524	3,965	3,783
Michigan......................	1,974	2,100	2,745	2,629	2,748	2,920	2,859
Minnesota.....................	1,210	1,450	1,377	1,534	1,692	1,683	1,866
Mississippi...................	662	809	843	968	1,039	911	1,040
Missouri......................	1,313	1,492	1,438	1,600	1,818	2,044	2,110
Montana.......................	388	379	378	434	474	469	535
Nebraska......................	578	611	589	681	745	661	867
Nevada........................	484	431	446	557	651	668	631
New Hampshire.................	328	360	371	416	387	445	522
New Jersey....................	2,102	2,247	2,513	2,905	4,503	4,276	4,863
New Mexico....................	535	546	570	753	1,162	1,119	983
New York......................	4,584	4,778	6,051	5,347	5,307	5,301	7,161
North Carolina................	1,871	2,099	2,352	2,441	2,621	2,868	3,001
North Dakota..................	270	326	306	413	385	358	385
Ohio..........................	2,637	2,940	3,327	3,158	3,351	3,493	3,580
Oklahoma......................	828	867	944	1,322	1,417	1,443	1,839
Oregon........................	888	992	1,051	1,009	1,010	984	1,029
Pennsylvania..................	3,153	3,764	3,902	4,143	4,517	4,875	5,365
Rhode Island..................	290	225	339	316	256	380	380
South Carolina................	668	741	766	885	970	1,104	1,201
South Dakota..................	286	349	305	371	466	463	437
Tennessee.....................	1,230	1,351	1,420	1,398	1,440	1,563	1,622
Texas.........................	3,593	4,253	4,295	4,840	5,665	5,716	5,960
Utah..........................	431	802	1,129	1,072	1,072	941	956
Vermont.......................	194	213	222	252	287	297	265
Virginia......................	2,107	2,358	2,619	2,771	2,678	2,909	3,185
Washington....................	1,909	1,851	1,805	1,780	1,871	2,042	2,276
West Virginia.................	781	940	893	930	1,170	1,289	1,210
Wisconsin.....................	1,252	1,354	1,398	1,614	1,663	1,793	2,204
Wyoming.......................	272	284	321	386	396	360	460

Source: U.S. Federal Highway Administration, *Highway Statistics*, annual. See Internet site <http://www.fhwa.dot.gov/policy/ohpi /hss/hsspubs.htm>.

No. 1079. State Motor Vehicle Registrations: 1980 to 2002

[In thousands (155,796 represents 155,796,000). Compiled principally from information obtained from state authorities, but it was necessary to draw on other sources and to make numerous estimates in order to complete series. Includes Alaska and Hawaii. See also Table 1082]

Item	1980	1990	1995	1999	2000	2001	2002
All motor vehicles	155,796	188,798	201,530	216,309	221,475	230,428	229,620
Private and commercial	153,265	185,541	197,941	212,474	217,567	226,646	225,772
Publicly owned	2,531	3,257	3,589	3,834	3,908	3,782	3,848
Automobiles [1]	121,601	133,700	128,387	132,432	133,621	137,633	135,921
Private and commercial	120,743	132,164	126,900	131,077	132,247	136,341	134,605
Publicly owned	857	1,536	1,487	1,355	1,374	1,293	1,316
Buses	529	627	686	729	746	750	761
Private and commercial	254	275	288	307	314	318	320
Publicly owned	275	351	398	422	432	432	441
Trucks [1]	33,667	54,470	72,458	83,148	87,108	92,045	92,939
Private and commercial	32,268	53,101	70,754	81,091	85,005	89,988	90,847
Publicly owned	1,399	1,369	1,704	2,057	2,103	2,058	2,091

[1] Trucks include pickups, panels and delivery vans. Beginning 1990, personal passenger vans, passenger minivans and utility-type vehicles are no longer included in automobiles but are included in trucks.
Source: U.S. Federal Highway Administration, Highway Statistics, annual. See Internet site <http://www.fhwa.dot.gov/policy/ohpi/hss/hsspubs.htm>

No. 1080. Alternative Fueled Vehicles in Use by Fuel Type: 2002 to 2004

[2004 data are projections. 378,589 represents 378,589,000]

Fuel type	Alternative fueled vehicles			Fuel consumption (1,000 gasoline-equivalent gallons)		
	2002	2003	2004	2002	2003	2004
Total	471,098	510,805	547,904	378,589	412,725	447,198
Liquified petroleum gases (LPG)	187,680	190,438	194,389	223,143	230,486	242,368
Compressed natural gas (CNG)	120,839	132,988	143,742	120,670	141,726	159,464
Liquified natural gas (LNG)	2,708	3,030	3,134	9,382	10,514	10,868
Methanol, 85 percent (M85) [1]	5,873	4,917	4,592	337	274	257
Ethanol, 85 percent (E85) [1]	120,951	133,776	146,195	17,783	20,092	22,405
Electricity [2]	33,047	45,656	55,852	7,274	9,633	11,836

[1] The remaining portion is gasoline. [2] Excludes gasoline-electric hybrids.
Source: Energy Information Administration, Alternatives to Traditional Transportation Fuels. See Internet site <http://www.eia.doe.gov/fuelalternate.html> (released February 2004)

No. 1081. Number of Households Leasing Vehicles and Number of Vehicles Leased Per Household: 1992 to 2001

[Based on the Survey of Consumer Finances; see Appendix III]

Item	Share of households leasing a vehicle for personal use (percent)				Average number of leased vehicles, among households having such vehicles			
	1992	1995	1998	2001	1992	1995	1998	2001
All households	2.9	4.5	6.4	5.8	1.1	1.1	1.2	1.2
Household income:								
Less than $10,000	(Z)	(Z)	(Z)	(Z)	(Z)	(Z)	1.1	(Z)
$10,000 to $24,999	(Z)	1.3	4.1	1.8	(Z)	1.0	1.1	1.1
$25,000 to $49,999	3.1	3.2	4.6	5.3	1.1	1.0	1.1	1.0
$50,000 to $99,999	3.7	9.2	9.2	7.6	1.1	1.1	1.2	1.2
$100,000 and over	9.5	12.6	13.8	12.9	1.1	1.3	1.3	1.3"
Age of household head:								
Less than 35 years	3.2	4.8	8.2	7.3	1.0	1.0	1.1	1.1
35 to 44 years	4.3	5.4	8.3	5.9	1.1	1.1	1.1	1.2
45 to 54 years	3.2	7.9	7.6	6.1	1.2	1.2	1.3	1.2
55 to 64 years	3.2	4.1	4.4	5.5	1.2	1.2	1.1	1.2
65 to 74 years	1.0	1.3	2.9	6.3	1.0	1.1	1.2	1.1
75 years and over	(Z)	0.5	1.9	1.6	(Z)	1.0	1.0	1.0
Race/ethnicity of respondent:								
White non-Hispanic	3.1	4.4	6.3	6.3	1.1	1.1	1.1	1.2
Non-White and Hispanic	2.3	4.9	6.5	4.2	1.1	1.1	1.3	1.1
Work status of household head:								
Work for someone else	3.4	6.0	8.1	6.2	1.1	1.1	1.2	1.2
Self employed	7.2	5.2	9.0	9.4	1.1	1.3	1.1	1.3
Retired	0.7	1.4	1.5	3.1	1.3	1.0	1.2	1.1
Other not working	(Z)	2.6	(Z)	(Z)	(Z)	1.0	(Z)	(Z)
Homeownership status:								
Owner	3.5	5.8	7.2	6.2	1.1	1.2	1.2	1.2
Renter or other	1.8	2.3	4.8	5.0	1.1	1.1	1.1	1.1
Net worth percentile:								
Bottom 25 percent	2.1	2.7	4.9	3.9	1.1	1.1	1.1	1.2
25 to 49.9 percent	1.6	4.2	5.4	4.4	1.0	1.0	1.1	1.1
50 to 74.9 percent	2.9	4.3	7.1	6.3	1.1	1.1	1.2	1.3
75 to 89.9 percent	3.7	6.2	7.0	7.6	1.0	1.1	1.2	1.2
Top 10 percent	6.5	8.2	9.9	10.2	1.2	1.3	1.2	1.2

Z Ten or fewer observations.
Source: Board of Governors of the Federal Reserve System, unpublished data. See Internet site <http://www.federalreserve.gov/pubs/oss/oss2/2001/scf2001home.html>.

Transportation 691

No. 1082. State Motor Vehicle Registrations, 1980 to 2002, and Licensed Drivers, and Motorcycle Registrations by State: 2002

[In thousands (155,796 represents 155,796,000). Motor vehicle registrations cover publicly, privately, and commercially owned vehicles. For uniformity, data have been adjusted to a calendar-year basis as registration years in states differ; figures represent net numbers where possible, excluding re-registrations and nonresident registrations. See also Table 1079]

| State | Motor vehicle registrations [1] | | | | | | | 2002 | | |
| | | | | | | 2002 | | | | |
	1980	1985	1990	1995	1999	2000	Total	Automobiles (incl. taxis)	Motorcycle registration (incl. official) [2]	Licensed drivers
U.S	155,796	171,689	188,798	201,530	221,475	230,428	229,620	135,921	4,963	194,296
AL......	2,938	3,383	3,744	3,553	3,960	4,235	4,428	1,802	62	3,578
AK......	262	353	477	542	594	598	620	255	18	480
AZ......	1,917	2,235	2,825	2,873	3,795	3,967	3,940	2,238	218	3,668
AR......	1,574	1,384	1,448	1,613	1,840	1,864	1,873	960	34	1,965
CA......	16,873	18,899	21,926	22,432	27,698	28,780	29,619	18,450	520	22,395
CO......	2,342	2,759	3,155	2,812	3,626	4,649	2,151	957	1	3,166
CT......	2,147	2,465	2,623	2,622	2,853	2,917	2,915	2,027	62	2,672
DE......	397	465	526	592	630	653	674	417	14	573
DC......	268	306	262	243	242	249	238	193	1	309
FL......	7,614	9,865	10,950	10,369	11,781	14,340	13,964	8,471	339	12,744
GA	3,818	4,580	5,489	6,120	7,155	7,305	7,648	4,212	108	6,013
HI......	570	651	771	802	738	868	893	532	20	815
ID......	834	854	1,054	1,043	1,178	1,324	1,386	598	43	907
IL......	7,477	7,527	7,873	8,973	8,973	9,861	9,577	6,100	232	8,033
IN......	3,826	3,824	4,366	5,072	5,571	5,625	5,665	3,216	135	4,221
IA......	2,329	2,696	2,632	2,814	3,106	3,318	3,310	1,862	140	1,993
KS......	2,007	2,148	2,012	2,085	2,296	2,331	2,337	843	53	1,935
KY......	2,593	2,615	2,909	2,631	2,826	3,626	3,601	2,088	49	2,773
LA......	2,779	3,012	2,995	3,286	3,557	3,609	3,660	1,989	53	3,168
ME	724	840	977	967	1,024	1,018	968	583	31	949
MD	2,803	3,276	3,607	3,654	3,848	3,939	3,884	2,523	57	3,523
MA	3,749	3,738	3,726	4,502	5,265	5,198	5,407	3,636	130	4,686
MI	6,488	6,727	7,209	7,674	8,436	8,454	8,534	4,874	203	7,025
MN	3,091	3,385	3,508	3,882	4,630	4,554	4,520	2,504	158	2,997
MS	1,577	1,746	1,875	2,144	2,289	1,954	1,955	1,136	27	1,861
MO	3,271	3,558	3,905	4,255	4,580	4,208	4,235	2,482	64	3,931
MT	680	652	783	968	1,026	1,033	1,056	466	30	695
NE......	1,254	1,258	1,384	1,467	1,619	1,633	1,656	841	25	1,275
NV......	655	709	853	1,047	1,220	1,280	1,253	650	35	1,461
NH	704	974	946	1,122	1,052	1,100	1,143	682	57	955
NJ......	4,761	5,164	5,652	5,906	6,390	6,580	6,688	4,503	134	5,712
NM	1,068	1,226	1,301	1,484	1,529	1,428	1,538	715	34	1,244
NY......	8,002	9,042	10,191	10,274	10,235	10,196	10,456	7,924	142	10,914
NC	4,532	4,501	5,162	5,682	6,223	6,180	6,149	3,687	91	5,943
ND	627	655	630	695	694	708	698	348	18	461
OH	7,771	8,102	8,410	9,810	10,467	10,555	10,470	6,553	270	7,706
OK	2,583	2,911	2,649	2,856	3,014	3,281	3,071	1,622	66	2,324
OR	2,081	2,204	2,445	2,785	3,022	3,039	3,069	1,560	74	2,564
PA	6,926	7,209	7,971	8,481	9,260	9,631	9,525	6,072	249	8,324
RI	623	610	672	699	760	764	776	539	23	721
SC......	1,996	2,222	2,521	2,833	3,095	3,143	3,202	1,960	62	2,919
SD......	601	657	704	709	793	803	814	389	34	546
TN......	3,271	3,754	4,444	5,400	4,820	5,139	4,777	2,805	84	4,206
TX......	10,475	12,444	12,800	13,682	14,070	14,359	14,664	7,809	232	13,185
UT......	992	1,099	1,206	1,447	1,628	1,752	1,847	968	41	1,530
VT......	347	398	462	492	515	534	537	298	27	529
VA......	3,626	4,253	4,938	5,613	6,046	6,171	6,273	4,011	70	5,158
WA	3,225	3,526	4,257	4,503	5,116	5,179	5,336	2,980	133	4,381
WV	1,320	1,143	1,225	1,425	1,442	1,452	1,463	782	30	1,325
WI	2,941	3,187	3,815	3,993	4,366	4,473	4,557	2,587	204	3,530
WY	467	500	528	601	586	573	603	220	25	303

[1] Automobiles, trucks, and buses. Excludes vehicles owned by military services.   [2] Private and commercial.

Source: U.S. Federal Highway Administration, *Highway Statistics*, annual; and *Selected Highway Statistics and Charts*, annual. See Internet site <http://www.fhwa.dot.gov/policy/ohpi/hss/hsspubs.htm>.

No. 1083. Roadway Congestion: 2001

[15,772 represents 15,772,000 Various federal, state, and local information sources were used to develop the data base with the primary source being the Federal Highway Administration's Highway Performance Monitoring System. Areas shown are rated the top 72 in annual per person hours of delay]

Urbanized areas	Freeway daily vehicle miles of travel		Annual person hours of delay		Annual congestion cost		
	Total miles (1,000)	Per lane-mile of freeway	Total hours (1,000)	Per person	Per person (dol.)	Delay and fuel cost (mil. dol.)	Fuel wasted (gal. per person)
Total, average	15,772	16,219	47,285	26	517	927	42
Albany-Schenectady-Troy NY	5,730	10,420	3,194	6	123	64	12
Albuquerque NM	3,650	15,210	10,835	18	352	208	29
Atlanta GA	43,000	18,695	101,169	34	676	2,021	58
Austin TX	9,400	16,070	22,627	30	590	449	50
Bakersfield CA	1,985	10,180	1,624	4	81	33	7
Baltimore MD	23,555	15,915	49,671	22	455	1,005	38
Beaumont TX	1,620	12,000	871	6	119	17	7
Birmingham AL	8,685	12,865	9,889	15	296	198	25
Boston MA	23,370	17,855	86,778	29	563	1,705	46
Boulder CO	490	9,800	566	5	97	11	.
Buffalo-Niagara Falls NY	6,380	10,045	5,487	5	100	111	8
Charleston SC	2,865	11,460	5,244	11	218	100	20
Charlotte NC	7,815	16,115	14,267	21	425	282	36
Chicago IL-Northwestern IN	49,865	18,780	220,265	27	513	4,163	42
Cincinnati OH-KY	15,945	15,945	26,000	20	406	524	36
Cleveland OH	16,750	13,085	13,704	7	149	278	13
Colorado Springs CO	2,530	10,765	5,988	13	243	114	19
Columbus OH	13,285	15,095	17,719	17	340	357	29
Corpus Christi TX	2,915	9,880	1,286	4	79	25	6
Dallas-Fort Worth TX	49,410	15,685	139,571	36	711	2,732	60
Denver CO	17,250	16,750	73,019	36	698	1,413	56
Detroit MI	30,955	17,100	108,253	27	523	2,107	43
El Paso TX-NM	4,115	14,440	7,410	11	222	146	20
Eugene-Springfield OR	1,325	12,045	1,236	5	107	25	9
Fort Myers-Cape Coral FL	405	9,000	2,183	7	133	40	13
Fresno CA	2,520	12,295	4,930	9	174	97	14
Ft. Lauderdale-Hollywood-Pompano Beach FL	13,340	18,400	46,292	28	532	864	43
Hartford-Middletown CT	8,445	13,510	6,622	10	221	142	19
Honolulu HI	5,740	14,000	7,329	10	216	151	17
Houston TX	41,000	16,665	127,590	37	711	2,470	59
Indianapolis IN	12,000	16,440	23,231	23	446	459	39
Jacksonville FL	9,750	13,540	13,709	15	309	275	26
Kansas City MO-KS	19,350	11,250	12,939	9	185	264	17
Laredo TX	430	5,735	803	4	77	15	-
Las Vegas NV	7,730	16,105	19,828	16	313	393	25
Los Angeles CA	129,755	23,130	667,352	52	1,005	12,837	78
Louisville KY-IN	10,000	14,925	15,733	19	370	311	31
Memphis TN-AR-MS	7,170	14,060	16,758	17	332	326	28
Miami-Hialeah FL	13,330	18,260	75,269	33	626	1,418	51
Milwaukee WI	9,545	15,775	19,852	14	282	395	24
Minneapolis-St. Paul MN	28,185	17,615	68,454	28	559	1,365	48
Nashville TN	10,485	13,795	14,103	21	424	284	36
New Orleans LA	5,585	13,460	11,406	10	202	221	17
New York NY-Northeastern NJ	103,675	15,335	421,856	25	491	8,434	41
Norfolk-Newport News-Virginia Beach VA	11,635	12,715	20,094	13	261	396	22
Oklahoma City OK	9,060	11,845	6,818	6	126	137	11
Omaha NE-IA	3,420	11,400	7,674	12	233	147	19
Orlando FL	9,950	13,535	40,417	33	626	764	51
Pensacola FL	1,150	10,455	3,042	10	184	56	13
Philadelphia PA-NJ	25,605	14,630	77,463	17	330	1,518	27
Phoenix AZ	21,600	18,945	80,603	28	536	1,553	44
Pittsburgh PA	11,310	9,505	13,205	7	142	255	12
Portland-Vancouver OR-WA	12,670	18,100	37,975	24	476	757	39
Providence-Pawtucket RI-MA	8,765	13,485	19,129	21	414	385	33
Richmond VA	7,975	11,000	7,118	10	204	143	17
Sacramento CA	12,650	18,335	26,993	19	401	563	33
Salem OR	1,190	11,900	1,432	7	135	28	10
Salt Lake City UT	7,800	14,855	10,169	11	231	211	21
San Antonio TX	15,600	14,650	22,544	18	356	449	30
San Bernardino-Riverside CA	17,400	19,440	49,285	34	694	1,003	57
San Diego CA	34,590	19,270	67,887	25	524	1,412	43
San Francisco-Oakland CA	46,700	20,000	168,681	42	835	3,376	67
San Jose CA	16,775	18,850	56,524	34	670	1,125	54
Seattle-Everett WA	24,450	17,220	65,173	32	637	1,315	53
Spokane WA	1,525	10,895	1,534	5	91	30	6
St. Louis MO-IL	25,155	14,170	36,761	18	359	738	31
Tacoma WA	5,505	18,660	9,526	15	317	195	26
Tampa-St. Petersburg-Clearwater FL	8,900	13,485	48,097	24	445	889	36
Tucson AZ	2,450	12,565	9,728	14	266	187	36
Tulsa OK	6,325	11,715	6,192	8	153	123	23
Washington DC-MD-VA	35,770	18,155	125,332	34	667	2,488	14
West Palm Beach-Boca Raton-Delray Beach FL	8,395	18,250	20,824	19	377	405	31

- Rounds to zero.

Source: Texas Transportation Institute, College Station, Texas; 2003 Urban Mobility Study (issued October 2003). (Copyright). See <http://mobility.tamu.edu/ums/>.

No. 1084. Commuting to Work by State: 2000

[In percent, except as indicated (128,279 represents 128,279,000). As of April 1. For workers 16 years old and over. Based on sample data from the 2000 Census of Population and Housing; see text Section 1, and Appendix III]

State	Total workers (1,000)	Commuted by car, truck, or van		Used public transportation[1]	Walked	Used other means	Worked at home	Mean travel time to work (min.)
		Drove alone	Car-pooled					
U.S.	128,279	75.7	12.2	4.7	2.9	1.2	3.3	25.5
AL...............	1,900	83.0	12.3	0.5	1.3	0.8	2.1	24.8
AK...............	291	66.5	15.5	1.8	7.3	4.8	4.1	19.6
AZ...............	2,210	74.1	15.4	1.9	2.6	2.3	3.7	24.9
AR...............	1,160	79.9	14.1	0.4	1.9	1.0	2.6	21.9
CA...............	14,525	71.8	14.5	5.1	2.9	1.9	3.8	27.7
CO	2,192	75.1	12.2	3.2	3.0	1.5	4.9	24.3
CT...............	1,641	80.0	9.4	4.0	2.7	0.7	3.1	24.4
DE...............	373	79.2	11.5	2.8	2.6	1.0	3.0	24.0
DC...............	261	38.4	11.0	33.2	11.8	1.9	3.8	29.7
FL...............	6,910	78.8	12.9	1.9	1.7	1.7	3.0	26.2
GA	3,833	77.5	14.5	2.3	1.7	1.1	2.8	27.7
HI...............	563	63.9	19.0	6.3	4.8	2.4	3.6	26.1
ID...............	595	77.0	12.3	1.1	3.5	1.4	4.7	20.0
IL...............	5,746	73.2	10.9	8.7	3.1	1.0	3.1	28.0
IN...............	2,911	81.8	11.0	1.0	2.4	0.9	2.9	22.6
IA	1,470	78.6	10.8	1.0	4.0	0.9	4.7	18.5
KS...............	1,311	81.5	10.6	0.5	2.5	0.9	4.0	19.0
KY...............	1,782	80.2	12.6	1.2	2.4	0.9	2.7	23.5
LA...............	1,831	78.1	13.6	2.4	2.2	1.6	2.1	25.7
ME...............	615	78.6	11.3	0.8	4.0	0.9	4.4	22.7
MD...............	2,592	73.7	12.4	7.2	2.5	0.8	3.3	31.2
MA...............	3,103	73.8	9.0	8.7	4.3	1.0	3.1	27.0
MI...............	4,540	83.2	9.7	1.3	2.2	0.7	2.8	24.1
MN...............	2,542	77.6	10.4	3.2	3.3	0.9	4.6	21.9
MS	1,164	79.4	15.2	0.6	1.9	1.0	1.9	24.6
MO	2,629	80.5	11.6	1.5	2.1	0.8	3.5	23.8
MT...............	422	73.9	11.9	0.7	5.5	1.7	6.4	17.7
NE...............	873	80.0	10.5	0.7	3.2	0.9	4.6	18.0
NV...............	923	74.5	14.7	3.9	2.7	1.6	2.6	23.3
NH...............	639	81.8	9.8	0.7	2.9	0.8	4.0	25.3
NJ...............	3,876	73.0	10.6	9.6	3.1	0.9	2.7	30.0
NM...............	759	75.8	14.8	0.8	2.8	1.6	4.2	21.9
NY...............	8,212	56.3	9.2	24.4	6.2	0.8	3.0	31.7
NC...............	3,838	79.4	14.0	0.9	1.9	1.1	2.7	24.0
ND...............	319	77.7	10.0	0.4	5.0	0.8	6.0	15.8
OH...............	5,308	82.8	9.3	2.1	2.4	0.7	2.8	22.9
OK...............	1,540	80.0	13.2	0.5	2.1	1.1	3.1	21.7
OR...............	1,601	73.2	12.2	4.2	3.6	1.9	5.0	22.2
PA...............	5,556	76.5	10.4	5.2	4.1	0.8	3.0	25.2
RI...............	491	80.1	10.4	2.5	3.8	1.0	2.2	22.5
SC...............	1,823	79.4	14.0	0.8	2.3	1.3	2.1	24.3
SD...............	373	77.3	10.4	0.5	4.5	0.8	6.5	16.6
TN...............	2,618	81.7	12.5	0.8	1.5	0.8	2.6	24.5
TX...............	9,158	77.7	14.5	1.9	1.9	1.3	2.8	25.4
UT...............	1,033	75.5	14.1	2.2	2.8	1.2	4.2	21.3
VT...............	312	75.2	11.9	0.7	5.6	0.9	5.7	21.6
VA...............	3,482	77.1	12.7	3.6	2.3	1.2	3.2	27.0
WA...............	2,785	73.3	12.8	4.9	3.2	1.4	4.3	25.5
WV...............	718	80.3	12.7	0.8	2.9	0.9	2.4	26.2
WI...............	2,691	79.5	9.9	2.0	3.7	0.9	3.9	20.8
WY...............	240	75.4	13.2	1.4	4.4	1.3	4.3	17.8

[1] Including taxicabs.

Source: U.S. Census Bureau, "2000 Census of Population and Housing, Profiles of General Demographic Characteristics"; <http://www.census.gov/Press-Release/www/2002/demoprofiles.html>.

No. 1085. Commuting to Work—25 Largest Metropolitan Areas: 2000

[For workers 16 years old and over. Based on sample data from the 2000 Census of Population and Housing; see text Section 1, and Appendix III. Covers metropolitan statistical areas (MSA's) and consolidated metropolitan statistical areas (CMSAs) as defined by the U.S. Office of Management and Budget as of June 30, 1999. For definitions of metropolitan areas see Appendix II. For definition of median, see Guide to Tabular Presentation]

Metropolitan area	Total workers (1,000)	Percent of workers who—						Mean travel time to work (min.)
		Commuted by car, truck, or van		Used public transportation[1]	Walked	Used other means	Worked at home	
		Drove alone	Car-pooled					
Atlanta, GA MSA	2,060.6	77.0	13.6	3.7	1.3	1.0	3.5	31.2
Boston-Worcester-Lawrence, MA-NH-ME-CT CMSA	2,898.7	73.9	8.8	9.0	4.1	1.0	3.2	27.8
Chicago-Gary-Kenosha, IL-IN-WI CMSA	4,218.1	70.5	11.0	11.5	3.1	1.0	2.9	31.0
Cincinnati-Hamilton, OH-KY-IN CMSA	951.7	81.4	10.0	2.9	2.3	0.6	2.7	24.3
Cleveland-Akron, OH CMSA	1,375.8	82.3	8.7	3.4	2.1	0.7	2.7	24.0
Dallas-Fort Worth, TX CMSA	2,527.6	78.8	14.0	1.8	1.5	1.0	3.0	27.5
Denver-Boulder-Greeley, CO CMSA	1,346.0	75.6	11.5	4.3	2.4	1.4	4.7	25.9
Detroit-Ann Arbor-Flint, MI CMSA	2,482.5	84.2	9.3	1.8	1.8	0.7	2.3	26.1
Houston-Galveston-Brazoria, TX CMSA	2,081.6	77.0	14.2	3.3	1.6	1.3	2.5	28.8
Kansas City, MO-KS MSA	881.3	82.8	10.4	1.3	1.4	0.7	3.4	22.9
Los Angeles-Riverside-Orange County, CA CMSA	6,767.6	72.4	15.2	4.7	2.6	1.6	3.6	29.1
Miami-Fort Lauderdale, FL CMSA	1,642.9	76.6	13.4	3.9	1.8	1.5	2.8	28.9
Minneapolis-St. Paul, MN-WI MSA	1,595.6	78.3	10.0	4.5	2.4	0.9	3.8	23.7
New York-Northern New Jersey-Long Island, NY-NJ-CT-PA CMSA	9,319.2	56.3	9.4	24.9	5.6	0.9	3.0	34.0
Philadelphia-Wilmington-Atlantic City, PA-NJ-DE-MD CMSA	2,815.4	73.3	10.3	8.7	3.9	1.0	2.8	27.9
Phoenix-Mesa, AZ MSA	1,466.4	74.6	15.3	2.0	2.1	2.2	3.7	26.1
Pittsburgh, PA MSA	1,057.4	77.4	9.7	6.2	3.6	0.7	2.4	25.3
Portland-Salem, OR-WA CMSA	1,105.1	73.1	12.1	5.7	3.0	1.5	4.6	24.4
Sacramento-Yolo, CA CMSA	800.0	75.3	13.5	2.7	2.2	2.2	4.0	25.6
St. Louis, MO-IL MSA	1,239.0	82.6	9.9	2.4	1.6	0.6	2.8	25.5
San Diego, CA MSA	1,299.5	73.9	13.0	3.4	3.4	1.9	4.4	25.3
San Francisco-Oakland-San Jose, CA CMSA	3,432.2	68.1	12.9	9.5	3.3	2.2	4.1	29.3
Seattle-Tacoma-Bremerton, WA CMSA	1,776.2	71.6	12.8	6.8	3.2	1.4	4.2	27.7
Tampa-St. Petersburg-Clearwater, FL MSA	1,064.0	79.7	12.4	1.4	1.7	1.7	3.1	25.6
Washington-Baltimore, DC-MD-VA-WV CMSA	3,839.1	70.4	12.8	9.4	3.0	0.9	3.5	31.7

[1] Includes taxicabs.

Source: U.S. Census Bureau, "2000 Census of Population and Housing, Profiles of General Demographic Characteristics"; <http://www.census.gov/Press-Release/www/2002/demoprofiles.html>.

No. 1086. Commuting to Work—25 Largest Cities: 2000

[In percent, except as indicated (353.1 represents 353,100). As of April 1. For workers 16 years old and over. Based on sample data from the 2000 Census of Population and Housing; see text Section 1, and Appendix III]

City	Total workers (1,000)	Percent of workers who—						Mean travel time to work (min.)
		Commuted by car, truck, or van		Used public transportation[1]	Walked	Used other means	Worked at home	
		Drove alone	Car-pooled					
Austin, TX	353.1	73.6	13.9	4.5	2.5	2.1	3.4	22.4
Baltimore, MD	249.4	54.7	15.2	19.5	7.1	1.1	2.3	31.1
Boston, MA	278.5	41.5	9.2	32.3	13.0	1.6	2.4	28.8
Chicago, IL	1,192.1	50.1	14.5	26.1	5.7	1.3	2.4	35.2
Columbus, OH	367.4	79.0	10.8	3.9	3.2	0.8	2.3	21.9
Dallas, TX	537.0	70.8	17.8	5.5	1.9	1.2	2.8	26.9
Denver, CO	278.7	68.3	13.5	8.4	4.3	1.8	3.7	24.5
Detroit, MI	319.4	68.6	17.1	8.7	2.8	1.1	1.8	28.4
El Paso, TX	208.1	76.5	15.8	2.3	2.0	1.2	2.2	22.4
Houston, TX	841.7	71.8	15.9	5.9	2.3	1.7	2.3	27.4
Indianapolis, IN[2]	385.2	80.0	12.3	2.4	2.0	0.8	2.5	22.7
Jacksonville, FL	350.5	79.2	13.4	2.1	1.8	1.6	1.9	25.2
Los Angeles, CA	1,494.9	65.7	14.7	10.2	3.6	1.6	4.1	29.6
Memphis, TN	274.9	76.6	15.7	3.0	1.9	1.0	4.1	29.6
Milwaukee, WI	249.9	68.8	13.6	10.3	4.7	0.9	1.7	22.5
Nashville-Davidson, TN[2]	274.0	78.5	13.5	1.8	2.4	0.9	3.0	23.3
New York, NY	3,192.1	24.9	8.0	52.8	10.4	1.0	2.9	40.0
Philadelphia, PA	569.8	49.2	12.8	25.4	9.1	1.6	1.9	32.0
Phoenix, AZ	599.6	71.7	17.4	3.3	2.2	2.2	3.3	26.1
San Antonio, TX	491.4	75.6	15.2	3.8	2.2	1.1	2.2	23.8
San Diego, CA	580.3	74.0	12.2	4.2	3.6	2.0	4.0	23.2
San Francisco, CA	418.6	40.5	10.8	31.1	9.4	3.6	4.6	30.7
San Jose, CA	428.0	76.4	14.1	4.1	1.4	1.5	2.5	27.8
Seattle, WA	316.5	56.5	11.2	17.6	7.4	2.7	4.6	24.8
Washington, DC	260.9	38.4	11.0	33.2	11.8	1.9	3.8	29.7

[1] Includes taxicabs. [2] Represents the portion of a consolidated city that is not within one or more separately incorporated places.

Source: U.S. Census Bureau, "2000 Census of Population and Housing, Profiles of General Demographic Characteristics"; <http://www.census.gov/Press-Release/www/2002/demoprofiles.html>.

Transportation 695

No. 1087. Motor Vehicle Distance Traveled by Type of Vehicle: 1970 to 2002

[1,110 represents 1,110,000,000,000. Travel estimates based on automatic traffic recorder data.]

Year	Vehicle-miles of travel (bil.)					Avg. miles per vehicle (1,000)				
	Passenger cars				Trucks [3]	Passenger cars				Trucks [3]
	Total [1]	Cars [1]	Buses [2]	Vans, pickups, SUVs		Total [1]	Cars [1]	Buses [2]	Vans, pickups, SUVs	
1970	1,110	920	4.5	123	62	10.0	10.0	12.0	8.7	13.6
1975	1,328	1,040	6.1	201	81	9.6	9.3	13.1	9.8	15.2
1980	1,527	1,122	6.1	291	108	9.5	8.8	11.5	10.4	18.7
1981	1,555	1,144	6.2	296	109	9.5	8.9	11.5	10.2	19.0
1982	1,595	1,172	5.8	306	111	9.6	9.1	10.4	10.3	19.9
1983	1,653	1,204	5.2	328	116	9.8	9.1	8.9	10.5	21.1
1984	1,720	1,236	4.6	358	122	10.0	9.2	8.0	11.2	22.6
1985	1,775	1,256	4.5	391	124	10.0	9.4	7.5	10.5	20.6
1986	1,835	1,280	4.7	424	127	10.1	9.5	7.9	10.8	22.1
1987	1,921	1,325	5.3	457	134	10.5	9.7	8.9	11.1	23.3
1988	2,026	1,380	5.5	502	138	10.7	10.0	8.9	11.5	22.5
1989	2,096	1,412	5.7	536	143	10.9	10.2	9.1	11.7	22.9
1990	2,144	1,418	5.7	575	146	11.1	10.3	9.1	11.9	23.6
1991	2,172	1,367	5.8	649	150	11.3	10.3	9.1	12.2	24.2
1992	2,247	1,381	5.8	707	153	11.6	10.6	9.0	12.4	25.4
1993	2,296	1,385	6.1	746	160	11.6	10.5	9.4	12.4	26.3
1994	2,358	1,416	6.4	765	170	11.7	10.8	9.6	12.2	25.8
1995	2,423	1,438	6.4	790	178	11.8	11.2	9.4	12.0	26.5
1996	2,486	1,470	6.6	817	183	11.8	11.3	9.4	11.8	26.1
1997	2,562	1,503	6.8	851	191	12.1	11.6	9.8	12.1	27.0
1998	2,632	1,550	7.0	868	196	12.2	11.8	9.8	12.2	25.4
1999	2,691	1,569	7.7	901	203	12.2	11.9	10.5	12.0	26.0
2000	2,747	1,600	7.6	923	206	12.2	11.9	10.2	11.7	25.7
2001	2,797	1,628	7.1	943	209	11.9	11.8	9.4	11.2	26.6
2002	2,856	1,659	6.8	966	215	12.2	12.2	9.0	11.4	27.1

[1] Motorcycles included with cars through 1994; thereafter in total, not shown separately.   [2] Includes school buses.
[3] Includes combinations.

Source: U.S. Federal Highway Administration, *Highway Statistics*, annual. See Internet site <http://www.fhwa.dot.gov/policy/ohpi/hss/hsspubs.htm>.

No. 1088. Domestic Motor Fuel Consumption by Type of Vehicle: 1970 to 2002

[92.3 represents 92,300,000,000. Comprises all fuel types used for propulsion of vehicles under state motor fuels laws. Excludes federal purchases for military use. Minus sign (-) indicates decrease]

Year	Annual fuel consumption (bil. gal)					Average miles per gallon				
	All vehicles [1]	Avg. annual percent change [2]	Cars [1]	Buses [3]	Vans, pickups, SUVs	Trucks [4]	All vehicles [1]	Cars [1]	Buses [3]	Vans, pickups, SUVs	Trucks [4]
1970	92.3	4.8	67.8	0.8	12.3	11.3	12.0	13.5	5.5	10.0	5.5
1975	109.0	2.5	74.3	1.1	19.1	14.6	12.2	14.0	5.8	10.5	5.6
1980	115.0	-5.9	70.2	1.0	23.8	20.0	13.3	16.0	6.0	12.2	5.4
1981	114.5	-0.4	69.3	1.1	23.7	20.4	13.6	16.5	5.9	12.5	5.3
1982	113.4	-1.0	69.3	1.0	22.7	20.4	14.1	16.9	5.9	13.5	5.5
1983	116.1	2.4	70.5	0.9	23.9	20.8	14.2	17.1	5.9	13.7	5.6
1984	118.7	2.2	70.8	0.8	25.6	21.4	14.5	17.4	5.7	14.0	5.7
1985	121.3	2.2	71.7	0.8	27.4	21.4	14.6	17.5	5.4	14.3	5.8
1986	125.2	3.2	73.4	0.9	29.1	21.9	14.7	17.4	5.3	14.6	5.8
1987	127.5	1.8	73.5	0.9	30.6	22.5	15.1	18.0	5.8	14.9	5.9
1988	130.1	2.0	73.5	0.9	32.7	22.9	15.6	18.8	5.8	15.4	6.0
1989	131.9	1.4	74.1	0.9	33.3	23.5	15.9	18.0	6.0	16.1	6.1
1990	130.8	-0.8	69.8	0.9	35.6	24.5	16.4	20.3	6.4	16.1	6.0
1991	128.6	-1.7	64.5	0.9	38.2	25.0	16.9	21.2	6.7	17.0	6.0
1992	132.9	3.3	65.6	0.9	40.9	25.5	16.9	21.0	6.6	17.3	6.1
1993	137.3	3.3	67.2	0.9	42.9	26.2	16.7	20.6	6.6	17.4	6.1
1994	140.8	2.5	68.1	1.0	44.1	27.7	16.7	20.8	6.6	17.3	6.1
1995	143.8	2.1	68.1	1.0	45.6	29.0	16.8	21.1	6.6	17.3	6.2
1996	147.4	2.5	69.2	1.0	47.4	29.6	16.9	21.2	6.6	17.2	6.2
1997	150.4	2.0	69.9	1.0	49.4	29.9	17.0	21.5	6.7	17.2	6.4
1998	155.4	3.3	71.7	1.1	50.5	32.0	16.9	21.6	6.7	17.0	6.1
1999	161.4	3.9	73.2	1.1	52.8	33.9	16.7	21.4	6.7	17.4	6.0
2000	162.5	0.7	73.1	1.1	52.9	35.2	16.9	21.9	6.8	17.6	5.8
2001	163.5	0.6	73.6	1.0	53.5	35.2	17.1	22.1	6.9	17.6	5.9
2002	167.7	2.6	74.9	1.0	54.8	36.8	17.0	22.1	6.9	17.6	5.8

[1] Motorcycles included with through 1994; thereafter in total, not shown separately.   [2] Change from immediate prior year.
[3] Includes school buses.   [4] Includes combinations.

Source: U.S. Federal Highway Administration, *Highway Statistics*, annual. See Internet site <http://www.fhwa.dot.gov/policy/ohpi/hss/hsspubs.htm>.

No. 1089. Motor Vehicle Accidents—Number and Deaths: 1980 to 2002

[17.9 represents 17,900,000]

Item	Unit	1980	1985	1990	1995	1998	1999	2000	2001	2002
ACCIDENTS										
Motor vehicle accidents [1]	Million.	17.9	19.3	11.5	10.7	12.7	11.4	13.4	12.5	18.3
Vehicles involved:										
Cars	Million.	22.8	25.6	14.3	12.3	13.8	11.6	15.9	13.6	18.1
Trucks	Million.	5.5	6.1	4.4	4.5	7.3	6.2	8.8	7.4	12.2
Motorcycles	1,000	560	480	180	152	100	70	130	119	190
DEATHS										
Motor vehicle deaths within 1 yr. [2]	1,000	53.2	45.9	46.8	43.4	43.5	43.0	43.0	43.7	44.0
Noncollision accidents	1,000	14.7	12.6	4.9	4.4	4.2	4.3	4.6	5.2	5.5
Collision accidents:										
With other motor vehicles	1,000	23.0	19.9	19.9	19.0	18.5	18.8	20.6	18.4	18.2
With pedestrians	1,000	9.7	8.5	7.3	6.4	5.9	5.8	5.3	6.1	5.7
With fixed objects	1,000	3.7	3.2	13.1	12.1	12.0	11.1	11.2	12.8	13.5
Deaths within 30 days [3]	1,000	51.1	43.8	44.6	41.8	41.5	41.7	41.9	42.2	42.8
Occupants	1,000	41.9	36.0	37.1	35.3	35.4	35.9	36.3	36.4	37.2
Passenger cars	1,000	27.4	23.2	24.1	22.4	21.2	20.9	20.7	20.3	20.4
Light trucks	1,000	7.5	6.7	8.6	9.6	10.7	11.3	11.5	11.7	12.2
Large trucks	1,000	1.3	1.0	0.7	0.6	0.7	0.8	0.8	0.7	0.7
Motorcycles [4]	1,000	5.1	4.6	3.2	2.2	2.3	2.5	2.9	3.2	3.2
Buses	1,000	(Z)	0.1	(Z)	(Z)	(Z)	0.1	(Z)	(Z)	(Z)
Other/unknown	1,000	0.5	0.5	0.5	0.4	0.4	0.4	0.5	0.5	0.7
Nonoccupants	1,000	9.2	7.8	7.5	6.5	6.1	5.8	5.6	5.8	5.6
Pedestrians	1,000	8.1	6.8	6.5	5.6	5.2	4.9	4.8	4.9	4.8
Pedicyclist	1,000	1.0	0.9	0.9	0.8	0.8	0.8	0.7	0.7	0.7
Other/unknown	1,000	0.1	0.1	0.1	0.1	0.1	0.1	0.1	0.1	0.1
Traffic death rates: [3][5]										
Per 100 million vehicle miles	Rate	3.3	2.5	2.1	1.7	1.6	1.6	1.5	1.5	1.5
Per 100,000 licensed drivers	Rate	35.2	27.9	26.7	23.7	22.4	22.3	22.0	22.1	22.0
Per 100,000 registered vehicles	Rate	34.8	26.4	24.2	21.2	20.0	19.6	19.3	19.1	19.0
Per 100,000 resident population	Rate	22.5	18.4	17.9	15.9	15.4	15.3	14.9	14.8	14.8

Z Fewer than 50. [1] Covers only accidents occurring on the road. Data are estimates. Year-to-year comparisons should be made with caution. [2] Deaths that occur within 1 year of accident. Includes collision categories not shown separately. [3] Within 30 days of accident. Source: U.S. National Highway Traffic Safety Administration, *Traffic Safety Facts*, annual; and unpublished data. See Internet site <http://www.nhtsa.dot.gov/people/Crash/Index.html> [4] Includes motorized cycles. [5] Based on 30-day definition of traffic deaths.

Source: Except as noted, National Safety Council, Itasca, IL, *Injury Facts*, annual (copyright). See Internet site <http://www.nsc.org/>.

No. 1090. Traffic Fatalities by State: 1980 to 2002

[For deaths within 30 days of the accident]

State	1980	1990	2000	2002	Fatality rate [1] 1980	2002	State	1980	1990	2000	2002	Fatality rate [1] 1980	2002
U.S. [1]	51,091	44,599	41,945	42,815	3.3	1.5	MO	1,175	1,097	1,157	1,208	3.4	1.8
AL	940	1,121	996	1,033	3.2	1.8	MT	325	212	237	270	4.9	2.6
AK	88	98	106	87	3.3	1.8	NE	396	262	276	307	3.5	1.6
AZ	947	869	1,036	1,117	5.3	2.2	NV	346	343	323	381	5.7	2.1
AR	588	604	652	640	3.6	2.1	NH	194	158	126	127	3.0	1.0
CA	5,496	5,192	3,753	4,078	3.5	1.3	NJ	1,120	886	731	773	2.2	1.1
CO	709	544	681	742	3.2	1.7	NM	606	499	432	449	5.4	2.0
CT	575	385	341	322	3.0	1.0	NY	2,610	2,217	1,460	1,522	3.4	1.1
DE	153	138	123	124	3.6	1.4	NC	1,503	1,385	1,557	1,575	3.6	1.7
DC	41	48	48	47	1.2	1.3	ND	151	112	86	97	2.9	1.3
FL	2,825	2,891	2,999	3,132	3.6	1.8	OH	2,033	1,638	1,366	1,418	2.8	1.3
GA	1,508	1,562	1,541	1,523	3.5	1.4	OK	959	641	650	734	3.5	1.6
HI	186	177	132	119	3.3	1.3	OR	646	579	451	436	3.4	1.3
ID	331	244	276	264	4.8	1.9	PA	2,089	1,646	1,520	1,614	2.9	1.5
IL	1,975	1,589	1,418	1,411	3.0	1.3	RI	129	84	80	84	2.4	1.0
IN	1,166	1,049	886	792	3.0	1.1	SC	852	979	1,065	1,053	3.8	2.2
IA	626	465	445	404	3.3	1.3	SD	228	153	173	180	3.7	2.1
KS	595	444	461	512	3.4	1.8	TN	1,153	1,177	1,307	1,175	3.4	1.7
KY	820	849	820	915	3.2	2.0	TX	4,366	3,250	3,779	3,725	3.8	1.7
LA	1,219	959	938	875	5.0	2.0	UT	334	272	373	328	3.1	1.3
ME	265	213	169	216	3.5	1.5	VT	137	90	76	78	3.7	0.8
MD	756	707	588	659	2.6	1.2	VA	1,045	1,079	929	914	2.7	1.2
MA	881	605	433	459	2.5	0.9	WA	971	825	631	659	3.4	1.2
MI	1,750	1,571	1,382	1,277	2.8	1.3	WV	523	481	411	439	4.9	2.2
MN	848	566	625	657	3.0	1.2	WI	972	769	799	803	3.1	1.4
MS	695	750	949	885	4.2	2.4	WY	245	125	152	176	4.9	2.0

[1] Deaths per 100 million vehicle miles traveled.

Source: U.S. National Highway Safety Traffic Administration, *Traffic Safety Facts*, annual. See Internet site <http://www.nhtsa.dot.gov/people/Crash/Index.html>.

No. 1091. Fatal Motor Vehicle Accidents—National Summary: 1990 to 2002

[Based on data from the Fatality Analysis Reporting System (FARS). FARS gathers data on accidents that result in loss of human life. FARS is operated and maintained by National Highway Traffic Safety Administration's (NHTSA) National Center for Statistics and Analysis (NCSA). FARS data are gathered on motor vehicle accidents that occurred on a roadway customarily open to the public, resulting in the death of a person within 30 days of the accident. Collection of these data depend on the use of police, hospital, medical examiner/coroner, and Emergency Medical Services reports; State vehicle registration, driver licensing, and highway department files; and vital statistics documents and death certificates. See source for further detail]

Item	1990	1995	1997	1998	1999	2000	2001	2002
Fatal crashes, total	39,836	37,241	37,324	37,107	37,140	37,526	37,862	38,309
One vehicle involved	23,445	21,250	20,807	20,900	20,911	21,117	21,510	22,086
Two or more vehicles involved.	16,391	15,991	16,517	16,207	16,229	16,409	16,352	16,223
Persons killed in fatal crashes	44,599	41,817	42,013	41,501	41,717	41,945	42,196	42,815
Occupants	37,134	35,291	35,725	35,382	35,875	36,348	36,440	37,232
Drivers.	25,750	24,390	24,667	24,743	25,257	25,567	25,869	26,549
Passengers	11,276	10,782	10,944	10,530	10,521	10,695	10,469	10,571
Other	108	119	114	109	97	86	102	112
Nonmotorists	7,465	6,526	6,288	6,119	5,842	5,597	5,756	5,583
Pedestrians	6,482	5,584	5,321	5,228	4,939	4,763	4,901	4,808
Pedalcyclists.	859	833	814	760	754	693	732	662
Other/unknown	124	109	153	131	149	141	123	113
Occupants killed by vehicle type:								
Passenger cars	24,092	22,423	22,199	21,194	20,862	20,699	20,320	20,416
Mini-compact (95 inches)	3,556	2,207	1,763	1,480	1,224	1,113	887	806
Subcompact (95 to 99 inches)	4,753	4,584	4,457	4,034	3,663	3,660	3,571	3,420
Compact (100 to 104 inches)	5,310	6,899	7,195	6,804	6,942	7,022	6,731	7,002
Intermediate (105 to 109) inches . . .	4,849	4,666	4,794	4,617	4,721	5,204	5,402	5,473
Full size (110 to 114) inches	2,386	2,116	2,242	2,014	2,179	2,287	2,344	2,412
Largest (115 inches and over)	2,249	1,297	1,239	1,092	708	897	864	821
Unknown	989	654	509	1,153	1,425	516	521	482
Motorcycles	3,129	2,114	2,028	2,186	2,374	2,783	3,077	3,126
Other motorized cycles	115	113	88	108	109	114	120	118
Light Trucks.	8,601	9,568	10,249	10,705	11,265	11,526	11,723	12,182
Pickup.	5,979	5,938	5,887	5,921	6,127	6,003	6,139	6,057
Utility.	1,214	1,935	2,380	2,713	3,026	3,358	3,530	3,995
Van	1,154	1,639	1,914	2,042	2,088	2,129	2,019	2,095
Other	254	56	68	29	24	36	35	35
Mediumn trucks	134	96	122	99	90	106	82	87
Heavy trucks	571	552	601	643	669	648	620	597
Buses	32	33	18	38	59	22	34	45
Other vehicles	296	307	343	336	355	401	401	422
Unknown.	164	85	77	73	92	49	63	239
Persons involved in fatal crashes.	107,777	102,102	102,197	101,100	100,666	100,716	101,175	101,195
Occupants.	99,297	94,621	95,050	94,241	93,959	94,325	94,706	94,869
Drivers.	58,893	56,164	56,688	56,604	56,502	57,280	57,586	57,803
Passengers	40,229	38,252	38,184	37,448	37,280	36,889	36,892	36,858
Other	175	205	178	189	177	156	228	208
Nonoccupants	8,480	7,481	7,147	6,859	6,707	6,391	6,469	6,326
Vehicle miles traveled (VMT) (100 mil)	21,444	24,227	25,617	26,315	26,911	27,469	27,973	28,558
Licensed drivers (1,000)	167,015	176,628	182,709	184,861	187,170	190,625	191,276	194,296
Registered vehicles (1,000)	184,275	197,065	203,568	208,076	212,685	217,028	221,230	225,685
Percent distribution of fatal accidents by the highest blood alcohol concentration (BAC) in accident:								
0.00 percent	49.5	57.7	60.3	59.8	60.2	58.7	58.9	59.2
0.01 to 0.07 percent	6.5	5.7	5.3	5.8	5.5	5.9	5.9	5.6
0.08 percent and over	44.0	36.7	34.3	34.4	34.3	35.4	35.2	35.2
Fatalities per 100,000 population:								
Under 5 years old	4.9	4.3	4.1	4.0	3.9	3.7	3.4	3.1
5 years to 15 years old	6.4	6.0	5.6	5.2	5.1	4.7	4.3	4.3
16 years to 24 years old	35.2	30.7	29.3	28.5	28.9	28.5	28.6	29.3
25 years to 44 years old	19.7	17.2	16.6	16.4	16.4	16.1	16.2	16.1
45 years to 64 years old	14.9	13.6	14.2	14.0	13.8	13.8	13.5	13.7
65 years to 79 years old	18.8	18.5	19.2	18.7	18.3	17.1	17.1	16.9
80 years old and over	26.8	28.0	29.2	28.4	27.3	25.0	24.5	23.0
Fatalities per 100 million VMT [1]	2.1	1.7	1.6	1.6	1.6	1.5	1.5	1.5
Fatalities per 100,000 licensed drivers	26.7	23.7	23.0	22.4	22.3	22.0	22.1	22
Licensed driver per person.	0.7	0.7	0.7	0.7	0.7	0.7	0.7	0.7
VMT [1] per registered vehicle	11,637	12,294	12,584	12,647	12,653	12,657	12,644	12,654
Fatalities per 100,000 registered vehicles . .	24.2	21.2	20.6	19.9	19.6	19.3	19.1	19.0
Fatal crashes per 100 million VMT [1]	1.9	1.5	1.5	1.4	1.4	1.4	1.4	1.3
Involved vehicles per fatal crash.	1.5	1.5	1.5	1.5	1.5	1.5	1.5	1.5
Fatalities per fatal crash	1.1	1.1	1.1	1.1	1.1	1.1	1.1	1.1
Average occupants per fatal crash.	2.5	2.5	2.5	2.5	2.5	2.5	2.5	2.5
Fatalities per 100,000 population.	17.9	15.9	15.7	15.4	15.3	14.9	14.8	14.8

[1] VMT = vehicle miles of travel.

Source: U.S. National Highway Traffic Safety Administration, *Fatality Analysis Reporting System*, annual. See Internet site <http://www.nhtsa.dot.gov/people/Crash/Index.html>.

No. 1092. Motor Vehicle Occupants and Nonoccupants Killed and Injured: 1985 to 2002

[For deaths within 30 days of the accident. (3,416 represents 3,416,000)]

Year	Total	Occupants Total	Passenger cars	Light trucks [1]	Large trucks [1]	Motor-cycles [2]	Buses	Other/ un-known [3]	Nonoccupants Total	Pedes-trian	Pedal-cyclist	Other/ un-known [3]
KILLED												
1985	43,825	36,043	23,212	6,689	977	4,564	57	544	7,782	6,808	890	84
1988	47,087	39,170	25,808	8,306	911	3,662	54	429	7,917	6,870	911	136
1989	45,582	38,087	25,063	8,551	858	3,141	50	424	7,495	6,556	832	107
1990	44,599	37,134	24,092	8,601	705	3,244	32	460	7,465	6,482	859	124
1991	41,508	34,740	22,385	8,391	661	2,806	31	466	6,768	5,801	843	124
1992	39,250	32,880	21,387	8,098	585	2,395	28	387	6,370	5,549	723	98
1993	40,150	33,574	21,566	8,511	605	2,449	18	425	6,576	5,649	816	111
1994	40,716	34,318	21,997	8,904	670	2,320	18	409	6,398	5,489	802	107
1995	41,817	35,291	22,423	9,368	648	2,227	33	392	6,526	5,584	833	109
1996 [4]	42,065	35,695	22,505	9,932	621	2,161	21	455	6,368	5,449	765	154
1997	42,013	35,725	22,199	10,249	723	2,116	18	420	6,288	5,321	814	153
1998	41,501	35,382	21,194	10,705	742	2,294	38	409	6,119	5,228	760	131
1999	41,717	35,875	20,862	11,265	759	2,483	59	447	5,842	4,939	754	149
2000	41,945	36,348	20,699	11,526	754	2,897	22	450	5,597	4,763	693	141
2001	42,196	36,440	20,320	11,723	702	3,197	34	464	5,756	4,901	732	123
2002	42,815	37,232	20,416	12,182	684	3,244	45	661	5,583	4,808	662	113
INJURED (1,000)												
1988	3,416	3,224	2,585	478	37	105	15	4	192	110	75	8
1989	3,284	3,088	2,431	511	43	83	15	5	196	112	73	11
1990	3,231	3,044	2,376	505	42	84	33	4	187	105	75	7
1991	3,097	2,931	2,235	563	28	80	21	4	166	88	67	11
1992	3,070	2,908	2,232	545	34	65	20	12	162	89	63	10
1993	3,149	2,978	2,265	601	32	59	17	4	171	94	68	9
1994	3,266	3,102	2,364	631	30	57	16	4	164	92	62	9
1995	3,465	3,303	2,469	722	30	57	19	4	162	86	67	10
1996	3,483	3,332	2,458	761	33	55	20	4	151	82	58	11
1997	3,348	3,201	2,341	755	31	53	17	6	146	77	58	11
1998	3,192	3,061	2,201	763	29	49	16	4	131	69	53	8
1999	3,236	3,097	2,138	847	33	50	22	7	140	85	51	3
2000	3,189	3,055	2,052	887	31	58	18	10	134	78	51	5
2001	3,033	2,901	1,927	861	29	60	15	9	131	78	45	8
2002	2,926	2,800	1,805	879	26	65	19	6	126	71	48	7

[1] See footnotes 2 and 3 in Table 1093. [2] Includes motorized cycles. [3] Includes combination trucks. [4] Includes two fatalities of unknown type.

Source: U.S. National Highway Traffic Safety Administration, *Traffic Safety Facts, 2002*; and unpublished data. See Internet site <http://www.nhtsa.dot.gov/people/Crash/Index.html>

No. 1093. Vehicles Involved in Crashes by Vehicle Type, Rollover Occurrence, and Crash Severity: 2002

[Numbers in thousands (11,107.8 represents 11,107,800]

Vehicle type	Total Number	Total Percent	Rollover Yes Number	Yes Percent	Rollover No Number	No Percent
All crashes [1]	11,107.8	100.0	276.3	2.5	10,831.5	97.5
Passenger cars	6,606.1	100.0	113.5	1.7	6,492.6	98.3
Light trucks: [2]	3,988.5	100.0	145.0	3.6	3,843.5	96.4
Pick-up	1,742.0	100.0	64.9	3.7	1,677.1	96.3
Utility	1,330.7	100.0	63.4	4.8	1,267.3	95.2
Van	847.7	100.0	14.7	1.7	833.0	98.3
Other	68.1	100.0	2.0	2.9	66.1	97.1
Large truck [3]	434.5	100.0	16.6	3.8	417.9	96.2
Bus	58.3	100.0	(Z)	(Z)	58.3	100.0
Other/unknown	20.4	100.0	1.2	5.9	19.2	94.1
Fatal crashes	54.8	100.0	11.3	20.6	43.5	79.4
Passenger cars	27.1	100.0	4.5	16.6	22.6	83.4
Light trucks: [2]	21.5	100.0	6.0	27.9	15.5	72.1
Pick-up	11.0	100.0	2.9	26.4	8.1	73.6
Utility	6.7	100.0	2.4	35.8	4.3	64.2
Van	3.7	100.0	0.7	18.9	3.0	81.1
Other	0.1	100.0	(Z)	(Z)	0.1	100.0
Large truck [3]	4.5	100.0	0.6	13.3	3.9	86.7
Bus	0.3	100.0	(Z)	(Z)	0.3	100.0
Other/unknown	1.4	100.0	0.2	14.3	1.2	85.7

Z Less than 500 or 0.05 percent. [1] Includes injury and property only crashes, not shown separately. [2] Trucks of 10,000 pounds gross vehicle weight rating or less. [3] Trucks over 10,000 pounds gross vehicle weight rating.

Source: U.S. National Highway Safety Traffic Administration, *Traffic Safety Facts, 2002*; and unpublished data. See Internet site <http://www.nhtsa.dot.gov/people/Crash/Index.html>.

[Speeding consists of exceeding the posted speed limit or driving too fast for the road conditions or any speed related violation charged (Racing, driving above speed limit, speed greater than reasonable, exceeding special speed limit)]

State	Traffic fatalities, total	Speeding-related fatalities by road type and speed limit								
		Interstate			Non-Interstate					
		Total [1]	Over 55 mph	At or under 55 mph	55 mph	50 mph	45 mph	40 mph	35 mph	Under 35 mph
United States.......	42,815	13,713	1,350	424	3,832	524	1,755	883	1,512	1,512
Alabama............	1,033	411	40	2	104	8	138	24	51	27
Alaska.............	87	33	10	4	4	-	9	1	2	2
Arizona............	1,117	436	55	7	71	19	74	44	44	40
Arkansas...........	640	125	9	1	64	1	16	12	11	9
California..........	4,078	1,468	228	15	389	46	123	113	168	155
Colorado...........	742	319	30	24	43	17	39	31	40	46
Connecticut.........	322	154	9	19	5	6	7	16	21	68
Delaware...........	124	40	1	-	4	17	2	1	-	8
District of Columbia.....	47	17	-	-	-	-	-	-	3	14
Florida............	3,132	558	55	20	92	16	137	26	69	81
Georgia	1,523	313	13	5	96	5	58	16	78	20
Hawaii	119	41	1	5	2	-	6	2	10	13
Idaho	264	88	10	-	17	9	8	-	14	3
Illinois............	1,411	530	29	58	205	6	42	47	82	61
Indiana............	792	185	12	8	69	5	21	21	22	24
Iowa..............	404	49	2	2	27	2	2	1	4	8
Kansas............	512	300	24	-	93	8	10	13	9	36
Kentucky...........	915	179	26	3	98	3	16	1	19	8
Louisiana	875	107	5	2	47	3	13	6	16	4
Maine.............	216	83	4	3	1	7	23	4	16	6
Maryland...........	659	213	11	17	19	30	12	30	35	52
Massachusetts.......	459	176	16	2	4	10	11	21	32	71
Michigan...........	1,277	287	27	3	161	7	20	9	20	18
Minnesota..........	657	179	18	13	92	7	3	10	2	21
Mississippi..........	885	232	31	1	82	8	40	15	20	13
Missouri	1,208	509	57	8	171	5	49	17	66	31
Montana	270	102	16	1	2	2	4	1	8	5
Nebraska...........	307	44	10	4	7	14	-	-	4	3
Nevada............	381	148	26	4	29	3	25	2	18	19
New Hampshire	127	38	1	2	3	6	1	5	11	8
New Jersey..........	773	49	3	2	2	5	1	9	3	19
New Mexico..........	449	177	33	10	25	12	11	8	15	19
New York	1,522	486	13	32	185	15	26	39	14	85
North Carolina.......	1,575	601	38	7	351	4	115	2	-	7
North Dakota........	97	33	4	-	17	-	1	-	-	5
Ohio..............	1,418	245	14	9	112	3	20	4	38	37
Oklahoma..........	734	306	48	3	41	8	73	9	13	12
Oregon............	436	135	5	3	67	-	12	10	10	13
Pennsylvania........	1,614	729	40	19	151	17	150	109	132	66
Rhode Island........	84	46	4	10	1	4	1	3	7	16
South Carolina.......	1,053	495	51	-	142	11	121	19	46	37
South Dakota........	180	78	9	-	27	2	5	3	8	6
Tennessee..........	1,175	293	16	12	61	9	69	32	25	54
Texas.............	3,725	1,546	153	69	278	56	132	98	120	153
Utah..............	328	100	28	-	13	5	3	9	7	13
Vermont...........	78	36	2	-	-	27	-	2	3	-
Virginia	914	251	36	14	101	6	43	4	27	14
Washington.........	659	260	25	-	25	65	15	11	53	39
West Virginia........	439	136	7	-	58	3	25	16	10	12
Wisconsin..........	803	276	20	1	167	-	20	7	21	30
Wyoming...........	176	71	25	-	7	2	3	-	-	1

- Represents zero.   [1] Includes fatalities that occurred on roads for which the speed limit was unknown.

Source: U.S. National Highway Traffic Safety Administration, Traffic Safety Facts, Speeding, annual; and unpublished data. See Internet site <http://www.nhtsa.dot.gov/people/Crash/Index.html>

No. 1095. Traffic Fatalities by State and Highest Blood Alcohol Concentration (BAC) in the Crash: 2002

[BAC means blood alcohol concentration; g/dl means grams per deciliter]

State	Traffic fatalities, total	No alcohol (BAC=0.00 g/dl) Number	No alcohol (BAC=0.00 g/dl) Percent	Any alcohol (BAC=0.01 g/dl) or more — Number	Any alcohol (BAC=0.01 g/dl) or more — Percent	Low alcohol (BAC=0.01-0.07 g/dl) Number	Low alcohol (BAC=0.01-0.07 g/dl) Percent	High alcohol (BAC=0.08 g/dl or more) Number	High alcohol (BAC=0.08 g/dl or more) Percent
United States.....	42,815	25,396	59	17,419	41	2,401	6	15,019	35
Alabama	1,033	620	60	413	40	43	4	370	36
Alaska	87	52	59	35	41	2	2	34	39
Arizona	1,117	640	57	477	43	58	5	420	38
Arkansas	640	398	62	242	38	35	5	207	32
California	4,078	2,466	60	1,612	40	300	7	1,312	32
Colorado	742	435	59	307	41	39	5	268	36
Connecticut	322	182	57	140	43	17	5	123	38
Delaware	124	73	59	51	41	8	6	43	34
District of Columbia	47	22	48	25	52	3	5	22	47
Florida	3,132	1,856	59	1,276	41	177	6	1,099	35
Georgia	1,523	994	65	529	35	90	6	439	29
Hawaii	119	69	58	50	42	10	8	41	34
Idaho	264	173	66	91	34	17	7	74	28
Illinois	1,411	763	54	648	46	97	7	552	39
Indiana	792	523	66	269	34	46	6	223	28
Iowa	404	273	68	131	32	24	6	107	27
Kansas	512	283	55	229	45	23	5	205	40
Kentucky	915	614	67	301	33	39	4	263	29
Louisiana	875	462	53	413	47	62	7	351	40
Maine	216	165	76	51	24	4	2	47	22
Maryland	659	394	60	265	40	49	7	216	33
Massachusetts	459	238	52	221	48	30	6	192	42
Michigan	1,277	787	62	490	38	68	5	422	33
Minnesota	657	402	61	255	39	46	7	209	32
Mississippi	885	553	62	332	38	41	5	292	33
Missouri	1,208	683	57	525	43	68	6	457	38
Montana	270	143	53	127	47	21	8	106	39
Nebraska	307	190	62	117	38	21	7	97	31
Nevada	381	210	55	171	45	23	6	148	39
New Hampshire	127	76	60	51	40	5	4	46	36
New Jersey	773	474	61	299	39	45	6	254	33
New Mexico	449	234	52	215	48	27	6	189	42
New York	1,522	1,044	69	478	31	77	5	400	26
North Carolina	1,575	974	62	601	38	67	4	533	34
North Dakota	97	49	50	48	50	8	8	40	41
Ohio	1,418	856	60	562	40	66	5	496	35
Oklahoma	734	485	66	249	34	35	5	215	29
Oregon	436	257	59	179	41	26	6	153	35
Pennsylvania	1,614	958	59	656	41	88	5	568	35
Rhode Island	84	38	45	46	55	8	9	38	45
South Carolina	1,053	502	48	551	52	64	6	487	46
South Dakota	180	88	49	92	51	13	7	80	44
Tennessee	1,175	704	60	471	40	61	5	410	35
Texas	3,725	1,980	53	1,745	47	194	5	1,551	42
Utah	328	255	78	73	22	7	2	67	20
Vermont	78	51	65	27	35	5	6	22	28
Virginia	914	544	59	371	41	48	5	323	35
Washington	659	361	55	298	45	32	5	265	40
West Virginia	439	259	59	180	41	20	5	160	36
Wisconsin	803	440	55	364	45	39	5	325	40
Wyoming	176	107	61	70	39	7	4	62	35

Source: U.S. National Highway Traffic Safety Administration, *Traffic Safety Facts*, annual; and unpublished data. See Internet site <http://www.nhtsa.dot.gov/people/Crash/Index.html>

No. 1096. Fatalities by Highest Blood Alcohol Concentration in the Crash: 1985 to 2002

[BAC means blood alcohol concentration; g/dl means grams per deciliter]

Item	1985	1990	1995	1998	1999	2000	2001	2002
Total fatalities........	43,825	44,599	41,817	41,501	41,717	41,945	42,196	42,815
Fatalities in alcohol-related crashes .	23,167	22,587	17,732	16,673	16,572	17,380	17,400	17,419
Percent.............	52.9	50.6	42.4	40.2	39.7	41.4	41.2	40.7
BAC = 0.01-0.07 g/dl: Number..............	3,081	2,980	2,490	2,465	2,321	2,511	2,542	2,401
Percent.............	7.0	6.7	6.0	5.9	5.6	6.0	6.0	5.6
BAC = 0.08 g/dl or more: Number..............	20,086	19,607	15,242	14,207	14,250	14,870	14,858	15,019
Percent.............	45.8	44.0	36.5	34.2	34.2	35.5	35.2	35.1
Fatalities with BAC = 0.00 g/dl: Number..............	20,659	22,012	24,085	24,828	25,145	24,565	24,796	25,396
Percent.............	47.1	49.4	57.6	59.8	60.3	58.6	58.8	59.3

Source: U.S. National Highway Traffic Safety Administration, *Traffic Safety Facts*, annual; and unpublished data. See Internet site <http://www.nhtsa.dot.gov/people/Crash/Index.html>.

No. 1097. Crashes by Crash Severity: 1990 to 2002

[6,471 represents 6,471,000. A crash is a police-reported event that produces injury and/or property damage, involves a vehicle in transport and occurs on a trafficway or while the vehicle is in motion after running off the trafficway]

Item	1990	1995	1996	1997	1998	1999	2000	2001	2002
Crashes (1,000)............	6,471	6,699	6,770	6,624	6,335	6,279	6,394	6,323	6,316
Fatal......................	39.8	37.2	37.5	37.3	37.1	37.1	37.5	37.9	38.3
Nonfatal injury...........	2,122	2,217	2,238	2,149	2,029	2,054	2,070	2,003	1,929
Property damage only	4,309	4,446	4,494	4,438	4,269	4,188	4,286	4,282	4,348
Percent of total crashes:									
Fatal.................	0.6	0.6	0.6	0.6	0.6	0.6	0.6	0.6	0.6
Nonfatal injury........	32.8	33.1	33.1	32.4	32.0	32.7	32.4	31.7	30.5
Property damage only	66.6	66.4	66.4	67.0	67.4	66.7	67.0	67.7	68.8

Source: U.S. National Highway Safety Traffic Administration, *Traffic Safety Facts,* annual. See Internet site <http://www.nhtsa.dot.gov/people/Crash/Index.html>.

No. 1098. Alcohol Involvement for Drivers in Fatal Crashes: 1992 and 2002

[BAC = blood alcohol concentration]

Drivers involved in fatal crashes	1992		2002	
	Number of drivers	Percentage with BAC of .08% or greater	Number of drivers	Percentage with BAC of .08% or greater
Total drivers [1]	51,901	25	57,803	21
Drivers by age group:				
16 to 20 years old.................	7,192	21	8,082	17
21 to 24 years old.................	6,323	35	6,285	33
25 to 34 years old.................	13,049	35	11,416	28
35 to 44 years old.................	9,284	27	10,896	26
45 to 64 years old.................	9,360	17	13,580	17
65 years old and over	5,474	7	6,271	5
Drivers by sex:				
Male.............................	38,598	28	42,134	25
Female	12,596	15	14,911	12
Drivers by vehicle type:				
Passenger cars	29,670	25	26,966	22
Light trucks	14,540	28	21,373	23
Large trucks......................	3,980	2	4,508	2
Motorcycles......................	2,435	40	3,337	31

[1] Includes age, sex, and types of vehicles unknown.

Source: U.S. National Highway Safety Traffic Administration, *Traffic Safety Facts, 2002.* See Internet site <http://www.nhtsa.dot.gov /people/Crash/Index.html>.

No. 1099. Licensed Drivers and Number in Accidents by Age: 2002

[193,300 represents 193,300,000]

Age group	Licensed drivers		Drivers in accidents				Accidents per number of drivers	
			Fatal		All			
	Number (1,000)	Percent	Number	Percent	Number (1,000)	Percent	Fatal [1]	All [2]
Total..............	193,300	100.0	52,700	100.0	30,700	100.0	27	16.0
Under 16 years old........	48	(Z)	400	0.8	120	0.4	(3)	(3)
16 years old	1,382	0.7	1,300	2.5	740	2.4	94	54
17 years old	2,228	1.2	1,300	2.5	910	3.0	58	41
18 years old	2,674	1.4	1,600	3.0	940	3.1	60	35
19 years old	3,176	1.6	1,500	2.8	910	3.0	47	29
19 years old and under	9,508	4.9	6,100	11.6	3,620	11.8	64	38
20 years old	3,305	1.7	1,700	3.2	840	2.7	51	25
21 years old	3,421	1.8	1,000	1.9	580	1.9	29	17
22 years old	3,401	1.8	1,100	2.1	540	1.8	32	16
23 years old	3,284	1.7	1,000	1.9	490	1.6	30	15
24 years old	3,357	1.7	1,100	2.1	440	1.4	33	13
20 to 24 years old	16,768	8.7	5,900	11.2	2,890	9.4	35	17
25 to 34 years old	33,734	17.5	10,300	19.5	7,020	22.9	31	21
35 to 44 years old	41,040	21.2	10,300	19.5	6,670	21.7	25	16
45 to 54 years old	38,711	20.0	8,300	15.7	5,130	16.7	21	13
55 to 64 years old	25,609	13.2	5,300	10.1	2,760	9.0	21	11
65 to 74 years old	15,812	8.2	2,800	5.3	1,490	4.9	18	9
75 years old and over	12,118	6.3	3,700	7.0	1,120	3.6	31	9

Z Less than 0.05. [1] Per 100,000 licensed drivers. [2] Per 100 licensed drivers. [3] Rates for drivers under age 16 are substantially overstated due to the high proportion of unlicensed drivers involved.

Source: National Safety Council, Itasca, IL, *Injury Facts, 2003,* (copyright). See Internet site <http://www.nsc.org/>.

No. 1100. Passenger Transit Industry—Summary: 1980 to 2002

[6,510 represents $6,510,000,000. Includes Puerto Rico. Includes aggregate information for all transit systems in the United States. Excludes nontransit services such as taxicab, school bus, unregulated jitney, sightseeing bus, intercity bus, and special application mass transportation systems (e.g., amusement parks, airports, island, and urban park ferries). Includes active vehicles only]

Item	Unit	1980	1985	1990	1995	2000	2001	2002
Operating systems	Number	1,044	4,972	5,078	5,973	6,000	6,000	6,000
Motor bus systems	Number	1,040	2,631	2,688	2,250	2,262	2,264	2,264
Passenger vehicles, active	Number	75,388	94,368	92,961	115,874	131,493	134,271	135,282
Motor bus	Number	59,411	64,258	58,714	67,107	75,013	76,075	76,190
Trolley bus	Number	823	676	832	885	951	600	600
Heavy rail	Number	9,641	9,326	10,419	10,157	10,591	10,718	10,718
Light rail	Number	1,013	717	913	999	1,577	1,366	1,445
Commuter rail	Number	4,500	4,035	4,415	4,565	5,073	5,124	5,300
Demand response	Number	(NA)	14,490	16,471	29,352	33,080	34,661	34,699
Other	Number	(NA)	867	1,197	2,809	5,208	5,727	6,330
Operating funding, total	Mil. dol.	6,510	12,195	16,053	18,241	24,243	25,288	26,632
Passenger funding	Mil. dol.	2,557	4,575	5,891	6,801	8,746	8,891	8,649
Other operating funding [1]	Mil. dol.	248	702	895	2,812	4,217	3,580	4,602
Operating assistance	Mil. dol.	3,705	6,918	9,267	8,628	11,280	12,817	13,382
Federal	Mil. dol.	1,094	940	970	817	994	1,130	1,319
Local [2]	Mil. dol.	2,611	5,979	5,327	3,981	5,319	5,986	5,344
State [2]	Mil. dol.	(NA)	(NA)	2,970	3,830	4,967	5,701	6,719
Total expense	Mil. dol.	6,711	14,077	17,979	21,540	28,194	29,279	30,918
Operating expense	Mil. dol.	6,247	12,381	15,742	17,849	22,646	23,517	24,834
Vehicle operations	Mil. dol.	3,248	5,655	6,654	8,282	10,111	10,439	11,057
Maintenance	Mil. dol.	1,774	3,672	4,631	5,047	6,445	6,638	6,999
General administration	Mil. dol.	1,224	2,505	3,450	2,590	3,329	3,463	3,808
Purchased transportation	Mil. dol.	(NA)	549	1,008	1,930	2,761	2,977	2,970
Reconciling expense	Mil. dol.	464	1,696	2,237	3,691	5,548	5,762	6,084
Capital and planning grants, federal [3]	Mil. dol.	2,787	2,559	2,428	5,534	7,366	6,795	7,323
Capital expenditures	Mil. dol.	(NA)	(NA)	(NA)	7,230	9,587	11,419	12,848
Vehicle-miles operated	Million	2,287	2,791	3,242	3,550	4,081	4,196	4,277
Motor bus	Million	1,677	1,863	2,130	2,184	2,315	2,377	2,411
Trolley bus	Million	13	16	14	14	14	13	14
Heavy rail	Million	385	451	537	537	595	608	621
Light rail	Million	18	17	24	35	53	54	61
Commuter rail	Million	179	183	213	238	271	277	284
Demand response	Million	(NA)	247	306	507	759	789	803
Other	Million	15	15	18	37	74	78	83
Passengers carried	Million	8,567	8,636	8,799	7,763	9,363	9,653	9,623
Motor bus	Million	5,837	5,675	5,677	4,848	5,678	5,849	5,868
Trolley bus	Million	142	142	126	119	122	119	116
Heavy rail	Million	2,108	2,290	2,346	2,033	2,632	2,728	2,688
Light rail	Million	133	132	175	251	320	336	337
Commuter rail	Million	280	275	328	344	413	419	414
Demand response	Million	(NA)	59	68	88	105	105	103
Other	Million	67	63	79	80	93	97	97
Avg. funding per passenger	Cents	29.8	53.0	66.9	87.6	93.4	92.1	89.0
Employees, number (avg.) [4]	1,000	187	270	273	311	360	371	373
Payroll, employee	Mil. dol.	3,281	5,843	7,226	8,213	10,400	10,627	11,197
Fringe benefits, employee	Mil. dol.	1,353	2,868	3,986	4,484	5,413	5,706	6,247

NA Not available. [1] Beginning 1995, includes taxes levied directly by transit agency and other dedicated funds, formerly included in Local. [2] Includes other operating revenue, nonoperating revenue, and auxiliary income. Data for 1985 are state and local combined. [3] 1980, capital grants only. [4] Through 1990, represents employee equivalents of 2,080 hours = one employee; beginning 1995, equals actual employees.

Source: American Public Transportation Association, Washington, DC, Public Transportation Fact Book, annual. See Internet site <http://www.apta.com/>.

No. 1101. Class I Intercity Motor Carriers of Passengers: 1990 to 2002

[943 represents $943,000,000. For carriers whose adjusted annual gross operating revenues are $5 million or more. Intercity carriers have intercity revenues which are 50 percent or more of their total operating revenues. Minus sign (-) indicated deficit]

Item	Unit	1990	1994	1995	1996	1997	1998	1999	2000	2001	2002
Number of intercity carriers [1]	Number	21	20	20	17	17	15	14	12	12	12
Operating revenue	Mil. dol.	943	870	917	912	1,000	999	1,014	1,088	1,076	1,070
Intercity regular route	Mil. dol.	739	718	767	771	834	860	864	920	917	907
Other	Mil. dol.	204	152	150	141	165	139	150	168	158	163
Operating expenses	Mil. dol.	1,026	919	899	878	948	947	1,014	1,035	1,039	1,046
Operating income	Mil. dol.	-83	-48	18	33	52	52	0.2	53	36	25
Revenue passengers	Million	44	41	43	37	52	47	43	33	32	32
Intercity regular route passengers	Million	37	36	38	34	41	37	33	31	30	30
Other passengers	Million	7	4	5	4	12	10	10	2	2	2
Average fare, intercity regular route	Dol.	20.22	19.77	20.10	22.85	20.57	23.14	26.16	29.46	30.27	30.11

[1] Excludes carriers preponderantly in local or suburban service and carriers engaged in transportation of both property and passengers.

Source: U.S. Bureau of Transportation Statistics, Selected Earnings Data, Class I Motor Carriers of Passengers. Carriers of Passengers, 1988-1997, 1998, 1999, 2000 and 2001; and unpublished data. See Internet site <http://www.bts.gov/mcs/prod.html>.

No. 1102. Characteristics of Rail Transit by Transit Authority: 2001

Mode and transit agency	Primary city served	States served	Directional route-miles [1]	Number of crossings	Number of stations	Number of ADA accessible stations [2]
Total [3]	(X)	(X)	9,486.0	5,820	2,816	1,363
Heavy rail	(X)	(X)	1,572.0	27	1,019	359
Chicago Transit Authority	Chicago	IL	206.3	25	144	64
Greater Cleveland Regional Transit Authority	Cleveland	OH	38.2	-	18	8
L.A. County Metropolitan Transportation Authority	Los Angeles	CA	31.9	-	16	16
Maryland Transit Administration	Baltimore	MD	29.4	-	14	14
Massachusetts Bay Transportation Authority	Boston	MA	76.3	-	53	38
Metropolitan Atlanta Rapid Transit Authority	Atlanta	GA	96.0	-	38	38
Miami-Dade Transit Agency	Miami	FL	42.2	-	21	-
MTA New York City Transit	New York	NY	493.8	-	468	41
MTA Staten Island Railway	New York	NY	28.6	-	23	3
Port Authority Trans-Hudson Corp	New York	NY, NJ	25.0	2	13	6
Port Authority Transit Corporation	Philadelphia	PA, NJ	31.5	-	13	5
San Francisco Bay Area Rapid Transit District	San Francisco	CA	190.1	-	39	39
Southeastern Pennsylvania Transportation Authority	Philadelphia	PA	76.1	-	76	4
Washington Metropolitan Area Transit Authority	Washington	DC, MD, VA	206.6	-	83	83
Commuter rail	(X)	(X)	6,988.7	2,525	1,159	587
Alaska Railroad Corporation	Anchorage	AK	275.0	27	3	3
Altamont Commuter Express Authority	San Jose	CA	172.0	127	10	10
Central Puget Sound Regional Transit Authority	Seattle	WA	78.6	39	7	7
Connecticut Department of Transportation	New Haven	CT	101.2	3	8	8
Maryland Transit Administration	Baltimore	MD, DC, WV	373.4	40	40	19
Massachusetts Bay Transportation Authority	Boston	MA, RI	710.0	-	121	75
MTA Long Island Rail Road	New York	NY	638.2	402	124	97
MTA Metro-North Railroad	New York	NY, CT	545.7	162	108	28
New Jersey Transit Corporation	New York	NY, NJ, PA	975.2	329	162	46
North San Diego County Transit Development Board	San Diego	CA	82.2	34	8	8
NE Illinois Regional Commuter Rail Corporation	Chicago	IL, WI	940.4	512	227	125
Northern Indiana Commuter Trans District	Chicago	IL, IN	179.8	117	18	7
ON TRACK	Syracuse	NY	3.5	(NA)	3	3
Peninsula Corridor Joint Powers Board	San Francisco	CA	153.6	49	34	22
Pennsylvania Department of Transportation	Philadelphia	PA	144.4	7	14	4
South Florida Regional Transportation Authority	Miami	FL	142.2	72	18	18
Southeastern Pennsylvania Transportation Authority	Philadelphia	PA	449.2	116	177	30
Southern California Regional Rail Authority	Los Angeles	CA	770.0	442	49	49
Trinity Railway Express	Dallas	TX	51.6	24	7	7
Vermont Transportation Authority	Burlington	VT	25.0	(NA)	3	3
Virginia Railway Express	Washington	DC, VA	177.5	23	18	18

- Represents zero.   NA Not available.   X Not applicable.   [1] The mileage in each direction over which public transportation vehicles travel while in revenue service. The mileage is computed without regard to the number of traffic lanes or rail tracks existing in the right-of-way.   [2] Number of stations that comply with the American with Disabilities Act of 1992 (ADA). Some stations may be wheelchair accessible and not comply with the ADA.   [3] Includes light rail, not shown separately.

Source: U.S. Bureau of Transportation Statistics, *State Transportation Profile: Summary, 2003.* See Internet site: <https://www.bts.gov:443/pdc/index.xml>.

No. 1103. Transit Ridership in 50 Largest Urbanized Areas: 2001

[Areas ranked by 2000 population size]

Urbanized area	2000 Population[1] Total (1,000)	Rank	Annual unlinked passenger trips[2] (mil.)	Percent Motor bus	Heavy rail[3]	Light rail[4]	Commuter rail[5]	Other[6]
U.S., urbanized total[7]	**195,984**	(X)	**9,007.8**	**57.9**	**30.3**	**3.7**	**4.6**	**3.5**
Top 50 Total	127,900	(X)	8,333.7	55.3	32.7	4.0	5.0	2.9
Percent of U.S. total	65.3	(X)	92.5	88.4	100.0	100.0	100.0	78.1
Atlanta, GA	3,500	11	167.0	50.5	49.3	-	-	0.2
Austin, TX	902	40	34.0	98.2	-	-	-	1.8
Baltimore, MD	2,076	18	109.4	77.1	12.4	7.1	2.7	0.6
Boston, MA-NH-RI	4,032	7	372.4	31.4	36.9	20.2	9.7	1.8
Bridgeport-Stamford, CT-NY	889	41	39.6	62.4	-	-	36.8	0.9
Buffalo, NY	977	38	26.2	75.6	-	24.2	-	0.2
Charlotte, NC-SC	759	47	15.5	96.4	-	-	-	3.6
Chicago, IL-IN	8,308	3	600.4	56.4	30.3	-	12.6	0.7
Cincinnati, OH-KY-IN	1,503	26	29.7	98.5	-	-	-	1.5
Cleveland, OH	1,787	21	68.0	80.4	12.1	6.5	-	1.0
Columbus, OH	1,133	36	18.8	97.9	-	-	-	2.1
Dallas-Fort Worth-Arlington, TX	4,146	6	85.1	80.5	-	13.6	3.3	2.6
Denver-Aurora, CO	1,985	20	80.1	88.0	-	11.3	-	0.7
Detroit, MI	3,903	9	56.4	94.3	-	0.1	-	5.6
Hartford, CT	852	45	18.7	95.8	-	1.5	-	2.6
Houston, TX	3,823	10	101.2	98.0	-	-	-	2.0
Indianapolis, IN	1,219	33	10.7	97.2	-	-	-	2.8
Jacksonville, FL	882	43	9.2	86.9	-	-	-	13.1
Kansas City, MO-KS	1,362	29	16.0	96.4	-	-	-	3.6
Las Vegas, NV	1,314	31	50.2	98.7	-	-	-	1.3
Los Angeles-Long Beach-Santa Ana, CA	11,789	2	614.6	88.1	5.1	5.0	0.9	0.9
Louisville, KY-IN	864	44	16.6	97.6	-	-	-	2.4
Memphis, TN-MS-AR	972	39	13.1	81.7	-	16.7	-	1.6
Miami, FL	4,919	5	126.4	81.4	10.9	-	2.0	5.7
Milwaukee, WI	1,309	32	73.0	98.3	-	-	-	1.7
Minneapolis-St. Paul, MN	2,389	16	78.5	97.8	-	-	-	2.2
Nashville-Davidson, TN	750	48	7.1	98.3	-	-	-	1.7
New Orleans, LA	1,009	37	61.3	85.9	-	8.4	-	5.7
New York-Newark, NY-NJ-CT	17,800	1	3,402.0	38.8	53.6	0.2	6.6	0.7
Oklahoma City, OK	747	49	5.7	97.1	-	-	-	2.9
Orlando, FL	1,157	35	26.5	94.8	-	-	-	5.2
Philadelphia, PA-NJ-DE-MD	5,149	4	337.5	51.1	28.9	7.4	9.2	3.5
Phoenix-Mesa, AZ	2,907	13	41.0	95.7	-	-	-	4.3
Pittsburgh, PA	1,753	22	78.7	85.5	-	9.6	-	5.0
Portland, OR-WA	1,583	23	97.4	73.3	-	25.7	-	1.0
Providence, RI-MA	1,175	34	15.6	91.2	-	-	4.7	4.1
Richmond, VA	819	46	16.2	98.2	-	-	-	1.8
Riverside-San Bernardino, CA	1,507	25	24.5	90.2	-	-	6.0	3.8
Sacramento, CA	1,393	28	29.6	69.8	-	29.1	-	1.1
Salt Lake City, UT	888	42	25.9	73.3	-	23.4	-	3.3
San Antonio, TX	1,328	30	47.0	97.8	-	-	-	2.2
San Diego, CA	2,674	15	103.3	68.9	0.0	28.0	1.4	1.7
San Francisco-Oakland, CA	3,229	12	451.6	44.0	23.0	11.0	1.2	20.8
San Jose, CA	1,538	24	63.7	75.4	-	14.5	8.7	1.4
Seattle, WA	2,712	14	144.7	66.1	-	0.3	0.3	33.3
St. Louis, MO-IL	2,078	17	53.0	71.7	-	26.9	-	1.3
Tampa-St. Petersburg, FL	2,062	19	19.8	98.1	-	-	-	1.9
Tucson, AZ	720	50	15.9	98.1	-	-	-	1.9
Virginia Beach, VA	1,394	27	16.7	94.2	-	-	-	5.8
Washington, DC-VA-MD	3,934	8	418.4	42.1	56.3	-	1.3	0.2

- Represents zero. X Not applicable. [1] As of April 1. Based on the 2000 decennial census. [2] The number of times passengers board public transportation vehicles. [3] Also called metro, subway, rapid transit, or rapid rail. [4] Also called streetcar, tramway, or trolley. [5] Also called metropolitan rail or regional rail. [6] Includes such modes as trolley bus, ferry, cable car, vanpool, and demand service. [7] Includes Puerto Rico.

Source: U.S. Bureau of Transportation Statistics, *State Transportation Profile: Summary, 2003*. See Internet site: <https://www.bts.gov:443/pdc/index.xml>.

No. 1104. Truck Transportation, Couriers and Messengers, and Warehousing and Storage—Estimated Revenue: 2000 to 2002

[In millions of dollars (237,783 represents $237,783,000,000). For taxable and tax-exempt employer firms. Estimates have been adjusted to the results of the 1997 Economic Census. Based on the North American Industry Classification System, 1997; see text, Section 15]

Kind of business	1997 NAICS code [1]	2000	2001	2002
Selected transportation industries.	48, 49	237,783	235,659	237,485
Truck transportation	484	172,258	169,069	169,443
General freight trucking	4841	109,914	108,655	110,607
General freight trucking, local	48411	15,152	14,919	15,143
General freight trucking, long-distance	48412	94,762	93,736	95,464
General freight trucking, long-distance, truckload. . . .	484121	61,909	62,526	64,749
General freight trucking, long-distance, less than truckload	484122	32,852	31,210	30,715
Specialized freight trucking.	4842	62,344	60,414	58,835
Used household and office goods moving	48421	15,875	14,578	13,853
Specialized freight (except used goods) trucking, local. . .	48422	25,332	25,360	25,876
Specialized freight (except used goods) trucking, long-distance	48423	21,138	20,476	19,106
Couriers and messengers	492	52,738	53,317	53,101
Couriers	4921	48,258	49,068	48,888
Local messengers and local delivery	4922	4,480	4,248	4,213
Warehousing and storage	493	12,787	13,273	14,941
General warehousing and storage	49311	7,004	7,429	8,726
Refrigerated warehousing and storage	49312	2,426	2,336	2,472
Farm product warehousing and storage	49313	647	688	636
Other warehousing and storage.	49319	2,710	2,819	3,106

[1] Based on the 1997 North American Industry Classification System; see text Section 15.

Source: U.S. Census Bureau, 2002 Service Annual Survey, *Truck Transportation, Messenger Services and Warehousing.* Internet site: <http://www.census.gov/econ/www/servmenu.html> (published 10 February 04).

No. 1105. Truck Transportation—Summary: 2000 to 2002

[In millions of dollars (172,258 represents $172,258,000,000). For taxable and tax-exempt employer firms. Covers NAICS 484. Estimates have been adjusted to the results of the 1997 Economic Census. Based on the North American Industry Classification System, 1997; see text, Section 15]

Item	2000	2001	2002
Total operating revenue	172,258	169,069	169,443
Total motor carrier revenue	160,860	158,494	158,782
Local trucking [1]	51,854	52,071	53,224
Long-distance trucking [1]	109,006	106,423	105,559
Size of shipments:			
Less-than-truckload	48,183	47,171	47,869
Truckload	112,677	111,323	110,913
Commodities handled:			
Agricultural and fish products	12,062	11,770	11,114
Grains, alcohol, and tobacco products.	5,715	6,370	7,217
Stone, nonmetallic minerals, and metallic ores . . .	10,292	10,629	11,224
Coal and petroleum products.	5,913	6,076	5,954
Pharmaceutical and chemical products	9,328	8,460	7,693
Wood products, textiles, and leathers	16,120	16,408	14,829
Base metal and machinery	12,520	12,376	12,593
Electronic, motorized vehicles, and precision instruments	9,900	9,907	11,226
Used household and office goods.	10,297	9,670	8,681
New furniture and miscellaneous manufactured products	15,524	15,737	15,741
Other goods	53,187	51,091	52,510
Hazardous materials	9,999	9,734	9,581
Origin and destination of shipments:			
U.S. to U.S.	154,842	153,148	153,714
U.S. to Canada.	1,750	1,611	1,634
U.S. to Mexico	1,283	1,160	1,108
Canada to U.S.	1,223	1,065	1,007
Mexico to U.S.	1,116	981	783
All other destinations	647	531	537
Inventory of revenue generating equipment (1,000):			
Trucks	210	211	219
Owned	178	179	195
Leased	33	32	23
Truck-tractors.	935	955	915
Owned	790	813	768
Leased	145	142	147
Trailers	1,923	1,991	1,937
Owned	1,599	1,668	1,630
Leased	324	323	308
Highway miles traveled (mil.):			
Total.	86,252	86,350	86,927
By loaded or partially loaded vehicles	68,404	68,625	68,850
By empty vehicles	17,848	17,725	18,076

$del

[1] Local trucking is the carrying of goods within a single metro area and its adjacent nonurban areas; long-distance trucking is the carrying of goods between metro areas.

Source: U.S. Census Bureau, 2002 Service Annual Survey, *Truck Transportation, Messenger Services and Warehousing.*

[As of Dec. 31, or calendar year data, except as noted (216 represents 216,000). Compiled from annual reports of class I railroads only, except where noted. Minus sign (-) indicates deficit]

Item	Unit	1990	1995	1997	1998	1999	2000	2001	2002
Class I line-hauling companies [1]	Number.	14	11	9	9	9	8	8	8
Employees [2]	1,000..	216	188	178	178	178	168	162	157
Compensation	Mil. dol.	8,654	9,070	9,235	9,938	9,603	9,623	9,430	9,387
Average per hour.	Dollars.	15.83	19	20.3	21.3	21	21.5	22.1	22.7
Average per year.	Dollars.	39,987	48,188	51,882	55,764	54,082	57,157	58,153	59,650
Mileage:									
Railroad line owned [3]	1,000..	146	137	133	132	122	121	119	118
Railroad track owned [4]	1,000..	244	228	225	224	207	205	204	200
Equipment:									
Locomotives in service.	Number.	18,835	18,812	19,684	20,261	20,256	20,028	19,745	20,506
Average horsepower	1,000 lb.	2,665	2,927	3,060	3,126	3,200	3,261	3,275	3,378
Cars in service:									
Freight train [5]	1,000..	1,212	1,219	1,270	1316	1,369	1,381	1,314	1,300
Freight cars [6]	1,000..	659	583	568	576	579	560	500	478
Income and expenses:									
Operating revenues.	Mil. dol.	28,370	32,279	33,118	33,151	33,521	34,102	34,576	35,327
Operating expenses.	Mil. dol.	24,652	27,897	27,291	27,916	28,011	29,040	29,164	29,592
Net revenue from operations.	Mil. dol.	3,718	4,383	5,827	5,235	5,510	5,062	5,412	5,735
Income before fixed charges.	Mil. dol.	4,627	5,016	6,168	5,803	6,001	5,361	5,517	6,179
Provision for taxes [7]	Mil. dol.	1,088	1,556	1,886	1,573	1,664	1,430	1,614	1,823
Ordinary income.	Mil. dol.	1,961	2,439	3,156	2,807	2,976	2,501	2,740	3,201
Net income.	Mil. dol.	1,977	2,324	3,156	2,807	2,971	2,500	2,740	3,201
Net railway operating income	Mil. dol.	2,648	2,858	3,984	3,698	4,047	3,924	4,111	4,248
Total taxes [8]	Mil. dol.	3,780	4,075	4,514	4,411	4,459	4,379	4,673	4,724
Indus. return on net investment	Percent.	8.1	7	7.6	7	6.9	6.5	6.9	7
Gross capital expenditures	Mil. dol.	3,591	5,720	6,737	7,357	6,193	5,290	5,113	5,605
Equipment	Mil. dol.	996	2,343	2,146	2,321	2,183	1,508	1,013	1,021
Roadway and structures	Mil. dol.	2,644	3,651	4,121	4,875	4,446	4,549	4,421	4,645
Other	Mil. dol.	-49	-275	471	161	-436	-767	-321	-61
Balance sheet:									
Total property investment	Mil. dol.	70,348	86,186	96,058	102,171	103,424	106,136	108,588	117,770
Accrued depreciation and amortization	Mil. dol.	22,222	23,439	21,862	23,338	23,177	23,989	24,635	26,649
Net investment.	Mil. dol.	48,126	62,746	74,196	78,832	80,247	82,147	83,953	91,121
Shareholder's equity	Mil. dol.	23,662	31,419	34,996	32,976	30,478	32,401	34,822	39,675
Net working capital	Mil. dol.	-3,505	-2,634	-3,434	-4,443	-4,834	-5,783	-6,282	-6,037
Cash dividends.	Mil. dol.	2,074	1,518	995	1,521	2,084	819	2,120	870
AMTRAK passenger traffic:									
Passenger revenue.	Mil. dol.	941.9	734.1	792.1	821.5	1067.8	1201.6	1299.9	1304.3
Revenue passengers carried.	1,000..	22,382	20,349	20,200	21,248	21,544	22,985	23,444	23,269
Revenue passenger miles.	Million.	6,125	5,401	5,166	5,325	5,289	5,574	5,571	5,314
Averages:									
Revenue per passenger	Dollars.	42.1	36.1	39.2	38.7	49.6	52.3	55.4	56.1
Revenue per passenger mile	Cents..	15.4	13.6	15.3	15.4	20.2	21.6	23.3	24.5
Freight service:									
Freight revenue	Mil. dol.	24,471	31,356	32,322	32,247	32,680	33,083	33,533	34,110
Per ton-mile	Cents..	2.7	2.4	2.4	2.3	2.3	2.3	2.2	2.3
Per ton originated	Dollar..	19.3	20.2	20.4	19.6	19	19	19.3	19.3
Revenue-tons originated	Million..	1,425	1,550	1,585	1,649	1,717	1,738	1,742	1,767
Revenue-tons carried	Million..	2,024	2,322	2,114	2,158	2,155	2,179	2,187	2,207
Tons carried one mile	Billion..	1,034	1,306	1,349	1,377	1,433	1,466	1,495	1,507
Average miles of road operated	1,000..	133	122	122	120	121	121	121	123
Revenue ton-miles per mile of road	1,000..	7,763	10,439	11,087	11,491	11,848	12,156	12,358	12,245
Revenue per ton-mile	Cents..	3	2	2	2	2	2	2	2
Train miles	Million..	380	458	475	475	490	504	500	500
Net ton-miles per train-mile [9]	Number.	2,755	2,870	2,861	2,923	2,947	2,923	3,005	3,030
Net ton-miles per loaded car-mile [9]	Number.	69.1	73.6	74	73.2	73.8	73.1	72.4	71.5
Train-miles per train-hour	Miles..	23.7	21.8	19.2	19	20	21	21	21
Haul per ton, U.S. as a system	Miles..	726	843	851	835	835	843	858	853
Accidents/incidents: [10]									
Casualties—all railroads:									
Persons killed	Number.	1,297	1,146	1,063	1,008	932	937	971	951
Persons injured	Number.	25,143	14,440	11,767	11,459	11,700	11,643	10,985	11,103
Class I railroads:									
Persons killed	Number.	1,166	994	895	900	808	778	805	796
Persons injured	Number.	19,284	9,571	7,439	7,532	7,805	7,655	7,232	7,722

[1] See text, this section, for definition of Class I. [2] Average midmonth count. [3] Represents the aggregate length of roadway of all line-haul railroads. Excludes yard tracks, sidings, and parallel lines. (Includes estimate for class II and III railroads.) [4] Includes multiple main tracks, yard tracks, and sidings owned by both line-haul and switching and terminal. (Includes estimate for class II and III railroads.) [5] Includes cars owned by all railroads, private car companies, and shippers. [6] Class I railroads only. [7] Includes State income taxes. [8] Includes payroll, income, and other taxes. [9] Revenue and nonrevenue freight. [10] Source: Federal Railroad Admin., Accident Bulletin, annual. Includes highway grade crossing casualties. See Internet site <http://www.fra.dot.gov/>

Source: Except as noted, Association of American Railroads, Washington, DC, Railroad Facts, Statistics of Railroads of Class I, annual, and Analysis of Class I Railroads, annual. See Internet site <http://www.aar.org/AboutTheIndustry/AboutTheIndustry.asp>.

[In thousands (27,160 represents 27,160,000). Figures are 52-week totals]

Year	Carloads[1]	Commodity group	Carloads 2002[3]	Carloads 2003[3]	Commodity group	Carloads 2002[3]	Carloads 2003[3]
1970 . .	27,160	Coal	6,735	6,631	Metals and products	607	599
1980 . .	22,598	Metallic ores	265	252	Stone, clay, and glass products . .	491	512
1990 . .	16,177	Chemicals, allied products. . . .	1,440	1,464	Crushed stone, gravel, sand	863	889
1995 . .	16,706	Grain.	1,079	1,095	Nonmetalic minerals	375	380
1996 [2]	16,521	Motor vehicles and equipment .	1,245	1,216	Waste and scrap materials	443	471
1997 [2]	16,568	Pulp, paper, allied products . . .	425	442	Lumber, wood products	277	277
1998 [2]	16,914	Primary forest products.	189	185	Coke.	183	247
1999 [2]	16,407	Food and kindred products . . .	439	432	Petroleum products	291	282
2000 [3]	16,354	Grain mill products.	476	471	All other carloads	279	305
2001 [3]	16,286						
2002 [3]	16,101						
2003 [3]	16,150						

[1] Beginning 1990 excludes intermodal.   [2] Excludes 2 Class I railroads.   [3] Excludes 3 Class I railroads. 2003 data preliminary.

Source: Association of American Railroads, Washington, DC, *Weekly Railroad Traffic*, annual. See Internet site <http://www.aar.org/AboutTheIndustry/AboutTheIndustry.asp>

No. 1108. Railroads, Class I Line-Haul-Revenue Freight Originated by Commodity Group: 1990 to 2003

[21,401 represents 21,401,000]

Commodity group	1990	1995	1997	1998	1999	2000	2001	2002	2003
Carloads (1,000) [1]	21,401	23,726	25,016	25,705	27,096	27,763	27,205	27,901	28,870
Farm products	1,689	1,692	1,408	1,404	1,477	1,437	1,461	1,471	1,519
Metallic ores	508	463	327	311	295	322	251	328	331
Coal.	5,912	6,095	6,703	7,027	6,965	6,954	7,295	7,088	7,037
Nonmetalic minerals.	1,202	1,159	1,160	1,256	1,306	1,309	1,280	1,310	1,370
Food and kindred products	1,307	1,377	1,295	1,282	1,354	1,377	1,446	1,472	1,478
Lumber and wood products	780	719	669	645	673	648	603	619	612
Pulp, paper, allied products	611	628	582	547	612	633	601	646	667
Chemicals, allied products	1,531	1,642	1,674	1,653	1,814	1,820	1,777	1,866	1,913
Petroleum and coal products . . .	573	596	534	510	543	565	547	533	606
Stone, clay, and glass products. . .	539	516	485	475	538	541	528	559	581
Primary metal products	477	575	604	644	682	723	642	656	648
Fabricated metal products	31	32	29	27	27	30	51	38	36
Machinery, exc. electrical.	39	41	43	37	34	35	46	38	38
Transportation equipment	1,091	1,473	1,485	1,671	1,896	1,984	1,777	1,831	1,811
Waste and scrap materials.	439	623	608	581	624	619	591	617	651
Tons (mill) [1]	1,425	1,550	1,585	1,649	1,717	1,738	1,742	1,767	1,799
Farm products	147	154	126	129	139	136	137	138	141
Metallic ores	47	44	32	31	29	32	25	31	33
Coal.	579	627	705	749	751	758	801	785	784
Nonmetalic minerals.	109	110	109	120	125	126	123	126	133
Food and kindred products	81	91	86	87	92	94	98	102	102
Lumber and wood products	53	51	48	47	50	49	46	48	47
Pulp, paper, allied products	33	36	32	31	35	36	34	37	39
Chemicals, allied products	126	138	140	139	154	155	150	157	162
Petroleum and coal products . . .	40	43	39	38	40	42	42	42	49
Stone, clay, and glass products. . .	44	43	41	41	47	48	46	49	51
Primary metal products	38	47	50	53	56	60	53	55	54
Fabricated metal products	1	1	1	1	1	1	1	1	1
Machinery, exc. electrical.	1	1	1	1	1	1	1		
Transportation equipment	23	30	31	36	40	42	37	38	36
Waste and scrap materials.	28	38	37	36	40	40	37	39	41
Gross revenue (mil. dol.) [1]	29,775	33,782	34,964	34,898	35,441	36,331	36,063	36,742	38,434
Farm products	2,422	3,020	2,645	2,529	2,720	2,673	2,741	2,711	2,870
Metallic ores	408	394	399	373	336	338	288	285	289
Coal.	6,954	7,356	7,698	7,997	7,739	7,794	8,181	7,797	7,890
Nonmetalic minerals.	885	875	899	920	955	969	945	967	1,041
Food and kindred products	2,188	2,464	2,385	2,378	2,400	2,424	2,579	2,657	2,760
Lumber and wood products	1,390	1,385	1,471	1,487	1,528	1,524	1,519	1,628	1,745
Pulp, paper, allied products	1,486	1,543	1,507	1,472	1,457	1,457	1,457	1,567	1,646
Chemicals, allied products	3,933	4,553	4,764	4,610	4,616	4,636	4,504	4,658	4,779
Petroleum and coal products . . .	918	997	1,028	991	980	1,010	1,014	1,026	1,123
Stone, clay, and glass products. . .	931	1,044	1,063	1,056	1,089	1,113	1,090	1,149	1,211
Primary metal products	979	1,199	1,294	1,304	1,289	1,371	1,292	1,288	1,349
Fabricated metal products	42	44	41	37	38	48	65	61	47
Machinery, exc. electrical.	67	69	73	64	55	61	73	61	60
Transportation equipment	3,100	3,269	3,462	3,339	3,582	3,843	3,590	3,731	3,707
Waste and scrap materials.	504	685	711	693	689	706	685	717	799

[1] Includes commodity groups and small packaged freight shipments, not shown separately.

Source: Association of American Railroads, Washington, DC, *Freight Commodity Statistics*, annual. See Internet site <http://www.aar.org/AboutTheIndustry/AboutTheIndustry.asp>.

No. 1109. Railroad Freight—Producer Price Indexes: 1990 to 2003

[Dec. 1984=100. Reflects prices for shipping a fixed set of commodities under specified and unchanging conditions]

Commodity	1990	1995	1998	1999	2000	2001	2002	2003
Railroad line-haul operating	107.5	111.7	113.4	113.0	114.5	116.6	118.9	121.4
Coal	104.2	107.3	108.7	107.3	108.7	110.6	110.1	111.3
Farm products	110.4	115.6	123.9	121.7	123.1	124.5	125.5	132.0
Food products	105.4	111.2	107.4	99.7	100.4	102.8	102.7	101.7
Metallic ores	106.5	101.9	104.4	103.8	105.9	107.0	107.0	105.9
Chemicals and allied products	111.7	120.0	120.1	119.1	121.3	122.3	126.2	131.6
Nonmetallic minerals	111.7	119.5	121.5	121.7	122.1	123.0	124.3	125.8
Lumber and wood products	107.5	110.0	110.3	109.8	109.0	112.2	120.5	123.3
Transportation equipment	107.5	112.8	113.4	113.3	112.6	118.7	130.5	136.6
Pulp, paper, and allied products	108.0	108.7	113.7	115.5	119.0	122.4	122.4	124.4
Primary metal products	113.1	115.6	116.1	118.4	124.1	128.8	132.5	136.0
Stone, clay, glass, and concrete products	114.1	121.4	121.8	122.6	128.7	129.0	124.3	127.1
Petroleum and coal products	109.2	114.3	122.5	123.0	124.6	126.8	127.5	129.6

Source: U.S. Bureau of Labor Statistics, *Producer Price Indexes*, monthly and annual. See Internet site <http://www.bls.gov/ppi/>

No. 1110. Petroleum Pipeline Companies—Characteristics: 1980 to 2002

[173 represents 173,000. Covers pipeline companies operating in interstate commerce and subject to jurisdiction of the Federal Energy Regulatory Commission]

Item	Unit	1980	1985	1990	1995	1998	1999	2000	2001	2002
Miles of pipeline, total	1,000	173	171	168	177	157	154	152	155	150
Gathering lines	1,000	36	35	32	35	21	20	18	17	16
Trunk lines	1,000	136	136	136	142	136	134	134	138	133
Total deliveries	Mil. bbl . . .	10,600	10,745	11,378	12,862	12,914	13,317	14,450	13,352	13,343
Crude oil	Mil. bbl . . .	6,405	6,239	6,563	6,952	7,639	7,551	6,923	7,082	7,019
Products	Mil. bbl . . .	4,195	4,506	4,816	5,910	5,275	5,766	7,527	6,270	6,324
Total trunk line traffic	Bil. bbl-miles.	3,405	3,342	3,500	3,619	3,442	3,738	3,508	3,505	3,563
Crude oil	Bil. bbl-miles.	1,948	1,842	1,891	1,899	1,747	1,815	1,602	1,566	1,620
Products.	Bil. bbl-miles.	1,458	1,500	1,609	1,720	1,696	1,923	1,906	1,939	1,943
Carrier property value	Mil. dol . . .	19,752	21,605	25,828	27,460	30,181	33,780	29,648	32,148	32,605
Operating revenues	Mil. dol . . .	6,356	7,461	7,149	7,711	6,890	7,220	7,483	7,730	7,812
Net income	Mil. dol . . .	1,912	2,431	2,340	2,670	2,051	2,928	2,705	3,007	3,409

Source: PennWell Publishing Co., Houston, Texas, *Oil & Gas Journal*, annual (copyright).

No. 1111. U.S. Postal Service Rates for Letters and Post Cards: 1958 to 2002

[Domestic airmail letters discontinued in 1973 at 13 cents per ounce; superseded by express mail. Prior to February 3, 1991, international airmail rates were based on international zones which have been discontinued. Rates exclude Canada and Mexico]

	Surface mail						Letters				
Domestic mail date rate of change	Letters					International air mail date of rate change	Letters				
	Each ounce	First ounce	Each added ounce	Post cards	Express mail [1]		First 1/2 ounce	Second 1/2 ounce	Each added 1/2 ounce	Post cards	Aero-grammes
1958 (Aug. 1) . .	0.04	(X)	(X)	0.03	(X)	1961 (July 1) . .	(X)	(X)	(X)	0.11	0.11
1963 (Jan. 7) . .	0.05	(X)	(X)	0.04	(X)	1967 (May 1) . .	(X)	(X)	(X)	0.13	0.13
1968 (Jan. 7) . .	0.06	(X)	(X)	0.05	(X)	1971 (July 1) . .	(X)	(X)	(X)	0.13	0.13
1971 (May 16) . .	0.08	(X)	(X)	0.06	(X)	1974 (Mar. 2) . .	(X)	(X)	(X)	0.18	0.18
1974 (Mar. 2). .	0.10	(X)	(X)	0.08	(X)	1976 (Jan. 3) . .	(X)	(X)	(X)	0.21	0.22
1975 (Sept. 14) .		0.10	0.09	0.07	(X)	1981 (Jan. 1) . .	(X)	(X)	(X)	0.28	0.30
1975 (Dec. 31). .	[2](X)	[2]0.13	[2]0.11	[2]0.09	(X)	1985 (Feb. 17) .	(X)	(X)	(X)	0.33	0.36
1978 (May 29) . .	(X)	0.15	0.13	0.10	(X)	1988 (Apr. 17) .	(X)	(X)	(X)	0.36	0.39
1981 (Mar. 22). .	(X)	0.18	0.17	0.12	(X)	1991 (Feb. 3) . .	0.50	0.45	[3]0.39	0.40	0.45
1981 (Nov. 1) . .	(X)	0.20	0.17	0.13	9.35	1995 (July 9) . .	0.60	[3]0.40	(X)	0.40	0.45
1985 (Feb. 17) . .	(X)	0.22	0.17	0.14	10.75	1999 (Jan. 10) . .	0.60	[3]0.40	(X)	0.50	0.50
1988 (Apr. 3) . .	(X)	0.25	0.20	0.15	[4]12.00	2001 (Jan. 7) . .	[3] [5]0.80	[3] [5]1.70	(X)	0.70	0.70
1991 (Feb. 3) . .	(X)	0.29	0.23	0.19	[4]13.95	2002 (June 30) . .	[3]0.80	[3]1.70	(X)	0.70	0.70
1995 (Jan. 1) . .	(X)	0.32	0.23	0.20	[4]15.00						
1999 (Jan. 10) . .	(X)	0.33	0.22	0.20	[4]15.75						
2001 (Jan. 7) . .	(X)	0.34	0.21	0.20	[4]16.00						
2002 (June 30) .	(X)	0.37	0.23	0.23	[4]17.85						

X Not applicable.   [1] Post Office to addressee rates. Rates shown are for weights up to 2 pounds, all zones. Beginning Feb. 17, 1985, for weights between 2 and 5 lbs, $12.85 is charged. Prior to Nov. 1, 1981, rate varied by weight and distances. Over 5 pounds still varies by distance.   [2] As of October 11, 1975, surface mail service upgraded to level of airmail.   [3] Up to the limit of 64 ounces.   [4] Over 8 ounces and up to 2 pounds.   [5] The rate increments changed to 1 ounce.

Source: U.S. Postal Service, "United States Domestic Postage Rate: Recent History," and unpublished data. See Internet site <http://www.usps.com/common/category/postage.htm>

No. 1112. U.S. Postal Service—Summary: 1980 to 2003

[106.311 represents 106,311,000,000. For years ending Septmeber 30. Includes Puerto Rico and all outlying areas. See text, this section]

Item	1980	1990	1995	2000	2001	2002	2003
Offices, stations, and branches	39,486	40,067	39,149	38,060	38,123	37,683	37,579
Number of post offices	30,326	28,959	28,392	27,876	27,876	27,791	27,556
Number of stations and branches	9,160	11,108	10,757	10,184	10,247	9,892	10,023
Delivery Points (mil.)	(NA)	(NA)	(NA)	135.9	137.7	139.5	141.4
Residential	(NA)	(NA)	(NA)	123.9	125.4	127.0	128.7
City	(NA)	(NA)	(NA)	76.1	76.6	77.0	77.5
P.O. Box	(NA)	(NA)	(NA)	15.9	15.8	15.8	15.7
Rural/highway contract	(NA)	(NA)	(NA)	31.9	33.0	34.2	35.5
Business	(NA)	(NA)	(NA)	12.1	12.3	12.5	12.7
Pieces of mail handled (mil.)	106,311	166,301	180,734	207,882	207,463	202,822	202,185
Domestic [1]	105,348	165,503	179,933	206,782	206,381	201,918	201,248
First class [2]	60,276	89,270	96,296	103,526	103,656	102,379	99,059
Express Mail	17	59	57	71	69	61	56
Priority Mail	248	518	869	1,223	1,118	998	860
Periodicals (formerly 2d class)	10,220	10,680	10,194	10,365	10,077	9,690	9,320
Standard A (formerly 3d class)	30,381	63,725	71,112	90,057	89,938	87,231	90,359
Standard B (formerly 4th class)	633	663	936	1,128	1,093	1,075	1,129
Mailgram	39	14	5	4	3	3	3
U.S. Postal Service	(NA)	538	412	363	381	425	391
Free for the blind	28	35	52	47	45	57	70
International surface	450	166	106	79	60	39	30
International air	513	632	696	1,021	1,022	865	909
Employees, total (1,000)	667	843	875	901	891	854	827
Career	643	761	753	788	776	753	729
Headquarters	3	2	2	2	2	2	2
Headquarters support	(NA)	6	4	6	6	4	4
Inspection Service	5	4	4	4	4	4	4
Inspector General	(X)	(X)	(X)	1	1	1	1
Field Career	635	747	745	775	764	743	719
Postmasters	29	27	27	26	26	26	26
Supervisors/managers	36	43	35	39	39	38	35
Professional, administrative, and technical	5	10	11	10	10	10	9
Clerks	263	290	274	282	270	257	242
Mail handlers	37	51	57	61	60	59	57
City carriers	187	236	240	241	240	234	229
Motor vehicle operators	6	7	8	9	9	9	9
Rural carriers	33	42	46	57	60	61	62
Special delivery messengers	3	2	2	(X)	(X)	(X)	(X)
Building and equipment maintenance	27	33	38	42	43	42	41
Vehicle maintenance	5	5	5	6	6	6	6
Other [3]	4	1	2	2	1	2	2
Noncareer	25	83	122	114	115	101	98
Casuals	5	27	26	30	30	19	17
Transitional	(X)	(X)	32	13	14	13	11
Rural substitutes	20	43	50	58	58	56	56
Relief/Leave replacements	(X)	12	13	12	12	12	12
Nonbargaining temporary	(X)	(Z)	1	1	1	1	1
Compensation and employee benefits (mil. dol.)	16,541	34,214	41,931	49,532	51,351	51,557	50,428
Avg. salary per employee (dol.) [4]	24,799	37,570	45,001	50,103	54,481	54,225	57,051
Pieces of mail per employee, (1,000)	159	197	207	231	233	237	244
Total revenue (mil. dol.) [5]	19,253	40,074	54,509	64,540	65,834	66,463	68,529
Operating postal revenue	17,143	39,201	54,176	64,476	65,766	66,415	68,499
Mail revenue [6]	16,377	37,892	52,490	62,284	63,425	63,761	65,701
First class mail	10,146	24,023	31,955	35,510	35,876	36,483	37,048
Priority mail [7]	612	1,555	3,075	4,837	4,916	4,723	4,494
Express mail [8]	184	630	711	996	996	911	888
Mailgram	15	8	2	2	1	1	1
Periodicals (formerly 2d class)	863	1,509	1,972	2,171	2,205	2,165	2,235
Standard mail A (formerly 3d class)	2,412	8,082	11,792	15,193	15,705	15,819	17,203
Standard mail B (formerly 4th class)	805	919	1,525	1,912	1,994	2,080	2,216
International surface	154	222	205	180	178	150	146
International air	442	941	1,254	1,477	1,554	1,429	1,469
Service revenue	765	1,310	1,687	2,191	2,341	2,655	2,798
Registry [9]	157	174	118	98	98	87	82
Certified [9]	120	310	560	385	495	606	624
Insurance [9]	55	47	52	109	123	135	138
Collection-on-delivery	21	26	21	22	15	14	11
Special delivery [10]	73	6	3	(X)	(X)	(X)	(X)
Money orders	95	155	196	235	225	239	231
Other [9]	244	592	737	1,342	1,384	1,574	1,711
Operating expenses (mil. dol.) [11]	19,413	40,490	50,730	62,992	65,640	65,234	63,902

NA Not available. X Not applicable. Z Fewer than 500. [1] Data for 1980 includes penalty and franked mail, not shown separately. [2] Items mailed at 1st class rates and weighing 11 ounces or less. [3] Includes discontinued operations, area offices, and nurses. [4] For career bargaining unit employees. Includes fringe benefits. [5] Net revenues after refunds of postage. Includes operating reimbursements, stamped envelope purchases, indemnity claims, and miscellaneous revenue and expenditure offsets. Shown in year which gave rise to the earnings. [6] For 1980, includes penalty and franked mail, not shown separately. [7] Provides 2 to 3 day delivery service. [8] Overnight delivery. Later years have that mail distributed into the appropriate class. [9] Beginning 1998, return receipt revenue broken out from registry, certified, insurance and included in "other". [10] Special delivery discontinued June 8, 1997. [11] Shown in year in which obligation was incurred.

Source: U.S. Postal Service, Annual Report of the Postmaster General and Comprehensive Statement on Postal Operations, annual; and unpublished data.

Section 24
Information and Communications

This section presents statistics on the various information and communications media: publishing, including newspapers, periodicals, books, and software; motion pictures, sound recordings, broadcasting, and telecommunications; and information services, such as libraries. Statistics on computer use and Internet access are also included. Data on the usage, finances, and operations of the Postal Service previously shown in this section are now presented in Section 23, Transportation.

Information industry—The U.S. Census Bureau's *Service Annual Survey, Information Services Sector,* provides estimates of operating revenue of taxable firms and revenues and expenses of firms exempt from federal taxes for industries in the information sector of the economy. Similar estimates were previously issued in the *Annual Survey of Communications Services.* Data beginning 1998 are based on the North American Industry Classification System (NAICS), 1997 and the information sector is a newly created economic sector. It comprises establishments engaged in the following processes: (a) producing and distributing information and cultural products, (b) providing the means to transmit or distribute these products as well as data or communications, and (c) processing data. It includes establishments previously classified in the Standard Industrial Classification (SIC) in manufacturing (publishing); transportation, communications, and utilities (telecommunications and broadcasting); and services (software publishing, motion picture production, data processing, online information services, and libraries).

This new sector is comprised of industries which existed previously, were revised from previous industry definitions, or are completely new industries. Among those which existed previously are newspaper publishers, motion picture and video production, and online information services.

Revised industries include book publishers and libraries and archives. Newly created industries include database and directory publishers, record production, music publishers, sound recording studios, cable networks, wired telecommunications carriers, paging, and satellite telecommunications. The following URL contains detailed information about NAICS and provides a comparison of the SIC and NAICS <http://www.census.gov /epcd/www/naics.html>. See also the text in Section 15, Business Enterprise.

Beginning 2001, the Service Annual Survey estimates reflect the introduction of the provisional North American Product Classification System (NAPCS) for the information sector. Data for prior years are not comparable. See <http://www.census.gov/eos/www /napcs/napcs.htm>.

The 1997 Economic Census was the first economic census to cover the new information sector of the economy. The census, conducted every 5-years, for the years ending "2" and "7," provides information on the number of establishments, receipts, payroll, and paid employees for the United States and various geographic levels. The most recent reports are from the 2002 Economic Census. This census was conducted in accordance with the 2002 NAICS.

The Federal Communications Commission (FCC), established in 1934, regulates wire and radio communications. Only the largest carriers and holding companies file annual financial reports which are publically available. The FCC has jurisdiction over interstate and foreign communication services but not over intrastate or local services. The gross operating revenues of the telephone carriers reporting publically available data annually to the FCC, however, are estimated to cover about 90 percent of the revenues of all U.S. telephone companies. Data are not comparable with Census Bureau *Annual*

Information and Communications   711

Survey because of coverage and different accounting practices for those telephone companies which report to the FCC.

Reports filed by the broadcasting industry cover all radio and television stations operating in the United States. The private radio services represent the largest and most diverse group of licensees regulated by the FCC. These services provide voice, data communications, point-to-point, and point-to-multipoint radio communications for fixed and mobile communicators. Major users of these services are small businesses, the aviation industry, the maritime trades, the land transportation industry, the manufacturing industry, state and local public safety and governmental authorities, emergency medical service providers, amateur radio operators, and personal radio operations (CB and the General Mobile Radio Service). The FCC also licenses entities as private and common carriers. Private and common carriers provide fixed and land mobile communications service on a for-profit basis. Principal sources of wire, radio, and television data are the FCC's *Annual Report* and its annual *Statistics of Communications Common Carriers.*

Statistics on publishing are available from the Census Bureau, as well as from various private agencies. Editor & Publisher Co., New York, NY, presents annual data on the number and circulation of daily and Sunday newspapers in its *International Year Book.* Data on book production and prices are available from Information Today, Medford, NJ. The Book Industry Study Group, New York, NY, collects data on books sold and domestic consumer expenditures. Book purchasing data are from Ipsos, NPD, Inc., Rosemont, IL. Data on academic and public libraries are collected by the U.S. National Center for Education Statistics. Public library data are also gathered by Information Today, Medford, NJ, and the National Commission on Libraries and Information Science, Washington, DC.

Advertising—Data on advertising previously shown in this section are now presented in Section 27, Accommodation, Food Services, and Other Services.

Statistical reliability—For a discussion of statistical collection and estimation, sampling procedures, and measures of statistical reliability applicable to Census Bureau data, see Appendix III.

U.S. Census Bureau, Statistical Abstract of the United States: 2004-2005

[2002 preliminary. For establishments with payroll. (623,214 represents $623,214,000,000). Based on the 1997 and 2002 Economic Censuses; See Appendix III]

Kind of business	1997 NAICS code [1]	Number of establish-ments	Receipts (mil. dol.)	Annual payroll (mil. dol.)	Paid employees (1,000)
Information: [2]					
1997	51	114,475	623,214	129,482	3,066.2
2002	51	137,276	904,614	189,658	3,845.6
Publishing industries:					
1997	511	33,896	179,035	43,358	1,006.2
2002		32,239	235,300	64,064	1,132.4
Motion picture and sound recording industries:					
1997	512	22,204	55,926	9,392	276.0
2002	512	22,831	76,732	11,696	334.4
Broadcasting and telecommunications:					
1997	513	43,480	346,316	63,480	1,434.5
2002	513	57,277	499,061	83,690	1,740.4
Information services and data processing services: [2]					
1997	514	14,895	41,937	13,252	349.5
2002	514	24,929	93,521	30,209	638.5

[1] North American Industry Classification System, 1997; see text, Section 15. [2] 2002 data include enterprise support establishments, not included in 1997.

Source: U.S. Census Bureau, 2002 Economic Census, *Advance Report*, issued March 2004. See Internet site: <http://www.census.gov/econ/census02/>.

No. 1114. Information Sector Services—Estimated Revenue: 2000 to 2002

[In millions of dollars (852,886 represents $852,886,000,000), except percent. For taxable and tax-exempt employer and nonemployer firms. Except as indicated, estimates adjusted to the results of the 1997 Economic Census]

Industry	1997 NAICS code [1]	2000	2001	2002	Percent change, 2001-02
Information industries	51	852,886	878,387	885,081	0.8
Publishing industries	511	233,935	233,625	232,869	-0.3
Newspaper, periodical, book, database, and other publishers [2]					
Newspaper publishers	5111	145,774	142,445	143,435	0.7
Periodical publishers	51111	51,711	47,357	47,731	0.8
Book publishers	51112	40,314	39,765	39,341	-1.1
Database and directory publishers	51113	25,481	26,347	27,471	4.3
Other publishers	51114	15,956	16,614	16,665	0.3
Software publishers	51119	12,312	12,361	12,227	-1.1
	5112	88,161	91,180	89,434	-1.9
Motion picture and sound recording industries	512	69,378	70,525	75,672	7.3
Motion picture and video [3]	5121	55,298	56,914	61,735	8.5
Motion picture and video production and distribution	51211,12	40,045	41,207	45,707	10.9
Motion picture and video exhibition	51213	9,956	10,424	11,138	6.8
Sound recording [2]	5122	14,080	13,609	13,937	2.4
Integrated record production/distribution	51222	10,908	10,270	10,466	1.9
Broadcasting and telecommunications	513	470,920	489,328	486,204	-0.6
Radio and television broadcasting	5131	52,992	48,149	52,256	8.5
Radio broadcasting	51311	15,001	13,922	15,069	8.2
Radio networks	513111	1,640	1,555	1,816	16.8
Radio stations	513112	13,361	12,367	13,253	7.2
Television broadcasting	51312	37,991	34,227	37,187	8.6
Cable networks and program distribution [2]	5132	68,110	74,598	80,729	8.2
Cable networks	51321	20,906	21,899	24,073	9.9
Cable and other program distribution	51322	47,203	52,698	56,656	7.5
Telecommunications [3]	5133	349,819	366,581	353,220	-3.6
Wired telecommunications carriers	51331	266,018	262,921	240,134	-8.7
Wireless telecommunications carriers (except satellite) [2]	51332	64,612	83,441	94,884	13.7
Paging	513321	6,908	5,152	3,596	-30.2
Cellular and other wireless telecommunications	513322	57,705	78,288	91,289	16.6
Telecommunications resellers	51333	9,042	8,838	8,806	-0.4
Satellite telecommunications	51334	8,419	9,649	8,058	-16.5
Information services and data processing services	514	78,653	84,908	90,336	6.4
Information services [3]	5141	35,813	36,779	36,397	-1.0
Libraries and archives	51412	1,289	1,267	1,368	8.0
Other information services	51419	32,452	33,458	33,020	-1.3
Online information services	514191	27,515	29,651	28,925	-2.4
Data processing services	5142	42,841	48,129	53,939	12.1

[1] North American Industry Classification System, 1997; see text, this section and Section 15. [2] Estimates not adjusted to the 1997 Economic Census. [3] Includes other industries, not shown separately.

Source: U.S. Census Bureau, *Service Annual Survey: 2002*, SAS/02. See <http://www.census.gov/econ/www/servmenu.html> (released February 2004).

Information and Communications 713

No. 1115. Information Industries—Establishments, Employees, and Payroll: 2000 and 2001

[For establishments with payroll (3,545.7 represents 3,545,700.) Excludes most government employees, railroad employees, and self-employed persons]

Industry	1997 NAICS code [1]	Establishments (number) 2000	2001	Paid employees [2] (1,000) 2000	2001	Annual payroll (mil. dol) 2000	2001
Information industries	51	133,590	137,293	3,545.7	3,754.7	209,394	207,124
Publishing industries	511	32,545	32,111	1,080.7	1,100.9	75,348	68,981
Newspaper, periodical, book, & database publishers.	5111	21,946	21,758	749.2	747.6	31,258	32,026
Newspaper publishers.	51111	8,586	8,540	412.6	414.0	14,216	14,747
Periodical publishers.	51112	6,252	6,248	135.6	133.2	7,676	7,544
Book publishers	51113	2,661	2,698	87.2	89.7	4,310	4,803
Database & directory publishers	51114	1,370	1,394	46.2	45.1	2,418	2,328
Other publishers	51119	3,077	2,878	67.5	65.6	2,637	2,604
Greeting card publishers	511191	112	102	17.8	17.4	631	688
All other publishers	511199	2,965	2,776	49.7	48.2	2,006	1,916
Software publishers	5112	10,599	10,353	331.5	353.3	44,090	36,955
Motion picture & sound recording industries. .	512	22,899	22,782	304.2	297.1	11,736	11,986
Motion picture & video industries	5121	19,730	19,532	276.6	270.1	9,806	10,156
Motion picture & video production	51211	10,018	10,595	84.5	96.9	5,723	6,816
Motion picture & video distribution	51212	678	537	13.9	5.9	1,119	307
Motion picture & video exhibition.	51213	5,884	5,353	144.0	132.7	1,130	1,189
Motion picture theaters (except drive-ins)	512131	5,593	5,050	142.3	130.9	1,107	1,162
Drive-in motion picture theaters	512132	291	303	1.7	1.7	23	26
Post production & other motion picture & video industries	51219	3,150	3,047	34.2	34.7	1,834	1,846
Teleproduction & other postproduction services.	512191	2,816	2,702	29.7	30.2	1,591	1,589
Other motion picture & video industries.	512199	334	345	4.5	4.6	243	257
Sound recording industries	5122	3,169	3,250	27.6	27.0	1,930	1,830
Record production	51221	276	270	1.1	1.2	55	73
Integrated record production/distribution . .	51222	310	305	9.0	8.8	1,100	1,043
Music publishers	51223	670	645	5.1	5.1	283	277
Sound recording studios	51224	1,516	1,621	8.1	8.4	327	313
Other sound recording industries.	51229	397	409	4.3	3.5	166	123
Broadcasting & telecommunications	513	54,971	59,675	1,631.8	1,777.0	88,766	93,960
Radio & television broadcasting	5131	8,492	9,234	253.6	269.4	12,292	12,740
Radio broadcasting.	51311	6,442	7,297	121.5	142.7	4,841	5,381
Radio networks	513111	334	359	9.3	12.2	516	375
Radio stations	513112	6,108	6,938	112.1	130.5	4,325	5,006
Television broadcasting	51312	2,050	1,937	132.2	126.7	7,451	7,359
Cable networks & program distribution . . .	5132	5,270	6,692	212.7	245.4	10,084	11,730
Cable networks	51321	689	887	39.1	41.0	2,654	2,964
Cable & other program distribution	51322	4,581	5,805	173.6	204.4	7,430	8,767
Telecommunications.	5133	41,209	43,749	1,165.5	1,262.2	66,389	69,490
Wired telecommunications carriers	51331	26,223	27,509	870.2	905.5	49,010	50,210
Wireless telecommunications carriers (except satellite).	51332	10,424	11,610	202.5	256.6	11,027	13,368
Paging	513321	4,098	3,900	72.4	72.5	3,396	3,488
Cellular & other wireless telecommunications.	513322	6,326	7,710	130.1	184.1	7,631	9,880
Telecommunications resellers	51333	2,458	2,475	54.6	59.9	3,342	3,218
Satellite telecommunications	51334	728	737	21.3	21.3	1,680	1,492
Other telecommunications	51339	1,379	1,418	16.9	18.9	1,330	1,202
Information services & data processing services.	514	23,175	22,725	529.0	579.6	33,544	32,197
Information services.	5141	14,139	13,437	232.5	262.1	19,023	16,709
News syndicates	51411	567	540	11.3	12.2	648	680
Libraries & archives	51412	2,754	2,725	33.8	36.1	679	920
Other information services	51419	10,818	10,172	187.4	213.7	17,696	15,109
Online information services.	514191	10,257	9,608	177.3	202.1	15,690	14,410
All other information services	514199	561	564	10.1	11.6	2,006	700
Data processing services	5142	9,036	9,288	296.6	317.5	14,521	15,488

[1] North American Industry Classification System, 1997; see text this section. [2] For employees on the payroll for the pay period including March 12.

Source: U.S. Census Bureau, County Business Patterns; 2001 data published 10 April 2003; <http://www.census.gov/epcd/cbp/view/cbpview.html>.

No. 1116. Gross Domestic Income in Information Technologies (IT) Industries: 1999 to 2003

[In millions of dollars (821,683 represents $821,683,000,000), except as noted]

Industry	1997 NAICS [1] code	1999	2000	2001	2002 est.	2003 est.
Total IT-Producing Industries	(X)	821,683	877,813	828,911	831,573	871,875
Percent share of the economy	(X)	8.8	8.8	8.1	7.9	7.9
Hardware	(X)	252,207	244,132	189,362	189,261	208,029
Computers and equipment, calc. machines	(²)	62,263	54,967	46,390	43,700	46,234
Computers and equipment wholesale sales	421430pt.	77,212	72,212	58,796	55,401	58,614
Computer and equipment retail sales	443120pt.	6,431	6,410	5,581	5,785	6,121
Electron tubes	334411	1,758	1,362	1,181	1,324	1,562
Printed circuit boards	334412	5,557	6,627	4,732	5,307	6,259
Semiconductors	334413	68,022	67,897	44,118	49,485	58,360
Passive electronic components	334414,5,6,9	12,658	14,779	11,037	12,380	14,600
Industrial instruments for measurement	334513	4,581	4,802	4,567	4,138	4,242
Instruments for measuring electricity	334515	9,010	10,347	8,237	7,462	7,650
Laboratory analytical instruments	334516	4,715	4,730	4,723	4,279	4,387
Software and services [3]	(X)	278,275	316,600	320,336	323,652	328,798
Computer programming services	541511	56,405	63,262	61,145	61,818	62,693
Prepackaged software	5112,334611	69,063	75,961	77,709	78,564	80,201
Computer integrated system design	541512	66,115	75,137	73,733	74,544	75,600
Computer processing, data preparation	5142	30,029	33,603	37,850	38,266	38,809
Information retrieval services	51419	16,354	25,313	26,156	26,443	26,818
Computer services management	541513	11,883	12,780	14,891	15,055	15,268
Office equipment rental and leasing	532420	7,292	7,847	6,636	6,708	6,804
Computer maintenance and repair	811212	8,480	8,494	8,652	8,747	8,871
Computer related services, n.e.c. [4]	541519	7,497	9,330	9,548	9,653	9,790
Communications hardware [3]	(X)	60,625	67,262	54,890	46,601	43,452
Telephone equipment, exc. ext. modems	334210	32,745	35,843	28,005	23,776	22,087
Radio & TV communications equipment	334220, 90	23,123	26,757	22,752	19,316	17,944
Communications services	(X)	230,576	249,820	264,323	272,058	291,597
Telephone and telegraph communications	5133	193,700	208,000	218,500	224,846	240,980
Cable and other pay TV services	5132	36,876	41,820	45,823	47,212	50,617

X Not applicable. [1] North American Industry Classification System, 1997; see text, Section 15. [2] NAICS 334111,2,3,9,334418pt.,333311.,3pt. [3] Includes industries not shown separately. [4] N.e.c. means not elsewhere classified.

No. 1117. Information Technologies (IT)—Employment and Wages: 2000 to 2002

[110,996 represents 110,996,000]

Industry	2002 NAICS [1] code	Employment (1,000)			Annual wages per worker (dol.)	
		2000	2001	2002	2001	2002
Total private	(X)	110,996	110,707	108,886	36,160	36,520
IT producing industries	(X)	5,381.6	5,350.4	4,779.0	68,330	67,440
Total computer hardware [2]	(X)	1,679.6	1,596.4	1,376.4	69,160	68,740
Electronic computers	334111	168.6	159.3	138.4	95,050	93,020
Computer and software wholesalers	423430	298.4	280.0	251.4	88,530	84,840
Computer and software retailers	443120	191.4	178.9	162.0	53,700	52,870
Bare printed circuit boards	334412	139.5	120.2	83.9	38,680	40,020
Semiconductors and related devices	334413	289.2	292.1	254.8	78,820	75,780
Printed circuit assemblies	334418	64.4	60.8	51.2	47,950	48,010
Miscellaneous electronic components	334415,6,9	121.7	115.1	96.2	43,990	43,820
Industrial process variable instruments	334513	70.1	71.4	61.2	52,290	53,500
Electricity and signal testing instruments	334515	65.8	65.1	54.8	70,240	73,900
Total software and computer services [2]	(X)	2,127.5	2,160.8	1,961.0	75,520	72,940
Software publishers	511210	260.6	268.9	256.0	104,810	99,440
Data processing and related services	518210	315.7	316.8	305.3	55,650	55,820
Custom computer programming services	541511	540.0	562.9	511.8	77,540	76,080
Computer systems design services	541512	502.9	520.3	462.4	75,950	75,070
Computer facilities management services	541513	64.9	64.6	58.4	63,620	60,770
Total communications equipment [2]	(X)	322.0	301.5	248.4	63,420	65,390
Telephone apparatus	334210	106.5	97.2	70.6	70,740	72,940
Broadcast and wireless communications equipment	334220	107.3	102.5	89.1	61,240	63,010
Audio and video equipment	334310	52.1	47.4	41.6	46,790	48,850
Total communications services [2]	(X)	1,252.5	1,291.8	1,193.1	56,390	57,220
Wired telecommunications carriers	517110	719.2	732.2	662.4	59,270	60,810
Telecommunications resellers	517310	213.6	214.1	185.7	55,110	56,790
Cable and other program distribution	517510	123.0	129.2	128.0	42,560	43,430

X Not applicable. [1] North American Industry Classification System, 2002; see text, Section 15. [2] Includes other industries, not shown separately.

Source of tables 1116 and 1117: U.S. Department of Commerce, Economics and Statistics Administration, *The Digital Economy 2003*, December 2003. See Internet site: <http://www.esa.doc.gov/DigitalEconomy2003.cfm>.

Information and Communications 715

No. 1118. Communications Industry—Finances: 1999 to 2002

[In millions of dollars (242,512 represents $242,512,000,000). Covers 299 publicly reporting media and communications companies with revenues of over $1 million in 12 media and communication industry segments. Minus sign (-) indicates loss]

Industry	Revenue				Operating income			
	1999	2000	2001	2002	1999	2000	2001	2002
Total	242,512	280,506	288,670	308,597	27,831	30,707	12,393	-14,243
Advertising, marketing services and specialty media [1]	39,546	45,016	46,422	47,250	7,624	7,347	7,481	7,570
Marketing services holding companies	22,011	24,656	25,640	26,389	2,403	3,052	2,281	2,221
Telephone directory publishing	10,275	10,654	10,978	10,936	4,907	4,567	4,919	4,696
Specialty media	2,716	3,084	3,310	3,340	331	422	430	350
Broadcast television	27,119	31,902	31,660	34,318	4,815	6,126	4,850	5,660
Television network companies	20,430	24,282	24,674	26,697	2,956	3,892	3,411	3,498
Television station broadcasters	6,689	7,620	6,986	7,622	1,859	2,234	1,439	2,162
Cable and satellite television	40,343	54,091	62,734	69,068	981	4,638	-7,418	-12,296
Cable and satellite providers	27,882	39,640	46,942	52,166	-825	4,436	-7,944	-12,308
Cable and satellite networks	12,461	14,451	15,792	16,901	1,806	202	526	13
Radio broadcasting	5,729	8,024	10,212	10,824	1,276	1,293	368	3,605
Entertainment	47,367	49,166	45,742	52,408	3,119	2,023	1,400	2,459
Filmed entertainment	28,137	28,707	29,167	32,935	1,203	1,247	1,187	2,292
Recorded music	10,639	11,404	9,315	9,995	434	34	-341	-1,138
Consumer Internet	6,685	10,872	11,574	12,381	-714	835	-490	-33,135
Internet service providers	5,581	8,640	9,912	10,491	-176	1,632	2,280	-32,623
Newspaper publishing	24,418	25,440	23,905	23,703	5,374	5,419	4,010	5,005
Consumer book publishing	4,355	4,531	4,837	4,861	262	484	547	495
Consumer magazine publishing	8,644	8,634	8,867	9,441	345	226	381	1,278
Business-to-business communications	2,370	2,545	2,272	1,999	18	374	5	-192
Professional, educational and training media [1]	12,018	13,683	12,030	13,505	1,236	1,379	969	1,516
Professional and educational media	8,084	9,162	6,738	7,455	991	1,223	726	1,131
Business information services [1]	23,917	26,604	28,417	28,837	3,495	563	290	3,791
Financial information	13,676	14,684	15,463	15,812	2,619	2,360	2,656	2,585
Healthcare information	3,861	4,564	4,829	5,027	174	-2,220	-2,388	549

[1] Includes other industries, not shown separately.

No. 1119. Media Usage and Consumer Spending: 1999 to 2007

[Estimates of time spent were derived using rating data for television, cable and satellite television and radio, survey research and consumer purchase data (units, admissions, access) for books, home video, Internet, interactive TV, magazines, movies in theaters, newspapers, recorded music, and video games. Adults 18 and older were the basis for estimates for television, cable & satellite television, daily newspapers, consumer books, consumer magazines, home video and interactive TV. Persons 12 and older were the basis for estimates for radio, recorded music, movies in theaters, video games and consumer Internet]

Item	1999	2000	2001	2002	2003, proj.	2004, proj.	2005, proj.	2006, proj.	2007, proj.
HOURS PER PERSON PER YEAR									
Total	3,444	3,505	3,534	3,599	3,660	3,732	3,789	3,811	3,874
Television	1,588	1,640	1,672	1,701	1,726	1,749	1,770	1,763	1,785
Broadcast TV [1]	867	865	828	786	778	773	772	756	759
Network stations [1]	706	805	766	724	715	711	709	693	697
Independent stations [1]	162	61	62	62	62	62	63	63	63
Cable & satellite TV	720	774	844	914	949	976	999	1,007	1,026
Basic cable and satellite TV [1]	617	638	697	758	789	812	830	834	845
Premium cable and satellite TV [1]	103	137	147	156	159	164	168	173	180
Sateulite radio	939	945	953	994	1,013	1,046	1,068	1,074	1,098
Box office [2][3]	13	12	13	14	13	13	14	14	14
Home video [2][3]	55	57	60	58	67	73	83	91	98
Interactive TV [4]	1	2	2	2	2	3	4	4	5
Recorded music [2]	281	258	229	201	188	179	166	163	152
Video games [2]	53	59	60	67	75	84	90	98	109
Consumer Internet [2]	80	107	136	154	169	182	193	205	216
Daily newspapers [2]	183	180	177	176	173	171	171	169	168
Consumer books [2]	119	109	106	109	110	107	109	109	108
Consumer magazines [2]	134	135	128	125	123	122	122	121	119
CONSUMER SPENDING PER PERSON PER YEAR (dol.)									
Total	611.17	632.83	673.38	721.03	764.83	809.44	851.44	895.26	941.07
Television	177.67	187.93	202.73	222.20	235.52	249.18	258.74	271.55	283.09
Cable and satellite TV [1]	177.67	187.93	202.73	222.20	235.52	249.18	258.74	271.55	283.09
Basic cable & satellite networks [1]	132.60	144.24	155.16	170.47	181.12	192.68	198.98	208.18	217.96
Premium cable & satellite services [2]	45.08	43.70	47.57	51.73	54.41	56.51	59.77	63.37	65.13
Satellite radio [2]	-	-	-	0.07	0.52	1.40	2.98	4.82	6.47
Box office [2][3]	32.15	32.75	35.45	39.68	39.35	41.07	43.99	46.46	50.26
Home video [2][3]	95.17	100.72	108.40	113.88	126.86	136.38	147.92	156.86	169.02
Interactive TV [4]	2.14	2.38	2.90	3.47	4.72	6.21	7.43	8.34	9.53
Recorded music [2]	62.95	61.24	57.92	52.58	50.23	47.62	45.21	44.40	41.06
Video games [2]	26.34	25.89	26.89	30.47	34.95	39.14	42.45	46.48	51.58
Consumer Internet [2]	40.55	49.64	68.70	84.73	97.76	110.46	122.67	134.25	145.26
Daily newspapers [2]	52.63	52.48	52.84	53.35	53.22	54.02	54.61	55.15	56.06
Consumer books [2]	87.34	86.13	84.45	87.89	90.07	91.26	92.27	93.80	95.62
Consumer magazines [2]	47.98	47.70	46.96	42.01	46.43	47.91	48.55	48.54	48.66

- Represents zero. [1] UPN, WB, and PAX affiliates included in network-affiliated stations, superstations included in basic cable, and pay-per-view included in premium service. [2] Does not include Internet-related use of traditional media. Some examples include: listening to downloaded music directly on the computer or from a burned disc on a MP3 player, reading a downloaded e-book, listening to a radio station transmitted by a Windows media player, and reading a Web-based newspaper article. Such activities are included in the time spent data under consumer Internet, which was originally provided on a traditional media. [3] Playback of prerecorded VHS cassettes and DVDs only. [4] Video-on-demand (VOD) only. Personal video recorders (PVRs) included in total TV.

Source of tables 1118 and 1119: Veronis Suhler Stevenson, New York, NY, Communications Industry Forecast & Report, annual (copyright).

716 Information and Communications

No. 1120. Utilization of Selected Media: 1970 to 2002

[62.0 represents 62,000,000]

Item	Unit	1970	1980	1990	1995	1997	1998	1999	2000	2001	2002
Households with—											
Telephone service [1]	Percent	87.0	93.0	93.3	93.9	93.9	94.1	94.0	94.6	94.6	95.5
Radio [2]	Millions	62.0	78.6	94.4	98.0	98.0	(NA)	(NA)	(NA)	(NA)	(NA)
Percent of total households	Percent	98.6	99.0	99.0	99.0	99.0	99.0	99.0	99.0	99.0	99.0
Average number of sets	Number	5.1	5.5	5.6	5.6	5.6	5.6	5.6	5.6	(NA)	(NA)
Television [3]	Millions	59	76	92	95	97	98	99	101	102	106
Percent of total households	Percent	95.3	97.9	98.2	98.3	98.4	98.3	98.2	98.2	98.2	98.2
Television sets in homes	Millions	81	128	193	217	229	235	240	245	248	254
Average number of sets per home	Number	1.4	1.7	2.0	2.3	2.4	2.4	2.4	2.4	2.4	2.4
Color set households	Millions	21	63	90	94	97	98	99	101	102	105
Cable television [4]	Millions	4	15	52	60	64	66	67	69	69	73
Percent of TV households	Percent	6.7	19.9	56.4	63.4	66.5	67.2	67.5	68.0	68.0	69.4
VCRs [4]	Millions	(NA)	1	63	77	82	83	84	86	88	96
Percent of TV households	Percent	(NA)	1.1	68.6	81.0	84.2	84.6	84.6	85.1	86.2	91.2
Commercial radio stations: [2]											
AM	Number	4,323	4,589	4,987	4,909	4,762	4,793	4,783	4,685	4,727	4,804
FM	Number	2,196	3,282	4,392	5,296	5,542	5,662	5,766	5,892	6,051	6,161
Television stations: [5] Total	Number	862	1,011	1,442	1,532	1,564	1,589	1,615	1,663	1,686	1,714
Commercial	Number	677	734	1,092	1,161	1,195	1,221	1,243	1,288	1,309	1,333
VHF	Number	501	516	547	562	555	561	561	567	572	581
UHF	Number	176	218	545	599	640	660	682	721	737	752
Cable television:											
Systems [6]	Number	2,490	4,225	9,575	11,218	10,950	10,845	10,700	10,243	9,924	9,339
Households served [7]	Millions	4.5	17.7	54.9	63.0	65.9	67.0	74.9	76.5	79.5	85.5
Daily newspaper circulation [8]	Millions	62.1	62.2	62.3	58.2	56.7	56.2	56.0	55.8	55.6	55.2

NA Not available. [1] For occupied housing units. 1970 and 1980 as of April 1; all other years as of March. Source: U.S. Census Bureau, *1970* and *1980 Census of Housing*, vol. 1; thereafter Federal Communications Commission, *Trends in Telephone Service*, annual. [2] 1970-1995 as of December 31. Source: M Street Corp. as reported by Radio Advertising Bureau New York, NY, through 1990, *Radio Facts*, annual (copyright); 1995, *Radio Marketing Guide and Fact Book for Advertisers*, annual (copyright). Number of stations on the air compiled from Federal Communications Commission reports. Beginning 1997, Federal Communications Commission, unpublished data as of Sept. 30. See Internet site <http://www.fcc.gov/mb/audio/totals>. [3] 1970, as of September of prior year; all other years as of January of year shown. Excludes Alaska and Hawaii. Source: Television Bureau of Advertising, Inc., *Trends in Television*, annual (copyright). [4] As of February. Excludes Alaska and Hawaii. Source: See footnote 3. [5] Source: Beginning 1997, Federal Communications Commission, unpublished data. See Internet site <http://www.fcc.gov/mb/audio/totals>. 1997 and 1998 as of December; beginning 1999, as of September. For prior years data, see footnote 3. [6] As of January 1. Source: Warren Communications News, Washington DC, *Television and Cable Factbook* (copyright). [7] Source: Nielsen Media Research, New York, NY, (copyright). [8] As of September 30. Source: Editor & Publisher, Co., New York, NY, *Editor & Publisher International Year Book*, annual (copyright).
Source: Compiled from sources mentioned in footnotes.

No. 1121. Multimedia Audiences—Summary: 2003

[In percent, except total (206,900 represents 206,900,000). As of fall. For persons 18 years old and over. Represents the percent of persons participating during the prior week, except as indicated. Based on sample and subject to sampling error; see source for details]

Item	Total population (1,000)	Television viewing	Television prime time viewing	Cable viewing [1]	Radio listening	Newspaper reading	Accessed Internet [2]
Total	206,900	94.3	83.3	76.6	84.2	79.8	59.8
18 to 24 years old	27,172	93.0	77.0	73.3	90.0	74.8	73.1
25 to 34 years old	38,085	93.0	81.4	76.1	91.3	77.4	71.9
35 to 44 years old	44,563	93.1	82.2	77.5	90.3	80.8	68.5
45 to 54 years old	38,789	94.2	84.9	78.8	85.3	82.0	66.2
55 to 64 years old	24,854	96.0	86.2	81.0	81.6	81.9	53.6
65 years old and over	33,437	97.2	87.8	72.5	64.1	81.4	20.9
Male	99,258	94.6	83.5	76.9	85.9	80.0	60.6
Female	107,642	94.0	83.0	76.3	82.7	79.7	59.1
White	173,897	94.1	83.2	77.6	84.6	79.8	60.8
Black	24,218	96.4	86.0	71.4	84.0	83.4	48.2
Asian	5,366	90.5	75.7	68.3	78.5	69.8	76.4
Other	3,419	92.4	78.8	72.3	78.3	75.0	67.9
Spanish speaking [3]	25,792	94.4	81.4	69.9	85.9	64.7	47.4
Not high school graduate	34,784	94.0	81.3	64.7	74.0	61.7	21.1
High school graduate	66,320	95.4	85.4	78.3	83.0	79.8	45.8
Attended college	56,111	94.2	83.0	79.2	88.2	83.8	74.9
College graduate	49,685	92.9	82.0	79.5	88.7	88.1	88.5
Employed:							
Full time	110,707	93.6	82.5	79.5	91.0	81.8	72.0
Part time	21,788	93.1	81.3	76.4	88.8	80.5	70.0
Not employed	74,405	95.6	84.9	72.3	72.9	76.7	38.7
Household income:							
Less than $10,000	12,433	91.3	78.7	55.3	69.1	63.3	24.4
$10,000 to $19,999	21,824	95.8	84.4	63.5	73.4	69.4	26.0
$20,000 to $29,999	23,868	94.3	83.3	68.2	79.0	74.2	37.1
$30,000 to $34,999	11,797	94.4	83.6	70.4	79.8	74.2	45.9
$35,000 to $39,999	11,209	95.3	83.9	73.5	83.1	78.5	52.1
$40,000 to $49,999	20,895	94.6	83.4	76.6	87.6	81.0	58.4
$50,000 or more	104,874	94.1	83.4	84.7	89.4	85.7	78.9

[1] In the past 7 days. [2] In the last 30 days. [3] English-capable household.
Source: Mediamark Research Inc., New York, NY, *Multimedia Audiences*, fall 2003 (copyright).

Information and Communications 717

No. 1122. Newspapers and Periodicals—Number by Type: 1980 to 2002

[Data refer to year of compilation of the directory cited as the source, i.e., generally to year preceding year shown. Data for 1995 and prior years include Canada and Mexico]

Type	1980	1985	1990	1995	1997	1998	1999	2000	2001	2002
Newspapers [1]	9,620	9,134	11,471	12,246	10,042	10,504	10,530	10,696	10,739	10,855
Semiweekly	537	517	579	705	558	557	560	558	573	555
Weekly	7,159	6,811	8,420	9,011	7,191	7,267	7,471	7,594	7,622	7,440
Daily	1,744	1,701	1,788	1,710	1,582	1,461	1,647	1,661	1,656	1,507
Periodicals [1]	10,236	11,090	11,092	11,179	8,530	12,448	11,751	13,019	13,878	13,846
Weekly	1,716	1,367	553	513	350	382	366	402	407	393
Monthly	3,985	4,088	4,239	4,067	3,067	3,378	3,204	3,572	3,636	3,605
Bimonthly	1,114	1,361	2,087	2,568	1,943	2,184	2,034	2,294	2,358	2,328
Quarterly	1,444	1,759	2,758	3,621	2,893	3,386	3,158	3,578	3,814	3,826

[1] Includes other items not shown separately.

Source: Gale Group, Farmington Hills, MI, Gale Directory of Publications and Broadcast Media, annual (copyright).

No. 1123. Newspaper, Periodical, Database and Directory Publishers—Estimated Revenue, Printing Expenses and Inventories: 2000 to 2002

[In millions of dollars (51,507 represents $51,507,000,000). For taxable and tax-exempt employer firms. Estimates have not been adjusted to the results of the 1997 Economic Census. Based on the North American Industry Classification System, 1997; see text, this section and Section 15]

Item	Newspaper publishers (NAICS 51111)			Periodical publishers (NAICS 51112)			Database and directory publishers (NAICS 51114)		
	2000	2001	2002	2000	2001	2002	2000	2001	2002
Revenue [1]	51,507	47,153	47,524	39,834	39,266	38,844	16,657	16,512	15,564
Print	(NA)	42,134	42,099	(NA)	31,033	30,404	(NA)	11,856	11,748
Subscription and sales	(NA)	9,314	9,436	(NA)	13,073	12,971	(NA)	693	622
Advertising	(NA)	32,820	32,664	(NA)	17,960	17,434	(NA)	11,162	11,126
Internet	(NA)	410	597	(NA)	1,302	1,333	(NA)	433	(S)
Subscription and sales	(NA)	(S)	(S)	(NA)	888	928	(NA)	(S)	(S)
Advertising	(NA)	303	466	(NA)	(S)	(S)	(NA)	192	(S)
Contract printing	(NA)	1,770	1,749	(NA)	922	690	(NA)	201	(S)
Distribution of flyers, inserts, etc.	(NA)	930	1,020	(NA)	105	118	(NA)	(NA)	(NA)
Graphic design services	(NA)	(S)	(S)	(NA)	(S)	(S)	(NA)	98	(S)
Sales or licensing of rights of content	(NA)	69	45	(NA)	221	240	(NA)	1,051	1,162
Rental or sales of mailing lists	(NA)	13	(S)	(NA)	160	168	(NA)	31	29
Publishing services for others	(NA)	11	12	(NA)	339	(S)	(NA)	(S)	(S)
Expenses: Purchased printing	3,352	2,639	2,412	4,981	4,426	4,246	1,112	1,229	(S)
Inventories at end of year	786	748	717	1,340	1,634	1,671	398	374	(S)
Finished goods and work-in-process	51	63	80	879	1,223	1,252	370	355	(S)
Materials, supplies, fuel, etc	736	685	636	462	411	419	(S)	19	(S)

NA Not available.   S Data do not meet publication standards.   [1] Includes other sources of revenue, not shown separately.

Source: U.S. Census Bureau, Service Annual Survey: 2002, SAS/02 and prior issues. See <http://www.census.gov/econ/www/servmenu.html> (released February 2004).

No. 1124. Daily and Sunday Newspapers—Number and Circulation: 1970 to 2003

[Number of newspapers as of February 1 the following year. Circulation figures as of September 30 of year shown (62.1 represents 62,100,000). For English language newspapers only]

Type	1970	1975	1980	1985	1990	1995	1998	1999	2000	2001	2002	2003
NUMBER												
Daily: Total [1]	1,748	1,756	1,745	1,676	1,611	1,533	1,489	1,483	1,480	1,468	1,457	1,456
Morning	334	339	387	482	559	656	721	736	766	776	777	787
Evening	1,429	1,436	1,388	1,220	1,084	891	781	760	727	704	692	680
Sunday	586	639	736	798	863	888	898	905	917	913	913	917
CIRCULATION (mil.)												
Daily: Total [1]	62.1	60.7	62.2	62.8	62.3	58.2	56.2	56.0	55.8	55.6	55.2	55.2
Morning	25.9	25.5	29.4	36.4	41.3	44.3	45.6	46.0	46.8	46.8	46.6	46.9
Evening	36.2	35.2	32.8	26.4	21.0	13.9	10.5	10.0	9.0	8.8	8.6	8.3
Sunday	49.2	51.1	54.7	58.8	62.6	61.5	60.1	59.9	59.4	59.1	58.8	58.5
PER CAPITA CIRCULATION [2]												
Daily: Total [1]	0.30	0.28	0.27	0.26	0.25	0.22	0.20	0.20	0.20	0.20	0.19	0.19
Morning	0.13	0.12	0.13	0.15	0.17	0.17	0.17	0.16	0.17	0.16	0.16	0.16
Evening	0.18	0.16	0.14	0.11	0.08	0.05	0.04	0.04	0.03	0.03	0.03	0.03
Sunday	0.24	0.24	0.24	0.25	0.25	0.23	0.22	0.21	0.21	0.21	0.20	0.20

[1] All-day newspapers are counted in both morning and evening columns but only once in total. Circulation is divided equally between morning and evening.   [2] Based on U.S. Census Bureau estimated resident population as of July 1, except 2000, enumerated resident population as of April 1.

Source: Editor & Publisher Co., New York, NY, Editor & Publisher International Year Book, annual (copyright).

U.S. Census Bureau, Statistical Abstract of the United States: 2004-2005

No. 1125. Daily Newspapers—Number and Circulation by Size of City: 1980 to 2003

[Number of newspapers as of February 1 the following year. Circulation as of September 30 (29,413 represents 29,413,000). For English language newspapers only. See Table 26 for number of cities by population size. All-day newspapers are counted in both morning and evening columns; circulation is divided equally between morning and evening]

Type of daily and population-size class	Number					Net paid circulation (1,000)				
	1980	1990	1995	2000	2003	1980	1990	1995	2000	2003
Morning dailies, total . .	**387**	**559**	**656**	**766**	**787**	**29,413**	**41,311**	**44,310**	**46,772**	**46,930**
In cities of—										
1,000,001 or more	20	18	25	26	27	8,795	6,508	10,173	10,820	10,937
500,001 to 1,000,000.	27	22	22	25	32	5,705	4,804	5,587	5,412	6,625
100,001 to 500,000.	99	138	153	163	158	8,996	20,051	17,214	17,469	16,618
50,001 to 100,000.	75	100	138	162	160	2,973	4,373	5,602	5,887	5,477
25,001 to 50,000	64	102	115	141	149	1,701	3,209	3,150	3,899	3,906
Less than 25,000	102	179	203	249	261	1,243	2,365	2,584	3,285	3,366
Evening dailies, total . .	**1,388**	**1,084**	**891**	**727**	**680**	**32,788**	**21,017**	**13,883**	**9,000**	**8,255**
In cities of—										
1,000,001 or more	11	7	3	1	1	2,984	1,423	390	1	1
500,001 to 1,000,000.	23	12	7	3	6	4,101	1,350	1,017	519	812
100,001 to 500,000.	123	71	45	32	27	8,178	4,687	2,529	1,603	1,324
50,001 to 100,000.	156	94	72	54	44	4,896	2,941	2,029	1,332	1,122
25,001 to 50,000	246	204	158	124	116	5,106	4,278	2,819	1,898	1,709
Less than 25,000	829	696	606	513	486	7,523	6,338	5,099	3,648	3,286

Source: Editor & Publisher Co., New York, NY, *Editor & Publisher International Year Book*, annual (copyright).

No. 1126. Daily and Sunday Newspapers—Number and Circulation, 1991 to 2002 and by State, 2003

[Number of newspapers as of February 1 the following year. Circulation as of September 30 (60,687 represents 60,687,000). For English language newspapers only. California, New York, Massachusetts, and Virginia Sunday newspapers include national circulation]

State	Daily			Sunday		State	Daily			Sunday	
		Circulation [1]			Net paid circulation			Circulation [1]			Net paid circulation
	Number	Net paid (1,000)	Per capita [2]	Number	(1,000)		Number	Net paid (1,000)	Per capita [2]	Number	(1,000)
Total, 1991	1,586	60,687	0.24	875	62,068	Louisiana	26	698	0.16	21	770
Total, 1992	1,570	60,164	0.23	891	62,160	Maine.	7	229	0.18	4	193
Total, 1993	1,556	59,812	0.23	884	62,566	Maryland	13	595	0.11	9	808
Total, 1994	1,548	59,305	0.23	886	62,294	Massachusetts. .	32	1,571	0.24	16	1,520
Total, 1995	1,533	58,193	0.22	888	61,529	Michigan.	48	1,655	0.16	27	1,893
Total, 1996	1,520	56,983	0.21	890	60,798	Minnesota.	25	864	0.17	15	1,155
Total, 1997	1,509	56,728	0.21	903	60,484	Mississippi	23	367	0.13	18	369
Total, 1998	1,489	56,182	0.20	898	60,066	Missouri	43	936	0.16	23	1,155
Total, 1999	1,483	55,979	0.20	905	59,894	Montana.	11	186	0.20	7	185
Total, 2000	1,480	55,773	0.20	917	59,421	Nebraska	17	408	0.23	6	390
Total, 2001	1,468	55,578	0.19	913	59,090	Nevada	8	297	0.13	4	326
Total, 2002	1,457	55,186	0.19	913	58,780	New Hampshire .	11	219	0.17	8	227
						New Jersey	18	1,316	0.15	15	1,619
Total, 2003	1,456	55,185	0.19	917	58,495	New Mexico . . .	18	280	0.15	13	286
Alabama.	24	631	0.14	20	708	New York . . .	59	6,985	0.36	38	5,494
Alaska.	7	107	0.16	5	124	North Carolina. .	47	1,311	0.16	39	1,448
Arizona.	16	768	0.14	11	881	North Dakota. . .	10	161	0.25	7	165
Arkansas	28	468	0.17	16	539	Ohio	84	2,324	0.20	41	2,607
California	91	5,853	0.16	62	6,724	Oklahoma.	43	623	0.18	36	764
Colorado.	30	1,021	0.22	15	1,177	Oregon.	19	663	0.19	12	702
Connecticut. . . .	17	685	0.20	13	793	Pennsylvania. . .	82	2,656	0.21	41	3,065
Delaware	2	133	0.16	2	165	Rhode Island. . .	6	220	0.20	3	266
District of Columbia	2	835	1.48	2	1,077	South Carolina. .	16	614	0.15	14	704
Florida	40	3,029	0.18	37	3,839	South Dakota. .	11	154	0.20	4	135
Georgia	32	977	0.11	27	1,264	Tennessee	25	828	0.14	17	1,012
Hawaii	6	267	0.21	6	303	Texas.	84	2,851	0.13	81	3,772
Idaho	12	206	0.15	8	228	Utah	6	332	0.14	6	360
Illinois	66	2,350	0.19	31	2,457	Vermont	8	119	0.19	3	93
Indiana	68	1,266	0.20	25	1,253	Virginia.	25	3,154	0.43	17	1,159
Iowa	37	601	0.20	12	620	Washington. . . .	23	1,077	0.18	17	1,227
Kansas	43	410	0.15	14	369	West Virginia. . .	20	337	0.19	12	346
Kentucky	23	583	0.14	14	620	Wisconsin.	35	877	0.16	18	1,068
						Wyoming	9	87	0.17	5	70

[1] Circulation figures based on the principal community served by a newspaper which is not necessarily the same location as the publisher's office.   [2] Per capita based on estimated resident population as of July 1, except 2000, enumerated resident population as of April 1.

Source: Editor & Publisher Co., New York, NY, *Editor & Publisher International Year Book*, annual (copyright).

U.S. Census Bureau, Statistical Abstract of the United States: 2004-2005

No. 1127. Periodicals—Average Retail Prices: 2000 to 2004

[In dollars. Reflects prices for an annual subscription]

Subject	2000	2001	2002	2003	2004
Agriculture	519	546	583	638	714
Anthropology	244	237	259	291	319
Art and architecture	108	113	116	125	136
Astronomy	1,153	1,213	1,396	1,451	1,602
Biology	998	1,062	1,137	1,253	1,377
Botany	785	826	875	947	1,048
Business and economics	412	457	501	555	614
Chemistry	1,995	2,137	2,337	2,501	2,695
Education	248	275	301	330	371
Engineering and technology	1,076	1,170	1,274	1,377	1,491
Food science	787	855	898	969	1,080
General science	678	732	803	887	962
General works	82	84	88	99	116
Geography	592	633	711	774	859
Geology	789	846	906	982	1,071
Health sciences	702	758	812	889	975
History	116	124	131	148	166
Language and literature	107	115	124	138	153
Law	157	169	187	203	222
Library and information science	254	271	290	319	354
Math and computer science	881	946	1,010	1,080	1,171
Military and naval science	289	315	310	337	365
Music	80	83	92	100	106
Philosophy and religion	143	150	164	182	200
Physics	1,865	1,996	2,180	2,351	2,543
Political science	226	257	279	312	360
Psychology	306	336	368	399	446
Recreation	113	126	144	154	167
Sociology	274	306	336	371	422
Technology	958	1,044	1,140	1,241	1,350
Zoology	701	743	803	870	918

Source: Library Journal, New York, NY, *Library Journal*, April 15, 2004. (Copyright 2004, used with permission of Library Journal, a publication of Reed Business Information, a division of Reed Elsevier).

No. 1128. Quantity of Books Sold and Value of U.S. Domestic Consumer Expenditures: 2000 to 2004

[2,332 represents 2,332,000,000. Includes all titles released by publishers in the United States and imports which appear under the imprints of American publishers. Multivolume sets, such as encyclopedias, are counted as one unit]

Type of publication	Net publishers shipments [1] (mil.)					Domestic consumer expenditures (mil. dol.)				
	2000	2001	2002	2003	2004, proj.	2000	2001	2002	2003	2004, proj.
Total	2,332	2,221	2,245	2,222	2,249	36,136	36,060	36,796	37,908	38,999
Trade	1,156	1,080	1,089	1,071	1,102	11,583	11,277	11,496	11,786	12,284
Adult	564	546	550	536	530	8,124	8,062	8,288	8,401	8,540
Hardback	279	265	267	266	263	4,754	4,650	4,914	4,989	5,079
Paperback	286	281	283	270	267	3,370	3,411	3,374	3,411	3,461
Juvenile	592	535	539	535	572	3,459	3,215	3,208	3,386	3,745
Hardback	234	175	177	184	194	2,126	1,644	1,601	1,762	1,926
Paperback	358	359	362	350	377	1,333	1,571	1,607	1,624	1,819
Mass market paperbacks-rack sized	421	407	411	406	404	2,935	2,911	2,967	2,998	3,052
Bookclubs	112	112	113	112	112	1,753	1,795	1,800	1,843	1,904
Hardback	36	36	37	37	37	1,387	1,418	1,420	1,454	1,502
Paperback	75	75	76	75	75	366	377	380	389	402
Mail order publications	68	54	55	56	54	577	491	510	531	531
Religious	133	136	138	138	137	2,783	2,913	2,970	3,208	3,260
Hardback	52	53	54	54	54	1,665	1,745	1,765	1,905	1,931
Paperback	81	83	84	84	84	1,118	1,168	1,205	1,303	1,329
Professional	187	169	170	171	171	6,340	5,858	6,104	6,295	6,446
Hardback	72	65	65	65	65	4,622	4,264	4,334	4,470	4,578
Paperback	116	104	105	106	106	1,718	1,593	1,770	1,825	1,869
University press	18	18	18	18	18	541	533	534	539	560
Hardback	6	5	5	5	5	263	258	262	264	271
Paperback	13	12	12	12	12	275	275	272	276	289
Elhi text	152	159	162	161	161	4,373	4,714	4,497	4,568	4,698
Hardback	58	61	62	57	62	2,383	2,565	2,445	2,281	2,554
Paperback	94	98	100	104	100	1,991	2,150	2,052	2,287	2,143
College text	83	86	88	89	89	4,265	4,571	4,899	5,086	5,236
Hardback	37	39	39	40	40	2,851	3,085	3,287	3,408	3,508
Paperback	46	48	49	49	49	1,414	1,486	1,612	1,678	1,727
Subscription reference	1	1	1	1	1	986	999	1,020	1,045	1,067

[1] Net, after returns.

Source: Book Industry Study Group, Inc., New York, NY, *Book Industry Trends, 2004*, annual (copyright).

No. 1129. American Book Title Production: 2000 and 2002

[Data compiled from R.R. Bowker's Books in Print database. Includes the output of small presses and self publishers]

Subject	Total		Hardcover		Mass market [1]		Trade [2]	
	2000	2002, prel.	2000	2002, prel.	2000	2002, prel.	2000	2002, prel.
Total	122,117	120,106	53,947	51,897	7,350	5,447	60,820	62,762
Agriculture	1,073	888	563	453	8	1	502	434
Art	4,980	4,483	2,447	2,195	19	23	2,514	2,265
Biography	3,899	5,052	2,017	2,444	96	74	1,786	2,534
Business	4,069	4,571	1,588	1,869	20	6	2,461	2,696
Education	3,379	3,658	1,107	1,202	15	32	2,257	2,424
Fiction	14,615	15,133	4,250	4,309	4,020	2,384	6,345	8,440
General works	1,318	1,470	639	699	12	19	667	752
History	7,931	6,827	4,137	3,122	36	47	3,758	3,658
Home economics	2,513	2,161	1,081	902	48	24	1,384	1,235
Juvenile	8,691	9,545	5,119	6,346	2,358	2,183	1,214	1,016
Language	2,535	2,420	1,143	936	35	66	1,357	1,418
Law	3,070	2,206	1,400	1,112	5	3	1,665	1,091
Literature	3,372	3,946	1,776	1,982	64	62	1,532	1,902
Medicine	6,235	5,949	2,845	2,652	77	41	3,313	3,256
Music	1,582	1,615	619	582	17	11	946	1,022
Philosophy, psychology	5,556	6,012	2,321	2,331	127	112	3,108	3,569
Poetry and drama	2,479	2,812	708	844	39	17	1,732	1,951
Religion	6,210	6,664	2,629	2,532	85	111	3,496	4,021
Science	8,465	7,043	5,222	4,098	52	56	3,191	2,889
Sociology, economics	14,909	13,829	6,981	6,786	89	74	7,839	6,969
Sports, recreation	3,483	3,569	1,254	1,219	91	62	2,138	2,288
Technology	8,582	7,926	3,449	2,799	16	17	5,117	5,110
Travel	3,171	2,327	652	483	21	22	2,498	1,822

[1] "Pocket-sized" books sold primarily through magazine and news outlets, supermarkets, variety stores, etc. [2] All paperbound books, except mass market.

Source: Information Today, Inc., Medford, NJ, *The Bowker Annual Library and Book Trade Almanac, 2004.* (Copyright 2004 by Information Today, Inc.)

No. 1130. Average Per Volume Book Prices: 2000 and 2002

[In dollars. Data compiled from R.R. Bowker's Books in Print database. Includes the output of small presses and self publishers]

Subject	Hardcover		Mass market [1]		Trade [2]	
	2000	2002, prel.	2000	2002, prel.	2000	2002, prel.
Total	60.84	59.80	5.77	6.48	31.07	29.42
Agriculture	66.52	63.88	7.48	7.95	41.31	26.31
Art	50.31	53.86	7.26	8.27	26.96	27.23
Biography	45.31	44.00	6.71	6.61	19.47	21.55
Business	93.84	93.14	8.41	7.80	52.00	50.81
Education	62.23	55.22	7.30	6.51	28.43	29.20
Fiction	25.75	28.01	5.78	6.81	15.90	17.20
General works	165.39	155.05	6.57	8.11	39.84	46.25
History	54.01	54.44	7.36	6.81	27.24	25.44
Home economics	39.76	31.75	7.07	7.69	18.95	18.72
Juvenile	22.71	21.18	5.21	5.72	20.78	18.44
Language	57.27	66.12	6.92	6.50	26.52	30.92
Law	101.50	94.66	8.77	7.66	51.87	42.59
Literature	55.17	64.70	6.71	7.94	20.53	25.28
Medicine	90.32	95.52	6.70	7.33	35.72	44.16
Music	42.91	53.80	7.24	7.52	22.49	21.91
Philosophy, psychology	52.02	59.73	7.24	7.41	21.60	22.95
Poetry and drama	39.90	46.32	6.09	7.23	16.26	16.96
Religion	41.61	44.17	8.16	8.40	18.38	19.43
Science	90.11	96.35	6.58	6.29	40.29	45.51
Sociology, economics	66.79	68.29	6.99	7.67	41.22	29.53
Sports, recreation	40.64	41.85	6.66	8.18	20.76	20.81
Technology	102.40	88.16	6.71	7.92	56.22	54.40
Travel	40.27	41.71	8.65	9.04	22.45	19.52

[1] "Pocket-sized" books sold primarily through magazine and news outlets, supermarkets, variety stores, etc. [2] All paperbound books, except mass market.

Source: Information Today, Inc., Medford, NJ, *The Bowker Annual Library and Book Trade Almanac, 2004.* (Copyright 2004 by Information Today, Inc.)

No. 1131. Book Publishers—Estimated Revenue, Printing Expenses, and Inventories: 1998 to 2002

[In millions of dollars (22,480 represents $22,480,000,000). For taxable and tax-exempt employer firms. For NAICS 51113. Estimates have not been adjusted to the results of the 1997 Economic Census. Based on the North American Industry Classification; System, 1997; see text, this section and Section 15]

Item	1998	1999	2000	2001	2002
Revenue, total	22,480	24,129	25,236	21,211	22,436
Books, print, total	(NA)	(NA)	(NA)	1499	1,404
Books, internet, total	(NA)	(NA)	(NA)	819	992
Books, other media, total	(NA)	(NA)	(NA)	298	274
Sale or licensing of rights to content	(NA)	(NA)	(NA)	186	235
Contract printing services	(NA)	(NA)	(NA)	141	144
Fulfillment services	(NA)	(NA)	(NA)	(S)	7
Rental or sale of mailing lists	(NA)	(NA)	(NA)	37	52
Publishing services for others	(NA)	(NA)	(NA)	1,896	1,657
Other services revenue	(NA)	(NA)	(NA)		
Expenses: Purchased printing	3,908	4,104	4,229	4,212	4,631
Inventories at end of year	2,737	2,984	3,463	4,092	4,325
Finished goods and work-in-process. . . .	2,510	2,723	3,200	3,936	4,154
Materials, supplies, fuel, etc.	227	261	263	156	171

NA Not available.   S Data do not meet publication standards.
Source: U.S. Census Bureau, *Service Annual Survey: 2002*, SAS/02 and prior issues . See <http://www.census.gov/econ/www /servmenu.html> (released February 2004).

No. 1132. Book Purchasing for Adults: 1998 and 2003

[In percent. Excludes all books purchased for children under age 14. Based on an ongoing survey of 12,000 households conducted over 12 months ending in December of year shown. For details, see source]

Characteristic	Total		Mass market [1]		Trade [2]		Hardcover		Audio [3] 2003
	1998	2003	1998	2003	1998	2003	1998	2003	
Total	100.0	100.0	100.0	100.0	100.0	100.0	100.0	100.0	100.0
Age of purchaser:									
Under 25 years old	5.0	3.9	4.4	2.9	6.6	5.9	3.9	2.9	2.8
25 to 34 years old	15.2	12.1	14.3	9.8	16.8	14.3	14.4	12.4	7.4
35 to 44 years old	24.6	17.8	19.4	14.2	28.3	21.9	26.2	17.5	14.9
45 to 54 years old	24.4	24.2	24.2	23.1	23.2	24.7	25.8	24.7	32.1
55 to 64 years old	15.0	22.4	17.8	25.2	12.9	18.8	14.3	23.2	21.3
65 years old and over	15.9	19.6	20.0	24.8	12.3	14.4	15.4	19.3	21.5
Education of household head:									
Not a high school graduate	7.4	6.3	9.0	8.4	6.6	5.8	6.5	4.8	4.3
High school graduate	56.4	54.3	62.1	60.0	53.2	49.2	53.6	53.5	56.5
College graduate	18.8	22.4	16.6	19.0	19.9	24.7	19.9	23.5	25.4
Post college	17.5	16.9	12.3	12.6	20.4	20.4	20.0	18.2	13.8
Occupation of household head:									
Professional/managerial	37.9	35.3	33.4	28.8	40.3	40.8	40.0	36.8	30.1
Sales/service	8.8	8.1	8.1	7.0	9.4	9.0	9.1	8.5	5.8
Blue collar	19.6	19.1	20.2	19.2	19.7	18.4	18.9	19.4	27.0
Retired/unemployed	29.9	35.0	35.9	42.8	25.4	28.9	28.3	33.1	35.6
Other	3.8	2.5	2.4	2.1	5.2	3.0	3.7	2.3	1.5
Household income:									
Under $30,000	30.8	25.2	35.8	31.5	29.3	22.8	26.9	20.9	23.5
$30,000 to 49,999	32.8	22.0	32.0	22.2	33.9	22.5	32.4	21.6	17.2
$50,000 to 74,999	11.6	18.9	12.5	17.7	10.5	19.3	11.7	19.8	21.6
$75,000 and over	24.8	33.8	19.8	28.6	26.2	35.4	28.9	37.7	37.8
Household size:									
One member	18.3	17.1	19.8	18.2	17.4	16.7	17.5	16.3	19.1
Two members	43.7	46.0	44.5	45.8	41.7	44.0	45.2	48.3	44.9
Three or more members	38.0	36.9	35.7	35.9	40.9	39.3	37.4	35.3	36.0
Age of intended reader:									
Under 25 years old	8.3	7.1	5.7	4.8	11.8	10.6	7.0	6.1	4.2
25 to 34 years old	15.8	12.6	14.4	10.1	17.5	15.3	15.3	12.8	7.9
35 to 44 years old	23.3	16.9	19.0	13.1	25.8	20.7	25.0	17.2	15.0
45 to 54 years old	22.9	22.4	23.5	22.1	21.1	21.9	24.2	22.9	30.5
55 to 64 years old	14.0	21.4	17.5	24.9	11.3	17.2	13.3	21.9	21.2
65 years old and over	15.8	19.6	19.8	25.0	12.5	14.3	15.2	19.1	21.2
Category of book:									
Popular fiction.	49.1	57.3	92.2	93.3	15.7	29.6	38.6	47.2	63.8
General nonfiction	7.8	7.9	2.6	2.3	8.7	9.9	12.6	11.7	12.3
Cooking/crafts.	9.5	7.2	0.2	0.1	14.5	13.1	14.2	9.0	0.7
Other	33.6	27.6	5.0	4.3	61.1	47.4	34.6	32.1	23.2
Where purchased (channel):									
Book stores [4]	45.0	44.8	37.8	41.3	53.0	51.8	43.9	41.9	29.4
Mass merchandisers	6.0	6.3	12.1	12.6	2.2	2.1	3.4	3.7	11.9
Book clubs	17.9	16.9	20.1	19.3	13.5	12.7	20.6	18.6	20.1
Online retailer/Internet	(NA)	9.4	(NA)	5.5	(NA)	11.2	(NA)	11.9	10.3
Other [5]	31.1	22.6	30.0	21.3	31.3	22.2	32.1	23.9	28.3

NA Not available.   [1] "Pocket size" books sold primarily through magazine and news outlets, supermarkets, variety stores, etc.   [2] All paperbound books, except mass market.   [3] Audio and digital books were added to questionnaire in January 2001. Sample size for digital book purchasing (i.e. eBooks) was too small to show detailed breaks.   [4] Includes independent, chain and used bookstores.   [5] Includes mail order, price clubs, discount stores, food/drug stores, multimedia, and other outlets.
Source: Ipsos-NPD, Inc., Rosemont IL., *Ipsos BookTrends*, a service mark of Ipsos-NPD, Inc. (copyright).

No. 1133. Software Publishers—Estimated Revenue, Expenses, and Inventories: 1999 to 2002

[In millions of dollars (80,959 represents $80,959,000,000). For taxable and tax-exempt employer firms. Covers NAICS 5112. Estimates have been adjusted to the results of the 1997 Economic Census. Based on the North American Industry Classification System, 1997; see text this section, and Section 15]

Item	1999	2000	2001	2002	Percent change, 2001-02
Revenue	80,959	88,042	90,591	88,846	-1.9
System software publishing, total	(NA)	(NA)	31,842	31,459	-1.2
Operating system software	(NA)	(NA)	9,217	10,010	8.6
Network software	(NA)	(NA)	7,543	7,963	5.6
Database management software	(NA)	(NA)	9,929	8,602	-13.4
Development tools and programming languages software	(NA)	(NA)	3,717	3,535	-4.9
Other systems software	(NA)	(NA)	1,437	1,348	-6.1
Application software publishing, total	(NA)	(NA)	37,297	37,473	0.5
General business productivity and home use applications	(NA)	(NA)	16,980	17,940	5.7
Cross-industry application software	(NA)	(NA)	11,580	10,643	-8.1
Vertical market application software	(NA)	(NA)	7,414	7,717	4.1
Utilities software	(NA)	(NA)	943	850	-9.9
Other application software	(NA)	(NA)	380	323	-15.0
Custom application design and development services	(NA)	(NA)	(S)	(S)	(S)
Customization and integration of packaged software ...	(NA)	(NA)	4,045	4,029	-0.4
Information technology consulting services	(NA)	(NA)	5,847	5,004	-14.4
Application service provisioning.	(NA)	(NA)	(S)	(S)	(S)
Business process management services	(NA)	(NA)	(S)	(S)	(S)
Re-sale of computer hardware and software	(NA)	(NA)	(S)	(S)	(S)
Information technology related training services	(NA)	(NA)	1,245	1,173	-5.8
Other services revenue	(NA)	(NA)	7,667	7,459	-2.7
Expenses: Selected purchases, total	5,460	6,060	(S)	(S)	(S)
Purchased printing	693	769	(S)	(S)	(S)
Purchased software reproduction	2,413	2,777	(S)	(S)	(S)
Purchased programming services	2,354	2,514	(S)	(S)	(S)
Inventories at end of year.............	863	1,020	1,671	2,072	24.0
Finished goods and work-in-process	697	864	1,310	1,691	29.1
Materials, supplies, fuel, etc.	167	157	361	381	5.5

NA Not available.   S Data do not meet publication standards.
Source: U.S. Census Bureau, *Service Annual Survey: 2002*, SAS/02 and prior issues. See <http://www.census.gov/econ/www/servmenu.html> (released February 2004).

No. 1134. Motion Picture and Sound Recording Industries—Estimated Revenue and Inventories: 1998 to 2002

[In millions of dollars (59,404 represents $59,404,000,000), except percent. For taxable and tax-exempt employer firms. Except where indicated, estimates have been adjusted to results of the 1997 Economic Census. Based on the North American Industry Classification System 1997, see text, this section, and Section 15. Minus sign (-) indicates decrease]

Item	1998	1999	2000	2001	2002	Percent change, 2001-02
Motion picture and recording industries (NAICS 512):						
Operating revenue........................	59,404	63,906	67,325	68,529	73,525	7.3
Total inventories.....................	14,384	15,423	15,813	15,780	16,657	5.6
Finished goods and work-in-process	14,218	15,241	15,605	15,554	16,455	5.8
Materials, supplies, fuel, etc.	168	181	208	225	202	-10.3
Motion picture and video (NAICS 5121):						
Operating revenue.....................	48,002	51,330	53,619	55,315	59,990	8.5
Total inventories	14,068	15,117	15,454	15,387	16,243	5.6
Finished goods and work-in-process	13,952	14,994	15,319	15,242	16,115	5.7
Materials, supplies, fuel, etc.	117	123	135	(S)	(S)	(S)
Sound recording (NAICS 5122): [1]						
Operating revenue.....................	11,403	12,575	13,705	13,215	13,535	2.4
Total inventories.....................	317	306	359	393	414	5.5
Finished goods and work-in-process	266	248	286	313	340	8.9
Materials, supplies, fuel, etc.	51	58	73	80	74	-7.6

S Data do not meet publication standards.   [1] Estimates not adjusted to the results of the 1997 Economic Census.
Source: U.S. Census Bureau, *Service Annual Survey: 2002*, SAS/02. See <http://www.census.gov/econ/www/servmenu.html> (released February 2004).

No. 1135. Recording Media—Manufacturers' Shipments and Value: 1990 to 2003

[865.7 represents 865,700,000. Based on reports of RIAA member companies who distributed about 84 percent of the prerecorded music in 2003. These data are supplemented by other sources. Minus sign (-) indicates returns greater than shipments]

Medium	1990	1995	1998	1999	2000	2001	2002	2003
UNIT SHIPMENTS [1] (mil.)								
Total [2]	865.7	1,112.7	1,123.9	1,160.6	1,079.2	968.5	859.7	798.4
CD's	286.5	722.9	847.0	938.9	942.5	881.9	803.3	745.9
CD singles	1.1	21.5	56.0	55.9	34.2	17.3	4.5	8.3
Cassettes	442.2	272.6	158.5	123.6	76.0	45.0	31.1	17.2
Cassette singles	87.4	70.7	26.4	14.2	1.3	-1.5	-0.5	(NA)
Albums—LPs and EPs	11.7	2.2	3.4	2.9	2.2	2.3	1.7	1.5
Vinyl singles	27.6	10.2	5.4	5.3	4.8	5.5	4.4	3.8
Music video	9.2	12.6	27.2	19.8	18.2	17.7	14.7	19.9
DVD video	(X)	(X)	0.5	2.5	3.3	7.9	10.7	17.5
DVD audio	(X)	(X)	(X)	(X)	(X)	0.3	0.4	0.4
VALUE (mil. dol.)								
Total [2]	7,541.1	12,320.3	13,711.2	14,584.7	14,323.7	13,740.9	12,614.2	11,854.4
CD's	3,451.6	9,377.4	11,416.0	12,816.3	13,214.5	12,909.4	12,044.1	11,232.9
CD singles	6.0	110.9	213.2	222.4	142.7	79.4	19.6	35.9
Cassettes	3,472.4	2,303.6	1,419.9	1,061.6	626.0	363.4	209.8	108.1
Cassette singles	257.9	236.3	94.4	48.0	4.6	-5.3	-1.6	(NA)
Albums—LPs and EPs	86.5	25.1	34.0	31.8	27.7	27.4	20.5	21.7
Vinyl singles	94.4	46.7	25.7	27.9	26.3	31.4	24.9	21.5
Music video	172.3	220.3	508.0	376.7	281.9	329.2	288.4	399.9
DVD video	(X)	(X)	12.2	66.3	80.3	190.7	236.3	369.6
DVD audio	(X)	(X)	(X)	(X)	(X)	6.0	8.5	8.0

X Not applicable. [1] Net units, after returns. [2] Includes discontinued media. Beginning 2003 includes super audio compact disks (SACD), not shown separately.

Source: Recording Industry Association of America, Washington, DC, *2003 Yearend Statistics* and earlier issues (copyright). See Internet site <http://www.riaa.com> (accessed 28 April 2004).

No. 1136. Profile of Consumer Expenditures for Sound Recordings—Percent Distribution: 1990 to 2003

[In percent. Based on monthly telephone surveys of the population 10 years old and over]

Item	1990	1995	1998	1999	2000	2001	2002	2003
Total [1]	100.0	100.0	100.0	100.0	100.0	100.0	100.0	100.0
Age: 10 to 14 years	7.6	8.0	9.1	8.5	8.9	8.5	8.9	8.6
15 to 19 years	18.3	17.1	15.8	12.6	12.9	13.0	13.3	11.4
20 to 24 years	16.5	15.3	12.2	12.6	12.5	12.2	11.5	10.0
25 to 29 years	14.6	12.3	11.4	10.5	10.6	10.9	9.4	10.9
30 to 34 years	13.2	12.1	11.4	10.1	9.8	10.3	10.8	10.1
35 to 39 years	10.2	10.8	12.6	10.4	10.6	10.2	9.8	11.2
40 to 44 years	7.8	7.5	8.3	9.3	9.6	10.3	9.9	10.0
45 years and over	11.1	16.1	18.1	24.7	23.8	23.7	25.5	26.6
Sex: Male	54.4	53.0	48.7	50.3	50.6	48.8	49.4	49.1
Female	45.6	47.0	51.3	49.7	49.4	51.2	50.6	50.9
Sales outlet:								
Record store	69.8	52.0	50.8	44.5	42.4	42.5	36.8	33.2
Other store	18.5	28.2	34.4	38.3	40.8	42.4	50.7	52.8
Tape/record club	8.9	14.3	9.0	7.9	7.6	6.1	4.0	4.1
Ad or 800 number	2.5	4.0	2.9	2.5	2.4	3.0	2.0	1.5
Internet [2]	(NA)	(NA)	1.1	2.4	3.2	2.9	3.4	5.0
Music type: [3]								
Rock	36.1	33.5	25.7	25.2	24.8	24.4	24.7	25.2
Rap/Hip Hop	8.5	6.7	9.7	10.8	12.9	11.4	13.8	13.3
R&B/Urban	11.6	11.3	12.8	10.5	9.7	10.6	11.2	10.6
Country	9.6	16.7	14.1	10.8	10.7	10.5	10.7	10.4
Pop	13.7	10.1	10.0	10.3	11.0	12.1	9.0	8.9
Religious	2.5	3.1	6.3	5.1	4.8	6.7	6.7	5.8
Classical	3.1	2.9	3.3	3.5	2.7	3.2	3.1	3.0
Jazz	4.8	3.0	1.9	3.0	2.9	3.4	3.2	2.9
Soundtracks	0.8	0.9	1.7	0.8	0.7	1.4	1.1	1.4
Oldies	0.8	1.0	0.7	0.7	0.9	0.8	0.9	1.3
New age	1.1	0.7	0.6	0.5	0.5	1.0	0.5	0.5
Children's	0.5	0.5	0.4	0.4	0.6	0.5	0.4	0.6
Other	5.6	7.0	7.9	9.1	8.3	7.9	8.1	7.6
Media type: CDs	31.1	65.0	74.8	83.2	89.3	89.2	90.5	87.8
Cassettes	54.7	25.1	14.8	8.0	4.9	3.4	2.4	2.2
Singles (all types)	8.7	7.5	6.8	5.4	2.5	2.4	1.9	2.4
Music video [4]	(NA)	0.9	1.0	0.9	0.8	1.1	0.7	0.6
DVD audio	(NA)	(NA)	(NA)	(NA)	(NA)	1.1	1.3	2.7
Digital download	(NA)	(NA)	(NA)	(NA)	(NA)	0.2	0.5	1.3
SACD [5]	(NA)	(NA)	(NA)	(NA)	(NA)	(NA)	(NA)	0.5
Vinyl LPs	4.7	0.5	0.7	0.5	0.5	0.6	0.7	0.5

NA Not available. [1] Percent distributions exclude nonresponses and responses of don't know. [2] Excludes record club purchases over the Internet. [3] As classified by respondent. [4] Beginning 2001 includes video DVDs. [5] Super audio compact disks.

Source: Recording Industry Association of America, Inc., Washington, DC, *2003 Consumer Profile* and earlier issues (copyright). See Internet site <http://www.riaa.com> (accessed 28 April 2004).

No. 1137. Radio and Television Broadcasting—Estimated Revenue and Expenses: 2000 to 2002

[In millions of dollars (52,668 represents $52,668,000,000). For taxable and tax-exempt employer firms. Estimates have been adjusted to the results of the 1997 Economic Census. Based on the North American Industry Classification System, 1997 see text, this section, and Section 15]

Item	Total (NAICS 5131) 2000	2001	2002	Radio broadcasting (NAICS 51311) 2000	2001	2002	TV broadcasting (NAICS 51312) 2000	2001	2002
Operating revenue	52,668	47,840	51,918	14,811	13,740	14,870	37,858	34,100	37,048
Station time sales	(NA)	28,820	31,335	(NA)	11,489	12,258	(NA)	17,331	19,077
Network compensation	(NA)	514	487	(NA)	91	97	(NA)	424	390
National/regional advertising	(NA)	9,502	10,738	(NA)	2,538	2,816	(NA)	6,964	7,922
Local advertising revenue	(NA)	18,803	20,110	(NA)	8,861	9,345	(NA)	6,964	7,922
Network time sales	(NA)	14,322	15,655	(NA)	935	1,122	(NA)	9,943	10,766
Program rights	(NA)	177	272	(NA)	171	259	(NA)	13,387	14,535
Production and post-production services	(NA)	(S)	67	(NA)	(S)	22	(NA)	(S)	(S)
Public and non-commercial programming rights	(NA)	1,751	1,621	(NA)	(S)	(S)	(NA)	(S)	44
Other operating services revenue	(NA)	2,715	2,968	(NA)	619	697	(NA)	1,229	1,109
Expenses [1]	40,366	39,714	41,432	11,406	11,242	12,000	(NA)	2,095	2,271
Annual payroll	11,280	11,242	11,943	4,458	4,476	4,683	28,960	28,472	29,432
Employer contributions to employee benefit plans	1,535	1,541	1,475	590	566	582	6,821	6,766	7,261
Contract labor	(NA)	(NA)	419	(NA)	(NA)	314	945	975	893
Broadcast rights and music license fees	12,754	11,898	12,750	713	728	657	(NA)	(NA)	105
Depreciation	3,648	4,048	3,045	1,638	1,572	1,095	12,041	11,170	12,092
Lease and rental	655	787	871	294	386	354	2,010	2,475	1,951
Purchased repairs	276	266	327	91	94	104	362	401	517
Purchased communications	(NA)	(NA)	350	(NA)	(NA)	156	185	172	223
Purchased utilities	(NA)	(NA)	380	(NA)	(NA)	157	(NA)	(NA)	194
Purchased advertising	1,534	1,445	1,559	455	523	624	(NA)	(NA)	223
Purchased materials, parts, and supplies	(NA)	(NA)	316	(NA)	(NA)	124	1,079	923	934
							(NA)	(NA)	192

NA Not available.   S Does not meet publication standards.   [1] Includes other expenses, not shown separately.

Source: U.S. Census Bureau, *Service Annual Survey: 2002*, SAS/02; and prior issues. See <http://www.census.gov/econ/www/servmenu.html> (released February 2004).

No. 1138. Cable and Pay TV—Summary: 1975 to 2003

[9,800 represents 9,800,000. Cable TV for calendar year. Pay TV as of Dec. 31 of year shown]

Year	Cable TV: Avg. basic subscribers (1,000)	Avg. monthly basic rate (dol.)	Revenue [1] (mil. dol.) Total	Basic	Pay TV: Units [2] (1,000) Total pay [3]	Pay cable	Non-cable delivered premium	Monthly rate (dol.) All pay weighted average [3]	Pay cable	Non-cable delivered premium
1975	9,800	6.50	804	764	194	194	(NA)	(NA)	7.85	(NA)
1980	17,500	7.69	2,609	1,615	8,581	7,336	(NA)	8.91	8.62	(NA)
1984	32,800	8.98	7,738	3,534	28,815	27,754	(NA)	10.03	9.96	(NA)
1985	35,440	9.73	8,831	4,138	29,885	29,418	(NA)	10.29	10.25	(NA)
1986	38,170	10.67	9,955	4,887	31,033	30,668	(NA)	10.35	10.31	(NA)
1987	41,160	12.18	11,563	6,016	33,528	33,232	(NA)	10.25	10.23	(NA)
1988	44,160	13.86	13,409	7,345	37,085	36,777	(NA)	10.25	10.23	(NA)
1989	47,500	15.21	15,378	8,670	39,055	38,916	(NA)	10.24	10.17	(NA)
1990	50,520	16.78	17,582	10,174	39,902	39,751	(NA)	10.25	10.20	(NA)
1991	52,570	18.10	19,426	11,418	39,983	36,569	(NA)	10.35	10.30	(NA)
1992	54,300	19.08	21,079	12,433	40,893	36,879	(NA)	10.35	10.27	(NA)
1993	56,200	[4] 19.39	22,809	13,528	42,010	37,113	(NA)	10.29	10.17	(NA)
1994	58,373	21.62	21,531	15,144	47,478	42,528	4,950	9.27	9.11	(NA)
1995	60,550	23.07	23,338	16,763	55,723	46,798	8,925	8.19	8.33	6.99
1996	62,300	24.41	25,371	18,249	63,705	49,728	13,977	7.59	7.70	6.99
1997	63,600	26.48	27,895	20,213	72,785	51,933	20,852	7.28	7.36	6.99
1998	64,650	27.81	30,486	21,574	80,605	55,280	25,325	7.14	7.20	6.99
1999	65,500	28.92	33,599	22,732	88,455	59,005	29,450	7.02	7.03	6.99
2000	66,250	30.37	36,757	24,142	102,590	65,918	36,672	6.73	6.60	6.99
2001	66,732	32.87	42,273	26,324	115,325	75,433	39,892	6.67	6.49	6.99
2002	66,472	34.71	47,896	27,690	125,662	81,128	44,534	6.45	6.13	7.06
2003 est.	65,883	36.59	53,050	28,926	123,558	81,236	42,322	6.14	5.56	7.20
								5.99	5.28	7.35

NA Not available.   [1] Includes installation revenue, subscriber revenue, and nonsubscriber revenue; excludes telephony and high-speed access.   [2] Individual program services sold to subscribers.   [3] Includes multipoint distribution service (MDS), satellite TV (STV), multipoint multichannel distribution service (MMDS), satellite master antenna TV (SMATV, C-band satellite, and DBS satellite. Includes average pay unit price based on data for major premium pay movie services.   [4] Weighted average representing 8 months of unregulated basic rate and 4 months of FCC rolled-back rate.

Source: Kagan Research LLC. From the *Broadband Cable Financial Databook 2002* (copyright); *The Pay TV Newsletter*, June 28, 2002, July 31, 2002; and *Cable Program Investor*, Dec. 23, 2003 and various other publications.

No. 1139. Cable Networks and Program Distribution Services—Estimated Revenue and Expenses: 1999 to 2002

[In millions of dollars (59,895 represents $59,895,000,000). For taxable and tax-exempt employer firms. Covers NAICS 5132. Estimates have not been adjusted to the results of the 1997 Economic Census. Based on the North American Industry Classification System, 1997 see text, this section, and Section 15. Minus sign (-) indicates decrease]

Item	1999	2000	2001	2002	Percent change, 2001-02
Operating revenue	59,895	67,930	74,420	80,536	8.2
Air time (advertising).	(NA)	(NA)	12,225	13,825	13.1
Special programming service	(NA)	(NA)	12,466	13,097	5.1
Basic programming service	(NA)	(NA)	32,148	34,340	6.8
Premium cable programming packages	(NA)	(NA)	5,215	5,253	0.7
Pay-per-view service.	(NA)	(NA)	1,927	2,133	10.7
Program distribution installation services.	(NA)	(NA)	512	504	-1.6
Program distribution equipment sales and rentals.	(NA)	(NA)	1,779	1,725	-3.0
Other program distribution related services	(NA)	(NA)	2,350	2,203	-6.3
Internet access services	(NA)	(NA)	2,127	3,400	59.8
Basic fixed local telephony.	(NA)	(NA)	1,031	1,112	7.9
Basic fixed long-distance	(NA)	(NA)	128	163	26.7
Other communication services	(NA)	(NA)	399	340	-14.8
Other operating revenue	(NA)	(NA)	2,113	2,441	15.5
Operating expenses [1].	52,952	62,039	70,821	74,885	5.7
Annual payroll	8,388	9,696	10,640	10,705	0.6
Employer contributions to employee benefit plans	1,666	1,929	2,019	1,993	-1.3
Contract labor	(NA)	(NA)	(NA)	958	(NA)
Program and production costs	16,525	19,077	22,177	24,430	10.2
Depreciation	11,498	13,965	16,869	17,935	6.3
Lease and rental	878	1,005	1,058	974	-7.9
Purchased repairs and maintenance	721	684	865	688	-20.5
Purchased communications	(NA)	(NA)	(NA)	607	(NA)
Purchased advertising.	1,836	2251	2,319	2,703	16.6
Taxes and licence fees	(NA)	(NA)	(NA)	878	(NA)
Purchased legal and accounting services	(NA)	(NA)	(NA)	461	(NA)

NA Not available. [1] Includes other expenses, not shown separately.
Source: U.S. Census Bureau, *Service Annual Survey: 2002*, SAS/02; and prior issues . See <http://www.census.gov/econ/www /servmenu.html> (released February 2004).

No. 1140. Telecommunications—Estimated Revenue and Expenses: 2000 to 2002

[In millions of dollars (349,109 represents $349,109,000,000), except percent. For taxable and tax-exempt employer firms. Except for NAICS 51332, wireless telecommunications carriers (except satellite), estimates have been adjusted to the results of the 1997 Economic Census. Based on the North American Industry Classification System, 1997; see text, this section, and Section 15. Minus sign (-) indicates decrease. See Table 1141 wireless telecommunications carriers, NAICS 51332]

Item	Telecommunucations (NAICS 5133)			Wired telecommunications carriers (NAICS 51331)		
	2000	2001	2002	2000	2001	2002
Operating revenue	349,109	365,540	352,198	265,704	262,615	239,850
Fixed total.	(NA)	188,155	171,670	(NA)	178,150	161,890
Fixed local.	(NA)	87,980	83,540	(NA)	86,657	82,049
Basic service.	(NA)	72,687	69,859	(NA)	71,480	68,538
Fixed long-distance	(NA)	75,346	64,597	(NA)	71,203	60,962
Outbound service.	(NA)	64,701	55,389	(NA)	61,357	52,397
Fixed all distance	(NA)	5,146	4,294	(NA)	4,943	3,922
Dedicated network services.	(NA)	11,525	11,212	(NA)	8,130	7,811
Data transmission services	(NA)	8,159	8,027	(NA)	7,216	7,147
Mobile total	(NA)	74,008	84,145	(NA)	857	907
Mobile telephony services.	(NA)	69,089	80,504	(NA)	(NA)	(NA)
Local access and use.	(NA)	49,684	59,174	(NA)	(NA)	(NA)
Messaging services	(NA)	194	214	(NA)	(NA)	(NA)
Mobile dispatch services.	(NA)	61,366	58,604	(NA)	54,926	53,722
Carrier services	(NA)	52,992	52,286	(NA)	50,329	49,467
Network access	(NA)	10,518	10,618	(NA)	5,934	4,712
Other telecommunications services	(NA)	31,493	27,161	(NA)	22,748	18,618
Other services revenue [1]						
Telecommunications network installation services.	(NA)	3,026	2,047	(NA)	2,720	1,860
Telecommunications equipment sales	(NA)	8,013	8,199	(NA)	1,889	1,776
Sales of directory advertising space	(NA)	1,245	1,156	(NA)	1,072	1,026
Other revenue	(NA)	18,034	14,486	(NA)	16,057	12,898
Operating expenses [1]	306,706	331,423	302,653	230,098	235,716	202,885
Annual payroll	65,306	66,433	56,613	52,517	51,039	42,958
Employer contributions to Social Security and other supplemental benefits	14,119	15,467	15,748	11,414	12,489	13,013
Access charges	40,530	40,654	37,604	32,891	31,472	29,006
Depreciation	59,725	73,892	61,687	44,075	52,737	43,058
Lease and rental	8,010	8,995	9,202	4,476	4,949	4,688
Purchased communications	(NA)	(NA)	7,713	(NA)	(NA)	5,790
Purchased utilities.	(NA)	(NA)	4,793	(NA)	(NA)	3,930
Purchased advertising.	(NA)	8,840	8,095	(NA)	4,366	3,325
Purchased materials, parts, and supplies	(NA)	(NA)	7,402	(NA)	(NA)	4,067
Taxes and licence fees	(NA)	(NA)	6,020	(NA)	(NA)	5,184

NA Not available. [1] Includes other revenue sources and expenses, not shown separately.
Source: U.S. Census Bureau, *Service Annual Survey: 2002*, SAS/02; and prior issues . See <http://www.census.gov/econ/www/servmenu.html> (released February 2004).

No. 1141. Wireless Telecommunications Carriers (Except Satellite)—Estimated Revenue and Expenses: 1999 to 2002

[In millions of dollars (53,485 represents $53,485,000,000). For taxable and tax-exempt employer firms. For NAICS 51332. Estimates have not been adjusted to the results of the 1997 Economic Census. Based on the North American Industry Classification System, 1997; see text, this section and Section 15. See Table 1140 for telecommunications total and wired carriers (NAICS 5133 and 51331). Minus sign (-) indicates decrease]

Item	1999	2000	2001	2002	Percent change, 2001-02
Operating revenue	53,485	64,309	83,145	94,605	13.8
Mobile total	(NA)	(NA)	71,596	81,531	13.9
Mobile telephony services	(NA)	(NA)	66,965	78,082	16.6
Local access and use	(NA)	(NA)	49,354	58,532	18.6
Mobile value-added services	(NA)	(NA)	2,277	2,762	21.3
Mobile long distance	(NA)	(NA)	4,820	5,697	18.2
Mobile all distance	(NA)	(NA)	8,258	9,480	14.8
Dedicated network services	(NA)	(NA)	(S)	(S)	(S)
Other mobile telephony revenue	(NA)	(NA)	2,257	1,610	-28.6
Messaging services	(NA)	(NA)	4,439	3,236	-27.1
Mobile dispatch services	(NA)	(NA)	192	213	11.0
Carrier services	(NA)	(NA)	2,743	2,610	-4.9
Network access	(NA)	(NA)	1,093	1,138	4.1
Other carrier services	(NA)	(NA)	1,650	1,472	-10.8
Other telecommunications services	(NA)	(NA)	2,526	3,051	20.8
Other services revenue	(NA)	(NA)	6,280	7,412	16.6
Operating expenses	50,381	59,214	78,156	85,189	9.0
Annual payroll	8,259	9,224	11,726	10,681	-8.9
Employer contributions to social security and other supplemental benefits	1,787	2,095	2,266	2,367	4.5
Contract labor	(NA)	(NA)	(NA)	1,659	(NA)
Access charges	3,371	5,038	6,745	6,302	-6.6
Depreciation	10,376	13,275	18,594	16,103	-13.4
Lease and rental	2,328	2,793	3,445	3,906	13.4
Purchased repairs and maintenance	660	846	988	932	-5.6
Purchased communications	(NA)	(NA)	(NA)	1,429	(NA)
Purchased utilities	(NA)	(NA)	(NA)	773	(NA)
Purchased advertising	2,343	3,330	4,211	4,539	7.8
Universal service, contributions, and other similar charges	441	526	624	591	-5.3
Purchased materials, parts, and supplies	(NA)	(NA)	(NA)	2,987	(NA)
Taxes and licence fees	(NA)	(NA)	(NA)	674	(NA)
Purchased legal and accounting services	(NA)	(NA)	(NA)	295	(NA)
Purchased computer services	(NA)	(NA)	(NA)	949	(NA)
Management consulting services	(NA)	(NA)	(NA)	411	(NA)
Other operating expenses	19,505	20,329	27,513	30,593	11.2

NA Not available. S Data do not meet publication standards.

Source: U.S. Census Bureau, *Service Annual Survey: 2002*, SAS/02; and prior isssue. See <http://www.census.gov/econ/www/servmenu.html> (released February 2004)

No. 1142. Telecommunications Industry—Carriers and Revenue: 1995 to 2002

[Revenue in millions of dollars (190,076 represents $190,076,000,000). Data based on carrier filings to the FCC. Because of reporting changes, data beginning 1999 are not strictly comparable with previous years; see source for details]

Category	Carriers					Telecommunications revenue				
	1995	1999	2000	2001	2002 [1]	1995	1999	2000	2001	2002
Total [2]	3,058	4,486	4,879	5,001	4,390	190,076	268,505	292,762	301,799	292,341
Local service providers	1,675	2,416	2,641	2,755	2,531	103,792	119,938	128,075	133,502	130,941
Incumbent local exchange carriers (ILECs)	1,347	1,318	1,335	1,335	1,310	102,820	112,216	116,158	117,885	114,990
Pay telephone providers	271	704	699	751	606	349	1,213	972	836	641
Competitors of ILECs	57	394	607	669	615	623	6,508	10,945	14,781	15,310
CAPs and CLECs [3]	57	298	479	511	451	623	5,652	9,814	12,998	13,043
Local resellers	(4)	73	105	132	100	(4)	511	879	1,393	1,538
Other local exchange carriers .	(4)	23	23	26	64	(4)	171	11	329	406
Private carriers	(4)	(4)	(4)	(4)	(4)	(4)	87	39	15	281
Shared tenant service providers	(4)	(4)	(4)	(4)	(4)	(4)	87	202	46	42
Wireless service providers [5]	930	1,419	1,430	1,306	927	18,627	50,152	63,280	74,596	80,467
Telephony [6]	792	784	783	670	422	17,208	46,513	59,823	71,887	78,568
Paging service providers	138	391	425	425	346	(4)	3,232	3,102	2,197	1,473
Toll service providers	453	651	808	940	932	76,447	98,414	101,407	93,702	80,934
Interexchange carriers	130	178	212	233	229	70,938	87,570	87,311	81,272	68,146
Operator service providers	25	15	20	19	18	500	337	635	611	554
Prepaid service providers	8	18	23	27	27	16	866	727	133	460
Satellite service carriers	(4)	17	25	34	33	(4)	280	336	373	406
Toll resellers	260	406	493	558	574	4,220	9,211	10,641	8,797	9,279
Other toll carriers	30	17	35	69	51	773	150	1,758	2,516	2,089

[1] Counts dropped in 2002 because many affiliated filers were allowed to file consolidated reports. [2] Revenue data include adjustments, not shown separately. For 1995, revenue data include some non-telecommunications revenue, formerly reported as local exchange wireless revenue. [3] Competitive access providers (CAPs) and competitive local exchange carriers (CLECs). [4] Data not available separately. [5] Beginning 2000, includes specialized mobile radio services and other services, not shown separately. [6] Cellular service, personal communications service, and specialized mobile radio.

Source: U.S. Federal Communications Commission, *Trends in Telephone Service*, annual.

Information and Communications **727**

No. 1143. Telephone Systems—Summary: 1985 to 2002

[112 represents 112,000,000. Covers principal carriers filing annual reports with Federal Communications Commission]

Item	Unit	1985	1990	1995	1997	1998	1999	2000	2001[1]	2002[1]
LOCAL EXCHANGE CARRIERS [2]										
Carriers [3]	Number	55	51	53	51	52	52	52	30	29
Access lines	Millions	112	130	166	194	205	228	245	253	262
Business access lines	Millions	31	36	46	53	57	57	58	54	54
Residential access lines	Millions	79	89	101	108	110	115	115	112	103
Other access lines (public, mobile, special)	Millions	2	6	19	33	38	55	72	87	105
Number of local calls (originating)	Billions	365	402	484	522	544	554	537	515	459
Number of toll calls (originating)	Billions	(NA)	63	94	101	97	102	106	98	90
Gross book cost of plant	Bil. dol	191	240	284	309	325	342	362	360	367
Depreciation and amortization reserves	Bil. dol	49	89	127	149	163	176	190	194	210
Net plant	Bil. dol	142	151	157	160	161	166	172	166	157
Total assets	Bil. dol	162	180	197	198	200	204	214	208	195
Total stockholders equity	Bil. dol	63	74	72	72	70	67	72	66	58
Operating revenues	Bil. dol	73	84	96	103	108	113	117	109	103
Local revenues	Bil. dol	32	37	46	52	55	58	60	55	51
Operating expenses [4]	Bil. dol	48	62	72	75	78	79	81	77	79
Net operating income [5]	Bil. dol	13	14	14	16	18	20	20	19	23
Net income	Bil. dol	9	11	11	12	12	13	15	11	8
Employees	(1,000)	(NA)	569	447	435	436	436	434	386	333
Compensation of employees	Bil. dol	(NA)	23	21	22	23	24	24	23	23
Average monthly residential local telephone rate [6]	Dollars	(NA)	19.24	20.01	19.88	19.76	19.93	20.78	22.62	23.38
Average monthly single-line business telephone rate [6]	Dollars	(NA)	41.21	41.80	41.67	41.29	41.21	41.80	42.43	43.59
LONG DISTANCE CARRIERS										
Number of carriers with presubscribed lines	Number	(NA)	325	583	(NA)	(NA)	(NA)	(NA)	(NA)	(NA)
Number of presubscribed lines	Millions	(NA)	132	153	(NA)	(NA)	(NA)	(NA)	(NA)	(NA)
Total toll service revenues [7]	Bil. dol	43	52	78	91	96	100	103	94	79
Interstate switched access minutes	Bil. min	167	307	432	497	519	553	567	538	486
INTERNATIONAL TELEPHONE SERVICE [8]										
Number of U.S. billed calls	Millions	425	984	2,830	4,259	4,477	5,305	5,742	6,265	5,926
Number of U.S. billed minutes	Millions	3,446	8,030	15,889	22,753	24,250	28,515	30,135	33,287	35,063
U.S. billed revenues	Mil. dol	3,487	8,059	14,335	15,662	14,726	14,980	14,909	11,380	9,773
U.S. carrier revenue net of settlements with foreign carriers	Mil. dol	2,332	5,188	9,397	10,232	10,242	10,379	10,982	8,034	6,931
Revenue from private-line service	Mil. dol	172	201	514	851	921	1,216	1,480	1,467	988
Revenue from resale service	Mil. dol	(NA)	167	1,756	4,112	4,798	4,528	7,600	5,341	4,871

NA Not available. [1] Beginning 2001, detailed financial data only filed by regional Bell operating companies. Access lines and calls reported by 50 reporting companies. [2] Gross operating revenues, gross plant, and total assets of reporting carriers estimated at more than 90 percent of total industry. New accounting rules became effective in 1990; prior years may not be directly comparable on a one-to-one basis. Includes Virgin Islands, and prior to 1995, Puerto Rico. [3] The reporting threshold for carriers is $100 million in annual operating revenue. [4] Excludes taxes. [5] After tax deductions. [6] Based on surveys conducted by FCC. [7] Starting 1995, includes other toll, wireless and CLECs (competitive local exchange carriers.) [8] Beginning 1995, data are for all U.S. points, and include calls to and from Alaska, Hawaii, Puerto Rico, Guam, the U.S. Virgin Islands, and offshore U.S. points. Beginning 1995, carriers first started reporting traffic to and from Canada and Mexico. Data for Canada and Mexico in prior years are staff estimates.

Source: U.S. Federal Communications Commission, *Statistics of Communications Common Carriers,* annual; *Trends in Telephone Service,* annual; and *Trends in the International Telecommunications Industry,* annual.

No. 1144. Cellular Telecommunications Industry: 1990 to 2003

[Calendar year data, except as noted (5,283 represents 5,283,000). Based on a survey mailed to all cellular, personal communications services, and enhanced special mobile radio (ESMR) systems. For 2003 data, the universe was 3,123 systems and the response rate was 87 percent. The number of operational systems beginning 2000 differs from that reported for previous periods as a result of the consolidated operation of ESMR systems in a broader service area instead of by a city-to-city basis]

Item	Unit	1990	1995	1998	1999	2000	2001	2002	2003
Systems	Number	751	1,627	3,073	3,518	2,440	2,587	2,846	3,123
Subscribers	1,000	5,283	33,786	69,209	86,047	109,478	128,375	140,766	158,722
Cell sites [1]	Number	5,616	22,663	65,887	81,698	104,288	127,540	139,338	162,986
Employees	Number	21,382	68,165	134,754	155,817	184,449	203,580	192,410	205,629
Service revenue [2]	Mil. dol	4,548	19,081	33,133	40,018	52,466	65,016	76,508	87,624
Roamer revenue [2]	Mil. dol	456	2,542	3,501	4,085	3,883	3,936	3,896	3,766
Capital investment	Mil. dol	6,282	24,080	60,543	71,265	89,624	105,030	126,922	145,867
Average monthly bill [3]	Dollars	80.90	51.00	39.43	41.24	45.27	47.37	48.40	49.91
Average length of call [3]	Minutes	2.20	2.15	2.39	2.38	2.56	2.74	2.73	2.87

[1] The basic geographic unit of a wireless PCS or cellular system. A city or county is divided into smaller "cells," each of which is equipped with a low-powered radio transmitter/receiver. The cells can vary in size depending upon terrain, capacity demands, etc. By controlling the transmission power, the radio frequencies assigned to one cell can be limited to the boundaries of that cell. When a wireless PCS or cellular phone moves from one cell toward another, a computer at the Switching Office monitors the movement and at the proper time, transfers or hands off the phone call to the new cell and another radio frequency. [2] Service revenue generated by subscribers' calls outside of their system areas. [3] As of December 31.

Source: Cellular Telecommunications & Internet Association, Washington, DC, *Semi-annual Wireless Survey* (copyright).

No. 1145. Information Services and Data Processing Services—Estimated Revenue: 1999 to 2002

[In millions of dollars (60,105 represents $60,105,000,000), except percent. For taxable and tax-exempt employer firms. Estimates have been adjusted to results of the 1997 Economic Census. Based on the 1997 North American Industry Classification System; see text, this section, and Section 15]

Item	1999	2000	2001	2002
Total (NAICS 514)	60,105	76,524	82,641	87,890
News syndicates (NAICS 51411):				
Revenue	1,823	1,986	1,960	1,917
Fees from supplying information	(NA)	(NA)	1,838	1,838
Other services revenue	(NA)	(NA)	122	79
Libraries and archives (NAICS 51412):				
Revenue	1,018	1,151	1,116	1,212
Subsidies, contributions, gifts, and grants	(NA)	(NA)	812	904
Fees from educational workshops and seminars	(NA)	(NA)	(S)	(S)
Fees and dues from providing access to collections	(NA)	(NA)	49	47
Sales of books and other educational materials	(NA)	(NA)	(S)	(S)
Other services revenue	(NA)	(NA)	246	250
On-line information services (NAICS 514191):				
Revenue	18,012	26,577	28,623	27,832
Internet access services	(NA)	(NA)	14,222	14,632
Advertising	(NA)	(NA)	3,516	2,866
Web site hosting	(NA)	(NA)	839	731
Internet backbone services	(NA)	(NA)	(S)	(S)
Internet telecommunications services	(NA)	(NA)	180	(S)
Information technology consulting services	(NA)	(NA)	201	(S)
Information technology design and development	(NA)	(NA)	(S)	(S)
Application service provisioning	(NA)	(NA)	(S)	(S)
Business process management	(NA)	(NA)	(S)	(S)
Video and audio streaming services	(NA)	(NA)	(S)	(S)
Other services revenue	(NA)	(NA)	(S)	36
All other information services (NAICS 514199):				
Revenue [1]	2,109	4,861	4,429	4,315
Advertising	(NA)	(NA)	3,724	4,011
Web hosting and design	(NA)	(NA)	1,670	1,408
Information search services	(NA)	(NA)	(S)	48
Stock photo services	(NA)	(NA)	713	849
Data processing services (NAICS 5142):				
Revenue	37,143	41,950	47,219	52,920
Business process management	(NA)	(NA)	15,953	20,124
Information and document transformation	(NA)	(NA)	1,183	(S)
Information technology design and development	(NA)	(NA)	13,660	13,441
Data storage services	(NA)	(NA)	224	214
Data management services	(NA)	(NA)	3,238	4,321
Collocation services	(NA)	(NA)	(S)	(S)
Information technology consulting services	(NA)	(NA)	1,161	(S)
Web site hosting	(NA)	(NA)	771	743
Software publishing	(NA)	(NA)	(S)	(S)
Rental and leasing of computer hardware	(NA)	(NA)	973	1,066
Application service provisioning	(NA)	(NA)	43	39
Video and audio streaming services	(NA)	(NA)	(S)	19
Other services revenue	(NA)	(NA)	8,476	8,713

NA Not available. S Data do not meet publication standards. [1] Includes other sources of revenue, not shown separately.

Source: U.S. Census Bureau, Service Annual Survey: 2002, SAS/02; and prior issues. See <http://www.census.gov/econ/www/servmenu.html> (released February 2004).

No. 1146. Academic Libraries—Summary: 2000

[For fiscal year. (193,963 represents 193,963,000.) For 2- and 4-year degree granting institutions. Based on the Academic Libraries Survey; see source for details]

Item	Number of libraries	Circula-tion [1] (1,000)	Gate count [2] (1,000)	Volumes held [3] (1,000)	Staff [4] Total	Staff [4] Librarians (percent)	Expenditures Total (mil. dol.)	Expenditures Salary [5] (percent)	Percent with access from within library to— Electronic catalog	Percent with access from within library to— Internet
Total	3,527	193,963	16,457	913,547	95,665	26.3	5,026	50.1	93.7	98.6
Control: Public	1,566	127,848	10,890	544,917	58,277	25.6	3,080	51.5	98.9	99.6
Private	1,961	66,115	5,567	368,630	37,388	27.4	1,946	47.9	88.9	97.8
Level: [6]										
4-year degree and above [7]	2,148	166,442	12,563	856,414	81,800	25.9	4,473	48.0	95.6	98.7
Doctor's	568	117,186	7,449	605,978	55,090	24.9	3,284	46.6	98.0	98.6
Master's	884	34,228	3,667	179,758	19,193	27.3	859	52.4	96.1	99.1
Bachelor's	660	12,814	1,278	66,740	6,887	28.8	286	51.7	92.4	98.2
Less than 4-year	1,379	27,521	3,894	57,133	13,864	28.9	553	66.6	90.6	98.5
Enrollment: [4]										
Less than 1,500	1,910	25,131	2,982	117,713	14,385	30.2	596	53.4	87.9	97.6
1,500 to 4,999	1,051	39,563	4,395	176,512	22,355	27.5	1,041	53.0	99.4	99.8
5,000 or more	566	129,268	9,079	619,323	58,925	24.9	3,389	48.6	99.8	99.6

[1] Includes reserves. [2] In a typical week. [3] At end-of-year. [4] Full-time equivalent. [5] Salary and wages. [6] Level of highest degree offered. [7] Includes 36 institutions granting "other" degrees, not shown separately.

Source: U.S. National Center for Education Statistics, Academic Libraries: 2000, NCES 2004-317, November, 2003.

No. 1147. Libraries—Number by Type: 1980 to 2003

Type	1980	1990	2000	2003	Type	1980	1990	2000	2003
Total[1]	31,564	34,613	37,024	36,142	Junior college...	1,191	1,233	1,283	1,323
					Colleges, universities....	3,400	3,360	3,494	3,997
United States...	28,638	30,761	32,914	32,169	Departmental.	1,489	1,454	1,454	1,524
Public...	8,717	9,060	9,480	9,567	Law,				
Public branches...	5,936	5,833	6,957	7,181	medicine,				
Special[2]...	7,649	9,051	9,948	8,530	religious..	269	501	418	622
Medicine...	1,674	1,861	1,955	1,698	Government.....	1,260	1,735	1,411	1,261
Religious...	913	946	1,015	1,101	Armed Forces....	485	489	341	310
Law[3]...	417	647	1,172	1,001	Outlying areas...	113	110	(NA)	(NA)
Academic...	4,591	4,593	4,777	5,320					

NA Not available. [1] Includes Canadian libraries, and libraries in regions administered by the United States, not shown separately. Data are exclusive of elementary and secondary school libraries. Law libraries with fewer than 10,000 volumes are included only if they specialize in a particular field. [2] Includes other types of special libraries, not shown separately. Increase between 1980 and 1990 is due mainly to revised criteria for identifying special libraries and improved methods of counting. [3] Increase in 2000 due to increased effort in identifying special libraries.

Source: Information Today, Inc., Medford, NJ, *The Bowker Annual Library and Book Trade Almanac* and *American Library Directory*, annual. (Copyright 2004 by Information Today, Inc.)

No. 1148. Public Libraries by Selected Characteristics: 2001

[8,223 represents $8,223,000,000. Based on survey of public libraries. Data are for public libraries in the 50 states and the District of Columbia. The response rates for these items are between 96 and 97 percent]

Population of service area	Number of—		Operating income—	Source (percent)		Paid staff[3]		Libraries with Internet access
	Public libraries	Stationary outlets[1]	Total (mil. dol.)[2]	State government	Local government	Total	Librarians with ALA-MLS[4]	
Total..........	9,129	16,421	8,223	12.7	77.3	133,456	30,094	8,785
1,000,000 or more.....	24	977	1,223	9.2	78.7	16,608	4,757	24
500,000 to 999,000....	52	1,104	1,305	16.0	75.3	18,313	4,630	52
250,000 to 499,999....	95	1,099	946	13.1	79.0	14,794	3,695	95
100,000 to 249,999...	327	1,992	1,322	11.9	80.0	22,117	4,878	327
50,000 to 99,999.....	541	1,642	1,061	15.2	76.2	17,729	3,968	538
25,000 to 49,999.....	913	1,706	985	13.4	77.4	16,789	3,840	909
10,000 to 24,999.....	1,767	2,273	866	11.8	76.1	15,488	3,120	1,757
5,000 to 9,999.......	1,443	1,597	297	11.2	74.4	6,110	861	1,425
2,500 to 4,999.......	1,305	1,354	123	7.7	74.2	2,808	229	1,272
1,000 to 2,499.......	1,621	1,631	74	6.0	67.0	2,003	94	1,548
Fewer than 1,000.....	1,041	1,046	21	7.6	66.0	697	22	838

[1] The sum of central and branches libraries. The total number of central libraries was 8,971; the total of branch libraries was 7,450. [2] Includes income from the federal government (0.6%) and other sources (9.4%), not shown separately. [3] Full-time equivalents. [4] Librarians with master's degrees from a graduate library education program accredited by the American Library Association (ALA). Total librarians, including those without ALA-MLS, were 44,428.

Source: U.S. National Center for Education Statistics, *Public Libraries in the United States: 2001*, NCES ɔ03-399, June 2003.

No. 1149. Public Library Use of the Internet: 2002

[In percent, except number of outlets. As of spring. Based on sample survey; see source for details]

Item		Metropolitan status[1]			Poverty status[2]		
	Total	Urban	Sub-urban	Rural	Less than 20 percent	20 to 40 percent	More than 40 percent
All libraries outlets[3]..................	16,004	2,742	4,764	8,498	12,847	2,832	325
Connected to the Internet...............	98.7	100.0	99.7	97.8	99.0	97.4	100.0
Connected with public access...........	95.3	100.0	95.3	93.7	94.4	98.9	100.0
Average number of workstations..........	10.8	20.6	11.7	6.7	9.8	15.1	10.6
Speed of access:[4]							
56kpbs dial-up.......................	6.5	-	2.8	11.0	7.7	2.2	-
56kpbs direct connect................	14.8	6.6	10.6	20.1	14.3	15.8	23.7
64kbps to 1.5mbps...................	16.6	11.9	19.7	16.5	16.8	16.7	7.2
1.5mbps (T1) or greater..............	49.1	77.2	59.3	33.2	48.0	53.9	47.2
Public access database subscription services available on—							
All workstations...................	65.0	75.5	61.7	63.3	64.5	69.0	53.2
Some workstations.................	25.6	21.8	31.0	23.8	25.5	24.4	36.2
No workstations...................	9.4	2.7	7.3	12.9	10.0	6.6	10.6
Database subscription services offered remotely to off-site users............	44.3	61.9	41.2	40.0	44.7	43.1	42.5
Public access Internet content filtering/blocking on—							
All workstations...................	24.4	38.9	19.5	22.1	21.6	36.9	23.2
Some workstations.................	17.5	18.1	23.8	13.7	18.5	12.7	23.2
No workstations...................	58.1	43.0	56.7	64.2	59.9	50.4	53.6

- Represents or rounds to zero. [1] Urban = inside central city; Suburban = in metro area, outside of a central city; Rural = outside a metro area. [2] Determined by the 1990 poverty status of the service area of the outlet. [3] Central libraries and branches; excludes bookmobiles. [4] Less than 56kbps accounts for 1.7 percent of public libraries connected to the Internet. Don't know responses are 10.5 percent total.

Source: Information Use Management and Policy Institute, School of Information Studies, Florida State University, Tallahassee, FL, *Public Libraries and the Internet 2002: Internet Connectivity and Networked Services*, by John Carlo Bertot and Charles R. McClure, Florida State University, Tallahassee, FL.

No. 1150. Internet Access and Usage and Online Service Usage: 2003

[For persons 18 years old and over (209,657 represents 209,657,000). As of fall. Based on sample and subject to sampling error; see source for details]

Item	Total adults	Any Online/ Internet usage	Have Internet access			Used the Internet in the last 30 days			Used any online service in the past 30 days
			Home or work or other	Home only	Work only	Home or work or other	Home only	Work only	
Total adults (1,000).	209,657	131,839	165,898	128,549	73,315	128,417	107,604	62,159	118,133
PERCENT DISTRIBUTION									
Age:									
18 to 34 years old	31.5	37.2	34.3	32.1	33.8	37.6	34.7	34.2	37.7
35 to 54 years old	40.0	45.6	43.1	46.2	54.0	45.7	47.2	54.4	45.3
55 years old and over	28.5	17.2	22.7	21.6	12.2	16.8	18.1	11.4	17.0
Sex:									
Male	48.0	48.4	48.3	49.3	50.2	48.3	49.0	49.9	47.9
Female	52.0	51.6	51.7	50.7	49.8	51.7	51.0	50.1	52.1
Household size:									
1 to 2 persons	46.3	40.4	42.3	38.8	41.3	40.6	39.4	42.0	40.1
3 to 4 persons	38.2	44.3	41.9	45.1	45.1	44.2	45.5	45.4	44.5
5 or more persons	15.5	15.3	15.8	16.1	13.6	15.2	15.1	12.7	15.4
Any child in household	42.0	47.1	45.1	47.1	47.8	47.0	47.7	47.6	47.0
Marital status:									
Single	24.4	26.7	25.6	22.8	23.7	26.9	24.3	23.5	27.5
Married	56.7	60.7	59.3	64.6	63.8	60.7	64.1	64.5	60.2
Other	18.9	12.5	15.2	12.7	12.5	12.4	11.5	12.0	12.4
Educational attainment:									
Graduated college plus.	24.3	35.0	29.6	34.1	45.3	35.7	37.9	49.5	34.6
Attended college	26.9	33.0	30.7	31.5	32.2	33.3	32.9	31.6	33.4
Did not attend college	48.8	31.9	39.7	34.4	22.6	31.0	29.2	18.9	32.0
Employed full time	53.0	63.9	59.0	60.9	87.5	64.2	63.1	88.9	64.1
Employed part time	10.8	12.3	11.9	12.4	12.1	12.4	12.9	10.7	12.1
Occupation of employed persons:									
Professional	10.4	15.6	13.0	14.7	24.4	15.9	16.7	25.4	15.3
Exec./manager/administrator	9.8	14.2	12.0	13.7	22.9	14.4	14.9	25.2	14.1
Clerical/sales/technical	18.2	23.9	21.3	21.9	32.5	24.2	23.1	33.4	24.3
Precision/crafts/repair.	6.8	6.5	6.9	6.7	6.8	6.4	6.2	5.6	6.3
Other	18.7	16.0	17.7	16.3	13.1	15.7	15.1	10.1	16.3
Household income:									
Less than $50,000.	49.1	33.8	39.8	31.7	22.5	33.3	29.5	20.2	33.4
$50,000 to $74,999	20.3	23.7	23.1	24.4	24.0	23.7	24.0	23.6	23.9
$75,000 to $149,999	24.0	33.1	29.1	34.0	41.0	33.4	35.7	42.8	33.5
$150,000 or more	6.5	9.4	8.1	9.8	12.4	9.6	10.8	13.4	9.2

Source: Mediamark Research Inc., New York, NY, CyberStats, fall 2003 (copyright). Internet site <http://www.mriplus.com/pocketpiece.html>.

No. 1151. Programs for Adults in Public Library Outlets: 2000

[In percent. For activities offered during a typical week during the prior year. Represents programs for which the outlet provided funding, materials, or staff to support the program or the library system ran the program within or on behalf of of the outlet. Based on the Fast Response Survey System and subject to sampling error; see source for details]

Program and group	All outlets	Number of visits per week			Metropolitan status [1]		
		Less than 300	300 to 1,400	1,500 or more	Urban	Suburban	Rural
GENERAL PROGRAMS							
Computer/Internet instruction	56	36	59	77	68	59	49
Book/film discussions or presentations	43	22	45	69	56	50	34
Cultural performances	41	11	48	71	60	51	28
Recreational activities [2]	39	24	40	59	52	50	29
Parenting skills.	20	6	22	38	28	24	15
Financial planning/investment information . . .	18	4	19	38	30	26	11
Employment/career guidance	17	8	20	24	31	18	12
College/continuing education guidance	15	9	18	18	21	14	13
Citizenship preparation	5	5	4	5	7	6	3
PROGRAMS FOR SPECIFIC GROUPS							
Senior citizens.	24	12	25	38	35	29	18
Parents.	24	10	27	38	32	31	17
Limited English speaking and/or recent immigrants.	9	1	11	19	20	11	5
Adults with physical disabilities	6	4	7	9	7	5	6
Adults with learning disabilities	5	2	6	6	8	3	5

[1] Urban = inside central city; Suburban = In metro area, outside of a central city; Rural = outside a metro area. [2] Such as crafts and hobbies.

Source: U.S. National Center for Education Statistics, Fast Response Survey System, Programs for Adults in Public Library Outlets, NCES 2003-010, November 2002.

Information and Communications 731

No. 1152. Households With Computers and Internet Access by Selected Characteristic: 2003

[Percent of all households in specified group. As of October. Based on the Current Population Survey and subject to sampling error; for details see source. See also text Section 1, Population, and Appendix III]

Characteristic	Households with computers				Households with Internet access			
	Total	Rural [1]	Urban [1]	Central city [1]	Total	Rural [1]	Urban [1]	Central city [1]
All households	61.8	61.9	61.7	56.9	54.6	54.1	54.8	49.3
Age of householder:								
Under 25 years old	56.5	52.5	57.2	56.6	46.9	43.3	47.5	46.0
25 to 34 years old	68.6	71.6	67.8	64.3	60.2	62.1	59.7	56.1
35 to 44 years old	73.2	75.3	72.6	65.8	65.2	66.2	64.9	57.0
45 to 54 years old	71.9	71.5	72.1	65.3	65.1	63.9	65.6	58.4
55 years old or over	46.6	46.7	46.6	41.5	40.8	40.3	40.9	35.4
Sex:								
Male	65.6	64.2	66.2	61.3	58.6	56.3	59.5	54.2
Female	57.4	58.6	57.1	52.5	50.1	51.1	49.8	44.4
Education of householder:								
Elementary	20.6	18.1	21.6	20.7	14.0	12.7	14.5	13.2
Some high school	32.7	34.7	32.0	28.0	24.3	26.3	23.6	20.1
High school graduate or GED	51.1	56.5	48.7	43.0	43.0	47.5	41.1	34.6
Some college	70.6	73.3	69.7	65.4	62.4	64.8	61.6	56.7
BA degree or more	83.3	84.4	83.0	80.1	78.3	79.3	78.1	74.3
Household income:								
Under $5,000	35.6	29.8	37.0	33.6	26.8	20.0	28.4	24.3
$5,000 to $9,000	26.9	24.4	27.5	27.0	20.0	17.7	20.6	20.4
$10,000 to $14,999	31.7	31.7	31.7	32.2	23.7	23.6	23.7	23.2
$15,000 to $19,999	38.2	36.7	38.8	37.8	29.4	26.9	30.3	28.8
$20,000 to $24,999	46.1	47.7	45.5	45.6	36.7	36.6	36.7	37.8
$25,000 to $34,999	55.4	55.7	55.4	54.7	45.6	46.3	45.4	44.5
$35,000 to $49,999	71.1	72.6	70.6	70.0	62.8	62.3	63.0	62.0
$50,000 to $74,999	81.9	82.4	81.7	81.7	76.0	75.8	76.1	75.1
$75,000 to $99,999	88.1	87.9	88.2	85.6	84.1	84.1	84.1	81.7
$100,000 to $149,999	92.9	92.2	93.2	89.8	90.4	89.7	90.6	86.0
$150,000 or more	94.7	95.0	94.7	92.3	92.4	91.6	92.5	91.8

[1] See text, Section 1, Population, and Appendix II.
Source: US Department of Commerce, National Telecommunications and Information Administration, *A Nation Online, 2004,* forthcoming report. See Internet site <http://www.ntia.doc.gov/ntiahome/dn/index.html>.

No. 1153. Households With Computers and Internet Access: 1998 and 2003

[Percent of all households in specified group. As of October. Based on survey and subject to sampling error; for details, see source]

State	1998		2003		State	1998		2003	
	Computers	Internet access	Computers	Internet access		Computers	Internet access	Computers	Internet access
U.S..	42.1	26.2	61.8	54.6	MO	41.8	24.3	60.7	53.0
AL	34.3	21.6	53.9	45.7	MT	40.9	21.5	59.5	50.4
AK	62.4	44.1	72.7	67.6	NE	42.9	22.9	66.1	55.4
AZ	44.3	29.3	64.3	55.2	NV	41.6	26.5	61.3	55.2
AR	29.8	14.7	50.0	42.4	NH	54.2	37.1	71.5	65.2
CA	47.5	30.7	66.3	59.6	NJ	48.1	31.3	65.5	60.5
CO	55.3	34.5	70.0	63.0	NM	42.2	25.8	53.9	44.5
CT	43.8	31.8	69.2	62.9	NY	37.3	23.7	60.0	53.3
DE	40.5	25.1	59.5	53.2	NC	35.0	19.9	57.7	51.1
DC	41.4	24.2	64.3	56.8	ND	40.2	20.6	61.2	53.2
FL	39.5	27.8	61.0	55.6	OH	40.7	24.6	58.8	52.5
GA	35.8	23.9	60.6	53.5	OK	37.8	20.4	55.4	48.4
HI	42.3	27.9	63.3	55.0	OR	51.3	32.7	67.0	61.0
ID	50.0	27.4	69.2	56.4	PA	39.3	24.9	60.2	54.7
IL	42.7	26.5	60.0	51.1	RI	41.0	27.1	62.3	55.7
IN	43.5	26.1	59.6	51.0	SC	35.7	21.4	54.9	45.6
IA	41.4	21.8	64.7	57.1	SD	41.6	23.9	62.1	53.6
KS	43.7	25.7	63.8	54.3	TN	37.5	21.3	56.7	48.9
KY	35.9	21.1	58.1	49.6	TX	40.9	24.5	59.0	51.8
LA	31.1	17.8	52.3	44.1	UT	60.1	35.8	74.1	62.6
ME	43.4	26.0	67.8	57.9	VT	48.7	31.8	65.5	58.1
MD	46.3	31.0	66.0	59.2	VA	46.4	27.9	66.8	60.3
MA	43.4	28.1	64.1	58.1	WA	56.3	36.6	71.4	62.3
MI	44.0	25.4	59.9	52.0	WV	28.3	17.6	55.0	47.6
MN	47.6	29.0	67.9	61.6	WI	43.0	25.1	63.8	57.4
MS	25.7	13.6	48.3	38.9	WY	46.1	22.7	65.4	57.7

Source: U.S. Department of Commerce, National Telecommunications and Information Administration, *Falling through the Net: Defining the Digital Divide,* July 1999, and *A Nation Online, 2004,* forthcoming report. See Internet site <http://www.ntia.doc.gov/ntiahome/dn/index.html>.

Section 25
Banking, Finance, and Insurance

This section presents data on the nation's finances, various types of financial institutions, money and credit, securities, insurance, and real estate. The primary sources of these data are publications of several departments of the federal government, especially the Treasury Department, and independent agencies such as the Federal Deposit Insurance Corporation, the Federal Reserve Board, and the Securities and Exchange Commission. National data on insurance are available primarily from private organizations, such as the American Council of Life Insurers and the Insurance Information Institute.

Flow of funds—The flow of funds accounts of the Federal Reserve Board bring together statistics on all of the major forms of financial instruments to present an economy-wide view of asset and liability relationships. In flow form, the accounts relate borrowing and lending to one another and to the nonfinancial activities that generate income and production. Each claim outstanding is included simultaneously as an asset of the lender and as a liability of the debtor. The accounts also indicate the balance between asset totals and liability totals over the economy as a whole. Several publications of the Board of Governors of the Federal Reserve System contain information on the flow of funds accounts: Summary data on flows and outstandings, in the *Statistical Supplement to the Federal Reserve Bulletin*, and *Flow of Funds Accounts of the United States* (quarterly); and concepts and organization of the accounts, in *Guide to the Flow of Funds Accounts* (2000). Data are also available at the Board's Web site <http://www.federalreserve.gov/releases/>.

Survey of Consumer Finances (SCF)—The Federal Reserve Board in cooperation with the Department of the Treasury sponsors this survey, which is conducted every 3 years to provide detailed information on the finances of U.S. families. Among the topics covered are the balance sheet, pension, income,

and other demographic characteristics of U.S. families. The survey also gathers information on the use of financial institutions. Since 1992, data for the SCF have been collected by the National Organization for Social Science and Survey Research at the University of Chicago. Data from the survey are published periodically in the *Federal Reserve Bulletin*. The latest survey is available in the January 2003 issue of the Bulletin. More data and information on the survey are available at the following Web site of the Federal Reserve Board, <http://www.federalreserve.gov/pubs/oss/oss2/scfindex.html>.

Banking system—Banks in this country are organized under the laws of both the states and the federal government and are regulated by several bank supervisory agencies. National banks are supervised by the Comptroller of the Currency. *Reports of Condition* have been collected from national banks since 1863. Summaries of these reports are published in the Comptroller's *Annual Report*, which also presents data on the structure of the national banking system.

The Federal Reserve System was established in 1913 to exercise central banking functions, some of which are shared with the U.S. Treasury. It includes national banks and such state banks that voluntarily join the system. Statements of state bank members are consolidated by the Board of Governors of the Federal Reserve System with data for national banks collected by the Comptroller of the Currency into totals for all member banks of the system. Balance sheet data for member banks and other commercial banks are published quarterly in the *Statistical Supplement to the Federal Reserve Bulletin*. The Federal Deposit Insurance Corporation (FDIC), established in 1933, insures each depositor up to $100,000. Major item balance sheet and income data for all insured financial institutions are published in the *FDIC Quarterly Banking Profile*. This publication is also available on

Banking, Finance, and Insurance 733

U.S. Census Bureau, Statistical Abstract of the United States: 2004-2005

the Internet at the following address: <http://www.fdic.gov>. Balance sheet and income data for individual institutions are also available at this site in the Institution Directory (ID) system.

Credit unions—Federally chartered credit unions are under the supervision of the National Credit Union Administration. State-chartered credit unions are supervised by the respective state supervisory authorities. The administration publishes comprehensive program and statistical information on all federal and federally insured state credit unions in the *Annual Report of the National Credit Union Administration*. Deposit insurance (up to $100,000 per account) is provided to members of all federal and those state credit unions that are federally-insured by the National Credit Union Share Insurance Fund which was established in 1970. Deposit insurance for state chartered credit unions is also available in some states under private or state-administered insurance programs.

Other credit agencies—Insurance companies, finance companies dealing primarily in installment sales financing, and personal loan companies represent important sources of funds for the credit market. Statistics on loans, investments, cash, etc., of life insurance companies are published principally by the American Council of Life Insurers in its *Life Insurers Fact Book*. Consumer credit data are published currently in the *Statistical Supplement to the Federal Reserve Bulletin*.

Government corporations and credit agencies make available credit of specified types or to specified groups of private borrowers, either by lending directly or by insuring or guaranteeing loans made by private lending institutions. Data on operations of government credit agencies, along with other government corporations, are available in reports of individual agencies; data on their debt outstanding are published in the *Statistical Supplement to the Federal Reserve Bulletin*.

Securities—The Securities and Exchange Commission (SEC) was established in 1934 to protect the interests of the public and investors against malpractices in the securities and financial markets and to provide the fullest possible disclosure of

information regarding securities to the investing public. Statistical data are published in the *SEC Annual Report*.

Data on the securities industry and securities transactions are also available from a number of private sources. The Securities Industry Association, New York, NY, <http://www.sia.com/>, publishes the *SIA Annual Report, Securities Industry Yearbook*, and the periodic *Securities Industry Trends*. The Investment Company Institute, Washington, DC, <http://www.ici.org/> publishes a reference book, research newsletters, and a variety of research reports that examine the industry, its shareholders, or industry issues. The annual *Mutual Fund Fact Book* is a guide to trends and statistics observed in the investment company industry. *Fundamentals* is a newsletter summarizing the findings of major Institute research projects. Institute research reports provide a detailed examination of shareholder demographics and other aspects of fund ownership.

Among the many sources of data on stock and bond prices and sales are the New York Stock Exchange, New York, NY, <http://www.nyse.com/>; NASDAQ, Washington, DC, <http://www.nasdaq.com/>; Global Financial Data, Los Angeles, CA, <http://www.globalfindata.com/>; Dow-Jones & Company, Inc., New York, NY, <http://www.dj.com/>; and the Bond Market Association, New York, NY, <http://www.bondmarkets.com/>.

Insurance—Insuring companies, which are regulated by the various states or the District of Columbia, are classified as either life or property. Both life and property insurance companies may underwrite health insurance. Insuring companies, other than those classified as life, are permitted to underwrite one or more property lines provided they are so licensed and have the necessary capital or surplus.

There are a number of published sources for statistics on the various classes of insurance—life, health, fire, marine, and casualty. Organizations representing certain classes of insurers publish reports for these classes. The American Council of Life Insurers publishes statistics on life insurance purchases, ownership, benefit payments, and assets in its *Life Insurers Fact Book*.

No. 1154. Gross Domestic Product in Finance, Insurance, Real Estate, Rental and Leasing in Current and Real (2000) Dollars: 2000 to 2003

[In billions of dollars, except percent (741 represents $741,000,000,000). Represents value added by industry. For definition of gross domestic product and explanation of chained dollars, see text, Section 13]

Industry	NAICS code [1]	Current dollars				Chained (2000) dollars			
		2000	2001	2002	2003	2000	2001	2002	2003
Finance & insurance, total	52	**741**	**770**	**804**	**864**	**741**	**762**	**774**	**830**
Percent of gross domestic product . . .		7.5	7.6	7.7	7.9	7.5	7.7	7.7	8.0
Monetary authorities—central bank, credit intermediation & related activities	521,522	319	352	375	(NA)	319	338	337	(NA)
Security, commodity contracts & like activity	523	168	165	163	(NA)	168	181	188	(NA)
Insurance carriers & related activities	524	238	235	249	(NA)	238	228	234	(NA)
Funds, trusts, & other financial vehicles (part)	525	16	18	18	(NA)	16	15	16	(NA)
Real estate & rental & leasing, total . .	53	**1,191**	**1,258**	**1,322**	**1,365**	**1,191**	**1,215**	**1,236**	**1,258**
Percent of gross domestic product . . .		12.1	12.5	12.6	12.4	12.1	12.3	12.3	12.1
Real estate	531	1,082	1,150	1,210	(NA)	1,082	1,106	1,120	(NA)
Rental & leasing services [2]	532,533	108	108	112	(NA)	108	109	116	(NA)

NA Not available.   [1] See footnote 1, Table 1155.   [2] Includes lessors of other nonfinancial intangible asset.

Source: U.S. Bureau of Economic Analysis, "Gross-Domestic-Product-by-Industry Accounts;" published 17 June 2004; <http://www.bea.gov/bea/dn2/home/gdpbyindy.htm>.

No. 1155. Finance and Insurance, and Real Estate and Rental and Leasing—Establishments, Revenue, Payroll, and Employees by Kind of Business (1997 NAICS Basis): 1997 and 2002

[2,198 represents $2,198,000,000,000. For establishments with payroll. Data for 2002 are preliminary. Based on the 1997 and 2002 Economic Censuses; see Appendix III]

Kind of business	NAICS code [1]	Number of establishments		Revenue (bil. dol.)		Annual payroll (bil. dol.)		Paid employees (1,000)	
		1997	2002	1997	2002	1997	2002	1997	2002
Finance & insurance	52	**395,203**	**449,134**	**2,198**	**2,616**	**264.6**	**343.5**	**5,835**	**6,664**
Monetary authorities-central bank . . .	521	42	47	25	29	0.9	1.2	22	22
Credit intermediation & related activities	522	166,882	194,822	809	923	98.7	127.0	2,745	3,055
Security, commodity contracts & like activity .	523	54,491	80,493	275	316	71.3	95.6	706	976
Insurance carriers & related activities .	524	172,299	170,795	1,073	1,320	92.2	118.0	2,327	2,579
Funds, trusts, and other financial vehicles (part) .	525	1,489	2,977	17	27	1.4	1.6	35	30
Real estate & rental & leasing . . .	53	**288,273**	**325,590**	**241**	**348**	**41.6**	**61.8**	**1,702**	**2,136**
Real estate	531	221,650	258,639	153	238	27.9	42.8	1,117	1,450
Rental & leasing services.	532	64,472	64,624	76	95	12.6	17.5	559	658
Lessors of other nonfinancial intangible asset	533	2,151	2,327	11	14	1.1	1.5	26	28

[1] North American Industry Classification System, 1997; see text, section 15.

Source: U.S. Census Bureau, 2002 Economic Census, Advance Report, issued March 2004. See Internet site: <http://www.census.gov/econ/census02/>

No. 1156. Finance and Insurance—Nonemployer Establishments and Receipts by Kind of Business: 1997 to 2002

[679.2 represents 679,200. Includes only firms subject to federal income tax. Nonemployers are businesses with no paid employees. Data originate chiefly from administrative records of the Internal Revenue Service; see Appendix III]

Kind of business	NAICS code [1]	Establishments (1,000)			Receipts (mil. dol.)		
		1997	2000	2002	1997	2000	2002
Finance and insurance	52	**679.2**	**691.8**	**660.3**	**36,966**	**49,058**	**44,139**
Credit intermediation & related activities	522	163.7	165.3	66.0	8,693	4,848	3,796
Depository credit intermediation.	5221	6.5	6.5	(NA)	215	197	(NA)
Nondepository credit intermediation	5222	142.7	134.1	(NA)	7,920	3,624	(NA)
Activities related to credit intermediation	5223	14.5	24.7	(NA)	557	1,028	(NA)
Security, commodity contracts & like activity	523	188.4	181.5	240.5	16,438	29,379	24,172
Scrty & comdty contracts interm & brokerage. . . .	5231	29.3	29.6	(NA)	6,159	6,395	(NA)
Securities & commodity exchanges	5232	1.2	1.6	(NA)	315	1,495	(NA)
Other financial investment activities	5239	158.0	150.2	(NA)	9,965	21,488	(NA)
Insurance carriers & related activities	524	327.1	345.0	353.8	11,834	14,831	16,171
Insurance carriers	5241	0.9	1.0	(NA)	76	98	(NA)
Agencies & other insurance related activities	5242	326.2	344.0	(NA)	11,758	14,733	(NA)
Insurance agencies & brokerages.	52421	258.0	245.5	(NA)	9,718	11,570	(NA)
Other insurance related activities	52429	68.1	98.5	(NA)	2,040	3,163	(NA)

NA Not available.   [1] North American Industry Classification System, 1997; see text, section 15.

Source: U.S. Census Bureau, "Nonemployer Statistics"; <http://www.census.gov/epcd/nonemployer/> and 2002 Economic Census: Advance Nonemployer Statistics; published 21 May 2004; <http://www.census.gov/epcd/nonemployer/2002/us/US000.HTM>.

Banking, Finance, and Insurance   **735**

[423.7 represents 423,700. Covers establishments with payroll. Employees are for the week including March 12. Most government employees are excluded. For statement on methodology, see Appendix III]

Kind of business	NAICS code[1]	Establishments (1,000)		Employees (1,000)		Payroll (bil. dol.)	
		2000	2001	2000	2001	2000	2001
Finance & insurance, total	52	423.7	425.0	5,963.4	6,248.4	346.8	373.6
Monetary authorities—central bank	521	0.1	0.1	22.3	23.6	1.1	1.2
Credit intermediation & related activities	522	176.3	180.8	2,753.2	2,917.6	116.1	130.4
Depository credit intermediation [2]	5221	105.6	107.2	1,934.7	2,062.5	78.5	85.3
Commercial banking	52211	73.9	75.8	1,492.8	1,603.2	63.6	69.2
Savings institutions	52212	15.9	15.7	243.6	253.1	9.2	9.8
Credit unions	52213	15.6	15.5	192.3	200.4	5.4	6.0
Nondepository credit intermediation [2]	5222	49.3	49.8	620.9	646.4	29.6	35.2
Real estate credit	522292	19.8	19.8	237.7	251.5	10.8	14.8
Activities related to credit intermediation	5223	21.4	23.7	197.6	208.7	7.9	9.9
Security, commodity contracts & like activity	523	72.9	76.9	866.2	947.1	119.5	125.0
Scrty & comdty contracts intermed & brokerage [2]	5231	38.1	39.6	539.0	575.3	80.2	84.7
Investment banking & securities dealing	52311	6.3	7.0	138.5	172.7	31.2	35.2
Securities brokerage	52312	29.5	30.3	377.7	381.1	47.0	47.5
Securities & commodity exchanges	5232	(Z)	0.1	6.8	6.5	0.5	0.6
Other financial investment activities [2]	5239	34.8	37.2	320.4	365.2	38.8	39.8
Portfolio management	52392	11.6	11.3	156.2	171.5	24.9	23.7
Insurance carriers & related activities	524	172.2	164.8	2,290.2	2,326.1	108.1	114.8
Insurance carriers [2]	5241	37.4	30.9	1,489.2	1,505.0	74.7	78.5
Direct life/health/medical insurance carriers	52411	13.9	13.5	813.4	821.9	40.0	41.8
Direct life insurance carriers	524113	10.7	10.6	491.1	500.0	25.7	26.9
Direct health & medical insurance carriers	524114	3.1	3.0	322.3	321.8	14.3	15.0
Other direct insurance carriers [2]	52412	23.0	16.8	660.4	668.6	33.5	35.4
Direct property & casualty insurance carriers	524126	19.8	12.2	609.4	592.6	31.1	31.3
Agencies & other insurance related activities [2]	5242	134.8	134.0	801.0	821.1	33.3	36.3
Insurance agencies & brokerages	52421	121.5	120.9	596.2	613.0	24.7	27.1
Other insurance related activities	52429	13.3	13.1	204.8	208.1	8.6	9.1
Funds, trusts, & other financial vehicles (part)	525	2.3	2.4	31.5	34.0	2.1	2.1

Z Less than 50.   [1] North American Industry Classification System, 1997; see text, Section 15.   [2] Includes industries not shown separately.

Source: U.S. Census Bureau, County Business Patterns, annual, <http://www.census.gov/prod/2003pubs/01cbp/cbp01-1.pdf>, (issued April 2003).

No. 1158. Flow of Funds Accounts—Financial Assets of Financial and Nonfinancial Institutions by Holder Sector: 1990 to 2003

[In billions of dollars (36,715 represents $36,715,000,000,000). As of Dec. 31]

Sector	1990	1995	1996	1997	1998	1999	2000	2001	2002	2003
All sectors	36,715	54,378	60,442	68,356	77,003	87,847	91,200	92,228	90,970	101,402
Households [1]	14,861	21,646	24,105	27,574	30,521	34,990	33,950	32,653	30,410	34,341
Nonfinancial business	3,979	5,568	6,162	6,644	7,873	9,335	11,260	11,554	11,850	12,705
Farm business	47	61	61	62	64	65	65	67	72	77
Nonfarm noncorporate	356	548	643	774	993	1,177	1,423	1,578	1,720	1,879
Nonfinancial corporations	3,575	4,959	5,458	5,809	6,816	8,094	9,772	9,909	10,058	10,748
State and local government	963	994	1,008	1,033	1,180	1,258	1,296	1,388	1,474	1,544
U.S. Government	442	442	447	442	445	561	514	615	613	634
Monetary authorities	342	472	495	534	567	697	636	683	754	797
Commercial banking	3,337	4,494	4,710	5,175	5,629	5,982	6,469	6,829	7,329	7,812
U.S.-chartered commercial banks	2,644	3,322	3,445	3,742	4,081	4,431	4,774	5,015	5,427	5,840
Foreign banking offices in U.S.	367	666	715	811	806	751	789	792	801	733
Bank holding companies	298	467	511	575	686	741	842	942	1,026	1,152
Banks in U.S.-affiliated areas	28	39	40	46	56	59	63	80	75	88
Savings institutions	1,323	1,013	1,032	1,029	1,089	1,150	1,218	1,299	1,357	1,475
Credit unions	217	311	330	354	391	415	441	506	561	617
Bank personal trusts, estates	522	775	842	918	976	1,104	1,068	929	808	899
Life insurance	1,351	2,064	2,246	2,515	2,770	3,068	3,136	3,225	3,335	3,823
Other insurance	533	740	770	843	876	873	862	858	919	1,043
Private pension funds	1,627	2,889	3,207	3,689	4,105	4,541	4,423	4,063	3,533	4,194
State and local government employee retirement funds	801	1,303	1,495	1,817	2,054	2,227	2,290	2,180	1,964	2,284
Federal government retirement funds	340	541	606	659	718	776	799	862	897	960
Money market funds	493	741	887	1,043	1,330	1,579	1,812	2,241	2,224	2,016
Mutual funds	608	1,853	2,342	2,989	3,613	4,538	4,435	4,135	3,639	4,665
Closed-end funds	53	136	144	146	149	152	142	140	151	215
Exchange-traded funds	-	1	2	7	16	34	66	83	102	151
Government-sponsored enterprises	478	897	989	1,099	1,404	1,721	1,900	2,301	2,543	2,819
Federally-related mortgage pools	1,020	1,570	1,711	1,826	2,018	2,292	2,492	2,830	3,158	3,488
Asset-backed securities issuers	286	793	938	1,140	1,468	1,678	1,881	2,174	2,432	2,712
Finance companies	547	672	717	764	853	1,004	1,140	1,160	1,196	1,381
Mortgage companies	49	33	41	32	32	32	32	32	32	32
Real estate investment trusts	28	33	38	64	71	68	62	70	93	115
Security brokers and dealers	262	568	636	779	921	1,001	1,221	1,466	1,335	1,602
Funding corporations	251	394	499	613	740	1,000	1,141	1,205	1,193	1,274
Rest of the world	1,998	3,435	4,042	4,627	5,195	5,772	6,446	6,750	7,070	7,803

- Represents zero.   [1] Includes nonprofit organizations.

Source: Board of Governors of the Federal Reserve System, "Federal Reserve Statistical Release, Z.1, Flow of Funds Accounts of the United States"; published: 4 March 2004; <http://www.federalreserve.gov/releases/Z1/20040304/data.htm>.

No. 1159. Flow of Funds Accounts—Credit Market Debt Outstanding: 1990 to 2003

[In billions of dollars (13,772 represents $13,772,000,000,000). As of Dec. 31]

Item	1990	1995	1996	1997	1998	1999	2000	2001	2002	2003
Credit market debt	13,772	18,499	19,867	21,329	23,507	25,650	27,389	29,409	31,699	34,449
U.S. Government	2,498	3,637	3,782	3,805	3,752	3,681	3,385	3,380	3,637	4,033
Nonfederal domestic nonfinancial	8,352	10,046	10,631	11,384	12,489	13,621	14,781	15,923	17,038	18,362
Households [1]	3,598	4,885	5,230	5,552	6,006	6,499	7,077	7,722	8,498	9,401
Corporations	2,533	2,910	3,092	3,382	3,775	4,181	4,543	4,767	4,806	4,971
Nonfarm noncorporate business	1,093	1,062	1,129	1,224	1,406	1,595	1,788	1,948	2,097	2,227
Farm business	135	145	150	156	164	169	180	188	196	201
State and local government	992	1,045	1,029	1,071	1,138	1,177	1,192	1,298	1,442	1,561
Rest of the world	289	454	542	608	639	652	709	660	666	652
Financial sectors	2,632	4,363	4,913	5,532	6,626	7,695	8,514	9,447	10,358	11,403
Commercial banking	198	251	264	309	382	449	509	562	612	661
Savings institutions	140	115	141	160	212	260	288	295	281	281
Credit unions	-	-	-	1	1	3	3	5	7	9
Life insurance companies	-	1	2	2	2	3	2	3	5	8
Government-sponsored enterprises	399	807	897	995	1,274	1,592	1,826	2,114	2,340	2,583
Federally-related mortgage pools	1,020	1,570	1,711	1,826	2,018	2,292	2,492	2,830	3,158	3,488
Asset-backed securities issuers	288	796	947	1,151	1,481	1,688	1,887	2,181	2,437	2,718
Finance companies	374	484	534	568	625	696	778	780	823	932
Mortgage companies	25	17	21	16	16	16	16	16	16	16
Real estate investment trusts	28	45	56	96	159	165	168	170	190	213
Security brokers and dealers	15	29	27	35	43	25	41	42	41	47
Funding corporations	147	249	312	373	413	504	504	448	448	446

- Represents or rounds to zero.   [1] Includes nonprofit organizations.

Source: Board of Governors of the Federal Reserve System, "Federal Reserve Statistical Release, Z.1, Flow of Funds Accounts of the United States"; published: 4 March 2004; <http://www.federalreserve.gov/releases/Z1/20040304/data.htm>.

No. 1160. Flow of Funds Accounts—Financial Assets and Liabilities of Foreign Sector: 1990 to 2003

[In billions of dollars (1,998 represents $1,998,000,000,000). As of Dec. 31]

Type of instrument	1990	1995	1996	1997	1998	1999	2000	2001	2002	2003
Total financial assets [1]	1,998	3,435	4,042	4,627	5,195	5,772	6,446	6,750	7,070	7,803
Net interbank assets	53	229	177	173	146	140	161	116	120	125
U.S. checkable deposits and currency	107	194	214	244	258	298	294	318	341	368
U.S. time deposits	49	50	61	74	87	102	103	83	95	87
Security RPs [2]	20	68	71	91	72	80	91	151	190	460
Credit market instruments	889	1,493	1,840	2,098	2,273	2,307	2,477	2,724	3,131	3,742
Open market paper	11	43	58	78	115	102	112	118	135	153
U.S. government securities	488	966	1,222	1,375	1,413	1,381	1,471	1,594	1,884	2,171
Official holdings	291	507	631	648	670	694	750	799	898	1,056
Treasury	286	490	606	615	623	618	625	651	711	838
Agency	5	18	25	33	47	76	125	148	187	218
Private holdings	197	459	591	727	743	687	721	795	986	1,114
Treasury	152	330	441	551	562	463	401	389	504	651
Agency	45	129	150	176	181	224	320	406	482	463
U.S. corporate bonds [3]	217	361	433	502	603	704	776	897	986	1,294
Loans to U.S. corporate business	172	122	126	143	142	120	117	116	126	125
U.S. corporate equities	244	550	672	953	1,250	1,612	1,626	1,534	1,223	1,618
Trade receivables	45	53	58	59	53	47	47	44	47	44
Miscellaneous assets	591	799	950	937	1,056	1,186	1,647	1,780	1,922	1,358
Foreign direct investment in U.S [4]	505	680	746	824	1,001	1,216	1,316	1,383	1,521	1,619
Other	86	119	204	113	55	-30	331	397	401	-261
Total liabilities [1]	1,389	2,012	2,317	2,562	2,776	3,148	3,488	3,567	3,757	3,508
U.S. official foreign exchange and net IMF position	61	64	54	49	60	50	46	47	56	62
U.S. private deposits	298	419	522	618	625	686	820	851	875	847
Credit market instruments [1]	289	454	542	608	639	652	709	660	666	652
Commercial paper	75	56	67	65	73	89	121	107	143	165
Bonds	115	299	366	428	451	453	468	443	410	385
Bank loans n.e.c. [5]	19	35	44	52	59	59	71	63	69	61
Miscellaneous liabilities [1]	713	1,030	1,156	1,238	1,407	1,710	1,862	1,962	2,123	1,899
U.S. direct investment abroad [3][4]	629	886	990	1,068	1,196	1,414	1,530	1,598	1,752	1,890

[1] Includes other items not shown separately.   [2] Repurchase agreements.   [3] Through 1992, corporate bonds include net issues by Netherlands Antillean financial subsidiaries; U.S. direct investment abroad excludes net inflows from those bond issues.   [4] Direct investment is valued on a current-cost basis.   [5] Not elsewhere classified.

Source: Board of Governors of the Federal Reserve System, "Federal Reserve Statistical Release, Z.1, Flow of Funds Accounts of the United States"; published: 4 March 2004; <http://www.federalreserve.gov/releases/Z1/20040304/data.htm>.

No. 1161. Flow of Funds Accounts—Assets of Households: 1990 to 2003

[As of December 31 (14,861 represents $14,861,000,000,000). Includes nonprofit organizations]

Type of instrument	Total (bil. dol.)							Percent distribution		
	1990	1995	1999	2000	2001	2002	2003	1990	2000	2003
Total financial assets	14,861	21,646	34,990	33,950	32,653	30,410	34,341	100.0	100.0	100.0
Deposits	3,259	3,298	4,023	4,352	4,835	5,063	5,253	21.9	12.8	15.3
Foreign deposits	13	23	44	59	54	64	68	0.1	0.2	0.2
Checkable deposits and currency . .	412	544	346	226	315	279	215	2.8	0.7	0.6
Time and savings deposits	2,465	2,281	2,811	3,100	3,350	3,644	3,985	16.6	9.1	11.6
Money market fund shares	369	450	822	968	1,116	1,076	986	2.5	2.9	2.9
Credit market instruments	1,556	1,940	2,558	2,473	2,433	2,433	2,510	10.5	7.3	7.3
Open-market paper	63	48	68	73	42	48	46	0.4	0.2	0.1
U.S. Government securities	538	843	1,108	935	757	478	688	3.6	2.8	2.0
Treasury issues	471	783	807	586	487	382	418	3.2	1.7	1.2
Agency issues	67	59	301	348	270	95	270	0.5	1.0	0.8
Municipal securities	575	431	450	461	512	618	681	3.9	1.4	2.0
Corporate and foreign bonds	236	509	822	892	1,010	1,175	980	1.6	2.6	2.9
Mortgages	144	109	110	113	113	114	115	1.0	0.3	0.3
Corporate equities [1]	1,781	4,141	9,052	7,474	6,184	4,601	5,709	12.0	22.0	16.6
Mutual fund shares	457	1,153	3,115	3,036	2,870	2,539	3,292	3.1	8.9	9.6
Security credit	62	128	324	412	454	413	466	0.4	1.2	1.4
Life insurance reserves	392	566	784	819	880	921	1,005	2.6	2.4	2.9
Pension fund reserves	3,376	5,671	9,068	9,071	8,681	8,003	9,304	22.7	26.7	27.1
Investment in bank personal trusts . . .	552	803	1,130	1,096	961	841	932	3.7	3.2	2.7
Equity in noncorporate business	3,183	3,629	4,571	4,847	4,965	5,178	5,414	21.4	14.3	15.8
Miscellaneous assets	243	316	364	371	389	418	455	1.6	1.1	1.3

[1] Only those directly held and those in closed-end and exchange-traded funds. Other equities are included in mutual funds, life insurance and pension reserves, and bank personal trusts.

Source: Board of Governors of the Federal Reserve System, "Federal Reserve Statistical Release, Z.1, Flow of Funds Accounts of the United States"; published: 4 March 2004; <http://www.federalreserve.gov/releases/Z1/20040304/data.htm>.

No. 1162. Financial Assets Held by Families by Type of Asset: 1995 to 2001

[Median value in thousands of constant 2001 dollars (18.0 represents $18,000). All dollar figures are adjusted to 2001 dollars using the "current methods" version of the consumer price index for all urban consumers published by U.S. Bureau of Labor Statistics. Families include one-person units; for definition of family, see text, Section 1. Based on Survey of Consumer Finance; see Appendix III]

Age of family head and family income	Any financial asset [1]	Transac-tion accounts [2]	Certifi-cates of deposit	Savings bonds	Stocks [3]	Mutual funds [4]	Retirement accounts [5]	Life insur-ance [6]	Other man-aged [7]
PERCENT OF FAMILIES OWNING ASSET									
1995, total	91.0	87.0	14.3	22.8	15.2	12.3	45.2	32.0	3.9
1998, total	92.9	90.5	15.3	19.3	19.2	16.5	48.8	29.6	5.9
2001, total	93.1	90.9	15.7	16.7	21.3	17.7	52.2	28.0	6.6
Under 35 years old	89.2	86.0	6.3	12.7	17.4	11.5	45.1	15.0	2.1
35 to 44 years old	93.3	90.7	9.8	22.6	21.6	17.5	61.4	27.0	3.1
45 to 54 years old	94.4	92.2	15.2	21.0	22.0	20.2	63.4	31.1	6.4
55 to 64 years old	94.8	93.6	14.4	14.3	26.7	21.3	59.1	35.7	13.0
65 to 74 years old	94.6	93.8	29.7	11.3	20.5	19.9	44.0	36.7	11.8
75 years old and over	95.1	93.7	36.5	12.5	21.8	19.5	25.7	33.3	11.2
Percentiles of income: [8]									
Less than 20 ($10,300) . .	74.8	70.9	10.0	3.8	3.8	3.6	13.2	13.8	2.2
20-39.9 ($24,400)	93.0	89.4	14.7	11.0	11.2	9.5	33.3	24.7	3.3
40-59.9 ($39,900)	98.3	96.1	17.4	14.1	16.4	15.7	52.8	25.6	5.4
60-79.9 ($64,800)	99.6	98.8	16.0	24.4	26.2	20.6	75.7	35.7	8.5
80-89.9 ($98,700)	99.8	99.7	18.3	30.3	37.0	29.0	83.7	38.6	10.7
90-100 ($302,700)	99.7	99.2	22.0	29.7	60.6	48.8	88.3	41.8	16.7
MEDIAN VALUE [9]									
1995, total	18.0	2.5	11.6	1.2	10.4	23.1	19.6	5.8	34.7
1998, total	24.5	3.3	16.3	1.1	19.0	27.2	26.1	7.9	34.3
2001, total	28.0	4.0	15.0	1.0	20.0	35.0	29.0	10.0	70.0
Under 35 years old	6.3	1.8	4.0	0.3	5.7	9.0	6.6	10.0	40.0
35 to 44 years old	26.9	3.4	6.0	1.0	15.0	17.5	28.5	9.0	50.0
45 to 54 years old	45.7	4.6	12.0	1.0	15.0	38.5	48.0	11.0	60.0
55 to 64 years old	56.6	5.5	19.0	2.5	37.5	60.0	55.0	10.0	55.0
65 to 74 years old	51.4	8.0	20.0	2.0	85.0	70.0	60.0	8.8	120.0
75 years old and over	40.0	7.3	25.0	3.0	60.0	70.0	46.0	7.0	100.0

[1] Includes other types of financial assets, not shown separately, money market mutual funds, and call accounts at brokerages. [2] Checking, savings, and money market deposit accounts, money market mutual funds, and call accounts at brokerages. [3] Covers only those stocks that are directly held by families outside mutual funds, retirement accounts and other managed assets. [4] Excludes money market mutual funds and funds held through retirement accounts or other managed assets. [5] The tax-deferred retirement accounts consist of IRAs, Keogh accounts, and certain employer-sponsored accounts. Employer-sponsored accounts include 401(k), 403(b), and thrift saving accounts from current or past jobs; other current job plans from which loans or withdrawals can be made; and accounts from past jobs from which the family expects to receive the account balance in the future. [6] Cash value. [7] Includes personal annuities and trusts with an equity interest and managed investment accounts. [8] Value in parentheses represents median income for that percentile group. Percentile: A value on a scale of zero to 100 that indicates the percent of a distribution that is equal to or below it. For example, a family with income in the 80th percentile has income equal to or better than 80 percent of all other families. [9] Median value of financial asset for families holding such assets.

Source: Board of Governors of the Federal Reserve System, Federal Reserve Bulletin, January 2003, and unpublished revisions.

No. 1163. Flow of Funds Accounts—Liabilities of Households: 1990 to 2003

[As of December 31 (3,720 represents $3,720,000,000,000). Includes nonprofit organizations.]

Type of instrument	1990	1995	1999	Total (bil. dol.) 2000	2001	2002	2003	Percent distribution 1990	2000	2003
Total liabilities	3,720	5,082	6,877	7,466	8,077	8,812	9,757	100.0	100.0	100.0
Credit market instruments	3,598	4,885	6,499	7,077	7,722	8,498	9,401	96.7	94.8	96.4
Home mortgages [1]	2,505	3,353	4,524	4,900	5,389	6,063	6,821	67.3	65.6	69.9
Consumer credit	824	1,168	1,543	1,719	1,857	1,938	2,040	22.2	23.0	20.9
Municipal securities	87	98	137	143	157	170	184	2.3	1.9	1.9
Bank loans, n.e.c. [2]	18	57	67	74	58	55	96	0.5	1.0	1.0
Other loans	82	116	118	120	120	120	120	2.2	1.6	1.2
Commercial mortgages	83	92	110	121	142	153	141	2.2	1.6	1.4
Security credit	39	79	228	235	196	148	181	1.0	3.1	1.9
Trade payables	67	101	131	135	135	146	154	1.8	1.8	1.6
Unpaid life insurance premiums [3] . . .	16	18	19	20	19	20	21	0.4	0.3	0.2

[1] Includes loans made under home equity lines of credit and home equity loans secured by junior liens. [2] Not elsewhere classified. [3] Includes deferred premiums.

Source: Board of Governors of the Federal Reserve System, "Federal Reserve Statistical Release, Z.1, Flow of Funds Accounts of the United States"; published: 4 March 2004; <http://www.federalreserve.gov/releases/Z1/20040304/data.htm>.

No. 1164. Financial Debt Held by Families by Type of Debt: 1995 to 2001

[Median debt in thousands of constant 2001 dollars (25.0 represents $25,000). See headnote, Table 1162]

Age of family head and family income	Any debt	Home-secured debt [1]	Other residential property	Installment	Credit card balances [2]	Other lines of credit	Other debt [3]
PERCENT OF FAMILIES HOLDING DEBTS							
1995, total	74.5	41.0	4.9	45.9	47.3	1.9	8.5
1998, total	74.1	43.1	5.1	43.7	44.1	2.3	8.8
2001, total	75.1	44.6	4.7	45.2	44.4	1.5	7.2
Under 35 years old	82.7	35.7	2.7	63.8	49.6	1.7	8.8
35 to 44 years old	88.6	59.6	4.9	57.1	54.1	1.7	8.0
45 to 54 years old	84.6	59.8	6.5	45.9	50.4	1.5	7.4
55 to 64 years old	75.4	49.0	8.0	39.3	41.6	3.1	7.4
65 to 74 years old	56.8	32.0	3.4	21.1	30.0	(B)	5.0
75 years old and over	29.2	9.5	2.0	9.5	18.4	(B)	3.6
Percentiles of income: [4]							
Less than 20 ($10,300)	49.3	13.8	(B)	25.5	30.3	1.3	5.9
20-39.9 ($24,400)	70.2	27.0	1.8	43.2	44.5	1.5	5.6
40-59.9 ($39,900)	82.1	44.4	3.2	51.9	52.8	1.5	7.7
60-79.9 ($64,800)	85.6	61.8	5.4	56.7	52.6	1.5	7.7
80-89.9 ($98,700)	91.4	76.9	10.3	55.7	50.3	2.6	9.3
90-100 ($302,700)	85.3	75.4	14.9	41.2	33.1	1.4	8.8
MEDIAN DEBT [5]							
1995, total	25.0	59.1	34.7	7.0	1.7	4.0	2.3
1998, total	35.4	67.5	43.5	9.5	1.9	2.7	3.3
2001, total	38.8	70.0	40.0	9.7	1.9	3.9	3.0
Under 35 years old	24.9	77.0	52.0	9.5	2.0	0.5	2.0
35 to 44 years old	61.5	80.0	45.5	11.1	2.0	0.7	3.1
45 to 54 years old	54.3	75.0	33.5	9.6	2.3	5.3	5.0
55 to 64 years old	34.6	55.0	40.0	9.0	1.9	20.5	5.0
65 to 74 years old	13.1	39.0	77.0	7.0	1.0	(B)	2.5
75 years old and over	5.0	44.8	42.0	5.8	0.7	(B)	2.5

B Base figure too small. [1] First and second mortgages and home equity loans and lines of credit secured by the primary residence. [2] Families that had an outstanding balance on any of their credit cards after paying their most recent bills. [3] Includes loans on insurance policies, loans against pension accounts, borrowing on margin accounts and unclassified loans. [4] Value in parentheses represent median income for that percentile group. See footnote 8, Table 1162. [5] Median amount of financial debt for families holding such debts.

No. 1165. Percent Distribution of Amount of Debt Held by Families: 1998 and 2001

[See headnote, Table 1162]

Type of debt	1998	2001	Purpose of debt	1998	2001	Type of lending institution	1998	2001
Total	100.0	100.0	Total	100.0	100.0	Total	100.0	100.0
Home-secured debt. .	71.3	75.1	Home purchase	67.7	70.7	Commercial bank	32.8	34.1
Installment loans.	13.0	12.3	Home improvement . .	2.1	1.9	Savings and loan	9.7	6.1
Credit card balances . .	3.9	3.4	Investment, excluding real estate	3.3	2.8	Credit union	4.2	5.5
Other lines of credit. . .	0.3	0.5	Vehicles.	7.6	7.8	Finance or loan company.	4.2	4.3
Other residential property	7.7	6.4	Goods and services . .	6.1	5.7	Brokerage	3.8	3.1
Other debt	3.7	2.3	Other residential property	7.9	6.6	Real estate lender	35.5	38.0
			Education.	3.4	3.1	Individual lender	3.3	2.0
			Other loans	1.9	1.4	Other nonfinancial	1.3	1.4
						Government	0.6	1.1
						Credit and store cards . .	3.9	3.7
						Other loans	0.7	0.8

Source of Tables 1164 and 1165: Board of Governors of the Federal Reserve System, *Federal Reserve Bulletin*, January 2003, and unpublished revisions.

No. 1166. Ratios of Debt Payments to Family Income: 1995 to 2001

[In percent. All dollar figures are adjusted to 2001 dollars using the "current methods" version of the consumer price index for all urban consumers published by U.S. Bureau of Labor Statistics. Families include one-person units; for definition of family, see text, Section 1. Based on Survey of Consumer Finance; see Appendix III. For definition of median, see Guide to Tabular Presentation]

Age of family head and family income (constant (2001) dollars)	Ratio of debt payments to family income						Percent of debtors with—					
	Aggregate			Median			Ratios above 40 percent			Any payment 60 days or more past due		
	1995	1998	2001	1995	1998	2001	1995	1998	2001	1995	1998	2001
All families	13.6	14.4	12.5	15.6	17.1	16.1	10.6	12.8	11.0	7.1	8.1	7.0
Under 35 years old.	17.1	16.6	16.6	16.2	16.1	16.7	11.4	11.8	10.8	8.7	11.1	11.9
35 to 44 years old	16.7	17.1	14.7	17.6	19.4	17.3	9.3	11.8	9.4	7.7	8.4	5.9
45 to 54 years old	14.7	15.9	12.4	16.1	17.2	16.8	10.6	11.5	10.9	7.4	7.4	6.2
55 to 64 years old	11.5	13.0	10.7	13.9	16.5	13.8	14.4	13.9	12.2	3.2	7.5	7.1
65 to 74 years old	6.9	8.5	8.8	11.1	12.6	15.1	7.8	17.5	13.9	5.3	3.1	1.5
75 years old and over	2.4	3.9	3.8	2.0	8.1	7.4	7.4	20.9	14.3	5.4	1.1	0.8
Percentiles of income:[1]												
Less than 20 ($10,300) . . .	18.0	17.9	15.3	12.1	15.8	17.2	26.2	28.2	27.0	10.2	12.9	13.4
20-39.9 ($24,400)	16.1	15.7	15.1	16.1	16.7	15.9	16.0	17.2	16.0	10.1	12.3	11.7
40-59.9 ($39,900)	14.9	17.8	16.5	15.1	18.5	16.9	8.1	15.3	11.7	8.7	10.0	7.9
60-79.9 ($64,800)	17.4	18.5	16.3	18.3	18.8	17.9	7.1	8.6	5.6	6.6	5.9	4.0
80-89.9 ($98,700)	16.2	16.4	16.5	16.5	17.2	17.0	4.6	3.4	3.5	2.8	3.9	2.6
90-100 ($302,700)	9.3	10.2	8.0	12.2	13.4	11.1	2.0	2.6	2.0	1.0	1.6	1.3

[1] Value in parentheses represents median income for that percentile group. See footnote 8, Table 1162.

Source: Board of Governors of the Federal Reserve System, *Federal Reserve Bulletin*, January 2003, and unpublished revisions.

No. 1167. Household Debt-Service Payments and Financial Obligations as a Percentage of Disposable Personal Income: 1980 to 2002

[Household debt service ratio is an estimate of the ratio of debt payments to disposable personal income. Debt payments consist of the estimated required payments on outstanding mortgage and consumer debt. Financial obligations ratio (FOR) is a broader measure than the debt service ratio. The FOR includes automobile lease payments, rental payments on tenant-occupied property, homeowners' insurance, and property tax payments]

Year	Household debt service ratio	Financial obligations ratio			Year	Household debt service ratio	Financial obligations ratio		
		Total	Home-owner	Renter			Total	Home-owner	Renter
1980. . .	10.60	15.32	11.20	23.67	1998. . .	12.12	17.48	13.27	28.14
1990. . .	11.99	17.31	13.35	24.68	1999. . .	12.44	17.85	13.56	29.20
1995. . .	11.88	17.43	13.10	26.95	2000. . .	12.86	18.16	13.83	30.41
1996. . .	12.13	17.65	13.39	27.22	2001. . .	13.33	18.76	14.24	31.38
1997. . .	12.12	17.62	13.44	27.23	2002. . .	13.32	18.73	14.13	32.29

Source: Board of Governors of the Federal Reserve System, "Household Debt Service and Financial Obligations Ratios;" <http://www.federalreserve.gov/releases/housedebt/default.htm>.

No. 1168. Selected Financial Institutions—Number and Assets by Asset Size: 2003

[As of December. (7,602.5 represents $7,602,500,000,000).) FDIC=Federal Deposit Insurance Corporation]

Asset size	Number of institutions			Assets (bil. dol.)		
	F.D.I.C.-insured			F.D.I.C.-insured		
	Commercial banks	Savings institutions	Credit unions [1]	Commercial banks [2]	Savings institutions	Credit unions [1]
Total	7,769	1,413	9,369	7,602.5	1,474.3	610.2
Less than $25.0 million	701	94	6,358	11.9	1.3	45.8
$25.0 million to $49.9 million	1,253	138	1,114	46.8	5.2	39.5
$50.0 million to $99.9 million	1,957	247	776	142.0	18.4	54.2
$100.0 million to $499.9 million . . .	3,055	633	889	649.4	150.0	188.3
$500.0 million to $999.9 million. . .	379	144	150	260.7	100.7	102.5
$1.0 billion to $2.9 billion	246	92	72	405.7	150.0	113.0
$3.0 billion or more.	178	65	10	6,086.1	1,048.8	66.9
	Percent distribution					
Total	100.0	100.0	100.0	100.0	100.0	100.0
Less than $25.0 million	9.0	6.7	67.9	0.2	0.1	7.5
$25.0 million to $49.9 million	16.1	9.8	11.9	0.6	0.4	6.5
$50.0 million to $99.9 million	25.2	17.5	8.3	1.9	1.2	8.9
$100.0 million to $499.9 million . . .	39.3	44.8	9.5	8.5	10.2	30.9
$500.0 million to $999.9 million. . .	4.9	10.2	1.6	3.4	6.8	16.8
$1.0 billion to $2.9 billion	3.2	6.5	0.8	5.3	10.2	18.5
$3.0 billion or more.	2.3	4.6	0.1	80.1	71.1	11.0

[1] Source: National Credit Union Administration, *National Credit Union Administration Yearend Statistics 2003*. Excludes nonfederally insured state chartered credit unions and federally insured corporate credit unions.   [2] Includes foreign branches of U.S. banks.

Source: Except as noted, U.S. Federal Deposit Insurance Corporation, *Statistics on Banking, 2003*.

No. 1169. FDIC-Insured Financial Institutions—Number, Assets, and Liabilities: 1990 to 2003

[In billions of dollars, except as indicated (4,649 represents $4,649,000,000,000). As of Dec. 31. 2003 data preliminary. Includes outlying areas. Except as noted, includes foreign branches of U.S. banks]

Item	1990	1995	1997	1998	1999	2000	2001	2002	2003
All banking offices	84,353	81,350	83,641	84,587	86,040	85,952	86,506	87,837	89,096
Commercial bank offices, total [1]	62,723	65,888	68,810	70,052	71,534	71,911	72,458	74,072	75,159
Number of main offices	12,376	9,971	9,165	8,793	8,597	8,331	8,095	7,887	7,769
Number of branches	50,347	55,917	59,645	61,259	62,937	63,580	64,363	66,185	67,390
Savings institutions offices, total	21,630	15,462	14,831	14,535	14,506	14,041	14,048	13,765	13,937
Number of main offices	2,815	2,030	1,780	1,690	1,642	1,589	1,534	1,467	1,413
Number of branches	18,815	13,432	13,051	12,845	12,864	12,452	12,514	12,298	12,524
Number of financial institutions reporting	15,158	11,970	10,923	10,464	10,222	9,905	9,613	9,354	9,182
Assets, total [2]	4,649	5,338	6,045	6,531	6,884	7,462	7,868	8,436	9,077
Net loans and leases	2,867	3,198	3,611	3,896	4,187	4,576	4,687	4,968	5,349
Real estate loans	1,586	1,690	1,877	1,990	2,181	2,396	2,561	2,850	3,143
1-4 family residential mortgages	859	1,006	1,110	1,170	1,251	1,340	1,380	1,513	1,611
Commercial real estate	328	349	389	418	471	525	570	628	682
Construction and development	171	90	108	130	165	197	232	245	272
Home equity loans [3]	86	98	116	113	121	151	184	256	346
Commercial and industrial loans	646	674	811	920	996	1,086	1,020	954	922
Loans to individuals	451	576	613	624	618	672	701	772	848
Credit cards and related plans	142	224	246	242	227	266	250	292	339
Farm loans	33	40	45	47	46	49	48	47	47
Other loans and leases	245	294	332	385	416	448	440	434	477
Less: Reserve for losses	65	60	62	64	66	71	80	85	86
Less: Unearned income	29	15	5	4	4	3	3	4	3
Securities	890	1,099	1,121	1,249	1,338	1,361	1,465	1,633	1,771
Domestic office assets	4,259	4,753	5,297	5,807	6,144	6,702	7,119	7,684	8,253
Foreign office assets	390	585	748	724	740	760	749	752	824
Liabilities and capital, total	4,649	5,338	6,045	6,531	6,884	7,462	7,868	8,436	9,077
Noninterest-bearing deposits	511	641	710	761	745	802	927	1,001	1,003
Interest-bearing deposits	3,127	3,129	3,416	3,625	3,793	4,113	4,262	4,567	4,951
Other borrowed funds	569	849	1,043	1,171	1,376	1,467	1,496	1,571	1,736
Subordinated debt	28	46	65	76	79	90	99	99	107
Other liabilities	128	238	304	341	315	356	377	422	448
Equity capital	286	436	507	557	575	634	707	776	831
Domestic office deposits	3,344	3,315	3,600	3,814	3,882	4,208	4,560	4,910	5,213
Foreign office deposits	293	454	526	572	656	707	630	658	741
Estimated insured deposits [4]	2,629	2,662	2,745	2,849	2,868	3,054	3,210	3,384	3,451

[1] Includes insured branches of foreign banks that file a Call Report. [2] Includes other items not shown separately. [3] For one- to four-family residential properties. [4] Excludes foreign office deposits which are uninsured.

No. 1170. FDIC-Insured Financial Institutions—Income and Selected Measures of Financial Condition: 1990 to 2003

[In billions of dollars, except as indicated (437.7 represents $437,700,000,000). 2003 data preliminary. Includes outlying areas. Includes foreign branches of U.S. banks]

Item	1990	1995	1997	1998	1999	2000	2001	2002	2003
Interest income	437.7	373.4	408.7	433.1	441.5	512.2	486.8	429.5	404.6
Interest expense	295.9	190.7	205.6	221.2	218.0	276.5	235.0	152.9	122.6
Net interest income	141.8	182.7	203.1	211.9	223.5	235.7	251.8	276.6	282.0
Provisions for loan losses	41.4	14.7	22.0	24.0	23.4	32.0	46.3	51.5	37.3
Noninterest income	62.2	89.5	111.5	132.9	154.2	164.8	168.8	183.7	202.6
Percent of net operating revenue [1]	30.5	32.9	35.4	38.5	40.8	41.1	40.1	39.9	41.8
Noninterest expense	144.2	171.6	191.1	217.7	228.2	241.6	251.1	263.7	279.7
Income taxes	9.1	30.3	36.7	37.2	45.5	43.7	44.0	52.0	58.9
Net income	11.3	56.4	67.9	72.0	82.4	81.7	87.2	105.1	120.6
PERFORMANCE RATIOS									
Return on assets [2] (percent)	0.24	1.10	1.18	1.16	1.25	1.14	1.14	1.30	1.38
Return on equity [3] (percent)	3.95	13.63	14.03	13.49	14.71	13.55	12.99	14.14	15.04
Net interest margin [4] (percent)	3.47	4.05	4.04	3.91	3.90	3.78	3.78	3.96	3.73
Net charge-offs [5]	34.8	14.4	19.9	22.2	21.6	26.3	38.9	47.0	40.7
Net charge-offs to loans and leases, total (percent)	1.19	0.46	0.57	0.59	0.53	0.59	0.83	0.97	0.78
Net charge-off rate, credit card loans (percent)	3.39	3.39	5.11	5.17	4.40	4.37	5.15	5.47	5.78
CONDITION RATIOS									
Equity capital to assets (percent)	6.16	8.16	8.39	8.52	8.35	8.49	8.99	9.20	9.15
Noncurrent assets plus other real estate owned to assets [6] (percent)	3.16	0.92	0.71	0.66	0.63	0.71	0.88	0.90	0.75
Percentage of banks losing money	16.5	3.1	4.7	6.0	7.6	7.5	8.2	6.7	5.7
Number of problem institutions	1,492	193	92	84	79	94	114	136	116
Assets of problem institutions	640	31	6	11	10	24	40	39	30
Number of failed/assisted institutions	169	6	1	3	8	7	4	11	3

[1] Net operating revenue equals net interest income plus noninterest income. [2] Net income (including securities transactions and nonrecurring items) as a percentage of average total assets. [3] Net income as a percentage of average total equity capital. [4] Interest income less interest expense as a percentage of average earning assets (i.e. the profit margin a bank earns on its loans and investments). [5] Total loans and leases charged off (removed from balance sheet because of uncollectibility), less amounts recovered on loans and leases previously charged off. [6] Noncurrent assets: the sum of loans, leases, debt securities and other assets that are 90 days or more past due, or in nonaccrual status. Other real estate owned: Primarily foreclosed property.

Source of Tables 1169 and 1170: U.S. Federal Deposit Insurance Corporation, Annual Report; Statistics on Banking, annual; FDIC Quarterly Banking Profile; and FDIC Quarterly Banking Profile Graph Book.

No. 1171. FDIC-Insured Financial Institutions by Asset Size: 2003

[In percent, except as indicated (7,602 represents $7,602,000,000,000). Preliminary. See headnote, Table 1170]

Item	Total	Less than $100 million	$100 million to $1 billion	$1 billion to $10 billion	Greater than $10 billion
COMMERCIAL BANKS					
Number of institutions reporting.	7,769	3,911	3,434	341	83
Assets, total (bil. dol.).	7,602	201	910	947	5,544
Deposits (bil. dol.)	5,029	169	737	646	3,477
Net income (bil. dol.).	103	2	11	13	77
Return on assets	1.40	0.94	1.27	1.46	1.42
Return on equity	15.31	8.19	12.80	14.00	16.37
Equity capital to assets	9.10	11.27	9.91	10.58	8.64
Noncurrent assets plus other real estate owned to assets	0.77	0.83	0.71	0.65	0.80
Net charge-offs to loans and leases.	0.89	0.33	0.42	0.65	1.04
Percentage of banks losing money	5.7	9.5	1.9	1.2	1.2
SAVINGS INSTITUTIONS					
Number of institutions reporting.	1,413	479	777	130	27
Assets, total (bil. dol.).	1,474	25	251	365	833
Deposits (bil. dol.)	925	20	190	236	479
Net income (bil. dol.).	18.0	0.3	2.0	4.5	11.2
Return on assets	1.28	1.07	0.88	1.31	1.40
Return on equity	13.66	8.25	8.36	13.60	15.87
Equity capital to assets	9.41	13.24	10.59	9.75	8.79
Noncurrent assets plus other real estate owned to assets	0.62	0.82	0.57	0.56	0.65
Net charge-offs to loans and leases.	0.30	0.12	0.13	0.22	0.39
Percentage of banks losing money	5.7	10.6	3.3	2.3	-

- Represents zero.
Source: U.S. Federal Deposit Insurance Corporation, *Annual Report; Statistics on Banking*, annual; and *FDIC Quarterly Banking Profile.* <http://www.fdic.gov/bank/index.html>.

No. 1172. Retail Fees and Services of Depository Institutions: 2001 and 2002

[In dollars, except as noted. As of June. For most services, fees are reported in terms of (1) the proportion of those institutions offering a service that charge for the service and (2) the average fee charged by the institutions that charge for the service. Based on a random sample of depository institutions belonging to the Bank Insurance Fund, whose members are predominantly commercial banks, or the Savings Association Insurance Fund, whose members are predominantly savings and loans associations]

Type of account or service	2001	2002	Type of account or service	2001	2002
NONINTEREST CHECKING ACCOUNT			**AUTOMATED TELLER MACHINES (ATMs)**		
Percent offering.	96.7	96.1	Percent offering.	90.9	93.4
Single-balance, single-fee account: [1]			Annual fee:		
Percent offering.	29.6	32.3	Percent charging	10.7	10.3
Monthly fee (low balance)	7.12	7.35	Average	10.35	11.65
Minimum balance to avoid fee	527	591	Fees for customer withdrawals on us: [4]		
Fee-only account: [2]			Percent charging	3.6	2.7
Percent offering	37.7	39.9	Average	0.81	0.56
Monthly fee	4.74	5.27	Fees for customer withdrawals on others: [4]		
NOW ACCOUNTS [3]			Percent charging	78.5	69.0
Percent offering.	96.2	95.6	Average	1.17	1.14
			Surcharge: [5]		
Single-fee account: [1]			Percent charging	88.5	89.4
Percent offering.	49.5	40.9	Average	1.32	1.36
Monthly fee (low balance)	8.15	8.71			
Minimum balance to avoid fee	1,132	1,091			

[1] A monthly fee for balances below the minimum, no monthly fee for balances above the minimum, and no other charges. [2] A monthly fee, no minimum balance to eliminate the fee, and a charge per check in some cases. [3] NOW (negotiable order of withdrawal) accounts are checking accounts that pay interest and often have fee structures that differ from those of noninterest checking accounts. [4] An institution's "customer" is one who has an account at the institution. A customer's ATM transactions in which the machine used is that of the customer's institution are called "on us"; a customer's transactions in which the machine used is that of another institution are called "on others." [5] An ATM surcharge is a fee imposed by the ATM's institution, typically on every transaction by the machine's noncustomer users.
Source: Board of Governors of the Federal Reserve System, *Annual Report to the Congress on Retail Fees and Services of Depository Institutions*, June 2003.

No. 1173. U.S. Banking Offices of Foreign Banks—Summary: 1990 to 2003

[In billions of dollars, except as indicated (791 represents $791,000,000,000). As of December. Data cover foreign-bank branches and agencies in the 50 states and the District of Columbia, New York investment companies (through September 1996) and U.S. commercial banks of which more than 25 percent is owned by foreign banks, and International Banking Facilities. Foreign banks are those owned by institutions located outside of the United States and its affiliated insular areas]

Item	1990	1995	1998	1999	2000	2001	2002	2003	Share [1]			
									1990	1995	2000	2003
Assets	791	984	1,118	1,228	1,299	1,385	1,338	1,369	21.4	21.7	19.9	17.6
Loans, total	398	461	494	499	531	523	471	445	18.0	17.3	13.7	10.2
Business	193	249	280	279	296	271	238	192	30.8	35.1	27.1	21.5
Deposits	384	523	558	697	709	743	665	686	14.5	17.6	17.6	14.4

[1] Percent of "domestically owned" commercial banks plus U.S. offices of foreign banks.
Source: Board of Governors of the Federal Reserve System, "Share Data for U.S. Offices of Foreign Banks"; published 10 March 2004; <http://www.federalreserve.gov/releases/Iba/Share/SHRTBL1.html>.

No. 1174. FDIC-Insured Financial Institutions—Number and Assets by State: 2003

[In billions of dollars, except as indicated (9,076.8 represents $9,076,800,000,000). As of Dec. 31. Information is obtained primarily from the Federal Financial Institutions Examination Council (FFIEC) Call Reports and the Office of Thrift Supervision's Thrift Financial Reports. Data are based on the location of each reporting institution's main office. Reported data may include assets located outside of the reporting institution's home state]

State	Number of institutions	Assets by asset size of bank				State	Number of institutions	Assets by asset size of bank			
		Total	Less than $1 bil.	$1 bil. to $10 bil.	Greater than $10 bil.			Total	Less than $1 bil.	$1 bil. to $10 bil.	Greater than $10 bil.
Total	9,182	9,076.8	1,386.2	1,312.6	6,377.9	NV	37	59.2	6.9	33.4	19.0
AL	162	214.8	23.5	5.3	185.9	NH	31	29.7	7.1	8.8	13.8
AK	7	3.9	1.7	2.2	-	NJ	146	152.2	31.4	76.5	44.3
AZ	50	60.7	6.8	5.5	48.5	NM	60	20.5	8.6	12.0	-
AR	170	38.2	27.5	10.7	-	NY	206	1,733.6	42.7	125.5	1,565.4
CA	318	962.9	62.1	130.0	770.8	NC	104	1,101.9	25.6	6.8	1,069.5
CO	180	35.3	26.5	8.8	-	ND	104	20.8	10.5	10.3	-
CT	63	55.9	15.5	14.3	26.1	OH	304	648.2	46.2	35.8	566.2
DE	34	216.2	4.5	29.5	182.2	OK	278	56.8	27.3	18.4	11.1
DC	5	0.8	0.8	-	-	OR	38	21.4	6.7	14.7	-
FL	304	110.7	55.0	55.7	-	PA	270	297.1	61.1	69.3	166.7
GA	345	214.1	53.3	36.3	124.5	RI	15	216.5	2.5	11.5	202.5
HI	8	31.9	0.9	31.0	-	SC	97	40.7	14.4	26.3	-
ID	18	4.7	4.7	-	-	SD	94	85.4	13.2	15.7	56.5
IL	769	575.5	115.0	68.6	391.8	TN	208	118.6	35.1	4.8	78.7
IN	206	117.4	37.6	37.3	42.5	TX	698	200.2	87.2	82.0	31.0
IA	422	55.9	44.5	11.4	-	UT	64	150.9	10.3	8.1	132.6
KS	380	53.1	35.0	18.1	-	VT	19	7.5	4.5	3.0	-
KY	243	47.5	32.2	15.2	-	VA	141	181.6	33.9	12.8	134.9
LA	170	53.7	23.7	11.5	18.5	WA	100	78.4	21.9	27.2	29.3
ME	40	40.3	12.2	1.6	26.4	WV	74	19.0	9.7	9.3	-
MD	122	42.7	23.7	19.0	-	WI	311	109.4	44.1	22.6	42.7
MA	209	214.2	52.6	52.8	108.7	WY	46	5.6	5.6	-	-
MI	178	197.4	30.8	19.8	146.7						
MN	486	108.7	44.6	3.9	60.2	AS	1	0.1	0.1	-	-
MS	103	40.1	14.8	14.9	10.3	GU	3	0.9	0.9	-	-
MO	377	86.8	47.2	27.6	12.1	FM	1	0.1	0.1	-	-
MT	80	13.5	9.7	3.9	-	PR	11	78.1	0.6	31.3	46.2
NE	270	45.6	22.0	11.4	12.2	VI	2	0.1	0.1	-	-

- Represents zero.

Source: U.S. Federal Deposit Insurance Corporation, *Statistics on Banking*, annual.

No. 1175. FDIC-Insured Financial Institutions—Number of Offices and Deposits by State: 2003

[As of June 30 (5,132.1 represents $5,132,100,000,000). Includes insured U.S. branches of foreign banks. The term "offices" includes both main offices and branches. "Banking office" is defined to include all offices and facilities that actually hold deposits, and does not include loan production offices, computer centers, and other nondeposit installations, such as automated teller machines (ATMs). Several institutions have designated home offices that do not accept deposits; these have been included to provide a more complete listing of all offices. The figures for each geographical area only include deposits of offices located within that area. Based on the Summary of Deposits survey]

State or other area	Number of offices	Total deposits (bil. dol.)	State or other area	Number of offices	Total deposits (bil. dol.)	State or other area	Number of offices	Total deposits (bil. dol.)
Total ..	87,792	5,132.1	LA	1,511	52.6	RI	230	17.8
U.S.	87,151	5,087.9	ME	507	16.1	SC	1,261	44.9
			MD	1,689	77.9	SD	444	15.7
AL	1,431	60.3	MA	2,090	172.4	TN	2,029	86.7
AK	129	5.7	MI	2,975	137.1	TX	5,145	297.3
AZ	993	56.0	MN	1,682	97.4	UT	574	85.0
AR	1,302	37.7	MO	2,153	91.6	VT	265	8.8
CA	6,318	614.7	MT	360	11.3	VA	2,429	129.7
CO	1,345	61.1	NE	970	31.5	WA	1,784	81.5
CT	1,175	69.6	NV	445	31.9	WV	642	22.3
DE	246	96.8	NH	418	29.7	WI	2,201	95.9
DC	193	15.6	NJ	3,102	196.3	WY	204	7.8
FL	4,732	268.2	NM	486	16.7	AS	5	0.1
GA	2,476	124.9	NY	4,655	580.7	GU	36	1.7
HI	297	21.2	NC	2,462	147.0	MH	3	(Z)
ID	468	12.6	ND	412	11.0	FM	6	0.1
IL	4,167	281.8	OH	3,915	211.0	MP	12	0.5
IN	2,215	80.3	OK	1,223	44.3	PW	3	0.1
IA	1,519	52.1	OR	999	37.3	PR	553	40.3
KS	1,461	44.9	PA	4,606	208.0	VI	23	1.3
KY	1,703	56.1						

Z Less than $50 million.

Source: U.S. Federal Deposit Insurance Corporation, *Bank and Thrift Branch Office Data Book*, annual.

Banking, Finance, and Insurance 743

No. 1176. Federal and State-Chartered Credit Unions—Summary: 1990 to 2003

[Except as noted, as of December 31 (36,241 represents 36,241,000).. Federal data include District of Columbia, Puerto Rico, Guam, and Virgin Islands. Excludes state-insured, privately-insured, and noninsured state-chartered credit unions and corporate central credit unions which have mainly other credit unions as members]

Year	Operating credit unions Federal	Operating credit unions State	Number of failed institutions[1]	Members (1,000) Federal	Members (1,000) State	Assets (mil. dol.) Federal	Assets (mil. dol.) State	Loans outstanding (mil. dol.) Federal	Loans outstanding (mil. dol.) State	Savings (mil. dol.) Federal	Savings (mil. dol.) State
1990 ...	8,511	4,349	164	36,241	19,454	130,073	68,133	83,029	44,102	117,892	62,082
1995 ...	7,329	4,358	26	42,163	24,927	193,781	112,860	120,514	71,606	170,300	99,838
1996 ...	7,152	4,240	19	43,546	25,652	206,695	120,193	134,127	79,661	180,969	105,743
1997 ...	6,981	4,257	16	43,491	27,921	215,104	136,074	140,104	92,117	187,822	119,359
1998 ...	6,814	4,181	17	43,865	29,674	231,890	156,811	144,849	100,890	202,651	137,348
1999 ...	6,566	4,062	23	44,076	31,308	239,316	172,086	155,578	116,366	207,614	149,305
2000 ...	6,336	3,980	29	43,883	33,705	242,881	195,363	163,851	137,485	210,188	169,053
2001 ...	6,118	3,866	22	43,817	35,560	270,123	231,432	170,326	152,112	235,201	201,923
2002 ...	5,953	3,735	15	44,600	36,300	301,238	255,837	181,768	160,881	261,819	222,372
2003 ...	5,776	3,593	13	46,153	36,287	336,611	273,572	202,898	173,236	291,484	236,856

[1] 1990 for year ending September 30; 1995 reflects 15-month period from October 1994 through December 1995; beginning 1996 reflects calendar year. A failed institution is defined as a credit union which has ceased operation because it was involuntarily liquidated or merged with assistance from the National Credit Union Share Insurance Fund.

Source: National Credit Union Administration, *Annual Report of the National Credit Union Administration*, and unpublished data.

No. 1177. Mortgage Debt Outstanding by Type of Property and Holder: 1990 to 2003

[In billions of dollars (3,808 represents $3,808,000,000,000). As of Dec. 31. Includes Puerto Rico and Guam]

Type of property and holder	1990	1994	1995	1996	1997	1998	1999	2000	2001	2002	2003
Mortgage debt, total..........	3,808	4,381	4,577	4,864	5,202	5,712	6,315	6,883	7,582	8,463	9,477
Residential nonfarm	2,908	3,571	3,754	4,008	4,280	4,694	5,156	5,606	6,184	6,951	7,829
One- to four-family homes.....	2,620	3,301	3,478	3,720	3,979	4,363	4,787	5,205	5,739	6,463	7,292
Savings institutions..........	600	478	482	514	521	534	548	594	621	631	703
Mortgage pools or trusts[1]...	1,046	1,656	1,768	1,935	2,099	2,375	2,690	2,925	3,340	3,755	4,223
Government National Mortgage Association	392	441	461	494	523	522	565	593	569	512	445
Federal Home Loan Mortgage Corp.	308	488	512	552	577	643	745	817	941	1,073	1,148
Federal National Mortgage Assoc	291	521	570	633	688	804	925	1,016	1,238	1,479	1,787
Private mortgage conduits[2].....	55	206	224	256	311	405	455	500	591	692	843
Commercial banks[3]...........	430	590	647	678	746	797	880	966	1,024	1,224	1,347
Individuals and others[4]......	377	341	343	367	393	432	456	492	507	558	635
Federal and related agencies[4]	153	228	229	220	213	218	208	223	242	291	380
Farmers Home Administration.....	19	18	18	17	17	17	17	16	16	15	14
Federal National Mortgage Assoc	94	159	164	155	150	148	141	144	155	176	215
Federal Home Loan Mortgage Corporation..................	19	39	40	42	43	49	44	43	40	36	34
Life insurance companies......	13	9	9	7	7	6	5	5	5	4	4
Five or more units...........	288	270	276	288	301	331	368	401	445	488	537
Nonfarm, nonresidential......	821	727	739	769	832	921	1,057	1,168	1,281	1,387	1,516
Farm.......................	79	83	85	87	90	97	103	109	116	125	132
TYPE OF HOLDER											
Savings institutions.........	802	596	597	628	632	644	668	723	758	781	871
Commercial banks............	849	1,013	1,090	1,145	1,245	1,337	1,495	1,660	1,790	2,058	2,256
Life insurance companies.....	268	216	213	208	207	214	231	236	243	250	260
Individuals and others.......	562	515	520	550	600	644	655	697	717	776	867
Mortgage pools or trusts[1]...	1,088	1,726	1,849	2,038	2,232	2,581	2,947	3,226	3,701	4,161	4,692
Government National Mortgage Assoc....	404	451	472	506	537	537	582	612	591	538	474
Federal Home Loan Mortgage Corp.....	316	491	515	554	579	646	749	822	948	1,082	1,157
Federal National Mortgage Association	300	530	583	651	710	835	961	1,058	1,290	1,538	1,857
Private mortgage conduits....	68	254	279	326	407	562	654	734	870	1,003	1,203
Federal and related agencies[4]...	239	316	308	294	285	292	320	341	373	436	532
Federal National Mortgage Association	105	174	178	168	160	156	149	153	166	189	235
Farmers Home Administration....	41	42	42	42	41	41	74	73	72	72	70
Federal Land Banks..............	29	29	28	30	31	33	34	36	41	46	50
Federal Home Loan Mortgage Corp....	22	42	44	47	48	57	57	59	63	64	60
Federal Housing and Veterans Admin....	9	11	10	6	(X)	(X)	(X)	(X)	(X)	(X)	(X)
Resolution Trust Corporation..........	33	10	2	(X)	(X)	(X)	(X)	(X)	(X)	(X)	(X)
Federal Home Loan Bank...........	-	-	-	-	(Z)	1	2	16	28	61	113

- Represents zero.   X Not applicable.   Z Less than $500 million.   [1] Outstanding principal balances of mortgage pools backing securities insured or guaranteed by the agency indicated. Includes other pools not shown separately.   [2] Includes securitized home equity loans.   [3] Includes mortgage companies, real estate investment trusts, state and local retirement funds, noninsured pension funds, state and local credit agencies, credit unions, and finance companies.   [4] Includes other agencies not shown separately.

Source: Board of Governors of the Federal Reserve System, *Statistical Supplement to the Federal Reserve Bulletin*, monthly.

No. 1178. Characteristics of Conventional First Mortgage Loans for Purchase of Single-Family Homes: 1990 to 2003

[In percent, except as indicated (154.1 represents $154,100). Annual averages. Covers fully amortized conventional mortgage loans used to purchase single-family nonfarm homes. Excludes refinancing loans, nonamortized and balloon loans, loans insured by the Federal Housing Administration, and loans guaranteed by the Veterans Administration. Based on a sample of mortgage lenders, including savings and loans associations, savings banks, commercial banks, and mortgage companies]

Loan characteristics	New homes						Previously occupied homes					
	1990	1995	2000	2001	2002	2003	1990	1995	2000	2001	2002	2003
Contract interest rate, [1] all loans	9.7	7.7	7.4	6.9	6.3	5.7	9.8	7.7	7.9	7.0	6.3	5.7
Fixed-rate loans	10.1	8.0	8.0	7.0	6.6	5.9	10.1	8.0	8.2	7.0	6.6	5.8
Adjustable-rate loans [2]	8.9	7.2	6.5	6.4	5.6	5.1	8.9	7.0	7.2	6.3	5.6	5.0
Initial fees, charges [3]	1.98	1.20	0.69	0.67	0.61	0.63	1.74	0.93	0.66	0.51	0.44	0.32
Effective interest rate, [4] all loans	10.1	7.9	7.5	7.0	6.4	5.8	10.1	7.8	8.1	7.0	6.5	5.7
Fixed-rate loans	10.4	8.2	8.2	7.1	6.7	6.0	10.4	8.2	8.3	7.1	6.7	5.9
Adjustable-rate loans [2]	9.2	7.4	6.5	6.4	5.6	5.1	9.2	7.1	7.2	6.4	5.7	5.0
Term to maturity (years)	27.3	27.7	29.2	28.8	28.9	28.7	27.0	27.4	27.4	26.6	27.5	26.5
Purchase price ($1,000)	154.1	175.4	234.9	244.8	261.7	275.3	140.3	137.3	191.8	211.5	227.5	237.0
Loan to price ratio	74.9	78.6	77.4	77.3	77.7	77.9	74.9	80.1	77.9	76.0	74.8	72.6
Percent of number of loans with adjustable rates	31	37	40	18	27	21	27	31	21	11	16	17

[1] Initial interest rate paid by the borrower as specified in the loan contract.   [2] Loans with a contractual provision for periodic adjustments in the contract interest rate.   [3] Includes all fees, commissions, discounts and "points" paid by the borrower, or seller, in order to obtain the loan. Excludes those charges for mortgage, credit, life or property insurance; for property transfer; and for title search and insurance.   [4] Contract interest rate plus fees and charges amortized over a 10-year period.

Source: U.S. Federal Housing Finance Board, *Rates & Terms on Conventional Home Mortgages, Annual Summary.*

No. 1179. Mortgage Delinquency and Foreclosure Rates: 1990 to 2003

[In percent. Covers one- to four-family residential nonfarm mortgage loans]

Item	1990	1995	1997	1998	1999	2000	2001	2002	2003
Delinquency rates: [1]									
Total	4.7	4.3	4.3	4.7	4.5	4.5	5.3	5.2	4.8
Conventional loans	3.0	2.8	2.8	3.4	3.2	3.2	3.8	3.8	3.5
VA loans	6.4	6.4	6.9	7.1	6.8	6.8	7.7	7.9	8.0
FHA loans	6.7	7.6	8.1	8.5	8.6	9.1	10.8	11.5	12.2
Foreclosure rates: [2]									
Total	0.9	0.9	1.1	1.3	1.3	1.2	1.4	1.5	1.3
Conventional loans	0.7	0.7	0.8	0.9	1.0	1.0	1.3	1.3	1.1
VA loans	1.2	1.3	1.8	1.9	1.7	1.2	1.3	1.6	1.6
FHA loans	1.3	1.3	2.1	2.4	2.0	1.7	2.2	2.8	2.8

[1] Number of loans delinquent 30 days or more as percentage of mortgage loans serviced in survey. Annual average of quarterly figures.   [2] Percentage of loans in the foreclosure process at yearend, not seasonally adjusted.

Source: Mortgage Bankers Association of America, Washington, DC, *National Delinquency Survey,* quarterly.

No. 1180. Insured Commercial Banks—Delinquency Rates on Loans: 1990 to 2003

[In percent. Annual averages of quarterly figures, not seasonally adjusted. Delinquent loans are those past due 30 days or more and still accruing interest as well as those in nonaccrual status. They are measured as a percentage of end-of-period loans]

Type of loan	1990	1995	1997	1998	1999	2000	2001	2002	2003
Total loans	5.33	2.48	2.27	2.18	2.13	2.18	2.61	2.69	2.33
Real estate	6.10	2.94	2.37	2.16	1.93	1.89	2.13	1.99	1.76
Residential [1]	(NA)	2.20	2.31	2.16	2.08	2.11	2.29	2.11	1.83
Commercial [2]	(NA)	3.94	2.39	2.04	1.69	1.49	1.79	1.71	1.54
Consumer	3.83	3.08	3.72	3.73	3.61	3.55	3.67	3.51	3.27
Credit cards	(NA)	3.73	4.69	4.70	4.54	4.50	4.86	4.87	4.47
Other	(NA)	2.67	3.08	3.13	3.09	2.98	3.03	2.79	2.67
Leases	1.97	0.79	1.08	1.04	1.28	1.59	2.11	2.24	1.91
Commercial and industrial	5.34	1.95	1.66	1.68	1.91	2.22	3.08	3.84	3.34
Agricultural	3.84	2.50	2.64	2.73	3.00	2.54	2.63	2.51	2.50

NA Not available.   [1] Residential real estate loans include loans secured by one- to four-family properties, including home equity lines of credit.   [2] Commercial real estate loans include construction and land development loans, loans secured by multifamily residences, and loans secured by nonfarm, nonresidential real estate.

Source: Federal Financial Institutions Examination Council (FFIEC), *Consolidated Reports of Condition and Income* (1990-2000: FFIEC 031 through 034; beginning 2001: FFIEC 031 & 041).

Banking, Finance, and Insurance   745

No. 1181. Percent of U.S. Households That Use Selected Payment Instruments: 1995 and 2001

[In percent. Based on Survey of Consumer Finance conducted by the Board of Governors of the Federal Reserve System; see Appendix III]

Age and education of head of household	Any of these instruments		ATM [1]		Debit card		Direct deposit		Automatic bill paying		Smart card [1]	
	1995	2001	1995	2001	1995	2001	1995	2001	1995	2001	1995	2001
All households	76.5	88.4	61.2	69.8	17.6	47.0	46.8	67.3	21.8	40.3	1.2	2.9
Under 30 years old	75.2	83.0	71.1	78.1	24.5	60.6	31.1	48.8	17.9	32.1	1.8	2.6
30 to 60 years old	77.4	89.3	67.2	76.8	19.7	53.4	42.9	64.8	24.5	44.1	1.5	3.3
61 years old and over	75.2	89.2	43.1	48.9	9.6	24.6	63.2	83.2	18.2	35.9	0.3	2.1
No college degree	69.8	84.7	52.8	63.7	14.3	42.3	40.4	61.8	18.2	33.7	0.8	2.4
College degree	91.5	95.6	80.1	81.6	25.2	56.2	61.0	78.0	30.1	53.2	2.1	3.8

[1] The questions on ATMs and smart cards asked whether any member of the household had an ATM card or a smart card, not whether the member used it. The other questions asked about usage.

Source: Mester, Loretta J., "Changes in the Use of Electronic Means of Payment: 1995-2001," *Business Review*, Third Quarter 2003, published by Federal Reserve Bank of Philadelphia. See also <http://www.phil.frb.org/files/br/brq303lm2.pdf>.

No. 1182. Consumer Payment Systems by Method of Payment, 2000 and 2002, and Projections, 2005

[112.3 represents 112,300,000,000]

Method of payment	Transactions						Volume					
	Number (bil.)			Percent distribution			Amount (bil. dol.)			Percent distribution		
	2000	2002	2005, proj.	2000	2005, proj.		2000	2002	2005, proj.	2000	2005, proj.	
Total	112.3	120.7	132.4	100.0	100.0		5,183	5,660	6,465	100.0	100.0	
Paper [1]	80.2	80.7	76.0	71.5	57.4		3,371	3,439	3,180	65.0	49.2	
Direct check payments [1]	30.2	29.5	28.2	26.9	21.3		2,276	2,206	2,081	43.9	32.2	
Cash	48.8	49.9	46.4	43.5	35.0		978	1,103	947	18.9	14.6	
Money orders	0.9	1.0	1.1	0.8	0.9		82	94	114	1.6	1.8	
Travelers cheques	0.2	0.2	0.2	0.2	0.1		13	12	12	0.3	0.2	
Official checks [2]	0.1	0.1	0.1	0.1	0.1		22	23	26	0.4	0.4	
Cards [3]	30.0	37.0	50.2	26.7	37.9		1,593	1,904	2,570	30.7	39.7	
Credit cards [3]	19.9	21.2	24.4	17.7	18.5		1,238	1,361	1,683	23.9	26.0	
Debit cards [4]	8.3	13.3	22.7	7.4	17.1		309	477	801	6.0	12.4	
Stored value cards [5]	1.3	1.8	2.0	1.1	1.5		31	48	59	0.6	0.9	
EBT cards and food stamps [6]	0.6	0.7	1.0	0.5	0.8		15	18	27	0.3	0.4	
Electronic [7]	2.1	2.9	6.3	1.8	4.7		219	317	715	4.2	11.1	
Preauthorized payments [7]	1.5	2.0	3.2	1.4	2.5		166	229	379	3.2	5.9	
Remote payments [8]	0.5	0.9	3.0	0.5	2.3		53	88	337	1.0	5.2	

[1] Excludes consumer check repayments and prepayments involving other payment systems as well as all commercial and government checks. [2] Official checks include cashier's checks, teller checks, and certified checks purchased from financial institutions. Excludes those purchased by businesses. [3] Credit cards include general purpose cards usable at all kinds of merchants and proprietary cards usable only at selected outlets. Includes some purchases on personal cards for government, commercial, and business-related spending. Cash advances are excluded. [4] Debit cards include general purpose cards carrying the Visa or MasterCard brand, electronic funds transfer (EFT) brands of regional EFT systems, proprietary commercial cards issued by private firms to drivers in the long-haul trucking and business aviation industry, and proprietary consumer cards issued by supermarkets. Cash withdrawals at ATM's and cash back over the counter are excluded. [5] Stored value cards are used primarily for gift certificates and telephone calls. [6] Electronic benefits transfer cards are replacements for paper scrip food stamps. [7] Preauthorized payments are handled electronically "end-to-end" through an automated clearing house. [8] Remote payments are made using a telephone or a computer and include point-of-sale check conversions and utility-bill payments made at ATMs, self-service clerk-assisted electronic banking machines kiosks and clerk-assisted machines at supermarkets.

Source: HSN Consultants Inc., Oxnard, CA, *The Nilson Report*, twice-monthly. (Copyright used by permission.)

No. 1183. Debit Cards—Holders, Number, Transactions, and Volume, 2000 and 2002, and Projections, 2005

[168 represents 168,000,000]

Type of debit card	Cardholders (mil.)		Number of cards (mil.)			Number of transactions (mil.)			Volume (bil. dol.)		
	2002	2005, proj.	2000	2002	2005, proj.	2000	2002	2005, proj.	2000	2002	2005, proj.
Total [1]	168	181	235	260	283	9,834	15,585	25,550	448	700	1,137
Bank [2]	150	156	137	175	205	6,797	10,332	14,093	327	496	712
EFT systems [3]	167	180	223	249	271	2,979	5,235	11,439	119	203	425
Other [4]	11	11	11	11	11	59	18	19	1	1	1

[1] Cardholders may hold more than one type of card. Bank cards and EFT cards are the same pieces of plastic that carry multiple brands. The total card figure shown does not include any duplication. [2] Visa Check Card and MasterCard MasterMoney. [3] Cards issued by financial institution members of regional and national switches. EFT=Electronic funds transfer. [4] Commercial fuel cards issued by private-label firms plus retail cards such as those issued by supermarkets and oil companies.

Source: HSN Consultants Inc., Oxnard, CA, *The Nilson Report*, twice-monthly. (Copyright used by permission.)

No. 1184. Consumer Credit Outstanding and Finance Rates: 1990 to 2003

[In billions of dollars, except percent (808 represents $808,000,000,000). Covers most short- and intermediate-term credit extended to individuals, excluding loans secured by real estate. Estimated amounts of seasonally adjusted credit outstanding as of end of year; finance rates, annual averages]

Type of credit	1990	1995	1996	1997	1998	1999	2000	2001	2002	2003
Total.	808	1,141	1,242	1,305	1,400	1,513	1,686	1,822	1,903	2,002
Revolving	239	443	499	522	563	590	659	704	717	745
Nonrevolving [1]	570	698	743	783	837	922	1,027	1,118	1,186	1,257
FINANCE RATES (percent)										
Commercial banks:										
New automobiles (48 months)	11.78	9.57	9.05	9.02	8.73	8.44	9.34	8.50	7.62	6.93
Other consumer goods (24 months)	15.46	13.94	13.54	13.90	13.76	13.39	13.90	13.22	12.54	11.95
Credit-card plans.	18.17	15.90	15.63	15.77	15.71	15.21	15.71	14.89	13.42	12.74
Finance companies:										
New automobiles.	12.54	11.19	9.84	7.12	6.30	6.66	6.61	5.65	4.29	3.40
Used automobiles	15.99	14.48	13.53	13.27	12.64	12.60	13.55	12.18	10.74	9.72

[1] Comprises automobile loans and all other loans not included in revolving credit, such as loans for mobile homes, education, boats, trailers, or vacations. These loans may be secured or unsecured.

Source: Board of Governors of the Federal Reserve System, *Statistical Supplement to the Federal Reserve Bulletin*, monthly.

No. 1185. Credit Cards—Holders, Number, Spending, and Debt, 2000 and 2002, and Projections, 2005

[159 represents 159,000,000]

Type of credit card	Cardholders (mil.)			Number of cards (mil.)			Credit card spending (bil. dol.)			Credit card debt outstanding (bil. dol.)		
	2000	2002	2005, proj.	2000	2002	2005, proj.	2000	2002	2005, proj.	2000	2002	2005, proj.
Total [1].	159	163	173	1,425	1,452	1,430	1,458	1,638	2,022	680	764	922
Bank [2]	107	112	120	455	525	580	938	1,095	1,359	480	560	683
Phone.	125	126	128	181	182	184	21	20	22	3	2	3
Store	114	115	118	597	547	464	120	127	147	92	91	97
Oil company	76	75	73	98	97	90	50	54	71	5	5	7
Other [3]	7	7	7	94	100	111	330	342	423	101	105	133

[1] Cardholders may hold more than one type of card. [2] Visa and MasterCard credit cards. Excludes debit cards. [3] Includes Universal Air Travel Plan (UATP), also known as Air Travel Card; automobile rental, and miscellaneous cards. Except for data on cardholders, also includes Discover, American Express, and Diners Club.

Source: HSN Consultants Inc., Oxnard, CA, *The Nilson Report*, twice-monthly. (Copyright used by permission.)

No. 1186. Usage of General Purpose Credit Cards by Families: 1992 to 2001

[General purpose credit cards include Mastercard, Visa, Optima, and Discover cards. Excludes cards used only for business purposes. All dollar figures are given in constant 2001 dollars based on consumer price index data as published by U.S. Bureau of Labor Statistics. Families include one-person units; for definition of family, see text, Section 1, Population. Based on Survey of Consumer Finance; see Appendix III. For definition of median, see Guide to Tabular Presentation]

Age of family head and family income	Percent having a general purpose credit card	Median number of cards	Median new charges on last month's bills (dol.)	Percent having a balance after last month's bills	Median balance (dol.) [1]	Percent of cardholding families who—		
						Almost always pay off the balance	Some-times pay off the balance	Hardly ever pay off the balance
1992, total	62.4	2	100	52.6	1,200	53.0	19.6	27.4
1995, total	66.5	2	200	56.0	1,700	52.4	20.1	27.5
1998, total	67.5	2	200	54.7	2,000	53.8	19.3	26.9
2001, total	72.7	2	200	53.7	1,800	55.3	19.1	25.6
Under 35 years old	64.2	2	100	68.2	1,800	40.6	24.1	35.4
35 to 44 years old.	76.9	2	200	62.9	2,000	47.0	22.8	30.2
45 to 54 years old.	80.0	2	200	57.3	2,000	54.3	19.3	26.4
55 to 64 years old.	76.0	2	300	48.2	2,000	59.8	17.8	22.3
65 to 74 years old.	76.5	2	200	30.0	1,100	75.8	11.0	13.2
75 years old and over	59.7	2	200	24.2	700	81.2	9.3	9.4
Less than $10,000	28.5	1	-	67.4	1,000	45.3	23.0	31.7
$10,000 to $24,999	56.1	2	100	57.0	1,000	49.5	19.9	30.6
$25,000 to $49,999	76.1	2	100	61.3	1,700	46.7	19.7	33.6
$50,000 to $99,999	87.9	2	200	53.9	2,000	55.2	20.8	24.0
$100,000 and more	95.8	2	1,000	36.1	3,000	75.2	13.9	10.9

- Represents zero. [1] Among families having a balance.

Source: Board of Governors of the Federal Reserve System, unpublished data.

No. 1187. Money Stock: 1980 to 2003

[In billions of dollars (408 represents $408,000,000,000). As of December. Seasonally adjusted averages of daily figures]

Item	1980	1985	1987	1988	1989	1990	1991	1992	1993	1994	1995	1996	1997	1998	1999	2000	2001	2002	2003
M1, total [1]	408	620	750	787	793	825	897	1,025	1,130	1,151	1,127	1,079	1,073	1,096	1,124	1,088	1,177	1,215	1,293
Currency [1]	115	168	197	212	222	246	267	292	332	354	372	384	425	460	518	532	582	627	664
Travelers checks [2]	3	6	7	7	7	8	8	8	8	9	9	9	8	9	9	8	8	8	8
Demand deposits [3]	261	267	288	287	279	277	290	340	386	384	389	401	394	378	355	310	330	301	312
Other checkable deposits [4]	28	180	259	281	285	294	332	385	415	404	357	275	245	249	243	238	257	279	310
M2, total	1,600	2,496	2,831	2,994	3,158	3,278	3,378	3,432	3,484	3,496	3,640	3,815	4,031	4,384	4,649	4,933	5,453	5,806	6,071
M1	408	620	750	787	793	825	897	1,025	1,130	1,151	1,127	1,079	1,073	1,096	1,124	1,088	1,177	1,215	1,293
Non-M1 components in M2	1,192	1,876	2,081	2,208	2,365	2,453	2,481	2,407	2,354	2,346	2,513	2,736	2,958	3,288	3,525	3,845	4,276	4,591	4,778
Money market funds, retail	64	175	223	244	320	357	371	352	353	380	448	516	591	732	833	925	993	928	810
Savings deposits (including MMDAs [5])	400	815	937	926	894	923	1,044	1,187	1,219	1,149	1,134	1,273	1,399	1,604	1,738	1,876	2,309	2,769	3,159
Commercial banks	186	457	535	542	541	582	665	754	785	752	775	906	1,022	1,187	1,287	1,422	1,736	2,053	2,328
Thrift institutions	215	359	403	384	353	342	380	433	434	397	359	367	377	417	451	454	573	716	831
Small time deposits [6]	729	886	921	1,037	1,151	1,173	1,066	868	782	816	931	947	968	952	954	1,044	973	894	809
Commercial banks	286	386	392	451	534	611	602	508	468	503	575	593	625	626	635	700	634	591	536
Thrift institutions	442	499	529	586	618	563	463	360	314	314	357	354	343	326	319	345	339	302	272
M3, total	1,996	3,208	3,687	3,929	4,077	4,153	4,206	4,217	4,278	4,360	4,625	4,972	5,446	6,036	6,535	7,102	8,012	8,541	8,814
M2	1,600	2,496	2,831	2,994	3,158	3,278	3,378	3,432	3,484	3,496	3,640	3,815	4,031	4,384	4,649	4,933	5,453	5,806	6,071
Non-M2 components in M3	396	713	855	935	919	875	828	785	794	864	985	1,157	1,415	1,653	1,886	2,169	2,559	2,735	2,743
Large time deposits [7]	260	422	462	512	528	480	415	350	332	370	428	509	618	669	744	820	785	677	859
Commercial banks	215	270	299	338	366	358	331	283	270	305	354	431	533	581	652	717	670	677	739
Thrift institutions	45	152	163	175	161	121	83	67	62	65	74	78	85	88	92	103	115	117	120
Repurchase agreements [8]	58	121	178	197	169	151	131	142	173	196	199	211	254	294	337	366	379	481	505
Eurodollars [8]	61	104	121	132	109	103	92	80	73	86	94	115	147	150	170	194	209	228	280
Money market funds, institution only [9]	16	65	94	94	112	140	190	214	217	211	265	323	396	539	635	708	1,187	1,232	1,099

[1] Currency outside U.S. Treasury, Federal Reserve Banks and the vaults of depository institutions. [2] Outstanding amount of nonbank issuers. [3] At commercial banks and foreign-related institutions. [4] Consists of negotiable order of withdrawal (NOW) and automatic transfer service (ATS) accounts at all depository institutions, credit union share draft balances, and demand deposits at thrift institutions. [5] Money market deposit accounts (MMDA). [6] Issued in amounts of less than $100,000. Excludes individual retirement accounts (IRA's) and Keogh accounts. [7] Issued in amounts of $100,000 or more. Excludes those booked at international banking facilities. [8] Excludes those held by money market mutual funds, depository institutions, U.S. Government, foreign banks and official institutions. [9] Excludes those held by depository institutions and money market mutual funds.

Source: Board of Governors of the Federal Reserve System, Statistical Supplement to the Federal Reserve Bulletin, monthly, and Money Stock Measures, Federal Reserve Statistical Release H.6, weekly.

No. 1188. Money Market Interest Rates and Mortgage Rates: 1980 to 2003

[Percent per year. Annual averages of monthly data, except as indicated]

Type	1980	1985	1990	1991	1992	1993	1994	1995	1996	1997	1998	1999	2000	2001	2002	2003
Federal funds, effective rate	13.35	8.10	8.10	5.69	3.52	3.02	4.21	5.83	5.30	5.46	5.35	4.97	6.24	3.88	1.67	1.13
Prime rate charged by banks	15.26	9.93	10.01	8.46	6.25	6.00	7.15	8.83	8.27	8.44	8.35	8.00	9.23	6.91	4.67	4.12
Discount rate [1]	11.77	7.69	6.98	5.45	3.25	3.00	3.60	5.21	5.02	5.00	4.92	4.62	5.73	3.40	1.17	2.12
Eurodollar deposits, 3-month	14.00	8.27	8.16	5.86	3.70	3.18	4.63	5.93	5.38	5.61	5.45	5.31	6.45	3.70	1.73	1.14
Large negotiable CDs:																
3-month, secondary market	13.02	8.04	8.15	5.83	3.68	3.17	4.63	5.92	5.39	5.62	5.47	5.33	6.46	3.71	1.73	1.15
6-month, secondary market	12.94	8.24	8.17	5.91	3.76	3.28	4.96	5.98	5.47	5.73	5.44	5.46	6.59	3.66	1.81	1.17
Taxable money market funds [2]	12.68	7.71	7.82	5.71	3.36	2.70	3.75	5.48	4.95	5.10	5.04	4.64	5.89	3.67	1.29	0.64
Tax-exempt money market funds [2]	(NA)	4.90	5.45	4.13	2.58	1.97	2.38	3.39	2.99	3.14	2.94	2.72	3.54	2.24	0.94	0.53
Certificates of deposit (CDs): [3]																
6-month	(NA)	8.05	7.79	5.80	3.51	2.88	3.42	4.92	4.68	4.86	4.58	4.27	5.09	3.43	1.67	1.02
1-year	(NA)	8.53	7.92	6.03	3.78	3.16	4.01	5.39	4.95	5.15	4.81	4.56	5.46	3.60	1.98	1.20
2½-year	(NA)	9.32	7.96	6.46	4.56	3.80	4.58	5.69	5.14	5.40	4.93	4.74	5.64	3.97	2.74	1.77
5-year	(NA)	9.99	8.06	7.02	5.76	4.98	5.42	6.00	6.46	5.66	5.08	4.93	5.97	4.58	3.96	2.92
U.S. Government securities: [4]																
Secondary market:																
3-month Treasury bill	11.39	7.47	7.50	5.38	3.43	3.00	4.25	5.49	5.01	5.06	4.78	4.64	5.82	3.40	1.61	1.01
6-month Treasury bill	11.32	7.65	7.46	5.44	3.54	3.12	4.64	5.56	5.08	5.18	4.83	4.75	5.90	3.34	1.68	1.05
Auction average: [5]																
3-month Treasury bill	11.51	7.48	7.51	5.42	3.45	3.02	4.29	5.51	5.02	5.07	4.81	4.66	5.85	3.45	1.62	1.02
Home mortgages:																
New-home mortgage yields [6]	12.66	11.55	10.05	9.32	8.24	7.20	7.49	7.87	7.80	7.71	7.07	7.04	7.52	7.00	6.43	5.80
Conventional, 15 yr. fixed [3]	(NA)	11.48	9.73	8.76	7.80	6.65	7.77	7.39	7.28	7.16	6.58	7.09	7.76	6.53	6.02	5.25
Conventional, 30 yr. fixed [3]	(NA)	11.85	9.97	9.09	8.27	7.17	8.28	7.86	7.76	7.57	6.92	7.46	8.08	7.01	6.56	5.89

NA Not available. [1] Rate for the Federal Reserve Bank of New York. Beginning 2003, the rate charged for discounts made and advances extended under the Federal Reserve's primary credit discount window program, which became effective January 9, 2003. The rate replaced that for adjustment credit, which was discontinued after January 8, 2003. [2] 12 month return for period ending December 31. Source: iMoneyNet, Inc., Westborough, MA, Money Market Insight, monthly, <http://www.imoneynet.com> (copyright). [3] Annual averages. Source: Bankrate, Inc., North Palm Beach, FL, Bank Rate Monitor, weekly (copyright). [4] Averages based on daily closing bid yields in secondary market, bank discount basis. [5] Averages computed on an issue-date basis; bank discount basis. Source: U.S. Council of Economic Advisors, Economic Indicators, monthly. [6] Effective rate (in the primary market) on conventional mortgages, reflecting fees and charges as well as contract rate and assumed, on the average, repayment at end of ten years. Source: U.S. Federal Housing Finance Board, Rates & Terms on Conventional Home Mortgages, Annual Summary.

Source: Except as noted, Board of Governors of the Federal Reserve System, Statistical Supplement to the Federal Reserve Bulletin, monthly.

No. 1189. Bond Yields: 1980 to 2003

[Percent per year. Annual averages of daily figures, except as indicated]

Type	1980	1985	1990	1995	1997	1998	1999	2000	2001	2002	2003
U.S. Treasury, constant maturities: [1][2]											
1-year	12.00	8.42	7.89	5.94	5.63	5.05	5.08	6.11	3.49	2.00	1.24
2-year	11.73	9.27	8.16	6.15	5.99	5.13	5.43	6.26	3.83	2.64	1.65
3-year	11.51	9.64	8.26	6.25	6.10	5.14	5.49	6.22	4.09	3.10	2.10
5-year	11.45	10.12	8.37	6.38	6.22	5.15	5.55	6.16	4.56	3.82	2.97
7-year	11.40	10.50	8.52	6.50	6.33	5.28	5.79	6.20	4.88	4.30	3.52
10-year	11.43	10.62	8.55	6.57	6.35	5.26	5.65	6.03	5.02	4.61	4.01
20-year	(NA)	(NA)	(NA)	6.95	6.69	5.72	6.20	6.23	5.63	5.43	4.96
State and local govt. bonds, Aaa	7.84	8.60	6.96	5.79	5.32	4.93	5.29	5.58	5.01	4.87	4.52
State and local govt. bonds, Baa	8.99	9.59	7.30	6.05	5.50	5.14	5.70	6.19	5.75	5.64	5.20
Municipal (Bond Buyer, 20 bonds)	8.55	9.11	7.27	5.95	5.52	5.09	5.43	5.71	5.15	5.04	4.75
High-grade municipal bonds (Standard & Poor's) [3]	8.51	9.18	7.25	5.95	5.55	5.12	5.43	5.77	5.19	5.05	4.73
Corporate Aaa seasoned [4]	11.94	11.37	9.32	7.59	7.27	6.53	7.05	7.62	7.08	6.49	5.66
Corporate Baa seasoned [4]	13.67	12.72	10.36	8.20	7.87	7.22	7.88	8.37	7.95	7.80	6.76
Corporate seasoned, all industries [4]	12.75	12.05	9.77	7.83	7.54	6.87	7.45	7.98	7.49	7.10	6.24

NA Not available. [1] Yields on actively traded non-inflation-indexed issues adjusted to constant maturities. Data from U.S. Treasury. [2] Through September 1996, yields are based on closing bid prices quoted by at least five dealers. Beginning October 1996, yields are based on closing indicative prices quoted by secondary market participants. [3] Source: U.S. Council of Economic Advisors, *Economic Indicators*, monthly. [4] Source: Moody's Investors Service, New York, NY.

Source: Except as noted, Board of Governors of the Federal Reserve System, *Statistical Supplement to the Federal Reserve Bulletin*, monthly.

No. 1190. Volume of Debt Markets by Type of Security: 1990 to 2003

[In billions of dollars (2,764 represents $2,764,000,000,000). Covers debt markets as represented by the source]

Type of security	1990	1995	1999	2000	2001	2002	2003
NEW ISSUE VOLUME							
Total	2,764	6,789	11,169	12,637	15,969	16,915	19,722
U.S. Treasury securities [1]	1,531	2,331	2,028	2,038	2,743	3,812	4,249
Federal agency debt	637	3,531	7,077	8,746	10,496	9,236	10,496
Municipal	163	198	264	241	343	430	452
Mortgage-backed securities [2]	235	269	687	483	1,089	2,296	3,197
Asset-backed securities [3]	50	143	359	387	420	489	584
Corporate debt [4]	149	317	754	742	879	652	744
DAILY TRADING VOLUME							
Total	111.2	246.3	316.5	357.7	508.8	613.4	733.8
U.S. Treasury securities [1][5]	111.2	193.2	186.5	206.6	297.9	366.4	433.5
Federal agency debt [5]	(NA)	23.7	54.6	72.8	90.2	81.8	81.7
Municipal [6]	(NA)	(NA)	8.3	8.8	8.8	10.7	12.6
Mortgage-backed securities [2][5]	(NA)	29.4	67.1	69.5	112.0	154.5	206.0
VOLUME OF SECURITIES OUTSTANDING							
Total	7,745	11,229	15,951	16,969	18,500	20,224	21,954
U.S. Treasury securities [1]	2,196	3,307	3,281	2,967	2,968	3,205	3,575
Federal agency debt [7]	435	845	1,617	1,852	2,143	2,359	2,637
Municipal	1,184	1,294	1,457	1,481	1,604	1,765	1,884
Mortgage-backed securities [2]	1,333	2,352	3,334	3,565	4,126	4,705	5,309
Asset-backed securities [3][7]	90	316	901	1,072	1,281	1,543	1,694
Money market instruments [8]	1,157	1,177	2,339	2,661	2,542	2,551	2,418
Corporate debt [4][7]	1,350	1,938	3,023	3,372	3,836	4,096	4,437

NA Not available. [1] Marketable public debt. [2] Includes only Government National Mortgage Association (GNMA), Federal National Mortgage Association (FNMA), Federal Home Loan Mortgage Corporation (FHLMC) mortgage-backed securities (MBS) and collateralized mortgage obligations (CMOs) and private-label MBS/CMOs. [3] Excludes mortgage-backed assets. [4] Includes non-convertible corporate debt, Yankee bonds, and MTNs (Medium-Term Notes), but excludes federal agency debt and all CDs. [5] Primary dealer transactions. [6] Beginning September 1998 includes customer-to-dealer and dealer-to-dealer transactions. [7] The Bond Market Association estimates. [8] Commercial paper, bankers acceptances, and large time deposits.

Source: The Bond Market Association, New York, NY. Copyright. Based on data supplied by Board of Governors of the Federal Reserve System, U.S. Dept. of Treasury, Thompson Financial Securities Data Company, Inside MBS & ABS, FHLMC, FNMA, GNMA, Federal Home Loan Banks, Student Loan Marketing Association, Federal Farm Credit Banks, Tennessee Valley Authority, and Municipal Securities Rulemaking Board.

No. 1191. Commercial Paper Outstanding by Type of Company: 1990 to 2003

[In billions of dollars (563 represents $563,000,000,000). As of December 31. Seasonally adjusted. Commercial paper is an unsecured promissory note having a fixed maturity of no more than 270 days]

Type of company	1990	1994	1995	1996	1997	1998	1999	2000	2001	2002	2003
All issuers	563	595	675	775	967	1,163	1,403	1,619	1,459	1,348	1,265
Financial companies [1]	415	431	487	591	766	936	1,124	1,276	1,234	1,194	1,160
Dealer-placed paper [2]	215	223	276	361	521	636	824	994	976	1,015	963
Directly-placed paper [3]	200	208	211	230	245	300	300	282	258	179	197
Nonfinancial companies [4]	148	165	188	185	201	227	279	343	225	154	105

[1] Institutions engaged primarily in commercial, savings, and mortgage banking; sales, personal, and mortgage financing; factoring, finance leasing, and other business lending; insurance underwriting; and other investment activities. [2] Includes all financial company paper sold by dealers in the open market. [3] As reported by financial companies that place their paper directly with investors. [4] Includes public utilities and firms engaged primarily in such activities as communications, construction, manufacturing, mining, wholesale and retail trade, transportation, and services.

Source: Board of Governors of the Federal Reserve System, *Statistical Supplement to the Federal Reserve Bulletin*, monthly.

No. 1192. Total Returns of Stocks, Bonds, and Treasury Bills: 1970 to 2003

[In percent. Average annual percent change. Stock return data are based on the Standard & Poor's 500 index. Minus sign (-) indicates loss]

Period	Stocks				Treasury bills, total return	Bonds (10-year), total return
	Total return	Capital gains	Dividends and reinvestment	Total return after inflation		
1970 to 1979...........	5.88	1.60	4.20	-1.38	6.48	5.94
1980 to 1989...........	17.55	12.59	4.40	11.85	9.13	13.01
1990 to 1999...........	18.21	15.31	2.51	14.85	4.95	8.02
2000 to 2003...........	-5.34	-6.73	1.49	-8.82	2.97	9.39
2001	-11.89	-13.04	1.32	-13.68	3.32	5.51
2002	-22.10	-23.37	1.65	-23.91	1.61	15.15
2003	28.68	26.38	1.82	26.31	1.03	0.54

Source: Global Financial Data, Los Angeles, CA, "GFD Guide to Total Returns"; <http://www.globalfindata.com/articles/totalreturnworksheet.xls>; and unpublished data. (copyright).

No. 1193. Equities, Corporate Bonds, and Municipal Securities—Holdings and Net Purchases by Type of Investor: 1990 to 2003

[In billions of dollars (3,543 represents $3,543,000,000,000). Holdings as of Dec. 31. Minus sign (-) indicates net sales]

Type of investor	Holdings					Net purchases				
	1990	1995	2000	2002	2003	1990	1995	2000	2002	2003
EQUITIES [1]										
Total [2]...........:	3,543	8,475	17,627	11,871	15,498	-45.7	1.5	5.3	47.0	107.8
Household sector [3]	1,781	4,141	7,474	4,601	5,709	-48.6	-102.8	-470.0	-72.5	-183.1
Rest of the world [4] ...	244	550	1,626	1,223	1,618	-16.0	16.5	193.6	53.2	35.5
Bank personal trusts and estates ...	190	225	357	181	213	0.5	1.6	-2.5	-39.4	-18.7
Life insurance companies	82	310	887	705	956	-5.7	28.2	111.2	52.5	58.3
Other insurance companies......	80	134	194	152	187	-7.0	-0.6	0.7	-1.1	2.1
Private pension funds	606	1,278	2,138	1,418	1,873	0.6	-72.1	-55.1	-66.8	21.3
State and local retirement funds....	285	679	1,335	1,002	1,319	22.5	18.2	-18.4	20.0	19.0
Mutual funds	233	1,025	3,227	2,188	3,062	14.4	87.4	189.1	31.1	136.4
CORPORATE & FOREIGN BONDS										
Total [2]..........:	1,722	2,932	5,068	6,190	6,840	141.1	344.1	379.5	495.8	650.6
Household sector [3]	236	509	892	1,175	980	74.8	93.9	65.8	165.3	-116.6
Rest of the world [4] ...	217	361	776	986	1,294	5.3	50.1	72.0	89.3	307.7
Commercial banking	89	111	279	379	506	4.6	8.4	58.1	2.7	49.3
Life insurance companies	567	870	1,222	1,449	1,597	56.5	90.7	49.0	106.8	147.8
Other insurance companies......	89	123	188	199	219	10.4	12.7	6.4	2.4	20.3
Private pension funds	158	240	318	332	341	19.8	13.1	18.7	8.0	8.5
State and local retirement funds....	142	189	340	361	363	-10.5	10.1	29.7	9.4	2.0
Money market mutual funds	2	22	162	171	186	-1.7	6.4	38.2	7.7	15.2
Mutual funds	59	196	362	471	548	4.7	23.3	-6.2	50.9	77.4
Government-sponsored enterprises .	-	31	117	140	157	-	10.3	25.8	7.0	17.6
Brokers and dealers...........	29	76	113	192	228	-4.0	12.0	19.3	30.7	35.5
MUNICIPAL SECURITIES [5]										
Total [2]............	1,184	1,268	1,481	1,763	1,899	49.3	-57.6	23.6	159.4	136.3
Household sector [3]	575	431	461	618	681	27.6	-53.0	10.4	106.4	62.3
Other insurance companies......	137	161	184	183	201	1.8	7.0	-14.9	9.2	17.6
Money market mutual funds	84	128	245	283	297	13.9	14.3	34.3	1.8	14.6
Mutual funds	113	210	230	277	291	13.9	3.2	-8.9	24.0	13.7

- Represents or rounds to zero.   [1] Excludes mutual fund shares.   [2] Includes other types not shown separately.   [3] Includes nonprofit organizations.   [4] Holdings and net purchases of U.S. issues by foreign residents.   [5] Includes loans.

Source: Board of Governors of the Federal Reserve System, "Federal Reserve Statistical Release, Z.1, Flow of Funds Accounts of the United States"; published: 4 March 2004; <http://www.federalreserve.gov/releases/Z1/20040304/data.htm>.

No. 1194. New Security Issues of Corporations by Type of Offering: 2000 to 2003

[In billions of dollars (1,079.7 represents $1,079,700,000,000). Represents gross proceed of issues maturing in more than one year. Figures are the principal amount or the number of units multiplied by the offering price. Excludes secondary offerings, employee stock plans, investment companies other than closed-end, intracorporate transactions, and Yankee bonds. Stock data include ownership securities issued by limited partnerships]

Type of offering	2000	2002	2003	Type of offering	2000	2002	2003
Total [1]	1,079.7	1,429.3	1,810.2	Stocks, total	311.9	170.9	182.1
Bonds, total	944.8	1,318.9	1,686.9	Public.	134.9	110.4	123.3
Sold in the United States	822.0	1,232.6	1,574.0	Nonfinancial	118.4	62.1	44.4
Sold abroad	122.8	86.2	112.9	Financial	16.5	48.3	78.9
Nonfinancial	258.8	282.5	362.1	Private placement	177.0	60.5	58.8
Financial.	686.0	1,036.4	1,324.8				

[1] Excludes private placements of stocks.

Source: Board of Governors of the Federal Reserve System, *Statistical Supplement to the Federal Reserve Bulletin*, monthly.

No. 1195. Purchases and Sales by U.S. Investors of Foreign Bonds and Stocks, 1990 to 2003, and by Selected Country, 2003

[In billions of dollars (31.2 represents $31,200,000,000). Covers transactions in all types of long-term foreign securities as reported by banks, brokers, and other entities in the United States. Data cover new issues of securities, transactions in outstanding issues, and redemptions of securities. Includes transactions executed in the United States for the account of foreigners, and transactions executed abroad for the account of reporting institutions and their domestic customers. Data by country show the country of location of the foreign buyers and sellers who deal directly with reporting institutions in the United States. The data do not necessarily indicate the country of beneficial owner or issuer. The term "foreigner" covers all institutions and individuals domiciled outside the United States, including U.S. citizens domiciled abroad, and the foreign branches, subsidiaries and other affiliates abroad of U.S. banks and businesses; the central governments, central banks, and other official institutions of foreign countries; and international and regional organizations. "Foreigner" also includes persons in the United States to the extent that they are known by reporting institutions to be acting on behalf of foreigners. Minus sign (-) indicates net sale by U.S. investors or a net inflow of capital into the United States]

Year and country	Net purchases			Total transactions [1]			Bonds		Stocks	
	Total	Bonds	Stocks	Total	Bonds	Stocks	Purchases	Sales	Purchases	Sales
1990	31.2	21.9	9.2	907	652	255	337	315	132	123
1991	46.8	14.8	32.0	949	675	273	345	330	153	121
1992	47.9	15.6	32.3	1,375	1,043	332	529	514	182	150
1993	143.1	80.4	62.7	2,126	1,572	554	826	746	308	245
1994	57.3	9.2	48.1	2,526	1,706	820	858	848	434	386
1995	98.7	48.4	50.3	2,569	1,827	741	938	890	396	346
1996	110.6	51.4	59.3	3,239	2,279	960	1,165	1,114	510	450
1997	89.1	48.1	40.9	4,505	2,952	1,553	1,500	1,452	797	756
1998	11.1	17.3	-6.2	4,527	2,674	1,853	1,346	1,328	923	930
1999	-10.0	5.7	-15.6	3,941	1,602	2,339	804	798	1,162	1,177
2000	17.1	4.1	13.1	5,539	1,922	3,617	963	959	1,815	1,802
2001	19.6	-30.5	50.1	5,135	2,290	2,845	1,130	1,160	1,448	1,398
2002	-27.0	-28.5	1.5	5,253	2,716	2,537	1,344	1,372	1,269	1,268
2003, total [2]	36.6	-25.7	62.3	7,108	4,281	2,828	2,127	2,153	1,445	1,383
United Kingdom	2.5	-4.5	7.0	3,363	2,297	1,067	1,146	1,151	537	530
Cayman Islands	8.5	10.7	-2.2	743	499	243	255	244	121	123
Japan	31.9	-5.5	37.3	577	209	368	102	107	203	165
Bermuda	1.0	0.9	0.1	369	280	89	141	140	44	44
Canada	-7.4	-10.1	2.6	331	203	128	96	107	65	63
Germany	-4.4	-2.0	-2.3	212	167	45	82	84	21	24
Hong Kong	3.9	1.2	2.7	170	45	125	23	22	64	61
France [3]	3.2	2.0	1.1	119	34	85	18	16	43	42
Taiwan [3]	9.6	-3.9	13.5	118	7	111	1	5	62	49
Bahamas, The	-0.8	-1.1	0.3	116	79	37	39	40	19	19
Australia	1.1	0.3	0.8	86	24	62	12	12	31	31
Switzerland	-3.5	-4.3	0.7	69	23	45	10	14	23	22
Brazil	2.0	0.1	1.9	67	54	13	27	27	7	5
Singapore	-1.8	-0.8	-1.1	60	24	37	11	12	18	19
Netherlands	-0.7	0.1	-0.8	56	19	36	10	10	18	19
Mexico	1.2	1.6	-0.4	49	34	14	18	16	7	7

[1] Total purchases plus total sales. [2] Includes other countries, not shown separately. [3] See footnote 3, Table 1198.

Source: U.S. Dept. of Treasury, *Treasury Bulletin*, quarterly.

No. 1196. U.S. Holdings of Foreign Stocks and Bonds by Country: 2001 to 2003

[In billions of dollars (1,612.7 represents $1,612,700,000,000)]

Country	Stocks			Country	Bonds		
	2001	2002	2003		2001	2002	2003
Total holdings	1,612.7	1,345.1	1,972.2	Total holdings	502.1	501.8	502.1
Western Europe [1]	942.2	785.0	1,101.7	Western Europe [1]	240.9	236.4	239.2
United Kingdom	354.6	303.3	450.5	United Kingdom	73.4	67.1	65.9
Finland	51.3	42.4	57.1	France	24.3	28.7	32.4
France	112.2	94.1	128.8	Germany	43.5	49.1	49.9
Germany	72.2	58.1	76.5	Italy	27.9	26.3	27.6
Ireland	28.4	23.0	30.8	Netherlands	12.5	12.6	18.3
Italy	33.7	27.5	36.9	Sweden	8.8	9.5	9.7
Netherlands	112.8	89.9	119.9	Canada	104.6	111.0	106.9
Spain	32.5	26.8	35.0	Japan	24.7	34.5	30.9
Sweden	24.3	19.3	27.6	Latin America [1]	49.8	49.0	53.3
Switzerland	75.6	65.5	89.6	Brazil	11.0	10.1	10.6
Canada	89.6	69.7	97.3	Mexico	21.2	22.7	25.7
Japan	170.7	141.4	233.7	Other Western Hemisphere [1]	30.2	26.9	38.8
Latin America [1]	59.3	53.2	84.3	Cayman Islands	21.9	19.1	32.1
Argentina	0.7	0.6	0.9	Other countries [1]	41.0	33.6	21.5
Brazil	21.8	20.0	33.5	Australia	14.2	14.7	15.8
Mexico	26.3	23.9	36.7	Korea, South	4.7	8.0	4.5
Other Western Hemisphere [1]	172.3	148.7	206.8	International organizations	10.9	10.4	11.5
Bermuda	118.9	98.3	133.3				
Netherlands Antilles	14.5	10.7	14.7				
Other countries [1]	178.6	147.1	248.4				
Australia	37.1	30.4	44.8				
Hong Kong	30.2	21.8	33.8				
Singapore	21.4	17.0	21.7				

[1] Includes other countries not shown separately.

Source: U.S. Bureau of Economic Analysis, *Survey of Current Business*, July 2004.

752   Banking, Finance, and Insurance

No. 1197. Foreign Purchases and Sales of U.S. Securities by Type of Security, 1990 to 2003, and by Selected Country, 2003

[In billions of dollars (18.7 represents $18,700,000,000). Covers transactions in all types of long-term domestic securities by foreigners as reported by banks, brokers, and other entities in the United States (except nonmarketable U.S. Treasury notes, foreign series; and nonmarketable U.S. Treasury bonds and notes, foreign currency series). See headnote, Table 1195. Minus sign (-) indicates net sales by foreigners or a net outflow of capital from the United States]

Year and country	Net purchases					Total transactions [4]				
	Total	Trea-sury bonds and notes [1]	U.S. Govt. corpora-tions [2] bonds	Corpo-rate bonds [3]	Corpo-rate stocks	Total	Trea-sury bonds and notes [1]	U.S. Govt. corpora-tions [2] bonds	Corpo-rate bonds [3]	Corpo-rate stocks
1990	18.7	17.9	6.3	9.7	-15.1	4,204	3,620	104	117	362
1991	58.1	19.9	10.2	16.9	11.1	4,706	4,016	124	155	411
1992	73.2	39.3	18.3	20.8	-5.1	5,282	4,444	204	187	448
1993	111.1	23.6	35.4	30.6	21.6	6,314	5,195	263	239	618
1994	140.4	78.8	21.7	38.0	1.9	6,562	5,343	297	222	699
1995	231.9	134.1	28.7	57.9	11.2	7,243	5,828	222	278	915
1996	370.2	232.2	41.7	83.7	12.5	8,965	7,134	241	422	1,169
1997	388.0	184.2	49.9	84.4	69.6	12,759	9,546	469	617	2,126
1998	277.8	49.0	56.8	121.9	50.0	14,989	10,259	992	641	3,097
1999	350.2	-10.0	92.2	160.4	107.5	14,617	8,586	880	577	4,574
2000	457.8	-54.0	152.8	184.1	174.9	16,910	7,795	1,305	775	7,036
2001	520.8	18.5	164.0	222.0	116.4	20,003	10,517	2,239	1,260	5,986
2002	547.6	119.9	195.1	182.3	50.2	25,498	14,409	3,261	1,459	6,369
2003, total [5]	744.5	273.0	162.9	271.1	37.5	30,707	18,216	4,488	1,810	6,193
United Kingdom	164.4	30.5	25.2	108.0	0.7	8,833	6,542	338	693	1,260
Cayman Islands	37.0	-10.4	12.6	32.9	1.9	6,574	2,225	2,516	480	1,353
Bermuda	44.0	25.4	8.4	14.3	-4.0	2,613	1,363	369	99	783
France	4.0	-6.8	0.9	3.6	6.2	1,558	1,004	12	31	511
Japan	181.3	148.9	22.4	12.2	-2.2	1,343	1,015	179	49	100
Canada	27.9	10.8	-1.4	6.9	11.7	1,311	904	45	39	323
Norway	20.7	8.3	1.6	5.8	5.0	805	747	27	8	23
Bahamas, The	1.1	-6.0	4.8	2.1	0.¹	763	475	75	52	161
Ireland	25.1	3.8	4.1	9.5	7.8	726	526	39	40	122
China [6]	64.7	30.5	29.6	4.6	-0.1	695	505	176	10	4
Netherlands Antilles	7.3	6.8	-1.0	0.7	0.8	543	299	103	8	133
Germany	9.7	7.9	-1.1	3.8	-0.9	440	299	22	31	88
Netherlands	1.4	0.2	-0.1	1.3	0.1	412	279	49	13	71
Hong Kong	23.3	6.0	11.9	4.5	0.9	325	248	46	12	19
Singapore	6.1	-1.3	0.7	3.3	3.4	289	170	26	23	69

[1] Marketable bonds and notes. [2] Includes federally-sponsored agencies. [3] Includes transactions in directly placed issues abroad by U.S. corporations and issues of states and municipalities. [4] Total purchases plus total sales. [5] Includes other countries, not shown separately. [6] See footnote 3, Table 1198.

Source: U.S. Dept. of Treasury, *Treasury Bulletin*, quarterly.

No. 1198. Foreign Holdings of U.S. Securities by Country: 2001 to 2003

[In billions of dollars (1,063.1 represents $1,063,100,000,000). Covers only private holdings of U.S. securities, except as noted]

Country	U.S. Treasury securities [1]			Country	Corporate and agency bonds			Corporate stocks		
	2001	2002	2003		2001	2002	2003	2001	2002	2003
Total holdings [2]	1,063.1	1,254.1	1,499.2	Total holdings	1,343.1	1,600.4	1,853.0	1,478.3	1,186.2	1,538.1
Japan	330.1	385.3	542.2	Europe [2]	935.7	1,086.0	1,225.9	915.9	714.5	929.7
China [3]	89.7	124.3	168.1	United Kingdom	593.2	648.2	749.2	289.2	213.4	269.3
Korea, South	29.1	48.0	61.9	France	14.3	17.5	22.6	44.3	35.2	51.4
United Kingdom	28.6	67.0	58.3	Germany	34.4	31.5	33.3	84.1	58.3	72.5
Taiwan [3]	37.9	40.5	50.4	Italy	4.0	5.2	7.6	34.4	26.9	34.4
Hong Kong	47.7	44.4	48.9	Netherlands	25.8	29.0	28.7	111.3	93.8	118.7
Switzerland	28.6	37.7	45.3	Canada	30.6	37.1	49.4	165.0	142.3	192.5
Germany	42.9	38.0	43.8	Japan	136.9	174.1	169.3	126.9	109.9	136.4
Bermuda	11.6	12.6	39.3	Latin America	12.3	16.6	28.2	30.2	23.3	29.2
Mexico	22.1	27.5	31.9	Other Western Hemisphere	159.4	191.7	260.0	148.0	109.2	134.9
				Other countries	68.2	94.9	120.2	92.3	87.0	115.4

[1] Includes foreign official holdings. [2] Includes other countries not shown separately. [3] With the establishment of diplomatic relations with China on January 1, 1979, the U.S. government recognized the People's Republic of China as the sole legal government of China and acknowledged the Chinese position that there is only one China and that Taiwan is part of China.

Source: U.S. Bureau of Economic Analysis, *Survey of Current Business*, July 2004.

No. 1199. Stock Prices and Yields: 1990 to 2003

[Closing values as of end of December, except as noted]

Index	1990	1995	1999	2000	2001	2002	2003
STOCK PRICES							
Standard & Poor's indices: [1]							
S&P 500 composite (1941-43=10)	330.2	615.9	1,469.3	1,320.3	1,148.1	879.8	1,111.9
S&P 400 MidCap Index (1982=100)	100.0	217.8	444.7	516.7	508.3	429.8	576.0
S&P 600 Small Cap Index (Dec. 31, 1993=100)..	(NA)	121.1	197.8	219.6	232.2	196.6	270.4
S&P 500/Barra Value Index (Dec. 31, 1974=35)..	177.7	325.1	610.6	636.2	552.0	428.0	551.9
S&P 500/Barra Growth Index (Dec. 31, 1974=35).	159.9	302.0	887.3	687.6	594.6	448.8	555.9
Russell indices: [2]							
Russell 1000 (Dec. 31, 1986=130)	171.2	328.9	768.0	700.1	604.9	466.2	594.6
Russell 2000 (Dec. 31, 1986=135)...	132.2	316.0	504.8	483.5	488.5	383.1	556.9
Russell 3000 (Dec. 31, 1986=140)...	180.9	351.9	793.3	725.8	634.2	489.5	630.1
N.Y. Stock Exchange common stock index:							
Composite (Dec. 31, 2002=5000)...	1,908.5	3,484.2	6,876.1	6,945.6	6,236.4	5,000.0	6,440.3
Yearly high...	2,126.7	3,501.7	7,011.7	7,164.6	7,048.1	6,445.0	6,469.5
Yearly low...	1,715.1	2,651.2	6,092.3	6,094.9	5,331.4	4,452.5	4,418.6
American Stock Exchange Composite Index (Dec. 29, 1995=550)	(NA)	550.0	877.0	897.8	847.6	824.4	1,173.6
NASDAQ composite index (Feb. 5, 1971=100)	373.8	1,052.1	4,069.3	2,470.5	1,950.4	1,335.5	2,003.4
Nasdaq-100 (Jan. 31, 1985=125).	200.5	576.2	3,708.0	2,341.7	1,577.1	984.4	1,467.9
Industrial (Feb. 5, 1971=100) ...	406.1	964.7	2,239.0	1,483.0	1,389.2	1,029.7	1,603.7
Banks (Feb. 5, 1971=100) ...	254.9	1,009.4	1,691.3	1,939.5	2,134.9	2,231.3	2,899.2
Computers (Oct. 29, 1993=200)...	(NA)	366.1	2,325.4	1,295.0	980.5	622.6	934.9
Transportation (Feb. 5, 1971=100)...	417.1	816.4	999.1	1,160.4	1,285.0	1,297.6	1,754.4
Telecommunications (October 29, 1993=200)....	84.0	208.4	1,015.4	463.4	236.6	108.8	183.6
Biotech (Oct. 29, 1993=200)...	(NA)	304.3	881.8	1,084.5	908.8	496.9	724.1
Dow-Jones and Co., Inc.:							
Composite (65 stocks)...	920.6	1,693.2	3,214.4	3,317.4	2,892.2	2,375.0	3,000.8
Industrial (30 stocks)...	2,633.7	5,117.1	11,497.1	10,786.9	10,021.5	8,341.6	10,453.9
Transportation (20 stocks)...	910.2	1,981.0	2,977.2	2,946.6	2,640.0	2,310.0	3,007.1
Utility (15 stocks)...	209.7	225.4	283.4	412.2	293.9	215.2	266.9
Wilshire 5000 Total Market Index [3] (Dec. 31, 1980=1404.596)...	3,101.4	6,057.2	13,812.7	12,175.9	10,818.6	8,343.2	10,799.4
COMMON STOCK YIELDS (percent)							
Standard & Poor's composite index (500 stocks): [4]							
Dividend-price ratio [5]...	3.61	2.56	1.25	1.15	1.32	1.61	1.77
Earnings-price ratio [6]...	6.47	6.09	3.17	3.63	2.95	2.92	3.85

NA Not available. [1] Standard & Poor's Indices are market-value weighted and are chosen for market size, liquidity, and industry group representation. The S&P 500 index represents the 500 largest publicly traded companies. The S&P MidCap Index tracks mid-cap companies. The S&P SmallCap Index consists of 600 domestic small-cap stocks. [2] The Russell 1000 and 3000 indices show respectively the 1000 and 3000 largest capitalization stocks in the United States. The Russell 2000 index shows the 2000 largest capitalization stocks in the United States after the first 1000. [3] The Wilshire 5000 Total Market Index measures the performance of all U.S. headquartered equity securities with readily available prices. [4] Source: U.S. Council of Economic Advisors, *Economic Report of the President*, annual. [5] Aggregate cash dividends (based on latest known annual rate) divided by aggregate market value based on Wednesday closing prices. Averages of monthly figures. [6] Averages of quarterly ratios which are ratio of earnings (after taxes) for 4 quarters ending with particular quarter to price index for last day of that quarter.

Source: Except as noted, Global Financial Data, Los Angeles, CA, <http://www.globalfindata.com/trial/index2.html>; (copyright).

No. 1200. Dow-Jones U.S. Equity Market Index by Industry: 1995 to 2003

[As of end of year]

Industry	1995	1998	1999	2000	2001	2002	2003
U.S. Equity Market Index, total	147.49	281.61	341.57	306.88	266.71	204.51	262.68
Basic materials	139.19	150.23	187.16	154.49	153.22	136.97	181.10
Consumer, cyclical	140.36	282.76	341.88	277.68	278.19	209.66	278.49
Consumer, noncyclical..............	134.03	246.00	244.64	215.56	217.96	204.19	242.73
Energy............................	134.54	186.15	219.71	272.96	236.74	200.29	246.08
Financial..........................	176.60	356.05	354.55	440.91	404.50	346.36	445.96
Healthcare	127.77	277.52	263.62	360.18	310.76	242.87	286.04
Industrial.........................	156.39	245.89	308.19	276.11	245.14	179.78	235.69
Technology	229.18	648.08	1,188.60	749.01	535.89	327.84	493.02
Telecommunications	154.84	305.76	356.97	210.38	180.62	115.04	119.12
Utilities...........................	109.07	141.84	118.12	177.80	127.04	95.75	114.54

Source: Dow Jones & Company, Inc., New York, NY, *Dow Jones Indexes*, (copyright).

No. 1201. Sales of Stocks on Registered Exchanges: 1990 to 2003

[1,752 represents $1,752,000,000,000. Excludes over-the-counter trading]

Exchange	Unit	1990	1995	1996	1997	1998	1999	2000	2001	2002	2003
Market value of all sales, all exchanges [1][2]	Bil. dol . .	1,752	3,690	4,735	6,879	8,698	11,220	14,552	13,315	13,715	14,670
New York	Bil. dol . .	1,394	3,078	4,013	5,848	7,275	9,087	11,217	10,738	10,793	10,050
American	Bil. dol . .	65	105	131	204	355	543	915	884	730	682
Chicago	Bil. dol . .	74	114	136	213	326	540	1,038	702	526	448
CBOE [3]	Bil. dol . .	81	107	130	179	214	271	330	197	157	159
Pacific	Bil. dol . .	53	94	108	151	182	255	248	96	69	1,441
Philadelphia	Bil. dol . .	41	59	68	89	97	103	165	130	86	116
STOCKS [4]											
Shares sold, all exchanges [2] . .	Billion . . .	53.3	106.4	125.7	159.7	206.4	244.1	317.7	371.1	479.5	568.9
New York.	Billion . . .	43.8	90.1	108.2	138.8	178.9	207.7	265.7	313.4	376.7	379.3
American	Billion . . .	3.1	4.8	5.3	6.2	7.6	8.7	11.9	15.3	17.3	19.9
Chicago	Billion . . .	2.5	3.9	4.2	6.0	9.5	14.4	24.1	27.3	24.0	24.2
Pacific.	Billion . . .	1.7	2.7	3.0	3.2	4.0	4.9	4.1	1.5	1.1	63.8
Market value, all exchanges [2] . .	Bil. dol . . .	1,612	3,507	4,511	6,559	8,307	10,680	13,691	12,721	13,230	14,131
New York.	Bil. dol . . .	1,390	3,076	4,011	5,847	7,274	9,087	11,216	10,737	10,793	10,050
American	Bil. dol . . .	36	73	86	139	280	446	758	807	684	644
Chicago	Bil. dol . . .	74	114	136	213	326	540	1,038	702	526	448
Pacific.	Bil. dol . . .	45	79	92	123	148	206	163	46	47	1,422

[1] Includes market value of stocks, rights, warrants, and options trading. [2] Includes other registered exchanges, not shown separately. [3] Chicago Board Options Exchange, Inc. [4] Includes voting trust certificates, American Depository Receipts, and certificate of deposit for stocks.

Source: U.S. Securities and Exchange Commission, *Annual Report*.

No. 1202. Volume of Trading on New York Stock Exchange: 1990 to 2003

[39,946 represents 39,946,000,000. *Round lot*: A unit of trading or a multiple thereof. On the NYSE the unit of trading is generally 100 shares in stocks. For some inactive stocks, the unit of trading is 10 shares. *Odd lot*: An amount of stock less than the established 100-share unit or 10-share unit of trading]

Item	Unit	1990	1995	1996	1997	1998	1999	2000	2001	2002	2003
Shares traded	Million . .	39,946	87,873	134,404	171,188	206,299	265,499	311,290	369,069	356,767	
Round lots	Million . .	39,665	87,218	133,312	169,745	203,914	262,478	307,509	363,135	352,398	
Average daily shares	Million . .	157	346	527	674	809	1,042	1,240	1,441	1,398	
High day	Million . .	292	653	1,201	1,216	1,350	1,560	2,368	2,813	1,886	
Low day	Million . .	57	118	155	247	312	403	414	462	360	
Odd lots	Million . .	282	656	1,091	1,443	2,384	3,021	3,781	5,934	4,370	
Value of shares traded . .	Bil. dol .	1,336	3,110	5,833	7,395	9,073	11,205	10,645	10,491	9,846	
Round lots	Bil. dol .	1,325	3,083	5,778	7,318	8,945	11,060	10,489	10,278	9,692	
Odd lots	Bil. dol . .	11	27	56	77	128	145	155	213	154	
Bond volume [1] **. . . . . . .**	Mil. dol .	10,893	6,979	5,046	3,838	3,221	2,328	2,668	3,625	2,503	
Daily average	Mil. dol .	43.1	27.7	19.9	15.2	12.8	9.2	10.8	14.4	9.9	

[1] Par value.

Source: New York Stock Exchange, Inc., New York, NY, *Fact Book*, annual (copyright).

No. 1203. Securities Listed on New York Stock Exchange: 1990 to 2003

[As of December 31, except cash dividends are for calendar year (1,689 represents $1,689,000,000,000)]

Item	Unit	1990	1994	1995	1996	1997	1998	1999	2000	2001	2002	2003
BONDS												
Number of issuers	Number .	743	583	564	563	533	474	416	392	369	343	340
Number of issues	Number .	2,912	2,141	2,097	2,064	1,965	1,858	1,736	1,627	1,447	1,323	1,300
Face value	Bil. dol . .	1,689	2,526	2,773	2,845	2,625	2,554	2,402	2,125	1,654	1,378	1,350
STOCKS												
Companies	Number .	1,774	2,570	2,675	2,907	3,047	3,114	3,025	2,862	2,798	2,783	2,750
Number of issues	Number .	2,284	3,060	3,126	3,285	3,358	3,382	3,286	3,072	2,984	2,966	2,943
Shares listed	Billions . .	90.7	142.3	154.7	176.9	207.1	239.3	280.9	313.9	341.5	349.9	359.7
Market value	Bil. dol . .	2,820	4,448	6,013	7,300	9,413	10,864	12,296	12,372	11,714	9,603	12,200
Average price	Dollars . .	31.08	31.26	38.86	41.26	45.45	45.40	43.77	42.14	34.11	28.39	27.50

Source: New York Stock Exchange, Inc., New York, NY, *Fact Book*, annual (copyright).

U.S. Census Bureau, Statistical Abstract of the United States: 2004-2005

No. 1204. Stock Ownership by Age of Head of Family and Family Income: 1995 to 2001

[Median value in thousands of constant 2001 dollars (16.9 represents $16,900). Constant dollar figures are based on consumer price index data published by U.S. Bureau of Labor Statistics. Families include one-person units; for definition of family, see text, Section 1. Based on Survey of Consumer Finance; see Appendix III. For definition of median, see Guide to Tabular Presentation]

Age of family head and family income (constant (2001) dollars)	Families having direct or indirect stock holdings [1] (percent)			Median value among families with holdings			Stock holdings' share of group's financial assets (percent)		
	1995	1998	2001	1995	1998	2001	1995	1998	2001
All families	40.4	48.9	51.9	16.9	27.2	34.3	39.9	53.9	56.0
Under 35 years old	36.6	40.8	48.9	5.9	7.6	7.0	27.2	44.8	52.6
35 to 44 years old	46.4	56.7	59.5	11.6	21.8	27.5	39.5	54.6	57.3
45 to 54 year: old	48.9	58.6	59.2	30.0	41.4	50.0	42.6	55.7	59.1
55 to 64 years old	40.0	55.9	57.1	35.8	51.2	81.2	44.2	58.4	56.1
65 to 74 years old	34.4	42.7	39.2	39.3	61.0	150.0	35.8	51.3	55.1
75 years old and over	27.9	29.4	34.2	23.1	65.3	120.0	39.8	48.7	51.4
Percentiles of income: [2]									
Less than 20 ($10,300)	6.5	10.0	12.4	4.3	5.4	7.0	14.2	20.4	36.9
20-39.9 ($24,400)	24.7	30.8	33.5	7.3	10.9	7.5	26.7	29.7	34.9
40-59.9 ($39,900)	41.5	50.2	52.1	7.2	13.1	15.0	28.4	37.9	46.4
60-79.9 ($64,800)	54.3	69.3	75.7	14.6	20.4	28.5	35.6	45.7	51.7
80-89.9 ($98,700)	69.7	77.9	82.0	28.9	49.0	64.6	41.3	50.4	57.4
90-100 ($302,700)	80.0	90.4	89.6	69.3	146.5	247.7	45.4	62.5	60.4

[1] Indirect holdings are those in mutual funds, retirement accounts, and other managed assets. [2] See footnote 8, Table 1162.
Source: Board of Governors of the Federal Reserve System, *Federal Reserve Bulletin*, January 2003, and unpublished data.

No. 1205. Household Ownership of Equities: 2002

[52.7 represents 52,700,000. Based on a national probability sample of 4,009 household financial decision-makers. Further questions about equity ownership were asked of those 1,986 decision-makers who indicated they owned equities]

Type of holding	Households owning equities		Number of individual investors (mil.)
	Number (mil.)	Percent of all households	
Any type of equity (net) [1]	52.7	49.5	84.3
Any equity inside employer-sponsored retirement plans	36.2	34.0	57.9
Any equity outside employer-sponsored retirement plans	35.9	33.7	57.4
Individual stock (net) [1]	25.4	23.9	38.1
Individual stock inside employer-sponsored retirement plans	8.8	8.3	12.3
Individual stock outside employer-sponsored retirement plans	21.0	19.7	31.5
Stock mutual funds (net) [1]	47.0	44.2	70.5
Stock mutual funds inside employer-sponsored retirement plans	33.2	31.2	46.5
Stock mutual funds outside employer-sponsored retirement plans . . .	28.7	27.0	43.1

[1] Multiple responses included.

No. 1206. Characteristics of Equity Owners: 2002

[In percent, except as indicated. See headnote, Table 1205. For definition of median, see Guide to Tabular Presentation]

Item	Total	Age					Household income		
		18 to 34 years old	35 to 44 years old	45 to 54 years old	55 to 64 years old	65 years old and over	Less than $50,000	$50,000 to $99,999	$100,000 and over
Median age of owner (years)	47	29	40	50	59	73	46	44	47
Median household income (dol.) [2]	62,500	60,000	70,000	68,000	62,500	45,000	34,000	70,000	125,000
Median household financial assets [1] (dol.) .	100,000	32,500	99,100	136,800	274,300	415,100	37,500	100,000	421,500
Equity investments owned:									
Individual stock (net) [2]	49	41	49	50	50	56	39	48	64
Inside retirement plans [3]	17	18	21	18	16	6	11	18	22
Outside retirement plans [3]	41	33	40	42	44	50	31	40	57
Stock mutual funds (net) [2]	89	85	90	93	93	83	88	90	91
Inside retirement plans [3]	66	67	76	77	61	28	57	73	73
Outside retirement plans [3]	56	47	54	52	67	67	50	50	67
Non-equity investments owned: [2]									
Savings accounts, MMDAs, or CDs [4] . . .	86	88	87	84	82	86	78	89	87
Bond investments (net) [2]	36	28	31	35	44	48	26	35	43
Individual bonds	17	13	15	16	21	28	13	15	21
Bond mutual funds	26	19	23	25	31	34	17	25	31
Fixed or variable annuities	23	13	19	25	31	33	21	23	24
Hybrid mutual funds	52	43	51	55	60	52	43	51	61
Money market mutual funds	35	27	35	35	43	36	25	33	44
Investment real estate	24	15	20	29	32	30	17	22	40
Have retirement plan coverage [3]	79	81	87	84	78	58	75	87	83
Have Individual Retirement Account (IRA) . .	57	46	56	62	66	55	43	58	72

[1] Includes assets in employer-sponsored retirement plans but excludes value of primary residence. [2] Multiple responses included. [3] Employer-sponsored. [4] MMDA=money market deposit account; CD=certificate of deposit.
Source of Tables 1205 and 1206: Investment Company Institute, Washington, DC, and Securities Industry Association, New York, NY, *Equity Ownership in America, Fall 2002* (copyright).

No. 1207. Households Owning Mutual Funds by Age and Income: 2000 and 2003

[In percent. Includes money market, stock, bond and hybrid, variable annuity, IRA, Keogh, and employer-sponsored retirement plan fund owners. In 2003, an estimated 53,300,000 households own mutual funds. Based on a sample survey of 3,000 households; for details, see source]

Age of household head and household income	Percent distri-bution, 2003	As percent of all households		Age of household head and household income	Percent distri-bution, 2003	As percent of all households	
		2000	2003			2000	2003
Total	100	49	48				
Less than 25 years old .	4	23	27	Less than $25,000	7	17	15
25 to 34 years old.	16	49	44	$25,000 to $34,999	9	37	33
35 to 44 years old.	26	58	54	$35,000 to $49,999	14	49	41
45 to 54 years old.	25	59	57	$50,000 to $74,999	29	66	59
55 to 64 years old.	16	54	59	$75,000 to $99,999	18	77	77
65 years old and over . .	13	32	34	$100,000 and over	23	79	83

Source: Investment Company Institute, Washington, DC, *Fundamentals, Investment Company Institute Research in Brief*, Vol. 9, No. 4, August 2000 and Vol. 12, No. 4, October 2003 (copyright).

No. 1208. Characteristics of Mutual Fund Owners: 2001

[In percent, except as indicated. Mutual fund ownership includes holdings of money market, stock, bond, and hybrid mutual funds; and funds owned through variable annuities, Individual Retirement Accounts (IRAs), Keoghs, and employer-sponsored retirement plans. Based on a national probability sample of 2,592 primary financial decisionmakers in households with mutual fund investments. For definition of median, see Guide to Tabular Presentation]

Characteristic	Total	Age			Household income		
		Under 40 years old	40 to 64 years old	65 years old and over	Less than $50,000	$50,000 to $100,000	Over $100,000
Median age (years).	46	33	49	72	43	45	46
Median household income (dol.)	62,100	60,000	70,000	50,000	32,500	65,000	130,000
Median household financial assets [1] (dol.).	100,000	50,000	150,000	243,000	40,000	100,000	300,000
Own an IRA.	60	59	60	58	51	60	66
Household has a defined contribution retirement plan(s), net [2]	81	87	84	58	75	88	86
401(k) plan.	64	75	67	20	55	68	72
403(b) plan.	11	12	11	10	9	12	13
State, local, or federal government plan.	35	31	36	42	34	38	38
Median mutual fund assets (dol.).	40,000	20,000	60,000	59,500	17,500	44,800	120,000
Median number of mutual funds owned	4	4	4	3	3	4	6
Own: [2]							
Equity funds	88	90	89	80	86	87	96
Bond funds	37	31	39	41	31	34	44
Hybrid funds.	34	33	34	34	33	32	43
Money market mutual funds	48	41	52	50	44	44	53
Own mutual funds bought: [2]							
Outside employer-sponsored retirement plan(s).	69	59	71	89	60	60	75
Inside employer-sponsored retirement plan(s). .	62	71	66	24	57	69	76

[1] Includes assets in employer-sponsored retirement plans but excludes value of primary residence. [2] Multiple responses included.

Source: Investment Company Institute, Washington, DC, *2001 Profile of Mutual Fund Shareholders*, 2001 (copyright).

No. 1209. Mutual Funds—Summary: 1990 to 2003

[Number of funds and assets as of December 31 (1,065 represents $1,065,000,000,000). A mutual fund is an open-end investment company that continuously issues and redeems shares that represent an interest in a pool of financial assets. Excludes data for funds that invest in other mutual funds. Minus sign (-) indicates net redemptions]

Type of fund	Unit	1990	1995	1997	1998	1999	2000	2001	2002	2003
Number of funds, total	Number. .	3,079	5,725	6,684	7,314	7,791	8,155	8,305	8,244	8,126
Equity funds	Number. .	1,099	2,139	2,951	3,513	3,952	4,385	4,716	4,748	4,601
Hybrid funds	Number. .	193	412	501	525	532	523	483	474	509
Bond funds	Number. .	1,046	2,177	2,219	2,250	2,262	2,208	2,091	2,033	2,043
Money market funds, taxable [1] . . .	Number. .	506	674	682	685	702	703	689	679	661
Money market funds, tax-exempt [2] . .	Number. .	235	323	331	341	343	336	326	310	312
Assets, total	Bil. dol .	1,065	2,811	4,468	5,525	6,846	6,965	6,975	6,390	7,414
Equity funds	Bil. dol. .	240	1,249	2,368	2,978	4,042	3,962	3,418	2,663	3,685
Hybrid funds	Bil. dol. .	36	210	317	365	379	346	346	330	437
Bond funds	Bil. dol. .	291	599	724	831	812	811	925	1,125	1,241
Money market funds, taxable [1] . . .	Bil. dol. .	415	630	898	1,163	1,409	1,607	2,013	1,997	1,763
Money market funds, tax-exempt [2] . .	Bil. dol. .	84	123	161	189	204	238	272	275	288
Equity, hybrid and bond funds:										
Sales	Bil. dol. .	149	475	869	1,058	1,274	1,630	1,383	1,434	1,430
Redemptions	Bil. dol. .	98	313	541	748	1,021	1,330	1,177	1,228	1,148
Net sales	Bil. dol. .	51	163	328	310	252	300	206	206	282
Money market funds, taxable: [1]										
Sales	Bil. dol. .	1,219	2,729	4,395	5,534	7,083	8,691	10,701	11,011	10,149
Redemptions	Bil. dol. .	1,183	2,617	4,265	5,289	6,866	8,499	10,314	11,075	10,401
Net sales	Bil. dol. .	36	112	129	244	217	192	387	-64	-252
Money market funds, tax-exempt: [2]										
Sales	Bil. dol. .	197	396	536	639	687	788	783	750	873
Redemptions	Bil. dol. .	190	385	518	612	675	757	751	736	866
Net sales	Bil. dol. .	7	11	18	27	12	31	31	14	7

[1] Funds invest in short-term, high-grade securities sold in the money market. [2] Funds invest in municipal securities with relatively short maturities.

Source: Investment Company Institute, Washington, DC, *Mutual Fund Fact Book*, annual (copyright).

Banking, Finance, and Insurance 757

No. 1210. Mutual Fund Shares—Holdings and Net Purchases by Type of Investor: 1990 to 2003

[In billions of dollars (608 represents $608,000,000,000). Holdings as of Dec. 31. Minus sign (-) indicates net sales]

Type of investor	Holdings					Net purchases				
	1990	1995	2000	2002	2003	1990	1995	2000	2002	2003
Total	608	1,853	4,435	3,639	4,665	53.7	147.4	235.0	182.7	288.2
Households, nonprofit organizations	457	1,153	3,036	2,539	3,292	22.5	75.5	171.6	118.8	293.1
Nonfinancial corporate business...	10	46	123	90	128	-1.0	4.6	5.0	9.3	9.3
State and local governments.....	5	35	26	33	31	3.3	5.9	0.8	2.0	-3.0
Commercial banking	2	2	15	20	17	-0.3	0.3	2.5	1.7	-6.2
Credit unions	1	3	2	4	4	0.2	0.2	-0.3	-0.2	0.5
Bank personal trusts and estates..	63	254	397	339	391	9.7	11.9	48.5	37.3	-15.0
Life insurance companies	31	33	102	81	107	12.6	3.9	5.7	2.8	7.6
Private pension funds	40	327	734	533	696	6.6	45.0	1.2	11.0	1.9

Source: Board of Governors of the Federal Reserve System, "Federal Reserve Statistical Release, Z.1, Flow of Funds Accounts of the United States"; published: 4 March 2004; <http://www.federalreserve.gov/releases/Z1/20040304/data.htm>.

No. 1211. Mutual Fund Retirement Assets: 1990 to 2003

[In billions of dollars, except percent (206 represents $206,000,000,000). Based on data from the Institute's Annual Questionnaire for Retirement Statistics. The 2003 survey gathered data from 14,059 mutual fund share classes representing approximately 83 percent of mutual fund industry assets. Assets were estimated for all non-reporting funds. Estimates of retirement assets in street name and omnibus accounts were derived from data reported on the Annual Questionnaire for Retirement Statistics and the Annual Institutional Survey]

Type of account	1990	1995	1998	1999	2000	2001	2002	2003
Mutual fund retirement assets ...	206	913	1,948	2,535	2,478	2,342	2,078	2,662
Percent of total retirement assets.	5	13	19	22	21	21	20	22
Individual retirement accounts (IRAs) ...	139	470	968	1,259	1,230	1,160	1,032	1,306
Employer-sponsored defined contribution retirement plans	67	443	980	1,276	1,248	1,182	1,046	1,356
401(k) plans [1]	35	266	619	814	820	799	711	922
Percent of total 401(k) assets [2]	9	31	40	45	46	47	47	49
403(b) plans [3]	15	119	233	289	264	238	200	263
457 plans [4]	2	8	24	40	38	37	31	38
Other defined contribution plans [5]	15	50	104	133	127	109	105	133
Percent of all mutual funds:								
Mutual fund retirement assets	19	32	35	37	36	34	33	36
Individual retirement accounts (IRAs) ...	13	17	18	18	18	17	16	18
Employer-sponsored retirement plans ...	6	16	18	19	18	17	16	18

[1] A 401(k) plan is a qualified retirement plan that allows participants to have a portion of their compensation (otherwise payable in cash) contributed pretax to a retirement account on their behalf. Predominantly 401(k) assets, but may also include some profit-sharing plan assets that do not have a 401(k) feature. [2] Beginning 2000 percents are estimated. [3] Section 403(b) of the Internal Revenue Code permits employees of certain charitable organizations, nonprofit hospitals, universities, and public schools to establish tax-sheltered retirement programs. These plans may invest in either annuity contracts or mutual fund shares. [4] These plans are deferred compensation arrangements for government employees and employees of certain tax-exempt organizations. [5] Includes Keoghs; target benefit plans; thrift savings plans, stock bonus plans, and money purchase plans without a 401(k) feature; and all other defined contribution plans not specified elsewhere.

Source: Investment Company Institute, Washington, DC, Fundamentals, Investment Company Institute Research in Brief, "Mutual Funds and the Retirement Market in 2003"; Vol. 13, No. 2, June 2004; <http://www.ici.org> (copyright).

No. 1212. Individual Retirement Accounts (IRA) Plans—Value by Institution: 1990 to 2003

[As of December 31 (637 represents $637,000,000,000). Estimated]

Institution	Amount (bil. dol.)								Percent distribution		
	1990	1995	1998	1999	2000	2001	2002	2003	1990	2000	2003
Total IRA assets	637	1,288	2,150	2,651	2,629	2,619	2,445	3,007	100	100	100
Bank and thrift deposits [1]	266	261	249	244	252	255	263	268	42	10	9
Life insurance companies [2]	40	81	156	202	202	210	267	315	6	8	10
Mutual funds................	139	470	968	1,259	1,230	1,160	1,032	1,306	22	47	43
Securities held in brokerage accounts [3]......	191	477	776	947	945	994	883	1,117	30	36	37

[1] Includes Keogh deposits. [2] Annuities held by IRAs, excluding variable annuity mutual fund IRA assets. [3] Excludes mutual fund assets held through brokerage accounts, which are included in mutual funds.

Source: Investment Company Institute, Washington, DC, Fundamentals, Investment Company Institute Research in Brief, "Mutual Funds and the Retirement Market in 2003"; Vol. 13, No. 2, June 2004; <http://www.ici.org> (copyright).

No. 1213. Assets of Private and Public Pension Funds by Type of Fund: 1990 to 2003

[In billions of dollars (3,337 represents $3,337,000,000,000). As of end of year. Except for corporate equities, represents book value. Excludes social security trust funds, see Table 526]

Type of pension fund	1990	1995	1997	1998	1999	2000	2001	2002	2003
Total, all types	3,337	5,614	7,251	8,125	8,975	8,968	8,569	7,885	9,181
Private funds	2,197	3,769	4,775	5,353	5,972	5,879	5,528	5,024	5,937
Insured [1]	570	881	1,086	1,248	1,431	1,456	1,465	1,492	1,743
Noninsured [2][3]	1,627	2,889	3,689	4,105	4,541	4,423	4,063	3,533	4,194
Credit market instruments [3]	464	608	647	621	635	666	673	701	701
U.S. Government securities [3]	255	335	330	280	288	301	303	309	304
Agency	133	214	211	195	209	225	237	242	237
Corporate and foreign bonds	158	240	277	298	299	318	324	332	341
Corporate equities	606	1,278	1,667	1,948	2,269	2,138	1,860	1,418	1,873
Mutual fund shares	40	327	570	668	754	734	652	533	696
Unallocated insurance contracts [4]	215	332	382	385	393	378	369	363	398
State and local pension funds [3]	801	1,303	1,817	2,054	2,227	2,290	2,180	1,964	2,284
Credit market instruments [3]	402	530	632	705	751	806	788	802	815
U.S. Government securities	231	291	340	360	376	399	366	364	367
Corporate and foreign bonds	142	189	245	280	310	340	351	361	363
Corporate equities	285	679	1,085	1,234	1,343	1,335	1,222	1,002	1,319
Federal government retirement funds [5]	340	541	659	718	776	799	862	897	960

[1] Annuity reserves held by life insurance companies, excluding unallocated contracts held by private pension funds. [2] Private defined benefit plans and defined contribution plans (including 401(k) type plans). [3] Includes other types of assets not shown separately. [4] Assets at life insurance companies (e.g., guaranteed investment contracts (GICs), variable annuities). [5] Includes the Federal Employees Thrift Savings Plan, the National Railroad Retirement Investment Trust, and nonmarketable government securities held by federal government retirement funds.

Source: Board of Governors of the Federal Reserve System, "Federal Reserve Statistical Release, Z.1, Flow of Funds Accounts of the United States"; published: 4 March 2004; <http://www.federalreserve.gov/releases/Z1/20040304/data.htm>.

No. 1214. Annual Revenues of Selected Securities Industries: 1999 to 2002

[In millions of dollars (285,317 represents $285,317,000,000). Covers taxable employer firms only. Based on the North American Industry Classification System (NAICS), 1997; see text, Section 15. Based on Service Annual Survey; see Appendix III]

Kind of business	NAICS code	1999	2000	2001	2002
Total	523x	285,317	331,497	288,417	256,879
Securities and commodity contracts intermediation and brokerage	5231	193,759	227,841	191,007	163,080
Investment banking & securities dealing	52311	104,154	116,244	97,479	79,083
Securities brokerage	52312	85,050	106,933	88,757	79,257
Commodity contracts dealing	52313	1,807	1,920	1,980	1,985
Commodity contracts brokerage	52314	2,748	2,744	2,791	2,754
Other financial investment activities [1]	5239x	91,558	103,656	97,410	93,799
Portfolio management	52392	76,275	86,395	81,855	77,247
Investment advice	52393	15,283	17,261	15,555	16,553

[1] Excludes NAICS 52391 (miscellaneous intermediation) and NAICS 52399 (all other financial investment activities).

Source: U.S. Census Bureau, Service Annual Survey: 2002.

No. 1215. Securities Industry—Financial Summary: 1990 to 2002

[In billions of dollars, except as indicated (71.4 represents $71,400,000,000)]

Type	1990	1995	1996	1997	1998	1999	2000	2001	2002
Number of firms	8,437	7,722	7,774	7,796	7,685	7,461	7,258	7,002	6,768
Revenues, total	71.4	143.4	172.4	207.2	235.0	266.8	349.5	280.1	221.8
Commissions	12.0	23.2	27.9	32.7	36.7	45.9	54.1	44.8	45.0
Trading/investment gains	15.7	29.0	30.8	36.0	32.8	55.5	70.8	39.0	24.2
Underwriting profits	3.7	8.9	12.6	14.6	16.2	17.8	18.7	16.9	14.7
Margin interest	3.2	6.5	7.4	10.6	12.7	15.2	24.5	13.9	6.4
Mutual fund sales	3.2	7.4	10.1	12.4	14.8	16.7	19.4	16.4	15.7
Other	33.4	68.5	83.7	101.0	121.7	115.7	161.9	149.1	115.8
Expenses, total	70.6	132.1	155.4	187.3	217.8	237.7	310.4	260.7	206.5
Interest expense	28.1	56.9	64.7	80.7	98.1	87.5	131.9	98.9	56.4
Compensation	22.9	41.5	51.0	58.6	65.0	81.7	95.2	83.5	74.9
Commissions/clearance paid	3.0	5.7	7.4	8.9	10.3	13.5	15.5	14.0	15.0
Other	16.6	28.0	32.3	39.2	44.3	55.0	67.8	64.2	60.3
Net income, pretax	0.8	11.3	17.0	20.0	17.2	29.1	39.1	19.4	15.3
Pre-tax profit margin (percent)	1.1	7.9	9.8	9.6	7.3	10.9	11.2	6.9	6.9
Pre-tax return on equity (percent)	2.2	20.1	27.3	27.1	19.4	27.8	31.1	13.8	10.7
Assets	657	1,494	1,748	2,079	2,187	2,537	2,866	3,371	3,261
Liabilities	623	1,435	1,682	1,997	2,092	2,423	2,728	3,227	3,119
Ownership equity	34	59	66	82	95	114	138	144	142

Source: U.S. Securities and Exchange Commission, Annual Report.

No. 1216. Life Insurance in Force and Purchases in the United States— Summary: 1990 to 2002

[As of December 31 or calendar year, as applicable (389 represents 389,000,000). Covers life insurance with life insurance companies only. Represents all life insurance in force on lives of U.S. residents whether issued by U.S. or foreign companies]

Year	Life insurance in force				Life insurance purchases [2]				
	Number of policies, total (mil.)	Value (bil. dol.)			Number (1,000)			Amount (bil. dol.)		
		Total [1]	Individual	Group	Total	Individual	Group	Total	Individual	Group
1990	389	9,393	5,391	3,754	28,791	14,199	14,592	1,529	1,070	459
1994	366	11,081	6,449	4,443	32,225	13,835	18,390	1,617	1,057	560
1995	370	11,696	6,890	4,605	31,999	12,595	19,404	1,577	1,039	538
1996	355	12,704	7,426	5,068	30,783	12,022	18,761	1,704	1,089	615
1997	351	13,364	7,873	5,279	31,707	11,734	19,973	1,892	1,204	689
1998	358	14,471	8,523	5,735	31,891	11,559	20,332	2,064	1,325	740
1999	367	15,496	9,172	6,110	38,584	11,673	26,912	2,367	1,400	967
2000	369	15,953	9,376	6,376	34,882	13,345	21,537	2,515	1,594	921
2001	377	16,290	9,346	6,765	40,095	14,059	26,036	2,773	1,600	1,172
2002	396	16,346	9,312	6,876	38,713	14,692	24,020	2,767	1,753	1,014

[1] Includes other types of policy not shown separately. [2] Excludes revivals, increases, dividend additions, and reinsurance acquired. Includes long-term credit insurance (life insurance on loans of more than 10 years' duration).

Source: American Council of Life Insurers, Washington, DC, *Life Insurers Fact Book*, annual (copyright).

No. 1217. U.S. Life Insurance Companies—Summary: 1990 to 2002

[As of December 31 or calendar year, as applicable (402.2 represents $402,200,000,000). Covers domestic and foreign business of U.S. companies. Beginning 1994 includes annual statement data for companies that primarily are health insurance companies]

Item	Unit	1990	1994	1995	1996	1997	1998	1999	2000	2001	2002
U.S. companies [1]	Number .	2,195	2,136	2,079	1,679	1,620	1,563	1,470	1,269	1,225	1,171
Income	Bil. dol.	402.2	492.6	528.1	561.1	610.6	663.4	726.9	811.5	724.4	734.0
Life insurance premiums	Bil. dol..	76.7	98.9	102.8	107.6	115.0	119.9	120.3	130.6	125.3	134.5
Annuity considerations [2]	Bil. dol..	129.1	153.0	158.4	178.4	197.5	229.5	270.2	306.7	251.3	269.3
Health insurance premiums....	Bil. dol..	58.3	86.2	90.0	92.2	92.7	94.9	100.0	105.6	103.4	108.7
Investment and other........	Bil. dol..	138.2	154.5	176.9	182.9	205.3	219.1	236.4	268.5	244.5	221.5
Payments under life insurance and annuity contracts	Bil. dol..	88.4	200.8	227.6	246.9	276.6	301.8	355.3	375.2	304.9	301.3
Payments to life insurance beneficiaries.............	Bil. dol..	24.6	32.6	34.5	36.3	37.5	40.1	41.4	44.1	46.5	48.2
Surrender values under life insurance [3]	Bil. dol..	18.0	18.0	19.5	24.5	24.0	26.8	32.8	27.2	30.7	32.9
Surrender values under annuity contracts [3][4]	Bil. dol..	(NA)	92.8	105.4	115.7	140.8	154.5	198.3	214.0	151.3	142.9
Annuity payments	Bil. dol..	12.0	15.9	17.8	18.1	18.0	18.9	19.1	20.0	20.0	21.0
Policyholder dividends	Bil. dol..	32.6	40.4	48.5	51.1	55.1	60.4	62.5	68.7	55.2	55.0
Matured endowments	Bil. dol..	0.7	0.6	1.0	0.7	0.6	0.6	0.5	0.6	0.5	0.6
Other payments	Bil. dol..	0.6	0.5	0.9	0.6	0.6	0.6	0.6	0.6	0.6	0.6
Health insurance benefit payments	Bil. dol..	40.0	60.1	64.7	66.7	67.4	70.0	74.5	78.8	76.3	78.7
BALANCE SHEET											
Assets.................	Bil. dol.	1,408	1,942	2,144	2,328	2,579	2,827	3,071	3,182	3,269	3,380
Government bonds	Bil. dol..	211	396	409	411	391	379	362	364	377	481
Corporate securities	Bil. dol..	711	1,072	1,241	1,416	1,658	1,898	2,180	2,238	2,263	2,266
Percent of total assets ...	Percent .	50	55	58	61	64	67	71	70	69	67
Bonds	Bil. dol..	583	791	869	962	1,060	1,140	1,190	1,241	1,354	1,475
Stocks..............	Bil. dol..	128	282	372	454	598	758	990	997	909	791
Mortgages.............	Bil. dol..	270	215	212	212	210	216	230	237	244	251
Real estate	Bil. dol..	43	54	52	50	46	41	38	36	32	33
Policy loans	Bil. dol..	63	85	96	102	105	105	99	102	104	105
Other	Bil. dol..	110	120	133	137	169	187	163	204	248	244
Interest earned on assets [5] ...	Percent ..	8.89	7.14	7.41	7.25	7.35	6.95	6.71	7.05	6.31	5.38
Obligations and surplus funds [6] ..	Bil. dol..	1,408	1,942	2,144	2,328	2,579	2,826	3,071	3,182	3,269	3,380
Policy reserves	**Bil. dol.**	1,197	1,644	1,812	1,966	2,165	2,377	2,610	2,712	2,446	2,507
Annuities [7]	Bil. dol..	798	1,095	1,213	1,312	1,455	1,608	1,781	1,841	1,516	1,550
Group	Bil. dol..	516	612	619	690	762	845	907	960	571	570
Individual	Bil. dol..	282	482	594	622	693	763	874	881	945	980
Supplementary contracts [8] ..	Bil. dol..	17	23	25	28	28	31	32	34	13	14
Life insurance	Bil. dol..	349	468	511	556	606	656	705	742	816	833
Health insurance	Bil. dol..	33	58	63	70	75	82	92	96	101	111
Liabilities for deposit-type contracts [9]	Bil. dol..	18	20	20	20	20	21	21	21	338	364
Capital and surplus	Bil. dol..	91	137	151	147	160	173	181	188	191	202

NA Not available. [1] Beginning 1994 includes life insurance companies that sell accident and health insurance. [2] Beginning 2001 excludes certain deposit-type funds from income due to codification. [3] Beginning with 1994, "surrender values" include annuity withdrawals of funds, which were not included in prior years. [4] Beginning 2001 excludes payments under deposit-type contracts. [5] Net rate. [6] Includes other obligations not shown separately. [7] Beginning 2001, excludes reserves for guaranteed interest contracts (GICs). [8] Through 2000 includes reserves for contracts with and without life contingencies; beginning 2001 includes only reserves for contracts with life contingencies. [9] Policyholder dividend accumulations for all years. Beginning 2001 also includes liabilities for guaranteed interest contracts, supplementary contracts without life contingencies, and premium and other deposits.

Source: American Council of Life Insurers, Washington, DC, *Life Insurers Fact Book*, annual (copyright).

No. 1218. Property and Casualty Insurance—Summary: 1990 to 2002

[In billions of dollars (217.8 represents $217,800,000,000). Minus sign (-) indicates loss]

Item	1990	1995	1997	1998	1999	2000	2001	2002
Premiums, net written [1]	217.8	263.7	279.7	284.2	289.6	303.2	329.2	377.2
Automobile, private [1][2]	78.4	102.0	113.8	117.4	118.6	119.6	127.9	139.5
Automobile, commercial [1][2]	17.0	17.2	18.0	18.1	18.1	19.5	21.7	24.5
Liability other than auto [3]	22.1	23.4	25.0	27.8	27.4	28.2	31.1	41.4
Fire and allied lines [1]	7.1	8.1	7.9	7.7	7.4	7.5	8.6	11.9
Homeowners' multiple peril [1]	18.6	24.0	26.9	29.0	30.6	32.4	35.2	40.0
Commercial multiple peril [4][5]	17.7	9.7	10.0	10.2	10.3	11.5	13.0	15.1
Workers' compensation [1]	31.0	29.5	26.5	25.7	24.6	28.1	31.4	36.5
Marine, inland and ocean [3]	5.7	7.1	7.6	8.6	7.7	8.1	8.5	9.4
Accident and health [3]	5.0	7.8	8.3	9.8	11.1	13.3	14.4	14.1
Other lines [1]	15.2	34.9	35.7	29.9	33.8	35.0	37.4	44.8
Losses and expenses [4]	234.7	268.4	272.6	289.7	302.6	326.3	368.5	387.2
Underwriting gain/loss [3]	-18.6	-14.2	-1.1	-12.6	-20.5	-28.3	-51.0	-29.7
Net investment income [3]	32.9	36.8	41.5	41.1	40.0	41.9	39.0	40.0
Operating earnings after taxes [4]	9.0	20.6	36.8	30.8	21.9	26.1	-6.7	40.0
Assets [3]	556.3	765.2	870.1	930.1	940.0	935.4	977.6	1,042.1
Policyholders' surplus [3]	138.4	230.0	308.5	338.8	339.8	322.9	295.4	291.1

[1] Includes state funds after 1992. [2] Includes premiums for automobile liability and physical damage. [3] Includes state funds after 1997. [4] Includes state funds after 1999. [5] Nonliability portion only.
Source: Insurance Information Institute, New York, NY, The Fact Book, Property/Casualty Insurance Facts, annual (copyright).

No. 1219. Automobile Insurance—Average Expenditures Per Insured Vehicle by State: 1995 to 2001

[In dollars. Average expenditure equals total premiums written divided by liability car-years. A car-year is equal to 365 days of insured coverage for a single vehicle. The average expenditures for automobile insurance in a state are affected by a number of factors, including the underlying rate structure, the coverages purchased, the deductibles and limits selected, the types of vehicles insured, and the distribution of driver characteristics]

State	1995	2000	2001	State	1995	2000	2001	State	1995	2000	2001
U.S.	667	687	718	KS	474	540	556	ND	381	477	498
AL	549	594	605	KY	555	616	645	OH	531	579	614
AK	730	770	826	LA	788	806	839	OK	526	603	622
AZ	727	792	822	ME	472	528	545	OR	565	625	643
AR	500	606	621	MD	732	757	784	PA	667	699	726
CA	794	661	689	MA	898	946	936	RI	870	825	880
CO	722	755	808	MI	645	702	735	SC	582	620	617
CT	881	871	912	MN	628	696	735	SD	428	482	510
DE	784	849	851	MS	579	654	638	TN	519	592	611
DC	959	996	1,012	MO	573	612	634	TX	711	678	735
FL	739	746	788	MT	468	530	572	UT	547	620	640
GA	597	674	703	NE	452	533	554	VT	512	568	603
HI	963	702	705	NV	759	829	851	VA	553	576	610
ID	447	505	523	NH	609	665	686	WA	650	722	750
IL	612	652	683	NJ	1,013	977	1,028	WV	646	680	707
IN	542	570	615	NM	639	674	662	WI	506	545	573
IA	429	479	513	NY	906	939	1,015	WY	433	496	528
				NC	501	564	565				

Source: National Association of Insurance Commissioners (NAIC), Kansas City, MO, State Average Expenditures and Premiums for Personal Automobile Insurance, annual (copyright). Reprinted with permission of the NAIC. Further reprint or distribution strictly prohibited without prior written permission of the NAIC.

No. 1220. Average Premiums for Renters and Homeowners Insurance by State: 2000

[In dollars. Average premium equals premiums divided by exposure per house-years. A house-year is equal to 365 days of insured coverage for a single dwelling and is the standard measurement for homeowners insurance]

State	Renters [1]	Home-owners [2]	State	Renters [1]	Home-owners [2]	State	Renters [1]	Home-owners [2]
U.S.	175	508	KS	165	593	ND	107	426
AL	163	476	KY	141	414	OH	142	334
AK	164	607	LA	239	721	OK	207	612
AZ	197	438	ME	115	352	OR	154	343
AR	192	494	MD	135	389	PA	136	418
CA	265	592	MA	186	542	RI	165	533
CO	173	571	MI	158	439	SC	168	527
CT	184	571	MN	129	420	SD	109	380
DE	135	329	MS	223	592	TN [3]	188	474
DC	158	635	MO	158	457	TX [3]	233	880
FL	223	666	MT	141	451	UT	144	378
GA	202	458	NE	131	499	VT	122	426
HI	194	554	NV	235	479	VA	136	371
ID	142	326	NH	140	425	WA	161	428
IL	164	410	NJ	168	510	WV	135	393
IN	149	397	NM	192	450	WI	104	287
IA	128	358	NY	199	611	WY	152	484
			NC	169	449			

[1] Based on the HO-4 renters insurance policy for tenants. Includes broad named-peril coverage for the personal property of tenants. [2] Based on the HO-3 homeowner package policy for owner-occupied dwellings, 1-4 family units. Provides "all risks" coverage (except the most common package written. [3] The Texas Insurance Commissioner promulgates residential policy forms which are similar but not identical to the standard forms. Insurers can use State-promulgated or standard forms.
Source: National Association of Insurance Commissioners (NAIC), Kansas City, MO, Dwelling Fire, Homeowners Owner-Occupied, and Homeowners Tenant and Condominium/Cooperative Unit Owners Insurance (copyright). Reprinted with permission of the NAIC. Further reprint or distribution strictly prohibited without prior written permission of the NAIC.

No. 1221. Real Estate, Rental, and Leasing—Nonemployer Establishments and Receipts by Kind of Business: 1997 to 2002

[1,397 represents 1,397,000. Includes only firms subject to federal income tax. Nonemployers are businesses with no paid employees. Data originate chiefly from administrative records of the Internal Revenue Service; see Appendix III. Based on the North American Industry Classification System 1997 (NAICS), see text, Section 15]

Kind of business	NAICS code	Establishments (1,000)			Receipts (mil. dol.)		
		1997	2000	2002	1997	2000	2002
Real estate & rental & leasing, total	53	1,397	1,696	1,880	101,704	133,398	161,790
Real estate	531	1,336	1,616	1,799	98,845	127,862	156,150
Lessors of real estate	5311	572	714	(NA)	68,718	86,934	(NA)
Offices of real estate agents & brokers	5312	530	522	(NA)	17,556	22,623	(NA)
Activities related to real estate	5313	235	380	(NA)	12,571	18,305	(NA)
Rental & leasing services	532	60	79	80	2,806	5,440	5,519
Automotive equipment rental & leasing	5321	15	19	(NA)	591	995	(NA)
Consumer goods rental	5322	14	17	(NA)	521	766	(NA)
General rental centers	5323	1	3	(NA)	53	252	(NA)
Commercial/industrial equip rental & leasing	5324	31	41	(NA)	1,641	3,426	(NA)
Lessors of other nonfinancial intangible assets	533	(Z)	1	1	53	96	121

NA Not available.   Z Less than 500.

Source: U.S. Census Bureau, "Nonemployer Statistics"; <http://www.census.gov/epcd/nonemployer/> and *2002 Economic Census: Advance Nonemployer Statistics*; published 21 May 2004; <http://www.census.gov/epcd/nonemployer/2002/us/US000.HTM>.

No. 1222. Real Estate, Rental and Leasing—Establishments, Employees, and Payroll: 2000 and 2001

[300.2 represents 300,200. Covers establishments with payroll. Employees are for the week including March 12. Most government employees are excluded. For statement on methodology, see Appendix III]

Kind of business	NAICS code [1]	Establishments (1,000)		Employees (1,000)		Payroll (bil. dol.)	
		2000	2001	2000	2001	2000	2001
Real estate & rental & leasing, total	53	300.2	307.0	1,942	2,014	59.2	64.0
Real estate	531	234.9	241.1	1,280	1,335	40.4	44.4
Lessors of real estate	5311	108.2	108.0	501	513	12.5	13.9
Offices of real estate agents & brokers	5312	65.1	68.9	271	284	10.6	11.1
Activities related to real estate	5313	61.6	64.2	507	538	17.3	19.5
Rental & leasing services	532	63.2	63.8	636	653	17.2	18.0
Automotive equipment rental & leasing	5321	11.1	12.1	182	189	5.1	5.3
Passenger car rental & leasing	53211	5.2	5.5	129	136	3.4	3.6
Truck, utility trailer & RV rental & leasing	53212	5.8	6.6	53	53	1.7	1.8
Consumer goods rental [2]	5322	33.1	32.3	255	256	4.2	4.4
Video tape & disk rental	53223	19.6	18.6	152	150	1.6	1.6
General rental centers	5323	6.4	6.4	42	41	1.2	1.2
Commercial/industrial equip rental & leasing	5324	12.6	13.0	157	166	6.7	7.0
Lessors of other nonfinancial intangible assets	533	2.1	2.1	26	26	1.6	1.6

[1] North American Industry Classification System, 1997; see text, Section 15.   [2] Includes other kinds of business not shown separately.

Source: U.S. Census Bureau, *County Business Patterns*, annual; <http://www.census.gov/prod/2003pubs/01cbp/cbp01-1.pdf> (issued April 2003).

No. 1223. Rental and Leasing Services—Revenue by Kind of Business: 2000 to 2002

[In millions of dollars (106,628 represents $106,628,000,000). Based on the North American Industry Classification System (NAICS) 1997; see text, Section 15. Estimates have been adjusted using the results of the 1997 Economic Census. Based on Service Annual Survey; see Appendix III]

Kind of business	NAICS code	Employer and nonemployer firms			Employer firms		
		2000	2001	2002	2000	2001	2002
Rental & leasing services	532	106,628	104,794	106,081	101,188	99,126	100,507
Automotive equipment rental & leasing	5321	37,496	36,373	36,203	36,501	35,367	35,174
Passenger car rental & leasing	53211	24,357	23,882	24,121	23,769	23,288	23,500
Truck, utility trailer, & RV rental & leasing	53212	13,139	12,491	12,081	12,732	12,079	11,674
Consumer goods rental [1]	5322	18,794	19,233	19,079	18,029	18,445	18,265
Video tape & disk rental	53223	9,427	9,431	9,240	9,159	9,174	8,962
General rental centers	5323	5,504	5,094	5,176	5,252	4,819	4,892
Commercial/industrial equip rental & leasing	5324	44,833	44,094	45,624	41,407	40,495	42,176

[1] Includes other kinds of business not shown separately.

Source: U.S. Census Bureau, *Service Annual Survey: 2002*.

Section 26
Arts, Entertainment, and Recreation

This section presents data on the arts, entertainment, and recreation economic sector of the economy, and personal recreational activities, the arts and humanities, and domestic and foreign travel.

Arts, Entertainment, and Recreation Industry—The U.S. Census Bureau's *Service Annual Survey, Arts, Entertainment, and Recreation Sector,* provides estimates of operation revenue of taxable firms and revenues and expenses of firms exempt from federal taxes for industries in this sector of the economy. Data beginning 1998 are based on the North American Industry Classification System (NAICS). Most establishments were previously classified in the Standard Industrial Classification (SIC) in services, some in retail trade.

This new sector is comprised of industries which existed previously, were revised from previous industry definitions, or are completely new industries. Among those which existed previously are amusement and theme parks. Revised industries include museums. New industries include theater companies and dinner theaters. The following URL contains detailed information about NAICS and provides a comparison of the SIC and NAICS <http://www.census.gov/epcd/www /naics.html>. See also the text in Section 15, Business Enterprise.

The 1997 Economic Census was the first economic census to cover the new Information Sector of the economy. The Census, conducted every 5-years, for the years ending "2" and "7," provides information on the number of establishments, receipts, payroll and paid employees for the U.S. and various geographic levels.

Recreation and leisure activities— Data on the participation in various recreation and leisure time activities are based on several sample surveys. Data on participation in fishing, hunting, and other forms of wildlife-associated recreation are published periodically by the U.S. Department of Interior, Fish and Wildlife Service. The most recent data are from the 2001 survey. Data on participation in various sports recreation activities are published by the National Sporting Goods Association. Mediamark, Inc. also conducts periodic surveys on sports and leisure activities, as well as other topics.

Parks and recreation—The Department of the Interior has responsibility for administering the national parks. The National Park Service publishes information on visits to national park areas in its annual report, *National Park Statistical Abstract. The National Parks: Index (year)* is a biannual report which contains brief descriptions, with acreages, of each area administered by the service, plus certain "related" areas. The annual *Federal Recreation Fee Report* summarizes the prior year's recreation fee receipts and recreation visitation statistics for seven federal land managing agencies. Statistics for state parks are compiled by the National Association of State Park Directors.

Travel— Statistics on arrivals to the United States are reported by the International Trade Administration (ITA). Statistics on departures from the United States include the Department of Transportation's *International Air Travel Statistics* and other sources. Data on domestic travel, business receipts and employment of the travel industry, and travel expenditures are published by the U.S. Travel Data Center, which is the research department of the Travel Industry Association and the national nonprofit center for travel and tourism research located in Washington, DC. Other data on household transportation characteristics are in Section 23, Transportation.

Statistical reliability—For a discussion of statistical collection and estimation, sampling procedures, and measures of statistical reliability applicable to Census Bureau data, see Appendix III.

Arts, Entertainment, and Recreation   763

No. 1224. Arts, Entertainment and Recreation Services—Estimated Revenue: 2001 and 2002

[In millions of dollars (128,904 represents $128,904,000,000), except percent. For taxable and tax-exempt employer firms. Except as indicated, estimates adjusted to the results of the 1997 Economic Census. Minus sign (-) indicates decrease. See Appendix III]

Industry	NAICS Code [1]	Total			Taxable		
		2001	2002	Percent change, 2001-2002	2001	2002	Percent change, 2001-2002
Arts, entertainment, and recreation	71	128,904	137,236	6.5	105,730	114,129	7.9
Performing arts, spectator sports	711	46,391	50,086	8.0	40,522	44,217	9.1
Performing arts companies [2]	7111	9,252	9,321	0.7	5,389	5,568	3.3
Spectator sports.	7112	18,416	20,224	9.8	18,416	20,224	9.8
Sports teams and clubs	711211	11,104	12,619	13.6	11,104	12,619	13.6
Racetracks	711212	5,337	5,526	3.5	5,337	5,526	3.5
Other spectator sports	711219	1,975	2,078	5.2	1,975	2,078	5.2
Promoters of performing arts, sports and similar events	7113	8,131	9,117	12.1	6,125	7,000	14.3
Agents and managers for artists, athletes, entertainers and other public figures.	7114	3,468	3,672	5.9	3,468	3,672	5.9
Independent artists, writers, and performers	7115	7,125	7,753	8.8	7,125	7,753	8.8
Museums, historical sites, and similar institutions.	712	8,173	7,735	-5.4	844	913	8.1
Amusement, gambling, and recreation industries	713	74,341	79,415	6.8	64,363	68,999	7.2
Amusement parks and arcades.	7131	9,664	9,295	-3.8	9,664	9,295	-3.8
Amusement and theme parks	71311	8,542	8,084	-5.4	8,542	8,084	-5.4
Amusement arcades	71312	1,122	1,211	7.9	1,122	1,211	7.9
Gambling industries	7132	21,510	24,300	13.0	21,510	24,300	13.0
Casinos (except casino hotels)	71321	15,230	16,923	11.1	15,230	16,923	11.1
Other gambling industries.	71329	6,280	7,378	17.5	6,280	7,378	17.5
Other amusement and recreation industries	7139	43,167	45,820	6.1	33,189	35,404	6.7
Golf courses and country clubs	71391	16,090	16,738	4.0	9,745	10,258	5.3
Skiing facilities	71392	1,569	1,729	10.2	1,569	1,729	10.2
Marinas [3]	71393	3,264	3,228	-1.1	3,264	3,228	-1.1
Fitness and recreational sports centers	71394	13,617	15,079	10.7	10,770	12,016	11.6
Bowling centers	71395	3,106	3,315	6.7	3,106	3,315	6.7
All other amusement and recreation. . .	71399	5,520	5,731	3.8	4,735	4,858	2.6

[1] Based on the North American Industry Classification System 1997; see text, this section and Section 15, Business Enterprise. [2] Estimates for NAICS 71113 and 71119, not shown separately, have not been adjusted to the 1997 Economic Census. [3] Estimates not adjusted to the 1997 Economic Census.

Source: U.S. Census Bureau, *2002 Service Annual Survey, Arts, Entertainment, and Recreation Services.* See <http://www.census.gov/econ/www/servmenu.html>; (accessed 7 June 2004).

No. 1225. Arts, Entertainment and Recreation—Establishments, Revenue, Payroll, and Employees by Kind of Business (1997 NAICS Basis): 1997 and 2002

[For establishments with payroll. (104,715 represents $104,715,000,000). 2002 data are preliminary. Numbers in parentheses represent North American Industry Classification System 1997 codes, see text, section 15. Based on the 1997 and 2002 Economic Census; See Appendix III]

Kind of business	Number of establishments	Revenue (mil. dol.)	Annual payroll (mil. dol.)	Paid employees
Arts, entertainment and recreation (71):				
1997	99,099	104,715	32,787	1,587,660
2002	111,128	137,782	43,075	1,895,724
Performing arts, spectator sports, and related industries (711):				
1997	30,566	37,619	14,456	326,757
2002	38,770	55,124	19,571	437,938
Museums, historical sites, and similar institutions (712):				
1997	5,580	6,764	1,837	91,776
2002	6,712	8,656	2,900	123,597
Amusement, gambling, and recreational industries (713):				
1997	62,953	60,332	16,494	1,169,127
2002	65,646	74,002	20,603	1,334,189

Source: U.S. Census Bureau, 2002 Economic Census, *Advance Report,* issued March 2004. See Internet site: <http://www.census.gov/econ/census02/>

No. 1226. Arts, Entertainment, and Recreation—Nonemployer Establishments and Receipts by Kind of Business (NAICS Basis): 1997 to 2002

[693.3 represents 693,300. Includes only firms subject to federal income tax. Nonemployers are businesses with no paid employees]

Kind of business	NAICS code [1]	Establishments (1,000)			Receipts (mil. dol)		
		1997	2000	2002	1997	2000	2002
Arts, entertainment, and recreation ..	71	693.3	781.7	866.0	14,366.1	17,713.4	19,999.8
Performing arts, spectator sports, and related industries	711	536.0	645.4	732.9	10,251.8	13,008.4	14,808.0
Performing arts companies	7111	10.8	19.3	26.0	320.2	575.9	676.6
Spectator sports	7112	65.8	67.3	95.7	1,433.4	1,480.7	1,773.7
Promoters of performing arts, sports, and similar events	7113	12.8	23.1	29.3	513.1	850.6	1,100.1
Agents/managers for artists, athletes, and other public figures	7114	15.5	27.1	28.1	529.0	856.8	968.8
Independent artists, writers and performers	7115	431.1	508.6	553.8	7,456.1	9,244.4	10,288.8
Museums, historical sites, and similar institutions	712	1.8	3.6	4.4	37.5	51.5	66.3
Amusement, gambling, and recreation ffindustries	713	155.6	132.7	128.7	4,076.8	4,653.5	5,125.5
Amusement parks and arcades	7131	7.2	5.4	5.2	463.1	291.4	321.6
Gambling industries	7132	2.7	5.9	7.3	196.6	532.1	875.2
Other amusement and recreation services	7139	145.7	121.3	116.2	3,417.0	3,829.9	3,928.7

[1] Based on the North American Industry Classification System (NAICS), see text, Section 15.

Source: U.S. Census Bureau, "Nonemployer Statistics"; <http://www.census.gov/epcd/nonemployer/>. 2002 Economic Census, Advance Nonemployer Statistics; published 21 May 2004; <http://www.census.gov/epcd/nonemployer/2002/us/US000.HTM>

No. 1227. Arts, Entertainment, and Recreation—Establishments, Payroll, and Employees by Kind of Business (NAICS Basis): 2000 and 2001

[For establishments with payroll. (1,741.5 represents 1,741,500). See Appendix III]

Kind of Business	NAICS code [1]	Establishments		Paid employees [2] (1,000)		Annual payroll (mil. dol.)	
		2000	2001	2000	2001	2000	2001
Arts, entertainment, and recreation......	71	103,816	105,961	1,741.5	1,780.4	43,204	46,133
Performing arts, spectator sports	711	33,859	34,840	351.9	361.7	19,090	20,393
Performing arts companies	7111	9,253	9,327	126.4	127.8	3,251	3,344
Theater companies & dinner theaters	71111	3,367	3,354	63.4	66.4	1,469	1,517
Dance companies	71112	584	604	10.7	10.9	216	218
Musical groups & artists	71113	4,497	4,562	44.0	43.0	1,341	1,349
Other performing arts companies	71119	805	807	8.3	7.5	226	260
Spectator sports	7112	4,461	4,584	100.2	104.4	9,215	9,955
Sports teams & clubs	711211	684	735	36.3	40.1	7,587	8,268
Racetracks	711212	899	881	45.8	45.2	994	989
Other spectator sports	711219	2,878	2,968	18.1	19.1	633	697
Promoters of performing arts, sports, and similar events	7113	4,394	4,456	71.8	73.9	1,917	2,010
Promoters of performing arts, sports, & similar events with facilities	71131	1,107	1,184	44.3	48.3	787	942
Promoters of performing arts, sports, & similar events without facilities	71132	3,287	3,272	27.6	25.6	1,130	1,068
Agents/managers for artists, athletes, and other public figures	7114	3,048	3,107	16.0	16.2	1,117	1,139
Independent artists, writers, & performers	7115	12,703	13,366	37.5	39.4	3,589	3,946
Museums, historical sites, & similar institutions	712	5,777	6,032	110.4	113.5	2,549	2,781
Museums	71211	3,988	4,140	75.4	76.8	1,765	1,907
Historical sites	71212	892	893	8.3	8.4	143	154
Zoos & botanical gardens	71213	414	459	20.5	21.8	509	558
Nature parks & other similar institutions	71219	483	540	6.2	6.5	133	162
Amusement, gambling, & recreation industries	713	64,180	65,089	1,279.2	1,305.1	21,564	22,958
Amusement parks & arcades	7131	2,879	2,783	124.0	119.3	2,277	2,314
Amusement & theme parks	71311	716	700	102.8	98.8	2,011	2,044
Amusement arcades	71312	2,163	2,083	21.3	20.5	266	270
Gambling industries	7132	2,191	2,175	202.6	215.6	4,757	5,400
Casinos (except casino hotels)	71321	537	562	150.2	156.2	3,592	4,007
Other gambling industries	71329	1,654	1,613	52.4	59.5	1,165	1,392
Other amusement & recreation services	7139	59,110	60,131	952.6	970.1	14,531	15,244
Golf courses & country clubs	71391	11,885	11,861	297.9	295.1	6,243	6,472
Skiing facilities	71392	389	404	56.9	63.9	452	495
Marinas	71393	4,126	4,121	24.8	24.7	640	675
Fitness & recreational sports centers	71394	23,003	24,068	382.8	399.4	4,499	4,844
Bowling centers	71395	5,234	5,059	87.9	84.6	888	889
All other amusement & recreation industries	71399	14,473	14,618	102.4	102.5	1,808	1,870

[1] North American Industry Classification System code; see text, this section and Section 15, Business Enterprise. [2] For employees on the payroll for the period including March 12.

Source: U.S. Census Bureau, "County Business Patterns"; 2001 data published April 2003; <http://www.census.gov/prod/www/abs/cbptotal.html>.

[Data are annual averages. In dollars, except as indicated. Based on Consumer Expenditure Survey; see text, Section 13, Income, Expenditures, and Wealth for description of survey. See also headnote, Table 660. For composition of regions, see map, inside front cover]

Year and characteristic	Entertainment and reading		Entertainment				Reading
	Total	Percent of total expenditures	Total	Fees and admissions	Television, radios, and sound equipment	Other equipment and services [1]	
1985	1,311	5.6	1,170	320	371	479	141
1986	1,289	5.4	1,149	308	371	470	140
1987	1,335	5.5	1,193	323	379	491	142
1988	1,479	5.7	1,329	353	416	560	150
1989	1,581	5.7	1,424	377	429	618	157
1990	1,575	5.6	1,422	371	454	597	153
1991	1,635	5.5	1,472	378	468	627	163
1992	1,662	5.6	1,500	379	492	629	162
1993	1,792	5.8	1,626	414	590	621	166
1994	1,732	5.5	1,567	439	533	595	165
1995	1,775	5.5	1,612	433	542	637	163
1996	1,993	5.9	1,834	459	561	814	159
1997	1,977	5.7	1,813	471	577	766	164
1998	1,907	5.4	1,746	449	535	762	161
1999	2,050	5.5	1,891	459	608	824	159
2000	2,009	5.3	1,863	515	622	727	146
2001	2,094	5.3	1,953	526	660	767	141
2002, total	2,218	5.5	2,079	542	692	845	139
Age of reference person:							
Under 25 years old	1,269	5.2	1,212	313	457	442	57
25 to 34 years old	2,130	5.3	2,027	490	750	788	103
35 to 44 years old	2,820	5.8	2,685	743	817	1,125	135
45 to 54 years old	2,732	5.6	2,565	662	806	1,097	167
55 to 64 years old	2,478	5.6	2,297	584	717	997	181
65 to 74 years old	1,532	4.8	1,371	382	546	443	161
75 years old and over	1,030	4.3	896	216	372	308	134
Origin of reference person:							
Hispanic	1,469	4.2	1,409	289	565	555	60
Non-Hispanic	2,295	5.6	2,148	568	705	876	147
Race of reference person:							
White and other	2,359	5.6	2,211	588	699	924	148
Black	1,191	4.0	1,124	203	640	281	67
Region of residence:							
Northeast	2,452	5.8	2,287	657	725	905	165
Midwest	2,292	5.6	2,143	538	688	917	149
South	1,808	4.8	1,705	419	643	643	103
West	2,598	5.8	2,436	644	747	1,044	162
Size of consumer unit:							
One person	1,301	5.4	1,193	320	467	407	108
Two or more persons	2,599	5.5	2,448	634	786	1,027	151
Two persons	2,277	5.4	2,115	532	694	889	162
Three persons	2,451	5.1	2,308	547	812	949	143
Four persons	3,078	5.7	2,928	817	902	1,209	150
Five persons or more	3,170	5.7	3,038	831	871	1,335	132
Income before taxes:							
Total complete reporting [2]	2,312	5.4	2,167	562	710	895	145
Quintiles of income:							
Lowest 20 percent	882	4.6	813	183	384	247	69
Second 20 percent	1,200	4.4	1,103	225	497	382	97
Third 20	1,764	4.8	1,644	348	663	633	120
Fourth 20	2,827	5.6	2,659	615	867	1,178	168
Highest 20	4,879	6.2	4,608	1,436	1,140	2,032	271
Incomplete reporting of income	1,852	5.6	1,745	448	608	689	107

[1] Other equipment and services includes pets, toys, and playground equipment; sports, exercise, and photographic equipment; and recreational vehicles. [2] Income values derived from "complete income reporters" only. Represents the combined income of all consumer unit members 14 years or over during the 12 months preceding the interview. A complete reporter is a consumer unit providing values for at least one of the major sources of income.

Source: U.S. Bureau of Labor Statistics, Consumer Expenditure Survey, annual.

No. 1229. Personal Consumption Expenditures for Recreation: 1990 to 2002

[In billions of dollars (290.2 represents $290,200,000,000), except percent. Represents market value of purchases of goods and services by individuals and nonprofit institutions. See also headnote table 420]

Type of product or service	1990	1995	1998	1999	2000	2001	2002
Total recreation expenditures	290.2	418.1	505.8	546.1	585.7	603.4	633.9
Percent of total personal consumption[1]	7.6	8.4	8.6	8.7	8.7	8.6	8.6
Books and maps	16.2	23.2	28.8	31.5	33.7	34.6	35.8
Magazines, newspapers, and sheet music	21.6	27.5	32.1	33.5	35.0	34.5	34.2
Nondurable toys and sport supplies	32.8	44.4	51.3	54.7	56.6	58.0	59.7
Wheel goods, sports and photographic equipment[2]	29.8	39.5	48.2	52.7	57.5	58.9	70.7
Video and audio products, computer equipment, and musical instruments	53.0	81.5	99.7	108.1	116.6	115.5	120.8
Video and audio products, including musical instruments	44.1	57.2	62.7	67.8	72.8	73.5	76.7
Computers, peripherals, and software	8.9	24.3	37.0	40.4	43.8	42.0	44.2
Radio and television repair	3.2	3.6	4.1	4.1	4.2	4.0	4.0
Flowers, seeds, and potted plants	10.9	14.0	16.4	17.1	18.0	18.0	18.2
Admissions to specified spectator amusements	15.1	21.1	26.2	28.4	30.4	32.8	35.3
Motion picture theaters	5.1	5.6	7.2	7.9	8.6	9.0	9.6
Legitimate theaters and opera, and entertainments of nonprofit institutions[3]	5.2	8.1	9.2	9.9	10.3	11.4	12.1
Spectator sports[4]	4.8	7.4	9.8	10.6	11.5	12.4	13.6
Clubs and fraternal organizations except insurance[5]	13.5	17.4	17.1	18.0	19.0	20.0	22.4
Commercial participant amusements[6]	25.2	48.8	63.1	68.8	75.8	79.4	83.7
Pari-mutuel net receipts	3.5	3.7	4.4	4.9	5.0	5.1	5.3
Other	65.4	93.4	114.4	124.3	133.9	142.6	152.6

[1] See Table 649. [2] Includes boats and pleasure aircraft. [3] Except athletic. [4] Consists of admissions to professional and amateur athletic events and to racetracks, including horse, dog, and auto. [5] Consists of current expenditures (including consumption of fixed capital) of nonprofit clubs and fraternal organizations and dues and fees paid to proprietary clubs. [6] Consists of billiard parlors; bowling alleys; dancing, riding, shooting, skating, and swimming places; amusement devices and parks; golf courses; sightseeing buses and guides; private flying operations; casino gambling; and other commercial participant amusements. [7] Consists of net receipts of lotteries and expenditures for purchases of pets and pet care services, cable TV, film processing, photographic studios, sporting and recreation camps, video cassette rentals, and recreational services, not elsewhere classified.

Source: U.S. Bureau of Economic Analysis, *Survey of Current Business*, January 2004. See also <http://www.bea.doc.gov/bea/dn/nipaweb/selecttable.asp?selected=N> (released as 16 December, 2003).

No. 1230. Performing Arts—Selected Data: 1985 to 2002

[Sales, receipts and expenditures in millions of dollars (209 represents $209,000,000). For season ending in year shown, except as indicated]

Item	1985	1990	1995	1996	1997	1998	1999	2000	2001	2002
Legitimate theater:[1]										
Broadway shows:										
New productions	33	40	33	38	37	33	39	37	28	37
Attendance (mil.)[2][3]	7.3	8.0	9.0	9.5	10.6	11.5	11.7	11.4	11.9	11.0
Playing weeks[2][3]	1,078	1,070	1,120	1,146	1,349	1,442	1,441	1,464	1,484	1,434
Gross ticket sales	209	282	406	436	499	558	588	603	666	643
Broadway road tours:										
Attendance (mil.)	8.2	11.1	15.6	18.1	17.6	15.2	14.6	11.7	11.0	11.7
Playing weeks	993	944	1,242	1,345	1,334	1,127	1,082	888	823	863
Gross ticket sales	226	367	701	796	782	721	707	572	541	593
Nonprofit professional theatres:[4]										
Companies reporting[5]	217	185	215	228	197	189	313	262	363	1,146
Gross income	234.7	307.6	444.4	450.7	565.0	570.0	740.0	791.0	961.1	1,436.0
Earned income	146.1	188.4	281.2	274.0	349.9	342.0	442.0	466.0	554.5	761.0
Contributed income	88.6	119.2	163.1	176.7	215.1	228.0	298.0	325.0	406.6	675.0
Gross expenses	239.3	306.3	444.9	439.5	526.6	518.5	701.0	708.0	923.6	1,405.0
Productions	2,710	2,265	2,646	3,074	2,295	2,135	3,921	3,241	4,787	10,000
Performances	52,341	46,131	56,608	56,954	51,453	46,628	64,556	66,123	81,828	157,000
Total attendance (mil.)	14.2	15.2	18.6	17.1	17.2	14.6	18.0	22.0	21.1	32.2
OPERA America professional member companies:[6]										
Number of companies reporting[7]	97	98	88	83	91	89	95	98	96	(NA)
Expenses[7]	216.4	321.2	435.0	466.7	534.1	556.3	591.1	636.7	685.1	(NA)
Performances[8]	1,909	2,336	2,251	2,019	2,137	2,222	2,200	2,153	2,031	(NA)
Total attendance (mil.)[8][9]	6.7	7.5	6.5	6.5	6.9	6.6	6.6	6.7	6.5	(NA)
Main season attendance (mil.)[8][10]	3.3	4.1	3.9	3.9	4.0	3.7	4.0	4.3	4.2	(NA)
Symphony orchestras:[11]										
Concerts	19,573	18,931	29,328	28,887	26,906	31,766	31,549	33,154	36,437	37,118
Attendance (mil.)	24.0	24.7	30.9	31.1	31.9	32.2	30.8	31.7	31.5	30.3
Gross revenue	252.4	377.5	536.2	558.9	575.5	627.6	671.8	734.0	774.7	763.6
Operating expenses	426.1	621.7	858.8	892.4	937.1	1,012.0	1,088.0	1,126.3	1,311.9	
Support	188.1	257.8	351.0	382.8	401.7	459.7	486.0	521.0	559.6	580.0

NA Not available. [1] Source: The League of American Theaters and Producers, Inc, New York, NY. For season ending in year shown. [2] All shows (new productions and holdovers from previous seasons). [3] Eight performances constitute one playing week. [4] Source: Theatre Communications Group, New York, NY. For years ending on or prior to Aug. 31. [5] Beginning in 2002, nonprofit theatre data is based on survey responses and extrapolated data from IRS Form 990. [6] Source: OPERA America, Washington, DC. For years ending on or prior to Aug 31. [7] United States companies. [8] Prior to 1993 and for 1999, United States and Canadian companies; 1993 to 1998, U.S. companies only. [9] Includes educational performances, outreach, etc. [10] For paid performances. [11] Source: American Symphony Orchestra League, Inc., New York, NY. For years ending Aug. 31. Prior to 1995 represents 254 U.S. orchestras; beginning 1995, represents all U.S. orchestras, excluding college/university and youth orchestras. Also, beginning 1995, data based on 1,200 orchestras.

Source: Compiled from sources listed in footnotes.

U.S. Census Bureau, Statistical Abstract of the United States: 2004-2005

[In millions of dollars (188.1 represents $188,100,000), except as indicated. For fiscal year ending September 30]

Type of fund and program	1980	1990	1995	1997	1998	1999	2000	2001	2002
National Endowment for the Arts:									
Funds available [1]	188.1	170.8	152.1	98.4	85.3	85.0	85.2	94.0	98.6
Program appropriation	97.0	124.3	109.0	65.8	64.3	66.0	66.0	86.7	95.8
Matching funds [2]	42.9	32.4	28.5	16.8	16.8	14.5	13.0	-	-
Grants awarded (number)	5,505	4,475	3,685	1,098	1,459	1,675	1,882	2,093	2,138
Funds obligated [3][4]	166.4	157.6	147.9	94.4	82.3	82.6	83.5	92.5	96.2
National Endowment for the Humanities:									
Funds available [1]	186.2	140.6	152.3	94.8	94.0	95.5	102.6	106.8	110.1
Program appropriation	100.3	114.2	125.7	80.0	80.0	80.0	82.7	86.4	89.9
Matching funds [2]	38.4	26.3	25.7	13.9	13.9	13.9	15.1	15.6	16.1
Grants awarded (number)	2,917	2,195	1,871	900	852	874	1,230	1,290	1,252
Funds obligated [3]	185.5	141.0	151.8	94.8	92.7	92.1	100.0	105.7	106.1
Education programs	18.3	16.3	19.2	10.5	10.8	10.3	13.0	12.1	12.1
State programs	26.0	29.6	32.0	29.5	29.1	29.3	30.6	32.1	32.8
Research grants	32.0	22.5	22.2	8.5	7.7	6.6	6.9	7.0	7.0
Fellowship program	18.0	15.3	16.5	5.6	5.7	5.6	6.1	7.0	7.7
Challenge [5]	53.5	14.6	13.8	9.9	9.9	9.9	10.8	11.9	13.4
Public programs	25.1	25.4	25.8	12.6	11.1	12.2	11.8	16.3	13.2

-Represents zero.   [1] Includes other funds, shown separately. Excludes administrative funds.   [2] Represents federal funds obligated only upon receipt or certification by Endowment of matching nonfederal gifts.   [3] Includes obligations for new grants, supplemental awards on previous years' grants, and program contracts.   [4] Beginning with 1997 data, the grantmaking structure changed from discipline-based categories to thematic ones.   [5] Program designed to stimulate new sources and higher levels of giving to institutions for the purpose of guaranteeing long-term stability and financial independence. Program usually requires a match of at least 3 private dollars to each federal dollar. Funds for challenge grants are not allocated by program area because they are awarded on a grant-by-grant basis.

Source: U.S. National Endowment for the Arts, Annual Report; and U.S. National Endowment for the Humanities, Annual Report.

No. 1232. Attendance Rates for Various Arts Activities: 2002

[In percent. For persons 18 years old and over. Represents attendance at least once in the prior 12 months. Excludes elementary and high school performances. Based on the 2002 household survey Public Participation in the Arts. Data are subject to sampling error; see source. See also Tables 1233 and 1234]

Item	Jazz performance	Classical music performance	Opera	Musical plays	Non-musical play	Ballet	Art museum	Historic parks	Arts/craft fairs
Total	11	12	3	17	12	4	27	32	33
Sex:									
Male	11	10	3	14	10	3	25	31	27
Female	11	13	4	20	14	5	28	33	39
Race and ethnicity:									
Hispanic	6	6	2	7	6	2	16	17	20
White alone	11	14	4	20	14	5	30	36	38
African American alone	13	5	1	10	7	2	15	18	10
Other alone	7	10	3	12	10	2	33	30	26
Age:									
18 to 24 years old	11	8	2	15	11	3	24	28	29
25 to 34 years old	11	9	3	15	11	4	27	33	34
35 to 44 years old	13	11	3	19	13	5	27	36	37
45 to 54 years old	14	15	4	19	15	5	33	38	39
55 to 64 years old	9	16	4	20	14	3	28	32	35
65 to 74 years old	8	13	4	17	13	2	23	24	31
75 years old and older	4	10	2	10	5	2	13	13	16
Education:									
Grade school	1	2	-	2	1	-	5	6	8
Some high school	3	2	1	4	4	1	8	11	14
High school graduate	5	5	1	9	6	1	14	20	26
Some college	12	12	3	19	13	4	29	37	38
College graduate	19	22	6	30	23	7	47	51	49
Graduate school	24	34	11	38	32	13	59	57	52

- Represents or rounds to zero.

Source: U.S. National Endowment for the Arts, Research Division Report #45. 2002 Survey of Public Participation in the Arts.

No. 1233. Participation in Various Leisure Activities: 2002

[In percent, except as indicated (205.9 represents 205,900,000). For persons 18 years old and over. Covers activities engaged in at least once in the prior 12 months. See headnote, Table 1232. See also Table 1234]

Item	Adult population (mil.)	Attendance at—			Participation in—				
		Movies	Sports events	Amusement park	Exercise program	Playing sports	Charity work	Home improvement/repair	Gardening
Total	205.9	60	35	42	55	30	29	42	47
Sex:									
Male	98.7	60	41	40	55	39	26	46	37
Female	107.2	61	29	43	55	23	32	39	57
Race and ethnicity:									
Hispanic	22.7	53	26	39	40	22	15	28	35
White alone	150.1	63	38	43	59	33	33	48	52
African American alone . . .	23.7	49	27	37	46	23	23	26	30
Other alone	9.5	58	22	44	50	27	23	34	41
Age:									
18 to 24 years old	26.8	83	46	58	61	49	25	21	21
25 to 34 years old	36.9	73	42	56	60	40	26	41	41
35 to 44 years old	44.2	68	42	53	60	37	33	53	52
45 to 54 years old	39.0	60	36	37	59	29	33	55	55
55 to 64 years old	25.9	47	26	27	48	16	28	45	57
65 to 74 years old	17.6	32	20	18	47	14	29	38	57
75 years old and over . . .	15.5	20	11	10	31	6	21	22	48
Education:									
Grade school	11.6	20	9	17	21	7	8	20	33
Some high school	20.1	39	17	31	33	17	13	25	31
High school graduate	63.8	52	28	38	46	23	20	36	44
Some college	56.9	69	40	49	62	35	33	47	50
College graduate	36.1	77	51	50	73	45	43	56	56
Graduate school	17.4	78	48	44	77	44	53	62	63
Income:									
$9,999 or less	14.4	39	17	30	37	15	16	20	32
$10,000 to $19,999	22.7	42	20	31	42	19	19	24	39
$20,000 to $29,999	25.0	48	23	35	45	21	21	28	41
$30,000 to $39,999	24.2	58	30	39	53	27	27	42	47
$40,000 to $49,999	17.6	63	35	43	55	29	29	46	49
$50,000 to $74,999	34.7	69	45	50	63	36	35	54	54
$75,000 or More	45.8	79	53	54	73	48	42	61	56
Not reported	21.5	51	28	31	45	23	23	34	43

Source: U.S. National Endowment for the Arts, *Research Division Report #45. 2002 Survey of Public Participation in the Arts.*

No. 1234. Participation in Various Arts Activities: 2002

[In percent. For persons 18 years old and over. Covers activities engaged in at least once in the prior 12 months. See headnotes in Tables 1232 and 1233]

Item	Playing classical music	Other dancing[1]	Drawing	Pottery work[2]	Weaving	Photography[3]	Creative writing	Buying art work	Singing in groups
Total	2	4	9	7	16	12	7	30	5
Sex:									
Male	2	3	6	5	2	11	6	30	5
Female	2	5	11	9	29	12	8	30	4
Race and ethnicity:									
Hispanic	1	4	7	5	13	7	4	38	3
White alone	2	4	9	8	18	13	8	29	5
African American alone . .	-	4	6	4	9	8	7	36	9
Other alone	2	6	7	7	15	12	5	26	4
Age:									
18 to 24 years old	3	6	15	9	10	13	13	41	5
25 to 34 years old	1	5	10	8	13	12	8	39	4
35 to 44 years old	2	4	8	7	15	14	7	31	5
45 to 54 years old	3	4	8	8	19	12	7	28	5
55 to 64 years old	2	3	7	6	19	11	5	26	6
65 to 74 years old	1	4	5	5	21	8	4	24	5
75 years old and older . .	1	3	3	2	18	4	4	11	4
Education:									
Grade school	-	1	2	2	12	2	2	23	1
Some high school	-	4	5	4	11	5	3	24	3
High school graduate . . .	1	3	6	6	15	8	4	23	3
Some college	2	6	12	9	18	13	9	28	6
College graduate	4	5	11	8	17	17	11	31	6
Graduate school	5	6	11	7	18	20	13	34	7
Income:									
$9,999 or less	2	3	7	7	16	7	8	23	3
$10,000 to $19,999	1	3	7	6	18	7	6	22	5
$20,000 to $29,999	1	5	7	6	16	7	6	27	4
$30,000 to $39,999	2	5	10	7	17	11	8	27	6
$40,000 to $49,999	3	4	9	7	18	14	7	24	5
$50,000 to $74,999	3	5	8	8	17	13	7	31	5
$75,000 or More	2	4	11	8	17	17	9	34	5
Not Reported	1	5	7	5	12	12	9	26	4

- Represents or rounds to zero. [1] Dancing other than ballet (e.g. folk and tap). [2] Includes ceramics, jewelry, leatherwork, and metalwork. [3] Includes making movies or video as an artistic activity.

Source: U.S. National Endowment for the Arts, *Research Division Report #45. 2002 Survey of Public Participation in the Arts.*

Arts, Entertainment, and Recreation 769

No. 1235. Retail Sales and Household Participation in Lawn and Garden Activities: 1999 to 2003

[For calendar year. (33,519 represents $33,519,000,000). Based on national household sample survey conducted by the Gallup Organization. Subject to sampling variability; see source]

Activity	Retail sales (mil. dol.)					Percent households engaged in activity				
	1999	2000	2001	2002	2003	1999	2000	2001	2002	2003
Total..............	33,519	33,404	37,734	39,635	38,371	64	72	80	79	78
Lawn care..............	8,986	9,794	12,672	11,963	10,413	43	50	56	55	54
Indoor houseplants........	1,270	1,332	1,784	2,128	1,571	32	39	46	44	41
Flower gardening.........	3,976	4,167	3,926	3,131	3,025	45	45	43	41	38
Insect control..........	1,214	1,232	2,058	2,281	2,053	23	27	33	32	30
Shrub care............	1,376	1,429	1,298	1,072	1,042	29	31	30	27	27
Vegetable gardening......	2,595	2,169	1,535	1,270	1,408	29	27	25	25	24
Tree care.............	1,732	1,872	2,121	2,790	2,359	20	23	25	26	25
Landscaping...........	8,585	6,809	6,310	8,854	10,507	25	30	37	34	33
Flower bulbs...........	657	912	1,188	1,191	1,036	23	28	31	29	26
Fruit trees............	264	284	748	695	635	13	13	15	12	12
Container gardening......	1,020	1,257	1,202	1,362	1,219	15	18	22	23	24
Raising transplants [1]......	302	334	291	262	230	12	11	12	12	10
Herb gardening.........	185	204	413	444	345	11	12	14	15	14
Growing berries........	87	147	227	171	345	7	8	8	7	6
Ornamental gardening.....	464	519	756	580	831	6	8	9	8	9
Water gardening........	806	943	1,205	1,441	1,565	7	10	13	14	15

[1] Starting plants in advance of planting in ground.

Source: The National Gardening Association, Burlington, VT, National Gardening Survey, annual (copyright).

No. 1236. Household Pet Ownership: 2001

[Based on a sample survey of 80,000 households in 2001; for details, see source]

Item	Unit	Dogs	Cats	Birds	Horses
Percent of households owning companion pets [1].........	Percent ...	36.1	31.6	4.6	1.7
Average number owned......................	Number ...	1.6	2.1	2.1	2.9
Households obtaining veterinary care [2].............	Percent ...	85.0	66.8	12.9	56.7
Average visits per household per year.............	Number ...	2.7	1.8	0.3	2.1
PERCENT OF HOUSEHOLDS OWNING PETS					
Annual household income:					
Under $20..........................	Percent ...	29.7	28.1	5.1	1.0
$20,000 to $34,999...................	Percent ...	33.9	30.9	4.5	1.3
$35,000 to $54,999...................	Percent ...	37.9	32.2	4.8	2.0
$55,000 to $84,999...................	Percent ...	40.5	34.3	4.4	2.1
$85,000 and over....................	Percent ...	39.7	33.7	4.2	2.1
Household size: [1]					
One person........................	Percent ...	20.8	23.5	2.8	0.7
Two persons.......................	Percent ...	34.3	31.3	4.0	1.6
Three persons......................	Percent ...	46.2	37.4	5.9	2.2
Four persons.......................	Percent ...	50.6	38.2	6.3	2.3
Five or more persons..................	Percent ...	53.0	39.7	8.3	3.2
Veterinary Expenditures:					
Per household per year (mean).............	Dollars ...	261	160	18	263
Per animal (mean)...................	Dollars ...	179	85	9	112

[1] As of December 31, 2001. [2] During 2001.

Source: American Veterinary Medical Association, Schaumburg, IL, U.S. Pet Ownership and Demographics Sourcebook, 2002 (copyright).

U.S. Census Bureau, Statistical Abstract of the United States: 2004-2005

No. 1237. Adult Attendance at Sports Events by Frequency: 2003

[In thousands (9,438 represents 9,438,000), except percent. For fall 2003. Based on survey and subject to sampling error; see source]

Event	Attend one or more times a month		Attend less than once a month		Event	Attend one or more times a month		Attend less than once a month	
	Number	Percent	Number	Percent		Number	Percent	Number	Percent
Baseball	9,438	4.50	17,063	8.14	Golf	1,642	0.78	4,167	1.99
Basketball:					High school sports	11,501	5.49	7,892	3.76
College games	4,264	2.03	6,583	3.14	Horse racing:				
Professional games	3,517	1.68	7,767	3.70	Flats, runners	1,004	0.48	2,920	1.39
Bowling	1,721	0.82	2,849	1.36	Trotters/harness	455	0.22	2,109	1.01
Boxing	865	0.41	2,335	1.11	Ice hockey	2,542	1.21	6,717	3.20
Equestrian events	857	0.41	2,456	1.17	Motorcycle racing	792	0.38	2,392	1.14
Figure skating	626	0.30	2,407	1.15	Pro beach volleyball	338	0.16	1,903	0.91
Fishing tournaments	685	0.33	2,210	1.05	Rodeo	633	0.30	4,304	2.05
Football:					Soccer	3,220	1.54	3,403	1.62
College games	5,620	2.68	9,371	4.47	Tennis	810	0.39	2,847	1.36
Monday night professional games	2,038	0.97	3,458	1.65	Truck and tractor pull/mud racing	606	0.29	3,450	1.65
Weekend professional games	3,939	1.88	7,936	3.79	Wrestling—professional	1,071	0.51	2,781	1.33

Source: Mediamark Research, Inc., New York, NY *Top-line Reports* (copyright). Internet site <http://www.mediamark.com/mri/docs/TopLineReports.html>.

No. 1238. Adult Participation in Selected Leisure Activities by Frequency: 2003

[In thousands (13,058 represents 13,058,000), except percent. For fall 2003. Based on sample and subject to sampling error; see source]

Activity	Participated in the last 12 months		Frequency of participation							
			Two or more times a week		Once a week		Two to three times a month		Once a month	
	Number	Percent	Number	Percent	Number	Percent	Number	Percent	Number	Percent
Adult education courses	13,058	6.2	2,583	1.2	2,494	1.2	618	0.3	743	0.4
Attend auto shows	16,317	7.8	202	0.1	376	0.2	252	0.1	811	0.4
Attend country music performances	10,607	5.1	105	0.1	36	(Z)	257	0.1	399	0.2
Attend dance performances	7,561	3.6	211	0.1	339	0.2	240	0.1	341	0.2
Attend horse races	5,356	2.6	136	0.1	226	0.1	164	0.1	174	0.1
Attend music performances [1]	29,897	14.3	265	0.1	542	0.3	1,583	0.8	3,131	1.5
Attend rock music performances	19,292	9.2	222	0.1	172	0.1	619	0.3	1,030	0.5
Backgammon	4,863	2.3	650	0.3	137	0.1	477	0.2	358	0.2
Baking	36,904	17.6	7,406	3.5	5,734	2.7	7,875	3.8	5,414	2.6
Barbecuing	68,906	32.9	11,608	5.5	10,474	5.0	16,250	7.8	9,038	4.3
Billiards/pool	19,473	9.3	1,791	0.9	1,658	0.8	2,299	1.1	2,516	1.2
Birdwatching	9,108	4.3	4,506	2.2	897	0.4	750	0.4	379	0.2
Board games	37,084	17.7	2,473	1.2	3,122	1.5	6,069	2.9	7,330	3.5
Book clubs	7,747	3.7	519	0.3	414	0.2	474	0.2	2,450	1.2
Ceramics/pottery	2,993	1.4	318	0.2	223	0.1	306	0.2	183	0.1
Chess	9,540	4.6	1,112	0.5	558	0.3	844	0.4	1,404	0.7
Concerts on radio	7,504	3.6	1,412	0.7	896	0.4	908	0.4	678	0.3
Cooking for fun	33,028	15.8	11,085	5.3	4,885	2.3	5,919	2.8	2,856	1.4
Crossword puzzles	33,118	15.8	14,479	6.9	4,259	2.0	3,496	1.7	2,138	1.0
Dance/go dancing	22,300	10.6	1,997	1.0	2,310	1.1	2,779	1.3	3,278	1.6
Dining out	103,033	49.1	20,700	9.9	23,511	11.2	25,169	12.0	12,619	6.0
Electronic games (not TV)	19,611	9.4	5,556	2.7	2,704	1.3	2,672	1.3	2,048	1.0
Entertain friends or relatives at home	83,734	39.9	7,862	3.8	9,742	4.7	19,007	9.1	17,645	8.4
Fly kites	6,650	3.2	50	(Z)	210	0.1	158	0.1	619	0.3
Furniture refinishing	8,762	4.2	463	0.2	201	0.1	346	0.2	904	0.4
Go to bars/night clubs	43,060	20.5	3,705	1.8	5,286	2.5	6,385	3.1	6,759	3.2
Go to beach	48,979	23.4	2,636	1.3	2,586	1.2	4,351	2.1	4,327	2.1
Go to live theater	30,061	14.3	292	0.1	564	0.3	1,299	0.6	3,726	1.8
Go to museums	30,793	14.7	216	0.1	288	0.1	578	0.3	3,083	1.5
Model making	3,633	1.7	563	0.3	164	0.1	188	0.1	377	0.2
Painting, drawing	14,089	6.7	2,826	1.4	1,463	0.7	2,071	1.0	1,639	0.8
Photography	23,794	11.4	3,070	1.5	2,500	1.2	4,930	2.4	4,433	2.1
Picnic	24,354	11.6	322	0.2	527	0.3	1,775	0.9	3,450	1.7
Play bingo	9,169	4.4	918	0.4	995	0.5	803	0.4	928	0.4
Play cards	49,326	23.5	6,038	2.9	5,383	2.6	7,664	3.7	7,423	3.5
Play musical instrument	15,828	7.6	6,607	3.2	1,679	0.8	1,360	0.7	1,266	0.6
Reading books	79,205	37.8	43,668	20.8	7,981	3.8	6,419	3.1	5,511	2.6
Surf the Net	58,601	28.0	36,870	17.6	7,525	3.6	4,133	2.0	1,937	0.9
Trivia games	13,731	6.6	1,650	0.8	1,420	0.7	2,034	1.0	1,749	0.8
Video games	29,429	14.0	10,394	5.0	4,030	1.9	3,588	1.7	2,203	1.1
Woodworking	11,323	5.4	2,451	1.2	1,069	0.5	1,765	0.8	1,619	0.8
Word games	16,112	7.7	5,626	2.7	1,743	0.8	1,478	0.7	1,578	0.8
Zoo attendance	25,861	12.3	136	0.1	203	0.1	553	0.3	1,477	0.7

Z Represents less than 0.05.   [1] Excluding country and rock.

Source: Mediamark Research, Inc., New York, NY, *Top-line Reports* (copyright). Internet site <http://www.mediamark.com/mri/docs/TopLineReports.html>

Arts, Entertainment, and Recreation 771

No. 1239. Selected Spectator Sports: 1985 to 2003

[47,742 represents 47,742,000]

Sport	Unit	1985	1990	1995	1999	2000	2001	2002	2003
Baseball, major leagues: [1]									
Attendance............	1,000..	47,742	55,512	51,288	71,558	74,339	73,881	69,428	69,501
Regular season........	1,000..	46,824	54,824	50,469	70,139	72,748	72,267	67,859	67,568
National League.......	1,000..	22,292	24,492	25,110	38,323	39,851	39,558	36,949	36,661
American League	1,000..	24,532	30,332	25,359	31,817	32,898	32,709	30,910	30,908
Playoffs [2]	1,000..	591	479	533	1,202	1,314	1,247	1,262	1,568
World Series..........	1,000..	327	209	286	216	277	366	306	365
Players' salaries: [3]									
Average	$1,000.	371	598	1,111	1,607	1,896	2,139	2,296	2,372
Basketball: [4] [5]									
NCAA—Men's college:									
Teams	Number.	753	767	868	926	932	937	936	967
Attendance	1,000..	26,584	28,741	28,548	28,505	29,025	28,949	29,395	30,124
NCAA—Women's college:									
Teams	Number.	746	782	864	940	956	958	975	1,009
Attendance	1,000..	2,072	2,777	4,962	8,010	8,698	8,825	9,533	10,164
Pro: [6]									
Teams	Number.	23	27	27	29	29	29	29	29
Attendance, total [7]	1,000..	11,534	18,586	19,883	13,450	21,503	21,436	21,571	21,760
Regular season	1,000..	10,506	17,369	18,516	12,135	20,059	19,956	20,182	20,074
Average per game...	Number.	11,141	15,690	16,727	16,738	16,870	16,784	16,974	16,883
Playoffs............	1,000..	985	1,203	1,347	1,315	1,427	1,460	1,370	1,685
Average per game...	Number.	14,479	16,704	18,457	19,926	19,202	20,565	19,296	19,152
Football:									
NCAA College: [5]									
Teams	Number.	509	533	565	601	606	608	617	617
Attendance	1,000..	34,952	35,330	35,638	39,483	39,059	40,481	44,556	46,145
National Football League: [8]									
Teams	Number.	28	28	30	32	31	31	32	32
Attendance, total [9]	1,000..	14,058	17,666	19,203	20,763	20,954	20,590	21,505	21,639
Regular season......	1,000..	13,345	13,960	15,044	16,207	16,387	16,166	16,833	16,914
Average per game.. [10]	Number.	59,567	62,321	62,682	65,349	66,078	65,187	65,755	66,328
Postseason games ...	1,000..	711	848	(NA)	794	809	767	782	806
Players' salaries: [11]									
Average	$1,000.	217	354	584	708	787	986	1,180	1,259
Median base salary ...	$1,000.	160	275	301	400	441	501	568	590
National Hockey League: [12]									
Regular season attendance..	1,000..	11,634	12,580	9,234	17,152	18,800	20,373	20,615	20,409
Playoffs attendance	1,000..	1,108	1,356	1,329	1,472	1,525	1,584	1,691	1,636
Horseracing: [13] [14]									
Racing days...........	Number.	13,745	13,841	13,243	11,398	11,348	(NA)	(NA)	(NA)
Attendance............	1,000..	73,346	63,803	38,934	(NA)	(NA)	(NA)	(NA)	(NA)
Pari-mutuel turnover......	Mil. dol..	12,222	7,162	14,592	15,828	16,040	(NA)	(NA)	(NA)
Revenue to government	Mil. dol..	625	624	456	392	368	(NA)	(NA)	(NA)
Greyhound: [13]									
Total performances	Number.	9,590	14,915	16,110	14,455	14,403	(NA)	(NA)	(NA)
Attendance............	1,000..	23,853	28,660	(NA)	(NA)	(NA)	(NA)	(NA)	(NA)
Pari-mutuel turnover......	Mil. dol..	2,702	3,422	2,730	2,130	2,054	(NA)	(NA)	(NA)
Revenue to government	Mil. dol..	201	235	157	101	98	(NA)	(NA)	(NA)
Jai alai: [13]									
Total performances	Number.	2,736	3,620	2,748	2,119	2,034	(NA)	(NA)	(NA)
Games played	Number.	32,260	(NA)	37,052	28,706	27,461	(NA)	(NA)	(NA)
Attendance............	1,000..	4,722	5,329	3,208	(NA)	1,959	(NA)	(NA)	(NA)
Total handle	Mil. dol..	664	546	296	119	(NA)	(NA)	(NA)	(NA)
Revenue to government	Mil. dol..	50	39	13	5	4	(NA)	(NA)	(NA)
Professional rodeo: [15]									
Rodeos	Number.	617	754	739	700	688	668	666	657
Performances	Number.	1,887	2,159	2,217	2,128	2,081	2,015	2,207	1,949
Members.............	Number.	5,239	5,693	6,894	7,403	6,255	5,913	6,209	6,158
Permit-holders (rookies)	Number.	2,534	3,290	3,835	3,511	3,249	2,544	2,543	3,121
Total prize money	Mil. dol..	15.1	18.2	24.5	31.1	32.3	33.1	33.3	34.3

NA Not available. [1] Source: Major League Baseball (previously, The National League of Professional Baseball Clubs), New York, NY, *American League Green Book;* and The American League of Professional Baseball Clubs, New York, NY, *American League Red Book.* [2] Beginning 1997, two rounds of playoffs were played. Prior years had one round. [3] Source: Major League Baseball Players Association, New York, NY. [4] Season ending in year shown. [5] Source: National Collegiate Athletic Assn., Indianapolis, IN (copyright). For women's attendance total, excludes double-headers with men's teams. [6] Source: National Basketball Assn., New York, NY. [7] Includes All-Star game, not shown separately. [8] Source: National Football League, New York, NY. [9] Beginning 1987 includes preseason attendance, not shown separately. [10] Includes Pro Bowl, a nonchampionship game and Super Bowl. [11] Source: National Football League Players Association, Washington, DC. [12] Source: National Hockey League, Montreal, Quebec. [13] Source: Association of Racing Commissioners International, Inc., Lexington, KY. [14] Includes thoroughbred, harness, quarter horse, and fairs. [15] Source: Professional Rodeo Cowboys Association, Colorado Springs, CO., *Official Professional Rodeo Media Guide,* annual (copyright).

Source: Compiled from sources listed in footnotes.

No. 1240. Selected Recreational Activities: 1985 to 2003

[41 represents 41,000,000]

Activity	Unit	1985	1990	1995	1999	2000	2001	2002	2003
Softball, amateur: [1]									
Total participants [2]	Million..	41	41	42	35	31	31	31	30
Youth participants	1,000 ..	712	1,100	1,350	1,411	1,370	1,355	1,365	1,351
Adult teams [3]	1,000 ..	152	188	187	163	155	149	143	119
Youth teams [3]	1,000 ..	31	46	74	83	81	80	80	79
Golfers (one round or more) [4][5]	1,000 ..	17,520	23,000	23,700	25,200	25,400	25,800	26,200	27,400
Golf rounds played [4][5]	1,000 ..	414,777	421,200	431,400	496,400	518,400	518,100	502,400	494,900
Golf facilities [4]	Number.	12,346	12,846	14,074	15,195	15,489	15,689	15,827	15,899
Classification:									
Private	Number.	4,861	4,810	4,324	4,285	4,290	4,313	4,326	4,353
Daily fee	Number.	5,573	6,024	7,491	8,470	8,761	8,972	9,113	9,156
Municipal	Number.	1,912	2,012	2,259	2,440	2,438	2,404	2,388	2,390
Tennis: [6]									
Players	1,000 ..	13,000	21,000	17,820	20,000	22,900	22,000	23,200	(NA)
Courts	1,000 ..	220	220	240	(NA)	(NA)	(NA)	(NA)	(NA)
Indoor	1,000 ..	14	14	15	(NA)	(NA)	(NA)	(NA)	(NA)
Tenpin bowling: [7]									
Establishments	Number.	8,275	7,611	7,049	6,398	6,247	6,022	5,973	5,811
Lanes	1,000 ..	155	148	139	128	125	123	122	120
Membership, total [8]	1,000 ..	8,064	6,588	4,925	4,156	3,756	3,553	3,382	3,246
American Bowling Congress	1,000 ..	3,657	3,036	2,370	2,027	1,866	1,767	1,694	1,635
Women's Bowling Congress	1,000 ..	3,714	2,859	2,036	1,678	1,481	1,373	1,291	1,226
Young American Bowling Alliance [9]	1,000 ..	693	693	519	451	409	413	397	385
Motion picture screens [10]	1,000 ..	21	24	28	38	38	37	36	37
Indoor	1,000 ..	18	23	27	37	37	37	35	36
Drive-in	1,000 ..	3	3	1	1	1	1	1	1
Receipts, box office	Mil. dol..	3,749	5,022	5,494	7,448	7,661	8,413	9,520	9,489
Admission, average price	Dollars	3.55	4.23	4.35	5.08	5.39	5.66	5.81	6.03
Boating: [11]									
Recreational boats owned [12]	1,000 ..	13,778	15,987	15,375	16,820	17,030	17,200	17,360	17,490
Retail expenditures on boating [13]	Mil. dol..	13,284	13,731	17,226	21,736	27,870	28,556	30,362	29,997
Retail units purchased:									
Total all boats [14]	1,000 ..	675	525	664	586	577	883	845	842
Outboard boats	1,000 ..	305	227	231	230	241	218	212	207
Inboard boats	1,000 ..	17	15	12	19	24	22	22	20
Sterndrive boats	1,000 ..	115	97	94	80	78	72	69	69
Jet boats	1,000 ..	(NA)	(NA)	15	8	7	6	5	6
Personal watercraft	1,000 ..	(NA)	(NA)	200	106	92	81	79	81
Canoes [15]	1,000 ..	79	75	98	121	112	106	100	87
Kayaks [15]	1,000 ..	(NA)	(NA)	(NA)	(NA)	(NA)	357	340	324
Inflatable boats	1,000 ..	34	27	(NA)	(NA)	(NA)	(NA)	(NA)	31
Boat trailers	1,000 ..	192	165	207	168	159	136	141	131
Outboard motors	1,000 ..	392	352	317	332	349	299	302	305
Sterndrive and inboard engines	1,000 ..	155	134	120	109	110	104	105	101

NA Not available. [1] Source: Amateur Softball Association, Oklahoma City, OK. [2] Amateur Softball Association teams and other amateur softball teams. [3] Amateur Softball Association teams only. [4] Source: National Golf Foundation, Jupiter, FL. [5] Prior to 1990, for persons 5 years of age and over; thereafter for persons 12 years of age and over. [6] Source: Tennis Industry Association, Hilton Head, SC. Players for persons 12 years old and over who played at least once. [7] Source: Bowling Headquarters, Greendale, WI. [8] Membership totals are for U.S., Canada and for U.S. military personnel worldwide. [9] Prior to 1985, represents American Jr. Bowling Congress and ABC/WIBC Collegiate Division. [10] Source: Motion Picture Association of America, Inc., Encino, CA. [11] Source: National Marine Manufacturers Association, Chicago, IL. (copyright). [12] 2003 data is estimated. [13] Represents estimated expenditures for new and used boats, motors and engines, accessories, safety equipment, fuel, insurance, docking, maintenance, launching, storage, repairs, and other expenses. [14] 1985 through 1990 includes other boats, not shown separately. [15] Kayak category added in 2001.

Source: Compiled from sources listed in footnotes.

U.S. Census Bureau, Statistical Abstract of the United States: 2004-2005

No. 1241. Participation in Selected Sports Activities: 2002

[In thousands (253,729 represents 253,729,000), except rank. For persons 7 years of age or older. Except as indicated, a participant plays a sport more than once in the year]

Activity	All persons		Sex		Age								Household income (dol.)					
	Number	Rank	Male	Female	7-11 years	12-17 years	18-24 years	25-34 years	35-44 years	45-54 years	55-64 years	65 years and over	Under 15,000	15,000-24,999	25,000-34,999	35,000-49,000	50,000-74,999	75,000 and over
SERIES I SPORTS [1]																		
Total	253,729	(X)	123,459	130,271	20,095	24,264	27,548	36,923	44,224	39,260	26,112	35,303	28,431	28,683	30,813	40,320	54,199	71,284
Number participated in—[2]																		
Aerobic exercising [2] . .	29,038	11	7,786	21,253	737	2,284	4,744	6,613	5,386	4,507	2,220	2,546	2,236	2,266	3,240	4,527	6,227	10,541
Backpacking [3]	15,501	18	9,490	6,012	1,145	2,694	2,732	3,395	2,970	1,700	408	456	1,847	1,441	1,631	2,602	3,368	4,612
Baseball	15,623	17	11,526	4,097	5,070	3,937	1,939	1,488	1,606	847	450	285	979	963	1,433	2,695	4,150	5,402
Basketball	28,947	12	19,389	9,558	6,240	7,787	4,274	4,615	3,151	1,945	588	346	1,582	2,362	2,843	5,125	6,315	10,720
Bicycle riding [2] . . .	41,387	7	22,464	18,923	9,378	7,405	3,188	5,856	7,013	4,300	2,207	2,039	2,568	3,822	4,289	6,658	10,253	13,798
Billiards	35,263	9	21,516	13,747	1,649	4,081	8,545	9,136	6,728	3,437	1,011	677	2,435	3,389	4,427	6,152	7,433	11,427
Bowling	43,910	6	22,438	21,472	6,206	6,738	7,938	8,184	7,545	4,230	1,575	1,494	2,981	3,841	4,618	7,969	9,988	14,514
Camping [4]	55,436	2	28,760	26,676	6,451	6,831	7,822	10,712	10,667	7,267	3,008	2,678	4,412	5,233	7,015	10,611	14,044	14,121
Exercising with equipment [2]	50,227	4	23,109	27,117	785	5,069	6,983	9,020	9,702	9,209	4,749	4,709	3,034	3,616	5,139	7,626	11,366	14,445
Exercise walking [2] . .	82,183	1	30,568	51,615	3,005	4,482	8,084	13,167	15,679	15,395	9,988	12,384	8,200	8,421	9,391	12,766	17,504	25,900
Fishing (Net)	44,221	5	29,262	14,959	5,027	4,906	5,498	7,234	8,551	6,174	3,533	3,298	3,058	4,615	6,042	8,257	10,166	12,085
Fishing—fresh water . .	38,511	8	25,570	12,941	4,783	4,446	4,718	6,485	7,380	5,276	2,961	2,462	2,673	4,222	5,528	7,103	8,823	10,162
Fishing—salt water [2] .	12,240	22	8,509	3,731	766	1,117	1,821	1,680	2,613	1,845	1,192	1,206	817	784	1,443	2,515	2,471	4,209
Football—tackle	7,400	26	6,682	719	1,334	3,171	1,366	627	462	221	99	120	561	474	1,072	1,379	1,569	2,346
Football—touch	10,319	25	8,156	2,163	2,139	2,924	2,025	1,835	772	357	137	132	730	748	955	1,999	2,086	3,802
Golf	28,257	13	22,408	5,849	968	2,405	2,920	6,130	5,949	4,706	2,765	2,414	685	1,879	2,166	4,173	6,612	12,741
Hiking	30,531	10	15,376	15,155	2,487	3,321	4,110	6,468	5,793	4,754	2,020	1,578	2,387	2,680	3,234	4,868	6,522	10,840
Hunting with firearms . .	19,473	16	16,864	2,610	869	2,118	3,216	3,685	4,182	3,044	1,339	1,020	1,819	1,979	2,920	3,846	4,313	4,598
Martial arts	4,192	28	2,397	1,795	1,299	650	585	684	579	317	8	69	420	225	665	914	750	1,218
Running/jogging [2] . .	24,748	15	13,356	11,392	2,068	4,387	4,911	5,794	4,003	2,493	718	375	1,890	1,554	2,984	3,520	4,883	9,917
Soccer	14,543	19	9,043	5,499	5,851	3,722	1,663	1,526	1,048	259	173	300	762	728	1,265	2,467	2,690	6,630
Softball [2]	13,630	21	6,901	6,729	2,169	3,078	1,795	2,755	2,201	1,118	274	240	831	846	1,208	2,293	3,601	4,851
Swimming	54,657	3	25,447	29,210	9,267	8,567	6,863	8,391	9,249	6,383	2,914	3,022	3,104	4,546	5,866	8,467	12,277	20,397
Tai Chi/Yoga	7,058	27	1,456	5,602	244	228	1,270	2,188	1,121	955	404	649	746	829	845	1,225	1,385	2,027
Tennis	10,970	24	6,199	4,771	976	2,048	1,751	1,824	2,023	1,367	450	532	598	615	595	1,594	2,165	5,403
Volleyball	11,450	23	5,212	6,238	1,382	3,091	1,724	2,638	1,521	749	262	84	855	982	1,225	1,844	2,782	3,763
Weightlifting	28,050	14	18,355	9,695	311	4,965	5,130	7,174	4,948	3,522	1,199	802	1,425	1,985	3,035	3,981	6,445	11,180

See footnotes at end of table.

U.S. Census Bureau, Statistical Abstract of the United States: 2004-2005

SERIES II SPORTS [5]

Activity	All persons		Sex		Age								Household income (dol.)					
	Number	Rank	Male	Female	7-11 years	12-17 years	18-24 years	25-34 years	35-44 years	45-54 years	55-64 years	65 years and over	Under 15,000	15,000-24,999	25,000-34,999	35,000-49,999	50,000-74,999	75,000 and over
Total	253,734	(X)	123,455	130,279	20,094	24,265	27,548	36,922	44,227	39,261	26,114	35,304	29,503	27,425	30,765	38,897	57,303	69,841
Number participating in—																		
Archery (target)	4,173	17	3,207	966	625	795	629	412	807	601	160	143	337	471	488	707	1,320	849
Boating, motor/power	26,626	2	15,029	11,596	2,303	3,024	3,105	4,668	5,775	3,984	2,015	1,753	1,128	1,717	2,163	4,254	6,660	10,704
Canoeing	7,592	11	4,341	3,250	685	862	827	1,567	1,523	1,230	365	534	450	592	675	1,211	1,932	2,731
Darts-metal tip	9,951	8	6,164	3,787	502	925	2,266	2,475	1,961	1,161	333	329	1,202	1,070	1,083	1,383	2,443	2,771
Darts-soft tip	11,026	7	6,363	4,662	1,029	970	1,726	3,292	2,138	1,237	295	338	1,036	1,044	1,762	2,640	2,755	1,788
Hockey (Ice)	2,085	21	1,633	453	132	539	417	572	210	121	-	95	128	80	157	249	518	952
Hunting with bow and arrow	4,639	16	4,193	446	65	377	625	943	1,262	810	389	168	359	430	586	923	1,317	1,024
In-line Roller skating	18,845	4	9,054	9,790	6,734	4,789	2,201	2,378	1,911	454	151	228	972	1,271	1,890	3,233	5,389	6,089
Mountain biking-on road	15,265	5	8,701	6,564	1,839	2,469	1,566	3,785	3,308	1,551	467	280	848	522	1,297	1,944	4,897	5,014
Mountain biking-off road	7,770	10	4,859	2,911	1,448	823	869	1,918	1,606	753	208	144	442	1,265	623	1,233	2,300	2,650
Muzzleloading	3,552	19	3,282	270	-	208	550	708	716	761	452	157	197	468	407	722	940	818
Paintball games	6,910	13	5,480	1,430	505	2,209	2,055	1,002	701	256	72	110	438	499	666	1,445	1,725	2,136
Scooter riding	13,384	6	7,816	5,568	7,552	3,694	314	460	485	259	293	326	761	921	1,466	2,107	3,366	4,763
Skateboarding	9,664	9	7,776	1,888	4,023	3,834	710	480	283	101	74	160	581	908	1,135	1,588	2,192	3,261
Skiing—alpine	7,402	12	4,491	2,910	895	1,276	1,073	1,245	1,715	740	262	195	135	146	453	495	2,100	4,071
Skiing—cross country	2,202	20	1,179	1,023	280	185	123	241	321	717	232	102	73	62	100	194	524	1,249
Snowboarding	5,589	15	4,305	1,284	969	1,659	1,149	997	440	279	24	71	128	381	581	861	1,475	2,163
Target shoot	18,906	3	14,306	4,600	926	1,859	3,390	3,723	3,879	2,898	1,267	965	1,423	1,562	2,473	3,440	4,992	5,015
Target shoot-airgun	4,094	18	3,217	877	600	909	458	510	653	513	248	203	345	499	528	760	737	818
Water skiing	6,870	14	4,042	2,829	457	1,174	1,657	1,491	1,181	688	191	32	431	260	488	975	1,847	1,224
Work-out at club	28,913	1	13,294	15,619	512	1,405	4,432	7,584	5,805	4,511	2,413	2,251	1,302	1,695	2,226	3,858	6,585	13,247

- Represents or rounds to zero. X Not applicable. [1] Based on a sampling of 15,000 households. [2] Participant engaged in activity at least six times in the year. [3] Includes wilderness camping. [4] Vacation/overnight. [5] Based on a sampling of 20,000 households

Source: National Sporting Goods Association, Mt. Prospect, IL., Sports Participation in 2002:Series 1 and Series II (copyright)

Arts, Entertainment, and Recreation 775

No. 1242. High School Students Engaged in Organized Physical Activity by Sex, Race and Hispanic Origin: 2003

[In percent. For students in grades 9 to 12. Based on the Youth Risk Behavior Survey, a school-based survey and subject to sampling error; for details see source]

Characteristic	Enrolled in physical education class		Exercised 20 minutes or more per class [1]	Played on a sports team
	Total	Attended daily		
All students............	**55.7**	**28.4**	**80.3**	**57.6**
Male.....................	58.5	30.5	84.5	64.0
Grade 9	70.8	37.7	84.8	65.0
Grade 10...............	63.0	33.5	83.2	62.0
Grade 11...............	50.5	26.0	83.7	66.3
Grade 12...............	44.5	21.4	87.2	62.3
Female	52.8	26.4	75.3	51.0
Grade 9	71.2	38.0	75.7	55.2
Grade 10...............	58.0	29.1	77.0	53.9
Grade 11...............	40.8	19.2	71.6	47.8
Grade 12...............	34.6	15.2	74.9	45.9
White, non-Hispanic	53.7	24.9	81.5	60.8
Male....................	55.9	26.8	85.8	65.4
Female	51.5	23.1	76.6	55.9
Black, non-Hispanic	56.0	33.0	74.0	53.2
Male....................	63.1	37.1	80.0	67.5
Female	49.3	29.0	66.7	39.6
Hispanic	58.8	36.7	78.2	49.5
Male....................	61.4	39.5	82.5	56.2
Female	56.1	34.0	73.5	42.8

[1] For students enrolled in physical education classes.

Source: U.S. Centers for Disease Control and Prevention, Atlanta, GA, Youth Risk Behavior Surveillance—United States, 2003, Morbidity and Mortality Weekly Report, Vol. 53, No. SS 02, May 21, 2004.

No. 1243. Participation in High School Athletic Programs by Sex: 1972 to 2003

[Data based on number of state associations reporting and may underrepresent the number of schools with and participants in athletic programs]

Year	Participants [1]		Sex and sport	Most popular sports, 2002-2003 [2]	
	Males	Females		Schools	Participants
1972-73	3,770,621	817,073	**MALE**		
1973-74	4,070,125	1,300,169			
1975-76	4,109,021	1,645,039	Football (11-player)	13,642	1,023,142
1977-78	4,367,442	2,083,040	Basketball	17,333	540,874
1978-79	3,709,512	1,854,400	Track & field (outdoor)	15,195	498,027
1979-80	3,517,829	1,750,264	Baseball	14,988	453,792
1980-81	3,503,124	1,853,789	Soccer	10,103	345,156
1981-82	3,409,081	1,810,671	Wrestling	9,543	239,845
1982-83	3,355,558	1,779,972	Cross country.............	12,574	191,833
1983-84	3,303,599	1,747,346	Golf	13,120	162,805
1984-85	3,354,284	1,757,884	Tennis.................	9,411	144,844
			Swimming & diving	5,588	94,612
1985-86	3,344,275	1,807,121			
1986-87	3,364,082	1,836,356	**FEMALE**		
1987-88	3,425,777	1,849,684			
1988-89	3,416,844	1,839,352	Basketball	17,028	457,165
1989-90	3,398,192	1,858,659	Track & field (outdoor)	15,032	415,602
1990-91	3,406,355	1,892,316	Volleyball................	14,244	396,682
1991-92	3,429,853	1,940,801	Softball (fast pitch)...........	14,007	357,912
1992-93	3,416,389	1,997,489	Soccer	9,299	301,450
1993-94	3,472,967	2,130,315	Cross country.............	12,083	163,360
1994-95	3,536,359	2,240,461	Tennis...............	9,332	162,810
			Swimming & diving	6,120	141,468
1995-96	3,634,052	2,367,936	Competitive spirit squads	4,644	111,191
1996-97	3,706,225	2,474,043	Golf	8,106	62,159
1997-98	3,763,120	2,570,333			
1998-99	3,832,352	2,652,726			
1999-00	3,861,749	2,675,874			
2000-01	3,921,069	2,784,154			
2001-02	3,960,517	2,806,998			
2002-03	3,988,738	2,856,358			

[1] A participant is counted in the number of sports participated in.   [2] Ten most popular sports for each sex in terms of number of participants.

Source: National Federation of State High School Associations, Indianapolis, IN, The 2002-2003 High School Athletics Participation Survey (copyright).

U.S. Census Bureau, Statistical Abstract of the United States: 2004-2005

No. 1244. Participation in Selected Major NCAA Sports: 2001-2002

Sport	Males			Females		
	Teams	Athletes	Average squad	Teams	Athletes	Average squad
Total [1]	8,151	212,140	(X)	8,920	155,513	(X)
Baseball	866	26,343	30.4	(X)	(X)	(X)
Basketball	990	15,883	16.0	1,017	14,524	14.3
Bowling [2]	2	7	3.5	39	325	8.3
Cross country	858	10,840	12.6	928	12,008	12.9
Equestrian [2]	8	87	10.9	46	1,031	22.4
Fencing [3]	38	586	15.4	46	633	13.8
Field hockey	(X)	(X)	(X)	252	5,296	21.0
Football	617	58,090	94.1	(X)	(X)	(X)
Golf	754	7,631	10.1	451	3,447	7.6
Gymnastics	23	371	16.1	89	1,440	16.2
Ice hockey [4]	134	3,708	27.7	69	1,433	20.8
Lacrosse [5]	211	6,551	31.0	249	5,326	21.4
Rifle [3]	43	227	5.3	46	240	5.2
Rowing [2]	57	1,557	27.3	140	6,191	44.2
Sailing [2]	24	285	11.9	(X)	(X)	(X)
Skiing [3]	41	539	13.1	45	496	11.0
Soccer	734	18,559	25.3	868	19,467	22.4
Softball	(X)	(X)	(X)	895	15,514	17.3
Squash [2]	22	306	13.9	27	380	14.1
Swimming/diving	388	7,307	18.8	478	10,279	21.5
Synchronized swimming [4]	(X)	(X)	(X)	9	101	11.2
Tennis	770	7,441	9.7	898	8,378	9.3
Track, indoor	553	17,483	31.6	595	16,334	27.5
Track, outdoor	657	20,382	31.0	697	18,433	26.4
Volleyball	81	1,115	13.8	974	13,107	13.5
Water polo	48	891	18.6	55	1,055	19.2
Wrestling	231	5,943	25.7	(X)	(X)	(X)

X Not applicable. [1] Includes other sports, not shown separately. [2] Sport recognized by the NCAA but does not have an NCAA championship. [3] Co-ed championship sport. [4] Sport recognized by the NCAA but does not have an NCAA championship for women. [5] Sport recognized by the NCAA but does not have an NCAA championship for men.
Source: The National Collegiate Athletic Association (NCAA), Indianapolis, IN, 2001-02 Participation Study (copyright).

No. 1245. Participants in Wildlife Related Recreation Activities: 2001

[Preliminary. In thousands (37,805 represents 37,805,000). For persons 16 years old and over engaging in activity at least once in 2001. Based on survey and subject to sampling error; see source for details]

Participant	Number	Days of participation	Trips	Participant	Number	Days of participation
Total sportsmen	37,805	785,762	636,787	Wildlife watchers [1]	66,105	(X)
Total anglers	34,071	557,394	436,662	Nonresidential [2]	21,823	372,006
Freshwater	28,439	466,984	365,076	Observe wildlife	20,080	295,345
Excluding Great Lakes	27,913	443,247	349,188	Photograph wildlife	9,427	76,324
Great Lakes	1,847	23,138	15,888	Feed wildlife	7,077	103,307
Saltwater	9,051	90,838	71,586			
Total hunters	13,034	228,368	200,125	Residential [3]	62,928	(X)
Big game	10,911	153,191	114,445	Observe wildlife	42,111	(X)
Small game	5,434	60,142	46,450	Photograph wildlife	13,937	(X)
Migratory birds	2,956	29,310	24,155	Feed wildlife	53,988	(X)
Other animals	1,047	19,207	15,074	Visit public parks	10,981	(X)
				Maintain plantings or natural areas	13,072	(X)

X Not applicable. [1] Detail does not add to total due to multiple responses and nonresponse. [2] Persons taking a trip of at least 1 mile for activity. [3] Activity within 1 mile of home.

No. 1246. Expenditures for Wildlife Related Recreation Activities: 2001

[Preliminary. (35,632 represents $35,632,000,000). See headnote, Table 1245.]

Type of expenditure	Fishing			Hunting			Wildlife watching		
	Expenditures (mil. dol.)	Spenders Number (1,000)	Percent of anglers	Expenditures (mil. dol.)	Spenders Number (1,000)	Percent of hunters	Expenditures (mil. dol.)	Spenders Number (1,000)	Percent of watchers
Total [1]	35,632	31,950	94	20,611	12,585	97	38,414	52,083	79
Food and lodging	5,881	25,603	75	2,450	10,073	77	4,819	15,365	70
Food	4,141	25,406	75	1,980	10,057	77	2,836	15,263	70
Lodging	1,740	6,473	19	470	1,701	13	1,983	5,648	26
Transportation	3,516	25,146	74	1,789	10,502	81	2,596	17,091	78
Public	400	1,254	4	186	452	3	702	1,986	9
Private	3,115	24,816	73	1,603	10,421	80	1,893	16,495	76
Other trip-related costs	5,259	25,658	75	1,013	3,479	27	7,354	45,802	69
Sport specific equipment [2]	4,618	21,228	62	4,562	9,516	73	748	6,350	29
Auxiliary equipment [3]	721	4,347	13	1,203	4,584	35	717	3,807	6
Special equipment [4]	11,625	2,319	7	4,597	573	4	15,469	1,410	2
Other expenditures [5]	4,013	(NA)	(NA)	4,997	(NA)	(NA)	6,712	(NA)	(NA)

NA Not available. [1] Total not adjusted for multiple responses or nonresponse. [2] Items owned primarily for each specific activity, such as rods and reels for fishing and guns and rifles for hunting. [3] Equipment such as camping gear owned for wildlife-associated recreation. [4] "Big ticket" equipment such as campers and boats owned for wildlife-associated recreation. [5] Books, magazines, membership dues and contributions, land leasing and ownership, licenses and plantings.
Source of Tables 1245 and 1246: U.S. Fish and Wildlife Service, 2001 National Survey of Fishing, Hunting, and Wildlife Associated Recreation, May 2002.

Arts, Entertainment, and Recreation 777

Sporting Goods Sales by Product Category: 1990 to 2003

[In millions of dollars (50,725 represents $50,725,000,000), except percent. Based on a sample survey of consumer purchases of 80,000 households, (100,000 beginning 1995), except recreational transport, which was provided by industry associations. Excludes Alaska and Hawaii. Minus sign (-) indicates decrease]

Selected product category	1990	1995	1997	1998	1999	2000	2001	2002	2003, proj.
Sales, all products	50,725	59,794	67,333	69,848	71,161	74,442	74,337	77,917	79,810
Annual percent change [1]	(NA)	6.5	7.2	3.7	1.9	4.6	-0.1	4.8	5.9
Percent of retail sales	(NA)	2.6	2.7	2.6	2.5	2.4	2.4	2.4	2.3
Athletic and sport clothing [2]	10,130	10,311	12,035	12,844	10,307	11,030	10,217	9,979	10,179
Athletic and sport footwear [2]	11,654	11,415	13,319	13,068	12,546	13,026	13,814	14,107	14,445
Aerobic shoes	611	372	380	334	275	292	281	239	238
Basketball shoes	918	999	1,134	1,000	821	786	761	789	812
Cross training shoes	679	1,191	1,450	1,402	1,364	1,528	1,476	1,421	1,449
Golf shoes	226	225	239	220	208	226	223	243	245
Gym shoes, sneakers	2,536	1,741	1,980	2,010	1,936	1,871	2,004	2,042	2,083
Jogging and running shoes	1,110	1,043	1,482	1,469	1,502	1,638	1,670	1,733	1,774
Tennis shoes	740	480	545	515	505	533	505	503	508
Walking shoes	2,950	2,841	3,236	3,192	3,099	3,317	3,280	3,415	3,531
Athletic and sport equipment [2]	14,439	18,809	19,033	19,192	20,343	21,608	21,594	21,748	22,200
Archery	265	287	270	255	262	259	276	276	285
Baseball and softball	217	251	290	304	329	319	316	306	315
Billiards and pool	192	304	242	347	354	516	528	543	559
Camping	1,072	1,205	1,153	1,204	1,265	1,354	1,371	1,415	1,458
Exercise equipment	1,824	2,960	2,968	3,233	3,396	3,610	3,889	4,336	4,553
Fishing tackle	1,910	2,010	1,891	1,903	1,917	2,030	2,058	2,024	2,028
Golf	2,514	3,194	3,703	3,658	3,567	3,805	3,871	3,339	3,372
Hunting and firearms	2,202	3,003	2,562	2,200	2,437	2,274	2,206	2,470	2,495
In-line skating and wheel sports	150	646	562	509	473	1,074	726	494	469
Optics	438	655	690	710	718	729	783	826	850
Skin diving and scuba	294	328	332	345	363	355	348	331	337
Skiing, alpine	475	562	723	718	648	495	515	528	539
Tennis	333	297	319	318	338	383	371	397	401
Recreational transport	14,502	19,259	22,946	24,743	27,965	28,779	28,712	32,083	32,986
Bicycles and supplies	2,423	3,390	4,860	4,957	4,770	5,131	4,725	4,961	4,763
Pleasure boats	7,644	9,064	10,208	10,539	11,962	13,224	14,558	15,382	15,690
Recreational vehicles	4,113	5,895	6,904	8,364	10,413	9,529	8,598	10,960	11,722
Snowmobiles	322	910	975	883	820	894	831	780	811

NA Not available. [1] Represents change from immediate prior year. [2] Includes other products not shown separately.

Source: National Sporting Goods Association, Mt. Prospect, IL, *The Sporting Goods Market in 2003*; and prior issues (copyright).

Consumer Purchases of Sporting Goods by Consumer Characteristics: 2002

[In percent. Based on sample survey of consumer purchases of 100,000 households. Excludes Alaska and Hawaii]

Characteristic	Total house-holds	Footwear					Equipment				
		Aero-bic shoes	Gym shoes/ sneak-ers	Jog-ging/ run-ning shoes	Skate-board-ing shoes	Walk-ing shoes	Multi pur-pose home gyms	Rod/ reel combi-nation	Golf club set	Rifles	Soccer balls
Total	100	100	100	100	100	100	100	100	100	100	100
Age of user:											
Under 14 years old	20	10	50	12	36	6	1	6	3	-	56
14 to 17 years old	6	4	9	9	41	3	5	1	4	1	14
18 to 24 years old	10	8	6	10	15	5	2	6	5	5	8
25 to 34 years old	13	23	12	25	4	12	35	23	22	24	4
35 to 44 years old	16	24	10	20	4	15	25	27	14	27	3
45 to 64 years old	23	26	10	22	1	40	29	29	46	38	1
65 years old and over	13	6	3	2	-	19	2	5	8	5	-
Multiple ages	-	-	-	-	-	-	2	5	-	-	14
Sex of user:											
Male	49	17	56	56	82	39	68	80	77	90	66
Female	51	83	44	44	18	61	22	13	23	10	28
Both sexes	-	-	-	-	-	-	10	7	-	-	6
Education of household head:											
Less than high school	8	4	6	4	5	6	2	13	1	8	3
High school	23	16	21	15	22	21	26	21	10	24	16
Some college	36	38	38	34	39	37	30	40	32	38	42
College graduate	33	42	35	48	34	36	42	26	58	30	40
Annual household income:											
Under $15,000	14	3	8	5	4	9	-	6	1	6	5
$15,000 to $24,999	13	8	9	8	8	11	10	7	5	7	11
$25,000 to $34,999	12	8	11	8	11	11	19	10	5	14	11
$35,000 to $49,999	15	18	16	14	12	14	17	15	14	14	16
$50,000 to $74,999	19	23	26	22	30	23	23	31	10	31	23
$75,000 to $99,999	13	21	15	17	20	14	14	13	29	20	17
$100,000 and over	13	19	16	27	15	19	17	18	34	16	18

- Represents or rounds to zero.

Source: National Sporting Goods Association, Mt. Prospect, IL, *The Sporting Goods Market in 2002* (copyright).

No. 1249. National Park System—Summary: 1990 to 2002

[For year ending September 30, except as noted. (986 represents $986,000,000) Includes data for five areas in Puerto Rico and Virgin Islands, one area in American Samoa, and one area in Guam]

Item	1990	1995	1997	1998	1999	2000	2001	2002
Finances (mil. dol.): [1]								
Expenditures reported	986	1,445	1,473	1,604	1,530	1,833	1,985	2,161
Salaries and wages	459	633	683	721	733	799	840	876
Improvements, maintenance	160	234	246	255	289	299	305	311
Construction	109	192	188	191	62	215	199	296
Other	259	386	356	437	446	520	641	678
Funds available	1,506	2,225	2,301	2,658	2,972	3,316	3,642	3,940
Appropriations	1,053	1,325	1,625	1,765	1,867	1,881	2,241	2,257
Other [2]	453	900	676	893	1,105	1,435	1,401	1,683
Revenue from operations	79	106	175	203	215	234	246	245
Recreation visits (millions): [3]								
All areas	258.7	269.6	275.3	286.7	287.1	285.9	279.9	277.3
National parks [4]	57.7	64.8	65.3	64.5	64.3	66.1	64.1	64.5
National monuments	23.9	23.5	24.1	23.6	24.3	23.8	21.8	20.3
National historical, commemorative, archaeological [5]	57.5	56.9	63.0	74.2	72.6	72.2	66.7	70.2
National parkways	29.1	31.3	31.6	32.8	34.6	34.0	34.4	35.7
National recreation areas [4]	47.2	53.7	51.6	53.0	52.8	50.0	48.3	48.2
National seashores and lakeshores	23.3	22.5	22.4	22.6	22.7	22.5	22.2	23.3
National Capital Parks	7.5	5.5	5.1	4.2	3.9	5.4	4.6	3.8
Recreation overnight stays (millions)	17.6	16.8	15.8	15.6	15.9	15.4	15.3	14.7
In commercial lodgings	3.9	3.8	3.6	3.6	3.7	3.7	3.6	3.5
In Park Service campgrounds	7.9	7.1	6.3	6.1	6.2	5.9	5.7	5.8
In backcountry	1.7	2.2	2.2	2.1	2.0	1.9	2.0	1.9
Other	4.2	3.7	3.8	3.9	4.1	3.8	3.9	3.5
Land (1,000 acres): [6]								
Total	76,362	77,355	77,457	77,654	78,166	78,153	78,943	78,811
Parks	46,089	49,307	49,384	49,416	49,859	49,785	49,862	49,639
Recreation areas	3,344	3,353	3,329	3,361	3,404	3,388	3,388	3,390
Other	26,929	24,695	24,744	24,877	24,903	24,980	25,693	25,782
Acquisition, net	21	27	61	95	44	222	20	17

[1] Financial data are those associated with the National Park System. Certain other functions of the National Park Service (principally the activities absorbed from the former Heritage Conservation and Recreation Service in 1981) are excluded. [2] Includes funds carried over from prior years. [3] For calendar year. Includes other areas, not shown separately. [4] For 1990, combined data for North Cascades National Park and two adjacent National Recreation Areas are included in National Parks total. [5] Includes military areas. [6] Federal land only, as of Dec. 31. Federal land acreages, in addition to National Park Service administered lands, also include lands within national park system area boundaries but under the administration of other agencies. Year-to-year changes in the Federal lands figures include changes in the acreages of these other lands and hence often differ from "net acquisition."

Source: U.S. National Park Service, Visits, *National Park Statistical Abstract*, annual; and unpublished data. Other data are unpublished.

No. 1250. State Parks and Recreation Areas by State: 2002

[For year ending June 30 (13,162 represents 13,162,000). Data are shown as reported by state park directors. In some states, park agency has under its control forests, fish and wildlife areas, and/or other areas. In other states, agency is responsible for state parks only]

State	Acreage (1,000)	Visitors (1,000)[1]	Revenue Total ($1,000)	Percent of operating expenditures	State	Acreage (1,000)	Visitors (1,000)[1]	Revenue Total ($1,000)	Percent of operating expenditures
United States	13,162	758,216	667,715	35.4	Missouri	139	17,760	4,555	15.1
Alabama	50	5,163	24,095	78.5	Montana	66	1,219	1,255	20.8
Alaska	3,326	4,283	1,949	34.7	Nebraska	134	9,802	11,652	59.1
Arizona	59	2,410	3,017	17.7	Nevada	133	3,286	2,177	25.5
Arkansas	51	8,218	12,837	42.2	New Hampshire	85	6,779	7,595	100.0
California	1,457	85,665	71,380	21.4	New Jersey	377	15,040	3,133	8.5
Colorado	365	11,098	17,371	64.6	New Mexico	91	3,923	4,318	25.6
Connecticut	22	3,207	8,575	46.2	New York	1,159	56,864	47,522	29.2
Delaware	200	9,001	3,741	38.5	North Carolina	168	12,758	3,703	11.9
Florida	592	17,735	31,925	45.4	North Dakota	17	1,097	1,103	41.7
Georgia	81	14,623	27,415	46.4	Ohio	205	57,246	29,030	44.4
Hawaii	28	6,340	1,642	23.5	Oklahoma	72	14,057	24,008	53.4
Idaho	45	2,497	3,427	16.7	Oregon	95	39,439	15,425	42.2
Illinois	306	43,623	6,988	12.6	Pennsylvania	289	36,627	16,925	21.2
Indiana	179	16,879	33,514	78.7	Rhode Island	9	7,270	3,839	67.1
Iowa	63	15,439	3,386	33.4	South Carolina	80	8,151	16,537	69.0
Kansas	32	7,991	5,000	69.3	South Dakota	105	8,822	7,624	63.6
Kentucky	44	7,873	55,457	66.6	Tennessee	144	26,275	31,824	49.6
Louisiana	38	2,008	253	1.4	Texas	668	17,090	14,860	25.6
Maine	97	2,554	2,214	30.6	Utah	115	5,941	8,213	36.5
Maryland	266	10,340	14,299	31.4	Vermont	69	994	5,827	93.1
Massachusetts	294	11,884	2,904	9.1	Virginia	62	6,856	5,207	28.8
Michigan	285	25,297	27,654	51.4	Washington	262	48,864	10,229	23.6
Minnesota	267	8,076	7,549	24.9	West Virginia	196	7,318	19,214	63.3
Mississippi	24	4,225	6,645	43.5	Wisconsin	133	15,528	8,498	43.3
					Wyoming	119	2,784	1,269	23.1

[1] Includes overnight visitors.

Source: National Association of State Park Directors, Tucson, AZ, *2003 Annual Information Exchange*.

No. 1251. Domestic Travel by U.S. Resident Households—Summary: 1997 to 2003

[In millions (644.5 represents 644,500,000). See headnote, Table 1252]

Type of trip	1997	1998	1999	2000	2001	2002	2003
All travel: [1]							
Household trips	644.5	656.3	640.8	637.7	645.6	637.0	643.5
Person-trips	1,101.8	1,108.0	1,089.5	1,100.8	1,123.1	1,127.0	1,140.0
All overnight travel:							
Household trips	469.7	479.4	475.5	477.5	483.7	482.7	491.2
Person-trips	794.9	800.0	804.9	822.4	839.2	855.4	871.6
Business travel:							
Household trips	188.8	195.8	192.9	184.9	179.0	166.6	163.5
Person-trips	239.0	245.4	240.9	235.1	227.6	214.7	210.5
Leisure travel: [2]							
Household trips	455.7	460.5	447.9	452.8	466.6	470.4	480.0
Person-trips	862.8	862.6	848.6	865.7	895.5	912.3	929.5

[1] Includes personal and other trips (e.g. medical, funerals, weddings), not shown separately.   All domestic travel included. 95% of U.S. resident person-trips are domestic.   [2] Includes visiting friends/relatives, outdoor recreation, entertainment and travel for other pleasure/personal reasons, etc.

Source: Travel Industry Association of America, Washington, DC, *TravelScope*, annual (copyright).

No. 1252. Characteristics of Domestic Overnight Leisure Trips by U.S. Resident Households: 1998 to 2003

[In millions (335.4 represents 335,400,000). Represents household trips to destinations 50 miles or more, one-way, away from home and including one or more overnights. Based on a monthly mail panel survey of 25,000 U.S. households. For details, see source.]

Overnight leisure trip characteristics	Unit	1998	1999	2000	2001	2002	2003
Total overnight leisure trips [1]	Millions	335.4	331.1	337.1	349.1	354.0	360.3
Average nights per trip	Number	4.2	4.2	4.2	4.2	4.2	4.1
Traveled primarily by auto/truck/RV rental car	Percent	75	74	74	74	75	74
Traveled primarily by air	Percent	17	18	18	18	17	17
Stayed in a hotel/motel/B&B while on trip.	Percent	41	42	43	42	43	44
Household income:							
Less than $50,000	Percent	(NA)	(NA)	48	44	45	43
$50,000 or more	Percent	(NA)	(NA)	52	56	55	57

NA Not available.   [1]"Leisure" includes visiting friends/relatives, outdoor recreation, entertainment, and travel for other pleasure/personal reasons etc. Other pleasure/personal trips are trips such as for medical reasons, funerals, weddings etc.

Source: Travel Industry Association of America, Washington, DC, *TravelScope*, annual (copyright).

No. 1253. Domestic Travel Expenditures by State: 2001

[479,016 represents $479,016,000,000. Represents U.S. spending on domestic overnight trips and day trips of 50 miles or more, one way, away from home. Excludes spending by foreign visitors and by U.S. residents in U.S. territories and abroad. Includes travelers' expenditures in Indian casino gaming. Due to data revisions, 2001 travel expenditure estimates are not comparable to travel expenditure estimates in previous publications.]

State	Total (mil. dol.)	Share of total (per- cent)	Rank	State	Total (mil. dol.)	Share of total (per- cent)	Rank	State	Total (mil. dol.)	Share of total (per- cent)	Rank
U.S., total	479,016	100.0	(X)	KS	3,637	0.8	38	ND	1,167	0.2	50
				KY	5,116	1.1	31	OH	12,490	2.6	11
AL	5,348	1.1	29	LA	8,701	1.8	18	OK	4,206	0.9	33
AK	1,343	0.3	49	ME	1,920	0.4	43	OR	5,451	1.1	28
AZ	8,686	1.8	19	MD	8,683	1.8	20	PA	14,714	3.1	8
AR	3,921	0.8	36	MA	10,074	2.1	15	RI	1,414	0.3	47
CA	60,560	12.6	1	MI	11,785	2.5	13	SC	6,845	1.4	24
CO	9,121	1.9	17	MN	7,702	1.6	22	SD	1,463	0.3	46
CT	6,602	1.4	26	MS	5,174	1.1	30	TN	10,126	2.1	14
DE	1,067	0.2	51	MO	9,313	1.9	16	TX	31,922	6.7	3
DC	4,129	0.9	34	MT	1,964	0.4	42	UT	3,788	0.8	37
FL	40,525	8.5	2	NE	2,692	0.6	39	VT	1,351	0.3	48
GA	14,349	3.0	9	NV	18,760	3.9	6	VA	13,138	2.7	10
HI	7,073	1.5	23	NH	2,606	0.5	40	WA	7,891	1.6	21
ID	2,164	0.5	41	NJ	14,732	3.1	7	WV	1,707	0.4	44
IL	20,949	4.4	5	NM	3,949	0.8	35	WI	6,841	1.4	25
IN	6,456	1.3	27	NY	27,072	5.7	4	WY	1,538	0.3	45
IA	4,415	0.9	32	NC	12,375	2.6	12				

X Not applicable.

Source: Travel Industry Association of America, Washington, DC, *Impact of Travel on State Economies*, 2001 (copyright).

International Travelers and Expenditures: 1990 to 2003

[In millions (47,880 represents $47,880,000,000). For coverage, see Table 1255. Some traveler data revised since originally issued]

Year	Travel and passenger fare (mil. dol.) Payments by U.S. travelers Total[1]	Expenditures abroad	Receipts from foreign visitors Total[1]	Travel receipts	U.S. net travel and passenger payments (mil. dol.)	U.S. travelers to foreign countries (1,000)	International visitors to the U.S. (1,000)
1990	47,880	37,349	58,305	43,007	10,425	44,623	39,363
1995	59,579	44,916	82,304	63,395	22,725	50,835	43,318
1996	63,887	48,078	90,231	69,809	26,344	52,311	46,489
1997	70,189	52,051	94,294	73,426	24,105	52,944	47,752
1998	76,454	56,483	91,423	71,325	14,969	56,288	46,396
1999	80,278	58,963	94,586	74,801	14,308	57,598	48,492
2000	88,979	64,705	103,087	82,400	14,108	60,891	50,945
2001	82,833	60,200	89,819	71,893	6,986	57,963	44,898
2002	78,013	58,044	83,593	66,547	5,580	56,359	41,892
2003 [2]	76,754	56,190	80,652	65,054	3,898	(NA)	40,356

[1] Includes passenger fares not shown separately. [2] Preliminary estimates
Source: U.S. Dept. of Commerce, International Trade Administration, Tourism Industries & Bureau of Economic Analysis (BEA)
Internet site <http://www.tinet.ita.doc.gov> Released: April 2004

No. 1255. Foreign Travel: 1990 to 2002

[In thousands (44,623 represents 44,623,000). U.S. travelers cover residents of the United States, its territories and possessions. Foreign travelers to the U.S. include travelers for business and pleasure, international travelers in transit through the United States, and students; excludes travel by international personnel and international businessmen employed in the United States]

Item and area	1990	1995	1997	1998	1999	2000	2001	2002
U.S. travelers to foreign countries....	44,623	50,835	52,944	56,288	57,598	60,891	57,963	56,359
Canada..................	12,252	13,005	13,401	14,880	15,276	15,188	15,561	16,161
Mexico..................	16,381	18,771	17,909	18,338	17,743	18,849	17,153	16,810
Total overseas..........	15,990	19,059	21,634	23,069	24,579	26,853	25,249	23,397
Europe.................	8,043	8,596	9,800	11,143	11,577	13,373	11,438	10,131
Foreign travelers to the U.S.........	39,363	43,318	47,752	46,396	48,492	50,945	44,898	41,892
Canada..................	17,263	14,662	15,127	13,422	14,110	14,648	13,507	12,968
Mexico..................	7,041	8,016	8,431	9,276	9,915	10,322	9,558	9,807
Total overseas..........	15,059	20,639	24,194	23,698	24,466	25,975	21,833	19,117
Europe.................	6,659	8,793	10,390	10,675	11,243	11,597	9,496	8,603
South America............	1,328	2,449	2,831	2,957	2,733	2,941	2,531	1,815
Central America..........	412	509	564	697	731	822	771	704
Caribbean...............	1,137	1,044	1,189	1,161	1,258	1,331	1,202	1,053
Far East................	4,360	6,616	7,756	6,724	6,935	7,554	6,316	5,689
Middle East..............	365	454	552	587	625	702	644	483
Oceania................	662	588	680	639	667	731	586	483
Africa.................	137	186	234	258	274	295	287	241

Source: U.S. Dept. of Commerce, International Trade Administration, Tourism Industries, Internet site<http://www.tinet.ita.doc.gov>

No. 1256. Top States and Cities Visited by Overseas Travelers: 2000 and 2003

[25,975 represents 25,975,000. Includes travelers for business and pleasure, international travelers in transit through the United States, and students; excludes travel by international personnel and international businessmen employed in the United States]

State	Overseas visitors[1] (1,000) 2000	2003	Market share (percent) 2000	2003	City	Overseas visitors[1] (1,000) 2000	2003	Market share (percent) 2000	2003
Total overseas travelers [2].	25,975	18,026	100.0	100.0	New York City, NY	5,714	3,984	22.0	22.1
Florida	6,026	4,200	23.2	23.3	Los Angeles, CA	3,533	2,127	13.6	11.8
New York	5,922	4,200	22.8	23.3	Miami, FL.............	2,935	2,073	11.3	11.5
California.............	6,364	3,984	24.5	22.1	Orlando, FL...........	3,013	1,767	11.6	9.8
Hawaiian Islands........	2,727	1,947	10.5	10.8	San Francisco, CA......	2,831	1,694	10.9	9.4
Nevada...............	2,364	1,370	9.1	7.6	Oahu/Honolulu, HI.....	2,234	1,622	8.6	9.0
Guam................	1,325	847	5.1	4.7	Las Vegas, NV	2,260	1,298	8.7	7.2
Illinois...............	1,377	829	5.3	4.6	Washington, DC	1,481	865	5.7	4.8
Massachusetts..........	1,429	829	5.5	4.6	Chicago, IL.	1,351	775	5.2	4.3
Texas................	1,169	829	4.5	4.6	Boston, MA	1,325	757	5.1	4.2
New Jersey	909	685	3.5	3.8	San Diego, CA	701	433	2.7	2.4
Pennsylvania	649	613	2.5	3.4	Houston, TX	442	397	1.7	2.2
Arizona	883	487	3.4	2.7	Philadelphia, PA	390	397	1.5	2.2
Georgia	805	451	3.1	2.5	Atlanta, GA.	701	379	2.7	2.1
Michigan	494	361	1.9	2.0	Ft. Lauderdale, FL......	468	342	1.8	1.9
Washington............	468	342	1.8	1.9	San Jose, CA	494	324	1.9	1.8
Ohio.................	390	324	1.5	1.8	Tampa/St. Petersburg, FL .	519	324	2.0	1.8
Colorado	519	288	2.0	1.6	Dallas/Ft. Worth, TX.....	494	306	1.9	1.7
Connecticut	260	252	1.0	1.4	Seattle, WA.	416	306	1.6	1.7
North Carolina	416	252	1.6	1.4	Anaheim, CA	494	288	1.9	1.6
Utah.................	416	252	1.6	1.4	Florida Keys	284	252	1.3	1.4
Virginia	364	234	1.4	1.3	Detroit, MI	338	234	1.3	1.3
Louisiana	390	216	1.5	1.2	New Orleans, LA	364	198	1.4	1.1

[1] Excludes Canada and Mexico. [2] Includes other states and cities, not shown separately.
Source: U.S. Dept. of Commerce, International Trade Administration, Internet site <http://www.tinet.ita.doc.gov>.

Arts, Entertainment, and Recreation 781

No. 1257. Impact of International Travel on States' Economies: 2000

[Preliminary. (79,265.9 represents $79,265,900,000)]

State	Travel expenditures (mil. dol.)	Travel generated payroll (mil. dol.)	Travel generated employment (1,000)	Travel generated tax receipts (mil. dol.)	State	Travel expenditures (mil. dol.)	Travel generated payroll (mil. dol.)	Travel generated employment (1,000)	Travel generated tax receipts (mil. dol.)
U.S., total...	79,265.9	21,628.8	1,003.8	13,665.5	MO	177.7	49.0	2.6	32.9
AL	90.2	21.0	1.4	12.3	MT	101.4	24.3	2.0	13.8
AK	162.9	67.4	3.0	32.0	NE	63.7	17.7	1.2	11.2
AZ	1,746.9	494.9	25.4	288.2	NV	2,865.2	915.4	41.9	393.3
AR	50.3	13.2	0.9	7.6	NH	122.0	28.8	1.7	14.8
CA	15,079.7	3,999.0	179.1	2,417.1	NJ	933.0	252.6	10.8	188.3
CO	877.5	293.9	14.6	204.2	NM	114.9	27.4	1.9	16.0
CT	211.8	46.9	2.1	34.0	NY	10,271.5	2,793.5	108.1	2,164.9
DE	90.8	21.6	1.2	15.4	NC	584.3	185.3	9.2	107.6
DC	1,961.0	431.8	16.6	288.5	ND	46.4	12.2	1.0	10.7
FL	18,171.9	4,767.7	235.9	2,899.3	OH	620.9	176.5	9.6	121.6
GA	1,246.6	475.1	19.3	318.2	OK	90.1	34.5	1.7	16.0
HI	7,436.1	1,773.4	78.1	1,053.7	OR	371.5	104.5	6.2	61.6
ID	113.6	28.6	1.9	21.1	PA	1,246.2	364.8	17.7	227.4
IL	1,796.4	490.6	22.5	354.2	RI	119.4	26.1	1.5	15.8
IN	244.0	75.6	4.1	45.1	SC	491.8	124.2	7.7	76.3
IA	143.3	35.5	2.5	21.7	SD	40.1	10.7	0.9	5.6
KS	104.9	25.2	1.7	15.8	TN	442.2	197.3	7.7	105.2
KY	130.6	55.2	2.7	28.3	TX	3,751.3	1,162.0	54.3	705.2
LA	514.9	118.4	7.1	72.7	UT	381.1	130.2	8.0	76.5
ME	193.6	44.9	3.2	26.4	VT	144.5	35.5	2.2	20.5
MD	447.3	130.1	5.7	91.3	VA	500.8	151.7	8.1	82.1
MA	2,178.3	564.4	25.1	359.5	WA	909.3	249.4	12.3	172.7
MI	764.7	205.4	11.2	141.5	WV	32.2	8.0	0.5	5.0
MN	620.6	231.0	10.7	195.6	WI	334.4	90.2	6.0	57.9
MS	57.2	26.4	1.4	9.5	WY	75.1	19.7	1.6	9.3

Source: Travel Industry Association of America, Washington, DC, *Impact of Travel on State Economies, 2000* (copyright).

No. 1258. Foreign Visitors for Pleasure Admitted by Country of Last Residence: 1990 to 2002

[In thousands (13,418 represents 13,418,000). For years ending September 30. Represents non-U.S. citizens admitted to the country for a temporary period of time (also known as nonimmigrants)]

Country	1990	1995	2000	2002	Country	1990	1995	2000	2002
All countries [1]	13,418	17,612	30,511	19,967	United Arab Emirates ...	7	14	36	11
Europe [1]	5,383	7,012	11,806	7,403	Africa [1]	105	137	327	178
Austria	87	146	182	78	Egypt	16	16	44	18
Belgium	95	153	254	129	Nigeria	11	10	27	25
Czech Republic	(X)	12	44	19	South Africa	26	59	114	52
Denmark	75	78	150	87	Oceania [1]	562	478	748	538
Finland	83	47	95	45	Australia [1]	380	327	535	356
France	566	738	1,113	685	New Zealand [4]	153	115	170	150
Germany [2]	969	1,550	1,925	933	North America [1]	2,463	2,240	6,501	5,275
Greece	43	44	60	29	Canada	119	127	277	228
Hungary	15	29	58	26	Mexico	1,061	893	3,972	3,429
Iceland	10	14	27	15	Caribbean [1]	963	831	1,404	984
Ireland	81	126	325	242	Aruba	10	19	24	22
Italy	308	427	626	341	Bahamas, The	332	234	377	287
Netherlands	214	308	559	327	Barbados	34	36	57	35
Norway	80	71	144	84	British Virgin Islands	8	9	31	21
Poland	55	36	116	88	Cayman Islands	31	31	53	37
Portugal	30	40	86	46	Dominican Republic	137	138	195	124
Russia	(X)	33	74	33	Haiti	57	43	72	52
Spain	183	248	370	270	Jamaica	132	130	240	160
Sweden	230	142	321	138	Netherlands Antilles	31	32	43	38
Switzerland	236	321	400	217	Trinidad and Tobago	81	64	133	99
United Kingdom	1,899	2,342	4,671	3,443	Central America [1]	320	387	792	603
Asia [1]	3,830	5,666	7,853	4,528	Costa Rica	62	91	172	109
China [3]	187	378	656	267	El Salvador	46	63	175	171
Hong Kong	111	162	195	84	Guatemala	91	99	177	130
India	75	75	253	151	Honduras	52	37	87	71
Indonesia	28	44	62	29	Nicaragua	13	28	47	35
Israel	128	160	319	201	Panama	43	54	106	69
Japan	2,846	3,986	4,946	2,963	South America [1]	1,016	1,978	2,867	1,622
Korea	120	427	606	409	Argentina	136	320	515	159
Malaysia	27	40	64	19	Bolivia	14	16	48	22
Pakistan	27	27	47	30	Brazil	300	710	706	346
Philippines	76	85	163	142	Chile	54	117	194	98
Saudi Arabia	33	45	67	13	Colombia	122	174	411	273
Singapore	32	61	131	46	Ecuador	57	77	122	124
Thailand	25	59	76	35	Peru	97	98	190	144
Turkey	20	27	93	47	Uruguay	16	37	66	46
					Venezuela	199	400	570	377

X Not applicable.   [1] Includes other countries and countries unknown, not shown separately.   [2] Data for 1990 are for former West Germany.   [3] Includes People's Republic of China and Taiwan.   [4] Prior to fiscal year 1995, data for Niue are included in New Zealand.

Source: U.S. Dept. of Homeland Security, Office of Immigration Statistics, *2002 Yearbook of Immigration Statistics,*. See also <http://www.uscis.gov/graphics/shared/aboutus/statistics/ybpage.htm>.

U.S. Census Bureau, Statistical Abstract of the United States: 2004-2005

No. 1259. Summary of Travel Trends: 1977 to 2001

[108,826 represents 108,826,000,000. Data obtained by collecting information on all trips taken by the respondent on a specific day (known as travel day), combined with longer trips taken over a 4-week period (known as travel period). For comparability with previous survey data, all data are based only on trips taken during travel day. Be aware that terminology changes from survey to survey. See source for details. 1995 and 2001 not comparable directly with prior years due to methodology changes]

Characteristics	Unit	1977	1983	1990	1995	2001
Vehicle trips	Millions . . .	108,826	126,874	158,927	229,745	233,040
Vehicle miles of travel (VMT)	Millions . . .	907,603	1,002,139	1,409,600	2,068,368	2,274,797
Person trips	Millions . . .	211,778	224,385	249,562	378,930	407,262
Person miles of travel	Millions . . .	1,879,215	1,946,662	2,315,300	3,411,122	3,972,749
Average annual VMT per household [1]	Miles.	12,036	11,739	15,100	20,895	21,188
To or from to work	Miles.	3,815	3,538	4,853	6,492	5,724
Shopping	Miles.	1,336	1,567	1,743	2,807	3,062
Other family or personal business	Miles.	1,444	1,816	3,014	4,307	3,956
Social and recreational	Miles.	3,286	3,534	4,060	4,764	5,186
Average annual vehicle trips per household [1]	Number. . .	1,442	1,486	1,702	2,321	2,171
To or from to work	Number. . .	423	414	448	553	479
Shopping	Number. . .	268	297	345	501	458
Other family or personal business	Number. . .	215	272	411	626	537
Social and recreational	Number. . .	320	335	349	427	441
Average vehicle trip length [1]	Miles.	8.35	7.90	8.98	9.06	9.87
To or from to work	Miles.	9.02	8.55	10.97	11.80	12.08
Shopping	Miles.	4.99	5.28	5.10	5.64	6.74
Other family or personal business	Miles.	6.72	6.68	7.43	6.93	7.45
Social and recreational	Miles.	10.27	10.55	11.80	11.24	11.94
Average vehicle occupancy [1]	Persons. . .	1.9	1.8	1.6	1.6	1.6
To or from to work	Persons. . .	1.3	1.3	1.1	1.1	1.1
Shopping	Persons. . .	2.1	1.8	1.7	1.7	1.8
Other family or personal business	Persons. . .	2.0	1.8	1.8	1.8	1.8
Social and recreational	Persons. . .	2.4	2.1	2.1	2.0	2.0
Workers by usual mode to work	Percent . .	100.0	100.0	100.0	100.0	100.0
Auto	Percent . .	93.0	92.4	87.8	91.0	91.0
Public transit	Percent . .	4.7	5.8	5.3	5.1	5.0
Other	Percent . .	2.3	1.8	6.9	3.9	4.0

[1] Includes other purposes not shown separately.

Source: 1995 and prior years—U.S. Federal Highway Administration, Summary of Travel Trends, 1995 National Personal Transportation Survey, December 1999; 2001—U.S. Federal Highway Administration and the U.S. Bureau of Transportation Statistics, 2001 National Household Travel Survey, January 2004 Release. See Internet site <http://nhts.ornl.gov/2001>.

No. 1260. Travel in the United States by Selected Trip Characteristics: 2001

[In thousands (2,554,068 represents 2,554,068,000). Trips of 50 miles or more, one way. U.S. destinations only. Data based on a sample and subject to sampling variability.]

Characteristics	Person trips Number (1,000)	Person trips Per-cent	Person miles Number (1,000)	Person miles Per-cent	Personal use vehicle trips Number (1,000)	Personal use vehicle trips Per-cent	Personal use vehicle miles Number (1,000)	Personal use vehicle miles Per-cent
Total	2,554,068	100.0	1,138,322,697	100.0	1,470,475	100.0	434,764,422	100.0
Principal means of transportation:								
Personal use vehicles	2,310,376	90.5	735,882,255	64.7	1,470,475	100.0	434,764,422	100.0
Airplane	165,039	6.5	367,888,741	32.3	(X)	(X)	(X)	(X)
Commercial airplane	158,880	6.2	361,717,015	31.8	(X)	(X)	(X)	(X)
Bus [1]	52,962	2.1	23,747,433	2.1	(X)	(X)	(X)	(X)
Intercity bus	3,456	0.1	1,765,696	0.2	(X)	(X)	(X)	(X)
Charter, tour, or school bus	45,952	1.8	21,019,942	1.9	(X)	(X)	(X)	(X)
Train	20,672	0.8	9,266,373	0.8	(X)	(X)	(X)	(X)
Ship, boat, or ferry	(B)	(B)	(B)	(B)	(X)	(X)	(X)	(X)
Other	(B)	(B)	(B)	(B)	(X)	(X)	(X)	(X)
Round trip distance:								
100 to 300 miles	1,688,358	66.1	284,586,370	25.0	1,086,375	73.9	179,729,832	41.3
300 to 499 miles	373,550	14.6	143,571,597	12.6	207,377	14.1	79,094,901	18.2
500 to 999 miles	261,802	10.3	180,669,482	15.9	126,324	8.6	85,265,168	19.6
1,000 to 1,999 miles	125,665	4.9	178,629,838	15.7	36,180	2.5	48,308,222	11.1
2,000 miles or more	104,694	4.1	350,865,409	30.8	14,219	1.0	42,366,300	9.7
Mean (miles)	446	(X)	(X)	(X)	296	(X)	(X)	(X)
Median [2] (miles)	206	(X)	(X)	(X)	180	(X)	(X)	(X)
Main purpose of trip:								
Commuting	329,395	12.9	65,877,968	5.8	273,779	18.6	49,068,646	11.3
Other business	405,866	15.9	242,353,212	21.3	268,688	18.3	82,157,090	18.9
Personal/leisure	1,406,411	55.1	667,471,358	58.7	708,145	48.2	235,475,184	54.2
Personal business	322,645	12.6	130,020,982	11.4	162,832	11.1	48,761,452	11.2
Other	88,230	3.5	32,031,679	2.8	56,085	3.8	19,062,128	4.4
Mean travel party size:								
Household members	2.1	(X)	(X)	(X)	1.8	(X)	(X)	(X)
Non-Household members	1.0	(X)	(X)	(X)	-	(X)	(X)	(X)
Nights away from home:								
Household members	1,454,847	57.0	304,469,524	26.8	955,138	65.0	185,433,307	42.7
1 to 3 nights	808,281	31.7	414,219,147	36.4	406,995	27.7	153,687,767	35.4
4 to 7 nights	214,464	8.4	269,265,597	23.7	82,548	5.6	59,427,600	13.7
8 or more nights	76,475	3.0	150,368,429	13.2	25,793	1.8	36,215,748	8.3
Mean excluding none (nights)	3.3	(X)	(X)	(X)	2.9	(X)	(X)	(X)

-Represents or rounds to zero.   B Base figure too small to meet statistical standards for reliability of a derived figure.   X Not applicable.   [1] Includes other types of buses.   [2] For definition of median, see Guide to Tabular Presentation.

Source: U.S. Bureau of Transportation Statistics and the U.S. Federal Highway Administration, 2001 National Household Travel Survey.

Arts, Entertainment and Recreation   783

No. 1261. U.S.-Canadian and U.S.-Mexican Border Land-Passenger Gateways: 2002

[(32,539 represents 32,539,000)]

Item and gateway	Entering the U.S. (1,000)	Item and gateway	Entering the U.S. (1,000)
All U.S.-Canadian land gateways [1]		**All U.S.-Mexican land gateways**	
Personal vehicles	32,539	Personal vehicles	89,849
Personal vehicle passengers	70,008	Personal vehicle passengers	199,021
Buses	161	Buses	309
Bus passengers	4,213	Bus passengers	3,926
Train passengers	255	Train passengers	15
Pedestrians	1,082	Pedestrians	50,278
Personal vehicles—top 5 gateways:		**Personal vehicles—top 5 gateways:**	
Champlain-Rouses Point, NY	7,570	San Ysidro, CA	16,442
Detroit, MI	6,857	El Paso, TX	13,095
Blaine, WA	2,385	Hidalgo, TX	8,136
Port Huron, MI	2,187	Brownsville, TX	7,897
Massena, NY	1,163	Laredo, TX	6,922
Personal vehicle passengers—top 5 gateways:		**Personal vehicle passengers—top 5 gateways:**	
Buffalo-Niagara Falls, NY	17,031	San Ysidro, CA	36,172
Detroit, MI	12,319	El Paso, TX	26,363
Blaine, WA	4,794	Hidalgo, TX	17,614
Port Huron, MI	4,189	Laredo, TX	15,916
Champlain-Rouses Point, NY	3,766	Brownsville, TX	15,821
Buses—top 5 gateways:		**Buses—top 5 gateways:**	
Buffalo-Niagara Falls, NY	51	San Ysidro, CA	97
Detroit, MI	37	Otay Mesa, CA	65
Blaine, WA	16	Laredo, TX	39
Champlain-Rouses Point, NY	10	El Paso, TX	32
Sault Ste. Marie, MI	9	Hidalgo, TX	32
Bus passengers—top 5 gateways:		**Bus passengers—top 5 gateways:**	
Buffalo-Niagara Falls, NY	1,557	San Ysidro, CA	1,200
Detroit, MI	916	Laredo, TX	757
Blaine, WA	337	Hidalgo, TX	633
Champlain-Rouses Point, NY	283	Otay Mesa, CA	546
Port Huron, MI	147	El Paso, TX	351
Train passengers—top 5 gateways:		**Train passengers—top 5 gateways:**	
Blaine, WA	61	Eagle Pass, TX	7
Buffalo-Niagara Falls, NY	47	Nogales, AZ	2
Champlain-Rouses Point, NY	34	Calexico East, CA	2
Skagway, AK	30	El Paso, TX	2
Port Huron, MI	27	Tecate, CA	2
Pedestrians—top 5 gateways:		**Pedestrians—top 5 gateways:**	
Buffalo-Niagara Falls, NY	819	El Paso, TX	9,301
Sumas, WA	64	San Ysidro, CA	7,903
Portland, ME (ferry crossing)	39	Calexico, CA	6,895
Calais, ME	35	Nogales, AZ	5,912
International Falls, MN	24	Laredo, TX	4,648

[1] Data reflects all personal vehicles, buses, passengers, and pedestrians entering the U.S.-Canadian border, regardless of nationality.

Source: U.S. Department of Transportation, Bureau of Transportation Statistics, special tabulations, July 2003. Based on the following primary data source: U.S. Department of Treasury, U.S. Customs Service, Office of Field Operations, Operations Management Database (Washington, D.C. 2002) <http://www.bts.gov/publications/nationaltransportationstatistics/2003/>; (accessed: 10 June 2004).

Accommodation, Food Services, and Other Services

This section presents statistics relating to services other than those covered in the previous few sections (22 to 26) on domestic trade, transportation, communications, financial services, and recreation services. Data shown for the services are classified by kind of business and cover sales or receipts, establishments, employees, payrolls, and other items. The principal sources of these data are from the Census Bureau and include the *2002 Economic Census* reports, annual surveys, and the *County Business Patterns* program. These data are supplemented by data from several sources such as the National Restaurant Association on food and drink sales (Table 1271), the American Hotel & Motel Association on lodging (Table 1268), and Universal McCann and Publishers Information Bureau on advertising (Tables 1274 and 1275, respectively).

Data on these services also appear in several other sections. For instance, labor force employment and earnings data appear in Section 12, Labor Force; gross domestic product of the industry (Table 660) appear in Section 13, Income, Expenditures, and Wealth; and financial data (several tables) from the quarterly *Statistics of Income Bulletin,* published by the Internal Revenue Service, appear in Section 15, Business Enterprise.

Censuses—Limited coverage of the service industries started in 1933. Beginning with the 1967 census, legislation provides for a census of each area to be conducted every 5 years (for years ending in "2" and "7"). For more information on the most current census, see the *History of the 1997 Economic Census* found at <http://www.census.gov/prod/ec97/pol00-hec.pdf>. The industries covered in the censuses and surveys of business are those classified in 13 sectors defined in the *North American Industry Classification System,* called NAICS (see below). All Census Bureau tables in this section are utilizing the new NAICS codes, which replaced the Standard Industrial Classification (SIC) system. NAICS makes substantial structural improvements and identifies over 350 new industries. At the same time, it causes breaks in time series far more profound than any prior revision of the previously used SIC system. For information on this system and how it affects the comparability of statistics historically, see text, Section 15, Business Enterprise, and especially the Census Web site at <http://www.census.gov/epcd/www/naics.html>.

The *Accommodation and Food Services sector* (NAICS sector 72) comprises establishments providing customers with lodging and/or prepared meals, snacks, and beverages for immediate consumption. The *Other Services (Except Public Administration) sector* (NAICS sector 81) covers establishments with payroll engaged in providing services not specifically provided for elsewhere in the NAICS. Establishments in this sector are primarily engaged in activities such as repair and maintenance of equipment and machinery, personal and laundry services, and religious, grantmaking, civic, professional, and similar organizations. Establishments providing death care services, pet care services, photofinishing services, temporary parking services, and dating services are also included. Private households that employ workers on or about the premises in activities primarily concerned with the operation of the household are included in this sector but are not included in the scope of the census. In general, the 2002 Economic Census has two series of publications and documents for these two sectors: 1) subject series with reports on such as commodity line sales and establishment and firm sizes and 2) geographic reports with individual reports for each state. For information on these series, see the Census Web site at <http://www.census.gov/econ/census02>.

Current surveys—The Service Annual Survey provides annual estimates of nationwide receipts for selected personal, business, leasing and repair, amusement and entertainment, social and health, and other professional service industries in the United States. For selected accommodation, social, health, and other professional service industries, separate estimates are developed for receipts of taxable firms and revenue and expenses for firms and organizations exempt from federal income taxes. Several service sectors from this survey are covered in other sections of this publication. The estimates for tax exempt firms in these industries are derived from a sample of employer firms only. Estimates obtained from annual and monthly surveys are based on sample data and are not expected to agree exactly with results that would be obtained from a complete census of all establishments. Data include estimates for sampling units not reporting.

Statistical reliability—For a discussion of statistical collection and estimation, sampling procedures, and measures of statistical reliability applicable to Census Bureau data, see Appendix III.

Figure 27.1
Advertising Expenditures: 1990 to 2003

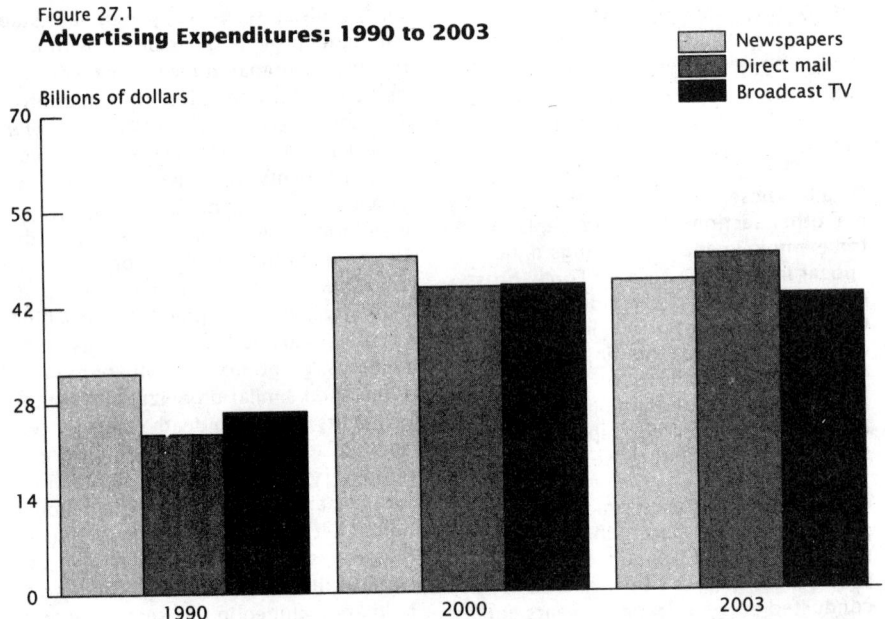

Source: Chart prepared by U.S. Census Bureau. For data, see Table 1274.

U.S. Census Bureau, Statistical Abstract of the United States: 2004-2005

Service Related Industries—Establishments, Sales, Employees, and Payroll: 2002

[917,006,982 represents $917,006,982,000 except as indicated. Covers establishments with payroll. These data are preliminary and are subject to change. For statement on methodology, see Appendix III]

Kind of business	NAICS code [1]	Estab-lishments (number)	Sales, receipts, revenue, or shipments ($1,000)	Annual payroll ($1,000)	Paid employees (number)
Professional, scientific, and technical services . .	54	778,612	917,006,982	381,437,040	7,791,084
Management of companies and enterprises	55	(S)	(S)	(S)	(S)
Administrative and support and waste management and remediation services	56	353,559	449,563,340	204,966,326	8,886,637
Administrative and support services	561	335,088	398,250,265	192,860,409	8,544,579
Waste management and remediation services . .	562	18,471	51,313,075	12,105,917	342,058
Accommodation and food services	72	562,059	463,375,143	128,683,108	10,836,365
Accommodation	721	(S)	(S)	(S)	(S)
Food services and drinking places	722	(S)	(S)	(S)	(S)
Other services (except public administration) . . .	81	539,476	319,554,700	84,434,989	3,621,780
Repair and maintenance.	811	232,075	119,308,233	35,106,918	1,325,657
Personal and laundry services.	812	200,530	74,475,393	23,060,868	1,346,636
Religious, grantmaking, civic, professional, and similar organizations.	813	106,871	125,771,074	26,267,203	949,487

S Estimates did not meet publication standards. [1] North American Industry Classification System, 2002; see text, Section 15.

Source: U.S. Census Bureau, 2002 Economic Census, Advance Summary Statistics for the United States 2002 NAICS Basis, issued March 2004 See also: <http://www.census.gov/econ/census02/advance/TABLE/.htm>.

No. 1263. **Services Related Industries—Establishments, Sales, Employees, and Payroll: 1997 and 2002**

[595,251 represents $595,251,000,000 except as indicated. Covers establishments with payroll. These data are preliminary and are subject to change. For statement on methodology, see Appendix III]

Kind of business	NAICS code [1]	1997				2002			
		Estab-lish-ments (number)	Sales, receipts, revenue, or ship-ments (mil. dol.)	Annual payroll (mil. dol.)	Paid employ-ees	Estab-lish-ments (number)	Sales, receipts, revenue, or ship-ments (mil. dol.)	Annual payroll (mil. dol.)	Paid employ-ees
Professional, scientific, and technical services	54	621,129	595,251	231,399	5,361,210	746,964	896,343	374,515	7,508,866
Professional, scientific, and technical services . . .	541	621,129	595,251	231,399	5,361,210	746,964	896,343	374,515	7,508,866
Administrative and support and waste management and remediation services. .	56	276,393	295,936	137,337	7,347,366	276,040	413,623	193,517	8,344,783
Administrative and support services.	561	260,025	256,591	128,438	7,066,658	257,569	362,310	181,411	8,002,725
Waste management and remediation services	562	16,368	39,346	8,899	280,708	18,471	51,313	12,106	342,058
Accommodation and food services	72	545,068	350,399	97,007	9,451,226	562,059	463,375	128,683	10,836,365
Accommodation	721	58,162	98,457	26,674	1,696,659	(S)	(S)	(S)	(S)
Food services and drinking places.	722	486,906	251,942	70,334	7,754,567	(S)	(S)	(S)	(S)
Other services (except public administration)	81	519,715	265,898	65,520	3,256,178	527,508	315,049	82,670	3,527,621
Repair and maintenance . .	811	235,466	105,154	29,875	1,276,389	232,949	120,365	35,459	1,366,997
Personal and laundry services.	812	185,484	57,879	18,577	1,217,185	192,333	72,893	22,591	1,311,387
Religious, grantmaking, civic, professional, and similar organizations	813	98,765	102,864	17,068	762,604	102,226	121,790	24,619	849,237

S Estimates did not meet publication standards. [1] North American Industry Classification System, 1997; see text, Section 15.

Source: U.S. Census Bureau, 2002 Economic Census, Advance Comparative Statistics for the United States, issued March 2004 See also: <http://www.census.gov/econ/census02/advance/table2.htm>.

Accommodation, Food Services, and Other Services **787**

No. 1264. Service-Related Industries—Nonemployer Establishments and Receipts by Kind of Business: 2000 to 2002

[2,420 represents 2,420,000. Includes only firms subject to federal income tax. Nonemployers are businesses with no paid employees. Based on the North American Industry Classification System, 1997 (NAICS), see text, Section 15]

Kind of business	NAICS code	Establishments (1,000)			Receipts (mil. dol.)		
		2000	2001	2002[1]	2000	2001	2002[1]
Professional, scientific & technical services . . .	54	2,420	2,446	2,553	90,272	91,292	96,395
Management, sci & tech consulting services .	5416	383	380	465	17,123	16,947	18,637
Admin/support waste mgt/remediation services .	56	1,032	1,076	1,263	23,754	24,851	26,910
Administrative & support services	561	1,017	1,061	1,244	22,858	23,940	25,826
Accommodation & food services	72	218	226	242	13,418	13,472	14,178
Accommodation	721	51	52	52	3,528	3,554	3,766
Food services & drinking places	722	167	174	190	9,890	9,917	10,412
Other services (except public administration) [2] . .	81	2,350	2,433	2,459	55,056	57,653	60,468
Repair & maintenance [2]	811	624	632	643	21,139	21,844	22,817
Automotive R&M	8111	263	265	271	11,492	11,915	12,182
Personal & household goods R&M	8114	264	271	274	6,109	6,344	6,831
Personal & laundry services	812	1,562	1,632	1,642	31,459	33,234	35,127
Personal care services	8121	598	631	666	11,631	12,643	13,582

[1] Preliminary data.   [2] Includes other kinds of business not shown separately.

Source: U.S. Census Bureau, "Nonemployer Statistics"; published May 2004; <http://www.census.gov/epcd/nonemployer/>.

No. 1265. Service-Related Industries—Establishments, Employees, and Payroll by Industry: 2000 and 2001

[7,070 represents 7,070,000. Covers establishments with payroll. Employees are for the week including March 12. Excludes most government employees, railroad employees, and self-employed persons. Kind-of-business classification based on North American Industry Classification System, 1997 (NAICS); see text, Section 15. For statement on methodology, see Appendix III]

Kind of business	NAICS code	Establishments (1,000)		Employees (1,000)[1]		Payroll (bil. dol.)	
		2000	2001	2000	2001	2000	2001
All industries, total	(X)	7,070	7,095	114,065	115,061	3,879	3,989
Professional, scientific, & technical services	54	723	736	6,816	7,157	362	374
Professional, scientific, & technical services	541	723	736	6,816	7,157	362	374
Legal services	5411	177	177	1,089	1,110	62	67
Accounting/tax prep/bookkeep/payroll services. .	5412	100	102	1,164	1,191	38	38
Architectural, engineering & related services . .	5413	102	104	1,213	1,286	65	69
Specialized design services	5414	28	29	140	148	6	6
Computer systems design & related services . . .	5415	100	101	1,171	1,255	85	85
Management, sci & tech consulting services . . .	5416	97	108	712	806	44	47
Scientific R&D services	5417	13	14	359	387	25	25
Advertising & related services.	5418	40	39	472	464	23	22
Other professional/scientific/technical services . .	5419	65	64	496	509	14	15
Management of companies & enterprises.	55	47	48	2,874	2,879	211	213
Admin/support waste mgt/remediation services . .	56	352	363	9,138	9,062	210	221
Administrative & support services [2]	561	336	346	8,847	8,761	200	210
Employment services	5613	42	45	4,573	4,364	98	101
Temporary help services.	56132	28	30	3,013	2,676	59	57
Business support services	5614	35	34	702	711	17	18
Travel arrangement & reservation services	5615	33	32	308	313	10	10
Waste management & remediation services	562	16	17	291	301	11	11
Accommodation & food services.	72	542	549	9,881	9,972	126	129
Accommodation [2].	721	60	60	1,768	1,753	35	34
Traveler accommodation	7211	50	50	1,714	1,698	34	33
RV parks & recreational camps	7212	7	7	38	39	1	1
Food services & drinking places	722	483	488	8,113	8,220	91	95
Full-service restaurants	7221	192	193	3,897	3,963	47	49
Limited-service eating places	7222	211	216	3,385	3,407	33	35
Special food services	7223	29	29	502	514	7	8
Drinking places (alcoholic beverages).	7224	51	50	329	335	3	3
Other services (except public administration). . . .	81	723	719	5,293	5,370	110	115
Repair & maintenance [2]	811	233	231	1,334	1,343	37	38
Automotive R&M	8111	164	164	856	871	21	21
Electronic & precision equipment R&M	8112	15	15	144	141	7	6
Personal and laundry services	812	199	197	1,293	1,312	23	24
Religious/grantmaking/prof/like organizations. . . .	813	291	292	2,666	2,716	50	53

X Not applicable.   [1] Includes employees on the payroll for the pay period including March 12.   [2] Includes other kinds of business not shown separately.

Source: U.S. Census Bureau, County Business Patterns, annual. See also <http://www.census.gov/epcd/cbp/view/cbpview.html>.

No. 1266. Service-Related Industries—Establishments, Employees, and Annual Payroll by State: 2001

[374,409,080 represents $374,409,080,000. Covers establishments with payroll. Employees are for the week including March 12. Excludes most government employees, railroad employees, and self-employed persons. Kind-of-business classification based on North American Industry Classification System, 1997 (NAICS); see text, Section 15. For statement on methodology, see Appendix III]

State	Professional, scientific, & technical services (NAICS 54)			Admin/support waste mgt/remediation services (NAICS 56)			Accommodation and food services (NAICS 72)		
	Establishments	Employees [1]	Annual payroll ($1,000)	Establishments	Employees [1]	Annual payroll ($1,000)	Establishments	Employees [1]	Annual payroll ($1,000)
United States..	736,454	7,156,579	374,409,080	362,665	9,061,987	221,385,956	548,569	9,972,301	128,649,922
Alabama.........	8,375	76,061	3,334,028	4,089	123,738	2,454,774	6,870	127,776	1,304,633
Alaska..........	1,651	11,404	588,333	965	11,258	365,267	1,793	21,926	402,301
Arizona..........	12,785	117,366	4,729,182	7,141	189,748	4,135,469	9,429	205,693	2,540,445
Arkansas	4,872	31,999	1,082,341	2,274	63,007	1,053,946	4,464	76,932	748,423
California	96,210	1,177,669	65,613,606	42,499	1,108,895	29,507,772	64,337	1,137,789	16,119,057
Colorado.........	18,201	149,387	8,198,312	7,579	185,708	5,237,450	10,311	206,313	2,673,618
Connecticut......	10,174	95,724	5,900,336	5,598	104,122	2,869,296	6,755	95,378	1,437,101
Delaware........	2,223	19,564	1,114,496	1,225	30,194	713,008	1,608	27,263	378,750
District of Columbia ..	4,249	80,331	6,334,238	1,094	31,489	963,847	1,692	44,054	913,132
Florida	52,752	371,157	17,142,317	28,023	1,043,426	24,169,798	28,978	613,432	8,065,587
Georgia	22,446	205,699	10,806,397	10,880	334,934	8,538,482	15,047	303,213	3,631,958
Hawaii	2,838	19,500	852,402	1,751	34,208	751,384	3,036	85,949	1,648,747
Idaho...........	3,074	29,655	1,112,024	1,718	30,140	580,241	2,888	44,741	444,164
Illinois..........	35,518	353,262	20,607,684	16,192	476,766	11,507,622	23,573	416,554	5,245,707
Indiana..........	11,462	91,045	3,421,507	6,928	146,328	3,170,650	11,577	221,665	2,349,436
Iowa	5,601	38,349	1,314,886	3,341	62,223	1,231,595	6,436	102,977	1,003,054
Kansas..........	6,492	52,362	2,152,937	3,421	65,681	1,416,480	5,551	96,466	960,196
Kentucky	7,271	56,400	1,930,604	3,702	74,841	1,398,158	6,609	137,195	1,518,009
Louisiana	10,280	79,445	3,005,486	4,351	105,432	2,135,350	7,294	164,550	1,981,242
Maine...........	3,160	22,612	900,725	1,793	27,438	620,884	3,624	44,004	606,124
Maryland........	17,030	207,526	11,103,513	7,527	165,733	4,190,891	9,099	168,647	2,225,229
Massachusetts.....	21,182	257,577	17,195,835	9,561	211,977	6,559,907	14,578	236,346	3,610,981
Michigan.........	21,522	212,598	10,174,034	12,274	298,865	7,868,602	18,793	329,888	3,647,178
Minnesota........	15,077	123,646	6,395,833	6,994	145,826	3,595,188	9,947	194,845	2,270,143
Mississippi	4,180	28,387	1,012,486	2,163	48,137	790,952	4,127	98,228	1,233,085
Missouri	12,273	121,844	5,768,099	6,817	151,422	3,367,258	10,927	210,613	2,400,977
Montana.........	2,707	16,191	500,952	1,289	12,340	211,374	3,148	39,599	398,472
Nebraska	3,719	35,738	1,471,557	2,427	51,261	1,166,660	3,918	61,095	590,672
Nevada	5,858	42,395	1,948,112	3,316	67,938	1,718,061	3,982	267,436	6,161,122
New Hampshire	3,779	26,701	1,338,803	1,948	41,320	1,079,160	3,062	47,926	656,091
New Jersey.......	30,489	282,874	16,720,205	13,535	312,917	8,089,023	16,725	253,626	4,388,690
New Mexico	4,217	30,545	1,259,843	1,837	35,462	776,046	3,641	69,852	767,717
New York	53,393	554,444	34,403,364	23,188	493,679	14,524,839	38,526	511,955	8,243,386
North Carolina.....	18,150	158,447	7,072,529	10,571	233,720	4,858,832	15,234	281,651	3,155,774
North Dakota......	1,271	9,200	279,339	787	10,912	217,052	1,723	26,361	241,049
Ohio...........	23,921	236,447	10,357,324	13,931	340,181	7,034,161	22,352	416,681	4,385,546
Oklahoma........	8,074	53,702	2,084,032	3,870	90,510	1,767,527	6,444	109,271	1,102,456
Oregon..........	9,694	69,510	3,096,272	4,653	81,322	1,813,015	8,408	126,746	1,559,433
Pennsylvania......	27,210	302,487	16,003,065	14,071	294,291	6,933,411	24,144	367,312	4,237,861
Rhode Island......	2,795	19,490	834,791	1,678	27,119	678,086	2,604	36,976	483,796
South Carolina	8,039	65,784	2,709,892	4,862	138,534	2,691,051	7,887	154,358	1,751,199
South Dakota	1,526	8,108	252,229	881	10,393	171,126	2,213	31,020	303,361
Tennessee	9,954	96,986	3,997,260	6,302	180,803	3,940,517	9,736	198,727	2,306,052
Texas	49,728	479,969	25,726,093	23,388	775,682	20,496,765	35,508	717,945	8,765,822
Utah	5,731	58,516	2,297,077	2,970	78,145	1,656,982	4,028	81,135	863,074
Vermont	1,957	11,533	463,806	910	8,246	189,987	1,865	28,533	350,726
Virginia..........	21,733	305,927	17,790,511	9,507	226,279	5,484,917	12,500	251,664	3,087,098
Washington.......	16,331	141,642	7,309,247	8,153	125,282	3,561,751	13,258	203,038	2,682,071
West Virginia......	2,893	20,679	629,289	1,428	29,927	580,063	3,231	52,958	557,600
Wisconsin........	10,848	92,118	3,863,327	6,521	117,893	2,442,282	12,958	199,482	1,969,379
Wyoming	1,539	6,577	208,520	742	6,295	108,997	1,731	24,517	282,198

[1] Includes employees on the payroll for the pay period including March 12.

Source: U.S. Census Bureau, County Business Patterns, annual. See also <http://www.census.gov/epcd/cbp/view/cbpview.html>.

No. 1267. Selected Service Industries—E-Commerce Revenue: 2001 and 2002

[36,045 represents $36,045,000,000. Includes data only for businesses with paid employees, except for accommodation and food services, which also includes businesses with and without paid employees. Except as noted, based on the Service Annual Survey]

Kind of business	NAICS code [1]	E-commerce revenue (mil. dol.) 2001	E-commerce revenue (mil. dol.) 2002	E-commerce as percent of total revenue, 2002	E-commerce revenue, percent distribution, 2002
Selected service industries, total	(X)	36,045	41,463	0.9	100
Selected transportation and warehousing [2]	48-49	2,810	3,429	1.4	8.3
Information [3]	51	10,438	11,059	1.3	26.6
Publishing industries	511	4,941	5,362	2.3	12.9
Online information services.	51419	1,850	1,823	5.7	4.4
Selected finance [4]	52	3,754	4,191	1.6	10.1
Securities and commodity contracts intermediation and brokerage	5231	3,570	4,071	2.5	9.8
Rental and leasing services	532	(S)	(S)	(S)	(S)
Selected professional, scientific, and technical services [5].	54	5,237	6,490	0.8	15.6
Computer systems design and related services	5415	3,526	4,267	2.6	10.3
Selected administrative and support and waste management and remediation services [6].	56	9,612	10,463	2.5	25.2
Health care and social assistance services	62	(S)	(S)	(S)	(S)
Arts, entertainment, and recreation services	71	(S)	(S)	(S)	(S)
Accommodation and food services [7]	72	(S)	(S)	(S)	(S)
Selected other services [8].	81	656	1,097	0.3	2.6

S Data do not meet publication standards because of high sampling variability or poor response quality. X Not applicable. [1] North American Industry Classification System, 1997; see text, Section 15. [2] Excludes NAICS 481 (air transportation), 482 (rail transportation), 483 (water transportation), 485 (transit and ground passenger transportation), 487 (scenic and sightseeing transportation), 488 (support activities for transportation) and 491 (postal service). [3] Includes other industries not listed separately. [4] Excludes NAICS 521 (monetary authorities-central bank), 522 (credit intermediation and related activities), 5232 (securities and commodity exchanges), NAICS 52391 (miscellaneous intermediation), 52399 (all other financial investment activities), 524 (insurance carriers and related activities) and 525 (funds and trusts). [5] Excludes NAICS 54112 (offices of notaries) and 54132 (landscape architectural services). [6] Excludes NAICS 56173 (landscaping services). [7] Based on Annual Retail Trade Survey. [8] Excludes NAICS 81311 (religious organizations), 81393 (labor and similar organizations), 81394 (political organizations) and 814 (private households).

Source: U.S. Census Bureau, "E-Stats"; published 15 April 2004; <http://www.census.gov/eos/www/ebusiness614.htm>.

No. 1268. Lodging Industry Summary: 1990 to 2002

Year	Average occupancy rate (percent)	Average room rate (dol.)	Room size of property	2002 Establishments	2002 Rooms (mil.)	Item	2002 Business traveler	2002 Leisure traveler
1990	63.3	57.96	Total	47,040	4.4	Typical night:		
1995	65.5	66.65				Made reservations (percent)	91	83
1996	65.2	70.93	Percent:			Amount paid	$93.00	$85.00
1997	64.5	75.31	Under 75 rooms. . .	57.1	25.6	Length of stay (percent):.		
1998	64.0	78.62	75-149 rooms	30.1	34.4	One night	42	46
1999	63.2	81.33	150-299 rooms . . .	9.4	20.1	Two nights	25	27
2000	63.7	85.89	300-500 rooms . . .	2.3	9.3	Three or more	33	27
2001	60.3	88.27	Over 500 rooms. . .	1.1	10.6			
2002	59.1	83.54						

Source: American Hotel & Motel Association, Washington, DC, Lodging Industry Profile (copyright).

No. 1269. National Nonprofit Associations—Number by Type: 1980 to 2003

[Data compiled during last few months of year previous to year shown and the beginning months of year shown]

Type	1980	1985	1990	1995	1997	1998	1999	2000	2001	2002	2003
Total	14,726	19,121	22,289	22,663	22,901	22,049	22,474	21,840	22,449	22,141	22,464
Trade, business, commercial .	3,118	3,719	3,918	3,757	3,755	3,714	3,815	3,880	3,922	3,883	3,818
Agriculture and environment. .	677	882	940	1,122	1,124	1,107	1,113	1,103	1,120	1,125	1,137
Legal, governmental, public admin., military	529	658	792	776	780	755	778	790	807	814	832
Scientific, engineering, tech . .	1,039	1,270	1,417	1,355	1,381	1,306	1,332	1,302	1,317	1,309	1,326
Educational.	[1]2,376	[1]2,822	1,291	1,290	1,310	1,274	1,321	1,297	1,346	1,307	1,301
Cultural	(¹)	(¹)	1,886	1,918	1,918	1,841	1,876	1,786	1,812	1,766	1,749
Social welfare	994	1,450	1,705	1,885	1,934	1,896	1,913	1,829	1,925	1,917	1,941
Health, medical	1,413	1,886	2,227	2,348	2,453	2,383	2,481	2,495	2,574	2,601	2,808
Public affairs	1,068	1,935	2,249	2,148	2,113	1,855	1,877	1,776	1,857	1,808	1,836
Fraternal, nationality, ethnic . .	435	492	573	552	541	542	552	525	537	529	557
Religious	208	281	462	686	745	861	877	835	834	785	802
Veteran, hereditary, patriotic. .	910	1,311	1,475	1,549	1,548	1,468	1,463	1,330	1,408	1,380	1,435
Hobby, avocational	504	737	840	838	836	765	782	717	762	730	760
Athletic sports	235	252	253	245	245	235	235	232	233	218	211
Labor unions	235	252	168	168	162	129	146	143	142	141	139
Chambers of Commerce [2] . . .	105	142									
Greek and non-Greek letter societies	318	331	340	336	335	313	313	296	312	301	309
Fan clubs	(NA)	(NA)	581	460	491	449	449	381	373	348	

NA Not available. [1] Data for cultural associations included with educational associations. [2] National and binational. Includes trade and tourism organizations.

Source: Gale Group, Farmington Hills, MI. Compiled from Encyclopedia of Associations, annual (copyright).

No. 1270. Accommodation and Food Services—Establishments, Employees, and Payroll by Kind of Business: 2000 and 2001

[9,881 represents 9,881,000. Covers establishments with payroll. Employees are for the week including March 12. Excludes most government employees, railroad employees, and self-employed persons. Kind-of-business classification based on North American Industry Classification System, 1997 (NAICS); see text, Section 15. For statement on methodology, see Appendix III]

Kind of business	NAICS code	Establishments (number) 2000	Establishments (number) 2001	Employees (1,000) 2000	Employees (1,000) 2001	Payroll (mil. dol.) 2000	Payroll (mil. dol.) 2001
Accommodation & food services, total	72	542,411	548,569	9,881	9,972	125,582	128,650
Accommodation	721	59,851	60,196	1,768	1,753	34,708	34,096
Traveler accommodation	7211	49,736	50,206	1,714	1,698	33,661	32,986
Hotels (exc casino hotels) & motels....	72111	45,554	45,972	1,379	1,377	25,181	24,807
Casino hotels	72112	288	304	312	297	8,143	7,837
Other traveler accommodation	72119	3,894	3,930	24	24	337	342
Bed & breakfast inns	721191	2,999	3,042	19	20	254	265
All other traveler accommodation....	721199	895	888	5	5	83	77
RV parks & recreational camps	7212	6,975	7,000	38	39	843	901
RV parks & campgrounds	721211	3,691	3,750	18	18	334	351
Recreational/vacation camps (exc campgrounds)	721214	3,284	3,250	20	21	509	550
Rooming & boarding houses	7213	3,140	2,990	16	16	204	209
Food services & drinking places	722	482,560	488,373	8,113	8,220	90,874	94,554
Full-service restaurants	7221	192,342	193,262	3,897	3,963	46,707	48,702
Limited-service eating places	7222	210,895	215,793	3,385	3,407	33,454	34,789
Limited-service restaurants	722211	170,565	173,753	2,968	2,997	28,852	30,134
Cafeterias	722212	4,199	4,464	70	70	875	890
Snack & nonalcoholic beverage bars..	722213	36,131	37,576	348	341	3,728	3,765
Special food services	7223	28,745	29,345	502	514	7,367	7,576
Food service contractors	722231	16,894	17,330	377	385	5,632	5,771
Caterers	722232	8,714	9,058	109	113	1,470	1,543
Mobile food services	722233	3,137	2,957	16	16	265	262
Drinking places (alcoholic beverages)....	7224	50,578	49,973	329	335	3,345	3,486

Source: U.S. Census Bureau, County Business Patterns, annual. See also <http://www.census.gov/epcd/cbp/view/cbpview.html>.

No. 1271. Commercial and Noncommercial Groups—Food and Drink Establishments and Sales: 1990 to 2004

[238,149 represents $238,149,000,000. Excludes military. Data refer to sales to consumers of food and alcoholic beverages. Sales are estimated. For details, see source]

Type of group	Establishments, 2000	Sales (mil. dol.) 1990	1995	2000	2001	2002	2003	2004[1]
Total	868,581	238,149	294,631	377,652	392,175	406,334	419,876	438,405
Commercial restaurant services [2][3]	685,932	211,606	265,910	345,345	358,990	373,632	385,442	403,178
Eating places [2]	444,830	155,552	198,293	259,743	271,797	283,594	293,263	306,262
Full-service restaurants	205,838	77,811	96,396	133,834	139,990	146,149	150,976	157,921
Limited-service restaurants [4]	183,223	[5]69,798	[5]92,901	107,147	111,648	116,113	119,253	123,904
Snack and nonalcoholic beverage bars	45,179	(5)	(5)	12,867	14,227	15,350	17,196	18,589
Bars and taverns [6]	51,303	9,533	9,948	12,412	12,673	13,270	13,418	13,848
Managed services [2]	19,430	14,149	18,186	24,841	25,832	26,841	27,584	29,304
Manufacturing and industrial plants .	(NA)	3,856	4,814	6,223	6,236	6,185	6,142	6,440
Colleges and universities	(NA)	2,788	3,989	5,879	6,343	6,762	7,324	7,836
Lodging places	13,276	13,568	15,561	19,438	18,432	18,458	18,771	19,875
Retail hosts [2][7]	133,526	9,513	12,589	14,869	15,624	16,443	16,971	17,781
Department store restaurants	4,111	876	1,038	903	910	(NA)	(NA)	(NA)
Grocery store restaurants [7]	60,541	5,432	6,624	7,116	7,440	(NA)	(NA)	(NA)
Gasoline service stations	52,441	1,718	2,520	4,693	4,969	(NA)	(NA)	(NA)
Recreation and sports	15,485	2,871	3,866	4,772	4,995	5,105	5,349	5,615
Noncommercial restaurant services [2]	182,649	26,543	28,722	32,307	33,185	32,702	34,434	35,227
Employee restaurant services	4,049	1,864	1,364	986	902	826	708	676
Industrial, commercial organizations	1,812	1,603	1,129	717	628	(NA)	(NA)	(NA)
Educational restaurant services	102,087	7,671	9,059	9,977	10,094	9,990	(NA)	(NA)
Elementary and secondary schools .	97,925	3,700	4,533	5,039	5,080	4,974	5,075	5,024
Hospitals	5,791	8,968	9,219	9,982	10,484	10,006	11,181	11,494
Miscellaneous [3]	33,966	2,892	3,673	4,898	5,008	5,096	(NA)	(NA)
Clubs	10,514	1,993	2,278	3,164	3,196	3,196	(NA)	(NA)

NA Not available. [1] Projection. [2] Includes other types of groups, not shown separately. [3] Data for establishments with payroll. [4] Fast-food restaurants. [5] Snack and nonalcoholic beverage bars included in limited service restaurants. [6] For establishments serving food. [7] Includes a portion of delicatessen sales in grocery stores.

Source: National Restaurant Association, Washington, DC, Restaurant Numbers: 25 Year History, 1970-1995, 1998; Restaurant Industry in Review, annual; and National Restaurant Association Restaurant Industry Forecast, December 2003 (copyright).

Accommodation, Food Services, and Other Services   791

[In millions of dollars. (813,217 represents $813,217,000,000). Estimates are based on data from the 2002 Service Annual Survey and administrative data. Estimates for 2001 are revised to reflect the latest administrative data for nonemployers. Except where indicated, estimates have been adjusted using the results of the 1997 Economic Census]

Kind of business	NAICS code	Employer and nonemployer firms				Taxable employer firms			
		1999	2000	2001	2002	1999	2000	2001	2002
Professional, scientific, and technical services (except notaries and landscape architectural services)	54	813,217	894,781	932,172	940,970	710,314	786,451	822,472	826,867
Legal services (except notaries)	5411	157,916	164,573	175,621	184,305	144,912	151,082	161,340	169,257
Offices of lawyers	54111	151,847	158,603	168,964	177,107	139,330	145,617	155,263	162,742
Other legal services [1]	54119	6,069	5,970	6,656	7,198	5,581	5,465	6,077	6,515
Accounting, tax preparation, bookkeeping, and payroll services	5412	72,263	79,398	84,158	84,890	66,783	73,561	77,960	78,424
Architectural, engineering, & related services (except landscape architectural services)	5413	148,240	166,709	174,823	176,142	141,191	159,105	166,993	168,343
Specialized design services	5414	20,786	23,120	23,018	21,953	16,478	18,276	18,133	17,311
Computer systems design and services	5415	163,554	185,501	184,162	172,138	154,286	175,338	174,367	162,175
Management, scientific, and technical consulting services	5416	96,530	105,663	115,026	121,511	79,973	88,540	98,079	104,022
Scientific research and development services	5417	45,739	51,428	57,473	63,006	28,743	33,221	38,796	42,917
Advertising and related services	5418	65,605	73,593	71,884	69,553	60,436	68,267	66,753	64,535
Advertising agencies	54181	22,419	26,350	25,937	25,740	21,253	25,149	24,780	24,589
Public relations agencies	54182	7,026	8,693	8,248	8,283	6,061	7,699	7,290	7,348
Display advertising	54185	6,244	6,701	6,363	6,523	5,960	6,409	6,081	6,226
Direct mail advertising	54186	9,929	10,359	10,708	10,531	9,415	9,830	10,198	10,013
All other advertising	5418x	19,987	21,489	20,629	18,475	17,747	19,181	18,405	16,360
Other professional, scientific, and technical services (except veterinary services)	5419	42,584	45,246	46,046	47,472	17,512	19,026	20,052	19,884
Marketing research and public opinion polling	54191	9,572	10,177	9,947	9,526	8,936	9,478	9,257	8,834
Photographic services	54192	7,901	8,238	8,286	7,984	5,783	6,000	6,125	5,883

[1] Estimates for NAICS 541191 (title abstract and settlement offices), not shown separately, have not been adjusted using the results of the 1997 Economic Census.

Source: U.S. Census Bureau, "Service Annual Survey 2002"; published February 2004; <http://www.census.gov/prod/2004pubs/sas-02.pdf>.

[In millions of dollars (162,175 represents $162,175,000,000). See headnote Table 1272]

Kind of business	Amount	Kind of business	Amount
Computer systems design and related services (NAICS 5415) total	162,175	Information technology infrastructure (computer) and network management services	3,509
Information tech. design and development total	70,505	Information technology technical support services	4,539
Custom application design and development.	30,166	Information technology consulting services	6,786
Computer systems disign, development, and integration services.	32,996	Software publishing	3,250
Network design and development services	7,343	Other services revenue	2,974
Information technology infrastructure (computer) and network management services	20,926	**Computer systems design services (NAICS 541512) total**	77,166
Information technology technical support services	16,990	Information technology design and development, total	36,669
Information technology consulting services	14,316	Custom application design and development.	8,329
Software publishing	7,300	Computer systems design, development, and integration services.	22,590
Data storage services	1,293	Network design and development services	5,751
Data management services	3,080	Information technology infrastructure (computer) and network management services	5,229
Information technology related training services	2,552	Information technology technical support services	9,283
Internet access services	705	Information technology consulting services	4,731
Application service provisioning	3,197	Software publishing	3,134
Re-sale of computer hardware and software	7,993	Data storage services	690
Other services revenue	9,537	Data management services	1,890
Custom computer programming services (NAICS 541511) total revenue	58,406	Information technology related training services	958
Information technology design and development, total	30,315	Internet access services	528
Custom application design and development.	20,763	Web site hosting services	601
Computer systems design, development, and integration services.	8,489	Application service provisioning	2,337
Network design and development services	1,153	Re-sale of computer hardware and software	4,879
		Other services revenue	5,589

Source: U.S. Census Bureau, "Service Annual Survey 2002"; published January 2004; <http://www.census.gov/prod/2004pubs/sas-02.pdf>.

No. 1274. Advertising—Estimated Expenditures by Medium: 1990 to 2003

[In millions of dollars (129,968 represents $129,968,000,000). See source for definitions of types of advertising]

Medium	1990	1995	1997	1998	1999	2000	2001	2002	2003 [1]
Total	129,968	165,147	191,307	206,697	222,308	247,472	231,287	236,875	249,156
National	73,638	96,933	112,809	122,271	132,170	151,664	141,797	145,429	154,882
Local	56,330	68,214	78,498	84,426	90,138	95,808	89,490	91,446	94,274
Newspapers	32,281	36,317	41,670	44,292	46,648	49,050	44,255	44,031	45,438
National	3,867	3,996	5,016	5,402	6,358	7,229	6,615	6,806	7,282
Local	28,414	32,321	36,654	38,890	40,290	41,821	37,640	37,225	38,156
Magazines	6,803	8,580	9,821	10,518	11,433	12,370	11,095	10,995	11,765
Broadcast TV	26,616	32,720	36,893	39,173	40,011	44,802	38,881	42,068	43,247
Four TV networks	9,863	11,600	13,020	13,736	13,961	15,888	14,300	15,000	15,525
Syndication	1,109	2,016	2,438	2,609	2,870	3,108	3,102	3,034	3,489
Spot (National)	7,788	9,119	9,999	10,659	10,500	12,264	9,223	10,920	10,647
Spot (Local)	7,856	9,985	11,436	12,169	12,680	13,542	12,256	13,114	13,586
Cable TV	2,631	6,166	8,750	10,340	12,570	15,455	15,536	16,297	18,983
Cable TV networks	2,000	4,500	6,450	7,640	9,405	11,765	11,883	12,071	14,123
Spot (Local)	631	1,666	2,300	2,700	3,165	3,690	3,653	4,226	4,860
Radio	8,726	11,338	13,491	15,073	17,215	19,295	17,861	18,877	19,493
Network	482	480	560	622	684	780	711	775	822
Spot (National)	1,635	1,959	2,455	2,823	3,275	3,668	2,956	3,340	3,540
Spot (Local)	6,609	8,899	10,476	11,628	13,256	14,847	14,194	14,762	15,131
Yellow Pages	8,926	10,236	11,423	11,990	12,652	13,228	13,592	13,776	13,914
National	1,132	1,410	1,711	1,870	1,986	2,093	2,087	2,087	2,108
Local	7,794	8,826	9,712	10,120	10,666	11,135	11,505	11,689	11,806
Direct mail	23,370	32,866	36,890	39,620	41,403	44,591	44,725	46,067	49,061
Business papers	2,875	3,559	4,109	4,232	4,274	4,915	4,468	3,976	3,857
Out of home [2]	1,084	1,263	1,455	1,576	1,725	5,176	5,134	5,175	5,304
National	640	701	795	845	925	2,068	2,051	2,061	2,112
Local	444	562	660	731	800	3,108	3,083	3,114	3,192
Internet	(NA)	(NA)	800	1,383	2,832	6,507	5,752	4,883	5,615
Miscellaneous [3]	16,656	22,102	26,005	28,500	31,545	32,083	29,988	30,730	32,479
National	12,074	16,147	18,745	20,312	22,264	24,418	22,829	23,414	24,936
Local	4,582	5,955	7,260	8,188	9,281	7,665	7,159	7,316	7,543

NA Not available. [1] Preliminary data. [2] Prior to 2000, represents only "outdoor" billboards. Beginning 2000 includes other forms of outdoor advertising (i.e. transportation vehicles, bus shelters, telephone kiosks, etc.) previously covered under "Miscellaneous." [3] Beginning 2000, part of miscellaneous now included under "Out of home" advertising. See footnote 2.

Source: Universal McCann, New York, NY (copyright). See also <http://www.universalmccann.com>.

No. 1275. Magazine Advertising Revenue by Category: 2000 to 2003

[17,052 represents $17,052,000,000. Represents the volume of advertising in the consumer magazines belonging to the Publishers Information Bureau]

Category	Pages			Volume (mil. dol.)		
	2000	2002	2003	2000	2002	2003
Total [1]	269,016	228,224	226,049	17,052	16,182	18,318
Automotive	22,295	20,469	22,403	1,730	1,819	2,088
Automotive accessories and equipment	22,012	20,242	22,023	1,711	1,799	2,049
Technology [1]	26,536	13,994	13,684	1,736	1,100	1,134
Telecommunications	4,812	2,375	2,699	311	197	243
Computers and software	17,156	7,942	7,786	1,205	705	729
Home furnishings and supplies [1]	16,611	15,984	16,978	1,197	1,427	1,554
Household furnishings and accessories	4,597	3,801	3,838	272	289	313
Audio and video equipment and supplies	4,507	4,426	4,567	284	353	397
Toiletries and cosmetics [1]	15,741	16,776	17,492	1,218	1,544	1,699
Cosmetics and beauty aids [2]	8,781	9,060	9,448	640	820	893
Personal hygiene and health [2]	2,818	2,779	3,078	271	296	338
Hair products and accessories [2]	2,837	3,433	3,513	217	304	329
Direct response companies	19,554	18,802	17,443	1,034	61	1,112
Apparel and accessories [1]	26,575	22,700	22,434	1,295	1,411	1,513
Ready-to-wear	13,648	10,165	10,302	586	615	674
Footwear	4,058	3,964	3,912	218	211	232
Jewelry and watches	5,021	4,584	4,453	282	302	319
Financial, insurance and real estate	16,976	11,877	10,547	1,154	970	896
Financial	13,453	8,583	7,678	894	694	671
Insurance and real estate [1]	3,524	3,293	2,868	260	276	226
Food and food products	10,693	10,988	10,574	1,140	1,337	1,391
Prepared foods	1,961	2,110	2,038	212	268	270
Dairy, produce, meat and bakery goods	2,858	3,206	3,470	315	398	465
Beverages	1,981	1,768	1,716	197	194	209
Drugs and remedies	12,470	13,899	15,407	1,121	1,418	1,663
Medicines and proprietary remedies	10,506	11,924	13,500	965	1,234	1,476
Media and advertising	15,328	11,872	11,713	1,145	1,080	1,146
Retail stores	19,263	14,166	14,208	1,056	949	986
Retail stores [3]	15,869	10,984	10,515	863	737	753
Public transportation, hotels, and resorts	15,421	14,212	12,797	743	736	714
Cigarettes, tobacco and accessories	4,677	2,025	2,400	388	216	269
Beer, wine and liquor	5,016	4,828	4,342	360	414	394
Liquor	3,874	3,495	2,889	286	308	271
Miscellaneous services and amusements	5,803	4,954	4,198	310	301	254
Sporting goods	13,752	12,849	11,209	263	268	253

[1] Includes other categories, not shown separately. [2] Women's, men's, and unisex. [3] Includes apparel, business, drugs and toiletries, and food and beverage.

Source: Publishers Information Bureau, Inc., New York, NY, as compiled by Competitive Media Reporting.

No. 1276. Administrative and Support and Waste Management and Remediation Services—Estimated Revenue: 2000 to 2002

[In millions of dollars (408,315 represents $408,315,000,000), except percent. For taxable and tax-exempt employer firms. Except as indicated, estimates adjusted to the results of the 1997 Economic Census. Based on the Service Annual Survey; see Appendix III]

Kind of business	NAICS code [1]	2000	2001	2002	Percent change, 2001-2002
Admin/support waste mgt/remediation services	56	408,315	409,984	421,107	2.7
Administrative & support services	561	362,246	363,764	375,343	3.2
Office administrative services	56111	48,732	54,729	59,263	8.3
Facilities support services	56121	9,271	9,037	9,093	0.6
Employment services [2]	5613	125,181	113,724	114,728	0.9
Temporary help services	56132	74,054	63,857	63,421	-0.7
Employee leasing services	56133	42,855	40,981	41,449	1.1
Business support services [2]	5614	47,412	50,856	51,478	1.2
Telephone call centers	56142	16,115	16,647	14,818	-11.0
Business service centers	56143	10,173	10,257	10,099	-1.5
Travel arrangement & reservation services [2]	5615	26,611	26,487	26,545	0.2
Travel agencies	56151	10,940	9,607	8,824	-8.1
Other travel arrangement & reservation services	56159	12,616	14,029	14,994	6.9
Investigation and security services	5616	25,869	27,062	29,654	9.6
Investigation, guard, & armored car services	56161	14,895	14,869	16,517	11.1
Security systems services	56162	10,975	12,193	8,962	7.7
Services to buildings & dwellings	5617	41,065	43,744	45,809	4.7
Janitorial services	56172	30,097	32,089	33,054	3.0
Other support services	5619	38,107	38,125	38,774	1.7
Waste management & remediation services	562	46,068	46,220	45,765	-1.0
Waste collection	5621	25,498	25,313	24,863	-1.8
Waste treatment & disposal [3]	5622	10,261	10,380	9,830	-5.3
Remediation & other waste management services	5629	10,310	10,527	11,072	5.2

[1] North American Industry Classification System, 1997; see text, Section 15.   [2] Includes other kinds of business not shown separately.   [3] Estimates have not been adjusted to the results of the 1997 Economic Census.

No. 1277. Other Services—Estimated Revenue for Employer and Nonemployer Firms: 2000 to 2002

[In millions of dollars (374,249 represents $374,249,000,000), except percent. Except where indicated, results have been adjusted to the results of the 1997 Economic Census. Based on the Service Annual Survey. See text, this section and Appendix III.]

Kind of business	NAICS code [1]	2000	2001	2002	Percent change, 2001-2002
Other services (except public administration, religious, labor, and political organizations, and private households)	81	374,249	380,208	381,850	0.4
Repair & maintenance	811	146,151	152,326	153,307	0.6
Automotive R&M	8111	85,775	89,667	88,612	-1.2
Electronic and precision equipment R&M [2]	8112	18,776	19,141	19,110	-0.2
Commercial equipment (exc auto elec) R&M	8113	22,898	24,411	26,478	8.5
Personal and household goods R&M	8114	18,703	19,107	19,109	2.0
Personal & laundry services	812	99,631	103,426	107,162	3.6
Personal care services	8121	28,782	30,481	32,589	6.9
Hair, nail, & skin care services	81211	24,568	25,654	27,056	5.5
Other personal care services	81219	4,213	4,827	5,534	14.6
Death care services	8122	13,918	14,475	14,434	-0.3
Drycleaning & laundry services	8123	22,629	23,239	23,233	(Z)
Coin-operated laundries & drycleaners	81231	4,303	4,453	4,456	0.1
Drycleaning and laundry services, (exc coin-op)	81232	9,043	9,019	8,992	-0.3
Linen & uniform supply	81233	9,282	9,768	9,786	0.2
Other personal services	8129	34,302	35,230	36,905	4.8
Photofinishing	81292	5,873	5,767	5,958	3.3
Parking lots & garages	81293	7,658	8,126	8,274	1.8
All other personal services	81299	20,772	21,337	22,673	6.3
Religious/grantmaking/prof/like organizations (except religious, labor, and political organizations)	813	128,467	124,457	121,381	-2.5
Grantmaking and giving services [3]	8132	63,057	55,978	51,006	-8.9
Social advocacy organizations	8133	10,438	10,871	11,668	7.3
Civic & social organizations	8134	12,175	12,526	13,043	4.1
Business, professional, and other organizations (except labor and political organizations)	8139	42,798	45,083	45,664	1.3

[1] North American Industry Classification System, 1997; see text, Section 15.   [2] Estimates for NAICS 811219 (other electronics and precision equipment repair and maintenance) have not been adjusted to the results of the 1997 Economic Census.   [3] Estimates for NAICS 813211 (grantmaking foundations) have not been adjusted to the results of the 1997 Economic Census.

Source of Tables 1276 and 1277: U.S. Census Bureau, "Service Annual Survey 2002"; published February 2004. See also <http://www.census.gov/prod/2004pubs/sas-02.pdf>

Section 28
Foreign Commerce and Aid

This section presents data on the flow of goods, services, and capital between the United States and other countries; changes in official reserve assets of the United States; international investments; and foreign assistance programs.

The Bureau of Economic Analysis publishes current figures on U.S. international transactions and the U.S. international investment position in its monthly *Survey of Current Business*. Statistics for the foreign aid programs are presented by the Agency for International Development (AID) in its annual *U.S. Overseas Loans and Grants and Assistance from International Organizations* and by the Department of Agriculture in its *Foreign Agricultural Trade of the United States*.

The principal source of merchandise import and export data is the U.S. Census Bureau. Current data are presented monthly in *U.S. International Trade in Goods and Services* report Series FT 900. The *Guide to Foreign Trade Statistics*, found on the Census Bureau Web site at <http://www.census.gov/foreign-trade /guide/index.html>, lists the Bureau's monthly and annual products and services in this field. In addition, the International Trade Administration and the Bureau of Economic Analysis present summary as well as selected commodity and country data for U.S. foreign trade in the *U.S. Foreign Trade Highlights* and the *Survey of Current Business*, respectively. The merchandise trade data in the latter source include balance of payments adjustments to the Census Bureau data. The Treasury Department's *Monthly Treasury Statement of Receipts and Outlays of the United States Government* contains information on import duties. The International Trade Commission, U.S. Department of Agriculture, U.S. Department of Energy, and the U.S. Geological Survey release various reports and specialized products on U.S. trade.

International accounts—The international transactions tables (Nos. 1279 and 1280) show, for given time periods, the transfer of goods, services, grants, and financial assets and liabilities between the United States and the rest of the world. The international investment position table (No. 1281) presents, for specific dates, the value of U.S. investments abroad and of foreign investments in the United States. The movement of foreign and U.S. capital as presented in the balance of payments is not the only factor affecting the total value of foreign investments. Among the other factors are changes in the valuation of assets or liabilities, including changes in prices of securities, defaults, expropriations, and write-offs.

Direct investment abroad means the ownership or control, directly or indirectly, by one person of 10 percent or more of the voting securities of an incorporated business enterprise or an equivalent interest in an unincorporated business enterprise. Direct investment position is the value of U.S. parents' claims on the equity of and receivables due from foreign affiliates, less foreign affiliates receivables due from their U.S. parent's. Income consists of parents' shares in the earnings of their affiliates' plus net interest received by parents on intercompany accounts, less withholding taxes on dividends and interest.

Foreign aid—Foreign assistance is divided into three major categories— grants (military supplies and services and other grants), credits, and other assistance (through net accumulation of foreign currency claims from the sale of agricultural commodities). *Grants* are transfers for which no payment is expected (other than a limited percentage of the foreign currency "counterpart" funds generated by the grant), or which at most involve an obligation on the part of the receiver to extend aid to the United States or other countries to achieve a common objective. *Credits* are loan disbursements or transfers under other agreements which give rise to specific obligations to repay, over a period of years, usually with interest. All known returns to the U.S. government stemming from grants and credits (reverse grants, returns of grants, and payments of principal) are taken into account in net grants and net credits, but no allowance is made for interest or commissions. *Other assistance* represents the transfer of U.S. farm products in exchange for foreign currencies (plus, since enactment of Public Law 87-128, currency claims from principal and interest collected on credits extended under the farm products program), less the government's disbursements of the currencies as grants, credits, or for purchases. The net acquisition of currencies represents net transfers of resources to foreign countries under the agricultural programs, in addition to those classified as grants or credits.

The basic instrument for extending military aid to friendly nations has been the Mutual Defense Assistance Program authorized by the Congress in 1949. Prior to 1952, economic and technical aid was authorized in the Foreign Assistance Act of 1948, the 1950 Act for International Development, and other legislation which set up programs for specific countries. In 1952, these economic, technical, and military aid programs were combined under the Mutual Security Act, which in turn was followed by the Foreign Assistance Act passed in 1961. Appropriations to provide military assistance were also made in the Department of Defense Appropriation Act (rather than the Foreign Assistance Appropriation Act) beginning in 1966 for certain countries in Southeast Asia and in other legislation concerning program for specific countries (such as Israel). Figures on activity under the Foreign Assistance Act as reported in the *Foreign Grants and Credits* series differ from data published by AID or its immediate predecessors, due largely to differences in reporting, timing, and treatment of particular items.

Exports—The Census Bureau compiles export data primarily from Shipper's Export Declarations required to be filed with customs officials for shipments leaving the United States. They include U.S.

exports under mutual security programs and exclude shipments to U.S. Armed Forces for their own use.

The value reported in the export statistics is generally equivalent to a free alongside ship (f.a.s.) value at the U.S. port of export, based on the transaction price, including inland freight, insurance, and other charges incurred in placing the merchandise alongside the carrier at the U.S. port of exportation. This value, as defined, excludes the cost of loading merchandise aboard the exporting carrier and also excludes freight, insurance, and any other charges or transportation and other costs beyond the U.S. port of exportation. The country of destination is defined as the country of ultimate destination or country where the merchandise is to be consumed, further processed, or manufactured, as known to the shipper at the time of exportation. When ultimate destination is not known, the shipment is statistically credited to the last country to which the shipper knows the merchandise will be shipped in the same form as exported.

Effective January 1990, the United States began substituting Canadian import statistics for U.S. exports to Canada. As a result of the data exchange between the United States and Canada, the United States has adopted the Canadian import exemption level for its export statistics based on shipments to Canada.

Data are estimated for shipments valued under $2,501 to all countries, except Canada, using factors based on the ratios of low-valued shipments to individual country totals.

Prior to 1989, exports were based on Schedule B, Statistical Classification of Domestic and Foreign Commodities Exported from the United States. These statistics were retabulated and published using Schedule E, Standard International Trade Classification, Revision 2. Beginning in 1989, Schedule B classifications were based on the Harmonized System and made to coincide with the Standard International Trade Classification, Revision 3. This revision will affect the comparability of most export series beginning with the 1989 data for commodities.

Imports—The Census Bureau compiles import data from various customs forms required to be filed with customs officials. Data on import values are presented on two valuations bases in this section: The c.i.f. (cost, insurance, and freight) and the customs import value (as appraised by the U.S. Customs Service in accordance with legal requirements of the Tariff Act of 1930, as amended). This latter valuation, primarily used for collection of import duties, frequently does not reflect the actual transaction value. Country of origin is defined as country where the merchandise was grown, mined, or manufactured. If country of origin is unknown, country of shipment is reported.

Imports are classified either as "General imports" or "Imports for consumption." *General imports* are a combination of entries for immediate consumption, entries into customs bonded warehouses, and entries into U.S. Foreign Trade Zones, thus generally reflecting total arrivals of merchandise. *Imports for consumption* are a combination of entries for immediate consumption, withdrawals from warehouses for consumption, and entries of merchandise into U.S. customs territory from U.S. Foreign Trade Zones, thus generally reflecting the total of the commodities entered into U.S. consumption channels.

Prior to 1989, imports were based on the Tariff Schedule of the United States Annotated. The statistics were retabulated and published using Schedule A, Standard International Trade Classification, Revision 2. Beginning in 1989, the statistics are based on the Harmonized Tariff Schedule of the United States, which coincides with the Standard International Trade Classification, Revision 3. This revision will affect the comparability of most import series beginning with the 1989 data.

Area coverage—Except as noted, the geographic area covered by the export and import trade statistics is the United States Customs area (includes the 50 states, the District of Columbia, and Puerto Rico), the U.S. Virgin Islands (effective January 1981), and U.S. Foreign Trade Zones (effective July 1982). Data for selected tables and total values for 1980 have been revised to reflect the U.S. Virgin Islands' trade with foreign countries, where possible.

Statistical reliability—For a discussion of statistical collection and estimation, sampling procedures, and measures of statistical reliability applicable to Census Bureau data, see Appendix III.

U.S. Census Bureau, Statistical Abstract of the United States: 2004-2005

Figure 28.1
U.S. International Transaction Balances: 1990 to 2003

Source: Chart prepared by U.S. Census Bureau. For data, see Table 1280.

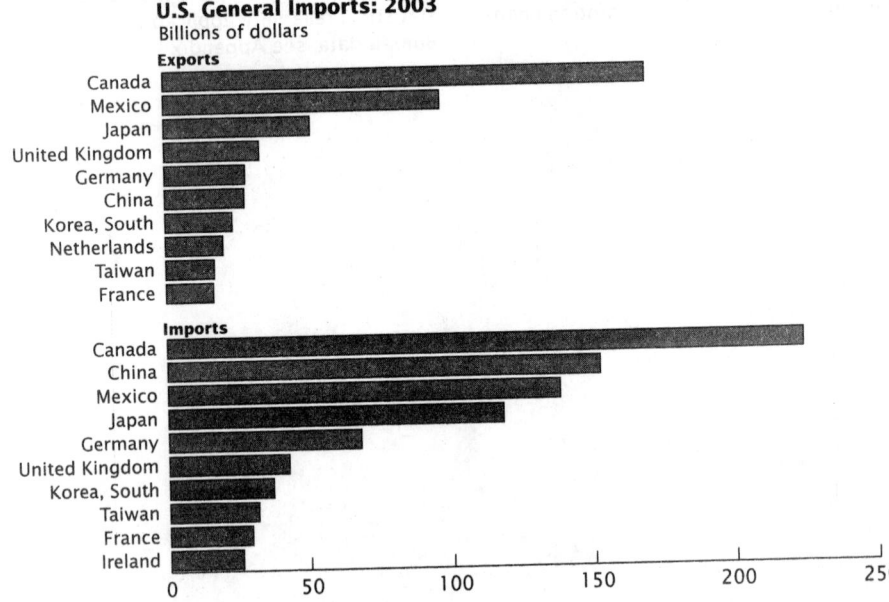

Figure 28.2
Top Purchasers of U.S. Exports and Suppliers of U.S. General Imports: 2003

Source: Chart prepared by U.S. Census Bureau. For data, see Table 1298.

U.S. Census Bureau, Statistical Abstract of the United States: 2004-2005

No. 1278. U.S. International Transactions by Type of Transaction: 1990 to 2003

[In millions of dollars ($706,975,000,000). Minus sign (-) indicates debits. N.i.e.=Not included elsewhere]

Type of transaction	1990	1994	1995	1996	1997	1998	1999	2000	2001	2002	2003
Exports of goods and services and income receipts	**706,975**	**869,775**	**1,004,631**	**1,077,731**	**1,191,441**	**1,194,803**	**1,259,665**	**1,421,429**	**1,293,345**	**1,242,739**	**1,314,888**
Exports of goods and services	535,233	703,254	794,387	851,602	934,637	933,495	966,443	1,070,980	1,006,653	975,940	1,020,503
Goods, balance of payments basis[1]	387,401	502,859	575,204	612,113	678,366	670,416	683,965	771,994	718,712	681,833	713,122
Services[2]	147,832	200,395	219,183	239,489	256,271	263,079	282,478	298,986	287,941	294,107	307,381
Transfers under U.S. military agency sales contracts[3]	9,932	12,787	14,643	16,446	16,675	17,405	15,928	13,790	12,539	11,943	12,491
Travel	43,007	58,417	63,395	69,809	73,426	71,325	74,801	82,400	71,893	66,728	64,509
Passenger fares	15,298	16,997	18,909	20,422	20,868	20,098	19,785	20,687	17,926	17,046	15,693
Other transportation	22,042	23,754	26,081	26,074	27,006	25,604	26,916	29,803	28,442	29,195	31,833
Royalties and license fees[4]	16,634	26,712	30,289	32,470	33,228	35,626	39,670	43,233	40,696	44,219	48,227
Other private services	40,251	60,841	65,048	73,340	84,113	92,095	104,493	108,287	115,614	124,181	133,818
U.S. Government miscellaneous services	668	887	818	928	955	926	885	786	831	795	810
Income receipts	171,742	166,521	210,244	226,129	256,804	261,308	293,222	350,449	286,692	266,799	294,385
Income receipts on U.S.-owned assets abroad	170,570	164,578	208,065	223,948	254,534	258,871	290,474	347,614	283,761	263,861	291,354
Direct investment receipts	65,973	77,344	95,260	102,505	115,323	103,963	131,626	151,839	128,665	147,291	187,522
Other private receipts	94,072	83,106	108,092	116,852	135,652	151,307	155,651	191,929	151,535	113,267	99,135
U.S. Government receipts	10,525	4,128	4,713	4,591	3,559	3,601	3,197	3,846	3,561	3,303	4,697
Compensation of employees	1,172	1,943	2,179	2,181	2,270	2,437	2,748	2,835	2,931	2,938	3,031
Imports of goods and services and income payments	**-759,290**	**-951,008**	**-1,080,005**	**-1,159,355**	**-1,287,010**	**-1,355,917**	**-1,509,732**	**-1,779,188**	**-1,632,465**	**-1,657,301**	**-1,778,117**
Imports of goods and services	-616,097	-801,633	-890,652	-955,544	-1,042,815	-1,098,363	-1,229,695	-1,449,324	-1,369,345	-1,397,675	-1,517,011
Goods, balance of payments basis	-498,438	-668,690	-749,374	-803,113	-876,470	-917,103	-1,029,980	-1,224,408	-1,145,900	-1,164,728	-1,260,674
Services	-117,659	-132,943	-141,278	-152,431	-166,345	-181,260	-199,715	-224,916	-223,445	-232,947	-256,337
Direct defense expenditures	-17,531	-10,217	-10,043	-11,061	-11,707	-12,185	-13,335	-13,473	-14,835	-19,101	-25,117
Travel	-37,349	-43,782	-44,916	-48,078	-52,051	-56,483	-58,963	-64,705	-60,200	-58,044	-56,613
Passenger fares	-10,531	-13,062	-14,663	-15,809	-18,138	-19,971	-21,315	-24,274	-22,633	-19,969	-20,957
Other transportation	-24,966	-26,019	-27,034	-27,403	-28,959	-30,363	-34,139	-41,425	-38,682	-38,407	-44,768
Royalties and license fees[4]	-3,135	-5,852	-6,919	-7,837	-9,161	-11,235	-13,107	-16,468	-16,538	-19,235	-20,049
Other private services	-22,229	-31,451	-35,080	-39,556	-43,567	-48,174	-56,035	-61,688	-67,675	-75,271	-85,829
U.S. Government miscellaneous services	-1,919	-2,560	-2,623	-2,687	-2,762	-2,849	-2,821	-2,883	-2,882	-2,920	-3,004
Income payments	-143,192	-149,375	-189,353	-203,811	-244,195	-257,554	-280,037	-329,864	-263,120	-259,626	-261,106
Income payments on foreign-owned assets in the U.S.	-139,728	-143,423	-183,090	-197,511	-237,529	-250,560	-272,082	-322,345	-255,034	-251,246	-252,573
Direct investment payments	-3,450	-22,150	-30,318	-33,093	-42,950	-38,418	-53,437	-56,910	-12,783	-46,460	-68,657
Other private payments	-95,508	-77,081	-97,149	-97,878	-112,878	-127,988	-138,120	-180,918	-159,825	-128,672	-111,874
U.S. Government payments	-40,770	-44,192	-55,623	-66,618	-81,701	-84,154	-80,525	-84,517	-82,426	-76,114	-72,042
Compensation of employees	-3,464	-5,952	-6,263	-6,300	-6,666	-6,994	-7,955	-7,519	-8,086	-8,380	-8,533
Unilateral current transfers, net	**-26,654**	**-36,799**	**-34,104**	**-38,583**	**-40,410**	**-48,443**	**-46,755**	**-55,684**	**-46,581**	**-59,382**	**-67,439**
U.S. Government grants[1]	-10,359	-14,978	-11,190	-15,401	-12,472	-13,270	-13,774	-16,714	-11,517	-17,097	-21,865
U.S. Government pensions and other transfers	-3,224	-4,556	-3,451	-4,466	-4,191	-4,305	-4,406	-4,705	-5,798	-5,125	-5,341
Private remittances and other transfers[5]	-13,070	-17,265	-19,463	-18,716	-23,747	-30,868	-28,575	-34,265	-29,266	-37,160	-40,233

See footnotes at end of table.

No. 1278. U.S. International Transactions by Type of Transaction: 1990 to 2003—Con.

[See headnote, Page 799]

Type of transaction	1990	1994	1995	1996	1997	1998	1999	2000	2001	2002	2003
Capital account transactions, net	-6,579	-1,723	-927	-654	-1,044	-740	-4,843	-809	-1,083	-1,260	-3,079
U.S. assets abroad, net (increase/financial outflow) (-)	**-81,234**	**-178,937**	**-352,264**	**-413,409**	**-485,475**	**-347,829**	**-503,640**	**-569,798**	**-366,768**	**-198,014**	**-283,414**
U.S. official reserve assets, net	-2,158	5,346	-9,742	6,668	-1,010	-6,783	8,747	-290	-4,911	-3,681	1,523
Gold	-192	-441	-808	370	-350	-147	10	-722	-630	-475	601
Special drawing rights	731	494	-2,466	-1,280	-3,575	-5,119	5,484	2,308	-3,600	-2,632	1,494
Reserve position in the International Monetary Fund	-2,697	5,293	-6,468	7,578	2,915	-1,517	3,253	-1,876	-681	-574	-572
Foreign currencies	2,317	-390	-984	-989	68	-422	2,750	-941	-486	345	537
U.S. Government assets, other than official reserve assets, net	-8,410	-5,383	-4,859	-5,025	-5,417	-4,678	-6,175	-5,182	-4,431	-5,251	-7,279
Repayments on U.S. credits and other long-term assets	10,856	5,088	4,125	3,930	5,438	4,111	9,559	4,265	3,873	5,701	7,981
U.S. foreign currency holdings and U.S. short-term assets, net	-130	-95	-250	106	47	145	-634	-24	72	-105	-165
U.S. private assets, net	-81,393	-183,893	-341,538	-419,088	-484,533	-340,624	-515,137	-568,567	-361,371	-194,678	-285,474
Direct investment	-37,183	-80,167	-98,750	-91,885	-104,803	-142,644	-224,934	-159,212	-142,349	-134,835	-173,799
Foreign securities	-28,765	-63,190	-122,394	-149,315	-116,852	-124,204	-116,236	-121,908	-84,644	15,889	-72,337
U.S. claims on unaffiliated foreigners reported by U.S. nonbanking concerns	-27,824	-36,336	-45,286	-86,333	-121,760	-38,204	-97,704	-138,790	-8,520	-45,425	-28,932
U.S. claims reported by U.S. banks, not included elsewhere	12,379	-4,200	-75,108	-91,555	-141,118	-35,572	-76,263	-148,657	-125,858	-30,307	-10,406
Foreign-owned assets in the U.S., net (increase/financial inflow (+))	**141,571**	**305,989**	**438,562**	**551,096**	**706,809**	**423,569**	**740,210**	**1,046,896**	**782,859**	**768,246**	**829,173**
Foreign official assets in the U.S., net	33,910	39,583	109,880	126,724	19,036	-19,903	43,543	42,758	28,059	113,990	248,573
U.S. Government securities	30,243	36,827	72,712	120,679	-2,161	-3,589	32,527	35,710	54,620	89,016	194,568
Other U.S. Government liabilities	1,868	1,564	-105	-982	-881	-3,326	-2,863	-1,825	-2,309	137	-564
U.S. liabilities reported by U.S. banks, n.i.e.	3,385	3,665	34,008	5,704	22,286	-9,501	915	5,746	-29,978	21,221	49,420
Other foreign official assets	-1,586	-2,473	3,265	1,323	-208	-3,487	12,964	3,127	5,726	3,616	5,149
Other foreign assets in the U.S., net	107,661	266,406	328,682	424,372	687,773	443,472	696,667	1,004,138	754,800	654,256	580,600
Direct investment	48,494	46,121	57,776	86,502	105,603	179,045	289,444	321,274	167,021	72,411	39,890
U.S. Treasury securities	-2,534	34,274	91,544	147,022	130,435	28,581	-44,497	-69,983	-14,378	100,432	113,432
U.S. securities other than U.S. Treasury securities	1,592	56,971	77,249	103,272	161,409	156,315	298,834	459,889	393,885	285,500	250,981
U.S. currency flows	18,800	23,400	12,300	17,362	24,782	16,622	22,407	5,315	23,783	21,513	16,640
U.S. liabilities to unaffiliated foreigners reported by U.S. nonbanking concerns	45,133	1,302	59,637	53,736	116,518	23,140	76,247	170,672	66,110	77,990	84,014
U.S. liabilities reported by U.S. banks, n.i.e.	-3,824	104,338	30,176	16,478	149,026	39,769	54,232	116,971	118,379	96,410	75,643
Statistical discrepancy	25,211	-7,297	24,107	-16,826	-84,311	134,557	65,095	-62,846	-29,307	-95,028	-12,012
Balance on goods	-111,037	-165,631	-174,170	-191,000	-198,104	-246,687	-346,015	-452,414	-427,188	-482,895	-547,552
Balance on services	30,173	67,452	77,905	87,058	89,926	81,819	82,763	74,070	64,496	61,160	51,044
Balance on income	28,550	17,146	20,891	22,318	12,609	3,754	13,185	20,585	23,572	7,173	33,279
Balance on current account [8]	-78,968	-118,032	-109,478	-120,207	-135,979	-209,557	-296,822	-413,443	-385,701	-473,944	-530,668

- Represents or rounds to zero. [1] Excludes exports of goods under U.S. military agency sales contracts identified in Census export documents, excludes imports of goods under direct defense expenditures identified in Census import documents, and reflects various other adjustments (for valuation, coverage, and timing) of Census statistics to balance of payments basis. [2] Includes some goods: Mainly military equipment; major equipment, other materials, supplies, and petroleum products purchased abroad by U.S. military agencies; and fuels purchased by airline and steamship operators. [3] Includes transfers of goods and services under U.S. military grant programs. [4] These lines are presented on a gross basis. The definition of exports is revised to exclude U.S. affiliates' payments to foreign affiliates and to include U.S. affiliates' receipts from foreign parents. [5] The "other transfers" component includes taxes paid by U.S. private residents to foreign governments and taxes paid by private nonresidents to the U.S. Government. [6] At the present time, all U.S. Treasury-owned gold is held in the United States. Includes sales by U.S. private residents to foreign governments. The definition of imports is revised to include U.S. parents' payments to foreign affiliates and to exclude U.S. affiliates' receipts from foreign parents. [7] In the national income and product accounts (NIPA's). However, the foreign transactions account in the NIPAs (a) includes adjustments to the international transactions accounts for the different geographical treatment of transactions with U.S. territories and Puerto Rico, and (b) includes adjustments to the international transactions accounts for the treatment of gold, (c) includes services furnished without payment by financial intermediaries except life insurance carriers and private noninsured pension plans. [8] Conceptually, "Balance on current account" is equal to "net foreign investment" in the national income and product accounts.

Source: U.S. Bureau of Economic Analysis, *Survey of Current Business*, July 2004, and <http://www.bea.gov/bea/international/bpweb/list.cfm?anon=71&registered=0> (released 18 June 2004).

No. 1279. U.S. Balances on International Transactions by Area and Selected Country: 2002 and 2003

[In millions of dollars (-482,895 represents -$482,895,000,000). Minus sign (-) indicates debits]

Area or country	2002, balance on— Goods [1]	Services	Income	Current account	2003, balance on— Goods [1]	Services	Income	Current account
All areas	-482,895	61,160	7,173	-473,944	-547,552	51,044	33,279	-530,668
Europe	-101,047	11,370	-11,787	-104,399	-116,459	7,884	-1,031	-111,365
European Union [2]	-85,024	10,686	-11,064	-83,527	-97,611	8,053	-3,906	-92,797
Belgium-Luxembourg	3,524	1,858	-7,126	-2,082	4,928	1,442	-3,949	2,244
France	-9,407	707	218	-8,435	-12,401	682	2,401	-9,346
Germany	-36,447	-4,768	7,192	-32,804	-39,719	-5,197	2,598	-42,431
Italy	-14,389	11	1,568	-13,073	-15,105	-160	2,159	-13,529
Netherlands	8,308	1,581	8,409	18,148	9,009	1,299	8,206	17,246
United Kingdom	-8,379	4,821	-27,556	-29,944	-9,705	3,484	-26,637	-30,859
Canada	-50,862	6,438	16,053	-28,711	-54,344	7,588	14,883	-32,063
Latin America, other Western Hemisphere	-57,106	9,976	4,166	-66,655	-69,024	4,463	9,106	-81,587
Mexico	-38,274	5,072	-2,352	-42,273	-41,771	4,732	-1,235	-45,582
Venezuela	-11,128	2,366	25	-8,891	-14,357	1,761	-96	-12,885
Japan [3]	-71,757	12,014	-24,306	-83,676	-67,784	11,154	-19,010	-75,581
Australia	6,311	2,254	1,920	10,251	6,300	2,695	3,425	12,289
Other Asia and Africa	-208,434	16,363	3,561	-213,886	-246,241	14,947	6,997	-256,002
South Africa	-1,519	365	289	-1,095	-1,809	160	520	-1,403
International and unallocated	(NA)	2,745	17,566	13,132	(NA)	2,313	18,909	13,641

NA Not available.   [1] Adjusted to balance of payments basis; excludes exports under U.S. military sales contracts and imports under direct defense expenditures.   [2] Includes Denmark, Greece, Ireland, Spain, Portugal, European Atomic Energy Community, European Coal and Steel Community, and European Investment Bank, not shown separately.   [3] Includes Ryukyu Islands.

Source: U.S. Bureau of Economic Analysis, Survey of Current Business, July 2004, and <http://www.bea.gov/bea/international/bpweb/list.cfm?anon=71&registered=0> (released 18 June 2004).

No. 1280. Private International Service Transactions by Selected Type of Service and Country: 2000 to 2003

[In millions of dollars ($284,410 represents $284,410,000,000). For all transactions, see Table 1278]

Type of service and country	Exports 2000	2001	2002	2003	Imports 2000	2001	2002	2003
Total private services	284,410	274,571	281,369	294,080	208,560	205,728	210,926	228,216
TYPE								
Travel	82,400	71,893	66,728	64,509	64,705	60,200	58,044	56,613
Passenger fares	20,687	17,926	17,046	15,693	24,274	22,633	19,969	20,957
Other transportation	29,803	28,442	29,195	31,833	41,425	38,682	38,407	44,768
Freight	12,547	11,731	12,289	14,099	27,388	25,736	25,973	31,775
Port services	17,256	16,711	16,906	17,734	14,037	12,946	12,434	12,995
Royalties and license fees	43,233	40,696	44,219	48,227	16,468	16,538	19,235	20,049
Other private services	108,287	115,614	124,181	133,818	61,688	67,675	75,271	85,829
Affiliated services	35,857	39,262	43,329	48,450	28,776	29,845	31,848	35,497
Unaffilated services	72,431	76,352	80,852	85,368	32,912	37,830	43,423	50,332
Education	10,348	11,476	12,628	13,399	2,031	2,251	2,451	2,696
Financial services	15,522	14,819	16,091	17,637	4,564	4,171	3,823	4,236
Insurance, net	3,631	3,423	4,515	4,877	11,284	16,706	22,116	26,702
Telecommunications	3,883	4,332	5,016	5,477	5,428	4,770	4,647	4,799
Business, professional, and technical services	25,318	28,364	28,488	29,084	8,973	9,297	9,617	10,960
AREA AND COUNTRY								
Canada	24,528	24,303	24,676	26,725	17,861	17,387	18,151	19,146
Europe	108,066	104,097	110,468	117,465	90,314	90,124	92,513	101,311
Belgium-Luxembourg	3,299	3,326	4,244	4,150	2,389	2,272	2,380	2,380
France	10,562	10,043	10,938	11,061	10,667	9,973	10,082	10,281
Germany	16,152	14,925	16,045	16,409	12,599	12,824	15,637	16,409
Italy	5,443	5,077	5,300	5,474	5,048	5,173	4,516	4,655
Netherlands	7,050	6,886	7,397	7,584	5,682	6,088	6,000	6,354
United Kingdom	31,935	30,740	32,254	34,533	28,236	27,337	27,128	30,552
Latin America and other Western Hemisphere	54,524	54,490	52,900	53,672	38,697	41,226	42,614	48,974
Mexico	14,333	15,180	16,258	16,606	10,773	10,524	11,018	11,681
Venezuela	3,310	3,300	2,830	2,187	610	664	464	419
Australia	5,567	4,859	5,218	5,835	3,488	2,993	3,160	3,160
Japan	33,391	30,196	30,064	29,784	17,387	16,459	17,132	17,363
Int'l organizations and unallocated	6,205	5,708	6,205	5,952	3,947	3,368	3,459	3,635

Source: U.S. Bureau of Economic Analysis, Survey of Current Business, October 2003 and July 2004.

No. 1281. International Investment Position by Type of Investment: 1990 to 2003

[In millions of dollars (-245,347 represents -$245,347,000,000). Estimates for end of year; subject to considerable error due to nature of basic data. Unless otherwise specified, types below refer to current-cost method. For information on current-cost method and market value, see article cited in source]

Type of investment	1990	1995	1999	2000	2001	2002	2003
U.S. net international investment position:							
Current cost	-245,347	-458,462	-775,488	-1,388,745	-1,889,680	-2,233,018	-2,430,682
Market value	-164,495	-305,836	-1,046,688	-1,588,556	-2,308,161	-2,553,407	-2,650,990
U.S.-owned assets abroad:							
Current cost	2,178,978	3,486,272	5,965,143	6,231,236	6,270,408	6,413,535	7,202,692
Market value	2,294,085	3,964,558	7,390,427	7,393,643	6,898,707	6,613,320	7,863,968
U.S. official reserve assets	174,664	176,061	136,418	128,400	129,961	158,602	183,577
Gold	102,406	101,279	75,950	71,799	72,328	90,806	108,866
Special drawing rights	10,989	11,037	10,336	10,539	10,783	12,166	12,638
Reserve position in IMF	9,076	14,649	17,950	14,824	17,869	21,979	22,535
Foreign currencies	52,193	49,096	32,182	31,238	28,981	33,651	39,538
U.S. Government assets, other	84,344	85,064	84,227	85,168	85,654	85,309	84,772
U.S. loans and other long-term assets	83,716	82,802	81,657	82,574	83,132	82,682	81,980
Repayable in dollars	82,602	82,358	81,367	82,293	82,854	82,406	81,706
Other	1,114	444	290	281	278	276	274
U.S. foreign currency holdings and short-term assets	628	2,262	2,570	2,594	2,522	2,627	2,792
U.S. private assets:							
Current cost	1,919,970	3,225,147	5,744,498	6,017,668	6,054,793	6,169,624	6,934,343
Market value	2,035,077	3,703,433	7,169,782	7,180,075	6,683,092	6,369,409	7,595,619
Direct investments abroad:							
Current cost	616,655	885,506	1,414,355	1,531,607	1,686,635	1,839,995	2,069,013
Market value	731,762	1,363,792	2,839,639	2,694,014	2,314,934	2,039,780	2,730,289
Foreign securities	342,313	1,203,925	2,525,341	2,385,353	2,114,734	1,846,879	2,474,374
Bonds	144,717	413,310	521,625	532,511	502,061	501,762	502,130
Corporate stocks	197,596	790,615	2,003,716	1,852,842	1,612,673	1,345,117	1,972,244
U.S. claims on unaffiliated foreigners [1]	265,315	367,567	704,517	836,559	839,303	908,024	614,672
U.S. claims reported by U.S. banks [2]	695,687	768,149	1,100,285	1,264,149	1,414,121	1,574,726	1,776,284
Foreign-owned assets in the U.S.:							
Current cost	2,424,325	3,944,734	6,740,631	7,619,981	8,160,088	8,646,553	9,633,374
Market value	2,458,580	4,270,394	8,437,115	8,982,199	9,206,868	9,166,727	10,514,958
Foreign official assets in the U.S	373,293	682,873	951,088	1,030,708	1,082,296	1,212,723	1,474,161
U.S. Government securities	291,228	507,460	693,781	756,155	831,459	954,896	1,145,029
U.S. Treasury securities	285,911	489,952	617,680	639,796	704,603	796,449	956,663
Other	5,317	17,508	76,101	116,359	126,856	158,447	188,366
Other U.S. Government liabilities	17,243	23,573	21,141	19,316	17,007	17,144	16,580
U.S. liabilities reported by U.S. banks	39,880	107,394	138,847	153,403	123,425	144,646	190,601
Other foreign official assets	24,942	44,446	97,319	101,834	110,405	96,037	121,951
Other foreign assets in the U.S:							
Current cost	2,051,032	3,261,861	5,789,543	6,589,273	7,077,792	7,433,830	8,159,213
Market value	2,085,287	3,587,521	7,486,027	7,951,491	8,124,572	7,954,004	9,040,797
Direct investments:							
Current cost	505,346	680,066	1,101,709	1,421,017	1,513,514	1,505,171	1,553,955
Market value	539,601	1,005,726	2,798,193	2,783,235	2,560,294	2,025,345	2,435,539
U.S. Treasury securities	152,452	326,995	440,685	381,630	358,483	457,670	542,542
U.S. securities other than U.S. Treasury securities	460,644	969,849	2,351,291	2,623,014	2,821,372	2,786,647	3,391,050
Corporate and other bonds	238,903	459,080	825,175	1,068,566	1,343,071	1,600,414	1,852,971
Corporate stocks	221,741	510,769	1,526,116	1,554,448	1,478,301	1,186,233	1,538,079
U.S. currency	85,933	169,484	250,657	255,972	279,755	301,268	317,908
U.S. liabilities to unaffiliated foreigners [1]	213,406	300,424	578,046	738,904	798,314	864,632	466,543
U.S. liabilities reported by U.S. banks [2]	633,251	815,043	1,067,155	1,168,736	1,306,354	1,518,442	1,887,215

[1] Reported by U.S. nonbanking concerns.   [2] Not included elsewhere.

Source: U.S. Bureau of Economic Analysis, *Survey of Current Business*, July 2004.

No. 1282. U.S. Reserve Assets: 1990 to 2003

[In billions of dollars ($83.3 represents $83,300,000,000). As of end of year]

Type	1990	1995	1997	1998	1999	2000	2001	2002	2003
Total	83.3	85.8	70.0	81.8	71.5	67.6	68.7	79.0	85.9
Gold stock	11.1	11.1	11.0	11.0	11.0	11.0	11.0	11.0	11.0
Special drawing rights	11.0	11.0	10.0	10.6	10.3	10.5	10.8	12.2	12.6
Foreign currencies	52.2	49.1	30.8	36.0	32.2	31.2	29.0	33.8	39.7
Reserve position in IMF [1]	9.1	14.6	18.1	24.1	18.0	14.8	17.9	22.0	22.5

[1] International Monetary Fund.

Source: Board of Governors of the Federal Reserve System, *Federal Reserve Bulletin*, monthly; and Department of the Treasury, *Treasury Bulletin*, monthly.

No. 1283. Foreign Direct Investment Position in the United States on a Historical-Cost Basis by Industry and Selected Country: 1990 to 2003

[In millions of dollars (394,911 represents $394,911,000,000)]

Country	1990	2000	2001	2002	2003 Total[1]	2003 Manufacturing	2003 Wholesale	2003 Information
All countries	394,911	1,256,867	1,343,987	1,340,011	1,378,001	475,475	182,176	120,122
Canada	29,544	114,309	92,420	96,437	105,255	29,046	2,640	5,160
Europe	247,320	887,014	999,069	982,062	1,000,532	376,603	106,670	97,928
Austria	625	3,007	2,743	4,030	4,104	2,317	255	-2
Belgium	3,900	14,787	15,623	10,096	10,678	3,391	1,619	(D)
Denmark	819	4,025	1,857	2,433	2,860	2,420	(D)	-1
Finland	1,504	8,875	7,620	6,320	5,700	3,926	(D)	312
France	18,650	125,740	154,984	141,400	143,341	54,978	12,156	26,159
Germany	28,232	122,412	162,314	139,620	148,774	52,514	12,589	21,427
Ireland	1,340	25,523	25,632	26,339	26,793	2,711	3,186	(D)
Italy	1,524	6,576	6,826	6,807	6,695	1,047	1,043	(D)
Luxembourg	2,195	58,930	95,299	97,822	104,452	23,940	1,373	4,012
Netherlands	64,671	138,894	145,554	153,679	146,117	63,608	7,882	7,426
Norway	773	2,665	2,574	3,424	3,218	2,135	440	(D)
Spain	792	5,068	4,659	4,475	5,520	1,696	187	(D)
Sweden	5,484	21,991	20,804	21,006	19,823	8,092	5,295	76
Switzerland	17,674	64,719	129,478	119,338	112,856	72,274	4,013	11,715
United Kingdom	98,676	277,613	197,651	218,175	230,374	70,795	55,723	16,909
Latin America and Other Western Hemisphere	20,168	53,691	64,842	66,366	69,557	8,302	9,669	3,443
South and Central America	6,140	13,384	15,498	18,198	20,636	-924	6,163	163
Mexico	575	7,462	6,645	7,483	6,680	442	1,292	119
Panama	4,188	3,819	4,385	5,394	8,383	(D)	12	-6
Other Western Hemisphere	14,028	40,307	49,344	50,167	48,921	9,226	3,506	3,281
Bahamas	1,535	1,254	1,203	1,151	1,120	(D)	423	1
Netherlands Antilles	12,974	3,807	4,384	4,014	4,048	680	389	(D)
United Kingdom Islands, Caribbean	-2,979	15,191	25,620	28,260	28,949	1,928	2,302	(D)
Africa	505	2,700	2,346	2,298	2,187	653	448	(D)
Middle East	4,425	6,506	6,082	7,456	7,931	1,518	2,889	(D)
Israel	640	3,012	2,882	3,699	3,834	1,540	127	(D)
Kuwait	1,805	908	964	986	1,155	-18	(D)	-
Saudi Arabia	1,811	(D)	(D)	(D)	(D)	(D)	(D)	6
Asia and Pacific	92,948	192,647	179,228	183,392	192,539	59,353	59,860	13,222
Australia	6,542	18,775	19,465	23,136	24,652	3,665	515	(D)
Hong Kong	1,511	1,493	1,292	1,879	1,981	619	498	(D)
Japan	83,091	159,690	149,859	150,499	159,258	54,293	56,625	(D)
Singapore	1,289	5,087	1,221	650	-162	-856	-92	(D)
Taiwan	836	3,174	2,520	2,569	2,708	980	657	34

- Represents or rounds to zero. D Suppressed to avoid disclosure of data of individual companies. [1] Includes other industries not shown separately.

Source: U.S. Bureau of Economic Analysis, *Survey of Current Business*, September 2004.

No. 1284. U.S. Affiliates of Foreign Companies—Assets, Sales, Employment, Land, Exports, and Imports by Industry: 2001

[5,466,000 represents $5,466,000,000,000. A U.S. affiliate is a U.S. business enterprise in which one foreign owner (individual, branch, partnership, association, trust, corporation, or government) has a direct or indirect voting interest of 10 percent or more. Estimates cover the universe of nonbank affiliates. These data are now on a NAICS (North American Industry Classification System) basis]

Industry	Total assets (mil. dol.)	Sales (mil. dol.)[1]	Employment (1,000)[2]	Employee compensation (mil. dol.)	Gross book value (mil. dol.) P & E[3]	Gross book value (mil. dol.) Land	Merchandise exports[4] (mil. dol.)	Merchandise imports[4] (mil. dol.)
All industries[5]	5,466,000	2,354,136	6,371.9	350,575	1,141,711	58,353	163,641	369,488
Manufacturing	1,151,660	952,003	2,569.8	160,926	527,247	20,504	99,394	144,995
Petroleum and coal products	53,607	95,232	26.5	2,973	44,603	1,160	1,732	12,317
Chemicals	263,557	174,681	385.2	30,337	118,103	5,857	16,935	20,704
Computers and electronic products	111,804	98,870	256.6	19,407	38,273	685	17,421	24,184
Transportation equipment	206,515	198,389	389.2	25,157	104,781	1,134	29,788	50,651
Wholesale trade[5]	411,476	653,230	596.6	41,671	178,062	4,982	58,099	213,468
Motor vehicles and motor vehicle parts and supplies	74,125	129,589	56.5	4,692	32,766	765	2,720	79,576
Petroleum and petroleum products	114,506	182,075	72.9	5,648	(D)	(D)	13,514	24,530
Retail trade	83,705	137,142	776.5	20,024	38,193	2,778	1,443	5,114
Information	334,134	98,779	307.4	21,270	67,773	791	(D)	242
Finance (except depository institutions) and insurance	2,922,634	253,305	336.5	36,503	69,935	1,356	(Z)	4
Real estate and rental and leasing	118,683	24,197	44.6	2,730	79,348	15,322	(D)	455
Professional, scientific, and technical services	60,319	45,396	202.4	14,208	12,099	242	405	313
Other industries	383,390	190,084	1,538.1	53,244	169,055	12,378	3,370	4,897

D Withheld to avoid disclosure of data of individual companies. Z Less than $500,000. [1] Excludes returns, discounts, allowances, and sales and excise taxes. [2] Average number of full-time and part-time employees. [3] Plant and equipment (P & E). Includes mineral rights and minor amounts of property other than land. [4] F.a.s. value at port of exportation. [5] Includes industries not shown separately.

Source: U.S. Bureau of Economic Analysis, *Survey of Current Business*, August 2003; and *Foreign Direct Investment in the United States: Operations of U.S. Affiliates of Foreign Companies*, Preliminary 2001 Estimates.

No. 1285. Foreign Direct Investment in the United States—Gross Book Value and Employment of U.S. Affiliates of Foreign Companies by State: 1990 to 2001

[(578,355 represents $578,355,000,000. A U.S. affiliate is a U.S. business enterprise in which one foreign owner (individual, branch, partnership, association, trust corporation, or government) has a direct or indirect voting interest of 10 percent or more. Estimates cover the universe of nonbank U.S. affiliates]

State and other area	Gross book value of property, plant, and equipment (mil. dol.)				Total employment				
								2001, prel.	
	1990	1995	2000	2001, prel.	1990 (1,000)	1995 (1,000)	2000 (1,000)	Total (1,000)	Percent of all businesses
Total	578,355	769,491	1,175,628	1,200,064	4,734.5	4,941.8	6,524.6	6,371.9	(X)
United States	552,902	733,089	1,070,422	1,083,463	4,704.4	4,898.9	6,498.3	6,343.9	5.6
Alabama	7,300	10,598	16,646	17,379	55.7	60.6	77.9	92.2	5.8
Alaska	19,435	25,558	28,964	29,591	13.2	9.8	12.0	12.1	5.5
Arizona	7,234	6,699	10,716	10,241	57.1	51.9	73.2	72.3	3.7
Arkansas	2,344	3,666	4,613	5,891	29.2	32.1	40.9	41.0	4.1
California	75,768	96,576	121,040	120,009	555.9	548.6	749.4	713.5	5.6
Colorado	6,544	8,602	15,319	12,915	56.3	72.2	102.6	93.4	4.8
Connecticut	5,357	8,466	13,604	14,417	75.9	73.3	118.0	123.9	8.3
Delaware	5,818	2,919	6,114	8,229	43.1	15.8	31.8	29.8	8.1
District of Columbia	3,869	4,983	4,247	5,620	11.4	13.4	17.1	18.0	3.9
Florida	18,659	24,865	38,755	35,839	205.7	210.0	312.1	303.3	4.7
Georgia	16,729	22,432	29,510	31,115	161.0	180.1	227.9	243.8	7.1
Hawaii	11,830	15,972	10,369	9,950	53.0	48.9	44.8	41.8	9.1
Idaho	776	1,026	2,749	2,740	11.7	11.3	14.2	13.9	2.9
Illinois	23,420	34,305	48,425	49,553	245.8	237.0	325.8	320.9	6.0
Indiana	13,426	18,782	30,179	29,331	126.9	136.9	168.2	163.0	6.3
Iowa	2,712	4,527	7,186	7,400	32.8	35.8	40.9	47.0	3.7
Kansas	5,134	3,233	9,036	5,343	29.6	34.0	61.0	39.6	3.5
Kentucky	9,229	15,136	22,091	22,911	65.7	83.4	106.0	101.5	6.6
Louisiana	17,432	20,543	31,160	32,990	61.4	51.0	61.3	59.5	3.7
Maine	2,080	3,885	5,087	5,352	26.6	29.1	33.9	34.2	6.6
Maryland	5,713	9,197	13,157	13,017	79.6	95.0	112.9	112.3	5.4
Massachusetts	8,890	12,707	23,875	25,725	131.2	141.5	226.8	220.8	7.3
Michigan	12,012	21,370	39,238	53,826	139.6	170.3	249.9	244.2	6.1
Minnesota	11,972	8,688	13,472	13,224	89.8	79.8	106.2	108.4	4.6
Mississippi	2,989	3,055	4,121	4,885	23.6	22.6	24.2	27.6	3.0
Missouri	5,757	8,327	15,773	15,120	73.7	79.3	107.4	114.0	4.8
Montana	2,181	1,938	3,099	3,099	5.1	4.4	6.8	7.5	2.3
Nebraska	776	1,320	2,737	2,467	14.9	15.7	21.7	23.6	3.0
Nevada	5,450	8,242	10,128	8,281	22.7	25.0	36.3	32.5	3.4
New Hampshire	1,446	2,212	5,124	5,442	25.9	30.0	46.5	45.2	8.1
New Jersey	18,608	26,175	35,115	38,626	227.0	205.2	272.2	270.8	7.8
New Mexico	4,312	4,363	5,801	5,625	17.4	16.2	16.7	14.8	2.5
New York	36,424	52,992	68,522	71,225	347.5	343.8	479.1	480.8	6.6
North Carolina	15,234	21,475	29,931	23,062	181.0	225.3	264.8	237.7	7.1
North Dakota	1,251	915	1,824	1,845	3.1	3.2	7.7	9.4	3.5
Ohio	20,549	29,932	37,530	35,303	219.1	222.1	260.3	242.2	4.9
Oklahoma	6,049	5,448	7,635	7,940	43.6	34.2	41.9	41.6	3.4
Oregon	3,427	5,807	13,178	12,018	39.1	49.7	62.1	56.4	4.1
Pennsylvania	16,587	24,432	34,106	34,188	221.6	231.6	283.4	267.1	5.2
Rhode Island	1,120	2,240	3,394	3,945	13.3	16.2	24.2	24.1	5.7
South Carolina	10,067	13,438	23,563	23,238	104.7	111.6	138.4	136.7	8.8
South Dakota	553	665	1,011	1,051	4.5	4.6	6.9	6.7	2.1
Tennessee	10,280	14,227	20,842	21,330	116.9	136.3	153.2	157.0	6.7
Texas	57,079	68,142	110,032	112,106	299.5	326.4	445.2	428.1	5.3
Utah	3,918	5,612	14,340	13,666	21.0	28.6	38.1	37.6	4.1
Vermont	631	1,037	2,146	2,618	7.7	10.4	11.5	11.6	4.4
Virginia	10,702	15,129	23,570	21,445	113.3	141.4	181.9	171.3	5.8
Washington	7,985	11,462	22,257	19,244	77.5	83.0	106.8	103.9	4.5
West Virginia	7,975	7,809	7,061	7,128	34.9	31.9	28.1	27.7	4.8
Wisconsin	5,088	7,415	13,961	15,844	81.4	71.5	110.3	110.1	4.5
Wyoming	2,782	4,544	8,072	10,118	5.8	6.9	7.8	7.7	4.1
Puerto Rico	1,499	2,174	2,169	2,306	16.1	27.4	17.9	18.5	(NA)
Other territories and offshore	18,484	17,798	34,105	34,582	9.0	13.1	7.9	9.2	(NA)
Foreign	5,470	16,430	2,406	3,012	5.0	2.4	0.5	0.3	(NA)
Unspecified[1]	(NA)	(NA)	66,526	76,701	(NA)	(NA)	(NA)	(NA)	(NA)

NA Not available.   X Not applicable.   [1] Covers property, plant, and equipment not located in a particular state, including aircraft, railroad rolling stock, satellites, undersea cable, and trucks engaged in interstate transportation.

Source: U.S. Bureau of Economic Analysis, *Survey of Current Business*, August 2003 issue, and *Foreign Direct Investment in the United States, Operations of U.S. Affiliates of Foreign Companies,* annual.

No. 1286. U.S. Businesses Acquired or Established by Foreign Direct Investors— Investment Outlays by Industry of U.S. Business Enterprise and Country of Ultimate Beneficial Owner: 1990 to 2003

[In millions of dollars (65,932 represents $65,932,000,000). Foreign direct investment is the ownership or control directly or indirectly, by one foreign individual branch, partnership, association, trust, corporation, or government of 10 percent or more of the voting securities of a U.S. business enterprise or an equivalent interest in an unincorporated one. Data represent number and full cost of acquisitions of existing U.S. business enterprises, including business segments or operating units of existing U.S. business enterprises and establishments of new enterprises. Investments may be made by the foreign direct investor itself, or indirectly by an existing U.S. affiliate of the foreign direct investor. Covers investments in U.S. business enterprises with assets of over $1 million, or ownership of 200 acres of U.S. land]

Industry and country	1990	1995	1998	1999	2000	2001	2002	2003, prel.
Total	65,932	57,195	215,256	274,956	335,629	147,109	54,519	60,320
U.S. businesses acquired	(NA)	47,179	182,357	265,127	322,703	138,091	43,442	52,580
U.S. businesses established	(NA)	10,016	32,899	9,829	12,926	9,017	11,077	7,741
By type of investor:								
Foreign direct investors	(NA)	11,927	120,828	120,878	105,151	23,134	13,650	26,974
U.S. affiliates	(NA)	45,268	94,428	154,078	230,478	123,975	40,869	33,347
INDUSTRY								
Manufacturing	(NA)	(NA)	149,243	73,122	143,285	37,592	16,446	9,538
Wholesale trade	(NA)	(NA)	3,321	(D)	8,561	3,982	871	623
Retail trade	(NA)	(NA)	1,153	3,458	1,672	1,913	551	964
Information....................	(NA)	(NA)	13,399	90,855	67,902	27,599	14,181	10,015
Depository institutions	(NA)	(NA)	1,563	(D)	(D)	2,636	613	5,416
Finance, (except depository institutions) and insurance	(NA)	(NA)	21,057	46,380	44,420	40,780	4,344	21,622
Real estate and rental and leasing	(NA)	(NA)	6,299	5,206	4,526	3,572	5,266	2,607
Professional, scientific, and technical services	(NA)	(NA)	4,289	9,366	32,332	7,044	4,012	1,397
Other industries	(NA)	(NA)	14,932	32,680	30,264	18,917	8,234	8,139
COUNTRY [1]								
Canada	3,430	8,029	22,635	9,271	28,346	16,646	4,333	6,858
Europe	36,011	38,195	170,173	196,288	249,167	78,328	39,644	39,076
France	10,217	1,129	14,493	23,750	26,149	5,772	15,196	1,135
Germany	2,363	13,117	39,873	21,514	18,452	12,733	3,067	9,034
Netherlands	2,247	1,061	19,009	22,265	47,686	14,879	3,476	712
Switzerland	3,905	7,533	4,525	7,512	22,789	16,468	2,656	534
United Kingdom...............	13,096	9,094	84,995	109,226	110,208	17,095	12,188	22,492
Other Europe	4,183	6,261	7,278	12,021	23,883	11,381	3,061	5,169
Latin America and other Western Hemisphere	796	1,550	11,354	33,046	15,400	15,274	3,487	644
South and Central America	399	1,283	920	1,622	5,431	431	373	172
Other Western Hemisphere	397	267	10,433	31,424	10,066	14,843	3,144	472
Africa	(D)	(D)	212	(D)	(D)	(D)	(D)	(D)
Middle East	472	447	2,810	848	947	(D)	(D)	198
Asia and Pacific	23,170	8,688	7,329	15,100	40,282	11,383	5,131	13,518
Australia.....................	1,412	2,270	(D)	(D)	(D)	4,869	1,565	11,313
Japan	19,933	3,602	4,862	11,696	26,044	5,345	3,275	1,487
Other Asia and Pacific	1,825	2,816	(D)	(D)	(D)	1,169	291	718

NA Not available. D Suppressed to avoid disclosure of data of individual companies. [1] For investments in which more than one investor participated, each investor and each investor's outlays are classified by country of each ultimate beneficial owner. Source: U.S. Bureau of Economic Analysis, *Survey of Current Business*, June 2004, and previous June issues.

No. 1287. U.S. Direct Investment Position Abroad, Capital Outflows, and Income by Industry of Foreign Affiliates: 2000 to 2003

[In millions of dollars (1,316,247 represents $1,316,247,000,000). See headnote, Table 1288]

Industry	Direct investment position on a historical-cost basis			Capital outflows (inflows (-))			Income		
	2000	2002	2003	2000	2002	2003	2000	2002	2003
All industries, total ...	1,316,247	1,601,414	1,788,911	142,627	115,340	151,884	133,692	126,694	164,712
Mining.................	72,111	86,564	98,669	2,174	7,949	9,816	13,164	9,503	12,786
Utilities...............	21,964	24,330	26,907	2,466	-835	-213	1,610	1,902	1,991
Manufacturing..........	343,899	339,391	378,033	43,002	28,000	28,370	42,230	26,733	36,531
Food	23,497	18,340	22,717	2,014	2,210	2,793	2,681	2,674	3,172
Chemicals.............	75,807	81,449	90,341	3,812	6,332	6,178	11,552	9,093	10,620
Primary and fabricated metals	21,644	21,926	22,970	1,233	1,244	-169	1,536	898	1,607
Machinery.............	22,229	18,612	21,380	2,659	220	2,405	2,257	1,974	2,043
Computer and electronic products	59,909	53,601	57,596	17,303	1,179	3,061	8,860	2,504	5,394
Electrical equipment, appliances, and components	10,005	9,030	9,657	2,100	269	772	1,079	522	739
Transportation equipment..	49,887	44,820	45,322	7,814	2,471	1,517	4,107	612	1,802
Wholesale trade........	93,936	124,686	140,579	11,938	3,841	12,802	14,198	12,905	19,583
Information............	52,345	39,812	47,525	16,531	-1,886	5,578	-964	535	5,474
Depository institutions.....	40,152	56,595	63,655	-1,274	-1,976	693	2,191	1,288	2,356
Finance and insurance	217,086	264,680	299,805	21,659	14,643	30,149	15,210	13,946	19,165
Professional, scientific, and technical.............	32,868	34,907	40,599	5,441	1,167	4,497	3,548	2,481	4,623
Other industries........	441,886	630,450	693,138	40,690	64,434	60,191	42,504	57,401	62,203

Source: U.S. Bureau of Economic Analysis, *Survey of Current Business*, July 2003 issue. See also <http://www.bea.doc.gov/bea/ARTICLES/2004/07July/0704DirectInvest.pdf> (released July 2004).

No. 1288. U.S. Direct Investment Position Abroad on a Historical-Cost Basis by Selected Country: 1990 to 2003

[In millions of dollars (430,521 represents 430,521,000,000). U.S. investment abroad is the ownership or control by one U.S. person of 10% or more of the voting securities of an incorporated foreign business enterprise or an equivalent interest in a unincorporated foreign business enterprise. Negative position can occur when a U.S. parent company's liabilities to the foreign affiliate are greater than its equity in, and loans to the foreign affiliate]

Country	1990	1995	1998	1999	2000	2001	2002	2003
All countries	430,521	699,015	1,000,703	1,215,960	1,316,247	1,460,352	1,601,414	1,788,911
Canada	69,508	83,498	98,200	119,590	132,472	152,601	170,169	192,409
Europe	214,739	344,596	518,433	627,754	687,320	771,936	848,599	963,087
Austria	1,113	2,829	3,856	3,848	2,872	3,964	4,514	5,139
Belgium	9,464	18,706	17,899	21,756	17,973	22,589	24,868	25,804
Denmark	1,726	2,161	2,764	3,846	5,270	5,160	6,132	7,329
Finland	544	965	1,628	1,379	1,342	1,686	1,838	2,271
France	19,164	33,358	42,328	43,120	42,628	40,125	42,999	47,914
Germany	27,609	44,242	47,685	53,399	55,508	63,396	67,404	80,163
Greece	282	533	648	760	795	835	1,017	1,106
Ireland	5,894	7,996	21,825	25,157	35,903	39,541	46,617	55,463
Italy	14,063	17,096	15,548	17,889	23,484	22,883	24,886	30,417
Luxembourg	1,697	5,929	14,571	22,148	27,849	50,771	59,496	66,919
Netherlands	19,120	42,113	89,978	121,315	115,429	147,687	164,217	178,933
Norway	4,209	4,741	6,897	5,944	4,379	4,446	6,307	8,325
Portugal	897	1,413	1,360	2,188	2,664	2,746	3,402	3,480
Spain	7,868	10,856	14,221	19,970	21,236	28,174	33,735	38,215
Sweden	1,787	6,816	5,237	10,624	25,959	26,374	29,359	28,905
Switzerland	25,099	31,125	38,225	40,532	55,377	63,768	71,454	86,435
Turkey	522	973	1,014	1,792	1,826	1,641	1,880	1,989
United Kingdom	72,707	106,332	183,035	216,638	230,762	228,230	239,219	272,640
Latin America and other Western Hemisphere	71,413	131,377	196,755	253,928	266,576	279,611	284,561	304,023
South America	22,933	49,170	72,593	83,477	84,220	76,809	67,133	69,942
Argentina	2,531	7,660	12,327	18,865	17,488	15,535	11,247	11,026
Brazil	14,384	25,002	37,195	37,184	36,717	32,027	27,615	29,915
Chile	1,896	6,216	9,029	10,177	10,052	10,526	9,991	9,986
Colombia	1,677	3,506	3,749	3,775	3,693	3,122	2,557	2,751
Ecuador	280	889	904	1,116	832	579	1,179	1,446
Peru	599	1,335	2,148	3,148	3,130	3,197	2,809	2,659
Venezuela	1,087	3,634	5,912	7,385	10,531	10,069	10,330	10,859
Other	479	928	1,329	1,828	1,778	1,755	1,406	1,299
Central America	20,415	33,493	56,035	73,761	73,841	60,716	64,840	71,507
Costa Rica	251	921	2,074	1,493	1,716	1,835	1,802	1,831
Honduras	262	68	111	347	399	227	181	270
Mexico	10,313	16,873	26,657	37,151	39,352	52,544	55,724	61,526
Panama	9,289	15,123	25,924	33,493	30,758	5,141	5,844	6,497
Other	299	506	1,269	1,277	1,618	970	1,290	1,382
Other Western Hemisphere	28,065	48,714	68,127	96,690	108,515	142,086	152,587	162,574
Barbados	252	698	929	3,030	2,141	2,240	1,571	1,766
Bermuda	20,169	28,374	41,908	50,847	60,114	84,969	80,048	84,609
Dominican Republic	529	330	645	968	1,143	1,116	983	860
Africa	3,650	6,017	14,061	13,118	11,891	15,574	16,290	18,960
Egypt	1,231	1,093	1,963	2,210	1,998	2,557	2,859	3,018
Nigeria	-401	629	1,686	233	470	260	1,753	2,082
South Africa	775	1,422	2,344	3,474	3,562	3,070	3,366	3,902
Other	2,045	2,873	8,068	7,202	5,861	9,687	8,312	9,958
Middle East	3,959	7,198	10,739	10,950	10,863	13,212	14,671	16,942
Israel	746	1,831	2,837	4,777	3,735	5,690	5,632	6,208
Saudi Arabia	1,899	2,741	4,672	3,336	3,661	3,570	3,823	4,217
United Arab Emirates	409	500	674	540	683	834	1,277	1,430
Other	905	2,126	2,556	2,298	2,784	3,118	3,939	5,087
Asia and Pacific	64,716	122,712	159,678	190,621	207,125	227,418	267,125	293,490
Australia	15,110	24,328	31,483	35,386	34,838	27,778	34,409	40,985
China	354	2,765	6,350	9,401	11,140	12,081	10,499	11,877
Hong Kong	6,055	11,768	17,548	22,759	27,447	32,494	41,571	44,323
India	372	1,105	1,592	2,390	2,379	2,496	3,283	3,609
Indonesia	3,207	6,777	8,104	8,402	8,402	10,511	10,341	10,387
Japan	22,599	37,309	41,423	55,120	57,091	55,651	65,939	73,435
Korea, South	2,695	5,557	7,365	7,474	8,968	9,977	12,178	13,318
Malaysia	1,466	4,237	5,629	6,222	7,910	7,489	6,954	7,580
New Zealand	3,156	4,601	6,021	4,852	4,271	4,273	4,004	3,849
Philippines	1,355	2,719	3,931	3,517	3,638	5,436	4,642	4,700
Singapore	3,975	12,140	17,550	20,665	24,133	40,764	52,449	57,589
Taiwan	2,226	4,293	6,295	6,744	7,836	9,301	10,153	10,961
Thailand	1,790	4,283	5,209	5,500	5,824	6,176	7,608	7,393
Other	356	830	1,177	2,190	2,746	2,990	3,094	3,484

Source: U.S. Bureau of Economic Analysis, *Survey of Current Business*, July 2003, and earlier issues. See also <http://www.bea.doc.gov/bea/ARTICLES/2004/07July/0704DirectInvest.pdf> (released July 2004).

[In millions of dollars (14,396 represents $14,396,000,000). See text, this section. Negative figures (-) occur when the total of grant returns, principal repayments, and/or foreign currencies disbursed by the U.S. Government exceeds new grants and new credits utilized and/or acquisitions of foreign currencies through new sales of farm products]

Country	1990	1995	1998	1999	2000	2001	2002	2003
Total, net	14,396	12,666	14,029	18,559	17,858	12,601	17,505	23,662
Investment in financial institutions	1,304	1,517	1,580	1,451	1,500	1,704	1,778	2,169
Western Europe	-103	177	317	431	183	220	104	387
Austria	-10	-1	(Z)	-	-	-	-	-
Belgium and Luxembourg	-9	-	-	-	-	-	-	-
Denmark	-	-	-	-	-	-	-	-
Finland	-	-	-	-	-	-	-	46
France	-8	-1	(Z)	-	-	-	-	-
Germany	-15	-	-	-	-	-	-	-
Iceland	-338	(Z)	-	-	-	-	-	-
Ireland	(Z)	-	-	-	-	-	-1	-
Italy	2	-	8	-	-	-	-	-
Netherlands	-30	(Z)	-	-	-	-	(Z)	44
Norway	-	-	-	-	-	-	-	-
Portugal	-	-	-	-	-	-	-	-
Spain	56	-16	26	4	-79	-28	-27	-75
Sweden	-122	-59	-37	-28	-19	-19	-19	-19
United Kingdom	-	-	-	-	-	-	-	-
Yugoslavia [1]	-111	-120	-130	-136	-135	-56	-66	-68
Former Yugoslavia [1]:	-39	(X)	-1	-	1	-	-51	231
Bosnia and Hercegovina	(X)	94	236	188	52	115	64	46
Croatia	(X)	9	-11	1	3	18	36	52
Macedonia	(X)	1	7	20	50	29	15	57
Slovenia	(X)	-24	-15	2	2	2	7	7
Former Yugoslavia - Regional [3]	(X)	(Z)	8	21	74	87	128	66
Other and unspecified [3]	520	293	229	355	234	72	17	(Z)
Eastern Europe	973	1,979	1,790	2,152	1,830	1,300	1,464	1,267
Albania	-	15	16	4	26	38	40	41
Bulgaria	-	6	14	26	46	54	34	46
Czechoslovakia	(Z)	-	-	-	-	-	-	-
Czech Republic	(X)	3	5	8	11	11	23	8
Estonia	(X)	2	6	4	6	3	-2	18
Hungary	1	36	13	13	12	8	16	7
Latvia	(X)	2	8	9	6	1	11	9
Lithuania	(X)	28	15	4	-16	(Z)	3	12
Poland	912	6	38	24	40	-1	16	19
Romania	79	9	28	10	38	43	48	65
Slovakia	-	2	6	8	7	10	10	13
Soviet Union	-30	(X)	-	-	-	-	-	-
Newly Independent States:								
Armenia	(X)	102	39	35	20	52	54	74
Azerbaijan	(X)	19	6	6	8	15	32	34
Belarus	(X)	50	3	6	1	4	2	(z)
Georgia	(X)	89	28	23	36	49	97	65
Kazakhstan	(X)	17	70	45	42	58	52	49
Kyrgyzstan	(X)	33	30	15	15	32	36	34
Moldova	(X)	19	5	32	32	60	28	22
Russia	(X)	465	444	968	797	280	266	191
Tajikistan	(X)	34	30	6	8	34	18	24
Turkmenistan	(X)	16	3	3	4	8	6	5
Ukraine	(X)	171	172	318	138	195	118	95
Uzbekistan	(X)	1	7	19	22	41	39	51
Former Soviet Union - Regional [3]	(X)	613	603	506	501	295	510	364
Other and unspecified [3]	11	241	200	61	29	10	7	21
Near East and South Asia	6,656	3,025	5,045	4,378	7,658	2,520	5,656	9,811
Afghanistan	57	10	-	2	5	6	140	548
Bangladesh	181	87	24	65	43	89	45	28
Cyprus	16	6	14	-	-	-	-	-
Egypt	4,976	1,639	2,018	2,093	3,091	1,296	1,689	2,023
Greece	282	261	-240	-145	-169	-153	-218	-318
India	13	48	167	-79	-64	-56	-122	-151
Iran	-	-	-	-	-	-	-	-
Iraq [4]	-7	128	-	-	(Z)	1	(Z)	3,220
Israel	4,380	420	2,842	2,221	3,932	589	3,061	2,742
Jordan	155	129	217	186	317	298	483	1,340
Kuwait	-2,506	-	-	-	-	-	-	-
Lebanon	9	5	2	9	22	60	28	75
Nepal	20	20	20	19	15	27	28	24
Oman	4	4	20	-6	-6	-10	-8	42
Pakistan	531	-187	-82	79	366	170	445	-2
Saudi Arabia	-1,614	-	-	-	-	-	-	-
Sri Lanka	72	27	1	-6	-15	-6	-10	222
Syria	(Z)	-	-	-	-	-	-	-16
Turkey	367	147	-159	-259	-86	-5	-138	-324
United Arab Emirates	-361	-	-	-	-	-	-	-
Yemen (Sanaa)	(X)	(X)	-	-	-	-	-	-
Yemen	43	3	5	10	16	7	5	17
UNRWA [5]	7	103	78	93	97	77	71	124
West Bank-Gaza	1	58	80	88	64	115	143	195
Other and unspecified [3]	29	118	39	10	30	15	14	22

See footnotes at end of table.

No. 1289. U.S. Government Foreign Grants and Credits by Type and Country: 1990 to 2003—Con.

[In millions of dollars. See headnote, p. 807]

Country	1990	1995	1998	1999	2000	2001	2002	2003
Africa	1,883	2,217	1,366	841	1,042	1,562	2,015	2,781
Algeria	59	755	45	-46	-53	182	-73	-123
Angola	-15	37	38	21	31	43	87	27
Benin	5	14	14	23	22	38	23	23
Botswana	17	18	5	3	1	1	12	(Z)
Burkina	15	23	17	9	7	9	12	2
Burundi	18	39	9	6	3	6	3	18
Cameroon	42	4	6	2	1	3	6	3
Cape Verde	8	11	6	1	1	2	3	1
Chad	24	14	3	2	2	7	3	1
Congo (Kinshasa)	242	1	1	2	9	16	33	1,078
Cote d'Ivoire	18	16	8	11	9	2	32	52
Eritrea	-	9	21	7	48	45	36	23
Ethiopia	57	127	162	44	142	98	87	137
Ghana	14	63	40	38	40	86	48	49
Guinea	16	28	18	22	19	45	41	30
Kenya	115	35	37	31	44	108	50	57
Lesotho	16	13	3	1	1	1	1	1
Liberia	32	67	19	26	19	19	10	13
Madagascar	34	33	44	30	21	63	36	31
Malawi	35	64	23	30	45	41	46	42
Mali	31	31	36	36	50	9	49	50
Mauritania	13	2	4	2	2	5	4	3
Morocco	96	-48	-48	-28	-9	-29	760	-59
Mozambique	83	115	81	74	119	133	105	107
Niger	34	31	13	7	5	5	9	3
Nigeria	156	1	-4	-38	-17	17	45	468
Rwanda	13	138	32	29	26	57	32	36
Senegal	61	24	18	26	27	51	42	44
Sierra Leone	2	11	14	5	10	11	29	36
Somalia	80	26	4	12	7	1	6	10
South Africa	20	112	90	91	68	119	98	113
Sudan	150	11	28	16	17	13	11	41
Swaziland	14	13	14	-	-	-	-	-
Tanzania	51	19	27	22	15	50	44	48
Togo	10	3	2	2	2	2	4	5
Tunisia	44	-4	-19	-22	-19	-18	-12	-17
Uganda	43	56	19	51	92	55	71	85
Zambia	63	27	14	27	44	42	34	51
Zimbabwe	10	29	47	18	23	24	21	23
Other and unspecified[3]	157	246	475	248	168	200	168	269
Far East and Pacific	39	753	759	1,145	550	725	331	760
Australia	-34	-	-	-	-	1	4	6
Burma	1	-2	-2	-	-	-	-	-
Cambodia	5	39	35	16	23	42	35	32
China	71	136	248	293	167	132	45	4
Hong Kong	-8	73	17	-17	-15	-24	-20	-23
Indonesia	46	25	24	483	270	488	221	821
Japan and Ryukyu Islands	-635	(Z)	-	-	-	1	-	-
Korea, Republic of	-192	-49	-52	330	-132	-215	-134	-137
Laos	(Z)	3	5	4	5	6	7	6
Malaysia	-1	(Z)	2	23	134	184	11	1
Mongolia	-2	-	-	-	-	-	-	14
New Zealand	-	-	-	-	-	-	-	-
Pacific Islands, Trust Territory of the[6]	220	209	175	145	145	206	193	103
Philippines	557	56	297	-34	20	-17	-46	-41
Singapore	(Z)	1	-	-	-	-	-	-
Taiwan	-7	-5	-1	-1	-1	-1	-1	-
Thailand	-19	205	-63	-120	-102	-118	-27	-50
Vietnam	1	(Z)	-9	-6	1	10	7	9
Other and unspecified[3]	38	51	58	36	26	12	16	15
Western Hemisphere	2,025	485	1,033	5,120	1,173	1,380	710	639
Argentina	64	-26	-84	-96	-73	-55	4	18
Bolivia	114	101	97	104	136	189	152	207
Brazil	261	-204	90	38	195	119	106	-80
Canada	-41	-	-	-	-	-	-	-5
Chile	-32	-24	5	-8	-22	-19	-19	-5
Colombia	-30	5	43	173	33	71	76	148
Costa Rica	108	-28	-27	-37	-34	-31	-27	-42
Dominican Republic	28	-15	-14	-13	-58	-41	-65	-61
Ecuador	61	5	3	14	14	38	75	17
El Salvador	303	119	41	38	27	78	45	53

See footnotes at end of table.

U.S. Census Bureau, Statistical Abstract of the United States: 2004-2005

[In millions of dollars. See headnote, p. 807]

Country	1990	1995	1998	1999	2000	2001	2002	2003
Western Hemisphere—Continued:								
Guatemala	98	39	36	45	49	106	54	41
Guyana	42	10	12	5	5	9	4	4
Haiti	54	156	88	86	63	106	66	64
Honduras	226	77	31	82	100	258	85	49
Jamaica	108	30	-21	-24	-34	-21	-15	-9
Mexico	140	-198	-127	-118	-123	14	-13	-9
Nicaragua	105	41	50	53	53	152	60	40
Panama[7]	102	8	-20	4,100	-13	-9	(Z)	3
Paraguay	(Z)	1	2	6	4	9	9	11
Peru	93	151	113	101	87	133	109	83
Trinidad and Tobago	5	-14	205	-39	-19	-21	-26	-31
Uruguay	-3	1	1	2	-2	(Z)	-2	-
Venezuela[8]	-18	-2	5	4	133	2	-8	-7
Other[8] and unspecified[3]	236	251	505	605	652	292	40	145
Other international organizations and unspecified areas[3]	1,619	2,513	2,138	3,141	3,942	3,191	5,447	5,848

X Not applicable. - Represents zero or rounds to zero. Z Less than $500,000. [1] Includes European Atomic Energy Community, European Coal and Steel Community, European Payments Union, European Productivity Agency, North Atlantic Treaty Organization, and Organization for European Economic Cooperation. [2] In 1992, some successor countries assumed portions of outstanding credits of the former Yugoslavia (assignment of the remaining portions is pending). Subsequent negative totals reflect payments to the United States on these assumed credits which were greater than the extension of new credits and grants to these countries. [3] In recent years, significant amounts of foreign assistance has been reported on a regional, inter-regional, and worldwide basis. Country totals in this table may understate actual assistance to many countries. [4] Foreign assistance to Iraq during the 1991-96 period was direct humanitarian assistance to ethnic minorities of Northern Iraq after the conflict in the Persian Gulf. [5] United Nations Relief and Works Agency for Palestine refugees. [6] Excludes transactions with Commonwealth of the Northern Mariana Islands after October 1986; includes transactions with Federated States of Micronesia, Republic of the Marshall Islands, and Republic of Palau. [7] Includes transfer of Panama Canal to the Republic of Panama on December 1999. [8] Includes Andean Development Corporation, Caribbean Development Bank, Central American Bank for Economic Integration, Eastern Caribbean Central Bank, Inter-American Institute of Agricultural Science, Organizations of American States, and Pan American Health Organization.

Source: U.S. Bureau of Economic Analysis, press releases, and unpublished data.

No. 1290. U.S. Foreign Economic and Military Aid Programs: 1980 to 2000

[In millions of dollars (9,695 represents $9,695,000,000). For years ending September 30. Economic aid shown here represents U.S. economic aid—not just aid under the Foreign Assistance Act. Major components in recent years include AID, Food for Peace, Peace Corps, and paid-in subscriptions to international financial institutions, such as IBRD, and IDB. Annual figures are gross unadjusted program figures]

Year and region	Total economic and military aid	Economic aid			Military aid		
		Total	Loans	Grants	Total	Loans	Grants
1980	9,695	7,573	1,993	5,580	2,122	1,450	672
1981	10,550	7,305	1,460	5,845	3,245	2,546	699
1982	12,324	8,129	1,454	6,675	4,195	3,084	1,111
1983	14,202	8,603	1,619	6,984	5,599	3,932	1,667
1984	15,524	9,038	1,621	7,417	6,486	4,401	2,085
1985	18,128	12,327	1,579	10,748	5,801	2,365	3,436
1986	16,739	10,900	1,330	9,570	5,839	1,980	3,859
1987	14,488	9,386	1,138	8,248	5,102	953	4,149
1988	13,792	8,961	852	8,109	4,831	763	4,068
1989	14,688	9,860	694	9,166	4,828	410	4,418
1990	15,727	10,834	756	10,078	4,893	404	4,489
1991	16,663	11,904	354	11,550	4,760	428	4,332
1992	15,589	11,242	494	10,748	4,347	345	4,002
1993	28,196	24,054	462	23,593	4,143	855	3,288
1994	15,870	11,940	887	11,053	3,931	770	3,161
1995	15,108	11,295	190	11,105	3,813	558	3,255
1996	13,559	9,589	329	9,260	3,970	544	3,426
1997	13,037	9,171	218	8,953	3,866	298	3,568
1998	13,907	10,318	271	10,047	3,589	100	3,489
1999	15,987	12,308	408	11,899	3,679	152	3,527
2000, total	16,943	11,740	304	11,436	5,204	-	5,204
Near East	6,860	2,180	10	2,170	4,680	-	4,680
Sub Saharan Africa	1,553	1,499	9	1,490	54	-	54
Latin America	1,977	1,960	23	1,937	17	-	17
Asia	862	845	45	800	18	-	18
Eastern Europe	9	9	-	9	1	-	1
Western Europe	1,141	1,124	212	911	17	-	17
Eurasia	899	748	5	744	150	-	150
Oceania and other	3	-	-	-	3	-	3
Nonregional	3,639	3,375	-	3,375	263	-	263

- Represents zero.

Source: U.S. Agency for International Development, *U.S. Overseas Loans and Grants and Assistance from International Organizations*, annual.

No. 1291. U.S. Foreign Economic and Military Aid by Major Recipient Country: 1996 to 2000

[In millions of dollars (13,559.8 represents $13,559,800,000), except as indicated. For years ending Sept. 30]

Recipient country	1996	1997	1998	1999	2000 Total (mil. dol.)	Rank	Military aid (mil. dol.)	Economic aid (mil. dol.)
Total [1]	13,559.8	13,034.7	13,907.0	15,986.5	16,943.0	(X)	5,204.0	11,740.0
Afghanistan	15.2	28.3	-	19.2	30.1	55	-	30.1
Albania	21.8	8.4	34.3	53.8	65.0	28	2.2	62.8
Angola	83.5	49.4	62.8	48.5	92.3	17	-	92.3
Armenia	70.7	16.8	74.3	74.3	93.0	16	-	93.0
Azerbaijan	5.6	2.1	24.7	28.9	48.9	37	-	48.9
Bangladesh	55.5	78.2	97.7	190.6	71.9	25	0.5	71.5
Benin	16.7	17.3	22.8	29.0	21.1	67	0.4	20.7
Bolivia	90.6	131.7	109.5	135.7	232.4	7	0.5	231.9
Bosnia Hercegovina	245.6	184.1	283.5	189.6	149.4	13	51.9	97.5
Bulgaria	33.3	12.4	48.2	36.7	44.3	41	5.8	38.5
Cambodia	28.9	36.5	-	14.6	24.0	63	-	24.0
Colombia	16.9	35.1	61.8	212.8	1,027.0	3	0.9	1,026.1
Congo (Kinshasa)	1.3	-	-	19.1	22.4	65	-	22.4
Croatia	15.8	2.6	17.8	16.3	54.4	33	4.5	49.9
East Timor	(X)	(X)	(X)	-	35.4	48	8.5	26.9
Ecuador	14.1	15.5	15.3	26.9	61.6	30	0.5	61.1
Egypt	2,125.3	2,111.7	2,129.4	2,161.3	2,042.4	2	1,301.0	741.4
El Salvador	79.0	31.6	40.7	49.4	34.0	51	0.5	33.5
Eritrea	13.8	25.0	18.5	11.2	25.7	59	-	25.7
Ethiopa	111.1	79.5	114.1	126.6	241.0	6	0.2	240.8
Georgia	20.3	2.0	81.2	101.3	105.0	15	3.4	101.6
Ghana	43.8	47.5	48.9	74.8	62.5	29	0.5	62.0
Guatemala	37.3	61.6	82.7	101.7	66.5	27	0.2	66.2
Guinea	15.7	31.7	45.9	27.5	32.4	53	0.2	32.3
Haiti	99.5	101.7	103.0	94.6	86.2	19	4.3	81.9
Honduras	26.3	29.0	21.6	105.6	38.4	47	0.5	37.8
India	157.5	126.0	126.9	172.8	168.6	12	0.5	168.1
Indonesia	34.0	34.9	99.2	205.1	201.2	8	-	201.2
Iraq	7.2	7.4	-	-	25.0	61	25.0	-
Israel	3,000.0	3,000.0	3,000.0	2,940.0	4,069.1	1	3,120.0	949.1
Jordan	133.7	184.4	139.6	290.1	473.2	4	226.4	246.9
Kazakhstan	30.1	10.1	31.0	49.0	51.6	36	2.1	49.6
Kenya	16.4	29.2	67.4	78.8	79.8	21	0.4	79.4
Korea, North	0.0	-	70.4	156.6	79.4	22	-	79.4
Kyrgyzstan	17.3	5.5	18.6	42.7	38.7	46	1.4	37.3
Lebanon	1.5	11.6	15.0	13.8	27.5	57	0.6	26.9
Macedonia	9.9	1.6	50.6	43	56.7	31	0.5	56.2
Madagascar	19.8	18.8	28.2	24.6	27.1	58	0.2	26.9
Malawi	31.5	37.3	39.5	29	44.4	40	0.3	44.0
Mali	31.1	38.5	46.8	40.8	42.9	42	0.3	42.7
Mexico	26.3	11.6	24.8	20.3	24.2	62	0.9	23.3
Moldova	32.0	4.8	31.4	48.8	45.3	38	1.7	43.5
Morocco	16.7	19.7	21.3	18.1	41.5	44	2.4	39.1
Mozambique	59.5	55.2	72.4	78.6	82.2	20	0.2	82.0
Nicaragua	27.3	26.9	54.4	65.8	32.2	54	0.2	32.0
Nigeria	1.8	1.3	9.6	23.7	89.1	18	10.5	78.5
Peru	103.7	126.7	168.5	196.8	191.0	10	0.5	190.5
Philippines	58.3	41.7	69.6	69.1	78.2	23	4.9	73.3
Romania	29.8	4.9	51.3	64.9	44.9	39	7.1	37.8
Russia	178.8	65.8	138.2	689.1	439.7	5	0.7	438.9
Rwanda	120.8	87.2	40.7	47.7	35.2	50	0.2	35.0
Senegal	20.4	21.7	22.8	30.2	29.1	56	0.8	28.3
Sierra Leone	28.3	16.5	32.6	17.4	25.7	60	-	25.7
South Africa	117.2	80.1	76.0	58.8	52.6	35	0.9	51.7
Sudan	23.5	27.2	64.1	84.2	42.8	43	-	42.8
Tajikistan	3.4	10.6	11.6	25.8	21.1	66	-	21.1
Tanzania	11.9	12.2	36.4	66.3	40.9	45	0.2	40.7
Uganda	39.7	65.3	85.3	73.1	75.2	24	0.2	75.0
Ukraine	121.8	50.7	164.7	227.9	178.3	11	4.6	173.7
Uzbekistan	11.2	4.7	15.3	34.8	33.8	52	2.3	31.5
West Bank/Gaza	63.4	67.0	60.7	79.6	121.4	14	-	121.4
Yemen, Republic of	1.4	8.4	60.5	23.0	55.2	32	0.1	55.0
Yugoslavia (Montenegro)	(X)	(X)	(X)	1.7	195.6	9	33.4	162.3
Serbia	(X)	(X)	9.9	-	71.3	26	-	71.3
Yugoslavia (Serbia/Montenegro)	(X)	(X)	(X)	45.2	22.8	64	-	22.8
Zambia	11.1	16.3	33.5	31.0	54.3	34	-	54.3
Zimbabwe	19.7	11.5	21.3	12.3	35.3	49	0.1	35.2

- Represents or rounds to zero. X Not applicable. [1] Includes countries not shown separately.

Source: U.S. Agency for International Development, U.S. Overseas Loans and Grants, annual.

No. 1292. U.S. International Trade in Goods and Services: 1996 to 2003

[In millions of dollars (-102,689 represents $-102,689,000,000). Data presented on a balance of payments basis and will not agree with the following merchandise trade Tables 1293 to 1302]

Category	1996	1997	1998	1999	2000	2001	2002	2003
TRADE BALANCE								
Total	-102,869	-107,047	-163,153	-261,201	-375,384	-357,819	-418,038	-489,377
Goods	-191,000	-198,119	-246,696	-346,022	-452,423	-427,215	-482,872	-549,409
Services	88,131	91,072	83,543	84,821	77,039	69,396	64,834	60,032
Travel	21,731	21,375	14,842	15,838	17,695	11,693	8,503	8,761
Passenger fares	4,613	2,730	127	-1,530	-3,587	-4,707	-2,923	-4,871
Other transportation	-1,329	-1,953	-4,759	-7,223	-11,622	-10,240	-9,361	-13,179
Royalties, license fees	24,633	24,067	24,391	26,563	26,765	24,385	24,884	28,878
Other private services	34,857	41,692	45,645	50,516	49,568	52,752	53,158	53,618
Other [1]	5,385	4,968	5,220	2,593	317	-2,436	-7,302	-10,982
U.S. govt miscel. services	-1,759	-1,807	-1,923	-1,936	-2,097	-2,051	-2,125	-2,193
EXPORTS								
Total	850,877	933,873	932,558	965,473	1,070,054	1,007,580	974,107	1,018,572
Goods	612,113	678,366	670,416	683,965	771,994	718,712	681,874	713,761
Services	238,764	255,507	262,142	281,508	298,060	288,868	292,233	304,811
Travel	69,809	73,426	71,325	74,801	82,400	71,893	66,547	65,767
Passenger fares	20,422	20,868	20,098	19,785	20,687	17,926	17,046	15,690
Other transportation	26,074	27,006	25,604	26,916	29,803	28,442	29,166	31,699
Royalties, license fees	32,470	33,228	35,626	39,670	43,233	41,098	44,142	48,084
Other private services	72,615	83,349	91,158	103,523	107,361	116,139	122,594	130,047
Other [1]	16,446	16,675	17,405	15,928	13,790	12,539	11,943	12,713
U.S. govt miscel. services	928	955	926	885	786	831	795	811
IMPORTS								
Total	953,746	1,040,920	1,095,711	1,226,674	1,445,438	1,365,399	1,392,145	1,507,949
Goods	803,113	876,485	917,112	1,029,987	1,224,417	1,145,927	1,164,746	1,263,170
Services	150,633	164,435	178,599	196,687	221,021	219,472	227,399	244,779
Travel	48,078	52,051	56,483	58,963	64,705	60,200	58,044	57,006
Passenger fares	15,809	18,138	19,971	21,315	24,274	22,633	19,969	20,561
Other transportation	27,403	28,959	30,363	34,139	41,425	38,682	38,527	44,878
Royalties, license fees	7,837	9,161	11,235	13,107	16,468	16,713	19,258	19,206
Other private services	37,758	41,657	45,513	53,007	57,793	63,387	69,436	76,429
Other [1]	11,061	11,707	12,185	13,335	13,473	14,975	19,245	23,695
U.S. govt miscel. services	2,687	2,762	2,849	2,821	2,883	2,882	2,920	3,004

[1] Represents transfers under U.S. military sales contracts for exports and direct defense expenditures for imports.
Source: U.S. Census Bureau, *U.S. International Trade in Goods and Services*, December 2003, Series FT-900(03-12) See also <http://www.census.gov/foreign-trade/Press-Release/2003pr/12/#ft900> (released 13 February 2004).

No. 1293. U.S. Exports, General Imports, and Trade Balance in Goods: 1980 to 2003

[In billions of dollars (225.7 represents $225,700,000,000). Domestic and foreign exports, are f.a.s. value basis; general imports are on customs value basis]

Year	Total goods [1]			Manufactured goods [2][3]			Agricultural products [4]			Mineral fuels [3][5]		
	Exports	Imports	Balance	Exports	Imports	Balance	Exports	Imports	Balance	Exports	Imports	Balance
1980	225.7	245.3	-19.5	160.7	133.0	27.7	41.8	17.4	24.3	8.2	78.9	-70.7
1981	238.7	261.0	-22.3	171.7	149.8	22.0	43.8	17.2	26.6	10.3	81.2	-70.9
1982	216.4	244.0	-27.5	155.3	151.7	3.6	37.0	15.7	21.3	12.8	65.3	-52.5
1983	205.6	258.0	-52.4	148.5	171.2	-22.7	36.5	16.5	19.9	9.8	57.8	-48.0
1983	205.6	258.0	-52.4	148.7	170.9	-22.2	36.1	16.0	20.2	9.8	57.8	-48.0
1984	224.0	330.7	-106.7	164.1	230.9	-66.8	37.9	19.3	18.6	9.7	60.8	-51.1
1985	218.8	336.5	-117.7	168.0	257.5	-89.5	29.3	19.5	9.8	10.3	53.7	-43.4
1986	227.2	365.4	-138.3	179.8	296.7	-116.8	26.3	20.9	5.4	8.4	37.2	-28.8
1987	254.1	406.2	-152.1	199.9	324.4	-124.6	28.7	20.3	8.4	8.0	44.1	-36.1
1988	322.4	441.0	-118.5	255.6	361.4	-105.7	37.1	20.7	16.4	8.5	41.0	-32.5
1989	363.8	473.2	-109.4	287.0	379.4	-92.4	41.6	21.1	20.5	9.9	52.6	-42.7
1990	393.6	495.3	-101.7	315.4	388.8	-73.5	39.6	22.3	17.2	12.4	64.7	-52.3
1991	421.7	488.5	-66.7	345.1	392.4	-47.3	39.4	22.1	17.2	12.3	54.1	-41.8
1992	448.2	532.7	-84.5	368.5	434.3	-65.9	43.1	23.4	19.8	11.3	55.3	-43.9
1993	465.1	580.7	-115.6	388.7	479.9	-91.2	42.8	23.6	19.2	9.9	55.9	-46.0
1994	512.6	663.3	-150.6	431.1	557.3	-126.3	45.9	26.0	20.0	9.0	56.4	-47.4
1995	584.7	743.4	-158.7	486.7	629.7	-143.0	56.0	29.3	26.8	10.5	59.1	-48.6
1996	625.1	795.3	-170.2	524.7	658.8	-134.1	60.6	32.6	28.1	12.4	78.1	-65.7
1997	689.2	870.7	-181.5	592.5	728.9	-136.4	57.1	35.2	21.9	13.0	78.3	-65.3
1998	682.1	911.9	-229.8	596.6	790.8	-194.2	52.0	35.7	16.3	10.4	57.3	-47.0
1999	695.8	1,024.6	-328.8	611.6	882.7	-271.1	48.2	36.7	11.5	9.9	75.2	-65.3
2000	781.9	1,218.0	-436.1	691.5	1,012.9	-321.3	53.0	39.2	13.8	13.4	135.4	-122.0
2001	729.1	1,141.0	-411.9	640.2	950.7	-310.4	55.2	39.5	15.7	12.7	121.9	-109.2
2002	693.1	1,164.7	-471.6	606.3	974.6	-368.3	54.8	42.0	12.8	11.7	115.7	-104.0
2003	724.0	1,263.2	-539.2	626.1	1,027.4	-401.3	61.5	53.1	8.3	14.0	155.6	-141.5

[1] Includes nonmonetary gold, military grant aid, special category shipments, trade between the U.S. Virgin Islands and foreign countries and undocumented exports to Canada. Adjustments were also made for carryover. Import values are based on transaction prices whenever possible. [2] Manufactured goods include commodity sections 5-9 under Schedules A and E for 1980-1982 and SITC Rev. 3 for 1983-forward. Manufactures include undocumented exports to Canada, nonmonetary gold (excluding gold ore, scrap, and base bullion), and special category shipments. [3] Data for 1980 exclude trade between the U.S. Virgin Islands and foreign countries. Census data concordances link the 1980-92 trade figures into time series that are as consistent as possible. Import values are for Customs value; these values are based on transaction prices while maintaining a data series as consistent as possible over time. 1991 Imports include revisions for passenger cars, trucks, petroleum and petroleum products not included elsewhere. [4] Agricultural products for 1983-forward utilize the latest census definition that excludes manufactured goods that were previously classified as manufactured agricultural products. [5] Mineral fuels include commodity section 3 under SITC Rev. 2 for 1980-1982 and SITC Rev. 3 for 1983-forward.
Source: U.S. International Trade Administration, through 1996, *U.S. Foreign Trade Highlights*, annual; and thereafter, <http://www.ita.doc.gov/td/industry/otea/usfth/aggregate/H02t03.pdf> (released 24 February 2004).

Foreign Commerce and Aid 811

No. 1294. U.S. Exports and Imports for Consumption of Merchandise by Customs District: 1990 to 2003

[In billions of dollars (393.0 represents $393,000,000,000). Exports are f.a.s. (free alongside ship) value all years; imports are on customs value basis. These data reflect revisions not found in tables 1293, 1298, and 1299. For methodology, see Foreign Trade Statistics in Appendix III.]

Customs district	Exports					Imports for consumption				
	1990	2000	2001	2002	2003	1990	2000	2001	2002	2003
Total [1]	393.0	780.0	731.0	693.1	723.7	490.6	1,205.6	1,132.6	1,152.5	1,250.1
Anchorage, AK........	3.7	5.9	7.7	7.3	8.4	0.7	13.4	11.5	11.3	9.2
Baltimore, MD	6.7	6.2	5.7	5.1	6.0	11.2	18.6	18.4	19.5	22.7
Boston,.............	5.6	7.0	7.0	6.8	7.0	12.2	18.7	16.8	15.4	16.4
Buffalo, NY	15.8	38.2	31.1	25.7	28.8	19.2	38.4	34.7	34.3	35.9
Charleston, SC [2]	6.7	12.6	13.5	11.9	13.6	6.8	16.9	17.2	17.5	21.0
Chicago, IL.........	10.2	21.7	21.5	19.6	21.3	18.3	51.1	49.1	53.0	58.3
Cleveland, OH	4.0	22.7	18.0	16.5	17.2	11.3	36.5	35.2	33.3	36.1
Dallas/Fort Worth, TX	3.4	11.5	10.2	11.5	12.3	4.8	18.8	19.7	19.2	22.4
Detroit, MI..........	35.6	79.4	77.2	86.2	87.6	37.8	97.6	91.3	93.7	98.8
Duluth, MN	0.8	1.5	1.3	1.6	1.7	3.9	7.0	6.4	6.6	7.6
El Paso, TX..........	3.9	18.0	16.3	16.5	17.5	5.0	24.1	23.9	24.7	25.3
Great Falls, MT	2.4	5.0	6.1	4.6	5.4	4.7	14.3	17.6	14.8	17.5
Honolulu, HI.........	0.5	0.7	0.6	2.7	2.5	2.1	2.9	2.3	2.1	2.0
Houston/Galveston, TX ...	17.6	29.7	29.5	29.5	32.1	21.6	40.9	39.3	39.9	48.4
Laredo, TX..........	15.2	57.7	52.1	48.9	48.6	10.0	62.7	62.3	64.6	66.1
Los Angeles, CA.......	42.1	77.6	69.1	63.3	67.7	64.1	150.1	141.7	149.5	165.4
Miami, FL	11.2	31.0	29.9	26.3	26.3	7.1	23.3	22.5	22.4	25.0
Milwaukee, WI	0.1	0.1	0.2	0.2	0.2	1.1	1.5	1.3	1.4	1.8
Minneapolis, MN.	0.9	1.4	1.4	1.5	1.5	2.0	4.3	3.8	4.4	5.4
Mobile, AL [2]........	1.9	4.0	4.8	4.3	4.6	3.4	7.9	7.3	8.1	8.9
New Orleans, LA	18.0	35.9	33.1	32.7	33.6	24.1	54.0	47.8	51.0	59.2
New York, NY	50.9	79.5	76.2	68.4	71.9	68.0	145.6	137.8	140.7	147.5
Nogales, AZ.........	2.1	7.3	6.2	5.3	5.0	4.2	14.1	12.9	11.7	11.6
Norfolk, VA [2]	11.7	12.4	12.4	11.9	12.3	7.4	13.6	12.8	15.0	17.7
Ogdensburg, NY.......	7.9	12.4	11.6	10.5	10.4	9.8	23.7	22.0	21.0	21.3
Pembina, ND........	3.4	8.7	8.2	7.8	9.2	4.1	11.0	10.3	9.7	9.6
Philadelphia, PA	4.0	6.0	8.0	7.1	7.3	18.3	28.3	28.1	27.3	29.8
Port Arthur, TX	0.9	1.2	1.0	1.1	1.4	3.2	10.9	9.0	10.9	13.7
Portland, ME	1.7	2.6	2.3	2.4	2.8	4.3	8.7	9.2	8.2	8.8
Portland, OR	5.8	7.2	6.1	6.0	6.2	5.6	12.5	12.4	12.7	11.8
Providence, RI	(Z)	(Z)	(Z)	(Z)	0.1	1.3	1.3	1.4	1.5	3.1
San Diego, CA........	3.4	12.7	12.3	12.9	12.7	4.3	22.2	21.2	22.9	22.8
San Francisco, CA	23.1	58.3	45.8	35.1	33.1	28.0	68.6	49.1	44.3	46.2
San Juan, PR	2.5	4.8	5.8	5.7	8.9	5.4	11.8	12.9	14.8	19.0
Savannah, GA	7.4	15.9	15.5	15.7	17.0	9.8	26.1	25.2	29.5	30.8
Seattle, WA	32.6	40.4	41.4	39.9	39.8	20.9	40.5	38.0	35.9	35.7
St. Albans, VT	4.0	4.5	3.1	3.0	3.0	5.2	9.4	9.2	8.4	9.8
St. Louis, MO.	0.3	1.3	0.8	0.8	0.6	3.0	7.9	7.1	6.6	7.9
Tampa, FL	4.3	4.8	4.7	5.8	6.2	7.0	14.7	13.4	14.1	14.6
Virgin Islands of the U.S. ...	0.2	0.3	0.3	0.4	0.4	2.1	4.8	3.9	3.6	5.0
Washington, DC	1.1	2.8	3.0	2.5	2.4	0.8	2.6	2.3	2.3	2.4
Wilmington, NC	3.0	2.5	2.3	1.7	1.7	3.3	10.6	10.8	11.9	13.2

Z Less than $50 million. [1] Totals shown for exports reflect the value of estimated parcel post and Special Category shipments, and beginning 1990, adjustments for undocumented exports to Canada which are not distributed by customs district. The value of bituminous coal exported through Norfolk, VA; Charleston, SC; and Mobile, AL is reflected in the total but not distributed by district. [2] Excludes exports of bituminous coal, which are included in the "Total" line.

Source: U.S. Census Bureau, 1990, *U.S. Merchandise Trade: Selected Highlights*, Series FT 920, monthly; beginning 2000, *U.S. Export History* and *U.S. Import History* on compact disc.

No. 1295. Export and Import Unit Value Indexes—Selected Countries: 2000 to 2003

[Indexes in U.S. dollars, 2000=100. A unit value is an implicit price derived from value and quantity data]

Country	Export unit value				Import unit value			
	2000	2001	2002	2003	2000	2001	2002	2003
United States	100.0	99.2	98.2	99.7	100.0	96.5	94.1	96.9
Australia	100.0	98.2	100.0	109.9	100.0	94.3	94.5	103.8
Belgium....................	100.0	99.3	103.4	120.2	100.0	99.5	102.2	118.3
Canada	100.0	97.8	95.1	105.6	100.0	98.8	98.2	102.0
Finland	100.0	88.3	90.3	104.9	100.0	91.0	96.6	114.7
France	100.0	96.8	98.0	117.6	100.0	95.1	94.7	113.5
Germany...................	100.0	104.9	112.3	134.8	100.0	106.1	112.1	135.8
Greece	100.0	98.3	103.2	114.7	100.0	100.0	102.7	115.1
Ireland	100.0	94.3	91.9	(NA)	100.0	96.4	103.7	(NA)
India	100.0	101.3	104.5	(NA)	100.0	99.1	100.5	(NA)
Italy	100.0	101.3	104.5	(NA)	100.0	90.9	86.8	93.1
Japan	100.0	91.4	87.6	90.9	100.0	91.0	87.5	95.6
Korea	100.0	86.9	83.1	85.1	100.0	99.7	103.0	(NA)
Netherlands	100.0	100.4	99.2	(NA)	100.0	93.9	97.0	107.5
New Zealand	100.0	100.7	99.3	111.0	100.0	98.2	102.8	116.1
Norway	100.0	93.1	93.3	104.3	100.0	96.5	95.9	99.7
Singapore	100.0	92.5	90.5	93.9	100.0	96.6	98.4	117.5
Spain	100.0	99.7	105.1	124.9	100.0	94.8	95.9	(NA)
United Kingdom	100.0	95.3	99.2	(NA)				

NA Not available.

Source: International Monetary Fund, Washington, DC, *International Financial Statistics*, monthly, (copyright).

U.S. Census Bureau, Statistical Abstract of the United States: 2004-2005

No. 1296. U.S. Exports by State of Origin: 2000 to 2003

[In millions of dollars (782,429 represents $782,429,000,000). Exports are on a f.a.s. value basis. Exports are based on origin of movement]

State and other area	2000	2002	2003 Total	Rank	State and other area	2000	2002	2003 Total	Rank
Total	782,429	693,517	724,006	(X)	Montana	541	386	361	50
United States . .	712,055	648,800	675,827	(X)	Nebraska	2,511	2,528	2,724	34
Alabama	7,317	8,267	8,340	24	Nevada	1,482	1,177	2,033	42
Alaska	2,464	2,516	2,739	33	New Hampshire	2,373	1,863	1,931	43
Arizona	14,334	11,871	13,323	16	New Jersey	18,638	17,002	16,818	11
Arkansas	2,599	2,804	2,962	32	New Mexico	2,391	1,196	2,326	39
California	119,640	92,214	93,995	2	New York	42,846	36,977	39,181	3
Colorado	6,593	5,522	6,109	27	North Carolina	17,946	14,719	16,199	15
Connecticut	8,047	8,313	8,136	25	North Dakota	626	859	854	46
Delaware	2,197	2,004	1,886	44	Ohio	26,322	27,723	29,764	6
District of Columbia . .	1,003	1,066	809	(X)	Oklahoma	3,072	2,444	2,660	35
Florida	26,543	24,544	24,953	8	Oregon	11,441	10,086	10,357	23
Georgia	14,925	14,413	16,286	14	Pennsylvania	18,792	15,768	16,299	13
Hawaii	387	514	368	49	Rhode Island	1,186	1,121	1,178	45
Idaho	3,559	1,967	2,096	41					
Illinois	31,438	25,686	26,473	7	South Carolina	8,565	9,656	11,773	18
Indiana	15,386	14,923	16,402	12	South Dakota	679	597	672	47
Iowa	4,466	4,755	5,236	28	Tennessee	11,592	11,621	12,612	17
Kansas	5,145	4,988	4,553	30	Texas	103,866	95,396	98,846	1
Kentucky	9,612	10,607	10,734	22	Utah	3,221	4,543	4,115	31
Louisiana	16,814	17,567	18,390	10	Vermont	4,097	2,521	2,627	36
Maine	1,779	1,973	2,188	40	Virginia	11,698	10,796	10,853	21
Maryland	4,593	4,474	4,941	29	Washington	32,215	34,627	34,173	4
Massachusetts	20,514	16,708	18,663	9	West Virginia	2,219	2,237	2,380	38
Michigan	33,845	33,775	32,941	5	Wisconsin	10,508	10,684	11,510	19
Minnesota	10,303	10,402	11,266	20	Wyoming	503	553	582	48
Mississippi	2,726	3,058	2,558	37	Puerto Rico	9,735	9,732	11,914	(X)
Missouri	6,497	6,791	7,234	26	Virgin Islands	174	258	253	(X)
					Other[1]	60,464	34,727	35,457	(X)

X Not applicable. [1] Includes unreported, not specified, special category, estimated shipments, re-exports, and any timing adjustments.

Source: U.S. Census Bureau, *U.S. International Trade in Goods and Services*, series FT-900, December issues. For most recent release, see <http://www.census.gov/foreign-trade/Press-Release/2003pr/12/#ft900> (released 13 February 2004).

No. 1297. U.S. Agriculture Exports by State: 1999 to 2003

[In millions of dollars (49,043 represents $49,043,000,000). Fiscal years]

State	1999	2000	2001	2002	2003	State	1999	2000	2001	2002	2003
U.S.	49,043	50,744	52,698	53,291	56,186	MT	347	350	326	288	400
						NE	2,843	3,013	2,771	3,020	3,041
AL	373	392	396	415	381	NV	13	16	33	39	32
AK	(Z)	(Z)	1	1	1	NH	5	6	8	7	7
AZ	389	439	461	418	476	NJ	116	104	121	117	119
AR	1,301	1,371	1,188	1,213	1,435						
CA	7,366	7,982	7,226	7,112	8,210	NM	81	97	239	228	225
CO	807	919	880	898	843	NY	469	476	492	494	454
CT	95	110	88	70	46	NC	1,349	1,318	1,430	1,468	1,294
DE	106	107	143	138	119	ND	1,483	1,180	1,735	2,032	1,767
FL	1,177	1,277	1,212	1,247	1,280	OK	1,282	1,174	1,265	1,287	1,171
GA	831	909	949	1,005	964	OH	531	531	521	537	586
HI	81	79	82	77	82	OR	648	626	718	683	704
ID	748	776	789	768	847	PA	903	929	1,041	955	1,012
IL	2,969	3,026	3,107	3,254	3,363	RI	2	2	5	4	3
IN	1,419	1,402	1,593	1,751	1,622	SC	255	263	309	311	248
IA	3,091	3,177	2,957	3,136	3,638						
KS	2,930	3,156	2,953	3,018	2,970	SD	1,067	1,067	1,079	1,038	894
KY	809	740	1,013	970	981	TN	468	488	562	609	649
LA	375	427	417	411	486	TX	2,569	3,137	2,892	2,881	3,428
ME	58	60	62	59	58	UT	134	248	253	247	256
MD	221	224	264	234	204	VT	15	16	11	10	15
						VA	430	459	471	465	436
MA	134	157	146	137	168	WA	1,726	1,562	1,836	1,794	1,912
MI	763	831	778	720	842	WV	30	31	43	38	37
MN	2,320	2,275	2,300	2,167	2,637	WI	1,309	1,378	1,505	1,453	1,584
MS	546	605	603	665	778	WY	42	43	60	55	44
MO	1,118	1,074	1,248	1,178	1,239	Unallocated .	1,939	1,906	2,122	2,170	2,196

Z Less than $500,000.

Source: U.S. Dept. of Agriculture, Economic Research Service, *Foreign Agricultural Trade of the United States (FATUS)*, annual. See also <http://www.ers.usda.gov/publications/fau/jul04/fau9001/fau9001.pdf> (released 29 June 2004).

Foreign Commerce and Aid 813

No. 1298. U.S. Exports, Imports, and Merchandise Trade Balance by Country: 1999 to 2003

[In millions of dollars (695,797.2 represents $695,797,200,000). Includes silver ore and bullion. Country totals include exports of special category commodities, if any. Data include nonmonetary gold and includes trade of Virgin Islands with foreign countries. For methodology, see Foreign Trade Statistics in Appendix III. Minus sign (-) denotes an excess of imports over exports]

Country	Exports, domestic and foreign					General imports					Merchandise trade balance				
	1999	2000	2001	2002	2003	1999	2000	2001	2002	2003	1999	2000	2001	2002	2003
Total [1]	695,797.2	781,917.7	729,100.3	693,103.2	724,006.3	1,024,618.2	1,218,022.0	1,140,999.4	1,161,366.0	1,259,705.2	-328,821.0	-436,104.3	-411,899.1	-468,262.8	-535,698.9
Afghanistan	18.0	8.2	5.8	80.0	60.7	9.3	0.8	0.8	3.3	56.1	8.8	7.4	5.0	76.7	4.6
Albania	24.8	20.9	15.5	14.8	9.7	9.0	7.8	7.3	5.8	4.4	15.8	13.1	8.2	9.0	5.3
Algeria	458.8	861.8	1,037.8	984.4	487.3	1,824.4	2,724.3	2,701.9	2,360.2	4,752.9	-1,365.5	-1,862.5	-1,664.1	-1,375.8	-4,265.6
Andorra	7.8	10.2	8.2	11.0	8.2	0.1	0.3	0.2	0.8	0.3	7.7	9.9	8.0	10.2	7.9
Angola	252.0	225.3	275.9	374.0	491.9	2,418.3	3,555.3	3,095.9	3,122.7	4,264.3	-2,166.3	-3,330.0	-2,820.0	-2,748.7	-3,772.4
Anguilla	22.2	29.9	20.1	19.9	21.3	2.3	1.7	3.7	1.0	1.3	19.9	28.2	18.3	18.9	20.0
Antigua and Barbuda	95.2	138.0	95.5	81.4	127.3	1.8	2.3	3.7	3.5	12.7	93.4	135.7	91.8	77.9	114.6
Argentina	4,949.9	4,695.6	3,920.2	1,585.4	2,435.4	2,598.3	3,099.5	3,013.4	3,187.3	3,169.3	2,351.5	1,596.1	906.8	-1,601.9	-733.9
Armenia	51.2	55.6	49.9	111.8	102.8	15.3	23.0	32.9	30.7	37.6	35.9	32.6	17.0	81.1	65.2
Aruba	307.2	291.4	276.5	464.6	355.0	674.8	1,535.5	1,034.0	773.7	963.9	-367.6	-1,244.1	-757.5	-309.1	-608.9
Australia	11,818.4	12,482.3	10,930.5	13,085.0	13,103.8	5,280.1	6,438.1	6,477.9	6,478.8	6,413.9	6,538.2	6,044.2	4,452.6	6,606.2	6,689.9
Austria	2,588.2	2,591.5	2,604.7	2,427.4	1,792.5	2,909.3	3,226.6	3,968.5	3,814.9	4,489.2	-321.1	-635.1	-1,363.8	-1,387.5	-2,696.7
Azerbaijan	54.8	209.6	64.3	69.6	121.2	26.3	20.9	20.6	34.4	9.5	28.6	188.7	43.7	35.2	111.7
Bahamas, The	842.0	1,069.3	1,026.3	975.3	1,084.3	195.3	275.0	313.9	449.7	479.4	646.7	794.3	712.4	525.6	604.9
Bahrain	347.8	449.0	432.7	419.3	508.8	225.4	337.6	424.1	394.9	378.3	122.3	111.4	8.6	24.4	130.5
Bangladesh	274.2	239.1	306.9	269.1	226.5	1,918.2	2,417.6	2,359.0	2,134.2	2,073.6	-1,644.0	-2,178.5	-2,052.1	-1,865.1	-1,847.1
Barbados	304.9	306.9	286.6	267.6	301.8	58.9	38.6	39.5	34.4	43.5	246.0	268.3	247.1	233.2	258.3
Belarus	26.1	31.1	34.9	19.1	84.1	93.6	104.0	108.2	125.5	215.4	-67.6	-72.9	-73.3	-106.4	-131.3
Belgium	12,381.4	13,925.7	13,502.3	13,325.8	15,217.9	9,196.1	9,929.3	10,158.4	9,806.8	10,140.7	3,185.4	3,996.4	3,343.9	3,519.0	5,077.2
Belize	135.8	208.4	173.2	137.7	199.4	80.6	93.6	97.4	77.7	101.4	55.2	114.8	75.8	60.0	98.0
Benin	31.4	26.4	32.2	35.2	30.2	17.8	2.4	1.3	0.7	0.6	13.5	24.0	30.9	34.5	29.6
Bermuda	343.8	428.5	371.0	415.1	401.2	24.6	39.0	65.6	22.9	15.2	319.2	389.5	305.4	392.2	386.0
Bolivia	298.3	253.0	215.9	192.1	181.8	223.7	184.8	166.4	160.4	184.8	74.6	68.2	49.5	31.7	-3.0
Bosnia and Herzegovina	43.7	44.1	43.1	31.7	21.2	14.9	17.8	11.9	15.5	11.7	28.8	26.3	31.2	16.2	9.5
Brazil	13,202.6	15,320.9	15,879.5	12,376.0	11,218.3	11,313.8	13,852.5	14,466.4	15,780.6	17,884.0	1,888.8	1,468.4	1,413.1	-3,404.6	-6,665.7
Brunei	66.7	156.3	104.0	46.3	35.8	388.7	383.8	398.9	287.1	422.5	-322.0	-227.5	-294.9	-240.8	-386.7
Bulgaria	102.8	114.0	108.4	108.4	155.8	198.8	235.6	337.0	339.7	441.4	-96.0	-121.6	-228.6	-238.3	-285.6
Burkina Faso	10.9	15.9	4.4	10.1	11.0	2.8	2.5	5.0	2.9	0.9	8.1	13.4	-0.6	7.2	10.1
Burma	8.6	17.1	11.4	10.3	6.9	232.1	470.7	469.9	356.4	275.7	-223.5	-453.6	-458.5	-346.3	-268.8
Cameroon	37.0	59.3	184.0	155.8	90.8	77.4	155.1	101.6	172.1	214.0	-40.4	-95.8	82.4	-16.3	-123.2
Canada	166,600.0	178,941.0	163,424.1	160,922.6	169,770.0	198,711.1	230,838.3	216,267.8	209,087.6	224,166.1	-32,111.1	-51,897.3	-52,843.7	-48,165.0	-54,396.1
Cayman Islands	368.8	354.5	261.8	231.6	309.6	9.4	6.6	6.8	8.8	11.8	359.4	347.9	255.0	222.8	297.8
Chad	2.7	10.8	137.0	127.3	64.4	6.9	4.6	5.7	5.7	22.4	-4.3	6.2	131.3	121.6	42.0
Chile	3,078.3	3,460.0	3,118.4	2,609.0	2,719.3	2,953.1	3,269.0	3,495.3	3,784.5	3,703.1	125.2	191.3	-376.9	-1,175.5	-983.8
China	13,111.0	16,185.3	19,182.3	22,127.8	28,418.5	81,788.2	100,018.4	102,278.3	125,192.5	152,379.2	-68,677.2	-83,833.1	-83,096.0	-103,064.7	-123,960.7
Colombia	3,559.5	3,671.2	3,583.1	3,582.5	3,754.7	6,259.0	6,968.1	5,710.3	5,604.3	6,385.5	-2,699.4	-3,296.9	-2,127.2	-2,021.8	-2,630.8
Congo (Brazzaville)	47.0	81.7	90.0	52.4	78.8	414.6	531.7	473.8	182.1	432.8	-367.6	-450.0	-383.8	-129.7	-354.0
Congo (Kinshasa)	21.0	21.0	18.6	18.8	30.6	229.0	214.8	154.0	204.1	174.5	-207.9	-204.8	-135.4	-176.0	-143.9
Costa Rica	2,380.6	2,460.4	2,502.3	3,116.5	3,414.2	3,967.8	3,538.7	2,886.1	3,141.8	3,361.6	-1,587.2	-1,078.3	-383.8	-25.3	52.6
Cote d'Ivoire	151.4	89.9	96.8	76.2	102.8	425.9	383.9	333.1	376.4	489.7	-274.5	-289.1	-236.3	-300.2	-386.9
Croatia	107.5	89.9	109.8	78.1	196.8	110.0	141.0	139.0	145.6	180.7	-2.5	-51.1	-29.2	-67.5	16.1
Cyprus	191.7	190.1	267.9	193.4	326.9	31.4	23.4	35.1	25.6	25.6	160.2	166.7	232.8	167.8	302.1
Czech Republic	609.7	735.8	706.1	653.7	672.3	753.6	1,070.2	1,116.2	1,233.4	1,394.3	-143.9	-334.4	-410.1	-579.7	-722.0

See footnotes at end of table.

No. 1298. U.S. Exports, Imports, and Merchandise Trade Balance by Country: 1999 to 2003—Con.

[See headnote, page 814]

Country	Exports, domestic and foreign					General imports					Merchandise trade balance				
	1999	2000	2001	2002	2003	1999	2000	2001	2002	2003	1999	2000	2001	2002	2003
Denmark	1,725.6	1,506.8	1,609.2	1,495.9	1,548.4	2,818.7	2,965.0	3,406.7	3,237.3	3,718.4	-1,093.1	-1,458.2	-1,797.5	-1,741.4	-2,170.0
Djibouti	26.4	16.8	18.6	58.6	34.3	0.1	0.4	1.0	1.9	0.6	26.3	16.4	17.6	56.7	33.7
Dominica	38.6	37.5	30.7	45.0	34.4	19.1	6.9	5.3	4.7	5.3	19.5	30.6	25.4	40.3	29.1
Dominican Republic	4,100.4	4,472.8	4,397.6	4,250.1	4,213.6	4,286.7	4,383.3	4,183.4	4,168.9	4,455.1	-186.3	89.5	214.2	81.2	-241.5
Ecuador	909.9	1,037.8	1,412.1	1,605.7	1,448.4	1,821.3	2,237.8	2,009.7	2,143.4	2,720.9	-911.4	-1,200.0	-597.6	-537.7	-1,272.5
Egypt	3,000.8	3,333.9	3,564.4	2,868.4	2,660.2	617.6	887.7	882.0	1,356.0	1,143.8	2,383.2	2,446.2	2,682.4	1,512.4	1,516.4
El Salvador	1,519.1	1,780.2	1,759.5	1,664.1	1,823.8	1,605.0	1,932.9	1,880.2	1,982.3	2,019.4	-85.9	-152.7	-120.7	-318.2	-195.6
Estonia	162.9	88.0	57.7	81.5	120.6	237.0	572.9	241.1	163.6	181.6	-74.0	-484.9	-183.4	-82.1	-61.0
Ethiopia	163.5	165.3	61.1	60.5	409.1	30.2	28.7	29.1	25.7	30.5	133.3	136.6	32.0	34.8	378.6
Fiji	126.4	23.0	19.4	16.9	19.6	99.8	146.8	182.3	156.3	175.4	26.6	-123.8	-162.9	-139.4	-155.8
Finland	1,668.8	1,570.9	1,554.0	1,534.9	1,713.8	2,907.7	3,250.8	3,393.8	3,447.0	3,598.0	-1,238.9	-1,679.9	-1,839.8	-1,912.1	-1,884.2
France	18,877.4	20,361.5	19,864.5	19,016.2	17,068.2	25,708.6	29,800.1	30,408.2	28,240.1	29,221.2	-6,831.2	-9,438.6	-10,543.7	-9,223.9	-12,153.0
French Guiana	194.2	17.0	129.9	249.7	155.7	4.2	2.3	0.4	7.5	3.4	190.0	14.7	129.5	242.2	152.3
French Polynesia	93.5	93.9	83.0	78.9	91.5	42.7	43.9	48.0	44.1	47.9	50.9	49.9	35.0	34.8	43.6
Gabon	45.4	63.5	73.0	65.5	63.0	1,543.2	2,196.5	1,659.7	1,587.5	1,969.5	-1,497.8	-2,133.0	-1,586.7	-1,522.0	-1,906.5
Gambia, The	9.6	9.1	8.4	9.6	26.7	0.2	0.4	0.5	0.3	0.1	9.4	8.7	7.9	9.3	26.6
Georgia	83.5	109.5	105.9	98.8	131.5	18.3	31.9	30.7	17.5	54.0	65.3	77.6	75.2	81.3	77.5
Germany	26,800.2	29,448.4	29,995.3	26,629.6	28,847.9	55,228.4	58,512.8	59,076.7	62,505.7	68,047.0	-28,428.2	-29,064.4	-29,081.4	-35,876.1	-39,199.1
Ghana	232.7	191.2	199.6	192.6	209.4	208.6	204.5	186.9	116.3	81.9	24.1	-13.3	12.7	76.3	127.5
Gibraltar	4.1	15.1	10.4	14.0	14.0	9.5	1.4	2.6	1.4	2.9	-5.5	13.7	7.8	12.6	11.1
Greece	995.5	1,221.8	1,293.6	1,151.8	1,191.1	563.1	591.4	505.2	546.2	616.0	432.3	630.4	788.4	605.6	575.1
Greenland	3.1	1.1	4.7	4.0	3.0	13.3	15.7	28.8	22.6	13.9	-10.1	-14.6	-24.1	-18.6	-10.9
Grenada	66.2	79.5	59.9	56.4	68.4	19.8	27.1	24.1	6.9	7.6	46.4	52.4	35.8	49.5	60.8
Guadeloupe	54.6	85.9	58.8	44.4	45.4	2.8	9.6	10.6	15.2	2.8	51.8	76.3	48.2	29.2	42.6
Guatemala	1,811.9	1,900.7	1,869.6	2,044.4	2,273.6	2,265.2	2,607.4	2,588.6	2,796.4	2,945.3	-453.2	-706.7	-719.0	-752.0	-671.7
Guyana	145.1	159.2	141.3	128.2	117.2	125.8	179.6	140.3	142.7	150.6	19.3	-20.4	1.0	-14.5	-33.4
Haiti	613.8	576.6	550.4	573.2	639.8	301.1	296.9	263.1	255.0	640.9	312.7	279.7	287.3	318.2	-1.1
Honduras	2,369.8	2,584.0	2,415.9	2,571.1	3,311.5	2,713.3	3,090.2	3,126.5	3,261.3	3,004.0	-343.5	-506.2	-710.6	-690.2	307.5
Hong Kong	12,651.8	14,582.0	14,027.5	12,594.4	13,542.1	10,527.9	11,449.0	9,646.3	9,328.2	8,850.4	2,123.9	3,133.0	4,381.2	3,266.2	4,691.7
Hungary	504.1	569.1	685.5	687.9	933.8	1,892.6	2,715.2	2,964.6	2,637.4	2,699.3	-1,388.5	-2,146.1	-2,279.1	-1,949.5	-1,765.5
Iceland	297.6	255.6	225.4	219.0	242.3	303.7	259.8	232.5	296.9	282.8	-6.0	-4.2	-7.1	-77.9	-40.5
India	3,687.8	3,667.2	3,757.0	4,101.1	4,986.3	9,070.8	10,686.6	9,737.2	11,818.3	13,052.8	-5,383.0	-7,019.4	-5,980.2	-7,717.2	-8,066.5
Indonesia	2,038.3	2,401.9	2,520.6	2,555.8	2,520.1	9,525.4	10,367.0	10,103.6	9,643.3	9,520.0	-7,487.0	-7,965.1	-7,583.0	-7,087.5	-6,999.9
Iran	48.1	16.8	8.1	31.8	98.8	2.4	168.8	143.4	156.3	161.2	45.7	-152.0	-135.3	-124.5	-62.4
Iraq	9.5	10.4	4.7	31.6	315.7	4,226.4	6,065.9	5,778.8	3,548.2	4,573.8	-4,216.9	-6,055.5	-5,774.1	-3,516.6	-4,258.1
Ireland	6,383.6	7,713.5	7,144.0	6,745.1	7,698.5	10,994.3	16,463.6	18,499.3	22,437.7	25,840.8	-4,610.7	-8,750.1	-11,355.3	-15,692.6	-18,142.3
Israel	7,690.8	7,745.9	7,475.3	7,026.7	6,878.4	9,864.3	12,964.4	11,959.0	12,415.7	12,770.2	-2,173.5	-5,218.5	-4,483.7	-5,389.0	-5,891.8
Italy	10,090.6	11,060.3	9,915.6	10,056.8	10,570.1	22,356.5	25,042.7	23,789.9	24,220.3	25,436.7	-12,265.9	-13,982.4	-13,874.3	-14,163.5	-14,866.6
Jamaica	1,292.9	1,375.8	1,405.1	1,420.2	1,469.6	648.2	648.2	460.2	396.3	494.7	644.7	727.6	944.9	1,023.9	974.9
Japan	57,465.7	64,924.4	57,451.6	51,449.3	52,063.8	130,863.9	146,479.4	126,473.5	121,428.7	118,029.0	-73,398.2	-81,555.0	-69,021.9	-69,979.4	-65,965.2
Jordan	275.6	316.7	339.0	412.3	492.0	30.9	73.3	229.1	420.2	673.5	244.7	243.4	109.9	-7.9	-181.5
Kazakhstan	179.5	124.2	160.3	604.6	168.3	229.1	429.0	351.8	334.6	392.3	-49.6	-304.8	-191.5	270.0	-224.0
Kenya	189.2	237.6	577.7	271.2	196.7	106.3	110.1	128.3	188.6	249.2	82.8	127.5	449.4	82.6	-52.5

See footnotes at end of table.

Foreign Commerce and Aid 815

No. 1298. U.S. Exports, Imports, and Merchandise Trade Balance, by Country: 1999 to 2003—Con.

[See headnote, page 814]

Country	Exports, domestic and foreign					General imports					Merchandise trade balance				
	1999	2000	2001	2002	2003	1999	2000	2001	2002	2003	1999	2000	2001	2002	2003
Korea, South	22,958.4	27,830.0	22,180.6	22,575.8	24,098.6	31,178.6	40,307.7	35,181.4	35,571.8	36,963.3	-8,220.2	-12,477.7	-13,000.8	-12,996.0	-12,864.7
Kuwait	864.4	787.0	902.4	1,014.7	1,509.1	1,439.2	2,781.2	1,990.7	1,940.4	2,276.8	-574.9	-1,994.2	-1,088.3	-925.7	-767.7
Kyrgyzstan	22.8	22.8	27.7	31.1	39.1	0.5	1.9	3.3	4.8	11.0	22.3	20.9	24.4	26.3	28.1
Latvia	218.2	133.6	110.5	90.8	124.0	228.8	287.7	144.5	197.0	377.4	-10.6	-154.1	-34.0	-106.2	-253.4
Lebanon	356.5	354.7	418.2	317.4	314.3	51.4	76.8	89.6	61.7	92.3	305.1	277.9	328.6	255.7	222.0
Lesotho	0.7	0.9	0.8	2.0	5.1	110.8	140.3	215.3	321.7	393.3	-110.1	-139.4	-214.5	-319.7	-388.2
Liberia	44.7	43.1	36.8	27.7	33.4	30.3	45.4	42.6	45.8	59.5	14.4	-2.3	-5.8	-18.1	-26.1
Liechtenstein	9.1	13.9	7.1	14.5	15.9	276.8	278.2	224.2	237.7	261.9	-267.8	-264.3	-217.1	-223.2	-246.0
Lithuania	66.0	59.4	99.8	102.8	162.6	96.8	135.0	164.2	299.6	347.3	-30.8	-75.6	-64.4	-196.8	-184.7
Luxembourg	983.4	397.4	548.6	480.1	279.1	313.9	331.6	305.6	300.0	264.9	669.5	65.8	243.0	180.1	14.2
Macau	41.9	70.5	70.1	79.0	54.6	1,124.4	1,266.3	1,225.1	1,231.7	1,355.9	-1,082.5	-1,195.8	-1,155.0	-1,152.7	-1,301.3
Macedonia	56.2	68.5	32.9	18.6	26.3	136.5	151.8	111.6	73.2	60.8	-80.3	-83.3	-78.7	-54.6	-34.5
Madagascar	105.8	15.4	21.0	15.4	46.4	80.3	157.8	271.6	215.8	383.7	25.5	-142.4	-250.6	-200.4	-337.3
Malawi	7.4	13.7	12.8	30.1	16.6	72.5	55.4	77.9	70.8	76.9	-65.1	-41.7	-65.1	-40.7	-60.3
Malaysia	9,060.0	10,937.5	9,357.7	10,343.7	10,920.6	21,424.9	25,568.2	22,340.3	24,008.9	25,437.7	-12,364.3	-14,630.7	-12,982.6	-13,665.2	-14,517.1
Maldives	8.5	6.1	6.4	4.1	6.6	54.9	94.1	97.7	113.6	94.4	-46.4	-88.0	-91.3	-109.5	-87.8
Mali	29.8	32.0	32.7	11.2	31.5	9.0	9.8	6.1	2.6	2.4	20.8	22.2	26.6	8.6	29.1
Malta	190.4	334.7	258.9	210.1	201.6	325.0	482.4	368.9	309.9	372.8	-134.6	-147.7	-110.0	-99.8	-171.2
Marshall Islands	35.8	60.2	26.5	28.7	28.1	9.8	5.0	5.5	9.4	27.1	26.0	55.2	21.0	19.3	1.0
Martinique	34.9	21.6	23.2	23.7	21.7	0.8	1.7	0.6	0.7	0.6	34.1	19.9	22.6	23.0	21.1
Mauritania	25.2	16.2	25.4	22.9	34.9	0.8	0.4	0.3	0.9	0.9	24.4	15.8	25.1	22.0	34.0
Mauritius	39.0	23.9	29.0	27.5	32.0	259.3	285.9	277.9	280.6	298.1	-220.3	-262.0	-248.9	-253.1	-266.1
Mexico	86,908.9	111,349.0	101,296.5	97,470.3	97,457.4	109,720.6	135,926.4	131,337.9	134,615.8	138,073.3	-22,811.6	-24,577.4	-30,041.4	-37,145.5	-40,615.9
Micronesia, Federated States of	25.0	29.1	30.0	27.2	23.6	10.1	13.7	20.8	15.2	14.3	14.9	15.4	9.2	12.0	9.3
Moldova	10.6	27.3	35.5	30.7	25.2	87.1	105.4	68.3	39.1	42.9	-76.6	-78.1	-32.8	-8.4	-17.7
Monaco	12.6	28.2	15.0	11.4	50.3	14.3	22.9	15.0	15.1	21.6	-1.7	5.3	0.0	-3.7	28.7
Mongolia	10.1	17.7	12.1	66.3	20.7	60.8	116.7	143.8	161.7	183.4	-50.7	-99.0	-131.7	-95.4	-162.7
Morocco	565.8	523.2	282.2	565.4	465.1	386.4	440.8	434.6	392.4	385.2	179.5	82.4	-152.4	173.0	79.9
Mozambique	34.8	57.0	28.4	94.6	62.5	10.3	24.4	7.1	8.5	8.4	24.5	32.6	21.3	86.1	54.1
Namibia	195.6	80.4	255.6	57.8	35.4	29.7	45.0	37.3	57.4	123.2	165.9	35.4	218.3	0.4	-87.8
Netherlands	19,436.6	21,836.0	19,484.7	18,310.7	20,702.9	8,475.0	9,670.6	9,515.3	9,848.5	10,971.9	10,961.6	12,165.4	9,969.4	8,462.2	9,731.0
Netherlands Antilles	597.4	673.9	816.4	741.4	747.1	384.3	718.7	484.6	361.7	620.4	213.1	-44.8	331.8	379.7	126.7
New Caledonia	41.7	19.3	25.1	36.6	43.2	8.7	31.4	14.6	9.6	12.6	33.0	-12.1	10.5	27.0	30.6
New Zealand	1,923.4	1,970.3	2,110.5	1,813.1	1,848.8	1,748.2	2,080.2	2,199.2	2,281.6	2,403.4	175.2	-109.9	-88.7	-468.5	-554.6
Nicaragua	373.7	380.1	443.1	437.0	502.8	495.2	588.5	603.6	679.6	769.3	-121.5	-208.4	-160.5	-242.6	-266.5
Niger	18.5	36.5	63.4	40.9	33.6	12.1	7.0	4.6	0.9	4.0	6.4	29.5	58.8	40.0	29.6
Nigeria	627.8	721.8	955.1	1,057.8	1,029.0	4,385.1	10,537.6	8,774.8	5,945.4	10,393.6	-3,757.3	-9,815.8	-7,819.7	-4,887.6	-9,364.6
Norway	1,439.4	1,547.2	1,834.7	1,406.5	1,467.5	4,042.6	5,706.1	5,202.8	5,842.6	5,212.4	-2,603.2	-4,158.9	-3,368.1	-4,436.1	-3,744.9
Oman	188.2	199.8	306.2	356.0	323.1	219.5	257.5	420.1	400.6	694.8	-31.3	-57.7	-113.9	-44.6	-371.7
Pakistan	496.7	462.2	541.3	693.4	839.6	1,740.7	2,166.8	2,249.4	2,305.0	2,531.5	-1,244.0	-1,704.6	-1,708.1	-1,611.6	-1,691.9
Panama	1,742.3	1,612.4	1,330.5	1,406.7	1,848.0	364.8	307.0	290.7	302.6	301.2	1,377.5	1,305.4	1,039.8	1,104.1	1,546.8
Papua New Guinea	37.1	22.2	22.2	23.2	30.3	144.5	33.7	39.3	90.2	66.1	-107.3	-11.5	-17.1	-67.0	-35.8
Paraguay	514.7	445.8	388.8	432.9	488.8	48.1	40.9	32.6	43.7	53.3	466.6	404.9	356.2	389.2	435.5
Peru	1,696.5	1,659.9	1,564.3	1,562.5	1,706.8	1,928.4	1,994.9	1,843.8	1,939.3	2,406.8	-231.9	-335.0	-279.5	-376.8	-700.0
Philippines	7,222.1	8,799.2	7,660.0	7,276.0	7,992.2	12,352.8	13,934.7	11,325.4	10,979.9	10,060.9	-5,130.6	-5,135.5	-3,665.4	-3,703.9	-2,068.7
Poland	826.2	757.2	787.7	686.3	758.7	816.2	1,041.3	952.6	1,108.5	1,325.8	10.0	-284.1	-164.9	-422.2	-567.1

See footnotes at end of table.

U.S. Census Bureau, Statistical Abstract of the United States: 2004-2005

No. 1298. U.S. Exports, Imports, and Merchandise Trade Balance by Country: 1999 to 2003—Con.

[See headnote, page 814]

Country	Exports, domestic and foreign					General imports					Merchandise trade balance				
	1999	2000	2001	2002	2003	1999	2000	2001	2002	2003	1999	2000	2001	2002	2003
Portugal	1,091.8	984.2	1,239.7	861.3	862.8	1,355.8	1,578.5	1,555.4	1,672.6	1,967.3	-264.0	-594.3	-315.7	-811.3	-1,104.5
Qatar	145.5	191.1	335.9	313.9	408.5	272.2	485.6	502.0	484.7	331.3	-126.7	-294.5	-166.3	-170.8	77.2
Romania	176.0	232.7	374.5	248.2	366.9	442.4	472.8	519.9	695.1	730.2	-266.4	-240.1	-145.4	-446.9	-363.3
Russia	2,059.8	2,092.4	2,716.1	2,397.0	2,450.2	5,920.8	7,658.7	6,264.4	6,870.2	8,598.2	-3,861.0	-5,566.3	-3,548.3	-4,473.2	-6,148.0
Western Samoa	12.4	64.0	69.9	7.6	11.1	5.3	5.5	7.3	6.4	4.4	7.0	58.5	62.6	1.2	6.7
Saudi Arabia	7,911.9	6,234.1	5,957.5	4,780.7	4,596.0	8,253.5	14,364.7	13,272.2	13,149.9	18,068.9	-341.6	-8,130.6	-7,314.7	-8,369.2	-13,472.9
Senegal	63.4	81.7	79.5	74.6	102.0	9.2	4.2	103.8	3.6	4.5	54.3	77.5	-24.3	71.0	97.5
Serbia and Montenegro (Yugoslavia)	58.6	29.9	66.2	78.1	50.0	4.5	2.3	6.1	9.6	14.6	54.1	27.6	60.1	68.5	35.4
Singapore	16,247.3	17,806.3	17,651.7	16,217.9	16,575.7	18,191.4	19,178.3	15,000.0	14,802.2	15,158.2	-1,944.1	-1,372.0	2,651.7	1,415.7	1,417.5
Slovakia	127.2	110.1	69.8	92.7	115.2	169.3	240.8	237.6	260.3	1,013.0	-42.1	-130.7	-167.8	-167.6	-897.8
Somalia	2.8	4.9	6.6	6.2	7.0	0.2	0.5	0.3	0.3	0.2	2.6	4.4	6.3	5.9	6.8
South Africa	2,585.5	3,089.5	2,959.6	2,525.5	2,821.2	3,194.4	4,210.1	4,432.6	4,034.1	4,637.6	-609.0	-1,120.6	-1,473.0	-1,508.6	-1,816.4
Spain	6,133.4	6,322.3	5,756.0	5,297.9	5,935.3	5,059.2	5,713.3	5,197.3	5,733.0	6,707.8	1,074.2	609.0	558.7	-435.1	-772.5
Sri Lanka	167.1	204.7	183.0	171.9	154.8	1,742.2	2,001.9	1,984.2	1,810.4	1,807.4	-1,575.1	-1,797.2	-1,801.2	-1,638.5	-1,652.6
St. Lucia	98.1	107.4	86.7	99.5	121.2	28.0	22.3	28.9	19.2	13.0	70.1	85.1	57.8	80.3	108.2
St. Vincent and the Grenadines	92.1	37.9	38.8	40.4	46.5	8.2	8.9	22.5	16.5	4.1	83.8	29.0	16.3	23.9	42.4
Sudan	8.8	17.4	17.0	10.8	26.1	0.1	1.8	3.4	1.4	2.8	8.8	15.6	13.6	9.4	23.3
Suriname	143.8	134.2	155.3	124.8	192.9	122.9	135.2	142.9	132.7	140.1	20.9	-1.0	12.4	-7.9	52.8
Sweden	4,250.5	4,553.7	3,541.0	3,153.0	3,225.5	8,102.7	9,597.1	8,908.5	9,216.3	11,124.6	-3,852.2	-5,043.4	-5,367.5	-6,063.3	-7,899.1
Switzerland	8,371.3	9,953.6	9,807.3	7,782.5	8,660.1	9,538.6	10,159.8	9,669.6	9,382.0	10,667.9	-1,167.4	-206.3	137.7	-1,599.5	-2,007.8
Syria	173.1	226.0	231.4	274.1	214.0	94.9	158.6	158.5	160.8	258.9	78.2	67.4	72.9	113.3	-44.9
Taiwan	19,131.4	24,405.9	18,121.6	18,381.8	17,487.9	35,204.4	40,502.8	33,374.5	32,147.9	31,599.9	-16,073.1	-16,096.9	-15,252.9	-13,766.1	-14,112.0
Tajikistan	13.8	12.1	28.6	33.1	11.1	22.7	9.0	5.2	1.1	7.3	-8.9	3.1	23.4	32.0	3.8
Tanzania	68.4	44.7	64.0	62.7	66.0	35.4	32.2	27.9	24.8	24.2	33.0	12.5	36.1	37.9	41.8
Thailand	4,984.6	6,617.5	5,989.4	4,860.2	5,841.7	14,329.9	16,385.3	14,727.2	14,792.9	15,180.7	-9,345.3	-9,767.8	-8,737.8	-9,932.7	-9,339.0
Togo	25.7	10.6	16.3	13.8	15.2	3.2	6.0	12.6	2.7	5.6	22.5	4.6	3.7	11.1	9.6
Trinidad and Tobago	785.3	1,099.6	1,087.1	1,020.2	1,064.0	1,286.7	2,228.8	2,380.0	2,440.3	4,321.7	-501.4	-1,129.2	-1,292.9	-1,420.1	-3,257.7
Tunisia	280.2	288.9	276.0	194.8	170.5	74.6	93.9	121.7	93.2	100.1	205.6	195.0	154.3	101.6	70.4
Turkey	3,217.1	3,720.1	3,094.7	3,113.0	2,904.3	2,629.4	3,041.5	3,054.8	3,516.0	3,787.9	587.7	678.6	39.9	-403.0	-883.6
Turkmenistan	18.4	84.4	248.4	47.1	34.2	8.5	28.0	45.5	59.6	76.4	9.9	56.4	202.9	-12.5	-42.2
Turks and Caicos Islands	94.8	88.6	77.1	53.6	71.9	6.3	5.9	8.1	15.3	6.1	88.5	82.7	69.0	38.3	65.8
Uganda	25.0	28.2	31.7	24.0	42.7	20.3	29.1	17.7	15.3	7.8	4.7	-0.9	14.0	8.7	34.9
Ukraine	204.6	191.0	200.1	254.8	230.8	528.9	872.2	673.6	362.4	282.0	-324.3	-681.2	-473.5	-107.6	-51.2
United Arab Emirates	2,707.8	2,284.7	2,637.9	3,593.2	3,510.4	714.3	971.8	1,194.2	922.9	1,129.0	1,993.5	1,312.9	1,443.5	2,670.3	2,381.4
United Kingdom	38,407.1	41,570.4	40,714.2	33,204.7	33,895.4	39,237.2	43,345.1	41,368.8	40,744.9	42,666.9	-830.1	-1,774.7	-654.6	-7,540.2	-8,771.5
Uruguay	494.5	536.9	406.3	208.6	326.8	198.6	313.0	227.7	193.2	255.8	295.9	223.9	178.6	15.4	71.0
Uzbekistan	339.0	157.7	144.9	138.5	256.7	25.6	41.2	53.5	77.1	83.7	313.4	116.5	91.4	61.4	173.0
Venezuela	5,353.5	5,549.9	5,642.1	4,429.7	2,839.5	11,334.5	18,623.2	15,250.5	15,093.5	17,144.2	-5,981.0	-13,073.3	-9,608.4	-10,663.8	-14,304.7
Vietnam	291.5	367.6	460.3	580.2	1,324.4	608.3	821.4	1,052.9	2,394.7	4,554.9	-316.8	-453.8	-592.6	-1,814.5	-3,230.5
Virgin Islands, British	60.1	63.4	74.7	67.4	70.5	22.3	30.9	11.9	40.5	35.0	37.8	32.5	62.8	26.9	35.5
Yemen	157.0	189.4	185.4	366.1	195.3	23.6	255.6	202.4	246.3	66.1	133.4	-66.2	-17.0	119.8	129.2
Zambia	19.8	19.1	31.2	35.7	19.5	37.7	17.7	15.6	7.9	12.5	-17.8	1.4	15.6	27.8	7.0
Zimbabwe	60.9	52.4	31.2	49.3	41.7	132.8	112.4	90.8	102.8	56.6	-71.9	-60.0	-59.6	-53.5	-14.9

¹ Includes timing adjustment and unidentified countries, not shown separately.

Source: U.S. Census Bureau, *U.S. International Trade in Goods and Services, December 2003*, Series FT-900(03-12); and annual revisions. See also <http://www.census.gov/foreign-trade/Press-Release/2003pr/12/#ft900>> (released 13 February 2004).

No. 1299. U.S. Exports and General Imports by Selected SITC Commodity Groups: 2000 to 2003

[In millions of dollars (781,918 represents $718,918,000,000). SITC=Standard International Trade Classification. For methodology, see Foreign Trade Statistics in Appendix III. N.e.s.=Not elsewhere specified]

Selected commodities	Exports [1]				General imports [2]			
	2000	2001	2002	2003	2000	2001	2002	2003
Total	781,918	729,100	693,103	724,006	1,218,022	1,140,999	1,161,366	1,259,705
Agricultural commodities [3]	51,296	53,705	53,115	59,495	39,186	39,544	42,012	47,419
Animal feeds	3,780	4,221	3,824	3,885	597	574	605	635
Coffee.	9	16	8	5	2,350	1,357	1,369	1,612
Corn.	4,695	4,755	5,108	4,963	160	135	137	151
Cotton, raw and linters.	1,893	2,174	2,031	3,219	28	27	25	27
Hides and skins	1,426	1,813	1,594	1,653	109	100	84	74
Meat and preparations.	7,004	7,231	6,356	7,261	3,841	4,254	4,269	4,403
Soybeans	5,284	5,429	5,734	7,935	31	31	28	47
Sugar.	4	3	13	6	461	480	495	535
Tobacco, unmanufactured.	1,204	1,269	1,050	1,035	569	710	701	690
Vegetables and fruits.	7,477	7,415	7,607	8,123	9,286	9,517	10,194	11,454
Wheat.	3,374	3,375	3,630	3,955	229	282	266	141
Manufactured goods [3]	625,894	577,714	544,913	556,800	1,012,855	950,679	974,576	1,027,358
ADP equipment, office machinery . .	46,595	39,240	30,368	28,852	92,133	75,859	76,877	80,826
Airplane parts.	15,062	15,735	14,309	14,524	5,572	6,287	4,986	4,474
Airplanes.	24,777	26,961	27,115	23,418	12,412	14,884	12,329	12,327
Alcoholic bev, distilled	424	489	505	551	2,946	3,063	3,273	3,693
Aluminum	3,780	3,253	2,947	2,941	6,949	6,406	6,757	7,238
Artwork/antiques.	1,387	1,637	977	1,157	5,864	5,458	5,194	4,398
Basketware, etc	3,309	3,579	3,842	4,692	4,840	5,591	6,564	7,854
Chemicals, cosmetics	5,292	5,825	5,870	6,557	3,539	3,750	4,195	5,611
Chemicals, dyeing.	4,089	3,782	3,860	4,137	2,667	2,478	2,357	2,480
Chemicals, fertilizers	2,249	2,077	2,106	2,341	1,684	1,890	1,619	2,130
Chemicals, inorganic	5,359	5,578	5,464	5,577	6,108	6,153	6,018	7,419
Chemicals, medicinal.	12,893	15,031	15,732	18,775	14,685	18,628	24,748	31,516
Chemicals, n.e.s.	12,264	12,382	12,348	12,986	5,725	5,927	6,168	6,857
Chemicals, organic	17,990	16,424	16,406	20,105	28,578	29,712	30,366	32,876
Chemicals, plastics	19,519	18,485	19,380	21,069	10,647	10,401	10,760	12,161
Cigarettes	3,304	2,118	1,466	1,403	258	238	316	300
Clothing	8,191	6,510	5,485	4,960	64,296	63,856	63,803	68,162
Cork, wood, lumber.	4,320	3,533	3,364	3,387	8,227	7,968	7,872	7,276
Crude fertilizers	1,724	1,654	1,520	1,582	1,401	1,318	1,275	1,340
Electrical machinery	89,917	72,055	66,948	69,772	108,747	84,670	81,158	82,433
Fish and preparations	2,806	3,069	2,976	3,084	9,907	9,742	10,000	10,930
Footwear.	663	639	518	495	14,842	15,234	15,387	15,603
Furniture and parts	4,744	4,255	3,814	3,608	18,923	18,610	21,577	24,356
Gem diamonds.	1,289	1,714	1,182	386	12,068	10,616	12,088	12,931
General industrial machinery.	33,094	32,153	30,075	30,115	34,667	33,264	35,200	38,467
Gold, nonmonetary	5,898	4,872	3,244	4,820	2,657	2,079	2,428	2,932
Iron and steel mill products.	5,715	5,482	5,252	6,268	15,807	12,449	12,951	11,112
Lighting, plumbing.	1,384	1,321	1,333	1,347	5,104	4,895	5,566	6,003
Metal manufactures, n.e.s.	13,453	11,365	11,170	11,218	16,204	15,510	16,681	17,985
Metal ores; scrap	4,234	4,420	4,626	5,646	3,817	3,237	3,101	3,142
Metalworking machinery.	6,191	4,703	4,140	4,108	7,726	6,587	5,104	5,335
Optical goods.	3,246	3,036	2,132	2,249	4,019	3,455	2,836	2,992
Paper and paperboard.	10,640	10,042	9,551	9,814	15,185	14,815	14,435	14,849
Photographic equipment.	4,236	3,281	3,529	3,330	6,896	5,596	5,325	5,046
Plastic articles, n.e.s..	7,607	7,065	6,820	6,778	8,034	8,257	9,138	10,216
Platinum	888	962	723	481	5,566	5,240	2,830	2,624
Power generating machinery.	32,743	33,577	32,430	31,495	33,773	36,118	33,922	32,485
Printed materials.	4,776	4,746	4,429	4,607	3,680	3,721	3,960	4,148
Pulp and waste paper	4,576	3,690	3,842	4,096	3,381	2,630	2,363	2,597
Records/magnetic media	5,395	4,611	4,414	4,473	5,172	4,883	5,279	5,852
Rubber articles, n.e.s..	1,673	1,569	1,423	1,412	1,962	1,979	2,139	2,358
Rubber tires and tubes	2,379	2,287	2,232	2,200	4,785	4,209	4,765	5,258
Scientific instruments.	30,984	29,123	27,087	27,998	22,007	21,356	20,884	23,661
Ships, boats.	1,070	1,801	1,200	1,172	1,178	1,209	1,325	1,592
Silver and bullion	227	234	262	177	775	530	687	801
Spacecraft.	158	201	509	142	217	71	310	188
Specialized industrial machinery . . .	30,959	25,747	23,532	23,371	22,711	19,554	18,401	20,841
Television, VCR, etc.	27,921	24,230	19,374	16,851	70,468	62,836	66,212	71,137
Textile yarn, fabric.	10,534	10,074	10,263	10,457	15,171	14,616	16,097	17,257
Toys/games/sporting goods.	3,609	3,217	2,985	3,155	20,011	20,901	22,067	21,566
Travel goods	351	308	277	291	4,430	4,300	4,402	4,842
Vehicles.	57,421	54,347	57,698	60,521	161,544	157,400	168,073	172,578
Watches/clocks/parts.	348	277	236	242	3,481	3,048	3,203	3,600
Wood manufactures	1,842	1,568	1,564	1,578	7,228	6,998	7,853	9,289
Mineral fuel [3]	13,179	12,494	11,541	13,691	135,367	121,923	115,748	155,561
Coal	2,162	1,915	1,673	1,621	805	1,022	966	1,176
Crude oil	463	187	92	155	89,876	74,293	79,252	101,722
Petroleum preparations	5,746	5,034	6,009	7,057	25,673	24,620	20,748	26,735
Natural gas	411	536	995	1,300	12,594	15,417	10,974	20,621
Reexports.	68,203	64,780	63,792	72,319	(X)	(X)	(X)	(X)

X Not applicable. [1] F.a.s. basis. Exports by commodity are only for domestic exports. [2] Customs value basis. [3] Includes other commodities not shown separately.

Source: U.S. Census Bureau, *U.S. International Trade in Goods and Services*, Series FT-900(03), and previous final reports. See also <http://www.census.gov/foreign-trade/Press-Release/2002pr/FinalRevisions2002/02final.pdf> (released 13 June 2003) and <http://www.census.gov/foreign-trade/Press-Release/2003pr/12/#ft900> (released 13 February 2004).

No. 1300. United States Total and Aerospace Foreign Trade: 1980 to 2003

[In millions of dollars (-19,696 represents -$19,696,000,000), except percent. Data are reported as exports of domestic merchandise, including Department of Defense shipments and undocumented exports to Canada, f.a.s. (free alongside ship) basis, and imports for consumption, customs value basis. Minus sign (-) indicates deficit]

Year	Merchandise trade			Aerospace trade						
				Exports						
								Civil		
	Trade balance	Imports	Exports	Trade balance	Imports	Total	Percent of U.S. exports	Total	Trans-ports	Military
1980	-19,696	245,262	225,566	11,952	3,554	15,506	6.9	13,248	6,727	2,258
1981	-22,267	260,982	238,715	13,134	4,500	17,634	7.4	13,312	7,180	4,322
1982	-27,510	243,952	216,442	11,035	4,568	15,603	7.2	9,608	3,834	5,995
1983	-52,409	258,048	205,639	12,619	3,446	16,065	7.8	10,595	4,683	5,470
1984	-106,703	330,678	223,976	10,082	4,926	15,008	6.7	9,659	3,195	5,350
1985	-117,712	336,526	218,815	12,593	6,132	18,725	8.6	12,942	5,518	5,783
1986	-138,279	365,438	227,159	11,826	7,902	19,728	8.7	14,851	6,276	4,875
1987	-152,119	406,241	254,122	14,575	7,905	22,480	8.8	15,768	6,377	6,714
1988	-118,526	440,952	322,426	17,860	9,087	26,947	8.4	20,298	8,766	6,651
1989	-109,399	473,211	363,812	22,083	10,028	32,111	8.8	25,619	12,313	6,492
1990	-101,718	495,311	393,592	27,282	11,801	39,083	9.9	31,517	16,691	7,566
1991	-66,723	488,453	421,730	30,785	13,003	43,788	10.4	35,548	20,881	8,239
1992	-84,501	532,665	448,164	31,356	13,662	45,018	10.0	36,906	22,379	8,111
1993	-115,568	580,659	465,091	27,235	12,183	39,418	8.5	31,823	18,146	7,596
1994	-150,630	663,256	512,626	25,010	12,363	37,373	7.3	30,050	15,931	7,322
1995	-158,801	743,543	584,742	21,561	11,509	33,071	5.7	25,079	10,606	7,991
1996	-170,214	795,289	625,075	26,602	13,668	40,270	6.4	29,477	13,624	10,792
1997	-180,522	869,704	689,182	32,239	18,134	50,374	7.3	40,075	21,028	10,299
1998	-229,758	911,896	682,138	40,960	23,110	64,071	9.4	51,999	29,168	12,072
1999	-328,821	1,024,618	695,797	37,381	25,063	62,444	9.0	50,624	25,694	11,820
2000	-436,104	1,218,022	781,918	26,734	27,944	54,679	7.0	45,566	19,615	9,113
2001	-411,899	1,140,999	729,100	26,035	32,473	58,508	8.0	49,371	22,151	9,137
2002	-468,263	1,161,366	693,103	29,534	27,242	56,775	8.2	47,348	21,661	9,427
2003	-535,455	1,259,485	724,030	27,111	25,393	52,504	7.3	44,060	19,434	8,445

Source: Aerospace Industries Association of America, Washington, DC, *Aerospace Facts and Figures*, annual.

No. 1301. U.S. Exporting Companies Profile by Company Type and Employment-Size Class: 1992 and 2001

[348,960 represents $348,960,000,000. Data are based on economic census and survey data on file at the Census Bureau, administrative records from other government agencies, and documents filed for export clearances]

Company type and employment-size-class	Number of exporters		Known export value [1] (mil. dol.)		Percent of—			
					Number of exporters		Known export value	
	1992	2001	1992	2001	1992	2001	1992	2001
All companies, total	112,854	238,284	348,960	623,394	100.0	100.0	100.0	100.0
No employees	15,534	70,818	9,178	48,586	13.8	29.7	2.6	7.8
1 to 19 employees	51,186	94,171	29,397	43,629	45.4	39.5	8.4	7.0
20 to 49 employees	18,501	30,822	17,005	19,863	16.4	12.9	4.9	3.2
50 to 99 employees	10,505	16,757	13,840	17,533	9.3	7.0	4.0	2.8
100 to 249 employees	8,679	13,067	18,371	29,011	7.7	5.5	5.3	4.7
250 to 499 employees	3,621	5,101	15,055	23,600	3.2	2.1	4.3	3.8
500 or more employees	4,828	7,548	246,114	441,171	4.3	3.2	70.5	70.8
Manufacturers	(NA)	69,134	(NA)	444,122	(NA)	29.0	(NA)	71.2
No employees	(NA)	12,772	(NA)	17,130	(NA)	5.4	(NA)	2.7
1 to 19 employees	(NA)	20,075	(NA)	5,233	(NA)	8.4	(NA)	0.8
20 to 49 employees	(NA)	13,868	(NA)	6,474	(NA)	5.8	(NA)	1.0
50 to 99 employees	(NA)	9,009	(NA)	7,298	(NA)	3.8	(NA)	1.2
100 to 249 employees	(NA)	7,344	(NA)	16,154	(NA)	3.1	(NA)	2.6
250 to 499 employees	(NA)	2,720	(NA)	13,998	(NA)	1.1	(NA)	2.2
500 or more employees	(NA)	3,346	(NA)	377,835	(NA)	1.4	(NA)	60.6
Wholesalers	(NA)	72,570	(NA)	93,488	(NA)	30.5	(NA)	15.0
No employees	(NA)	17,013	(NA)	9,515	(NA)	7.1	(NA)	1.5
1 to 19 employees	(NA)	39,402	(NA)	23,826	(NA)	16.5	(NA)	3.8
20 to 49 employees	(NA)	8,843	(NA)	8,085	(NA)	3.7	(NA)	1.3
50 to 99 employees	(NA)	3,515	(NA)	6,609	(NA)	1.5	(NA)	1.1
100 to 249 employees	(NA)	2,305	(NA)	8,534	(NA)	1.0	(NA)	1.4
250 to 499 employees	(NA)	766	(NA)	4,960	(NA)	0.3	(NA)	0.8
500 or more employees	(NA)	726	(NA)	31,958	(NA)	0.3	(NA)	0.8
Other companies	(NA)	85,866	(NA)	76,945	(NA)	36.0	(NA)	12.3
No employees	(NA)	33,771	(NA)	18,264	(NA)	14.2	(NA)	2.9
1 to 19 employees	(NA)	33,383	(NA)	13,494	(NA)	14.0	(NA)	2.2
20 to 49 employees	(NA)	7,114	(NA)	4,472	(NA)	3.0	(NA)	0.7
50 to 99 employees	(NA)	3,646	(NA)	3,196	(NA)	1.5	(NA)	0.5
100 to 249 employees	(NA)	3,135	(NA)	4,019	(NA)	1.3	(NA)	0.6
250 to 499 employees	(NA)	1,501	(NA)	4,134	(NA)	0.6	(NA)	0.7
500 or more employees	(NA)	3,316	(NA)	29,366	(NA)	1.4	(NA)	4.7
Unclassified companies	(NA)	10,714	(NA)	8,839	(NA)	4.5	(NA)	1.1

NA Not Not available. [1] Known value is defined as the value of exports by known exporters, i.e., those export transactions that could be matched to specific companies. Export values are on f.a.s. or "free alongside ship basis." Total export value was $251 billion in 1987 and $448 billion in 1992 and $729 billion in 2001.

Source: U.S. Census Bureau, *A Profile of U.S. Exporting Companies. 1992* and *2000-2001*. See also <http://www.census.gov/foreign-trade/aip/edbrel-0001.pdf> (released 20 February 2003).

Foreign Commerce and Aid 819

No. 1302. Domestic Exports and Imports for Consumption of Merchandise by Selected NAICS Product Category: 2000 to 2003

[In millions of dollars (712,285 represents $712,285,000,000). Includes nonmonetary gold. For methodology, see Foreign Trade Statistics in Appendix III. NAICS=North American Industry Classification System; see Text, Section 15]

Product category	2000	2001	2002	2003
Domestic exports, total	712,285	666,021	629,599	651,687
Agricultural, forestry and fishery products	29,153	29,666	30,068	34,699
Agricultural products, total	23,596	24,068	24,827	29,194
Livestock and livestock products	1,255	1,309	1,020	1,177
Forestry products, not elsewhere specified	1,644	1,436	1,419	1,462
Fish, fresh or chilled; and other marine products	2,658	2,854	2,802	2,866
Mining, total	6,187	5,403	5,585	6,117
Oil and gas	1,706	1,261	1,725	2,143
Minerals and ores	4,481	4,141	3,860	3,973
Manufacturing, total	644,440	597,101	562,834	577,789
Food and kindred products	24,966	26,486	25,175	26,795
Beverages and tobacco products	5,568	4,334	3,559	3,648
Textiles and fabrics	7,010	7,098	7,397	7,557
Textile mill products	2,236	1,991	1,875	1,881
Apparel and accessories	8,104	6,469	5,462	4,923
Leather and allied products	2,322	2,285	2,049	2,035
Wood products	4,854	3,944	3,777	3,818
Paper products	15,539	14,045	13,640	13,965
Printed, publishing & similar products	4,869	4,867	4,509	4,706
Petroleum and coal products	8,862	8,214	7,897	9,349
Chemicals	77,649	76,837	78,049	88,384
Plastics and rubber products	16,970	15,745	15,383	15,661
Nonmetallic mineral products	7,830	7,378	6,025	6,069
Primary metal products	20,126	18,150	15,371	17,877
Fabricated metal products	21,737	19,547	18,893	18,848
Machinery, except electrical	85,038	76,572	70,178	69,285
Computers and electronic products	161,449	134,263	116,243	115,883
Electrical equipment, appliances and components	25,401	22,764	20,587	20,632
Transportation equipment	121,701	122,877	123,970	122,246
Furniture and fixtures	2,882	2,419	2,158	2,349
Miscellaneous manufactured commodities	19,327	20,815	20,640	21,591
Special classification provisions	32,505	33,852	31,112	33,109
Waste & scrap	4,948	4,738	5,081	6,456
Used or second-hand merchandise	1,950	2,169	1,562	1,808
Goods returned or reimported	333	310	241	205
Special classification provision, not elsewhere specified	25,274	26,635	24,228	24,640
Imports for consumption, total	1,205,339	1,132,635	1,154,811	1,250,097
Agricultural, forestry and fishery products	24,378	23,598	24,327	26,197
Agricultural products, total	11,771	11,290	11,773	13,035
Livestock and livestock products	3,085	3,445	3,455	2,782
Forestry products, not elsewhere specified	1,409	1,158	1,288	1,612
Fish, fresh or chilled; and other marine products	8,113	7,706	7,811	8,768
Mining, total	79,841	76,243	76,288	105,662
Oil and gas	76,166	72,690	72,830	101,800
Minerals and ores	3,675	3,553	3,458	3,862
Manufacturing, total	1,040,329	972,669	995,103	1,060,349
Food and kindred products	18,944	19,646	21,110	23,769
Beverages and tobacco products	8,350	8,723	9,772	10,925
Textiles and fabrics	7,042	6,336	6,778	6,791
Textile mill products	7,347	7,580	8,643	9,857
Apparel and accessories	62,928	62,429	62,313	66,499
Leather and allied products	21,463	21,865	22,104	22,627
Wood products	15,388	14,968	15,720	16,581
Paper products	19,080	18,170	17,528	18,414
Printed, publishing & similar products	4,197	4,143	4,432	4,699
Petroleum and coal products	40,156	35,222	31,976	39,161
Chemicals	76,606	80,681	87,311	102,078
Plastics and rubber products	17,362	16,887	18,554	20,504
Nonmetallic mineral products	14,740	13,552	13,547	14,428
Primary metal products	43,833	36,350	34,356	34,065
Fabricated metal products	27,974	26,386	28,607	30,068
Machinery, except electrical	79,366	72,124	68,645	77,344
Computers and electronic products	250,694	204,950	205,564	212,201
Electrical equipment, appliances and components	39,567	38,949	39,707	41,914
Transportation equipment	213,110	212,013	219,186	223,304
Furniture and fixtures	15,607	15,266	17,492	19,636
Miscellaneous manufactured commodities	56,577	56,427	61,759	65,484
Special classification provisions	60,791	60,125	59,093	57,889
Waste & scrap	1,875	1,590	1,613	1,810
Used or second-hand merchandise	6,345	5,902	5,668	4,752
Goods returned or reimported	33,851	34,682	34,981	33,605
Special classification provision, not elsewhere specified	18,720	17,951	16,831	17,723

Source: U.S. Census Bureau, *U.S. International Trade in Goods and Services*, series FT-900, December issues. For most recent, see <http://www.census.gov/foreign-trade/Press-Release/2003pr/12/#ft900> (released 13 February 2004).

Puerto Rico and the Island Areas

This section presents summary economic and social statistics for Puerto Rico, the U.S. Virgin Islands, Guam, American Samoa, and the Northern Mariana Islands. Primary sources are the decennial censuses of population and housing, county business patterns, and the censuses of agriculture, business, manufactures, and construction (taken every 5 years) conducted by the U.S. Census Bureau; the annual *Vital Statistics of the United States*, issued by the National Center for Health Statistics; and the annual *Income and Product* of the Puerto Rico Planning Board, San Juan.

Jurisdiction—The United States gained jurisdiction over these areas as follows: the islands of *Puerto Rico* and *Guam*, surrendered by Spain to the United States in December 1898, were ceded to the United States by the Treaty of Paris, ratified in 1899. Puerto Rico became a commonwealth on July 25, 1952, thereby achieving a high degree of local autonomy under its own constitution. The *U.S. Virgin Islands*, comprising 50 islands and cays, was purchased by the United States from Denmark in 1917. *American Samoa*, a group of seven islands, was acquired by the United States in accordance with a convention among the United States, Great Britain, and Germany, ratified in 1900 (Swains Island was annexed in 1925). By an agreement approved by the Security Council and the United States, the Northern Mariana Islands, previously under Japanese mandate, was administered by the United States between 1947 and 1986 under the United Nations trusteeship system. The Northern Mariana Islands became a commonwealth in 1986.

Censuses—Because characteristics of the Puerto Rico and the Island Areas differ, the presentation of census data for them is not uniform. The 1960 Census of Population covered all of the places listed above except the Northern Mariana Islands (their census was conducted in April 1958 by the Office of the High Commissioner), while the 1960 Census of Housing also excluded American Samoa. The 1970, 1980, 1990, and 2000 Censuses of Population and Housing covered all five areas. The 1959, 1969, and 1978 Censuses of Agriculture covered Puerto Rico, American Samoa, Guam, and the Virgin Islands; the 1964, 1974, and 1982 censuses covered the same areas except American Samoa; and the 1969, 1978, 1987, 1992, and 1997 censuses included the Northern Mariana Islands. Beginning in 1967, Congress authorized the economic censuses, to be taken at 5-year intervals, for years ending in "2" and "7." Prior economic censuses were conducted in Puerto Rico for 1949, 1954, 1958, and 1963 and in Guam and the U.S. Virgin Islands for 1958 and 1963. In 1967, the census of construction industries was added for the first time in Puerto Rico; in 1972, the U.S. Virgin Islands and Guam were covered. For 1982, 1987, 1992, and 1997 the economic censuses covered the Northern Mariana Islands.

Information in other sections—In addition to the statistics presented in this section, other data are included as integral parts of many tables showing distribution by states in various sections of the *Abstract*. See "Puerto Rico and the Island Areas" in the Index. For definition and explanation of terms used, see Section 1, Population; Section 4, Education; Section 17, Agriculture; Section 20, Construction and Housing; Section 21, Manufactures; and Section 22, Domestic Trade.

Figure 29.1
Selected Island Areas of the United States

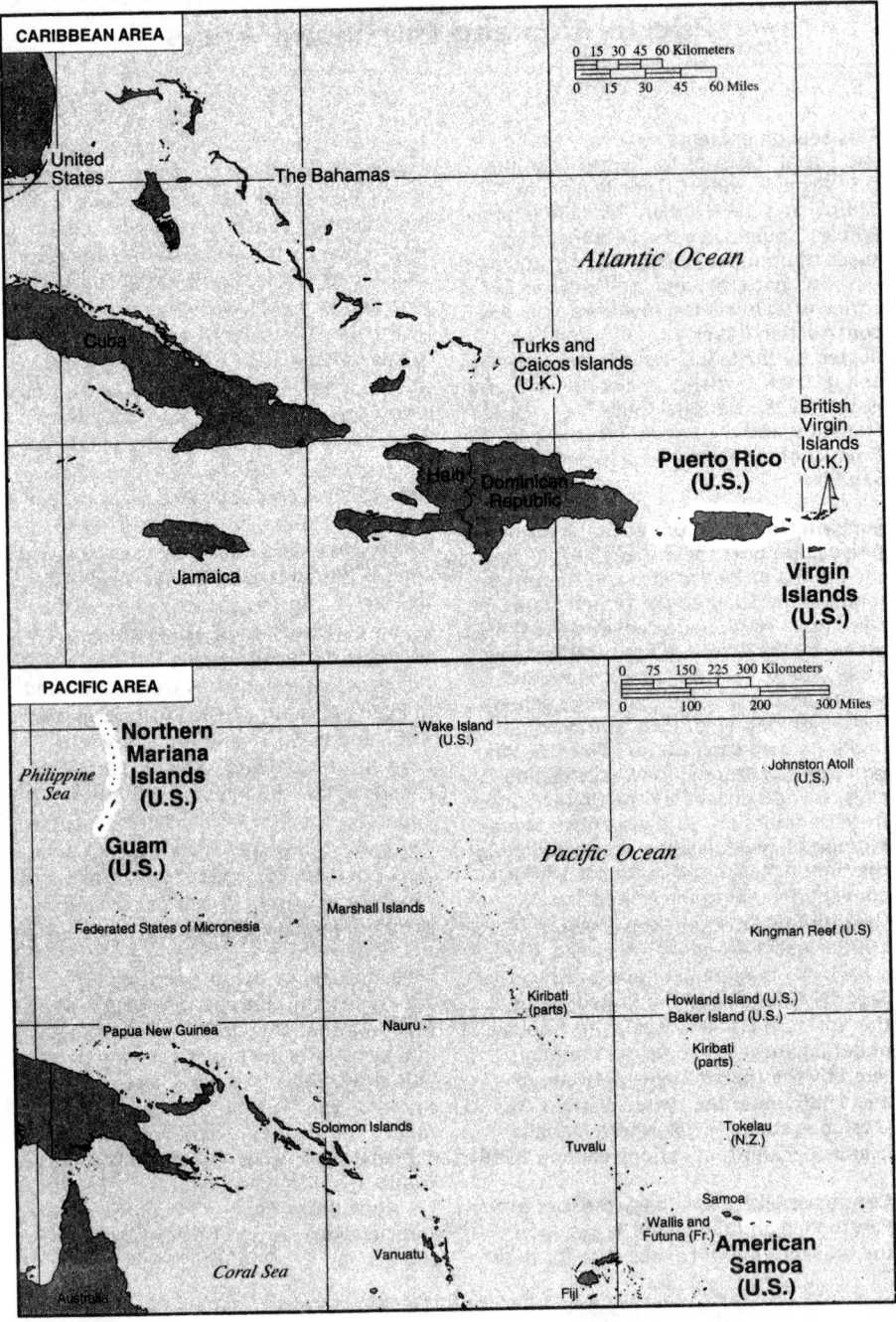

U.S. Census Bureau, Statistical Abstract of the United States: 2004-2005

No. 1303. Estimated Resident Population With Projections: 1970 to 2010

[In thousands (2,722 represents 2,722,000). Population as of July 1. Population data generally are de-facto figures for the present territory. Data for 1990 to 2000 are adjusted to the 2000 Census of Population for Puerto Rico only. See text, Section 30, for general comments regarding the data. For details of methodology, coverage, and reliability, see source]

Area	1970	1980	1990	1995	1999	2000	2001	2002	2003	2010, proj.
Puerto Rico	2,722	3,210	3,537	3,683	3,800	3,816	3,838	3,859	3,879	4,001
American Samoa	27	32	47	57	64	57	57	58	58	57
Guam	86	107	134	144	152	155	158	158	58	57
Virgin Islands	63	98	104	114	120	109	109	161	164	181
Northern Mariana Islands	12	17	44	58	69	70	72	74	76	91

Source: U.S. Bureau of the Census, International Data Base. See Internet site: <http://census.gov/ipc/www/idbnew.html>

No. 1304. Vital Statistics—Specified Areas: 1980 to 2002

[Births, deaths, and infant deaths by place of residence. Rates for 1980, 1990 and 2000 based on population enumerated as of April 1; for other years, on population estimated as of July 1]

Area and year	Births Number	Births Rate [1]	Deaths Number	Deaths Rate [1]	Infant deaths Number	Infant deaths Rate [2]
Puerto Rico:						
1980	72,986	22.8	20,413	6.4	1,351	18.5
1990	66,417	18.8	25,957	7.3	888	13.4
1995	63,425	17.0	30,032	8.1	804	12.7
2000	59,333	15.2	28,369	7.2	574	9.7
2001	55,866	14.2	29,082	7.6	517	9.3
2002 [3]	52,747	13.7	27,927	7.2	505	(NA)
Guam:						
1980	2,945	27.8	393	3.7	43	14.6
1990	3,839	28.6	520	3.9	31	8.1
1995	4,180	29.0	592	4.1	38	9.4
2000	3,766	24.4	648	4.2	22	5.8
2001	3,564	22.6	663	4.2	35	9.8
2002 [3]	3,212	19.9	639	4.0	20	(NA)
Virgin Islands:						
1980	2,504	25.9	504	5.2	61	24.4
1990	2,267	21.8	480	4.6	33	14.6
1995	2,063	18.1	664	5.8	34	16.6
2000	1,564	12.9	641	5.3	21	13.4
2001	1,669	13.7	605	5.6	13	(NA)
2002 [3]	1,634	15.0	623	5.7	5	(NA)
American Samoa:						
1997	1,634	27.1	257	4.3	17	(B)
2002 [3]	1,627	28.2	294	5.1	25	(NA)
Northern Marianas:						
1998	1,462	21.9	162	2.4	13	(B)
2002 [3]	1,290	17.4	163	220.3	9	(NA)

B Base figure too small to meet statistical standards of reliability. NA Not available. [1] Per 1,000 population. [2] Rates are infant deaths (under 1 year) per 1,000 live births. [3] Mortality data for 2002 is preliminary.
Source: U.S. National Center for Health Statistics, *Vital Statistics of the United States*, annual; and *National Vital Statistics Reports (NSVR)* and unpublished data.

No. 1305. Population Characteristics by Area: 2000

[As of April 1. Based on the Census of Population; see Appendix III. See Table 346 for land area. For definition of median, see Guide to Tabular Presentation]

Item	United States	Puerto Rico	Virgin Islands	Guam	American Samoa	Northern Mariana Islands
Total resident population	281,421,906	3,808,610	108,612	154,805	57,291	69,221
Percent increase, 1990-2000	13.2	8.1	6.7	16.3	22.5	59.7
Male	138,053,563	1,833,577	51,864	79,181	29,264	31,984
Female	143,368,343	1,975,033	56,748	75,624	28,027	37,237
Males per 100 females	96.3	92.8	91.4	104.7	104.4	85.9
Median age (years)	35.3	32.1	33.4	27.4	21.3	28.7
Marital status, persons 15 years and over	221,148,671	2,903,329	80,207	107,649	35,079	53,632
Never married	59,913,370	813,784	32,764	37,711	12,741	22,462
Now married, excludes separated	120,231,273	1,509,403	31,223	57,505	19,519	28,224
Separated	4,769,220	104,897	2,639	1,453	437	916
Widowed	14,674,500	197,123	4,078	4,253	1,570	1,121
Divorced	21,560,308	278,122	9,503	6,727	812	909
Households and families:						
Households	105,480,101	1,261,325	40,648	38,769	9,349	14,055
Family households (families) [1]	71,787,347	1,004,080	26,636	32,367	8,706	9,407
With own children under 18 years	34,588,368	486,409	14,107	19,678	6,297	6,569
Married-couple family	54,493,232	682,804	13,498	22,693	6,596	6,445
With own children under 18 years	24,835,505	337,190	5,905	13,964	5,261	4,526
Female household, no husband present	12,900,103	268,476	10,132	6,284	1,398	1,663
With own children under 18 years	7,561,874	131,584	6,450	3,753	640	1,106
Nonfamily households	33,692,754	257,245	14,012	6,402	643	4,648
Average household size	2.59	2.98	2.64	3.89	6.05	3.66
Average family size	3.14	3.41	3.34	4.27	6.24	4.16

[1] Includes other family types, not shown separately.
Source: U.S. Census Bureau, United States and Puerto Rico: DP-1, "Profile of General Demographic Characteristics: 2000 (area)" and DP-2, "Profile of Selected Social Characteristics Characteristics: 2000 (area)"; Virgin Islands, Guam, and Northern Mariana Islands: "Population and Housing Profile: 2000 (area)". See Internet sites: <http://www.census.gov/population/www/cen2000/ islandareas.html> and <http://www.census.gov/census2000/states/pr.html>

Puerto Rico and the Island Areas 823

No. 1306. Puerto Rico, Guam, Virgin Islands, American Samoa, and Northern Mariana Islands—Population: 1990 and 2000

[As of April 1. Minus sign (-) indicates decrease]

Area	1990	2000	Percent change, 1990 to 2000	Area	1990	2000	Percent change, 1990 to 2000
PUERTO RICO				Trujillo Alto zona urbana	44,336	50,841	14.7
Municipio:				Arecibo zona urbana.	49,545	49,318	-0.5
San Juan	437,745	434,374	-0.8	Fajardo zona urbana.	31,659	33,286	5.1
Bayamon	220,262	224,044	1.7	Levittown comunidad zona			
Ponce	187,749	186,475	-0.7	urbana	30,807	30,140	-2.2
Carolina	177,806	186,076	4.7	Catano zona urbana	34,587	30,071	-13.1
Caguas	133,447	140,502	5.3				
Arecibo.	93,385	100,131	7.2	**GUAM**			
Guaynabo.	92,886	100,053	7.7	Dedido District	31,728	42,980	35.5
Mayaguez.	100,371	98,434	-1.9	Yigo District	14,213	19,474	37.0
Toa Baja.	89,454	94,085	5.2	Mangilao District	10,483	13,313	27.0
Trujillo Alto	61,120	75,728	23.9				
Aguadilla	59,335	64,685	9.0	**U.S. VIRGIN ISLANDS**			
Toa Alta	44,101	63,929	45.0	St Croix Island	50,139	53,234	6.2
Vega Baja	55,997	61,929	10.6	St Thomas Island	48,166	51,181	6.3
Humacao	55,203	59,035	6.9	Charlotte Amalie subdistrict . . .	20,589	18,914	-8.1
Rio Grande	45,648	52,362	14.7	St John Island.	3,504	4,197	19.8
Place:							
San Juan zona urbana	426,832	421,958	-1.1	**AMERICAN SAMOA**			
Bayamon zona urbana	202,103	203.499	0.7	Eastern District	21,175	23,441	10.7
Carolina zona urbana	162,404	168,164	3.5	Ma'oputasi County	10,640	11,695	9.9
Ponce zona urbana	159,151	155,038	-2.6	Western District.	23,868	32,435	35.9
Caguas zona urbana.	92,429	88,680	-4.1	Tualauta County.	14,724	22,025	49.6
Guaynabo zona urbana.	73,385	78,806	7.4	**NORTHERN MARIANA ISLANDS**			
Mayaguez zona urbana.	83,010	78,647	-5.3	Saipan Municipality	38,896	62,392	60.4

No. 1307. Selected Social and Economic Characteristics by Area: 2000

[As of April 1. Based on the Census of Population and Housing; see Appendix III]

Characteristic	United States	Puerto Rico	Virgin Islands	Guam	American Samoa	Northern Mariana Islands
EDUCATIONAL ATTAINMENT						
Persons 25 years and over.	182,211,639	2,288,326	65,603	83,281	25,380	42,123
Less than 9th grade	13,755,477	581,225	12,133	7,843	3,120	5,794
9th to 12th grade, no diploma.	21,960,148	335,179	13,743	11,862	5,476	7,181
High school graduate	52,168,981	509,856	17,044	26,544	9,983	14,986
Some college or associate degree. . . .	49,864,428	443,813	11,694	20,398	4,928	7,634
Bachelor's degree or higher	44,462,605	418,253	10,989	16,634	1,873	6,528
EMPLOYMENT STATUS						
Persons, 16 years old and over. . . .	217,168,077	2,842,876	78,265	105,014	33,945	52,898
In labor force.	138,820,935	1,156,532	51,042	68,894	17,664	44,471
Percent of total	63.9	40.7	65.2	65.6	52.0	84.1
Armed forces	1,152,137	4,669	109	4,442	37	6
Civilian labor force	137,668,798	1,151,863	50,933	64,452	17,627	44,465
Employed.	129,721,512	930,865	46,565	57,053	16,718	42,753
Unemployed	7,947,286	220,998	4,368	7,399	909	1,712
Percent of civilian labor force .	5.8	19.2	8.6	11.5	5.2	3.9
Not in labor force	78,347,142	1,686,344	27,223	36,120	16,281	8,427
FAMILY INCOME IN 1999						
Families	72,261,780	1,008,555	26,636	32,367	8,706	9,407
Less than $10,000	4,155,386	316,675	5,584	3,955	2,107	1,553
$10,000 to $14,999	3,115,586	150,199	2,142	1,734	1,449	1,162
$15,000 to $24,999	7,757,397	202,824	4,203	3,923	1,995	1,864
$25,000 to $34,999	8,684,429	123,810	3,529	4,082	1,146	1,280
$35,000 to $49,999	12,377,108	101,047	4,011	5,400	969	1,301
$50,000 to $74,999	16,130,100	64,839	3,782	6,267	677	1,191
$75,000 or more	20,041,774	49,161	3,385	7,006	363	1,056
Median family income (dollars)	50,046	16,543	28,553	41,229	18,357	25,853
RESIDENCE IN 1995						
Persons 5 years and over	262,375,152	3,515,228	100,059	138,020	49,471	63,429
Same house	142,027,478	2,560,034	61,879	73,120	37,103	23,989
Different house in this area	112,851,828	820,514	27,688	40,945	5,763	15,576
Outside area	7,495,846	134,680	10,492	23,955	6,605	23,864
LANGUAGE SPOKEN AT HOME						
Persons 5 years and over	262,375,152	3,515,228	100,059	138,020	49,471	63,429
Speak only English at home.	215,423,557	506,661	74,740	52,831	1,440	6,819

Source of Tables 1306 and 1307: U.S. Census Bureau, United States and Puerto Rico: DP-1, "Profile of General Demographic Characteristics: 2000 (area)" and DP-2, "Profile of Selected Social Characteristics: 2000 (area)"; Virgin Islands, Guam, and Northern Mariana Islands: "Population and Housing Profile: 2000 (area)". See Internet sites: /<http://www.census.gov/census2000/states/pr.html/> <http://www.census.gov/population/www/cen2000/islandareas.html>

No. 1308. Public Elementary and Secondary Schools by Area: 2001

[For school year ending in year shown, unless otherwise indicated. (2,257,837 represents $2,257,837,000)]

Item	Puerto Rico	Guam	Virgin Islands	American Samoa	Item	Puerto Rico	Guam	Virgin Islands	American Samoa
Enrollment, fall	604,177	31,992	18,780	15,897	School staff	51,247	3,210	(NA)	1,316
Elementary (kindergarten-grade 8)	438,053	23,133	13,421	11,911	Teachers	42,906	1,918	(NA)	914
					Student support staff	3,854	53	(NA)	73
Secondary (grades 9-12 and post graduates)	166,124	8,859	5,359	3,986	Other support services staff	18,082	140	(NA)	172
Staff, fall	75,254	3,765	(NA)	1,686	Current expenditures [1]				
School district staff	2,071	362	(NA)	125	($1,000)	2,257,837	(NA)	125,252	40,642

NA Not available   [1] Public elementary and secondary day schools.

Source: U.S. National Center for Education Statistics, *Digest of Education Statistics*, annual; and unpublished data. See Internet site <http://nces.ed.gov/edstats>.

No. 1309. Puerto Rico—Summary: 1980 to 2003

[3,184.0 represents 3,184,000]

Item	Unit	1980	1990	1995	1999	2000	2001	2002	2003
POPULATION									
Total [1]	1,000	3,184.0	3,512.4	3,641.1	3,790.6	3,808.0	3,827.5	3,849.3	3,869.0
Persons per family	Number	4.3	3.7	3.5	3.4	3.4	3.4	3.4	3.3
EDUCATION [2]									
Enrollment, total	1,000	941.4	953.0	932.7	907.1	971.4	993.3	1,067.1	1,172.3
Public (except public colleges or universities)	1,000	716.1	651.2	621.4	613.9	612.3	610.8	603.5	596.3
Private schools	1,000	95.2	145.8	145.9	118.7	183.7	197.5	272.9	376.2
College and university	1,000	130.1	156.0	165.4	174.5	175.4	185.0	190.7	199.8
Expenses	Mil. dol.	825.0	1,686.4	2,555.8	3,950.6	4,254.1	4,646.6	4,608.7	5,090.1
As percent of GNP	Percent	7.5	7.8	9.0	10.3	10.3	10.5	10.2	10.7
Public	Mil. dol.	612.2	1,054.2	1,689.4	2,970.0	3,160.4	3,298.9	3,459.3	3,934.5
Private	Mil. dol.	212.8	644.2	866.4	980.6	1,093.7	1,105.1	1,149.4	1,155.6
LABOR FORCE [3]									
Total [4]	1,000	907	1,124	1,219	1,310	1,303	1,293	1,330	1,378
Employed [5]	1,000	753	963	1,051	1,147	1,159	1,158	1,170	1,211
Agriculture [6]	1,000	38	36	34	27	24	22	23	25
Manufacturing	1,000	143	168	172	159	159	159	139	136
Trade	1,000	138	185	211	229	239	242	240	257
Government	1,000	184	222	232	246	249	251	261	274
Unemployed	1,000	154	161	168	163	143	135	160	167
Unemployment rate [7]	Rate	17.0	14.0	14.0	12.5	11.0	10.5	12.0	12.1
Compensation of employees	Mil. dol.	7,200	13,639	17,773	22,098	23,504	24,389	24,933	25,876
Average compensation	Dollar	9,563	14,854	16,911	19,266	20,280	21,061	21,310	21,368
Salary and wages	Mil. dol.	7,200	13,639	17,773	22,098	23,504	24,389	24,933	25,876
INCOME [8]									
Personal income:									
Current dollars	Mil. dol.	11,002	21,105	27,378	36,614	38,856	41,079	42,225	43,639
Constant (1954) dollars	Mil. dol.	3,985	5,551	6,547	8,250	8,491	8,714	8,919	9,118
Disposable personal income:									
Current dollars	Mil. dol.	10,403	19,914	25,591	34,042	36,239	38,405	39,437	40,537
Constant (1954) dollars	Mil. dol.	3,768	5,238	6,119	7,671	7,919	8,147	8,331	8,470
Average family income:									
Current dollars	Dollar	14,858	22,232	26,316	32,842	34,693	36,491	37,296	37,221
Constant (1954) dollars	Dollar	5,381	5,847	6,293	7,400	7,581	7,741	7,878	7,777
BANKING [9]									
Assets	Mil. dol.	10,223	27,902	39,859	53,338	58,813	55,701	66,294	74,315
TOURISM [8]									
Number of visitors	1,000	2,140	3,426	4,087	4,221	4,566	4,908	4,364	4,402
Visitor expenditures	Mil. dol.	619	1,366	1,828	2,138	2,388	2,728	2,486	2,677
Average per visitor	Dollar	289	399	447	507	523	556	570	608
Net income from tourism	Mil. dol.	202	383	499	577	615	663	645	678

[1] 1980, and 1990 enumerated as of April 1; all other years estimated as of July 1.   [2] Enrollment for the first school month. Expenses for school year ending in year shown. "Public" includes: Public Preschool, Public Elementary, Public Intermediate, Public High School, Public Post-High School, Public Technological, Public Adult Education, Public Vocational Education, and Public Special Education. "College and university" includes both public and private colleges and universities.   [3] Annual average of monthly figures. For fiscal years.   [4] For population 16 years old and over.   [5] Includes other employment not shown separately.   [6] Includes forestry and fisheries.   [7] Percent unemployed of the labor force.   [8] For fiscal years.   [9] As of June 30. Does not include federal savings banks and international banking entities.

Source: Puerto Rico Planning Board, San Juan PR, *Income and Product* annual; and *Socioeconomics Statistics*, annual.

Puerto Rico and the Island Areas   **825**

No. 1310. Puerto Rico—Gross Product and Net Income: 1990 to 2003

[In millions of dollars (21,619 represents $21,619,000,000). For fiscal years ending June 30. Data for 2003 are preliminary]

Item	1990	1995	1999	2000	2001	2002	2003
Gross product.	21,619	28,452	38,281	41,419	44,047	45,008	47,354
Agriculture	434	318	336	529	348	228	203
Manufacturing.	12,126	17,867	23,312	24,079	29,037	30,527	31,297
Contract construction and mining [1] . .	720	1,006	1,668	1,875	1,802	1,814	1,760
Transportation & other public services [2]	2,468	3,276	4,032	4,237	4,698	4,934	5,145
Trade	4,728	5,989	8,112	8,340	8,339	8,409	8,622
Finance, insurance, real estate.	3,896	5,730	8,183	9,977	11,294	11,590	12,732
Services.	3,015	4,724	6,140	6,603	6,982	7,169	7,391
Government	3,337	4,440	5,530	5,478	5,992	6,303	7,147
Commonwealth	2,884	3,793	4,693	4,601	5,084	5,364	6,147
Municipalities.	453	647	836	877	908	939	1,000
Rest of the world	-8,985	-14,195	-19,560	-20,283	-25,162	-26,298	-27,009
Statistical discrepancy	-121	-703	529	585	717	333	66
Net income.	17,941	23,653	29,908	32,610	34,582	35,509	38,229
Agriculture	486	442	619	669	613	544	570
Manufacturing.	11,277	16,685	21,662	22,348	27,390	28,668	29,595
Mining	26	30	34	41	45	40	40
Contract construction	679	903	1,474	1,691	1,578	1,569	1,517
Transportation and other public services [2] . .	1,778	2,360	2,632	2,968	3,159	3,364	3,516
Trade	3,420	4,108	5,462	5,752	5,730	5,802	5,908
Finance, insurance, and real estate.	3,280	4,735	6,743	8,264	9,252	9,402	10,647
Services.	2,643	4,146	5,313	5,682	5,986	6,114	6,297
Commonwealth government [3]	3,337	4,440	5,530	5,478	5,992	6,303	7,147
Rest of the world	-8,985	-14,195	-19,560	-20,283	-25,162	-26,298	-27,009

[1] Mining includes only quarries. [2] Includes other public utilities, and radio and television broadcasting. [3] Includes public enterprises not elsewhere classified.

No. 1311. Puerto Rico—Transfer Payments: 1990 to 2003

[In millions of dollars (4,871 represents $4,871,000,000). Data represent transfer payments between federal and state governments and other nonresidents. See headnote, Table 1310]

Item	1990	1995	1999	2000	2001	2002	2003
Total receipts	4,871	6,236	8,627	8,659	9,501	9,824	10,374
Federal Government.	4,649	5,912	8,057	7,966	8,712	9,047	9,764
Transfers to individuals [1]	4,577	5,838	7,866	7,868	8,606	8,922	9,637
Veterans benefits.	349	440	479	491	490	519	514
Medicare	368	661	1,112	1,196	1,262	1,433	2,045
Old age, disability, survivors (social security) . .	2,055	2,912	3,556	3,863	4,336	4,643	4,644
Nutritional assistance	880	1,063	1,088	1,193	1,208	1,194	1,237
Industry subsidies	72	74	191	98	106	124	127
Other nonresidents	18	18	17	15	11	17	22
U.S. state governments	205	307	553	679	778	760	588
Total payments.	1,801	2,301	2,565	2,763	2,900	2,988	3,081
Federal Government.	1,756	2,132	2,499	2,693	2,845	2,884	2,937
Transfers from individuals	817	1,052	1,237	1,326	1,408	1,444	1,470
Contribution to Medicare	97	162	182	191	205	227	227
Employee contribution for social security . .	720	888	1,053	1,133	1,200	1,215	1,240
Transfers from industries	16	49	47	51	52	59	54
Unemployment insurance	247	184	216	234	233	228	228
Employer contribution for social security . . .	675	847	999	1,081	1,152	1,153	1,184
Other nonresidents [2]	45	164	66	70	55	104	144
Net balance	3,070	3,935	6,062	5,897	6,602	6,835	7,293
Federal government	2,893	3,780	5,558	5,273	5,868	6,162	6,827
U.S. state governments	16	13	12	10	6	-32	-53
Other nonresidents	162	143	492	614	728	705	519

[1] Includes other receipts and payments not shown separately. [2] Includes U.S. state governments.

Source of Tables 1310 and 1311: Puerto Rico Planning Board, San Juan, PR, *Economic Report of the Governor,* annual.

No. 1312. Puerto Rico—Merchandise Imports and Exports: 1980 to 2003

[In millions of dollars (9,018 represents $9,018,000,000). Imports are imports for consumption; see text, Section 28]

Item	1980	1985	1990	1995	1996	1997	1998	1999	2000	2001	2002	2003
Imports.	9,018	10,162	16,200	18,969	19,422	21,928	21,706	26,697	27,199	27,690	30,511	35,945
From U.S . . .	5,345	6,130	10,792	12,213	12,220	13,904	13,318	15,949	15,171	14,718	15,675	16,949
From other. . .	3,673	4,032	5,408	6,756	7,202	8,024	8,388	10,754	11,834	12,972	14,824	18,996
Exports	6,576	11,087	20,402	23,573	22,379	26,653	31,501	37,779	43,191	46,689	50,641	55,814
To U.S	5,643	9,873	17,915	20,986	19,907	25,045	28,109	33,173	38,335	40,981	44,907	46,880
To other	933	1,214	2,487	2,587	2,472	1,608	3,392	4,785	4,856	5,708	5,734	8,934

Source: U.S. Census Bureau, *Foreign Commerce and Navigation of the United States,* annual; *U.S. Trade with Puerto Rico and U.S. Possessions, FT 895;* and, through 1985, *Highlights of U.S. Export and Import Trade, FT990;* thereafter, *FT920* supplement. <http://www.census.gov/prod/www/avs/ftdpr895.html> accessed 25 June 2004.

No. 1313. Puerto Rico—Economic Summary by Industry: 2001

[13,700.7 represents 13,700,700,000. Covers establishments with payroll. Employees are for the pay period including March 12. See headnote Table 730. Based on the County Business Patterns. This annual series is used as a benchmark for statistical series, surveys, and databases between economic censuses. For a description of County Business Patterns; see Appendix III]

Industry	1987 SIC code [1]	Total number of establishments	Number of employees	Annual payroll (mil. dol.)
Total industry	(X)	44,372	723,998	13,700.7
Construction industries [2]	C	2,261	64,369	970.8
General contractors and operative builders	15	848	33,800	497.6
Manufacturing [2]	D	1,938	135,857	3,542.4
Food and kindred products	20	278	15,091	326.6
Tobacco products.	21	4	1,423	37.7
Textile mill products	22	23	1,843	21.3
Apparel and other textile products.	23	187	13,221	162.3
Lumber & wood products	24	90	1,555	15.4
Furniture and fixtures	25	128	1,639	22.5
Paper and allied products	26	40	2,019	46.3
Printing and publishing	27	190	5,520	154.9
Chemicals and allied products	28	169	34,920	1,390.3
Petroleum and coal products	29	28	1,345	46.7
Rubber and misc. plastic products.	30	62	3,906	80.0
Leather and leather products	31	17	2,296	32.0
Stone, clay, and glass products	32	150	4,734	109.7
Fabricated metal products	34	212	6,521	117.7
Industrial machinery and equip.	35	80	6,065	172.1
Electronic and other electronic equip.	36	76	17,068	396.4
Transportation equipment	37	26	1,118	20.5
Instruments and related products	38	66	13,025	316.0
Miscellaneous manufacturing products.	39	60	1,613	28.5
Wholesale trade [2]	F	2,674	41,454	1,107.7
Durable goods.	50	1,490	19,376	523.7
Nondurable goods	51	1,166	21,322	555.6
Retail trade [2]	G	14,529	172,619	2,104.3
Building materials, garden supplies	52	956	8,136	108.9
General merchandise stores	53	464	23,030	285.9
Food stores	54	1,921	28,526	295.5
Automotive dealers and service stations.	55, ex. 554	2,215	13,371	240.6
Gasoline service stations.	554	1,037	5,326	52.2
Apparel and accessory stores	56	1,870	17,300	183.3
Furniture and home furnishings	57	1,096	8,046	125.2
Eating and drinking places.	58	3,226	45,142	420.1
Drug stores & proprietary stores	591	768	8,990	148.9
Miscellaneous retail	59, ex. 591	1,932	10,871	148.3
Service industries [2]	I	15,913	223,149	3,685.5
Arrangement of passenger transportation	472	309	1,904	24.6
Hotels, paradores & motels	701	234	14,044	249.6
Personal services.	72	959	5,327	66.1
Business services	73	2,040	61,539	891.4
Auto repair, services, and parking	75	1,208	6,169	88.6
Miscellaneous repair services.	76	479	3,655	62.4
Motion pictures	78	179	1,867	24.3
Amusement and recreation services	79	357	3,565	52.7
Dental laboratories	80	5,108	53,122	914.7
Legal services.	81	1,358	6,008	143.6
Engineering and management services	87, ex. 872	1,240	14,707	340.5

X Not Applicable.   [1] 1987 Standard Industrial Classification (SIC) code; see text, Section 12.   [2] Includes other industries not shown separately.

Source: U.S. Census Bureau, *County Business Patterns, Puerto Rico*, series CBP/01-53. See also <http://www.census.gov/prod/2003pubs /01cbp/cbp01-53.pdf> (released May 2003).

No. 1314. Puerto Rico—Farms and Market Value of Agricultural Products Sold: 2002

[581,544 represents $581,544,000]

Type of product	Number of farms	Market value ($1,000)	Average value per farm (dol.)	Type of product	Number of farms	Market value ($1,000)	Average value per farm (dol.)
Total	17,659	581,544	32,932	Horticultural specialties .	471	66,519	141,229
Crops, including horticultural specialties . .	14,101	250,429	(NA)	Grasses and other crops	499	11,012	22,069
Sugarcane	24	614	25,603	Livestock, poultry, and	5,098	331,115	64,950
Coffee	9,108	42,095	4,622	their products	5,098	331,115	64,950
Pineapples	39	5,754	147,547	Cattle and calves.	3,353	36,507	10,888
Plantains	5,498	47,460	8,632	Poultry and poultry			
Bananas	3,456	14,426	4,174	products	923	78,784	85,357
Grains	935	5,471	5,851	Dairy products.	363	194,194	534,971
Root crops or tubers. . .	2,236	8,610	3,850	Hogs and pigs.	1,083	9,728	8,983
Fruits and coconuts . . .	3,884	17,940	4,619	Sheep and goats	456	680	1,491
Vegetables or melons . .	1,288	30,528	23,702	Other.	706	11,221	15,893

NA Not available.

Source: U.S. Dept. of Agriculture, National Agricultural Statistics Service, *2002 Census of Agriculture*, Volume 1, Geographic Area Series Part 52, (AC-02-A-52).

Puerto Rico and the Island Areas   827

No. 1315. Puerto Rico—Agricultural Summary: 1998 and 2002

[1 cuerda = .97 acre]

All farms	Unit	1998	2002	All farms	Unit	1998	2002
Farms.	Number. . .	19,951	17,659	Average size of farm by operator:			
Farm land	Cuerdas . .	865,478	690,687	Full owners	Cuerdas . .	29.3	26.8
Average size of farm .	Cuerdas . .	43.4	39.1	Part owners	Cuerdas . .	111.7	96.3
				Tenants	Cuerdas . .	75.9	61.1
Approximate land area.	Cuerdas . .	2,254,365	2,254,365	Farms by type of organization:			
Proportion in farms . .	Percent. . .	38.4	30.6	Individual or family. . .	Number. . .	17,887	15,843
Farms by size:				Partnership	Number. . .	211	162
Less than 10 cuerdas.	Number. . .	7,759	7,943	Corporation	Number. . .	437	595
10 to 19 cuerdas. . . .	Number. . .	4,473	3,847	Other	Number. . .	1,416	1,059
20 to 49 cuerdas	Number. . .	4,023	3,228	Farms by value of sales:			
50 to 99 cuerdas. . . .	Number. . .	1,792	1,282	Less than $1,200 . .	Number. . .	3,307	3,977
100 to 174 cuerdas .	Number. . .	809	590	$1,200 to $2,499. . . .	Number. . .	3,633	3,471
175 to 259 cuerdas . .	Number. . .	421	281	$2,500 to $4,499. . . .	Number. . .	3,900	3,044
260 cuerdas or more .	Number. . .	674	488	$5,000 to $7,499. . . .	Number. . .	2,408	1,575
				$7,500 to $9,999. . . .	Number. . .	1,233	1,087
Tenure of operator:				$10,000 to $19,999 . .	Number. . .	2,366	1,781
Operators	Number. . .	19,951	17,659	$20,000 to $39,999 . .	Number. . .	1,247	1,062
Full owners	Number. . .	15,620	13,693	$40,000 to $59,999 . .	Number. . .	405	375
Part owners	Number. . .	2,207	2,330	$60,000 or more . .	Number. . .	1,452	1,287
Tenants	Number. . .	2,124	1,636				

Source: U.S. Dept. of Agriculture, National Agricultural Statistics Service, *2002 Census of Agriculture-Geographic Area Series* Part 52, Puerto Rico, Volume 1, Series AC-02-A-52.

No. 1316. Guam, Virgin Islands, American Samoa, and Northern Mariana Islands—Economic Summary: 1997

[Sales and payroll in millions of dollars (4,640 represents $4,640,000,000). Based on the 1997 and 2002 Economic Census; see Appendix III]

Item	Guam [2]	Virgin Islands [2]	Northern Mariana Islands [3]	Item	Guam [2]	Virgin Islands [2]	Northern Mariana Islands [3]
Total: Establishments:	2,707	2,032	1,276	Annual payroll.	77	27	9
Sales	4,640	2,296	1,832	Paid employees [1]	3,393	1,144	849
Annual payroll.	750	382	382	Retail trade:			
Paid employees [1]	42,477	21,216	32,790	Establishments	1,091	973	297
Construction: Establish-				Sales	1,840	1,058	312
ments:	354	203	63	Annual payroll.	221	136	29
Sales	506	185	50	Paid employees [1]	15,334	8,966	2,916
Annual payroll.	139	52	11	Services:			
Paid employees [1]	7,094	2,623	1,013	Establishments	932	667	(X)
Manufacturing:				Sales	1,188	655	(X)
Establishments	60	74	78	Annual payroll.	280	139	(X)
Sales	165	146	666	Paid employees [1]	15,336	7,289	(X)
Annual payroll.	33	28	185	Accommodation & Food			
Paid employees [1]	1,320	1,194	16,941	Service Establishments . . .	(X)	(X)	151
Wholesale trade:				Sales	(X)	(X)	197
Establishments	270	115	78	Annual payroll.	(X)	(X)	47
Sales	941	252	123	Paid employees [1]	(X)	(X)	4,304

X Not applicable. [1] For pay period including March 12. [2] Data based on 1997 Census. [3] Data based on the 2002 Census. Selected kinds of businesses displayed.

Source: U.S. Census Bureau, *1997 Economic Census of Puerto Rico and the Island Areas*, OA97-E-5 to OA97-E-7. 2002 Economic Census of Northern Mariana Islands. IA02-00A-NMI. Accessed 22 June 2004. See internet site<http://www.census.gov/csd/ia/index.html>.

No. 1317. Federal Direct Payments: 2002

[In thousands of dollars (5,281,765 represents $5,281,765,000). For fiscal years ending September 30]

Selected program payments	Puerto Rico	Guam	Virgin Islands	American Samoa	Northern Mariana Islands
Direct payments to individuals for retirement and disability [1]	5,281,765	198,143	138,036	39,395	20,995
Social Security:					
Retirement insurance	2,140,073	61,279	77,965	9,692	4,910
Survivors insurance	951,565	25,533	21,093	10,405	4,206
Disability insurance	1,469,432	12,798	16,587	10,215	1,140
Federal retirement and disability:					
Civilian [2]	201,060	59,290	15,019	1,556	4,827
Military.	88,265	29,137	4,548	3,290	1,497
Veterans benefits:					
Service connected disability.	232,426	7,392	1,412	3,309	462
Other	172,984	1,777	618	885	69
Other direct payments [1].	2,657,610	78,121	89,694	2,303	3,206
Medicare:					
Hospital insurance	541,283	772	13,569	-	-
Suplemental medical insurance . .	874,790	535	9,610	-	-
Food stamp payments [3]	-	51,816	17,431	-	-
Other	704,589	8,353	7,327	2,303	3,198

- Represents zero or rounds to zero. [1] Includes other payments, not shown separately. [2] Includes retirement and disability payments to former U.S. Postal Service employees. [3] Food stamp program in Puerto Rico was replaced by the Nutrition Assistance Grant Program in 1982.

Source: U.S. Census Bureau, *Consolidated Federal Funds Report for Fiscal Year, 2002* (issued May 2003). See also <http://www.census.gov/govs/www/cffr02.html>

Comparative International Statistics

This section presents statistics for the world as a whole and for many countries on a comparative basis with the United States. Data are shown for population, births and deaths, social and industrial indicators, finances, agriculture, communication, and military affairs.

Statistics of the individual nations may be found primarily in official national publications, generally in the form of year-books, issued by most of the nations at various intervals in their own national languages and expressed in their own or customary units of measure. (For a listing of selected publications, see Guide to Sources.) For handier reference, especially for international comparisons, the United Nations Statistics Division compiles data as submitted by member countries and issues a number of international summary publications, generally in English and French. Among these are the *Statistical Yearbook*; the *Demographic Yearbook*; *International Trade Statistics Yearbook*; *National Accounts Statistics: Main Aggregates and Detailed Tables*; *Population and Vital Statistics Reports* (quarterly); the *Monthly Bulletin of Statistics*; and the *Energy Statistics Yearbook*. Specialized agencies of the United Nations also issue international summary publications on agricultural, labor, health, and education statistics. Among these are the *Production Yearbook* and *Trade Yearbook* issued by the Food and Agriculture Organization, the *Yearbook of Labour Statistics* issued by the International Labour Office, *World Health Statistics* issued by the World Health Organization, and the *Statistical Yearbook* issued by the Educational, Scientific, and Cultural Organization.

The U.S. Census Bureau presents estimates and projections of basic demographic measures for countries and regions of the world in the *World Population Reports* (WP) series. The *International Population Reports* (Series IPC), and *International Briefs* (Series IB) also present population figures for many foreign

countries. Detailed population statistics are also available from the Census Bureau's International Data Base (http://www.census.gov/ipc/www/idbnew.html>.

The International Monetary Fund (IMF) and the Organization for Economic Cooperation and Development (OECD) also compile data on international statistics. The IMF publishes a series of reports relating to financial data. These include *International Financial Statistics*, *Direction of Trade*, and *Balance of Payments Yearbook*, published in English, French, and Spanish. The OECD publishes a vast number of statistical publications in various fields such as economics, health, and education. Among these are *OECD in Figures*, *Main Economic Indicators*, *Economic Outlook*, *National Accounts*, *Labour Force Statistics*, *OECD Health Data*, and *Education at a Glance*.

Statistical coverage, country names, and classifications—Problems of space and availability of data limit the number of countries and the extent of statistical coverage shown. The list of countries included and the spelling of country names are based almost entirely on the list of sovereign nations, dependencies, and areas of special sovereignty provided by the U.S. Department of State.

In recent years, several important changes took place in the status of the world's nations. In 1990, a unified Germany was formed from the Federal Republic of Germany (West) and the German Democratic Republic (East). The Republic of Yemen was formed by union of the Yemen Arab Republic and the People's Democratic Republic of Yemen. Also in 1990, Namibia, once a United Nations mandate, realized its independence from South Africa.

In 1991, the Soviet Union broke up into 15 independent countries: Armenia, Azerbaijan, Belarus, Estonia, Georgia, Kazakhstan, Kyrgyzstan, Latvia, Lithuania, Moldova, Russia, Tajikistan, Turkmenistan, Ukraine, and Uzbekistan.

Comparative International Statistics 829

In the South Pacific, the Marshall Islands, Micronesia, and Palau gained full independence from the U.S. in 1991.

Following the breakup of the Socialist Federal Republic of Yugoslavia in 1992, the United States recognized Bosnia and Herzegovina, Croatia, Slovenia, and The Former Yugoslav Republic of Macedonia as independent countries.

On January 1, 1993, Czechoslovakia was succeeded by two independent countries: the Czech Republic and Slovakia. Eritrea announced its independence from Ethiopia in April 1993 and was subsequently recognized as an independent nation by the United States. In May of 2002, East Timor won independence from Indonesia, making it the world's newest independent state.

The population estimates and projections used in Tables 1318, 1319, 1321, 1322, and 1325 were prepared by the Census Bureau. For each country, the data on population, by age and sex, fertility, mortality, and international migration were evaluated and, where necessary, adjusted for inconsistencies and errors in the data. In most instances, comprehensive projections were made by the component method, resulting in distributions of the population by age and sex and requiring an assessment of probable future trends of fertility, mortality, and international migration.

Economic associations—The Organization for European Economic Co-Operation (OEEC), a regional grouping of Western European countries established in 1948 for the purpose of harmonizing national economic policies and conditions, was succeeded on September 30, 1961, by the Organization for Economic Cooperation and Development (OECD). The member nations of the OECD are Australia, Austria, Belgium, Canada, Czech Republic, Denmark, Finland, France, Germany, Greece, Hungary, Iceland, Ireland, Italy, Japan, Luxembourg, Mexico, the Netherlands, New Zealand, Norway, Poland, Portugal, Slovakia, South Korea, Spain, Sweden, Switzerland, Turkey, the United Kingdom, and the United States.

Quality and comparability of the data—The quality and comparability of the data presented here are affected by a number of factors:

(1) The year for which data are presented may not be the same for all subjects for a particular country or for a given subject for different countries, though the data shown are the most recent available. All such variations have been noted. The data shown are for calendar years except as otherwise specified.

(2) The bases, methods of estimating, methods of data collection, extent of coverage, precision of definition, scope of territory, and margins of error may vary for different items within a particular country, and for like items for different countries. Footnotes and headnotes to the tables give a few of the major time-periods and coverage qualifications attached to the figures; considerably more detail is presented in the source publications. Many of the measures shown are, at best, merely rough indicators of magnitude.

(3) Figures shown in this section for the United States may not always agree with figures shown in the preceding sections. Disagreements may be attributable to the use of differing original sources, a difference in the definition of geographic limits (the 50 states, conterminous United States only, or the United States including certain outlying areas and possessions), or to possible adjustments made in the United States figures by other sources in order to make them more comparable with figures from other countries.

International comparisons of national accounts data—In order to compare national accounts data for different countries, it is necessary to convert each country's data into a common unit of currency, usually the U.S. dollar. The market exchange rates, which are often used in converting national currencies, do not necessarily reflect the relative purchasing power in the various countries. It is necessary that the goods and services produced in different countries be valued consistently if the differences observed are meant to reflect real differences in the volumes of goods and services produced.

U.S. Census Bureau, Statistical Abstract of the United States: 2004-2005

The use of purchasing power parities (see Table 1337) instead of exchange rates is intended to achieve this objective.

The method used to present the data shown in Table 1337 is to construct volume measures directly by revaluing the goods and services sold in different countries at a common set of international prices. By dividing the ratio of the gross domestic products of two countries expressed in their own national currencies by the corresponding ratio calculated at constant international prices, it is possible to derive the implied purchasing power parity (PPP) between the two currencies concerned. PPPs show how many units of currency are needed in one country to buy the same amount of goods and services that one unit of currency will buy in the other country. For further information, see *National Accounts, Main Aggregates, Volume I,* issued annually by the Organisation for Economic Cooperation and Development, Paris, France.

International Standard Industrial Classification—The original version of the International Standard Industrial Classification of All Economic Activities (ISIC) was adopted in 1948. Wide use has been made both nationally and internationally in classifying data according to kind of economic activity in the fields of production, employment, national income, and other economic statistics. A number of countries have utilized the ISIC as the basis for devising their industrial classification scheme.

Substantial comparability has been attained between the industrial classifications of many other countries, including the United States and the ISIC by ensuring, as far as practicable, that the categories at detailed levels of classification in national schemes fitted into only one category of the ISIC. The United Nations, the International Labour Organization, the Food and Agriculture Organization, and other international bodies have utilized the ISIC in publishing and analyzing statistical data. Revisions of the ISIC were issued in 1958, 1968, and 1989.

International maps—A series of regional world maps is provided on pages 832-838. References are included in Table 1321 for easy location of individual countries on the maps. The Robinson map projection is used for this series of maps. A map projection is used to portray all or part of the round Earth on a flat surface, but this cannot be done without some distortion. For the Robinson projection, distortion is very low along the Equator and within 45 degrees of the center but is greatest near the poles. For additional information on map projections and maps, please contact the Earth Science Information Center, U.S. Geological Survey, 507 National Center, Reston, VA 22092.

U.S. Census Bureau, Statistical Abstract of the United States: 2004-2005

World

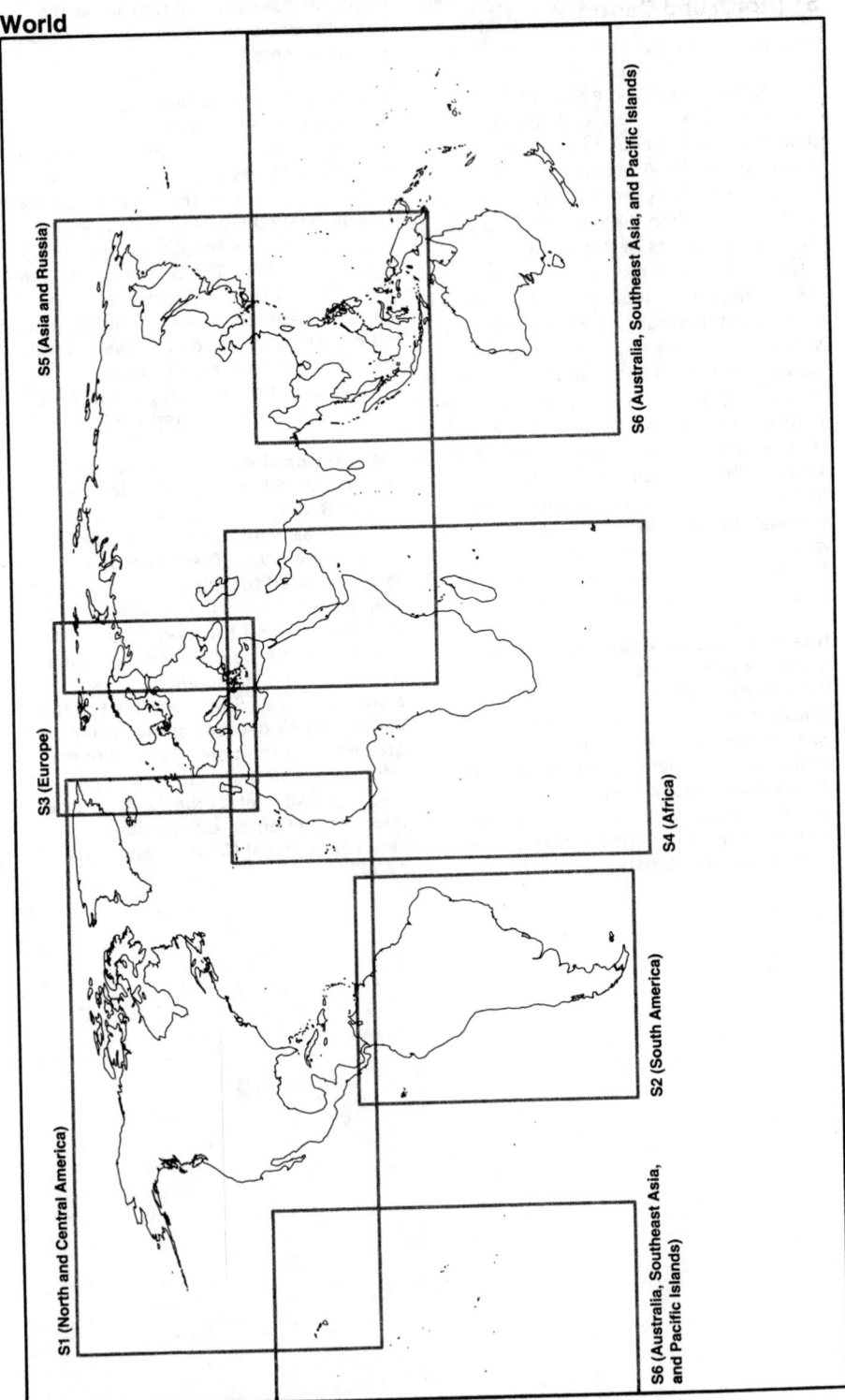

S5 (Asia and Russia)

S6 (Australia, Southeast Asia, and Pacific Islands)

S3 (Europe)

S4 (Africa)

S1 (North and Central America)

S2 (South America)

S6 (Australia, Southeast Asia, and Pacific Islands)

Caribbean Sea

Venezuela

Guyana
Suriname
French Guiana

Colombia

Ecuador (part)
(Galapagos Islands)

Ecuador
(part)

Peru

Brazil

Bolivia

Paraguay

Pacific Ocean

Atlantic Ocean

Uruguay

Chile

Argentina

United Kingdom (part)
(Falkland Islands)

U.S. Census Bureau, Statistical Abstract of the United States: 2004-2005

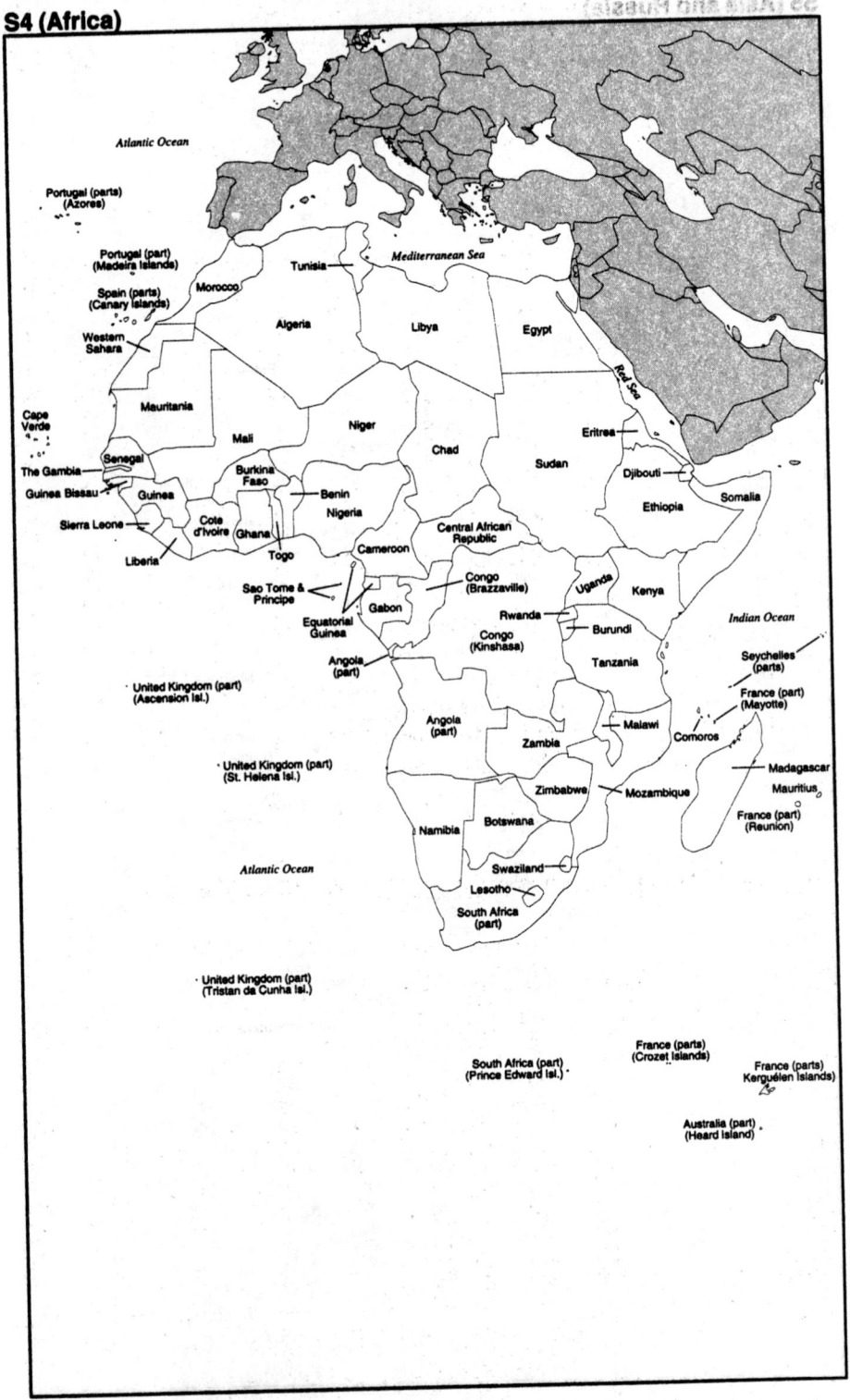

Atlantic Ocean

Portugal (parts)
(Azores)

Portugal (part)
(Madeira Islands)

Spain (parts)
(Canary Islands)

Western
Sahara

Cape
Verde

Mediterranean Sea

Tunisia

Morocco

Algeria

Libya

Egypt

Mauritania

Mali

Niger

Chad

Sudan

Eritrea

Djibouti

Somalia

Ethiopia

Red Sea

Senegal

The Gambia

Guinea Bissau

Guinea

Sierra Leone

Cote
d'Ivoire

Ghana

Liberia

Burkina
Faso

Benin

Nigeria

Togo

Cameroon

Central African
Republic

Sao Tome &
Principe

Equatorial
Guinea

Gabon

Congo
(Brazzaville)

Congo
(Kinshasa)

Uganda

Kenya

Rwanda

Burundi

Tanzania

Indian Ocean

United Kingdom (part)
(Ascension Isl.)

Angola
(part)

Angola
(part)

Zambia

Malawi

Comoros

Seychelles
(parts)

France (part)
(Mayotte)

United Kingdom (part)
(St. Helena Isl.)

Zimbabwe

Mozambique

Madagascar

Mauritius

France (part)
(Reunion)

Namibia

Botswana

Atlantic Ocean

Swaziland

Lesotho

South Africa
(part)

United Kingdom (part)
(Tristan da Cunha Isl.)

South Africa (part)
(Prince Edward Isl.)

France (parts)
(Crozet Islands)

France (parts)
Kerguélen Islands

Australia (part)
(Heard Island)

Figure 30.1
Net Additions to the World: 2003
In 2003, the world gained 2⅓ people per second

Per Minute

139 people
A Boeing 737 airplane

Per Day

Per Second

2⅓ people

199,790 people
Two large sports stadiums

Over the Next 5 Years

Per Month

Per Year

6.1 million people
Nearly the population of
Indiana, USA in 2003
(6.2 million)

362 million people
Nearly the population of
Western Europe
in 2003 (394 million)

73 million people
About the population of
Egypt in 2003 (75 million)

Source: U.S. Census Bureau, International Programs Center, International Data Base and
unpublished tables.

U.S. Census Bureau, Statistical Abstract of the United States: 2004-2005

No. 1318. Total World Population: 1980 to 2050

[As of midyear (4,454 represents 4,454,000,000)]

Year	Average annual [1] Population (mil.)	Growth rate (percent)	Population change (mil.)	Year	Average annual [1] Population (mil.)	Growth rate (percent)	Population change (mil.)
1980	4,454	1.68	75.4	2015	7,171	0.97	69.8
1985	4,853	1.71	83.6	2020	7,511	0.86	65.0
1990	5,285	1.58	84.1	2025	7,824	0.76	59.3
1995	5,696	1.38	79.3	2030	8,112	0.67	54.7
2003	6,305	1.14	72.5	2035	8,378	0.60	50.7
2004	6,378	1.13	72.6	2040	8,623	0.54	46.7
2005	6,450	1.12	72.5	2045	8,848	0.48	42.3
2010	6,812	1.05	72.2	2050	9,050	(NA)	(NA)

NA Not available. [1] Represents change from year shown to immediate succeeding year.

Source: U.S. Census Bureau, "Total Midyear Population for the World: 1950-2050," updated 30 April 2004; <http://www.census.gov/ipc/www/worldpop.html>.

No. 1319. Population by Continent: 1980 to 2050

[In millions, except percent (4,454 represents 4,454,000,000)]

Year	World	Africa	North America	South America	Asia	Europe	Oceania
1980	4,454	473	372	242	2,651	694	23
1990	5,285	627	425	296	3,189	721	27
2000	6,085	803	487	348	3,686	730	31
2010	6,812	977	541	392	4,138	728	35
2020	7,511	1,153	595	431	4,572	722	38
2030	8,112	1,344	647	461	4,912	707	41
2040	8,623	1,554	695	481	5,166	684	43
2050	9,050	1,784	738	490	5,340	654	45
PERCENT DISTRIBUTION							
1980	100.0	10.6	8.4	5.4	59.5	15.6	0.5
2000	100.0	13.2	8.0	5.7	60.6	12.0	0.5
2050	100.0	19.7	8.2	5.4	59.0	7.2	0.5

Source: U.S. Census Bureau, "International Data Base" (as of 30 April 2004); <http://www.census.gov/ipc/www/idbagg.html>.

No. 1320. Population and Population Change, by Development Status: 1950 to 2051

[In millions, except percent (2,555 represents 2,555,000,000). The "less developed" countries include all of Africa, all of Asia except Japan, the Transcaucasian and Central Asian republics of the New Independent States, all of Latin America and the Caribbean, and all of Oceania except Australia and New Zealand. This category matches the "less developed country" classification employed by the United Nations]

Year	World	Less developed countries	More developed countries	Percent of world Less developed countries	More developed countries
POPULATION					
1951	2,555	1,749	807	68.4	31.6
1961	3,040	2,129	910	70.1	29.9
1971	3,708	2,705	1,003	72.9	27.1
1981	4,454	3,374	1,081	75.7	24.3
1991	5,285	4,142	1,143	78.4	21.6
2001	6,085	4,892	1,193	80.4	19.6
2011	6,812	5,588	1,224	82.0	18.0
2021	7,511	6,265	1,246	83.4	16.6
2031	8,112	6,858	1,254	84.5	15.5
2041	8,623	7,369	1,254	85.5	14.5
2051	9,050	7,805	1,245	86.2	13.8
POPULATION CHANGE					
1950-1960	484	381	104	78.6	21.4
1960-1970	668	576	93	86.1	13.9
1970-1980	746	669	78	89.6	10.4
1980-1990	830	768	62	92.5	7.5
1990-2000	801	750	50	93.7	6.3
2000-2010	727	696	31	95.8	4.2
2010-2020	698	677	21	96.9	3.1
2020-2030	601	592	9	98.5	1.5
2030-2040	511	511	-	100.0	-
2040-2050	427	436	-9	102.1	-2.1

- Represents zero.

Source: U.S. Census Bureau, "International Data Base" (as of April 2004).

No. 1321. Population by Country: 1990 to 2010

[5,284,679 represents 5,284,679,000. Population data generally are de facto figures for the present territory. Population estimates were derived from information available as of spring 2002. East Timor became independent of Indonesia, but population data will not be available until the next update of the International Data Base. See text of this section for general comments concerning the data. For details of methodology, coverage, and reliability, see coverage, and reliability, see source. Minus sign (-) indicates decrease]

Country or area	Map refer- ence	Mid-year population (1,000) 1990	2000	2003	2010, proj.	Popu- lation rank, 2003	Annual rate of growth,[1] 2000- 2010 (percent)	Popu- lation per sq. mile, 2003	Area (sq. mile)
World	S0	5,284,679	6,085,479	6,305,145	6,812,248	(X)	1.1	125	50,580,305
Afghanistan	S5	14,669	23,898	27,060	34,505	39	3.7	108	250,000
Albania	S3	3,251	3,474	3,527	3,660	128	0.5	333	10,579
Algeria	S4	25,093	30,409	31,714	34,555	35	1.3	34	919,591
Andorra	S3	53	67	69	74	203	1.0	397	174
Angola	S4	8,049	10,132	10,766	12,250	72	1.9	22	481,351
Antigua and Barbuda	S1	63	66	68	71	204	0.6	400	170
Argentina	S2	33,022	37,498	38,741	41,405	30	1.0	37	1,056,637
Armenia	S5	3,377	3,043	3,002	2,967	131	-0.3	261	11,506
Australia	S6	17,022	19,165	19,732	20,925	52	0.9	7	2,941,285
Austria	S3	7,723	8,113	8,163	8,214	87	0.1	256	31,942
Azerbaijan	S5	7,200	7,748	7,831	8,221	89	0.6	234	33,436
Bahamas, The	S1	257	290	297	311	176	0.7	77	3,888
Bahrain	S4	500	634	667	737	162	1.5	2,792	239
Bangladesh	S5	109,897	130,407	138,448	159,765	8	2.0	2,678	51,703
Barbados	S1	263	274	277	283	178	0.3	1,670	166
Belarus	S3	10,215	10,367	10,322	10,294	77	-0.1	129	80,154
Belgium	S3	9,969	10,264	10,331	10,423	76	0.2	885	11,672
Belize	S1	191	247	266	312	179	2.3	30	8,803
Benin	S4	4,662	6,428	7,041	8,504	94	2.8	165	42,710
Bhutan	S5	1,598	2,005	2,140	2,476	142	2.1	118	18,147
Bolivia	S2	6,574	8,153	8,586	9,499	86	1.5	21	418,683
Bosnia and Herzegovina	S3	4,424	3,836	3,989	4,103	120	0.7	202	19,741
Botswana	S4	1,312	1,578	1,573	1,420	147	-1.1	7	226,012
Brazil	S2	151,084	175,553	182,033	195,580	5	1.1	56	3,265,061
Brunei	S6	258	336	358	408	174	1.9	176	2,035
Bulgaria	S3	8,894	7,818	7,588	7,149	91	-0.9	178	42,683
Burkina Faso	S4	9,090	12,217	13,228	15,748	63	2.5	125	105,714
Burma	S5	38,526	41,772	42,511	43,721	27	0.5	167	253,954
Burundi	S4	5,285	5,714	6,096	7,296	100	2.4	616	9,903
Cambodia	S5	9,271	12,433	13,125	14,902	64	1.8	193	68,154
Cameroon	S4	11,685	14,792	15,746	17,938	59	1.9	87	181,251
Canada	S1	27,791	31,278	32,207	34,253	34	0.9	9	3,560,219
Cape Verde	S1	349	401	412	431	172	0.7	265	1,556
Central African Republic	S4	2,803	3,501	3,684	4,073	126	1.5	15	240,533
Chad	S4	6,030	8,419	9,253	11,302	82	2.9	19	486,178
Chile	S2	13,128	15,153	15,663	16,720	60	1.0	54	289,112
China [2]	S5	1,148,364	1,268,853	1,291,496	1,347,563	1	0.6	359	3,600,930
Colombia	S2	32,859	39,686	41,662	46,109	28	1.5	104	401,042
Comoros	S4	429	578	633	773	163	2.9	755	838
Congo (Brazzaville) [3]	S4	2,240	2,809	2,954	3,209	133	1.3	22	131,853
Congo (Kinshasa) [3]	S4	37,969	51,810	56,625	69,577	23	2.9	65	875,521
Costa Rica	S2	3,027	3,711	3,896	4,306	123	1.5	199	19,560
Cote d'Ivoire	S4	11,901	15,866	16,962	19,485	57	2.1	138	122,780
Croatia	S3	4,508	4,411	4,498	4,487	116	0.2	206	21,829
Cuba	S1	10,545	11,134	11,269	11,507	69	0.3	263	42,803
Cyprus	S5	681	758	772	801	159	0.5	216	3,568
Czech Republic	S3	10,310	10,270	10,251	10,202	79	-0.1	338	30,365
Denmark	S3	5,141	5,337	5,394	5,516	108	0.3	330	16,359
Djibouti	S4	366	431	457	526	166	2.0	54	8,486
Dominica	S1	73	72	70	70	202	-0.2	240	290
Dominican Republic	S1	7,076	8,354	8,716	9,521	85	1.3	467	18,680
East Timor	S6	746	847	998	1,153	156	3.1	177	5,641
Ecuador	S2	10,318	12,505	13,074	14,245	65	1.3	122	106,888
Egypt	S4	56,694	70,492	74,719	84,348	15	1.8	194	384,344
El Salvador	S1	5,100	6,123	6,470	7,293	98	1.7	809	8,000
Equatorial Guinea	S4	368	474	510	604	164	2.4	47	10,830
Eritrea	S4	2,944	4,243	4,362	5,128	118	1.9	93	46,842
Estonia	S3	1,569	1,380	1,351	1,291	150	-0.7	78	17,413
Ethiopia	S4	47,958	62,651	66,558	75,066	18	1.8	154	432,310
Fiji	S6	738	832	869	958	157	1.4	123	7,054
Finland	S3	4,986	5,169	5,204	5,255	111	0.2	44	117,942
France	S3	56,735	59,382	60,181	61,638	20	0.4	286	210,668
Gabon	S4	938	1,223	1,322	1,562	151	2.5	13	99,486
Gambia, The	S4	962	1,367	1,501	1,833	148	2.9	389	3,861
Georgia	S5	5,426	4,777	4,711	4,601	114	-0.4	175	26,911
Germany	S3	79,380	82,188	82,398	82,283	13	(Z)	609	135,236
Ghana	S4	15,400	19,509	20,468	22,230	50	1.3	230	88,811
Greece	S3	10,130	10,559	10,626	10,750	73	0.2	210	50,502
Grenada	S2	92	89	89	91	197	0.2	682	131
Guatemala	S1	9,654	12,820	13,909	16,589	62	2.6	332	41,865
Guinea	S4	6,280	8,642	9,030	10,800	83	2.2	95	94,927
Guinea-Bissau	S4	996	1,278	1,361	1,566	149	2.0	126	10,811
Guyana	S2	742	698	702	732	161	0.5	9	76,004
Haiti	S1	6,075	7,177	7,528	8,555	92	1.8	707	10,641
Honduras	S1	4,757	6,201	6,670	7,686	97	2.1	154	43,201
Hungary	S3	10,372	10,137	10,058	9,880	80	-0.3	282	35,653
Iceland	S3	255	281	291	309	177	0.9	8	38,707
India	S5	841,655	1,002,708	1,049,700	1,155,011	2	1.4	914	1,147,950
Indonesia	S6	188,005	224,138	234,893	258,825	4	1.4	336	699,548

See footnotes at end of table.

U.S. Census Bureau, Statistical Abstract of the United States: 2004-2005

[See headnote, page 841]

Country or area	Map refer- ence	Mid-year population (1,000)			Popu- lation 2010, proj.	Popu- lation rank, 2003	Annual rate of growth,[1] 2000- 2010 (percent)	Popu- lation per sq. mile, 2003	Area (sq. mile)
		1990	2000	2003					
Iran	S5	57,036	65,660	68,018	71,861	17	0.9	106	631,660
Iraq	S5	18,135	22,676	26,075	29,672	44	2.7	147	167,556
Ireland	S3	3,508	3,792	4,016	4,250	122	1.1	148	26,598
Israel	S4	4,512	5,842	6,277	6,645	99	1.3	779	7,849
Italy	S3	56,743	57,719	58,103	58,091	22	0.1	511	113,521
Jamaica	S1	2,463	2,653	2,732	2,851	137	0.7	645	4,181
Japan	S5	123,537	126,700	127,417	127,195	10	(Z)	845	152,411
Jordan	S4	3,262	4,999	5,760	6,486	105	2.6	154	35,344
Kazakhstan	S5	16,398	15,032	15,186	15,460	61	0.3	14	1,049,150
Kenya	S4	23,934	30,310	32,368	33,654	37	1.0	144	219,788
Kiribati	S6	71	92	103	115	195	2.3	356	277
Korea, North	S5	20,019	21,648	22,912	23,802	48	0.9	483	46,490
Korea, South	S5	42,869	47,261	48,893	50,180	24	0.6	1,274	37,911
Kuwait	S5	2,142	1,974	2,336	2,788	141	3.5	317	6,880
Kyrgyzstan	S5	4,382	4,851	5,146	5,509	112	1.3	65	76,641
Laos	S5	4,210	5,498	6,217	6,994	102	2.4	66	89,112
Latvia	S3	2,664	2,376	2,290	2,218	139	-0.7	93	24,903
Lebanon	S4	3,147	3,578	3,826	4,056	125	1.3	944	3,950
Lesotho	S4	1,693	1,847	1,867	1,862	146	0.1	159	11,718
Liberia	S4	2,189	3,149	3,482	3,935	130	2.2	89	37,189
Libya	S4	4,140	5,115	5,766	6,447	104	2.3	8	679,359
Liechtenstein	S3	29	32	34	35	213	0.8	533	62
Lithuania	S5	3,695	3,654	3,597	3,545	127	-0.3	144	25,174
Luxembourg	S3	383	439	469	498	167	1.3	458	998
Macedonia, The Former Yugoslav Republic of.	S3	1,893	2,041	2,079	2,115	143	0.4	208	9,928
Madagascar	S4	11,522	15,506	18,040	20,993	56	3.0	76	224,533
Malawi	S4	9,215	10,874	12,159	13,416	67	2.1	321	36,324
Malaysia	S6	17,504	21,793	23,953	26,144	46	1.8	182	126,853
Maldives	S5	216	301	349	400	175	2.8	2,846	116
Mali	S4	8,228	10,665	12,292	14,012	68	2.7	25	471,042
Malta	S4	359	390	399	407	173	0.4	3,189	124
Marshall Islands	S6	46	53	59	66	208	2.2	807	70
Mauritania	S4	1,984	2,668	3,087	3,561	134	2.9	7	397,838
Mauritius	S4	1,074	1,179	1,231	1,280	153	0.8	1,696	714
Mexico	S1	84,914	99,927	106,203	112,469	11	1.2	140	742,486
Micronesia, Federated States of	S6	109	108	108	107	193	-0.1	399	271
Moldova	S5	4,398	4,431	4,455	4,535	117	0.2	341	13,012
Monaco	S3	30	32	32	33	214	0.4	41,608	1
Mongolia	S5	2,216	2,601	2,791	3,004	136	1.4	4	604,247
Morocco	S4	24,686	30,122	32,726	35,301	36	1.6	184	172,317
Mozambique	S4	12,649	17,673	19,027	19,721	54	1.1	61	302,737
Namibia	S4	1,409	1,826	1,976	2,036	145	1.1	6	317,873
Nauru	S6	9	12	13	14	223	1.9	1,550	8
Nepal	S5	19,325	24,702	27,677	30,758	40	2.2	501	52,819
Netherlands	S3	14,952	15,908	16,407	16,783	58	0.5	1,238	13,104
New Zealand	S6	3,360	3,820	4,035	4,228	121	1.0	38	103,734
Nicaragua	S2	3,684	4,932	5,465	5,990	110	1.9	113	46,430
Niger	S4	7,630	10,174	11,666	13,220	70	2.6	23	489,073
Nigeria	S4	92,566	123,750	140,602	156,787	9	2.4	381	351,649
Norway	S3	4,242	4,492	4,593	4,676	115	0.4	38	118,865
Oman	S5	1,773	2,533	3,002	3,523	135	3.3	34	82,031
Pakistan	S5	114,578	146,343	162,420	179,592	6	2.0	519	300,664
Palau	S6	15	19	20	22	219	1.4	112	177
Panama	S2	2,388	2,836	3,039	3,220	132	1.3	101	29,340
Papua New Guinea	S6	3,825	4,927	5,545	6,171	109	2.3	30	174,405
Paraguay	S2	4,236	5,586	6,348	7,162	101	2.5	39	153,398
Peru	S2	21,511	25,980	27,926	29,758	38	1.4	55	494,208
Philippines	S6	64,318	79,740	87,857	95,868	12	1.8	735	115,124
Poland	S3	38,119	38,646	38,635	38,691	31	(Z)	329	117,571
Portugal	S3	9,923	10,336	10,566	10,736	75	0.4	296	35,382
Qatar	S5	481	744	863	970	158	2.6	192	4,247
Romania	S5	22,866	22,452	22,330	22,181	49	-0.1	252	88,934
Russia	S5	147,931	146,673	143,155	140,581	7	-0.4	22	6,592,817
Rwanda	S4	6,962	7,405	8,099	8,821	90	1.7	811	9,633
Saint Kitts and Nevis	S1	41	39	39	40	212	0.4	279	139
Saint Lucia	S1	140	156	166	177	190	1.3	687	236
Saint Vincent and the Grenadines	S1	107	115	118	119	191	0.3	892	131
Samoa	S0	170	179	177	176	187	-0.2	162	1,100
San Marino	S3	23	27	29	31	215	1.3	1,214	23
Sao Tome and Principe	S4	119	160	187	219	188	3.1	475	371
Saudi Arabia	S4	16,061	23,153	26,418	29,222	43	2.3	30	829,996
Senegal	S4	7,362	9,784	11,127	12,534	74	2.5	143	74,131
Serbia and Montenegro	S3	9,935	10,850	10,829	10,839	71	(Z)	274	39,435
Seychelles	S4	73	79	81	83	198	0.4	457	176
Sierra Leone	S4	4,226	5,203	6,018	6,688	103	2.5	207	27,653
Singapore	S6	3,047	4,037	4,426	4,701	119	1.5	17,751	241
Slovakia	S3	5,263	5,400	5,431	5,470	107	0.1	287	18,842
Slovenia	S3	1,991	2,011	2,011	2,003	144	(Z)	257	7,819
Solomon Islands	S6	335	466	538	610	165	2.7	48	10,633
Somalia	S4	6,675	7,253	8,592	9,922	88	3.1	33	242,216

See footnotes at end of table.

No. 1321. Population by Country: 1990 to 2010—Con.
[See headnote, page 841]

Country or area	Map refer- ence	Mid-year population (1,000) 1990	2000	2003	2010, proj.	Popu- lation rank, 2003	Annual rate of growth,[1] 2000- 2010 (percent)	Popu- lation per sq. mile, 2003	Area (sq. mile)
South Africa	S4	37,191	42,351	42,552	40,608	26	-0.4	91	471,444
Spain	S3	39,351	40,016	40,217	40,549	29	0.1	209	192,819
Sri Lanka	S5	17,193	19,239	19,742	20,832	51	0.8	790	24,996
Sudan	S4	26,627	35,080	38,114	45,485	32	2.6	42	917,375
Suriname	S2	395	429	435	441	170	0.3	7	62,344
Swaziland	S4	885	1,120	1,161	1,170	154	0.4	175	6,641
Sweden	S3	8,601	8,924	8,970	9,074	84	0.2	56	158,927
Switzerland	S3	6,837	7,267	7,408	7,623	93	0.5	482	15,355
Syria	S4	12,436	16,306	17,586	20,606	55	2.3	247	71,062
Tajikistan	S5	5,332	6,441	6,864	8,007	95	2.2	124	55,251
Tanzania	S4	25,651	33,768	35,922	41,197	33	2.0	105	342,100
Thailand	S5	55,250	62,352	64,265	68,058	19	0.9	325	197,595
Togo	S4	3,705	5,033	5,429	6,256	106	2.2	259	21,000
Tonga	S0	92	102	108	123	194	1.8	391	277
Trinidad and Tobago	S2	1,198	1,125	1,104	1,042	155	-0.8	557	1,981
Tunisia	S4	8,207	9,564	9,873	10,583	81	1.0	165	59,985
Turkey	S5	56,085	65,667	68,109	73,322	16	1.1	229	297,591
Turkmenistan	S5	3,668	4,518	4,776	5,431	113	1.8	25	188,456
Tuvalu	S6	9	11	11	13	224	1.5	1,126	10
Uganda	S4	17,242	23,496	25,633	31,570	42	3.0	332	77,108
Ukraine	S5	51,658	49,153	48,055	46,193	25	-0.6	206	233,089
United Arab Emirates	S5	1,951	2,369	2,485	2,763	138	1.5	77	32,278
United Kingdom	S3	57,493	59,522	60,095	61,285	21	0.3	644	93,278
United States	S1	250,132	282,339	290,343	309,163	3	0.9	82	3,539,227
Uruguay	S2	3,106	3,324	3,382	3,491	129	0.5	50	67,035
Uzbekistan	S5	20,624	24,756	25,982	29,280	41	1.7	150	172,741
Vanuatu	S6	154	190	199	221	184	1.5	35	5,699
Venezuela	S2	19,325	23,543	24,655	27,134	45	1.4	72	340,560
Vietnam	S5	66,637	78,518	81,625	89,223	14	1.3	650	125,622
Yemen	S5	12,416	17,479	19,350	24,637	53	3.4	95	203,849
Zambia	S4	7,876	9,799	10,307	11,286	78	1.4	36	285,992
Zimbabwe	S4	10,154	12,186	12,577	12,926	66	0.6	84	149,293
OTHER									
Taiwan [2]	S5	20,279	22,151	22,603	23,562	47	0.6	1,815	12,456
AREAS OF SPECIAL SOVEREIGNTY AND DEPENDENCIES									
American Samoa	S0	47	57	58	57	207	(Z)	753	77
Anguilla	S1	8	12	13	14	222	1.8	363	35
Aruba	S1	67	70	71	73	201	0.5	951	75
Bermuda	S1	58	63	64	67	206	0.7	3,408	19
Cayman Islands	S1	26	38	42	50	211	2.7	418	100
Cook Islands	S0	18	20	21	22	218	0.9	226	93
Faroe Islands	S3	47	45	46	48	210	0.6	86	541
French Guiana	S2	116	173	187	214	185	2.1	5	34,421
French Polynesia	S0	202	249	262	291	180	1.5	185	1,413
Gaza Strip [4]	S4	643	1,132	1,275	1,651	152	3.8	8,666	147
Gibraltar	S3	29	28	28	28	216	0.2	11,990	2
Greenland	S1	56	56	56	56	209	(Z)	-	131,931
Guadeloupe	S1	378	426	440	468	169	0.9	647	680
Guam	S6	134	155	164	181	189	1.5	783	209
Guernsey	S3	63	64	65	66	205	0.3	865	75
Hong Kong	S5	5,688	6,659	6,810	7,090	96	0.6	17,833	382
Jersey	S3	84	89	90	92	196	0.3	1,996	45
Macau	S6	352	431	441	468	168	0.8	71,466	6
Man, Isle of	S3	69	73	74	77	200	0.5	327	227
Martinique	S1	374	415	426	448	171	0.8	1,042	409
Mayotte	S4	90	156	178	231	186	3.9	1,229	145
Montserrat	S1	11	6	9	10	225	4.3	233	39
Netherlands Antilles	S2	189	210	216	228	182	0.8	583	371
New Caledonia	S6	168	202	211	230	183	1.3	29	7,243
Northern Mariana Islands	S6	44	70	76	91	199	2.6	413	184
Puerto Rico	S1	3,537	3,816	3,879	4,001	124	0.5	1,121	3,459
Reunion	S4	597	721	755	829	160	1.4	783	965
Saint Helena	S4	7	7	7	8	226	0.6	47	158
Saint Pierre and Miquelon	S1	6	7	7	7	227	0.2	75	93
Turks and Caicos Islands	S1	12	18	19	24	220	3.0	117	166
Virgin Islands	S1	104	109	109	108	192	-0.1	805	135
Virgin Islands, British	S1	16	20	22	25	217	2.0	375	58
Wallis and Futuna	S6	14	15	16	17	221	0.9	149	106
West Bank [4]	S4	1,255	2,020	2,237	2,765	140	3.1	1,027	2,178
Western Sahara	S4	191	245	262	301	181	2.1	3	102,703

- Represents or rounds to zero.   X Not applicable.   Z Less than 0.05 percent or less than one person per square mile.
[1] Computed by the exponential method. For explanation of average annual percent change, see Guide to Tabular Presentation.
[2] With the establishment of diplomatic relations with China on January 1, 1979, the U.S. government recognized the People's Republic of China as the sole legal government of China and acknowledged the Chinese position that there is only one China and that Taiwan is part of China.   [3] "Congo" is the official short-form name for both the Republic of Congo and the Democratic Republic of the Congo. To distinguish one from the other, the U.S. Dept. of State adds the capital in parentheses. This practice is unofficial and provisional.   [4] The Gaza Strip and West Bank are Israeli occupied with interim status subject to Israeli/Palestinian negotiations. The final status is to be determined.

Source: U.S. Census Bureau, "International Data Base" (as of 30 April 2004); <http://www.census.gov/ipc/www/idbnew.html>.

[In percent. Covers countries with 5 million or more population in 2003]

Country or area	2003 Under 15 years old	2003 65 years old and over	2010, proj. Under 15 years old	2010, proj. 65 years old and over	Country or area	2003 Under 15 years old	2003 65 years old and over	2010, proj. Under 15 years old	2010, proj. 65 years old and over
World	28.6	7.1	26.5	7.7	Laos	42.2	3.2	40.5	3.1
Afghanistan	44.8	2.4	44.4	2.4	Libya	34.5	4.1	32.9	4.4
Algeria	30.8	4.6	24.8	5.0	Madagascar	44.9	3.1	44.5	2.9
Angola	43.5	2.8	43.1	2.8	Malawi	46.7	2.7	46.9	2.8
Argentina	26.2	10.4	24.1	11.0	Malaysia	33.7	4.4	31.0	5.1
Australia	20.2	12.7	18.7	13.9	Mali	47.2	3.0	46.4	2.8
Austria	16.1	15.7	14.3	18.1	Mexico	32.1	5.3	28.7	6.4
Azerbaijan	27.7	7.6	24.5	6.9	Morocco	33.2	4.8	29.6	5.2
Bangladesh	34.1	3.4	33.8	3.7	Mozambique	43.8	2.7	41.3	3.1
Belarus	16.8	14.3	15.6	13.6	Nepal	39.7	3.6	37.3	3.9
Belgium	17.2	17.2	16.0	17.8	Netherlands	18.4	13.8	17.2	15.2
Benin	47.0	2.3	45.2	2.4	Nicaragua	38.8	3.0	33.1	3.4
Bolivia	37.1	4.5	32.1	4.9	Niger	47.6	2.2	46.1	2.2
Brazil	27.1	5.7	24.0	6.8	Nigeria	43.6	2.8	42.5	3.0
Bulgaria	14.7	17.1	13.8	17.9	Pakistan	40.7	4.0	36.7	4.2
Burkina Faso	46.1	2.9	45.6	2.8	Papua New Guinea	38.4	3.8	36.6	4.1
Burma	28.1	4.9	25.4	5.3	Paraguay	38.4	4.7	36.5	5.1
Burundi	46.7	2.7	44.7	2.5	Peru	32.6	5.0	28.5	5.8
Cambodia	39.3	3.0	33.1	3.1	Philippines	36.2	3.9	33.2	4.4
Cameroon	42.3	3.2	40.5	3.4	Poland	17.5	12.7	15.7	13.1
Canada	18.5	12.9	16.7	14.2	Portugal	16.8	16.7	16.3	17.8
Chad	47.9	2.8	47.4	2.7	Romania	16.8	14.2	15.5	14.7
Chile	26.4	7.7	22.7	9.2	Russia	15.7	13.3	14.3	13.3
China [1]	23.1	7.4	19.6	8.3	Rwanda	42.5	2.7	43.0	2.5
Colombia	31.3	4.9	28.5	5.7	Saudi Arabia	38.4	2.3	38.0	2.5
Congo (Kinshasa) [2]	48.3	2.5	47.2	2.4	Senegal	43.7	3.1	40.8	3.0
Cote d'Ivoire	45.4	2.2	43.9	2.4	Serbia and Montenegro	18.6	14.7	17.5	15.0
Cuba	20.5	9.9	18.2	11.7	Sierra Leone	44.8	3.2	43.8	3.4
Czech Republic	15.3	14.0	13.5	15.9	Slovakia	17.9	11.6	15.7	12.6
Denmark	18.9	14.9	17.9	16.6	Somalia	44.8	2.7	45.0	2.5
Dominican Republic	33.6	5.2	31.1	6.0	South Africa	30.0	5.0	26.7	6.3
Ecuador	34.4	4.8	31.0	5.4	Spain	14.4	17.6	14.5	18.4
Egypt	33.9	4.2	31.0	4.9	Sri Lanka	25.2	6.9	22.6	8.2
El Salvador	37.1	5.1	35.0	5.4	Sudan	44.0	2.2	40.7	2.7
Ethiopia	44.8	2.8	43.4	2.9	Sweden	17.8	17.2	15.5	19.3
Finland	17.7	15.5	16.2	17.2	Switzerland	16.9	15.3	15.4	16.6
France	18.6	16.3	18.0	16.7	Syria	38.6	3.2	35.5	3.4
Germany	14.9	17.8	13.5	20.4	Taiwan [1]	20.1	9.3	18.4	10.4
Ghana	38.9	3.6	32.7	4.0	Tajikistan	39.8	4.7	36.9	4.1
Greece	14.5	18.3	14.2	19.4	Tanzania	44.3	2.6	42.9	2.7
Guatemala	42.9	3.3	41.2	3.4	Thailand	24.2	7.0	22.4	8.5
Guinea	44.5	3.2	44.1	3.2	Togo	44.5	2.5	40.2	2.9
Haiti	42.7	3.7	39.7	3.7	Tunisia	26.7	6.4	22.3	7.2
Honduras	41.6	3.6	38.6	4.0	Turkey	27.2	6.4	23.5	7.3
Hungary	16.2	14.8	14.8	16.0	Uganda	50.8	2.4	49.0	2.2
India	32.2	4.8	29.2	5.3	Ukraine	16.3	15.0	15.4	14.8
Indonesia	29.7	5.0	27.6	5.8	United Kingdom	18.3	15.7	16.5	16.4
Iran	29.4	4.8	23.4	5.1	United States	20.9	12.4	20.0	13.0
Iraq	40.7	3.0	38.5	3.0	Uzbekistan	34.7	4.7	31.7	4.3
Israel	26.9	9.9	25.4	10.0	Venezuela	31.0	4.9	26.6	5.7
Italy	14.0	18.8	13.4	20.3	Vietnam	30.2	5.6	26.0	5.6
Japan	14.4	18.6	14.1	22.1	Yemen	46.8	2.8	46.1	2.5
Jordan	35.9	3.6	30.5	4.3	Zambia	46.3	2.8	44.4	2.8
Kazakhstan	25.3	7.3	21.6	7.6	Zimbabwe	39.7	3.5	38.7	4.1
Kenya	41.3	2.8	36.5	3.2					
Korea, North	25.0	7.2	22.2	9.5					
Korea, South	20.6	7.9	18.3	9.9					
Kyrgyzstan	33.0	6.0	29.4	5.5					

[1] See footnote 2, Table 1321.   [2] See footnote 3, Table 1321.

Source: U.S. Census Bureau, "International Data Base" (as of 30 April 2004); <http://www.census.gov/ipc/www/idbnew.html>.

No. 1323. Foreign or Foreign-Born Population and Labor Force in Selected OECD Countries: 1990 and 2001

[31,811 represents 31,811,000. In Australia, Canada, and the United States the data refer to people present in the country who are foreign born. In the European countries and Japan they generally refer to foreigners and represent the nationalities of residents]

Country	Foreign population [1]				Foreign labor force [2]			
	Number (1,000)		Percent of total population		Number (1,000)		Percent of total labor force	
	1990	2001	1990	2001	1990	2001	1990	2001
United States [3]	(NA)	31,811	(NA)	11.1	11,565	20,014	9.4	13.9
Australia [3]	(NA)	4,482	(NA)	23.1	(NA)	2,367	25.7	24.2
Austria	456	764	5.9	9.4	230	360	7.4	11.0
Belgium	905	847	9.1	8.2	289	(NA)	7.1	(NA)
Canada [3]	(NA)	5,449	(NA)	18.2	(NA)	3,151	(NA)	19.9
Denmark	161	267	3.1	5.0	69	101	2.4	3.5
France	3,597	(NA)	6.3	(NA)	1,550	1,618	6.2	6.2
Germany	5,343	7,319	8.4	8.9	(NA)	3,616	(NA)	9.1
Italy	781	1,363	1.4	2.4	(NA)	801	(NA)	3.8
Japan	1,075	1,779	0.9	1.4	(NA)	169	(NA)	0.2
Luxembourg	113	167	29.4	37.5	85	171	45.2	61.7
Netherlands	692	690	4.6	4.3	197	(NA)	3.1	(NA)
Spain	279	1,109	0.7	2.7	85	607	0.6	3.4
Sweden	484	476	5.6	5.3	246	227	5.4	5.1
Switzerland	1,100	1,419	16.3	19.7	670	739	18.9	18.1
United Kingdom	1,723	2,587	3.2	4.4	882	1,229	3.3	4.4

NA Not available. [1] Data are from population registers except for France (census), the United Kingdom (labor force survey), Japan and Switzerland (register of foreigners), and Italy and Spain (residence permits). [2] Includes unemployed except for Italy, Luxembourg, Netherlands, and United Kingdom. Data for Austria, Germany, and Luxembourg are from social security registers, and for Denmark, from the register of population. Data for Italy, Spain, and Switzerland are from residence or work permits. Figures for Japan and Netherlands are estimates. Data for other countries are from labor force surveys. [3] Census data from Current Population Survey.

Source: Organization for Economic Cooperation and Development, Paris, France, Trends in International Migration (2003 Editions) (copyright).

No. 1324. Medical Doctors and Inpatient Care—Selected Countries: 1990 to 2001

Country	Medical doctors per 1,000 population			Inpatient care					
				Acute care beds per 1,000 population			Average length of stay (days)		
	1990	2000	2001	1990	2000	2001	1990	2000	2001
United States	2.4	(NA)	(NA)	3.7	2.9	2.9	9.1	6.8	6.7
Australia	2.2	2.4	2.5	(NA)	3.8	(NA)	(NA)	15.9	(NA)
Austria	2.2	3.1	3.2	7.0	6.2	6.2	12.8	8.6	(NA)
Belgium	3.3	3.9	(NA)	4.9	(NA)	(NA)	13.8	(NA)	(NA)
Canada	2.1	2.1	2.1	4.0	3.2	(NA)	13.0	(NA)	(NA)
Czech Republic	2.7	3.4	3.4	8.5	6.6	6.5	15.4	11.4	11.3
Denmark	3.1	3.4	3.4	4.1	(NA)	(NA)	8.2	6.0	5.9
Finland	2.4	3.1	3.1	4.3	2.4	2.4	18.2	10.3	10.6
France	3.1	3.3	3.3	8.5	6.7	(NA)	15.1	13.1	(NA)
Germany	(NA)	3.3	3.3	7.5	6.4	6.3	17.2	11.9	11.6
Greece	3.4	4.5	4.4	4.0	(NA)	(NA)	9.9	(NA)	(NA)
Hungary	2.9	(NA)	2.9	7.1	6.3	6.0	12.6	9.7	8.7
Iceland	2.8	3.4	3.5	4.3	(NA)	(NA)	18.3	(NA)	(NA)
Ireland	(NA)	2.2	2.4	3.3	3.0	3.0	7.9	7.4	7.5
Italy	(NA)	4.1	4.3	6.2	4.3	(NA)	11.7	7.7	(NA)
Japan	1.7	1.9	(NA)	(NA)	(NA)	(NA)	50.5	(NA)	(NA)
Korea, South	0.8	1.3	1.4	2.7	5.2	5.2	13.0	14.0	13.0
Luxembourg	2.0	2.5	2.5	7.0	6.7	6.6	17.6	(NA)	(NA)
Mexico	(NA)	1.4	1.5	(NA)	1.0	1.0	4.4	4.3	4.2
Netherlands	2.5	3.2	3.3	4.3	3.5	3.3	34.1	33.4	33.0
New Zealand	1.9	2.2	(NA)	8.0	(NA)	(NA)	9.4	7.7	7.7
Norway	(NA)	2.9	3.0	3.8	3.1	3.1	(NA)	8.9	8.7
Poland	2.1	2.2	2.2	6.3	5.1	5.0	12.5	8.9	8.4
Portugal	2.8	3.2	3.2	3.4	(NA)	(NA)	10.8	10.4	10.1
Slovak Republic	(NA)	3.7	3.6	(NA)	5.9	5.6	(NA)	(NA)	(NA)
Spain	(NA)	3.3	3.1	3.3	(NA)	(NA)	12.2	(NA)	(NA)
Sweden	2.9	3.0	(NA)	4.1	2.4	(NA)	18.0	6.4	6.4
Switzerland	3.0	3.5	3.5	6.5	4.1	3.9	(NA)	12.8	12.7
Turkey	0.9	1.3	1.3	2.0	2.2	2.1	6.9	5.9	5.8
United Kingdom	1.5	2.0	(NA)	(NA)	3.9	3.9	15.6	(NA)	(NA)

NA Not available.

Source: Organization for Economic Cooperation and Development, Paris, France, OECD Health Data 2003 (copyright).

No. 1325. Vital Statistics, by Country: 2003 and 2010

[Covers countries with 12 million or more population in 2003]

Country or area	Crude birth rate [1] 2003	2010, proj.	Crude death rate [2] 2003	2010, proj.	Expectation of life at birth (years) 2003	2010, proj.	Infant mortality rate [3] 2003	2010, proj.	Total fertility rate per woman [4] 2003	2010, proj.
United States	14.1	14.2	8.4	8.3	77.1	78.4	6.8	6.2	2.07	2.11
Afghanistan	47.5	45.1	21.5	18.8	42.0	45.1	168.9	149.3	6.81	6.47
Algeria	18.3	16.7	4.6	4.7	72.5	74.3	33.4	25.7	2.16	1.76
Argentina	17.5	15.8	7.6	7.5	75.5	76.9	16.2	13.1	2.28	2.03
Australia	12.6	11.7	7.3	7.7	80.1	81.0	4.8	4.4	1.76	1.75
Bangladesh	29.9	27.8	8.6	7.7	61.3	63.9	66.1	54.3	3.17	3.04
Brazil	17.7	15.5	6.1	6.3	71.1	73.0	31.7	24.9	2.01	1.81
Burkina Faso	44.8	42.4	18.8	18.6	44.5	43.6	99.8	92.1	6.34	5.92
Burma	19.2	16.9	12.2	12.0	55.8	57.7	70.4	59.7	2.15	1.86
Cambodia	27.3	26.6	9.3	8.5	57.9	60.6	75.9	61.9	3.58	3.10
Cameroon	35.5	32.5	15.3	15.5	48.1	47.9	70.1	62.7	4.63	4.08
Canada	11.0	10.7	7.6	8.0	79.8	80.7	4.9	4.5	1.61	1.62
Chad	47.1	43.4	16.4	16.8	48.5	46.2	95.7	88.6	6.44	5.97
Chile	16.1	14.5	5.7	6.1	76.2	77.5	9.3	7.7	2.09	1.90
China [5]	13.0	14.3	6.9	7.1	71.6	73.8	26.4	19.4	1.68	1.80
Colombia	21.6	19.3	5.6	5.6	71.1	73.1	22.5	17.8	2.61	2.44
Congo (Kinshasa) [6]	45.1	42.4	14.9	13.4	48.9	50.5	96.6	83.2	6.69	6.11
Cote d'Ivoire	40.0	36.8	18.4	19.0	42.7	41.7	98.3	88.4	5.51	4.79
Ecuador	23.7	20.8	4.3	4.2	75.8	77.2	25.4	19.9	2.83	2.50
Egypt	24.4	21.3	5.4	5.2	70.4	72.4	35.3	26.7	3.02	2.61
Ethiopia	39.8	35.6	20.2	20.7	41.2	40.1	103.2	94.9	5.55	4.76
France	12.5	11.5	9.1	9.4	79.3	80.3	4.4	4.0	1.85	1.83
Germany	8.6	8.2	10.3	11.0	78.4	79.4	4.2	4.0	1.37	1.42
Ghana	25.8	21.4	10.5	11.5	56.5	55.6	53.0	47.6	3.32	2.54
Guatemala	35.1	32.0	6.8	6.6	65.2	65.9	37.9	31.4	4.67	4.19
Hungary	9.8	9.4	13.1	12.9	72.1	73.7	8.8	7.7	1.30	1.36
India	23.3	20.7	8.5	7.9	63.6	66.1	59.6	48.5	2.91	2.55
Indonesia	21.5	18.7	6.3	6.3	68.9	71.1	38.1	30.0	2.50	2.28
Iran	17.2	17.3	5.6	5.6	69.4	71.4	44.2	35.6	1.95	1.73
Iraq	33.7	29.4	5.8	4.9	67.8	70.3	55.2	42.2	4.52	3.76
Italy	9.2	8.0	10.1	10.8	79.4	80.3	6.2	5.4	1.26	1.32
Japan	9.6	8.7	8.6	10.0	80.9	81.6	3.3	3.2	1.38	1.42
Kazakhstan	15.3	16.7	9.7	9.4	65.6	68.2	31.9	24.9	1.90	1.87
Kenya	28.8	23.6	16.0	18.3	45.2	43.7	63.4	58.0	3.47	2.63
Korea, North	17.6	13.8	6.9	7.5	70.8	72.7	25.7	20.5	2.25	1.90
Korea, South	12.6	11.0	6.0	6.8	75.4	76.8	7.3	6.5	1.56	1.58
Madagascar	42.2	40.5	11.9	10.1	56.1	58.9	80.2	68.7	5.73	5.47
Malaysia	23.7	22.1	5.1	5.1	71.7	73.6	19.0	15.0	3.13	2.92
Mexico	21.9	19.4	4.7	4.8	74.7	76.3	22.5	17.8	2.53	2.31
Morocco	23.3	20.6	5.8	5.4	70.0	72.1	44.9	34.7	2.89	2.46
Mozambique	36.9	32.9	23.0	29.1	38.2	32.4	137.8	133.0	4.87	4.29
Nepal	32.5	28.8	9.8	8.7	59.0	61.7	70.6	58.7	4.39	3.73
Netherlands	11.7	10.3	8.7	8.8	78.6	79.6	5.2	4.7	1.66	1.66
Nigeria	38.8	35.3	13.8	15.7	51.0	47.3	71.4	65.8	5.40	4.79
Pakistan	32.0	26.9	8.9	7.5	62.2	64.9	76.6	63.1	4.44	3.46
Peru	21.7	18.9	6.3	6.2	68.9	71.0	34.0	27.2	2.66	2.32
Philippines	26.3	23.2	5.6	5.2	69.3	71.4	25.0	20.2	3.29	2.89
Poland	10.5	10.9	10.0	10.3	73.9	75.6	9.0	7.6	1.37	1.42
Romania	10.7	10.4	11.6	11.9	70.9	72.7	28.1	22.1	1.35	1.40
Russia	9.4	10.4	15.3	14.6	66.1	68.3	17.4	14.6	1.25	1.31
Saudi Arabia	29.9	28.2	2.7	2.5	75.0	76.5	14.2	11.3	4.17	3.77
South Africa	18.9	16.4	18.4	30.1	46.6	36.5	60.8	65.1	2.24	1.96
Spain	10.1	9.5	9.5	10.1	79.2	80.2	4.5	4.2	1.26	1.32
Sri Lanka	16.1	14.8	6.5	6.6	72.6	74.4	15.2	12.5	1.90	1.78
Sudan	36.5	31.8	9.6	8.3	57.7	60.5	65.6	55.2	5.10	4.21
Syria	29.5	25.2	5.0	4.6	69.4	71.5	31.7	25.0	3.72	3.02
Taiwan [5]	12.7	12.0	6.2	6.9	76.9	78.1	6.7	5.9	1.57	1.59
Tanzania	39.5	35.7	17.4	17.1	44.6	44.6	103.7	92.3	5.24	4.62
Thailand	16.4	14.2	6.9	7.3	71.2	73.0	21.8	17.4	1.91	1.83
Tunisia	16.0	15.3	5.0	5.3	74.4	76.0	26.8	20.4	1.83	1.71
Turkey	17.6	15.6	6.0	6.1	71.8	73.7	44.2	34.3	2.03	1.82
Uganda	46.6	45.0	17.0	15.2	44.9	46.8	87.9	76.6	6.72	6.12
Ukraine	9.9	11.6	16.4	15.7	66.5	68.5	20.9	17.5	1.34	1.58
United Kingdom	11.0	10.7	10.2	10.0	78.2	79.2	5.3	4.8	1.66	1.66
Uzbekistan	26.1	26.1	8.0	7.4	64.0	66.2	71.5	65.6	3.00	2.80
Venezuela	19.8	17.8	4.9	5.0	73.8	75.5	23.8	18.9	2.36	2.13
Vietnam	19.6	18.7	6.2	6.0	70.1	72.1	30.8	24.7	2.24	2.10
Yemen	43.2	41.8	9.0	7.4	61.0	63.6	65.0	53.4	6.82	6.23
Zimbabwe	30.3	27.8	22.0	27.4	39.0	34.6	66.5	69.0	3.66	3.26

[1] Number of births during 1 year per 1,000 persons (based on midyear population). [2] Number of deaths during 1 year per 1,000 persons (based on midyear population). [3] Number of deaths of children under 1 year of age per 1,000 live births in a calendar year. [4] Average number of children that would be born if all women lived to the end of their childbearing years and, at each year of age, they experienced the birth rates occurring in the specified year. [5] See footnote 2, Table 1321. [6] See footnote 3, Table 1321.

Source: U.S. Census Bureau, "International Data Base" (as of 30 April 2004); <http://www.census.gov/ipc/www/idbnew.html>.

No. 1326. Births to Unmarried Women by Country: 1980 to 2001

[Percent of all live births. For U.S. figures, beginning 1980, marital status is inferred from a comparison of the child's and parents' surnames on the birth certificate for those States that do not report on marital status. No estimates are included for misstatements on birth records or failures to register births]

Country	1980	1990	1995	2001 [1]
United States	18.4	28.0	32.2	33.2
Canada	12.8	24.4	27.6	28.3
Japan	0.8	1.1	1.2	1.6
Denmark	33.2	46.4	46.5	44.6
France . . . [2]	11.4	30.1	37.6	42.6
Germany [2]	(NA)	15.1	16.1	23.4
Ireland	5.0	14.6	22.3	31.8
Italy	4.3	6.5	8.1	9.6
Netherlands	4.1	11.4	15.5	24.9
Spain	3.9	9.6	11.1	17.0
Sweden	39.7	47.0	53.0	55.3
United Kingdom	11.5	27.9	33.6	39.5

NA Not available. [1] Data for Ireland, Italy, and Spain are either provisional or estimated by Eurostat. For all other countries, data are final. [2] Data are for 1991 instead of 1990.

Source: U.S. Bureau of Labor Statistics, *Monthly Labor Review*, September 2003.

No. 1327. Marriage and Divorce Rates by Country: 1980 to 2000

[Per 1,000 population aged 15-64 years]

Country	Marriage rate				Divorce rate			
	1980	1990	1995	2000 [1]	1980	1990	1995	2000 [1]
United States [2]	15.9	14.8	13.6	12.8	7.9	7.2	6.8	6.2
Canada.	11.5	10.0	8.1	7.4	3.7	4.2	3.9	3.4
Japan.	9.8	8.4	9.1	9.3	1.8	1.8	2.3	3.1
Denmark.	8.0	9.1	9.9	10.8	4.1	4.0	3.7	4.0
France [3]	9.7	7.7	6.7	7.5	2.4	2.8	3.2	3.1
Germany [4]	(NA)	8.2	7.8	7.5	(NA)	2.5	3.1	3.5
Ireland	10.9	8.3	6.7	7.6	[5]	[5]	[5]	1.0
Italy	8.7	8.2	7.5	7.2	0.3	0.7	0.7	1.0
Netherlands.	9.6	9.3	7.7	8.2	2.7	2.8	3.2	3.2
Spain	9.4	8.5	7.5	7.7	(NA)	0.9	1.2	1.4
Sweden	7.1	7.4	6.0	7.0	3.7	3.5	4.0	3.8
United Kingdom	11.6	10.0	8.5	7.8	4.4	4.4	4.5	4.0

NA Not available. [1] Marriage data for Ireland and Italy are either provisional or estimated by Eurostat. The U.S. divorce rate is estimated by the Bureau of Labor Statistics. [2] U.S. data include unlicensed marriages in California. [3] Data are for 1999 instead of 2000. [4] Data are for 1991 instead of 1990. [5] Divorce not allowed by law prior to 1997.

Source: U.S. Bureau of Labor Statistics, *Monthly Labor Review*, September 2003.

No. 1328. Single-parent Households: 1980 to 2002

[In thousands (6,061 represents 6,061,000). For the United Kingdom in 1981, children are defined as those under 15 and those who are 15, 16, or 17 and attended school full time; for later years, children are defined as those under 16 and those who are 16 or 17 and attend school full time. For Ireland, children are defined as those under 15. For all other countries, children are defined as children living at home, or away from school, under the age of 18]

Country and year	Number	Percent of all households with children	Country and year	Number	Percent of all households with children
United States:			Ireland: [1]		
1980	6,061	19.5	1981	30	7.2
1990	7,752	24.0	1991	44	10.7
1995	9,055	26.4	1996	56	13.8
2001	9,374	26.5	2002	69	16.7
Canada:			Germany:		
1981	437	12.7	1991	1,429	15.2
1991	572	16.2	1995	1,674	17.6
1996	690	18.7	2000	1,963	21.2
2000	707	19.3	Netherlands:		
Japan:			1988	179	9.6
1980	796	4.9	1993 [2]	180	10.0
1990	934	6.5	1995 [2]	208	11.7
1995	884	6.9	2000	240	13.0
2000	1,003	8.3	Sweden:		
Denmark: [1]			1985	117	11.2
1980	99	13.4	1990	151	14.8
1990	117	17.8	1991 [2]	166	15.2
1995	120	18.6	1995	189	17.4
2001	120	18.4	2000	251	23.1
France:			United Kingdom: [3] . .		
1988	761	11.9	1981	1,010	13.9
1990	755	11.9	1991	1,344	19.4
1995	874	14.0	1994-95	1,617	21.9
2000	1,039	17.1	2001	1,446	20.7

[1] Data are from family-based, rather than household-based, statistics. [2] Break in series. [3] Great Britain only (excludes Northern Ireland).

Source: U.S. Bureau of Labor Statistics, *Monthly Labor Review*, September 2003.

Comparative International Statistics 847

No. 1329. Percent Distribution of Households by Type and Country: 1980 to 2002

Year		Married-couple households [1]				One-person	Other [3]
	Total	Total	With children [2]	Without children [2]	Single parent [2]		
United States:							
1980	100.0	60.8	30.9	29.9	7.5	22.7	9.0
1990	100.0	56.0	26.3	29.8	8.3	24.6	11.1
1995	100.0	54.4	25.5	28.9	9.1	25.0	11.5
2001	100.0	52.3	24.0	28.3	8.7	26.1	13.0
Canada:							
1981	100.0	66.8	36.3	30.5	5.3	20.3	7.6
1991	100.0	62.8	29.6	33.2	5.7	22.9	8.6
1996	100.0	60.5	27.8	32.7	6.4	24.2	8.9
2001	100.0	59.4	25.6	33.8	6.1	25.7	8.8
Japan:							
1980	100.0	68.4	42.9	25.6	2.2	19.8	9.5
1990	100.0	65.2	33.1	32.1	2.3	23.1	9.4
1995	100.0	62.8	27.4	35.4	2.0	25.6	9.6
2000	100.0	61.1	23.8	37.4	2.2	26.5	10.3
Denmark: [4]							
1980	100.0	50.3	25.0	25.3	3.9	44.9	1.0
1990	100.0	45.6	19.5	26.1	4.2	49.6	0.6
1995	100.0	44.9	18.2	26.6	4.2	50.4	0.5
2001	100.0	45.7	18.5	27.2	4.2	49.6	0.6
France:							
1982	100.0	67.0	39.7	27.3	4.3	24.6	4.1
1990	100.0	64.9	38.6	26.2	6.6	26.1	2.5
1995	100.0	62.2	35.9	26.3	6.7	28.9	2.3
2000	100.0	60.0	32.8	27.1	7.2	30.8	2.0
Germany:							
1991	100.0	55.3	31.6	23.7	7.1	33.6	4.0
1995	100.0	53.3	28.8	24.4	7.3	34.9	4.5
2000	100.0	51.1	25.9	25.2	7.7	36.1	5.2
Ireland:							
1981	100.0	(NA)	(NA)	(NA)	(NA)	16.9	(NA)
1991	100.0	61.6	47.9	13.7	10.6	20.2	7.6
1996	100.0	59.6	44.5	15.1	11.2	21.5	7.7
2002	100.0	59.2	41.4	17.7	11.7	21.6	7.6
Netherlands:							
1988	100.0	64.7	37.3	27.4	5.4	28.7	1.2
1993	100.0	63.1	33.3	29.9	5.0	30.9	1.0
1995 [5]	100.0	61.2	32.6	28.5	5.6	32.6	0.7
2000	100.0	60.2	30.6	29.6	5.6	33.4	0.7
Sweden:							
1985	100.0	54.8	23.8	31.0	3.2	36.1	5.9
1990	100.0	52.1	21.9	30.2	3.9	39.6	4.4
1991 [5]	100.0	52.6	22.4	30.2	4.1	41.2	2.2
1995	100.0	50.7	21.2	29.4	4.6	42.3	2.4
2000	100.0	45.8	19.1	26.7	5.8	46.5	1.9
United Kingdom: [6]							
1981	100.0	65.0	31.0	34.0	5.0	22.0	8.0
1991	100.0	61.0	25.0	36.0	6.0	27.0	6.0
1994-95	100.0	58.0	25.0	33.0	7.0	27.0	8.0
2001	100.0	58.0	23.0	35.0	6.0	29.0	7.0

NA Not available. [1] May include unmarried cohabiting couples. Such couples are explicitly included under married couples in Canada, Denmark, Ireland, France, and the Netherlands. For Sweden, all cohabitants are included as married couples. In other countries, some unmarried cohabitants are included as married couples, while some are classified under "other households," depending on responses to surveys and censuses. [2] Children are defined as unmarried children living at home according to the following age limits: under 18 years old in the United States, Canada, Japan, Denmark, Sweden, and the United Kingdom, except that the United Kingdom includes 15-, 16-, and 17-year-olds in 1981and 16- and 17-year-olds thereafter only if they are attending school full-time; under 25 years old in France; and children of all ages in Germany, Ireland, and the Netherlands. [3] Includes both family and nonfamily households not elsewhere classified. These households comprise, for example, siblings residing together, other households composed of relatives, and households made up of roommates. Some unmarried cohabiting couples may also be included in the "other" group. See footnote 1. [4] From family-based statistics. However, one person living alone constitutes a family in Denmark. In this respect, the Danish data are closer to household statistics. [5] Break in series. [6] Great Britain only (excludes Northern Ireland).

Source: U.S. Bureau of Labor Statistics, *Monthly Labor Review*, September 2003.

Health Expenditures as Percent of GDP by Country: 1980 to 2001

[In percent. G.D.P.=gross domestic product; for explanation, see text, Section 13, Income]

Country	Total health expenditures					Public health expenditures				
	1980	1990	1999	2000	2001	1980	1990	1999	2000	2001
United States	8.7	11.9	13.0	13.1	13.9	3.6	4.7	5.7	5.8	6.2
Australia	7.0	7.8	8.7	8.9	(NA)	4.4	5.2	6.0	6.1	(NA)
Austria	7.6	7.1	7.8	7.7	7.7	5.2	5.2	5.4	5.4	5.3
Belgium	6.4	7.4	8.5	8.6	9.0	(NA)	(NA)	6.2	6.2	6.4
Canada	7.1	9.0	9.1	9.2	9.7	5.4	6.7	6.4	6.5	6.9
Czech Republic	(NA)	5.0	7.1	7.1	7.3	(NA)	4.9	6.5	6.5	6.7
Denmark	9.1	8.5	8.5	8.3	8.6	8.0	7.0	7.0	6.9	7.1
Finland	6.4	7.8	6.9	6.7	7.0	5.0	6.3	5.2	5.0	5.3
France	(NA)	8.6	9.3	9.3	9.5	(NA)	6.6	7.1	7.1	7.2
Germany [1]	8.7	8.5	10.6	10.6	10.7	6.8	6.5	8.0	7.9	8.0
Greece	6.6	7.4	9.6	9.4	9.4	3.7	4.0	5.1	5.3	5.2
Hungary	(NA)	(NA)	6.8	6.7	6.8	(NA)	(NA)	5.3	5.1	5.1
Iceland	6.2	8.0	9.5	9.3	9.2	5.5	6.9	8.0	7.8	7.6
Ireland	8.4	6.1	6.2	6.4	6.5	6.8	4.4	4.6	4.7	4.9
Italy	(NA)	8.0	7.8	8.2	8.4	(NA)	6.4	5.6	6.0	6.3
Japan	6.4	5.9	7.5	7.6	(NA)	4.6	4.6	5.8	6.0	(NA)
Korea, South	(NA)	4.8	5.6	5.9	(NA)	(NA)	1.7	2.4	2.6	(NA)
Luxembourg	5.9	6.1	6.1	5.6	(NA)	5.5	5.7	5.4	4.9	(NA)
Mexico	(NA)	4.5	5.5	5.6	6.6	(NA)	2.0	2.7	2.7	3.0
Netherlands	7.5	8.0	8.7	8.6	8.9	5.2	5.4	5.5	5.5	5.7
New Zealand	5.9	6.9	7.9	8.0	8.1	5.2	5.7	6.1	6.2	6.2
Norway	6.9	7.7	8.5	7.6	8.0	5.9	6.4	7.3	6.5	6.8
Poland	(NA)	5.3	6.2	6.0	6.3	(NA)	4.8	4.4	4.2	4.6
Portugal	5.6	6.2	8.7	9.0	9.2	3.6	4.1	5.9	6.2	6.3
Slovak Republic. . . .	(NA)	(NA)	5.8	5.7	5.7	(NA)	(NA)	5.2	5.1	5.1
Spain	5.4	6.7	7.5	7.5	7.5	4.3	5.3	5.4	5.3	5.4
Sweden	8.8	8.2	8.4	8.4	8.7	8.2	7.4	7.2	7.1	7.4
Switzerland	7.6	8.5	10.7	10.7	10.9	(NA)	4.5	5.9	5.9	(NA)
Turkey	3.3	3.6	(NA)	(NA)	(NA)	0.9	2.2	(NA)	(NA)	(NA)
United Kingdom	5.6	6.0	7.2	7.3	7.6	5.0	5.0	5.8	5.9	6.2

NA Not available.   [1] Data prior to 1991 are for former West Germany.

Source: Organization for Economic Cooperation and Development, Paris, France, *OECD Health Data 2003*, 2nd ed. (copyright).

Average Temperatures and Precipitation—Selected International Cities

[In degrees Fahrenheit, except as noted. Data are generally based on a standard 30-year period; for details, see source. For data on U.S. cities, see Tables 377-380]

City	January					July				
	Average high	Average low	Warmest	Coldest	Average precipitation (inches)	Average high	Average low	Warmest	Coldest	Average precipitation (inches)
Amsterdam, Netherlands	41	34	57	3	3.1	69	55	90	39	2.9
Athens, Greece.	55	44	70	28	1.9	89	73	108	61	0.2
Baghdad, Iraq.	58	38	75	25	1.1	110	78	122	61	-
Bangkok, Thailand.	89	71	95	54	0.4	90	78	99	72	6.2
Beijing, China.	34	17	54	1	0.2	86	72	104	63	8.8
Berlin, Germany	35	26	58	-11	(NA)	73	56	95	41	(NA)
Bogota, Colombia	66	43	84	27	1.9	64	47	82	32	1.8
Brasilia, Brazil	81	64	95	54	(NA)	79	52	97	37	(NA)
Buenos Aires, Argentina	85	64	104	44	4.2	58	41	88	23	2.3
Cairo, Egypt.	65	49	86	32	0.2	93	72	108	63	-
Frankfurt, Germany	38	30	56	-4	1.8	75	57	97	38	2.4
Geneva, Switzerland	39	29	57	-2	2.2	77	56	96	41	2.8
Hong Kong, China.	67	58	79	43	1.1	89	81	97	70	14.3
Istanbul, Turkey	46	37	64	16	3.7	82	66	100	50	0.7
Jakarta, Indonesia	83	75	92	72	(NA)	88	74	92	67	(NA)
Kabul, Afghanistan	36	23	64	-4	1.3	88	67	102	49	0.2
Karachi, Pakistan	76	55	93	39	0.3	89	83	109	68	3.5
Lagos, Nigeria	82	79	93	64	(NA)	79	76	88	70	(NA)
London, England	45	36	61	15	2.4	72	56	93	45	1.8
Madrid, Spain	51	32	68	14	1.8	90	61	104	46	0.4
Manila, Philippines	86	71	95	61	0.8	88	76	99	70	15.9
Mexico City, Mexico.	70	45	86	26	0.3	74	56	86	37	5.1
Montreal, Canada	21	7	52	-31	2.8	79	61	93	43	3.4
Moscow, Russia	21	11	46	-33	1.4	71	55	95	41	3.2
Nairobi, Kenya	77	58	88	45	1.8	71	54	85	43	0.5
New Delhi, India	68	48	85	32	0.9	93	81	111	70	7.9
Paris, France	43	34	59	1	(NA)	75	58	95	41	(NA)
Rio De Janeiro, Brazil	91	74	109	64	5.3	81	64	102	52	1.8
Rome, Italy	55	39	64	19	3.2	83	66	100	55	0.6
Seoul, Korea	33	21	55	-1	(NA)	82	71	97	55	(NA)
Singapore, Singapore	85	73	100	66	9.4	86	76	99	55	5.9
Sydney, Australia	79	65	109	49	4.0	62	44	80	32	2.5
Tel Aviv, Israel	62	46	84	32	(NA)	87	69	100	50	(NA)
Tokyo, Japan	48	35	66	25	2.0	82	71	95	55	5.3
Toronto, Canada	28	15	59	-24	1.9	79	60	99	45	2.8

- Represents zero.   NA Not available.

Source: U.S. National Oceanic and Atmospheric Administration, *Climates of the World*.

Comparative International Statistics   849

No. 1332. Selected Environmental Data—OECD Countries

[Figures are for 1998 or the latest available year. Varying definitions and survey methods can limit the comparability across countries]

Country	Air pollutant emissions per capita			Waste generated			
					Nuclear [3]		
	Sulfur oxides (kilograms)	Nitrogen oxides (kilograms)	Carbon dioxide [1] (tons)	Municipal [2] (kilograms per capita)	Amount (tons)	Per unit of energy (tons per Mtoe [4])	Per 1,000 persons (kilograms)
United States	63	84	21	760	1,900	0.9	7.1
Australia............	96	135	17	690	-	-	-
Austria.............	5	23	8	560	-	-	-
Belgium	20	36	12	550	165	1.3	16.2
Canada	82	67	17	350	1,515	5.0	50.0
Czech Republic	26	39	12	330	43	1.1	4.2
Denmark..........	5	39	9	660	-	-	-
Finland............	15	46	11	460	72	2.2	14.0
France	14	28	6	510	1,165	4.5	19.8
Germany	10	20	10	[5]540	450	1.3	5.5
Greece............	51	36	8	430	-	-	-
Hungary...........	59	22	6	450	80	1.9	7.9
Iceland............	33	92	8	700	-	-	-
Ireland............	42	32	11	560	-	-	-
Italy...............	16	26	7	500	897	1.9	7.1
Japan.............	7	13	9	410	370	2.7	8.0
Korea, South........	25	23	10	360	-	-	-
Luxembourg	7	39	18	640	22	0.1	0.2
Mexico............	12	12	4	320	12	0.2	0.8
Netherlands	6	27	11	610	-	-	-
New Zealand........	12	53	8	[6]380	-	-	-
Norway............	6	54	8	620	-	-	-
Poland............	39	22	8	290	(NA)	(NA)	(NA)
Portugal...........	38	37	6	450	-	-	-
Spain.............	40	33	7	660	97	1.2	2.5
Sweden...........	8	30	5	450	238	4.7	26.9
Switzerland.........	4	15	6	650	64	2.4	9.0
Turkey............	33	14	3	390	-	-	-
United Kingdom	20	27	9	560	865	3.4	14.6

- Represents zero.   NA Not available.   [1] Carbon dioxide from energy use only. Excludes international marine bunkers. [2] Municipal waste is that which is collected and treated by or for municipalities: household waste and bulky waste as well as comparable waste from small communities or industrial enterprises; and market and garden residue.   [3] Wastes from spent fuel arising in nuclear power plants, measured in terms of heavy metal.   [4] Mtoe=million tons of oil equivalent (primary energy supply).   [5] Includes separate collection by private sector.   [6] Household waste only.

Source: Organization for Economic Cooperation and Development, Paris, France, OECD Environmental Data Compendium, 2002 (copyright).

No. 1333. Carbon Dioxide Emissions from Consumption of Fossil Fuels by Country: 1990 to 2002

[In million metric tons of carbon equivalent (5,901 represents 5,901,000,000). Includes carbon dioxide emissions from the consumption of petroleum, natural gas, and coal, and the flaring of natural gas]

Country	1990	1995	1996	1997	1998	1999	2000	2001	2002
World, total.	5,901	6,029	6,157	6,244	6,225	6,310	6,516	6,608	6,691
Australia...............	72	80	81	89	90	96	98	107	112
Brazil.................	69	82	84	87	88	90	92	95	94
Canada	130	135	138	146	148	151	157	157	161
China [1]...............	617	788	803	824	805	795	823	866	906
France	102	101	106	104	110	109	112	112	111
Germany	(NA)	239	240	239	235	223	230	235	229
India	162	236	226	238	245	255	272	275	280
Indonesia	41	58	64	67	65	72	75	80	82
Iran	55	71	71	79	81	88	87	92	98
Italy..................	113	118	118	113	116	115	122	122	122
Japan.................	270	299	308	310	299	310	323	322	322
Korea, South...........	64	109	112	118	101	106	115	118	123
Mexico................	84	87	92	95	104	97	103	100	99
Netherlands	58	61	62	64	62	61	68	75	70
Poland	89	83	78	91	85	88	79	75	73
Russia	(NA)	433	428	392	396	416	421	424	415
Saudi Arabia	59	69	73	72	70	76	81	85	90
South Africa	81	94	95	104	99	102	104	103	103
Spain.................	62	67	64	72	74	80	87	88	93
Taiwan [1]..............	32	49	53	56	60	59	64	59	63
Thailand	23	43	46	48	44	49	47	49	51
Turkey	35	41	46	49	50	49	55	52	52
Ukraine	(NA)	122	109	102	100	101	98	103	106
United Kingdom	164	153	159	153	149	146	151	156	151
United States	1,367	1,442	1,494	1,512	1,521	1,542	1,587	1,558	1,568

NA Not available.   [1] See footnote 2, Table 1321.

Source: U.S. Energy Information Administration, International Energy Annual, 2002. See also <http://www.eia.doe.gov/emeu/iea/contents.html>.

[Percent of adult population (persons 25 to 64 years old). Tertiary-type A includes education leading to a BA, Masters or equivalent degree, and advanced research programs]

Country	Upper secondary education or higher	Tertiary type-A attainment	Country	Upper secondary education or higher	Tertiary type-A attainment
United States	87.7	28.3	Japan	83.1	19.2
Australia	58.9	19.2	Luxembourg	52.7	11.4
Austria	75.7	6.6	Korea, South	68.0	17.5
Belgium	58.5	12.1	Mexico	21.6	13.3
Canada.	81.9	20.4	Netherlands.	65.0	21.0
Czech Republic . . .	86.2	11.1	New Zealand	75.7	13.9
Denmark.	80.2	7.5	Norway	85.2	25.6
Finland	73.8	14.8	Poland	45.9	11.9
France	63.9	11.9	Portugal	19.9	6.6
Germany.	82.6	13.5	Spain	40.0	16.9
Greece	51.4	12.4	Sweden	80.6	16.9
Hungary	70.2	14.1	Switzerland	87.4	15.8
Iceland	56.9	18.8	Turkey	24.3	8.9
Ireland	57.6	14.0	United Kingdom . . .	63.0	18.0
Italy	43.3	10.0			

Source: Organization for Economic Cooperation and Development, Paris, France, OECD in Figures, 2003, (copyright).

No. 1335. Participation in Job-Related Continuing Education and Training by Country

[Percentage of the employed population 25 to 64 years old. Data refer to all job-related education and training organized, financed, or sponsored by authorities, provided by employers, or self-financed. Job-related continuing education and training refers to all organized, systematic education and training activities in which people take part in order to obtain knowledge and/or learn new skills for a current or a future job, to increase earnings, improve job and/or career opportunities in current or other fields, and generally to improve their opportunities for advancement and promotion. Data are based on International Adult Literacy Survey 1994-1998 and national household surveys on adult education and training]

Country	Time period	Total	Male	Female
United States [1].	2001.	40	39	41
Australia.	1996-97.	47	46	50
Canada	1997.	28	26	30
Czech Republic	1998-99.	27	31	23
Denmark.	1998-99.	55	52	58
Finland [1].	2000.	43	41	45
Germany [1]	2000.	29	34	23
Hungary	1998-99.	20	17	23
Ireland	1995-96.	24	21	29
Italy	1998-99.	25	25	25
Netherlands	1994-95.	33	35	29
New Zealand.	1995-96.	47	46	47
Norway.	1998-99.	51	49	54
Poland	1994-95.	17	16	17
Switzerland	1998-99.	37	39	35
United Kingdom	1995-96.	52	51	53

[1] Includes the unemployed population.

Source: Organization for Economic Cooperation and Development, Paris, France, Education at a Glance, 2002 (copyright).

U.S. Census Bureau, Statistical Abstract of the United States: 2004-2005

No. 1336. Gross National Income by Country: 1990 and 2002

[61 represents $61,000,000,000. GNI (gross national product, or GNP, in the terminology of the 1968 United Nations System of National Accounts) measures the total domestic and foreign value added claimed by residents. GNI comprises GDP plus net receipts of primary income (compensation of employees and property income) from nonresident sources]

Country	Gross national income [1]				GNI on purchasing power parity basis [2]			
	Total (bil. dol.)		Per capita (dol.)		Total (bil. dol.)		Per capita (dol.)	
	1990	2002	1990	2002	1990	2002	1990	2002
Algeria	61	54	2,440	1,720	107	173	4,280	5,530
Angola	8	9	820	710	15	24	1,570	1,840
Argentina	104	154	3,220	4,220	227	387	6,990	10,190
Australia	302	384	17,720	19,530	278	539	16,320	27,440
Bangladesh	31	51	280	380	107	241	970	1,770
Belarus	(NA)	14	(NA)	1,360	44	55	4,310	5,500
Belgium	185	237	18,520	22,940	181	291	18,140	28,130
Brazil	415	495	2,800	2,830	757	1,300	5,120	7,450
Bulgaria	20	14	2,260	1,770	48	56	5,480	7,030
Burkina Faso	3	3	330	250	6	13	700	1,090
Cambodia	(NA)	4	(NA)	300	(NA)	25	(NA)	1,970
Cameroon	11	9	950	550	19	30	1,600	1,910
Canada	551	702	19,840	22,390	511	907	18,400	28,930
Chile	29	66	2,190	4,250	58	147	4,450	9,420
China [3]	368	1,234	320	960	1488	5,792	1,310	4,520
Colombia [4]	42	80	1,190	1,820	159	269	4,550	6,150
Congo (Kinshasa) [4]	2	2	880	610	2	3	650	710
Cote d'Ivoire	9	10	780	620	15	24	1,270	1,450
Czech Republic	(NA)	56	(NA)	5,480	112	152	10,790	14,920
Ecuador	9	19	900	1,490	26	43	2,510	3,340
Egypt	42	98	810	1,470	121	253	2,310	3,810
Ethiopia	9	7	170	100	27	52	520	780
France [5]	1,142	1,362	19,620	22,240	1011	1,609	17,820	27,040
Germany	1,601	1,876	20,160	22,740	1427	2,226	17,960	26,980
Ghana	6	6	380	270	20	42	1,300	2,080
Greece	79	124	7,770	11,660	114	200	11,260	18,770
Guatemala	8	21	970	1,760	24	48	2,760	4,030
Hong Kong	71	168	12,520	24,690	91	187	15,980	27,490
Hungary	30	54	2,880	5,290	90	133	8,640	13,070
India	331	495	390	470	1156	2,778	1,360	2,650
Indonesia	111	150	620	710	313	650	1,760	3,070
Iran	141	113	2,590	1,720	204	438	3,740	6,690
Iraq	39	(NA)	2,170	(NA)	(NA)	(NA)	(NA)	(NA)
Italy	988	1,101	17,420	19,080	984	1,510	17,360	26,170
Japan	3,349	4,324	27,110	34,010	2339	3,481	18,930	27,380
Kazakhstan	(NA)	23	(NA)	1,520	76	84	4,620	5,630
Kenya	9	11	380	360	20	32	880	1,010
Korea, South	246	473	5,740	9,930	317	808	7,390	16,960
Madagascar	3	4	240	230	9	12	740	730
Malawi	2	2	200	160	3	6	410	570
Malaysia	43	86	2,380	3,540	78	207	4,290	8,500
Mali	2	3	270	240	5	10	550	860
Mexico	236	597	2,830	5,920	491	887	5,890	8,800
Morocco	25	35	1,030	1,170	63	111	2,630	3,730
Mozambique	2	4	170	200	7	18	480	990
Nepal	4	6	220	230	15	33	840	1,370
Netherlands	280	378	18,710	23,390	264	458	17,670	28,350
Niger	2	2	310	180	5	9	710	800
Nigeria	26	40	270	300	62	106	650	800
Pakistan	43	61	390	420	143	284	1,320	1,960
Peru	17	54	780	2,020	66	130	3,050	4,880
Philippines	45	82	740	1,030	191	356	3,140	4,450
Poland	(NA)	177	(NA)	4,570	215	404	5,640	10,450
Portugal	64	109	6,450	10,720	105	181	10,630	17,820
Romania	40	42	1,730	1,870	124	145	5,340	6,490
Russia	(NA)	307	(NA)	2,130	1234	1,165	8,320	8,080
Saudi Arabia	118	187	7,490	8,530	162	277	10,240	12,660
Senegal	5	5	720	470	8	15	1,100	1,540
Serbia and Montenegro	(NA)	12	(NA)	1,400	(NA)	(NA)	(NA)	(NA)
Singapore	36	86	11,840	20,690	37	99	12,170	23,730
South Africa	102	113	2,890	2,500	276	445	7,840	9,810
Spain	454	596	11,680	14,580	498	868	12,810	21,210
Sri Lanka	8	16	490	850	31	67	1,880	3,510
Sudan	14	12	570	370	23	57	930	1,740
Sweden	226	232	26,390	25,970	144	230	16,820	25,820
Switzerland	225	264	33,510	36,170	165	232	24,550	31,840
Syria	11	19	940	1,130	25	59	2,090	3,470
Tanzania	5	10	190	290	10	20	410	580
Thailand	84	123	1,520	2,000	199	425	3,580	6,890
Turkey	127	173	2,270	2,490	242	438	4,300	6,300
Uganda	6	6	320	240	12	33	700	1,360
Ukraine	(NA)	38	(NA)	780	368	234	7,080	4,800
United Kingdom	932	1,511	16,190	25,510	940	1,574	16,330	26,580
United States	5,846	10,207	23,440	35,400	5768	10,414	23,120	36,110
Uzbekistan	(NA)	8	(NA)	310	30	41	1,480	1,640
Venezuela	52	102	2,650	4,080	89	131	4,580	5,220
Vietnam	9	35	130	430	61	185	920	2,300
Yemen	(NA)	9	(NA)	490	6	15	520	800
Zimbabwe	9	(NA)	880	(NA)	22	28	2,140	2,180

NA Not available.   [1] Gross national income calculated using the World Bank Atlas method; for details, see source.   [2] See footnote 2, Table 1337.   [3] See footnote 2, Table 1321.   [4] See footnote 3, Table 1321.   [5] GNI and GNI per capita estimates include the French overseas departments of French Guiana, Guadeloupe, Martinique, and Reunion.
Source: The World Bank, Washington, DC, World Development Indicators CD-ROM, annual (copyright).

No. 1337. Gross Domestic Product (GDP) by Country: 1995 to 2002

[23,686 represents $23,686,000,000,000. Except as noted, based on the System of National Accounts, 1993; for details, see source]

Country	Current price levels and exchange rates (bil. dol.)					Constant (1995) price levels and exchange rates [1] (bil. dol.)					GDP per capita, 2001 based on current	
	1995	1999	2000	2001	2002	1995	1999	2000	2001	2002	Exchange rates	PPPs [2]
OECD, total [3][4]	23,686	24,857	25,233	24,874	25,959	23,686	26,465	27,435	27,687	28,119	24,012	25,808
OECD Europe [3][4]	9,253	9,175	8,511	8,502	9,283	9,253	10,202	10,570	10,724	10,845	20,049	23,228
Australia	373	406	388	369	409	373	443	450	468	481	20,706	28,069
Austria	235	210	190	190	206	235	260	269	271	275	25,516	28,872
Belgium	277	251	228	227	245	277	305	317	319	321	23,689	27,717
Canada	582	651	714	705	725	582	678	714	727	751	23,074	30,303
Czech Republic	52	55	51	57	70	52	54	55	57	58	6,811	15,102
Denmark	180	173	159	159	173	180	200	206	209	213	32,167	29,328
Finland [5]	130	128	120	121	132	130	155	163	165	169	25,282	26,478
France [5]	1,553	1,444	1,308	1,320	1,431	1,553	1,708	1,773	1,810	1,832	23,375	27,217
Germany	2,458	2,108	1,870	1,856	1,986	2,458	2,613	2,688	2,711	2,715	24,080	25,917
Greece	118	126	114	117	133	118	133	139	145	150	12,149	18,439
Hungary	45	48	47	52	65	45	52	54	57	58	6,391	13,894
Iceland	7	8	8	8	9	7	8	9	9	9	29,553	28,399
Ireland	67	96	95	103	122	67	97	106	113	121	31,144	32,646
Italy	1,097	1,180	1,075	1,092	1,184	1,097	1,171	1,208	1,230	1,234	20,409	25,568
Japan	5,304	4,470	4,764	4,176	3,988	5,304	5,529	5,684	5,707	5,715	31,291	26,954
Korea, South	489	406	462	427	477	489	568	620	640	680	10,006	17,016
Luxembourg	18	20	20	20	21	18	23	26	28	29	47,237	49,150
Mexico	286	481	581	624	637	286	350	373	372	375	6,342	9,215
Netherlands [6]	415	399	371	384	419	415	482	498	504	506	25,915	29,009
New Zealand [6]	61	57	52	51	58	61	67	69	72	75	14,680	21,783
Norway	148	158	167	170	191	148	172	177	180	182	41,965	35,482
Poland	132	162	164	183	189	132	164	170	172	174	4,946	10,716
Portugal	107	115	107	110	122	107	125	130	132	133	11,728	18,394
Slovakia	19	20	20	21	24	19	23	23	24	25	4,497	12,255
Spain	584	602	562	585	655	584	677	706	726	740	16,160	22,406
Sweden [6]	248	251	240	219	241	248	279	291	294	300	26,956	27,209
Switzerland [6]	307	259	240	245	268	307	326	336	339	340	36,722	29,940
Turkey	169	185	199	146	183	169	191	206	190	205	2,629	6,408
United Kingdom [6]	1,135	1,462	1,439	1,431	1,565	1,135	1,276	1,324	1,353	1,376	26,426	27,976
United States	7,338	9,213	9,762	10,020	10,383	7,338	8,629	8,965	8,978	9,196	36,121	36,121

[1] Based on constant (1995) price data converted to U.S. dollars using 1995 exchange rates. [2] The goods and services produced in different countries should be valued consistently if the differences observed are meant to reflect real differences in the volumes of goods and services produced. The use of purchasing power parities (PPP) instead of exchange rates is intended to achieve this objective. PPP's show how many units of currency are needed in one country to buy the same amount of goods and services which one unit of currency will buy in the other country. See text of this section. [3] Excluding Czech Republic, Hungary, Poland, and Slovakia. [4] European Union: Austria, Belgium, Denmark, Finland, France, Germany, Greece, Ireland, Italy, Luxembourg, Netherlands, Portugal, Spain, Sweden, and United Kingdom. OECD Europe: Austria, Belgium, Denmark, Finland, France, Germany, Greece, Iceland, Ireland, Italy, Luxembourg, Netherlands, Norway, Portugal, Spain, Sweden, Switzerland, Turkey, United Kingdom. Includes overseas departments. [6] Based on System of National Accounts, 1968.

Source: Organization for Economic Cooperation and Development, Paris, France, National Accounts of OECD Countries annual, Vol. 1; published July 2004.

No. 1338. Selected International Economic Indicators by Country: 1980 to 2002

[Data cover gross domestic product (GDP) at market prices. Gross fixed capital formation covers private and government sectors except military. Savings data are calculated by deducting outlays—such as personal consumption expenditures, interest paid, and transfer payments to foreigners—from disposable personal income]

Year	United States	France	Ger-many	Italy	Nether-lands	United Kingdom	Japan	Canada
Ratio of gross fixed capital formation to GDP (current prices):								
1980	20.0	23.8	22.6	25.2	22.7	18.7	31.8	23.1
1985	19.4	20.3	19.5	21.8	20.9	18.1	27.8	20.2
1990	17.2	22.6	20.9	21.5	22.5	20.5	32.2	21.3
1995	17.5	18.8	22.4	18.3	20.3	16.3	27.7	17.6
2000	19.9	20.2	21.6	19.8	22.5	16.7	26.2	19.3
2001	19.1	20.1	20.1	19.8	21.9	16.5	25.6	19.9
2002	18.0	19.5	18.4	19.7	21.0	16.1	24.1	19.7
Ratio of savings to disposable personal income:								
1980	10.2	17.2	13.4	27.9	7.8	12.4	19.9	15.6
1985	9.2	14.1	12.1	30.7	5.6	9.8	16.5	15.8
1990	7.8	13.1	13.9	27.8	11.6	8.0	14.0	13.0
1995	5.6	16.0	11.2	22.5	14.9	10.0	11.9	9.2
2000	2.8	15.7	9.8	14.5	6.7	4.3	9.8	4.6
2001	2.3	16.2	10.1	15.4	9.6	5.7	6.9	4.5
2002	3.7	16.7	10.4	16.0	10.7	4.7	5.8	4.2

Source: U.S. Dept. of Commerce, International Trade Administration, Office of Trade and Economic Analysis, based on official statistics of listed countries.

No. 1339. International Economic Composite Indexes by Country: 1980 to 2003

[Average annual percent change from previous year; derived from indexes with base 1990=100. The coincident index changes are for calendar years and the leading index changes are for years ending June 30 because they lead the coincident indexes by about 6 months, on average. The G-7 countries are United States, Canada, France, Germany, Italy, United Kingdom, and Japan. Minus sign (-) indicates decrease]

Country	1980	1985	1990	1995	1996	1997	1998	1999	2000	2001	2002	2003
LEADING INDEX												
Total, 13 countries	-0.4	2.2	2.1	5.9	1.1	3.4	2.5	1.1	5.6	-0.4	-3.9	2.5
12 countries, excluding U.S.	2.7	4.6	3.8	6.3	1.8	2.8	2.1	1.6	6.7	1.7	-3.2	1.8
G-7 countries	-0.4	2.0	2.0	5.8	1.0	3.3	2.5	0.9	5.3	-0.5	-4.4	2.3
North America	-4.2	-1.0	-0.9	5.4	-	4.3	3.3	0.6	4.1	-3.4	-4.8	3.7
United States	-4.7	-1.4	-1.0	5.2	-0.1	4.4	3.1	0.3	3.8	-4.0	-5.1	3.8
Canada	3.7	4.2	-1.1	7.4	1.1	4.6	6.1	4.0	6.9	3.7	-1.1	2.0
Four European countries	3.1	3.6	1.8	6.3	0.4	1.3	5.7	2.7	4.1	0.5	-5.0	-0.8
France	2.0	0.9	1.5	6.6	-1.1	1.2	6.8	2.0	1.9	-3.7	-7.8	-1.9
Germany	3.1	4.1	4.5	7.3	-0.1	1.9	6.3	5.4	5.7	1.5	-3.6	-0.4
Italy	5.1	6.1	0.2	10.8	0.7	-2.0	10.1	0.4	8.0	2.9	-5.6	-1.3
United Kingdom	1.8	2.9	-0.3	4.1	2.1	1.8	2.0	2.9	2.5	1.5	-1.3	0.5
Seven Pacific region countries	2.2	5.8	6.1	6.2	3.2	4.1	-1.5	0.2	9.3	3.0	-2.0	4.3
Australia	0.7	7.0	-1.4	6.4	0.9	2.1	4.5	4.5	8.1	-0.8	1.1	2.9
Taiwan [1]	1.1	5.3	4.9	6.6	1.7	8.3	7.4	3.1	8.6	-0.4	2.4	6.7
Thailand	1.3	4.4	12.1	8.7	4.6	-0.7	-3.6	1.0	9.1	2.9	7.0	6.2
Japan	2.3	5.9	6.6	6.0	3.3	4.2	-2.4	-0.9	9.0	3.7	-3.4	4.1
Korea, South	0.6	6.0	6.5	10.5	6.1	4.7	1.3	8.8	15.9	2.6	6.1	6.6
Malaysia	4.8	-1.3	-0.8	4.1	-0.8	1.6	-5.0	-5.6	12.0	-4.8	-1.0	5.6
New Zealand	2.3	3.2	0.8	1.4	1.6	2.9	1.0	1.7	1.7	0.3	2.8	0.9
COINCIDENT INDEX												
Total, 13 countries	0.2	3.7	4.5	2.4	1.9	3.4	1.7	2.6	5.2	-0.7	-1.4	0.6
12 countries, excluding U.S.	2.4	3.6	6.8	1.6	1.3	2.1	-0.7	1.7	5.7	0.5	-0.8	0.9
G-7 countries	-	3.6	4.5	2.0	1.8	3.3	1.9	2.5	5.1	-1.0	-1.9	0.3
North America	-3.8	4.1	-0.2	4.0	3.2	5.6	6.2	5.2	4.9	-3.1	-2.0	0.2
United States	-4.3	3.7	-0.1	3.8	3.4	5.6	6.1	4.9	4.4	-3.4	-2.2	-0.1
Canada	2.5	10.1	-1.7	5.0	0.3	7.5	7.5	9.4	9.6	-0.7	4.1	2.1
Four European countries	0.8	2.2	5.9	2.5	1.4	3.2	6.1	6.2	9.9	5.2	0.8	0.2
France	-2.0	-1.6	5.7	2.5	0.2	3.5	9.4	8.8	14.2	7.4	-0.2	-1.7
Germany	1.0	2.0	7.2	2.9	-0.4	-	5.0	5.8	7.6	2.0	-2.3	-3.1
Italy	8.7	5.5	9.3	-	4.2	6.2	5.9	8.6	15.1	10.9	6.6	5.3
United Kingdom	-1.2	4.2	0.9	4.1	4.0	6.2	5.0	2.3	4.5	2.9	2.3	3.7
Seven Pacific region countries	3.9	4.4	8.1	0.8	1.3	1.0	-6.2	-2.5	1.6	-3.7	-2.8	1.5
Australia	3.9	8.7	-0.4	8.1	3.5	4.1	6.8	7.9	4.8	1.6	6.7	6.3
Taiwan [1]	10.2	1.8	5.1	3.8	1.2	6.0	7.8	3.1	4.5	-6.4	1.3	3.1
Thailand	2.9	2.0	11.6	9.7	5.2	-1.6	-6.4	12.6	9.6	7.0	9.6	9.1
Japan	4.3	4.4	8.6	-0.4	0.6	0.6	-6.8	-4.7	0.0	-5.0	-4.9	0.7
Korea, South	-4.2	7.1	9.9	8.0	7.1	3.9	-14.7	11.8	13.7	5.3	8.6	2.0
Malaysia	-1.6	-8.5	1.5	3.6	1.3	-1.4	-12.6	-1.9	3.4	-7.8	-7.2	-2.5
New Zealand	0.2	7.4	-1.2	9.5	6.7	1.2	-3.4	5.6	2.7	3.7	6.9	6.4

- Represents or rounds to zero. [1] See footnote 2, Table 1321.

Source: Foundation for International Business and Economic Research, New York, NY, International Economic Indicators, monthly.

No. 1340. Index of Industrial Production by Country: 1980 to 2003

[Annual averages of monthly data. Industrial production index measures output in the manufacturing, mining, and electric, gas and water utilities industries. Minus sign (-) indicates decrease]

Country	Index (1995=100)								Annual percent change				
	1980	1985	1990	1999	2000	2001	2002	2003	1998-99	1999-00	2000-01	2001-02	2002-03
OECD, total	(NA)	(NA)	(NA)	114.4	121.2	118.2	118.3	119.7	3.4	5.9	-2.5	0.1	1.2
Australia	70.1	77.8	92.9	112.5	116.8	116.5	119.8	119.9	4.5	3.8	-0.3	2.8	0.1
Austria	70.2	76.6	92.3	123.2	134.1	137.9	139.0	141.7	6.0	8.8	2.8	0.8	1.9
Belgium [1]	83.4	86.8	99.3	109.7	115.6	113.1	114.8	114.7	0.8	5.4	-2.2	1.5	-0.1
Canada	71.8	83.0	88.4	116.7	122.9	123.0	125.3	125.6	7.8	5.3	0.1	1.9	0.2
Czech Republic [1] . . .	(X)	(X)	144.9	104.8	110.5	117.7	128.8	136.4	-3.2	5.4	6.5	9.4	5.9
Denmark	63.0	77.0	86.0	113.0	120.0	118.0	119.0	120.0	2.7	6.2	-1.7	0.8	0.8
Finland	66.4	76.7	86.9	129.0	144.3	144.4	146.9	147.8	5.3	11.9	0.1	1.7	0.6
France	89.5	89.5	100.4	112.4	116.3	115.8	114.2	113.8	2.2	3.5	-0.4	-1.4	-0.4
Germany	85.6	88.3	103.2	110.4	117.2	114.8	113.5	114.1	1.8	6.2	-2.0	-1.1	0.5
Greece	92.6	99.2	101.9	114.1	114.7	116.3	116.8	118.3	3.9	0.5	(NA)	0.4	1.3
Hungary [1]	116.7	128.1	113.8	142.4	168.3	174.3	179.1	190.5	10.3	18.2	3.6	2.8	6.4
Ireland	34.2	43.9	63.2	174.6	201.5	222.1	239.5	255.0	22.7	15.4	10.2	7.8	6.5
Italy	77.2	73.9	93.2	102.9	107.5	106.3	104.8	104.4	-	4.5	-1.1	-1.4	-0.4
Japan [1]	69.9	82.8	103.2	99.8	105.4	98.2	97.1	100.1	0.8	5.6	-6.8	-1.1	3.1
Korea, South [1]	22.0	36.2	66.4	131.9	154.0	155.0	167.6	176.1	24.2	16.8	0.6	8.1	5.1
Luxembourg [2]	71.0	79.8	97.1	118.0	123.0	125.2	126.4	129.6	11.5	4.2	1.8	1.0	2.5
Mexico [1]	80.3	85.0	95.7	133.3	141.3	136.6	136.1	135.1	4.2	6.0	-3.3	-0.4	-0.7
Netherlands	78.7	83.1	90.6	106.8	110.6	110.6	109.5	107.2	1.6	3.6	0.0	-1.0	-2.1
New Zealand	74.0	85.0	87.0	101.0	105.0	105.0	109.0	110.0	-3.8	4.0	0.0	3.8	0.9
Norway	50.6	61.5	78.6	108.1	111.2	109.3	110.3	105.7	-0.3	2.9	-1.7	0.9	-4.2
Poland	(X)	107.3	87.7	133.5	143.5	144.1	146.0	158.8	4.8	7.5	0.4	1.3	8.8
Portugal	62.1	71.7	97.0	117.6	115.3	118.9	118.6	118.9	3.1	-2.0	3.1	-0.3	0.3
Spain	80.1	82.7	96.6	114.2	119.2	117.9	118.0	119.6	2.5	4.4	-1.1	0.1	1.4
Sweden [3][4]	73.0	80.5	88.0	115.6	122.2	118.5	118.9	122.1	3.1	5.7	-3.0	0.3	2.7
Switzerland	77.0	80.0	96.0	112.0	122.0	121.0	115.0	115.0	3.7	8.9	-0.8	-5.0	0.0
Turkey	38.2	57.2	81.3	116.0	124.0	113.2	123.9	134.8	-3.7	6.9	-8.7	9.5	8.8
United Kingdom	76.8	83.0	94.1	104.1	105.9	105.4	102.5	102.0	1.3	1.7	-0.5	-2.8	-0.5
United States	69.6	76.9	86.4	121.9	129.1	124.9	124.2	124.5	4.0	5.9	-3.3	-0.6	0.2

- Represents or rounds to zero.   NA Not available.   X Not applicable.   [1] Not adjusted for unequal number of working days in the month.   [2] Including construction.   [3] Mining and manufacturing.   [4] Annual figures correspond to official annual figures and differ from the average of the monthly figures.

Source: Organization for Economic Cooperation and Development, Paris, France, *Main Economic Indicators*, monthly (copyright).

No. 1341. Labor Productivity and Hours Worked by Country: 1995 to 2003

[Annual percent change for period shown. Data are derived from an annual database maintained by the Groningen Growth and Development Centre at the University of Groningen, Netherlands, in association with The Conference Board. For OECD countries and Eastern Europe, estimates are based on gross domestic product per hour worked, converted at purchasing power parities of 1999. Hence, estimates expressed in U.S. dollars at the price level of 1999 are corrected for differences in relative price levels]

Country	Labor productivity		Total hours worked		Country	Labor productivity		Total hours worked	
	1995-2000	2000-2003	1995-2000	2000-2003		1995-2000	2000-2003	1995-2000	2000-2003
All OECD	2.1	1.5	1.2	0.2	Cyprus	2.9	1.9	0.9	0.8
All OECD, excl. United States	2.0	1.3	0.8	0.2	Czech Republic	1.9	3.8	-0.7	-1.3
United States	1.9	1.9	2.2	0.1	Estonia	5.2	6.4	-0.3	-1.7
European Union (EU-15, present) [1]	1.6	0.9	1.1	0.3	Hungary	2.4	3.8	1.6	-0.4
Austria	3.2	0.8	-0.5	0.1	Latvia	5.3	8.3	-0.7	-1.9
Belgium	2.8	-0.2	(-Z)	0.9	Lithuania	4.9	7.1	-0.2	-1.4
Denmark	1.6	1.9	1.0	-0.6	Malta	3.5	-0.2	1.0	0.4
Finland	3.1	1.8	1.6	-0.4	Poland	5.2	4.6	(-Z)	-2.6
France	1.3	1.3	1.4	-0.1	Slovakia	3.8	3.9	-0.1	0.1
Germany	2.2	1.5	-0.3	-1.2	Slovenia	3.4	2.7	0.9	-0.3
Greece	2.8	3.6	0.6	0.5	European Union (EU-25, enlarged) [3]	1.9	1.4	0.9	-0.1
Ireland	5.8	3.5	3.9	1.4	Japan	2.3	2.0	-0.9	-0.8
Italy	1.0	-0.3	1.0	1.2	Other OECD members . . .	2.3	1.1	1.4	1.1
Luxembourg	2.9	-1.9	4.0	3.2	Australia	2.1	2.1	1.7	1.1
Netherlands	0.6	0.6	3.1	-0.3	Canada	1.6	1.4	2.5	0.9
Portugal	2.5	0.2	1.4	0.3	Iceland	2.4	2.1	2.5	-0.7
Spain	-0.3	-0.3	4.2	2.6	Mexico	2.4	-0.6	2.9	1.4
Sweden	2.2	1.8	1.0	-0.3	New Zealand	1.6	1.1	1.0	2.5
U.K.	2.1	1.4	1.0	0.6	Norway	2.3	1.9	1.3	-0.7
European Union (EU-10, new) [2]	4.0	4.5	(Z)	-1.7	South Korea	4.2	2.8	0.6	1.2
					Switzerland	1.6	0.3	0.2	-0.1
					Turkey	3.3	0.6	0.7	0.9

Z Less than .05 percent.   [1] Referring to membership of the European Union until April 2004.   [2] Referring to new membership of the European Union as of 1 May 2004.   [3] Referring to all members of the European Union as of 1 May 2004.

Source: The Conference Board, New York, NY, *Performance 2004: Productivity, Employment, and Income in the World's Economies*, by Robert H. McGuckin and Bart van Ark, 2004 (copyright). See also <http://www.conference-board.org/>.

No. 1342. Annual Percent Changes in Consumer Prices, by Country: 1995 to 2003

[Change from previous year. See text of this section for general comments concerning the data. For additional qualifications of the data for individual countries, see source. Minus sign (-) indicates decrease]

Country	1995	2000	2001	2002	2003	Country	1995	2000	2001	2002	2003
United States	2.8	3.4	2.8	1.6	2.3	Kenya	0.8	10.0	5.7	2.0	9.8
Argentina	3.4	-0.9	-1.1	25.9	13.4	Korea, South	4.5	2.2	4.1	2.7	3.6
Australia	4.6	4.5	4.4	3.0	2.8	Malaysia	5.3	1.5	1.4	1.8	1.1
Austria	2.3	2.4	2.7	1.8	1.4	Mexico	35.0	9.5	6.4	5.0	4.5
Bangladesh	5.8	2.4	1.9	3.4	4.6	Netherlands	1.9	2.5	4.5	3.5	2.1
Belgium	1.5	2.5	2.5	1.6	1.6	Nigeria	72.8	14.5	13.0	12.9	14.0
Bolivia	10.2	4.6	1.6	0.9	3.3	Norway	2.5	3.1	3.0	1.3	2.5
Brazil	66.0	7.0	6.8	8.4	14.7	Pakistan	12.3	4.4	3.1	3.3	2.9
Canada	2.2	2.7	2.5	2.2	2.8	Peru	11.1	3.8	2.0	0.2	2.3
Chile	8.2	3.8	3.6	2.5	2.8	Philippines	8.0	4.4	6.1	2.9	3.1
Colombia	21.0	9.2	8.0	6.3	7.1	Portugal	4.1	2.8	4.4	3.5	3.3
Egypt	15.7	2.7	2.3	2.7	4.2	Romania	32.2	45.7	34.5	22.5	15.3
France	1.8	1.7	1.7	1.9	2.1	Russia	197.4	20.8	21.5	15.8	13.7
Germany	1.8	1.5	2.0	1.4	1.0	South Africa	8.6	5.4	5.7	8.1	6.0
Ghana	59.5	25.2	32.9	14.8	26.7	Spain	4.7	3.4	3.6	3.1	3.0
Greece	8.9	3.1	3.4	3.6	3.6	Sri Lanka	7.7	6.2	14.2	9.6	6.3
Guatemala	8.4	6.0	7.6	8.0	5.5	Sweden	2.5	0.9	2.4	2.2	1.9
India	10.2	4.0	3.7	4.4	3.8	Switzerland	1.8	1.5	1.0	0.6	0.6
Indonesia	9.4	4.5	12.0	11.5	5.8	Thailand	5.8	1.6	1.7	0.6	1.8
Iran	49.6	14.5	11.3	14.3	16.5	Turkey	88.1	54.9	54.4	45.0	25.3
Israel	10.0	1.1	1.1	5.6	-0.6	United Kingdom	3.4	2.9	1.8	1.6	2.9
Italy	5.2	2.5	2.8	2.5	2.7	Venezuela	59.9	16.2	12.5	22.4	31.1
Japan	-0.1	-0.7	-0.7	-0.9	-0.3						

Source: International Monetary Fund, Washington, DC, International Financial Statistics, monthly (copyright).

No. 1343. Comparative Price Levels—Selected OECD Countries: 2003

[Example of data: An item that costs $1.00 in the United States would cost $1.54 (U.S. dollars) in Japan]

Country	United States (U.S. dollar)	Canada (Canadian dollar)	Mexico (Mexican peso)	Japan (yen)	France (euro)	Germany (euro)	Italy (euro)	United Kingdom (pound)
United States	100	102	144	65	83	83	90	84
Australia	110	113	159	72	91	91	99	93
Austria	117	119	168	76	96	96	105	98
Belgium	117	119	168	76	97	97	105	98
Canada	98	100	141	64	81	81	88	83
Czech Republic	60	61	86	39	50	50	54	51
Denmark	150	152	215	97	124	124	135	126
Finland	137	140	197	89	113	114	124	116
France	121	123	174	79	100	100	109	102
Germany	121	123	174	79	100	100	109	102
Greece	100	102	144	65	83	83	90	84
Hungary	63	65	91	41	52	53	57	53
Iceland	148	151	213	97	123	123	134	125
Ireland	138	140	198	90	114	114	124	116
Italy	111	113	160	72	92	92	100	94
Japan	154	156	221	100	127	127	138	129
Korea, South	71	72	102	46	59	59	64	60
Luxembourg	118	120	170	77	97	98	106	99
Mexico	70	71	100	45	57	58	63	59
Netherlands	120	122	172	78	99	99	108	101
New Zealand [1]	100	102	143	65	82	83	90	84
Norway	146	149	210	95	121	121	132	123
Poland	56	57	80	36	46	46	50	47
Portugal	88	90	127	57	73	73	79	74
Slovakia	40	41	58	26	33	33	36	34
Spain	100	101	143	65	82	82	90	84
Sweden	133	135	191	87	110	110	120	112
Switzerland	157	160	226	102	130	130	141	132
Turkey	66	67	95	43	55	55	60	56
United Kingdom	119	121	171	77	98	98	107	100

[1] Estimates based on quarterly consumer prices.

Source: Organization for Economic Cooperation and Development, Paris, France, Main Economic Indicators, January 2004 (copyright).

856 Comparative International Statistics

No. 1344. Gross Public Debt, Expenditures, and Receipts by Country: 1990 to 2003

[Percent of nominal gross domestic product. 2003 data estimated. Expenditures cover current outlays plus net capital outlays. Receipts cover current receipts but exclude capital receipts. Non-tax current receipts include operating surpluses of public enterprises, property income, fees, charges, fines, etc]

Country	Gross debt			Expenditures			Receipts		
	1990	1995	2003	1990	1995	2003	1990	1995	2003
United States [1]	-4.3	-3.1	-4.9	36.5	36.4	35.9	32.1	33.3	31.0
Australia	-1.5	-3.9	0.8	36.3	39.7	36.2	34.8	35.9	37.0
Austria	-2.4	-5.3	-1.3	53.1	57.3	51.6	50.6	52.0	50.4
Belgium [2]	-6.8	-4.3	0.2	53.4	52.8	49.7	46.6	48.5	49.9
Canada [2]	-5.9	-5.3	1.0	48.8	48.5	40.1	42.9	43.2	41.2
Czech Republic	(X)	-1.1	-6.6	(X)	43.9	47.1	(X)	42.8	40.5
Denmark	-1.0	-2.3	0.8	57.0	60.3	56.6	56.0	58.0	57.4
Finland	5.5	-3.9	2.6	48.6	59.6	51.0	54.0	55.7	53.6
France	-2.1	-5.5	-4.0	50.7	55.0	54.4	48.6	49.5	50.4
Germany [3]	-2.0	-3.3	-4.1	44.4	49.4	49.4	42.5	46.1	45.3
Greece	-15.7	-10.2	-1.6	50.2	50.0	46.7	34.5	39.9	45.1
Hungary	(NA)	-7.6	-5.2	(NA)	56.9	48.4	(NA)	49.3	43.1
Iceland	-3.3	-3.0	-1.0	42.4	43.7	46.5	39.1	40.7	45.5
Ireland	-2.8	-2.1	-1.0	43.2	41.5	35.2	40.4	39.4	34.2
Italy	-11.8	-7.6	-2.7	54.4	53.4	48.5	42.6	45.8	45.8
Japan [4]	2.0	-4.7	-7.4	32.1	36.1	38.3	34.2	31.4	30.9
Korea, South	3.5	4.2	3.5	19.5	20.6	29.1	23.0	24.8	32.6
Netherlands	-5.3	-4.2	-2.4	54.8	51.4	48.6	49.4	47.3	46.2
New Zealand	-4.3	3.0	2.6	53.3	41.9	39.8	48.9	44.9	42.5
Norway	2.6	3.4	9.8	52.8	51.6	48.4	55.4	55.0	58.2
Portugal	-6.6	-5.5	-2.9	42.1	45.0	46.8	35.5	39.6	43.9
Spain	-3.9	-6.6	0.1	43.4	45.0	39.3	39.5	38.4	39.4
Sweden	3.7	-7.4	0.2	59.4	67.6	59.0	63.1	60.2	59.3
United Kingdom	-1.6	-5.8	-2.9	42.2	44.6	42.8	40.7	38.9	39.9

NA Not available. X Not applicable. [1] Includes funded part of central government employee pension liabilities amounting to 8.3 percent of GDP in 1999. Expenditures data includes outlays net of surpluses of public enterprises. Receipts exclude the operating surpluses of public enterprises. [2] Includes funded government employee pension liabilities amounting to 19 percent of GDP in 1999. This overstates the Canadian debt position relative to countries that have large unfunded liabilities for such pensions which are not counted in those countries' debt figures. [3] Debt data include accounts of the Inherited Debt Fund from 1995 on. The 1995 outlays are net of the debt taken on this year from the Inherited Debt funds. [4] Debt data include debt of the Japan Railway Settlement Corporation and the National Forest Special Account from 1998 on. The 1998 expenditures would have risen by 5.4 percentage points of GDP if account were taken of the assumption by the central government of the debt of these two entities. Receipts data includes deferred tax payments on postal savings accounts in 2002.

Source: Organization for Economic Cooperation and Development, Paris, France, OECD Economic Outlook, December 2003 (copyright).

No. 1345. Percent Distribution of Tax Receipts by Country: 1980 to 2001

Country	Total [1]	Income and profits taxes [2]			Social security contributions			Taxes on goods and services [5]		
		Total [3]	Individual	Corporate	Total [4]	Employees	Employers	Total [3]	General consumption taxes [6]	Taxes on specific goods, services [7]
United States:										
1980	100.0	49.8	39.1	10.8	21.9	9.2	11.9	17.6	7.0	8.3
1990	100.0	45.4	37.7	7.7	25.9	11.0	13.4	17.3	8.0	7.1
2001	100.0	48.8	42.3	6.5	24.6	10.8	12.5	16.1	7.8	6.3
Canada:										
1980	100.0	46.6	34.1	11.6	10.5	3.7	6.6	32.6	11.5	13.0
1990	100.0	48.6	40.8	7.0	12.2	4.4	7.6	25.8	14.1	10.3
2001	100.0	48.1	37.1	10.0	14.7	6.0	8.3	24.7	14.5	8.9
France:										
1980	100.0	16.8	11.6	5.1	42.7	11.1	28.4	30.4	21.1	8.4
1990	100.0	17.2	11.8	5.3	44.1	13.2	27.2	28.4	18.8	8.7
2001	100.0	25.4	17.7	7.7	36.3	9.0	24.9	25.2	16.7	7.9
Germany [8]:										
1980	100.0	35.1	29.6	5.5	34.4	15.3	18.4	27.1	16.6	9.3
1990	100.0	32.4	27.6	4.8	37.5	16.2	19.1	26.7	16.6	9.2
2001	100.0	28.8	27.1	1.7	39.8	17.5	19.5	28.8	18.2	9.4
Italy:										
1980	100.0	31.1	23.1	7.8	38.0	6.9	28.4	26.5	15.6	9.7
1990	100.0	36.5	26.3	10.0	32.9	6.3	23.6	28.0	14.7	10.6
2001	100.0	34.2	25.9	8.6	29.0	5.5	20.1	25.6	14.8	8.5
Japan:										
1980	100.0	46.1	24.3	21.8	29.1	10.2	14.8	16.3	-	14.1
1990	100.0	48.5	26.9	21.6	29.0	11.0	15.0	13.2	4.3	7.3
2001	100.0	32.8	20.1	12.7	37.7	15.1	18.8	19.0	8.9	7.8
United Kingdom:										
1980	100.0	37.8	29.4	8.4	16.7	6.4	10.1	29.2	14.7	13.3
1990	100.0	38.3	27.1	11.2	16.7	6.5	9.7	30.5	16.4	12.4
2001	100.0	39.6	30.2	9.5	17.0	6.8	9.6	31.3	18.3	11.8

- Represents zero. [1] Includes property taxes, employer payroll taxes other than Social Security contributions, and miscellaneous taxes, not shown separately. [2] Includes taxes on capital gains. [3] Includes other taxes not shown separately. [4] Includes contributions of self-employed not shown separately. [5] Taxes on the production, sales, transfer, leasing, and delivery of goods and services and rendering of services. [6] Primary value-added and sales taxes. [7] For example, excise taxes on alcohol, tobacco, and gasoline. [8] Data are for former West Germany.

Source: Organization for Economic Cooperation and Development, Paris, France, Revenue Statistics of OECD Member Countries, annual (copyright).

No. 1346. Household Tax Burden by Country: 2003

[Percent of gross earnings equivalent to the average production worker. The tax burden reflects income tax plus employee contributions less cash benefits]

Country	Single person without children	One earner family with two children	Country	Single person without children	One earner family with two children
Australia	24.0	15.6	Luxembourg	22.5	-2.6
Austria	28.9	8.9	Mexico	4.4	4.4
Belgium	40.6	20.3	Netherlands	34.0	23.3
Canada	24.6	14.5	New Zealand	20.6	20.4
Czech Republic	24.1	6.3	Norway	28.8	18.3
Denmark	42.4	29.7	Poland	31.2	29.2
Finland	31.2	22.8	Portugal	16.6	5.6
France	26.8	15.1	Slovak Republic	19.1	6.6
Germany	41.9	19.5	Spain	18.5	9.7
Greece	15.9	15.9	Sweden	30.8	21.6
Hungary	25.5	4.8	Switzerland	21.2	8.5
Iceland	25.3	3.6	Turkey	29.9	29.9
Ireland	16.4	-2.6	United Kingdom	24.3	10.3
Italy	27.2	14.2	**United States**	**24.1**	**9.1**
Japan	17.4	13.2			
Korea	6.8	6.2			

Source: Organization for Economic Cooperation and Development, Paris, France, *Taxing Wages, 2002-2003*, (copyright).

No. 1347. Income Tax and Social Security Contributions as Percent of Labor Costs: 2003

[Data are for single individual at the income level of the average production worker]

Country	Labor costs [1] (dol.)	Percent of labor costs			
		Total [2]	Income tax	Social security contributions	
				Employee	Employer [3]
Belgium	45,187	54	20	11	23
Germany	42,949	52	17	17	17
Australia	39,639	28	23	-	6
Netherlands	39,045	43	7	22	14
Switzerland	38,447	29	9	10	10
Norway	38,065	37	19	7	11
Denmark	37,453	43	32	11	1
Luxembourg	37,294	32	8	12	12
Canada	36,694	32	16	6	10
Korea, South	36,488	14	2	4	8
United States	**36,019**	**29**	**15**	**7**	**7**
Finland	36,276	44	20	5	19
Italy	35,690	45	14	7	25
France	34,537	48	9	10	29
Austria	34,068	45	8	14	23
United Kingdom	34,004	31	14	8	9
Japan	33,881	27	5	10	12
Sweden	33,352	48	18	5	25
Iceland	30,112	29	24	-	5
New Zealand	28,568	21	21	-	-
Ireland	28,367	25	10	5	10
Spain	27,999	38	9	5	23
Czech Republic	20,812	44	9	9	26
Greece	19,825	34	-	12	22
Turkey	18,596	42	12	12	18
Poland	17,475	43	5	21	17
Portugal	15,011	33	5	9	19
Hungary	12,770	46	10	9	27
Mexico	10,743	17	2	1	13

- Represents or rounds to zero. [1] Adjusted for purchasing power parities, see text of this section. Labor costs include gross wages plus employers compulsory social security contributions. [2] Due to rounding total may differ one percentage point from aggregate columns for income tax and social security contributions. [3] Includes reported payroll taxes.

Source: Organization for Economic Cooperation and Development, Paris, France, *Taxing Wages, 2002-2003* (copyright).

No. 1348. U.S. Patents by Country: 2003

[Includes only U.S. patents granted to residents of areas outside of the United States and its territories]

Country	Total [1]	Inventions	Designs	Country	Total [1]	Inventions	Designs
Total	**88,454**	**81,127**	**6,529**	Sweden	1,629	1,521	106
				Netherlands	1,570	1,325	79
Japan	37,250	35,517	1,567	Switzerland	1,433	1,308	123
Germany	12,140	11,444	509	Israel	1,260	1,193	47
Taiwan [2]	6,676	5,298	1,370	Australia	1,047	900	120
Korea, South	4,132	3,944	186	Finland	944	865	77
France	4,127	3,869	227	Belgium	727	622	64
United Kingdom	4,031	3,627	354	Austria	639	592	43
Canada	3,893	3,426	446	Denmark	611	529	55
Italy	2,022	1,722	292	Other countries	4,323	3,425	864

[1] Includes patents for botanical plants and reissues, not shown separately. [2] See footnote 2, Table 1321.
Source: U.S. Patent and Trademark Office, Technology Assessment and Forecast Database.

U.S. Census Bureau, Statistical Abstract of the United States: 2004-2005

No. 1349. Civilian Labor Force, Employment, and Unemployment by Country: 1980 to 2002

[106,940 represents 106,940,000. Data based on U.S. labor force definitions (see source) except that minimum age for population base varies as follows: United States, Canada, France, Sweden, and United Kingdom, 16 years; Australia, Japan, Netherlands, Germany, and Italy (beginning 1995), 15 years; and Italy (1980 and 1990) 14 years]

Year	United States	Canada	Austra-lia	Japan	France	Ger-many [1]	Italy	Nether-lands	Swe-den	United King-dom
Civilian labor force (1,000):										
1980	106,940	11,707	6,693	55,740	22,930	27,260	21,120	5,870	4,312	26,520
1995	[2]132,304	14,517	8,995	65,990	[2]24,760	38,980	[2]22,460	7,210	4,460	[2]28,157
2000	[2]142,583	15,789	9,590	66,990	26,070	[2]39,302	23,340	8,150	4,489	28,930
2001	143,734	16,027	9,752	66,870	26,350	39,459	23,540	8,340	4,530	29,053
2002	144,863	16,475	9,907	66,240	26,590	39,413	23,750	8,300	4,544	29,288
2003	[2]146,510	16,819	10,092	66,010	26,730	39,276	23,880	8,330	4,567	29,490
Labor force participation rate: [3]										
1980	63.8	64.9	62.1	62.6	57.5	54.7	48.2	55.4	66.9	62.5
1995	[2]66.6	64.9	64.5	62.9	[2]55.4	57.1	[2]47.1	58.8	64.1	[2]62.4
2000	[2]67.1	65.9	64.4	62.0	56.6	[2]56.6	48.1	64.5	63.8	62.9
2001	66.8	66.0	64.4	61.6	56.8	56.6	48.3	65.8	63.7	62.7
2002	66.6	66.8	64.4	60.8	57.0	56.3	48.6	65.0	64.0	62.9
2003	[2]66.2	67.3	64.6	60.3	57.0	56.1	48.8	64.6	64.0	62.9
Civilian employment (1,000):										
1980	99,303	10,857	6,284	54,600	21,440	26,490	20,200	5,520	4,226	24,670
1995	[2]124,900	13,271	8,256	63,890	21,960	35,780	[2]19,820	6,730	4,056	[2]25,718
2000	[2]136,891	14,827	8,989	63,790	23,690	[2]36,236	20,840	7,910	4,229	27,350
2001	136,933	14,997	9,091	63,470	24,140	36,350	21,270	8,130	4,303	27,570
2002	136,485	15,325	9,271	62,650	24,280	36,018	21,580	8,070	4,310	27,768
2003	[2]137,736	15,660	9,481	62,510	24,250	35,615	21,790	8,010	4,303	28,011
Employment-population ratio: [4]										
1980	59.2	60.2	58.3	61.3	53.8	53.1	46.1	52.1	65.6	58.1
1995	[2]62.9	59.4	59.2	60.9	49.1	52.4	[2]41.5	54.9	58.3	[2]57.0
2000	[2]64.4	62.1	60.3	59.0	51.4	[2]52.2	42.9	62.6	60.1	59.4
2001	63.7	61.9	60.1	58.4	52.0	52.2	43.6	64.2	60.5	59.5
2002	62.7	62.4	60.3	57.5	52.0	51.5	44.1	63.2	60.7	59.6
2003	[2]62.3	63.0	60.7	57.1	51.7	50.9	44.6	62.1	60.3	59.8
Unemployment rate:										
1980	7.1	7.3	6.1	2.0	6.5	2.8	4.4	6.0	2.0	7.0
1995	[2]5.6	8.6	8.2	3.2	[2]11.3	8.2	[2]11.8	6.7	9.1	[2]8.7
2000	[2]4.0	6.1	6.3	4.8	9.1	[2]7.8	10.7	2.9	5.8	5.5
2001	4.7	6.4	[2]6.8	5.1	8.4	7.9	9.6	2.5	5.0	5.1
2002	5.8	7.0	6.4	5.4	8.7	8.6	9.1	2.8	5.1	5.2
2003	[2]6.0	6.9	6.1	5.3	9.3	9.3	8.8	3.8	5.8	5.0
Under 25 years old	12.4	12.9	12.2	10.0	(NA)	(NA)	27.5	(NA)	14.0	12.4
Teenagers [5]	17.5	17.3	16.0	12.1	(NA)	(NA)	35.7	(NA)	19.3	(NA)
20 to 24 years old	10.0	10.2	9.4	9.6	(NA)	(NA)	25.6	(NA)	11.7	(NA)
25 years old and over	4.8	5.8	4.6	4.8	(NA)	(NA)	6.9	(NA)	4.8	3.7

NA Not available. [1] Unified Germany for 1991 onward. Prior to 1991, data relate to the former West Germany. [2] Break in series. Data not comparable with prior years. [3] Civilian labor force as a percent of the civilian working age population. Germany and Japan include the institutionalized population as part of the working age population. [4] Civilian employment as a percent of the civilian working age population. [5] 16-to 19-year-olds in the United States, Canada, France, Sweden, and the United Kingdom; 15-to 19-year-olds in Australia, Japan, Germany, and Italy.

Source: U.S. Bureau of Labor Statistics, *Comparative Civilian Labor Force Statistics, Ten Countries, 1959-2003*, February 2004. Also see <http://stats.bls.gov/fls/flslforc.pdf>.

No. 1350. Percent of Persons 15 to 24 Years Old Not in Education or at Work by Age Group and Sex: 2001

[Represents those persons not in education and either unemployed or not in the labor force]

Country	15 to 19 years old			20 to 24 years old		
	Total	Male	Female	Total	Male	Female
Australia	7.6	7.9	7.2	13.9	11.4	16.5
Belgium	6.3	6.0	6.5	13.0	10.9	15.2
Canada	5.9	6.7	5.0	14.3	14.4	14.2
Czech Republic	6.9	6.4	7.3	18.0	12.7	23.7
Denmark	3.7	4.7	2.7	6.5	3.8	9.3
Finland	8.0	12.0	3.7	14.4	16.0	12.9
France	3.4	3.4	3.5	13.4	10.9	15.8
Germany	5.1	4.9	5.3	16.4	14.3	18.7
Greece	7.5	5.6	9.6	23.3	17.7	28.4
Hungary	8.4	8.8	7.9	20.2	15.6	24.5
Italy	12.2	11.8	12.5	25.6	23.9	27.3
Luxembourg	1.8	1.6	2.0	9.0	7.2	10.8
Mexico	17.9	7.2	28.3	27.1	5.6	46.1
Netherlands	4.1	3.8	4.4	8.7	5.7	11.8
Poland	5.8	6.3	5.3	27.1	25.6	28.5
Portugal	7.7	5.5	10.0	10.7	8.3	13.0
Spain	9.0	8.6	9.5	14.3	10.7	17.9
Sweden	5.2	6.4	3.7	10.2	10.2	10.1
Switzerland	(NA)	(NA)	(NA)	8.4	(NA)	(NA)
United States	7.5	7.0	8.0	15.6	12.1	18.9

NA Not available.

Source: Organization for Economic Cooperation and Development, Paris, France, *Education at a Glance 2003* (copyright).

Comparative International Statistics **859**

No. 1351. Unemployment Rates by Country: 1995 to 2003

[Annual averages. The standardized unemployment rates shown here are calculated as the number of unemployed persons as a percentage of the civilian labor force. The unemployed are persons of working age who, in the reference period, are without work, available for work and have taken specific steps to find work]

Country	1995	2001	2002	2003	Country	1995	2001	2002	2003
OECD, total	7.5	6.5	7.0	7.1	Ireland	12.3	3.9	4.3	4.6
European Union[1]	10.7	7.4	7.7	8.0	Italy	11.9	9.4	9.0	8.6
					Japan	3.1	5.0	5.4	5.3
United States	5.6	4.7	5.8	6.0	Korea, South	(NA)	4.0	3.3	3.6
Australia	8.6	6.8	6.4	6.1	Luxembourg	2.9	2.1	2.8	3.7
Austria	3.9	3.6	4.3	4.4	Netherlands	6.9	2.5	2.7	3.8
Belgium	9.9	6.7	7.3	8.1	New Zealand	6.3	5.3	5.2	4.7
Canada	9.5	7.2	7.7	7.6	Norway	5.0	3.6	3.9	4.5
Czech Republic	(NA)	8.0	7.3	7.8	Poland	(NA)	18.5	19.8	19.2
Denmark	7.2	4.3	4.6	5.6	Portugal	7.3	4.1	5.1	6.4
Finland	16.2	9.1	9.1	9.0	Spain	22.9	10.6	11.3	11.3
France	11.7	8.5	8.8	9.4	Sweden	8.8	4.9	4.9	5.6
Germany	8.2	7.8	8.6	9.3	Switzerland	3.5	2.6	3.2	4.1
Hungary	(NA)	5.6	5.6	5.8	United Kingdom	8.7	5.0	5.1	5.0

NA Not available.   [1] See footnote 4, table 1337.

Source: Organization for Economic Cooperation and Development, Paris, France, *Main Economic Indicators*, April 2004 and earlier releases.

No. 1352. Female Labor Force Participation Rates by Country: 1980 to 2001

[In percent. Female labor force of all ages divided by female population 15-64 years old]

Country	1980	1990	1995	2001	Country	1980	1990	1995	2001
Australia	52.7	62.1	64.8	66.2	Korea, South	(NA)	51.2	53.2	55.6
Austria	48.7	55.4	62.3	63.3	Luxembourg	39.9	50.7	58.0	77.5
Belgium	47.0	52.4	56.1	58.7	Mexico	33.7	(NA)	40.1	41.6
Canada	57.8	67.6	67.6	70.5	Netherlands	35.5	[1]53.1	[1]59.0	66.3
Czech Republic	(X)	69.1	[1]65.4	64.1	New Zealand	44.6	[1]63.0	63.3	67.9
Denmark	(NA)	78.5	73.6	76.0	Norway	62.3	71.2	72.4	76.4
Finland	70.1	73.8	70.3	72.7	Poland	54.3	62.9	62.4	68.3
France[2]	54.4	57.8	59.4	63.8	Portugal	(NA)	(NA)	61.1	59.6
Germany[2]	52.8	56.7	61.7	64.5	Slovak Republic	(NA)	(NA)	(NA)	63.6
Greece	33.0	43.6	45.9	49.2	Spain	32.2	41.2	45.1	50.9
Hungary	(NA)	(NA)	50.5	52.0	Sweden	74.1	[1]80.4	76.1	75.5
Iceland	(NA)	65.6	81.9	82.6	Switzerland	54.1	65.7	[1]67.8	77.4
Ireland	36.3	43.8	47.8	56.5	Turkey	(NA)	36.7	34.2	26.5
Italy	39.6	45.9	[1]43.3	47.8	United Kingdom	58.3	66.5	66.6	67.5
Japan	54.8	60.3	62.2	64.4	United States	59.7	[1]68.5	70.7	70.7

NA Not available.   X Not applicable.   [1] Break in series. Data not comparable with prior years.   [2] Prior to 1991 data are for former West Germany.

Source: Organization for Economic Cooperation and Development, Paris, France, *OECD in Figures*, annual (copyright).

No. 1353. Civilian Employment-Population Ratio: 1980 to 2003

[Civilian employment as a percent of the civilian working age population. See headnote, Table 1349]

Country	Women					Men				
	1980	1990	1995	2002	2003	1980	1990	1995	2002	2003
United States	47.7	[1]54.3	[1]55.6	[1]56.3	[1]56.1	72.0	[1]72.0	[1]70.8	[1]69.7	[1]68.9
Canada	46.8	54.1	52.8	56.9	57.7	74.0	70.6	66.2	68.2	68.5
Australia	41.9	[1]49.5	50.5	52.9	53.6	75.1	[1]71.4	68.2	67.8	68.1
Japan	45.7	48.0	47.7	45.4	45.3	77.9	75.4	75.0	70.4	69.9
France[2]	40.3	[1]41.5	41.7	45.5	45.3	68.9	[1]61.3	57.3	59.2	58.7
Germany[2]	38.9	[1]40.9	42.7	[1]44.5	44.4	69.6	[1]65.6	63.1	[1]59.0	57.8
Italy	27.9	[1]29.2	[1]28.0	32.2	32.7	66.0	[1]60.0	[1]56.5	57.2	57.5
Netherlands	31.0	[1]39.4	44.1	54.1	54.0	74.1	[1]67.0	65.9	72.6	70.5
Sweden	58.0	[1]61.8	54.7	57.1	57.2	73.6	[1]70.6	62.1	64.4	63.9
United Kingdom	44.8	[1]50.2	[1]49.8	53.0	53.2	72.8	[1]70.4	[1]64.8	66.7	66.9

NA Not available.   [1] Break in series. Data not comparable with previous years.   [2] Unified Germany for 1991 onward. Prior to 1991, data relate to the former West Germany.

Source: U.S. Bureau of Labor Statistics, *Comparative Civilian Labor Force Statistics, Ten Countries, 1959-2004*, February 2004. Also see <http://stats.bls.gov/fls/flsforc.pdf>.

No. 1354. Civilian Employment by Industry and Country: 1990 and 2003

[118,793 represents 118,793,000. Data based on U.S. labor force definitions except that minimum age for population base varies as follows: United States, Canada, France, Sweden, and United Kingdom, 16 years; Australia, Germany, Italy, Japan, 15 years; and Italy (1990), 14 years. Industries based on International Standard Industrial Classification; see text of this section]

Industry	United States	Canada	Austra- lia	Japan	France	Ger- many [1]	Italy	Sweden	United Kingdom
TOTAL EMPLOYMENT (1,000)									
1990, total	[2]118,793	13,084	7,877	61,700	[2]22,081	27,952	21,080	4,501	26,818
Agriculture, forestry, fishing [3]	[2]3,394	559	441	4,270	[2]1,262	965	1,879	178	573
Industry [4]	[2]29,834	3,063	1,880	20,890	[2]6,344	10,875	6,842	1,268	8,128
Manufacturing	[2]21,346	2,053	1,184	15,010	(NA)	8,839	4,755	943	[5]5,971
Services [6]	[2]85,565	9,462	5,557	36,540	[2]14,475	16,112	12,355	3,056	18,117
2003, total	[2]137,736	15,746	9,481	62,510	(NA)	(NA)	21,785	4,290	(NA)
Agriculture, forestry, fishing [3]	[2]2,275	447	374	2,780	(NA)	(NA)	1,067	107	(NA)
Industry [4]	[2]27,565	3,408	1,932	17,800	(NA)	(NA)	6,850	944	(NA)
Manufacturing	[2]16,902	2,294	1,085	11,750	(NA)	(NA)	5,019	696	(NA)
Services [6]	[2]107,896	11,891	7,175	41,930	(NA)	(NA)	13,868	3,239	(NA)
PERCENT DISTRIBUTION									
1990, total	100.0	100.0	100.0	100.0	100.0	100.0	100.0	100.0	100.0
Agriculture, forestry, fishing [3]	[2]2.9	4.3	5.6	6.9	[2]5.7	3.5	8.9	4.0	2.1
Industry [4]	[2]25.1	23.4	23.9	33.9	[2]28.7	38.9	32.5	28.2	30.3
Manufacturing	[2]18.0	15.7	15.0	24.3	(NA)	31.6	22.6	20.9	[5]22.3
Services [6]	[2]72.0	72.3	70.5	59.2	[2]65.6	57.6	58.6	67.9	67.6
2003, total	100.0	100.0	100.0	100.0	(NA)	(NA)	100.0	100.0	(NA)
Agriculture, forestry, fishing [3]	1.7	2.8	3.9	4.4	(NA)	(NA)	4.9	2.5	(NA)
Industry [4]	20.0	21.6	20.4	28.5	(NA)	(NA)	31.4	22.0	(NA)
Manufacturing	12.3	14.6	11.4	18.8	(NA)	(NA)	23.0	16.2	(NA)
Services [6]	78.3	75.5	75.7	67.1	(NA)	(NA)	63.7	75.5	(NA)

NA Not available. [1] Data for 1990 are for former West Germany (prior to unification); later data are for unified Germany. [2] Break in series. [3] Includes hunting. [4] Includes manufacturing, mining and construction. [5] Includes mining. [6] Transportation, communication, public utilities, trade, finance, public administration, private household services, and miscellaneous services.

Source: U.S. Bureau of Labor Statistics, *Comparative Civilian Labor Force Statistics, Ten Countries, 1959-2003*, February 2004. Also see http://stats.bls.gov/fls/flsforc.pdf>.

No. 1355. World Food Production by Commodity: 1990 to 2003

[In millions of metric tons (1,768.8 represents 1,768,800,000)]

Commodity	1990	1995	1997	1998	1999	2000	2001	2002	2003
Grains, total	1,768.8	1,710.3	1,879.5	1,875.5	1,871.5	1,839.5	1,872.1	1,809.3	1,830.6
Wheat	588.0	538.0	610.1	589.9	585.3	581.5	581.1	563.0	549.4
Coarse grains	828.7	801.3	882.8	891.2	877.5	859.9	892.3	867.9	890.3
Corn [1]	482.5	559.0	592.7	574.1	605.4	606.9	589.5	598.8	601.0
Rice, milled	352.0	371.0	386.7	394.4	408.7	398.1	398.7	378.3	391.0
Oils [1]	58.1	76.5	82.1	87.7	86.4	89.9	92.8	94.5	101.0
Soybeans [1]	104.1	137.7	132.2	158.1	159.8	159.9	175.2	184.9	197.3
Rapeseed [1]	25.1	30.3	31.5	33.2	35.9	42.6	37.6	36.1	32.5
Pulses [2]	58.3	55.5	54.7	56.0	57.0	54.8	53.8	56.7	56.5
Vegetables and melons [2]	461.8	564.6	613.5	640.3	695.1	745.6	776.4	815.6	842.2
Fruits [2]	352.6	410.6	443.7	438.8	459.2	471.7	472.2	477.9	480.2
Nuts [2]	4.7	5.6	6.4	6.4	7.1	7.3	7.4	8.2	8.2
Beef and pork	117.2	117.9	128.2	131.4	131.4	132.1	137.0	137.6	139.3
Poultry	37.4	47.1	49.5	52.3	54.9	56.6	58.5	58.8	60.5
Milk	441.3	(NA)	373.7	378.1	382.4	386.2	393.5	394.1	398.5

NA Not available. [1] Data from U.S. Dept. of Agriculture, Foreign Agricultural Service, *Production, Supply, & Distribution (PSD) Online*. See also <http://www.fas.usda.gov/psd/psdselection.asp>. [2] Data from Food and Agriculture Organization of the United Nations, Rome, Italy.

Source: Except as noted, U.S. Dept. of Agriculture, Economic Research Service, *Agricultural Outlook*, monthly.

No. 1356. Fisheries—Commercial Catch by Country: 1990 to 2001

[In thousands of metric tons, live weight (97,854 represents 97,854,000). Catch of fish, crustaceans, mollusks (including weight of shells). Does not include marine mammals and aquatic plants]

Country	1990	1995	2000	2001	Country	1990	1995	2000	2001
World [1]	97,854	116,042	130,927	130,207	Thailand	2,786	3,573	3,643	3,606
China [2]	12,095	28,418	41,568	42,579	Norway	1,745	2,803	3,191	3,199
Japan	10,354	6,787	5,734	5,521	Korea, South	1,745	2,688	2,117	2,282
India	3,794	4,906	5,685	5,965	Philippines	2,210	2,222	2,287	2,380
United States	5,868	5,638	5,174	5,405	Iceland	1,508	1,616	1,986	1,985
Russia	7,808	4,374	4,048	3,718	Vietnam	960	1,394	1,961	2,010
Indonesia	3,044	4,139	4,858	5,068	Denmark	1,518	2,044	1,578	1,552
Peru	6,875	8,943	10,665	7,996	Bangladesh	848	1,173	1,661	1,687
Chile	5,195	7,591	4,692	4,363	Spain	1,380	1,391	1,358	1,397
					Mexico	1,401	1,355	1,369	1,475

[1] Includes other countries, not shown separately. [2] See footnote 2, Table 1321.

Source: U.S. National Oceanic and Atmospheric Administration, National Marine Fisheries Service, *Fisheries of the United States*, annual. Data from Food and Agriculture Organization of the United Nations, Rome, Italy.

No. 1357. Meat Production by Type and Country: 2001 to 2002

[In thousands of metric tons (48,958 represents 48,958,000). Carcass weight basis for beef, veal, and pork. Excludes offals and rabbit]

Country	Beef and veal 2001	Beef and veal 2002, prel.	Country	Pork [1] 2001	Pork [1] 2002, prel.	Country	Poultry meat 2001	Poultry meat 2002, prel.
World [2]	48,958	51,033	World [2]	83,158	86,030	World [2]	51,695	52,825
United States	11,983	12,427	China [3]	41,845	43,266	United States	14,033	14,467
European Union	6,896	7,456	European Union	17,419	17,825	European Union	6,822	5,950
Brazil	6,895	7,240	United States	8,691	8,929	Brazil	6,567	7,449
China [3]	5,488	5,846	Brazil	2,230	2,565	China [3]	9,278	9,558
Argentina	2,640	2,700	Canada	1,729	1,854	Mexico	2,067	2,157
Australia	2,049	2,089	Russia	1,560	1,630	India	1,250	1,400
Mexico	1,925	1,930	Poland	1,550	1,640	Thailand	1,230	1,205
India	1,770	1,810	Japan	1,245	1,260	Japan	1,074	1,107
Russia	1,760	1,740	Korea, South	1,077	1,153	Canada	927	932
Canada	1,250	1,295	Mexico	1,065	1,085	Argentina	870	640

[1] Includes edible pork fat, but excludes lard and inedible greases (except United States). [2] Includes other countries, not shown separately. [3] See footnote 2, Table 1321.

Source: U.S. Dept. of Agriculture, National Agricultural Statistics Service, *Agricultural Statistics*, annual.

No. 1358. Meat Consumption by Type and Country: 2002 to 2003

[In thousand metric tons (12,738 represents 12,738 represents 12,738,000). Carcass weight basis for beef, veal, and pork. Broiler (chicken 16 week-old) weight based on ready to cook equivalent]

Country	Beef and veal 2002	Beef and veal 2003 [1]	Country	Pork 2002	Pork 2003 [1]	Country	Poultry meat 2002	Poultry meat 2003 [1]
United States	12,738	12,341	China [2]	43,195	44,467	United States	12,269	12,534
European Union [3]	7,507	7,640	European Union [3]	16,621	16,750	China [2]	9,559	10,066
Brazil	6,437	6,273	United States	8,684	8,833	European Union [3]	6,311	6,216
China [2]	5,586	6,116	Russia	2,429	2,309	Brazil	5,872	5,742
Russia	2,465	2,255	Japan	2,377	2,372	Mexico	2,424	2,634
Mexico	2,409	2,308	Brazil	1,975	1,957	Japan	1,830	1,842
Argentina	2,362	2,428	Poland	1,600	1,670	Russia	1,697	1,699
India	1,394	1,495	Mexico	1,349	1,423	Canada	915	918
Japan	1,285	1,324	South Korea	1,199	1,296	Thailand	915	(NA)
Canada	977	1,013	Philippines	1,116	1,155	South Korea	525	(NA)
Australia	704	726	Canada	1,072	1,026	Poland	483	(NA)
Colombia	693	(NA)	Taiwan	932	(NA)	Hong Kong [2]	255	(NA)

NA Not available. [1] Preliminary data. [2] Hong Kong & China data series has been revised to more accurately reflect actual demand and not just transshipments. [3] See footnote 3, Table 1337.

Source: U.S. Department of Agriculture, Foreign Agricultural Service, *Livestock and Poultry: World Markets and Trade*, annual. Also see <http://www.fas.usda.gov/dlp/circular/2004/04-03LP/toc.htm>.

No. 1359. World Crop Production Summary: 2002 to 2004

[In millions of metric tons, (566.87 represents $566,870,000), except as indicated]

Commodity	Unit	World	North America			Other Europe			Asia				South America		Selected Other		
			United States	Canada	Mexico	EU-25	Russia	Ukraine	China	India	Indo-nesia	Pakistan	Argen-tina	Brazil	Australia	South Africa	Turkey
Wheat:																	
2002-2003	Mil. metric tons . .	566.87	43.71	16.20	2.90	124.48	50.55	20.56	90.29	71.81	-	18.23	12.30	2.93	10.06	2.32	16.80
2003-2004, prel. . .	Mil. metric tons . .	550.48	63.59	23.50	2.90	106.59	34.10	3.60	86.49	65.10	-	19.19	13.50	5.85	24.92	1.43	16.80
Coarse grains:																	
2002-2003	Mil. metric tons . .	871.72	243.72	19.89	26.49	137.45	33.40	17.11	130.62	25.66	6.10	1.85	19.45	47.10	6.55	10.13	9.96
2003-2004, prel. . .	Mil. metric tons . .	899.43	275.70	26.31	28.70	121.36	30.50	15.60	125.13	35.00	6.30	1.85	16.10	44.27	12.39	8.33	10.34
Rice (milled): [1]																	
2002-2003	Mil. metric tons . .	378.16	6.54	-	0.13	1.65	0.31	0.05	122.18	72.70	33.41	4.48	0.47	7.02	0.28	-	0.23
2003-2004, prel. . .	Mil. metric tons . .	386.63	6.37	-	0.20	1.68	0.30	0.06	112.46	86.40	34.25	4.90	0.64	8.60	0.38	-	0.26
Total grains [1]:																	
2002-2003	Mil. metric tons . .	1,816.75	293.96	36.09	29.52	263.58	84.26	37.72	343.09	170.17	39.51	24.56	32.21	57.04	16.89	12.45	26.99
2003-2004, prel. . .	Mil. metric tons . .	1,836.55	345.66	49.81	31.80	229.62	64.90	19.26	324.08	186.50	40.55	25.94	30.24	58.72	37.70	9.76	27.40
Oilseeds [2]:																	
2002-2003	Mil. metric tons . .	329.70	83.94	6.67	0.24	16.84	4.22	3.46	52.59	18.83	1.88	3.80	39.62	54.18	1.49	0.87	2.35
2003-2004, prel. . .	Mil. metric tons . .	335.88	75.62	9.09	0.34	16.21	5.44	4.54	51.48	28.60	1.97	3.76	37.70	55.04	2.29	0.85	2.05
Cotton:																	
2002-2003	Mil. 480 lb. bales . .	88.28	17.21	-	0.21	0.28	-	-	17.21	10.60	0.04	7.80	0.29	3.89	1.70	0.07	4.18
2003-2004, prel. . .	Mil. 480 lb. bales . .	93.89	18.26	-	0.36	0.24	-	-	18.26	13.20	0.04	7.75	0.50	5.80	1.50	0.11	4.10

- Indicates no reported or insignificant production.   [1] Includes wheat, coarse grains, and rice (milled) shown above.   [2] Includes soybean, cottonseed, peanut (in shell), sunflowerseed, rapeseed for individual countries. Copra and palm kernel are added to world totals.

Source: U.S. Department of Agriculture, Foreign Agricultural Service, World Agricultural Production, July 2004. Also see <http://www.fas.usda.gov/wap/circular/2004/04-08/toc.html>.

No. 1360. Wheat, Rice, and Corn—Exports and Imports of Leading Countries: 1995 to 2003

[In thousands of metric tons (33,778 represents 33,778,000). Wheat data are for trade year beginning in July of year shown; rice data are for calendar year; corn data are for trade year beginning in October of year shown. Countries listed are the ten leading exporters or importers in 2003]

Leading exporters	Exports			Leading importers	Imports		
	1995	2000	2003		1995	2000	2003
WHEAT				**WHEAT**			
United States	33,778	28,904	31,842	EU-25[1]	2,545	4,704	7,000
Australia............	13,311	15,930	17,500	Egypt	5,932	6,050	7,000
Canada	16,342	17,316	15,500	Brazil	5,809	7,201	5,600
EU-25[1]............	13,242	16,792	9,500	Japan	6,101	5,885	5,600
Argentina	4,483	11,272	8,000	Indonesia..........	3,632	4,069	4,100
Kazakhstan	4,279	3,972	6,200	Mexico	1,581	3,066	3,700
India	1,500	1,569	5,500	Ukraine	183	686	3,500
Russia............	206	696	3,500	Algeria	3,782	5,600	3,300
China[2]............	496	623	2,500	Korea.............	2,554	3,127	3,300
Syria	364	-	1,500	China[2]............	12,531	195	3,000
RICE				**RICE**			
Thailand............	5,281	7,521	8,750	Nigeria	350	1,906	1,600
Vietnam	3,040	3,528	3,750	China[2]............	852	270	1,300
United States	2,625	2,541	3,300	Indonesia..........	1,081	1,500	1,250
India	3,676	1,936	2,500	EU-25[1]............	952	1,189	1,200
Pakistan	1,668	2,417	2,000	Iraq	234	959	1,100
China[2]............	265	1,847	1,200	Saudi Arabia	814	1,053	1,050
Uruguay	597	806	775	Iran	1,574	765	950
Egypt.............	338	705	700	Philippines	699	1,175	900
Argentina	366	368	375	Cote d'Ivoire........	291	654	750
EU-25[1]............	318	265	351	Senegal............	604	874	750
CORN				**CORN**			
United States	56,589	49,313	52,072	Japan	15,976	16,340	16,800
Argentina	7,494	9,676	8,500	Korea	8,963	8,743	9,500
China[2]............	157	7,276	8,000	Mexico	6,433	5,928	6,300
Brazil.............	267	6,261	4,000	EU-25[1]............	4,486	3,800	5,000
South Africa	2,650	1,281	1,000	Taiwan[2]...........	5,734	4,924	4,800
Ukraine	58	397	1,000	Egypt	2,257	5,268	4,500
India	42	95	500	Malaysia	2,309	2,588	2,400
EU-25[1]............	388	1,016	400	Colombia	1,430	1,857	2,100
Paraguay	124	465	400	Canada	823	2,746	2,000
Canada	604	122	300	Algeria	488	1,600	1,500

- Represents zero. [1] European Union (EU) has been updated to EU-25 for 2000-2003, but 1995 remains EU-15 data. EU-15: Austria, Belgium, Denmark, Finland, France, Germany, Greece, Ireland, Italy, Luxembourg, Netherlands, Portugal, Spain, Sweden, and United Kingdom. EU-25 added: Poland, Czech Republic, Hungary, Slovakia, Slovenia, Latvia, Lithuania, Estonia, Cyprus, and Malta. [2] See footnote 2, Table 1321.
Source: U.S. Department of Agriculture, Economic Research Service, unpublished data from the PS&D (Production, supply and distribution) database.

No. 1361. Unmanufactured Tobacco and Cigarettes—Selected Countries: 1995 to 2003

[5,546 represents 5,546,000. Tobacco is on dry weight basis]

Country	Unmanufactured tobacco (1,000 metric tons)			Country	Cigarettes (bil. pieces)		
	1995	2000	2003		1995	2000	2003
PRODUCTION				**PRODUCTION**			
World, total.......	5,546	6,097	5,371	World, total	5,599	5,609	5,536
China[1]............	2,083	2,295	1,918	China[1]............	1,735	1,699	1,735
India	528	599	595	United States	746	595	500
Brazil	324	493	516	Russia............	141	341	380
United States	513	408	339	Japan	263	258	224
Indonesia	(NA)	157	135	Germany	221	207	211
				Indonesia..........	186	233	186
				Turkey............	100	128	135
EXPORTS							
World, total........	1,767	1,962	2,089				
Brazil	256	342	458	**EXPORTS**			
United States	209	180	155	World, total	987	843	762
China[1]............	(NA)	113	146	Netherlands	82	102	136
Malawi	99	101	121	United States	231	136	117
Italy	(NA)	101	121	Germany	85	91	105
				United Kingdom	85	111	100
IMPORTS				Singapore	50	59	59
World, total........	1,781	2,011	2,033	Hong Kong	74	28	28
Russia............	148	285	293	Korea, South	(NA)	7	25
United States	199	197	261	Switzerland	(NA)	23	23
Germany	210	263	195				
Netherlands	89	112	102	**IMPORTS**			
United Kingdom	141	108	88	World, total	668	714	721
				Japan	72	83	83
CONSUMPTION				Italy	39	56	65
World, total.......	6,305	5,136	5,906	France	51	68	60
China[1]............	2,209	1,235	2,232	Singapore	38	49	49
India	464	474	488	United Kingdom	20	69	44
United States	699	499	444	Spain	(NA)	25	38
Russia............	142	301	294	Germany	(NA)	34	36
Japan	197	165	147				

NA Not available. [1] See footnote 2, Table 1321.
Source: U.S. Dept. of Agriculture, Foreign Agricultural Service, Tobacco: World Markets and Trade, June 2004.

No. 1362. Wood Products—Production, Exports, and Consumption for Selected Countries: 1990 to 2003

[In thousand cubic meters (5,830 represents 5,830,000)]

Country	Production 1990	Production 2002	Production 2003	Exports 1990	Exports 2002	Exports 2003	Consumption 1990	Consumption 2002	Consumption 2003
SOFTWOOD LOGS									
Australia	5,830	16,477	16,500	(NA)	900	900	5,830	15,578	15,601
Canada	122,000	168,000	170,000	800	4,200	4,500	125,289	167,800	167,500
China [1]	69,080	27,335	27,362	8	1	1	72,836	39,645	43,469
Finland	19,600	26,000	26,000	161	500	500	19,734	31,500	31,500
France	14,189	13,000	13,000	477	400	500	13,969	12,720	12,650
Germany [2]	(NA)	18,000	17,500	1,947	3,500	3,100	(NA)	17,500	17,100
Japan	16,775	12,800	12,500	11	2	2	33,446	24,098	23,498
New Zealand	8,361	16,000	16,000	2,931	6,975	7,000	5,435	9,029	9,005
Russia	(NA)	66,000	68,000	(NA)	21,500	22,500	(NA)	44,500	45,500
Sweden	24,700	30,000	30,000	336	2,000	2,000	24,787	37,000	37,000
SOFTWOOD LUMBER									
Canada	53,777	69,000	73,000	37,008	43,900	48,000	17,767	25,600	25,400
China [1]	17,650	4,830	5,229	15	88	88	17,733	5,510	6,101
Finland	7,400	13,000	13,500	4,152	8,500	8,800	3,261	4,700	4,900
Germany [2]	12,145	14,600	15,000	839	3,500	3,500	15,551	15,600	15,500
Japan	26,551	14,300	14,000	7	5	5	33,854	22,295	21,995
Russia	(NA)	14,100	14,665	(NA)	4,400	4,750	(NA)	9,700	9,915
Sweden	11,785	16,000	16,300	6,500	11,300	11,600	5,431	4,850	4,850
TEMPERATE HARDWOOD LOGS									
China [1]	42,340	14,127	14,410	83	12	11	42,286	19,703	20,713
France	10,157	7,000	6,500	1,655	958	700	8,621	6,266	6,050
Russia	(NA)	23,500	24,000	(NA)	9,600	10,000	(NA)	13,900	14,000
TEMPERATE HARDWOOD LUMBER									
China [1]	10,819	3,059	3,606	65	350	367	10,755	5,622	6,444
France	3,303	2,320	2,100	646	540	370	2,767	1,979	1,880
Russia	(NA)	4,700	4,795	(NA)	380	400	(NA)	4,320	4,395
TROPICAL HARDWOOD LOGS									
Brazil	33,000	28,835	29,700	(NA)	14	20	33,146	28,821	29,680
Indonesia	27,000	26,500	25,000	(NA)	(NA)	(NA)	27,068	26,500	25,000
Malaysia	39,655	19,500	19,000	20,378	4,300	3,000	19,286	15,500	16,050
TROPICAL HARDWOOD LUMBER									
Brazil	8,500	15,300	15,912	525	370	425	8,252	14,963	15,517
Indonesia	9,000	6,500	6,250	561	(NA)	(NA)	8,439	6,500	6,250
Malaysia	8,780	5,000	5,200	5,247	2,500	2,400	3,568	4,000	4,800

NA Not available. [1] See footnote 2, Table 1321. [2] Data for 1990 do not include East Germany.

Source: U.S. Dept. of Agriculture, Foreign Agricultural Service, *Wood Products: International Trade and Foreign Markets, Biennial Production, Consumption, and Trade Edition*, Circular Series WP-1-01, March 2001, year 1990; thereafter Production, Supply & Distribution Online <http://www.fas.usda.gov/psd/completetables/FO-table2-40.htm> (accessed January 2004).

No. 1363. World Production of Major Mineral Commodities: 1990 to 2002

[5,348 represents 5,348,000,000]

Commodity	Unit	1990	1995	2001	2002	Leading producers, 2001
MINERAL FUELS						
Coal	Mil. short tons	5,348	5,079	5,227	5,252	China, United States, India
Dry natural gas	Tril. cu. ft.	73.6	78.0	90.5	92.3	Russia, United States, Canada
Natural gas plant liquids [1]	Mil. barrels [2]	1,691	2,005	2,458	2,570	United States, Saudi Arabia, Canada
Petroleum, crude	Mil. barrels [2]	22,107	22,752	24,799	24,397	Saudi Arabia, Russian, United States
NONMETALLIC MINERALS						
Cement, hydraulic	Mil. metric tons	1,160	1,444	1,700	1,800	China, India,United States (inc. Puerto Rico)
Diamond, gem and industrial	Mil. carats	111	113	(NA)	(NA)	(NA)
Nitrogen in ammonia	Mil. metric tons	97.5	100.0	106.0	109.0	China, United States, India
Phosphate rock	Mil. metric tons	162	130	126	135	United States, Morocco and Western Sahara, China
Potash, marketable	Mil. metric tons	27.5	24.6	26.4	26.3	(NA)
Salt	Mil. metric tons	183	192	225	210	Canada, China, Germany
Sulfur, elemental basis	Mil. metric tons	57.8	53.2	57.3	57.7	Canada, United States, Russia
METALS						
Aluminum [3]	Mil. metric tons	19.3	19.7	24.4	25.9	Russia, China, United States
Bauxite, gross weight	Mil. metric tons	113.0	112.0	138.0	144.0	Australia, Guinea, Brazil
Chromite, gross weight [1]	1,000 metric tons	13,200	14,300	12,100	13,500	South Africa, Kazakhstan, India
Copper, metal content [4]	1,000 metric tons	8,950	10,100	13,700	13,600	Chile, United States, Indonesia
Gold, metal content	Metric tons	2,180	2,210	2,570	2,550	South Africa, United States, Australia
Iron ore, gross weight [5]	Mil. metric tons	983	1,031	1,060	1,080	China, Brazil, Australia
Lead, metal content [4]	1,000 metric tons	3,370	2,820	3,100	2,910	Australia, China, United States
Nickel, metal content [4]	1,000 metric tons	974	1,030	1,330	1,340	Russia, Australia, Canada
Tin, metal content [4]	1,000 metric tons	221	193	222	249	China, Indonesia, Peru

NA Not available. [1] Excludes China. [2] 42-gallon barrels. [3] Unalloyed ingot metal. [4] Mine output. [5] Includes iron ore concentrates and iron ore agglomerates.

Source: Mineral fuels, U.S. Energy Information Administration *International Energy Annual, 2004;* nonmetallic minerals and metals, 1990, U.S. Bureau of Mines; thereafter, U.S. Geological Survey, Minerals Yearbook; Annual Reports; and *Mineral Commodity Summaries, 2003.*

No. 1364. World Primary Energy Production by Region and Type: 1980 to 2002

[In quadrillion Btu (289.1 represents 289,100,000,000,000,000). Btu=British thermal units. For Btu conversion factors, see source]

Region and type	1980	1985	1990	1995	1997	1998	1999	2000	2001	2002 [1]
World total [2]	289.1	308.6	351.1	363.8	380.3	383.9	384.8	396.3	402.9	405.0
North America	83.3	87.6	91.8	96.0	98.9	99.5	98.4	98.7	99.1	98.6
United States	67.3	67.7	70.7	71.2	72.4	72.8	71.7	71.2	71.4	70.8
Central and South America	12.1	13.7	16.7	21.1	24.1	24.8	24.5	26.0	25.9	25.4
Western Europe	30.5	37.3	38.4	41.6	44.0	43.8	44.2	44.2	44.6	44.3
Eastern Europe and former U.S.S.R.	67.6	77.0	81.8	59.5	58.1	57.5	59.9	62.1	64.1	66.0
Middle East	42.3	25.8	41.0	48.0	51.3	54.5	53.4	57.1	55.9	54.1
Africa	17.4	18.4	21.6	24.1	26.2	26.4	26.6	27.8	28.1	28.0
Far East and Oceania	36.0	48.9	59.6	73.4	77.6	77.4	77.8	80.4	85.3	88.5
Petroleum	133.2	121.2	136.4	141.5	149.0	151.9	149.8	155.9	155.3	153.4
Natural gas	54.7	64.2	75.9	80.2	83.9	85.6	87.5	91.0	93.4	95.3
Coal	72.5	83.5	92.0	88.7	92.4	91.1	90.6	91.4	96.7	97.4
Hydroelectric power	18.0	20.6	22.5	25.4	26.2	26.2	26.7	27.1	26.0	26.6
Nuclear electric power	7.6	15.3	20.3	23.2	23.8	24.3	25.1	25.5	26.4	26.9
Geothermal, solar, wind, wood, and waste	0.5	0.8	1.7	2.2	2.5	2.5	2.7	2.9	3.0	3.3

[1] Preliminary. [2] Includes geothermal, solar, and wood and waste energy produced in the United States and not used for generating electricity, not shown separately by type.

No. 1365. World Primary Energy Consumption by Region and Type: 1980 to 2002

[In quadrillion Btu (284.9 represents 284,900,000,000,000,000). Btu=British thermal units. For Btu conversion factors, see source]

Region and type	1980	1985	1990	1995	1997	1998	1999	2000	2001	2002 [1]
World total [2]	284.8	310.1	348.2	365.9	380.3	381.5	388.8	399.1	403.9	411.2
North America	91.8	91.2	100.9	108.8	113.0	113.4	115.5	118.2	115.2	117.4
United States	78.3	76.4	84.6	91.2	94.7	95.1	96.8	98.9	96.3	97.6
Central and South America	11.5	12.4	14.5	17.6	19.4	20.1	20.3	20.9	21.2	21.2
Western Europe	58.5	59.6	64.1	66.2	68.8	70.2	70.3	71.5	72.6	72.3
Eastern Europe and former U.S.S.R.	61.3	70.5	74.1	52.6	49.8	48.8	50.1	50.5	51.8	51.9
Middle East	5.9	8.6	11.1	13.9	15.4	16.2	16.6	17.3	18.0	18.9
Africa	6.8	8.5	9.3	10.6	11.4	11.3	11.4	12.0	12.5	12.7
Far East and Oceania	49.1	59.4	74.2	96.0	102.5	101.4	104.4	108.7	112.7	116.9
Petroleum	131.0	123.1	136.0	142.6	148.6	150.2	153.7	155.6	158.0	159.4
Natural gas	54.0	63.6	75.0	81.0	84.6	85.5	87.6	91.0	92.2	94.7
Coal	71.3	83.9	90.5	89.0	92.3	90.4	90.8	94.8	96.3	98.3
Hydroelectric power	18.0	20.6	22.5	25.4	26.2	26.2	26.7	27.1	26.0	26.6
Nuclear electric power	7.6	15.3	20.3	23.2	23.8	24.3	25.1	25.5	26.4	26.9
Geothermal, solar, wind, wood, and waste	0.5	0.8	1.7	2.2	2.5	2.5	2.7	2.9	3.0	3.3

[1] Preliminary. [2] See footnote 2, Table 1364.

Source of Tables 1364 and 1365: U.S. Energy Information Administration, *International Energy Annual, 2002.*
Also see <http://www.eia.doe.gov/emeu/iea/contents.html>.

No. 1366. World Energy Consumption by Region and Energy Source, 1990 to 2001, and Projections, 2010 to 2025

[In quadrillion Btu (348.4 represents 348,400,000,000,000,000). Btu=British thermal units. For Btu conversion factors, see source. Energy totals include net imports of coal coke and electricity generated from biomass in the United States. The electricity portion of the national consumption values consists of generation for domestic use plus an adjustment for electricity trade based on a fuel's share of total generation in the exporting country]

Region and energy source	1990	2000	2001	Projections			
				2010	2015	2020	2025
World, total	348.4	398.9	403.9	470.8	517.3	567.8	622.9
North America	100.6	118.7	115.6	134.5	144.6	155.0	166.6
United States	84.6	99.3	97.0	111.8	119.7	127.9	136.5
Western Europe	59.9	66.8	68.2	71.2	73.8	76.7	79.7
Industrialized Asia	22.3	27.5	27.7	30.6	32.0	33.4	35.1
Eastern Europe and former Soviet Union	76.3	52.2	53.3	59.0	64.3	70.3	75.6
Developing Asia	52.5	80.5	85.0	110.6	129.7	150.5	173.4
Middle East	13.1	20.3	20.8	25.0	27.7	30.7	34.1
Africa	9.3	11.9	12.4	14.6	16.7	19.0	21.5
Central and South America	14.4	21.0	20.9	25.4	28.4	32.2	36.9
Oil	135.1	155.9	156.5	185.4	204.0	223.8	245.3
Natural gas	75.0	91.4	93.1	108.5	122.0	138.8	156.5
Coal	91.6	93.6	95.9	108.0	116.6	126.8	140.2
Nuclear	20.3	25.5	26.4	29.8	31.4	31.8	30.4
Other	26.4	32.8	32.2	39.0	43.2	46.6	50.4

Source: U.S. Energy Information Administration (EIA), *International Energy Outlook 2004.* Also see <http://www.eia.doe.gov/oiaf/ieo/pdf/appa1a8.pdf>.

No. 1367. Energy Consumption and Production by Country: 1995 and 2002

[365.9 represents 365,900,000,000,000,000. See text of this section for general comments about the data. For data qualifications for countries, see source]

Country	Primary energy consumed Total (quad. Btu) 1995	2002 prel.	Per capita (mil. Btu) 1995	2002, prel.	Dry natural gas production (tril. cu. ft) 1995	2002, prel.	Crude petroleum production (1,000 barrels per day) 1995	2002, prel.	Coal production (mil. short tons) 1995	2002, prel.
World Total..........	365.9	411.2	64	66	78.0	92.3	62,335	66,842	5,079	5,252
United States	91.2	97.6	64	66	18.6	19.0	6,560	5,746	1,033	1,094
Algeria.....................	1.3	1.3	47	41	2.1	2.8	1,202	1,306	(Z)	(Z)
Argentina...................	2.3	2.5	66	65	0.9	1.3	715	757	(Z)	(Z)
Australia	4.0	5.6	224	286	1.0	1.3	562	626	267	378
Austria	1.3	1.4	159	172	0.1	0.1	23	19	1	2
Bahrain	0.3	0.4	489	587	0.2	0.3	41	35	(Z)	(Z)
Bangladesh	0.4	0.6	3	4	0.3	0.4	1	6	(Z)	(Z)
Belarus	1.0	1.2	99	116	(Z)	(Z)	38	37	(Z)	(Z)
Belgium....................	2.3	2.7	230	265	(Z)	(Z)	(Z)	(Z)	1	(Z)
Brazil	7.0	8.6	44	49	0.2	0.3	695	1,455	5	5
Bulgaria...................	0.9	0.9	109	107	(Z)	(Z)	1	1	30	28
Burma.....................	0.1	0.2	3	3	0.1	0.3	10	15	(Z)	(Z)
Canada....................	12.1	13.1	412	418	5.6	6.6	1,805	2,171	83	73
Chile. ¹	0.8	1.1	54	68	0.1	(Z)	11	6	1	(Z)
China ¹....................	35.2	43.2	29	33	0.6	1.2	2,990	3,390	1,537	1,521
Colombia.................. ²	1.1	1.2	28	28	0.2	0.2	585	577	28	48
Congo (Kinshasa) ²	0.1	0.1	2	2	(Z)	(Z)	30	23	(Z)	(Z)
Cuba	0.4	0.5	38	42	(Z)	(Z)	26	47	(Z)	(Z)
Czech Republic	1.7	1.6	165	154	(Z)	(Z)	3	7	83	70
Denmark	0.9	0.8	168	155	0.2	0.3	186	371	(Z)	(Z)
Ecuador	0.3	0.4	27	29	(Z)	(Z)	392	393	(Z)	(Z)
Egypt.....................	1.6	2.3	26	33	0.4	0.9	920	631	(Z)	(Z)
Finland	1.1	1.2	220	236	(Z)	(Z)	(Z)	(Z)	(Z)	(Z)
France	10.1	11.0	173	184	0.1	0.1	50	27	11	2
Germany..................	14.3	14.3	175	173	0.7	0.8	59	69	274	231
Greece	1.1	1.4	108	126	(Z)	(Z)	9	3	64	75
Hong Kong	0.6	0.9	102	122	(Z)	(Z)	(Z)	(Z)	(Z)	(Z)
Hungary	1.0	1.1	101	106	0.2	0.1	35	24	16	14
India.....................	11.5	14.0	12	13	0.6	0.9	703	665	321	393
Indonesia.................	3.3	4.5	16	21	2.2	2.5	1,503	1,267	45	112
Iran	3.8	5.9	61	86	1.2	2.6	3,643	3,444	1	1
Iraq	1.1	1.2	56	47	0.1	0.1	560	2,023	(Z)	(Z)
Ireland	0.4	0.6	120	161	0.1	(Z)	(Z)	(Z)	(Z)	(Z)
Israel	0.6	0.8	116	126	(Z)	(Z)	(Z)	(Z)	(Z)	(Z)
Italy	7.1	7.6	124	133	0.7	0.5	93	85	(Z)	(Z)
Japan	20.9	22.0	166	172	0.1	0.1	11	5	7	3
Korea, North	1.2	1.1	52	49	(Z)	(Z)	(Z)	(Z)	35	37
Korea, South	6.6	8.4	147	177	(Z)	(Z)	(Z)	(Z)	6	4
Kuwait....................	0.6	1.0	347	390	0.2	0.3	2,057	1,894	(Z)	(Z)
Libya	0.6	0.7	117	123	0.2	0.2	1,390	1,319	(Z)	(Z)
Malaysia	1.5	2.3	72	97	1.0	1.7	682	698	(Z)	1
Mexico	5.5	6.6	60	65	1.0	1.3	2,618	3,177	10	12
Morocco	0.4	0.5	14	15	(Z)	(Z)	(Z)	1	1	(Z)
Netherlands	3.6	3.9	231	244	3.0	2.7	66	46	(Z)	(Z)
New Zealand	0.8	0.9	224	228	0.2	0.2	32	30	4	5
Nigeria...................	0.8	0.9	8	8	0.2	0.5	1,993	2,118	(Z)	(Z)
Norway...................	1.8	2.0	410	442	1.1	2.4	2,768	2,990	(Z)	2
Pakistan..................	1.6	1.8	13	12	0.6	0.8	57	50	3	4
Peru	0.5	0.6	20	21	(Z)	(Z)	130	97	(Z)	(Z)
Philippines................	1.0	1.2	14	15	(Z)	0.1	3	24	1	2
Poland	3.7	3.3	96	87	0.2	0.2	5	17	220	178
Portugal	0.8	1.1	85	107	(Z)	(Z)	(Z)	(Z)	(Z)	(Z)
Romania..................	2.0	1.7	89	77	0.7	0.5	135	120	45	34
Russia....................	27.9	27.5	189	191	21.0	21.0	5,995	7,408	271	259
Saudi Arabia	3.9	5.1	203	219	1.3	2.0	8,231	7,634	(Z)	(Z)
Serbia and Montenegro	0.5	0.7	44	65	(Z)	(Z)	22	14	45	35
South Africa	4.1	4.5	100	102	0.1	0.1	(Z)	19	227	245
Spain	4.3	5.9	108	143	(Z)	(Z)	13	7	31	24
Sweden...................	2.2	2.2	254	251	(Z)	(Z)	(Z)	(Z)	(Z)	(Z)
Switzerland	1.2	1.3	174	177	(Z)	(Z)	(Z)	(Z)	(Z)	(Z)
Syria.....................	0.7	0.9	45	49	0.1	0.2	575	511	(Z)	(Z)
Taiwan	2.9	4.1	134	182	(Z)	(Z)	1	1	(Z)	(Z)
Thailand	2.2	3.1	38	49	0.4	0.7	51	127	20	22
Trinidad and Tobago	0.3	0.5	258	386	0.3	0.6	131	122	(Z)	(Z)
Tunisia	0.2	0.3	24	35	(Z)	0.1	89	76	(Z)	(Z)
Turkey....................	2.5	3.1	39	44	(Z)	(Z)	67	47	61	59
Ukraine	7.2	6.5	140	134	0.6	0.6	65	75	95	93
United Arab Emirates	1.6	2.1	642	720	1.1	1.5	2,233	2,082	(Z)	(Z)
United Kingdom	9.4	9.6	163	162	2.7	3.6	2,489	2,292	52	33
Venezuela	2.5	2.9	113	115	0.9	1.1	2,750	2,604	4	10
Vietnam...................	0.5	0.9	7	11	(Z)	0.1	173	340	9	14

Z Less than 50 billion cubic feet, 500 barrels per day, or 500,000 short tons. ¹ See footnote 2, Table 1321. ² See footnote 3, Table 1321.

Source: U.S. Energy Information Administration, *International Energy Annual.*

No. 1368. Net Electricity Generation by Type and Country: 2001

[14,813.3 represents 14,813,300,000,000]

Country	Total[1] (bil. kWh)	Thermal[2]	Hydro	Nuclear	Country	Total[1] (bil. kWh)	Thermal[2]	Hydro	Nuclear
World, total	14,813.3	64.1	17.3	17.0	Korea, South	265.9	58.2	1.5	40.1
Argentina	86.4	49.4	42.4	7.6	Malaysia	67.7	89.3	10.7	-
Australia	204.7	91.3	7.9	-	Mexico	198.6	78.7	14.2	4.2
Austria	60.8	28.5	68.1	-	Netherlands	88.2	90.7	0.1	4.3
Belgium	74.4	38.2	0.6	59.2	New Zealand	38.6	33.9	55.0	-
Brazil	323.0	9.4	82.1	4.4	Norway	120.0	0.4	99.3	-
Bulgaria	41.3	50.6	5.2	44.2	Pakistan	68.9	69.9	27.2	2.9
Canada	570.1	28.1	57.8	12.8	Paraguay	44.9	(Z)	99.9	-
China[3]	1,409.3	80.3	18.3	1.2	Poland	135.2	97.7	1.7	-
Colombia	42.5	24.6	74.1	-	Romania	51.3	61.4	28.8	9.8
Czech Republic	70.0	76.1	2.9	20.0	Russia	843.5	64.1	20.6	14.9
Denmark	35.4	82.7	0.1	-	Saudi Arabia	129.1	100.0	-	-
Egypt	78.4	82.2	17.8	-	Serbia and Montenegro	30.5	62.3	37.7	-
Finland	71.0	39.4	18.4	30.5	South Africa	199.6	93.6	1.0	5.4
France	522.1	8.4	14.1	76.8	Spain	223.4	50.4	18.2	27.1
Germany	547.9	62.5	3.7	29.7	Sweden	153.9	3.9	50.4	42.7
Greece	50.0	94.1	4.2	-	Switzerland	68.7	1.2	59.6	37.1
Hungary	34.4	60.1	0.5	39.0	Taiwan[3]	151.1	71.4	6.0	22.6
India	545.6	82.6	13.4	3.3	Thailand	96.8	92.2	6.4	-
Indonesia	96.1	86.1	11.0	-	Turkey	116.6	79.3	20.4	-
Iran	124.2	96.0	4.0	-	Ukraine	163.3	48.7	7.4	43.9
Italy	258.0	78.7	18.0	-	United Kingdom	361.6	73.6	1.1	23.7
Japan	978.3	58.9	8.5	31.0	United States	3,736.6	71.6	5.6	20.6
Kazakhstan	52.4	84.7	15.3	-	Uzbekistan	45.4	86.9	13.1	-
Korea, North	31.6	28.5	71.5	-	Venezuela	87.6	31.7	68.3	-

- Represents zero. Z Less than 0.05 percent. [1] Includes geothermal, solar, wind, and wood and waste generation, not shown separately. [2] Electricity generated from coal, oil, and gas. [3] See footnote 2, Table 1321.

Source: U.S. Energy Information Administration, *International Energy Annual 2002*.

No. 1369. Commercial Nuclear Power Generation by Country: 1990 to 2003

[Generation for calendar years; other data as of December (1,743.9 represents 1,743,900,000,000).
kWh=kilowatthours.kW=kilowatts]

Country	Reactors 1990	1995	2002	2003	Gross electricity generated (bil. kWh) 1990	1995	2002	2003	Gross capacity (1,000 kW) 1990	1995	2002	2003
Total	368	423	436	436	1,743.9	2,271.7	2,666.7	2,597.1	301,745	358,414	380,261	381,110
United States	112	109	104	104	606.4	705.7	811.9	797.0	105,998	105,810	104,209	104,350
Argentina	2	2	2	2	7.0	7.0	5.8	1.9	1,005	1,005	1,005	1,005
Armenia	(NA)	1	1	1	(NA)	0.3	2.2	1.7	(NA)	408	408	408
Belgium	7	7	7	7	42.7	41.3	47.3	47.4	5,740	5,911	6,050	6,050
Brazil	1	1	2	2	2.0	2.5	13.8	13.3	657	657	2,007	2,007
Bulgaria	(NA)	6	6	4	(NA)	17.1	20	17	(NA)	3,760	3,760	2,880
Canada	19	22	21	21	74.0	100.2	75.9	75.7	13,855	16,699	15,795	15,396
China	(NA)	(NA)	2	2	(NA)	(NA)	14.7	15.0	(NA)	(NA)	1,968	1,968
Czech Republic	(NA)	(NA)	4	6	(NA)	(NA)	13.3	24.4	(NA)	(NA)	1,760	3,722
Finland	4	4	4	4	18.9	18.9	18.9	22.7	2,400	2,400	2,760	2,760
France	58	56	59	59	314.1	377.2	434.7	441.1	58,862	60,674	66,042	66,042
Germany	22	21	19	19	147.2	154.1	164.8	165.1	23,973	24,035	22,365	22,365
Great Britain	42	34	25	25	68.8	82.7	89.6	88.6	15,274	14,022	14,240	14,240
Hungary	4	4	4	4	13.6	14.0	13.9	11.0	1,760	1,840	1,866	1,866
India	6	10	14	14	6.0	7.6	19.5	18.3	1,330	2,270	2,720	2,720
Italy	2	(NA)	(NA)	-	(NA)	(NA)	(NA)	-	1,132	(NA)	(NA)	(NA)
Japan	40	50	53	53	191.9	286.0	313.5	227.1	31,645	41,356	45,907	45,907
Korea, South	9	10	18	18	52.8	63.9	116.5	129.6	7,616	8,615	15,768	15,768
Lithuania	(NA)	2	2	2	(NA)	9.6	13.2	15.5	(NA)	3,000	3,000	3,000
Mexico	2	2	1	1	2.1	7.9	9.7	10.5	540	540	480	480
Netherlands	2	1	2	1	3.4	4.0	3.9	4.0	137	137	462	462
Pakistan	1	1	2	2	0.4	0.5	1.9	1.9	(NA)	(NA)	706	706
Romania	(NA)	(NA)	1	1	(NA)	(NA)	5.5	4.9	(NA)	(NA)	707	707
Russia	(NA)	29	30	30	(NA)	98.7	139.7	148.6	(NA)	21,266	22,266	22,266
Slovakia	(NA)	(NA)	6	6	(NA)	(NA)	18.2	17.9	(NA)	(NA)	2,640	2,640
Slovenia	1	1	1	1	4.6	4.7	5.5	5.2	664	664	707	707
South Africa	2	2	2	2	8.9	11.9	12.6	13.2	1,930	1,930	1,930	1,930
Spain	10	9	9	9	54.3	55.4	63.0	61.9	7,984	7,400	7,870	7,895
Sweden	12	12	11	11	68.2	69.9	68.5	68.4	10,344	10,442	9,844	9,844
Switzerland	5	5	5	5	23.6	24.8	27.1	27.3	3,079	3,200	3,352	3,352
Taiwan[1]	6	6	6	6	32.9	35.3	39.5	38.9	5,146	5,144	5,144	5,144
Ukraine	(NA)	15	13	13	(NA)	70.5	77.9	81.4	(NA)	13,880	11,880	11,880

- Represents zero. NA Not available. [1] See footnote 2, Table 1321.

Source: McGraw-Hill, Inc., New York, NY, *Nucleonics Week*, March issues (copyright).

U.S. Census Bureau, Statistical Abstract of the United States: 2004-2005

No. 1370. Selected Indexes of Manufacturing Activity by Country: 1980 to 2002

[1992=100. Data relate to employees (wage and salary earners) in Belgium and Italy, and to all employed persons (employees, self-employed workers, and unpaid family workers) in the other countries. Minus sign (-) indicates decrease. For explanation of average annual percent change, see Guide to Tabular Presentation]

Index	United States	Canada	Japan	Belgium	France	Germany	Italy	Netherlands	Norway	Sweden	United Kingdom
Output per hour:											
1980.	70.5	72.9	63.2	65.4	61.6	(NA)	78.6	69.1	77.9	73.1	54.4
1990.	96.9	93.4	94.4	96.8	93.9	(NA)	96.6	98.7	98.1	94.6	89.2
1995.	113.8	112.4	111.0	113.2	114.4	112.3	107.9	117.3	100.7	124.5	106.5
2000.	142.1	129.3	135.9	130.8	143.2	127.0	113.6	132.7	106.6	175.5	121.9
2001.	142.7	127.0	135.9	132.6	148.0	127.8	115.9	132.3	108.9	170.3	126.4
2002.	155.9	130.5	139.5	141.7	152.1	131.0	114.3	133.1	110.9	184.3	127.6
Average annual percent change:											
1995-2000.	4.5	2.8	4.1	2.9	4.6	2.5	1.0	2.5	1.1	7.1	2.7
2000-2001.	0.4	-1.8	-0.1	1.4	3.4	0.6	2.0	-0.3	2.2	-3.0	3.7
2001-2002.	9.2	2.8	2.7	6.8	2.7	2.5	-1.4	0.5	1.8	8.2	1.0
Compensation per hour, national currency basis: [1]											
1980.	55.6	47.5	58.5	52.5	41.2	(NA)	30.4	60.5	39.0	37.3	32.1
1990.	90.8	88.3	90.6	90.1	90.9	(NA)	87.6	89.8	92.3	87.8	82.9
1995.	107.9	106.0	108.3	109.2	110.4	117.6	111.3	112.1	109.2	106.8	109.5
2000.	131.1	119.6	113.7	120.6	123.4	137.4	127.8	132.0	140.5	136.8	137.7
2001.	134.3	123.8	114.6	127.2	128.2	142.0	132.4	138.9	148.2	143.8	144.2
2002.	140.6	126.8	122.8	136.5	132.4	145.5	135.6	146.0	157.2	149.2	149.2
Average annual percent change:											
1995-2000.	4.0	2.5	1.0	2.0	2.3	3.2	2.8	3.3	5.2	5.1	4.7
2000-2001.	2.4	3.4	0.8	5.5	3.8	3.4	3.6	5.2	5.5	5.1	4.8
2001-2002.	4.7	2.4	7.1	7.3	3.3	2.5	2.5	5.1	6.0	3.7	3.4
Real hourly compensation: [1] [2]											
1980.	91.4	91.6	75.3	86.5	80.5	(NA)	85.3	82.2	86.0	87.7	66.7
1990.	96.4	94.7	95.1	95.2	96.3	(NA)	98.0	95.6	97.7	97.6	91.0
1995.	100.7	101.7	106.3	102.3	104.6	107.8	97.4	104.2	102.7	97.8	101.7
2000.	109.0	105.0	110.9	104.1	110.1	118.3	99.1	110.2	118.0	120.1	112.0
2001.	108.6	106.0	111.6	107.1	112.4	119.9	99.9	111.0	120.8	123.3	115.3
2002.	112.0	106.2	120.6	113.1	113.9	121.2	99.9	112.6	126.5	125.2	117.3
Average annual percent change:											
1995-2000.	1.6	0.6	0.7	0.3	1.0	1.9	0.3	1.1	2.8	4.2	1.9
2000-2001.	-0.4	1.0	1.5	2.9	2.1	1.4	0.8	0.7	2.4	2.7	2.9
2001-2002.	3.1	0.2	8.1	5.6	1.3	1.1	-	1.4	4.7	1.5	1.7
Unit labor costs, national currency:											
1980.	78.8	65.2	92.6	80.3	67.0	(NA)	38.7	87.6	50.0	51.0	59.0
1990.	93.7	94.6	95.9	93.0	96.8	(NA)	90.7	91.1	94.2	92.9	92.9
1995.	94.8	94.3	97.5	96.4	96.5	104.7	103.2	95.6	108.4	85.8	102.8
2000.	92.3	92.5	83.6	92.2	86.2	108.1	112.5	99.5	131.9	77.9	113.0
2001.	94.1	97.4	84.4	95.9	86.6	111.2	114.2	105.0	136.1	84.4	114.2
2002.	90.2	97.1	88.0	96.4	87.1	111.1	118.7	109.7	141.8	80.9	116.9
Average annual percent change:											
1995-2000.	-0.5	-0.4	-3.0	-0.9	-2.2	0.6	1.7	0.8	4.0	-1.9	1.9
2000-2001.	2.0	5.3	0.9	4.0	0.4	2.8	1.5	5.5	3.2	8.4	1.1
2001-2002.	-4.1	-0.3	4.3	0.5	0.5	-	3.9	4.5	4.2	-4.1	2.4
Unit labor costs, U.S. dollar basis: [3]											
1980.	78.8	67.4	51.8	88.3	83.9	(NA)	55.7	77.5	62.9	70.2	77.7
1990.	93.7	98.0	83.9	89.5	94.1	(NA)	93.3	87.9	93.6	91.3	93.8
1995.	94.8	83.0	131.6	105.2	102.5	114.2	78.0	104.8	106.4	70.0	91.8
2000.	92.3	75.3	98.4	67.8	64.2	79.7	66.1	73.3	93.0	49.5	96.9
2001.	94.1	76.0	88.0	68.4	62.6	79.5	65.1	75.0	94.0	47.6	93.0
2002.	90.2	74.8	89.1	72.6	66.4	83.9	71.4	82.8	110.3	48.5	99.4
Average annual percent change:											
1995-2000.	-0.5	-2.0	-5.7	-8.4	-8.9	-6.9	-3.3	-6.9	-2.7	-6.7	1.1
2000-2001.	2.0	1.0	-10.5	0.9	-2.6	-0.3	-1.6	2.3	1.1	-3.9	-4.0
2001-2002.	-4.1	-1.7	1.3	6.1	6.2	5.6	9.7	10.4	17.4	2.0	6.9
Employment:											
1980.	111.6	115.1	88.9	119.3	124.7	(NA)	115.7	107.4	134.2	130.9	151.5
1990.	105.4	113.2	97.5	102.5	105.2	(NA)	103.7	100.0	105.2	117.2	115.5
1995.	102.5	104.8	90.1	91.9	92.8	86.2	95.8	92.1	107.0	98.0	99.3
2000.	101.8	120.4	81.7	88.9	91.3	82.7	96.1	93.1	107.5	98.0	94.0
2001.	97.0	119.5	79.6	89.6	92.4	83.0	95.9	92.6	106.0	97.0	89.8
2002.	90.4	119.8	75.8	86.4	90.8	81.2	96.7	90.6	104.8	94.3	85.2
Average annual percent change:											
1995-2000.	-0.1	2.8	-1.9	-0.7	-0.3	-0.8	0.1	0.2	0.1	-	-1.1
2000-2001.	-4.7	-0.8	-2.6	0.8	1.2	0.4	-0.3	-0.5	-1.4	-1.1	-4.5
2001-2002.	-6.8	0.3	-4.7	-3.6	-1.7	-2.2	0.9	-2.2	-1.1	-2.8	-5.0
Aggregate hours:											
1980.	107.5	114.6	95.6	119.7	132.5	(NA)	107.4	111.2	134.7	124.0	160.5
1990.	104.8	113.5	102.9	104.3	105.6	(NA)	102.9	100.3	103.4	116.4	118.1
1995.	104.0	106.4	89.1	92.0	91.7	84.8	94.9	92.3	106.6	105.9	101.2
2000.	102.8	123.1	80.3	91.7	86.8	78.8	100.1	92.5	105.9	105.9	94.3
2001.	96.3	120.9	77.7	90.8	86.5	78.2	98.9	91.9	104.1	107.3	89.8
2002.	89.7	121.1	74.2	85.8	84.2	76.1	99.5	89.9	101.6	102.7	85.7
Average annual percent change:											
1995-2000.	-0.2	3.0	-2.0	-0.1	-1.1	-1.5	0.1	-	-0.1	0.3	-1.4
2000-2001.	-6.4	-1.8	-3.3	-1.0	-0.4	-0.8	-1.2	-0.6	-1.7	0.2	-4.8
2001-2002.	-6.8	0.1	-4.5	-5.5	-2.6	-2.7	0.7	-2.2	-2.4	-4.5	-4.5

- Represents or rounds to zero.   NA Not available.   [1] Compensation includes, but real hourly compensation excludes, adjustments for payroll and employment taxes that are not compensation to employees, but are labor costs to employers.   [2] Index of hourly compensation divided by the index of consumer prices to adjust for changes in purchasing power.   [3] Indexes in national currency adjusted for changes in prevailing exchange rates.

Source: U.S. Bureau of Labor Statistics, *International Comparisons of Manufacturing Productivity and Unit Labor Cost Trends*, March 26, 2004.

Comparative International Statistics   869

No. 1371. Indexes of Hourly Compensation Costs for Production Workers in Manufacturing by Country: 1980 to 2002

[United States=100. Compensation costs include pay for time worked, other direct pay (including holiday and vacation pay, bonuses, other direct payments, and the cost of pay in kind), employer expenditures for legally required insurance programs and contractual and private benefit plans, and for some countries, other labor taxes. Data adjusted for exchange rates. Area averages are trade-weighted to account for difference in countries' relative importance to U.S. trade in manufactured goods. The trade weights used are the sum of U.S. imports of manufactured products for consumption (customs value) and U.S. exports of domestic manufactured products (f.a.s. value) in 1992; see source for detail]

Area or country	1980	1985	1990	1995	2001	2002	Area or country	1980	1985	1990	1995	2001	2002
United States	100	100	100	100	100	100	Austria [7]	90	58	119	147	94	99
Total [1]	66	51	80	89	66	66	Belgium	133	69	129	161	102	107
OECD [2]	72	55	86	95	71	71	Denmark	110	62	121	145	107	114
Europe	99	61	115	127	90	95	Finland [8]	84	63	142	141	96	101
Asian newly industrial-							France	91	58	104	113	77	82
izing economies [3]	12	13	25	38	33	33	Germany [7][9]	124	73	146	184	118	123
Brazil	(NA)	(NA)	(NA)	(NA)	14	12	Greece	38	28	45	53	(NA)	(NA)
Canada	88	84	107	94	77	75	Ireland	61	46	79	80	64	71
Mexico	22	12	11	10	11	11	Italy	83	59	117	94	67	70
Australia [4]	86	63	89	90	65	73	Luxembourg	117	58	108	136	84	89
Hong Kong [5]	15	13	22	29	29	27	Netherlands	122	67	121	140	96	102
Israel	38	31	57	61	66	57	Norway	117	80	144	142	112	128
Japan	56	49	85	138	95	88	Portugal	21	12	25	31	(NA)	(NA)
Korea, South	10	9	25	42	38	43	Spain	60	36	76	74	53	56
New Zealand	53	34	55	58	38	42	Sweden	127	74	140	125	89	95
Singapore	15	19	25	43	37	34	Switzerland	112	74	140	170	106	113
Sri Lanka	2	2	2	3	2	(NA)	United Kingdom	77	48	85	80	78	82
Taiwan [6]	10	11	26	34	28	25							

NA Not available. [1] From 1975 to 1998, the 28 foreign economies shown below less Brazil; thereafter all 29 foreign economies. [2] Organization for Economic Cooperation and Development; see text of this section. [3] Hong Kong, South Korea, Singapore, and Taiwan. [4] Includes non-production workers, except in managerial, executive, professional, and higher supervisory positions. [5] Average of selected manufacturing industries. [6] See footnote 2, Table 1321. [7] Excludes workers in establishments considered handicraft manufactures (including all printing and publishing and miscellaneous manufacturing in Austria). [8] Includes workers in mining and electrical power plants. [9] Former West Germany.

Source: U.S. Bureau of Labor Statistics, News Release USDL 03-507, September 26, 2003. Also see <ftp://ftp.bls.gov/pub/special.requests/ForeignLabor/supptab.txt>.

No. 1372. Key Global Telecom Indicators for the World Telecommunication Service Sector: 1995 to 2002

[[In billions U.S. dollars (779 represents $779,000,000,000), except where noted. All data were converted by annual average exchange rates. Country fiscal year data was aggregated to obtain calendar year estimates]

Indicators	1995	1996	1997	1998	1999	2000	2001	2002, prel.
Telecom market total revenue	779	885	946	1,015	1,123	1,210	1,232	1,295
Telecom telephone services revenue [1]	428	444	437	456	476	477	472	465
Other statistics:								
Main telephone lines (mil.)	689	738	792	846	905	983	1,053	1,129
Mobile cellular subscribers (mil.)	91	145	215	318	490	740	955	1,155
International telephone traffic minutes [2] (bil.)	63	71	79	89	100	118	127	135
Personal computers (mil.)	235	275	325	375	435	500	555	615
Internet users (mil.)	40	74	117	183	277	399	502	580

[1] Revenue from installation, subscription and local, trunk and international call charges for fixed telephone service. [2] From 1995 including traffic between countries of former Soviet Union.

Source: International Telecommunication Union, Geneva Switzerland, 2003; <http://www.itu.int/ITU-D/ict/statistics/atglance/Key Telecom99.html>.

No. 1373. Telephones and Computers by Country: 2002

[Rates per 100 persons. See text of this section for general comments about the data. For data qualifications for countries, see source]

Country	Telephone main lines	Cellular phone subscribers	Personal computers [1]	Country	Telephone main lines	Cellular phone subscribers	Personal computers [1]
Australia	53.86	63.98	56.51	Italy	48.07	93.87	23.07
Austria	48.88	78.62	36.93	Japan	55.83	63.65	38.22
Belgium	49.44	78.56	24.14	Korea, South	48.86	67.95	55.58
Brazil	22.32	20.06	7.48	Mexico	14.67	25.45	8.20
Canada	63.55	37.72	48.70	Netherlands	61.77	74.47	46.66
China [2]	16.69	16.09	2.76	Norway	73.44	84.36	52.83
Colombia	17.94	10.62	4.93	Pakistan	2.50	0.85	(NA)
Czech Republic	36.23	84.88	17.74	Poland	(NA)	36.26	10.56
Ecuador	11.02	12.06	3.11	Russia	24.22	12.01	8.87
Egypt	11.49	6.68	1.66	Saudi Arabia	15.11	22.80	13.67
Finland	52.35	86.74	44.17	Singapore	46.29	79.56	62.20
France	56.89	64.70	34.71	South Africa	10.66	30.39	7.26
Germany	65.09	72.75	43.13	Spain	50.62	82.42	19.60
Guatemala	7.05	13.15	1.44	Switzerland	74.42	78.93	70.87
Hungary	36.12	67.60	10.84	Taiwan [2]	58.17	106.15	39.46
India	3.98	1.22	0.72	Thailand	10.50	26.04	3.98
Indonesia	3.65	5.52	1.19	United Kingdom	59.06	84.07	40.57
Iraq	2.78	0.08	0.83	United States	64.58	48.81	65.89
Israel	45.30	95.45	24.26				

- Represents or rounds to zero. NA Not available. [1] In many countries mainframe computers are used extensively, and thousands of users can be connected to a single mainframe computer; thus the number of PCs understates the total use of computers. [2] See footnote 2, Table 1321.

Source: International Telecommunications Union, Geneva, Switzerland, World Telecommunication Indicators, (copyright).

No. 1374. Dow-Jones World Stock Index by Country and Industry: 1995 to 2003

[Index figures shown are as of December 31. Based on share prices denominated in U.S. dollars. Stocks in countries that impose significant restrictions on foreign ownership are included in the world index in the same proportion that shares are available to foreign investors]

Country and industry	1995	2001	2002	2003	Country and industry	1995	2001	2002	2003
World, total.........	132.4	175.7	140.5	187.0	Asia/Pacific	118.5	73.2	66.5	92.2
Americas............	145.3	259.5	199.8	259.8	Australia	132.9	154.1	149.4	218.1
United States	147.5	266.7	204.5	262.7	Hong Kong........	201.9	195.2	156.3	216.8
Canada..........	112.9	180.1	157.5	238.7	Indonesia........	174.7	25.4	33.1	55.0
Mexico..........	79.0	157.4	133.6	175.6	Japan............	111.1	62.3	56.5	77.7
Europe............	131.0	189.2	152.6	207.9	Malaysia.........	224.3	91.6	86.1	108.6
Austria	103.5	86.2	104.4	165.2	New Zealand	178.8	102.7	119.8	180.8
Belgium..........	144.0	170.5	154.3	217.3	Singapore	187.8	108.4	97.7	133.2
Denmark.........	113.0	187.3	160.1	239.1	Thailand	196.6	28.4	33.5	80.0
Finland	267.1	955.0	671.5	788.0					
France	117.9	193.4	153.8	213.9	Basic materials......	128.1	109.8	107.6	154.1
Germany.........	133.9	165.8	112.1	180.9	Consumer, cyclical	131.7	171.4	136.9	184.8
Ireland..........	155.6	301.0	236.7	341.4	Consumer, noncyclical ..	125.5	173.2	166.0	199.0
Italy.............	80.3	137.8	123.6	171.0	Energy	132.7	206.4	187.3	234.7
Netherlands	176.0	257.2	199.5	249.8	Financial	134.9	175.5	147.7	201.6
Norway	129.8	125.0	110.8	155.8	Healthcare........	133.3	281.7	224.6	270.3
Spain	111.2	167.3	142.6	221.9	Industrial.........	124.0	138.5	106.6	146.2
Sweden	157.0	236.1	163.3	261.4	Technology	188.1	377.3	229.6	347.8
Switzerland	225.7	293.9	259.1	344.9	Telecommunications ...	146.8	208.6	147.9	185.6
United Kingdom	122.5	166.7	137.9	177.3	Utilities	118.8	123.3	101.9	128.5

Source: Dow Jones & Company, Inc., New York, NY, *Dow Jones Indexes*, (copyright).

No. 1375. Foreign Stock Market Activity—Morgan Stanley Capital International Indexes: 2000 to 2003

[Index figures shown are as of December 31. January 1, 1970=100, except as noted. Based on share prices denominated in U.S. dollars. EM=Emerging Markets]

Index and country	Index			Percent change[1]		Index and country	Index			Percent change[1]	
	2000	2002	2003	2002	2003		2000	2002	2003	2002	2003
ALL COUNTRY (AC) INDEXES						Sweden	4,240	2,088	3,361	-31.5	61.0
AC World index[2]......	289.8	190.8	251.1	-20.5	31.6	Switzerland	2,695	1,874	2,480	-11.0	32.4
AC World index except USA[2]......	195.4	127.6	175.5	-16.6	37.5	United Kingdom	1,146	791.1	1,006.1	-17.8	27.2
AC Asia Pacific[2]	92.7	63.1	87.2	-9.8	38.2	Hong Kong	5,475	3,424	4,536	-20.6	32.5
AC Europe[2]	376.5	238.1	321.9	-19.9	35.2	Japan	2,552	1,593	2,144	-10.9	34.6
European Union[2]......	361.5	224.1	302.6	-21.2	35.0	Singapore	2,081	1,356	1,820	-13.1	34.2
						EMERGING MARKETS					
DEVELOPED MARKETS						EM Far East index[4] ..	123.8	130.0	187.9	-7.1	44.5
World index[3]........	1,221	792.2	1,036	-21.1	30.8	India[6]	114.5	95.6	166.4	5.9	74.0
EAFE index[3].......	1,492	952.7	1,289	-17.5	35.3	Indonesia	78.2	95.8	162.8	38.0	70.0
Europe index........	1,378	867.4	1,169	-20.1	34.8	Korea, South.......	78.7	123.4	163.6	7.5	32.6
Pacific index........	1,832	1,241	1,651	-10.4	36.3	Malaysia..........	160.9	160.0	196.9	-2.6	23.1
Far East index.......	2,583	1,615	2,171	-11.9	34.4	Pakistan[6]	44.3	64.4	84.5	122.1	31.2
United States	1,250	824.6	1,045	-24.0	26.8	Philippines[6]	142.2	81.9	113.8	-30.5	38.9
Canada	832.5	560.1	853.2	-14.4	52.3	Sri Lanka[6]	36.3	64.1	91.0	29.8	42.0
Australia...........	317.7	303.9	441.1	-3.8	45.1	Taiwan[7]	191.7	155.6	217.9	-25.4	40.0
New Zealand[4].......	56.4	71.5	107.3	20.0	50.1	Thailand	56.9	75.4	176.6	24.4	134.2
Austria	708.3	749.8	1,158	14.4	54.5	EM Latin America	1,002	658.9	1,101	-24.8	67.1
Belgium............	1,222	880.5	1,151	-17.2	30.7	Argentina	1,233	470.3	933.6	-51.0	98.5
Denmark...........	2,201	1,535	2,252	-17.0	46.7	Brazil	869.9	395.4	802.0	-33.8	102.8
Finland[4]...........	921.8	386.3	450.9	-31.2	16.7	Chile	604.7	445.5	800.6	-21.7	79.7
France	1,509	902.1	1,243	-22.2	37.8	Colombia[6]	42.1	68.3	108.6	18.4	59.0
Germany...........	1,436	724.9	1,161	-34.0	60.1	Mexico...........	1,197	1,443	1,873	-15.0	29.8
Greece[4]...........	475.8	234.6	382.8	-28.2	63.2	Peru[6]	125.0	182.7	344.1	26.8	88.4
Ireland[4]...........	308.4	212.7	296.5	-28.0	39.4	Venezuela[6]	106.1	77.7	103.8	-18.6	33.6
Italy..............	447.2	290.2	391.2	-10.0	34.8	Czech Republic[8]	79.9	107.9	166.4	40.9	54.2
Luxembourg[5]	491.9	(NA)	(NA)	(NA)	(NA)	Hungary[8]	233.6	269.5	352.9	28.9	31.0
Netherlands.........	2,177	1,290	1,607	-22.5	24.5	Jordan	55.1	72.9	113.4	2.5	55.5
Norway............	1,181	926.2	1,332	-9.0	43.8	Poland[8]	499.0	354.0	471.1	-0.5	33.1
Portugal[4]	127.8	83.2	115.8	-15.4	39.2	Russia[8]	155.2	270.7	461.1	13.8	70.3
Spain.............	347.1	251.6	388.1	-16.9	54.3	South Africa[6]	157.6	154.9	216.6	23.3	39.8
						Turkey	247.7	104.2	231.8	-36.5	122.5

NA Not available. [1] Percent change during calendar year (e.g. December 31, 2002 through December 31, 2003). Adjusted for foreign exchange fluctuations relative to U.S. dollar. [2] January 1, 1988=100. [3] Europe, Australasia, Far East Index. Comprises all European and Far East countries listed under developed markets plus Australia and New Zealand. [4] January 1, 1988=100. [5] MSCI Luxembourg Index discontinued as of March 29, 2002. [6] January 1, 1993=100. [7] See footnote 2, Table 1321. [8] January 1, 1995=100.

No. 1376. Foreign Stock Market Indices: 1980 to 2003

[As of year end. The DAX index is a total return index which includes dividends, whereas the other foreign indices are price indices which exclude dividends]

Year	London FTSE 100	Tokyo Nikkei 225	Hong Kong Hang Seng	Germany DAX-30	Paris CAC-40	Dow Jones Europe STOXX 50
1980	647	7,116	1,477	481	(X)	(X)
1985	1,413	13,113	1,752	1,366	(X)	(X)
1990	2,144	23,849	3,025	1,398	1,518	835
1991	2,493	22,984	4,297	1,578	1,766	1,000
1992	2,847	16,925	5,512	1,545	1,858	1,058
1993	3,418	17,417	11,888	2,267	2,268	1,429
1994	3,066	19,723	8,191	2,107	1,881	1,299
1995	3,689	19,868	10,073	2,254	1,872	1,538
1996	4,119	19,361	13,452	2,889	2,316	1,850
1997	5,136	15,259	10,723	4,250	2,999	2,634
1998	5,883	13,842	9,507	5,002	3,943	3,320
1999	6,930	18,934	16,962	6,958	5,958	4,742
2000	6,223	13,786	15,096	6,434	5,926	4,557
2001	5,217	10,543	11,397	5,160	4,625	3,707
2002	3,940	8,579	9,321	2,893	3,064	2,408
2003	4,477	10,677	12,576	3,965	3,558	2,660

X Not applicable.

Source: Global Financial Data, Los Angeles, C, <http://www.globalfindata.com>, unpublished data (copyright).

No. 1377. United States and Foreign Stock Markets—Market Capitalization and Value of Shares Traded: 1990 to 2003

[In billions of U.S. dollars (3,059.4 represents $3,059,400,000,000). Market capitalization is the market value of all domestic listed companies at the end of the year. The market value of a company is the share price times the number of shares outstanding. Value of shares traded is the annual total turnover of listed company shares]

Country	Market capitalization				Value of shares traded			
	1990	1995	2002	2003	1990	1995	2002	2003
United States	3,059.4	6,857.6	11,052.4	14,266.3	1,751.3	5,108.6	25,371.3	15,547.4
Argentina	3.3	37.8	103.4	38.9	0.9	4.6	1.4	4.9
Australia	107.6	245.2	381.0	585.5	40.1	98.7	294.7	369.8
Austria	11.5	32.5	31.7	54.5	18.6	25.8	5.8	10.8
Belgium	65.4	105.0	127.6	173.6	6.4	15.2	33.8	37.5
Brazil	16.4	147.6	123.8	234.6	5.6	79.2	48.2	60.4
Canada	241.9	366.3	575.3	894.0	71.3	183.7	406.1	467.8
Chile	13.6	73.9	47.6	86.3	0.8	11.1	3.1	6.5
China [1]	(NA)	42.1	463.1	681.2	(NA)	49.8	333.4	476.8
Denmark	39.1	56.2	76.8	128.0	11.1	25.9	51.6	67
Egypt	1.8	8.1	26.1	27.1	0.1	0.7	2.6	3.3
Finland	22.7	44.1	138.8	170.3	3.9	19.0	176.5	163.5
France	314.4	522.1	967.0	1,355.6	116.9	364.6	934.8	995.4
Germany	355.1	577.4	686.0	1,079.0	501.8	573.5	1,233.10	1,147.2
Greece	15.2	17.1	68.7	106.8	3.9	6.1	24.9	38.6
Hong Kong	83.4	303.7	463.1	714.6	34.6	106.9	210.7	331.6
India	38.6	127.2	131.0	279.1	21.9	13.7	197.1	284.8
Indonesia	8.1	66.6	30.0	54.7	4.0	14.4	13	14.8
Iran	(NA)	6.6	14.3	34.4	(NA)	0.7	1.9	5.3
Ireland	(NA)	25.8	59.9	85.1	(NA)	13.2	32.9	44
Israel	3.3	36.4	45.4	75.7	5.5	9.2	55.3	41.6
Italy	148.8	209.5	477.1	614.8	42.6	86.9	539.9	663.2
Japan	2,917.7	3,667.3	2,126.1	3,040.7	1,602.4	1,231.6	1,573.3	2,273.00
Korea, South	110.6	182.0	249.6	329.6	75.9	185.2	826.6	682.7
Luxembourg	10.5	30.4	24.6	37.3	0.1	0.2	0.3	0.3
Malaysia	48.6	222.7	123.9	168.4	10.9	76.8	27.6	50.1
Mexico	32.7	90.7	103.1	122.5	12.2	34.4	27.7	23.5
Morocco	1.0	6.0	8.6	13.2	0.1	2.4	0.6	0.7
Netherlands	119.8	356.5	401.5	488.6	40.2	248.6	462.3	463.5
New Zealand	8.8	32.0	21.7	33.1	1.9	8.4	7.5	10.5
Norway	26.1	44.6	67.3	94.7	14.0	24.4	48.9	70
Philippines	5.9	58.9	39.0	23.6	1.2	14.7	3.1	2.6
Poland	(NA)	4.6	28.8	37.2	(NA)	2.8	5.8	8.5
Portugal	9.2	18.4	42.8	58.3	1.7	4.2	20.3	21.4
Russia	(NA)	15.9	124.2	230.8	(NA)	0.5	36.1	81
Saudi Arabia	(NA)	40.9	74.9	157.3	(NA)	6.2	35.7	159.1
Singapore	34.3	148.0	101.9	145.1	20.3	60.5	56.1	87.9
Sweden	97.9	178.0	177.1	287.5	17.6	93.2	218.5	263.8
Switzerland	160.0	433.6	553.8	725.7	(NA)	310.9	656.7	575.6
Taiwan [1]	100.7	187.2	261.5	379.0	715.0	383.1	631.9	592
Thailand	23.9	141.5	46.1	118.7	22.9	57.0	47.6	96.6
Turkey	19.1	20.8	34.0	68.4	5.8	51.4	70.7	99.6
United Kingdom	848.9	1,407.7	1,864.1	2,412.4	278.7	510.1	2,721.3	2,150.8

NA Not available.   [1] See footnote 2, Table 1321.

Source: Standard and Poor's, New York, NY, Standard & Poor's Emerging Stock Markets Factbook 2004 (copyright).

U.S. Census Bureau, Statistical Abstract of the United States: 2004-2005

No. 1378. Foreign Exchange Rates: 2002

[**Foreign currency units per U.S. dollar.** Rates shown include market, official, principal, and secondary rates, as published by the International Monetary Fund in *International Financial Statistics*]

Country	Currency	2002	Country	Currency	2002
Afghanistan [1]	Afghanis	3,000.00	Laos	Kip	10,056.3
Albania	Leks	140.15	Latvia	Lats	0.62
Algeria	Algerian Dinar	79.68	Lebanon	Lebanese Pounds	1,507.50
Antigua and Barbuda	E.Caribbean Dollar	2.70	Lesotho	Maloti	10.54
Argentina	Argentine Pesos	3.06	Liberia	Liberian Dollar	61.75
Armenia	Dram	573.35	Libya [1]	Libyan Dinars	1.21
Aruba	Aruban Florins	1.79	Lithuania	Litai	3.68
Australia	Australian Dollar	1.68	Luxembourg [2]	Euro	(NA)
Austria [2]	Euro	(NA)	Macedonia, The Former		
Bahamas, The	Bahamian Dollar	1.00	Yugoslav Republic of	Denar	64.35
Bahrain	Bahrain Dinars	0.38	Madagascar	Malagasy Francs	6,832.00
Bangladesh	Taka	57.89	Malaysia	Ringgit	3.80
Barbados	Barbados Dollar	2.00	Mali	Cfa Francs	696.99
Belarus [2]	Belarusian Rubel	1,790.92	Malta	Maltese Liri	0.43
Belgium [2]	Euro	(NA)	Mauritania	Ouguiyas	255.63
Belize	Belize Dollar	2.00	Mauritius	Mauritian Rupees	29.96
Benin	Cfa Francs	696.99	Mexico	Mexican Pesos	9.66
Bolivia	Bolivianos	7.17	Moldova	Lei	13.57
Botswana	Pula	6.33	Mongolia	Togrogs	1,110.31
Brazil	Reais	2.92	Morocco	Dirhams	11.02
Bulgaria	Leva	2.08	Mozambique	Meticais	23,678.0
Burkina Faso	Cfa Francs	696.99	Namibia	Namibia Dollar	10.54
Burma [1]	Kyat	6.64	Nepal	Nepalese Rupees	77.88
Cambodia	Riels	3,912.10	Netherlands [2]	Euro	(NA)
Cameroon	Cfa Francs	696.99	Netherlands Antilles	Euro	(NA)
Canada	Canadian Dollar	1.57	New Zealand	New Zealand Dollar	2.15
Central African Republic	Cfa Francs	696.99	Nicaragua	Cordobas	14.25
Chad	Cfa Francs	696.99	Niger	Cfa Francs	696.99
Chile	Chilean Pesos	688.94	Nigeria	Naira	120.58
China [3]	Yuan	8.28	Norway	Norwegian Kroner	7.98
Colombia	Colombian Pesos	2,504.24	Oman	Rials Omani	0.38
Comoros	Comorian Francs	522.74	Pakistan	Pakistan Rupees	59.72
Congo (Brazzaville) [4]	Cfa Francs	696.99	Panama	Balboas	1.00
Costa Rica	Colones	359.82	Papua New Guinea	Kina	3.89
Cote d'Ivoire	Cfa Francs	696.99	Paraguay	Guaranies	5,716.30
Croatia	Kuna	7.87	Peru	Nuevos Soles	3.52
Cyprus	Cyprus Pounds	0.61	Philippines	Philippine Pesos	51.60
Czech Republic	Koruny	32.74	Poland	Zlotys	4.08
Denmark	Kroner	7.90	Portugal [2]	Euro	(NA)
Djibouti	Djibouti Francs	177.72	Qatar	Qatar Riyals	3.64
Dominica	E.Caribbean Dollar	2.70	Romania	Lei	33,055.4
Dominican Republic	Dominican Pesos	18.61	Russia	Russian Rubles	31.35
Ecuador	U.S. Dollar	25,000.0	Rwanda	Rwanda Francs	475.37
Egypt	Egyptian Pounds	4.50	Saint Kitts and Nevis	E.Caribbean Dollar	2.70
El Salvador	Colones	8.75	Saint Lucia	E.Caribbean Dollar	2.70
Equatorial Guinea	Cfa Francs	696.99	Saint Vincent and the		
Estonia	Krooni	16.61	Grenadines	E.Caribbean Dollar	2.70
Ethiopia [1]	Birr	8.57	Saudi Arabia	Saudi A. Riyals	3.75
Euro area (EMU-11) [2]	Euro	1.06	Senegal	Cfa Francs	696.99
Fiji	Fiji Dollar	2.19	Sierra Leone	Leones	2,099.03
Finland [2]	Euro	(NA)	Singapore	Singapore Dollar	1.79
France [2]	Euro	(NA)	Slovakia	Koruny	45.33
Gabon	Cfa Francs	696.99	Slovenia	Tolars	240.25
Georgia	Lari	2.20	South Africa	Rand	10.54
Germany [2]	Euro	(NA)	Spain [2]	Euro	(NA)
Greece	Euro	(NA)	Sri Lanka	Sri Lanka Rupees	95.66
Guatemala	Quetzales	7.82	Sudan [1]	Sudanese Dinars	263.31
Guyana	Guyana Dollar	190.70	Suriname [1]	Suriname Guilders	2,346.75
Haiti	Gourdes	29.25	Swaziland	Emalangeni	10.48
Honduras	Lempiras	16.43	Sweden	Swedish Kronor	9.74
Hong Kong	Hong Kong Dollar	7.80	Switzerland	Swiss Francs	1.56
Hungary	Forint	257.89	Syria	Syrian Pounds	11.23
Iceland	Kronur	91.66	Tanzania	Tanzania Shilling	966.58
India	Indian Rupees	48.61	Thailand	Baht	42.96
Indonesia	Rupiah	9,311.20	Togo	Cfa Francs	696.99
Iran	Rials	6,906.96	Trinidad and Tobago	Tt Dollars	6.25
Iraq [2]	Dinars	0.31	Tunisia	Tunisian Dinars	1.42
Ireland [2]	Euro	(NA)	Turkey	Liras	1,507,226
Israel	New Sheqalim	4.74	Uganda	Uganda Shilling	1,797.60
Italy [2]	Euro	(NA)	Ukraine	Hryvnias	5.33
Jamaica	Jamaica Dollars	48.42	United Arab Emirates	Dirhams	3.67
Japan	Yen	125.39	United Kingdom	Pounds Sterling	0.67
Jordan	Jordinian Dinars	0.71	Uruguay	Uruguayan Pesos	21.26
Kazakhstan	Tenge	153.28	Vanuatu	Vatu	139.20
Kenya	Kenya Shillings	78.75	Venezuela	Bolivares	1,160.95
Korea, South	Won	1,251.09	Yemen	Rials	175.63
Kuwait	Kuwaiti Dinars	0.30	Zambia	Zambian Kwacha	4,398.60
Kyrgyzstan	Soms	46.94	Zimbabwe	Zimbabwe Dollar	55.05

NA Not available. [1] End-of year values were used if annual averages were unavailable. Some values were estimated using partial year data. [2] The euro is the official currency of the 11 Euro Area (EMU) nations. [3] See footnote 2, Table 1321. [4] See footnote 3, Table 1321.

Source: U.S. Dept. of Commerce, International Trade Administration, "Foreign Exchange Rates, 1994-02"; accessed September 2003. Also see <http://www.ita.doc.gov/td/industry/otea/usfth/aggregate/H02T34.html>.

[In millions of U.S. dollars (57,630 represents $57,630,000,000). Assets include holdings of convertible foreign currencies, special drawing rights, and reserve position in International Monetary Fund and exclude gold holdings. Minus sign (-) indicates debits]

Country	Total reserve assets		2003		Current account balance			Merchandise trade balance		
	2001	2002	Total	Currency holdings[1]	2001	2002	2003	2001	2002	2003
United States	57,630	67,960	74,890	39,720	-393,740	-480,860	-541,830	-424,110	-479,380	-546,160
Algeria	18,081	23,238	33,125	32,942	(NA)	(NA)	(NA)	(NA)	(NA)	(NA)
Argentina........	14,553	10,489	14,153	13,145	-3,982	9,559	(NA)	7,385	17,236	(NA)
Australia	17,955	20,689	32,189	29,966	-8,712	-17,386	-30,675	1,786	-5,431	-15,369
Austria	12,509	9,683	8,470	7,144	-3,636	575	-2,392	-1,269	3,572	1,932
Bangladesh	1,275	1,683	2,578	2,574	-535	739	(NA)	-2,049	-1,678	(NA)
Belgium [2].......	11,266	11,855	10,989	7,651	9,392	(NA)	(NA)	3,707	(NA)	(NA)
Brazil	35,739	37,683	49,111	49,108	-23,215	-7,696	(NA)	2,650	13,143	(NA)
Burma..........	401	470	550	550	-309	(NA)	(NA)	-271	(NA)	(NA)
Cameroon	332	630	640	637	(NA)	(NA)	(NA)	(NA)	(NA)	(NA)
Canada.........	33,962	36,984	36,222	31,537	17,422	14,909	18,630	45,864	36,838	42,989
Chile..........	14,379	15,341	15,840	15,211	-1,100	-885	-594	1,844	2,256	3,015
China [3].........	215,605	291,128	408,151	403,251	17,401	35,422	(NA)	34,017	44,167	(NA)
Colombia........	10,154	10,732	10,784	10,188	-1,212	-1,488	-1,417	563	234	265
Congo (Brazzaville) [4].	69	32	35	33	-28	-35	(NA)	1,374	1,598	(NA)
Cote d'Ivoire......	1,019	1,863	2,231	2,229	-60	767	(NA)	1,528	2,735	(NA)
Denmark	17,110	26,986	37,105	36,004	4,920	4,991	(NA)	7,451	8,308	(NA)
Ecuador	840	715	813	786	-800	-1,222	(NA)	-462	-1,004	(NA)
Egypt	12,926	13,242	13,589	13,400	-388	622	(NA)	-6,935	-5,762	(NA)
Finland	7,983	9,285	10,515	9,545	8,704	10,148	9,295	12,659	12,882	13,390
France	31,749	28,365	30,186	23,122	23,120	25,740	(NA)	2,840	8,990	(NA)
Germany	51,404	51,171	50,694	41,095	1,710	43,440	53,510	89,250	128,210	149,370
Ghana..........	298	540	1,353	1,306	-325	-33	(NA)	-1,101	-692	(NA)
Greece	5,154	[5]8,083	4,361	3,843	-9,400	-10,405	(NA)	-19,087	-21,452	(NA)
Hungary	10,727	10,348	12,737	12,015	-1,754	-2,644	(NA)	-2,237	-2,119	(NA)
India	45,870	67,665	98,938	97,617	1,761	4,656	(NA)	-12,833	-12,416	(NA)
Indonesia........	27,246	30,969	34,962	34,742	6,899	7,823	(NA)	22,695	23,513	(NA)
Ireland	5,587	5,415	4,079	3,425	-690	-925	-2,990	27,263	34,898	36,313
Israel	23,379	24,083	26,315	25,778	-1,776	-1,226	-174	-3,004	-3,560	-2,560
Italy	24,419	28,603	30,366	26,056	-652	-6,741	-21,942	15,540	16,533	9,700
Japan	395,155	461,186	663,289	652,790	87,800	112,450	136,220	70,210	93,830	106,400
Kenya	1,065	1,068	1,482	1,461	-340	-137	(NA)	-1,347	-997	(NA)
Korea, South	102,753	121,345	155,284	154,509	8,239	6,092	(NA)	9,192	7,249	(NA)
Kuwait..........	9,897	9,208	7,577	6,641	8,324	4,192	(NA)	(NA)	(NA)	(NA)
Malaysia	30,474	34,222	44,515	43,466	7,287	7,190	(NA)	18,383	18,135	(NA)
Mexico	44,741	50,594	58,956	57,740	-18,182	-14,070	-9,166	-9,954	-7,916	-5,603
Morocco	8,474	10,133	13,851	13,634	1,606	1,472	(NA)	-3,022	-3,061	(NA)
Nepal	1,038	1,018	1,223	1,213	-339	(NA)	(NA)	-765	(NA)	(NA)
Netherlands	9,034	9,563	11,012	7,180	7,830	10,116	16,467	20,840	19,944	26,570
Nigeria	10,457	7,331	7,128	7,128	(NA)	(NA)	(NA)	(NA)	(NA)	(NA)
Norway	15,488	20,682	22,997	21,667	26,171	24,769	28,643	26,472	24,339	28,109
Pakistan	3,640	8,078	10,941	10,693	1,878	3,854	3,597	-610	-596	-100
Peru	8,672	9,339	9,777	9,776	-1,184	-1,206	-1,116	-267	207	710
Philippines.......	13,429	13,135	13,457	13,326	1,323	4,197	(NA)	-743	408	(NA)
Poland	25,648	28,650	32,579	31,725	-5,357	-5,007	(NA)	-7,660	-7,249	(NA)
Portugal	9,667	11,179	5,876	5,249	-10,403	-8,118	-7,549	-13,301	11,882	12,444
Romania	5,442	7,211	8,999	8,998	-2,229	-1,525	(NA)	-2,969	-2,611	(NA)
Saudi Arabia	17,596	20,610	22,620	17,662	9,366	11,889	(NA)	39,418	42,897	(NA)
Singapore	75,375	82,021	95,746	94,975	16,137	18,704	(NA)	14,768	18,549	(NA)
South Africa	6,045	5,904	6,496	6,164	56	610	-1,456	5,180	4,631	3,701
Spain	29,582	34,536	19,788	17,513	-16,404	-16,044	-23,676	-32,539	32,841	42,923
Sri Lanka........	1,287	1,631	(NA)	(NA)	-265	-290	(NA)	-1,158	-1,407	(NA)
Sudan..........	118	441	848	847	-618	-1,008	-727	304	-345	-297
Sweden.........	13,977	17,127	19,681	18,015	6,696	10,624	(NA)	13,832	15,469	(NA)
Switzerland	32,006	40,155	47,652	45,560	23,898	26,011	(NA)	1,564	6,432	(NA)
Syria...........	(NA)	(NA)	(NA)	(NA)	1,221	1,440	(NA)	1,424	2,210	(NA)
Thailand	32,355	38,046	41,077	40,965	6,192	7,014	7,965	8,543	9,081	11,606
Trinidad and Tobago .	1,907	2,028	2,451	2,258	416	(NA)	(NA)	718	(NA)	(NA)
Turkey..........	18,879	27,069	33,991	33,793	3,390	-1,521	(NA)	-4,543	-8,337	(NA)
United Kingdom	37,280	39,360	41,850	35,150	-33,740	-26,710	(NA)	-58,440	-70,150	(NA)
Venezuela	9,239	8,487	16,035	15,546	2,062	7,423	(NA)	7,592	13,034	(NA)

NA Not available. [1] Holdings of convertible foreign currencies. [2] Balance of payments current account and trade balance data prior to 2002 is for Belgium-Luxembourg. Thereafter, data is for Belgium only. [3] See footnote 2, Table 1321. [4] See footnote 3, Table 1321. [5] Break in series. Data not comparable to earlier years.

Source: International Monetary Fund, Washington, DC, *International Financial Statistics*, monthly, (copyright).

No. 1380. Foreign Trade—Destination of Exports and Source of Imports for Selected Countries: 2002

[In billions of dollars (1,161.2 represents $1,161,200,000,000)]

Country	United States		Canada		Australia		Japan		France		Germany		Italy		United Kingdom	
	Imports	Exports	Imports	Exports	Imports	Exports	Imports	Exports	Imports	Exports	Imports	Exports	Imports	Exports	Imports	Exports
World [1]	1,161.2	693.1	222.2	252.4	69.5	65.0	337.6	416.7	303.8	304.9	490.1	615.6	242.7	251.0	351.7	288.6
Canada	209.0	160.9	—	—	0.9	1.0	7.8	7.3	1.7	2.5	1.7	5.2	1.2	2.3	5.5	4.7
Mexico	134.6	97.5	3.5	1.5	0.3	0.2	1.8	3.8	0.5	1.4	1.2	4.9	0.2	1.8	0.8	1.1
United States	—	—	139.2	220.1	12.6	6.3	57.9	118.9	24.3	24.7	36.3	63.4	11.7	24.4	39.1	42.6
Australia	6.5	13.1	1.1	0.7	—	—	14.0	8.3	0.8	1.6	1.1	3.7	1.2	2.1	2.7	3.2
Japan	121.4	51.4	9.8	5.4	8.6	12.1	—	—	9.9	5.2	18.7	11.6	5.0	4.2	12.7	5.4
Korea	35.6	22.6	3.1	1.3	2.6	5.4	15.5	28.6	1.6	2.3	4.4	5.1	1.5	2.0	4.3	2.2
Czech Republic	2.6	0.7	0.1	0.1	(Z)	(Z)	0.2	0.3	2.1	2.0	15.2	14.6	1.8	2.6	1.3	1.1
Hungary	2.6	1.4	0.1	(Z)	(Z)	(Z)	0.4	0.8	1.6	1.8	11.4	10.5	1.2	1.1	1.9	1.1
Norway	5.8	0.7	0.1	0.6	(Z)	(Z)	0.1	0.7	5.7	1.2	6.6	4.3	2.3	4.0	8.4	2.7
Poland	1.1	2.4	0.1	0.1	(Z)	(Z)	0.1	0.4	2.3	3.6	13.3	15.0	2.3	8.8	1.9	2.0
Switzerland	9.4	7.8	0.2	0.2	0.7	0.2	3.3	1.6	6.6	9.9	17.6	24.2	9.2	8.8	3.0	5.0
Russia	6.9	2.9	0.2	0.3	(Z)	(Z)	3.3	0.9	4.9	2.2	8.6	10.6	4.7	3.6	0.6	1.5
Algeria	2.4	1.0	—	0.3	(Z)	(Z)	0.1	0.2	2.6	3.5	0.9	1.3	1.1	1.2	0.6	0.2
Egypt	1.4	2.9	0.2	0.1	(Z)	0.4	0.7	0.5	0.3	1.0	0.3	0.8	0.5	1.1	0.1	0.7
Nigeria	5.9	1.1	1.1	0.1	(Z)	(Z)	2.9	0.3	1.1	0.9	0.5	0.7	1.9	0.5	4.2	1.3
South Africa	4.0	2.5	(Z)	0.2	0.5	0.7	2.7	1.6	0.9	1.3	3.0	4.1	0.3	0.9	2.1	2.4
Columbia	5.6	3.6	0.1	0.5	(Z)	(Z)	0.4	0.3	0.2	0.2	0.5	0.4	1.0	0.3	0.3	0.1
Brazil	15.8	12.4	0.3	0.2	0.3	0.2	0.8	1.8	2.2	2.6	3.6	4.6	0.7	1.9	1.4	1.3
Argentina	3.2	1.6	0.2	0.1	0.1	(Z)	0.8	0.7	0.5	0.3	0.9	0.5	1.8	0.3	1.1	0.2
Israel	12.4	7.0	0.2	0.2	0.3	0.2	0.8	0.8	0.8	1.5	1.4	2.1	1.8	1.4	0.7	2.1
Saudi Arabia	13.1	4.8	0.5	0.1	0.7	0.2	11.6	3.8	2.1	1.4	0.8	3.2	0.3	1.7	0.7	2.1
Iran	0.2	(Z)	(Z)	0.4	0.1	0.1	4.7	0.7	0.8	0.9	0.5	2.0	1.5	1.7	0.1	0.6
Pakistan	2.3	0.7	0.2	0.3	(Z)	0.3	0.2	0.7	0.4	0.7	0.3	0.5	0.8	0.3	2.8	0.4
India	11.8	4.1	0.8	0.3	0.5	1.3	2.1	1.9	1.4	0.8	2.4	2.0	0.5	0.6	2.4	2.7
Thailand	14.8	4.9	1.1	1.4	1.7	1.4	10.5	13.2	1.4	0.5	2.2	2.0	0.9	0.6	2.7	0.8
Malaysia	24.0	10.3	1.3	1.2	2.1	1.2	11.2	11.0	1.9	0.7	3.2	2.4	0.9	0.9	2.7	1.3
Indonesia	9.6	2.6	0.6	1.7	2.3	1.7	14.2	6.2	1.2	0.8	2.1	1.4	0.9	0.5	1.6	0.5
China [2]	125.2	22.1	10.2	2.6	7.0	4.6	61.8	39.8	10.7	3.3	20.0	13.7	7.8	3.8	10.5	2.3
European Union:																
Denmark	3.2	1.5	0.7	0.3	0.4	0.1	2.2	0.6	2.4	2.4	8.2	10.4	1.7	1.9	4.0	4.0
Sweden	9.2	3.2	1.2	0.8	0.9	0.1	2.0	1.4	4.1	4.4	8.3	12.5	3.3	2.4	6.3	5.6
United Kingdom	40.7	33.2	6.2	2.8	3.2	3.0	5.4	12.0	22.2	31.3	30.8	50.0	12.1	17.2	—	—
Austria	3.8	2.4	0.6	0.2	0.4	(Z)	0.9	0.9	3.1	2.9	19.6	31.2	10.5	5.5	3.4	1.9
Belgium-Luxembourg	9.8	13.3	0.9	1.2	1.8	0.8	1.5	4.6	20.0	22.0	23.0	28.7	10.5	7.6	17.3	14.9
France	28.5	19.0	3.7	1.3	1.8	0.9	6.5	6.1	—	—	45.3	63.8	27.3	30.2	27.6	27.3
Germany	62.5	26.6	5.3	1.9	4.0	0.2	12.4	14.1	52.2	44.2	—	—	42.8	34.1	45.3	32.1
Finland	3.4	1.5	0.4	0.2	0.4	0.1	1.0	1.1	2.5	2.4	5.8	6.2	1.5	1.3	4.1	2.1
Ireland	22.4	6.7	2.8	0.9	0.8	0.2	3.2	1.5	6.1	2.4	12.7	3.6	3.4	1.3	13.9	23.3
Italy	24.2	10.1	1.1	1.1	2.1	0.1	5.4	4.5	27.4	27.6	31.4	43.9	—	—	15.8	12.4
Netherlands	9.8	18.3	0.9	1.1	0.5	0.8	1.8	10.6	14.4	12.2	35.2	36.3	13.5	6.4	22.5	20.4
Spain	5.7	5.3	0.7	0.6	0.5	0.4	1.1	2.7	21.8	29.6	14.6	27.4	11.1	15.8	12.1	12.4

- Represents zero.   Z Less than 50,000,000.   [1] Includes other countries not shown separately.   [2] See footnote 2, Table 1321.

Source: Organization for Economic Cooperation and Development, Paris, France, OECD International Trade by Commodities Statistics, 2002.

Comparative International Statistics **875**

No. 1381. International Tourism Arrivals, Expenditures, and Receipts—Leading Countries: 1990 to 2002

[Expenditures and receipts in millions of dollars; arrivals in thousands of visitors (455,946 represents 455,946,000). Receipts are dollars spent by foreign tourists inside the country shown. Expenditures are dollars visitors (same-day visitors and tourists) from a given origin spend on tourism outside their country of residence. Excludes international transport receipts]

Country	Arrivals 1990	1995	1999	2000	2001	2002	Expenditures 2001	2002	Receipts 1990	1995	1999	2000	2001	2002
World, total [1]	455,946	550,354	643,329	687,281	684,108	702,636	459,451	474,189	264,142	404,625	454,953	473,383	459,451	474,189
France	52,497	60,033	73,147	77,190	75,202	77,012	17,718	19,460	20,184	27,527	31,507	30,754	29,979	32,329
Spain	34,085	34,920	46,776	47,898	50,094	51,748	5,974	6,638	18,593	25,388	32,497	31,454	32,873	33,609
United States	39,362	43,318	48,491	50,945	44,898	41,892	60,200	58,044	43,007	63,395	74,801	82,400	71,893	66,547
Italy	26,679	31,052	36,516	41,181	39,563	39,799	14,802	16,935	16,458	28,729	28,359	27,500	25,796	26,915
China [2]	(NA)	20,034	27,047	31,229	33,167	36,803	13,909	15,398	2,218	8,733	14,099	16,224	17,792	20,385
United Kingdom	18,013	23,537	25,394	25,209	22,835	24,180	36,483	40,409	13,762	18,554	20,223	19,544	16,283	17,591
Canada	15,209	16,932	19,411	19,627	19,810	20,057	10,250	9,929	6,339	7,882	10,190	10,839	10,774	9,700
Mexico	17,176	20,241	19,043	20,641	19,679	19,667	5,702	6,060	5,467	6,179	7,223	8,295	10,401	8,858
Austria	19,011	17,173	17,467	17,982	18,180	18,611	8,886	9,391	13,417	12,927	11,035	9,931	10,118	11,237
Germany	17,045	14,847	17,116	18,983	17,861	17,969	51,933	53,196	14,288	17,243	17,210	18,479	18,422	19,158
Hong Kong	6,581	10,200	11,328	13,059	13,725	16,566	12,316	12,417	5,032	9,604	7,210	7,886	8,282	10,117
Hungary	20,510	20,690	14,401	15,571	15,340	15,870	1,456	1,722	824	2,929	3,563	3,445	3,770	3,273
Greece	8,873	10,130	12,164	13,096	14,057	14,180	4,181	2,450	2,587	4,136	8,783	9,221	9,447	9,741
Poland	(NA)	19,215	17,950	17,400	15,000	13,980	3,500	3,200	358	4,614	6,100	6,100	4,815	4,500
Malaysia	7,446	7,469	7,931	10,222	12,775	13,292	2,614	2,618	1,667	3,909	3,242	4,562	6,374	6,785
Turkey	4,799	7,083	6,893	9,586	10,784	12,782	1,738	1,881	3,225	4,957	5,203	7,636	7,386	9,010
Portugal	8,020	9,511	11,632	12,097	12,167	11,666	2,153	2,274	4,326	4,339	5,261	5,282	5,505	5,919
Thailand	5,299	6,952	8,651	9,579	10,133	10,873	2,923	3,303	4,155	8,043	7,040	7,489	7,077	7,902
Switzerland	13,200	11,500	10,700	11,000	10,800	10,000	6,088	6,427	(NA)	9,365	7,769	7,576	7,310	7,628
Netherlands	5,795	6,574	9,874	10,003	9,500	9,595	12,016	12,919	(NA)	6,252	6,996	7,217	6,723	7,706
Russia	(NA)	(NA)	(NA)	7,030	7,400	7,943	9,960	12,005	(NA)	4,312	3,723	3,429	3,560	4,188
Saudi Arabia	2,209	3,325	(NA)	6,585	6,727	7,511	(NA)	7,356	(NA)	(NA)	(NA)	(NA)	3,420	(NA)
Sweden	(NA)	2,310	2,595	2,746	7,154	7,459	6,926	7,241	2,906	3,434	4,151	4,079	4,275	4,496
Singapore	4,842	6,422	6,258	6,917	6,726	6,996	4,647	5,213	4,937	3,390	5,859	6,018	5,081	4,932
Croatia	7,049	1,485	3,805	5,831	6,544	6,944	606	781	1,704	1,349	2,493	2,758	3,335	3,811
Belgium	(NA)	5,560	5,369	6,457	6,452	6,724	9,782	10,435	3,721	4,548	6,472	6,592	6,903	6,892
Macao	2,513	4,202	5,050	5,197	5,842	6,565	(NA)	(NA)	992	3,233	2,598	3,205	3,745	4,415
South Africa	1,029	4,684	6,026	6,001	5,908	6,550	2,869	1,798	1,459	2,126	2,637	2,513	2,501	2,719
Ireland	3,666	4,818	6,403	6,646	6,353	6,476	2,179	3,743	(NA)	2,211	2,637	2,608	2,790	3,089
Ukraine	(NA)	3,716	(NA)	(NA)	(NA)	6,326	(NA)	2,087	(NA)	632	2,124	2,207	2,725	2,992
United Arab Emirates	973	2,315	3,393	3,907	4,134	5,445	(NA)	(NA)	315	(NA)	893	1,012	1,064	1,328
Republic of Korea	2,959	3,753	3,660	5,322	5,147	5,347	6,547	7,642	3,559	5,587	6,802	6,811	6,373	5,277
Japan	3,236	3,345	4,438	4,757	4,772	5,239	26,530	26,681	3,578	3,226	3,428	3,373	3,301	3,499
Tunisia	3,204	4,120	4,832	5,058	5,387	5,064	273	(NA)	948	1,393	1,560	1,496	1,605	1,422
Indonesia	2,178	4,324	4,728	5,064	5,154	5,033	3,406	(NA)	2,105	5,229	4,710	5,749	5,411	(NA)

NA Not available. [1] Includes other countries not shown separately. [2] See footnote 2, Table 1321.

Source: World Tourism Organization, Madrid, Spain, Yearbook of Tourism Statistics, 2003 (copyright).

No. 1382. Net Flow of Financial Resources to Developing Countries and Multilateral Organizations: 1995 to 2002

[165,182 represents $165,182,000,000. Net flow covers loans, grants, and grant-like flows minus amortization on loans. Military flows are excluded. GNP=gross national product]

Country	Amount (mil. dol.)					Percent of GNP	
	1995	1999	2000	2001	2002	2001	2002
Total net flows....................	165,182	193,740	133,788	107,926	85,893	0.45	0.35
United States........................	46,984	50,138	25,252	38,618	24,410	0.38	0.23
Australia.............................	2,536	1,279	1,491	1,290	834	0.37	0.22
Austria...............................	906	1,963	1,067	882	1,866	0.47	0.92
Belgium..............................	-234	5,528	2,281	304	1,337	0.13	0.54
Canada..............................	5,724	6,992	6,483	1,538	2,046	0.22	0.28
Denmark.............................	1,799	1,992	2,176	2,645	1,577	1.67	0.93
Finland..............................	604	858	1,087	1,334	-200	1.11	-0.15
France...............................	12,477	9,160	5,557	16,327	4,729	1.24	0.33
Germany.............................	21,197	20,006	12,331	6,345	8,733	0.34	0.44
Greece..............................	-	195	229	202	322	0.17	0.24
Ireland..............................	247	251	741	735	1,469	0.85	1.49
Italy.................................	2,800	11,337	10.846	-189	1,399	-0.02	0.12
Japan................................	42,295	20,794	11,264	13,714	4,659	0.32	0.11
Luxembourg	72	124	129	144	148	0.78	0.78
Netherlands..........................	6,795	7,985	6,947	-3,432	-1,487	-0.89	-0.36
New Zealand.........................	166	163	142	139	164	0.32	0.30
Norway..............................	1,670	2,060	1,437	1,485	2,279	0.88	1.19
Portugal.............................	395	2,457	4,622	1,775	171	1.66	0.14
Spain................................	2,025	29,029	23,471	11,523	8,171	2.01	1.25
Sweden..............................	2,224	2,892	3,952	3,077	2,211	1.42	0.93
Switzerland	1,118	3,241	2,054	-158	2,234	-0.06	0.75
United Kingdom	13,382	15,299	10,230	9,627	18,820	0.67	1.18

- Represents zero.

Source: Organization for Economic Cooperation and Development, Paris, France, *Annual Reports of the Development Assistance Committee* (copyright).

No. 1383. External Debt by Country: 1990 to 2002

[In millions of dollars (28,149 represents $28,149,000,000). Total external debt is debt owed to nonresidents repayable in foreign currency, goods or services. Total external debt is the sum of public, publicly guaranteed, and private nonguaranteed long-term debt, use of IMF credit, and short-term debt. Short-term debt includes all debt having an original maturity of one year or less and interest in arrears on long-term debt]

Country	1990	1995	2001	2002	Country	1990	1995	2001	2002
Algeria	28,149	33,042	22,581	22,800	Mexico	104,442	165,379	145,674	141,264
Angola	8,594	11,502	9,297	10,134	Morocco........	25,017	23,821	19,308	18,601
Argentina	62,233	98,802	136,729	132,314	Nigeria.........	33,439	34,093	31,042	30,476
Bangladesh......	12,439	15,924	15,236	17,037	Pakistan........	20,663	30,229	31,692	33,672
Brazil...........	119,964	160,505	226,358	227,932	Panama	6,506	6,107	8,246	8,298
Bulgaria	(NA)	10,379	9,638	10,462	Peru	20,064	30,859	27,645	28,167
Cameroon.......	6,657	9,425	8,367	8,503	Philippines	30,580	39,382	57,822	59,343
Chile	19,226	22,038	38,398	41,945	Poland.........	49,364	44,263	63,275	69,521
China [1]	55,301	118,090	170,059	168,255	Romania........	1,140	6,805	11,529	14,683
Colombia .....[2] .	17,222	25,048	36,699	33,853	Russia	(NA)	121,451	152,491	147,541
Congo (Kinshasa)[2] .	4,947	6,004	4,491	5,152	Serbia and Monte-				
Cote d'Ivoire	17,251	18,899	11,618	11,816	negro	(NA)	11,137	12,516	12,688
Croatia..........	(NA)	3,830	11,360	15,347	Slovakia	(NA)	5,744	11,154	13,013
Czech Republic	(NA)	16,218	22,339	26,419	South Africa	(NA)	25,358	24,050	25,041
Ecuador	12,107	13,994	14,481	16,452	Sri Lanka	5,863	8,395	8,658	9,611
Egypt...........	33,017	33,499	29,331	30,750	Sudan	14,762	17,603	15,414	16,389
Ghana	3,837	5,888	6,735	7,338	Syria	17,259	21,415	21,341	21,504
Hungary	21,202	31,651	30,305	34,958	Tanzania........	6,459	7,425	6,679	7,244
India	83,628	94,464	97,516	104,429	Thailand........	28,095	100,039	67,211	59,212
Indonesia	69,872	124,398	134,044	132,208	Tunisia	7,690	10,820	10,877	12,625
Iran	9,021	21,879	7,483	9,154	Turkey	49,424	73,781	113,437	131,556
Jordan	8,333	7,661	7,516	8,094	Ukraine	(NA)	8,429	12,816	13,555
Kazakhstan......	(NA)	3,750	14,372	17,538	Uruguay........	4,415	5,318	9,706	10,736
Korea, South.....	(NA)	(NA)	(NA)	(NA)	Venezuela.......	33,171	35,538	34,960	32,563
Lebanon........	1,779	2,966	12,416	17,077	Vietnam	23,270	25,428	12,580	13,349
Malaysia........	15,328	34,343	44,612	48,557					

NA Not available. [1] See footnote 2, Table 1321. [2] See footnote 3, Table 1321.

Source: The World Bank, Washington, DC, *2004 World Development Indicators CD-ROM* (copyright).

U.S. Census Bureau, Statistical Abstract of the United States: 2004-2005

No. 1384. Military Budget, by Country: 2002

[Figures are for latest year available, usually 2002, except where noted. Expenditures are used in a few cases where official budgets are significantly lower than actual spending]

Country	Amount (bil. dol.)	Country	Amount (bil. dol.)
Argentina [1]	3.3	Luxembourg	0.2
Australia	7.6	Netherlands	6.6
Belgium	2.7	North Korea	1.4
Brazil [1]	10.5	Norway	3.8
Canada	7.6	Pakistan	2.6
China [1]	47.0	Philippines	1.4
Colombia	1.7	Poland	3.5
Cuba	0.8	Portugal	1.3
Czech Republic	1.6	Russia	65.0
Denmark	2.4	Saudi Arabia	21.3
Egypt	3.0	Singapore	4.8
France	29.5	South Korea	14.1
Germany	24.9	Spain	8.4
Greece	3.5	Sudan	0.6
Hungary	1.1	Sweden	4.5
India	15.6	Syria	1.0
Iran	4.1	Taiwan	7.0
Iraq	1.4	Turkey	5.8
Israel	9.4	United Arab Emirates [1]	3.1
Italy	19.4	United Kingdom	38.4
Japan	42.6	United States	399.1
Kuwait	3.9	Vietnam	2.4
Libya	1.2	Yugoslavia	0.7

[1] 2001 Funding.

Source: Data from U.S. Dept. of Defense and International Institute for Strategic Studies, Center for Defense Information, Washington, DC, "Last of the Big Time Spenders: U.S. Military Budget Still the World's Largest, and Growing" (published 3 February, 2003). Also see <http://www.cdi.org/issues/wme/spendersFY04.html>.

No. 1385. Military Manpower Fit for Military Service, by Country: 2003

[Covers male ages 15-49]

Country	Number	Country	Number
Afghanistan	3,837,646	Ireland	821,378
Albania	742,837	Israel [3]	1,279,277
Algeria	5,646,418	Italy	12,349,356
Argentina	7,942,837	Jamaica	528,689
Australia	4,339,011	Japan	25,405,779
Austria	1,725,123	Kazakhstan	3,658,815
Bahrain	121,739	Korea, North	3,654,223
Bangladesh	22,807,339	Korea, South	8,994,941
Belarus	2,158,875	Kuwait	508,399
Belgium	2,059,131	Laos	759,499
Bolivia	1,380,883	Lebanon	630,657
Bosnia and Herzegovina	897,856	Libya	914,649
Brazil	34,347,078	Malaysia	3,672,517
Bulgaria	1,551,485	Mexico	20,123,970
Burma [1]	6,566,122	Morocco	5,411,846
Cambodia	1,829,535	Mozambique	2,373,444
Canada	7,158,016	Netherlands	3,536,586
Chile	3,070,140	New Zealand	859,505
China	206,000,000	Nicaragua	825,906
Colombia	7,403,433	Nigeria	18,259,696
Congo (Kinshasa)	6,267,752	Norway	910,628
Congo (Brazzaville)	381,556	Oman	438,326
Cote d'Ivoire	2,110,276	Pakistan	23,328,575
Croatia	856,946	Peru	5,045,619
Cuba [2]	1,923,967	Philippines	15,428,043
Czech Republic	2,002,202	Poland	8,077,706
Denmark	1,094,611	Russia	24,000,000
Dominican Republic	1,453,705	Saudi Arabia	3,431,281
Ecuador	2,395,178	Sierra Leone	596,617
Egypt	12,867,160	Singapore	1,012,498
El Salvador	973,884	South Africa	7,211,075
Ethiopia	8,040,381	Spain	8,391,612
Finland	1,016,693	Sudan	5,558,462
France	12,079,413	Sweden	1,800,376
Germany	17,399,936	Switzerland	1,552,728
Greece	2,026,409	Syria	2,629,148
Guatemala	2,167,270	Thailand	10,724,565
Honduras	948,957	Turkey	11,801,267
Hungary	2,026,912	Ukraine	9,597,172
Iceland	62,552	United Arab Emirates	416,963
India	169,000,000	United Kingdom	12,353,942
Indonesia	38,290,550	United States	(NA)
Iran	12,094,551	Venezuela	4,870,751
Iraq	3,541,467	Vietnam	14,366,732

NA Not available. [1] 6,553,458 females ages 15-49 fit for service. [2] 1,875,412 females ages 15-49 fit for service. [3] 1,237,926 females ages 15-49 fit for service.

Source: Central Intelligence Agency, The World Factbook, 2003. See also <http://www.cia.gov/cia/publications/factbook/index.html> (accessed June 2004).

Guide to—Sources of Statistics, State Statistical Abstracts, and Foreign Statistical Abstracts

Alphabetically arranged, this guide contains references to important primary sources of statistical information for the United States. Secondary sources have been included if the information contained in them is presented in a particularly convenient form or if primary sources are not readily available. Nonrecurrent publications presenting compilations or estimates for years later than 1990 or types of data not available in regular series are also included. Much data are also available in press releases.

Much valuable information may also be found in state reports, foreign statistical abstracts, which are included at the end of this appendix and in reports for particular commodities, industries, or similar segments of our economic and social structures, many of which are not included here.

Publications listed under each subject are divided into two main groups: "U.S. Government" and "Nongovernment." The location of the publisher of each report is given except for federal agencies located in Washington, DC. Most federal publications may be purchased from the Superintendent of Documents, U.S. Government Printing Office, Washington, DC 20402, tel. 202-512-1800, (Web site <http://www.access. gpo.gov> or from Government Printing Office bookstores in certain major cities. In some cases, federal publications may be obtained from the issuing agency.

U.S. GOVERNMENT

Administrative Office of the United States Courts
http://www.uscourts.gov
Calendar Year Reports on Authorized Wiretaps. (State and Federal.)
Federal Court Management Statistics. Annual.
Federal Judicial Caseload Statistics. Annual.
Judicial Business of the United States Courts.
Statistical Tables for the Federal Judiciary. Semiannual.

Agency for International Development
http://www.usaid.gov
U.S. Overseas Loans and Grants and Assistance From International Organizations. Annual.

Army, Corps of Engineers
http://www.usace.army.mil
Waterborne Commerce of the United States (in five parts). Annual.

Board of Governors of the Federal Reserve System
http://www.federalreserve.gov
Assets and Liabilities of Commercial Banks in the United States. H.8. Weekly.
Federal Reserve Banks. Monthly review published by each Bank with special reference to its own Federal Reserve District.

Board of Governors of the Federal Reserve System —Con.
Federal Reserve Bulletin. Quarterly.
Flow of Funds Accounts of the United States: Flows and Outstandings. Z.1. Quarterly.
Industrial Production and Capacity Utilization G.17. Monthly.
Money Stock and Debt Measures. H.6. Weekly.
Statistical Digest. (Formerly Annual Statistical Digest). Quinquennial.

Bureau of Economic Analysis
http://www.bea.gov
National Income and Product Accounts of the United States, 1929-1997: Statistical Tables, early 2001.
Survey of Current Business. Monthly. (January, April, July, and October issues contain data on U.S. international transactions. Articles on foreign direct investment in the United States, U.S. direct investment abroad, and other topics appear periodically in other issues.)
U.S. Direct Investment Abroad: 1999 Benchmark Survey, 2004.

Bureau of Justice Statistics
http://www.ojp.usdoj.gov/bjs
Age Patterns in Violent Victimizations, 1976-2000. February 2002.

Bureau of Justice Statistics —Con.

Alcohol and Crime: An Analysis of National Data on the Prevalence of Alcohol Involvement in Crime. April 1998.

Background Checks for Firearm Transfers, 2002. September 2003. Annual.

Campus Law Enforcement Agencies, 1995. December 1996.

Capital Punishment, 2002. Annual.

Carjackings in the United States, 1992-96. March 1999.

Census of State and Local Law Enforcement Agencies, 2000. October 2002.

Characteristics of Adults on Probation, 1995, December 1997.

Characteristics of Drivers Stopped by Police, 1999. March 2002.

Child Victimizers: Violent Offenders and Their Victims. March 1996.

Civil Rights Complaints in U.S. District Courts, 2000. July 2002.

Civil Trial Cases and Verdicts in Large Counties, 2001. April 2004.

Community Policing in Local Police Department Departments, 1997 and 1999. February 2001.

Compendium of Federal Justice Statistics, 2001. Annual.

Crime and the Nation's Households, 2002. Annual.

Crimes Against Persons Age 65 or Older, 1992-97. January 2000.

Criminal Victimization, 2002. Annual.

Defense Counsel in Criminal Cases. November 2000.

Education and Correctional Populations. January 2003.

Federal Criminal Case Processing, 2001: With Trends 1982-01. January 2003.

Federal Law Enforcement Officers, 2002. July 2003.

Federal Tort Trials and Verdicts, 1996-97. March 1999.

Felony Defendants in Large Urban Counties, 2000. November 2003. Biennial.

Firearm Injury and Death From Crime, 1993-97. October 2000.

Firearm Use by Offenders. November 2001.

Hispanic Victims of Violent Crime, 1993-2000. April 2002.

HIV in Prisons, 2001. January 2004.

Homicide Trends in the United States: 2000 update. January 2003.

Immigration Offenders in the Federal Criminal Justice System, 2000. August 2002.

Incarcerated Parents and Their Children. August 2000.

Indicators of School Crime and Safety, 2003. October 2003. Annual.

Indigent Defense Services in Large Counties, 1999. November 2000.

Injuries From Violent Crime, 1992-98. June 2001.

Bureau of Justice Statistics —Con.

Intimate Partner Violence, 1993-2001. February 2003.

Jails in Indian Country, 2002. November 2003.

Justice Expenditure and Employment in the United States, 2001. April 2004.

Juvenile Felony Defendants in Criminal Courts: Survey of 40 Counties, 1998. May 2003.

Local Police Departments, 2000. January 2003.

Medical Problems of Inmates, 1997. January 2001.

Money Laundering Offenders, 1994-2001. July 2003.

National Corrections Reporting Program. June 2003. Annual. Electronic.

Police Departments in Large Cities, 1990-2000. May 2002.

Prevalence of Imprisonment in the U.S. Population, 1974-2001. August 2003.

Prior Abuse Reported by Inmates and Probationers. April 1999.

Prison and Jail Inmates at Midyear, 2002. April 2003. Annual.

Prisoners in 2002, July 2003. Annual.

Probation and Parole in the United States, 2002. August 2003.

Profile of State Prisoners Under Age 18, 1985-97. February 2000.

Prosecutors in State Courts, 2001. May 2002.

Rape and Sexual Assault: Reporting to Police and Medical Attention, 1992-2000. August 2002.

Recidivism of Sex Offenders Released From Prison in 1994. November 2003.

Reentry Trends in the United States. Current Data. Electronic.

Sex Offenses and Offenders: An Analysis of Data on Rape and Sexual Assault. February 1997.

Sheriffs' Office, 2002. January 2003.

Sourcebook of Criminal Justice Statistics, 2002. CD-ROM. Annual.

State Court Sentencing of Convicted Felons. February 2000. Through 1986, Biennial. Thereafter, electronic.

Substance Abuse and Treatment of State and Federal Prisoners, 1997. January 1999.

Summary of State Sex Offender Registries, 2001. March 2002.

Survey of DNA Crime Laboratories, 2001. January 2002.

Survey of State Criminal History Information Systems, 2001. Biennial.

Survey of State Procedures Related to Firearm Sales, May 2004. Annual.

Traffic Stop Data Collection Policies for State Police, 2001. December 2001.

Truth in Sentencing in State Prisons. January 1999.

Bureau of Justice Statistics —Con.

Urban, Suburban, and Rural Victimization, 1993-98. October 2000.

Veterans in Prison or Jail. January 2000.

Violence in the Workplace, 1993-99. December 2001.

Bureau of Labor Statistics
http://www.bls.gov

College Enrollment and Work Activity of High School Graduates. Annual.

Comparative Labor Force Statistics, Ten Countries. Annual.

Compensation and Working Conditions. Quarterly. 1996-2001, prints. Thereafter, electronic only.

Consumer Expenditure Survey, Integrated Diary and Interview Survey data.

Consumer Prices: Energy and Food. Monthly.

CPI Detailed Report. Monthly.

Employee Benefits in Medium and Large Firms. Biennial.

Employee Benefits in Small Private Establishments. Biennial.

Employee Benefits in State and Local Governments. Biennial.

Employer Costs for Employee Compensation. Annual.

Employment and Earnings. Monthly.

Employment and Wages. Annual.

Employment Characteristics of Families. Annual.

Employment Cost Index. Quarterly.

Employment Cost Indexes and Levels. Annual.

The Employment Situation. Monthly.

Geographic Profile of Employment and Unemployment. Annual.

International Comparisons of Hourly Compensation Costs for Production Workers in Manufacturing. Annual.

International Comparisons of Manufacturing Productivity and Unit Labor Cost Trends. Annual.

Metropolitan Area Employment and Unemployment. Monthly.

Monthly Labor Review.

Occupational Injuries and Illnesses in the United States by Industry. Annual.

Occupational Projections and Training Data. Biennial.

Producer Price Indexes. Detailed report. Monthly, with annual supplement.

Productivity Measures for Selected Industries and Government Services. Annual.

Real Earnings. Monthly.

Regional and State Employment and Unemployment. Monthly.

Relative Importance of Components in the Consumer Price Indexes. Annual.

Union Members. Annual.

U.S. Import and Export Price Indexes. Monthly.

Bureau of Labor Statistics —Con.

Usual Weekly Earnings of Wage and Salary Workers. Quarterly.

Work Experience of the Population. Annual.

Bureau of Land Management
http://www.blm.gov

Public Land Statistics. Annual.

Census Bureau
http://www.census.gov

Major reports which consist of many volumes, are listed by their general, all-inclusive titles. In most cases, separate reports of the most recent censuses are available for each state, subject, industry, etc.

1997 Economic Census.

Comparative Statistics.

Bridge Between NAICS and SIC.

Business Expenses.

Nonemployer Statistics.

Minority- and Women-Owned Business Enterprises.

Annual Benchmark Report for Retail Trade and Food Services.

Annual Benchmark Report for Wholesale Trade and Food Service.

Annual Survey of Manufactures.

Census of Governments. Quinquennial.

Compendium of Public Employment. Series GC, Vol. 3.

Employee-Retirement Systems of State and Local Governments. Series GC, Vol. 4.

Employment of Major Local Governments. Series GC, Vol. 3.

Finances of County Governments. Series GC, Vol. 4.

Government Organization. Series GC, Vol. 1.

Public Education Finances. Series GC, Vol. 4.

Census of Housing. Decennial. (2000, most recent.)

Census of Population. Decennial. (2000, most recent.)

CFFR Consolidated Federal Funds Report. Annual.

Volume I County Areas

Volume II Subcounty Areas

County Business Patterns. Annual.

Current Construction Reports: New Residential Construction and New Residential Sales: Press Releases and Web sites. Value of Construction Put in Place, C30 (monthly with occasional historical supplement); Residential Improvements and Repairs, C50 (quarterly and annual).

Current Housing Reports: Housing Vacancies, H111 (quarterly and annual); Who Can Afford to Buy a House, H121 (biennial) Market Absorption of Apartments, H130 (quarterly and annual); Characteristics of Apartments Completed, H131 (annual); American Housing Survey for

Census Bureau —Con.

the United States, H150 (biennial); American Housing Survey for Selected Metropolitan Areas, H170; Survey for Selected Metropolitan Areas, H171.

Current Population Reports. (Series P20.)

Consumer Income and Poverty, P60 and Household Economic Studies, P70.

Economic Census. Quinquennial.

Economic Census of Outlying Areas. Quinquennial.

FAS Federal Aid to States for Fiscal Year. Annual.

Global Population Profile: 2002 (Series WP)

International Briefs. (Series IB.)

International Population Reports. (Series IPC.)

Manufacturing Profiles. (Series MP-1.) Annual. 1994-1998.

Manufacturers' Shipments, Inventories, and Orders. Monthly.

Manufacturers' Shipments, Inventories, and Orders: 1992-2002.

Population Profile of the United States. (Biennial Series P23.)

Quarterly Financial Report for Manufacturing, Mining, and Trade Corporations.

Service Annual Survey Report.

Survey of Plant Capacity Utilization. (Current Industrial Reports MQ-C1.)

U.S. International Trade in Goods and Services: includes cumulative data. (FT 900.)

U.S. Trade with Puerto Rico and U.S. Possessions. Monthly and Annual. (FT 895.)

Vehicle Inventory and Use Survey. Quinquennial.

Centers for Disease Control and Prevention, Atlanta, GA
http://www.cdc.gov

Injury Fact Book, 2001-2002.

Morbidity and Mortality Weekly Report. Annual.

Centers for Medicare and Medicaid Services (CMS)
http://www.cms.hhs.gov

Centers for Medicare and Medicaid Services (CMS)

Health Care Financing Review. Medicare and Medicaid Statistical Supplement. Annual.

Health Care Financing Research Reports. Occasional.

Health Care Financing Review. Quarterly.

Coast Guard (See Department of Homeland Security)

Comptroller of the Currency
http://www.occ.treas.gov

Quarterly Journal.

Congressional Clerk of the House
http://clerkweb.house.gov

Statistics of the Presidential and Congressional Election Years. Biennial.

Council of Economic Advisers
http://www.whitehouse.gov

Economic Indicators. Monthly.

Economic Report of the President. Annual.

Council on Environmental Quality
http://www.whitehouse.gov/ceq

Environmental Quality. Annual.

Department of Agriculture
http://www.usda.gov

Agricultural Chemical Usage. Field crops, vegetables (fruits and vegetables alternate years), restricted use pesticides. Chemical application rates and acres treated, selected states and U.S. Annual.

Agricultural Income and Finance. Situation and Outlook Report. Quarterly.

Agricultural Price Reports. Reports on prices received for farm commodities, prices paid for farm supplies, indexes and parity ratios. Monthly and annual.

Amber Waves, periodic.

Catfish Production. Annual.

Census of Agriculture. Quinquennial. (2002, most recent.)

Cotton Ginnings and Winter Wheat Seedings.

Crop Production Reports. Acreage, yield, and production of various commodities. Monthly and annual.

Crop Values Report. Price and value of various commodities. Annual.

Dairy Product Prices. U.S. cheddar cheese, butter, nonfat dry milk, and dry whey prices and sales volumes. Regional cheddar cheese prices and sales volumes. Weekly.

Farm Labor. Quarterly.

Farm Numbers, Value. Farm numbers and land in farms, agricultural cash rents, agricultural land values, foreign ownership of U.S. Agricultural Land (ERS). Annual.

Food Consumption, Prices, and Expenditures, 1970-97. (Statistical Bulletin No. 928.)

Food Marketing Review, (Agricultural Economic Report No. 743). Revised annually.

Food Spending in American Households. (Statistical Bulletin No. 824.) Annual.

Fruit and Vegetable Reports. Acreage, yield, production, value, and utilization of various fruits and vegetables. Periodic.

Geographic Area Series (Internet, CD-ROM, Print), Volume 1.

Income, Wealth, and the Economic Well-Being of Farm Households. (ERS).

Journal of Agricultural Economics Research. Quarterly.

Livestock Reports. Cattle, Cattle on Feed, Hogs and Pigs. Sheep, Goats, Wool, and Mohair. Monthly, Quarterly, and Annual.

Milk and Dairy Products Reports. Milk cows, milk production, and dairy products. Monthly and Annual.

882   Appendix I

Department of Agriculture —Con.

Other Reports. Reports on varied items including cold storage, catfish, cherries, cranberries, trout, farm employment and wages, farm production expenditures, mink, mushrooms, and floriculture crops. Monthly and annual.

Poultry and Egg Reports. Reports covering eggs, chickens, turkeys, hatcheries, egg products, and poultry slaughter. Weekly, monthly, annual.

Rural Conditions and Trends. Quarterly.

Rural Development Perspectives. Three issues per year.

Situation and Outlook Reports. Issued for agricultural exports, cotton and wool, dairy, feed, fruit and tree nuts, agricultural resources, livestock and poultry, oil crops, rice, aquaculture, sugar and sweeteners, tobacco, vegetables, wheat, and world agriculture. Periodic.

Stock Reports. Stocks of grain, hops, peanuts, potatoes, rice, and soybeans. Quarterly, annual, periodic.

Trout Production. Annual.

Usual planting and harvesting dates. Dates for major field crops. Periodic.

Weekly Weather and Crop Bulletin. Report summarizing weather and its effect on crops the previous week. Weekly.

Winter Wheat Seedings.

Department of Agriculture, Food and Nutrition Service

http://www.fns.usda.gov

Annual Historical Review:

Food and Consumer Service Programs.

Department of Agriculture, Natural Resources and Conservation Service.

http://www.nrcs.usda.gov

National Resources Inventory. Periodic.

Department of Defense

http://www.defenselink.mil

Foreign Military Sales and Military Assistance Facts. Annual.

Department of Education

http://www.ed.gov

Rehabilitation Services Administration. Annual Report.

Caseload Statistics of State Vocational Rehabilitation Agencies in Fiscal Year. Annual.

Department of Health and Human Services

http://www.os.hhs.gov

Annual Report.

Department of Homeland Security (DHS)

http://www.dhs.gov

Coast Guard

http://www.uscg.mil

Office of Immigration Statistics

http://uscis.gov/graphics/shared/aboutus/statistics/index.htm

Yearbook of Immigration Statistics. Annual.

Department of Housing and Urban Development

http://www.hud.gov

Survey of Mortgage Lending Activity. Monthly and quarterly press releases.

Department of Labor

http://www.dol.gov

Annual Report of the Secretary.

Department of State

http://www.state.gov

United States Contribution to International Organizations. Issued in the House Documents series. Annual.

Department of Transportation

http://www.dot.gov

Airport Activity Statistics of Certified Route Air Carriers. Annual.

Annual Report of the Secretary of Transportation.

Condition and Performance Report. 1999. Biennial.

National Transportation Statistics, 1998.

Report of Passenger Travel Between the United States and Foreign Countries. Annual, semiannual, quarterly. Monthly.

Transportation Safety Information Report. Quarterly.

U.S. International Air Travel Statistics. Annual.

Wage Statistics of Class I Railroads in the United States. Annual. (Statement No. 300.)

Department of the Treasury

http://www.treasury.gov

Department of the Treasury, Alcohol and Tobacco Tax and Trade Bureau (formerly Bureau of Alcohol, Tobacco, and Firearms).

http://www.atf.treas.gov

Alcohol and Tobacco Summary Statistics. Annual.

Tobacco Products Monthly Statistical Releases.

Department of the Treasury, Bureau of Public Debt

http://www.publicdebt.treas.gov

Monthly Statement of the Public Debt of the United States.

Department of the Treasury, Financial Management Services

http://www.fms.treas.gov

Active Foreign Credits of the United States Government. Quarterly.

Combined Statement of Receipts, Outlays, and Balances.

Monthly Treasury Statement of Receipts and Outlays of the United States Government.

Treasury Bulletin. Quarterly.

Financial Report of the United States Government.

Department of Veterans Affairs
http://www.va.gov

Disability Compensation, Pension, and Death Pension Data. Annual.

Government Life Insurance Programs for Veterans and Members of the Service. Annual.

Selected Compensation and Pension Data by State of Residence. Annual.

Veterans Affairs Annual Accountability Report.

Drug Enforcement Administration
http://www.whitehousedrugpolicy.gov

Drug Abuse and Law Enforcement Statistics. Irregular.

Employment and Training Administration
http://www.doleta.gov

Unemployment Insurance Claims. Weekly.

Energy Information Administration
http://www.eia.doe.gov

Annual Energy Outlook. 2004.

Annual Energy Review. 2002.

Coal Industry. 2000. Annual.

Cost and Quality of Fuels for Electric Utility Plants, 2001. Annual.

Electric Power Annual, 2002. Annual.

Electric Power Monthly.

Electric Sales and Revenue, 2002. (Discontinued after 2002 Report.

Electric Trade in the United States, 1996.

Electric Utility Demand-Side Management, 2000.

Emissions of Greenhouse Gases in the U.S. 2002. Annual

Financial Statistics of Major U.S. Investor-Owned Electric Utilities. (Discontinued after 1996 Report)

Financial Statistics of Major U.S. Publicly-Owned Electric Utilities. 2000. (Discontinued after 2000 Report)

Financial Statistics of Selected Electric Utilities. Annual

Foreign Direct Investment in U.S. Energy. 2001. (Web only).

International Energy Annual, 2002. Annual.

International Energy Outlook, 2004.

Inventory of Electric Utility Power Plants in the United States. 2000. Annual. (Discontinued after 2000 Report)

Inventory of Nonutility Power Plants in the United States. 2000. (Discontinued after 2000 Report)

Monthly Energy Review, 2004.

Natural Gas. 2002. Annual.

Natural Gas. 2000. Issues & Trends. (Web Only)

Natural Gas, 2004. Monthly.

Performance Profiles of Major Energy Producers. Annual.

Petroleum Marketing, 2003. Annual.

Petroleum Marketing, 2004. Monthly.

Energy Information Administration —Con.

Petroleum Supply, 2002. Volume 1. Annual.

Petroleum Supply. 2002 Volume 2. Annual. (Web Only).

Petroleum Supply Monthly, 2004.

Quarterly Coal Report, 2004.

Renewable Energy, 2002. Annual.

Residential Energy Consumption Survey: Housing Characteristics. Triennial.

Residential Transportation Energy Consumption Survey. Triennial.

Short-Term Energy Outlook, 2004. Quarterly. (Web Only)

State Electricity Profiles, 2002.

State Energy Data Consumption, 2000.

State Energy Data, Price and Expenditure, 2000.

Uranium Industry. 2002. Annual.

U.S. Crude Oil, Natural Gas, and Natural Gas Liquids Reserves. 2002. Annual.

Weekly Coal Production, 2004. (Web Only)

Environmental Protection Agency
http://www.epa.gov

Air Quality Data. Annual.

Cost of Clean Water. Annual.

Drinking Water Infrastructure Needs Survey. Second Report to Congress (EPA 816-R-01-004, February 2001).

Federal Certification Test Results for Motor Vehicles. Annual.

Municipal Water Facilities Inventory. Quinquennial.

National Air Quality and Emissions Trends Report. 1999. Annual

Needs Survey, Conveyance and Treatment of Municipal Wastewater Summaries of Technical Data. Biennial.

Pesticides Monitoring Journal. Quarterly.

Radiation Data and Reports. Monthly.

Sewage Facility Construction. Annual.

Summary of Water Enforcement Actions Pursued by EPA since December 3, 1970. (Updated continuously)

Toxics Release Inventory (EPA 260-R-01-001). Annual (Most Recent 1999).

Water Quality Report to Congress, 1998. Biennial.

Export-Import Bank of the United States
http://www.exim.gov

Annual Report.

Report to the U.S. Congress on Export Credit Competition and the Export-Import Bank of the United States. Annual.

Farm Credit Administration.
http://www.fca.gov

Annual Report on the Work of the Cooperative Farm Credit System.

Loans and Discounts of Farm Credit Banks and Associations. Annual.

Production Credit Association: Summary of Operations. Annual.

Farm Credit Administration. —Con.
Report to the Federal Land Bank Associations. Annual.

Federal Bureau of Investigation
http://www.fbi.gov
Bomb Summary. Annual.
Crime in the United States. Annual.
Hate Crime Statistics. Annual.
Law Enforcement Officers Killed and Assaulted. Annual.

Federal Communications Commission
http://www.fcc.gov
Annual Report.
Statistics of Communications Common Carriers. Annual.

Federal Deposit Insurance Corporation
http://www.fdic.gov
Annual Report.
Data Book-Operating Banks and Branches. Annual.
Quarterly Banking Profile.
Quarterly Banking Review.
Statistics on Banking. Annual, and Historical.
Trust Assets of Financial Institutions. Annual.

Federal Highway Administration
http://www.fhwa.dot.gov
Highway Statistics. Annual.

Federal Railroad Administration
http://www.fra.dot.gov
Accident/Incident Bulletin. Summary, statistics, and analysis of accidents on railroads in the United States. Annual.
Rail-Highway Crossing Accident/Incident and Inventory Bulletin. Annual.

Fish and Wildlife Service
http://www.fws.gov
Federal Aid in Fish and Wildlife Restoration. Annual.
National Survey of Fishing, Hunting, and Wildlife Associated Recreation.

Forest Service
http://www.fs.fed.us
An Analysis of the Timber Situation in the United States. 1996-2050.
Land Areas of the National Forest System. Annual.
The 1993 RPA Timber Assessment Update. Forthcoming.
U.S. Timber Production, Trade, Consumption, and Price Statistics. 2001.

General Services Administration
http://www.gsa.gov
Inventory Report on Real Property Leased to the United States Throughout the World. Annual.

General Services Administration —Con.
Inventory Report on Real Property Owned by the United States Throughout the World. Annual.

Geological Survey
http://ask.usgs.gov
A Statistical Summary of Data from the U.S. Geological Survey's National Water Quality Networks. (Open-File Report 83-533.)
Mineral Commodity Summaries. Annual.
Mineral Industry Surveys. (Monthly, quarterly, or annual report.)
Minerals Yearbook. (Monthly, quarterly, or annual report.)

Immigration and Naturalization Service (See Department of Homeland Security)

Internal Revenue Service
http://www.irs.ustreas.gov
Corporation Income Tax Returns. Annual.
Individual Income Tax Returns. Annual.
IRS Data Book.
Statistics of Income Bulletin. Quarterly.
Statistics of Income Division. (Annual report on Corporation Income Tax Returns. Periodic compendiums on Studies of International Income and Taxes.)

International Trade Administration
http://www.ita.doc.gov
U.S. Foreign Trade Highlights. (Print discontinued 1997.) Available electronically at http:www.ita.doc.gov/td/industry/otea/usfth/
U.S. Industry and Trade Outlook. (Discontinued, 2000, most recent.)

International Trade Commission
http://www.usitc.gov
Synthetic Organic Chemicals, U.S. Production and Sales. Annual.

Library of Congress
http://www.loc.gov
Annual Report.

Maritime Administration
http://www.marad.dot.gov
Annual Report.
Cargo-Carrying U.S. Flag Fleet by Area of Operation. (Semiannual)
Merchant Fleet Ocean-Going Vessels 1,000 Gross Tons and Over. Quarterly.
Seafaring Wage Rates. Biennial.

Mine Safety and Health Administration
http://www.msha.gov
Informational Reports by Mining Industry: Coal; Metallic Minerals; Nonmetallic Minerals (except stone and coal); Stone, Sand, and Gravel. Annual.
Mine Injuries and Worktime. (Some preliminary data.) Quarterly.

National Aeronautics and Space Administration
http://ifmp.nasa.gov

U.S. Census Bureau, Statistical Abstract of the United States: 2004-2005

National Aeronautics and Space Administration —Con.
Annual Procurement Report.
The Civil Service Work Force.

National Center for Education Statistics
http://nces.ed.gov
College and University Library Survey.
The Condition of Education. Annual.
Digest of Education Statistics. Annual.
Earned Degrees Conferred. Annual.
Education Statistics. Quarterly.
Faculty Salaries, Tenure, and Benefits. Annual.
Fall Enrollment in Degree-Granting Institutions. Annual.
Fall Staff in Postsecondary Institutions. Biennial.
Financial Statistics of Higher Education. Annual.
National Assessment of Educational Progress.
Private School Survey. Biennial.
Projections of Education Statistics. Annual.
Revenues and Expenditures for Public Elementary and Secondary Education. Annual.
School and Staffing Survey. Quadrennial.
Statistics of Public Elementary and Secondary School Systems. Fall. Annual.

National Center for Health Statistics
http://www.cdc.gov/nchs/
Ambulatory Care Visits to Physician Offices, Hospital Outpatient Departments and Emergency Departments. Annual.
Health: United States. Annual. (DHHS Pub. No. PHS year-1232.)
National Hospital Discharge Survey: Annual Summary. Annual.
National Vital Statistics Reports (NVRS.) Monthly.
Vital and Health Statistics. (A series of statistical reports covering health-related topics.)
Series 10: Health Interview Survey Statistics.
Attention Deficit Disorder and Learning Disability.
Current Estimates from the Health Interview Survey. Annual.
Injury and Poisoning Episodes and Conditions.
Summary Health Statistics for U.S. Adults. Annual.
Summary Health Statistics for U.S. Children. Annual
Series 11: Health and Nutrition Examination Survey Statistics. Irregular.
Series 13: Data from National Health Care Survey.
Series 14: Data on Health Resources: Manpower and Facilities.
Series 20: Mortality Data. Irregular.

National Center for Health Statistics —Con.
Series 21: Natality, Marriage, and Divorce Data. Irregular.
Series 23: Data from the National Survey of Family Growth.
Vital Statistics of the United States. Annual.
Volume I, Natality
Volume II, Mortality
Volume III, Marriage and Divorce

National Credit Union Administration
http://www.ncua.gov
Annual Report.
Midyear Statistics.
Yearend Statistics.

National Guard Bureau
http://www.ngb.army.mil/
Annual Review of the Chief.

The National Library of Medicine (for clinical medical reports)
http://www.nlm.nih.gov
Annual Report.

National Oceanic and Atmospheric Administration
http://www.lib.noaa.gov
Climates of the World, HCS 6-4. Monthly and annual.
Climatological Data. Issued in sections for states and outlying areas. Monthly with annual summary.
Climatography of the United States, No. 20, Supplement No. 1, Freeze/Frost Data.
Comparative Climatic Data. Annual.
Daily Normals of Temp, Precip, HDD, & CDD/Clim 84. Periodic.
General Summary of Tornadoes. Annual.
Hourly Precipitation Data. Monthly with annual summary; for each state.
Local Climatological Data. Monthly with annual summary; for major cities.
Monthly Climatic Data for the World. Monthly.
Monthly Normals of Temp, Precip, HDD, & CDD/Clim 84. Periodic.
Our Living Oceans. Periodic.
Storm Data. Monthly.
Weekly Weather and Crop Bulletin. National summary.

National Park Service
http://www.nps.gov
Federal Recreation Fee Report. Annual.
National Park Statistical Abstract. Annual.

National Science Foundation
http://www.nsf.gov
Academic Research and Development Expenditures. Detailed Statistical Tables. Annual
Academic Science and Engineering: Graduate Enrollment and Support: Detailed Statistical Tables. Annual

National Science Foundation —Con.

Characteristics of Doctoral Scientists and Engineers in the United States. Detailed Statistical Tables. Biennial.

Characteristics of Recent Science/Engineering Graduates. Detailed Statistical Tables. Biennial.

Federal Funds for Research and Development. Detailed Statistical Tables. Annual.

Federal R&D Funding by Budget Function. Report. Annual.

Federal Science and Engineering Support to Universities, Colleges, and Nonprofit Institutions. Detailed Statistical Tables. Annual.

Federal Support to Universities, Colleges, and Nonprofit Institutions. Detailed Statistical Tables. Annual.

Graduate Students and Post-doctorates in Science and Engineering. Annual.

Immigrant Scientists, Engineers, and Technicians. Detailed Statistical Tables. Annual.

International Science and Technology Data Update. Report. Annual.

National Patterns of R&D Resources. Report. Annual.

Planned R&D Expenditures of Major U.S. Firms. Special Report. (NSF 91-306.)

Research and Development in Industry. Detailed Statistical Tables. Annual.

Science and Engineering Degrees. Annual.

Science and Engineering Degrees, by Race/Ethnicity of Recipients. Detailed Statistical Tables. Annual.

Science and Engineering Doctorates Awards. Detailed Statistical Tables. Annual.

Science and Engineering Indicators. Report. Biennial.

Science and Engineering Personnel: A National Overview. Report. Biennial.

Science and Engineering Profiles. Annual.

Science and Technology Pocket Data Book. Report. Annual.

Science Resources Studies. Data Brief. Frequent.

Scientific and Engineering Research Facilities at Universities and Colleges. Report. Biennial.

Scientists, Engineers, and Technicians in Manufacturing Industries. Detailed Statistical Tables. Triennial.

Scientists, Engineers, and Technicians in Nonmanufacturing Industries. Detailed Statistical Tables. Triennial.

Scientists, Engineers, and Technicians in Trade and Regulated Industries. Detailed Statistical Tables. Triennial.

Survey of Direct U.S. Private Capital Investment in Research and Development Facilities in Japan. Report. (NSH 91-312.)

U.S. Scientists and Engineers. Detailed Statistical Tables. Biennial.

National Science Foundation —Con.

Women, Minorities, and Persons with Disabilities. Report. Biennial

Women, Minorities in Science and Engineering. Report. Biennial.

National Transportation Safety Board
http://www.ntsb.gov

Accidents; Air Carriers. Annual.

Accidents; General Aviation. Annual.

Office of Management and Budget
http://www.whitehouse.gov/omb

The Budget of the United States Government. Annual.

Office of Personnel Management
http://www.opm.gov

Civil Service Retirement and Disability Fund. Report. Annual.

Demographic Profile of the Federal Workforce. Biennial. (Even years.)

Employment and Trends. Bimonthly. (Odd months.)

Employment by Geographic Area. Biennial. (Even years.)

The Fact Book. Annual.

Federal Employment Statistics. Annual.

Occupations of Federal White-Collar and Blue-Collar Workers. Biennial. (Odd years.)

Pay Structure of the Federal Civil Service. Annual.

Statistical Abstract for the Federal Employee Benefit Programs. Annual.

Work Years and Personnel Costs. Annual.

Patent and Trademark Office
http://www.uspto.gov

Commissioner of Patents and Trademarks Annual Report.

Technology Assessment and Forecast Reports

All Technologies. Annual.

Patenting Trends in the United States. Annual.

State Country. Annual.

Railroad Retirement Board, Chicago, IL
http://www.rrb.gov

Annual Report.

Monthly Benefit Statistics.

Statistical Supplement to the Annual Report.

Securities and Exchange Commission
http://www.sec.gov

Annual Report.

Small Business Administration
http://www.sbaonline.sba.gov

Annual Report.

Handbook of Small Business Data.

The State of Small Business.

Social Security Administration
http://www.ssa.gov

Social Security Administration —Con.
Income of the Population 55 and over,
1994, 1996, 1998, 2000.
Social Security Beneficiaries by State and
County Data. Annual.
Social Security Bulletin. Quarterly with
annual statistical supplement. (Data on
Social Security Benefits, OASDI, Supple-
mental Security Income, Aid to Families

Social Security Administration —Con.
with Dependent Children, Medicare, Medicaid, Low Income Home Energy Assistance, Food Stamps, Black Lung benefits,
and other programs.)
State Assistance Programs for SSI Recipients. Annual.
Supplemental Security Income, State and
County Data. Annual.

NONGOVERNMENT

**AAFRC Trust For Philanthropy,
Indianapolis, IN**
http://www.aafrc.org
Giving USA. Annual.

**Aerospace Industries Association,
Washington, DC**
http://www.aia-aerospace.org
Aerospace Facts and Figures. Annual.
Aerospace Industry Year-End Review and
Forecast. Annual.
Commercial Helicopter Shipments. Quar-
terly.
Employment in the Aerospace Industry.
Monthly, Tabulated Quarterly.
Exports of Aerospace Products. Quarterly.
Imports of Aerospace Products. Quarterly.
Manufacturing Production, Capacity, and
Utilization in Aerospace and Aircraft and
parts. Monthly, Tabulated Quarterly.
Orders, Shipments, Backlog and inventories
for Aircraft, Missiles, & Parts. Monthly,
Tabulated Quarterly.

**Air Transport Association of America,
Inc., Washington, DC**
http://www.airlines.org
Air Transport Association, Annual Report.

**The Alan Guttmacher Institute, New York,
NY**
http://www.guttmacher.org
Perspectives on Sexual and Reproductive
Health. Bimonthly.

**American Bureau of Metal Statistics, Inc.,
Secaucus, NJ**
http://www.abms.com
Non-Ferrous Metal Yearbook.

**American Council on Education,
Washington, DC**
http://www.acenet.edu
A Fact Book on Higher Education. Quarterly.
National Norms for Entering College Fresh-
men. Annual.

**American Council of Life Insurers,
Washington, DC**
http://www.acli.com
Life Insurers Fact Book. Annual.

American Dental Association, Chicago, IL
http://www.ada.org
Dental Statistics Handbook. Triennial.
Dental Students' Register. Annual.
Distribution of Dentists in the United States
by Region and State. Triennial.
Survey of Dental Practice. Annual.

**American Forest & Paper Association,
Washington, DC**
http://www.afandpa.org
Annual Statistical Summary of Recovered
Paper Utilization.
Statistical Roundup.
Statistics of Paper, Paperboard, and Wood
Pulp. Annual.
U.S. Wood Pulp Data Report. Annual.
U.S. Forest Facts and Figures.

**American Frozen Food Institute,
Burlingame, CA**
http://www.affi.com
Frozen Food Pack Statistics. Annual.

**American Gas Association, Washington,
DC**
http://www.aga.org
Gas Facts. Annual.

**American Iron and Steel Institute,
Washington, DC**
http://www.steel.org
Annual Statistical Report.

**American Jewish Committee, New York,
NY**
http://www.ajc.org
American Jewish Year Book.

American Medical Association, Chicago, IL
http://www.ama-assn.org
Physician Characteristics and Distribution in
the U.S. Annual.
Physician Marketplace Statistics. Annual.
Physician Socioeconomic Statistics. 1991-
2000.
Socioeconomic Characteristics of Medical
Practice. 1997/98.
U.S. Medical Licensure Statistics, and
License Requirements. Annual.

American Metal Market, New York, NY
http://www.amm.com
Metal Statistics. Annual.

American Osteopathic Association, Chicago, IL
http://www.aoa-net.org
Yearbook and Directory of Osteopathic Physicians. Annual.

American Petroleum Institute, Washington, DC
http://www.api.org
The Basic Petroleum Data Book. Annual.
Joint Association Survey on Drilling Costs (JA5). Annual.
Petroleum Industry Environmental Report. Annual.
Quarterly Well Completion Report.

American Public Transportation Association, Washington, DC
http://www.apta.com
Public Transportation Fact Book. Annual.

Association for Manufacturing Technology
http://www.amtonline.org
Economic Handbook of the Machine Tool Industry 2003-2004.

Association of American Railroads, Washington, DC
http://www.aar.org
Analysis of Class I Railroads. Annual.
Cars of Revenue Freight Loaded. Weekly with annual summary.
Freight Commodity Statistics, Class I Railroads in the United States. Annual.
Yearbook of Railroad Facts.

Association of Racing Commissioners International, Inc., Lexington, KY
http://www.arci.com
Statistical Reports on Greyhound Racing in the United States. Annual.
Statistical Reports on Horse Racing in the United States. Annual.
Statistical Reports on Jai Alai in the United States. Annual.

Book Industry Study Group, Inc., New York, NY
http://www.bisg.org
Book Industry Trends. Annual.
Consumer Research Study on Book Purchasing. Annual.

Boy Scouts of America, Irving, TX
http://www.scouting.org
Annual Report.

The Bureau of National Affairs, Inc., Washington, DC
http://www.bna.com
Basic Patterns in Union Contracts. Annual.
BNA's Employment Outlook. Quarterly.
BNA's Job Absence and Turnover. Quarterly.

The Bureau of National Affairs, Inc., Washington, DC —Con.
Briefing Sessions on Employee Relations Workbook. Annual.
Calendar of Negotiations. Annual.
Directory of U.S. Labor Organizations. Annual.
National Labor Relations Board Election Statistics. Annual.
NLRB Representation and Decertification Elections Statistics. Quarterly.
PPF Survey (Personnel Policies Forum.) Three times a year.

Carl H. Pforzheimer & Co., New York, NY
(No Web site)
Comparative Oil Company Statistics, 1999. Annual.

Chronicle of Higher Education, Inc., Washington, DC
http://chronicle.com
Almanac. Annual.

College Board, New York, NY
http://www.collegeboard.com
National Report on College-Bound Seniors.

Commodity Research Bureau, Logical Systems, Inc., Chicago, IL
http://www.crbtrader.com
Commodity Year Book Update Disk. (Three editions annually.)
CRB Commodity Index Report. Weekly.
CRB Commodity Year Book. Annual.
CRB Futures Perspective. Weekly.
CRB Infotech. CD
Electronic Futures Trend Analyzer. Daily.
Final Markets. End of day.
Futures Market Service. Weekly.
Futures Market Service Fundamental & Technical Commentary. Daily and weekly.
Price Service. Daily

The Conference Board, New York, NY
http://www.conference-board.org
http://www.globalindicators.org
Business Cycle Indicators, Monthly.
Corporate Contributions in 2002, December 2003. Annual.
Productivity, Employment, and Income in the World's Economies. Annual.

CQ Press, Washington, DC
http://www.cqpress.com
America Votes. A handbook of contemporary American election statistics, compiled and edited by Richard M. Scammon, Alice V. McGillivray and Rhodes Cook. Biennial.

Consumer Electronics Association (Electronic Industries Alliance), Arlington, VA
http://www.ce.org
Electronic Market Data Book. Annual.

U.S. Census Bureau, Statistical Abstract of the United States: 2004-2005

Consumer Electronics Association (Electronic Industries Alliance), Arlington, VA —Con.
Electronic Market Trends. Monthly.
Electronics Foreign Trade. Monthly.

The Council of State Governments, Lexington, KY
http://www.statesnews.org
The Book of the States. Annual.
State Administrative Officials Classified by Function. Annual.
State Elective Officials and the Legislatures. Annual.
State Legislative Leadership, Committees, and Staff. Annual.

Credit Union National Association, Inc., Madison, WI
http://www.cuna.org
The Credit Union Ranking Report. Annual.
Credit Union Services Profile. Annual.
Operating Ratios and Spreads. Semiannual.

Dow Jones & Co., New York, NY.
http://www.dj.com
Wall Street Journal.
Daily except Saturdays, Sundays, and holidays.

Edison Electric Institute, Washington, DC
http://www.eei.org
Statistical Yearbook of the Electric Utility Industry. Annual.

Editor & Publisher Co., New York, NY
http://www.editorandpublisher.com
Editor & Publisher. Monthly.
International Year Book. Annual.
Market Guide. Annual.

ENO Transportation Foundation, Leesburg, VA
http://www.enotrans.com
Transportation in America, 2000, with Historical Compendium 1939-1999. 2001.

Euromonitor International, London, England
http://www.euromonitor.com
Consumer Asia. Annual.
Consumer China. Annual.
Consumer Eastern Europe. Annual.
Consumer Europe. Annual.
Consumer International. Annual.
Consumer Latin America. Annual.
European Marketing Data and Statistics. Annual.
International Marketing Data and Statistics. Annual.
Latin America Marketing Data and Statistic. Annual.
World Consumer Expenditure Patterns. Annual.
World Consumer Income Patterns. Annual.

Euromonitor International, London, England —Con.
World Economic Factbook. Annual.
World Retail Data and Statistics. Annual.

Federal National Mortgage Association, Washington, DC
http://www.fanniemae.com
Annual Report.

Food and Agriculture Organization of the United Nations, Rome, Italy
http://www.fao.org
Fertilizer Yearbook.
Production Yearbook.
Trade Yearbook.
Yearbook of Fishery Statistics.
Yearbook of Forest Products.

The Foundation Center, New York, NY
http://www.fdncenter.org
Foundation Giving Trends. Annual.
Foundation Yearbook. Annual.

Gale Group Inc., Farmington Hills, MI
http://www.galegroup.com
Gale Directory of Publications and Broadcast Media. 1999.

General Aviation Manufacturers Association, Washington, DC
http://www.gama.aero/home.php
Shipment Report. Quarterly and Annual.
Statistical Databook. Annual.

Girl Scouts of the USA, New York, NY
http://www.girlscouts.org
Annual Report.

Health Forum, L.L.C.,an American Hospital Association Company, Chicago, IL.
http://www.healthforum.com
Annual Report.

America's Health Insurance Plans, Washington, DC
http://www.ahip.org
Source Book of Health Insurance Data. Annual.

Independent Petroleum Association of America, Washington, DC
http://www.ipaa.org
Domestic Oil and Gas Trends. Monthly.
Oil & Natural Gas Production in Your State. Annual.
U.S. Petroleum Statistics. Annual.

Information Today, Inc., Medford, NJ
http://www.infotoday.com
American Library Directory. Annual.
Bowker Annual Library and Book Trade Almanac.

Institute for Criminal Justice Ethics, New York, NY
http://www.lib.jjay.cuny.edu/cje/html/institute.html
Criminal Justice Ethics. Semiannual.

U.S. Census Bureau, Statistical Abstract of the United States: 2004-2005

Insurance Information Institute, New York, NY
http://www.iii.org
The Fact Book, Property/Casualty Insurance Facts. Annual.

Inter-American Development Bank, Washington, DC
http://www.iadb.org
Annual Report.
Economic and Social Progress in Latin America. Annual Survey.

International Air Transport Association
http://www.iata.org
World Air Transport Statistics.

International City Management Association, Washington, DC
http://www.icma.org
Compensation: An Annual Report on Local Government Executive Salaries and Fringe Benefits.
Municipal Year Book. Annual.

International Labour Organizaion, Geneva, Switzerland
http://www.ilo.org
Yearbook of Labour Statistics.

International Monetary Fund, Washington, DC
http://www.imf.org
Annual Report.
Balance of Payments Statistics. Monthly with annual yearbook.
Direction of Trade Statistics. Monthly with annual yearbook.
Government Finance Statistics Yearbook.
International Financial Statistics. Monthly with annual yearbook.

Investment Company Institute, Washington, DC
http://www.ici.org
Mutual Fund Fact Book. Annual.

Jane's Information Group, Coulsdon, UK and Alexandria, VA
http://www.janes.com
Jane's Air-Launched Weapons. (Binder-4 monthly update.)
Jane's All the World's Aircraft. Annual.
Jane's Armour and Artillery. Annual.
Jane's Avionics. Annual.
Jane's Fighting Ships. Annual.
Jane's Infantry Weapons. Annual.
Jane's Merchant Ships. Annual.
Jane's Military Communications. Annual.
Jane's Military Logistics. Annual.
Jane's Military Training Systems. Annual.
Jane's NATO Handbook. Annual.
Jane's Spaceflight Directory. Annual.

Joint Center for Political and Economic Studies, Washington, DC
http://www.jointcenter.org
Black Elected Officials: A Statistical Summary. Annual.

McGraw-Hill Construction Dodge, a Division of the McGraw-Hill Companies, New York, NY
http://www.fwdodge.com
Dodge Construction Potential, Monthly.

Moody's Investors Service, New York, NY
http://www.moodys.com

National Academy of Sciences, Washington, DC
http://www.pnas.org
Science, Engineering, and Humanities Doctorates in the United States. Biennial.
Summary Report. Doctorate Recipients from United States Universities. Annual.

National Association of Home Builders, Washington, DC
http://www.nahb.org
Home Builders Forecast. Monthly.
Housing Economics. Monthly
Housing Market Statistics. Monthly.

National Association of Latino Elected and Appointed Officials, Washington, DC
http://www.naleo.org
National Roster of Hispanic Elected Officials. Annual.

National Association of Realtors. Washington, DC
http://www.realtor.org
Real Estate Outlook: Market Trends & Insights. Monthly.

National Association of State Budget Officers, Washington, DC
http://www.nasbo.org
State Expenditure Report. Annual.
Fiscal Survey of the States. Semi-annual.

National Association of State Park Directors, Tucson, AZ
http://www.naspd.org
Annual Information Exchange.

National Catholic Educational Association, Washington, DC
http://www.ncea.org
Catholic Schools in America. Annual.
United States Catholic Elementary and Secondary Schools. Staffing and Enrollment. Annual.
U.S. Catholic Elementary Schools and their Finances. Biennial.
U.S. Catholic Secondary Schools and their Finances. Biennial.

National Center for State Courts, Williamsburg, VA
http://www.ncsconline.org
State Court Caseload Statistics. Annual.

National Council of the Churches USA, New York, NY
http://www.ncccusa.org
Yearbook of American and Canadian Churches. Annual.

U.S. Census Bureau, Statistical Abstract of the United States: 2004-2005

National Council of Savings Institutions, Washington, DC
Now, America's Community Bankers.
http://www.acbankers.org
Fact Book of National Council of Savings Institutions. Annual.

National Education Association, Washington, DC
http://www.nea.org
Rankings of the States and Estimates of School Statistics. Annual.
Status of the American Public School Teacher, 2000-2001. Quinquennial

National Fire Protection Association, Quincy, MA
http://www.nfpa.org
NFPA Journal. Bimonthly.

National Golf Foundation, Jupiter, FL
http://www.ngf.org
A Beginner's Guide to Golf.
Careers in Golf: An Insider's Guide to Careers in the Golf Industry.
Development & Operations Manual: How to Plan, Build & Operate a Successful Golf Range.
Easy Way to Learn Golf.
Easy Way to Learn Golf Rules.
Golf Course Directory.
Golf Course Etiquette Brochure.
Golf Course Operations Policy Manual.
Golf Facilities in the U.S.
Golf Manager's Handbook.
Golf Participation in the U.S.
Marketing Your Golf Course: Big Hits Marketing.
Operating & Financial Performance Profiles of 18-hole Golf Facilities in the U.S.
Twelve Golf Lessons.
Welcome Programs That Work.
Welcome to Golf.
Women Welcome Here.

National Marine Manufacturers Association, Chicago, IL
http://www.nmma.org
Boating. (A Statistical Report on America's Top Family Sport.) Annual.
State Boat Registration. Annual.

National Restaurant Association, Washington, DC
http://www.restaurant.org
Compensation for Salaried Personnel in Restaurants. 2001.
Ethnic Cuisines II. 2000.
Holiday Dining. 2001.
Meal Consumption Behavior. 2001.
Quick-Service Restaurant Trends. Annual.
Restaurant Economic Trends. Monthly.
Restaurant Industry Forecast. Annual.
Restaurant Industry in Review. Annual.

National Restaurant Association, Washington, DC —Con.
Restaurant Industry Operations Report. Annual.
Restaurant Industry Pocket Factbook. Annual.
Restaurant Industry 2010. 1999.
Restaurant Numbers: 25-Year History, 1970-95. 1998.
Restaurant Performance Index. Monthly.
Restaurant Spending. Annual. Restaurants USA. Monthly.
State of the Restaurant Industry Work Force. Annual.
Tableservice Restaurant Trends. Annual
Takeout Foods: A Consumer Study of Carry-out and Delivery. 1998
The Economic Impact of the Nation's Eating and Drinking Places. Annual.

National Safety Council, Itasca, IL
http://www.nsc.org
Injury Facts. Annual.

National Sporting Goods Association, Mt. Prospect, IL
http://www.nsga.org
Fitness in America 2001.
The Sporting Goods Market in 2004. Annual.
Sports Participation in 2003. Annual.
Sports Equipment Purchases in 2003. Annual.

New York Stock Exchange, Inc., New York, NY
http://www.nyse.com
Fact Book. Annual.

The New York Times Almanac, 2004.

Organisation for Economic Cooperation and Development, Paris, France
http://www.sourceoecd.org
Agricultural Outlook, 2003-2008. Annual.
Bank Profitability: Financial Statements of Banks, 2002. Annual.
Central Government Debt: Statistical Yearbook. Annual.
Coal Information. Annual.
CO2 Emissions From Fuel Combustion, 1971-2001. 2003 Edition. Annual.
Communications Outlook, 2003 Edition. Annual.
Creditor Reporting System on Aid Activities. Quarterly.
Economic Outlook. Bi-ennial.
Economic Studies. Annual for Member Countries.
Economic Surveys. Annual for Member Countries.
Education at a Glance: OECD Indicators, 2003. Annual.
Electricity Information, 2003 Edition. Annual.
Employment Outlook, 2004. Annual.
Energy Balances of Non-OECD Countries, 2000-2001. 2003 Edition. Annual.

Organization for Economic Cooperation and Development, Paris, France —Con.

Energy Balances of OECD Countries, 2000-01. 2003 Edition. Annual.

Energy Prices and Taxes. Quarterly.

Energy Statistics of NON-OECD Countries, 2000-2001. 2003 Edition. Annual.

Energy Statistics of OECD Countries 2000-01. 2003 Edition. Annual.

Environmental Outlook.

External Debt Statistics, 1998-02. 2003 Edition. Annual.

Financial Market Trends. Triennial.

Geographical Distribution of Financial Flows to Aid Recipients, 1998-02. 2004 Edition. Annual.

Health Data, 2003 CD-ROM. Annual.

Historical Statistics, 1970-2000. 2001 Edition.

Information Technology Outlook, 2002 Edition. Biannual.

Insurance Statistics Yearbook, 1994-2001. 2003 Edition. Annual.

International Development Statistics CD-ROM and Online Database, 2004. Annual.

International Trade by Commodities. Annual.

Iron and Steel Industry in 2002. 2004 Edition.

Labour Force Statistics. 1982-2002. 2003 Edition. Annual.

Main Economic Indicators. Monthly.

Main Science and Technology Indicators, Vol. 2003. Biennial.

Measuring Globalisation: The Role of Multinationals in OECD Countries. 2001 Edition. Biannual.

Monthly Statistics of International Trade. Series A. Monthly.

National Accounts of OECD Countries. Annual.

Vol. I: Main Aggregates.

Vol. II: Detailed Tables.

Natural Gas Information. 2003 Edition. Annual.

Nuclear Energy Data. 2004 Edition. Annual.

OECD Observer. Bimonthly.

Oil Information. 2003 Edition. Annual.

Oil, Gas, Coal, and Electricity Quarterly Statistics. Quarterly.

Quarterly Labor Force Statistics.

Quarterly National Accounts.

Policies in OECD Countries. Annual.

Research and Development Statistics CD-ROM.

Revenue Statistics of OECD Member Countries, 1965-2002. 2003 Edition. Annual.

Review of Fisheries in OECD Member Countries. Annual.

Organization for Economic Cooperation and Development, Paris, France —Con.

Science, Technology and Industry: Scoreboard, 2003. Bi-ennial.

Small and Medium Enterprise Outlook. 2002 Edition. Bi-ennial.

Statistical Report on Road Accidents, 1999-2000.

Structural Statistics for Industry and Services, 1993-2000. 2003 Edition. Annual.

Taxing Wages, 2003. Annual.

The DAC Journal. Quarterly.

Trends in International Migration. 2003 Edition. Annual.

Trends in the Transport Sector, 1970-2002. 2004 Edition.

Uranium Resources Production and Demand, 2001. Biennial.

Pan American Health Organization, Washington, DC

http://www.paho.org

Health Conditions in the Americas. Quadrennial.

PennWell Corporation, Tulsa, OK

http://www.pennwell.com

Offshore. Monthly.

Oil and Gas Journal. Weekly.

Population Association of America, Washington, DC

http://www.popassoc.org

Demography. Quarterly.

Puerto Rico Planning Board, San Juan, PR

http://www.jp.gobierno.pr

Balance of Payments—Puerto Rico. Annual.

Economic Activity Index. Monthly.

Economic Indicators. Monthly.

Economic Projections. Annual.

Economic Report to the Governor. Annual.

External Trade Statistics-Puerto Rico. Annual.

Income and Product. Annual.

Input-Output—Puerto Rico. Every five years.

Statistical Appendix to the Economic Report to the Government. Annual.

Radio Advertising Bureau, New York, NY

http://www.rab.com

Radio Facts. Annual.

Radio Marketing Guide and Fact Book. Annual.

Reed Business Information, New York, NY

http://www.cahners.com

Library Journal. Semimonthly.

Publishers Weekly.

School Library Journal. Monthly.

Regional Airline Association, Washington, DC

http://www.raa.org

Statistical Report.

Magazine. Quarterly.

Research Associates of Washington, Arlington, VA
http://www.rschassoc.com
Inflation Measures for Schools, Colleges, and Libraries. Periodic.

Securities Industry Association, New York, NY
http://www.sia.com
Foreign Activity Report. Quarterly.
Securities Industry Trends. Periodic.
Securities Industry Yearbook. Annual.

Standard and Poor's Corporation, New York, NY
http://www.standardandpoors.com
Analyst's Handbook. Annual with monthly cumulative supplements.
Corporation Records. Six basic volumes; News Supplements, daily; Dividend Record, daily; and cumulative monthly and annual.
Daily Stock Price Records. Quarterly.
Security Owner's Stock Guide. Monthly.
Standard and Poor's Global Stock Market Factbook. Annual with data on 78 equity markets around the world.
Statistical Service. (Security Price Index Record; business and financial basic statistics with monthly supplement.)

UNESCO Institute for Statistics
http://www.uis.unesco.org

United Nations Statistics Division, New York, NY
http://unstats.un.org/unsd/
Compendium of Human Settlements Statistics. (Series N.)
Demographic Yearbook. (Series R.)
Energy Balances and Electricity Profiles. (Series W.)
Energy Statistics Yearbook. (Series J.)
Industrial Statistics Yearbook: (Series P.)
Commodity Production Statistics.
International Trade Statistics Yearbook. (Series G.)
Monthly Bulletin of Statistics. (Series Q.)
National Accounts Statistics: (Series X, Annually.)
Main Aggregates and Detailed Tables.
Analysis of Main Aggregates.
Population and Vital Statistics Report. (Series A, Quarterly.)
Social Statistics and Indicators: (Series K, Occasional.)
The World's Women: Trends and Statistics.
Women's Indicators and Statistics Database (CD and diskette only.)

United Nations Statistics Division, New York, NY —Con.
Statistical Yearbook. (Series; also available in CD-ROM, Series S/CD)
World Statistics Pocketbook. (Series V, Annually.)

United States League of Savings Institutions, Washington, DC
Now, America's Community Bankers.
http://www.acbankers.org
Savings Institutions Sourcebook. Annual.

United States Telecom Association, Washington, DC
http://www.usta.org
Statistics of the Local Exchange Carriers. Annual.

United Way of America, Alexandria, VA
http://www.unitedway.org
Annual Directory.

University of Michigan, Center for Political Studies, Institute for Social Research, Ann Arbor, MI
http://www.umich.edu
National Election Studies Cumulative Datafile. Biennial.

Warren Communications News, Washington, DC
http://www.warren-news.com
Cable and Station Coverage Atlas. Annual.
Television and Cable Action Update. Weekly.
Television and Cable Factbook. Annual.

World Almanac, New York, NY
http://www.worldalmanac.com
The World Almanac and Book of Facts. Annual.

The World Bank Group, Washington, DC
http://www.worldbank.org
Global Development Finance, 2003. Annual.
The Little Data Book.
World Bank Atlas, 2003. Annual.
World Development Indicators, 2003. Annual.

World Health Organization, Geneva, Switzerland
http://www.who.int
Epidemiological and Vital Statistics Report. Monthly.
World Health Statistics. Quarterly and annual.

894   Appendix I

Guide to State Statistical Abstracts

This bibliography includes the most recent statistical abstracts for states published since 1995 plus those that will be issued in late 2004. For some states, a near equivalent has been listed in substitution for, or in addition to, a statistical abstract. All sources contain statistical tables on a variety of subjects for the state as a whole, its component parts, or both. Internet sites also contain statistical data.

Alabama

University of Alabama, Center for Business and Economic Research, Box 870221, Tuscaloosa, AL 35487-0221. 205-348-6191. Fax: 205-348-2951. Internet site <http://cber.cba.ua.edu/>
Economic Abstract of Alabama, 2000. Alabama Economic Outlook, 2004. (Revised annually.)

Alaska

Department of Community and Economic Development, Division of Community Advocacy, 550 W. 7th Avenue. Suite 1770, Anchorage, AK 99501-2341. 907-269-4580. Fax: 907-269-4539. Internet site <http://www.dced.state.ak.us/>
The Alaska Economic Performance Report, 2003. On line.

Arizona

Economic and Business Research, University of Arizona, McClelland Hall, Rm. 103, P.O. Box 210108, Tucson, AZ 85721-0108. 520-621-2155. Fax: 520-621-2150. Internet site <http://www.ebr.eller.arizona.edu/>
Arizona Statistical Abstract, 2003. Arizona's Economy. Quarterly newsletter.
Arizona Economic Indicators. Online.

Arkansas

University of Arkansas at Little Rock, Institute for Economic Advancement, Economic Research, 2801 South University Avenue, Little Rock, AR 72204. 501-569-8521. Internet site <http://www.aiea.ualr.edu/>
Arkansas State and County Economic Data, 2003. (Revised annually.)
Arkansas Personal Income Handbook, 2003.

University of Arkansas at Little Rock, Institute for Economic Advancement, Census State Data Center, 2801 South University, Little Rock 72204. 501-569-8530. Internet site <http://www.aiea.ualr.edu/>
Arkansas Statistical Abstract, 2004. Revised biennially.

California

Department of Finance, 915 L Street, 8th Floor, Sacramento, CA 95814. 916-322-2263. Internet site <http://www.dof.ca.gov/HTML/FS_DATA/STAT-ABS/Sa_home.htm>
California Statistical Abstract, 2003. Annual.

Colorado

University of Colorado, University Libraries, 184 VCB, 1720 Pleasant St., Boulder, CO 80309-0184. 303-492-8834. Internet site <http://www.colorado.edu/libraries/govpubs/online.htm>
Colorado by the Numbers. online only.

Connecticut

Connecticut Department of Economic & Community Development, 505 Hudson St., Hartford, CT 06106. 1-860-270-8000. Internet site <http://www.ct.gov/ecd/site/default.asp>
Connecticut Town Profiles, 2002-2003.

Delaware

Delaware Economic Development Office, 99 Kings Highway, Dover, DE 19901. 302-739-4271. FAX 302-739-2028. Internet site <http://www.state.de.us/dedo/>
Delaware Statistical Overview, 2002-2003.

District of Columbia

Office of Planning, Data Management Division, 801 North Capitol St., N.E., Suite 4000, Washington, DC 20002. 202-442-7632
Indices—A Statistical Index to DC Services, Dec. 1997-98.

Florida

University of Florida, Bureau of Economic and Business Research, P.O. Box 117145, 221 Matherly Hall, Gainesville, FL 32611-7145. 352-392-0171, ext. 219. Internet site <http://www.bebr.ufl.edu/>
Florida Statistical Abstract, 2003. 37th ed. Annual. Also available on CD-ROM. *Florida County Perspective, 2003.* One profile for each county. Annual. Also available on CD-ROM. *Florida County Rankings, 2003.* 10th edition. Annual. Also available on CD-ROM. *Florida and the Nation, 2004.* Annual. Also available on CD-ROM.

Georgia

University of Georgia, Selig Center for Economic Growth, Terry College of Business, Athens, GA 30602-6269. 706-542-4085. Internet site <http://www.selig.uga.edu/>

Georgia Statistical Abstract, 2002-03.

University of Georgia, Center for Agribusiness and Economic Development, 202 Lumpkin House, Athens, GA 30602-7509. 706-542-8938 or 706-542-0760. Fax: 706-542-8934. Internet sites <http://www.georgiastats.uga.edu/> and <http://www.agecon.uga.edu>

The Georgia County Guide, 2003. Annual.

Hawaii

Hawaii State Department of Business, and Economic Development & Tourism, Research and Economic Analysis Division, Statistics and Data Support Branch P.O. Box 2359, Honolulu, HI 96804. 808-586-2423. Internet site <http://www2.hawaii.gov/DBEDT/index.cfm>

The State of Hawaii Data Book 2002: A Statistical Abstract.

Idaho

Department of Commerce, 700 West State St., P.O. Box 83720, Boise, ID 83720-0093. 208-334-2470. Internet site <http://www.idoc.state.id.us/data/community/>

County Profiles of Idaho, 2003.
Idaho Community Profiles, 2003.
Profile of Rural Idaho, 1999.

Illinois

Institute of Government and Public Affairs,1007 W. Nevada Street, Urbana, IL, 61801 MC-037. 217-333-3340. Internet site <http://www.igpa.uiuc.edu/default.htm>

Illinois Statistical Abstract, 2003. Online only.

Indiana

Indiana University, Indiana Business Research Center, Kelley School of Business, Ste 3110, 1275 E. 10th Street, Bloomington, IN 47405-1703. 812-855-5507. Internet site <http://www.ibrc.indiana.edu>

STATS Indiana. Online only.

Iowa

Office of Social and Economic Trend Analysis, 303 East Hall, Ames, IA 50010-1070. 515-294-9903. Internet site <http://www.seta.iastate.edu/>

State Library of Iowa, State Data Center, Ola Babcock Miller Building, East 12th and Grand, Des Moines, IA 50319. 800248-4483. Internet site <http://www.silo.lib.ia.us/specialized-services/datacenter/>

Kansas

University of Kansas, Policy Research Institute, 1541 Lilac Lane, 607 Blake Hall, Lawrence, KS 66044-3177. 785-864-3701. Internet site <http://www.ku.edu/pri/>

Kansas Statistical Abstract, 2002. 37th ed. Online only.

Kentucky

Kentucky Cabinet for Economic Development, Division of Research, 500 Mero Street, Capital Plaza Tower, Frankfort, KY 40601. 502-564-7670. Internet site <http://www.thinkkentucky.com/kyedc/resandstat.asp>

Kentucky Deskbook of Economic Statistics. Online only.

Louisiana

University of New Orleans, Division of Business and Economic Research, New Orleans, LA 70148. 504-280-6240. Internet site <http://leap.ulm.edu/>

Statistical Abstract of Louisiana, 1997. 10th ed.

Louisiana State Census Data Center, Office of Electronic Services, P.O. Box 94095, Baton Rouge, LA 70804. 225-219-4025. Internet site <http://www.louisiana.gov/wps/portal/.cmd/cs/.ce/155/.s/1133>

Maine

Maine State Planning Office,#38 State House Station, Augusta, ME 04333. 800-662-4545. Internet site <http://www.state.me.us/spo/economics/economics/>

Maryland

RESI, Towson University 8000 York Road, Towson, MD 21252-7097. 410-704-7374. Fax 410-704-4115. Internet site <http://www.resiusa.org/>

Maryland Statistical Abstract. 2003.

Massachusetts

Massachusetts Institute for Social and Economic Research, University of Massachusetts, 128 Thompson Hall, 200 Hicks Way, Amherst, MA 01003-9277. 413-545-3460. FAX 413-5453686. Internet site <http://www.umass.edu/miser/>

Michigan

Michigan Economic Development Coporation, 300 North Washington Square, Lansing, MI 48913. 517-373-9808. Internet Site <http://medc.michigan.org/miinfo/>

Michigan Info. Online only.

Minnesota

Minnesota Department of Employment and Economic Development, 500 Metro Square Building, 121 East 7th Place, St. Paul, MN 55101-2146. 800-657-3858. Internet site <http://www.deed.state.mn.us/facts/index.htm>

Compare Minnesota: Profiles of Minnesota's Economy and Population, 2002-2003.

State Demographic Center, Department of Administration, Centennial Bldg., 658 Cedar Street, St. Paul, MN 55155. 651-296-2557. Internet Site <http://www.demography.state.mn.us/>

Mississippi

Mississippi State University, College of Business and Industry, Division of Research, P.O. Box 5288, Mississippi State, MS 39762. 662-325-3817. Fax 662-325-8686.

Mississippi Statistical Abstract, 2003.

Missouri

University of Missouri, Economic and Policy Analysis Research Center, 10 Professional Bldg., Columbia, MO 65211. 573-882-4805. Internet site <http://econ.missouri.edu/eparc/SAM_2003/Index.html>

Statistical Abstract for Missouri, 2003. Biennial. Online only.

Montana

Census and Economic Information Center, Montana Department of Commerce, 301 S. Park, P.O. Box 200505, Helena, MT 59620-0505. 406-841-2740. Internet site <http://ceic.commerce.state.mt.us/>

Nebraska

Nebraska Department of Economic Development, P.O. Box 94666,301 Centennial Mall South, Lincoln, NE 68509-4666. 402-471-3111. Fax 402-471-3778. Internet site <http://info.neded.org/>

Nebraska Data Book. Online only.

Nevada

Department of Administration, Budget and Planning Division, 209 East Musser Street, Suite 200, Carson City, NV 89701. 775-684-0222. Internet site <http://www.budget.state.nv.us/>

Nevada Statistical Abstract, 2004. Biennial Report 2001-2002.

New Hampshire

NH Office of Energy and Planning, 57 Regional Drive, Suite 3, Concord, NH 03301. 603-271-2155. Fax 603-271-2615. Internet site <http://www.nh.gov/oep>

New Jersey

New Jersey State Data Center, NJ Department of Labor, P.O. Box 388, Trenton, NJ 08625-0388. 609-984-2595. Internet site <http://www.state.nj.us/labor/lra/>

Labor Market Information. Online only.

New Mexico

University of New Mexico, Bureau of Business and Economic Research, MSC02 1720, Albuquerque, NM 87131-0001. 505-277-2216. Fax 505-277-7066. Internet site <http://www.unm.edu/~bber/>

New Mexico Business, Current Economic Report Monthly.

FOR-UNM Bulletin Quarterly.

New York

Nelson A. Rockefeller Institute of Government, 411 State Street, Albany, NY 12203-1003. 518-443-5522. Internet site <http://www.rockinst.org/>

New York State Statistical Yearbook, 2003. 28th ed.

North Carolina

Office of Governor, Office of State Budget and Management, Management Section, Data Services Unit, 116 West Jones Street, Raleigh, NC 27699-8005. 919-733-7061. Fax 919-7330640. Internet site <http://www.osbm.state.nc.us/osbm/>

How North Carolina Ranks, 2004. Online only.

North Dakota

University of North Dakota, Bureau of Business and Economic Research, P.O. Box 8369, Grand Forks, ND 58202. 701-7776219. Fax 701-777-3365. Internet site <http://business.und.edu/bber/>

North Dakota Statistical Abstract.

Ohio

Office of Strategic Research, Ohio Department of Development, P.O. Box 1001, 77 S. High Street, Columbus, OH 43216-1001. 1-800-848-1300. Internet site <http://www.odod.state.oh.us/research>

Research products and services. Updated continuously.

Ohio County Profiles; Ohio County Indicators Updated periodically.

Oklahoma

University of Oklahoma, Center for Economic and Management Research, Michael F. Price College of Business, 307 West Brooks Street, Norman, OK 73019. 405-325-2931. Fax 405-3257688. Internet site <http://cemr.ou.edu/>

Statistical Abstract of Oklahoma, 1999.

Oregon

Secretary of State, Archives Division, Archives Bldg., 800 Summer Street, NE Salem, OR 97310. 503-373-0701. Internet site <http://www.sos.state.or.us/>

Oregon Blue Book. 2003-2004. Biennial.

Pennsylvania

Pennsylvania State Data Center, Institute of State and Regional Affairs, Penn State Harrisburg, 777 West Harrisburg Pike, Middletown, PA 17057-4898. 717-948-6336. Internet site <http://pasdc.hbg.psu.edu>

Pennsylvania Abstract, A Statistical Fact Book, 2004.

Rhode Island

Rhode Island Economic Development Corporation, 1 West Exchange Street, Providence, RI 02903. 401-222-2601. Internet site <http://www.riedc.com/>

Rhode Island Annual Economic Trends, 2002.

South Carolina

Budget and Control Board, Office of Research and Statistics, 1919 Blanding Street, Columbia 29201. 803-898-9940. Internet site <http://www.ors2.state .sc.us/abstract/index.asp>

South Carolina Statistical Abstract, 2004.

South Dakota

South Dakota State Data Center, Business Research Bureau, The University of South Dakota, 414 E. Clark Street, Vermillion, SD 57069. 605-677-5287. Fax: 605-677-5427. Internet site <http://www.usd.edu/brbinfo/>

2002 South Dakota Community Abstracts.

Tennessee

University of Tennessee, Center for Business and Economic Research, College of Business Administration, 100 Glocker Bldg., Knoxville, TN 37996-4170. 865-974-5441. Internet site <http://cber.bus.utk.edu/Default.htm>

Tennessee Statistical Abstract, 2003.

Texas

Dallas Morning News, Communications Center, P.O. Box 655237, Dallas, TX 75265-5237. 214-977-8261. Internet Site <http://www.texasalmanac.com/>

Texas Almanac, 2004-2005.

Utah

Governor's Office of Planning and Budget, Demographic & Economic Analysis, State Capitol Complex, Suite 210, East Office Building, Salt Lake City, UT 84114-2210. 801-538-1027.

2001 Economic Report to the Governor. Annual.

Utah Data Guide Newsletter. Quarterly.

Vermont

Labor Market Information, Department of Employment and Training, P.O. Box 488, Montpelier, VT 05601-0488. 802-828-4202. Internet site <http://www.vtlmi.info/>

Vermont Economic-Demographic Profile. Annual.

Virginia

Weldon Cooper Center, P.O. Box 400206, Charlottesville, VA 22904-4206. 434-982-5582. Internet site <http://www.ccps.virginia.edu /demographics/>

Virginia Statistical Abstract. Online only.

Washington

Washington State Office of Financial Management, Forecasting Division P.O. Box 43113 Olympia, WA 98504-3113. 360-902-0555. Internet site <http://www.ofm.wa.gov/>

Washington State Data Book, 2003. Biennial.

West Virginia

West Virginia University, College of Business and Economics, Bureau of Business and Economic Research, P.O. Box 6025, Morgantown, WV 26506-6025. 304-293-7835. Internet site <http://www.bber.wvu.edu/>

2003 West Virginia County Data Profiles.

West Virginia Economic Outlook, 2004. Annual.

West Virginia Research League, Inc., P.O. Box 11176, Charleston, WV 25339. 304-766-9495. Internet site <http://www.wvrl.org/>

The 2001 Statistical Handbook. Annual.

Wisconsin

Wisconsin Legislative Reference Bureau, P.O. Box 2037, Madison, WI 53701-2037. 608-266-0341 Internet site <http://www.legis.state.wi.us/lrb/bb/>

2003-2004 Wisconsin Blue Book. Biennial.

Wyoming

Department of Administration and Information, Economic Analysis Division, 1807 Capitol Avenue, Suite 206, Cheyenne, WY 82002-0060. 307-777-7504. Internet site <http://eadiv.state.wy.us/>

The Equality State Almanac, 2002.

Guide to Foreign Statistical Abstracts

This bibliography presents recent statistical abstracts for member nations of the Organisation for Economic Cooperation and Development and Russia. All sources contain statistical tables on a variety of subjects for the individual countries. Many of the following publications provide text in English as well as in the national language(s). For further information on these publications, contact the named statistical agency which is responsible for editing the publication.

Australia

Australian Bureau of Statistics, Canberra. http://www.abs.gov.au.

Year Book Australia. Annual. 2004. 872 pp. (In English.)

Austria

Statistik Austria, A-1033 Wien. http://www.statistik.at/index.shtml.

Statistisches Jahrbuch Osterreichs. Annual. 2004. 620 pp. With CD-ROM. (In German.) With English translations of table headings.

Belgium

Institut National de Statistique, Rue de Louvain; 44-1000 Bruxelles. http://statbel.fgov.be/info/linksen.asp.

Annuaire statistique de la Belgique. Annual. 1995. 820 pp. (In French.)

Canada

Statistics Canada, Ottawa, Ontario, KIA OT6. http://www.statcan.ca/start.html.

Canada Yearbook: A review of economic, social and political developments in Canada. 2001. 563 pp. Irregular. (In English.)

Czech Republic

Czech Statistical Office, Sokolovska 142, 186 04 Praha 8; http://www.czso.cz/.

Statisticka Rocenka Ceske Rpubliky 2003. 739 pp. (In English and Czech.)

Denmark

Danmarks Statistik, Sejrogade 11, 2100 Kobenhavn O. http://www.dst.dk/665.

Statistisk ARBOG. 2004. Annual. 600 pp. (Printed version - In Danish only.)

Finland

Statistics Finland, Helsinki. http://www.stat.fi/

Statistical Yearbook of Finland, Annual. 2003. 704 pp. with CD-ROM (In English, Finnish, and Swedish.)

France

Institut National de la Statistique et des Etudes Economiques, Paris 18, Bld. Adolphe Pinard, 75675 Paris (Cedex 14). http://www.insee.fr/fr/home/home_page.asp.

Annuaire Statistique de la France. Annual. 2003. 586 pp. (In French.) 2004 CD-ROM only.

Germany

Statistische Bundesamt, D-65180 Wiesbaden. http://www.destatis.de.

Statistisches Jahrbuch fur die Bundesrepublic Deutschland. Annual. 2003. 738 pp. (In German.)

Statistisches Jahrbuch fur das Ausland. 2003. 368 pp.

Greece

National Statistical Service of Greece, Athens. http://www.statistics.gr/.

Concise Statistical Yearbook 2002. 277 pp. (plus 11 pages of graphs) (In English and Greek).

Statistical Yearbook of Greece. Annual. 2002. 565 pp. (plus 6 pages of graphs). (In English and Greek.)

Hungary

Hungarian Central Statistical Office, 1024 Budapest. http://www.ksh.hu.

Statistical Yearbook of Hungary, 2002 with CD-ROM. 617 pp. (In English and Hungarian.)

Iceland

Hagstofa Islands/Statistics Iceland; http://www.hagstofa.is/template41.asp?PageID=251.

Statistical Yearbook of Iceland. 2003 with CD-ROM. Irregular. 346 pp. (In English and Icelandic.)

Ireland

Central Statistics Office, Skehard Road, Cork. http://www.cso.ie.

Statistical Yearbook of Ireland. Annual. 2003. 449 pp. (In English.)

Italy

ISTAT (Istituto Centrale di Statistica); http://www.istat.it. Via Cesare Balbo 16 Roma.

Annuario Statistico Italiano. Annual. 2003 with CD-ROM. 747 pp. (In Italian.)

Japan

Statistics Bureau, Ministry of Public Management, Home Affairs Posts and Telecommunications, Japan. www.stat.go.jp/english/data/index.htm.

Japan Statistical Yearbook. Annual. 2004. 951 pp. (In English and Japanese.)

U.S. Census Bureau, Statistical Abstract of the United States: 2004-2005

Korea, South
National Statistical Office, Government Complex, #920 Dunsan-dong Seo-gu Daejeon 302-701. http://www.nso.go.kr/.
Korea Statistical Yearbook. Annual. 2003 with CD-ROM. 856 pp. (In Korean and English.)

Luxembourg
STATEC (Service Central de la Statistique et des Etudes), B.P. 304, L-2013, Luxembourg. http://statec.gouvernement.lu/.
Annuaire Statistique. Annual. 2002. (In French.) (Alphabetical numbering system.)

Mexico
Instituto Nacional de Estadistica Geografia e Informatica, Av. Heroe Nacozari Num. 2301 Sur Fracc. Jardines del Parque, CP 20270 Aguascalientes, Ags. http://www.inegi.gob.mx.
Anuario estadistico de los Estados Unidos Mexicanos. Annual. 2002. 727 pp. Also on disc. (In Spanish.) *Agenda Estadistica 2001.* 149 pp.

Netherlands
Statistics Netherlands, R L Vellekoop. Prinses Beatrixiaan 428, 2273 X Z Voorburg; http://www.cbs.nl/en/.
Statistical Yearbook 2004 of the Netherlands. 520 pp. (In English.)
Statistisch Jaarboek 2004 529 pp. with CD-ROM.

New Zealand
Department of Statistics, Wellington. http://www.stats.govt.nz/.
New Zealand Official Yearbook. Annual. 2002. 627 pp. (In English.)

Norway
Statistics Norway, Oslo/Kongsvinger. http://www.ssb.no/english/subjects/.
Statistical Yearbook. Annual. 2002. 539 pp. (In English.)

Poland
Central Statistical Office al. Niepodleglosci 208, 00-925 Warsaw. http://www.stat.gov.pl/english/index.htm.
Concise Statistical Yearbook 2003. (In Polish and English.) Statistical Yearbook of the Republic of Poland 2002. (In Polish and English.)

Portugal 2
INE (Instituto Nacional de Estatistica). http://www.ine.pt/index_eng.htm. Avenida Antonio Jose de Almeida P-1000-043 Lisboa.
Anuario Estatistico de Portugal. 2002. (In Portuguese and English.)

Russia
State Committee of Statistics of Russia, Moscow. http://www.gks.ru/eng/.
Statistical Yearbook. 2003. 705 pp. (In Russian.)

Slovakia
Statistical Office of the Slovak Republic, Bradacova 7, 852 86 Bratislava. http://www.statistics.sk/webdata/english/index2a.htm.
Statisticka Rocenka Slovenskej Republik. 2000. 719 pp. Plus 16 pages of graphs. (In English and Slovak.)

Spain
INE (Instituto Nacional de Estadistica); Paseo de la Castellana, 183, Madrid 16. http://www.ine.es/welcoing.htm.
Espana Anuaria Estadistico Annual. 2002-2003. 768 pp. 16 pages of graphs (In Spanish.)

Sweden
Statistics Sweden, S-11581 Stockholm. http://www.scb.se/indexeng.asp.
Statistisk Arsbok for Sverige. Annual. 2004 with CD-ROM.. 725 pp. (In English and Swedish.)

Switzerland
Bundesamt fur Statistik, Hallwylstrasse 15, CH-3003, Bern
Statistisches Jahrbuch der Schweiz. Annual. 2004. 901 pp. with CD-ROM (In French and German.)

Turkey
State Institute of Statistics, Prime Ministry, 114 Necatibey Caddesi, Bakanliklar, Yenisehir, Ankara
Statistical Yearbook of Turkey. 1999. 721 pp. (In English and Turkish.)
Turkey in Statistics 1999 144 pp. (In English only.)

United Kingdom
The Stationary Office; P.O. Box 29, Norwich, NR3 1GN. http://www.statistics.gov.uk/.
Annual Abstract of Statistics. Annual. 2002. 429 pp. (In English.)

Metropolitan and Micropolitan Statistical Areas: Concepts, Components, and Population

The United States Office of Management and Budget (OMB) defines metropolitan and micropolitan statistical areas according to published standards that are applied to Census Bureau data. The general concept of a metropolitan or micropolitan statistical area is that of a core area containing a substantial population nucleus, together with adjacent communities having a high degree of economic and social integration with that core. Currently defined metropolitan and micropolitan statistical areas are based on application of 2000 standards (which appeared in the Federal Register on December 27, 2000) to 2000 decennial census data. Current metropolitan and micropolitan statistical area definitions were announced by OMB effective June 6, 2003 and subsequently updated as of December 2003.

Standard definitions of metropolitan areas were first issued in 1949 by the then Bureau of the Budget (predecessor of OMB), under the designation "standard metropolitan area" (SMA). The term was changed to "standard metropolitan statistical area" (SMSA) in 1959 and to "metropolitan statistical area" (MSA) in 1983. The term "metropolitan area" (MA) was adopted in 1990 and referred collectively to metropolitan statistical areas (MSAs), consolidated metropolitan statistical areas (CMSAs), and primary metropolitan statistical areas (PMSAs). The term "core based statistical area" (CBSA) became effective in 2000 and refers collectively to metropolitan and micropolitan statistical areas.

OMB has been responsible for the official metropolitan areas since they were first defined, except for the period 1977 to 1981, when they were the responsibility of the Office of Federal Statistical Policy and Standards, Department of Commerce. The standards for defining metropolitan areas were modified in 1958, 1971, 1975, 1980, 1990, and 2000.

Defining Metropolitan and Micropolitan Statistical Areas—The 2000 standards provide that each CBSA must contain at least 1 urban area of 10,000 or more population. Each metropolitan statistical area must have at least 1 urbanized area of 50,000 or more inhabitants. Each micropolitan statistical area must have at least 1 urban cluster of at least 10,000 but less than 50,000 population.

Under the standards, the county (or counties) in which at least 50 percent of the population resides within urban areas of 10,000 or more population, or that contain at least 5,000 people residing within a single urban area of 10,000 or more population, is identified as a "central county" (counties). Additional "outlying counties" are included in the CBSA if they meet specified requirements of commuting to or from the central counties. Counties or equivalent entities form the geographic "building blocks" for metropolitan and micropolitan statistical areas throughout the United States and Puerto Rico.

If specified criteria are met, a metropolitan statistical area containing a single core with a population of 2.5 million or more may be subdivided to form smaller groupings of counties referred to as "metropolitan divisions."

As of December 2003, there are 361 metropolitan statistical areas and 573 micropolitan statistical areas in the United States. In addition, there are eight metropolitan statistical areas and five micropolitan statistical areas in Puerto Rico.

Principal Cities and Metropolitan and Micropolitan Statistical Area Titles— The largest city in each metropolitan or micropolitan statistical area is designated a "principal city." Additional cities qualify if specified requirements are met concerning population size and employment. The title of each metropolitan or micropolitan statistical area consists of the names of up to three of its principal cities and the name of each state into which the metropolitan or micropolitan statistical area extends. Titles of metropolitan divisions also typically are based on principal city names but in certain cases consist of county names.

Text continued on page 906.

Appendix II 901

Figure A1

Metropolitan and Micropolitan Statistical Areas of the United States

As defined by the U.S. Office of Management and Budget, December 2003

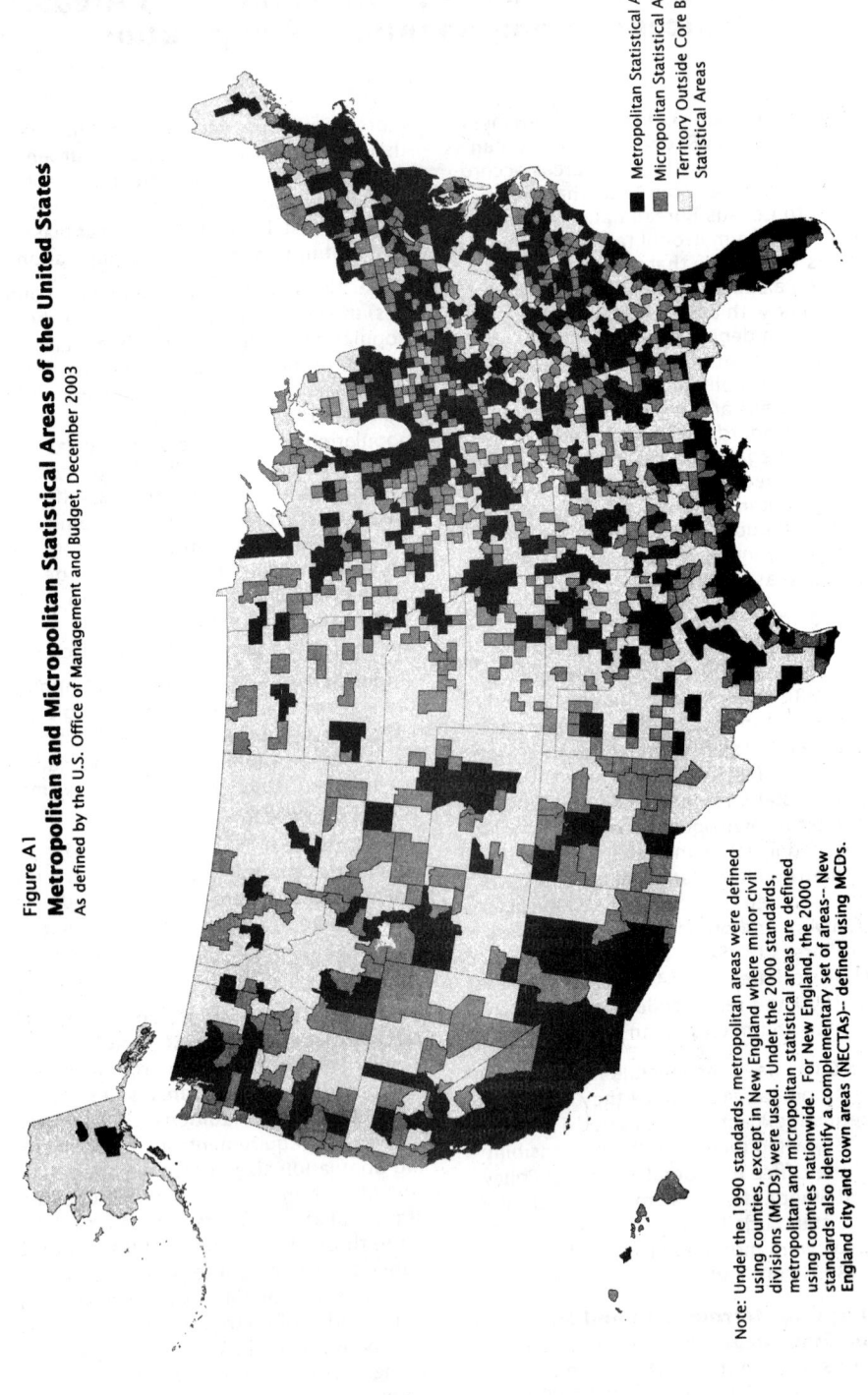

Metropolitan Statistical Area
Micropolitan Statistical Area
Territory Outside Core Based
Statistical Areas

Note: Under the 1990 standards, metropolitan areas were defined using counties, except in New England where minor civil divisions (MCDs) were used. Under the 2000 standards, metropolitan and micropolitan statistical areas are defined using counties nationwide. For New England, the 2000 standards also identify a complementary set of areas-- New England city and town areas (NECTAs)-- defined using MCDs.

Metropolitan Areas of the United States

Metropolitan Statistical Areas (MSAs) and Consolidated Metropolitan Statistical Areas (CMSAs) defined by the U.S. Office of Management and Budget, June 30, 1999

Metropolitan Area (CMSAs and MSAs)

Territory Outside Metropolitan Areas

Note: Under the 1990 standards, metropolitan areas were defined using counties, except in New England where minor civil divisions (MCDs) were used. Under the 2000 standards, metropolitan and micropolitan statistical areas are defined using counties nationwide. For New England, the 2000 standards also identify a complementary set of areas-- New England city and town areas (NECTAs)-- defined using MCDs.

Metropolitan and Micropolitan New England City and Town Areas (NECTAs)
As defined by the U.S. Office of Management and Budget, December 2003

Metropolitan NECTA

Micropolitan NECTA

Territory Outside NECTAs

Note: Under the 1990 standards, metropolitan areas were defined using counties, except in New England where minor civil divisions (MCDs) were used. Under the 2000 standards, metropolitan and micropolitan statistical areas are defined using counties nationwide. For New England, the 2000 standards also identify a complementary set of areas-- New England city and town areas (NECTAs) -- defined using MCDs.

New England Metropolitan Areas

Metropolitan Statistical Areas (MSAs) and Consolidated Metropolitan Statistical Areas (CMSAs) defineɑ
by the U.S. Office of Management and Budget, June 30, 1999

■ Metropolitan Area (CMSAs and MSAs)

☐ Territory Outside Metropolitan Areas

Note: Under the 1990 standards, metropolitan areas were defined using counties, except in New England
where minor civil divisions (MCDs) were used. Under the 2000 standards, metropolitan and
micropolitan statistical areas are defined using counties nationwide. For New England, the 2000
standards also identify a complementary set of areas-- New England city and town areas (NECTAs)
-- defined using MCDs.

U.S. Census Bureau, Statistical Abstract of the United States: 2004-2005

Defining New England City and Town Areas—In view of the importance of cities and town in New England, the 2000 standards also provide for a set of geographic areas that are defined using cities and towns in the six New England states. The New England city and town areas (NECTAs) are defined using the same criteria as metropolitan and micropolitan statistical areas and are identified as either metropolitan or micropolitan, based, respectively, on the presence of either an urbanized area of 50,000 or more population or an urban cluster of at least 10,000 but less than 50,000 population. If the specified criteria are met, a NECTA containing a single core with a population of at least 2.5 million may be subdivided to form smaller groupings of cities and towns referred to as New England city and town area divisions.

Changes in Definitions Over Time—Changes in the definitions of these statistical areas since the 1950 census have consisted chiefly of (1) the recognition of new areas as they reached the minimum required city or urbanized area population and (2) the addition of counties (or cities and towns in New England) to existing areas as new decennial census data showed them to qualify.

In some instances, formerly separate areas have been merged, components of an area have been transferred from one area to another, or components have been dropped from an area. The large majority of changes have taken place on the basis of decennial census data. However, Census Bureau data serve as the basis for intercensal updates in specified circumstances.

Because of these historical changes in geographic definitions, users must be cautious in comparing data for these statistical areas from different dates. For some purposes, comparisons of data for areas as defined at given dates may be appropriate; for other purposes, it may be preferable to maintain consistent area definitions. Historical metropolitan area definitions are available for 1999, 1993, 1990, 1983, 1981, 1973, 1970, 1963, 1960, and 1950.

Excluding Table 24 in the Population section; Table 655 in the Income section, and the tables that follow in this appendix, the tables presenting data for metropolitan areas in this edition of the *Statistical Abstract* are based on the 1999 or earlier metropolitan area definitions. For a list of component counties according to the 1999 definition, see Appendix II in the 2002 edition of the *Statistical Abstract* or <http://www.census.gov/population/www/estimates/pastmetro.html>.

Table A. Metropolitan Statistical Areas and Components as of December 2003

[Population as of **July 2003**. **158** represents 158,000. All metropolitan areas are arranged alphabetically]

Metropolitan statistical area Metropolitan division Component county	Population, 2003 (1,000)	Metropolitan statistical area Metropolitan division Component county	Population, 2003 (1,000)	Metropolitan statistical area Metropolitan division Component county	Population, 2003 (1,000)
Abilene, TX	**158**	Henderson County, NC .	94	**Barnstable Town, MA**	**230**
Callahan County, TX . . .	13	Madison County, NC . . .	20	Barnstable County, MA. .	230
Jones County, TX	20	**Athens-Clarke County, GA** .	**172**	**Baton Rouge, LA**	**723**
Taylor County, TX	125	Clarke County, GA	104	Ascension Parish, LA. . .	84
Akron, OH	**702**	Madison County, GA . . .	27	East Baton Rouge	
Portage County, OH. . . .	155	Oconee County, GA. . . .	28	Parish, LA	412
Summit County, OH. . . .	547	Oglethorpe County, GA .	13	East Feliciana Parish,	
Albany, GA	**161**	**Atlanta-Sandy Springs-**		LA	21
Baker County, GA	4	**Marietta, GA**	**4,610**	Iberville Parish, LA. . .	33
Dougherty County, GA. .	96	Barrow County, GA	53	Livingston Parish, LA . .	102
Lee County, GA.	28	Bartow County, GA	85	Pointe Coupee Parish,	
Terrell County, GA	11	Butts County, GA.	22	LA	23
Worth County, GA	22	Carroll County, GA. . . .	99	St. Helena Parish, LA . .	10
		Cherokee County, GA . .	167	West Baton Rouge	
Albany-Schenectady-Troy,		Clayton County, GA. . . .	260	Parish, LA	22
NY	**841**	Cobb County, GA	651	West Feliciana Parish,	
Albany County, NY	298	Coweta County, GA	101	LA	15
Rensselaer County, NY .	154	Dawson County, GA . . .	19	**Battle Creek, MI**	**139**
Saratoga County, NY . . .	210	DeKalb County, GA	674	Calhoun County, MI. . . .	139
Schenectady County,		Douglas County, GA . . .	102		
NY	147	Fayette County, GA	99	**Bay City, MI**	**109**
Schoharie County, NY . .	32	Forsyth County, GA	124	Bay County, MI	109
Albuquerque, NM	**765**	Fulton County, GA. . . .	818	**Beaumont-Port Arthur, TX**. .	**383**
Bernalillo County, NM. . .	581	Gwinnett County, GA . . .	673	Hardin County, TX.	50
Sandoval County, NM . .	99	Haralson County, GA . . .	27	Jefferson County, TX . . .	249
Torrance County, NM . .	17	Heard County, GA	11	Orange County, TX	84
Valencia County, NM . . .	68	Henry County, GA	150	**Bellingham, WA**	**177**
Alexandria, LA	**146**	Jasper County, GA	13	Whatcom County, WA . .	177
Grant Parish, LA	19	Lamar County, GA	16	**Bend, OR**	**129**
Rapides Parish, LA	127	Meriwether County, GA .	23	Deschutes County, OR. .	129
Allentown-Bethlehem-		Newton County, GA. . . .	76		
Easton, PA-NJ	**768**	Paulding County, GA . . .	100	**Billings, MT**	**143**
Warren County, NJ	109	Pickens County, GA . . .	27	Carbon County, MT	10
Carbon County, PA	60	Pike County, GA	15	Yellowstone County, MT.	133
Lehigh County, PA.	321	Rockdale County, GA. . .	75	**Binghamton, NY**	**251**
Northampton County,		Spalding County, GA. . .	60	Broome County, NY. . . .	199
PA	278	Walton County, GA	69	Tioga County, NY	52
Altoona, PA	**127**	**Atlantic City, NJ**	**263**	**Birmingham-Hoover, AL** . . .	**1,073**
Blair County, PA	127	Atlantic County, NJ	263	Bibb County, AL	21
Amarillo, TX	**233**	**Auburn-Opelika, AL**	**120**	Blount County, AL	54
Armstrong County, TX . .	2	Lee County, AL	120	Chilton County, AL.	41
Carson County, TX	7	**Augusta-Richmond County,**		Jefferson County, AL . . .	658
Potter County, TX	117	**GA-SC**	**511**	St. Clair County, AL. . . .	69
Randall County, TX	107	Burke County, GA	23	Shelby County, AL.	159
Ames, IA	**83**	Columbia County, GA. . .	98	Walker County, AL.	70
Story County, IA	83	McDuffie County, GA . . .	21	**Bismarck, ND**	**97**
Anchorage, AK	**339**	Richmond County, GA . .	198	Burleigh County, ND . . .	72
Anchorage Borough, AK .	271	Aiken County, SC	147	Morton County, ND	25
Matanuska-Susitna		Edgefield County, SC. . .	25	**Blacksburg-Christiansburg-**	
Borough, AK	68	**Austin-Round Rock, TX**. . . .	**1,378**	**Radford, VA**	**153**
Anderson, IN	**131**	Bastrop County, TX	67	Giles County, VA	17
Madison County, IN	131	Caldwell County, TX. . . .	36	Montgomery County, VA.	86
Anderson, SC	**172**	Hays County, TX	114	Pulaski County, VA	35
Anderson County, SC. . .	172	Travis County, TX	857	Radford city, VA	15
Ann Arbor, MI	**339**	Williamson County, TX . .	304	**Bloomington, IN**	**179**
Washtenaw County, MI. .	339	**Bakersfield, CA**	**713**	Greene County, IN.	33
Anniston-Oxford, AL	**112**	Kern County, CA	713	Monroe County, IN.	123
Calhoun County, AL. . . .	112	**Baltimore-Towson, MD**	**2,616**	Owen County, IN.	23
Appleton, WI	**211**	Anne Arundel County,		**Bloomington-Normal, IL** . . .	**157**
Calumet County, WI. . . .	43	MD	507	McLean County, IL.	157
Outagamie County, WI . .	167	Baltimore County, MD . .	777	**Boise City-Nampa, ID**	**511**
Asheville, NC	**382**	Carroll County, MD	163	Ada County, ID	325
Buncombe County, NC. .	213	Harford County, MD	232	Boise County, ID	7
Haywood County, NC. . .	55	Howard County, MD. . . .	264	Canyon County, ID	152
		Queen Anne's County,		Gem County, ID	16
		MD	44	Owyhee County, ID	11
		Baltimore city, MD	629		
		Bangor, ME	**147**		
		Penobscot County, ME. .	147		

Appendix II **907**

Metropolitan statistical area / Metropolitan division / Component county	Population, 2003 (1,000)
Boston-Cambridge-Quincy, MA-NH	**4,440**
Boston-Quincy, MA	**1,823**
Norfolk County, MA	654
Plymouth County, MA	488
Suffolk County, MA	681
Cambridge-Newton-Framingham, MA	**1,472**
Middlesex County, MA	1,472
Essex County, MA	**738**
Essex County, MA	738
Rockingham County-Strafford County, NH	**408**
Rockingham County, NH	290
Strafford County, NH	118
Boulder, CO	**278**
Boulder County, CO	278
Bowling Green, KY	**108**
Edmonson County, KY	12
Warren County, KY	96
Bremerton-Silverdale, WA	**241**
Kitsap County, WA	241
Bridgeport-Stamford-Norwalk, CT	**899**
Fairfield County, CT	899
Brownsville-Harlingen, TX	**363**
Cameron County, TX	363
Brunswick, GA	**96**
Brantley County, GA	15
Glynn County, GA	70
McIntosh County, GA	11
Buffalo-Niagara Falls, NY	**1,159**
Erie County, NY	941
Niagara County, NY	218
Burlington, NC	**137**
Alamance County, NC	137
Burlington-South Burlington, VT	**204**
Chittenden County, VT	149
Franklin County, VT	47
Grand Isle County, VT	7
Canton-Massillon, OH	**407**
Carroll County, OH	30
Stark County, OH	378
Cape Coral-Fort Myers, FL	**492**
Lee County, FL	492
Carson City, NV	**55**
Carson City, NV	55
Casper, WY	**68**
Natrona County, WY	68
Cedar Rapids, IA	**243**
Benton County, IA	26
Jones County, IA	20
Linn County, IA	196
Champaign-Urbana, IL	**217**
Champaign County, IL	187
Ford County, IL	14
Piatt County, IL	16
Charleston, WV	**307**
Boone County, WV	26
Clay County, WV	10
Kanawha County, WV	195
Lincoln County, WV	22
Putnam County, WV	53

Metropolitan statistical area / Metropolitan division / Component county	Population, 2003 (1,000)
Charleston-North Charleston, SC	**572**
Berkeley County, SC	146
Charleston County, SC	321
Dorchester County, SC	104
Charlotte-Gastonia-Concord, NC-SC	**1,437**
Anson County, NC	25
Cabarrus County, NC	143
Gaston County, NC	193
Mecklenburg County, NC	752
Union County, NC	146
York County, SC	178
Charlottesville, VA	**182**
Albemarle County, VA	88
Fluvanna County, VA	23
Greene County, VA	17
Nelson County, VA	15
Charlottesville city, VA	39
Chattanooga, TN-GA	**486**
Catoosa County, GA	58
Dade County, GA	16
Walker County, GA	63
Hamilton County, TN	310
Marion County, TN	28
Sequatchie County, TN	12
Cheyenne, WY	**84**
Laramie County, WY	84
Chicago-Naperville-Joliet, IL-IN-WI	**9,334**
Chicago-Naperville-Joliet, IL	**7,807**
Cook County, IL	5,352
DeKalb County, IL	94
DuPage County, IL	925
Grundy County, IL	40
Kane County, IL	457
Kendall County, IL	67
McHenry County, IL	286
Will County, IL	587
Gary, IN	**685**
Jasper County, IN	31
Lake County, IN	487
Newton County, IN	14
Porter County, IN	153
Lake County-Kenosha County, IL-WI	**841**
Lake County, IL	685
Kenosha County, WI	156
Chico, CA	**211**
Butte County, CA	211
Cincinnati-Middletown, OH-KY-IN	**2,047**
Dearborn County, IN	48
Franklin County, IN	23
Ohio County, IN	6
Boone County, KY	97
Bracken County, KY	8
Campbell County, KY	88
Gallatin County, KY	8
Grant County, KY	24
Kenton County, KY	152
Pendleton County, KY	15
Brown County, OH	44
Butler County, OH	343
Clermont County, OH	186
Hamilton County, OH	823
Warren County, OH	182
Clarksville, TN-KY	**237**
Christian County, KY	70
Trigg County, KY	13
Montgomery County, TN	141
Stewart County, TN	13

Metropolitan statistical area / Metropolitan division / Component county	Population, 2003 (1,000)
Cleveland, TN	**106**
Bradley County, TN	90
Polk County, TN	16
Cleveland-Elyria-Mentor, OH	**2,140**
Cuyahoga County, OH	1,364
Geauga County, OH	94
Lake County, OH	229
Lorain County, OH	291
Medina County, OH	162
Coeur d'Alene, ID	**117**
Kootenai County, ID	117
College Station-Bryan, TX	**193**
Brazos County, TX	160
Burleson County, TX	17
Robertson County, TX	16
Colorado Springs, CO	**572**
El Paso County, CO	550
Teller County, CO	22
Columbia, MO	**151**
Boone County, MO	141
Howard County, MO	10
Columbia, SC	**671**
Calhoun County, SC	15
Fairfield County, SC	24
Kershaw County, SC	54
Lexington County, SC	227
Richland County, SC	332
Saluda County, SC	19
Columbus, GA-AL	**287**
Russell County, AL	49
Chattahoochee County, GA	19
Harris County, GA	26
Marion County, GA	7
Muscogee County, GA	186
Columbus, IN	**72**
Bartholomew County, IN	72
Columbus, OH	**1,675**
Delaware County, OH	133
Fairfield County, OH	133
Franklin County, OH	1,089
Licking County, OH	151
Madison County, OH	41
Morrow County, OH	34
Pickaway County, OH	52
Union County, OH	44
Corpus Christi, TX	**407**
Aransas County, TX	24
Nueces County, TX	315
San Patricio County, TX	68
Corvallis, OR	**79**
Benton County, OR	79
Cumberland, MD-WV	**101**
Allegany County, MD	74
Mineral County, WV	27
Dallas-Fort Worth-Arlington, TX	**5,590**
Dallas-Plano-Irving, TX	**3,740**
Collin County, TX	597
Dallas County, TX	2,284
Delta County, TX	5
Denton County, TX	511
Ellis County, TX	124
Hunt County, TX	81
Kaufman County, TX	82
Rockwall County, TX	55

U.S. Census Bureau, Statistical Abstract of the United States: 2004-2005

Metropolitan statistical area / Metropolitan division / Component county	Population, 2003 (1,000)	Metropolitan statistical area / Metropolitan division / Component county	Population, 2003 (1,000)	Metropolitan statistical area / Metropolitan division / Component county	Population, 2003 (1,000)
Fort Worth-Arlington, TX .	**1,850**	**Duluth, MN-WI . . . .**	**276**	**Fort Collins-Loveland, CO. .**	**267**
Johnson County, TX. . . .	139	Carlton County, MN	33	Larimer County, CO. . . .	267
Parker County, TX.	97	St. Louis County, MN. . .	199		
Tarrant County, TX.	1,559	Douglas County, WI. . . .	44	**Fort Smith, AR-OK . . . .**	**280**
Wise County, TX	54			Crawford County, AR . . .	56
		Durham, NC	**447**	Franklin County, AR. . . .	18
Dalton, GA	**127**	Chatham County, NC. . .	55	Sebastian County, AR . . .	117
Murray County, GA	39	Durham County, NC. . . .	237	Le Flore County, OK . . .	49
Whitfield County, GA . . .	88	Orange County, NC	118	Sequoyah County, OK . . .	40
		Person County, NC	37		
Danville, IL	**83**			**Fort Walton Beach-**	
Vermilion County, IL. . . .	83	**Eau Claire, WI. . . . .**	**151**	**Crestview-Destin, FL. . . . .**	**178**
		Chippewa County, WI. . .	57	Okaloosa County, FL . . .	178
Danville, VA	**109**	Eau Claire County, WI . .	94		
Pittsylvania County, VA. .	62			**Fort Wayne, IN . . . .**	**400**
Danville city, VA	47	**El Centro, CA . . . .**	**149**	Allen County, IN	340
		Imperial County, CA. . . .	149	Wells County, IN	28
Davenport-Moline-Rock				Whitley County, IN.	32
Island, IA-IL	**375**	**Elizabethtown, KY. . . . .**	**109**		
Henry County, IL.	51	Hardin County, KY.	96	**Fresno, CA. . . . .**	**850**
Mercer County, IL.	17	Larue County, KY	13	Fresno County, CA	850
Rock Island County, IL. .	148				
Scott County, IA	159	**Elkhart-Goshen, IN . . . .**	**189**	**Gadsden, AL. . . . .**	**103**
		Elkhart County, IN.	189	Etowah County, AL	103
Dayton, OH.	**846**				
Greene County, OH. . . .	151	**Elmira, NY . . . .**	**90**	**Gainesville, FL . . . .**	**239**
Miami County, OH.	100	Chemung County, NY . .	90	Alachua County, FL. . . .	224
Montgomery County,				Gilchrist County, FL. . . .	16
OH.	552	**El Paso, TX. . . . .**	**705**		
Preble County, OH. . . .	42	El Paso County, TX	705	**Gainesville, GA. . . . .**	**156**
				Hall County, GA	156
Decatur, AL.	**147**	**Erie, PA . . . .**	**280**		
Lawrence County, AL. . .	35	Erie County, PA.	280	**Glens Falls, NY. . . . .**	**127**
Morgan County, AL	113			Warren County, NY	65
		Eugene-Springfield, OR. . . .	**331**	Washington County, NY .	62
Decatur, IL	**111**	Lane County, OR.	331		
Macon County, IL	111			**Goldsboro, NC . . . .**	**113**
		Evansville, IN-KY	**346**	Wayne County, NC	113
Deltona-Daytona Beach-		Gibson County, IN	33		
Ormond Beach, FL	**469**	Posey County, IN	27	**Grand Forks, ND-MN. . . . . .**	**96**
Volusia County, FL. . . .	469	Vanderburgh County, IN .	172	Polk County, MN	31
		Warrick County, IN.	55	Grand Forks County,	
Denver-Aurora, CO	**2,301**	Henderson County, KY. .	45	ND.	65
Adams County, CO	380	Webster County, KY. . . .	14		
Arapahoe County, CO . .	516			**Grand Junction, CO . . . . . .**	**125**
Broomfield County, CO. .	42	**Fairbanks, AK. . . . .**	**86**	Mesa County, CO	125
Clear Creek County, CO.	10	Fairbanks North Star			
Denver County, CO . . .	557	Borough, AK	86	**Grand Rapids-Wyoming, MI.**	**762**
Douglas County, CO . . .	223			Barry County, MI	59
Elbert County, CO	22	**Fargo, ND-MN. . . . .**	**179**	Ionia County, MI	64
Gilpin County, CO	5	Clay County, MN.	52	Kent County, MI	590
Jefferson County, CO. . .	529	Cass County, ND.	127	Newaygo County, MI . . .	49
Park County, CO.	16				
		Farmington, NM	**122**	**Great Falls, MT. . . . .**	**80**
Des Moines, IA	**503**	San Juan County, NM . .	122	Cascade County, MT . . .	80
Dallas County, IA.	46				
Guthrie County, IA.	12	**Fayetteville, NC . . . .**	**342**	**Greeley, CO . . . .**	**211**
Madison County, IA	15	Cumberland County, NC.	304	Weld County, CO.	211
Polk County, IA	389	Hoke County, NC.	38		
Warren County, IA	42			**Green Bay, WI. . . . .**	**291**
		Fayetteville-Springdale-		Brown County, WI	234
Detroit-Warren-Livonia, MI. .	**4,484**	**Rogers, AR-MO . . . .**	**378**	Kewaunee County, WI . .	20
Detroit-Livonia-Dearborn,		Benton County, AR	172	Oconto County, WI	37
MI.	**2,029**	Madison County, AR . . .	14		
Wayne County, MI	2,029	Washington County, AR .	170	**Greensboro-High Point, NC.**	**662**
Warren-Farmington Hills-		McDonald County, MO. .	22	Guilford County, NC. . . .	434
Troy, MI.	**2,455**			Randolph County, NC . .	135
Lapeer County, MI	91	**Flagstaff, AZ . . . .**	**121**	Rockingham County,	
Livingston County, MI. . .	173	Coconino County, AZ . .	121	NC.	93
Macomb County, MI. . . .	814				
Oakland County, MI. . . .	1,208	**Flint, MI . . . .**	**442**	**Greenville, NC . . . .**	**159**
St. Clair County, MI . . .	169	Genesee County, MI . . .	442	Greene County, NC	20
				Pitt County, NC	139
Dothan, AL.	**133**	**Florence, AL . . . .**	**141**		
Geneva County, AL. . . .	25	Colbert County, AL	55	**Greenville, SC. . . . .**	**578**
Henry County, AL	16	Lauderdale County, AL. .	87	Greenville County, SC. . .	395
Houston County, AL. . . .	91			Laurens County, SC. . . .	70
		Florence-Muscle Shoals,		Pickens County, SC. . . .	113
Dover, DE	**134**	**SC . . . .**	**196**		
Kent County, DE	134	Darlington County, SC . .	68	**Gulfport-Biloxi, MS . . . .**	**249**
		Florence County, SC . . .	128	Hancock County, MS . . .	45
Dubuque, IA	**90**			Harrison County, MS . . .	190
Dubuque County, IA. . . .	90	**Fond du Lac, WI . . . .**	**98**	Stone County, MS	14
		Fond du Lac County, WI.	98		

U.S. Census Bureau, Statistical Abstract of the United States: 2004-2005

Metropolitan statistical area / Metropolitan division / Component county	Popu-lation, 2003 (1,000)	Metropolitan statistical area / Metropolitan division / Component county	Popu-lation, 2003 (1,000)	Metropolitan statistical area / Metropolitan division / Component county	Popu-lation, 2003 (1,000)
Hagerstown-Martinsburg, MD-WV	**238**	**Indianapolis, IN**	**1,595**	Wyandotte County, KS..	157
Washington County, MD.	137	Boone County, IN	49	Bates County, MO	17
Berkeley County, WV...	85	Brown County, IN	15	Caldwell County, MO...	9
Morgan County, WV....	16	Hamilton County, IN....	217	Cass County, MO	89
		Hancock County, IN....	59	Clay County, MO	194
Hanford-Corcoran, CA	**139**	Hendricks County, IN ...	119	Clinton County, MO....	20
Kings County, CA	139	Johnson County, IN	123	Jackson County, MO...	660
		Marion County, IN	863	Lafayette County, MO ..	33
Harrisburg-Carlisle, PA	**517**	Morgan County, IN	69	Platte County, MO	79
Cumberland County, PA.	220	Putnam County, IN	37	Ray County, MO	24
Dauphin County, PA....	253	Shelby County, IN	44		
Perry County, PA	44			**Kennewick-Richland-Pasco, WA**	**210**
		Iowa City, IA	**137**	Benton County, WA....	154
Harrisonburg, VA	**111**	Johnson County, IA	116	Franklin County, WA ...	56
Rockingham County, VA.	69	Washington County, IA..	21		
Harrisonburg city, VA...	41			**Killeen-Temple-Fort Hood, TX**	**343**
		Ithaca, NY	**101**	Bell County, TX	249
Hartford-West Hartford-East Hartford, CT	**1,178**	Tompkins County, NY...	101	Coryell County, TX	75
Hartford County, CT....	871			Lampasas County, TX ..	19
Middlesex County, CT ..	161	**Jackson, MI**	**162**		
Tolland County, CT	145	Jackson County, MI....	162	**Kingsport-Bristol-Bristol, TN-VA**	**300**
				Hawkins County, TN	55
Hattiesburg, MS	**129**	**Jackson, MS**	**510**	Sullivan County, TN	153
Forrest County, MS....	74	Copiah County, MS	29	Scott County, VA	23
Lamar County, MS.....	42	Hinds County, MS	249	Washington County, VA .	51
Perry County, MS	12	Madison County, MS ...	80	Bristol city, VA	17
		Rankin County, MS ...	125		
Hickory-Lenoir-Morganton, NC	**350**	Simpson County, MS ...	28	**Kingston, NY**	**181**
Alexander County, NC..	35			Ulster County, NY	181
Burke County, NC	90	**Jackson, TN**	**110**		
Caldwell County, NC...	79	Chester County, TN....	16	**Knoxville, TN**	**637**
Catawba County, NC...	147	Madison County, TN ...	94	Anderson County, TN...	72
				Blount County, TN	112
Hinesville-Fort Stewart, GA.	**70**	**Jacksonville, FL**	**1,203**	Knox County, TN	393
Liberty County, GA....	59	Baker County, FL	23	Loudon County, TN	42
Long County, GA.....	11	Clay County, FL	158	Union County, TN	19
		Duval County, FL	817		
Holland-Grand Haven, MI ..	**249**	Nassau County, FL	62	**Kokomo, IN**	**101**
Ottawa County, MI.....	249	St. Johns County, FL ...	143	Howard County, IN	85
				Tipton County, IN	16
Honolulu, HI	**903**	**Jacksonville, NC**	**148**		
Honolulu County, HI....	903	Onslow County, NC	148	**La Crosse, WI-MN**	**129**
				Houston County, MN ...	20
Hot Springs, AR	**91**	**Janesville, WI**	**155**	La Crosse County, WI ..	109
Garland County, AR....	91	Rock County, WI	155		
				Lafayette, IN	**185**
Houma-Bayou Cane-Thibodaux, LA	**197**	**Jefferson City, MO**	**143**	Benton County, IN	9
Lafourche Parish, LA...	91	Callaway County, MO...	42	Carroll County, IN	20
Terrebonne Parish, LA ..	106	Cole County, MO	72	Tippecanoe County, IN..	155
		Moniteau County, MO ..	15		
Houston-Baytown-Sugar Land, TX	**5,076**	Osage County, MO	13	**Lafayette, LA**	**244**
Austin County, TX	25			Lafayette Parish, LA ...	194
Brazoria County, TX....	263	**Johnson City, TN**	**186**	St. Martin Parish, LA ...	50
Chambers County, TX..	28	Carter County, TN	58		
Fort Bend County, TX ..	420	Unicoi County, TN	18	**Lake Charles, LA**	**194**
Galveston County, TX ..	267	Washington County, TN .	110	Calcasieu Parish, LA ...	184
Harris County, TX	3,596			Cameron Parish, LA ...	10
Liberty County, TX....	74	**Johnstown, PA**	**149**		
Montgomery County, TX.	345	Cambria County, PA....	149	**Lakeland, FL**	**510**
San Jacinto County, TX .	24			Polk County, FL	510
Waller County, TX.....	35	**Jonesboro, AR**	**110**		
		Craighead County, AR ..	85	**Lancaster, PA**	**483**
Huntington-Ashland, WV-KY-OH	**287**	Poinsett County, AR....	25	Lancaster County, PA...	483
Boyd County, KY	50				
Greenup County, KY ...	37	**Joplin, MO**	**162**	**Lansing-East Lansing, MI ..**	**456**
Lawrence County, OH ..	63	Jasper County, MO	108	Clinton County, MI	68
Cabell County, WV	95	Newton County, MO....	54	Eaton County, MI	106
Wayne County, WV	42			Ingham County, MI	282
		Kalamazoo-Portage, MI	**320**		
Huntsville, AL	**358**	Kalamazoo County, MI..	242	**Laredo, TX**	**214**
Limestone County, AL ...	68	Van Buren County, MI ..	78	Webb County, TX	214
Madison County, AL....	290				
		Kankakee-Bradley, IL	**106**	**Las Cruces, NM**	**182**
Idaho Falls, ID	**107**	Kankakee County, IL ...	106	Dona Ana County, NM ..	182
Bonneville County, ID...	87				
Jefferson County, ID ...	20	**Kansas City, MO-KS**	**1,905**	**Las Vegas-Paradise, NV ...**	**1,577**
		Franklin County, KS....	26	Clark County, NV	1,577
		Johnson County, KS....	487		
		Leavenworth County, KS	72	**Lawrence, KS**	**103**
		Linn County, KS	10	Douglas County, KS....	103
		Miami County, KS	29		

910　Appendix II

U.S. Census Bureau, Statistical Abstract of the United States: 2004-2005

Metropolitan statistical area Metropolitan division Component county	Popu- lation, 2003 (1,000)	Metropolitan statistical area Metropolitan division Component county	Popu- lation, 2003 (1,000)	Metropolitan statistical area Metropolitan division Component county	Popu- lation, 2003 (1,000)
Lawton, OK	114	**Macon, GA**	226	**Missoula, MT**	99
Comanche County, OK. .	114	Bibb County, GA	154	Missoula County, MT. . .	99
Lebanon, PA	123	Crawford County, GA ...	13		
Lebanon County, PA ...	123	Jones County, GA	25	**Mobile, AL**	400
		Monroe County, GA	23	Mobile County, AL	400
Lewiston, ID-WA	58	Twiggs County, GA	10		
Nez Perce County, ID ..	38			**Modesto, CA**	492
Asotin County, WA.....	21	**Madera, CA**	133	Stanislaus County, CA ..	492
		Madera County, CA	133		
Lewiston-Auburn, ME	106			**Monroe, LA**.............	171
Androscoggin County,		**Madison, WI**	527	Ouachita Parish, LA. . . .	148
ME.	106	Columbia County, WI ...	54	Union Parish, LA......	23
		Dane County, WI	449		
Lexington-Fayette, KY.....	422	Iowa County, WI	23	**Monroe, MI**	151
Bourbon County, KY ...	20			Monroe County, MI	151
Clark County, KY......	34	**Manchester-Nashua, NH** ...	395		
Fayette County, KY	267	Hillsborough County,		**Montgomery, AL**	353
Jessamine County, KY. .	42	NH.	395	Autauga County, AL....	46
Scott County, KY......	37			Elmore County, AL.....	71
Woodford County, KY. . .	24	**Mansfield, OH**	128	Lowndes County, AL ...	13
		Richland County, OH . . .	128	Montgomery County, AL .	222
Lima, OH	108				
Allen County, OH.	108	**McAllen-Edinburg-Pharr,**		**Morgantown, WV**	114
		TX	636	Monongalia County, WV. .	84
Lincoln, NE..............	278	Hidalgo County, TX	636	Preston County, WV ...	30
Lancaster County, NE ..	261				
Seward County, NE....	17	**Medford, OR**.............	190	**Morristown, TN**..........	127
		Jackson County, OR ...	190	Grainger County, TN . . .	21
Little Rock-North Little				Hamblen County, TN ...	59
Rock, AR	628	**Memphis, TN-MS-AR**......	1,239	Jefferson County, TN ...	47
Faulkner County, AR ...	92	Crittenden County, AR . .	51		
Grant County, AR	17	DeSoto County, MS....	124	**Mount Vernon-Anacortes,**	
Lonoke County, AR	57	Marshall County, MS ...	35	**WA**	109
Perry County, AR......	10	Tate County, MS	26	Skagit County, WA.....	109
Pulaski County, AR	365	Tunica County, MS	10		
Saline County, AR	88	Fayette County, TN	32	**Muncie, IN**	117
		Shelby County, TN.....	906	Delaware County, IN ...	117
Logan, UT-ID............	108	Tipton County, TN	54		
Franklin County, ID	12			**Muskegon-Norton Shores,**	
Cache County, UT.....	96	**Merced, CA**	232	**MI**	173
		Merced County, CA	232	Muskegon County, MI . .	173
Longview, TX	198				
Gregg County, TX	114	**Miami-Fort Lauderdale-**		**Myrtle Beach-Conway-North**	
Rusk County, TX......	47	**Miami Beach, FL**........	5,289	**Myrtle Beach, SC**	211
Upshur County, TX	37	**Fort Lauderdale-**		Horry County, SC	211
		Pompano Beach-			
Longview, WA...........	95	**Deerfield Beach, FL**....	1,731	**Napa, CA**	132
Cowlitz County, WA	95	Broward County, FL....	1,731	Napa County, CA	132
		Miami-Miami Beach-			
Los Angeles-Long Beach-		**Kendall, FL**	2,341	**Naples-Marco Island, FL** ...	287
Santa Ana	12,829	Miami-Dade County, FL .	2,341	Collier County, FL	287
Los Angeles-Long		**West Palm Beach-Boca**			
Beach-Glendale, CA. ...	9,872	**Raton-Boynton Beach,**		**Nashville-Davidson-**	
Los Angeles County, CA.	9,872	**FL**..................	1,216	**Murfreesboro, TN**	1,371
Santa Ana-Anaheim-		Palm Beach County, FL .	1,216	Cannon County, TN....	13
Irvine, CA	2,958			Cheatham County, TN ..	37
Orange County, CA	2,958	**Michigan City-La Porte, IN.** .	110	Davidson County, TN . .	570
		La Porte County, IN....	110	Dickson County, TN....	45
Louisville, KY-IN	1,190			Hickman County, TN ...	23
Clark County, IN	99	**Midland, TX**	119	Macon County, TN.....	21
Floyd County, IN	71	Midland County, TX	119	Robertson County, TN ..	58
Harrison County, IN	36			Rutherford County, TN..	202
Washington County, IN..	28	**Milwaukee-Waukesha-West**		Smith County, TN	18
Bullitt County, KY......	65	**Allis, WI**	1,514	Sumner County, TN....	139
Henry County, KY	16	Milwaukee County, WI ..	933	Trousdale County, TN ..	7
Jefferson County, KY ...	699	Ozaukee County, WI ...	85	Williamson County, TN..	141
Meade County, KY.....	28	Washington County, WI .	122	Wilson County, TN.....	95
Nelson County, KY	40	Waukesha County, WI ..	374		
Oldham County, KY	51			**New Haven-Milford, CT**	842
Shelby County, KY.....	36	**Minneapolis-St. Paul-**		New Haven County, CT .	842
Spencer County, KY ...	14	**Bloomington, MN-WI**.....	3,084		
Trimble County, KY	9	Anoka County, MN.....	314	**New Orleans-Metairie-**	
		Carver County, MN	79	**Kenner, LA**	1,318
Lubbock, TX............	257	Chisago County, MN ...	46	Jefferson Parish, LA ...	452
Crosby County, TX	7	Dakota County, MN	373	Orleans Parish, LA	469
Lubbock County, TX. ...	250	Hennepin County, MN ..	1,121	Plaquemines Parish, LA.	28
		Isanti County, MN	35	St. Bernard Parish, LA..	66
Lynchburg, VA	231	Ramsey County, MN ...	506	St. Charles Parish, LA ..	49
Amherst County, VA....	32	Scott County, MN	109	St. John the Baptist	
Appomattox County, VA .	14	Sherburne County, MN..	75	Parish, LA.	45
Bedford County, VA	63	Washington County, MN..	214	St. Tammany Parish, LA.	208
Campbell County, VA. . .	51	Wright County, MN	103		
Bedford city, VA.	6	Pierce County, WI	38	**New York-Northern New**	
Lynchburg city, VA....	65	St. Croix County, WI ...	71	**Jersey-Long Island,**	
				NY-NJ-PA	18,641

U.S. Census Bureau, Statistical Abstract of the United States: 2004-2005

Metropolitan statistical area / Metropolitan division / Component county	Population, 2003 (1,000)
Edison, NJ	**2,271**
Middlesex County, NJ	781
Monmouth County, NJ	632
Ocean County, NJ	546
Somerset County, NJ	312
Nassau-Suffolk, NY	**2,808**
Nassau County, NY	1,339
Suffolk County, NY	1,468
Newark-Union, NJ-PA	**2,140**
Essex County, NJ	796
Hunterdon County, NJ	128
Morris County, NJ	483
Sussex County, NJ	151
Union County, NJ	529
Pike County, PA	52
New York-Wayne-White Plains, NY-NJ	**11,422**
Bergen County, NJ	898
Hudson County, NJ	607
Passaic County, NJ	498
Bronx County, NY	1,363
Kings County, NY	2,473
New York County, NY	1,565
Putnam County, NY	100
Queens County, NY	2,225
Richmond County, NY	460
Rockland County, NY	293
Westchester County, NY	940
Niles-Benton Harbor, MI	**163**
Berrien County, MI	163
Norwich-New London, CT	**264**
New London County, CT	264
Ocala, FL	**280**
Marion County, FL	280
Ocean City, NJ	**102**
Cape May County, NJ	102
Odessa, TX	**123**
Ector County, TX	123
Ogden-Clearfield, UT	**469**
Davis County, UT	256
Morgan County, UT	8
Weber County, UT	206
Oklahoma City, OK	**1,133**
Canadian County, OK	93
Cleveland County, OK	220
Grady County, OK	47
Lincoln County, OK	32
Logan County, OK	35
McClain County, OK	29
Oklahoma County, OK	676
Olympia, WA	**222**
Thurston County, WA	222
Omaha-Council Bluffs, NE-IA	**793**
Harrison County, IA	16
Mills County, IA	15
Pottawattamie County, IA	88
Cass County, NE	25
Douglas County, NE	477
Sarpy County, NE	132
Saunders County, NE	20
Washington County, NE	20
Orlando, FL	**1,803**
Lake County, FL	246
Orange County, FL	965
Osceola County, FL	206
Seminole County, FL	386
Oshkosh-Neenah, WI	**159**
Winnebago County, WI	159
Owensboro, KY	**111**
Daviess County, KY	93
Hancock County, KY	8
McLean County, KY	10
Oxnard-Thousand Oaks-Ventura, CA	**791**
Ventura County, CA	791
Palm Bay-Melbourne-Titusville, FL	**506**
Brevard County, FL	506
Panama City-Lynn Haven, FL	**155**
Bay County, FL	155
Parkersburg-Marietta, WV-OH	**163**
Washington County, OH	63
Pleasants County, WV	8
Wirt County, WV	6
Wood County, WV	87
Pascagoula, MS	**154**
George County, MS	20
Jackson County, MS	134
Pensacola-Ferry Pass-Brent, FL	**429**
Escambia County, FL	296
Santa Rosa County, FL	133
Peoria, IL	**366**
Marshall County, IL	13
Peoria County, IL	182
Stark County, IL	6
Tazewell County, IL	128
Woodford County, IL	36
Philadelphia-Camden-Wilmington, PA-NJ-DE-MD.	**5,773**
Camden, NJ	**1,225**
Burlington County, NJ	444
Camden County, NJ	514
Gloucester County, NJ	267
Philadelphia, PA	**3,875**
Bucks County, PA	613
Chester County, PA	457
Delaware County, PA	554
Montgomery County, PA	771
Philadelphia County, PA	1,479
Wilmington, DE-MD-NJ	**673**
New Castle County, DE	515
Cecil County, MD	93
Salem County, NJ	65
Phoenix-Mesa-Scottsdale, AZ	**3,593**
Maricopa County, AZ	3,389
Pinal County, AZ	204
Pine Bluff, AR	**106**
Cleveland County, AR	9
Jefferson County, AR	83
Lincoln County, AR	14
Pittsburgh, PA	**2,410**
Allegheny County, PA	1,261
Armstrong County, PA	72
Beaver County, PA	179
Butler County, PA	180
Fayette County, PA	146
Washington County, PA	204
Westmoreland County, PA	368
Pittsfield, MA	**133**
Berkshire County, MA	133
Pocatello, ID	**83**
Bannock County, ID	76
Power County, ID	7
Portland-South Portland-Biddeford, ME	**505**
Cumberland County, ME	271
Sagadahoc County, ME	36
York County, ME	198
Portland-Vancouver-Beaverton, OR-WA	**2,040**
Clackamas County, OR	357
Columbia County, OR	46
Multnomah County, OR	678
Washington County, OR	479
Yamhill County, OR	89
Clark County, WA	380
Skamania County, WA	10
Port St. Lucie-Fort Pierce, FL	**349**
Martin County, FL	135
St. Lucie County, FL	213
Poughkeepsie-Newburgh-Middletown, NY	**654**
Dutchess County, NY	291
Orange County, NY	363
Prescott, AZ	**184**
Yavapai County, AZ	184
Providence-New Bedford-Fall River, RI-MA	**1,623**
Bristol County, MA	547
Bristol County, RI	51
Kent County, RI	171
Newport County, RI	86
Providence County, RI	639
Washington County, RI	129
Provo-Orem, UT	**407**
Juab County, UT	9
Utah County, UT	398
Pueblo, CO	**149**
Pueblo County, CO	149
Punta Gorda, FL	**153**
Charlotte County, FL	153
Racine, WI	**192**
Racine County, WI	192
Raleigh-Cary, NC	**884**
Franklin County, NC	52
Johnston County, NC	137
Wake County, NC	696
Rapid City, SD	**117**
Meade County, SD	25
Pennington County, SD	92
Reading, PA	**385**
Berks County, PA	385
Redding, CA	**176**
Shasta County, CA	176
Reno-Sparks, NV	**374**
Storey County, NV	4
Washoe County, NV	371
Richmond, VA	**1,138**
Amelia County, VA	12
Caroline County, VA	23
Charles City County, VA	7
Chesterfield County, VA	277
Cumberland County, VA	9
Dinwiddie County, VA	25
Goochland County, VA	18
Hanover County, VA	94
Henrico County, VA	271
King and Queen County, VA	7
King William County, VA	14
Louisa County, VA	28
New Kent County, VA	15
Powhatan County, VA	25

912   Appendix II

Metropolitan statistical area Metropolitan division Component county	Population, 2003 (1,000)	Metropolitan statistical area Metropolitan division Component county	Population, 2003 (1,000)	Metropolitan statistical area Metropolitan division Component county	Population, 2003 (1,000)
Prince George County, VA	34	Washington County, MO .	24	Chatham County, GA . . .	235
Sussex County, VA	12	St. Louis city, MO	332	Effingham County, GA . .	43
Colonial Heights city, VA.	17	Salem, OR	363	Scranton—Wilkes-Barre,	
Hopewell city, VA.	22	Marion County, OR	297	PA	552
Petersburg city, VA	33	Polk County, OR	66	Lackawanna County, PA.	210
Richmond city, VA	195	Salinas, CA.	414	Luzerne County, PA. . . .	314
Riverside-San Bernardino-Ontario, CA.	3,642	Monterey County, CA. . .	414	Wyoming County, PA . . .	28
Riverside County, CA. . .	1,783	Salisbury, MD	113	Seattle-Tacoma-Bellevue,	
San Bernardino County, CA.	1,860	Somerset County, MD . .	25	WA	3,142
Roanoke, VA.	290	Wicomico County, MD . .	87	Seattle-Bellevue-Everett, WA	2,401
Botetourt County, VA. . .	31	Salt Lake City, UT.	1,005	King County, WA	1,761
Craig County, VA.	5	Salt Lake County, UT. . .	924	Snohomish County, WA .	639
Franklin County, VA . . .	49	Summit County, UT	33	Tacoma, WA	741
Roanoke County, VA . . .	87	Tooele County, UT.	48	Pierce County, WA.	741
Roanoke city, VA.	93	San Angelo, TX.	105	Sheboygan, WI	113
Salem city, VA.	25	Irion County, TX	1	Sheboygan County, WI. .	113
Rochester, MN	172	Tom Green County, TX. .	104	Sherman-Denison, TX	115
Dodge County, MN	19	San Antonio, TX	1,821	Grayson County, TX. . . .	115
Olmsted County, MN . . .	131	Atascosa County, TX . . .	42	Shreveport-Bossier City,	
Wabasha County, MN . .	22	Bandera County, TX. . . .	19	LA	378
Rochester, NY.	1,041	Bexar County, TX	1,472	Bossier Parish, LA.	102
Livingston County, NY . .	65	Comal County, TX	88	Caddo Parish, LA	250
Monroe County, NY	737	Guadalupe County, TX. .	97	De Soto Parish, LA	26
Ontario County, NY	102	Kendall County, TX	26	Sioux City, IA-NE-SD.	143
Orleans County, NY	44	Medina County, TX	42	Woodbury County, IA . . .	103
Wayne County, NY	94	Wilson County, TX.	35	Dakota County, NE	20
Rockford, IL	331	San Diego-Carlsbad-San Marcos, CA.	2,931	Dixon County, NE	6
Boone County, IL.	46	San Diego County, CA . .	2,931	Union County, SD	13
Winnebago County, IL . .	284	Sandusky, OH.	79	Sioux Falls, SD.	198
Rocky Mount, NC	145	Erie County, OH	79	Lincoln County, SD	29
Edgecombe County, NC .	55	San Francisco-Oakland-Fremont, CA	4,157	McCook County, SD . . .	6
Nash County, NC.	90	Oakland-Fremont-Hayward, CA	2,462	Minnehaha County, SD .	155
Rome, GA.	93	Alameda County, CA . . .	1,461	Turner County, SD.	9
Floyd County, GA	93	Contra Costa County, CA.	1,001	South Bend-Mishawaka, IN-MI.	318
Sacramento—Arden-Arcade—Roseville, CA . . .	1,975	San Francisco-San Mateo-Redwood City, CA	1,695	St. Joseph County, IN . .	266
El Dorado County, CA . .	169	Marin County, CA	246	Cass County, MI	51
Placer County, CA.	292	San Francisco County, CA.	752	Spartanburg, SC	261
Sacramento County, CA.	1,331	San Mateo County, CA. .	697	Spartanburg County, SC.	261
Yolo County, CA	183	San Jose-Sunnyvale-Santa Clara, CA	1,735	Spokane, WA	431
Saginaw-Saginaw Township North, MI.	209	San Benito County, CA .	56	Spokane County, WA. . .	431
Saginaw County, MI. . . .	209	Santa Clara County, CA .	1,678	Springfield, IL.	204
St. Cloud, MN	174	San Luis Obispo-Paso Robles, CA	253	Menard County, IL.	13
Benton County, MN	37	San Luis Obispo County, CA.	253	Sangamon County, IL. . .	192
Stearns County, MN	137	Santa Barbara-Santa Maria-Goleta, CA	403	Springfield, MA.	688
St. George, UT	104	Santa Barbara County, CA.	403	Franklin County, MA . . .	72
Washington County, UT .	104	Santa Cruz-Watsonville, CA.	252	Hampden County, MA . .	461
St. Joseph, MO-KS	123	Santa Cruz County, CA .	252	Hampshire County, MA .	155
Doniphan County, KS. . .	8	Santa Fe, NM	136	Springfield, MO.	385
Andrew County, MO. . . .	17	Santa Fe County, NM. . .	136	Christian County, MO. . .	62
Buchanan County, MO. .	85	Santa Rosa-Petaluma, CA . .	467	Dallas County, MO.	16
DeKalb County, MO. . . .	13	Sonoma County, CA . . .	467	Greene County, MO. . . .	246
St. Louis, MO-IL	2,759	Sarasota-Bradenton-Venice, FL.	634	Polk County, MO	28
Bond County, IL	18	Manatee County, FL . . .	287	Webster County, MO . . .	33
Calhoun County, IL	5	Sarasota County, FL . . .	347	Springfield, OH.	143
Clinton County, IL	36	Savannah, GA.	304	Clark County, OH	143
Jersey County, IL	22	Bryan County, GA	26	State College, PA	142
Macoupin County, IL . . .	49			Centre County, PA.	142
Madison County, IL	262			Stockton, CA	633
Monroe County, IL.	30			San Joaquin County, CA.	633
St. Clair County, IL	259			Sumter, SC	106
Crawford County, MO. . .	24			Sumter County, SC	106
Franklin County, MO . . .	97			Syracuse, NY	654
Jefferson County, MO . .	207			Madison County, NY . . .	70
Lincoln County, MO	44			Onondaga County, NY . .	461
St. Charles County, MO .	312			Oswego County, NY . . .	123
St. Louis County, MO. . .	1,013				
Warren County, MO. . . .	27				

U.S. Census Bureau, Statistical Abstract of the United States: 2004-2005

Metropolitan statistical area Metropolitan division Component county	Population, 2003 (1,000)
Tallahassee, FL	**328**
Gadsden County, FL ...	45
Jefferson County, FL ...	14
Leon County, FL	243
Wakulla County, FL	26
Tampa-St. Petersburg-Clearwater, FL	**2,532**
Hernando County, FL...	143
Hillsborough County, FL .	1,073
Pasco County, FL	389
Pinellas County, FL	926
Terre Haute, IN	**170**
Clay County, IN.......	27
Sullivan County, IN	22
Vermillion County, IN ...	17
Vigo County, IN.......	105
Texarkana, TX-Texarkana, AR	**132**
Miller County, AR......	42
Bowie County, TX	90
Toledo, OH	**661**
Fulton County, OH.....	42
Lucas County, OH	454
Ottawa County, OH	41
Wood County, OH	123
Topeka, KS.............	**226**
Jackson County, KS.....	13
Jefferson County, KS ...	19
Osage County, KS......	17
Shawnee County, KS...	171
Wabaunsee County, KS .	7
Trenton-Ewing, NJ	**362**
Mercer County, NJ.....	362
Tucson, AZ	**893**
Pima County, AZ	893
Tulsa, OK	**880**
Creek County, OK	69
Okmulgee County, OK ..	40
Osage County, OK.....	45
Pawnee County, OK ...	17
Rogers County, OK	77
Tulsa County, OK	570
Wagoner County, OK...	62
Tuscaloosa, AL	**195**
Greene County, AL	10
Hale County, AL	18
Tuscaloosa County, AL..	166
Tyler, TX...............	**184**
Smith County, TX	184
Utica-Rome, NY	**298**
Herkimer County, NY...	64
Oneida County, NY	234
Valdosta, GA	**122**
Brooks County, GA	16
Echols County, GA	4
Lanier County, GA.....	7
Lowndes County, GA...	95
Vallejo-Fairfield, CA	**412**
Solano County, CA	412

Metropolitan statistical area Metropolitan division Component county	Population, 2003 (1,000)
Vero Beach, FL	**120**
Indian River County, FL .	120
Victoria, TX	**113**
Calhoun County, TX....	20
Goliad County, TX	7
Victoria County, TX	85
Vineland-Millville-Bridgeton, NJ	**149**
Cumberland County, NJ .	149
Virginia Beach-Norfolk-Newport News, VA-NC....	**1,637**
Currituck County, NC...	21
Gloucester County, VA..	37
Isle of Wight County, VA.	32
James City County, VA..	53
Mathews County, VA ...	9
Surry County, VA......	7
York County, VA	61
Chesapeake city, VA ...	211
Hampton city, VA......	147
Newport News city, VA..	182
Norfolk city, VA.......	242
Poquoson city, VA	12
Portsmouth city, VA	100
Suffolk city, VA	74
Virginia Beach city, VA..	439
Williamsburg city, VA ...	12
Visalia-Porterville, CA	**391**
Tulare County, CA.....	391
Waco, TX	**220**
McLennan County, TX ..	220
Warner Robins, GA.......	**120**
Houston County, GA ...	120
Washington-Arlington-Alexandria, DC-VA-MD-WV. Bethesda-Frederick-Gaithersburg, MD	**5,090** **1,133**
Frederick County, MD ..	214
Montgomery County, MD	919
Washington-Arlington-Alexandria, DC-VA-MD-WV	**3,958**
District of Columbia, DC.	563
Calvert County, MD....	84
Charles County, MD....	133
Prince George's County, MD	839
Arlington County, VA ...	188
Clarke County, VA	13
Fairfax County, VA.....	1,000
Fauquier County, VA...	61
Loudoun County, VA ...	222
Prince William County, VA	325
Spotsylvania County, VA.	108
Stafford County, VA	111
Warren County, VA	34
Alexandria city, VA.....	129
Fairfax city, VA	22
Falls Church city, VA ...	10
Fredericksburg city, VA..	20
Manassas city, VA	37
Manassas Park city, VA .	11
Jefferson County, WV ..	46

Metropolitan statistical area Metropolitan division Component county	Population, 2003 (1,000)
Waterloo-Cedar Falls, IA ...	**162**
Black Hawk County, IA..	126
Bremer County, IA.....	23
Grundy County, IA.....	12
Wausau, WI	**127**
Marathon County, WI...	127
Weirton-Steubenville, WV-OH	**129**
Jefferson County, OH...	72
Brooke County, WV	25
Hancock County, WV...	32
Wenatchee, WA..........	**102**
Chelan County, WA	68
Douglas County, WA ...	34
Wheeling, WV-OH	**150**
Belmont County, OH ...	70
Marshall County, WV ...	35
Ohio County, WV......	46
Wichita, KS.............	**583**
Butler County, KS	61
Harvey County, KS	34
Sedgwick County, KS...	463
Sumner County, KS....	25
Wichita Falls, TX.........	**150**
Archer County, TX	9
Clay County, TX	11
Wichita County, TX	129
Williamsport, PA	**118**
Lycoming County, PA...	118
Wilmington, NC	**293**
Brunswick County, NC ..	82
New Hanover County, NC	168
Pender County, NC	44
Winchester, VA-WV	**110**
Frederick County, VA...	65
Winchester city, VA	24
Hampshire County, WV .	21
Winston-Salem, NC.......	**438**
Davie County, NC	37
Forsyth County, NC	318
Stokes County, NC	45
Yadkin County, NC	37
Worcester, MA	**777**
Worcester County, MA..	777
Yakima, WA	**227**
Yakima County, WA....	227
York-Hanover, PA	**395**
York County, PA	395
Youngstown-Warren-Boardman, OH-PA.......	**593**
Mahoning County, OH ..	252
Trumbull County, OH ...	222
Mercer County, PA.....	120
Yuba City, CA	**148**
Sutter County, CA	85
Yuba County, CA.......	63
Yuma, AZ	**171**
Yuma County, AZ	171

Source: U.S. Census Bureau, unpublished data.

[Population as of **July 2003. 54 represents 54,000.** All micropolitan areas are arranged alphabetically]

Micropolitan statistical area Component county	Popu- lation, 2003 (1,000)	Micropolitan statistical area Component county	Popu- lation, 2003 (1,000)	Micropolitan statistical area Component county	Popu- lation, 2003 (1,000)
Abbeville, LA	54	**Ashtabula, OH**	103	**Bennington, VT.**	37
Vermilion Parish, LA	54	Ashtabula County, OH	103	Bennington County, VT . . .	37
Aberdeen, SD	39	**Astoria, OR.**	36	**Berlin, NH-VT**	40
Brown County, SD.	35	Clatsop County, OR.	36	Coos County, NH	33
Edmunds County, SD	4			Essex County, VT	7
		Atchison, KS	17		
Aberdeen, WA	69	Atchison County, KS	17	**Big Rapids, MI**	42
Grays Harbor County, WA .	69			Mecosta County, MI.	42
		Athens, OH.	64		
Ada, OK	35	Athens County, OH	64	**Big Spring, TX**	33
Pontotoc County, OK.	35			Howard County, TX.	33
		Athens, TN	51		
Adrian, MI.	101	McMinn County, TN.	51	**Bishop, CA.**	18
Lenawee County, MI	101			Inyo County, CA	18
		Athens, TX	77		
Alamogordo, NM.	62	Henderson County, TX. . . .	77	**Blackfoot, ID.**	43
Otero County, NM.	62			Bingham County, ID	43
		Auburn, IN	41		
Albany-Lebanon, OR.	106	De Kalb County, IN	41	**Bloomsburg-Berwick, PA** . .	83
Linn County, OR	106			Columbia County, PA.	65
		Auburn, NY.	82	Montour County, PA	18
Albemarle, NC	59	Cayuga County, NY.	82		
Stanly County, NC.	59			**Bluefield, WV-VA.**	106
		Augusta-Waterville, ME. . . .	120	Tazewell County, VA	44
Albert Lea, MN	32	Kennebec County, ME. . . .	120	Mercer County, WV	62
Freeborn County, MN	32				
		Austin, MN	39	**Blytheville, AR**	49
Albertville, AL.	84	Mower County, MN	39	Mississippi County, AR . . .	49
Marshall County, AL	84				
		Bainbridge, GA.	28	**Blytheville, AR** ...	
Alexander City, AL	12	Decatur County, GA	28	**Bogalusa, LA**	44
Coosa County, AL.	12			Washington Parish, LA . . .	44
		Baraboo, WI	56		
Alexandria, MN	34	Sauk County, WI.	56	**Boone, IA**	26
Douglas County, MN	34			Boone County, IA	26
		Barre, VT	59		
Alice, TX.	40	Washington County, VT . . .	59	**Boone, NC**	43
Jim Wells County, TX	40			Watauga County, NC.	43
		Bartlesville, OK.	49		
Allegan, MI	110	Washington County, OK. . .	49	**Borger, TX**	23
Allegan County, MI	110			Hutchinson County, TX . . .	23
		Bastrop, LA	31		
Alma, MI.	43	Morehouse Parish, LA. . . .	31	**Bozeman, MT**	73
Gratiot County, MI.	43			Gallatin County, MT.	73
		Batavia, NY.	60		
Alpena, MI	31	Genesee County, NY.	60	**Bradford, PA.**	45
Alpena County, MI.	31			McKean County, PA	45
		Batesville, AR.	34		
Altus, OK	27	Independence County, AR .	34	**Brainerd, MN**	87
Jackson County, OK	27			Cass County, MN	28
		Bay City, TX	38	Crow Wing County, MN . . .	58
Americus, GA	37	Matagorda County, TX. . . .	38		
Schley County, GA	4			**Branson, MO**	71
Sumter County, GA	33	**Beatrice, NE**	23	Stone County, MO.	30
		Gage County, NE	23	Taney County, MO	41
Amsterdam, NY.	49				
Montgomery County, NY . .	49	**Beaver Dam, WI**	87	**Brenham, TX.**	31
		Dodge County, WI.	87	Washington County, TX . . .	31
Andrews, TX.	13				
Andrews County, TX	13	**Beckley, WV**	79	**Brevard, NC**	29
		Raleigh County, WV	79	Transylvania County, NC . .	29
Angola, IN	34				
Steuben County, IN	34	**Bedford, IN.**	46	**Brigham City, UT**	45
		Lawrence County, IN.	46	Box Elder County, UT	45
Arcadia, FL.	34				
DeSoto County, FL	34	**Beeville, TX**	32	**Brookhaven, MS**	34
		Bee County, TX	32	Lincoln County, MS	34
Ardmore, OK	55				
Carter County, OK.	46	**Bellefontaine, OH**	46	**Brookings, OR**	22
Love County, OK.	9	Logan County, OH	46	Curry County, OR	22
Arkadelphia, AR	24	**Bemidji, MN**	42	**Brookings, SD**	28
Clark County, AR	24	Beltrami County, MN	42	Brookings County, SD	28
Ashland, OH.	54	**Bennettsville, SC**	28	**Brownsville, TN**	20
Ashland County, OH	54	Marlboro County, SC.	28	Haywood County, TN.	20

U.S. Census Bureau, Statistical Abstract of the United States: 2004-2005

Micropolitan statistical area Component county	Population, 2003 (1,000)	Micropolitan statistical area Component county	Population, 2003 (1,000)	Micropolitan statistical area Component county	Population, 2003 (1,000)
Brownwood, TX	**38**	**Chillicothe, OH**	**74**	**Crawfordsville, IN**	**38**
Brown County, TX.......	38	Ross County, OH	74	Montgomery County, IN....	38
Bucyrus, OH...........	**46**	**City of The Dalles, OR.**	**24**	**Crescent City, CA**........	**28**
Crawford County, OH	46	Wasco County, OR	24	Del Norte County, CA	28
Burley, ID.............	**41**	**Claremont, NH**	**42**	**Crossville, TN**...........	**49**
Cassia County, ID.......	22	Sullivan County, NH	42	Cumberland County, TN...	49
Minidoka County, ID	19				
		Clarksburg, WV.	**92**	**Crowley, LA**	**59**
Burlington, 'A-IL........	**49**	Doddridge County, WV ...	7	Acadia Parish, LA........	59
Henderson County, IL	8	Harrison County, WV.....	68		
Des Moines County, IA ...	41	Taylor County, WV	16	**Cullman, AL**............	**78**
				Cullman County, AL......	78
Butte-Silver Bow, MT	**33**	**Clarksdale, MS**	**30**		
Silver Bow County, MT ...	33	Coahoma County, MS	30	**Danville, KY**	**52**
				Boyle County, KY	28
Cadillac, MI.	**46**	**Clearlake, CA**...........	**63**	Lincoln County, KY	25
Missaukee County, MI....	15	Lake County, CA.	63		
Wexford County, MI.....	31			**Daphne-Fairhope, AL**	**152**
		Cleveland, MS.	**39**	Baldwin County, AL......	152
Calhoun, GA.	**48**	Bolivar County, MS	39		
Gordon County, GA......	48			**Decatur, IN**	**34**
		Clewiston, FL	**37**	Adams County, IN.......	34
Cambridge, MD..........	**31**	Hendry County, FL	37		
Dorchester County, MD ...	31			**Defiance, OH**	**39**
		Clinton, IA	**50**	Defiance County, OH.....	39
Cambridge, OH..........	**41**	Clinton County, IA.......	50		
Guernsey County, OH	41			**Del Rio, TX.**	**47**
		Clovis, NM	**45**	Val Verde County, TX	47
Camden, AR	**33**	Curry County, NM	45		
Calhoun County, AR	6			**Deming, NM**	**26**
Ouachita County, AR.....	28	**Coffeyville, KS**	**35**	Luna County, NM	26
		Montgomery County, KS ..	35		
Campbellsville, KY	**23**			**De Ridder, LA.**	**34**
Taylor County, KY.......	23	**Coldwater, MI**	**46**	Beauregard Parish, LA ...	34
		Branch County, MI	46		
Canon City, CO.	**48**			**Dickinson, ND.**	**23**
Fremont County, CO	48	**Columbia, TN**	**73**	Billings County, ND	1
		Maury County, TN.......	73	Stark County, ND	22
Canton, IL.	**38**				
Fulton County, IL........	38	**Columbus, MS**	**61**	**Dillon, SC.**	**31**
		Lowndes County, MS....	61	Dillon County, SC	31
Cape Girardeau-Jackson,					
MO-IL...............	**92**	**Columbus, NE**	**31**	**Dixon, IL.**	**36**
Alexander County, IL.....	9	Platte County, NE	31	Lee County, IL	36
Bollinger County, MO....	12				
Cape Girardeau County,		**Concord, NH.**	**144**	**Dodge City, KS**	**33**
MO	70	Merrimack County, NH....	144	Ford County, KS	33
Carbondale, IL	**59**	**Connersville, IN**	**25**	**Douglas, GA**	**47**
Jackson County, IL	59	Fayette County, IN	25	Atkinson County, GA.....	8
				Coffee County, GA	39
Carlsbad-Artesia, NM	**51**	**Cookeville, TN**	**96**		
Eddy County, NM	51	Jackson County, TN	11	**Dublin, GA**	**56**
		Overton County, TN.....	20	Johnson County, GA	9
Cedar City, UT	**36**	Putnam County, TN.....	65	Laurens County, GA	46
Iron County, UT	36				
		Coos Bay, OR.	**63**	**DuBois, PA.**	**83**
Cedartown, GA.	**40**	Coos County, OR	63	Clearfield County, PA.....	83
Polk County, GA........	40				
		Corbin, KY	**37**	**Dumas, TX**	**20**
Celina, OH	**41**	Whitley County, KY	37	Moore County, TX.......	20
Mercer County, OH	41				
		Cordele, GA.	**22**	**Duncan, OK**	**42**
Central City, KY	**32**	Crisp County, GA	22	Stephens County, OK	42
Muhlenberg County, KY...	32				
		Corinth, MS	**35**	**Dunn, NC**	**99**
Centralia, IL	**41**	Alcorn County, MS	35	Harnett County, NC......	99
Marion County, IL	41				
		Cornelia, GA.	**38**	**Durango, CO.**	**46**
Centralia, WA	**70**	Habersham County, GA...	38	La Plata County, CO	46
Lewis County, WA.......	70				
		Corning, NY	**99**	**Durant, OK**	**37**
Chambersburg, PA	**133**	Steuben County, NY	99	Bryan County, OK.......	37
Franklin County, PA.....	133				
		Corsicana, TX	**47**	**Dyersburg, TN**	**37**
Charleston-Mattoon, IL	**63**	Navarro County, TX......	47	Dyer County, TN	37
Coles County, IL........	52				
Cumberland County, IL ...	11	**Cortland, NY.**	**49**	**Eagle Pass, TX**	**50**
		Cortland County, NY	49	Maverick County, TX	50
Chester, SC	**34**				
Chester County, SC......	34	**Coshocton, OH.**	**37**	**East Liverpool-Salem, OH** ..	**112**
		Coshocton County, OH ...	37	Columbiana County, OH ..	112

U.S. Census Bureau, Statistical Abstract of the United States: 2004-2005

Micropolitan statistical area / Component county	Population, 2003 (1,000)
Easton, MD.	35
Talbot County, MD.	35
East Stroudsburg, PA	154
Monroe County, PA	154
Edwards, CO	54
Eagle County, CO	46
Lake County, CO	8
Effingham, IL	35
Effingham County, IL	35
El Campo, TX	41
Wharton County, TX	41
El Dorado, AR.	45
Union County, AR	45
Elizabeth City, NC	56
Camden County, NC	8
Pasquotank County, NC. . .	36
Perquimans County, NC. . .	12
Elk City, OK	20
Beckham County, OK	20
Elko, NV.	46
Elko County, NV	44
Eureka County, NV	2
Ellensburg, WA.	35
Kittitas County, WA	35
Emporia, KS	39
Chase County, KS.	3
Lyon County, KS.	36
Enid, OK.	57
Garfield County, OK	57
Enterprise-Ozark, AL.	94
Coffee County, AL.	45
Dale County, AL	49
Escanaba, MI	38
Delta County, MI.	38
Espanola, NM	41
Rio Arriba County, NM. . . .	41
Eufaula, AL-GA	31
Barbour County, AL.	29
Quitman County, GA	2
Eureka-Arcata-Fortuna, CA .	128
Humboldt County, CA	128
Evanston, WY.	20
Uinta County, WY	20
Fairmont, MN	21
Martin County, MN	21
Fairmont, WV	56
Marion County, WV	56
Fallon, NV.	25
Churchill County, NV	25
Faribault-Northfield, MN . . .	60
Rice County, MN.	60
Farmington, MO	58
St. Francois County, MO . .	58
Fergus Falls, MN.	59
Otter Tail County, MN	59
Findlay, OH.	73
Hancock County, OH.	73
Fitzgerald, GA.	27
Ben Hill County, GA	17
Irwin County, GA.	10

Micropolitan statistical area / Component county	Population, 2003 (1,000)
Forest City, NC	64
Rutherford County, NC . . .	64
Forrest City, AR	29
St. Francis County, AR . . .	29
Fort Dodge, IA	40
Webster County, IA	40
Fort Leonard Wood, MO . . .	45
Pulaski County, MO.	45
Fort Morgan, CO.	28
Morgan County, CO.	28
Fort Payne, AL.	66
DeKalb County, AL	66
Fort Polk South, LA	51
Vernon Parish, LA.	51
Fort Valley, GA	24
Peach County, GA	24
Frankfort, IN	34
Clinton County, IN.	34
Frankfort, KY	68
Anderson County, KY	20
Franklin County, KY.	48
Freeport, IL.	48
Stephenson County, IL . . .	48
Fremont, NE	36
Dodge County, NE	36
Fremont, OH.	62
Sandusky County, OH	62
Gaffney, SC	54
Cherokee County, SC	54
Gainesville, TX	38
Cooke County, TX.	38
Galesburg, IL	73
Knox County, IL	54
Warren County, IL.	18
Gallup, NM	73
McKinley County, NM	73
Garden City, KS	39
Finney County, KS	39
Gardnerville Ranchos, NV. .	44
Douglas County, NV	44
Georgetown, SC	59
Georgetown County, SC . .	59
Gettysburg, PA.	96
Adams County, PA	96
Gillette, WY	36
Campbell County, WY	36
Glasgow, KY.	49
Barren County, KY	39
Metcalfe County, KY	10
Gloversville, NY	55
Fulton County, NY.	55
Granbury, TX	52
Hood County, TX	45
Somervell County, TX	7
Grand Island, NE	69
Hall County, NE	54
Howard County, NE.	7
Merrick County, NE.	8
Grants, NM.	26
Cibola County, NM	26

Micropolitan statistical area / Component county	Population, 2003 (1,000)
Grants Pass, OR.	79
Josephine County, OR. . . .	79
Great Bend, KS.	27
Barton County, KS	27
Greeneville, TN.	64
Greene County, TN.	64
Greensburg, IN	25
Decatur County, IN	25
Greenville, MS	60
Washington County, MS. . .	60
Greenville, OH	53
Darke County, OH.	53
Greenwood, MS	47
Carroll County, MS	10
Leflore County, MS	36
Greenwood, SC.	68
Greenwood County, SC . . .	68
Grenada, MS.	23
Grenada County, MS.	23
Guymon, OK.	20
Texas County, OK	20
Hammond, LA.	104
Tangipahoa Parish, LA. . . .	104
Hannibal, MO	38
Marion County, MO.	28
Ralls County, MO	10
Harriman, TN	52
Roane County, TN	52
Harrisburg, IL	26
Saline County, IL.	26
Harrison, AR.	43
Boone County, AR.	35
Newton County, AR	9
Hastings, NE.	38
Adams County, NE	31
Clay County, NE.	7
Havre, MT.	16
Hill County, MT.	16
Hays, KS	27
Ellis County, KS.	27
Heber, UT.	18
Wasatch County, UT	18
Helena, MT.	68
Jefferson County, MT	10
Lewis and Clark County, MT	57
Henderson, NC.	44
Vance County, NC.	44
Hereford, TX.	18
Deaf Smith County, TX . . .	18
Hilo, HI.	158
Hawaii County, HI	158
Hilton Head Island-Beaufort, SC.	154
Beaufort County, SC	133
Jasper County, SC	21
Hobbs, NM	56
Lea County, NM	56
Homosassa Springs, FL . . .	126
Citrus County, FL	126

U.S. Census Bureau, Statistical Abstract of the United States: 2004-2005

Micropolitan statistical area Component county	Population, 2003 (1,000)	Micropolitan statistical area Component county	Population, 2003 (1,000)	Micropolitan statistical area Component county	Population, 2003 (1,000)
Hood River, OR	21	**Kearney, NE**	50	**Lawrenceburg, TN**	41
Hood River County, OR . . .	21	Buffalo County, NE	43	Lawrence County, TN	41
		Kearney County, NE	7		
Hope, AR	33			**Lebanon, MO**	33
Hempstead County, AR . . .	23	**Keene, NH**	76	Laclede County, MO	33
Nevada County, AR.	10	Cheshire County, NH.	76		
				Lebanon, NH-VT	171
Houghton, MI	38	**Kendallville, IN**	47	Grafton County, NH.	84
Houghton County, MI.	36	Noble County, IN.	47	Orange County, VT	29
Keweenaw County, MI. . . .	2			Windsor County, VT	58
		Kennett, MO	33		
Hudson, NY	63	Dunklin County, MO	33	**Levelland, TX**	23
Columbia County, NY	63			Hockley County, TX.	23
		Keokuk-Fort Madison,			
Humboldt, TN	48	**IA-MO**	44	**Lewisburg, PA**	43
Gibson County, TN	48	Lee County, IA	37	Union County, PA	43
		Clark County, MO	7		
Huntingdon, PA	46			**Lewisburg, TN**	28
Huntingdon County, PA . . .	46	**Kerrville, TX**	45	Marshall County, TN	28
		Kerr County, TX	45		
Huntington, IN	38			**Lewistown, PA**	46
Huntington County, IN	38	**Ketchikan, AK.**	13	Mifflin County, PA	46
		Ketchikan Gateway			
Huntsville, TX.	62	Borough, AK.	13	**Lexington, NE.**	27
Walker County, TX	62			Dawson County, NE	25
		Key West-Marathon, FL. . . .	79	Gosper County, NE.	2
Huron, SD.	16	Monroe County, FL	79		
Beadle County, SD	16			**Lexington Park, MD**	93
		Kill Devil Hills, NC	33	St. Mary's County, MD. . . .	93
Hutchinson, KS.	64	Dare County, NC.	33		
Reno County, KS	64			**Liberal, KS**	23
		Kingsville, TX	32	Seward County, KS.	23
Hutchinson, MN	36	Kenedy County, TX.	(Z)		
McLeod County, MN	36	Kleberg County, TX.	31	**Lincoln, IL.**	31
				Logan County, IL.	31
Indiana, PA.	89	**Kinston, NC**	59		
Indiana County, PA	89	Lenoir County, NC.	59	**Lincolnton, NC**	67
				Lincoln County, NC	67
Indianola, MS	33	**Kirksville, MO**	29		
Sunflower County, MS. . . .	33	Adair County, MO	25	**Lock Haven, PA**	37
		Schuyler County, MO.	4	Clinton County, PA	37
Iron Mountain, MI-WI.	32				
Dickinson County, MI.	27	**Klamath Falls, OR.**	65	**Logansport, IN**	40
Florence County, WI	5	Klamath County, OR	65	Cass County, IN	40
Jackson, WY-ID	26	**Kodiak, AK**	13	**London, KY**	55
Teton County, ID.	7	Kodiak Island Borough, AK.	13	Laurel County, KY.	55
Teton County, WY.	19				
		Laconia, NH	60	**Los Alamos, NM**	19
Jacksonville, IL.	41	Belknap County, NH	60	Los Alamos County, NM. . .	19
Morgan County, IL.	36				
Scott County, IL	6	**La Follette, TN**	40	**Lufkin, TX.**	81
		Campbell County, TN	40	Angelina County, TX	81
Jacksonville, TX	48				
Cherokee County, TX	48	**La Grande, OR**	25	**Lumberton, NC**	126
		Union County, OR.	25	Robeson County, NC.	126
Jamestown, ND.	21				
Stutsman County, ND	21	**LaGrange, GA**	60	**Macomb, IL.**	33
		Troup County, GA	60	McDonough County, IL . . .	33
Jamestown-Dunkirk-					
Fredonia, NY.	138	**Lake City, FL**	60	**Madison, IN**	32
Chautauqua County, NY . .	138	Columbia County, FL.	60	Jefferson County, IN	32
Jasper, IN	53	**Lake Havasu City-Kingman,**		**Madisonville, KY.**	47
Dubois County, IN.	40	**AZ**	171	Hopkins County, KY	47
Pike County, IN.	13	Mohave County, AZ.	171		
				Magnolia, AR	25
Jennings, LA	31	**Lamesa, TX**	14	Columbia County, AR	25
Jefferson Davis Parish, LA.	31	Dawson County, TX.	14		
				Malone, NY.	51
Jesup, GA	28	**Lancaster, SC**	63	Franklin County, NY	51
Wayne County, GA	28	Lancaster County, SC	63		
				Manhattan, KS	107
Juneau, AK.	31	**Laramie, WY**	32	Geary County, KS	26
Juneau Borough, AK	31	Albany County, WY	32	Pottawatomie County, KS. .	19
				Riley County, KS.	62
Kahului-Wailuku, HI	136	**Las Vegas, NM**	30		
Maui County, HI	136	San Miguel County, NM. . .	30	**Manitowoc, WI**	82
				Manitowoc County, WI. . . .	82
Kalispell, MT.	79	**Laurel, MS**	83		
Flathead County, MT.	79	Jasper County, MS	18	**Mankato-North Mankato,**	
		Jones County, MS.	65	**MN**	88
Kapaa, HI	61			Blue Earth County, MN . . .	57
Kauai County, HI.	61	**Laurinburg, NC**	36	Nicollet County, MN.	31
		Scotland County, NC.	36		

918   Appendix II

Micropolitan statistical area Component county	Popu-lation, 2003 (1,000)	Micropolitan statistical area Component county	Popu-lation, 2003 (1,000)	Micropolitan statistical area Component county	Popu-lation, 2003 (1,000)
Marinette, WI-MI	68	**Midland, MI**.	84	**Natchez, MS-LA**	53
Menominee County, MI . . .	25	Midland County, MI	84	Concordia Parish, LA.	20
Marinette County, WI.	43			Adams County, MS	33
		Milledgeville, GA.	55		
Marion, IN.	72	Baldwin County, GA	45	**Natchitoches, LA**	39
Grant County, IN.	72	Hancock County, GA	10	Natchitoches Parish, LA. . .	39
Marion, OH.	66	**Minden, LA.**	41	**New Bern, NC.**	115
Marion County, OH	66	Webster Parish, LA	41	Craven County, NC.	92
				Jones County, NC.	10
Marion-Herrin, IL.	62	**Mineral Wells, TX**	27	Pamlico County, NC	13
Williamson County, IL	62	Palo Pinto County, TX	27		
				Newberry, SC	37
Marquette, MI	65	**Minot, ND.**	65	Newberry County, SC	37
Marquette County, MI	65	McHenry County, ND.	6		
		Renville County, ND	2	**New Castle, IN**	48
Marshall, MN.	25	Ward County, ND	57	Henry County, IN	48
Lyon County, MN	25				
		Mitchell, SD	22	**New Castle, PA**.	93
Marshall, MO	23	Davison County, SD	19	Lawrence County, PA	93
Saline County, MO	23	Hanson County, SD.	4		
				New Iberia, LA.	74
Marshall, TX	63	**Moberly, MO.**	25	Iberia Parish, LA.	74
Harrison County, TX	63	Randolph County, MO	25		
				New Philadelphia-Dover,	
Marshalltown, IA.	39	**Monroe, WI.**	34	**OH**	92
Marshall County, IA.	39	Green County, WI	34	Tuscarawas County, OH . .	92
Martin, TN.	34	**Montrose, CO**	36	**Newport, TN**	34
Weakley County, TN	34	Montrose County, CO	36	Cocke County, TN.	34
Martinsville, VA.	72	**Morehead City, NC**	61	**Newton, IA**	38
Henry County, VA	57	Carteret County, NC	61	Jasper County, IA	38
Martinsville city, VA	15				
		Morgan City, LA	52	**New Ulm, MN**	27
Maryville, MO	22	St. Mary Parish, LA.	52	Brown County, MN	27
Nodaway County, MO	22				
		Moscow, ID.	35	**Nogales, AZ**	40
Mason City, IA	53	Latah County, ID.	35	Santa Cruz County, AZ . . .	40
Cerro Gordo County, IA . . .	45				
Worth County, IA.	8	**Moses Lake, WA.**	79	**Norfolk, NE.**	50
		Grant County, WA	79	Madison County, NE	36
Mayfield, KY	37			Pierce County, NE.	8
Graves County, KY	37	**Moultrie, GA**	43	Stanton County, NE.	7
		Colquitt County, GA.	43		
Maysville, KY	31			**North Platte, NE**	36
Lewis County, KY	14	**Mountain Home, AR**	39	Lincoln County, NE	35
Mason County, KY	17	Baxter County, AR.	39	Logan County, NE.	1
				McPherson County, NE . . .	1
McAlester, OK.	44	**Mountain Home, ID**	29		
Pittsburg County, OK.	44	Elmore County, ID.	29	**North Vernon, IN.**	28
				Jennings County, IN	28
McComb, MS	53	**Mount Airy, NC**	72		
Amite County, MS	14	Surry County, NC	72	**North Wilkesboro, NC**	67
Pike County, MS.	39			Wilkes County, NC	67
		Mount Pleasant, MI	65		
McMinnville, TN	39	Isabella County, MI	65	**Norwalk, OH**	60
Warren County, TN	39			Huron County, OH.	60
		Mount Pleasant, TX	29		
McPherson, KS.	29	Titus County, TX	29	**Oak Harbor, WA**	76
McPherson County, KS . . .	29			Island County, WA.	76
		Mount Sterling, KY	42		
Meadville, PA	90	Bath County, KY	11	**Oak Hill, WV**	47
Crawford County, PA.	90	Menifee County, KY.	7	Fayette County, WV	47
		Montgomery County, KY . .	24		
Menomonie, WI.	41			**Ocean Pines, MD**	50
Dunn County, WI.	41	**Mount Vernon, IL**	49	Worcester County, MD. . . .	50
		Hamilton County, IL.	8		
Meridian, MS.	106	Jefferson County, IL	40	**Ogdensburg-Massena, NY.** .	112
Clarke County, MS	18			St. Lawrence County, NY. .	112
Kemper County, MS	10	**Mount Vernon, OH**	57		
Lauderdale County, MS . . .	78	Knox County, OH	57	**Oil City, PA.**	57
				Venango County, PA	57
Merrill, WI.	30	**Murray, KY**	35		
Lincoln County, WI	30	Calloway County, KY.	35	**Okeechobee, FL**	37
				Okeechobee County, FL . .	37
Mexico, MO	26	**Muscatine, IA**	54		
Audrain County, MO	26	Louisa County, IA	12	**Olean, NY.**	83
		Muscatine County, IA.	42	Cattaraugus County, NY . .	83
Miami, OK.	33				
Ottawa County, OK.	33	**Muskogee, OK**	70	**Oneonta, NY.**	62
		Muskogee County, OK. . . .	70	Otsego County, NY.	62
Middlesborough, KY	30				
Bell County, KY	30	**Nacogdoches, TX**	60	**Ontario, OR-ID**	53
		Nacogdoches County, TX. .	60	Payette County, ID	21
				Malheur County, OR	31

U.S. Census Bureau, Statistical Abstract of the United States: 2004-2005

Micropolitan statistical area Component county	Popu- lation, 2003 (1,000)	Micropolitan statistical area Component county	Popu- lation, 2003 (1,000)	Micropolitan statistical area Component county	Popu- lation, 2003 (1,000)
Opelousas-Eunice, LA.	89	**Pierre Part, LA**	23	**Rochelle, IL**	53
St. Landry Parish, LA	89	Assumption Parish, LA . . .	23	Ogle County, IL.	53
Orangeburg, SC	91	**Pittsburg, KS**	38	**Rockingham, NC.**	47
Orangeburg County, SC. . .	91	Crawford County, KS.	38	Richmond County, NC	47
Oskaloosa, IA	22	**Plainview, TX**	36	**Rockland, ME.**	40
Mahaska County, IA	22	Hale County, TX	36	Knox County, ME	40
Ottawa-Streator, IL	153	**Platteville, WI**	49	**Rock Springs, WY.**	37
Bureau County, IL.	35	Grant County, WI	49	Sweetwater County, WY . .	37
La Salle County, IL	112	**Plattsburgh, NY**	81	**Rolla, MO**	42
Putnam County, IL	6	Clinton County, NY	81	Phelps County, MO.	42
Ottumwa, IA	36	**Plymouth, IN.**	46	**Roseburg, OR.**	102
Wapello County, IA	36	Marshall County, IN.	46	Douglas County, OR	102
Owatonna, MN	35	**Point Pleasant, WV-OH**	57	**Roswell, NM**	61
Steele County, MN	35	Gallia County, OH.	31	Chaves County, NM	61
Owosso, MI	73	Mason County, WV	26	**Russellville, AR**	77
Shiawassee County, MI . . .	73	**Ponca City, OK.**	47	Pope County, AR	55
Oxford, MS	40	Kay County, OK	47	Yell County, AR.	21
Lafayette County, MS	40	**Pontiac, IL**	39	**Ruston, LA**	58
Paducah, KY-IL.	98	Livingston County, IL.	39	Jackson Parish, LA	15
Massac County, IL	15	**Poplar Bluff, MO**	41	Lincoln Parish, LA.	42
Ballard County, KY	8	Butler County, MO.	41	**Rutland, VT**	64
Livingston County, KY	10	**Portales, NM.**	18	Rutland County, VT.	64
McCracken County, KY . . .	65	Roosevelt County, NM. . . .	18	**Safford, AZ.**	41
Pahrump, NV	36	**Port Angeles, WA**	67	Graham County, AZ.	33
Nye County, NV	36	Clallam County, WA	67	Greenlee County, AZ.	8
Palatka, FL.	72	**Portsmouth, OH**	77	**St. Marys, GA**	45
Putnam County, FL	72	Scioto County, OH	77	Camden County, GA	45
Palestine, TX	55	**Pottsville, PA**	148	**St. Marys, PA**	34
Anderson County, TX	55	Schuylkill County, PA.	148	Elk County, PA	34
Palm Coast, FL.	62	**Price, UT**	20	**Salina, KS.**	60
Flagler County, FL.	62	Carbon County, UT	20	Ottawa County, KS	6
Pampa, TX	22	**Prineville, OR**	21	Saline County, KS.	54
Gray County, TX.	21	Crook County, OR.	21	**Salisbury, NC**	134
Roberts County, TX.	1	**Pullman, WA.**	41	Rowan County, NC	134
Paragould, AR	38	Whitman County, WA. . . .	41	**Sanford, NC**	49
Greene County, AR	38	**Quincy, IL-MO.**	78	Lee County, NC	49
Paris, TN	31	Adams County, IL.	68	**Sault Ste. Marie, MI.**	39
Henry County, TN	31	Lewis County, MO.	10	Chippewa County, MI	39
Paris, TX	49	**Raymondville, TX**	20	**Sayre, PA**	63
Lamar County, TX.	49	Willacy County, TX	20	Bradford County, PA	63
Parsons, KS	22	**Red Bluff, CA**	59	**Scottsbluff, NE.**	38
Labette County, KS.	22	Tehama County, CA	59	Banner County, NE	1
Payson, AZ.	51	**Red Wing, MN.**	45	Scotts Bluff County, NE . . .	37
Gila County, AZ	51	Goodhue County, MN	45	**Scottsboro, AL.**	54
Pecos, TX.	12	**Rexburg, ID**	42	Jackson County, AL.	54
Reeves County, TX.	12	Fremont County, ID.	12	**Scottsburg, IN**	24
Pella, IA	32	Madison County, ID.	30	Scott County, IN	24
Marion County, IA	32	**Richmond, IN**	70	**Seaford, DE**	168
Pendleton-Hermiston, OR . .	84	Wayne County, IN.	70	Sussex County, DE	168
Morrow County, OR.	12	**Richmond-Berea, KY.**	91	**Searcy, AR**	70
Umatilla County, OR	72	Madison County, KY	75	White County, AR	70
Peru, IN	36	Rockcastle County, KY . . .	17	**Sebring, FL.**	91
Miami County, IN	36	**Rio Grande City, TX**	58	Highlands County, FL	91
Phoenix Lake-Cedar Ridge,		Starr County, TX.	58	**Sedalia, MO**	39
CA	57	**Riverton, WY**	36	Pettis County, MO.	39
Tuolumne County, CA	57	Fremont County, WY.	36	**Selinsgrove, PA**	38
Picayune, MS	51	**Roanoke Rapids, NC.**	78	Snyder County, PA	38
Pearl River County, MS . . .	51	Halifax County, NC	56	**Selma, AL.**	45
Pierre, SD.	19	Northampton County, NC . .	22	Dallas County, AL.	45
Hughes County, SD.	17				
Stanley County, SD.	3				

U.S. Census Bureau, Statistical Abstract of the United States: 2004-2005

Micropolitan statistical area / Component county	Population, 2003 (1,000)
Seneca, SC	69
Oconee County, SC	69
Seneca Falls, NY	35
Seneca County, NY	35
Sevierville, TN	76
Sevier County, TN	76
Seymour, IN	42
Jackson County, IN	42
Shawnee, OK	67
Pottawatomie County, OK	67
Shelby, NC	98
Cleveland County, NC	98
Shelbyville, TN	40
Bedford County, TN	40
Shelton, WA	52
Mason County, WA	52
Sheridan, WY	27
Sheridan County, WY	27
Sidney, OH	49
Shelby County, OH	49
Sierra Vista-Douglas, AZ	122
Cochise County, AZ	122
Sikeston, MO	41
Scott County, MO	41
Silver City, NM	30
Grant County, NM	30
Silverthorne, CO	25
Summit County, CO	25
Snyder, TX	16
Scurry County, TX	16
Somerset, KY	58
Pulaski County, KY	58
Somerset, PA	79
Somerset County, PA	79
Southern Pines-Pinehurst, NC	79
Moore County, NC	79
Spearfish, SD	22
Lawrence County, SD	22
Spencer, IA	17
Clay County, IA	17
Spirit Lake, IA	16
Dickinson County, IA	16
Starkville, MS	43
Oktibbeha County, MS	43
Statesboro, GA	58
Bulloch County, GA	58
Statesville-Mooresville, NC	133
Iredell County, NC	133
Staunton-Waynesboro, VA	112
Augusta County, VA	67
Staunton city, VA	24
Waynesboro city, VA	20
Stephenville, TX	33
Erath County, TX	33
Sterling, CO	21
Logan County, CO	21
Sterling, IL	60
Whiteside County, IL	60

Micropolitan statistical area / Component county	Population, 2003 (1,000)
Stevens Point, WI	67
Portage County, WI	67
Stillwater, OK	71
Payne County, OK	71
Storm Lake, IA	20
Buena Vista County, IA	20
Sturgis, MI	63
St. Joseph County, MI	63
Sulphur Springs, TX	33
Hopkins County, TX	33
Summerville, GA	26
Chattooga County, GA	26
Sunbury, PA	93
Northumberland County, PA	93
Susanville, CA	34
Lassen County, CA	34
Sweetwater, TX	15
Nolan County, TX	15
Tahlequah, OK	44
Cherokee County, OK	44
Talladega-Sylacauga, AL	80
Talladega County, AL	80
Tallulah, LA	13
Madison Parish, LA	13
Taos, NM	31
Taos County, NM	31
Taylorville, IL	35
Christian County, IL	35
The Villages, FL	59
Sumter County, FL	59
Thomaston, GA	28
Upson County, GA	28
Thomasville, GA	44
Thomas County, GA	44
Thomasville-Lexington, NC	152
Davidson County, NC	152
Tiffin, OH	58
Seneca County, OH	58
Tifton, GA	40
Tift County, GA	40
Toccoa, GA	25
Stephens County, GA	25
Torrington, CT	188
Litchfield County, CT	188
Traverse City, MI	138
Benzie County, MI	17
Grand Traverse County, MI	82
Kalkaska County, MI	17
Leelanau County, MI	22
Troy, AL	29
Pike County, AL	29
Truckee-Grass Valley, CA	96
Nevada County, CA	96
Tullahoma, TN	96
Coffee County, TN	50
Franklin County, TN	41
Moore County, TN	6

Micropolitan statistical area / Component county	Population, 2003 (1,000)
Tupelo, MS	128
Itawamba County, MS	23
Lee County, MS	78
Pontotoc County, MS	28
Tuskegee, AL	23
Macon County, AL	23
Twin Falls, ID	86
Jerome County, ID	19
Twin Falls County, ID	67
Ukiah, CA	88
Mendocino County, CA	88
Union, SC	29
Union County, SC	29
Union City, TN-KY	40
Fulton County, KY	7
Obion County, TN	32
Urbana, OH	40
Champaign County, OH	40
Uvalde, TX	27
Uvalde County, TX	27
Valley, AL	36
Chambers County, AL	36
Van Wert, OH	29
Van Wert County, OH	29
Vermillion, SD	13
Clay County, SD	13
Vernal, UT	26
Uintah County, UT	26
Vernon, TX	14
Wilbarger County, TX	14
Vicksburg, MS	49
Warren County, MS	49
Vidalia, GA	35
Montgomery County, GA	9
Toombs County, GA	26
Vincennes, IN	39
Knox County, IN	39
Wabash, IN	34
Wabash County, IN	34
Wahpeton, ND-MN	25
Wilkin County, MN	7
Richland County, ND	18
Walla Walla, WA	57
Walla Walla County, WA	57
Walterboro, SC	39
Colleton County, SC	39
Wapakoneta, OH	47
Auglaize County, OH	47
Warren, PA	43
Warren County, PA	43
Warrensburg, MO	50
Johnson County, MO	50
Warsaw, IN	75
Kosciusko County, IN	75
Washington, IN	30
Daviess County, IN	30
Washington, NC	45
Beaufort County, NC	45
Washington, OH	28
Fayette County, OH	28

U.S. Census Bureau, Statistical Abstract of the United States: 2004-2005

Micropolitan statistical area Component county	Popu- lation, 2003 (1,000)	Micropolitan statistical area Component county	Popu- lation, 2003 (1,000)	Micropolitan statistical area Component county	Popu- lation, 2003 (1,000)
Watertown, SD	32	**West Point, MS**	22	**Winona, MN**	49
Codington County, SD	26	Clay County, MS	22	Winona County, MN	49
Hamlin County, SD	6	**Whitewater, WI**	97	**Wisconsin Rapids-**	
Watertown-Fort Atkinson,		Walworth County, WI	97	**Marshfield, WI**	75
WI.	77	**Willimantic, CT**	113	Wood County, WI	75
Jefferson County, WI	77	Windham County, CT	113	**Woodward, OK**	18
Watertown-Fort Drum, NY . .	115	**Williston, ND.**	19	Woodward County, OK . . .	18
Jefferson County, NY.	115	Williams County, ND	19	**Wooster, OH**	113
Wauchula, FL	28	**Willmar, MN**	41	Wayne County, OH	113
Hardee County, FL	28	Kandiyohi County, MN	41	**Worthington, MN.**	21
Waycross, GA.	52	**Wilmington, OH**	42	Nobles County, MN.	21
Pierce County, GA	16	Clinton County, OH	42	**Yankton, SD**	21
Ware County, GA	36	**Wilson, NC**	75	Yankton County, SD	21
West Helena, AR.	25	Wilson County, NC	75	**Yazoo City, MS**	28
Phillips County, AR	25	**Winfield, KS**	36	Yazoo County, MS	28
West Plains, MO	37	Cowley County, KS	36	**Zanesville, OH**	85
Howell County, MO	37			Muskingum County, OH. . .	85

Z Less than 500.

Source: U.S. Census Bureau, unpublished data.

U.S. Census Bureau, Statistical Abstract of the United States: 2004-2005

Appendix III
Limitations of the Data

Introduction The data presented in this *Statistical Abstract* came from many sources. The sources include not only Federal statistical bureaus and other organizations that collect and issue statistics as their principal activity, but also governmental administrative and regulatory agencies, private research bodies, trade associations, insurance companies, health associations, and private organizations such as the National Education Association and philanthropic foundations. Consequently, the data vary considerably as to reference periods, definitions of terms, and, for ongoing series, the number and frequency of time periods for which data are available.

The statistics presented were obtained and tabulated by various means. Some statistics are based on complete enumerations or censuses while others are based on samples. Some information is extracted from records kept for administrative or regulatory purposes (school enrollment, hospital records, securities registration, financial accounts, social security records, income tax returns, etc.), while other information is obtained explicitly for statistical purposes through interviews or by mail. The estimation procedures used vary from highly sophisticated scientific techniques, to crude "informed guesses."

Each set of data relates to a group of individuals or units of interest referred to as the *target universe* or *target population*, or simply as the *universe* or *population*. Prior to data collection the target universe should be clearly defined. For example, if data are to be collected for the universe of households in the United States, it is necessary to define a "household." The target universe may not be completely tractable. Cost and other considerations may restrict data collection to a *survey universe* based on some available list; such a list may be inaccurate or out of date. This list is called a *survey frame* or *sampling frame*.

The data in many tables are based on data obtained from all population units, *a census,* or on data obtained from only a portion, or *sample,* of the population units. When the data presented are based on a sample, the sample is usually a scientifically selected *probability sample.* This is a sample selected from a list or sampling frame in such a way that every possible sample has a known chance of selection, and usually each unit selected can be assigned a number, greater than zero and less than or equal to one, representing its likelihood or probability of selection.

For large-scale sample surveys, the probability sample of units is often selected as a multistage sample. The first stage of a multi-stage sample is the selection of a probability sample of large groups of population members, referred to as primary sampling units (PSUs). For example, in a national multi-stage household sample, PSUs are often counties or groups of counties. The second stage of a multi-stage sample is the selection, within each PSU selected at the first stage, of smaller groups of population units, referred to as secondary sampling units. In subsequent stages of selection, smaller and smaller nested groups are chosen until the ultimate sample of population units is obtained. To qualify a multi-stage sample as a probability sample, all stages of sampling must be conducted using probability sampling methods.

Prior to selection at each stage of a multi-stage (or a singlestage) sample, a list of the sampling units or sampling frame for that stage must be obtained. For example, for the first stage of selection of a national household sample, a list of the counties and county groups that form the PSUs must be obtained. For the final stage of selection, lists of households and sometimes persons within the households have to be compiled in the field. For surveys of economic entities and for the economic censuses the Bureau generally uses a frame constructed from the Bureau's Business Register. The Business Register contains all establishments with payroll in the United States, including small single-establishment firms as well as large multi-establishment firms.

Wherever the quantities in a table refer to an entire universe, but are constructed from data collected in a sample survey, the table quantities are referred to as *sample estimates*. In constructing a sample estimate, an attempt is made to come as close as is feasible to the corresponding universe quantity that would be obtained from a complete census of the universe. Estimates based on a sample will, however, generally differ from the hypothetical census figures. Two classifications of errors are associated with estimates based on sample surveys: (1) *sampling error* the error arising from the use of a sample, rather than a census, to estimate population quantities; and (2) *nonsampling error* those errors arising from nonsampling sources. As discussed below, the magnitude of the sampling error for an estimate can usually be estimated from the sample data. However, the magnitude of the nonsampling error for an estimate can rarely be estimated. Consequently, the actual error in an estimate typically exceeds the error that can be estimated.

The particular sample used in a survey is only one of a large number of possible samples of the same size that could have been selected using the same sampling procedure. Estimates derived from the different samples would, in general, differ from each other. The *standard error* is a measure of the variation among the estimates derived from all possible samples. The standard error is the most commonly used measure of the sampling error of an estimate. Valid estimates of the standard errors of survey estimates can usually be calculated from the data collected in a probability sample. For convenience, the standard error is sometimes expressed as a percent of the estimate and is called the relative standard error or *coefficient of variation* (CV). For example, an estimate of 200 units with an estimated standard error of 10 units has an estimated CV of 5 percent.

A sample estimate, together with an estimate of its standard error or CV, can be used to construct an interval estimate. This "confidence interval" has a prescribed confidence that it includes the average of the estimates derived from *all* possible samples conducted under the same sampling design. To illustrate, suppose that all possible samples were selected under essentially the same general conditions, using the same sample design, and a sample estimate and its estimated standard error were calculated from each sample. Then the average estimate derived from *all possible* samples would be included in approximately 90 percent of the intervals from 1.65 standard errors below the sample estimate to 1.65 standard errors above the sample estimate, or in approximately 95 percent of the intervals from two standard errors below the sample estimate to two standard errors above the sample estimate.

Thus, for a particular sample, one can say with the appropriate level of confidence (e.g., 90 percent or 95 percent) that the average of all possible samples is included in the constructed interval. As an example of a confidence interval, suppose that an estimate is 200 units with a standard error of 10 units. An approximate 95 percent confidence interval (plus or minus 2 standard errors) is from 180 to 220.

Care should be taken before making inferences from data in tables that were derived from a sample. In some cases, what appears to be a change from one time period to another, or a difference between two states or other categories, might not be statistically significant; that is, the estimated difference may be small relative to the sampling error of that difference. Similar caution should be taken regarding the rankings of states or other categories in the tables. The order of the categories might not be statistically significant. More complex statistical methods may be required before making inferential statements.

All surveys and censuses are subject to nonsampling errors, which can arise in various ways. A common source is missing data, such as unit nonresponse (when no usable data are obtained from a sampled unit) or item nonresponse (when only a portion of a response may be usable) due to failure to reach the respondent or the respondent's unwillingness or inability to provide information. In addition, the interpretation of questions by respondents or interviewers can induce response error; errors can arise when respondents must estimate; the actions of coders and keyers can lead to processing error. Sometimes a serious source of error is undercoverage (missing units) or overcoverage (duplication) of the target universe. Nonsampling errors often result in an understatement of the error and thus an overstatement of the precision of survey estimates. Estimating the magnitude of nonsampling errors typically requires special experiments or access to independent data; consequently, their magnitudes are seldom available.

Most types of nonsampling errors that affect surveys also occur in complete censuses. Because surveys can be conducted on a smaller scale than censuses, nonsampling errors can sometimes be controlled more tightly in surveys. Relatively more funds and effort can perhaps be expended toward eliciting responses, detecting and correcting response error, and reducing processing errors. As a result, survey results can sometimes be more accurate than census results.

To compensate for suspected nonsampling errors, adjustments are often made to the sample estimates. For example, procedures are frequently applied to address nonresponse, both unit and partial. In many surveys, unit nonresponse is treated by means of a noninterview adjustment, whereby the sampling weights of responding units are increased to represent those of nonresponding units. Such an adjustment is usually made separately within various groups of sample units, formed by placing together respondents and nonrespondents that have similar design or ancillary characteristics.

In some data collection programs, unit nonresponse is handled by imputing (substituting) all the replies of a respondent for those of a nonrespondent. For example, in some censuses, nearestneighbor imputation is used. That is, the data from the closest (in some sense, perhaps geographic) responding unit satisfying some criterion usually based on similarity to the nonresponding unit are substituted into the record of the nonrespondent. Imputation is more commonly applied to address item nonresponse. When one or more data items are missing from a unit that has responded, the missing item is often filled using a statistical procedure that may be based on other information available on that unit, or on data obtained from other units in the sample or population.

For an estimate calculated from a sample survey, the *total error* in the estimate is composed of the sampling error, which can usually be estimated from the sample, and the nonsampling error, which usually cannot be estimated from the sample. The total error present in a population quantity obtained from a complete census is composed of only nonsampling errors. Ideally, estimates of the total error associated with data given in the *Statistical Abstract* tables should be given. However, due to the unavailability of estimates of nonsampling errors, only estimates of the levels of sampling errors, in terms of estimated standard errors or coefficients of variation, are available. To obtain estimates of the estimated standard errors from the sample of interest, obtain a copy of the referenced report that appears at the end of each table.

Source of Additional Material: The Federal Committee on Statistical Methodology (FCSM) is an interagency committee dedicated to improving the quality of Federal statistics. <http://fcsm.ssd.census.gov>

Principal data bases Beginning below are brief descriptions of 37 of the sample surveys and censuses that provide a substantial portion of the data contained in this *Abstract*.

U.S. DEPARTMENT OF AGRICULTURE, National Agricultural Statistics Service

Basic Area Frame Sample

Universe, Frequency, and Types of Data: June agricultural survey collects data on planted acreage and livestock inventories. The survey also serves to measure list incompleteness and is subsampled for multiple frame surveys.

U.S. Census Bureau, Statistical Abstract of the United States: 2004-2005

Type of Data Collection Operation: Stratified probability sample of about 11,000 land area units of about 1 sq. mile (range from 0.1 sq. mile in cities to several sq. miles in open grazing areas). Sample includes 42,000 parcels of agricultural land. About 20 percent of the sample replaced annually.

Data Collection and Imputation Procedures: Data collection is by personal enumeration. Imputation is based on enumerator observation or data reported by respondents having similar agricultural characteristics.

Estimates of Sampling Error: Estimated CVs range from 1 percent to 2 percent for regional estimates to 3 percent to 6 percent for state estimates of major crop acres and livestock inventories.

Other (nonsampling) Errors: Minimized through rigid quality controls on the collection process and careful review of all reported data.

Sources of Additional Material: U.S. Department of Agriculture, National Agricultural Statistics Service, USDA's National Agricultural Statistics Service: The Fact Finders of Agriculture, September 1994.

Census of Agriculture

Universe, Frequency, and Types of Data: Complete count of U.S. farms and ranches conducted once every 5 years with data at the national, state, and county level. Data published on farm numbers and related items/characteristics.

Type of Data Collection Operation: Complete census for number of farms; land in farms; agriculture products sold; total cropland; irrigated land; farm operator characteristics; livestock and poultry inventory and sales; and selected crops harvested. Market value of land and buildings, total farm production expenses, machinery and equipment, fertilizer and chemicals, and farm labor are estimated from a sample of farms.

Data Collection and Imputation Procedures: Data collection is by mailing questionnaires to all farmers and ranchers. Nonrespondents are contacted by telephone and correspondence followups. Imputations were made for all

nonresponse item/characteristics. Coverage adjustments were made to account for missed farms and ranches.

Estimates of Sampling Error: Variability in the estimates is due to the sample selection and estimation for items collected by sample and census nonresponse and coverage estimation procedures. The CVs for national and state estimates are generally very small. Approximately 81 percent response rate.

Other (nonsampling) Errors: Nonsampling errors are due to incompleteness of the census mailing list, duplications on the list, respondent reporting errors, errors in editing reported data, and in imputation for missing data. Evaluation studies are conducted to measure certain nonsampling errors such as list coverage and classification error. Results from the evaluation program for the 2002 census indicate the net under coverage amounted to about 18 percent of the nation's total farms.

Sources of Additional Material: U.S. Department of Agriculture (NASS), 2002 Census of Agriculture, Volume 1, Subject Series C Part 1, Agriculture Atlas of the U.S.; Part 2, Coverage Evaluation; Part 3, Rankings of States and Counties; Part 4, History; Part 5, ZIP Code Tabulation of Selected Items; and Volume 3 Special Studies, Part 1, Farm and Ranch Irrigation Survey; Part 2, Census of Horticultural Specialties; Part 3, Census of Aquaculture.

Multiple Frame Surveys

Universe, Frequency, and Types of Data: Surveys of U.S. farm operators to obtain data on major livestock inventories, selected crop acreage and production, grain stocks, and farm labor characteristics; farm economic data and chemical use data.

Type of Data Collection Operation: Primary frame is obtained from general or special purpose lists, supplemented by a probability sample of land areas used to estimate for list incompleteness.

Data Collection and Imputation Procedures: Mail, telephone, or personal interviews used for initial data collection. Mail nonrespondent followup by phone and personal interviews. Imputation based on average of respondents.

Estimates of Sampling Error: Estimated CV for number of hired farm workers is about 3 percent. Estimated CVs range from 1 percent to 2 percent for regional estimates to 3 percent to 6 percent for state estimates of livestock inventories and crop acreage.

Other (nonsampling) Errors: In addition to above, replicated sampling procedures used to monitor effects of changes in survey procedures.

Sources of Additional Material: U.S. Department of Agriculture, National Agricultural Statistics Service), USDA's National Agricultural Statistics Service: The Fact Finders of Agriculture, September 1994.

Objective Yield Surveys

Universe, Frequency, and Types of Data: Surveys for data on corn, cotton, potatoes, soybeans, and wheat, to forecast and estimate yields.

Type of Data Collection Operation: Random location of plots in probability sample. Corn, cotton, soybeans, spring wheat, and durum wheat selected in June from Basic Area Frame Sample (see above). Winter wheat and potatoes selected from March and June multiple frame surveys, respectively.

Data Collection and Imputation Procedures: Enumerators count and measure plant characteristics in sample fields. Production measured from plots at harvest. Harvest loss measured from post harvest gleanings.

Estimates of Sampling Error: CVs for national estimates of production are about 2-3 percent.

Other (nonsampling) Errors: In addition to above, replicated sampling procedures used to monitor effects of changes in survey procedures.

Sources of Additional Material: U.S. Department of Agriculture, National Agricultural Statistics Service), USDA's National Agricultural Statistics Service: The Fact Finders of Agriculture, September 1994.

U.S. BUREAU OF JUSTICE STATISTICS (BJS)

National Crime Victimization Survey

Universe, Frequency, and Types of Data: Monthly survey of individuals and households in the United States to obtain data on criminal victimization of those units for compilation of annual estimates.

Type of Data Collection Operation: National probability sample survey of about 42,000 interviewed households in 203 PSUs selected from a list of addresses from the 1990 census, supplemented by new construction permits and an area sample where permits are not required.

Data Collection and Imputation Procedures: Interviews are conducted every 6 months for 3 years for each household in the sample; 7,000 households are interviewed monthly. Personal interviews are used in the first interview; the intervening interviews are conducted by telephone whenever possible.

Estimates of Sampling Error: CVs for 2002 estimates are: 3.7 percent for personal crimes (includes all crimes of violence plus purse snatching crimes), 3.8 percent for crimes of violence; 12.6 percent for estimate of rape/sexual assault counts; 9.3 percent for robbery counts; 4.0 percent for assault counts; 15.5 percent for purse snatching (it refers to purse snatching and pocket picking); 2.0 percent for property crimes; 4.0 percent for burglary counts; 2.2 percent for theft (of property); and 6.2 percent for motor vehicle theft counts.

Other (nonsampling) Errors: Respondent recall errors which may include reporting incidents for other than the reference period; interviewer coding and processing errors; and possible mistaken reporting or classifying of events. Adjustment is made for a household noninterview rate of about 7 percent and for a within-household noninterview rate of 10 percent.

Sources of Additional Material: U.S. Bureau of Justice Statistics, Criminal Victimization in the United States, annual.

U.S. Bureau of Labor Statistics

Consumer Expenditure Survey

(CES) Universe, Frequency and Types of Data: Consists of two continuous components: a quarterly Interview survey and a weekly Diary or record keeping survey. They are nationwide surveys that collect data on consumer expenditures, income, characteristics, and assets and liabilities. Samples are national probability samples of households that are representative of the civilian noninstitutional population. The surveys have been ongoing since 1980.

Type of Data Collection Operation: The Interview Survey is a panel rotation survey. Each panel is interviewed for five quarters and then dropped from the survey. About 7,500 consumer units are interviewed each quarter. The Diary Survey sample is new each year and consists of about 7,500 consumer units. Data are collected on an ongoing basis in 105 PSUs since 1996.

Data Collection and Imputation Procedures: For the Interview Survey, data are collected by personal interview with each consumer unit interviewed once per quarter for five consecutive quarters. Designed to collect information that respondents can recall for 3 months or longer, such as large or recurring expenditures. For the Diary Survey, respondents record all their expenditures in a self-reporting diary for two consecutive one-week periods. Designed to pick up items difficult to recall over a long period, such as detailed food expenditures. Missing or invalid attributes or expenditures are imputed. Income, assets, and liabilities are not imputed. The U.S. Census Bureau collects the data for the Bureau of Labor Statistics.

Estimates of Sampling Error: Standard error tables are available since 2000.

Other (nonsampling) Errors: Includes incorrect information given by respondents, data processing errors, interviewer errors, and so on. They occur regardless of whether data are collected from a sample or from the entire population.

Sources of Additional Material: Bureau of Labor Statistics, Internet site <http://www.bls.gov/cex>

Consumer Price Index (CPI)

Universe, Frequency, and Types of Data: Monthly survey of price changes of all types of consumer goods and services purchased by urban wage earners and clerical workers prior to 1978, and urban consumers thereafter. Both indexes continue to be published.

Type of Data Collection Operation: Prior to 1978, and since 1998, sample of various consumer items in 87 urban areas; from 1978 - 1997, in 85 PSUs, except from January 1987 through March 1988, when 91 areas were sampled.

Data Collection and Imputation Procedures: Prices of consumer items are obtained from about 50,000 housing units, and 23,000 other reporters in 87 areas. Prices of food, fuel, and a few other items are obtained monthly; prices of most other commodities and services are collected every month in the three largest geographic areas and every other month in others.

Estimates of Sampling Error: Estimates of standard errors are available.

Other (nonsampling) Errors: Errors result from inaccurate reporting, difficulties in defining concepts and their operational implementation, and introduction of product quality changes and new products.

Sources of Additional Material: U.S. Bureau of Labor Statistics, Internet site <http://stats.bls.gov/cpi> and BLS Handbook of Methods, Chapter 17, Bulletin 2490.

Current Employment Statistics (CES) Program

Universe, Frequency, and Types of Data: Monthly survey drawn from a sampling frame of over 8 million Unemployment Insurance tax accounts in order obtain data by industry on employment, hours, and earnings.

Type of Data Collection Operation: In 2003, the CES sample included about 160,000 businesses and government agencies, which represent approximately 400,000 individual worksites.

Data Collection and Imputation Procedures: Each month, the State agencies cooperating with BLS, as well as BLS Data Collection Centers, collect data through various automated collection modes and mail. BLS-Washington staff prepares national estimates of employment, hours, and earnings while States use the data to develop State and area estimates.

Estimates of Sampling Error: The relative standard error for total nonfarm employment is 0.2 percent.

Other (nonsampling) Errors): Estimates of employment adjusted annually to reflect complete universe. Average adjustment is 0.3 percent over the last decade, ranging from less than 0.1 percent to 0.7 percent.

Sources of Additional Material: U.S. Bureau of Labor Statistics, Employment and Earnings, monthly, Explanatory Notes and Estimates of Errors, Tables 2-A through 2-F.

National Compensation Survey

Universe, Frequency, and Types of Data: Nationwide sample survey of establishments of all employment size classes, stratified by geographic area, in private industry and state and local government. Data collected include wages and salaries, and employer costs of employee benefits. Data produced include percent changes in the cost of employment cited in the Employment Cost Index (ECI) and costs per hour worked for individual benefits cited in the Employer Costs for Employee Compensation (ECEC). The survey provides data by ownership (Private industry and state and local government), industry sector, major industry divisions, major occupational groups, bargaining status, metropolitan area status, and census region. ECEC also provides data by establishment size class.

Type of Data Collection Operation: Probability proportionate to size sample of establishments. The sample is replaced on a continual basis. Establishments are in the survey for approximately 5 years.

Data Collection and Imputation Procedures: For the initial visit, data are primarily collected in a personal visit to the establishment. Quarterly updates are obtained primarily by mail, fax, and telephone. Imputation is done for individual benefits.

Estimates of Sampling Error: Because standard errors vary from quarter to quarter, the ECI uses a 5-year moving average of standard errors to evaluate published series. These standard errors are available at <http://www.bls.gov/ncs/ect/home.htm>

Other (nonsampling) Errors: Nonsampling errors have a number of potential sources. The primary sources are (1) survey nonresponse and (2) data collection and processing errors. Nonsampling errors are not measured. Procedures have been implemented for reducing nonsampling errors, primarily through quality assurance programs. These programs include the use of data collection reinterviews, observed interviews, computer edits of the data, and systematic professional review of the reports on which the data are recorded. The programs also serve as a training device to provide feedback to the field economists, or data collectors, on errors. And, they provide information on the sources of error which can be remedied by improved collection instructions or computer processing edits. Extensive training of field economists is also conducted to maintain high standards in data collection.

Sources of Additional Material: Bureau of Labor Statistics, BLS Handbook of Methods, Chapter 8 (Bulletin 2490) and <http://www.bls.gov/ncs>

Producer Price Index (PPI)

Universe, Frequency, and Types of Data: Monthly survey of producing companies to determine price changes of all commodities produced in the United States for sale in commercial transactions. Data on agriculture, forestry, fishing, manufacturing, mining, gas, electricity, public utilities, and a few services.

Type of Data Collection Operation: Probability sample of approximately 30,000 establishments that result in about 100,000 price quotations per month.

Data Collection and Imputation Procedures: Data are collected by mail and facsimile. If transaction prices are not supplied, list prices are used. Some prices are obtained from trade publications, organized exchanges, and government agencies. To calculate index, price changes are multiplied by their relative weights taken from 1997 shipment values from the Census of Manufactures.

Estimates of Sampling Error: Not applicable.

Other (nonsampling) Errors: Not available at present.

Sources of Additional Material: U.S. Bureau of Labor Statistics, BLS Handbook of Methods, Chapter 14, Bulletin 2490. U.S. Bureau of Labor Statistics Internet sites <http://stats.bls.gov/ppi>

BOARD OF GOVERNORS OF THE FEDERAL RESERVE SYSTEM

Survey of Consumer Finances

Universe, Frequency, and Types of Data: Periodic sample survey of families. In this survey a given household is divided into a primary economic unit and other economic units. The primary economic unity, which may be a single individual, is generally chosen as the unit that contains the person who either holds the title to the home or is the first person listed on the lease. The primary unit is used as the reference family. The survey collects detailed data on the composition of family balance sheets, the terms of loans, and relationships with financial institutions. It also gathered information on the employment history and pension rights of the survey respondent and the spouse or partner of the respondent.

Type of Data Collection Operation: The survey employs a two-part strategy for sampling families. Some families were selected by standard multistage area probability sampling methods applied to all 50 states. The remaining families in the survey were selected using statistical records derived from tax returns, under the strict rules governing confidentiality and the rights of potential respondents to refuse participation.

Data Collection and Imputation Procedures: NORC at the University of Chicago has collected data for the survey since 1992. Since 1995, the survey has used computer-assisted personal interviewing. Adjustments for nonresponse

are made through multiple imputation of unanswered questions and through weighting adjustments based on data used in the sample design for families that refused participation.

Estimates of Sampling Error: Because of the complex design of the survey, the estimation of potential sampling errors is not straightforward. A replicate-based procedure is available.

Other (nonsampling) Errors: The survey aims to complete 4,500 interviews, with about twothirds of that number deriving from the area-probability sample. The response rate is typically about 70 percent for the area-probability sample and about 35 percent over all strata in the tax-data sample. Proper training and monitoring of interviewers, careful design of questionnaires, and systematic editing of the resulting data were used to control inaccurate survey responses.

Sources of Additional Material: Board of Governors of the Federal Reserve System, "Recent Changes in U.S. Family Finances: Evidence from the 1998 and 2001 Survey of Consumer Finances," Federal Reserve Bulletin, January 2003.

U.S. CENSUS BUREAU

American Housing Survey

Universe, Frequency, and Types of Data: Conducted nationally in the fall in odd numbered years to obtain data on the approximately 121 million occupied or vacant housing units in the United States (group quarters are excluded). Data include characteristics of occupied housing units, vacant units, new housing and mobile home units, financial characteristics, recent mover households, housing and neighborhood quality indicators, and energy characteristics.

Type of Data Collection Operation: The national sample was a multistage probability sample with about 61,000 units eligible for interview in 2003. Sample units, selected within 394 PSUs, were surveyed over a 4-month period.

Data Collection and Imputation Procedures: For 2003, the survey was conducted by personal interviews. The interviewers obtained the information from the occupants or, if the unit was vacant, from informed persons such as landlords, rental agents, or knowledgeable neighbors.

Estimates of Sampling Error: For the national sample, illustrations of the S.E. of the estimates are provided in the Appendix D of the 2003 report. As an example, the estimated CV is about 0.2 percent for the estimated percentage of owner occupied units with two persons.

Other (nonsampling) Errors: Response rate was about 92 percent. Nonsampling errors may result from incorrect or incomplete responses, errors in coding and recording, and processing errors. For the 2003 national sample, approximately 2.2 percent of the total housing inventory was not adequately represented by the AHS sample.

Sources of Additional Material: U.S. Census Bureau, Current Housing Reports, Series H-150 and H170, American Housing Survey. <http://www.census.gov /hhes/www/ahs.html>

Census of Population

Universe, Frequency, and Types of Data: Complete count of U.S. population conducted every 10 years since 1790. Data obtained on number and characteristics of people in the U.S.

Type of Data Collection Operation: In 1980, 1990 and 2000 complete census for some items; age, sex, race, and relationship to householder. In 1980, approximately 19 percent of the housing units were included in the sample; in 1990 and 2000, approximately 17 percent.

Data Collection and Imputation Procedures: In 1980, 1990, and 2000, mail questionnaires were used extensively with personal interviews in the remainder. Extensive telephone and personal followup for nonrespondents was done in the censuses. Imputations were made for missing characteristics.

Estimates of Sampling Error: Sampling errors for data are estimated for all items collected by sample and vary by characteristic and geographic area. The CVs for national and state estimates are generally very small.

Other (nonsampling) Errors: Since 1950, evaluation programs have been conducted to provide information on the magnitude of some sources of nonsampling errors such as response bias and undercoverage in each census. Results from the evaluation program for the 1990 census indicate that the estimated net under coverage amounted to about 1.5 percent of the total resident population. For Census 2000, the evaluation program indicates a net overcount of 0.5% of the resident population.

Sources of Additional Material: U.S. Census Bureau, The Coverage of Population in the 1980 Census, PHC80-E4; Content Reinterview Study: Accuracy of Data for Selected Population and Housing Characteristics as Measured by Reinterview, PHC80-E2; 1980 Census of Population, Vol. 1, (PC801), Appendixes B, C,and D. 1990 Census of Population & Housing, Content Re-Interview Study, CPH-E-1, 1990 Census of Population & Housing, Effectiveness of Quality Assurance, CPH-E-2, 1990 Census of Population & Housing, Programs to Improve Coverage, CPH-E-3. For 2000 Census see <http://www.census.gov/pred/www>

Current Population Survey (CPS)

Universe, Frequency, and Types of Data: Nationwide monthly sample survey of civilian noninstitutional population, 15 years old or over, to obtain data on employment, unemployment, and a number of other characteristics.

Type of Data Collection Operation: Multistage probability sample of about 50,000 households in 754 PSUs in 1996 expanded to about 60,000 households in July 2001. Over-sampling in some states and the largest MSAs to improve reliability for those areas of employment data on annual average basis. A continual sample rotation system is used. Households are in sample 4 months, out for 8 months, and in for 4 more. Month-to-month overlap is 75 percent; year-to-year overlap is 50 percent.

Data Collection and Imputation Procedures: For first and fifth months that a household is in sample, personal interviews; other months, approximately 85 percent of the data collected by phone. Imputation is done for both item and

U.S. Census Bureau, Statistical Abstract of the United States: 2004-2005

total nonresponse. Adjustment for total nonresponse is done by a predefined cluster of units, by MSA size and residence; for item nonresponse imputation varies by subject matter.

Estimates of Sampling Error: Estimated CVs on national annual averages for labor force, total employment, and nonagricultural employment, 0.2 percent; for total unemployment and agricultural employment, 1.0 percent to 2.5 percent. The estimated CVs for family income and poverty rate for all persons in 1986 are 0.5 percent and 1.5 percent, respectively. CVs for subnational areas, such as states, would be larger and would vary by area.

Other (nonsampling) Errors: Estimates of response bias on unemployment are not available, but estimates of unemployment are usually 5 percent to 9 percent lower than estimates from reinterviews. Six to 7.0 percent of sample households unavailable for interviews.

Sources of Additional Material: U.S. Census Bureau and Bureau of Labor Statistics, Current Population Survey; Design and Methodology, (Tech. Paper 63), available on the Internet at <http://www.census.gov/prod/2002pubs/tp63rv.pdf> and Bureau of Labor Statistics, Employment and Earnings, monthly, Explanatory Notes and Estimates of Error, Household Data and BLS Handbook of Methods, Chapter 1, available on the internet at <http://www.bls.gov/opub/hom/homch1a.htm>

2002 Economic Census (Geographic Area Series and Subject Series Reports) (for NAICS sectors 22, 42, 44-45, 48-49, and 51-81)

Universe, Frequency, and Types of Data: Conducted every 5 years to obtain data on number of establishments, number of employees, total payroll size, total sales/receipts/revenue, and other industry specific statistics. In 2002, the universe was all employer and nonemployer establishments primarily engaged in wholesale, retail, utilities, finance & insurance, real estate, transportation & warehousing, and other service industries.

Type of Data Collection Operation: All large employer firms were surveyed (i.e. all employer firms above the payroll size cutoffs established to separate large from small employers) plus a 5 percent to 25 percent sample of the small employer firms. Firms with no employees were not required to file a census return.

Data Collection and Imputation Procedures: Mail questionnaires were used with both mail and telephone followups for nonrespondents. Data for nonrespondents and for small employer firms not mailed a questionnaire were obtained from administrative records of other federal agencies or imputed. Nonemployer data were obtained exclusively from IRS 2002 income tax returns.

Estimates of Sampling Error: Not applicable for basic data such as sales, revenue, receipts, payroll, etc.

Other (nonsampling) Errors: Establishment response rates in 2002 ranged from 80 percent to 89 percent. Item response rates ranged from 50 percent to 90 percent with lower rates for the more detailed questions. Nonsampling errors may occur during the collection, reporting, and keying of data, and due to industry misclassification.

Sources of Additional Material: U.S. Census Bureau, 2002 Economic Census: Geographic Area Series and Subject Series Reports (by NAICS sector), Appendix C and http://www.census.gov/econ/census02/guide/index.html>

1997 Economic Census - Manufacturing Sector

Universe, Frequency, and Types of Data: Conducted every 5 years to obtain information on labor, materials, capital input and output characteristics, plant location, and legal form of organization for all plants in the United States with one or more paid employees. Universe was 36,000 manufacturing establishments in 1997.

Type of Data Collection Operation: Complete enumeration of data items obtained from 200,000 firms. Administrative records from Internal Revenue Service (IRS) and Social Security Administration (SSA) are used for 166,000 smaller single-location firms, which were determined by various cutoffs based on size and industry.

Data Collection and Imputation Procedures: Four mail and telephone followups for larger nonrespondents. Data for small single-location firms (generally those with fewer than 10 employees) not mailed census questionnaires were estimated from administrative records of IRS and SSA. Data for nonrespondents were imputed from related responses or administrative records from IRS and SSA. Approximately 9 percent of total value of shipments was represented by fully imputed records in 1997.

Estimates of Sampling Error: Not applicable.

Other (nonsampling) Errors: Based on evaluation studies, estimates of nonsampling errors for 1972 were about 1.3 percent for estimated total payroll; 2 percent for total employment; and 1 percent for value of shipments. Estimates for later years are not available.

Sources of Additional Material: U.S. Census Bureau, 1997 Economic Census - Manufacturing Sector, Industry Series, Geographic Area Series, Subject Series and Summary Series.

Annual Survey of Manufactures

Universe, Frequency, and Types of Data: The Annual Survey of Manufactures (ASM) is conducted annually, except for years ending in 2 and 7 for all manufacturing establishments having one or more paid employees. The purpose of the ASM is to provide key intercensal measures of manufacturing activity, products, and location for the public and private sectors. The ASM provides statistics on employment, payroll, worker hours, payroll supplements, cost of materials, value added by manufacturing, capital expenditures, inventories, and energy consumption. It also provides estimates of value of shipments for 1,800 classes of manufactured products.

Type of Data Collection Operation: The ASM includes approximately 55,000 establishments selected from the census universe of 366,000 manufacturing establishments. Some 25,000 large

establishments are selected with certainty, and some 30,000 other establishments are selected with probability proportional to a composite measure of establishment size. The survey is updated from two sources Internal Revenue Service administrative records are used to include new singleunit manufacturers and the Company Organization Survey identifies new establishments of multi-unit forms.

Data Collection and Imputation Procedures: Survey is conducted by mail with phone and mail follow-ups of nonrespondents. Imputation (for all nonresponse items) is based on previous year reports, or for new establishments in survey, on industry averages.

Estimates of Sampling Error: Estimated standard errors for number of employees, new expenditure, and for value added totals are given in annual publications. For U.S. level industry statistics, most estimated standard errors are 2 percent or less, but vary considerably for detailed characteristics.

Other (nonsampling) Errors: Response rate is about 85 percent. Nonsampling errors include those due to collection, reporting, and transcription errors, many of which are corrected through computer and clerical checks.

Sources of Additional Material: U.S. Census Bureau, Annual Survey of Manufactures, and Technical Paper 24. <http://www.census.gov/econ/www/mancen.html>

Annual Surveys of State and Local Government

Universe, Frequency, and Types of Data: Sample survey conducted annually to obtain data on revenue, expenditure, debt, and employment of state and local governments. Universe is all governmental units in the United States (about 87,500).

Type of Data Collection Operation: Sample survey includes all state governments, county governments with 100,000+ population, municipalities with 75,000+ population, townships with 50,000+ population, all school districts with

10,000+ enrollment in March 2000, and other governments meeting certain criteria; probability sample for remaining units.

Data Collection and Imputation Procedures: Field and office compilation of data from official records and reports for states and large local governments; central collection of local governmental financial data through cooperative agreements with a number of state governments; mail canvass of other units with mail and telephone follow-ups of nonrespondents. Data for nonresponses are imputed from previous year data or obtained from secondary sources, if available.

Estimates of Sampling Error: State and local government totals are generally subject to sampling variability of less than 3 percent.

Other (nonsampling) Errors: Nonresponse rate is less than 15 percent for local governments. Other possible errors may result from undetected inaccuracies in classification, response, and processing.

Sources of Additional Material: Publications <http://www.census.gov/prod /www/abs/govern.html>: U.S. Census Bureau, Public Employment in 1992, GE 92, No. 1, Governmental Finances in 1991-1992, GF 92, No. 5, and Census of Governments, 1997 and 2002, various reports. Web site references: Census of Governments <http://www.census.gov /govs/www /cog2002.html> <http://www.census.gov/govs/www /cog.html> Employment - state and local site: <http://www.census.gov/govs /www/apes.html> Finance - state and local site: <http://www.census.gov /govs/www/financegen.html>

Census of Governments

Universe, Frequency, and Types of Data: Survey of all governmental units in the United States conducted every 5 years to obtain data on government revenue, expenditures, debt, assets, employment and employee retirement systems, property values, public school systems, and number, size, and structure of governments.

Type of Data Collection Operation: Complete census. List of units derived through classification of government

units recently authorized in each state and identification, counting, and classification of existing local governments and public school systems.

Data Collection and Imputation Procedures: Data collected through field and office compilation of financial data from official records and reports for states and large local governments; mail canvass of selected data items, like state tax revenue and employee retirement systems; and collection of local government statistics through central collection arrangements with state governments.

Estimates of Sampling Error: Not applicable.

Other (nonsampling) Errors: Some nonsampling errors may arise due to possible inaccuracies in classification, response, and processing.

Sources of Additional Material: Publications <http://www.census.gov/prod /www/abs/govern.html>: U.S. Census Bureau, Public Employment in 1992, GE 92, No. 1, Governmental Finances in 1991-1992, GF 92, No. 5, and Census of Governments, 1997 and 2002, various reports. Web site references: Census of Governments <http://www.census.gov /govs/www/cog2002.html> <http://www.census.gov/govs/www /cog.html> Employment - state and local site: <http://www.census.gov/govs /www/apes.html>. Finance - state and local site: <http://www.census.gov /govs/www/financegen.html>.

County Business Patterns

Universe, Frequency, and Types of Data: County Business Patterns is an annual tabulation of basic data items extracted from the Business Register, a file of all known single and multi location companies maintained and updated by the Census Bureau. Data include number of establishments, number of employees, first quarter and annual payrolls, and number of establishments by employment size class. Data are excluded for self-employed persons, domestic service workers, railroad employees, agricultural production workers, and most government employees.

Type of Data Collection Operation: The annual Company Organization Survey provides individual establishment data for multi location companies. Data for single establishment companies are obtained from various Census Bureau programs, such as the Annual Survey of Manufactures and Current Business Surveys, as well as from administrative records of the Internal Revenue Service and the Social Security Administration.

Estimates of Sampling Error: Not applicable.

Other (nonsampling) Error: The data are subject to non-sampling errors, such as industry classification errors, as well as errors of response, keying, and non-reporting.

Sources of Additional Material: U.S. Census Bureau, General Explanation of County Business Patterns.

Foreign Trade - Export Statistics

Universe, Frequency, and Types of Data: The export declarations collected by U.S. Bureau of Customs and Border Protection are processed each month to obtain data on the movement of U.S. merchandise exports to foreign countries. Data obtained include value, quantity, and shipping weight of exports by commodity, country of destination, district of exportation, and mode of transportation.

Type of Data Collection Operation: Shipper's Export Declarations (paper and electronic) are generally required to be filed for the exportation of merchandise valued over $2,500. U.S. Bureau of Customs and Border Protection officials collect and transmit the documents to the Census Bureau on a flow basis for data compilation. Data for shipments valued under $2,501 are estimated, based on established percentages of individual country totals.

Data Collection and Imputation Procedures: Statistical copies of Shipper's Export Declarations are received on a daily basis from ports throughout the country and subjected to a monthly processing cycle. They are fully processed to the extent they reflect items valued over $2,500. Estimates for shipments

valued at $2,500 or less are made, based on established percentages of individual country totals.

Estimates of Sampling Error: Not applicable.

Other (nonsampling) Errors: The goods data are a complete enumeration of documents collected by the U.S. Bureau of Customs and Border Protection and are not subject to sampling errors; but they are subject to several types of non-sampling errors. Quality assurance procedures are performed at every stage of collection, processing and tabulation; however the data are still subject to several types of nonsampling errors. The most significant of these include reporting errors, undocumented shipments, timeliness, data capture errors, and errors in the estimation of low-valued transactions.

Sources of Additional Material: U.S. Census Bureau, U.S. International Trade in Goods and Services, FT 925 (discounted after 1996), U.S. Imports of Merchandise, and U.S. Exports of Merchandise. <http://www.census.gov/foreign-trade/guide/sec2.html>

Foreign Trade - Import Statistics

Universe, Frequency, and Types of Data: The import entry documents collected by U.S. Bureau of Customs and Border Protection are processed each month to obtain data on the movement of merchandise imported into the United States. Data obtained include value, quantity, and shipping weight by commodity, country of origin, district of entry, and mode of transportation.

Type of Data Collection Operation: Import entry documents, either paper or electronic, are required to be filed for the importation of goods into the United States valued over $2,000 or for articles which must be reported on formal entries. U.S. Bureau of Customs and Border Protection officials collect and transmit statistical copies of the documents to the Census Bureau on a flow basis for data compilation. Estimates for shipments valued under $2,001 and not reported on formal entries are based on estimated established percentages for individual country totals.

Data Collection and Imputation Procedures: Statistical copies of import entry documents, received on a daily basis from ports of entry throughout the country, are subjected to a monthly processing cycle. They are fully processed to the extent they reflect items valued at $2,001 and over or items which must be reported on formal entries.

Estimates of Sampling Error: Not applicable.

Other (nonsampling) Errors: The goods data are a complete enumeration of documents collected by the U.S. Bureau of Customs and Border Protection and are not subject to sampling errors; but they are subject to several types of nonsampling errors. Quality assurance procedures are performed at every stage of collection, processing and tabulation; however the data are still subject to several types of nonsampling errors. The most significant of these include reporting errors, undocumented shipments, timeliness, data capture errors, and errors in the estimation of low-valued transactions.

Sources of Additional Material: U.S. Census Bureau, U.S. International Trade in Goods and Services, FT 900 (discounted after 1996), U.S. Imports of Merchandise, and U.S. Exports of Merchandise. <http://www.census.gov/foreigntrade/guide/sec2.html>

Monthly Retail Trade and Food Service Survey

Universe, Frequency, and Types of Data: Provides monthly estimates of retail and food service sales by kind of business and end of month inventories of retail stores.

Type of Data Collection Operation: Probability sample of all firms from a list frame. The list frame is the Bureau's Business Register updated quarterly for recent birth Employer Identification (EI) Numbers issued by the Internal Revenue Service and assigned a kind of business code by the Social Security Administration. The largest firms are included monthly; a sample of others is included every month also.

Data Collection and Imputation Procedures: Data are collected by mail questionnaire with telephone followups and fax reminders for nonrespondents. Imputation is made for each nonresponse item and each item failing edit checks.

Estimates of Sampling Error: For the 2003 monthly surveys, CV's are about 0.5 percent for estimated total retail sales and 1.0 percent for estimated total retail inventories. Sampling errors are shown in monthly publications.

Other (nonsampling) Errors: Imputation rates are about 20 percent for monthly retail and food service sales, and 28 percent for monthly retail inventories.

Sources of Additional Material: U.S. Census Bureau, Current Business Reports, Annual Benchmark Report for Retail Trade and Food Services.

Monthly Survey of Construction

Universe, Frequency, and Types of Data: Survey conducted monthly of newly constructed housing units (excluding mobile homes). Data are collected on the start, completion, and sale of housing. (Annual figures are aggregates of monthly estimates.)

Type of Data Collection Operation: For permit issuing places probability sample of 850 housing units obtained from 19,000 permit issuing places. For nonpermit places, multistage probability sample of new housing units selected in 169 PSUs. In those areas, all roads are canvassed in selected enumeration districts.

Data Collection and Imputation Procedures: Data are obtained by telephone inquiry and field visit.

Estimates of Sampling Error: Estimated CV of 3 percent to 4 percent for estimates of national totals, but may be higher than 20 percent for estimated totals of more detailed characteristics, such as housing units in multiunit structures.

Other (nonsampling) Errors: Response rate is over 90 percent for most items. Nonsampling errors are attributed to definitional problems, differences in interpretation of questions, incorrect reporting, inability to obtain information about all cases in the sample, and processing errors.

Sources of Additional Material: All data are available on the Internet at <http://www.census.gov/const/www/newsresconstindex.html> Further documentation of the survey is also available at that site.

Nonemployer Statistics

Universe, Frequency, and Types of Data: Nonemployer statistics are an annual tabulation of economic data by industry for active businesses without paid employees that are subject to federal income tax. Data showing the number of establishments and receipts by industry are available for the U.S., states, counties, and metropolitan areas. Most types of businesses covered by the Census Bureau's economic statistics programs are included in the nonemployer statistics. Tax-exempt and agricultural-production businesses are excluded from nonemployer statistics.

Type of Data Collection Operation: The universe of nonemployer establishments is created annually as a byproduct of the Census Bureau's Business Register processing for employer establishments. If a business is active but without paid employees, then it becomes part of the potential nonemployer universe. Industry classification and receipts are available for each potential nonemployer business. These data are obtained primarily from the annual business income tax returns of the Internal Revenue Service (IRS). The potential nonemployer universe undergoes a series of complex processing, editing, and analytical review procedures at the Census Bureau to distinguish nonemployers from employers, and to correct and complete data items used in creating the data tables.

Estimates of Sampling Error: Not applicable.

Other (nonsampling) Errors: The data are subject to nonsampling errors, such as errors of self-classification by industry on tax forms, as well as errors of response, keying, nonreporting, and coverage.

Sources of Additional Material: U. S. Census Bureau, Nonemployer Statistics: 2000 (Introduction; Coverage and Methodology). See also <http://www.census.gov/epcd/nonemployer/view/cov&meth.htm>

Service Annual Survey

Universe, Frequency, and Types of Data: The U.S. Census Bureau conducts the Service Annual Survey to provide national estimates of revenues, expenses, and e-commerce revenues for taxable and tax-exempt firms classified in selected service industries. Estimates are summarized by industry classification based on the 1997 North American Industry Classification System (NAICS). Industries covered by the Service Annual Survey include all or part of the following NAICS sectors: Transportation and Warehousing (NAICS 48-49); Information (NAICS 51); Finance and Insurance (NAICS 52); Real Estate and Rental and Leasing (NAICS 53); Professional, Scientific, and Technical Services (NAICS 54); Administrative and Support and Waste Management and Remediation Services (NAICS 56); Health Care and Social Assistance (NAICS 62); Arts, Entertainment, and Recreation (NAICS 71); and Other Services, except Public Administration (NAICS 81). Data items collected include total revenue, revenue from e-commerce transactions; and for selected industries, revenue from detailed service products, total expenses, and expenses by major type, revenue from exported services, and inventories. Questionnaires are mailed in January and request annual data for the prior year. Estimates are published approximately 12 months after the initial survey mailing.

Type of Data Collection Operation: The Service Annual Survey estimates are developed using data from a probability sample and administrative records. Service Annual Survey questionnaires are mailed to a probability sample that is periodically re-selected from a universe of firms located in the United States and having paid employees. The sample includes firms of all sizes and covers both taxable firms and firms exempt from Federal income taxes. Updates to the sample are made on a quarterly basis to account for new businesses. Firms without paid employees, or nonemployers, are included in the estimates through imputation and/or administrative records data provided by other Federal agencies. Links to additional information about confidentiality protection, sampling error, nonsampling error, sample design, definitions, and copies of the questionnaires may be found on the Internet at <ttp://www.census.gov /econ/www/servmenu.html>

Estimates of Sampling Error: Coefficients of variation for the 2002 Service Annual Survey estimates range from 0.5% to 2.2% for total revenue estimates computed at the NAICS sector (2-digit NAICS code) level. Sampling errors for more detailed industries are shown in the corresponding publications. The full 2002 Service Annual Survey results, including coefficients of variations, can be found at <http://www.census.gov/econ /www/servmenu.html> Links to additional information regarding sampling error may be found at: <http://www.census.gov/svsd/www /cv.html>

Other (nonsampling) Errors: Data are imputed for unit nonresponse, item nonresponse, and for reported data that fails edits. The percent of imputed data for total revenue for the 2002 Service Annual Survey is approximately 13%.

Sources of Additional Material: U.S. Census Bureau, Current Business Reports, Service Annual Survey, Census Bureau Website: <http://www.census.gov/econ /www/servmenu.html>

U.S. DEPARTMENT OF EDUCATION National Center for Education Statistics

Higher Education General Information Survey (HEGIS), Degrees and Other Formal Awards Conferred. Beginning 1986, Integrated Postsecondary Education Data Survey (IPEDS), Completions

Universe, Frequency, and Types of Data: Annual survey of all institutions and branches listed in the Education Directory, Colleges and Universities to obtain data on earned degrees and other formal awards, conferred by field of study, level of degree, sex, and by racial/ethnic characteristics (every other year prior to 1989, then annually).

Type of Data Collection Operation: Complete census.

Data Collection and Imputation Procedures: Data are collected through a web-based survey in the fall of every year. Missing data are imputed by using data of similar institutions.

Estimates of Sampling Error: Not applicable.

Other (nonsampling) Errors: For 2001-02, approximately 98.9 percent response rate for degreegranting institutions.

Sources of Additional Material: U.S. Department of Education, National Center for Education Statistics, Postsecondary Institutions in the United States: Fall 2002 and Degrees and Other Awards Conferred: 2001-02. <http://www.nces.ed.gov/ipeds>

Higher Education General Information Survey (HEGIS), Fall Enrollment in Institutions of Higher Education; beginning 1986, Integrated Postsecondary Education Data Survey (IPEDS), Fall Enrollment

Universe, Frequency, and Types of Data: Annual survey of all institutions and branches listed in the Directory to obtain data on total enrollment by sex, level of enrollment, type of program, racial/ethnic characteristics (every other year prior to 1989, then annually) and attendance status of student, and on first-time students.

Type of Data Collection Operation: Complete census.

Data Collection and Imputation Procedures: The data are collected through a web-based survey in the spring of every year. Missing data are imputed by using data of similar institutions.

Estimates of Sampling Error: Not applicable.

Other (nonsampling) Errors: For degreegranting institutions approximately 97.9 percent response rate for fall 2001 data.

Sources of Additional Material: U.S. Department of Education, National Center for Education Statistics, Enrollment in Postsecondary Institutions, Fall 2001 and Financial Statistics, Fiscal Year 2001. <http://www.nces.ed.gov/ipeds>

National Household Education Surveys Program

Universe, Frequency, and Types of Data: The National Household Education Surveys Program (NHES) is a system of telephone surveys of the noninstitutionalized civilian population of the United States. Surveys in NHES have varying universes of interest depending on the particular survey. Specific topics covered by each survey are at the NHES web site <http://nces.ed.gov/nhes>. A list of the surveys fielded as part of NHES, each universe, and the years they were fielded is provided below. 1. Adult Education Interviews were conducted with a representative sample of civilian, noninstitutionalized persons age 16 and older who were not enrolled in grade 12 or below (1991, 1995, 1999, 2001, 2003). 2. Before-and After-School Programs and Activities Interviews were conducted with parents of a representative sample of students in grades K through 8 (1999, 2001). 3. Civic Involvement Interviews were conducted with a representative sample of parents, youth, and adults(1996, 1999). 4. Early Childhood Program Participation Interviews were conducted with parents of a representative sample of children from birth through grade 3, with the specific age groups varying by survey year (1991, 1995, 1999, 2001). 5. Household and Library Use Interviews were conducted with a representative sample of U.S. households (1996). 6. Parent and Family Involvement in Education Interviews were conducted with parents of a representative sample of children age three through grade 12 or in grades K through 12 depending on the survey year.(1996, 1999, 2003). 7. School Readiness Interviews were conducted with parents of a representative sample of 3- to 7-year-old children (1993, 1999). 8. School Safety and Discipline Interviews were conducted with a representative sample of students in grades 6 12, their parents, and the parents of a representative sample of students in grades 3 through 5 (1993).

Type of Data Collection Operation: NHES uses telephone interviews to collect data.

Data Collection and Imputation Procedures: Telephone numbers are selected using random digit dialing techniques. Approximately 45,000 to 64,000 households are contacted in order to identify persons eligible for the surveys. Data are collected using computer-assisted telephone interviewing (CATI) procedures. Missing data are imputed using hot-deck imputation procedures.

Estimates of Sampling Error: Unweighted sample sizes range between 2,500 and 21,000. The average root design effects of the surveys in NHES range from 1.1 to 4.5.

Other (nonsampling) Errors: Because of unit nonresponse and because the samples are drawn from households with telephone instead of all households, nonresponse and/or coverage bias may exist for some estimates. However, both sources of potential bias are adjusted for in the weighting process. Analyses of both potential sources of bias in the NHES collections have been studied and no significant bias has been detected.

Sources of Additional Material: Please see the NHES website at <http://nces.ed.gov/nhes>

U.S. FEDERAL BUREAU OF INVESTIGATION

Uniform Crime Reporting (UCR) Program

Universe, Frequency, and Types of Data: Monthly reports on the number of criminal offenses that become known to law enforcement agencies. Data are collected on crimes cleared by arrest; by age, sex, and race of arrestees and for victims and offenders for homicides, on fatal and nonfatal assaults against law enforcement officers, and on hate crimes reported.

Type of Data Collection Operation: Crime statistics are based on reports of crime data submitted either directly to the FBI by contributing law enforcement agencies or through cooperating state UCR programs.

Data Collection and Imputation Procedures: States with UCR programs collect data directly from individual law enforcement agencies and forward reports, prepared in accordance with UCR standards, to FBI. Accuracy and consistency edits are performed by FBI.

Estimates of Sampling Error: Not applicable.

Other (nonsampling) Errors: Coverage of 93 percent of the population (94 percent in MSA's, 86 percent in "other cities," and 85 percent in rural areas) by UCR program, though varying number of agencies report.

Sources of Additional Material: U.S. Federal Bureau of Investigation, Crime in the United States, annual, Hate Crime Statistics, annual, Law Enforcement Officers Killed & Assaulted, annual, <http://www.fbi.gov/ucr.htm>

U.S. INTERNAL REVENUE SERVICE

Corporation Income Tax Returns

Universe, Frequency, and Types of Data: Annual study of unaudited corporation income tax returns, Forms 1120, 1120-A, 1120-F, 1120-L, 1120-PC, 1120-REIT, 1120-RIC, and 1120S, filed by corporations or businesses legally defined as corporations. Data provided on various financial characteristics by industry and size of total assets and business receipts.

Type of Data Collection Operation: Stratified probability sample of approximately 145,093 returns for Tax Year 2001, allocated to sample classes which are based on type of return, size of total assets, size of net income or deficit, and selected business activity. Sampling rates for sample classes varied from .25 percent to 100 percent.

Data Collection and Imputation Procedures: Computer selection of sample of tax return records. Data adjusted during editing for incorrect, missing, or inconsistent entries to ensure consistency with other entries on return and to comply with statistical definitions.

Estimates of Sampling Error: Estimated CVs for Tax Year 2001: Returns with assets over $250 million are self-representing. For other returns grouped by assets, CVs ranged from 0.03 percent to 2.87 percent; for amount of net income CV is 0.19 percent.

Other (nonsampling) Errors: Nonsampling errors include coverage errors, processing errors, and response errors.

Sources of Additional Material: U.S. Internal Revenue Service, Statistics of Income, Corporation Income Tax Returns, annual.

Partnership Income Tax Returns

Universe, Frequency, and Types of Data: Annual study of unaudited income tax returns of partnerships, Form 1065. Data provided on various financial characteristics by industry.

Type of Data Collection Operation: Stratified probability sample of approximately 36,200 partnership returns from a population of 2.3 million filed during calendar year 2001. The sample is classified based on combinations of gross receipts, net income or loss, and total assets, and on industry. Sampling rates vary from 0.12 percent to 100 percent.

Data Collection and Imputation Procedures: Computer selection of sample of tax return records. Data are adjusted during editing for incorrect, missing, or inconsistent entries to ensure consistency with other entries on return. Data not available due to regulations are not imputed.

Estimates of Sampling Error: Estimated CVs for tax year 2001 (latest available): For number of partnerships, 0.28 percent; business receipts, 0.35 percent; net income, 0.73 percent; net loss, 1.45 percent.

Other (nonsampling) Errors: Processing errors and errors arising from the use of tolerance checks for the data.

Sources of Additional Material: U.S. Internal Revenue Service, Statistics of Income, Partnership Returns and Statistics of Income Bulletin, Vol. 23, No. 2 (fall 2003).

Sole Proprietorship Income Tax Returns

Universe, Frequency, and Types of Data: Annual study of unaudited income tax returns of nonfarm sole proprietorships, form 1040 with business schedules. Data provided on various financial characteristics by industry.

Type of Data Collection Operation: Stratified probability sample of approximately 51,000 sole proprietorships for tax year 2001. The sample is classified based on presence or absence of certain business schedules; the larger of total income or loss; and size of business plus farm receipts. Sampling rates vary from 0.05 percent to 100 percent.

Data Collection and Imputation Procedures: Computer selection of sample of tax return records. Data adjusted during editing for incorrect, missing, or inconsistent entries to ensure consistency with other entries on return.

Estimates of Sampling Error: Estimated CVs for tax year 2001 are available. For sole proprietorships, business receipts, 0.66 percent; net income, (less loss), .89 percent; depreciation 1.25 percent.

Other (nonsampling) Errors: Processing errors and errors arising from the use of tolerance checks for the data.

Sources of Additional Material: U.S. Internal Revenue Service, Statistics of Income, Sole Proprietorship Returns (for years through 1980) and Statistics of Income Bulletin, Vol. 22, No. 1 (summer 2003).

Individual Income Tax Returns

Universe, Frequency, and Types of Data: Annual study of unaudited individual income tax returns, forms 1040, 1040A, and 1040EZ, filed by U.S. citizens and residents. Data provided on various financial characteristics by size of adjusted gross income, marital status, and by taxable and nontaxable returns. Data by state, based on 100 percent file, also include returns from 1040NR, filed by nonresident aliens plus certain self employment tax returns.

Type of Data Collection Operation: Annual 2001 stratified probability sample of approximately 192,000 returns broken into sample strata based on the larger of total income or total loss amounts as well as the size of business plus farm receipts. Sampling rates for sample strata varied from 0.05 percent to 100 percent.

Data Collection and Imputation Procedures: Computer selection of sample of tax return records. Data adjusted during editing for incorrect, missing, or inconsistent entries to ensure consistency with other entries on return.

Estimates of Sampling Error: Estimated CVs for tax year 2001: Adjusted gross income less deficit 0.11 percent; salaries and wages 0.21 percent; and tax exempt interest received 1.75 percent. (State data not subject to sampling error.)

Other (nonsampling) Errors: Processing errors and errors arising from the use of tolerance checks for the data.

Sources of Additional Material: U.S. Internal Revenue Service, Statistics of Income, Individual Income Tax Returns, annual.

U.S. NATIONAL CENTER FOR HEALTH STATISTICS (NCHS)

National Health Interview Survey (NHIS)

Universe, Frequency, and Types of Data: Continuous data collection covering the civilian noninstitutional population to obtain information on demographic characteristics, conditions, injuries, impairments, use of health services, health behaviors, and other health topics.

Type of Data Collection Operation: Multistage probability sample of 49,000 households (in 198 PSUs) from 1985 to 1994; 36 - 40,000 households (358 design PSUs) from 1995 on.

Data Collection and Imputation Procedures: Some missing data items (e.g., race, ethnicity) are imputed using a hot deck imputation value. Unit nonresponse is compensated for by an adjustment to the survey weights.

Estimates of Sampling Error: Estimates of Standard Error (SE): For 2002 medically attended injury episodes rates in the past 12 months by falling for: females 27.26 (1.69), and males 23.42 (1.56) per 1,000 population; for 2002 injury episodes rates during the past 12 months inside the home - 20.50 (1.04) per 1,000 population.

Other (nonsampling) Errors: The response rate was 93.8 percent in 1996; in 2002, the total household response rate was 89.6 percent, with the final family response rate of 88.1 percent, and the final sample adult response rate of 74.3 percent. (Note: The NHIS sample redesign was conducted in 1995, and the NHIS questionnaire was redesigned in 1997.)

Sources of Additional Material: National Center for Health Statistics, Summary Health Statistics for the U.S. Population: National Health Interview Survey, 2002, Vital and Health Statistics, Series 10 #220; National Center for Health Statistics, Summary Health Statistics for U.S. Children: National Health Interview Survey, 2002, Vital and Health Statistics, Series 10 #221; National Center for Health Statistics, Summary Health Statistics for U.S. Adults: National Health Interview Survey, 2002, Vital and Health Statistics, Series 10 #222; U.S. National Center for Health Statistics, Design and Estimation for the National Health Interview Survey, 1995-2004, Vital and Health Statistics, Series 2 #130.

National Vital Statistics System

Universe, Frequency, and Types of Data: Annual data on births and deaths in the United States.

Type of Data Collection Operation: Mortality data based on complete file of death records, except 1972, based on 50 percent sample. Natality statistics 1951-71, based on 50 percent sample of birth certificates, except a 20 percent to 50 percent sample in 1967, received by NCHS. Beginning 1972, data from some states received through Vital Statistics Cooperative Program (VSCP) and complete file used; data from other states based on 50 percent sample. Beginning 1986, all reporting areas participated in the VSCP.

Data Collection and Imputation Procedures: Reports based on records from registration offices of all states, District of Columbia, New York City, Puerto Rico, Virgin Islands, Guam, American Samoa, and Northern Marianas.

Estimates of Sampling Error: For recent years, CVs for births are small due to large portion of total file in sample (except for very small estimated totals).

Other (nonsampling) Errors: Data on births and deaths believed to be at least 99 percent complete.

Sources of Additional Material: U.S. National Center for Health Statistics, Vital Statistics of the United States, Vol. I and Vol. II, annual, and National Vital Statistics Reports. NCHS web site at <http://www.cdc.gov/nchs/nvss.htm>

National Highway Traffic Safety Administration (NHTSA)

Fatality Analysis Reporting System (FARS)

Universe, Frequency, and Types of Data: Census of all motor vehicle traffic crashes involving at least one person killed as a result of the crash. The crash must be reported to the state and the death of the involved person must be within thirty days of the crash date. These fatal crashes occur throughout the United States (includes the District of Columbia), Puerto Rico, Virgin Islands and American Pacific Territories.

Type of Data Collection Operation: Each state provides an analyst(s) who extracts data from the official documents and enters it into a standardized database.

Data Collection and Imputation Procedures: Detailed data describing the characteristics of the fatal crash, the vehicles and persons involved are obtained from police crash reports, driver and vehicle registration records, autopsy reports, highway department, etc. Computerized edit checks monitor that accuracy and completeness of the data. The FARS incorporates a sophisticated mathematical multiple imputation model to impute missing blood alcohol concentration (BAC) in the database for drivers, pedestrians, and bicyclists only.

Estimates of Sampling Error: Since this is census data, there are no sampling errors.

Other (nonsampling) Errors: Data on the fatal motor vehicle traffic crashes is more than 97 percent complete.

Sources of Additional Material: The FARS Coding and Validation Manual, ANSI D16.1 Manual on Classification of Motor Vehicle Traffic Accidents (Sixth Edition).

Appendix IV
Weights and Measures

[For assistance on metric usage, call or write the National Institute of Standards and Technology, Metric Program, 100 Bureau Drive, Stop 2600, Gaithersburg, MD 20899-2600 (301-975-3690) Internet site <http://www.nist.gov/> E-mail: metric_prg@nist.gov]

Symbol	When you know conventional	Multiply by	To find metric	Symbol
in	inches	2.54	centimeters	cm
ft	feet	30.48	centimeters	cm
yd	yards	0.91	meters	m
mi	miles	1.61	kilometers	km
in^2	square inches	6.45	square centimeters	cm^2
ft^2	square feet	0.09	square meters	m^2
yd^2	square yards	0.84	square meters	m^2
mi^2	square miles	2.59	square kilometers	km^2
	acre	0.41	hectare	ha
oz	ounces [1]	28.35	grams	g
lb	pounds [1]	.45	kilograms	kg
oz (troy)	ounces [2]	31.10	grams	g
	short tons (2,000 lb)	0.91	metric tons	t
	long tons (2,240 lb)	1.02	metric tons	t
fl oz	fluid ounces	29.57	milliliters	mL
c	cups	0.24	liters	L
pt	pints	0.47	liters	L
qt	quarts	0.95	liters	L
gal	gallons	3.78	liters	L
ft^3	cubic feet	0.03	cubic meters	m^3
yd^3	cubic yards	0.76	cubic meters	m^3
F	degrees Fahrenheit (subtract 32)	0.55	degrees Celsius	C

Symbol	When you know metric	Multiply by	To find conventional	Symbol
cm	centimeters	0.39	inches	in
cm	centimeters	0.03	feet	ft
m	meters	1.09	yards	yd
km	kilometers	0.62	miles	mi
cm^2	square centimeters	0.15	square inches	in^2
m^2	square meters	10.76	square feet	ft^2
m^2	square meters	1.20	square yards	yd^2
km^2	square kilometers	0.39	square miles	mi^2
ha	hectares	2.47	acre	
g	grams	.035	ounces [1]	oz
kg	kilograms	2.21	pounds	lb [1]
g	grams	.032	ounces [2]	oz (troy)
t	metric tons	1.10	short tons (2,000 lb)	
t	metric tons	0.98	long tons (2,240 lb)	
mL	milliliters	0.03	fluid ounces	fl oz
L	liter	4.24	cups	c
L	liters	2.13	pints (liquid)	pt
L	liters	1.05	quarts (liquid)	qt
L	liters	0.26	gallons	gal
m^3	cubic meters	35.32	cubic feet	ft^3
m^3	cubic meters	1.32	cubic yards	yd^3
C	degrees Celsius (after multiplying, add 32)	1.80	degrees Fahrenheit	F

[1] For weighing ordinary commodities.   [2] For weighing precious metals, jewels, etc.

U.S. Census Bureau, Statistical Abstract of the United States: 2004-2005

2003
number

Sec. 1. **POPULATION**

22   Resident Population by Hispanic or Latino Origin and State: 2000 and 2002
25   Metropolitan and Nonmetropolitan Area Population by State: 1980 to 2000
27   Metropolitan Areas With 600,000 or More Inhabitants in 2000— Selected Racial Groups:
       2000
28   Metropolitan Areas With 600,000 or More Inhabitants in 2000— Hispanic and Non-
       Hispanic Groups: 2000
32   Cities With 250,000 or More Inhabitants in 2000—Selected Racial Groups: 2000
33   Cities With 250,000 or More Inhabitants in 2000—Hispanic and Non-Hispanic Groups:
       2000
45   Selected Native Hawaiian Home Lands: 2000
49   Nativity and Place of Birth of Resident Population—25 Largest Metropolitan Areas: 2000
53   Foreign-Stock Population by Nativity and Parentage: 1960 to 2000
55   Ancestry of Resident Population by State: 2000
56   Language Spoken at Home by Nativity: 2000
59   Language Spoken at Home by Resident Population—25 Largest Metropolitan Areas: 2000
68   Households—States: 2000
78   Population in Group Quarters—States: 2000
80   Religious Preference, Church Membership, and Attendance: 1980 to 2002

Sec. 3. **HEALTH AND NUTRITION**

198   Disability Status of Population—25 Largest Metropolitan Areas: 2000
199   Disability Status of Population—25 Largest Cities: 2000

Sec. 4. **EDUCATION**

257   Advanced Telecommunications in Private Schools: 1995 and 1999
259   Public School Teachers Using Computers or the Internet for Classroom Instruction During
       Class Time: 1999
260   Children's Access to Home Computer and Use of the Internet at Home: 2000
286   Undergraduates in Postsecondary Institutions Taking Any Distance Education Courses:
       1999-2000

Sec. 6. **GEOGRAPHY AND ENVIRONMENT**

361   Nonfederal Developed Land Use by State and Other Area: 1997

Sec. 7. **ELECTIONS**

423   Political Party Financial Activity by Major Political Party: 1981 to 2000
424   National Party Nonfederal Activity: 1996 to 2000

Sec. 9. **FEDERAL GOVERNMENT FINANCES AND EMPLOYMENT**

484   Government-Sponsored Enterprise Participation in the Credit Market: 1980 to 2002
485   Federal Government Debt by Type and Maturity: 1990 to 2002
505   Accessions to and Separations From Employment in the Federal Government: 2001 and
       2002
506   Federal Agencies Employing 500 or More Full-Time Officers With
       Authority to Carry Firearms and Make Arrests—Number of Officers: 1996 to 2002

U.S. Census Bureau, Statistical Abstract of the United States: 2004-2005

2003
number

Sec. 11. **SOCIAL INSURANCE AND HUMAN SERVICES**

553   401(k) Plans—Summary: 1985 to 1998
558   Vocational Rehabilitation—Summary: 1980 to 1999
586   Community Service Participation of Students in Grades 6 Through 12: 1996 and 1999

Sec. 12. **LABOR FORCE, EMPLOYMENT AND EARNINGS**

637   Annual Percent Changes in Earnings and Compensation: 1980 to 2002

Sec. 13. **INCOME, EXPENDITURES, AND WEALTH**

681   Household Income—Distribution by Income Level and 25 Largest Metropolitan Areas:
        1999
682   Household Income—Distribution by Income Level and State: 1999
698   Families and People Below Poverty Level by 25 Largest Metropolitan Areas: 1999
699   Families and People Below Poverty Level by State: 1999

Sec. 15. **BUSINESS ENTERPRISE**

752   Hispanic-Owned Firms by Industry Division: 1997
753   Black-Owned Firms by Industry Division: 1997
754   Asian- and Pacific Islander-Owned Firms by Industry Division: 1997
755   American Indian- and Alaska Native-Owned Firms by Industry Division: 1997

Sec. 16. **SCIENCE AND TECHNOLOGY**

801   NASA Space Shuttle Operations Expenditures: 1996 to 2001

Sec. 17. **AGRICULTURE**

821   Indexes of Farm Production, Input Use, and Productivity: 1980 to 1999

Sec. 19. **ENERGY**

906   Manufacturing Energy Consumption for all Purposes by Type of Fuel and Major Industry
        Group: 1998
907   Energy Prices: 1980 to 2001
921   Nonutility Electric Power Producers—Summary by Type of Fuel: 1998 to 2000
923   Major Investor-Owned Electric Utilities—Balance Sheet and Income Account of Privately
        Owned Companies: 1995 to 2000

Sec. 20. **CONSTRUCTION AND HOUSING**

932   Construction—Establishments, Employees, and Payroll by Kind of Business (NAICS Basis):
        1997
936   Value of New Construction Put in Place by Type: 1990 to 2002

Sec. 22. **DOMESTIC TRADE**

1026   Retail Trade—Establishments, Sales, Payroll, and Employees by Kind of Business: 1997
1037   Toy Industry—Retail Sales by Type of Product: 2001 and 2002
1044   Retail E-Commerce Sales, Number of Orders, and Average Purchase Amount in Key Cat-
        egories: 2001 and 2002
1050   Wholesale Trade—Establishments, Sales, Payroll, and Employees by Kind of Business:
        1997

Sec. 23. **TRANSPORTATION**

1055   Transportation Revenues by Level of Government and Mode: 1990 to 2001
1073   Jobs on U.S. Deep Sea Commercial Fleet and Typical Basic Monthly Wage for Able-Bodied
        Seamen: 1980 to 2002

Appendix V   945

2003
number

1078	Hazardous Material Shipment Characteristics: 1997
1094	Urban Travel by Sex of Traveler and Purpose of Trip: 2001

Sec. 24. **INFORMATION AND COMMUNICATIONS**

1119   Information Industries—Establishments, Receipts, Payroll, and Employees by Kind of Business (NAICS Basis): 1997

Sec. 25. **BANKING, FINANCE, AND INSURANCE**

1165	Flow of Funds Accounts—Business Credit Market Debt Outstanding by Type of Instrument: 1990 to 2002
1206	NASDAQ—Securities Listed and Volume of Trading: 1990 to 2002

Sec. 26. **ARTS, ENTERTAINMENT, AND RECREATION**

1238   Public School Supplemental Arts Education Programs by School Characteristic: 1998-99

Sec. 27. **ACCOMMODATION, FOOD SERVICES, AND OTHER SERVICES**

1278   Religious, Grantmaking, Civic, and Professional Service Firms—
Revenue and Expenses for Tax-Exempt Employer Firms: 1999 to 2001 (combined with Table 1277).

Sec. 29. **PUERTO RICO AND THE ISLAND AREAS**

1308   Puerto Rico—General Demographic Characteristics: 1990 and 2000

Sec. 30. **COMPARATIVE INTERNATIONAL STATISTICS**

1321	World Summary: 1980 to 2002
1346	Age of Withdrawal From Labor Force and Retirement Duration: 1999
1370	Motor Vehicle Transportation Indicators for Selected Countries: 2000
1383	Military Expenditures and Armed Forces Personnel by Country: 1990 and 1999

Sec. 31. **CONGRESSIONAL DISTRICT PROFILES**

1384   Congressional District Profiles—108th Congress: 2000

946 Appendix V

Appendix VI
New Tables

Table number		Page number
	Sec. 1. **POPULATION**	1
39	Social and Economic Characteristics of the Native Hawaiian and Other Pacific Islander Alone Population: 2000	40
47	Population by Selected Ancestry Group and Region: 2000.	46
	Sec. 4. **EDUCATION**	133
227	Selected Statistics for the Largest Public School Districts: 2001-2002	150
244	Computer and Internet Use by Children and Adolescents: 2001	160
270	Distance Education in Degree-Granting Postsecondary Institutions: 2000-01 .	174
	Sec. 5. **LAW ENFORCEMENT, COURTS, AND PRISONS**	183
310	Percentage of Students in Grades 9-12 Who Reported Carrying a Weapon: 1993 to 2001	197
311	Number of School-Associated Violent Deaths Occurring at and Away From School: 1992 to 2003	197
327	Computer Related Crime Prosecuted by Prosecutor's Offices: 2001	203
	Sec. 6. **GEOGRAPHY AND ENVIRONMENT**	211
348	Land Cover/Use by Type: 1982 to 2002.	214
349	Developed Land by Type: 1982 to 2001.	214
	Sec. 9. **FEDERAL GOVERNMENT FINANCES AND EMPLOYMENT**	305
468	Federal Trust Fund Receipts, Outlays, and Balances: 2001 to 2003	312
	Sec. 10. **NATIONAL DEFENSE AND VETERANS AFFAIRS**	325
514	Veterans by Sex, Race, and Hispanic Origin: 2000	337
	Sec. 11. **SOCIAL INSURANCE AND HUMAN SERVICES**	339
568	Volunteers by Type of Main Organization: 2003	366
	Sec. 12. **LABOR FORCE, EMPLOYMENT, AND EARNINGS**	367
614	Private Sector Job Gains and Losses: 1992 to 2003	404
	Sec. 13. **INCOME, EXPENDITURES, AND WEALTH**	421
662	Average Annual Expenditures of All Consumer Units by Income Level: 2001-2002	441
664	Median Income of Households in Constant (2001) Dollars by State: 3-Year Averages for 1990 to 2001.	442
668	Money Income of Households—Number and Distribution by Race and Hispanic Origin: 2002.	445
669	Money Income of Families—Number and Distribution by Race and Hispanic Origin: 2002	445
681	Money Income of People—Number by Income Level and by Sex, Race, and Hispanic Origin: 2002	451

U.S. Census Bureau, Statistical Abstract of the United States: 2004-2005

Table number		Page number
691	Asset Ownership Rates for Households by Type of Asset and Household Characteristic: 2000.	456
692	Asset Ownership Rates for Households and Median Value by Type of Asset: 2000	456
	Sec. 15. **BUSINESS ENTERPRISE**	481
722	Nonfarm Noncorporate Business-Sector Balance Sheet: 1990 to 2003	486
	Sec. 16. **SCIENCE AND TECHNOLOGY**	509
773	Science and Engineering Degree Recipients: 1999 to 2001	514
	Sec. 17. **AGRICULTURE**	521
787	Farms by Size and Type of Organization: 1974 to 2002	524
791	Farms—Number, Acreage, and Value by Type of Organization: 1997 and 2002	525
792	Corporate Farms—Characteristics by Type: 2002	526
793	Farms—Number, Acreage, and Value of Sales by Size of Sales: 2002	526
794	Number of Farms by Economic Class of Farm: 2002	526
795	Farms—Number, Acreage and Value by State: 1997 and 2002	527
816	Top 10 U.S. Export Markets for Selected Commodities: 2003	536
	Sec. 18. **NATURAL RESOURCES**	547
842	Natural Resource-Related Industries—Establishments, Sales, Payroll, and Employees: 1997 and 2002	550
	Sec. 19. **ENERGY AND UTILITIES**	569
905	Electric Energy Price by Class of Service and State: 2002	585
907	Revenue and Expense Statistics for Major U.S. Investor-Owned Electric Utilities: 1995 to 2002	586
	Sec. 20. **CONSTRUCTION AND HOUSING**	591
919	Construction—Establishments, Value of Work Done, Payroll, and Employees by Kind of Business (NAICS Basis): 2002	594
931	Average Length of Time From Start to Completion of New Privately Owned 1 Unit Residential Buildings: 1971 to 2003	601
932	Price Indexes of New One-Family Houses Sold, Including the Value of Lot by Region: 1979 to 2003	601
	Sec. 21. **MANUFACTURES**	625
975	Manufactures—Establishments, Employees, Payroll, and Value of Shipments by Industry (NAICS Basis): 1997 and 2002	630
978	Manufacturing Industries—Export-Related Shipments and Employment by Industry: 2000	632
979	Manufacturing Industries—Export-Related Shipments and Employment by State: 2002	632
982	Manufacturing Industries—Employment by Industry: 1990 to 2003	634 & 635
	Sec. 22. **DOMESTIC TRADE**	651
1016	Retail Trade—Establishments, Employees, and Payroll: 2002	654
1017	Retail Trade—Establishments, Employees, and Payroll: 1997 and 2002	654
1028	Retail Sales—New Passenger Cars: 1990 to 2001	661
1029	Retail Sales of New Cars by Sector: 1990 to 2002	662
1032	Annual U.S. Motor Vehicle Production and Factory (Wholesale) Sales: 1990 to 2001	662

948   Appendix VI

Table number		Page number
	Sec. 23. **TRANSPORTATION**.	669
1046	Transportation System Mileage Within the U.S.: 1980 to 2001	674
1047	U.S. Aircraft, Vehicles, and Other Conveyances: 1980 to 2001	674
1050	Transportation and Warehousing—Establishments, Revenue, Payroll, and Employees by Kind of Business (NAICS Basis): 1997 and 2002.	676
1072	Shipment Characteristics, by Distance and Weight Shipped: 1997 and 2002 .	687
1102	Characteristics of Rail Transit by Transit Authority: 2001	704
1103	Transit Ridership in 50 Largest Urbanized Areas: 2001	705
	Sec. 24. **INFORMATION AND COMMUNICATIONS**.	711
1113	Information—Establishments, Receipts, Payroll, and Employees by Kind of Business (NAICS Basis): 1997 and 2002	713
	Sec. 25. **BANKING, FINANCE, AND INSURANCE**	733
1155	Finance and Insurance, and Real Estate and Rental and Leasing—Establish-. . ments, Revenue, Payroll, and Employees by Kind of Business (1997 NAICS Basis): 1997 and 2002.	735
1156	Finance and Insurance—Nonemployer Establishments and Receipts by Kind of Business: 1997 to 2002	735
	Sec. 26. **ARTS, ENTERTAINMENT, AND RECREATION**	763
1225	Arts, Entertainment and Recreation—Establishments, Revenue, Payroll, and Employees by Kind of Business (1997 NAICS Basis): 1997 and 2002. . . , ...	764
1260	Travel in the U.S. by Selected Trip Characteristics: 2001	783
1261	U.S. Canadian and U.S. Mexican Border Land-Passenger Gateways: 2002	784
	Sec. 27. **ACCOMMODATION, FOOD SERVICES, AND OTHER SERVICES**. . .	785
1262	Service Related Industries—Establishments, Employees, and Payroll: 2002. . .	787
1263	Retail Trade—Establishments, Employees, and Payroll: 1997 and 2002	787
	Sec. 29. **PUERTO RICO AND THE ISLAND AREAS**.	821
1314	Puerto Rico—Farms and Market Value of Agricultural Products Sold: 2002 . . .	827
1315	Puerto Rico—Agricultural Summary: 1998 and 2002	828
	Sec. 30. **COMPARATIVE INTERNATIONAL STATISTICS** . . . . ,	829
1320	Population and Population Change, by Development Status: 1950 to 2051 . .	840
1326	Births to Unmarried Women, by Country: 1980 to 2001	847
1327	Marriage and Divorce Rates, by Country: 1980 to 2000.	847
1328	Single-parent Households: 1980 to 2002.	847
1329	Percent Distribution of Households by Type and Country: 1980 to 2002	848
1384	Military Budget, by Country: 2002	878
1385	Military Manpower Fit for Military Service, by Country: 2003	878

U.S. Census Bureau, Statistical Abstract of the United States: 2004-2005

Index

Table

A

Abortions 89, 90, 91
Abrasives, stone 860
Accidents and fatalities . 174, 1053, 1089, 1090, 1097, 1106
Age of driver 1099
Aircraft 1053, 1058, 1060
Alcohol involvement 1095, 1096, 1098
Costs 176
Deaths and death rates . 102, 104, 105, 106, 1089, 1090, 1106
Infants 70, 100, 101
Fires 345
Industrial 631, 632, 633, 634
Injuries 174, 175
Motor vehicles . 102, 105, 1053, 1089, 1090, 1091, 1092, 1093, 1094, 1097
Motorcycle 1089
Police officers assaulted, killed 322
Railroad 1106
Transportation 1053
Vehicle rollovers 1093
Work fatalities 636
Work time lost 632
Accommodation and food services industry:
Capital 751
Earnings 611, 613, 618, 728, 731, 732, 1265, 1266, 1270
Electronic commerce 1267
Employees . 611, 613, 728, 1265, 1266, 1270
Establishments . 728, 729, 732, 1264, 1265, 1266, 1270
Finances 718, 721
Gross domestic product 642
Hours 611
Nonemployers 729, 1264
Productivity 615
Profits 758
Sales .. 718, 721, 726, 727, 728, 729, 1264, 1270
Accountants and auditors 597, 599
Accounting, tax preparation, bookkeeping, and payroll services:
Earnings 613, 1265
Employees 613, 1265
Establishments 1265
Finances 718
Receipts 718
Acquired immuno-deficiency syndrome (AIDS) .. 177, 179, 180, 181
Acquisition of territory by the U.S. 347
Activities of daily living (ADLs) 172, 183
Activity limitation caused by chronic conditions . 182, 183
Administrative & support & waste management & remediation services industry:
Capital 751
Earnings 611, 613, 618, 728, 731, 732, 1265, 1266
Electronic commerce 1267
Employees . 611, 613, 728, 731, 732, 1265, 1266

Table

Administrative & support & waste management & remediation services industry: —Con.
Establishments . 728, 729, 731, 1264, 1265, 1266
Finance 718, 721
Gross domestic product 642
Hours 611
Nonemployers 729, 1264
Profits 728
Sales, shipments, receipts ... 718, 721, 726, 727, 728, 729, 1264, 1276, 1277
Adult education 288
Advertising and related services:
Earnings 613
Employees 613
Establishments 1265
Finances 1274, 1275
Productivity 615
Receipts 742
Aerobics 1241, 1248
Aeronautics, civil. See Air transportation.
Aerospace engineering:
Degrees conferred 773
Aerospace industry:
Earnings 613, 733, 976
Employees 613, 733, 976, 1064
Foreign trade 1300
Industrial production 754
Productivity 615
New orders, backlog 1011
Research and development 776, 777
Sales 1011, 1014
Shipments 976, 1011, 1012, 1013, 1014
Afghanistan. See Foreign countries.
Africa. See Foreign countries.
African American. See Black population.
Age of population. See Population.
Aggravated assault 289, 290, 291, 292
Agricultural loans. See Farm mortgage loans.
Agricultural products. See Farms and individual products.
Agricultural sciences:
Degrees conferred 284, 285, 286, 775
Agriculture (see also Farms and Farmers and farm workers):
Employees 597
Federal aid to state and local governments . 424
Foreign trade . 811, 812, 815, 816, 817, 818
Value added 800
Agriculture, forestry, and fishing industry:
Capital 748, 751
Earnings 618, 731, 738, 841
Employees 601, 731, 738, 841
Establishments 731, 841
Finances 716, 718, 721
Gross domestic product 642, 843
Mergers and acquisitions 742
Occupational safety 631, 634, 636
Profits 716, 758
Sales, shipments, receipts ... 716, 718, 721, 726, 727, 738, 758
Women-owned businesses 738

NOTE: Index citations refer to **table** numbers, not page numbers.

U.S. Census Bureau, Statistical Abstract of the United States: 2004-2005

Agriculture, construction, and mining machin-
ery manufacturing 613, 615, 976
Aid to families with dependent children (See
Temporary assistance for needy families pro-
gram)
AIDS (acquired immuno-deficiency syndrome) ..
177, 179, 180, 181
Air conditioning, homes with 947, 965
Air Force, Department of, personnel .. 500, 501
Air pollution:
Air pollution control equipment 372
Emissions ... 359, 360, 361, 362, 366, 367,
1332
Expenditures 371, 370
Greenhouse gases 362
Industry 371, 372
States 370
Air transportation:
Accidents and deaths 1053, 1058, 1060
Airline markets 1057
Airport summary 1056, 1061
Flight on-time performance 1061
Bomb threats 1059
Civil aviation 1064
Consumer complaints 1062
Cost indexes 1055
Employees 1054
Federal outlays 461
Finances 1054
Fleet size 1047, 1064
Freight 1049, 1054
Manufacturing orders booked/announced. 1012
Passenger outlays 1048
Passenger screening 1059
Price indexes 700
Regional airlines 1063
Traffic carried 1049, 1054, 1063
Air transportation industry:
Earnings 613, 1050, 1051, 1052, 1265
Employees ... 613, 1050, 1051, 1052, 1265
Establishments 1050, 1052, 1265
Finances 1054, 1055
Gross domestic product 642
Occupational safety 634
Productivity 615
Profits 1054
Revenues 1050, 1054
Aircraft manufacturing. See Aerospace industry.
Airline operations (see also Air transportation) ..
1054, 1057
Airmail service 1111
Airplanes 1299
Airports or airfields 1064
Federal aid to state and local government ...
424
Serving regional airlines 1063
Traffic 1056, 1061
Alaska Native. See American Indian, Alaska
Native population
Alcoholic beverages (see also Liquors and bev-
erages):
Advertising 1275
Alcoholism treatment 163, 185
Consumer expenditures . 658, 660, 661, 1035
Consumption 186, 201
"Binge" use 186, 187
Foreign trade 1299
Price indexes 700
Sales 1038

Alcohol involvement in fatal crashes . 1095, 1096,
1098
Alcohol treatment 163, 185
Aleut population (See American Indian, Alaska
Native population)
Algeria. See Foreign countries.
Aliens deported 313
Alimony 521
Almonds 801, 846
Altitudes, geographical 351
Aluminum:
Consumption 861
Employment 861
Foreign trade 861, 866, 1299
Prices 861
Production 998
Recycling 364
World production 864
Ambulatory health care services industry:
Earnings 145, 613, 728
Employees 613, 728
Establishments 728
Finances 718
Gross domestic product 642
Sales, receipts 718, 728
American College Testing Program 249
American Indian, Alaska Native population . 14,
13, 16, 21, 218, 775, 788
Age and/or sex 13, 14, 15, 16
Business owners 737
Charter schools 224
Cities 27
College enrollment 262
Disability 269
Commuting to work 37
Computer use 244
Crime 309
Degrees conferred 283
Disability status 37
Educational attainment 37
Farm operators 788
Food stamp participants 553
Foreign born 37
Health care visits to professionals . 152, 154
Hospital visits 154, 162
Immunization of children 178
Income 663, 676
Mobility status 37
Nativity 37
Nurses 148
Occupation 37
Poverty 682
Reservation and Trust Lands population . 36
States 21
Tribes 35
Veterans 514
American Samoa. See Island areas of the U.S.
American sign language 267
American Stock Exchange 1201
Composite index 1199
AMTRAK 1106
Amusement and recreation services. See Arts,
entertainment and recreation.
Amusement, gambling, and recreation industry:
Earnings 613, 728, 1225, 1226, 1227
Employees 613, 728, 1225
Establishments 728, 1226, 1227
Gross domestic product 642
Nonemployers establishments 1226

NOTE: Index citations refer to **table** numbers, not page numbers.

U.S. Census Bureau, Statistical Abstract of the United States: 2004-2005

Amusement, gambling, and recreation indus-
try: —Con.
Receipts, revenue 728, 1225, 1226
Amusement parks 1224, 1225, 1226, 1227,
                                                    1233
Analgesics 186
Ancestry 47
Anchovies 854
Andorra. See Foreign countries.
Anemias, deaths 102
Anesthesiologists 149
Angiocardiography 165
Angola. See Foreign countries.
Anguilla. See Foreign countries.
Animal oils and fats. See Oils, animal.
Animal slaughtering and processing industry ...
                                                613, 615
Animals, domestic (see also individual classes):
Inventory and production 832
Annuities. See Pensions and retirement benefits.
Antigua and Barbuda. See Foreign countries.
Antimony 861, 866
Apparel manufacturing:
Earnings 613, 973, 976, 984
Electronic commerce 980
Employees ... 613, 973, 976, 978, 982, 984
Establishments 976
Finances 760
Foreign trade 978, 1302
Gross domestic product 642, 972
Industrial production index 754
Mergers and acquisitions 742
Occupational safety 634
Pollution abatement 371
Productivity 615
Profits 760
Shipments 976, 978, 980
Toxic chemical releases 367
Apparel goods:
Advertising 1275
Consumer expenditures . 658, 659, 660, 661
Foreign trade 1299
Prices 698, 700, 706
Sales 1038
Apples . 200, 700, 712, 798, 801, 813, 821, 830
Appliances, household:
Consumer expenditures 660, 661
Homes with 965
Price indexes 700
Sales and shipments 1015, 1038
Appliances (household) manufacturing:
Inventories 987
Shipments 987
Apricots 830
Aquaculture 801, 855
Archery 1241, 1247
Architects and engineers 597
Architectural services. See Engineering and
architectural services.
Area of:
Developed land 348, 349
Federal land 347
Foreign countries 1321
Forest land 844
Island areas of the U.S. 346
Parks 1249, 1250
States 346
United States 1, 346, 1321
Cities 27

Area of: —Con.
Water 1, 346, 353
World 1321
Argentina. See Foreign countries.
Arizona. See State data.
Arkansas. See State data.
Armed Forces ... 500, 502, 503, 504, 506, 507,
                                                    510
Foreign countries 502, 1385
Armenia. See Foreign countries.
Army personnel 500
Arrests (see also Law enforcement) ... 309, 312,
                                                314, 315
Arsenic 861
Arson 309, 345
Arteriography 165
Arteriosclerosis, deaths 102, 105, 106
Artists 597
Arts, entertainment, and recreation:
Capital 751
Earnings 611, 613, 618, 728, 731, 732,
                                            1225, 1226
Employees . 611, 613, 728, 731, 732, 1225,
                                            1226, 1227
Establishments . 728, 729, 731, 1225, 1226,
                                                    1227
Finances 718, 721, 1224, 1226
Gross domestic product 642
Hours 611
Mergers and acquisitions 742
Nonemployers 729, 1227
Occupational safety 634
Profits 758
Receipts, revenue . 718, 721, 726, 727, 728,
                            729, 1224, 1225, 1226, 1227
Arts and humanities:
Aid to 1231
Attendance 1230, 1232
Charitable contributions 562
Federal aid 1231
Grants, foundations 566
Philanthropy 563
Public confidence 404
Aruba. See Foreign countries.
Asbestos 324, 372, 861, 864, 866
Asia. See Foreign countries.
Asian and Pacific Islander population . 775, 788
Births 71, 78
Business owners 737
College enrollment 262
College costs 271
Disability 269
Computer use 1152
Congress, members of 396
Crime 319
Educational attainment 212, 213
Food stamp participants 553
Foreign-born population 211
Health insurance coverage 139, 141
Hospital visits 154, 162
Immunization of children 178
Income 663, 668, 669, 676, 680, 681
Overweight 194
Poverty 683, 684, 689
School enrollment 211, 233, 266, 269
Charter schools 224
States 21
Asian Indian population 22, 737, 1152

NOTE: Index citations refer to **table** numbers, not page numbers.

Asian population . 13, 14, 15, 38, 71, 218, 775, 788
  Commuting to work 37
  Computer use 244
  Disability status 37
  Educational attainment 37, 38, 212, 213
  Family type 38
  Farm operators 788
  Foreign born 37
  Health care visits to professionals 152
  Housing tenure 38
  Income 38
  Labor force ... 38, 570, 571, 573, 576, 597, 603, 608, 623, 627, 639
    Multiple job holders 590
    Occupation 600
    Industry 601
  Mobility status 37
  Nativity 37
  Nurses 148
  Occupation 37
  Poverty .. 38, 682, 683, 684, 686, 689, 690
  Veterans 514
Asparagus 200
Asphalt 860, 920
Assault ... 289, 290, 291, 292, 305, 306, 307
Asset-backed securities 1158, 1159, 1190
Assets, personal 693, 694, 695, 1162
Associations, national, nonprofit 1269
Asthma 102, 104, 106, 155, 163
Atherosclerosis, deaths 102, 105
Athletic goods. See Sporting and athletic goods.
Athletes 597
Atomic energy defense activities, expenditures . 493
Attention deficit disorder 155
Audio equipment 1007
Auditing. See Accounting, tax preparation, bookkeeping, and payroll services.
Australia. See Foreign countries.
Austria. See Foreign countries.
Authors 597
ATMs (automated teller machines) . 1034, 1172, 1181
Automatic bill paying 1181
Automobile loans 1184
Automobile rentals and leasing. Automotive equipment rental and leasing and Rental and leasing services.
Automobiles (see also Motor vehicles):
  Advertising 1275
  Consumer expenditures . 658, 659, 660, 661, 662
  Expenditure per new car 1031
  Foreign trade 1299
  Imports 1031
  Insurance 1219
  Leases 1030
  Price indexes 700
  Production 1031
  Sales 1031, 1030
Automobile dealers:
  Earnings 613, 1018, 1019
  Employees 613, 1018, 1019
  Establishments 1018, 1019
  Inventories 1024
  Productivity 615
  Sales 1020

Automotive equipment rental and leasing . 613, 615
Automotive products. See Motor vehicles, Tires and tubes, etc.
Automotive repair and maintenance service:
  Earnings 613
  Establishments 1264, 1265
  Mergers and acquisitions 742
  Nonemployers 1264
  Productivity 615
  Receipts/revenue 1264, 1277
Avocados 801, 830
Azerbaijan. See Foreign countries.

B

Backpacking 1241
Bacon 700, 712
Bahamas, The. See Foreign countries.
Bahrain. See Foreign countries.
Bakeries and tortilla manufacturing .. 613, 615, 976
Bakery products 660, 661, 700
Balance of payments 1278, 1279, 1292
Balance sheet 469, 722, 723, 725
Ballet 1231
Bananas 200, 700, 712, 810, 812
Bangladesh. See Foreign countries.
Bankruptcies 739, 740
Banks, commercial:
  ATM's 1172
  Checking accounts 1172
  Consumer credit finance rates 1184
  Credit cards 1169, 1180, 1185
  Debit cards 1183
  Delinquency rates, repossessions, loans . 1180
  Deposits 1169, 1173
  Earnings 613, 1157
  Employees 613, 1157
  Establishments 1157, 1168, 1169
  Finances ... 1158, 1159, 1168, 1169, 1170, 1171, 1173, 1174, 1175, 1177, 1187, 1210
  Flow of funds 1158, 1159, 1210
  Foreign banking offices in United States . 1173
  Gross domestic product 642, 1154
  Home equity loans 1169
  Individual Retirement Accounts 1212
  Insured banks 1168, 1174
  Loans to families 1165
  Mergers and acquisitions 742
  Occupational safety 634
  Productivity 615
  Profits 1170, 1171
  Robbery 303
  State data 1174, 1175
  Stock and bond prices and yields 1199
Barbados. See Foreign countries.
Barbecuing 1238
Barber shops 1277
Barite 860, 861, 864
Barium 801, 866
Barley 798
Bars. See Food Services and drinking places.
Base, military closings 501
Baseball . 1237, 1239, 1241, 1243, 1244, 1247
Basketball . 1237, 1239, 1241, 1243, 1244, 1247
Bauxite 860, 864
  Consumption 861
  Employment 861
  Foreign trade 861

NOTE: Index citations refer to **table** numbers, not page numbers.

U.S. Census Bureau, Statistical Abstract of the United States: 2004-2005

Bauxite —Con.
Prices 861
Production 864
Strategic and critical materials inventory . 865
World production 864, 1363
Beans 200, 798, 801, 806, 813, 829
Beauty shops 1277
Price indexes 700
Beef (see also Meat and meat products):
  Consumer expenditures 658, 660, 661
  Consumption 199, 813, 831, 1358
    Foreign countries 1358
  Foreign trade 812, 813, 831
  Price indexes 700
  Prices 700, 712
  Production 831
    Foreign countries 1357
  Supply 831
Beer. See Malt beverages.
Beer, wine, and liquor stores:
  Earnings 613, 1019
  Employees 613, 1019
  Establishments 1019, 1026
  Nonemployers 1026
  Productivity 615
  Sales 1020, 1026, 1035
Belarus. See Foreign countries.
Belgium. See Foreign countries.
Belize. See Foreign countries.
Benin. See Foreign countries.
Bermuda. See Foreign countries.
Beryllium 861
Beverages and tobacco product manufacturing:
  Earnings 613, 973, 976
  Employees 613, 973, 976, 978, 982
  Finances 760
  Foreign trade 978
  Gross domestic product 642
  Industrial production index 754
  Multinational companies 762, 763
  Pollution abatement 371
  Productivity 615
  Profits 760
  Shipments 976, 978, 986, 987
Beverages (see also Alcoholic beverages):
  Advertising expenditures 1275
  Consumption 201
  Price indexes 700
Bhutan. See Foreign countries.
Bicycles 303, 1241, 1247, 1248
Billiards 1241
Biological sciences:
  Degrees conferred 775
  Employment 597
Bird ownership 1236
Birth and birth rates .. 4, 70, 71, 72, 74, 75, 77,
         78, 79, 80, 81, 82, 83, 86, 87
  American Indian, Eskimo, and Aleut popula-
    tion 71
  Asian and Pacific Islander population 71
  Births to mothers who smoked 84
  Births to single or unmarried women . 71, 79,
         86, 91, 1326
  Births to teenage mothers 73, 91
  Birth weight 71, 81, 82
  Black, African American population . 71, 72,
         74, 82, 86
  Cesarean section deliveries 83, 165
  Characteristics of mother 72, 83, 86, 87

Birth and birth rates —Con.
Delivery procedures 165
First births 85, 86, 87
Foreign countries 1325, 1326
Hispanic population 71, 74
Island areas of the U.S. 1304
Low birthweight by smoking status 84
Prenatal care 71, 82
Projections 76
Race 72, 74, 77, 79
States 19, 74, 81
Birth control 88
Birth weights 71, 81, 82
Bismuth 861
Black lung benefit program 542
Black, African American population . 13, 16, 21,
              46
Abortions 89, 90
Activity limitation 182, 183
Adult education 288
Age and/or sex 11, 13, 15, 16, 33
AIDS 179, 180
Birth and birth rates . 71, 72, 74, 77, 78, 82,
              86
  Births to teenage mothers 78
  Births to unmarried women 79
Business owners 737
Cancer 104, 105, 191
Charity contributions 561
Child care 559
Children under 18 years old . 11, 15, 16, 33
  Literacy activities 220, 223
  Poverty 684, 686
  School readiness 220, 223
Cigarette smoking 188
Community service 567, 568
Commuting to work 34
Computer use 244, 1152
Congress, members of 396
Consumer expenditures 660, 661
Contraceptive use 88
Crime (arrests) 308, 309
Criminal victimizations 217, 218, 308
Deaths and death rates .. 95, 100, 101, 104,
              105
Disabled persons 34, 269, 540
Educational attainment 34
Elderly 11, 15, 33, 686
Elected officials 396, 405
Elections, voter registrations and turnout ...
             407
Families, characteristics 59, 60, 61, 62
Farm operators, workers 788, 809
Fertility, fertility rate 75, 76
Food stamp participants 553
Foreign-born population 34, 211
Health care, visits to professionals . 152, 154
Health insurance coverage ... 132, 139, 141
High school graduates and dropouts 256
Home health and hospice care 169
Homeschooled 229
Homicides 297
Hospital use 154, 162
Households, characteristics .. 58, 60, 61, 62
Housing 950, 954, 962, 964
Immunization of children 178
Income .. 33, 521, 665, 666, 667, 668, 669,
      670, 671, 672, 673, 677, 681

NOTE: Index citations refer to **table** numbers, not page numbers.

U.S. Census Bureau, Statistical Abstract of the United States: 2004-2005

Black, African American population —Con.
Infant deaths 100, 101
Internet access 244, 1121, 1152
Jail inmates 334
Job search 604
Labor force 570, 571, 573
Displaced workers 594
Earnings 623
Employed . 571, 587, 588, 589, 590, 591,
597, 600, 601
Employment status 571
Educational attainment 573, 608
High school graduates and dropouts,
employment status 257
School enrollment, persons 16 to 24
years old 576
Unemployed 603, 608
Job search 604
Persons working at home 587
Language proficiency 221
Life expectancy 92, 93, 94
Living arrangements 54
Marital status 51
Media users 1121
Minimum wage workers 627
Mobility status 34
Nativity 34
Nurses 148, 516
Occupation 34, 597, 600
Overweight 194
Pension plan coverage 535
Physical activity 195
Poverty 33, 683, 684, 686, 690
Prisoners 338
Property owners 954, 961, 964
Recreation activities 1232, 1233, 1234
School dropouts, high school 255, 257
Schools and education:
Adult education 288
American College Testing Program .. 249
Attainment 212, 213, 214
Enrollment 207, 211, 233, 266
Charter schools 224
College costs 271
College enrollment 262, 263, 264
Disability 269
Preprimary enrollment 222
Higher education institutions:
Degrees conferred 775
Enrollment 211, 262, 263, 264
High school dropouts 254, 255, 257
High school graduates 257
Homeschooled 229
Scholastic Assessment Test 248
Sports participation 1242
Teachers 235, 247, 597
Senior citizen communities 962
States 21
Suicides 102, 103, 104, 105, 106, 110
Union membership 639
Veterans 514
Volunteers 567, 568
Voter registration and turnout 407
**Blast furnace and basic steel products. See Iron
and steel products.**
Blind persons 543
Medicaid payments and recipients 133
Blood alcohol concentration . 1095, 1096, 1098

Blue collar workers 455, 620, 625
Bluefish 854
Board and care homes 171
Accidents 1053
Bolivia. See Foreign countries.
Bolts, nuts, etc. See Iron and steel products.
Bonds:
Foreign 1196, 1197
Holdings by sector . 1159, 1160, 1161, 1193,
1196, 1198
Life insurance companies 1193, 1217
New issues 1194
Ownership by equity holders 1206
Prices, yields, sales, and issues .. 470, 1189,
1192, 1195, 1197, 1203
Rating 437, 438
U.S. savings 470, 1162
**Bookkeeping. See Accounting, tax preparation,
bookkeeping, and payroll services.**
Book, periodical and music stores 613, 615,
1020
Book publishing industry 1131
**Books (see also Information industry, Publishing
industry, and Libraries):**
Prices 1130
Production 1129
Reading 1119
Sales 1036, 1038, 1118, 1128, 1132
Boots. See Footwear.
Border Patrol activities 313
Boron 860, 861
Bosnia and Herzegovina. See Foreign countries.
Botswana. See Foreign countries.
Botulism 177
Bowling 1240, 1241, 1247
Bowling center industry 1224, 1226
Boxing 1237
Brazil. See Foreign countries.
Bread 700, 712
Bridge inventory 1073
British Virgin Islands. See Foreign countries.
Broadcasting and telecommunications industry:
Earnings 613, 728, 1113, 1115
Employees 613, 728, 1113, 1115
Establishments 728, 1113, 1115
Finances 1137, 1139, 1140, 1141
Gross domestic product 642
Multinational companies 762, 763
Receipts, revenue .. 728, 1113, 1114, 1137,
1139, 1140, 1141
World 1372
Broadway and off-Broadway shows 1230
Broccoli 200, 801, 813, 829
Broilers (see also Poultry) .. 798, 801, 831, 839,
840
Bromine 861
Bronchitis, emphysema, etc. 102, 104, 105,
106, 155, 156
Brunei. See Foreign countries.
Buckwheat, organic acreage 798
Buddhist population. See Religion.
Budget, Federal:
Outlays 461, 462, 463, 464, 465
Receipts 461, 467
Revenue losses (tax expenditures) 471
Tax expenditures 471
Taxes 467
Building contractors, general:
Earnings 613, 918, 919
Employees 613, 918, 919

NOTE: Index citations refer to **table** numbers, not page numbers.

U.S. Census Bureau, Statistical Abstract of the United States: 2004-2005

Building contractors, general: —Con.
Establishments 918, 919
Occupational safety 634
Value of work 919
Building materials, and garden supplies, retail
stores:
Earnings 613, 728, 1019
Electronic commerce 1039
Employees 613, 728, 1019
Establishments 728, 1019, 1026
Inventories 1024
Nonemployers 1026
Productivity 615
Purchases 1023
Sales 728, 1020, 1022, 1025, 1026
Building permits. See Construction industry, and
Housing and housing units.
Buildings (see also Construction industry, and
Housing and housing units):
Characteristics 970
Construction value 922, 923, 924, 925
Correctional facilities 335
Energy consumption and expenditures . 893
Federal 490, 491
Fires and property loss 344
Floorspace 490, 491, 893, 970
Office vacancy rate 969, 971
Principal activity 893, 970
Bulgaria. See Foreign countries.
Burglary 289, 290, 291, 292, 303, 308, 309
Burkina Faso. See Foreign countries.
Burma. See Foreign countries.
Burundi. See Foreign countries.
Buses and bus transportation (see also Passen-
ger transit and Motor vehicles):
Finances 1101
Passenger traffic and outlays ... 1048, 1049
Receipts 1101
Business enterprise (see also individual types of
business and industry):
American Indian and Alaska Native owned
businesses 737
Asian and Pacific Islander owned businesses .
737
Bankruptcies filed 739, 740
Black owned businesses 737
Capital, fixed by industry 748
Corporations:
Philanthropy 563
Profits and sales 719
Corporations, partnerships, and proprietor-
ships . 716, 718, 719, 720, 721, 726, 727
Cycles 753
Divestitures 741
Economic indicators 752
Employees 730, 733, 735, 761
Establishments 728, 730, 731, 733
Failures and starts 734
Finances . 716, 719, 720, 722, 723, 759, 760,
762, 763, 990, 991
Firms 733, 735
Flow of funds 1158
Foreign investment in the U.S. . 1283, 1284,
1285, 1286
Hispanic owned businesses 737
Leading indicators 752
Leveraged buy-outs 741
Loans to minority-operated small businesses
.... 736

**Business enterprise (see also individual types
of business and industry): —Con.**
Mergers and acquisitions 741, 742
Multinational companies 761, 762
Patents 744, 745, 746, 1348
Payroll 730, 733, 735
Profits 757, 758, 759, 760, 990, 991
Sales, shipments, receipts ... 985, 987, 988,
991
Small business 733, 734, 735, 736
Venture capital 743
Women owned businesses 737
Business management, degrees conferred . 284,
285, 286
Salary offers 281
Business services (see individual types of serv-
ice):
Gross domestic product 993
Mergers and acquisitions 742
Multinational companies 763
Occupational safety 634
Receipts 1118
Butter 199, 837
Butterfish 854

C
Cabbage 829
Cable and other pay television services 700,
1108, 1120
Advertising expenditures 1274
Price indexes 700
Viewing 1119, 1121
Cable TV industry:
Earnings 613, 1117
Employees 613, 1117, 1139
Finances 1118, 1139
Gross domestic product 1116
Receipts 1118, 1139
Cadmium 861, 864, 866
Cafeterias. See Eating and drinking places.
Calcium, dietary 197, 198
Calcium chloride 860
California. See State data.
Calisthenics 1241
Calves 801, 831, 832, 835
Cambodia. See Foreign countries.
Cambodian population 22
Cameroon. See Foreign countries.
Campaigns, fund raising ... 411, 412, 413, 414,
415, 416
Camping 1241, 1247
Canada. See Foreign countries.
Cancer (malignancies) . 102, 104, 106, 112, 155,
163, 169, 191, 192
Deaths 105, 106, 107, 180, 192
Cantaloupe 829
Capacity utilization, index 755
Cape Verde. See Foreign countries.
Capital (see individual industries):
Banking 1169, 1170
Expenditures . 371, 370, 749, 750, 751, 976
New security issues 1194
Pollution abatement 371, 370
Residential 966
Stocks 748, 985
Utilities 907, 913, 1143
Capital equipment, producer price indexes . 704
Capital punishment 341, 342
Carbon dioxide emissions 362, 1333

NOTE: Index citations refer to **table** numbers, not page numbers.

U.S. Census Bureau, Statistical Abstract of the United States: 2004-2005

Carbon dioxide (natural), production and value .
  860
Cardiac catheterization 165
Cardiovascular disease. See Heart disease.
Cargo tonnage. See Tonnage U.S. Flag fleet.
Carrots 200, 801, 829
Cars. See automobiles
Cash usage 1182
Cassettes 1135
Casualties, military conflicts 506
Casualty insurance 1218
Catalog and mail order sales . 1020, 1023, 1026,
  1038, 1039
Catfish 801, 855
Catholic population. See Religion.
CAT scan 165
Cat ownership 1236
Cattle:
  Farm marketings, sales 801, 804, 807
  Imports 812
  Number on farms 832, 833, 835
  Organic 798
  Prices 832
  Production 832, 835
  Slaughter 835
  Value on farms 832
Cauliflower 200
Cayman Islands. See Foreign countries.
Celery 200, 829
Cellular telephones (See also Telephone carriers)
  .... 965, 1372
Cement (see also Nonmetallic mineral product
  manufacturing) 860, 935
  Consumption 861
  Earnings 613
  Employment 613, 861
  Foreign trade 861
  Price indexes 867
  Prices 861
  Production and value 860
  Productivity 615
  World production 1363
Central African Republic. See Foreign countries.
Central America. See Foreign countries.
Central and South American population (His-
  panic origin) 40, 41, 71
Cereal and bakery products:
  Advertising 1112
  Expenditures, prices ... 658, 660, 661, 700,
  808
  Foreign trade 1299
Cerebrovascular diseases, deaths . 102, 104, 105,
  106, 156, 163, 1206
Certificates of deposit 1162, 1188
Cesarean section deliveries 83, 165
Cesium 861
CFC (Chloroflurocarbon) gases 362
Chad. See Foreign countries.
Charitable contributions (see also Philanthropy) .
  475, 477, 562, 563
Charter schools 224
Checking accounts . 691, 692, 1162, 1172, 1182
Cheese (see also Dairy products) . 198, 199, 712,
  813, 837
Chemical engineering:
  Degrees conferred 773
  Employment 773
  Salary 773
Chemical products 1299
  Producer price indexes 700

Chemical products —Con.
  Production 996
  Toxic chemical releases 366, 367, 368
Chemicals manufacturing (see also individual
  chemicals):
  Capital 371
  Earnings 613, 973, 976, 984
  Electronic commerce 980
  Employees ... 613, 973, 976, 978, 982, 984
  Establishments 973
  Finances 760
  Foreign trade 978, 1302
  Gross domestic product 642, 972
  Industrial production index 754
  Inventories 986, 987
  Mergers and acquisitions 742
  Multinational companies 762, 763
  Occupational safety 634
  Patents 745
  Pollution abatement 371
  Productivity 615
  Profits 759, 760
  Research and development 776, 777
  Shipments 976, 978, 986, 987
  Toxic chemical releases 367
Chemistry (see also Physical sciences):
  Employment 597
  Nobel prize laureates 786
  Salary offers 281
Cherries 830
Chicken pox 177
Chickens. See Poultry.
Child abuse 331, 332
Child care .. 559, 560, 597, 599, 602, 700, 962
  Expenditures for 657
Child day care services:
  Earnings 555, 556, 613
  Employees 555, 556, 597, 613
  Establishments 555, 556
  Finances 555, 556, 557
Child support 521, 548, 549
Children (see also Population and Vital statis-
  tics):
  Activity limitation 182
  Age and/or sex 11, 12, 16
  Aid, social welfare programs 524
  AIDS 179, 180
  Alcohol use 186
  Child abuse 331, 332
  Child day care 559, 560, 700
  Child support 521, 548, 549
  Cigarette smoking 186
  College dormitories 66
  Computer use 242, 243, 244
  Congenital abnormalities 163
  Correctional institutions 66
  Cost of raising 657
  Crime, arrests 306, 312
  Deaths and death rates . 100, 101, 104, 105,
  180
  Disability status 245
  Drug use 186
  Families with .. 57, 59, 60, 61, 62, 63, 1328
  Food insecurity 196
  Food stamp program 552, 553
  Foreign born population 46
  Foreign country 1328
  Foster care 524
  Group quarters population 66

NOTE: Index citations refer to **table** numbers, not page numbers.

U.S. Census Bureau, Statistical Abstract of the United States: 2004-2005

Children (see also Population and Vital statistics): —Con.
Head start program 554
Health insurance coverage .. 132, 135, 139, 140, 141, 524
High school dropouts 254, 255
High school graduates 225, 253, 259
Hispanic origin population 14, 15, 16
Homeschooled 229
Hospital use 66, 155, 156, 162, 163
Hunger 196
Immigrants 6
Immunization against diseases 178
Income, families with children 673
Injuries 174
Internet access 244
Juvenile delinquency institutions 66, 329
Labor force (16 to 19 years old), ... 570
Employed 582, 583, 590, 592
Employment status 576
Minimum wage workers 627
Multiple job holders 590
Participation rates 577
Sex 570, 572
Unemployed 603, 609
Language proficiency 221
Literacy activities 220, 223
Literacy skills 220, 223
Missing children 333
Mobility status 28
Mothers in the labor force, by age of children 579
Music purchases 1136
Parental involvement 219
Physician visits 152, 154, 155
Pneumonia 163
Poverty 684, 686
Projections 12
Respiratory infection, acute 163
School crimes 217, 218
School enrollment . 202, 204, 206, 207, 208, 209, 210, 225, 230, 232
Homeschooled 229
Parental involvement 219
Preprimary school enrollment 222
Projections 202
School readiness 223
Social Security beneficiaries and payments .. 527
Suicides 104
Chile. See Foreign countries.
China. See Foreign countries.
Chinese population 22, 737
Chiropractors' offices 145
Chloroflurocarbon (CFC's) gases 362
Chocolate. See Cocoa and Confectionery products.
Cholelithiasis, deaths 102
Cholera 177
Cholesterol 198
Christian population. See Religion.
Christmas trees 801
Chromite 1363
Chromium 861, 865, 866
Churches (see also Religion):
Construction value 925
Grants, foundations 566
Number and membership 68

Churches (see also Religion): —Con.
Volunteers 567, 568
Cigar usage 186
Cigarettes (see also Tobacco products):
Advertising 1275
Consumption 992
Foreign trade 1299, 1361
Production 992, 1361
Smokers and use 186, 187, 188, 189
Circuit boards 1003, 1004, 1005
Circulation of newspapers and periodicals . 1120, 1122, 1124, 1125
Foreign countries 1373
Cirrhosis of liver, deaths 102, 104, 105
Cities (see also Metropolitan areas):
Climate . 377, 378, 379, 380, 381, 382, 383
Foreign cities 1331
Commuting to work 1086
Crime 290, 292
Debt 450
Drug use 314
Employees, earnings, payrolls 459
Finances of city governments 449, 450
Foreign born 43
Foreign travel to 1256
Governmental units 417, 419
Housing 945, 957, 960
Language spoken at home 50
Office vacancy rates 971
Officials elected 405
Population 26, 27
Property tax rates 446
Taxes paid, by family income level 445
Citrus fruits:
Consumption 200, 201, 813, 827
Foreign trade 813, 827
Pesticide usage 821
Production 827, 830
Civil and architectural engineering 773
Civil aviation. See Air transportation.
Civil cases, U.S. District Courts 324
Civil service employees. See Government.
Clams 854, 856, 857
Clergymen 68
Employment 597
Climate, selected cities 377, 378, 379, 380, 381, 382, 383, 1331
Precipitation 380, 381, 382, 1331
Temperature . 376, 377, 378, 379, 383, 1331
Clocks and watches 1299
Clothing and accessory stores, retail:
Earnings 613, 728, 1019
Electronic commerce 1039
Employees 613, 728, 1019
Establishments 728, 1019, 1026
Finances 760
Inventories 1024
Nonemployers 1026
Productivity 615
Profits 760
Purchases 1023
Sales 728, 1020, 1022, 1025, 1026
Coal (see also Petroleum and coal products and Coal mining):
Car loadings 1107, 1108
Consumption 884, 885, 887, 901, 1365, 1366
Expenditures 889, 890
Foreign trade 878, 885, 895, 896, 1299

NOTE: Index citations refer to **table** numbers, not page numbers.

U.S. Census Bureau, Statistical Abstract of the United States: 2004-2005

Coal (see also Petroleum and coal products and Coal mining): —Con.
Net generation 901
Net summer capacity 901
Prices 704, 862, 878
Production 860, 878, 884, 885, 1111
World production . 864, 879, 1363, 1364, 1367
Reserves 880, 881
Coal mining:
   Capital 859
   Earnings 841, 859
   Employment 693, 841, 859, 878
   Establishments 841, 859
   Gross domestic product 642
   Mines 878
   Occupational safety 634
   Output 858, 860, 884, 887
   Productivity 878
   Shipments 859
   Supply 877
   Value added 859
Coast Guard personnel 504
Coastal population 23
Cobalt 865, 866
Cocaine (see also Drugs (illegal)), arrests and use 186, 315, 316
Cocoa 199, 812, 1299
Cod 854, 857
Coffee:
   Consumption 199, 201
   Foreign trade 810, 812, 1299
   Price indexes 700
   Prices 700, 712
Cogeneration of electricity 901
Coke. See Coal.
College:
   Aid received 275
   Costs 271
   Price index 700
   State appropriations 274
   Tuition 276
Colleges and universities. See Education, higher education institutions.
Colombia. See Foreign countries.
Colorado. See State data.
Columbium-tantalum 861, 864, 866
Commerce:
   Domestic, by rail 1107
   Domestic, by water 1065, 1066
   Foreign. See Foreign trade.
Commerce and housing credit 462, 465
Commercial buildings:
   Characteristics 970
   Construction value 925
   Cost of construction 921
   Crime incidents 307
   Energy characteristics 970
   Floor space 925, 970
   Inventory 970
   Vacancy rates 969, 971
Commercial paper 723, 1191
Commodities. See individual types of commodities.
Commodity flow 1071, 1072
Communicable diseases 177
Communications, degrees conferred . 284, 285, 286

Communications equipment manufacturing:
   Earnings 613, 973, 976
   Employees 613, 973, 976
   Establishments 973
   Inventories 987
   Mergers and acquisitions 742
   Productivity 615
   Shipments 976, 987, 1008
Communications industry. See Information industry.
Community care facilities for the elderly industry 145
Community development, federal outlays .. 465
Community food, housing services ... 555, 556, 557
Community service 567, 568
Commuting to work .. 34, 37, 630, 1084, 1085, 1086
Comoros. See Foreign countries.
Compact disks (CD-ROM) 1007, 1135
Computer:
   Advertising expenditures 1275
   Foreign trade 1299
   Sales 1007, 1036, 1037, 1038
   Use ... 242, 243, 244, 604, 617, 965, 1121, 1150, 1152, 1153, 1372, 1373
Computer programming and data processing services:
   Earnings 613, 773, 1117
   Employees 613, 1117
   Gross domestic product 1116
Computer specialists:
   Degrees conferred . 284, 285, 286, 773, 775
   Labor force 597, 599
   Salary offers 281, 773
Computer systems design:
   Earnings 1265
   Employees 1265
   Establishments 1265
   Gross domestic product 642
   Multinational companies 762, 763
   Receipts 1273
Computers and electronic product manufacturing:
   Capital 371
   Earnings 613, 973, 976, 1117
   Electronic commerce 980
   Employees .. 613, 973, 976, 978, 982, 1117
   Establishments 973
   Finances 760
   Foreign trade 975
   Gross domestic product 642, 972, 1116
   Industrial production index 754
   Inventories 986, 987
   Mergers and acquisitions 742
   Multinational companies 763
   Pollution abatement 371
   Productivity 615
   Profits 760
   Shipments . 976, 978, 980, 986, 987, 1004, 1005, 1006
Computer related crimes 203
Computerized axial tomography (CAT scan) . 165
Concerts, symphony orchestras 1230
Condensed and evaporated milk 199, 837
Confectionery products 813
Congo (Brazzaville). See Foreign countries.
Congo (Kinshasa). See Foreign countries.
Congestion on road 1083

NOTE: Index citations refer to **table** numbers, not page numbers.

U.S. Census Bureau, Statistical Abstract of the United States: 2004-2005

Congress, U.S.:
Asian, Pacific Islander members 396
Bills, acts, resolutions 397, 398
Black members 396
Campaign finances 415, 416
Composition 393, 394
Congressional apportionment 390
Congressional districts:
Candidates, votes cast 391
Hispanic members 396
Members, characteristics 396
Public confidence 404
Representatives, vote cast ... 391, 392, 410
Senators, vote cast 389
Seniority 396
Time in session 397
Women members 396
Connecticut. See State data.
Construction industry (see also Building materials and Highways):
Building authorized 927
Building permits, value 927
Capital 748, 751
Construction contracts 925, 926
Cost 921
Earnings . 611, 613, 618, 619, 728, 731, 732,
738, 918, 919, 1316
Employees .. 587, 601, 611, 612, 613, 635,
728, 731, 732, 738, 765, 918, 919, 1316,
Establishments ... 728, 729, 731, 918, 919,
1316
Finances 718, 721, 1310
Gross domestic product 642, 646, 1310
Hours 611
Mergers and acquisitions 742
Nonemployers 729
Occupational safety 631, 634, 636
Producer price indexes 920
Profits 716, 758
Residential 927, 928, 929, 930
Shipments, receipts 716, 718, 721, 726,
727, 728, 729, 738, 1316
Unions 639
Value, work 919, 922, 923, 924
Women-owned businesses 738
Construction machinery, manufacturing:
Earnings 613, 976
Employees 613, 976
Inventories 987
Productivity 615
Shipments 987
Construction materials. See Building materials.
Consumer:
Consumer complaints against airlines . 1062
Consumer goods 704
Credit . 723, 1163, 1164, 1165, 1167, 1184,
1185, 1186
Delinquency rates 1180
Electronics 1006, 1007, 1036
Expenditures 658, 659, 662
Books 1128
Communications 1119
Entertainment 1228
Food ...., 658, 659, 662, 808
Housing ...., 658, 659, 662
Medical care .. 116, 117, 119, 120, 125,
658, 659, 661, 662
Metropolitan areas 659
Reading material 1132, 1228

Consumer: —Con.
Sporting goods 1247
Consumer payment systems 1182
Consumer price indexes 697, 698, 699, 700
By commodity group 698, 700
Foreign countries 702, 1342
Medical care 124, 698, 700
Purchasing power of the dollar 697
Year-to-year changes 698
Consumption. See individual commodities.
Contraception use 88
Convenience stores 1033
Cook Islands. See Foreign countries.
Cookies 700
Cooking oils consumption 199
Copper:
Consumption 861
Foreign trade 861, 866
Prices 861, 862
Production and value 860
World production 864, 1363
Copyrights registration 747
Corn:
Acreage 822, 823
Genetically modified seed plantings . 820
Organic 798
Consumption 199, 200
Farm marketings, sales 801, 804, 807
Foreign trade 814, 816, 817, 822, 1299,
1360
Pesticide usage 821
Prices 822, 823
Production 814, 822, 823, 829
World production 814, 1355
Supply and disappearance 822
Coronary procedures 165
Corporate business sector 723, 724
Political action committees ... 411, 412, 413
Corporations:
Capital 725
Dividend payments 757
Finances . 716, 717, 718, 719, 720, 721, 723,
724, 725, 726, 727, 1158, 1159, 1210
Manufacturing 990
Nonfinancial 723, 724
Philanthropy 563
Profits .. 716, 757, 758, 759, 760, 989, 990
Public confidence 404
Receipts 716
Sales 721, 726, 727, 989
Stocks and bonds 1189, 1190
Taxes:
Corporate income tax 757
Returns 716, 717, 725
Correctional institutions (see also Prisons and prisoners):
Employment 597
Expenditures 440, 441
Facilities 335
Prisoners 66, 335, 336
Cosmetics, perfume, etc.:
Advertising expenditures 1275
Foreign trade 1299
Costa Rica. See Foreign countries.
Cost-of-living indexes 701
Cote d'Ivoire. See Foreign countries.
Cotton:
Acreage 822, 823
Genetically modified seed plantings . 820

NOTE: Index citations refer to **table** numbers, not page numbers.

U.S. Census Bureau, Statistical Abstract of the United States: 2004-2005

Cotton: —Con.
Organic 798
Consumption 993
Farm marketings, sales 801, 805, 807
Foreign trade . 810, 814, 816, 817, 822, 993,
1299
Pesticide usage 821
Prices 806, 822, 823
Production 814, 822, 823
World 814, 1359
Supply and disappearance 822
County governments 417, 418, 419
Debt 452
Elected officials 405, 406
Employees, earnings, payroll 460
Finances of county government ... 451, 452
Couriers and messengers:
Earnings 613, 1050, 1051, 1052
Employees 613, 1050, 1051, 1052
Establishments 1050, 1052
Revenue 1050, 1104
Courts 323, 324
District courts, U.S. 324, 325
Juvenile court cases handled 329
Public officials, prosecutions 326
Sentencing 325
Supreme Court, U.S. 323
Cows (see also Dairy products) .. 833, 836, 837
Crabs 854, 856, 857
Crack cocaine 186
Cranberries 830
Credit cards ... 1034, 1164, 1165, 1180, 1182,
1184, 1185, 1186
Credit intermediation industry:
Earnings 1155, 1157
Employees 1155, 1157
Establishments 1155, 1156, 1157
Nonemployers 1156
Receipts 1155, 1156
Credit markets 1159, 1184
Credit unions:
Earnings 1157
Employees 1157
Establishments 1157, 1168, 1176
Finances 1158, 1168, 1176, 1184, 1210
Individual Retirement Accounts 1212
Crew 1244
Crime (see also Criminal victimization and Law
enforcement):
Assault 289, 290, 291, 292
Average value lost 303
Burglary 289, 290, 291, 292, 303, 308
Child abuse and neglect 331, 332
DNA crime laboratories 321
Drug abuse violations 315, 325
Hate crimes 301, 302
Homicides, race and sex 297
Larceny-theft 289, 290, 291, 292, 303
Motor vehicle theft . 289, 290, 291, 292, 293,
303, 308
Murder, murder circumstances 289, 290,
291, 292, 293, 300
Place and time of occurrence 308
Police officers assaulted, killed 322
Property crime 289, 290, 291, 292
Rape, forcible 289, 290, 291, 292, 298
Robbery 289, 290, 291, 292, 303
Shoplifting 303

**Crime (see also Criminal victimization and
Law enforcement): —Con.**
Students and schools 217, 218
Violent crime . 289, 290, 291, 292, 293, 300
Workplace 635, 636
Criminal victimization . 217, 218, 304, 305, 306,
307, 308
Households 308
Place of occurrence 308
Violent 307, 300
Weapons involved 305, 307, 308
Workplace 635, 636
Croaker 854
Croatia. See Foreign countries.
Crops (see also Farms and individual crops):
Acreage 819, 822, 1315
Farm marketings, sales 800, 801, 805
Foreign trade 815, 817, 822
Prices 806, 822
Production 822
Productivity 819
Supply and disappearance 822
Cross country (running) 1243, 1244
Crossword puzzles 1238
Crude materials:
Producer price indexes 703, 704
Production 898
Crude oil (see also Petroleum and products):
Foreign trade 868, 885, 896, 897, 898
Prices 860, 868, 894
Production 867, 868
World production 872
Cryptosporidiosis 177
Cuba. See Foreign countries.
Cuban population 22, 40
Business owners 737
Commuting to work 41
Disability status 41
Educational attainment 41, 212
Foreign born 41
Labor force 571
Mobility status 41
Nativity 41
Occupation 41
Cucumbers 200, 801, 813, 829
Currency:
Foreign exchange rate 1378
Personal saving component 650
Supply 1187
Customs outlays 465
Customs regions, imports and exports 1295
Cyclones 374
Cyprus. See Foreign countries.
Czech Republic. See Foreign countries.

D

Dairy products (see also individual products):
Calcium source 198
Cholesterol source 198
Consumer expenditures 658, 661
Consumption 199, 201, 813
Farm marketings, sales 801, 813, 837
Foreign trade 812, 813, 815, 1299
Iron source 198
Manufacture 837
Prices 806
Production 837
Dairy products manufacturing 615, 976
Dance 1232, 1234

.**NOTE:** Index citations refer to **table** numbers, not page numbers.

U.S. Census Bureau, Statistical Abstract of the United States: 2004-2005

Dart throwing 1241
Data processing services. See Computer pro-
gramming and data processing services.
Day care. See Child day care services.
Death care services 613, 1277
Death penalty 341, 342
Deaths and death rates (see also Accidents and
fatalities):
  Age and sex . 94, 95, 96, 97, 104, 107, 112
  AIDS 102, 180
  Black, African American population . 100, 104,
                                      180
  Cancer 102, 104, 106, 112
  Cause .. 102, 103, 104, 105, 106, 107, 108,
               109, 180, 1053, 1106
  Fetal and neonatal 100
  Foreign countries 1325
  Heart disease . 102, 104, 105, 106, 107, 112
  Industrial 631, 632
  Infant 100, 101
  Injuries 112
  Island areas of the U.S. 1304
  Maternal 100
  Military deaths 505
  Race 94, 95, 100, 101, 104, 107
  States 19
  Suicide 102, 104, 105, 106, 110
  Summary 70
  Traffic fatalities ... 1053, 1089, 1090, 1091,
           1092, 1094, 1095, 1096
  Weather related 375
  Workers deaths 632
Debit cards 1181, 1182, 1183
Debt (see also Loans and mortgages):
  City 447, 450
  Consumer 1167, 1184
  County governments 452
  Farm 802, 803
  Federal government 461, 477
  Foreign countries 1383
  Households 1159, 1164
  Local governments . 428, 429, 434, 435, 436,
                                        444
  State and local government 428, 435
  Highways 1077
  State government 440, 442
Deductions (taxes) 475, 477, 561
  Businesses 719, 720, 721, 725
Defense, Department of (see also Army, Navy,
and Air Force):
  Budget authority, outlays 462, 463, 465,
                        492, 493, 494
  Contract awards, by states 496
  Employees, civilian 496, 501
  Expenditures 492, 493, 494, 496, 499
    Health and medical care .. 115, 116, 118
  Funds available and outlays 494
  Military bases 501
  Military personnel . 500, 501, 502, 507, 508
  Military retirees 508
  Property, real and personal 490
Degrees conferred (see also individual field) ....
  282, 283, 284, 285, 286, 287, 773, 775
  Salary offers 281, 773
Delaware. See State data.
Delinquency. See Juveniles.
Denmark. See Foreign countries.
Dentists 147, 597

Dentists —Con.
  Charges and expenditures for 116, 117,
                                      120, 124
  Dental schools, students, and graduates . 151,
                                           287
  Medicaid payments, recipients 133
  Offices 145, 146
Deoxyribonucleic acid (DNA) crime laboratories .
                                          321
Department stores:
  Earnings 613, 1019, 1022
  Employees 613, 1019, 1022
  Establishments 1019, 1022
  Inventories 1024
  Productivity 615
  Sales 1020, 1022, 1024, 1025, 1271
Deposits. See banks.
Dermatologists 149
Diabetes 102, 104, 105, 106, 155, 163
Diagnostic health procedures 165
Diamonds 861, 1363
  Foreign trade 1299
  World production 1363
Diatomite 860, 861
Dietitians and nutritionists 597
Diphtheria 178
Direct deposit 1181
Direct mail advertising expenditures 1274
Disability 175
  American Indian, Alaska Native population ..
                                     37, 184
  Asian population 37
  Beneficiaries 521, 527
  Benefits paid 526, 527
  Black, African American population 34
  Children 184
  Elderly 32, 184
  Food stamp participants 552, 553
  Government transfer payments ... 518, 519,
                                       520
  Labor force status 595
  Medicaid payments and or recipients .. 133,
                                       540
  Native Hawaiian, Other Pacific Islander
    population 37
  Payments 526
  Persons with disability 32, 184, 540
  Poverty 689
  Public assistance recipients and/or pay-
    ments 540, 543
  Social Security recipients 527, 528
  States 184
  Students with disabilities 245, 269
  Supplemental Security Income recipients and
    payments 543
  Veterans receiving compensation .. 515, 517
Disability Insurance Trust Fund (Social Security) .
                                          526
Disasters (tornadoes, floods, etc.) 374
Discount rates, Federal Reserve Bank of New
  York 1188
Diseases (see also specific diseases and Deaths
  and death rates) 163, 177
  Deaths from 102, 104, 105, 106, 107
Dishwashers 965
Diskettes 1004, 1006, 1007
Disposable personal income (see also Income
  and National income) 648, 654, 1167

NOTE: Index citations refer to **table** numbers, not page numbers.

Distance education 270
District Courts, U.S. 324, 325
District of Columbia. See State data.
Dividends:
  Corporation 757
  Individual income tax returns 478
  National and/or personal income compo-
    nents 650
  Persons receiving income 521
  Railroad stock 1106
Divorce. See Marriage and divorce and Marital
  status.
Djibouti. See Foreign countries.
DNA crime laboratories 321
Doctors, M.D.'s. See Physicians.
Dogs 1236, 1239
Dominica. See Foreign countries.
Dominican Republic. See Foreign countries.
Dormitories, college 66
Dow-Jones stock indices 1199, 1200
Drinking places. See Food services and drinking
  places.
Driving (see also Motor vehicles and Transporta-
  tion):
  Crashes 1093, 1097
  Fatal accidents 1053, 1091
  Intoxicated 309, 1098
  Licensed drivers 1082
  Traffic offense 309
Drug stores and proprietary stores. See Pharma-
  cies and drug stores.
Drugs (illegal):
  Arrests 309, 313, 315
  Court cases 325
  Enforcement activities 313, 316, 1286
  Juveniles 329, 330
  Usage 186, 187, 314, 315
Drugs and medicines (see also Pharmaceutical
  and medicine manufacturing):
  Advertising expenditures 1275
  Consumer price indexes 124, 700
  Expenditures for .. 114, 116, 117, 118, 120,
    123, 125
  Foreign trade 1299
  Medicaid payments 133
  Outpatient prescription benefits 143
  Price indexes 124, 700
  Retail sales 122, 1038
Drunk driving, arrests 309
Drycleaning and laundry services:
  Earnings 613, 1265
  Employees 613, 1265
  Establishments 1265
  Productivity 615
  Receipts 1277
Dryers, clothes 965
Dwellings. See Housing and housing units and
  Households or families.

E
Earnings:
  Agriculture, forestry, fisheries 731
  Airlines 1054
  College faculty 278
  College graduates, starting salaries 281
  Construction industry 731, 732
  Educational attainment 215, 679
  Employment covered by social insurance ....
    525, 538, 541
  Family type 521

Earnings: —Con.
  Foreign born population 46
  Government employees:
    Federal 453, 454, 482, 483
    State and local 453, 454, 458
  Income tax returns (reported totals) 475,
    476, 477, 478
  Industry 618, 731, 732
  Manufacturing 731, 732, 973, 976, 983
  Metropolitan areas 622
  Mineral industries 859
  Minimum wage workers 626, 627
  Mining industry 731
  Minority-owned businesses 737
  Municipal employees 459
  Occupations 620, 623, 624
  Personal income ... 650, 652, 653, 654, 655
  Physicians 153
  Private employer firms 732, 733, 735
  Railroads 1106
  Retail trade 731, 732
  School teachers 225, 235, 236, 247
  States 621
  Telephone systems, employees . 1142, 1143
  Transportation 731, 732
  Union members 620, 639
  Wholesale trade 731, 732
  Women-owned businesses 737, 738
Earth sciences, degrees conferred 775
Eating and drinking places. See Food services
  and drinking places:
E-commerce. See Electronic commerce.
E coli O157:H7 177
Economic assistance, foreign 1290
Economic growth rates 644, 1338
Economic indicators 752, 753, 1339
  Foreign countries 1338, 1339
Ecuador. See Foreign countries.
Education:
  Adult education 288
  Advanced placement exams 251
  Alternative school 226, 231
  American College Testing (ACT) Program ....
    249
  Attainment 31, 33, 212, 213, 214, 216
  American Indian, Alaska Native popula-
    tion 37
  Asian population 37, 38
  Asian and Pacific Islander population . 212,
    213
  Black, African American population .. 33,
    34, 212, 213, 214, 255, 256
  Cigarette smoking 188
  Elderly 31, 46
  Foreign born 44, 46
  Foreign countries 1334
  General Education Development certifi-
    cates (GED's) 258
  Hispanic origin population . 33, 40, 212,
    213, 214, 255, 263
  Income 667, 673
  Internet access 1121, 1150, 1152
  Island area of the U.S. 1308
  Labor force status 573, 583, 608
  Media users 1121
  Native Hawaiian, Other Pacific Islander
    population 37
  Occupation 600

NOTE: Index citations refer to **table** numbers, **not page numbers.**

U.S. Census Bureau, Statistical Abstract of the United States: 2004-2005

Education: —Con.
Poverty 689
Race 33, 256
Recreation activities 1241
States 216
Women 213, 214
Catholic schools 246
Charitable contributions 562
Charter schools 224
Computer use in schools 242, 243
Construction, value 923, 924
Continuing education 1335
Credit card use 218
Crime incidents 217, 307
Degrees conferred . 282, 283, 284, 285, 286, 287
   Non-resident aliens 283
   Salary offers 281, 773
Dental schools, students, graduates 151
Disabled students 245, 269
Distance education 270
Employment, state and local government ... 457
Employment status of high school graduates and dropouts 257
Enrollment .. 202, 204, 206, 207, 208, 209, 210, 222, 225, 228, 230, 232, 233, 260, 261, 263, 266, 773
   Catholic schools 246
   Foreign-born students 211
   Homeschooled 229
   Island areas of U.S. 1308, 1309
   Preprimary schools 208, 222
   States 230, 263
Expenditure (see also Finances):
   Assistance for persons with limited income 523, 524
   City government 450
   County government 452
   Local government 444
   Private 203
   State and local government ... 428, 440, 442
Federal aid .. 205, 273, 419, 462, 518, 519, 520, 767
Federal assistance to families 521
Foreign language enrollment 252, 267
General Education Development (GED's) . 258
Grants to institutions from foundations . 566
Handicapped students 245
Higher education institutions:
   Aid received 275
   Beginning salary offers, college graduates 281
   Charges for room and board 276
   Costs 271
   Degrees conferred .. 204, 282, 283, 284, 285, 286, 287, 773, 775
   Non-resident aliens 283
   Dormitories 66
   Enrollment 202, 204, 208, 209, 210, 260, 261, 262, 263, 265, 773
   College freshmen 268
   Disabled 269
   Distance education 270
   Foreign-born students 211
   Foreign languages 267

Education: —Con.
   Foreign students 262, 265
   Projections 202, 204
   States 263
   U.S. service schools 263
   Expenditures 203, 204, 261
   Price indexes 272
   Scientific purposes, by type 770
   Faculty 261, 278, 279, 280
   Finances 203, 204, 261, 274
   Financial aid 273
   Libraries 1147, 1148
   Number 261, 263
   Price indexes 272
   Tuition and fees 276
   State appropriations 274
   Voluntary financial support 277
High school dropouts ... 216, 255, 256, 257
Homeschooled 229
Internet access 242, 243
Island areas of the U.S. 1308, 1309
Loans and grants, federal government . 273
Medical schools, students, graduates ... 151
Montessori schools 246
National Assessment of Educational Progress Tests (NAEP) 250
Nursing programs, students, graduates . 151
Optometry schools, students, graduates . 151
Parental involvement 219
Pharmacy schools, students, graduates . 151
Philanthropy 562, 563, 566
Price indexes 700
Private elementary and secondary schools:
   Computer use 243
   Elementary and secondary . 202, 203, 208, 210, 234, 246
   Expenditures 203
   Internet access 243
   Teachers 246, 247
Public elementary and secondary schools:
   Alternative education 226, 231
   Charter schools 224
   Computer use 242, 243
   Crimes against students 217
   Enrollment 202, 204, 208, 210, 225, 230, 232
   Projections 202, 204
   Size 228
   States 230
   Finances 203, 204, 240, 241
   High school graduates 204, 253
   Internet access 242
   Number 228
   Personnel 238
   Salaries 237
   Price indexes 239
   School districts 227, 418
   Special education programs 226, 245
   Teachers 204, 225, 235, 236, 238
   Projections 204
   Vocational education 226
Scholastic Assessment Test 248
School activities 219
School districts 227, 418
School years completed. See Education attainment.
Special education programs 245, 246

NOTE: Index citations refer to **table** numbers, not page numbers.

U.S. Census Bureau, Statistical Abstract of the United States: 2004-2005

Education: —Con.
State data:
 Elementary and secondary . 230, 236, 241, 253
 Higher education 263, 274
Teachers:
 Catholic schools 246
 Elementary and secondary . 225, 234, 236
 Employment projections 204, 599
 Higher education 261, 278
Tests:
 Advanced placement exams 251
 American College Testing (ACT) Program . 249
 National Assessment of Educational Progress (NAEP) Tests 250
 Scholastic Assessment Tests (SAT) ... 248
 Vocational education 226
 Volunteers 567, 568
Educational expense indexes 700
Educational services:
 Advertising expenditures 1275
 Capital 751
 Earnings 618, 728, 731
 Employees 602, 611, 613, 728, 731
 Establishments 728, 729, 731
 Finances 718, 721
 Gross domestic product 642
 Industry 728
 Mergers 742
 Nonemployers 729
 Occupational safety 634
 Profits 758
 Receipts 718, 721, 726, 727, 728, 729
Education and health services:
 Earnings 611, 613, 619
 Employees 611, 612, 613
 Hours 611
Eggs (see also Poultry):
 Cholesterol source 198
 Consumption 199
 Farm marketings, sales 801
 Iron (dietary), source 198
 Prices 700, 712, 839
 Production 839
Egypt. See Foreign countries.
Elderly (see also Population):
 Activity limitation 182, 183
 Adult education 288
 Age and/or sex 11, 12, 14, 16, 31
 AIDS 179
 Assets 694, 1162
 Black, African American population . 16, 31, 33
 Book purchasing 1132
 Cancer 104, 105, 163
 Cerebrovascular disease 105, 163
 Charitable contributions 561
 Children under 18 years old living with eld-
  erly parents 72
 Cigarette smoking 188
 Community care facilities 145
 Computer use 1121, 1150
 Correctional institutions 66
 Deaths and death rates 105, 107
 Disability population 32, 184
 Education, attainment 31, 214
 Elections, voter registration and turnout . 407

Elderly (see also Population): —Con.
Food stamps, programs 524, 552, 553
Foreign-born population 46
Group quarters population 66
Health care expenditures 125
Health insurance coverage ... 132, 139, 141
Heart disease 104, 107, 163
Height distribution 193
Hispanic origin population 14, 16, 40
Home health and hospice care 169, 170
Homeownership .. 942, 951, 954, 961, 962, 964
Homes for the aged 171, 172
Hospital use 66, 155, 156, 162, 163
Households 58, 64
Income 521
Internet access 604, 1121, 1152
Job search 604
Labor force 570, 572, 577, 603
 Disabled 595
 Displaced workers 594
 Employed . 582, 583, 588, 589, 590, 592
 Participation rates 570, 577
 Reason not in 596
 Tenure with employer 592
 Unemployed 603
Library programs 1151
Living arrangements 54
Marital status 31, 53
Media users 1121
Medicaid payments and recipients . 132, 133, 134
Medicare program 126, 127, 129
Mobility status 28
Mutual fund owners 1207, 1208
Nurses 148
Nursing homes 66, 167, 172
Overweight 194
Persons living alone (one-person house-
 holds) 65
Physical activity 195
Physician visits 152, 154, 155, 156
Pneumonia 104, 105, 163
Poverty 31, 686
Projections 12
Property owners 951, 954, 961, 964
Public assistance 521
Recreation activities . 1228, 1232, 1233, 1234, 1241, 1248
Senior citizens communities 962
Social Security beneficiaries, payments . 527
States 20
Stock ownership 1204, 1206
Suicide 104
TV viewing 1121
Victimization 306
Volunteer work 567
Voter registration and turnout 407
Elections:
 Black elected officials 405
 Campaign finances . 411, 413, 414, 415, 416
 Congressional 389, 391, 392
 Gubernatorial 399, 400
 Hispanic origin officials 406
 Political action committees (PAC) . 411, 412, 413
 Political party identification 409
 Presidential .. 384, 385, 386, 387, 388, 413

NOTE: Index citations refer to **table** numbers, not page numbers.

U.S. Census Bureau, Statistical Abstract of the United States: 2004-2005

Elections: —Con.
State legislatures 401, 402
Voter registration 407, 408, 409, 410
Voter turnout 407, 408, 410
Votes cast 386, 387, 389, 391, 392, 408
Voting-age population 407, 408, 410
Women in public office 403
Electric light and power industry (see also Utilities and Electricity):
Capital expenditures 371, 749
Construction costs 921
Customers 906, 914
Emissions 361, 362
Finances 907
General capacity 901, 902, 903
Industrial production index 754
Multinational companies 763
Ownership, class of 901
Peak load 903
Pollution abatement 371
Water use 356
Electricity (see also Electric light and power industry):
Capability 901, 902, 903
Commercial buildings 893, 970
Consumption . 891, 892, 893, 901, 904, 906
Expenditures ......, 661, 889, 890, 891, 895
Foreign countries 1368, 1369
Hydroelectric power 884, 887, 901, 912
Nuclear 884, 887, 901, 909, 910, 1125, 1368, 1369
Price indexes 700, 706
Prices 901, 905
Production 901, 902, 906
World production 1368
Residential 874, 891, 892, 906
Sales 901, 904, 906
Service, class of 905
Electrical engineering 773
Electrical equipment and manufacturing (See also Computer and electronic products manufacturing):
Capital 371
Earnings 613, 973, 976, 984, 1117
Electronic commerce 980
Employees .. 613, 973, 976, 977, 978, 982, 984, 1117
Establishments 973
Finances 758, 760
Foreign trade 978, 1302
Gross domestic product 642, 972, 1116
Industrial production index 754
Inventories 986, 987
Mergers and acquisitions 742
Multinational companies 763
Occupational safety 634
Pollution abatement 371
Productivity 615
Profits 759, 760
Research and development 776, 777
Shipments 976, 978, 980, 986, 987
Toxic chemical releases 367
Value added 987
Electronic commerce (e-commerce):
Business sales 1036
Consumer sales 1036, 1037
Manufacturing 980
Retail trade 1038, 1039

Electronic commerce (e-commerce): —Con.
Services 1267
Wholesale 1043
Electronic funds transfer payment 1182
Electronic goods:
Foreign trade 1299
Sales, shipments, receipts . 1003, 1006, 1007, 1038
Electronic instruments manufacturing . 613, 615
Electronic shopping and mail order houses . 613, 615, 1020
Electronics and appliance stores:
Earnings 613, 728, 1019
Electronic commerce 1039
Employees 613, 728, 1019
Establishments 728, 1019, 1026
Nonemployers 1026
Productivity 615
Purchases 1023
Sales 728, 1020, 1022, 1026, 1039
El Salvador. See Foreign countries.
Emergency medicine, departments ... 149, 154, 156
Emphysema 104
Employee benefits 142, 144, 629, 630
Government employees 455, 456
Employees. See Business enterprise and individual industries.
Employment service industry 613
Endangered species 373
Energy (see also Electric light and power industry and various fuel types):
Air pollutant emissions 362
Foreign countries 1332, 1333
Assistance for persons with limited income . 523, 524
Commercial buildings 891, 970
Consumption . 884, 886, 887, 888, 891, 892, 1365
Characteristic of household 891, 892
End-use sector 886, 887
Foreign countries 1365, 1367
Renewable sources 888, 912
Source 884
End-use sector 886, 887, 890
Expenditures 889, 890, 891, 892, 893
Commercial 889, 890, 940
Residential 889, 890, 891, 892
Type of structure 891, 892
Federal outlays 465
Price indexes:
Consumer 698, 699, 700
Export ....:........... 714
Import 713
Producer 704, 705
Prices 894
Solar collectors, manufacturer's shipments .. 911
Engineering and architectural services:
Earnings 613, 773, 1265
Employees 613, 773, 1265
Establishments 1265
Engineers and scientists (see also individual fields):
Degrees conferred . 284, 285, 286, 773, 775
Employment 597, 773, 779
Research and development 770
Salary offers 281, 773

NOTE: Index citations refer to **table** numbers, not page numbers.

Entertainment (see also Arts, entertainment, and recreation):
Consumer expenditures 660, 661, 1228
Consumer price indexes 700
Personal expenditures . 649, 660, 661, 700, 1228
Environment (see also pollution)
Environmental industry, agencies 372
Wetlands 352
Volunteers 567, 568
Environmental Protection Agency:
Employment 485
Waste treatment facilities, Federal aid to state and local governments 425
Equatorial Guinea. See Foreign countries
Eritrea. See Foreign countries.
Eskimo population. See American Indian, Alaska Native population.
Establishments. See Business enterprise and individual industries.
Estate and gift taxes 467, 474
Estonia. See Foreign countries.
Ethane 873
Ethiopia. See Foreign countries.
Europe. See Foreign countries.
European Union. See Foreign countries.
Evaporated and condensed milk 199, 837
Excise taxes 467, 473, 474
Executions 341, 342
Executive Office of the President (federal) . 483, 485
Exercise equipment 1229, 1247, 1248
Expectation of life (average lifetime) . 92, 93, 94
Foreign countries 1325
Projections 92
Expenditures. See individual subjects.
Expenditures of state and local government. See individual governmental units.
Expenditures of U.S. Government . 420, 421, 422, 423, 424, 425, 465, 1075, 1289, 1290, 1291
Aid to the arts and humanities 1231
Aid to Island areas 425, 1317
Aid to state and local government . 423, 424, 425
By function 424
Highway trust fund 425, 1075
Atomic energy defense activities 493
Budget outlays 461, 462, 463, 465
By function 465, 523, 524
By source of funds 467
Capital outlay 430, 431
Contract awards 495, 496
Education. See federal aid to education.
Food programs, federal 523, 524
Health 118, 523, 524
Hospitals 157
Justice 328
Land and buildings 490
Military personnel 499
National defense 492, 493, 494
Outlays, by agency 464
Outlays, by function 465
Payments for public assistance ... 523, 524, 539
Payrolls 453, 454, 482, 483, 484, 488
Public debt 461
Public roads 425, 1075
Research and development .. 764, 765, 766, 767, 769
Schools 205

Expenditures of U.S. Government —Con.
Science/space 782
Space programs 781, 784
Veterans benefits. See Veterans affairs.
Exports. See Foreign trade.
Express mail 1111, 1112
Eye care price indexes 700
Eyeglasses and contact lenses ... 116, 117, 120

F

Fabricated metal product manufacturing:
Capital 371, 1288
Earnings 613, 973, 976, 984
Electronic commerce 980
Employees ... 613, 973, 976, 978, 982, 984
Establishments 973
Finance 760, 999
Foreign trade 978, 999, 1302
Gross domestic product 642, 972
Industrial production index 754
Occupational safety 634
Pollution abatement 371
Productivity 615
Profits 759, 760
Shipments 976, 978, 980, 986, 987
Toxic chemical releases 367
Fabrics. See Textile mill products.
Families. See Households.
Farm mortgage loans 510, 1177
Farmers and farm workers:
Employment 597, 809
Unemployment 607
Farms:
Acreage . 787, 789, 790, 791, 792, 793, 795, 796, 797, 798
Cropland 348, 350, 798, 819
Crops harvested (see also individual crops) 819, 822, 823, 829, 1362
Agrichemicals 806
Agricultural products:
Exports 1293
Foreign countries, production . 1357, 1359
Prices. See Prices received by farmers.
Railroad car loadings 1107, 1108
Waterborne commerce 1066
World production 1355, 1357, 1359
Assets and liabilities 802, 803, 1158
Capital stocks, farm housing 966
Contracts 807
Corporate 787, 791, 792, 794, 1315
Crops (see also individual crops):
Acreage 819, 822
Fruits and nuts 830, 1314
Income 801, 805, 1315
Production 807, 814, 819, 822
World 1357, 1359
Vegetables 829
Debt 802, 803
Mortgages outstanding 1177
Economic class 794
Expenses 800
Farm products sold, marketing receipts . 799, 800, 801, 804, 805, 807
Government payments to farmers . 799, 800, 805
Gross farm product 642, 799
Housing, rental value 799, 800
Income 799, 800, 801, 803, 805

NOTE: Index citations refer to **table** numbers, not page numbers.

U.S. Census Bureau, Statistical Abstract of the United States: 2004-2005

Table

Farms: —Con.
Individual or family 787, 791, 794
Inventories, change in 799
Labor expenses 800, 806
Labor inputs 809
Machinery and motor vehicles 800, 802
Mortgage loans 1177
National income, origin in 799
Number of farms . 787, 789, 790, 791, 792,
793, 794, 795, 796, 797
Operator characteristics 788
Organic acreage, livestock 798
Parity ratio 806
Partnerships 787, 791, 794
Prices:
    Crops 806, 822
    Livestock and products 806, 832
    Taxes 799, 806
Tenure of operator 788, 790, 794
Value:
    Farm land and buildings . 791, 792, 795,
802
Farm products sold, marketing receipts
791, 792, 793, 794, 795, 799, 800, 801,
805, 807
Faroe Islands. See Foreign countries.
Fatalities. See Accidents and fatalities.
Fat, nutrient for consumption 197
Fats. See Lard, Margarine, and Oils.
Federal agency debt 1190
Federal aid to education 205, 424, 425, 428
Elementary and secondary education ... 205
Higher education institutions 205, 261
Research and development .. 765, 771, 772
Science and engineering 770, 771
Federal aid to state and local government . 423,
424, 425, 428
Federal budget. See Expenditures of U.S. Government.
Federal debt 461
Federal employees retirement trust fund. See
Government.
Federal funds, summary distribution by state ...
472
Federal government. See Government.
Federal Government finances. See Receipts and
Expenditures of U.S. Government.
Federal Housing Administration, mortgage
loans 1177, 1179
Federal National Mortgage Association loans ....
1177
Federal real property 347
Federal trust fund 468
Feed. See Grain.
Feldspar 860, 861, 864
Female householder. See Households or families.
Female population. See Women.
Fencing 1244
Fertility rate 75, 76
Fertilizers:
    Farm expenditures for 800
    Foreign trade 1299
    Prices 806
    Shipments 999
Fetal deaths 100
Fibers 993
Fiber, dietary 197
Fiji. See Foreign countries.
Filberts 830

Table

Field hockey 1243, 1244
Figure skating 1237, 1241
Filipino population 22, 737
Filling stations. See Gasoline stations.
Finance 656, 1158, 1159, 1161
    Consumer installment credit 1184
    Corporate funds 724
Finance, insurance, and real estate industry:
    Capital 748, 751, 1194
    Earnings . 611, 613, 618, 619, 728, 731, 732,
738, 1155, 1157
    Employees .. 583, 587, 601, 611, 612, 613,
728, 731, 732, 738, 765, 1155, 1157
    Establishments . 728, 729, 731, 1155, 1156,
1157
    Finances . 716, 718, 721, 1158, 1168, 1184,
1310
    Foreign investments in U.S. 1283, 1284
    Gross domestic product 642, 646, 1154,
1310
    Hours 611
    Industry 728
    Mergers and acquisitions 742
    Multinational companies 762, 763
    Nonemployers 729, 1156
    Profits 716, 758
    Sales or receipts .. 718, 721, 726, 727, 728,
729, 738, 1155, 1156
    Union membership 639
    Women-owned businesses 738
Financial institution. See Banks, commercial;
Credit unions; and Savings institutions.
Finished consumer goods, producer price
indexes 704
Finland. See Foreign countries.
Firearms 319, 1059, 1241, 1247
    Deaths 319
Fire departments. See Public safety.
Fire insurance 1218
Fires and property loss 343, 344, 345
    Accidental deaths 345
Firms. See Business enterprise, and individual
types of business and industry.
Fish (see also individual species):
    Aquaculture 801, 855
    Canning and preserving 857
    Catch, quantity and value ... 852, 853, 854,
1356
    Cholesterol source 198
    Consumer expenditures 658, 660, 661
    Consumption 199
    Foreign trade 813, 852, 1302
    Iron (dietary), source 198
    Prices 700, 853
    Production and value, processed products ..
855, 857
    Supply 852
Fishing, commercial:
    Catch, quantity, value . 852, 853, 854, 1356
    Foreign trade 1357
    Products 852, 857
Fishing and hunting ... 1241, 1245, 1246, 1247
Floods 374, 375
Floriculture 801, 826
Florida. See State data.
Florists:
    Earnings 613, 1019
    Employees 613, 1019
    Establishments 1019

NOTE: Index citations refer to **table** numbers, not page numbers.

U.S. Census Bureau, Statistical Abstract of the United States: 2004-2005

Florists: —Con.
Productivity 615
Flounder 854, 857
Flour 199, 813
Flowers 826, 1235
Flu 102, 104
Fluorspar 860, 861, 864
Food (see also individual commodities and
industry data below):
Car loadings 1108
Commercial vegetables 829
Consumption 199, 200, 201, 813
Expenditures . 658, 660, 661, 662, 808, 1035
Fish products 658
Food costs 701, 711, 712
Hunger, insecurity 196
Prices (see also individual commodities) . 698,
700, 706, 711, 712
Sales 1038
World production 1355, 1357
Food and beverage stores:
Earnings 613, 728, 1018, 1019
Electronic commerce 1039
Employees 613, 728, 1018, 1019
Establishments . 728, 1018, 1019, 1026, 1033
Finances 718, 760
Inventories 1024
Mergers 742
Nonemployers 1026
Productivity 615
Profits 760
Purchases 1023
Sales ... 718, 728, 1018, 1020, 1022, 1024,
1025, 1026, 1033, 1035
Prescription drugs 122
Food insecurity 196
Food manufacturing:
Capital 367, 371
Earnings 613, 973, 976, 984
Employees ... 613, 973, 976, 978, 982, 984
Establishments 973
Finances 760
Foreign trade 978, 1302
Gross domestic product 642, 972
Industrial production index 754
Mergers and acquisitions 742
Multinational companies 762, 763
Occupational safety 633, 634
Patents 745
Pollution abatement 371
Profits 759, 760
Research and development 777
Sales or shipments . 976, 978, 980, 986, 987
Toxic chemical releases 367
Food services and drinking places:
Earnings 613, 728, 1265
Employees 613, 728, 1265
Establishments 728, 1018, 1265
Finances 718
Productivity 615
Sales 718, 728, 1020, 1035
Food stamps, programs ... 519, 522, 523, 524,
550, 551, 552, 553, 1182
Football 1237, 1239, 1243, 1244
Footwear:
Consumer expenditures 660, 661
Foreign trade 995, 1299
Sales or shipments 995

Foreign aid or assistance 1289, 1291, 1382
Foreign born population 42, 44, 45, 46
Age 44, 46
American Indian, Alaska Native population ..
37
Asian population 37
Black, African American population 34
Cities 43
Earnings 46
Educational attainment 44, 46
Foreign countries 1323
Households 46
Housing tenure 46
Income 44, 46
Marital status 46
Native Hawaiian, Other Pacific Islander
population 37
Poverty status 44, 46
States 42
Foreign companies, U.S. affiliates .. 1284, 1285,
1286
Foreign countries:
Agricultural trade 818, 1297
Aid to developing countries 1289, 1290,
1291, 1382
Air pollution emissions 1332
Area 1321
Armed Forces personnel 1385
Balance of payments 1379
Births and birth rates 1325, 1326
Border crossings 1261
Carbon dioxide emissions 1333
Cigarettes 1361
Coal production . 878, 879, 1364, 1365, 1366,
1367
College students enrolled in U.S. 265
Communications 1372, 1373
Consumer price index 702, 1342
Crude oil 896, 897
Death and death rates 1325
Debt 1383
Economic indicators 1338, 1339
Education 1334, 1335
Electricity generation 1368
Employment and labor force ... 1339, 1349,
1350, 1351, 1352, 1353, 1354
Energy production, consumption, and prices .
1364, 1365, 1366, 1367
Exchange rates 1378
Export and imports 1296, 1360, 1380
Financial assets, liabilities (flow of funds) ...
1160
Fish catches 1356
Food consumption 1358
Forest products 1362
Geothermal energy 1364, 1365
Government finances 1344, 1345
Gross domestic product 1337, 1338
Gross national product 1336
Health care expenditures 1330
Households and families 1328, 1329
Hydroelectric power 1364, 1365, 1368
Immigrant population 1323
Immigration to U.S. 8, 9, 10
Income tax 1347
Inpatient care 1324
International transactions, balances .. 1279,
1280

NOTE: Index citations refer to **table** numbers, not page numbers.

U.S. Census Bureau, Statistical Abstract of the United States: 2004-2005

Foreign countries: —Con.
Investment in U.S. . 1197, 1198, 1281, 1283,
    1284, 1285, 1286
Labor costs 1347, 1370, 1371
Labor force 1323, 1349, 1352
Labor productivity 1341
Lumber 1362
Manufacturing 1371
    Productivity 1370
Marital status 1326, 1327, 1328, 1329
Marriage and divorce 1327, 1329
Meat 1357, 1358
Military expenditures 1384
Military manpower 1385
Military personnel, U.S. on active duty .. 502
Military sales 498
Municipal waste 1332
Natural gas .. 876, 1364, 1365, 1366, 1367
Nobel prize laureates 786
Nuclear power generation . 1364, 1365, 1366,
    1368, 1369
Nuclear waste 1332
Patents 1348
Petroleum production . 872, 1364, 1365, 1366,
    1367
Physicians 1324
Population 1321, 1322, 1323
Precipitation (cities) 1331
Prices 712, 1342, 1343
Production:
    Crops 1359
    Indexes 1340
    Meat 1357
    Minerals 864, 1367
Rainfall (cities) 1331
Refugees admitted to U.S. 9
Research and development expenditures . 766
Reserve assets 1379
Sales and assistance by U.S. government ....
    497, 498
Securities .. 1195, 1196, 1197, 1198, 1374,
    1375, 1377
Single-parent households 1328, 1329
Social security contributions 1347
Space launches 783
Tax burden 1346
Taxes (revenue) 1344, 1345
Telecommunication services 1372
Temperature (cities) 1331
Tobacco 1361
Trade with United States ... 817, 1280, 1298
Travelers and expenditures 1254, 1255
U.S. investment abroad .. 1195, 1196, 1288
Visitors from 1258
Vital statistics 1325
Weather 1331
Foreign currency holdings 1379
Foreign exchange rates 1378
Foreign grants and credits, U.S. government ....
    1289
Foreign investments .. 1160, 1197, 1283, 1284,
    1285, 1287
Foreign languages:
    Degrees conferred 284, 285, 286
    Persons speaking 49, 50, 221
    Students enrolled 252, 267
Foreign military sales trust fund 457

Foreign sales and assistance by U.S. govern-
    ment 1290, 1291
    Economic assistance 1291
    Military sales and assistance 497, 1291
Foreign students, college 265
Foreign trade (see also Foreign aid, Foreign
    countries, and individual commodities) . 1293,
    1294, 1295, 1296, 1297, 1298, 1302
    Aerospace products 1299, 1300
    Agricultural products .. 810, 811, 812, 813,
    815, 817, 818, 827, 828, 1293, 1297
    Aircraft and aircraft parts 1012, 1299
    Automobiles 1299
    Balance of trade ... 1278, 1279, 1293, 1298
    Coal 878, 896
    Companies exporting 1301
    Countries 1298, 1380
    Crude oil 867, 896, 897, 898
    Customs and districts 1295
    Fish products 852
    Indexes, unit value 1296
    Industry 978, 1302
    International transactions, balances, U.S. . 1278,
    1279, 1280, 1292
    Manufacturing 978, 979
    Mineral imports 866
    Services 1278, 1280
    Timber products 847, 1299
    U.S. affiliates of foreign companies 1284
Forest products (see also individual products):
    Car loadings 1107, 1108
    Consumption 846
    Foreign countries 1362
    Foreign trade 846, 847
    Producer prices 704, 705, 849
    Sales 800
    Shipments 1071
Forests:
    Land, acreage, and ownership 348, 350
    National 844
Forgery and counterfeiting (arrests) 309
Foster care 524
Foundations, philanthropic . 563, 564, 565, 566
Foundries 613, 615
401(k) plans 533, 537, 1211
France. See Foreign countries.
Franchised establishments 1027
Freezers, home 965
Freight traffic. See Air transportation, Railroads,
    Rivers, and Waterways.
French Guiana. See Foreign countries.
French Polynesia. See Foreign countries.
Fruit juices 200, 201, 810, 813
Fruits:
    Consumer expenditures 658, 660, 661
    Consumption 200, 813, 827
    Farm marketings and sales 801, 807
    Foreign trade . 810, 813, 815, 817, 827, 1299
    Iron (dietary), source 198
    Pesticide usage 821
    Prices 700, 712, 714, 806
    Production 827, 830, 1355
Fruit and vegetable preserving manufacturing ..
    613, 615, 976
Fuel (see also individual types, and energy):
    Commercial building use 892, 893, 970
    Consumer expenditures 660, 661
    Consumption, motor vehicles 1088
    Electricity generated by 901

NOTE: Index citations refer to **table** numbers, not page numbers.

Fuel (see also individual types, and energy): —Con.
Prices .. 698, 700, 704, 705, 710, 713, 714, 715, 806, 889, 894
  Retail 710
  Production and value 860, 864, 884
  Residential use 888, 889, 915
  World production 864
Funds, trusts and other financial assets 613, 1157
Funeral service and crematories. See Death care services.
Furniture 660, 661, 700, 706, 1299
Furniture and related product manufacturing:
  Capital 371
  Earnings 613, 973, 976, 984
  Electronic commerce 980
  Employees 613, 973, 976, 978, 984
  Establishments 973
  Finances 760
  Foreign trade 978, 1302
  Gross domestic product 642, 972
  Industrial production index 754
  Mergers and acquisitions 742
  Occupational safety 634
  Pollution abatement 371
  Productivity 615
  Profits 760
  Shipments 976, 978, 980, 986, 987
  Toxic chemical releases 367
Furniture and home furnishing stores:
  Earnings 613, 728, 984, 1019
  Electronic commerce 1039
  Employees 613, 728, 984, 1019
  Establishments 728, 1019, 1026
  Inventories 1024
  Nonemployers 1026
  Productivity 615
  Purchases 1023
  Sales .. 728, 1020, 1022, 1024, 1026, 1038
Futures price indexes, selected commodities 708

G

Gabon. See Foreign countries.
Gallbladder disorders, deaths 102
Gallium 861
Gambia, The. See Foreign countries.
Gambling, arrests 309
Garages. See Gasoline service stations, and Automobile repair and maintenance service.
Garden activities and equipment 1235
Garden supplies. See Building materials and garden supplies.
Garnet (abrasive) production and value 860
Garnet (industrial) 861
Gas (see also Petroleum, Gas utility industry and Gasoline):
  Liquefied petroleum gases 873
  Natural 859, 860, 875
    Consumption .. 875, 884, 887, 891, 892
    Energy expenditures 889, 890
    Foreign trade 885, 895, 896, 1302
    Offshore lease revenues 869
    Prices 862, 884
    Production and value 860, 869, 875, 884, 1363, 1364
      Foreign countries 1363, 1367
      Indexes 858

Gas (see also Petroleum, Gas utility industry and Gasoline): —Con.
  Reserves 875
  Residential 891, 892, 915
  World production 876, 1363, 1364
Natural gas plant liquids 870
Price indexes 700
Gas and electric utilities. See Utilities.
Gas utility industry (see also Utilities):
  Accidents and deaths 1053
  Capital expenditures 749
  Construction expenditures 914
  Customers 914, 915
  End users 914
  Finances 913
  Mains, mileage 914
  Prices 914
  Revenues 883, 913, 914, 915
  Sales 914, 915
Gasoline (see also motor fuel):
  Blending components 868
  Consumer expenditures . 658, 659, 660, 661, 662
  Excise taxes 715, 1076
  Finished motor gasoline 868
  Prices 715
  Supply 706
Gasoline stations, retail:
  Earnings 613, 728, 1019
  Electronic commerce 1039
  Employees 613, 728, 1019
  Establishments 728, 1019, 1026
  Finances 718
  Nonemployers 1026
  Productivity 615
  Purchases 1023
  Sales ... 718, 728, 1020, 1022, 1025, 1026, 1271
Gastroenterology 149
Gaza Strip. See Foreign countries.
Gem stones 860, 861
General merchandise stores:
  Earnings 613, 728, 1019
  Electronic commerce 1039
  Employees 613, 728, 1019
  Establishments 728, 1019, 1026
  Finances 760
  Inventories 1024
  Mergers and acquisitions 742
  Nonemployers 1026
  Productivity 615
  Profits 760
  Purchases 1023
  Sales .. 728, 1020, 1022, 1023, 1025, 1026, 1039, 1271
Genetically modified seed plantings 820
Geography and cartography. See Land.
Georgia. See Foreign countries.
Georgia, state of. See State data.
Geothermal energy 884, 888, 1364, 1365
Germanium 861
Germany. See Foreign countries.
Germany DAX-30 stock market index 1376
Ghana. See Foreign countries.
Gibraltar. See Foreign countries.
Gift, novelty, and souvenir stores 1019
Gift and estate taxes 429, 474
Gold:
  Consumption 861

NOTE: Index citations refer to **table** numbers, not page numbers.

Gold: —Con.
Employment 859, 861
Foreign trade 861, 1299
Prices 861, 862
Production and value 860, 861
　World production 864, 1363
Reserve assets 1282
Golf . 962, 1237, 1240, 1241, 1243, 1244, 1247,
　　　　　　　　　　　　　　　　1248
Golf courses, industry 1224, 1227
Gonorrhea 177
Government (see also Expenditures of U.S. government, and Receipts, and individual governmental units):
　Buildings 490, 491
　Capital stock 696
　Earnings 458, 618
　Employees 487, 611, 612, 613, 765
　　Benefits 455
　　City government 459
　　County government 460
　　Federal, civilian 453, 485, 486
　　　Accessions and separations 488
　　　Pay increases 488
　　　Salaries 482
　　　Turnover 489
　　Local government .. 320, 453, 454, 457,
　　　　　　　　　　　　　　　　458
　　Retirement systems . 521, 529, 530, 531
　　State government .. 320, 453, 454, 457,
　　　　　　　　　　　　　　　　458
　　States 457, 458, 484
　Employment cost index 625
　Expenditures:
　　Capital outlay 430, 431
　　City government 450, 455
　　Consumption 420, 421, 422
　　County government 452, 455
　　Federal .. 429, 430, 431, 461, 463, 465,
　　　　　　　　　　　　　　467, 471
　　　Aid to state and local government ....
　　　　　423, 424, 425, 458, 1075
　　　Capital outlay 430, 431
　　　Public assistance programs . 523, 524
　　Local government 430, 431, 443,
　　　　　　　　　　　　　　　　444
　　State and local government ... 426, 427,
　　　　　428, 429, 430, 431, 523
　　State government .. 429, 430, 431, 439,
　　　　　　　　　　　　　　440, 442
　　Transfer payments 518, 519, 520
　Federally owned land 347, 490, 491
　Flow of funds 1158, 1159, 1161
　Gross domestic product . 421, 422, 426, 427,
　　　　　　　　　　　　　642, 646
　Highways .. 1069, 1074, 1075, 1076, 1077,
　　　　　　　　　　　　　　　　1078
　Hospitals 157
　Insurance. See Social insurance.
　Land. See Public lands.
　Local government:
　　Cities:
　　　Employees, earnings, payroll 459
　　　Finances 449, 450
　　Counties:
　　　Employees, earnings, payroll 460
　　　Finances 451, 452
　　　Earnings 458

Government (see also Expenditures of U.S. government, and Receipts, and individual governmental units): —Con.
　Employees 320, 453, 454, 457, 458
　Number, by type 417, 418, 419
　Payroll 453, 454, 457, 458
　Population, by size-group 419
　Number of units, by type of government ....
　　　　　　　　　　　　　　417, 418
　Occupational safety 631, 636
　Payrolls 453, 454, 459, 460
　Purchases of goods and services . 426, 641,
　　　　　　　　　　　　　　　　644
　Salaries and wages (see also Income, and individual industries):
　　Federal 472, 482
　　National income component .. 426, 427,
　　　　　　　　　　　　　　　　618
　　State and local government employees ..
　　　　　　　　　　　　　　　　458
　Securities 436, 1188, 1189, 1197
　State and local governments . 440, 453, 454,
　　　　　　　　　　　　　457, 458
　　Benefits 455
　　Bond ratings 437, 438
　　Employees 335, 453, 454, 457, 458
　　Federal aid 423, 424, 425, 1075
　　Finances . 425, 426, 427, 428, 429, 430,
　　　　　431, 432, 433, 434, 435
　　Payroll 453, 454, 457, 458
　State government 439, 441, 442
　Strategic and critical materials, summary ....
　　　　　　　　　　　　　　　　822
Government National Mortgage Association
　loans 1177
Governors, number and vote cast 399, 400
Graduates:
　College 282, 285, 286, 287
　High school 204, 253, 256, 257
Grain (see also individual classes):
　Car loadings 1107
　Consumption 199
　Farm marketings, sales 801
　Foreign trade 810, 812, 815, 817
　Iron (dietary), source 198
　Prices 806
　Production 1355, 1359
Grandparents 32
Grants, by foundations 566
Grapefruit 200, 801, 830
Grapes 200, 798, 801, 813, 830
Graphite 861
Grazing:
　National forests, livestock, and receipts . 844
　Public lands, leases 490
Great Britain. See Foreign countries.
Great Lakes:
　Area 353
　Commerce 1065
　Water quality 357
Greece. See Foreign countries.
Greenhouse and nursery crops 801, 826
Greenhouse gases 362
Greenland. See Foreign countries.
Grenada. See Foreign countries.
Grocery stores (See also Food and beverage stores):
　Earnings 613, 1019
　Employees 613, 1019

NOTE: Index citations refer to **table** numbers, not page numbers.

U.S. Census Bureau, Statistical Abstract of the United States: 2004-2005

Grocery stores (See also Food and beverage stores): —Con.
Establishments 1020, 1026, 1033
Nonemployers 1026
Productivity 615
Sales 1025, 1026, 1033
Services, products offered 1034
Gross domestic product:
Components, annual growth rates . 426, 427,
641, 643, 644, 1045, 1116
Foreign countries 1337, 1338
Implicit price deflators for 641
Industry 642
National defense outlays 492
Per capita 648
Relation to national and personal income ....
647
State 645, 646
Gross national product 648
Foreign countries 1336
Gross private domestic investment ... 641, 644,
707, 739
Ground water used 355
Group health insurance plans 137
Group quarters population 66
Guadeloupe. See Foreign countries.
Guam. See Island areas of the U.S.
Guamanian population 22
Guatemala. See Foreign countries.
Guernsey. See Foreign countries.
Guinea. See Foreign countries.
Guinea-Bissau. See Foreign countries.
Guns. See Firearms.
Guyana. See Foreign countries.
Gymnastics 1244
Gypsum and gypsum products .. 860, 861, 864,
866, 920

H

Haddock 854, 857
Haemophilus influenza 177
Haiti. See Foreign countries.
Hake, pacific whiting, imports 854
Halibut 854
Hallucinogenic drugs 186
Ham price indexes 700
Ham prices 712
Handguns 293, 318, 1059
Handicapped (See Disability)
Hawaii. See State data.
Hawaiian population. See Native Hawaiian and
Other Pacific Islander population.
Hay 798, 801, 822
Hazardous waste/materials:
Abatement expenditures 370
Superfund sites 369
Transportation 1053
Waste management 372
Hazelnuts (filberts) 830
Head start program 554
Health and education service industries . 61, 601,
606, 611, 612, 639
Health and Human Services, Department of . 767
Health and personal care stores:
Earnings 613, 728, 1019
Electronic commerce 1039
Employees 613, 728, 1019
Establishments 728, 1019, 1026
Nonemployers 1026
Productivity 615

Health and personal care stores: —Con.
Purchases 1023
Sales .. 728, 1020, 1022, 1024, 1026, 1039
Health care and social assistance industry:
Earnings 611, 618, 728, 1265
Electronic commerce 1267
Employees 611, 728, 1265
Establishments 728, 729, 1265
Gross domestic product 642
Hours 611
Nonemployers 729
Profits 758
Receipts 728, 729
Health clubs 1241
Health insurance (see also Health services,
Insurance carriers, Medicaid, and Medicare):
Coverage . 132, 137, 139, 140, 141, 142, 144
Enrollment and payments ... 129, 134, 135,
136, 138
Expenditures . 114, 115, 116, 117, 119, 120,
121, 125, 142, 658, 659, 660, 661, 662
Premiums and expenses 142, 144
Premiums and policy reserves, life insurance
companies 1217
State Children's Health Insurance program ..
135, 524
Health insurance industry, employees 147
Health Maintenance Organizations ... 137, 138,
142
Health sciences, degrees conferred ... 151, 284,
285, 286, 287
Health services:
Buildings and floor space 970
Charitable contributions 562
Construction, value 923, 924
Coverage 126, 129, 132, 134, 139, 517
Employment benefits 142
Expenditures 123
Federal government . 114, 115, 118, 121,
424, 523, 524
Private expenditures . 114, 115, 116, 117,
119, 120, 121, 125, 660
Public expenditures . 114, 115, 116, 117,
118, 119, 120, 121, 523, 524
State and local government ... 114, 121,
428, 523, 524
City government 450
County government 452
State government 440, 442
Foreign countries 1330
Government employment and payrolls . 454
Hospitals . 157, 158, 159, 160, 161, 162, 163
Industry:
Capital expenditures 749, 751
Earnings 613, 731, 732
Employees 147, 613, 731, 732
Establishments 731
Finances 718, 721
Mergers and acquisitions 742
Occupational safety 634
Sales or receipts 718, 721, 726, 727
Medicaid . 121, 132, 133, 134, 136, 139, 424,
524
Medicare 115, 118, 121, 126, 129, 526
Mental health facilities 173
Nursing homes 116, 117, 120, 167, 171
Occupations 149, 150, 151, 597
Philanthropy 120, 563

NOTE: Index citations refer to **table** numbers, not page numbers.

Health services: —Con.
Price indexes 124, 700
Veterans health care 115, 118
Volunteers 567, 568
Hearing impaired 172
Heart disease 102, 104, 106, 107, 155, 163
Deaths 102, 104, 106, 107
Heat pumps 947
Heating and plumbing equipment 911, 930,
947, 967
HVAC and commercial refrigeration equipment
manufacturing 613, 615
Heating oil 710, 868, 869, 911
Heights, average, by age and sex 193
Helium 860
Hepatitis 177
Hernia and intestinal obstruction 102
Heroin 186, 315, 316
Herring, sea 854
Hides and skins (see also Leather and leather
products), foreign trade 817, 1299
Highways:
Accidents 1097
Bridge inventory 1073
Construction costs 921
Value of new construction 923, 924
Debt, state and local government 1077
Employees, government 454, 457
Expenditures: ·
City government 450
County government 452
Local government 444
State and local government ... 425, 428,
429, 430, 431, 433
State government 440, 442
U.S. government 1075
Aid to state and local governments ..
424
Highway trust fund 425, 1075
Federal-aid systems 1069, 1070, 1075
Mileage 1069, 1070
Motor fuel consumption 1088
Motor fuel tax 1076
Type and control 1069, 1070
Types of roads traveled 1070
Hiking 1241
Hindu population. See Religion.
Hispanic origin population ... 13, 16, 21, 22, 46
Activity limitation 182, 183
Adult education 288
Age and/or sex 13, 14, 15, 16, 40
AIDS 179, 180
Births and birth rates 71, 74, 86
Business owners 737
Charity contributions 561
Child care 559
Children under 18 years old . 13, 14, 15, 16
Literacy activities 220, 223
College enrollment 262
Community service 567, 568
Commuting to work 41
Computer use 244, 1152
Congress, members of 396
Criminal victimization rates . 217, 218, 306,
308
Death rates 96, 98
Degrees conferred 775
Disability status 41, 269, 540

Hispanic origin population —Con.
Educational attainment ... 40, 41, 212, 213,
214
Elderly 13, 14, 15, 16, 686
Elected officials 396, 406
Elections, voter registration and turnout . 407
Families, characteristics .. 40, 59, 60, 61, 62
Farm operators, workers 788, 809
Food stamp participants 553
Foreign-born populations 41, 211
Health insurance coverage ... 132, 139, 141
High school dropouts 254, 255, 256
Homeschooled 229
Household or family characteristics . 40, 52,
58, 59, 60, 62
Housing 40, 950, 954, 961, 964
Immunization of children 178
Income:
Family 669, 670, 671, 673, 676
Household 665, 666, 667, 668
Persons 659, 663, 665, 681
Internet access 244
Jail inmates 334
Job search 604
Labor force and employment 570
Displaced workers 594
Earnings 623
Employed . 40, 571, 587, 588, 589, 590,
591, 597, 601
By industry, occupation 597, 600,
601
Minimum wage workers 627
Job search 604
Persons working at home 587
Unemployed 40, 571, 603
Union membership 639
Language proficiency 221
Living arrangements 54
Marital status 51
Media users 1121
Mobility status 41
Nativity 41
Nurses 148, 597
Occupation 41, 597, 600
Overweight 194
Pension plan coverage 535
Physical activity 195
Poverty .. 40, 132, 682, 683, 684, 686, 690
Projections 16
School enrollment . 207, 211, 233, 256, 262,
266
Adult education 288
Charter schools 224
Homeschooled 229
Preprimary school 222
Senior citizen communities 962
Sports participation 1242
States 21
Teachers 235, 247
Union membership 639
Volunteers 567, 568
Voter registration and turnout 407
HIV infection (see also AIDS) . 103, 105, 106, 111
Hmong population 22
Hockey 1239, 1241, 1243, 1244
Hogs 798, 801, 807, 831, 832, 833, 834
Home economics, degrees conferred . 284, 285,
286

NOTE: Index citations refer to **table** numbers, not page numbers.

U.S. Census Bureau, Statistical Abstract of the United States: 2004-2005

Home equity loans/lines of credit ... 961, 1164, 1169
Home furnishings stores 613, 615, 1020
Home furnishings. See Appliances.
Home health care . 128, 168, 169, 170, 597, 599
Home health care services:
  Earnings 613
  Employees 613
  Expenditures 116, 117, 118, 120
  Finances 145
Homeland Security, Department of 466
Home remodeling 968, 1165
Homeowners insurance 1218, 1220
Homes. See Housing and housing units.
Homeschooling 229
Homicides . 102, 105, 106, 289, 290, 291, 292, 293, 294, 295, 296, 297
Honduras. See Foreign countries.
Hong Kong. See Foreign countries.
Hong Kong Hong Seng stock market index . 1376
Horses:
  Ownership 1236
  Racing 1237, 1239
  Riding 1237
Horses and mules 801
Hospices 128, 168, 169
Hospitals:
  Average daily room charge 158
  Beds 157, 159
  Charges and personal expenditure for . 116, 117, 118, 119, 120, 121, 123, 133
  Construction 925
  Consumer price index 124
  Cost to hospital per patient 158
  Diagnostic procedures 165
  Discharges from 161, 162, 163, 166
  Earnings 613, 728
  Emergency departments 154, 156
  Employees 147, 157, 457, 613, 728
  Establishments 157, 159, 728
  Finances 145, 146, 157, 1271
  Grants, foundations 566
  Gross domestic product 642
  Medicare program 126, 127, 128, 131
  Mental hospitals 157, 160, 173
  National expenditures . 114, 115, 116, 117, 118, 119, 120, 121, 123
  Outpatient visits ... 154, 155, 157, 159, 160
  Patients 157, 159
  Public expenditures 115, 116, 117, 119, 120, 121
  City governments 450
  County governments 452
  State governments 440
  Receipts 145, 146, 728
  States 159
  Surgery 165
  Organ transplants 164
  Use, admissions, and patient days . 157, 159, 160, 161, 162, 163
Veterans, expenditures and patients 173
Hotels and other lodging places (see also Accommodation and food services):
  Buildings and floor space 970
  Earnings 613, 1270
  Employees 613, 1270
  Establishments 1268, 1270
  Mergers and acquisitions 742
  New construction 936

Hotels and other lodging places (see also Accommodation and food services): —Con.
  Occupancy rate 1268
  Occupational safety 634
  Productivity 615
  Receipts 1035, 1271
  Travel summary 1268
House of Representatives .. 390, 391, 392, 393, 394, 395, 396, 397
Household workers. See Domestic service.
Households or families (see also Housing and housing units) . 54, 57, 56, 58, 59, 61, 62, 63, 64, 65, 1161
  Age of householder . 58, 62, 667, 1162, 1164, 1166, 1207
  Asian population 38
  Assets . 695, 1158, 1161, 1162, 1193, 1210
  Automobiles, ownership 964, 965
  Balance sheet 695
  Black, African American population . 33, 58, 59, 60, 61, 62, 64, 665, 666, 667, 670, 671, 672, 673
  Book purchasing 1132
  Characteristics ... 57, 58, 59, 60, 61, 62, 63
  Children under 18 years . 57, 59, 60, 61, 62, 63, 657, 673
  Computer use . 244, 965, 1121, 1150, 1152, 1153
  Consumer expenditures . 658, 659, 660, 661, 662
  Criminal victimization 308
  Debt .. 695, 1163, 1164, 1165, 1166, 1167
  Educational attainment 667
  Elderly 58, 62, 64, 65, 667
  Employment of parents 581
  Female householder . 57, 56, 58, 59, 61, 62, 63, 64, 65
  Finances, financial services . 1158, 1159, 1161, 1162, 1163, 1165, 1166, 1193, 1207, 1210
  Flow of funds 1158, 1159, 1161, 1163
  Food insecurity 196
  Food stamp program 552, 553
  Foreign born population 46
  Hispanic origin population .. 40, 52, 58, 59, 60, 62
  Hunger 196
  Income . 665, 666, 667, 668, 669, 670, 671, 672, 673, 674, 675, 1162, 1164, 1166, 1207
  Individual retirement accounts (IRAs) ... 536
  Internet access . 244, 965, 1119, 1121, 1152, 1153
  Interracial married couples 52
  Living arrangements 54
  Marital status of householder . 62, 65, 1326, 1327, 1328, 1329
  Media users 1121
  Mobility status 29
  Mutual fund ownership 1207
  Native Hawaiian, Other Pacific Islander population 39
  Net worth 693, 695
  Persons living alone (one-person households) 54, 57, 56, 58, 64, 65
  Poverty 690
    Asian and Pacific Islander population . 690
    Black, African American population . 690
    Hispanic origin population 690

NOTE: Index citations refer to **table** numbers, not page numbers.

U.S. Census Bureau, Statistical Abstract of the United States: 2004-2005

Table

Households or families (see also Housing and housing units) —Con.

Public assistance to families 522, 524
Race 33, 62, 673
Region of householder 673
Single-parent 33, 39, 56, 59, 60, 62, 63, 1326, 1328, 1329
Size 46, 56, 58, 61
Stock ownership 1204
Taxes paid 666
Telephones 1120
Types:
  Male householder 57, 62, 63
  Married couples with or without own children . 52, 57, 56, 58, 60, 61, 62, 63
  Non-family 57, 56, 64, 65
  One-person households . 57, 56, 58, 64, 65
  Unmarried partners 55
Wealth 693, 694
Housekeeping supplies expenditures . 660, 661
Housing and household operations, price indexes 700, 706
Housing and housing units (see also Households or families):
Age of housing stocks 947
Amenities 964
Appliances 965
Building permit value 927
Capital 966
City data 945, 957, 960
Condominiums 939
Construction:
  Apartments completed and rented .. 940
  Cost indexes 921
  New units 927, 928, 929
  Time to completion 931
  Value 922, 925
Consumer expenditures . 658, 659, 660, 661, 662
Consumer price indexes 698, 700
Costs 946, 954
Deficiencies 964
Elderly 951, 954, 964
Energy:
  Characteristics 930
  Consumption 886, 887, 891, 892
  Expenditures 889, 890, 891, 892
Fires and property loss 344
Floorspace 930
Government expenditures ... 428, 429, 440, 450, 465
Heating equipment used . 930, 947, 951, 963
Kitchen equipment 947
Loans and mortgages . 930, 933, 961, 1177, 1178, 1179
  Federal Housing Administration (FHA) ... 930, 933, 961
  Veterans Administration (VA) .. 930, 933, 961
Lot size 949
Maintenance and repair expenditures .. 660, 661, 967
Metropolitan area data .. 937, 946, 956, 959
Mobile homes 935, 946, 947, 948
Neighborhood indicators 962
New privately owned homes, characteristics . 930

Table

Housing and housing units (see also Households or families): —Con.

Ownership (see tenure)
Plumbing 951
Price indexes 932
Prices, or costs ... 921, 934, 935, 936, 937, 939, 953, 954
Public housing, low rent units 522
  Federal aid to state and local governments 424, 425
  Government expenditures 523, 524
Remodeling 968
Rent, rental value 953, 954
Rooms 949
Sales 933, 936, 938
Senior citizen communities 962
Square footage 949
State data 952
Structural type 928, 943, 947, 967, 948
Tenure. 28, 33, 38, 39, 40, 46, 667, 941, 942, 944, 945, 946, 947, 950, 951, 952, 953, 954, 1214
Vacancies 941, 943, 944, 945, 946
Value 695, 953, 955, 956, 957
Year built 892, 943, 951
Housing and Urban Development, Dept. of:
Employment 485
Federal aid to state and local governments .. 424, 425
Housing assistance 522, 523, 524
Human immunodeficiency virus (HIV) infection (see also AIDS) 105, 106, 177, 179, 180
Hungary. See Foreign countries.
Hunger 196
Hunting and fishing ... 1241, 1245, 1246, 1247
Hurricanes 374, 375
Hydroelectric power 888, 912
Capacity 901, 912
Consumption 884, 887, 888, 1365
Net generation 901, 912
Production 884, 901, 1364, 1368
Hypertension 155
Hysterectomy 165

I

Ice cream 199, 712, 837
Ice hockey 1237, 1241, 1244
Ice skating 1241
Iceland. See Foreign countries.
Idaho. See State data.
Illegal immigration. See Immigrants.
Illinois. See State data.
Immigrants (see also Foreign born population) .. 5, 6, 8, 9, 10
Area of residence 10
Class of admission 6
Country of birth 8, 9, 10
Foreign countries 1323
Refugees 6, 9
Unauthorized 7
Immunization of children 178
Imports. See Foreign trade.
Income (see also Poverty, Consumer expenditures, and Earnings):
Adult education 288
Aggregate income 663, 672
American Indian, Alaskan Native population . 663, 676

NOTE: Index citations refer to **table** numbers, not page numbers.

U.S. Census Bureau, Statistical Abstract of the United States: 2004-2005

Income (see also Poverty, Consumer expenditures, and Earnings): —Con.
Asian and Pacific Islander population .. 663, 666, 668, 669, 676, 681
Asian population 38
Black, African American population . 33, 521, 663, 670, 671, 672, 673, 676, 678, 690
Consumer expenditures 662
Corporate 716, 718, 725, 726
Disposable personal 648, 650, 654
Distribution . 663, 665, 667, 670, 672, 673, 676, 677
Energy consumption 892
Families 33, 31, 40, 669, 670, 671, 672, 673, 674, 675, 676
Asian families 38
Computer use 244
Island areas 1309
Native Hawaiian, Other Pacific Islander population 39
Type of family . 670, 671, 672, 673, 674, 675
Farm 799, 803, 805
Foreign born 44, 46
Hispanic origin population 40, 521, 665, 666, 667, 668, 669, 680, 681
Household ... 652, 663, 665, 666, 667, 668, 676, 678
Age 667, 679
Black, African American population . 663, 665, 666, 667, 668, 676
Book purchasing 1132
Computer use 1150, 1152
Educational attainment 667
Elderly 667
Hispanic origin population . 663, 665, 666, 667, 668, 676
Homeschooling 229
Mobility status 29
Native Hawaiian and Other Pacific Islander 663, 676
Recreation activities, physical activity . 195, 1241, 1248
Stock, mutual fund ownership . 1204, 1206, 1208
Taxes 1345, 1347
Tenure 667
National income ... 641, 643, 644, 647, 648
By type of income 647
Originating in farming 799
Native Hawaiian, other Pacific Islander population 39
Per capita 648, 680
Personal 650, 652, 653
Persons 46, 677, 678, 680, 681
Educational attainment 677, 679
Source of income 521
Savings 651, 656
Sports participation, goods 1241, 1248
Income security outlays 462
Income tax (see also Tax receipts):
Average tax by income level 473
Corporation 473, 474, 725
Deductions 475, 477, 561
Foreign countries 1347
State collections 441
Index numbers. See individual subjects.
India. See Foreign countries.

Indiana. See State data.
Indian, American population. See American Indian, Alaska Native population.
Indian, Asian population. See Asian Indian population.
Indium 861, 1162
Individual retirement accounts (IRA's) . 536, 691, 692, 1206, 1208, 1211, 1212
Indonesia. See Foreign countries.
Industrial and commercial enterprises, failures . 730
Industrial engineering:
Degrees conferred 773
Employment 773
Salary 773
Industrial minerals 860
Industrial production indexes 754
Foreign countries 1340
Industry. See Corporations and individual industries.
Infant deaths (see also Deaths and death rates) . 70, 100, 101
Island areas of the U.S. 1304
Inflation. See Prices, consumer, and Consumer price indexes.
Information industry:
Capital 749, 751
Earnings . 611, 613, 618, 619, 650, 728, 731, 732, 1113, 1115, 1117, 1265
Electronic commerce 1267
Employees .. 611, 612, 613, 728, 731, 732, 1113, 1115, 1117, 1265
Establishments .. 728, 729, 731, 973, 1113, 1115, 1117, 1265
Finances 718, 721
Foreign countries 1373
Gross domestic product 642, 1116
Hours 611
Multinational companies 762, 763
Nonemployers 729
Occupational safety 634
Productivity 615
Profits 718, 758, 759
Shipments, revenue 718, 721, 726, 727, 728, 729, 1113, 1114, 1118, 1123, 1131, 1133, 1134, 1145
Infrastructure expenditures. See government.
Influenza 102, 104
Inhalants, persons using 186
Injuries (see also Accidents and Occupational safety) . 112, 156, 163, 169, 174, 1053, 1106
Associated with consumer products 175
Costs 176
Crime victimization 305, 306, 307, 308
Industrial 631, 632, 633, 634
Work time lost 632
Inmates (see also Correctional institutions) . 334, 338
Installment loans (see also Loans and mortgages) 1164, 1184
Institutional care facilities (see also Hospitals and Nursing and related care facilities) . 157, 160, 167, 171, 172, 173
Institutional population 66
Mentally ill, retarded 173
Prisoners 336, 338
Institutions. See Hospitals and other individual facilities.
Institutions of higher education. See Education.
Instrumental activities of daily living (IADLs) . 172

NOTE: Index citations refer to **table** numbers, not page numbers.

Instruments and related products, manufacturing:
Earnings 613, 984
Employees 613, 984
Foreign trade 1302
Gross domestic product 972
Mergers and acquisitions 742
Occupational safety 634
Patents 745
Productivity 615
Profits 760
Toxic chemical releases 367
Insurance. See individual forms of insurance.
Insurance agents, brokers, and service:
Earnings 1157
Employees 1157
Establishments 1157, 1169
Finances 1193, 1218
Foreign investments in the U.S. 1286
Gross domestic product 1154
Mergers and acquisitions 742
Occupational safety 634
Insurance carriers:
Earnings 613, 1155, 1157
Employees 613, 1155, 1157
Establishments 1155, 1156, 1157
Finances 1158, 1218
Gross domestic product 1154
Multinational companies 762, 763
Nonemployers 1156
Occupational safety 634
Profits 1218
Receipts 1155, 1156
Insurance, government. See Social insurance.
Insurance, medical care 115, 119, 120
Interactive digital media 1118
Inter-American Development Bank 1289
Intercity traffic 1049, 1101
Interest:
Payments, federal government 462, 465
Persons receiving income 521
Receipts, by source:
Individual income tax returns .. 475, 478
National and personal income component 650
Interest rates 1188
Mortgages 1178, 1188
Intermediate goods, price indexes, producer 704
Internal revenue collections (see also Tax receipts) 474
Internal waterways, traffic 1065
International affairs:
Balance of trade 1293
Commerce .. 1293, 1294, 1295, 1298, 1312
Federal outlays 465
Foreign exchange rates 1378
Foreign investments in U.S. 1197, 1198, 1283
International transactions, U.S. . 1278, 1279, 1280, 1282
U.S. government aid 1289, 1290, 1291
U.S. investments .. 1195, 1196, 1278, 1288
International Bank for Reconstruction and Development 1289
International Development Association ... 1289
International Finance Corporation 1289
International investment position, U.S. ... 1278, 1281, 1288

International mail (U.S. postal) 1111
Internet access/use . 242, 604, 965, 1119, 1121, 1132, 1136, 1149, 1150, 1152, 1153, 1238, 1372
Internet publishing and broadcasting 613
Interracial married couples 52
Intracity transportation price indexes 700
Inventories (see also Stocks, commodity) .. 985, 986, 987, 988, 1024, 1027, 1042
Business (GDP) 641
Investments (see also Capital stock and Securities):
Foreign, in U.S. ... 1197, 1198, 1278, 1281, 1283, 1285, 1286, 1287
Private domestic, gross 641, 651
U.S. government obligations 1169
U.S. international . 1195, 1196, 1278, 1281, 1288
Venture capital 743
Iowa. See State data.
Iran. See Foreign countries.
Iraq. See Foreign countries.
Ireland (Eire). See Foreign countries.
Iron (see also Steel):
Foreign trade 866, 936, 1299
Mining industry 859
Productivity 933
Prices 862
Production 860, 864, 936
World production 864, 1363
Iron (nutritional), available for human consumption 197, 198
Iron and steel mills (see also Primary metal manufacturing):
Capital 999
Earnings 613, 973, 976
Electronic commerce 980
Employees 613, 973, 976, 999
Establishments 973
Foreign trade 999
Occupational safety 634
Productivity 615
Shipments 976, 980, 999
Iron and steel products 864, 878, 1000
Production and value 860
Scrap 861
Irrigation 355, 356
Islamic population. See Religion.
Island areas of the U.S.:
Agriculture 1314, 1315
Aid by U.S. government 1317
Area 346, 1305
Banks and banking 1309
Births and deaths 1304
Business, summary 1316
Climate (Puerto Rico) ... 378, 379, 380, 381, 382, 383
Commerce 1312
Education 1309
Attainment 1307
Enrollment 1308
Employees 1313, 1316
Establishments 1313, 1316
Federal payments 1317
Finances 1310, 1311
Foreign investment 1285
Foreign trade 1312
Geography 346
Gross product 1310

NOTE: Index citations refer to **table** numbers, not page numbers.

Table

Island areas of the U.S.: —Con.
Hospital facilities 159
Income 1307, 1309
Industry 1313, 1316
Labor force and employment ... 1307, 1309
Language spoken 1307
Marital status 1305
Marriage and divorce 1304
Mobility 1307
Payroll by industry 1313, 1316
Population and/or area ... 346, 1303, 1305,
1306, 1309, 1321
Public aid 544
Public libraries 1147
Sales, shipments, receipts 1316
Social insurance 528
Tourism 1309
Unemployment insurance 539
Vital statistics 1304
Isle of Man. See Foreign countries.
Israel. See Foreign countries.
Italy. See Foreign countries.
Itemized deductions (taxes) 475, 477, 561

J

Jails 334, 337
Jamaica. See Foreign countries.
Japan. See Foreign countries.
Japanese population 22, 737
Jazz 1136, 1232
Jersey. See Foreign countries.
Jewelry, luggage and leather goods stores . 613,
615
Jewelry sales 1020
Jewish population. See Religion.
Job Corps 524
Job gains and losses 614
Jogging 1241, 1247, 1248
Jordan. See Foreign countries.
Judicial service (Federal):
Employees and payrolls 483
Federal outlays 465
Juices 201
Juveniles:
Arrest 312
Court cases 329

K

Kansas. See State data.
Kazakhstan. See Foreign countries.
Kentucky. See State data.
Kenya. See Foreign countries.
Keogh plans 477, 1162
Kidney disease and infections, deaths 102
Kiribati. See Foreign countries.
Korea. See Foreign countries.
Korean population 22, 737
Kuwait. See Foreign countries.
Kyrgyzstan. See Foreign countries.

L

Laboratories, medical and dental 145
Labor force, employment, and earnings (see
also individual industries or occupations):
Accidents and fatalities . 631, 632, 633, 634,
635, 636
Work time lost 632
Average pay, States 621
Commuting to work 1084, 1085, 1086
Metro areas 622

Table

**Labor force, employment, and earnings (see
also individual industries or occupations):
—Con.**
City government 459
Civilian labor force:
Asian and Pacific Islander population . 570,
571, 573, 603, 608, 623
Asian population . 38, 570, 571, 573, 576,
590, 597, 600, 601, 603, 608, 623, 627,
639
Black, African American population .. 33,
570, 571, 573, 576, 587, 588, 589, 597,
608
Displaced workers 573, 594, 608
Educational attainment ... 573, 600, 608
Employed . 569, 571, 574, 575, 576, 579,
581, 583, 584, 587, 588, 589, 590, 591,
593, 600, 601
Female ... 571, 572, 573, 574, 576, 577,
578, 579, 580, 587, 588, 589, 608
Age of children 579
Marital status 577, 578, 579
Multiple job holders 590
Foreign-born population 46
High school graduates, dropouts ... 257
Hispanic origin population . 40, 570, 571,
587, 588, 589, 597, 601
Home-based work 587
Metropolitan areas 575
Minimum wage workers 627
Multiple job holders 590
Not at work 585
Part-time 593
Participation rates .. 570, 571, 573, 574,
577, 578, 579, 580
Selected countries 1349, 1352
Wives, by age of youngest child . 580
Projections 570, 599, 602
Race . 33, 570, 571, 573, 576, 587, 588,
589, 597, 608
Reason not in 596
School enrollment, persons 16 to 24
years old 576
Self-employed workers 586
States 574
Unemployed .. 569, 571, 574, 575, 576,
579, 603, 605, 606, 607, 608, 609, 610
Women who gave birth in previous year .
86, 87
Computer use 1121
Disabled persons 540, 595
Displaced workers 594
Earnings 618, 621, 622, 623, 624
Educational attainment 214, 573, 608
Elderly 31, 570, 572, 577, 582, 603
Employee benefits . 142, 144, 532, 629, 630
Government employees 455
Employee training 1335
Employees 611, 612, 613, 982
States 612
Employer costs 628
Employment cost index ... 625, 1347, 1370,
1371
Employment projections 599, 602
Employment taxes and contributions ... 467

NOTE: Index citations refer to **table** numbers, not page numbers.

Labor force, employment, and earnings (see also individual industries or occupations): —Con.
Female . 571, 572, 573, 574, 576, 577, 578, 579, 580, 597, 601, 605, 606, 608, 609, 623, 624
Flexible schedules 588
Foreign countries . 1341, 1349, 1351, 1352, 1353, 1354
Foreign-owned firms 1284, 1285
Government. See Government.
High school graduates and dropouts 257
Hispanic origin population 40, 570, 571, 601, 603
Hours 1341, 1370
Indexes of compensation 616, 1371
Internet access 1121
Job gains and losses 614
Job search 604
Metropolitan areas 575, 622
Minimum wage workers 626, 627
Mobility status 28
Occupational groups. See Occupations and individual occupations.
Occupational safety 631, 632, 633, 634, 635, 636
Persons working at home 587
Poverty status 687
Production workers 976, 977
Productivity 616, 1341, 1370
Self-employed 586
Shift work 589
Social insurance coverage 525
State data 574, 598, 610, 621
Tenure with employer 592
Unemployed workers:
Age 576, 603
Asian and Pacific Islander population . 571, 603, 608
Black, African American population .. 33, 571, 576, 603, 608
Educational attainment 214, 608
Foreign-born population 46
Foreign countries 1349, 1351
High school graduates and dropouts . 257
Hispanic origin population . 40, 570, 603
Industry 606
Occupation 607
Race 33, 571, 576, 603, 608
Reason 605, 609
Sex . 571, 574, 576, 579, 603, 605, 606, 607, 608, 609
States 574, 610
Union membership 638, 639, 640
Work stoppages 637
Youth employment programs 524
Labor organizations or unions:
Membership 638, 639, 640
Political action committees (PAC) . 411, 412, 413
Public confidence 404
Labor strikes 637
Lacrosse 1244
Lakes 353, 357
Lamb and mutton (see also Meat and meat products) 199, 831
Lambs. See Sheep and lambs.

Land (see also Farms and Public lands):
Area:
Cities 27
Coastal 23
Foreign countries 1321
Island areas 346, 1305
National parks 1249
States 346
United States 1, 346
Farmland 348, 787, 789, 790, 791, 792, 793, 795, 796, 797
Federal land 347, 348, 490
Foreign investors 1284, 1285
Forest, area and ownership 343, 348
Parks 1249, 1250
Use 348, 349, 350
Landfills (see also Solid waste) .. 362, 363, 912, 1332
Languages spoken at home . 32, 48, 49, 50, 221
Laos. See Foreign countries.
Laotian population 22
Larceny, larceny-theft . 289, 290, 291, 292, 303, 305, 308
Lard 199
Latex. See Rubber.
Latvia. See Foreign countries.
Laundry, cleaning, and garment services. See Dry-cleaning and laundry services.
Law degrees conferred 284, 285, 286, 287
Law enforcement (see also Courts, crime, and correctional institutions):
Arrests 309, 314, 315
Drug enforcement 314, 315, 316
Employees 454
Expenditures 428, 429, 440, 442
Handgun checks 318
Police officers 320, 322, 454, 597
Wiretaps 317
Workplace violence 635, 636
Lawn care 1235
Lawyers (see also Legal services) 597
Lead 861
Air quality 359, 360, 361
Consumption 861
Employment 861
Foreign trade 861
Prices 861, 862
Production and value 860
World production 864, 1363
Leather and allied product, manufacturing (see also Hides and skins, and Footwear):
Earnings 613, 973, 976, 984
Electronic commerce 980
Employees ... 613, 973, 976, 978, 982, 984
Establishments 973
Foreign trade 978, 1302
Gross domestic product 642, 972
Industrial production index 754
Occupational safety 633, 634
Pollution abatement 371
Shipments 976, 978, 980, 987
Toxic chemical releases 367
Lebanon. See Foreign countries.
Legal assistants 597
Legal, governmental, public administrative associations 291
Legal services:
Earnings 613, 1265
Employees 613, 1265

NOTE: Index citations refer to **table** numbers, not page numbers.

Legal services: —Con.
Establishments 1265
Finances 718
Gross domestic product 642
Occupational safety 634
Receipts 718
Legionellosis 177
Legislatures, State party composition . 401, 402
Leisure and hospitality industry:
Earnings 611, 613, 619
Employees 611, 612, 613
Hours 611
Leisure activities. See Recreation.
Lemons 801, 830
Leprosy 177
Lesotho. See Foreign countries.
Letters (postal) 1111, 1112
Lettuce 200, 712, 798, 801, 829
Leveraged buy-outs 741
Liberia. See Foreign countries.
Libraries and librarians . 1146, 1147, 1148, 1149
Adult programs 1151
Degrees conferred 284, 285, 286
Employees 597
Grants, foundations 566
Internet use 1149
Public employment 446
Revenue 1145
Libya. See Foreign countries.
Licenses, permits, etc.:
Public lands 490
Taxes 440
Liechtenstein. See Foreign countries.
Life expectancy 92, 93, 94
Foreign countries 1325
Projections 92
Life insurance 1216, 1217
Capital 1217
Cash value 1162
Consumer expenditures 658, 660
Establishments 1217
Finances 1158, 1177, 1193, 1210, 1217
Flow of funds 1193, 1210
In force 1216
Individual Retirement Accounts 1212
Mortgage loans outstanding 1177
Purchases, policies 1161, 1216
Reserves 1161, 1217
Sales 1216, 1217
Life sciences 773, 775
Degrees conferred 284, 285, 286, 773
Employment 773, 779
Life years lost 112
Light and power. See Electric light and power
industry.
Lightning 374
Lime 860, 861
Liquefied petroleum gases, consumption ... 873
Liquor stores, retail. See Beer, wine, and liquor
stores.
Liquors and beverages:
Alcoholism treatment 185
Consumption 186, 201
Government revenues .. 428, 429, 432, 443,
440, 441
Literacy activities 220, 223
Lithuania. See Foreign countries.
Livestock and livestock products (see also Ani-
mals, domestic, and individual classes):
Commodity futures trading 708

Livestock and livestock products (see also
Animals, domestic, and individual classes):
—Con.
Consumption 199, 831
Farm marketings, sales 800, 801, 805
Foreign trade . 810, 812, 815, 817, 831, 1302
Number and value on farms 832, 835
Prices 806, 832
Production 831, 832, 835
Purchases 800
Supply 831
Value on farms 832
Living cost. See Consumer price indexes and
Prices.
Loans and mortgages (see also Debt):
Automobile loans 1184
Banks, commercial 1169, 1180
Commercial paper 1191
Consumer credit .. 1163, 1164, 1165, 1167,
1169, 1180, 1183, 1184
Credit market, flow of funds 1159, 1163
Credit unions 1157
Delinquency rates 1179, 1180
Farm. See Farm mortgage loans.
Federal Housing Administration (FHA) . 1179
Foreclosure rates 1179
Home mortgage/equity loans . 695, 961, 1164,
1167, 1177, 1180
Installment loans 1164
Interest rates 1178, 1188
Life insurance 1217
Minority-operated small businesses 736
Mortgage-backed securities 1190
Mortgage pools 1159
Mortgages . 695, 722, 723, 1159, 1161, 1163,
1164, 1165, 1177
Personal loans 1184
Savings institutions 1176
Veterans Administration (VA) 1179
Lobsters 854, 856
Local and suburban transit. See Passenger tran-
sit industry.
Local government. See individual governmental
units and State and local government.
Locomotives (railroad) 1106
Lodging industries. See Hotels and other lodg-
ing places.
London FTSE 100 stock market index 1376
Long term care insurance 630
Lotteries 447, 448
Louisiana. See State data.
Low birth weight 71, 78, 81, 84
LSD usage 186
Lumber (see also Forest products and Wood
products manufacturing):
Consumption 846, 848
Foreign countries 1362
Foreign trade 846, 847
Prices 849
Production 846
Railroad car loadings 1107, 1108
Waterborne commerce 1066
Luxembourg. See Foreign countries.
Lyme disease 177

M

Macadamia nuts 830
Macau. See Foreign countries.

NOTE: Index citations refer to **table** numbers, not page numbers.

Macedonia, the Former Yugoslav Republic of. See Foreign countries.
Machine tools 1002, 1042
Machinery manufacturing:
    Capital 371
    Earnings 613, 973, 976, 1117
    Employees .. 613, 973, 976, 978, 982, 1117
    Establishments 973
    Finances 760
    Foreign trade 978, 1302
    Gross domestic product 642, 972, 1116
    Industrial production index 754
    Inventories 987
    Mergers and acquisitions 742
    Multinational companies 762, 763
    Occupational safety 633
    Patents 745
    Pollution abatement 371
    Productivity 615
    Profits 759, 760
    Research and development 776, 777
    Shipments 976, 978, 980, 986, 987
    Toxic chemical releases 367
Mackerel, Pacific 857
Madagascar. See Foreign countries.
Magazines:
    Advertising expenditures 1274
    Prices 1127
    Reading 1119
    Receipts 1118
Magnesium 860, 864
Mail 1111, 1112
Mail order houses (including electronic shopping):
    Earnings 613, 1019
    Employees 613, 1019
    Establishments 1019, 1026
    Productivity 615
    Purchases 1023
    Sales 1020, 1026, 1038, 1039
Maine. See State data.
Malaria 177
Malawi. See Foreign countries.
Malaysia. See Foreign countries.
Maldives. See Foreign countries.
Male householder. See Households or families.
Mali. See Foreign countries.
Malt beverages (see also Beverages) .. 201, 810, 812, 813
    Advertising 1275
    Beer 201, 700
Malta. See Foreign countries.
Mammography testing 190
Managed care, health plans 128, 136
Management of companies and enterprises:
    Capital 751
    Earnings 613, 731
    Employees 613, 731
    Establishments 731
    Finances 718, 721, 726
    Gross domestic product 642
    Profits 728
    Receipts 718, 721, 726, 727
Managers. See Proprietors, etc.
Manganese 859, 865, 866
Manganiferous ore 860
Manmade fibers and fabrics (see also Foreign trade and specific items) 993
Manufactured products (see also individual products):

Manufactured products (see also individual products): —Con.
    Production indexes 754
Manufacturers' excise taxes 474
Manufacturing industry (see also individual industries):
    Capital 749, 751, 991, 1194
    Earnings . 611, 613, 618, 619, 728, 731, 732, 738, 976, 983, 1316
    Economic indicators 752
    Electronic commerce 980
    Employees .. 587, 601, 611, 612, 613, 716, 728, 731, 732, 738, 977, 978, 979, 982, 1316
    Establishments ... 728, 729, 731, 976, 983, 1316
    Finances 718, 721, 760, 990, 991, 1310
    Foreign countries 1370, 1371
    Foreign investments in U.S. 1283
    Form of organization 976
    Gross domestic product . 642, 646, 972, 1310
    Hours 611
    Industrial production index 754
    Inventories 986, 987
    Investment abroad 1288
    Island areas of the United States . 1313, 1316
    Multinational companies 762, 763
    Nonemployers 729
    Occupational safety 631, 634, 636
    Productivity 615, 616, 755
        Foreign countries 1370
    Profits 716, 759, 760, 991
    Sales, shipments, receipts ... 716, 718, 721, 726, 727, 728, 729, 738, 769, 976, 978, 983, 985, 986, 987, 991
    State data 974, 977, 979, 983
    Toxic chemical releases 367
    Union membership 639
    Value added 983
    Women-owned businesses 738
Maple syrup, organic tree acreage 798
Margarine 199, 712
Marihuana (see also Drugs (illegal)):
    Arrests, seizures 315, 316
    Use 186, 187
Marine Corps 500, 501
Marital status of population 51, 53
    Black, African American population 51
    By presence of children 57
    Computer use 1150
    Couples with or without own household . 52, 56
    Elderly 31, 53
    Employed persons 582
    Female householder 62, 1326
    Foreign born population 46
    Foreign countries 1327, 1329
    Hispanic origin population 51
    Household status 62, 1328, 1329
    Internet access 1150
    Island areas 1305
    Labor force participation rates 577, 578, 579, 580
    Male householder 62
    Nonfamily householder 64
    Unmarried partners 55
    Women in the labor force 578, 579
    Work schedules 590

NOTE: Index citations refer to **table** numbers, not page numbers.

Marriage and divorce (see also Marital status) ...
      70, 113
  Foreign countries 1327, 1329
  Island areas of the U.S. 1304
Married couples. See Households or families.
Married persons. See Marital status.
Marshall Islands. See Foreign countries.
Martial arts 1241
Martinique. See Foreign countries.
Maryland. See State data.
Massachusetts. See State data.
Maternal and child health service, expenditures
  for 115
Mathematics:
  Degrees conferred . 284, 285, 286, 773, 775
  Employment 779
  Salary offers 281, 773
Mauritania. See Foreign countries.
Mauritius. See Foreign countries.
Mayotte. See Foreign countries.
Measles 177, 178
Measuring, analyzing, and controlling instru-
  ments. See Instruments and related products,
  manufacturing.
Meat and meat products (see also Food manu-
  facturing and individual meats):
  Cholesterol, source 198
  Consumer expenditures 658, 660, 661
  Consumption 199, 813, 832
  Expenditures 808
    Food at home 658
  Foreign trade . 810, 813, 815, 817, 831, 1299
  Iron (dietary), source 198
  Price indexes 700, 712
  Production 831, 1355, 1357
  Supply 831
Mechanical engineering:
  Degrees conferred 773
  Employment 773
  Salary 773
Media (see also individual medium) . 404, 1119,
      1120, 1121
Medicaid:
  Coverage, recipients ... 132, 133, 134, 136,
      139, 522, 524
  Expenditures 121, 134, 146, 519, 524
  Nursing homes 133, 171, 172
  State data 134, 136
Medical care (see also Health services):
  Budget outlays 462
  Expenditures for .. 115, 116, 117, 118, 119,
      120, 518, 519, 520, 523, 524, 658, 660,
      661
  Insurance benefits 115, 119
  Price indexes, consumer 124, 698, 700
    Fixed-weighted 706
  Products and shipments 988
Medical equipment and supplies manufacturing .
      613, 615, 976
Medical research 115
Medical schools 151, 287
  Foreign graduates 149
  Number, students, graduates 151, 287
Medical sciences, employment 597
Medical services. See Health services.
Medicare:
  Ambulatory care visits 154
  Benefit payments, expenditures .. 115, 121,
      127, 130, 131, 146, 519
  Contributions 131

Medicare: —Con.
  Enrollees 126, 129
  Hospital visits 154
  Nursing homes 171, 172
  State data 129, 130
  Trust funds 131
  Utilization and charges 127, 128
Medicines. See Drugs and medicines, and Phar-
  maceutical and medicine manufacturing.
Melons 200, 801, 813, 829
Membership organizations:
  Earnings 613
  Employees 613
  Establishments 1265
  Revenue 1277
Members of Congress. See Congress, U.S.
Menhaden 854
Meningitis 102, 177
Mental hospitals 157, 160, 173
Merchandise. See Foreign trade and General
  merchandise stores.
Mercury 860, 861, 864, 866
Mergers and acquisitions 741, 742
Metals . 859, 860, 861, 862, 863, 864, 866, 1108
  Foreign trade 1299, 1302
  Production and value 860
    Indexes of production 858
  Railroad, car loadings of 1107, 1108
  Spot market price indexes 709
  Strategic and critical materials 865
  World production 864, 1363
Metal ore mining industry:
  Capital 859
  Earnings 859
  Employees 756, 859
  Establishments 859
  Gross domestic product 642
  Occupational safety 634
  Production indexes 858
  Shipments 859
  Value added 859
Metalworking manufacturing 613, 615, 976
Methamphetamine, illegal use 186
Methane gases 362
Metropolitan areas:
  Airline markets 1057
  Civilian labor force 575
  Commuting to work 1085
  Consumer expenditures 659
  Consumer price index 701
  Earnings 622
  Housing 640, 957, 959
  Housing prices 937
  Income 655
  Population 24
Mexican origin population 22, 40
  Births and birth rates 74
  Business owners 737
  Commuting to work 41
  Disability status 41
  Educational attainment 41, 212
  Foreign born 41
  Labor force 571
  Nativity 41
  Occupation 41
Mexico. See Foreign countries.
Mica 860, 864, 866
  Foreign trade (sheet) 866
  Production and value 860

NOTE: Index citations refer to **table** numbers, not page numbers.

U.S. Census Bureau, Statistical Abstract of the United States: 2004-2005

Mica —Con.
World production 864
Mica, scrap and flake 861
Micronesia, Federated States of, See Foreign countries.
Michigan. See State data.
Microcomputers (see Computers)
Migration 18, 28, 30
Military bases 501
Military expenditures, worldwide 1384
Foreign countries 1384
Military manpower 1385
Military outlays 462
Military sciences, degrees conferred .. 284, 285, 286
Military services:
Basic pay 507
Casualties 506
Contract awards 495, 496, 499
Expenditures 492, 493, 494, 499
Military force structure 511
National Guard 510
Pay grades 507
Payroll 496, 499
Personnel 496, 499, 503
By war 506
Foreign countries 502
Rank 507
Reserves, by branch 508
Sex and age 509
Retirees 500, 521, 529
Retirement system 529
Milk, cream and other dairy products:
Calcium, source ....., ... 198
Cholesterol, source 198
Consumption 199, 838
Prices 712
Production 836, 837, 838, 1355
Sales 837
Millet, organic acreage 798
Milo. See Sorghum for grain.
Mineral fuels 860
Mineral leases, public 499
Minerals and mineral products (see also Mining and individual minerals):
Foreign trade 866
Waterborne commerce 1066
Imports as percent of consumption 866
Price indexes 713, 714
Prices 862
Production and value ... 858, 860, 863, 864
Foreign countries 1367
Strategic and critical materials 865
World production 864, 1363
Mining industry (see also Minerals and mineral products and individual minerals):
Capital 371, 748
Expenditures 751, 859
Earnings . 613, 618, 728, 731, 738, 841, 859
Employees .. 587, 601, 613, 728, 731, 738, 841, 859
Establishments 728, 729, 731, 841, 859
Finances 718, 721, 760, 1310
Foreign investments in the U.S. 1285
Gross domestic product 642, 1310
Industrial production index 754
Mergers and acquisitions 742
Multinational companies 762, 763
Nonemployers 729

Mining industry (see also Minerals and mineral products and individual minerals): —Con.
Occupational safety 631, 634, 636
Pollution abatement 371
Productivity 615
Profits 716, 760
Receipts . 716, 718, 721, 726, 727, 728, 729, 859
Union membership 639
Value added 859
Women-owned businesses 738
Mining machinery, manufacturing 613, 976
Minnesota. See State data.
Mississippi. See State data.
Mississippi River traffic 1065
Missouri. See State data.
Mobile homes 935, 946, 947, 948
Mobility status of population . 28, 29, 30, 34, 37
Moldova. See Foreign countries.
Molybdenum 860, 861, 864
Monaco. See Foreign countries.
Monetary system and banks, flow of funds . 1158
Money market accounts, funds . 722, 1158, 1161, 1190
Families using 1161, 1162, 1206, 1208
Money market rates 1188
Money orders 1112, 1182
Money supply (stock) 1187
Mongolia. See Foreign countries.
Monitors 1013
Montana. See State data.
Montenegro. See Foreign countries.
Montserrat. See Foreign countries.
Morocco. See Foreign countries.
Mortality costs 112
Mortgage pools and trusts ... 1158, 1159, 1177
Mortgages. See Loans and mortgages.
Motion picture and sound recording industry:
Earnings 613, 728, 1113, 1115
Employees 613, 728, 1113, 1115
Establishments 728, 1113, 1115
Gross domestic product 642
Inventory 1134
Mergers and acquisitions 742
Productivity 613
Receipts, revenue .. 728, 1113, 1114, 1118, 1134
Motor freight transportation and warehousing. See Trucking and warehousing.
Motor fuel taxes 440, 1076, 1088
Motor vehicle and parts dealers, retail:
Earnings 613, 728, 1019, 1027
Electronic commerce 1039
Employees 613, 728, 1019, 1027
Establishments . 728, 1018, 1019, 1026, 1027
Finances 718, 1027
Franchises 1027
Inventories 1024, 1027
Nonemployers 1026
Productivity 615
Profits 1027
Purchases 1023
Sales ... 718, 728, 1018, 1020, 1022, 1025, 1026, 1027, 1039
Motor vehicles:
Accidents/deaths .. 106, 1053, 1089, 1091, 1097
Air pollutant emissions 361
Alternative fueled vehicles in use 1080
Common carriers 1049, 1100, 1101

NOTE: Index citations refer to **table** numbers, not page numbers.

Motor vehicles: —Con.
Consumer expenditures . 658, 659, 660, 661
Crashes 1093
Drivers licenses 1082
Expenditure per new car 1031
Foreign trade 1299
Fuel consumed 1088
Imports 1031
Insurance 1218
Leases 1030
Miles of travel 1082, 1259, 1260
Number 1047
Ownership 691, 692, 964, 965
Passenger outlays 1048
Price indexes, consumer 700
    Fixed-weighted 706
Production 1032
Railroad car loadings 1107
Registrations 1079, 1082
Sales 1031, 1030
Service and repair shops. See Automotive
    repair and maintenance service.
Taxes, licenses and motor fuel 440
Theft 289, 290, 291, 303, 308, 309
Traffic fatalities ... 1089, 1090, 1091, 1092,
                        1094, 1095, 1096
Trucks 1087, 1088
Motor vehicle manufacturing:
Earnings 613, 984
Employees 613, 982, 984, 1009, 1010
Foreign trade 1302
Gross domestic product 642, 972
Industrial production index 754
Inventories 987
Multinational companies 762, 763
Occupational safety 634
Productivity 615
Research and development 776, 777
Sales, shipments, receipts .. 976, 988, 1000,
                    1009, 1010, 1028, 1029, 1032
State data 1010
Motorcycles 1082, 1089, 1299
Accidents and deaths 1089
Foreign trade 1299
Racing 1237
Mountain biking 1241
Movie theaters 1119, 1233, 1240
Mozambique. See Foreign countries.
Mullet, catch 854
Multinational companies 761, 762, 763
Multiple births 80
Multiple jobholders 590
Mumps 177, 178
Municipal and State bonds 722, 723, 1161,
                        1163, 1189, 1190, 1199
Municipal waste 363, 364
Foreign countries 1332
Municipalities. See Cities and Metropolitan
areas.
Murders . 289, 290, 291, 292, 293, 294, 297, 309
Museums 1231, 1232
Museums, botanical, zoological gardens. See
Museums, historical sites.
Museums, historical sites:
Earnings 613, 728
Employees 613, 728, 1226
Establishments 728, 1226
Federal aid 1231
Finances 1226, 1231

Museums, historical sites: —Con.
Nonemployers 1227
Occupational safety 634
Receipts, revenue 728, 1224, 1227
Mushrooms 801, 813, 829
Music:
Industry receipts 1118, 1135
Listening and expenditures . 1036, 1119, 1136,
                        1232, 1234
Musicians and composers 597
Muslim population. See Religion.
Mutton (see also Meat and meat products) . 199,
                        831
Mutual funds . 691, 692, 723, 724, 1158, 1161,
1162, 1193, 1205, 1206, 1207, 1208, 1209,
                        1210, 1211, 1212, 1215

N
Namibia. See Foreign countries.
National Aeronautics and Space Administration .
                        767, 783
Budget 783
Expenditures, research and development . 764
    Space program 784
Space launches 783, 785
National Association of Securities Dealers (NAS-
DAQ) 1199
NCAA sports participation 1244
National debt. See Debt.
National defense (see also individual military
services):
Contract awards and payrolls 496
Expenditures, world 1384
Federal employment and payrolls 454
Federal outlays 461, 465, 493
Military forces 502, 504
    Foreign countries 1385
Ready reserves 509
Outlays 492
National forests. See Forests.
National Guard 510
National health expenditures 115, 116, 117
National income (see also Gross domestic prod-
uct) 648
Native Hawaiian and Other Pacific Islander .. 13,
                        14, 15, 22, 39
Births 71
College costs 271
Commuting to work 37
Disability status 37, 269
Educational attainment 37
Farm operators 788
Foreign born 37
Head Start 554
Households 39
Housing tenure 39
Income 39, 663, 676
Minority businesses 737
Mobility status 37
Nativity 37
Nurses 148
Occupation 37
Poverty 39, 682
Veterans 514
Natural gas:
Consumption . 884, 885, 887, 891, 892, 893,
                        1365, 1366
Expenditures 889, 890, 891, 892, 893
Foreign trade 885, 895, 896, 1299

NOTE: Index citations refer to **table** numbers, not page numbers.

U.S. Census Bureau, Statistical Abstract of the United States: 2004-2005

Table		Table

Natural gas: —Con.
Prices 700, 704, 862, 875, 894
Production 870, 884, 885
  World . 864, 875, 876, 1363, 1364, 1367
Reserves 871
Natural gas distribution industry 613, 615
Natural gas plant liquids 870
Prediction 870
Reserves 871
Supply 868
Value 870
Natural resources:
Federal outlays 465
Governmental finances 429
Aid to State and local governments . 424
Government employment and payrolls ...
                                        454
Governmental revenue 429
State and local governments 428
State governments 439, 440
Natural resource industry 611, 619
Nauru. See Foreign countries.
Navy 500, 501
Nebraska. See State data.
Nectarines 200, 830
Neonatal deaths (see also Deaths and death
rates) 100
Nepal. See Foreign countries.
Netherlands. See Foreign countries.
Netherlands Antilles. See Foreign countries.
Neurologists 149
Nevada. See State data.
New Caledonia. See Foreign countries.
New Hampshire. See State data.
New Jersey. See State data.
New Mexico. See State data.
New York. See State data.
New York Stock Exchange 1199, 1201
New Zealand. See Foreign countries.
Newspapers (See also Publishing industry):
Advertising expenditures 1274
Expenditures, consumer 1119, 1229
Frequency of publication 1122
Number and circulation .. 1120, 1124, 1125
Public confidence in media 404
Reading 1119, 1121
Receipts 1118
Newspaper, book and directory publishers:
Earnings 613, 1115
Employees 613, 1115
Establishments 1115
Finances 1123
Inventory 1123
Revenue 1114, 1123
Newsprint 851
Producer prices 849
Nicaragua. See Foreign countries.
Nickel 860, 864, 866, 1299
Consumption 861
Employment 861
Foreign trade 861, 866, 1299
Prices 861
Production and value 860, 861, 864
World production 864, 1363
Niger. See Foreign countries.
Nigeria. See Foreign countries.
Nitrogen in ammonia, world production ... 861,
                                      864, 1363
Nobel prize laureates 786

Nonemployer establishments .. 558, 729, 1026,
                          1156, 1221, 1227, 1264
Nonfinancial corporations. See Corporations.
Nonmetallic mineral mining and quarrying,
except fuels:
Capital 859
Earnings 859
Employees 859
Establishments 859
Finances 760
Gross domestic product 843
Industrial production index 754
Occupational safety 634
Productivity 615
Shipments, receipts 859
Value added 859
Nonmetallic mineral product manufacturing (see
also Metals and metal products):
Earnings 613, 973, 976, 984
Electronic commerce 980
Employees ... 613, 973, 976, 978, 982, 984
Establishments 973
Foreign trade 978, 1302
Gross domestic product 642, 972
Occupational safety 633, 634
Patents 745
Pollution abatement 371
Productivity 615
Profits 760
Sales, shipments, receipts ... 976, 978, 980,
                                      986, 987
Stone, clay, and glass 1107, 1108
Toxic chemical releases 367
North Carolina. See State data.
North Dakota. See State data.
Northern Mariana Islands. See Island areas of
the U.S.
North Korea. See Foreign countries.
Norway. See Foreign countries.
Nuclear power 908, 909, 910
Capacity 901, 909, 910, 1369
Commercial generation, by country ... 1369
Consumption ... 884, 885, 887, 1365, 1366
Production . 901, 909, 910, 1364, 1368, 1369
Reactors 910, 1369
State data 909, 910
Waste discharged fuel 908, 1332
Nursery and greenhouse products 801, 826
Nursing personnel 148, 150
Employment 597
Projections 599
Nursing and residential care facilities:
Earnings 613, 728
Employees 147, 171, 613, 728
Establishments 167, 171, 728
Expenditures 114, 116, 117, 118, 123
Consumer 116, 117
Receipts 145, 146, 728
Residents 66, 171, 172
Nursing programs, students, and graduates . 151
Nutrition:
Consumption of major commodities ... 199,
                                      200, 201
Nutrients and nutritional intake 197
Nutritional deficiencies, deaths 102
Nuts:
Cash receipts, marketing 801
Consumption 813, 828
Foreign trade 815, 817, 828
Production 828, 1355

NOTE: Index citations refer to **table** numbers, not page numbers.

O

Oats 798, 813
Obstetricians (See also Physicians) 149
Occupational safety 633, 634
Occupations (see also individual occupations):
  Adult education 288
  American Indian, Alaska Native population ..
                                        37
  Asian population 37, 597, 600
  Black, African American population . 34, 597,
                                       600
  Computer use 617
  Earnings 620, 623, 624
  Employment . 587, 588, 589, 597, 598, 600
    Black, African American population . 597,
                                     600
    Employee benefits 630
    Flexible schedules 588
    Hispanic origin population 597
    Home-based work 587
    Projections 597
    Race 597
    Sex 597, 601
    Shift work 589
    State data 598
  Employment cost index 625
  Hispanic origin population 597
  Job search 604
  Labor union membership 639
  Mobility status 28
  Native Hawaiian, Other Pacific Islander
    population 37
  Pension plan/health plan coverage 629
  White-collar and blue-collar workers 625
Ocean perch, Atlantic 854
Office buildings (see also Commercial
  buildings) 970
  Construction 969
  Vacancy rates 969, 971
Office equipment. See Computer and office
  equipment.
Office supplies, stationary and gift stores . 613,
                                       615
Offshore leases 869
Ohio. See State data.
Oil. See Petroleum and products.
Oil and gas extraction industry:
  Capital 371, 859
  Earnings 613, 728, 859
  Employees 613, 728, 859
  Establishments 728, 859
  Gross domestic product 642, 843
  Mergers and acquisitions 742
  Multinational companies 763
  Occupational safety 634
  Output 858
  Patents 745
  Pollution abatement 371
  Production indexes 858
  Productivity 615
  Shipments, receipts 728, 859
  Value added 859
Oil crops 801, 806, 810, 812
Oilseeds 810, 1359
Oil spills 358
Oils:
  Animal (oils and fats) 199, 817
  Animal and vegetable, foreign trade ... 814,
                                       817

Oils: —Con.
  Vegetable:
    Foreign trade . 810, 813, 814, 815, 817,
                                 1299
    Production, consumption, and stocks . 199,
                        813, 814, 1355
Oklahoma. See State data.
Old-age pensions. See Pensions.
Old-age, survivors, disability, and health insur-
  ance. See Social insurance.
Olives 813, 830
Oman. See Foreign countries.
Onions 200, 712, 801, 813, 829
Opera 1230, 1232
Operations performed, medical 165
Ophthalmologists 149
Optical goods 116, 117
Optometrists 116, 117, 145
Optometry schools, students, graduates ... 151
Oranges 200, 801, 813, 830
Oregon. See State data.
Ores, crude. (see also individual ores):
  World production 864
Organ transplants 164
Organic farmland, livestock 798
Orphans 6
Osteopaths (see also Physicians) 149
Otolaryngology 149
Outdoor recreation activities (see also Recre-
  ation and specific forms of recreation) . 1233,
                          1241, 1245, 1246
Outlays, Federal budget ... 461, 462, 463, 464,
                                       465
Outpatient care centers industry 145
Outpatient hospital visits 157, 159
Overweight 194
Oysters 854, 856, 857

P

Pacific Islander population (See also Native
  Hawaiian, Other Pacific Islander population) ..
                                    22, 218
Pagers 1007
Pain relievers, illegal use 186
Pakistan. See Foreign countries.
Pakistani population 22
Palau. See Foreign countries.
Panama. See Foreign countries.
Paper and paperboard products:
  Foreign trade 1299
  Producer prices 849
  Production 851
  Railroad car loadings 1107, 1108
  Recycling 364
Paper products, manufacturing:
  Capital 371
  Earnings 613, 973, 976, 984
  Electronic commerce 980
  Employees ... 613, 973, 976, 978, 982, 984
  Establishments 973
  Finances 760
  Foreign trade 978, 1302
  Gross domestic product 642, 843, 972
  Industrial production index 754
  Mergers and acquisitions 742
  Occupational safety 634
  Output 851
  Pollution abatement 371
  Productivity 615

NOTE: Index citations refer to **table** numbers, not page numbers.

U.S. Census Bureau, Statistical Abstract of the United States: 2004-2005

Paper products, manufacturing: —Con.
Profits 760
Research and development 777
Sales, shipments, receipts ... 830, 976, 978,
980, 986, 987
Toxic chemical releases 367
Papua New Guinea. See Foreign countries.
Paraguay. See Foreign countries.
Paris CAC-40 stock market index 1376
Parks 1249, 1250
Finances 1249, 1250
Government employment and payrolls . 454
National 1249
State 1250
Parolees (see also Correctional institutions, and
Prisons and prisoners) 337
Parties, political. See Political parties.
Partnerships, establishments and finances . 716,
717, 718, 720, 721
Passenger transit industry (see also Passengers):
Earnings 613
Employees 615
Occupational safety 634
Passengers (see also Passenger transit industry
and various transportation modes):
Arriving from overseas ... 1254, 1255, 1256
Border crossings 1261
Carrier operation, summary 1054, 1100,
1101, 1106
Air 1054, 1063
Rail 1106
Outlays, by type of transport 1048
Passenger traffic, volume 1049
Railroads 1106
Patents and trademarks ... 744, 745, 746, 1348
Pathologists 149
Payrolls. Earnings and individual industries.
PCP usage 186
Peaches 200, 801, 830
Peanuts 199, 801
Peanut butter 712
Pears 200, 712, 830
Peas 829
Peat 860, 861
Pecans 801, 830
Pediatricians (see also Physicians) 149, 153
Pennsylvania. See State data.
Pensions and retirement benefits (see also
Social insurance):
Expenditures 529, 658
Families receiving 521, 536
Funds (flow of funds) 1158, 1161, 1213
Government employees . 521, 529, 530, 531
Plans 534, 537
Railroad 521
Retirement and pension plans 529, 532,
533, 629, 1193, 1210, 1211, 1212
Veterans 512, 521
Peppers 712, 801, 813, 829
Perch 857, 972
Performing arts 1227, 1230, 1238
Performing arts, spectator sports industry:
Earnings 613, 728, 1226
Employees 613, 728, 1226
Establishments 728, 1226
Nonemployers 1227
Receipts, revenue 728, 1224, 1227
Periodical prices. (See also Information industry
and Publishing industry) 1127

Periodical publishing 1123
Perlite 860, 861
Personal care workers 597
Personal care price indexes 700
Personal computers. See Computers.
Personal consumption expenditures .. 641, 644,
648, 706, 707, 1229
Chain-type price indexes 706
Recreation 1229
Personal health care:
Expenditures 116, 117, 119, 120
Practices 186, 188
Personal income 650, 652, 653, 654, 655
Personal savings 651, 656
Personal and laundry services (formerly per-
sonal supply services):
Earnings 613, 728, 1265
Employees 613, 728, 1265, 1277
Establishments 728, 1265
Finances 718
Occupational safety 634
Productivity 615
Receipts 718, 728, 1277
Pertussis 177
Peru. See Foreign countries.
Pesticides 821
Pet ownership 1236
Petroleum and coal product manufacturing:
Capital 371
Earnings 613, 973, 984
Employees 613, 973, 978, 982, 984
Establishments 973
Finances 760, 900
Foreign investments in U.S. 1283, 1284,
1286
Foreign trade 978, 1302
Gross domestic product 642, 972
Industrial production index 754
Mergers and acquisitions 742
Multinational companies 762
Occupational safety 634
Pollution abatement 371
Productivity 615
Profits 759, 760, 899, 900
Research and development 776, 777
Sales, shipments 859, 978, 986, 987
Toxic chemical releases 367
Petroleum products:
Consumption 866, 884, 885, 887, 1365,
1366
Foreign trade . 866, 867, 885, 895, 896, 897,
898, 899, 1293, 1302
Lease revenues 869
Oilspills 358
Prices 862, 894
Production .. 860, 862, 864, 867, 869, 872,
876, 884, 885
World 864, 872, 1363, 1364, 1367
Railroad, car loadings of 1107, 1108
Refineries 867
Reserves 867, 871
Stocks 898
Strategic reserve 898
Value 868, 870
Wells 867, 868
Drilling costs 868
Leases and production 869
Pharmaceutical and medicine manufacturing:
Earnings 613, 973, 976

NOTE: Index citations refer to **table** numbers, not page numbers.

Pharmaceutical and medicine manufacturing: —Con.
Employees 613, 785, 973, 976
Mergers and acquisitions 742
Multinational companies 763
Productivity 615
Shipments 976, 997
Pharmacies and drug stores:
Earnings 1019, 1022
Employees 1019, 1022
Establishments 1019, 1022
Sales 1020, 1022
Pharmacists 597
Pharmacy schools, students, graduates 151
Philanthropy 561, 562, 563, 565, 566
Philippines. See Foreign countries.
Phonograph records and tapes 1135
Phosphate rock:
Consumption 861
Employment 861
Foreign trade 861
Prices 861
Production and value 860
World production 864, 1363
Photographic equipment and supplies 1299
Physical activity 195
Physical sciences:
Degrees conferred . 284, 285, 286, 773, 775
Employees 597, 773, 779
Physicians 147, 149, 150, 152
Degrees conferred 287
Earnings 153
Employment 149, 150, 597
Expenditures for .. 114, 116, 117, 118, 119,
120, 121, 123
Foreign countries 1324
Foreign medical school graduates 149
Medical schools, students and graduates ...
151, 287
Offices 145, 146
Patient care activities 153
Price index 124
Specialty and professional activity 149
State data 150
Type of practice 149
Visits to 152, 154, 155
Physics (see also Physical sciences):
Nobel prize laureates 786
Salary offers 281
Physiology:
Degrees conferred 773
Employment 773
Nobel prize laureates 786
Salary 773
Pig iron. See Iron.
Piggyback, railroad carloads 1062
Pigs. See Hogs.
Pilchard. See Sardines.
Pineapples 200, 830
Pipe (smoking), usage 186
Pipeline, freight and mileage 1046, 1110
Pipelines, transportation industry:
Capital 1110
Earnings 613, 1050, 1051, 1052
Employees 613, 1050, 1051, 1052
Establishments 1050, 1052
Finances 1110
Gross domestic product 642
Occupational safety 634

Pipelines, transportation industry: —Con.
Output 1110
Revenue 1050
Pistachios 801, 830
Pistols. See Firearms.
Plague 177
Plants 826, 1235
Plastic and rubber products manufacturing:
Capital 371
Earnings 613, 973, 976, 984
Electronic commerce 980
Employees .. 587, 613, 973, 976, 978, 982,
984
Establishments 973
Finances 760
Foreign trade 978, 1302
Gross domestic product 642, 972
Industrial production index 754
Inventories 987
Mergers and acquisitions 742
Occupational safety 633, 634
Patents 745
Pollution abatement 371
Productivity 615
Profits 760
Sales, shipments, receipts ... 976, 978, 980,
986, 987
Toxic chemical releases 367
Plastic surgeons 149
Plastics 1299
Platinum-group metals 861
Consumption 861
Employment 861
Foreign trade 861, 866
Prices 861, 862
Production 861
Strategic and critical materials 865
Plumbing 967
Plums and prunes 200, 830
Plural births 80
Plywood:
Consumption 846
Foreign trade 846, 847
Output 846
Producer price indexes 849
Pneumonia 102, 104, 105, 156, 163
Poland. See Foreign countries.
Police. See Law enforcement and Public safety.
Poliomyelitis 178
Political action committees (PAC) . 411, 412, 413,
416
Political parties, organizations:
Campaign finances 414, 415, 416
Political action committees (PAC) ... 413,
416
Congress, composition of 393, 394
Congressional districts 391
Governors, by party affiliation 399
Public confidence 404
State legislatures, composition of . 401, 402
Volunteers 567, 568
Voter identification 409
Votes ... 384, 386, 387, 388, 389, 392, 400
Pollock 854, 857
Pollution:
Abatement expenditures 370, 371
Air 359, 360, 361, 370, 371
Hazardous waste sites 369
Industry 372

NOTE: Index citations refer to **table** numbers, not page numbers.

U.S. Census Bureau, Statistical Abstract of the United States: 2004-2005

Pollution: —Con.
Motor vehicle emissions 361
Oilspills 356, 358
Toxic releases 366, 367, 368
Wastewater treatment 917
Water 358, 371
Poor persons. See Income and Poverty.
Population (see also Vital statistics):
  Age:
    American Indian, Alaska Native popula-
      tion 14, 15, 16
    Asian population 14, 15, 16, 38
    Black, African American population .. 11,
                        14, 15, 16, 33
    Distribution 11, 12, 14, 16, 20, 46
    Foreign born 44
    Hispanic origin population . 14, 15, 16, 40
    Island areas 1305
    Native Hawaiian, Other Pacific Islander ..
                          14, 15
    Race 11, 14, 15, 16, 33
    School enrollment 204, 207
    Sex 11, 12, 22
    Voting-age population 407, 410
  American Indian, Alaska Native. See Ameri-
    can Indian, Alaskan Native population.
  Ancestry 47
  Asian, Pacific Islander population. See Asian,
    Pacific Islander population.
  Asian population. See Asian population.
  Black. See Black, African American popula-
    tion.
  Cities 26, 27
  Civilian 2
  Coastal 23
  Components of change 4, 19
  Continents 1319
  Density 1, 17
    Foreign countries 1321
  Developed countries 1320
  Elderly 11, 14, 15, 16, 20, 31, 65
  Ethnic origin 47
  Fertility 75
  Foreign born 42, 45, 46
    Students 211
  Foreign countries 1320, 1321, 1322
  Group quarters 66
  Hispanic origin. See Hispanic origin popula-
    tion.
  Households and/or families. See Households
    or families.
  Immigrants 5, 6, 8, 9, 10
  Island areas of the U.S. .. 1303, 1305, 1306,
                            1309
  Labor force. See Labor force, employment
    and earnings.
  Less developed countries 1320
  Marital status. See Marital status of popula-
    tion.
  Metropolitan areas 24
  Migration 28, 29
  Mobility 28, 29
  Native Hawaiian, Other Pacific Islander
    population. See Native Hawaiian, Other
    Pacific Islander population.
  Nativity 42, 46
  Place of birth 42
  Projections 3, 4, 12, 16

Population (see also Vital statistics): —Con.
Race 13, 14, 15, 16
  States 21
Resident 1, 2, 3, 4, 11, 20, 23
Rural 25
Sex 11, 12, 13, 46
States 17, 18, 19, 20, 21
  American Indian, Alaska Native popula-
    tion 21
  Asian 21
  Black, African American population ... 21
  Density 18
  Hispanic origin population 21
  Native Hawaiian, Other Pacific Islander ..
                             21
  Race 21
  Voting age 407, 410
Total, including Armed Forces overseas ... 2
Townships and special districts 419
Veterans 514
Urban 25
World 1318, 1320, 1321, 1322
Pork (see also Meat and meat products):
  Consumption 199, 813, 831
  Foreign trade 812, 813, 831
  Production 831, 832, 1357
  Supply 831
Pork chops 712
Portland cement 860
Ports, U.S. 1068
Portugal. See Foreign countries.
Postal rates 1111
Postal Service 1112, 1122
  Productivity 615
Potash (potassium salts) 860, 861, 864
Potassium, foreign trade 866
Potatoes:
  Acreage 822, 829
  Consumption 200, 813, 827
  Farm marketings, sales 801
  Foreign trade 827
  Pesticide usage 821
  Prices 712, 806, 822
  Production 822, 827, 829
Poultry (see also Eggs):
  Cholesterol source 198
  Consumer expenditures 660, 661
  Consumption 199, 831
  Farm marketings, sales 801, 804
  Foreign trade 815, 817, 831
  Iron (dietary), source 198
  Number on farms 839
  Organic 798
  Prices 712, 806, 839
  Production and sales ... 807, 831, 839, 840,
                            1355
    Foreign countries 1357
  Value 839
Poverty:
  Asian and Pacific Islander population .. 683,
                             684
  Asian population 38, 682, 683, 684, 686
  Black, African American population:
    Families 33, 682, 690
    Persons ... 33, 672, 682, 683, 684, 686,
                             689
    Children 684, 686
    Families 689, 690, 55

NOTE: Index citations refer to **table** numbers, not page numbers.

U.S. Census Bureau, Statistical Abstract of the United States: 2004-2005

Table

Poverty: —Con.
Asian and Pacific Islander population . 689
Asian population 38, 689, 690
Black, African American population .. 33,
682, 690
Educational attainment 690
Elderly 673
Hispanic origin population 40, 690
Housing 920
Labor force 687, 690
Native Hawaiian, Other Pacific Islander
population 39
Foreign born 44, 46
Hispanic origin population:
Families 40, 690
Persons 40, 672, 682, 683, 684, 686
Native Hawaiian, Other Pacific Islander
population 39
Persons 682
Age 686, 687
American Indian, Alaska Native 682
Asian population 38, 682
Black, African American population .. 33,
672, 682, 683, 684, 686, 689
Children 684, 686
Elderly 31, 686
Hispanic origin population . 40, 672, 682,
683, 684, 686
Native Hawaiian and Other Pacific
Islander 39, 682
State 688
Threshold 685
Power (see also Electric light and power indus-try):
Electric . 901, 902, 903, 904, 906, 907, 910
Hydro 901
Nuclear 901, 1369
Prices 710, 889
Water 356, 912
Power generation and supply industry . 613, 615
Power plants. See Electric light and power
industry.
Precipitation, selected cities 380, 381, 382,
1331
Pregnancies 84, 155
Smoking during pregnancy 84
Teen pregnancies 71, 72, 73, 78, 79, 81
Prenatal care 71, 78, 82
Prescription drugs 114, 116, 117, 118, 119,
120, 122, 123, 124, 143, 700
President, U.S., elections for . 384, 385, 386, 387,
388, 410
Campaign finances 413, 414
Prices (see also individual commodities):
Bonds 1199, 1203
Books and periodicals 1127, 1130
Electricity 710, 889, 905
Energy 894
Fish, by species 853
Food 711, 712
Foreign countries 702, 1342, 1343
Housing 934, 935, 936, 937, 939
Indexes:
Airline cost 1055
Construction materials 920
Consumer price 698, 700, 1342
Foreign countries 1342
Medical care 124

Table

Prices (see also individual commodities): —Con.
Metropolitan areas 699, 701
Exports 714
Imports 708, 713
Producer prices 703
Construction materials 920
Railroad freight 1109
Stage-of-processing 703
Timber 849
Purchasing power of the dollar 697
Received by farmers 806
School expenditures 239
Spot market price 709
Lumber and stumpage 850
Mineral products (see also individual miner-als) 862
Received by farmers:
Crops 822
Indexes 806
Livestock and products, poultry . 832, 839
Stocks 1199, 1203
Primaries, Presidential preference 414
Primary metal manufacturing:
Capital 371
Earnings 613, 973, 976, 984
Electronic commerce 980
Employees ... 613, 973, 976, 978, 982, 984
Establishments 973
Finance 760, 999
Foreign trade 978, 999, 1302
Gross domestic product 642, 972
Industrial production index 754
Mergers and acquisitions 742
Occupational safety 634
Patents 745
Pollution abatement 371
Productivity 615
Profits 759, 760
Research and development 777
Shipments . 976, 978, 980, 986, 987, 1000,
1001
Toxic chemical releases 367
Printing and related support activities. See Pub-lishing industry.
Prisons and prisoners (see also Correctional institutions) ... 335, 336, 338, 339, 340, 341,
342, 343
Death sentence 339, 340, 341, 342
Executions 341, 342
Expenditures 440, 442
Inmate characteristics 335
Sentence, by offense 325
Probation 337
Producer price indexes 703, 704, 705
Construction materials 920
Railroad freight 1109
Stage-of-processing 703
Timber 849
Productivity (see also individual industries):
Capacity utilization 755
Farm output 819
Labor 616, 1341, 1370, 1371
Mining industries 878
Professional and business services:
Earnings 611, 613, 619
Employees 611, 612, 613
Hours 611

NOTE: Index citations refer to **table** numbers, not page numbers.

U.S. Census Bureau, Statistical Abstract of the United States: 2004-2005

Professional, scientific and technical services:
  Capital 751
  Earnings ... 611, 613, 728, 731, 732, 1266,
                                            1272
  Employees .. 611, 613, 728, 731, 732, 1266
  Establishments . 728, 729, 731, 1264, 1266
  Finances 718, 721
  Gross domestic product 642
  Hours 611
  Multinational companies 762
  Nonemployers 729, 1264
  Profits 758
  Sales, receipts . 718, 721, 726, 727, 728, 729,
                                            1264
Profits 725, 1027, 1170, 1171, 1215, 1218
  Corporations . 651, 716, 757, 758, 759, 760,
                                             989
  Partnerships and proprietorships . 716, 719,
                                             720
Projections:
  Births 76, 1325
  College enrollment 202, 204
  Deaths 1325
  Degrees conferred 204
  Employment 599, 602
  Energy 885
  Health expenditures 114, 116, 119
  High school graduates 204
  Labor force 570, 599, 602
  Life expectancy 92, 1325
  Population 3, 12, 16, 1321
  School enrollment 202, 204
  Teachers 204
Property and casualty insurance 1218
  Fire losses 343, 344, 345
Property tax 429, 440
  Rates, selected cities 446
  State and local government 428
Proprietors' income 650
Proprietorships 716, 718, 719
Prostitution and commercialized vice, arrests ..
                                             309
Protective service workers. See Public safety.
Protein available for consumption 197
Protestants. See Religion.
Prunes and plums 200, 830
Psychiatric care and institutions. See Mental
  hospitals.
Psychology:
  Degrees conferred 284, 285, 286, 775
  Employment 597
  Research, U.S. government obligations for ..
                                             768
Psychotherapeutic drugs, nonmedical use .. 186
Public administration. See Government.
Public aid, assistance ../............. 523, 544
  Benefits paid ..../.................... 544
  Federal aid to State and local governments ..
                                         424, 425
  Federal expenditures ... 115, 118, 129, 133,
                      134, 522, 523, 524, 545, 546
  Health expenditures 115, 118, 129, 133,
                      134, 522, 523, 524
  Recipients 521, 522, 524, 544, 545, 546
Public domain. See Public lands.
Public housing 425, 522, 523, 524
Public lands (see also Forests):
  Area 347, 350, 490
  Cost and usage 490

Public lands (see also Forests): —Con.
  Leases, permits, licenses 490, 869
  National forests 844
  National park system 1249
  Ownership 490
  Recreation 1249
Public officials, prosecutions 326
Public roads. See Highways.
Public safety (see also Law enforcement):
  Employment 597
  City government 459
  Fire protection 454
  Police protection and correction 454,
                                             457
  Expenditures 320
  City government 450
  Construction, value 923, 924
  Local government 444
  State and local government 428
  State government 440
  Volunteers 567, 568
Public schools. See Education.
Public transportation indexes 700
Publishing. See Books, Newspapers and Print-
  ing.
  Books 1128, 1129, 1132
  Newspapers 1122, 1124, 1125, 1126
  Periodicals 1127
Publishing industries:
  Capital 371
  Earnings 613, 728, 1113, 1115
  Employees 613, 728, 1113, 1115
  Establishments 728, 1113, 1115
  Finances 760
  Gross domestic product 642, 972
  Industrial production index 754
  Pollution abatement 371
  Profit 760
  Receipts, revenue .. 728, 1113, 1114, 1123,
                                       1131, 1133
Puerto Rico. See Island areas of the U.S.
Puerto Rican population (see also Hispanic ori-
  gin population) 22, 40
  Agriculture 1314, 1315
  Business owners 703, 737
  Commuting to work 41
  Disability status 41
  Educational attainment 41, 194, 213
  Foreign born 41
  Labor force 544, 571
  Mobility status 41
  Nativity 41
  Occupation 41
  Population 22, 23, 29, 34
Pulmonary diseases ... 102, 104, 106, 163, 177
Pulpwood 846, 847
Pulses 200, 1355
Pumice and pumicite 860, 861
Purchasing power of the dollar 697
Pyrites 860

Q

Qatar. See Foreign countries.
Quarries. See Mining industries.
Quicksilver (mercury) 860

R

Rabies 177
Racetrack operations 1239

NOTE: Index citations refer to **table** numbers, not page numbers.

Racquetball 1241
Radiologists 149
Radio broadcasting:
  Advertising expenditures 1274
  Public confidence in media 404
Radio broadcasting industry (See Broadcasting
and telecommunications):
  Earnings 613, 1115
  Employees 613, 1115, 1137
  Establishments 1115
  Finances 1118, 1137
  Mergers and acquisitions 742
  Productivity 615
  Revenue 1114, 1118, 1137
  Stations 1120
Radios:
  Audience characteristics 1119, 1121
  Households with 1120
  Listening 1119
Railroad employees retirement funds 519
Rail transportation industry (See also Railroads):
  Earnings 613, 1106
  Employees 613, 1106, 1106
  Finances 1106, 1189
  Gross domestic product 642
  Productivity 615, 1106
Railroads:
  AMTRAK 1106
  Carloadings, by commodity 1107, 1108
  Equipment in service 1106
  Freight price indexes 1109
  Freight traffic 1049, 1106, 1107, 1108
  Mileage owned and operated 1106
  Occupational safety 1053, 1106
  Passenger traffic and revenue .. 1049, 1106
  Piggyback 1107, 1108
  Vehicles 1047
Rainfall, selected cities 380, 381, 1331
Raisins 801
Rankings:
  Airport traffic 1056
  Cities:
    Population 26, 27
    Residential property tax 446
  Countries:
    Consumption of beef, pork, poultry . 1358
    Exports and imports of wheat, rice, corn .
                                         1360
    Population 1321
  Exports 1296
  Federal R&D obligations to higher education .
                                         772
  Hazardous waste sites 368
  Sports participation 1241
  State:
    Domestic travel expenditures 1253
    Farm marketings 805
    Foreign trade 1294
    Government finances 441
    Personal income per capita 653
      Disposable 654
    Population 18
    Public elementary/secondary school
      finances 241
Rape, forcible ... 289, 290, 291, 292, 298, 299,
                        305, 306, 307, 308
Rapeseed 1355
Rare-earth minerals 861
Raw materials. See Crude materials.

Reading (see also Books and Libraries) . 660, 661,
                         1228, 1232, 1238
  Consumer price indexes 700
Real estate and rental and leasing industry:
  Capital 751, 766
  Earnings 611, 613, 618, 728, 731, 732,
                                   1155, 1222
  Employees .. 597, 611, 613, 728, 731, 732,
                                   1155, 1222
  Establishments . 728, 729, 731, 1155, 1221,
                                         1222
  Finances 718, 721
  Gross domestic product 642, 1154
  Hours 611
  Mergers and acquisitions 742
  Nonemployers 729, 1221
  Receipts 718, 721, 726, 727, 728, 729,
                             1155, 1221, 1222
Receipts (see also individual industries and Tax
receipts):
  Corporations, partnerships, and proprietor-
    ships . 716, 717, 718, 719, 720, 721, 725,
                                    726, 727
  International transportation 1278
  Minority-owned businesses 737
  Revenue:
    Local governments 429, 443
      City governments 449, 450
      County governments 451
    State and local governments combined ..
                             427, 428, 434
    State governments .. 429, 439, 440, 441
    Tax collections 441
  United States Government ... 420, 429, 461,
                                    467, 474
  Women-owned businesses 737, 738
Recreation (see also Arts, entertainment, and
recreation and Sports):
  Activities 195, 1119, 1230, 1232, 1233,
    1234, 1235, 1238, 1239, 1240, 1241, 1249,
                                         1250
  Building construction, value 925
  Consumer expenditures . 1119, 1128, 1228,
                             1229, 1247, 1248
  Consumer price indexes 700
  Employment and expenditures, government .
                                         465
    City governments 454
    County governments 451
  Parks:
    Government expenditures 428, 430
    National 1249
    Visits 1249, 1250
  Performing arts 1230
  Spectator sports 1239
  Travel . 1251, 1252, 1253, 1254, 1255, 1259,
                                         1261
  Volunteers 567, 568
RV parks and recreational camps 613
Recreational vehicles 1047, 1240, 1247
Recycling waste 363, 364, 365, 366
Refrigerators and refrigeration equipment . 1015
Refugees 6, 9
Refuse collection 365, 700
Religion 67, 68, 69
  Charitable contributions 562
  Philanthropy 563, 566

NOTE: Index citations refer to **table** numbers, not page numbers.

Religious, grantmaking, civic, professional orga-
nizations:
  Employees 728, 1265
  Establishments 728, 1265
  Revenues 728, 1277
  Volunteers 567, 568
Religious identification 67
Rental and leasing services:
  Earnings 1155, 1222, 1265
  Electronic commerce 1267
  Employees 1155, 1222, 1265
  Establishments 1155, 1222, 1265
  Revenues 1155, 1223, 1267
Rental property 691, 692
Renters insurance 1220
Rents 700, 958, 959, 960
Repair services. See Automobile repair and
  maintenance service.
Representatives, U.S. See Congress, U.S.
Research and development:
  Employment 778
  Expenditures:
    College and universities 765, 770
    Federal .. 764, 765, 766, 767, 769, 771,
                                          772
    Foreign countries 766
    Industry 765
    National defense 493, 764
  Services 1265
Residential buildings. See Construction industry,
  and Housing and housing units.
Residential capital 966
Restaurants. See Food services and drinking
  places.
Retail trade:
  Capital expenditures 748, 751
  Earnings . 611, 613, 618, 619, 728, 731, 732,
                          738, 1018, 1316
  Electronic commerce 1036, 1037
  Employees .. 587, 601, 611, 613, 728, 731,
    732, 738, 1016, 1017, 1018, 1313, 1316
  Establishments . 728, 729, 731, 1018, 1026,
                              1313, 1316
  Finances ... 716, 718, 721, 760, 1184, 1310
  Foreign investments in the U.S. . 1284, 1286
  Gross domestic product 642, 646, 1310
  Hours 611
  Industry 728
  Inventories 756, 1024
  Mergers and acquisitions 742
  Multinational companies 762, 763
  Nonemployers 729, 1026
  Occupational safety 634
  Productivity 615
  Profits 760
  Sales, receipts . 718, 721, 726, 727, 728, 729,
    738, 1018, 1020, 1021, 1023, 1024, 1025,
                      1026, 1036, 1037, 1316
  Women-owned businesses 738
Retirement systems:
  Benefits paid 529
  Civil service 529, 530, 1213
  Defined benefit retirement plans 534
  Federal government .. 529, 530, 1158, 1213
  Government transfer payments ... 518, 519,
                                          520
  Old-age, survivors, disability, and health
    insurance. See Social insurance.
  Pension plans 529, 532, 1213

Retirement systems: —Con.
  Public employees 529
  Railroad 1213
  Social security trust funds 526
  State and local government . 428, 458, 1213
Reunion. See Foreign countries.
Revolvers. See Firearms.
Rhode Island. See State data.
Rice:
  Acreage, organic 798
  Consumption 199, 813
  Farm marketings, sales 801
  Foreign trade 810, 813, 814, 817, 1299
  Production 814
    World 814, 1355
Rifle (NCAA) 1244
Rivers, canals, harbors, etc.:
  Commerce, domestic and foreign 1065
  Drainage area and flow 354
  Length of principal rivers 354
  Water quality 357
Roads, public. See Highways.
Roadway congestion 1083
Robbery ... 289, 290, 291, 292, 303, 305, 306,
                                          307
Rockfish 854, 857
Rodeos 1237, 1239
Roller skating 1241
Romania. See Foreign countries.
Rowing 1244
Rubber, crude natural 810, 812
Rubber and misc. plastics manufacturing. See
  Plastics and rubber products manufacturing.
Rubber products 1299
Rubella 177, 178
Rugs 175, 993
Running/jogging 1241
Rural population. 25
Russell stock indices 1199
Russia. See Foreign countries.
Rwanda. See Foreign countries.

                      S

Sablefish 854
Safflower 801
Sailing 1241
Saint Kitts and Nevis. See Foreign countries.
Saint Lucia. See Foreign countries.
Saint Vincent and the Grenadines. See Foreign
  countries.
Salad and cooking oils, consumption 199
Salaries and wages. See Earnings.
Sales. See individual commodities and indus-
  tries.
Salesworkers 597, 607, 623, 624
Salmon 854
  Canned 856, 857
Salmonellosis 177
Salt (common), production/value 860, 1363
Samoa. See Foreign countries.
Samoa, American. See Island areas of the U.S.
Samoan population 22
Sand and gravel industry (see also Mining
  industry) 859, 860, 861
Sanitation. See Health and Sewage treatment.
San Marino. See Foreign countries.
Sao Tome and Principe. See Foreign countries.
Sardines 857
Saudi Arabia. See Foreign countries.
Sausages 712

NOTE: Index citations refer to **table** numbers, not page numbers.

Savings:
  Credit unions 1176
  Deposits 656, 1161
  Gross savings, sources and uses 651
  Personal 650, 651
Savings banks. See Savings institutions.
Savings bonds 470, 691, 692, 1162
Savings institutions:
  Earnings 1157
  Employees 1157
  Establishments 1157, 1168, 1169
  Finances ... 1158, 1159, 1168, 1171, 1177,
                                          1187
  Individual Retirement Accounts 1212
  Mergers and acquisitions 742
Saw logs 846, 849
Scallops 854, 856
Scenic and sightseeing transportation industry:
  Earnings 613, 1050, 1051, 1052
  Employees 613, 1050, 1051, 1052
  Establishments 1050, 1052
  Revenue 1050
Scholastic Assessment Test (SAT) 248
Schools (see also Education):
  Activities for parents 219
  Alternative 226, 231
  Boards, elected officials 405, 406
  Charter schools 224
  Crimes 217, 229
  Districts 225, 418
  Internet access 242, 243
  Lunch programs 522, 524, 550, 551
  Number 228, 246, 261, 263
  Special education 226
  Violence 310, 311
  Vocational 226
Scientific instruments. See Instruments.
Scientific research. See Research and develop-
  ment.
Scientists and engineers (see also individual
  fields):
  Degrees conferred 284, 285, 286, 775
  Employment 597, 768, 771, 772, 779
  By industrial sector 779
Scrap metal. See individual commodities.
Scuba diving 1241, 1247
Scup, catch 854
Sea bass 854
Seafoods 855
Sea trout 854
Securities:
  Foreign holdings .. 1160, 1198, 1278, 1281,
                                          1377
  Foreign purchases and sales ... 1195, 1197,
                                1374, 1375, 1377
  Government 436, 722, 723, 1160, 1190,
                                    1197, 1198
  Held by life insurance 1217
  Holdings of banks 722, 723, 1169
  Holdings of individuals and businesses . 1161
  New issues 1190, 1194
  Prices, indexes, yields and issues . 1189, 1199,
                          1200, 1203, 1375
  Sales, stocks and bonds . 1190, 1195, 1197,
                                1374, 1375, 1377
  Savings of individuals 651, 656
  State and local government . 417, 722, 723,
                                          1190

Security and commodity brokers:
  Earnings 613, 1155, 1157
  Electronic commerce 1267
  Employees 613, 1155, 1157
  Establishments 1155, 1156, 1157
  Finances 1158, 1214, 1215
  Gross domestic product 1154
  Mergers and acquisitions 742
  Multinational companies 762, 763
  Nonemployers 1156
  Occupational safety 634
  Profits 1215
  Receipts 1155, 1156
Sedatives, persons using 186
Seeds 800
Selenium 866
Selenium, dietary 197
Semiconductors (see also Computer and elec-
  tronic product components) 1003
Senators, U.S. 389, 393, 394, 395, 396
Senegal. See Foreign countries.
Septicemia 102
Serbia and Montenegro. See Foreign countries.
Service industries (see also specific sectors and
  Professional and business services):
  Capital 748
  Earnings 613, 618, 619, 738, 1316
  Electronic commerce 1267
  Employees .. 147, 587, 601, 612, 613, 738,
              756, 765, 1262, 1263, 1313, 1316
  Establishments 716, 1313, 1316
  Finances 1310
  Foreign trade 1278, 1280, 1292
  Gross domestic product 646, 1310
  Industry 728
  Multinational companies 762, 763
  Occupational safety 631, 634, 636
  Productivity 615
  Profits 716, 758
  Sales or receipts 716, 738, 1262, 1263,
                                          1316
  Women-owned businesses 738
Service occupations:
  Benefits 629
  Earnings 623, 624
  Employment 597
    Projections 599
    States 598
  Unemployment 607
  Union membership 639
Service stations. See Gasoline service stations.
Service workers. See Service industries and
  Service occupations.
Sewage treatment systems 425, 917
  Construction 425
  Employment 454
  Expenditures 428
  Residences 947, 951
Sexual assault (see Rape and assault).
Seychelles. See Foreign countries.
Sheep and lambs 798, 801, 831, 832
Shellfish:
  Canned, quantity and value 857
  Catch, quantity and value 854
  Consumption 199
Shelter (see also Housing and housing units),
  consumer price indexes 698, 700
Shigellosis 177
Ship and boat building and repairing:
  Earnings 977

NOTE: Index citations refer to **table** numbers, not page numbers.

U.S. Census Bureau, Statistical Abstract of the United States: 2004-2005

Ship and boat building and repairing: —Con.
Productivity 615
Shipments, manufacturers' (see also individual
products or industries) ... 976, 977, 987, 988
Shipping. See Merchant vessels and Tonnage,
U.S. Flag Fleet.
Ships, U.S. Flag fleet 1067:
Shoes. See Footwear.
Shoe stores 613, 615, 1020
Shoplifting 303
Shopping centers 1040, 1041
Shortening 199
Shrimp 854, 856, 857
Sickness. See Illness.
Sierra Leone. See Foreign countries.
Silicon 861
Silver 860, 864, 866, 867
Consumption 861
Employment 861
Foreign trade 861, 866
Prices 861, 862
Production and value 860, 864, 867
Strategic and critical material 865
World production 864
Silverware. See Jewelry.
Singapore. See Foreign countries.
Single persons. See Marital status.
Single-parent households . 33, 39, 56, 59, 60, 62,
63, 1326, 1328, 1329
Sinusitis 155
Skate boarding 1241
Skiing 1241, 1244, 1247
Skins. See Hides, etc.
Skilled nursing facilities, services 128, 167
Slaughtering and meat-packing industry. See
Meat and meat products.
Slovakia. See Foreign countries.
Slovenia. See Foreign countries.
Small business:
Budget outlays 461
Employees 732, 733, 734, 735
Firms 732, 733, 734, 735
Loans 736
Payroll 732, 733, 735
Smart card 1181
Smoking 84, 186, 188, 189
Snapper 854
Snorkeling 1241
Snow and ice pellets, selected cities 382
Snowboarding 1241
Snowmobiles 1247
Soccer 1237, 1241, 1243, 1244
Social assistance industry:
Earnings 555, 556, 613, 728
Employees 555, 556, 613, 728
Establishments 555, 556, 558, 728
Gross domestic product 642
Nonemployers 558
Receipts 555, 556, 557, 558, 728
Social insurance (see also Medicare, Retirement
systems, and Social Security):
Employment covered 525
Expenditures 518, 519, 520
Government insurance trust funds 429
Federal receipts and expenditures .. 526
State and local receipts, expenditures ....
428, 440, 531
Government transfer payments ... 518, 519,
520

Social insurance (see also Medicare, Retirement systems, and Social Security): —Con.
Individual programs:
Beneficiaries and benefits 527, 528
Coverage 525, 531
Federal retirement insurance . 530, 1213
Civil service 530
Old-age, survivors, disability, and health
insurance:
Contributions 526
Coverage, workers, and earnings . 525
Payments 519, 526, 527, 528
Tax collections 474
Trust funds 526
Railroad insurance 519, 1213
State and local public retirement systems ...
531
Trust funds 1213
Unemployment insurance (federal and State) .
518, 519, 520, 538, 539
Workers' compensation . 115, 118, 519, 541,
542
Social sciences:
Degrees conferred . 284, 285, 286, 773, 775
Employment 597, 773, 779
Salary offers 281
Social Security (Old-age survivors, disability,
and health insurance) (see also Social insurance):
Beneficiaries and payments 527, 528
Contributions, rates 526
Foreign countries 1347
Coverage, workers and earnings 525
Families receiving 521
Food stamp participants 553
Outlays 462
Payments 519, 527, 528
Trust funds 526
Social services:
Capital expenditures 749
Employees 555
Occupational safety 634
Social welfare (see also individual programs):
Charitable contributions 562
Employees (State and local government) . 457
Expenditures:
City government 450
County government 452
State and local government 428
State government 440, 442
Volunteers 567, 568
Sodium, dietary 197
Sodium carbonate 860, 861
Sodium sulfate 860, 861
Soft drinks (see also Beverages) 201
Softball 1241, 1243, 1244
Software publishing industry (see also Publishing) 1007
Earnings 613, 1115
Employees 613, 1115
Establishments 1115
Finances 1133
Inventory 1133
Productivity 615
Revenue 1114, 1133
Software sales 1007
Solar energy 888, 911
Solid waste:
Abatement expenditures 371

NOTE: Index citations refer to **table** numbers, not page numbers.

Solid waste: —Con.
Disposal 363, 364, 431
Industry 372
Landfills 363
Recycling 364, 365
Solomon Islands. See Foreign countries.
Somalia. See Foreign countries.
South Africa. See Foreign countries.
South Carolina. See State data.
South Dakota. See State data.
South Korea. See Foreign countries.
Soybeans:
Acreage 822, 824
Genetically modified seed plantings . 820
Organic 798
Farm marketings, sales 801, 807
Foreign trade 814, 816, 817, 822, 1299
Pesticide usage 821
Prices 822, 824
Production 814, 822, 824
World production 814, 1355
Supply and disappearance 822
Space expenditures, private 780
Space program:
Finances 781, 782, 784
Launches 783
NASA 767, 782
Space shuttle 784, 785
Vehicle systems 781, 1299
Space research and technology, Federal outlays .
465, 781, 784, 1014
Spain. See Foreign countries.
Speeding 1094
Spices, imports 813
Spinach 829
Sporting and athletic goods (see also Sports and
Retail trade) 1247, 1248, 1299
Advertising 1275
Consumer price indexes 700
Retail stores 1020
Sales 430
Sporting goods, hobby, book, and music stores:
Earnings 613, 728, 1019
Electronic commerce 1039
Employees 613, 728, 1019
Establishments 728, 1019, 1026
Nonemployers 1026
Purchases 1023
Productivity 615
Sales .. 728, 1020, 1022, 1024, 1026, 1039
Sports ... 1237, 1238, 1240, 1241, 1242, 1243,
1244
Expenditures 1229, 1247
NCAA 1244
Volunteers 567, 568
Sports associations 72
Sports industry 1224, 1226
Spot market price index 709
Squash (NCAA) 1244
Squid 854, 857
Sri Lanka. See Foreign countries.
Stamps, postage, receipts from 1112
Standard & Poor's stock indices 1199
State and local governments, combined data
(see also individual governmental units):
Component of gross domestic product . 426,
427
Debt 428, 434, 435
Highways 1077

**State and local governments, combined data
(see also individual governmental units):
—Con.**
Employees 335, 453, 454, 457, 458
Benefits 455
Expenditures (see also Finances) .. 427, 428,
429, 430, 431, 434
By type 429, 430
Capital outlay 430, 431
Construction, value 924
Hospitals and medical care 118, 157,
434
Federal aid 423, 424, 425, 463
By function 424, 426, 427
Finances 429
Intergovernmental 424, 428, 432
Flow of funds 1158, 1159
Gross domestic product 642
Hospitals 157, 158
Number of units 417
Payrolls 453, 454
Purchases of goods and services . 426, 427,
641, 643
Receipts 427
By source 429
Retirement systems . 529, 531, 1158, 1193,
1213
Securities issued 436
Women holding public office 403
State Children's Health Insurance program . 135,
524
State data:
Abortions 91
Agriculture:
Farms 795, 797
Income, farm 803, 805
AIDS.................................... 181
Alcohol use 187
Altitudes 351
American Indian, Alaska Native population ..
21
Apparel and accessory stores, sales ... 1025
Area 346
Asian population 21
Assets and liabilities, farm 803
Automotive dealers 1018, 1025
Automobile insurance expenditures ... 1219
Bankruptcies 740
Births and birth rates 19
Birth weight 81
Births to single or unmarried women . 81
Black elected officials 405
Black, African American population 21
Blood alcohol concentration (BAC) 1095
Border crossings 1261
Building materials and garden supplies,
sales 1025
Building permits 927
Cancer 192
Capital punishment 342
Child abuse cases 332
Cigarette smoking 187, 189
Civilian labor force 574
Climate 378, 379, 380, 381, 382, 383
Coal and coke production 878, 881
Commuting to work 1084
Computer use 1153
Congress, U.S., composition 394

NOTE: Index citations refer to **table** numbers, not page numbers.

U.S. Census Bureau, Statistical Abstract of the United States: 2004-2005

State data: —Con.

Congressional apportionment 390
Construction contracts 926
Corrections 433, 457
Crime rates 291
Crops, principal 812, 819, 823, 830
Deaths and death rates 19, 99, 101, 106
Infant 101
Defense contracts 496
Department stores, sales 1025
Disabled population 184
Domestic travel expenditures 1253
Drivers licenses 1082
Drug use 187
Earnings 621, 974, 1018
Eating and drinking places, sales . 1018, 1025
Elections . 386, 387, 389, 392, 394, 400, 401,
                                     408, 410
Voter registration 408
Electrical power 902, 904, 905
Elevations 351
Employees .. 457, 458, 484, 612, 735, 974,
                     977, 979, 1010, 1018
Energy consumption 887
Energy expenditures 890
Energy, renewable 912
Establishments 974, 1018
Exports 979, 1296, 1297
Farms 795, 797
Assets and liabilities 803
Income 803, 805
Federal funds 472
Financial institutions 1174, 1175
Fire protection 444, 457
Food stamp program 551
Food stores 1018, 1025
Foreign born 42
Foreign investment in the U.S. 1285
Foreign trade 979, 1296, 1297
Foreign travel to 1256
Fuel production 868
Furniture, home furnishing stores 1025
Gas utility industry 915
Gasoline prices 715
Gasoline service stations 1025
Gasoline tax rates 1076
General merchandise stores, sales 1025
Government finances:
  Federal aid to State and local govern-
  ments 425
  Federal (income tax collections) 479
  State and local governments .. 368, 432,
                                     433
  State governments .. 439, 440, 441, 442
  Tax collections 447
  Transfer payments 520
Governors, vote cast 400
Gross State product 645, 646
Hazardous waste sites 368
Health care expenditures 123
Health insurance coverage 135, 140
Health maintenance organizations (HMO) . 138
Highway funds 1078
Highway mileage 1070
Highway trust fund 1075
Hispanic elected officials 406
Hispanic population 21
Hospitals 123, 159, 433, 457

State data: —Con.

Housing . 927, 929, 938, 944, 948, 952, 955,
                                         958
Sold 938
Immigrants admitted 10
Income 803
  Disposable personal 652, 654
  Household 664
  Personal 652, 653
Internet access 1153
Land 347
  Federal 490
Language spoken at home 49
Legislatures, composition 401, 402
Livestock 835, 836
Local government units 418
Lotteries, revenue from 447
Manufactures, summary statistics . 979, 983
Marriage and divorce 113
Medicaid 134
Medicare 129
Migration 18, 30
Milk production 836
Mining, mineral production value 863
Motorcycles 1082
Motor fuel tax 1076
Motor vehicle dealers 1018, 1025
Motor vehicle manufacturing 1010
Motor vehicle registrations 1082
National forests 844
Native Hawaiian, Other Pacific Islander
  population 21
Newspapers, number and circulation .. 1126
Nurses 150
Nursing home care expenditures 123
Occupations 598
Parks 1249, 1250
Patents 746
Physicians, physician services 123, 150
Police protection 442, 444, 457
Pollution abatement 371
Population 17, 18, 19, 20, 21
  Age distribution 20
  American Indian, Alaska Native 21
  Asian 21
  Black 21
  Components of change 19
  Density 18
  Hispanic origin population 21
  Native Hawaiian, Other Pacific Islander
  population 21
Poultry 840
Poverty 655
Prescription drug expenditures 123
President, vote cast 384, 386
Prisons and prisoners 309
Public aid 544
Public road and street mileage 1082
Recreational areas 1250
Representatives, U.S. vote cast for 391
Retail trade, sales 1018, 1025
Roads and highways 1070, 1075, 1078
Rural population 25
Sales 1018, 1025, 1041
Schools and education:
  Colleges, number 263
  Educational attainment 216

NOTE: Index citations refer to **table** numbers, not page numbers.

State data: —Con.
Elementary/secondary teachers, public .. 236
Enrollment:
  Elementary and secondary . 226, 230
  Higher education 263
Finances:
  Elementary and secondary, public . 241
  High school graduates, public 253
  Higher education appropriations 274
  Teachers 236
Senators, vote cast for 389
Services industry 1266
Shopping centers 1041
Small businesses 735
Social Security program 129, 528
Supplemental Security Income 544
Taxation 441, 447, 479
Temperatures (highs and lows) 376
Temporary assistance for needy families program 546, 547
Toxic chemical releases 368
Traffic fatalities 1090, 1095
Travel expenditures 1253, 1257
Unemployment 574, 610
Unemployment insurance 520, 538
Union membership 640
Urban population 25
Vehicle miles of travel 1082
Veterans, number and expenditures 512, 520
Voter registration 408
Voter turnout 410
Votes cast 386, 387, 389, 400, 410
Voting age population 408, 410
Water, sewage, and other services 917
Women holding public office 403
State government (see also State and local governments):
  Debt 435, 440, 442
  Public highways 1077
  Employees and payrolls . 453, 454, 457, 458
  Finances . 427, 429, 431, 439, 440, 441, 442
  Revenue from lotteries 447, 448
  Tax collections 441, 447
  Highway funds, disbursements of 1078
  Park systems 1250
  Public confidence 404
  Receipts, highways 1074
  Taxes 441,
State highways. See Highways.
State park systems 1250
Steak 712
Steam engines and turbines, electric, locomotive (railroad) 1106
Steel (see also Iron and steel) ... 864, 999, 1000
  Scrap 999
  World production 864
Steel works and rolling mills. See Iron and steel.
Stimulants, persons using 186
Stock exchanges:
  Prices 1199, 1203
  Volume of trading 1201, 1202, 1203
Stockholders' equity, profit rates on 1170
Stockpiles, government, strategic and critical materials 865
Stocks:
  Corporate, flow of funds 1158, 1193
  Foreign 1196, 1197

Stocks: —Con.
Foreign market indices 1376
Holdings by sector . 1160, 1162, 1193, 1196, 1198
Households 691, 692, 693
Life insurance 1193, 1217
New issues 1194
Ownership 1204, 1205, 1206
Prices, yield, sales, issues, etc. . 1189, 1192, 1199, 1201, 1374, 1375, 1377
Stone 860
Stone, clay, and glass products 1107, 1108
Stone, clay, and concrete products manufacturing. See Nonmetallic mineral product manufacturing.
Stone (crushed) 861
Stoves or ranges 1015
Strategic and critical materials 865
Strategic petroleum reserves 868
Strawberries 801, 813, 829
Strokes (see also Cerebrovascular diseases) . 102, 104, 106, 163
Strontium, foreign trade 866
Students. See Education, enrollment.
Subways and urban railways 1100
Sudan. See Foreign countries.
Sugar and sugar cane (see also Food and kindred products):
  Beet 801, 807
  Consumption 199, 813
  Farm marketings 801
  Foreign trade 812, 813, 1299
  Prices 712
Suicides 102, 104, 105, 106
Sulfur:
  Consumption 861
  Employment 861
  Foreign trade 861, 866
  Prices 861, 862
  Production and value 860, 864
  World production 1363
Sunflowers 798, 801
Supermarkets. See Grocery stores.
Supplemental Security Income .. 519, 521, 524, 543, 544, 553
  States 544
Supreme Court, U.S. 323
Surgeons (See also Physicians) 153
Surgical procedures 165
  Organ transplants, facilities 164
Suriname. See Foreign countries.
Swaziland. See Foreign countries.
Sweden. See Foreign countries.
Sweet potatoes 200, 829
Swimming 1241, 1243, 1244
Swine. See Hogs.
Switzerland. See Foreign countries.
Swordfish, imports 854
Symphony orchestras 1230
Synagogues. See Religion.
Syphilis 177, 181
Syria. See Foreign countries.

T
Taiwan. See Foreign countries.
Tajikistan. See Foreign countries.
Talc, pyrophyllite, and soapstone 860
Tangelos 830
Tangerines 830
Tantalum 866

NOTE: Index citations refer to **table** numbers, not page numbers.

U.S. Census Bureau, Statistical Abstract of the United States: 2004-2005

Tanzania. See Foreign countries.
Target shooting 1241
Tariff. See Customs receipts.
Taxes:
  Corporate 717, 725, 757
  Deductions 475, 477, 561
  Partnerships 720
  Proprietorships 719
Tax burden, expenditures, revenue loss esti-
  mates 471, 1375
Tax receipts:
  Foreign countries 1344, 1345
  Governmental revenue, by type of tax .. 429
  Motor-fuel taxes and motor-vehicle fees . 1076
  National (internal revenue) 429, 474
    Adjusted gross income 476
    By type of tax 429
    Collections by source 474
  Corporation income tax:
    Federal budget receipts 467
    Internal revenue collections . 473, 474
    Tax liabilities 725
    Tax returns filed 473, 725
  Employment taxes 467, 473, 474
  Estate and gift taxes 467, 473, 474
  Excise taxes 467, 473, 474
  Individual income tax 429, 441, 467,
    473, 474, 475, 476, 477, 478, 479
    Average tax by income level 476
    Rates 480, 481
Property tax:
  City government 449
  Rates, selected cities 446
  State and local government 428, 429
State and local government:
  By households 445
  By type of tax 428, 429, 440
  City government 446, 449
  County government 451
  Local government 443
  State government 440, 441, 442
Tea 201
Teachers:
  Catholic schools 246
  Degrees conferred 284, 285, 286
  Employment . 225, 234, 261, 279, 280, 597
    Projections 204, 599
  Private schools 246, 247
  Public schools 204, 225, 236
    Experience, and degrees held .. 235, 247
    Higher education institutions .. 261, 278
    Number 204, 225, 234, 235, 236
    Salaries 225, 236
    States 236
Technicians 598
Teenagers:
  Abortions 90
  AIDS 179
  Alcohol use 186
  Births/birth rates . 72, 73, 76, 78, 79, 81, 85
  Child abuse 331
  Cigarette smoking 186
  Computer use 242, 244, 273, 604
  Cost of raising 657
  Crimes, arrests 217, 218, 306, 312
    Homicide rates 289, 290, 291, 297
  Deaths and death rates 104
  Disabled 269
  Drug use 186

Teenagers: —Con.
  Education:
    College costs 271
    College freshmen, characteristics ... 268
    Enrollment 202, 204, 206, 207, 208,
      209, 225, 230, 232, 233, 246, 259, 260,
                                          266
      Projections 202, 204
    High school dropouts 254, 255
    High school graduates 225, 253, 259
    School crimes 217, 218
    Test scores 248, 249, 250, 251
  Health insurance coverage 139
  Hispanic origin population 14, 15, 16
  Job search 604
  Juvenile delinquency 329, 330
  Labor force 570
    Employed . 582, 583, 588, 589, 590, 592
    Enrollment status 576, 1350
    Minimum wage workers 627
    Multiple job holders 590
    Participation rates 577
    Sex 570, 572
    Unemployed 603, 609
  Life expectancy 94
  Marital status 53
  Mobility status 28
  Music purchases 1136
  Population 11, 14, 15
    Foreign born 16
    Hispanic origin 16, 40
    Projections 12, 16
    Race 14, 15, 16
  Sports activity participation 1241, 1242,
                                          1243
  Sporting goods purchasers 1248
  Suicides 104
  Victimization 306
Telecommunications . 1008, 1142, 1275, 1299,
                                          1372
Telecommunications indicators (Global) ... 1372
Telecommunications industry (See also Broad-
  casting and telecommunications):
  Earnings 613, 1115
  Employees 613, 1115
  Establishments 1115
  Finances 1114, 1140, 1141, 1142
  Productivity 615
Telegraph and other communications . 1142, 1143
Telemarketers 597
Telephone carriers 1142
  Cellular 1144, 1373
Telephone communication:
  Earnings 613, 1142, 1143
  Employees 613, 1143, 1144
  Finances 1143, 1144
  Price indexes 700
  Productivity 615
  Receipts 1143
Telephones (see also Telegraph, etc.):
  Access lines 1143, 1372
  Calls 1143, 1372
  Consumer expenditures 660, 661
  Consumer price index 698
  Households with service .. 951, 1120, 1153
  Number 1143
    Foreign countries 1373
  Sales or shipments 1007, 1008

NOTE: Index citations refer to **table** numbers, not page numbers.

U.S. Census Bureau, Statistical Abstract of the United States: 2004-2005

Television broadcasting (see also Cable and other pay TV services):
  Advertising expenditures 1274
  Mergers and acquisitions 742
  Public confidence in media 404
Television broadcasting industry:
  Earnings 613, 1115, 1117
  Employees 613, 1115, 1117
  Finances 1114, 1115, 1118, 1137, 1139
  Gross domestic product 1116
  Productivity 615
Televisions:
  Consumer expenditures 1228, 1229
  Households with 1120
  Injuries associated 175
  Sales or shipments 1007
  Viewing 1119, 1121
Temperature:
  Cities 378, 379, 380, 383
  Foreign cities 1331
  States (highs and lows) 376
Temples (fruit) 830
Temporary assistance for needy families pro-
  gram . 519, 521, 524, 545, 546, 547, 549, 553
Tennessee. See State data.
Tennis ... 1237, 1240, 1241, 1243, 1244, 1247
Tenure. See Housing and housing units and
  Farms.
Tetanus 177
Texas. See State data.
Textile mill products:
  End-use 993
  Foreign trade 994, 1299, 1302
  Production 994
  World ....
Textile mills and product manufacturing:
  Capital 371
  Earnings 613, 973, 976, 984
  Electronic commerce 976, 980
  Employees ... 613, 973, 976, 978, 982, 984
  Establishments 973
  Finances 760
  Foreign trade 978, 1302
  Gross domestic product 642, 972
  Industrial production index 754
  Inventories 987
  Mergers and acquisitions 742
  Occupational safety 634
  Patents 745
  Pollution abatement 371
  Productivity 615
  Profits 760
  Shipments 976, 978, 980, 986, 987
  Toxic chemical releases 367
Thai population 22
Thailand. See Foreign countries.
Theaters:
  Attendance and receipts 1230, 1238
  Federal aid 1231
  Personal expenditures 1127
Theft. See Crime and criminals.
Theology, degrees conferred 287
Thread. See Yarn, thread, etc.
Thrift Savings Plan 529, 691, 692
Timber (see also Lumber and wood products):
  Consumption 846
  Foreign trade 846, 847
  Producer prices 849, 850
  Production 846
  Roundwood products 846

Tin:
  Foreign trade 866
  Prices 862
  Production 864
    World 1363
  Strategic and critical materials 865
Tires and tubes 1299
Titanium:
  Production 860, 864, 874
  Strategic and critical material 865
  World production 864
Tobacco (see also Tobacco products, manufac-
  turing, and Cigarettes):
  Consumer expenditures 658, 660, 661
  Consumption and use .. 186, 188, 189, 992
    During pregnancy 84
  Farm marketings, sales 801
  Foreign countries 1361
  Foreign trade 810, 814, 1299, 1361
  Prices 700, 806
  Production 1361
  Taxes 440, 474
Tobacco manufacturing (see also Beverage and
  tobacco product manufacturing):
  Earnings 984
  Employees 984
  Foreign trade 1302
  Inventories 987
  Mergers 742
  Occupational safety 634
  Price indexes 700
  Shipments 986, 987
  Toxic chemical releases 367
Togo. See Foreign countries.
Tokyo Nikkei 225 stock market index 1376
Tomatoes 200, 712, 801, 813, 829
Tonga. See Foreign countries.
Tonnage, U.S. Flag fleet 1067
Tools. See Machine tools.
Tornadoes 374
Tourism, foreign (see also Travel) .. 1254, 1255,
                                   1256, 1258, 1261
Townships and special districts 417, 418
Toxic-shock syndrome 177
Toys and sporting goods:
  Consumer expenditures 1229
  Foreign trade 1299
  Price indexes 700
Track 1243, 1244
Trade (business). See Commerce, Foreign trade,
  Retail trade, and Wholesale trade.
Trade, transportation and utilities:
  Earnings 611, 613, 619
  Employees 611, 612, 613
  Hours 611
Traffic fatalities . 1053, 1089, 1090, 1091, 1092,
                                   1094, 1095, 1096
Tranquilizers ..⁻............................ 186
Transit and ground transportation industry. Also
  see, Passenger transit industry.
  Earnings 613, 1050, 1051, 1052
  Employees 613, 1050, 1051, 1052
  Establishments 1050, 1052
  Gross domestic product 642
  Revenue 1050
Transit systems:
  Characteristics 1102
  Cities served 1102
  Mileage 1046
  Trips taken 1103

NOTE: Index citations refer to **table** numbers, not page numbers.

U.S. Census Bureau, Statistical Abstract of the United States: 2004-2005

Table

Transit systems: —Con.
Vehicles 1047
Transportation (see also Motor vehicles, and individual modes):
Accidents 1053, 1058, 1060
Carriers of passengers .. 1049, 1054, 1100, 1101, 1106, 1260
Carriers of property 1049, 1107, 1108
Commodity flow 1071, 1072
Commuting to work . 1084, 1085, 1086, 1259
Construction, value 923, 924
Consumer complaints 1062
Consumer expenditures . 658, 659, 660, 661, 662
Consumer price indexes 698, 700
Motor fuel 700
New cars and new trucks 700
Cost indexes 1090
Airlines 1055
Railroad 1109
Energy consumption 886, 887, 889, 890
Expenditures 649, 1048
Federal government:
Aid to State and local governments . 424
Outlays 462, 465, 769
Freight 1048
Government employees and payrolls ... 454
Government finances .. 428, 429, 431, 441, 442, 465
Metropolitan areas 1057, 1085
Occupations 597, 607, 1054
Outlays, by type of transport 1048
Port traffic 1068
Securities 1199
Stock and bond prices and yields 1199
System mileage 1046
Travel trends 1259
Travel volume 1049, 1054, 1063
Transportation and warehousing:
Capital 371, 748, 751
Earnings 611, 613, 619, 728, 731, 732, 1050, 1051, 1052
Employees .. 587, 611, 613, 728, 731, 732, 1050, 1051, 1052
Establishments . 728, 729, 731, 1050, 1052
Finances 718, 721
Hours 611
Multinational companies 762, 763
Nonemployers 729
Occupational safety 634
Pollution abatement 371
Productivity 615
Revenue 1050, 1104
Sales, receipts . 718, 721, 726, 727, 728, 729
Transportation equipment manufacturing (see also Motor vehicle and Aerospace):
Earnings 613, 973, 976, 984
Electronic commerce 980
Employees ... 613, 973, 976, 978, 982, 984
Establishments 973
Finances 760
Foreign trade 978, 1293, 1302
Gross domestic product 642
Inventories 987
Mergers and acquisitions 742
Multinational companies 762, 763
Occupational safety 633, 634
Producer prices 705, 706

Table

Transportation equipment manufacturing (see also Motor vehicle and Aerospace): —Con.
Productivity 615
Profits 760
Research and development 776, 777
Shipments 976, 978, 980, 986, 987
Toxic chemical releases 367
Transportation, communications, and public utilities industry (see also Energy and utilities, Information, and Transportation and warehousing):
Capital 748, 749
Construction cost indexes 921
Earnings 618, 738
Employees 601, 738
Gross domestic product 646
Mergers and acquisitions 742
Occupational safety 631, 634, 636
Profits 716, 758
Union membership 639
Women-owned businesses 738
Transportation support services industry . 1050, 1051, 1052
Travel:
Accidents 1053
Air carriers 1058, 1060
Border crossings 1261
Business, pleasure travelers 1251, 1252
Domestic expenditures by State 1253
Foreign 1254, 1255, 1256
Highway mileage 1069, 1070
Household trips 1251, 1252
International expenditures 1254
States 1257
Passengers 1054, 1063, 1254, 1255
Person trips 1250, 1251, 1259
Recreation 1251, 1252
Services 1292
Tourists 1254, 1255, 1256, 1381
Volume 1049, 1054, 1063
Travel accommodations industry 613, 615
Travel arrangement industry 613
Travel in the United States ... 1259, 1260, 1261
Travelers checks 1182, 1187
Treasury bonds:
Foreign purchases and sales, holdings . 1197, 1198
Sales, prices, and yields 1189, 1190
Trichinosis 177
Trinidad and Tobago. See Foreign countries.
Tripoli 860
Trips. See Travel.
Truck and tractor pull 1237
Truck transportation industry:
Commodities handled 1105
Earnings 613, 1050, 1051, 1052
Employees 613, 1050, 1051, 1052
Establishments 1050, 1052
Finances 1105
Gross domestic product 642
Productivity 615
Revenue 1050
Trucks:
Factory sales (trucks and buses) 1031
Imports 1031
Motor-fuel consumption 1088
Registration (trucks and buses) 1082
Tuberculosis 177, 181
Deaths 102

NOTE: Index citations refer to **table** numbers, not page numbers.

Table

Tuberculosis —Con.
Hospitals 157
Tuition 276
  Consumer price indexes 700
Tuna 854, 857
  Catch 854
  Prices 712
  Supply 856
Tungsten:
  Foreign trade 866
  Production and value 860
  Strategic and critical material 865
  World production 864
Tunisia. See Foreign countries.
Turbines. See Steam engines.
Turkey. See Foreign countries.
Turkeys 712, 798, 801, 831, 840
Turkmenistan. See Foreign countries.
Turks and Caicos Islands. See Foreign countries.
Tuvalu. See Foreign countries.
Typhoid fever 177
Typhus fever 177

U

Uganda. See Foreign countries.
Ukraine. See Foreign countries.
Ulcer of stomach and duodenum, deaths ... 102
Ultrasound, diagnostic 165
Unemployment. See Labor force, unemployed workers.
Unemployment insurance:
  Beneficiaries 521, 538, 539
  Coverage, workers and earnings 538
  Governmental finances 428, 440, 467
  Payments 518, 519, 520, 538, 539
Union membership 638, 639, 640
  Employee benefits 630
United Arab Emirates. See Foreign countries.
United Kingdom. See Foreign countries.
United States securities (see also Debt):
  Foreign purchases and sales, holdings . 1197, 1198
  Held by banks 1169
  Holdings by households 1161
  Prices, sales, and yields 1189
  Taxable yields 1188
Universities. See Education, higher education institutions.
Unmarried-partner households 55
Unmarried women, births 1326
Uranium (see also Nuclear power) . 860, 881, 908
Urban population 25
Uruguay. See Foreign countries.
Utah. See State data.
Utilities (formerly Electric, gas, and sanitary services). See also Gas utility industry and Electric light power industry:
  Capital 751
  Customers and bills 906
  Earnings . 611, 613, 618, 619, 728, 731, 732, 883
  Employees ... 611, 613, 728, 731, 732, 883
  Establishments 728, 729, 731, 883
  Expense 907
  Finances 718, 721, 1189, 1199
  Gross domestic product 642
  Hours 611
  Income 907
  Industrial production index 754
  Industry 728, 882, 883, 903

Table

Utilities (formerly Electric, gas, and sanitary services). See also Gas utility industry and Electric light power industry: —Con.
  Investor owned 907
  Mergers and acquisitions 742
  Multinational companies 762, 763
  Net generation 903, 906
  Net summer capacity 903
  Nonemployers 729
  Occupational safety 634
  Productivity 615
  Revenue 906, 907
  Sales, shipments, receipts ... 718, 721, 726, 727, 728, 729, 906
  States 906
Urban transit systems industry 1052
Uzbekistan. See Foreign countries.

V

Vacancy rates:
  Housing 941, 943, 944, 945
  Office buildings 969, 971
Value added (see also individual manufacturing and mining industries):
  States 983
Vanadium 860, 864, 866
Vanuatu. See Foreign countries.
Veal (see also Beef and Meat and meat products) . 199, 831, 1358
Vegetable oils. See Oils.
Vegetables (see also individual commodities):
  Acreage 829
  Calcium source 198
  Consumer expenditures 660, 661
  Consumption 200, 813, 827
  Farm marketings, sales 801, 804, 807
  Foreign trade . 810, 812, 813, 815, 817, 827, 1299
  Gardens 1235
  Iron (dietary) source 198
  Pesticide usage 821
  Prices 700, 705, 806
  Production 827, 829, 1355
Vehicles. See Motor vehicles, Tractors, etc.
Venereal diseases (see also AIDS) 177
Venezuela. See Foreign countries.
Venture capital 743
Vermiculite 860
Vermont. See State data.
Vessels. See Ships.
Veterans Affairs, Dept. of:
  Budget outlays 462
  Expenditures . 115, 516, 517, 518, 519, 520
  Hospital, medical care 115
  Home loans 1177, 1179
  Land and buildings 490
Veterans:
  Characteristics 514
  Number 512, 513
  Pensions and other benefits:
    Disability, service-connected compensation 515
    Disbursements 492, 517, 519
    Federal aid to State and local governments 424
    Health expenditures 115, 118
    Veterans or dependents receiving .. 515, 517, 521
Vetoed bills, Congressional 398

NOTE: Index citations refer to **table** numbers, not page numbers.

U.S. Census Bureau, Statistical Abstract of the United States: 2004-2005

VCR's 1007, 1120
Video games 1036, 1119
Vietnam. See Foreign countries.
Vietnamese population 22, 737
Violent crime. See Crime.
Virgin Islands. See Island areas of the U.S.
Virginia. See State data.
Visual arts 1234
Visual impairment 172
Vital statistics (see also Births and Deaths):
   Fertility and fertility rate 75
   Foreign countries 1325
   Island areas 1304
   Life expectancy 92, 93, 94
   Marriage and divorce 70, 113
   Rates, summary 70
   World 1325
Vitamins 197
Vocational education 424
   Medical payments 115
   Service industry 555, 556, 557
Volleyball 1237, 1241, 1243, 1244
Volunteer workers 567, 568, 1233
Voter registration 407, 408
Voter turnout 407, 408, 410
Votes:
   Congressional 389, 391, 392, 410
   Gubernatorial 400
   Presidential .. 384, 385, 386, 387, 388, 410
Voting-age population 407, 408, 410

W

Wage earners. See Labor force, employment,
  and earnings, and individual industries.
Wages and wage rates. See Earnings.
Wallis and Futuna. See Foreign countries.
Walnuts 830
Warehouses (see Trucking and warehousing) ....
                                970
Warehousing and storage industry:
   Earnings 613, 1050, 1051, 1052
   Employees 613, 1050, 1051, 1052
   Establishments 1050, 1052
   Gross domestic product 642
   Revenue 1050, 1104
Wars, U.S. troops and casualties 506
Washing machines, homes with 965
Washington. See State data.
Waste management & remediation services :
   Earnings 728
   Employees 728
   Establishments 728
   Receipts 728
Wastepaper 849
Wastewater treatment 883, 917
Watches. See Clocks and watches, etc.
Water (see also Water transportation industry
  and Wastewater treatment):
   Area 1, 346
   Consumption 355, 356
   Freight 1049, 1065, 1066
   Pollution:
      Abatement expenditures 371
      Oil spills 358
      Rivers and streams 358
      Toxic releases 366
   Power 356, 901, 912
   Public supply . 355, 356, 883, 916, 947, 951
   Vessels 1047, 1240
Water heater 1015

Watermelons 829
Water polo 1244
Water skiing 1241
Water transportation industry:
   Earnings 613, 1050, 1052
   Employees 613, 1050, 1051, 1052
   Establishments 1050, 1052
   Foreign trade 1066
   Freight 1048, 1049, 1065, 1066
   Gross domestic product 642
   Occupational safety 634, 1053
   Outlays 465
   Revenue 1050
Water utility 882, 883, 916
Water, sewage and other systems 613, 917
Waterways 1065
Wealth:
   Business 696
   Families 693, 694
   Government 696
   Households 691, 692, 696
Weather 375, 378, 379, 380, 381, 382, 383
   Foreign countries 1331
Welfare services. See Social welfare; Public aid,
  assistance; and individual programs.
West Bank. See Foreign countries.
West Virginia. See State data.
Western Sahara. See Foreign countries.
Wetlands 352
Wheat:
   Acreage 822, 825
      Organic 798
   Farm marketings, sales 801
   Farm prices 822, 825
   Foreign trade 810, 813, 814, 817, 822,
                           1299, 1360
   Pesticide usage 821
   Production 814, 822, 825
      World production 1355
   Supply and disappearance 822
Wheat flour 199
Wheelchair usage 172
White-collar workers:
   Earnings 620
   Employment cost index 625
   State and local government workers 455
Whiting, quantity and value of catch 854
Wholesale trade:
   Capital expenditures 748, 751
   Companies exporting 1301
   Earnings . 611, 613, 618, 619, 728, 731, 732,
                             738, 1316
   Employees .. 587, 601, 611, 613, 728, 731,
                 732, 738, 1313, 1316
   Establishments . 728, 729, 731, 1313, 1316
   Finances 718, 721, 760
   Foreign investments in U.S. 1284
   Gross domestic product 642, 646
   Hours 611
   Industry 728
   Inventories 1042
   Mergers and acquisitions 742
   Multinational companies 762, 763
   Nonemployers 729
   Occupational safety 634
   Productivity 615
   Profits 716, 760
   Sales, receipts . 716, 718, 721, 726, 727, 728,
           729, 738, 1036, 1042, 1316

NOTE: Index citations refer to **table** numbers, not page numbers.

Wholesale trade: —Con.
Women-owned businesses 738
Whooping cough 177
Wildlife:
  Endangered species 373
  Related recreation activities 1245, 1246
Wilshire equity index 1199
Wind:
  Energy source 888
  Selected cities 383
  Solar energy 888
  Velocity 888
Wind surfing 1241
Wines (see also Alcoholic beverages) . 201, 810,
                                          812, 813
Wiretaps 317
Wisconsin. See State data.
Women:
  Abortions 89, 90, 91
  Activity limitation 182, 183
  Adult education 288
  Advanced placement exams 251
  Age 11, 12
  AIDS 179, 180
  American Indian, Alaska Native population ..
                                          13
  Asian population 13
  Births and birth rates . 70, 71, 72, 77, 79, 82,
                             83, 86, 87, 1325
    Births to single women ... 78, 79, 81, 86
    Cesarean section deliveries 83, 165
    Characteristics, selected 72, 86, 87
    First births 86
  Black, African American population 13
  Business owners 737, 738
  Cancer 191
  Child day care 559
  Child support 548
  Cigarette smoking 84, 188, 189
  Community service 567, 568
  Computer use 617, 1121, 1150
  Contraceptive use 88
  Correctional institutions 66
  Criminal victimization .. 217, 218, 300, 306
  Deaths and death rates .. 95, 104, 107, 180
  Delivery procedures, births 83, 165
  Education:
    Adult education 288, 1335
    American College Testing program .. 249
    Attainment 212, 214, 256, 257, 259
      Labor force status 257
    College costs 271
    College dormitories 66
    College enrollment . 204, 209, 259, 260,
                          261, 262, 774
      By age 260
      By State 263
      Disabled 269
    Degrees conferred .. 282, 284, 285, 286,
                         287, 775
    Enrollment by level 209, 233, 266
    High school dropouts 254, 256, 257
    Teachers 235, 247, 279, 597
    SAT tests 248
  Elections, voter registration and turnout . 407
  Farmworkers 809
  Fertility, fertility rate 75, 76
  Food stamp participants 553

Women: —Con.
  Group quarters population 66
  Gynecological services 155, 165
  Health insurance coverage 139, 141
  Height distribution 193
  Hispanic origin population 13
  Home health and hospice care 169
  Homicides 297
  Hospital use ... 66, 155, 156, 161, 163, 165
  Householders . 57, 56, 58, 60, 62, 63, 64, 65
  Illness/injury 174
  Income 677, 678, 679
  Injuries 174
  Internet access 604, 1121, 1150
  Job search 604
  Juvenile institutions 66
  Labor force and employment:
    Age 570, 572
    Computer use 617
    Displaced workers 594
    Earnings 623, 624
    Educational attainment ... 573, 591, 608
    Employed . 571, 574, 576, 579, 583, 585,
                587, 588, 589, 590, 592, 597, 601
    Foreign countries 1350, 1352, 1353
    Industry 601
    Marital status 577, 578, 579, 580
    Occupation 597, 624
    Participation rates .. 570, 571, 573, 574,
                           577, 578, 579, 580
    Persons working at home 587
    Projections 570
    Reason not in 596
    School enrollment 576
    States 574
    Tenure with employer 592
    Unemployed .. 571, 574, 576, 579, 603,
                   605, 606, 607, 608, 609
    Union membership 639
  Life expectancy 92, 93, 94
  Mammography 190
  Marital status 51, 52, 53
  Marriage and divorce 113
  Military quarters 66
  Music purchases 1136
  Native Hawaiian, Other Pacific Islander
    population 13
  Nursing home residents 66, 172
  Overweight 194
  Pension plan coverage 535
  Persons living alone (one-person house-
    holds) 65
  Physical activity 195
  Physicians 149
    Visits to 152, 154, 155
  Pilots 1064
  Population 11, 12, 13
  Property owners 951
  Race 13
  Rape 289, 290, 291, 292, 298, 309
  Recreational activities ... 1232, 1233, 1234,
                              1241, 1248
  Social Security beneficiaries and payments ..
                                            527
  Sports participation in school .. 1242, 1243,
                                     1244
  Surgical procedures 165

NOTE: Index citations refer to **table** numbers, not page numbers.

U.S. Census Bureau, Statistical Abstract of the United States: 2004-2005

Women: —Con.
  Unemployment ... 571, 574, 576, 579, 603,
                    605, 606, 607, 608, 609
    Age 603
    Reason 605, 609
  Union membership 639
  Unmarried-partner households 55
  Volunteers 567, 568
  Voter registration and turnout 407
Wood and wood products. See Lumber.
Wood products manufacturing:
  Earnings 613, 973, 976, 984, 1285
  Electronic commerce 980
  Employees .. 613, 973, 976, 978, 982, 984,
                                          1285
  Establishments 973, 1285
  Finances 760
  Foreign trade 978, 1302
  Gross domestic product 642, 843, 972
  Industrial production index 754
  Mergers and acquisitions 742
  Occupational safety 633, 634
  Prices 849
  Productivity 615
  Profits 760
  Railroad car loadings 1107, 1108
  Renewable energy 912
  Shipments 976, 978, 980
  Toxic chemical releases 367
Woodpulp (see also Paper and paperboard prod-
  ucts):
  Foreign trade 847
  Producer price indexes 849

Work stoppages 637
Workplace violence 631, 635, 636
Workers. See Employment and labor force.
Workers' compensation program . 115, 146, 519,
                                521, 541, 542
Workstations. See Computer.
World summary statistics 878
  Comparative data (area, population, etc.) ....
                                       1321, 1322
  Energy 1364, 1365
  Farm commodities 814, 1355, 1359
  Mineral production 875, 878
  Population 1318, 1319, 1321, 1322
  Telecommunication service sector 1372
Wrestling 1237, 1243, 1244
Wyoming. See State data.

                    Y

Yemen. See Foreign countries.
Yogurt consumption/production 199, 837
Youth employment programs 524

                    Z

Zambia. See Foreign countries.
Zimbabwe. See Foreign countries.
Zinc 1299
  Foreign trade 866, 1299
  Mining industry 859
  Prices 862
  Production and value (mine and smelter) ....
                                          860, 864
    World 864, 1363
  Strategic and critical materials 865

NOTE: Index citations refer to **table** numbers, not page numbers.

U.S. Census Bureau, Statistical Abstract of the United States: 2004-2005